RUDOLF II AND PRAGUE

Hans von Aachen
Portrait of Rudolf II

RUDOLF II AND PRAGUE

THE COURT AND THE CITY

Edited by

Eliška Fučíková

James M. Bradburne, Beket Bukovinská, Jaroslava Hausenblasová,
Lumomír Konečný, Ivan Muchka, Michal Šroněk

PRAGUE CASTLE ADMINISTRATION
THAMES AND HUDSON
SKIRA

This book has been published on the occasion of the exhibition
*Rudolf II and Prague: The Imperial Court and Residential
City as the Cultural and Spiritual Heart of Central Europe,*
30 May 1997–7 September 1997

First published in Great Britain in 1997 by Thames and Hudson Ltd, London

First published in the United States of America in hardcover in 1997 by
Thames and Hudson Inc., 500 Fifth Avenue, New York, New York 10110

The texts in this catalogue were supplied in Czech, German and English by
the Contributors listed on page xii. The Publishers take sole and full
responsibility for their form and wording in this English-language edition.

Library of Congress Catalog Card Number 97 - 60327

British Library Cataloguing-in-Publication Data
A catalogue record for this book is available from the British Library

ISBN 0-500-23737-9

Printed and bound in Italy

VÁCLAV HAVEL
President of the Czech Republic

During the reign of Emperor Rudolf II, the city of Prague became one of the most fascinating centres of spiritual life in the history of Europe. I am delighted that this great exhibition is taking place here, since it successfully evokes the Rudolfine era and the wealth of inspiration slumbering within it, which, I am firmly convinced, can address contemporary humanity in fundamental ways.

IMPERIAL COURT

RESIDENTIAL CITY

CATALOGUE

ELIŠKA FUČÍKOVÁ
Curatorial Director of the Exhibition

The 300th anniversary of the death of Emperor Rudolf II in 1912 inspired the Society for the Patriotic Friends of Art in the Czech Lands, a forerunner of the Narodni galeri v Praze, to 'honour the memory of the ruler, so important for domestic art, with an exhibition of paintings and engravings and portraits of the artists who were active at his court or were especially recognized by that court'. The halls of the Prague Rudolfinum contained 262 exhibits – in reality around 350 objects, paintings, sculptures, drawings, miniatures, graphics, decorative arts, astronomical and measuring instruments, medals, coins, books and archival materials. Eighty years on, Prague has the honour once again to present the works of masters whom Karel Chytil described in the introduction to the 1912 exhibition catalogue as 'the most exquisite talents' of the Rudolfine era. This time, however, the exhibition is being held within the halls of Prague Castle – the authentic environment in which these artists were active.

The difference between the two exhibitions does not lie only in the number of exhibits. Chytil also wrote that many of the Rudolfine talents 'were, of course, eclectics and mannerists'. Although the last decades of the nineteenth and beginning of the twentieth centuries saw the publication of monographs on the most important artists at the court of Rudolf II and the gradual unveiling of archival sources on the Rudolfine era, the period was indeed considered to have been eclectic and Mannerist and to have contributed little to the future development of art and science. It was not until later, when Mannerism was being reappraised, that Rudolfine art was recognized as one of its closing phases. The exhibition Prag um 1600: Kunst und Kultur am Hofe Rudolfs II, *held in 1988 in Essen and Vienna, was the first presentation of these new findings, including characteristic examples of works by Rudolfine masters and outlining the reasons why they deserved a respected place in the history of fine art.*

The success of Prag um 1600 *provided the organizers of the present exhibition with the incentive to create a show which would evoke the memory of one of the most important, unjustly neglected periods in Czech history.* Rudolf II and Prague *is not meant as a mere repetition of the 1988 exhibition. It has taken advantage of the authentic environment of Prague by installing the works not only at Prague Castle but also in the city itself, which, thanks to the presence of the imperial court for more than 30 years, was transformed into a major European metropolis. When Rudolf II died and his successors moved back to Vienna, the dignified Wallenstein Palace saw itself as a fitting competitor for Prague Castle. Its architecture and interior decoration have, for the most part, survived in their original form; thus the Wallenstein Riding Hall provides the ideal space for the City section of the exhibition, with the palace itself becoming one of the exhibits. The Court section of the exhibition will allow visitors to see some of the most fascinating examples of Castle architecture from the sixteenth and early seventeenth centuries, reflections of the industrious building activities commissioned by the first Habsburgs on the Czech throne.*

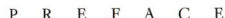
Visitors to these halls will discover the functions of the imperial court and its illustrious figures, artists and scholars and the results of their work, the music of the era and so on. The situation of Rudolf II and Prague is therefore reminiscent of its famous predecessor of 1912; however, the basic approach is not only complemented by a far greater selection of exhibits but also provides much more detailed and extensive information about Rudolf II as a monarch, patron of the arts and collector, about the learned and artistic colony at his court and about his collections and the works created under his liberal patronage.

Despite the fact that this is the largest project to date to concern itself with Rudolf II and his era – a project which would not have been possible without enthusiastic international co-operation – it does not claim to be exhaustive, nor could it be. The organizers of the 1912 exhibition were able to show Dürer's Feast of the Rosaries *without having considered whether the painting might be damaged during transport and installation. Today Hans van Aachen's wonderful paintings executed on alabaster, Roelandt Savery's bouquets painted on wooden panels and Joris Hoefnagel's illuminated manuscripts remain safely in storage due to the dangers of transporting them over large distances, as do the bronze statues of Adriaen de Vries. Despite these gaps, the exhibition's organizers have endeavoured to put together the widest and most diverse selection of exhibits possible in order to present the most complete picture of the period.*

Exhibitions such as this will always bring to light new works, unfamiliar names, fresh knowledge; they will initiate further research which will take our awareness considerable steps forwards. And if Rudolf II and Prague *also delights and fascinates visitors, then the enormous amount of work involved in its preparation will not have been in vain.*

Organizing Institutions: Správa Pražského hradu, Kancelář prezidenta republik, Ministerstvo kultury České republiky, Hlavní město Praha, Uměleckoprůmyslové muzeum v Praze

Curatorial Director of the Exhibition: Eliška Fučíková

Exhibition Curators: Duna Panenková (Imperial Court), Olga Drahotová (Residential City)

Assistants: Veronika Hulíková, Jana Skálová

Exhibition Committee: James M. Bradburne, Milena Bravermannová, Beket Bukovinská, Petr Danék, Olga Drahotová, Eliška Fučíková, Jaroslava Hausenblasová, Petr Chotěbor, Luboš Konečný, Ivan Muchka, Michal Šroněk, Antonín Švejda

Exhibition Design: Vladimir Hora, Martin Vopálka, Emil Zavadil, Studio Najbrt Lev, Pavel Lev

Exhibition Arrangements: C.H. expo, atypexpo, Kusttrans Praha, Vídeň Dagmar Stará, ZdenĚk Hojda, Lenka Zapletalová

The following organizations participated in the exhibition:

Ústav dějin umění Akademie věd České republiky
Uměleckoprůmyslové muzeum
Národní galerie v Praze
Národní muzeum v Praze
Národní technické muzeum v Praze
Národní knihovna v Praze
Státní ústřední archiv
Archiv hlavního města Prahy
Klášter premonstrátů na Strahove
Kunsthistorisches Museum Wein

List of Lenders

Amsterdam, Rijksmuseum, Rijksprentenkabinet
Antwerp, Koninklijk Museum voor Schone Kunsten
Antwerpen, Stedelijk Prentenkabinet
Arcibiskupský seminář, Praha
Arcibiskupství pražké
Archiv hlavního města Prahy
Archiv města Plzně
Archiv Národní galerie v Praze, fond pražská malířská bratrstva
Archiv Národního muzea, Praha
Archiv Univerzity Karlovy - ústav dějin UK, Praha
Augsburg / München, Privatbesitz
Augsburg, Stadt Augsburg Kunstsammlungen
Baltimore, The Baltimore Museum of Art
Basel, Oeffentliche Kunstsammlung Basel, Kupferstichkabinett
Balsta, Skokloster Castle
Belgium, P. Verhagen
Benediktinské arciopatství sv. Vojtěcha a sv. Markéty, Praha
Berlin, Staatliche Museen
  Kunstbibliothek
  Kunstgewerbemuseum
  Kupferstichkabinett
  Münzkabinett
Bern, Kunstmuseum (Eigentum der Gottfried Keller-Stiftung)
Bonn, Rheinisches Landesmuseum
Bratislava, Slovenská národná galéria
Bremen, Kunsthalle, Kupferstichkabinett
Brno, Klášter augustiniánů na Starém Brně
Brno, Moravská galerie
Brno, Moravské zemské muzeum
Brussels, Musées royaux des Beaux-Arts de Belgique
Bucharest, The National Museum of Art of Romania
Budapest, Szépmüvészeti Múzeum
Cambridge, Lent by Syndics of the Fitzwilliam Museum
Canada, Frank and Marianne Seger

Chlumec nad Cidlinou, Městský úřad
Copenhagen, Den kgl. Malerei- og Skulptursamling Statens Museum for Kunst
  Den Kongelige Kobberstiksamling, Statens Museum for Kunst
Copenhagen, Nationalmuseum
Copenhagen, The Royal Danish Collection at Rosenborg Palace
Corning, N.Y., The Corning Museum of Glass
Čechy, soukromá sbírka
Darmstadt, Hessisches Landesmuseum
Dessau, Anhaltische Gemäldegalerie
Dortmund, Museum für Kunst und Kulturgeschichte der Stadt Dortmund
Dresden, Staatliche Kunstsammlungen
  Gemäldegalerie Alte Meister
  Grünes Gewölbe
  Kunstgewerbemuseum
  Kupferstich-Kabinett
  Rüstkammer
  Skulptursammlung
Duchcov, státní zámek
Düsseldorf, Graphische Sammlung, Kunstmuseum Düsseldorf, Sammlung der Kunstakademie (NRW)
Edinburgh, National Gallery of Scotland
Florence, Gabinetto Disegni e Stampe degli Uffizi Firenze, Galleria degli Uffizi
Florence, Museo dell' Opificio delle Pietre Dure
Frankfurt, Städtische Galerie in Städelschen Kunstinstitut
  Graphische Sammlung im Städelschen Kunstinstitut
Freiburg im Breisgau, Augustinermuseum
Gdansk, Muzeum Narodowe
Geneva, private collection
Göttingen, Kunstsammlung der Universität
Göttweig, Kunstsammlungen des Stiftes Göttweig
Graz, Alte Galerie des Steiermärkischen Landesmuseum Joanneum
Hamburg, Hamburger Kunsthalle
Hamburg, Museum für Kunst und Gewerbe

Hanover, Niedersächsisches Landesmuseum
Hrádek u Nechanic, Zapůjčeno Památkovým ústavem v Pardubicích z evidence mobiliáře státního zámku Hrádek u Nechanic
Jaroměř, Městské muzeum
Kancelář Metropolitní kapituly u sv. Víta, Praha
Kancelář prezidenta republiky, Archiv Pražského hradu
Kassel, Staatliche Museen Kassel, Graphische Sammlung
Katedrála sv. Víta, Správa Pražského hradu
Klášter benediktinů, Rajhrad
Klášter premonstrátů na Strahově, Praha
Klášter premonstrátů, Teplá
Knihovna Národního muzea, Praha
Kostel Panny Marie před Týnem, Praha
Cologne, Wallraf-Richartz-Museum
Cracow, The Wawel Royal Castle - State Collection of Art
Kremsmünster, Benediktinerstift Kremsmünster Kunstsammlungen
Kroměříž, Arcibiskupství olomoucé, Arcibiskupský zámek a zahrady v Kroměříži
Lambach, Sammlungen der Benediktinerabtei
Leiden, Prentenkabinet der Rijksuniversiteit
Leipzig, Museum der bildenden Künste
Liberec, Státní Okresní archiv
London, College Art Collections, University College London
London, The Board of Trustees of the Victoria and Albert Museum
London, The British Museum
Loreta, Řád Menších bratří kapucínů
Lyon, Museé des arts décoratifs
Metropolitní kapitula u sv. Víta, Pražský hrad
Město Žlutice, okres Karlovy Vary
Městské muzeum a galerie v Poličce
Městské muzeum, Týn nad Vltavou
Moravská galerie Brno
Moscow, Pushkin State Museum of Fine Arts
Muzeum hlavního města Prahy
Muzeum jihovýchodní Moravy, Obuvnické muzeum, Zlín

Muzeum skla a bižuterie, Jablonec nad Nisou
Muzeum Šumavy v Sušici
Muzeum Vysočiny v Jihlavě, pobočka Polná
Munich, Bayerische Staatsgemäldesammlungen,
    Alte Pinakothek
Munich, Bayerisches Nationalmuseum
Munich, Deutches Museum
Munich, Staatliche Graphische Sammlung
Münster, Stadtmuseum - Leihgabe aus Privatei-
    gentum
Münster, Westfälisches Landesmuseum für
    Kunst und Kulturgeschichte
New York, The Metropolitan Museum of Art
Nürnberg, Germanisches Nationalmuseum
Okresní muzeum ve Vysokém Mýtě
Okresní muzeum Chrudim
Okresní muzeum v Lounech
Okresní vlastivědné muzeum, Česká Lípa
Olomouc, soukromá sbírka
Olomouc, Státní vědecká knihovna
Opava, Slezské muzeum
Osnabrück, Kulturgeschichtliches Museum
Ottawa, National Gallery of Canada
Oxford, The Visitors of Ashmolean Museum
Památková správa Buchlovice, hrad Buchlov
Památkový ústav České Budějovice, Státní zámek
    Český Krumlov
Památkový ústav České Budějovice, Zámek Hlu-
    boká nad Vltavou
Památkový ústav České Budějovice, zámek
    Jindřichův Hradec
Památkový ústav středních Čech, Praha
Památkový ústav středních Čech, zámek Dobříš
Památkový ústav středních Čech, zámek
    Jemniště
Památkový ústav středních Čech, zámek Kono-
    piště
Památkový ústav středních Čech, zámek Veltrusy
Památkový ústav v Pardubicích, Hrádek u
    Nechanic
Památkový ústav v Plzni, zámek Kozel
Památník národního písemnictví
Paris, Bibilothéque nationale de France
Paris, Collection Frits Lugt, Institut Néerlandais
Paris, Musée du Louvre
    Département des Arts Graphiques
    Département des Objets d'Art
    Département des Peintures
Paris, Observatoire de Paris
Plzeň, Západočeské muzeum
Prachatice, Prachatické muzeum
Prague, Archeologický ústav AV ČR v Praze
Prague, Archiv hl. města Prahy
Prague, Archiv Pražského hradu
Prague, Arcibiskupství pražské
Prague, Knihovna Národního muzea
Prague, Konzervatoř, archiv a knihovna
Prague, Metropolitní kapitula u sv. Víta
Prague, Muzeum hl. m. Prahy
Prague, Národní galerie v Praze

Grafická sbírka
    Sbírka starého umění
Prague, Národní knihovna České republiky
Prague, Národní muzeum- minearologické od-
    dělení
- zoologické oddělení
- numismatické oddělení
- oddělení starších českých dějin
- Archiv Národního muzea
Prague; Muzeum české hudby
Prague, Náprstkovo muzeum
Prague, Národní technické muzeum
Prague, Obrazárna Kláštera premonstrátů na
    Strahově
Prague, Památník národního písemnictví
Prague, Rentiérský investiční fond l. IN, a. s.
Prague, Řád Menších bratří kapucínů, Pražská
    Loreta
Prague, Sbírky Pražského hradu
Prague, soukromá sbírka
Prague, Státní ústav památkové péče, sbírka
    plánů
Prague, Státní ústřední archiv v Praze
Prague, Strahovská knihovna
Prague, Uměleckoprůmyslové muzeum v Praze
Prague, Ústav dějin umění AV ČR, odd. doku-
    mentačních a sbírkových fondů
Prague, Zapůjčeno rytířským řádem křižovníků s
    červenou hvězdou v Praze
Privatsammlung, Dr. Helmut Seling
Rakovník, Okresní muzeum
Rokycany, Děkanský úřad církve římsko-ka-
    tolické
Rotterdam, Museum Boijmans Van Beuningen
Roudnická lobkowiczká sbírka
Rožmberk, státní zámek (Památkový ústav České
    Budějovice)
Rychnov nad Kněžnou, ze sbírek rychnovské vět-
    ve Kolowratů
Římskokatolická duchovní správa u kostela sv.
    Ignáce, Praha
Římskokatolická duchovní správa u kostela
    Panny Marie Vítězné, Praha
Římskokatolický farní úrad, Vejprnice
Římskokatolická farnost, Děkanství Most
Římskokatolická farnost, kostel Navštívení
    Panny Marie, Milevsko
Římskokatolická farnost u kostela sv. Štěpána,
    Praha
Římskokatolická farnost Matky před Týnem, Pra-
    ha
Římskokatolická farnost u kostela Nejsvětějšího
    Salvátora, Praha
Římskokatolická farnost u kostela sv. Havla, Pra-
    ha
Římskokatolická farnost u kostela sv. Mikuláše,
    Praha
Římskokatolická farnost u kostela sv. Václava,
    Stará Boleslav
Římskokatolický děkanský úřad Polná

Sbírka Holšan
Senát Parlamentu České republiky, Praha
Severočeské muzeum v Liberci
Schwerin, Staatliches Museum, Kupferstichkabi-
    nett
Sibiu, The National Brukenthal Museum
Správa Pražského hradu
Státní hrad Křivoklát
Státní hrad Šternberk
Státní oblastní archiv v Praze
Státní ústřední archiv v Praze
Státní zámek Telč
Stockholm, Nationalmuseum
Stockholm, Riksarkivet
Stockholm, The Royal Collections of Sweden
Stahovská knihovna, Praha
Stuttgart, Staatsgalerie
    Graphische Sammlung der Staatsgalerie
Stuttgart, Württembergisches Landesmuseum
Sv. Mikuláš na Malé Straně, Praha
Třeboň, Státní oblastní archiv
Uměleckoprůmyslové muzeum v Praze
Ústí nad Labem, Muzeum města Ústí nad Labem
Verona, Private Collection
Warsaw, Muzeum Narodowe
Washington, D.C., National Gallery of Art
Weimar, Kunstsammlungen zu Weimar
Weimar, Stiftung Weimarer Klassik / Herzogin
    Anna Amalia Bibliothek
Vienna, Finanz- und Hofkammerarchiv
Vienna, Graphische Sammlung Albertina
Vienna, Handschriften- und Inkunabeln Samm-
    lung der ÖNB
Vienna, Haus-, Hof- und Staatsarchiv
Vienna, Kunsthistorisches Museum
    Gemäldegalerie
    Hofjagd und Rüstkammer
    Kunstkammer
    Münzkabinett
    Sammlung alter Musikinstrumente
    Sammlungen Schloss Ambras
Vienna, MAK - Österreichisches Museum für an-
    gewandte Kunst
Vienna, Museen der Stadt Wien
Vienna, Museum und Schatzkammer des Deut-
    schen Ordens
Vienna, Österreichische Nationalbibliothek
Vienna, Österreichisches Staatsarchiv, Allgemei-
    nes Verwaltungsarchiv
Vienna, Österreichisches Staatsarchiv, Kriegsar-
    chiv
Vienna, Private collection
Wroclaw, Biblioteka Uniwersytecka
Wroclaw, Muzeum Narodowe
Západočeské muzeum v Plzni
Zdeněk Sternberk, hrad Český Šternberk
Zdice, Římskokatolická farnost
Zürich, Graphische Sammlungen der ETH
Židovské muzeum, Praha

Contributors to the Catalogue

M.A.	Miloš Anděra	Hf.	Václav Houfek	Ma.P.	Markéta Procházková
L.A.	Luboš Antonín	Hz.	Jan Hozák	V.P.	Věra Přenosilová
N.B.	Nina Bažantová	JHr.	Jakub Hrdlička	Přk.	Miroslava Přikrylová
Bm.	Jutta Bäumel	V.H.	Václav Huml	J.R.	Jan Royt
K.B.	Karel Beránek	I.G.	Günter Irmscher	M.R.	Marie Ryantová
Be.	Věra Beránková	I.J.	Igor A. Jenzen	H.Sch.	Holger Schuckelt
U.B.	Ursel Berger	J.Ka.	Josef Kandert	K.Sch.	Karl Schulz
S.B.	Szilvia Bodnar	Kpp.	Jutta Kappel	R.A.S.	Rudolf Alexander Schütte
M.Bo.	Mirjam Bohatcová	D.K.	Daniela Karasová	P.S.	Pavel Sedláček
J.B.	James Bradburne	T.C.K.	Thomas Kaufmann-DaCosta	H.S.	Helena Sedláčková
M.Br.	Milena Bravermannová	H.Kn.	Hana Knfžková	H.Sg.	Helmut Seling
V.B.	Vladimír Brych	L.K.	Lubomír Konečný	Sm.	Věra Smolová
B.B.	Beket Bukovinská	I.K.	Ivo Kořán	J.S.	Joaneath Spicer
P.B.	Pavla Burdová	H.K.	Helena Königsmarková	E.Sp.	Elisabeth Springer
J.Ch.	Jan Chlíbec	J.Kr.	Jiří Kropáček	L.Sr.	Lubomír Sršeň
P.Ch.	Petr Chotěbor	K.K.	Květa Křížová	D.St.	Dagmar Stará
K.C.	Kateřina Cichrová	J.Kc.	Jaroslava Kuncová	M.St.	Manfred Staudinger
L.Č.	Ladislav Čepička	J.Ky.	Jana Kybalová	W.S.	Wolfgang Steguweit
Z.Č.	Zlata Černá	I.Ky.	Ivana Kyzourová	D.S.	Dana Stehlíková
BČ	Bohuslav Čížek	L.O.L.	Lars Olof Larsson	F.S.	Filip Suchomel
I.Č.	Ivana Čornejová	M.L.J.	Manfred Leithe-Jasper	J.Š.	Jiřina Šedinová
D.Č.	Denko Čumlivski	J.H.L.	H. John Leopold	E.Š.	Eduard Šimek
P.D.	Petr Daněk	D.L	Dorothy Limouze	E.Šn.	Evženie Šnajdrová
R.D.	Rudolf Distelberger	I.v.M.	Ivan Martinovský	M.Š.	Michal Šroněk
J.D.	Jan Diviš	M.M.	Martin Mádl	Št.	Miroslava Štýbrová
O.D.	Olga Drahotová	J.Me.	Jaroslava Mendelová	A.Š.	Antonín Švejda
F.F.	František Frýda	M.Ě.	Václav Měřička	D.T.	Dora Thornton
E.F.	Eliška Fučíková	Z.M.	Zdenka Míková	H.T.	Helmut Trnek
T.G.	Teréz Gerszi	J.M.	Jan Mohr	E.T.	Eva Turek
L.G.	Libor Gottfried	J.R.tM.	J. R. ter Molen	E.U.	Eva Uchalová
Gbl.	Michael Göbl	G.M.	Gottfried Mraz	L.U.	Libuše Urešová
S.H.	Sabine Haag	I.M.	Ivan Muchka	J.V.	Jarmila Vacková
G.H.	Gisela Haase	M.Mž.	Marie Mžyková	V.V.	Věra Vávrová
H.B.	Marion Hagenmann-Bischoff	J.N.	Jiří Nimrichter	Th.V.W.	Thea Vignau-Wilberg
M.H.	Martin Halata	J.P.	Jan Pařez	A.V.	Alena Vlasáková
Hr.	Gerhard Hartl	J.Ps.	Jana Pasáková	V.Vo.	Věra Vokáčová
H.H.	Herbert Haupt	M.Pe.	Miroslav Pertl	R.V.	Radim Vondráček
J.Ha.	Jaroslava Hausenblasová	Ptr.	Ernst Petrisch	J.W.	Johannes Wienninger
J.He.	Jürgen Hein	MPf.	Matthias Pfaffenbichler	J.Z.	Jürgen Zimmer
B.H.	Bernhard Heitmann	M.P.	Milan Plášil		
Hol.	Karel Holešovský	P.P.	Pavel Pokorný		

IMPERIAL COURT

Prague Castle under Rudolf II,
His Predecessors and Successors

ELIŠKA FUČÍKOVÁ

When, in 1575, the Bohemian Estates approved the election of the young Archduke Rudolf as King of the Bohemian lands, they asked Emperor Maximilian II [fig. 1.1] for assurance that his son and successor would learn Czech and remain in Prague to devote himself to ruling the crown lands. It was not the first time that the Habsburgs had heard this sort of request. Hardly anybody at the time, however, could have suspected that within only a few years the request would be more than met. In 1583, Prague, as decided by Rudolf (no longer simply King of Bohemia but now also Emperor of the Holy Roman German nation), officially became the residential city. The transfer of the imperial residence to the metropolis of the Kingdom of Bohemia did not mean, though, that the young monarch had complied with a categoric demand of the Czech side.[1] There seem to be many reasons for this.

As early as 1531, Ferdinand I had moved his residence to Vienna, but he had no intention of omitting Prague from his plans. He had to vie for the favour of the Bohemian Estates in order to obtain the rule of the crown lands for his son. He did not consider his title of King of Bohemia to be a mere formality. King Wladislaw II Jagiellon and his son Louis had begun medieval Prague Castle's gradual transformation into a modern residence. Ferdinand, aware of the imposing nature of this site, decided to continue the Jagiellons' efforts in Renaissance style. Perhaps he also believed that having his residence in Prague would provide him greater security against the Turks than Vienna, closer to Turkish incursions, could offer.

Ferdinand (Alcalá de Henáres 1503–Vienna 1564) was said to be a kind and approachable man who became withdrawn only after the death of his beloved wife, Anne.[2] He was interested in botany, zoology, scholarship and music. In the Netherlands, where he was brought up, his education emphasized foreign languages as preparation for his state duties. The young Ferdinand was apparently very inquisitive, astounding others with his knowledge in all imaginable fields, and he was also good with his hands. Architecture was one area in which he was extraordinarily interested. He played an active part in planning the buildings he commissioned and reserved the right to decide every detail. He was intensely interested in history, and this is perhaps why the only scholar to obtain a permanent position at his court was the historian Wolfgang Lazius.

Thanks to Ferdinand, three collections were assembled at the Viennese court; they later became a permanent part of the Habsburg patrimony. It was he who established the tradition of collecting in the Central European branch of the house of Habsburg.[3] The Emperor's love of learning about the past was kindled by a collection of coins and medals, whose basis was, apparently, formed by inherited pieces or gifts. Later, however, it grew with systematic acquisitions made around the world. The coin collection was gradually augmented by a collection of ancient fragments, inscriptions and torsos. A sort of 'Roman museum' emerged at the Hofburg in Vienna in the 1550s, 10 years before the renowned Münzhof in Munich.

The court historian, Lazius, deserves the credit for its professional organization. If Archimboldo's painting representing *The Scholar* is truly a portrait of Lazius, then he has also been depicted in an additional important role at Ferdinand's court, namely as an expert who shared in the creation of another of Ferdinand's collections, the library. Lazius travelled to Austrian convents and monasteries in search of interesting and rare books and manuscripts for Ferdinand. Apart from purchases and bequests, it was largely thanks to the consignment of free copies of books, made possible by imperial prerogative, that the library grew. Interest in the world's knowledge led Ferdinand to support generously a variety of scholarly publications. In connection with his title of King of Bohemia one ought especially to recall his financial contribution to the publishing of two important works in Czech, *Cosmographie* by Sebastian Münster, translated into Czech by Zikmund z Puchova in 1554, and Pierandrei Mattioli's *Herbarium*.[4] Mattioli, an Italian botanist and physician, came to Bohemia in 1554, and attended to the health not only of Ferdinand I, but also of Archduke Ferdinand II and of Maximilian II. Mattioli became famous for his commentararies on the work of Pedanius Dioscorides (fl. c. A. D. 50), and then assembled his own botany. It was written in Latin but he lived to see the first Czech edition, titled *Herbář, jinak Bylinář velmi užitečný* [Herbarium, or An herbal most useful], with a dedication to Maximilian II, who, heeding his father Ferdinand's wishes, financed the printing of the book.

In the 1550s also appeared the first mention of the *Kunstkammer*, Ferdinand's third collection. Not merely an assembly of jewels and insignia, it contained objects of art, pictures, miniatures and other items. Like the Emperor's other collections, it was given its own space thanks to the alterations and construction work Ferdinand had carried out at the Hofburg in Vienna. Among these other collections was the imperial armoury, which had stored not only the earlier set of items which Ferdinand had inherited from Archduke Sigismund and Emperor Maximilian I, but also those items he had commissioned for himself and his sons from renowned armourers in Innsbruck, Nuremberg and Augsburg. He ordered his son, Archduke Ferdinand II, to establish an armourer's workshop at Prague Castle, which would carry out his commissions.[5]

Many Builders who had worked for Ferdinand in Vienna and who found employment at Prague Castle included Pietro Ferrabosco, Hans Tschert and Bonifác Wolmut.[6] In 1535, Giovanni Spazio, who had relatives working as builders for the Emperor in other Austrian towns, was sent from Vienna to the Bohemian metropolis. In Prague, it seems, Ferdinand built more than in the towns of the other countries he ruled.[7] In the immediate vicinity of the Castle there was sufficient space for him to realize his bold architectural plans. On land he purchased on the far side of the Castle's Stag Moat, he established a grandly conceived garden. Gardeners from Italy, Spain, Flanders, Alsace and even from Byelorussia created botanical gardens, a herb garden and orchards with various exotic trees. The most ornate parts of the garden were the decoratively designed *giardinetto*, with rare flowers often imported from the Orient.[8] A new bridge, begun in 1534, connected the sides of the Stag Moat and provided visitors with easy access to the garden. At the far end of the garden, running lengthwise, a splendid Renaissance summerhouse appeared in 1538, built by Ferdinand for Anne of Jagiellon. The builder was Spazio, followed by Giovanni Maria and Giovanni Battista Aostalli. The name of the architect is unknown,

though it was perhaps the builder and sculptor Paola della Stella, a native of Melide on Lake Como, who had created the model in Genoa in 1537–38. Sebastian Serlio's treatise on architecture (1537) provided the inspiration in its discussion of the ground plans of Antique temples and Greco-Roman-style porticoed villas. From the same source, apparently, came the impetus to forge an effective link between architecture and nature by means of delicate arcades decorated with ornate sculptural reliefs which accentuate the play of light and shadow on the building's surface.[9] The relief was designed by della Stella in collaboration with a large group of Italian masons, and the subjects were selected from Classical mythology and history.

The creation of the Royal Garden and of the buildings within it was delayed by a fire in the Lesser Town and at Hradčany in 1541, which also severely damaged Prague Castle. Construction work concentrated only for a time on the damaged parts of the summerhouse, such as the royal bedroom in the Old Palace above the Green Room, so that they could again serve their original purpose. Construction work expanded even further in the 1550s, though Ferdinand's relationship to the Bohemian Crown Lands changed significantly after the suppression of the Estates' rebellion of 1547. That year was not on the whole happy for the Roman king. It saw the death of Ferdinand's wife Anne Jagiellon, Charles V began to question the accession to the imperial thrown of Ferdinand's son, Maximilian, in favour of Philip. By naming his second son, Archduke Ferdinand II, regent in the Bohemian Lands Ferdinand I made clear his intention to maintain order in the eternally rebelling kingdom. At Prague Castle a man had been raised to the throne who for more than twenty years (from 1547 to 1567) attentively supervised the realization of his plans and his love of art, and who, with his collecting markedly, contributed to the formation of both court culture and the style and taste of the nobles and burghers of Prague and throughout the kingdom.

The first stage of construction work there during Ferdinand's reign came to a close in 1552 with the death of della Stella. Hans Tyrol, employed for a short time, was replaced by Wolmut (Überlingen ?–Prague 1579), who had come to Prague from Vienna probably in 1555 and who became the court builder.[10] Wolmut had been trained as a mason; he knew how to build Gothic arches and had become acquainted with the architecture of the Italian Renaissance mostly through architectural essays. In Prague, the Emperor overwhelmed him with great and sundry tasks. From 1556 to 1563, he built the first storey of the Summerhouse, surrounded by a wide terrace. The copper roof was covered with red and white stripes and painted escutcheons; the ceiling of the upper rooms were meant to be ornamented with the stars, planets and signs of the zodiac.

From 1556 to 1557, Wolmut worked out his plan for a choir on the provisional western wall of St Vitus' cathedral. The monumental classicizing façade, inspired by Serlio's model, hid, like stage scenery, the late Gothic choir and was finished in 1560. It is not the only example at Prague Castle of Wolmut using Gothic and Renaissance elements in the same building. In late 1558 and early 1559, he made plans for the reconstruction of the parliament which had been destroyed in the fire of 1541. Wolmut's solution was favoured by Emperor Ferdinand I and Archduke Ferdinand II as well as by two Italian specialists from Vienna, despite its pronouncedly Gothicizing quality. Into this historicizing space Wolmut placed, between 1563 and

1.1 WORKSHOP OF NICOLAS
NEUFCHATEL
Maximilian II (Father of
Rudolf II)
Ca. 1566
[Vienna, Kunsthistorisches
Museum, Gemäldegalerie]

1564, a tribune of writers and orators, whose architectural morphology could serve as a text-book example of Palladian building. This combination of old and new styles can be understood as embodying the builder's intention to base his work clearly on that of his predecessors.

Ferdinand I also sent his painters and sculptors to Prague to create new interiors. From 1531 onwards, his court painter was Jakob Seisenegger, whose tasks included the execution of portraits of the Emperor and his family.[11] The painter travelled a great deal in the service of the Emperor and came to know the art of northern Italy, though this is not apparent from his portraits. Reports of his work for Prague Castle date only from 1535, when he painted a large portrait of Ferdinand I and one of the Emperor's wife. Following the Emperor's lead, the Bohemian nobility also commissioned portraits from Seissenegger.[12]

Apart from a design for the Melantrich Bible, published in 1570, no other work by Florian Abel, who appeared in Prague sometime before 1550, is known.[13] Though he was employed at the court, he entered the Old Town painters' guild and trained a number of young painters. His ability is clear from his designs for Maximilian I's tomb in Innsbruck, on which the Abel brothers began to work in marble. After their deaths, Alexander Collin took over the project. From 1539, another court painter was employed at Prague Castle, Giovanni Battista Ferro, but nothing of his work remains. Lastly, the unrealized cycle of forty portraits of Bohemian monarchs and the family of Ferdinand I, which was to replace the older monarchical gallery destroyed by fire in 1541, must also be mentioned. Ferro began working but stopped for fear that painting on walls damaged by fire would soon flake off.[14] It was commissioned from Domenico Pozzo of Milan, a painter who also took part in the ornamentation of the organ-case in St Vitus'. Pozzo began work on the cycle in 1563, and, as is clear from the letters of Ferdinand II written the following year, some of the figures had already been realized by that time.[15] This information is related to several remarkably painted monarchs on what was originally the outside wall of the parliament building, something which continues to be overlooked by experts. The monumental figures, painted with confidence and elegance, testify to Pozzo's talent, a man knowledgeable about late Italian Renaissance painting and who himself was educated in the new Mannerist canon.

From the moment when Archduke Ferdinand II made Prague the seat of his imperial regency, court artists began work on the decoration of Prague Castle. Francesco Terzio (Bergamo 1520–Rome 1600), trained in Venice, had been in the Archduke's service from 1551, and came to Prague three years later.[16] He worked mainly on the organ in St Vitus', which is no longer extant. Only his design for a bronze fountain in front of the Summerhouse was realized. One other painter worked on the decoration of the organ-case: Hans Gersching of Salzburg. He also worked on the Summerhouse.[17]

Thirteen Italian sculptors and masons worked on the relief ornamentation of the Summerhouse under the direction of della Stella, after coming with him to Prague in May 1538. Among them may have been his brother, Giovanni Maria, who in 1550 worked on the stone escutcheons on the corners of the terrace. Though the quality of the sculptural work is uneven, it is clear that Paolo della Stella designed it; its quality is unprecedented in Bohemia.[18] Only the splendid bronze fountain, realized by several artists from 1562 to 1568, could compete in quality with the Sum-

merhouse. The fountain was probably modeled by the sculptor Antonio Brocco, following Terzio's design, while the wooden forms were made by the carver Hans Peysser. The bronze was poured by the gunsmith Tomáš Jaroš in Brno, Moravia, and the final engraving work was carried out by Brocco.

Ferdinand I also employed at Prague Castle representatives of various crafts such as upholsters, goldsmiths and cabinet-makers, though even less is known about their work than about that of painters and sculptors. It seems that then more than in later years, the services of the town's guild masters were used, and, if certain specialists were hired for the court, they were, perhaps for financial reasons, called *trabant* - that is, lacking a speciality.[19]

The list of the building, painting and sculpting work carried out in the reign of Ferdinand I is impressive and leaves one convinced that the Emperor considered his residence just as important as the Hofburg in Vienna. Otherwise, he and his wife Anne would hardly have made their final resting place St Vitus' cathedral.[20] When in 1562 the young Prince Rudolf came with his parents to Prague Castle on a visit, he saw a residence truly fit for an emperor. The Stag Moat and the lovely Renaissance garden opposite completed the harmony of the precinct.

The hunting lodge known as the Star Summerhouse Hunting Lodge (Hvězda) must have left a pleasant impression on Rudolf. Within less than an hour's walk from Prague Castle, it had been built according to the wishes of Archduke Ferdinand II in the middle of a game preserve.[21] The six-pointed plan was clearly inspired by designs for ideal fortified towns. The Star Summerhouse was built between 1555 and 1556 by Giovanni Maria Aostalli and Giovanni Luchese under the supervision of Bonifác Wolmut. The sloping terrain below the hunting lodge was arranged into terraces. On the highest of them, a ball-games house or 'gallery' was built. The severe exterior betrayed nothing of the villa's complexly articulated interior. The vaulting of the ground floor was covered with ornate stucco work executed between 1556 and 1560 by Italian stuccoers.[22] Though their names have long been forgotten, Brocco, who would later work for Archduke Ferdinand of the Tyrol, might have been among them. The classicizing look of the stucco relief and the Mannerist canon of the individual figures hint on the one hand at being inspired by Roman stucco of imperial times, and on the other hand suggest the influence of cinquecento palazzo decoration, similar to that of the Salla deglli stucchi in the Palazzo del Te. Similar to the plans of Giulio Romano for the Mantua building are the profiles of the fireplaces in the Star Hunting Lodge, which suggests that the cartoons for the sculptural decoration might have been the work of Jacopo Strada, who, from 1556, corresponded with Archduke Ferdinand and offered him his services as a designer.[23] The stucco ornamentation, no matter who designed it, was unprecedented in Bohemia at that time, and, together with the relief ornamentation of the summerhouse in the Royal Garden, it set the tone for the decoration of many a palazzo and chateau in Bohemia.

Archduke Ferdinand II (Linz 1529–Innsbruck 1595)[24] was a person who in the Bohemian environment was inspiring in many other respects. Ferdinand I's second son and favourite child, he was sent to Prague at the age of eighteen and entrusted with ruling the Bohemian Lands, a task undoubtedly difficult for such a young man.24 His manner of handling his twenty-years in the royal residence and the political problems he faced in a way which inspired others, and not only the members of his family.

1.2 GIUSEPPE ARCIMBOLDO
Summer
1563
[Vienna, Kunsthistorisches
Museum, Gemäldegalerie]

While endeavouring to ensure the young archduke sufficient esteem as his successor in Bohemia, Ferdinand I provided him with enough finances to be able to keep up with the rich Bohemian aristocrats. Archduke Ferdinand II established himself comfortably in Prague and was soon setting the tone in Bohemian society. In November 1558, on the occasion of Ferdinand I's ceremonial entry into Prague, he organized a huge spectacle, a costume play, in which Jupiter fought giants, devils and monstrous beasts. The Jesuits erected a triumphal arch in front of the Clementinum; fishermen acted out the conquest of a moated castle. The whole town took part in these festivities.[25]

In 1557 the Archduke secretly married Philippina Welser, a girl of lesser birth, with whom, however, he would have a loving and harmonious marriage. In their residence at Křivoklát Castle, where Philippina lived in seclusion, Ferdinand II began to indulge in another one of his passions, the building of his collection.[26] He specialized in certain areas, including the armour of famous men, which he called 'ehrliche Gesellschaft' (esteemed society), undoubtedly the reason he wanted to have close at hand the portraits of those to whom the armour had once belonged.[27] The Archduke's interest in portraits surpassed his father's many times over. In this he inspired many noble families. When in 1600 the French envoy visited Paul Sixt Trautson at his home on Hradčany Square, a dinner was given in a room hung with four hundred portraits of the most famous personages of the ages.[28]

In his book on the establishment of the imperial collection, Alfons Lhotsky complains of the unfortunate lack of a list of the treasures accumulated at Křivoklát by Archduke Ferdinand II.[29] The same can be said, of course, about his palace at Prague Castle. He had taken to Innsbruck not only collections assembled in Bohemia but also Bohemian servants and many artists and artisans who had worked on imperial commissions. Some of them stayed in Prague while continuing to work for the Archduke. Matyáš Hutský, as a token of his gratitude to the Archduke for having recognized his talent at an early age, taken him from his native Křivoklát to Prague and had him trained in the Tyrol, painted for Ferdinand miniature reproductions of scenes from the life of St Wenceslas, with which a master painter from Litoměřice had adorned the St Wenceslas chapel in St Vitus' cathedral.[30] Because he was apparently a good portraitist, Hutský supplied Innsbruck with the portraits of high-born Bohemians.

For political and dynastic reasons, the Archduke, his father and his nephew were often at odds. As an art lover and collector, however, the Emperor's uncle was a model for the young monarch. When after seven years in Spain Rudolf and his brother Ernest returned to Vienna in 1571, they travelled by way of Innsbruck, where they undoubtedly had the opportunity to peruse Ferdinand's collections. These were not yet in Ambras, but in the Archduke's Innsbruck palace; none the less, they must have stuck in the memory of the future Emperor, who, after the Archduke's death, went to great lengths to get them from his son, Karl von Burgau.[31]

In 1562, Maximilian II became king of Bohemia. A monarch well known for his sympathy for Protestantism was now on the throne. The non-Catholic estates in the Bohemian lands therefore saw him as their white hope. They were disappointed, however. Maximilian was rarely in Bohemia, and when he was, it was with evident reluctance, perhaps because of the eternal religious disputes shaking the country.

As the first-born son of Ferdinand I, he was from the beginning prepared for his future career as ruler. He was educated in Innsbruck by Velius and Tannstetter and, later, by Wolfgang August Schiefer, a man who sympathized with Lutheranism. Maximilian had been excellently equipped with languages: apart from German, Latin, French, Italian and Spanish, he also knew Hungarian and Czech. He devoted most of his attention, however, to the natural sciences. He tried to attract representatives of their individual branches to his court in Vienna. These scholars often travelled to Bohemia, where they left traces of their work. Maximilian made Pierandrea Mattioli (who had served Maximilian's father) his personal physician and supported his botanical research. Angerius (Ongier) Ghislain de Busbecq, who had for years served as Ferdinand I's envoy to Constantinople, was Maximilian's favourite diplomat. On his return to the Emperor's court from Turkey in 1562, he was able to apply his knowledge of botany; he brought with him many hitherto unknown plants, including the first tulips, the snowflake genus of amaryllis and, in particular, lilac trees, which both the Emperor's garden in Vienna and the Royal Garden in Prague could now boast. Busbecq also impressed Maximilian with his interest in archaeology, antiques and old manuscripts. It is not surprising, then, that he became, albeit only for a short time, the teacher of the young Prince Rudolf.[32] The head of the imperial gardens and famous botanist Carolus Clusius (Charles de l'Ecluse), interested in comparative botany, studied the flora of Bohemia and Hungary; he carried on a lively correspondence with many colleagues at the court in Prague. Johannes Crato (Kraft), one of the most important physicians of his day, was employed at the court by Emperor Ferdinand I already in 1560. He faithfully served Maximilian II, tended to his health and, as he himself said, was also the monarch's adviser on religious and political affairs. Rudolf valued his service, and Crato remained in Prague till 1581 - that is, almost till the end of his life.[33]

Hugo Blotius became the first official court librarian, cataloguing Ferdinand's older collection of manuscripts and prints and seeing to its expansion; he remained in this post until 1608.[34] Lazio's successor as court historian was Johannes Sambucus (Ján Sambocký), a trained physician, botanist, publisher of classical literature and author of a book on emblems which in its day became very popular and inspired many, including Shakespeare. It also became an important manual in the workshops of the artists at Rudolf's court. Until his death in 1584, Sambucus remained in Rudolf's service.[35]

In 1558, the goldsmith and antiquary Jacopo Strada (Mantua 1515–Vienna 1588) was hired at the imperial court.[36] He would serve three monarchs while doing a great deal of work for other nobles. Well versed in architecture, numismatics and history, and familiar with linguistics, he could offer an incredibly wide range of knowledge and abilities. He designed the court festivities, the gardens and the waterworks. Ferdinand I had named him court architect, and Maximilian named him imperial antiquary and head custodian of the *Kunstkammer*. Strada had hardly any time left for the goldsmithery he had been trained in. As an architect, he worked on plans for the Munich Antiquarium, and he contributed significantly to the architectural form of the Vienna Neugebäude. He published a number of books and had his workshop produce illustrated volumes with reproductions of Antique coins, portraits of Roman emperors and designs for vessels for the nobility. He stayed mostly in Vienna, and when he came to Prague or other cities it was primarily as an

adviser on conceptual work and iconography. It was mostly probably Strada who began work on the set of symbols which his son Ottavio completed and published.[37]

One of Strada's journeys took him to Prague for the funeral of Ferdinand I in 1565. This event had been prepared by Archduke Ferdinand II. Strada was perhaps also meant to design the tomb in St Vitus' cathedral, which Maximilian commissioned from the sculptor Collin the following year. Collin had come to Prague to acquaint himself with the site chosen for the tomb, and upon his return to Innsbruck began work on the commission.[38] Strada was also his consultant on a work commissioned by Ferdinand I, namely Maximilian's tomb in Innsbruck. As curator of the imperial collections, he mainly looked after new acquisitions, and he tried to accommodate the Emperor's love of Classical sculpture. A great deal of his time was, of course, devoted to his own work as publisher and antiques dealer, which is probably why Rudolf consented to his quitting the court in 1579.

Though he preferred Vienna, where he enlarged the imperial residence substantially and where he was surrounded by his scholarly 'Academy', Maximilian II continued with the plans his father had initiated in Prague. In 1567, Wolmut began to build a wing to link the two houses of Count von Thurn, which Maximilian had bought two years earlier, with the new building of Archduke Ferdinand II. That same year, construction of the Little Ball-Games Hall at the entrance to the Royal Garden was finished, and in 1567–69 the Large Ball-Games Hall was built. The Royal Garden thus acquired 'the most remarkable composition of central European Classicism from the mid-sixteenth century, of even a Palladian calibre', which was already considerably marked by a Mannerist tendency.[39] It now had everything that a place intended for recreation required: a hall for social gatherings and dancing in the Summerhouse, a ball-games house, a shooting range and gardens which were both functional and decorative, with a labyrinth, an orangery, a large bronze fountain, large wooden tubs with fish both for decoration and for eating, a wooden menagerie and an aviary. The wooden corridors were painted green and connected the individual rooms with each other and with the Castle. The Stag Moat was intended for hunting, as was the nearby Star Hunting Lodge, which provided more space and extra game.

The well-equipped areas of Prague's Royal Garden and of the Star Hunting Lodge evidently inspired Maximilian II to have a similarly grandly conceived precinct close to his seat in Vienna. Not far from his summer residence in Ebersdorf he began to build the Neugebäude summer palace and garden, which were to bring together all his passions: the outdoors, animals and, of course, his collections.[40] Master builders and artisans worked on its construction and decoration. Though his agents in Italy were unsuccessful in their search for a capable architect, the Emperor himself was more fortunate in his hiring of skilled painters and sculptors.

In 1562, Giuseppe Arcimboldo (Milan 1527–1593) entered the service of the Emperor. He had briefly worked for Ferdinand I, mainly in the area for which he had been summoned to the court, namely to paint portraits of the Emperor's family. Maximilian was to discover that he had other, exceptional abilities. The Emperor admired Arcimboldo's composite heads, paintings composed of shapes and colours from the organic and inorganic worlds. Together with *The Four Seasons* and *The Four Elements*, which he presented to the Emperor on New Year's Day 1569, Arcimboldo included a poem by Giovanni Battista Fonteo as a kind of commentary on the com-

1.3 GIUSEPPE ARCIMBOLDO
Winter
1563
[Vienna, Kunsthistorisches Museum, Gemäldegalerie]

plicated message of these cycles.[41] They are allegories of imperial office, based on a complex system of correspondence between macrocosm, microcosm and the institutions of government, and they glorify the house of Habsburg [figs 1.2, 1.3]. The pictures, which Maximilian valued greatly and which he must have kept in his collections in Vienna till the end of his life, made their way to Prague only during the reign of Rudolf. Arcimboldo had, however, found a place for himself in Prague even before that, as an organizer of court festivities. For Carnival in 1570, Maximilian organized a magnificent pageant in Prague, at which, apart from the sumptuous decoration, there was also a live elephant. Old Town Square was dominated by a model of Mt Etna which sputtered fire and brimstone. A costume procession represented the various heroes of Classical mythology and history. Perseus rode Pegasus with the head of the Medusa, and horses dressed as dragons drew a chariot bearing Jason and Medea. The procession also included a Theseus, an Argos, and Furies astride black horses. King Porus commanded his elephant to kneel before the imperial couple. The procession also included Czech mythology in the form of Vlasta and her retinue of maidens. The wizard Zifreo on his six-legged dragon, by tapping on Mt Etna, conjured up other figures including a rustic wedding with comically attired villagers, the Queen of Sheba, hussars jousting and a huntsman with a live vulture and hare. At the end of the procession was the set designer himself, the painter Arcimboldo, in a black robe and black beard. A description of the festivities in a poem by Adam Cholossio explains the symbolism of the individual scenes and can be linked to some of the painter's original designs for the costumes and props, which Arcimboldo brought together with others in a single volume and dedicated to Rudolf in 1585. In festivities at the wedding of Charles of Styria and Maria of Bavaria, in Vienna in 1571, Maximilian himself performed together with the young Rudolf, who had just returned from Spain.[42]

After painting the chapel at the castle in Pressburg, Giulio Licinio (Venice 1527–1591?) was taken into the service of the court.[43] He is often mentioned in archival records as a portrait painter, but no portrait connected with his name has survived. Maximilian used Licinio's services mainly in the decoration of the Neugebäude. While there, the painter met Bartholomeus Spranger and Hans Mont, who were employed by the Emperor on the recommendation of the famous Florentine sculptor Giambologna. All three eventually appeared in Prague during the reign of Rudolf, and while Licinio seems to have dedicated himself mainly to acquisitions, the young painter and the sculptor became the founders of a large colony of artists at the new imperial residence.

An important person whom Maximilian took into his service in 1566 was the medalist Antonio Abondio (Riva di Trento 1538–Vienna 1591).[44] He was a virtuoso modeller in wax, from which he made superb forms for medals and coins. He was also involved in independent work, predominantly wax reliefs. The best known is a circular medallion celebrating his sovereign, Maximilian II, as Roman emperor and general, while the reverse seems to be a celebration of the initial successes of the imperial forces in the campaign in Transylvania led by Lazarus von Schwendi in 1565.[45] Apart from superb models for coins and medals, which preserve the likenesses of a number of important people of the time, Abondio devoted himself to modelling small sculptures which he then cast in bronze. He and his son Alessandro found work at the court of Rudolf in Prague, to where they moved their workshops.

1.4 MARTINO ROTA
Archduke Ernst (Brother of
Rudolf II)
1577–80
[Vienna, Kunsthistorisches
Museum, Gemäldegalerie]

Most of the goldsmiths, clockmakers, cutters of gems and other artisans worked for Maximilian in Vienna. But orders also made their way to the traditional centres of handicrafts. Wenzel Jamnitzer worked in Nürnberg on the famous silver fountain for the Emperor.[46] This work, which was not finished until after Maximilian's death, made its way not to Vienna but to the imperial collections in Prague. It was undoubtedly an extraordinary commission. The work of Nicholas Müller (d. Prague 1586), mentioned in the archival records as the court goldsmith at Prague Castle,[47] would have been particularly interesting for Prague, but he sent it to the Emperor in Vienna. Müller managed to advance from being an impoverished artisan to being a merchant and owner of houses who was so wealthy that he could lend money to princes. Though his work is now unknown, his epitaph was painted by his son-in-law, Bartholomeus Spranger. In the enumeration in Maximilian's *Hofstaat* (court list) from 1567, the gilder Lorenz de Negran is also mentioned; he might be Lorenc Nero, a gilder and court swordsmith who later worked in Prague.[48]

It is now clear that a number of members of Maximilian's court, artists and scholars, also found employment in the service of Rudolf. Maximilian's activity had a positive influence on the young prince upon his return from Spain. He captured Rudolf's imagination as a collector who used his diplomats to acquire works of art. This method of acquisition was most noticeable in the growing collection of Classical sculpture which Maximilian particularly admired.[49] From his father he seems to have inherited a love of numismatics and old manuscripts and an interest in contemporary art, particularly from Italy. He prepared the ground for Rudolf, not only as concerned the titles of Emperor and King but also in his tolerance, respect for learning and love of art, which were meant to help one forget violence, intolerance and the thankless duties of a monarch.

Rudolf was born of a loveless marriage between Maximilian and his cousin, Maria of Spain, the daughter of Charles V.[50] Maximilian's sympathies for Protestantism and Maria's bigoted Roman Catholicism both manifested themselves in their approach to the young prince's upbringing. Fearing for his faith, Maria of Spain, her brother King Philip II and their uncle Ferdinand I were able to convince Maximilian to entrust the education of the young pretender to the imperial throne to a responsible person at the Spanish court. The 11-year-old Prince Rudolf, together with his brother Ernest, a year younger [fig. 1.4], thus left Vienna to spend almost 8 years at the court of their uncle, King Philip, in Madrid. Their sojourn there influenced the brothers for life, by no means in a negative sense.[51] Their humanistically orientated education, provided by two highly qualified teachers who had come from Vienna with the two princes, alternated with hunting, dancing and tourneys. Philip saw to their faith, and with his sincerity and friendly approach tried to compensate for their being far from home. Through him they were prepared for their future duties of state, and it was also thanks to him that they were initiated into the beauty of art. They saw in him a generous patron and passionate collector. Philip's majestic appearances in public and the tremendous reverence and respect which he elicited during audiences made a great impression on them. A restrained manner towards one's surroundings was adopted by both princes – to such an extent, in fact, that they suffered for it at home; in Vienna, where the relationship between Emperor and courtiers was far more hearty, and where mores were looser, the princes were considered haughty. Rudolf maintained his Spanish manners and fashion to the end of his days, thus earning the sobriquet 'Rudolfo di pocche parole'. Though he elicited reverence and respect and appeared majestic in public, he was still approachable. The Venetian envoy Soranzo, a skilled diplomat who met the Emperor, provided in 1607 a singular characterization of Rudolf, which is all the more precious in that it concerns a period when fate had ceased to favour the Emperor. Rudolf, he wrote,

> was a rather small figure, of quite pleasing stature and relatively quick movements. His pale face, nobly formed forehead, fine wavy hair and beard and large eyes looking around with a certain forbearance, made a deep impression on all who met him. The Habsburg family likeness was evident in the largish lips which curled towards the right. There was nothing haughty in his comportment; he behaved rather shyly, avoided all noisy society and took no part in the usual amusements; jokes pleased him not, and only rarely was he seen to laugh: these were the characteristics he had in common with his brother Ernest, with Philip II and with Philip III. Apart from hunting, he also enjoyed a game with a ball and riding on horseback, but the older he became, the more he made it clear that he did this not for amusement but for the needed physical movement. During audiences he was patient, and otherwise he was kindly disposed towards his surroundings, open to conversation, though he himself rarely spoke, and if so, then with an evident ease. He had mastered several languages: German, Latin, French and some Czech; and Spanish, being the language he was brought up in, was entirely normal for him; none the less he had a special affection for German, and used it almost exclusively.[52]

1.5 GIUSEPPE ARCHIMBOLDO
Reversible Head with Meats
Ca. 1570 (?)
[Stockholm, National-museum]

When in St Vitus' cathedral in 1575 the archbishop of Prague placed the crown of St Wenceslas upon Archduke Rudolf's head, Maximilian still reigned. Rudolf, however, as Bohemian king, had already to consider where he would rule from once he replaced his father on the imperial throne. Maximilian had built the Rudolfsburg (later Amalienburg) for him in Vienna, but construction was also underway to provide the monarch with a place to live when at Prague Castle. Because Maximilian suddenly died in October 1576, the need for a decision on the future residence became urgent. That same year, Rudolf had rooms above the Green Room and in the Ludwig Wing redone for himself and his mother; these were to provide a temporary home until more dignified rooms could be completed.

Immediately after his accession to the imperial throne, Rudolf visited the countries he ruled; in order to hold his ground in his duties, he familiarized himself with the structures of the state administration and, mainly, with the complicated tangle of imperial and international politics. The choice of a location for the future imperial seat was a highly political question, not to be hurried, and the young monarch evidently considered it carefully from all sides in order to choose one that would best suit him. In 1576 and 1577, he was often in Prague and could therefore supervise the building of his summerhouse and study, a residential wing and the west end of the south façade of Prague Castle, plans for which had probably been drawn up for Maximilian II.[53] Unfortunately, very little is known about Rudolf's accommodations during his visits to Prague, because neither written records, plans, nor pictures of them have survived. At the Castle, there was a three-gabled palace (clearly visible on a vista of Prague from 1562), the residence of Archduke Ferdinand II.[54] The court also had at its disposal the two houses

bought from Count Thurn and the wing connecting them with Ferdinand's building.

In 1579, construction work on the new palace under Ulric Aostalli had reached a point where it was possible to begin decorating the interiors. From 1580 onwards, Rudolf remained in Prague on a more or less permanent basis; thus it seems reasonable to believe that he had them altered according to his own taste. An act of 1583 established Prague Castle as the imperial seat. The Emperor had asked the Bohemian Estates to contribute finances for the building of a dignified permanent residence for him, loftily setting out the reasons why he had chosen Prague. Apart from the venerable age of the town and its erstwhile glory, practical reasons must have been behind the Emperor's decision. Thanks to Maximilian, Rudolf had become absolute ruler of the Empire and had only to pay his siblings ample annual allowances. His attempts to increase his power were frustrated by his brothers' lack of understanding and unsatisfied ambitions, however. In their attempt to rule in other countries, they plunged into dangerous adventures and caused Rudolf political, financial and personal problems by continually emphasizing his inability to rule and forcing him to name his successor. Even Rudolf's mother refused him moral support. She suspected him (like his father) of secretly sympathizing with the Protestants and of neglecting the duties of a Roman Catholic monarch. Rudolf perceived his mother's ordering him about and his brothers' ambitions as an erosion of his own power, and he therefore tried to distance himself as much as possible from his family. They felt at home in Vienna, but out of place in Prague. With the move to the metropolis of the kingdom of Bohemia, Rudolf won the favour of the Bohemian Estates, and distanced himself not only from his family but also from the Papal court, whose influence in Bohemia (considered to be in confessional chaos) was less than in Austria. Though the kingdom of Bohemia was not an oasis of peace and quiet, the mountains at its frontiers did provide greater protection against the Turkish peril than did the open Hungarian plains leading to Vienna.

Thanks to the magnanimous architectural achievements of Ferdinand I at Prague Castle and to the intense building activity of its nobles and burghers, Prague was gradually being transformed into an imposing metropolis. The skyline of the vast area of the Castle dominated the town, and its most important buildings, St Vitus' cathedral and the old Royal Palace, recalled the glorious past when Emperor Charles IV had had his royal seat here. Prague Castle was a town within a town, isolated from Prague's daily life, but satisfying all the wishes of a demanding imperial court. It was the residence of the Bohemian king and of the archbishop of Prague, and here stood the imposing palazzi of Bohemian nobles, the houses of court officials and of the canons of St Vitus', as well as the dwellings of servants and artisans working for the court. The mighty ramparts and the deep Stag Moat gave Prague Castle the appearance of inaccessibility, security, calm and reserved majesty. All of these qualities convinced Rudolf that Prague was where he wanted to live.

If he was going to feel happy, he was going to have to furnish his new residence comfortably and with objects which would be in keeping with his station. His model was probably not so much the Hofburg in Vienna as it was the splendidly furnished palaces he had known during his sojourn at the Spanish court and his long journeys through Italy. At the beginning of his reign, he visited the ornate residences of the Wittelsbachs and Fuggers in Bavaria. In his biography of Bartholomeus Spranger, Karel van Mander writes that early on Rudolf did not seem

1.6 BARTHOLOMEUS SPRANGER
Cybele and Minerva
After 1590
[Düsseldorf, Graphische
Sammlung, Kunstmuseum
Düsseldorf, Sammlung der
Kunstakademie (NRW)]

to be particularly interested in art.[55] This was evidently a bit of invective against a man whom van Mander otherwise considered the greatest living patron of the arts. He could thus explain why the Emperor had not enlisted Spranger's services immediately upon ascending the throne. Duties of state, of course, had priority, and Rudolf, particularly at the beginning, devoted himself to them with great intensity. If construction of the new palace at Prague Castle was sufficiently advanced in 1579 to allow cabinet-makers, locksmiths and gilders to begin work, then now was the time for painters and sculptors to decorate the new abode. By the autumn of 1580, Spranger had definitively settled in Prague, and on 1 January 1581 he was named court painter.[56]

Many of the scholars, artists and artisans who had worked for Ferdinand I and Maximilian II now followed their new patron to Prague Castle and formed the basis of a colony of scholars and artists. As early as 1584, when the merchant Hans Ulrich Krafft arrived and, thanks to the kindness of Spranger, visited the imperial palace, he was able to have a look at several rooms ornately decorated with works of art. In the first room, he saw Spranger's paintings, which, he says, were quite large. These might have been the cycle based on Ovid's *Metamorphoses*, which the painter had been working on at the time. In adjacent rooms hung the work of Spanish painters and many nudes from Rome and elsewhere in Italy.[57] Were Veronese's allegories and mythologies, which had been commissioned by Rudolf from the famous Venetian painter, already amongst them? Krafft's descriptions seem to suggest this. His report also provides important information about life at Prague Castle at a time when it has been throught that there was no great activity in the arts. Spranger had to interrupt the tour because the time was approaching when His Majesty would return to the rooms. He told his guest that he would not be able to give him more of his time because he himself had to be back in his studio for one of the Emperor's regular visits.

Rudolf's building activity at Prague Castle ran from the mid-1570s through the 1580s. The chapel of St Vojtěch (St Adalbert), for example, was built in front of the west façade of St Vitus' cathedral; it was based on plans by Wolmut and carried out under Ulrico Aostalli on a commission from Archbishop Brus, and had the financial backing of the Emperor.[58] Similarly, the reconstruction of All Saints' chapel also received Rudolf's support; the project had, in 1580, been initiated by his sister Elizabeth, the widow of the French king Charles IX. Apart from the final work on the Summer Palace (specifically, on the Emperor's residential wing), other landscaping was carried out, stables were built and the Castle buildings were linked by covered passages. For his grand building plans, Rudolf acquired, in 1585, the services of the Florentine architect Giovanni Gargiolli (d. 1603). Antonio Valenti also stayed for a short time before being entrusted with work outside Bohemia.[59]

The Emperor's residence was not to be outdone by the two imposing palazzi already standing in the Prague Castle precinct and belonging to the Pernštejns (from 1554) and the Rožmberks (built 1545-56; reconstructed 1573-74).[60] The precinct could also boast the royal summer palace and the game preserves near the Castle. In 1578 and 1579, Ulrico Aostalli rebuilt the late Gothic summerhouse in Stromovka in the Renaissance style. In its halls hung rare paintings, and the vaulted arcade around the building looked onto the gardens and game preserve.[61] The large fish-pond with a small, man-made island at its centre was supplied with water

1.7 BARTHOLOMEUS SPRANGER
Allegory of Faithfulness Triumphant Over Fate
(Allegory of The Fate of Sculptor Hans Mont)
1607
[Prague, Sbírky Pražského hradu]

1.9 BARTHOLOMEUS SPRANGER
Triumph of Wisdom
Ca. 1605
[Vienna, Kunsthistorisches Museum, Gemäldegalerie]

1.8 BARTHOLOMEUS SPRANGER
Allegory of the Turkish Wars
Ca. 1610
[Münster, Stadtmuseum, loan from private collection]

1.10 BARTHOLOMEUS SPRANGER
Mars and Venus in the Smithy of Vulcan
After 1607
[Vienna, Kunsthistorisches Museum, Gemäldegalerie]

from the Moldau which flowed through an almost kilometre-long aqueduct under Letná plain.[62] It had been dug from 1583 to 1593 and was one of the extraordinary technical achievements of the period.

The Royal Garden was, from the beginning, the object of Rudolf's attention. In 1577, Aostalli had made improvements to the two terraces in its western part, and in 1582 and 1583 he built the Lion Yard. It seems that solid-walled buildings for housing tropical plants during the winter were already being considered. The Garden of Paradise, first built by Archduke Ferdinand II, was connected by a stairway with the imperial apartments.

Apart from work for the architects, an enormous range of tasks awaited painters at Prague Castle. Martino Rota (ca.1520 Šibenik/Sibenico–before 23 September 1583) trained in Italy, where he first worked; from 1586 onwards he was employed by the Habsburgs at the court.[63] His portraits of Rudolf and Archduke Ernst are not exceptional, but they are well executed and fairly idealized, and provide good likenesses. Rota was also a good draughtsman and engraver, but left no significant trace of this at the imperial court, where he worked only till 1582.

Portraits at Rudolf's court were also made by Arcimboldo. In two drawings he recorded the young monarch, warts and all, wearing the Bohemian and imperial crowns.[64] We can get a better idea of his work from his self-portraits,[65] interesting psychological studies which reveal much about a painter whose ambitions and abilities went far beyond those of a typical court portraitist. He was said to have also excelled as a builder of hydraulic machines, and he created a secret code and invented a form of musical notation using colours. All of this undoubtedly intrigued the Emperor as much as his pictures. The reversible still-lifes (which when rotated 180 degrees turn into composite heads) and the Primavera paintings might be from his work in Prague [fig. 1.5].[66] For Rudolf he also arranged various court festivities, such as those for the coronation in 1575 and others in 1578 and 1579, above all in 1585, when the Emperor was presented with the Order of the Golden Fleece. Connected with that date is a book containing 145 designs for costumes and decorations created by Arcimboldo for various occasions and devoted to his patron.[67] He was by then old and ill and was considering going to Milan. This was perhaps because younger artists had appeared at Rudolf's court, who were orientated towards other styles and who had won the attention of the Emperor. In 1587, Arcimboldo returned to Italy, from where, a few years later, he paid homage to the Emperor by sending him a painting of *Vertumnus*, in fact a hidden portrait of Rudolf.[68] Arcimboldo used the same symbolism as in his *Elements* and *Four Seasons*. Comanini's poem, which accompanied the portrait, explained its subject matter: Vertumnus (the Emperor) is the god of metamorphoses in nature and in human life. The fruit and flowers which comprise the Emperor's face symbolize the peace, prosperity and harmony of his wise and magnanimous rule, from which was born the eternal spring of a new golden age. The Emperor, who was delighted by the portrait, conferred on Arcimboldo the title 'comes palatinus'. The painter, however, was not to enjoy the honour for long; he died in Milan the following year.

Giulio Licinio was taken into the service of the court as a painter.[69] After he finished his work for the Neugebäude, he followed the Emperor to Prague, though he often spent long periods in Italy, particularly in Venice, where he bought works of art for Rudolf. It might have been he who mediated the Emperor's commissions for

1.11 BARTHOLOMEUS SPRANGER
Sophonisba
1603–07
[Prague, Národní galerie v Praze]

Veronese, Tintoretto and Fiammingo. In Prague, he seems seldom to have devoted himself to painting, and if the altarpiece *Dead Christ with Angels* in St Vitus' cathedral is Licinio's work, it is safe to assume that there his style began to change under the influence of Spranger.[70]

By the time he settled in Prague, Bartholomeus Spranger (Antwerp 1546–Prague 1611) already had behind him a difficult but successful career.[71] From his native Netherlands, where he had trained as a landscape painter, he set out on a journey through Europe in order to learn other techniques and genres. During a brief sojourn in France, he practised portrait painting and chalk drawing. In Italy, which became his home for a number of years, he first acquainted himself with fresco technique. Giulio Clovio initiated him into the mysteries of the miniature, and thanks to a commission from Pope Pius V, he became a virtuoso in pen-and-ink drawing. In Caprarola, where he worked on the villa of Cardinal Farnese, he came to understand the importance of perfectly combining the elements of painting and sculpture. At the invitation of Maximilian II, he went to Vienna to work on the decoration of the Neugebäude, which for him and his friend, the sculptor Hans Mont, must have been a challenge they could not refuse. It afforded them the opportunity to apply themselves independently to a similar project, albeit probably not as demanding as the one in Caprarola.[72] But it was only in Prague that Spranger attained a position he could hardly have been dreaming of when he had left Antwerp.

Perhaps like every transmontane artist who arrived in Italy, Spranger tried to absorb inspiration from a wide variety of sources. He studied Parmigianino's paintings and was fascinated by Michelangelo's compositions. In Caprarola, he became acquainted with the work of Bertoja, the Zuccari brothers and Salviati. Apart from the Caprarolian models, Marco Pino and Jacopo Zucchi also had an influence on him, and he was in close contact with the artists of the Netherlands who were working in Italy, particularly Jan Speckaert. Spranger managed to make use of all these inspirations for the creation of his own expressive style. In *The Resurrection*, he provided an account of his Italian experiences through his dynamic composition, exciting movement, clear and ample variety of colour and supreme execution.[73] At this time, he also demonstrated his virtuosity in the drawing of an original manuscript which engrossed his compatriots so much that they drew inspiration from it even though they had only heard about it from others. Karel van Mander took Spranger's drawings to the Netherlands, and Hendrik Goltzius reproduced them as prints. Thanks to Goltzius, Spranger's *Knollen-* or *Teigsstil* spread throughout the Netherlands and Central Europe at the end of the sixteenth and beginning of the seventeenth centuries, and it was an important influence on the formation of Mannerism.

Spranger's first works in Prague were evidently intended for the decoration of the chambers in the Emperor's new palace. At the time, a cycle of paintings was created inspired by Ovid's *Metamorphoses* and, sometime after 1585, the frescoes representing Mercury and Minerva were executed on the ceiling of the White Tower.[74] Apart from large canvasses intended for the decoration of interiors, he also created smaller cabinet pieces, intended for the Emperor's collection. The large and the small paintings, with mythological, religious and allegorical themes, excelled in their interesting and often complicated subject matter, elaborate composition and

1.12 BARTHOLOMEUS SPRANGER
The Resurrection
1575–80
[Prague, Obrazárna kláštera premonstrátu na Strahové]

1.14 BARTHOLOMEUS SPRANGER
Venus, Ceres and Bacchus
After 1590
[Graz, Alte Galerie des Steiermärkischen Landesmuseum Joanneum]

1.13 JOSEPH HEINTZ THE ELDER
Cupid's Departure From Psyche
Probably ca. 1603–05
[Nürnberg, Germanisches Nationalmuseum]

1.16 JOSEPH HEINTZ THE ELDER
Adoration of Shepherds
Ca. 1599
[Prague, Obrazáma kláštera
premonstrátů na Strahově]

1.15 BARTHOLOMEUS SPRANGER
Bacchus and Venus
After 1590
[Hannover, Niedersächsisches
Landesmuseum]

1.17 HANS VON AACHEN
The Annunciation
1613
[Prague, arcibiskupství
pražské]

effective use of colour [figs 1.6, 1.14, 1.15, 1.19, 1.21, 1.25, 1.26]. This was true of the cycle devoted to the adventures of Venus.[75] Under the influence of his colleagues at the court, Spranger developed his own style with a greater emphasis on colour (from von Aachen and Heintz) and form (from Adrian de Vries). Among his best works are two paintings in which he celebrates two men with whom he had a very strong bond: Rudolf II, in the *Allegory of Wisdom*,[76] and his own father-in-law, the goldsmith Müller, in the epitaph for his tombstone.[77] Apart from his work for the Emperor, Spranger occasionally was busy with commissions from other sources, in particular the large cycle of saints for St George's convent, which he managed only with the assistance of a large workshop.[78] In the final 10 years of his professional life, Spranger devoted himself increasingly to unusual iconographic themes, indulging in visual polemics, moralizing and remarking on the vanity of human endeavour [fig. 1.18]. This is why he chose a more dramatic form of expression in which light breaks up forms and underscores the phantasmic nature of the scenes. Such is the case in his paintings *Venus and Adonis* and *The Suicide of Sophonisba*.[79]

In the 1580s, other significant artists worked at the imperial court. Above all one should mention the sculptor Hans Mont (dates unknown), a student of Giambologna [fig. 1.30]. His sojourn in Prague was a short one, because an eye injury prevented him from continuing as a sculptor.[80] The only pieces which bear his signature are drawings, which are stylistically close to Spranger's. The sculptures attributed to Mont seem to be counterparts to Spranger's paintings, and the small marble *Mars and Venus* is the sculptural form of a small painting of Vulcan and Maia; a similar analogy can be found in the charming *Venus Callipyge* or the bronze *Venus and Adonis*.[81] When in 1607 Spranger painted a picture in which he recalled a lost friend, he used, as he himself admitted, Mont's composition.[82]

In 1582, a painter of miniatures, Frabrizio Martinengo, appeared in Prague, but he died too early (in 1586) to be able to make a great impression at the imperial court.[83] Hans Hoffmann (Nürnberg ? ca. 1530?–Prague ca. 1591-92), however, made his mark in Prague.[84] The Emperor had, in 1585, enlisted his services as an expert on the work of Dürer and as a master copyist of that great German master. At the opposite pole to Spranger's Mannerist expression, Hoffmann intrigued the Emperor with his watercolour studies of flora and fauna [fig. 1.23], painted from nature, which he rather artificially set into his paintings. For Hoffmann's *Hare in the Clearing*, the Emperor paid what was then an unusually high sum of 200 guldens.[85] Rudolf made use of Hoffmann's expertise when in 1588 he was offered the famous Imhoff collection of Dürer's work. Hoffmann was able to distinguish the originals from copies, which he often had authored himself, and he thus saved his patron unnecessary expenses.[86]

In the 1580s, new acquisitions arrived at Prague Castle from all over Europe. Hans Khevenhüller, an envoy to the Spanish court, obtained for Rudolf Correggio's *Io, Danaë and Ganymede*, Parmigianino's *Cupid Carving His Bow*, and also sculptures, *Handsteine*, bezoars and rare objects brought back from the New World on Spanish and Portuguese ships. The Emperor entrusted his court artists, including Arcimboldo, with the acquisition of art objects and turned to specialized agents who knew the market well and provided reliable information on interesting offers. Among these agents in the 1580s was Jakob König, a German goldsmith who had settled in Italy, where he made a living selling works of art and precious stones.[87] This friend

of Veronese, Tintoretto and Giambologna, a collector of self-portraits and portraits of important Italian artists, visited Prague on several occasions. He befriended the Emperor and bought and commissioned art for him from Italian artists. After his death, the Emperor acquired König's portrait collection.[88]

The Emperor followed the whole range of creative human activity closely. A particularly large group of craftsmen at his court comprised goldsmiths who, apart from making the obligatory gifts, created works of extraordinary quality intended for Rudolf's collections. From 1581 to 1607, Zacharias Glockner worked at the court.[89] And from 1582, Erasmus Hornick, whose work we know from numerous sets of extant drawings, was employed at the Castle,[90] as was Georg Lencker, who worked both in Prague and Augsburg from 1578 to 1589.[91] A truly important person was Anton Schweinberger (active in Prague 1587-1603), a goldsmith whose work was of exceptional quality.[92] The superb transformation of hard material into softly flowing and dramatically interwoven shapes places him at the head of a number of master artisans at Rudolf's court who followed the same principle in their work. A vessel he made with Neptune astride a hippocampus is a classic example of the superb setting of natural materials in gold, including a Seychelle-nut decorated with bas-reliefs by Nikolaus Pfaff.[93] Schweinberger's small sculptures in silver were listed in the inventory of Rudolf's *Kunstkammer*.

Not all goldsmiths, however, were willing to abandon their prosperous workshops and move to Prague. Wenzel Jamnitzer and his grandson Christoph worked on important commissions for the Emperor whilst remaining in Nürnberg, travelling to Prague only when necessary. David Altenstetter and Christoph Lencker remained at home in Augsburg to create their works for the Emperor's *Kunstkammer*.[94] Augsburg was also where Georg Roll created for the Emperor one of the most complicated globes of the period.[95]

From the late 1580s, the Emperor sponsored systematic exploration for pre-

1.19 BARTHOLOMEUS SPRANGER
Judith Lays the Head of Holofernes into a Sack
[Paris, Musée du Louvre, Depártement des Arts Graphiques]

1.18 BARTHOLOMEUS SPRANGER
Memento mori (Vanitas)
After 1600
[Cracow, The Wawel Royal Castle. State Collection of Art]

1.21 BARTHOLOMEUS SPRANGER
The Judgement of Paris
After 1575
[Prague, Národní galerie v
Praze, Grafická sbírka]

cious stones in the Bohemian lands.[96] In an attempt to ensure access to the most important deposits, he issued a patent in 1598 ordering that all important finds be presented to the Bohemian Chamber. He also appointed prospectors who had the right to look for this valuable raw material; Mathes Krätsch, Kryštof Krebs and Jan Plejskař were some of the men granted a patent. Well-equipped workshops and experts were required to turn these rare finds into works of art. In 1584, therefore, the Bohemian Chamber purchased a mill at the confluence of the Bubeneč Stream and the Moldau to serve as both a sawmill and a cutting room. This was the beginning of the extensive reconstruction of the area next to Stromovka, which for the next two decades would serve industrial purposes; it also became a sort of imperial refuge. Today, the imperial Water Mill barely resembles one of Rudolf's important building projects. From the late 1580s till the early 1600s, not only was the cutting room expanded to cut and polish precious stones, but a glassworks was added for the production of high-quality, hard material to be decorated with figural engraving. The Emperor's water mill also had a grotto with a fountain, as well as a long, open, columned gallery which afforded a lovely view, and fish ponds. Today, only the grotto and entrance gates remain.

Until he obtained the services of suitable master artisans, the Emperor would send unfinished Bohemian stones to the Medici workshops in Florence. As early as 1588, Ottavio Miseroni (Milan? ca .1560–Prague 1624), a member of the famous Milan family of stone-cutters, found employment at the imperial court.[97] In Prague, he made his mark with a signed cameo with Rudolf II's portrait.[98] For the Emperor he created a number of vessels of precious stones and crystal. He made the most of the coloured layers of stones in the modelling of figures and to engrave hard materials so as to give them the appearance of soft, supple forms [figs 1.27, 1.28]. Vessels shaped by Ottavio and finished with gems mounted by the best court goldsmiths were among the strongest examples of the European gem-engraver's art at the end of the sixteenth and beginning of the seventeenth centuries. Ottavio was later joined in Prague by his brothers, Giovanni Ambroggio and Alessandro. The Miseroni settled at the Emperor's residence, and their workshop was busy there well into the seventeenth century. It is depicted by Karel Škréta in his portrait of Dionysio Miseroni and his family.[99]

1.20 BARTHOLOMEUS SPRANGER
Hercules and Omphale
1599
[Prague, Národní galerie,
Grafická sbírka]

[25]

In 1588, Caspar Lehmann (Uelzen 1563–1622) first appeared in Prague. He introduced at the Emperor's court the new technique of cut glass.[100] From 1590, he was classified as a *trabant*, one of the Emperor's underlings and only after 1601 became an official court glass-cutter. He probably made the greatest use of the raw materials from the Bubeneč glassworks, which were suitable for figurative cutting, for which Rudolf eventually granted him a privilege in 1607. He celebrated the Emperor with a representative portrait engraved into a small glass tablet. A goblet ornamented with allegories even bears his signature, a way of demonstrating that he was among the pioneers of this technique.[101]

At the express wish of the Emperor, the outstanding medallist Antonio Abondio moved to Prague from Vienna for a while and continued working for Rudolf in the same fields as he had done for Maximilian II.[102] He created a number of superb portraits on medallions and coins, modelled in wax and made small sculptures out of metal. When he died in Vienna in 1591, his son Alessandro Abondio (Trent 1570–Munich 1648) continued his work at the imperial court. So far, only medals are connected with his name, but thanks to the *Kunstkammer's* inventory we know that he also modeled small sculptures and reliefs out of wax.

From 1581, Ottavio Strada (Nürnberg? 1550–Prague 1606) was in the Emperor's employ.[103] He had probably learned the antiquary's trade from his father, and he undoubtedly knew how to draw well. It seems that his principal task was to look after Rudolf's collections, a role he took over from his father Jacopo. Though originally disinherited, Ottavio acquired his father's collection and immediately put it up for sale. He also took over Jacopo's workshop, where he continued to produce volumes of portraits of Roman emperors, designs for vessels and collections of emblems. The latter were published as *Symbola Divina et Humana*.[104] His rather enigmatic activity and great influence at the court can be explained by the fact that his daughter, Anna Marie, became Rudolf's mistress and bore the Emperor several children. Ottavio was a man of the world, and he associated and corresponded with important persons from all over Europe. He met many of them in Prague, because from the 1580s the Emperor's residence was already attracting many interesting figures.

The focus of attention was undoubtedly the Emperor himself, but his interesting visitors were also drawn by the many scholars, artists and artisans employed at the court. An exceptional position was occupied by Tadeáš Hájek z Hájku (Thadeus Hagecius), who had been the personal physician of Rudolf's father and grandfather.[105] He served the new Emperor from 1576 till his death in 1600 and took part in many important debates on cosmology, astronomy, medicine and alchemy. Rudolf had several other personal physicians in the 1580s, most of whom had also attended his father. Among them were Johann Crato, Peter Monau, Julius Alexandrinus, Rembert Dodoens and Bartholomeus Guarinoni. Each of them, like Hájek, had some other interest apart from medicine; Dodoens, for example, was a botanist, and Martin Ruland published medical works and some dictionaries.[106] When the Emperor's historian Sambucus died, Rudolf and his court librarian, Blotius, endeavoured to obtain his library for the imperial collection, because it was one of the most extensive of its day.[107] As the Emperor's envoy to the French court, Busbecq remained in frequent correspondence with Rudolf and till 1585 sent detailed reports from France about Henry III and his politics. He also saw to the fulfilling of many of Rudolf's wishes, including the purchase of clocks and hermetic literature.[108]

1.22 HANS MONT
Sacrifice Scene
1577 (?)
[Budapest, Szépmüvészeti Múzeum]

1.23 HANS HOFFMANN
Thistle
1583
[Budapest, Szépmüvészeti Múzeum]

1.24 DAVID ALTENSTETTER
CORNELIUS GROß
HANS SCHLOTTHEIM (watch)
Table Clock
Ca. 1585
[Vienna, Kunsthistorisches Museum, Kunstkammer]

1.25 BARTHOLOMEUS SPRANGER
Saint Wenceslav and Saint Vitus
After 1585
[Prague, Národní galerie v Praze]

1.27 OTTAVIO MISERONI
Lady with a Fan
Ca. 1610
[Vienna, Kunsthistorisches
Museum, Kunstkammer]

1.28 OTTAVIO MISERONI
Standing Cup
Between 1600–05
[Dresden, Staatliche
Kunstsammlungen, Grünes
Gewölbe]

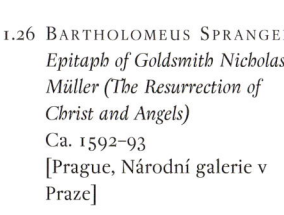

1.26 BARTHOLOMEUS SPRANGER
*Epitaph of Goldsmith Nicholas
Müller (The Resurrection of
Christ and Angels)*
Ca. 1592–93
[Prague, Národní galerie v
Praze]

The educated society of the court maintained close contact with traditional centres of education (Wroclaw/Breslau, Leipzig),[109] and important and interesting figures came to Prague. The Elizabethan poet Philip Sydney visited the city in 1575 and, two years later, as Queen Elizabeth's envoy conveying her condolences upon the death of Maximilian II.[110] Sydney's teacher was the famous Dr John Dee, a mathematician, astronomer, occultist and magician, who came to Prague with his student, Edward Kelly, in 1584.[111] They stayed for a while at the house of Hájek, organized various esoteric meetings and had the sympathy of the Emperor. Both men, however, fell into disfavour, Dee in 1586 and Kelly in 1591, and had to leave Rudolf's court. In 1588, one of the most original minds of his day, the philosopher, emblematist, devotee of the cabbala and Ramon Llull Giordano Bruno, was in Prague for several months. This is where he finished and published two of his works, one of which, *Articuli centum et sexaginta adversus hujus tempestatis mathematicos atque philosophos*, was dedicated to the Emperor. Rudolf rewarded Bruno with the substantial sum of 300 thalers.[113]

Music also had its place at the Emperor's court.[114] It had an important role in the social life of the court, accompanying many festivities and the extremely popular ballets with masques.[115] An important position was held by the *Kapellmeister* and composer Filippe de Monte (Mechelen 1521–Prague 1603), a master of the Italian madrigal, motet and mass, who had also served Maximilian. With his own book of madrigals, dedicated to the young *re di Hungaria*, another musician, Jacques de Regnart (Douai 1540–Prague 1599), sought a position at Rudolf's court. Thanks to his versatility and talents, he became Monte's *Vizekappelmeister*, just like Camillo Zanotti (Cesena 1545–Prague 1591), a master of the madrigal and villanelle. Rudolf, in keeping with his love of music, maintained one of the largest orchestras in Europe at the time.

In the late 1570s and throughout the 1580s, the Emperor's residence at Prague Castle was the hub of social and cultural life. The Turkish Wars, religious conflicts, succession struggle in the Empire and many other problems throughout Europe seems to have accelerated this development. Prague became accustomed to the variegated national composition of its population, its busy life, its public spectacles, the ceremonial arrivals of the Emperor's relatives and the visits of delegations from Europe and the Orient. It attracted nobles and soldiers, merchants, tradesmen, artists and scholars, but also beggars and thieves. At the beginning of the 1590s, Rudolf's court grew significantly as an increasing number of interesting figures sought and found work there.

After the arrival of the architect Gargiolli from Florence in 1585, large building projects, mostly under his supervision, were prepared and carried out in the 1590s. Buildings along the Romanesque western rampart were purchased and then demolished in 1590, and in the following years a narrow, approximately hundred-metre-long wing, called the 'Langbau' or 'Gangbau' Corridor Wing was built.[116] If in 1598 Hans and Paul Vredemann de Vries worked on the wall paintings on the second floor, the building must have been virtually completed, though the stairway to the Bishop's (later known as the Mathematician's) Tower was still under construction in 1603. The ground floor contained, among other things, the saddlery, which served for the storage of rare harnesses rather than as workshops. The Emperor's *Kunstkammer* was on the first floor, divided into two separate parts by a stairwell

and a connecting corridor in the Bishop's Tower. It comprised three smaller vaulted rooms called 'vordere Kunstkammer (erstes, zweites und drittes Gewölbe)' and one large, unvaulted room called the *Kunstkammer*.[117] On the second floor were two halls divided by the tower space; they served as a picture gallery. We only know the external appearance of this building from a drawing of the façade from the reconstruction in the 1640s; we know what the interiors looked like only from their description in the inventories of the *Kunstkammer*. The collections were accessible from the second floor of the imperial palace or directly from the imperial apartments, because the first floors of the two buildings were on different levels.

On the north side, a great hall was connected to the Corridor Wing; built above the Spanish stables and completed in 1597, it was named the Spanish Hall. Hans and Paul Vredemann de Vries worked on the decoration of its ceiling. Hans probably also worked on the gallery rooms, if we can judge from the information that he presented the Emperor with his elevations (*Visierungen*) for the two buildings for the picture collections.[118] At that time, the Spanish Hall was intended only for the exhibition of pictures, which was probably a first among the collections of the European nobility. The long (48.5 metres) and relatively narrow (10 metres) space seems to have been divided horizontally by three rows of ledges upon which the paintings were placed. The same principle was used in the galleries of the Corridor Wing. Hans Vredemann, who worked on the decoration of both spaces, had probably been asked to come up with a practical and easy way of installing the paintings in them.

Apart from the imposing buildings for the Emperor's collections, construction took place on many other parts of Prague Castle.[119] At the Powder Bridge entrance, an impressive single-storey gate was built with a rusticated portal, similar to those leading to the stables on the west side, to the Castle park on the east, and to Rudolf's aqueduct on the Letná side. From 1594 to 1596, Aostalli rebuilt in Renaissance style the house of the burgrave. He levelled and paved the grounds on the second courtyard and those between the cathedral and St George's convent. The Castle area was also improved by the addition of various industrial buildings. In 1594, a 'secret armoury' was built in Vikářská ulička, and the foundry by the Spanish Hall was repaired and enlarged. The following year a beautiful portal designed by Gargiolli connected the Vladislav Hall with All Saints' chapel, and construction began on the farm in the Castle park on the northwest side; in 1594, the upper part of the Stag Moat with an orchard and part of the vineyards above it had been joined to the Castle precinct. A large fish pond was established, and the so-called 'new garden', as well as a carpenters' hatch, a blacksmith's shop, stables and a gamekeeper's lodge. In 1597, Rudolf granted the Castle fusileers permission to build their homes in the aprons of the north fortifications, thus giving rise to the little street so popular today, Golden Lane.

The enormous rooms for the Emperor's collections began to fill up quickly, particularly because of the many new artists who were employed by the court in the 1590s. In 1589, Dirk de Quade van Ravesteyn came to Prague; little is known about him except that he was a painter from the northern Netherlands and a disciple of one of Floriso's students.[120] His inclination to oversized decorative detail, ornateness, expressive stylization and stereotyping can perhaps be explained by his contact with the art of the French court. A single signed painting and one signed draw-

1.29 JAN VERMEYEN (mounting)
MISERONI WORKSHOP (cameo)
Covered Goblet from the Horn of a Narwhal
Ca. 1600
[Vienna, Kunsthistorisches Museum, Kunstkammer]

1.31 DIRK DE QUADE VAN RAVESTEYN
Allegory of the Reign of Rudolf II
1603
[Prague, Obrazáma Kláštera premonstrátů na Strahově]

1.30 GIAMBOLOGNA
Rudolf II on Horse
Ca. 1595
[Stockholm, Nationalmuseum]

ing enable us to credit Ravesteyn with a relatively large body of unsigned work [figs 1.33, 1.34]. At first, he remained strongly orientated to Flemish art in his compositions, figural types and execution, as is clear from his painting *St Veronica with Angels Bearing the Symbols of the Passion*.[121] Under the influence of his colleagues at the court, his brushwork became more refined and his colours more striking, and his figures acquired more sinuous poses. These features are clear in his best-known painting, *Allegory of Peace, Justice and Prosperity*, which extols the virtues of Rudolf as the empire's protector from the Turkish peril [fig. 1.31].[122] Ravesteyn repeated some of his compositions with small variations and on different scales for patrons outside the court. Ravesteyn provided figural staffage and various animals for the architectural fantasies of the Vredemann brothers. His figural work does not rank with the best painting produced during Rudolf's reign; his attempts at refinement and elegance miss their mark and result in a strange affectedness. All the more surprising, then, are his zoological illustrations for Rudolf's bestiary, which are on a completely different level.[123]

At the imperial court, this level was represented outstandingly by Joris Hoefnagel (Antwerp 1542–Vienna 1600), a miniaturist who was named court painter in 1590 [figs 1.36, 1.37].[124] This erudite man, humanist and excellent poet was actually only an amateur painter. From his childhood, he had enjoyed drawing, and on journeys through Europe he recorded the landscapes, towns and people he saw. He was brilliant with watercolours and body-colours and raised the half-forgotten technique of the medieval miniature to new heights. His topographical studies were used by Braun and Hogenberg in their five-volume *Civitates orbis terrarum*, which mostly contains depictions of European towns.[125] Before entering the Emperor's employ, Hoefnagel lived for several years in England and Spain, but also spent time in Italy and Bavaria. For Archduke Ferdinand II, from 1582 to 1590, he illustrated the *Missale romanum* by setting its texts into decorative frames composed of Classical grotesques, human figures, various flora, fauna and sundry objects, thus imbuing them with a bountiful symbolic content.[126] When Rudolf bought a large zoological compendium from Hoefnagel, together with four books of the Elements, he probably realized that they were not studies from nature.[127] Hoefnagel's pictures nonetheless caught his attention because of their profound philosophical and allegorical content. The painter accompanied them with quotations from the Bible and from works of Classical Antiquity so as to give the illustrations a moral message. Hoefnagel also illustrated for Rudolf two volumes of calligraphy samples which the imperial secretary and scribe Georg Bocskay had originally made for Maximilian.[128] Miniatures painted from 1591 to 1593 represent various topographical illustrations and portraits, elaborate grotesques and also the most voluminous collection of symbolism related to Rudolf. Hoefnagel's separate little pictures of flowers and still-lifes painted on parchment are complex allegories often recalling the vanity of human endeavour. As an emblematist, he significantly influenced Rudolfine iconography, because as early as his Munich sojourn in the late 1580s and early 1590s he had been preparing ideas for the prints which Hans von Aachen then realized in drawings and Aegidius Sadeler transferred to engravings.[129] Because all three men met again several years later in Prague, it is safe to assume that Hoefnagel advised them and others on matters of iconography. Hoefnagel stayed in Prague only temporarily; it seems that he preferred Vienna. His son Jakob (Antwerp 1575–Hol-

1.32 KONRAD SEIFERT OF FRIBITZ (presumably) Torse of an organ cabinet 1606 [Ústí nad Labem, Muzeum města Ústí nad Labem]

1.33 DIRK DE QUADE VAN RAVESTEYN *Cupid Stung by Bees Running to Venus* Before 1608 [Budapest, Szépmüvészeti Múzeum]

1.34 Dirk de Quade van
Ravesteyn
Flute Player (Allegory of Music?)
Ca. 1600
[Vienna, Kunsthistorisches
Museum, Gemäldegalerie]

land ca. 1630), on the other hand, had become so at home in Prague that he even took part in the Estates' rising, and after the Battle of the White Mountain (1620) he had to flee Bohemia to avoid the death penalty.[130] He had studied under his father, and in 1592 he published *Archetypa*, a series of prints based on his father's drawings. He worked closely with his father throughout the 1590s, as is clear from the print with a scene of *Diana and Actaeon*, lavishly framed with flowers, snails, butterflies and other insects, evidently the work of Jakob.[131] In 1599, he sojourned in Prague, where he drew the *Allegory of Humanist Virtue* [fig. 1.38], but his official court title was conferred on him only in 1602, two years after his father's death.[132] Apart from the significant influence of his father, we can also observe in Jacob's work inspiration from Rudolfine figurative painters, in particular Josef Heintz.

Josef Heintz the Elder (Basle 1564–Prague 1609) learned the art of building from his father, Daniel, and painting from Hans Bock the Elder.[133] Not satisfied with the results of his training, he went to Italy to complete his education by studying the work of the great Italian masters. He obtained good training there in painting

ECCE. HOMO.

[34]

1.36 JORIS HOEFNAGEL
An Arrangement of Flowers with Insects
1594
[Oxford, The Visitors of Ashmolean Museum]

1.35 JOSEPH HEINTZ THE ELDER
Christ at the Column
Probably ca. 1590–95
[Dresden, Staatliche Kunstsammlungen, Gemäldegalerie Alte Meister]

1.37 JORIS HOEFNAGEL
Shell, Lobster and Crab
[Prague, Národní galerie v Praze, Grafická sbírka]

and drawing, inspired mainly by the works of Correggio, Barocci and Muziano. He collaborated with the transmontane artists who had settled in Rome and also met von Aachen, who later helped him gain employment at Rudolf's court. Heintz captured the Emperor's attention precisely because of what he had learned from Correggio, namely the application of light and colour. He was accepted into the Emperor's service in 1591 and only a few months later was sent back to Italy to record in drawings important relics from Antiquity and other periods. Thanks to this, he worked his way to a genuine mastery of drawing. In Italy, he carried out other tasks, including looking for works of art for the Emperor's gallery and *Kunstkammer*. When four years later he returned to Prague, he tended to devote himself to painting, including such pictures as *The Holy Family with Angels and SS Catherine and Barbara* for the convent of St Thomas.[134] An expressive brush-stroke, individual figurative style and effective use of light and colour are the principal features of Heintz's work from this period. Comparing his small paintings representing the *The Adoration of the Shepherds* [fig. 1.16] and *Satyrs and Nymphs* [fig. 1.41] demonstrates that he did not differentiate between mythological and devotional compositions.[135] His portraits are another matter [fig. 1.40]; in conformity with the Central European fashion of the time, they go beyond the usual conventions only when the painter had a closer relationship with his subject, for example when they were members of his family.[136] Heintz's untimely death occurred while he was finishing work on his large *Last Judgment*. This painting had been intended for another patron, but the Emperor decided to keep it for his own collection.[137] Explicitly inspired by Venetian art, it sums up all of Heintz's qualities as a painter, including theatrical compositions, a stylized figural type and the effective use of light and colour [figs 1.35, 1.39, 1.42]. Heintz (like Hoefnagel) often sojourned away from Prague, mainly in Augsburg, whence he used to return to see his family and to work. In southern Germany, he found work as a painter and mostly as an architect; evidently he did not have an opportunity to practise architecture at Prague Castle.[138]

Hans von Aachen (Cologne 1551/2–Prague 1615), like Heintz, was trained at home.[139] His teacher was an unknown painter of Flemish origin who provided his student with a solid grounding in painting and cultivated his talent for portraiture. Aachen, too, decided to complete his education in Italy because he felt certain shortcomings, particularly in drawing. He copied the work of the Italian masters and befriended artists from the Netherlands who were living in Rome. As a portraitist in Italy, he obtained a position which more than one Italian artist could envy. His *Self-portrait with 'donna venusta'* gained him the recognition of connoisseurs, commissions from the court of the Medici and his colleagues' interest in portraits by him [figs 1.48, 1.51].[140] Aachen reacted sensitively to all the impulses around him, Roman and Florentine in figure type, Venetian in use of colour and in composition. He grafted them onto a Flemish base, and thus created a very individual form of expression in painting and drawing, which attracted attention not only in Italy, but also caught the eye of the Wittelsbachs and the Fuggers in Bavaria. For several years, Rudolf had been trying to entice him to Prague; the Emperor had probably learned of von Aachen from his antiquary Jakob König. From 1588 onwards, when he was evidently first in Prague, von Aachen provided the imperial collection with his work. Though he became a court painter in 1592, he did not settle permanently in Prague until about four years later, after he had completed his commissions in

Munich and Augsburg. For Rudolf he painted large mythological pictures [figs 1.49, 1.50], allegories of all types [figs 1.43, 1.44, 1.47], small cabinet pictures with various subjects, paintings on stone, portraits, devotional works and genre scenes. He was an important representative of late Mannerist painting at Rudolf's court, as is clear from his *Road to Calvary* or *Rape of Proserpine*.[141]

Gradually, however, his compositions became calm and the figures more monumental. Examples of this are *Bacchus, Ceres and Cupid* and *The Three Graces* [fig. 1.46].[142] In the portraits, he managed to capture more than mere physical form. This is clear in his portrait of Rudolf or in the touchingly recorded face of his own young daughter [fig. 1.45].[143] In these, as in his genre paintings, von Aachen applied his Flemish schooling, free brushwork and realistic (at times even harsh) reproduction of reality - for example, when he painted his own face or lent it to an actor in his mythological or allegorical compositions. In his later paintings, he worked his way to the very threshold of the early Baroque: in the *Annunciation* altarpiece, light changes a balanced composition into an irrational revelation [fig. 1.17].[144]

Von Aachen, more than other court painter, had various responsibilities while in the employ of the Emperor. As Rudolf's friend and confident, he was entrusted with various diplomatic missions, mainly in Italy, where he made more acquisitions for the Emperor's collections than any other agent. He negotiated audiences, passed on intelligence, provided advice and arranged for everything Rudolf desired.[145] At the imperial court, he was the kind soul who looked after unexpected visitors and people coming to offer their services; they were welcome to stay in his home on the little square behind the convent of St George. His fame spread to neighbouring countries, which is why people from many noble houses were sent to study under him.

Around 1593, the sculptor Adrian de Vries (The Hague 1545–Prague 1626) appeared in Prague for a while.[146] De Vries' permanent period of work in Prague fell in the next decade. Just as von Aachen and Heintz's arrival is reflected in Spranger's work in a change in the use of colour and a greater emphasis on the effect of light, so too all three painters reacted immediately to de Vries' work in Prague. His little sculptures *Mercury and Psyche* and *Psyche Borne by Cupids onto Olympus* directed their attention to the careful perception of plastic forms and their reproduction in painting.[147] The work of de Vries, Spranger, von Aachen and Heintz began to harmonize in a special way, and the time came when they dared to collaborate. One example of this collaboration is the epitaph of the goldsmith Müller, painted by Spranger and decorated with angels by de Vries (unfortunately, the sculptures are no longer extant).[148]

In another collective effort, the three were joined by two more painters, Hans Vredemann de Vries (Leeuwarden 1526?–Amsterdam 1606) and Paul Vredemann de Vries (Antwerp 1567?–Amsterdam after 1630), who had come to Prague in 1596 [figs 1.52, 1.53, 1.58].[149] They were typical itinerant artists with an abundant list of work to their names. They had published a book of samples of architecture of all sorts, had designed fortifications, triumphal arches, interiors and fountains, and had executed wall paintings and canvases. In his altarpiece for the Emperor's chapel, Aachen painted *The Resurrection*, which we know only from his preparatory drawing.[150] The wings of the altar have fortunately been preserved. On one, Spranger painted *The Three Marys by the Sepulchre*; the other bears *The Road to Em-*

1.38 JACOB HOEFNAGEL
Allegory of the Humanist Virtue
1599
[Budapest, Szépmüvészeti Múzeum]

1.40 JOSEPH HEINTZ THE ELDER
Archduke Maximilian Ernst
1604
[Vienna, Kunsthistorisches Museum, Gemäldegalerie]

1.39 JOSEPH HEINTZ THE ELDER
Pieta with Angels
1607
[London, College Art Collections, University College London]

MAXIMI: ERNEST: ER: HER: ZU ÖSTEREI

maus by Heintz. When it was closed, one saw *The Annunciation* by the Vredemanns - imposing, fantastic architecture, high vaulted arcades in which the actual scene is almost lost.¹⁵¹ The Vredemanns were masters of optical illusion and brought to Prague Castle a new manner of interior decoration. The walls of the palace, which had hitherto been decorated with wood panelling, leather, tapestries and pictures, were covered with painted gateways into imaginary spaces. On the ceiling of the Spanish Hall they stretched a canvas of enormous dimensions (48.5 by 10 metres) with painted illusory vaulting, a large perspective vista in the middle and many grotesques. Jupiter, the Four Elements and the twelve months decorated the gallery hall on the second floor of the Corridor Wing near the entrance to the residential palace.¹⁵² There, in accordance with the express wishes of the Emperor, arcades with a view of the garden and fountain were painted on the wall to deceive the eye. In their easel paintings, they created fantastic historicizing architectures and apparently weightless buildings with lace-like façades. The staffage of these pictures was often executed by figurative painters, in particular Dirk de Quade van Ravestyn and Pieter Isaacks.¹⁵³ The two Vredemanns remained in Prague only three years, probably because the buildings whose interiors they were meant to decorate remained under construction.

In the collections of his uncle, Philip II, Rudolf had discovered the works of Pieter Bruegel the Elder, and he was taken by their peculiar and sometimes brutal statements on the world. Bruegel also earned Rudolf's admiration as a landscape painter who imbued his work with a profound philosophical content. Landscape for Bruegel was not only a back-drop for a figurative scene, as it was understood by the Italian masters; it was a reflection of the cosmic order. The Emperor longed to have Bruegel's work in his collections because the painter, like Rudolf, sought answers to questions about the meaning of life, about human beings relationship

1.42 JOSEPH HEINTZ THE ELDER
Venus, Cupid and Apollo
[Dresden, Staatliche Kunst-
sammlungen, Gemäldegalerie
Alte Meister]

1.41 JOSEPH HEINTZ THE ELDER
Satyrs and Nymphs
1599
[Munich, Bayerische Staats-
gemäldesammlungen, Alte
Pinakothek]

1.43 HANS VON AACHEN
*Allegory of the Turkish Wars:
Rudolf II as Imperator
Romanorum*
1603–04
[Basel, Öffentliche Kunst-
sammlung Basel, Kupfer-
stichkabinett]

with nature, about microcosm and macrocosm. Rudolf was also interested in land-scapes which were not ennobled by higher concepts; he collected Dürer's land-scape, botanical and zoological studies, in which he found evidence that nature's creations can, even without human help, provide the highest aesthetic experience. He also followed the work of contemporary Northern landscape painters who had devoted themselves to this genre in Italy.

Pieter Stevens (Mecheln 1567?–Prague after 1624) was, in 1594, the first North-ern landscapist to come to Prague [figs 1.55, 1.56, 1.59, 1.62, 1.65, 1.66].[154] He had probably received his training in Antwerp. At the beginning of the 1590s, he had travelled through Italy, where he associated with Paul Bril. During his travels, he may also have visited Frankenthal and become acquainted with the work of its school of landscape painting. At the imperial seat, he presented himself as an expe-rienced painter and draughtsman whose style of landscape had been formed under the influence of Bril, Bol and Cleefe. He painted village festivities, scenes which projected deep into the landscape, and were often made unusual by the addition of Antique ruins [fig. 1.61] and numerous figures. In Prague, his style began to change, becoming more expressive, less broad in scope, and losing their distant horizons, but also with a greater emphasis on the use of light as a space-creating element. In his drawings, he was able to capture light and atmospheric phenomena with much greater immediacy and effect. The sharp, linear strokes of his Italian sketches were replaced by fine lines and lush washes. Stevens was inspired by land-scape painters who had entered the service of the court at the beginning of the sev-enteenth century and by Jan Brueghel the Elder, who had visited Prague in 1604.

Stevens was attracted by the city as a motif [fig. 1.70]. His collection of views of European cities was made – judging by the numbering and similarity of tech-nique – after 1604 as an album probably intended for the Emperor.[155] They were not classical city vistas, but rather interesting scenes of city quarters, riverside spots and the outskirts. They were not made in the open air, but were composed (like Stevens's paintings) and refined in the studio. Despite the influence of his 're-alist' colleagues, Stevens did not abandon completely the compositional schemes and means of expression he had come to know in the Netherlands and had culti-vated in Italy. He even passed them on to other generations of painters in his fam-ily, which had settled in Prague and, with the title von Steinfels, worked there till the eighteenth century.[156]

Another painter who found employment at the imperial court with his land-scape drawings was Aegidius Sadeler (Antwerp ca. 1570–Prague 1629), who settled in Prague in 1597.[157] Sadeler made his name mostly as an outstanding engraver and draughtsman and also, it seems, as an interesting painter. He had received his training under his uncles Jan and Raphael, and had moved with them from Antwerp to Frankfurt and Munich, where he settled with Hans von Aachen and Joris Hoefnagel; for several years beginning in 1588, he collaborated closely with them. At the beginning of the 1590s, Sadeler went to Italy, where he spent much time drawing alone; he learned the art of the landscape by copying Bril's landscapes as engravings, and practised the art of figurative painting by copying the composi-tions of the well-known Italian painters Raffael, Parmigianino, Titian and Tintoret-to. Sandrart, who was his student, wrote that Sadeler even back then excelled at transcribing with a burin all the subtleties of the brush-work of other masters. In

1.44 HANS VON AACHEN
Curriculum vitae christianae
1589
[Prague, Národní galerie v
Praze, Grafická sbírka]

[39]

[41]

Prague, Sadeler applied himself in a variety of areas. Working from his own models and those of his colleagues at the court, he seems to have been able to transfer motifs to metal plates as mirror images without using the usual technique of engraving through; as a result, the prints were the same way round as their models. Rudolf considered the copper plates from which Sadeler printed to be works of art in their own right and thus, together with Dürer's plates, they occupied a special place in the *Kunstkammer*. Among them was a portrait of Rudolf from 1603 based on a model by von Aachen.[158] Sadeler himself was an excellent portraitist, and in his drawings and prints he captured the likenesses of a number of important personalities who came through Prague [fig. 1.60]. Particularly when he was portraying a person to whom he was bound by friendship (for example, J. M. Wacker), or if he was taken with an interesting face (as in the case of S. Bathory), he managed to capture more than a merely physical likeness. Under the influence of Rudolfine painters, Sadeler's figurative style also changed gradually, developing very individually and, mainly in the final two decades, taking on an increasingly expressive 'Flemish' form [fig. 1.63]. A similar transformation of style seems to have occured in his painting, judging from works which have been attributed to him.[159] Apart from Sadeler's own oeuvre, his reproductions of the work of his colleagues at the imperial court are essential for understanding Rudolfine art, particularly in the cases where the originals are no longer extant.

In the final two decades of the sixteenth century, painters at the court covered the majority of genres which interested the Emperor. The distinguishing features of its members were their transmontane origin, Italian training, the ability to influ-

1.48 HANS VON AACHEN
Portrait of an Unknown Nobleman (Hermann Christoph von Rusworm?)
Ca. 1604
[Budapest, Szépmüvészeti Múzeum]

1.47 HANS VON AACHEN
Allegory of the Turkish Wars: The Conquest of Györ (Raab) 29 March 1598
1603–04
[Budapest, Szépmüvészeti Múzeum]

[Preceding pages]

1.45 HANS VON AACHEN
Head of a Girl (Portrait of the Artist's Daughter)
1612
[Prague, Sbírky Pražského hradu]

1.46 HANS VON AACHEN
The Three Graces
1604
[Bucharest, The National Museum of Art of Romania]

1.49 HANS VON AACHEN
Tarquinius and Lucretia
1600–05
[Vienna, Kunsthistorisches
Museum, Gemäldegalerie]

ence one another and their friendships which preceded their arrival in Prague. The Emperor granted them extraordinary freedom in their work. He so valued painting that in 1595, he used his prerogative to raise it to one of the liberal arts. Most of the work of his court painters was intended to decorate the palace, particularly the new rooms for his collections.

Painters, however, were not the only ones to gain the Emperor's favour. From 1593 onwards, Erasmus Habermel (?–Prague 1606) was employed at the court. He was a maker of 'astronomical and geometrical' instruments [fig. 1.64].[160] We do not know where he trained, but this outstanding mechanic and mathematician (and talented engraver) came to Prague even before obtaining a position at the court. Only a part of the more than 140 pieces signed by him ended up in the Emperor's collections, because Habermel had other patrons as well. But his largest work, a sextant which served astronomers at Prague Castle, never left Prague [fig. 1.67].[161] He married Suzanne Solis, sister-in-law of the painter Virgil Solis; she had a house and a shop with clocks at Prague Castle. The link with Solis might have been important in Habermel's other work. His instruments excel in their simplicity and elegance. The engraved numbers, letters and technical data were executed with such virtuosity that they comprise the instruments' natural decoration and are in perfect harmony with the finely engraved ornamentation which might have found its inspiration in Solis' prints.[162]

Christoph Margraf (in Prague 1595-1612), a court clockmaker, was among the Rudolfine master craftsmen who formed a link between the artists' colony at the

1.51 HANS VON AACHEN
Rudolf II
After 1602
[Budapest, Szépmüvészeti
Múzeum]

1.50 HANS VON AACHEN
Bacchus, Ceres and Cupid
Ca. 1600
[Vienna, Kunsthistorisches
Museum, Gemäldegalerie]

imperial court and its learned sister, and in their work combined technical inventions with superb artistic work.[163] All we know about him is that he was the inventor of the so-called 'Kugellaufuhr' based on Galileo's discovery that a ball on a slanted surface moves constantly with the same speed. Margraf used this principle to measure time and made clocks in which the motion of an ivory ball moving along a precisely calculated track of stretched-out wires is only one of the many spectacles on offer. The clocks' opulent and surprising ornamentation is the work of Margraf in collaboration with the court painters and sculptors. He was also rewarded for the invention of a pump used in mining and is listed in the inventory of the *Kunstkammer* as the maker of a musical automaton.

Musical automata were imported mostly from Augsburg for the imperial collection; Hans Schlottheim was one of the importers.[164] One automaton, the most advanced musical machine of its time, was built by the organist and composer Hans Leo Hassler, who was granted an imperial privilege for his invention.[165]

Also working with complicated techniques were members of the Castrucci family, who came to Prague in the 1590s to make so-called *commessi in pietre dure*.[166] They laid together, according to colour and shape, small (barely half a centimetre thick) yet strong polished tablets of precious stone, to make pictures of landscapes [fig. 1.71], animals, figures and decorative elements of all kinds. These small stone pictures adorned the doors of cabinets, the sides of little chests and table-tops, but also existed independently as works to be hung on the wall. Sending Bohemian stones to Florence for preparation took too long and deprived Rudolf of the opportunity of watching the production of these elaborate works. The imperial Water Mill in Bubeneč was technically well equipped for this task. Thus in 1596, Cosimo Castrucci appeared in Prague and was joined two years later by his son Giovanni.

1.52 HANS VREDEMAN DE VRIES
*Palace Architecture with
Musicians*
1596
[Vienna, Kunsthistorisches
Museum, Gemäldegalerie]

[45]

They mostly made landscapes, and their names are linked especially with views of Prague Castle. A round table with the imperial eagle in its centre was still being worked on when the French lawyer Esprinchard visited Prague in 1597; he wrote that it was also the work of the Castruccis.[167] The last mention of Giovanni Castrucci in Prague is from 1615, but it seems that his workshop remained in operation under his son Cosimo, who is recorded as still being in Prague in 1622.[168]

At Rudolf's court, goldsmiths also had high status. Apart from the obligatory gifts, they also created masterpieces for the imperial collections. At the end of the sixteenth century, Rudolf prepared an extraordinary order for them: a new imperial crown was to be constructed. Zacharias Glockner had been involved mostly in the making of gold chains, and Anton Schweinberger had been creating extraordinarily plastic decoration. For such a weighty task, they therefore enlisted a third artisan, Jan Vermeyen (Brussels before 1559–Prague 1606).[169] Vermeyen came from a family of painters and had studied in Antwerp; in 1589, he moved to Frankfurt and in 1597 became a goldsmith to the court of Rudolf [figs 1.68, 1.69]. He is usually called *Juwelier* (jeweller), which means that he was ideally qualified to work on the Emperor's crown. There no longer exists a direct source of information about its construction; we have only indirect evidence from information concerning the search for suitable stones, the summoning of the diamond-cutters to Prague and the doubling of Vermeyen's pay in 1602, when the crown was completed.[170]

The crown represented a genuine *Gesamtkunstwerk*, a perfect whole of masterfully set stones, opulent enamelling and adept goldsmith's work. The lappets were formed by four convex triangles decorated with reliefs whose subjects are unique

1.54 MATTHÄUS GUNDELACH
The Vision of Ezechiel
By tradition, ca. 1610
[Zdice, ňímskokatolická farnost]

1.55 PIETER STEVENS
*Landscape with Woodcutters
(January)*
1607
[Prague, Národní galerie v
Praze, Grafická sbírka]

1.56 PIETER STEVENS
Landscape with a Bridge
Ca. 1600
[Prague, Národní galerie v
Praze, Grafická sbírka]

on an object of this sort. They depicted Rudolf at his Hungarian, Bohemian and imperial coronations; in the fourth scene, he was celebrated as peace-maker and conqueror of the Turks. While the choice of stones corresponded to the usual symbolism of sovereigns' crowns, the reliefs were conceived with Rudolf himself as the central theme. The reliefs also demonstrated that the crown was intended as the personal symbol of Rudolf's power rather than the official insignia of state. The question of who the artist of the relief decoration might have been has led to speculation but to no convincing conclusion. In the inventory of the Rudolfine *Kunstkammer*, however, Vermeyen is mentioned as the maker of the little wax models; he was also a good draughtsman and thus was able to master without difficulty some of the parts of Rudolf's crown. He worked exclusively with gold, so today most of the mounts of vessels crafted by Ottavio Miseroni and of cups made of bezoar and horn are ascribed to him [fig. 1.29]. Rudolf's crown, however, was unquestionably his most important work.[171]

In the 1590s, there was an even greater number of people buying *objets d'art* and rare materials for Rudolf from all over Europe. Rudolf's correspondence with his vice-chancellor, Rudolf Coraduz, during the latter's sojourn in Rome provides an interesting description of the complicated negotiations and tremendous range of interests involved in searching for appropriate objects for the imperial collections. Coraduz complained that many opportunities to buy things were being missed because the Emperor lacked a permanent representative in Rome. He sought a suitable informant and adviser who could obtain lists of collections being offered for sale, and he also saw to the quality of works of art, because the Emperor was satisfied with copies only if the original was absolutely unobtainable. Coraduz was advised by Adrian de Vries and Josef Heintz the Elder, who were living at the time in Italy and were themselves also active as buyers. Italy, of course, was not the only source of exhibits for the imperial collections. *Objets d'art* and rare creations of nature came from all over Europe and the New World. In Rudolf's *Kunstkammer*, there was also porcelain from China and all sort of objects from India, Persia, Turkey and Egypt, to name but a few of the countries of origin.[172] Rather unclear in

1.57 HANS VON AACHEN
A Deer Hunt
Ca. 1585 (?)
[Dresden, Staatliche Kunstsammlungen,
Kupferstich-Kabinett]

this respect is the role of Ottavio Strada, whose job as court antiquary undoubtedly also involved acquisitions.[173] More frequently, however, he was offering his own collections for sale, and because of his publishing activity he got along well with the group of scholars working at Rudolf's court in the 1590s.

Some of them worked in the bureaucracy, but felt drawn to the society of artists and scholars at the Castle. Among Rudolf's confidants was Johann Barvitius, who from the mid-1590s served as the Emperor's *Geheimsekretär*.[174] He was an extremely well-educated humanist born in the Netherlands, where he had also received his schooling; he had a brilliant mastery of Latin, which was the language he used for the Emperor's correspondence mainly with various men of learning. He arranged and undersigned privileges for the books whose publication Rudolf supported. He befriended and looked after Tycho Brahe, Kepler, the poetess Elisabeth Jane Weston (known as Westonia) and many others. Barvitius dedicated an altarpiece by Hans von Aachen to the church of St Salvator. His ability was also valued by Emperor Matthias. Like Barvitius, Johann Matthäus Wacker von Wackenfels was showered with gratitude and many dedications to interesting works.[175] This lawyer, who was a councillor to the Silesian Exchequer, interested the Emperor so much that Rudolf ennobled him and summoned him to Prague. Wacker became a court

1.58 HANS VREDEMAN DE VRIES
Palace Courtyard with Bathers
Ca. 1596
[Vienna, Kunsthistorisches
Museum, Gemäldegalerie]

1.61 PIETER STEVENS
Landscape with Roman Ruins
1604–07
[Dresden, Staatliche Kunstsammlungen, Gemäldegalerie
Alte Meister]

1.59 PIETER STEVENS
Landscape with Pond
Early 17th century
[Budapest, Szépmüvészeti
Múzeum]

1.60 AEGIDIUS SADELER
*Carlo Gaudenzio Madruzzi,
Bishop of Trento*
1610
[Budapest, Szépmüvészeti
Múzeum]

councillor and Rudolf's adviser on legal matters; he took part in all interesting state and political negotiations, in which he employed his diplomatic talent and tremendous knowledge of languages. Thanks to his great learning in various fields of science and scholarship he was a good partner in conversation with scholars at Rudolf's court; he loved history and art, and he wrote verse. One of his poem commemorates the death of Rudolf and was published with illustrations by Egidius Sadeler depicting two eagles and a lion leaving Earth with their master; they are bearing the Emperor up to heaven to be among the gods of Antiquity where, because of his deeds, he truly belongs.[176]

In 1598, Jakob Typotius, a Fleming who had studied in Italy and had published several books devoted to questions of the various forms of state, justice, ethics and legality arrived in Prague; he preferred a strong empire as the guardian of Christian culture.[177] His most important work from Prague comprised the commentaries to two volumes of emblems of emperors, kings, dukes, princes and members of the clergy; their prototypes were re-etched by Aegidius Sadeler and prepared and published by Ottavio Strada as *Symbola divina et humana*.[178] Only posthumously and thanks to Jessenius was Typotius's theory of emblematics, *De Hierographia libri duo*, published in 1618.[179] The emblems and sacred symbols are not accessible to every one. Everything profane contains a deeper meaning, asserted Typotius, and the wise are able to recognize, interpret, and thus reveal the mystery of divine creation. The imperial collections served as a fount of wisdom which Typotius was able to tap for his study of emblematics.

Several such studies of considerable importance emerged at Prague Castle at this time. In 1592, Adam Zálužanský published his *Methodi Herbarii libri III,* in which he endeavours to make a systematic ordering of botany and classification of plant species.[180] Rudolf's doctor Godefridus Steeghius (Versteegh) devoted himself in a similar way to medicine and appended his book with a detailed index to facilitate orientation in it.[181]

At the very end of the century, the famous Danish astronomer Tycho Brahe came to Prague, bringing with him not only rare instruments but also extensive records of his observations of celestial bodies. He did not accept Copernicus's teachings, but, thanks to his own observations, knew that not even the Ptolomeic system was not exact. His untimely death in Prague prevented him from drawing the correct conclusions. At the time of his death he was Kepler's assistant, and Kepler, using his observations, arrived at conclusions which have remained valid ever since. The Royal Summer Palace, which had for a short period served as the site of Brahe's astronomical observations, was turned by the Emperor into a sort of museum of astronomy; there, among the portraits of famous astronomers and their patrons, Tycho Brahe, too, received a place of honour.[182]

Johannes Kepler (Weil 1571–Regensburg 1630) came to Prague in 1600. Unlike the dignified Brahe, Kepler was not particularly assertive.[183] In terms of knowledge, however, he did not fall behind Kepler. Precise measuring enabled him to make great astronomical discoveries. Nor did he shun astrology, though he was aware of its pitfalls and feared its misuse, particularly concerning the Emperor. He demonstrated that the planets move along elliptical orbits, and he also became the founder of modern optics and discovered a star; at the same time, however, as a typical representative of Rudolfine pansophy he sought to discover the relationship between the profane and sacred worlds. It is remarkable that he, as the most brilliant scholar at Rudolf's court and linked by bonds of friendship with artists, men of learning and scholars in Prague and beyond, was unable to develop a more intimate relationship with the Emperor. And yet he admired Rudolf immensely as a charismatic figure who was gifted with great internal strength and was able to achieve the almost impossible in politics. According to Kepler, only a definitive victory over Turkey stood in the way of Rudolf becoming ruler of the world.[184]

1.63 PIETER STEVENS
Venus with the Lute Player
Ca. 1600
[Paris, Collection Frits Lugt, Institut Néerlandais]

1.62 PIETER STEVENS
Rocky Landscape with a Goat Hunt
After 1600
[Copenhagen, Den kgl. Malerei- og Skultursamling Statens Museum for Kunst]

1.65 PIETER STEVENS
Landscape with a Watermill
Ca. 1610
[Prague, Sbírky Pražského
hradu]

1.64 ERASMUS HABERMEL
Equinoctial Ring-Dial with a
Stand
Ca. 1600
[Prague, Uměleckoprůmyslové
muzeum v Praze]

The first twelve years of the new century, the last period of Rudolf's life, no matter how problematic and complicated politically, represented the full blossoming of the imperial seat at Prague Castle. In 1600, Rudolf exchanged a palazzo on Hradčany Square, which he had confiscated from Lobkovic, for the Rožmberk palazzo at the Castle, and thus gained another large complex with a beautiful garden, comparable with the imperial buildings. The following year he had renovations carried out and a new corridor built which would link it with the Vladislav Hall. While Rudolf's picture collection already had its own rooms, the sculpture collection still lacked a dignified place at the Castle. At the beginning of the century, therefore, planning began for the New Building in connection with the Spanish Hall. It comprised two floors of the architecturally imposing stables and enormous hall above it, which was divided by niches and decorated with ornate stucco work. It was most probably designed by Giovanni Maria Filippi, an architect who had entered the service of the court at the beginning of the seventeenth century.[185] Filippi, who came from Dasindo in upper Italy, had trained in Rome where he then worked for a period. He was evidently the person who had the final word in all the projects realized at the Castle till he left Prague in 1616. He has been attributed with having designed the New Hall, and also the architectural decoration of the upper floor of the New Stables, the Matthias Gateway, improvements to the Bishop's (Mathematician's) Tower and the arcade (only partly realized) on the north side of the second courtyard (an important building which, unfortunately, has for the most part not been preserved in its original form). The only work which can definitely be said to be Filippi's is the *castrum doloris* for Rudolf's tomb, whose appearance we know from a print.[186] Filippi was provided with an executive builder, the ex-patriot Italian Martin Gambarin (Martino Gambarini of Lugano), who worked at the Castle till

1618. The head of building at the Castle was Orazio Fontana of Brusato, who had also made Bohemia his home; he built a sort of small orangery, a 'room for an Indian bird' and a residence for the guard in the pheasantry, also under construction at that time. From 1602 to 1604, the *laboratorium* was built in the little street Vikářská ulička by the Spanish Hall. In 1607 the dome of the White Tower was taken down and replaced by a terrace with a balustrade. Building activity took place even in the Royal Garden, where, apart from the completion of projects already underway, some of the facilities were expanded – for example, the Lion Yard – and some new ones – for example, the Orangery – were begun. Beyond the Castle precinct, not far from the Premonstratensian monastery at Strahov, Rudolf had promised to build a votive church, commemorating the driving out of the plague in 1599 and dedicated to SS Roch and Sebastian.[187] In 1603 Giovanni Battista Bussi of Campione began work on it; later he became the Castle builder, but by the end of Rudolf's life he had completed only the rough structure of the church. The small, historicizing structure, especially the polygonal space ending in three apses, is one of the most interesting examples of church architecture in Bohemia during this period.

The colony of Rudolfine artists grew with the arrival of several important figures in the first decade of the new century; they completed the wide range of activity at the court by entering some of the existing fields of creative activity or providing expertise in hitherto absent ones. In 1603 or 1604, Roelandt Savery (Kortrijk 1576?–Utrecht 1639) arrived in Prague. Rudolf thus finally obtained a landscape artist who would creatively take up the work of the great Dutch master Pieter Bruegel the Elder [fig. 1.72].[188] Savery had trained in Amsterdam under his brother Jacques, a student of Hans Bol, and came to Prague as a mature artist with a wide range of means of expression. He painted village scenes, woodland and rocky country and animals [figs 1.76–1.78]; he was also among the first to paint flower still-lifes. Though the compositions of his early works may have comprised individual motifs along the traditional three-plane scheme, in Prague he was already orientated to smaller landscape scenes. He prepared for his paintings by means of studies drawn in the open air. These splendid ink and chalk drawings, often capturing the

1.67 ERASMUS HABERMEL
Sextant
1600
[Prague, Národní technické muzeum]

1.66 PIETER STEVENS
Rocky Landscape with an Inn
After 1604
[Rotterdam, Museum Boijmans van Beuningen]

1.70 PIETER STEVENS
*The Čertovka River under
Charles Bridge*
1604–07
[Prague, Muzeum hl. m.
Prahy]

1.68 MISERONI WORKSHOP
JAN VERMEYEN (mounting)
Covered Goblet
Ca. 1600
[Copenhagen, The Royal
Danish Collection at Rosen-
borg Palace]

1.69 MISERONI WORKSHOP
JAN VERMEYEN (mounting)
Moorish Girl
1560–1600; mounting 1602–08
[Vienna, Kunsthistorisches
Museum, Kunstkammer]

scenery of the Castle environs, Petřín and Divoká Šárka, inspired the Emperor to send Savery to the Tyrolean Alps to draw and thus perhaps record the places which Rudolf had travelled through years before on his way to Spain and then back to Vienna.[189] This wealth of drawings was then used by Savery in his paintings *Woodland Interiors* and *Rocky Landscapes*, whose only living subjects are the small-scale pilgrims, peasants, woodcutters and animals. His studies and paintings of animals were also drawn from live models provided by the imperial menagerie, the Stag Moat and the royal preserves rich in game and wildfowl.

Prague, too, became an interesting landscape motif for Savery [fig. 1.73]. In his drawings, apart from several typical vistas, he recorded scenes of daily life, various secluded parts of Prague, houses and their courtyards, riverbanks, and the ordinary people of the city. The painter studied them with the thoroughness of a modern-day ethnographer, noticing the material and colour of their clothing.[190] Savery's Prague studies are a unique cultural-historical document on life in the imperial seat and its appearance [fig. 1.75]. They were an inspiration to Václav Hollar in his similar unofficial scenes of Prague. Savery's floral still-lifes and animal paintings initiated the development of this genre in Netherlandish art of the first half of the seventeenth century.

In the same period as Savery, Paulus van Vianen (Utrecht ca. 1570–Prague 1613) arrived in Prague. He was an outstanding goldsmith, who after completing his training in his hometown set out for France, Italy and Germany in search of further knowledge.[191] Before entering the service of the Emperor in 1603, he worked for Archbishop Wolf Dietrich von Raitenau in Salzburg. The journey to Prague led van Vianen through Alpine country which enchanted him and inspired him to record some of the stops along the way, and his sketchbook is full of panoramas and fascinating places. These nearly photographic recollections of the journey were sometimes used by van Vianen as landscape motifs in the backgrounds of his goldsmith work. In Prague, his passion for recording his surroundings did not wane in his drawings, which were free of all conventions of the day. His landscape studies, with their woodland and city motifs, had an enormous influence on his colleagues

in the service of the court, especially on the landscape artists who were inspired not only by his range and efforts to capture local atmosphere but also by his subtlety. He was similarly influenced by the son of a famous father, Jan Brueghel the Elder, who visited Prague in 1604 and brought back from there a number of drawings with Prague motifs, which he later incorporated into his paintings.[192]

Van Vianen was active at the imperial court, however, mainly as a goldsmith; he excelled in the technique of beating gold and silver.[193] He was able to impose upon metal the softness and malleability of wax, as is shown by his numerous plaques with mythological and religious motifs in whose composition he sometimes used Prague motifs for his landscape backgrounds. For the imperial *Kunstkammer* he created vessels as well as plaques, and he was also a master of mounts conceived as sculpture. A jasper jug, cut perhaps by Ottavio Miseroni, has a lid decorated by van Vianen with a small sculpture of a Nereid; the base of the vessel is decorated with signs of the zodiac [fig. 1.79].[194] He was a surprisingly versatile artist who was also able to paint. Apart from a small painting in which he recorded himself at work on a portrait of Hans von Aachen in the presence of Adrian de Vries, he also recorded in paint an extraordinary historical event he had witnessed the Passau troops' attack on Prague's Lesser Town.[195]

The friendly relationship among the artists at Rudolf's court, close collaboration and mutual assistance were the predominant features of life at the imperial seat. At the end of 1601, Hans van Aachen presented the Emperor with several miniatures painted by Daniel Fröschl, an artist staying at von Aachen's home at that very moment [fig. 1.83]. Fröschl (Augsburg 1563–Prague 1613) had been trained at home, but had already spent several years in the service of the Medici, occupied predominantly with illustrations for a botanical and zoological compendium.[196] Using the subtle technique of the miniature painter, he was also able to copy the work of the great masters, for instance Correggio and Michelangelo. Fröschl's work intrigued the Emperor so much that he offered him a position at the court, while allowing him to continue to work in Florence for a few more years. In 1604, the painter settled permanently in Prague and continued making miniature copies of the work of foreign masters. New impulses to work were provided by the imperial collections, particularly the work of Dürer, which he transformed and 'improved' in a fascinating way. He was also influenced by the work of his colleagues at court, mainly by von Aachen [fig. 1.57].[197] From 1607 onwards, however, Fröschl had little

1.72 ROELANT SAVERY
Distant Valley
Ca. 1607
[Hamburg, Hamburger Kunsthalle]

1.73 ROELANT SAVERY
Inn and Cottages on the Outskirts of Prague
1603–05
[Edinburgh, National Gallery of Scotland]

1.71 GIOVANNI CASTRUCCI WORKSHOP
View of Hradčany and the Lesser Town
After 1601, frame dated later
[Prague, Uměleckoprůmyslové muzeum v Praze]

1.74 BARTOLOMEUS SPRANGER
JAN MULLER
The Adoration of the Shepherds
After 1606
[Prague, Národní galerie v Praze]

1.75 ROELANT SAVERY
The Invasion of Prague 15
February 1611
1611–12
[Belgium, P. Verhagen]

time left for painting; he had become the custodian of the imperial collections and apart from organizing them, he was entrusted with inventorying them. His records of objects stored in the so-called *Kunstkammer* are still extant in part.[198] In this, Fröschl showed himself not only to be a connoisseur of the material he managed and a supervisor of the comings and goings of individual works, but he also provided some objects with small drawings. It is only to be regretted that the same inventories for the other parts of the imperial collection have not survived.

On the recommendation of his colleagues, Matthäus Gundelach (Hesse 1566?– Augsburg 1654) entered the service of the Emperor [fig. 1.88]. He was a painter, probably trained in Cassel, who first appeared in Prague in 1593.[199] His arrival is usually seen in connection with the first visit to the imperial seat in 1592 of the outstanding clockmaker and mathematician Jost Bürgi. Gundelach's first engagement – judging from his early drawings – was in the studio of Bartholomeus Spranger, where he seems to have helped in the realization of large painting cycles, for example for the convent of St George. That is when the painted copy of Spranger's *Adoration of the Shepherds* might have been made, which Gundelach signed with his monogram.[200] After 1600, Gundelach probably found similar employment in Heintz's workshop. Under Heintz's supervision, Gundelach gradually worked his way to his own form of expression. His *Susanna and the Elders* is still greatly under Spranger's influence [fig. 1.85]; the small *Adam and Eve*, though, is already in the spirit of Heintz [fig. 1.82].[201] When Heintz died in 1609, Gundelach obtained his position as court painter, inherited his studio, married his widow and became the guardian of his children. He remained in Prague for a few years after the death of Rudolf, and apart from working for Emperor Matthias, he also had other patrons. *Ezekiel's Vision*, with its effective treatment of light, and the altarpiece depicting the *Assumption* for the Fürstenbergs demonstrate that already in Prague Gundelach was inclining towards a new early Baroque style, whose rep-

1.76 ROELANT SAVERY
Forest Path beside a Stream
1611–13
[Prague, Národní galerie v
Praze]

1.77 ROELANT SAVERY
Deer Chased by Hunters
1610–13
[Prague, Národní galerie v
Praze]

resentative he then became in Augsburg, where he settled permanently in 1617.[202]

From 1604, another painter, Jeremias Günther (dates unknown), found employ at Rudolf's court.[203] One of his signed drawings is a precise copy of Heintz's print with *Artistotle and Phyllis*, and is dated 1600.[204] Günther, like Gundelach, had been in Prague before he entered the Emperor's service, and he had also worked as an assistant in the studio of an established master. Two signed paintings, *Rudolf II* and *Empress Anna*, show him as a portraitist.[205] Günther started from the prototypes of Hans von Aachen, and he saw to the production of official portraits which made their way to various courts as gifts. The rest of his work we know only from various inventories and requests for payment. It must, however, have been extremely interesting, because Günther painted not only copies, including some of works by Bruegel and Bassano, but also miniatures on parchment and ivory, large mythological paintings of his own invention, still lifes and genre scenes.[206] In an inventory from 1620, there is mention of his painting on wood covered with fine grooves painted on both sides. Looking at it from one side yielded an allegory of Rome, and from the other the imperial eagle.[207] This type of deceptive painting may possibly have been the invention of Günter's colleague at the court, Paul de Roy (Rog?), whose proudly signed and dated painting of Rudolf, from one side, and Ferdinand I and Maximilian II, from the other, is one of the oldest existing examples of this pe-

culiar *trompe-l'oeil* technique.[208] Judging from the subject, this painting might be the key that opened the way for the painter to employment in the service of the Emperor.

At the beginning of the century, Rudolf finally convinced a sculptor whose work already enhances the imperial collection to make Prague his home.[209] Adrian de Vries (The Hague ca. 1545–Prague 1626) was recommended to the Emperor by Giambologna, in whose employ de Vries had been in the late 1570s and early 1580s. Vries completed his first works for the Emperor in 1593, the date of Jan Muller's engravings based on some of them. Two sculptures of *Psyche*, which in 1602 still adorned the lower hall of the Royal Summer Palace, were moved together with others to the new sculpture gallery, after the completion of the New Hall.[210] After he had definitively settled in Prague de Vries began to concentrate on more intimate sculptures [figs 1.89, 1.90] which found their place in the *Kunstkammer*. Among them are the allegory of the triumphant Empire, reliefs with scenes of the Turkish Wars [fig. 1.91] and Rudolf introducing the arts into Bohemia, as well as little sculptures of horses, whose live models were in the nearby imperial stables.[211] Rudolf was portrayed by de Vries three times, twice heroically in large busts, and once in a smaller bust with a more civil, intimate air.[212] Vries got on well with his painter colleagues; his works [fig. 1.86] influenced them and theirs influenced him, particularly in cases where he transferred the prototypes into sculptures.[213] After the death of Rudolf, de Vries received a superb offer whose realization kept him in Prague till his death in 1626. He returned to monumental work when he made a set of sculptures to decorate the fountains in the garden of the Waldstein Palace.[214]

Another sculptor employed by Rudolf in 1605 remained at court after the death of his patron. Giovanni Battista Quadri (d. Vienna 1618) was evidently also a disciple of Giambologna. In collaboration with Hans Reichl in Brixen, he became a specialist in terracotta and stucco.[215] He was summoned to Prague for the specific task of decorating the New Hall, where, together with his assistants, he carried out the stucco work of the walls and created larger-than-lifesize sculptures of plaster, stucco and terracotta for the niches. The only extant work of his, a stucco relief of the *Adoration of the Magi* intended for the chapel at the imperial country seat in Brandýs nad Labem, is testimony to the stylistic affinity with de Vries's work [fig. 1.87]. The 1607–11 *Kunstkammer* inventory mentions a number of his sculptures which are unfortunately no longer extant. Quadri worked in his studio located between the *Kunstkammer* and the New Hall. His assistant and successor in the service of the Emperor, Heidelberger, left us the information that Quadri modeled in wax.[216] Possibly under Quadri's supervision, Heidelberger carried out the upper part of the inscription plaque at the Matthias Gateway which, unlike the older, lower part carved in stone, is of stucco.[217]

Rudolf's interest in small sculpture was also satisfied by other masters, for example Ottavio Miseroni with his little sculptures carved out of precious stones, the two Abondios who worked in wax and bronze, and some goldsmiths. At the court there were, of course masters especially oriented to sculpture, for example Nikolaus Pfaff (Nürnberg 1566–Prague after 1610), who was Rudolf's court carver from 1601 onwards.[218] He worked in ivory, horn and amber, and in the inventory of the *Kunstkammer* he is listed as the maker of an ivory relief of *Danaë* and a little sculpture of *Venus with Cupid*.[219] This source also mentions a *Mercury* in a chariot drawn by

1.78 ROELANT SAVERY
Forest Cascade with Tobias and the Angel
1605
[Dessau, Anhaltische Gemäldegalerie]

1.79 OTTAVIO MISERONI (?)
PAULUS VAN VIANEN (mounting)
Ewer
1608; ewer ca. 1600
[Vienna, Kunsthistorisches Museum, Kunstkammer]

1.81 PAULUS VAN VIANEN
River Landscape with a Bridge
1604–05
[Budapest, Szépmüvészeti
Múzeum]

1.80 PAULUS VAN VIANEN
River Landscape with Raftsmen
(verso: Roman Ruins)
1603
[Budapest, Szépmüvészeti
Múzeum]

two cocks, which rested on a high, turned stem. Pfaff's name is not mentioned, but the fact that it is this was work is clear from the fine, supple modelling of the human figure and the head of the monster decorating the chariot of this superb composition.[220] The base of the sculpture is most likely the work of a specialist in using the lathe to turn and carve objects of the most whimsical shapes. In 1599, Georg Wecker, the court turner to the elector of Saxony, set up a workshop for the Emperor at Prague Castle, which served for the shaping of ivory, wood and jasper.[221] This was used by Wecker's son, Hans, who during the last ten years of Rudolf's life worked at the imperial court on various vessels, small boxes and toys.[222] Turning was a pastime of the rich and the powerful – for example, Christian II of Saxony, who gave the Emperor a set of his own hand-made work.[223]

In the inventory of the *Kunstkammer* are listed several paintings of flowers in vases and of landscapes which were finely embroidered with silk thread. They were the creations of the court embroiderer Philipp van den Bossche, who lived in Prague from 1604 to 1615.[224] His daughter Elisabeth and her husband H. Cappelmann worked together with Bossche for the court. Bossche was known as an excellent draughtsman who, apart from executing landscape studies, made his name with a prototype for a splendid large panorama of Prague, engraved by Johannes Wechter and published in 1606 by Aegidius Sadeler.[225] Bossche's drawings are constructed of fine parallel lines, and in their manner of capturing light and atmospheric effects link up with similar studies by van Vianen and Savery. They do not imitate them, though; rather, they have their own specific 'handwriting' which corresponds to their purpose: many of them served as models for embroidery work. Recently, by using them for comparison, it has finally been possible to find the one which formed the background for a wax relief of the *Pietà*.[226] The parallel pen strokes were replaced substituted with tiny stitches, almost invisible to the naked eye, and are reminiscent of light touches of the brush such as one finds on miniatures of the period. The result is a masterpiece of embroidery unsurpassed by any painting. Individual landscapes and flowers from Bossche's workshop must have

1.83 DANIEL FRÖSCHL
Venus and Cupid
1613
[Canada, Frank and Marianne
Seger]

1.82 MATTHÄUS GUNDELACH
Adam and Eve
1605–14 (?)
[Olomouc, soukromá sbírka]

1.84 MATTHÄUS GUNDELACH
Mercury and Herse
1613
Budapest, Szépmüvészeti
Múzeum]

had an even greater effect than the little altar whose veristic wax relief so captures our attention. Its author was certainly a master of modelling in wax, which was the speciality of several artists at Rudolf's court, for example Alessandro Abondio and Hans Vermeyen.[227] Daniel Mignot (Minnot), an engraver of ornaments from Augsburg, is also mentioned as the maker of a small wax portrait of Rudolf, found only recently and hitherto known only from several bronze casts.[228]

Apart from the superb goldsmiths Vermeyen and van Vianen, other outstanding figures appeared in this field before 1612. One was Andreas Osenbruck, a goldsmith who worked in Prague till 1622.[229] His signature adorns the sceptre which went with Rudolf's crown, but which was not finished till the reign of Emperor Matthias and thus carries the latter's monogram. Osenbruck, like Vermeyen, seems mainly to have been a jeweller; apart from work on the imperial insignia he devoted himself to setting in gold cameos from the workshops of the Milanese Miseronis and of Alessandro Masnago. The high quality of his jewellery is evident from the pendants which originally formed a splendid chain and were later used to decorate a monstrance. His masterpiece, however, is undoubtedly Matthias' sceptre, in the fashioning of where continued in the tradition of Vermeyen.

Winter's list of Prague goldsmiths is full of names of those working at the court, of whom we should at least mention Herzig van Bein, Gerhart de Bois, Hans Bull and Hans Hensell, for whom there was no room in the official court planning of personnel, and whose employment was often made legal by ranking them among members of the Emperor's lifeguards, the *Leibtrabanten*.[230] Among them were also some clockmakers [fig. 1.24] – for example, Vilém Thyrhammer of Öttingen and Christoph Schüssler of Augsburg.[231] The clockmaker Michael Schneeberger came to Prague from Schwarzwald, and obtained freedom of the city in 1602; he worked for the Emperor till the end of the decade.[232] The originality and high quality of his clocks suggest that he moved in the circle of the pre-eminent clockmaker Jost Bürgi (Lichtensteig 1552–Cassel 1632), a Swiss who had spent a quarter of a century in Cassel working for the great patron of astronomy, Landgrave Wilhelm IV of Hesse-Cassel, before coming to the court in Prague in 1604.[233] Bürgi was an outstanding clockmaker, an excellent mathematician and constructor of instruments [fig. 1.92]. His clocks excelled in their extraordinary precision, their many technical innovations and superior construction [fig. 1.93], as did his astronomical instruments. On the recommendation of Kepler, Bürgi made a functional model of a valveless pump, the prototype of the water-pump in the decorative fountain at the imperial court. Bürgi and Kepler, however, had mainly mathematics and astronomy in common. In an attempt to simplify astronomical calculations Bürgi discovered the principle of logarithms, but is not credited with this because his tables, completed in Prague, were only published in 1620. When making his observations, Kepler had used Bürgi's sextant, which remained in the *Kunstkammer* until the Josephine auction in 1782. Bürgi's workshop was in Vikárská ulička till the beginning of the 1620s, when he left Prague. The information about it is one of the few pieces of data we have concerning the studios and workshops of court artists and artisans.[234] Most of them were in the Castle precinct so that the Emperor could visit them without difficulty. Also important was their link to the rooms housing the collections, where the court artists went to look for suitable material to work on. That was also where unfinished works were stored till capable artists arrived to finish them.[235] In the last ten

years of the Emperor's life, the collections also acted as a source of information and study material for authors of scholarly publications.

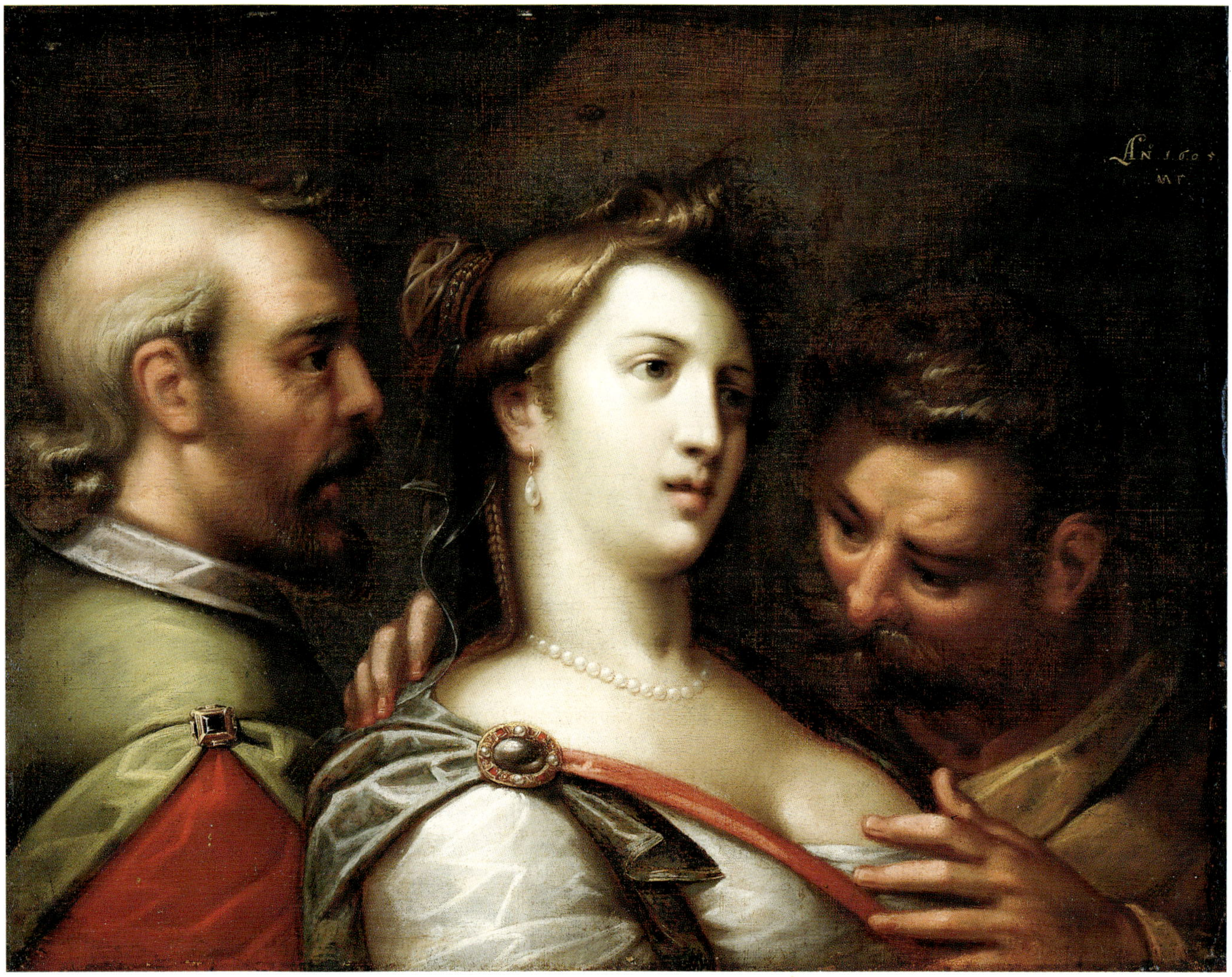

Beginning in 1604, after ten years in the service of Vilém of Rožmberk, Anselmus Boetius de Boodt (Brugge 1550–1632) became personal physician to Rudolf.[236] By studying materials largely by the Emperor's mineral collections, he systematically classified about 600 minerals and described their medicinal qualities and potential magical effects in his book *Gemmarum et Lapidum Historia* (1609).[237] Boodt was, however, also interested in botany and zoology, as is clear from an album of drawings, many of which he made himself. He was also responsible for the commentaries and publishing of a third volume of *Symbola Divina et Humana*, where he shows himself to have been an experienced emblematist.[238]

The imperial collections were an inspiration to Oswald Croll (from 1602 onwards another of Rudolf's physicians) for his *Basilica Chymica* (1608). The first part of this work comprises pansophical speculation on the relationship between microcosm and macrocosm, but its second part provided the basis for modern pharmacology.[239] In a much more speculative and mystical spirit is the book *Atalanta Fugiens* (1619), written by yet another of the Emperor's physicians, Michael Meier (1568–1622). Meier endeavoured here to reveal the way in which the message of an-

1.85 MATTHÄUS GUNDELACH
Susanna and the Elders (Allegory of Touch?)
1605
[Augsburg/Munich, private collection]

[62]

1.86 ADRIAN DE VRIES
Hercules with the Apples of the Hesperides
Ca. 1615
[Prague, Národní galerie v Praze]

cient Egyptian knowledge and the symbolism of Antique myths had been projected into the science and music of his day.[240] This typically pansophical work stands at the opposite pole to the practical textbook of hygiene which Hippolytus Guarinoni dedicated to the Emperor in 1610. It was written in German so as to be accessible to the widest range of readers.[241] A textbook on surgery and the rudiments of anatomy was dedicated to the Emperor by the physician Johann Jessenius (1566–1621), known, among other things, for having performed the first public autopsy in Prague. In 1601, he settled there permanently and befriended the learned men of the court and members of Charles University. In 1617, he became the university's rector. After the death of the Emperor in 1612, Jessenius performed the autopsy and embalmed him. As one of the leaders of the Estates' rebellion, he was executed in Prague in 1621.[242]

Among the numerous physicians at Rudolf's court, a special place was occupied by Johannes Pistorius (Nidda 1546–Prague 1608).[243] He, too, was a figure of many professions and interests. This lawyer, physician, theologian and adept in the cabbala, was originally a Lutheran, then a Calvinist, and finally a Roman Catholic prelate. After the death of Tadeáš Hájek, he was sent to Prague by the Papal court to be Rudolf's confessor and also physician to the Emperor's soul. The Emperor and his 'psychoanalyst' shared an interest in the arts and sciences; their intimate friendship was manifested not only in matters of the Emperor's health but also in the court environment in general. It is thanks to Pistorius that we have a reliable diagnosis of Rudolf's illness: he wrote to Rome that the Emperor was not obsessed, only melancholic, and that there were many malevolent types around him taking advantage of his condition in order to make things worse.[244] Pistorius, though an exponent of the Papal court, was a man of tremendous tolerance and, like the Emperor, did not distinguish between people on the basis of their religion, but according to their knowledge and abilities. He befriended the Lutheran Kepler, and once ended a heated debate about faith with the words 'I shall nevertheless remain your friend and servant because your mathematical talent and exceptional genius deserve as much.'[245]

Like to Pistorius, Heinrich Julius, duke of Brunswick, stood by the Emperor in his last years.[246] From 1607, he settled permanently in Prague; he was president of the privy council and a confident of Rudolf who the delicate political negotiations with, for example, the Emperor's brother Matthias, the Bohemian Estates and with the Passavian troops who invaded Prague in 1610. Duke Heinrich Julius was a great art lover; he loved the theatre and fine arts and provided generous support to artists. He provided Hans von Aachen with regular remuneration on behalf of his court office, and he sent gifted young people from his estate to von Aachen's studio to learn painting.[247]

The last years of Rudolf's life, no matter how connected with the greatest cultural and social heyday of his court, were certainly not among his happiest ones. Under systematic pressure from members of his family, he was forced to yield to Matthias first the Hungarian crown in 1608 and, three years later, the Bohemian crown as well. He was left with only the imperial title, stripped of all power; the ill-considered decision which led to the Passavian troops being invited to Prague only worsened his situation further. Closed within the walls of Prague Castle, he considered moving to Austria and thought about building a large new palace in Stromov-

1.87 GIOVANNI BATTISTA QUADRI
The Adoration of the Magi
Before 1611
[Prague, Sbírky Pražského hradu]

1.88 MATTHÄUS GUNDELACH
Cupid and Psyche
1613
[Munich, Bayerische Staats-
gemäldesammlungen
(Barockgalerie Augsburg)]

ka. He was, however, probably unable to imagine that his collections, which were now finally respectably housed and had in Daniel Fröschl an experienced curator, would have to be moved. When Rudolf died on 20 January 1612, his passing was mourned by those who knew that they had lost one of the most educated and art-loving sovereigns of all time, who, thanks to his special ability to achieve a balance of power between inimical political factions, had been able to maintain a relative cessation of hostilities in the empire during the thirty years of his reign.[248] He was laid to rest without the usual pomp, and within no time his successor, Matthias, had clandestinely begun to move the most valuable items of Rudolf's collections to Vienna for fear that the Bohemian Estates would soon prevent him from doing so. The collections were invaluable; the Venetian envoy Soranzo estimated the number of paintings alone to be over 3,000. During the inventory ordered by Emperor Matthias shortly after the death of Rudolf, the other treasures were (according to Pavel Skála of Zhoř) valued at 17 million ducats.[249]

What Matthias was unable to take to Vienna fell, in 1619, into the hands of the so-called 'Directors', who wanted to sell what they could to finance the Estates' armies.[250] The unexpectedly quick defeat at the Battle of the White Mountain and the flight of the 'Winter King', Friedrich V, prevented them from doing this, yet Rudolf's treasures were not left in peace. Ferdinand II, who had succeeded Matthias on the imperial throne, used them to pay off debts, for example to Maximilian I of Bavaria for his help in putting down the Estates' revolt. Karl von Liechtenstein, the governor of Bohemia (after 1620), borrowed some of the treasures, on a permanent basis, for his own collection. Paintings with erotic subject matter were sold to Daniel de Briers in 1623.[251] Saxon troops took their booty in 1632,[252] and when in 1648 the Swedish army occupied the Lesser Town and Hradčany, their principle destination was Prague Castle and its collections. Queen Christina was disappointed

1.89 ADRIAN DE VRIES
Fawn and Nymph (Venus?)
Before 1588
[Dresden, Staatliche Kunst-
sammlungen, Grünes
Gewölbe]

1.90 ADRIAN DE VRIES
Hercules
1625–26
[Prague, Muzeum hl. m.
Prahy]

with the bountiful booty brought to her – it was missing works by renowned Italian masters which, without her having been informed, had ended up in the imperial collections in Vienna.[253] The rooms of the Castle which had housed the collections were abandoned; all that remained was what the custodians had managed to hide, what had been damaged (Dürer's *Feast of the Rosaries*), what was hidden in the *Kunstkammer* or what could not be transported because of fragility (for example, the sculptures of stucco and terracotta in the New Hall). The majority of these objects remained in the rooms until the Josephine auction in 1782, but some of them still grace Prague Castle to the present day.[254]

The woeful events vexing the Bohemian lands during the Thirty Years' War and the transfer of the imperial seat to Vienna did not mark the end of Prague Castle, however. From 1613 to 1615, during the reign of Emperor Matthias, it underwent reconstruction, and a storey was added to the south city wing and the walled, vaulted gateway above the entrance to the Castle Stairs was completed. The sculptural decoration of the Matthias Gateway was also finished, as well as the Emperor's and Empress's monogram adorning the pavilion (completed in 1617) in the Garden of Paradise. Ferdinand II completed the purchasing of houses by the Gallery Wing and entrusted Giuseppe Mattei, an architect from Vienna, with their reconstruction and incorporation into the existing buildings. Mattei, from 1638 to 1642, constructed, in connection with the imperial palace, a building for the Empress above Maximilian's kitchens. He also proposed the excavation of the so-called New Way, which linked Prague Castle with the street known today as Nerudova. The builder Santino Bossi deserves the credit for its realization. In 1644, the Emperor's chapel was finished in the Romanesque White Tower and dedicated to St Wenceslas.[255]

1.91 ADRIAN DE VRIES
Allegory of the Turkish Wars
Ca. 1603
[Vienna, Kunsthistorisches
Museum, Kunstkammer]

The artists who had worked for Rudolf either died before their patron (for example, Heintz and Spranger) or left Prague immediately upon his death or shortly thereafter (for example, von Aachen, Gundelach, Savery and Alessandro Abondio). Those who remained mostly found other demanding patrons; de Vries, for example, had commissions from Waldstein,[256] and Stevens seems to have worked for Liechtenstein. Emperor Matthias, Ferdinand II and other patrons provided work for Aegidius Sadeler, who, apart from his extensive engraving work, devoted himself for seventeen more years to the training of young engravers (such as Marco Sadeler and Isaac Major) and at the very least influenced the young Václav Hollar.[257] Well into the second half of the seventeenth century, stonecutters from the Miseroni family were still active at Prague Castle. The reason seems to have been that their workshop's superior technical equipment for the rough and fine cutting of stones could not be transported to Vienna without difficulty; Dionysio and Ferdinand Eusebius Miseroni thus continued to provided the court in Vienna from Prague with vessels, vases, candelabra, tabernacles and other objects of crystal and precious stone [figs 1.96, 1.97].[258] The kinds of work they were now involved in, however, had increased in variety. They supervised various building projects at the Castle, and, after the death of Hans Karl König, they also assumed the office of Custodian. Only at the beginning of the 1620s did Jost Bürgi quit the Emperor's service, remaining in Prague to continue the production of his remarkable clocks.[259] We do not know in what capacity either Giovanni Battista Quadri or his helper Ernst Johann Heidelberger (ca. 1590–ca. 1660)[260] were employed at Prague Castle in the 1620s. The court painters were not assigned particularly important tasks and had fewer opportunities to develop their talents. Two large altarpieces in St Vitus' cathedral are the best examples of the work of Matthias Mayer (his *Crucifixion* with Bohemian patrons and depiction of Ferdinand II with his family)[261] and of Hans Georg Hering (his *Annunciation*).[262] The focal point of their work, as with Heidelberger's, shifted to a different setting, the city.[263]

With the death of Rudolf II, the imperial court lost the powerful magic which had attracted interesting and talented people from all over Europe and which had made the imperial seat into a shrine of the muses and centre of learning [figs 1.94, 1.95]. None of his successors on the imperial throne was as able as Rudolf to create such an inspirational environment or such splendid conditions for creative work, or to appreciate talent and convey a longing for the mysteries of the world to be revealed. Prague Castle, its renowned collections and artists' workshops became a reality for Rudolf's contemporaries, but for the next generation it has already become unattainable. In the centuries to come, the magic of a powerful creative milieu never returned to Prague Castle.

1.92 JOST BÜRGI
Sextant
Ca. 1600
[Prague, Národní technické muzeum]

1.93 JOST BÜRGI
Globe with a Clockwork
Ca. 1585
[Weimar, Stiftung Weimarer Klassik/Herzogin Anna Amalia Bibliothek]

1.94 Funerary Shield of Rudolf II
1612 (?)
[Prague, Sbírky Pražského hradu]

1.95 Inventory of the Tomb of Rudolf II – Cloak
Most likely 1612
[Prague, Sbírky Pražského hradu]

1. On Rudolf II, see, for example, A. Gindely, *Rudolf II. und seine Zeit 1600–1612*, vols I and II (Prague, 1863–65); J. B. Novák, *Rudolf II. a jeho pád* (Prague, 1931); G. von Schwarzenfeld, *Rudolf II.: Der saturnische Kaiser* (Munich, 1961); P. Erlanger, *L Empereur insolite Rudolphe II de Habsbourg (1552–1612)* (Paris, 1971); R. J. W. Evans, *Rudolf II and His World: A Study in Intellectual History, 1576–1612* (Oxford, 1973); K. Vocelka, *Die politische Propaganda Kaiser Rudolfs II. (1576–1612)* (Vienna, 1981); J. Janáček, *Rudolf II. a jeho doba* (Prague, 1987).

2. G. Stöckl, 'Kaiser Ferdinand I. (1503–1564)' in *Gestalter der Geschichte Österreichs* (Innsbruck, Vienna and Munich, 1967), pp. 127–41; W. Hilger, *Ikonographie Kaiser Ferdinands I. (1503–1564)* (Vienna, 1969); P. Sutter Fichtner, *Ferdinand I of Austria: The Politics of Dynasticism in the Age of Reformation* (New York, 1982).

3. Lhotsky, pp. 137–56; E. Scheicher, *Die Kunst- und Wunderkammern der Habsburger* (Vienna, Munich and Zurich, 1979), pp. 62–67.

4. Lhotsky, p. 176; Evans (note 1), p. 118.

5. Winter, pp. 491–92.

6. Lhotsky, p. 149.

7. J. Krčálová, 'Der Prager Hof Ferdinands I. und Maximilians II.' in *Die Kunst der Renaissance und Manierismus in Böhmen* (Prague, 1979), pp. 50–74; J. Krčálová, 'Renesanční architektura v Čechách a na Moravě', *Dějiny českého výtvarného umění*, II:1 (Prague, 1989), pp. 6–29 (contains all the earlier literature).

8. J. Krčálová, 'Die Gärten Rudolfs II.', *Leids Kunsthistorisch Jaarboek*, I (1982): 149–60.

9. Krčálová 1979 (note 7), p. 51; Krčálová 1989 (note 7), pp. 7–9.

10. Krčálová 1979 (note 7), pp. 55–57, 68–73; Kyčálová 1989 (note 7), pp. 9, 13–18.

11. Winter, pp. 163–64; K. Löcher, *Jacob Seisenegger, Hofmaler Kaiser Ferdinands I.* (Munich and Berlin, 1962).

12. The portrait of the young Rudolf in the Picture Gallery, Prague Castle (inv. no. O 311), may also orignate from this period; see J. Neumann, *Obrazárna Prazského hradu* (Prague, 1966), pp. 222–24, cat. no. 57, 223.

13. Winter, pp. 166–67.

14. *Ibid.*, pp. 164–65.

15. *Ibid.*, p. 167.

16. A. Ilg, 'Francesco Terzio, der Hofmaler Erzherzog Ferdinands von Tirol', *JKSAK*, IX (1889): 235–373; Winter, pp. 165–66; Lhotsky, p. 191.

17. Winter, p. 165.

18. Kyčálová 1979 (note 7), p. 52; I. Kořán, 'Renesanční sochařství v Čechách a na Moravě', *Dejiny českého výtvarného umení*, II:1 (Prague, 1989), pp. 116–35 (117).

19. See note 5.

20. Kyčálová 1979 (note 7), p. 74; Korán (note 18), pp. 119–20.

21. Kyčálová 1979 (note 7), p. 53; Kyčálová 1989 (note 7), pp. 9–10.

22. M. Suchomel, 'Štuková výzdoba letohrádku Hvězda', *Umění*, XXI, (1973): 99–116.

23. Winter, pp. 170–71; D. J. Jansen, 'Jacopo Strada (1515–1588): Antiquario della Sacra Cesarea Maesta', *Leids Kunsthistorisch Jaarboek*, I (1982): 57–69 (59).

24. J. Hirn, *Erzherzog Ferdinand II. von Tirol*, vols I and II (Innsbruck, 1885–88).

25. *Dějiny českého divadla*, I (Prague, 1968), pp. 139–40.

26. Lhotsky, pp. 179–202; Scheicher (note 3), pp. 73–135.

27. F. Kenner, 'Die Porträtsammlung des Erzherzogs Ferdinand von Tirol', *JKSAK*, XIV (1893): 35; XV (1894): 147; XVII: 135; XIX (1898): 6.

28. *Tři francouzští kavalíři v rudolfínské Praze* (Prague, 1989), p. 57.

29. Lhotsky, pp. 180–81.

30. Winter, pp. 167–70.

31. Lhotsky, pp. 184–85, 286–89.

32. V. Bibl, *Maximilian II.: der rätselhafte Kaiser* (Hellerau bei Dresden, 1929) (cites all the earlier literature); Katharina Podewils, 'Kaiser Maximilian II. (1564–1576) als Mazen der bildenden Künste und der Goldschmiedekunst', Ph.D. diss., Vienna, 1992; Evans (note 1), pp.118 (Mattioli), 121 (Busbecq).

33. Evans (note 1), pp. 119–120 (Clusius), 89–90 (Crato); von Schwarzenfeld (note 1), pp. 19, 42, 57–59 (Crato).

34. Lhotsky, p. 164.

35. Evans (note 1), pp. 123–28; A. Vantuch, *Ján Sambucus* (Bratislava, 1975); A. Buck (intro.), *J. Sambucus, Emblemata, Antverpiae 1564* (Budapest, 1982).

36. R. von Busch, 'Studien zu deutschen Antikensammlungen des 16. Jahrhunderts', Ph.D. diss., Tübingen, 1973, pp. 193–219 (Jacopo Strada); Jansen (note 23), pp. 57–69; J. Jansen, 'Example and Examples: The Potential Influence of Jacopo Strada on the Development of Rudolphine Art' in *Prag um 1600: Beiträge zur Kunst und Kultur am Hofe Rudolfs II.* (Freren, 1988), pp. 132–46.

37. A. C. van der Boom, ' Tra Principi e Imprese: The Life and Works of Ottavio Strada', in *Prag um 1600* (note 36), pp. 19–23.

38. H. Dressler, 'Alexander Collin', Ph.D. diss., Freiburg, 1969.

39. Kyčálová 1989 (note 7), p. 14.

40. H. Lietzmann, *Das Neugebäude in Wien* (Munich and Berlin, 1987).

41. S. Alfons, *Giuseppe Arcimboldo*, Tidskrift för Konstvetenskap 31 (Malmö, 1957); P. Preiss, *Giuseppe Arcimboldo* (Prague, 1967); T. DaCosta Kaufmann, *Variations on the Imperial Theme in the Age of Maximilian II and Rudolf II* (New York and London, 1978); *Effetto Arcimboldo*, exh. cat. ed. J. David (Milan, 1987); Kaufmann 1988, pp.164–72.

42. *Dějiny českého divadla*, I (Prague, 1968), p.140.

43. L. Vertova, 'Giulio Licinio' in *I pittori Bergamaschi dal XIII al XIX secolo: Il Cinquecento* (Bergamo, 1976), pp. 513–89; Lietzmann (note 40), pp. 148–51.

44. F. Dworschak, *Antonio Abondio* (Trento, 1958).

45. Vienna, Kunsthistorisches Museum, Kunstkammer, inv. no. 3074.

46. R. Schürer, 'Wenzel Jamnitzers Brunnen für Maximilian II.: Überlegungen zu Ikonographie und Zweck', *Anzeiger des Germanischen Nationalmuseums* (1986): 55–59.

47. Winter, pp. 401–2, 441.

48. *Ibid.*, p. 423.

49. Lhotsky, pp. 158–60.

50. For Rudolf II, see *Prag um 1600* (note 36); *Prag um 1600: Kunst und Kultur am Hofe Rudolfs II.*, exh. cat. (Essen and Vienna, 1988).

51. E. Mayer-Löwenschwert, *Der Aufenthalt der Erzherzoge Rudolf und Ernst in Spanien 1564–1571*, Sitzungsberichte der phil.-histor. Klasse der Akademie der Wissenschaften in Wien, CCVI (1927), 5. Abhandlung.

52. German translation: A. Gindely, *Rudolf II. und seine Zeit 1600–1612*, 2nd edn (Prague, 1868), p. 27.

53. E. Fučíková, B. Bukovinská, and I. Muchka, *Umění na dvore Rudolfa II.* (Prague, 1988).

54. Jan Kozel and Michael Petrle z Annabergu, *View of Prague*, woodcut, 1562.

55. Carel van Mander, *Das Leben der niederländischen und deutschen Maler*, trans. and ed. Hanns Floerke (Munich and Leipzig, 1906, vol. II, pp. 153–57.

56. Muchka (note 53), p. 182.

57. *Reisen und Gefangenschaft Hans Ulrich Kraffts*, from a manuscript by Dr. K. D. Haszler, Bibliothek des Literarischen Vereins in Stuttgart, LXI (Stuttgart, 1861), p. 388.

58. Krcálova 1979 (note 7), pp. 71–73; Kyčálová1989 (note 7), p. 171.

59. Kyčálová1989 (note 7), p.176; Muchka (note 53), pp. 185, 186.

60. Kyčálová1989 (note 7), pp. 21–22.

61. Kyčálová1989 (note 7), pp. 164–65.

62. Essen and Vienna 1988, cat. no. 439.

63. G. Heinz, 'Studien zur Porträtmalerei an den Höfen der österreichischen Erblande', *JKSW*, LIX (1963): 99–224.

64. Prague, Národní muzeum v Praze, inv. no. 40155; Essen–Vienna 1988, cat. no. 193.

65. Národní galerie v Praze, inv. no. K 5338; Essen–Vienna 1988, cat. no. 188.

66. Kaufmann 1988, cat. nos 2.18–2.21.

67. A. Beyer, *Giuseppe Arcimboldo: Figurinnen, Kostüme und Entwürfe für höfische Feste* (Frankfurt am Main, 1983).

68. T. DaCosta Kaufmann, 'Arcimboldo and Propertius: A Classical Source for Rudolf II as Vertumnus', *Zeitschrift für Kunstgeschichte*, XXXVIII (1985): 117–23; Essen–Vienna 1988, cat. no. 111.

69. On Licinio, see above, note 43; Winter, p. 23.

70. Prague Castle, St Vitus' cathedral, Thun chapel; Fučíková (note 53), p. 182, pl. 127.

71. E. Diez, 'Der Hofmaler Bartholomäus Spranger', *JKSAK*, XXVIII (1909–10): 93–151; A. Niederstein, 'Das graphische Werk des Bartholomäus Spranger', *Repertorium für Kunstwissenschaft*, LII (1931): 7–33; K. Oberhuber, 'Die stilistische Entwicklung im Werk Bartholomäus Sprangers', Ph.D. diss., Vienna, 1958; M. Henning, *Die Tafelbilder Bartholomäus Sprangers (1546–1611)* (Essen, 1987); Kaufmann 1988, pp. 249–79.

72. Lietzmann (note 40), pp. 151–58.

73. Prague, Premonstratensian Monastery at Strahov, inv. no. 542; Essen–Vienna 1988, cat. no. 152.

74. J. Neumann, 'Kleine Beiträge zur rudolfinischen Kunst und ihre Auswirkungen', *Umění*, XIII (1970): 142–51.

75. Fučíková (note 53), pp. 191–92; Essen–Vienna 1988, cat. nos 156, 157.

76. Essen–Vienna 1988, cat. no. 159.

77. Essen–Vienna 1988, cat. no.158.

78. Kaufmann 1988, cat. nos 20.14–20.17.

79. *Venus and Adonis*: Duchcov château; *The Suicide of Sophonisba*: Prague, Národní galerie v Praze, inv. no. 1593.

80. L. O. Larsson, 'Hans Mont', *Konsthistorik Tidskrift*, XXXVI (1967): 7–8; Essen-Vienna 1988, p. 130; Lietzmann (note 40).

81. Essen-Vienna 1988, cat. no. 73 (*Mars and Venus*); Essen-Vienna 1988, cat. no. 74 (*Venus Callipyge*).

82. Essen-Vienna 1988, cat. no. 162.

83. Kaufmann 1988, p. 220.

84. K. Pilz, 'Hans Hoffmann, ein Nürnberger Dürer-Nachahmer der 2. Hälfte des 16. Jahrhunderts', *Mitteilungen des Vereins für Geschichte der Stadt Nürnberg*, LI (1962): 236–72; K. Achilles, 'Naturstudien von Hans Hoffmann in der Kunstsammlung des Nürnberger Kaufmannes Paulus II. Praun', *JKSW*, LXXXII–LXXXIII (1986–87): 243–59.

85. Pilz (note 84), p. 241.

86. E. Fučíková, 'Umělci na dvoře Rudolfa I. a jejich vztah k tvorbě Albrechta Dürera', *Umění*, XX (1972): 149–66.

87. E. Fučíková, 'Studien zur rudolfinischen Kunst: Addenda et Corrigenda', *Umění*, XXVII (1979): 489–514 (497–98).

88. A. J. Martin, 'Eine unbekannte Sammlung bedeutender Portraits der Renaissance aus dem Besitz des Hans Jakob König', *Kunstchronik*, IIL (1995): 46–54.

89. Winter, pp. 407, 435; Lhotsky, pp. 251–52.

90. Lhotsky, p. 252; J. F. Hayward, *Virtuoso Goldsmiths and the Triumph of Mannerism* (London, 1976), pp. 241–51.

91. Winter, pp. 413, 439; Lhotsky, p. 252.

92. Lhotsky, p. 252; R. Distelberger, 'Die Kunstkammerstücke', in Essen-Vienna 1988, pp. 437–66 (440).

93. Essen-Vienna 1988, cat. no. 340.

94. Distelberger (note 92), p. 464; Bukovinská (note 53), pp. 151, 153, 154.

95. Essen-Vienna 1988, cat. no. 447.

96. Distelberger (note 92), pp. 457–62; Bukovinská (note 53), pp. 158–68.

97. Distelberger (note 92), pp. 457–59 and literature cited there; Bukovinská (note 53), pp. 163–64, and literature cited there.

98. Essen-Vienna 1988, cat. nos 379–81.

99. Prague, Národní galerie v Praze, inv. no. O 560.

100. F. Röver, 'Caspar Lehman aus Uelzen: Zur Biographie und Herkunft des ersten europäischen Glasschneiders der Neuzeit', *Niederdeutsche Beiträge zur Kunstgeschichte*, IV (1965): 251–67; Distelberger (note 92), pp. 460–62; Bukovinská (note 53), p. 167.

101. Prague, Uměleckoprůmyslové muzeum, inv. no. Z 279/1, dat. 1605.

102. F. Dworschak, *Antonio Abondio* (Trento, 1958).

103. Van der Boom (note 37), pp. 19–23.

104. Essen-Vienna 1988, cat. no. 335.

105. Von Schwarzenfeld (note 1), pp. 42, 70; Evans (note 1), pp. 152, 203–4; E. Trunz, 'Pansophie und Manierismus im Kreise Kaiser Rudolfs II.' in *Die österreichische Literatur: Ihr Profil von den Anfängen im Mittelaler bis ins 18. Jahrhundert (1050–1750)*, ed. H. Zeman (Graz, 1986), pp. 865–986 (886).

106. Evans (note 1), pp. 204–5; Trunz (note 105), p. 890.

1.96 (Attributed to) DIONYSIO MISERONI
Vase with Cover
Ca. 1647
[Vienna, Kunsthistorisches Museum, Kunstkammer]

1.97 DIONYSIO MISERONI
Tabernacle
1644–50
[Prague, Metropolitní kapitula u sv. Víta]

107. Evans (note 1), pp. 119, 123, 146.

108. Von Schwarzenfeld (note 1), pp. 19, 161; Evans (note 1), p. 121.

109. Evans (note 1), pp. 203-5.

110. Von Schwarzenfeld (note 1), pp. 85-86, 134; Evans (note 1), pp. 218-22; Trunz (note 105), p. 886.

111. Von Schwarzenfeld (note 1), pp. 85-86; Evans (note 1), pp. 218-28; Trunz (note 105), p. 886.

112. F. A. Yates, *Giordano Bruno and the Hermetic Tradition* (Chicago, 1978), pp. 313-15; Trunz (note 105), pp. 888-89.

113. Evans (note 1), p. 231.

114. For music at the court of Rudolf II, see R. Lindell, 'Das Musikleben am Hof Rudolfs II.' in Essen-Vienna 1988, pp. 75-83; G. Stradner, 'Die Klangwelt der Musikinstrumente in Prag um 1600' in Essen-Vienna 1988, pp. 28-31; *Prag um 1600* (note 36), essays by C. P. Comberiati, P. Danek and R. Lindell.

115. *Dejiny ceského divadla*, vol. I (Prague, 1968), p. 140.

116. J. Krcálová, 'Die rudolfinische Architektur', *Leids Kunsthistorisch Jaarboek*, I (1982): 274-75; Muchka (note 53), pp. 186-87.

117. E. Fučíková, 'The Collection of Rudolf II at Prague: Cabinet of Curiosities or Scientific Museum' in *The Origin of Museums*, ed. O. Impey and A. MacGregor (Oxford, 1985), pp. 47-53.

118. Muchka (note 53), pp. 198-99.

119. *Ibid.*, pp. 186-87.

120. Fučíková (note 87), pp. 492-95; Kaufmann 1988, pp. 220-25.

121. Prague, Národní galerie v Praze, inv. no. DO 5351.

122. Essen-Vienna 1988, cat. no. 140, once again the property of the Premonstratensian Monastery at Strahov.

123. *Le Bestiaire de Rodolphe II: Cod.min 129 et 130 de la Bibliotheque nationale d' Autriche* (Paris, 1990).

124. T. Wilberg Vignau-Schuurman, *Die emblematischen Elemente im Werke Joris Hoefnagels*, 2 vols (Leiden, 1969), and literature cited there; M. L. Hendrix, 'Joris Hoefnagel and the Four Elements: A Study in Sixteenth-Century Nature Painting', Ph.D. diss., Princeton University, 1984; Kaufmann 1988, pp. 202-10.

125. *Civitates orbis terrarum ...* , collaborantibus Francisco Hohenbergio et Georgio Hoefnagel, ed. Georg Braun (Cologne, 1572-1618).

126. Vienna, Österreichische National-Bibliothek, Cod. 1784.

127. Essen-Vienna 1988, cat. no. 219.

128. Essen-Vienna 1988, cat. no. 599, 600.

129. Essen-Vienna 1988, cat. no. 176.

130. Winter, pp. 178-79.

131. T. Vignau-Wilberg, *Archetypa Studiaque patris Georgii Hoefnagelii: Natur, Dichtung und Wissenschaft in der Kunst um 1600* (Munich, 1994).

132. Lhotsky, p. 266.

133. J. Zimmer, *Joseph Heintz der Ältere als Maler*, Weissenhorn, 1971, xxxkde vsechna starsí literatura; J. Zimmer, *Joseph Heintz der Ältere: Zeichnungen und Dokumente*, Munich-Berlin, 1988.

134. Essen-Vienna 1988, cat. no. 137.

135. *Ibid.*, cat. nos 126, 132.

136. *Ibid.*, cat. nos 128-30.

137. *Ibid.*, cat. no. 136.

138. J. Zimmer, 'Joseph Heintz als Architekt' in *Elias Holl und das Augsburger Rathaus* (Regensburg, 1985), pp. 98-118.

139. R. A. Peltzer, 'Der Hofmaler Hans von Aachen, seine Schule und seine Zeit', *JKSAK*, XXX (1911-12): 59-182; R. an der Heiden, 'Die Porträtmalerei des Hans von Aachen', *JKSW*, LXVI (1970): 135-227; Kaufmann 1988, pp. 133-63 and the literature cited there.

140. E. Fučíková, *Hans von Aachen: Bakchus a Silén*, exh. cat. (Prague, 1996), pp. 10-11, pls 3, 4.

141. Essen-Vienna 1988, cat. no. 89 – *The Road to Calvary*; Sibiu, Muzeul Bruckenthal, inv. no. 1 – *The Rape of Proserpine*.

142. Essen-Vienna 1988, cat. no. 547 – *Bacchus, Ceres and Cupid*; Bucharest, Muzeul National, inv. no. 8395/429 – *The Three Graces*.

143. Essen-Vienna 1988, cat. nos 105, 108.

144. *Ibid.*, cat. no. 110.

145. Pelzer (note 139), pp. 158, 172, 174

146. L. O. Larsson, *Adrian de Vries: Adrianus Fries Hagiensis Batavus* (Vienna and Munich, 1967).

147. *Ibid.*, cat. nos 31, 36.

148. Essen-Vienna 1988, cat. no. 158.

149. H. Mielke, 'Hans Vredeman de Vries: Verzeichnis der Stichwerke', Ph.D. diss., Berlin, 1967; J. Ehrmann, 'Hans Vredeman de Vries', *Gazette des Beaux-Arts*, XCIII (1979): 13-26; G. Irmscher, 'Hans Vredeman de Vries als Zeichner' – I, *Kunsthistorisches Jahrbuch Graz*, XXI (1985): 123-45; – II, XXII (1986): 79-119; Kaufmann 1988, pp. 287-91.

150. Essen-Vienna 1988, cat. no. 180.

151. *Ibid.*, cat. no. 589.

152. *JKSAK*, XXII (1891), II. T., Reg. 8309, 8320.

153. Fučíková (note 87), pp. 493-94.

154. A. Zwollo, 'Pieter Stevens, ein vergessener Maler des Rudolfinischen Kreises', *JKSW*, LXIV (1968): 119-80; *idem*, 'Pieter Stevens: Neue Zuschreibungen und Zusammenhänge', *Umění*, XVIII (1970): 246-59; *idem*, 'Ein Beitrag zur Niederländischen Landschaftsmalerei um 1600. Stadtansichten und antike Ruinen unter besonderer Berücksichtigung des Rudolfinischen Kreises', *Umění*, XXXI (1983): 399-412.

155. Zwollo 1970 (note 154), pp. 246-59.

156. M. Šroněk, 'Barokní malířství 17. století v Čechách' in *Dějiny českého výtvarného umění*, II/1 (Prague, 1989), pp. 337-39.

157. D. Limouze, 'Aegidius Sadeler (c. 1570-1629): Drawings, Prints and Art History', Ph.D. diss., Princeton University, 1990, and literature cited there.

158. Bauer-Haupt 1976, no. 1987.

159. Limouze (note 157), pp. 315-22.

160. W. Eckhart, 'Erasmus Habermel: Zur Biographie des Instrumentenmachers Kaiser Rudolfs II.', *Jahrbuch der Hamburger Kunstsammlungen*, XXI (1976): 55-92; *idem*, 'Erasmus und Josua Habermel: Kunstgeschichtliche Anmerkungen zu den Werken der beiden Instrumentenmacher', *Jahrbuch der Hamburger Kunstsammlungen*, XXII (1977): 13-74.

161. Before the auction of 1782, it was stored in the *Kunstkammer*, rather than being auctioned off, it was donated to the Polytechnical Institute.

162. Distelberger (note 92), p. 464.

163. H. von Bertele and E. Neumann, 'Der kaiserliche Kammeruhrmacher Christoph Margraf und die

Erfindung der Kugellaufuhr', *JKSW*, LIX (1963): 39-98.

164. Essen-Vienna 1988, cat. no. 448.

165. Bukovinská (note 53), p.174.

166. Distelberger (note 92), p. 460; Bukovinská (note 53), pp. 165-66.

167. *Tři francouzští kavalíři v rudolfínské Praze* (Prague, 1989).

168. C. Przyborowski, 'Die Ausstattung der Fürtenkapelle an der Basilika von San Lorenzo in Florenz: Versuch einer Rekonstruktion', Ph.D. diss., Berlin, 1982.

169. Distelberger (note 92), pp. 449-52; Bukovinská (note 53), pp. 145-48.

170. Distelberger (note 92), p. 449.

171. Vermeyen was also a good draughtsman, as is demonstrated by his only extant drawing; Essen-Vienna 1988, cat. no. 280.

172. The 1607-11 inventory of Rudolf's *Kunstkammer* contains many items of this sort and often mentions their sources.

173. Van der Boom (note 37), p. 20.

174. Trunz (note 105), pp. 877-88.

175. Evans (note 1), pp.154-57; Trunz (note 105), pp. 878-89.

176. Limouze (note 157), pp. 215-16; Hollstein 320.

177. Trunz (note 105), pp. 883-84, 899-903.

178. Essen-Vienna 1988, cat. no. 335.

179. Trunz (note 105), pp. 902-3.

180. Evans (note 1), p. 138; Trunz (note 105), p. 889.

181. Trunz (note 105), pp. 889-90.

182. F. J. Studnička, *Bericht über die astrologischen Studien des Reformators der beobachtenden Astronomie Tycho Brahe* (Prague, 1901); von Schwarzenfeld (note 1), pp. 136-44; Trunz (note 105), p. 889.

183. Evans (note 1), pp. 152-53, 187-90, 245, 280; Z. Horsky, *Kepler v Praze* (Prague, 1980); Trunz (note 105), p. 889.

184. M. Caspar und W. von Dyck, *Johannes Kepler in seinen Briefen* (Munich and Berlin, 1930), pp. 77-78.

185. Kyčálová(note 116), pp. 273-88; Muchka (note 53), p. 190.

186. Essen-Vienna 1988, cat. no. 326.

187. Kyčálová(note 116), pp. 291-92.

188. K. Erasmus, *Roelant Savery, sein Leben und seine Zeit* (Halle, 1908); J. Spicer -Durham, 'The Drawings of Roelandt Savery', Ph.D. diss., Yale University, New Haven, 1979; K. J. Müllenmeister, *Roelant Savery: Die Gemälde, mit kritischem Oevrekatalog* (Freren, 1988); Kaufmann 1988, pp. 228-48.

189. See J. Spicer's essay on Roelandt Savery in the present volume.

190. J. Spicer, 'Roelandt Savery's Studies in Bohemia', *Umění*, XVIII (1970): 270-75; *idem*, 'The`naer het leven' Drawings: By Pieter Bruegel or Roelandt Savery?', *Master Drawings*, VIII (1970): 3-30.

191. T. Gerszi, *Paulus van Vianen: Handzeichnungen* (Hanau, 1982); J. R. ter Molen, *Van Vianen: een Utrechtse familie van zilversmeden met een internationale faam*, 2 vols (Leiden, 1984), and literature cited there.

192. A. Zwollo, 'Pieter Stevens: Nieuw werk, contact met Jan Brueghel op Kerstiaen Keunink', *Leids Kunsthistorisch Jaarboek*, I (1982): 95-118; see also the essay by T. Gerszi in the present volume; ter Molen (note 191), vols I, pp. 17-28; II, pp. 13-79.

194. Essen-Vienna 1988, cat. no. 353.

195. Both pictures come from the Fürstenberg collection and as early as the mid-seventeenth century were listed as by van Vianen; both are included in this exhibition.

196. Fučíková (note 86), pp.154-57; Fučíková (note 87), pp. 496-98; L. Tongiorgi-Tomasi, 'Daniel Fröschl before Prague: His Artistic Activity in Tuscany at the Medici Court' in *Prag um 1600* (note 50), pp. 289-98.

197. Essen-Vienna 1988, cat. no. 118.

198. Bauer-Haupt 1976, XXII-XXVII.

199. E. Bender, 'Matthäus Gundelach: Leben und Werk', Ph.D. diss., Frankfurt am Main, 1981, and literature cited there; Kaufmann 1988, pp. 180-83.

200. Essen-Vienna 1988, cat. no. 120.

201. *Ibid.*, cat. no. 121.

202. Bender (note 199), pp. 37-148.

203. Fučíková (note 87), pp. 495-96; Kaufmann 1988, pp. 224-26.

204. Essen-Vienna 1988, cat. no. 198.

205. *Rudolf II*: Chapel Hill, Ackland Museum; *Empress Anna*: Vienna, Kunthistorisches Museum, inv. no. 3092.

206. Fučíková (note 87), pp. 495-96.

207. H. Zimmermann, 'Das Inventar der Prager Schatz- und Kunstkammer vom 6. Dezember 1621 nach Akten des k. und k. Reichsfinanzarchivs in Vienna', *JKSAK*, XXV (1905), II. T., no. 1162.

208. H. Seifertová and M. Šroněk, 'Rastrový obraz z rudolfínskych sbírek', *Bulletin Národní galerie v Praze*, V-VI (1995-96): 253-57.

209. Larsson (note 146); *idem*, 'Bildhauerkunst und Plastik am Hofe Rudolfs II.' in Essen-Vienna 1988, pp. 131-37.

210 E. Fučíková, 'Zur Konzeption der rudolfinischen Sammlungen' in *Prag um 1600* (note 50), pp. 59-62 (59).

211. Essen-Vienna 1988, cat. nos 59, 539, 538, 63.

212. *Ibid.* cat. no. 57, 59.

213. See, for example, the reliefs *Allegory of the Turkish Wars* (Essen-Vienna 1988, cat. no. 58) and *Bacchus and Ariadne* (Amsterdam, Rijksmuseum).

214. Larsson (note 146), pp. 91-98.

215. E. Fučíková, 'Giovanni Battista Quadri a socharství počátku 17. století na Pražském hrade' in *Barokní umění a jeho význam v české kultuře* (Prague, 1991), pp. 28-34.

216. O. Blažíček and V. Husa, 'Materiálie k dějinám barokního výtvarnictví v Cechách I.' in *Ročenka kruhu pro pěstování dějin umění za rok 1935* (Prague, 1936), pp. 61-2.

217. The plaque on the Matthias Gateway is comprised of two pieces. The lower one, of sandstone, was carved with great skill, and the upper one is made of stucco. It appears that working the stone took a long time and so the quicker method of working in stucco was chosen. This was also a good opportunity to change the name of the builder to Matthias; he was at odds with the man who had actually commissioned the work (Rudolf). This work was not prestigious enough to warrent the attention of court sculptors and so was probably entrusted to their assistants.

218. Haupt-Bauer 1976, XXIV; Distelberger (note 92), p. 463.

219. Essen–Vienna 1988, cat. nos 394, 395.

220. Zimmermann (note 207), II. T., LXII, no. 254.

221. Distelberger (note 92), p. 463, cat. no. 411.

222. J. Kappel, *Die Elfenbeindrechsler am Kurfürstlichen Hof zu Dresden in Wiedergewonnen*, exh. cat. (Erbach, 1995), pp. 14–19.

223. Haupt-Bauer 1976, nos 907–9, 973, 982.

224. *Ibid*. nos 618, 626, 632–36; E. Fučíková, 'Veduta v rudolfínském krajinárství', *Umění*, XXXI (1983): 395, and literature cited there; Essen–Vienna 1988, cat. nos 194, 195.

225. Limouze (note 157), pp. 357–58.

226. London, British Museum, inv. no. 52.3-27.12, listed as an Augsburg master of the first half of the seventeenth century.

227. No small sculptures or reliefs by Alessandro Abondio or Hans Vermeyen have so far been identified; it is therefore impossible to determine who the artist of this relief might have been.

228. Haupt-Bauer 1976, no. 2107.

229. Bukovinská (note 53), pp.148–53; Distelberger (note 92), pp. 452–54.

230. Winter, pp. 432–47; B. Bukovinská, 'Zu den Goldschmiedearbeiten der Prager Hofwerkstätte zur Zeit Rudolfs II.', *Leids Kunsthistorisch Jaarboek*, I (1982): 71–82.

231. Winter, pp. 505–7.

232. Winter, p. 506; Bukovinská (note 53), p. 169.

233. Winter, pp. 479–81; Distelberger (note 92), 465; Bukovinská (note 53), pp. 171–72, and literature cited there.

234. In addition to Bürgi's workshop, another place is known where the sculptor worked and where a foundary was located. Research in archives in Vienna has yielded information to be published soon by Dr. Staudinger.

235. Bauer-Haupt 1976, no. 1556.

236. Evans (note 1), pp. 216–17; Trunz (note 105), p. 889.

237. C. Parkhurst, 'A Color Theory from Prague: Anselm de Boot, 1609', *Bulletin Allen Memorial Art Museum*, XXIX (1971): 3–10; M.-C. Maselis, A. Balis and R. H. Marijnissen, *De Album van Anselmus de Boot* (Lannoo, 1989).

238. Essen–Vienna 1988, cat. no. 335, and literature cited there.

239. Evans (note 1), p. 142; Trunz (note 105), pp. 891–92.

240. Evans (note 1), pp. 206–7; Trunz (note 105), pp. 887–88.

241. Evans (note 1), p. 204; Trunz (note 105), p. 890.

242. J. Polisensky, *Jan Jesenský – Jessenius* (Prague, 1965); Evans (note 1), pp. 136–38; Trunz (note 105), p. 890.

243. Von Schwarzenfeld (note 1), pp. 150–51, 177; Evans (note 1), 89–91; Essen–Vienna 1988, cat. no. 29.

244. Von Schwarzenfeld (note 1), p. 151.

245. Caspar and von Dyck (note 184), p. 285.

246. A. H. J. Knight, *Heinrich Julius, Duke of Brunswick* (Oxford, 1948); F. Thöne, *Wolfenbüttel, Geist und Glanz einer alten Residenz* (Munich, 1963), pp. 55–77; Trunz (note 105), p. 876; Essen-Vienna 1988, cat. no. 17.

247. Peltzer (note 139), pp.106–7.

248. Sigmund von Birken, *Ostländischer Lorbeerhäyn* (Nürnberg, 1657).

249. *JKSAK*, XX (1899), II. T., Reg. 17099; *Pavla Skály ze Zhore Historie ceská od r.1602 do roku 1623*, ed. K. Tieftunk (Prague, 1865), I. díl, p. 336.

250. J. Morávek, *Nově objevený inventář rudolfinských sbírek na Hradě pražském* (Prague, 1937), pp. III.-VII.

251. Zimmermann (note 158), Reg. 19422.

252. J. Svátek, *Culturhistorische Bilder aus Böhmen* (Vienna, 1879), pp. 253–54.

253. *Christina Queen of Sweden. A Personality of European Civilisation*, exh. cat. (Stockholm, 1966), pp. 416–21.

254. K. Köppl, 'Urkunden, Acten, Regesten und Inventare aus dem K.K. Statthalterei-Archiv in Prag', *JKSAK*, X (1889), Reg. 6231.

255. V. Naňková, 'Architektura 17. století v Čechách' in *Dějiny českého výtvarného umění*, II/1 (Prague, 1989), pp. 249–92 (254).

256. Larsson (note 146), pp. 91–98.

257. Limouze (note 157), pp. 363–66.

258. R. Distelberger, 'Dionysio und Ferdinand Eusebio Miseroni', *JKSW*, LXXV (1979): 109–88.

259. Essen and Vienna 1988, cat. no. 745.

260. O. J. Blažíček, 'Barokní sochařství 17. století v Čechách' in *Dejiny ceského vytvarného umení* (note 255), pp. 293–314 (295); Fučíková (note 215), pp. 30–31.

261. Seifertová and Šroněk (note 208), p. 324.

262. *Ibid.*, pp. 324–25.

263. See Seifertová and Šroněk's article on Baroque painting in seventeenth- century Bohemia (note

In the Name of God:
Religious Struggles in the Empire, 1555–1648

HERBERT HAUPT

The coronation of Charlemagne on Christmas Day 800 coincided with the creation of the Holy Roman Empire, seen at the time as a continuation of the *Imperium Romanum*[1] and embracing notions of universalism that survived into the Christian Middle Ages in the West. However, after the Middle Ages, the idea of one overriding Western centre of power met with increasing resistance from the ruling classes, which included the new regional lords (*Landesherren*). During the fifteenth and sixteenth centuries, the Holy Roman Empire became the Holy Roman Empire of German Nations. By the time the treaty of religious peace was negotiated in the Imperial Diet in Augsburg in 1555, the empire had become a loose union of more or less independent Estates, a weak structure something like a German nation. The overarching authorities were the Imperial Diet, the Supreme Court, the Privy Council and the organization of imperial districts. Despite these links, the different parts of the empire drifted even further apart. This was largely due to Martin Luther (1483–1546), the Reformation his teachings inspired and an increasing level of unresolvable social unease.[2] The empire nonetheless continued to live on in the German consciousness in the sixteenth and seventeenth centuries and, through the humanist influence of Emperor Maximilian I, acquired a new 'national-romantic' popularity. People were drawn together by the memory of shared greatness and the awareness of present shared suffering, all of which coloured the literature, art and social structures of the time. The Augsburg Treaty was a recognition of the reality of religious divisions: the Estates and the Emperor granted the Augsburg Confession of 1530 legal recognition under imperial law. Lutheran teachings acquired the status of an officially approved religion just like the Roman Catholic Church.

No one questioned the fact that regional rulers dictated the religion of their subjects ('cuius regio, eius religio'), but not all the provisions of the Augsburg Treaty were so unambiguous. Many were open to interpretation, and all parties were concerned to interpret them to their own advantage. Among the debatable points was the status of Calvinism, the Reformation in the free cities and the secularization of the religious foundations and monasteries outside the towns in the larger Protestant territories. However, the most volatile cause of conflict was the so-called 'religious exclusion' order, which stated that Imperial Diet members who had become Protestant should relinquish their authority, territories and income to the Catholic church. This effectively prevented any Protestants becoming prince-bishops. The fight against 'religious exclusion' dominated the politics of the Evangelical Diet members. Not only did they view the imperial bishoprics which were leaving the Catholic fold as ideal homes for members of the Protestant nobility; they also saw this as a chance to extend their own territories by absorbing these same lands, which had hitherto been under the jurisdiction of the Catholic church. The stage for these disputes was the Diet itself, which reflected the empire's changing balance of power in its decisions. Religious matters became an increasingly welcome political lever to be employed in any struggle against authority. Just as the

Emperor had to fight to hold his own in the Diet against its increasingly confident members, so the Estates had to fight their own battle against the provincial delegates. The rich burghers with hereditary rights set themselves against the town fathers, but were not prepared to concede rights to new burghers coming into the towns. Religion became a pretext for personal interest, a tool in the pursuit of self-advancement. The cry for religious freedom was almost always linked to the demand for enhanced political rights. In order to achieve a particular goal, it was by no means unheard of for warring parties to enter into alliances with those who were of a different religious persuasion but who shared the same political aims.

The close links between territory and religious persuasion repeatedly led to disputes and armed conflict. Streams of refugees poured across Europe seeking a home where they could worship as they wished. The situation was complicated by the fact that the different religious groups all had external connections with members of the same faith in other lands. These individuals were only too ready to respond to cries for help from their brethren and to intervene in the empire's affairs, incidentally extending their own power. While the Habsburg and Wittelsbach Protestant camp could count on the support of Spain and the Vatican, the Lutherans could rely on Sweden and Denmark. The Calvinists, on the other hand, could call on the Netherlands and the Swiss Confederation as well as sections of the French nobility. Thus a conflict ostensibly in the future was already becoming effectively internationalized.

And yet there were still princely rulers in place who were perfectly satisfied with the Augsburg Treaty and who, without abandoning their own faith, put what united them with others above what divided them. Although unbending in matters of religion, nevertheless these rulers had respect for each other's achievements, seeing their counterparts in the first instance as their peers, and only in the second instance as members of another religion. Thus friendly contact was maintained between members of the higher aristocracy until around 1600. Elector Johann of Brandenburg's (1571–1598) exhortation to support the crumbling fabric of the empire rather than to break it up completely[3] sums up the guiding principle behind the usual political attitudes and behaviour of the majority of his peers. Repeated violations of the Augsburg Peace were not played up, just resolved pragmatically. Evangelical and Catholic imperial rulers alike approved the Emperor's Turkish tax and, at the appointed time, elected a son of the Emperor as King of the Romans (Maximilian II in 1562 and Rudolf II in 1575). The concept of mutual religious understanding without conflict was still alive, and the proceedings of the Diet of 1566 under Emperor Maximilian II are characteristic of the time in their reference to new negotiations on the question of church unity.

This willingness to make reasonable compromises and sincere desire for peace had its roots in the memory, still fresh, of the Schmalkaldic War of 1546–47. People temporized and hoped that the opposition would be prepared to talk. In itself, this approach produced no real results. Additionally, Emperor Maximilian's undogmatic Christianity, with its humanist-liberal flavour, was not acceptable to both parties. A crucial role in the redistribution of power was played by the threat of the Ottoman Turks to the east. The need to resist them dominated imperial politics throughout this period. In coupling their acceptance of a Turkish tax with religious concessions, the Protestant nobility achieved their aims simply by applying the pressure of political necessity. The Religious Concession of 1568, the Assecura-

tion Acts for Donauösterreich of 1571 and the so-called 'Brucker Libell' of 1578 marked highpoints of Habsburgs–Protestantism co-operation. But as Protestant influence grew, the Catholic church began to make efforts to recover lost territories. Bolstered by the Council of Trent (1545–63), self-confident popes began to resist all forms of Protestantism. First and foremost these included Pius V, Gregory XIII, Clement VII and Paul V. Above all, they drew support from the Society of Jesus (the Jesuits), formed by the Basque Ignatius of Loyola (1491–1556)[4] and from the Catholic Habsburg emperors. Visits by the authorities, the establishment of a general order for religious foundations and monasteries in 1567 and the *Klosterrat* of 1568 were the first moves on the part of the established church to revitalize the decayed and depopulated monastic communities. The church's mission to the people was in the hands of the Franciscans and the Capuchins. The reinstatement of the Corpus Christi procession was a visible signal of the reinvigorated Catholic authorities' willingness to hold their ground, seemingly seeking rather than avoiding confrontation with Protestantism. Throughout the land, armies were formed in God's name, ready to strike out and do their part in securing victory for their particular faith.

The increasingly belligerent tone taken by some Protestants caused a split in their ranks. While the electorates of Saxony and Brandenburg and other Lutherans broadly supported the empire's politics, to their own considerable benefit, the Calvinist Rhine Palatinate was, from the outset, determined to confront the Catholic Habsburg emperors. As the sixteenth century drew to a close, the peace-loving signatories from Augsburg in 1555 died one after the other – Duke Albrecht V of Bavaria in 1579, Elector August I of Saxony in 1586 and Elector Johann Georg of Brandenburg in 1598 – and Diet members on both sides turned militant. The first warnings of escalation were the disputes surrounding the spiritual electorate in Cologne (1582–83) and the Strasbourg *Kapitelstreit* (1583–1604). In both cases, the Catholic side was able to force the implementation of the 'religious exclusion' orders against Protestant-Calvinist claims. Both bishoprics remained Catholic.

Another extremely significant factor in further political developments was the dissolution of various imperial authorities. The fact was that the Diet members could not decide on the make-up of the *Visitationskommission* of the Imperial Court of Justice. Trouble flared up when Joachim Friedrich (1546–1608), later elector of Brandenburg, expressed the wish, in his role as Evangelical administrator of the archbishopric of Magdeburg, to be present with voting rights at the Augsburg Diet of 1582. His attempt was resolutely thwarted by the Catholic members. In 1588, they also prevented Magdeburg becoming one of the rotating members of the *Visitationskommission*, which meant that this important review body no longer met. The significance of this development was highlighted by the so-called 'Four Monasteries' Feud'. This involved the successful appeal to the Imperial Court of Justice[5] by four[6] father superiors whose properties had been secularized by the Protestant Estates in contravention of the – admittedly controversial – Augsburg decrees. The Protestants contested the judgment. Now that there was no review body, the so-called '*Deputationstag*', which had been formed in 1597–98 to lighten the load of the Imperial Court of Justice, was elevated to become a court of appeal against decisions made by the imperial court. When it looked increasingly likely that the imperial court's decision was going to be upheld, the Rhine Palatinate declared that the

Deputationstag had no legal powers and, together with the Rhine Palatinate and the electorate of Brandenburg and Wolfenbüttel, blocked any further decisions. From then on the *Deputationstag* also ceased meeting.

The collapse of the imperial system of justice was one of the major factors leading to the outbreak of the Thirty Years' War. Outstanding legal disputes remained unresolved. As the channels of justice dried up, litigants turned to political solutions or, increasingly, to military ones. The Diet itself suffered a similar fate, as it was rendered powerless by warring factions. In 1605, the Rhine Palatinate refused to agree to the Emperor's proposed Turkish tax. This was tantamount to abolishing the principle of majority voting in the imperial financial committees. It was now becoming increasingly clear that the intention of the Rhine Palatinate was to undermine the powers of the Diet even to the point of eliminating it altogether. For the time being, the Palatinate lacked the support of the moderate Protestant centre parties, who held the majority in the Diet. However, this changed at a stroke when Duke Maximilian I of Bavaria (1573–1651) executed a pitiless imperial proscription order against the Protestant free imperial town of Donauwörth. The electorate of Saxony now made their approval of the Emperor's Turkish tax dependent on the withdrawal of Bavarian troops from the town. However, even before negotiations aimed at alleviating the crisis had been completed, the Rhine Palatinate delegation left the Diet. The Diet went into recess without having come to any decision which could be issued as a decree. So the Diet members started to take charge of their own affairs. In order to do this, the different denominations founded bodies to defend their interests: in 1608, the Protestant Union was founded, with the Catholic League following a year later. They also strengthened their connections abroad, hoping for help in the event of war.

The external and internal threats to the empire had to be met by decisive action. Since the election of Rudolf I in 1273, the position of head of the empire had been held almost exclusively by members of the house of Habsburg. The only exceptions had occurred in the fourteenth century. After the death of Charles V, in 1558 the imperial crown went to his brother Ferdinand (1503–1564). The death of King Ludwig II (1506–1526) in the Battle of Mohács against the Turks meant that Ferdinand, married to Ludwig's sister, Anna of Hungary (1503–1547), inherited the crowns of both Bohemia and Hungary. Ferdinand, brought up and educated in Spain, arrived in Vienna in 1522 at the age of nineteen, thus marking the beginning of one of the most extraordinary periods of change seen in modern times. On his death, after ruling for forty-two years, the 'Spaniard' had become a successful and committed defender of the lands of the Habsburg-Austrians, having laid the foundations for the later super-power status of the monarchy along the Danube.

No less Catholic in fact than his brother Karl, Ferdinand was nevertheless pragmatic enough to recognize the religious divisions which beset the empire as a political reality. He strove, albeit in vain, to achieve some kind of settlement between the different denominations. As much as he was prepared to listen to the Protestant Diet members, he also energetically promoted the reorganization and reinstatement of Catholicism in the empire and in the lands he had inherited, inviting Jesuits to settle there, for example, in 1551. In his will, Ferdinand divided his realm among his three sons: Ferdinand received the Tyrol with Sundgau and Breisgau; Karl inherited Inner Austria (Carinthia, Styria, Carniola and Görz); all the rest went

to Maximilian, who was also elected king of the Romans in 1562. Maximilian, interested in the arts and widely educated himself, turned the newly finished Hofburg in Vienna into his residence, but still maintained close contacts with Prague. The Italianate belvedere which he had built between 1538 and 1563 for Queen Anna in the Prague Castle, intended to proclaim the house of Habsburg as the new possessors of the Bohemian crown, is one of the earliest and most beautiful Renaissance constructions north of the Alps. With a similar end in mind, in 1555–56 Archduke Ferdinand (1529–1595) built a belvedere to his own plans outside the town, with a plan in the form of a six-pointed star – hence the name Schloss Stern (Star Summer Palace). Like his father, Emperor Maximilian II had a peace-loving nature. His friendship with influential Protestant princes of the Holy Roman Empire initially appeared to benefit the cause of religious harmony. Although officially Catholic by virtue of his office and position, his personal situation as regards religion remained obscure. His manoeuvrings between the different religious camps reflected both his own leanings and political necessity, but did not go far towards resolving conflict. In the end, both denominations, disappointed, turned their backs on their supposed supporter. Maximilian's attempts at a 'general Christian reformation' foundered, each side being convinced of the unique truth of its own beliefs.

When Maximilian's son Rudolf II (1552–1612) came to the throne, he thus found an uneasy peace. Even his contemporaries found Rudolf's personality baffling. Their responses to him ranged from respect to scepticism to outright rejection. A key to understanding his character is found in the time, between 1564 and 1571, which he spent at the court of his uncle King Philip II in Spain. Rudolf's experiences there left a lasting impression and strengthened various aspects of his character as a Habsburg. Torn between imperial expectations and the reality of his situation, tormented by the fear that he might not be equal to the demands of his high office and plagued by illness and depression, he found comfort in pansophy[7] and art. Under his regency, Prague for the second time became the much-admired centre of the empire ('Praga caput regni').[8] While the first twenty years of his reign saw him energetically involved in the affairs of the empire, repeated bouts of depression left him increasingly indecisive. Since he also did not marry, the continued existence of the dynasty was in jeopardy. In view of threatening developments in the Turkish Wars (1593–1606), the situation appeared to become untenable.[9] When Rudolf and his brother Matthias settled their feud in 1608, the real winners were the nobles, who negotiated privileges in return for their help (as enshrined in the Bohemian Imperial Charter of 1609). In 1611, Rudolf was forced to abdicate as king of Bohemia, and Prague was plundered by the troops of Archduke Leopold V (1586–1632),[10] whom Rudolf had already chosen as his successor. All that was left to him was the imperial title. Yet this, too, was in danger. The electors had decided they must end the leadership crisis in the empire by electing a new king in spring 1612. Rudolf was only spared this final humiliation by his death on 20 January of that year.

Rudolf's successor, Matthias, did not have the personality to overcome the national crisis which was partially of his own making. His attempt in 1611 to revive the functions of the Diet were just as unsuccessful as the efforts by his most influential adviser, Cardinal Khlesl (1553–1630), to resolve the complaints of the two opposing denominations by reaching some form of mutual understanding. It looked

increasingly likely that force would be used to decide contentious constitutional issues and the arguments surrounding religious co-existence.

It was not a matter of chance that the war which was to inflict thirty years of indescribable misery on the population broke out in Bohemia. Nowhere else did so many antagonistic denominations live so closely together, nor were religion and nationalism (in this case entrenched since the Hussite Wars) so inextricably intertwined as in Rudolfine Prague. Whether Hussites, Taborites, Utraquists, Calvinists, Catholics or Jews, they all believed that they alone followed the true faith. It seemed that anything was justified when it came to political self-protection. In addition to this, there was the uncertain legal relationship between the ruling family and the Bohemian nobility. In this context, little help was to be had from the grudging Imperial Charter issued by Rudolf II in 1609 with its freedoms for Protestants and Jews. The distance between the two sides was too great and the self-confidence of the Protestant nobility too strong.

To the Protestants, this seemed the right moment to rid themselves of the hated Catholic Habsburgs. Clashes between Protestants and Catholics in 1611 in Braunau in Bohemia (Broumov) and in 1614 in Klostergrab (Hrob) along with the second Prague Defenestration[11] carried out by Protestant delegates in 1618 led to the uprising of the established, largely Protestant nobility against their Catholic rulers. The results are well known: a new provincial diet, a government with thirty 'directors' and an army to serve their cause. Moravia joined the uprising, which ultimately spilled over and involved the Protestant Estates in Austria.[12] The Calvinist Georg Erasmus von Tschernembl, the spokesman for the uprising, described the provincial diet as an organ of the sovereignty of the people with its own authorization to act independently. The Confederation Act of 31 July 1619 proposed the linking of all the lands under Habsburg rule along the lines of arrangements in the Netherlands and Switzerland. At the height of their powers in August 1619, the provincial Bohemian diet, in alliance with the Protestant Estates of Austria, deposed Emperor Ferdinand II (1578–1637) and in his place elected the leader of the Protestant Union, Elector Friedrich V from the Rhine Palatinate, as king of Bohemia (the 'Winter King'). Ferdinand's reaction was predictable: he was neither prepared to accept his deposition as king of Hungary nor simply to stand by as Protestantism flexed its muscles in Bohemia and the neighbouring lands. Ferdinand found support in the Catholic League under the leadership of Duke Maximilian I of Bavaria. With the defeat on 8 November 1620 of the Bohemian army by the combined forces of the emperor and the Catholic League at the Battle of the White Mountain, the uprising was finally over. Friedrich V fled, and the government stepped down.[13] The Catholic advance carried the war on into the empire and introduced foreign powers into the scene.

What had started as a localised dispute grew inexorably until it had spread right across Europe, affecting almost every country with the exception of Turkey and the British Isles. The lands of the empire and the Habsburg crown and hereditary territories were the setting for conflicts of varying intensity and length. Mercenaries spread fear and terror. While fortified houses offered at least limited protection, the countryside was hopelessly exposed to the ravages of the *Soldateska*. The international aspect of the war is underlined by the composition of the armies. With the outbreak of war in the empire, the close contacts between the courts in Vienna and

Madrid meant that the Spanish entered battle at the Rhine on Ferdinand II's side. The Danes came to the assistance of the Protestant princes under pressure in northern Germany, but were paid for their trouble with a heavy defeat. The victories won by the imperial army under Albrecht of Wallenstein (1583–1634) caused a further internationalization of the war. Religious considerations apart, no European power wanted the Habsburgs to become too strong. Emperor Ferdinand II met with increasing opposition from within his own Catholic party. The main focus of the Catholic League's anger was, however, directed at the figure of Wallenstein. His rapid rise and the almost kingly powers he wielded had made him into a dangerous enemy. The *Kurfürstentag* called by the Emperor in Regensburg in 1630 offered an opportunity to take action. Led by Duke Maximilian of Bavaria, the Electors issued an ultimatum demanding that Wallenstein be dismissed and that the imperial army should be scaled down. Ferdinand II agreed to both demands. This weakening of his power proved to be the turning point of the war. At almost exactly the same time, King Gustav Adolf II (1594–1632) landed with a Swedish army in Upper Pomerania and took this distant region on the German coast without opposition. With Sweden's intervention, the emerging Baltic powers came very much to the fore. How little the propaganda of a religious 'mission of mercy' had to do with reality is evident from the fact that Gustav Adolf's campaign was financed by Catholic France under Richelieu (1585–1642).[14] The unexpectedly decisive military successes of the King of Sweden, whose troops advanced as far as Bavaria in 1631–32, were alarming to his allies. However, his death in the Battle of Lützen in 1632 brought the Swedish advance to a halt. Suspicions on the part of the Protestant Estates and the European dimensions of the war mitigated against the final expulsion of the Swedish forces from the empire. The following years were coloured by the tragedy of Wallenstein, who had been recalled when the Swedish threat was at its most dangerous. Having been found guilty of high treason, the *Generalissimus* was murdered in Eger on 25 February 1634.

After the Swedish had been defeated by the imperial army at Nördlingen in 1634, it seemed as though the fortunes of war might be turning in Ferdinand's favour once again. As his own resources ran out and war fatigue set in all around, the opposing sides came to the negotiating table. The Emperor could be satisfied with the outcome: his superior position with regard to the Estates was secured, and his new-found strength was reflected in the election of his son Ferdinand (III). Apart from the Electorate of Saxony, all the dignitaries of the Imperial Diet signed the Prague Peace Treaty in 1635. However, this peace was not to be realized, because France viewed it as a weakening of its own position. Cardinal Richelieu moved from covert to overt warfare and did his utmost to maintain Sweden's presence on the battlefields of Germany and Bohemia. This new escalation of hostilities marked the start of the final and most terrible phase of the war. Despite initial successes with Spain's help, after 1640 the French and Swedes had the upper hand. Ferdinand III (1608–1657), who had succeeded his father in 1637, found himself in an increasingly precarious military situation. Now, despite the terms of the Prague Peace Treaty, the secular electors deserted Friedrich one after the other and entered into separate agreements with the opposite side. The enemy made increasingly frequent forays into the heartlands of the empire: the French laid Bavaria waste and in 1648 advanced as far as the Inn. In the same year, the defeat of Prague gave the

Swedes their chance to plunder Rudolf II's famous *Kunstkammer*. Then in the winter of 1648–49, the Westphalian Peace Treaty granted the foreign powers the territories they wanted. Sweden was given the bishopric of Verden and archbishoprics of Bremen, Wismar and Upper Pomerania with Rügen. France took advantage of the Habsburg territories in Alsace. The Lorrainese bishoprics of Metz, Toul and Verdun seceded from the empire and were handed over to France. The terms of the treaty took on a constitutional function, and their observance was strictly guarded by the victors. The politics of Richelieu and his successor Cardinal Mazarin emerged triumphant and laid the foundation for the future status and strength of France.

1. There is no point in overloading a short article like this one with quotations and notes. Therefore, I have restricted myself to a minimum of explanations and references.

2. These were evident in the Peasants' Wars which plagued the empire in 1524–25, the Austrian territories in 1595–97 and Upper Austria in 1626; see H. Buszello, 'Der deutsche Bauernkrieg von 1525 als politische Bewegung', *Studien zur europäischen Geschichte*, 8 (1969); H. Feigl, 'Der niederösterreichische Bauernaufstand 1596/97', *Militärhistorische Schriftenreihe*, 22 (1978).

3. '... das alte bruchfällige reichsgebeu lieber stützen als vollends brechen' (quoted in E. W. Zeeden, 'Das Zeitalter der Glaubenskämpfe' in Gebhardt, *Handbuch der deutschen Geschichte*, vol. 9 [1970], p. 50).

4. In 1540, Pope Paul III ratified the formation of the Society of Jesus, which Ignatius had founded in Paris in 1534. This was an order of clerics that had neither lay associates nor female members; see B. Duhr, *Geschichte der Jesuiten in den Ländern deutscher Zunge*, 4 vols (1907–28).

5. Since 1527, the Imperial Court of Justice had met in Speyer; from 1693 until its dissolution in 1806, it met in Wetzlar.

6. The margrave of Baden-Durlach, Count von Öttingen, the imperial city of Strasbourg and the Reichsritter von Hirschhorn; see M. Ritter, *Deutsche Geschichte im Zeitalter der Gegenreformation und des dreißigjährigen Krieges*, vol. 2 (1895), pp. 160ff.

7. An umbrella term for a typical late humanist attitude prevalent around 1600. Pansophists believe that a single overarching form of science is both possible and desirable; see Erich Trunz, *Weltbild und Dichtung im deutschen Barock* (1992), pp. 40ff.

8. Charles IV (1316–1378) was the first emperor (beginning in 1346) to reside in Prague. His son and heir, Wenzel IV (1361–1419), also ruled the empire from Prague.

9. W. Leitsch, 'Rudolph II. und Südosteuropa 1593-1606', *East European Quarterly*, 6 (1974): 301ff.; see also the detailed account by A. Loebl, *Prager Studien aus dem Gebiet der Geschichtswissenschaften 6, 10: Zur Geschichte des Türkenkriegs von 1593–1606*, 3 vols (Prague, 1899–1904).

10. Archduke Leopold, bishop of Strasbourg and Passau, was the younger brother of the later emperor Ferdinand II from the Styrian line of the house of Habsburg. The notorious 'Passau men of war' whom he had recruited were to defend the interest of the imperial family in the disputes surrounding Jülich-Cleve-Berg according to Rudolf II's wishes and by force if need be.

11. The first Prague Defenestration, on 30 June 1419, had been the start of the Hussite uprising. A group of militant Hussites had forced their way into the council rooms of the Neustädt town hall and had thrown the Catholic councillors out of the window down into the street, where they were killed by an incensed mob.

12. The members of the Protestant Estates of the archdukedoms on and below the River Enns came together on 6 October 1608 as the so-called 'Horner Bund' and, having been granted additional religious rights, swore allegiance to King Matthias in March 1609.

13. Friedrich first fled to Silesia, then to the Netherlands and finally to the court in London. The military support which he had expected from his father-in-law King James I of England never materialized.

14. Zeeden (note 3), p. 99.

King Ferdinand I of Bohemia, Archduke Ferdinand II and the Prague Court, 1527–1567

MADELON SIMONS

The decision by the Czech nobility to crown Ferdinand Habsburg (1503–64) king of Bohemia in 1527 was not only significant for the Czech power structure. Ferdinand I, as the royal patron, had a pronounced influence on the appearance of the Bohemian court. During his time at Prague Castle, the seat may not have lost its aspect as a stronghold, but its gates were thrown open.

Why is it that interest in the Habsburg contribution to the Bohemian court is once again concentrated on Ferdinand's grandson, Emperor Rudolf II, whose political position was not strong?[1] One possible explanation is the openness of Rudolf's court to research by art historians. Rudolf II's move to Prague in 1583 gave rise to a unique and immediately discernible court culture.[2]

What had the culture of the royal court of Ferdinand I been like? That is the question which this study will try to answer. There are many sources which document the workings of the Prague court between 1527 and 1564, and a number of remarkable buildings were constructed then, both within Prague Castle and outside it. Research based on these sources does not automatically provide a coherent picture of the ways in which people thought and worked at the royal court, however. In order to find out more, we need written sources about the artists and scientists who shaped the Prague court – sources from which it would be possible to find out at least something about their ideas and opinions. That sort of period material is almost non-existent, however, and this is the main reason why our knowledge of the court culture of the time remains hypothetical.

Ferdinand I was born in Spain, the son of Philip I Habsburg and Joan of Castile. In 1521, he married Anna of Jagellon (1503–1547), the only sister of the king of Bohemia and Hungary Louis II of Jagellon. The wedding was the result of a concentrated and unusually successful marriage policy by the Habsburgs established by Ferdinand's grandfather Emperor Maximilian I (1459–1519). After the sudden death of his brother-in-law at the Battle of Mohács in 1526, Ferdinand thought that he could make a claim for the Czech throne, based on his relationship to Louis. However, the Czech nobles were against this, and Prague became the scene of intensive talks between representatives of the three Czech Estates: the nobles, the knights and the burghers. In the end, they decided to elect Ferdinand I king of Bohemia. This is not the place for a detailed analysis of the reasons why the Estates finally agreed to Ferdinand I despite their initial resistance.[3] Their political position is relevant, however. They did not believe that the royal title was hereditary, and it was not therefore of key importance in their eyes. What was more important for the Estates was the role of the ruler as the head of the Estates Parliament (*Landtag*). During its meetings, which took place twice a year, Ferdinand I had to be personally present in Prague, but he did not have to settle in Prague permanently. This function gave the King the right to revenue from various taxes, but this was not enough to maintain an expensive royal court in Prague.

The most important residences of Ferdinand I and Queen Anna after 1526 re-

mained their seats in Innsbruck and Vienna. The Viennese court gained in importance as an influential political centre for the eastern part of the Habsburg empire, especially after 1533, while Ferdinand's first children were born in Innsbruck – Maximilian II in 1527 and Ferdinand II in 1529.

It is symptomatic of our present state of information about life in the courts of Ferdinand I that we know little about his living arrangements. All we know is that he and Queen Anna had separate quarters in the 'Western Palace' in Prague, which bordered on the White Tower. The building was two-storeyed, and its south façade was part of the castle ramparts. Although Ferdinand complained of a lack of comfort, no notable alterations were made to the palace during his reign.[4] The Royal Palace, on the other hand, had been altered considerably during the reigns of Ferdinand's predecessors, Vladislav and Louis Jagellon. The imposing public rooms were added under the supervision of architect Benedict Ried, who died in 1534. The biggest room was the Vladislav Hall, also known as the throne room, but its use was much more varied and above all more dynamic than that term might imply. It was used for various meetings, assemblies and banquets, and even jousting tournaments were held there.[5]

The distinctions between styles which have been drawn by architectural historians are somewhat too rigid for a clear understanding of the history of Prague Castle's construction.[6] The point of reference for style labels has been Italian architecture of the fifteenth century. The work of Benedict Ried is not, for that reason, considered by many authors to be Renaissance, and although it is possible to recognize forms in his work which are taken from Italian models, Ried's buildings tend to be labelled Gothic. Although it is quite certain that Ried was acquainted with building types based on Vitruvius' writings, he clearly did not feel obliged to adhere strictly to this theoretical model. Wagner-Rieger believes that so many Italian architects were capable of creating or translating 'real Renaissance architecture' that no Italians can have worked for Ried.[7] Given the lack of written sources, our knowledge of Ried's opinions on Classical architecture and theoretical models is weak. From the material sources, however, it can be seen that the head of building activity at the Prague court was an individual and notable architect. With the arrival of Ferdinand I, pure Renaissance architecture arrived in Bohemia.

Ferdinand's activity as royal patron can be divided into two periods. During the first period, the King made decisions about a number of buildings, but these were only partially implemented, one of the causes being the extensive fire in the Lesser Town district in 1541, in which a large part of the Castle burnt down. Restoration work took precedence over new building. During the second period, after 1547, there was a revival at the royal court and a good deal more building work was ordered and started.

The first building commissioned by Ferdinand I dates from 1534, the year of Ried's death.[8] It may have been that the latter's demise opened up room for new projects. I am more inclined to believe, however, that the beginning of a big project in this year was connected with the strengthening of Ferdinand I's influence in Bohemia. It was only in the eighth year of his reign that the possibility presented itself of creating new public rooms for the Bohemian court.[9] On the north side of the Castle, he had the ramparts knocked down so that a large garden could be built. In the exhaustive biographical literature devoted to Ferdinand I in the nineteenth cen-

PRAGA BOHEMIÆ METROPOLIS,

tury, the creation of this area is explained by a love of gardens dating from his childhood in the Spanish court with his grandparents, Ferdinand and Isabella of Aragon. Although the King's personal interest in garden-making shines through in his correspondence,[10] it is more probable that personal considerations were not at the forefront when the character of his courts was created. What Ferdinand was aiming to do in the 1530s was to give Prague Castle, as well as his Vienna seat, the sort of royal stateliness and recreational possibilities which were growing in favour all over Europe. The gardens and parks of an aristocratic chĈteau or a palace in a natural setting following the Italian model became essential accoutrements at countless European courts in the first half of the sixteenth century.

Italian models were undoubtedly also of great importance for the Prague design, both for the overall ground plan of the garden complex and for the *Lusthof*, or summer palace, inside it.[11] However, no records of garden designs, animal enclosures, areas for sport and games or a summer palace by any famous Italian architect are preserved in either the Prague or Vienna archives.[12] It is characteristic that the creator of Ferdinand's gardens is unknown and that the plans have not been preserved. It almost seems as if Ferdinand I as king of Bohemia had no architect at the Prague court whose work was worthy of documentation.

In fact, the designs for the Prague Castle gardens were probably not made in Prague, but at the Vienna court. Vienna was the home of Ferdinand's financial chancellor, the court architect Hans Tscherte and also of several Germans and Italians, including members of the Spazio family. They were behind Ferdinand's great

CCVRATISSIME EXPRESSA.1.5.6.2.

3.1 JAN KOZEL
MICHAEL PETERLE
View of Prague
1562

building plans, which were never actually implemented to the extent originally intended because of lack of money. It is known that Hans Tscherte was also interested in architectural theory,[13] and he was probably capable of coping with the infrastructure of the Prague project, but whether he became the chief architect of the garden project remains uncertain.[14]

Work on the gardens proceeded slowly. Although eleven masons went to Prague from Vienna to work under Hans Spazio on the perimeter wall and the stone pillars for the bridge which was to connect the Castle with the gardens, the construction of the bridge itself took several years.[15] We do know a little about the way in which the gardens were divided up. Near the bridge, there were various wooden sheds and a gardener's house. Not far from the path leading from the Castle, there was also an area for exotic animals. There was a lion cage, at least one aviary and a wooden enclosure for an elk, which unfortunately had only a very short life in captivity.[16] Wild game wandered in the moat between the Castle and the gardens and could be hunted there.[17]

A large part of the gardens was taken up by fruit trees and vineyards. The ornamental gardens, herb gardens and exotic plants were probably on the sunny south side. These areas were certainly surrounded by wooden walls, or perhaps even roofed over with wooden galleries, which may be considered the precursors of the later enclosed orangeries for plants which could not be exposed to winter frosts.[18] Either this protection was not sufficient for the citrus trees or the gardener Francesco did not give them enough care, because by 1538 they had still not borne

[83]

fruit.[19] Although the King employed a number of gardeners and a botanist to oversee them, there are no signs that in the first years of their existence the gardens were used for study and research as they were in later times.[20]

In 1547, fundamental changes took place at the Prague court. King Ferdinand I gained a political victory over his Czech adversaries and managed to put a large number of the rebel Estates out of the power struggle. One result of this victory was that he made the throne safe for his heirs by unilaterally proclaiming his son Maximilian II the future king of Bohemia.[21] Ferdinand also strengthened his day-to-day contacts with Prague by appointing his younger son Archduke Ferdinand II governor of Bohemia. Before that, the king's representative in Bohemia had always been a Czech nobleman.

The arrival of the young Archduke Ferdinand II in Prague is very important for our picture of Bohemian court culture. This is not only because much of the correspondence between father and son has been preserved in the archives of the Prague governor's office, but because Ferdinand I documented many of his activities himself.[22]

Archduke Ferdinand II played a special role in Habsburg governing policy, because he did not give his life entirely to the crown. In 1557, he entered into a morganatic marriage with Philippina Welser, thus debarring himself from the throne. On finishing his studies in Innsbruck, he undertook a number of journeys across Europe, and from 1544 he lived partly in Prague, where his mother resided permanently.[23] From 1547 onwards, the Archduke, as governor of Bohemia, had a much larger court than his father. He frequently entertained numerous guests, and the number and diversity of his festivities and entertainments were greatly admired, as his biographer Josef Hirn describes at length. Visitors were amazed by the endless stream of high-born aristocrats, musicians and bodyguards. They praised Ferdinand's large and well-stocked stables, the extensive buildings and beautifully made gardens. According to Hirm, looking after the Castle buildings and ornamental gardens was one of his favourite activities.[24] Also famous were the large grounds in which the Archduke and his friends from the Czech nobility hunted game. Hirn says Ferdinand was in his element when preparing exceptional celebrations. He participated personally in the organization of various processions, welcoming ceremonies and allegorical theatre performances. He had the directions for such festivities written down in detail, making his own maps to accompany them.[25]

In describing the royal court and the Archduke, Hirn used mostly contemporary sources, but these, of course, had to meet the strict criteria of the Habsburg view of the world. We thus cannot expect to find any critical judgment of Prague court life in these written sources.[26] The chroniclers Collinus and Chutenus, for example, describe at length how in 1588 Ferdinand II directed all the details of the ceremonial arrival of his father in Prague. From their description – however exaggerated – it is clear what the extent of this reception was. The authors write that thousands of people lined the streets of Prague to cheer the King after his appointment as Holy Roman Emperor. In several places, he was addressed by a representative of a certain office or group. Houses were decorated with banners, flags and tapestries, and in many places there were triumphal arches and other decorations made especially for the occasion. These details reveal only a few of the many commissions which the royal court made from Prague craftsmen. Chutenus and Collinus themselves be-

longed to a group of Classically trained artists who created ideas and designs for theatrical performances.[27] However, they say nothing about the relationship between the 'intellectuals' who created the ceremonies and the craftsmen who made the decorations, and the decorations themselves have disappeared without trace.[28]

The iconography of the triumphal arches and the sculptures which decorated the fountains or of the theatre performances was definitely not complicated – this at least is clear from the writings of Chutenus and Collinus. Proof also exists in the description of a theatrical performance on the occasion of Emperor Ferdinand's arrival. Both Chutenus and Collinus took their accounts from Pietro Andrea Mattioli (1500–1577), Ferdinand II's court doctor, who unlike the chroniclers was an important guest. The performance, held in the garden near the Summer Palace, featured a struggle between Jupiter, personifying Habsburg power, and some giants, representing the Habsburgs' enemies. At the end, the huge paper figures of the giants went up in flames as part of a magnificent fireworks, and Jupiter's power was confirmed.[29]

The activities of the humanists Collinus and Chutenus and the residence of Mattioli at Ferdinand II's court in Prague are an indication that in the 1550s the court included a circle of scholars who engaged in research at the Archduke's bidding. Mattioli had an interest in botany and carried out various medical experiments.[30] The circle also included the unusually versatile Georg Hanch, the Archduke's personal doctor. Hanch did not publish much, but from the large number of manuscripts which have been preserved in Ferdinand's library, it can be seen that in addition to his medical work he had literary aspirations.[31] Hanch had received a humanist education, and his writings make it possible to understand at least something of the intellectual climate in which opinions were exchanged and ideas formed. Let us hope that in the future a deeper acquaintance with the written sources will bring deeper knowledge of Habsburg court culture under Ferdinand II.

The transient nature of the decorations for the Habsburg ceremonies in Prague means that they can tell us nothing about their form and quality, and so we have to turn to objects which have been preserved in their original form and which are the best-known results of Ferdinand's role as royal commissioner. The Summer Palace in the Royal Gardens and the Star (Hvězda) Villa on White Mountain still exist unchanged.

The building of the Royal Summer Palace started in 1538 with the arrival of Italian architect Paolo Stella.[32] Stella brought with him Italian masons and a model of the building. The long, narrow structure with its arcaded gallery is generally labelled Renaissance. Krčálová has called it the first fully preserved Renaissance garden building in central Europe.[33] For a survey of the culture of the Prague court, however, what is much more interesting than the question of the building's architectural style is the problem of who designed it. The model of the Summer Palace is attributed to Stella because it was he who brought it from Genoa. According to Wagner-Rieger, however, he was not its author.[34] On the basis of his reliefs for the Summer Palace, Wagner-Rieger calls Stella an eclectic who was not himself capable of developing Classical architectural theory in a creative way. Something else which makes it unlikely that Stella was the architect is the fact that he was not entrusted with overseeing the building in 1538, only from 1545 onwards.

Who, then, did design the Summer Palace? Did Ferdinand I use the services of

Italian architects who provided plans to order, but otherwise did not work directly on the project? I have no answers to these questions as yet. Our ignorance of the architect of the Royal Summer Palace is merely proof of the lack of links between royal commissions and Prague court culture. The King did not use Czech artists or craftsmen, and he introduced a new type of building into the country, one which could only be used in the summer months, however.[35]

Paolo Stella did not finish the Summer Palace. When he died in 1552, only the ground floor and the first storey with its arcaded gallery had been completed.[36] Some of the sandstone reliefs on the walls between the arches are, Wagner-Rieger believes, undoubtedly Stella's work.[37] After 1552, the Prague building projects were overseen by Germans. On Stella's death, the master builder became Hans Tirol, and in 1555 the function was taken over by Bonifaz Wohlmut. Under his supervision, the roof was completed according to his own design.[38] The first floor with its gallery was decorated with wall paintings including portraits of kings of Bohemia.

In 1555, work on the summer residence in the new royal enclosure on White Mountain, six kilometres to the west of Prague Castle, was started. I consider this summer palace the most remarkable project to have taken place under Ferdinand I. The building of the villa known as the Star, or Golden Star, embodies our fragmentary knowledge of court culture during the reign of Ferdinand I.

At the Star Villa, Tirol was again superseded by Bonifaz Wohlmut, in the autumn of the year in which construction began. The Italian craftsmen were headed by Giovanni Lucchese. Officially, the Star is not ascribed to any of these architects, but to Archduke Ferdinand himself.[39] The text which says that he was the author is understandably written in the form of a *laudatio*, but it is likely that it is genuine proof of his direct participation in the design of the building.

Who, together with the Archduke, drew the plans for the six-pointed star? Was it the same Italian who gave the different storeys of the Royal Summer Palace such diverse appearances? What is certain is that the walls of the Star Villa were laid in the Italian fashion.[40] From this it is possible to conclude that, like the Royal Summer Palace, it was built by a group of foreign builders. Its stucco interior is also the work of Italian craftsmen. Was its unknown architect one of the fortification designers who worked for Ferdinand in Hungary and Vienna? Did he, together with Tscherte, experiment with various geometric forms, often used in the construction of star-shaped city fortifications?[41] Did he make use of these skills when he worked with Ferdinand on the plans for a building which was to serve as a museum?[42] In expressing the belief that Archduke Ferdinand was working in 1555 in Prague on plans for premises in which he could house his collections, as he later did in Ambras, I am perhaps letting myself be overwhelmed by the amazement which the unusual design of the Star Villa provokes.[43] The countless niches on the ground and first floors simply cry out for sculptures and suits of armour to be placed within them.[44]

Of the building's four storeys, only the function of the top one is clear. It has a tiled floor with a surface which is not very slippery, making it suitable for dancing. The Archduke ordered a similar floor for the Summer Palace at Prague Castle.[45] The Star Villa thus must have had the same function. A building for relaxation and court pastimes, it definitely was not meant as a residence or magic centre for the study of cosmology, numerology or other such phenomena.[46] The perfectly pre-

served stucco decoration in the ground-floor vaults clearly shows the public function of the whole building.[47] Whether or not the armour of courageous members of the Habsburg family stood in the niches of the Star Villa, the ruler could certainly have shown his guests the heroes of Classical myth. In the centre of the dodecagonal hall was the figure of Aeneas leaving the burning Troy with his father on his shoulders. However, the theory that the stucco decoration is programmatic or that there is a connection between the various scenes has, I believe, to be abandoned. A deliberate pictorial programme would have asked too much of visitors to the villa. After all, they would just have returned from hunting.

1. See *Prag um 1600: Kunst und Kultur am Hofe Rudolfs II.*, exh. cat., 2 vols (Freren, 1988).

2. See R. J. W. Evans, *Rudolf and His World: A Study In Intellectual History 1576–1612* (Oxford, 1973), pp. 116–95, Eliška Fučíková, Beket Bukovinská and Ivan Muchka, *Die Kunst am Hofe Rudolf II* (Prague, 1988).

3. F. B. von Buchholtz, *Geschichte der Regierung Ferdinands des Ersten*, 9 vols (Vienna 1831–38), vol, 2, sect. 7, pp. 395–425. Karl Bosl has summarized the demands and conditions regarding the King's choice in a different way from Buchholtz; see Karl Bosl, *Die Geschichte der Böhmischen Länder*, vol. 2 (Stuttgart, 1974), p. 148. In not taking up residence in Prague, Ferdinand was breaking his word. On his policies, see Buchholtz, sects 4 and 6, 'Innere Verwaltung Böhmens', pp. 417–538.

4. Martin Mandlmayr, 'Die Beschreibung der Krönungen durch Hans Habersack' in *Fontes Rerum Austriacarum 13: Scriptores* (Vienna, 1990), p. 47. Milada Vilímková, *Praha na úsvitu nových déjin* (Prague, 1988), p. 46, describes the alterations to the Royal Palace and Louis' wing.

5. For example, on 26 February 1527, to celebrate the coronation of Ferdinand I and Queen Anna, a tournament was held in the Vladislav Hall. The King entered the ring in the company of twelve Czech and German lords, while the master of ceremonies Pietro Cordoba led a group of Spanish and Dutch lords. In the Vladislav Hall, there was a standing tribune with thirty benches on which the Queen and twenty-three noblewomen stood. The jousters had slanting saddles (high at the front, low at the back) and small horses. See Buchholtz (note 3), vol. 2, sect. 7, pp. 444–47.

6. See O. Pollak, 'Studien zur Geschichte der Architektur Prags 1520–1600', *Jahrbuch der kunsthistorischen Sammlungen*, 29 (1910–11), pp. 85–170; O. Schürer, *Prag, Kultur, Kunst, Geschichte* (Vienna, 1935), p. 1; Eva Samanková, 'Über die Anfänge der Tschechische Renaissance-Architektur', *Acta Hist. Art. Hung.*, 13 (1967), pp. 115–22. Jarmila Krčálová, *Die Kunst der Renaissance und des Manierismus* (Prague, 1979), pp. 51–76.

7. Renate Wagner-Rieger, 'Die Renaissancearchitektur in Österreich, Böhmen und Ungarn in ihrem Verhältnis zu Italien bis zur Mitte des 16. Jahrhunderts' in *Arte e artisti dei laghi lombardi*, vol. 1 (Como, 1964), pp. 463–65.

8. Karl Köpel, 'Urkunden, Akten, Regesten und Inventare aus dem K.K. Statthalterei-Archiv in Prag 1529–1600', *Jahrbuch des Allerhöchsten Kaiserhauses*, 10 (1889), sect. 63–200, reg. 5959. It is interesting that Bonifaz Wohlmut, later to become court architect, was already in Prague in 1534. His position at this time was not yet such that he could play an important role in Ferdinand I's building plans for Prague.

9. Work on the gardens was financed from, among other sources, revenues from Prague's Jews; see Köpel (note 8), reg. 6048.

10. Jarmila Krčálová, 'Die Gärten Rudolfs II', *Leids Kunsthistorisch Jaarboek* (1982), p. 149.

11. See Egon Verheyen, *The Palazzo del Te in Mantua* (Baltimore and London, 1982), pp. 16–19.

12. Amedeo Belluzi and Kurt W. Forster, 'Giulio Romano al corte dei Gonzaga' in exh. cat. *Giulio Romano* (Milan, 1989), pp. 177–226, 317–83.

13. Hans Tscherte was a friend of Albrecht Dürer, to whom he sent mathematical precepts, probably in connection with Dürer's publication *Unterricht zur Befestigung der Städte, Märkte und Schlösser*; see Hans Rupprich, *Albrecht Dürer schriftlicher Nachlass*, vol. 1 (Berlin, 1956), p. 94, n. 40. In 1534, Tscherte was commissioned to design a water conduit for the Hofburg. See Harry Kuehnel, 'Die landesfuerstlichen Baumeister der Wiener Hofburg, 1494–1564' in *Forschungsergebnisse zur Geschichte der Wiener Hofburg*, vol. 3 (Vienna, 1960).

14. Despite the problems which occurred between the Czech overseers and the Italian masons during the construction of the bridge (under the leadership of Hans Spazio) and the Summer Palace (under the leadership of Paolo Stella), Tscherte is frequently cited as a very knowledgeable architect. Whether he actually went to Prague remains unclear, however (Köpel [note 8], reg. 6004 27.6.1538: 'Dieweil dann disz gepeu, wie der Tscherte und er selbst anfenkhlich angezaigt...'; reg. 6007, 3.8.1538: '...liese eur maj. prunmaister von Wienn den Tscherte ... noch ain rais herein thuen...').

15. Köpel (note 8), reg. 5959, 5962.

16. Buchholtz (note 3), vol. 4, p. 535 (no source given).

17. Köpel (note 8), reg. 6043 on partridges in the moat. In his notes, Archduke Ferdinand calls this area a hunting ground – 'der alte Tiergarten'.

18. Krčálová (note 10), p. 152, n. 8.

19. Köpel (note 8), 1889, reg. 6004. Without giving a source, Buchholtz (note 3) wrote about a supply of saplings, apricot grafts for plums, rosebushes and plant seeds which were ordered from Naples and Genoa.

20. For the arrival of the Dutch botanist Dr H. Velius in March 1539 and his departure in November 1539, see Köpel (note 8), reg. 6035. Velius worked on the area of the gardens in the moat under the bridge. It is open to question whether this part of the garden was 'Dutch' in character, as Z. Winter claims in *Řemeslnictvo a Živnosti XVI. věku v Čechách, 1526-1620* (Prague, 1909), p. 575. Velius was more likely to have offered advice on an enclosed terraced garden.

21. Berthold Bretholz, *Neuere Geschichte Böhmens* (Gotha, 1929), pp. 213-22; Paula Sutter Fichner: 'When Brothers Agree: Bohemia, the Habsburgs and the Schmalkaldic Wars, 1546-47', *Austrian History Yearbook*, 11 (1975). The Prague parliament (Landtag) only agreed with this decision in 1549 (Buchholtz [note 3], vol. 7, p. 486).

22. 'Hochzeitsturnier in München' (KK5346). See Alfred Auer and Eva Irblich, '*Natur und Kunst': Handschriften und Alben aus der Ambraser Sammlung Erzherzog Ferdinand II. (1529-1595)*, exh. cat. (Vienna, 1995).

23. Queen Anna died in Prague in 1547 during the birth of her fifteenth child. She spent the last three years of her life in Prague because of the danger of Turkish attacks on Vienna. She was buried in St Vitus' cathedral in Prague Castle.

24. Joseph Hirn, *Erzeherzog Ferdinand von Tirol*, vol. 1 (Innsbruck, 1885), p. 35. Hirn follows a work by Laurentius Spanus, *Ferdinando Pyrgum* (Vienna, Hofbibliothek, 9902, Ms. Ambras 473).

25. That Ferdinand I kept detailed records is clear from his notes, which were preserved in his library. For example, in his *Jagdtagebücher* (Hunting Diary), he recorded how many animals he had killed and where. Hirn vol. 2, p. 486. See also Auer and Irblick (note 22).

26. Martinus Chutenus and Mattheus Collinus, *Brevis descriptio pompae...* (Prague, 1558); *Ignaz Cornova: Beschreibung des feyerlichen Einzugs Kaiser Ferdinand I in die Hauptstadt Prag des 8sten Nov. 1559, aus den lateinischen einer gleichzeitigen Feders übersetzt mit Anmerkungen begleitet* (Prague, 1802).

27. Chutenus and Collinus were humanists from the circle of Jan Hodějovský of Hodějov. See Hans-Bernd Harder, 'Zentren des Humanismus in Böhmen und Mähren im 16. Jahrhundert' in A. Buck *et al.* (eds), *Europäische Hofkultur im 16. und 17. Jahrhundert*, vol. 2 (Hamburg, 1979), pp. 161-62; Z. Horský: 'Die Europäische Bedeutung der Böhmischen Tradition der "Neuen Wissenschaft" im 16. Jahrhundert' in H. B. Harder (ed.), *Studien zum Humanismus in den Böhmischen Ländern* (Cologne and Vienna, 1988), pp. 281-84.

28. The decorations were kept, but clearly not carefully enough. The three huge figures used during the celebrations of Emperor Ferdinand I's arrival were stored in a shed in the Castle gardens. See Jahrbuch 5, Franz Kreyczi, K. und K. Reichs Finanz Archiv, reg. 4340, 5.4.1563.

29. Cornova (note 26), p. 94.

30. Harry Kühnel, 'Pietro Andrea Mattioli, Leibartz und Botaniker des 16. Jahrhunderts', *Mitteilungen des Öster. Staatsarchiv*, 15 (1962).

31. There are over forty-five manuscripts by Hanch in the Hofbibliothek, Vienna, with various titles, including medical diaries (e.g., 11204, 1, 2, 4), descriptions of animals (*Historia animalum* 1 [11143]-5 [11142]) and collections of poetry (*Poemata latina* [9821]). A more detailed analysis of his diary notes could provide much information about the Prague court.

32. Köpel (note 8), reg. 6007.

33. Krčálová (note 10), p. 51. This purity of style is shown by the use of characteristic forms which can be identified in theoretical writings on architecture. The Summer Palace's door and window frames are said to have been taken from the fourth book of Serlius, published in 1537.

34. Wagner-Rieger (note 7), p. 468.

35. Collinus and Chutenus noted the Royal Summer Palace was unusually suited for walks in hot summer weather (Cornova [note 26], p. 92).

36. Much more of the groundwork of the Summer Palace was visible than it is today. See Erich Hubala, 'Palast und Schlossbau, Villa und Gartenarchitektur (...)' in F. Seibt (ed.), *Renaissance in Böhmen* (1985), pp. 53-55.

37. Wagner-Rieger (note 7), p. 468.

38. D. von Schönherr, 'Urkunden und Regesten aus dem K. K. Statthaltereiarchiv in Innsbruck', *Jahrbuch d. A. Kh.*, 11 (1890). On the interior of the Summer Palace, see reg. 7463. Ferdinand wanted paintings of stars, planets and the signs of the zodiac on the wooden ceiling. The copper roof was to be executed in the Habsburg colours of white and red.

39. Schönherr (note 38), 7143, 25.6.1555; 'David von Schönherr, 'Erzherzog Ferdinand von Tirol als Architekt', *Repertorium für Kunstwissenschaft*, 1 (1876), 28-44; R. von Falke, *Schloss Stern* (Wenen, 1879). One of the five epitaphs: 'Abgemessen, gemacht und circuliert, von einem Fürsten lobeleich, Ferdinand Erzherzog von Österreich'.

40. See Schönherr (note 38), 7175, on the shortage of bricks. The existence of bricks in the wall was (re)confirmed during restoration work by architect B. Kozánková in 1993.

41. Leone A. Maggirotti, *Architetti e Architettura Militari* (Rome, 1937), pp. 97-197.

42. This hypothesis can be backed up by similar designs. See, for example, Marcin Fabianski, 'Iconography of the Architecture of Ideal Musea in the Fifteenth to Eighteenth Centuries', *Journal of the History of Collections*, 2:2 (1990), pp. 95-134; Liliane Chatelet-Lange, 'Le Museo di Vanves (1560)', *Zeitschrift für Kunstgeschichte*, 38 (1975), p. 272; Cabinet d'Antiques in the tower of the chateau at Tanlay.

43. During Ferdinand's time as governor, there was an increase in the number of remarkable commissions which the Archduke made, for example with goldsmiths (including Wenzel Jamnitzer), embroiderers, tapestry workshops (Brussels) and portrait painters. The biggest commissions were for armour. On the collections of Archduke Ferdinand II and their installation at Schloss Ambras, see L. Luchner, *Denkmal eines Renaissancefürsten, Versuch einer Rekonstruktionen des Ambraser Museums von 1583* (Vienna, 1958); Elisabeth Scheicher, 'The Collection of Archduke Ferdinand II at Schloss Ambras: Its Purpose, Composition and Evolution' in O. Impey and A. MacGregor (eds), *The Origins of*

Museums (Oxford, 1985), pp. 29–38.

44. E. Scheicher, 'Historiography and Display: The "Heldenrüstkammer" of Archduke Ferdinand II in Schloss Ambras', *Journal of the History of Collections*, 2:1 (1990), pp. 69–79. The idea that the Star Villa or at least its ground floor was intended as 'exhibition space' is also found in Christian Gries, 'Erzherzog Ferdinand von Tirol, Kontouren einer Sammlerpersönlichkeit', *Frühneuzeit-Info*, 4:2 (1993).

45. Schönherr (note 38), reg. 7463.

46. Martin Stejskal's hypothesis. In '*Hvězda', pokus o vymezení pražského letohrádku jako filosofického obydlí* (Prague, no date) he tries to connect various kinds of magic cosmological symbols with the iconography of the Star Villa. However, his hypotheses are not sufficiently backed up by written sources.

47. Milada Lejsková, 'K ikonologii figurálních štuků Hvězdy', *Umění*, 11 (1963), 209–11; Miloš Suchomel, 'Štuková vyzdoba letohrádku Hvězda', *Umění*, 21 (1973), 112–16.

Architectural Styles in the Reign of Rudolf II: Italian and Hispanic Influences

IVAN MUCHKA

The oscillation between the personal wishes of the builder and the general spirit of the times provokes constant questions of the history of architecture. A work of architecture is, of course, shaped by many factors, and it is very difficult and misleading to single out one of them as being dominant. Questions as to whether a building is new or a conversion, how it relates to its surroundings and terrain, and how it is configured and in what context put architecture in a completely different category from paintings or even works of applied art. To talk about someone 'giving priority' to painting over architecture is also misleading. The architect cannot 'merely' be ostentatious or 'merely' aim to fit something in somewhere gently and modestly, simply to fill existing space.

Site naturally played a much greater role in Prague, on the rocky heights of Hradčany, than it might have in a flat landscape. Even Rome's seven hills, to which Prague is sometimes compared, are far from being as dramatic as the area in which the developments we are now tracing took place. The configuration of Hradčany, the 'town of a hundred houses', as the Protestant priest Martinides described it in 1615, does not correspond to our normal idea of a 'castle' or 'ruler's residence'. Demolishing and replacing everything which already existed on the site was never anyone's intention.

Rudolf II is one of history's distinctive individuals, swathed in conjecture, impression and rumour. Because the nature of Rudolfine painting, sculpture and applied art is well known, it has understandably been tempting to speculate as to whether its introverted, closed, precious nature was carried over into architecture – whether there exist, for example, 'Archimboldesque' composite forms in Rudolfine buildings. The answer to this question is no less paradoxical than the period itself. There is the example of the 'Archimboldesque herms',[1] but these are very unlikely to have ever been used by the architects of Prague Castle. A whole treatise on architecture by Wendel Dietterlin[2] was published, full of bizarre, extravagant and original shapes and forms which correspond perfectly to what we might expect Mannerist architecture to look like. However, these were not used in Prague either. One treatise was even published in Prague itself in 1600, but it too failed to have any direct influence on architectural style at the court.[3]

Until now, all study of Rudolfine architecture has been marked by the fact that researchers were to some extent inhibited by the traditional assertions that architecture was not of interest to Rudolf and that no architecture of note was produced during his reign. The first thing scholars felt they had to show, therefore, was that under Rudolf a lot of building did go on. The question of what sort of building this might have been was pushed into the background.[4] Although these researchers were undoubtedly successful, it is a sad fact that the degree of preservation of buildings initiated by Rudolf is very low, owing to several unfavourable circumstances. Most analyses therefore have to take place on the basis of 'imaginative reconstructions' of Rudolfine buildings. This means maximum use of analogy and

comparison – in other words, mediated information – while stylistic analysis requires primary information.

At Prague Castle, for example, research is permanently frustrated by missing parts, without which the picture is incomplete. The list of 'losses' includes the portal of the Mathematics Tower in the middle wing, which appears on eighteenth-century plans but only in summary form, and the portal of the building with the New Room – now the Spanish Room – on the west side, from the garden on the ramparts.[5]

The portal of the Mathematics Tower, elevated by four degrees because of the terrain, consisted of columns or half-columns at the front and pilasters at the back. It was much like the portal of the church in Smečno; its fairly slender proportions could indicate that the columns were also Ionic. However, in the case of the portal in Smečno, the semicircular entrance ends under the entablature, whereas the Mathematics Tower portal had a taller entrance, reducing the architrave and cornice to mere sections above the columns. What is almost identical is the split pediment, which inside has characteristic shell-shaped sections, and in the Prague case a vase or urn, while at Smečno the pediment contains a further form, a small aedicule with an inscription. The church in Smečno, built under Jiří Bořita of Martinice and Eliška of Vrbno, was finished in 1587, and the portal is one of the most advanced examples of Italianate masonry in central Bohemia. Interestingly, a split triangular pediment can be found both at Prague Castle and at Rudolf's Castra Doloris, including similar turned sections and a central motif, in this case the Habsburg coat of arms. A segmented but unbroken pediment was used by the architect of the portal of St Adalbert's chapel in 1575, and this could be called a prologue to the Italianate character of the architecture of Rudolf II's reign.

The reason portals are so important in analyses of architectural style is that in sixteenth-century architecture, they represent a certain conscious *pars pro toto* – an embodiment, visualization or compression of what the architecture was meant to express. Architects considered the portal to be of central importance, not just to serve a practical function. This can be seen in the case of both portals on the All Saints' chapel, on which outstanding care was lavished by both architect and mason. Even surfaces which cannot be directly seen from the front were worked in detail. The portal from the Vladislav Hall to the All Saints' chapel is at a disadvantage partly because of its height – a result of the floor of the hall and that of the choir being at different levels – partly by being next to windows, which originally led out of the hall to the east, and partly because of the lack of natural lighting today. One of the consummate works of Czech architecture at the end of the sixteenth century, this portal thus does not show some of its details to best advantage.

When inquiring into the character of Rudolfine architectural style, we should start by ascertaining whether Rudolf II's own opinions provide any clue. Probably the only direct ones are in the correspondence between him and his envoy to the Spanish court, Khevenhüller, whom he repeatedly asked to send views of Spanish buildings. The assiduousness with which Rudolf went about this suggests that the issue had genuine importance for him.[6]

Rudolf sent the first letter to his envoy in Madrid in February 1588, repeating his request in November. It is interesting to note that he used the word *abriß*, a term used in the 'technical' documentation of buildings. This seems to indicate that

Rudolf wanted to have as detailed an idea as possible of buildings which he had only been able to see in their embryonic states when he was in Spain. The original request concerns the Escorial and other, unspecified royal buildings. In November, the name Aranjuez was added. In April of the following year, ten engravings of the Escorial arrived in Prague with the promise that other buildings – summer palaces in Aranjuez and Segovia – would be added in the form of oil paintings.[7] These could have been further summer residences of Philip II, such as the Pardo and Balsain palaces. We shall return to the Escorial in more detail later; what concrete inspiration Rudolf could have drawn from Philip II's summer palaces is difficult to evaluate.

A hitherto unknown project by Rudolf was situated in the Stromovka Park ('Im alten Thiergarten'), most probably just to the south of the large lake, approximately where the Mitrovský summer pavilion, known in this century as the Šlechta restaurant, was later built. The design for this project was not made until 1604. Costing a remarkable 41,115 guilders, it was to be a three-storey building of 48 by 44 paces (approximately 91 by 84 metres) with a central courtyard, five 'various' corridors, two halls and eighty rooms.[8] The drawing of Aranjuez from the sixteenth century, preserved in the Österreichische Nationalbibliothek (Sig. Cod. 6481), shows a small three-storey palace around a central, enclosed courtyard with an arcaded cloister surrounding it. The extent – both spatial and financial – of this undertaking shows that Rudolf's aims remained, surprisingly, just as grandiose as they had been earlier in his life. Almost thirty years after he had ascended the throne, and at a relatively advanced age, he did not consider his building plans to be finished.

The building about which Rudolf had most wanted information was, of course, the Escorial.[9] It was built on a terrace on the south slope of the Sierra del Guadarrama, and thus partly in the same situation as Prague Castle, but on more moderate terrain. Construction had started in 1562 under the direct supervision of Philip II, according to a 'general design' by Juan Bautista de Toledo. From 1569 onwards, the architect was Juan de Herrera. The building was finished in about 1574, but various alterations, mostly interior ones, continued for some years afterwards.

We must ask ourselves how the architecture of the Escorial – an austere monastery-like stronghold embracing the church of Saint Lawrence – could have been of significance for the creation of Prague Castle or other Prague buildings which Rudolf initiated. The perfectly symmetrical Escorial, with its grid plan of sixteen courtyards and the church 'placed' within it in a manner reminiscent of the end met by its patron, Lawrence the Martyr, was certainly not a direct model for Prague Castle, a structure which developed organically.

It clearly was influential on Rudolf, however. San Lorenzo el Real de El Escorial, the embodiment of Spanish power, had been built from scratch to commemorate the great victory over French troops in the Battle of San Quentino on 10 August 1557, St Lawrence's Day. That date had a direct influence on the huge building, which is about 215 by 210 metres in size. Its main axis runs through the church of St Lawrence on only an approximate east–west axis, since it is rotated 16 degrees to meet the setting on 10 August. This orientation was established by astrologers, just as philosophers and mystics had a say in its design – the ground plan alludes to the life of the saint, and the form is connected with the new Temple of Solomon. Another factor in the building's design was that Charles V had ended his days in the

Jeronymite monastery in Yusta. The Escorial, where Philip II intended to die, was given to the same order. Because the Escorial was built as a magnificent monument to the Habsburgs, monks were meant to pray for the family's salvation. At the same time, however, it was a huge religious training institution, with dormitories and school buildings. Its educational ambitions determined the form of the entrance side to the west, with its largest room, a library, being placed immediately behind the central motif of the façade, which combined the Vignolaesque façade of Il Gesu with an Antique triumphal arch. Anyone seeking an embodiment of the Latin motto 'temple and tower' would find it here.

The fact that the Escorial is one of the most remarkable works of European architecture is not due merely to its originality and purely aesthetic qualities but to the non-transferable spirit of the place, which must have affected Rudolf even across the borders of countries. Its style was also important, however. Juan Bautista de Toledo had worked as Michelangelo's assistant on the Vatican, and Juan de Herrera was Spain's most Italian-orientated architect of the sixteenth century. The Italo-Dutch style, the term sometimes used to describe the Escorial, included barrel vaults, Italian fireplaces and Vredeman portals. Perhaps the only specifically Spanish element were the wonderful ceramic floor and wall tiles, but even these have a 'standard European' acanthus pattern. The Italianate style of the Escorial essentially mirrors the case of the Alhambra in Grenada at the beginning of the sixteenth century. That building, begun in 1526 by Pedro Machuca for Charles V, is such a textbook example of Italian orientation in a country dominated by the 'Moorish' style that it could be mistaken for Raphael's Villa Madama in Rome or a building by Giulio Romano.[10]

The interiors of the Escorial present an interesting paradox. Although this was the richest and most powerful royal family in Europe (Philip II was king of Naples, Sicily and Milan, and from 1555 also ruler of the Netherlands), the living quarters of the Habsburgs are not at all magnificent, but of almost striking modesty. This is not true, however, as far as their siting is concerned – the placement of Philip's bedroom in immediate proximity to the main altar is architecturally unique.[11]

If we compare the Escorial with Prague Castle, in a general way, certain factors such as *genius loci* played a fundamental role in both cases. For example, the creation of formalized, symmetrical courtyards in Prague, which Rudolf may have wanted and which formed part of the alterations carried out mostly in the Teresian period, encountered natural resistance in the medieval character of the existing buildings (the cathedral, monastery and royal palace). The captivating charm and picturesque beauty of the Castle definitely did not support attempts to create open courtyards. However, two important parts of both buildings do merit comparison.

If we forget the colossal nature of the Escorial and compare the western main entrance with the main entrance, also to the west, of Prague Castle, the Matthias Gate, interesting and surprising affinities can be found. Both gates are multi-levelled, with Doric columns at ground level and Ionic ones above. The Ionic aedicules have triangular pediments with quarter-circle wings at each side, terminating in obelisks. The ground-level configurations actually have rows of columns – in the Escorial three of them, in Prague two – as is shown by the rectangular windows between the Doric supports. The Escorial entrance is wider and has eight half-columns below and four on the first level. The Prague entrance is more vertically

developed and has only four pilasters at ground level and two up above. The difference is perhaps most striking in the obelisks. In both cases, they rest on bases and stone balls, with their tips 'piercing' other balls. However, while the Prague obelisks are slender and elegant, the Spanish ones are bulky, almost paunchy. The doubling of the half-column travée at the Escorial gives the impression of a cathedral façade, while the Prague entrance is more of a gate in the city walls, with typical rustic-work.

In both cases, the aedicule contains a carved coat of arms, but in Prague this is much larger and more monumental, given emphasis partly by the perfectly sculpted griffins which hold it. However, the coat of arms and griffins have to compete with the upper part of the stuccowork, where there is a doubtful inscription about the construction made by Emperor Matthias in 1614 and held by stucco ephebes.[12]

At the Escorial, the upper part of the aedicule is filled, logically and in keeping with the coat of arms there, by a statue of the patron, which thus crowns the construction both literally and figuratively. A comparison of the two constructions indicates the probable time difference between them – the Prague entrance is, despite the use of pilasters, more dynamic and more interesting from the point of view of tectonics. The main emphasis falls on the semicircular entrance, whereas the rectangular doors at the Escorial command little attention. The Prague construction is two-layered, and the cornice between the upper and lower parts breaks up the vertical elements. The pilasters have no bases, in contrast to the nearby obelisks. The most movement, however, is in the rustic-work, which contrasts with the smooth surface and is formed into bands alternating in groups of two and three. This complicated rhythm even occurs in the rustic-work voussoirs, which in the case of the rectangular windows form an entirely 'unclassical' joke because in the bottom parts they are turned upside down.

The Escorial's entrance façade, in which the frames of the rectangular windows only sometimes protrude from the smooth surface, might have been echoed in the façade of the unpreserved middle wing at Prague Castle, just as the interesting, but also unpreserved, Mathematics Tower could have been reminiscent of the prismatic corner tower of the Escorial. This tower rises four storeys above the crowing cornice and ends in balustraded attic gables. All of these architectural forms are so general in character that to search for their prototypes would be to ignore historical logic, however. Perhaps Rudolf's interest in the Escorial was linked with a policy which involved favouring Spain over France, the Habsburgs' eternal rival. In this connection, we might explore the reason for the use of the adjective *Spanish* to describe the stables and halls in the north wing at Prague Castle, which have been known as 'Spanish' since the time of their construction. This difficult question was posed by Peter Fiedler, who was struck by the relatively frequent use of the term by the Habsburg monarchy.[13] Unfortunately, in the case of the oldest occurrence – the hall at Ambras – the term is not recorded in the archives at the time of construction. Nonetheless, further analysis would be worthwhile.

However misleading it might be to connect political and social aspects too closely with artistic ones, the hypothesis that Spanish forms were more 'politically correct' than Protestant or French ones sounds generally credible. In the case of Rudolf II, it can be taken as a working theory that a certain amount of solidarity between the Habsburgs was reality, although from a purely geographical point of

view it seems improbable. With a little exaggeration, it is possible to say that in Prague we can see the rejection of all styles and modalities which might be too suggestive of the Northern, largely 'Protestant', style of Mannerist architecture.

1. Daniel Meyer, *Architectura* (Frankfurt, 1609).

2. Wendel Dietterlin, *Architectura Von Austheilung, Symmetria und Proportion der Funff Seulen* (Nürnberg, 1598).

3. Gabriel Krammer, *Architectura* (Prague, 1600). With this work the usual rules were followed, namely that the Emperor banned any further editions for five years under the usual conditions and that three copies were sent to the Imperial Court Office. Compare reg. 12 459 of 20 February 1599.

4. A brief survey of the literature on the subject of this essay is given in the notes to Ivan Muchka, 'Rudolf II jako stavbiník' in *Uměni na dvoře Rudolfa II* (Prague, 1988), pp. 180–212.

5. Kunz's plan of Prague Castle shows the façade of the Spanish Room before its alteration under Empress Maria Theresa – with three window axes, which on the unbroken façade seem odd, almost minute. On the southermost axis, there is a summarily executed portal, connected to the structure by a window above it. However, the form of the portal – for example, its compressed entrance arch and balustrade and the indented door space – makes it unlikely to be from around 1600, and we can only reconstruct the form of the original portal with great difficulty.

6. For Khevenhüller compare Georg Khevenhüller-Metsch, *Hans Khevenhüller, kaiserlicher Botschafter bei Philipp II: Geheimes Tagebuch 1548–1605* (Graz, 1971). This publication has reproductions of drawings of the Escorial, the Aranjuez summer palace (both Vienna, Österreichische Nationalbibliothek, Cod. 6461) and the hunting lodge called 'La Casa De Bosco De Segovia' (Österreichische Nationalbibliothek, Cod. Min. 41), which could have a connection with the above-mentioned correspondence.

7. *Jahrbuch ... Wien*, 13 (1892), Reg. 9547, 4.2.1588: 'Rudolf II beauftragt den Hans Freiherrn von Khevenhüller, nachdem er von des Königs von Spanien fürnemeren heuser und lustheuser als Escurial und anderer abriss haben wolte, ihm solche zu übersenden'; Conc. Pap. Spanische Acten. Reg. 9583 11.11.1588: 'Was dann die disgenos Aranjuez und san Lorenzo el Real betrufft, die sollen nicht fällen und möcht's vileicht obberwerter mein diener auch mitzufuehren', Reg. 9590, 10.12.1588: 'Die Zeichnungen von Aranjuez und dem Escurial werde er nächstens übersenden'; 29.4.1589: 'übersendet das gegen de sanct Lorenco el Real in khupfer gestochen. Dero seien 10. Stück. Aranjuez y la case des bosques de Segovia läßt der khünig in Ölfarben stellen, hat aber darumben, das vill weil bedarf, auf dies mall nicht khunen fertig werden; solle, geliebt's gott, volgen.'

8. 'Bemachter Überschlag Wegen Erbauung eines Neuen wonhaus Im alten thiergarten 19.10.1604 (Actum Bauschreiber amt) ... 48 Klafter lang und 44 Klafter breit, in der mitte ein ziemblich grosser Platz oder Hof 3 Gaden Hoch mit 5 underschiedlichen Gängen, 2 Sall und 80 Zimmern erbaut daran vonnäthen ... 41 115 Gld' (SUA, sign. SM B 110 1/L).

9. The interests which Rudolf may have formed during his Spanish stay and which probably had to do with his relationship to Philip II, above all his interest in alchemy and the esoteric, are dealt with by Pavel Štěpánek in a manuscript study, 'Španělský dvůr v době Rudolfa II – zdroj jeho zájmů a zálib'. In this country, as distorted a view used to be held of Rudolf II's uncle as of Rudolf himself, and just as modern research has rehabilitated Rudolf, it is beginning to appreciate Philip's huge intellectual abilities and his support for art and architecture. See also Georg Kubler, *Building the Escorial* (Princeton, 1981); José Luis Sancho, *Das Kloster San Lorenze el Real de El Escorial* (Madrid, 1991); Anton Dieterich, 'El Escorial' in Boekhoff, Hermann (eds), *Paläste, Schlösser, Residenzen, Zentren europäischer Geschichte* (Erlangen, 1971), pp. 75–89.

10. Nikolaus Pevsner *An Outline of European Architecture* (Harmondsworth, 1964), p. 215.

11. 'Wider Erwarten haben die Wohnzimmer des Habsburgs nicht Großartiges an sich. Sie sind äußerst bescheiden, berühren jedoch menschlich. Da sie unmittelbar um den Chor der Kirche angeordnet sind, konnte der König vom Bett aus auf den Hochaltar sehen' [see Dieterich (note 9), p. 82].

12. On the question of the date of the Matthias Gate, see Muchka (note 4), p. 190.

13. Peter Fidler, 'Spanische Säle – Architekturtypologie oder semiotik?' in Wolfram Krämer (ed.), *Spanien und Österreich in der Renaissance: Akten des Fünften Spanisch-Österreichischen Symposions 21–25. September 1987 in Wien* (Innsbruck, 1989).

Perspective on Prague: Rudolfine Stylistics Reviewed

THOMAS DACOSTA KAUFMANN

What is distinctive about Rudolfine art? In the context of the present exhibition, Rudolfine works are being exhibited in the capital of Bohemia, its historic commercial and religious centre, in which they were made and for which in many instances they were intended. Yet that milieu has changed, not just over the course of centuries but most radically in the past few years. One obvious sign of change is the very venue of the exhibition. In the present Czech Republic, the process of reintegration of Rudolfine art into Czech cultural history which has been going on for three decades is being continued, but in a public forum.[1]

Much as the present Czech Republic is also being reintegrated into a broadening definition of Europe and Prague once again has become a centre, the question of the characteristics of Rudolfine art suggests even broader perspectives. Numerous monographs, studies and other exhibitions have established that Prague in the era of Rudolf II had an international, even intercontinental, importance for the arts.[2] It can be argued, moreover, that in effect Rudolf II's Prague was the only real metropolis for art in (East) Central Europe in the period between 1400 and 1650.[3]

Artistic metropolis, imperial residence, Bohemian capital, commercial centre, archbishopric – this plethora of descriptions indicates the wide range of possibilities for interpretation. Depending on perspective, different answers can be given to the question of what is characteristic about Rudolfine art.

Take issues of patronage and collecting. Legends have long depicted Rudolf II as the strangeling of the Prague castle, a melancholic, even mad, ruler who shut himself up with his treasures and ignored the world outside. Consequently, the Emperor's idiosyncrasies were long said to have shaped the character of the arts in Prague. Scholarship has confirmed some aspects of these legends, in providing evidence that the Emperor was indeed one of the greatest collectors and patrons in the history of his time, even in European history, and demonstrating that Rudolf was personally involved in the arts. But were his interest and involvement so unique? If Rudolf II is not to be regarded simply as a peculiar individual case, or judged according to some inappropriate ideal of rulership, the supposedly personal aspects of his collecting and patronage may in fact be assigned a political and social rationale. Rudolf II can be seen as but one of many contemporary rulers who engaged in artistic activities, patronized and collected on a large scale and employed the arts in matters of state.[4] A good deal of attention has for instance recently been paid not only to the other German courts of the time, but to the patronage and collecting of the Emperor's Spanish relations as well as to his Austrian predecessors and descendants.[5]

The court's interests can also be related to those of others in Prague itself. In a well-known passage the Netherlandish artist and art theorist Karel van Mander singled out the collections of Rudolf II, whom he called the 'greatest art patron in the world at the present time', to be sure. But attention should be called to another point in the same passage, where van Mander also mentioned the collections of other great art lovers elsewhere in Prague.[6] That the leader of Europe in protocol

5.1 FEDERICO BAROCCI
The Flight from Troy
[Rome, Galleria Borghese]

was a great collector and set a tone that many princes and collectors throughout Europe emulated must also have been pertinent for other social groups, including those in Bohemia. Recent research in Prague, re-emphasized in the present exhibition and publications associated with it, has indeed indicated that a taste for paintings extended not only to aristocratic households, but throughout bourgeois milieus in Prague, no less than they did elsewhere in Europe.[7]

Consideration of a genre patronized by both court and city, namely works of art and architecture made for religious purposes in Prague, takes us directly to a central problem of perspective, however. Epitaphs and altarpieces by court artists were designed for local clients as well as members of the court. Major projects of redecoration went on. The Emperor contributed to some of these local projects and paid for a major votive offering of his own, the St Roch's chapel at Strahov. Like the other churches that were constructed in Prague in the late sixteenth and early seventeenth centuries, Rudolfine religious art constitutes part of the local artistic legacy. Such works, and the portraits frequently found in local collections, also provide a connection with the activities and creations of other local artists, both in earlier and later times. Even technical elements in the works of artists who had been associated with the court may be compared with those found in the early paintings of an artist like Škarel Kréta.[8] Because making religious works was an honoured task, these may seem to 'rank among the most important achievements of the Prague artists'.[9]

But when Rudolfine religious works are assessed in the larger context of the total production of art at court, or when Prague court art of this sort is compared either with that of other contemporary centers or with subsequent Habsburg patronage, a different picture may emerge. No doubt, Rudolf II or servitors of the imperial court on occasion paid for works with a religious function, but it cannot be stated that this was the kind of painting which the Emperor usually desired to own. It is significant that he commissioned what is the unique composition of a secular subject other than

portraits in the oeuvre of Federico Barocci, an artist most notable for his religious compositions, expressly asking for something that did not correspond to a taste for the devotional object [fig. 5.1].[10] His tastes as a collector ran similarly. While the Emperor may have tried to obtain pictures with religious content like Dürer's *Madonna of the Rose Garden* [fig. 5.2], such a work had literally to be taken out of context (from the church of San Bartolommeo in Venice), and transported as a precious object of delectation, carried by hand to Prague. Dürer's painting was treated like a work of art, not an altarpiece, in a manner that evokes a vision of contemporary curators carrying objects to exhibitions. In other instances, the Emperor eschewed acquisition of objects specifically because he thought them to be of religious character.[11]

Thus while imperial taste and patronage certainly did not determine all that was done in Prague, they nevertheless may have been related to a decline in the number of commissions for religious paintings from court artists that can still be observed in comparison with the numbers of surviving or recorded works in other genres; religious paintings form a relatively small percentage of their whole oeuvres. Com-

5.2 ALBRECHT DÜRER
Madonna of the Rose Garden
[Prague, Národní galerie v Praze]

pared with Philip II of Spain's Escorial, Emperor Ferdinand II's (or even Ferdinand III's) later Austrian court, or Wilhelm V's or Maximilian I of Bavaria's at Munich, where such activity dominated the artistic scene, the making of religious art does not stand at the centre either of the major patron's interest or, consequently, of court artistic production. Questions of quantity aside, religious painting was not a site of innovation in Prague, as were other genres: this situation may also be contrasted with that of other contemporary centres in Italy.[12] Whatever its accomplishments and interests – and it is to be hoped that one result of the present exhibition will be to illuminate these more clearly – religious works, while related to the local scene, are surely not what can be taken to be most characteristic of Prague court art.

Rather, mythological paintings, often of an erotic quality; complicated allegories, often glorifying the Emperor; and *Kunstkammerstücke*, splendid specimens of the goldsmith's and stonecutter's art, often, as in the case of Seychelles nuts, transformed by Nicholas Pfaff not for use but for the collection, are what are usually noted as characteristically Rudolfine. Many of these items have also been regarded as exemplars of Mannerism. Objects, whether in gold or on canvas, carry an overabundance of distracting ornament; mythologies, especially those of erotic themes, display wildly gesticulating nudes in complicated poses in compressed space.

Again, however, these sorts of objects, while undoubtedly striking and distinctive, are not exclusively Rudolfine. *Kunstkammerstücke* were staples of many collections, and artists who provided them for Prague served other courts as well. The elements of Mannerist art just mentioned were in fact adapted from a recent essay on Cardinal Gabriele Paleotti's comments on religious painting in Italy.[13] And what has been said about the specific and the idiosyncratic, aspect of this sort of art made for the Emperor can be questioned, especially in considering the supposedly erotic character of Rudolfine painting. Painting with erotic content in Prague has antecedents and parallels in art made for many Italian courts that earlier overidealization of Italian art had obscured, but that is now becoming recognized as a not inconsiderable part of Renaissance painting.[14] It has recently been argued that pagan erotic subjects were important for Northern courts such as Fontainebleau as well.[15]

Emphasis on Mannerism, as on the erotic, also ignores many significant, indeed contrasting, aspects of art in Prague. These tendencies cannot easily be called 'Mannerist', but rather can be described as 'naturalistic'. Prague produced innovations in nature painting – that is, the painting of *naturalia*; some of the origins of independent still life, animal painting and landscape based on nature studies are all to be found in Prague. The Emperor also was personally interested in this kind of art. Important nature studies and depictions of creatures by Jacques de Gheyn, Joris and Jakob Hoefnagel, and Daniel Fröschl, as well as the so-called Museum manuscript (or Bestiary) of Rudolf now attributed to Dirck de Quade van Ravesteyn and other painters, were all sold to or made for the emperor. Emanuel Sweerts called the Emperor the greatest lover of flowers in the world. Joachim van Sandart reports that Rudolf II sent Roelandt Savery out to draw the rare wonders of nature; motifs gained therefrom later appeared in his art.[16]

In sum, it would be difficult to point out any one set of forms which is characteristically Rudolfine. An effort fully to characterize Rudolfine art by reference to the personal style of any one artist who worked in Prague would also come up short. Individual artists could work in a variety of seemingly contradictory modes.

The problem of perspective nevertheless does not mean that 'perspectivism' is the solution – that is to say a recourse to the interpretive relativism of the sort favoured by a radical hermeneutics. Many efforts at synthesis are still possible: in order to reconcile the discrepancies that exist between the genres and the multiple forms of art which artists developed, I have previously proposed one such solution: that they be related to a conception of stylistics. While Prague lacked a writer on art like van Mander, it did have a rich humanistic intellectual culture with which artists were intimately involved, as the complicated content of their works often suggests. The verbal and written statements of Rudolf's artists, their allegories made on the arts and an analysis of their works all can be used to suggest that a basic structure underlay the situation in which they made choices in their work. This can be called their stylistics, the system that underlay the determination of individual stylistic choices.[17]

To summarize earlier arguments: the existence of some sort of stylistic matrix in Prague is suggested by the court painters' adherence to an ideal symbolized by the figure of Hermathena, a recurring image in Rudolfine iconography [fig. 5.3]. This is the image of the academic ideal, the symbol of learned or wise eloquence, or eloquent wisdom. Rudolfine images show Mercurial (pertaining to Hermes) painters placed under the aegis of Minerva (Athena). In the thinking implied by this ideal, the visual arts approximately assume the principles of rhetoric, whose goal was eloquence; as the notion has been current since Antiquity, paintings may also be considered visual poems. Inasmuch as rhetorical and poetic notions were fused at the time, these are indeed often conjoined in their application; they pertain in turn to the visual arts.[18] Artistic ideals may consequently have been related to rhetorical considerations, involving matters of decorum, that would determine the choice of mode according to the subject, and poetic ones, involving the form of artistic imitation appropriate to the matter depicted. Inasmuch, moreover, as rhetorical (and poetic) considerations would also have involved questions of function in relation to audience, these ideas may also be extended to help deal with questions of patronage and location.

Like any other explication that tries to analyze complicated cultural phenomena by rational explanation, this exegesis necessarily involves methodological abstraction. But it has other advantages, heuristic as well as hermeneutic. Stylistics is meant to envisage the whole of Rudolfine artistic production, not just assume a perspective gained from an understanding of one aspect. A notion of pictorial poetics helps to reconcile the plethora of perspectives on the interpretation of style. A notion of pictorial poetics helps us to see how Prague paintings are also visual *poésie* – so in fact were they described in a number of contemporary sources – if of a variety and character different from the Italian Renaissance paintings to which this term, and the related idea of 'ut pictura poesis', is generally applied. A notion of visual eloquence allows for variation in forms of imitation, between the idealized forms associated with Mannerism in the higher genres such as religious or mythological painting, and naturalism in the lower genres such as still life. A notion of visual rhetoric also helps to account for the varying amounts of what may be described as visual ornament found in elements such as contrapposto (between old and young, etc.) or antithesis, chiasmus, and anaphora in Prague painting. Since a notion of visual poetics involves considerations of imitation of art as well as of nature, it helps to allow for an explanation of what I have called the 'modern' stance of Prague artists: how

5.3 AEGIDIUS SADELER
(after Hans von Aachen
after Joris Hoefnagel)
Hermathena
1615
[Vienna, Graphische
Sammlung Albertina]

their efforts to emulate, rather than simply to copy or imitate, may have led them on to various sorts of artistic innovations.[19]

This conceptualization of Prague stylistics has other heuristic benefits as well. By presenting a model whereby forms can be related to function, and thus to their audience, it allows for insights into the social context of art: forms are adapted to the commission they fulfil. This hypothesis has also had a certain predictive value for the assimilation of new material: information has subsequently come to light that supports the association between humanistic rhetorical and poetic models and Prague painters, particularly Spranger.[20] It has provided methods of analysis that other scholars have found useful.[21] And finally, it may help to provide a further European perspective for art in Prague.

Here the comparison with Dutch art of the period between 1580 and 1620 may be elaborated. This comparison supplies a broader perspective for Prague painting, in which similarities and differences may ultimately be understood in relation to differences in stylistics.[22] Art in Prague has often been taken as a source for Netherlandish Mannerism, but more is involved in the association. This may be seen in regard to the turning point in Northern Netherlandish art that has been described as occurring in the period of the reigns of Rudolf II and Matthias, when ecclesiastical commissions were replaced, as it were, by a market for other sorts of painting. In new genres supposedly 'realistic' scenes appear, where nevertheless a range of ideas which may be called moralizing are embodied. This turning point in Dutch art has thus been described as one that involves the painting of landscape, still life, gallant companies and peasant scenes, everyday subjects that developed into specializations and that posterity identified with something innately Dutch.

Yet many of the traits that are associated with the transformation of Northern Netherlandish painting, not only 'Mannerist' art, may also be found in painting of the Prague school. While, as noted, the relative significance of religious works seems to have declined in Prague, at the same time moralizing elements entered into other kinds of paintings there as in the Northern Netherlands; these include a fairly large number of scenes of 'everyday life', which also have a 'realistic' component. Artists other than Netherlanders executed these kinds of works in Prague. Similar scenes are recorded in the work of Jeremias Günther, and represented in the work of Hans von Aachen, who frequently depicts ill-matched couples, or 'gallant' scenes, with a naturalistic component. Von Aachen also frequently depicted his own portrait in such paintings. As in Holland, these images also clearly evoke the idea of vanity. Paintings of merry companies are also found in the oeuvres of Rudolfine artists. For example, van Mander describes von Aachen's painting as the artist with the Donna Venusta; this work, as the name indicates, surely preserved some kind of moralizing, allegorical content. Peasant scenes are introduced both in von Aachen's work and in Savery's executed in Prague. Van Ravesteyn did single-length figures, associated with kitchen scenes, as even Spranger is recorded to have done.[23] It may also be remembered that the first surviving independent floral still lifes by a Northern Netherlandish artist may actually have been done in Prague by Savery. Independent animal paintings were also done by him there, as they were by the German painters Hans Hoffmann and Daniel Fröschl. Architectural views were executed by Vredeman de Vries in Prague as elsewhere, including the Netherlands.[24] And Savery's and Stevens's landscapes were not only renewals of mid-century tradi-

tions. As noted, they were based on observations of the artists' surroundings in Central Europe, much as Netherlanders turned to such subjects at home. Whatever the term may mean, Savery's 'naer het leven' drawings in Bohemia clearly served him for paintings done in Prague. Even the move towards Caravaggism in Netherlandish art that occurred in the second decade of the seventeenth century was anticipated in Prague, if we mean by Caravaggism the introduction of tenebrism, exclusive of the treatment of subject matter, such as the introduction of apparently low-life and naturalistic elements into history painting. Rudolf II owned a painting of Joseph and Potiphar's wife by Caravaggio, and tenebrist tendencies are found in the later works of artists at his court.[25]

It may thus be argued that not only Dutch Mannerism, but many of the other supposed innovations of Northern Netherlandish art, were directly sponsored simultaneously, if not even earlier, at the Prague court. Artistic specialization itself, a feature that came to be associated with the artistic scene in the seventeenth-century Netherlands, may also have been anticipated to a degree in Prague. Because a large group of artists was to be found at the imperial court, artists tended to concentrate more on one genre than another. On the other hand, the fact that someone like Goltzius executed both 'Mannerist' history paintings and 'naturalistic' landscapes does not seem so surprising when we know that the oeuvres of the same Prague painters also displayed a comparable range of works.

Where does this leave us with the problem of a specifically Rudolfine art? Obviously, Prague was not the sole contemporary site of innovation, regardless of its tendency towards emulation and invention. We can look as well to other spots where Netherlanders were present, such as Frankfurt am Main, for the origins of several types of modern still life.[26] Prague was nevertheless not the same sort of centre as Frankfurt, nor Amsterdam or Haarlem.

The social conditions in which art was made, the demands of production and consumption, the place and function of art – all obviously differed in the Netherlands and in Prague. The difference with the Netherlands thus appears to have been that in a place like Haarlem the strict divisions which may have been imposed in a hierarchical court society were broken. Whatever activities may actually have been carried on by the artists who frequented the Haarlem 'academy', this group operated under a different aegis of the Hermathenic ideal than did the Prague court circle, taken symbolically as well as socially. Goltzius' own drawing of Mercury and Minerva, dated to the time of his breaking away from Spranger's influence around 1590, seems to stand symbolically for this difference, since his ideal gods apparently are based on studies from nature, or at least we may claim that observation stands behind them. No such drawings from the nude like the startling sheets by Goltzius have been identified by any Prague court artist. Certainly, none would have been used by them for paintings in the way that Goltzius, again for a Hermathenic painting, seems to have used drawings from the nude, for his figure of Minerva/Athena.[27]

Not the development of new genres in themselves, therefore, but the way that they were handled, and the way older genres such as history painting (the painting of significant human or divine action) are treated seem to differentiate Northern Netherlandish from Prague painting. The hierarchy of stylistic decorum upheld in Rudolfine Prague seems to have broken down in Holland. Ideal figures came to be eschewed in favour of the observable. As in Prague painting, ancient or Renaissance

models did not merely provide sources, but were transformed, struggled with or even distorted, in a move toward what would have been understood as the 'modern'. But the process of emulation found in both centres is different. The Dutch artists never went so far as to leave aside the observable or the ideal source as found in the Antique or the Renaissance. In the Netherlands, the direction taken was away from the abstract or ideally gracious – a difference from Prague, as a comparison of Spranger's with Goltzius' nudes makes clear.[28]

If only briefly, a similar point may be made for differences between Prague and other sites of innovation in Italy, such as Bologna or Rome. As in Rudolfine mythologies, the imagery of the Carracci often displays considerable wit in scenes with erotic content.[29] The Carracci, like the Rudolfine artists, were also capable of varying theirmodes of presentation according to the subject depicted, or the function of the work. Their art includes religious painting inspired by Raphael and other masters of the High Renaissance, Classical subjects drawn from the Antique and corrected against the nude, as well as naturalistic landscapes and pictures of subjects such as butcher shops. Again however, as in Holland, but unlike in Prague, their histories, their scenes of Classical or religious subject matter, both derived directly from drawings from the Antique and from the model (see the multiple drawings for the Farnese Gallery).[30] In Italy, the reform of painting – against a 'Mannerism' comparable to aspects of Rudolfine figural painting and graphic art – identified with the Carracci thus encompassed both the observation of nature and the emulation of the Antique and the Renaissance.

Furthermore, for the Carracci, another aspect of what may be called the rhetoric or poetics of painting was important. The notion of visual rhetoric implied by stylistics brings along with it considerations of the ends of art. Traditionally, these were conceived of as instruction and delight. Looking at Prague painting with these ideas in mind has helped to decipher what otherwise had seemed to be irreconcilable differences in painting, since both aspects can be found in pictures like Arcimboldo's seemingly scurrilous, but actually imperial, allegories.[31]

There is, however, traditionally another central aim demanded by artistic rhetoric – to move. And it was precisely because the forms of religious art produced by the painters of the so-called *maniera*, with their gesticulating figures, distorted space and complicated poses, in Italy failed to move beholders, that the desire for 'visual reality' after the Council of Trent came to demand a newer sort of art, a reform of painting like that of religion. And this is what was furnished by the Carracci, with their striving for verisimilitude in art, or, on the other hand, Caravaggio, with his figures taken from what could be observed.

For all of the Emperor's interest in a variety of artistic forms, for all of the apparent similarity in having a basic structure of visual stylistics, a major transformation of religious art, as at the hands of a Carracci, a Caravaggio – or a Bernini – is something that the Rudolfine artists did not achieve. Where a work like von Aachen's *Annunciation*, or even Spranger's late *St. Sebastian*, may display some of the darker palette and strong shadows that we associate with Italian tenebrism, and a reduced number of figures, they are lacking in the qualities of the Italians. They adhere more to the characteristics decried by the Italian reformers, as seen the distorted nude of Spranger's *St Sebastian*, the reduced space in which the saint stands, the disjunction with the background. In other later Rudolfine works with religious content, such as

Joseph Heintz's *Mystic Marriage of St Catherine*, Mannerist elegance of form and elegance, seen in the poses of the angels, the languid grace of the saints and the Virgin and their striking coloring, is paramount. Rudolfine artists never sought, as did the Carracci, to incorporate idealism and naturalism in the same work. With their adherence to a stricter hierarchy of stylistics, they did not break through to the newer forms of the Baroque, as in the works of the Carracci – much less than the rough 'naturalism' of Caravaggio's religious painting. And whereas in Post-Tridentine Italy, a new conception of hierarchies in art evolved, as Cardinal Paleotti envisioned them, these also were not the same as those in Prague: what was desired in Italy around 1600, in Milan and Bologna as well as Rome, differed not only in religious art, but in the approach taken by artists to many of the themes, including landscape, still life and history, that were also present in Prague painting.[32]

One final image may suggest that the seemingly heady world in which Minervan intellectualization dominated the stylistics of the Prague school[33] was not restricted to the Hradčany. A recently published drawing by Spranger depicts Minerva/Athena as protector of painting. This signed sheet appears to be the first version of a familiar drawing (Vienna, Graphische Sammlung Albertina) in which the goddess holds a maulstick in her left hand and rests on a shield adorned with the triple escutcheon of the painter's guild of St Luke. But in the unpublished drawing, the message may be taken not only to apply to the painters' guild, or even more broadly to the position of painters. The device on the shield is replaced with a city tower, resembling that of the city arms of Prague: the *matka měst*, the *mater urbium*, is a city of the arts under Minerva's aegis.[34]

1. I have discussed the issue of the interpretation of the art of Central Europe in relation to its changed historical circumstances more extensively in the introduction to *Court, Cloister and City: The Art and Culture of Central Europe, 1450–1800* (London and Chicago, 1995). For the circumstances before 1988, and the change represented by the Essen and Vienna exhibition 'Prag um 1600: Kunst und Kultur am Hofe Rudolfs II' (exh. cat., 2 vols, Freren, 1988), see the comments in my review in *Kunstchronik* (October 1988), pp. 553ff.

2. *Prag um 1600* (note 1) and the present volume contain references to the extensive and growing monographic literature on Rudolfine Prague. Among the books published in 1988 or subsequently are: Eliška Fučíková (ed.), *Prag um 1600: Beiträge zur Kunst und Kultur am Hofe Rudolfs II.* (Freren, 1988); J. Dvorský (ed.), *Die Kunst am Hofe Rudolfs II* (Hanau, 1988; also in other editions); Thomas Da-Costa Kaufmann, *The School of Prague: Painting at the Court of Rudolf II* (Chicago and London, 1988), *Prag um 1600: Die Beiträge des vom 25. bis 27. Februar 1989 vom Kunsthistorischen Museum in Wien veranstalteten Symposiums, Jahrbuch der Kunsthistorischen Museums in Wien* 85/86 (1989/90; published 1992). Exhibitions and publications subsequent to *Prag um 1600* include *The Parnassus of the Arts: The Prague Court in the Elizabethan Era*, exh. cat. (St Andrews, n.d.); 'The Sadelers: Engravers from the Golden Age of Antwerp and Prague' (see Dorothy Limouze, 'Aegidius Sadeler Imperial Printmaker', *Bulletin* (Philadelphia Museum of Art), vol.

8, [Spring 1989]); *The Stylish Image: Printmakers to the Court of Rudolf II*, exh. cat. by Mungo Campbell with intro. by R. J. W. Evans and Eliška Fučíková (Edinburgh, 1991); *Eros und Mythos: Kunst am Hof Rudolfs II*, exh. cat. (Vienna, 1995). Also of note is François Antonovich, *L'Art à la cour de Rodolphe II empereur du Saint Empire Romain Germanique: Prague et son rayonnement* (Paris, 1992).

3. See my 'Das Problem der Kunstmetropolen im frühneuzeitlichen Ostmitteleuropa' in Evamaria Engel, Karen Lambrecht, and Hanna Nogossek (eds) *Metropolen im Wandel: Zentralität in Ostmitteleuropa an der Wende vom Mittelalter zur Neuzeit* (Berlin, 1995), pp. 33–46; also 'The Problem of Artistic Metropolises in East Central Europe from the Fifteenth to the Twentieth Century', in *The Historical Metropolis. A Hidden Potentia*, ed. Jacek Purchla (Cracow, 1996), pp. 109–20.

4. See the review of the conflict of interpretations presented in my *The Mastery of Nature: Aspects of Art, Science and Humanism in the Renaissance* (Princeton, 1993), chap. 7, 'From Mastery of the World to Mastery of Nature: The *Kunstkammer*, Politics, and Science', pp. 174–94, where some of the literature on the other German courts of the time in the next sentence is also adduced.

5. Among the literature on these topics, increasing in recent years, see for Philip II, Fernando Checa Cremades, *Felipe II: Mecenas de las Artes* (Madrid, 1992); for Philip IV, Leopold Wilhelm and other seventeenth-century monarchs, Jonathan Brown, *Kings and Connoisseurs. Collecting Art in Seventeenth-Centu-*

ry Europe (Princeton, 1995); for Archduke Ferdinand (of Tyrol), Christian Gries, 'Erzherzog Ferdinand von Tirol: Konturen einer Sammlerpersönlichkeit', *Früh Neuzeit-Info*, 4 (1993), pp. 162–73, and Erzherzog Ferdinand II. Von Tirol und die Sammlungen auf Schloß Ambras', *Früh Neuzeit-Info*, 5 (1994), pp. 7–37, and, more recently, *Natur und Kunst: Handschriften und Alben aus der Ambraser Sammlung Erzherzog Ferdinands II (1529–1595)*, exh. cat. (Vienna, 1995).

6. See the translation of this passage from *Het Schilderboeck* (Haarlem, 1604), Voorreden iiiiv, by R. J. W. Evans, *Rudolf II and his World. A Study in Intellectual History 1578–1612*, Oxford, 1984 (2nd edn), p. 162.

7. Among earlier publications, see, for example, the essays by Jaroslav Pánek, 'Zwei Arten böhmischen Adelsmäzenatentums in der Zeit Rudolfs II', and Jiří Pešek, 'Porträts in den Bürgerhäusern des rudolfinischen Prags', in Fučíková (ed.) (note 2), pp. 218–31, 244–48, as well as *idem*, 'Obrazy a grafiky a jejich majitelé ve pedblohorské Praze', *Umění* 39 (1991), pp. 369–83. See further James R. Palmitessa, 'House, Home & Neighborhood on the Eve of White Mountain: Material Culture and Daily Life in the New City of Prague' (Ph.D. dissertation, New York University, 1995).

8. Věra Frömlova, 'Malířská technika Karla Škréty (S prihlédnutím maleb v čechách v letech 1581–1631)', in *Karel kréta 1610–1674*, exh. cat. Prague, 1974, pp. 270–6. The present exhibition will doubtless adduce both more data of this nature, as well as pointing out connnections with subject matter and mode of presentation of other earlier and later artists in Prague.

9. Eliška Fučíková, review of *The School of Prague*, in *Burlington Magazine*, 132:1042 (January 1990), p. 40; Fučíková makes some of the other points in this paragraph.

10. See Kaufmann (note 2), pp. 18, fig. 15; 120 n. 40; 63.

11. For the sculpture in Várad, see Gyöngyi Török, 'Bilderstürme durch die Türken in Ungarn', in *L'Art et les révolutions*, XVIIIe Congrès International d'Histoire de l'Art 4, Strasbourg, 1989: *Les Iconoclasmes* (Strasbourg, 1992), p. 272, n. 19, with further reference. The other material discussed here is familiar from the literature on Rudolfine art and repeats information from Kaufmann (note 2), for example on Barocci.

12. The treatment of Rudolfine religious art offered here depends on that in Kaufmann (note 2), pp. 63–5, 'Religious Painting in Prague'. The evaluation of the quantity of work is based on calculations derived from the surviving and recorded works tabulated in the catalogues of the individual artists, *ibid*. Much more evidence will have to come to light to indicate that religious painting constituted more than a small portion of the Rudolfine painters' output or that it was innovative in the way that contemporary Italian painting was – or that Rudolfine still life and landscape were. A comparison with contemporary painting in Munich will indicate that it would be false to overestimate the typicality of religious painting in Prague.

13. Pamela M. Jones, 'Art Theory as Ideology: Gabriele Paleotti's Hierarchical Notion of Painting's Universality and Reception' in Claire Farago (ed.), *Reframing the Renaissance: Visual Culture in Europe and Latin America 1450–1650* (New Haven and London, 1995), p. 131.

14. For the problem of erotic art in Prague in relation to Italian images, see most extensively my 'Eros et poesia: La Peinture à la cour de Rodolphe II', *Revue de l'art*, 69 (1985), pp. 29–46; see further comments in Kaufmann (note 2), pp. 59–63. A strong, albeit ahistorical argument has been made about erotic imagery by David Freedberg, in *The Power of Images: Studies in the History and Theory of Response* (Chicago and London, 1989), pp. 317ff. See, however, *Eros und Mythos* (note 2), and the more balanced comments by R. J. W. Evans in 'Culture and Politics at the Court of Rudolf II', in Campbell (note 2), pp. 9–10.

15. See Janet Cox-Rearick, 'Sacred to Profane: Diplomatic Gifts of the Medici to Francis I', *Journal of Medieval and Renaissance Studies*, 24:2 (Spring 1994), esp. pp. 255ff.

16. For these sorts of works see *Prag um 1600*. These activities correspond to another important part of Rudolfine culture: Prague was a centre for the new observational science, and the new mathematics that restructured its results. The new astronomy that Paulus Fabritius, Johannes Kepler, Tycho de Brahe (the latter particularly involving observations) carried on was sponsored by the Emperor, as was the work of the Netherlandish gemmologist Anselmus Boethius de Boodt, who is now proved also to have been an animal and flower painter (see Marie-Christiane Maselis *et al.*, *De Albums van Anselmus de Boodt (1550–1632). Geschilderde natuurobsevatie aan het Hof van Rudolf II te Praag*, Tielt, 1989). The emperor provided the specific stimulus for Kepler to develop a telescope, as he read Galileo before the German astronomer did. Rudolf lent Kepler Galileo's *Sidereal Messenger*, and a looking glass in order to verify the Italian's observations, as well as telling Kepler to develop one. For the sources of information on these subjects, and my interpretation of them, see *The Mastery of Nature* and *The School of Prague*.

17. The thesis presented here was first articulated in 'The Eloquent Artist: Towards an Understanding of the Stylistics of Painting at the Court of Rudolf II', *Leids Kunsthistorisch Jaarboek*, 1 (1982), pp. 119–48, and elaborated in Kaufmann (note 2), pp. 90ff. These ideas can obviously be extended, *mutatis mutandis*, to other genres.

18. See the comment made recently by Brian Vickers, in his review of Julius Caesar Scaliger, *Poetices libri septem*, ed. Luc Deitz and Gregor Vogt-Spira, in *Bulletin of the Society for Renaissance Studies*, 13:1 (October 1995), p. 27:

   > Although the *Poetics* [of J. C. Scaliger – the most extensive such work of the sixteenth century] might seem to belong to what we now call poetics or literary theory, it is typical of all Renaissance writings on literature in making no distinction between poetics and rhetoric.

19. See my 'Ancients and Moderns in Prague: Arcimboldo's drawings for Silk Manufacture', in *Mastery of Nature*, pp. 151–74, first published in *Leids Kunsthistorisch Jaarboek* 2, 1983 (published 1984), pp.

179–207; see further *The School of Prague*, pp. 96–9.

20. See *The Mastery of Nature*, pp. 147–50. This material was originally presented slightly differently in 'Astronomy, Technology, Humanism and Art at the Entry of Rudolf II into Vienna, 1577', *Jahrbuch der Kunsthistorischen Sammlungen in Wien* 85/86, 1989/90 (published 1992), especially pp. 107–11.

    More attention should perhaps be given to the reception accorded Spranger by the Old Chamber of Rhetoricians in Haarlem, who on the artist's visit there in 1602 to honour him put on a play in praise of the art of painting: see the account in Karel van Mander, now conveniently available in facsimile and translation as *Karel van Mander. The Lives of the Illustrious Netherlandish and German Painters, from the first edition of the Schilder-boeck, etc.*, intro. and trans., ed. Hessel Miedema (Doornspijk, 1994), 1, pp. 354–5.

21. See Lubomír Konečný, 'Sources and Significance of Two Mythological Paintings by Bartholomäus Spranger', *Jahrbuch der Kunsthistorischen Sammlungen in Wien* 85/86, 1989/90 (published 1992), pp. 47–56.

22. These comparisons with Dutch art are taken from a lecture, 'Dutch Mannerism in an International Context', delivered on 14 February 1994, at the Rijksmuseum, Amsterdam, on the occasion of the exhibition from which this term is derived, 'Dawn of the Golden Age: Northern Netherlandish Art 1580–1620' (exh. cat. ed. Ger Luijten *et al.* [Zwolle, 1993], containing the most extensive bibliography of treatments of this subject). The interpretation of Dutch art presented in this and the following paragraphs summarizes especially the essays published in *ibid.* by J. Bruyn, 'A Turning-Point in the History of Dutch Art' (pp. 112–21), and Wouter Kloek, 'Northern Netherlandish Art 1580–1620: A Survey', (pp. 15–111).

23. See further for these subjects my '"Gar lecherlich": Low-life painting in Rudolfine Prague', in *Prag um 1600. Beiträge zur Kunst und Kultur am Hofe Rudolfs II*, pp. 33–8.

24. For the continued collaboration on similar sorts of works by artists from the Prague circle back in the Netherlands, see my 'Addenda Rudolphina', in *Études sur l'histoire de l'art en honneur du soixantième anniversaire de Miklós Mojzer (Annales de la Galerie Nationale Hongroise)* (1991), pp. 141–47.

25. See *The School of Prague* for further discussion of these genres of painting.

26. See now *Georg Flegel 1566–1638: Stilleben*, exh. cat. ed. Kurt Wettengl (Frankfurt, 1993).

27. See E. K. J. Reznicek, *Die Zeichnungen von Hendrick Goltzius* (Utrecht, 1961), pp. 217ff. Interesting attempts to relate the history of art in specific centres in the Low Countires to the characters of cities have been made by Elisabeth de Bièvre, 'Violence and Viture: History and Art in the City of Haarlem', *Art History*, 11:5 (September 1988), pp. 305–34, and 'The Urban Sub-conscious in the Art of Delft and Leiden', *Art History*, 18:2 (June, 1995), pp. 222–52. Were one to attempt to expand beyond the questions of court and city, it might be useful to extend this sort of approach to Prague.

28. These points were first adumbrated in Kaufmann (note 17). I have treated the differences between Goltzius and Spranger more recently in 'Reading Van Mander on the Reception of Rome: A Crux in the Biography of Spranger in the *Schilder-Boeck*', *Bolletino d'arte*, forthcoming.

    Recently Christopher Wood, 'Curious Pictures and the Art of Decription', *Word & Image* 11, 1995, p. 352, has criticized this distinction and characterization of the Netherlandish tradition. Wood's interpretation seems however to rely on a view of a coherent and distinctive, independent Netherlandish tradition of an art of description which I do not accept: see my 'An Independent Dutch Art? A View from Central Europe', *De Zerentiende Eeuw*, 13:1 (1997), pp. 355–65, and, with Anthony Grafton, 'Holland without Huizinga: Dutch Visual Culture in the Seventeenth Century', *Journal of Interdisciplinary History* 16, 1985, pp. 255–65.

29. For bases for the account of the Carracci offered in these pages, see A. W. A. Boschloo, *Annibale Carracci in Bologna: Visual Reality in Art after the Council of Trent* ,2 vols. (The Hague, 1974), to which allusion is made below; Charles Dempsey, *Annibale Carracci and the Beginnings of Baroque Style*, Villa i Tatti Monographs, no. 3) (Gluckstadt, 1977); *idem*, 'Some Observations on the Education of Artists in Florence and Bologna during the Later Sixteenth Century', *Art Bulletin*, 62:4 (1980), pp. 552–69; *idem*, 'The Carracci Reform of Painting', in *The Age of Correggio and the Carracci: Emilian Painting of the Sixteenth and Seventeenth Centuries*, exh. cat. (Washington, New York and Bologna, 1986), pp. 237–54; *idem*, 'The Carracci Academy', in *Academies of Art between Renaissance and Romanticism (Leids Kunsthistorisch Jaarboek* 5–6, [1986–87; published 1989]), pp. 33–43.

30. See John Rupert Martin, *The Farnese Gallery* (Princeton, 1965), for a still valuable survey of the Carracci's working procedure on this monument.

31. For this interpretation, see the revised statement in Kaufmann (note 4), pp. 100–35; see further 'Arcimboldo's Serious Jokes: "Mysterious but Long Meaning"' in Karl-Ludwig Selig and Elizabeth Sears (eds.), *The Visual and the Verbal: Essays in Honor of William Sebastian Heckscher* (New York, 1990), pp. 59–86.

32. See Jones (note 11), and *eadem, Federico Borromeo and the Ambrosiana: Art Patronage and Reform in Seventeenth-century Milan* (Cambridge, 1993).

33. It should be clear that in employing this word here, I am not intending that this nomenclature should be more than evocative, as continuing polemics about it are moot.

34. For the Prado drawing, see 'Some Drawings of the Late Sixteenth and Early Seventeenth Century from Northern and Central Europe in the Museo del Prado', in V. Vlnas (ed.) *Ars Baculum Vitae* (Prague, 1996), pp. 108–12. For the Vienna sheet, see *Prag um 1600* (note 1), vol. 2, pp. 175f, cat. no. 645.

Picturing the Artist in Rudolfine Prague

LUBOMÍR KONEČNÝ

Recurring like variations on a theme throughout literature about the court of Rudolf II is the assertion that the arts and artists in Prague enjoyed a high degree of prestige.[1] The keystone of this argument is the fact that on 27 April 1595 the Emperor issued a Letter of Majesty not only reaffirming the existing privileges of the Prague painters' guild but also adding a new one: 'Because their art and mastery [i.e., painting] is very different from other handicrafts ... it shall, from the date of this letter ... no longer be regarded or described as a craft by anybody, but rather shall be termed altogether the art of painting.' At the same time as this official elevation in status, the coat of arms of the Prague painters' guild was also improved by ruling of the Emperor. The main novelty was the replacement of the figure of a Moorish woman with that of the goddess Athena 'in antique armour down to her thighs, with a billowing red or ruby-coloured cloak, wearing on her head a morion yellow or gold in colour with three ostrich plumes red on the sides and white in the middle, upright but slightly bent at the top, holding in her outstretched right hand a small rod, and in her left hand a round shield depicting the head of the virgin Medusa wreathed in snakes instead of hair ...'[2] This version of the guild coat of arms was painted in 1631 by Georg Gabriel Mayer after a lost original by Bartholomeus Spranger, to whom the addition of the figures of Mercury to the left and Fame to the right is most probably to be attributed.[3] Whether or not this is so, what is certain is that the 'art' of painting of the Prague masters thus came to be placed under the auspices of Pallas Athena or Minerva and hence characterized as intellectual activity.

The improved coat of arms of the painters' guild is the first of a large group of art works which represent these circumstances so favourable to the arts with much greater sophistication. Perhaps the most significant of these works is the engraving by Aegidius Sadeler after a model by Hans von Aachen, depicting *Minerva* introducing Painting to the Liberal Arts (Hollstein 114) – a work which is not only crucial to any discussion of the status of painting at Rudolf II's court, but which has moreover become to some degree an advertisement for Rudolfine art as a whole.[4] Although the engraving is dedicated to the Bavarian duke (later elector) Maximilian and was probably produced in 1595/96 when von Aachen and Sadeler were resident in Munich, it is highly probable that its iconography was inspired by the decree of April 1595 and its message reflects the situation in Prague around the mid-1590s.[5] Von Aachen had been a painter to the imperial court since January 1592, though he was not obliged to live there (being a *Kammermaler von Haus aus*); consequently, it is not impossible that, after frequent visits to the imperial court, he should have endeavoured through his oeuvre to induce the Bavarian Duke to follow the example of Rudolf's decree. Our belief that the 'intellectual conception' of this engraving did not take place in Munich, where it was executed, but in Prague is further supported by the fact that von Aachen's other Munich works are virtually without exception portraits and altar pieces, whereas this is a profane allegory.[6] Its iconogra-

phy can be relatively easily deciphered with the aid of the appended quatrain and its meaning is readily comprehensible from a text dating from April 1595. Under the patronage of Hercules, whose statue is visible in the top left of the picture, a personification of Painting is led by Minerva towards the Liberal Arts, who fill the right half of the composition, above which a winged genius hovers holding a laurel wreath and palm frond.[7] Or, put another way: painting, founded on intellectual ability (Minerva) and virtue (Hercules), belongs with the liberal arts and leads to deserved success and reward (the laurel and palm).

It would be possible to cite further works which reveal the intellectual prestige and social status of artists in Rudolfine Prague. But let us instead return to the Letter of Majesty of April 1595 and attempt to interpret it from a perspective different from that customarily evoked. In my opinion, this key document represents less some sort of spontaneous recognition of painting than an astute reaction on the part of the imperial court to the evident tension then existing in relations between municipal and court painters. The history of the conflict between the ambitious individual artist and the guilds is one of the central themes of all sociological analyses of Renaissance art, so there is no need to recapitulate it here. It is enough to note that this conflict escalated wherever a third party entered the game – that is, a monarch's court with its 'court artists'.[8] In Prague, this situation arose in the 1580s when the imperial court moved from Vienna to Hradčany Castle. We can assume that, initially, any discrepancies between guild and court were neither frequent nor serious. This may partially have been due to the fact that one leading figure among the court painters, Spranger himself [fig. 6.1], belonged both to the court and to the guild. This *Hofmaler* (from the start of 1581) married the daughter of Prague goldsmith Jan Muller [fig. 6.3] and in June 1584 was admitted to the guild and played an active role in municipal affairs in general.[9] If it was Spranger who was chosen to propose an improvement to the guild emblem, then this was not just because he was an expert in depicting mythological gods but also on account of his role as reliable mediator between the court and the city. It was a very good tactic – all the more so when the number of court artists independent of the guild began to rise: Joseph Heintz joined the court in 1591, von Aachen just one year later as already mentioned, and Pieter Stevens in 1594. In contrast to Spranger, none of these new court painters became members of the guild. The same is true of the court painters already active in Prague in the 1580s – Giuseppe Arcimboldo and the lesser-known Giovanni Contarini. Arcimboldo, who had been court painter since the first half of the 1560s, left Prague probably in 1587; Contarini lived there from about 1579/80 until the start of the nineties.[10] Their independence from the guild had been ensured by their ennoblement.[11] Both were elevated to the nobility in 1580; in 1592, Arcimboldo attained the title of *Comus Palatinus*. Their aristocratic rank and attendant social standing of course guaranteed them independence from municipal structures. This solution ultimately also proved preferable for Spranger, who was ennobled in October 1595, hence a short while after the decree was issued. The ennoblement of other artists followed (Heintz in 1602). This congruence of dates is no coincidence and suggests that the year 1595 was critical for relations between court and municipal artists.

If we review all these facts and circumstances, we must agree with Hessel Miedema's conclusion: 'This privilege was intended to deprive the guild of its power in

6.1 BARTHOLOMEUS SPRANGER
Self-portrait
1580–85
[Vienna, Kunsthistorisches
Museum, Gemäldegalerie]

favour of the court painters: if art was explicitly declared the antithesis of craft, then that had to mean that creating art was no longer to be subject to guild rules.'[12] This interpretation corresponds perfectly with our assumption that the imperial decree of April 1595 was nothing other than an artful attempt to prevent an imminent or inevitable conflict. It was merely a formal act, and we ought to view it from two angles. Seen from below, from the viewpoint of the guild, the fact of becoming 'artists' was of no practical significance to the municipal painters because those who were in the service of the court – and especially those who had been ennobled – were at any rate more or less independent of the guild. Seen from above, from the court's point of view, it was a formal gesture, merely confirmation of the *status quo*. The guild, even after 1595, associated not only painters and glaziers but also embroiderers. The members soon realized that, in a situation where the market with lucrative commissions was dominated by court artists, their newly accorded freedom was of little actual value. When in June 1602 guild representatives went to the court office to complain of the advantages enjoyed by court artists, they received the answer that the recently confirmed guild privileges could not prevent the Emperor from granting favours as he chose.[13] This incident, I think, confirms the correctness of Miedema's interpretation: Rudolf's decree was not meant to be a reward for those who thought membership of the guild beneath them, but a well considered means of placating the guild.[14]

We must therefore realize that the meaning of documents like the text of April 1595 is circumscribed by the situations in which they originated and by the specific interests of their authors and the people to whom they were addressed. This implies the need to analyze the question of the status of art and artists at the court of Rudolf on the basis of different material than official pronouncements, such as, in my opinion, the self-portraits and portraits of court artists.[15] These works better than any others give us an idea of how Rudolfine artists saw themselves and their art, and how they wanted others to see them. Ideal of course for analyses of this type are *Selbstdarstellungen* – i.e., 'portraits of artists ... which through amplifications, attributes or additions go beyond the representation of the person in question and thereby place the individual in a wider context'.[16] But we do not need to restrict ourselves to 'programmed' self-portraits. Portraits are of similar significance, especially those in which the artist and model belonged to the same (relatively closed) cultural and social circle. In our case, painter and model both were employed as artists at the court of a monarch, and one may therefore assume that they had more or less identical attitudes to life and views on art. What is more, the self-portraitist is generally in some fashion stylized. By self-stylization I mean not merely the momentary pose the model strikes in front of the artist or the facial expression he or she adopts (though these do say something about the model's personality), but the phenomenon for which Stephen Greenblatt coined the term 'self-fashioning'.[17] This, he believes, involves a conscious attempt by the individual to form an attitude *vis-à-vis* the world or a manner of behaviour – in short, to present himself as a unique personality. This process, particularly characteristic of the modern era, occurred in both life and art. According to Greenblatt, who was writing about literature (though his conclusions apply also *mutatis mutandis* to the fine arts), self-fashioning 'crosses the boundaries between the creation of literary characters, the shaping of one's own identity, the experience of being moulded by forces outside one's con-

trol, the attempt to fashion other selves'. In art and in life, the same symbolic structures exist because people too, as Clifford Geertz has observed, are 'cultural artefacts'. And last but not least, culture is nothing but 'a set of control mechanisms –
plans, recipes, rules, instructions … – for the governing of behavior'. The following
brief analysis of self-portraits and portraits of artists working at Rudolf II's court in
Prague is intended to help us understand what mechanisms of self-fashioning were
in operation there. On no account will we attempt to present an exhaustive list of
these artists' portraits or propose a psychological interpretation of them, since – as
is often emphasized – attempts to surmise the character of the subjects of portraits
on the basis of physiognomy are generally futile.[18]

The oldest known self-portrait by Bartholomeus Spranger was painted some
time in the first half of the 1580s and is known today through two later versions.
One of these is in Vienna [fig. 6.1]; the other, perhaps painted in association with
the artist's workshop, is in the Prince of Liechtenstein's collection in Vaduz.[19]
Spranger portrayed himself *en buste* with his cap rather carelessly askew and his collar loosened. In Rudolfine art, this is a relatively rare example of informal self-portraiture, but in spite – or because – of this, the picture radiates Spranger's self-as-
surance. This effect is not achieved by using special symbols or attributes of dignity, but by the resolute placement of the figure. We see Spranger from the side; his
shoulder is at right angles to the canvas; his head is turned slightly towards the
viewer. As Hans-Joachim Raupp recently demonstrated convincingly, this type of
self-portrait can be traced back to Giorgione's *Self-Portrait* of circa 1510 (Braunschweig, Herzog Anton Ulrich-Museum), in which the Venetian master appears in
the role of the Old Testament hero David.[20] Somewhat less persuasive is Raupp's interpretation of the way the hero looks over his shoulder at the viewer. He describes
this posture as 'geniale Kopfwendung', a turning of the head that signifies artistic
genius in the moment of inspiration.[21] This interpretation has been contested on a
number of counts, one being that the position of head and shoulder is a necessary
consequence of self-portraiture, because the easel cannot be placed between the
artist and the mirror.[22] Yet there are further issues to consider. First, most self-portraits conceived in this way show the model painting either his own likeness (for instance, Luca Cambiaso, ca. 1570) or another picture (Anthonis Mor, 1558; Jacopo
Palma il Giovane, ca. 1585/90), possibly with painter's tools in his hands (Alessandro Allori, ca. 1555).[23] But in Spranger's painting, we see only the bust, not the
hands, and were it not for the inscription *IPSE F*, nothing would suggest that the
subject was the painter himself. Additionally, this formula was used not only for
self-portraits but for portraits of artists; consequently, some special significance appears to have been attached to it. Raupp's interpretation of this significance appears to me to be too narrow. In my opinion, it can be inferred from the interaction
between portrait and viewer. The posture chosen by Spranger creates a sense of distance between the viewer and the subject of the portrait, who thus gives a very self-
confident, reserved, even aloof impression. It is not by mere chance that the idiom
exists of 'giving someone the cold shoulder', meaning to look at someone with an
awareness of one's own superiority, with indifference and even disrespect.

A closely related composition can be found in a slightly later likeness of
Spranger that was engraved in 1597 by Goltzius' pupil Jan Muller (Bartsch 21) after
a work by Hans von Aachen.[24] Von Aachen was evidently following the example of

6.2 AEGIDIUS SADELER
*Bartholomäus Spranger and his
Deceased Wife Christina*
[Hollstein 322]

6.3 JOSEPH HEINTZ
Aegidius Sadeler
[Munich, Staatliche
Graphische Sammlung]

Spranger's earlier *Self-Portrait*. The only substantial difference is that the dress in the 1597 engraving is formal. The model – a painting, or more probably, a drawing – was sent to Muller in Amsterdam; he engraved the portrait and set it against an allegorical background. While this allegorization extends the meaning of the work, it seems to have come about without the involvement of Spranger or von Aachen. The idea of placing the portrait of an artist in a surround of professional attributes and personifications derives from the portraits printed in the second edition of Giorgio Vasari's *Le vite de' piu eccelenti pittori, scultori ed architettori* (1568) and became popular especially in Dutch graphic art of the last third of the sixteenth century.[25] Good examples of this type of graphic portrait are Goltzius' *Johannes Stradanus* of around 1583 (Bartsch 187) and, in particular, the *Portrait of Hans Bol* by the same artist of 1593 (Bartsch 161), in which the element of portraiture is virtually identical in conception to that of von Aachen's Spranger in Muller's engraving of 1597.[26] The most distinctive feature of Muller's engraving are the two geniuses with the attributes of Minerva and Fame, a *bucranium* under the portrait and garlands of fruit. The meaning of the surround can be paraphrased as follows: the art of painting which imitates the richness of nature, resides in work and is executed under the patronage of Minerva, leads to glory.[27]

It seems that Aegidius Sadeler used the same formula as Jan Muller for his portrait of Spranger three years later, in 1600; he made the engraving (Hollstein 322) on the occasion of the death of the painter's wife, Christine[fig. 6.2].[28] The allegorical content of the composition, the antithesis of death and fame, is conveyed by using a whole range of attributes and personifications, but the dominant element is the artist on the left and his late wife on the right. Spranger again surveys the viewer from over his (cold) shoulder, but this time – in contrast to the early *Self-Portrait*

– we see his arms; the right one, the elbow of which appears to be jutting out of the picture towards the viewer, can be seen as the logical extension of the 'aggressive' shoulder position of Spranger's *Self-Portrait*. This is the 'Renaissance elbow' which Joaneath Spicer recently interpreted as a gesture typical for the early modern era, the gesture of the confident individual who thus sets himself apart from the surrounding world.[29]

Perhaps the most splendid Rudolfine elbow is the one Sadeler himself leans on in a drawing by Joseph Heintz in Munich [fig. 6.3].[30] In Jürgen Zimmer's view, this portrait was most probably made in Rome at the beginning of the 1590s – i.e., before Sadeler was made engraver to the court (Kupferstecher) in 1597. It nonetheless shows a man well aware of his own abilities and confidently staking out his territory. It is particularly revealing to compare this drawn portrait with the etched *Self-Portrait* Rembrandt made in 1639 [fig. 6.4].[31] Both artists, Sadeler and Rembrandt, are shown leaning on their left elbows; both sport rather extravagant headgear and a defiantly curled moustache and look self-confidently over their shoulders at the spectator. Rembrandt's etching and the kindred mirror-image picture of 1640 (London, National Gallery) belong to a series of self-portraits from the 1640s in which the artist styled himself as a 'haughty, self-confident, elegant' gentleman.[32] It was at this time more than any other in his life – writes Eddy de Jongh – that Rembrandt behaved like a 'social climber', his self-portraits demonstrating 'not only ... the dignity of his profession in general, but his own social eminence in particular'. I consider Heintz's *Sadeler* also to be a depiction of a young man who aspired to high social standing. And again, as in Spranger's early *Self-Portrait* and other works related to it, there is nothing to indicate that the subject of the painting is an artist.

Writers on Rembrandt have naturally paid close attention to the question of possible sources for these two Rembrandt self-portraits.[33] It is more than likely that their immediate model was Titian's *Man in Blue* of around 1512, a painting which in the seventeenth century was thought to be a portrait of the poet Ariosto and was moreover in Amsterdam at the time.[34] In it, an unknown man leans on a parapet with his right elbow, recalling the Rembrandt picture of 1640 and Sadeler's *Spranger* of 1600. While it is possible that Heintz and Sadeler drew their inspiration from Titian's so-called *Ariosto*, it is extremely unlikely that Rembrandt knew Heintz's drawing (though he may have known Sadeler's engraving). This web of relationships is interesting not just for the possible filiation of the works under discussion, but for the fact that it places the (self-)portraits of Rudolfine artists in a broader European context of the visual depiction of creative genius.

All the works analyzed so far represent a type of portrait bust whose dominant feature is the regard over the shoulder at right angles to the viewer. We shall call this formula from now on the 'Rudolfine shoulder' and bear in mind its connection in terms of form and meaning with the 'Renaissance elbow'. It may come as a surprise that this motif was introduced into the repertoire of Rudolfine portrait formulae by Spranger, who particularly in comparison with von Aachen never really stood out as an inventive portrait artist. But it is not surprising if we consider the circumstances in which Spranger's oldest known self-portrait was painted. They correspond closely to those Stephen Greenblatt has identified as being fertile soil for self-fashioning. This happens, he says, when the individual is confronted with something he feels to be foreign, strange or even hostile.[35] Newly installed as court

6.4 REMBRANDT VAN RIJN
Self-portrait
[Bartsch 21]

6.5 JAN SAENREDAM
(after Pieter Isaacsz and Hans von Aachen)
Hans von Aachen
[Bartsch 105]

6.6 GIUSEPPE ARCIMBOLDO
Self-portrait
[Prague, Národní galerie v
Praze]

painter and furthermore a foreigner in Prague, Spranger could have perceived the authority of the guild in these ways and protected himself by showing his cold Rudolfine shoulder to his environment.

The formula had thus come into being and began to lead its own life. It became the dominant type for Rudolfine artists' (self-)portraits. Apart from the examples already mentioned, there was the *Portrait of Hans von Aachen* (Bartsch 105) engraved by Jan Saenredam in 1601 [fig. 6.5].[36] The engraving was made in Amsterdam after a lost self-portrait which von Aachen sent from Prague to his former pupil and assistant Pieter Isaacsz. It was the latter who devised the allegorical surround. The portrait itself therefore is conceived in the Prague style: a finely dressed artist is depicted again with his shoulder towards us, the left shoulder this time, and the fingers of his right hand lightly touch his chest.[37] Finally, the category also includes Heintz's *Portrait of the Sculptor Giovanni da Bologna* (Washington, D.C., National Gallery of Art), a drawing Zimmer has dated to around 1587.[38]

Although the Rudolfine shoulder can be said to dominate the Prague (self-)portraits, it is a conceptual dominance rather than a spiritual one. Other portrayals of court artists are known, but they do not constitute a homogeneous group. Instead they tend to document individual experiments or a specific purpose. Among them is the well-known and often reproduced drawing by Giuseppe Arcimboldo in the Národní Galerie v Praze in which the artist portrayed himself symmetrically *en face*, his gaze fixed almost hypnotically on the viewer [fig. 6.6].[39] Except for the inscription in the top left of the picture (apparently in his own hand), there seems once more to be no suggestion that what we have before us is a self-portrait. That it is one is indicated, in spite of the total absence of attributes, by the very type of portrayal. The symmetrical bust seen frontally was reserved in the Middle Ages for renderings of Christ; it was first used for an artist's portrait by Albrecht Dürer in his famous *Self-Portrait* of 1500 (Munich, Alte Pinakothek), in which the Nürnberg master styled himself as the 'divine creator'. Arcimboldo, whose drawing follows on from Dürer and the style of self-portraiture he evolved, thus provided personal testimony of the meaning and sublimity of art.[40]

In the corpus of Rudolfine (self-)portraits, the work of Hans von Aachen constitutes a special chapter. Only the work which formed the basis of Saenredam's engraving of 1601 represents the Rudolfine shoulder. Von Aachen's earliest self-portrait – painted around 1574 (Cologne, Wallraf-Richartz-Museum) – is highly conventional in type, since the artist shows himself face-on, only very slightly turned in the direction of his right arm.[41] Just ten years later, around 1586, von Aachen painted *Self-Portrait with 'Donna venusta'*, which until recently – when the original was discovered in a private collection in Italy – was known only from one preparatory sketch and workshop productions and copies.[42] The painting shows an elegant female lutenist and a laughing singer who raises a goblet of wine in his left hand, while the forefinger of his right hand, resting on a sheet of music, taps to the rhythm. There is an inscription which indicates, but does not completely elucidate, the meaning of this original double portrait: *Vinum et musica laetificant cor meum* [Wine and music gladden my heart; Ecclesiasticus 40:20). The Apocryphal text continues: 'but moreover both are love of wisdom'. E. Fučíková has written that this painting is an antecedent to Rembrandt's *Self-Portrait with Saskia* (Dresden), in which the Dutch master depicted himself in jubilant mood, with Saskia on his lap and a goblet of wine in

his hand.[43] One other von Aachen painting reveals kinship with this work: *A Young Couple* in Vienna [fig. 6.7].[44] The laughing man, who holds a purse in his right hand and points to the spectator with his left, is again easily recognized as the artist himself, although this time at a more advanced age than in *Self-Portrait with 'Donna venusta*. His partner, tugging fondly at his ear, is his wife Regina (daughter of the composer Orlando di Lasso), whom he married in Munich on 1 July 1596. Both of von Aachen's canvases display traits that in iconographical tradition are inseparably associated with illustrations of the biblical parable of the Prodigal Son as we know it especially from Dutch art of the sixteenth century: the drinking of wine, dalliance with women of easy virtue, and the setting of a public house or brothel, which is indicated in Rembrandt and von Aachen (in the top right-hand corner) by a table with a customer's bill.[45] Whereas the specific reasons which induced Rembrandt to make use of this iconographic scheme have been analyzed in detail in specialist literature, von Aachen's motivation has not been adequately examined. It would appear that this painting, too, reveals the artist's tendency to give other figures in his canvases his own likeness – as with *Joking Couple with Mirror*[46] and *Bacchus, Venus and Cupid* (both Vienna, Kunsthistorisches Museum),[47] *Two Laughing Youths* (in the gallery of the archbishop's residence in Kroměříž)[48] and the painting of Bacchus and Silenus newly on loan to the Národní Galerie v Praze.[49] Only further research will reveal the meaning of these works, but today it is clear that their interpretation will fall somewhere between two extremes. Either they are scenes in which von Aachen's self-portraits play the obviously predetermined role of 'portraits within a particular story' (*stellvertretende Bildnisse* or *portraits historiés*), or the widespread belief that 'all artists paint themselves' will find further confirmation.[50]

While we do not know for whom and what reason these paintings were made, another group of Rudolfine (self-)portraits has on the whole a clearly definable purpose. These are the official portraits intended for the Medici gallery of self-portraits by famous artists in Florence, the Galleria degli Autoritratti.[51] The three Rudolfine portraits in this category all show their subject face-on and slightly turned to the right. This standard formula for official portraits can be seen in its purest form in von Aachen's *Self-Portrait,* painted around 1595.[52] Giovanni Contarini's *Self-Portrait* is evidently contemporary. But the latter artist is more finely dressed and has placed his left hand in a rhetorical gesture on his chest, around which hangs a gold chain, possibly an allusion to his ennoblement in 1580.[53] A massive gold chain also decorates the chest of the aging Spranger in the portrait by von Aachen from before 1610.[54] Such chains were often presented to artists on their ennoblement, but in time they came to be a general attribute representing not only the aristocratic rank of the bearers but also the nobility of their profession.[55] Both connotations should be perceived in the gold chains worn by Spranger in Sadeler's engraving of 1600 and by von Aachen in Saenredam's portrait of 1601.

A final group of (self-)portraits by Rudolfine artists comprises works whose content was augmented by the additional use of attributes and personifications. A good example of this category is the *Portrait of Joris Hoefnagel* (Hollstein 599), an engraving which Jan Sadeler produced after his own drawing in 1591 – thus when the subject was still working in Munich [fig. 6.8].[56] Underneath the preparatory drawing, made in Munich on July 28(?) according to the inscription, is an eight-line dedication written in Sadeler's own hand, and above it there is a short motto: *Ars est*

6.7   HANS VON AACHEN
A Young Couple
[Vienna, Kunsthistorisches
Museum, Gemäldegalerie]

DVM EX — TENDAR.

GEORGIVS HOVFNAGLIVS ANTVERP:
QVI PICTVRAM DELICATIOREM GENIO DVCE
AMPLEXVS, EO PROMOVIT SVMMIS VT PRINCIP:
PLACEAT ALBERTO ET GVILIELMO BOIARICIS.
FERDINAND.ᵉ AVSTRIACO IPSI IMP:
RVDOLPHO AVGVST.
Ioann. Sadelerus Amicus Amico et Posteritati.

6.8   JAN SADELER
Joris Hoefnagel
[Hollstein 587]

5.9   AEGIDIUS SADELER
Allegory of Painting
[Leiden, Prentenkabinet der
Rijksuniversiteit]

contenta doceri. There are a number of differences between the drawing and the engraving. One of them is that in the engraving, the motto has been replaced by Hoefnagel's own impresa, DVM EXTENDAR and a representation of a hammer striking a nail on an anvil. In the emblematics of the period, the best-known variant of this motif is a heart being struck by the hammer of fate on the anvil of life. But Hoefnagel has as it were 'customized' the device by substituting the heart for an object which alludes to his name – a nail (*nagel* in Dutch). Nota bene: most often it is a horseshoe that is wrought on the anvil and then nailed to the hoof (*hoef* in Dutch).[57]

This survey of portraits and self-portraits of artists working at the court of Rudolf II in Prague was not intended to be an inventory of all the works in this category or a thorough analysis of the examples cited. The aim was instead to highlight certain fundamental types and their chief characteristics and thereby to prepare the ground for the final part of this chapter. Whether the Rudolfine artists show their shoulder *urbi et orbi* or whether the (self-)portraits are of some different type, they all have one thing in common: the Rudolfine artist does not portray himself at work, does not paint or hold the tools of his trade. Exceptions of course exist, but they have such clear motivations that they serve merely to confirm the rule. Of these there are above all two group portraits by Heintz. In the first one, Heintz portrayed himself with his brother, as he (Heintz) painted their sister Salome.[58] The painting is dated 1596 and apparently originated in Bern, which the artist visited briefly after the death of his father. The painting is thus an intimate family document which the artist left his kin to remind them of him during his absence. The portrait's function is chiefly commemorative, and in composing it Heintz innovatively combined two iconographic traditions: 1) the family portrait, and 2) the self-portrait of the painter creating a likeness of others, like a picture within a picture. Heintz's *Self-Portrait with Family*, on the other hand, painted around 1608 and now in Pommersfelden, follows only the first tradition. The artist, who at this time was working mainly in architecture, portrayed himself with a compass in his hand.[59]

The last Rudolfine work in which the artist showed himself 'in action' is of similarly intimate character. It is not a family portrait, but a *Freudschaftsbild*, in which goldsmith Paulus van Vianen depicted himself painting Hans von Aachen in the presence of Adriaen de Vries.[60] This small painting on copper of 1608, not demanding in execution but interesting in conception, has the private commemorative function which Alberti postulated when he wrote: 'Painting contains a divine force which ... makes men present, as friendship is said to do.'[61]

Apart from these three pictures, which anyway are wholly private in character (concerning family or friends), one cannot find in the Rudolfine oeuvre a single portrait or self-portrait which shows the artist in his normal professional environment – i.e., the atelier. Only biblical and mythological figures or personifications were depicted – such as, for instance, St Luke in Spranger's painting of 1582 in Munich,[62] Venus in Sadeler's *Allegory of Painting* of 1600 in Leiden [fig. 6.9],[63] and the artist in Heintz's allegorical drawing of around 1592–4 in Dresden, which is a general representative of the art of painting, not a specific artist's portrait.[64] We never see the artist holding the attributes of his profession; at best, we find them elsewhere in the work. In Sadeler's allegorical portrait of Spranger of 1600, Painting is personified to the left behind the artist; she holds a maulstick in her right hand, and a palette and brushes in her left hand defend him from the assaults of time, repre-

sented by the god Cronus. The same three objects appear again in the lower right-hand corner of the engraving.

All of the foregoing observations lead inevitably to a seemingly paradoxical conclusion. The creators of the (self-)portraits in question, these representatives of the art of painting *par excellence*, working at a court considered to be an artists' paradise, preferred to portray themselves as if they were not artists at all. These representatives of an art famous for allegories, personifications, symbols, attributes, emblems – in a word, iconography based on learning – preferred the kind of *Selbstdarstellungen* that got by perfectly well without any intellectual apparatus. The most distinctive feature of these portraits and self-portraits was what we have called the Rudolfine shoulder (sometimes with the elbow, too), hence pure body language. Bar the mentioned exceptions, these men presented themselves not as artists or scholars, but as high-born, self-aware and self-assured courtiers.[65] In its essential characteristics, this tendency on the one hand reflects a general attempt evident at that time elsewhere in Europe to heighten the prestige of the fine arts and elevate artists' social status. But on the other hand, the tendency seems to have been nowhere as pronounced as in Rudolfine Prague or, more precisely, at the court of Rudolf II. The word *court* is crucial in this connection, and I cannot help but sympathize with those writers who see the phenomenon of the court artist as an important stage on the way to the 'modern' artist, or who advocate a 'return to history from above' for further study of Rudolfine art.[66] Only thus can we explain the fact that Rudolfine artists, when seeking their social identity and artistic formulae to convey it, hit upon the same solutions as Rembrandt did a few decades later in some of his self-portraits. Similarly, the set of (self-)portraits by Rudolfine masters, with their assertive body language and almost total absence of professional paraphernalia, can be compared with van Dyck's *Iconography*, the first folios of which were published in Antwerp around 1635.[67] From the title page of this collection, van Dyck himself gazes over his shoulder at us. Later, on folio 61, the Antwerp painter Theodor Rombouts is shown in a position which appears to emulate the portraits of the court of Rudolf II (Hollstein 587; fig. 6.10).[68] Virtually everything commonly thought to characterize the portrait of the artist in *Iconography* holds true, with slight modifications, for the portrayal of Rudolfines. The models display the dress and bearing of aristocrats; they carry none of the accessories of their profession; there is no trace of the workmanly aspects of art. On the contrary, 'the artistic activity of the virtuoso is expressed only by posture, gesture, the arrangement of garments, and physiognomy'.[69] This concept of the artist as a gentleman who creates masterpieces out of sheer innate virtuosity derives chiefly from van Dyck's experience at Charles I's court in London and was subsequently transferred to those working outside the sphere of the court.

In Rudolfine art, there is no better expression of this ideal than von Aachen's apparently inconspicuous but prophetic drawing of a man standing, convincingly identified as the sculptor Adriaen de Vries by Fučíková [fig. 6.11].[70] The graceful figure with an emphasized shoulder leans nonchalantly on his right elbow against the bust of a statue on a pedestal. Van Dyck himself could have been proud of such a portrait! A total antithesis, at least in terms of Rudolfine art, is the drawing by van Vianen of 1603 picturing two artists drawing in the woods [fig. 6.12].[71] If we compare the curly-haired man under the tree on the right with van Vianen's slightly lat-

6.10 PAULUS PONTIUS
Theodor Rombouts
[Hollstein 587]

6.11 HANS VON AACHEN
Adrian de Vries
[Zürich, Eidgenössische Technische Hochschule, Graphische Sammlung]

6.12 PAULUS VAN VIANEN
Two Painters in the Woods
[Berlin, Stiftung Preußischer
Kulturbesitz, Kupferstich-
kabinett]

er triple portrait, it seems likely that the artist here recorded himself sitting on the ground sketching trees. In spite of the entirely private character of the drawing, I think we can speculate that a man immortalizing himself in this way could only have been a goldsmith and landscape artist in the pay of the Emperor but not ennobled – an employee of the court, not a courtier.

This detour brings us back again, but for the last time, to the question of self-fashioning, of which – as I have tried to demonstrate – the Rudolfine shoulder is an exemplary manifestation. I have quoted Stephen Greenblatt's view that this phenomenon results whenever the individual is confronted by an authority which lies beyond him and to which he must submit. This authority may be God, military command, or a monarch's court. It is above all in the court environment that the individual is subjected to the formative pressure of external authority with its hegemonic interests, group strategies and requirements of etiquette. If my interpretation is correct, the Rudolfine shoulder, which came about as Spranger's means of delimiting himself in relation to the authority of the guild, served not only him but also other court artists as a formula whereby they identified with the court's ideals but at the same time preserved their own identity vis-à-vis the court. Seen in this context, the (self-)portraits of Rudolfine artists arc in fact typical pictorial representations of wishful thinking, *Wunschbilder*. They are not a record of idylls, but the expression of a utopia.[72]

The notes to this chapter have been kept to the absolute minimum (appearances notwithstanding) except for notes 2, 4 and 15. References to literature on the artworks cited are generally limited to two key works: Prag um 1600: Kunst und Kultur am Hofe Kaiser Rudolfs II., exh. cat. (Freren, 1988), 2 vols. (henceforth Prag um 1600) and T. DaCosta Kaufmann, The School of Prague: Painting at the Court of Rudolf II (Chicago and London, 1988) (henceforth The School of Prague). Older literature is cited only occasionally, later works only if they offer new facts or views.

1. For a respresentative statement of this opinion, see *The School of Prague*, pp. 40–45.

2. For the Czech wording of this document, see K. Chytil, *Malířstvo pražské XV. a XVI. věku a jeho cechovní kniha staroměstská z let 1490–1582* (Prague, 1906), pp. 310–14 (313); a German translation of 1732 is quoted in *Jahrbuch der kunsthistorischen Sammlungen des allerhöchsten Kaiserhauses*, 7:2 (1888): xl–xli, ref. no. 4607. For partial quotations and commentaries, see also K. Chytil, *Umění v Praze za Rudolfa II* (Prague, 1904), pp. 22, 24 (ill. 11), 61 (n. 18); R. Kuchynka, 'Manuál pražského pořádku malířského z let 1600–1656', *Památky archeologické*, 27 (1915): 26; Chytil, 'Apotheosa umění od B. Sprangera', *Ročenka Kruhu pro pěstování dějin umění za rok 1918* (1919): 7; av [Hana Volavková], 'Privilegium Rudolfa II.', *Výtvarné umění*, 2:3 (1969): 60–61 (ill.); J. Neumann, 'Rudolfské umění I.', *Umění*, 25 (1977): 414–15, 405 [ill. 3]; J. Zimmer, *Josef Heintz der Ältere als Maler (1564–1609)* (Bamberg, 1967), p. 74. See also below, notes 3, 12 and 14.

3. This information was first published in Kuchynka (note 2), 26. The symbol has been much debated and reproduced; see *The School of Prague*, p. 269, cat. no. 20.61; *Prag um 1600*, vol. 1, pp. 209 (cat. no. 88), 195 (pl. 11). For the best colour reproductions, see E. Fučíková, B. Bukovinská and I. Muchka, *Die Kunst am Hofe Rudolfs II* (Prague/Hanau, 1988), p. 60 (ill. 47).

4. L. O. Larson, *Adrian de Vries - Adrianus Fries Hagiensis Batavus 1545–1626* (Vienna and Munich, 1967), p. 50; he describes this engraving as an 'illustration of the Emperor's decree'. The following bibliographical references, which are extensive but hardly exhaustive, show how often this document is reproduced and discussed: R. A. Peltzer, 'Der Hofmaler Hans von Aachen, seine Schule und seine Zeit', *Jahrbuch der kunsthistorischen Sammlungen des allerhöchsten Kaiserhauses*, 30 (1911/12): 100, 101 [ill. 32], 166 [cat. no. 43]; K. Oberbuber, 'Die stilistische Entwicklung im Werk Bartholomäus Spranger' (Ph.D. dissertation, Vienna, 1958), p. 148; *idem, Zwischen Renaissance und Barock: Das Zeitalter von Bruegel und Bellange*, exh. cat. (Vienna, 1967), pp. 232–33, no. 345; K. van Mander, *Den grondt der edel vry schilder-const*, ed. H. Miedema (Utrecht, 1973), vol. 2, pp. 331–32, ill. 1; Neumann (note 2), pp. 424, 408, ill. 6; W. Prinz, 'Das Motiv "Pallas Athena führt die Pictura in den Kreis der septem artes liberales ein" und die sogenannte Cellini-Schale' in *Festschrift für Peter Wilhelm Meister zum 65. Geburtstag am 16. Mai 1974* (Berlin, 1975), pp. 165–73; T. DaCosta Kaufmann, 'The Eloquent Artist: Towards an Understanding of the Stylistics of Painting at the Court

of Rudolf II', *Leids Kunsthistorisch Jaarboek*, 1 (1982): 127, 128, ill. 7; *idem*, 'The Nature of Imitation: Hoefnagel on Dürer', *Jahrbuch der Kunsthistorischen Sammlungen in Wien*, 82–83(66–67) (1986–87) (*Albrecht Dürer und die Tier- und Pflanzenstudien der Renaissance: Symposium*): 168, 169, ill. 176; *idem, The School of Prague*, pp. 53, 44, ill. 37; E. Fučíková, *Rudolfínská kresba* (Prague, 1986), no. 23 (German edn, 1987); H. P. Chapman, 'A Hollandse Pictura: observations on the title page of Philips Angel's *Lof der schilder-konst*', *Simiolus*, 16 (1986): 237–38, ill. 3; G. Luijten, 'De Triomf van de Schilderkunst: een titeltekening van Gesina ter Borch en een toneelstuk', *Bulletin van het Rijksmuseum*, 36 (1988): 287–88, 290, ill. 8; H. U. Asemissen and G. Schweikhart, *Malerei als Thema der Malerei* (Berlin, 1994), pp. 32–33, 31, ill. 7; D. Limouze, 'Taking the High Road: Netherlandish Engravers at the Courts of Munich and Prague', *BlockPoints: The Annual Journal and Report of the Mary and Leigh Block Gallery*, 2 (1995): 37. The engraving is reproduced in *Prag um 1600*, p. 431, as cat. no. 319, but the corresponding text on pp. 425–26 in fact relates to a different work. See also below, note 5.

5. L. Konečný, 'Hans von Aachen and Lucian: An Essay in Rudolfine Iconography', *Leids Kunsthistorisch Jaarboek*, 1 (1982): 237–40.

6. On von Aachen's Munich period, see esp. E. Fučíková, 'Über die Tätigkeit Hans von Aachens in Bayern', *Münchner Jahrbuch der bildenden Kunst*, 3, ser. 1 (1970): 129–42; T. Vignau-Wilberg, 'Künstlerische Beziehungen zwischen Prag und München zur Zeit Rudolfs II.' in *Prag um 1600: Beiträge zur Kunst und Kultur am Hofe Rudolfs II.* (Freren, 1988), pp. 299–308.

7. A detailed interpretation of the individual figures can be found in Prinz (note 4), p. 168; Asemissen and Schweikhart (note 4), p. 32.

8. On this phenomenon, see above all M. Warnke, *Hofkünstler: Zur Vorgeschichte des modernen Künstlers* (Cologne, 1985).

9. A good overview is provided in M. Šroněk, *Pražští malíři 1600–1656: Mistři, tovaryži, učedníci v žtolíři v Knize Staroměstského malířského cechu. Biograficky slovník* (Prague, 1996), *s.v.* Spranger.

10. Zimmer, 'Giovanni Contarini – ein "rudolfinischer" Künstler?' in *Prag um 1600* (note 6), p. 314; Warnke (note 8), p. 219.

11. A list of ennobled artists has been compiled by Warnke (note 8), pp. 217–23. On the same topic, see S. Schütze, 'Arte Liberalissima e Nobilissima: Die Künstlernobilitierung im päpstlichen Rom – Ein Beitrag zur Sozialgeschichte des Künstlers in der frühen Neuzeit', *Zeitschrift für Kunstgeschichte*, 55 (1992): 319–52.

12. H. Miedema, 'Over de waaedering van architekt en beeldende kunstenaar in de zestiende eeuw', *Oud Holland*, 96 (1980), p. 83.

13. Warnke (note 8), pp. 91–92.

14. Kaufmann, 'The Elegant Artist' (note 4), p. 144, n. 31, rejects Miedema's interpretation, asserting that the aim of the decree was to consolidate the rights of the guild. Although Miedema took sufficient note of this criticism ('Kunstschilders, gilde en academie: Over het probleem van de emanciptie van de kunstschilders in de Noordelijke Nederlan-

den van de 16de en 17de eeuw', *Oud Holland*, 101 [1987]: 27, n. 111), I am inclined to share his opinion that it was 'nothing more than a slight decoration for those who thought guild membership was beneath them'. I think the situation in Prague requires thorough study, for which good groundwork has been laid by the recent work by M. Šroněk (note 9) and M. Halata, *Kniha protokolů pražského malířského cechu z let 1600–1656* (Prague, 1996).

15. For the history and a broader context for this material, see the following works: E. Benkard, *Das Selbstbildnis vom 15. bis zum Beginn des 18. Jahrhunderts* (Berlin, 1927); L. Goldscheider, *Fünfhundert Selbstporträts von der Antike bis zur Gegenwart (Plastik, Malerei, Graphik)* (Vienna, 1936); M. Masciotta, *Autoritratti del Quattrocento e del Cinquecento* (Florence, 1949); M. Gasser, *Das Selbstbildnis* (Zurich, 1961); G.-W. Költzsch, *Maler und Modell*, exh. cat. (Baden-Baden, 1969); S. Holsten, *Das Bild des Künstlers: Selbstdarstellungen*, exh. cat. (Hamburg, 1978); *Selbstbildnisse und Künstlerporträts von Lucas van Leyden bis Anton Raphael Mengs*, exh. cat. (Braunschweig, 1980), pp. 7–35; H.-J. Raupp, 'Selbstbildnisse und Künstlerporträts -- ihre Funktion und Bedeutung' in J. Kinner and D. Piper, *The Artist by Himself: Self-Portrait Drawings from Youth to Old Age* (London, 1980); *idem, Untersuchungen zu Künstlerbildnis und Künstlerdarstellung in den Niederlanden im 17. Jahrhundert* (Hildesheim, Zurich and New York, 1984); P. Bonafoux, *Le Métier d'artiste: Les Peintres et l'autoportrait* (Geneva, 1984); P. Georgel and A.-M. Lecoq, *La Peinture dans la Peinture* (Paris, 1987); M. Koortbojian, *Self-Portraits* (London, 1991); M. Winner (ed.), *Der Künstler über sich in seinem Werk* (Internationales Symposium der Bibliotheca Hertziana, Rome, 1989) (Weinheim, 1992); Asemissen and Schweikhart (note 4). Some specialized works are cited in notes 24, 25, 31 and 65 below. See also L. Freedman, *Titian's Independent Self-Portraits* (Florence, 1990).

16. Asemissen and Schweikhart (note 4), p. 18.

17. S. Greenblatt, *Renaissance Self-Fashioning: From More to Shakespeare* (Chicago and London, 1980), esp. pp. 2–4.

18. E. de Jongh, 'Reticent informants: seventeenth-century portraits and the limits of intelligibility' in K.-L. Selig (ed.), *Plyanthea: Essays on Art and Literaure in Honor of William Sebastian Heckscher* (The Hague, 1993), p. 59.

19. Vienna, Kunsthistorisches Museum, Gemäldegalerie, 1137. See Oberhuber (note 4), pp. 204–5; *Prag um 1600*, vol. 1, p. 275 (no. 153) 2, 3 (no. 581); *The School of Prague*, pp. 256–57, cat. no. 20, 24, 25; *Eros und Mythos: Kunst am Hof Rudolfs II.*, exh. cat. (Vienna, 1995), pp. 66 (no.19), 18 (ill.).

20. See at least *Selbstbildnisse und Künstlerporträts* (note 15), pp. 38–42; Raupp, *Untersuchungen ...* (note 15), pp. 182–83; Asemissen and Schweikhart (note 4), pp. 76–78. For a broader perspective on the issue, see J. Andersen, 'The Giorgionesque Portrait: from Likeness to Allegory' in *Giorgione (Atti del Convegno Internazionale di Studio)* (Venice, 1979), pp. 154–55; W. S. Sheard, 'Giorgione's Portrait Inventions c. 1500: Transfixing the Viewer (With Observations on Some Florentine Antecedents)' in M. A. Di Cesare

(ed.), *Reconsidering the Renaissance* (Binghampton, 1992), pp. 141–76.

21. Raupp, *Untersuchungen ...* (note 15), p. 82. This view is based on an interpretation of F. Zuccaro's composition *Lamento della pittura*; for a more recent work on this – and one often offering different conclusions – see I. Gerards-Nelissen, 'Frederigo Zuccaro and the *Lament of Painting*', *Simiolus*, 13 (1983): 44–53.

22. Gerards-Nelissen in his review of Raupp's 1984 book (note 15), *Simiolus*, 16 (1986): 263.

23. See Asemissen and Schweikhart (note 4), pp. 86 (ill. 14), 84 (ill. 11), 87 (ill. 17), 83 (ill. 10).

24. *Prag um 1600*, vol. 1, p. 414, no. 300; *The School of Prague*, p. 31 (ill. 26); J. P. Filedt Kok, 'Jan Harmensz: Muller as Printmaker', *Print Quarterly*, 11(1994): 223–64, 351–78; 12 (1995): 3–29 (244–45 [ills 125–26], 9); *idem*, 'Artists Portrayed by their Friends: Goltzius and His Circle', *Simiolus*, 24 (1996): 166–67, ill. 5.

25. On this, see W. Prinz, *Vasaris Sammlung von Künstlerbildnissen* (Florence, 1966); Filedt Kok, 'Artists Portrayed ...' (note 24), p. 162.

26. See Filedt Kok, 'Artists Portrayed ...' (note 24), pp. 162 (ill. 1), 166 (ill. 4). It is worth mentioning that the way Goltzius' Stradanus writes an inscription around his own portrait could have inspired Aegidius Sadeler, in his engraving after Spanger's *Triumph of Wisdom* (Hollstein 115), to make Clio, the muse of history, write the text herself under the portrait; see Limouze (note 4), pp. 39, 41 (ill. 6).

27. Filedt Kok, 'Artists Portrayed ...' (note 24), p. 168, interprets *bucranium* (the skull of an ox or bull) as 'an allusion to St Luke, the patron saint of painters', whereas it is a symbol of physical labour. On this, see G. P. Valeriano, *Hieroglyphica* (Lyon, 1602), pp. 30–31, and particularly K. Hermann-Fiore, 'Il tema "Labor" nella creazione artistica del Rinascimento' in Winner (ed.) (note 15), pp. 245–92. R. an der Heiden, 'Die Porträtmalerei des Hans von Aachen' in *Jahrbuch der Kunsthistorischen Sammlungen in Wien*, 66 (1970): 213, believes that the allegorical surround is connected with Spranger's ennoblement.

28. *Prag um 1600*, vol. 1, pp. 420–21, no. 313; *The Stylish Image: Printmakers to the Court of Rudolf II*, exh. cat. (Edinburgh, 1991), p. 28, no. 9; Filedt Kok, 'Artists Portrayed ...' (note 24), pp. 170–71. I have not had the opportunity of acquainting myself with the same author's study 'Aegidius Sadeler: Portrait allégorique de Bartholomeus Spranger et sa femme Christina Müller' in M. van Berge, Gerbaud and H. Buijs (eds), *Morceaux choisis* (Paris, 1994), no. 74.

29. J. Spicer, 'The Renaissance elbow' in *A Cultural History of Gesture*, ed. J. Bremmer and H. Roodenburg (Ithaca, 1991), pp. 84–128.

30. Munich, Staatliche Graphische Sammlung, 34.825. See *Prag um 1600*, vol. 1, pp. 348–49, no. 206; J. Zimmer, *Joseph Heintz der Ältere: Zeichnugen und Dokumente* (Munich, 1988), pp. 132–33, cat. no. A 49, ill. 91.

31. On this etching in the context of artists' self-portraits, see most recently H. P. Chapman, *Rembrandt's Self-Portraits: A Study in Seventeenth-Century Identity* (Princeton, 1990), pp. 71–78.

32. E. de Jongh, 'The Spur of Wit: Rembrandt's Re-

sponse to an Italian Challenge', *Delta*, 12:2 (1969): 49–67.

33. Besides the literature cited in notes 31 and 32 above, see C. Brown, *Second Sight: Portrait of a Man, Rembrandt's Self-Portrait at the Age of 34* (London, 1980).

34. For a good colour reproduction, see *Tiziano*, exh. cat. (Venice, 1990), p. 102 (ill.). Filedt Kok, 'Artists Portrayed ...' (note 24), p. 170 (n. 38), remarks on the evident similarity between Sadeler's Spranger, Titian's 'Ariosto' and Rembrandt in the etching of 1639.

35. Greenblatt (note 17), p. 9.

36. An der Heiden (note 27), pp. 209–10 (cat. no. B 12), 201 (ill. 170); Raupp, *Untersuchungen ...* (note 15), p. 82; Gerards-Nelissen (note 22), pp. 265–66, 264 (ill. 1); *The School of Prague*, p. 146, cat. no. I.37; *The Stylish Image* (note 28), p. 29, no. 10; Filedt Kok, 'Artists Portrayed ...' (note 24), pp. 168–70, ill. 8.

37. On this gesture and its meaning, see F. Graf, 'Gestures and Conventions: the Gestures of Roman Actors and Orators' in Bremmer and Roodenburg (eds) (note 20), p. 50; L. Konečný, 'L'accord interrompu: An Emblematic Source for Matthieu Le Nain' in K.-L. Selig and E. Sears (eds), *The Verbal and the Visual: Essays in Honor of William Heckscher* (New York, 1990), pp. 103–04.

38. The complex problem of the portraits of this sculptor, who never belonged to the court of Rudolf II, still awaits thorough analysis. In the meantime, see an der Heiden (note 27), pp. 221–22 (cat. no. D 1); J. Foucart, 'A propos du portrait de Jean Bologne (1529–1608) déposé par le Louvre au Musée de Douai' in *'Il se rendit en Italie': Etudes offertes à André Chastel* (Paris and Rome, 1987), pp. 311–19; Zimmer (note 30), pp. 117–19 (cat. no. A 16), ills 50, 1.

39. Prague, Národní Galerie v Praze, K 5338. For further and more recent bibliography, see L. Konečný, 'Arcimboldo, Christ and Dürer', *Bulletin of the National Gallery in Prague*, 5 (1995): 132–37.

40. This interpretation is given by Konečný (note 39). For Arcimboldo's 'paper' self-portrait recently discovered in the Palazzo Rosso, Genoa, and for a review of questions relating to other portraits, see G. Berra, 'Un *Autoritratto cartaceo* di Giuseppe Arcimboldo', *Arte Lombardo*, 116 (1996): 53–62.

41. Cologne, Wallraf-Richartz-Museum, 5211. See above all E. Fučíková, '"Quae praestat iuvenis vix potuere viri": Hans von Aachens Selbstbildnis in Köln', *Wallraf-Richartz-Jahrbuch*, 33 (1971): 115–24. Similar in character are other likenesses von Aachen painted of artists during his stay in Italy – Gaspar Rem, Jakob Bilivert and Ludwig Toeput – on which see an der Heiden (note 27), pp. 177–81, ills 144, 146, 147. A marked deviation from this standard bust type is represented by the *Portrait of Josef Heintz* (Prague, Národni Galeri v Praze, 4326), usually published as a work of von Aachen's (see an der Heiden, pp. 182–83 [cat. no. A9]. 146 [ill. 126]) but also attributed to Annibale Carracci: D. S. Pepper, 'Annibale Carracci ritrattista', *Arte illustrata*, 6:53 (1973): 130–31; Zimmer (note 30), pp. 26–27.

42. While the copies have been reproduced several times, for the original see *Hans von Aachen: Bakchus a Silén* (Prague, 1996), p. 12, ill. 3.

43. *Ibid.*, p. 23, n. 33.

44. Vienna, Kunsthistorisches Museum, Gemäldegalerie, 1134. See *Prag um 1600*, vol. 1, pp. 211–12, no. 92; *The School of Prague*, pp. 134–35, cat. no. I.6.

45. This iconographical kinship was first discerned by L. Konečný, 'Albrechta Dürera "Laus bombardae"', *Umění*, 20 (1972): 341, n. 19; see also *The School of Prague*, pp. 134–35. For a broader context, see I. Bergström, 'Rembrandt's Double Portrait of Himself and Saskia at the Dresden Gallery: A Tradition Transformed', *Nederlands Kunsthistorisch Jaarboek*, 27 (1966), 143–69.

46. Vienna, Kunsthistorisches Museum, Gemäldegalerie, 1155. See *The School of Prague*, pp. 135–36, cat. no. I.7; *Eros und Mythos* (note 19), pp. 62 (cat. no. 2), 22 (ill.).

47. Vienna, Kunsthistorisches Museum, Gemäldegalerie, 1132. See *Prag um 1600*, vol. 1, p. 212, no. 93; *The School of Prague*, p. 136, cat. no. I.9.

48. Kroměříž, Obrazárna Arcibiskupského zámku. See Fučíková (note 41), p. 116 (ill. 77).

49. Rentiérsky investiční fond I.IN, a.s.; on loan to Prague, Národní Galeri v Praze, VO 1809. See Fučíková (note 42), p. 8, ill. 1.

50. On the former theory, see A. Reinle, *Das stellvertretende Bildnis: Plastiken und Gemälde von der Antike bis ins 19. Jahrhundert* (Zürich and Munich, 1984); R. Wishnevsky, 'Studien zum "portrait historié" in den Niederländen' (Ph.D. dissertation, Munich, 1967). See also G. F. Hartlaub, 'Das Selbstbildnerische in der Kunstgeschichte: "Ogni dipintore dipinge se"', *Zeitschrift für Kunstwissenschaft*, 9 (1955): 97–124; E. Kris and O. Kurz, *Legend, Myth and Magic in the Image of the Artist: A Historical Experiment* (New Haven and London, 1979), pp. 114–20; M. Kemp, '"Ogni dipintore dipinge se": A Neoplatonic Echo in Leonardo's Art Theory?' in *Cultural Aspects of the Italian Renaissance: Essays in Honour of Paul Oskar Kristeller* (Manchester, 1976), pp. 311–23; F. Zöllner, 'Ogni Pittore Dipinge Sé: Leonardo da Vinci and "Automimesis"' in Winner (note 15), pp. 137–50.

51. On this specialized collection, see Prinz, *Die Sammlung der Selbstbildnisse in den Uffizien*, I: *Geschichte der Sammlung* (Berlin, 1971); K. Langedijk, *Die Selbstbildnisse der holländischen und flämischen Künstler in der Galleria degli Autoritratti der Uffizien in Florenz* (Florence, 1992); A. Cechi, *Painters by Portraits*, exh. cat. (Houston, 1988); *Autoritratti dagli Uffici da Andrea del Sarto a Chagall*, exh. cat. (Florence, 1990).

52. Florence, Galleria Palatina, Palazzo Pitti, 329. See *Prag um 1600*, vol. 1, pp. 212–13, no. 94.

53. Florence, Galleria degli Uffizi, 428. See Zimmer (note 10), pp. 314, 315 (ill. 1).

54. Florence, Galleria degli Uffizi, 1890. See *The School of Prague*, p. 159, cat. no. I.78.

55. On this question, see J. S. Held, *Rembrandt's Aristotle and Other Rembrandt Studies* (Princeton, 1969), pp. 32–41; Chapman (note 31), pp. 50–52.

56. Bremen, Kunstverein, A 262. The drawing is referred to but not reproduced in *Prag um 1600*, vol. 2, p. 164, no. 630; see also T. Vignau-Wilberg, *Archetypa studiaque patris Georgii Hoefnagelii, 1592: Natur, Dichtung und Wissenschaft in der Kunst um 1600* (Munich, 1994), p. 18, ill. 4. The most complicated case of a graphic likeness is that of the *Portrait of Pieter Breugel* which Aegidius Sadeler made

in 1606 after Spranger's original (Hollstein 279); see J. B. Bedaux amd A. van Gool, 'Bruegel's Birthyear, Motive of an Ars/Natura Transmutation', *Simiolus*, 7 (1974): 133–56; Filedt Kok, 'Artists Portrayed ...' (note 24), pp. 171–72.

57. *Die emblematischen Elemente im Werke Joris Hoefnagels* (Leiden, 1969), vol. 1, pp. 3–4, 257–58.

58. Bern, Kunstmuseum, 243. See *Prag um 1600*, vol. 1, pp. 236–37, no. 128; *The School of Prague*, p. 186, cat. no. 7.6. See also J. W. Salomonson, 'A Self-portrait by Michiel van Mierevelt: The History, Subject and Context of a Forgotten Painting', *Simiolus*, 20 (1990–1991): 241, 244–45; Asemissen and Schweikhart (note 4), pp. 87–88, ill. 19.

59. Pommerfelden, Schloss Weisenstein, Schönborn-Wiesentheid Collection, 233. See *The School of Prague*, p. 200, cat. no. 7.56. For the category of the family portrait, see above all E. de Jongh, *Portretten van echt en trouw: Huwelijk en gezin in de Nederlandse kunst van de zeventiende eeuw*, exh. cat. (Zwolle and Haarlem, 1986).

60. Herdingen, Fürstenberg Collection, 42. See an der Heiden (note 27), pp. 225 (cat. no. D 13), 224 (ill. 195); *The School of Prague*, p. 286, cat. no. 23.1. For the early phase of the 'picture of friendship', see H. Keller, 'Entstehung der Blütezeit des Freundschaftsbildes' in *Essays in the History of Art presented to Rudolf Wittkower* (London, 1967), pp. 161–73.

61. Leon Battista Alberti, *On Painting*, trans. and ed. J. R. Spencer (New Haven and London, 1966), p. 63. Alberti's source was Cicero, *De amicitia*, VII.23.

62. Munich, Alte Pinakothek, 14357. See *The School of Prague*, p. 255, cat. no. 20.18.

63. Leiden, Prentenkabinet der Rijksuniversiteit, AW 1110. See *Prag um 1600*, vol. 1, p. 376, cat. no. 238; *The School of Prague*, p. 95, ill. 59.

64. Dresden, Staatliche Kunstsammlungen, Kupferstichkabinett, C 6383. See Zimmer (note 30), p. 131 (cat. no. A 46), ill. 84.

65. See G. Schweikhart, 'Künstler als Gelehrte: Selbstdarstellungen in der Malerei des 16. Jahrhunderts' in *Begegnungen: Festschrift für Peter Anselm Riedl zum 60. Geburtstag* (Worms, 1993), pp. 18–27.

66. Cf. Warnke (note 8) and, with regard to Rudolfine art, esp. Limouze (note 4).

67. On this publication, see M. Mauquoy-Hendrickx, *L'iconographie d'Antoine van Dyck* (Brussels, 1956). The most recent information is available in J.

Spicer, 'Anthony van Dyck's Iconography: An Overview of its Preparation' in *Studies in the History of Art 46: Van Dyck* 350 (Hanover and London, 1994), pp. 327–64.

68. See D. Preising, *Anthonis van Dyck: Porträts in Radierung und Kupferstich*, exh. cat. (Aachen, 1988), pp. 38 (no. 45), 97 (ill.). The drawing for this portrait was published and attributed to Paulus Pontius by Spicer in 'Unrecognized studies for Van Dyck's Iconography in the Hermitage', *Master Drawings*, 23-24 (1985–1986): 540–41.

69. Preising (note 67), p. 11. For an exemplary analysis of some van Dyck formulae, see L. Vergara, 'Steenwyck, De Momper and Snellinx: Three Painters' Portraits by Van Dyck' in *Essays in Northern European Art Presented to Egbert Havercamp-Begemann on his Sixtieth Birthday* (Doornspijk, 1983), pp. 283–86.

70. Zürich, Eidgenössische Technische Hochschule, Graphische Sammlung, 1925.36. See *Prag um 1600*, vol. 1, p. 335, cat. no. 185. For further portraits of this artist, see Larsson (note 4), p. 18, ills 1–3. The most interesting of these is the sixty-sixth engraving in the set *Pictorum aliquot celebrium praecipue germaniae inferioris effigies*, which was published in The Hague by Hendrick Hondius in 1610; see Larsson, ill. 2; Asemissen and Schweikhart (note 4), p. 92, ill. 3. In it, de Vries is portrayed as 'Pictor Hagiensis' and holds a statuette symbolizing painting. Hondius's publication – on which, see Raupp, *Untersuchungen ...* (note 15), pp. 18–36, and Filedt Kok, 'Artists Portrayed ...' (note 24) – also contains copies of the graphic portraits of Spranger and von Aachen listed above.

71. Staatliche Museen zu Berlin, Stiftung Preußischer Kulturbesitz, Kupferstichkabinett, 13612. See T. Gerszi, *Paulus van Vianen: Handzeichnungen* (Hanau, 1982), cat. no. and ill. 10. The drawing is dated 1603, but because van Vianen moved from Salzburg to Prague some time in the second half of that year, it is not clear where it was made. It tends, however, to be automatically classed with his Salzburg works; see T. Gerszi and H. Klein, *Die Salzburger Skizzenbücher des Paulus van Vianen: Landschaftszeichnungen und Stadtansichten des Hofgoldschmiedes von Erzbischof Wolf Dietrich von Raitenau*, exh. cat. (Salzburg, 1983), pp. 70 (no. 20), 11 (ill.).

72. See Schweikhart (note 64), p. 18.

Portraits of Emperor Rudolf II

LARS OLOF LARSSON

On 7 September 1575, Archduke Rudolf II, king of Hungary since 1572, was crowned king of Bohemia in St Vitus' cathedral in Prague. On 1 November of the same year, he was elected king of the Romans in Regensburg. Giuseppe Arcimboldo, court painter in the service of Emperor Maximilian II, was present on both occasions. In the drawings which Arcimboldo subsequently made [fig. 7.1],[1] he seems to have paid particular attention to the two crowns which were used, the Wenceslas crown and the imperial crown, but the young King's features also give the impression of being true to life. The scene looks all the more authentic in that the artist did not try to hide the fact that the imperial crown was too large for Rudolf – 'two fingers' width on all sides' according to a note on the print. The wording of the signature underlines the fact that this is the work of an eye-witness: *io Giuseppe Arcimboldo fui presente*. These drawings are in many ways a moving image of the discrepancy between the frailty of the individual and the burden being imposed on him. No other portraits allow the viewer to approach Rudolf so closely.

Since Arcimboldo's duties at court included painting portraits of the royal family, it is likely that he made these drawings to use for later portrait work. The coronation of a prince was an opportunity to add to the more usual portraits in circulation. However, these drawings could only serve as the basis for an official commission: in contemporary eyes, the portrait of a king or emperor had to achieve something beyond mere portrayal, as will be seen in this examination of various more or less contemporaneous portraits of Rudolf intended for public view.

The first is an engraving by Martino Rota which may have been made in connection with the election of the King in Regensburg in that it shows Rudolf as a half-length figure in his coronation robes. The inscription describes him as the

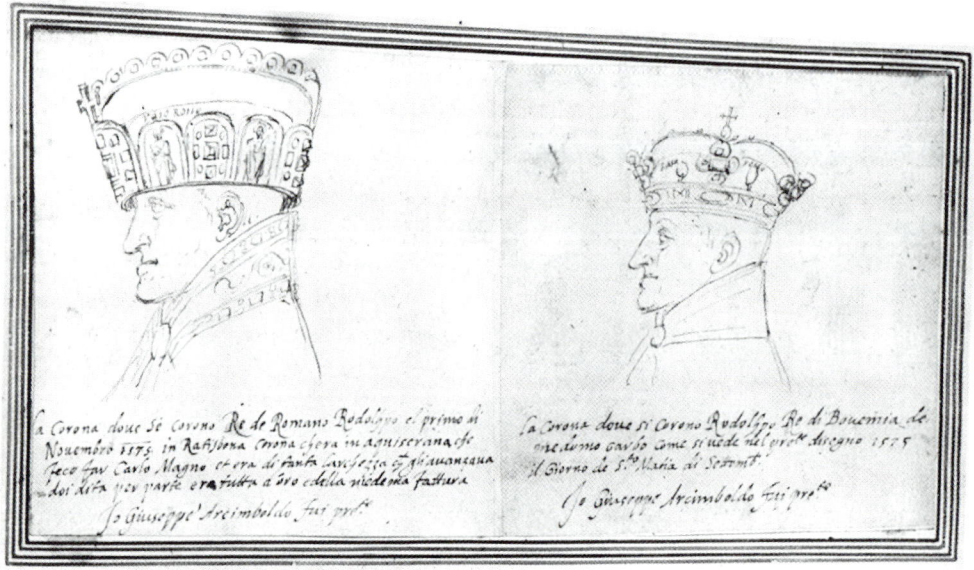

7.1 GIUSEPPE ARCIMBOLDO
Rudolf II as Holy Roman Emperor and King of Bohemia
1575–76
[Prague, Národní muzeum, oddělení starších českých dějin]

7.2   ANTONIO ABONDIO
Rudolf II
After 1576
[Prague, Národní muzeum,
numizmatické odděleni]

'Son of Maximilian II, Roman, Hungarian and Bohemian King' and not as Emperor. The crown is probably meant to be the Bohemian crown, but the engraver allowed himself a certain freedom in the matter. Rudolf's features are smooth and almost expressionless.[2] In 1574, Rota had engraved a half-length portrait of Rudolf in his armour (Bartsch 97). The features in the two portraits are almost identical. It seems likely that the coronation portrait was based on the earlier engraving.

This portrait may have been commissioned to mark the coronation of Rudolf as king of Hungary, although the event itself had taken place two years previously.[3] In 1577, shortly after the imperial coronation, Rota brought out a slightly changed, somewhat updated version.[4] Rudolf's moustache is thicker, and he now has fine side-whiskers. This engraving became one of the most widely circulated prints of the young Emperor. It may be regarded as his official portrait, a state portrait, and was not replaced by newer versions for about 20 years.

The same may be said of the medal which Alessandro Abondio made at much the same time [fig. 7.2].[5] Abondio showed the Emperor in profile, again in armour. If we compare the profiles by Arcimboldo and Abondio, it becomes evident how subtly the physiognomy has been heroized although without detracting from the work's function as a portrait conveying a likeness of the subject: his forehead, nose and chin have been brought into line, transforming the obviously jutting chin, clearly visible in the drawing, into an expression of strength of will and determination. Rota stylized the Emperor's head in a similar manner, only in his case it is less noticeable because he did not show the head in profile. In general terms, these alterations can be seen as 'idealization', yet this says little about the intentions behind these manipulations and what they involved. In order to understand better what the artist and his employer had in mind, we should draw some comparisons with other sources.

Despite its major social and political importance, the art of portraiture occupied a relatively menial position in art theory of the time. However, Giovanni Paolo Lomazzo, who was in contact with Arcimboldo and who may be taken as the mouthpiece of ideas which were also current in Viennese court art circles at the time, devoted a whole chapter of his 1584 tract to portraiture.[6] Lomazzo emphasized the necessity of clearly defining the subject's qualities and social status for the viewer. He specified the means to do this as being costume, attributes or symbols of office, facial expression and body language. About the portrait of a prince, he wrote:

> l'Imperatore sopra tutto, siccome ogni re e principe vuol maestà, ed avere un'aria a tanto grado conforme, si che spiri nobiltà e gravità, ancora che naturalmente non fosse talc. Consciosia chè al pittore conviene che sempre accresca nelle faccie grandessa e maestà, coprendo il defetto del naturale ...[7]

Thus it was not a matter of idealization in the sense of beautification, but of suitable characterization, although this may in itself have included an element of beauty.

Both Abondio and Rota carried out their imperial portraits in the spirit of Lomazzo's writings. The young Rudolf radiates that *gravità* which should mark a portrait's subject out as a ruler – even if 'this is not his nature.' His costume and attributes (armour and baton) are also in keeping with Lomazzo's thinking, although the latter did prefer costume *all'antica*. Clearly, however, in order that an official

portrait met the demands of authenticity, the subject had to be dressed in contemporary clothing. In the sixteenth and seventeenth centuries, a ruler would wear armour for official occasions such as court tournaments and similar events. In addition, armour points to the ruler's role as a leader on the battlefield, underlining his valour and at times no doubt sending out a hostile message.[8] In Lomazzo's view, armour on a prince was the ultimate expression of his claim to power. The virtuosic depiction of the highlights on the gleaming steel with its elegant decorations demonstrates its ceremonial importance. The fact that Rota showed Rudolf in the very armour which he wore for the coronation in Pressburg underlines the portrait's claims to authenticity.

In laying down what should be expected of a portrait, Lomazzo made a few brief references to the methods used by poets to write hymns of praise. In poetics of the time, and above all in contemporary thinking on rhetoric, there is a theory which, *mutatis mutandis*, perfectly fits Lomazzo's ideas. This in itself provides a good reason to analyze some portraits of Rudolf in the light of the art of rhetoric.

The portrait of Rudolf II that Rota engraved for the coronation in Regensburg in 1576 may certainly be seen as a solemn 'hymn of praise'. The subject's head is seen as a picture within a picture in an oval medallion in front of a double eagle. The portrait is framed by the imperial insignia: above the image, the imperial crown and stole, below it, the imperial globe, the sceptre and the sword, the latter above a cross. The eagles are extremely life-like and aggressive. The portrait of Rudolf is on a different level of reality to that of the figures surrounding it. He seems somehow distant, as though in another world. As motifs referring to the *image* of the Emperor and not to his *person*, the heraldic eagles and insignia could be portrayed much more expressively – in order to glorify and elevate the Emperor – than if portrait and attributes had occupied the same picture space.

In terms of the art of rhetoric, it is essential that the form and expression of an address should match the occasion, the subject and the intended audience. In terms of portraiture, this means analyzing the portrayal itself, the setting and medium used for the portrait with respect to the social status of the subject, the reason for the portrait's being commissioned and those who might be expected to view it. The analogy between rhetoric and portraiture can, however, be drawn even more closely. In the sense that a person in a portrait is presenting him- or herself to the viewer (whether contemporaneous or later), then that person is in a situation which can be precisely expressed in rhetorical terms. The subject of the portrait turns to the viewer and 'talks to him – or her'. Therefore the subject of a portrait can be compared to an orator. In the rhetorical concept of *actio*, we find the relevant criteria for judging the way speakers present themselves. This therefore lays down a yardstick by which the subject of a portrait may similarly be judged for his or her pose, gesture and clothing.

There is, however, yet another angle from which we may view the relationship of portraiture and rhetoric. If we see the artist and not the sitter as the speaker, then the portrait is the artist's 'address'. This opens up the possibility of analyzing the work by means of the full range of rhetorical devices, applying them to its making, mode of expression and style. The close links between rhetoric and social standards can be seen in the central significance which both attach to what is fitting, to *decorum*, whatever the situation. A good example of the validity of the notion of *deco-*

7.3 HANS VON AACHEN
Portrait of Emperor Rudolf II
1606–08
[Vienna, Kunsthistorisches
Museum, Gemäldegalerie]

rum for the society of Rudolf's time may be found in the numerous dress codes
which were laid down with pedantic exactitude, decreeing what clothes a person
was allowed to wear, according to their status, age and sex.

The relevance of the theory of rhetoric as a key to understanding the social
norms of the early modern era is further confirmed by well-known and widely consulted treatises on courtly behaviour such as Baldassare Castiglione's *Il Cortegiano*,
which is, in fact, based on the rules and standards of rhetoric.[9]

If one views portraits of Rudolf from this standpoint, they may seem at first to
say less than the portraits of some other contemporary princes and members of the
nobility. Amongst other things, this has to do with the fact that there are few
full-length portraits with the greater creative potential of that form. Furthermore,

as a rule, his portraits are rarely immediately appealing to the viewer. The one extant full-length portrait of Rudolf was painted by Hans von Aachen [fig. 7.3].[10] It fits exactly the conventions of state portraits which were to be found all over Europe at that time.[11] An early and extremely influential example of the style may be seen in Madrid in Titian's portrait of Prince Philip (later to be Philip II).[12] The work by Titian also shows a young prince dressed in armour, standing at a table. He is turning round as though he has been surprised by the viewer coming into the room. In comparison, Rudolf II would appear to be expecting the viewer. Rudolf presents himself face on, feet planted firmly apart and gesturing expansively with his arms. While Titian has given the viewer the impression of witnessing a moment in time, von Aachen has represented Rudolf in a much more formal pose. Rudolf has the same clothing and weaponry here as in Rota's engraving: breast-plate, baton and dagger. He is crowned with a laurel wreath. Von Aachen replaced the helmet with a crown which Rudolf touches with his left hand: his helmet and gauntlets lie on the ground.

7.4 AEGIDIUS SADELER
(after Hans von Aachen and Martino Rota)
Emperor Rudolf II in Armour
1604
[Prague, Národní galerie v Praze]

The viewer stands before this portrait of Rudolf as though attending an audience. Yet the situation has little to do with a real audience. It is hardly likely that Rudolf would have received visitors clad in armour and with his baton in his hand, and it is just as unlikely that during an audience he would have laid his hand on the crown in this possessive manner – an affront to the dignity of the regalia. Like any other prince, the Emperor would have granted audiences wearing court dress. The regalia, if on view at all, would have been laid out next to the throne in a strict order.[13] Thus the situation shown in this portrait is wholly fictional. Laurel leaves, armour, baton, crown and curtain (denoting a castle) should be seen as symbols of the various aspects of the Emperor's status, with the artist at pains to unite them in such a way that the viewer would, as far as possible, have the sense of standing before a living image of the Emperor.

We do not know the purpose for which this portrait was intended, so it is idle to ask to what extent it achieved its intended impact. However, there are many examples in which the clothes and attributes of a subject are clearly governed by the importance of the viewer – that is to say, what the subject's intentions were with regard to the latter. Thus it was hardly by chance that for the life-size portrait which Rudolf gave to the 'Freie Reichsstadt' of Nürnberg, he wore court dress and not armour.[14] A further example is the engraving which Domenicus Custos brought out during the Imperial Diet in Regensburg in 1594. Rudolf depended on the loyalty of the Diet and on this occasion was hoping to win support for his campaign against the Turks, so he appeared before them without imperial attributes or weapons, simply wearing court dress, as *primus inter pares*, one might say. Only the inscription at the edge of the print tells the viewer that this is the Emperor.

The propaganda value and the function of a portrait are closely linked to how widely it will become known, which in turn rests on the medium used. Public memorials, paintings, engravings and medallions all have distinct types and numbers of target viewers, and function differently according to circumstances. There were never any public memorials to Rudolf II. A large painting in a town hall would presumably only be seen by a limited number of people and then mostly only the members of the élite. A further important consideration here is that a portrait in a town hall would seem to indicate a connection between the picture's subject and

whoever was in power at the time. A portrait of this kind would represent an authority greater than the town itself, to which the town owed loyalty. In a private residence or castle, another quite different set of conditions would prevail. Here too the portrait could be a declaration of allegiance. On the other hand, it might simply have been acquired because the subject was famous, although perhaps feared as well.

Engravings were printed in large numbers and circulated widely. Since they were often copied by painters, they were indirectly instrumental in making the portrait of the Emperor a familiar sight to a great many individuals.[15] These engravings, which themselves met the highest artistic standards, almost always had an inscription in Latin. This, above all, may be seen as evidence that they were intended for an international public. However, the use of Latin did mean that they would be incomprehensible to the vast majority of the population.

Mention of the inscriptions leads us to the question of who initiated engravings. It seems fair to assume, at least in principle, that in the case of these prints, the Emperor was the client, although painted replicas may have been produced and further prints made without any further imperial initiative. On other occasions, the artist clearly declared himself to be the initiator by dedicating a work to the Emperor. This is exemplified in Aegidius Sadeler's reworking – or updated copy – of Rota's 1604 portrait of the Emperor, which Sadeler dedicated to the Emperor as 'Subjectissimus cliens' [fig. 7.4].[16] Hardly less respectful is the dedication on the famous print with the portrait of Rudolf II surrounded by allegorical figures alluding to his victories over the Turks [fig. 7.5].[17] This work is, in fact, a visual hymn of praise to the Emperor and, as such, worthy of closer examination.

In this composition, the portrait of the Emperor again appears as a picture within a picture. Thus Rudolf appears to be on a different level of reality – in a different world to the seemingly lively allegorical figures round the edges. This print is a good example of the close relationship between allegorical portraiture and epideictic rhetoric. The function of panegyric and portrait alike is to present the good deeds and qualities of the subject in the best possible light.[18] According to Aristotle and other authorities on the subject, this includes reference to the subject's superior origins and good education. However, the good deeds are the most important matter, particularly those which are personal achievements and therefore specially worthy of praise. Bearing this in mind, the same intentions are clearly recognizable in this print by Sadeler. The goat and the eagle, 'poised' above the Emperor as the highpoint of the surrounding frame, indicate his spiritual descent from Emperor Augustus and the ancient god Jupiter. In the lower part of the composition below the portrait, crouching Turks in chains, trophies and the battle scene on the plinth tell of his achievements. Bellona and Fortuna stand by as his associates, portrayed here as constant and reliable. The goddess of victory is enthroned above the portrait and forms the link, as it were, between the historical figure with all he has done and his 'mythological' origins. The goddess holds the palm of victory above Rudolf's head and gazes calmly down at Bellona, as though to reassure herself of the latter's constancy.

A composition of this kind was naturally helpful to imperial propaganda even if – or perhaps precisely because – it was self-evidently an artist's tribute to the Emperor. The term *propaganda* should not be interpreted here in its narrow modern

7.5   AEGIDIUS SADELER
(after Hans von Aachen)
Emperor Rudolf II
1603
[Prague, Národní galerie v Praze]

sense.[19] It was not a matter of winning over broad swathes of the public to the Emperor's cause: codified, intricate inventions with allegorical figures and inscriptions in Latin would not have been the best way to achieve that. Thus the message was directed first and foremost at the Emperor himself, confirming his own self-image as specially chosen amongst men and victorious in battle. Beyond this, the message was also directed at a relatively restricted circle of the political elite whose support and loyalty towards the Emperor were crucial at that particular time, when the power struggle between Rudolf and his brother Matthias was beginning to come to a head. Furthermore, it is important not to underestimate the extent to which works of this kind might have enhanced the artist's own reputation – his reputation, that is, in the eyes of the Emperor, his paymaster, whom he was thus flattering, and equally in the eyes of the artistically aware public, who would have appreciated the rich 'inventio' and its virtuosic realization.

Easier to understand as a piece of propaganda is Sadeler's engraved portrait of Rudolf on horseback [fig. 7.6] after Adriaen de Vries.[20] Here the message is proclaimed loud and clear in the powerful portrayal: the Emperor's impresa, the eagle with the arrow and the motto *Adsit*, are merely complementary extras and a substitute for the Emperor's name, which is not spelled out. The fact that Rudolf II never personally went into battle was evidently not a hindrance when it came to portraying him as a victorious leader on the battlefield.

With regard to propaganda, the busts and portrait relief which de Vries made of Rudolf are particularly interesting. The most striking is the more than life-size bust of 1603 [fig. 7.7].[21] More so than in any other portraits, here Rudolf impresses the viewer with his energetic, majestic pose, which could not provide a more startling contrast to reports by contemporary observers. De Vries, however, did not stop at this proud, dynamic image of the Emperor: he adorned his work with mythological and symbolical figures to add to the Emperor's *amplificatio*. The bust is carried by two gods from antiquity, Jupiter and Mercury, and by two creatures, the eagle and the goat. Jupiter, the eagle and the goat, already familiar from Sadeler's allegorical engraving, fulfil the same function as before; Mercury may be interpreted here as symbolizing wisdom. The ceremonial armour, an invention of the artist and not a copy of any real armour, is decorated with reliefs, which add yet another dimension to the meaning of the work. In the *Kunstkammer*, the bust could be seen alongside Leone Leoni's similarly structured portrait of Emperor Charles V. This juxtaposition in turn opens up a further important layer of meaning: Rudolf II on a level with Charles V – a theme that mattered a great deal to Rudolf.

The motif of *comparatio* underpinning the whole composition takes on a somewhat different tone to that in Sadeler's work. The Antique gods and mythological creatures with whom Rudolf is compared, at the same time as they represent his idealized origins, are not set above him, as in the engraving, for here they carry his portrait. Here the theme would appear to be not only *comparatio* but also *superatio* – as in the relationship to the bust of Charles V, which is much less effective than the dynamic portrait of Rudolf II.

In the portrait relief of Rudolf II made in 1609, the *amplificatio* concentrates on the comparison of Emperor and lion.[22] The large lion mask on the shoulder-piece of the armour forces the viewer to make the comparison with the Emperor's head; here the physiognomic implication is that the Emperor possesses

7.6 AEGIDIUS SADELER
(after Adrian de Vries)
Emperor Rudolf II on Horseback
Ca. 1603
[Prague, Národní galerie v Praze]

7.7 ADRIAN DE VRIES
Bust of Rudolf II
1603
[Vienna, Kunsthistorisches Museum, Kunstkammer]

the character of a lion. The depiction on Rudolf's armour of Hercules with a lion's skin over his head and a terrestrial globe in his arms adds yet another aspect to the whole.

Cast in bronze, these 'memorials' were intended 'for eternity'. However, they were kept in the imperial *Kunstkammer*, where only the chosen few can have had access to them. This vividly demonstrates the complexity of the propaganda question. Perhaps the addressee at the time of their making was primarily the Emperor himself, who might have seen in them the confirmation of his own role. However, above all, they were addressed to posterity, that it might recognize in these works the Emperor's true character, as yet untarnished by failure and slander.

1. *Prag um 1600: Kunst und Kultur am Hofe Kaiser Rudolfs II.*, 2 vols, exh. cat. (Freren, 1988), no. 193.

2. This portrait may well have been engraved on the occasion of Rudolf's coronation in Prague, with the inscription being added after the royal election, which took place only 2 months later.

3. Bruno and Christiane Thomas, 'Die sogenannte Dreiprinzengarnitur in Wien', *Jahrbuch der Kunsthistorischen Sammlungen in Wien*, 79 (1983): 19ff., 26f. Preparatory studies by Rota for this engraving and two further engravings, showing Archduke Ernst and Emperor Maximilian II, are held in the Szépmüvészeti Múseum, Budapest. See *Meisterzeichnungen des Künstlerkreises um Rudolf II. aus dem Museum der schönen Künste in Budapest*, exh. cat. (Salzburg, 1987), nos. 33–35.

4. After his coronation as king of the Romans, Rudolf also bore the title of emperor, which meant that it was necessary to update his titles on official portraits. In addition, he was clearly concerned at the time that his portraits should give an accurate impression of his age.

5. See Georg Habich, *Die deutsche Schaumünze des 16 Jahrhunderts* (Munich, 1929–34), vols 2:1, pp. 374f.; 2:2, pp. 499f., 519ff.

6. Giovanni Paolo Lomazzo, *Trattato dell'arte della pittura* (1584); 1844 Rome edn, vol. 2, pp. 369ff.

7. *Ibid.*, p. 370.

8. In the face of defeat by his nobles, the Emperor was, however, obliged to behave 'peacefully and in a neighbourly manner towards the rebels and Christian powers, neither starting nor undertaking quarrels, feuds or war, either in or outside the empire ...' On the other hand, 'when anyone attacks or makes war on the empire or the Holy Roman Empire, then we shall defend ourselves as best we may' (Karl Vocelka, *Die Politische Propaganda Kaiser Rudolfs II.* [Vienna, 1981], p. 125). Thus defensive action was permitted.

9. *Il Libro del Cortegiano del Conte Baldesar Castiglione* (Venice, 1528).

10. *Prag um 1600* (note 1), no. 98.

11. Mariana Jenkins, *The State Portrait: College Art Association*, 3 (New York, 1947).

12. Harold E. Wethey, *The Paintings of Titian 2: The Portraits* (London, 1971), pp. 41ff., 126ff., cat. no. 78.

13. Jenkins (note 10), p. 34. Anthonis Goeteeris from the Netherlands gives a vivid description of an au- dience with King Gustav Adolf II of Sweden in 1616, which was probably conducted in much the manner of an audience with the Emperor. See A. Goeteeris, *En holländsk beskicknings resor 1615–1616*, ed. S. Hildebrand (Stockholm, 1917).

14. Rüdiger an der Heiden, 'Die Porträtmalerei des Hans von Aachen', *Jahrbuch der kunsthistorischen Sammlungen in Wien*, 66 (1970): 218, cat. no. C.13.

15. Larsson in *Prag um 1600* (note 1), p. 163.

16. Jürgen Zimmer, *Joseph Heintz als Maler* (Weißenhorn, 1971), pp. 117f.

17. An der Heiden (note 14), pp. 170ff., 194ff.

18. *Ibid.*, p. 194, no. A 24.

19. Many Prague burghers owned portraits of the Emperor. It is largely impossible to establish to what extent these were paintings and not simply framed engravings, however. It does seem that there were considerable numbers of painted portraits, replicas from the studios of the court painters and copies from engravings. See Jiří Pešek, 'Porträts in den Bürgerhäusern des rudolfinischen Prag' in *Prag um 1600* (note 1), pp. 244–48.

20. An der Heiden, op. cit., p.199, cat. no., A 25d; Larsson in *Prag um 1600* (note 1), p.164.

21. An der Heiden (note 14), pp. 196ff., cat. no. A 25a.

22. O. B. Hardison Jr, *The Enduring Moment: A Study of the Idea of Praise in Renaissance Literary Theory and Practise* (Chapel Hill, 1962), pp. 29ff; Theodor Vermeyen, 'Barockes Herrscherlob: Rhetorische Tradition, Sozialgeschichtliche Aspekte, Gattungsprobleme', *Der Deutschunterricht*, 28 (1976): 24–25. The 1594 portrait of the Emperor by Domenicus Custos may of course also be interpreted in a similar manner.

23. Vocelka (note 8) discusses in detail the notion of propaganda at the beginning of the modern era.

24. *Prag um 1600* (note 1), no. 87; L. Larsson, 'Antonio Tempesta och ryttarporträttet under 1600-talet', *Konsthistorisk tidskrift*, 37 (1968): 34ff. A finely worked, hitherto unpublished drawing (brown pen and ink over black chalk, 5.12 x 3.78 cm), which seems to have been intended for engraving appeared recently on the American art market.

25. *Prague um 1600* (note 1), no. 57; L. O. Larsson, *Adrian de Vries. Adrianus Fries Hagiensis Batavus 1545–1626* (Vienna and Munich, 1967), pp. 36ff.; Larsson, pp.166f.

26. *Prague um 1600* (note 1), no. 59; Larsson 1967, p. 48; Larsson in *Prag um 1600* (note 1), pp.166ff.

Landscapes and City Views of Prague

TERÉZ GERSZI

Around 1600, Prague became famous for both the landscapes and the townscapes which artists living there were producing. Landscape painting had captured the imperial patron's interest not only as a new form but also as a way of studying Nature other than by means of conventional scientific observation.

Inventories of only a fraction of the imperial collection have survived, but even these show that there was a wealth of landscape paintings and drawings in the *Kunstkammer*.[1] Most numerous were works by the Netherlandish masters, specifically those following the Breugel tradition, including Hans Bol, Jacob Grimmer, Gillis Mostaert, Jan Breugel, David Vinckboons, Tobias Verhaeght, Joos de Momper and Savery (it is not certain whether this referred to Jacob or Roelandt). There were many works by Pieter Breugel which Rudolf II had inherited from his brother Ernst, the governor of the Netherlands. Besides numerous figural compositions, *Landscape with the Fall of Icarus* and the *Months* series which Ernst had received as a gift from the town of Antwerp in 1594 went to Prague. The 1621 inventory also contains a large number of works by the Valckenborch brothers. As far as the early masters are concerned, there are frequent references to Herri met de Bles. Amongst the German masters, certain references point to Lucas Cranach, while the Italians included Giovanni Bellini, Paolo Veronese, Titian and Bassani. From the inventories of 1607-11, it is clear that the holdings of books also included bound albums of drawings and prints by various artists. Amongst those named are Pieter Breugel, Hendrik van Cleve, Hans Bol and Pieter Stevens. On the basis of these inventories, it is fair to conclude that landscapes both by contemporary artists and by leading exponents of the art from the past were systematically collected, ultimately leading to a richly diverse collection of this genre.

That Emperor Rudolf II seems to have made equally systematic efforts to attract these landscape artists to the imperial court confirms his interest in this art form. However, there were far fewer landscape artists than figurative artists at the court in Prague. In fact, Pieter Stevens and Roelandt Savery were the only two to work there, although there were others who produced landscape drawings and engravings. The first to go to Prague was Pieter Stevens from Mechelen, probably via Italy and perhaps as a result of meeting one of the Rudolfine painters, possibly Joseph Heintz. In 1594, Stevens was appointed painter to the court of Rudolf, although he had presumably already been living in Prague for a while; he remained until his death 30 years later. The second to arrive, in 1597, was Aegidius Sadeler, who also remained until his death in 1629. Although Sadeler was not a landscape painter, as an engraver he played a crucial part in the reproduction of landscape works. In fact, his function as an engraver was no less important than his role as a mediator: on the one hand through his connections with other, leading art centres and on the other hand through the impact in Prague of the prints (possibly also drawings and paintings) which he brought with him from Italy. By the summer of 1603, Paulus van Vianen, a native of Utrecht, may well also have been in Prague.

8.1 PIETER STEVENS
*Mountain Landscape with
Waterfall*
[Frankfurt, Städelsches
Kunstinstitut]

One of the most gifted goldsmiths and landscape artists of his day, he stayed until his death in 1613. Before settling in Prague, he had worked in many different places: probably in Nürnberg for a while, then definitely in Munich and, between 1601 and 1603, in Salzburg, in the service of the prince-bishop. Not long after him, Roelandt Savery from Kortrijk also moved to Prague. In his youth, he had fled from Spain to the Netherlands with his family; he went relatively directly from Amsterdam to Prague. His invitation to the imperial court may have been as a result of Bartholomeus Spranger's visit to the Netherlands in 1602. In 1613, Savery visited the Netherlands briefly, and in 1616 he returned there to stay. Alongside these outstanding artists, there was also the silk-embroiderer Philipp van den Bossche, whose name crops up in the court accounts between 1604 and 1612, as well as Isaac Major from Frankfurt, an engraver who also produced landscape drawings in the style of Roelandt Savery.

These artists, who came from different towns and who had worked in a variety of places, all went to Prague with their own experience of landscape art, but were importantly linked as artists by their Netherlandish origins. Their art was to a greater or lesser degree in the Breugel tradition, and their work was influenced by the artistic ideals of late Mannerism, which still held sway north of the Alps in the 1590s and early 1600s, in both figurative and landscape art. In both genres, the artist would stylize certain elements of reality: some he would ignore entirely whilst exaggerating others. The difference between the two genres was that in figurative composition, there was a long and glorious history of idealization and stylization that had developed by means of a lengthy process dating back to Antiquity. This process was, however, entirely absent in landscape art, since landscape was a relatively new genre with few forerunners in Antiquity. Examples from the Middle Ages were largely symbolic, and it was not until the Renaissance that illusionistic means were developed to portray distance and space. The Mannerist landscape painters – just like their figurative counterparts – drew their ideas from their imaginations, from observation and from past masters, only the balance was weighted more heavily in favour of observation. Works by Rudolfine landscape artists sum the entire gamut from reality to fantasy, ranging from detailed studies of nature to expressive, purely decorative compositions. On the one hand, their works strive for ever greater naturalism and accuracy in the portrayal of details, while on the other hand, there is also a tendency to heighten the decorative aspects of compositions and to reflect the romantic atmosphere of the landscape, which can become positively monumental in later works.

During the Prague years, Stevens and Savery came fully into their own as artists. Over a period of 30 years in Stevens' case and of 10 years in Savery's, their work underwent significant changes, similar to those seen in Rudolfine figurative art. At first, they continued to explore the same themes they had used elsewhere. Stevens, still working through his impressions of Italy, made paintings and drawings[2] of Roman ruins, while Savery painted village scenes in the manner of Bruegel. In both cases, however, change came very quickly. Between 1594 and 1596, Stevens started to produce drawings of woods, rocky landscapes and streams plunging over stones.[3] And soon Savery's many-figured, Bruegelesque compositions were replaced by landscapes with cliffs and woods as well as views of the city of Prague. These changes would seem to bear witness to the inspirational effect

which the wild beauty of the woods around Prague and even the town itself had on the two Netherlandish painters.

These drawings of woods by Stevens are not only worthy of attention as evidence of his changed interests, but display qualities which gave direction to his subsequent output. They usually focus on one motif, usually observed close up. A rich web of foreground motifs prevents the viewer seeing any further into the distance. When, however, there is a longer view, this is only ever through a very small opening and only occupies a small part of the picture space. (Two drawings in which this can be seen are *Mountain Landscape with Waterfall* [Frankfurt, Städelsches Kunstinstitut; fig. 8.1], and *Rocky Landscape* [University of Göttingen].)[4] This form of composition presupposes an intimate knowledge of Nature that is virtually unique amongst European landscape artists in the period 1594-96. There are indeed paintings and drawings of wooded landscapes from the 1590s by Hans Bol, Paul Brill and Jan Bruegel, but these are somewhat different from Stevens' work in that their views are not so detailed, depth is important, the compositions are airier, and there is an emphasis on the foreground structure. In Stevens' drawings, the decorative framework has been abandoned in favour of a dense myriad of motifs that evokes the element of chance.

As well as this kind of woodland scene with a view seen through a small opening, Stevens also produced more traditional compositions which employ a single view like *Landscape with the Temptation of Christ* (Budapest, Szépmüvészeti Museum). And there are other works in which he employed the conventional method of creating spatial tension by depicting clear foreground motifs against a blurred background landscape, as in the case of *Landscape with the Fall of Icarus* (Vienna, Nationalbibliothek).[5] In both of these methods of composition, however, the spatial relationship between individual motifs is uncertain.

After 1597, a new theme entered Stevens' work, and considerable changes ensued in his portrayal of space. It was at this time that he began to take an interest in the sea and the seashore, a subject which had been wholly absent from his œuvre up until that point. This widening of his repertoire and the new life it breathed into his work were clearly connected with the arrival of Aegidius Sadeler in Prague.[6] The engravings and possibly drawings which Sadeler brought with him from Italy must have made a deep impression on Stevens, who had been the only landscape artist working in Prague until then. These landscapes in fact informed him of the most important innovations in the 1590s. In Rome in the mid 1590s, Paul Brill and Jan Bruegel had developed a new style of landscape art showing the sea, the coast and woods, which had in turn been engraved by the Sadeler brothers and had become famous throughout Europe.[7] It cannot be chance that Stevens' *Seascape*[8] of 1597 (Berlin, Kupferstichkabinett) has so much in common with Raphael Sadeler's *Bay with Cliffs*[9] after Paul Brill – from its basic construction and motifs to the billowing clouds and shimmering light. Similarly, Stevens' *Landscape with Wood* of 1597 was clearly influenced by Aegidius Sadeler's *Landscape with Wood*[10] after Paul Brill (Frankenthal, private collection). He even adopted the trees from Brill's composition. Instead of the flatter, more penetrable treetops from his earlier paintings and drawings, the crowns are now denser and more plastic. Besides this work, Paul Brill's[11] seashores influenced a number of Stevens' drawings: *Harbour Landscape*, also of 1597 (Darmstadt, Hessisches Landesmuseum); *Fort on a Rocky Island* of the

late 1590s (Leiden, Prentenkabinet der Rijksuniversiteit); the painting *Landscape with Fishing Catch* (Vienna); the watercolour *Landscape with Stream* of 1600 (Moscow, Pushkin Museum) and various other works[12] known only as engravings. However, Stevens took this form a stage further by portraying atmospheric phenomena and light conditions. In particular, his moonlit landscapes at night demonstrate new, painterly qualities.[13]

Stevens' reaction to Paul Brill's recent innovations is understandable in that Brill's compositions and style of drawing had already had a major impact on him once before, when he was staying in Rome from 1590 to 1591.[14] In later years, he continued to draw on the motifs and compositional aspects of these prints by the Sadeler brothers, with the result that the impulses he had absorbed became an organic part of his own work. This may be seen in Aegidius Sadeler's engraving *Wooded Landscape with Bridge* [fig. 8.2][15] after Stevens: the composition of this work clearly goes back to Jan Sadeler's engraving after Matthys Brill.[16] Although all the main motifs are the same, Stevens handled them very much in his own style: the vegetation is richer, and the background is barely visible. In fact, he altered the composition to such an extent that the connection between the two works has hitherto gone unnoticed.[17]

Paintings by Stevens from around 1600, like *Village Scene with Fishermen* (location unknown) and *Landscape with Avenue* (Madrid, Museo del Prado) seem more natural than earlier works, due to a greater sense of space and depth, a clearer compositional structure and the way light is portrayed.[18] Stevens had retained his preference for foreground detail, but the whole composition had become airier and acquired greater depth. From this time onwards, his interest in monumental trees became clear. *Landscape with Stream* (two versions: Paris, Fondation Custodia; Beck Collection; fig. 8.3) and the related paintings in Madrid[19] have tiny figures next to mighty trees, somewhat romantically demonstrating Nature's size and power.

An example of Stevens' openness to all kinds of influences is his series depicting the seasons of 1600-1, engraved by H. Hondius.[20] In a move away from traditional depictions of the seasons, here architecture dominates, and there is an emphasis on the geometric construction of depth. This tendency is most noticeable in the depiction of *Spring*, in which the illusion of space is created by the double diagonal of a geometric garden stretching away into the picture and by the buildings which extend the sense of space yet further. This structure is completely new in Stevens' work and clearly implies inspiration from elsewhere. Between 1596 and 1598, Hans Vredemann de Vries, an architect and theorist born in Leeuwarden, worked in Prague along with his son. He acquired a considerable reputation for his emphasis on perspective in his portrayal of buildings in his paintings, drawings and engravings. Stevens' *Spring* shows the influence of Vredemann de Vries, as does his *Landscape with Watch Tower*[21] in the engraving by Aegidius Sadeler, which was specifically influenced by Vredemann's etching *Water-Castle*.[22]

A valuable addition to art circles in Prague came in 1603 in the form of the goldsmith Paulus van Vianen.[23] His landscape drawings were particularly inspirational for the Prague landscape artists. He had come from Salzburg bringing with him astonishingly realistic and at the same time extraordinarily artistic drawings of the mountains of the Salzkammergut. These were mostly drawn from nature in pen and ink, usually with a wash, and showed topographically identifiable mountain panora-

mas, townscapes and studies of landscape motifs. This uninhibited response to nature must have seemed utterly new and bold to Stevens, and van Vianen's drawings spurred him on to new experiments. He copied his colleague's nature studies, attempting to adapt his own style to accord with the fine, subtle lines of the originals.[24] Stevens was also interested in van Vianen's drawings of woods and in his own drawings worked hard to express what he himself had observed. However, unlike van Vianen, he did not make any studies directly from nature. In the years around 1600, Mannerism, with its interest in ideal compositions and stylized forms, did not favour detailed studies, and few artists made drawings directly from nature. Apart from van Vianen, the only ones who are known to have done this are Hendrick Goltzius, Jacques de Gheyn, Jan Bruegel and Roelandt Savery.[25]

From 1600 onwards, forms in Stevens' work became more expressive and less schematic, he used finer lines and subtler, airier washes, not least as a result of the influence of van Vianen's drawings. At this time, Stevens' compositions also became better balanced and less dense; the transitions between light and shade are richer and thus all the more effective when it comes to conveying atmospheric phenomena. These developments may be seen particularly well in his watercolours from between 1604 and 1607 showing towns in Flanders and townscapes of Rome and Prague in landscape settings.[26] Although these townscapes are not topographically wholly accurate, nevertheless they are easily identifiable by the most important buildings. The individual works in this series have numbers which show that originally there was a total of over fifty, of which fewer than half are known to have survived. Particularly attractive are the views of Prague (Paris, Fondation Custodia; Prague, Muzeum hl. mešta Prahy), with their varied viewpoints, sense of intimacy, naturalism and depictions of atmospheric conditions. Only one of these, the view of the New Town, was engraved: in 1607 for the series depicting the months.[27]

Jan Bruegel's visit to Prague in 1604 was a major event. Presumably, as one of the outstanding landscape artists of his day, he went in order to commission Aegidius Sadeler to make engravings of the drawings he had brought with him. The finished prints, for which many studies still exist, provide an excellent cross-section both of the broad thematic range of landscape art at the time and of Jan Bruegel's own stunning, most recent work.[28] No doubt, Stevens was inspired by the skilful, light graphic style of these studies and their subtle washes.[29] At the time when Bruegel visited Prague, Sadeler may well already have been engaged upon his important re-working of the extremely popular 1575 series of engravings by Etienne Duperac,[30] *Vestigi delle Antichite di Roma Tivoli Pozzuolo et Altri Luochi*. In 1606, Sadeler brought out his own version with an additional 12 prints,[31] including 10 for which Jan Bruegel had made the studies – presumably in Prague – in turn using Stevens' own drawings of Roman ruins of 1590-91.[32] It is likely that it was Jan Bruegel's visit to Prague that inspired the idea of adding to the *Vestigi* series.

Following the *Vestigi* prints and Stevens' *Months*, Aegidius Sadeler undertook more wide-ranging engraving work after Stevens and after Roelandt Savery, who had arrived in Prague in 1604. Stevens brought out three series of landscapes at different stages in his career, and these reflect developments in his style. The series bring together works with a variety of themes.[33] Inspiration for motifs and composition can be traced to the works of Matthys and Paul Brill, Jan Bruegel, Hendrik van Cleve and Hans Vredemann de Vries.[34] In many of these works, plant motifs crowd

8.2 AEGIDIUS SADELER
(after Pieter Stevens)
Wooded Landscape with Bridge
[Hollstein 254]

the foreground of a dense compositional structure, but there are also some with more spacious views of river-banks and mountains. The most notable examples of both approaches are contained in the third series, which most likely came out at some point between 1615 and 1620. *Landscape with Mill on a River* shows vegetation, trees and mill inextricably intertwined, demonstrating Stevens' love of tightly packed forms and impenetrable tangles of foliage and plants.[35] The other engraving seems to show the mill from another side: much more of it is visible; there are figures fishing in the foreground, and a town is can been seen in the distance.[36] In these works, Stevens conveys everyday reality by means of a more realistic portrayal of the rich earth of the river bank, the burgeoning vegetation, nature bursting with vitality and the small figures going about their business. *Bridge over a Cataract* is particularly worthy of attention with its generous, even robust composition: it is as though the diagonal bridge, seen from below, unites all the various motifs into a seamless whole.[37] A similar move towards monumentalism is evident in *Nocturnal Landscape with Fishermen*, where the striking silhouette of the stone bridge constitutes the main focus of the composition.[38] In terms of Stevens' customary style, an unusually idyllic mood pervades his engraving of fishermen's houses by the water, showing the gleaming, silvery rays of the setting sun.[39] Examples of Stevens' late style may be seen in two watercolours painted after 1610: *Rocky Landscape with Bridge* of 1613 (Munich, Staatliche Graphische Sammlung) and *Stream with Huntsmen* of 1614 (Amsterdam, Rijksprentenkabinet, P. de Boer Collection). Both of these works would seem to have been partly inspired by Roelandt Savery's picturesque, rocky compositions.[40] The last decade of Stevens' time in Prague is lost in obscurity.[41]

Roelandt Savery's art, on the other hand, was more firmly rooted in the Bruegel school than Stevens'. His brother, Jacob Savery, with whom he also served his apprenticeship, was one of the leading guardians of this tradition in Amsterdam. As recent research by Hans Mielke has shown, Jacob Savery had so completely absorbed Pieter Bruegel's graphic style that until recently his own so-called *Little*

Landscapes had been assumed to be by Pieter Bruegel.[42] It seems likely that Jacob Savery owned works by the great Flemish master and, thanks to his outstanding technical skills, was able to reproduce their style extremely accurately. Some alpine scenes, which have similarly hitherto been attributed to Pieter Bruegel, are also – on the evidence of the watermark in the paper used – clearly by Jacob Savery and were produced around 1600.[43]

8.3 AEGIDIUS SADELER
(after Pieter Stevens)
Landscape with Stream
[Hollstein 231]

Bearing these circumstances in mind, Pieter Bruegel's influence was clearly even greater than has been previously thought. It is likely that his close connection with Bruegel led to Roelandt Savery's invitation to go to Prague – Rudolf II's enthusiasm for Bruegel's work is well documented. Thus Savery went to Prague with a deep and extensive knowledge of Bruegel's work, which is perfectly clear in the paintings and drawings he produced during his first years there. Mention has already been made of his richly populated village scenes and their allegiance to the Bruegel school.[44] This is less evident in his rocky landscapes of around 1606, although they do display features which can be traced back to Pieter Bruegel, Jacob Savery and Jan Bruegel.[45] At the same time, however, Savery's own individuality comes into play: instead of the broad perspectives and desire for monumentalism that are characteristic of Pieter Bruegel's work, Roelandt Savery's is not so expansive and shows a leaning towards the picturesque. Compared to work by Jacob Savery and Jan Bruegel, Roelandt Savery's oeuvre may be seen as a more extreme version of late Mannerism. This is most evident in the confused, restless accumulation of forms in the foreground and the fantastic vertical forms of the cliffs, with their overtones of late Gothic architecture. Savery's works from between 1606 and 1608 bear the stamp of his fanatical interest in rocks and stones. In the first half of the sixteenth century, fantastic rocky landscapes were a favourite motif in Netherlandish painting. In the 1590s, Joos de Momper, for example, was just as passionate as Savery in his portrayal of panoramic rocky landscapes almost entirely bereft of vegetation.[46] Few such mountain panoramas by Savery are known, just one work in Lugano and some other drawings which clearly show that the artist came from the Bruegel school.[47] Rocks also played an important part in Savery's early Prague works, and rocky landscapes in the Graphische Sammlung Albertina, Vienna, and in a New York private collection almost create the impression of competing in their invention of fantastic forms with the rocky landscapes of Herri met de Bles,[48] many of whose works were to be found in the imperial collection in Prague. *Mesa* (St Petersburg, Hermitage), with its strange cliff face and *arco naturale*, looks like some fantastic vision.[49] On the other hand, some of Savery's drawings – *Hilly Landscape with Rocks in the Foreground* (Amsterdam, Rijksprentenkabinet) and *Mountainous Landscape with Rocks* (Paris, Musée du Louvre) – clearly depict the hilly surroundings of Prague in the background.[50] It is significant, both in terms of the period and of Savery's own work, that he should have created these two different views in quite different styles as part of one and the same work. The chance element in these background landscapes lends a feeling of objectivity to what is seen, while the mass of rocks fulfills the need for decorative forms and ornament. *River Valley* (Amsterdam, Rijksprentenkabinet) has neither rocks nor foreground repoussoir; it is simply a depiction of a river landscape, going into the finest of detail and, in that sense, reminiscent of Pieter Bruegel's works.[51] These works from Savery's early years in Prague show that, amongst the landscape artists developing out of the Bruegel school, he

stood out from the rest for his lively imagination and the sheer wealth of the forms he created.

Savery's so-called Tyrol drawings, imbued with his experience of the Alps, display these qualities all the more strongly.[52] According to Sandrart, between 1606 and 1608 Savery made drawings of the Tyrol for an imperial commission. These drawings, most of which are now in the Nationalbibliothek, Vienna, are mostly in black and coloured chalks, some with a watercolour wash. In the strict sense, they are neither nature studies nor studies for engravings, but works of art in their own right. Bound as a single volume, they could easily have found their way into the *Kunstkammer* to delight Savery's imperial client. The majority depict a waterfall plunging down a rocky face, without doubt one of the most impressive sights of any mountain landscape, partly because it is so picturesque but also because it is so dynamic. This miracle of nature occupied and inspired Savery's imagination, and he gave expression to his experiences, multiplying and intensifying them and employing a whole variety of forms. Most of these carefully composed drawings with side repoussoirs show only a small section of sky. Extremely complex rocky cliff faces, set somewhat diagonally across the picture plane, cut off the view in any other direction. Here Savery was using a particular compositional structure in order to convey how he had been affected by the wild, gigantic cliffs high up in the mountains. His work is utterly convincing in its portrayal of natural forces, particularly the erosion which cuts deep into the cliffs, washes boulders away and tears trees out by their roots; all of which lends a high degree of dynamism to his compositions. When these drawings are compared to depictions by Pieter Bruegel and Jan Bruegel of the Tivoli[53] or with smaller woodland waterfalls by Stevens, it becomes clear how innovative Savery was in choosing to depict the immense power of nature. In contrast to Jan Bruegel's waterfalls, Savery's work is much more stylized and greater importance is attached to the ornamental aspect of the composition. Between observation and ornament on the one hand, and stylization in the cause of imagination on the other, it is the latter which dominates in these works.

From 1608 to 1609, Savery produced his woodland scenes – partly recollecting his time in the Alps and partly responding to his discovery of the woods of Bohemia. These were then engraved by Aegidius Sadeler.[54] Vegetation has a more important part to play in these depictions of mixed woods than in earlier works, and the detail is subtler. It is, however, noticeable that this detail is even finer in Sadeler's reworking of them as engravings and that the prints are consequently even more convincing in their depiction of nature. On the other hand, their composition still owes a clear debt to Pieter Bruegel. By and large, their schema is scarcely different from the type developed by Pieter Bruegel, Paul Brill and Jan Bruegel in the early 1590s in Rome, which formed the basis for the work and further development of Gillis van Coninxloo, David Vinckboons, Gillis de Hondecoeter and others. This by now 'classical' schema consisted of trees on either side (sometimes on a rise), a stream flowing away into the distance, water plants in the foreground, a rotting tree-trunk and a small amount of sun-drenched landscape in the background. Savery's wooded landscapes draw on his own knowledge of mountains and woodlands as well as on his thorough acquaintance with this schema; in his case, the main motif is placed beyond a shadowy foreground repoussoir, not too far away, half in shadow and with the sun-filled landscape in the background. Some of these prints

8.4 ROELANT SAVERY
Wild Boar Hunt
[Dresden, Gemäldegalerie;
DaCosta 19.41]

also show a rise in the middle ground 'borrowed' from Jacob Savery.[55] Less of nature is to be seen in Roelandt's works in portrait format,[56] which ultimately look back to Pieter Bruegel's drawings of woodland scenes (these have mostly only survived as copies,[57] like Jan Bruegel's paintings in the same format and with a similar theme).[58] One of these portrait-format wooded landscape paintings stands out in particular. Once owned by B. Houthakker in Amsterdam (now private collection), it has a simplicity and grandeur which already point the way towards the monumentalism of the next stage of Savery's creative output.[59]

Between 1609 and 1610, Savery produced a number of innovative hunting scenes: paintings, drawings and engravings.[60] These various depictions of wild boar hunts show little of the natural setting, and the huntsman grasping the boar is seen somewhat from below [fig. 8.4]. The decorative foliage and thorny twigs in the lower centre foreground are reminiscent of Pieter Bruegel's painting *Winter Landscape with Bird Trap* (Brussels, Koninklijke Musea voor Schone Kunsten van België), while the branches inclined towards one another and the view between them of a sun-drenched landscape remind the viewer of Jan Bruegel's *Wooded Landscape with the Temptation of Christ* (Paris, Foundation Custodia).[61] (Aegidius Sadeler's engraving of the latter work is one of a number he made in Prague after Jan Bruegel.) Of course, the allusion to Bruegel's work in no sense diminishes the originality of the bold innovation of Savery's works on the theme of hunting. This degree of intimacy and proximity was without parallel in contemporary paintings. Savery's *Deer Hunt* of 1610 (location unknown) shows more of the wood itself and is more romantic in its aspect than his earlier wooded landscapes.[62] The trees, plants and toppled treetrunks in the foreground recall the dense profusion of plants in Stevens' works, and it would be fair to assume that Stevens was an influence here because, in the 1590s, he had already attempted close views of complex woodland scenes. In Sav-

ery's case, however, the foreground motifs do not cut off the view beyond, and the middle ground, with its portentous light effects, heightens the romantic mood of the landscape. Savery reached the highpoint of his wooded landscapes with his series of engravings and related paintings with gnarled trees.[63] Here the emphasis is on the picturesque group of trees that stands out in the foreground. The depiction of the individual qualities of different trees was a consequence of detailed observation. At the same time, the trees tend to be stylized so that they appear both heroic and more ornamental. The idea of a close view of a monumental group of trees – alive, fallen and damaged – may have been inspired by Jan Bruegel, specifically by his *Wooded Landscape with the Temptation of Christ* and *Wooded Landscape with Fallen Tree*[64] in the form of an engraving by Raphael Sadeler. The inspiration for the depiction of the individual trees came from Pieter Bruegel and is also seen in works by Jacob Savery, Gillis van Coninxloo, Jan Bruegel and others. Jan Bruegel, in particular, increased the monumental aspect of the mighty tree in the centre by heightening its plasticity and intensifying the contrast of light and shade. Savery, who was specially attracted by extraordinary, singular forms, went even further along the route taken by Jan Bruegel and simply intensified everything. The forms of twisted, fallen trees took on a bizarre appearance and acquired new silhouettes which – along with the dramatic play of light and shade – seemed to transport the scene into a fantastic, fairy-tale realm. Savery's rich invention, formal power and fantastic painterly vision are seen here at their most intense and artistic in works which preempt the wealth of forms and dynamism of Baroque art. His inspiration, drawing on tradition and innovative composition combining observation and imagination, naturally provided a major impetus for the heroic creations of the greatest master of wooded landscapes, Jacob van Ruisdael.[65]

Savery's wooded landscapes may well have been preceded by detailed studies of nature. This would certainly seem to have been the case on the evidence of several chalk and some pen and ink drawings showing a fir tree, a rotten tree stump, snake-like roots and foliage reflected in water. The style of these drawings is extremely varied; this becomes particularly evident when one compares Savery's various studies of fir trees. These include one in New York [fig. 8.5], with echoes of the airy brushwork of Paulus van Vianen; an extremely detailed chalk drawing (Berlin, Kupferstichkabinett); a fleeting sketch (Oberlin, Allen Memorial Art Museum) and a version so stylized as to be decorative (Dresden, Kupferstichkabinett).[66] Savery's close-up studies of roots are particularly appealing, conveying the life force within the trees and the wonderful variety of natural forms.[67] Probably dating from his later Prague period, these works do not display the same desire for decorative expressiveness as does, for example, the chalk drawing of a hollow oak tree of 1606-7 (Vienna, Nationalbibliothek).[68]

After he settled in Prague, Savery found his interest in nature matched by a lively interest in the town he had moved to. A relatively large number of his drawings of Prague have survived, from panoramic views to particular neighbourhoods to individual houses and even parts of individual houses. The drawings were evidently intended for his own private use and were not made to be sold or engraved. Savery's intention does not seem to have been to produce informative, topographically exact illustrations of the sort which were so popular at the time. Instead, he simply seems to have been recording images which had caught his artist's eye. Relatively few of these mostly pen and ink drawings in the tradition of the Bruegel school portray famous parts of the town or important buildings. Instead the artist was clearly much more interested in small, simple, often dilapidated houses with decaying roofs.

Three of his cityscapes show characteristic views of Prague from different angles, but only one of these (New York, private collection) is topographically accurate in the conventional manner.[69] The other two (Amsterdam, Rijksprentenkabinet; Copenhagen, Kobberstiksamling) are more painterly depictions of a town in a landscape setting.[70] The drawings of various parts of the town are unconventional in the sense that the artist chose a variety of often surprising viewpoints, his favourite one being the picturesque layering of complicated buildings one behind the other. An example of this may be seen in the drawing of a group of buildings of the Lesser Town at the head of the Charles Bridge (Prague, Národní Galeri v Praze). It is intimate and picturesque in its effect, just like the view of the Lesser Town Square (Leipzig, Museum der bildenden Künste), in which the strangely formed roofs occupy the centre of the composition.[71] Many of these drawings with their wealth of detail also bear witness to Savery's preference for coming in close to his subject matter, which increases the sense of intimacy between viewer and viewed. Often a house, cut off at the edge of the picture plane, creates an impression of chance and spontaneity. Savery loved courtyards, with haphazard little houses clinging to the main buildings, adding to the wealth of different shapes and forms.[72] In his view, a collapsed mill (Paris, Fondation Custodia) was worth recording for posterity, because of the intriguing arabesque of the forms and the confused tangle of structural parts.[73] At the time, there was nothing to equal these town views. Examples by Joris Hoefnagel, Lodewijk Toeput and Frederick van Valckenborch are much more conventionally descriptive and informative.[74] Only Toeput in one of his views of Venice achieved a more subjective level of representation, concentrating on the picturesque aspect of the scene before him. The emergence of houses – above all of peasant dwellings – in Netherlandish art around 1600 may be attributed to the increasing interest in everyday life and surroundings. In many artistic centres, peasant dwellings first appeared in the backgrounds of scenes from mythology and the Bible before coming into their own later on. In Prague, for the first time, town houses and groups of houses appeared in drawings by Savery and Paulus van Vianen as identifiable components of the town.

Although significantly fewer townscapes by van Vianen have survived than by Savery, they are amongst the most important examples of the genre from the period[75] and include his mainly panoramic views from his time in Salzburg. During his time in Prague, he really only produced drawings of smaller, more intimate scenes: a mill from various angles, an inn and a larger group of houses. His views of Hradschin and Vysehrad are the exception to this rule.[76] The approach and, to a certain extent, the style of these intimate drawings is so similar to Savery's that one must assume that there was a lively interchange of ideas between these two artists. Of the two, Savery's work is more romantic and decorative, while van Vianen's is more objective and painterly. Van Vianen presumably began to use chalks as a result of his contact with Savery, yet the difference between the two is also evident in their use of this medium. Savery's houses are more strongly stylized, while van Vianen's are more accurate in their depiction, and the shading is subtler.

8.5 ROELANT SAVERY
Fir Tree
[New York, private collection]

The same intimacy and lack of inhibition that characterize van Vianen's town houses are present in his landscape drawings. The innovative quality particularly of his nature studies has already been mentioned – his combining of the specialist knowledge of the scholar with the aesthetic gifts of the artist. As a goldsmith, van Vianen was not hampered by the unwritten rules of landscape painting and could therefore approach the subject with less prejudice and draw what he saw with a greater degree of freedom and individuality [fig. 8.7]. During his stay in Germany, he had had the opportunity to study and be inspired by Dürer's fresh, naturalistic drawings and watercolours which are the earliest detailed studies of nature in art history.[77] Van Vianen recognized that it is possible to produce a convincing representation of the true nature of a landscape by the meticulous characterization of its uniqueness and the materiality of its detail. His time in Salzburg also led him along the path to a natural, unforced form of expression, because travel – in this case through one of the most beautiful landscapes in Europe – generally awakens an artist's interest in the representation of reality.

Van Vianen continued his nature studies in Prague, always taking visual reality as his starting point and characterizing its qualities with the most suitable means available to him. His studies of rocks and trees are marked by objectivity, precise observation, an awareness of their inner essence and artistic execution.[78] In Salzburg, he had already developed his graphic skills to the extent that now he was able to depict the complexity of natural forms, the different textures and materials and the sheer variety of light with sensitivity and subtlety. His style, which ultimately goes back to Pieter Bruegel, bears witness to his own approach as an artist. His light lines with all their nuances are not merely playfully calligraphic or decorative. Fine, broken outlines, small dots deepening the shadows and delicate parallel lines all lend his drawings – even without wash – an airy, painterly aspect. He often used a brush to add the subtlest possible shading to his works. These nature studies were clearly not entirely unconnected to the growing interest in research into the natural world around 1600; these were two sides of the same coin. All over Europe, it had become fashionable to depict natural objects, and in Prague there were some outstanding exponents of the art: Hans Hoffmann, Daniel Fröschl, Joris and Jacob Hoefnagel. However, in the work of all these masters, the emphasis is on description and analysis rather than independent, artistic expression. Van Vianen's drawings, on the other hand, take account of both, harmoniously balancing almost scientific exactitude with artistic expression.

The beauty and realism of van Vianen's drawings were not only an inspiration to Savery and Stevens, but also to the silk-embroiderer Philipp van den Bossche.[79] Although not a landscape artist himself, like his goldsmith colleague, he was nevertheless extremely interested in landscape art. Some pen and ink drawings known to be by him bear witness to this, as do a silk print (London, Victoria and Albert Museum)[80] and a reference in a letter, written by Philip Hainhofer, to landscapes on handwork produced by van den Bossche. The diversity of his talent is demonstrated by the fact that he was to draw the most important panoramic view of Prague of the time; it was engraved in 1606 by Johannes Wechter and brought out by Aegidius Sadeler.[81] Only a fragment of the preparatory study for this print has survived (Göttingen, Kunstsammlungen der Universität). However, the huge print itself gives us an impression of the superior skill and graphic accuracy

8.6 PHILIPP VON DEN BOSSCHE
Mountain Landscape with Stream and Figures
[Vienna, Österreichisches Nationalbibliothek; Spicer C 29]

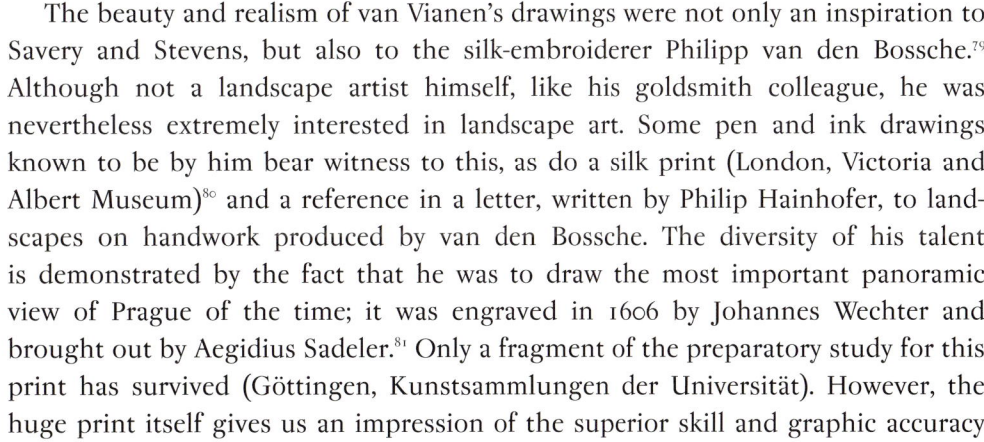

of this panorama as compared to those produced by professional topographic artists.

The themes of van den Bossche's drawings are similar to those of his Rudolfine colleagues: rocky mountain scenes, romantic mountain streams, ruins high up in the mountains.[82] His interest in rocks belies the strong influence of Savery, yet his motifs also owe much to Stevens.[83] His drawings, which show van Vianen's influence in their style, were probably produced in Prague between 1604 and 1614. In his compositions, he depicted details, for example trees, very much in the style of van Vianen, yet their structure was more 'additive' in the style of the Mannerists [fig. 8.6]. The somewhat schematic parallel lines of his shading also show a slight lack of originality. His most harmonious work, one which also comes closest to van Vianen's ideals, is *Decayed Water Mill in the Woods* (Weimar, Schlossmuseum) in which the objectivity and intimacy of the landscape elements are matched by the sensitive portrayal of the overall atmosphere.[84] After 1614, he moved to Augsburg. However, the work which he produced there, much of it dated 1615, does not reach the same standard as his earlier work and is also not as close in style to van Vianen.

Aegidius Sadeler lent landscape art a particular importance by virtue of the amount and quality of his work.[85] His engravings are amongst the very best graphic work of the time. One of his foremost skills was the extremely subtle graphic reproduction of stylistic differences. Having learnt his technique in the best traditional manner, he had the ability to reproduce individual stylistic qualities with the greatest accuracy. In his engravings of landscapes by Pieter Stevens and Roelandt Savery, he was not only able to express the different styles of the two artists, but was also able to mirror the changes which their work underwent as it developed and progressed. By differentiating the thickness and direction of lines and increasing the transitional range from light to shade, he became ever more skilled in portraying detail which appeared realistic and physical and in conveying a convincing sense of light and atmosphere. At the same time, responding to the originals laid before him, after 1610 he heightened the decorative quality of Savery's work by emphasizing the outlines and plasticity of forms.

Sadeler's pupil of Flemish descent, Isaac Major,[86] who lived in Prague in the early 1600s, was not only his assistant on the print series after Jan Bruegel, Stevens and Savery but also produced landscapes of his own in the manner of Savery and created his own engravings after Stevens and Savery.[87] His prints and landscape drawings are typical of those of an epigone. His technique was less highly developed than Sadeler's, which means that his engravings are somewhat monotonous. The same might also be said of his landscape drawings, in which his pen and ink style is reminiscent of that of engraving, as in his drawing of Prague, *Town on the Banks of a River* (Vienna, Albertina).[88]

Not only did the less illustrious landscape artists benefit from their contact with the masters in the field; these same masters also worked productively together.[89] For a fresh, uninhibited, but accurate view of reality, artists would look to van Vianen's work; Stevens showed the way in the representation of intimate scenes with the addition of watercolour washes to enhance the impression of atmospheric conditions; Savery, on the other hand, spurred the others on with his dynamic, decorative style of composition and use of chalks. But as has been shown here, their success owed much to the impulses coming from various Netherlandish masters working in different artistic centres in Europe. Thanks to the intermediary role of Aegid-

8.7 PAULUS VAN VIANEN
Pasture on the Bank of a Lake
[Berlin, Küpferstichkabinett]

ius Sadeler, Savery was able to take up ideas from Paul Brill, while Stevens could do the same with Jan Bruegel's work. Von Vianen's links with the Northern Netherlands meant that artists in Prague were informed about the new national and bourgeois directions developing in the urban centres there.[90] Hans Vredemann de Vries' stay of some years' duration in Prague, as he toured Europe, and Jan Bruegel's shorter visit were also instrumental in bringing news of what was going on in art elsewhere.

These masters of landscape art in Prague did much to contribute to the hegemony of Netherlandish landscape art. If their activities are viewed from a longer perspective, three main directions may be seen to emerge from landscape painting in the sixteenth century: realistic, decorative Baroque and classicizing. It is clear that the Prague artists played a major part in the development of the first two. In their own different ways and on their own different levels, all three styles achieved, by means of a relaxed, intimate portrayal of detail, a more expressive, realistic depiction of nature, which could thus convey the individual quality of a landscape. At the same time, observation and the study of nature led to a re-integration and restructuring of conventional schemas of composition. Stevens concentrated on close views of dense vegetation in small areas of landscape; Savery created a new style of composition with his picturesque foreground motifs. Stevens contributed to townscapes throughout Europe with his atmospheric watercolours; Savery and van Vianen, with their intimate drawings of groups of houses, left a significant mark on the development of subjective, painterly townscapes.

1. H. Zimmermann, 'Das Inventar der Prager Schatz- und Wunderkammer vom 6. Dezember 1621', *JKSW*, 25 (1905), pt 1: XXXVIII–XLIX; R. Bauer and H. Haupt (eds), 'Die Kunstkammer Kaiser Rudolfs II. in Prag: Ein Inventar aus den Jahren 1607–1611', *JKSW*, 72 (1976): 138.

2. A. Zwollo, 'Pieter Stevens: Ein vergessener Maler des Rudolfinischen Kreises', *JKSW*, 64 (1968): ills 166–68, 170.

3. T. DaCosta Kaufmann, *The School of Prague: Paintings at the Court of Rudolf II* (Chicago and London, 1988), 19.3, 19.4, 19.9.

4. Both are dated 1594. See H. G. Franz, 'Meister der spätmanieristischen Landschaftsmalerei in den Niederlanden', *Jahrbuch des Kunsthistorischen Instituts der Universtät Graz*, 3–4 (1968–69): ills 29, 30.

5. Zwollo (note 2), ills 181, 178; *Prag um 1600: Kunst und Kultur am Hofe Rudolfs II.*, 2 vols (Freren, 1988), cat. no. 268.

6. D. Limouze, 'Aegidius Sadeler (c. 1570–1629) Drawings, Prints and Art Theory' (Ph.D. dissertation, 1990; Ann Arbor, 1992), p. 139.

7. T. Gerszi, 'Bruegels Nachwirkung auf die niederländischen Landschaftsmaler um 1600', *Oud Holland*, 90:4 (1976): 212–21; idem, 'Pieter Bruegels Einfluss auf die Herausbildung des niederländischen See- und Küstenlandschaftsdarstellung', *JBM*, 24 (1982): 152–71.

8. Zwollo (note 2), ill. 217; *Prag um 1600* (note 5), cat. no. 269.

9. Hollstein (Dutch), XXI–XXII, 217.

10. *Ibid.*, XXI; XXII, 204; Franz (note 4), ill. 29.

11. Gerszi, 'Pieter Bruegels Einfluss' (note 7), ills 6, 7,

24–26. Stevens' drawing *Sea Harbour with Sailing Ships* (Vienna, Albertina) was perhaps influenced by Frans Huys' engraving after Pieter Bruegel's *Sea Battle at Messina*.

12. G. Bergstrasser, *Niederländische Zeichnungen des 16 Jahrhunderts im Hessischen Landesmuseum Darmstadt*, exh. cat. (1979), cat. no. 94; Zwollo (note 2), ills 196, 199, 203; Hollstein XXI–XXII, 258, 265.

13. His nocturnal compositions were perhaps influenced by Gillis Mostaert and Jan Bruegel's nighttime scenes.

14. Zwollo (note 2), 127, ill. 163; 131–37, ills 170, 172; A. Zwollo, 'Pieter Stevens: Nieuw werk, contact met Jan Bruegel, invloed op Kerstiaen de Keuninck', *LKJ* (1982): 95–118, ill. 13. On the evidence of the paper used and the style, twenty of the items now in Vienna belong together and are certainly by the artist himself. On the top edge of the sheets, the place and date are written in ink different from that used for the drawing. Their style resembles that of the Brill brothers.

15. Hollstein XXI–XXII, 254.

16. Hollstein XXI–XXII, 577.

17. The main motifs of the same engraving are found again on the *Landscape with Mill* (Warsaw, Muzeum Narodowe), reversed and with additional motifs. See Kaufmann (note 3), 21.16.

18. Kaufmann (note 3), 21.10, 21.14. The last composition with an avenue leading into the far distance is by Hans Bol (Paris, Fondation Custodia). See K. G. Boon, *The Netherlandish and German Drawings of the XVth and XVIth Centuries of the Lugt Collection* (Paris, 1992), cat. no. 18, pl. 104.

19. Zwollo (note 4), ills 200–202.
20. Hollstein IX, 66–69.
21. *Ibid.*, XXI–XXII, 250; Zwollo (note 14), 96–99, ill. 3.
22. *Zwischen Renaissance und Barock: Das Zeitalter von Bruegel und Bellange*, exh. cat. by K. Oberhuber (Vienna, 1968), cat. no. 149, pl. 29. Zwollo also pointed out the links between the drawing *Boats in a Southern Harbour* (Amsterdam, Rijksprentenkabinet, P. de Boer Collection) and an etching by Hans Vredemann de Vries (Zwollo [note 2], ills 228, 229).
23. T. Gerszi, *Paulus van Vianen: Handzeichnungen* (Hanau, 1982); *idem, Die Salzburger Skizzenbücher des Paulus van Vianen* (Salzburg, 1983).
24. T. Gerszi, 'Le Problème de l'influence réciproque des paysagistes Rodolphins', *BMHBA*, 48–49 (1977): ills 75, 77.
25. Only one pen and ink drawing by Stevens has survived (Dresden, Kupferstichkabinett). This would appear to be a study directly from nature, but may equally well have been made after a drawing by Paulus van Vianen or drawing on the inspiration provided by his studies.
26. Zwollo (note 2), 174–75, ills 231, 232, 243; *idem*, 'Pieter Stevens en Jacob Savery enige kanttekeningen', *Oud Holland* (1969): 298–301, ill. 35; *idem*, 'Ein Beitrag zur niederländischen Landschaftsmalerei um 1600', *Umění*, 31:5 (1983): 399–40l, ill. 1; Boon (note 18), cat. nos 193–96, pls 236–39.
27. Hollstein XXI–XXII, 129–41. The depiction of February in the *Months* series contains several motifs from *Jänner* by A. and J. Collaert after Joos de Momper. The depiction of May has links with the engraving *April* by A. and J. Collaerts (Hollstein IV, 559, 562).
28. Hollstein XXI–XXII, 209, 210, 212–18; Limouze (note 6), pp. 186–88; M. Winner, 'Zeichnungen des Älteren Jan Brueghel', *JBM*, III (1961), ills 6, 9, 11; *idem*, 'Neubestimmtes und Unbestimmtes im zeichnerischen Werk von Jan Brueghel D.Ä', *JBM*, 14 (1972), ill. 16.
29. *The Stigmatization of St Francis in the Wilderness* by Jan Bruegel (London, British Museum), engraved by Aegidius Sadeler (Hollstein XXI–XXII, 212), could have been the model for the landscape with 'arco naturale' by Stevens which we know from prints by Aegidius Sadeler (Hollstein XXI–XXII, 261).
30. Hollstein XXI–XXII, 151–201.
31. The forty-eighth print in the series with the representation of the 'Forum Vulcani' was engraved after a drawing by Joris Hoefnagel (Washington, D.C., National Gallery of Art, A. Mellon Bruce Fund, B–26, 778).
32. Some of Stevens' drawings of Roman ruins (inv. 3162, 3149, 3140, 3168) bearing a striking resemblance to depictions of ruins in the *Vestigi* series (nos 42, 45–47). The studies by Jan Bruegel for nos 45 and 46 still exist. This has led people to conclude that Stevens based his drawings of ruins on Jan Bruegel's sketches (which date from his Italian period). It is likely that Stevens based his drawings on works that no longer exist. It is, however, certain that the preparatory studies by Jan Bruegel are in a style which he used in 1604, whereas Stevens' series of ruins must date from around 1590. The last twelve *Vestigi* engravings do not bear the name

of the maker, perhaps because Jan Bruegel made use in the preparatory studies of the drawings of Roman ruins that Stevens had made in Prague. This would mean that the compositions were not entirely his own work.
33. Hollstein XXI–XXII, 247–70; Limouze (note 6), pp. 190, 194, 287–290.
34. The following prints by Aegidius Sadeler have connections with works by other masters: Hollstein XXI–XXII, 34, with Jan Sadeler's engraving after Matthys Brill (Hollstein XXI–XXII, 577); Hollstein XXI–XXII, 256, with a drawing by van Vianen (Gerszi, *Paulus van Vianen* [note 23], cat. no. 29); Hollstein XXI–XXII, 258 and 265, with Raphael Sadeler's engraving after Paul Brill (Hollstein XXI–XXII, 217); Hollstein XXI–XXII, 261, with Aegidius Sadeler's engraving after Jan Breughel (Hollstein XXI–XXII, 212); Hollstein XXI–XXII, 264, with Aegidius Sadeler's engraving after Roelandt Savery (Hollstein XXI–XXII, 226); Hollstein XXI–XXII, 267, with Aegidius Sadeler's engraving after Jan Bruegel (Hollstein XXI–XXII, 210); Hollstein XXI–XXII, 270, with an engraving after Hendrik van Cleve (Hollstein IV, 1).
35. Hollstein XXI–XXII, 249.
36. *Ibid.*, 247.
37. *Ibid.*, 263.
38. *Ibid.*, 251; *Prag um 1600* (note 5), cat. no. 323a.
39. *Ibid.*, 252.
40. W. Wegner: *Die niederländischen Handzeichnungen des 15.–18. Jahrhunderts* (Berlin, 1973), cat. no. 125; Zwollo (note 2), ill. 225; *Prag um 1600* (note 5), cat. no. 276.
41. Hollstein XXI–XXII, 142–45. For his depiction of spring, Stevens used Jan Sadeler's engraving after Hendrik van Cleve (Hollstein XXI–XXII, 581); for *Summer*, he used a drawing by van Vianen (Gerszi, *Paulus van Vianen* [note 23], cat. no. 54); for *Autumn* (the movement in the foreground figures), he used an engraving by Aegidius Sadeler after Paul Brill (Hollstein XXI–XXII, 122).
42. See Hans Mielke's discussion of the catalogue by K. G. Boon, *L'Epoque de Lucas de Leyde et Pierre Bruegel: Dessins des anciens Pays–Bas: Collection Frits Lugt* (Paris, 1981), in *Master Drawings*, 23–24:1 (1985–86): 75–81.
43. See H. Mielke's 'Noch einmal zum Problem von Pieter Bruegels Landschaftszeichnungen', *Münchner Jahrbuch der bildenden Kunst*, 42 (1991): 137–47; *idem*, 'Pieter Bruegel D. Ä: Probleme seines zeichnerisches Oeuvres', *JBM* (1991): 129–34.
44. Kaufmann (note 3), 19.3, 19.4, 19.9; *Roelant Savery in seiner Zeit (1576–1639)*, exh. cat. by E. Mai *et al.* (Cologne and Utrecht, 1986), pp. 39–45; K. J. Mullenmeister, *Roelant Savery: Kortrijk 1576–1639* (Freren, 1988).
45. Kaufmann (note 3), 19.10–19.12. *The Landscape with the Flight to Egypt* (St Petersburg, Hermitage) may be seen as a modernized version of the engraving after Pieter Bruegel's *Hieronymus in the Desert*. The painting also in St Petersburg, *Mountainous Landscape with St Hieronymus*, was influenced by Aegidius Sadeler's engraving after Jan Bruegel on the same theme (Hollstein XXI–XXII, 211). The composition of *Rocky Landscape with the Temptation of Christ* (location unknown) is related to that of Ja-

cob Savery's drawing *Sunrise over a Valley* (L. Munz, *The Drawings of Bruegel* [London, 1961], cat. no. 41).

46. T. Gerszi, 'Zur Gestaltungsmethode von Joos de Momper', *Die Malerei. Antwerpens: Gattungen. Meister. Wirkungen* (international colloquium) (Vienna, 1993), pp. 85–88.

47. Kaufmann (note 3), 19.34; J. Spicer (Durham), 'The Drawings of Roelandt Savery' (Ph.D. dissertation, Yale University, 1979; Ann Arbor, 1986), C 21, C 22, C 35.

48. Spicer (note 47), C 9, C 10 1968, ill. 235.

49. *Ibid.*, C 7; *Dessins flamands et hollandais du XVIIe siècle du musée de l'Ermitage, Leningrad et du musée Pouschkin, Moscou*, exh. cat. (St Petersburg, 1972–3), cat. no. 95.

50. Spicer (note 47), C 14, C 17; M. Schapelhouman, *Netherlandish Drawings circa. 1600* (Amsterdam, 1987), cat. no. 76; F. Lugt, *Inventaire général des écoles du Nord: Ecole hollandaise* (Paris, 1931), cat. no. 710.

51. Spicer (note 47), C 8; Schapelhouman (note 50), cat. no. 75.

52. Spicer (note 47), I, pp. 52–71 (C 15, C 16, C 23–C 33, C 49, C 55); H. G. Franz, 'Roelandt Savery im rudolfinischen Kunstlerkreis: Landschaftszeichnungen im Atlas Blaeu der Österreichischen Nationalbibliothek Wien', *Kunsthistorisches Jahrbuch Graz*, 23 (1987): 60–79.

53. Winner (note 28), ill. 15.

54. Hollstein XXI–XXII, 225–30.

55. *Ibid.*, 229 and 230 are connected with Jacob Savery's engraving, *Landscape with Castle* (Hollstein XXIII, 9).

56. Kaufmann (note 3), 19.19–19.22, 19.29, 19.30.

57. K. Arndt, 'Pieter Bruegel D. Ä. und die Geschichte der "Waldlandschaft"', *JBM*, 14 (1972): 69–121; H. Mielke, 'La Question des paysages dans l'oeuvre de Pieter Bruegel' in *Le Paysage en Europe du XVIe au XVIIIe siècle*, Actes du colloque organisé au musée du Louvre par le Service Culturel du 25 au 27 janvier 1990 (Paris, 1993), pp. 15–23.

58. Mielke (note 57), ills 6, 10; K. Ertz, *Jan Breughel D. Ä. (1568–1625): Die Gemälde mit kritischem Oeuvrekatalog* (Cologne, 1979), cat. nos 126, 130.

59. Kaufmann (note 3), 19.29. Savery's painting *Rocky Wooded Landscape with Goats and Lambs* (ibid., 19.49) shows the influence of Aegidius Sadeler's engraving after Jan Bruegel's *Stigmatization of St Francis* (Hollstein XXI–XXII, 212).

60. Kaufmann (note 3), 19.39–19.42, 19.53.

61. Hollstein XXI–XXII, 210.

62. Kaufmann (note 3), 19.43.

63. Hollstein XXI–XXII, 231–36; Kaufmann (note 3), 19.44, 19.45, 19.57.

64. Hollstein XXI–XXII, 210, 53.

65. T. Gerszi, 'Jacob Ruisdael und die Bruegel-Nachwirkung' in *Orient und Okzident im Spiegel der Kunst: Festschrift Heinrich Gerhard Franz zum 70 Geburtstag* (Graz, 1986), pp. 139–46, 546–52.

66. F. Stampfle with R. S. Kraemer and J. Shoaf Turner, *Netherlandish Drawings of the Fifteenth and Sixteenth Centuries and Flemish Drawings of the Seventeenth and Eighteenth Centuries* (New York and Princeton, 1991), cat. no. 89; Spicer (note 47), C 50, C 53, C 51; *Prag um 1600* (note 5), cat. no. 248.

67. Spicer (note 47), C 57–C 60; *Prag um 1600* (note 5), cat. no. 249.

68. Spicer (note 47), C 55; Franz (note 52), ill. 19.

69. Spicer (note 47), C 95.

70. *Ibid.*, C 93, C 94; *Prag um 1600* (note 5), cat. no. 635.

71. Spicer (note 47), C 65, C 78; *Prag um 1600* (note 5), ill. 250, 254.

72. Spicer (note 47), C 75.

73. *Ibid.*, C 84; Boon (note 18), cat. no. 177.

74. L. Nuti, 'The Mapped Views by Georg Hoefnagel: The Merchant's Eye, the Humanist's Eye', *Word and Image*, 4:2 (1988), 545–70; T. Gerszi 'The Draughtsmanship of Lodewijk Toeput', *Master Drawings*, 30:4 (1992): 367–95; *idem*, 'Quelques problèmes que pose l'art du paysage de Frederik van Valckenborch', *BMHBA*, 42 (1947): 63–89.

75. Gerszi, *Paulus van Vianen* (note 23), cat. nos 53–55, 58–63; *Prag um 1600* (note 5), cat. nos. 286, 659.

76. Gerszi, *Paulus van Vianen* (note 23), cat. nos 56, 57; *Prag um 1600* (note 5), cat. nos. 289, 661.

77. T. Gerszi, 'Les Attaches de Paulus van Vianen avec l'art allemand', *BMHBA*, 44 (1975): 71–90.

78. Gerszi, *Paulus van Vianen* (note 23), cat. nos 39–42, 43.

79. H. Modern, 'Eine Landschaft von Philipp van den Bossche', *Mitteilungen der Gesellschaft für Vervielfältigende Kunst* (1902): 50–53; *Prag um 1600* (note 5), cat. nos 194, 195.

80. Thanks to Eliška Fučíková for kindly sharing this information.

81. E. Fučíková, 'Veduta v rudolfinském krajinarstvi', *Umění*, 31 (1983): 391–99; Limouze (note 6), pp. 356–58.

82. Gerszi, *Paulus van Vianen* (note 23), ills 127, 133; Wegner 1973 (note 40), cat. no. 10, pl. 62; *Prag um 1600* (note 5), cat. no. 195; Mak van Waay, auction cat. 301a (1979), no. 204.

83. *Prag um 1600* (note 5), cat. no. 194.

84. *Ibid.*, cat. no. 195.

85. *Engravers from the Golden Age of Antwerp and Prague*, exh. cat. (Philadelphia, 1989); D. Limouze, 'Aegidius Sadeler: Imperial Printmaker', *Bulletin of the Philadelphia Museum of Art*, 85:362 (1989); *The Stylish Image: Printmakers to the Court of Rudolf II*, exh. cat. by R. J. W. Evans, E. Fučíková and M. Campbell (Edinburgh, 1991).

86. Limouze (note 6), pp. 358–62.

87. Hollstein (German) XXIII, 8–32.

88. H. Geissler, *Zeichnungen in Deutschland: Deutsche Zeichnungen 1540–1640*, exh. cat., (Stuttgart, 1979), I,C 16.

89. Gerszi (note 24), pp. 105–28.

90. Gerszi, *Paulus van Vianen* (note 23), pp. 29–30.

Roelandt Savery and the 'Discovery' of the Alpine Waterfall

JOANEATH SPICER

Waterfall with Artist Sketching [fig. 9.1][1] is one of many studies drawn by Roelandt Savery in the Alps,[2] very likely in the warmer months of 1607. It is not only one of the artist's finest drawings, but the product of what could be called a remarkable 'discovery'. Obviously, alpine waterfalls existed before Savery drew them, but the striking absence of precedent *representations* suggests that the falls were just not recognized as worthy of portrayal by earlier artists who travelled through the Alps. Some of Savery's contemporaries, such as Jan Brueghel, Hendrick Goltzius, Pieter Lastman, and Josse de Momper among others, represented the occasional waterfall or cascade, but no one focused on their attractions as Savery did nor drew them repeatedly from life. Therefore, as a subject for artistic meditation, the alpine waterfall could be said to have been 'discovered' by Savery.

While rushing mountain waterfalls and foaming cataracts provided later Western landscapists with some of their most dramatic material, the early development of the subject has received little scholarly attention.[3] This essay will explore two factors behind this discovery: the importance of patronage in providing the impetus for Savery to search out these waterfalls, and the accessibility of related visual models, both thematic and stylistic, that fostered Savery's recognition of the falls' pictorial potential.

Waterfall with Artist Sketching is executed in black chalk with washes made from red and ochre chalks, introducing a hazy, atmospheric quality to the study. Like many of the related drawings, this sheet is large, over 60 centimetres high and its dimensions contribute to the impact of the subject. While the guide gestures towards the falls, the draughtsman, at once Savery's alter ego and our surrogate as observer, is absorbed in transposing from life his intimate experience of the falls. He is perched precariously close to his subject, close enough to feel the spray. In the actual drawing, Savery added what his alter ego could not see, the slender exposed roots on the left, cantilevered out from the bank, and the jumble of fallen trees, which provide an intricate, static foil for the thrust of the onrushing water. The human presence encourages our approach, but the falls, cutting through the jagged rock, are the artist's true subject.

The drawing under discussion is one of the well-known group of 13 mountainous landscapes and 2 tree studies by Savery which was subsequently incorporated into volumes XIII and XLVI of the *Atlas van der Hem*[4] now in the Österreichische Nationalbibliothek, Vienna. The mountain views – 2 pen drawings made in Bohemia in 1606 and 11 black and coloured chalk compositions made in the Swiss and Tyrolean Alps in the warmer months of 1606 and 1607 – can be traced back to those which, along with the two tree studies[5] and a few other drawings, were put into an album that Savery took back to Amsterdam in 1613 after a decade in the service to Emperor Rudolf II in Prague. Savery made numerous landscape drawings in the same years, but those in this album have gained particular renown from having been documented in Rembrandt's collection and copied by his follower Lambert Doomer.[6]

Savery's first biographer, the German painter and writer Joachim von Sandrart, who in the 1620s worked in Prague and Utrecht (where Savery was then living), wrote in *Teutsche Academie* (1675) that because Savery was so good at depicting cliffs, crags, rocks, mountains and waterfalls,

> Emperor Rudolf sent him into the Tyrol in order to search for rare wonders of nature. As a result, over two years he made drawings of the most wondrous mountains and valleys ... in a large book which were later of great use for his landscapes that were to be enjoyed in the gallery of the Emperor (for whom he worked for many years).[7]

9.1 ROELANT SAVERY
Waterfall with Artist Sketching
Ca. 1607
[Vienna, Österreichische
Nationalbibliothek]

Sandrart's claims for Savery are generally consistent with other evidence. Most of the mountain landscape drawings are indeed fully worked, pictorially conceived compositions, and a number of Savery's extant landscape drawings, including two in the *Atlas*, were used for extant paintings of approximately the same dimensions. For example, one drawing of a waterfall [fig. 9.2][8] is the basis for *Waterfall with Fishermen* [fig. 9.3].[9] Although Savery drew some sensitive and dramatic mountainous views before 1606, only two imaginary views[10] among these include cascades, rather flaccid ones ignored by the passing travellers. In consequence, I suspect that it was Savery's skill in depicting dramatic landscapes in general, not specifically waterfalls, that prompted the imperial commission.

Sandrart's intriguing comment that Savery was searching for 'wonders of nature' can be assessed in relation to Rudolf's interest in obtaining new rarities for his *Kunst- und Wunderkammer*.[11] While most attention has been devoted to his *artificialia*, Rudolf's collection of *naturalia* was substantial, including both objects and books of drawings.

In this context, there is real significance to Savery's choice of motifs. Besides the 'wondrous mountains and valleys', there are more specific motifs: bizarre rock formations, rainbows, as well as alpine waterfalls.[12] These are all wonders or marvels of nature, *naturalia*, examples of the divine handiwork that could not be physically collected and displayed [fig. 9.1]. Such motifs are absent from the subtle alpine landscapes drawn from life a few years earlier by Savery's colleague in Prague, the goldsmith Paulus van Vianen.[13] Surely van Vianen passed by torrential alpine waterfalls, but he simply did not see them as worthy of artistic attention. He probably just thought of them the way most travellers did, as threatening. Besides the many startling, often exaggerated outcroppings or pinnacles of eroded limestone, Savery also captured features curiously suggesting a human face in *Monstrous Rocks* [fig. 9.4],[14] thereby evoking the monstrously deformed natural objects found in collections of curiosities[15] that underline the unknowableness of the divine plan. Savery's mischievous sense of humour often resulted in plays on forms. In his 1604 *Landscape with Deer Hunters*,[16] mounds of earth mimic the bodies of the deer. In *Mountainside with Waterfalls, Rainbow, and Artist Sketching* [fig. 9.6],[17] Savery's guide gestures towards the rainbow that arches through the dark rain clouds. In all likelihood, it was the nature of his commission that prompted Savery even to attempt to capture on paper this ephemeral phenomenon. It is difficult to sketch a rainbow; Doomer just left it out of his copy.[18] A rainbow also animates the sky of a contemporary alpine view in Hamburg.

The most spectacular of the natural wonders Savery recorded was the alpine wa-

9.2 ROELANT SAVERY
Waterfall
Ca. 1607
[Vienna, Österreichische
Nationalbibliothek,
Kartensammlung]

terfall. His large chalk compositions of waterfalls and cascades are often depicted from an oblique angle for greater drama, allowing a thrilling rush into the foreground, frequently throwing up froth and boulders as well as limbs of dead trees. It is important to try to recall the intense awe – the awful as well as the awe-some – found in contemporary travellers' descriptions of the momentous power and terrifying noise of surging water. Savery, sent out to record such wonders, saw them from a different perspective, both figuratively (as an artist) and literally (up close).[19]

In 1606, there was one place where the play of a great waterfall was considered an aesthetic experience: at Tivoli just outside Rome. Savery never went to Italy, but I will propose that this experience could be accessed through acquaintance with engravings of Tivoli. In consequence, the appreciation of the aesthetic properties of the falls and cascades at Tivoli as a vehicle of artistic expression was apparently instrumental in creating a paradigm for the recognition of the aesthetic potential of the truly fearsome, torrential alpine falls. The mountain waterfall, once 're-vealed', entered the permanent expressive vocabulary of the visual arts.

The tumbling waterfall, which would seem an obvious vehicle for composi-tional drama, played a remarkably small role in the sixteenth-century evolution of landscape into an independent specialty. Waterfalls as opposed to springs, foun-tains, rivers, seas or, on the other hand, trees, mountains or caves, played no real role in Christian narratives, Greco-Roman history and mythology or Renaissance pastoral poetry,[20] the prime sources for the subjects of early landscape painting. The waterfall was almost unique among the elements of nature introduced by six-teenth-century landscapists in having practically no literary, much less pictorial, prehistory (i.e., before the advent of landscapes as such) in which the conventions were formulated.

In the first half of the sixteenth century, the 'stupefying experience', to use a re-curring phrase, of contemplating an alpine waterfall was apparently not translat-able into an aesthetic experience. Waterfalls were seemingly invisible to the land-scapists of the Danube River school, who preferred to depict the mountains of Central Europe from a distance, set off by a single, heroic pine. In Italy, the *locus amoenus*, the pleasure garden, is the primary setting. Leonardo da Vinci's interest in violent deluges of water was more technical than artistic and remain isolated.[21] It is possible that before mid-century, few Netherlandish landscapists had even seen a mountain waterfall.

The portrayal of a rushing, violent waterfall seems to have made its artistic de-but in the mid-sixteenth century, at least as far as existing works of art give evidence, at Tivoli outside Rome, in works by the Venetian Giulio Muziano and the Fleming Pieter Bruegel, whose original lost compositions are recorded in contemporary engravings. For reasons to be discussed, it is very likely that Savery knew Bruegel's composition, but much less likely that he knew Muziano's. These two archetypes reflect different approaches to the representation of nature. Muziano's *St Francis in Ecstasy on Mt Alvernia* [fig. 9.5] provides a contemporary summation of traditional notions of wilderness as a natural setting where human character or faith is tested. Descriptions of St Francis receiving the stigmata on Mount Alvernia do not include a waterfall, and the motif is here an outgrowth of the earlier use of barren rock or foam-flecked streams for such settings. Bruegel's *Prospectus Tyburtinus*, of which we will discuss a version re-engraved

9.3 ROELANT SAVERY
Waterfall with Fishermen
Ca. 1608
[Gent, Museum voor Schone Kunsten]

9.4 Roelant Savery
Monstrous Boulders
Ca. 1607
[Paris, Institut Néerlandais, Fondation Custodia]

9.5 CORNELIUS COURT
(after Girolamo Muziano)
*St Francis in Ecstasy on
Mt Alvernia*
1567

in Prague in 1606, is an expression of the new interest in the representation of sites noteworthy for geographical (cartographic) or historical reasons.

Giulio Muziano's composition *St Francis in Ecstasy on Mt Alvernia*,[22] engraved by Cornelius Cort in 1567, is based on drawings made of the cascades at Tivoli in the years 1560–66, when the artist was in residence at Tivoli in the service of Cardinal Ippolito d'Este, a man fascinated with the beauty of flowing water, who created the fabulous series of fountains there. Muziano's extant landscape drawings exhibit the artist's Mannerist taste for undulating, linear visual patterns, inherited in part from his mentor Titian. A leaping stream of water or dramatic fall with its unique blend of twisting, turning forms, insubstantial, infinitely subtle, unexpected, unbridled in its power, could hold great attractions for an artist receptive to contemporary stylistic currents. In contrast, it is hard to imagine it attracting a contemporary of Piero della Francesca.

This is not the delightful, fostering atmosphere of the *locus amoenus* or the aspect of Tivoli which inspired the sixteenth-century poet Tarquato Tasso in *La Gerusalemme Liberata* (1581), but a place where the forces of nature challenge the saint to conquer himself.[23] Conflicts of body and soul, tensions and exhilarating spiritual release, are here magnificently evoked. The print was re-engraved in reverse with St Narcissus, patriarch of Jerusalem, substituted for St Francis and the inscription with the names of Muziano and Cort replaced by *Sadeler excud.*[24] Savery could have seen this engraving through his contacts with Aegidius Sadeler, court engraver in Prague to the Emperor and Savery's colleague, but there is no evidence that he did. Whether or not he knew it is not critical to our discussion. Other Sadeler prints are more important.

In 1606, shortly before Savery set off from Prague on his travels in the Alps, Aegidius Sadeler[25] published two views of the falls at Tivoli in a series of famous antiquities found in Italy and Northern Europe entitled *Vestigi della Antichita di Roma, Tivoli, Pozzuolo et altri Luochi*.[26] One is a re-engraved version [fig. 9.8] of the etching and engraving of the falls on the Tibur near Tivoli, entitled *Prospectus Tybertinus*, initially published by Hieronymus Cock around 1558 with the famous series after Pieter Bruegel known collectively as the *Large Landscapes*. It has traditionally been presumed to be based on a lost drawing made by Pieter Bruegel during his travels to and in Italy between 1552 and 1554.[27] The second view of the falls at Tivoli [fig. 9.7] is one of the views in the series after drawings made by Jan Brueghel, who had been at Tivoli in July 1593 and whose visit to Prague in 1604 may have prompted Sadeler's publication.

Prospectus Tyburtinus reflects both the humanist interest among sixteenth-century Northern artists visiting Italy in documenting Roman sites and the contemporary cartographic interest in atlas views. On the one hand, it and the view of Tivoli after Jan Brueghel are among the 11 views that Sadeler added to the 38 copies after E. Dupérac's 1575 *Vestigi...* (with its own view of Tivoli *sans* falls) to make up the publication of 1606. On the other hand, Bruegel's composition can be compared with the engraving after Joris Hoefnagel's drawing of the falls at Tivoli made on his visit in February 1578 which is inserted in a corner of his panoramic view of the site, *Tiburtum vulgo Tivoli*, included in the atlas *Civitates orbis terrarum* published by Georg Braun and Frans Hogenberg (Cologne, 1572-1618).

Other compositions within Bruegel's *Large Landscapes* incorporating mountains are essentially imaginary, including in some cases passages of extant drawings made in the Alps. While the authorship of some mountain landscapes traditionally attributed to Bruegel is currently disputed,[28] it remains clear that his alpine drawings are concerned with expressing the awesome, dominating mass of these mountain ranges, which are therefore portrayed from considerable distance. Scholars of Bruegel landscape drawings have shown that the foreground must, in nearly all cases, have been drawn in later. None of the extant studies made in the Alps or as imaginary reconstructions of that experience include cascades or in fact any closely scrutinized natural detail. It is almost as if he never left the road.

In Bruegel's day, the wise traveller unacquainted with the upland passes, but aware of their dangers, would rarely have left the road for something so nonessential. Contemporary texts help to characterize this perspective.

De Alpibus, the first specialized, systematic treatise on the Alps, was published in Zürich in 1574 by Josias Simler.[29] As a crystallization of the age-old fears of those who travelled the land routes between Northern Europe and Italy across this terrifying natural barrier, this text on the Alps is in fact on the *passes*, the roads through the Alps. No 'Alps', used to mean both peak or range, without a major pass are included. The first and major portion of the book is on the passes themselves. The next describes the difficulties: narrow road, falling rocks, danger of plunging off the path or into a snow-covered crevasse, and other hazards. Only then is there a discussion of the terrain itself, the flora and fauna and the water. It is in the preface that Simler drops his pragmatic compilations of travel information and comments on the 'stupor' that he notes overcomes strangers upon first seeing the Alps. While there are mountains elsewhere, nowhere are there the

9.6 ROELANT SAVERY
Mountainside with Waterfalls, Rainbow and Artist
Ca. 1607
[Vienna, Österreichische Nationalbibliothek, Kartensammlung]

9.7 JAN BRUEGEL
Cascades at Tivoli
1606

9.8 PIETER BREUGEL
Falls on the Tibor (Prospectus
Tyburtinus)
1606

extremes of the gigantic or the menacing which here 'strike the spirit', as he puts it. The same tone pervades one of the few contemporary evocations of contemporary life which involve waterfalls. The hero of *Don Quixote* (1610) is faced with proving his chivalric manliness before the terrors of a night adventure that is made more fearsome by 'the dreadful noise of water ... which seems to precipitate itself headlong down the steep mountains'.[30]

In contrast, the first extended description of the *joys* of alpinism[31] that I know of is found in a letter of 1541 written by the famous Swiss naturalist Konrad Gesner:

> Each year I ascend various mountains, or at least one, at the season when plants are in full bloom in order to examine them and to procure for my body a noble exercise at the same time as an enrichment for my spirit ... What delights for the soul rightly moved to admire the spectacular effect of the enormous mass of these mountains and to hold up one's head in the bosom of the clouds. Without being able to explain myself I feel my spirit struck by these astonishing heights and delighted in the contemplation of the Sovereign Architect.[32]

Gesner was Swiss and a naturalist; he was not passing through the Alps but climbing them, with anticipation of gratification and with an attention to the particular.

Did the waterfalls of the Alps not appeal to Bruegel's imagination? While he 'looked at' them as a traveller, as an artist he apparently did not 'see' them. In the environs of Rome, where the reverence and description of famous sites of Antiquity had long been acknowledged by a humanist, antiquarian culture as 'worthy' in their own right, as inherently beautiful, Bruegel's eyes were opened. Here one might leave the road; indeed it was encouraged. Hadrian, as well as more recent members of the élite such as Cardinal Ippolito d'Este, had built their country villas here. There were tourist sites to be visited. On the other hand, there were no glaciers; one would not be swept away by a suddenly engorged cataract. There was no threat; the force of the moving water could be viewed with detachment.

In April 1581, after an arduous passage through the Alps, the great French essayist and humanist Michel de Montaigne visited Tivoli. His lyric description of the falls there contrasts markedly with the terse characterization of the alpine falls taken down by his secretary the previous October. While Montaigne demonstrates little interest in the scenery on his passage through Switzerland, devoting more attention to the costs of meals and the cultural level of his hosts, in one striking paragraph he acknowledges the 'savage crags, some massive, others interrupted by great crevasses and torrents of water'. He notes rock falls and the sight of entire forests ripped up by their roots. At Tivoli, however, with its layered literary and historical associations for the humanist at his ease in the d'Este gardens already famous beyond the borders of Italy, Montaigne's mood relaxes. He writes gracefully of the Teverone, a tributary of the Tibur which at the crest of the hill 'takes a marvellous leap, descends the mountain and hides in a little hole in the rock. Five or six hundred steps further it reappears, plays about in a diverting manner and joins the Tibur a little below the town'.[32]

9.9   ROELANT SAVERY
Mountainous Landscape with Castles and Waterfall
1606/07
[Washington D.C., National Gallery]

All the representations that I have identified of waterfalls based on studies from life during the closing decades of the sixteenth century seem to be connected directly or indirectly with visits to Tivoli, with one telling exception. This is a panoramic view of the appropriately named town of Aquapendente (l'Aquila) with a waterfall which goes back to a drawing by Lodewijk Toeput, redrawn by Joris Hoefnagel for inclusion in *Civitates orbis terrarum*, volume 63. Thus all the waterfalls are associated with 'sites'. Even with this conventional common denominator, some of the studies of individual cascades at Tivoli – those by Paul Brill[34] and Jan Brueghel[35] – are immensely sensitive. Brueghel's delicate interpretations of the falls are adroitly incorporated into compositions such as his 1595 *Flight of the Holy Family into Egypt* (Germany, private collection),[36] painted shortly after his return from Italy, or his *Allegory of Water* of around 1614 (Milan, Ambrosiana).[37]

Savery's *Mountainous Landscape with Castles and Waterfall* [fig. 9.9],[38] drawn in black and coloured chalk on grey-green paper, can be considered one of the artist's earliest treatments of this theme for reasons of style. It was probably studied in part from life, but fantasy and formula are the determinants. At the crest of this alpine ridge, one sees not only ruins of a generalized Roman type, but, more specifically, arcades and what appears to be a circular temple roughly paralleling those overlooking the precipices at Tivoli. Thus the authority of Tivoli is acknowledged.

Savery's imaginative treatment depends on a second-hand acquaintance with a received formula which he expanded through personal experience. If my chronology of his waterfall drawings is correct, the artist quickly moved away from a hesitant use of a borrowed vocabulary to develop this theme in all the heightened naturalism and bravura of the Baroque. Compositionally, there is a consistent use of the oblique or diagonal to emphasize the movement of the water as it sweeps across the picture plane. While in most of these studies, the artist presents his protagonist in heroic profile, and many of the individual forms are surely exaggerated, there is an underlying sense of natural detail closely observed.

A complement is found in an exactly contemporary publication of the Dutch art theorist, painter and poet Carel van Mander. His equally personal, if brief, reaction to an alpine waterfall does not appear among his pastoral poems, but rather

9.10 ROELANT SAVERY
Falls on the Rhine at Schaffhausen
Ca. 1607
[Vienna, Österreichische Nationalbibliothek, Kartensammlung]

in chapter 8 of his didactic poem *Grondt der Edel vry Schilderconst* (Basics of the Noble Art of Painting) (Haarlem, 1604), 'Van het landschap'. Van Mander's poetry frequently describes some aspect of nature, but the imagery is usually conventional. Here, however, there was no real precedent, and van Mander showed himself capable of enjoying nature spontaneously, not only with his eyes but with his pen. The experience may have been quite old by 1600-1603, possibly from the 1570s, but the moment recorded must have been one of intense feeling intensely recalled. All his other descriptions of potential landscape subject matter were developed from the contemporary landscape school in Holland. The spontaneity is unfortunately lost in my prose rendering of stanzas 33-35:

> But let us ... climb for a moment on the steep rocks dampened by the moist lips of the scurrying clouds, which wash as well the highest summits. In general, their colour is rather light ash; sometimes their bare pinnacles thrust up amidst dense forests of fir trees. Ah, those horrifying rock formations that fill the land of the Swiss and that separate the French from the Italians, those targets of the north wind, full of white flashes, from those, peaks sometimes rise up into the clouds as well as under castles. Oh paint-brushes, become Echo here and imitate the roar of the water that throws itself furiously down between withered rocks. Mark how in that waterfall rock formations hang down like icicles, all green and mossy and unruly, and how the stream, as if drunk, runs helter-skelter down rambling, crooked byways; once below, it becomes as snakes. See how these evergreens grow tall here and how mysterious they seem. Who could ever dream this?[39]

Who could ever dream this? That is the heart of the matter. Once established as an aesthetic experience, as picture-worthy, the waterfall spread with amazing rapidity, becoming almost a commonplace by the 1620s.

Savery's *Falls on the Rhine at Schaffhausen* [fig. 9.10],[40] where travellers in Simler's day were 'stupefied' at seeing the 'river fall from the rocks',[41] can be compared with one of Jacob van Ruisdael's trademark cataract compositions of the mid-1660s, *Waterfall with a Castle and a Cottage* [fig. 9.11],[42] to demonstrate the direction the theme would take in the hands of the artist whose work may be said to epitomize Baroque landscape. Ruisdael never travelled in mountainous terrain, but once acquainted with the alpine imagery of Savery and Allart van Everdingen's views of Scandinavia, he was able to discover breathtaking drama in the cataracts of the hill country in the eastern Netherlands.

Apart from the question of increased safety of travel, why was it only in the mid-sixteenth century, gathering momentum around 1590 to 1610, that European artists were first truly receptive to the waterfall, much less the mountain waterfall, as a subject worthy of study? A comparison can be made with shifting preferences for types of trees. The straight, vertically soaring pine trees preferred by the early sixteenth-century Danube River school can be contrasted with the new taste around 1600 for great gnarled trees, commanding the diagonal, which appear among the drawings of the Carracci and other Italian landscapists as well as of a number of Netherlanders such as Savery, whose extravagant *Hollow Oak* [fig. 9.12][43] from 1608/10 perfect expresses contemporary aesthetic sensitivities.

In conclusion, while the challenge of responding to Rudolf's appetite for wonders not only prompted Savery's travel in the Alps, but probably prodded his

9.11 JACOB VAN RUISDAEL
Waterfall with a Castle and Cottage
Early 1660s
[Cambridge (MA), Harvard University Art Museum, Gift of Helen Clay Frick]

openness to new subjects, the thematic model that he needed to appreciate the alpine waterfall as awesome rather than simply awful, as a subject worthy of pictorial treatment, was provided by the famous falls and cascades at Tivoli, known to him through Sadeler's prints. Finally, he had to be able to appreciate them aesthetically. It is no accident that these vigorous, shifting, onrushing obliques and diagonals, often on the point of spilling into the viewer's space, first caught the imagination of artists schooled in the attractions of contrapposto,[44] imbued with the compositional and gestural dynamics of Mannerism and early Baroque art. While the Tivoli falls first 'appeared' at the height of the *maniera*, it was only to a member of the generation of Caravaggio or of Peter Paul Rubens, the latter's compositional bravura epitomized by his *Prometheus* of circa 1612 [fig. 9.13], that the alpine waterfall was first revealed.[45]

9.12 ROELANT SAVERY
Hollow Oak
1608–10
[Österreichische Nationalbibliothek, Kartensammlung]

1. Österreichisches Nationalbibliothek, Vienna, Kartensammlung, Atlas van der Hem, XLVI, fol. 14 (Joaneath Spicer [Durham], 'The Drawings of Roelandt Savery' [Ph.D. diss., Yale University, 1979; Ann Arbor, 1986], no. C32). Aspects of this essay were developed there. A revised monograph on Savery's drawings is in preparation.

2. For Savery's alpine drawings, see Spicer (note 1), pp. 51–89 (and related entries); *idem. in Prag um 1600: Kunst und Kultur am Hofe Rudolfs II.* (Freren, 1988), nos. 244–46, 636 (*Falls on the Rhine at Schaffhausen* [wrongly labelled]). H. G. Franz, 'Roelandt Savery im rudolfinischen Künstlerkreis, Landschaftszeichnungen im Atlas Blaeu der Österreichischen Nationalbibliothek Wien', *Kunsthistorisches Jahrbuch Graz*, 23 (1987–88), 60–78, cites Spicer (note 1), but is unfamiliar with the findings discussed there.

3. Spicer (note 1), pp. 57–67. Other approaches: A. C. Steland, 'Wasserfälle, Die Emanzipation eines Bildmotivs in der holländischen Malerei um 1640', *Niederdeutsche Beiträge zur Kunstgeschichte*, 24 (1985), 85–104; E. J. Walford, *Jacob van Ruisdael and the Perception of Landscape* (New Haven, 1991), pp. 34–35, 104–6, 141–46; M. Schefford, 'Der Wasserfall als Bildmotiv, Anregungen zu einer Ikonographie', *Aachener Kunstblätter* 41: *Festschrift für Wolfgang Krög*, (1971), 274ff. Chapters on water in S. Schama, *Landscape and Memory* (New York, 1995), throw light on many sixteenth- and seventeenth-century texts and motifs, except for waterfalls. On wilderness in general, see J. Wozniakowski, *Die Wildnis: Zur Deutungsgeschichte des Berges in der europäischen Neuzeit* (Frankfurt, 1987).

4. A 'large parchment book of drawings made in the Tyrol from life by Roelandt Savery' was in Rembrandt's collection at the time of his 1656 bankruptcy proceedings. Rembrandt may have purchased them from Roelandt or from his nephew Hans Savery. As the Utrecht landscapist Antonie Waterloo incorporated motifs from these into his own compositions, he may have owned the drawings before Rembrandt. Lambert Doomer probably bought the album at Rembrandt's bankruptcy sale, made copies of at least seven of the sheets and sold most but not all of them around 1665 to Laurens

van der Hem, who incorporated them into his atlas of 46 volumes based on Bleau's 11-volume *Atlas Major*. See Spicer (note 1), under no. C24 with literature; Franz (note 2), 60 (details incomplete).

5. *Pine Tree*, fol. 1 (Spicer [note 1], no. C49), and *Hollow Oak*, fol. 5 (fig. 12; Spicer [note 1], no. C55), can be dated slightly later.

6. For Doomer's copies, see Spicer (note 1), under nos. C24, C29, with literature.

7. Eben so grosse Erfahrung liess er auch merken in Steinfelsen, Klippen, Rotzen, Bergen und Wasserfällen, dahero Kayser Rudolphus bewogen, ihm in Tyrol verschickt, um darinnen der Natur seltsame Wunder mehr zu erkundigen. Also zeichnete er alle schönste und verwunderlichste Gebürge und Thäler dieses Landes aufs fleissigste mit der Feder, die grosse Bäume mit Kohle, die weit-aussehende Werke aber mit Wasserfarben in zweyen Jahren in eine grosses Buch, dass ihm hernach in seinen Landschaften sehr wol zu Nutzen kame, wie hiervon in der Galerie zu Prag (allwo er in Diensten Ihro Kays. Majestät viel Jahre gearbeitet) der Genüge nach zu sehen, die nachmals von Egidio Sadeler und desselben Discipel Isaac Major meistentheils in Kupfer gebracht worden [*Teutsche Academie*, ed. A. R. Peltzer (Munich, 1925), pp. 175–76].

8. Atlas van der Hem (note 1), XLVI, fol. 2; Spicer (note 1), no. C23.

9. Spicer (note 1), under C23; T. Kaufmann, *The School of Prague: Painting at the Court of Rudolf II* (Chicago 1985/88), no. 19.28; K. Müllenmeister, *Roelant Savery: Die Gemälde* (Freren, 1988), no. 73. The large size of these drawings suggests that Savery chose to compose on a scale roughly parallel to the anticipated paintings; indeed fol. 2 is 42 cm high, 3 cm higher than the subsequent painting.

10. Spicer (note 1), nos. C9 (Albertina), 10 (Christies, London, 30 November 1965, lot 59, ill.).

11. For Rudolf's collection, see, for example, E. Scheicher, *Die Kunst- und Wunderkammern der Habsburger* (Vienna, 1979), pp. 142–78; more generally, J. Kenseth (ed.), *The Age of the Marvelous*, exh. cat. (Hannover, NH, 1991).

12. Identifying the location of *Mountainside with Ten Caves* (Atlas van der Hem, [note 1], XLVI, fol. 12;

9.13 PIETER PAUL RUBENS
Prometheus
Ca. 1612
[Philadelphia, Philadelphia Museum of Art, Purchased with the W.P. Wilstach Fund]

Spicer [note 1], no. C31; Franz [note 2], fig. 11) might reveal that it was considered a wonder.

13. For van Vianen's drawings of the mountains and streams around Salzburg, see T. Gerszi, *Paulus van Vianen: Hanzeichnungen* (Hanau, 1982); idem, *Die Salzburger Skizzenbücher des Paulus van Vianen*, exh. cat. (Salzburg, 1983).

14. Spicer (note 1), no. C39.

15. For example, in the 1621 inventory in Vienna of objects removed from Rudolf's collection in Prague, chest 6 includes a mix of objects among which is no. 65, '1 monster mit 2 köpfen' (*JKSAK*, 25 [1905], pt 2, xxi). One is reminded of Giambologna's gigantic stone, brick and lava statue *The Apennines* of ca. 1583 in the garden of the villa of Pratolino (C. Avery, *Giambologna* [London, 1987], pl. XI; also Kenseth (ed.) (note 11), no. 179. Jacques de Gheyn did at least three curious studies of faces in rocks (J.Q. van Regteren Altena, *Jacques de Gheyn: Three Generations* [The Hague, 1983], nos. 529, 531, 1004). For another contemporary traveller's observation of a face in a boulder, see J. van der Waals, *De Prentschat van Michiel Hinloopen* (Amsterdam, 1988), fig. 203.

16. Kaufmann (note 9), no. 19.5; Müllenmeister (note 9), no. 73; *Prag um 1600* (note 2), no. 572

17. Spicer (note 1), no. C29.

18. See under *ibid.*, no. C24, 29.

19. Franz (note 2) justly calls attention to the emphasis on foreground detail in Savery's drawings.

20. For example, Ovid's 'foam-flecked waters' of the Peneus running through the Vale of Tempe in his *Metamorphoses* I.570-1, describes cataracts in a river, not a waterfall. A mid-sixteenth-century visualization of the river is found in Abraham Ortelius' panoramic view of the 'Vale of Tempe' in *Theatrum Orbis Terrarum* of 1570. Ovid's river may be the prototype for Jacopo Sannazaro's stream Erymanthus (*Arcadia*, 1490s), which, issuing from the foot of a mountain, 'hurls itself forth with a mighty and fearful uproar'. See W. H. Herendeen, *From Landscape to Literature: The River and the Myth of Geography* (Pittsburgh, 1986), chap. III.

21. M. Schneider, *Leonardo da Vinci: Das Wasserbuch: Schriften und Zeichnungen* (Munich, 1996).

22. M. Sellink, *Cornelius Cort*, exh. cat. (Rotterdam, 1994), p. 61 (with literature).

23. In Italian art before Muziano, swiftly flowing water already appears in evocations of wilderness as a place of spiritual testing, as in Polidoro da Caravaggio's *Scenes from the Life of Mary Magdalene* in S. Silvestro in Rome, painted before 1527. Such imagery is susceptible to a reading as representative of a hostile environment with which the protagonist must contend, or as an expression of the tumult of the human soul and the transience of life. One of the few explicitly emblematic images by Savery's contemporaries to draw on the waterfall is found in F. Schoonhoven, *Emblemata* (Gouda, 1618), where Embl. XLVI, 'Voluptatis praemium', is illustrated by a snake swallowing the head of another snake before a waterfall, expressing the tumult of the soul tempted by worldly pleasures and pursuits. Efforts to give emblematic readings to non-narrative paintings of waterfalls have centered on Ruisdael. The chapter on his waterfalls in W.

Wiegand, '*Ruisdael-Studien, Ein Versuch zur Ikonologie der Landschaftsmalerei*' (Ph.D. diss., Hamburg, 1971), pp. 87-91, is not very convincing, in the first place because hardly any of his literary sources are actually about waterfalls. Wiegand appears to be the point of inspiration for the moral interpretation of Ruisdael's waterfalls in J. Bruyn, 'Toward a Scriptural Reading of Seventeenth-Century Dutch Landscape Paintings', in P. Sutton (ed.), *Masters of 17th-Century Dutch Landscape Painting* (Boston, 1987).

24. Hollstein (Sadeler excudit) 16, ill.

25. For Sadeler and on his interest in landscape, see D. Limouze, '*Aegidius Sadeler (c.1570-1629): Drawings, Prints and Art Theory*' (Ph.D. diss., Princeton University, 1990); I. de Ramaix, *Les Sadeler*, exh. cat. (Brussels, 1992).

26. Hollstein 151-201; Limouze (note 25), pp. 188-89.

27. For the *Large Landscapes*, see D. Freedberg (ed.), *The Prints of Pieter Bruegel the Elder* (Tokyo, 1989), pp. 103-5. Hans Mielke's new monograph on Bruegel's drawings was not yet available at this writing.

28. The monograph by H. Mielke is expected to address this.

29. Josias Simler, *De Alpibus commentarius: Die Alpen* (ed. A. Steinitzer, Munich, 1931); W. A. B. Coolidge, *Josias Simler et les origines de l'alpinisme jusqu'en 1600* (Grenoble, 1904). Simler's approach is an outgrowth of that found in Jacques Signot's *La Totale et Vraie Description de tous les passaiges, lieux et destroictz par lesquelz on peut passer et entrer des Gaules es ytalies ...* (Paris, 1518). See further E. S. Bates, *Touring in 1600* (London, 1911); G. R. de Beer, *Early Travelers in the Alps* (London, 1930).

30. Miguel de Cervantes Saavedra, *Don Quixote de La Mancha* (1605), chap. xx.

31. Petrarch, who ascended Mount Ventoux in 1336, is frequently signalled as the first European to climb a mountain to see the view, but, as he described in a letter to a friend (*De rebus familiaribus*), upon reaching the top, he was overwhelmed by his own self-indulgence.

32. Letter from Gesner to Jacques Vogel printed at the beginning of Gesner's brochure 'Libellus de lacte et operibus lactariis', Zürich, 1541.

33. F. Rigolot (ed., *Journal du voyage de Michel de Montaigne en Italie par la Suisse et l'Allemagne en 1580 et 1581* (Paris, 1992), pp. 55-56 (between Brixen and Trente), 128 (Tivoli). Montaigne travelled with a secretary who wrote down his comments, except in Italy, where he did it himself.

34. For example, *Tivoli Waterfall Seen from a Cave* of 1595/99 (Amsterdam, Rijksmuseum); for this and related studies, see L. Oehler, 'Einige frühe Naturstudien von Paul Bril', *Marburger Jahrbuch für Kunstwissenschaft*, 16 (1955), 199-206.

35. For example, his *Waterfall of the River Anio at Tivoli* (Leiden, Prentenkabinet der Rijksuniversiteit), for which see M. Winner, 'Neubestimmtes und Unbestimmtes im zeichnerischen Werk von Jan Brueghel d. Ä.', *Jahrbuch der Berliner Museen*, 14 (1972), 133-36, fig. 15; idem., 'Zeichnungen des Älteren Jan Brueghel', *JdBM*, 3 (1961).

36. K. Ertz, *Jan Brueghel der Ältere: Die Gemälde* (Cologne, 1979), no. 10, ill. For the related engraving published by A. Sadeler (Hollstein 209), and the Tivoli-inspired drawing (Rotterdam) behind it,

see Winner, 'Zeichnungen ...' (note 35), fig. 9-10.

37. Ertz (note 36), no. 302, ill.

38. Spicer in M. M. Grasselli (ed.), *The Touch of the Artist: Master Drawings from the Woodner Collections*, exh. cat. (Washington, D.C., 1995), no. 64. Among Paulus van Vianen's landscape drawings made around Salzburg in 1601–3 before arriving in Prague is an imaginary view (Budapest) that is a similar combination of Central European fortifications and motifs from Tivoli, though the fall of water is reduced to a thin stream (Gerszi, *Die Salzburger Skizzenbücher* [note 13], no. 19).

39. Karel van Mander, *Den grondt der edel vry schilderconst* (Haarlem, 1604); edn by Hessel Miedema, Utrecht, 1973, vol. VIII, pp. 33–35 (no commentary on waterfalls). This is complemented in chap. VII, 'Van de Reflecty' (On Reflections), by verses describing a deafening stream in Italy which bear the gloss *over a mooie waterval* (about a beautiful waterfall).

40. Atlas van der Hem (note 1), XLVI, fol. 11; Spicer (note 1), no. 31; Franz (note 2), p. 68; Spicer in *Prag um 1600* (note 2), no. 636.

41. Simler (note 29), chap. XVI, 'De Alpinis aquis'.

42. Cambridge, MA, Fogg Art Museum, Gift of Miss Helen Clay Frick; see S. Slive, *Jacob van Ruisdael*, exh. cat. (The Hague, 1982), no. 34. On Ruisdael's cataracts in general, see Walford (note 3), pp. 104–6, and note 3 above.

43. Spicer (note 1), C55.

44. One of the most famous cases of artistic accessibility involves the *Belvedere Torso*, physically discovered decades before its aesthetic potential was truly revealed, first of all by Michelangelo.

45. For a related Baroque 'gesture', see J. Spicer, 'The Renaissance Elbow' in J. Bremmer and H. Roodenburg (eds), *A Cultural History of Gesture* (Oxford, 1991).

Natural History Illustration at the Court of Rudolf II

LEE HENDRIX

10.1 ALBRECHT DÜRER
Hare
[Vienna, Graphische
Sammlung Albertina]

10.2 GIORGIO LIBERALE
Page from Cod. min. 2669
(an octopus)
[Vienna, Österreichische
Nationalbibliothek,
Handschriften- und
Inkunabelsammlung]

In surveying Rudolf's collection, one is struck by the extent and quality of the natural history illustration it contained. Indeed the works of this type once owned by the Emperor include a number of the most renowned nature illustrations ever made: Dürer's *Hare* [fig. 10.1], Hoefnagel's manuscripts *The Four Elements* (Washington, D.C., The National Gallery of Art) and *Mira calligraphiae monumenta* (Los Angeles, The J. Paul Getty Museum) and de Gheyn's album of nature studies (Paris, Fondation Custodia).

The antecedents for Rudolf's interest in natural history illustration go back several generations. In 1551, Emperor Charles V issued a privilege to Pier Andrea Mattioli to produce an illustrated commentary in Latin on one of the central medical texts of Classical Antiquity, *De materia medica* by the Greek physician Pedianos Dioscorides. Mattioli (1501–1577) practised medicine in Trent and Görz before coming to Vienna as imperial physician to Emperor Ferdinand I in 1554, the year that his extensively illustrated commentary on Dioscorides was published with a dedication to the Emperor.[1] Earlier that year, while still in Görz, Mattioli had supervised the hand-colouring of a copy presented to Emperor Ferdinand, which may be identical to a sumptuous hand-coloured example with extensive use of gold and silver in the Österreichische Nationalbibliothek.[2] The Habsburg involvement with *De materia medica* continued into the reign of Emperor Maximilian II, who with the aid of the ambassador to Constantinople Olgier Giselin de Busbecq procured the magnificent illuminated *De materia medica* dating to the sixth century AD and produced for the daughter of the Byzantine Emperor.[3] The acquisition of this precious manuscript makes clear the Habsburg awareness of the Antique imperial precedent for patronizing lavishly illustrated treatises on natural history.

Mattioli seems to have been especially appreciated by Emperor Ferdinand's son and namesake, Archduke Ferdinand of the Tyrol, who eventually employed him as his personal physician. While *Statthalter* of Bohemia, Archduke Ferdinand continued the tradition of Habsburg patronage of illustrated botanical treatises by supporting the publication in 1562 of the Czech edition of Mattioli's *Commentaries*.[4] Through his patronage of Mattioli, Ferdinand came into contact with the artist whom Mattioli had met in Görz and hired to execute the illustrations for the Dioscorides Commentaries, Giorgio Liberale.[5] In 1558, Liberale went to Prague to assist with the illustrations for the Bohemian edition of the *Commentaries*, and the following year at the suggestion of Mattioli, the Archduke issued a commission to depict all the fish of the Adriatic, which he entrusted to Liberale.[6] From 1562, Liberale was active as an animal painter for the Archduke for a period of seventeen years.[7] Liberale's work on the fish of the Adriatic is probably to be identified with an elephant folio volume in the Österreichisches Nationalbibliothek [fig. 10.2], consisting of a hundred vellum leaves painted on both sides, beginning with a series of dogs and consisting of ninety-two fish, with additional creatures such as snakes and other reptiles, insect and crustaceans.[8] This large-scale, colourful work, free of text and destined for Archduke

Ferdinand's *Kunstkammer* at Schloss Ambras, is important as a precedent for the large natural history albums, the so-called *Museum*, that would be produced for Emperor Rudolf II (Vienna, Österreichisches Nationalbibliothek).

Another key figure in stimulating Rudolf's taste for nature illustration was Giuseppe Arcimboldo. Called to the imperial court by Maximilian II in 1562, Arcimboldo soon began to produce his famous paintings of composite heads, presenting the Emperor with two series depicting the four seasons and four elements on New Year's Day, 1569.[9] The agglomeration of species of sea creatures in *Water* of 1566 (Vienna, Kunsthistorisches Museum) and of mammals in *Earth* of circa 1570 [fig. 10.3] suggest that Arcimboldo knew and was stimulated by natural history illustration such as that in Mattioli's Dioscorides *Commentaries*, as well as the other massive illustrated nature compendia published during the mid-sixteenth century, and give evidence of the importance of scientific treatises in popularizing the appreciation of the encyclopaedic bounty of creation.[10] Additionally, Arcimboldo's paintings breathe tremendous animation into the individual specimens, treating each as an expressive countenance within the overall composite head of which they are a part. It is logical to assume that Arcimboldo made a fund of nature studies upon which he based his paintings, and this is confirmed by the recent discovery that several in a number of animal studies by the same hand, which are mounted in an album of nature studies by various artists which once belonged to Rudolf II, appear to have served as models for specimens in Arcimboldo's paintings.[11] One such example is the cheetah dated 1570 at the top of folio 13r of this album [fig. 10.4], upon which is ultimately based the head of the cheetah towards the 'brow' in Arcimboldo's *Earth*. If Arcimboldo is the author of these studies, as the connection with his painting suggests, this would establishe him both as the first major producer of natural history illustration employed directly by Rudolf II and as a figure of larger importance for Rudolfine nature illustration as it would develop.

Arcimboldo's composite heads of animals and flowers point directly to the imperial taste for amassing rare specimens of flora and fauna, both living and dead. In addition to Mattioli, Maximilian II employed two other major figures in the revival and advancement of botanical studies in the sixteenth century, the Netherlanders Carolus Clusius, who worked for Emperors Maximilian II and Rudolf II in Vienna from 1573 intermittently until 1588, and Rembert Dodoens, who was in Vienna in 1574 and served Rudolf II in Prague in 1575–77.[12] Maximilian kept menageries at the imperial retreats of Ebersdorf and the Neugebäude outside Vienna, while Rudolf created gardens for exotic plants and animals on the slopes of the imperial castle in Prague, which included a botanical garden, fish pond, pheasant garden, aviary with rare birds, a lions' den and moats with deer, and maintained the gardens of the Belvedere villa on the Hradčany, that had been built by Archduke Ferdinand of the Tyrol. Additionally, Rudolf kept a menagerie at Villa Hvězda.[13]

Rudolf's patronage and collecting of art gained momentum in the early 1580s.[14] With his own seat of patronage not yet fully formed, he looked to more established centres from whence to procure artists, most notably the Munich court of Duke Wilhelm V of Bavaria. In 1585, he hired Hans Hoffmann, whom the Duke had called to Munich in 1584. During the later 1570s, Hoffmann, who was then living in Nürnberg, had made a specialty of making copies and adaptations of drawings by Dürer for the Nürnberg collectors Willibald Imhoff and Paulus Praun.[15] Although he

10.3 GIUSEPPE ARCIMBOLDO
Earth
[Vienna, private collection]

10.4   Cod.min. 42
(cheetahs, a lynx and a tiger
by various artists)
[Vienna, Österreichische
Nationalbibliothek,
Handschriften- und
Inkunabelsammlung]

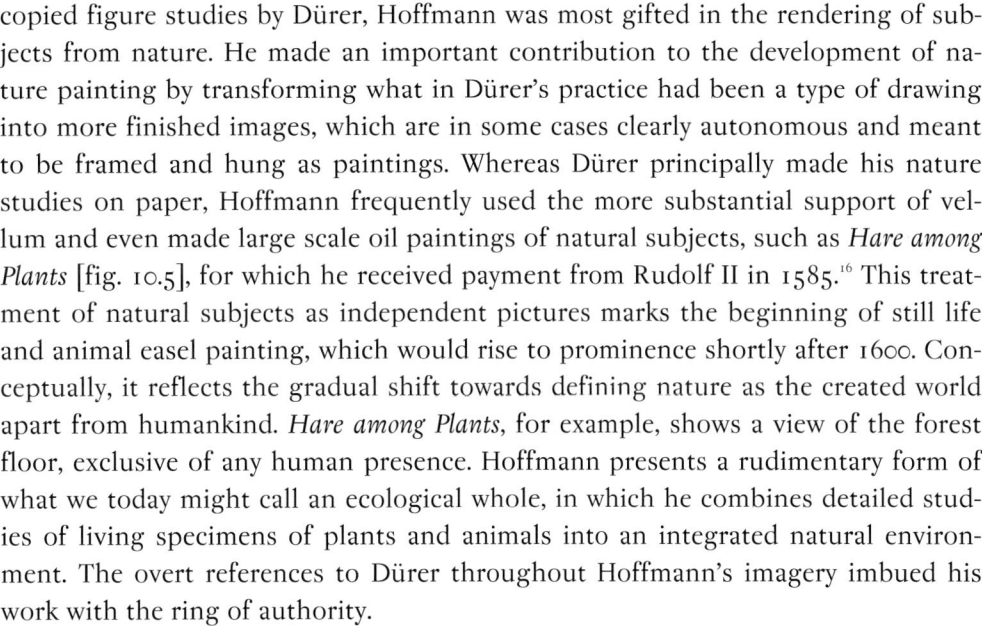

copied figure studies by Dürer, Hoffmann was most gifted in the rendering of subjects from nature. He made an important contribution to the development of nature painting by transforming what in Dürer's practice had been a type of drawing into more finished images, which are in some cases clearly autonomous and meant to be framed and hung as paintings. Whereas Dürer principally made his nature studies on paper, Hoffmann frequently used the more substantial support of vellum and even made large scale oil paintings of natural subjects, such as *Hare among Plants* [fig. 10.5], for which he received payment from Rudolf II in 1585.[16] This treatment of natural subjects as independent pictures marks the beginning of still life and animal easel painting, which would rise to prominence shortly after 1600. Conceptually, it reflects the gradual shift towards defining nature as the created world apart from humankind. *Hare among Plants*, for example, shows a view of the forest floor, exclusive of any human presence. Hoffmann presents a rudimentary form of what we today might call an ecological whole, in which he combines detailed studies of living specimens of plants and animals into an integrated natural environment. The overt references to Dürer throughout Hoffmann's imagery imbued his work with the ring of authority.

Dürer's watercolour nature studies form only a limited part of his vast and varied graphic oeuvre. In the context of the burgeoning interest in natural history during the later sixteenth century, however, they became objects of particular fascination. This, as well as Dürer's having served his forebears, Emperors Maximilian I and Charles V, must have shaped Rudolf's taste for works by Hoffmann and by Dürer himself. Indeed, Hoffmann may have advised the Emperor on the acquisition of examples by Dürer. A major success in the Emperor's pursuit of works by Dürer was his purchase of a block of objects by him from the Nürnberg Imhoff collection in 1588, which included a number of Dürer's watercolour nature studies such as the renowned *Hare* [fig. 10.1].[17] The entry into the Rudolfine collection of this, *Dead Blue Roller*, *Wing of a Blue Roller*, *Lion*,[18] and other nature watercolours by Dürer probably further fueled the Emperor's taste for this type of imagery, and also would have given definition to nature imagery as a segment within the broader imperial collection, anchoring it in an authoritative core of works by Dürer himself.

In Munich, Hoffmann met the Netherlandish manuscript illuminator and topographical draughtsman Joris Hoefnagel, who had left his native Antwerp after the so-called Spanish Fury of 1576 and been hired as court painter by Duke Albrecht V of Bavaria in 1577, continued to serve Duke Wilhelm V, who succeeded his father in 1579.[19] Among Hoefnagel's projects in Munich was the illumination of a missal for Archduke Ferdinand of the Tyrol.[20] He was also working on a four-volume manuscript illustrating the creatures of the earth divided according to the Four Elements.[21] This set includes copies of Dürer's *Hare* and *Stag Beetle*, indicating that Hoefnagel followed Hoffmann's lead in framing his own work as continuing Dürer's tradition.[22]

In 1590/91, Hoefnagel entered the service of Rudolf II, although he moved not to Prague but to Frankfurt am Main. These included the botanist Carolus Clusius, who is likely to have had an impact upon Hoefnagel's artistic and intellectual approach to the natural world.[23] While in Frankfurt, Hoefnagel illuminated for the Emperor a writing model book by the great Hungarian writing master Georg Bocskay, decorating it with an amalgam of natural, political, religious and other types of imagery, embedded with deeply learned symbolic and emblematic content [fig. 10.6].[24] Hoef-

10.5   HANS HOFFMANN
Hare among Plants
[London, private collection
(Ellen Melas Kyriazi)]

nagel's son Jacob, an artist who himself entered Rudolf's employ in 1602, published a series of engravings of 'archetypes' after his father's models in 1592 entitled *Archetypa studiaque patris Georgii Hoefnagelii* [fig. 10.7].[25] Focusing on plants, insects and other natural minutiae, elements that form the most distinctive and captivating part of Hoefnagel's imagery, the *Archetypa* was widely influential upon painting, graphic art and the decorative arts and spread Hoefnagel's fame throughout Europe.

Hoefnagel left Frankfurt in 1594 and settled in Vienna, where he died in 1601.[26] This was a particularly fertile period for him, during which he executed one of the major monuments of Rudolfine nature painting, *Mira calligraphiae monumenta*.[27] It consists of two parts – 129 folios comprising a writing model book, inscribed by Georg Bocskay like the previously mentioned Vienna codex [fig. 10.7], and 21 folios forming a constructed alphabet with grotesque borders, with the final folio inscribed by Hoefnagel *1596*, the only date he wrote in the manuscript.[28] As a florilegium of sorts, the first part of the manuscript points to Clusius' probable impact on Hoefnagel during his Frankfurt period, as well as to the taste for floriculture at the Habsburg court itself, which had been fuelled by Clusius and Dodoens' residences and had witnessed the importation of ornamentals from the Levant, most notably the tulip. Also bearing witness to this is the engraved Florilegium published in Frankfurt in 1612 by the erstwhile imperial gardener-turned-flower-dealer Emanuel Sweerts, in which the author described the Emperor as the 'greatest most enthusiastic admirer and lover' of flowers.[29] Hoefnagel's manuscript laid the groundwork for the emergence of independent floral still-life painting as it would later be practised at the Prague court by Roelandt Savery, who arrived there in 1603.[30]

The Four Elements [figs 10.9, 10.10] is Hoefnagel's other major contribution to Rudolfine nature painting. He dated it variously 1575, 1576, 1580 and 1582, indicating that his principal engagement with it was during these years, although he could well have continued working on it after entering imperial service.[31] Although it is not known whether the Emperor commissioned the manuscript, he eventually owned it, paying Hoefnagel a reputed thousand gold crowns, according to Carel van Mander.[32] *The Four Elements* was the most extensive and representative compendium of painted nature illustrations to enter Rudolf's collection prior to 1600. Illustrating hundreds of species of flora and fauna, and interleaved with paper singletons inscribed with Antique and humanist texts pertaining to the various animals, it was also apparently accompanied by an explanatory text, as a source of reference for natural history.[33]

With its scope, astonishing beauty and brilliance and knowledge of nature, Hoefnagel's imagery raised nature painting to an altogether new level of accomplishment. Indeed Hoefnagel's ambitious artistic goals and virtuosic mastery of his means, fit into the larger trend among Rudolfine artists to aggrandize the nobility and humanistic stature of their profession.[34] One of the salient features of the ambitiousness of Hoefnagel's art is its encyclopaedic striving towards complete representation of the natural world. Integral to this encyclopaedism was his copying of the nature imagery of other artists. In addition to those after Dürer, Hoefnagel's *Four Elements* contains copies after many other images, including the woodcut illustrations to Conrad Gessner's multi-volume *Historia animalium*, perhaps from a three-volume manuscript by his purported teacher, Hans Bol, and other watercolour and gouache nature studies by the so-called 'mute of Antwerp', Hans Verha-

10.6 JORIS HOEFNAGEL
GEORG BOCSKAY
Model Book of Calligraphy
[Vienna, Kunsthistorisches
Museum]

10.8 Jacob Hoefnagel
(after Joris Hoefnagel)
*Archetypa studiaque patris
Georgii Hoefnagelii*
Part 2, fol. 8
[Munich, Staatliche
Graphische Sammlung]

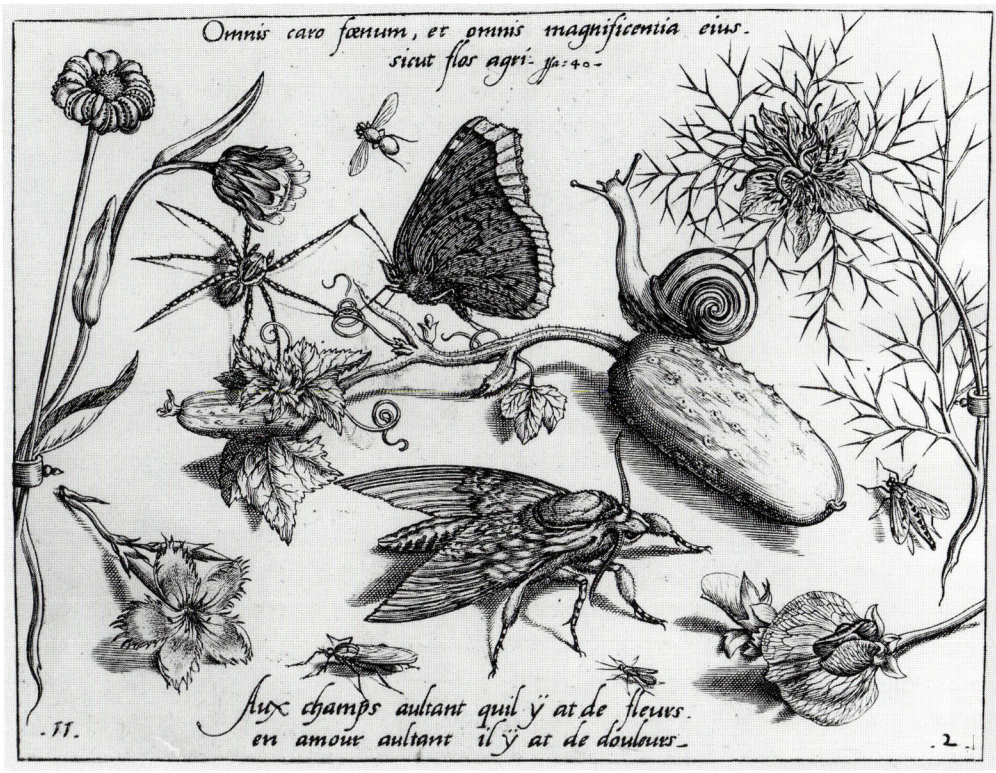

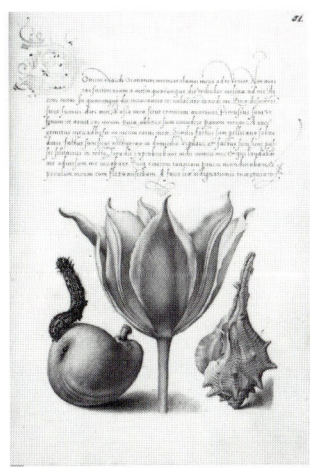

10.7 Joris Hoefnagel
George Bocskay
Mira Calligraphiae monumenta
Fol. 51 (a tulip, pear,
caterpillar and purple snail)
[Los Angeles, J. Paul Getty
Museum]

gen [fig. 10.11].[35] The *Four Elements* forms a seamless whole. The extent of the copying underscores the distance between Hoefnagel's enterprise and twentieth-century expectations of artistic originality and empirical observation of nature. Copying was ubiquitous in printed illustrated nature treatises and hand-painted compendia of nature illustrations of the sixteenth century and also played a significant role in the growth of scientific knowledge. In those days, part of the value of a treatise rested upon the comprehensiveness of its coverage of nature. Striving to demonstrate absolute mastery of nature in the *Four Elements*, Hoefnagel may be described as having combined the functions of scientist and artist. In his capacity as naturalist, he sought to demonstrate an intellectual knowledge of nature expressed through a level of encyclopaedic coverage rivalling monumental printed treatises such as those of Gessner. In his capacity as artist, he did not pursue a modern standard of empirically based accuracy, but rather followed a course that emphasized the role of artifice in the imitation of nature. He appears to have sought to use his artistic skill to make his specimens seem 'alive' or 'lively', adjectives that one encounters in late sixteenth- and seventeenth-century descriptions of nature imagery.[36] Hoefnagel's astonishing ability to imbue his specimens with lifelike motion in turn implies a larger mimetic goal. This is in harmony with the authoritative ability to imitate nature that he proclaimed through the motto *Natura sola magistra* with which he sometimes inscribed his work.[37]

One aspect of the influence of Hoefnagel's art, in particular the *Four Elements*, upon Rudolfine nature illustration is felt in an increased striving towards encyclopaedism.[38] An equal if not greater impetus to this development, however, was Rudolf's own high ambition for his *Kunstkammer*. Comprising *artificialia*, things made by human hands, and *naturalia*, things made by nature, it contained an array

of artefacts pertaining to the natural world, as well as texts on nature and compendia of painted nature illustrations.[39] Indeed the monumental compendium of natural history illustrations produced for the Emperor during his later reign, the so-called *Museum of Rudolf II*, would appear to represent the natural world as it was embodied in and defined by his own collections. The *Museum* consists of two large volumes of nature studies executed principally in oil (with other media) on vellum and comprising collectively 179 folios.[40] Creatures represented in volume I (Cod.min. 129) include mammals, reptiles, fish, birds and coral as well as other creatures, and those in volume II (Cod.min. 130) comprise birds and a few insects.

The *Museum*'s link with the Rudolfine *Kunstkammer* is most explicit in those illustrations that depict objects displayed on a green surface, such as the arrangement of a rhinoceros's horn, tooth, part of a foot and a turned vessel of rhinoceros horn on folio 10r of Cod.min. 129 [fig. 10.12].[41] This display surface parallels the description in the inventory of the collection compiled in 1621 of a 'long green table' in the middle of the *Kunstkammer* on which objects were arranged.[42] The *Museum* contains other illustrations of the remains of animals, such as narwhal horns, also displayed on a green surface, a remarkable hanging skin of a hippopotamus (Cod.min. 129, fols. 14r, 81r) and preserved birds of paradise (Cod.min. 130, fol. 12r).[43] These are interspersed amongst the majority of illustrations which show 'living' animals, usually one or two per folio. Most of the quadrupeds stand on earthen mounds or flat patches of grass, while the birds primarily perch on branches or stand on mounds. The animals are set off by a coloured ground, and the varying of these colours from folio to folio enhances the visual interest of the work as a whole. Greens, ochres and earth tones predominate among the quadrupeds, with a few of the sea creatures appearing against aqueous grounds, and blues, mauves and lavenders used frequently in the volume on birds.

The comprehensiveness of the Emperor's *Museum* appears to be of a somewhat different type than that of Hoefnagel's *Four Elements*, for while the latter strives to encompass all the animal species of creation, the former records many animals remains or living specimens actually in the imperial collections and provides a pictorial records of other individual specimens that either interested the Emperor or that he tried and failed to acquire. The history of the specimens recorded in the *Museum* vividly conveys the Emperor's involvement in the collecting of natural rarities. Among the most notable such examples in the *Museum* are the learned hirsute Petrus Gonzales and his family, memorialized on the first folio of volume 1 of the *Museum*; the rhinoceros that arrived in Lisbon in 1577, which the Emperor tried unsuccessfully to obtain; the cassowary, the first to be seen in Europe, that Rudolf received as a gift in 1601; and the dodo that appears to have been taken alive to Prague between 1599 and 1609.[44] With these specimens plus others, the *Museum* forms a compendium of nature's rare and wondrous manifestations. Its large size, together with its unusual use of oil paint on a vellum support, lend it monumentality, suggesting that it was predicated on the imperial collection itself and conceived as a painted counterpart to it. The *Museum* thus provides a permanent record of the wonders actually in the collection and posthumously brings into imperial possession other wonders of exceptional not.

The *Museum* is probably identical to the objects described in the 1607–11 inventory of the imperial *Kunstkammer* as 'His Majesty's book of animals with all manner

10.9 JORIS HOEFNAGEL
Ignis. Animalia Rationalia et Insecta from the *Four Elements*
Fol. LI (grasshoppers, a caterpillar and a morning glory)
[Washington, D.C., The National Gallery of Art, Gift of Mrs Lessing J. Rosenwald, 1987]

10.10 JORIS HOEFNAGEL
Aier. Animalia Volatilia et Cochiliata from the *Four Elements*
Fol. VI (a hawk and various accipiters)
[Washington, D.C., The National Gallery of Art, Gift of Mrs Lessing J. Rosenwald, 1987]

10.11 HANS VERHAGEN
Cod. Min. 42 (an eagle)
[Vienna, Österreichische
Nationalbibliothek,
Handschriften- und
Inkunabelsammlung]

of four-footed beasts, all painted in oil after life by Dieterich Raffenstein, on vellum, bound in red leather'; 'the other part is the book of birds, which also includes fish and other reptiles'.[45] The Netherlander Dirck de Quade van Ravesteyn was active as a painter at the imperial court from 1589 to at least 1608, and in addition to the entry in the 1607–11 inventory, his authorship of at least a portion of the images in the Museum is supported by animal staffage that he added to several architectural paintings of 1596 done by Hans Vredeman de Vries for the Emperor.[46] There were several hands involved in the Museum, however. Another one was probably that of Daniel Fröschl, the Augsburg-born miniature painter who was also imperial antiquarius, and who in this capacity himself probably compiled the Kunstkammer inventory in question.[47] The pervasive knowledge of the contents and display of the imperial Kunstkammer and the grandiosity of the imagery of the Museum befitting the imperial milieu bespeak Fröschl's participation in its execution, and perhaps even his contribution to its overall conception. He was a learned artist, particularly in the field of natural history. During the 1590s, he worked as a natural history illustrator at the Botanical Garden at Pisa and at the court of Grand Duke Ferdinand I de Medici in Florence, in concert with naturalists such as Francesco Malocchi, Director of the Botanical Garden at Pisa. The latter sent Fröschl's illustration of a cardinal to the Bolognese naturalist Ulisse Aldrovandi, who published it in the second volume of his Ornithologia, which appeared in 1600.[48] Fröschl visited Prague in 1601 and was named imperial miniature painter in 1603 and antiquarius, or keeper of the Kunstkammer, in 1607.[49]

Another artist whose name should be mentioned in connection with the Museum is Roelandt Savery.[50] He is an important figure because of the role he played in adapting the subject matter of natural history illustration for use in oil easel paintings. His floral still life in oil on copper dated 1603, which he probably made in Prague (New York, private collection), is the earliest extant dated independent floral still life by a Dutch artist and builds upon Hoefnagel's legacy of floral imagery, as in the Mira calligraphiae monumenta, the Four Elements, and the independent floral still lifes on vellum that Hoefnagel began to make during the 1590s.[51] Savery made oil paintings of horses, such as Stallion and Groom of 1605 (The Netherlands, private collection), imagery that calls to mind the series of stallions in the Museum and that collectively reflects the Emperor's love of horses expressed by his collecting of them and by his building of the famed 'Spanish Stables' above which he placed his art collections.[52] Additionally, by the second decade of the seventeenth century, Savery was producing the kind of painting for which he is arguably most famous, paradisiacal assemblages of animals in landscape settings. The range of the animals that Savery represented, the prominence of exotica, as well as the appearance in his paintings of birds such as parrots and cockatoos, perched on branches against an azure sky, suggest an interrelation between his work and the Museum. Indeed he may even have contributed a few folios to it, although this remains conjectural.[54] In any event, the Museum was in production while Savery was in Prague, as is indicated by the date of 1610 that occurs on folios 17r [fig. 10.13] and 69r of Cod.min. 130 (the only dated folios in the Museum). This possibly marks the date of the completion of this massive project, which was probably begun during the early years of the seventeenth century.[55]

Many of the animals in the Museum are in turn based upon drawings found in a fascinating album into which are mounted natural history illustrations by various

artists, Cod.min. 42 in the Österreichisches Nationalbibliothek. It contains a wide range of material, stretching from fifteenth-century images, such as the hoopoe bird inscribed as 'by the hand' of Simon Marmion (ca. 1420/25–1489), to later depictions, such as a study of a basket of flowers in oil on paper by Ludger Tom Ring the Younger (1522–1584), who was active in Münster.[56] The Drawings have been roughly systematized into quadrupeds followed by birds, fish, then insects.[57] Towards the end are plants as well as the above-mentioned still life by Ring. The album appears to have been assembled around 1600 or shortly thereafter and was almost certainly part of the Rudolfine *Kunstkammer*.[58]

10.12 Cod.min. 129
(the *Museum of Rudolf II*)
Fol 10r (the horn, tooth, foot
of a rhinoceros and a turned
vessel of rhinoceros horn)
[Vienna, Österreichische
Nationalbibliothek,
Handschriften- und
Inkunabelsammlung]

The material copied from Cod.min. 42 in the *Museum* ranges from a highly worked series of images depicting an elephant, a rhinoceros and a wolf in landscape settings, probably by Hans Hoffmann (Cod.min 42, fols. 1, 2, 4), to images possibly of Italian origin, some of which are dated to the 1570s, such as the cheetah (dated 1570) that, as previously mentioned, also appears in Arcimboldo's composite head, *Earth* [fig. 10.4].[59] The *Museum* also contains copies of some of the most beautifully rendered images in Cod.min. 42.[60]

Cod.min. 42 seems to bring together nature drawings that had accumulated in the imperial collection over a period of time, at least some and perhaps most of which had been taken there by various artists active at the imperial court. There is the aforementioned Italian material that might be associated with Arcimboldo, and images by Various artists that Hoefnagel appears to have collected as source material for the *Four Elements*, such as those by Hans Verhagen.[61] Among its contents are also several signed studies by Daniel Fröschl, such as the beautiful Düreresque woodpeckers dated 1589, when the artist was only sixteen years old [fig. 10.15].[62]

The appearance in Cod.min. 42 of nature illustrations by a range of artists underscores the Emperor's interest in this kind of material. He was probably assisted in its acquisition by his own artists. Hoffmann's probable role in the acquisition of drawings by Dürer has already been mentioned. Hans Bol's three-volume natural history manuscript now in Copenhagen, which is mentioned in Fröschl's inventory, could have been procured by Hoefnagel [fig. 10.14].[63] Similarly, the two albums of fish and bird illustrations, mentioned in Fröschl's inventory as by Jacopo Ligozzi, could have been acquired through the mediation of Fröschl [fig. 10.16].[64] Artists beyond Prague were certainly aware of Rudolf's taste for nature imagery. Jacques de Gheyn's astonishing album in watercolour and gouache on vellum illustrating flowers and natural minutiae and dated 1600–1604, which van Mander reports as having been purchased by the emperor, is clearly inspired by Hoefnagel's work of the type exemplified by *Mira calligraphiae monumenta* [fig. 10.17].[65] De Gheyn, who was active in The Hague when he painted it, would have known Hoefnagel's work both through the *Archetypa* and Hoefnagel's easily portable miniatures. De Gheyn's album as well as Hoefnagel's work in turn inspired the exquisite marginalia in the *Prayerbook of Elector Maximilian I of Bavaria* (Munich, Bayerische Staatsbibiothek), which appear to have been painted between 1604 and 1612 by an artist at the Rudolfine court.[66]

10.13 Cod.min. 130
(the *Museum of Rudolf II*)
Fol. 17r (parrot [Ara macao])
[Vienna, Österreichische
Nationalbibliothek,
Handschriften- und
Inkunabelsammlung]

The decision to organize and mount all of the diverse material in Cod.min. 42 would seem to manifest the increasingly systematic approach to collecting witnessed in the *Museum* and in the inventorization of the *Kunstkammer* in 1607–11. This approach in turn suggests a conscious impetus to impart a sense of wholeness and permanence to the *Kunstkammer* as a reflection of imperial majesty. The *Museum*,

10.15 DANIEL FRÖSCHL
Cod.min 42
Fol. 54r (two woodpeckers)
[Vienna, Österreichische
Nationalbibliothek,
Handschriften- und
Inkunabelsammlung]

10.14 HANS BOL
Icones ... animalium
Fol. 2 (an ostrich)
[Copenhagen, Konelige
Bibliotek]

moreover, seems to have been conceived in this way and as such, took nature paint-ing in a new direction. Aspects of the *Museum* which appear to manifest its character as an imperial project include it monumentality and its execution in oil paint, in-stead of watercolour and gouache, the normal media for nature illustration at that time. Hoefnagel and Hoffmann, for example, appear to have worked in oil only rarely, as opposed to van Ravesteyn, who worked principally in oil as a figure painter. The specimens in the *Museum* are not only painted in oil, but appear against a solid coloured ground, as contrasted with the blank ground commonly found in nature illustrations in watercolour and gouache on paper or vellum. The *Museum* thus manifests an oil painter's practice of working towards the goal of the finished painting. In the hands of Hoefnagel or of artists who worked for naturalists such as Liberale, nature illustration was associated with the production of books and with manuscript illumination; when it was taken up by oil painters, it was transformed in-to a different enterprise. The production of the *Museum* coincided with the efflores-cence after 1600 of easel paintings depicting landscapes, floral still lifes and animal scenes, such as those of Savery. The *Museum* is thus an important transitional monument, pointing retrospectively to the tradition of nature painting as defined by drawing, book illustration, and manuscript illumination, and prospectively to the newly ascendant practice of producing oil paintings treating floral and animal subjects. This development should also be seen as part of the larger dominance of oil painting as an artistic goal in Northern and Central Europe during the late six-teenth and early seventeenth centuries, manifested for example by both Hendrick Goltzius and Jacques de Gheyn's eventual abandonment of the graphic arts for painting. Hoefnagel, on the other hand, was not sympathetic to oil and continued to prefer water-soluble pigments on vellum, which he employed on a miniaturistic scale.

This narrative has sketched an account of the Emperor's strong and consistent

interest in nature painting throughout his reign. His patronage and collecting of nature painting parallels the expansion of the *Kunstkammer*, with its dualistic emphasis upon natural and human artifice, as well as that of the imperial collections of living specimens of animals and plants. As a microcosmic reflection of the greater whole, the imperial collections gave a large place to nature, with its sense of its vast extent strongly informed by the mounting weight of scientific research.

The Notion of the Wondrous in Rudolfine Nature Painting

The sixteenth-century explosion of exploratory travel and research into natural history produced a new awareness of the vastness of the global domain. So pervasive was this sense of discovery that often the concept of nature as a whole was identified with that part of the creation which was seen to exist outside the bounds of the normative – curiosities, marvels and wonders.[67] The tendency to frame the concept of nature in terms of the wondrous was common throughout Europe during the sixteenth and seventeenth centuries, but it seems to have had especially pointed meaning within Rudolfine nature painting.

10.16 JACOPO LIGOZZI
Cod.min 83
Fol. 3r (crabs)
[Vienna, Österreichische Nationalbibliothek, Handschriften- und Inkunabelsammlung]

Rudolfine nature painting is populated by actual natural wonders. The opening image of *Ignis: Animalia rationalia et insecta*, the first volume of Hoefnagel's *Four Elements*, presents Petrus Gonzales, a man inflicted with hirsutism, and his wife [fig. 10.18].[68] As both a human being, the pinnacle of creation, and a wonder, or exceptional natural phenomenon, Gonzales appears to function in the *Four Elements* as a herald of the wondrous character of nature as it will unfold throughout the rest of the manuscript.[69] While the *Four Elements* celebrates wondrous nature, it does not explicitly link the notion of the wondrous to the imperial setting. This, however, would seem to be the import of the portrait of Gonzales and his family which appears on the first folio of the *Museum* (Cod.min. 129, fol. 1r). Compared with Hoefnagel's image, in which Gonzales wears a grim expression, is well but not opulently dressed and is shown in a landscape setting that hints at his association with the mythic wild man, that in the *Museum* shows him smiling, at ease, clad in a splendid robe and gathered with his family in a grand, columned space. The image appears to assimilate the notion of the wondrous to the grandiosity of the imperial setting, and reciprocally characterizes this setting as itself home to the exceptional. The Emperor's collection, as displayed on the folios that follow, encompasses both the exotica discussed above and exceptional natural phenomena which, in addition to those already mentioned, include a snake whose tail sprouted a branch of leaves (Cod.min. 129, fol. 79r) and birds with two heads or three legs (Cod.min. 130, fols. 61r, 76r).[70] Another image of this type is Hans Hoffmann's rendering of a stag with monstrous horns, inscribed by the artist as having been drawn in Prague in 1589 [fig. 10.20].[71]

Key to the period fascination with wondrous nature was the pursuit of the sensations of shock, disquiet, surprise and delight evoked by confrontation with the new and the unexpected. The notion of the wondrous in turn shaped natural history illustrators' conception of their own artistic practice. In general, their imagery displays consciousness that the task constituted more than the detailed rendering of the specimen. Such imagery thus appears to have been calculated to exhibit wondrousness on two levels – that of the subject matter *per se*, and that of art.

Illusionism is thus a common feature of nature painting. Approaches to illusionism took various forms. That of Joris Hoefnagel grew directly out of 'strewn-

10.17 JACQUES DE GHEYN II
Album of Nature Studies
Fol. 15r (Two roses and a lily)
[Paris, Fondation Custodia,
Frits Lugt Collection]

'pattern' marginalia of late fifteenth-century Flemish manuscript illumination, which created the *trompe l'oeil* effect of insects alighting on blossoms that had been strewn on the page surface. Hoefnagel's debt to earlier manuscript illumination is particularly clear in the insect illustrations of *Ignis: Animalia rationalia et insecta*, in which the insects are never shown dead and pinned to the page, but alive and frequently alighting upon flowers.

Ligozzi, on the other hand, employed a quite different form of illusionism. The 'lifelike' quality of his specimens rests less with animation than with an effect of physical presence. His fish album (Cod.min. 83) and the bird album (Cod.min. 131), which if not by him is by a close follower, are large scaled. Ligozzi had a distinctive swelling, expansive way of modelling the specimens, which together with their large scale causes them to come forward in space dynamically, in a powerful, indeed confrontational, manner. In contrast to Hoefnagel's love of minutiae, which draws the eye inward, Ligozzi tended to treat larger specimens that expand outward, with their visual impact enhanced by his highly plastic form of illusionism. His approach is close to that of Giorgio Liberale in Archduke Ferdinand's dog and fish album (Cod.min.ser.nov. 2669), which itself contains copies after the illustrations for Ippolyto Salviani's treatise on fish, *Aquatilium animalium historiae*, published in Rome in 1554 [fig. 10.19]. Named in the author's preface as Bernardo Aretino, the creator of these illustrations is otherwise unknown.[72] The illustrations differ markedly from those in Northern European nature treatises of the period. They are engravings instead of woodcuts, are large scaled and take advantage of engraving's capacity to lend plasticity to forms through swelling, curvilinear modelling. Salviani's artist accentuated the strange, often grotesque forms of the fish, with this plus their effect of high relief calculated to create the effect of confronting an actual specimen. The styles of both Liberale and Ligozzi owe a large debt to this precedent.[73] In turn, the comparatively large scale of the specimens in the *Museum* seems to have been a continuation of the format preferred by Liberale and Ligozzi, as contrasted to the miniaturistic approach of Hoefnagel.

The two methods of illusionism described above also share certain features. One of these is the use of the blank ground, the brilliance of which strikes the viewer's eye. Silhouetted against the white ground, Ligozzi's specimens dynamically project off of the page. This contrasts with the grounds in the *Museum*, in which the colour reduces by comparison the contrast between specimen and ground and creates a mild sense of spatial recession rather than projection. Whereas the indeterminacy of the blank ground supports the effect that the painted specimen occupies a space contiguous with that of the viewer, the painted ground hints at the existence of a fictive pictorial space separate from the 'real' space of the viewer. In Hoefnagel's *Four Elements* and *Model Book of Calligraphy*, the brilliant white ground that sets off blooming plants and animated insects is both indeterminate and heightens the effect of their having magically materialized from a void.

Another important component of illusionism in natural history illustration is the exploitation of the vivid, jewel-like hues of water-based pigment. Their unadulterated brilliance, like that of the blank ground, strikes the eye and thus strengthens the illusionistic effect that the viewer is confronting nature. Brilliant colour in nature, moreover, appears to have been a source of wonderment. The close visual study of a specimen in order to capture the actual colours of nature was a strong

10.18 JORIS HOEFNAGEL
Ignis. Animalia Rationalia et Insecta from the *Four Elements*
Fol. I (Petrus Gonzales and his wife)
[Washington, D.C., The National Gallery of Art, Gift of Mrs Lessing J. Rosenwald, 1987]

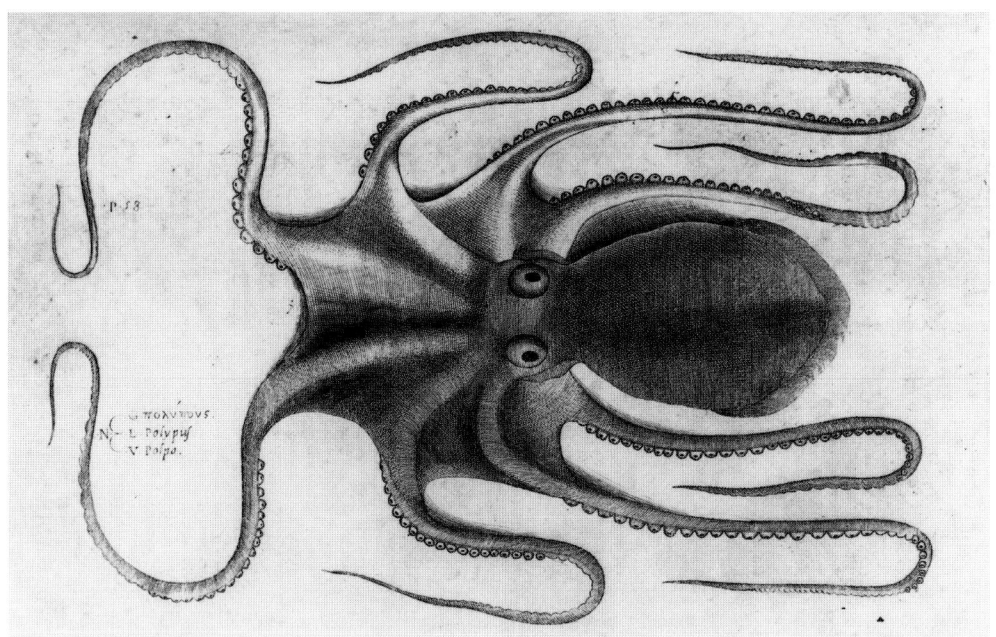

10.19 IPPOLYTO SALVIANI
Aquatilium animalium historiae
P. 159v (an octopus)
[Los Angeles, The Getty
Research Institute for the
History of Art and the
Humanities]

theme in the natural history illustration surveyed above. Groundbreaking in this respect was Dürer's *Wing of a Blue Roller*, which as much as it is a study in the anatomy of a bird's wing is an exploration of natural colour in its vast extent and variety.
With its focus on flowers, Hoefnagel's *Mira calligraphiae monumenta* forms an extended essay on natural colour and brings home the degree to which European
eyes were astonished by the world of colour opened up by newly imported ornamentals. Another high point in this exploration of natural colour is de Gheyn's previously mentioned album in Paris.[74] While Hoefnagel's manuscript consistently
seeks after brilliant hue and thereby points to nature's spontaneous creation of
colour and his own artistic ability to replicate the splendours of natural colour, de
Gheyn's album depicts vivid colour to be sure, but shows it in greater detail, broken down in individual specimens, even quite tiny ones, into myriad components.
De Gheyn's effort would appear to have been dictated by the spirit of intensive objective observation characteristic of evolving empiricism during the early seventeenth century. His rendering of the coloration of his specimens demonstrates observational powers so exacting as to call to mind microscopy as it was then developing in Holland and England.

The creation of the powerful illusion of confronting nature visually thus impart-
ed wondrousness to the artistic dimension of nature imagery, just as its subject
matter characterized nature in this way by showing the exotic, the extraordinary
and the newly recognized variety of creation. As such, the natural history imagery
discussed here at once fits into the context of Rudolfine art and broadens its scope.
In its quest for newness and the aura of the exceptional, this imagery parallels the
tendency of Spranger and other Rudolfine figure painters to strive towards new
and surprising heights of artistic virtuosity. Additionally, nature painting would
have functioned symbolically as enhancing the Emperor's power by bringing the
wondrousness of nature itself under the imperial aegis.

By appreciating its glorification of wondrous nature, one can envision the particular way in which nature painting enhanced the image of the Prague court. This
emphasis upon the wondrous suggests a larger effort on the Emperor's part to con-

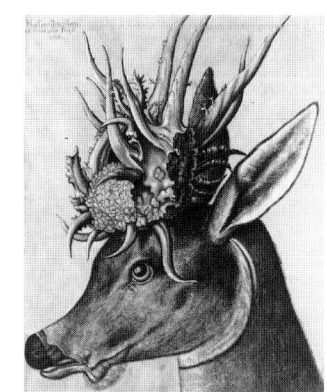

10.20 HANS HOFFMANN
A Stag with Monstrous Horns
[Berlin, Kupferstichkabinett,
Preussischer Kulturbesitz]

struct and advertise his own privileged relationship to nature, which in turn appears to have been expressed by his well-known occultism and his patronage of science, most notably the researches of the astronomers Kepler and Brahe.[75] There is a thread running through Hoefnagel's art as well as through the *Museum* that emphasizes nature's ultimate estrangement from normalcy and its identity as a vessel of secrets and mysteries.[76] This type of imagery could possibly have appealed to the emperor as an indication of his own access to nature's innermost secrets.

1. W. Blunt and S. Raphael, *The Illustrated Herbal* (New York, 1979), pp. 132–36; *Commentarii in libros sex Pedacii Dioscorides de Medica Materia. Adjectis quam plurimis plantarum et animalium imaginibus eodem authore* (Venice, Valgris, 1554), with 562 woodcuts; see. C. Nissen, *Die Botanische Buchillustration* (Stuttgart, 1951), p. 119, no. 1305.

2. Call no. 69.P.32. The book is mentioned in a letter from Mattioli written in Görz on 17 February 1554 to Ulisse Aldrovandi in Bologna. See C. Raimondo, 'Lettere di P.A. Mattioli ad Ulisse Aldrovandi', *Bollotino Senese di Storia Patria*, 23 (1906), letter 1554, 17.II. A hand-coloured example of 1558 (Vienna, Österreichisches Nationalbibliothek) and other hand-coloured examples in Prague and Dresden are mentioned in G. C. Cronberg, 'Giorgio Liberale e I Suoi Fratelli' in *Studi di Storia dell'Arte in Onore de Antonio Morassi* (Venice, 1971), p. 87 and in Nissen (note 1), p. 119, no. 1305.

3. Vienna, Österreichisches Nationalbibliothek, Handschriften- und Inkunabelsammlung, Codex Vindobonensis Med. Gr. 1; Blunt and Raphael (note 1), p. 16; O. Mazal, *Pflanzen, Wurzeln, Säfte, Samen: Antike Heilkunst in Miniaturen des Wiener Dioskurides* (Graz, 1981), p. 42 (for further bibliography).

4. *Herbarž*, Prague, 1562; Nissen (note 1), p. 119, no. 1314; D. Landau and P. Parshall, *The Renaissance Print* (New Haven and London, 1994), pp. 253–56.

5. Cronberg (note 2), pp. 85–96.

6. D. Ritter von Schönherr, 'Urkunden und Regesten aus dem k.k. Statthalterei-Archiv in Innsbruck', *Jahrbuch der Kunsthistorischen Sammlungen des Allerhöchsten Kaisershauses*, 11(1884): CLXXVII, Reg. nos. 7374, 10323; Cronberg (note 1), p. 86, n. 12.

7. H. Trnek in *Prag um 1600: Kunst und Kultur am Hofe Kaiser Rudolfs II.*, exh. cat. (Freren, 1988), vol 2, p. 138, under no. 602; Cronberg (note 1), pp. 90ff.

8. Vienna, Österreichisches Nationalbibliothek, Codex Miniatus S.N. 2669; Cronberg (note 1), pp. 89–90; *Prag um 1600* (note 7), vol. 2, pp. 135–38, no. 602; M. Staudinger in E. Irblick (ed.), *Thesaurus Austriacus: Europas Glanz im Spiegel der Buchkunst, Handschriften und Kalbstalben von 800 bis 1600*, exh. cat. (Vienna, 1996), pp. 210–25 (for further bibliography), no. 45.

9. *Summer* and *Winter* from the *Four Seasons* are dated 1563; *Fire* from the *Four Elements* is dated 1566; see T. DaCosta Kaufmann, *The School of Prague*, 2nd rev. edn (Chicago, 1988), pp. 164–67 (with further bibliography), nos 2.1–2.7; *idem*, 'The Allegories and Their Meaning' in P. Hulton *et al.*, *The Arcimboldo Effect: Transformations of the Face from the Sixteenth to the Twentieth Century*, exh. cat. (Venice, 1987), pp. 88–109; *idem*, 'Metamorphoses of Nature: Arcimboldo's Imperial Allegories' in *The Mastery of Nature: Aspects of Art, Science, and Humanism in the Renaissance* (Princeton, 1993), pp. 100–28.

10. Other important illustrated treatises of the era include Konrad Gessner, *Historia animalium lib. I* (Zürich, 1551); *Icones animalium quadrupedum* (Zürich, 1553); *De avium natura* (Zurich, 1555); *Historia animalium lib. IIII qui est de piscium...* (Zurich, 1558); Pierre Belon, *De aquatilibus libri duo* (Paris, 1553); Ippolyto Salviani, *Aquatilium animalium historia* (Rome, 1554); Guillaume Rondelet, *Libri de piscibus marinis* (Lyon, 1554); *Universae aquatilium historiae...* (Lyon, 1555). For a list of specimens in Arcimboldo's *Water* (Vienna, Kunsthistorisches Museum), see Hulton *et al.* (note 9), pp. 96–97.

11. Vienna, Österreichisches Nationalbibliothek, Handschriften- und Inkunabelsammlung, Cod.min. 42. See T. Vignau-Wilberg, 'Le "Muséum de l'empereur Rodolphe II" et le Cabinet des arts et curiosités' in H. Haupt *et al.*, *Le Bestiaire de Rodolphe II: Cod.min. 129 et 130 de la Bibliothèque nationale d'Autriche* (Paris, 1990), pp. 40–41.

12. R. J. W. Evans, *Rudolf II and His World: A Study in Intellectual History 1576–1612*, 2nd edn (Oxford, 1984), pp. 120–21; F. de Nave and D. Imhof, *Botany in the Low Countries (End of the 15th Century-ca. 1650)*, exh. cat. (Antwerp, 1993), pp. 98, 109.

13. J. Krcálová, 'Die Gärten Rudolfs II', *Leids Kunsthistorisch Jaarboek* (1982): 149–60; Staudinger in Haupt *et al.* (note 11), p. 340; Kaufmann, *The School of Prague* (note 9), p. 76.

14. Kaufmann, *The School of Prague* (note 9), p. 30.

15. H. Budde, 'Das "Kunstbuch" des Nürnberger Patriziers Willibald Imhoff und die Tier- und Pflanzenstudien Albrecht Dürers und Hans Hoffmanns', *Jahrbuch der Kunsthistorischen Sammlungen in Wien*, 82–83 (1986–87): 213–42; K. Achilles, 'Naturstudien von Hans Hoffmann in der Kunstsammlung des Nürnberger Kaufmanns Paulus II. Praun', *Jahrbuch der Kunsthistorischen Sammlungen in Wien*, 82–83 (1986–87): 243–60.

16. F. Koreny, *Albrecht Dürer and the Animal and Plant Studies of the Renaissance* (New York, 1988), pp. 148–49, no. 49; Kaufmann, *The School of Prague* (note 9), p. 215, no. 11.1.

17. Koreny (note 16), pp. 15–16, 136–37, 261–62; no. 43.

18. Vienna, Graphische Sammlung Albertina, 3133, 4840, 3173; Koreny (note 16), pp. 54–55, 84–85, 170–71, nos. 10, 22, 58.

19. See T. Vignau-Wilberg, 'Joris Hoefnagel's Tätigkeit in München', *Jahrbuch der Kunsthistorischen Sammlungen in Wien*, 81 (1985): 103ff.; T. Vignau-Wilberg, 'Joris Hoefnagel, The Illuminator', in L. Hendrix and T. Vignau-Wilberg, *Mira calligraphiae monumenta: A Sixteenth-Century Calligraphic Manuscript Inscribed by Georg Bocskay and Illuminated by Joris Hoefnagel* (Malibu, 1992), pp. 15–28.

20. Vienna, Österreichische Nationalbibliothek, Hand-schriften- und Inkunabelsammlung, Cod. 1784; see T. A. G. Wilberg Vignau-Schuurman, *Die emblematischen Elemente im Werke Joris Hoefnagels* (Leiden, 1969), vols I–II.

21. Washington, D.C., The National Gallery of Art, Gift of Mrs Lessing J. Rosenwald, 1987; watercolour and gouache on vellum, all four volumes bound in red leather; approximate page size 145 × 185 mm; collectively 274 miniatures plus six unfinished folios. There are also excised folios in various public and private collections. See M. Lee Hendrix, 'Joris Hoefnagel and "The Four Elements:" A Study in Sixteenth-Century Nature Painting' (Ph.D. dissertation, Princeton University, 1984); Kaufmann, *The School of Prague* (note 9), pp. 202–3, no. 9.1.

22. See further T. DaCosta Kaufmann, 'The Nature of Imitation: Hoefnagel on Dürer' in Kaufmann, *The Mastery of Nature* (note 9), pp. 79–99; Koreny (note 16), pp. 124–25, no. 38; pp. 138–39, no. 44.

23. Vignau-Wilberg in Hendrix and Vignau-Wilberg (note 19), p. 20.

24. Vienna, Kunsthistorisches Museum, 975; written by Bocskay in 1571–73 and illuminated by Hoefnagel in 1591–94; see Wilberg Vignau-Schuurman (note 20). Born at an unknown date in Razinia, a part of Croatia then belonging to Hungary, Bocskay served Emperors Ferdinand I and Maximilian II and died in Vienna in 1575; see T. Vignau-Wilberg, 'Georg Bocskay, The Calligrapher' in Hendrix and Vignau-Wilberg (note 19), pp. 7–14.

25. Kaufmann, *The School of Prague* (note 9), pp. 211–14; T. Vignau-Wilberg, *Archetypa Studiaque Patris Georgii Hoefnagelii 1592: Natur, Dichtung und Wissenschaft in der Kunst um 1600* (Munich, 1994).

26. Vignau-Wilberg in Hendrix and Vignau-Wilberg (note 19), pp. 21–23.

27. Los Angeles, The J. Paul Getty Museum, Ms. 20 (86.MV.527).

28. Bocskay's writing samples are dated 1561–62; approximate folio size 16.6 × 12.4 cm; written by Bocskay in a variety of inks including brown, carbon black and blue, with gold and silver leaf and painted gold; illuminated by Hoefnagel in watercolour and gouache, painted gold and silver; see Hendrix and Vignau-Wilberg (note 19).

29. E. F. Bleier (trans. and ed.), *Early Floral Engravings. All 1010 Prints from the "Florilegium" by Emanuel Sweerts* (New York, 1976), p. xi.

30. See J. A. Spicer-Durham, 'The Drawings of Roelandt Savery' (Ph.D. dissertation, Yale University, 1979), vol. 1, p. 19; Kaufmann, *The School of Prague* (note 9), p. 228.

31. *Ignis*, f. I, '1582'; *Terra*, ff. XXIX, '1575', and XXXIX, '1580'; *Aier*, ff. II, '1576', and IV, '1580'. There is disagreement about whether Hoefnagel was in contact with the Emperor as early as 1576 as well as whether he completed the major work on the *Four Elements* before entering imperial service or afterwards. For the fullest summary of the various points of view concerning these issues, see Kaufmann, *The School of Prague* (note 9), pp. 202–3, no. 9.1; Vignau-Wilberg in Haupt *et al.* (note 11), p. 34.

32. Carel van Mander, *Het Schilderboek* (Haarlem, 1604), fol. 263r.

33. As recognized by Kaufmann, *Drawings from the Holy Roman Empire 1540–1680: A Selection from North American Collections*, exh. cat. (Princeton, 1982), p. 156, no. 56; p. 157, no. 6; R. Bauer and H. Haupt (eds), 'Das Kunstkammerinventar Kaiser Rudolfs II.', *Jahrbuch der Kunsthistorischen Sammlungen in Wien*, 72 (1976), 14, inv. 230, 231.

34. Kaufmann, *The School of Prague* (note 9), pp. 40–54.

35. P. Dreyer discovered Verhagen, a major sixteenth-century nature illustrator, and noted Hoefnagel's reliance upon his work. The largest body of his work is in the Staatliche Museen Preussischer Kulturbesitz, Kupferstichkabinett, Berlin. It was presumed that another source of Hoefnagel's imagery was Hans Bol's three-volume series of albums in Copenhagen (see below, note 63) (see Hendrix [note 21], p. 40), but Dreyer has argued that both artists in fact copied from Verhagen. See P. Dreyer, 'Zeichnungen von Hans Verhagen dem Stummen von Antwerpen, Ein Beitrag zu den Vorlagen der Tierminiaturen Hans Bols und Georg Hoefnagels', *Jahrbuch der Kunsthistorischen Sammlungen in Wien*, 82–83 (1986–87): 115–144, esp. 129–30.

36. See, for example, Adrian Collaert's series of animal engravings entitled *Avium vivae icones* and *Piscium vivae icones* (Hollstein 616–47, 648–78) or Joost van den Vondel's prefatory description of the etched illustrations to his edition of Aesop's fables, in which he beckons his readers to 'note in particular the inspired hand of the artful painter, who has imitated the character (*wesen*) of things in such a pleasing and lively (*levendich*) manner, that nature herself seems to be surpassed' (my translation). See J. van den Vondel, *Vorstelijke warande der dieren* (Amsterdam, 1617), p. iii; Hendrix (note 21), pp. 74–80. The taste for illustrated fables was manifested at the Rudolfine court in Aegidius Sadeler's edition of Aesop's fables entitled *Theatrum Morum* (Prague, 1608), whose etched illustrations demonstrate the influence of the elder Hoefnagel, Savery, and other artists. See D. A. Limouze, 'Aegidius Sadeler (c. 1570–1629): Drawings, Prints, and Art Theory' (Ph.D. dissertation, Princeton University, 1989), pp. 198–202.

37. For example, in *View of Seville*, dated 1570 and 1573 (Brussels, Bibliotèque Royale), and in his entry in the *album amicorum* of Abraham Ortelius in Pembroke College, Cambridge; see J. Puraye (ed.), *Abraham Ortelius, Album Amicorum* (Amsterdam, 1969), fol. 12v, p. 21.

38. Also important in this regard are the encyclopaedic nature albums assembled by the doctor and naturalist Anselmus Boetius de Boodt, which reflect strong influence from the *Four Elements*; see M-C. Maselis, A. Balis and R.H. Marijnissen, *De Albums van Anselmus de Boodt (1550–1632). Geschilderde natuurobservatie aan het Hof van Rudolf II te Praag* (Tielt, 1989).

39. Kaufmann, *The School of Prague* (note 9), pp. 16, 76.

40. Vienna, Österreichisches Nationalbibliothek, Hand-schriften- und Inkunabelsammlung, Cod.min. 129 and 130; Vignau-Wilberg and Irblich in Haupt *et al.* (note 11), pp. 36–39, 65–66. The average folio measurement is 40 × 30–30.5 cm; cf. Staudinger (note 8), pp. 230–77, no. 47.

41. See Staudinger in Haupt *et al.* (note 11), p. 114, no. 9.

42. Bauer and Haupt (eds) (note 33), p. XXVII, nn. 58–59; Vignau-Wilberg and Irblich in Haupt *et al.* (note 11), pp. 38, 68; E. Fučíková, 'The Collection of

Rudolf II at Prague: Cabinet of Curiosities or Scientific Museum?' in O. Impey and A. MacGregor (eds), *The Origins of Museums: The Cabinet of Curiosities in Sixteenth- and Seventeenth-Century Europe* (Oxford, 1985), pp. 47–53.

43. Staudinger in Haupt *et al.* (note 11), pp. 122–23, 258–59, 302–3, nos. 13, 80, 101.

44. *Ibid.*, pp. 92–97, 109–10, 340–49. For more on Gonzales, see L. Hendrix, 'Of Hirsutes and Insects: Joris Hoefnagel and the Art of the Wondrous', *Word and Image*, 11:4 (October–December 1995): 373–90.

45. Bauer and Haupt (eds) (note 33), p. 135, inv. nos 2689, 2690, fol. 381r. The connection of these entries with the *Museum* was made by T. Vignau-Wilberg; see Haupt *et al.* (note 11), pp. 55–59.

46. Vienna, Kunsthistorisches Museum, 2334, 2335; see Vignau-Wilberg in Haupt *et al.* (note 11), pp. 56–57; Kaufmann, *The School of Prague* (note 9), pp. 287–89, cat. nos. 25.1, 25.3.

47. L. Tongiorgi Tomasi, 'Daniel Froeschl before Prague; His Artistic Activity in Tuscany at the Medici Court' in E. Fučíková (ed.), *Prag um 1600: Beiträge zur Kunst und Kultur am Hofe Rudolfs II* (Freren, 1988), pp. 289–98; Vignau-Wilberg and Staudinger in Haupt *et al.* (note 11), pp. 52–53, 376–77; and, for a broader account of Fröschl's oeuvre, Kaufmann, *The School of Prague* (note 9), pp. 173–77.

48. Tongiorgi Tomasi (note 47), pp. 295–96; Staudinger in Haupt *et al.* (note 11), p. 376.

49. Kaufmann, *The School of Prague* (note 9), p. 173.

50. Vignau-Wilberg in Haupt *et al.* (note 11), pp. 54–55.

51. See, for example, Hoefnagel's floral still life on vellum in the Ashmolean Museum, Oxford, inv. no. 56E; see Koreny (note 16), pp. 248–49, no. 91. That by Savery is in a private collection, New York; there is an autograph replica, also dated 1603, in Utrecht, Centraal Museum; see Spicer-Durham (note 30), vol. 1, p. 246; Kaufmann, *The School of Prague* (note 9), pp. 229–30, nos. 19.1, 19.2.

52. The parallel between the *Museum* and Savery's equine imagery was suggested by Vignau-Wilberg in Haupt *et al.* (note 11), p. 55; see *Stallion and Groom*, private collection, The Netherlands; Spicer-Durham (note 30), vol. 1, p. 161; Kaufmann, *The School of Prague* (note 9), pp. 230–31, no. 19.7; for the *spanischen Stallungen* ('Spanish Stables') see J. Krčálová, 'Die rudolfinische Architektur', *Leids Kunsthistorisch Jaarboek*, 1 (1982), 271–308; I. Muchka, 'Die Architektur unter Rudolf II., gezeigt am Beispiel der Prager Burg' in *Prag um 1600: Kunst und Kultur am Hofe Rudolfs II*, exh.cat. (Freren, 1988), pp. 81–9.

53. See Vignau-Wilberg in Haupt *et al.* (note 11), p. 55; Spicer-Durham (note 30), vol. 1, p. 162; Kaufmann, *The School of Prague* (note 9), p. 242, no. 19.46.

54. For comparison, see for example *Paradise*, signed and dated 1618 (Prague, Národní Galeri v Praze, DO 4245); *Landscape with Birds*, signed and dated 1628 (Kortrijk, Museum voor Schone Kunsten, 783); K. J. Müllenmeister *et al.*, *Roelandt Savery in Seiner Zeit (1576–1639)*, exh. cat. (Cologne, 1985), p. 95, no. 21; p. 145, no. 58; pp. 148–49; see Vignau-Wilberg and Staudinger in Haupt *et al.* (note 11), pp. 45, 162–63. A few folios in the *Museum*, which appear to be by the same hand, are sufficiently close to Savery's style to warrant consideration of his authorship. Cod.min. 128, fol. 48r, and Cod.min. 130, fols 17r, 69r, have a

55. Vignau-Wilberg in Haupt *et al.* (note 11), p. 41.

56. Koreny (note 16), pp. 28–29, no. 1; pp. 240–43, no. 88; Vignau-Wilberg in Haupt *et al.* (note 11), pp. 40–43.

57. Vignau-Wilberg in Haupt *et al.* (note 11), p. 41.

58. Koreny (note 16), p. 66.

59. Vignau-Wilberg in Haupt *et al.* (note 11), pp. 40–41. Copies of the images by Hoffmann appear in the *Museum* on fols 6r, 8r and 9r of Cod.min. 129 and of the cheetah on fol. 5r of the same manuscript.

60. Cod.min. 130, fols 20r, 36r, 45r; see Staudinger in Haupt *et al.* (note 11), pp. 320–21, 360–61, 378–79.

61. Dreyer (note 35), pp. 115–44; Koreny (note 16) pp. 130–31, no. 41.

62. See Koreny (note 16), pp. 66–67, no. 16.

63. Hans Bol, *Icones ... animalium*, Copenhagen, Kongelige Bibliothek, G. Kg. Samlg. 3471, I–III 8£; See Bauer and Haupt (eds) (note 33), p. 135, no. 2706, fol. 381; T. Vignau-Wilberg, 'Qualche disegni d'importancia: Joris Hoefnagel als Zeichnungssammler', *Münchner Jahrbuch der bildenden Kunst*, 38 (1987): 185ff.

64. Vienna, Österreichisches Nationalbibliothek, Handschriften- und Inkunabelsammlung, Cod.min. 83 and 131; Bauer and Haupt (eds) (note 33), p. 135, nos 2693, 2696; H. Trnek in *Prag um 1600* (note 52), vol. 2, pp. 138–43, nos. 603, 604. The attribution to Ligozzi of the album of bird illustrations (Cod.min. 131) is questionable; see Vignau-Wilberg in Haupt *et al.*(note 11), p. 35.

65. Inv. 5655; see K. G. Boon, *The Netherlandish and German Drawings of the XVth and XVIth Centuries of the Frits Lugt Collection* (Paris, 1992), vols 1, pp. 147ff, no. 80; 2, pls 162–83.

66. T. Vignau-Wilberg *et al.*, *Das Gebethuch Kurfürst Maximilians I. von Bayern: Bayerische Staatsbibliothek München, Clm 23640* (Frankfurt am Main, 1986), esp. pp. 106–16.

67. See Fučíková (note 42); J. Kenseth, *The Age of the Marvelous* (Hannover, NH, 1992); *Word and Image*, 11:4 (October–December, 1995) (issue entitled *Art and Curiosity*).

68. See the excellent account of him and further bibliography provided by Staudinger in Haupt *et al.* (note 11), pp. 90–97.

69. Hendrix (note 44).

70. Staudinger in Haupt *et al.* (note 11), pp. 254–55, 410–11, 440–41.

71. Berlin, Staatliche Museen Preussischer Kulturbesitz, Kupferstichkabinett, Hz. 2048; for further discussion and bibliography, see Kaufmann, *The School of Prague* (note 9), p. 216, no. 11.3.

72. C. Nissen, *Die Zoologischen Buchillustration* (Stuttgart, 1976), vol. II, p. 117; *idem*, *Schöne Fischbücher, Kurze Geschichte der ichthyologischen Illustration* (Stuttgart, 1951), p. 13.

73. Hendrix (note 21), p. 140.

74. See the research on the album by F. Hopper (forthcoming, as cited in Boon [note 65]); C. Swann, '"Ad vivum, naer het leven," From the Life: Defining a Mode of Representation', *Word and Image*, 11:4 (October–December 1995): 353–72.

75. See Evans (note 12), pp. 196–274.

76. Hendrix in Hendrix and Vignau-Wilberg (note 19), pp. 50–52.

Engraving at the Court of Prague

DOROTHY LIMOUZE

The reign of Rudolf II was contemporaneous with a period of great virtuosity and innovation in the field of engraving. His years of rule ran parallel to the careers of a number of gifted engravers: Hendrik Goltzius and his followers; Jan, Raphael and Aegidius Sadeler; Dominicus Custos and Lukas Kilian. These circumstances reflect more than a mere historical coincidence. Developments in the graphic media suggest that court patronage helped to stimulate the outpouring of talent between the 1580s and the early seventeenth century. The impact of that patronage was not only seen in the work of Aegidius Sadeler and other engravers in imperial service: in fact, artists across Northern Europe responded to the magnet of the Rudolfine court by producing novel and ambitious prints.[1]

11.1 AEGIDIUS SADELER
(after Pieter Stevens)
September, October
(from a series of The Twelve
Months)
[Prague, Národní galerie v
Praze]

The force of Rudolfine patronage extended well beyond the attraction of imperial wealth. It seems also to have shaped both the appearance and content of prints. Prague patronage gave rise to an expanded range of themeó and imagery because of the broader need for engravings within the spectrum of court representation. Engravings came to be microcosmic reflections of the court, describing its culture in ways not achievable by other artistic media. As multiples, prints were a favoured means of disseminating information about personages and events. And as with other products of court society, they were not merely documents but also expressions of imperial ideologies.[2]

It is possible to trace the beginnings of this development in printmaking to one Habsburg patron, Rudolf's great-great-grandfather Maximilian I. Selecting the woodcut medium, already widely used for broadcasting political and religious ideas, Maximilian initiated a number of print projects that would create a grandiose, quasi-mythological image of the Emperor for posterity. Maximilan engaged Hans Burgkmair, Albrecht Altdorfer, Lukas Cranach the Elder and Albrecht Dürer, as well as a series of talented woodblock cutters and publishers.[3] Yet these artists worked not from the court, but from their independent shops in Augsburg, Regensburg, Nürnberg and Wittenberg. The phenomenon of an engraver in residence at a court seems to have begun during the reign of Emperor Maximilian II with the appointment of Martino Rota.

Rota (Sibenik, Dalmatia, ca. 1520–Vienna 1583) was the first official engraver of Emperors Maximilian II and Rudolf II. Active in Venice, Florence and Rome in the 1550s and 1560s, he had acquired the titles of *canterfeeter* and *maller* (portraitist and painter) at Emperor Maximilian's court by 1573.[4] While the services for which we have payment records include the purchase of wood-carvings and an iron portrait for casting coinage, he left behind several engraved portraits of Habsburgs and members of the court in Vienna. A series of three portraits of Maximilian II in ceremonial armour and other regalia dates from between 1573 and 1575. His eldest sons, Rudolf and Ernst, were engraved in 1574 and 1576, respectively, wearing festive armour that is still partly intact and in the Habsburg treasury.[5] This group of portraits initiated a longer tradition of Hab-

sburg court portraiture which would occupy Rota's successor, Aegidius Sadeler.

Rota's 1574 portrait of Rudolf II (Bartsch 97) commemorates his coronation as king of Hungary, the first stage in his succession to the imperial throne. Wearing parade armour that reflects Roman models and carrying a baton of rule, Rudolf is shown in a similar pose to the three-quarter-length portrait of Julius Caesar in Titian's famous series for the Gonzaga of Mantua. The allusions to Caesar may have been intended to promote Rudolf as a worthy successor in the ongoing struggle with the Ottoman Turks. Rota's second engraving of Rudolf, from 1575, portrays him in the coronation regalia of his new position as king of Bohemia. In 1577, Rota re-engraved his 1574 portrait of Rudolf in armour to reflect the latter's new status as Holy Roman Emperor (Bartsch 97). In April of that same year, Rota was appointed to Rudolf's court, as a *conterfetter* and *pildhauer* (sculptor)[6], a post he held until his death in 1583.

Rota's rarely discussed prints include other subjects undertaken for Habsburg patrons. In addition to portraits, Rota composed and etched two allegories that show the Habsburgs victorious in their struggle against the Turks (Bartsch 107, 112). In the year of Rudolf's coronation as Holy Roman Emperor, Rota engraved an ambitious *Last Judgment* of his own composition (Bartsch 29), a work in the manner of his famous reproductive engraving after Michelangelo's painting in the Sistine Chapel (1569; Bartsch 28).[7]

From the 1580s on, Rudolf's growing reputation as a patron and the allure of Prague as an artistic centre drew the notice of engravers living abroad. Furthermore, the impressive group of painters and sculptors employed at the court, above all Bartholomeus Spranger, Hans von Aachen, Joseph Heintz the Elder and Adriaen de Vries, provided printmakers with inspired models for reproductive engravings. Jan Sadeler (Brussels 1550–Venice 1600), the gifted founder of a dynasty of Antwerp engravers, began engraving after Spranger's designs in 1580, five years before the earliest print by Goltzius after that artist. Two religious subjects that Sadeler engraved after Spranger, the striking *Christ Appearing to Mary Magdalen* and *Holy Family with Three Angels* (Hollstein 255, 300), were dedicated to members of the Prague court. While the dedications were authored by the court artist Spranger, the prints no doubt introduced Jan Sadeler's virtuosity to potential patrons. In 1580, Sadeler himself applied to the imperial court for permission to work within the empire.[8] His application was supported by Count Otto Heinrich von Schwarzenberg, a Bohemian noble whose majestic portrait was engraved by Sadeler in the same year. In 1588, Jan Sadeler brought his brother Raphael and cousin Aegidius from war-torn Antwerp to work, first in Frankfurt, and then for Rudolf's Wittelsbach relations at the courts of Cologne and Munich. The prints produced by this family in Munich are the most important and immediate precedents for Emperor Rudolf's patronage of reproductive engraving.[9]

The premier Dutch engraver Hendrick Goltzius (Mülbracht 1558–Haarlem 1617) also began to engrave after drawings by the imperial painter Spranger as early as 1585. Both prints after Goltzius' own design and prints after Spranger's drawings and reliefs bore dedications to members of the court. In 1586, Goltzius published a series of Roman Heroes after his own designs (Bartsch 94–103), with a dedication to Rudolf II. This significant series contains allusions to the house of Habsburg and to the concept of a world monarchy rivalling that of ancient Rome. Its title

page makes wistful references to harmony between the Habsburgs and the house of Orange.[10]

In 1587, Goltzius dedicated two extraordinary prints after Spranger models, the *Lamentation* (after a terracotta relief; Bartsch 273) and *The Wedding of Cupid and Psyche* (after a drawing; Bartsch 277), to Paul Sixt Trautson, marshal of the Imperial Curia, and to the powerful high steward, Wolfgang Rumpff. Further, Goltzius dedicated the second state of another engraving after Spranger, the elegant *Mars and Venus* (Bartsch 276), to another member of the Privy Council, Ottavio Spinola.[11]

The awarding of imperial *privilegia* became a further draw for engravers working within the Holy Roman Empire and the Dutch Provinces. These decrees served as copyrights against the pirating of one engraver's works by others. Jan Sadeler's application to the court from 1580 contained a request for a *privilegium*, which was granted him for a 10-year period beginning in 1581.

A *privilegium* was also applied for by the Antwerp engraver Dominicus Custos (Antwerp after 1550–Augsburg 1612), who settled in Augsburg and built an enterprise that would include three sons and his two stepsons, Lukas and Wolfgang Kilian. Custos was present at the Diet of Regensburg of 1594, where he began an engraved portrait of the Emperor.[12] He also dedicated a book of engravings to Rudolf's cousin, Archduke Ferdinand of Styria.[13] In October 1607, Custos and Lukas Kilian, travelled to Prague to request from the Emperor a *privilegium* – an official protection of ten years against the copying of their prints. The request was granted by the Emperor in January 1608.[14]

Hendrick Goltzius and his followers also enjoyed the use of imperial *privilegia*. In 1595, Goltzius was guaranteed the protection of his work for the coming six years.[15] Prints inscribed with this *privilegium* include not only engravings by Goltzius himself but also prints by his pupils Jacob Matham and Jan Saenredam, indicating that the *privilegium* covered his entire workshop. His stepson Matham's application for a *privilegium* in 1601[16] was clearly an extension of the first, which expired in that year. In 1606, an imperial decree granted the Dutch engraver Jan Muller a *privilegium* of six years, mentioning in particular his large and "elegantly engraved" *Adoration of the Shepherds* after Spranger (Bartsch 65).[17]

These engravers of international reputation had further incentives for acquiring *privilegia*. The provisions attached to them involved the submission of two or more impressions of each print to the imperial court. By this means, an artist's new work was continually brought before a large group of wealthy patrons.

By far the most significant printmaker at the court was Rudolf's imperial engraver, Aegidius (Gilis Sadeler; Antwerp ca. 1568–Prague 1628). Sadeler had emigrated to Germany and Italy with his cousins, Jan and Raphael, who were in contact with the Rudolfine court as early as 1580.[18] The activities of the Sadelers at the court of Wilhelm V in Munich, from around 1588 to 1595, anticipated the diverse and ambitious projects with which Aegidius would be engaged in Prague.[19] In 1597, during a second trip to Italy, Aegidius Sadeler was called to Prague, where he began a lifetime post as *Kaiserlicher Kupferstecher* (imperial engraver).[20] He continued in this capacity under Rudolf's successors, Emperors Matthias and Ferdinand II.

Living near Prague castle in the Mala Strana, Sadeler set up a workshop for engraving and etching, assisted at various times by Isaac Major, Johan Bara and a further family member, Marco Sadeler, who inherited many of Aegidius' printing

11.2 AEGIDIUS SADELER
*The Great (Vladisdlav) Hall of
Prague Castle*
1607
[Hollstein 150]

plates. While Aegidius, like his cousins Jan and Raphael, produced an enormous output, his work is distinguished by its innovations in subject matter and graphic technique. Often referred to as a reproductive engraver, he did make numerous prints after drawings and paintings by Renaissance and Mannerist artists. However, a significant part his oeuvre are the many engravings he made after his own compositions. He made several finished drawings and paintings as well, many of these dating from the period of Rudolf's reign.[21]

A major facet of Sadeler's activity involved the engraving of portraits, not only of Rudolf II, whom he portrayed in four different and equally striking images, but also of numerous other court dignitaries. With the exception of a few drawn from von Aachen, Spranger and de Vries, many of these portraits were made after Sadeler's own grisaille drawings of the sitters. The elegant formats he designed, as well as his great skill at capturing likenesses, made these prints models for many seventeenth-century engravers.

Sadeler's first portrait of Rudolf II, from 1603 (Hollstein 323), sets a likeness of the Emperor copied from Hans von Aachen in an ornate architectural frame adorned with personifications and devices. The allegorical frame was drawn from a type developed by Hans von Aachen and Pieter Isaacs. Sadeler's second dated portrait, of 1604 (Hollstein 322), revived the format of Rota's print *Rudolf II as King of Hungary*. The image looks back to Titian's portraits of Charles V in Armour and Julius Caesar, evoking a longer tradition of Habsburgian references to the Roman Empire. Sadeler's third portrait of Rudolf II on horseback (fig. 5) sets a lost model by Adriaen de Vries against a battle scene inspired by Tempesta's engraving *King Henri IV on Horseback*. Sadeler's fourth work is a small etching done at the time of the Emperor's death and showing him floating up to heaven in a carriage drawn by his symbols, the eagle and the lion.[22]

Sadeler's prints after and in the manner of Albrecht Dürer played a significant role among his works for Rudolf II. An avid collector of Dürer's paintings, prints and drawings, the Emperor even kept a number of engraving plates by Dürer and his contemporary Lucas van Leyden, along with several plates by Sadeler.[23] Rudolf's patronage of the 'Dürer Renaissance' has been discussed, not only as an example of his informed habits of collecting but also as an emulation of the grand patronage of his forerunner, Emperor Maximilian I. The wave of copies and imitations of Dürer has also been seen as the pictoral expression of Renaissance imitation theory and as the sign of a new interest in art-historical traditions.[24] Sadeler made exquisite engravings after several drawings acquired by the Emperor from the estate of Cardinal Granvelle. Sadeler also composed Düreresque works, after the fashion of the *Meesterstukjes* of Goltzius.

As imperial engraver, Sadeler was given the task of reproducing works by other court artists, although his artistic contacts with three of these figures predate his arrival in Prague. During periods of activity in Munich and Rome, Sadeler had engraved compositions by Joris Hoefnagel, Hans von Aachen and Joseph Heintz. In Prague, Sadeler made one further engraving after a Heintz composition in the Emperor's collection: the *Diana and Actaeon*, a print that is remarkable for its delicate burin work and rich modulations of tone.

In fact, the artist with whom Aegidius Sadeler worked most closely during his first years in Prague was Bartholomeus Spranger. The two artists produced five dra-

matic prints, each a model of its genre. The engraved *Wisdom Conquering Ignorance*
(Hollstein 115) draws multilayered meanings from a larger body of court imagery
and both Christian and pagan sources. It combines Rudolfine references to the
flourishing of the arts and intellectual pursuits at Rudolf's court, and at the same
time, it evokes the medieval *psychomachia*, found in many Renaissance princely allegories, as well as the theme of Christ's Resurrection.[25] Two other prints after
Spranger, the portraits *Pieter Brueghel* and *Bartholomeus Spranger with His Deceased
Wife Christina Müller* (Hollstein 279, 332), are profound tributes to artists of the
past and present. The finely conceived and executed allegorical portraits involved
Sadeler and Spranger in an extraordinary intellectual and artistic collaboration.[26]

During Sadeler's service as court engraver, the Rudolfine artists also employed
other printmakers to reproduce their work.[27] If so, this may reveal that the artists in
question favoured the more obviously mannered burin techniques of these engravers, both of whom were close followers of Goltzius. On the other hand, an examination of Sadeler's circumstances suggests a different reason. The great quantity and variety of prints which he produced under Rudolf II indicate that he did not
have the luxury of working exclusively with a given court artist.

By far Sadeler's most extensive collaborations with Prague artists involved the cycles of landscape prints which he and his assistants engraved between ca. 1604 and
the end of his career. The models for these series were drawings by the court artists
Roelandt Savery, Pieter Stevens and the Flemish painter Jan Brueghel, who visited
Prague in 1604.[28] The engravings after Savery and Stevens contain not only views of
Prague [fig. 11.1], but also many references to woodlands, swamps, mountains and
villages of Bohemia and the Tyrol, the regions in which these artists travelled. As
they are idealized distillations of sketches from life, the landscapes are imaginary
views of these regions. At the same time, the cultural specificity of the farms, mining
towns and alpine forests may have had propagandistic intent, each image a celebration of Rudolf's hereditary domains. The concepts behind these print cycles, as well
as the virtuoso engraving technique, made them important models for the landscapes of Rubens and the seventeenth-century Dutch printmakers.

A rare document reveals the Emperor's interest in the topographical, documentary and ultimately political value of landscape engravings. In 1604, the Augsburg
engraver Wilhelm Peter Zimmermann was paid for prints of 'Hungarian cities, fortifications, castles and houses, from the beginning of his majesty's reign up to the
present'. This project seems to have been directed towards asserting the imperial
claim to lands under continual threat of Turkish conquest. Sadeler acted as a go-
between in this project.[29] Sadeler served also as an intermediary and mentor to
another printmaker when he published the extraordinary, topographically precise
View of Prague engraved by Johannes Wechter after drawings by the court embroiderer Philipp van den Bossche.[30]

The tribute to the imperial city in the *View of Prague* was complemented by
Sadeler's print of the grandest interior within Prague castle, the celebrated *Vladislav
Hall* of 1607 (Hollstein 150; fig. 11.2). Labelling his print a *sciographia*, or architectural perspective, Sadeler captured the spatial expanse of the hall with its complex
ribbed vaulting. The scene is filled with clusters of courtiers, including the Emper-
or himself in the background at the left, and is lined with booths for selling art
objects, among them an engravings stall, in which a bearded figure, perhaps Sadel-

11.3 AEGIDIUS SADELER
Ferdinand II on Horseback
1629
[Hollstein 287]

er himself, stands behind the counter. Sadeler's print is seen as a symbol of the centrality of the arts to daily life at the court and to the imperial enterprise.[31]

Sadeler and other court artists also made significant sets of book illustrations, which reflect the intellectual and political interests of the court. Notable among these were the *Archetypa* of Joris and Jacob Hoefnagel, the *Symbola divina*, an encyclopaedia of the imprese of rulers, past and present, engraved by Sadeler after Ottavio Strada, and the *Theatrum morum*, Sadeler's expanded edition of an earlier illustrated Aesop.

Aegidius Sadeler remained in Prague after the death of Rudolf II, retaining his post as imperial engraver to Rudolf's successors Matthias and Ferdinand II. The character of his official engravings changed to reflect the increasingly reactionary climate of the court. Concentrated doses of traditional Habsburg iconography inform Sadeler's four portraits of Emperor Matthias and Empress Anna (Hollstein 273, 309, 310), while his last known print, *Emperor Ferdinand on Horseback* (Hollstein 287; fig. 11.3), reflects the militarism and hatred of Protestant insurgents which fuelled the Thirty Years' War.[32]

Less in demand as a court artist, Sadeler was freer to establish contacts with artists working outside the court, notably Joachim von Sandrart. A relaxation of imperial patronage also allowed him to develop new types of subject matter. His late work had a demonstrable impact not only upon figures of the Bohemian Baroque, such as Wenceslaus Hollar and Karel Skréta, but upon Rubens and other artists from Sadeler's native Antwerp.[33]

The career of Aegidius Sadeler best illustrates the impact of Rudolfine patronage upon the art of engraving. Rudolf II was not only an avid collector of the graphic arts; he also became an ideal patron, sought after by engravers across Northern Europe. The special efforts made by engravers to attract his patronage affected both the physical appearance and content of engraving in the late sixteenth century. Prints designed for court dedications increasingly reflected the luxury of large, expensive sizes of paper. This expanded format gave artists greater freedom to improvise with burin techniques, innovating with linear patterns and increasing their tonal ranges to a degree only surpassed by the mezzotint.

Arguably, Rudolfine patronage also added new categories and levels of meaning to the subject matter of prints. The symbolic repertory found in prints from the time of Maximilian I and Charles V was revived and greatly augmented. Allegories that had earlier incarnations at the courts of France, Italy and Bavaria – such as the mystical Hermathena motif, or the theme of the ruler as protector of the arts – were given magnificent new form in the prints of Aegidius Sadeler and Jan Muller. The new court of Prague called for ever new discourses of ennoblement, which had profound consequences for the artistic, intellectual and propagandistic content of the print media.

1. On this general subject, see R. J. W. Evans and Eliska Fučíková, *The Stylish Image: Printmakers to the Court of Rudolf II*, exh. cat. (Edinburgh, 1991); Teréz Gerszi, 'Zeichnung und Druckgraphik,' in *Prag um 1600: Kunst und Kultur am Hofe Rudolfs II.*, exh. cat. (Freren, 1988), pp. 301–27. On print imagery generated by court patronage, see Dorothy Limouze, 'Taking the High Road: Netherlandish Engravers at the Courts of Munich and Prague', *Blockpoints: Annual Journal of the Block Gallery, Northwestern University* (1993; in press), 28–45.

2. R. J. W. Evans, *Rudolf II and His World: A Study in Intellectual History, 1576–1612* (Oxford, 1973), p. 128; Thomas DaCosta Kaufmann, *The School of Prague: Painting at the Court of Rudolf II* (Chicago, 1988); Dorothy Limouze, 'Aegidius Sadeler (c. 1570–1629):

Drawings, Prints and Art Theory' (Ph.D. dissertation, Princeton, 1990), chap. 1, 5; Herbert Haupt, 'Der Türkenkrieg Kaiser Rudolfs II. 1593-1606' in *Prag um 1600* (note 1), pp. 87-125.

3. Most recently discussed by David Landau and Peter Parshall, in *The Renaissance Print, 1470-1550* (New Haven, 1994), pp. 206-13, 217-18.

4. Luigi Servolini in *Allgemeines Lexikon der bildenden Künstler*, vol. XXIX (Leipzig, 1935), p. 82; Szilvia Bodnár in *Meisterzeichnungen des Künstlerkreises um Kaiser Rudolf II. aus dem Szépmüvészeti Múzeum in Budapest*, exh. cat. (Salzburg, 1987), pp. 62-67. Both date Rota's court appointment to 1568. Documents beginning in 1573 were published by W. Boeheim in 'Urkunden und Regesten aus der K. K. Hofbibliothek', *Jahrbuch der Kunsthistorischen Sammlungen des Allerhöchsten Kaiserhauses*, 9 (1888).

5. Bruno and Christiane Thomas, 'Die Sogenannte Dreiprinzengarnitur in Wien: Neue Erkenntnisse und Ergebnisse', *Jahrbuch der Kunsthistorischen Sammlungen in Wien*, 79 (1983), pp. 19-42; the drawings discussed in Bodnár (note 4).

6. Boeheim (note 4), p. clxix, no. 5369.

7. Rota dedicated his other prints on this theme to Emanuelo Philiberto, duke of Savoy, and to Rudolf's physician, Anselmus Boetius de Boodt, in thanks for medical care.

8. Hans von Voltelini, 'Urkunden und Regesten aus dem K. und K. Haus-, Hof-, und Staats-Archiv in Wien', *Jahrbuch der Kunsthistorischen Sammlungen des Allerhöchsten Kaiserhauses*, 15 (1894), lxxx-lxxxii, nos. 11938, 11939, 11949. All Sadeler documents cited here are reprinted in Limouze (note 2) Appendix I.

9. On the Sadelers in Cologne and Frankfurt, see Dorothy Limouze, 'Protestant Madonnas Revisited: Iconographic Duality in Works by Jan Sadeler and Joos van Winghe' in *A Tribute to Robert A. Koch* (Princeton, 1994), pp. 115-25. On artistic connections between Munich and Prague, see Eliška Fučíková, 'Über die Tätigkeit Hans von Aachens in Bayern', *Münchener Jahrbuch der Bildenden Kunst*, 21 (1970), pp. 129-42.

10. See E. K. J. Reznicek, *Die Zeichnungen von Hendrik Goltzius*, 2 vols (Utrecht, 1961); Lawrence W. Nichols, 'The "Pen Works" of Hendrick Goltzius', *Bulletin of the Philadelphia Museum of Art* (Winter, 1992), 14, 17.

11. Discussed as reflections of court patronage in Limouze, 'Taking the High Road' (note 1), 30-31, 35. Note that the present essay revises the information on print dedications given in that article.

12. See Mungo Campbell in Evans and Fučíková (note 1), cat. 2.

13. Hans von Voltelini, 'Urkunden und Regesten aus dem K. und K. Haus-, Hof-, und Staats-Archiv zu Wien', *Jahrbuch der Kunsthistorischen Sammlungen des Allerhöchsten Kaiserhauses*, 19 (1898), cix, no. 17000.

14. *Ibid.* lxxix, lxxxiii, nos. 16748, 16787.

15. Lawrence W. Nichols, citing earlier publications, in 'Hendrick Goltzius – Documents and Printed Literature Concerning His Life', *Nederlands Kunsthistorisch Jaarboek*, 42-43 (1991-92), 82, 91.

16. The document is mentioned in Lena Widerkehr 'Jacobus Matham Goltzij Privignus: Jacob Matham graveur et ses rapports avec Hendrick Goltzius', *Nederlands Kunsthistorisch Jaarboek*, 42-43 (1991-92),

232, 255, n. 48.

17. Voltelini (note 13), lxiv, no. 16602. On Muller's association with the Prague court, see Jan Piet Filedt Kok, 'Jan Harmensz. Muller as Printmaker – I', *Print Quarterly*, 11:3 (September 1994), 223-63; Lars Olof Larsson, 'Bildhauerkunst und Plastik am Hofe Rudolfs II' in *Prag um 1600* (note 1), pp. 174-76.

18. For the revised birth date of Aegidius and new information regarding his relationship to Jan and Raphael Sadeler, see Isabelle de Ramaix, 'Les Sadeler: De damasquineur à graveur et marchand d'estampes: Quelques documents inédits', *Le Livre & l'estampe*, 35 (1989), 7-46. The death date of Aegidius is from a previously unnoticed reference in Otto Doering (ed.), 'Hainhofers Reisen nach Innsbruck und Dresden', *Quellenschriften für Kunstgeschichte*, 10 (1910) 91.

19. See Fučíková (note 9); Limouze (note 2) chap. 4, 5.

20. See documents cited in Limouze (note 2), pp. 424-26, 434.

21. An initial oeuvre of drawings and paintings is discussed in Limouze (note 2), chaps 3-5, and pp. 465-73.

22. The current attribution of this work to Johann Matthias Wacker von Wackenfels in discussed by Eliš-ka Fučíková in 'Studien zur rudolfinischen Kunst: Addenda und Corrigenda', *Umění* 27:6 (1979), 507. Limouze (note 2), pp. 215-16, argues on the basis of the inscriptions that Wackenfels' initials indicate him to be the author of the poem beneath the image.

23. See Rotraud Bauer and Herbert Haupt (eds) 'Das Kunstkammerinventar Kaiser Rudolfs II., 1607-1611', *Jahrbuch der Kunsthistorischen Sammlungen in Wien*, 36 (1976), 104-6.

24. Limouze (note 2), pp. 143-48, 220-21, n. 11, with citations of earlier literature.

25. Most recently discussed by Fučíková in *Prag um 1600* (note 1), pp. 281-82. See also Kaufmann, (note 2), pp. 265-66.

26. See Limouze (note 2), pp. 152-55, 388ff.

27. Kok (note 17) discusses Muller's prints after Spranger and de Vries (see p. 224). Jürgen Zimmer, *Joseph Heintz der Ältere als Maler* (Weissenhorn, 1971), esp. pp. 60ff., discusses Heintz's collaboration with Lukas Kilian.

28. See the catalogue entries on landscape prints by Joaneath Spicer and An Zwollo in *Prag um 1600* (note 1), pp. 418-19, 426-28, and the discussions in Limouze (note 2), pp. 185-97, 285-92.

29. W. Boeheim, 'Urkunden und Regesten aus der K. K. Hofbibliothek', *Jahrbuch der Kunsthistorischen Sammlungen des Allerhöchsten Kaiserhauses* (1889), xiv, no. 5629. A further payment for unspecified work was made to Zimmermann in 1613 (see Heinrich Zimmerman in *Jahrbuch der Kunsthistorischen Sammlungen des Allerhöchsten Kaiserhauses* [1910-11], vii, no. 19548). Also see Géza Galavics, 'Die Rudolfinische Kunst und Ungarn' in E. Fučíková (ed.), *Prag um 1600: Beiträge zur Kunst und Kultur am Hofe Rudolfs II* (Freren, 1988), pp. 63-69.

30. Fučíková, 'Veduta v rudolfínském krajinárství', *Umění*, 31 (1983), 391-99; Limouze (note 2), pp. 353-58.

31. Evans (note 2), pp. 183-84; Kaufmann (note 2), pp. 102-3; Limouze (note 2), pp. 176-80.

32. See Limouze (note 2), pp. 277-79. The print was completed posthumously (see above, note 18).

33. Limouze (note 2), pp. 363-69.

Pictor Doctus: Drawing and the Theory of Art around 1600

THEA VIGNAU-WILBERG

12.1 JAN MULLER
(after Bartholomeus
Spranger)
*Mercury Takes the Young Artist
to Minerva*
1628

In 1628, Jan Muller made the engraving entitled *Mercury Takes the Young Artist to Minerva* [fig. 12.1].[1] According to the text below the image, Muller based his work on a design which Bartholomeus Spranger had made in 1592 for a relative of his, the young painter G. (Georgius?) Spranger; a generation later, the latter in turn left the engraving to his eldest son, Matthias Spranger, who apparently was also to become a painter.[2] The young artist, kneeling and dressed in an ox's hide, is shown being crowned with a laurel wreath by Minerva, who also holds a palm frond in readiness. Behind the young man stands Mercury, who speaks on his behalf to the goddess. In his right hand, he has a quill; an ink bottle and writing tools lie by him on the ground; a book is propped open. Minerva's aegis is secured to the back of her throne. Taut ropes lead from it to the vices she has conquered. Scaling Mount Helicon in the left background are the Arts, recognizable by their attributes. Poised above the central scene, the allegorical figure of Fame holding two sackbuts proclaims the artist's glory.[3]

The two lines of old Dutch above the image[4] are a free rendering of the six lines of Latin below it:

Impigro Iuveni specioso pelle bovina
condecorat caput & lauro Palmaque Minerva

Mercurio ductore, opibus ditatur abunde

Quem labor & studium ingenuas conducit ad artes,
Famaque eum super Aetherea & Mortalia tollit!
Invide, segnis, Iners arctis froenabers habenis.
A[ugerius] Clutius[5]

(Minerva decorates the zealous youth, beautiful in his ox's hide,[6] with a laurel wreath for his head and also a palm frond. Thus rich treasures are showered on the one who, with Mercury's guidance, is led to the arts by diligent work and the practice of his natural talent, and fame raises him above heaven and earth. O Envy, Sloth and Ignorance, you are restrained by taut bindings).

Using both text and image, the print declares in no uncertain terms that art will only bestow immortal fame on the artist if he pursues his talent with diligence, tirelessly extending his knowledge and avoiding feelings of envy.

Another work from the 1590s is an engraving by Aegidius Sadeler, *Minerva Leads Painting to the Liberal Arts* [fig. 12.2],[7] after a drawing by Hans von Aachen. Here, too, the interpretation of the image is assisted by an accompanying text. Von Aachen is named as having made the drawing, with Sadeler as the maker of the engraving.[8] Four couplets describe the image:

Nobile si quid humus, si quid tenet Amphitrite
Spectatu dignum si quid olympus habet

Aemula naturae dextra pictura potenti
Semper victuras transtulit in tabulas.

Sed rudis est omnis culta sine Pallade forma;
Si coniurarint pulchrius hic quid erit

Et comes ambabus si venerit inclyta virtus
Undique perfectum laurea cinget opus

(When the earth is home to something noble, when the sea, when the heavens contain something worthy of sight, then skilled Painting, competing with mighty Nature, has transferred it to wooden panels, which will live on forever. Indeed every
form is raw without cultured Minerva: when Pictura and Minerva unite – what is
there more beautiful? And when Virtue, renowned far and wide, comes to lend her
company to the other two, she will crown the wholly perfect work with laurel leaves).

12.2 AEGIDIUS SADELER
(after Hans von Aachen)
*Mercury Leads Painting to the
Liberal Arts*
1595/97
[Hollstein 114]

Pictura, recognizable by her palette, paintbrush and maulstick, is led by
Minerva[9] to a gathering of the Liberal Arts. Grammar (who is writing), Arithmetic
(counting on her fingers) and Geometry (with compasses and globe) together
forming the so-called trivium. Also identifiable are Music (musical instruments),
Astronomy (armillary sphere), Dialectic (reading a book and gesticulating) and
Rhetoric (caduceus), forming the so-called quadrivium.[10] Painting is moving away
from Sculpture's unfinished work (one arm is missing, a hammer and a chisel are
lying on the ground). Virtue, moral perfection, is not represented as a female allegory but by Hercules, standing on a podium in the left background. The work is
dedicated to Duke Maximilian of Bavaria (later Elector), who by 1595 had already
largely taken over from his father, Wilhelm V, before officially succeeding him in
1597.[11] This engraving cannot, therefore, have been made before 1595. Since the
post of court engraver to Rudolf II was conferred on Sadeler in 1597, the engraving
must have been made at some point between 1595 and 1597.[12]

The meaning of this print is also clear: amongst the visual arts, painting is the
most universal. It alone has the capacity to represent accurately the world as we
perceive it. However, only intellectual activity will raise it above the level of a craft
and allow it to join the circle of Liberal Arts. Individual works will only achieve perfection if and when a gifted, skilled, learned artist is, in addition to all of this, a person of high moral standing.

These engravings are not hard to interpret for all their intricate composition,
varied foreshortening, virtuosic representation of human bodies and limbs, elegant
movement and lively drapery. They are more like clear manifestos on the notion of
painting as an art form and on the self-image of the painter as an artist.

These two profound allegorical works are the easier to understand and contex-
tualize if they are viewed against the background of contemporary international
discourse regarding the status of painting. This debate, which had been restricted
in the fifteenth and early sixteenth centuries to Italy, moved northwards in the second half of the sixteenth century.

By 1590, over 50 years had elapsed since Leon Battista Alberti's tract *De Pictura*,
completed in 1435, had appeared in print.[13] Once published, this work had a far-
reaching influence on ideas as to what painting was. First and foremost, it disseminated the notion of painting as an art form, which in turn made new demands on

painters. Alberti's approach differed markedly from the traditional view of painting and painters. In the sixteenth century south of the Alps, the status of painting was already high. North of the Alps, however, it was regarded primarily as a craft. The Netherlandish and German artists of the time were practically all firmly locked into guilds and 'worshipful companies'. Whereas the more or less contemporary *Commentarii* by Lorenzo Ghiberti (unpublished) still reflects the practices of the artist-craftsman in his workshop, the painter in Alberti's tract is seen as a creative artist, and importance is laid on his education, social standing and ethical and moral behaviour. Alberti himself, versed in humanist culture, was both artist and theorist, with a concept of art firmly rooted in Classical traditions.[14]

The basic line of thought of the tract is not new. It goes back to the writings of Antiquity, in which Nature is the mistress of all things[15] and in which the two poles of *ingenium* and *industria*, natural talents and diligence, are required in any creative activity.[16] After a discussion in the first book of the technical problems of drawing for the painter, in Book II Alberti comes to his main concern – that is, the question of what painting actually is. He arrives at the conclusion that painting has divine powers in its capacity to represent people and objects which are absent (Book II, 25). The painter is like a divine creator; thus painting is the mistress of all the arts (Book II, 26). Alberti declares that it is not his intention to write a history of art as Pliny did, but rather to fathom its being by looking at examples from Antiquity. The art of painting was then held in particularly high esteem in Greece and Rome.[17] Greek slaves, on the other hand, were not allowed to receive instruction in painting, which was only worthy of free spirits and noble intellects.[18] According to Alberti, the painter's highest goal was the *historia*. A *historia* worthy of admiration would captivate both the learned and the unlearned viewer by virtue of the variety of objects and beings it represented. The poses and garments of the figures should be varied, and there was to be no ugliness. The movements of the figures should be diverse, convincing and true to nature. The same kind of accuracy should also be the aim in the portrayal of inanimate objects (Book II, 40ff.).

In Alberti's view, the painter had to possess outstanding technical skills (Book I). His paintings must captivate and enrich the viewer (Book II). However, he believed that the necessary prerequisites of painting as an art form were intellectual and ethical. These are the subject of the third book of his tract.[19] The painter had to be educated in the liberal arts, particularly in geometry. He had to study poets and orators, for their use of ornament was closely related to his own.[20] *Inventio*, as the most important component of poetry, was crucial in the preparation of the *historia*, which could even be pleasing without pictorial representation, as could be seen from Lucian's description of the painting of Calumny by Apelles.[21] All those who wanted their work to be valued by future generations had first of all to plan it thoroughly and then to carry it out with the utmost diligence. For diligence was just as essential as natural ability (Book III, 61).[22] Like Apelles, one had to submit oneself to the criticism of friends and other spectators, for painting had a social role, namely to please the public (Book III, 62).[23]

Alberti understood art as an exceptional activity; in his view, the artist was chosen amongst men and, although mortal, nevertheless re-created and re-interpreted living beings and nature. His beliefs about the necessary achievements and interests of artists were wholly relevant to art in Italy in the fifteenth and sixteenth centuries. Alberti's *De Pictura* laid the foundations of the image of the artist and his role in society that typified the late Renaissance both south and north of the Alps.

Alberti was the first writer to define painting as an art form, an idea which was to have a deep and lasting effect on the way painters saw themselves. The first theoretical work on art written outside of Italy, Karel van Mander's *Grondt der edel vry schilder-const*, was wholly influenced by *De Pictura*, even if the text rarely refers directly to Alberti's work – as Hessel Miedema showed in his thought-provoking edition – but rather to the German version by Walther Rivius (Ryff). Van Mander wrote his *Grondt* between 1596 and 1603, and it was not published until 1603/4. He had returned from a journey to Italy in 1577 and had settled in Haarlem in 1583. Here, as in Prague, there were strict rules and directives which ranked painting no higher than a craft, and painters were in the same guild as tinkers and others of that ilk.[24] Despite the presence of such forward-looking artists as Jan Muller's teacher, Hendrick Goltzius, conditions in Haarlem were not to change to any significant degree until 1631.[25]

12.3 PIETER BREUGEL THE ELDER
Landscape with Mercury Carrying off Psyche
1553

Van Mander laid down even more clearly than Alberti the skills which were essential if one were to become a good artist.[26] The main requirement was a natural gift (*ingenium*); this talent was then to be developed (*ars*, skill) and practised (*exercitatio, usus*). As the Netherlandish title of his book shows, van Mander already regarded painting without restrictions as a noble, liberal art, as one of the 'artes liberales'. As far as he was concerned, only nobly born children who lived honourable, virtuous lives could practise this art; *Wellevenheit* – that is to say, morally impeccable behaviour – was the *sine qua non*.[27] The young, talented painter had to apply himself zealously and not let himself be drawn into indolence or envy.[28]

From this vantage point, the interpretations suggested above for the engravings by Jan Muller after Spranger and by Aegidius Sadeler after von Aachen appear all the more compelling. In both cases, there is a pictorial representation of an intellectual programme which was current in advanced art circles – first in Italy, then, in the sixteenth century, north of the Alps as well – and which had first been laid down in Alberti's *De Pictura*.

There are other engravings which may be seen as part of the theoretical debate about art in the late sixteenth century. First, however, mention might be made of two texts from Antiquity which exercised a major influence on Alberti's tract and on the whole area of art theory in the 1500s. Although about poetry rather than painting, Aristotle's *Poetics* and Horace's *Ars Poetica*[29] nevertheless left their mark on almost all theoretical writing about art in the sixteenth and seventeenth centuries. They were read not only by literary scholars, but by humanists, art theorists and visual artists and formed, so to speak, the Antique foundations for new developments. The later of the two, Horace's *Ars Poetica*, was also the more influential; it is as though Aristotle's earlier demands were embedded in it. For the main issue in the *Ars Poetica* is less literature than the question of attitudes to art in general. This is not a descriptive volume of poetics, but a programmatic text with what we might today call a particular agenda.[30] This explains the work's influence on other art forms, particularly on painting, to which Horace often refers in his text.

These two works by Aristotle and Horace seemed to confirm and complement each other. When humanists then attempted to gather together the knowledge of Antiquity into a coherent whole, there were attempts to integrate elements of the

one into the theory of the other, although, in terms of value and authority, the *Ars Poetica* occupied the leading position from the outset.[31]

Aristotle's *Poetics* (and his *Rhetorics*) analyze true art – all the while referring exclusively to poetry – as a result of natural ability (*physis*), skill which may be learnt (*mathèsis*) and practice (*askèsis*). This triad, the necessary basis for the success of any creative work,[32] lived on as *Natura-Ars-Exercitatio* in the writings of Cicero and Quintilian; in Horace's writings, it emerges as *natura*, *vena* or *ingenium* (natural ability), as *ars* or *disciplina* (skill which may be learnt) and as *exercitatio* or *usus* (practice). Horace's work repeatedly draws on descriptive parallels to painting, of which 'ut pictura poesis' (V. 361) is the best known.[33] In Horace's view, art in its highest manifestation was a fine balance between talent and skill: 'Natura fieret laudabile carmen an arte, quaesitum est: ego nec studium sine divite vena nec rude quid prosit video ingenium: alterius sic alter poscit opem res et coniurat amice'[34] (People have asked whether a poem was successful because of natural talent or acquired skill. I cannot see what the use is of effort without an inventive vein or talent which is still raw; thus the one needs the help of the other, and the two unite as allies).

Two engravings which should be seen in the context of the theoretical discussions of the sixteenth century about art are prints of landscapes drawn, according to the inscription, by Pieter Breughel the Elder in Rome in 1553. Cornelis Cort etched and engraved them, and Joris Hoefnagel published them as *Landscape with Mercury Carrying off Psyche*[35] and *Landscape with the Fall of Icarus* [figs. 12.3, 12.4].[36] Both works portray expansive, mountainous river landscapes – world landscapes – and in their compositions look back to other well-known landscape drawings by Breughel.[37] The first reveals two figures with their backs to the viewer – a traditional motif. In both cases, there are also two small figures in the sky, hardly affecting the overall composition, but relating to the message contained in the inscription. A flying Mercury with Psyche is accompanied by the words *Arte et ingenio stat sine morte decus* (Through skill and natural gifts the shining work is immortal). The flying Daedalus and falling Icarus are accompanied by the words *Inter utrunque vola*[38] – *medio tutissimus ibis* (Fly between the two worlds – you will be safest in the middle.)

The introduction of a small *historia* is not unusual. In Hans Bol's landscapes, which van Mander saw as an influence on Hoefnagel, it is often barely possible to discover the *historia* in the landscape. With these mottos, it is as if Hoefnagel, the publisher, was emblematizing Breughel's work. The *Landscape with Mercury* has an explanation in two couplets:

Pulcher Atlantiades Psychen ad Sydera tollens,
Ingenio scandi Sydera posse docet
Ingenio liquidum possum conscendere Coelum,
Si mundi curas fata levare velint.

(The fair grandson of Atlas [= Mercury] who carries Psyche towards the heavens shows that through his natural gifts he can ascend to the stars. I can rise up into the bright skies if Fate wants to relieve the cares of the world).

The second print, *Landscape with the Fall of Icarus*, has the following couplets:

Qui fuit ut tutas agitaret Daedalus alas?
Icarus immensas nomine signet aquas?

12.4 PIETER BREUGEL THE
ELDER
Landscape with the Fall of Icarus
1553

Nempe quod hic alte, demissius ille volabat:
Nam pennas ambo non habuere suas.

(How can it be that Daedalus could safely move his wings back and forth? And that Icarus inscribed his name on the endless waters? It was of course because the one flew high while the other flew lower: for neither had his own wings).

Neither of these works is primarily concerned with the retelling of mythological events. The motto on the first print refers explicitly to the two figures in the sky, Mercury and Psyche, representing Ars and Ingenium and standing for acquired artistic skills and natural ability. The mythological figures serve a similar allegorical purpose to that of Minerva as an allegory of wisdom. The mottos of both engravings allude to the theory of art based on Horace's *Ars Poetica*. It is as though these mottos were the very cornerstones of that theory: true art arises only out of natural ability (*ingenium*) and acquired skills (*ars*). The artist must steer a middle course between his own inclinations (*furor poeticus*) and strive for greater skill. Without this balance, the artwork is doomed to failure. The fact that the two prints are sequential[39] makes it all the more evident that the motto on the second one also alludes to the artist.

In mythological terms, the abduction of Psyche by Mercury is part of the final episode of the well known story of Amor and Psyche as told in *The Golden Ass* by Apuleius. This story has been interpreted in many different ways. At the end of it, the gods decide that Psyche, with whom Amor is in love, should be brought to Mount Olympus, where she is to be granted immortality. The final scene, the feast of the gods, during which immortality is bestowed on Psyche, becomes the apotheosis; in Apuleius' account, the abduction does not receive particular attention.[40] In the engraving after Breughel, Psyche stands triumphantly upright with an olive branch and is carried up into the heavens by Mercury. On an allegorical level, this could be interpreted as Psyche-Ingenium – that is to say, natural ability with learning (the olive branch) – carried by Mercury-Ars – that is to say, acquired skill – to her ultimate destiny amongst the immortal gods – *ad astra, ad sydera* – where she will become one of their number: true art achieving immortality.

It seems likely that Hoefnagel published these programmatic works in the late 1580s. This was the only period when he enjoyed imperial protection and was active both publishing drawings and as the 'inventor hieroglyphicus' of drawings. Further programmatic graphic works also include the moral-philosophical engraving *Nikomachie vitae* of 1588[41] as well as a series in which the individual works are linked by their titles: *Occasio*, *Cursus* and *Praemium*.

As one of his first works for Rudolf II, in 1576/77 Bartholomeus Spranger executed an easel painting which shows the abduction of Psyche by Mercury.[42] Van Mander was enthusiastic in his praise of this work: 'Den Sprangher maeckte hier nae een stucxken passelijcken groot / daer Mercurius in den Raedt der Goden Psyche brengt / het welck met eem aerdich doorsien der wolcken uytnemende wel geordineert / en wel ghedaen was.'[43] Thus in art circles at the court of Rudolf II, Mercury and Psyche became popular in and of themselves, which is surprising in view of how little importance was attached to them in the myth. While a signed copy of the painting, in which Psyche holds aloft the jug with embrocating oils for Venus, is still to be seen in Budapest,[44] a print ascribed to Spranger in Hamburg

12.5 ADRIAEN DE VRIES
Mercury and Psyche
1593

shows only the two figures.[45] Usually, Psyche is placed close to Mercury; often she bears a jug with oils for Venus and can be identified by this attribute, as in the case of the bronze by Adriaen de Vries,[46] which led to three engravings by Joris Hoefnagel [fig. 12.5].[47] It is clear that around 1590, the combination of the two figures of Mercury and Psyche established itself as a new idea and that people read a particular significance into it. In Alberti's view, the *inventio*[48] of a pictorial theme, its inception, ranked much higher than the execution of an idea. This can be the only possible explanation for the popularity of the theme of Mercury and Psyche in Rudolf's time. In the sculpture by de Vries, as in the miniature *Mercury and Psyche* by Daniel Fröschl [fig. 12.6],[49] it is not the insignificant mythological event that counts, but rather its allegorical meaning, in which Mercury represents Ars and Psyche represents Ingenium.[50] This new interpretation is very much in the spirit of concealment and the search for hidden meanings that was characteristic of Rudolfine art in general. The jug in Psyche's hand had no other function than to show her to be Psyche; however, since the link between Mercury and Ars and between Psyche and Ingenium was well established in Rudolfine circles, in his miniature (which was, after all, for those in the know, perhaps even for Rudolf himself), Fröschl took the liberty of placing the olive branch of Minerva in her hand.[51] Mercury and Psyche as a pair are probably equivalent in theoretical terms to Minerva and Mercury in the hybrid figure of Hermathena. Apart from this, the new *inventio* also corresponded to van Mander's approach. He repeatedly referred to the teachings of Macrobius, according to whom the artist's soul, his *ingenium*, descended to earth from the heavenly spheres;[52] thus it was now returning to its place of origin.

Before 1600, painting and artists were nowhere in Europe valued as highly as at the court of Rudolf II.[53] The Emperor had outstanding artists in his service, including Giuseppe Arcimboldo (who had been court painter to Emperor Maximilian II since 1564), Bartholomeus Spranger (since 1581), Joseph Heintz (since 1591), Hans von Aachen (since 1592, without the obligation to be in residence) and others. Following the example of Antiquity, Rudolf had personal contact with his painters and exercised considerable influence over their choice of subject matter.[54] Van Mander describes how Spranger had to work in the Emperor's private chambers and how the latter took a lively interest in what the artist was doing.[55] The Emperor is known to have favoured complicated allegorical and mythological themes, *historias* dominated by personifications, symbols and emblems – that is to say, an intellectualized form of art. Similarly, when it came to the portrayal of nature – as may be seen in the *Four Elements* by Hoefnagel – he was not simply interested in faithful representation, but in the implied metaphysical content of the subject.

Most court painters had had a training as guild members, but it was serving at court that gave them the best chance of achieving artistic freedom. If a person, by the strength of his own talent – *natura, ingenium* – and by diligent application – *studium* – acquired the ability to achieve great things in the field of painting, then he had created the conditions for himself to become a painter of renown, conditions which were at considerable variance with the rules governing the activities of painters tied to the guilds and worshipful companies. This new concept of painting as a liberal art which was no longer bound to a guild could only be put into practice by artists in the service of the court. Here they enjoyed protection, freedom and a right of residence. This new mode of artistic existence, first described by Alberti,

also laid particular emphasis on the artist's good manners, social skills, broad awareness of culture and learning.

For those involved in the art of painting at the court of Rudolf II, the cultural aspect of their work was of paramount importance. The Emperor's interest in the occult, his tendency to seek out the actual essence and truth behind a picture, rather than merely view its surface, the intellectualism of the art he preferred – all this placed the highest of demands on both the technical accomplishment and the learning of the court artists. It was, after all, hardly voyeuristic pleasure in the sight of beautiful, naked human forms that prompted Rudolf's interest in scenes from Antiquity; as has been shown, in such scenes allegory could barely be separated from mythology. The *historia*, which Alberti maintained should be constructed with the greatest possible degree of variety and beauty, simply used various human forms. It was the task of the 'pictor doctus' to develop this kind of *historia*; he was to be both inventive and capable of uncovering the deeper meaning in images.[56]

12.6 DANIEL FRÖSCHL
Mercury and Psyche
[Vienna, Kunsthistorisches
Museum]

Already during the first half of Rudolf's reign, artists had risen to become privileged members of society. As early as 1588, the Emperor conferred a coat of arms on Spranger as a liegeman, and in 1595 he elevated him into ranks of the hereditary nobility, as he did that same year to Hans von Aachen.[57] It is true that in 1584, Spranger was admitted into the Painters' Guild in Prague, but the position occupied by painters in the town was very different from that of craftsmen. Thus in April 1595, Rudolf was, if anything, acting somewhat after the event when he issued a royal charter renewing the privileges of the guilds in Prague and, at the same time, declared that painters were from now on to be regarded as artists and not as craftsmen associated with bead-workers and glaziers. Significantly, the coat of arms of the new society depicts the goddess Minerva.[58]

North of the Alps, this special dispensation for painters on the part of Rudolf II was quite exceptional. It largely followed developments in Italy, where artists had enjoyed higher social status than in the rest of Europe since the fifteenth century.[59] Since the second half of the sixteenth century, numerous artists' academies had even been established in Italy, the earliest being the Accademia del Disegno in Florence in 1562. Since Rudolf occupied a position as Emperor which set him above other rulers, his attitude to the art of painting may be seen as having set an example for other courts. Perhaps this means that Aegidius Sadeler's engraving of 1595/97 [fig. 12.2], dedicated to Maximilian of Bavaria, should be seen as an attempt to encourage the promising young Duke to develop a similar respect for painting. However, the Duke, who inclined to Mars rather than Minerva, does not seem to have taken the artist's message to heart quite as it was meant, and so in 1597 Sadeler accepted the imperial invitation and went to Prague as court engraver to Rudolf II.

1. Bartsch 67; Hollstein 55. See Albrecht Niederstein, 'Das graphische Werk des Bartholomäus Spranger', *Repertorium für Kunstwissenschaft*, 52:1/2 (1931): 15f., 26; Konrad Oberhuber, 'Die stilistische Entwicklung im Werk Bartholomäus Sprangers' (Ph.D. dissertation, Vienna, 1958), pp. 155f.; Thomas Dacosta Kaufmann, 'The Eloquent Artist: Towards an Understanding of the Stylistics of Painting at the Court of Rudolf II', *Leids Kunsthistorisch Jaarboek*

    (1982): 126; *Prag um 1600: Beitrage zur Kunst und Kultur am Hof Rudolfs II*. (Freren 1988), vols 1, no. 319; 2, no. 646; Thomas Dacosta Kaufmann, *The School of Prague: Painting at the Court of Rudolf II* (Chicago and London, 1988), p. 92, ill. 58.

2. 'B. Spranger Schidia haec pro themate G. Spranger MDXCII adulescenti D[onum] D[edit]. Qui postmodum ea divulgans maiori filio suo Math Sprang[er] C[onsecratum?] D[edit] sculptore I.

Mullero MDCXXVIII' (In the year 1592, Bartholo-
meus Spranger gave these 'fragments' of a picture
design to the young G. Spranger as a gift. In his
turn, the latter gave them to his eldest son
Matthias Spranger and published them. Jan Muller
engraved them in 1628.)

3. Lubomír Konečný (in *Prag um 1600* [note 1], vol. 1,
no. 319) discusses this work in the context of other
Spranger drawings.

4. 'd'Ondeugt, luy, Nyt, onconst met Schaemt beloont,
hier blycklyck leyt gebonden / de Ieugt door vlyt in
Const, befaemt ghecroont, wort Rycklyck opgeson-
den.'

5. This text was composed for the printing of the engraving. Augerius Clutius lived in Leiden.

6. On the ox as labour or work see Karel van Mander,
Den grondt der edel vry schilder-const, ed. Hessel
Miedema, 2 vols (Utrecht, 1973), vol. II, p. 315: 'Met
het Ossen hoofs, oft met t'hooft en huydt, wort den
arbeydt beteeckent.'

7. 50.3 × 39.1 cm; Hollstein 114. On this engraving, see
van Mander (note 6), vol. II, pp. 331f., ill. 1; Kaufmann, 'The Eloquent Artist' (note 1): 127; *idem*,
Kaufmann, *The School of Prague* (note 1), p. 44;
Dorothy Limouze, 'Aegidius Sadeler (1570–1629):
Drawings, Prints and Art Theory' (Ph.D. dissertation, Princeton University, 1990), pp. 99f., 128. Related works on this theme are discussed in *ibid.*
(with earlier bibliography).

8. *S:C.M^{tis} pict. Johan ab ach pinxit G Sadler scalpsit
Monachii.*

9. Miedema has described this figure as a maiden resembling Virtue; see Hessel Miedema, 'Tekst en af-
beelding als bronnen bij historisch onderzoek' in
Herman Vekeman and Justus Muller Hofstede (eds),
*Wort und Bild in der Niederländischen Kunst und Lit-
eratur des 16. und 17. Jahrhunderts* (Erftstadt, 1984),
p. 8. However, although she is without armour or
aegis, in light of the text she can only be interpreted as Minerva.

10. See Miedema (note 9), p. 15, n. 16.

11. *Sereniss^{mo} Principi Ac Domino D. Maximiliano Comiti
Palatino Rheni Utriusque Bavariae Duci Domino Suo
Clementissimo D.*

12. For an overview of the question of dating, see
Limouze (note 7).

13. *De pictura praestantissima et nunquam satis laudata
arte libri tres absolutissimi Leonis Baptistae de Albertis
…* (Basel: Th. Venatorius, 1540). Manuscripts exist in
Latin and Italian. The first edition of the Latin text
appeared in 1540. An edition based on the Italian
manuscript did not appear until 1847. However, in
1547 an Italian edition had been translated from
the Latin. This essay uses the Latin–English edition
by Cecil Grayson (Leon Battista Alberti, *On Painting
and On Sculpture: The Latin Texts of De Pictura and
De Statua*, ed. with translations, introduction and
notes by Cecil Grayson (London and New York,
1972).

14. Alberti (note 13), p. 9.

15. In the dedication to Filippo Brunelleschi; see *ibid.*,
p. 32.

16. '…quantum ingenio et industria luminis et doctri-
nae attulerim ex libris ipsis' (dedication to Giovan
Francesco Illustrious Prince of Mantua; see *ibid.*, p.
34).

17. 'Non pauci Romani cives filios inter bonas artes ad
bene beateque vivendum picturam edocerent' (Alberti [note 13], p. 64).

18. 'Pingendi ars profecto liberalibus ingeniis et no-
bilissimis animis dignissima' (Alberti [note 13],
p. 64).

19. 'Sed cupio pictorem … in primis esse virum et bon-
um et doctum bonarum artium' (Alberti [note 13]),
p. 94.

20. 'Proxime non ab re erit se poetis atque rhetoribus
delectabuntur. Nam hi quidem multa cum pictore
habent ornamenta communia' (Alberti [note 13]),
p. 94.

21. '…quae omnis laus praesertim in inventione consis-
tit. Atqui ea quidem hanc habet vim, ut etiam sola
inventio sine picture delectet' (Alberti [note 13]),
p. 94.

22. 'Nam omnes qui sue posteris grata et accepta fore
opera cupiunt, multo ante meditari opus oportet,
quod multa diligentia perfectum reddant. Siquidem
non paucis in rebus ipsa diligentia grate non minus
est quam omne ingenium' (Alberti [note 13], p.
104).

23. 'Pictoris enim opus multitudini gratum futurum
est. Ergo multitudinis censuram et iudicium tum
non aspernetur, cum adhuc satisfacere opinionibus
liceat' (Alberti [note 13]), p. 104.

24. Van Mander (note 6), vol. II, p. 301. For more on
van Mander and his concept of art, see other works
by Miedema, which contain a wealth of material
and information on art and attitudes at that time.

25. Van Mander (note 6), vol. II, p. 302.

26. *Ibid.*, vol. I, pp. 70–75, Exhortatio 1–12.

27. *Ibid.*, vol. I, pp. 78–83, Exhortatio 25–36.

28. Van Mander says little about the content of paintings. Instead he gives instructions as to how to
overcome the technical problems involved in painting.

29. Horace, *Ars Poetica*, ed. with introduction by Eckart
Schäfer (Stuttgart, 1984).

30. *Ibid.*, p. 61

31. *Ibid.*, p. 61

32. See J. A. Emmens, 'Natuur, onderwijzing en oefen-
ing: Bij een drieluik van Gerrit Dou' in *Album Dis-
cipulorum aangeboden aan Professor Dr J.G. van
Gelder* (Utrecht, 1963), pp. 125ff., in particular pp.
130 ff.

33. Rensselaer W. Lee, 'Ut picture poesis: The Humanistic Theory of Painting', *Art Bulletin*, 17 (1940):
197ff.

34. Vs. 408–11.

35. Etching with engraving; 27 × 33 cms; René van
Bastelaer, *Les Estampes de Peter Bruegel l'Ancien*
(Brussels, 1908), 2; with *Petrus Breugel fec. A° 1553*
and *Excud.Houf: cum prae Caes* below the image
(first state of three).

36. Etching with engraving; 27 × 33 cm; Bastelaer (note
35), 2; with *Petrus Breugel fed:: Romae A° 1553* and
Excud Houfs cum pra^e Cae^s below the image (first
state of two).

37. Nina Eugenia Serebrennikov gave a paper at the
Fourth International Emblem Conference in
Löwen, 18–23 August 1996, on these two prints,
with particular reference to the landscapes, drawing
a quite different conclusion.

38. Ovid, *Metamorphoses*, VIII.206.

39. See Serebrennikov (note 37). There are two further prints of similar construction, engraved by Cornelis Cort. The first shows a shipwreck from which allegories of virtue and wisdom are escaping, with the motto 'Omnia mea mecum porto'. The second shows a shipwreck with the living and the dead and the motto 'Nonne ille est mortis stipendiarium, qui morte quaerit unde vivat.' Both have two couplets of commentary and are inscribed with the words *Cornelius Cort Batavus fec.* and *excud. Hoef: cum prae. Caes.*

40. VI.23.4: 'et ilico per Mercurium arripi Psychen et in caelum perduci iubet.'

41. Hollstein 113, 116–18.

42. This is generally taken to be the work held in the Gurlitt Collection, Munich, until 1965 and auctioned on 18 November of that year in Cologne. See Michael Henning, *Die Tafelbilder Bartholomäus Sprangers (1546–1611): Höfische Malerei zwischen 'Manierismus' und 'Barock'* (Essen, 1987), pp. 28–95, 178, A 8. See also Kaufmann, *The School of Prague* (note 1), nos. 20–23, including further bilbliography. Other sources take the *Gathering of the Gods* at Hampton Court to be the work in question.

43. *Leben von Spranger*, in van Mander (note 6), fol. 272r.

44. Grey ink with wash, white highlights; 12.2 × 16.6 cm; Budapest, Szépmüvészeti Müzeum, 58.420. See Teréz Gerszi, *Netherlandish Drawings in the Budapest Museum: Sixteenth Century Drawings* (Amsterdam, 1971), no. 238, ill.

45. Red chalk and white body colour on paper with a reddish ground; 18.1 × 14.4 cm; cut all round; Hamburg, Kunsthalle, 22540. See Wolf Stubbe, *Hundert Meisterzeichnungen aus der Hamburger Kunsthalle 1500–1800* (Hamburg, 1967), no. 56, ill. 55.

46. Paris, Musée du Louvre, made in 1593.

47. Engraving; 50.7 × 25.9 cm; Bartsch 82–84; Hollstein 56–58.

48. A term from *Ars Rhetorica*.

49. Body colour on vellum, initialled; 13.5 × 8.6 cm; Vienna, Kunsthistorisches Museum, 6645. Also illustrated in Vladimír Denkstein, 'K prvním pocatkum Hollarava umeleckého rustu', *Umění*, 29 (1981): 389, as 'Merkur und Psyche' by Jacob Hoefnagel; and in Kaufmann, *The School of Prague* (note 1), p. 174, 3.5, as an allegory of Peace.

50. This *inventio* is only found north of the Alps. Ripa did not make this connection between Ingenium and Psyche.

51. See Vicenzo Cartari, *Imagini delli Dei de gl'Antichi* (Venice, 1647), p. 193: 'Imagine di Minerva ... inventrice dell'ulivo simbolo el lungo e necessario studio.'

52. Hessel Miedema, *Kunst, kunstenaar en kunstwerk bij Karel van Mander: Een analyse van zijn levensbeschrijvingen* (Alphen aan den Rijn, 1981) , p. 1.

53. For a detailed account, see Kaufmann, *The School of Prague* (note 1), pp. 40ff. and elsewhere.

54. Kaufmann, *The School of Prague* (note 1), pp. 17ff.

55. Van Mander (note 6), fol. 273r.

56. The description of Joris Hoefnagel as 'inventor hieroglyphicus et allegoricus' says a lot about the role of the artist in this respect.

57. Karl Chytil, *Die Kunst in Prag zur Zeit Rudolf II.* (Prague, 1904), p. 24.58. '...und denen mahlern darbei aus ursach, weilen ihre kunst und meisterschaft von alles anderen handwerkn sehr unterschieden, diese besondere gnadt erzeigen und selbte, damit sie von dato dieses unsern briefs und ertheilter confirmation von keinem mehr fur ein handwerkh gehalten noch genennt werdn, sondern sich der mahler kunst sambt und sonderlich, welche die sothanne kunst bei ordentlichen und mit denen mahlern in der Alt- und kleinen stadt Prag einstimmenden meistern erlehrnet, schreiben und nennen mogen, hiemit gnadiglich begnaden' (text of the Royal Charter in the Regestenteil (chronological list plus summaries), *Jahrbuch der Kunsthistorischen Sammlungen des Allerhöchsten Kaiserhauses*, 7 (1888): II, pp. XXXIX–XLI, no. 4607 (quote, p. XL).

58. '...anstadt der mohrin die sogenante göttin Pallas' (*ibid.*). See also Chytil (note 57), pp. 23f., ill. 11.

59. Anthony Blunt, *Artistic Theory in Italy 1450–1600*, 2nd edn (Oxford, 1956), pp. 48ff.

Thoughts on Rudolfine Art in the 'Court Workshops' in Prague

RUDOLF DISTELBERGER

The important exhibitions in Essen and Vienna in 1988 showed that sculptures by Adriaen de Vries and 'applied arts' from the court workshops had major significance in the context of European art around 1600. The painters, sculptors and goldsmiths at the court of Rudolf II were well travelled and knew what was going on elsewhere. Those who settled in Prague did so because of the evident affinity between their way of working and both the Emperor's attitude to art and the intellectual climate that surrounded the court. The Emperor's personality, his view of the world and his keen collector's eye united the court artists, whether salaried or 'by appointment', in their artistic ambitions. Even though they worked as individuals without supervision, as in the court at Florence, each of course knew what the others were doing and how they were doing it.

Once before, in the Middle Ages, Prague, under Emperor Charles IV (1346–1378), had occupied a leading position as a European city with a flourishing artistic life. The appearance of the city today still bears witness to this. When Rudolf II took up residence in the old imperial castle in 1583, he saw himself very much cast in the role of successor to Charles IV. Incrustations of agate, jasper and amethysts in the chapels at Burg Karlstein near Prague and in the Wenceslas Chapel in St Vitus' cathedral; exquisite vessels carved from semi-precious stones in the cathedral's collection of treasures: evidence could be found on all sides both of Charles IV's immense aspirations and of the wealth of semi-precious stones to be found in Bohemia. On his arrival, Rudolf kept on the most important painters from his father's day, namely Spranger and Arcimboldo, and directed his energy towards re-introducing the art of hardstone carving to Prague. As early as 1583, the goldsmith and hardstone carver Valentin Drausch (1546–1610; afflicted by mental illness in 1589) entered the service of Rudolf II.[1] Along with the goldsmith Friedrich Krug, Drausch

13.1 OTTAVIO MISERONI
Cup with a Mascaron
Ca. 1590-1600
[Vienna, Kunsthistorisches
Museum, Kunstkammer]

13.2 OTTAVIO MISERONI
JAN VERMEYEN (mounting)
Cup
Ca. 1600–05
[Vienna, Kunsthistorisches
Museum, Kunstkammer]

was commissioned to search for semi-precious stones in Silesia, at a by then neglected site in Cibousov near Klosterle on the Eger in the Bohemian Erzgebirge. The two were apparently extremely successful, but in 1585 Drausch had to return to Munich at the insistence of Duke Wilhelm V of Bavaria. Rudolf continued the search for semi-precious stones and initially sent the finest examples to Milan to have them carved there as vessels and cameos. In the seventeenth century, Bohemia became known again as a land where the stones which the cowherd threw at his cow were worth much more than the cow.[2]

The Prague school of hardstone carving began with the young Ottavio Miseroni (1567–1624) from Milan, who entered the Emperor's service on 22 January 1588. Over time, he persuaded three of his brothers to join him in Prague, and at least two of them, Giovanni Ambrogio and Alessandro, also worked as hardstone carvers.[3] They presumably worked in Ottavio's workshop, which would account for the fact that no works are specifically attributable to them. Ottavio's oeuvre covers a span of more than three and a half decades and underwent the changes one might expect. There are two strands to his first period, which lasted until around 1600: on the one hand, he was still working very much in the tradition of his father's workshop in Milan, while on the other, he was at pains to convince the Emperor of his own technical virtuosity. Examples from this period include the so-called *Lion's Skin*, the Jade Bowl [fig. 13.1] and a statuette, the *Repentant Magdalene*.

In his middle period, which lasted approximately until Rudolf II's death in 1612, Ottavio developed his own new, unmistakable style, which is unparalleled in glyptic art anywhere. He was by now established in court art circles and knew other artists' work. The sculptor Adriaen de Vries (1545–1626), the ivory carver Nikolaus Pfaff (1556?–1612) and the goldsmith Paulus van Vianen (ca. 1570–1613) had also settled in Prague. Their works are characterized by soft, sensual surfaces. In Ottavio's hands, hard stone became similarly soft and rounded, as though it might yield to any manipulation. This softening of form, which at the same time played on the ungiving quality of the stone, subtly intensifies its sensual effect. A good example of this is the oval Bowl in Coloured Jasper [fig. 13.2]. At its centre, it is as though a fluid substance is forming into a mascaron – an early example of auricular style. The viewer is amazed by the miracle of nature in the beauty of the stone and the sheer

virtuosity of the artist. That is, of course, the intention. The main work of this period is the large Heliotrope Bowl of 1608: asymmetrical, like the Jasper Bowl, and with an irregular form that somehow seems to move of its own accord. The soft outlines of the edge give the impression of being on the point of melting away altogether.

Ottavio Miseroni was particularly inspired during this time by his work with the goldsmith and jeweller Jan Vermeyen (before 1559–1608) and his assistants. Vermeyen had, in fact, developed a recognizable Prague style of gold and enamel work. As far as surface decoration went, he admittedly did draw on various current ornamental designs, but in the matter of colour and formal invention – for example, in his cameo settings – he was completely independent and stood out for the particular delicacy of his technique. Vermeyen created settings fit for the coloured stones they contained. Generally, his function was secondary. Occasionally, however, the hardstone carver and goldsmith would collaborate as equals, producing stunningly beautiful collectors' items for the *Kunstkammer*. In the case of the perfectly polished Chalcedony Bowl, the two artists were concerned above all to show the unusually beautiful stone at its outstanding best. In the case of the renowned Prase Bowl, the hardstone carver allowed the goldsmith to take the lead. Both pieces demanded the highest technical perfection from the hardstone carver and the suppression of his own personal style. The Bacchus Bowl [fig. 13.5] must already have brought the two master craftsmen together at the design stage, for the stone had to be prepared for the specific type of goldsmithing needed for the Bacchus figure seated on a vine leaf. Collaborative work of this immensely high standard was only possible on the basis of the close links between the various imperial workshops. With pieces of this kind, the court in Prague was laying down a challenge to the artists and artist-craftsmen of the house of Medici, who probably had the highest reputation at the time. The use of such varied and colourful stones was a significant innovation in the art of vessel carving. Interest was focused on the aesthetics of the materials themselves. The Prague school had created an identifiable style – that is to say, it was pursuing an artistic course which must properly be called 'Rudolfine' and which was independent of Milan and Florence.

Alongside vessels, the Miseroni workshop also produced cameos and relief *commes-*

13.3 JAN VERMEYEN
Tazza with Cover
Ca. 1600–05
[Vienna, Kunsthistorisches
Museum, Kunstkammer]

13.4 OTTAVIO MISERONI (?)
JAN VERMEYEN (mounting)
Cup
Ca. 1600–05
[Vienna, Kunsthistorisches
Museum, Kunstkammer]

si, as well as individual statuettes. The latter were probably the work of Giovanni Ambrogio because they bear no trace of Ottavio's style. It is striking that cameos should have played such a modest part in Ottavio's oeuvre. It may well be that competition from Milan was too overwhelming in this area. It is known that Alessandro Masnago worked almost exclusively for Rudolf [figs 13.6, 13.7], and the cameos from the Miseroni workshop in Milan were artistically far superior to those produced in Prague [fig. 13.8]. Perhaps this was also the reason why Ottavio turned instead to developing the relief *commesso*, in the process achieving utterly new, painterly effects.

13.5 OTTAVIO MISERONI Heliotrope Vessel with a Statue of a Little Bacchus 1600–05 [Vienna, Kunsthistorisches Museum, Kunstkammer]

How much the Emperor was personally involved in glyptic art in Prague may be seen in Ottavio's situation during his late period following Rudolf's death. Suddenly, there were many unfinished works lying around in the hardstone carver's workshop which were of little interest. In 1613, Ottavio, clearly seeing no great future for himself, sent four vessels in exceptionally beautiful Bohemian jasper to Florence to be used in the decoration of the ducal chapel.[4] His financial situation was becoming difficult by 1621, the Emperor owed him the enormous sum of 13,701 guilders.[5] The following year, he took numerous vessels to Vienna which were not set until much later – and even then only by a somewhat uncomprehending goldsmith.[6] Around 1620, Ottavio received some new commissions from the pious Empress Anna – that is to say, from her estate. He produced a small altar, altar candlesticks and two monstrances for relics [fig. 13.9], although it was stipulated that he should use an existing Milanese design for the altar. This work most likely brought him into close contact with the *commesso* workshop. As circumstances decreed, Ottavio's style became much sparser, stricter and abstracter towards the end of his life. The Small Smoky Quartz Bowl with faceted sides could hardly be a greater contrast to the work Ottavio had been producing at the height of his powers. 'Rudolfine' style no longer existed.

Once the potential abundance of semi-precious stones in Bohemia was discovered, Rudolf II's interest turned first to the new art of *commessi di pietre dure*, although it was some time before he managed to introduce this technique into Prague. The complex interplay of natural materials and the artist's creative representation of 'the world' was particularly in tune with the Emperor's pansophic world view. The new technique could therefore achieve a far greater degree of 'truth' in the representations of landscapes than landscape painters such as Pieter Stevens and Roelandt Savery. The famous table-top which Rudolf II had made in Florence from Bohemian stones, and which was six and a half years in the making (completed in 1597), already contained landscapes, although this was not usual in Florence at the time. In the centre of the table, rows of garnets set in gold formed Rudolf's monogram. The only typical Florentine motifs on the table were the birds and flowers. Thus Prague certainly exerted considerable influence on the table's design. This presupposes that there was a master craftsman in Rudolf's service who played a decisive part in the work's creation. Such a person may well have overseen the project, though it is hard to imagine why (or even to understand how) it was that artists in a Florentine workshop devoted their attention to a commission from so far away. The Emperor's man may have been Cosimo Castrucci. It is not known when he entered Rudolf's service, but a pass letter of 1592 already describes him as a semi-precious stone carver to His Majesty.[7] This explains how it was that when the Bavarian heir to the throne, Maximilian I (1573/1598–1651), visited Prague in 1593, Rudolf II was proudly able to present him with a work in the new technique. It seems that this gift

13.6 ALESSANDRO MASNAGO
(manner of)
JAN VERMEYEN (mounting)
Cameo of Leda and the Swan
Ca. 1600; mounting 1603–08
[Vienna, Kunsthistorisches
Museum, Kunstkammer]

13.7 ALESSANDRO MASNAGO
JAN VERMEYEN (mounting)
Jupiter and Io
Ca. 1600; mounting 1600–08
[Vienna, Kunsthistorisches
Museum, Kunstkammer]

may have been the octagonal plate in the table-top which is now in the Schatzkammer in the Munich Residence and which bears all the hallmarks of Cosimo's work.[8]

Information on Cosimo is cryptic at best and ceases altogether in 1600. In 1596, when he married for the second time, he received a special gift from the Emperor of 10 guilders, the equivalent of one month's salary. The key work in Cosimo's artistic output is the *Landscape with Chapel and Bridge*, which is signed on the back and dated 1596 [fig. 13.11]. The large *Sacrifice of Isaac* in Vienna, a true 'world landscape', is composed and constructed in a similar manner and may be seen as Cosimo's *chef d'oeuvre*. Both pieces present an elevated view of a broad, ideal landscape with astounding aerial perspectives. Cosimo achieved this by the subtlest differentiation in his choice of stones: the foregrounds are constructed from large, strongly coloured stones, while progressively smaller and paler stones recede into the distance. Thus he used stones to create both form and space. The composition consists of criss-crossing diagonals – a scheme familiar from Dutch landscape painting.

Giovanni Castrucci, Cosimo's son from his first marriage, was in Prague by 1598 at the latest. However, he could not match his father's outstanding artistic prowess. On 5 October 1604, the overseer of the Florentine workshop, Costantino de'Servi, wrote from Prague to the secretary of state Belisario Vinta in Florence that in the matter of *commesso* work there was only 'il Castruccio', and he did not greatly value the latter's work.[9] This can only have been a reference to Giovanni, since Cosimo, whose life art history has traditionally extended to 1610, had already died by then. Giovanni's hand alone is evident in the small domestic altar which Rudolf II gave to Zdenek Adalbert von Lobkowitz and Polyxena von Pernstein on the occasion of their marriage in 1603. In 1602, the acting master of the Florentine workshop, Jaques Bylivelt, considered recalling Giovanni Castrucci to Florence. However, in the end he decided to employ apprentices or assistants because they would work harder than master craftsmen.[10] In the same year work was started – presumably for Giovanni – on renovating the cutting mill in Bubenec, where plates for the *commessi* were prepared.[11] The Prague workshop's continued existence was evidently in the balance at the time, perhaps because of Cosimo's death. After this, all financial transactions were handled by Giovanni, who would appear to have supplemented his income from his work for the Prague court by some stone trading with Florence.[12] On 1 April 1610, the Emperor granted him the position of hardstone carver to the court with a secure salary of 20 guilders, and the Florentine court rewarded him for his services in August of the same year by entering him into the Grand Duke's *ruolo*, without stipend but with certain privileges. In 1613, Giovanni travelled in Italy, and it is known that from there he intended to return to Prague to look for jasper to use for some work in Milan.[13] It is clear from all of this that his entrepreneurial activities extended far and wide and – as Bylivelt rightly assumed – that this must have prevented him from doing very much in the workshop itself. It is therefore hardly surprising that the workshop was producing replicas of old motifs and pieces of widely differing quality. The *Kunstkammer* inventory of 1607–11 lists several *commessi* under Giovanni's name, including the *Landscape with Obelisk* [fig.13.12], *Landscape with a Well* and *Landscape with Seated Peasants*. His compositions consist of series of planes, parallel to the picture plane, without any real plastic effect or sense of space. Individual forms are largely schematic because Giovanni was not skilled in positioning stones to create the impression of forms in space.

The simplification of objects, formal abstraction and only minimal lightening of colours into the distance render the pieces no more than flatly decorative. The illusion of depth has vanished. Various sources show that Giovanni died in 1615.

In the meantime, the reputation of the Prague atelier had improved again. This may be inferred from the fact that in 1615, the Grand Duke Cosimo II sent a drawing by the painter Bernardo Pocetti showing Abraham and the Three Angels to Cosimo di Giovanni Castrucci – that is, Giovanni's son. Some time between 1606 and 1610, Pocetti had already done a coloured study from which Giovanni was to have made a *commesso* for a tabernacle frieze for the Capella dei Principi, but it seems that little progress had as yet been made on this.[14] Cosimo the Younger, who receives mention in contemporary sources only up until 1619, was a gifted artist, as can be seen from his beautiful depiction of Fame – probably to a design by Pocetti – now in the Museo dell'Opificio delle Pietre Dure.[15] There was little time for him to develop his talents. The Abraham *commesso* was, in fact, completed by Giovanni's son-in-law, Guiliano di Piero Pandolfini, who took it to Florence in 1622.[16] This late stage in the life of the Prague workshop also saw the making of the *Landscape with Repentant Magdalene* and *Landscape with Fiery Heavens*, which mark the beginnings of a new style. The atmospheric sense of depth comes from Cosimo, while the layered picture planes and schematization of architectural elements come from Giovanni. These works reflect the new Prague style of landscape art, which draws the viewer into a small, convincingly rendered section of landscape with details of ruins, houses and rocky cliffs.[17] It is not possible to say conclusively whether these two pieces were by Cosimo the Younger or whether they are early works by Pandolfini.

In its last years, the so-called Castrucci workshop barely worked at all for the court, which had by now moved back to Vienna. On the one hand, there was constant demand from Florence for panels with figurative *commessi*, while on the other hand there were commissions from Charles I of Liechtenstein (1597-1627) for a table and a chest in the form of a cabinet. It was only in 1627, after Charles I's death, and when his debts had been settled, that Pandolfini was paid 449 guilders owing to him, and a certain Hans Bartzels received the balance of 25 guilders for his work on the table.[18] The workshop probably no longer existed by this time, for it may well have been closed in 1624 after the death of Ottavio Miseroni, who had some form of overall responsibility for it in the end. Pandolfini moved back to Florence, where he was to make the panels for the Viennese cabinet which was previously thought to have been made in Prague.[19] He must have acquired a leading position in Florence. Charles Eusebius of Liechtenstein (1611-1648), Charles' son, bought a large table top from Pandolfini in Florence for which he paid 1,700 *scudi* in 1637.[20] In its centre is the Liechtenstein coat of arms charged with weapons in an elegantly styled quatrefoil, which matches exactly the design for Cosimo the Younger's Fame. This typifies the way in which forms created in Prague were re-used in Florence. The same can be seen in the geometric figures based on Jamnitzer's *Prospectiva corporum reglarium*, which Pandolfini came to know in Prague and used again in Florence. The roses, tulips, jasmine and other flowers which decorate the second Liechtenstein table appeared first on the lid of the Liechtenstein chest and then on the front of the Vienna cabinet. As before when Rudolf's 'miracle table' was made, Pandolfini's move to Florence meant that Prague again exerted considerable influence on the Grand Duke's atelier. This influence was probably most significant in the depiction of land-

13.8 Ottavio Miseroni
Cameo of Mary Magdalen
Ca. 1602–05
[Vienna, Kunsthistorisches
Museum, Kunstkammer]

13.9 OTTAVIO MISERONI
Monstrance with Madonna
and Child
Ca. 1620
[Vienna, Kunsthistorisches
Museum, Kunstkammer]

13.10 ANTON SCHWEINBERGER
NIKOLAUS PFAFF
Ewer of Seychelle-Nut
1602
[Vienna, Kunsthistorisches
Museum, Kunstkammer]

scape, which, as a motif, only came to Florence via Prague. As a variety of sources report, the Medici workshop repeatedly acquired stones from Bohemia, which means that their presence may not be taken as proof of a work's place of origin. Yet it must be the materials used that explain the attribution of so many works to Prague when there must be doubt as to whether production on this scale would have been technically possible. The Rudolfine *macchia* continued to dominate Florentine landscape *commessi* until well into the seventeenth century.[21] As yet, there is no way of drawing a clear distinction between pieces produced in Prague and those made in seventeenth-century Florence.

The landscape *commesso* was an original invention of the Prague Castrucci workshop. The ground must have been prepared for this by Rudolf II's pansophic world view. The *commesso* encompasses both macrocosm and microcosm. At this time, a pictorial representation of a landscape did not depict nature as such; it was always an ideal landscape standing for Nature as the macrocosm. The human being was the microcosm. The sense of *one* spirit pervading all things is scarcely intenser than in the representation of the landscape in a *commesso*. It is evident in the beauty of the stones, which come from the macrocosm of Nature, and in the work of the artist, who formed and arranged them to create meaning. Anselmus Boetius de Boodt was justified in his admiration of the *commessi di pietre dure* for the miraculous way in which they united the artistry of Nature with the creative gifts of the artist.

In the sixteenth century, the leading master goldsmiths also strove to go beyond the conventions of the *ars mechanica* of their craft and dignify their work as art on a level with philosophy.[22] The main opportunity to do this was provided by princely collectors seeking richly inventive items to display. The more discriminating and sophisticated collectors became, the more was asked of the master artist-craftsmen. At the highest level, these *Kunstkammer* pieces from the individual collections at rival courts cease to be interchangeable, because they have been defined by the artistic climate of one particular place. One example suffices to demonstrate this.

The first goldsmith whom we can positively identify at the court of Rudolf II was Anton Schweinberger from Augsburg. From 1587 until his death in March 1603, he was active in Prague. His one extant signed work is the renowned Ewer of Seychelle-Nut, made in 1602 [fig. 13.10]. The basin which went with the jug did enter the *Kunstkammer*, but it was unfinished and has not survived; it would be interesting to know its design. In total, ten Seychelle-nuts with mounts have been preserved. Schweinberger's work is so vastly superior in its artistry to all the rest that one must ask oneself why. There was no long tradition of mounting Seychelle-nuts in this way. Goldsmiths would either treat them like coconuts and make them into giant goblets (the nuts were always used as halves) or the halves could be made into ships or animals' bodies, namely dragons. Number 297 in the inventory of Rudolf II's *Kunstkammer* reads as follows: '1 other large "cocco de maldiva" set in silver, like a ship or a barque'; number 293 reads: '1 large Indian "cocco de maldiva" set in silver being in the shape of a dragon'. Schweinberger's design may have been inspired by the Iberian Seychelle-nut which is now in the Schatzkammer des Deutschen Ordens, Vienna, and which itself also came from Rudolf II's *Kunstkammer*. In both cases, the powerful horizontal axis is balanced by a strong vertical cutting through the nut. There are handles on either side, and the foot is relatively short in height. Schweinberger harmonized

13.11 COSIMO CASTRUCCI
Landscape with a Bridge and Chapel
1596
[Vienna, Kunsthistorisches Museum, Kunstkammer]

the various elements, lent them meaning and created unusually plastic forms.

These rare nuts were reputedly found washed up on the beaches of the Maldive Islands – hence their name, 'cocco de maldiva' – and were assumed to be some kind of sea fruit. Everything about the jug, therefore, is linked to the theme of water. Schweinberger's composition is contained within a rhombus, the sides of which run upwards through the handles and horizontally along the edge of the nut from spout to handle. Scrollwork softens the crossing point. The solid, protruding handle culminating in a female head, which matches the volute behind the spout, is set on the shorter half of the nut, thereby creating the necessary visual balance. Two tritons, crouching back to back, appear to support the hefty vessel; at the same time, they constitute the transition to the dominant horizontals of the jug's 'hull'. Silvery arms, heads and fish-legs emerge from soft, golden ornamental draperies reminiscent of the prints of Cornelis Bos. The waves lapping by the tritons are in purest auricular style. The plastic power of these figures is echoed on the lid by the dynamic silver Neptune on a golden hippocampus (the trident is missing), thus maintaining the traditional relationship of lid and foot. The combination of gold and silver creates an impression of complex layering at the same time as it clarifies the shifting boundaries between abstract scrollwork and zoomorphic representation. The scrollwork on the handle on the lid turns into fins while silver herms appear from out of the side handles. All the various details of the piece contribute to the rhythm and the dynamism of the cast forms, which are well served by the sense of their sheer weight. It is as though goldsmith had become sculptor, creating a work which is intrinsically monumental, a memorial to Neptune, god of the sea.

In finely balanced contrast to the plasticity of the silver and goldwork, the nut itself is carved with low reliefs by Nikolaus Pfaff. The erotic scenes with sea gods in couples and as families with sea-god children could well be allegories of the life-giving and -sustaining power of water.[23] These reliefs bear such a striking stylistic resemblance to Bartholomeus Spranger's work that they could almost be his designs. Whatever the case, Spranger was certainly the inspiration for their style. None of the other Seychelle-nut jugs have figurative carvings on the nut, although these are frequently found on coconuts.

On the underside of the jug is the signature *A. Schweinberger [fecit]*. The question is whether the master could equally well have written 'invenit et fecit' if this had been the custom of the day. The silver and gold forms are firmly rooted in the context of Rudolfine art. Neptune's upper body and arms could be a variation on the Mercury on Adriaen de Vries's first Augsburg fountain of 1599. De Vries had already used this positioning of the arms – one raised and one lowered forwards with a slight twist of the body – for his Hercules with the Dragon in Drottningholm (ca. 1590/93), and he used it again for his Hercules with the Hydra on his second Augsburg fountain, which was completed in 1602. On the other hand, there was a small Italian bronze warrior in the Emperor's *Kunstkammer* from the second quarter of the sixteenth century whose gestures are even closer to those of Neptune, although the other way round. And apart from this, Neptune's strength lies in his raised arm, while the warrior's lies in his lowered one. De Vries made a free copy of this warrior that proves his interest in the motif.[24] The tritons, too, on the foot of our jug had close forebears. In 1600, Rudolf II acquired a bust of Charles V by Leone Leoni (of 1555) that is supported by two figures crouched back to back, a motif which Leoni he is known to have adapted for his bust of Rudolf completed in 1603. The links between the jug and Leoni's work are so close that one might justifiably ask whether the designs for the plastic decoration of the jug might not, in fact, be his. He certainly did not form the models which were used, because they have their own distinctive style, yet he could well have played a part in the early stages of their making. However, the fact remains that the creative dialogue behind Schweinberger's work was with sculpture rather than with goldsmithing. His collaboration with the

13.12 GIOVANNI CASTRUCCI
*Landscape with an Obelisk and
the Imperial Coat of Arms*
Before 1611
[Vienna, Kunsthistorisches
Museum, Kunstkammer]

ivory- and wood-carver Pfaff, who in turn looked back to Spranger; his connections with the work of de Vries; and his knowledge of the contents of the *Kunstkammer* all place the jug in a much wider artistic context than that usually enjoyed by a goldsmith. This jug could not have been made anywhere other than in Prague.

Thus 'Rudolfine' style had many strands. In glyptic art, it is striking that it was the aesthetic of the stone itself that led to the making of a vessel: the result is a collection of minerals in the guise of a collection of skilfully crafted objects. As we know from Boetius de Boodt, the stone had to be worth the work expended on it. As far as form is concerned, many of the innovations were the result of the influence of one technique on another. The situation in Prague may perhaps be compared with that of Fontainebleau some decades previously. The demands on artists were of the highest order. Yet at the same time, these court artists, dependent as they were on their patron, were not able to break away from convention as Caravaggio dared to do in Rome. The future was to be made elsewhere.

1. On Drausch, see H. Lietzmann, 'Der Edelsteinschneider Valentin Drausch 1546–1610' in *Fest-schrift fur Brigitte Klesse* (Berlin, 1994), pp. 47–54.

2. Balbín in the *Miscellanea historica regni Bohemiae*.

3. Until recently, the fact that Giovanni Ambrogio must have been at least 15 years older than Ottavio has been overlooked, but in 1573 he was already of age and in a position to sign a contract (R. Distelberger, 'Nuove ricerche sulla biografia dei fratelli Gasparo e Girolamo Miseroni' in *Firenze e la Toscana dei Medici nell'Europa del '500, 3: Relationi artistiche: Il linguaggio architettonico europeo* (Florence, 1983), pp. 877–84. As may be seen from his patent of nobility of 1608, a third brother, Aurelio, must also have served the Emperor in some form. Later, however, he became a monk.

4. C. Przyborowski, 'Die Ausstattung der Fursten-kapelle an der Basilika von San Lorenzo in Florenz. Versuch einer Rekonstruktion' (Ph.D. dissertation, Berlin, 1982), p. 400.

5. *Jahrbuch der kunsthistorischen Sammlungen des A.H. Kaiserhauses*, 33 (1913–14), Regest 20.316.

6. *Jahrbuch der kunsthistorischen Sammlungen des A.H. Kaiserhauses*, 33 (1916), Regest 20.608; R. Distelberger, 'Beobachtungen zu den Steinschneidewerkstätten der Miseroni in Mailand und Prag', *Jahrbuch der kunsthistorischen Sammlungen in Wien*, 74 (1978), pp. 79–152.

7. Information generously passed on by Manfred Staudinger; Haus-, Hof- und Staatsarchiv, Reichshofkanzlei, Tax Books, vol. 72 (1592), fol. 42r.

8. H. Brunner (ed.), *Schatzkammer der Residenz München: Catalogue*, 3rd edn (Munich, 1970), no. 519; L. Seelig, 'Scagliola und Pietra dura. Farbige Stein- und Stuckintarsien in Münchner Schlössern und Museen', *Kunst & Antiquitäten*, 1 (1987), 34, ill. 6; A. M. Giusti, *Pietre Dure. Hardstone in Furniture and Decorations* (London, 1992), p. 174, ill. 58.

9. J. Krčálová and K. Aschengreen-Piacenti, 'Castrucci', *Dizionario Biografico degli Italiani*, vol. 22 (Rome, 1979), p. 251; Giusti 1992 (note 8), p. 140.

10. C. W. Fock, 'Pietre Dure Work at the Court of Prague: Some Relations with Florence', *Leids Kunsthistorisch Jaarboek*, 1 (1982), 261; idem, 'Pietre Dure Work at the Court of Prague: Some Relations', in *Prag um 1600: Beiträge zur Kunst und Kultur am Hofe Rudolfs II.* (Freren, 1988), p. 52.

11. B. Bukovinská, 'Kunsthandwerk', in *Die Kunst am Hofe Rudolfs II.* (Prague, 1988), p. 161.

12. Fock (note 10), p. 52.

13. Przyborowski (note 4), p. 410.

14. *Ibid.*, pp. 276–77, 579–80, 593–94.

15 A. M. Giusti, P. Mazzoni and A. Pampaloni Martelli, *Il Museo dell'Opificio delle Pietre Dure a Firenze* (Milan, 1978), pp. 290–91, no. 81, pl. 67; Giusti (as note 8), p. 170, pl. 82.

16. Przyborowski (note 4), pp. 276–77. The work is in the Museo dell'Opificio delle Pietre Dure, Florence. Giusti *et al.* (note 15), p. 290, no. 75, pl. 79; Giusti (note 8), pp. 140, 160–61, pl. 86.

17. See E. Fučíková in *Prag um 1600: Kunst und Kultur am Hofe Rudolfs II.*, exh. cat., 2 vols (Freren, 1988), vol. 1, p. 190.

18. H. Haupt, Quellen und Studien zur Geschichte des Furstenhauses Liechtenstein 1 (in 2 parts): *Fürst Karl I. von Liechtenstein, Obersthofmeister Kaiser Rudolfs II. und Vizekönig von Böhmen: Hofstaat und Sammeltätigkeit* (Graz and Vienna, 1983), p. 287, nos. 738, 739.

19. Vienna, Kunsthistorisches Museum, Kunstkammer, 3392. See *Prag um 1600* (note 17), no. 732. The entire cabinet was made in Florence. A publication is in preparation on this subject.

20. *Liechtenstein: The Princely Collections*, exh. cat. (New York, 1986), pp. 48–50, no. 27 (C. Vincent).

21. *Macchia*, which is untranslatable, refers to the depiction of objects by means of the colour and marbling of stones. A Florentine letter of 1622 uses the phrase *con bellisime macchie* to describe the Abraham commesso. See Przyborowski (note 4), p. 593.

22. See N. Gramaccini, 'Das genaue Abbild der Natur – Riccios Tiere und die Theorie des Naturabgusses seit Cennini', in *Natur und Antike*, exh. cat. (Frankfurt, 1986), p. 220.

23. E. Scheicher, 'Zur Ikonologie von Naturalien im Zusammenhang der enzyklopädischen Kunstkammer', *Anzeiger des Germanischen Nationalmuseums* (1995), 115–16.

24. Circumstances would seem to point to an early date for the warrior.

The *Kunstkammer* of Rudolf II: Where it Was and What It Looked Like

BEKET BUKOVINSKÁ

14.1 ANTONIO SUSINI
(after Giambologna)
CASTRUCCI WORKSHOP
Pacing Horse on a Pedestal with Paneling
Horse ca. 1605; pedestal
ca. 1610
[Dresden, Staatliche Kunst-sammlungen, Grünes Gewölbe]

14.2 UNKNOWN MASTER
Table Clock
Ca. 1610; pendulum ca. 1700
[Vienna, Kunsthistorisches Museum, Kunstkammer]

The *Kunstkammer* of Rudolf II has interested many scholars and will remain an inexhaustible subject for some time to come. Rudolf's contemporaries understood the significance of his collections, and they were never forgotten despite their fate following his death. To begin with, some items were removed to Vienna, then others were sold, taken as spoils by the Swedes at the end of the Thirty Years' War. Finally, some were sold at auction at the end of the eighteenth century. The collections in their entirety were therefore only experienced by contemporaries of the Emperor, and those who actually saw them were few in number. A memory of boundless wealth lived on, but its content remained elusive. The lack of information influenced J. Schlosser's negative evaluation, which had a substantial impact and in some places still holds to this day.[1]

The discovery of the *Kunstkammer* inventory brought about a fundamental change in the way the collection was seen. Compiled during the Emperor's life,[2] the inventory commenced in 1607 and continued up to 1611. Today, it is universally presumed to have been drawn up by the Emperor's miniature painter and court antiquarian Daniel Fröschl. A methodical edition of the inventory made in 1976 opened up a wide range of possibilities for studying the selection, composition, processing and arrangement of the collections. The foreword to this edition contains a summary of the state of knowledge and indentifies works which could be matched to particular entries. Since 1976, the inventory has supported a good deal of further research. Yet we still know comparatively little about the *Kunstkammer*; many aspects of it have failed to attract any interest at all. In future, detailed study of these will doubtless advance the fields of ethnography, Oriental studies and particularly the art of the Near East. This essay does not try to reconstruct the ideal programme of *Kunstkammer*; rather, it will attempt to clarify the location and arrangement of the *Kunstkammer*; at the same time, it will try to provide an outline of the collection's content based on a study of the inventories.

If we want to know where the *Kunstkammer* was located and what it looked like, we must refer to written sources, primarily inventories and the oldest extant plans from the first half of the eighteenth century. In this respect, the complete Zimmerman edition of the inventory of 1621, including other documents and especially the 1635 list, is important,[3] as is the Morávek edition of the *Kunstkammer* list procured by the Estates in 1619.[4] It is evident from the information contained in these inventories that the *Kunstkammer* occupied four adjoining rooms denoted as the 'Kunstkammer' proper and as the 'erstes, zweites und drittes Gewölb' or 'vordere Kunstkammer'. Zimmermann did not attempt to discover their location, while Morávek presumed that the 'Kunstkammer' proper is the same as the present-day Rudolfine Gallery. This was a distortion which confused the position and identification of a number of other rooms, including the 'New Room' (today the 'Spanish Room'). The authors of the edition of the 1607–1611 inventory devoted one sentence to the location of the collections: 'Die Kunstkammer bestand aus drei aufeinanderfolgenden Räumen, wovon ein Raum die eigentliche *kunstcammer* war, welcher zwei *gewelbe* oder *vorkamern* (*fördere kunstcammer*) vorgelagert waren.' They missed one room altogether.[5]

A correct identification of the *Kunstkammer*'s rooms that corresponds to the inventories was discovered by I. Muchka and supported by architectural research in the Prague Castle itself.[6] A more detailed study of the collections' location and content was made by E. Fučíková.[7] We now know that the Emperor's *Kunstkammer* was located on the first floor of the connecting wing between his living rooms in the palace's south wing facing the city and both the Spanish Room (now known as the Rudolfine Gallery) and the New Room (today called the Spanish Room) in the northern part of the Castle. This wing, called 'Gangbau' or 'Langbau' in sources of the time, was built against the wall of the former ramparts, onto which little houses, facing St Vitus' cathedral, abutted to the east. It had a large number of windows on its western side, looking onto today's second courtyard, and their number has remained practically unchanged to this day. The original division of the wing, which is today connected to a broad corridor on the first floor, can still be seen in part in plans from the first half of the eighteenth century. At the time, there was no connection from the south on the first floor, as the arch of the White Tower gateway, which was then the entrance point to the third courtyard, rose up to first-floor level. A single-flight staircase ran from the Emperor's rooms, which were on the second floor of the south palace, to the first floor, leading into the first room of the anterior *Kunstkammer*. This was the first of the three spaces which are consistently described in the inventories as 'erstes, zweites, drittes Gewölb'. These vaulted rooms occupied the Corridor Wing as far as the Mathematics Tower, which rose up through every floor and whose oval staircase connected the floors and allowed access from the courtyard. The main room, corresponding to the description 'Kunstkammer', evidently had a flat ceiling, was adjacent to the Mathematics Tower and ended at the north wing. There was another staircase here which the Emperor could descend from the second floor to reach the level of the *Kunstkammer* and both ceremonial rooms occupying two floor levels. The full length of the Corridor Wing was approximately 100 metres, of which around 60 were taken up by the three rooms of the anterior *Kunstkammer* and around thirty-three by the main *Kunstkammer*. It was 5.5 metres wide. During the Theresian renovations, the first floor was raised at the expense of the gallery floor. So originally, the ratio was the opposite of what it is today: the gallery corridor on the second floor was 5 metres high, and the *Kunstkammer* had a lower ceiling.

The appearance and layout of the *Kunstkammer* are not recorded anywhere, nor do we know anything of its basic furnishings. Here, too, we can get some idea of its appearance from the inventories. The most valuable information naturally comes from the original 1607–11 list. We know that this list was made systematically, so items are not recorded here on the basis of local grouping, but by affinity of material and provenance. In some cases, we learn about how these were spread out or placed in cases directly from the text or, more frequently, from the additional notes. These are in pencil and in a uniform hand, and it is presumed that they more or less coincide with the time of the records themselves.[8] In any case, they enable us to make a partial reconstruction of the area. In a number of cases, these diverse data also provide important information about the furnishings and their arrangement.

14.3 ERASMUS HABERMEL
Noctural and Sundial
1585–86
[Prague, Národní technické muzeum]

14.4 NIKOLAUS PFAFF
UNIDENTIFIED GOLDSMITH
Covered Goblet made from a Rhinoceros Horn
1611
[Vienna, Kunsthistorisches Museum, Kunstkammer]

14.6 (Attributed to)
DANIEL FRÖSCHL
Page with Horn of a Narwhal
from the *Museum of Rudolf II*
1598–1611
[Vienna, Handschriften- und
Inkunabeln Sammlung der
ÖNB]

14.5 CASTRUCCI WORKSHOP
Casket with Pietre Dure
Mosaics
1610–15
[Dresden, Staatliche Kunstsammlungen, Kunstgewerbe-
museum]

Based on a comparison with later sources, Fučíková pointed out that the 1607–11 inventory does not depict the entire *Kunstkammer*, merely the part denoted as the 'Kunstkammer' in the inventories.[9] In fact, there are whole groups of articles which we know to have been Rudolf's property and which are recorded in one of the two later lists. This is true of the collection of Italian and French faience, for example, which is recorded in the 1621 inventory as numbering 178 pieces in case number 2 in the first room of the anterior *Kunstkammer*.[10] The inventory also does not show a large quantity of worked and unworked precious stones which in 1621 were described as being in case number 14 in the third room of the anterior *Kunstkammer* and which apparently numbered hundreds of pieces, arranged by type in boxes and caskets.[11]

The first list made after the Rudolfine inventory was that drawn up on the order of the Estates before the arrival of Friedrich Falcký in 1619. Like its predecessor from 1607–11, it does not include the picture gallery, but it does record an extensive collection of arms as well as all four rooms of the *Kunstkammer*. The aim of this list was to value the collection, and so items are treated in groups according to type and furnished with an estimated price. At the end, there is a brief outline of the items' location in which the number of cases, cabinets and chests is summarized and their contents partially indicated. This outline starts in the three anterior vaulted rooms and ends with the *Kunstkammer* proper. Although the information is scanty, it does tell us something about the cases, for example.

The 1621 inventory is the first list which records the collections in their entirety, that is to say not just the *Kunstkammer* but also the picture gallery, and the furnishings of both the Spanish Room and New Room, adjacent chambers and even, to some extent, the living quarters. The description of the *Kunstkammer* starts from

the opposite end to the 1619 list, but the sequence of cabinets is consistent. A number of details are more specific and a clearer outline of the furniture is provided. The basic details of the *Kunstkammer*'s furnishings in fact concur in all the inventories, which allows us to presume that they were not changed fundamentally until the second decade of the seventeenth century. By combining the information from these three sources, we can form a picture of the *Kunstkammer* from the time of its founder.

The main room was furnished with twenty cases which are identically described not only in the two later inventories but also in the original 1607–11 list. Here they are mentioned in relation to the items which stood inside and between them.[12] These included globes and rare antlers, but consisted mainly of sculptures, a whole series of which have been preserved and identified. For example, in the first case there was a famous bust of Charles V by Leone Leoni,[13] in the second the sculpture *Lion Clawing a Horse* today ascribed to Antonio Susini.[14] Works by Giambologna, including the sculpture *Hercules and Antheus*[15] which stood in the fourth case, with *Hercules with the Boar of Erymanthus*[16] in the fifth. On the last case was a bust of Rudolf II by Adriaen de Vries from 1607.[17] The first of the twenty cases in the main room is labelled *A* and the last *B*, with the rest numbered from 1 to 18. In the later lists, they are numbered from 1 to 20, and their numbers and content correspond exactly. We have no report of their placement, but Muchka held that in the vaulted spaces – that is to say, in all the rooms of the anterior *Kunstkammer* – cases could only have stood against a full wall, whilst in the *Kunstkammer* proper, which evidently had a flat ceiling, they most probably also stood between the windows. A question remains as to why two of the cases were given letters and what can be inferred from this. It would seem that the case lettered *A* corresponds to case number 1 in the later inventories, which had two shelves, and it is most likely that the bust of Charles V which stood on it was not moved until 1621.[18] The last in the sequence, lettered *B* in the earliest inventory, is evidently the same as number 20 in the later lists. It also had two shelves, and at the time of Rudolf II the Emperor's bust stood on it. Did these cases face each other on the two shorter walls, or did they form symmetrical counterparts in the group of cabinets along the full east wall? Doubt is cast on this idea by the fact that the case listed as number 4 also had two shelves, and the bust of Rudolf II, which Adriaen de Vries had created as a counterpart to the portrait of Charles V, is placed in the Rudolfine inventory between 'Metalline bilder, so hin und her uff der tafel, tisch und studioln stehn und gefungen werden' – that is, between sculptures which stood on a large table or on other stands and cabinets. A note made in pencil tells us that this large bust was in the third room of the anterior *Kunstkammer* and it was also recorded there in 1621.[19]

All that we can garner about the appearance of the cases is that they had between two and six shelves each. It is difficult to judge whether they were the same height and whether they were adapted to suit their contents. It is likely that at least some of them were fairly large, if we imagine that, for example, cabinet number 18 (1621 inventory) with four shelves housed a total of 389 large and small pieces of porcelain. In some armoires, items were stored in various boxes and chests. In case number 6 (1621 inventory), for example, thirteen boxes and fourteen caskets were arranged on three shelves. Their contents correspond roughly to case number 5 in the Rudolfine inventory, described in folios 18–28, where the writer carefully de-

14.7 ANTONIO ABONDIO
Mary, Wife of Maximilian II
Ca. 1568
[Berlin, Staatliche Museen,
Münzkabinett]

14.8 JAN VERMEYEN
*Emperor Rudolf II on Horse-
back*
Ca. 1594
[Berlin, Staatliche Museen,
Münzkabinett]

scribes tortoises, crabs, fish and fossils of sea creatures, often with a note that they were stored in painted boxes.

A long table stood in the middle of the *Kunstkammer*, described in several places as a 'lange grüne Tafel'. In 1621, it was covered with globes, clocks, mechanical devices, caskets, mirrors, musical instruments – for example, 'eine ganze silberne lauten'[20] – silver vases with flowers of coloured silver or so-called '*handstein*' pieces, which are igneous rocks with figural decoration. In the Rudolfine inventory, we only find mention of what was on the table in certain places, for example in the entry on folio 338: 'Ein groß uhrwerk mit einem *astrolabio* sambt dem jahrzeiger herumb, darauf ein *sphera* sambt ihren *circulis planetarium* sambt anderer zugehor und ein geschribens tractelin darzu, steht auff der tafel in der kunstkammer, hat Jobst Bürgius gemacht, von h. von Braunschw: Ihr Mt: verehrt' (no. 2138). This is a clock with an astrolabe and globe with planets including instructions by Jost Bürgi, which was a gift from the Duke of Brunswick to the Emperor. Later on in the text is a description of a mechanical device in the form of a peacock, which walked, turned around and fanned its tail of real feathers: 'Ein uhr oder rederwerckh, ist ein pfaw, geht und wendt sich ringsum, schreitt und macht eine wannen mit seinem schwaiff von rechten federn, steht auff der tafel der kc:' (no. 2142). There were also musical instruments here; folio 332 mentions that 'Ein *spinet* oder *clavicimbolum* von glaßwerck, steht auf der tafel' (no. 2093). This glass instrument might be the same as the one which also stood on the table nine years later and was furnished with a black velvet case: '1 ganz gläsern instrument in einem schwarzensammaten futteral'.[21]

In the locations list attached to the Estates' inventory, the furniture count is followed by a number of individual objects. These were evidently free-standing pieces, many of which were situated on the large central table.[22] Here we also find the objects which are recorded as being on the table two years later – for example, a large crystal casket, a silver lute, a glass instrument, a mechanical device in the shape of a ship and particularly *handstein* pieces. One of these, depicting St George and the dragon, certainly corresponds to the 1621 entry number 338 and evidently also to an object recorded in the Rudolfine inventory among *handstein* pieces, but without any specification of its placement.[23] We also find corresponding descriptions in the Rudolfine inventory for other objects, but if their position is not given in the Estates' inventory we cannot be certain that they were also on the table then. That is why the mention of the mechanical device in the form of a peacock is gratifying, as it is indubitably the one which we have described above, and this demonstrates that certain items did indeed remain in the same place for at least another seven years after the Emperor's death. One object discovered in the revision of 1635 on the green table is 'Ein hohe gedrähete saul von helfenbein, darauf ist ein Mercurius', which is most likely to be the *Mercury* in the Národní Muzeum, Prague, and ascribed by Fučíková to Nikolaus Pfaff.[24]

The belief has been expressed by several scholars that the green table mentioned in the inventories is recorded among the pages of the so-called *Museum of Rudolf II,* in which zoological exhibits from the Emperor's collections are illustrated.[25] One page of this compendium shows two pieces of narwhal horn lying on a green desk; another page shows a goblet with a lid made from a rhinoceros horn another shows two pieces of bezoar (gastric calculuses found in antelopes); a page depicts two rhinoceros horns, one of which is mounted in gold.[26] The last piece has

been identified as the horn of an African rhinoceros now in a Viennese collection.[27] If this object corresponds to the entry in the Rudolfine inventory on folio 2 (no. 29), then at the time when the marginal pencil annotations were made this horn had a velvet case and was kept in chest number 22 along with the other nine pieces which follow in the inventory – together they are numbered independently from 1 to 10. It was therefore not displayed on the table.

In addition to the cases and the long table, the *Kunstkammer* also housed a number of other furnishings. There were tables, chests of a wide variety of sizes and 'schreibtische und studioli'. These terms must refer to various types of cabinets, jewellery cases and boxes which may have been so big that that they stood alone or on tables, or may have been so small that they were kept in cabinets and chests. For example, we read in the Estates' inventory that two chests contained a further six such pieces with many drawers in which gold, silver and copper Antique medals were kept: 'Zwo lange truhen, in deren jeder sechs schreibtisch mit vielen schublädeln, in deren meisten guldene, silberne und kupfern antiquische medailen'.[28]

The inventory of 1621 gives the best sense of how the pieces were arranged. A number of them stood on the floor by the large central table: 'Truhen und schreibtische, so an der erden an bemelter grünen tafel nacheinander stehen'.[29] There were seven cabinets placed around the table and four chests. The chest which was covered in leather and held knives and daggers in both 1619 and 1621 can be matched to chest number 71 in the Rudolfine inventory. The additional notes on folios 66–68 tell us that they held altogether 105 knives and daggers of a wide variety of provenances. As well as a large number of Turkish knives with handles richly decorated with gold, silver, ivory and precious stones, there was also supposedly the dagger with which Caesar was murdered and a knife which in 1602 had been swallowed by a peasant in Prague and remained inside him for nine months before being cut out. The contents of this chest were no longer so rich in 1621, but that inventory includes a description of the aforementioned swallowed knife and even adds the detail that it was cut out by a Master Florian, barber.[30]

Other tables, which are numbered at ten in the 1621 inventory, stood by the windows and supported cabinets or chests and also marble, bronze, plaster and wax sculptures or mirrors. There were other pieces of furniture, statues and globes placed between these tables and on the floor. Two chairs are also mentioned: one of them, an iron chair with rich figural decoration 'mit figurn durchbrochene arbeit' (1621, no. 509), can be matched to an entry in the Rudolfine inventory: '*Ein gantz eyserner sessel* mit vil außgehawenen bildern und historien *triumphen*, ganz künstliche und sehr verwunderliche mhüesame arbeitt daran' (no. 1154). This chair was still in Prague Castle in 1648 and is now at Longford Castle, near Salisbury in England.[1]

In the Rudolfine inventory, there are a number of cabinets and chests listed on folios 354–388 and numbered. If we consolidate all the information on the chests and cabinets found in various places in the oldest list and in the marginal notes, we discover that the numbering forms a sequence from 1 to 101. It starts with the chests (1–16, 18, 20, 22, 26, 28, 37, 53, 55, 58, 60–62, 70–73, 78, 93, 94–98); other numbers denote 'schreibtische' (21, 80–92 and 100–101). Some numbers do not appear in the sequence (17, 19, 23–25, 27, 29–36, 38–52, 54, 56–57, 59, 63–69, 74–77, 79, 99), and so it is not clear to which piece of furniture they relate. The additional notes showing positions are not consistently given for every item, so we do not

14.9 MISERONI WORKSHOP (Milan [?])
Crystal Vessel in the Shape of a Bucket
Ca. 1575–80
[Vienna, Kunsthistorisches Museum, Kunstkammer]

14.10 OTTAVIO MISERONI (?)
Tazza
Early 17th century
[Stockholm, The Royal Collections of Sweden]

14.11 HUBERT GERHARD
Mars, Venus and Cupid
Ca. 1605
[Vienna, Kunsthistorisches
Museum, Kunstkammer

know whether the missing numbers belonged to furniture which is not mentioned or to furniture which may have been in other rooms. The numbers of chests and cabinets are not included in the later lists, so it is impossible to state whether the numbering referred to one room (as was true for cases) or whether it was a system of designation used before the furniture was placed in the Corridor Wing.[32]

The chests are not described in detail, and there are only a few mentions of their being iron or covered in leather. The contents of a number of them are clear, however, particularly in the section where books, drawings and graphic art are assembled. None of the later inventories specifically record chests containing books and graphic art. We find more interesting information relating to cabinets, particularly in various places in the Rudolfine inventory. On folio 363, for example, there is a description of a cabinet decorated with precious stones, cameo glass and miniatures by H. Bol: 'Ist der schöne schreibkasten so zu *Milano* gemacht worden, von jaspis und mehrerley stainen und groß *camefey* und von 6 stuckh *miniatura von H. Boln*, umbher alles mit geschnitnen *granaten* eingefasst ...' (no. 2384) A number of other cabinets were made of ebony or walnut, many inlaid with ivory or decorated with silver. Some of these, described as 'indianisch schreibtischlein', may also have been Japanese works of black or red lacquer, painted with gold and inlaid with mother-of-pearl. Another cabinet described in this way was adorned with carved foliage and completely gilded. The dimensions of this cabinet are also given: '... ist lang 1 eln 8 zoll, breit 19 zoll, hoch 16 1/2 zoll'.[39] Some cabinets are described very extensively, such as a small piece gilded on the outside and white inside with painted golden birds and foliage, whose drawers held sea- and snail shells: 'Schriebtisch No. 87. Ein klein, aussen gantz vergult schreibtischl, inwendig weiß und guldene vögel und laubwerckh darauf gemalt, ist in seinem 6 schubladen anderst nichts also außgelesen mermuscheln und scheggen' (no. 2400).

The 'schreibtisch' containing the most items would seem to be number 100, called 'des elsässers'.[33] It was a cabinet of ebony combined with brown wood that had three drawers, the bottom one being large: 'In der understen grossen schubladen'. The brief introductory list of contents shows that it held precious small clocks and mechanical devices made of gold, adorned with gemstones, tiny portraits and miniatures, rings, earrings, medals and portraits in gold and silver. The detailed description of the entire contents by drawer follows, covering nine folios. Among the precious trinkets we find a large spider which could be wound up and sent running across the table, or a small jewel figure of St Jerome which moved its head and beat its breast with a stone. This cabinet also held a large opal set in gold, which we know was taken in 1631 to Vienna, where it remains today.[34] The small items were laid in boxes and cases and sometimes had their own numbering. For example, gold and silver medals with portraits of sovereigns are listed under numbers 1–70.

In the Estates' inventory, cabinets are individually described at the beginning and also on folios 96v and 97r. The first of these was decorated with jasper, chalcedony, gold and pearls ('Ain schön herlicher schreibtisch von schönem künstlischem geschnittenen jaspiß, chalcedon und andern steinen, mit gold, perln und edlgestäin gezirt'), and its value was estimated at 6 million groschen. One of the other cabinets, all of ebony or walnut, is described separately as '... wie ein pyramis zu antiquischen medalien' (fol. 97r). This is evidently the same as the one described

14.12 GASPARO MISERONI
WORKSHOP
Tazza
Ca. 1560; mounting ca.
1550–75
[Vienna, Kunsthistorisches
Museum, Kunstkammer]

in the Rudolfine inventory under number 91: 'Das ebani gestaffelt *da pyramide antiquarium*, darinnen allerley *antische medalien* gelegen sein ...' (no. 2404). This cabinet in the shape of a pyramid was specially adapted for storing medals and coins. Another detail which refers to this cabinet in the Rudolfine inventory is to be found in an entirely different context. On folio 320, which lists bronze statues standing on furniture, the writer draws attention to the fact that this piece of furniture was topped by a statue whose outstretched hands held a medal showing Caesar Augustus: 'Uff dem ebnin gestaffelten *piramide* oder *antiquario* mit No. 91 ist oben auff dem gipfel ein weiblin von metal, welches ein *Imp: Augusto* pfenning inn der rechten hand von silber endtpot hebt.'[35]

The composition and arrangement of furniture in the first three vaulted rooms of the anterior *Kunstkammer* was similar. There were in total seventeen cases altogether,[36] and also tables, chests, cabinets and free-standing objects. We learn from the Estates' inventory that two cases were open and the remaining fifteen closed. Numbers 16 and 17 were double cases. The fact that the armoires are here described as open and closed, sometimes double, may mean that they were different from the cases in the main *Kunstkammer*, where there was no such differentiation, or that a more detailed description may be missing, or that all the armoires there were the same, perhaps open.[37]

14.13 OTTAVIO MISERONI,
PRAGUE WORKSHOP
(mounting)
Goblet with a Swan
Ca. 1600
[Stockholm, The Royal
Collections of Sweden]

The *Kunstkammer* of Rudolf II was intended to be encyclopaedic; it conformed to the theoretical ideas of the time, and its composition was not so different from contemporary collections of the kind, such as those in Munich or Ambras. Nevertheless, it would seem, as Fučíková has demonstrated, that in Prague it was not only the quantity and breadth of its founder's interests that distinguished it but also the grouping of the objects and the way they were presented.[38]

The *Kunstkammer*s in Munich and Ambras were arranged so that the assembled objects, grouped according to particular criteria, could be viewed easily and bore clear witness to the founders' intentions. E. Seelig demonstrated that the objects in the Munich *Kunstkammer* were displayed predominantly on large rectangular tables in the middle of halls and on smaller square tables under windows. They were most often grouped by material so as to form units, intended primarily to make their ar-

14.14 MISERONI, PRAGUE
WORKSHOP
JAN VERMEYEN WORKSHOP
(mounting)
Covered Goblet
Ca. 1600
[Stuttgart, Württembergis-
ches Landesmuseum]

rangement impressive. The founder's main aim was for the visitor to look briefly around on entering the room, to perceive the entire space and to be moved by the unbelievable preciousness and splendour of the pieces on display.[39]

The *Kunstkammer* of Rudolf's uncle Archduke Ferdinand II, in Ambras Castle, had a strict order in which the aesthetic aspect played an important part. E. Scheicher demonstrated that on the central axis there were eighteen cases reaching up to the ceiling. Their contents were methodically arranged on the basis of material affinity, irrespective of the age, origin or significance of individual pieces. Objects of gold were kept together, as were silver, wood, stone and iron items, and the colour of the backgrounds was made to suit the collected objects and varied from case to case. Blue backgrounds were reserved for gold, green for silver and so on. Free-standing items placed on shelves were protected from dust and sunlight by cloth curtains. The same principle applied to both the Munich and Ambras collections: they were meant for presentation, to enchant and enlighten the viewer. Visitors were expected, and there were many of them. Access was granted to numerous, albeit élite, applicants.[40]

If we can rely on marginal notes to reveal the true arrangement of the objects in the Prague *Kunstkammer* during the life of Rudolf II or immediately after his death, it is evident that a large number of objects were arranged in such a way that viewing them required time and a knowledge of the material. It is striking that if we use these pencilled notes to piece together the contents of the chests and cabinets, we discover that even ostentatious works we would expect to have been displayed on tables or shelves were shut away in chests and, often, additionally in small gilded leather cases.

Chest number 2, for example, contained all the crystal vessels, including two magnificent crystal boxes, together with bezoar vessels. Chest number 3 held vessels made of walnut and conch in intricate silver-gilt mountings: we have a good idea of their magnificence as two works by anonymous goldsmiths[41] have been preserved and also a masterpiece by Anton Schweinberger which today ranks among the supreme pieces of Rudolfine craftsmanship.[42] Similarly, the contents of chest number 4 included van Vianen and Christoph Jamnitzer pots and bowls, including Jamnitzer's famous set, now in Vienna.[43] Chests numbers 6 and 8 are meant to have held vessels made of precious stones with gold mounts, a number of which have been successfully matched to existing pieces.

The inventories permit us to form a picture of the *Kunstkammer*'s location and a partial idea of how it was arranged; sometimes we even learn what individual pieces probably looked like. In many instances, we know which objects were stored together and how they were organized. The picture is incomplete, however, and a number of questions remain unanswered. We cannot rule out the possibility that there was a system in the arrangement of the cases, their relation to one another, their colour and so on. At present, we are chiefly able to deduce the purpose of the *Kunstkammer* and the system on which it was based from the system and composition of its original inventory. The information which this source can provide on the possible order of the collection's arrangement is still far from being exhausted, and it is therefore still too early to close off this path of enquiry with the claim that the arrangement of items had no method. It is evident that the inventories have much more to reveal.

1. J. von Schlosser, *Kunst und Wunderkammern der Spätrenaissance* (Leipzig, 1908), pp. 76–82.

2. First information about the finding is in E. Neumann, 'Das Inventar der rudolfinischen Kunstkammer von 1607–11' in *Analecta Reginensia* 1, *Queen Christina of Sweden: Documents and Studies* (Stockholm 1966); Bauer-Haupt 1976.

3. H. Zimmermann, 'Das Inventar der Prager Schatz und Kunstkammer vom 6. Dezember 1621', in *JKSAK*, XXX/2 (1905), pp. XV–LXXV.

4. J. Morávek, 'Nově objevený inventář rudolfínských sbírek na Hradě Pražském' (Prague, 1937).

5. Bauer-Haupt 1976, p. XXVII. In the relevant note there is a reference to the inventory issued by Morá-vek. E. Scheicher, *Die Kunst und Wunderkammern der Habsburger* (Vienna, 1979), p. 144 also gives one room less.

6. I. Muchka, 'Podoba Pražského hradu v rudolfínské době z hlediska veduty', *Umění* XXXI (1983), pp. 447–50.

7. E. Fučíková, B. Bukovinská, I. Muchka *Umění na dvoře Rudolfa II.* (Prague, 1988), pp. 214–48. 8.

8. E. Irblich (ed.) in *Thesaurus Austriacus: Europas Glanz im PSpiegel der Buchkunst*, (Vianna, 1996), p. 279, is of the opinion that the pencil notes are by Fröschl: 'Auch die marginalen Notizen und Lokationsbezeichnungen für die Standorte der Kunstgegenstände in Truhen oder Schränken (Almaren) in Bleistift stammen von Fröschl, wie Vergleiche mit der Schreibweise der Zahlen und mit der Abkürzung No. für die Nummer in Register bestätigen ...'

9. E. Fučíková, 'The Collection of Rudolf II at Prague: Cabinet of Curiosities or Scientific Museum?' in O. Impley and A. MacGregor (eds), *The Origins of Museums: The Cabinet of Curiosities in Sixteenth- and Seventeent Europe* (Oxford, 1985), pp. 47–53

10. Zimmermann (note 3), p. XXXIII, no. 608. The fact that the inventory does not contain everything in the *Kunstkammer* is obvious. In several places there are records of objects with a note that they are located in one of the rooms of the anterior *Kunstkammer*. Compare Bauer-Haupt 1976, nos 1832–33 (I. gw.), 1834–35 (II. gw.), 1846–47 (II. gw.), 1975–76 (III. gw), 1977–1978 (II. gw.) (all sculptures displayed on tables). These notes are amongst the penciled additions.

11. *Ibid.*, p. XXXVI, nos 746–62.

12. Bauer-Haupt 1976, nos 1874–1921.

13. *Ibid.* 1976, no. 1874; Vienna, Kunsthistorisches Museum, inv. no. 5404.

14. *Ibid.* 1976, no. 1878; Vienna, Kunsthistorisches Museum, inv. no. 6018.

15. *Ibid.* 1976, no. 1885; Vienna, Kunsthistorisches Museum, inv. no. 5845.

16. *Ibid.* 1976, no. 1887; Vienna, Kunsthistorisches Museum, inv. no. 5846.

17. *Ibid.* 1976, no. 1920; Vienna, Kunsthistorisches Museum, inv. no. 5491.

18. Zimmermann (note 3), p. XXXII, no. 541. Among the objects which stood on cases this portrait took first place.

19. *Ibid.*, no. 763.

20. *Ibid.*, no. 353.

21. *Ibid.*, no. 352.

22. Morávek (note 4), p. 33.

23. Bauer-Haupt 1976, no. 1616.

24. Zimmermann (note 3), p. LXII, no. 254. Prague, Národní muzeum v Praze, inv. no. H2–3685. The identification is not quite certain, because in the 1607–11

inventory there is another description of Mercury, which differs from the existing object. It mentions a standing figure, Bauer-Haupt, no. 953.

25. T. Vignau-Wilberg (Essen-Vienna, 1988), no. 605

26. *Le Bestiaire de l'empereur Rodolphe II* (Paris, 1989), nos 9, 11, 13, 16.

27. Vienna, Kunsthistorisches Museum, Kunstkammer, inv. no. 3702. R. Distelberger (Essen-Wien 1988, cat. no. 408) does not believe that this piece is the same as the one on fol. 12 of the aforementioned compendium. M. Staudinger believes the two are the same, however (Essen-Wien 1988, cat. no. 605).

28. Morávek (note 4), p. 32

29. Zimmermann (note 3), p. XXVIII.

30. *Ibid.*, no. 473.

31. B. Dudík, 'Die Rudolphinische Kunst- und Raritätenkammer in Prag', *Mitteilungen K.K. Central-Commission zur Erforschung und Erhalung der Baudebkmale*, XII (1867), p. XLIII: '1. ganz eiserner Sessel, so in der ersten Kunst Kammer stehet.'

32. Fučíková 1988 (note 7), pp. 230–31, presumes that 'the explicit listing of iron furniture in various parts of the *Kunstkammer* suggests that they might have been part of its older furnishings from the time when it was still situated in the palace'.

33. Bauer-Haupt 1976, no. 2408. The designation 'Elsassers', which relates to this piece of furniture in three places in the Rudolfine inventory, may be a clue to determining the master craftsman who made it. The brothers Bernhard and Wigelius Elsässer were in the services of Rudolf II. Wigelius was the Emperor's rifle maker (*Büchsenspanner*) and was paid 15 guldens a month, Bernhard made butts (*Büchsenschäfter*) and received 8 guldens a month. However, as A. Lhotsky in *Festschrift des Kunsthistorisches Museums zur Feier des fünfzigjärigen Bestandes: Die Geschichte der Sammlungen* (Vienna, 1941–45), p. 215 states, in 1594 he received 446 guldens and 40 kreutzers for a chest and 'schreibtisch'. Z. Winter in *Řemeslnictvo a živnosti XVI věku v Čechách (1526–1620)* (Prague, 1909), p. 467 states that this master craftsman made an inlaid table for Rudolf II.

34. Vienna, Kunsthistorisches Museum, Kunstkammer, inv. no. 1825.

35. Bauer-Haupt, no. 1963.

36. It is interesting that the cases are numbered from 1 to 17 and that in the first three rooms the 1621 inventory mentions another two cases: 'in einer grünen almar' and 'in der kleineren grünen almar'. Both contained stuffed birds.

37. In this essay I have concentrated on the main room of the *Kunstkammer*. In the near future I hope to be able to prepare a separate study which will enable me to put together similar information in greater depth.

38. Fučíková 1988 (note 7), pp. 236–43.

39. J. Seelig, 'The Munich Kunstkammer, 1565–1807' in O. Impley and A. MacGregor (eds) (note 9) pp. 76–89.

40. Scheicher (note 5), pp. 72–136.

41. Bauer-Haupt 1976, no. 298; Vienna, Kunsthistorisches Museum, Kunstkammer, inv. no. 6848 (Essen-Vienna 1988, no 686); Bauer-Haupt, no. 295; Schatzkammer des Deutschen Ordens, Inventarliste no. 74 (Essen-Vienna, no. 687)

42. Bauer-Haupt 1976, no. 296; Vienna, Kunsthistorisches Museum, Kunstkammer, inv. no. 6872.

43. *Ibid.* no. 1536, Vienna, Kunsthistorisches Museum, Kunstkammer, inv. nos 1104, 1128.

Cabinets, Collecting and Natural Philosophy

PAULA FINDLEN

15.1 **Armillary Sphere**
Ca. 1600
[Prague, Národní technické muzeum]

Shortly after Rudolf II moved from Vienna to Prague in 1583, court architects and engineers began to construct long galleries in Hradcany Castle to house several thousand paintings and equally vast numbers of sculptures, coins, vases, gems, natural rarities, precious medicines, scientific instruments, clocks, books and other curiosities that became the imperial *Kunstkammer*. Slowly the spaces known as the Spanish Room and the New Room emerged on the first floor, above the stalls on the ground level. In this northern part of the palace, Rudolf placed the majority of his artistic possessions – Titians, Correggios, Brueghels, Dürers, the best that Renaissance Europe had to offer – and an antiquarium. Court artists and craftsmen decorated the galleries, creating elegant chests to display the Habsburg treasures and embellishing the rooms with appropriate motifs that portrayed Rudolf as a new Maecenas who commanded the world from the vaults of his museum.

Construction of the rooms which housed Rudolf II's marvels took somewhat longer; these artefacts remained in the southern wing of the palace until approximately 1605–6. By then, the imperial artisans had completed the three vaulted rooms on the first floor known as the 'anterior *Kunstkammer*'. Just on the other side of the Mathematics Tower lay the *Kunstkammer* itself, containing an extensive display of some of Europe's finest scientific instruments, a handful of books and manuscripts and a desk where the Holy Roman Emperor sat amidst his treasures. Nearby was the library; below lay the workshops in which the imperial artisans laboured and possibly an alchemical laboratory. Visitors usually entered the *Kunstkammer* through an antechamber decorated with images of the four elements and twelve months, a microcosm of nature supervised by Jupiter, Rudolf's mythological alter-ego.[1] Thus in the last decade of Rudolf II's reign, he epitomized the image of the learned monarch who created and consumed all forms of knowledge, inhabiting a setting that the English statesman and philosopher Francis Bacon might have described as the realization of his image of a palace fit for a 'philosopher's stone' had he ever made the voyage from London to Prague.[2] In fact, this was an apt image for the castle of the 'German Hermes' whose library contained many alchemical and cabbalistic treatises and whose rooms were the site of many attempts to engender the philosopher's stone.

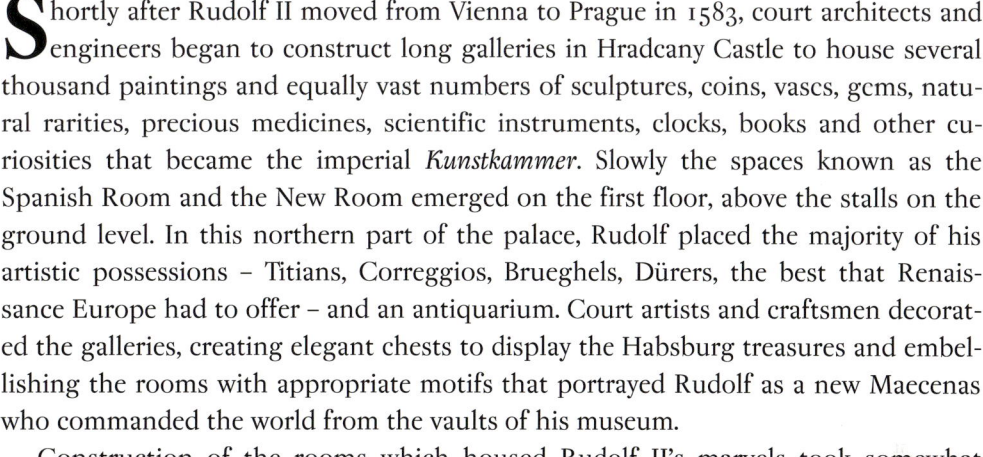

15.2 WILLEM JANSZOON BLAEU
Celestial Globe
1603
[Prague, Národní technické muzeum]

Few visitors enjoyed the privilege of seeing these rooms of wonders, yet word of their contents spread throughout Europe, so that many travelled to Prague with the aspiration of gaining an audience with the Holy Roman Emperor by presenting him with a gift worthy of his collection. By the time of Rudolf's death in 1612, it was hard to distinguish his own reputation from that of his artefacts. They had come to represent the Emperor perhaps better than the Emperor himself: 'Rudolf of few words', as the Venetian ambassador described him, spoke best through the objects in the imperial *Kunstkammer*.[3] Even after the dispersion of the collection in the seventeenth century, it continued to serve as a talisman of Rudolf's reputation as a learned and cultured ruler who saw the world as a precious cabinet of curiosities to be commanded and possessed at will.

The function of Rudolf II's collection continues to be a lively subject of debate. Early interpretations envisioned the *Kunstkammer* as a melancholic solitarium for an increasingly isolated and emotionally unstable emperor, who found solace in the works of nature and art and in the promises of alchemists as the tense political climate destroyed his vision of a universal peace for Christendom: 'Hiding himself in his great palace at Prague, with its libraries, its wonder rooms of magico-mechanical marvels, Rudolph withdrew in alarm from the problems raised by the fanatical intolerance of his frightening nephew.'[4] More recently such scholars as Eliška Fučíková, Georg Kugler and Thomas DaCosta Kaufmann have argued that Rudolf II's collection played an integral role in his political and diplomatic activities from the moment he ascended to the imperial throne. It served as a repository for gifts from princes, ambassadors, courtiers and scholars who, even if they rarely saw the collection, knew that they might enjoy the emperor's favour if they could place a trinket or two within his grasp.

The *Kunstkammer* also became a powerful symbol of the Emperor's vision of the world – an extended allegory of his earthly reign as Jupiter.[5] Celestial and terrestrial globes [figs 15.1, 15.2], astrolabes, quadrants, geometric compasses and a covered dish known as the *Weltallschale*, which contained an image of Europa in its basin, complemented the presence of such books as Ptolemy's *Geography* and a hand-coloured edition of Abraham Ortelius' *Theatrum orbis terrarum* (1570). Similarly, large quantities of Turkish and Indian daggers, a Turkish-Arabic dictionary, an Arabic Bible and a sketch of Constantinople defined the immediate political context for such objects as an 'old, long double-edged sword' inscribed with the words *Ubi regnat odium ibi cecum est iuditium* (Where hatred reigns, justice is blind).[6] Rather than being the folly of a delusory prince, the *Kunstkammer* was a calculated part of Rudolf's persona as an omniscient ruler and a logical expansion of the Habsburg tradition of patronizing the arts and sciences.[7]

The Mysteries of State Revealed

Rumours about the *Kunstkammer* abounded throughout the palace and in the streets of Prague. What exactly lay within those long hallways and vaulted chambers? 'Every day one finds new curiosities in the Imperial Palace', remarked Girolamo Soranzo to the Venetian Doge in 1612.[8] Early in Rudolf's reign, his passion for art became common knowledge. Princes openly competed in the depletion of their galleries to provide the Holy Roman Emperor with an adequate supply of ancient statues, bas-reliefs and canvases to sate his passion for beautiful objects. In July 1604, the ambassador for the Duke of Savoy, Carlo Francesco Manfredi, reported with glee that Rudolf had spent 'two and a half hours sitting motionless, looking at the paintings of fruit and fish markets sent by Your Highness'. Touring the Spanish Room in February 1605, he noted that they now enjoyed a place of honour in the imperial gallery.[9] One wonders if part of the attraction of these two paintings lay in their subject. Surely, they fit well in a collection that boasted the elaborate heads by the Milanese court painter Giuseppe Arcimboldo, who turned virtually every aspect of nature into a symbolic allegory of Habsburg rule [fig. 15.3].[10] Such gifts reflected some awareness of Rudolf's predilection for objects that intermingled art and nature.

Of course, Manfredi had no direct knowledge of Rudolf's initial reaction to the two paintings. He acquired his information from a court artist who had been with

15.3 GIUSEPPE ARCIMBOLDO
Water
1566
[Vienna, Kunsthistorisches Museum, Gemäldegalerie]

Rudolf at the time. Such a distinction raises important questions about the activities surrounding Rudolf's collection. We know that ceremonial visits played a central if infrequent role in the uses of the *Kunstkammer*. When other rulers visited, Rudolf personally showed them his collection, as occurred during the visits of Maximilian I of Bavaria and, later, of Christian II of Saxony in 1607.[11] On other occasions, Rudolf had his councillors, secretaries and attendants show visitors the rooms. During 1604–5, for instance, no less than three Italian ambassadors from the duchies of Modena and of Savoy toured the collections. On 23 August 1604, Girolamo Manzuolo followed the *cameriere maggiore* after a court banquet 'to see all the bejeweled treasures and His Majesty's other precious things'. Nine days earlier, no doubt in recognition of his higher social standing in the Este entourage from the duchy of Modena, Cardinal Alessandro d'Este saw Rudolf's paintings and the rooms filled with 'vases made of various kinds of precious stones, statues and clocks, a treasure worthy of its owner'.[12]

15.4 OTTAVIO MISERONI (?)
Cup with Cover
After 1600
[Bålsta, Skokloster Castle]

Manfredi, too, eventually got to see the *Kunstkammer*, no doubt as a reward for his role in the failed marital negotiations between Rudolf and the house of Savoy. His visit to the imperial art gallery had raised the question of seeing the rest of Rudolf's collection; in fact, Manfredi reported that the Emperor's advisors believed that he wanted to see the bejeweled Habsburg crown 'and other things that had now finished [in the hands of] the Emperor'. The second visit on 9 March 1605 commenced with an audience with Rudolf, the first Manfredi received after nine months of kicking his heels around the court. The Savoyard ambassador was not unprepared; he came bearing 'an Indian dagger', a ruby-encrusted rhinoceros horn, three bezoar stones, 'a large silver ship that contained inside it half of an Indian nut, larger than a man's head' and a crown. All of these objects harmonized well with the Emperor's taste for natural oddities, costly gems, sublime artisanry and exotica; numerous examples of similar artefacts appear in the 1607–11 inventory of the *Kunstkammer* composed by Rudolf's *antiquarius* Daniel Fröschl [figs 15.4, 15.5]. Apparently, Rudolf particularly admired the ship and the bezoar stones (precious antidotes for all manner of poisons according to ancient medical lore).[13] The former no doubt reminded him of the finely wrought automata that his artisans produced in the imperial workshops, while the latter made a fine addition to a collection of bezoar stones compiled by agents all over Europe which Rudolf used to ward off the 1599 plague. One court physician described a bezoar stone that was so large that Rudolf had it carved into a drinking cup.[14]

Just as Manfredi was about to leave, Rudolf summoned him back into his chamber. Two attendants then took the Savoyard ambassador on a tour of the *Kunstkammer*, where he beheld an array of jewelled boxes and necklaces, vases, a six-foot-long unicorn's horn (surely one of the narwhal horns Rudolf coveted), the imperial crown and a great agate basin, one of the most valued Habsburg treasures. Upon peering inside this last item, Manfredi discovered what made it so remarkable: 'and in the vein of the stone "Christ" was written by nature's hand in big letters'.[15] God himself seemed to have spoken to the imperial family through the work of nature, inscribing an object that gave testimony to all who beheld it that theirs was a divinely inspired reign. The importance of this natural hieroglyph helps to explain the value placed upon Giovanni Castrucci's paintings made with stone (*commessi in pietra dura*) that seemed to imitate this process [fig. 15.6].[16] These, in short, were the mysteries with which Rudolf surrounded himself every time he sat in his *Kunstkammer*.

Nature at the Center of the Realm

Accounts of official visits offer us a limited window through which to view Rudolf's passion for objects. Predictably, many ambassadors had eyes primarily for the most costly and wondrous objects in the collection; they viewed Rudolf's *Kunstkammer* with the practised gaze of art connoisseurs and the more traditional gaze of visitors to a medieval treasury. They did not mention, for instance, the following item which no visitor could have missed since it was one of the central objects in the room: 'A large clockwork with an astrolabe and an annual indicator round about it, and upon this a sphere with its *circulis planetarum* and other appurtenances, and a written treatise with it; it stands on the table in the *Kunstkammer*; Jost Bürgi made it, from the Duke of Braunschweig; presented to His Imperial Majesty.'[17] Rudolf's court physician Anselm Boetius de Boodt was right when he wrote in his *Gemmarum et lapidum historia* (1609), an imperial lapidary written from the objects in Rudolf's possession, that gems so often dazzled their beholders that they could see little beyond them.[18] Thus ambassadors such as Manfredi missed a great deal of the significance of the *Kunstkammer*, for all that they revealed.

A different sort of visitor would have readily discerned how much of the *Kunstkammer* pertained to scientific collecting (and might accordingly have appreciated the medical and philosophical value of Rudolf's gems, as de Boodt did, or the fantastic clocks, as Tycho Brahe and Johannes Kepler did). While it is hard to document these other sorts of visits, there is strong circumstantial evidence which suggests that court artists, scientists and craftsmen had more regular access to the collections that did princes and diplomats.[19] Recall the artist above who told ambassador Manfredi how Rudolf responded to the gift of two paintings. His presence in the *Kunstkammer* required no ceremonial visit, but was quite probably a regular part of the activities that expanded the collection between the 1580s and 1610s. Creating a collection of this size and scope demanded an extraordinary number of personnel to decorate and arrange the rooms and to produce new objects. By contrast, the *studiolo* of the Grand Duke of Tuscany, Francesco I de' Medici, was a somewhat modest affair that engaged the services of a handful of court artists and one humanist; it was probably never seen by anyone but the Grand Duke himself.[20] Many more people saw and contributed to the imperial collections in Prague. It was a privileged site, but not a personal site, allowing its visitors special access to *arcana imperii* (secrets of state) which derived from *arcana naturae* (secrets of nature).[21]

Even the most casual visitor to Prague could observe Rudolf's wide-ranging curiosity about nature. Around 1603, the physician Johan Eck, a member of the Roman Accademia de' Lincei, which ultimately included the magus Giovan Battista della Porta and the astronomer and mathematician Galileo Galilei among its luminaries, reported to his friends that 'His Majesty [is] inclined towards Lincean things'.[22] A few years later, the Venetian ambassador confirmed Rudolf's interest in 'the secrets of natural matters, as of artificial', observing that 'he who has the chance to treat of these things will always find the ears of the emperor ready'.[23]

In pursuit of these goals, Rudolf assembled a rich array of flora and fauna and an extensive collection of specialized instruments that might help him pursue knowledge of nature. At the height of his reign, a deer park surrounded Hradčany Castle, complemented by an aviary (in which one might glimpse the Emperor's birds of paradise and, after 1598, a dodo) and a botanical garden where distinguished naturalists

15.5 **Vase**
Ca. 1600
[Prague, Umělecko-
průmyslové muzeum v Praze]

such as Rembert Dodoens and Carolus Clusius tended exotic plants. From the 1580s onwards, a steady stream of visitors such as the English alchemists John Dee and Edward Kelley, the Italian mystic and Neoplatonist Giordano Bruno, and the physicians and occultists Oswald Croll and Michael Maier enjoyed audiences with Rudolf, bearing gifts of magic talismans, their own writings and promises to unlock the secrets of nature. At the same time, Rudolf looked to the heavens. By 1600, his interest in astronomy had become evident, as he willingly financed the expansion of various palaces to accommodate the astronomical instruments of the Danish noble Brahe and such assistants as astronomer Kepler.[24] Prague had become a microcosm of the scientific activities which characterized late Renaissance intellectual life and, accordingly, housed the artefacts necessary for such endeavours.

The 1607–11 inventory of the *Kunstkammer* reflects the fusion of these interests. Organizing the objects in the imperial collection, the antiquarian Fröschl began with *naturalia*, turned to *artificialia*, and ended with *scientifica*. The entries in the first category reflected the penchant for exotic creatures that characterized a great deal of Renaissance natural history [fig. 15.7]. Armadillos, chameleons and pelicans crowded between crocodiles, iguanas, tortoises, starfish, blowfish, seahorses and the ubiquitous birds of paradise. Not content to display the living examples in his aviary, Rudolf proudly collected as many dead birds as possible, often announcing the state of the specimen: 'One bird of paradise with its natural wings and feet'.[25] When specimens were inadequate or lacking, he called on painters such as his own artist Joris Hoefnagel or the Medici court artist Jacopo Ligozzi to produce images of natural objects.[26]

No naïve collector of New World nature – as the many books on the Americas in his *Kunstkammer* confirm – Rudolf understood, as many Renaissance naturalists did not, that birds of paradise did not *naturally* appear without feet. His collection allowed the discerning visitor to see the difference between the well-worn fable of a bird that flew continuously because it could not land and the *physical reality* of the bird that refuted this old tale.[27] In developing this assessment, Rudolf had surely been influenced by the work of his court naturalist Clusius, whose *Exoticarum libri decem* (1605) guided Fröschl in the naming of many animals in the collection.[28] Thus the collection tested contemporary knowledge about the natural world.

The condition of other objects further suggested the idea of a working collection that court physicians and naturalists regularly consulted. It is unlikely, for instance, that Rudolf created displays of 'two dissected frogs', 'seven teeth and one small [tooth] from a hippopotamus' or 'seventeen tigers' and leopards' claws' without the assistance of his naturalists.[29] Nor can we imagine Rudolf alone determining which *terrae sigillatae* (an ancient medicinal clay imprinted with seals), bezoar stones and amulets might be the most efficacious; we know that he lent samples of his medicinal earths to the Paracelsian physician Oswald Croll while Croll was completing his study of the hidden virtues of nature.[30] During his tenure as a court physician, Croll perfected plague remedies such as the Paracelsian *zenexton*, an amulet often presented in a bejewelled gold case containing a cake made of toads, virginal menstrual blood, white arsenic, orpiment, dittany, roots, pearls, coral and Eastern emeralds; the recipe appeared under imperial privilege in his *Basilica chymica* (1609).[31] Most of the ingredients and similar antidotes could be found in Rudolf's *Kunstkammer*.

Finally, Rudolf did not neglect the fabulous creatures of the medieval bestiary that made their way into early modern natural histories to join New World wonders.

15.6 GIOVANNI CASTRUCCI
WORKSHOP
Landscape
Early 17th century; frame
dated later
[Prague, Umělecko-
průmyslové muzeum v Praze]

Unicorns' horns, mandrakes and dragons also had a prominent role in his collection. Yet another court physician, de Boodt, saved a sketch with the following caption: 'This is the figure of a Dragon which the Emperor Rudolf II has; dried it is this exact size, where it is preserved'.[32] Lest we think that Rudolf was out of touch with contemporary developments in natural history, we should recall that such leading Renaissance naturalists as Conrad Gesner – whose books also were available in Rudolf's library[33] – and Ulisse Aldrovandi devoted lengthy pages to the anatomical, etymological and moral significance of dragons. The range of approaches to nature reflected in the imperial collections indicated the diversity of knowledge in the late sixteenth century. Examining the unicorn's horns in the *Kunstkammer* led de Boodt to the conclusion that the unicorn did *not* exist since such horns were inevitably from a rhinoceros or narwhal. We might imagine that he enjoyed a good argument or two with the emperor and other court intellectuals over this conclusion.[34] Far from being simply an intellectual relic, he was a ruler whose interests included the more modern sciences of chemical medicine, mathematical astronomy and zoology as well as a strong curiosity about ancient arts such as alchemy, astrology and prognostication. Inhabiting all of these different intellectual worlds, Rudolf commanded the empire of knowledge.

Magical Prague

Natural magic provided an important meeting ground for many of Rudolf's interests. It embodied the image of productive, encyclopaedic knowledge that emphasized the manipulation of nature and the creation of wondrous artefacts – both central images in the Rudolfine *Kunstkammer*. Natural magic occupied an important role in Rudolf's intellectual development. He was an avid reader of della Porta's *Natural Magic* (1558) and, in 1604, sent a courier to Naples to entreat the ageing magus to send an assistant to Prague to teach the Emperor natural magic. '[W]hen our arduous tasks of government permit,' Rudolf confessed, 'we enjoy the subtle knowledge of natural and artificial things in which you excel.'[35]

What exactly did the pursuit of natural magic entail? The spectrum of objects in the *Kunstkammer* reflected the breadth of della Porta's program for the reformation of knowledge. Symbolic knowledge figured prominently in Rudolf's library, in the form of readings about the Egyptian hieroglyphs (including a gift of a *Thesaurus hieroglyphicorum* by Kepler's friend, the imperial adviser Johan Matthaeus Wacker von Wackenfels), Achille Bocchi's *Symbolicarum questionum libri V* and various works on emblems and *imprese* such as the court historian Jacobus Typotius' *Symbola divina et humana* (1601–3), which included a rich assortment of imperial emblems. Such works suggest that the emperor was well read in the various subjects which were the hallmark of Renaissance Neoplatonism.[36] Next to these books lay more enigmatic texts such as 'an old philosophical book inscribed with figures'. Was it a work of alchemy or a cipher? Or was it perhaps the ancient book that the imperial physician Johann Altmanstedt allegedly found in a chest buried in a chamber beneath his house in Prague and presented to Rudolf around 1612?[37] The emperor supposedly had his alchemists decipher it, promising Altmanstedt 90,000 gulden for the recipe for gold tincture they uncovered.

Just as objects played an important role in della Porta's *Natural Magic*, they also gave testimony to the Emperor's command of natural and artificial secrets. The 'perspective instrument' created by the imperial clockmaker Burgi accompanied an entire category of crystal and glass mirrors as well as a square crystal and ebony table with cabbalistic symbols inscribed on parchment beneath it.[38] Elsewhere, the Venetian lenses for imperial telescopes lay safely tucked away, waiting to be put to use. And possibly an object described as a 'handsome silver cylinder covered with crystalline glass' may have been one of the telescopes built from the instructions in the *Natural Magic* or sent by Galileo to Prague.[39] Given the timing of the inventory, which Fröschl completed one year after Galileo announced his discovery of the moons of Jupiter with his new and improved telescope, it is hard to say which version would have prevailed. Since we know that Rudolf questioned Kepler extensively about his opinions of della Porta's *Natural Magic* in 1610, the sciences of natural magic – in which optics and ciphers figured prominently – were very much on his mind.[40]

As Rudolf's persistent questioning of Kepler suggests, he took an active interest in the production of artefacts that demonstrated power over nature. Natural magic made no clear division between the works of nature and those of humankind, suggesting that both participated in the act of creation. So great was Rudolf's engagement with these pursuits that he often spent afternoons perfecting his knowledge of various arts and crafts by participating in the activities of the imperial workshops. In 1609, the Tuscan ambassador commented unfavourably on this practice: 'For he himself tries alchemical experiments, and he himself is busily engaged in making clocks, which is against the decorum of a prince. He has transferred his seat from the imperial throne to the workshop stool'.[41] Yet Rudolf's decision to practise the sciences he patronized was not uncommon. Ironically, our best image of the 'prince-practitioner' comes from the Medici court that this particular ambassador represented . The image of the prince in his laboratory, surrounded by artisans and advised by an alchemist, evokes an important part of Rudolf's world. Certainly, his *Kunstkammer* in-

15.7 (Attributed to)
DANIEL FRÖSCHL
Page with *Raphus cucullatus*
from the *Museum of Rudolf II*
1601–09
[Vienna, Handschriften- und
Inkunabeln Sammlung der
ÖNB]

ventory echoed the same desire to perfect all sciences in the service of a common goal.

The level of Rudolf's interest in the mechanical arts has often been difficult to gauge. While we have scores of objects produced in Prague (often for the *Kunstkammer*), very little documentation remains regarding the extent of Rudolf's involvement in the production of the clocks and automata that often evoke the scientific artistry of the German courts [fig. 15.8]. An encounter with the astronomer Brahe provides a somewhat richer portrait. The Danish nobleman arrived in Prague towards the end of August 1599 and discovered, to his pleasure, that the Emperor wanted to meet him in a private audience. On 31 August, he arrived at the palace, bearing copies of three of his books – which joined such works as a Spanish geometry, a Jesuit mathematics textbook and a *Theatrum instrumentorum* in the *Kunstkammer*.[42] As Brahe left the room, the Emperor's secretary Johannes Barwitz stopped him:

> [T]he Emperor wished to have the mechanical device on my carriage shown to him (for he had seen it from the window when I drove up to the castle). I therefore had my son fetch the mechanism from the carriage, gave it to Barwitz, and showed him how to explain its construction to the emperor. When Barwitz had done this and returned to me, he said that the Emperor said he had one or two similar devices but none so large or made in exactly the same way. He did not want to accept mine from me but would have one made for himself by his astronomer, from the pattern of mine.[43]

Surely, the Danish astronomer's ascent as the highest-paid courtier in Prague had something to do with his ability to engage Rudolf as a collector of mechanical toys.[44]

Science in all its forms played a central role in the formation of the imperial *Kunstkammer*. The objects collected by and for the Emperor positioned him at the center of a complex intellectual world, enthralled by geographic and scientific novelties while actively pursuing the ancient tradition of *prisca sapientia* that occupied many natural philosophers at the dawn of a new millenium. Such a conjunction was particularly appropriate for a learned prince who owned copies of the *Pimander* and Galileo's *Sidereus Nuncius* – and read both carefully. He also saw no contradiction in employing the inventor of the Tychonic system of astronomy (geoheliocentrism) while having his clockmakers create models of the Copernican universe.[45] The *Kunstkammer* also connected the world of book learning to the realm of experience; just as art glided imperceptibly into science, objects never lay far from words. In this respect, too, Rudolf and his advisers mirrored the changes transforming scientific culture at the end of the Renaissance, when nature became a more sensory object to be anatomized and possessed by its interpretors.[46] Yet even in this new material world of learning, certain things remained intangible. In the almost three thousand entries made by Fröschl in the 1607–11 inventory, not one philosopher's stone appears. Despite numerous accounts of transmutations at the Rudolfine court, no tangible byproduct of these alchemical experiments found its way into the *Kunstkammer*.[47] Perhaps such secrets resided in the Emperor's private chambers, like the bell Rudolf allegedly used to summon spirits. Or perhaps there was none reliable enough to meet the test of authenticity that a berth in the imperial collections required. This one fascinating lacuna in the official possessions of the German Hermes suggests the complexity of the relationship between knowledge and objects at the end of the Renaissance, even in the hands of an emperor who aspired to possess the world.

15.8 JOHANN POETSDORFFER
Pendant with Watch
Most likely 1600
[Dresden, Staatliche Kunst-
sammlungen, Grünes
Gewölbe]

1. I have drawn upon a number of sources to create a composite portrait of the physical space of Rudolf's collection: Eliška Fučíková, 'The Collection of Rudolf II at Prague: Cabinet of Curiosities or Scientific Museum?' in Oliver Impey and Arthur MacGregor (eds), *The Origins of Museums: The Cabinet of Curiosities in Sixteenth- and Seventeenth-Century Europe* (Oxford, 1985), pp. 48–49; Thomas DaCosta Kaufmann, *Variations on the Imperial Theme in the Age of Maximilian II and Rudolf II* (New York, 1978), p. 114; *idem*, Kaufmann, *Court, Cloister, and City: The Art and Culture of Central Europe 1450–1800* (Chicago, 1995), pp. 179–81; and Georg Kugler, 'Rudolf II. als Sammler', in *Prag um 1600. Kunst und Kultur am Hofe Kaiser Rudolfs II* (Vienna, 1988), vol. 2, p. 11.

2. Francis Bacon, *Gesta Grayorum* (1594), in Impey and MacGregor (eds) (note 1), p. 1.

3. In Thomas DaCosta Kaufmann, *The School of Prague: Painting at the Court of Rudolf II* (Chicago, 1988), p. 20. This point is also raised in *idem*, 'Remarks on the Collections of Rudolf II: The *Kunstkammer* as a Form of *Representatio*', *Art Journal*, 38 (1978), 22.

4. This stereotypical view is found in Frances Yates, *The Rosicrucian Enlightenment* (Frogmore, St Albans, 1975), p. 45. See also H. C. Bolton, *The Follies of Science at the Court of Rudolf II* (Milwaukee, 1904); and G. von Schwarzenfeld, *Rudolf II, der saturnische Kaiser* (Munich, 1964).

5. See bibliography in note 1 above. Works such as R. J. W. Evans's marvellous *Rudolf II and His World: A Study in Intellectual History 1576–1612* (Oxford, 1973) and Erich Trunz's *Wissenschaft und Kunst im Kreise Kaiser Rudolfs II. 1576–1612* (Neumünster, 1992) occupy a middle ground in offering neither a negative portrait of the Emperor's collecting habits nor any strong statement about the role of collecting in Rudolf's political activities.

6. Rotrand Bauer and Herbert Haupt, 'Das Kunstkammerinventar Kaiser Rudolfs II., 1607–1611', *Jahrbuch der Kunsthistorischen Sammlungen in Wien*, 72 (1976), 39 (n. 697: sword), 40, 46 (n. 822: dictionary; n. 825: Bible), 110–16, 129–30 (globes and mathematical instruments). On the *Weltallschale*, see Kaufmann, *Variations …* (note 1), p. 120; *Court, City and Cloister* (note 1), p. 192. Jonas Silber made this dish for Rudolf in 1589.

7. For a discussion of the long Habsburg tradition of collecting, see Elisabeth Scheicher, *Die Kunst- und Wunderkammern der Habsburger* (Vienna, 1979); Horst Bredekamp, *The Lure of Antiquity and the Cult of the Machine: The Kunstkammer and the Evolution of Nature, Art and Technology*, trans. Allison Brown (Princeton, 1995), pp. 30–36.

8. Girolamo Soranzo to the Venetian doge, Prague, 5 March 1612, in Bauer and Haupt (note 6), XIV.

9. In Adolfo Venturi, 'Zur Geschichte der Kunstsammlungen Kaiser Rudolf II', *Repertorium für Kunstwissenschaft*, 8 (1885), 15.

10. On this subject, see particularly Giancarlo Maiorino, *The Portrait of Eccentricity* (London, ca. 1991); Thomas DaCosta Kaufmann, *Mastery of Nature: Aspects of Art, Science, and Humanism in the Renaissance* (Princeton, 1993), pp. 100–35; and the essays in *The Arcimboldo Effect: Transformations of the Face from the Sixteenth to the Twentieth Century*, exh. cat. (London, 1987).

11. Kaufmann, *Variations* (note 1), p. 108; *idem*, 'Remarks …' (note 3), p. 22. Archduke Maximilian II is also known to have seen the imperial collection.

12. Quotes in Kaufmann, *Variations* (note 1), p. 106; Kaufmann (note 10), p. 180. With the latter quote, I have added a little more of the original passage, as reproduced in Venturi (note 9), 19.

13. Vincenzo Promis (ed.), *Miscellanea di storia italiana per cura della Regia Deputazione di Storia Patria* 16:2:3 *Ambasciata di Carlo Francesco Manfredi di Luserna a Praga nel 1604* (1887), p. 593. For a list of similar artefacts, see Bauer and Haupt (note 6), pp. 19, 40, 93. Rudolf's predilection for bezoar stones is well documented in many sources. See Evans (note 5) p. 181; Scheicher (note 7), pp. 16–17, 93, 143.

14. Anselmus Boetius de Boodt, *Gemmarum et lapidum historia* (Prague, 1609).

15. *Ibid.*, p. 594. For more on these forms of natural artistry, see Paula Findlen, 'Jokes of Nature and Jokes of Knowledge: The Playfulness of Scientific Discourse in Early Modern Europe', *Renaissance Quarterly*, 43 (1990), 292–331; H. W. Janson, 'The "Image Made By Chance" in Renaissance Thought' in Millard Meiss (ed.) *De artibus opuscula XL: Essays in Honor of Erwin Panofsky* (New York, 1961); Horst Bredekamp (note 7), pp. 11–36, 63–80, *passim*.

16. Significantly, Giovanni Castrucci's works were the last items included in the 1607–11 inventory; see Bauer and Haupt, p. 140 (nn. 2809–14).

17. Kunstkammerinventar, p. 110 (n. 2138). See Klaus Maurice, 'Jost Bürgi, or On Innovation' in Klaus Maurice and Otto Mayr (eds) *The Clockwork Universe: German Clocks and Automata 1550–1650* (New York, 1980), pp. 87–102. I have reproduced the English translation of the inventory entry on p. 100.

18. De Boodt's preface to Rudolf is discussed in Lynn Thorndike, *A History of Magic and Experimental Science* (New York, 1941), vol. 6, p. 320, n. 94.

19. This point has already been suggested by Thomas Kaufmann in various publications, thought I hope to take it further by examining more closely Rudolf's interactions with some of the natural philosophers at his court; see especially Kaufmann (note 10).

20. The standard work on this subject is Luciano Berti, *Il Principe dello Studiolo. Francesco I dei Medici e la fine del Rinascimento fiorentino* (Florence, 1967).

21. For a more extended discussion of 'secrets' in early modern culture, see Carlo Ginzburg, 'High and Low: The Theme of Forbidden Knowledge in the Sixteenth and Seventeenth Centuries', *Past and Present*, 73 (1976), 28–41; William Eamon, *Science and the Secrets of Nature* (Princeton, 1994).

22. In M. E. H. N. Mout, 'Hermes Trismegistos Germaniae: Rudolf II en de arcane wetenschappen', *Leids Kunsthistorisch Jaarboek*, 1 (1982), 181.

23. Venetian ambassador, 1605–7, in Kaufmann, *The School of Prague* (note 3), p. 5.

24. This portrait of science in Rudolfine Prague is particularly indebted to Evans (note 5), pp. 196–242; Yates (note 4), Max Caspar, *Kepler*, trans. C. Doris Hellman, ed. Owen Gingerich and Alain Segonds (New York, 1993), pp. 116–208; Victor E. Thoren, *The Lord of Uraniborg: A Biography of Tycho Brahe* (Cambridge, 1990), pp. 416–70.

25. Bauer and Haupt (note 6), p. 10 (n. 140).

26. Ligozzi's watercolours of birds and fish are included in Bauer and Haupt (note 6), p. 135 (nn. 2693, 2696). In addition to his artistic talents, Hoefnagel must

obviously have been considered something of a taxonomic authority at court, since he is given the credit for naming various fish in Rudolf's collection; see Bauer and Haupt (note 6), p. 14 (nn. 230, 231). This intermingling of art and nature is the focal point of Kaufmann (note 10), esp. pp. 196–97.

27. The inventory of Rudolf's *Kunstkammer* included such works as Ptolemy's *Geography*, Columbus' *Voyages*, *Description of the Kingdom of Guiana* and various histories of Virgina, Florida and Peru. In addition, Rudolf also owned Joachim Camerarius the Younger's book of natural emblems, a standard source for legends about the animals in his collection; see Bauer and Haupt (note 6), p. 132 (nn. 2617–21, 2629); p. 133 (nn. 2654, 2663). On the various ways of viewing natural objects at this time, see William Ashworth, 'Natural History and the Emblematic World View' in David Lindberg and Robert Westman (eds), Reappraisals of the Scien-tific Revolution (Cambridge, 1990), pp. 303–32; *idem*, 'Remarkable Humans and Singular Beasts' in Joy Kenseth (ed.), *The Age of the Marvelous*, exh. cat. (Hanover, NH, 1991), pp. 113–44.

28. For Clusius' influence on the inventory, see Bauer and Haupt (note 6), pp. 6 (n. 42), 9 (n. 123), 10 (nn. 135, 143, 146, 148, 175). From Clusius came proper names for such creatures as the iguana and dodo.

29. Bauer and Haupt (note 6), pp. 8 (nn. 97, 108), 14 (n. 218). Rudolf found the hippopotamus teeth interesting enough to remove them to his private rooms, either for further study or to benefit from their supernatural powers. We should also consider the role of hunters in relation to the game animals in Rudolf's collection. The appearance of a number of anatomized specimens in the *Kunstkammer* further reinforces the idea of a working collection which made use of the most up-to-date skills of physicians and naturalists.

30. Oswald Croll, *A Treatise of ... Signatures of Internal Things* (London, 1669), sig. A.3v. Croll mentions receiving a gift of two samples of *Axungius*, similar to *terra lemnia*, from Rudolf. For the imperial collection of *terrae sigillatae*, see Bauer and Haupt (note 6), pp. 56–58.

31. This recipe is discussed in Martha Baldwin, 'Toads and Plague: Amulet Therapy in Seventeenth-Century Medicine', *Bulletin of the History of Medicine*, 67 (1993), 230–32.

32. *Albums de Boodt*, VII, 50, in Marie-Christiane Maselis, Arnout Balis and Roger H. Marijnissen, *De Albums van Anselmus de Boodt (1550–1632): Geschilderde natuurobservatie aan het Hof van Rudolf II te Praag* (Tielt, 1989), p. 73. For accounts of other dragons in early modern collections, see P. Findlen, *Possessing Nature: Museums, Collecting, and Scientific Culture in Early Modern Italy* (Berkeley, 1994), pp. 17–23.

33. Fröschl evidently consulted Gesner on several specimens; see Bauer and Haupt (note 6), p. 9 (n. 133).

34. Thorndike (note 18), vol. 6, pp. 323–24.

35. Rudolf II to della Porta, Prague, 20 June 1604, in Giuseppe Gabrieli, 'Giovan Battista Della Porta Linceo', *Giornale critico della filosofia italiana*, 8 (1927), 424. (I have followed the English translation by Edward Rosen in Kepler's *Conversation with Galileo's Sidereal Messenger* [New York, 1965], p. 83, n. 128.) For more on their interaction, see Luisa Muraro, *Giambattista Della Porta mago e scienziato* (Milan, 1978),

pp. 21–22. Della Porta was impressed enough by this letter to initially dedicate his *Taumatologia* to Rudolf, promising the Emperor exclusive access to these secrets. Rudolf's general interest in natural magic is discussed in Mout (note 22).

36. Bauer and Haupt (note 6), pp. 131 (n. 2602), 132 (nn. 2609, 2631, 2632), 133 (n. 2658), 136 (n. 2710). For a broader discussion of the sort of philosophical approach to knowledge that Rudolf may have found attractive, see Yates, *Giordano Bruno and the Hermetic Tradition* (Chicago, 1964). Yates aligned this way of thinking too strongly to an explicit reading of the Corpus Hermeticum, but her basic interpretation of Neoplatonic thought and its role in late Renaissance Europe is still a valuable introduction to this subject.

37. Bauer and Haupt (note 6), p. 131 (n. 2585). On Altmanstedt's discovery, see Moran, *The Alchemical World of the German Court: Occult Philosophy and Chemical Medicine in the Circle of Moritz of Hessen (1572–1632)* (Stuttgart, 1991), p. 151.

38. Bauer and Haupt (note 6), p. 118 (n. 2289), p. 69 (nn. 1277–81), p. 70 (n. 1288). The last entry reads: 'Ein viereggete tafel *in quadro* von crystall, in ebinholtz mit einer handheb gefasst, darunder ein *cabulistiche* schrifft mit vilen *characteribus* uff pergamen geschriben, dardurch mans lesen kan'.

39. *Ibid.*, pp. 70 (n. 1292), 115 (n. 2237).

40. As Kepler reports in his *Dissertatio cum Sidereus Nuncius* (1610): 'After I began to work on my "Optics," the Emperor questioned me frequently about Della Porta's aforementioned devices' in Rosen (note 35), pp. 17–18. This episode is also discussed in Kaufmann (note 10), pp. 191–92.

41. In Kaufmann, *The School of Prague*, p. 7. For a comparable image of the prince-practitioner, see Bruce Moran, 'German Prince-Practitioners: Aspects in the Development of Courtly Science, Technology and Procedures in the Renaissance', *Technology and Culture*, 22 (1981), 253–74.

42. Bauer and Haupt, pp. 136 (n. 2717), 137 (nn. 2748, 2749). The first entry, for Tycho's books, is as follows: 'Drey bucher, die 2 geschriben von der hand, das dritte gedruckht, *Anth: Tichonis Brahe*, sein alle drey in gulden stuckh gebunden mit seiden nestell und guldenen stefften.' Rudolf allegedly read these books with great pleasure at night.

43. Tycho Brahe to Holger Rosenkrantz, Prague, 30 August 1599 (old style), in Thoren (note 24), p. 413.

44. Tycho's recipe for a plague elixir, which he gave to Rudolf as an exclusive secret in 1599, may have been another reason for his popularity with the Emperor. See J. L. E. Dreyer, *Tycho Brahe: A Picture of Scientific Life and Work in the Sixteenth Century (1893)* (New York, 1963), pp. 130, 283. A closer inspection of Tycho's correspondence and writings would surely reveal greater detail about their relationship.

45. Mout (note 22), p. 178; Rosen (note 35), p. 11; Scheicher (note 7), p. 156.

46. These developments are discussed in greater detail in Findlen (note 32).

47. Physicians and natural philosophers from the infamous Kelley to de Boodt and Michael Sendivogius are reported to have performed successful transmutations before Rudolf. See Thorndike (note 18), vol. 6, pp. 318–24; vol. 7, p.158; Evans (note 5), Anm. 218.

The Court of Rudolf II and Humanist Culture

NICOLETTE MOUT

The Habsburg tradition of patronage of art and learning, well established by the time Emperor Rudolf II moved his court to Prague in 1583, played an important part in the development of humanist culture at the Rudolfine court. His father, Emperor Maximilian II, who had gathered around him a group of artists and learned men, had added to the imperial art collection and started building up an impressive imperial library. Noble patronage provided scholars with an income; thus it is not surprising that learned men flocked to Rudolf's court, especially from the early 1590s onwards, when his reputation as maecenas was firmly established.

The question arises whether all these learned men contributed to one consistent and distinct form of humanist culture which was typical of Rudolfine Prague. As court culture to a high degree revolved around the Emperor himself, we must consider the problem of whether Rudolf II had a clear concept of the ideal humanist culture at his court and a policy towards attaining this ideal.

Rudolf II saw and presented himself as the universal Emperor, like his grandfather Charles V before him, sole ruler of the Holy Roman Empire and heir to the world power of the ancient Romans. In his view, imperial majesty was universal and absolute, had sacral connotations and could not stand comparison to any other political position, including kingship. Court culture had to underpin and propagate this ideal image and stress the august position of the Emperor and his dynasty. It is not surprising, therefore, that Rudolf used the services of humanists in order to spread this message of universal and absolute majesty. In this he was advised by a small circle of courtiers who had a humanist background and were often themselves intellectually highly gifted, like the councillors Johann Matthias Wacker von Wackenfels and Johannes Barvitius, the imperial almoner Jacob Chimarrhaeus and, in the last years of Rudolf's life, Heinrich Julius Duke of Braunschweig.

It is obvious that any ruler, imperial or not, could highly profit from the fruits of humanist learning in the fields of law, history and literature in order to buttress his authority and augment his prestige. In the case of Rudolf II, many examples of humanist contributions to these eminently useful aspects of court culture could be given. The most authoritative writer on public law of the Holy Roman Empire, Melchior Goldast von Haiminsfeld, who, incidentally, also left an interesting Prague diary full of court gossip, not only served Rudolf for many years, but was even quite close to him. History played a prominent part in the extensive imperial political propaganda. The court historiographer, Jacobus Typotius, wrote a number of works on the Long War against the Turks (1593–1606), exhorting the Estates of the empire to pay extra taxes and eulogizing imperial policy and martiality in general and the occasional military victory in particular. In cooperation with the engraver Aegidius Sadeler and the antiquary Ottavio Strada, Typotius also produced *Symbola*, a book in which emblems dedicated to Rudolf extol his unique imperial dignity. Highly erudite Latin poetry served as an appropriate vehicle for praising the Emperor and his deeds. A host of humanist poets wrote Rudolfine panegyrics: Salamon Fren-

zelius, Hieronymus Arconatus and Caspar Dornavius may stand as examples. The lively circle of court officials with an interest in humanist poetry can be glimpsed through the works of the English poetess Elizabeth Weston (Westonia), who settled in Prague at the end of the sixteenth century and depicted literary life there.

In this practical use of humanist learning, Rudolf II did not differ from other rulers of his time. Nor was it unusual that he invoked the services of humanists and artists to create an image of his reign and his personal majesty. What is unusual is the large scale of these activities, through which the Prague court became a veritable centre of late humanist culture, the decisive influence of the scholarly and philosophical interests of the Emperor and his immediate entourage, and the fruitful interaction with intellectual traditions and mentalities already present in Bohemia before the court moved to Prague.

The magnificent scale of it all dazzled contemporaries as much as modern historians. Quantitative research would no doubt reveal that dozens of learned men, of which the names of only the most famous ones like Johannes Kepler or John Dee are familiar to us, were at one time or another, for longer or shorter periods, associated with the imperial court in Prague. The fact that attractive remunerations were readily promised but not always paid could not stem the stream of humanists and artists who were either actively recruited by the court or turned up there in order to try their luck. As cultural life at court and in the city were in many ways intertwined, trying one's luck could pay off: if no patronage was found in court circles, the economically thriving city offered many possibilities to earn a living.

Rudolf's devotion to art and learning expressed itself not only in financial inducement but also in the granting of patents of nobility or privileges of various kinds. Whoever worked for the Emperor was conscious of the fact that he was, in the general as well as the literal sense of the word, a privileged member of a society in which his work brought him recognition as well as responsibility. This responsibility comprised his role as communicator of truth and insight into the natural and supernatural world, and it is precisely at this point that Rudolf's personal interests became crucial to the development of humanist culture at his court.

As we have seen, the Emperor was fascinated by the Neoplatonic world-view, which was related to the scholarly pursuit of pansophy. The study of the microcosmos and macrocosmos was part of this philosophic approach, as was the idea that the study of biblical revelation and of nature were inseparable. The study of nature – which included medicine and natural philosophy, but also alchemy, astronomy and astrology – had made great progress since the beginning of the sixteenth century. This had been the work of such scholars as the astronomer Copernicus, the anatomist Vesalius and the many-sided natural philosopher Paracelsus, who founded an entirely new school of medical science that was closely related to alchemy and other arcane sciences. Magic also played a part in these pansophic efforts, because it could help to reveal the secrets of the universe and get into touch with divine forces that were responsible for the great universal harmony of creation.

When Rudolf II succeeded his father in 1576, he not only inherited a tradition of interest in these Neoplatonist ideas, but also a circle of exceptionally gifted scholars, among them the botanists Carolus Clusius and Pierandrea Matthioli, the physician Johannes Crato von Crafftheim, the librarian Hugo Blotius and the astronomer Tadeáš Hájek, who also wrote on mathematical, botanical and medical

subjects. They all moved in this world of pansophic, Neoplatonist scholarship. Their presence gave Rudolf a favourable start for his own activities in the field of patronage of learning. Court medicine, for instance, became more and more Paracelsian under their influence.

A decisive moment for the direction in which Rudolfine court culture was going to develop was the moving of the imperial court to Prague in 1583. It brought the learned men at court into close contact with Bohemian scholarship and – no less important – with the excellent Prague printers and publishers. Intellectual traditions in Bohemia at the time placed strong emphasis on practical sciences like mining, including metallurgy and geodesy, medicine and botany, but there were also excellent students of alchemy, natural magic, astronomy, astrology and prognostics. The Jewish ghetto in Prague housed David Gans, an eminent astronomer, geographer and historian; there are traces of contact between him and the court. No less important was the arrival of Tycho Brahe at the Prague court in 1599 and of Johannes Kepler in the following year. Astronomy – which was at the time still inseparable from astrology – was essential for the contemplation of the cosmos, indeed of the whole of creation. Brahe and Kepler had the best instrument-makers of Central Europe – among them the famous Erasmus Habermel and Jost Bürgi – at their disposal, because they all worked for Rudolf. For thirteen years, until Rudolf's death in 1612, Prague was the centre of astronomical studies.

The court attracted numerous alchemists and magicians. Contrary to popular belief, the making of gold was not the first interest of Rudolf or the majority of these men. Far more important was the quest for the philosopher's stone, which could eventually be used for transmutations of lesser metals into gold, but which would in the first place yield the secret wisdom necessary for understanding creation. Not many alchemists or magicians seemed to have stayed in Prague for long; they were more the travelling type of learned men, visiting one court after another. The English magicians John Dee and Edward Kelley and the Italian Giordano Bruno, who in Prague propagated his own interpretation of the Neoplatonist ideas of Hermes Trismegistos, belonged to this category.

The development of court culture was greatly helped by an atmosphere of religious toleration. On the one hand this was the result of the religious situation in Bohemia itself, where adherents to various brands of Protestantism – Hussite Utraquists, but also Lutherans and Calvinists – were allowed to live relatively undisturbed alongside the Catholics who were favoured by the Catholic dynasty but formed a minority – albeit a sizeable and influential one – in Bohemia. On the other hand, artists and scholars of every denomination were welcomed at court as long as they did not disturb the religious peace by writing against the Catholic church or any other polemical misdeed. Rudolf II himself was undoubtedly a Catholic, but a rather unusual one. He had, for political but also for spiritual reasons, a marked antipathy towards the papacy and almost certainly refused the last rites of the church on his deathbed. But he had no sympathy for Protestantism either and tried to steer clear of both camps. Personally, he was interested in mystical aspects of religion and in the occult spirituality magic had to offer. The flourishing of humanist culture at the court of Rudolf II in Prague was thus the result of a happy blend of very different elements.

Scientific and Magical Humanism at the Court of Rudolf II

GYÖRGY E. SZÖNYI

Although we refer to the 1500s as the period of the high Renaissance, it is clear that by the second half of the century the optimism and idealism which we normally associate with the Renaissance had given way to new ways of thinking. Contemporaries took note of this new intellectualism, which also produced a novel artistic style known as Mannerism.

If we look at the spectrum of European arts and sciences at this time, we can see that signs of crisis were appearing everywhere, not only in the visual arts. What we see is a proliferation of anticlassical tendencies; by the end of the century, the glorious ideals of the fifteenth century had been overshadowed by a sense of doubt, disappointment and frustration.[1] This crisis-ridden, exciting period provided the intellectual framework for the shift of philosophical paradigms and the emergence of the Scientific Revolution. Two radically oppositional world views – the *organic* and the *mechanistic* – polarized European thought at the time. It is exactly that eclecticism of thought that has perplexed historians of science the way religious, scientific and magical ideas could exist within the same scholarly head or set of scientific arguments.

An important feature of Mannerism was its exclusive nature, its aristocratic character. The victory of Realpolitik, growing religious intolerance (post-Tridentine Catholicism versus a more and more rigid and hysterical Protestantism), and uncertainties in the sciences revealed Renaissance ideals as mere utopias. Liberalism, magic, freethinking, esotericism – to mention just a few 'suspicious' directions in which intellectual investigation was moving – were never particularly encouraged, but the stakes which burned a Michael Servetus in Calvin's Geneva or Giordano Bruno in the Rome of the Inquisition were as horrifyingly new as the growing witch craze. While Europe gradually fell into a period of new authoritarianism, the representatives of free thought and the seekers of esoteric truths did not disappear. They formed an exciting layer of late Renaissance humanists who embraced all sorts of heterodoxy, from mystical enthusiasts and hermetic Neoplatonists through near-atheist sceptics.

These humanists can be regarded as a sort of international intellectual opposition, whose members desperately searched for shelter within the frontiers of the Continent. Such sheltering places might be some of the less conservative church-affiliated universities and, first and foremost, the late Renaissance or Mannerist courts. Many humanists found their ways to the East/Central European countries: Czech Prague, Polish Cracow, Hungarian Pozsony [=Bratislava/Pressburg] and Transylvania offered temporary asylum to heterodox intellectuals from Western Europe. This could happen because of the fairly high degree of tolerance and religious freedom (resulting largely from the anarchic political situation) and the underdeveloped educational infrastructure, which meant that humanists at court were little bothered by the authoritarian rivalry of the universities.

The Humanists of Rudolf

The international élite which prepared the way for the Scientific Revolution possessed both controversial social status and a controversial state of mind. A typical example is Bruno, who developed the concept of the infinity of worlds as part of his attempt to establish a mystical religion based on the wisdom of ancient Egypt. The court in Prague attracted scholars and humanists from both ends of Europe. One of the locals at the court in Prague was Johannes Jesensky (Jessenius, 1566–1621), a Slovak born in Breslau [= Wroclaw] who called himself 'eques Ungarus', a Hungarian nobleman. His thinking demonstrates the dichotomous world view of Mannerist intellectuals as well as the manner in which Eastern Europeans picked up and reprocessed ideas imported from Italy and other centres of the European Renaissance. He studied medicine in Padua, and while in Italy made friends with Francesco Patrizi, one of the late synthetizers of Neoplatonic hermeticism and magical philosophy. Later, Jessenius became the court physician of Friedrich Wilhelm, elector of Saxony, who helped him in the professorship of anatomy at the University of Wittenberg. There he became acquainted with Tycho Brahe, who subsequently attracted him to Prague. Jessenius visited there in 1600 and performed the first public anatomic dissection in the history of Charles University. The famous event was widely noted; Jessenius himself commemorated it in a published version of his five-day medical demonstration, the *Anatomia pragensis*.[2] He moved to Prague for good in 1602, and although (despite the often-repeated historical myth) he was never appointed as Rudolf's physician nor held a professorship at the university, he became one of Bohemia's most fashionable and sought-after private practitioners. This brought him into the colourful circle of humanists already described, including Kepler, who influenced him to devote more time to astronomy. Jessenius, who never confined himself to the study of medicine, wrote a great variety of treatises ranging from political pamphlets to mystical philosophy. An important early work in this genre was influenced by Patrizi's *Nova de universis Philosophia*. The title of Jessenius' book – which in fact is a compilation of Patrizi's work with the intention of popularizing the new Italian philosophy in more conservative Germany – was *Zoroaster, Nova, brevis veraque de universe Philosophia* (New, Short and True Philosophy about the Universe; Wittenberg, 1593) and defends Copernicus' heliocentrism, albeit with the vocabulary and rhetorics of hermetic-organic natural philosophy.[3] Reading this little book, one can see how the thought of Ficino and Pico found new expression through the pen of the Central European humanist, recreating old ideas as well as offering new insights. Although the conclusion of the work propagates the new world view of Mannerism, its beginning echoes Agrippa and the Renaissance magi, the old ambition to find lost primordial wisdom: 'We have named our little book Zoroaster because the oracles which we followed as guiding principles were the magic of Zoroaster and the theology of the Chaldeans. Not that sorcery which only mimics true magic and which was bred from the communion of sinful people and wicked demons ...' Like Ficino, Agrippa, Dee or Bruno, Jessenius stresses the importance of the ancient wisdom originating from the East which was in the custody of the magi. These magi, needless to say, were pious and devout Christians. The wisdom of *Zoroaster* springs from pure and perfect doctrines and reflects the whole world in its universality: a synthesis between Platonism and Christian philosophy embracing the great chain of being and

17.1 JOHN DEE
Monas Hieroglyphica
[Prague, Národní kninovna]

the world of ideas, the whole system being completed by a critique of Aristotelianism. This strange and controversial world of Jessenius can be compared with the contradictory thoughts of Dee, who turned Euclid's geometry into conjurings of angels, that of Bruno, who derived Egyptian wisdom from the new cosmology, or that of Kepler, who in his newly discovered laws sought the proofs of a universal theory of harmony.[4]

A look at the inner circle of humanists around Rudolf II – that is, his personal physicians, call the *Leibarzts*, his librarian and antiquarian, the court astrologer and mathematician – will give us a vivid picture of the versatile intellectual climate of the court. One of the oldest of the Emperor's doctors was Johannes Crato von Craftheim, who had also served his father, Maximilian II, in Vienna. To Prague Crato brought the continuing tradition of *eirenism*, religious attitude best defined by R. J. W. Evans as 'essentially an attempt to evade tightening religious antagonisms by calling on intellectual reserves which the practical world would not admit; the mentality of the earlier age of colloquy born out of its time, like the theories of political universalism which tended to accompany it'.[5] Another influential doctor and at the same time confessor to the Emperor was Johann Pistorius, a man of versatile convictions, who, before his conversion to Catholicism, tried Lutheranism as well as Calvinism. He was also interested in the occult arts, editing one of the major Renaissance compilations of cabbalist literature, *Artis Cabalisticæ, hoc est reconditæ theologiæ et philosophiæ scriptorum* (Basel, 1587). Among the court physicians, Tadeus Hájek (Hagecius) was a Bohemian, a graduate of Charles University. A friend of Girolamo Cardano, he contributed to the development of psychology. He was also a noted astronomer and promoted the invitation of Tycho Brahe to the royal court. One more court physician should be mentioned in this context: Martin Ruland, who, together with his son of the same name served the Emperor in the 1600s. This Bavarian family settled in Pozsony, Hungary, and besides medicine, became engaged in the study of mining. Having moved to the royal court in Prague, they continued alchemical experiments as documented in the famous Paracelsian dictionary, written by the father but edited by the son: *Lexicon Alchemiæ sive Dictionarium Alchemistarum* (Frankfurt, 1612). Ruland Jr also made himself famous with his studies of the *morbus hungaricus* – a kind of typhoid fever – but after having described the illness he himself died of it in 1611.[6]

The link between Rudolf's court and the Rosicrucian movement of the following decades is established by the obscure alchemist and emblematist Michael Maier (1568–1622), who held the official title of royal physician before 1612, when he moved to Germany and became one of the most prolific writers and publishers of Rosicrucian propaganda as well as theoretical literature on spiritual alchemy. Maier's lofty style, and his inclination to poetic symbolism, must have appealed to Rudolf and earned him the title of count palatine as well as a personal secretarial position. The setting of figure 3 powerfully evokes Rudolf's secret chambers of study and experiments; it is one of Maier's depictions of occult adepts.

Despite his melancholic and secluded personality, Rudolf's interests were wide-ranging. Consequently, one of the most important posts around his imperial person was that of librarian and antiquarian. Rudolf's favourite adviser in artistic matters was Jacopo Strada (1518–1588) originally an archaeologist from Mantua who had already served under Ferdinand I and Maximilian II. His son, Octavio

(1550–1616), continued the father's specialty and became the curator of Rudolf's different collections. Octavio's chief literary achievement was the publication of a three-volume emblem book – *Symbola divina et humana Pontificium, Imperatorum, Regum ...* (Prague, 1600) – which provided a rich gallery of popes, emperors and kings, the whole work suggesting, of course, the glory of the house of Habsburg. The collection was co-authored by the Dutchman Jakob Typotius, who was the chief orator of the Emperor, and Aegidius Sadeler (1570–1629), an Antwerp-born engraver who settled in Prague in 1597 and enjoyed Rudolf's utmost confidence. Sadeler made several portraits of the royal family, but his most famous works remain the superb panoramic view of Prague and etched map of Bohemia (1605–6).

One of the most secure types of 'passport' to the Emperor's court was a good reputation in alchemy, astrology and the occult arts. Some fortunate scholars received official titles such as court astronomer or court mathematician, while others enjoyed temporary payment or different favours, even the granting of nobility. The latter was actually the cheapest mode of promotion, since the Emperor claimed that alchemists needed neither money nor medicine as they themselves could make them, while the granting of social elevation was the sole privilege of the ruler. Most of the famous alchemists of late Renaissance Europe turned up in Rudolf's Prague during the long years of his reign.. The libraries and archives of Vienna, Prague, Budapest, Wolfenbüttel and other cities preserve many interesting alchemical books, collections of recipes and manuscripts of practical instructions dedicated to Rudolf or compiled and copied personally for him.[7]

Among the famous alchemists performing transmutations before the Emperor was the infamous Pole Michal Sedivoj (= Michael Sendivogius; 1556–ca. 1630). As Evans has clarified, Sedivoj lived in Prague during the 1590s and suffered more than one imprisonment. According to legend, he helped the Emperor in a very successful transmutation in Rudolf's private chamber in 1604, which the ruler commemorated by placing a marble plaque on the wall claiming: *Faciat hoc quispiam alius, Quod fecit Sendivogius Polonus* (Try to get someone to do what the Pole, Sendivogius, has done). Though this anecdote is of dubious origin, it is true that Sedivoj's treatise *Novum lumen chymicum* was published in that year and became one of the most revered alchemical texts of the seventeenth century.

Like other celebrated alchemists, Sedivoj was not only supported by Rudolf. He criss-crossed Europe, even securing other patrons in Bohemia. Among his sponsors one finds the Czech nobleman, Korálek z Tesín and the powerful magnate Vilém Vok Rožmberk, who had his residence adjoining that of Rudolf in the Hradčany Castle, but who also employed a great number of humanists and adepts on his estates, especially in Krumlov and Trebon (often referred to as Trebona).

Among the many famous and infamous visitors of Count Rožmberk one finds the two Englishmen Doctor John Dee and Edward Kelly, who made their way into innumerable historical and literary anecdotes, as well as a number of modern novels. Their activities in Prague and Trebon are so characteristic of this extraordinary world of late Renaissance humanism that it is worth looking at some of the details.

John Dee started his career in the 1540s as a promising scholar of Greek philology and mathematics, and in this capacity travelled in Europe and engaged in humanist editions of classical scientific texts. Following the accession of Elizabeth I, he rose to become an informal adviser and astrologer of the Queen, whose interests

ranged from mathematics through history, politics and antiquarianism, to magic and other aspects of the occult. Dee's all-embracing ambition was a typical Renaissance one: he wanted to regain the perfect, archetypal knowledge of Adam that had been lost with the fall. An ambition at the beginning, an obsession in Dee's later years – he tried in several ways to achieve this arcane wisdom. In 1558, he published a treatise in which he suggested an improved methodology for astrologers to refine their calculations. A few years later, he designed the magical sign he called *monas hieroglyphica* with which he aimed to bring scholars into perfect meditation in order to reveal and understand the hidden correspondences of the universe [fig. 17.1] shows the title page of the book with the mystical monad in the centre). The *monas* had geometrical, alchemical and astrological layers of meaning, and its message also employed a mystical-theological interpretation.[8] The publication of *Monas hieroglyphica* (Antwerp, 1564) was connected with the house of the Austrian Habsburgs. Prior to completing the book, in September 1563, Dee visited Austria and Hungary, and in Pozsony he participated in the coronation of Maximilian II as king of Hungary. He was so impressed with what he saw that he decided to dedicate his chief philosophical work to this learned and tolerant monarch.

Although his career seems to have been successful, Dee's ambitions were by no means satisfied in England. So he jumped at an invitation to Central Europe when he met and attracted the attention of the Polish nobleman Olbracht Laski in 1583. Laski, then visiting England, was for some time a figure of royal interest. He was escorted by Sir Philip Sidney, participated in Giordano Bruno's dispute with the professors of Oxford, appeared in several audiences before the Queen. It is not entirely clear what directed his attention to Dee, considering his wide range of interests it could have been any number of qualities of the magus-magician. Laski was a political adventurer, an amateur though rather serious student of the occult – on his estate he sponsored the publication of the works of Paracelsus – and, like most magnates, always in need of money. Thus he certainly was attracted by the prospects of making alchemical gold.

By that time, Dee's philosophical interests had taken a radical turn: he had come to the conclusion that the only way of recovering the lost archetypal knowledge he sought would be to learn it directly from the angels. In order to do so, from the late 1570s he engaged in angel magic in the form of séances with the help of mediums, through whom he tried to obtain information about the vocabulary and grammar of the *lingua adamica*. Dee's surviving protocols of the angelic conversations, the so-called 'spiritual diaries', make fascinating reading. Mystical speculations mix with political prophecies and personal meditations, embedded in a scattered chronology of travels and discourses through different courts of Central Europe.[9] At that time, Dee's medium was the infamous Edward Kelly, himself an alchemist who was reputed to have known the recipe of St Dunstan and, in possession of his red powder, the magic alchemical agent. Dee's political prophecies about Laski's becoming king of Poland, the doctor's scholarly reputation, and Kelly's practical alchemical skills seem to have been adequate reasons for the Polish lord to invite the Englishmen to his estate, together with their families and some servants. John Dee had the greatest private library in contemporary England (over 4,000 volumes), and he set out on his Continental journey with a travelling library of 500 books!

As the Englishman's doings did not entirely satisfy their Polish patron, tension

grew, and finally Dee proposed that they move to Prague in fall 1584 and try their fortune before Emperor Rudolf. Dee's ambition was to gain an official title as court 'Philosophus & mathematicus'.[10] He chanced to appear in front of the Emperor on 3 September 1584, after much preparation, and the audition lasted a full hour.[11] At the beginning of the conversation, Dee reviewed his major work, the *Monas hieroglyphica*, which he had dedicated to Rudolf's father. After Dee's introductory remarks, the Emperor admitted that he had difficulties in following the doctor's train of thought. Changing the subject, Dee explained how he had become disappointed in earthly sciences and how he had turned to angelic metaphysics. The openly magical program horrified the Emperor. On top of this, Dee poured out his personal mission:

> It pleased God to send me *his Light*; and his holy Angels, for these two years and a half, have used to inform me: yea, they have brought me *a Stone* of that value that no earthly Kingdom is of that worthinesse as to be compared to the vertue and dignity thereof, etc.
>
> The Angel of the Lord hath appeared to me, and rebuketh you for your sins. If you will hear me, and believe me, you shall Triumph: if you will not hear me, The Lord, the God that made Heaven and Earth, putteth his foot against your breast, and will throw you headlong down from your seat.
>
> Moreover, the Lord hath made his Covenant with me ... If you will forsake your wickednesse, and turn unto him, your Seat shall be the greatest that ever was: and the Devil shall become your prisoner: Which Devil, I did conjecture, to be the Great Turk. This my Commission, is from God.[12]

Hearing these prophecies, Rudolf could hardly contain himself. He assured Dee that he would consider his message and dismissed the doctor. However, in spite of all of Dee's efforts, he never again appeared before the Emperor, which contributed to his decision to move to Cracow and try his fortune with King Stephen Bathory.

During 1585, the Englishmen returned to Prague, but the eccentric Dee, prophesying religious tolerance and *eirenism*, became an object of suspicion on the part of the Emperor's Catholic, especially Jesuit, advisers. It is surprising that he was able to avoid arrest after voicing prophecies such as this one, delivered by the Holy Ghost on 10 April 1586: 'I shall preach penitence to you. Whosoever wishes to be wise may look neither to the right nor to the left; neither towards this man who is called a catholic, nor towards that one who is called a heretic; but may he look up to the god of heaven and earth and to his Son, Jesus Christ.'[13] A few days after this séance, pressed by the new apostolic nuncio, Filippo Sega, Rudolf banished Dee and Kelly from Bohemia and all Habsburg territories. They took shelter in German lands, but their exile had ended by August, when Count Rožmberk intervened on their behalf and settled them on his estate in Trebon. Dee stayed there for three years until he returned to England in 1589. He continued his angelic conversations, accomplished scientific experiments and met a great number of people: humanists, travellers, diplomats and merchants. Kelly's career prospered, he reappeared in the Emperor's court and performed transmutations, among others in the house of Tadeus Hájek, for which he was knighted and highly appreciated. But his fortune, as was often the case with alchemists, proved to be mercurial. He was rich and they poor; he married an English gentlewoman and provided a good education to his

step-daughter, who later became the noted poetess Westonia; he suffered several imprisonments and finally died in disgrace while trying to escape from Hradčany Castle in 1598.[14]

The Significance of Rudolfine Magical Humanism

For a pragmatist, the world of the late Renaissance humanists may seem a ludicrous theatre of dreams and delusions, but such a judgement would by no means be accurate. The opinion of the English historian Hugh Trevor-Roper pinpoints why that lost magical world is so compelling for the people of our (post-)modern age: 'The Rudolfine age, like the Elizabethan age, is an age in itself; it had its own philosophy, its own inner springs; and that philosophy is perhaps more intelligible to us, who live in a world of ideological tensions and ecumenical aspirations, than to our predecessors who looked for signs of "progress" and identified progress with particular parties in politics and ideas.'[15] Signs of progress can also be found in Rudolfine culture, among the scholars who found employment at court. 'Progress' embedded in a mixed and controversial intellectual atmosphere in which it is difficult to separate out old and new elements and in which diametrically opposing views united together more or less peacefully.

1. From the voluminous literature on Mannerism, I can recommend the following works: Max Dvorak, 'Über Greco und der Manierismus' (1920), in *Kunstgeschichte als Geistesgeschichte: Studien zur abendländischen Kunstentwicklung* (Munich, 1923), pp. 259–76; Gustav René Hocke, *Manierismus in der Literatur: Sprach-Alchimie und esoterische Kombinationskunst* (Hamburg, 1959); Arnold Hauser, *Der Ursprung der modernen Kunst und Literatur: Die Entwicklung des Manierismus seit der Krise der Renaissance* (1964; Munich, 1973); André Chastel, *La Crise de la Renaissance* (Geneva, 1968); Tibor Klaniczay, 'La Crise de la renaissance et le manicrisme', *Acta Litteraria*, 13 (1971), 269–314; Tibor Klaniczay, *A manierizmus* (Budapest,1975); Claude-Gilbert Dubois, *Le Manierisme* (Paris, 1979); Gerald Gillespie, 'Renaissance, Mannerism, Baroque', in G. Hoffmeister (ed.), *German Baroque Literature: The European Perspective* (New York, 1983), pp. 3–24; Maciej Zurowski, 'Aktualna problematyka manieryzmu', in B. Otwinowska and J. Pelc (eds), *Przelom wieków XVI i XVII w literaturze i kulturze Polskiej* (Wroclaw, Warsaw and Cracow, 1984); James V. Mirollo: *Mannerism and Renaissance Poetry* (New Haven and London, 1984); and Caroline Patey, *Manierismo* (Milan, 1996).
2. Johannis Jessenii, *Anatomiæ, Pragæ, Anno MDC abs se solenniter administratas historia. Accessis eiusdem de ossibus tractatus* (Wittenberg, 1601); J. Vinar, *Obrazy z minulosti ceského lekarstvi* (Prague, 1959), pp. 142ff.
3. On Jessenius, see Friedel Pick, *Johannes Jessenius de Magna Jessen, Arzt und Rektor in Wittenberg und Prag ...* (Leipzig, 1926); László Mátrai, *Régi magyar filozófusok* (Budapest, 1961), pp. 50–65; Mária Bokesová-Uherová, *Ján Jessenius* (Bratislava, 1966); László Ruttkay, *Jeszenszky (Jessenius) János és kora* (Budapest, 1971); R. J. W. Evans, *Rudolf II and His World* (Oxford, 1973), pp.136–8.
4. See Anthony Grafton, 'Humanism and Science in Rudolphine Prague: Kepler in Context', in James A. Parentes et al. (eds), *Literary Culture in the Holy Roman Empire, 1555–1720* (Chapel Hill, 1991), Josef Smolka, 'The Scientific Revolution in Bohemia', in Roy Porter and Mikulas Teich (eds), *The Scientific Revolution in National Context* (Cambridge, 1992), pp. 210–40.
5. Evans (note 3), p. 92.
6. See his poshoumusly published study, *De morbo ungarico peste cognoscendo* (Leipzig, 1619).
7. Vienna, Österreichische Nationalbibliothek, MS 11450; Prague, SÚA, SM A 72/1; Budapest, OSZK, MSS 9 Duod. Germ., 239 Quart. Germ.; Wolfenbüttel, Herzog August Bibiothek, MS 3338; etc.
8. Dee has been a favourite subject of English Renaissance cultural history. During the past few decades, several monographs and a great number of articles have been devoted to different aspects of his activities. See Peter J. French, *John Dee: The World of an Elizabethan Magus* (London, 1972); Frances Yates, *The Occult Philosophy in the Elizabethan Age* (London, 1979); Nicholas H. Clulee, *John Dee's Natural Philosophy: Between Science and Religion* (London, 1988); Geoffrey James, *The Enochian Magick of Dr. John Dee* (St. Paul, MN, 1994); William H. Sherman, *John Dee: The Politics of Reading and Writing in the English Renaissance* (Amherst, MA, 1995).
9. Dee's handwritten protocols fill many volumes in the British and Bodleian Libraries and have complicated textual interrelationships. A considerable portion of these diaries was published by Maric Casaubon in London in 1659 (*True and Faithful Relation of What Passed Between Doctor Dee ... and Some Spirits ...*). Recently, there has developed a vivid scholarly interest in the angelic conversations (see Stephen Clucas, Deborah Harkness, Christopher Whitby and others), but the only comprehensive (though brief) modern analysis is by Wayne Shu-

maker, in *Renaissance Curiosa* (Binghamton, NY, 1982), pp. 15–53.

10. On the Continental adventures of the Englishmen, apart from Evans (note 3), pp. 214–39, see, for example, the following articles: Luigi Firpo, 'John Dee, scienziato, negromante e avventuriero', *Rinascimento*, 3 (1952): 25–84; K. Zantuan, 'Olbracht Laski in Elizabethan England', *Polish Review*, 13 (1968): 3–22; Gy. E. Szonyi, 'John Dee i jego zwiazki ze Srodkowa Europa', *Odrodzenie I Reformacja W Polsce* 25 (1980): 99–111; *idem*, 'Traditions of Magic: From Faustus to Dee at European Universities and Courts', *Cauda Pavonis*, 10:2 (1991): 1–8; and two recent books published in Bohemia: Vaclav Kaplicky, *Zivot alchymistuv* (Prague, 1980); Jan Sviták, *Rudolfinská Trilogie: John Dee, Kouzelnlk z Londyna; Sir Edward Kelley, Cesky rytír; Elizabeth Johanna Weston* (Prague, 1994).

11. See Dee (note 9), pp. 230–1.

12. *Ibid.*, p. 231.

13. Published by C. H. Josten in 'An Unknown Chapter in the Life of John Dee', *Journal of the Warburg and Courtauld Institutes*, 28 (1965): 245.

14. On Kelley, Lady Jane Weston and Elizabeth Weston Leo, see the books of Kaplicky and Sviták, mentioned earlier, and Susan E. Bassnett, 'Revising a Biography: A New Interpretation of the Life of Elizabeth Jane Weston (Westonia), Based on Her Autobiographical Poem on the Occasion of the Death of Her Mother', *Cahiers elisabéthains*, 37 (1990): 1–8; Louise Schleiner, 'Elizabeth Weston, Alchemist's Step-Daughter and Published Poet', *Cauda Pavonis*, 10:2 (1991): 8–16.

15. Hugh Trevor-Roper, *Princes and Artists: Patronage and Ideology of Four Habsburg Courts, 1517–1633* (London, 1976), p. 96.

Natural Philosophy and Natural Magic

PENELOPE GOUK

Natural Magicke then is that, whiche having intentively behelde the forces of all natural thinges, and celestiall, and with curious search sought out their order, doth in such sorte publish abroade the hidden and secret powers of nature: coupling the inferiour things with the qualities of the superior as it were certaine enticements by a naturall joyninge of them together, that therof oftentimes doe arise marvellous miracles: not so much by Arte as nature whereunto this Arte dothe proffer herselfe a servaunte, when shee worketh these things.[1]

Magic: The Sixteenth-Century Background

In sixteenth-century Europe, magic as a whole was broadly understood as an art (*ars* in Latin, *techne* in Greek) that could bring about particular effects on things or people by 'occult' – that is, hidden – or insensible means. (The precise meaning of the term *occult* will be taken up below.) The art of magic encompassed a whole spectrum of practices which were not necessarily connected to each other in any systematic way, and these were seen as ranging from the activities of the most sophisticated practitioner to the lowliest and most ignorant charlatan. Although all magic was formally condemned by the Catholic church, its attraction as a source of power beyond that of ordinary mortals proved irresistible. Indeed those who became seriously involved in magic were often members of the clergy.[2]

Although magic was regarded as an essentially secret art, the subject became increasingly visible through the publication of many books on various aspects of magical practice. These included editions of ancient and medieval texts (often translated into the vernacular), as well as new works by Renaissance authors.[3] The increased visibility of the subject coincided with a widespread attempt to classify different forms of magic and to provide a coherent theoretical framework for them. Astrology and witchcraft were among the subjects that received most attention, but an unprecedented number of books explicitly on natural magic were published in Europe in the latter half of the sixteenth century.

There were many ways of classifying and ordering magic. One of the best known is that of Cornelius Agrippa, who distinguished between natural, celestial and ceremonial magic in his famous *De occulta philosophia* (1533). In contrast, Giordano Bruno identified at least ten different categories in his *De magia* (1590) that ranged from *sapientia* (the wise magic of the magus) to *maleficium* (demonic magic involving a pact with the devil). Between these were such categories as the natural magic of *medicina* and *chymia*; *praestigiatoria* or jugglery, and mathematical magic or occult philosophy, which relied on words, charms, numbers, images and characters.[4] In essence, all occult powers that could be harnessed by the magician fell into two basic categories, even if the distinction between them was not always clear. On the one hand, there was the kind of magic which relied on the intervention of supernatural, personified intelligences for bringing about particular effects: this was demonic magic, which everyone agreed was dangerous. On the other hand, natural, or

spiritual, magic supposedly avoided such intervention, since it concentrated on the investigation and manipulation of effects produced by occult *natural* causes. Although arguably still dangerous, this kind of magic seemed to gain an unprecedented level of respectability in the latter part of the sixteenth century.

Proponents of natural magic typically claimed that they were following an ancient tradition of the *prisca theologia*, or original theology.[5] According to this notion, God had revealed to Adam supernatural knowledge about the structure and processes of Creation. This secret wisdom had been transmitted through a select group of initiates which included Abraham and Moses, Hermes, Orpheus, Pythagoras and other *magi*. To conceal it from the vulgar, such knowledge was expressed hermetically through hidden symbols, myths and allegories that required correct interpretation. Nature (just like the Bible) was a book written in a secret language that could only be decoded by the spiritually pure. The doctrine of 'signatures' – the idea that the occult virtues of things were indicated through visible outward signs – was an important dimension of natural magic.

General Principles of Natural Magic

The terms *natural* and *occult* at this time both had quite different connotations than those understood today. Phenomena that were regarded as natural were only those that occur *most of the time*, in nature's habitual course. A rare event or astonishing feat might be considered unnatural, even though today we might consider it as being governed by natural laws. Likewise, occult forces were assumed to be of a different character from those of everyday experience. They included unknown properties of things, even though the effect might be perfectly 'natural' in modern terms.

At this time, the term *occult* was also used in a particular technical sense.[6] According to traditional Aristotelian natural philosophy, we cannot know anything outside the realm of the sensible. *Manifest* properties of bodies were those which were directly perceptible to the senses. Divided into primary and secondary qualities, these arose from the four elements and their combinations, and were the proper subject of physics. *Occult* qualities included anything that could not be explained in elemental terms, and were by definition excluded from scholastic physics. Within this intellectual framework, gravity, magnetism and musical resonance (to take but three examples) were all occult forces that acted at a distance, just as the more obviously 'magical' phenomena of fascination and binding exerted their influence.

In natural magic, occult forces were not only taken for granted, but it was assumed that they could be harnessed by the magician to bring about predictable effects. This manipulative approach is now accepted as characteristic of experimental science and technology, but in the sixteenth century it was most often recognized as a feature of magic. Medical practitioners, engineers, painters and musicians were among those who utilized a variety of empirical techniques to bring about effects on things or people by occult means. Many of these techniques were closely guarded secrets known only to initiates and therefore seemed almost miraculous to outsiders. The changes and effects wrought by these practitioners might be chemical, physical or mechanical, and especially included psychological and psychosomatic changes in human behaviour. The ability to manipulate emotions through the imagination, and to heighten desire, was a classic hallmark of the magician.[7]

A central figure in the development of magical doctrine was Marsilio Ficino

(1433–1499), a founder member of Cosimo de' Medici's Florentine Academy in the 1450s.[8] Ficino's learned editions of and commentaries on the works of Hermes Trismegistus and Plato, and above all his own *De triplici vita* (1489), provided the philosophical underpinnings for many later texts on magic.[9] Unknown to Ficino and his followers, however, all of the hermetic texts and many of the Platonic ones were actually Neoplatonic in origin and dated from the early centuries AD.

Few people would have actually read Ficino in full, yet his essentially Neoplatonic world-view was widely disseminated. One of the most accessible sources proved to be Agrippa's *De occulta philosophia* (first written in 1510 and enlarged in 1533), which went through many editions.[10] Another person who popularized Ficino's philosophy was Paracelsus, the famous Swiss-German physician and surgeon Philippus Aureolus Theophrastus Bombastus von Hohenheim (1493–1541).[11] An ardent reformer of medical learning (he was known as the 'Luther of medicine'), Paracelsus used Neoplatonic and Hermetic doctrine to support his attack on the traditional science that was being taught in medical faculties at the time. Although it had relatively little influence in his own lifetime, Paracelsus' belief that the medical practitioner should engage in the investigation and manipulation of the hidden powers of nature (especially through alchemy and astrology) was taken increasingly seriously fifty years later. Oswald Croll, Michael Maier, Heinrich Khunrath and Robert Fludd were among the physicians associated with Rudolf's court who engaged in Paracelsian alchemy and published highly influential works on the subject.

By the late sixteenth century, there seems to have been a remarkable degree of consensus about the core attributes of occult philosophy. These were first summarized by Agrippa, but it was Fludd who eventually provided the most memorable representations of the fundamental principles of magic in his *Utriusque cosmi. . . historia* (1617–19), or history of the macrocosm and microcosm [Figs 1 and 2].[12] First, there was a hierarchy of worlds which God created from the void. In descending order of perfection, these comprised the empyrean realm of angels and demons (intelligent beings with no corporeal bodies), the ethereal realm comprising the fixed stars and the seven planets and, finally, the elemental world, which extended from the earth to the moon. Connecting these realms is a network of correspondences, and actions or operations carried out at one level of the hierarchy could bring about effects on another level by means of sympathy, correspondence or harmony: 'as above, so below'. A favourite topos is how humans – the microcosm – were made in the image of the macrocosm. Thus the loftiest human faculty is the higher mind, or *mens*; the reason, will and imagination occupied the middle realms; the instincts and the body represented the elemental regions. The magus manipulated the correspondences between the macrocosm and the microcosm to bring about his desired ends. In theory at least, natural magic was confined to harnessing hidden forces in the elemental and ethereal realms, and when directed at a person it worked chiefly through the imagination and affected the body rather than addressing the intellect.

The effectiveness of all magic was based on several related principles. Arguably, the first and most important of these was the concept of *pneuma* or *spiritus mundi* (world spirit), an idea initially Stoic in origin that later became central to Neoplatonism. As Ficino explained, *spiritus* was a subtle fluid medium that permeated the entire cosmos and served as the principal mechanism for the influence of the stars on the earth. This invisible and extremely active substance (which was itself corpo-

real) intermingled with earthly matter and could bring about changes in its form. Sympathy – that is, the interaction and affinity of different parts of the cosmos – was maintained by *tonos*, or tension, a dynamic property of the *pneuma*. *Spiritus* was recognized as being similar, if not identical, to the medical spirits that effect the link between the body and soul. As Robert Burton explained in his *Anatomy of Melancholy* (1621): '*Spirit* is a most subtle vapour, which is expressed from the *Blood* and the instrument of the Soul, to perform all his Actions, a common type or *medium*, betwixt the Body and the soule.'

Many magical operations relied on the properties of both kinds of spirit. Alchemy, for example, manipulated the *spiritus* hidden in material substances through the process of distillation, and the medicinal effects of chemicals on the body were thought to rely chiefly on their affinity with the human spirits. The powerful effect that music can bring about on the passions relied on a similar correspondence between musical sound, moving air and the human spirits.[13]

The second magical principle lay in the potency of particular symbols, especially numbers, geometrical figures and letters. Much like *spiritus* (although not necessarily related to it), these entities mediated between the intellectual and material realms. Not only did they represent the elements of which the world is constructed; they actually were invested with the same qualities and powers as those elements. Hence as Agrippa explained, the magical power of names, incantations and mathematical formulae resided in the fact that they had a real relation to the concepts or things that they stood for. There were three initially distinct traditions that Renaissance philosophers drew on for understanding this aspect of magic: Pythagoreanism, the cabbala, and Lullism. According to the Pythagoreans (who had flourished as a mystic cult in the sixth century BC), numbers were the ultimate essence of reality and served as a means of rendering perceptible what would otherwise remain beyond the grasp of human sense experience. Pythagoras himself first demonstrated the correspondence between simple arithmetic ratios and musical consonances, and the same ratios were assumed to underly the structure of the entire cosmos, the 'harmony of the spheres'.

Similar beliefs about the generative power of letters were expressed in cabbala, a Jewish spiritual magic supposedly handed down through oral tradition from Moses himself. The cabbala taught that the letters of the Hebrew alphabet, the Sepiroth, formed the creative language of God, a language that Adam himself had spoken. The contemplation of these letters in their various combinations and permutations had a scientific and moral value, leading to union with the divine. It was Pico della Mirandola, a friend of Ficino and member of the Florentine Academy, who 'introduced Kabbalah into the Renaissance synthesis'.[14] However, the earliest exposition of its techniques and underlying principles was Johannes Reuchlin's *De arte cabalistica* (1517).[15] The Christian cabbalism of Pico and Reuchlin was in many respects similar to the mnemonic combinatory art of Raymon Lull, a thirteenth-century Christian mystic who sought to establish an infallible method of proving the truths of the Christian Trinity to Moslems and Jews.[16] There was a widespread revival of interest in Lull's art during the Renaissance, many of his extensive writings (and others mistakenly attributed to him) coming into print. Another influential text was Johannes Trithemius' *Steganographia* (written in 1499 and circulated in manuscript until printed in the early seventeenth century). Ostensibly a work simply dealing

with cryptography and the communication of messages by occult but natural means, it was widely recognized as a treatise on demonic magic concerned with the invocation and manipulation of spirits, demons and angels.[17]

The third important magical principle was the belief that artificial instruments could not only imitate nature but also serve to overcome the limits set on the unaided human senses. The 'artificial' magic of Roger Bacon and Albertus Magnus, which during the Middle Ages was popularly thought to rely on demonic agency, received renewed attention in the Renaissance. The distinction made between the natural and artificial initially arose as a consequence of the Aristotelian conception of natural and forced motions. Natural motions included those of heavy and light bodies moving to and from the earth in the sublunar realm, and the circular motion of heavenly bodies. Forced, or artificial, motion was any movement that was the result of constraining a body or forcing it against nature. This type of motion included most hydraulic, pneumatic and clockwork machinery. In the latter part of the sixteenth century, many devices of incredible sophistication were being constructed by clockmakers and mechanics (most notably those in Augsburg) which amply testified to the success of this artificial, manipulative approach to nature.[18]

The idea that both natural and artificial magic operated according to the same natural laws steadily gained ground. This view found support in the writings of Vitruvius, for example, who had stated that 'all machinery is generated by Nature, and the revolution of the universe guides and controls'.[19] The Renaissance philosopher-engineer, skilled in all aspects of the Vitruvian arts such as military technology, architecture and garden and theatre design, came to be widely regarded as a natural magician *par excellence*.[20] Giovan Battista della Porta's *Magia naturalis* (1589) was the most important modern work that addressed this kind of technological operation. Instruments and the effects they could produce were reputedly regarded with suspicion by scholastic philosophers who were mistrustful of the senses as a means of acquiring reliable or certain knowledge. Sight, for example, could be deceived by the use of lenses, mirrors and tricks of perspective, while the ear might be deluded by artificial birdsong. Instead of regarding them as mere toys, the natural magician saw such devices in a more positive light. On the one hand, they might be regarded as a means of controlling, and therefore understanding, nature. On the other, they might be used to arouse curiosity among patrons that could be channelled into profitable ends.

Why Natural Magic Is Interesting to Us Now

It was within the cultural milieu of the Rudolfine court that the fullest expression was given to 'occult philosophy' in the late sixteenth and early seventeenth centuries.[21] The experimental quest for higher truths and secret power, a possibly dangerous search involving communication with higher intelligences (i.e., demons and angels), was positively encouraged by the Emperor, whose court offered an unusually protected space within which conventional doctrinal, political and intellectual boundaries could be ignored. Both natural and demonic magic were attractive to individuals who were engaged in the development of new technologies and the effective exercise of political power. While his quest for secret knowledge may have been politically motivated, Rudolf's support of such practices had far-reaching cultural consequences. Bringing together practitioners with very different skills in a

search for universal truths meant that the many symbolic and technical correspondences between a whole range of arts and sciences were fruitfully explored.

The demise of Rudolf's court at Prague is seen as a critical turning-point in the status of magic during the seventeenth century. After his death, natural magic never again received such extensive patronage, and by the eighteenth century magic seems to have disappeared as a serious category of knowledge and practice altogether. There seems to be a direct correlation between this 'decline of magic' and the 'rise of science' embodied in the founding of the Royal Society and the achievements of Isaac Newton. But was it really such a straightforward process? Instead of accepting this linear view, we might instead focus on how a number of 'magical' beliefs and practices were mysteriously absorbed into the 'new science', while the category of magic remained dangerous and marginal.

Newton's natural philosophy, for example, assumed the existence of an extremely fine aether linking the sublunar realm with the cosmos that had a strong resemblance with *spiritus*. At the same time, he believed that the underlying structure of nature was mathematical, with the same laws operating throughout the cosmos: as above, so below. Similarly, the experimental philosophy promoted by the Royal Society relied on instruments such as the microscope to uncover realms normally invisible to the unaided senses. So thoroughly have we accepted these as examples of how scientific knowledge is created that it is difficult to accept that such practices were once unorthodox. The power of mathematical and mechanical models to uncover the secrets of nature has long been accepted as a part of modern science.

In contrast, the power of the imagination to visualize and change the world has only relatively recently become validated as a scientific process, chiefly due to unparalleled developments in communications technology, above all with the computer. As we become increasingly familiar with concepts such as 'virtual reality' and conceptualize the world as a network of invisible relationships mediated through the Internet, the magical cosmos and occult philosophy take on renewed significance. What even a generation ago seemed to be definitively 'non-scientific' about occult philosophy now seems to have anticipated recent developments in modern science and technology. Only now are we beginning to appreciate fully some of the resources that were explored in Rudolf's court.

If we think of natural magic as the production of extraordinary effects by little-understood techniques, and in terms of people deliberately trying to manipulate those effects to bring about particular ends, then natural magic clearly occupies a very significant space in present-day culture, just as it did in Rudolf's world. The entertainment industry, for example, deploys cutting-edge technology for the purpose of exciting, uplifting and transporting its audience into a world of fantasy. Through the manipulation of sounds, light and sophisticated devices, a virtual environment is created that can both imitate reality and move into the realm of pure imagination. At the same time, similar techniques are harnessed by the defence industry, whose principal goal is to achieve state security. Here the emphasis is on developing ever more powerful and secret technologies that can be used to defeat enemies and retain control of the state. Effective intelligence relies on devices that can allow rapid and secret communication among allies and the remote surveillance of enemies, while at the same time hopefully preventing the same techniques being used by others.

Natural magic continues to exist on the boundaries between legitimated practices and beliefs and those that are not, and is found in places where things are brought together that are normally kept apart. It mediates between the realms of the sacred and profane, between the immaterial and material worlds, between the invisible and the visible. Natural magic embraces activities that have an element of danger, secrecy or illegitimacy about them, but that also hold out the promise of fulfilling untold desires by natural means. Uncomfortable though it may be, the desire to unlock the hidden secrets of the universe and the higher search for ultimate truths are irrevocably yoked to the quest for ultimate power, the pursuit of pleasure, of beauty and even of eternal life.

1. H. C. Agrippa, *Of the Vanitie and Uncertaintie of Artes and Sciences*, trs. James Sandford (London, 1569), fol. 54r.

2. Among the most notorious sixteenth-century examples were Giordano Bruno and Tomasso Campanella, both of whom were Dominican friars. Friar Roger Bacon and Albertus Magnus were the most famous twelfth-century magicians.

3. W. Eamon, *Science and the Secrets of Nature: Books of Secrets in Medieval and Early Modern Culture* (Princeton, 1994).

4. L. Thorndike, *The Sixteenth Century*, vols V, VI, *A History of Magic and Experimental Science* (New York, 1941), vol. V, pp. 426–7; W. Schumaker, *Natural Magic and Modern Science: Four Treatises 1590–1657* (Binghamton, NY, 1989), p. 47; I. P. Couliano, *Eros and Magic in the Renaissance* (Chicago and London, 1987), pp. 157–9.

5. D. P. Walker, *The Ancient Theology: Studies in Christian Platonism from the Fifteenth to the Eighteenth Century* (London, 1972), pp. 1–25.

6. K. Hutchison, 'What happened to Occult Qualities in the Renaissance?', *Isis* 73 (1982), 233–53; J. Henry, 'Occult Qualities in the Experimental Philosophy: Active Principles in Pre-Newtonian Matter Theory', *History of Science*, 24 (1986), 335–81.

7. Couliano (note 4), esp. pp. 87–106.

8. On Ficino's theory of magic and its relationship to ancient texts, see D. P. Walker, *Spiritual and Demonic Magic* (London, 1958), esp. pp. 36–44 ('Sources of Ficino's Magic') and 75–84 ('General Theory of Natural Magic'); F. Yates, *Giordano Bruno and the Hermetic Tradition* (London, 1964; reprinted 1982), pp. 20–83; B. Copenhaver 'Astrology and Magic' in Charles B. Schmitt, Quentin Skinner and Jill Kraye, eds, *The Cambridge History of Renaissance Philosophy* (Cambridge, 1988), pp. 264–300, esp. the section on Ficino's philosophical theory of magic, pp. 274–85.

9. The publication of Ficino's *Opera Omnia* (Basel, 1576) seems to have given fresh impetus to the recovery of ancient secret learning in Rudolf's lifetime.

10. In the course of his varied career, the German philosopher Henricus Cornelius Agrippa (1486–1535) travelled widely as a physician, soldier and teacher. In 1524, he served as doctor and astrologer to the Queen Mother of France at Lyon and then as a librarian and historian to Margaret of Austria in Antwerp (1528–30). See Yates (note 8) and P. Zambelli, 'Magical and Radical Reformation in Agrippa of Nettesheim', *Journal of the Warburg and Courtauld Institutes*, 39 (1976), 69–103.

11. See Walter Pagel, *Paracelsus* (Basel, 1958).

12. H. C. Agrippa, *Three Books of Occult Philosophy*, tr. J. F. (London, 1651); R. Fludd, *Utriusque cosmi. . . historia*, 2 vols (Oppenheim, 1617–19). See also J. Godwin, *Robert Fludd: Hermetic Philosopher and Surveyor of Two Worlds* (London, 1979), esp. pp. 42–53.

13. Musical sound by the movement of the air moves the body: by purified air it excites the aerial spirit which is the bond of body and soul: by emotion it affects the senses and at the same time the soul: by meaning it works on the mind: finally, by the very movement of the subtle air it penetrates strongly; by its contemporation it flows smoothly: by the conformity of its quality it floods us with a wonderful pleasure: by its nature, both spiritual and material, it at once seizes, and claims as its own, man in his entirety (M. Ficino, *Commentary on the Timaeus*, cap. 28, in Walker [note 8], p. 9).

14. Yates (note 8), pp. 17–22 (17); see also C. Wirszubski, *Pico della Mirandola's Encounter with Jewish Mysticism* (Cambridge, MA, and London, 1989).

15. Yates (note 8), pp. 9–15; also *idem, The Art of Memory* (Harmondsworth, 1978), chap. 8, 'Lullism as an Art of Memory', pp. 175–19.

16. Yates (note 8), pp. 9–27; see also D. B. Ruderman, *Kabbalah, Magic and Science* (Cambridge, MA, and London, 1988).

17. On Trithemius, see Walker (note 8), pp. 86–90; Couliano (note 4), pp. 162–175; Nicholas H. Clulee, *John Dee's Natural Philosophy* (London, 1988), pp. 136–39.

18. S. A. Bedini, 'The Role of Automata in the History of Technology', *Technology and Culture*, 5 (1964), 24–42; W. Eamon, 'Technology as Magic in the Late Middle Ages and the Renaissance', *Janus*, 70 (1983), 171–212.

19. Vitruvius, *Ten Books on Architecture*, X.1.

20. Both R. Wittkower, *Architectural Principles*, and B. Gille, in *The Renaissance Engineers* (London, 1966), for example, discuss the Vitruvian characteristics of the philosopher-engineer without allusion to magic; the connection is made more explicit in F. Yates, *Theatre of the World*, pp. 20–59, and R. Strong, *The Renaissance Garden in England* (London, 1979), pp. 75–8.

21. R. Evans, *Rudolf II and His World* (Oxford, 1973), chaps 6, 7 (pp. 196–274).

From Feuding Brothers to a Nation at War with Itself

HERBERT HAUPT

Nothing was so galling to Emperor Rudolf II as the thought that he had not conclusively defeated the arch-enemy of Christendom and had thereby fallen miserably short of his own imperial standards.[1] As far as Rudolf was concerned, peace negotiations were a form of betrayal, which meant that the signatories of the peace treaty of Zsitva-Torok[2] on 11 November 1606 were now his personal enemies. The Emperor was convinced that the Regensburg Reichstag (spring 1608) would provide the necessary funds to pursue the war until the Turks were finally defeated. This was the thinking behind his refusal to sign the armistice agreement that his brother Matthias[3] (1557–1619) had negotiated. Above all, the Emperor was simply not prepared to accept the humiliation of handing over to the Turks such hard-won border posts as Gran (Esztergom), Erlau (Eger) and Kanischa (Nagykanizsa). He also refused to approve the Vienna Peace Treaty (23 June 1606) which had been reached with Grand Duke Stephan Bocskay of Transylvania (1555–1606). Yet, as so often in the Emperor's life, his own imperial aspirations had little to do with *realpolitik*.

The long, drawn-out Turkish Wars[4] and the Hungarian-Transylvanian uprising of 1604[5] had highlighted the weaknesses and insecure financial footing of the empire. As the Emperor lost his authority, so the nobility gained in strength. Now they were only prepared to underwrite the Turkish Wars in return for increased privileges and certain religious concessions.

During the Turkish Wars, Rudolf's long-standing mistrust of his brother Matthias[6] evolved into open enmity and hatred. Their characters could hardly have been more different: on the one hand, there was the Emperor, a proud ruler who was nevertheless indecisive, reclusive and increasingly threatened by depression; on the other hand, there was his ambitious brother, ready to promise anything when it came to bolstering his own position.

The feud between the two brothers entered a crucial phase when Rudolf attempted to dismantle the peace treaties of Zsitva-Torok and Vienna, which had been so hard to negotiate in the first place. The idea of revoking the Emperor's power took seed and grew. In secret talks in Vienna in April 1606, Archduke Maximilian III (1558–1618)[7] and Archdukes Ferdinand II (1578–1637) and Maximilian Ernst (1583–1616) from Graz recognized Matthias as head of the house of Habsburg. They also nominated him as their candidate in the election for the king of the Romans.[8] However, they rejected the suggestion coming from their advisers that the Emperor should be forcibly removed from the throne.

In the winter of 1607–8, Hungary was faced with the possibility of another uprising. Archduke Matthias, governor of Hungary since 1606, was alarmed. He knew that the aristocracy of Hungary and Austria shared his alarm, and in Pressburg on 1 February 1608, under Matthias' leadership, they set up a military alliance to preserve peace with the Turks. Messages were sent out to the aristocracy of Moravia, Silesia and Bohemia exhorting them to pledge their solidarity.

Emperor Rudolf II underestimated the significance of the Pressburg Confedera-

tion.[9] It still seemed inconceivable to him that his brother would allow himself to be persuaded to take up arms against him. Completely misinterpreting the facts, Rudolf reacted as though from a position of power. He was increasingly convinced by the advice of the imperial court secretary Andreas Hanewaldt to declare the Hungarian, Austrian and Moravian nobility guilty of high treason, expropriate their lands and arm the towns and cities which remained loyal to the Emperor. Even if it was far from clear how this could be achieved without an effective army and financial backing, the plan corresponded to his own way of thinking and seemed to him to be the perfect political lever. This was not lost on all concerned. Although the Emperor did not at that precise moment have the power to shatter the nobility, a speedy and energetic response was clearly essential.

On 7 March 1608, the noblemen Karl of Žerotín[10] (1564–1615) and Karl of Liechtenstein[11] (1569–1627), along with sixty knights and other noblemen, stormed a regular sitting of the Moravian Landrecht in Brno. They demanded that the leader of the Landtag, Ladislaus Berka von Duba, should call an extraordinary sitting of the house in view of the threatened attack by the haiducks. Žerotín and Liechtenstein's anxiety was also directed towards an invasion into Moravia by imperial troops under General Johann Tserclaes von Tilly (1559–1632). Berka refused: the Emperor alone had the power to convene an extraordinary sitting of the Landtag. The following day, Liechtenstein dismissed Berka for incompetence, relying as he did so on the support of the overwhelming majority in the Landtag. With only two exceptions, the members of the nobility supported Liechtenstein. The only opposition came from the towns and the prelates. Fearing Tilly's troops and the increasingly hostile attitude of the town of Brno, Liechtenstein and his entourage retreated to Austerlitz (Slavkov u Brna). A commission worked out what looked like suitable proposals: a thousand men should be recruited, and sweeping taxes should be imposed in Moravia. The Landtag was convened for 13 April 1608 in Eibenschütz (Ivančice).

Greatly disturbed by events in Moravia, Rudolf seized the initiative. He called a sitting of the Landtag for Bohemia and summoned Bishop Melchior Khlesl[12] (1552–1630), Matthias' most influential adviser, to Prague. In fact, in Bohemia the events in Hungary and Moravia were viewed with increasing disapproval, which was not unconnected with the kingdom of Bohemia's insistence on its supremacy over Moravia and Silesia. The only two individuals who made no secret of their support for Matthias were the crypto-Calvinist Petr Vok of Rožmberk (1539–1611) and the leader of the Czech Brethren, Václav Budovec (1547–1621). The sitting of the Landtag in Bohemia from 10 to 17 March 1608 strengthened Rudolf's position. The Emperor was authorized to issue a general decree and to call a sitting of the whole Landtag for 14 April in Prague which was to have equal representation from Bohemia, Moravia, Silesia and the Lausitz.

Now, at last, Bishop Khlesl's wait was over. After more than two weeks, during which time he had tried in vain to have an audience with the Emperor, Rudolf was prepared to receive the supposed instigator of the plot against him. The atmosphere was tense, and the Bishop may well have been glad that, before setting out for Prague, he had secured his safe-conduct for the return journey to Vienna. He spoke freely, reporting Matthias' determination to defend his right as a successor to the crown, with arms if need be. The Bishop explained that the Hungarians had

been forced to fall back on their own resources in view of the apparent imminence of war because Rudolf had left them unprotected. Nonetheless, in his view, the quarrel could be settled peacefully, if only Rudolf were to voluntarily abdicate his position and pass on the right of succession to Matthias. However, this was precisely what Rudolf did not want. He was utterly convinced that Matthias did not have the qualities required of a leader and that he had failed in his task as a military commander in the Turkish Wars. The Emperor was neither able to see nor to comprehend the *realpolitik* imperatives of the situation. His overriding concern was that the Turks should be defeated and the borders of the empire secured once and for all. Rudolf was pinning his hopes on the Reichstag in Regensburg, fully expecting financial support from there which would allow him to remain firm against the Turks and ultimately to emerge victorious.

However, the Emperor's first consideration was to dispel the unrest amongst the Moravian nobility by peaceful means. He therefore dispatched the privy councillor Cardinal Franz von Dietrichstein (1570–1636) to Brno. The mission proved to be harder than expected. Mistrust was deep-rooted on both sides. It was only after the Cardinal had pledged himself personally responsible for the safety of the renegade noblemen that the sitting of the Landtag called by him in the Emperor's name took place, on 29 March 1608. The Emperor's demand that the Moravian nobility should choose representatives for the general Landtag in Prague, and not meet for their planned Landtag in Eibenschütz (Ivančice), merely served to strengthen their conviction that the Emperor had no real understanding of the seriousness of the situation and was in no mood for concessions. The nobility therefore rejected the Emperor's demands as unacceptable, and the Landtag broke up inconclusively the next day. Not long after this Karl of Liechtenstein arrived in Vienna. He reported to Matthias on events in Brno and urged the Archduke to march against Rudolf. There had never been an opportunity like this to strip the Emperor of his authority and take the reins of power into his own hands. Yet even now, Matthias was not able to bring himself to launch a military attack on his imperial brother. The legal implications and the unpredictability of the way in which Bohemia and the empire would react to fratricidal war prevented him from taking that final step.

In fact, the decision to attack came in April 1608, when Cardinal von Dietrichstein repeated to Matthias the Emperor's demands that before the Peace Treaty could officially be signed, the Turks had to withdraw from the border forts at Gran (Esztergom), Erlau (Eger) and Kanischa (Nagykanizsa). It was clear that the sultan[13] would reject this and that the cease-fire, which had been so hard to set up, was now under serious threat. Rudolf seemed to have lost all sense of reality. In Matthias' eyes, the Emperor's evident inadequacy as a ruler was the justification he needed for a military attack on his brother. From now on, the legality of the campaign rested on the forcible imposition of peace on Rudolf.

In the middle of April 1608, the Reichstag in Regensburg went into recess without having sanctioned the monies required for Rudolf to continue to pursue the Turkish Wars.[14] Rudolf had been defeated in the diplomatic skirmishings. He had never been more ineffectual as a politician, military man and human being. However, he was still left with his unswerving faith in his own imperial vocation.

On 14 April 1608, when Archduke Matthias issued marching orders to the troops which had been in Vienna since the New Year, the feud between the two

brothers finally escalated into fratricidal war. In the Archduke's entourage there was a chronicler whose name has been lost to posterity. The following quotations are from his diary-like reports,[15] in which he gives a vivid description of the departure of the troops, the officers resplendent with red and white feathers on their caps. As they leave the town, they are seen off by crowds of townsfolk who wish them well, hold out their hands to them and make the sign of the cross:

Anno 1608 den 15. Aprillis umb halbe 3 uhr nachmitag, als nun alle herrn cammerer und officirn sich bei hoff versamblet hetten, zogen die fürstliche durchlaucht in hernach benander ordtnung von der kayserlichen purgg auß durch die Herrn gassen dem Schotten thor zue:

Alß erstlichen zu roß ein chavalriza oder roßbereitter in seiner klaidung allein, dem volgeten nacheinander 8 stall= oder reüttknecht in ierer liberei, als nemblich dunckl braune röckh mit erblen,[16] solche hüet mit rott und weißen federn etc., deren ein jeder wie gebraichig aines der fürstlichen durchlaucht leibroß, mit schönen rotten deckhen, schwarz rot undt weissen schniren geziert, bedeckt an der hand führete, dernach allain rite der reidtschmidt undt sattlkecht, dan nach einander 4 edlknaben, darauf volgete Neuhausar, der edlknab, so das scherfflin[17] sambt den helmblin, mit schönen federn der liberei geziert, führte.

Danach auch zu roß herr Colloredo,[18] der edl knab, so der fürstlichen durchlaucht leib ristung sambt den rot sameten schurtz, vergulden rappir und rot sameten mantiera führete ...

Hernach zu roß der höhr bauckher,[19] dan auch 8 trummeter in iherer liberei, alß schwartz, rot unnd weiß mit schönen federn, auch an den trummetten statliche von roten dammaschkh gemachte unnd der fürstlichen durchlaucht wappen, gemalte fahnen gantz schön unndt stadtlich sich höhren lassen.

Disen volgten etliche hoff unnd cammer diener, herrn und cammerer, auch kayserliche unnd der fürstlichen durchlaucht zugethan räth herrn unndt graffen, bey 40 pferdten ...

Hernach khommen zu fueß der fürstlichen durchlaucht leib quardia, die trabanden, zu mitten derer jeder belaidung[20] ritten zu rosse die fürstliche durchlaucht in gewöhlicher ertzhertzögischen bekleidung, ohne mandel, sondern mit aim schönnen fellt zaichen unndt stadtlichen foggi oder raigerbuschen[21] gezieret.

Alß dan auf ihr fürstliche durchlaucht volgete herrn obrist: cammerer herr von Meckhau[22] cammerdiener, die zwen edlknaben, der aine mit dem fueteral der hüet unnd der ander mit dem porso[23] oder falliso der mannttl.

Dan auch darauf etliche herrn aufwarter, aventuriri,[24] hoffmaister, der herrn diener unnd officirn, bey 40 pferdten. Hernacher der fürstlichen durchlaucht leib wagen, der herrn cammerer unndt cammer diener, hoff candzley, hoff controlohr, pfening maister unnd prediger, auch andere mehr wagen unndt troste ...

Alß man nun in bemeldter ordtnung fortruckhete, warte das stadt thor zum Schotten mit der stadt quardie durch herrn obristen leitenambt herrn Quarienten[25] mit seinen undergebenen soldaten zu baiderseits durch das thor, dardurch wir hinauszogen, gar uber die bruckhen hinauß, in ordtnung wolbestellet.

Ausserhalb der vorstadt unnd gar hinauß in die weingarten stunde sehr mechtig vill volckhes, wie dan auch herr burgermaister Lucas Lausser[26] unnd edliche herrn des raths zu wagen sich in solcher beklaidung befunden. Man spüerte und sah auch mit augen, wie das gemaine volckh der burger und inwonner alda von manns und

frauen perschonen mit hertzlicher söhnung und seuffzeten geberden diesen abzug beywohneten. Auch der maiste thaill mit mundt unnd hertzen, wie auch die lautern wordt gehört wurden, wünscheeden, das Gott der almechtige sein hülff, gnadt, seegen, glückh, haill unnd alle wolfahrt der fürstlichen durchlaucht mitthaillen unnd verleihen wölle, damidt sie ihr raiß unnd vorhaben glückhlichen unndt woll verrichten unnd mit triumph, friden unnd freüden wider anheimb gelangen möchten. Solche ihre hertzliche wünschung bezeig-eten der maiste thaill des volckes gantz offenbar mit außgestreckhter handt undt zeichen des heiligen creützes, welches dan den unserigen alß fordtraisenden nit allain gleichsam etwas wunderliches unnd selzam, sondern auch gar tröstlichen unnd annemblichen fürkam.

After breaking their march for four days in Klosternburg, the Archduke's men crossed the Danube on 19 April 1608. Matthias set up his own quarters in the finest house in the town. The burgomaster and council members received the Archduke with all due respect and provided his men with hospitality. The military visitation moved on the following day. Kreuzenstein and the noble seats of Schloss Göllersdorf[27] and Schloss Guntersdorf[28] were the next stations on their journey. On 23 April, the continuously increasing army arrived in Znaim (Znojmo) in Moravia. The same chronicler captured the scene, describing the sight which greeted the Archduke's men outside the town, with trumpeters and a tournament before they were welcomed again by the townspeople and council. For a week, Znaim was the scene of intense diplomatic activity with one delegation following the other. First came the leaders of the Moravian nobility, Karl of Žerotín and Karl of Liechtenstein. They reported to the Archduke on the recent Landtag in Eibenschütz (Ivančice) and urged him to proceed apace in the direction of Prague. Rudolf's psychological and military situation was worsening with every new company that joined Matthias' forces; in his despair he even thought about fleeing. However, Christian II (1583–1611), elector of Saxony, declined to afford him protection, explaining that in Dresden they were not prepared for such an illustrious visit. In addition, the Bohemian nobility implored the Emperor not to leave Prague. In order to hold up Matthias' progress, Rudolf, bowing to the influence of the Spanish envoy Don Guillén de San Clemente,[29] whom he had long known and admired, at last agreed to ratify the Turkish peace without pre-conditions.

Cardinal von Dietrichstein set out on the next imperial mission. On 27 April 1608, he rode into Znaim at the head of a high-powered delegation. San Clemente and the papal nuncio Antonio Caetano[30] were there to lend additional weight to the Emperor's case. Not only did the Cardinal come with news of the Emperor's readiness to sign the Peace Treaty of Zsitva-Torok; he also brought with him an invitation to a 'Fürstenkonvent', an assembly of all the leaders of the nobility. This was to be held in Prague. It would include all the Archdukes as well as the elector of Cologne[31] and duke of Bavaria,[32] and the intention would be to resolve the current disagreements between Rudolf and Matthias. It was proposed that this assembly meet at Whitsun.

Matthias was now under pressure. Rudolf's readiness to sign the Peace Treaty of Zsitva-Torok invalidated any legal justification for his continued advance, and yet the alliance amongst the nobility established by Matthias and his advisers had developed a momentum of its own, which the Archduke was increasingly unable to control. Thus peace with Turkey was no longer the central issue in the negotia-

tions with the imperial delegation. Now Matthias was insisting on an immediate transfer of power in all the crown lands, declaring that he would not be put off with promises and statements of intent any longer. On 28 April, only one day after their arrival, Dietrichstein and his entourage set out empty-handed on the return journey to Prague. Matthias issued a manifesto in which he reiterated the reasons for his campaign and allied himself to the cause of the different regions and the anxiety with which they viewed the threat to their own rights and freedoms, stating that he had been forced into this position by the Emperor's obduracy.[33] For the fourth time, the Archduke invited the Bohemian leaders to a joint meeting in Tschaslau (Čáslav). Before this, however, he continued his advance in the direction of Bohemia and strengthened his army further by the addition of Hungarian reserves, as described by our anonymous chronicler, who again emphasizes the sound of the trumpets, the sight of the beautiful feathers, and a hundred finely turned-out German horses:

> Den 1. Mai zogen abermals fort die wagen unndt stall pferdt. Damals kamme an herr Johann Eysebius Kuen,[34] der fürstlichen durchlaucht cammerer. Da umb 10 uhr also gleich die fürstliche durchlaucht zur taffl wahren, ritte durch herr obrist Nadasti Tomas unndt Duri Ferenz mit 5 hauffen der gränitzer hussaren[35] gar in schönner prechtiger ordtnung. Nach solchen zogen auch durch 4 fehnlein heiduckhen in ihrer ordnung, dan hernach, als die fürstliche durchlaucht gleich wolten zu roß sitzen, zoge durch ein Mährerisches heer, der herr von Lundenburg, so da fiehrette herrn von Zirotin volckh, nemblich 100 muschadir[36] zu fueß, mit trumbl pfeiffen und bevelchshaber ordenlich versehen, darauf kommen 3 bahr leib roß, 3 trummetter, 2 spieß knaben in gantzen küriß, mit schönnen federn geziert, als dan er, der herr von Lundenburg, stadtlich zu roß mit ainem wundt schuch,[37] hinder ime das cornet, nemblich 100 wol außgeriste teitsche pferdt. Nach solchen ruckhten die fürstliche durchlaucht fordth, die dan mit solcher quardia von teutschen reittern und hussarn heraus ins velt ringsweiß belaidet wurden.

After a short halt in Trebitsch (Trebic), the Archduke arrived in Iglau (Jihlava) on the Bohemian border on 3 May. The troops, cavalry and infantry alike, were then mustered in battle formation by Johann Siegmund Freiherr von Herberstein (d. 1611), commander-in-chief of the Archduke's army, which had in the meantime grown to a substantial 20,000 men. Matthias then swore in his men:

> Den 3. dito kamme an herr Wolff Sichmundt von Losnstain,[38] zogen fort die fueß knechte, dan auch nacher dem frue mahl in gar schöner zeit umb 10 uhr die fürstliche durchlaucht in gemainer ordtnung. Da sie nun auf ein meil wegs kommen, sahe man zuruckh alda zu Treditsch[39] eine starckhe prunst, die da durch verwahrlosung angangen. Alß sie aber uber die höhe durch etliche gestreiß unnd waldt kommen in ein thal ... hatte der herr obrist feldt martschalt von Herberstein[40] alles kriegs volckh von Hungern und Teitschen zu roß und zu fueß auff einer schönnen blossen hoche der velder in aine schöne schlacht ordnung gestellet; die da die stiern hohe warts gegen ir fürstliche durchlaucht, alß die gleich im hinauf ziehen waren, kerten sie also in ainer schönnen vista presentirten. Darauff die fürstliche durchlaucht von solchen obrist unndt bevelchs habern das juramentum und handt gelüebtnus empfingen.

The unmistakably threatening tone was not lost on the next imperial delegation, again under Dietrichstein and San Clemente, when it arrived in Iglau (Jihlava) on 6 May with a fourth message from the Emperor. Since the Emperor was not open to further negotiation, Matthias dismissed the delegation the same day, and resumed his advance towards Tschaslau (Čáslav). The same diarist reports on the army's entrance into the town on 10 May and on the diplomatic activities of the following days not forgetting to mention the difficult weather conditions:

Den 10. dito morgens umb 7 uhr zog man widerumb fort [sc. aus Habry] unndt wurden ire fürstliche durchlaucht mit den baiden corneten, der Lichtenstainischen und Zirotinischen, seer statlich bcklaittct in das schloß Janckowiz,[41] alda sie das frumall einnamben, nach solchem abermalß forth, unnd da sie gelangten auf eine meill wegs, hiltten auf ainer höhe nit weidt von Zschasslau herraußen herr Geörg Durso[42] mit allem Ungerischen kriegsvolckh ... In solcher wahrmen zeit unndt gewaldigen staub kamme die fürstliche durchlaucht umb 2 uhr in der stadt Zschasslau an und von solchen des raths auch mit freiden empfangen unndt in die fürnembste behausung alda einlosirt. In diser nacht gar spatt khome alda an herr cardinal von Diterrichstein unndt päbstliche nuncius sambt den dänischen herrn abgesandten.

Den 11. dito morgens umb 7 uhr hatten solche ankhombene herrn bey der fürstlichen durchlaucht audienza, wie auch nachmittag die herrn sexische unnd brandenburgerische abgesandte alda ankhomben unnd innen audienzza geben wurde, Disen verschinen tag war alzeit gar schen wetter, allein zur nacht thete es gar einnen stillen regen.

Den 12. khomben ihr hochfürstlich gnaden herr cardinal von Diterstein[43] gen hoff unnd sasse mit der fürstlichen durchlaucht zu taffell, die also in fürstlicher conversation das mittag mall einnamben. Des abents aber wurden die sexischen unnd brandenburgischen herrn abgesanten zu des herrn obristen cammerers tafel beruffen undt stadtlich tractirt. Wahr auch bey tag gar schöne zeit, bey nacht zimlicher regen.

Although the Archduke had summoned the Bohemian nobility to Tschaslau (Čáslav) for 4 May, when he arrived in the town he found only the Emperor's and the Electors' envoys. The Bohemian nobility refused to come to meet the Archduke, and Petr Vok of Rožmberk excused himself on the grounds of 'temporary indisposition'. Under extreme pressure from San Clemente and the papal nuncio, Rudolf had overcome his own reluctance and agreed to a further concession. He was prepared to concede sole governorship of Hungary and Austria to Matthias.[44] Yet this was not enough for the Archduke, who also wanted Rudolf to grant him the succession in Bohemia, a proposal that was in turn rejected by both the Emperor and the mighty Bohemian noblemen. Promises by San Clemente as well as his skills as a diplomat, however, persuaded the latter to rethink their position. Now leading members of the court, above all the court chancellor Zdenek Adalbert Popel of Lobkowicz (1568–1628), came to the Emperor and advised him to accept Matthias' claim to the crown of Bohemia. Bowing to necessity, Rudolf agreed.

But even this was not enough for Matthias. He demanded that the transfer of power in Bohemia should take place immediately, as he told the imperial delegation in Tschaslau (Čáslav) in no uncertain terms. Now the Emperor's advisers had reached the goal of their not disinterested political manoeuvrings. It was up to

them to strike while the iron was hot and to persuade the Emperor of the hopeless-ness of his situation. On 19 May 1608, Matthias advanced to Böhmisch Brod (Česky Brod). Only 25 kilometres lay between him and Hradschin. The troop movements filled our anonymous military chronicler with enthusiasm, and his text provides precise details as to numbers and equipment, including tigers' skins, kettledrums, weapons and flags.

Matthias's show of strength paid off. Rudolf's 4,500 men, whom he had financed himself, were badly equipped and without proper leadership. Again the Emperor thought about leaving Prague, but any plans to flee were dependent on the out-come of the Bohemian Landtag meeting there on 23 May 1608. For the first time in years, Rudolf appeared in public. Though marked by illness, he seemed determined to take up the fight against his brother. His general demeanour won the respect of the delegates. But just as in the case of the nobility from Austria, Hungary and Moravia, the Bohemian nobility were primarily interested in their own advantage. Václav Budovec put forward a twenty-five-point declaration on behalf of the Protes-tant nobility, demanding far-reaching religious and political freedoms. In the mean-time, envoys from the Archduke had arrived in Prague. Their attempts to persuade the Bohemian nobility to come over to Matthias' side remained unsuccessful. The Bohemians much preferred a weakened emperor who depended on them for help to an archduke who was obviously in a position to pursue his own ends in the struggle for power. After Count Joachim Andreas Schlick (1569–1621) issued an ul-timatum linking the support of the Bohemian Protestant nobility to the approval of the twenty-five-point declaration, Rudolf indicated that their requests would be granted, although any final decisions on matters of religion should be left to the next Landtag. Until then, all religious persecution was forbidden in Bohemia.[45] When the Emperor confirmed this in writing on 31 May, the Bohemian nobility were satisfied and declared their solidarity with him.

The subsequent negotiations with the archdukes' envoys took place in two tents on a hill near Schloß Lieben (Stará Líbena). Perhaps this accounts for our chroni-cler's references to the cold, wind and rain which did not let up for four days. The most important individuals who took up the negotiations on the Emperor's behalf in Dubeč near Böhmisch Brod (Česky Brod) were Cardinal Franz Dietrichstein, Adam von Sternberg (d. 1623), Václav Budovec and the counts Matthias Thurn (1577–1633) and Joachim Andreas Schlick (1569–1621). The Archduke's delegation was led by the Moravian noblemen Karl of Žerotín and Karl of Liechtenstein. The decisive breakthrough came when the imperial mandataries agreed to the separa-tion of Moravia from Bohemia and its secession to Matthias. Talks were continued on 18 June in Lieben (Stará Líbena) near Prague. Above all, the question of Matthias' succession in Bohemia was still a thorny issue. In the end, after repeated adjournments, on 25 June 1608 Rudolf signed the agreement which was to bring the conflict between the two brothers to an end. He relinquished his regencies in the kingdom of Hungary and archdukedoms of Austria and Moravia in favour of Matthias. In addition, the Archduke was granted succession rights in Bohemia. The Emperor finally sanctioned the Treaty of Zsitva-Torok, ending the Turkish Wars without pre-conditions. Both sides agreed to demobilize their troops.

Two days after the signing of the treaty, the Hungarian regal crown was ceremo-niously brought into the encampment at Sterbohol. In his address in Latin, Cardi-

nal Dietrichstein stressed the voluntary nature of this transfer of power from the Emperor to his brother. Again the chronicler reported the sights and the sounds, including the six greys drawing the imperial carriage and the salvos fired by musketeers and harquebusiers, all of which so impressed the citizens of Prague who had come to watch that they said they had never seen anything more beautiful in their lives:

Den 27. war ein schonner tag, allein es zu zeiten ainnen spreng regen thett. Morgens sambt den tag an zoge unser krüegs volckh zu roß unndt fueß das meiste, allein waß zur notturfft alß nemblich ein fendtlein zur haubt wacht vor ir fürstlichen durchlaucht zelt unndt sonsten aber alles hinaus uber die höhe gegen den thall nach Prag zu, nitt weit von dem schlösslein Liben, welche in einne schöne schlacht ordtnung nach dem besten gestellet unndt angeornet wurden ... Ungefehr umb 4 uhr ritten die fürstliche durchlaucht aus derselben quartir mit allen herrn röthen unndt chammer herrn, landt stendt und andern ... Khämen also in vorbemelte schlacht ordtnung, alda sie bey iherem vorbereitten leib oder chammer zelt ... verwarteten. Alß aber die herrn Pragerischen commissarien ungeferth ein viertl meill wegs uber die höche herein sich sehen lissen, wardt von der fürstlichen durchlaucht lein quardi haubtman ein gassen durch das volckh, welches unzelig vill baider thails von Prag herauß, dan auch der unserigen sich rundt herumb das zelt versamblet heten, gemacht, durch welche dan die herrn commissarien umb 7 uhr, da sie ankhommen mit zway compagnia reittern, so gleich woll an der landt strassen zuruckh verblieben, mit ieren wagen auch thails zu roß durchzogen in diser ordtnung:

Alß erstlich ir hochfürstliche durchlaucht herr cardinal von Ditterichstein, herr von Walstein,[46] kayserlicher obrister stallmaister, der von Donna unndt ander herrn mer ... Diese aber alle nach einander gingen der fürstlichen durchlaucht zu. Die stunden ein wenig vor der zelt, botten innen die handt, sonderlichen aber sie sich mit gantz schönner reverenz erzaigten, dan durch beider thails herrn commissarien gantz zirlichen nach einander empfingen. Darauff dan der khayserliche leib wagen mit 6 geferbten weißen schimmeln wurde fur das zelt gefürt. Da namen die zwen kayserliche cammer trabanten auß solchen wagen eine lange lichte truchen mit rottem sammet bedeckt. Darinnen lage der khönigliche ornat, zepter unndt chron. Trugen sie für das zelt, darnach die zwen cammerer gar hinein auff den tisch im zelt setzten. Desgleichen auch eine schwartze truhen, darin one zweiffell die sigill unndt andere sachen wahren. Solches wurde von den khaiserlichen abgesandten der khoniglichen würden herrn Matthiam, ertzherzogen zu Österreich, unsern genedigisten herrn, herrn mit schönner reverenz unndt gewaldigen oration presentiret, welches dan auch von der khoniglichen würden durch schön unndt anfelig beantwortet wurde. Verzogen sich bei einer halben stundte. Nach solchem alßbalden wurde durch herrn obristen feldt marschalten herrn von Herberstein angeornet unndt befollen, daß die muschcadirer schitzen sambt den reitern unndt archibusirern eine völlige salva machten ... Als solches 3 mall nach einander im zürckh herumb geschahe mit alle gregezza unndt freiden geschrey alß zirlich unndt schön, uber welches sich meniglich, sonderlich aber die Pragerischen, deren eine grosse anzall herauß khommen wahren, sich höchlich verwunderten mit vermeldten, sie die zeit ieres lebens kheinne schönnere sachen vorder gehördt noch gesehen ... Wan dem nun ir khonigliche würden die herrn khayserliche abgesandte zur taffl deß nachtmallß

beruffen woldten, als wurde in zwayen toppletn zelten zwu lange taffell zuberaitet unndt wie woll es spatt, darzu an ainnem fastag, dennoch mit serr statlichen speisen unndt edlesten tranckh besetzet unndt verfahren. Alß ir khonigliche würden sambt allen den khaiserlichen herrn commissarien solche malzeit soleniter unndt fröhlich volbrachten ... unndt nach verrichtung dessen allen die herrn khayserlichen commissarien ungeferte umb 11 uhr in der nacht von dannen nach Prag wendeten.

For the time being, civil war between the two brothers had been averted. The risk Archduke Matthias had taken had only partly paid off; he had gained much but not everything he and his troops had marched for. Rudolf II remained Emperor and could be sure of the kingdom of Bohemia as long as he left the nobility there a free hand. They were the real winners in the feud. This was a view already taken by a contemporary correspondent who reported to Archduke Ferdinand of Inner Austria, later to become Emperor Ferdinand II, that 'in truth now neither the Emperor nor King Matthias' was master.[47] Even as they were still in the encampment at Sterbohol, the Austrian and Moravian nobility made a secret pact that each would come to the other's assistance if their future ruler, King Matthias, should renege on the promised religious concessions. The agreement was signed by Johann Siegmund von Herberstein, Karl of Žerotín, Gotthard and Richard von Starhemberg, Georg Erasmus von Tschenembl[48] and the brothers Stanislaus and Nikolaus von Thurzo. Not only Rudolf's but also Matthias' room for political manoeuvre was considerably diminished by the events of 1608.[49] It seemed that the Habsburgs might soon be no more than the political plaything of the mighty nobility of their own crown lands.

1. On the Archduke, see Herbert Haupt, 'Kaiser Rudolf II. in Prag: Persönlichkeit und imperialer Anspruch' in *Prag um 1600: Kunst und Kultur am Hofe Rudolfs II.*, vol. 1 (Freren, 1988), pp. 45ff. (with extensive bibliography).

2. Town where the Zsitva joins the Little Danube, near Komorn on the border between Hungary and Slovakia (Hungarian: Komárom; Slovak: Komárno).

3. There are no up-to-date biographies on Matthias; see M. Ritter, 'Matthias, Österreichischer Erzherzog und Deutscher Kaiser' in *Allgemeine Deutsche Biographie*, vol. 20 (Leipzig, 1884), pp. 629–54; and, most recently, V. Press, 'Matthias. 1612–1619' in A. Schindling und W. Ziegler (eds), *Die Kaiser der Neuzeit 1519–1918: Heiliges Römisches Reich, Österreich, Deutschland* (Munich, 1990), pp. 114–123.

4. On the Turkish Wars waged by Rudolf II, see A. Loebl, *Zur Geschichte des Türkenkriegs von 1593–1606*, 3 vols; *Prager Studien aus dem Gebiet der Geschichtswissenschaften*, 6, 10 (1899–1904); see also W. Leitsch, 'Rudolph II. und Südosteuropa 1593–1606', *East European Quarterly*, 6 (1974): 301–20.

5. G. Lencz, *Der Aufstand Bocskays und der Wiener Friede* (Budapest, 1917).

6. Hans Sturmberger, 'Die Anfänge des Bruderzwists in Habsburg' in idem, *Land ob der Enns und Österreich* (Linz, 1979), pp. 32–75; Karl Vocelka, 'Matthias contra Rudolf: Zur politischen Propaganda in der Zeit des Bruderzwistes', *Zeitschrift für Historische Forschung*, 10 (1983): 341–51.

7. Heinz Noflatscher, 'Glaube, Reich und Dynastie: Maximilian der Deutschmeister (1558–1618)', *Quellen und Studien zur Geschichte des Deutschen Ordens*, 11 (1987).

8. Lothar Gross, 'Zur Geschichte des Wiener Vertrags vom 25. 4. 1606', *Mitteilungen des Instituts für österreichische Geschichtsforschung*, suppl. vol., 11 (1929): 574–87.

9. On what follows here, see: Franz Christoph Khevenhiller, *Annales Ferdinandei, Siebender und Achter Theil* (Leipzig, 1723), cols 6ff.; Anton Gindely, *Rudolf II. und seine Zeit. 1600–1612*, vol. 2, 2nd edn (Prague, 1863), pp. 205ff.; G. von Schwarzenfeld, *Rudolf II: Ein deutscher Kaiser am Vorabend des Dreißigjährigen Krieges*, 2nd edn (Munich, 1979), pp. 324ff.; Karl Vocelka, 'Die politische Propaganda Kaiser Rudolfs II. (1576–1612)', *Veröffentlichungen der Kommission für die Geschichte Österreichs*, 9 (Vienna, Graz and Cologne, 1981): 314ff. and bibliog. QV 446–QV 449.

10. Peter Ritter von Chlumecky, *Carl von Zierotin und seine Zeit: 1564–1615*, 2 vols (Brno, 1862–79).

11. Herbert Haupt, 'Fürst Karl I von Liechtenstein, Oberhofmeister kaiser Rudolfs II. und Vizekönig von Böhmen. Hofstaat und Sammeltätigkeit', *Quellen und Studien zur Geschichte des Fürstenhauses Liechtenstein*, I, 1–2 (Vienna, Cologne and Graz, 1983).

12. Joseph von Hammer-Purgstall, *Khlesl's des Cardinals, Director des geheimen Cabinetes Kaiser Mathias, Leben*, 4 vols (Vienna, 1847–51).

13. This would have been Sultan Ahmed I (1603–17).

14. The Reichstag was overshadowed by the unforgiving 'banning' of the Reichsstadt Donauwörth imposed by the troops of Duke Maximilian I of Bavaria.

15. Vienna, Österreichische Nationalbibliothek, Handschriftensammlung, Cod. 7647 (Hist. prof. 116), fols 1r–12v. The manuscript is incomplete.

16. Special cuffs (?).

17. Diminutive of Middle High German *Scherfe* or *Schärpe*, a ceremonial sash worn by officers over their tunics, either around the body or over the right shoulder and carrying on down to the left hip.

18. Christoph Freiherr von Colloredo, son of Ludwig Colloredo, Freiherr von Walsee. He died young, having served the Archduke and King Matthias in his youth as a page and later as an ensign.

19. A military kettle-drum player.

20. Company.

21. Heron feathers: The head feathers of certain kinds of heron were made into a bunch and used to decorate officers' headgear.

22. Leonhard Helfrid Freiherr (count, 1619) von Meggau (1577–1644); chief treasurer to the Archduke, 1608; chief treasurer to Emperor Matthias, 1612–19, 1626–37; 'Obersthofmeister' to Emperor Ferdinand II, 1626–37.

23. Italian *borso*, 'cover'.

24. Italian *avventuriere*, 'adventurers, courtiers, lansquenets'.

25. Hans Quariendt, 'ad interim' commander of the Vienna civil guard, 1596–97, 1599–1604; became 'Oberstleutnant', 1602; was 'Stellvertreter des Stadt-Obristen' until his death in 1609; see Alois Veltzé, 'Die Wiener Stadtguardia', *Berichte und Mittheilungen des Alterthums-Vereines zu Wien*, 36 (1902): 1–213, 297–309 (register).

26. Lucas Lausser (d. 1609). In 1608, he followed Augustin Haffner as leader of the council and was burgomaster of Vienna for a year.

27. Until 1710, Schloss Göllersdorf (BH. Hollabrunn) was in the ownership of the counts of Puchheim. It then transferred into the hands of the Schönborn family, who had the Renaissance castle rebuilt during the first half of the eighteenth century to designs by Johann Lukas von Hildebrandt.

28. In 1536, Georg von Roggendorf had the late Gothic Schloß Guntersdorf (BH. Hollabrunn) reshaped as a Renaissance structure. Since the late sixteenth century, the castle had been owned by a noble family whose members changed their name, Teufel, to von Guntersdorf after the castle.

29. For more on Clemente, see Herbert Haupt, 'Der Türkenkrieg Kaiser Rudolfs II. 1593–1606. Katalogteil 'Portraitstiche' in *Prag um 1600: Kunst und Kultur am Hofe Kaiser Rudolfs II.*, exh. cat. (Freren, 1988), pp. 123f.

30. Nuncio at the imperial court, 1607–11.

31. Prince Ernst, bishop of Freising, Hildesheim, Liège and Münster; archbishop and elector of Cologne, 1583–1612; b. 1554 son of Duke Albrecht V of Bavaria (1528–1590).

32. Duke (Elector after 1623) Maximilian I of Bavaria (1573–1651) ruled from 1595 onwards together with his father Wilhelm V (1548–1626) and alone after October 1597.

33. As in Hammer-Purgstall (note 12), doc. no. 217.

34. Johann Eusebius Freiherr Khuen von Belasy (1574–1622); delegate of the north Austrian nobility (1605–10); colonel; treasurer to Archduke Matthias; privy councillor, after 1612; imperial envoy in Constantinople, 1613.

35. Border hussars, mounted troops kitted out by Hungary; see the vivid description by Wilhelm Dilich (recte Schäfer), *Ungarische Chronica* (Kassel, 1600), p. 25: 'Es haben die Hussaren auf dem Haupte eine Sturmhaube, darnach einen Panzer mir Aermeln an, so ihnen auf die Beine reicht. An der linken Seite haben sie einen Säbel und unter dem rechten Schenkel einen Stecher. Führen in der rechten Faust ein Copey mit einem Fähnlein von 2 Zipfeln und Quasten' (quoted in Christian Beaufort-Spontin, 'Harnisch und Waffe Europas: Die militärische Ausrüstung im 17. Jahrhundert', *Bibliothek für Kunst- und Antiquitätenfreunde*, vol. 57 (Munich, 1982): 81.

36. Musketeers: infantrymen equipped with the lighter musket. Its accuracy was much improved by being set up on a portable forked pole, which was pointed at the foot. The musketeers' resulting increased mobility gave them the nickname 'mosquitoes'. See Paul Kalaus, 'Glossarium der waffentechnischen Fachausdrücke in den Inventaren des Bürgerlichen Zeughauses zu Wiener Neustadt', *Jahrbuch für Landeskunde von Niederösterreich*, n.s., 54–55 (1990): 49–58; and Beaufort-Spontin (note 39), 119ff.

37. Shoes with laces.

38. Wolf Sigmund von Losenstein (1567–1626), 'Obersthofmarschall', 1612–26.

39. Trebitsch (Trebic), a town in southern Moravia.

40. Johann Siegmund Freiherr von Herberstein (d. 1611), decorated several times on the field in Emperor Rudolf's 'long Turkish Wars', became 'Generalfeldzeugmeister' in 1602, and 'Generalfeldmarschall' and 'Hofkriegsratsdirektor' to King Matthias of Hungary in 1608.

41. The Renaissance Schloss Janowitz (Vrchotovy Janovice), not far from Prague in the Beneschau (Benesov) area, had been owned by the Rziczan family since the mid-16th century.

42. Count Georg Thurzo (1517–1616), Palatinate, magnate.

43. Cardinal Franz von Dietrichstein.

44. He stated that his brother should take over 'unter kaiserlicher Namenshoheit das Gubernament in Ungarn und Österreich absolut' (quoted in Schwarzenfeld [note 9], p. 228.

45. The twenty-five-point declaration formed the basis for the Bohemian Imperial Charter of 9 July 1609; see Anton Gindely, *Geschichte der Ertheilung des böhmischen Majestätsbriefes von 1609* (Prague, 1868).

46. Adam Freiherr (count after 1616) von Waldstein (1570–1638); 'Oberststallmeister', 1607–9; see Ernst Waldstein, 'Die Fürstenberger und die Familie der Grafen von Waldstein' in *Die Fürstenberger: 600 Jahre Herrschaft und Kultur in Mitteleuropa*, exh. cat. (Korneuburg, 1994), p. 285.

47. Vienna, Haus-, Hof- und Staatsarchiv, family documents, Facs. 2, fol. 1r.

48. Hans Sturmberger, *Georg Erasmus Tschernembl: Religion, Libertät und Widerstand* (Linz, 1953).

49. Only a few months after the Treaty of Lieben, the

Evangelical sections of the archdukedoms in Austria on and below the Enns formed the 'Horner Bund' (3 October 1608). They stated that their new ruler, King Matthias, must confirm that he agreed to the promised political and religious freedoms before they would swear their allegiance to him. The 'Horner Bundbrief' with its 166 signatures and seals is proof of the power of the nobility, who thus reinforced their claim to be the leading power in the region; see Gustav Reingrabner, 'Adel und Reformation: Beiträge zur Geschichte des protestantischen Adels im Lande unter der Enns während des 16. und 17. Jahrhunderts', *Forschungen zur Landeskunde von Niederösterreich*, 21 (1976): 14ff.

RESIDENTIAL CITY

Prague between 1550 and 1650

J I Ř Í   P E Š E K

Paradoxically, Prague became Rudolf II's splendid residential city and the most outstanding metropolis of Europe around 1600 as a consequence of the abolition of the Estates' power before the mid-1500s. From the Hussite period to the 1547 Lutheran conflict in Germany, which ended with the unsuccessful Czech uprising and the occupation of Prague by the army of Ferdinand I, Prague had been the leading centre of the burghers' Estate. The victory in 1547 enabled the King to break Prague's strength in the same manner as he had dealt with rebellious Vienna in 1522. Chosen representatives of the Prague 'towns' were executed in a spectacular manner, the Prague arsenal of weaponry was requisitioned, rich financial resources were confiscated (as was vast town property) and, of course, all the monarch's privileges were withdrawn. The city's self-government was curtailed drastically and henceforth became subject to the supervision of the royal administrators. In all the Prague towns, the guilds were temporarily abolished or given enormous fines, and harsh financial punishment was likewise imposed on individual burghers. This economic catastrophe culminated over a period of twenty years with the tax reform of 1567, whereby the tax burden was, in decisive part, shifted from the nobility to the towns.

The defeat of 1547 meant the loss of everything the people of Prague had gained in the course of the Hussite Revolution, gains that, for a hundred years, they had upheld in their conflicts with the nobility. The character of Prague was thus transformed in the mid-sixteenth century. The centre of power, where neither the King nor the nobles had felt safe, was turned into a modernized metropolis open to the wider world. From 1547, it was the residence of the governor-royal in Bohemia. It was this governor – the King's eldest son, Ferdinand of the Tyrol – who became the godfather of the gradual metamorphosis of Prague into a flourishing metropolis of greater than regional importance. The definition of a metropolis as a 'superior centre of activities in regard to management and dominance in the centre and in the area of the periphery dependent on it' was entirely accurate for Prague.

In the first instance, Prague was the capital city of the kingdom of Bohemia and all the lands of the Bohemian Crown, the essential and unique chief administrative centre of the country. Prague Castle was the residence of the governor and, whenever the King visited Bohemia, his own residence as well. At the same time, it was the seat of the highest and most important offices of the Estates in the land and, later, after the court had moved there, of the key authorities of the court and government. The Bohemian land rolls were deposited at Prague Castle, and a land roll authority existed there which kept records of the privileges of the Estates, of constitutional and legal regulations, personal privileges of the nobles and of free landed property in the country. Land Diets and courts of law were held here. The land constitution, which placed Prague at the forefront of the burghers' Estate, made the Old Town the court of appeal for the law courts of the individual royal burghs. After the 1547 defeat, Prague lost this status to a new-

20.1   AEGIDIUS SADELER
Portrait of Rudolf II
1603
[Prague, Uměleckoprůmyslové muzeum]

20.2 Jan Willenberg
View of Prague
1601
[Prague, Národní muzeum v
Praze]

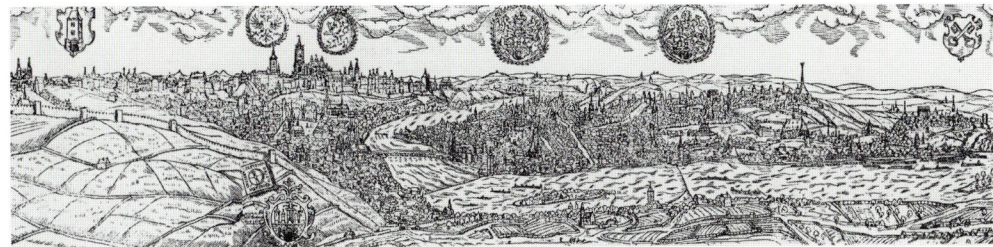

ly established royal court of appeal – which, however, ultimately had its seat there.

Prague was also the centre of the legal churches of the land – the Catholic church and that of the Utraquists. The Catholic church administration, the Consistory, had already resided at Prague Castle in the decade before 1561, when, after more than a century, the book-lover Antonín Brus of Mohelnice was appointed to the Prague Archepiscopal See thanks to the efforts of Ferdinand I. The Utraquist Consistory had been closely connected in person and residence with Prague University ever since the Hussite movement and continued to exist after 1478. It had its seat in the Old Town Carolinum, and the latter's main church, the leading confessional in the land, Our Lady before Týn, looked down upon the Old Town Circle.

The Czech lands were centred in Prague also in regard to education. Between fifteen and seventeen parish schools operated in the Prague towns, while the other Bohemian towns had only one such school, excepting Kutná Hora, which had two such schools. The Prague Utraquist university, founded by Charles IV in 1348 and reformed during the Hussite period, was drowsily conservative for long periods in the 1500s. In 1556, by way of competition, a church academy was opened as part of the Jesuit college, and from 1565 on it was granted the right to award lower academic degrees. The competition of the two academic centres for students and for influence on religious policies in Bohemia led to their many-sided development, finally stimulating the Protestant Academy to undertake modern reforms.

If we view the status of Prague in the broader Central European context of the sixteenth century, we find that despite the loss of internal power, its supranational importance evidently was on the rise. This trend culminated in the decades when Rudolf II resided in Prague, fading gradually in the subsequent period. The permanent high concentration of a broad scale of administrative and cultural functions within the walls of the Prague towns was an exceptional phenomenon in combination with the court and a weath of aristocratic palaces. It accounted for unusual levels of consumption of every kind: from food and fuel to cultural assets and information on foreign policy. Trade, finance and services of every imaginable kind characterized Prague in that period as much as its sophisticated and extensive cultural interests, which were entirely atypical for Central Europe of that time. Among the Bohemian state's eastern neighbours, there existed a number of exceptionally interesting cities, active in production and trade and of supranational significance, but none of them, not even the key royal cities of Cologne, Nürnberg or Augsburg, could compete with Prague at the time in regard to size, range of metropolitan functions, long-term wealth of social, political and cultural life, or artistic production and consumption. These aspects were not only linked with Prague during the period when Rudolf resided here. The lion's share of work in raising the quality of the Prague agglomeration, its social modernization and functional transformation,

fell to the governor, Ferdinand of the Tyrol, a Habsburg politician, cultured patron of the arts and good organizer.

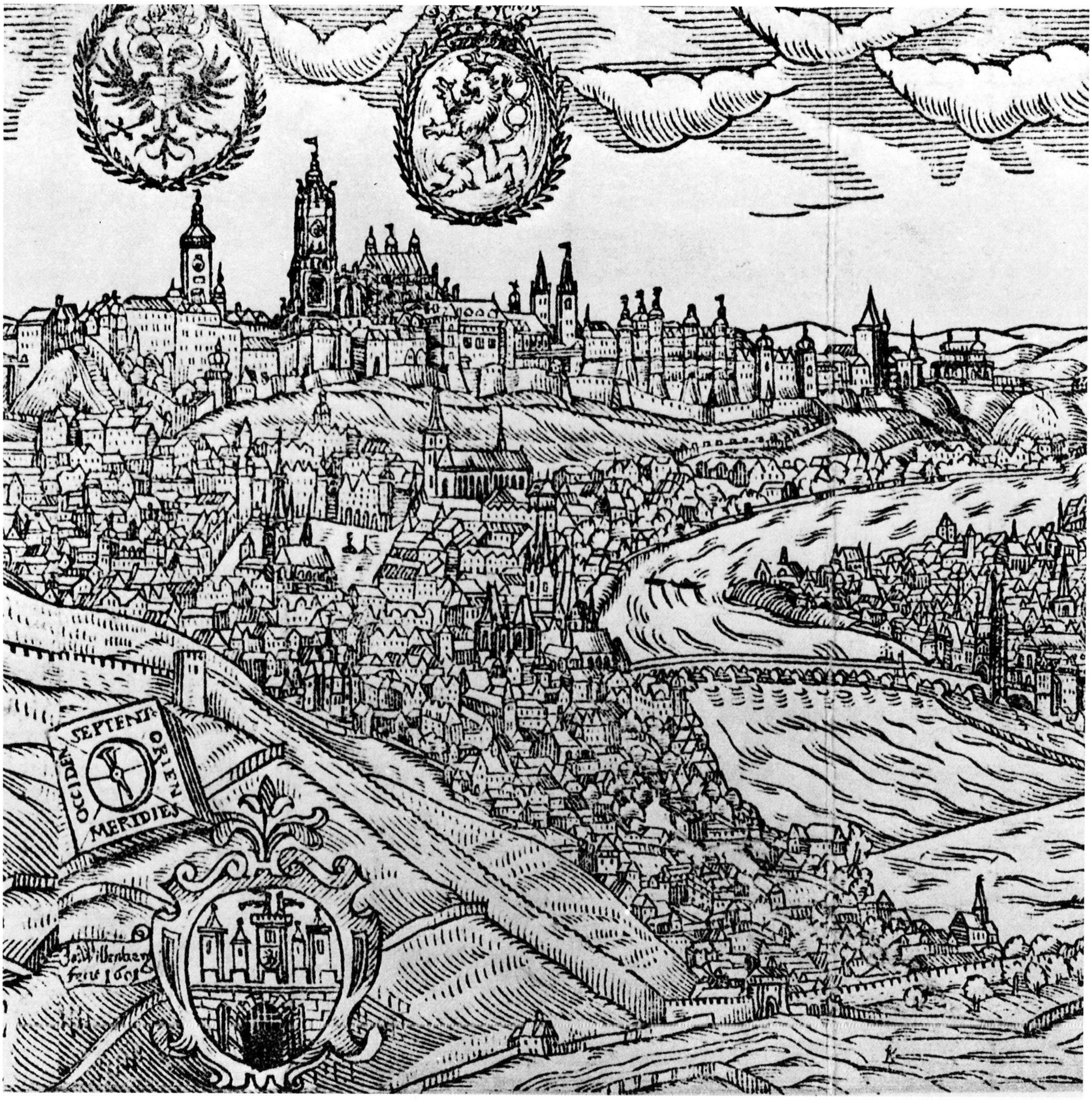

    To this day, Ferdinand remains a little-known Renaissance personality with a broad range of interests and activities. The eldest son of King Ferdinand I, he went to Prague with the intention of applying there, and in the surrounding area, a political model which was favourable to the aims of his royal father. After a none-too-successful pro-Catholic restoration, Ferdinand understood that stable support for the Habsburg government in Bohemia as the most important land of the monarchy could be established only by setting up a broader court circle among the Bohemian nobility, bound to the court residence in Prague. It is a credit to Ferdinand that he began to implement such a positive programme to benefit dynastic policies as well

20.3 JAN WILLENBERG
View of Prague (detail)
1601
[Prague, Národní muzeum v Praze]

[254]

as Prague and Bohemia themselves. During his stay in Prague in the years 1547–67, the face of the town underwent a transformation. An immense construction programme was undertaken at the Castle, on the lands of the aristocratic builders and the burghers' plots as well as on the estates immediately surrounding the town. Aristocratic residences became a normal feature of the urban landscape. Culture soon began to flourish, thanks to the tolerant attitudes of the governor's court. A number of humanists and intellectuals among the middle classes, who had traditionally been associated with the spiritually stagnating Utraquist University, found their way into the literary circles loosely connected with Ferdinand's court. Mention might be made of the literary fraternity of Jan Hodějovský of Hodějov.

Substantial and outstanding scientific and publishing establishments were connected with the court. Much went on at the printing house of the tolerant Lutheran Georg Melantrich of Aventinum, a member of the Old Town patriciate. Ferdinand, a Renaissance lover of science and the arts, a dilettante architect and owner of an extensive collection, acted as initiator and organizer of work in the sciences and arts, mediating commercial contacts and assuming the role of patron. His own collections and the scientists at his court (for example, the doctors and natural scientists Mattioli and Hájek) established a true centre of modern scientific life in Prague. Without Ferdinand's initiative and support, Mattioli's elaborate *Herbarium* would never have been published by Melantrich to become one of the most beautiful and valuable specialized books produced in Prague in the sixteenth century. Ferdinand's patronage gave rise to the establishment of a series of other publishing houses, to building activity and also to major public festivities. Changes in attitudes and in the cultural atmosphere of Prague in the 1550s can be seen, for example, in the broad participation of the people of Prague in the welcoming festivities held on the arrival of the recently crowned Emperor Ferdinand I in Prague in 1558. Mattioli's report, printed in several languages by the Melantrich publishing house, describes in colourful language the pageantry of this grand undertaking, which involved thousands of actors. Renaissance theatricality had become accepted in Prague, resembling in many respects contemporary Italian or French celebrations.

What do we actually mean when we speak of Prague at this time? Usually, we mean the Prague agglomeration. Each of the independent and heterogeneous towns on the banks of the Moldau and around Prague Castle had had its own legal status, independent authorities, property and town hall since the Middle Ages. Three and later four free royal towns were dominant: the Old Town (Staré Město), the New Town, the Lesser Town (Malá Strana) and, from 1598, Hradčany. The Jewish Town, or the ghetto, lay between the northern border of the Old Town and the Moldau.

Parts of Prague were exempt from the authority and jurisdiction of the town councils. The laws which applied there were relics of an older period and concerned enclaves associated mainly with ecclesiastical institutions. Civic laws likewise did not apply to the university and its parts, which came under the juridiction of academic law and the rector's office. Beyond the power of the town councils were the territories of aristocratic and patrician palaces and houses, registered in the land rolls as free property. This was no mere formality, since status outside civic law brought with it many economic and tax advantages. For that reason, this special status was jealously guarded by those who held it.

The prime place in the Prague agglomeration had belonged, from the Middle

Ages, to the Old Town, the holder of traditional privileges and the most powerful and richest town in the country. But the establishment of the governor's residence, the renewal of the archbishopric and the building of aristocratic palaces in and around the Castle can be said to have shifted the core of the agglomeration to the left bank of the Moldau. It was there that the majority of the courtiers found accommodation, as did court craftspeople and visitors. The entire agglomeration was seen by foreigners as a single unit, and in fact functioned as a unit in a number of social and economic respects.

At this time, Prague had some 20,000 to 25,000 inhabitants and was expanding rapidly. The new burghers, who purchased houses in the Prague towns and adopted civic rights, came primarily from Bohemian and German towns of the Czech lands and the neighbouring countries of the empire. Others who settled there were North Italian craftsmen from the Lugano area. Later, people from the Netherlands, France and Spain began to appear, as did – on isolated occasions – people from the British Isles. When the imperial court moved officially from Vienna, Prague had something over 40,000 inhabitants; by 1600, that number had risen to 50,000 or 60,000.

The oldest depictions of Prague show us that the parts of town were not evenly built up and inhabited. The individual parts retained their specific architectural, social and cultural characters. The Old Town was a municipality of rich patricians who did not allow themselves to be stopped by confiscation and fines from accumulating private property. They tried to match the aristocracy in their way of life, and so the town, was made up of several-storey, relatively narrow Gothic stone houses on deep plots. The Old Town burghers became aware of Renaissance modernization slightly later than the nobility, and the second half of the sixteenth and the early seventeenth centuries were a period of reconstruction or architectural renovation in the new Renaissance style. A number of burghers' palaces with ostentatious Renaissance and Mannerist fronts and arcaded courtyards came into being (examples include the House at the Two Golden Bears, and houses in Karlova and Melantrichova streets). Surviving remains, including the relatively complete House at the Minute beside the Old Town Hall, prove that the fashion of sgrafitto ornamentation was adopted by the Prague burghers around 1600.

Public buildings were likewise given the appropriate ostentatious appearance. This is true not only of the Gothic and Renaissance complex of the Old Town Hall, but equally of the Týn School with its arched gable in the style of the Venetian Renaissance. The various quarters prided themselves on their parish churches and gates. The Krocín Fountain, with its grand sculptural ornamentation, was placed in the Old Town Circle in 1596 and formed part of the city's supply of drinking water. The circle itself was used for annual fairs and ostentatiously staged aristocratic theatrical and sports events.

The New Town entered the new epoch with a far less pretentious aspect. Of the four New Town quarters, known by the names of the main parish churches, only the St Henry and St Steven districts partially attained the level of the Old Town. Both lay adjacent to the broad Horse Market (now Wenceslas Square). At the Golden Cross, where the two districts bordered on the Old Town, Bridge Street (ulice Na Můstku) linked the main New Town market with the key trading district in the Old Town. Here an integrated joint trading zone came into being in the early sixteenth

20.4 JOHANN WECHTER
PHILLIP VAN DER BOSCHE
AEGIDIUS SADELER
View of Prague (detail of
Prague Castle)
1606
[Prague, Archiv hl. města
Prahy]

century. It amounted to a concentration of booths, store houses and important patrician counting-houses.

St Peter's district, part of the New Town to the north, was not nearly as imposing. Its centre lay around the church of St Peter on the Riverside. The poorest part of the New Town was the Zderaz quarter, including the raftsmen and fishermen district 'Below the Rock' at Vyšehrad. Here the low houses were overshadowed by huge piles of rafting logs stored on the banks of the river and probably lying in heaps among the houses. The latter became more irregular in the direction of Karlov until they reached the gardens and vineyards which gave this part of the New Town a more rural character.

The crowded Jewish ghetto, with its densely packed dwellings, was administered by Jewish elders. The period we are concerned with here was a relatively favourable time in the history of the ghetto, if we leave aside such natural disasters as a major fire in 1567. On the one hand, profitable trade contacts with neighbouring Christians – burghers and, perhaps even more so, aristocrats – were possible. On the other hand, thanks to the protection of the monarch and tolerance towards the financially important Jewish community, it became the most important Central European centre of Hebrew scholarship, book printing and education.

A major conflagration in 1541 set the scene for rapid building activity in the Lesser Town and Hradčany, although the burghers could not afford to restore extensive burnt-out areas. Vacant building plots were snapped up by members of the aristocracy at the very time when the area around the Castle was being developed under Governor Ferdinand of the Tyrol. With money from country estates, new aristocratic palaces were constructed on them from the 1550s on. The house of Rožmberk built their imposing residence at the Castle itself, while the lords of Hradec, the Lobkowicz family and other aristocratic houses built their residences near the Castle grounds.

Another reason why the two towns on the left bank changed character in the century under discussion was that they were densely settled by courtiers and people working for the court. The settlement which had been overshadowed by the Old Town, with its control of the Stone Bridge and its Lesser Town bridgehead, now became the residential and service area of the royal residence and the permanent home of court craftsmen of foreign origin. The most important community was that of northern Italian building experts – stonemasons, bricklayers, stucco workers, painters. They were concentrated around the church of St Thomas and in the new streets laid out where gardens had been below Petřín Hill ('Italian Lane'). The Lesser Town Italians – craftsmen and representatives of Italian trading companies – gradually 'expanded' across the bridge to the Old Town. By 1590, some eighty Italian merchants, court tradesmen and firm factors were working in Prague. Their Italian congregation built the Mannerist Italian chapel inside the Old Town complex of the Jesuit Clementinum in the years 1590–1600. The most prestigious building of the Lesser Town Italians was the Lesser Town town hall, which was turned into an ostentatious Mannerist palace, the work of Italian stonemasons.

If, using the available literature, we trace the progress and scope of building activities in Prague in the second half of the sixteenth century, it might seem as though the activity and financial possibilities of the aristocrats and prospective house-owners among the common citizens far exceeded those of royalty. The

monarch's building activities at the Castle and in its vicinity progressed slowly. They had to be financed through the Bohemian Chamber, which did not always show the understanding required for such an undertaking. Thus the renovation of the royal palace, badly affected by the fire in 1541, went on far into the 1550s, when part of the reconstruction gave rise to the 'New Building' of Archduke Ferdinand. At the same time work, continued in the Royal Garden on the Summer Palace of Queen Anne, finished in 1562. And in the middle fifties the Star Summer Palace was erected in the White Mountain deer-park to a design by Archduke Ferdinand.

When, in 1567, Ferdinand moved his residence, extensive collections and part of a group of scholars from Prague to Ambras in the Tyrol, the wounds of Prague Castle had healed over, and the Renaissance palaces of Hradčany (primarily the Lobkowicz [now Schwarzenberg] Palace and Martinice Palace) and those in the Lesser Town (the first phase of the palace of the Lords of Hradec below the Castle Steps) were finished or close to completion. Shortly after Ferdinand's departure the large Renaissance Ball-Game Court was completed in the Royal Garden.

The onset of the Renaissance was not only apparent in the field of architecture. In the second half of the sixteenth century, there was an enormous expansion of private urban wealth and aristocratic culture. This can been seen in the growing comfort of home furnishings, in the opening of private galleries of family portraits and other pictures, and in the creation of large private libraries and rich treasuries containing jewellery and small works of sculpture. A specific feature was the gradual development of local instrumental music, which found its place among the musical activities of the court orchestra, the town's church organists and the singing fraternities attached to parish choirs. All these activities had reached their maximum potential by the turn of the century. Archival sources, on which this research into Prague's burghers is based, show that the beginnings of these developments date to the very years when Ferdinand of the Tyrol was playing a leading role in Prague.

If one realizes the scope of cultural activities and investments that was recorded for the Prague burghers, it is difficult to find an adequate comparison in any of the German towns of the empire. In Augsburg, Nürnberg and Cologne, we can find patricians who equalled the Prague burghers in their standard of culture, the quality of amassed property and breadth of cultural outlook, and some even surpassed them. But in numbers and breadth the cultural 'élite' of Prague and the scope of their interests, which went far beyond that of the traditional patrician éite, was unique in Central Europe.

Another unusual feature in Prague was religious tolerance, both between the two official churches and towards other Protestant faiths. Religious conflicts remained restricted to verbal and written polemics until the early seventeenth century. In this respect, Rudolf's Imperial Charter of 1609 did not mark a constitutional turning-point. It was more a legal confirmation of the existing situation.

The bourgeoisie of Prague, especially in the pre-Rudolfine period, was socially dynamic and involved in the town's rapid growth. (Between 1547 and 1583, the number of inhabitants doubled, and further rapid growth continued into the first decade of the seventeenth century.) The Prague town councils and the élite more generally were constantly being enlarged from among the ranks of the immigrants, and capable individuals had a good chance of rising socially. Education was also a means towards social advancement, which continued until the Battle of the White

20.5 JOHANN WECHTER
PHILLIP VAN DER BOSCHE
AEGIDIUS SADELER
View of Prague (detail of
Hradčany)
1606
[Prague, Archiv hl města
Prahy]

Mountain. Part of the merchant and financial élite stood aside from communal and boureois Estate politics and concentrated on developing trading operations between the court, the town and country aristocracy, foreign trade firms and financial houses. People like wholesale merchant and financier Hercules de Nova thus represented a new stratum, a group which could not have developed and settled in Prague before it became a residential city.

The flourishing period when Ferdinand held the office of Governor in Prague came to an end with the death of King and Emperor Ferdinand I in 1564. Ferdinand's successor, Emperor Maximilian II, showed little inclination to have his brother co-reign in Bohemia. He chose Vienna as the seat of his court, initiating interesting building activity there and surrounding himself with a group of artists and others, who – with the aid of Giuseppe Arcimboldo – implemented remarkable theatrical festivities. Assisted by Jacopo Strada, Maximilian began to build up his own art collections.

The departure of Archduke Ferdinand from Prague to the Tyrol was delayed until 1567. Meanwhile, the Prague agglomeration retained its character as a metropolis; the aristocratic officers of the government and the royal chancelleries had become used to officiating there; the flow of immigrants showed not sign of abating.

In this interim period, leading European artists settled in Prague. For example, from 1568 the conductor and composer Philipp de Monte was active there. Even without the court, there was ample impetus for investment and patronage. The Prague public, which had gradually acquired more sophisticated and exacting taste, began to differ strikingly from the more conservative consumers of culture in the country towns. As stimuli, they had access to grand tournaments, plays and costly staged events, for example, of the eruption of Etna or scenes from ancient and Czech mythology (the latter in the Old Town Square on the occasion of the Congress of the Imperial Nobility in 1570).

The most important event of Maximilian's reign was the preparation of the Bohemian Confession, an attempt to set up a church constitution which would permit Lutheranism and the Unity of Brethren to exist alongside the two traditional Christian denominations. A commission of representatives of the three Estates in the countryside, appointed by the Land Diet and meeting in the Lesser Town town hall in the spring of 1575, embodied in the text of the Confession many of the Estates' ideological demands. In the deliberations, the Prague towns were represented by four burghers, and the Prague Protestant university had two further representatives. It was these representatives of the burghers' Estate who tried to include in the Confession political demands of the royal towns. Although the monarch never officially acknowledged the Bohemian Confession, it became the basis of reform for the Estates until the beginning of the Thirty Years' War.

It was at exactly the time when the fate of the Bohemian Confession was being negotiated that, in September 1575, the Emperor's son Rudolf II of Habsburg was crowned with the St Vitus' Crown in St Vitus' cathedral. Rudolf's name is linked with the greatest florescence of the Prague metropolis since the time of Charles IV. From the moment he arrived in Bohemia, Rudolf made up his mind to move his residence to Prague. He did so even though one of his first encounters with the town on the Moldau in 1577 was somewhat dramatic. The grand funeral procession of Emperor Maximilian, brought from Vienna to Prague to be laid to rest under

Collin's tombstone in St Vitus', unexpectedly found itself in the narrow streets of the Old Town, where a group of spectators apparently staged an attack similar to Bartholomew Night in Paris. The aristocratic funeral guests scattered in terror, and the frightened twenty-four-year-old Rudolf remained in the Little Square for hours, alone except for his bodyguard.

Despite this experience, the young 'Saturnine Emperor' fell in love with the city on the Moldau. The atmosphere of a busy metropolis, combined with the splendid isolation of the Castle residence surrounded by gardens, suited his temperament. He was equally delighted with the surroundings of the town with royal deer-parks near the Star Summer Palace and at Bubeneč. He liked the château at Brandýs nad Labem and its enclosing parks. As early as 1577, preparatory work and construction began in preparation for the transfer of the court from Vienna. This was not simply a matter of putting into operation and renovating the living quarters and offices of the Castle, which had fairly recently been vacated by Archduke Ferdinand. Rudolf's Court was incomparably larger than that of the governor. In addition, he moved all the imperial authorities to Prague: the Court Chancellery and the Imperial Chancery. Furthermore, Prague had to be prepared to receive diplomatic deputations, which had previously only passed through on their way elsewhere, for long periods in the vicinity of the court.

In 1577, therefore, construction began at the Castle. Over The Renaissance stables, built to a design by Ulrico Avostalis between the second and the third court-yard, was a three-storey central wing. Known as Rudolf's *Kunstkammer*, it was designed by Orazzio Fontana for his extensive collections, between 1600 and 1602. For large-scale construction of imperial buildings to be undertaken in the neighbourhood of the Old Royal Palace, it became necesary to purchase and pull down a number of private houses. The monarch and his court were by no means the only inhabitants of the Castle grounds. In 1578, Avostalis likewise rebuilt an older hunting lodge in the Bubeneč royal deer-park in Renaissance style. The intense building activities at the Castle did not really stop until the final years of Rudolf's reign.

Other adaptations at the Castle which are not often mentioned include the repair and reconstruction of the chapel of All Saints, originally built by Peter Parler, which had suffered badly in the fire of 1541. One of Rudolf's guests at Prague Castle in 1579–80 was his sister Elizabeth, the widowed Queen of France. On her initiative, Avostalis carried out the adaptations at the chapel and ultimately renewed the link between it and Wladislav Hall inside the Castle.

Building and renovation continued everywhere in the Prague towns. A number of diplomats set up their permanent residences, among the most renowned being the papal nuncio and the ambassador of Venice. Thanks to their well-informed diplomatic reports from Prague, we know a great deal about life at the court and in the towns during Rudolf's reign. Court officials, aristocrats and aristocratic hangers-on who hoped to make their fortune at the court all had to live somewhere.

Legislation of the time shows how Prague prepared for the rapid growth in population and the number of visitors. On 28 July 1578, price regulations were issued for the Prague towns. They laid down rules for the systematic control of prices of food and craft products. These regulations harmed some of the small guild producers, but in view of the rapid rise in prices in the 1560s and especially 1570s, regulation was essential to keep the standard of living at a reasonable level.

20.6 Johann Wechter
Phillip van der Bosche
Aegidius Sadeler
View of Prague (detail of the
Old Town)
1606
[Prague, Archiv hl. města
Prahy]

Nevertheless, prices of food and other goods continued to rise until 1590s, when they became relatively stable, remaining so until the outbreak of the Thirty Years' War. The price of the basic food – beer – stayed more settled in the metropolis than did those of wine and beef. From 1579 on, only Prague beer could be on tap in Prague, the only exception being the renowned Rakovnice beer sold by the Emperor's privileged innkeepers.

A number of construction and sanitation regulations issued by the town councils underwent innovation at this time. In 1570, the Land Diet approved the unification of urban law in Bohemia on the basis of the laws of the Old Town of Prague. In 1579, the Urban Law of the Kingdom of Bohemia was printed in Prague by the renowned Melantrich printing house, having been elaborated by a former professor of Prague Utraquist University, now chancellor of the Old Town, Pavel Kristian of Koldín. Modernization had, of course, become necessary. The early metropolises suffered famine and were plagued by epidemics of infectious diseases at almost regular intervals, for example, the plague in 1568, 1582, 1585, 1598 and 1599. If the Prague agglomeration was to meet the demands made upon it as a residential city of the court, it had to try to ensure stability in food prices, regular sanitation, fire safety and police security day and night.

The rapid growth of the metropolis intensified its problems and at times made them virtually unmanageable. Period memoirs and literature present colourful descriptions of this dark side. The imperial residential town of the end of the sixteenth century inevitably included crowds of beggars, criminals and prostitutes, muddy streets, squares with piles of manure, channels of filthy water running from the courtyards of bourgeois and aristocratic residences and harsh police checks to ascertain whether some burgher or other had left a fire burning overnight in his workshop or kitchen.

Prague prepared in other ways for the arrival of the court. One of the great Mannerist artists of Rudolf's circle and one of the key organizers of the court ateliers and workshops, painter Bartolomeus Spranger settled there in 1580. He collaborated with Tadeáš Hájek of Hájek, the graduate of Prague University, doctor, natural scientist and astronomer who had belonged to the Prague circle of humanists at the court of Archduke Ferdinand of the Tyrol. Together they were at the heart of the court art and science until around 1600. Spranger was one of Rudolf's confidants.

Officially, the court moved to Prague on St Gall's Day (16 October) 1583. This was an ostentatious political act, and for that reason the Emperor requested the financial support of the Bohemian Land Diet, which approved special taxes for the occasion. It was one of the few taxes that the Estates gladly supported.

The idea that the monarch should live in the capital city of the most important land of the Czech crown had been voiced since Ferdinand since 1526. This was not simply a matter of prestige. In Prague, the King was more accessible to the Estates. He was more closely involved with local political problems, and in crisis situations might even become a 'hostage' of the dissatisfied Estates. Ferdinand I knew all this well and used various excuses to remain in Prague only temporarily. The defeat of the Estates and the quashing of the power of the towns in 1547, as well as the purposeful creation of a circle of Bohemian court aristocracy by Ferdinand of the Tyrol, changed this situation.

While Maximilian linked Prague with Ferdinand, for whom he felt no love, and

20.7 JOHANN WECHTER
PHILLIP VAN DER BOSCHE
AEGIDIUS SADELER
View of Prague (detail of the
New Town)
1606
[Prague, Archiv hl. města
Prahy]

with the demands of the Czech Estates, Rudolf had never felt attracted to Vienna, which was under permanent threat from Turkish offensives on the Hungarian battlefields near by. Thus he moved to the safe north-west, to the town which, with its organizational and geographical variety, enabled him to be present and, at the same time, remote, gave him detachment and a bird's eye view, offered prerequisites for a great cultural transformation, activities that were close to his heart. Having spent time at the court of Spain in the 1570s and 1580s, he did not give much thought to problems with the Estates. The court in Prague – directly and indirectly – became a gigantic consumer, client and investor, mainly in the areas of food, luxury goods, works of art and services of every kind. Money from the court and its im-

mediate surroundings spilt over into the pouches of merchants and craftsmen settled or temporarily staying in the Prague towns, and a substantial part, in consequence, ended up in the pockets of the town burghers.

Prague was an immense centre of consumption rather than production. In its time the immense agglomeration could sustain itself and provide supplies on its own only for a small part. Like all metropolitan, multi-functional centres of the time, the immense agglomeration could barely sustain itself. All imported commodities were meant to pass through customs in the Old Town Ungelt, but a number of merchants managed – legally and illegally – to avoid that duty. The nobility could import food, timber and other goods 'for their personal use' without paying duty. Most of these were brought on rafts on the river. The constant disputes as to the rights of the town craftsmen and free or quota imports were, in fact, arguments about how big their slices of court 'pie' should be.

In the sixteenth century, Prague was under the dominant influence of the financiers, merchants and middlemen of Nürnberg associated with whom were the manufactures and merchants of Augsburg. While Ferdinand of the Tyrol was governor in Prague, Italian merchants, mainly from Venice and Milan, began to arrive, and, occasionally, Austrian middlemen from Vienna, Salzburg and Linz. After Rudolf's court moved to Prague, the influence of Italian and Austrian merchants and financiers reached at least the same level as that of their competitors from the German region. Interest was shown also by merchants from Leipzig, Frankfurt, Cologne and even the Netherlands. Trade contacts concerned cloth, canvas, scrap iron, books and works of art. As the crossroads of these trade and information routes, Rudolfine Prague became a multicultural, poly-confessional and increasingly multinational environment. Its relatively high level of tolerance, judged by European standards, depended on the economic boom and political peace.

In the sixteenth century, Prague became an agglomeration of residential towns. This was primarily true of the Castle itself and its environs, especially the two towns on the left bank of the river, the Lesser Town and Hradčany, where the aristocrats lived in new palaces, apartments or rented accommodation. On important occasions, the burghers would even rent their own homes to members of the aristocracy. The imperial residence thus expanded beyond the narrow circle of the medieval walls to dominate the entire adjacent area.

We have far less information on the situation on the right bank of the Moldau. Yet it can be assumed that at least the Old Town was tied in to the rhythm of the Castle. Members of court society found dwellings on the Old Town side of Charles Bridge. The trading centre was there; certain crafts had been traditionally concentrated there. This was also the city's educational centre.

Just as the court expanded into the towns of the Prague agglomeration, the private studios of court artists moved into private burghers' houses. The Emperor, of course, reserved his right to priority purchase of works by his artists. Some artists and craftsmen were linked to the court by contracts or had loose relationships with it. Such people also worked for burghers, for various Prague corporations and, of course, for the nobility. Rudolfine court art thus influenced Prague culture both indirectly, in the form of rarely seen samples of the imperial collections or state rooms adorned with 'modern' works of art, and directly, in the competition of artists and their commissioned work.

If we look at the Prague élite, we find that it differed substantially from that in the rest of the Bohemian towns. It was not so much that Prague lacked the traditional upper class. Such a group did not exist elsewhere in Bohemia either in the sixteenth and early seventeenth centuries, nor in numerous important imperial towns of Germany. After 1547, there were no remaining local ruling élites. Those in charge of day-to-day running of Prague were intent on their individual prosperity and no longer bound to that of the town. They were, to a large extent, 'new people', who had only recently moved into the Prague towns and who sat on the town councils at the turn of the seventeenth century thanks to their property and personal connections. Among them there were fewer representatives of the intelligentsia than in other Bohemian towns. The majority of these people did not feel the need for great cultural involvement.

For a long time, no heavy demands were made on the town councils. They were not engaged in power politics. Only the dramatic years at the end of Rudolf II's reign forced the representatives of the town administrations to take political decisions. In June 1608, the conflict between Rudolf and his brother Matthias, supported by the Moravian and Hungarian Estates, came to an end outside the gates of the town, with the peace agreement signed in Libeň. A year later, on 1 May 1609, the Bohemian non-Catholic opposition Estates met at the New Town town hall to elect a committee of thirty directors to force the Emperor to implement the political and religious promises given the previous year. The Emperor had no choice but to capitulate and on 9 July issued a Letter of Majesty which guaranteed religious freedom in the Czech lands and thereby in the Prague towns. A Committee of Thirty Defenders, including three representatives of the people of Prague, was to supervise adherence to the Letter of Majesty. The first legal Lutheran and Union of Brethren (by that time de facto Calvinist) churches came into existence in the Prague towns. By the end of the sixteenth century, the Utraquist, quietly Catholicized Consistory had been turned into the management body of all Protestant churches. Prague University opened its gates to non-Utraquist, Protestant students.

The old, sick and deranged Rudolf tried to regain power over his country and capital city with the aid of the army of the Bishop of Passau, Archduke Leopold. On 15 February 1611, the Passau army occupied and looted the Lesser Town and Hradčany, but did not succeed in capturing the towns on the right bank of the river. The conflict was settled politically with the participation of the army of the Estates. The Passau army, paid off by Peter of Rožmberk out of his family treasury, left the country, and Rudolf abdicated in favour of Matthias, who was acceptable to the Estates. Matthias was crowned King of Bohemia on 23 May 1611. The old Emperor, politically powerless and isolated, died at Prague Castle on 20 January of the following year. Thus ended the long period of calm development of the residential city. Soon, in 1615, the first serious attempt at renewing the government policy of re-Catholicization was made in Prague, and certain burghers suffered persecution for having become involved in the policies of the Estate Defenders.

The situation continued to grow worse in 1617, when – still during the lifetime of the childless Emperor and King Matthias – the staunch Catholic Ferdinand of Styria was adopted and crowned King of Bohemia. When he realized that an easy political victory over the Estates was at hand, the monarch and the ruling group of the Catholic aristocracy undertook a decisive attack on the royal towns. Instruc-

20.8 **Martinic Palace**
Hradčany, Prague
Late sixteenth–early seven-
teenth centuries

tions issued to the royal magistrates in November 1617 abolished the political independence of town councils, strengthened the supervision of the royal magistrates
and, in the final instance, placed all decisions in the hands of the Bohemian Chancellery and the supreme chancellor Zdeněk Adalbert Popel of Lobkowicz.

Under these circumstances, the Prague towns did not dare to participate in
March 1618 in the congress of the non-Catholic Estates in the Old Town Carolinum, and they received the Emperor's thank for this in writing. But in the course
of the May congress (once again in the Carolinum), the radicals among the noblemen initiated the defenestration of the imperial governors Vilém Slavata of Chlum
and Jaroslav Bořita of Martinice from the Bohemian Chancellery at Prague Castle.
Now the representatives of the Prague towns had no choice but to join the
congress deliberations. They simply could not remain on the side of the Emperor at
the onset of the uprising of the Bohemian Estates. On 25 May, the Prague towns issued a written proclamation to the effect that they were joining the resistance
movement. Consequently, the Estates government included eight representatives of
the Prague towns among the ten burgher-members.

The Jesuits were expelled from Prague. In the summer of 1618, military preparations began, as did work on the modernization of the then basically medieval fortifications using early Baroque fortification architecture. In March 1619, the representatives of the Prague towns presented to those of the other royal towns a political programme which, in twenty points, aimed at the renewal of full constitutional
sovereignty and the equality of the royal towns as the free Third Estate. In June of
that year – i.e., a year after the beginning of the uprising – there followed the exchange of the existing pro-Emperor town councils, named in 1617 as representatives of the towns, and the new ones strongly supported the uprising.

At the General Diet of the Lands of the Czech Crown in July and August 1619, it

became possible to implement the renewal of full internal autonomy of the royal towns as demanded by the burghers' Estate and their recognition as the free Third Estate. But the aristocracy rejected the economic demands of the towns. The culmination of the uprising occurred in August with the dethronement of Ferdinand I of Habsburg and the election of Frederick of the Palatinate as king of Bohemia. On 4 November 1619, Frederick was solemnly crowned in St Vitus' cathedral. Three weeks later, the cathedral was ravaged – purified – instigation of Frederick's Calvinist preachers.

The inability of the aristocratic politicians to find a fitting compromise between the interests of the Estates and groups involved in the uprising, as well as the mighty onslaught of the imperial party supported by the Habsburg Catholic imperial and broader European 'lobby', led to the failure of the uprising. After a two-hour battle at the White Mountain outside Prague, the badly paid army of the Estates was routed and withdrew through Prague, which feared them more than the imperial soldiers. On 9 November, King Frederick fled the capital city, and without firing a shot the imperial army occupied the Prague towns on the left bank of the river. Nobody gave thought to defending the towns, and on 10 November the Prague towns capitulated unconditionally. Even though the imperial soldiers had occupied Prague without struggle, it was mercilessly ransacked between 11 and 15 November. The new imperial governor Karl of Liechtenstein took over and began arresting the supporters of the Estate government.

The military defeat at the Battle of the White Mountain, though perhaps no more than a scuffle, tends to be described by historians as a tragic turning point. But it should be said that, to a large extent, the uprising defeated itself. Neither the nobility nor the burghers were willing to lend the clumsy monarch the finances required for continuing the war. The burghers' militia did not in any way try to defend fortified Prague from the famished and wretched imperial army struggling through the autumnal slush. It was not a lack of weapons or fighting-fit soldiers. What was lacking was the conviction that the struggle made sense. And it was significant that the burghers believed that the town, taken over without struggle, would not be ransacked by the army, but that the imperial generals would impose discipline and order better than the officers of the Estate detachments.

The restoration of the old regime proceeded quickly. Prague and its inhabitants had to hand over all weapons, the leadership of the individual towns once again was taken over by the loyal councillors of 1617, and preparations went ahead for the trials of the uprising's leading personalities. At the trial, which ended with the proclamation of the verdict at Prague Castle on 19–20 June 1621, twenty-nine Prague citizens were sentenced, fifteen of these to death. The execution took place in the Old Town Square on 21 June 1621, and the heads of all those executed were displayed on the Old Town Bridge Tower. Other burghers were condemned to have their property confiscated or to pay high fines. The total fines imposed on Prague burghers was enormous.

The re-Catholicization of the Prague towns went ahead at great speed. At the end of 1621, all non-Catholic priests were exiled from Prague and Bohemia, and laymen were prohibited from taking communion *sub utraque*. In 1624, Catholicism was proclaimed as the only permitted religion. With the mandate of 31 July 1627, all non-Catholic burghers who did not wish to adopt Catholicism were exiled and had

20.9 Tombstone of Jaroslav Bořita and Jan Jiří of Martinic
St Vitus Cathedral, Prague
1624

to leave the Czech lands by the end of May 1628. Prague lost 620 families, roughly 5 per cent of its population. The families that left came primarily from the strata of the old Protestant élite. With their emigration, the spiritual atmosphere of the town underwent basic changes, rapidly acquiring a distinct Catholic character. An illustration of these trends can be found in the coronation of Ferdinand III in 1627, when Italian opera was heard for the first time in Prague. However, in the privacy of the burghers' houses, Protestant spiritual culture survived until the last third of the seventeenth century. Lists of burghers' libraries in legacy records are ample proof of this. The re-Catholicization seemed to bring a broadening of burghers' interests rather the replacing of one cultural model with another.

The Thirty Years' War, which began with the Prague uprising and showed most markedly in Prague with the ransacking after the Battle of the White Mountain, brought the Prague agglomeration not only hardship but also an important economic boom. Customs records reveal that, in the 1620s and 1630s, long-distance trade with Prague prospered. This trend was not changed even by the half year of the Saxon occupation (15 November 1631–5 May 1632). It is interesting that in Prague, from 1612 no longer the residential city of the monarch, there continued extensive building activity stimulated by ecclesiastical and secular, mainly aristocratic, customers. Building continued even at Prague Castle. Prague remained the country's only metropolis and its lively centre of political, social and cultural life. The renewal and establishment of higher and academic education went full speed ahead, though in a different direction than before, under the aegis of the archbishop and the Jesuits and other ecclesiastical orders. It is no surpise that under these circumstances, quite a few of Rudolf's artists and craftsmen remained in Prague and continued to work – for new customers.

Emperor Rudolf II had been a great collector and patron of the arts, but he did not wish to have aristocratic competition as a collector. On the contrary. He had 'presented as gifts' to him the best works from the aristocratic collections. After 1620, no such limitations existed, and Rudolf's former artists were able to attend fully to the commissions of the Prague aristocracy. The best proof of this is the construction and ornamentation of the vast Lesser Town residence which Albrecht of Wallenstein, Count of Frýdland, commissioned from Pierroni. Wallenstein, a *condotierre* of the imperial army, had grown rich from machinations with property confiscated after the Battle of the White Mountain and with Bohemian currency. His palace on the eastern edge of the Lesser Town, on the site of a number of burghers' houses and gardens, was more than proof of Pieroni's remarkable skill and high aims. It had exquisite interiors richly decorated with paintings, stucco and gold. It also housed Wallenstein's collections, and the spectacular garden was adorned with a collection of outstanding sculptures by Rudolf's leading sculptor, Adriaen de Vries.

The activities of the renowned glyptic workshop of the Miseroni family, summoned to Prague from Florence by Rudolf II, continued on a similarly grand scale. The Miseronis, while continuing their stone carving, now became curators of the imperial collections – the works which had remained at the Castle after part of the collections had been transferred to Vienna and choice pieces been sold by the Estates involved in the uprising and even by royal commissioners.

The continuity in the activities of the Rudolfine artists and their families was unusual at the time of the Thirty Years' War. It was the burghers' élite which had

20.10 GIOVANNI PIERRONI
Salla Terrena
Wallenstein Palace, Prague
Before 1629

the greatest chance of maintaining their names and family continuity. Otherwise, the Prague population changed in basic ways in the decades following the Battle of the White Mountain. This was due largely to repeated disastrous epidemics which befell Prague in the war years.

New inhabitants came to the metropolis at this time both from the Bohemian countryside and from other Central European and even more distant towns. Gradually, new foreign colonies grew up. The small communities speaking distinct languages grew into town minorities. By the side of communities speaking Czech and German, there existed a large Italian minority and a Jewish community. Early Baroque Prague prided itself on groups of French, Irish and Scottish people, with the odd Netherlander here and there. Most were merchants, artists, soldiers, even doctors. It is no surprise that this changing society took little interest in the ideas, ideals and traditions of the period before the Battle of the White Mountain. New stimuli, problems and dangers had to be addressed.

In the night of 25 July 1648, the Swedish army general Königsmark used treachery to occupy the Lesser Town and Hradčany. The Swedes, or rather their German mercenaries, thoroughly ransacked the two towns and the Castle. The attack on the Old Town and the New Town began on 30 July. But Prague defended itself. The fortifications and barricaded bridge were mounted by the imperial army aided by men of the town militia and the university student legion. They were not fighting for great ideas; they were simply defending the right-bank towns against an enemy which would loot and murder in their streets. The second wave of fierce Swedish attacks on Prague began on 11 October and lasted until 1 November – that is, a week after the Peace of Westphalia had been concluded. The people of Prague defended themselves literally to the last cask of gun powder. The Swedes abandoned the Prague towns on the left river-bank at the end of September 1649. They took valu-

able plunder as well as innumerable objects of artistic and intellectual value, among them Adriaen de Vries' statues from the Wallenstein Garden and the vast and precious Rožmberk library, kept in the 'security' of Prague Castle.

Emperor Ferdinand III made a fitting appraisal of the defence of Prague. The Imperial Charter of 1649 upgraded the Old Town and the New Town coats-of-arms. In the first place, it renewed the privileged status of the two largest Prague towns in the kingdom of Bohemia. It broadened court and police jurisdiction and patronage rights of the two town councils and confirmed the town charters and financial endowments. The Prague towns were granted tax reliefs, and certain honours – the formal raising to the aristocratic Estate – were conferred on a number of individual citizens. The Old Town then commissioned sculptor Bendl to make a memorial column with a statue of the Virgin Mary. The Marian Column, raised on 20 September 1650, symbolized for more than two and a half centuries the pleasure that the disastrous war had come to an end. The town now was different from what it had been 30 years before. Far more space was taken up by buildings and land belonging to Church institutions and, of course, aristocratic residences. Many had large gardens, which, to this day, render proof of the skill of the early Baroque architects and gardeners. The plan that surveyor Samuel Globic of Bučina drew in 1632 shows that, by the end of the first third of the seventeenth century, the face of the town had changed compared with its appearance at the turn of the seventeenth century, which can be guessed from vedute and small drawings by Rudolfine painters and draughtsmen.

The tax assessments of 1654 show in detail how the town, in the past inhabited mainly by burghers, had turned into one in which space was shared almost equally by the church and the aristocracy, and where other inhabitants were often second-rate citizens. Every new great ecclesiastical or aristocratic building erected on town land permanently removed some of the tax liability and income whereby the Prague towns ensured their own regeneration. It is no surprise that the town councils staunchly opposed the appropriation of town building plots for 'free' ecclesiastical or aristocratic building enterprise. These were quite different problems from those faced by the Prague agglomeration at the time of Archduke Ferdinand and in the Rudolfine period.

In the hundred years between 1550 and 1650, Prague changed from a late medieval cluster of communities of Czech burghers into an early Baroque, multicultural agglomeration, influenced by a number of nationalities, in which the government, the nobility and the church assumed, in most respects, roles as important as that of the burghers. As in other metropolises, development was attained at the cost of considerable losses, and not all that Prague lost could easily be dispensed with. But its status in the country and in the entire monarchy remained unique throughout the period under consideration. In the sphere of culture and the arts, we can state unequivocally that throughout this period Prague was an equal partner among the most important imperial cities in Europe.

The Nobility in the Czech Lands, 1550–1650

J A R O S L A V P Á N E K

21.1 **Tombstone of Vratislav of Pernštejn** (detail)
St Vitus Cathedral, Prague

A major European event that left a mark on the Bohemian and Moravian nobility is associated with Rudolf II in a very special way. Several dozen selected lords and knights gathered in Prague and then in Linz in June 1551, setting off from there for Genoa. Their aim was to welcome the titulary king of Bohemia, Maximilian II, and his wife, Maria, who were en route from Spain and to accompany them back to the Central European monarchy. Two other Habsburgs were behind this entire undertaking: Ferdinand I, the ruling German-Roman king of Bohemia and Hungary, and his second-born son Ferdinand, later called Ferdinand of the Tyrol. Together they had prepared the expedition of fifty-three nobles with a large escort of men-at-arms and men of lower birth, led by the twenty-one-year-old magnate Vratislav of Pernštejn. Clearly Ferdinand and his son wished to present the Bohemian-Austrian-Hungarian confederation to the rest of Europe in the best light. This confederation had come into being only a quarter of a century before, and its unstable foundations were constantly being threatened from the south-east by Ottoman expansion and shaken by internal conflicts between the monarch and the Estates. It was intended that the Central European Habsburg monarchy appear as a firm ally of powerful Spain (where Maria's father, Emperor Charles V, reigned) and as a serious contender in the European system of states.[1]

Under different circumstances, this expedition might have turned into a mere formality, providing support and protection for Maria, who found the journey from her country of birth to her new home barely endurable. For this long trip with the laborious crossing of the Alps caused hardship to each of the participants. The queen suffered especially, since she was in her third pregnanacy at the time. The noblemen of the Czech retinue will have been aware of this, but it will hardly have occurred to anyone that the child she was to bear would be their future monarch. Ferdinand – Maximilian and Maria's first-born son – died on 25 June 1552, and the right to rule passed to his younger brother Rudolf II, who was born three weeks later, on 18 July 1552, a mere two months after his mother's arrival in Vienna. Thus the future 'Sartunine Emperor' undertook his longest journey with an escort of Bohemian aristocrats even before his birth.[2]

The true significance of the aristocratic expedition to northern Italy lay elsewhere, however. This was the first time that representatives of the younger generation of leading seigniorial and knightly families had set out for Italy in such numbers. Among the youngest, there was, apart from Vratislav of Pernštejn, Vilém of Rožmberk, who, though only 16 years of age, was the richest Bohemian magnate; the twenty-four-year-old Zachariáš of Hradec and representatives of the Berkas of Dubé and the houses of Lobkowicz, Smiřický, Šternberk, Švamberk and Vartemberk. The knights included members of the houses of Bohdanecký of Hodkov, the Leskovecs, the rich Trčkas of Lípa and many others. These high-born men of tender age were torn away from their homes in a fading Gothic environment to spend

21.2 **Record, entry and coat-of-arms of Václav Budovec of Budov** (on a monument to Jiří of Švamberk)
1609

21.3 **Cup with the coat-of-arms of Vratislav of Pernštejn**
Before 1582
Glass covered with enamel
Buchlov Castle

long months in Italy during the late Renaissance. They encountered the dazzling phenomena of the new age in the princely residences of Mantua, Cremona, Milan, Pavia and Genoa.[3]

What most of the Bohemian nobles had, until that time, known only from narration or from Castiglione's work *The Courtier* they now had within their reach. The ostentatious setting of the Italian magnates – palaces, summer palaces and churches designed by Giulio Romano, with frescoes by Andrea Mantegna and Leonardo da Vinci; spectacular court life and banquets, with dancing and music – became a challenge to the Bohemians' social ambitions and financial possibilities. They met the local aristocracy, clergy and university students. Their tailors began to sew according to Italian fashion; their cooks cooked to Italian recipes.

The aesthetic impact of Italy was so strong that it influenced the cultural orientation of the expedition's participants for the whole of their lives. In the second half of the sixteenth century, these were the people who held leading positions in the Estates society of Bohemia and Moravia. Vilém of Rožmberk expressed his enchantment with Italy by rebuilding the largest country residence in Bohemia, his château at Český Krumlov, and by building a Renaissance summer palace called Kratochvíle (Pastime) as well as Rožmberk Palace (which could boldly compete with the Royal Palace) at Prague Castle. The ornamentation of these residences and the activities of the Rožmberk orchestra meant the introduction of Italian patterns into Bohemia shortly after the mid-sixteenth century and made its development possible even in the Rudolfine period. Other members of the expedition did likewise, though on a slightly more modest scale – Vratislav of Pernštejn at the château in Litomyšl, Zachariáš of Hradec at his château in Telč and Jaroslav Smiřický at Kostelec nad Černými lesy.[4]

The expedition to Italy did not simply influence culture and the way of life of the Bohemian nobility. The several months they spent in a foreign environment gave the future politicians a sense for European interconnections. It opened their eyes to the Spanish-French competition for hegemony in Western Europe, to the struggle between Spain and the Ottoman Empire for dominance in the Mediterranean, to the efforts of the Council of Trent to reform the Catholic church and even to the antagonism between the Spanish and the Bohemian-Austrian branches of the Habsburg dynasty. The links between Bohemian and European development, of which the preceding generation had not been sufficiently aware, became clear to every perceptive nobleman. The up-and-coming magnates understood that their ancestors' struggle for the autonomy of individual countries was not the only issue. The politically active nobles could not afford to ignore the weekly written reports which gave them insight into events in Europe and overseas. It was the end of the tranquil provincial period when politics had explicitly been determined by the Estates. The time was ripe to assert the importance of each individual in a changing society.[5]

The eight months' separation from home enabled the young magnates to get to know each other properly. In the course of the Italian journey, lifelong friendships were established, as were alliances and aversions. Shortly after their return, this polarization took the form of clashes between two groups of Bohemian noblemen, representing differing ambitions for power and a dissimilar attitude to the Habsburg concept of government. The struggle took place at the Land Diet, the Royal

Council and the Court of Justice in the years 1554–56, and the group composed of members of the ancient seigniorial houses won the upper hand. They were led by Vilém of Rožmberk, who, as supreme burgrave of Prague, became prime minister of the Bohemian land government in the years that followed. Jáchym of Hradec and Vratislav of Pernštejn assumed the office of supreme chancellor of the Bohemian Crown in succession.[6]

These magnates possessed a broad political outlook and high cultural standards. Together with followers from the next generation, they formulated and implemented a government programme that remained valid to the end of 1500s. This programme was based on respect for the Habsburg dynasty, balanced by protection of the independence of the state of Bohemia and a stabilized establishment based on the Estates. The programme's conservative character was manifested at the level of confessional politics. The Catholic members of the nobles' Estate, who were its creators and main bearers, tried to maintain their status at the expense of the Protestant majority – i.e., the noblemen who acknowledged the Neo-Utraquists (Hussites with a pro-Lutheran orientation), the Lutherans and the Unity of Brethren. The Catholics had no intention of persecuting the others, but they also did not intend to let them take a leading place in the land parliament. Basically, the Catholics insisted that only Catholicism, Old Utraquism or Hussitism in its pro-Catholic version should be legal in Bohemia. The highest Catholic officials tacitly ignored the fact that the majority of the noblemen acknowledged the illegal churches. Thanks to this tolerant attitude, the Rožmberks and their allies managed for a long time to maintain the balance of the Bohemian Estates community.

This balance was interrupted by the struggle for the Bohemian Confession in 1575. At that time, the Protestant wing of the Bohemian nobility, which was composed of Neo-Utraquists, open Lutherans and adherents of the Unity of Brethren, coalesced. At first, they vehemently demanded the legalization of their own creed, but after vague promises on the part of Maximilian II they accepted a compromise. The conflicts between the Habsburg court and the Catholic nobility, on the one side, and the Protestant opposition, on the other, never became irreconcilable. This was of great importance to Rudolf II, who, at the tempestuous Diet in 1575, was a pretender to the Bohemian Crown. It proved possible to maintain this compromise in confessional politics until the end of the 1500s, thanks to skillful balancing on the part of the leading conservative politicians, led by Vilém of Rožmberk until 1592 and then by his followers.[7]

During this outwardly calm period, the Bohemian Estates underwent a profound transformation in conformity with the general development of modern civilization. The aristocracy were both a subject of far-reaching changes and intent on impressing their own seal on these changes. The modernization of the nobility was especially apparent in property and social restructuring and in a new attitude to public activities, the government and religious orientation.

The Bohemian and Moravian nobility formed an insignificant fraction of Estates society as a whole; they were far exceeded by retainer peasantry, the citizens of the subject townships and towns and the privileged burghers in the royal towns. While the nobility in Hungary and Poland made up a 5- to 10-per-cent share, in Bohemia and Moravia only 1 per cent of the population could regard themselves as being of

21.4 **Sitting of the State Court at Prague Castle**
Ca. 1550

21.5 ANDREAS PLENNINGER
Horizontal sun dial
Late sixteenth century
[Prague, Umělecko-průmylsové muzeum]

21.6 THOMAS FRIDL
Figural table clock
Ca. 1620
[Prague, Umělecko-
průmyslové muzeum]

21.7 HANS STEINMEISEL
Table clock
1549
[Prague, Umělecko-
průmyslové muzeum]

noble birth, politically and legally privileged persons. Even this fraction was internally differentiated, especially in regard to status and property. Something on the order of thousands of members held the status of knight, making up the lower nobility, while only several hundred belonged to the highest rank of lords. Even they were divided into several dozen 'ancient' families, who aimed at acquiring and maintaining a monopoly in the influential authorities of the land and over the 'new' families.[8]

The lack of unity among the Bohemian and Moravian nobility was underlined by immense differences in property. The richest persons among the élite magnates, members of the lordly and, on exceptional occasions, knightly Estate, owned hundreds of villages, dozens of towns, townships, castles and châteaux with tens of thousands of subjects. The poor lords of the manor and most of the knights had to be satisfied with a better country manor and a few subject peasants from whom they levied tribute in money and kind. Between these two extremes stood the medium-wealthy nobility, who had a solid property background but could not compete in political ambitions and requirements for representation with the real magnates. However, the scope of property ownership and the number of subjects were not unchangeable, nor were they absolute measures of success.[9]

In fact, success depended least on good estate management. The magnates who evolved large-scale undertakings in the sphere of fish-farming and beer-brewing, in plant production on the manor farms and in trade, had incomes which were incomparably higher than those of people who were satisfied with the passive collection of cash rent according to late medieval custom. Certain knights showed organizational and commercial talent and they became increasingly rich money-lenders and officials in the services of the lords of the manors or the king. Regardless of their high-born status, the aristocratic members of Estates society were subject to constantly changing fortunes. Members of the ancient noble families became poorer or succumbed to bankruptcy, while formerly unknown *nouveaux riches* pushed ahead in public life. The growing importance of money served to shift social boundaries. Wealth, religious affiliation and adherence to the ruling house of Habsburg became decisive factors in the differentiation inside aristocratic society at the beginning of modern times.[10]

The 'higher Estates' – in particular, those who had political ambitions – reacted to the dynamic political, economic and cultural changes with a new attitude towards the basic coordinates of life, time and space. Abandoning the traditional orientation towards cyclical time, they began to think in linear terms. Clocks and watches in aristocratic dwellings and day-to-day records in calendars became tools with which to plan time as an immensely precious but irretrievably pass-ing value, with which whoever wanted to achieve success in public had to deal carefully.[11]

Likewise, the medieval perception of space was replaced gradually by territorialization. Living space ceased to be a set of – more or less isolated – fortified places of market or other importance. It became instead an interconnected, firmly ruled and systematically managed territory controlled by official bodies. From the point of view of the aristocracy, the basic organizational unit was the free homestead, in lesser cases, a fief or vassal farm and at a higher level, a larger manor and extensive demesne. Within the framework of his public activities, the nobleman took account,

apart from townships on his own property, of royal towns, the region, the land, the Bohemian crown and, possibly, other countries. Within this broad space, he set out to demarcate clearly the range of his own jurisdiction, not only on fertile plains, but in forests and mountains or along boundary streams. He did this at the risk of armed conflicts with adversaries and prolonged court cases.[12]

Viewed from the aristocrat's point of view, society was still organized to follow the medieval pattern: 'rule' from the top and 'servitude' from the bottom up, with the nobleman in the middle between the monarch and the peasant or burgher. At the beginning of modern times, shifts were occurring even here, however, for there arose around the nobleman's residence intricately intertwined relations between him and his courtiers, between him as patron and him as customer and between him as an insolvent aristocrat and his creditors. At the same time, horizontal pressures were brought to bear by legally equal members of the same Estate.[13]

The Bohemian and Moravian nobility was a body of high-born but differently situated persons. Multi-layered relations formed among these persons, families, groups and Estates and among each component of the nobility and the rest of society. Some high-born individuals lived in palaces or in more modest dwellings in Rudolfinian Prague, but almost all nobles had, at the same time or exclusively, residences and property in the countryside. Only the most important houses – the Rožmberks, Pernštejns, Lobkowiczes, Žerotíns, Lichtenštejns – established networks of residences, as did a few leading prelates of aristocratic origin, in particular the bishops of Olomouc. A complex network of aristocratic residences crystallized, in the second half of the sixteenth century, into a hierarchically laid out group of properties with two apexes – one in the countryside, the other in the capital city.

At the apex of this system was the chief country residence, which served as principal dwelling and fulfilled other functions, such as administrative management, political administration and law court, serving for representation and, to some extent, defence. This is true of the Pernštejns' Helfštejn and Tovačov, later Pardubice and Litomyšl, the Rožmberks' Český Krumlov, Horšovský Týn belonging to the house of Lobkowicz and Kroměříž, the central residence of the prince-bishop of Olomouc. At a slightly lower level were residences reserved for members of the second generation, in particular when the owner was not divided by property from the leading member of the family (for example, Petr Vok of Rožmberk owning Vimperk and Bechyně while Vilém of Rožmberk was the ruling head of the House). Below the primogenitary residences were those of a lower rank. Especially important among these was the second family residence, which could alternate with the first (for instance, the Rožmberks' residence at Třeboň near Český Krumlov). Then followed residences at the centre of estates – castles and châteaux – which served primarily for economic and administrative purposes and sometimes for defence. In isolated cases, these buildings were temporarily singled out to guarantee dowries or for use as widows' residences (the Rožmberks' Nové Hrady).

Alongside these administrative centres there occasionally came into being aristocratic residences in the subject towns (manorial houses or town halls with the best rooms reserved for travelling lordly families) or outside them (in architecturally imposing Renaissance mills). Such residences were used only to a limited extent

21.8 **Stock or choker watch**
Ca. 1600
[Prague, Umělecko-průmyslové muzeum]

21.10 A. SANCHEZ COELLO (a disciple)
Polyxena of Lobkowicz
After 1587
[Prague, Collection of W. Lobkowicz]

21.9 **Work in an office**
Sixteenth century

for short-term accommodation of the aristocrat who travelled about his own demesne, spending several nights at the most at a given place. Country-seats built in the style of Renaissance villas corresponded far better to the demands of the way of life at that time.[14]

The second apex in the network of aristocratic residences was the house or palace in the capital city of the land. In the case of Bohemian aristocrats, these were palaces at Prague Castle, at Hradčany, in the Lesser Town or in the Old Town, while wealthy Moravian noblemen had their central residences in Olomouc and in Brno, two towns that alternated as capital cities of Moravia. These town houses served the function of temporary dwelling places and, in particular, were available for political and social occasions. Farmsteads near the capital cities were of great economic significance. Outside the walls of Prague, for instance, there was Nová Libeň belonging to the house of Rožmberk and Butovice with Košíře, property of the lords of Hradec. Their function was to provide the Prague palace with food and forage and, at the same time, to give travelling magnates a night's rest before arriving in state in the metropolis. In the case of the leading magnates, such as the rulers of Rožmberk or the bishops of Olomouc, these two aspects of the residential set-up became linked in such a manner that on a journey between the capital city and faraway estates the aristocrat usually could stay or spend the night on lands belonging to him.[15]

Only a handful of magnates were able to build up such an extensive and firmly interconnected system of residences, composed of smaller estates and royal towns, reminiscent of the links between Rudolfine Prague Castle and the country residence at Brandýs nad Labem. Thousands of other nobles lived in far more modest settings. The majority had to be satisfied with one country residence, while some even gave this up and lived in their own or in rented houses in Prague or in the smaller towns.

The way of life of the Bohemian and Moravian nobility was determined, by way of example, by the magnates or at least the exceptionally wealthy noblemen who owned large property in the countryside. Socially and politically ambitious individuals went from there to the Habsburg court, but in case of the monarch's disfavour, ill health or financial or other difficulties, they were grateful to be able to withdraw to the safety of the countryside. The capital city with the official institutions, court tribunals and the monarch's court represented an attractive centre of public life and offered the most successful a dazzling career, but it also involved all manner of risks and threatened social disgrace, while the country residences formed a firm point in the aristocrat's existence in a material and legal sense.

In childhood, the country residences provided the setting for important family occasions. Renowned midwives were summoned long before the birth of a child, and the christenings that followed were the first social presentations of the offspring in this privileged society. While early childhood was spent in the narrow family circle, in the care of the mother and wet nurse or under the influence of other female family members, in subsequent years the home or host residences provided basic education. Males began to take an active part in the person of the preceptor or teacher from the local school, the priest or court servant. The young noble began to become aware of his own exclusiveness (children of the lordly Es-

21.11 **Cup with the coat-of-arms of Jiří Barthold Pontan of Breitenberk**
1595

21.12 **Cup with the coat-of-arms of Vratislav of Pernštejn**
Before 1582
[Buchlov Castle]

21.13 **Cup with two people dancing**
1582
[Buchlov Castle]

tate were addressed in the formal manner), and, in addition to literacy and religion, began to acquire elementary social graces, including etiquette, horse-riding, dancing and fencing.[16]

On the threshold of adulthood, the socially determined paths of aristocratic offspring separated according to gender. Unless she decided to take holy orders, the girl or young woman adopted the role of perpetuator of the family, and this limited her possibilities to a considerable extent. She could perfect her knowledge and skills either in the home or in other aristocratic women's settings (in the best cases, the queen's), where she learnt needlework, gardening and so on. Systematic schooling was not available to girls. In later years – as wife and particularly as widow – women acquired greater independence. They saw to the upbringing of the children, were in charge of the female servants, accompanied their husbands and, in addition, shared in the management of the property and could devote themselves to particular social and cultural interests. The surviving correspondence of aristocratic ladies of the sixteenth and seventeenth centuries reveals, in the case of a number of them, literary, musical, artistic and even economic and political interests.[17]

By contrast to the rather monotonous rhythm of life of the aristocratic ladies, noble men passed through different event-filled stages. On the threshold of adulthood, they usually left their home and set out to gain higher education and life experience, whenever possible abroad. They attended schools and universities and travelled and served as pages at the Habsburg court or at the courts of the local aristocracy. In this period, they developed their own cultural, political and religious personalities. After their return home, the young nobles would take over part of the family property or, should they have been orphaned in the meantime, assumed control of their fortunes.[18]

A period of social stablization then would set in. Not even the highest-born aristocrat regarded care for inherited property as unimportant. Writing instructions for clerks, checking accounts, supervising agricultural work – all that was respectable business. This led to increasingly bureaucratic methods. The furnishings of the residential areas in castles, châteaux and citadels at the turn of the seventeenth century consequently included bureaux, writing desks with office equipment, local regulations, Diet resolutions and other management literature.[19]

At the beginning of his independent life, sometimes even before inheriting his birthright, the wealthy aristocrat would begin to build up his own court. The nobleman who lacked means would seek service at such a court and become subject to the magnate's patronage. The leading aristocrats built their courts according to an established structure which followed that of the monarch's court, with a steward, a marshal, chamberlains and other courtiers, a chancellor and a secretary. The noble court comprised the management of the demesne, headed by a chief administrator and, subordinate to him, comptrollers, burgraves and specialized scribes. The young aristocrat would take over from his forebears and perfect or create a court and management model which enabled him to carry out the administrative and legal jurisdiction deriving from his status and place in Estates society.

The estate staff responsible for the running of the aristocratic residence differed considerably in numbers, composition, division of responsibilities and titles in di-

21.15 **Jug with the coat-of-arms of
Jan Vojtěch Šlik**
Ca. 1610
[Prague, Umélecko-
prûmyslové muzeum]

21.14 ANONYMOUS
Jakub Ludvík of Furstenberk
Ca. 1625
Oil on canvas
[Křivoklát, State Castle]

21.16 **Household altar**
Sixteenth century
[Prague, Umélecko-
prûmyslové muzeum]

verse categories of the nobility. This ranged from the precise hierarchical structure of the aristocratic court, in imitation of the pattern of the monarch's court, to a few domestic servants on poor gentlemen's freeholds. But one thing all these courts had was that they formed concrete personal links between the subjects, the noblemen as local lords of the manor and the public administration of the country, with which the less wealthy member of the 'higher Estates' kept contact through taxes and military service. The internal administration of property and establishment of a court did not only serve private functions. Within the range of their properties, the nobles ensured the effectiveness of the political system at regional, land and nation-wide levels.[20]

Economic independence and the certainty of regular income enabled the nobleman to explore areas he had discovered during his travels or his stay at the monarch's court or in other residences. By turning castles and fortresses into comfortable residences, constructing luxurious châteaux with furnishings in the spirit of the Renaissance and Mannerism, the nobility caught up with western and southern Europe in the course of the second half of the sixteenth and the early seventeenth centuries. There were strong social and cultural pressures on the aristocracy, and the activities of the court became especially important in this regard. Support for educational and artistic activities and the collecting and setting up of libraries occurred among all categories of the nobility, and in aristocratic residences a suitable environment was created for the activities of men of letters, artists, musicians, scholars and adherents of occult doctrines. Even before the arrival of Rudolf II in Prague, an appropriate environment had been created in the Bohemian and Moravian countryside to foster well-informed communication with artists and the intelligentsia at the court of archduke Ferdinand and later Rudolf II.[21]

The nobles who were firmly attached to their estates aimed to find their place in the higher spheres of the political system. While they regarded their participation in regional administration as something of a burden, partaking in the administration of the land held great attraction. They acted as assessors at land and magistrate courts and held Court, royal and higher land offices. Every year, they were away from their own residences for longer periods. This led to regular stays in the capital and forced them to speed up the rhythm of their work. At the same time, it involved increased demands which took the form of the ostentatious reconstruction of their country houses and those in the political centre. Interiors had to be furnished in a manner providing for the dignified reception and accommodation of the grandest of guests – representatives of the Habsburg dynasty. The 'imperial' and 'royal' rooms in Český Krumlov, at Bučovice, Velké Meziříčí, Moravská Třebová and other châteaux are proof of these efforts.[22]

The residences of aristocrats in public service assumed new functions. This was where they dealt with part of the political administration of the land and held official and secret negotiations. The country houses became secondary centres for gathering information and, at times of tension, assumed strategic importance. All this led to a great increase in demands for furnishings and services. Both country and town residences became the venue of festivities and banquets, hunts and gambling, entertainment that exceedeed the narrow social framework. The meetings of aristocrats and even members of the Habsburg dynasty with foreign princes thus could, and often did, turn into political consultations, in the course of

which links were formed between the local and foreign aristocracy. It was on such occasions that serious negotiations on the future of Central Europe took place.[23]

In the course of the sixteenth and the first two decades of the seventeenth centuries, tension was, indeed, growing in Central Europe. At its core was the problem of what order would prevail in the future, whether the Habsburgs would manage to suppress the efforts at decentralization of the Estates and whether Catholicism would prevail as the unifying religion. After the defeat of the Bohemian royal towns in 1547, the nobility assumed a decisive share in the Estates opposition and took full responsibility for its further development. During the reign of Rudolf II, who purposefully supported the nomination of Catholics to the Bohemian state parliament, the Estates opposition took a firm stand in favour of Protestantism.[24] Following the issuing of Rudolf's Letter of Majesty of 1609, the nobility took over the Protestant church organization (the Consistory, the Board of Defenders and Charles University).[25] Along with other privileges, this allowed the non-Catholic nobles to create 'their state within the state', and this inevitably led to conflict with the Habsburg rule. The disintegration of the political system of Bohemia resulted in the uprising of the Bohemian Estates in 1618–20.[26]

A group of radicals, led by Václav Budovec, Václav Vilém of Roupov and Jindřich Matthias of Thurn, responded to a government provocation with the defenestration of Governers Vílém Slavata and Jorslav Bořita of Martinic and prevailed upon the Bohemian and later the Moravian nobility to stage an uprising and start a war against the Habsburgs. During the interim government of the Estates Directors, it became possible to solve basic problems of constitutional law in the state of Bohemia and to pass a constitution in July 1619, which established a confederation of

21.17 **Album of Jiří Leopold von Stadl**
1606–14
[Prague, collection of W. Lobkowicz]

21.18 CASTRUCCI WORKSHOP
Household altar with the
Lobkowicz and Pernštejn
coat-of-arms
Before 1603
[Prague, collection of
W. Lobkowicz]

21.19 **Album of Jindřich
Biesenroth**
1612–17
[Prague, Praha Národní
knihovna]

countries and Estates communities. These, with the participation of Austrian and Hungarian Estates, were to become the crystallizing core of a new order in Central Europ – without the Habsburgs. This act was the culmination in the political and legal thinking of the Bohemian and Moravian nobility, but it did not receive sufficient support from the newly elected monarch, Frederick of the Palatinate. Likewise, the nobility of the confederate countries did not manage to mobilize their inner resources and follow up the international alliances that would have enabled them to resist the crushing superiority of the Habsburgs. The two-hour Battle of the White Mountain on 8 November 1620 revealed the weaknesses of the Estates uprising, which collapsed hopelessly after this defeat.

With the execution of the leaders of the uprising in the Old Town Square in Prague in June 1621, immense confiscations of aristocratic property and the re-Catholicization of the Czech lands, the hundred years of rivalry between the Habsburgs and the opposition party among the Czech nobility came to an end. It had been a time full of conflict but – in some respects at least – had offered possibilities of mutually beneficial co-existence. It was thanks to the Habsburgs in the sixteenth century that the relatively closed area of Bohemia had opened itself up to the rest of Europe. In foreign policy and cultural activities, the Bohemian nobility had been brought under the influence of Italian and Spanish patterns in particular. Under the governorship of Ferdinand of the Tyrol, the aristocrats helped to overcome the provincial limitations of Prague and formed a cosmopolitan society in which Austrian, German, Italian and other aristocrats existed by the side of Bohemian and Moravian nobles.[27]

During the reign of Rudolf, the links between the Habsburg court and the Bohemian nobility had become considerably closer. Individual titular major-domos, butlers and chamberlains had served at the court of Ferdinand I and Maximilian II, once the imperial residence had moved to Prague, the Bohemian nobility came to play a dominant part at court. The majority of the courtiers' ranks there were occupied by members of the houses of Lobkowicz, Pruskovský, Vchynský, Kolovrat, Valdštejn, Slavata, Berka, Vratislav of Mitrovice and other lords and knights. This increase in the Bohemian element did not mean that the court began to use the Czech language, however. It continued to be cosmopolitan in character with German holding the privileged position, but it brought the ruling Habsburg closer to the setting of the Bohemian and Moravian nobility, particularly its Catholic faction. After 1611, however, a reversal occurred which led to alienation between the monarch and the Bohemian nobility and lessened the hope for a conciliatory settling of the conflicts between them.[28]

At the end of the sixteenth and in the first half of the seventeenth centuries, the Habsburgs were able to take advantage of the fact that the nobility in Bohemia and Moravia were passing through an exceptionally dramatic period. This revealed itself in the biological exhaustion of a number of leading manorial families, who had until then determined the direction of political and cultural development. In the years 1597–1611 the lines of the lords of Boskovice, Šelmberk, Hasištejn of Lobkowicz, Krajíř of Krajek and those of Lomnice, Vartemberk, Hradec and Rožmberk became extinct, and this in itself involved immense shifts in property and power. The place of the ancient aristocrats was taken over by lords of lesser importance, by knights and families who were new arrivals in the country. Their ascent up the social ladder brought dynamic changes to the entire hierarchical structure of the aristocratic community.[29]

There was a greater influx of foreigners from the German speaking regions (Austria, Tyrol, Styria and the territorial states in the Empire), while immigrants from western and eastern Europe (Italy, Spain, Hungary and Croatia) remained a minority. As a whole, they could not change the local social situation, for few of them acquired outstanding landed properties, and the majority found their place in court service. Leading personalities assumed key positions in central institutions at the Court of Rudolf II (Ferdinand Hofmann, Paul Sixt Trautson), whereas the Land authorities remained closed to them.[30]

The situation changed fundamentally after the year 1620. Three waves of confiscations occurred in Bohemia, and, by stages, they completely altered the stratification of all aristocratic property in the country. Those who benefited most from the confiscations which immediately followed the defeat at the Battle of the White Mountain were the old Bohemian nobles. They acquired 69 per cent of the confiscated property, while the foreigners (the Buquoy, Eggerbergs and Marradas) took possession of the latifundia in South Bohemia. Albrecht of Wallenstein, one-time convert from the Unity of Brethren, showed by his giddy rise that opportunities for the acquisition of property and political career open to members of the ancient families of Bohemian lords, as long as they entered the services of the Habsburgs.[31] The Frydlant dukedom, with its dual centre – the château at Jičin and the monumental palace in Prague – followed the demesne of the house of Smiřický, thus establishing a network of residences belonging to Bohemian magnates in the early Baroque period.

The consequences of the emigration of non-Catholics were not yet catastrophic, for less than a quarter of the nobles accused of participation in the uprising emigrated. It was the second wave of confiscations that had a crushing effect on the hidden Estates opposition. This followed the brief occupation of Prague by the Saxons in 1631. What occurred now was the material uprooting of all forces of the opposition. This process reached its culmination with the subsequent purge of potential anti-Habsburg forces in the imperial army (following the assassination of Wallenstein in 1634). In the mid-1630s, the ancient Bohemian houses lost their decisive property position. With the break-up of the domains of the Wallensteins, Trčkas and Vchynskýs (Kinskýs), the most economically progressive landed property complexes in northern, north-eastern and eastern Bohemia disintegrated. The properties of the 'new' nobility of foreign origin (the Gallas, Piccolomini and others) grew up on these bases. The three waves of confiscations caused the complete restructuring of land ownership, and the foreign nobility, who acquired roughly two fifths of the confiscated property concentrated in large estates, now assumed leading positions in the country.[32]

The non-Czech nobility with citizen rights granted after 1620 achieved supremacy in the lordly Estate and among the wealthiest landowners. By contrast, the old Bohemian families maintained a numerical majority in the poorer categories and the Estate of knights, whose importance declined greatly. On the other hand, a dominant position was assumed by a narrow strata of magnates and wealthy landowners: a mere 5 per cent of all the nobility had at its disposition 55 per cent of all serfs, retainers and land. For them Bohemia became a 'paradise of the nobility', while the

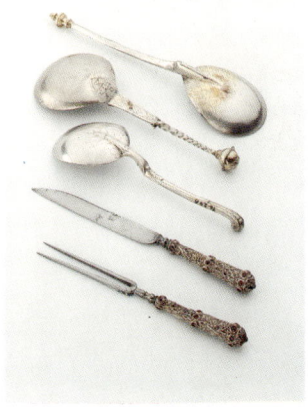

21.20 **Cutlery set**
First half of the seventeenth century
[Prague, Umělecko-průmyslové muzeum]

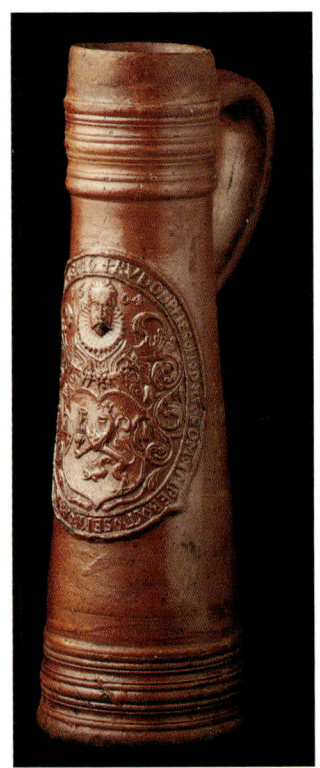

21.21 **Pint vessel with a portrait of Rudolf II**
1604
[Prague, Umělecko-průmyslové muzeum]

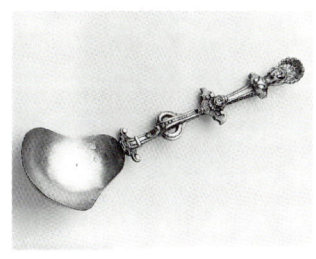

21.22 **Silver spoon**
After 1600
[Prague, Umělecko-
průmyslové muzeum]

majority of the old nobility sank into poverty and political insignificance.[33] In Moravia, the disestablishment of the old nobility took a slightly less dramatic course. Thanks to the adroitness of the bishop of Olomouc, Cardinal Franz of Dietrichstein, it became possible to convert members of the Protestant families to Catholicism and maintain the continuity of their property. Thus around the middle of the seventeenth century, members of the old (partly German-speaking) lineages were among the ten wealthiest magnates, while in Bohemia only three magnate houses (Slavata, Lobkowicz and Valdštejn) continued to belong to this élite. The arrival of foreigners (the Eggenburgs, Trauttmansdorffs, Buquoys, Gallas, Piccolomini and others) literally had a crushing effect on seventeenth-century Bohemia. In Moravia, only a few families of foreign origin (Forgách, Magnis, Collalto and Werdenberg) acquired larger property.[34]

However, the main trends of development were identical in both lands. Decisive groups of lords of the manor broke away from the Estates traditions of the main body of the Bohemian and Moravian noblemen and clearly identified themselves with the interests of the monarchy. (Some of them later claimed local patriotism to defend themselves against the excessive tax pressure from the government in Vienna.) By making use of the material resources of Bohemia and Moravia, the ambitious lords tried to achieve careers in Habsburg service. In contrast to the less and medium-wealthy nobility, which had virtually no political significance, the leading aristocrats were transformed into an all-Austrian nobility, the more so since some of them, such as the Lobkowiczes and Liechtensteins, owned estates in several countries of the monarchy. By accepting imperial titles of baron, count, prince and duke, the aristocrats expressed their parting of ways with the traditions of the once formally coherent lordly Estate. They were also aware, however, of the specific interests of the countries in which the property base of their power lay. The aristocracy's span of interests, ranging from the court in Vienna to individual countries, created a certain tension between the centre and the provinces, between the monarch and his most influential subjects. At the same time, it ensured constant settlement of interests by compromise on both sides and thereby the long-term stability of the Habsburg monarchy.[35]

The political assimilation to Austria and the adoption by the nobility in Bohemia and Moravia of the German language had not been completed by the mid-seventeenth century. But there was an indication of the direction developments would take. In the second half of the sixteenth and early seventeenth centuries, the Czech-speaking nobility to a large extent took over the cultural initiative from the humiliated burghers and with it responsibility for the broader cultural setting. Exceptional leading aristocrats did show great creative abilities, supporting schools and local artists, financing the publication and distribution of literature on their estates and becoming patrons at their courts, where the permanent staff or temporary guests included numerous culturally active personalities.[36]

National and cosmopolitan culture in the aristocratic setting rested on two pillars. The first was the interrelationship between the nobility, growing up at least partly in a Czech-speaking environment, and the larger social environment. The second was the possibility of using cultural activities to gain wider acknowledgement for the nobleman, his family and his court. The basic change in the political situation after 1620 severed these fine threads of cultural communication. The no-

21.23 **Pint vessel with the Hohen-**
lohe family coat-of-arms
Last quarter of sixteenth
century
[Prague, Umělecko-
průmyslové muzeum]

bility of foreign origin lacked the motivation to support works in the Czech language, but had unlimited scope in the sphere of cosmopolitan culture. In addition to activities which had been supported in earlier times, they supported the spread of religious art on a new level in the decades following the Peace of Westphalia.[37] In contrast, aristocrats of Czech origin – people who understood the Czech language and who might also have acted as patrons of the arts – lost public acceptance. Before 1620, a hierarchical structure had been typical for cultural life. In the subsequent period – leaving aside the specific cultural life of the burghers – there developed two layers: 'aristocratic' and 'non-aristocratic' culture. In the first, the hierarchical model, there was still an intermingling of national and cosmopolitan culture. In the second, parallel model, the two developed more or less independently. While the cultural life of the non-noble strata continued to be directed mainly by the Catholic church, aristocratic culture split off as the exclusive expression of the ruling strata of the Habsburg monarchy.[38]

21.24 **Saucer with the coat-of-arms of Jiří Zikmund of Zástřizly and Alěbžta Kotvrdovska of Volešnička**
1602
[Prague, Uměleckoprůmyslové muzeum]

1. This topic is dealt with in detail in Jaroslav Pánek,*Výprava české šlechty do Itálie v letech 1551–1552* (Prague, 1987). See also *idem*, 'The Expedition of Czech Noblemen to Italy within the Period 1551–1552 (A Contribution to the History of International Relations in the Field of Culture, Politics and Finances in the 16th Century)', *Historica*, 30 (1990), 29–95; 'Spedizione della nobiltà boema negli anni 1551–1552 e contatti tra le Terre boeme e il Mediterraneo', *Rapporti Genova – Mediterraneo – Atlantico nell'età moderna (Atti del IVo Congresso Internazionale di Studi Storici)* (Genoa, 1990), pp. 511–25.

2. For an understanding of the genealogical relationsips, see Franz Weihrich, *Stammtafel zur Geschichte des Hauses Habsburg* (Prague, Vienna and Leipzig, 1893); Wilhelm Karl Prinz von Isenburg, *Stammtafeln zur Geschichte der europäischen Staaten, Bd.1, Stammtafeln zur Geschichte der deutschen Staaten* (Berlin, 1936), tab.17.

3. A survey of the situation in Estates society and the nobility in the Czech lands is given in Josef Janáček, *České dějiny: Doba předbělohorská 1526-1547*, vol. I, 1–2 (Prague, 1968–84). See also Winfried Eberhard, *Konfessionsbildung und Stände in Böhmen 1478-1530* (Munich, Vienna, 1981); *idem, Monarchie und Widerstand. Zur ständischen Oppositionsbildung im Herrschaftssystem Ferdinands I in Böhmen* (Munich, 1985); Jaroslav Pánek, 'Das Ständewesen und die Gesellschaft in den Böhmischen Ländern in der Zeit vor der Schlacht auf dem Weissen Berg (1526–1620)', *Historica*, 25 (1985), 73–120; *Josef Macek, Jagellonský věk v českých zemích (1471–1526) 2: Šlechta* (Prague, 1994).

4. See Eva Šamánková, *Architektura české renesance* (Prague, 1961); Jarmila Krčálová, 'Palác pánů z Rožmberka', *Umění*, 18 (1970), 469–85; *eadem, Centrální stavby české renesance* (Prague, 1976). *eadem, Renesanční stavby B. Maggiho v Čechách a na Moravě* (Prague, 1986); Jaroslav Pánek, 'Renesanční velmož a utváření hudební kultury šlechtického dvora (K hudebnímu mecenátu Viléma z Rožmberka)', *Hudební věda*, 26 (1989), 4–17.

5. Zdeněk Šimeček, 'L'Amérique au 16e siècle à la lumière des nouvelles du service de renseignement de la famille de Rožmberk', *Historica*, 11 (1965), 53–93; 'Rožmberské zpravodajství o nových zemích Asie a Afriky v 16.století', *Československý časopis historický*, 13 (1965), 428–43; *idem*, 'Noviny z Prahy na sklonku 16.století' in *K soupisu cizojazyčných bohemik z let 1501–1800: Vědecké informace Základní knihovny ČSAV*, suppl. 1 (1970), pp. 34–79. *idem*, 'Osmanská expanze v českém zpravodajství 16. a počátku 17. století' in *Osmanská moc v střední a jihovýchodní Evropě II* (Prague, 1977), pp. 310–73.

6. Jaroslav Pánek, 'Zápas o vedení české stavovské obce v polovině 16. století (Knížata z Plavna a Vilém z Rožmberka 1547-1556)', *Československý časopis historický*, 31 (1983); *idem*, '"Výpověď krále Jana" – odraz politického programu české šlechty z poloviny 16. století' in M. Polívka and M. Svatoš (eds), *Historia docet, Festschrift for the 60th Birthday of Prof. Dr. Ivan Hlaváček* (Prague, 1992), pp. 341–55; *idem*, 'Konzervatismus a jeho úskalí v dramatické době (Český politický program z druhé poloviny 16. století)', *Střední Evropa*, 54-55 (1995), 67–72.

7. Ferdinand Hrejsa, *Česká konfese, její vznik, podstata a dějiny* (Prague, 1912); Rudolf Říčan, *Dějiny Jednoty bratrské* (Prague, 1957); Jaroslav Pánek, *Stavovská opozice a její zápas s Habsburky 1547–1577* (Prague, 1982); *idem, Zápas o Českou konfesi* (Prague, 1991).

8. For further details, see Jaroslav Pánek, 'Proměny stavovství v Čechách a na Moravě v 15. a v první polovině 16.století', *Folia Historica Bohemica*, 4 (1981), 179–219; *idem*, 'Stavovství v Čechách a na Moravě na prahu novověku (30 tezí se srovnávacím zřetelem k Říši a k Rakousům)' in *Morava na prahu nové doby* (Přerov, 1995), pp. 37–54.

9. See Alois Míka, 'Majetkové rozvrstvení české šlechty v předbělohorském období', *Sborník historický*, 15 (1967), 45–75.

10. Josef Válka, *Hospodářská politika feudálního velkostatku na předbělohorské Moravě* (Prague, 1962); Josef Petráň, *Poddaný lid v Čechách na prahu*

21.25 Portrait of Albrecht of Valdštejn
1643

třicetileté války (Prague, 1964); Václav Ledvinka, 'Rozmach feudálního velkostatku, jeho strukturální proměny a role v ekonomice českých zemí v předbělohorském období', *Folia Historica Bohemica*, 11 (1987), 103–32.

11. Jaroslav Pánek, 'Politický systém předbělohorského českého státu', *Folia Historica Bohemica*, 11 (1987), 41–101, esp. 54ff; Václav Bůžek, 'A tak jsem tam dlouho zdržován byl: Čas v životě předbělohorských rytířů', *Dějiny a současnost*, 15:3 (1993), 26–30.

12. A model example of a study of the territorial development of the demesne was written recently by Petr Vorel: 'Vývoj pozemkové držby pánů z Pernštejna v 15.-17. století' in Petr Vorel (ed.), *Pernštejnové v českých dějinách* (Pardubice, 1995), pp. 9–75.

13. Václav Ledvinka, *Úvěr a zadlužení feudálního velkostatku v předbělohorských Čechách (Finanční hospodaření pánů z Hradce 1560–1596)*, (Prague, 1985); Václav Bůžek, *Úvěrové podnikání nižší šlechty v předbělohorských Čechách* (Prague, 1989).

14. See Petr Vorel, 'Poddanská rezidenční města 16. století v Čechách a na Moravě' (Ph.D. dissertation, Institute of History of the Academy of Sciences of the Czech Republic, Prague, 1994).

15. See Václav Ledvinka, 'Palác pánů z Hradce (Příspěvek k poznání geneze a funkcí renesančního šlechtického paláce v Praze)', *Folia Historica Bohemica*, 10 (1986), 269–316; Václav Ledvinka, Bohumír Mráz and Vít Vlnas, *Pražské paláce* (Prague, 1995).

16. See Jaroslav Pánek, 'Rožmberští sirotci na jindřichohradeckém a českokrumlovském zámku (K otázce výchovy české renesanční aristokracie)', *Jindřichohradecký vlastivědný sborník*, 1 (1989), 1–20. Marie Koldinská, 'Šlechtické školy v předbělohorských Čechách' in L. Bobková (ed.) *Život na šlechtickém sídle v 16.-18. století* (Ústí nad Labem, 1992), pp. 217–22.

17. Josef Janáček, *Ženy české renesance*, 3rd edn (Prague, 1996).

18. Jaroslav Pánek, 'Čeští cestovatelé v renesanční Evropě (Cestování jako činitel kulturní a politické integrace)', *Český časopis historický*, 88 (1990), 661–82.

19. For more details, see Jaroslav Pánek, 'K úloze byrokratizace při přechodu od stavovské k absolutní monarchii', *Historická úloha absolutní monarchie ve střední Evropě*, AUC – Phil. et Hist. 3/1989 (*Studia Historica XXXVI*, [Praha 1991], 75–85).

20. Lenka Bobková (ed.), *Život na šlechtickém sídle v 16.-18. století* (Ústí nad Labem, 1992); Václav Bůžek (ed.), *Život na dvoře a v rezidenčních městech posledních Rožmberku* (České Budějovice, 1993); Václav Bůžek, *Rytíři renesančních Čech* (Prague, 1995).

21. Jaroslav Pánek, *Poslední Rožmberkové. Velmoži české renesance* (Prague, 1989); Václav Bůžek, *Nižší šlechta v politickém systému a kultuře předbělohorských Čech* (Prague, 1996).

22. František Hrubý, 'Selské a panské inventáře v době předbělohorské', *Český časopis historický*, 33 (1927), 293, 302; *Dějiny českého výtvarného umění*, vol II/1

(Praha, 1989), pp. 34ff.

23. Detailed documentation is provided in Václav Březan, *Životy posledních Rožmberků*, vols I–II (Prague, 1985). For an analysis of the issue under discussion here, see Jaroslav Pánek, *Poslední Rožmberkové* (note 21).

24 Josef Borovička, 'Obsazení nejvyšších zemských úřadů v Čechách v letech 1597–1599', *Český časopis historický* 28 (1922), pp. 277–304; Julius Glücklich, *Mandát proti Bratřím z 2. září 1602 a jeho provádění v letech 1602–1604* (Prague, 1904).

25. Anton Gindely, *Geschichte der Ertheilung des bömischen Majestätsbriefes von 1609* (Prague, 1859); Kamil Krofta, *Majestát Rudolfa I* (Prague, 1909); Jaroslav Pánek, 'Das politische System des böhmischen Staates im ersten Jahrhundert der habsburgischen Herrschaft (1526–1620)', *Mitteilungen des Instituts für österreichische Geschichtsforschung*, 97 (1989), 53–82.

26. Antonín Gindely, *Dějiny čeckého povstání léta 1618*, vols I–IV (Prague, 1870–1880); Noemi Rejchrtová, *Václav Budovec z Budova* (Prague, 1984); Karolina Adamová, 'K otázce konfederačních snah v čcském státě na počátku 17. století', *Právněhistorické studie*, 27 (1986), 57–96; Joachim Bahlcke, *Regionalismus und Staatintegration im Widerstreit: Die Länder der böhmischen Krone im ersten Jahrhundert der Habsburgherrschaft (1526–1619)* (Munich, 1994), esp. pp. 309–445; Josef Válka *Dějiny Moravy*, vol. 2, *Morava reformace, renescance a baroka* (Brno, 1996); Josef Petráň, *Staroměstská exekuce* (Prague, 1996).

27. Jaroslav Pánek, 'Der Adel im Turnierbuch Erzherzog Ferdinands II, von Tirol (Ein Beitrag zur Geschichte des Hoflebens und der Hofkultur in der Zeit seiner Statthalterschaft in Böhmen)', *Folia Historica Bohemica*, 16 (1993), 77–96.

28. Josef Janáček, *Rudolf II. a jeho doba* (Prague, 1987); Jaroslav Pánek, 'K povaze vlády Rudolfa II v Českém království', *Folia Historica Bohemica*, 18 (1996).

29. Jaroslav Honc, 'Populační vývoj šestí generací 125 českých panských rodů v letech 1502–1794', *Historická demografie*, 3 (1969), 20–51, esp. pp. 21ff.

30. Josef Polišenský and Frederik Snider, 'Změny ve složení české šlechty v 16. a 17. století', *Československý časopis historický*, 20 (1972), 515–26.

31. See Josef Janáček, *Valdštejn a jeho doba* (Prague, 1978) further literature is given. More recently, see Josef Polišenský and Josef Kollmann, *Valdštejn. Ani císař, ani král* (Prague, 1995).

32. Jiří A. Kovařík, 'Proměny feudální třídy v Čechách v předbělohorském období' in J. Petráň (ed.), *Pro-měny feudální třídy v Čechách v pozdním feudalismu*, AUC – Phil. et Hist. 1/1976 (*Studia Historica* 14 [Prague, 1976], 137–64); Petr Čornej, 'Vliv pobělohorských konfiskací na skladbu feudální třídy' in Petráň (ed.) pp. 165–94; Petr Čornej and Ondřej Felcman, 'Rozvrstvení feudální třídy v severovýchodních Čechách v letech 1603–1656', *Československý časopis historický*, 28 (1980), 559–89.

33. Volker Press, 'Adel in den österreichisch-böhmischen Erblanden und im Reich zwischen dem 15. und 17. Jahrhundert' in *Adel im Wandel: Politik – Kultur – Konfession 1500–1700* (Vienna, 1990) p. 27.

34. František Matějek, 'Bílá hora a moravská feudální společnosť, *Československý časopis historický*, 22 (1974), 81–104; Thomas Winkelbauer, 'Wandlungen des mährischen Adels um 1600' in K. Mack (ed.), *Jan Amos Comenius und die Politik seiner Zeit* (Vienna and Munich, 1992), pp. 16–36.

35. See Thomas Winkelbauer, 'Die Liechtenstein als "grenzüberschreitendes Adelsgeschlecht". Eine Skizze der Entwicklung des Besitzes der Herren und Fürsten von Liechtenstein in Niederösterreich und Mähren im Rahmen der politischen Geschichte' in V. Bůžek and S. Svátek (eds), *Kulturen an der Grenze. Waldviertel – Weinviertel – Südböhmen – Südmähren* (Vienna, 1995) pp. 219–26.

36. Josef Klik, *Národnostní poměry v Čechách od válek husitských do bitvy bělohorské* (Prague, 1922); Alois Míka, 'Národnostní poměry v českých zemích před třicetiletou válkou', *Československý časopis historický*,
20 (1972), 207–33; Jaroslav Pánek, 'K rozšiřování pražských tisků v předbělohorské době (Zprostředkovatelská úloha světských a církevních vrchností', *Documenta Pragensis*, 10 (1991), 239–55.

37. Jan Muk, *Po stopách národního vědomí české šlechty pobělohorské* (Prague, 1931); Alois Míka, 'K národnostním poměrům v Čechách po třicetileté válce', *Československý časopis historický*, 24 (1974), 535–63. Jaroslav Pánek, 'Česká a rakouská šlechta v počátcích habsburské monarchie', *Dějiny a současnost*, 12:3 (1990), 26–33.

38. Robert J. W. Evans, *Das Werden der Habsburgermonarchie 1550-1700. Gesellschaft, Kultur, Institutionen* (Vienna, Cologne and Graz, 1986); Jaroslav Pánek, 'Habsburská monarchie jako rámec rozvoje barokní kultury' in Z. Hojda (ed.), *Kultura baroka v Čechách a na Moravě* (Prague, 1992), pp. 43–52.

The Public and Private Lives of Prague's Burghers

VÁCLAV LEDVINKA AND JIŘÍ PEŠEK

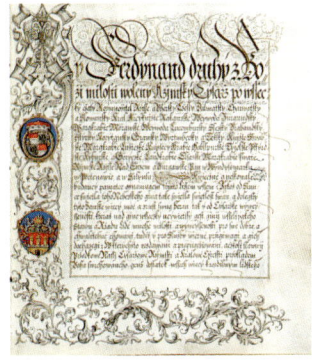

22.1 Privilege granted by Ferdinand II to the burghers of the Old Town
1627
[Prague, Archiv hl. města Prahy]

The long-term improvement in Prague's economy, together with the dynamic growth of its population and changing social structure, brought about a new way of life. This led, in turn, to the gradual transformation of the city's cultural and architectural aspects. For the second time in its history, Prague became one of Europe's most important metropolises and gained fame as an imperial city.

Between 1421 and 1547, the burghers' communities of Prague's Old Town, the New town and the Lesser Town had been at the forefront of the self-confident Commons' Estate, an equal of the Estate of aristocrats and knights in the kingdom of Bohemia. In the middle of the sixteenth century there existed thirty-nine free towns with a royal charter. This group had at its disposal economic, political and military forces which sufficed, even at the price of certain concessions and compromises, to uphold the interests of the townspeople in relation to both the weakening might of the monarch and the growing competitive pressure of the nobility and the propertied aristocrats. In this balancing act, the key role was played by the Prague towns, especially the Old Town, acknowledged as the head of the Commons' Estate. The Old Town town hall was the political centre, supreme court and court of appeal of the other Bohemian towns. It was the venue of their meetings and the seat of nation-wide associations and unions of townspeople. From the early sixteenth century on, the town councils of all three Prague towns were not subordinate to the royal or Land officials, only to the King, and during the long years when the monarch was absent from the country they were elected by the larger towns. Prior to 1500, only the Old Town had enjoyed this privilege. The broad administrative and political functions led to the raising of the number of aldermen from twelve to eighteen, in the Old Town for a time to as many as twenty-four. By the 1520s, there were also lower echelons of town self-government, which dealt with bridges, river, fishing, horses and stabling rights. The Old Town, furthermore, had an office of the master of the vineyards. This development culminated in the years 1518–28, when the Old Town and New Town merged into one unit. This unit probably represented the strongest power base in Bohemia at the time, a reality embodied in the new motto inscribed on the façade of the Old Town Hall: *Praga, caput regni*.

This trend derived partly from political and property acquisitions made by the Prague towns during the Hussite Revolution and from their active participation in internal power struggles during the reign of George of Poděbrady and the Jagellonian dynasty. It grew primarily out of the systematic growth in landed property of the Prague towns and their people between 1488 and 1544. At the same time, guild crafts production expanded greatly. Of exceptional importance was the revival of trade links with traditional partners in Nürnberg, Vratislav and the Austrian towns along the Danube; new contacts were established with the Netherlands, Venice and northern Italy. During the civil wars, there had been a major popula-

tion decline. From the last quarter of the fifteenth century on, the number of inhabitants began to grow again, and the renewal of building construction at the turn of the sixteenth century led to the extensive late Gothic restoration of Prague. This coincided with the simultaneous reconstruction of Prague Castle by King Vladislav II of the Jagiellonian dynasty. Within a short time, the parts of the Prague agglomeration that had been destroyed during the war and had lain waste for decades were built up. This was particularly true of the Lesser Town below Prague Castle, the western part of the subject town of Hradčany and the newly designated subject town at Vyšehrad in the eastern part of the grounds of the destroyed royal castle there.[1] It was at this time, then, that the foundations were laid for Rudolfine Prague.[2]

The self-confident ambitions for political power on the part of the free royal towns and the administrative concentration of left-bank towns of Prauge into a single strong unit, ruled from 1524 by Master Jan Pašek of Vrat, came into conflict immediatcly after 1526 with the centralism avowed by the first Habsburg monarch to sit on the throne of Bohemia, Ferdinand I. The determined monarch used the first opportunity (in 1528) to break up the unity of the Prague towns, which was was dangerous to his plans. He appointed new councils, excluding the former holders of power, and at the same time prohibited the establishment of large town units. Then, step by step, he began to impose his idea that the royal towns did not constitute a free political Estate, but were directly subordinate to the King, part of the 'Royal Chamber' – i.e., the sovereign sphere of the King's decision-making. This attitude was reflected in a number of political conflicts and religious dissensions between the Catholic ruler and the Utraquist Prague towns. In 1547, this led to the people of Prague heading up the Estates' uprising against Ferdinand and his imperial plans. The failure of this revolt had fatal consequences for the Commons' Estate. The people of Prague were condemned to the loss of all privileges, property and income, to disarmament and the surrender of weapons, and to lasting payment of taxes on the sale of beer and malt produced. They lost the right to appoint magistrates and a master of the vineyards, and the town ceased to be the court of appeal for the royal towns. The guilds were abolished, and all income from death duties, customs, local rates and the salt trade went to the monarch. The Commons' Estate was deprived of their vote in the Diets, and the town councils were subordinated to royal magistrates. New aldermen were appointed, and, in addition to being subordinate to magistrates summoned from among the loyal burghers, they came under the jurisdiction of royal district officers appointed from among the nobility.[3]

Some of these punishments proved only temporary. In order to prevent Prague from becoming bankrupt, in September 1547 King Ferdinand was forced to pardon the towns and give them back some of their privileges. In May 1549, he returned the town income and parish property. With a view to forming a balance to the Estate of aristocrats and knights at the Land Diet, he reestablished for the royal towns the right of a third vote on 28 September 1547 on condition that they did not rebel against the monarch's will again. In 1558, further property and privileges were returned to the Old and the New Town, and, where there was need, the guilds were permitted to function again. Despite these mea-

22.2 **Painters' emblem for a privilege granted by Rudolf II to the Old Town guild of painters**
1595
[Prague, Archiv Národní galerie]

sures, the public life of the townspeople had changed, since they no longer exercised the power to enforce their own political ideas and interests independently.

As a consequence of defeat in the anti-Habsburg rebellion of 1547, life in the Prague towns underwent an important transformation and assumed new dimensions. The dominant feature was the decline in political power, the importance placed on economic affairs and a general atmosphere of pragmatism. Individual burghers turned to their own private interests, abondoning public ambitions. Direct interference by King Ferdinand I and Ferdinand of the Tyrol penetrated the sphere of town authority. There was likewise an increase in the powers of the Estate of noblemen and knights. This increase manifested itself in the building of palaces on waste ground described in the preceding essay. It was not until 1588 that the townspeople of Prague managed to pass measures designed to put an end to the exemption of aristocratic buildings from taxes.[4]

While the forms of public representation of the town ostensibly remained unchanged (festivities and public demonstrations did not cease, for example, but were restricted to activities that suited the monarch), a hidden struggle continued for the restitution, or at least the maintenance, of the political positions of the Commons. This became apparent, though without any positive results, on the death of King Ferdinand I and at the end of the governorship of Ferdinand of the Tyrol. The restrictions placed on municipal politics after 1547 did not mean the end of public political activities on the part of Prague's townspeople. Their suppressed collective forms were simply replaced by individual actions whereby representatives of Prague's 'political patriciate' attempted to implement their concerns. Those most active during this period were simply replaced not by members of the old, rich families of merchants and craftsmen families, but by ambitous members of the intelligentsia, educated at the Prague Utraquist university and, increasingly, at foreign universities, who formed the most dynamic element of the Prague Commons of the time. They won both respect and capital by serving in the town or land offices and frequently grew rich as the result of advantageous marriages to the daughters or widows of rich patricians. From 1560s on, they were joined by assertive immigrants and merchants as well as pensioners from among the manorial officials of the royal or aristocratic Estates. These people were not primarily concerned with the public interest, pursuing their careers and interests outside the sphere of town politics and administration, in state and land services, and in land (and, at the time of Rudolf, in court) offices, including such institutions as the Bohemian Chancellery, the Office of the Land Rolls, the Court of Appeal and so on. Often, such individuals were raised to the lower ranks of the nobility, as reward for their services, through influential patrons or by the purchase of coats-of-arms and predicates. If they were not accepted as knights, they attained their highest political goals by appearing publically at Land Diets and and in the law courts among the ranks of the Commons' Estate. After 1575, one might also join boards of the Estate Defenders and Directors. A number of representatives of this patriciate played an important role in the political events surrounding Rudolf's Letter of Majesty in 1608–9, his abdication in 1611 and, especially, the uprising of 1618–20.

Beginning in the 1560s, numerous merchants, financiers and entrepreneurs

gained in importance among the Prague townspeople. They did not aim at political careers or leading positions on the town councils, devoting themselves fully to their entrepreneurial activities. Their social prestige derived from the weight of the property they had acquired and their financial links to the monarch, leading court circles and notable Bohemian Estate society. Most often, they came from among new immigrants from the imperial towns, from Italy, France, Savoy, England and the Netherlands. After the repeal of a number of restrictive medieval privileges and in view of the break-up of the guilds, conditions which weakened the town autonomy, these people found opportunities in Prague for bold projects and speculation, leading either to speedy downfall and disappearance from the public scene or to rapid accumulation of wealth and the adoption of leading places among the inhabitants of the capital.

As metropolis and permanent residence, first of the Habsburg governer Ferdinand of the Tyrol and, from 1583, of Rudolf himself, Prague became a significant consumer centre and the focus of a long-term trade boom Entrepreneurial risk was relatively low under both Ferdinand of the Tyrol and Rudolf, except during 1560s, when, for example, Simon de Genion of Naples met failure in attempts at setting up a factory for the production of fustian in the Prague Carolinum (1563). The same is true of Andreas Blau of Erfurt, Niklas Schwab and Paul Griemiller of Třebsko in their repeated endeavour to establish a monopoly on cultivating a dye plant (ca. 1565), and of Giovanni Olgiato of Como with his project to set up a factory for the production of Italian, Flemish and English cloth in Prague (1566). Throughout the subsequent three decades, Christoph and Eustachius Betengel of Neuenberg, Johann Netter of Glauch, Wolf and Thomas Hebenstrait of Straitenfeld, Johann Teufel of Zeilberg, Johann and Peter Nerhof of Holterberg, Hercules de Nova, Lorenz Stark of Starkenfels, Adam Myslich of Vilimstein, Valentin Kirchmaier of Rejchvice and many others conducted successful entrepeneurial and trade activities. For three generations, these successful merchants and financiers formed a rich and highly varied international stratum in Prague, a kind of new merchant or entrepreneur-money-lender patriciate. From the 1570s on, their members dominated the Old Town and Lesser Town merchant guild, and, beginning in the 1580s, they formed the core of a group of court merchants and purveyors to Emperor Rudolf II. They were, indeed, a link between the world at the imperial Court at Prague Castle and the town below it. They probably played a more important role in bringing the two circles closer together and creating a unique cultural atmosphere in the imperial metropolis than did the scholars and artists who worked at the court. Simultaneously, they maintained contacts with the university or joined local guilds. The way of life, cultural interests and building activity of members of this new patriciate proceeded along the same lines as those of the Bohemian aristocracy in their newly built Prague residences. Since they were copied immediately by the lower strata among the townspeople, the overall transformation of medieval Prague into a lively late Renaissance metropolis was encouraged. The world of the court and the aristocracy and that of the town at the foot of the Castle thus moved from contradiction to symbiosis. This was one of the leading features of Rudolfine Prague.[5]

22.3 **Cup of the guild of Lesser Town goldsmiths**
Third quarter of sixteenth century
[Prague, Národní muzeum]

22.4 Chest of the guild of Prague shearers
1609
[Prague, Muzeum hl. města Prahy]

The activities of the new patriciate is only partly recorded in archival documents, but one can draw some conclusions about them from the appearance and size of surviving Old Town houses belonging to the Hebenstraits, Nerhofs and Teufels. The size of the group is indicated by data on the numbers and significance of minorities of other nationalities among them. Around 1590, some eighty Italian merchants, stall-keepers and factors of trade firms were active in Prague. Together with Italian builders and stonemasons, they became founders of the local Italian Catholic community in 1575. They became the investors responsible for the construction of the chapel of the Assumption (1590) in the neighbourhood of the Clementinum and of the Italian Hospice (1600–17). The latter formed part of the newly founded Italian quarter on the site of one-time Lesser Town gardens below Petřín Hill. In 1609, the community of German Protestants in the Old and the New Town, set up and led by rich merchants, comprised as many as 385 families. It can be estimated that they made up some 15 to 20 per cent of the resident population of the two towns. The congregation was able to organize and carry out exacting building investments of their own, in particular the Church of St Saviour in the Old Town (1611–14), for which donations were acquired from the whole of Protestant Europe. The German Protestants in the Lesser Town took similar steps. At exactly the same time, they built their church of the Holy Trinity. Their impact was such that in 1613, the Lesser Town authorities had to pass a special bylaw that adjusted nationality relations and laid down rules for the use of the Czech and German languages in official business and during sermons.[6]

The Jews also benefited from the remarkable tolerance of Rudolfine Prague. In 1567, following repeated expulsions, they were granted an imperial charter which guaranteed them permanent domicile in the Czech lands and in the Prague ghetto. The formal acknowledgement of the jurisdiction of the Old Town in no way restricted their rapid economic rise, which was based on banking and other financial transactions. Any final obstacles were removed by a 1585 decree of the Court Chancellery that granted them permission for the free sale of merchandise and furs, which previously had been forbidden. The undisguised personal favour of Rudolf II contributed to the unique florescence of the Prague ghetto and the renown of Jewish representatives in the ranks of financiers and scholars. These matters are dealt with in more detail elsewhere in this publication.[7]

For a quarter century, Rudolf's residence at the Castle added lustre to the metropolis. This was a time of general development and substantial growth in the size of the Prague towns, which had no parallel in Europe. The towns, which around 1600 may have had as many as sixty thousand inhabitants, had many problems public health, religious conflict and politics. Contemporary sources speak eloquently of the urgency of the some of these. The cost of living had become unbearable for the lower strata of the population. There was an increase in the number of poor, tramps, beggars and homeless, without a means of subsistence, who sought refuge in the Prague towns. The reason they were admitted and tolerated can be found in reports about the long-term lack of seasonal labour, especially in the vineyards and on the burghers' suburban properties in the vicinity. In 1575 and 1585, the Diet repeatedly passed resolutions condemning the flight of rural serfs to the towns, especially to Prague. In 1585, this problem led to armed

Plebeia mulieris vestitus in Silesia.   Sponsa nubentis ornatus in Sibes.   Plebeia mulier in Bohemia.   Vir plebeius in Bohemia.

10

conflict and bloodshed between the town poor and the nobility, who came to collect their fugitive serfs from Prague. Another serious event during the early part of Rudolf's reign was the outbreak of the 'great Prague plague' in 1582. There allegedly were 30,000 casualties in Prague alone.

During Rudolf's reign, there was no substantial lessening of the contradiction between the outward appearance of prosperity and the continuing lack of political independence of the Prague towns. The monarch did make certain gestures of favour. For example, he reinstated the right to burghers' escheatage (1577), taken away in 1547, as well as the right (in the 1590s) to purchase free estate and record holdings in the land registers. But these were mere rewards for the loyalty of town representatives at the Land Diets. The same was true of the consent of the monarch and the Land Diet to the publication, in book form, of the new codification of Bohemian town law in 1579. While this publication was of considerable practical importance for the day-to-day legal life of the towns, it did not signify a substantial change in the non-independent political status of Prague.

Step by step, those to whom Rudolf II increasingly left the burden of rule once he moved to Prague began to enforce the direct subordination of the Prague towns and town councils to him and to the Court Chancellery. This was clearest in the highly sensitive area of religion. As early as in 1580, the papal nuncio, the Bishop of Piacenza, with the support of Archbishop Antonin Brus of Mohelnice, worked out a plan for the reintroduction of Catholicism in Bohemia, which was to

22.5 ABRHAAM BRUYN
Garments of the Czech and Silesian burghers
Sheet from *Imperii ac Sacerrdotii Ornatus*
Ca. 1600
[Prague, Uměleckoprůmyslové muzeum]

be initiated with a reform of Prague University. Brus' death on 28 August 1580 interrupted these plans. But no approval was given either to the 1581 demand of the Estate of knights to print, and thereby codify, the Protestant Bohemian Confession of 1575. Further conflicts occurred with the introduction of the Gregorian calendar in January 1584, which involved the intentional exclusion of the Day of Master Jan Hus and Master Jerome (6 July). In following years, this day was all the more ostentatiously celebrated in all Prague towns, which, with the exception of the Italian minority, almost exclusively acknowledged Protestantism

In Prague and in the other royal towns, public affairs grew steadily more complicated. The tendency of the people of Prague to lean towards the anti-centrist, non-Catholic Estates was to be weakened by filling the town councils of the Old and the New Town almost exclusively with aldermen chosen from the conservative Old Utraquists. Representing a minority among the townspeople, they could be persuaded to be loyal to the court and land authorities and the archbishop of Prague, and thereby to the efforts at administrative centralization and religious unification put forward by these institutions.

This approach was practised by the Prague town administration more or less consistently from 1584 until the uprising of 1618. Regularly, there would be between one and three Catholics on the Old Town Council. From 1599, the council was strenthened by exponents of the court and the Chancellery, most of them retired officials of manors or estates of the Catholic magnates, who bought property in the town and, with protection in high places, penetrated the town élite. Typical representatives included Kašpar Lukas of Lutenštejn (on the council 1599–1606), Jiří Heidelius of Razenštejn (1608–9) and František Ostrštok of Astfeld (1611–19). The new, energetic supreme chancellor, the Catholic Zdeněk Vojtěch Popel of Lobkowicz, soon after taking on the most important part in the land government (1598), managed to subordinate the town councils of the royal towns entirely to the Chancellery. In 1602, he began to interfere directly in town affairs, trying to support the re-introduction of Catholicism advocated by the monarch. The mayor of the Lesser Town, the town clerk and one of the aldermen were dismissed for not having taken part in the Corpus Christi procession. Finally, the printer Sixtus Palma Močidlanský was expelled from Bohemia for printing an anti-Catholic thesis and a song about Master Jan Hus.[8]

Despite these episodes, all attempts at re-Catholicization missed their target in the Prague towns and on the country estates of the non-Catholic nobility, for they were blocked by the Protestant majority among the Estates sitting on Land Diets and law courts. The non-Catholic Estates consistently held to the principle that 'each adhere to his religion and that on their estates each keep clergy and spiritual ministry at his own discretion'.[9] The efforts of the opposing camp and of the advocates of absolutism following the Spanish model did not even meet with unequivocal support from local Catholics until the defeat of the 1618–20 uprising. An event that occurred in 1586 speaks eloquently of the complicated situation of the time. Archbishop Martin Medek (1580–90) angered even the Emperor with his ill-considered radical attitude to such an extent that he was divested of the right to print and issue books and papal Bulls without Rudolf's consent.[10]

Nonetheless the Prague town government was, in this manner, turned into a

22.6 **Two jugs and plate in Beroun**
Second half of sixteeenth century
[Prague, Muzeum hl. města Prahy]

mere executor of orders from above or, in the best case, a herald and supporter of compromises. In this it sometimes found itself at odds with its own public. Ambitious members of the political patriciate were thus able to become spokesmen for radical opposition views and found themselves enthusiastically received even among members of both aristocratic Estates. These politicians took advantage of the crisis in 1608–9 and assumed influential positions in the organizations of Estate Defenders and Directors as representatives of the burghers' Estate.

Rudolf II's Letter of Majesty of 1609, and the accompanying political documents, expressly incorporated in its provisions the people of Prague, the burghers of other royal towns and the serfs and brought about a perceptible relaxation in the public life of the towns. But it did not mean a reversal of the existing trends in power politics. In the first place, it did not mean any change in the composition or status of the town governments. Their continuing subordination to the Chancellery and to Chancellor Lobkowicz soon caused further tension and renewed endeavours to change the religious and political conditions in the Prague towns, as we have seen. This struggle had many tragicomic episodes. For example, all members of the Old Town Guild of Furriers were imprisoned in 1615 for failing to take part in a Catholic procession. A year later, another episode proved more serious. A sentence of death for offending the monarch was pronounced, but not implemented, on a representative of the Committee of Thirty Defenders, Natanael Vodňanský of Uračov. Such episodes give an idea of the conflicts at a time when the centrist offensive against the freedoms of the Estates and what remained of self-government was intensifying.[11]

It would be incorrect to stress the negative aspects of life in the Prague towns at this time without paying appropriate attention to positive ones. For example, although acts of violence, street battles, robberies and looting were recorded by contemporary witnesses and appear in detail in older specialist publications and even in fiction,[12] public celebration and festivities more strikingly reflected the cultural face of the time. They occurred very frequently and in many forms and roused exceptional interest among the inhabitants.

Festive processions would pass through Prague whenever the monarch or his relatives, high-born guests or foreign embassies arrived, as well as on the occasion of aristocratic funerals. The numbers of horses and carriages involved were a closely observed matter of prestige. At times when foreign princes visited or during aristocratic weddings, the courtyards of Prague Castle and, chiefly, the Old Town Square became the venue of tournaments, attractions and allegorical presentations. These included the exhibition of exotic beasts, scenes from Antiquity, a staging of the War of the Czech Amazons and lifelike stagings of eruptions of Mount Etna. Among the participants were imperial courtiers and high-standing officers of state as well as ordinary burghers and crowds of the town poor. In the first period of his reign, Rudolf II himself liked to take part in these festivities – he would welcome prominent visitors outside the city walls, often going as far as the church of St Pancras. He would spend entire days watching the tournaments and plays as participant, spectator, guest of honour, patron and generous Maecenas. If we leave aside the no less frequent ecclesiastical and religious festivities, the sequence of Prague celebrations of this kind, initiated by the

22.7 **Tile with Miverva**
Second half of sixteenth
century
[Prague Národní muzeum]

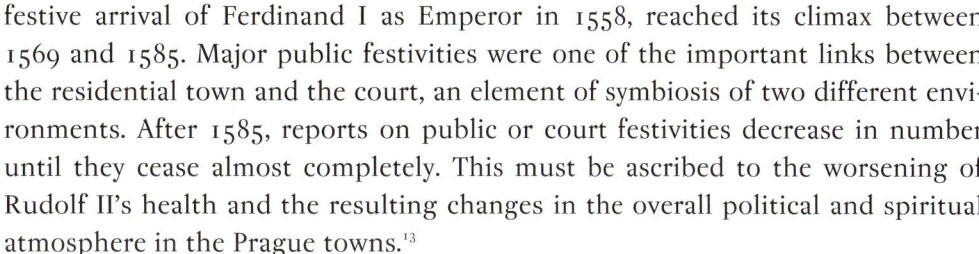

festive arrival of Ferdinand I as Emperor in 1558, reached its climax between 1569 and 1585. Major public festivities were one of the important links between the residential town and the court, an element of symbiosis of two different environments. After 1585, reports on public or court festivities decrease in number until they cease almost completely. This must be ascribed to the worsening of Rudolf II's health and the resulting changes in the overall political and spiritual atmosphere in the Prague towns.[13]

In contrast, there appears at that very time increasing information on public activities organized by the important foreign minorities. From the 1570s, these groups had begun to form associations in the imperial residential town. The Italian minority, in particular, gathered around the Italian Congregation and retained its language and religious and cultural exclusivity far into the seventeenth century.[14] The German minority underwent a somewhat different process. In the kindred cultural and religious atmosphere of the Protestant town agglomeration, they had undergone a long period of assimilation beginning with the Hussite Revolution. In the 1570s, they grew stronger as the result of major migration, acquiring property and increasing in influence without losing their language. They assumed active roles in public life, and in 1627 their Catholic members achieved full linguistic and political equality in the entire country through the Renewed Land Constitution.

All of these aspects of public life contributed to Prague becoming a city which, to a large extent, was unique in the century under discussion. People in the individual towns of the Prague agglomeration were affected differently as regards life style and culture. Prague was a city where various denominations, national groups and social strata came into contact (and conflict) to an extent scarcely attained elsewhere. This was due in part to the size of the city; no other city in the Czech lands came close in terms of population. There was space enough for various ways of life to develop side by side and to enrich and complement one another.

The smaller Central European towns were mostly mono-denominational or had only small and inconspicuous religious minorities, the Jews being one exception. The dominant denomination largely determined the way of life, as well as the pattern of private consumption and culture.[15] The burghers of the predominantly Lutheran towns of Bohemia and the surrounding countries based their private lives mainly on literary culture. Inventories of legacies and wills are the main sources for information about the townspeople's private life. They contain records of household goods and crockery, clothing and textiles of all kinds and furniture, as well as cash and often considerable collections of jewels. Many such documents include lists of books in burghers' libraries.[16] The cultivation of books was less important in the Catholic towns, and after the re-introduction of Catholicism in towns with a strong Protestant book tradition – for instance, in Austria – this rapidly dwindled. In such cases, the tradition of home picture galleries of various kinds asserted itself with greater intensity.[17]

Rudolfine Prague was unique in merging these two traditions and developing them intensively. It is remarkable that the Prague towns were perhaps the only place in the region we are dealing with where the culture of consort music developed broadly in burghers' homes. This synthesis of books, pictures and music,

22.8 **Pint vessel with figures of the apostles**
Ca. 1600
[Prague, Muzeum hlavního
města Prahy]

[295]

22.9 **Pint vessel with the coat-of-arms of the Old Town painters' guild and symbols of the planet**
1599
[Prague, Uměleckoprůmyslové muzeum]

common around 1600 especially in the Old Town and some circles of the New and the Lesser Town, existed otherwise only in the aristocratic setting. The wealth of cultural activities of the burghers of Prague renders proof of their individual and group self-confidence, which manifested itself in the spheres of culture, social prestige and luxury rather than politics.[18]

Cultural activity is further proof of how flexibly the Prague townspeople managed to avail themselves of the influences which came from the governor's and imperial court, as well as from the academic sector and centres of trade and information exchange with other countries. None of the important towns in the surrounding regions, such as Vratislav, Olomouc and Vienna, demonstrated a similar breadth of cultural activities. The burghers' flourishing private culture was not determined merely or primarily by property ownership. We can find remarkable cultural collections and traces of many-sided interests in Prague

among craftsmen. This conformed to the social and occupational stratification of cultural interests and activities in the smaller 'rural' towns of Bohemia.[19]

In the Prague agglomeration of the time, relatively few all-city cultural investments existed. This corresponds to the situation in other Czech towns and resulted from impoverishment following the repressions after 1547 and the harsh tax burden imposed after 1567. This low level of investment was also due to the loss of political power. It is entirely symptomatic that the most important official communal building – the Lesser Town town hall – was funded and built by the colony of Lesser Town Italians. Building construction was carried out by outstanding individuals (for example, the Krocín Fountain on the Old Town Square) or special interest groups (religious congregations as investors in Prague religious architecture).[20] The official representation of the Prague towns was limited to the preparation of public festivities or participation in festivities held at the instigation of others.[21]

Let us take a closer look at the cultural life of the Prague burghers. Descriptions of legacies tell us that in the Old Town in the mid-sixteenth century, books were to be found in a quarter of all households. By the time of the Battle of the White Mountain in 1621, they appeared in almost 60 per cent of those burghers' inventories which have been investigated. We have extensive source material also for the New Town. There slightly fewer volumes were found in burghers' libaries – roughly on the level of other Bohemian and Moravian royal towns – i.e., in between 10 to 38 per cent of households. That, in itself, indicates the burghers' exceptional interest in books, higher than, for example, in Cracow and comparable with Amiens, a rich town in northern France.[22]

The exceptional level of the Old Town burghers' interest in books becomes clear if we realize the considerable size of the burghers' libraries (10.6 per cent of libraries had more than a hundred volumes) and the relatively broad range of subject-matter. The greater part of the books had been printed recently, only a minimum number of books were several decades old, and they came from a variety of printing houses all over Europe. The respectable Bohemian publishing houses formed an important, but hardly dominant sector of suppliers on the book shelves. There were immense book imports, especially from German towns and also from Venice, the Netherlands and even France. It must be regarded as an outstanding achievement on the part of Prague printers and publishers that they managed to hold their place in this competition. The language barrier did not protect them. The burghers, most of whom had attended Prague, countryside and foreign Latin schools, enjoyed reading Latin and German. The popular German Lutheran literature – Martin Luther himself being relatively the most widely read author – was represented in the burghers' libraries around 1600, primarily in German editions.

In addition to the broad range of religious literature, the people of Prague read ancient literature, authors included in school and university teaching and, naturally, the works of the sixteenth-century European humanists. Among these, Erasmus and Melanchton enjoyed popularity. More than a tenth of the volume of libraries was taken up by history and political as well as geographical literature. This was especially true of large libraries, where the share of religious and

22.10 FABIÁN PULÉŘ
Copying workshop of Jan
Táborský
Illuminations from *Česky
Brod Hymn Book* (detail)
1552–57
[Prague, Národní knihovna]

moralist literature was the smallest. Unequivocally dominant in this category were key local works, in Czech translation and published in Prague, dealing with early modern European history and cosmography. Even though the horizon of literary thinking of the majority of the Prague burghers tended to be the borders of the Czech lands, the most educated among them were able to follow the dramatic development and transformation of Renaissance science around the world.

Dramatic political upheavals, emigration and devastating ransacking by the army left their powerful mark on the burghers' private culture between 1620 and 1648. However, recent research suggests that there was remarkable continuity in the character of their libraries in the period following the Battle of the White Mountain. Even religious literature shows few changes. Although the works of Luther and Jan Hus disappeared from the shelves, Protestant books continued to dominate, and the works of Catholic and anti-Reformation authors found their way into the Prague burghers' libraries only very slowly.

In the context of literary activities, records of Prague libraries are of little help, but use can be made of the bibliographies of small works of Latin poetry for special purposes. These were compiled and concentrated in *Festschrift*s (commemorative editions) and dedicated to patrons or honoured persons of different type. They represent the core proper of the literary activity of the burghers in the period prior to the Battle of the White Mountain. The intelligentsia at the Prague seats of higher learning collaborated with certain printers who had close relations with the University (Georg Melantrich of Aventinum, Daniel Adam of Veleslavín) in publishing translations and original works.[23]

Research about music in the sixteenth and early seventeenth centuries traditionally has focused on the specific role of the Czech Utraquist Brethren of Literates. We now know that these men of letters – chiefly in the Prague towns –

22.11 FABIÁN PULÉŘ
Copying workshop of Jan
Táborský
Illuminations from *Český
Brod Hymn Book* (detail)
1552–57
[Prague, Národní knihovna]

22.12 FABIÁN PULÉŘ
Copying workshop of Jan
Táborský
Illuminations from *Český
Brod Hymn Book* (detail)
1552–57
[Prague, Národní knihovna]

were far more involved in the supranational flow of European music than had been judged. The music centres of the imperial court strongly influenced the level of appreciation of listeners, and the Prague public took an interest in new trends in music. As a result, Prague musical life was not limited to the brethren choirs. There existed a rich structure of musical ensembles, ranging from Jewish orchestras to music groups of specialized schools, ad hoc burghers' orchestras and famous individual organists. In addition, a phenomenon developed which was so far unknown in Central Europe: burghers' home consort music, circles of players of instrumental music who performed in private for the burghers' families. All this points to a rich musical life in Rudolfine Prague.[24]

Important changes occurred in Prague musical life in the decades of the Thirty Years' War. Professionally performed Italian opera appeared during the 1620s, and there was the rapid development of Catholic church music. An indication of this is the rapid decline of the number of musical instruments recorded in burghers' legacies. Permanent changes in music appreciation were not recorded until after the middle of the seventeenth century, however.

About one fifth of Prague burghers in the period before the Battle of the White Mountain had pictures or graphics hanging in their homes.[25] At the beginning of the period under consideration, the sources reveal only occasional pictures. In the first decades of the seventeenth century, there already existed numerous larger picture galleries, more than a third of which held more than ten pictures, in isolated cases several dozen works. The fashion of setting up home galleries may have spread from the 1560s, and by the end of the 1580s quite large picture collections existed in burghers' houses. A key place of growing importance was reserved for the private burgher's portrait. There was an increasing enthusiasm for portraits of the monarch or public figures, including Rudolf himself, Luther, the Hussite General Jan Žižka and various ancient and contemporary European rulers. The first landscapes found their way into the burghers' homes around the year 1600. They were related to vedutas, which had been popular earlier, and to painted maps. By contrast, there was a radical decline in allegorical, historical or mythological paintings, and the greatest decrease is recorded in religious pictures for the period preceding the Battle of the White Mountain. In structure, themes and development, the picture collections in Prague differed considerably from those in Olomouc and even more so from those in Cracow, two metropolises for which comparable materials exist, since they were affected by the Counter-Reformation more harshly and earlier than Prague.

The Thirty Years' War did not restrict the development of art in the burghers' private lives. On the contrary, Prague became involved in the network of international trade in art, much to the displeasure of the strong local colony of painters, and this involvement intensified as time passed. In themes and types of pictures, Prague became linked more closely to the important centres of Italian, Netherlandish and French art.[26]

To this day, we know very little about the burghers' activities in commissioning and collecting small sculpture, medals and coins or about their interest in graphics. But it is clear that even in these spheres the Prague towns played an important role. Between 1550 and 1560 Prague was a very lively centre of culture. It reacted intensely and across a wide array of intellectual and artistic impulses coming from all sides and gave them novel shapes. This continued to be the case even after the Battle of the White Mountain, possibly due to the primarily private nature of patronage. After 1620, however, radical changes were introduced in the education system. Part of the town élite left, and many traditional cultural links with other countries were severed. It took a number of decades before the resulting changes were generally accepted.

22.13 FABIÁN PULÉŘ
Copying workshop of Jan Táborský
Illuminations from *Česky Brod Hymn Book* (detail)
1552-57
[Prague, Národní knihovna]

1. Basic facts are still only available in W. W. Tomek, *Dějepis města Prahy*, vols XI–XII (Prague, 1897-1901), and in the outdated survey by J. Janáček et al., *Dějiny Prahy* (Prague, 1964). No comprehensive bibliography of the numerous more recent studies of the history of modern Prague yet exists.

   The rapid renewal of the Prague towns on the left bank of the river in the Jagellonian period is convincingly evoked by the systematic research summed up in material by SÚRPMO (typewritten reports deposited at the Specialized Institute for the Reconstruction of Historical Towns and Places, Prague).

2. A sceptical evaluation of the economic and social situation in the Prague towns and their position in Central Europe in the first half of the sixteenth century is given by J. Janáček, 'Města v českých zemích v 16. století', *Hosp. Dějiny*, 4 (1979), 165-203; idem, 'Konec politické slávy pražských měst' in *Praha na úsvitu nových dějin: Čtvero knih o Praze* (Prague, 1988), pp. 8-9. A different theory is put forward by J. Pešek, 'Prag auf dem Weg zur kaiserlichen Residenz (1483-1583)' in E. Engel, K. Lambrecht, N. Nogossek (eds), *Metropolen im Wandel*, pp. 213-23.

3. J. Janáček, *České dějiny*, vol. I/2 (Prague, 1984), pp. 215-332; F. Roubík, 'Královští hejtmanů v městech pražských v letech 1546-1785' in *Miscellany on the History of the Capital City of Prague*, vol. VII (1933), pp. 121-89; idem, 'Královští rychtáři v pražských a jiných českých městech' in *Miscellany on the History of the Capital City of Prague*, VI (1930), pp. 265-356.

4. V. Ledvinka, 'Dům pánů z Hradce pod Stupni', *Folia Historica Bohemica*, 10 (Prague, 1986), 269-316; idem, 'Funkce venkovských rezidencí a pražských paláců jihočeské šlechty v 16. a 17. století', Acta Universitatis Purkynianae, Phil. et hist. I (*Opera historica* 1 [1992], pp. 28-41); V. Ledvinka, B. Mráz and V. Vlnas, *Pražské paláce* (Prague, 1995), pp. 14-19 passim.

5. The effect and importance of the social group here called the 'entrepreneur-money-lender patriciate' need to be studied further. Data were gathered by J. Janáček in *Dějiny obchodu v předbělohorské Praze* (Prague, 1955), pp. 298-375. Janáček called the group a 'merchant patriciate'. On this problem, see also A. Kostlán, V. Ledvinka and J. Pešek, 'Zemský prubíř Pavel Griemiller z Třebska', *Pražský sborník historický*, 19 (1986), 103-39.

6. While the Italian minority in Prague has received scholarly attention, the German (and other) minorities are mostly unstudied. See K. Chytil, 'Mistři lugánští v Čechách v XVI.století', *Ročenka Kruhu pro pěstování dějin umění za r.1924*, pp. 32-66; K. Šmrha, 'Vlašští stavitelé v Praze a jejich druzi (1510-1620)', *Umění*, 24 (1943), 159-84; J. Janáček, 'Italové v předbělohorské Praze (1526-1620)', *Pražský sborník historický*, 16 (1983), 77-118; P. Preiss, *Italští umělci v Praze. Renesance, manýrismus, baroko* (Prague, 1986); F. Hrejsa, 'U Salvátora: Z dějin evangelické církve v Praze (1609-1632)' (Prague, 1930); Janáček (note 5),pp. 344-74.

7. See the essay on the Jewish Town of Prague in the present volume.

8. For Rudolfine Prague. see J. Janáček, *Rudolf II a jeho doba* (Prague, 1987), pp. 206-21, 345-65; E. Fučíková, 'Praha v době vlády Rudolfa II' in E. Fučíková, B. Bukovinská and I. Muchka, *Umění na dvoře Rudolfa II* (Prague, 1988), pp. 29-59; Z. Hojda, 'Prag um 1600 als multikulturelle Stadt: Hof – Adel – Bürgertum – Kirche' in Engel, Lambrecht and Nogossek (eds) (see note 2), pp. 225-32. On the development of the town administration see, in addition to the older literature, J. Douša, 'Seznamy staroměstských konšelů z let 1547-1650', *Pražský sborník historický*, 14 (1981), pp.65-119.

9. This declaration by Vilém Malovec of Malovice, spokesman for the Estate of Knights at the Land Diet of 1585 is quoted in Tomek (note 1), vol. XII, p. 322.

10. Tomek (note 1) vol. XII, pp. 328-29.

11. J. Dvorský, 'Praha v českém stavovském povstání (1618-1620)', *Pražský sborník historický*, 10 (1977), pp. 51-120; F. Kavka, *Bílá hora a české dějiny* (Prague, 1962), pp. 95-102, 157-58.

12. The picture of the Rudolfine period as reflected in historiography, belles-lettres and so on has not been studied, although it is a topic of great interest.

13. One of the regular conferences of the Archives of the City of Prague was devoted to festivities in Prague history. A miscellany, *Pražské slavnosti a velké výstavy* was published as *Documenta Pragensia*, 12 (Prague, 1995).

14. See above, note 6. The maintenance of artistic traditions by several generations of Italian families living in Prague until almost the end of the seventeenth century is discussed in Preiss (note 6), pp. 134-41, 274-85.

15. See J. Pešek *Měšťanská vzdělanost a kultura v předbělohorských Čechách 1546-1620 (Všední dny*

kulturního života) (Prague, 1993). On the history of religion, see F. Hrubý, 'Luterství a kalvinismus na Moravě před Bílou horou', *Český časopis historický*, 40 (1934), 265-309; 41 (1935), 1-40; *idem*, 'Luterství a novoutrakvismus v českých zemích v 16. A 17. Století', *Český časopis historický*, 45 (1939), 31-44.

16. Lib.cit., pp. 64-103, where further literature regarding Bohemian towns is given.

17. See Roman Sandgruber, 'Alltag und materielle Kulture: Städtischer Lebensstil und bürgerliche Wohnkultur am Beispiel zweier oberösterreicher Städte des 16. Jahrhunderts', in Alfred Kohler abd Heinrich Lutz (eds), *Wiener Studien zur Geschichte der Neuzeit 14: Alltag im 16. Jahrhundert* (Vienna, 1987), pp. 23-44.

18. See J. Pešek (note 15), pp. 119-30.

19. See chiefly O. Fejtová, 'Lounské měšťanské knihovny v době předbělohorské, *Sborník okresního archivu v Lounech*, 4 (1991), 3-23.

20. See most recently, Preiss (note 6), pp. 99-101. For the Italian Chapel in the Old Town, the Italian Hospice with the church of St Charles Borromeo in the Lesser Town and the Lesser Town Lutheran church of the Holy Trinity, lib.cit. pp. 88-98 and note 6 above.

21. See above, note 13 and, in particular, V. Ledvinka, 'Šlechtická svatba v Praze r.1579 (K charakteru aristokratických slavností české renesance)', *Documenta Pragensia*, 12, 105-13; Janáček, (note 8), pp. 139-40, 157-68.

22. J. Pešek, 'Pražské knihy kšaftů a inventářů', *PSH*, 15 (1982), pp. 63-92; *idem* (note 15), J. Pešek, pp. 67ff; R. Žurek, 'Ksiegozbiory mieszczan Krakowskich XVII wieku', *Rocznik Biblioteki PAN w Krakowie*, 13 (1967), 21-51; A. Labarre, *Le Livre dans la vie aminoise du seizième siècle (1503-1576)* (Paris and Louvain, 1971).

23. See M. Svatoš (ed.), *Dějiny Univerzity Karlovy I, 1347/48-1622* (Prague, 1995), pp. 241-45.

24. See the essay by J. Koupa in J. Černý *et al.*, *Hudba v českých dějinách* (Prague, 1983), pp. 81-141; J. Pešek, 'Z pražské hudební kultury měšťanskho soukromí před Bílou horou', *Hudební věda*, 20 (1983), 242-56.

25. J. Pešek, 'Obrazy, Grafiky a jejich majitelé v předbělohorské Praze', *Umění*, 39 (1991), 269-83.

26. See Z. Hojda, 'Výtvarná díla v domech staroměstských měšťanů v letech 1627-1740 (Příspěvek k dějinám kultury barokní Prahy I-II)', *Pražský sborník historický*, 26 (1993), 38-102; 27 (1994), 47-104.

The Jewish Town in Prague

JIRINA ŠEDINOVÁ

No picture of Prague, its history and culture, would be complete without a mention of its Jewish quarter, which has formed an inextricable part of the city since the Middle Ages. A particularly important period in the history of Jewish Prague is the last third of the sixteenth and beginning of the seventeenth centuries, traditionally known as its Golden Age or Great Renaissance.

The Jewish settlement on the right bank of the Moldau, next to the Old Town, probably came into being in the middle of the twelfth century. The new settlement gradually grew up around the Old School in the district of the Holy Spirit and, from the thirteenth century onwards, around the Old-New synagogue and, later, around the Pinkas synagogue. These sites became the core of the district first known as the Jewish Street (Platea Judaeorum) and, from the seventeenth century onwards, as the Jewish Town, also referred to by the Italian title of 'the Ghetto'.[1]

During the sixteenth and seventeenth centuries, the Jewish Town continued to exist within the confines of its medieval boundaries. It consisted of one main street with several smaller ones leading from it, the whole quarter being separated from the surrounding areas by four gates. The dual purpose of these gates was to protect the Jews from attacks and to isolate the inhabitants of the ghetto from those outside in accordance with church regulations.

Over the centuries, the number of inhabitants of the original 'Jewish Street' grew, as did the number of houses and synagogues. In the final quarter of the thirteenth century, the Old-New synagogue, known in those times as the New, or Great, synagogue, was built. This was followed by several more prayer houses. In 1535, the synagogue built by the patrician Horowitz-Hořovský family, which later became known as the Pinkas synagogue, was completed. The High synagogue and the Maisel synagogue were built in 1568 and 1592, respectively. The building of both these Renaissance synagogues was paid for by the mayor Mordecai Maisel. At the very end of the sixteenth century, the Munka synagogue, later known as the Wechsler synagogue, was built, followed by the Cikán synagogue in 1613 and the Velkodvorská synagogue, built in 1627 by Jacob Bassevi of Treuenberg. Neither the Cikán synagogue nor the Velkodvorská synagogue, both of which contained Baroque features, survived the demolition of the ghetto at the turn of the nineteenth century. The only synagogue in the Baroque style to survive to this day is the Klaus synagogue.

Synagogues, which were always built in the latest style and only rebuilt or altered if damaged or ruined by fire, reflect the architectural development of the whole ghetto. Gothic architecture was gradually joined in the sixteenth and first half of the seventeenth centuries by buildings in the Renaissance and early Baroque styles, especially at the time when the Jewish community was run by Mordecai Maisel and Jacob Bassevi of Treuenberg. Both Maisel and Bassevi bought land and built for themselves as well as for the Jewish community. Maisel became part of Prague legend not only as a contemporary of Rabbi Loew but also as a public bene-

factor. After the year 1623, in which Jews were able, for a low price, to acquire houses and land which had been confiscated from non-Catholics and which lay outside the boundaries of the ghetto, Bassevi did, albeit on a smaller scale, what his powerful patron Albrecht of Wallenstein had done on the opposite bank of the Moldau. He built himself a Renaissance palace on open land where the original houses had been demolished.

With the exception of the Jewish Town Hall, Bassevi's palace was the grandest secular building in the Prague ghetto. The other inhabitants of the ghetto, including officials of the Jewish community and important scholars, lived in the cramped confines of the small houses built next to one another lining the narrow streets. Only on rare occasions did the wealthier Jews succeed in obtaining permission to buy a house situated outside the 'Jewish Street'. The council of the Old Town opposed such purchases as they ran contrary to their efforts to get rid of the Jews and the competition they posed. It was not until the 1620s, when the Czech Royal Chamber allowed the sale of thirty-nine confiscated, so-called Liechtenstein houses to Jews, that this strong opposition subsided. In spite of this temporary improvement of the housing situation, which was, however, only available to wealthier Jews, the Jewish Town remained overcrowded.[2]

Evidence of the existence of the Jewish Town in Prague and its alternating prosperity and stagnation is provided not only by the building of synagogues but also by the Old Jewish Cemetery, which was also situated within the grounds of the ghetto. Its inhabitants were buried here for almost 350 years, from the first half of the fifteenth century until 1787, when Josef II forbade burials within residential areas. The Hebrew inscriptions on grand tombstones and simple headstones alike tell of the families and social positions of those buried, of their material wealth, their professions and their involvement in public life. In some cases, they describe the sudden and often violent death met by the deceased during one of the tragic events in the ghetto's history. The headstones themselves gradually became small poetic works in which biblical and Talmudic language alternates with elements of everyday speech.

In 1541, Ferdinand I issued a decree on the expulsion of Jews from Prague. This did not, however, lead to a complete exodus. Nonetheless, many Jewish homes stood empty with the threat of further measures being taken against Jews by the city's authorities and the imperial court. This culminated in the issuing of a second decree ordering the eviction of Jews from the whole of the Bohemian kingdom. This lasted until 1564, when Ferdinand's successor Maximilian II abolished his father's decree. As soon as Maximilian's decision to abolish the eviction orders and formally confirm and even increase the existing privileges of the Jews was made known, life in the ghetto returned to its former pace.

It was then that the aforementioned 'Golden Age' occurred: during the last three decades of the sixteenth century and beginning of the seventeenth centuries. The favourable political, economic and cultural climate enabled considerable development within the Jewish community in Prague, and during this period it became one of the most important centres of the Jewish world. This relatively calm time, which was nevertheless interrupted by the Christian burghers' attempts to drive the Jews out of Prague, came to an end in 1618 during the uprising of the Bohemian Estates and the beginning of the Thirty Years' War. During that war, Jews were protected by the Emperor, for whom they presented a regular source of income which was need-

ed for military purposes. For this reason, Jews were also given certain privileges, but each adverse change in the fortunes of the Habsburgs meant fresh uncertainties for them.

The Jewish Town in Prague always held a leading position in relation to the other Jewish communities within the Bohemian kingdom. Prague's Jewish community had the largest population, its economy was the most developed, and in its organization it was the most stable. It had a traditionally strong self-governing body and a group of representatives with a mayor at its head, which represented the Jewish community in dealings with the municipal bodies and the state administration. Following the wave of evictions of Jews from Bohemian and Moravian towns commencing in the middle of the fifteenth century and continuing through to the beginning of the 1500s – a direct result of the weakening power of the ruler and pressure from city councils who desired the removal of the economic competition posed by Jewish tradesmen, craftsmen and financiers – Prague (apart from Kolín) was the only royal city in the Bohemian lands where Jews were permitted to live.

One of the main functions of the representatives of the Jewish community in Prague was the regular collection of Jewish taxes and special payments set by the parliament. The dominant administrative role of the Jewish community in Prague was thus reinforced and maintained until the second half of the seventeenth century, when the organization of rural Jewish communities in Bohemia became separate, although it took a long time for these communities to become wholly independent of their centre in Prague. There exist a number of documents connected with the practicalities of tax collecting which contain information about the structure of the Jewish communities, the social divisions within them and the conflicts between several wealthy groups on the one hand and, on the other hand, the majority of the inhabitants of the Jewish ghettos, who were becoming increasingly poorer.[3]

The central role of representing the Jewish communities was usually taken by wealthy business families who had approximately the same social standing as the Christian patriciate. As suppliers of imported luxury goods, tradesmen and moneylenders, they came into contact with burghers, the nobility and even the Royal Chamber. In return for their services, they were given special rights which enabled them to trade in markets at home as well as abroad, to expand their financial services and other business activities. They were also afforded special privileges which ensured them leading positions within the Jewish communities. The position of 'court factor' or 'court Jew' came into existence in the Bohemian lands in the sixteenth century. During Prague's Great Renaissance, the post of mayor was held by two court Jews: Mordecai Maisel, Rudolf II's financier, who died in 1601, and Jacob Bassevi of Treuenberg, who died in 1634. After the death of Rudolf II, Bassevi served his brother Matthias as well as Ferdinand II, who in 1622 made him the first Jew in the Bohemian lands to be promoted to the rank of nobleman.

The fate of Jacob Bassevi is typical of the rise and fall from favour which constantly threatened the position of court Jews. Bassevi provided valuable financial services not only to the Emperor but also to Albrecht of Wallenstein and the vice-regent in Bohemia the Prince of Liechtenstein. Together with Albrecht of Wallenstein and the Dutch banker Jan de Witte, Bassevi played a part in the coinage of counterfeit, so-called 'long' coins. As a result of this, he was imprisoned in 1631 and his property confiscated. Upon his release, he moved to Albrecht of Wallenstein's

23.1 PERLSTICKEER FAMILY
Embroidered curtains from
the Staronová (Old New)
Synagogue
1592
[Prague, Jewish Museum]

estate in Jičín, where he served as the Duke's court factor. Following Albrecht's murder in 1634, he fled to Mladá Boleslav, where he died. He was buried in the Jewish cemetery there. As mayor of Prague's Jewish community, Bassevi not only contributed to building activities and the improvement of life in the ghetto but also used his influence to protect Jews from the Emperor's armies.

The fortunes of Mordecai Maisel's life were somewhat more favourable. He soon reached a leading position in the representation of Prague's Jewish community and received a number of personal privileges in return for his services to Rudolf II. The most important of these included the building of his synagogue, permission to have his own banner and the right to manage his property as he wished. On the basis of this latter privilege bestowed upon him in 1598, Maisel, who had no children of his own, made a willleaving all his property to his wife and his brother's family. However, the Emperor lost no time in annulling his charter so that immediately after Maisel's death all his property, which according to various reports of the time amounted to half a million gold coins, was confiscated as escheat.[4]

Maisel and Bassevi became symbols of the prosperity of the wealthy and privileged few in contrast to the masses of shopkeepers, retailers and the poorest peddlars, as well as minor craftsmen in the ghettos, all of whom worked for the needs of the Jewish community. The situation in which the poorer Jewish people found themselves had its roots in the medieval church decrees which stated that Jews could only take an active part in the city's economic life in the spheres of trade and finance. The order forbidding Jews to carry out any other professions included the practising of crafts, with the exception of those which were essential for life within the ghetto. This meant that the Prague ghetto had its own Jewish butchers, tailors, shoemakers, glassmakers and other craftsmen who gradually set up their own guilds similar to Christian guilds. The Jews could only sell their wares outside the Jewish Town during exceptionally favourable times, and even then they soon encountered the hostile attitudes of the city's craft guilds and trade corporations. One such favourable period was the reign of Rudolf II, during which Jews were able to extend the sale of their goods beyond the confines of the ghetto. There were even several goldsmiths active in the ghetto at this time. A similar situation occurred during the Thirty Years' War, when the loyalty of the Jews and their financial support was of great importance to the ruler. Thus, in 1623 and 1627, Ferdinand II issued edicts enabling all Jews in Bohemia to expand their trading activities throughout the whole kingdom, as well as allowing them to learn and practise crafts which had previously been forbidden. The most important part of these edicts was the right to settle anywhere in the kingdom and the declaration that Jews should never be banished from the land.[5]

The differences in the social structure of the Jewish communities became even more pronounced during the political and accompanying economic changes in the 1600s. As well as the danger which Jewish inhabitants were faced with throughout the Thirty Years' War, the disruption of the production of agricultural produce and urban goods, the restriction of local trade and the stoppage or significant restrictions on international trade, Jews were put under increased financial pressure by the state, which required extra resources to conduct the war. With their permanent position of 'servants of the Chamber', more was demanded of the Jews. The privileges which were supposed to ensure them a high level of protection and support

their involvement in trade and other permitted branches of business were of no consequence when it came to paying the contributions set by the court's fiscal offices. The Jews' very existence was also under threat, not only from hostile soldiery but also from attacks by the poor from local towns. Such situations arose in Prague during the invasion by the Passau army in 1611 and then in 1620 in the days following the Battle of the White Mountain, when the inhabitants of the ghetto, considered to be allies of the enemy, became the victims of the angry Prague-dwellers' aggression. In November 1620, the ghetto was spared violent attacks and plundering thanks to the protection of the Emperor's triumphant army. The Jews had to pay for this protection and their relative security throughout the war.

The stance adopted by the Habsburg rulers towards Jews during the Thirty Years' War was two-sided. On the one hand, the Habsburgs granted them certain rights and privileges (it being in their own interests to do so), yet on the other hand Jews were subject to various restrictive measures which were increased after the victory of the Counter-Reformation following the Battle of the White Mountain. In the religious sphere, this meant the compulsory attendance of Jesuit sermons for Jews and - something which was a much more sensitive issue for the religious life of the Jewish community - the censorship and frequent confiscation of Hebrew books. These restrictions placed upon Prague Jewry were not lifted even when, just before the end of the war, the Emperor formally acknowledged the Jews' support by recognizing and extending their privileges, nor were they abolished after the end of the war, the last weeks of which were concentrated in Prague, which was surrounded by the Swedish army. The Jews played a significant part in defending the city while it was under Swedish siege, being actively involved in the building and repair of the city's ramparts and fortifications as well as providing ammunition and a firefighting service.[6]

The flourishing of the imperial court in Prague in the last quarter of the sixteenth and beginning of the seventeenth centuries during the reign of Rudolf II also provided a new impetus for the development of cultural life in Prague's Jewish Town. Prague, having the largest and most privileged Jewish community, being the administrative and representative centre of Jews in the Bohemian lands, the 'city and mother in Israel', soon became one of the main centres of Ashkenazi culture. Throughout the centuries, Prague was the base for a number of eminent scholars who were appointed to various posts in the chief rabbi's office or as rectors of the Talmudic school. Written works by authorities on religious matters often addressed questions of everyday life. This was particularly the case with sermons and collections of *Responsa*, which describe real cases from the standpoint of religious law, thus contributing to the creation of a complete picture of life in the ghetto, including cultural and artistic activity. A considerable number of these works became widely known thanks to the activities of several Jewish printers, working in Prague from the beginning of the 1500s, who were responsible for printing a wide range of books representing all genres of Ashkenazi literature. The works of leading authors have survived almost exclusively in book form. Manuscripts which were kept by the authors' descendants, students and successors were often destroyed during the unsettled times of war or in fires. It was during the great fire in the Prague ghetto on 21 June 1689 that Rabbi Loew's manuscripts were destroyed together with a number of first editions of his works.[7]

The favourable political situation during the reigns of Maximilian II and Rudolf II attracted a large number of people from various European countries to Prague, including Jews from Italy and the Netherlands, where a number of families from Sephardic communities settled following the eviction of Jews from the Pyrenese peninsula. The atmosphere of relative calm and tolerance during this period allowed Jews to establish contacts more freely with practitioners of Renaissance science and culture in the sphere of the Imperial court. Such contacts were established primarily by scholars as well as Jewish financiers, tradesmen and suppliers of goods. Apart from concentrating on the main discipline of religious law, scholars, who were the principal creators of traditional culture, also turned their attention to grammatical and philosophical studies, mysticism and, occasionally, poetry, although always within the boundaries of traditional Judaism. This sphere included synagogal poetry, such as Avigdor Kara's elegy commemorating the Easter pogrom of 1389, Abraham ben Avigdor Kara's invocatory psalm inspired by the eviction of Jews in 1541, Solomon Ephraim Luntshitz's elegy written in memory of the invasion by the Passau army in 1611, Yom Tov Lipman Heller's elegy commemorating the uprising of the Bohemian Estates and the Battle of the White Mountain in 1620, or the invocations written by Aaron Simon Spira for sermons when Prague was besieged by the Swedish army in 1648.[8] As is evident from the above examples, all of these works arose in response to unfortunate historical events. Through non-Jewish scholars and from their Sephardic co-believers whose cultural sphere had a stronger secular leaning, the Jews in Prague became acquainted with elements of Renaissance and humanist thought, which had hitherto been foreign and often unacceptable to the traditional disciplines of rabbinic culture in the Ashkenazi sphere.

Undoubtedly the best-known figure of Prague's Great Renaissance was Judah Liwa ben Bezalel, otherwise known as Rabbi Loew or the Prague Maharal, whose approximate dates are 1520-1609. Rabbi Loew became a symbol of the Golden Age of the Prague ghetto mainly due to the fact that together with Mayor Maisel, he became part of Prague legend as worker of wonders and creator of the Golem. Rabbi Loew's intellectual significance lies primarily in his work in religious philosophy, ethics and pedagogy. His pedagogical teachings and methods, which reflect his Renaissance view of human cognitive abilities, are in many ways similar to the ideas expressed later by J. A. Komenský (Comenius).[9]

David Gans (1541–1613), historian, mathematician, astronomer and contemporary of Rabbi Loew, also lived in Prague at this time. Gans was in direct personal contact with Tycho Brahe, Johannes Kepler and their assistants, and in his work *Nehmad ve-naim* he makes reference to his discussions and correspondence with them as well as mentioning his several observations of the night sky at Tycho's observatory in Benátky nad Jizerou. This work by Gans, which contains the geographical and astronomical findings of Jewish as well as non-Jewish scholars, was overlooked by conservative Judaism in Central Europe at the time and was not printed until the mid-eighteenth century. In contrast, Gans' two-part chronicle *Zemah David*, undoubtedly the most widely read secular Hebrew text written by a Central European Jewish author, was given a completely different reception by his contemporaries. It represents a breakthrough in the traditional perception of Hebrew literature, being the first secular literary work in the Ashkenazi sphere. It was also the first Ashkenazi work to concentrate on the non-Jewish world. Moreover, in its creation Gans was the first to employ Renaissance research methods and use sources following the model laid down by Italian humanist historiography. The introduction to the second part of the chronicle, dedicated to world history, is a true summary of the views of a Renaissance scholar on the human sciences. The chronicle also contains a brief mention of Rabbi Loew's audience with Rudolf II on 16 February 1592, which later formed the basis for the friendly relations between the Emperor and the Rabbi described in the Prague tales about the latter.[10]

One of the professions which the Jews in the Prague Ghetto were permitted to practise was medicine. At the end of the sixteenth century and in the first half of the seventeenth centuries, there were several physicians in Prague who are known to us by name (one was Isaac, father of Mordecai Maisel's wife Frumet). Amongst those who made their mark in the natural sciences and medicine were Joseph Solomon Delmedigo (1591–1655), who spent his last years in Prague. Delmedigo, physician, philosopher, mathematician, physicist and astronomer, was a pupil of Galileo Galilei, and during his time in Prague he had several pupils of his own, including Issachar Beer Teller (who died in 1687), author of the practical medical handbook *Beer mayim hayim*. Amongst other things, this distinguished surgeon held the important post of sworn physician of the Prague Burial Society.[11]

Apart from the traditional disciplines of rabbinic scholarship and sciences inspired by the Renaissance, the study of mysticism – the cabbala – was fast expanding in Prague. Rabbi Loew was amongst the important cabbalists of the sixteenth and seventeenth centuries, together with certain members of the Horowitz family, namely the physician Sabbatai Sheftl ben Akiba (who died in 1619) and Isaiah ben Abraham (who died in Palestine in the year 1630). Isaiah's book *Shne luhot ha-berit* became extremely popular and is still referred to today in the study of mysticism.

Literature, together with the activities of Hebrew printers, represents the main direction of Jewish Ashkenazi culture, which above all concentrated on the spiritual sphere of Judaism. This was also the case in Prague, even during its Golden Age. Jewish works of art were always closely connected with religion, worship and the synagogue. These works included the synagogues themselves as well as the objects within them which form an essential part of the furnishings, especially those connected with each synagogue's most precious treasure: the parchment scrolls of the Scriptures – the Torah. As long as the wealth of the Jewish communities and their members permitted it, the fabric as well as the metal ornaments on the Torah and parts of the tabernacle (the Ark of the Law), in which the scrolls were kept, were made from rare and precious materials just as representational objects were. The extent to which members of Jewish craft guilds were responsible for creating these works of art depended on the opportunities afforded them by the specific conditions in each individual Jewish community.

The opportunities for Jewish craftsmen to practise their crafts in Prague were limited; however, works made by those craftsmen whose crafts were permitted are of a high standard. This can be seen primarily in Renaissance and Baroque synagogue textiles made by members of Prague's Jewish guilds of embroiderers and tailors. Synagogue curtains and mantles for the scrolls of the Torah were made in their workshops using the latest techniques and were decorated with contemporary designs which frequently served as models for future creators of synagogal art. Above all, the Perlsticker family workshop was an important source of Jewish art,

23.2 **Mordechai Jafe, Levuš ir Šušan**
Leather-bound print
1609
[Prague, Jewish Museum]

several large synagogue textiles from this workshop, which date back to the end of the sixteenth century and first half of the seventeenth century, have survived. Even though Jews were allowed to pursue the craft of embroidery, including embroidery using gold and silver threads and pearls, only on rare occasions and only with the permission of the ruler were they allowed to produce works of art using precious metals. As a result, silver objects for use in religious ceremonies in the synagogue or in the home were usually commissioned by the Jewish community or its individual members from Christian silversmiths and goldsmiths in Prague, Brno and other Central European cities. Less frequently, objects made by Jewish craftsmen abroad were imported into the Bohemian lands.[12]

As with objects made of precious metals, the Jewish inhabitants of Prague had to order gravestones from the city's Christian stonemasons. However, Jewish calligraphers and engravers were most probably involved in producing the Hebrew inscriptions on the gravestones. The same was true of the inscriptions and decorative motifs on silverware and on silver appertainances of the Torah. Inevitably, the visual appearance of gravestones as well as synagogue textiles and silver was influenced to a certain degree by contemporary Hebrew book design, namely the decoration of books published by the Gersonide and Bak families. The actual shape of the Renaissance and Baroque gravestones corresponds closely to the architecture of the synagogues which were built and rebuilt nearby beyond the wall of the Old Jewish Cemetery.

1. A topography of the Jewish Town in Prague is provided in H. Volavková, *Zmizelé pražské ghetto* (Prague, 1961); M. Vilímková, *The Prague Ghetto* (Prague, 1993), pp. 9–43.

2. B. Nosek, 'Die judische Kultusgemeinde in Libeň (Lieben) im 16. bis 19. Jahrhundert', *Judaica Bohemiae* (hereafter *JB*), 16:2 (1980): 103–18.

3. In 1546, approximately 1,000 Jews lived in Prague. Approximately the same number of Jews were given special passes allowing them to reside in Prague in 1562. It is estimated that around 1600, Prague's Jewish population reached between 6,000 and 15,000(!). By 1638, this figure had dropped to 7,815, going down to 2,090 in 1653. Only a small proportion of this number consisted of wealthy people (T. Pěkný, *Historie v Čechách a na Moravě*. [Prague, 1993], pp. 272, 390). See also J. Hráský, *Sixteenth and Seventeenth Century Items in the Collections of the State Jewish Museum. Prague Ghetto in the Renaissance Period*. (Prague, 1965), p. 127; Vilímková (note 1), p. 80.

4. A. Kisch, *Das Testament Mordechai Maysels* (Frankfurt, 1893); Vilímková (note 1), pp. 93–95.

5. This final point was removed from the edicts in December 1650. According to a new parliamentary decree, Jews had to leave all places which they had not lived in before 1618. See Vilímková (note 1), pp. 75–76.

6. Judah Leb ben Joshua Porit-Porges, *Milhama bešalom* (Prague, [1650]). An analysis of this account of the Swedish siege of Prague is provided by J. Šedinová, 'Hebrew Literary Sources to the Czech History of the First Half of the 17th Century: The End of the *Thirty Years' War in the Testimonies of Contemporaries*', *JB*, 23:1 (1987): 38–57. The tradition of the 'Swedish Helmet' on the banner of Prague's Jewish community is disputed by A. Putík, 'The Origin of the Symbols of the Prague Jewish Town: The Banner of the Old-New Synagogue – David's Shield and the 'Swedish' Hat'. *JB*, 29 (1993): 4–37.

7. Moses Meir Perls, *Megillat yuhasin Maharal mi-Prag*. A description of this text from the early eighteenth century and its German translation were published by S. H. Lieben: 'Megillath Juchassin Mehral mi-Prag', *Jahrbuch der Judisch-Literarischen Gesellschaft*, 20 (1929): 315–36.

8. For the elegies of Luntshitz and Heller, see J. Šedinová, 'Hebrew Literature as a Source of Information on the Czech History of the First Half of the 17th century: The Reflection of the Events in Contemporary Hebrew Poetry', *JB*, 20:1 (1984): 3–30. Judah Leb ben Joshua refers to the lost elegy written by Spira (note 6).

9. A detailed study of the works of Rabbi Loew is provided by Vladimír Sadek in *Židovská mystika v Praze* (Prague, 1992), pp. 60–69.

10. David Gans, *Zemah David* (Prague, 1952), vol. 1, fol. 64.

11. Following its banishment, the Prague Burial Society was founded again in 1564. It was an important religious and charitable institution whose articles were devised by Rabbi Loew. It became a model for the foundation of other burial societies in a number of Jewish communities throughout Central Europe.

12. Hráský (note 3), pp. 108–20; Vilímková (note 1), pp. 205–6.

The Religious Situation in Rudolfine Prague

IVANA ČORNEJOVÁ

The religious situation in Prague and throughout the whole of the Bohemian kingdom during the second half of the sixteenth century was a complex one. Old Hussite Utraquism was undergoing changes caused by both inner and outer polarization. Under the ever-increasing pressure of expanding Lutheranism, the new Utraquist movement was gradually established, while the old Utraquists had stronger ties with the Catholic church. The Czech Brethren, who had once stood alone, were acquiring more followers, and their representatives were adopting Calvinist ideas. At the same time, there were efforts to strengthen the position of the Catholic faith. One success was the renewal of the archbishopric almost 150 years after it fell vacant. Even the Utraquists did not feel beyond the pale of the Catholic church, which enabled them to adhere to the *Compactata*. They also never gave up the acknowledgement of apostolic succession according to which only a priest officially ordained by a bishop can administer the sacraments.

The Catholic church received a significant boost from the Jesuits, who were members of a new and very active order concentrating on missionary work and education. Its first six delegates arrived in Prague in 1556 at the invitation of Ferdinand I, who was in close contact with the leading representatives of the Catholic church in Bohemia. At an earlier date, the renowned 'German apostle' Peter Canisius paved the way for the arrival of members of the Society of Jesus in Bohemia. While in Bohemia, Canisius chose the Dominican monastery of St Clement for his fellow fathers. Although conveniently situated on the Old Town side of the Stone Bridge, the St Clement monastery was in a considerable state of disrepair. The arrival of the Black Fathers in the capital city of the Bohemian kingdom, the majority of whose inhabitants belonged to non-Catholic confessions, was not entirely without problems: there were some stone-throwing incidents. Nevertheless, it was not long before the Jesuits had firmly established themselves with the help of powerful Catholic patrons. Even before the Battle of the White Mountain, they began building work on the grand foundations of the existing Clementine site.

Following protracted discussions, the archbishopric was once again occupied in 1562. The new metropolitan had already been chosen a year previously. The archbishopric was not given to the original candidate, Jindřich Písek (Scribonius), who had the support of Ferdinand I. Instead it was given to Antonín Brus of Mohelnice, a learned Moravian who was an outstanding orator well known for his previous services to the church as Grand Master of the Order of the Cross with the Red Star and bishop of Vienna and who had also gained the sovereign' favour. Ferdinand I's Golden Bull announcing the renewal of the archbishopric is dated 26 September 1562.[1]

Ferdinand I's Spanish education had made him, at the beginning of his reign, an implacable opponent of anything non-Catholic, but gradually he had to abandon his rigid stance, especially after his bitter experiences with the success of the Reformation throughout the empire and the Austrian lands. Forced also to change his attitude towards the Czech 'heretics', he began to fight for the official acceptance of lay communion (the offering of the chalice to the laity), continuing to do so for several

24.1 **Crucifix**
Ca. 1600
Wood, ivory
[Prague, Umělecko-
průmyslové muzeum]

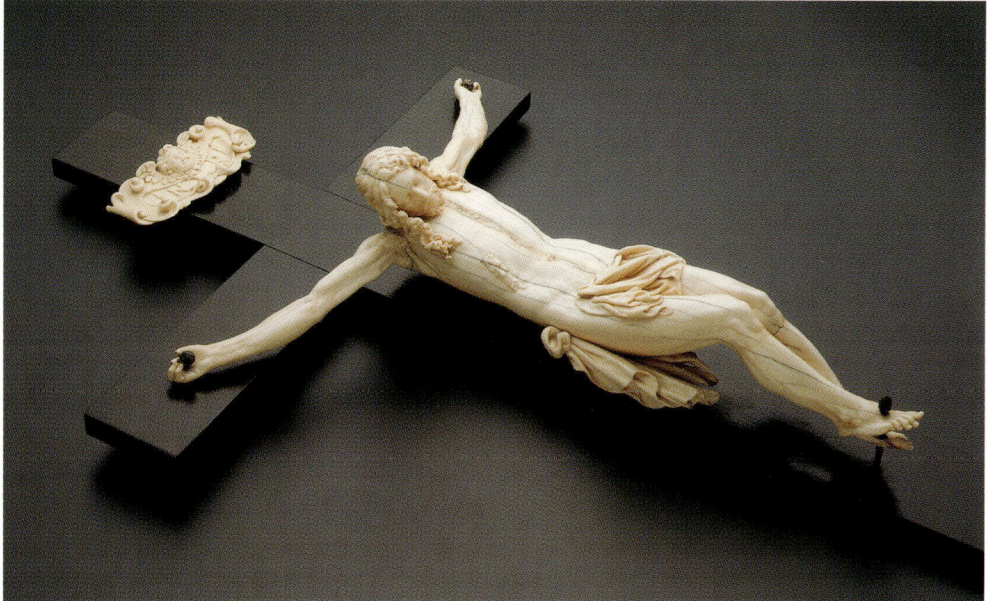

years until his death, even though unfortunately it was now too late: the mere acknowledgement of the chalice was no longer sufficient for most. It was Antonín Brus of Mohelnice who, as his chief orator, expressed Ferdinand's views on the matter at the Council of Trent, where his adversary was none other than Laýnez, the General of the Jesuit Order.[2]

The Council of Trent did not succeed in reaching an unequivocal conclusion regarding the question of lay communion and instead left the final decision to the Pope. In a brief dated 23 July 1564 the Bohemians received papal permission to offer the chalice to the laity. In accordance with this document, the Utraquists were then able to receive holy communion of both kinds following confession of sins and the declaration that 'Christ is wholly present in both kinds'.[3] Such restrictions were of course wholly unacceptable to the Lutherans and the Calvinists and could be accepted only by the old Utraquists, who, however, had a weaker position in the non-Catholic sphere at that time.

The papal brief, which in the eyes of the ruler was supposed to appease the situation in Bohemia, merely added fuel to the fire. On the one hand, it was inadequate for the non-Catholics; on the other, it reduced the willingness of strict Catholics to negotiate with and concede to the 'heretics' any further. In their view, enough concessions had already been made. The brief of Pius IV was ceremoniously proclaimed in St Vitus' cathedral. In Prague Archbishop Brus himself administered holy communion from the chalice, as did the Jesuits, who had to abide by the Pope's orders, although they administered holy communion in both kinds at side altars only.[4]

After the archbishopric had been restored, the Utraquists hoped that the metropolitan would confine himself to the ordaining of priests and refrain from interfering in their own internal affairs. By contrast, the Archbishop presumed that the Lower Consistory (that is, the highest Utraquist governing body residing at the church of Our Lady before Týn inPrague's Old Town) would prepare a full integration of the Utraquist faith within the framework of the Catholic church. After the old Utraquists and the Archbishop had failed to agree on honouring the memory of Jan Hus and Jerome of Prague and on the administering

of holy communion to infants, Brus refused outright to ordain Hussite priests.

Members of the Bohemian Estates bore the loss of their influence on the Lower Consistory badly, and in 1567 they asked Maximilian II for the restitution of the office of Estates' 'defenders'.[5] The request was denied although they had expected greater understanding from Maximilian, who was known for his pro-Protestant leanings. In his response, Maximilian pointed out the non-existence of privileges which would give the members of the Estates the right to appoint administrators or assessors of the Consistory. Members of the Estates met with more success at the parliamentary assembly of the same year, at which they demanded the withdrawal of the *Compactata* from the land records (tabulae terrae), something which at the time was unfavourable for non-Catholics.[6] Even though the Emperor refused to acknowledge this solution in its entirety, the Bohemian estates viewed the annulment of the *Compactata* as the end of jurisdiction of the Lower Consistory over non-Catholic confessions. The offensive begun by the Bohemian estates was to continue. The parliamentary assembly of 1571 was called in response to a request addressed to the sovereign in which the Estates asked him to acknowledge the Augsburg Confession with reference to the situation in the Austrian lands.

By the 1560s, the non-Catholic members of the Estates had realized that it was essential that an agreement about the internal organization of the Czech non-Catholic Church be reached, as divided standpoints would merely weaken, if not paralyse, any unified efforts. A joint approach was supported by the Czech Brethren, who were moving away from their ancient isolationism, having always belonged to the most persecuted of faiths and having been seen, in the eyes of the Habsburg rulers, whether Ferdinand I, the vice-regent Ferdinand of Tyrol or the pro-Lutheran sympathizer Maximilian II, as no more than highly dangerous and undesirable. The Czech Brethren thus felt the need for protection, although they continued to insist on the recognition of their dogmatic beliefs.

In the end, neither the Catholics nor the Evangelists were satisfied with Maximilian's reticent policies. The Evangelists had placed their hopes on the ruler, having been given certain positive expectations, but these soon began to disappear. In 1574, Maximilian II's authority was at its lowest, and an effective Estates opposition, in which the Czech nobility and the royal towns had at last come together, was formed. Inner tension meant that a power struggle was inevitable, and a suitable platform for this was provided by the forthcoming parliamentary assembly. After initial delays, partly due to Maximilian's ill health, the assembly was held in Prague at the end of February 1575. This assembly was of great importance to the Emperor, whose prime concern was the acceptance and subsequent coronation of his son Rudolf as king of Bohemia. However, he also wished to secure further funds to support the wars against the Turks. The Estates opposition was well aware that this was the right time for them to insist on their own requirements, which would balance their resistance to the sovereign.[7]

The Emperor came to Prague Castle with his whole family, court and a large number of members of parliament. This assembly was well attended by knights, as in the summer of the previous year suitable representatives from the lower nobility had been elected at the regional assemblies, and their stay was paid for with public funds set aside for this purpose. For several months, Prague became the true centre of the monarchy, including a social life worthy of a residential city with balls, banquets and resplendent church services. In contrast, the assembly dragged on.

24.2 **Chasuble**
Second half of the sixteenth century
Velvet, embroidery
[Prague, Umělecko-průmyslové muzeum]

24.3 ANONYMOUS
Drawing
Clemintinum – Jesuit College
in Prague's Old Town with
the church of the Holy
Saviour
First half of seventeenth
century

At the same time, talks concerning a unified programme for the Evangelical church took place in the Green Room at Prague Castle between March and May 1575. At first, because of internal disagreements, the Lutherans threatened to withdraw from these joint talks and draw up their own confession, which would reflect their standpoint. It was only after this that the Czech Brethren decided upon full cooperation. The joint efforts of the leading representatives of the various evangelical faiths, in which Pavel Pressius, Matěj Dvorský, Albrecht Kamejcký and Jiří Strejc were prominent, led to the emergence of the well-known document entitled *confessio Bohemica*. This document was not purely theological as its tone was dictated more by political considerations. The *confessio Bohemica* became a hitherto unheard-of compromise, which, in spite of its bias towards the Augsburg Confession, was eventually acceptable to both the Czech Brethren and the Utraquists and consequently led to a further understanding among Bohemian non-Catholics. Those responsible for creating the *confessio Bohemica* even agreed upon a joint organizational starting point and proposed that the Bohemian Evangelical church be managed by a consistory, whose members would be elected by the Estates, which would elect guardians or 'defenders' to oversee the consistory. 'The ecumenical significance of the *confessio Bohemica*, at a time when bloody battles were being fought for a single, universally acceptable expression of Christianity's relationship with God, resided in the fact that it preserved its human dimensions, its awareness of its own shortcomings and reference to the authority of the Scriptures.'[8]

The Estates presented Maximilian with the *confessio Bohemica* on 18 May 1575, and later a copy was also given to the Catholic opposition. It is not surprising that this document was also made available for scrutiny by the Jesuits, who had by this time gained an important place in Bohemian Catholic society; neither is it surprising to learn that their reaction was dismissive.[9] The Jesuits' opinion was published without delay. The old Utraquists, with Jan of Wallenstein at their head, also spoke out a-

24.4 WORKSHOP OF JAN
KANTOR
Illuminated manuscript
Songs in praise of God
1578

gainst the *confessio Bohemica*, agreeing only that the consistory should be under the direct supervision of the Estates. The protracted assembly discussions, which were not leading to the desired results, began to sow the seeds of discord in the camp of the Estates opposition. Thus in August 1575, there was conflict between the nobility and the royal towns, such that Maximilian threatened to rid the towns of their religious privileges if the conflict continued. He was able to do so as parliamentary recess was approaching; he knew too that the nobility had no intention of defending their town associates in any significant way.

The ruler announced that 16 August would be the beginning of the final parliamentary session and would incorporate voting. After the clear signs of a division within the evangelical ranks, Maximilian rightly felt that he had the upper hand. Realizing this, members of the opposition began to claim that they did not require explicit formal approval of the *confessio Bohemica*, but had in fact merely presented the ruler with the document to bring it to his attention.[10] After Maximilian had secured the support of the leader of the new Utraquists, Bohuslav Felix Hasištejn of Lobkovic, through lucrative proposals (including the office of the highest chamberlain, which he would take over from Jan of Wallenstein), it appeared that nothing could stand in the way of the ruler's outright victory. Other new Utraquist members of the Estates did not, however, share the new submissive stance adopted by the somewhat corrupt Hasištejn, and further discord within the Estates opposition merely played into the Emperor's hands.[11] In the end, the opposition had to accept a vague oral promise made by Maximilian that the *confessio Bohemica* would be tolerated. Rudolf II was crowned king of Bohemia, but Maximilian's tax demands were not met. Furthermore, the ruler had to take into account the fact that after the assembly, the power of the highest 'land' officials had in fact been strengthened and thus acknowledge the political victory of the Estates. A definitive solution of the religious situation was thus quietly deferred.

Maximilian reversed his concessions to the Bohemian non-Catholics in October 1575 in Regensburg when he issued a severe anti-Evangelist mandate, not only forbidding the publication of the *confessio Bohemica* but also adopting a strict stance against the religious reforms in the royal towns and prohibiting the activities of the Czech Brethren. It was also in Regensburg that Rudolf was crowned and that Maximilian made known his Protestant sympathies, hitherto hidden because of external pressure, when in his final hour on 12 October 1576 he apparently refused the last rites. His father's inconsistency faced Rudolf, as ruler, with a difficult task.[12]

The Bohemian question of religion gradually evolved into a conflict of Central European significance. Unfortunately, accurate research findings into the distribution of power of the different confessions in the Bohemian kingdom and in Prague itself at this time are still unavailable to us. We therefore have to rely on estimates according to which approximately 85 per cent of the population belonged to evangelical faiths. The exact proportion of believers from each confession within the individual social groups remains largely unknown. One thing we can be sure of is that the Catholic minority had influential representatives among the upper nobility, who succeeded in gaining important positions at the court of Rudolf II, who had been educated at the Catholic court in Spain. Even though it appeared that the *confessio Bohemica* had brought about a certain degree of understanding between the Evangelists, as early as 1576 the new Utraquists began to complain about the behaviour of the Consistory, which was in the hands of the old Utraquists, who, in turn, were un-

24.5 ABRAHAM LOTTER
Household altar showing the adoration of the shepherds
Before 1626
[Prague, Loreto]

happy about the introduction of preachers with a Lutheran orientation to the royal towns. Archbishop Brus frowned upon the expansion of new Utraquism and Luterism, and the Czech Brethren once again became unacceptable to strict Catholics and evangelists of a different orientation.

A further sign of the uncertain religious situation was the sheer panic which broke out in the procession accompanying Maximilian II's coffin to St Vitus' cathedral during his funeral. It was as though any large gathering containing people of different religious beliefs evoked fears of possible massacres, and, although events such as those on St Bartholomew's night did not take place in Prague, fear and suspicion were more powerful than rational argument. Such was the situation when the new ruler, Rudolf II, ascended the Czech throne.

Whereas during the reign of previous Habsburg rulers, Prague had been a somewhat neglected peripheral city, Rudolf turned it once again into a magnificent capital fit for the imperial residence. His interest in the sciences, including those which would today be described as obscure, together with his love of the arts in their various forms attracted numerous scientists and artists as well as a variety of charlatans to Prague. The hot-blooded Italians and Spaniards stirred up excitement in the recently renewed residential city, by fighting duels and by displaying their impassioned forms of exalted southern religiosity. Non-Catholics from the Netherlands also had their place in this multicultural atmosphere, as did others who came fromProtestant areas of the empire. Few recent researchers, including a number of professional historians, have realized that Prague at that time had a life of its own. The influence of the court of Rudolf II was felt mainly by those at the forefront of intellectual and artistic spheres while the rest of society was preoccupied with its own problems. These included religious disputes.

At the beginning of his reign, Rudolf, who is often remembered more as an eccentric ruler who paid more attention to his personal interests than to matters of state, approached the task ahead with enthusiasm. He toured his lands, allowing neither difficulties nor personal mood swings to deter him from his responsibilities. Rudolf II was undoubtedly a devout Catholic, but despite his strictly Catholic upbringing in Spain, he was not particularly interested in actively supporting the Catholic cause or taking action against the Evangelists. Probably it was not in his nature to do so. Instead it was his mother, Empress Maria, who adopted a rigid anti-Evangelist stance and who was unable to come to terms with the concessions her late husband had made to the non-Catholics. Thanks to her, the court at Prague became a welcome refuge for the pope's nuncios and militant representatives of the 'Spanish side', who together strengthened the Counter-Reformation movement, finding support among the young members of the Catholic nobility including new converts such as Vilém Slavata and Karel of Liechtenstein.

The papal nuncios worked also to oppose non-Catholic faiths, with some success. In 1590 for example, the old Utraquist administrator Fabián Rezek, under the influence of Nuncio Caetano, attempted to bring his church over to Catholicism. Failing to gain the support of his co-believers, he travelled in the end alone to Rome, where he denounced the 'Hussite heresies' before the Holy Office.[13] In Bohemia, the result of Rezek's action was a further fall in the prestige of the Lower Consistory. Rezek's place was taken by Václav Dačický, who was subordinate in many matters to the archbishop. While the old Utraquists were coming up against fundamental problems, the new Utraquists had difficulties of their own. Already a decade earlier, the

24.6. **Chasuble**
1615–25
Embroidered satin
[Prague, Umělecko-
průmyslové muzeum]

24..7 **The Flagellation**
1620–40
Marble
[Jemništž Chateau]

most enlightened new Utraquists had appealed to the non-Catholic Estates to put into practice the previous proclamation about taking a serious interest in the state of their own confession. An eloquent example of such efforts is the tract by Petr Codicillus of Tulechov, *Oraci M. Petra Codicilla aneb Spis k stavům pod oboji v království Českém, aby oni konzistoř dolejší pražskou k své správě navrácenou míti na sněmě obecném se snažili* ('The Oration of Petr Codicillus or the Tract Addressed to the Estates sub u-traque in the Bohemian Kingdom Entreating Them to Attempt to Have Prague's Lower Consistory Returned into Their Hands at the General Assembly).[14]

According to the latest historiographic findings, towards the end of the sixteenth century, out of a total of 1,600 parishes, the old Utraquist administrator had about 200 under him and the archbishop approximately the same number, while the remaining 1,200, the non-Catholic majority, proclaimed their loyalty to the *confessio Bohemica*.[15] The Catholics also had a few monasteries, of which some had survived the Hussite destruction and others had been restored at the end of the fifteenth century and beginning of the sixteenth century. Nevertheless, most of them were in a very poor state, and many buildings belonging to the order were inhabited only by individuals. According to a report sent by Archbishop Martin Medek to Pope Sixtus V in 1589, there were only forty monasteries in the whole diocese, 'the morale of which was rather low'.[16] The situation in Prague was not much better. The Bohemian Order of the Cross with the Red Star, whose monastery in Prague was supported by Grand Master Brus of Mohelnice, was under the direct patronage of the archbishop. In 1558, Brus reconsecrated the church of St Francis on the Old Town side of the Moldau. The monastery of Augustinian Canons in Karlov (Prague) existed in unusually quiet conditions for that time, and the monastic discipline of the order was subject to no complaints, unlike most of the other monasteries, which found themselves, both materially and spiritually, in an impoverished state.

The Dominicans, who moved from St Clements to St Agnes following the arrival of the Jesuits in Prague, were experiencing a period of decline, as were the Guardians of the Holy Sepulchre in Zderaz. The Benedictines at the church of St Margaret in Břevnov, where the once famous abbacy was reduced to a mere provostry, were not receiving the annuity due to them. The Jesuits were wealthier than all the others, and another new Counter-Reformation order, the Capuchins, who came to Bohemia at a later date, could also look forward to prosperous development. The Capuchins were invited to Bohemia in 1599 by Archbishop Zbyněk Berka of Dubé, who allotted them land for the construction of their order house in Hradčany in the vicinity of Prague Castle. The Capuchins enjoyed the special favour of the Lobkovic family, who became their generous patrons. The Emperor himself opposed the settlement of the Capuchins in Hradčany, as Tycho Brahe had apparently prophesied that the Emperor would die 'at the hands of a monk' – and who better to fulfil the prophecy than a member of a militant Catholic order?[17]

The restoration of certain old orders was another important factor contributing to the revival of monastic life. One such order was the Carmelites, who were assigned the church of the Holy Ghost in Prague's Old Town. The Italian and Spanish Franciscans meanwhile settled in the monastery of the Virgin Mary of the Snows.

In the late 1580s, Prague witnessed important Catholic celebrations, forerunners of the resplendent festivities which took place after the Battle of the White Mountain. On 29 May 1589, at the proposal of Archbishop Martin Medek, the remains of St Procopius were transferred from the abandoned Sázava monastery to

Prague. Prelates from St Vitus' cathedral, a large number of the Catholic clergy, members of the nobility, burghers and members of the lower echelons of society, as well as Rudolf II and his entourage, all took part in the procession. The saint's remains were reinterred in a new tomb in the All Saints collegiate chapel at the Castle.[18]

The gradual strengthening of the Catholic church created suitable conditions for the work of the papal nuncios, whose activities were inspired by Nuncio Bonhomini. The most successful of these was Nuncio Spinelli, the éminence grise who was behind the Catholic overthrow of the Bohemian Office and who had a significant influence on Rudolf II. The Emperor first stripped the Office of its supervision of church matters and then deposed the fervent evangelist Kryštof Želinský of Sebuzín and placed the young Zdeněk Vojtěch Popel of Lobkovic, a supporter of the Catholic cause, at the head of the Office.[19] A similar change occurred within the Czech Chamber. Furthermore, prominent places at the court were taken by active Catholics such as Kryštof Popel of Lobkovic, the archbishop's brother Václav Berka of Dubé, Adam of Šternberk and Volf Novohradský of Kolowrat. Rudolf then launched a further attack on the Czech non-Catholics when he renewed the mandate against the Czech Brethren, thus upsetting the already unstablenegotiations with the Evangelists.

Thus at the end of the seventeenth century, it seemed that there was not far to go before the Catholics gained a total victory. The Emperor, who was in poor health, was scarcely able to resist the increasing pressure of the Catholics around him, and Prague could thus become the centre of further Catholic offensives. Their hand was strengthened by the fact that the non-Catholic front was once again disrupted by internal disputes. The old Utraquists were virtually void of all influence, and in the eyes of other Evangelists they were compromised by their evident leanings towards Catholicism. The Czech Brethren again found themselves in a state of illegality following the renewal of the mandate, which was also directed against the new Utraquists and their priests. The Prague towns, the heart of the kingdom, naturally became the meeting point of the various conflicting interests.

The non-Catholic Estates awoke from their lethargy somewhat belatedly and attempted to protest against the new religious situation at the parliamentary assembly of 1603, at which Václav Budovec of Budov became the leading speaker for the Estates. The Estates argued that since the abolition of the *Compactata* they had not felt obliged to abide by the edicts of the Consistory, which was now under the direct supervision of the archbishop, and they referred to Maximilian's oral promise regarding the *confessio Bohemica*. However, they received a firm reply from the highest administrators, who said that they had found no mention of the *confessio Bohemica* or the Augsburg Confession in the 'land' privileges.[20] Discussions on religion were resumed at the parliamentary assembly of 1608. These were far from fruitful, and yet again the Evangelists were reminded of the importance of a unified approach. Disagreements between the Czech Brethren and the new Utraquists were to be forgotten, and both Evangelical faiths reminded themselves of the Mladá Boleslav agreement of 1595, which forbade mutual attacks and disruption of religious sermons.[21]

Favourable conditions for the support of the non-Catholics were created only after a change in the political situation, when in 1608 the Bohemian Estates took the side of Rudolf in the 'sibling rivalry' between the Habsburg brothers and secured the Bohemian crown for the Emperor in the Pact of Libeň. However, the support of the Bohemian Estates turned out to be a very heavy burden for the Emperor, as he

was then forced to defer to the pressure of the non-Catholic Estates, who had over-come the strong opposition of the Catholics, and sign the Letter of Majesty assuring religious freedom, which he did on 9 July 1609.

With this Letter of Majesty the Utraquists realized their aims: all that was required by the *confessio Bohemica* was now confirmed in writing, the Estates were able to take part in the management of the Consistory, they could elect 'defenders' and Prague University was once again in their hands.[22] There are other well-known documents connected with the Letter of Majesty through which the Czech Evangelical church at last acquired its own character, creating its own church organization without disrupting the identity of the Czech Brethren in any significant way. While the Evangelists had felt wronged after the Catholic overthrow in 1599, the effects of Rudolf's concessions to the non-Catholics were now felt still more strongly by followers of the Catholic Church.

However, even now the mutual tolerance of the Evangelists was not particularly consistent. As early as 1610, Adam Procházka, a priest from the church of St Gallus (Sv. Havel) in Prague's Old Town, wrote a paper entitled *Uvážení některých pilných věcí k obnově a reformaci konzistoře potřebných ...* (Considerations Regarding Certain Pressing Matters Necessary for the Renewal and Reformation of the Consistory ...), from a standpoint which was clearly against the Czech Brethren. The attack did not go unanswered. The Estates belonging to the Brethren put pressure on the 'defenders' to take action against Procházka, and he was put on trial, with Václav Budovec of Budov presiding. Procházka was reprimanded and warned that any further disruption of the peace would not go unpunished.[23]

In 1611, an event which, on the whole, unified Evangelists and Catholics occurred. Rudolf's ill-considered decision to call the Passau army to Prague and its aggressive, unruly behaviour provoked a strong reaction among almost all of the inhabitants of Prague's towns, and the highest district officers, who must have been taken by surprise by the Emperor's action, were plunged into confusion. Leopold of Passau had a meeting in the Capuchin monastery with the pope's envoy and the Spanish delegate, who realized the dangers of this delicate situation and immediately called for the disbandment of detachments, in spite of the fact that Leopold insisted that only by force could they achieve the submission of the Evangelists and rid them of their religious freedom. Added to the conquest of Prague's Lesser Town on 15 February and the unusually brutal behaviour of the mercenaries, the fact that the archduke of Passau found refuge with representatives of the Catholic church – the Capuchins – undoubtedly helped to trigger attacks on local monasteries by inhabitants of the Old Town. This was in spite of the fact that neither the Catholic Estates nor the majority of Bohemian church functionaries were in favour of the invasion of the Passau army.

The weary burghers saw a hidden 'fifth column' in the Catholic clergy, and thus they besieged and plundered churches and monasteries. They vented their anger upon the Jesuit College of St Clement, whose patres were saved thanks to the intervention of the cavalry. It must be remembered that the masses had vented their anger on Jesuit property in times of unrest even before the signing of the Letter of Majesty, when considerable damage was done to the chapel of St Michael in the Jesuit garden below Prague Castle. In 1611, most destruction was caused to the monastery of the Virgin Mary of the Snows, where fourteen Franciscan monks were alleged to have lost their lives, and the Augustinian monastery in Karlov, where the

abbot was tortured to death and the monastery property severely damaged.[24]

During the reign of Emperor Matthias, it was the non-Catholics who maintained their dominant position. The Lower Consistory was in the hands of the new Utraquists, Estates 'defenders' were responsible for the supervision of the Utraquist Charles Academy and the new Utraquists and Lutherans, whose pride and joy was the newly built church of St Salvador in the Old Town, were predominant amongst the Estates opposition. However, it is impossible to speak of any deep unity among the non-Catholics. The Czech Brethren came under severe attack from the dean of Chrudim, Blažej Borovský, who criticized the Brethren for taking over parishes in accordance with the wishes of 'certain members of the estates'.[25] The 'defenders' intervened, and Borovský's name was even struck off the Consistory register. In 1617, the Brethren were once again the subject of criticism in an anonymous tract written in Prague entitled '*Zdání o napravení církví evangelických v Čechách*' (About the Improvement of the Evangelical Confessions in Bohemia), in which the author accuses the Brethren of dogmatic deviation, claiming that a division of the Consistory was taking place. The Czech Brethren protested against the tract, demanding that its author be punished; this apparently did not happen, and it is quite possible that the author of the tract was someone close to the administrator.[26]

At approximately the same time, the Consistory came under attack from the other side – the old Utraquists – when twelve Prague priests wrote a petition, addressed to the Emperor, in which they requested that the supervisory role over the Consistory be withdrawn from the 'defenders' and returned to the archbishop. The priest of the church of St Gallus, Michal Pačuda, and probably even the priest of the church of St Nicholas in Prague's Old Town were prominent figures in this action; other signatories may have included Melchior Klesl, the bishop of Vienna and Matthias's confidential adviser. Jan Locika often spoke out against the 'defenders' from his pulpit, advocating old traditions of church sermons until, like Blažej Borovský's, his name was struck from the Consistory register. He was very popular with his parishioners, who pleaded for his pardon. This was the same Locika who, 5 years later, at the beginning of the post-White Mountain re-Catholicization process, was punished by Archbishop Lohelius for contravening strict orders by administering holy communion from the chalice in the Týn church at Easter 1622. He was interned at the monastery in Osek for being an obstinate heretic.[27]

This was a time when the religious situation had undergone significant changes. The former rivalry between the various denominations and even within individual faiths, which before the Battle of the White Mountain had often led to confrontations, with frequently beneficial outcomes, ceased, and the dominant position was occupied by the Catholic church. Later Catholicism became the only permitted religion, elevated to pride of place thanks to the interventions of the secular rulers in power at the time.

Discussions regarding the re-Catholicization of Bohemia began almost immediately after the Battle of the White Mountain. An important formal gesture, which also had profound practical repercussions, was the annulment of the Letter of Majesty in November 1620: this document, so despised by Catholics, is supposed to have been cut in half with a pair of scissors by Ferdinand II himself. Prague's archbishop, Jan Lohelius, the Jesuits, whose spiritual leader was the Emperor's confessor, William Lamormain, and a secular group, represented primarily by Karl of Liechtenstein, were at the forefront of the re-Catholicization debates. The clergy favoured a

swift, vigorous course of action, whereas Liechtenstein's followers, who included Pavel Michna of Vacínov, fearing a possible uprising, advocated a more gradual, cautious approach. In the end, it was the clergy's proposals which won. However, the swift pace of re-Catholicization did not mean, at least in theory, that force would be used. Instead emphasis was placed on missionary work, catechism and the reconstruction of the dense network of Catholic schools.

The first phase of re-Catholicization was carried out in areas under the direct influence of the Emperor – that is, the royal towns and, of course, Prague's towns. The first Counter-Reformation decrees of 1621 were aimed at the non-Catholic clergy, the Czech Brethren and the Calvinists. In December of the same year, Utraquist priests were targeted (only six old Utraquist priests converted to Catholicism). The German Lutherans were protected for a while by the Emperor's ally, the saxon Elector Jan Jiří, but were banished in October 1622.

In the next stage of re-Catholicization, the burghers of the royal towns were given a 'choice'. That is, they could either convert to Catholicism or face the confiscation of all their possessions and forced exile. The number of people emigrating from Prague's towns ran into thousands, and of the burghers who left Prague, the German Lutherans who settled in Saxony, for example, found better conditions in their new 'homelands'. However, the number of those who converted was not negligible and a cause of surprise even to contemporaries. Unfortunately, there has been no recent research into the subject, and therefore we must rely on older estimates. Václav Líva, whose prime source of information was the accounts by the mid eighteenth-century Jesuit historian, Jan Schmidl, wrote that in 1621-26 between 100 and 800 people were converted and that this figure rose rapidly to 3,538 in 1627 and to 23,728 in 1628. The sudden rise is explained by the fact that 1627 was the year in which the renewed Constitution, forbidding all faiths other than Catholicism, was proclaimed.[28] Besides repressive measures, the Catholics were above all seeking new ways to strengthen the position of their own faith, as had already been proposed in the initial concepts of re-Catholicization – that is the building and renovation of strictly Catholic schools of all levels and the restructuring of the Catholic administration as well as missionary work and catechism. There was often a shortage of clergy for filling vacant parishes, and it is here that, in the first phase of re-Catholicization in particular, the members of the various religious orders played an important role. In Prague, the Jesuits, the Dominicans at St Giles and St Mary Magdalene, the Franciscans at Virgin Mary of the Snows and the Capuchins at Hradčany were all very active in this area. In 1626, when the attempts at re-Catholicization in Bohemia appeared unsatisfactory to those in Vienna, Prague's towns served as 'guinea pigs' as new methods were introduced. Where there was no reliable priest, an instructor was appointed, and the archbishop issued an exact outline of the powers of priests in order to avoid complaints about their behaviour. A register of all young people, both Catholic and 'heretic', was kept, as the organizers of the re-Catholicization programme were well aware that influencing the younger generation was the alpha and omega of any future success.

From research done on the subject it is possible to deduce that the re-Catholicization of Prague's towns was, by and large, complete by the middle of the 1630s. The network of parishes was by then functioning fully, and priests regularly had to compile registers of parishioners, drawing attention to those suspected of heresy, and to keep a record of auricular confessions using testimonials of confessed sins.

The number of monastic institutions increased. For example, during the first half of the seventeenth century, Prague's towns became a true Jesuit bastion, for as well as having a base at St Clements in the Old Town, the Brotherhood of Jesus was also well established at the church of St Nicholas in the Lesser Town in 1625 and at the church of St Ignatius in the New Town in 1628. People were enticed into Catholic churches by attractive sermons and the numerous festivals of which they were sometimes active participants and at other times merely fascinated onlookers. One such event in 1627 was the transferral of the remains of St Norbert, founder of the Premonstratensian Order, from Magdeburg to Strahov (Prague).

The re-Catholicization of Bohemia was begun in Prague's towns, where it achieved greatest success. In 1631, Prague's newly converted inhabitants were still happy to revert to the faith of their fathers when they enthusiastically greeted the Protestant Saxon armies. However, in 1648 there was a wave of opposition to the Swedish mercenaries. Even though in this instance the question of religion was not dominant, there is no doubt that the Prague of 1648 was quite different from the Prague of 1631. By that time, graduates of Catholic schools, parishioners of famous priests, members of various devout brotherhoods and the more or less loyal subjects of the Catholic Habsburg ruler were all living in Prague.

1. A. Skýbová, 'Obnovení pražského arcibiskupství v letech 1561-1562 a jeho vztah k pražské univerzitě', *Acta Universitatis Carolinae – Historia Universitatis Carolinae Pragensis*, 7:1 (1966): 2-11; F. Kavka and A. Skýbová, *Husitský epilog na koncilu tridentském a původní koncepce habsburské rekatolisace Čech* (Prague, 1968), pp. 35-56.

2. J. Kadlec, 'Přehled českých církevních dějin II. Prague 1991' (Rome, 1987), pp. 33-34.

3. *Ibid.*, p. 40.

4. K. Borový, *Antonín Brus z Mohelnice, arcibiskup Pražský* (Prague, 1873), p. 89.

5. 'Defenders' were elected members of the non-Catholic estates who after 1909 were responsible for ensuring that the Letter of Majesty was adhered to and whose duties also included 'defending' the interests of Charles University.

6. J. Rak, 'Vývoj utrakvistické organizace v době před-bělohorské', *Sborník archivních prací*, 31:1 (1981): 179-204.

7. J. Pánek, *Stavovská opozice a její zápas s Habsburky 1547-1577*, Studie ČSAV č. 2 (Prague, 1982), pp. 101-19.

8. J. Pánek, *Zápas o Českou konfesi*, Slovo k historii 30 (Prague, 1991), p. 33.

9. F. Hrejsa, *Česká konfese, její vznik, podstata a dějiny* (Prague, 1912), p. 246.

10. Pánek (note 7), pp. 110-11.

11. K. Krofta, 'Boj o konsistoř pod obojí v letech 1562-1575 a jeho historický základ', *Český časopis historický*, 17 (1911): 410; K. Borový, *Jednání a dopisy konsistoře katolické a utrakvistické I-II* (Prague, 1868-69).

12. J. Janáček, *Rudolf II a jeho doba* (Prague, 1987), pp. 493-506.

13. J. Matoušek, 'Kurie a boj o konsistoř po obojí za administrátora Rezka', *Český časopis historický*, 37 (1931): 29.

14. *Sněmy české VI* (Prague, 1890), pp. 165-75.

15. Kadlec (note 2), p. 14.

16. K. Borový, *Martin Medek, arcibiskup Pražský: Historicko-kritické vypsání náboženských poměrů v Čechách od roku 1581-1590* (Prague, 1877), p. 48.

17. Z. Winter, *Život církevní v Čechách: Kulturně-historické vypsání náboženských poměrů v XV a XVI století* (Prague, 1895), p. 789.

18. Borový (note 16), pp. 157-58.

19. J. Borovička, 'Pád Želinského. (Obsazení nejvyšších zemských úřadů v Čechách 1597-1599)', *Český časopis historický*, 27 (1922): 277-304; K. Stloukal, *Papežská politika a císařský dvůr na předělu XVI. a XVII. věku* (Prague, 1925), pp. 103-95.

20. J. Glücklich, 'Mandát proti bratřím z 2. září 1602 a jeho provádění v letech 1602-1604', *Věstník Královské české společnosti nauk* (1904): 22-24.

21. F. Bareš, 'Snesení mezi jednotou bratrskou a stranou pod obojí, jež se stalo v Mladé Boleslavi 1. 1595', *Památky archeologické*, 16 (1893): 41-44.

22. J. Rak, 'Karlova univerzita v pravomoci defenzorů (1609-1622)', *Acta universitatis Carolinae – Historia Universitatis Carolinae Pragensis*, 17:1 (1977): 33-46.

23. Rak, (note 6), p. 201.

24. Winter (note 17), p. 765; M. Koldinská, 'Vpád pasovských a soudobé české myšlení', *Dějiny a současnost* (1991/6): 15-20.

25. K. Tieftrunk (ed.), *Pavla Skály ze Zhoře Historie česká od r. 1602 do r. 1623 II* (Prague, 1865), pp. 249-53.

26. Rak, (note 6), p. 202.

27. F. Tischer (ed.), *Dopisy konsistoře podobojí z let 1610-1619* (Prague, 1917), pp. 445-48.

28. V. Líva, Studie o době pobělohorské 2, *Sborník k dějinám hlavního města Prahy*, VII (1933), pp. 1-71.

Education in Rudolfine Prague

IVANA ČORNEJOVÁ

A characteristic feature of education in Europe after the onset of the Reformation was the separation of educational establishments according to religious denomination. This resulted in the end of the free 'wanderings' of students between various institutions as their movement was restricted to institutions which belonged to a single denomination. At the same time, the expansion of the Reformation and the newly awakened attempts at re-Catholicization led to a new competitiveness in the pedagogical world. New educational systems now emerged, which often drew from the same sources – that is, from the traditions of medieval universities, Classical scholarship and humanism. Following the Treaty of Augsburg, universities were also divided according to regional borders. It is from this period that the term *Landesuniversität* (regional university) originates. The students and teaching staff of these universities came predominantly from the region or country in which each university was situated.

A similar situation arose in the Bohemian lands more than a century earlier when, after the Hussite wars, the character of Prague University,[1] which had played an important political role during the Hussite period and whose representatives became leading ideologists, was altered considerably. The alma mater Pragensis remained true to Utraquism, thus becoming the first *Landesuniversität* in Europe. Its former international orientation, so typical of the medieval studium generale, came to an end before the Hussite revolution, immediately after the issuing of the Decree of Kutná Hora in 1409.[2] This important document expressed an explicit preference for Czech university members and resulted in the departure of most German teachers and students, which in turn led to a significant drop in the number of students at the university and a weakening of its intellectual base. The Decree of Kutná Hora later became the subject of numerous, often intricate, nationalistic interpretations on both the German and the Czech sides. The changes brought about by the decree led to the virtual collapse of the theological faculty before the Hussite revolution. A similar fate awaited the law and medical faculties. Consequently, university education in Prague became limited to a single faculty, the faculty of Arts.

The Utraquist exclusivity of Prague University did not diminish until the sixteenth century, when Prague began to establish links with other non-Catholic universities. Its position in Bohemia was further strengthened by its close ties with the lower *studium particulare* (the body of secondary schools) in various towns and cities in the Bohemian kingdom. Attempts at the re-Catholicization of *studium generale* in Prague had little success during the rule of the Jagellonians, achieving a greater, if still limited, impact following the arrival of Ferdinand I on the Czech throne. The influence Czech rulers had on the oldest university in Central Europe was reduced considerably during the Hussite period and was not restored until after the Battle of the White Mountain. In the post-Hussite period, the university's raison d'être was to meet the needs of the population of Prague and, later, the members of the Bohemian estates. The period of the second half of the fifteenth

century and the first decade of the sixteenth century is often referred to in special-
ist literature as a critical one for the old universities.[3] Nevertheless, in spite of its
changed religious orientation and the reduction of its scope, Prague University
continued to fulfil its main role as the prestigious centre of higher education in the
country with no significant drop in its standards.

After the middle of the sixteenth century, when Ferdinand I, with his experience
of the complex religious situation in the empire, had begun to distance himself
from the powerful pro-Catholic movement, Prague's Utraquist University stood at
the head of the educational hierarchy. Its students included a number of Catholics,
others of whom tended to apply for places at universities abroad. Graduates left the
university with a bachelor's degree and often went on to teach in *studia particularia*.
The knowledge they passed on to younger students no longer emanated solely
from a religious standpoint, but was influenced by the then fashionable humanism,
which laid greater emphasis on a classical Latin (and to a lesser degree Greek) education. This pattern is described by Zigmund Winter (who has yet to receive the
recognition he deserves) in his novels as well as his specialist works.[4]

Catholic town schools were to be found mainly in traditionally Catholic areas.[5]
The information in original sources about the lowest level of the school system, the
elementary level, where the basics of reading, writing and arithmetic were taught, is
very fragmentary. It would appear that the existence of such schools was largely dependent on individual teachers. Schools of the Czech Brethren were renowned for
their high standard of teaching.

The arrival of the Society of Jesus in 1556 brought about the most significant
changes to the school system in Prague. The Jesuits came to Bohemia at the invitation of the ruler Ferdinand I, who worked very closely with the Bohemian Catholics
in the matter of improving standards of education. The Jesuit Order strengthened
the position of the Catholics considerably prior to the renewal of the archbishopric. Moreover, its main mission was pedagogical. A principal feature of the
Catholic reformation endeavours was an emphasis on education. Those involved
were fully aware that a good school could significantly influence or even change
the traditional ideological outlook of a family. When the Jesuits arrived in Bohemia,
16 years after the Society of Jesus had been granted papal approval, they already
had, thanks to their founder, St Ignatius of Loyola, a basic educational system. This
was defined in more detail during the second half of the sixteenth century, being
codified at the general congregation of the Society of Jesus in 1599.[6]

In Prague, the Jesuits were allocated a place in the former Dominican monastery
of St Clement in the Old Town near the Moldau, where they founded a higher college[7] – that is, an order house – including both lower and upper schools. Lower
schools, known today as *gymnasia*, were Latin schools where grammar and the hu-
manities were taught. The upper schools included a philosophy faculty, a theological faculty and often a language faculty (*facultas linguarum*). The Jesuits began
teaching soon after their arrival in Prague, and their schools were formally inaugurated on 15 March 1562 with Ferdinand I's founding charter, which mentions lower
schools as well as higher education. Later their foundation was confirmed by privileges conferred upon them by Maximilian II in 1567 and Rudolf II on 1 April 1581.[8]
Ferdinand's Jesuit Academy was later promoted to *studium generale* by privileges
conferred by Matthias on 27 March 1616, even though it had been functioning as a

studium generale before then, awarding grades with reference to special privileges granted by Pope Pius V in 1561.

The main principles of the Jesuit college's teaching methods, as well as the organization and structure of the schools, were already in place before 1599, when the rules and regulations were formalized. Until 1618, the classes of the Jesuit schools at St Clement had never been full. Nevertheless, it did not take long for the schools to become established in society and for their attendance to increase. According to information contained in the schools' oldest register of students (*Album Academiae Pragensis Societas Iesu*)[9] – which cannot, however, be relied upon fully – the total number of students enrolled between 1573 and 1617 was 1,836, which means that the yearly average was almost 50 students. Unfortunately, we do not have any information regarding attendance at the lower schools, nor any precise figures which would permit a comparison with the level of attendance at the Utraquist Charles Academy. It may be said with reasonable certainty, however, that, after a somewhat unsteady start, the Jesuit schools were evidently successful.

In the first decades of the existence of the Jesuit schools, the duration of study at the *gymnasium* was 5 years. In 1578, another year was added, the lowest so-called *parva* year. The main element of the Jesuit educational system was the formal study of language, based on the study of Latin, with Greek as a secondary language. Students who had completed the lower stage of studies were expected to be able to read, write and debate in both languages. According to contemporary sources, Latin was the more popular of the two in the second half of the sixteenth century. A graduate of the college of St Clement, Jakub Pontanus, spoke rather contemptuously of Greek.[10] The classics were read, the works of Cicero in particular, as also the verse of Horace and Ovid, with the omission of all 'immoral' passages. The philosophy course was divided into 3 traditional years, logic, physics and metaphysics and philosophy (that is, the liberal arts or spiritual science), which prepared students for the highest aspiration – the study of theology.

Non-Catholics were able to study at the Jesuit schools under the same conditions as strict Catholics. This was, after all, a time when Ferdinand I had succeeded in gaining permission to offer the eucharist to the laity and when there was also a move towards the Catholic church by followers of the old Utraquist confession. Students who were followers of evangelical faiths could not partake in the catechism, which was compulsory for all Catholic students and, according to school regulations and explicit instructions given by Ignatius of Loyola, Jesuit teachers were not allowed to exert any pressure which could lead to a change in the religious faith of non-Catholic students. Despite these instructions, which were adhered to, many non-Catholic students under the influence of good Jesuit teachers converted to Catholicism.

The emergence of Catholic Jesuit schools in Prague's Old Town had the effect of revitalizing the activities of the Utraquist Charles Academy. Both seats of learning had more than half a century of fruitful co-existence, with intellectual and scholarly competition, ahead of them. However, it would be incorrect to assume that the Charles Academy was roused from any lethargy solely by fears of Jesuit competition. The narrow denominational introspection gradually began to disappear under the impact of Humanism, whose first proponent at the Prague University was Václav Písecký, who died in 1511, and, later, of Melanchthon's pupil Matouš Kolín –

Collinus of Chotěřiny (died 1566) – who was the founder of the Greek lectureship.[11] Contacts with reformed German universities also led to the opening up of the Charles Academy to the wider world.

Matouš Collinus felt the negative effects of the Jesuits' presence in Prague personally when, because of them, he lost the support of the court circles. This was mainly because of his friendship with Jakub Palaeologus, for whom he provided sanctuary in Prague when the Jesuits were in pursuit of him.[12] Palaeologus was a descendant of the last Byzantine dynasty and had been travelling throughout Europe, thus attracting the charge of heresy.

The Jesuit Academy of St Clement and the Charles Academy opened their doors to the public, especially for theatrical events. Such performances were the typical results of linguistic humanism and formed an active part of the Jesuit curriculum, being closely linked to the art of dialogue and declamation. They also provided an opportunity to present the students' achievements to the public, together with publicity or even propaganda, which often informed their artistic expression. These performances were mostly in Latin, and their themes were taken from the Bible, religious history, Antiquity and Bohemian history. In 1585, a play about St Wenceslas (Václav) performed in the Clementinum was a great success.[13]

Further attractions for the public were provided in the form of religious celebrations organized by the Jesuits at St Clements, in which students from the schools also took part. The most spectacular of these were the processions during Corpus Christi. These involved music, singing, pictures painted on banners, luxurious robes and young students dressed as angels, the most exceptional of which represented the archangel Gabriel. Wealthier parents bought their sons white robes decorated with gold and precious stones for the occasion. The carrying of the monstrance was reserved for dignitaries and special guests, so, for example, in 1575 the papal nuncio and Spanish envoy were invited for the occasion.[14] The highlight of the procession was the stop at the four altars facing the four corners of the earth, where the priests prayed to ward off disasters or for a good harvest. The Jesuits also organized pilgrimages to the miraculous picture of the Mother of God in Stará Boleslav. Such processions and other similar celebrations captured the attention of a considerable number of onlookers as well as the disapproval of various members of the evangelical Church, the Calvinists and the Czech Brethren in particular.

Charles University also organized renowned processions, which followed on from the medieval tradition of putting the holy relics of the saints on display in the Corpus Christi chapel at the Cattle Market. The Utraquist academics of the sixteenth century no longer adored the holy relics of the saints. Instead, the procession of teachers and students from the Carolinum to the Corpus Christi chapel was 'in memory of Charles IV' and took place every year until 1611.

An interesting anecdote based on original sources is told by Zigmund Winter, who describes a sacred doll known as the 'Bethlehem Infant', which in the early 1620s could still be found in the Bethlehem chapel and which was used to re-enact Herod's slaughter of the innocents. Even though such an example of superstitious worship is unusual in an evangelical context, the professors were apparently reluctant to part with the doll when in 1611 the Empress herself requested it.[15]

The Jesuit schools were also involved in establishing various congregations, most of which were connected with the adoration of the Virgin Mary. The first of

these were the Marian student sodalities founded at the Clementinum. Later there were burgher sodalities to which people outside the Jesuit Academy belonged and whose aims were to partake in spiritual exercises and to strengthen their piety. The members of such sodalities included important patrons who made donations of significant sums of money or even property to the Church and its schools. The Catholic patrons were far more generous than the patrons of the Utraquist Carolinum, who were never extravagant with their donations to the university.

The Clementinum enjoyed not only moral support but also the material and financial support of the leading members of Catholic society, which included its rulers. The Carolinum, for its part, benefited from its close links with lower schools, not only in Prague but throughout the whole of Bohemia (with the exception of border regions whose inhabitants were predominantly Lutheran). In Prague, the alma mater supervised the Týn School and the schools of St Gallus (Sv. Havel), St Castulus (Sv. Haštal) and St Nicholas (Sv. Mikuláš) in the Old Town. In the New Town, it was responsible for the prestigious school of St Henry (Sv. Jindřich) as well as the schools of St Stephen (Sv. Štěpán), St Adalbert (Sv.Vojtěch) in Jircháře and St Clement (Sv. Kliment) at na Poříčí. As in the lower Jesuit schools, lessons in the *studia particularia* were based on Latin.

The Charles Academy was also responsible for the regulations of the *studia particularia*. The paper drawn up by Petr Codicillus of Tulechov, based on the principles of Johann Sturm, became a model for school regulations. However, in practice it was rarely used owing to its highly theoretical nature. A more successful document was written in 1595 by Martin Bacháček of Nauměřice together with Vlaverin, and its regulations were first used in the private lower school which Bacháček had founded under the Academy. In 1598, they were made obligatory for all *studia particularia* which came under the jurisdiction of the university. Bacháček was also involved in the preparations for the regulations devised by Vavřinec Benedikt Nudožerský between 1607 and 1610.[16]

Rudolf II's Imperial Letter of Majesty declaring religious freedom had a great influence on Charles University, which was entrusted into the hands of the Estates' 'defenders',[17] and from then on it had very close ties with the Lower Consistory, of which the office, together with its archives, was located in the Carolinum itself. Under the management of the 'defenders', the university was to undergo gradual reforms, with improvements in the university's financial situation as well as the level of scholarship. This situation also had its negative side: the 'defenders' and the Consistory, through their close ties with the university, may well have tried to bring about an ideological subordination to new Utraquism as well as to interfere in academic autonomy. Eventually, a number of university teachers allowed themselves to be pulled into the maelstrom of high politics, as was the case during the Hussite period. Even though this increased the public reputation of *studium generale*, the effect of such political involvement on tuition was by and large unfavourable, not only at that time but throughout the entire history of the alma mater Pragensis.

It was clear to the main representatives of the Utraquist Estates that the university should become the spiritual centre of evangelism in Bohemia and that in order to achieve this the former fame and glory of the university would have to be restored, together with the restoration of all faculties, most notably the theological faculty. The only obstacle in the way of these ambitious plans was a lack of funds, a

problem that the university had been experiencing for a number of years, partly because members of the Estates were always reluctant to provide any financial support from their own resources. A committee, with Master Adam Zalužanský of Zalužany at its head, was set up in September 1609 to draft proposals for the university reforms. Members of the committee considered the option of selling off the university's scattered properties and earning interest on the money thus gained. This modern approach to the problem was not greeted with enthusiasm by the academics, who argued that the Jesuit Academy, which was a much younger institution, was able to exist without giving up its property. As a result, the committee's proposals were not realized, and the only change which came about was the creation of the post of economic manager or questor.[18] The university's villages were not sold until much later, in the middle of the eighteenth century.

In the end, the efforts of the members of the Estates to improve university standards had no far-reaching effects. The university property was not sold, the collection considered by the parliament in 1609 failed to take place and the Charles Academy continued to be limited to the single faculty of Arts. Other changes which occurred in the effort to reform were the long-awaited abolition of celibacy for the professors and the creation of the office of rector, to be held by a member of the aristocracy. In an attempt at a rapprochement with the Czech Brethren, the university, with its new Utraquist tendencies, allowed the Brethren use of the Bethlehem chapel, where in 1609 the preacher Matěj Cyrus was ceremoniously inaugurated. However, soon after this a dispute began between the university and the Brethren over a school the Brethren had founded at the Bethlehem chapel without the university's permission. The dispute lasted for two years until it was resolved on 7 March 1612, largely thanks to the intervention of Bacháček.[19]

The active Bacháček played a significant part in settling other conflicts, including the dispute between the university and a prestigious new school, which tried to evade the control of the university. This was a German Lutheran school at the church of St Salvador in Prague's Old Town. The school had aspirations to gain the status of an academy; naturally, such competition was not welcomed by the old university, which tried to put an end to the school's activities. Eventually, the school was formally subordinated to the Charles Academy, whose professors were quick to realize that the Lutherans could provide the school with financial and material support, which would promote further competition, no less dangerous than that offered by the Jesuit Clementinum.[20]

It was soon after the Utraquist University's dispute with the Lutherans that the Clementinum was once again afforded highest favour. In 1616, Emperor Matthias promoted Ferdinand's Academy at the church of St Clement to *studium generale*, thus bestowing on it the same privileges as those enjoyed by the *studium generale* in Paris, Bologna, Vienna, Ingolstadt and elsewhere in Germany, Italy, France and Spain.[21] The promotion was in fact no more than formal confirmation of the school's existing status; nevertheless, this expression of the ruler's support for the school was very important. The Clementine university expressed its gratitude the following year when, in the Emperor's honour, its students and teaching staff staged a performance celebrating Christian virtues and the significance of the Society of Jesus.[22]

The rivalry between the schools of various denominations came to an end short-

ly after the Battle of the White Mountain, after which only strict Catholic educational institutions were allowed to exist in Prague. As has been said, the standard of education in schools of the different denominations was very similar, both in their positive and their negative aspects. As well as leading to some friction, the co-existence of the various schools awoke a healthy ambition and competition in pedagogical and intellectual spheres. The quality of education was always dependent on the teaching staff who influenced the character of each institute, as is still very much the case today. The Jesuit schools boasted a better educational and organizational system, which had firm foundations in the rapidly developing order. However, there was a lack of prominent individuals at the Clementinum before the Battle of the White Mountain. Furthermore, foreigners prevailed at the Clementinum in the early years of its existence, and it was not until later that larger numbers of people from the Bohemian lands joined the institution. Individuals worth mentioning include Jindřich Blyssemius from Cologne, an outstanding theologian who, as well as teaching the Holy Scriptures, was an excellent teacher of Hebrew; and the Czech Václav Šturm, a swift-thinking polemic and preacher, and a fervent opponent of the Czech Brethren, who taught lower studies and philosophy.[23]

The Carolinum at that time could boast a larger number of exceptional individuals. The organizational abilities and activities of Martin Bacháček of Nauměřice have already been mentioned, and he is also remembered in the history of the alma mater as a professor at the faculty of Arts, as rector of the university and as a scientist who was in close contact with Johannes Kepler. Bacháček was responsible for arranging accommodation for Kepler and Tycho Brahe in Prague. Bacháček was a universally well-educated man, but it was in mathematics and astronomy that he excelled. He built himself an astronomical observatory in one of the towers of the Carolinum, and his mathematical tables, though they have not survived to the present, are referred to by his contemporaries. He built a globe and offered it to the university, which did not purchase it until the Clementine Jesuits expressed an interest in it. Martin Bacháček was also known for being temperamental and fond of wine.

Probably the best-known professor of the Charles University before the Battle of the White Mountain was Jan Jessenius, philosopher and physician, who performed the first public autopsy in Prague. Jessenius, however, found a political career more attractive than a career at the university, something for which he later paid dearly. Another professor at the Carolinum, Jan Campanus Vodňanský, an important humanist, Greek scholar, poet and playwright, was also a tragic victim of the Battle of the White Mountain. Jan Campanus Vodňanský's whole existence revolved around the Charles Academy, which he therefore found it virtually impossible to leave. He died soon after his conversion to Catholicism, was given a splendid funeral by the Jesuits and was buried in the chapel of Corpus Christi.[24]

The defeat of the non-Catholic armies at the Battle of the White Mountain, and its consequences, represented a turning point for education in Prague. The demise of non-Catholic schools came shortly after the dismissal of the clergy. Such was the fate of the Brethren's Bethlehem chapel and the Týn School as well as the Lutheran school of St Salvador. Following stormy discussions, the future of the alma mater Pragensis was decided in Vienna. Education was of great interest to the theoreticians of the re-Catholicization of the Bohemian lands, and the new character of the

highest seat of learning was one of the outstanding issues. In 1622, following a decision made by Ferdinand II and approved by a secret council, Charles University was given to the Jesuits, something which had previously been suggested by Archbishop Johann Lohelius and the ruler's adviser William Lamormain. The Jesuits began to reform the university according to their regulations. Ultimately, Jesuit universities were answerable to the General of the Society of Jesus in Rome. Somewhat later, in 1623-24, the medical and law faculties were re-opened; though in secular hands, they were under the control of the Jesuit rector of the university. The faculties of philosophy and theology were taken over by the Jesuits from the Clementinum.

Jesuit dominance over the university soon brought it to the centre of one of the most pronounced conflicts within the Catholic Church in the period after the Battle of the White Mountain.[25] The young archbishop Arnošt Vojtěch Harrach began making claims to his old rights as chancellor of the university of Prague. He had the support of the representatives of the so-called 'old orders' – that is, religious orders which had existed for more than a hundred years. The members of these orders felt that they had been equally wronged as they were not permitted to hold posts at the university faculties. The conflict between Archbishop Harrach and the Jesuits over the university, as well as over the censorship of religious literature, continued for over 30 years, even though the Archbishop had the papal throne on his side, while the Jesuits had the supreme support of the sovereign.

The sovereign did intervene in this matter – not Ferdinand II, but his son and successor Ferdinand III, who was not as dependent upon the Jesuits as his father had been. In 1638, he took the Carolinum away from the Jesuits, and the secular faculties were given independence. However, a final solution was not reached until 1654, when the Jesuit Clementinum was once again conjoined with the Carolinum, and according to the Emperor's wishes, Ferdinand's Charles University became the only *studium generale* in Bohemia.

Prague's Catholic schools flourished during the three decades following the Battle of the White Mountain, for, as a rule, all those involved in the re-Catholicization laid great emphasis on the education and upbringing of young people in a strictly Catholic manner. A network of elementary parish schools was created, and new *gymnasia* began to prosper in Prague's towns. As well as the Jesuit gymnasium in Prague's Old Town there was a college in the Lesser Town and another at the church of St Ignatius in the New Town, which was attended by dozens of students. Of the other *gymnasia* the well-known old Benedictine *gymnasium* in Břevnov is worth mentioning.

An important role in re-Catholicization was played by new priests who had received an appropriate education – that is, priests of Bohemian origin who had been educated in Bohemia. There were various schools belonging to the order, where, as well as receiving a secondary education, the priests attended philosophy and theology classes, similar to those at Prague University. These schools were, however, regarded as private schools and thus they did not possess the privileges of *studium generale*. In order to receive a universally recognized degree, the students of these schools had to complete the *studium generale* at Prague university. Unfortunately, not all students were able to do so. Dominicans, for example, could not graduate from the university as, in accordance with the regulations of their order, they were

not permitted to take the oath of the Immaculate Conception of the Virgin Mary.

The most important of the schools belonging to an order was the Dominican school at St Giles (Sv. Jiljí). This school played a particularly important role during the time of the Saxon invasion between 1631 and 1632, when it became a substitute for the university. Another important school was Ferdinand's Franciscan Minorite Academy of St James (Sv. Jakub). One of the most important institutions responsible for educating future priests was the archbishop's seminary, founded on the basis of the requirements of the Council of Trent. Archbishop Harrach, who even had a papal bull to support him, tried to found a second university, but did not succeed owing to strong opposition from the Emperor. The Cistercian Bernardinum and the Premonstratensian Norbertium, schools belonging to two other important orders, were also associated with the archbishop's seminary.

Thus, before the mid-seventeenth century, there were numerous élite schools in Prague's towns as well as elementary schools, all of which apparently provided a good standard of education, albeit in a Catholic vein. Unfortunately, there was no possibility for religious diversity of educational institutions at this time.

1. Prague University, also known as Charles University (after its founder Charles IV) is sometimes referred to in old sources as the Charles Academy or simply as the Carolinum (Karolinum).

2. *Bibliografie k dějinám pražské univerzity do roku 1622*, ed. M. Melanová and M. Svatoš (Prague, 1979), pp. 39-40.

3. *A History of the Universities in Europe I: University in the Middle Ages*, ed. H. de Ridder-Symeons (Cambridge, 1922), pp. 456-60.

4. Z. Winter, *Děje vysokých škol pražských od secessí cizích národů až po dobu bitvy bělohorské 1409-1622* (Prague, 1897); *O životě na vysokých školách pražských knihy dvoje. Kulturní obraz XV. a XVI. století* (Prague, 1899).

5. J. Šafránek, *Školy české: Obraz jejich vývoje a osudů I* (Prague, 1913), pp. 39-40.

6. I. Čornejová, 'Jezuitské školství a Jan Amos Komenský', in *Pocta Univerzity Karlovy J. A. Komenskému* (Prague, 1990), pp. 74-87.

7. The Jesuit University or College at St Clements is also known as the Ferdinand Academy (Ferdinandea) or the Clementinum.

8. K. Beránek, 'Kancelář university pražské na zlomku XVI. XVII. věku', *Sborník archivních prací*, 9:2 (1959), pp. 220-39.

9. *Album Academiae Pragensis Societatis Iesu 1573-1617 (1565-1624)*, ed. M. Truc (Prague, 1968).

10. I. Čornejová, 'Jezuitská akademie do roku 1622' in M. Svatoš. (ed.), *Dějiny Univerzity Karlovy I.* (Prague, 1995), p. 258.

11. J. Hejnic, 'Filip Melanchthon, Matouš Collinus a počátky měšťanského humanismu v Čechách', *Listy filologické*, 87 (1964): 361-78.

12. Winter, *O životě* (note 4), p. 267.

13. M. Cesnaková-Michalcová, 'První jezuitská představení v českých zemích' in F. Černý (ed.), *Dějiny českého divadla I. Od počátku do sklonku osmnáctého století* (Prague, 1968), pp. 132-39.

14. A. Podlaha, 'Dějiny kolejí jesuitských v Čechách a na Moravě', *Sborník historického kroužku*, 10 (1909): 46.

15. Z. Winter, *Život církevní v Čechách: Kulturně-historický obraz XV. a XVI. století I* (Prague, 1895), pp. 869, 875.

16. J. Pešek, 'M. Martin Bacháček z Nauměřic, rektor univerzity pražské', *Acta Universitatis Carolinae – Historia Universitatis Carolinae Pragensis*, 19:1 (1979): 73-94.

17. 'Defenders' were elected members of the non-Catholic estates who after 1609 were responsible for ensuring that the Letter of Majesty was adhered to and for 'defending' the interests of Charles University.

18. M. Svatoš, 'Pokusy o reformu a zánik karolinské akademie' in Svatoš (ed.) (note 10), pp. 282-84.

19. J. Rak, 'Karlova Univerzita v pravomoci defenzorů 1609-1622', *Historia Universitatis Carolinae – Historia Universitatis Carolinae Pragensis*, 17:1 (1977), pp. 33-46.

20. Pešek (note 16), p. 88.

21. J. Port, 'Divadlo řádových škol a náboženských bratrstev' in Černý (ed.) (note 13), p. 136.

22. Čornejová (note 8), pp. 167-69.

23. Z. Winter, 'Konec samostatné univerzity Karlovy', *Časopis českého muzea*, 71 (1897): 3-35, 97-109.

24. I. Čornejová, *Kapitoly z dějin pražské univerzity 1622-1773* (Prague, 1992), pp. 19-60.

25. I. Čornejová, *Dějiny Univerzity Karlovy II* (Prague, 1996), pp. 23-56.

Book-Printing and Other Forms of
Publishing in Prague, 1550–1650

M I R J A M B O H A T C O V Á

The victory in the Schmalkalden War of 1547 over the rebellious Czech Estates provided the Czech Habsburg king Ferdinand with a welcome and much desired opportunity to concentrate the poorly controlled, illegal print-shops strewn all over the Czech rural areas in Prague. This he achieved by banning all other book-printing activities in Bohemia (the ban did not affect Moravia, as it had not participated in the Estates' uprising). A single exception was made of the printer Bartoloměj Netolický, in order that he might be at the ruler's personal service.[1] Only gradually were the print-shops permitted to operate in Prague, and under altered conditions, notably prior censorship and the individual printers' willingness to modify their range of publishing activities.

From the second half of the sixteenth century to the end of the period of the Estates, approximately sixty-nine book-printers operated in Prague - that is, twenty-eight printers' families (often at least two generations) and their workshops, some of which were purely profit-oriented. Jiřík Nigrin (also called Černý – 'black' – or Schwarz) produced over six hundred printed items for the varied domestic and foreign clientele which passed through imperial Prague, as well as sheet music and emblematic prints.[2] Thirty-three other Czech and non-Czech printers (or perhaps they were simply booksellers and bookbinders) were working in Prague, printing limited numbers of topical items and eventually sinking into oblivion.[3]

Other Prague print-shops - especially that of Jiří Melantrich of Aventin - undertook a selective publishing programme, which sought some of their custom abroad and attempted to balance their budgets by accepting commissions of a commercial nature.[4] And finally there was the unconventional, inherited print shop of Melantrich´s son-in-law, Daniel Adam of Veleslavín, a former university professor and historian. His print-shop was deliberately oriented towards educating its Czech readers in the spirit of humanistic culture and responsible, patriotic ways of life.[5] Some printers followed a Protestant or Roman Catholic ideological programme. Several significant Prague printers of the epoch were Germans by origin, who had become fully assimilated into Bohemia and who, thanks to their foreign-language proficiency in the graphical spheres, also ensured sales of their output abroad. A notable example was Michal Peterle, originally an engraver).[6]

The great political change introduced in 1627 by the royal decree known as the Re-establishment of the State[7] put an end to the existence of those Prague print-shops which had been operating mostly on the basis of legal Utraquism. It also naturally liquidated the print-shops belonging to men who had sided with the anti-Habsburg uprising of 1618. Adam's son and successor, Samuel Adam of Veleslavín, for example, was sentenced to death for his sympathies with the Estates and survived only by fleeing the country. An alternative, opted for in exceptional cases, was to adapt to the changed conditions. The archbishop's and the Jesuit (university) print-shops were granted official status. Their administrations, too, were changed; henceforth they were to be operated by professional factors. Later these

26.1 Utraquist offering of the Eucharist 'sub utraque specie' with the symbolic figures of this and Luther

22.2 Serpent upright on a cross
and hailing the departing
people of Israel who had
made themselves an icon
while Moses was serving the
Lord, from the Czech Bible,
published by Jiří Melantrich

factors occasionally returned to individual book-printing activities limited to those
areas in which the archbishop's and the Jesuit print-shops took no interest and
which were acceptable from the religious standpoint.

The Art of Book-Printing

In those days, book-printing was considered an art, not a craft, which is why book-
printers did not form guilds. The Prague printers were commonly capable of typesetting in Latin (thanks largely to the town's specialized schools) and Greek, as well
as in living languages (primarily German, Italian and Spanish). They probably
sought assistance with the typesetting of Hebrew passages from prominent Prague
Jewish printers who, in turn, may occasionally have adopted some of the Prague
printers' ornamental motifs.

Books written in the Czech language were set (at least until the early nineteenth
century) in German Gothic type, mostly in various forms of black lettering acquired abroad. This type, however, poses some difficulty for modern 'editors' of
these texts, because the Czech diacritical marks were rendered by the joining of
several letters. The differences found in that type were thus not always of a philological but merely of a technical origin. Latin books were printed in Roman type. As
it was common for the educated patricians to know Latin, it became fashionable
and prestigious to incorporate laudatory Latin (humanistic) poetic dedications in
Czech-language books, or Latin (and even Greek) introductory phrases in a book's
title, heaping praise on the author, the printer or the work itself.

Until the end of the eighteenth century, typesetting was done manually. This
implied, among other things, that even during the actual printing procedure the
printer could make minor changes on the typeset sheets. This means that the dupli-
cating of old prints today presents a highly sensitive and delicate problem – even
an incomplete book copy may be unique. In 1828, Josef Dobrovský wrote an article[8]

entitled 'Rozličnosti v exemplářích Diadochu Bartholoměje Paprockého' (Differences in the Copies of the *Diadochos* of Bartholomēj Paprocký), relating that he had compared 15 or 16 copies; however, the typesetting of the *Diadochos* (the succession of Czech princes and kings) had dragged on for so long that changes might have occurred in the meantime in the honorifics of prominent personalities.

Xylographs were used as a decorative and illustrative graphic art technique; this technique was applied 'from the top', as was book-printing. Copper engraving was taken up only towards the end of the sixteenth century, initiating a major change: intaglio, a graphic technique 'from the depth'. As the metal-press plate required the exertion of greater pressure, the composition had to be placed under the press twice, which is why initially this process was seldom used. Illustrations were then inserted into the book as full-page unnumbered supplements. They were often produced outside the print-shops and, unlike xylographs, were usually presented along with information on the producer of both the copy and the metal plate. These single prints later became the rage among collectors and commercial buyers, to the detriment of the completeness of the books for which they had been destined. A result was the creation of the so-called frontispiece – a full-page, illustrated, inserted leaf which would either face or precede a book's title page. Some xylographs were coloured. This technique impaired the xylographs as it covered the lines engraved into the plate; these coloured pictures are thus not suitable for reproduction today. Paper was used for printing, an exception being illuminated books, which had a parchment title page; these were reserved mostly for printers' patrons.

Printers came into contact with unhealthy lead, which was why they died at a relatively early age. When a man had no adult heirs, his widow often married either one of her husband's apprentices, who was familiar with their printing process, or another printer. In this way, typographic, graphic and illustrative materials were passed on to other print-shops. This type of migration and the repeated use of materials form a significant factor in the identification and evaluation of individual printers' creative contribution and the aesthetic value of their books. Jan Kosořský of Kosoř, for example, inherited the xylographic materials owned by the Severin family into which he had married,[9] and Jiří Melantrich, for his re-edition of the publication *Rada všelikých nerozumných zvířat* (*Council of All Sorts of Unreasonable Animals*), dating from 1573 and 1578, obtained virtually all the 1528 illustrations from the long-abolished print-shop of the Pilsen printer Jan Pekk.[10] Thus, whether a printer can be identified by examining the appearance of sixteenth-century printed matter, on which no print-shop is named, depends on a detailed analysis of the forms and limitations of the materials used in the relevant print-shop.

Obtaining xylographic plates for book illustrations was largely a financial matter. The copying of original plates, loans of xylographic plates or even minor adaptations of older plates (such as the effacing of the year) were a pan-European phenomenon: the modern concept of 'plagiarism' was unknown. The use of other artists' illustrations and imitation of print-shops' signets and graphic book ornamentations on an international scale were viewed as manifestations of an admirable cultural outlook and an alignment alongside the masters of that art. An example worth mentioning in this respect was the second edition of Pierandrea Mattioli's *Czech Herbarium* of 1596, designed by Daniel Adam of Veleslavín, who borrowed the illustrating requisites from the printer of the German version of that work in Frankfurt am

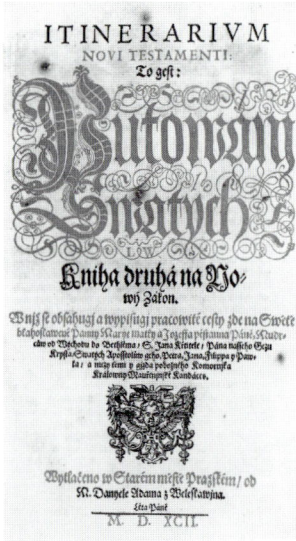

26.3   Itinerarium of the New Testament, the Pilgrimage of the Saints

26.5 Book of Judges; Samson
from the Czech Bible,
printed by Jiří Melantrich.

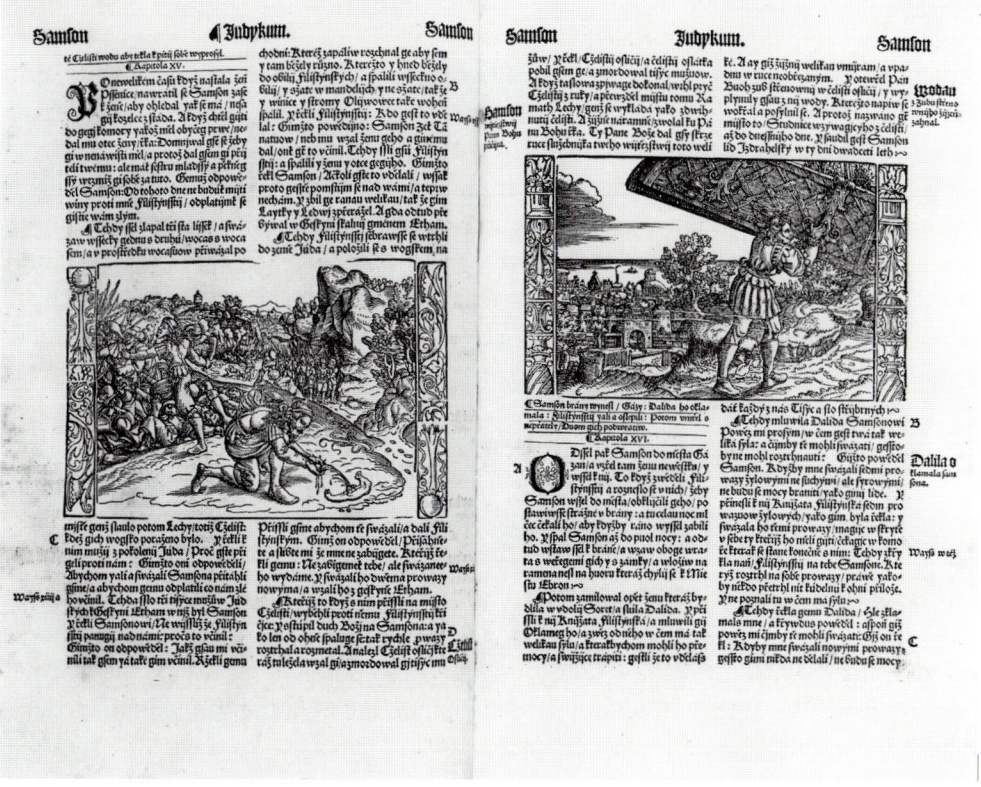

26.4 **Czech Bible**
First edition
1549

Main. The illustrations accompanying that edition (1586) had been prepared by Joachim Camerarius the Younger, using Konrad Gessner's illustrating equipment.[11]

This practice depended on the willingness of the books' readers to accept the secondary utilization of its illustrations and the repetition of the same xylographs within one book. Unless this had been so, the printers of those days could hardly have coped. This process had been handled with considerable sensitivity as early as the first half of the sixteenth century: in Hájek's *Kronika česká* (*The Czech Chronicle*; 1541), for instance, the scenes of rulers' enthronements were rendered with picturesque xylographs, while for the rulers' funerals, which were of lesser significance, four interchangeable plates sufficed. Throughout the text of the edition of Tovačovský's *Hádání Pravdy a Lži* (*The Dispute Between Truth and Falsehood*; 1539), two xylographs only were used interchangeably to depict the recurring scenes of the plaintiffs before the Holy Trinity, and of those two contending parties before the Last Judgment of the Holy Spirit. Yet the author of the original xylographs did not hesitate to create for this book additional illustrations of inconsequential yet socially interesting details.[12] It may be noted in passing that the first Czech illustrations serving not merely as decorative elements but as full accompaniments to a text came into being with the printing of authentic works by Czech authors, for which no usable foreign originals existed. At the other extreme was the practice resorted to by certain profit-oriented professional printers (such as Burian Valda), especially in the sphere of news dissemination, who would indiscriminately utilize any plates accessible. For example, the plate depicting the drowning of King Louis Jagellonian in the Mohács swamps (1526) was used to show the death of the king of Portugal in 1578, while the plates illustrating the murder of St Wenceslas and

one battle from Hájek's *Chronicle* were used as substitute scenes in the St Bartholomew's Day Massacre in 1572 in Paris.[13]

The relationships between authors and printers, the number of printed copies of books and their prices are not very clear. Such aspects are documented more in sporadic archival records (especially in wills) than in the books themselves. The paper used for printing books, especially in the sixteenth century, was of high quality. It was purchased at specialized stationery firms, and the sums owed both by printers and authors were often mentioned together with such transactions. It was common, chiefly in the second half of the sixteenth century, to reprint in the books themselves copies of the publication licences granted to authors and printers. The books were thus protected, for a given number of years, against pirate editions and unauthorized sellers. Offenders faced a fine. In an archival record dated 1566, the wording has been preserved of the contract concluded between the Prague Archbishop and the translator of Ferr's (Wild's) Latin postil into Czech. It includes information on the translator's fee, room and board, bed sheets, wood fuel and a servant.[14]

26.6 Emblem of the Old Town of Prague

The Books' Content and Editorial Supplements

Current research has ascertained that the content and editorial supplements of books printed in the sixteenth and seventeenth centuries consisted chiefly of the work of authors from the fifteenth century onwards and foreign publications selected for translation into Czech. The method of translation (then referred to as 'interpretation') developed considerably during the sixteenth century, becoming more accurate and refined. Such translations were quite easily accessible to Czech scholars, regardless of their financial situations. In their positions as teachers and chaperons of young noblemen travelling abroad for social experience, they could visit those countries' universities and meet prominent professors and learned men. With the support of domestic institutions and patrons, they could even study at universities abroad. Czech and foreign humanists did not often meet in person, but they would maintain close relations through correspondence and exchanges of specialized works.

The *Rukovět humanistického básnictví v Čechách a na Moravě* (*Handbook of Humanistic Poetry in Bohemia and Moravia*)[15] offers an ample survey indicating that, in the period 1550–1650, works by humanists in the lands of the Czech Crown were published in over seventy European countries and by more than two hundred print-shops. Most often, these were short, one- to two-sheet compositions, or individuals' contributions to humanistic volumes devoted, for example, to the honouring of friends, the observances of their deaths, or else to compositions praising rulers and prominent personalities. Links with foreign print-shops were often established by humanists from the Czech lands who were studying in those towns. Similarly, foreigners temporarily living and working in the Czech lands, for the most part in Prague, might permanently befriend their Czech humanistic counterparts, to whom they would dedicate their verses. Also worth noting are the Czech exiles who could no longer publish their works in their own country. The extensive works of poetry and prose written in Latin by Czech authors also found their places abroad, and were published there in first and subsequent editions. Such authors included Kašpar Cropacius, Jiří Barthold of Braitenberk, Matyáš Borbonius, Adam Zalužanský of Zalužany, Jan Campanus, Václav Budovec of Budov, Václav Clemens and Pavel Stránský.

Most books published in the Czech lands during the sixteenth and seventeenth

26.7 Excerpt from Moravian prints of the Unity of Czech Brethren

26.8 **Králice Bible**
The last Králice edition
printed before the Battle of
White Mountain
1596

centuries were of a specialized religious or moralistic nature. Also published, but on a lesser scale, were works of the kind referred to today as belles-lettres; very few have been preserved. Characteristic of the literary works of those days was the combining of disciplines. Moralistic writings were enlivened with amusing vignettes. Musical texts were often allied with spiritual songs and compositions. Astrology was applied in scientific circles alongside astronomy, prophecy next to history, and so on.

Editorial matter was accorded special importance. The frequent dedications to the book's patron immortalized his name, celebrating his financial generosity and his enterprise and foresight in the publication of the work. The ensuing forewords would express the author's and editor's, or the translator's, viewpoints and set out the factors which had directed and influenced them. Often these forewords also cited the reasons for publishing the book and the philological procedures adopted.[16] Latin epigrams dedicated to friends, literary figures and authorities were also extremely common in Czech books. Besides lists of persons and places, the contents and indexes at the end of a book provided lists of the subjects discussed therein. Lateral (marginal) summaries and references to Classical works quoted were also offered. Very common indeed were errata.

News Reporting

The printers themselves strove to obtain licences for the kind of output that would guarantee sales. This included textbooks (often Latin-Czech-German), official reports of parliamentary sessions, decrees of institutions such as universities and calendars. Nevertheless, single sheets in a folio or quarto format became the most effective medium. They were printed on one side only, so that they could be hung on a wall or door, posted in an inn, pasted on the inside of a trunk-top at home or filed as a document together with an official paper. There were also leaflets of several pages, most commonly the size of one quarto-format sheet. Together with religious themes, these leaflets provided information on various current events: individual news items, the forerunners of multi-item newspapers. Among other facts, they often provided information on the Turkish wars, coronations, journeys and deaths of rulers, natural disasters, mysterious occurrences in the sky and on earth, tragic and horrific events and God's punishments and warnings against an impious life (the so-called *memento mori*). These reports were disseminated in the form of translations and adapted versions, even beyond the frontiers of the state. Usually they consisted of two parts, which increased their popularity: illustrations depicting the essence of the information, and an accompanying explanatory text written in the language of the country for which they were intended. Their provenance was frequently anonymous, while the specific data on the place, time and persons affected by the events described lent these reports authenticity.[17]

In humanistic circles, graphic games of visual (figurative) poetry enjoyed particular popularity. These games, which originated in ancient manuscripts, assumed the creative collaboration of the author and printer. The arrangement of the type formed specific images, a congratulatory goblet, labyrinth, musical instrument, etc. At times, in order to be able to read them, the reader had to discern a sequence of various geometric lines and images running horizontally, vertically and diagonally, as all the letters together would spell out first names or symbolic maxims (Nigrin, in particular, was an expert in producing these single sheets).[18] Alternatively, the

letters of such mottoes might be numbered so that, when arranged in a particular sequence, they formed, say, the author's name. Sometimes the words in a phrase could be read backwards, providing an opposite meaning; for instance, in the composition *Encomia Bohemorum* dating from 1619, the phrase which begins 'Bohemi semper fideles in facto et re suis Regibus fuerunt...' can be read backwards as 'fuerunt Regibus suis re et facto infideles semper Bohemi...'). Also greatly enjoyed were rebuses, in which words (with the necessary spelling licence) were combined with pictures (so minute and often so blurred that they have become difficult to decipher). Rebuses appeared particularly frequently in German-language works and, during the episodic reign of Frederick of the Palatinate, reflected the political situation. These authors and types of printings were anonymous, perhaps even of foreign origin, yet their criticisms of the Czechs' choice of a ruler and the rebuses ridiculing that choice and its failure were surely aimed at Czech readers, and circulated among them. An example of this is: 'Der gr/Affe = aff/ von/ Turm = Turn/der fein g/Esel = esel/...' – ostensibly a phrase honouring the nobility of the duke but containing punning references to an ape and an ass. Czech-printed items defending Frederick and commentaries on the expulsion of the Jesuits from the Czech lands and Prague could hardly compete with such propaganda.[19]

Among the aristocratic and patrician classes, diverse personal congratulatory notes on the occasions of birthdays, births, weddings and professional promotions, or condolences on deaths in the family, oscillated between journalism and literature. Prosaic sermons to be handed out to funeral guests also come into this category. The author of such texts often expected a reward for his work, in the form either of money or of a career promotion. On the other hand, many truly sincere expressions of friendship also exist, occasionally compiled in the form of books (for example, following the sudden death of Daniel Adam of Veleslavín in 1599).

Times Past and Transitory

Even this brief survey of the different aspects of book-printing and other types of publishing in Prague during the predominance of the Estates testifies to the wealth, variety, graphic diversity and high quality of that production, as befitted the intense cultural life and thirst for written information of the aristocratic and educated urban classes of the capital. The clearest proof of the spiritual and social need for such information is the fact that biblical and legal publications especially were initiated and printed by the urban community.

It would be wrong to assume that the censorship imposed by the Re-establishment of the State decree (1627)[20] put an end to book-printing. Quite the contrary, the period between the Battle of the White Mountain and the year 1650 was a time of transition. The prominent figures of the Czech Baroque era had not yet embarked on their publishing activities to any degree; but the officially selected and authorized print-shops undertook on a substantial scale to substitute non-Catholic publications with new orthodox reading matter. It was believed that readers who had been raised to expect the broad choices provided by the Renaissance and Reformation could not be left, nor would it be advisable to leave them, starved of mental stimulation. According to Jungmann's *History of Czech Literature* (1849) – which, thanks to the author's classification according to topic, has not been surpassed even by the *Knihopis* (which lacks an index) – more than two hundred Czech

26.9 **Czech Bible**
Title page with Melantrich kneeling before the Crucifixion
Edition by Samuel Adam
1613

26.10 'Kronika Česká'
German translation by Václav Hájek of Libočan.
1596

works were published in the period 1621-50, mostly in octavo and pocket twelvemo formats. Most of these were religious writings, largely of a generally pastoral nature. Others were intended for the purposes of prayer; many were polemical and instructional works, or works acquainting their readers with the lives of certain saints and with the orders of new religious brotherhoods. Original works were scarce, so those printings included numerous translations from Latin or from living languages. New hymn books and the postil (with no mention of the place of publication or printer) had already appeared. The largest share of this production emanated from the Jesuit printing workshop, which published from 1635 on also under the title Academic (that is, university) workshop. There were also the the archbishop's print-shops, which began publishing in 1631. Among the private printers active during this period were Tobiáš Leopolt (Leopold), until 1623; Pavel Sessius, until 1631; the Bylina family, 1622–45; Zikmund Léva, 1624–31; and the Šípař family, 1639–52. A great deal of miscellaneous printed matter, but no information about the printer, place of printing or even the year, was published, probably in Prague and containing material of a 'good Catholic' nature. The threat of censorship was probably irrelevant in most cases, and this typographical anonymity may well have been intentional.

1. Petr Mašek, *Význam Bartoloměje Netolického pro český knihtisk 16. století* (Prague, 1987) Contributions to the Knikopis (note 7), vol. IV.

2. Mirjam Bohatcová and Josef Hejnic, 'Knihtiskař Jiří Nigrin a jednolistové "proroctví" Jindřicha Demetriana', *Sborník Národního muzea v Praze*, ser. A - History, 35:2 (1981).

3. See Karel Chyba, *Slovník knihtiskařů v Československu od nejstarších dob do roku 1860*, Appendix to the miscellany 'The Strahov Library', 1 (1966)-18/19 (1983/84).

4. Mirjam Bohatcová, Ivan Hlaváček, Josef Krása, Pravoslav Kneidl, Bohumil Nuska, *Česká kniha v proměnách staletí* (Prague, 1990): notably 214-27.

5. Mirjam Bohatcová and Josef Hejnic, 'O vydavatelské činnosti veleslavínské tiskárny', *Folia historica Bohemica*, 9 (1985): 291–388.

6. Pravoslav Kneidl, 'Michal Peterle, přední pražský dřevorytec a tiskař 16. století', *Bibliotheca Strahoviensis*, 1 (1995): 107-33.

7. See *Knihopis českých a slovenských tisků od doby nejstarší až do konce XVIII. století*, ed. Zdeněk Václav Tobolka and František Horák, pt II: *Tisky 16.–18. století*, no. 2447 (Prague, 1939-67).

8. *Časopis Českého musea 1828*, no. 2, sect. II, pp. 119-23.

9. Mirjam Bohatcová, 'Otázky nad publikační činností pražských Severinů', *Listy filologické 109* (1986): 97-115.

10. Probably through Bartoloměj Netolický's print-shop, which he purchased in the 1550s.

11. Mirjam Bohatcová, 'Prager Drucke der Werke Pierandrea Mattiolis aus den Jahren 1558-1602', in *Gutenberg-Jahrbuch* (Mainz, 1985), pp. 167-85. In Czech for *Sborník Národního muzea*, ser. C, 38, 1993, nos 3-4 (issued in 1997)

12. Mirjam Bohatcová, 'Wahrheit und Lüge in der Hand eines böhmischen Rechtsgelehrten (geschrieben 1467, gedruckt 1539)', in *Gutenberg-Jahrbuch* (Mainz, 1984), pp.25-35. In Czech as *Pravda a Lež v rukou právníka* (Přerov, 1995).

13. *Knihopis* (note 7), nos 1157, 6441 (herein with an incorrect description).

14. Bohatcová *et al.* (note 4), p. 206.

15. See Josef Hejnic and Jan Martínek, *Rukověť humanistického básnictví v Čechách a na Moravě; Enchridion renatae poesis Latinae in Bohemia et Moravia cultae*, 1–5 (Prague, 1966-82). For the list of 264 authors whose works were translated into Czech, see M. Bohatcová, 'Das Verhältnis der tschechischen und fremdsprachigen Drucke in Böhmen und Mähren vom 15. Jahrhundert bis zum Jahre 1621', in *Gutenberg-Jahrbuch* (Mainz, 1988), pp. 113-16.

16. Mirjam Bohatcová, 'Předmluva v českých předbělohorských tiscích', in František Šmahel (ed.), *Knihtisk a kniha v českých zemích od husitství do Bílé hory* (Prague, 1970), pp. 83-105.

17. Pravoslav Kneidl, *Lidová grafika v ilustracích novin, letáků a písniček* (Prague, 1983).

18. Mirjam Bohatcová, 'Farbige Figuralakrostichen aus der Offizin des Prager Druckers Georgius Nigrin (1574/1581)', in *Gutenberg-Jahrbuch* (Mainz, 1982), pp. 246-62.

19. Mirjam Bohatcová, 'Ein mährisches Labyrinth aus dem Jahre 1583', in *Gutenberg-Jahrbuch* (Mainz, 1989), pp. 149-56. In Czech as 'Setkali se v Labyrinthu žerotínský lev a boskovický hřeben' in *Husitství - reformace - renesance, Sborník k 60. narozeninám Františka Šmahela*, arranged by Jaroslav Pánek, Miloslav Polívka and Noemi Rejchrtová (Prague, 1994), vol. III, pp. 859-70; M. Bohatcová, *Irrgarten der Schicksale. Einblattdrucke vom Anfang des Dreissigjährigen Krieges* (Prague, 1966).

20. *Knihopis* (note 7), no. 2447.

Bookbinding: Style and Ornament

RADIM VONDRÁČEK

Bookbinding in the Czech lands went through a period of considerable stylistic change from the 1570s onwards. The increase in the number of books being produced – at the same time as books entered the lives of many town-dwellers, with the consequent increase in requests for bindings – was one of the causes of this transformation. This was a period of considerable prosperity for the bookbinding trade. Bookbinders from Bohemia, Silesia and Germany converged on Prague, which, profiting from its advantage in being the seat of the university and, later, the court, was the centre for the home market.[1] The number of Prague bookbinders multiplied in the second half of the sixteenth century. Out of 113 working there between 1526 and 1620, as listed by Zikmund Winter, only 11 were established before 1550.[2] Competition between bookbinders increased so much in the last quarter of the century that it was necessary to draw up guild regulations to afford some protection to those listed.[3]

Unfortunately the sources do not enable us to determine the exact number of craftsmen who concerned themselves primarily with the bookbinding trade, since the term *knihař* may refer not only to a bookbinder but also to one who sells books. The absence of any linguistic distinction reflects contemporary practice, especially in Prague, where the greater part of those who described themselves as *knihař* both bound books and sold them. The records of the estates of, for example, Jan Harovník and Tobiáš Fikar, bear witness to this. Both of them owned bookshops with workshops attached.[4] A particular specialization is clear from the use of the German terms *buchführer* and *buchhändler*, indicating those who exclusively or mainly traded in books and only arranged to have them bound as required.

Co-operation between printers and bookbinders was frequent, the bookbinder taking part of the edition for sale in his shop and binding it in a cheaper blind-stamped binding for stock. Evidence for this can be found in requests for payment for such book deliveries[5] and in surviving examples of books printed by Jiří Melantrich or Daniel Adam of Veleslavín in which uniform bindings were prepared for the same title.

Although bound books had become more available to a wider range of people, bindings which were artistically more demanding or required more expensive materials continued to count as luxury goods. For example, a gold-tooled binding with gauffered edges cost on average 60 groschen more per copy.[6] Consequently, neither the developing market in books nor the arrival of foreign craftsmen could in themselves have been the main influences on the transformation in style. The requirements of specialized book collectors – bibliophiles – who ordered artistic bindings which were individually produced were the decisive factor.

Book collectors of the Renaissance helped to shape the look of bookbinding in the Czech lands from at least the 1540s (for example, bindings with an heraldic *supralibros* for Jan Hodějovský of Hodějov dating from 1541). The requirements of the imperial court and of Emperor Rudolf II himself played an important role in

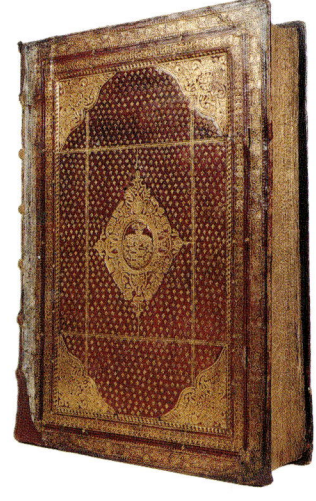

27.1 **Binding with supralibros of Rudolf of Teuffenbach**
Late 16th century–early 17th century
[Prague, Národní knihovna]

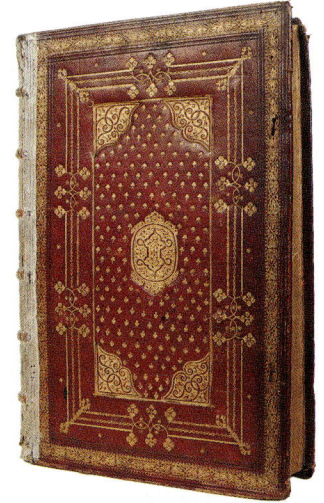

27.2 **Binding for Rudolf of Teuffenbach**
Late 16th century–early 17th century
[Prague, Národní knihovna]

the last quarter of the century. Several manuscripts and rare books acquired for the imperial collection were bound in the workshop of the Prague court, with which no specific craftsman known to us has so far been identified.[7] We know, for example, the binding of Albrecht Dürer's sketchbook, as well as those of manuscripts with illuminations of birds and sea creatures by Jacopo Ligozzi, and alchemists' manuscripts in Leiden (known as the Codices Vossiani Chymici).[8] With few exceptions, it was the content of rare books that was decisive for their inclusion in Rudolf's *Kunstkammer*, but the binding could emphasize their exclusivity and at the same time perform the important task of protecting the book. The Emperor or his entourage might also require bindings for an important occasion – for example, the richly decorated ceremonial binding of the charter of nobility for Jiří Pontanus of Breitenberk, the binding dedicated to Rudolf Colloredo-Wallsee, and others.[9]

Orders from bibliophiles amongst the courtiers and government officers were also carried out in the workshop (or workshops) of the Rudolfine court. In a consideration of the development of bookbinding (without regard to the scope and importance of particular libraries), our attention is especially drawn by the splendidly gold-tooled bindings for the Czech chancellor Zdeněk Vojtěch of Lobkovice, the president of the Court Chamber Ferdinand Hoffmann of Grünbüchl, the astronomer Tycho Brahe and the future general Rudolf of Teuffenbach; by the binding with painted coats of arms for Adam of Valdštejn and Kryštof Popel of Lobkovice; or by the less demanding work for the privy counsellor Leopold Strahlendorf and for Jaroslav Bořita of Martinice and Václav Práchenský of Flissenbach. There were a considerable number of orders from church circles (for the archbishop's library, for the abbot of Strahov Jan Lohelius, and for the capitular dean Pontanus of Breitenberk).

The spokesman for the Protestant opposition, Václav Budovec of Budov, had the volumes of his elegantly presented library bound by the court workshops or by craftsmen producing stylistically similar work in the city, as did bibliophiles amongst the burghers (Tomáš Teuffel of Cejlberk, Kryštof Kober of Kobersberk), lawyers (Václav Radnický of Zhoř), writers (Samuel Radešínský of Radešovice), university professors, doctors, clerks and tutors.[10]

Quality bookbinding to order was not only carried out in the Prague workshops. Another important centre of bookbinding was to be found on the Rožmberk estate, where Petr Vok had his own bookbinders working for him – for example, Jan Kemp in Český Krumlov.[11] The communities of the Unitas Fratrum in Ivančice, Kralice, Mladá Boleslav and Přerov also bound books to a technically advanced standard. Among the customers of the Unitas Fratrum workshops were the lords of Lipá, the Žerotíns, and the doctor Matyáš Borbonius of Borbenheim.

Bibliophile requirements considerably influenced the overall design of the book, the choice of material and the style and appearance of the ornamentation. The bookbinder substantially had to respect requirements such as the positioning of the owner's coat of arms or initials on the cover (the heraldic and initialled *supralibros*) and, as the case might be, the aesthetic demands of the customer. The treatment of the functional constituents might also depend on this. An example might be to increase the number of bands for aesthetic reasons, or to introduce false bands. Similar considerations governed the choice of material for the boards and covers. Some bibliophiles, such as Karel the Elder of Žerotín, found the leather for bindings

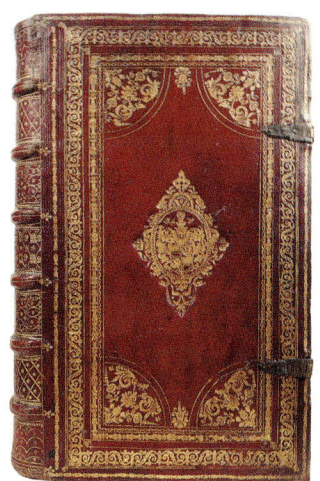

27.3 Binding with supralibros of Zdenek Vojtěch Popel of Lobkowicz
After 1605
[Prague, Lobkowicz collection]

27.4 Binding for the Archbishop of Prague, M. Medek
(back)
1583
[Prague, Uměleckoprůmyslové muzeum]

themselves and decided whether to use metal clasps or ribbon ties, and so forth.[12]

For the most demanding lovers of books it was possible to use hitherto un-known Oriental skins in unprecedented colours to cover the boards. We know about the use of red, black and blue saffian leather (for bindings for Petr Vok and Karel the Elder of Žerotín) and of morocco and cordovan leather. The green parch-ment often used for bindings for Hoffmann of Grünbüchl was a reference to his title. Bindings of green silk and blue satin made for Tycho Brahe still survive. In Fröschl's inventory of Rudolf's *Kunstkammer*, we find mention of rare books bound in red, yellow, orange, brown and black velvet and satin.[13] However, the most popu-lar material, next to red stained leather, remained white parchment, which was very suitable for gold-tooling.[14]

The more challenging process of gold-tooling the binding (often including gauf-fered edges and decoration of the borders) and the type of composition and decora-tion linked with it markedly differentiates this sort of bookbinding from the regular production of the Prague city workshops of Jan Komor, Adam the bookbinder, Sixt Stanhauer, Pavel Gutsch, Kryštof Meyšnar and others. They mostly brought out bindings stamped 'blind' – that is, without gold-tooling – with rolls and panel-stamps. Rolls with ornamental and figurative (usually Protestant) motifs covered the whole surface of the cover in concentric frames. Only in the centre was there left a small panel to be filled with the impression of a rectangular panel-stamp (with, for example, a religious scene) or with perpendicular rolls.

It was in comparison with the prevailing blind-stamped production that the spe-cial characteristic of the new stylistic trend stood out. From the 1570s onwards, Czech and Moravian bibliophile bindings were distinguished by the elegance of sim-ple open spaces instead of being crammed to the last corner with heavy decoration. The new style of composition allowed for the display of quality materials and the placing of dominants – usually a heraldic *supralibros* – in the middle of the open space.[15] The decoration at the border of the binding was also reduced; subtle lines and narrow bands of braided, linked, undulating or other ornament replaced moral-izing themes. Figurative and similar 'imitative' motifs were replaced by abstract, Ori-entally inspired decoration. If the middle of the cover was not taken up by a coat of arms, it would be filled by an oval or cartouche with a Moresque, arabesque or band-ed ornament. Sometimes the edges of the open space would be filled by similar dec-oration. In many cases, the execution indicates Saxon and central German patterns, stemming from the influence of French bindings and graphic precedents.[16]

Moresque ovals and cartouches on bindings of the Rudolfine period were often used, on the back cover for example, as an antithesis to or substitute to the heraldic emblem. An ornament thus placed is a direct suggestion to consider the original symbolic meaning. The magic oval mirror in which are fastened continuous undulat-ing and intertwining bands acted as a sign in itself, embodying the artifical world (contrasted with the natural world of the materials used in the preparation of the binding). The binding thus became an ideal spiritual construction presenting the principles of the universe. Cartouches with curling decoration (scrollwork) could be said to stand for 'fantastic-artistic' imagery (in the spirit of the Mannerist theory of Federico Zuccari). We come across them in the work of Czech bookbinders from the end of the 1580s, usually as a dominant motif into whose centre an oval has been set with a *supralibros* or motif of a vase with flowers. Curled, studded and auricular mo-

27.5– **Binding for the diary of**
6.   **Adam of Valdštejn**
    1606
    [Prague, Státní oblastní
    archiv]

27.7   **Binding with supralibros of**
    Václav Budovec of Budov
    1595
    [Prague, Umělecko-
    průmyslové muzeum]

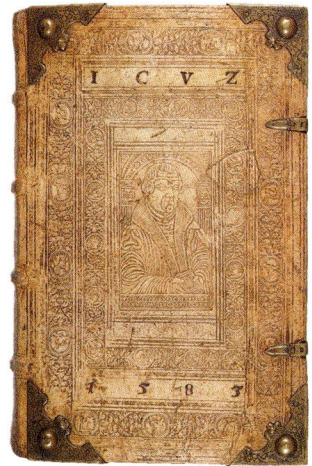

27.8 **Kryštof Meyšner, binding with initials ICVZ** (back)
1570s–90s
[Prague, Umělecko-průmyslové muzeum]

27.9 **Kryštof Meyšner, binding with initials ICVZ** (front)
1570s–90s
[Prague, Umělecko-průmyslové muzeum]

tifs are supplemented by festoons, mascarons, birds, baskets of fruit and allegorical figures. Here we find naturalistic quotations attached to the unreal cartouche ornament. Scrollwork cartouches also found their way into Czech bookbinding from imported German plates or from copies made by local carvers.[17] Their popularity is evidence of the influence of German and Dutch ornamentalists (Wendelin Dietterlin, Hans Vredeman de Vries, Virgil Solis). Book production from Ant-werp, Frankfurt and other workshops, with its rich illustrations, scrollwork printers' emblems and so forth, was clearly a greater influence on the ornament of bindings than were pattern albums. (We can call to mind remarkable publications from Christoph Plantini's workshop – for example, the atlases of Abraham Ortelius – or books from the Frankfurt shop of Sigmund Feyerabend with woodcuts by Jost Amman.)

The variety of influences at work on the creation of the new style of decoration reflected both the cosmopolitan environment of Rudolfine Prague and the multinational community of craftsmen at the court and in the city. Alongside gold-tooled bindings, plenty of blind-stamped bindings were still being produced, usually with a framework composition, a tradition which remained very strong in the Czech lands. It was current not only among the low-priced production for stock but also to order for bibliophiles.[18] Most Prague bookbinding workshops produced a variety of stylistically distinctive bindings at the same time. The plurality of stylistic levels flowed from the need to differentiate book production according to the financial, aesthetic and other requirements of customers. This applied not only to the Prague bookbinders but also to those on the Rožmberk estates and to the Unitas Fratrum, even though the more demanding nature of their work to order showed itself in a more conservative style when compared with that of the Prague bookbinders.[19]

1. Documentation exists concerning the immigration of bookbinders from Leipzig, Wittenberg, Stettin/Sczecin, Hamburg, Breslau/Wroclaw, Nürnberg, Nördlingen, Würzburg and Regensburg, and of journeymen from Freiburg, Rostock, Frydland (Mecklenburg), Heidelberg, Breslau/Wroclaw, Legnica and other towns. Bookbinders-sellers working in Prague came, for example, from Nürnberg, Linz, Wittenberg and Leipzig. See Zikmund Winter, *Řemeslnictvo a živností XVI. věku v Čechách* (Prague 1909), pp. 332–35; Bohumil Nuska, 'Die Beziehungen des böhmischen Renaissance-Bucheinbandes zu den Nachbarländern', *Zentralblatt für Bibliothekswesen*, 75:11 (1961), 481–94.

2. Winter (note 1), pp. 332–35. Winter's register records Prague bookbinders only on the basis of sources held in the City of Prague Archive (hereafter AHMP).

3. The town councillors of the Old Town issued guild regulations to bookbinders in 1596 (AHMP, rkp.č. 994, fol. 148); however, the beginnings of a trade organization of bookbinders in Prague go back to before this date, possibly to the 1570s (for example, the bookbinder Pavel Gutsch in the Old Town was Guild Master of the Bookbinders from 1574).

4. AHMP, rkp.č. 1174, 424–26, 1173, 387–88. The guild regulations also indicate a connection between the two professions, speaking out against abuses 'in the course of book binding and selling'. The Rožmberk accounts also record purchases of books

from bookbinders (Bohumil Nuska, 'Knihařské účty pana Petra Voka z Rožmberka', *Sborník Národního musea v Praze*, řada C – literární historie, IX, 1964, p. 67). The most recent documentation linking bookbinders and sellers (mainly Italian) comes from Anthony Hobson, 'Booksellers and Bookbinders' in Robin Myers and Michael Harris (eds), *A Genius for Letters* (St. Paul's Bibliographies, 1995), pp. 1–14.

5. AHMP, rkp.č. 1173, 85 (settlement of the estate of Jiří Melantrich the Younger in 1586).

6. Compare, for example, Ivan Vávra, 'Knižní vazby bratrské dílny ivančicko-kralické (1562–1620)' in *Historická knižní vazba* V-IX (1966-1970), Liberec 1970, p. 129; Zikmund Winter, *Český průmysl a obchod v XVI. věku* (Prague, 1913), p. 603.

7. Also to be considered, for example, is Görg Gebl, mentioned in the sources as 'J.M.Cís. buchbinder' (AHMP, rkp.č. 1064, 101). See Bohumil Nuska, 'České renesanční vazby ve východočeských sbírách, Práce musea v Hradci Králové', serie B, roč. V, Hradec Králové 1963, p. 123.

8. Ilse Schunke has drawn attention to some work by the craftsman known as the Master of the Dürer Sketchbook in 'Der Dürerbuch-Meister: Ein Buchbinder aus dem Rudolfinschen Prag', *Archiv für Buchbinderei*, 42 (1942), pp. 75–80. More detail on the Ligozzi manuscripts can be found in *Prag um 1600: Kunst und Kultur am Hofe Kaiser Rudolfs II.*, exh. cat. (Freren, 1988), vol. II, pp. 138–43. On the

Codices Vossiani, see Nicolette Mout, 'Books from Prague: The Leiden Codices Vossiani Chymici and Rudolf II' in *Prag um 1600: Beiträge zur Kunst und Kultur am Hofe Kaiser Rudolfs II.* (Freren, 1988), vol. II, p. 206. Further volumes to be found in Leiden are referred to in Rotraud Bauer and Herbert Haupt (eds), 'Das Kunstkammerinventar Kaiser Rudolfs II., 1607-1611', *Jahrbuch der kunsthistorischen Sammlungen* (Vienna), 72 (1976), pp. 133–34, 143.

9. Bohumír Lifka believes that Rudolf II may have dedicated the binding to his godson himself (Bohumír Lifka, *Exlibris a supralibros v ceskych korunních zemích v letech 1000–1900* [Prague, 1980], p. 96). Other dedications of Rudolfine bindings are noted in O. Walde, 'Bücher- und Bibliotheksgeschichtliche Forschungen in ausländischen Bibliotheken', *Nordisk tidskrift för bok-och biblioteksvasen* 17 (1930), p. 125, and Schunke (note 8), ill. 182.

10. For more work by the court workshops and the city masters, see, for example, *Knižní vazba sedmi století z fondů Strahovské knihovny*, exh. cat. ed. Pavlína Hamanová and Bohumil Nuska (Prague, 1966), pp. 15, 39-43

11. More detailed information can be found in Nuska, *Rozmberské účty* (note 4), pp. 62–63.

12. Vincenc Brandl, *Spisy Karla st. ze Žerotína* (Brno 1866-1872), letter no. 560 to Mikulás Petruš, p. 415.

13. Bauer and Haupt (eds) (note 8), pp. 130–39.

14. Fröschl's inventory gives data on the bindings of more than 120 volumes in the *Kunstkammer*. Approximately half of them were bound in red stained leather and in parchment; however, the share of parchment bindings was still greater, as the inventory does not note the more ordinary bindings.

15. This composition with a dominant motif on gold-tooled bindings could tie in with solutions of the early Renaissance, appearing in the Czech lands from the beginnings of the 1520s, and with domestic bindings with the ex-librises from the second third of the century (compare Schunke [note 8], p. 79). The Rudolfine period brought Czech bindings with *supralibros* close to contemporary bindings of this type from Rome with ceremonial papal and cardinal's ex-librises, France (for example, for Henri IV) and Saxony.

16. It is possible to find analogical motifs in graphic patterns in Jean Gourmont's *Livre de moresque*; also close is Jacques Androuet Ducerceau (*Livre contenant passement de moresques*), the anonymous Master GG and Virgil Solis. The expansion of Moresque ornamentation in bookbinding was helped by the migration of bookbinders and the importing of bindings and binding tools. Also evidence of the influence of bookbinders of the electorate of Saxony profiting from French patterns are a few Prague court bindings covered by small stamped floral and related ornaments.

17. We know of the almost identical use of tools on Prague bindings and on bindings from Augsburg, Würzburg and Dresden. Compare, for example, the Moresque oval on the binding for Archbishop Martin Medek of 1583 (Prague, Uměleckoprůmyslové muzeum) with the identical motif on the Würzburg binding published in O. Walde (note 9), pp. 14–30, or note the similarity between the scrollwork cartouche on the binding for the Lobkovicz family from after 1596 (Prague, Uměleckoprůmyslové muzeum) and on the binding for Philipp Eduard Fugger of 1577 (Vienna, Österreichische Nationalbibliothek; see Theodor Gottlieb, *Bucheinbände* [Vienna, 1909], pl. 88).

18. The tradition of blind-stamping left its mark on the production of Czech gilded bindings (with the space decorated almost exclusively by panel stamps) and led to the mutual influencing of these types of binding and their decoration (the types of mixed composition; the taking over of the composition by dominant motif for blind-stamped bindings; the use of identically carved rolls for both techniques).

19. Priority is more often given here to framed compositions and to figural motifs with allegorical or religious themes.

Architecture in Prague, 1550-1650

PAVEL VLČEK

With its complex architectural history, the small house known as U dvou zlatých medvědů (no.475/1) on the corner of Melantrichova and Kožní streets, with its beguiling grand portal, reflects the entire development of Czech architecture during the latter half of the sixteenth century. Its gradual and artistically demanding construction was carried out roughly between 1559 and 1575[1] and introduced new features into the medieval burgher's house.

The entrance portal, marked by northern decorativism, could not be contemporaneous with the elegant court arcades. At first glance, the portal is reminiscent of the early Renaissance style linked with the building enterprises of the powerful Pernštejn family. The Renaissance ornamentation, influenced by Northern architecture and covering all available space, the inlaid reliefs and the proportions all point to the work of an uncertain architect despite their obvious quality. The structure of the portal is at variance with what is almost a classical arcade. Its stylistically pure design was accredited to Bonifác Wolmut,[2] although its classicism, inspired by the Roman tradition, makes it clear that this attribution is incorrect. Even if we do not compare this arcade with the superb Griespekesque castle at Nelahozeves, for which Wolmut's authorship is only hypothetical,[3] we find it markedly different from his designs at Prague Castle for which documentation of his authorship exists. This difference stems chiefly from his misunderstanding of tectonics. A close look at details exposes his lack of proficiency. One has only to look at Wolmut's consoles set above the archivolts of the arches and not in the uppermost voussoir. They are therefore not structural, but instead, as in the choir in St Vitus' cathedral and the Ball-Game Hall, merely decorative. Compact, massive architectural expression is typical of Wolmut's works, devoid of Italian ethereality and grace. He rarely observed the proportional rules set by Renaissance theorists, having been guided instead by Cisalpine sensitivity.

The arcade of U dvou zlatých meděvdů,[4] pure and fragile like the Griespek chateaux, transcends the designs Wolmut created for the Castle. A few years later (before 1575), anonymous builders constructed further arcades on the north and south sides of the courtyard in a style influenced by the Tuscan Renaissance. The relatively slender columns were built on prism-shaped bases which reinforce the stone balustrade, and they highlight the individual arches, profiled by archivolts. As U dvou zlatých medvědů demonstrates, this Tuscan system, which appeared in Prague concurrently with the classical Roman style, became well established until the end of the sixteenth century. One cannot rule out the theory that this occurred under the influence of the architect appointed by the Castle, Ulrico Aostalli.[5]

An evidently earlier example of Tuscan arcades in Prague bourgeois architecture is the celebrated house owned by the Granovský family (no. 639/1), whose portals date the building to around 1559-60. Another house, U tří velbloudů (no. 471/1), stood in what is now Melantrichova Street (until its demolition at the end of the nineteenth century); it had been built after 1563 by Jiří Melantrich of Aventinum.

28.1 **Vault**
Church of the Virgin Mary
and Saint Charles the Great,
Prague
1575

The courtyard arcades there, with their small, slim pillars, were also complemented by elaborate relief ornamentation. Further Tuscan arcades completed the courtyard of U černého medvěda (no. 492/1) in Železná street; they were also used to great effect at U zlatého stromu (no. 729/1) in Dlouhá Street. The latter spanned three wings built during the period 1586-1608; the arcade of the fourth wing is part of a later extension (1648). Arcades were built at the beginning of the 1620s for the New Town house no. 1186/11 which existed on Petrské náměstí until its senseless demolition in 1936. The last two examples [6] from the early seventeenth century differ somewhat from the others. Evidently, the increasing drive to establish the Roman arcade system encouraged the architect to attempt to unify both styles, incorporating a classical Roman ground floor and adding subtle Tuscan arcades on the first floor. Thus a trait typical of Mannerism emerged in the endeavour to create, with a blend of heterogeneous yet exquisite individual features, a new, more exquisite style. A second type of arcade, simply known as a Roman arcade, began to make its mark on Prague architecture at a later stage; this is particularly noticeable at U svatych Tří králů (no. 463/1) in Melantrich street.[7] This feature was more typical of rural buildings and noble seats.

Before the advent of the bourgeois arcaded house during the 1560s, a new style of Prague noble palace had become established. The Pernštejn (formerly Krajířovský) and neighbouring Rožmberk palaces at Prague Castle were built before the middle of the century. The Lobkovic Palace (today the Schwarzenberg palace), however, standing on a prominent, attractive site, has a more positive quality. Although the construction of this palace was begun by Jan the Younger of Lobkovic before the mid-sixteenth century, it acquired its present appearance sometime during the 1560s. Its architect, ostensibly Agostino Galli, who also

worked for Lobkovic in Horšovský Týn, to a certain extent accommodated the northern way of thinking and taste of the owner. The sgraffito ornamentation (completed in 1567), imposing lunette cornice and striking tiered gables soon appeared on other buildings, especially those associated with Aostalli and known today as 'Czech Renaissance'. In Prague itself, the small U minuta (no. 3/1) on the Old Town Square could be considered a telling example. Palaces for the nobility were first built at Hradčany and later spread to the whole left bank of the Vltava; thus this part of the city acquired a slightly different character from the Old Town, particularly neighbourhoods inhabited by burghers.

Prague had very few important Renaissance palaces, or perhaps later structural improvements tended to overshadow many of them. Only the rear of the palace of the Lords of Hradec (no. 193/111) facing the New Castle Steps still has its Renaissance façades and gables which conceal original roofs. Stylistically, we cannot distinguish the central part of the palace (1562-64) from the wings added by Aostalli (1586-89). The Trčovský palace, built around 1583, was transformed into the Goltz-Kinský Palace (no. 606/1) following reconstruction work carried out in the late Baroque style. One of the last large Renaissance palaces, built on Malostranské náměstí (no. 6/111) and commissioned by the family, has preserved much of its period features despite late Baroque reconstruction. Apart from paired windows, these include polygonal bay windows at the corners, two of the most distinctive features of late Renaissance Bohemian architecture.

After the mid-sixteenth century, Prague opened its arms to the Renaissance when the last medieval residue disappeared from buildings of little (or no) importance. Exceptions included sacred buildings and projects in which Bonifác Wolmut had been closely involved. At the request of Emperor Ferdinand I,[8] Gothic rib vaulting was constructed over the organ choir in St Vitus' cathedral, but in a Renaissance manner. Wolmut also used transverse vaulting during the renovation of the New Town Hall after it was damaged by fire in 1559. Church Na Karlově (before 1575), still Gothic in style, may be ascribed to Wolmut due to its archaistic style. The construction of vaults with great distances between them presented Czech builders with almost insurmountable technical difficulties.

We might not be mistaken if we branded buildings which appeared as late as circa 1600 as consciously historicizing during a period when religious attitudes in the Czech lands were becoming increasingly intolerant. Historical influences are particularly apparent in the designs of Catholic churches, but can also be seen in many Protestant buildings. The Lutheran church of the Holy Saviour (no. 1045/1) was given a polygonal apse with a buttress; the high, narrow windows are Gothic in style. The apse of the presbytery, despite the use of Renaissance details, seems so heterogeneous that it must have been added as part of later renovation work. We also find Gothic features in the chapel of St Roch in Strahov, and Gothicizing traceries also appeared on the Premonstratensian monastery church there during its late Renaissance reconstruction by Giovanni Battista Bussi of Campione (1600-5). During the seventeenth century, historicizing details were used on the church of Sts Simon and Jude; the monks completely rebuilt this former church of the Czech Brethren sometime before 1632. This historicist programme, in which the Capuchin friars were following the teachings of St Francis of Assisi, was maintained in all of their buildings throughout the seventeenth and eighteenth centuries. The Ca-

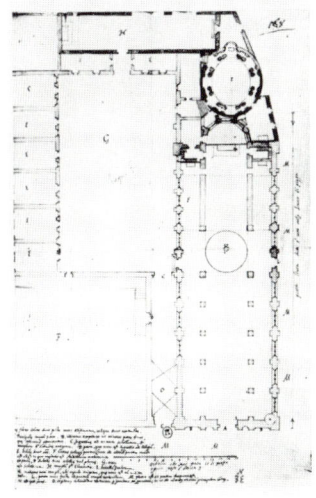

28.2 **Groundplan**
Church of the Holy Saviour (1578–1649), Valachian Chapel (1590–1597), Prague [Paris, Bibliothèque Nationale]

puchins built another monastery in Prague's New Town during the period 1636-42, this time under the supervision of court master-builder Melchior Meer. This building, demolished long ago, was similar to that at Hradčany conceived by the Venetian Capuchin P. Antonio of Pordenone in 1603.⁹

Before the arrival of the Capuchins, the Jesuits had already settled in Prague at the former Dominican monastery near the Charles Bridge, now the Clementinum. It was not until 1578 that the order decided to reconstruct the former Dominican church, or at least its presbytery (and perhaps part of its three aisles), by erecting two side spires. The reconstruction work, completed in 1583 and, according to the findings of Milada Vilímková, carried out by Master Fontana of Brusato,¹⁰ however, did not have much in common with the later Renaissance modifications (1600-1). The Jesuits were only able to extend the church after 1593, when they had purchased the land for it; the actual construction date was probably 1600, when they sent the new project for the church to Rome for approval. It was probably not until then that the dome was designed (undoubtedly without the tambour) and also the remarkable western façade, of which only three portals survive.¹¹ If we are to believe the ideal schematic view of the Clementinum from the beginning of the seventeenth century, the Jesuit church, the first in Bohemia, acquired a typical Italian façade divided into three axes by tall pilastered orders spanning several floors; the gable also corresponded to Italian models.

The number of Italians arriving in Prague increased rapidly during the latter half of the sixteenth century. Finding a fluid religious environment, they soon created their own congregation (1573) and built what was undeniably the most important sacred building of this period, the Marian chapel, behind the apse of the church of the Holy Saviour in the Clementinum. The significance of this small oval chapel, built as early as 1590, has been stressed frequently in recent times.¹² We find its echo in Prague in the chapel of St Mary Magdelen below Letná, which was completed around 1635.¹³ In the shadow of these Mannerist chapels stood another, larger building association formed by the Italian congregation. As early as 1600, to serve the emerging Italian colony, it founded a hospital in the region of Jánský Vršek in the Lesser Town; the chapel of the Assumption of Our Lady and St Charles Borromeo was built alongside it in 1611.¹⁴ Despite a traditional ground plan, its barrel vaulting, broken into segmented sections and highlighted with consoles, is fairly progressive.

The beginning of the seventeenth century was characterized in Prague by unprecedented construction activity which has received little scholarly attention. It was unusual if a Prague house did not undergo at least minimum renovation work during this period. The prices of properties began to rise beginning around the 1580s, and a sharp increase occurred at the beginning of the 1600s, both due to higher demand and increased construction activity. The houses being built were taller than before and were all the more noticeable for their high gables.

The beginning of this period was marked by a preference for vertical (i.e., Gothicizing) features, later replaced by robust horizontal cornices. At the beginning of the 1600s, gables were again altered to become more compact. The gable was conceived as a unified section, often complemented with scrolling wings and a split triangular pediment. An example of this could be seen on the tower of house no. 791/11, which stood on the corner of Wenceslas Square and Vodičková Street, built

28.3 **Townhall, Prague's Lesser Town**
View from the north west
1617-19

28.4 UNKNOWN ARCHITECT
Lutheran church of the Most
Holy Trinity
Prague's Lesser Town
[Prague, Museum of the City
of Prague]

in 1610, it was demolished in 1913. U císařskych (no. 832/11), on the corner of what is now Jindřišská Street and Wenceslas Square, built after 1606 and demolished in 1895, also acquired a number of gables of this kind. These houses were not unique for their era, as Morstadt's view of Žitná shows: several houses renovated in this manner were still being commissioned in 1873. A more pronounced example of the new type of gable may be seen on the Old Town house U pěti korun (no. 465/1) in Melantrichova Street, which is frequently mentioned in architecture books in connection with the Zwerchhaus in Augsburg and with Venetian buildings. A palace commissioned by Lazar Henkel the Younger of Donnersmark after 1609 has not survived (nor was it ever completed); it betrayed the influence of Venetian master-builders. A period illustration depicting the Passau invasion of Prague in 1611 captures this building in mid-construction with its colossal columns designed to break up the façade.[15] This house, on which such elements were used for the first time in Bohemia, derived from the work of Andrea Palladio and his successor Vincenzo Scamozzi and has been attributed to Giovanni Maria Filippi. A more alluring supposition suggests that it may be linked with an earlier (newly renovated) project by Scamozzi, who is known to have stayed in Prague. Similar columns were also incorporated into the architecture of the Clementinum after 1653. No less prominent, although different in expression, was the Lesser Town town hall, built after 1617 with gables added after 1628; these have since been dismantled. This building, whose design is attributed to Giovanni Battista Bussi of Campione,[16] represents a new compositional system despite its marked late Renaissance character. The architect focused on emphasizing the separate storeys and individual window axes, which were repeated across the entire façade. This additive principle applied to façades governed Prague architecture throughout the 1600s.

The issuing of Rudolf's Imperial Charter in 1609 was followed immediately by the construction in Prague of three Protestant churches: the traditional church of the Czech Brethren, of which only the north side aisle remains as part of the church of Sts Simon and Jude,[17] the German Lutheran church of the Holy Saviour in the Old Town, of similar design, and the church of the Most Holy Trinity in the Lesser Town. In 1611, the German Lutherans laid the foundations for a church whose design is fortunately preserved in surviving sketches and plans. It may thus be compared with the form it acquired after renovation work undertaken by the Carmelites during 1634–44. Whether the architect was G. M. Filippi, who built a

[349]

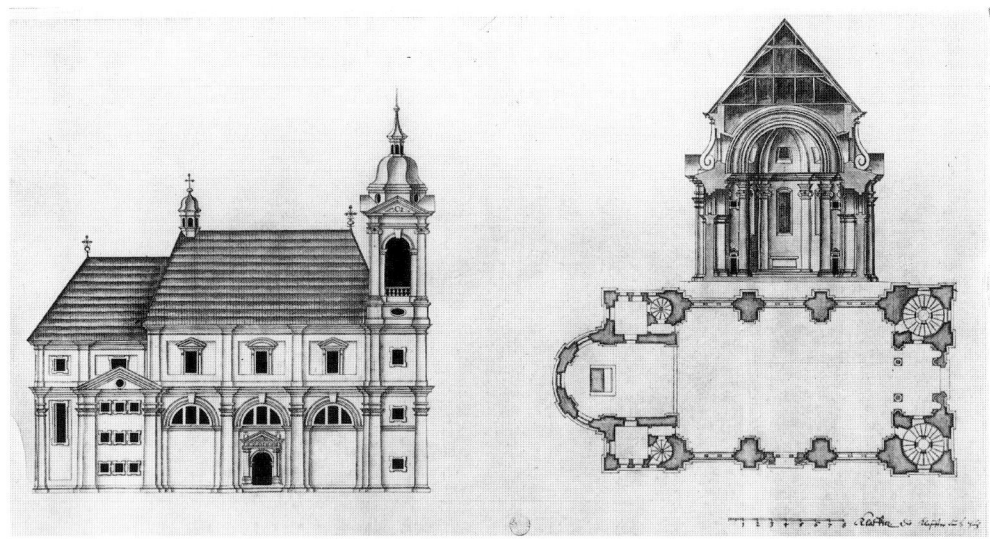

28.5 UNKNOWN ARCHITECT
Lutheran church of the Most
Holy Trinity
Prague's Lesser Town
[Prague, Museum of the City
of Prague]

similar edifice in Arc not far from his native town of Dasindo, or Josef Heintz,[18] it is considered an exceptional work of architecture, one of the first Baroque churches in Prague. The nave, symbolically divided into three vaulted bays, the modest side chapels, the narrow presbytery beneath one vaulted bay, and the semi-circular apse are all characteristic motifs of early Baroque churches. The Carmelite reconstruction was in no way governed by a change in stylistic sentiment, but by ideological purpose. The former Protestant role of the church was of key importance, but so were the needs of the Carmelites. They lacked an oratorium behind the presbytery, and the orientation of the church was also unsuitable. Furthermore, the façade was considered at the time to be typically Protestant and defied the building principles observed by strict mendicants like the Carmelites, who in 1614 established a commission to set down regulations dictating how churches should be constructed. This commission recommended that the church of Sta Maria della Scala[19] should serve as a model. By coincidence, the architect responsible for that building, Ottavio Mascherino, is mentioned in connection with the Italian chapel in the Clementinum. If the original Protestant church of the Holy Trinity had been designed to follow the Roman cathedral of Sta Trinita dei Monti[20] beginning around 1580, the new Carmelite church was inspired by a sanctuary built only slightly later, although still in the late Renaissance style.

While the defeat of the Czech Estates at the Battle of the White Mountain brought about enormous political and religious changes, it did not signify a turning point in architecture. It only marked the increasing influence of Italian craftsmanship on the work of the Italian congregation in Prague, which was not affected by Cisalpine taste. The war which broke out all over Europe after the Battle of the White Mountain hampered building work considerably; the need for housing in Prague was also reduced by a fall in the number of inhabitants.

We are able to document the architecture of this period chiefly through the buildings commissioned by the three most notable members of the newly rich sector of the community. Jakub Baševi of Treuenberk rose from the Prague Jewish ghetto, the bourgeois family of Pavel Michna of Vacínov had recently been awarded noble status, and Albrecht of Wallenstein had come from a relatively poor noble line. Baševi commissioned the building of a house in the Jewish Town after 1623 (no. 73/VI, now no longer in existence) which, from an architectural point of view, did not differ greatly from the bourgeois houses of the early 1600s. The date when the construction of the Michna Palace in the Lesser Town began is not known, although half of the garden wing, including its stucco decoration, was completed in 1644.[21] The intended design of the building is known from a recently discovered ground plan forming part of the so-called 'Dientzenhofer Sketch-Book'.[22] It would have been a challenging project, comparable with work undertaken in Rome at the time. Despite the fact that barely a quarter of the building was completed (whilst incorporating an earlier work by Aostalli), the resulting structure constituted the purest and most impressive example of secular Mannerism in the country. Perhaps this was the reason it was never imitated; on the contrary, the building soon underwent renovation work which did not do it justice.

The palace of Albrecht of Wallenstein in the Lesser Town had considerably greater influence on the shaping of Prague architecture, chiefly due to its spatial arrangement and decoration. The piano nobile, accessible via a grand staircase, comprises a main hall on two floors, a novel feature which became practically mandatory for all important Prague palaces and rural seats from the mid-seventeenth century onwards. The communication system of the palace indicates the importance ascribed to this space, which was decorated with the finest art works. Guests would have to pass through the main hall in order to reach adjacent reception rooms on the first floor and the great hall. The private rooms were situated in the wing which looks out onto Valdštejnská Street, where Wallenstein had access to the oratory in the palace chapel, his own dining room, his private apartments and his study.[23] Formally, the individual features were still Mannerist in character, although not taken directly from the Italian model, as was the case with the Michna Palace, but reworked in the Cisalpine tradition. The system used to distinguish the courtyard façades represents one of the last examples of the typical division of storeys, which disappeared during the latter half of the seventeenth century. The ground floor, in its Tuscan purity quite different from the rest of the palace, shows to what extent late Renaissance and Mannerist styles were formally applied. In addition to these qualities, however, this unusually spacious building also demonstrates a leaning towards the new Baroque style rooted in the owner's desire to create a truly princely residence. To this end, he even resorted to illusion to achieve his goals. This is evident from the entrance façade, which conceals diverse parts of the structure behind a single unified surface. Unlike buildings designed earlier, it was not possible to ascertain where the staircase led, nor where the great hall was located. The monumental main entrance itself is only a coulisse. Despite its late Renaissance (Mannerist) morphology, the principal façade of the Wallenstein Palace thus anticipated illusionism, one of the main traits of the approaching new style – the Baroque.

28.6 UNKNOWN ARCHITECT
Lutheran church of the Most Holy Trinity
Prague's Lesser Town
[Prague, Museum of the City of Prague]

1. J. Mayer, 'Dům u dvou medvědů', *Umění*, 6 (1958): 389–95.

2. *Ibid.*, J. Krčálová, 'Renesančí architektura v Čechách a na Moravě', *Dějiny Českého výtvarného umění*, 2:1 (1989): 47.

3. J. Krčálová (note 2):15 has most recently attributed the arcades at Nelahozeves Castle to Wolmut.

4. The arcade wall has apparently not survived in its entirety. The half-columns closely resemble those in the arcades at Nelahozeves, and it is probable that they were designed by the same architect.

5. In view of this fact, it would be strange to regard Aostalli as the pupil or successor of Wolmut, whose work is based on entirely different architectural principles.

6. D. Líbal recognized that both buildings were designed by the same architect (see M. Vilímková and D. Líbal, 'Architektura' in *Praha na úsvitu nových*

dějin, [Prague, 1988], p. 138).

7. J Mayer, 'Architektonické dílo Jana Dominika de Barifis', *Staletá Praha*, 5 (1971): 199–209.

8. J. Krčálová, 'Kostely České a moranské renesance, příspěvek k jejich typologii', *Umění* 29 (1981): 7.

9. Anna Salvini Cavazzana, 'I conventi capuccini in Lombardia', in *Il Francescanesimo in Lombardia, storia e arte* (Milan, 1983), p. 508.

10. Vilímkov and Líbal (note 6), p. 112.

11. P. Vlček, 'Dientzenhoferův skicář a česká architektura 1640–1670', *Umění* 37 (1989): 482–83. The attribution of the design of the church to B. Wolmut is questionable. The contrast between the parts is further emphasized by the differing widths of the presbytery and the nave of the original three-aisled basilica. The nave is surprisingly narrower, probably due to the use of different systems of measurement (Czech ells, in the case of the nave).

12. J. Krčálová, *Centrální stavby české renesance* (Prague, 1976), pp. 69–77.

13. J. Krčálová, 'Italští mistři Malé Strany na počátku 17. století', *Umění* 18 (1970), 565–66, credited the work to Domenico Bossi.

14. P. Preiss, *Italští umělci v Praze* (Prague, 1986), p. 92.

15. D. Líbal, 'Dvé dávno zaniklá architektonická díla pražské renesance', *Staletá Praha* 8 (1977): 263–73.

16. See above, note 13.

17. According to research carried out by J. Muk, we know that this side aisle once had a polygonal apse which was projected into the nave through semicircular arches. The interior of the church originally consisted of the nave and side aisle of the church of the Czech Brethren, which had the same length as the existing building.

18. J. Zimmer, 'Iosephus Heinzius architectus cum antiquis comparandus', *Umění* 17 (1969): 217–46.

19. B. J. Wanat, *Zakon karmelitów bosych w Polsce* (Cracow, 1979), p. 95.

20. V. Birnbaum, 'Původní průčelí kostela P. Marie Vítězné na Malé Straně', *Památky archeologické*, 34 (1924–25): 219–21.

21. The stucco-worker Domenico Galli amassed a debt of 3,319 gulden after the Michna estate was declared bankrupt; a document from 1644 states that he had been commissioned to do this work by the Count himself (V. Birnbaumov, *Tyršův dům v Praze* [Prague, 1948], p. 37).

22. Vlček (note 11): 474, 482–83.

23. *Ibid.*: 491–92.

Sculpture and Painting in Prague, 1550-1650

MICHAL ŠRONĚK

Sculpture

During the late sixteenth and early seventeenth centuries, heterogeneous trends from Italy, Saxony and Silesia began to influence Bohemian sculpture and stucco work. Also significant during this period were the wood-carving and stone-cutting practised predominantly in towns and cities. Diversity derived from the demands of patrons as well as the influences exerted by different social groups and religious denominations.[1]

The rise of Renaissance sculpture was closely associated with the building projects commissioned by Ferdinand I and Archduke Ferdinand, whose patronage inspired the relief decoration of Queen Anna's Summer Palace (1538–52) in the Royal Garden and the stucco work carried out on the Star Villa between 1555 and 1556. Work by sculptors in Saxony also had a marked influence on Bohemian sculpture.[2] This influence made itself felt for the most part along the borders of northern Bohemia, where work was commissioned by the Lutheran nobility, which had begun settling in the area during the sixteenth century.

29.1 **Tombstone of Jiří of Lobkowicz**
St Vitus Cathedral, Prague
1590

Sculptors from Dresden, Pirna and Freiburg in Saxony began to settle in the area between Most and Benešov nad Ploučnicí. This Saxon influence brought with it a new type of tombstone consisting of an aedicula framed by columns or pilasters normally topped by a triangular shield or smaller aedicula-like extension. A relief depicting the deceased kneeling before the cross was set between the columns. The making of tombstones, with few exceptions, provided the main source of work for sculptors in Bohemia in the sixteenth century. Styles employed ranged from late Gothic decorativism, with Saxon influences, to works inspired by realistic sculpture from the Netherlands. Instances of Italian influence were rare.

Only a fraction of the once vast collection of tombstones in Prague's churches has been preserved.[3] Figurative tombstones were more commonly commissioned by Utraquists and Lutherans, with catholics preferring simple lapidary inscriptions. The figurative tombstone style developed at the court presented, in so far as it was possible, a genuine depiction of the deceased, whereas in the towns and cities such representations remained more rustic and schematic. Court art was closely bound up with the construction of the so-called Habsburg mausoleum in St Vitus' cathedral in Prague, the design of which, particularly in its depiction of the deceased, had a noticeable influence on sculpture in the city during the last quarter of the sixteenth century. Responsible for the mausoleum's design and creation was the Netherlander Alexander Colin, who had been a sculptor at the court of Ferdinand I since 1562. In 1566, he was entrusted by Maximilian II with the design of the tombstone for Ferdinand I and Anna Jagellonská in Prague. Colin completed the work in 1573, and, following the death of Maximilian II, it was decided that the deceased Emperor would be buried in Prague beside his parents.

It is interesting to follow the design of the mausoleum from the initial drawings through to completion. It was originally intended that the recumbent sovereigns would be depicted in Roman fashion resting on an elbow, but this was later changed to a supine posture in which the figures assumed a majestic, if not unnatural, posture. Whether this was an attempt to give the Emperor a larger-than-life appearance, or whether Colin was influenced by Spanish regal portraiture, is not clear. Portraits of Rudolf II's ancestors were added to the mausoleum in 1587.[4]

Colin's impersonal depiction of the deceased influenced the design of several other tombstones commissioned by Catholics which were intended to be housed in the cathedral, for instance the tombstones by Bernardo Menesto from Toledo (after 1566) or the tomb slabs of the Prague archbishops Antonin Brus of Mohelnice and Nicholas Medek. There are also rare examples of tombstones with Italian influences in their design, such as that which the head steward Adam of Dietrichstein commissioned for his wife's parents, Antonio and Maria de Cardona, or the undated tombstone for twin infants, possibly the children of Hans Von Aachen. Saxon influence can be seen in the work of Vincent Strašryba, who came to Bohemia from Wroclaw via Saxony.[5] In 1581, he was commissioned to create an epitaph for the head steward Jan the Elder of Lobkovice; he designed it as a portal aedicula with the deceased kneeling inside it before the Holy Trinity. A relief of the Resurrected Christ is set in the extension between the figures of saints Peter and Paul. In view of the fact that Strašryba died in 1582 leaving the epitaph to be finished by his workshop in 1594, it is difficult to precisely define his style. The construction of the epitaph as a whole was carried out in strict accordance with Saxon style. By contrast, the unknown sculptor who created the tombstone for Jiří Popel of Lobkovice, while similarly adhering to the rules of Saxon figurative memorial sculpture, modified his work by using a refined combination of different-coloured marbles with a gracefully constructed figural representation of the deceased, acknowledging his debt to Colin and court art. The last direct influence wielded by Saxon sculpture over Prague before the Battle of the White Mountain was closely bound up with the activities of the Lutherans, who – following the issue of Rudolf's Imperial Charter – built the Holy Trinity and St Salvador churches in the Lesser Town and the Old Town, respectively. The Saxon sculptor Samuel Lorentz of Freiburg was entrusted with their ornamentation, adding an altar to the church of the Holy Trinity and a pulpit to that of St Salvador.[6]

Of the sculptors working in the city we know relatively little. By name alone we know of Jindřich Pražák known as Beránek (1576–1609) and the masons Václav Havelka (after 1592) and Havel Chrupavý (1595), who worked at the church of St Stephen.[7] Examples of city sculpture from this period are preserved in the church of Our Lady before Týn and those of saints Haštal, Henry and Stephen. As a sculpture by a city mason, the tomb slab of the astronomer Tycho Brahe (after 1600) in the church of Our Lady before Týn can be regarded as archetypal. While the unknown mason carefully reproduced the facial detail of the deceased, as well as the armour and ceremonial chain across his chest, the figure as a whole is somewhat awkwardly modelled and strangely shortened in its proportions. The figurative tombstone, so typical of Bohemian sculpture in the latter half of the sixteenth century, quickly disappeared following the Battle of the White Mountain.

The most important Renaissance sculptural commission involved the ornamentation of the fountain erected in the centre of the Old Town Square by the mayor Václav Krocín of Drahobejle, most likely carried out between 1591 and 1596.[8] The foun-

29.2 **Interior**
Church of the Holy Saviour
in the Clementinum
Old Town, Prague
1578–1649

tain, carved from solid red marble, was pointlessly destroyed in 1862; a fragment is on display in the Národní muzeum. The facets of the thirteen-sided basin were ornamented with signs of the zodiac and the coat of arms of the fountain's commissioner. A relief column of St Wenceslas and the city's coat of arms mounted below Neptune riding astride two dolphins was set at the head of the fountain. On the corner were allegories of the Virtues, and around the pilaster, statues of Neptune, Tellus, Jupiter and Minerva, intended to represent the elements of Water, Earth, Fire and Air. A vessel at the top of the pilaster was ornamented with animals and mermaids. The designer of this work was a sculptor who initialled it *LW*. It may well be that he was in fact a member of the Walther family of sculptors in Dresden. Krocín's fountain was not only a remarkable sculpture but was also an example of the then rare form of patronage for a public work, which was nonetheless designed to satisfy the aesthetics of a particular individual or family.

Such displays of patronage, linked to works which represented in various ways a particular religious faith, became increasingly common among the ranks of Bohemian Catholics in the 1570s.[9] Many sculptural monuments were not preserved. Works such as triumphal arches, 'Lord's tombs' and theatrical productions, though sculptural in nature, had only a transient existence. Particularly active in this area were the Jesuits, who on the occasion of the arrival of Ferdinand I in 1558, two years after their own arrival in Prague, staged an allegorical production in which Peace and Justice overpowered the bound figure of Mars. They similarly celebrated the arrival of Maximilian II by erecting a triumphal arch bearing the image of the Blessed Virgin attended by Jesuit pupils dressed up as angels. The thematic staging of 'The Divine Body', organized by the Jesuits in 1567, made use of forty-six boys as well as performances by the archangels Gabriel and Michael as symbols of the victorious church and was intended, by means of a 'dialogue with living statues', to convince the audience of the true presence of God in the Eucharist. Such productions often influenced the altar arrangement of churches during the early Baroque period. Besides these and other similar productions classifiable as something between religious parades and theatrical productions, Catholic patrons also commissioned works of a more permanent nature. Primarily, these included the construction of altars or tombstones for patron saints, the worship of whom had been systematically cultivated at the end of the sixteenth century by Jiří Bartold Pontanus of Breitenberk, a member of the Chapter of St Vitus. The number of newly erected altars grew significantly and provided a focal point in Catholic churches and chapels for the voicing of the church's ideas. These altars were in the main commissioned by the nobility, notably Rudolf's courtiers, the papal nuncio and a Spanish envoy. Maria Manrique de Lara, the widow of Vratislav of Pernštejn for example, commissioned the now lost altar of saints Cyril and Methodius to be built in St Vitus' cathedral. After 1600, a portal altar was built in the cathedral's Martinická chapel in a classical style; it was later removed to the Franciscan church in Slaný.

Unfortunately, the decoration of St Vitus' suffered serious damage at the hands of iconoclasts during the reign of Friedrich Falcký in 1619, and parts were destroyed by later reconstruction. Particularly active in building churches were the religious orders which had recently established themselves in Prague. The new altars of course combined painting and sculpture, but few examples have survived. The most active of these orders were probably the Jesuits, who in 1564 acquired a silver taber-

29.3 DOMENIC DE BARIFICE
Interior of the former
Lutheran church of the Holy
Saviour
Old Town, Prague
After 1609

nacle for the altar in the church of St Salvador and in 1581 added a main altar constructed out of alabaster. In 1600, Maria of Martinice commissioned the altar of Mary Magdalen, the central part of which contained a relief of the Resurrection by Bohuslav Balbín, and the sides of which carried depictions of Christ appearing before Mary Magdalen, and John the Baptist with Salome. A year later, four sculptures of saints were added to the main altar, including the as yet uncanonized saints Ignatius Loyola and Francis Xavier. In 1603, a new pulpit was added, as well as the altar of the Czech patron saints, and in 1604, the exceptionally active Spanish patron, the envoy Guillén de San Clemente, commissioned another altar. In 1608, he was also responsible for the building of a tomb of Prague Spaniards in the church of St Thomas belonging to the Augustinian Order, as well as the portal altar which has been preserved in the church's sacristy. His successor, Balthazar Zúniga, commissioned an altar to the newly canonized saint and supporter of the Counter-Reformation, Charles Borromeo. The Minorite church of St James in the Old Town was also richly ornamented, with fifteen altars, four epitaphs and an interior further decorated with standards and coats of arms,[10] all of which were unfortunately destroyed in a fire in 1689.

After 1600, new works were commissioned for the Premonstratensians' monastery in Strahov, including an altar to the Birth of the Blessed Virgin commissioned by the Spanish envoy San Clemente in 1606, and one to the Invention of the Holy Cross and St Helen commissioned by the imperial councillor Johan Matthaeus Wacker von Wackenfels.[11] In 1616, Konstancie, the sister of Abbot Caspar of Questernberk, commissioned the building of another altar on which work was done by Daniel Altman of Eydenburk, one of the few artists whose oeuvre, influenced by Bavarian sculpture, can be traced at least in part.[12] This altar was preserved in Litice u Plzně (1600), and his sculptures of the apostles Peter and Paul, originally set on the main altar of the church at the Strahov monastery (on which building began in 1618), were later transferred to the church of the Visitation of the Blessed Virgin. Altman also worked in the churches of St Stephen and Our Lady before Týn, and towards the end of his life participated in the interior redecoration of St Vitus'. There his Calvary figures, as with his sculpture of the Madonna in the Talmberg chapel of the Victorious Blessed Virgin, testify to the influence of late Gothic wood-carving. In 1583, as part of the worship of the Czech patron saints, the now lost alabaster tombstone of St Procopius, whose remains had recently been removed from Sásava to Prague, was built in the All Saints chapel at Hradčany Castle. The leading figures of Catholic society, the envoy San Clemente, Marshal Rusworm, gained recognition for their improvements to the altar and tombstone of St Ivan in the church of St John pod Skalou.[13]

The year 1620 did not so much herald a turning point in the style of sculpture in Prague as it did in the socio-historical milieu. With the take-over of all churches of different religious denominations by the Catholic church, the need increased to refit them with suitable interiors. As had been the case before the Battle of the White Mountain, however, commissions in the city were clearly Catholic. Albrecht of Wallenstein gathered around himself court artists with a level of training and ability way above that of artists then living in the city. The period between 1620 and 1650 was mixed stylistically and, also because of the fragmentary nature of the works preserved, is difficult to define. The basic line of development was based on Mannerism,

29.4 UNKNOWN MASON
Tombstone of Tycho de Brahe
Church of the Our Lady
before Týn
After 1601

which began to be combined with realistic elements. The attempt to envisage human beings as embodying clear spiritual meaning intensified and resulted in grandiose depictions. The first opportunity for these new demands to be implemented in the sculpture of the early Counter-Reformation, came with the interior redecoration of the cathedral of St Vitus. The project became a prestigious affair financed by Emperor Ferdinand II. Daniel Altman worked on the extensive commission along with the court's wood-carver Caspar Bechteler,[14] who made reliefs depicting the Calvinist desecration of the cathedral and the grave of St John Nepomuk, and the flight of Friedrich Falcký from Prague; these were mounted between the pilasters of the chancel sometime before 1623. The didactic, straightforward reliefs were intended to assuage the guilt which had led to the desecration of the cathedral and punishment by defeat in the Battle of the White Mountain. Bechteler included many realistic elements in his work on the cathedral's interior. The door panels begun in 1629 and completed in 1631, depicting the figures of the Czech patron saints in low relief, are similar in style. These works are important primarily from an iconographic point of view, in as much as they capture in an artistic form the conception of Bohemian national Catholicism at the turn of the seventeenth century and testify to the worship of St John Nepomuk.

The Premonstratensians continued fitting out their churches' interiors after the Battle of the White Mountain and in 1638 completed the main altar in their church in Strahov, begun by Daniel Altman in 1618.[15] Altman had built another altar for the Premonstratensians in the church of St Catherine, as well as a pontifical throne. Besides Altman, Mikuláš Pfaff also worked in Strahov, carving the altar of the Czech patron saints. His brother Jan, who worked on the altar in the chapel of the St Elizabeth hospital, also collaborated with him. The Strahov Premonstratensians' most ambitious project during the 1620s involved the transfer of St Norbert's remains to Prague.[16] These relics were brought to Bohemia and, in a ceremonial parade staged between 30 April and 2 May 1627, were taken to Strahov. The parade was routed through the streets of Prague, where triumphal arches had been erected and ornamented with allegories, paintings and emblems. In the church in Strahov, the remains were placed in a tomb enclosed by railings with angels at each corner, above which an enormous crown was hung in 1633. The celebrations accompanying the transfer of the saint's remains marked the first Baroque parade to be seen by Prague's citizens and symbolically marked the celebrations which accompanied the sanctification of St John Nepomuk a hundred years later.

Despite the fact that the church was the main source of commissions during this period, the patronage provided by the sovereign and nobility should not be discounted. When the so-called Empress' Wing of Hradčany Castle was constructed between 1638 and 1644, the living quarters for the Empress' female retinue were modified, and the chapel of St Wenceslas was built. Among those artists and wood-carvers working on the ornamentation of the newly constructed buildings were Abraham Melber, Jan Ernest Heidelberger, Elias Gutbier and Jan Jiří Bendl.[17] Given the character of the sovereign's projects for the Castle between the 1630s and 1640s, it is peculiar that work under the supervision of the treasurer Dionisio Miseroni was undertaken by artists who, though often calling themselves courtiers, were by and large connected with the city.

An aristocratic project which by its grandiose nature sought to compete with the

architectural and artistic projects of Rudolf II and his successors was the construction and decoration of Albrecht of Wallenstein's palace in the Lesser Town between 1623 and 1630. This complex was designed by Andrea Spezza in collaboration with Giovanni Pieroni and perhaps even Nicolo Sebregondi.[18] Though from a stylistic standpoint, Wallenstein palace's took its inspiration from north Italian and Mannerist architecture, its grandiose setting meant that it took on a somewhat Baroque appearance. That it was intended to counterbalance Hradčany Castle is clear not only from the architecture itself but also from the selection of renowned artists commissioned to work on it. In the early 1620s, Adriaen de Vries, at one time a sculpture in the court of Rudolf II, began working for Wallenstein.[19] For his palace gardens, the sculptor created the ornamentation for a fountain comprising a sculpture of Neptune, as well as statues of nymphs, tritons, horses and griffins. The four mythological themes of Venus and Adonis, the Wrestlers, Bacchus playing with a satyr, and Apollo provided the basis for the series of statues completed between 1624 and 1625 and set around the fountain. The statues' jagged silhouettes contrast to great effect with the stately *salla terrena*. Although de Vries' later work is often noted for its permissive content and exaggerated musculature, a feature of Baroque works, its other elements were foreign to the seriousness and expressiveness of early Baroque Bohemian sculpture. It was precisely for this reason that, following de Vries' death in 1626, his foundry failed to survive after completing its commissions for Wallenstein.

It is characteristic of the time that the bronze crucifix mounted on Charles Bridge in 1657 had been purchased abroad in Dresden by the Old Town council and made by the sculptor Wolf Brohn.[20] Wallenstein's liking for Mannerist art is further attested to by the fact that he acquired, for one of the fountains in his gardens, twin statues of Venus and Amor sculpted by the Nürnberg-based Benedict Wurzelbauer.[21] The works of the sculptor Ernest Jan Heidelberg provide a clear connection between Mannerist court art, Wallenstein's commissions, and works being made in the city.[22] Heidelberg may well have come to Prague from northern Saxony, but his works were unmistakably inspired by the Mannerist sculpture of southern Germany. Before 1618, he had worked on the ornamentation of the New Hall in Hradčany Castle. In 1628, he was made a court sculptor, and as such he designed Ferdinand II's and Ferdinand IV's *Castra Doloris* for St Vitus' and worked on the Empress' Wing of the Castle. Between 1630 and 1632, his services were at Wallenstein's disposal, and for the latter's palace he ornamented the altar in the chapel of St Wenceslas. At the sides of the altar, he positioned slender statues of angels whose posture, almost like that of dancers, leaves nothing to connect them with the altar painting's depiction of St Wenceslas' murder. The artistic quality of Heidelberg's work is attested to by the surface texture of his statues, which he created by combining white pigment and gilt, so as to imitate the much more expensive combination of gold and ivory known as chryselephantine. These angels are similar in style to the statues of the twelve Franciscan saints mounted on the wall supports of the main transept in the church of the Blessed Virgin Sněžná, completed between 1620 and 1640. It was without a doubt Heidelberg who sculpted the statues of saints Francis and Anthony, and the other statues of the series were clearly from his workshop.

One of Heidelberg's finest works is the sculpture of Francis of Paula, perhaps finished in 1625, which was originally intended for the Paulines' church in the Old Town. Today it can be found in the church of Our Lady before Týn. The work is no-

table for its stateliness and deep spirituality. Heidelberg is also associated with the sculptural decoration of the main altar in the Týn church, carried out between 1649 and 1651; figures of the apostles, St Francis and St John the Baptist are positioned either side of the main altar painting. On the altar's first level are standing female saints, on the second the figures of saints Wenceslas and Adalbert, and at the very top a depiction of Calvary and the archangel Gabriel. The statue of St Wenceslas is clearly Heidelberg's work, as can be seen from both its precision, reminiscent of his sculptures in Wallenstein's palace and the series of the Franciscan saints, and in its spirituality, also seen in his sculpture of St Francis of Paula. Heidelberg's work (evidently aiming to satisfy the demands of his patrons) highlights his ability to express himself in the spirit of Mannerist elegance while retaining the weighty sense of spirituality typical of the early Baroque.

The main altar in the church of Our Lady before Týn, completed between 1642 and 1649,[23] attests to the lack of poise of Prague sculpture. The altar statues are not the work of a single artist. The rather stiff figures of the patron saints at ground level are a product of the local wood-carving tradition, while the sculptures on the first level, with their slender proportions and high waists, are reminiscent of Heidelberg's work. The altar's figural decoration and conservative design on two levels contrast markedly with the dynamic character of its painted decoration by Karel Škréta.

In addition to these anonymous works, there are also many informative documents, both about artists to whom it is impossible to attach particular works, and about works which, though they have not survived, must have been outstanding. We know, for instance, that Abraham Melber from Leipzig and Stanislav Goldschneck from Styria were both working in Prague, as was one Jacob or Leopold Gemelin, who is recorded in a local sheriff's report of 1642 as having been involved in a street brawl. We cannot be absolutely sure, however, whether this was the same man who built the altar in the church of St Salvador in the early 1640s, to whom the Jesuits referred as the sculptor Gamelin. Of altars which have not survived, one in particular, as described by Baroque historians, deserves mention.[24] The main altar in the monasterial church of the Spanish Benedictine monks on Na Slovanech Street was commissioned by Count Balthazar Maradas, one of the Emperor's generals. A description of the altar was made by the monk and Benedictine historian J. Cechner, in which he explicitly claims that the altar was 'fashioned after the style of the altar in the church of the Blessed Virgin Sněžná'.[25] Above the tabernacle there was a statue of the Virgin Mary Montserrat surrounded by statues of saints Benedict and Scholasticus; above the altar's side entrance gates were the Emperor's emblematic eagles. The altar's main painting depicted Christ walking with two disciples to Emmaus. On the extension between the two statues was a painting of St Jerome set beneath a sculpture of the Resurrection. The overall configuration of the altar combined motifs celebrating the Benedictine saints Benedict and Scholasticus with the motif of the Virgin Mary Montserrat, while recalling the local tradition of Christ at Emmaus and St Jerome. The altar survived until 1726; all that remains is the statue of the Blessed Virgin, which today is housed in the chapel of the Czech patron saints in the church of St Ignatius.

The most renowned sculptor whose work falls partly into this period was Jan Jiří Bendl.[26] In terms of his training, he belonged to the southern German school of sculpture, but was also acquainted with the early Baroque style found in Rome. His

29.5 UNKNOWN MASON
Chrucin fountain
Central part showing an allegory of the elements
Ca. 1595
[Prague, Národní muzeum v Praze]

early works included the pulpit in St Wenceslas in Zderaz (1637) and the altar in the church of St Martin in the Old Town of Prague. His ability to work with stucco is attested to by the sculptures of angels in the dome of the Jesuit church of St Salvador (1648–49), which were influenced in style by stucco works found in the Borghese chapel of the church of Sta Maria Maggiore in Rome. However, Bendl's interpretation of that style is more earthy and realistic. In 1650, he was commissioned by the citizens of the Old Town, who were responding in turn to the wishes of Ferdinand III, to construct and decorate a column of the Blessed Virgin for the Old Town Square.[27] Although the Emperor wanted the work to be fashioned after a similar column in Vienna, Bendl went about his task in a relatively free manner. A statue of the Immaculate Virgin was mounted at the top of the column and below, on the corners of the balustrade, Bendl set four groups of angels fighting with devils. This work was intended not only to celebrate the successful defence of Prague against the invading Swedes during the Thirty Years' War, but equally, by giving expression to the Catholic dogma of the Immaculate Conception, to celebrate the victory of that faith. Bendl's work looks ahead in both style and content to the art of the Baroque.

Painting

No area of Renaissance art was more varied with regard to style and genre than painting. The list of privileges enjoyed by the painters' guild is in itself some proof of this; they included 'such things proper to them [artists] as tables, altars, standards, banners, emblazoned horse rugs, gilded and wooden candlesticks, lance small or large, pavis, round shield, and other like things connected with the use of colours'.[28] The different aspects of artists' work became so varied that in 1598 the guild attempted to enforce principles of specialization by which categories such as 'master painter' were created, which gave a person the right to undertake all types of free creative work, followed by *cuprejtíři* (gilders), *iluministi* (illuminators) and *lištáři*, craftsmen who decorated frames, varnished furniture and lacquered 'cottage dwelling rooms'. As a result of this specialization, the painting masters were set at the top of the hierarchy; working above one's prescribed artistic station was punishable by a fine. However, we know from surviving documents that this system of specialization was not adhered to.

As with the sculpture of the period, painting was often stylistically heterogeneous, thus making it difficult to plot a single line of development.[29] It was also heavily influenced by the facts that the Czech lands were separated along religious lines and that non-Catholics maintained a different approach to the fine arts. A major source of inspiration and employment for painters of this period, which frequently generated undesirable competition and conflict between the guild masters and the artists at the court, were the commissions for work on Hradčany Castle. Pattern books were an irreplaceable aid for the city artists and included patterns and designs by Albrecht Dürer, Jost Amman, Virgil Solis and the Sadeler family.[30]

In comparing historical documents of the period with what has survived of Renaissance and early Baroque painting in Prague, one is forced to accept the fact that losses were so far-reaching with regard to certain genres (for instance, city portraiture) that it is impossible to formulate any credible views about them.[31]

Examples of monumental painting only survive in fragmentary form. The practice of decorating façades with ornamental and figurative sgraffito, came to Prague

29.6 AEGIDIUS SADELER
View of Vladislav's Hall
(detail)
1606

29.7 NORTH ITALIAN
PAINTER (?)
*The vision of St Ignatius at
La Storta*
Church of the Holy Saviour
at the Clementinum
1610–20

from northern Italy. A good example of this is the gable of the Vladislav Hall completed in 1546 and the adornment of the Míčovna (game room) in the Royal Garden (1568–69), which includes rich ornament and allegories of the Elements, Fine Arts and Virtues.[32] The sgraffito decoration on the Lobkovic Palace in Hradčany (known today as the Schwarzenberg Palace) dates from between 1567 and 1568; its motifs took their form from northern Italy.[33] A typical example of sgraffito decoration in the city can be seen in the embellishment of the House at the Minute on the Old Town Square.[34] This house was decorated during the late sixteenth and early seventeenth centuries on the basis of the most varied compilation of designs, including allegories of the Virtues, figures and scenes taken from the Old Testament and Antiquity and a series of portraits of French kings. The artists who began the work were clearly Italians, but the technique was soon mastered by local artists such as Kinderman Kroch, who adorned one house in the Lesser Town with the figure of Goliath using the same method. [35] The decoration on the façade of the house known as The Three Ostriches near Charles Bridge on the Lesser Town side, carried out by Daniel Alexius, has also been partially preserved. The rich ornamentation of Martinický Palace in Hradčany, dating from the 1620s, bears witness to the fact that sgraffito façade decoration was not only a practice belonging to the period prior to the Battle of the White Mountain.[36] There the artist ingeniously broke up the rather monotonous façade by using illusionary porticos within which he composed scenes from the Old Testament. Worthy of special mention are the chiaroscuro paintings on the façade of the house in the Ungelt area of the Old Town which belonged to the tax-collector Jacob Granovský the Younger, which date from the 1560s.[37] In a style developed in Venice, where this type of decoration was most popular, these paintings depict mythological and Old Testament scenes, allegorical figures and a portrait of the owner's benefactor Emperor Ferdinand I. The quality of the paintings would certainly have required the guiding hand of one of the painters then working on Hradčany Castle.

Few interior decorations of nobles' palaces and town houses have survived. The friezes with gargoyles in rooms which were adjoined to the Michnovský Palace in the Lesser Town during its construction in the early Baroque period are of a very high standard.[38] The paintings in the burgrave's hall of Hradčany Castle, depicting the Senses as robust-looking women against a lightly sketched landscape, which an anonymous artist based on models from Marten de Vos and Rafael Sadeler, must also have been connected with the court artists.[39]

From the 1680s onwards, painted epitaphs (tombstone paintings) began to appear in abundance, commissioned predominantly by nobly descended oppidans of the Utraquist persuasion.[40] The formats for these were limited, depicting the family of the deceased kneeling at the Crucifixion or Resurrection or, more rarely, depicting the Last Judgment or Ezekiel's vision. Relatively rare by comparison are Catholic epitaphs, differing thematically from their Protestant counterparts in depicting saints and the Virgin Mary as intercessors for the dead. When Jarmila Vacková researched this group of relics in the 1960s, she claimed that they were 'in the field of fine art, witnesses of a state which may be characterised as the Bohemian urbanite's *Miserere mei Deus*'. This notion, expressed about other paintings which arose out of the context of Bohemian urban culture, was put forward to suggest that artistic work in the city during the latter half of the sixteenth and early seventeenth centuries was of a poor standard. In view of surviving relics and documents, some modification to this claim is definitely called for. Although it is true that many of the painted epitaphs are only of craft standard, there are nevertheless clear signs of the influences of the art of Rudolf's court, especially in the mining town of Jáchymov, for example. In Prague, only a very small number of painted epitaphs have survived, but it is certainly no accident that they testify without exception to the presence of court artists in the city. They include the epitaph of Nicholas Pykler (after 1579) in St Vitus'[41] and that of the Resurrection from the Strahov monastery's collection, which bear the hallmarks of Bartholomeus Spranger's work. Also attributable to him is the epitaph of the goldsmith Nicholas Müller (after 1586), originally intended for the church of St John in Obora and today housed in the Národní galerie in Prague,[42] and the epitaph of the printer Michael Peterle from Annaberk (after 1588) in the church of St Stephen in Prague's New Town.[43]

29.8 ANONYMOUS
The assumption of Our Lady
Chapel of St Sigmund, St
Vitus Cathedral
After 1620

Research by Jiří Pešek on the household inventories which have survived from this period has shown that homes contained numerous collections of paintings, including portraits of families and sovereigns, religious paintings and even landscapes.[44] The heads of these households were by and large members of the urban élite – city council members, merchants or artisans – and their collections of paintings were often complements to their libraries and other collections of cultural artefacts. Unfortunately, none of the collections of these urbanite cognoscenti have survived, and our knowledge of them is mostly limited to statistics. In contrast, a relatively large collection of portraits of a high standard of the Bohemian nobility has survived, which are often closely linked with the art of the court.[45] Jacob Seisenegger, a court painter during the reign of Ferdinand I who combined elements of drawing and north Italian sculpture, worked for the Pernštejns and Rožmberks from the 1540s onward.[46] His works, mainly in the Lobkovice collection, include portraits of Bohunka, Wilhelm of Rožmberk and, notably, a portrait of Vratislav of Pernštejn (1559). A similar style found in the Danube basin, which also drew its inspiration from north Italian art, was used by the painter known as the Master to the Lords of Rožmberk, who after the mid-sixteenth century painted five portraits of members of the Rožmberk family.[47]

In the mid-sixteenth century, Bohemian portraiture took a new direction. This new direction was influenced by the importation of portraits by the Spanish artists Alonso Sanches Coello and his pupil Juan Pantojo de la Cruz.[48] These works were brought to the Czech lands as a result of intermarriages between Bohemian and Spanish noble houses, in particular that between Vratislav of Pernštejn and Maria Manrique de Lara. The Spanish artists created hieratic figures at full length, with utmost compositional simplicity, clarity, intense colouring and careful detailing. These Spanish imports, together with Bohemian portraits, have been preserved in the well-rounded Lobkovice Collection in the castle in Nelahozeves and include the original treasures of the Pernštejn and Rožmberk family galleries. Bohemian imitators of the new Spanish style sought primarily to enliven their works and intensify their realism. Hans Krell the Younger from Leipzig, for example, combined the Saxon style of drawing with the Spanish use of colour. The closest he came to Spanish portraiture painting was in his portrait of Marie Magdalena Trčková.[49] The so-called Master to the Kolovrat Lords worked in Prague between 1569 and 1585. The geometric surfaces in his portraits are filled with rich ornamentation The so-called Master

to the Lords of Lobkovice, active from 1580 onwards, was also connected with Prague. He was influenced both by the Spanish portraiture which had made its way to Prague and by Dutch works, as can be seen from the animated way in which he painted faces and hands.[50] His best works are without a doubt the portraits of Ladislaus II of Lobkovice and Anna of Lobkovice. The strongest influence of Spanish portraiture can be observed in the works of two artists who worked outside Prague during the early seventeenth century, namely the Master to Elizabeth Těšínská and the Master to the Lady of Dobříše.

Renaissance portraiture, though artistically speaking Bohemia's most valuable product in the area of late sixteenth-century painting, has as yet been the subject of little research. In the light of this, it is no wonder that until recently illumination was considered the most worthwhile artistic production to have developed between 1550 and 1610, predominantly in the decoration of hymnals belonging to the choir singers of the Utraquist fraternities.[51] However, as with the painting of epitaphs and in accordance with the general scholarly consensus regarding the cultural decline in Bohemian cities in the latter half of the sixteenth century, the artistic standard of these decorations has not been valued at all highly. The illumination of hymn-books at a time when book-printing was flourishing was considered something of an anachronism. I would suggest, however, that it was a purposeful exercise by which certain patrons consciously sought to highlight their medieval heritage. This can also be seen in church architecture, which until the turn of the seventeenth century continued to use Gothic architectural morphology.

The centre for hymn-book decoration was Prague, home in the latter half of the sixteenth century to several different workshops. Almost fifty such books have survived. Between 1520 and 1562, the illuminator Fabian Puléř was employed at the workshop of Jan Táborský (1500–1572) of Klokotská Hora (1550–65).[52] Puléř combined styles found in southern Germany and the Danube basin with patterns taken from Dürer. The decoration is arranged so that each hymn begins with an initial and a scene from the New Testament. On the bottom of the page, there are scenes from the Old Testament, while the musical notation is adorned with ornate decoration and portraits of donors paired with the emblems of their trade. The slender figures are depicted in complex postures displaying Mannerist changes of colour and a traditional use of gilding. The various works commissioned in Prague include the *St Vitus Mass Gradual*, dating from between 1551 and 1552,[53] and the unfinished two-part *Hymn-Book for Our Lady before Týn*, dating after 1559.[54] In the 1560s the Prague illuminators began drawing their inspiration from Jost Amman's Nürnberg designs, as well as from illustrations found in the Bibles printed by Melantrich's printing house, consisting of a series of xylographs designed by the Italian artists Florian Abel and Francesco Terzio, then working at Hradčany Castle. In the last quarter of the sixteenth century, the illuminators Matthew Ornys from Lindperk, Matthew Hutský and Ambrose Ledecký worked at Jan Kantor's workshop in Prague. They had their own style and made use of numerous motifs from landscape painting as well as Flemish Mannerist designs.

In contrast to the number of surviving hymn-books, there are surprisingly few examples of illuminated secular manuscripts. These consist of a small number of travel books, including Frederick of Donín's publication (1588–94)[55] and Jindřich Hýzrle of Chody's travel book dating from 1612–46.[56] Unfortunately, their illustra-

tions have only documentary value. Popular amongst such secular works were albums which consisted mostly of coats of arms and amateur drawings and which rarely contain works by trained artists.[57]

Those artists working prior to the Battle of the White Mountain and about whose lives we know a little more include Matthew Hutský of Křivoklát (1546–1599), an artist at the court of Archduke Ferdinand.[58] According to Hutský's own account, he trained for a time in the Tyrol at the Archduke's bidding before being appointed a court artist. After Ferdinand's departure to Innsbruck, the artist remained behind in Prague and became a member of the Old Town painters' guild. He worked as an illuminator in Jan Kantor's workshop and in 1585 made a miniature copy for his benefactor of the paintings on the walls of the chapel of St Wenceslas in the cathedral of St Vitus.[59] We know of other works by Hutský which show that he was not simply a specialist in book illumination. In 1590, for instance, he painted the large altar in the church of St Benedict in the Old Town, and in 1594 his family's epitaph depicting the Nativity. While Hutský was head of the Old Town painters' guild between 1594 and 1596, Rudolf's famous *privilegium* was issued, raising the guild above others and granting it artistic distinction. The promotion of painting above other forms of art and craft led to divisions within the guild, which besides painters also included glass-blowers. The affair concluded with the dismissal of Hutský from his position as head of the guild; he died shortly afterwards. It was earlier thought that it was due to Hutský, as a one-time court artist, that the *privilegium* had been issued, but today it is considered more likely that Bartholomeus Spranger, an artist at the court of Rudolf II who had become a member of the painters' guild in 1584, was responsible.

Painters of universal significance include Jan Táborský from Klokotská Hora, Matthew Ornys from Lindperk[60] and Simon Podolský from Podolí.[61] Táborský, as well as being the owner of the workshop which illuminated hymn-books, was also keeper of the medieval horologe on the Old Town Square. In 1570, he wrote *Zpráva o orloji pražském*, which contained the history of the clock, a description of its mechanism and a calligraphic manuscript accompanied by detailed drawings.[62] Ornys and Podolský were renowned as surveyors. In 1562, in return for work carried out as a surveyor, Ornys was ennobled by Ferdinand I and granted a coat of arms bearing the symbol of a lion holding a measure and a lead weight. His artistic work includes the illumination of the *Staroměstský kancionál* (*Old Town Hymn-Book*),[63] completed between 1561 and 1567, and the *Graduál malostranský* (*Lesser Town Gradual*),[64] completed between 1569 and 1573. Ornys' works prior to 1575 also include a genealogy of Emperor Charles IV,[65] which together with Hutský's copies of the St Wenceslas legend, provide fine examples of painting during this period. Ornys was succeeded in his office of land surveyor by his one-time pupil Podolský, who also became keeper of the Old Town's horologe. Podolský also worked for Petr Vok making maps and reproducing portraits. As a surveyor, he wrote *Knížka o mírách zemských* (A Booklet on Land Measurements) in 1617 as an attempt to regulate the telemetry practices of the period.

Ambrose Ledecký, although primarily known for his skillful illumination, was also active at this time painting portraits and epitaphs.[66] When Ledecký died, the books recorded in the inventory of his estate included *Knihu velkou ... v níž figury všech arciknížat rakouských vytlačeny* (evidently a reference to Terzio's *Imagines gentis Austriacae* of 1588), *Kunstbuch z níž to se pacholata malovati učí* (a guide for teaching

29.9 H. G. HERING
Forest Landscape
1610–20
[Stuttgart, Graphische
Sammlung der Staatsgalerie]

children to paint), and *Landšraftů nydrlandských pět, od nebožtíka na paláci koupených* (Five landscapes from the Netherlands purchased from the estate of a deceased person in the palace).

A good account of the contact between the city and court artists can be found in a report about the painter Ferdinand from Eysern (1572–1624), who was commissioned to paint an altar at the Castle in 1604.[67] The only known work by Pavel Rogo (Roy), who appears in records between 1587 and 1608 – namely his portrait triptych of Ferdinand I, Maximilian II and Rudolf II, which belonged to Rudolph's collection – proves that some artists recorded in the documents of the period as city guild painters nevertheless succeeded in finding employment at the court.[68] A large collection of paintings recorded in 1612 as part of the estate of the then late and little known Lesser Town painter Jindřich Ekenperger also attests to the existence of close contact between court and city. This collection included forty-nine portraits, mainly of sovereigns but also of Rudolf's valet Caspar Rucký and the court wood-carver Pfaff, and a painting by Albrecht Dürer, which was reportedly sent by the citizens of the Lesser Town to the Castle.[69] Havel Graffer (1586–1615) is also known to have been in contact with the Castle circle. In 1605, he was asked to present a painting of the murdered Hanibal von Schönberg to be used as part of the corpus delicti in the trial of the accused, Adam Havel of Lobkovice. We also know that Graffer painted four now lost pictures in 1612, most probably for the decoration of a set of triumphal arches depicting a change-over of Bohemian sovereigns.[70]

Daniel Alexius (Lexa) from Květná, whose name appears in documents between 1599 and 1620, was commissioned to work on the St Vitus' cathedral (ca. 1600) and made the paintings for the chapel of St Sigismond. At roughly the same period, he decorated the chapel of the Archbishop's Palace for Archbishop Berka of Dubá.[71] As an artist, Alexius was familiar with the works of the court painters as well as those of the Venetian masters Veronese and Tintoretto, some of which could be viewed in the Emperor's collection.

The volume of commissions for work on Catholic churches, and in particular for work on the churches of religious orders, increased during the 1580s and benefited painters and sculptors alike. These commissions were financed in the main by nobles, courtiers and the Spanish and papal envoys. In 1587, Rudolf's personal doctor Guarinoni bore the cost of renovating the chapel of St Barbara in the Augustinian monastery in the Lesser Town and commissioned the court painter Josef Heintz to make a painting for the altar.[72] Together with his wife Polyxena, Chancellor Zdeněk Vojtěch Popel of Lobkovice financed the renovation of the church of St Thomas in 1593 and the Franciscan church of the Blessed Virgin Sněžná during the 1610s.[73] Numerous painters were commissioned to work on the Jesuit church of St Salvador, and in 1607 the papal nuncio Filipo Spinelli donated a picture of St Ignatius performing a miracle. The construction of the altars was financed by Bedřich of Donín, Apolonie of Šternberk and Marie of Wallenstein.[74] In contrast to many of the works which are anonymous or lost, this church houses one of the last well-preserved works by Hans von Aachen, donated by the court adviser Jan Barvitius for the altar of the Annunciation of Our Lady.[75]

In addition to employing Bohemian artists, the religious orders also engaged painters from abroad in a variety of ways. The Capuchins, for instance, sent one of their brethren, the painter Paolo Piazza, on a trip north of the Alps.[76] Piazza was

trained in the workshop of Palmo il Giovanne, and his works, which can be found in Venice, Prague, Linz and Munich, are good examples of late Venetian Mannerism. His altar painting of Christ and the Virgin appearing to St Francis of Assisi (1602) in the monasterial church of the Capuchins in Pohořelec in Prague shows the spirit of the new post–Council-of-Trent iconography. The painter of the fine picture showing the Vision of St Ignatius, now in the Jesuit church of St Salvador in the Clementinum, was also trained in northern Italy.

Monumental painting, whether mural or otherwise, was something of a rarity in Prague in the late sixteenth and early seventeenth centuries. Most commissions were intended to meet basic needs, and more grandiose projects were unlikely to gain financial approval. Several little-known memorials are worth mentioning, however. The late-sixteenth-century cycle of paintings in Strahov monastery, depicting the martyrdom of the apostles, vaguely recalls similar series of martyr paintings popular in Rome at the turn of the seventeenth century.[77] In 1613, the well-known patron Jiří Bartold Pontanus commissioned a painting for the chapel of St John the Baptist in St Vitus' cathedral which depicted the Virgin in a crescent, surrounded by choirs of angels and adored by hosts of heavenly figures and secular dignitaries. Although the painting was destroyed in 1863, a print made by Raphael Sadeler the Younger has survived. The unique monumental portrayal of the Assumption of the Virgin on the east wall of the cathedral's chapel of St Sigismond, which probably dates from after 1628, was inspired by Aegidius and Jan Sadeler's graphic designs. Both compositions, presentations of the Immaculate Conception and the Assumption of the Virgin, possess spectacular and didactic qualities, possibly in response to Protestant debates then seeking to cast doubt on Catholic dogma.[78]

Social changes following the Battle of the White Mountain had repercussions for both sculpture and painting.[79] The Catholic church became the main source for commissions. After the death of Rudolf II, the Habsburgs transferred their seat of power back to Vienna and were, by comparison, less involved in the financing of artworks. Ferdinand II and Ferdinand III both participated in the renovation of the cathedral interior, and in the early 1640s Ferdinand III decided to extend Hradčany Castle. Although some Prague artists in this period are referred to as court artists, they did not in fact work directly for the sovereign (with the exception of Dionisio Miseroni), but for the institutions which represented him, such as the vice-regency and the Bohemia Chamber. With the disintegration of the circle of court artists, the standing of the guild painters increased.[80] While in the period prior to the Battle of the White Mountain, several court artists (Bartholomeus Spranger, Pieter Stevens) had become members of the painters' guild, from 1620 onwards, the process was reversed. A number of artists of guild master painters were granted access to the court, but nevertheless maintained some degree of contact with the guild. Jonas Falk, a member of the guild in 1620, was commissioned in the 1630s to repair paintings in the Villa Hvězda. He was paid by the Bohemia Chamber and given the title of court artist.[81] Two other important representatives of city painting in Prague during this period, Jan Jiří Hering and Anthony Stevens, are also often recorded as court artists in the documentary sources of the period, although today we are unable to attribute any court works to them. In this period, the main source of work for artists shifted from the court to the city.

From a stylistic point of view, the period following the Battle of the White Moun-

29.10 H. G. HERING
Forest Landscape with Nude Woman
1610–20

tain may best be described as one of transition from the Renaissance and Mannerism to the early Baroque. Although the art produced by Rudolf's court artists used to be thought of as existing in isolation from the city of Prague, we know today that their art found its way into the city, both in the form of specific works by court artists and as influence wielded over a number of well-known and anonymous city painters and sculptors. The painter who initialled his works 'TR', for example, who is usually identified as the guild painter Thomas Ruhrweyd, recorded in historical sources in Prague between 1598 and 1604, was strongly influenced by the works of Bartholomeus Spranger. Four paintings of the Passion by this artist (Valdice and Prague, Národní galerie), which display a certain lightness almost to the point of caricature, are indebted to Spranger's late works.[82] Stylistic elements of the early Baroque can also be seen in the late works of some of Rudolf's court artists such as Hans von Aachen. His *Annunciation of the Virgin* of 1613 anticipates the later works of Karel Skřeta in its use of colour and realistic detail. A number of artists employed in von Aachen's workshop learnt his methods and incorporated his figurative themes and compositions into their own works. The painter known by the initials 'CS' made small paintings of the Passion and the dead Christ mourned by angels (housed in Kozel Castle) that were based directly on a design by von Aachen.[83] The painter of the *Crucifixion* in the Prague Národní galerie, also shows his indebtedness to von Aachen's schooling, particularly in his depiction of figures.[84]

A painter whose work provides a clear link between Rudolf's Mannerist artists and the early Baroque, openly displaying its support for the Counter-Reformation, was Jan Jiří Hering.[85] Originally from Hesse, Hering learnt his skill initially in Kassel, thereafter reportedly taking himself off to Italy for several years. His name first appears in historical sources from 1615 onward in Prague, where he became a member of the Old Town painters' guild in 1620. In 1626, he was raised to noble rank by Ferdinand II, possibly as a reward for services rendered as a court artist. He died in Prague in 1648, and an extensive collection of his drawings and paintings has been preserved. His drawings were influenced by Rudolf's court artists, in particular von Aachen and Stevens; this is highlighted by Hering's interest in landscapes and allegorical motifs. Unlike von Aachen and Stevens, he often preferred to work with a brush, using a liberal amount of water, which transformed what would otherwise have been sharp lines. From the period after 1620, we only know Hering's religious paintings, which were commissioned predominantly by the Strahov Premonstratensians and which include a series of five pictures depicting Premonstratensian saints, a collection of ten compositions depicting the life of St Norbert (in Milevsko) and a *Crucifixion* previously thought to have been the work of von Aachen, today housed in the Franciscan church in Slaný (previously in St Vitus' cathedral). While Hering sometimes composed his own paintings, usually as dramatic scenes employing realistic details, he often chose to base them on designs ranging from Albrecht Dürer's graphic collection (for example, the *Entombment* in the Premonstratensians' gallery in Strahov) to Italian Renaissance Mannerist works. His painting of the Visitation in St Vitus', for instance, was based in its composition and use of colour on a painting by Federico Barocci in the church of Sta Maria in Vallicella. Another of his paintings, depicting the Transfiguration, on the main altar of the Jesuit church of St Salvador, was based on Raphael's famous work in the Vatican.

An artist who drew his inspiration more from what was to be seen in his own

29.11 H. G: HERING
Roman ruins
1610–20

back yard was Matthias Mayer, who - though originally from Ybbs in southern Austria - lived in Prague from 1604 to 1648.[86] Recently, a successful reconstruction was completed of his quite considerable oeuvres. In 1629 and 1630, he worked on the renovation of the interior of St Vitus' and was responsible for the panelling on the pulpit depicting figures of the Evangelists and church fathers, as well as the large painting of the Crucifixion witnessed by the Czech patron saints, the Virgin, and Ferdinand II and his family (1631). In this work, Mayer adhered to the tradition of group portraiture, a recurrent feature of Bohemian epitaph painting during the Renaissance, but with iconography wholly in keeping with Baroque displays of reverence for the Czech patron saints and the Virgin. The earliest of Mayer's works is the altarpiece of St Wenceslas, the first Bohemian Baroque instance of the later common practice of depicting a saint between two angels. An example of Mayer's more mature work is the altarpiece in Our Lady of Victory, depicting Ferdinand II, Ferdinand III, the Carmelite monk Dominico, Christ, the Virgin and the Carmelite saints. This painting, which celebrates the Catholic victory at the Battle of the White Mountain, most probably dates from the late 1630s. Mayer's work is stylistically archetypal for this period of transition. In his portraits, he followed the group portrait tradition of the Renaissance and recreated qualities displayed in works by the court artists of Rudolf II. In his iconography, however, he used only Baroque motifs.

Another 'home-grown' artist was David Norbert Altman (brother of the sculptor Daniel Altman), whose name appears in records between 1617 and 1656.[87] He worked mainly for the Strahov Premonstratensians, decorating the altars in St Roch in collaboration with Jan Jiří Hering; he also gilded and decorated an altar carved by his brother there. Altman's most interesting work is the painting of the Virgin and Child, St Joseph, St Elizabeth and John the Baptist. The artist presented this work as part of his application for membership in the Old Town painters' guild, and it is, as the description on the back points out, a masterwork. The painting combines a Mannerist residue with realistic detail, which was particularly characteristic of the early Baroque period.

Anthony Stevens was connected to Rudolf II's circle of court artists through his father Pieter, the Emperor's landscape painter.[88] The precise year of Anthony's birth is not known, but it must have been sometime around 1610. In the 1630s and 1640s, the artist had close contact with the stone-cutter and royal treasurer Dionisio Miseroni. In 1643, he was raised to noble rank, and the title 'of Steinfels' was passed on to his son Jan Jacob, who was to become a renowned Bohemian fresco painter during the high Baroque period. Most of Anthony's paintings date from the 1660s, and many are preserved in the Premonstratensians' collections at Strahov. Of his early works, it is worth mentioning four unpreserved paintings depicting scenes from the life of St Augustine, which were housed at one time in the monasterial church of St Thomas in the Lesser Town. Attributable to the skills inherited from his father is a drawing, *Landscape with a Castle and River*, which dates from around 1630 and which in its use of sharp lines is reminiscent of Pieter's work from the 1590s. The tradition of Mannerist painting (inspired by the work of Bartholomeus Spranger) can be seen in Anthony's painting of St Sebastian on the main altar of the chapel at the country estate in Český Šternberk. Anthony Stevens further developed his father's style of landscape painting when decorating the ceiling of the pavilion in the garden of Strahov monastery.

29.12 ANTON STEVENS
Christ appearing to St Norbert and St Hugo
1660s
[Prague, Premonstratensian monastery at Strahov]

We know of many painters who worked in Prague following the Battle of the White Mountain only through written documents, which rarely give the reader any insight into the artists' life and only provide fragmentary information about their now lost works. Among those forced to leave the Czech lands for religious reasons after the Battle of the White Mountain was one Jan Živnůstka (recorded in documents between 1607 and 1631).[89] He remained in Prague until 1628, and his correspondence with Samuel Martinius, at one time the vicar of the church of St Haštal, provides a vivid account of conditions in Prague after the Catholic victory. In 1623, Živnůstka wrote of the removal of the chalices from the pulpit, altar and gable of the church of Our Lady before Týn. He also mentioned the defacing of memorials honouring Jan Hus.

Among those artists who followed the tradition of Rudolf's court painters, was Jiří Gabriel Majer from Cheb (documented in sources between 1613 and 1648). A drawing, *Landscape with a River*, dating from 1613, attests to his familiarity with the works of Pieter Stevens.[90] Another of Majer's surviving works is a coat of arms for the painters' guild, painted in response to Rudolf's *privilegium* and allegedly based on a design by Bartholomeus Spranger. Also worthy of mention is Gabriel Špindler from Erfurt, accounted for in documents between 1600 and 1632.[91] Špindler was head of the Old Town painters' guild between 1608 and 1631, and although we have little information about his work (we know only one of his drawings, depicting Minerva as a patron of the arts), it is clear that he must have been quite a character. Almost twenty apprentices and would-be artists applying to the Old Town painters' guild passed through his workshop and painted their masterwork under his watchful eye. In light of this, it must be assumed that he had a lasting influence on the up-and-coming generation of painters in Prague in the 1620s and 1630s.

An interesting report found in the records of the period involves Erasmus Schiller, originally from Nürnberg (in Prague between 1612 and 1631), who in 1624 registered the complaint that he was robbed while transporting 'portraits and other figures painted on canvas to Nürnberg and the Leipzig market'.[92] This is probably the only evidence from the 1620s of the export of paintings from Bohemia to the German states. Another artist worthy of mention is Bartholomeus Bolonin,[93] who settled in the Lesser Town, where his name appears in city records from 1634 onwards, and who by his own account was trained in Antwerp. We have no information about his work and can only speculate on the influence his Netherlands origin and training had on the Bohemian painting of the period.

As we have seen, in the period following the Battle of the White Mountain, the most important source of commissions after the church were high-ranking members of the nobility. In addition to Albrecht Wenzel Eusebius of Wallenstein, who will be mentioned again later, Karl of Liechtenstein, at one time an adviser to Rudolf II and later the vice-regent for Bohemia, was also an important patron of the arts.[94] It is known that he commissioned work from the artists of Rudolf's court and that he owned an extensive collection of their works. His accounts also record payments to city artists, for instance to Jan Christopher Kristl, who in 1624 received the considerable sum of almost fifteen hundred gold coins for work on the imperial *Kunstkammer*.[95] Another artist employed in the services of Liechtenstein was Hanuš of Felz, recorded in registers of the period between 1613 and 1619 as a court painter. In 1619, he was charged with the task of selecting which artworks in St Vitus' should be

saved from the Calvinist iconoclasm.[96] Perhaps the most famous of the city painters employed by Liechtenstein was Oldřich Musch.[97] It is known that he worked for Liechtenstein between 1611 and 1613 with the relatively high half-yearly pay of a hundred gold coins. In 1620, Musch applied for membership of the Old Town painters' guild in Prague, but due to defects in the masterwork he presented, he was only permitted to paint murals. In spite of this unflattering beginning, Musch was awarded commissions on some of the most important projects of the period, for instance the renovation of St Vitus', where he worked alongside Matthias Mayer. Unfortunately, it is impossible to delineate the parts of preserved works for which he was responsible. In 1631, Musch was made head of the Old Town painters' guild, and when he died in 1653 his 'funeral in a large churchyard ... [was attended] in great number by all the painters of the city of Prague and other citizens'.

By the mid-1620s, the construction of Wallenstein's palace had advanced to the point where interior decoration could begin. From those artists based in Bohemia, Wallenstein commissioned the painter Jan Schlemüller (circa 1666), one of Jan Jiří Hering's pupils, to work in Jičín and Stará Boleslav.[98] Unfortunately, none of these works have survived. Schlemüller has traditionally been connected with the altarpiece in the chapel in Wallenstein's palace which depicts the murder of St Vitus. That work, however, was by a different artist who also carried out a lion's share of the palace decorations, namely Bartolomeo Baccio del Bianco (1604-1655), a Florentine painter, stucco artist and designer.[99] From 1624 onwards, with the help of a group of assistants, he painted the main hall, the audience room, the mythological and astronomical corridor, the chapel and the *salla terrena*. In his fresco in the main hall, Bianco depicted Mars in a chariot, a composition clearly intended as an allusion to Wallenstein. Bianco drew inspiration from Italian Mannerism and Baroque painting (G. Romano, A. Campi, G. Reni and Guercino), but his fresh details and light brush strokes evoke a Baroque sense of dynamism and drama. The decoration of the other areas of the palace show an unusually wide thematic range. In the audience hall is a depiction of the Four Seasons and an allegory of the Four Times of Day, and in the mythological corridor, scenes from Ovid's *Metamorphoses* based on designs by V. Solis. The chapel walls are decorated with paintings based on the St Wenceslas cycle, while the oratorio has paintings of the Virgin. The finest of Bianco's works in the palace is the astronomical corridor located beside the main hall.. On the ceiling are allegories of the planets and the signs of the zodiac, and on the walls are allegories of the continents and elements. The continents are particularly interesting for their airy brushwork and selection of attributes inspired by the iconology of Cesare Ripa. The paintings in the *salla terrena*, besides depicting scenes from Virgil's *Aeneid* and other heroes of Antiquity, also include tritons, nereides and Neptune. If the decoration of the main hall was intended to celebrate Wallenstein's military prowess, and that of the astronomical hall and chapel to declare his love and respect for his patron saint, then the heroic, and in particular the *marine*, motifs of the *salla terrena* refer to Wallenstein's attempt to open a route to the Baltic, which brought him the title of 'general of Oceania and the Baltic Sea'.

Bianco's fine execution of Wallenstein's extensive commission had no peers in Prague after the Battle of the White Mountain. It was for this reason that he had been commissioned by Wallenstein, and although his work was predominantly inspired by Italian Mannerism, his dramatic, grand compositions in Prague have an al-

29.13 ANTON STEVENS
The Martyrdom of St Sebestian
1650s
[Český Šternberk, Šternberk
Castle]

most Baroque air about them. However, it was not only artists like Bianco, wandering around Europe from one commission to the next, who found themselves in Prague (Bianco himself returned to Italy upon completing Wallenstein's commission). Demanding patrons dissatisfied with local artists turned to artists from abroad. Imports of foreign works also attest to the daring of patrons, who - given the uncertainties of the Thirty Years' War - gave commissions to artists in Germany and Flanders. In 1649, for instance, the order of St Cyril in the Old Town commissioned a painting of the Invention of the Holy Cross for the main altar in their monasterial church from the Augsburg-based artist Mathias Strasser (today this picture is housed in the church of Our Lady before Týn).[100] Ten years earlier, the Augustinian abbot J. Svitavský had commissioned two paintings for the church of St Thomas in the Lesser Town from Peter Paul Rubens himself.[101] Rubens' painting of the martyrdom of St Thomas influenced several generations of painters in Prague, from Karel Škréta to representatives of the high Baroque style such as M. L. Wilmann and J. K. Liška.

An artist whose early paintings still bore traces of Rudolf's court style, but whose main corpus of work was stylistically Baroque, was Karel Škréta (1610-1674).[102] Born in Prague into a family which belonged to the Unity of Brethren religion, Škréta received his first formal artistic training in the 1620s, possibly from Aegidius Sadeler or J. J. Hering. Following the decree which permitted only the Catholic religion to be practised in the Czech lands, Škréta left his homeland and eventually made his way across Germany and probably Austria to Italy. While there, he visited the most important artistic centres, Venice, Bologna and Rome, acquainting himself with both sixteenth-century Venetian works by the likes of Veronese, Tintoretto and Titian, as well as with the works of the new Venetian school led by such painters as Liss, Strozzi and Fetti. In Bologna, he familiarized himself with compositions by the Carracci family and classically refined paintings by Guido Reni. In Rome, he acquainted himself with ornamental designs in the Palazzo Farnese by Annibale Carracci, as well as with work by Michelangelo, Claude Lorraine, Caravaggio and Poussin. He absorbed all the new techniques and styles, and, thanks to his own talent, succeeded in producing his own style, which modulated between Venetian colour and Baroque drama on the one hand and the Carracci's poise and Classicism on the other.

It was probably while in Italy that Škréta converted to Catholicism, and sometime before 1640 he returned to Prague, where he soon became the leading painter of his day. He painted altarpieces and wall-hung paintings and portraits and designed illustrations and university diplomas. His works dating from the 1640s in Prague derived much in their style and technique from his knowledge of Venetian and Roman paintings, as can be seen in his St Wenceslas series (1641-43) for the monastery of the discalced Augustinians in Na Zderaz. From the mid 1640s onwards, his altarpieces, while still strongly influenced by Venetian painting, began to display an increasing indebtedness to the Carraccis (for example, the *Crucifixion* with souls in purgatory for the church of St Nicholas in the Lesser Town and paintings showing St Martin sharing his cloak with a beggar and St Charles Boromeo visiting victims of the Plague [today Prague, Národní galerie]). On returning to Prague, Škréta began painting portraits in a style which accommodated the more conservative traditions which were still respected there. His portraiture as a whole, however, reflects the style and technique of Venetian painting, in particular the work of Bernardo Strozzi,

29.14 BACCIO BIANCO
Allegory of Europe
1620s
Astronomical corridor, Wallenstein Palace, Prague

whose influence is very noticeable in *Portrait of a Man with Long Fair Hair* (Prague, Národní galerie). All of Škréta's portraits are linked by the artist's attempt to capture the mental and psychological character of his subjects.

After the Thirty Years' War ended, Škréta was commissioned to paint the Assumption of the Virgin and the Holy Trinity for the church of Our Lady before Týn. This he did with Jan Jiří Bendl's column of the Virgin in mind, not simply in the sense that he conceived of the paintings as celebrating the triumph of the Catholic faith over its enemies but also in that he envisaged them, on the basis of the qualities they shared with works by Titian, the Carraccis and Reni, as being wholly Baroque. In Prague, the period of the Renaissance, of Rudolf's Mannerism, which had been an age of religious freedom and urban humanism as well as a time of war, finally came to a close. Into its place stepped the Baroque.

1. An overview of the history of Renaissance sculpture and painting in Bohemia and Prague is provided by I. Kořán, 'Sochařství. V odlesku cizích světel' in E. Poche (ed.), *Praha na úsvitu nových dějin (čtvero knih o Praze)* (Prague, 1988), pp. 151–79; idem, 'Renesanční sochařství v Čechách a na Moravě' in *Dějiny českého výtvarného umení: Od počátku renesance do závěru baroka II/1* (Prague, 1989), pp. 117–35. Art production in the period after the Battle of the White Mountain is also discussed in O. J. Blažíček, *Sochařství baroku v čechách: Plastika 17. a 18. věku* (Prague, 1958).

2. W. Hentschel, 'Sächsische Renaissancebildhauer in Nordwetböhmen' in *Nordwetböhmen in der Kunst von 1530–1680;* idem, *Dresdner Bildhauer des 16. und 17. Jahrhunderts* (Weimar, 1966).

3. The most detailed research on Prague tombstones can be found in Kořán in Poche (ed.) (note 1), pp. 160–65.

4. H. Dressler, *Alexander Colin* (Karlsruhe, 1973); Kořán in Poche (ed.) (note 1), pp. 158–59; Kořán (note 1), pp. 119–20.

5. For information on V. Strašryba, see P. Toman, *Nový slovník československých výtvarných umělců*, vol. II (Ostrava, 1993), p. 493.

6. For information on works by Saxon sculptors for the churches of the Holy Trinity and of St Salvador, see Kořán (note 1), p. 125. It is interesting to note that Adriaen de Vries also worked for the church of St Salvador.

7. Z. Winter, *řemeslnictvo a živnosti XVI. věku v čechách, 1526–1620* (Prague, 1909), pp. 95ff.

8. See V. Denkstein, Z. Drobná and J. Kybalová, *Lapidarium Národního muzea: Sbírka české architektonické plastiky XI. až XIX století* (Prague, 1958), pp. 74–75, 134–35. Kořán (note 1), pp. 127–29 considers the hypothesis that the sculptor was a member of the Walther family of Dresden.

9. Kořán in Poche (ed.) (note 1), pp. 165–73.

10. J. F. Hammerschmied, *Prodromus gloriae Pragenae: Vetero-Pragae* (1723), pp. 180–84.

11. Kořán in Poche (ed.) (note 1), p. 169; Kořán (note 1), p. 131.

12. For information on D. Altman, see Blažíček (note 1), pp. 58–59.

13. I. Kořán, 'Legenda a kult sv. Ivana', *Umění*, 35 (1987): 219–39.

14. On the question of authorship of the reliefs, see V. Kotrba, 'Georg neb Cajetan Bendl či Kašpar Bechteler', *Umění*, 22 (1974): 308–23; J. Lencová, 'Na okraj prací Kašpara Bechtelera pro Pražské hrad', *Umění*, 22 (1974): 548–43; L. Konečný, 'Esilio publico: Friedrich Falcký a Kašpar Bechteler', *Umění*, 31: 451–56.

15. Kořán in Poche (ed.) (note 1), pp. 169, 438; Kořán (note 1), p. 131.

16. The process of negotiations, the aspects of the event in Magdeburg and the transferral of the remains to Prague were researched in detail by C. Straka; see 'Ostatky a náhrobek sv. Norberta na Strahově', *Památky archeologické*, 28 (1916): 143–51; idem, *Přenesení ostatků sv. Norberta z Magdeburku na Strahov* (Prague, 1927); Kořán in Poche (ed.) (note 1), p. 439.

17. J. Morávek, 'Giuseppe Mattei a "Nová stavení" Pražského hradu 1638–1644', *Umění*, 5 (1957): 340–55.

18. I. Muchka and K. Křížová, *Valdštejnský palác* (Prague, 1996). From the older literature dealing with Wallenstein's relation to the fine arts, see Z. Wirth (ed.), *Albrecht z valdštejna a doba b člohorská*, exh. cat. (Prague, 1934); K. Křížová and A. Krutinová, 'Historické mobiliář Valdštejnského paláce v Praze – zpráva o novém soupisu', *Památky a příroda*, 9: 321–33.

19. O. Larson, *Adrian de Vries: Adrianus Fries Hagiensis Batavus: 1545–1626* (Vienna and Munich, 1967).

20. Blažíček (note 1), pp. 53–54.

21. J. Neumann, *Obrazárna Pražského hradu* (Prague, 1964), pp. 232–33; H. R. Weihrauch, 'Příspěvky k dílu Benedikta Wurzelbauera a Adriena de Vriese, *Umění*, 18: 60–73.

22. Blažíček (note 1), pp. 60–63; O. J. Blažíček, P. Preiss and D. Hejdová (eds.), *Kunst des Barock in Böhmen*, exh. cat. (Recklinghausen, 1977), p. 33; Kořán in Poche (ed.) (note 1) pp. 439–43; *Nová Encyklopedie českého výtvarného umění*, vols I–II (Prague, 1995) p. 251.

23. Blažíček (note 1), p. 62; Kořán in Poche (ed.) (note 1), p. 442.

24. M. Šroněk, 'Pražské oltáře v době třicetileté války', *Documenta Pragensia*, 9 (1991): 439–47.

25. J. Cechner, *Historiam Emausianem Neo Pragae Slavorum incolatu Celebrem sed adventu Hispanorum Mon-*

serratensium ... (1759), Central State Archive, ŘA Benediktini Emausy, ms. 5, pp. 362–64.

26. Blažíček (note 1), pp. 71–75; Blažíček, Preiss and Hejdová (eds) (note 22), pp. 34–41; O. J. Blažíček (ed.), *Výbér Řezeb pražského sochare raného baroka*, exh. cat. (Prague, 1982); Kořán in Poche (ed.) (note 1), pp. 446–49.

27. For detailed information on the origin of the column, see O. J. Blažíček, 'Jan Jiří Bendl, pražské sochař časného baroku', *Památky archeologické*, 40 (1934–35): 55–91. The works were overseen by D. Miseroni, and other unnamed sculptors were employed in addition to J. J. Bendl. In 1918, the column was demolished; a fragment is preserved in the Národní galerie, Prague; see Denkstein, Drobná) and Kybalová (note 8), pp. 140–41, which also includes earlier literature.

28. Published in K. Chytil, *Malířstvo pražské XV. a XVI. věku a jeho cechovní kniha staroměstská z let 1490–1582* (Prague, 1906), pp. 315–31.

29. A history of Renaissance murals has been compiled by J. Krčálová: 'Renesanční nástěnná malba v čechách a na Moravě' in *Dějiny* (note 1), pp. 63–92; this includes a list encompassing material found in minor periodical studies. For earlier literature, see Chytil (note 28); Winter (note 9); K. V. Herain, *české malířství od doby Rudolfínské do smrti Reinerovy. Příspěvek k dějinám jeho vnitřního vývoje v letech 1576–1743* (Prague, 1915).

30. See J. Krčálová, 'Renesanční nástěnná malba v čechách a na Moravě' in *Dějiny* (note 1), pp. 64–66 (p. 91, n. 8, for a review of the literature).

31. J. Pešek, 'Výtvarná díla s náboženskou tematikou v pražských předbělohorských interierech', *Umění*, 30 (1982): 163–67; *idem*, 'Veduty v pražských interierech doby předbělohorské', *Umění*, 21 (1983): 521–22; *idem*, 'Obrazy, grafiky a jejich majitelé v předbělohorské Praze', *Umění*, 39 (1991): 269–83.

32. P. Janák, 'Obnova sgrafit na Míčovně', *Umění*, 1 (1953): 215–25; *idem*, 'Míčovna v Královské zahradě a její sgrafita', *Ochrana památek*, 29 (1954): 9–12.

33. J. Brožová, 'Sgrafita Schwarzenberského paláce', *Ochrana památek* (1956): 42–46.

34. M. Lejsková-Matyášová, 'K tematice sgrafitové výzdoby domu U minuty v Praze', *Umění*, 17 (1969): 157–67; *idem*, 'Figurální sgrafito Arcibiskupského paláce v Praze' in *Staletá Praha*, vol. II, pp. 102–6.

35. M. Šroněk, *Pražští malíři 1600–1656: Mistři, tovaryši, úředníci a stolíři v Knize staroměstského malířského cechu: Biografický slovník* (Prague, 1996), entry 'K. Kroch'. This study collates all that is known about artists mentioned in *Kniha staroměstského malířského cechu*. Each biographical entry is accompanied by an exhaustive bibliography, and for this reason I will refer only to this work when discussing individual artists.

36. M. Lejsková-Matyášová, 'Samsonovy skutky v sgrafitech Martinického paláce v Praze', *Ochrana památek* (1961): 32–36.

37. For the most recent information on the decoration of the Granovských house, see P. Vlček (ed.), *Umělecké památky Prahy, Staré Město, Josefov* (Prague, 1996), pp. 421–32.

38. E. Poche and P. Preiss, *Pražské paláce* (1973), p. 128, also contains another example of Prague interior decoration.

39. J. Krčálová, 'Obnovené renesanční malby purkrabství Pražského hradu', *Památková péče*, 24 (1964): 275–84.

40. For a more detailed analysis of this material, see J. Vacková, 'Epitafní obrazy v předbělohorských čechách', *Umění*, 17 (1969): 131–56.

41. Krčálová, 'Renesance' in A. Merhautová (ed.), *Katedrála sv. Víta* (Prague, 1994), p. 154.

42. J. Kotalík (ed.), *Národní galerie v Praze: Sbírka starého evropského umění: Sbírka starého českého umění*, (Prague, 1984), pp. 284–85; T. DaCosta Kaufmann, *The School of Prague: Painting at the Court of Rudolf II* (Chicago and London, 1988), p. 264.

43. Kaufmann (note 42), p. 264.

44. Pešek (note 31); J. Pešek, *Mest'anská vzdělanost a kultura v předbělohorských čechách 1547–1620. (Všední dny kulturní života)* (Prague, 1993).

45. E. Bukolská, 'Renesanční portrét v čechách. 1520–1620' (Ph.D. dissertation, Prague, 1951); *idem*, 'Veduty na českých portrétech 16. a počátku 17. století', *Umění*, 31 (1983): 516–20; 'Malovaní portrét v čechách v období renesance' in *Seminaria niedzickie-Zwiazki artystczne polsko-czesko-slowacko-wegierskie II: Portret typu sarmackiego w weiku XVII* ... (Crakow, 1985), pp. 85–89.

46. K. Löcher, *Jakob Seisenegger, Hofmaler Ferdinands I* (Munich and Berlin, 1962). For information on artworks made for the Bohemian nobility, see J. Vacková, 'Závěsné malířství a knižní malba v letech 1526 až 1620' in *Dějiny* (note 1), p. 103.

47. Bukolská, 'Renesanční portrét' (note 45), pp. 53–54.

48. M. Dvořák and B. Matějka, *Soupis památek historických a uměleckých v politickém okrese roudnickém: Zámek roudnický*. (Prague, 1907); P. Štěpánek and E. Bukolská, 'Retratos espanoles en la colección Lobkowicz en Roudnice', *Archivo espanol de Arte* (1973): 319; *idem*, *španělské podobizny* (Prague, 1980).

49. Bukolská 'Renesanční portrét' (note 45), p. 64.

50. *Ibid*, pp. 65–66.

51. J. Vacková, 'Podoba a příčiny anachronismu (české utrakvistické kancionály druhé poloviny 16. století)', *Umění*, 16 (1968): 370–93, also cites older literature; see also *idem*. (note 46), pp. 95–99.

52. Vacková 1968 (note 51), pp. 380–82; J. Kropáček and P. Preiss, 'Malířství' in Poche (ed.) (note 1), pp. 199–201.

53. Prague, Kapitulní library, P 10.

54. Prague, Národní Knihovna.

55. Prague, Premonstratensians' monastery, Strahov, DG IV 23.

56. Prague, Národní Muzeum, Library, VI A 12; J. Vacková, 'Cestopis a životopis Jindřicha Hyzrleho z Chodova z let 1612–1648', *Umění*, 11 (1963): 112–23.

57. B. Hertlová, 'Úvod do problematiky památníků raného novověku' in *AUC–Phil. et Hist.* (1975), p. 5; *Z pomocných věd historických*, vol. III, pp. 117–46; L. Slavíček (ed.), *Artis pictoriae amatores: Evropa ve světle pražského barokního sběratelství*, exh. cat. (Prague, 1993), pp. 90–92.

58. Šroněk (note 35), entry 'M. Hutský'.

59. Today in Vienna, Österreichische Nationalbibliothek.

60. See most recently K. Stejskal, 'Matouš Ornys a jeho "Rod císaře Karla IV"', *Umění*, 24 (1976): 13-55.

61. Šroněk (note 35), entry 'Š. Podolský'.

62. Examined in detail in Z. Horský, *Pražské orloj* (Prague, 1988) p. 26. The original manuscript is stored in the Archív hl. města Prahy, inv. 1867, seventeenth-century transcript, inv. 7961.

63. Prague, Národní Khihovna, MS XVII A 40.

64. *Ibid*, A 3.

65. Prague, Národní galerie, Archive, Kodex Heidelbergský, AA 2015; original in Vienna, Österreichische Nationalbibliothek, Cod. 8330. Analyzed in detail in Stejskal (note 60), pp. 13-55. A similar example of the historicism of the period is the *Pulkavova kronika* from 1607, which belonged to Adam of Wallenstein. This manuscript is decorated with miniatures featuring portraits of the Czech kings up to Ferdinand I (Central State Archive, ČDK, 2452). I am indebted to Dr. J Hausenblasová for information about this work.

66. Šroněk (note 35), entry 'A. Ledecký'.

67. *Ibid.*, entry 'F. z Eysern'.

68. *Ibid.*, entry 'P. Rog'; H. Seifertová and M. Šroněk, 'Rastrový obraz z rudolfínských sbírek', *Bulletin Národní galeriee v Praze*, 5-6 (1995-96): 253-57; *idem.*, "'Gestraift doppelt Bild' from Prague's Rudolfine Collections', *Bulletin Národní galerie v Praze*, 5-6 (1995-96): 138-45.

69. Winter (note 7), pp. 209-10.

70. Šroněk (note 35), entry 'H. Graffer'.

71. *Ibid.*, entry 'D. Lexa'.

72. Kaufmann (note 7), p. 191.

73. B. Matějka, 'Přestavba a výzdoba chrámu sv. Tomáše při klášteře poustevníků řádu sv. Augustina na Menším Městě Pražském', *Památky archeologické*, 17 (1896-97): 81-152; F. Ekert, *Posvátná místa král. hl. města Prahy*, vol. II (Prague, 1883).

74. Kořán in Poche (ed.) (note 1), pp. 166-67.

75. Kotalik (ed.) (note 42), pp. 288-89; Kaufmann (note 42), pp. 159-60.

76. M. Šroněk, 'Paolo Piazza – ein malender kapuzier im rudolfinischen Prag' in *Prag um 1600: Beiträge zur Kunst und Kulturam Hofe Rudolfs II.* (Freren, 1988), pp. 284-89.

77. J. Neumann, *Malířství 17. století včechách. Barokní realismus* (Prague, 1951), p. 137.

78. For information about both paintings of the Virgin, see Merhantová (ed.) (note 41) pp. 148-151.

79. For the most recent summary of the development of Czech painting after 1620, see M. Šroněk, 'Barokní malířství 17. století v čechách' in *Dějiny* (note 1), pp. 324, 328; for the earlier literature, see Neumann (note 77), pp. 67-72.

80. For the history of the Old Town painters' guild, see M. Halata (ed.), *Kniha protokolů pražského malířského z let 1600-1656*, (Prague, 1996); Šroněk (note 35); R. Kuchynka, 'Manual pražského pořádku malířského z let 1600-1656', *Památky archeologické*, 27: 24-26.

81. Šroněk (note 35), entry 'J. Falk'.

82. E. Fučíková, 'Studien zur rudolfinischen Kunst: Addenda et corrigenda', *Umění*, 27: 489-519.

83. *Ibid.*, p. 504.

84. *Ibid.*

85. J. G. Dlabacž, *Allgemeines historisches Künstler-Lexikon für Böhmen und zum Teil auch für Mähren und Schlesien* (Prague, 1815), vol. I, pp. 613-14; Herrain (note 29), pp. 48-49; Neumann (note 77), pp. 70-71, 125; Fučíková (note 82), pp. 506-7; Šroněk (note 35), entry 'J. J. Hering'.

86. M. Šroněk, 'Matyáš Mayer, Oldřich Musch a David Altman-pražští malíři první poloviny 17. století', *Umění*, 40 (1992): 148-62; Šroněk (note 35), entry 'M. Mayer'.

87. Šroněk (note 86); Šroněk (note 35), entry 'D. Altman'.

88. Neumann (note 77), pp. 89-90, 127; *idem, český barok* (Prague, 1974), pp. 73-74; Šroněk (note 35), entry A. Stevens.

89. Šroněk (note 35), entry 'J. živnůstka'.

90. *Ibid.*, entry 'J. G. Majer'.

91. *Ibid.*, entry 'G. Špindler'.

92. *Ibid.*, entry 'E. Schiller'.

93. *Ibid.*, entry 'B. Bolonin'.

94. H. Haupt, *Fürst Karl I. von Liechtenstein, Obersthofmeister Kaisers Rudolfs II. und Vizekönig von Böhmen. Hofstaat und Sammeltätigkeit* (Vienna, Cologne and Graz, 1983).

95. Šroněk (note 35), entry 'J. K. Kristl'.

96. *Ibid.*, entry 'H. z Felzu'.

97. *Ibid.*, entry 'O. Musch', Šroněk (note 86).

98. Šroněk (note 35), entry 'J. Schlemüller'.

99. For a concise review of earlier literatur, see Šroněk (note 79), pp. 325-27, 355; P. Preiss, *Italští umělci v Praze* (Prague, 1986), pp. 235-50; for the most recent summary, see Muchka and Křížová (note 18).

100. Neumann (note 77), pp. 71-72; I. Kořán, 'Cyriacký klášter a chrám sv. Kříže Většího v baroku', *Umění*, 16 (1968): 175-76.

101. Kotalík (ed.) (note 42), pp. 134-35; L. Konečný, 'Rubensovo Umučení sv. Tomáše: Ikonografický komentář', *Umění*, 26 (1978): 211-47.

102. J. Neumann (ed.), *Karel Škréta. 1610-1674*, exh. cat. (Prague, 1974), includes references to all previous literature on the subject. The most important work is E. G. Pazaurek, *Carl Screta: 1610-1674: Ein Beitrag zur Kunstgeschichte des XVII. Jahrhunderts* (Prague, 1889. See also Neumann (note 77), pp. 72-88, 128-32. For a summary of recent literature, see Šroněk (note 35), entry 'K. Škréta'.

The Decorative Arts

JANA KYBALOVÁ

Initially, the socio-historical transformations which European society underwent during the first half of the sixteenth century were reflected only gradually in the area of the applied arts. The objects of material culture produced for manorial or urban interiors by artisans, who had been organized into specialized guilds since the late Middle Ages, remained rooted in the still-prevalent principles of the Gothic style.

The relocation of feudal lords into the city – and thus into greater proximity to the sovereign – and the abandonment of medieval fortresses in the countryside or their transformation into comfortable manors in the Italian style occurred in Prague as elsewhere. But in contrast to neighbouring Germany, where the Reformation and the tremendous concentration of bourgeois property led to the creation of the first truly Renaissance interior (the Fugger Burial Chapel)[1] in Augsburg as early as 1518, in Prague this stylistic transformation of the interior occurred only during the second quarter of the sixteenth century. Just as the disastrous fire of 1541 prevents us from having a clear picture of the interior decoration of the Old Royal Palace and other interiors built by Ferdinand I, so our information about the furnishings of the aristocratic residences which surrounded it is similarly scanty. On the other hand, the fire triggered a burst of feverish construction activity on the now-unified parcels of medieval houses. The instigators of this construction boom were the city's most prominent magnates. Journeys to Italy (and later to Heidelberg, Basel, etc.) by the members of the Czech and Moravian aristocracy during the 1550s also led, as we have seen, to an increased demand for all the comforts of life.[2]

According to contemporary reports, the interiors of these buildings were based on common principles. An increased need for display, new intellectual requirements and questions of comfort required the creation of new, specialized spaces: ceremonial and reception rooms, banquet halls, individual bedrooms for the lord and lady of the house, guests, children and servants, libraries, silver rooms, armouries and, by the end of the century, following the Emperor's example, *Kunstkammern* as well. The specialized purpose of these individual spaces was made clear by the built-in decoration of their interiors: stucco work, wall paintings and wooden ceilings of both the coffered and timbered type.

The stucco decoration of the ground floor of the Villa Hvězda (the Star Villa) in Prague dates from 1556–60; it is the oldest such work in Bohemia, and its exceptional quality makes it unique in the transalpine lands. In 334 subtly framed panels, Italian artists depicted cycles from ancient mythology and history using fragile, elongated figures based on Roman models from the first century A.D. The techniques of mural painting and stucco decoration of central- or barrel-vaulted spaces were adopted in Bohemia and Moravia during the second half of the sixteenth and the seventeenth centuries. Only slightly more recent than the Villa Hvězda is the stucco cycle of the Virtues at Nelahozeves Castle. Zachariáš of Hradec had the imposing interior of the burial chapel of the castle in Telč decorated with stucco. At the castle in Bučovice in Moravia, three-dimensional figural sculptures made of stucco were cre-

30.1 **Stucco decoration**
Main hall, Hvězda (Star)
Summer House
1556–1560

30.2 **Stucco decoration** (detail)
Main hall, Hvězda (Star)
Summer House
1556–60

30.3 **Winged altar**
Hasištejns and Lobkowicz
chapel
1532 and 1573–74
[Prague, collection of
W. Lobkowicz]

ated in the spirit of the Mannerist school of Fontainebleau and are attributed to the sculptor Hans Mont. The more robust stucco decoration of the front wing and the *salla terrena* of the Wallenstein Palace in Prague was executed during the period following the Battle of the White Mountain. The oldest carved Baroque altar in Prague, the work of A. J. Heidelberger for the chapel of the Wallenstein Palace, also dates from the period just prior to 1630.

Many of the painted wooden ceilings, both coffered and timbered, in Czech and Moravian Renaissance interiors tread the fine line between pure painting and applied art. In addition to coffered ceilings (the Schwarzenberg and Martinic palaces), most timbered ceilings were decorated with grotesque ornamentation depicting fruit, hunting trophies and drapery. In Prague, B. Spranger also participated in the painting of more involved figural decoration on ceilings. Wooden wall panelling of the type commonly found in Switzerland, France and England was more rare in Bohemia, however. The Czech interior more frequently featured the use of cloth or leather wall coverings – a custom imported from Spain and the Netherlands. The Rožmberk Palace in Hradčany was decorated not only with tapestries and imported Oriental rugs (which were used as covers for tables and benches) but also with upholstered red velvet and leather wall coverings featuring a silver design.[3] We know of cloth wall coverings with woven, embroidered and painted figures from the inventory of the castle in Moravská Třebová and leather wall coverings from Krumlov and Velké Meziříčí.[4] A fragment of the only leather wall coverings bearing the Žerotín coat-of-arms and dating between the late sixteenth and the early seventeenth centuries, has been preserved at the castle in Velké Losiny.[5] The walls of one of the rooms on the first floor of the Wallenstein Palace in Prague feature original leather wall coverings decorated with an embossed and polychromed large-format floral design dating from circa 1630.

The built-in fixtures of Prague interiors also included inset doors, which were

30.4 **Painted wooden ceiling**
Martinic Palace
Hradčany, Prague
First quarter of seventeenth
century

richly inlaid (the doors of the Old Town Hall) from the 1560s onwards, and windows filled with glass roundels embedded in lead; these windows were first imported from Venice and later made of locally manufactured clear glass on which heraldic devices and dates were painted with enamels.[6] Because climatic conditions in Bohemia differed from those in Italy, the fireplace appears only rarely in the Czech interior (Nelahozeves, before 1560); tile stoves of the kind found in Alpine countries were more common. The rather moderate domestic production of stoves was supplemented by imports from Salzburg or Nürnberg, but during the last quarter of the sixteenth century the tile stove began to be successfully manufactured in Moravian Anabaptist settlements.[7] Except for a single example in Prague, all of the extant Renaissance stoves are to be found in castles.

Inventories are also our only source of information about the quantity and richness of furniture. According to its inventory, the castle of the wealthiest aristocrat in Moravia, Ladislav Velen of Žerotín, was furnished with 'costly, partially gilded furniture'[8] before its confiscation. The inventory of Ladislav Berka of Dubá at Velké Meziříčí Castle also lists richly inlaid furniture. In both cases, the furniture in question was evidently imported from Italy and southern Germany. The lists also mention articles with painted stucco and gilt decoration, chests, benches (*cassapanca*),

30.5 Doors with an allegory of Justice and Strength
Prague, Old Town Townhall
Ca. 1560

30.6 Credenza
Second half of sixteenth century
[Prague, Umělecko-průmyslové muzeum]

chairs and stools of all types, cabinets (Spanish *vargueña*) and jewel cabinets In addition to imported objects, the testaments mention works by numerous domestic craftsmen as well. Adam of Hradec, for example, employed the cabinetmaker and carpenter Kryštof Henig of Hluboká, the locksmith Toman Šibík of Jindřichův Hradec and the carpenter Jiří Šulík of Kardášova Řečice in the extensive remodelling of the Hradčany Palace during the years 1580–84. Whatever was not destroyed in the fire of 1595, however, was irretrievably lost during repeated plundering in 1620, 1631 and 1648.[9]

In the period before the defeat at White Mountain, the Prague aristocracy and bourgeoisie owned a tremendous amount of wealth in the form of personal jewels and precious stones sewn into costly clothing made of imported Italian and Turkish brocades, velvets and samites. Here, too, we are forced to rely mainly on the accurate pictorial documentation of these objects provided by family portrait galleries. The luxury goods of the pre-White Mountain Prague aristocracy and bourgeoisie disappeared almost without a trace in the frenzied plundering of 1620.[10]

Regarding the furniture of the period 1550–1650, testaments and lists of the period provide some information about 'what went where' when enormous quantities of it were concerned, but the Prague testament books contain little information about the furniture's actual forms.[11] Our starting point must therefore be the fact that the late Gothic principle of building frame constructions and filling them with low-relief carved panelling persisted throughout the first half of the sixteenth century. A late example of this type of furniture is the archive case from 1567 in the Land Rolls Room of Prague Castle.[12] The adjoining rooms contain more examples of austere, functional furniture. This ascetic style is striking in its resemblance to the furnishings of certain rooms in the Escorial Palace in Spain. This similarity stems from the family relationship of the Habsburgs and is also evident in other branches of the applied arts. Other equally simple furnishings, such as small linden-wood tables with stools and austere beds, are mentioned in the inventory which was drawn up in Helfštejn Castle after the death of Jan of Pernštejn in 1552.[13]

Beginning in the late fifteenth century, the woodcarvers, cabinetmakers (*cistator*) and table-makers (*mercator*) of Prague, like their counterparts in economically prosperous cities such as Kutná Hora and Jindřichův Hradec, organized themselves into independent guilds. According to Z. Winter, these guilds unified 120 craftsmen during the years 1526–1620.[14] Artists from Italy, Switzerland and Germany worked alongside domestic craftsmen, but court cabinetmakers are not listed among them. Kryštof Hartwig of Wernigerode worked for Florian Griesbeck in Královice, Matthias Gandolf of Ulm and Jindrich Grodler of Zürich worked for Petr Vok in Bechyně.[15]

The preceding formulations make clear that the furniture in question was inlaid. Inlaying, a practice known in Italy since the end of the fifteenth century, was first employed in the Czech lands after the middle of the sixteenth century. It was used to decorate chests, cabinets and lavabos, as well as church interiors, pulpits and especially pews. In addition to primitive grotesque and floral ornamentation, this early inlay work often depicted simple architectural motifs and vistas, putting into practice new discoveries about perspective copied from foreign graphic models. As is confirmed by the inlaid doors in Nelahozeves, dated 1564, entire groups of chests with high pedestals and drawers (Prague, Uměleckoprúmyslové Muzeum and Duchcov) also date from the 1560s.[16]

Aristocratic interiors and the houses of the educated bourgeoisie also included a new type of furniture: bookcases. The chests previously used for storing manuscripts and incunabula were replaced by vertical cabinets in the same way that the medieval writing desk gave way to the 'Schreibtisch'. The volumes were placed in painted, carved, latticed or inlaid armoires or corner cupboards. Kateřina of Lokšany acquired a rare library, dated 1558, with chiaroscuro painting for the tower of her castle in Březnice. The wall decoration of the so-called 'green sitting rooms' of southern Bohemian castles was thus transferred onto massive, architecturally simple bookcases. More modest home furnishings also included open sideboards. The 'credenza' of the Žerotíns' castle in Velké Losiny is a three-tiered structure with carved and polychromed shelves with end panels. It also has a barrier at the front to foil poisoners. This domestic artefact combines the Italianate credenza type with Dutch-influenced studded ornamentation.[17]

In the early seventeenth century, the wooden guild coffers and caskets which replaced metal coffers placed particularly high demands on the cabinetmaker's art. Their inlaid surfaces, which were also painted and often richly carved, in a certain sense represent the culmination of the artistic ambition of domestic cabinetmaking.[18]

At the end of the sixteenth century, the ties between furniture production and goldsmithing were very close. The silver gilded chair of Zachariáš of Hradec (1557), a sketch of which has been preserved in the Třeboň archive, was evidently made by a goldsmith from Brno using silver from the mines of Přibyslav, which were owned by the lords of Hradec. Unfortunately, the chair, along with a silver table with five-leafed roses, was melted down at the beginning of the nineteenth century.[19]

Even after 1620, life in the cabinetmakers' workshops of Prague did not slow down. The high standard of filigree furniture for the court found its continuation in the production of cabinets whose drawers and interiors were decorated with individual polished stones and panelling made of more modest domestic minerals. Black ebony furniture was decorated with small, colourful enamel tablets. In addition to filling the orders of the new post-White Mountain aristocracy, Prague's cabinetmakers were employed in the creation of ecclesiastical furnishings for monasteries and church interiors, namely altars in the style of Italian portal architecture (parts of Týn cathedral, where the cabinetmaker Kotva and his assistant A. Wirkner worked from 1624 onwards; the altar of the church of the Virgin Mary of the Snows, dating from 1649–51). The pulpit, too, acquired a new importance during the Counter-Reformation (Bechteler's pulpit in St Vitus' cathedral from 1631), as did many other sacristy furnishings, pews and altar and picture frames.

In conclusion, among the activities outside Prague it is necessary to mention the work of the cabinetmakers' school of Cheb (Eger) in the area of sculptural and coloured figural inlay. The first products from the workshops of the Eck and Haberstumpf families can also be dated to before the mid-seventeenth century. The inlay work from Cheb features historical, military and hunting scenes after Dutch, German and French models, as well as reproductions of engravings by Václav Hollar.[20] Large quantities of products from the Cheb workshops were shipped to Prague.

During the period in question, metalwork had the same standing as furniture making. While few utilitarian household furnishings made of base metals and used mainly for food preparation have been preserved (the mortar with relief decoration after Peter Flötner in the City Museum of Prague), pewter was kept in the

30.8 **Cabinet**
First half of seventeenth
century
[Prague, Umělecko-
průmyslové muzeum]

30.9 **Drinking vessel with allegory of Charity and vessel with dancing couple**
Ca. 1600 and 1621
[Prague, Umělecko-průmyslové muzeum]

30.10 **Welcome vessel with hunting scene**
1627
[Prague, Umělecko-průmyslové muzeum]

sideboard and was used alongside faience dishes and silver for display purposes.

The mining of Czech tin is archivally documented from the thirteenth century onwards in the Krušné Mountains. In the sixteenth century as well, tin was mined and processed there (Jachýmov, Slavkov, Cheb). It was then transported to Prague and other workshops, mainly in the royal cities of Bohemia and Moravia.[21] During the period when urban crafts prospered, the processing of tin, or pewter-working (*konvářství*, as in Konvářská Street in Prague), became one of the most widespread of all the crafts. The irregular artistic quality of surviving artefacts was caused by the frequent reworking of this valuable raw material. The lifetime of an object almost never exceeded one generation. The most commonly preserved objects are large guild-produced jugs with engraved or bas-relief decorations and Gothic inscriptions. A number of bowls, plates, jugs, lavabos and bottles with stamped, engraved or hammered ornament following the pattern of Augsburg silver have been preserved. The craftsmen's stamps, or hallmarks, localize the workshops of master pewterers in Prague (Mrkvička, Brikcí, Křička), Pilsen (Laufer, Hořepický), České Budějovice (Hirsch), in Hradec Králové, Kutná Hora, Jindřichův Hradec and Písek, and in the Moravian cities of Jihlava, Brno, Opava and Olomouc. In the Czech border lands, craftsmen were mainly located in Litoměřice, Česká Lípa, Jáchymov (the Wildt family), Cheb (the Wildner family) and many other places. Z. Winter mentions over a hundred pewterers during the period 1526–1620.[22]

The so-called pewter treasure of Sušice provides testimony regarding the pewter furnishings of the bourgeois household. It was discovered in 1930 during the re-modelling of the house of the burgomaster čech, who had buried the treasure before emigrating in 1620.[23] The collection of eighty-six utilitarian objects demonstrates the high level of pewter-working in Renaissance Sušice (the stamp belongs to Master Jiřík), as well as in Horažďovice, Pilsen, Slavkov, and Kutná Hora. Some of the objects also come from faraway Žitava and of course from Nürnberg.

In addition to its secular uses, pewter was widely employed in the sixteenth and early seventeenth centuries for ecclesiastical purposes. It served as a substitute for precious metals in the manufacture of chalices, liturgical pitchers, candelabra and – last but not least – monumental baptismal fonts. These bell-shaped objects with lids and high lions' feet are among the most beautiful artefacts of domestic pewter-making (for example, the baptismal font of the church of St Giles in Prague). The relief on the font from Jachýmov, with its thirty-six arcaded panels depicting scenes from the Passion of Christ, is the work of Hans Wildt and is related to the Saxon tradition of relief-moulded pewter. In northern Bohemia, Jachýmov medals were often used for decoration, as were reliefs from plaques by P. Flötner. Other monumental pewter artefacts included epitaphs and coffins for prominent persons (such as Emperor Rudolf II himself).

The makers of bells and weapons were registered in the same guilds as pewterers. Entire family participated in the pouring of bells in Bohemia and Moravia. The best known is the Brikcí family of Cimperk: Bartoloměj (1553–1590) cast about eighty bells for churches in Prague,[24] while Tomáš Jaroš of Brno cast yet more bells for Prague during the years 1550-68; he was responsible for the execution of the Singing Fountain in the garden of the Royal Summer Palace. In Kutná Hora, the bell-making tradition was founded by Master Ondřej Ptáček and his sons Jakub and Michal; the bell-making workshops of Mladá Boleslav and Hradec Králové were also important.

Weaponry and armour enjoyed privileged positions among the applied arts of the Renaissance. Luxury weapons were supplied by armourers from Germany, and expensive ones were imported from Spain. In addition to decorative coats of arms, door knockers and locks with labyrinth mechanisms, the production of iron grilles represented the culmination of the blacksmith's art during this period. Such grilles were used mainly for exteriors and occasionally interiors (the grille of the knights' hall in the castle of Rožmberk) and in the context of stone tomb sculptures (the grille of the royal mausoleum in the cathedral of St Vitus). From the mid-sixteenth century onwards, table clocks of gilded bronze or copper were no longer a prerogative of the court circle. The oldest horizontal table clocks and tower clocks from the workshop of Prague clockmaker Jakub Steinmeissel are dated 1549.[24]

30.11 **Jug**
Last third of sixteenth century
[Prague, Umělecko-průmyslové muzeum]

In the area of Czech glass, the second half of the sixteenth century saw a flowering in the manufacture of stained glass, roundels and mirrors, but most of all in the production of blown glass. The rustic greenish forest glass, which had been produced since the late Middle Ages, became a utilitarian product for the middle class, aristocracy and court as early as the reign of the first Habsburgs.[25] Increasing contact with foreign countries and the need for ostentation, however, gradually created a demand for thin-walled, clear Venetian glass, classical in its proportions and often painted with enamel. Its import, however, was an expensive affair. Thus, in connection with the intensification of agriculture, pisciculture, and beer-brewing, glassworks were also founded on the feudal domains, particularly in areas where fuel wood was plentiful.[26] The most important of these early glassworks, both founded in 1530, were the north Bohemian manufactory in Chřibská (Kreibitz) and that in Falknov on the Sloup estate belonging to the Berka of Dubá family. Additional glassworks were founded in Mšeno (Grünwald) and Huť (Labau) around midcentury.[27] These manufactories were founded by the Schürer, Wander, Preussler and Friedrich families from the Ore Mountains in Saxony. But the southern Bohemian borderlands were not far behind in the production of glass, with kilns in Šumava and the glassworks of Rožmberk in the Novohradské Mountains. In 1571, Maximilian II exempted the glassworks from the land tax, so that by the end of the sixteenth century, over fifty glassworks were documented in Bohemia alone, and about half as many in Moravia and Silesia. These manufactories supplied Prague with fine glass for its tables.

30.12 **Bowl on stand**
Circa 1610
[Prague, Umělecko-průmyslové muzeum]

The necessity of competing with Venetian glass required above all significant technological progress in the quality of Czech glass, which became increasingly clear and colourless through the purification of raw materials and decolouration using manganese dioxide. This clear glass served as a base for enamel painting. The technique was mentioned in 1561, when Ferdinand of Tyrol ordered the production of 'etlich Glaswerch zum aussprennen'[28] from the glassworks of Sigmund Berka. A large number of cylindrical or conical beakers known as *Willkomms* or humpens (in accordance with their social significance and function) and dating from the mid-sixteenth through the mid-seventeenth century have been preserved in museums throughout the world. These beakers are decorated with enamel painting of aristocratic coats of arms and other decorations such as a painted double-headed eagle with the symbols of the Estates of the Holy Roman Empire, or the emperor and his electors, or Biblical or secular subjects with moralistic, satirical or hunting themes.[29] Ornamental friezes bordering the neck and foot of the vessel are also typical of

30.13 **Plate**
1611
[Prague, Umělecko-průmyslové muzeum]

30.14 Plate with the coat-of-arms of Trčka of Lípa
Between 1610 and 1620
[Prague, Umělecko-
průmyslové muzeum]

30.15 Dish with the coat-of arms of Dietrichstein
Ca. 1650
[Prague, Umělecko-
průmyslové muzeum]

30.16 Barrel
1610–1620
[Prague, Umělecko-
průmyslové muzeum]

Czech painted glass. A special group presents the small jugs and tankards of cobalt blue glass which were first produced at the Schürer glassworks. The techniques of diamond-point engraving and cold painting with oil and mastic paints came to the Czech lands from the Tyrolean town of Hall. One of the most beautiful examples of this technique is a tall beaker depicting the figure of Charity after a design by Jost Amman and bearing the Žerotín coat of arms. This exceptional technique is now associated with the Roěmberk glassworks at the foot of Vilemová Mountain.

It is the glass found in archaeological excavations at Prague Castle, particularly in the area of Vikářská Street, which bear the closest resemblance to Italian models. The shards include goblets with stems decorated with mascarons or mould-blown ornamentation, goblets with bell-shaped feet, and even some filigree glass.[30] This glass was produced either in the Schürer glassworks in Broumy, near Křivoklát, or in Prague itself, in the Bubeneč glassworks. Other finds have been unearthed in the northern Bohemian glassworks in Rejdice and on the grounds of the Convent of St Agnes of Bohemia in Prague,[31] as well as in the city centres of Pilsen, Hradec Králové and Olomouc.

The phenomenon of Renaissance engraved glass, however, was the most important in terms of the further development of Czech glass. Its creation is inextricably tied to the Mannerist atmosphere of Rudolf II's court and Rudolfine Prague. The city was home to numerous gem-cutters from Italy, the Netherlands and Germany. The production of Czech glass had to undergo a complex technological development in order to create the parisons necessary for the demanding cutting process. 'Czech crystal', which was created through the purification of potash and lime, became a substitute for precious minerals, in particular mountain crystal. The most famous glass engraver, Caspar Lehmann (1563/4–1622), was a native of the north German town of Uelzen and settled in Prague during the late 1580s. In 1609, the Emperor granted him an aristocratic title and an exclusive privilege for engraving glass.[32]

Although Lehmann's earliest signed work is a beaker made in 1605 for the Austrian noble Wolf Sigmund von Losenstein and his wife Susanne von Rogendorf, it has been demonstrated that he carved complex figural and ornamental compositions on flat glass panels in his studio prior to this date. These compositions include, for example, a small panel bearing a portrait of Christian II, Elector of Saxony, and numerous other unique works which are today scattered in collections throughout the world.[33] Lehmann's successors continued his glass engraving techniques mainly in Nürnberg. During the second half of the seventeenth century, Czech glass engravers took up the techniques of village stone cutters from the foothills of the Jizerské Mountains, but without the traditions of Rudolfine art, this technology would never have attained the breadth and quality of the well-known Czech work of the eighteenth and nineteenth centuries.

Throughout most of the sixteenth and early seventeenth centuries, ceramic products remained merely functional. Because of the danger of fires in heavily populated urban settlements, the potters' guilds which supplied Prague with ceramic goods were concentrated in many provincial cities in proximity to deposits of suitable clays; these towns included Rakovník, Levína, Kutná Hora, Pilsen and Beroun. Prague potters were definitely in the minority in comparison to other artisanal craftsmen. Of the Rošmberk towns, the most successful potters were in Bechyně and Třeboň, where they were granted special privileges by Vilém of Rožmberk in 1556.[34]

The discovery of lead glazes as well as tin glazes based on Italian models spread from Kutná Hora across Bohemia, apparently through the Hungarian lands under the reign of Mathias Corvinus In addition to a series of ceramic tiles depicting half-length portraits of the prophets with pairs of aristocrats in Renaissance arcades and cornices with Czech and Latin inscriptions, a fragment of a tile with a green-glazed relief portrait of Ferdinand I has been preserved. In the sphere of wheel-thrown pottery, the only extant object is a jug by Simon Nemazal of Beroun, dated 1572, which constitutes the oldest European pottery decorated in this style.

30.17 **Jugs**
1639 and 1650
[Prague, Umělecko-
průmyslové muzeum]

In the broader sense of the word, 'pottery' also includes terracotta construction elements. Complicated grotesque reliefs were produced by a fully developed ceramic workshop in the vicinity of the Pernštejns' construction projects in Pardubice as well as Prague (the Pernštejn/Lobkowicz Palace); towards the end of the sixteenth century, it was also used in other places such as in Horšovský Týn and in the roundel of the castle of Jindřichův Hradec. Czech construction ceramics, however, never attained such monumental forms as in the Austrian castle of Schallaburg, where terracotta figural consoles stand in the arcades of the courtyard.

The Czech aristocracy reacted to the shift from the use of precious metals and pewter to more hygienic majolica or faience for luxury banqueting by importing the goods from Italy. Probably the oldest of these is the fragmentary majolica set from Deruta which Vratislav of Perštejn acquired during a trip through Italy in 1551; the dishes in particular feature epic illustrations of the family legend of the conquering of the bison. Other faience sets in the 'bianchi di Faenza' style with the allied Pernštejn and Mendoza coats of arms and the Order of the Golden Fleece, as well as remnants of a set bearing the coat of arms of the Austrian branch of the Meggau family and dating from the late sixteenth-early seventeenth century, have been preserved in the Lobkowicz collections in Nelahozeves.

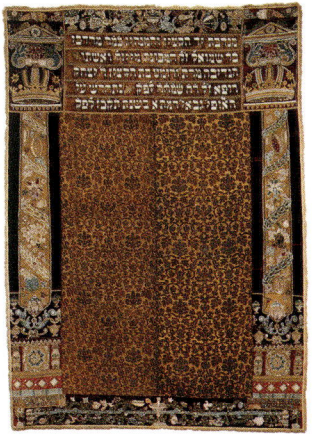

30.18 **Synagogue curtain**
[Prague, Jewish Museum]

During this period, equally refined and high-quality faiences were already being produced in the workshops of the Anabaptist settlements in Moravia.[35] After the first persecutions began in Switzerland in 1526, the members of this German-speaking Protestant group co-opted their equally persecuted brethren in Tyrol, northern Italy, Germany, Netherlands and, unified by the ideology of Jakub Huter, began to settle in isolated farmsteads on the estates of the tolerant Utraquist nobility in Moravia. Eighteen farmsteads of several hundred members each existed on the dominions of the Žerotíns alone. In addition to their artisanal and healing activities (in the early seventeenth century, an Anabaptist healer was even summoned to the Prague court), the Moravian Anabaptists (also known as Habaner) became renowned for their production of fine faience, pottery and stove-fittings. The beginning of production in Moravia is related to the larger wave of immigration during the years 1550–60. The shapes of the earliest Habaner faience betray a clear kinship with Italian majolica, for after the Battle of the White Mountain, the Anabaptists were forced to leave their lands and travel to the east. The harmonious forms of the open-work bowls, ball-shaped jugs, ewers, and plates are painted with unassuming decorations using either cobalt colour or the four high-temperature colours, and the subjects depicted are limited to heraldry, dates or floral motifs in accordance with the religious teachings of the brethren. The Premonstraterians of the Strahov monastery and the Benedictines in Břevnov ordered faience sets with these decorations. The various types of floral decoration show the dominant influence of Ottoman Turkey: in addition to

30.19 **Synagogue curtain**
[Prague, Jewish Museum]

carnations and pomegranates, the main motif is that of the tulip worked into scroll-work leaf patterns. Over the course of the seventeenth century, Habaner faience adhered conservatively to Renaissance principles and gradually became rusticated.

A scant number of small vessels made of *terra sigillata* produced during the years 1630–60 in northern Bohemia, today bear witness to a unique phenomenon in the history of European ceramics. In Jablonné v Podještědí, on the domain of Jindřich Berka of Dubá, an exclusive imperial privilege was granted for the production of smaller objects such as bowls, conical beakers, mugs and jugs with pewter tops. The thin-walled pottery, fired at the low temperature of 600–700 C°, was decorated with fine-quality Renaissance decorations using cold-painting techniques, which is why the colours often washed away. The background consisted of scrolling, black-outlined foliage with richly coloured lily-like flowers reminiscent of Habaner or Turkish pottery from Isnik. More rarely, we find depictions of St Elisabeth as well (on a tankard from 1649 in the Uměleckoprůmyslové Muzeum, Prague). Without exception, the most exposed place on the vessel always carries the stamp of Jindřich Wolf Berka, as do products made 20 years earlier in the Silesian town of Striegau.[36]

Since the Middle Ages, it was believed on the Greek islands, on Malta and in Turkey that these unique ceramic products, listed in all of the inventories of Mannerist *Kunstkammern*, were capable of curing almost any illness, including poisoning. This was reason enough for the miraculous *terra sigillata*, also known as 'Maltese' or 'St Paul's clay', to appear at the court of Rudolf II. The *Kunstkammer* inventory of 1607–11 lists *terra sigillata* in connection with the town of Brandýs nad Labem, but thus far, such a vessel has not been found in any of the collection's depositories known to us. [37]

Textiles represent an important part of material culture in Renaissance Bohemia. Tapestries are listed in almost all written inventories, but in spite of the efforts of King George of Poděbrady and, later, of Vladislav Jagellon to bring weavers from France, domestic tapestry production never took hold.[38] Thus from 1550 to 1650, tapestries were imported to Bohemia from France or Flanders. The number of objects preserved from this period does not correspond to contemporary reports. They can be thematically divided into three groups: *verdures*, tapestries with coats of arms, and figural subjects. Figural tapestries with wide borders, sometimes interwoven with gold or silver, were originally created in cycles and have been preserved in fragmentary form in Prague in the Archbishop's Palace and the Uměleckoprůmyslové Muzeum, as well as in a number of castles throughout Bohemia and Moravia.[39] Imported textiles also included Oriental rugs and expensive fabrics used for draperies and formal clothing.

It was above all embroidery which took root in the Czech environment. The traditionally high level of domestic embroidery dated from the reign of Charles IV and was manifested from the beginning of the sixteenth century in the ecclesiastical sphere, where the older practice of 'needle painting' was replaced by the technique of couching figures in high relief. In addition to a few surviving *casules* of this type, the Prague collections include a dorsal cross from the treasure of St Vitus. The other direction in domestic embroidery is represented by the technique of embroidering with river pearls, or passementerie – also traditional in the Czech lands. The mitre and gloves from the treasure of St Vitus are an eloquent testament to this tradition,[40] but the true masterpiece of this craft is the Hasištejnský-Lobkowicz wing altar

in the collections at Nelahozeves. The origin of this remarkable textile is complex and can be divided into roughly two time periods. The altar wings with the Annunciation and the predella were made in 1532 by Hans Plock, the Saxon court embroiderer. Between 1573 and 1574, the Prague embroiderer Filip Innderfelder completed the centre of the altar (irreparably damaged in 1939) with a depiction of the Triumphant Christ and a frame with the coat of arms of Eva Fictumová and Bohuslav Hasištejnský of Lobkowicz, who was then at the castle of Líčkov.[41]

The oldest Prague synagogue curtains (*parocot*) are also an important artefact of domestic embroidery. Their artistic and historic values reflect the atmosphere of the Prague ghetto and are important in helping to complete the colourful mosaic that was Rudolfine Prague. The curtains are usually composed of two portals framed by columns whose crown-shaped capitals are similar to the ends of the Torah. Over the course of the seventeenth century, these columns evolved into a decorative border finished off by a wide band of ornamental elements on the lower part of the rectangle. The models for this design were probably the title pages of contemporary prints.[42] The embroidery workshops of the Prague ghetto used fragments of imported Italian and Turkish brocades as well as embroideries made of pearls and gold thread to decorate the curtains.[43] In both Jakub Baschew's 1623 curtain and the even older curtain donated by Mordechai Maisel in 1592, the embroidered ornamentation clearly shows the influence of Ottoman culture, as do many ecclesiastical textiles of the post-White Mountain Catholic clergy.

1. G. Himmelheber 1972, pp. 55-61.
2. E. Poche–P. Preiss 1974.
3. J. Krčalová 1970, p. 439.
4. F. Hrubý 1927, pp. 227, 294: '...25 toperecaj kožených na stžny - 2.000 zl.' '...čalouný kožených pozlacených nových - 19 kusý' ('...25 leather wall coverings - 2.000 gold' '... new guilded leather upholstery - 19 items').
5. M. Lejsková - Matyášová 1972, pp. 34 ff.
6. O. Drahotová 1989, cat. nos 74-80.
7. J. Kybalová 1995, p. 207, ills 151-55, 164, tab. XII; cat. no 13.
8. F. Hrubý 1927, pp. 280ff.
9. V. Ledvinka–B. Mráz–V. Vlnas 1995, pp. 133-34.
10. J. Janáček 1987, pp. 230ff.
11. J. Pešek 1993, pp. 109ff.
12. E. Poche 1980, p. 156.
13. F. Hrubý 1927, pp. 285ff.
14. Z. Winter 1909, p. 543.
15. O. Herbenová 1988, manuscript.
16. J. Kybalová 1985, pp. 211-12.
17. *Ibid.*, pp. 212-13, tab. XII.
18. The coffers of the carpenters' guild, 1594; of the journeyman carpenters, 1596; of the shearers, 1609; of the glove-makers, 1612; and others in the City Museum of Prague.
19. O. Herbenová 1988, manuscript.
20. M. Mžyková 1986, pp. 7ff.
21. D. Stará 1972, p. 8.
22. Z. Winter 1909, pp. 136ff.
23. L. Lábek 1967, pp. 156ff.
24. E. Poche–L. Urešová, p. 31, ill. 4.
25. K. Hetteš 1962, ills 2-4; D. Hejdová 1975, pp.

142-50, tab. 14, 15.
26. E Poche 1980, pp. 158ff.
27. O. Drahotová 1981, p. 13.
28. M. Klante 1938, p. 598.
29. O. Drahotová 1989, pp. 55-57, 41-73.
30. Archaeological findings of Ivan Borkovský at Prague Castle, published by K. Hetteš, 1963.
31. D. Hejdová 1971, pp. 8-15; 1982, pp. 10-15.
32. E. Meyer–Heisig 1963, pp. 115ff.
33. O. Drahotová 1981 b, ills 4-11, 14.
34. Z. Winter 1909, pp. 531ff.
35. J. Kybalová 1992; 1995, pp. 18-19, cat. 1-8.
36. J. Horschik 1966, vol. 33, pp. 3-55.
37. *Das Kunstkammer Rudolfs II.* ... item 1069: 'Terrae sigillatae Geschirlein von Brandeis Ein bauchet niedere geschirlien auf die türkische art welche Ihr. May. aus den erden zu Brandeis Ao 1608 durch Ihren demaln laibapotheker N. Hegner machen lassen, ist von leibfarber erden.' I would like to thank Dr. B. Bukovinská for bringing this reference to my attention.
38. E. Poche 1980, p. 149.
39. J. Blážková 1957, pp. 19ff.
40. E. Šittler–A. Podlaha 1903, cat. no. 267.
41. L. Letošníková 1970, pp. 81-97. J. Rasmussen 1976, pp. 62, 94-95; L. Konečný 1990, vol. 38, pp. 504-10.
42. H. Volavková 1949, p. XI; O. Herbenová 1968, p. 112.
43. J. Polák 1931, p. 28. Ferdinand I collected part of his fees from the Jews in gold thread - 'gut gesprunnen Gold' - and sent them to his 'geliebten Döchtern gen Insprug'.

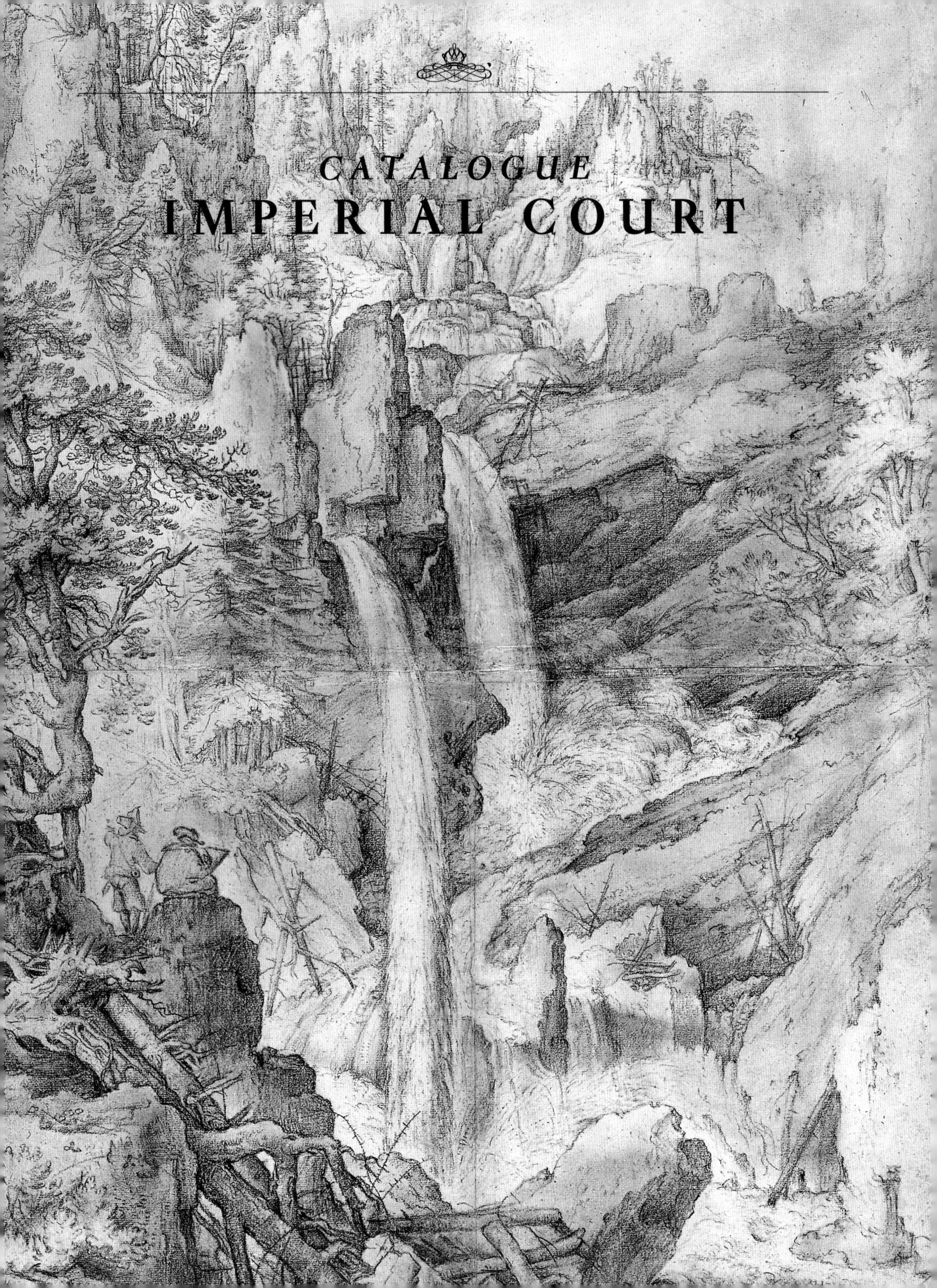

CATALOGUE
IMPERIAL COURT

Section I: Painting, Sculpture, Drawings and Engravings

Painting

Eliška Fučíková

Although painters constituted the largest group of artists at the Rudolfine court, this does not mean that the Emperor prefered painting to other forms of art. It comprised so many different genres which attracted the Emperor's interest that the presence of specialists in several fields was unavoidable. Pictures in the Emperor's collections, acquired through purchases and gifts, included works by all the important Italian, Dutch, German and other masters of earlier and contemporary generations. Rudolf II was, however, equally passionate about paintings executed under his patronage which involved direct contact with artists in their studios, where he would follow the creative process and supply ideas and comments. If in the beginning he had to content himself with artists who had worked for his father, he soon began to invite artists into his service according to his own taste and interests. These works of art created the environment through which he moved; they surrounded him in his apartments and reception rooms and in the halls built specially to exhibit them, where he undoubtedly spent much of his time.

Portrait painting was one of the most common genres at the court. Essential official portraits were executed in many variants and copies which travelled as obligatory state gifts to noble courts. They were impersonal, idealizing, often of average quality in view of the many times they were copied and the considerable share that workshops had in their execution. If, however, the subject and his faithful representation were important to the artist, an official portrait could be of exceptional quality. The self-portraits by Rudolfine artists and the portraits of family members and friends comprise a special chapter in the history of the genre and are fascinating in their immediacy. Hans von Aachen, who assumed a prominent position in this field, was a portrait painter by trade whose generally laughing expression, along with the faces of his wife and children, even appear in genre and mythological compositions. We also find examples of the so-called *Freundschaftsbild*, a portrait with friends, in the Rudolfine canon.

Paintings with mythological themes were the most numerous in palace interiors and in the imperial collections. Such compositions provided a wealth of opportunities for the depiction of the beauty of the human body or of sensuality, of which the Emperor was undoubtedly fond. Bartholomeus Spranger even painted whole series for him depicting Classical deities. It would be a mistake to think that Rudolf was ever content with the usual. Over time, the content of these paintings became more and more complex, involving several layers of interpretation whose message or moral lesson could be interpreted only by initiated viewers. Their painters found inspiration in Classical and contemporary literature, in books of emblems and symbols accompanied by learned interpretations. For their allegories, Rudolfine artists drew chiefly from the rich repertoire of period iconographic reference books. Many painters celebrated the Emperor and his wisdom; they responded to historical events such as the Turkish Wars; they expressed their awareness of the transience of human life and their hope that virtue would triumph over vice. None of these paintings, however, was intended for public presentation or propaganda or for the celebration of a noble line or ruler, as was the case at other royal courts. These works were aimed at a limited circle, mostly for the Emperor himself.

The Emperor reserved a special place in his collections for miniature paintings, which were a type of collector's jewel and which, in keeping with their location, were known as cabinet pieces or *Kunstkammerstücke* (works for the *Kunstkammer*). This meant that they were painted for those who appreciated both perfect execution and the elaborate treatment of themes. The motifs for these paintings were unlimited; they contained religious, mythological or allegorical motifs. They excel for their perfect compositions and unusual colours and demonstrate the virtuosity of their creators. Thus they resemble precious gems. Their small size made it possible for their owner to admire them close up and hold them in his hand.

The collection of altar paintings in this exhibition makes it clear that religious painting had an important place at the imperial court. Visitors will have the opportunity to see many of the altars in the very places for which they were painted – for example, in the churches of St Thomas (Heintz, Spranger), St James (Aachen) and Our Lady of the Capuchins (Piazza). Not all of these were imperial commissions, however; they may have been executed by artists close to the Rudolfine court who followed the Emperor's example, as, for instance, when several artists collaborated on single works. At first, these works were painted in the spirit of late Mannerism, but later they began to incorporate the ideas expressed at the Council of Trent, thus heralding the new style sooner than elsewhere. In this connection, we should also mention the small altars designed for private devotion, small paintings for worship in domestic chapels or use on journeys. More frequently than with other painting genres, these works contain references to famous earlier models, in the form of visual quotations or wholescale copying. The most frequent source of inspiration was Dürer, whose works were well represented in the imperial collections and therefore readily available.

Landscape artists were considered important members of the Rudolfine painters' community. They represented two prominent trends in European landscape painting: Pieter Stevens and the Dutch-Italian style of landscape composition, and Roelandt Savery, who continued the Bruegel tradition and focused on a realistic interpretation of nature. Stevens chose to depict distant views of the landscape, enlived in the beginning by Classical ruins, later incorporating features of the local environment. Influenced by Savery, he began to seek beauty in more detailed landscape scenes, secluded areas of forest and unusual rock formations. However, he never abandoned the traditional arrangement of the composition into three planes, and he never became part of the scene he was painting, remaining a distant observer. Savery, who was initially interested in village festivities and rural dwellings, perceived the landscape as an environment surrounding him in which he worked. Thus he devoted his time to drawing nature studies which he would transfer to canvas. He, too, chose vast Alpine valleys and high, craggy mountains as his subjects; he was also able to capture forest scenes with felled trees and the rapid currents of streams, which he knew from his excursions in Bohemia and the Tyrolean Alps. He also depicted the life he found there – animals, wanderers, woodcutters working in the forest, hunts for stag and wild boar. These motifs he brought to the Castle from his 'naert het leven' – studies of life.

Savery, of course, was not just a specialist in landscape painting. Unfortunately, we are unable to show visitors to the exhibi-

tion his floral still lifes, a field in which he was a pioneer, since transporting them would have exposed them to unacceptable risk. Similar works by Joris Hoefnagel, executed in miniature, may have provided him with inspiration. The so-called 'reversible head', a type of still life composed from all manner of objects, from one side forms a bizarre head, but, turned 180 degrees, forms a still life. Such pictures were painted by Giuseppe Arcimboldo, who executed the famous portrait of the Emperor and other composite heads and who evidently began working on this type of still life specifically for Rudolf II.

Savery is credited with other innovations. He was a pioneer in the area of animal painting, although at the imperial court he found a predecessor in Hans Hoffmann; Hoefnagel also studied this genre in his manuscripts and paintings. Savery was also one of the first to paint cityscapes, a venture in which he was success-fully aided by Paulus van Vianen. A new field of painting depicting architecture was also introduced to the imperial court by Vrede-man de Vries and his son Paul.

The Rudolfine painters did not form a unified group expressing a homogeneous style. The Emperor selected them according to their orientation in the same way a goldsmith would choose various precious stones for the ornamentation of a jewel so that, despite the different colours, they would complement each other perfectly. Each of these masters earned his place in the gaily coloured mosaic of the period's painting styles. They were not, however, indifferent to the works of their colleagues; they took their inspiration from all kinds of different sources, and they were open to experimentation. Thus there are occasions when the works of various Rudolfine artists come together in order to set off once more on their own journeys as new paintings.

I.1
Hans von Aachen
Double Portrait (Self-portrait)
Oil on oak
Before or ca. 1575
Public lottery in 1670, Vienna; collection of the Olomouc bishopric
Kroměříž, Arcibiskupství olomoucké, Arcibiskupský zámek a zahrady v Kroměříži, inv. no. O 288/KE 3177

This painting is the earliest of Aachen's surviving paintings. It was painted even before he left his native Cologne for Italy. He was trained in the workshop of the painter whom Karel van Mander in-troduces only by his Christian name (Georgie oft Jerrigh) and adds that he was Flemish, came from Antwerp and was a capable portraitist. Judging from the painting from Kroměříž, he instruct-ed his pupil primarily in this speciality, he acquainted him with genre painting, and he preferred a pastose painting tech-nique, modelling the forms softly. It is possible to read all of this from von Aachen's Kroměříž juvenilia. In this painting the painter's laughing counte-nance appears for the first time, even twice, for the head peeping out from be-hind what is undoubtedly von Aachen's self-portrait also belongs to him – in a sense an *alter ego* that is tugging on his ear, more in reproach than in playful-ness. But here von Aachen is not stylized in the role of a coarse, laughing peasant, as is common with Dutch painters from the first half of the sixteenth century. He chooses between two views of the world: over the crying Heraclitus he gives his preference to the laughing Democritus.

Peltzer 1911/1912, pp. 143, 161, cat. no. 26, ill. 63; An der Heiden 1970, pp. 140, 177, cat. no. A1, ill. 121, with earlier litera-ture; Fučíková 1971, pp. 118–119, ill. 77.

E.F.

I.2
Hans von Aachen
Self-portrait
Oil on oak
On the back, an old inscription: *Ritratto di Hans von Hachen fatto di sua propria mano fu Pittor celebre dell'imperatore Rodolfo 2o*; and further: *e.zenarzin Marg.te Rot.re*; on the pasted-on tag: *Baronesse Lupis*
Probably 1575 or shortly after 1575
Court Councillor Dr Jurié von Lavandal, Vienna; Dorotheum, Vienna, 1961; Dr En-gelmann, Vienna; purchased by the mu-seum in 1969
Cologne, Wallraf-Richartz-Museum, inv. no. 3 211

When von Aachen traveled around 1575 from his native Cologne to Venice to find a suitable atelier, Caspar Rem – a painter of Cisalpine origin who had already been waiting several years for recognition – re-fused to take him on. As we know from van Mander, von Aachen convinced him of his talent with his laughing self-por-trait. Rem was so taken with the painting that he refused to teach von Aachen be-cause there was no need for this, and ap-parently even prepared canvases for him. Von Aachen reciprocated by painting a portrait. The painting from Cologne de-picts von Aachen as serious, so it cannot be the one described by van Mander. It is, however, a rare document of von Aachen's production at the outset of his stay in Italy. In Cologne he had received a thorough training in portraiture from his Flemish teacher. The Cologne self-portrait already indicates a certain culti-vation gained from the Venetian environ-ment.

Mander 1906, p. 283; Peltzer 1911/1912, pp. 63, 164, cat. no. 73, ill. 3; An der Hei-den 1970, pp. 140, 178, cat. A3, pic. 122; Fučíková 1971, pp. 115–124.

E.F.

I.3
Hans von Aachen
Self-portrait, Smiling, with Woman Playing the Lute ('donna venusta')
Oil on canvas
114 x 87.5 cm
Ca.1585 or earlier
Astley-Corbett sale, Christie's, London, 8 July 1927; bought by W. Sabin for 75 guineas.
Verona, private collection

In 1602 Karel van Mander wrote that in Italy von Aachen had 'painted a smiling figure holding a glass of wine and a woman playing the lute – the *Madonna*
Venusta. . . connoisseurs of art said that they had never seen a better picture . . .' Recently discovered in an Italian private collection, von Aachen's picture had been thought lost. The drawing for it was pub-lished by An der Heiden, and contains, as well as the signature, the fragment of a date – 158- – which places the painting before 1585, by which time von Aachen was in Venice. Von Aachen repeated the composition in a more caricatured form without the garish features of the por-traits (likewise in an Italian private col-lection). In this picture von Aachen used his own face for the first time. This not merely the depiction of a happy young couple: the painter draws attention to a quotation from the Bible written on the music sheet, 'Vinum et musica laetificant cor meus' (Wine and music gladden the heart). The painter clearly intended a deeper moral for the work, because the quotation continues, 'but better still is the love of wisdom'.

Fučíková 1971, p. 125, ill. 82; An der Hei-den 1979, p. 453, pics 4–6; Kaufmann 1987, p. 108 (ill.); Kaufmann 1988, p. 72 (ill.); Fučíková 1996, pp. 10–14 (ill. also second Italian version).

E.F.

I.4
Hans von Aachen
Portrait of Joseph Heintz the Elder
Oil on canvas
57 × 44 cm
Ca. 1585
Nostická Collection no. 208, under
'Spranger'
Prague, Národní galerie v Praze, inv. no.
DO 4326

Peltzer correctly attributed this painting
to von Aachen in 1911, and a number of
decades later Jürgen Zimmer succeeded
in identifying the subject as Joseph
Heintz the Elder. Van Mander claimed

that the relationship between von Aachen
and Heintz was rather like that of master
to pupil, by which he no doubt meant that
Heintz, having arrived in Italy as a trained
artist, needed an atelier in which he could
continue his studies. Von Aachen himself
had been the beneficiary of a similar act of
kindness when he was allowed to join the
atelier of Casparo Remo and Anthonis
Santvoort on first arriving in Italy. Heintz
arrived in Italy in 1585, when von Aachen
already enjoyed a certain amount of fame,
and employed several helpers in his workshop. During this period von Aachen
painted a series of portraits of artists
working in Italy, for instance Giambo-

logna, Bylivelt (cat. no. I.5) and Toeput. It
seems more than likely that von Aachen
would have made a portrait of his young
colleague and helper, in the paintings for
Il Gesù in Rome. The technique and
brushstroke match those used in the portraits mentioned. For all these reasons,
the recent attribution to Domenico Fetti
seems highly unlikely to be correct.

Peltzer 1911–12, pp. 70–73, ill. 8; An der
Heiden 1970, pp. 148, 182–83, ill. 126, for
older literature.

E.F.

I.5
Hans von Aachen
Portrait of Jacques Bylivelt
Oil on canvas
On the back of the painting before relin-
ing there was an old inscription: *Rittrato
del Sig. Giaches Bilivert fia (mingo) Padre di
Giovanni Bilivert pitore … dipinto per mano
di Ans Vanach pittor Fiamingo anno 158 …*
1586
Florence, collection of Prince Corsini; art
market in Milan
Private collection

The portrait of the well-known Medici
goldsmith Jaques Bylivelt was already

published in 1893 by Frimmel. Before it
appeared on the art market, not long ago,
it was restored, and so the date of its origin – 1586 – is again legible. After the
overpainting and varnish were removed,
von Aachen's characteristic painting
handiwork is also more evident: more delicate, perfect modelling in the face, pastose and energetic in the dress. The
brownish background allows the figure to
stand out and amplifies the colour effect.
During his ten-year stay in Italy von
Aachen matured as a portraitist, gaining
the recognition of his colleagues and
even collectors. This painting can stand
up to the Dutch portrait paintings of the

first half of the seventeenth century, both
in its masterful execution and in the skill
in realistically depicting the human face.
Bylivelt was in Venice in 1586 to purchase
precious stones, so von Aachen could
have painted his portrait there, but it is
more likely to have been painted during
the artist's stay in Florence.

An der Heiden 1970, pp. 179–80, with all
the earlier literature; Frock 1974, p. 90, ill.
76.

E.F.

I.6
Hans von Aachen
Christ on the Way to Calvary
Oil on panel
42 × 59.6 cm
Bottom right: *HANS VON ACH 1587* (beneath this was originally *INVENIT 1587* -
a correction by the artist)
1587
Besançon, perhaps identical with the
painting from Thomas François Granvella's 1607 collection; 1967 purchased from
a private collection for the Slovenská
národná galéria in Bratislava
Bratislava, Slovenská národná galéria,
inv. no. O 1 742

Von Aachen's *Christ on the Way to Calvary*
is a masterly example of his artistic skill at
a time when he had decided to abandon
Italy to work on commissions in Bavaria.
The figures, full of a dramatic sense of
movement, highlight the influence of his
teachers in Rome, who were themselves
originally from the Netherlands, and their
use of colour similarly attests to his detailed knowledge of Venetian painting. All
these aspects are, however, suborned to
von Aachen's unique style, with his quick
brushstrokes and pentimenti brilliantly
working together with the colours. The
rich, relief-like composition filled with
figures is highlighted from behind by a

seemingly endless expanse of clear space,
so that the viewer is struck by the drama
of the scene apparently set against the
background of eternity. Rudolf II evidently never saw the painting, which dates
from the period when the Emperor first
met von Aachen in Prague.

Essen and Vienna 1988, cat. no. 89, for older literature.

Neumann 1978, p. 321 ill. 7; Neumann
1979, p. 206, ill. 181; Neumann 1985, p. 55,
ill. 11.

E.F.

I.7
Hans von Aachen
The Rape of Proserpina by Pluto
Oil on canvas
110 × 150 cm
Signed in the middle of the wheel: *HVA*
(lig.); on the wheel: *1589*
1589
Possibly identical with no. 817 in the in-
ventory of Rudolf's collections for 1621;
perhaps a gift of the Empress Maria
Theresa to Baron Brukenthal
Sibiu, National Brukenthal Museum, inv.
no. 1

The 1621 inventory lists under entry 817

*Ein Pluto mit Proserpino vom Hansen von
Acha. (Orig.)*, which most likely identifies
this picture. Even during his stay in
Bavaria, von Aachen worked for the Emperor, and *The Rape of Proserpina by Pluto*
could have been one of the works sent to
Prague from either Munich or Augsburg.
Peltzer doubted the authenticity of the
work, but he knew it only from pho-
tographs and did not know about the signature and the date, which classify the
painting among similar works such as the
Judgment of Paris from Douai (Musée de la
Chartreuse) or the *Carrying of the Cross*,
painted in 1587. These three paintings
share the same stylistic starting point.

They are significantly influenced by Venetian painting in their composition and
use of colour. The scenes are set within a
wonderfully freely painted landscape,
where again the Venetian inspiration is
unquestionable. Under softly blending,
palette-knifed paintwork, an obscure
brushed sketch shines through. It is very
characteristic of many of von Aachen's
pictures from that time that pentimenti
are visible to the naked eye.

Peltzer 1911–12, p. 168, III/9 (Hermannstadt).

E.F.

I.8
Hans von Aachen
A Young Couple
Oil on canvas
63 × 50 cm
Ca. 1596
? From the collection of Rudolf II; imperi-
al collection in Vienna; since 1781 housed
in a gallery
Vienna, Kunsthistorisches Museum,
Gemäldegalerie, inv. no. 1134

Von Aachen's self-portrait with Regina di
Lasso was evidently painted immediately
after their marriage in Munich in 1596.
This is not a simple portrait of two peo-

ple, but contains yet another level of understanding. The smiling faces, the affec-
tionate tugging at the ear, the small tablet
of stone with chalk transcripts, a pouch
with money are all motifs in sixteenth-
century Netherlandish painting that usually accompany the image of the prodigal
son, wasting time and money on loose
women in a tavern. Von Aachen knew this
symbolism well and undoubtedly used it
on purpose. Like the picture with '*donna
venusta*' (cat. no. I.3), this double portrait
is apparently believed to have a moral.
The evangelist Luke, in the parable of the
prodigal son, puts the following words into the mouth of the father (Luke 15): 'It

was meet that we should make merry and
be glad: for this thy brother was dead, and
is alive again; and was lost, and is found.'
In this picture, the father's challenge has
evidently passed over to the artist's wife,
who, with understanding and forgive-
ness, has brought him back to the true
path by marrying him.

Prague 1912, cat. no. 30; Essen and Vienna
1988, cat. no. 92.

Pellzer 1911–12, pp. 136, 163, ill. XVII; an
der Heiden 1970, pp. 189–191, ill. 130;
Kaufmann 1988, cat. no. 1.6.

E.F.

I.9
Hans von Aachen
Bacchus, Venus and Cupid
Oil on canvas
63 × 50 cm
On the plate, bottom left: *HVA (lig.)*
1595–1600
? From the collection of Rudolf II; imperial collection in Vienna; since 1781 housed in a gallery
Vienna, Kunsthistorisches Museum, Gemäldegalerie, inv. no. 1132

Many of von Aachen's mythological pictures are of multi-layered content; they tend to be genre works, moralities and al-

legories. This picture is one of those that might, Schnackenburg believed (1970, p. 146), have represented 'the rule of wine over love'. But Venus, represented by von Aachen's young wife, is dominant in the picture and Cupid, represented by his small son, touches her bared breast, from which he has barely been weaned. Love and fertility seem to play a decisive role in the picture. Von Aachen had a liking for a composition made up of half-figures and he used it several times, with variations, in pictures of various subjects. In the background of all of them can be seen his figure, with his characteristic smiling expression (cat. nos I.3, I.8, I.10). It is most in-

teresting to compare this with a picture of *Bacchus and Silenus* in which the wine must be acknowledged as the most significant element (cat. no. I.97).

Prague 1912, cat. no. 28; Essen and Vienna 1988, cat. no. 93 for older literature.

Pellzer 1911-12, p. 136, ill. XVI; Kaufmann 1988, cat. no. I.9; Fučíková 1996, p. 14, ill. 8.

E.F.

I.10
Hans von Aachen
Bacchus, Ceres and Cupid
Oil on canvas
Above right on the pillar: *HVA (lig.)*
Ca. 1600
From the collection of Rudolf II, inv. 1621, no. 970; imperial collection in Vienna
Vienna, Kunsthistorisches Museum, Gemäldegalerie, inv. no. 1098

In the inventory of 1621 this painting is described as 'Ein gausen [=eine Jause; 'a light meal'] vom Cerrere und Bacho vom Hansen von Acha'. The god of wine is rep-

resented by the painter himself, the goddess of fertility by his wife and the lad with the basket, possibly Cupid, by his son. Von Aachen often painted himself with a cup or grapes of the vine as Bacchus or Silenus. This picture was not, however, painted as a family portrait but for the imperial collection and may have been intended to illustrate the maxim from Terence's comedy *Eunuchus* (IV,732): 'Sine Cerere et Baccho friget Venus' ('Without Ceres and Bacchus, Venus freezes', meaning that 'without bread and wine, love freezes'). Venus, however, is missing from the picture. This perfectly composed and brilliantly executed work

resembles a superbly painted still life. Cupid and the basket of fruit in this picture recall Caravaggio's rendering of the same subject from the Galleria Borghese in Rome.

Nürnberg 1952, cat. no. K10; Vienna 1987, cat. no. III, 25; Essen and Vienna 1988, cat. no. 548, for older literature; Vienna 1995, p. 62, cat. no. 3.

Pellzer 1911-12, pp. 135, 163; Kaufmann 1988, cat. no. I.390; Konečný 1988, pp. 147-50.

E.F.

I.11
Hans von Aachen
The Suicide of Lucretia
Oil on canvas
67.7 × 48.2 cm
Above right: *HANS V.ACH.16.1.PINX*
1601
Auctioned by Christie's, 17 July 1988, cat. no. 145 as the successor to B. Spranger; Swiss private collection
Prague, Národní galerie v Praze, inv. no. o 17 169

The rape and suicide of Lucretia provided the theme for several of von Aachen's works. The earliest, which unfortunately

has not survived, was either a painted or a sketched design for one of Aegidius Sadeler's prints (Hollstein 146), made in the late 1580s or early 1590s. At the turn of the seventeenth century von Aachen approached the composition afresh, redrew it (cat. no. I.153) and with slight variations used it as the basis for this painting. During the same period he made both a painting and a further drawing of the rape of Lucretia (cat. nos I.12, I.154). Why such an inventive artist as von Aachen should have chosen to base the painting on one of his older works, which he had changed on the basis of someone else's graphic print, cannot be easily ex-

plained, unless it was at the Emperor's express command. According to an inventory drawn up in 1621 (no. 842), the painting was hung on the second floor of the main gallery in the so-called Long Corridor.

Essen and Vienna 1988, cat. no. 551.

Fučíková 1995-1996, pp. 36-38, ill. 1-3.

E.F.

I.12
Hans von Aachen
Tarquinius and Lucretia
Oil on canvas
121 × 185 cm
1600–1625
From the collection of Rudolf II, 1623 ? Daniel de Briers; central European private collection, sale Dorotheum 1994
Vienna, Kunsthistorisches Museum, Gemäldegalerie, inv. no. 9862

A painting listed in the inventory of 1621 under the number 1031 as *Tarquinius und Lucretia vom Hansen von Acha. (Orig.)*, which stood on the mantelpiece in the

second gallery of the Corridor building, is evidently identical to this work. Whether it was sold in 1623 to Daniel de Briers as lot no. 32, *Buhlschaft, Tarquino und Lucretia, copei*, for 400 thaler, is now less certain, although the high price and the location from which the picture had been removed lend support to the theory. (This theme was represented in the second gallery by this work alone.) The picture entitled *Pan and Selene* shared the same fate and had the same composition (Essen and Vienna 1988, cat. no. 101). A drawing from Stuttgart (cat. no. I.154) serves as a preparatory study for the Viennese picture, portraying two bodies caught in a

dramatic struggle. In the painted version, the scene is composed more elegantly and more theatrically. The two protagonists are accompanied by an indifferent witness to the violent spectacle, a servant who is drawing the curtains open while eagerly fixing an eye on the treacherous deed. The picture shows excellent use of colour and brilliant execution of the painting technique, and is one of the best painted by Aachen for the Emperor at the peak of his career. This recently discovered work will be elaborated on in greater detail elsewhere.

E.F.

I.13
Hans von Aachen
Portrait of Archduchess Anna
Oil on canvas
58 × 48 cm
Dated top left: *Ao 1604*
1604
From the collection of Rudolf II; imperial collection in Vienna
Vienna, Kunsthistorisches Museum, Gemäldegalerie, inv. no. 4410

In 1604 Rudolf II sent Hans von Aachen out to various, mostly Italian, courts to make portraits of young noblewomen so that he could choose a suitable bride from

among them. In Innsbruck the painter was to portray the likeness of the youngest daughter of Archduke Ferdinand II (of Tyrol). Thanks to the intrigues of a chamberlain named Lang, who had wanted to compromise von Aachen, Frans Pourbus the Younger had prepared a portrait of the Archduchess about one year earlier. Archduke Maximilian III, who was then the Governor of Tyrol, discovered this intrigue, and so von Aachen had the opportunity to create one of his most successful official portraits. This is also the only one of those portraits of potential imperial brides to have survived. Anna later married Archduke Matthias and von

Aachen portrayed her many times as Empress, but no portrait by von Aachen from that period has survived.

Heintz-Schütz 1976, cat. no. 87, ill. 155, for all older literature; Kaufmann 1988, cat. no. I.65.

E.F.

I.14
Hans von Aachen
The Three Graces
Oil on canvas
1604
Acquired in Prague in 1604 by Christian II, Elector of Saxony; from the end of the nineteenth century in the Rumanian Royal collection (as Padovanino and Varotari)
Bucharest, National Museum of Art of Romania, inv. no. 8 395/429

Aachen returned to the theme of the three daughters of Zeus and Eurynome twice, depicting the goddesses of charm, beauty, and festive joy in a miniature on copper from Braunschweig (Herzog Anton Ulrich-Museum, inv. no. 1088) and in this composition from Bucharest. Both works probably date from the same period and belonged to owners other than the Emperor. The miniature was perhaps a model for the painting. The figures of the Graces are identical down to the most minute detail (hair, movement of fingers, etc.). The high arch is covered by flying putti. There are fewer flowers here, but a monkey and parrot are included. In contrast to the Mannerist style characteristic of the Braunschweig miniature, the Bucharest painting is monumental not only in dimensions, but also by virtue of its sizeable figures, which are more dramatically arranged in the space, the effect of light, and the painterly technique. While the miniature was intended for a collector's *Kunstkammer*, this large canvas was designed for display in a gallery.

Catalogue of the Universal Art Gallery, Museum of the Socialist Republic of Romania, German and Austrian Painting, Bucharest, 1979; Kaufmann 1988, pp. 156-57, cat. no. I.69; Essen and Vienna 1988, cat. no. 100 (the picture from Braunschweig where mentioned is likewise from Bucharest).

E.F.

I.15
Hans von Aachen
A Boy with Grapes
Oil on canvas
45 × 36 cm
1600-75
Collection of Archduke Leopold Wilhelm, no.11
Vienna, Kunsthistorisches Museum, Gemäldegalerie, inv. 2504

In this painting, von Aachen returned to the story about the competition between two painters of Antiquity, Parrhasios and Zeuxis, known from Pliny's description in *Naturalis historia*. Von Aachen had first drawn the scene in 1589 (cat. no. I.142). It represents the occasion when, after losing a contest, Zeuxis paints a picture of a boy with grapes to prove his ability to copy nature perfectly, but then, having lost this contest too, angrily argues the matter over with bystanders. Von Aachen chose the same subject as Zeuxis in order to demonstrate his mastery over Zeuxis as a painter. L. Konečný has devoted detailed study to Zeuxis' story in von Aachen's work and has also demonstrated the relationship of his work to that of Caravaggio. Von Aachen chose as the model for the boy someone who was intimately known to him, namely his son, who had also appeared in several of his mythological works as the young Bacchus (cat. nos. I.9, 10). Von Aachen perhaps conceived of this work as a portrait, above all, a notion that is supported by a comparison with the portrait at Prague Castle of his daughter (cat. no. I.19). He also showed off his outstanding ability as a painter of still life.

Essen and Vienna 1988, cat. no. 95, for all older literature; Peltzer 1911-12, p. 161; An der Heiden 1970, pp. 201-02, ill. 138; Kaufmann 1988, cat. no. I.175; Konečný 1988, 147-53.

E.F.

I.16
Hans von Aachen
Portrait of Emperor Rudolf II
Oil on canvas
60 × 48 cm
1606-8
From the collection of Rudolf II
Vienna, Kunsthistorisches Museum, Gemäldegalerie, inv. no. 6438

Of the many portraits of Rudolf II mentioned in contemporary sources to come from the workshops of Hans von Aachen, the Emperor's official portrait artist, only two have survived that are the work of his own hand. A picture in London (Wellington Museum, see Essen and Vienna, cat. no. I.155) was a representative likeness in the true sense of the word; the Viennese portrait served as a model for this workshop reproduction. Von Aachen painted the model precisely as he was, without heroizing him and without stylization, but depicting wrinkles, pouches under the eyes and grizzled hair. The Emperor seems tired and a little melancholic; his sad eyes rest on the painter, whom he knew as a confidant and in front of whom he had no need to pretend. He looks even older than in the portrait by Jeremias Günther from 1606 (Chapel Hill, Ackland Art Museum), in which Rudolf is depicted in almost the same pose and dress, with a similar large dose of realism, but a trifle more superficially. Von Aachen's painted portrait is the counterpart to de Vries's bust from 1607, in which the sculpture likewise depicts the ageing face of the Emperor (Vienna, Kunsthistorisches Museum, inv. no. 5491).

Nürnberg 1952, cat. no. K 14; Salzburg 1986, cat. no. 183; Essen and Vienna 1988, cat. no. 105; Vienna 1995, cat. no. 4, for all older relevant literature; Vienna 1995, 62, cat. no. 4.

E.F.

I.17
Hans von Aachen
Bacchus and Silenus
Oil on canvas
65 × 53 cm
HVA (lig.) 1608
1608
Swiss private collection
Prague, Rentiérský investiční fond I. IN, a.s.; on loan to Národní galerie in Prague, inv. no. VO 809

The two half-figures of Bacchus and Silenus gave von Aachen the opportunity to make use of his favourite type of composition, which he had first used in his twin portrait in Kroměříž (cat. no. I.9), as well as later in the 1590s in his *Joking Couples* (cat. no I.8), *Bacchus, Venus and Cupid* in Vienna (cat. no. I.9), and during the first decade of the seventeenth century in his painting of *Bacchus and Ceres*, now in Bonn (cat. no. I.18). In the left corner of all these paintings a laughing face is depicted in an almost identical pose, and bearing physical features identifiable from von Aachen's self-portraits. Although von Aachen's wife and son are depicted in various disguises in the other paintings mentioned, here von Aachen is accompanied by a different figure, identifiable as Kryštof Popel of Lobkowicz. It was probably one of the first so-called *Freundschaftsbilder* to be painted in Bohemia and in a mythological guise. Von Aachen also made, or gave orders for his workshop to make, other versions of such lifelike portraits (see cat. no. I.13).

Hans von Aachen: Bacchus and Silenus, Prague, Národní galerie v Praze, collection of old art, the Rentiérský investiční fond I. IN, a.s., Prague, the Monastery of St George, 1996-97.

E.F.

I.18
Hans von Aachen
Bacchus and Ceres
Oil on canvas
After 1610
Auction at Christie's, 11 April 1986, cat. no. 38, private Swiss collection, bought in 1989
Bonn, Rheinisches Landesmuseum, inv. no. 91.0275

Von Aachen here portrays his wife and son in mythological guise. It was not the first time he had depicted family members as ancient gods: his wife Regina and eldest son also appear in a painting of the same theme, in which Aachen himself takes the role of Bacchus and his firstborn is Amor. The tough realism with which he captured his ageing wife and small fat son has parallels in Flemish painting of the sixteenth century. It also points to the future, to similar works by Rubens and Jordaens. During his frequent trips to Italy Aachen could have encountered Caravaggio's works and may have been inspired by them. Yet his own contribution to this development cannot be ruled out (see Konečný, 1988, pp. 78-84).

Kaufmann 1988, p. 160, ill. 1.82; Essen and Vienna 1988, cat. no. 552.

E.F.

I.19
Hans von Aachen
Head of a Girl (Portrait of The Artist's Daughter)
Oil on canvas
1612
Appears in Prague Castle inventory records from 1685 onwards
Prague, Sbírky Pražského hradu, inv. no. 138

In 1612, Melchior Gortzius, also known as Geldorp, made a drawing of the same girl as is depicted in this portrait (London, Witt Collection, inv. no. 4577). The drawing was not a copy from the painting be-cause it captures the girl's features from a slightly different angle. It must in fact have been sketched during the same sitting, which allows von Aachen's portrait to be dated precisely. Von Aachen was a brilliant portrait painter, with an obsession for painting real faces, as is shown by his preference for using his own facial features or the faces of his relatives on figures in mythological or genre scenes (cat. nos. I.9, 10, 18). Von Aachen's daughter, Maria Maximiliana, appears in the christening records several times as godmother to the children of court artists. She closely resembled her mother, which is perhaps why the artist made such an af-fectionate portrait of her. This work could justifiably be considered the best and most immediate portrait painted by any of the court artists, perhaps rivalled only by Spranger's portrait of his bride, the young Christina Müller (repr. in Essen-Vienna 1988, p. 187)..

Essen and Vienna 1988, cat. no. 108; Vienna 1996, cat. no. 1.

Neumann 1966, pp. 64-66; Kaufmann 1988, cat. no. I.76; Vienna 1996, p. 22, cat. no. 1, ill. 22.

E.F.

I.20
Hans von Aachen
Portrait of Emperor Matthias as King of Bohemia
Oil on canvas
184.5 × 116.5 cm
After 1611
The imperial collections in Vienna (Dep. V, 25/253-2741, Ev. B. 887); 1894 to Prague, Sbírky Pražského hradu, inv. no. O 304

One of von Aachen's own documents drawn up on 14 November 1612 listed the prices of works made for Emperor Matthias: 'ihr, maj. conterfect in Böhmis-chen königl. habit mit der königl. cron, die ganze leng ... 150 thaler'. This description fits the portrait housed in the Schatzkammer in Vienna, and not with the Czech portrait, in which the Emperor is depicted in royal Hungarian attire, with the Bohemian crown set beside him on a table. No doubt he received an equally high price for it. It is clear that his helpers took charge of minor aspects of the work only. The unusual combination of Hungarian regalia (with a rare Turkish brocade) and the Bohemian crown might have been intended to celebrate the occasion in 1611, in Hungary, when Matthias was to present himself as King of Bo-hemia. In the foreground of the Vienna painting the Emperor is in fact wearing the robes of King of Bohemia, while in the background scene he is depicted in royal Hungarian attire leading his armies against the Turks in defence of the Kingdom of Hungary (of which he was made King in 1608).

Peltzer 1911-12, pp. 142, 163, ill. T.XX; Neumann 1966, pp. 66-69; An der Heiden 1970, pp. 175-76, 203-4, ill. 141; Kaufmann 1988, cat. no. 1.84.

E.F.

See fig. 1.17

I.21
Hans von Aachen
The Annunciation
Oil on canvas
237 × 177 cm
1613
Prague, the church of St Salvador, until the end of the eighteenth century; the archiepiscopal seminary in Prague until 1953; the Jesuit church in Litoměřice; on permanent loan to Národní galerie in Prague since 1956, inv. no. VO 1 275
Prague, Národní galerie v Praze, V O 1275

In 1613, Johannes Barvitius, Rudolf II's private secretary, donated the painting to the church of St Salvador for its altar similarly consecrated to *The Annunciation*. The discovery of this fact makes it possible more accurately to date the painting, previously thought to be one of von Aachen's late works. Von Aachen returned to this subject several times. These works are reproduced in three engravings by Aegidius Sadeler, Lucas Kilian and Crispijn van de Passe. Important in this connection, however, is von Aachen's painting of 1605 (Munich, Bayerische Staatsgemälde-sammlungen, inv. no. 1244), which in its figurative style resembles the Prague altar. Its composition is made more dramatic, however, by the inscription of the main figures into an imaginary circle and the suggestion of a dialogue between them. The Prague painting is dominated by the verticality of the figures of the Virgin Mary and the archangel Gabriel with a reading stand between. The work, which is placid and filled with a sense of meditation, is an early harbinger of the new Baroque style, of which it already displays all the main characteristics.

Essen and Vienna 1988, cat. no. 110; Neumann 1957, pp. 119-32; Kaufmann 1988, cat. no. 1.80.

E.F.

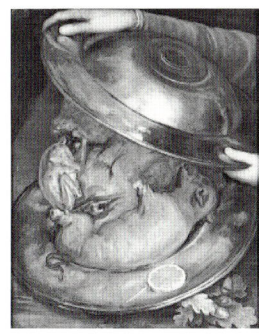

I.22
Giuseppe Arcimboldo
Milan 1527-Milan 1593
Reversible Head with Meats
Oil on wood
52.5 × 41 cm
Ca. 1570(?)
Imperial collection, Prague
Königsmarck 1648 (no. 311 ?); Finspöng Castle; Ax. Ekman Eollection; Djursholm, Commodore E. Braunerhjelm; private collection, Stockholm
Stockholm, Nationalmuseum, inv. no. NM 6897

Upside down, this painting of a compos-ite head becomes an image of two hands revealing a platter of meat. This represents an advance in sophistication in the development of Arcimboldo's composite heads, and therefore allows for a dating probably somewhat later than the series of seasons and elements of the 1560's. Yet the presence of the two hands suggests that this is not quite as advanced an image as Arcimboldo's *Reversible Head with Bowl of Vegetables*. It is possible that this painting is recorded as no. 1083 in the 1621 inventory. There is no inherent basis for assuming that this witty image is a hidden portrait.

Stockholm 1966; Venice 1987', 116, 119 ill.; Essen and Vienna 1988, cat. no. 114, ill. 206.

Granberg 1911; LeGrand and Sluys, 1954, p. 56, no. 19; Alfons 1957, p. 115; Preiss 1967, pp. 20-21, ill. no. 65; Porzio 1978, p. 1; De Mandiargues 1978, pp. 92-4, ill. 49, 53; Porzio, 1979, ill. 76, 77; Neumann 1978, ill. p.304; Barthes, 1980, pp. 28, 51, ill. 52, 53; Kaufmann, 1985, cat. 2-18 ill.; Kaufmann 1988, cat. 2-18 ill.; Kriegeskörte, 1988, p. 38, ill. 40, 41.

T.C.K.

I.23
Giovanni Contarini
Venice ? ca. 1548/49-Venice ca. 1504
The Fall of Saturn's Kingdom
Oil on canvas
225 × 157 cm
Probably before 1590
Prague, Obrazcrna Prazského hradu, inv. no. OPH 124

When this work was exhibited in Trieste, Ladislav Daniel named various figures with reference to Ovid's *Metamorphoses* (1, 113). The figures he identifies are Pluto on the right, Fama (above Chronos) in the centre and Rea (perhaps) to the right of Chronos and Fama. The female figures flying upwards to the left embody the dawn of the new age of Jupiter. If they have been correctly identified as Veritas and Iustitia, then they play a major part in defining the whole work, for Iustitia is the most important of the virtues. If this work was indeed painted for Rudolf II, then it would be of particular significance as a very early example of Rudolfine art, specifically in that it would clearly have a bearing on the Emperor's views on his own 'primacy' after his move to Prague. The links between this work and that of Tintoretto and his pupil Giovanni Pietro de Pomis are clear. The Emperor evidently favoured the Venetian style during his early years in Prague, as may be seen by the allegories made for Rudolf II by Veronese between 1576 and 1584. Al-though the Emperor never employed any of the Venetians directly at his own court, nevertheless Tintoretto's and Veronese's works constitute one of the most important elements of 'Rudolfine' art.

Essen and Vienna 1988, no. 115; Trieste 1996-97, no. 10.

Zimmer 1988, pp. 315, 317, ill. 3.

J.Z.

I.24
Daniel Fröschl
Madonna and Child with Grapes
Oil on panel
After 1605
Prague, řád Menších bratří kapucínů,
Pražská Loreta

As an administrator for Rudolf's collections, Fröschl had the opportunity to study Dürer's original paintings and drawings at length and drew inspiration from them. One of his drawings based on Dürer's painting of the *Madonna with a Pear*, owned by the Emperor, is housed in the Národní galerie in Prague (inv. no. K

25561). When transcribing from his model Fröschl used a relatively free interpretation, and gave the Madonna and the infant Jesus faces typical of his figures. Another step of this transformation can be seen in this painting of the *Madonna and Child with Grapes*, which Fröschl made as a painting on wood rather than as a miniature, as was his usual habit. He was inspired by the work of Hans von Aachen, thanks to whom he had found a place in the Emperor's service. The painting attests to the fact that Fröschl was also capable of 'great' art.

Essen and Vienna 1988, cat. no. 117.

Fučíková 1972, pp. 155–156, ills 5, 6; Kaufmann 1988, cat. no. 3.7.

E.F.

I.25
Matthäus Gundelach
Kassel ? ca. 1565/67–Augsburg 1653/54
Adam and Eve
Oil on copper
28.8 × 24.3 cm
Olomouc, private collection on loan in Oblastnigalerie, inv. no. D 454

This diagonal view of the first human beings and the god-like colour of their flesh, in itself reminiscent of figures from Antiquity, is far from conventional. On the contrary, it casts the theme in a late-humanistic mould and interprets it in terms of the affairs of the gods as described by

Ovid. In this sense it is close to Daniel Fröschl's fine parchment painting *Adam and Eve*, of 1604 (Vienna, Albertina, inv. no. 3352). The symbolic hare comes-doubled-from Dürer's famous engraving of 1504. The cool colouration of this small panel, its painterly 'handwriting' and the style itself are very much of the time of Rudolf II and of Gundelach's 'late Rudolfine' pictures: a date somewhere between 1605 and 1614 can therefore hardly be wrong. Kaufmann suggests narrowing it down to 1609–10.

Essen and Vienna 1988, cat. no. 121.

Kaufmann 1988, no. 6.4; Fučíková 1988, pp. 120 and 125, ill. 100.

J.Z.

I.26
Matthäus Gundelach
Diana with a Game-bird Trophy
Kassel ca. 1566–Augsburg 1654
Oil on canvas
86 × 68 cm
Spranger Pinxit (bottom left, inscribed later)
Ca. 1605 (?)
Sibiu, The National Brukenthal Museum, inv. no. 1119.

E.F.

I.27
Matthäus Gundelach
Kassel ? ca. 1565/67–Augsburg 1653/54
Susanna and the Elders (? Allegory of Touch)
Oil on canvas, laid down on wood
41.2 × 55.2 cm
An⁰ 1.6.0.5. / MG(lig.) F.
1605
Art market 1969
Augsburg/Munich, in private ownership

These three half-length views are unusual among the relatively large number of works portraying *Susanna and the Elders*. Generally, the viewer was allowed to see Susanna's entire body as she bathed. This

would seem to imply that the Bible story, even in the form of the 'Discussion of the Elders and the Distress of Susanna', as suggested by Bender, was not the only impulse behind this work, in which Gundelach is said to have drawn heavily on an engraving by Crispin de Passe the Elder after a work by the portraitist Geldorp Gortzius (Hollstein ? 44). According to Bender, Erich Herzog suggested Gundelach's theme might be *Tactus* (the sense of touch), one of the *Five Senses*. This is surely correct. Gundelach probably painted this in Prague. Whether this work was intended for the imperial collection is less certain; Gundelach was not appointed to

the court until 1609 and thus worked exclusively for the Emperor only from that point onwards. This is one of the earliest surviving paintings by Gundelach. The figure of Susanna, as a type, and the shadowy, foreshortened faces are typical of Gundelach's work both at that time and later.

Bender 1981, pp. 167–68, no. GA4; Neumeister, Munich, Auction 252, 20 September 1989; Munich 1989, p. 67, no. 450 with full-page ill.; Zwollo 1992, p. 38, ill. 3.

J.Z.

See fig. 1.85

I.28
Matthäus Gundelach
Kassel ? ca. 1565/67–Augsburg 1653/54
Cupid and Psyche
Oil on copper
33 × 45 cm
M / Gundelach / F. / 1613
1613
From the Prague *Kunstkammer*, sold in 1623 to the Frankfurt art dealer Daniel de Briers (no. 3: ein buhlschaft, *Cupido mit Psiche von Gundelach*. Taler 50); later in the gallery in Zweibrücken until 1779; since 1922 in the Städtische Kunstsammlungen in Augsburg
Augsburg, Städtische Kunstsammlun-

gen, Deutsche Barockgalerie, inv. no. L 724 (loan from Munich, Bayerische Staatsgemäldesammlungen, Alte Pinakothek, inv. no. 2386)

This finely painted *Kunstkammer* piece, done a year after Rudolf's death, confirms Gundelach as a fully fledged representative of Rudolfine taste, in choice of subject-matter and style alike. There are very close parallels between this work and that of Joseph Heintz the Elder. Here, as in the *Mystical Marriage of St Catherine*, Gundelach takes cool, restrained colouration right to the limits of its potential. It is clear that Gundelach is taking the mood

of Apuleius' *Metamorphoses* (V, 1–2) and depicting a love scene rather than illustrating any particular episode from the actual narrative. Bender suggested this might be the moment when Psyche first sees her spouse.

Bender 1981, pp. 168–69 (with earlier bibliography); *Deutsche Barockgalerie*, cat. of paintings, ed. Gode Krämer (2nd edn, 1984), p. 101, ill. 10; Kaufmann 1985, cat. no. 55, col. ill., Kaufmann 1988, p. 181, cat. no. 6.6.

J.Z.

I.29
Matthäus Gundelach
Kassel ? ca. 1565/67–Augsburg 1653/54
The Vision of Ezekiel
Oil on canvas, rounded, arched top
155 × 100 cm
Traditionally given as 'ca. 1610'
Perhaps painted as a commission for the Lobkowicz family
Prague, Prazské arcibiskupství

See fig. 1.54

The eight half-length figures across the bottom of this painting show that it was intended as a kind of epitaph. Earlier research has shown that this could well be the Lobkowicz family. Which of the

prophet's visions is depicted here is not entirely clear, but very likely it is that of the valley with the dried bones (Ezekiel 37:1–14) for this is always associated with the Last Judgment and therefore often to be found as an epitaph motif. This work recalls those other works where the main figures or ideas recede almost invisibly into the background (as in his *Gathering of the Gods*). In the *Vision of the Prophet Ezekiel* the main focus is clearly on the Resurrection. No date for this work is given and the only clues are the circumstances of the artist's own life. Kaufmann has narrowed the date down to 1613–14. In any case, the exhibition in Essen showed once

and for all that Gundelach was responsible for this work.

Essen and Vienna 1988, cat. no. 125.

Bender 1981, p. 226, no. GE 1 (with earlier bibliography); Kaufmann 1988, no. 6.8; Fučíková, pp. 121, 124, col. ill. 99.

J.Z.

I.30
Matthäus Gundelach
Kassel ? ca. 1565/67–Augsburg 1653/54
The Mystic Marriage of St Catherine
Oil on paper
40 × 31 cm
M. / Gundelach. / F. / 1614
1614
Vienna, Kunsthistorisches Museum, inv. no. 1103

The iconography of this relatively small panel suggests that it may well have been commissioned by Emperor Matthias: the Emperor himself as the apostle Matthew and his wife Anna as St Helena are attend-

ing the mystical nuptials. However, little more is known about the circumstances and purpose of this work. That the work was intended as a form of propaganda, as has been suggested, is hardly likely because it is simply too modest. Moreover, it does not seem to have reached a wider public as an engraving. This leaves only 'private' use for the imperial couple; and yet the painter has drawn on the full extent of the artistic skills he has acquired so far – perhaps in the – ultimately vain – hope of being taken on by Matthias as court painter.

Prague 1912, cat. no. 40; Nürnberg 1952,

cat. no. K 28a; Augsburg 1980, no. 464; Essen 1988, Vienna cat. no. 124.

Bender 1981, pp. 163–66, no. GA 3 (with earlier bibliography); Kaufmann 1988, cat. no. 6.10.

J.Z.

I.31
Joseph Heintz the Elder
Basel 1564–Prague 1609
Christ at the Column
Oil on canvas, laid down on wood
114 × 74 cm
IHE (lig.) *intz. F.* (fragmented); on the base of the pillar: *ECCE. HOMO.*
Perhaps ca. 1590–95
Transferred to the Gemäldegalerie 'from old stocks' of the Dresden *Kunstkammer* 1717
Dresden, Staatliche Kunstsammlungen, Gemäldegalerie Alte Meister, inv. no. 1973

The flagellation of Christ, portrayed as a beautiful youth, may strike the modern viewer strangely. In older iconography, however, the *Ecce Homo* is portrayed not as a narrative event, but as a symbol. Thus the flagellation is not the real subject of the picture: the viewer is presented not with Jesus racked with pain, but instead with his perfect, naked form against the pillar. This depiction of the human form is immediately recognizable as the fruit of Heintz's intensive study of the forms of Antiquity. Heintz also studied Michelangelo's works for the proportions of his figures (see cat. no. 1.189). The intricate cultural and historical background to this

painting makes it one of Heintz's most fascinating works. Unfortunately, nothing is known about the person who commissioned it nor of its purpose, although it may well have been painted for the court in Saxony.

Prague 1982, no. 79.

Zimmer 1971, pp. 76–77, no. A 3, ill. 8 (with earlier bibliography); Gemäldegalerie Alte Meister, Dresden, exh. cat., 1979, p. 205; Kaufmann 1985, p. 227, no. 7.1; Kaufmann 1988, p.184, no. 7.1.

J.Z.

I.32
Joseph Heintz the Elder
Basel 1564–Prague 1609
Portrait of Veronika Fugger
Oil on canvas
87 × 70 cm
On upper edge: *AETA. XX. ANO 1598 – IOHE* (in ligature) *intz.*
1598
Art market in Bern 1955
Bern, Kunstmuseum, inv. no. 1817 (Gottfried Keller-Stiftung, no. 999)

Heintz was the only artist at the court of Rudolf II to make substantial numbers of portraits of bourgeois subjects in addi-

tion to the expected state portraits (see cat. nos I.38, I.39). The fact that he divided his time between Prague and the Swabian Free Imperial Town of Augsburg no doubt accounts for the commissions that he executed for the patricians in the latter place. This portrait of a lady of about twenty years of age may well be of Veronika Fugger who married a distant relation, Albrecht Fugger, in 1597, and who is most probably the subject of the companion piece to this portrait (see cat. no. I.33). These portraits can be identified partly by comparison with engraved portraits of Veronika and Albrecht by Domenicus Custos. These two portraits may even

have been 'belated' wedding pictures, which would perhaps be in keeping with the pearl decorations on the cap worn by the lady.

Zimmer 1971, p. 116, no. A 31, ill. 74 (with earlier bibliography); Zimmer 1980, pp. 22–23, ill. 8, 9; Kaufmann 1985, p. 229, no. 7.9; Kaufmann 1988, p. 186, no. 7.9

J.Z.

I.33
Joseph Heintz the Elder
Basel 1564–Prague 1609
Portrait of Albrecht Fugger
Oil on canvas
87 × 70 cm
On upper edge: *AETA. XXVIII. ANO 1598 – IOHE* (lig.) *intz.*
1598
Art market 1955
Bern, Kunstmuseum, inv. no. 1816 (Gottfried Keller-Stiftung, no. 999)

Most probably a portrait of Albrecht Fugger von Kirchberg und Weißenhorn, Herr von Welden (1574–1614), where his epi-

taph still remains on his red marble gravestone in the parish church. Shown here at the age of twenty-eight, Albrecht Fugger died prematurely at the age of forty. This is a companion piece to the *Portrait of a Lady* (Veronika Fugger), cat. no. I.32 See further commentary under that number.

Zimmer 1971, pp. 115–16, no. A 30, ill. 73 (with earlier bibliography); Zimmer 1980, pp. 22–23, ill. 6, 7; Kaufmann 1985, no. 7.8; Kaufmann 1988, p. 186, no. 7.8.

J.Z.

I.34
Joseph Heintz the Elder.
Basel 1564–Prague 1609
The Adoration of the Shepherds
Oil on copper
29.7 × 21.8 cm
Unsigned, illegible writing on the back of
the copper panel
Not dated, probably ca. 1599
Unknown; at times exhibited in the
Národni galerie v Praze
Prague, Klášter Premonstrátu na Stra-
hove, inv. no. O 6813

This beautiful composition by Heintz exists in at least four versions, all, as it

would seem, in his own hand: one in
Freiburg i. Br. (as the *Beschneidung Jesu*,
Augustinermuseum inv. no. 2485), another in Basel (Öffentliche Kunstsammlungen, Kunstmuseum, inv. no. 1640, with
the remains of a signature by Heintz), the
present version in Prague and a fourth
version which has recently emerged out
of private ownership in Switzerland; this
alone has the full monogram *IOHE* (with
ligature) and is dated 1599. The resonance
that this intimate little work has always
found and still finds is well demonstrated
as much in its use on recent record
sleeves as in older copies by other masters. Heintz clearly also saw this picture as

a homage to his great compatriot Hans
Holbein the Younger: the figure of the
shepherd with the broad-brimmed hat
quotes a similar figure by Holbein on the
Oberried altar in Freiburg Cathedral, a
work that Rudolf tried in vain to acquire
for his own collection.

Essen 1988, no. 126

Zimmer 1971, p. no. illus.; Prag um 1600, I,
1988, pp. 234–235, no. 126 (Jürgen Zimmer, with older bibliography).

J.Z.

See fig. 1.16

I.35
Joseph Heintz the Elder
Basel 1564–Prague 1609
The Circumcision
Oil on copper
30 × 21.9 cm
On the lowest step of the altar: *IOHE*
(lig.) *intz 1599*
1599
Galerie Thum, St Gallen; acquired in
1958 from Erika Ritz, Binningen/Basel
Freiburg im Breisgau, Augustinermuse-
um, inv. no. M 58/1

The motif and format of this work link it
with cat. no. I.34 in this exhibition, but do

not mean that it is also part of a larger series of scenes from the life of Jesus as has
previously been thought. The companion
piece – both were evidently together in
Innsbruck at one time – is now held in
Freiburg im Breisgau (Augustinermuseum inv. no. 2485) and represented here by
a second version (out of a total of three in
the artist's own hand) from the Premon-
stratenian monastery at Strahov. Like the
Adoration of the Shepherds, this *Circumcision of Jesus* was also copied by the Servite
Father Bonaventura Rainer (Innsbruck,
Landesmuseum Ferdinandeum, inv. no.
1556). The picture derives its particular
quality from the contrast between calm,

perfect architecture (evidence of Heintz
the architect), the dynamic yet isocephalic
groups of people in the centre and the
few large, very dynamic foreground figures. At the same time this picture is also
fascinating for the sensitivity (*con gusto*) of
its intense coloration.

Heidelberg 1986, no. C 41.

Zimmer 1971, p. 75, no. A 2, ill. 6; Zinke
1990, pp. 126–27 (with earlier bibliography).

J.Z.

I.36
Joseph Heintz the Elder
Basel 1564–Prague 1609
Satyrs and Nymphs
Oil on copper
Centre of the oval: 24 × 32 cm
Signed bottom left: *IOHE* (lig.) *intz. F. /
1599* (in the artist's own hand)
1599
Probably from the collection of Rudolf II;
possibly went as part of the Prague inher-
itance to Archduke Albrecht in Brussels;
in ownership in the County Palatine in
1685 (Heidelberg, Schloß; Mannheim in
1756, then went from Zweibrücken to
Munich; in Schleißheim from 1863 until

1914)
Munich, Bayerische Staatsgemäldesammlungen, Alte Pinakothek, inv. no. 1579

As this work testifies, Joseph Heintz,
painter to the imperial court, must have
been at the height of his powers as an
artist in 1599. The painting shows Syrinx
(perhaps after Andrea dall'Anguillara I,
189–90), the nymph admired by Pan, with
a servant combing her long, flowing hair.
This painting, along with the *Circumcision
of Christ* (cat. no. I.35), demonstrates very
clearly that among artists at the court of
Rudolf II producing what one might call
'intimate mythologies' none could com-

pare with Heintz. Unlike other artists at
the court, Heintz used oval forms (see In-
grid Preussner, *Ellipsen und Ovale in der
Malerei des 15. und 16. Jahrhunderts*, Weinheim, 1987) on various occasions.

Nürnberg 1952, cat. no. K 17; Essen and
Vienna 1988, cat. no. 132.

Zimmer 1971, pp. 106–7, no. A 22, ill. 59,
col. pl. IV (with earlier bibliography);
Kaufmann 1985, p. 231, no. 7.19; Kaufmann 1988, no. 7.19.

J.Z.

I.37
Joseph Heintz the Elder
Basel 1564–Prague 1609
The Holy Family with an Angel
Oil on copper
17 × 20.7 cm
At the left on the pedestal under the
niche: *IOHE* (lig.) *intz ...* (fragmented)
Probably 1595–1605
London art market 1964
Stuttgart, Staatsgalerie, inv. no. 2728

Although this small copper panel is clearly Rudolfine in the accepted sense of the
term, it is likely that it was not painted for
the Emperor himself, but commissioned

by a member of the nobility in Augsburg
whose identity is now lost to us. However,
we do know that Wolfgang Kilian made a
fine copy of this work in Augsburg in
1639, on parchment and executed in the
style of an engraving (now in Vienna, Albertina), when the painting was still there
(Zimmer 1988, p. 299, no. E22, ill. 176).
The *Holy Family with Angel* shows Heintz's
outstanding skill – seen elsewhere only in
his *Circumcision of Christ* (cat. no. I.35) – in
portraying architectural spaces. So outstanding was his talent in this respect
that on his epitaph he is described as *architectus cum antiquis comparandus*, a designation that very clearly distinguishes him

from other 'figure painters' at the court in
Prague. More details on the particular
style of this work may be found in the catalogue *Prag um 1600*.

London 1965, no. 19; Essen and Vienna
1988, no. 134.

Zimmer 1971, pp. 77–78, no. A 5, ill. 10;
Zimmer 1985, p. 170; Kaufmann 1988, cat.
no. 7.21.

J.Z.

I.38
Joseph Heintz the Elder
Basel 1564–Prague 1609
Archduchess Constance
Oil on canvas
191.5 × 110 cm
Documented 1603/4
Originally in Graz Castle; on dissolution
of that collection taken in 1765 to the Im-
perial Collection in Vienna; in Schloß
Laxenburg in nineteenth century
Vienna, Kunsthistorisches Museum,
Gemäldegalerie, Porträtgalerie (Schloß
Ambras), inv. no. 9 452

Archduchess Konstanze, wife of Sigis-

mund III and thus Queen of Poland from
1605 to 1631, is portrayed here at the age
of about sixteen. According to a letter
written by Heintz in March 1604 (see Zimmer, p. 402, Q 126), Heintz was commissioned by Rudolf II in Graz to paint at
least six formal court portraits of the children of Archduke Karl II of Inner Austria
and Maria of Bavaria (see also cat. no.
I.39). He wrote to Duke Wolfgang Wilhelm
of Pfalz-Neuburg in March 1604 about
other court portraits of his – '*ettliche
Ertzherzoge zu Conterfehten für königl. Mayt:
in HISPANIEN*' – most probably referring
here, among others, to another, splendid
portrait of Konstanze, which originated

in Spain and is now in the Sterling and
Francine Art Institute, Williamstown, MA
(given by Julius S. Held).

Essen and Vienna 1988, cat. no. 565.

Zimmer 1971, cat. no. 135; Zimmer 1979,
pp. 9–13; Kaufmann 1988, cat. no. 7.37.

J.Z.

I.39
Joseph Heintz the Elder
Basel 1564–Prague 1609
Archduke Maximilian Ernst
Oil on canvas
191.5 × 105 cm
Signed: *IOHE* (lig.) *intz. F.*; inscribed:
*MAXIMI: ERNEST: ER: HER: ZU
ÖSTEREI.*; on the dog's collar: *M*[aximil-
ian] *E*[rnst]
Documented 1603/4
Originally in Graz Castle; on dissolution
of that collection taken to the Imperial
Collection in Vienna in 1765; in Schloß
Laxenburg in nineteenth century
Vienna, Kunsthistorisches Museum,

Gemäldegalerie, Porträtgalerie (Schloß
Ambras), inv. no. 9 495

This most splendid of the Graz 'state portraits' by Heintz (for more on its making
see cat. no. I.38) shows Archduke Maximilian Ernst, who died prematurely in 1616.
Here we see him at the age of twenty-one,
resplendent with his sword and his dog.
Later he was also to become a Commander of the Teutonic Order in Austria. Although Heintz's real strength perhaps lay
rather in exquisite 'intimate mythologies',
he was also evidently talented as a painter
of 'bourgeois' portraits (see cat. nos I.32,
I.33). This courtly portrait has a very per-

sonal, even, to some viewers, 'sinister'
quality. There is no reason to believe that
the portraitist has in any way 'improved'
his subject's physiognomy; he has merely
taken advantage of a certain natural dignity that attaches to the Duke's person by
virtue of his social standing.

Essen and Vienna 1988, cat. no. 563.

Zimmer 1971, cat. no. 138; Kaufmann
1988, cat. no. 7.39.

J.Z.

I.40
Joseph Heintz the Elder
Basel 1564–Prague 1609
Cupid's Departure From Psyche
Oil on canvas; cleaned, repaired, re-
touched and newly varnished in 1985–86
177.5 × 111.5 cm
Probably ca. 1603–05
Provenance unknown; acquired from Dr
Peltzer in 1926
Nürnberg, Germanisches Nationalmuse-
um, inv. no. GM 1 118

The story of Amor and Psyche as told in
the second century AD by Apuleius in his
Metamorphoses (V.23, 4) is well known. The

scene shown here links up with the scene
on the small copper panel that Heintz
painted in Augsburg (cat. no. I.42). Amor
has been hidden by the dark from Psyche
up until this point. However, when Psyche sees her lover by the light of her oil
lamp and inadvertently wakes him from
his sleep, he instantly flees without a
word, leaving the unhappy Psyche behind. This large-scale painting is less subtle than the small copper panel and the
light seems somehow extreme, even
harsh, quite unlike that on any other
painting on canvas by Heintz: the removal of the old, badly yellowed varnish
has given the work a certain brilliance,

but now there is a sense that a finishing
glaze would perhaps soften the startling
brightness of the naked back view.

Nürnberg 1952, no. K 12; Berlin and Hannover 1987; Carouge/Geneva and Zurich
1994, cat. no. 1.

Zimmer 1971, cat. no. 113; Kaufmann
1988, cat. no. 7.47.

J.Z.

I.41
Joseph Heintz the Elder
Basel 1564–Prague 1609
Venus, Cupid and Apollo
Oil on copper
40 × 27 cm
Recorded in the inventory as having been
acquired in 1741 from Bonaventura Rossi
in Italy as the work of G. C. Procaccini, although it may have been one of a number of paintings acquired from the Waldstein Collection in Duchcov in the same
year
Dresden, Staatliche Kunstsammlungen
Dresden, Gemäldegalerie Alte Meister,
inv. no. 646

In the ancient tales of the gods there do
not seem to be any accounts of any such
meeting between these three protagonists. Venus and Amor are easily identified, but there cannot be such certainty
about the figure in the background, although the laurel wreath and the
bow (*Apollo arquitenens*) do all point towards Apollo, the brother of Venus. Perhaps Heintz has followed the spirit rather
than the letter of Ovid's *Metamorphoses* (I,
463ff.): 'Then Venus' offspring said to
him: "Your bow, Phoebus, may wound everything, but mine wounds you: as certainly as one God rules over all beings, so
your fame pales into insignificance before

mine." Whatever the case, Venus does not
actually appear in the scene described by
Ovid. The influence of the art of Antiquity
on Heintz's work is evident not only in the
monumental pillar in the background but
also in the figure of Venus, which is based
on the much-copied *Aphrodite of Doidalsas*.

Zimmer 1971, pp. 109–10, no. A 25, ill. 61
(with earlier bibliography); Kaufmann
1988, cat. no. 7.34.

J.Z.

I.42
Joseph Heintz the Elder
Basel 1564–Prague 1609
Cupid and Psyche
Oil on copper
24.5 × 18.8 cm
IOHE (lig.) *intz. F.* (upper right, now
barely visible)
Probably 1605
Probably from the Speck-Sternburg Col-
lection in Lützschena, private collection
in Munich; on the art market in 1970
Augsburg, Städtische Kunstsammlun-
gen, Maximilianmuseum, inv. no. 12 336

This small, minutely detailed and subtly

coloured picture has all the attributes of a
work that a collector would want to have
in the *Kunstkammer*. It shows the moment
described by Apuleius (*Metamorphoses*, V.
22–23) when Psyche, with murderous intent, approaches the sleeping Amor who,
up until now, has been invisible to her because of the dark. When she sees him by
the light of her oil lamp she is overcome
by his beauty, but a moment later a drop
of oil wakes him and he disappears forever. The painter has captured this briefest
of moments, so that it is always there for
the viewer to contemplate and return to.
Nothing is known about the original destination of the work, whether it was for

the Emperor's *Kunstkammer*, or for a
high-ranking official of the court or perhaps for a member of the nobility in
Augsburg. What is certain is that in its intent and form this is a prime example of
the art of the court of Rudolf II.

Zimmer 1967, pp. 226–27, no. A 11; Zimmer 1971, p. 90, no. A 12, ill. 37, col. pl. II;
Katalog der Gemälde (Augsburg, Deutsche
Barockgalerie, 1984), pp. 112–13 (with earlier bibliography); Kaufmann 1988, cat.
no. 7.51.

J.Z.

I.43
Joseph Heintz the Elder
Basel 1564–Prague 1609
The Last Judgment
Oil on wood
102 × 274.5 cm
1606–9
From the collection of Rudolf II
Prague, Collection of Prague Castle, inv.
no. OPH 221

Although not signed, this is the best-doc-
umented work by Heintz, and was commissioned by Count Ernst of Schaum-
burg-Hollstein for the new chapel in his
castle in Bückeburg. It is incomplete

(which may explain its lukewarm reception among viewers today) and in 1609
the Emperor found it in his 'employee's'
estate after the latter's untimely death.
Rudolf decreed that the work should go
into the *Kunstkammer*, ignoring protests
by the Count, who had originally commissioned the work and already paid for half
of it. In the end the Count had to admit
defeat and commissioned a new *Last Judgment* from Christoph Gertner, painter to
the court at Wolfenbüttel. This work still
graces the back wall of the chapel.
Heintz's work was no doubt incomplete
partly because he had a huge workload in
his last years and partly because of the

composition of the work itself, which contained over a hundred largely naked figures. Heintz obviously intended to create
a mighty piece in the style of Tintoretto or
Palma's *Paradiso*, although his real
strength as a painter lay in his small-scale,
intimate cabinet pieces.

Essen and Vienna 1988, no. 136.

Zimmer 1971, p. 90, cat. no. 17 (with earlier bibliography); Neumann 1964, cat. no.
63; Kaufmann 1988, cat. no. 58.

J.Z.

I.44
Joseph Heintz the Elder (attributed)
Basel 1564–Prague 1609
Madonna and Child
Oil on wood
47 × 37 cm
In private ownership in Brno or Vienna,
acquired from Karlsbad in 1958
Prague, Národní galerie v Praze, Sbírka
Starého umění, inv. no. O 10 740 (DO
6804)

This is a relatively faithful copy (retaining
the original dimensions) of Correggio's
famous *Zingarella* ('Madonna in gypsy
dress'), which he painted in 1515 and

which is first documented in 1589 in the
inventory of Ottavio and Ranuccio Farnese. Today it is in the Museo Nazionale di
Capodimonte in Naples, having been
copied by numerous artists including
some of the most prominent. This version
differs from the original only in the somewhat less detailed background, but this
may be accounted for by the condition of
the varnish. In 1962 Eduard Šafařík tentatively attributed this work to Heintz. Lin-
gering doubts regarding this attribution
may be resolved when it is seen in this exhibition together with a large number of
originals by Heintz.

Prague 1962, no. 10.

Zimmer 1971, p. 147, no. C 3, ill. 116 (with
earlier bibliography).

J.Z.

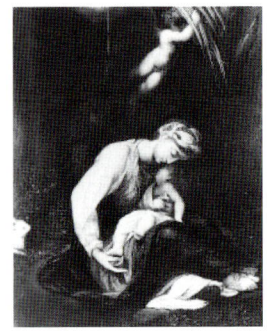

I.45
Joris Hoefnagel
Antwerp 1542–Vienna 1601
*Vase of Flowers Surrounded by Fruits and
Flowers*
Watercolour with body colour on parch-
ment
20.7 × 32 cm
In the cartouche: *Bis delectamur pictum
florem cum vivo decertantem videmus, in al-
tero miramur artificium naturae, in altero
pictoris ingenium*
1597
Sibiů, Muzeul Brukenthal, inv. no. 1510

The two miniatures from Sibiů are related

not only by virtue of text and image but
also by the similarity of their format. They
are outstanding examples of the kind of
cabinet miniatures showing natural objects in minute detail for which Hoefnagel was renowned throughout his life.
Around the ornamental vase with
grotesque decoration there is a loose arrangement of flowers, fruits and unusual
insects.

Frankfurt 1993/94, no. 108; Prague 1994,
no. 80.

Bergström 1963, pp. 2ff., ill.; Vignau-Schuurman 1969, vol. 2, p. 118, list of works 12;

Bergström, ed. Görel Cavalli-Björkman,
1985, pp. 178ff., ill. 4; Fučíková 1986, p. 26,
pl. 50; DaCosta Kaufmann 1988, p. 208,
no. 9.10; *Georg Flegel 1566–1638*, exh. cat.
ed. Kurt Wettengl (Stuttgart, 1993), p.
211, no. 108; *Georg Flegel 1566–1638*, exh.
cat. ed. Hana Seifertová (Prague, 1994), p.
145; *Archetypa* facsimile 1994, p. 33, ill. 9.

Th.V.W.

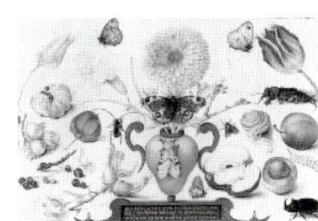

I.46
Joris Hoefnagel
Antwerp 1542–Vienna 1601
*Vase of Flowers Surrounded by Insects, Fruits
and Flowers*
Watercolour with body colour on parch-
ment
22 × 32 cm
On the cartouche: *In utroque benignitatem
Dei, qui in usum nostrum largitur haec om-
nia, nulla in re non admirabilis pariter et
amabilis. G. Houf. 97*
1597
Sibiů, Muzeul Brukenthal, inv. no. 1579

At a time of religious conflict an image of

nature may take on the role of a devotional picture. The text above the two miniatures in Sibiů is a quotation from the *Con-
vivium Religiosum* in Desiderius Erasmus's
Colloquia: 'Our delight is doubled when
we see the opposition of painted flower
and living flower. The latter fills us with
amazement at the artifice of nature while
the former astonishes us with the skills of
the artist. Both together fill us with
amazement at the Lord's unfailingly
miraculous and kind generosity, for he
has given us all these things to use.'

Frankfurt 1993/94, no. 108; Prague 1994,
no. 80.

Bergström 1963, pp. 2ff., ill.; Wilberg Vignau-Schuurman 1969, vol. 2, p. 118, list of
works 12; Fučíková 1986, p. 26, pl. 49;
Fučíková 1987, p. 28, pl. 40; DaCosta Kaufmann 1988, p. 208, no. 9.11; *Georg Flegel
1566–1638*, exh. cat. ed. Kurt Wettengl
(Stuttgart, 1993), p. 211, no. 108; *Georg
Flegel 1566–1638*, exh. cat. ed. Hana Seifertová (Prague, 1994), p. 145.

Th.V.W.

I.47
Jacob Hoefnagel
Antwerp 1572–Holland 1632/35
Triumph of Summer
Oil on copper
26.8 × 34.8 cm
Below left: [*J]ac: Hoefnagl [...R]oma*
1605–9
Kunstkammer of Emperor Rudolf II; 1619
in the inventory of the Vienna Hofburg;
since ca. 1948 in the Anhaltische
Gemäldegalerie, Dessau (Bodenreform
no. 15)
Dessau, Anhaltische Gemäldegalerie, inv.
no. 898

Research by Stephan Klingen has shown
that this painting, until now attributed to
Hans Rottenhammer, was in fact executed by Jacob Hoefnagel during his time in
Rome. Jacob Hoefnagel refers to it in a letter to Rudolf II as a *Triumph of Summer* (20
August 1610; Vienna, Hofkammerarchiv,
Hoffinanz, Akten Rote no. 140, without
folio no.). It is part of a series of *Four Seasons*, probably the same series listed as
'Auf vier taffeln die 4 zeiten des jahrs von
miniatur von Jakob Hueffnagl' (*Jahrbuch
des kunsthistorisches Sammlungen der Allerhöchsten Kaiserhauses*, vol. 26, no. 2
(1906/7), p. XI, no. 146). Three banners
waving above the procession show signs

of the zodiac, Cancer, Leo and Virgo. The
nymphs and satyrs in the foreground are
enjoying the gifts bestowed by Ceres in
her yearly triumph. Klingen points out
the influence on *Triumph of Summer* of the
series of seasons by Master AP in 1537
(Hollstein 1949, 1–4). The warrior accompanying Ceres' chariot is reminiscent of
the warrior on Tempesta's engraving of
summer (Bartsch 32, 805 [152]).

Harksen 1970, p. 11, no. 16, 1 (under Hans
Rottenhammer); Vignau-Willberg 1994, p.
27; Klingen 1996, I, p. 73, col ill. 10.

Th.V.W.

I.48
? Hans Hoffmann
The Mocking of Christ
Oil on panel
69 × 59 cm
1595–1600
Nosticka Collection
Prague, Národní galerie v Praze, inv. no.
DO 4 185

This painting, traditionally attributed to
Hans Hoffmann, is undoubtedly the work
of a late sixteenth-century Dürer imitator.
It differs from copies made in Bavaria during the revival of Dürer's popularity in the
1620s and 1630s. The *Mocking of Christ*

cannot, however, be linked to any particular design. It is an 'imitatio', a pastiche of
various elements taken from Dürer's
works, and possibly works of Netherlandish artists, which have been adapted to
lend the work an antique look. At the
same time, it is painted with the soft, fluid
brushstroke typical of the end of the century. In deciding the work's authorship,
the figure of Christ is essential, as it
would appear to have been the artist's
own invention and has similarities with
other heads drawn by Hoffmann, for instance his portrait of *Paul Pfinzing* (Nürnberg, Germanisches Nationalmuseum,
inv. no. Hz 4958), which is signed and dat-

ed 1591.

1988, p. 216, cat. no. 11.5; Fučíková 1988,
p. 82, ill. 64.

E.F.

I.49
Giulio Licinio (?)
The Dead Christ with Angels
Oil on panel
108 × 76.5 cm
After 1580
Prague, Metropolitní kapitula u sv. Víta,
inv. no. V 359

This as yet anonymous painting is the work of an artist who followed the figurative style of Andrea Schiavone and the colour techniques used by Veronese. The figure of Christ has a striking resemblance to Spranger's works dating from the beginning of his stay in Prague. It would appear that the work was by an Italian artist who must have been employed at the Emperor's court in the early 1580s, or thereabouts, and who must also have had the opportunity to acquaint himself with Spranger's work. In view of this, the artist is most likely to have been Giulio Licinio, who worked with Spranger on the Viennese Neugebäude and moved to Prague with him at roughly the same time. He painted a similar painting ten years earlier for the palace chapel in Graz, but between this painting and the altar in Prague there is a notable shift in style which can already be seen in his paintings for the Neugebäude. Luisa Vertová considers the attribution to Licinio as very probable.

Fučíková 1988, p. 182, ill. 127.

E.F.

I.50
Dirk de Quade Ravesteyn
St Veronica and Angels with Instruments of the Passion
Oil on panel
41 × 30 cm
1590s
From Wallenstein Palace in Prague
Prague, Národní galerie v Praze, inv. no. DO 5 351

The striking and characteristic faces of the cherubs are evidence enough to attribute this painting to Ravesteyn and to place it amongst his early works, at a period when he was still relatively free from the influence of the other artists at Rudolf's court. As Kaufmann has pointed out, the painting is an unusual treatment of a theme that had been common in paintings since the Middle Ages, namely the instruments of Christ's torture. In the bottom half of the painting the cherubs can be seen dancing and playing with the torture equipment, while above them St Veronica holds the veil bearing the impression of Christ's face. Ravesteyn positioned the Saint in the centre of the composition in order to ensure that the figure was the painting's main focus. The brushstrokes are subtle and slightly blurred compared with the smooth, sharp technique of his later works. It is not known if the painting was intended for purposes of private worship or for the imperial art collection.

Fučíková 1979, p. 494, for older literature; Kaufmann 1988, cat. no.16.9; Fučíková 1988, pp. 86–87, no. 68.

E.F.

I.51
Dirk de Quade Ravesteyn
The Mystic Marriage of St Catherine
Oil on canvas
29.5 × 21.5 cm
1590s
Collection of Pietro Fiorentini in Warsaw; brought to a museum 1879
Warsaw, Muzeum Narodowe, inv. no. M.Ob. 108 /f. 235

The picture in the National Museum at Warsaw was originally thought to be a work by Michiel Coxcie. Its ascription to Ravesteyn in 1979 by J. Zimmer has been generally accepted. It is apparently the earliest of Ravesteyn's works to have survived. It demonstrates the significant influence of Antwerp painting on the artist's work, particularly that of Frans Floris, Maerten de Vos and C. van den Broeck. (For Floris, see his *Holy Family* at the Louvre or in the royal collections in Brussels.) Ravesteyn's technique of palette-knifing the paint is also Flemish. The composition of the picture is not particularly noteworthy for its inventiveness: the figures fill in a field, which has been divided into simple geometric shapes. He is beginning here to formulate that unmistakable face type, with taunting, protruding eyes, a small nose and a hint of a smile on the lips. The picture contains, however, no trace of the influence of Rudolfine painting, which did not become manifest in his work until the end of the 1590s.

Warsaw 1963–64, cat. no. 24 (as M. Coxcie).

Zimmer 1979; Kaufmann 1988, pp. 220–22, 16.2.

E.F.

I.52
Dirk de Quade Ravesteyn
The Three Graces
Oil on canvas
197.5 × 126 cm
Ca. or after 1600
On loan from Germany L.M. 1234 as by J. Heintz the Elder
Münster, Westfälisches Landesmuseum für Kunst und Kulturgeschichte, inv. no. 69-316

This painting attests to Ravesteyn's habit of making several versions of a particular composition with only slight variations. This miniature from Baltimore (Baltimore Museum of Art, inv. no. 1948.171) could well have been a *bozzetto* for the large paintings in Münster and Poltava (State Museum, inv. no. 349). However, judging from its figurative nature, it would seem closer to Ravesteyn's early work influenced by Floris (cat. nos. I.50, 51) and pageantry, which he used to enrich the Vredemans' paintings. As with the painting in Poltava the painting lacks the usual flying amoretti. The painting in Münster is not only more complex in its composition but also in its iconography, and it pre-dates Ravesteyn's 1603 *Allegory of the Reign of Rudolf II* (cat. no. 54), which has just the kind of strong influence by von Aachen that is lacking in this painting. On a general level, as noted by Kaufmann, it is similar in theme to the allegory of Prosperity, Abundance and Peace often used to characterize the Emperor's reign. It was therefore more than likely painted for the Emperor's collection.

Essen and Vienna 1988, cat. no. 140 for the earlier literature; Kaufmann 1988, cat. no. 16.16.

E.F.

I.53
Dirk de Quade Ravesteyn
Justice and Peace
Oil on panel
44 × 32 cm
Ca. 1600
Osnabrück, Kulturgeschichtliches Museum, inv. no. 3628/13

Although this painting would appear to be a *bozzetto* for the *Allegory of the Reign of Rudolf II* from the Strahov monastery (cat. no. I.54), which is more complex in its composition and content, the relationship between the two paintings is in fact more complicated. In the technique employed and in its figurative style, the Osnabrück painting is closer to Ravesteyn's large painting of *The Three Graces* (cat. no. I.52), which dates from around 1600. Though in its choice of subject it is of course closer to the Strahov painting, its composition is nevertheless simpler and the theme is worked out on a general level. Flying amoretti sprinkle flowers on the two female figures of Justice (bearing a sword) and Peace (with two doves holding an olive branch perched on her shoulder, and an olive wreath above her head). It would appear that the painter had returned, after a gap of some time, to this more elegant and better balanced composition so as to enrich it and adapt it to the Emperor's requirements.

Essen and Vienna 1988, cat. no. 141 for earlier literature.

Kayser 1983; Kaufmann 1988, cat. no. 16.8.

E.F.

I.54
Dirk de Quade Ravesteyn
Allegory of the Reign of Rudolf II
Oil on panel
213 × 142 cm
Bottom right: *Did de Quade van Ravesteyn*
1603
1603
Rudolf II's collection; collection of the Premonstratensian Order in Strahov, Prague; in the Národní galerie in Prague from 1957; since returned to the Order Prague, Obrazárna Kláštera premonstrátů na Strahově, inv. no. O 786

The only signed and dated work by Ravesteyn, this dates from the period when the Emperor commissioned a series of allegories of himself as a peacemaker and victor in the war with the Turks. The painting in the Strahov monastery is also based on the same theme. The three embracing women represent Abundance (in the form of Ceres), Justice and Peace. The woman seen behind them forcing back Mars, who is being pressed forward by the Turk, was identified by Kaufmann as Knowledge (Scientia). The Emperor, as the embodiment of the empire, is represented by an eagle crowned with an olive wreath, a sceptre and an olive branch as symbols of his peace-loving reign and is bound by golden manacles to the main protagonists of the scene. The Habsburgs are here referred to by the less common combination of white–red–white in the coat of arms mounted by a ducal cap. This is undoubtedly one of the artist's best works, and it owes much in its style and execution to von Aachen and Spranger.

See fig. 1.31

Essen and Vienna 1988, cat. no. 140.

Kaufmann 1988, pp. 222–23, cat. no. 16.7; Kyzourová-Kalina 1993, cat. no. 32 (for earlier literature).

E.F.

I.55
Dirk de Quade Ravesteyn
Venus and Adonis
Oil on canvas
131 × 108
Ca. 1603
Previously Crépy-en-Valois, Musée de l'Archerie et du Valois
Paris, Musée du Louvre, Département des Peintures, inv. no. MNR 19

This painting, attributed to Ravesteyn by Kaufmann, is unique among the painter's works both in composition and in choice of theme. Scenes from Classical mythology are almost unknown in Ravesteyn's surviving works. In its technique the painting is very similar to the *Allegory of the Reign of Rudolf II* (cat. no. I.54). Its composition is however simpler, more synoptical, and it has less decorative detail. It would seem that after 1600 Ravesteyn began to be influenced by his fellow artists at the Emperor's court, in particular by Josef Heintz the Elder, and duly adapted his style and brushstrokes. This is first noticeable in his Prague *Allegory* dated 1603. The female figures have become more robust, the composition is calmer and a landscape view is included. Both paintings of *The Sleeping Venus* date from the same period (Vienna, Kunsthistorisches Museum, inv. no. 1104; Dijon, Musée des Beaux-Arts, inv. no. 135), as does the painting of *Venus, Cupid and Two Satyrs* from Brussels (Musées Royaux des Beaux-Arts).

Kaufmann 1988, cat. no. 16.11, for earlier literature.

E.F.

I.56
Martino Rota
Emperor Rudolf II
Oil on canvas
51 × 42 cm
? 1577
Imperial collection in Vienna; since 1781 in a gallery
Vienna, Kunsthistorisches Museum, Gemäldegalerie, inv. no. 2587

G. Heinz believed that this portrait might have been one of the first portraits of Rudolf to appear after his coronation as Emperor in 1576. He identified the artist on the basis of a comparison with an engraved portrait of the Emperor from 1577 by Martino Rota, who was a court painter. Rudolf's face has been caught on the picture and the engraving at approximately the same age. At that time Rota was the most experienced and competent portraitist at the imperial court. His somewhat dry and overcultivated style of painting corresponded perfectly to the requirements of court portraits. Since he rarely gave an account of a person whom he was portraying, evidence may come from comparison with Arcimboldo's drawing of Rudolf's head wearing the imperial crown (cat. no. III/46), where the Emperor is realistically depicted without any embellishment. It is no wonder, therefore, that the portrait of *Archduke Ernst*, which is the counterpart to this picture (inv. no. 2588), bears an overwhelming resemblance to Rudolf.

Essen and Vienna 1988, cat. no. 569.

Heinz 1963, pp. 115, 191, no. 37; Heintz and Schütz 1976, p. 106, cat. no. 74, ill. 130; Kaufmann 1988, cat. no. 17.1; Essen and Vienna 1988, cat. no. 569.

E.F.

I.57
Aegidius Sadeler
Antwerp ca. 1568–Prague 1628
Venus and Adonis
Oil on iron(?) panel
26 × 30.5 cm
Ca. 1606-10
Christoph Rosenkranz
Prague, Národní Galerie, sbírka starého umení (acquired 1939), inv. no. o 1642

This small, brightly coloured painting on iron, once connected with Bartholomeus Spranger, is here for the first time attributed to Aegidius Sadeler. While the figures in the painting show similarities to the drawings in the Pushkin Museum and Lugt collection, they are closest of all to Sadeler's drawings of *Venus and Cupid* (1614) in Schloss Friedenstein, Gotha, and *Narcissus* (1601). The sharp profile of Adonis seems to have been a favourite device of Sadeler, who used it not only in the abovementioned drawings, but also in the parchment drawing of *Hercules* in the Albertina, Vienna. While the face of Cupid reveals the influence of Spranger drawings, Venus' face has several counterparts in Sadeler's drawings from Toronto and Moscow (cf. Cupid's face) exhibited here, as well as those in Braunschweig and Groningen. Further, the branches and sprigs of foliage which form the enframing landscape relate closely to several Sadeler compositions from between 1593 and 1610. The closeness of the overgrown ruins to the right to background details in Sadeler's edition of the *Vestigi della antichità* suggests that this painting may date from around the same time as that series (1606).

Fucíková 1979, pp. 489–514; Národní galerie v Praze 1992.

D.L.

I.58
Aegidius Sadeler
Antwerp ca. 1568–Prague, 1628
Portrait of Jan Minckwitz
Oil on canvas
22 × 16 cm
Top left:
A[egidius] S[adeler] I[mperialis] P[ictor] F[ecit]
1616
Rudolfinum, Prague (acquired 1906)
Prague, Národní galerie v Praze, sbírka starého umění, inv. no. O 839

The initials *ASIPF* were first deciphered by Paul Bergner, who published this portrait and its pendant (cat. no. I.59), as a signature of Aegidius Sadeler, Imperial Painter. Sadeler, by many early accounts, was a skilled painter and is recorded as a painter of cabinet pictures (small paintings) in court records from 1615-17. In 1621, he joined the Painters' Guild of the Lesser Town, Prague, while still court engraver to Emperor Ferdinand II. However, recent scholarship has expressed scepticism about this and other attributions. A re-examination of these portraits reveals numerous connections with Sadeler's portrait drawings and prints, ranging from the fine and somewhat isolated treatment of the facial features and costume details to the chiaroscuro tonality, the style of the architectural enframements, and the inscriptions, which are analogous to those found in the engraved portraits. The sitter is identified by the inscription at top as an adviser to the imperial court of appeals under Emperor Matthias. Minckwitz held that post between 1613 and 1628, also serving Emperor Ferdinand II.

Bergner 1908, pp. 38–41; Limouze 1990 (cites previous arguments against the attribution).

D.L.

I.59
Aegidius Sadeler
Antwerp ca. 1568–Prague 1628
Portrait of Klara Minckwitz
Oil on canvas
22 × 16 cm
1616
Rudolfinum, Prague (acquired 1906)
Prague, Národní galerie v Praze, sbírka
starého umění, inv. no. O 840

This pendant to the above represents that
sitter's wife, Klara von Minckwitz. The inscription includes her maiden name, of
which only the initial S is legible, as well
as the beginning of a date: *16.Au[gust]*.

This raises the possibility that the portraits were made to commemorate the
couple's marriage. The inscription is partly cropped, suggesting that both canvases
have been cut down. Having the same
earth-toned architectural background as
its pendant, this painting shows great attention to detail, in the costume and jewelry of the sitter, as well as her facial features. As Bergner described it, the
paintings show a 'minute execution, that
would point to an engraver as opposed to
a painter by trade'. This painting has especially strong similarities to Sadeler's engraving of the same year of Empress Anna
(Hollstein 273).

Bergner 1908, pp. 38–41.

D.L.

I.60
Roelandt Savery
Kortrijk 1576–Utrecht 1639
Forest Cascade with Tobias and the Angel
Oil on wood
43.5 × 37 cm
*ROELANT SAVERY / FE IN PRAGA /
1605*
1605
Gotisches Haus, Wörlitz; Joachim-Ernst-
Stiftung no. 1424
Dessau, Schloss Georgium, Gemäldega-
lerie, inv. no. Gal. no. 386

The Old Testament story of Tobias and
the angel, like the New Testament Flight

into Egypt and St Jerome in the desert
from the Lives of the Saints, is among the
subjects treated by Savery in his first years
in Prague that were traditionally favoured
by Netherlandish landscape artists because they carried the richer resonance
of history painting and also allowed the
artist to explore the idea of wilderness.
Within a few years historical travellers
were largely replaced in Savery's mountain landscapes by ordinary peasants, as
in *Alpine Waterfall with Travellers* (cat. no.
I.62). This intriguing but immature composition is made up of exquisite vignettes
which are linked only superficially. The
grotto is not related to the woodland

from which it is separated by a rushing
stream, while the deer resting in foreground are undisturbed by the travellers.
This is the only extant painting that Savery inscribed as done in Prague. The significance is not clear since he had been
there since 1603.

Erasmus 1908, cat. no. 179; Bernt 1948, no.
727; Thiéry 1953, p. 189; Harksen 1968,
cat. no. 25-3; Bernt 1970, III, no. 1039;
Spicer 1979, p.54, 363; Kaufmann 1985,
cat. no. 19-9, 1988 cat. no. 19-8; Müllenmeister 1988, cat. no. 240.

J.S.

I.61
Roelandt Savery
Kortrijk 1576–Utrecht 1639
Bohemian Peasants Carousing before an Inn
Oil on canvas
46 × 50 cm
R. SAVERY / FE 1608
1608
W. Koller, 5.II.1872, lot 89; Gross
coll.(Fischoff, Vienna, 30.III.1896, lot 172);
Mesnier coll.; Heulens coll, Brussels; D.
Reder, Brussels; gift of the Amis des
Musées Royaux, Bruxelles, 1941
Brussels, Musées Royaux des Beaux Arts,
inv. no. 6216

This scene is surely meant to evoke peasant excess on a market day in Prague, although there is no identifiable city monument in view. Another undated version of
the composition (Paris, private collection;
Kaufmann 1985, cat. no. 19-28) has been
called 'Tyrolean', but the view to the rear is
identifiably Prague, and the present composition may be considered to represent
Prague as well. Like *Orpheus Charming the
Animals* (cat. no. I.66), this composition is
surely made up from studies from life of
the local 'fauna', Bohemian peasants, for
which studies see *Team of Horses* (cat. no.
I.246). Pieter Bruegel's contributions to
the tradition in Netherlandish and Ger-

man art of finding humour in scenes of
peasant excess were certainly in Savery's
consciousness in painting such scenes.
The signature and date are considered
'doubtful' in the 1984 Brussels catalogue
of the permanent collection.

Bialostocki 1958, p. 74; Spicer 1979, pp.
222, 231, 364, under cat. no. 77, p. 221; G.
Franz 1979/80, p. 175; Catalogue 1984, p.
266; Kaufmann 1985, no. 19-27, 1988. no.
19-26; Raubb 1985, p. 43; Thièry 1986 (2nd
edition), p. 60; Müllenmeister 1988, no. 9;
Schmidt 1988, p. 348.

J.S.

I.62
Roelandt Savery
Kortrijk 1576–Utrecht 1639
Alpine Waterfall with Travellers
Oil on copper
35 × 49 cm
R SAVERY / EE 1608 (last digit has been
read as 7)
1608
Weltliche Schatzkammer; 1819-1825 in
Paris
Vienna, Kunsthistorisches Museum, inv.
no. 1083 (exhibited at Schloss Ambras)

Although no drawing is known for this
composition, this *Alpine Waterfall* is cer-

tainly among the cabinet-size paintings
that Savery executed in Prague on the basis of drawings made in the Alps. While
the 'portrait' is surely idealized, passages
around the falls, the rocky grotto, the
abandoned sluice from a milling or mining operation, the shrine along the path,
all suggest a specific place. The copper
support contributes to the crisp, almost
dry delicacy of the execution; Savery has
here varied the sense of texture in passages such as the trees at the right by applying the paint in tiny, unmixed strokes.
The peasants were surely derived from
Savery's repertory, and the costumes reflect the practicalities of mountain life:

two men wear ponchos, and the women's
skirts have been hiked up for unencumbered walking (adapted from the Essen
and Vienna 1988 entry).

Essen and Vienna 1988, cat. no. 143 (with
further references).

Spicer 1979, pp. 57, 58, 363 (as dated
1607); Kaufmann 1985, cat. no. 19-24,
1988, cat. no. 19-23; Müllenmeister 1988,
cat. no. 60.

J.S.

I.63
Roelandt Savery
Kortrijk 1576–Utrecht 1639
Forest Clearing with Hermitage
Oil on copper
20 × 16 cm
R. SAVERY / 1608
1608
Gift of Graf Wallmoden-Gimborn to the
Verein f. d. off. Kunstsammlung, 1853
Hanover, Niedersächsische Landesga-
lerie, inv. no. KA 154/1967

Savery depicted a hermit living in self-im-
posed deprivation in a wilderness several
times during his Prague years, as in his

Pilgrims Leaving a Hermitage (cat. no. I.69).
The popularity of the subject with landscapists working in Catholic countries
may have been a response to the patrons'
desire for imagery of nature that reflects
and ennobles penance. The subject of hermit saints, especially St Jerome, was frequently chosen by early sixteenth-century
landscapists to give the resonance of history painting, with its higher intellectual
status, to landscape. This intimate interi-
or view of the deep forest offers a different perspective of wilderness from the
pendant *Waterfall*. A related drawing also
of 1608 of the same elements, which does
not necessarily precede it, in the Institut

Néerlandais (Spicer 1979, cat. no. 44), is
the incised model for the engraving dated
1609 published by A. Sadeler (Spicer 1979,
cat. no. Pr44; Hollstein Sad 225). Two pairs
of autograph replicas on copper of these
pendants are known; both were recently
in private collections in New York.

Essen and Vienna 1988, cat. no. 144 (with
further references).

Spicer 1979, pp. 75, 83, 363, under cat. no.
44; Kaufmann 1985, cat. no.19-20; Müllenmeister 1988, cat. no. 46.

J.S.

I.64
Roelandt Savery
Kortrijk 1576–Utrecht 1639
Waterfall in the Mountains
Oil on copper
20 × 16 cm
R. SAVERY / 1608
1608
History: see preceding entry
Hanover, Niedersächsische Landesga-
lerie, inv. no. KA 153/1967

Although the composition does not coincide with a known drawing, the combination of a rocky mountainside eroded by
falling water and a plateau to the side in
the foreground is roughly similar to various of Savery's Alpine chalk drawings. For
an extended discussion of the importance
of these waterfall drawings see the essay
'Roelandt Savery and the "Discovery" of
the Alpine Waterfall'. There is little discernible connection with its pendant, the
preceding *Forest Clearing with Hermitage*,
other than a similar range of earth tones
and hazy sky; however the existence of
two pairs of replicas leave no doubt that
Savery intended them as companion
pieces.

Essen and Vienna 1988, cat. no. 145 (with
further references).

Spicer 1979, pp. 75, 364; Kaufmann 1985,
cat. no. 19-21; Müllenmeister 1988, cat. no.
47.

J.S.

I.65
Roelandt Savery
Kortrijk 1576–Utrecht 1639
Mountain Vista with Fruitsellers
Oil on wood
40 × 32 cm (1 cm strip added at bottom)
. *R . SAVERY / 1609*
1609
Weltliche Schatzkammer
Vienna, Kunsthistorisches Museum, inv.
no. 1081 (927)

The apparent unreality of this scene –
fruitsellers casually chatting on the edge
of a mountain precipice – sets it apart
from Savery's usually more plausible
compositions. In contrast, the peasants
are depicted with realism and specificity
and must derive from life studies. The
standing woman is wearing the costume
of the Erzegebirge. The touch of red in
the costume of the seated woman provides a characteristic accent that Savery
introduced into the majority of his landscapes to bring out the richness of his
typically green-blue-brown palette. Indeed the vivid blue sky, reminiscent of
those of Jan Bruegel (in Prague in 1604) is
likely the reason the present painting was
once thought to have been a companion
to J. Bruegel's *Temptation of Christ* in the
same collection (inv 920). The deterioration of areas to the left characterized by a
mottled bluish tone may reflect Savery's
experimentation with pigments that
proved to be fugitive. His *Mountainside
with Woodcutters* of 1610 shows the same
problem (cat. no. I.67).

Ghent 1954, no. 13; Essen and Vienna
1988, cat. no. 146 (with further references).

Erasmus 1908, cat. no. 156; Spicer 1979, p.
364, cat. no. 229; Kaufmann 1985, cat. no.
19-38; Müllenmeister 1988, cat. no. 45.

J.S.

I.66
Roelandt Savery
Kortrijk 1576–Utrecht 1639
Animals Charmed by Orpheus
Oil on wood
51 × 61 cm
R. SAVERY . FE / ... (*1610* per catalogue
of 1900; *R. Savery FC. 1610*, per Spicker-
nagel)
1610
Possibly the 'indisch ross in gezelt allerlei
thier und dergleichen gemalt' cited in the
Prague inventory H of 1619, nr. 278; pur-
chased from Eberhardt-Winter, 1862
Frankfurt am Main, Städtische Galerie im
Städelschen Kunstinstitut, inv. no. 977

This exquisite little painting encapsulates
the interrelation of court painting and
natural science in Prague under the patronage of Rudolf II as few other works of
art do. Based on closely observed studies
made in the imperial menagerie, deer
parks, and stables, this image of Orpheus
provides a summation of the harmoniza-
tion of *naturalia* and *artificialia* within the
magic microcosm Rudolf sought to foster
within his court. While in this exhibition
Savery is well represented by his landscapes, he is best known to the public as a
painter of animal subjects, particularly of
'paradise' scenes in which wild and domestic animals, carnivores and their potential next meal, are peaceably assembled.

Erasmus 1908, cat. no. 48; Catalogue 1924,
cat. no. 977; Thièry 1953, pp. 33, 189;
Spickernagel; J. Spicer 1979, pp. 126, 162,
164, 244, 365, under cat. no. 134; Kaufmann 1985, cat. no.19-47, 1988, cat. no. 19-
46; Thièry 1986 (2nd edition), p. 72; Müllenmeister 1988, cat. no. 203.

J.S.

I.67
Roelandt Savery
Kortrijk 1576–Utrecht 1639
Mountainside with Woodcutters
Oil on copper
27 × 36 cm
R / SAVERY / 1610
1610
Schloss, Pressburg (Bratislava), trans-
ferred in 1781; 1809-15 in Paris
Vienna, Kunsthistorisches Museum, inv.
no. GG 957

A comparison of this painting of 1610 and
the Hamburg chalk drawing of a *Distant
Valley* (cat. no. I.259) of about 1607 makes
clear the tendency towards the domestica-
tion of the awesome in Savery's paintings,
especially those executed a few years after
his 1606/7 travels in the Alps. The majestic expanses and silence evoked by the
drawings made in the Alps may be
brought into focus by a lone figure, perhaps of the artist himself. Here this is replaced by the bustle of peasants busy at
everyday tasks; indeed even the scale of
the rocks relative to the humans have
been reduced and made less fearsome. See
further the essay 'Roelandt Savery and the
"Discovery" of the Alpine Waterfall'.

Vienna 1988, cat. no. 573 (with further references).

Spicer 1979, p. 365; Kaufmann 1985, cat.
no 19-48; Müllenmeister 1988, cat. no. 53.

J.S.

I.68
Roelandt Savery
Kortrijk 1576–Utrecht 1639
Deer Chased by Hunters
Oil on wood
24 × 34 cm
1610/13
Galerie Festetitz und Gsell, 1872; M.
Strauss, Vienna; gift of M. Oberländer,
1939
Prague, Národní galerie v Praze
inv. no. o-1655

Here, as in Savery's paintings of boar
hunts from these years, the prey is driven
towards the viewer, as it would be towards
the noble hunter. Thus the tensions of
the hunt, especially the moments just before the kill, are vicariously re-experi-
enced here. Síp was surely correct in
proposing that the artist intended to convey a setting in Bohemia, probably a royal
hunting preserve. A dating to 1610/13 is
suggested by the broad brushwork,
large individual forms and the striking diagonal bias to the composition,
in comparison with dated works such
as his 1610 *Deer Hunt* (Kaufmann
1988, cat. no. 19-43) and *Landscape
with Stag Hunt* of 1613 (Kaufmann
1988, pp. 19-64). A. Sadeler published
an engraving after this composition
(Hollstein Sad 231; Spicer 1979, cat.
no. Pr33).
Essen and Vienna 1988, cat. no. 149 (with
further references).

Spicer 1979, 73, 365, under Pr33; Kaufmann 1985, no.19-45, 1988; Müllenmeister 1988, no. 76.

J.S.

I.69

Roelandt Savery
Kortrijk 1576–Utrecht 1639
Pilgrims Leaving a Hermitage
Oil on wood
25 × 35 cm
R. SAVERY
1610/13
Wallenstein family; acquired in 1945
Prague, Národní Galerie, inv. no. o-10052

The subject of the landscape with a hermit, here visited by pilgrims, is discussed in connection with *Forest Clearing with Hermitage* (cat. no. I.72). While the composition is awkward and the surface is abraded, the painting is authentic and can be dated to the artist's last years in Prague, in comparison with such dated works as his 1610 *Deer Hunt* (Kaufmann 1988, cat. no. 19-43) or *River Landscape with Travellers* of 1613 (Kaufmann 1988, cat. no. 19-64).

Müllenmeister 1988, cat. no. 31 (ca.1605).

J.S.

See fig. 1.75

I.70

Roelandt Savery
Kortrijk 1576-Utrecht 1639
The Invasion of Prague 15 February 1611
Oil on wood
24.5 × 35 cm
.R. SAVERY. / 161(1?)
1611/12
Dr A. Berg, Frankfurt am Main, 1926; sale Christie's, London, 11.XII.1992, lot 82
Brussels, P. Verhagen

The view is from Mostecká Ulice into the Malostranske Namesti, the large square below the Hradčany. This is the only narrative painting by Savery, or any other court artist, to be focused on a specific street in Prague. There is a drawing of the same site by Savery in the Museum Mr Simon van Gijn in Dordrecht (Spicer 1979, cat. no. 76). There was only one pitched battle fought within the walls of Prague during Savery's years in the city; on 15 February 1611, troops assembled by Archduke Leopold, bishop of Passau, stormed Prague, and the most important skirmish of the ensuing struggle was played out exactly here. Having in 1608 been forced to relinquish other Habsburg domains in favour of Matthias, Rudolf attempted to consolidate his weakening hold on the crown of Bohemia by furthering the political aspirations of Leopold, his cousin and supporter. Leopold, with his army, entered Bohemia without permission of the Bohemian Estates and camped on White Mountain near Prague, hoping to secure the crown for himself and a victory over this Protestant stronghold for Rome.

Frankfurt 1926, cat. no. 187.

Spicer 1979, pp. 237, 363, under cat. no. 76; Spicer 1982, pp. 454-62; Kaufmann 1985, cat. no. 19-64; Müllenmeister 1988, cat. no. 23.

J.S.

I.71

Roelandt Savery
Kortrijk 1576–Utrecht 1639
Forest Path beside a Stream
Oil on wood
37 × 35.3 cm
1611/13
I. C. von Klinkosch, Vienna, 1889; purchased by Adalbert Ritter von Lanna for the Rudolfinum
Prague, Národní galerie v Praze, inv. no. 0611

The composition is a reworking of the central motifs in the drawing *Woodland Stream with Fallen Trees* in the Van Regetern Altena-van Royen collection (Spicer 1979, cat. no. 47). The additon of a path and heavy laden travellers, even one arguing couple, alters the wild seclusion of the drawing into a more domesticated intimacy. For another example of this transformation, see *Mountainside with Woodcutters* (cat. no. I.67). Kaufmann has plausibly suggested a dating to 1611/13.

Essen and Vienna 1988, cat. no. 148 (with further references).

Spicer 1979, p. 365, under cat. no. 47; Kaufmann 1985, cat. no.19-59, 1988, cat. no. 19-57; Müllenmeister 1988, cat. no. 55

(ca. 1606-08).

J.S.

I.72

Roelandt Savery (imitator of)
Kortrijk 1576–Utrecht 1639
Boar Cornered by Huntsmen
Oil on wood
25.5 × 35 cm
Early seventeenth century
Acquired from the Bohumila-Schramberková coll., 1943
Prague, Národní galerie v Praze, inv. no. O-2581

The snarling boar has been driven into brambles by the peasant huntsmen so that it can be killed by a nobleman. Only nobles were entitled to hunt boar, and this painting reflects the perspective of the noble. Rudolf's guests and members of his court would have hunted for boar in the imperial preserves; souvenirs of these hunts, as well as the stuffed trophy heads, may have been very desirable. Certainly, the present composition was much in demand since Savery painted various versions, the earliest known being that dated 1609 in Munich (Kaufmann 1985, cat. no. 19-40). This demand surely prompted the present work, the execution of which is very reductive in comparison with the autograph versions. It is not signed and appears to be by a contemporary imitator. Since there are other copies known of Savery's painting done in Prague and since copyists probably had access to his paintings for court patrons only in his shop, it is likely that the present painting was done under his supervision.

Spicer 1979, p. 326 (copy); Fučíková 1986, pl.73 (R.S.); Müllenmeister 1988, no.93 (early work).

J.S.

I.73

Bartholomeus Spranger
Antwerp 1546–Prague 1611
The Entombment of Christ
Oil on panel
16 × 11 cm
1575-80
Taken from the Národní fond obnovy (National Restoration Fund) in 1949
Prague, Národní galerie v Praze, inv. no. O 10 564

This small painting, although partly washed away, nevertheless provides an interesting record of Spranger's early work at the court of Rudolf II. Oberhuber thought the work to have been made in Italy, perhaps under the influence of Bertoja, and dated it at some time during the early 1570s. In his dissertation Henning, noting the work's connection with the Strahov painting of *The Resurrection*, gave it a somewhat later date. The figurative style and use of colour are also related to Spranger's other paintings made during the late 1570s, in particular the painting of *Mercury Brings Psyche to the Gods*, which is identical to a work that Spranger, according to van Mander, painted for the Emperor. Also similar is the miniature painting of the *Lamentation* (Munich, Bayerische Staatsgemäldesammlungen, inv. no. 2370), which without doubt dates from the same period, and, were it not painted on copper, could, in terms of its dimensions, be the pair of *The Entombment*. The most distant example of this style is the 1582 miniature painting of *St Luke Painting the Madonna* (cat. no. I.74), which links this series of Spranger's works with the mythology paintings made in Prague for the Emperor during the 1580s.

Oberhuber 1958, pp. 30-32, 225, cat. no. 24; Neumann 1984, p. 70, no. 26; Henning 1987, pp. 24-26, cat. no. A6.

E.F.

I.74
Bartholomeus Spranger
Antwerp 1546–Prague 1611
St Luke Painting the Virgin
Oil on copper
Signed on the back of the painting, on
the stand: *Barthollomeus Spranger den 24
september 1582*
1582
Acquired on the art market
Munich, Bayerische Staatsgemäldesamm-
lungen, Alte Pinakothek, inv. no. 14 357

When he published this miniature painting for the first time, An der Heiden called
it the oldest grisaille-painted design for a

graphic print (mirrored adaptation engraved by R. Sadeler). But Spranger obviously did not paint this miniature for
such a purpose, nor in order to present it
to the Prague or Antwerp painting guild.
The format and the 'hand' testify to the
fact that this jewel among Spranger's early Prague works was painted quickly, with
an emphasis on demonstrating technical
bravura, and was intended for someone
who could appreciate just such a quality.
The guild masters would not have been
likely to accept a master's work painted
thus. The exact date given indicates not
only the day of the work's origin but
perhaps even the day on which it was

delivered. It has more analogies among
Spranger's drawings from this time and is
very close, in a similarly grisaille spirit, to
the sketches of Hans Mont.

An der Heiden, R., 'Bartholomäus
Sprangers Lukas-Madonna Bild', *Pantheon*
XXIV, 1976, pp. 34–37; Henning 1987, pp.
48–49, cat. no. A17; Kaufmann 1988, p.
254, cat. and ill. no. 20.18.

E.F.

I.75
Bartholomeus Spranger
Antwerp 1546–Prague 1611
The Resurrection
Oil on panel
112.5 × 85 cm
1575–80
Usually identified as the epitaph for the
imperial hospital in Vienna referred to in
Karel van Mander's life of Spranger; Pre-
monstratensian collection in Strahov,
Prague; Národní galerie v Praze, Prague;
since returned to the Order
Prague, Obrazárna Kláštera premon-
strátů na Strahově

The Resurrection provides a masterful example of Spranger's style at the time
when he left Italy to work for the Habsburgs. It is characterized by subtle brushwork and a use of bright colours. The S-
shaped figures are full of movement and
the composition itself is very theatrical.
Oberhuber correctly drew attention to its
connection with the painting of cabinet
pictures and noted the change in proportions between the figure and the space
around it, diminishing its otherwise monumental dimensions. By comparing it
with the painting of *Mercury Brings Psyche
to the Gods* (since 1965 in the Gurlitt
Gallery in Munich, cat. no. 61), it can

clearly be seen that at that time Spranger
had already ceased to distinguish between painting religious and profane
scenes. *The Resurrection* would therefore
appear to have been intended as a *Kun-
stkammerstück*, to be housed in the imperial gallery rather than hung on an altar.

Prague 1912, cat. no. 12; Essen and Vienna
1988, cat. no. 152.

Diez 1909-1910, p. 115; Oberhuber 1958,
pp. 72, 225, cat. no. 25; Henning 1987, pp.
27–28, 178, cat. no. A7; Kaufmann 1988,
cat. no. 20.1.

E.F.

See fig. 1.12

I.76
Bartholomeus Spranger
Antwerp 1546–Prague 1611
Odysseus and Circe
Oil on canvas
108 × 72 cm
Ca. 1585
From the collection of Rudolf II; imperial
collection in Vienna, in the eighteenth
century in the treasury (*Schatzkammer*);
from 1781 in the gallery
Vienna, Kunsthistorisches Museum,
Gemäldegalerie, inv. no. 1 095

Odysseus and Circe is an example of
Spranger's compositions from the 1580s,

in which the protagonists' bodies, in elaborate poses, are surrounded by many accompanying elements, which cover the
entire surface of the canvas. The painting
is notable for its use of resplendent
colours and its perfect execution even of
minor details, which are reminiscent of
splendid jewellery decorated with enamel.
The subject of the picture comes from the
fourteenth book of Ovid's *Metamorphoses*.
It depicts the moment when Odysseus en-
ters Circe's chamber to take his revenge
on her for having transformed his men into swine. She is on the point of taking out
her magic wand to transform him as well.
Most of the animals in the picture belong

to Circe. They are tame and are fawning
towards Odysseus, the lioness. Only a pig,
who is one of his sailors, has seen how his
master has forced Circe to return his men
to human form. He narrates the tale.
Spranger's Ovidian cycle was evidently
destined for the imperial chambers.

Schallaburg 1974, cat. no. 488; Essen and
Vienna 1988, cat. no. 577; Vienna, 1995,
cat. no. 22.

Oberhuber 1958, p. 118, cat. no. G58; Henning 1987, pp. 58–60, 181, cat. no. A23;
Kaufmann 1988, cat. no. 20.23.

E.F.

I.77
Bartholomeus Spranger
Antwerp 1546–Prague 1611
Salmakis and Hermaphrodite
Oil on canvas
110 × 81 cm
Ca. 1585
From the collection of Rudolf II; imperial
collection in Vienna, since 1782 in the
gallery
Vienna, Kunsthistorisches Museum,
Gemäldegalerie, inv. no. 2 614

Spranger's Ovidian cycle was produced
over a long time and certain stylistic
changes in the artist's work can thus be

observed. Some of the pictures are influenced by the popular Mannerist practice
of depicting entangled bodies and by the
quantity of accompanying details (cat. no.
I.76). Some too resemble the artist's works
of the 1590s, in their peaceful and harmonious composition. One such work is
Hermaphrodite and Salmakis in which the
body of a nymph, slightly turned almost
in the manner of a screw, dominates the
left side of the picture. A landscape with a
pond, beautifully loosely painted, completes the right side. At the lake's edge sits
a charming boy, the son of Hermes and
Aphrodite. The picture portrays a scene
from Book IV of Ovid's *Metamorphoses*, in

which Salmakis, having been rejected by
the boy, secretly returns to watch him
bathing. Spranger depicts both characters when they have discarded their garments, in order to represent their perfect
nakedness.

Prague 1912, cat. no. 27; Naples 1952, cat.
no. 99; Essen and Vienna 1988, cat. no.
575; Vienna 1995, cat. no. 17.

Diez, 1909-1910, p. 120; Oberhuber 1958,
pp. 110-13, cat. no. G59; Henning 1987,
pp. 38–41, 178, cat. no. A11; Kaufmann
1988, cat. no. 20.8.

E.F.

I.78
Bartholomeus Spranger
St Catherine
Oil on wood
152 × 91.8 cm
Late 1580s
Prague, Sbírky Pražského hradu, inv. no.
J208

See the following entry.

I.79
Bartholomeus Spranger
Antwerp 1546–Prague 1611
St Monica
Oil on wood
150.5 × 92
After the mid-1580s
Painted for the Benedictine convent of St George at Prague Castle (at the beginning of the nineteenth century still in the basilica, later in the chapel of St Anne); since 1952 in the collection of Prague Castle
Prague, Sbírky Pražského hradu, inv. no. J70

Of the extensive cycle of saints that Spranger painted for the convent of St George, only four paintings have been preserved to this day (cat. no. I.78, SS *Elizabeth* and *Ursula* from the picture gallery of the Premonstratensian monastery at Strahov, inv. nos 0 540, 541). This picture must have originated at the time when Spranger had settled in Prague permanently and had acquired a sufficiently well-equipped workshop, which would have enabled him to accept more substantial commissions destined for the imperial court. He was able to entrust much of this work to his assistants, who followed his designs. The existence of these is indirect-

ly demonstrated by three pictures of saints from the Archer Huntington Gallery in Austin (inv no. 1984. 51-53), which are workshop replicas (or perhaps copies) and were originally planned for a more complicated set of compositions to come from Spranger's workshop.

Prague 1912, cat. nos 51, 52.

Oberhuber 1958, pp. 113–114, 227, cat. no. 33, 34; Neumann 1966, pp. 235-37, cat. no. 61; Henning 1987, pp. 41-46, cat. nos A 13, A 14; Kaufmann 1988, p. 254, cat. and picture nos 20.17 and 20.16.

E.F.

I.80
Bartholomeus Spranger
Antwerp 1546–Prague 1611
A Female Saint
Oil on wood, grisaille
93 × 73.5 cm
Late 1580s
From the Benedictine convent of St George at Prague Castle
Rožmberk, státné zámek, inv. no. 2100

Both [cat. nos. I.80 and I.81] panels originally formed the outer side of the altar wings, to which apparently belonged another two female saints: St Catherine (Karlsruhe, Kunsthalle, inv. no. 2587) and

St Barbara (Berlin-Dahlem, Staatliche Museen Preussischer Kulturbesitz, inv. no. KFMV 255). Unlike the paintings of female saints at Rožmberk, done in grisaille, these colourfully executed saints belonged to the internal part of the altar. (They were collectively auctioned off in Munich in 1913.) This altar may have been painted for the Benedictine nuns at St George's, which was a convent for women. Their abbesses, at least during the Middle Ages, tended to be of royal descent, and when the convent was discontinued in 1782, some of its furnishings were dispersed beyond the area of Prague Castle. The customer must have been

prestigious because, unlike similar plates of saints, Spranger did not entrust the execution of them to his workshop, although St Ursula, who could have formed the centre part of the altar, is more likely to be a workshop product. That plate, therefore, may be independent.

Prague 1912, cat. nos 54, 55.

Oberhuber 1958, p. 230, cat. no 43, 44; Henning 1987, pp. 51-56, cat. nos A19, A20; Kaufmann 1988, pp. 258-59, cat. and ill. no 20.32, 20.33.

E.F.

I.81
Bartholomeus Spranger
Antwerp 1546–Prague 1611
A Female Saint (Saint Margaret?)
Oil on wood, grisaille
94.5 × 59.5 cm
Late 1580s
From the Benedictine convent of St George at Prague Castle
Rožmberk, státné zámek, inv. no. 2101

See cat. no. I.80 for description.

E.F.

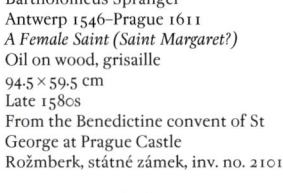

I.82
Bartholomeus Spranger
Antwerp 1546–Prague 1611
St Wenceslas and St Vitus
Oil on panel
127 × 72 cm
After 1585
Wallenstein collection, Doksy country estate; Duchcov country estate
Prague, Národní galerie v Praze, inv. no. O 11 160

During the 1580s, Spranger worked on a series of altar paintings depicting saints, mostly commissioned for the Benedictine nuns at the monastery of St George (cat.

nos I.78-81). The figures of four Bohemian patron saints painted on two large panels (St Sigismond and St Procopius are depicted on the other panel) may well have been intended as altar decoration, but since they were inspired by Dürer's compositions (cf. Fučíková 1972) they may have been intended for the Emperor's collection. DaCosta Kaufmann linked the work with Spranger's journey to the assembly in Augsburg as part of the imperial retinue, and suggests that in Prague at that time there were not enough of Dürer's works available. From 1585 onwards Hans Hoffmann worked at the Emperor's court and was not only the best copyist of

Dürer's works, but also the best 'improver' of them. Spranger had access not only to works of Dürer purchased by the court but also to works offered for sale, selected by the Emperor on the advice of Hoffmann, the acknowledged expert.

Fučíková 1972, pp. 158-62, 8-13; Neumann 1978, p. 372, no. 40; Henning 1987, pp. 46, 180, cat. no. A16 (where the saints are however incorrectly identified and the second panel wrongly dismissed); Kaufmann 1988, no. 20.20 (twin panel 20.21), for other literature.

E.F.

I.83
Bartholomeus Spranger
Antwerp 1546–Prague 1611
Self-Portrait
Oil on canvas
62.5 × 45 cm
On the left edge: *IPSE.F.*
1580-85
Collection of Archduke Leopold Wilhelm, inv. no. 1659, no 653; imperial collection in Vienna; since 1783 in the gallery
Vienna, Kunsthistorisches Museum, Gemäldegalerie, inv. no. I 137

When, in 1586, Jakob König visited Rudolf II in Prague, he undoubtedly met

the court painter Spranger. From him König acquired a self-portrait for his collection, which must be identical to the Viennese painting. The inscription *IPSE.F.* corresponds exactly to what König had sought for his collection. It agrees with a description of the picture in the register of König's estate from ca.1603 (no.12). An arrangement was made that after his death the collection would acquire the painting either as a gift or, rather, that it would be bought into the collection of Rudolf II. This explains the existence of two almost identical self-portraits by Spranger. One of them is in Vienna, the other is now kept in the Liechtenstein col-

lections (inv. no. 946). Spranger evidently held on to this for his collection.

Prague 1912, cat. no. 13; Nürnberg 1952, cat. no. K 8 ; Essen and Vienna 1988, cat. no. 153 (Liechtenstein) and 581 (Vienna).

Henning 1987, pp. 167-70, 191-92, cat. nos A66, A67; Kaufmann 1988, cat. nos 20.24, 20.25; Martin 1995, pp. 46-54.

E.F.

1.84
Bartholomeus Spranger
Antwerp 1546–Prague 1611
The Triumph of Wisdom
Oil on canvas
163 × 117 cm
Ca. 1595
From the collection of Rudolf II; imperial collection in Vienna, 1747/48 in the treasury, 1783 in the gallery
Vienna, Kunsthistorisches Museum, Gemäldegalerie, inv. no. 1133

This picture has been subject to iconographic analysis many times. Its dating is important for an interpretation of the work. Oberhuber dated the picture to about 1591, but a later origin seems more probable. In 1592 Spranger painted an allegory on Rudolf II (inv. no. 1192), in which the use of colour and of figural types was linked to his works from the 1580s. In the *Allegory of Wisdom*, however, the influence of de Vries, von Aachen and Heintz is already apparent, which means that it must have originated at the earliest in 1593 when all these artists met in Prague. L. Konečný interprets the main scene in the picture as Minerva being victorious over ignorance. The goddess of wisdom is thus surrounded by allegories of science and art. Two half-figures by the bottom edge are thought to be Bellona, the goddess of war (on the left), and History (on the right). Between 1593 and 1595 the imperial armies achieved several significant successes against the Turks. In 1595 Rudolf elevated painting to the status of the other arts.

Essen and Vienna 1988, cat. no. 159; Vienna 1995, cat. no. 27.

Oberhuber 1958, pp. 115-55, 235; Henning 1987, pp. 95-99, 185, cat. no. A37; Kaufmann 1988, cat. no. 20.50.

E.F.

1.85
Bartholomeus Spranger
Antwerp 1546–Prague 1611
Epitaph of Goldsmith Nicholas Müller
[*The Resurrection of Christ and Angels*]
Oil on canvas
Ca. 1592
243 × 160 cm
Cemetary chapel of St Matthias at the church of St John in the parish of Oborana Malá Strana, deconsecrated in 1784 and demolished in 1791
Prague, Národní galerie v Praze, inv. no. O 1 574

Karel van Mander, who heard about the epitaph for Müller on his journey to the Netherlands in 1602, claimed that, in addition to Spranger's painting, there were also amoretti by Adrian de Vries. Most scholars date the epitaph to the period immediately following Müller's death in 1588. But Müller died earlier than Winter claims; the inventory of his estate having been completed by 1 March 1586. The amoretti provide a more substantial clue to the date of the painting: de Vries was in Prague in the early 1590s and engravings based on his sculptures were made in 1593, which can therefore be taken as a date *ante quem*. Moreover, the figurative portrayal of Christ is identical to the sculptures in the *Venus* cycle, which again suggests a later date. Mander claimed that Spranger considered this painting his best work in terms of his use of colour, which changed significantly following the arrival of von Aachen and Heintz at the court (late 1591). Recent cleaning has revealed that the colours were originally brighter, showing Venetian influence.

Essen and Vienna 1988, cat. no. 158.

Mander (ed.) 1906, p. 159; Henning 1987, pp. 187–88, 184, cat. no. A34, for older literature; Kaufmann 1988, no. 20.47.

E.F.

1.86
Bartholomeus Spranger
Antwerp 1546–Prague 1611
Hercules and Omphale
Oil on panel
28 × 22.2 cm
Ca. 1595
Vienna, Dorotheum 1713, 1. auction on 1 March 1994, cat. no. 172, under Spranger-Schule
Geneva, Private Collection, on loan in the Národní galerie v Praze, inv. no. VO 1 825

This recently discovered painting is a classic example of scenes composed of half-figures, which became a very popular mode among other artists at Rudolf's court from the 1590s onwards. These compositions were not limited to particular themes, but were based in equal measure on mythological stories, allegories and religious themes. Common to all of them is their interesting style of composition and masterly brushwork, which makes them *sui generis*. Spranger's *Hercules and Omphale* is a typical example of the 'cabinet' painting of this period. Thanks to reflectographic techniques it is now known that the composition was first laid out in a very fine drawing. The striking outlines and short brushstrokes were a technique that Spranger developed by painting miniatures. The current painting is more reminiscent of Spranger's works on copper than on wood. The dating of this picture is estimated by comparison with two others of the same subject: it seems to have been made later than its Viennese counterpart, which dates from the early 1590s; but it was definitely done earlier than the Prague drawing of 1599 (cat. no. I.281).

Fučíková 1995-1996, pp. 40–43, ill. 12.

E.F.

1.87
Bartholomeus Spranger
Antwerp 1546–Prague 1611
Venus, Ceres and Bacchus
Oil on canvas
On the lower right: *B SPRANGERS Ant.us F.*
Ca. or after 1590 (Diez 1909/1910, p. 118, mentions the date 1590 by the signature, now missing)
The collection of Rudolf II, possibly identical with inv. 1621, no. 910; the imperial collection in Vienna, in 1872 donated by Emperor Franz Joseph I to the Graz museum
Graz, Alte Galerie des Steiermärkischen Landesmuseum Joanneum, inv. 68

Kaufmann and Henning considered this painting, together with the *Sine Cerere et Baccho Friget Venus* from Vienna, as counterparts illustrating a popular idiom from Terence's comedy *Eunuchus* (IV, 732). Also belonging to this oeuvre is the *Bacchus and Venus* from Hannover (cat. no. 42), the *Mars, Venus and Cupid* from Graz and the *Venus and Adonis* from Vienna. In the paintings from this cycle of Venus, Spranger abandoned complex compositions: individual figures are transformed into statues, into expressive verticals dominating the picture. Only what is most necessary for comprehension of the scene is delineated in the background, and decorative details are reduced to a minimum. The cycle, in which the painting from Graz occupied a central position, was probably destined for one of the imperial chambers rather than for the gallery, where alongside a number of others its compositional links would be lost.

Oberhauer 1958, pp. 145-146, 221, with all the earlier literature; Henning 1987, pp. 90-95, cat. no. A 36, ill. 23; Kaufmann 1988, p. 265, cat. and ill. no. 20.49.

E.F.

1.88
Bartholomeus Spranger
Antwerp 1546–Prague 1611
Bacchus and Venus
Oil on canvas
Ca. or after 1590
Collection of Rudolf II; on the Munich art market in 1940 as Goltzius; since 1966 on permanent loan to the FRG in Hannover
Hannover, Niedersächsisches Landesmuseum, inv. no. PAM 956

When, in 1970, B. Schnackenburg published this previously unknown painting, he presented a detailed iconographic analysis and suggested its moralizing content. He pointed out the connection with N. Reusner's book of emblems, from which not only the likeness of a leopard, but the message of the painting as a whole, is borrowed. The motto 'abstinuit Venere et Baccho' admonishes, among other things, that love and wine may cause more damage than violence and the sword. He who is wise maintains moderation. Likewise Schnackenburg mentions the possible sources of inspiration for both figures, the Venus of Antiquity and Giambologno's *Bacchus* from the fountain in Borgo San Jacopo, Florence. In this context, it is necessary to recall de Vries's drawing of the strutting youth (Apollo) from Gdansk (cat. no. 39), the figure of which is turned and straddled in the same manner as Spranger's Bacchus; it may serve as evidence of the sculptor's influence on the painter, possibly also of an exchange of designs. It may also aid in dating it to the period when de Vries was first living in Prague, around 1593.

Essen and Vienna 1988, cat. no. 157.

Schnackenburg 1970, pp. 143-160; Fučíková 1972, pp. 248, 258, ill. 3; Kaufmann 1988, p. 269, cat. and ill. no. 20.59.

E.F.

I.89
Bartholomeus Spranger
Antwerp 1546–Prague 1611
Venus and Adonis
Oil on canvas
163 × 104.3 cm
Ca. 1595
From the collection of Rudolf II; imperial collection in Vienna, since 1781 in the gallery
Vienna, Kunsthistorisches Museum, Gemäldegalerie, inv. no. 2 526

Three of Spranger's pictures portray the amorous adventure of Venus and Adonis. The oldest (Amsterdam, Rijksmuseum,

inv. no. N 2224.Ei) corresponds to Ovid's description of Venus following her lover like a hunter. In the Viennese picture, as in the Duchcov one (cat. no. I.89), Spranger turned for inspiration to other literary sources, which give a cosmological interpretation of Adonis' tragic death: Venus will not allow her lover to disappear for ever into the underworld. It is decided that he will always return to her each spring. The dusky landscape to the back of the picture acts as a view into the kingdom of Persephone, with whom Venus must share Adonis' presence. The special magic of this picture by Spranger derives from its restrained use of colour.

Against the dominant browns and greys, a single other colour is expressively asserted: the superb red oriental robe of Adonis. It is, of course, also the colour of Adonis' blood and of the flower into which the drops of his blood were transformed.

Essen and Vienna 1988, cat. no. 587; Vienna 1995, cat. no. 31.

Oberhuber 1958, p. 166, cat. no. G 60; Schnachenberg 1970, p. 150; Henning 1987, pp.116–18, 187, cat. no. A45; Kaufmann 1988, cat. no. 20.63.

E.F.

I.90
Bartholomeus Spranger
Antwerp 1546–Prague 1611
Sine Cerere et Baccho friget Venus (Venus Saddens when Bacchus and Ceres Abandon her)
Oil on canvas
Inscribed later bottom right: *B. Spranger*
Ca. 1595
From the collection of Rudolf II, inv. no. 1621, no. 981; imperial collection in Vienna; since 1783 housed in gallery
Vienna, Kunsthistorisches Museum, Gemäldegalerie, inv. no. 2435

Together with other depictions of Venus'

amorous adventure, this picture was also executed before or around the mid-1590s. Inspired by de Vries' statues of ca.1593, Spranger abandoned the complex tangle of human bodies and let statuesquely conceived and perfectly painted figures stand out against the dark background. These figures entirely dominate the surface of the picture. The related use of colour, refined by enamel, enhances their magical qualities and underlines the brilliance of the unbelievably smoothly painted bodies. In this picture Spranger illustrated the celebrated quotation from Terence's comedy *Eunuchus* (IV, 732), 'sine Cerere et Baccho friget Venus', which may

be interpreted as meaning that 'without bread and wine, love freezes'. K. Renger found the model for this unusual composition and its allegorical interpretation in an emblem from the book *Parvus mundus*, which was printed by L. Haechtanus in 1579.

Essen and Vienna 1988, cat. no. 156.

Essen and Vienna 1988, cat. no. 156, for older literature; Henning 1987, pp. 90–92, 184, cat. no. A35; Kaufmann 1988, cat. no. 20.48.

E.F.

I.91
Bartholomeus Spranger
Antwerp 1546–Prague 1611
Recumbent Diana after the Hunt
Before 1600
Ex Esterházy collection (as Frans Floris)
Budapest, Szépmüvészeti Múzeum, inv. no. 351

Spranger's paintings, like those of other Rudolfine artists, reflected the works of older German and Italian masters. This painting shows Venetian inspiration: the composition, which includes a background landscape, recalls Palma Vecchio's Dresden *Venus*, and the almost Rubensian

figure of Diana was probably modelled on the works of Paris Bordon. Spranger acknowledges his models to some extent, but without abandoning his individual expression: he surrounds his own inventions with citations from other masters. The painting has a smooth elegance, with an emphasis on perfectly executed detail (e.g., fur), and the composition is balanced and uncluttered. The Budapest picture is among the works in which Spranger concentrated on the plasticity of human figures, such as the series with *Venus and Bacchus*, and thus dates from the late 1590s.

Essen and Vienna 1988, cat. no. 160.

Fučíková 1980, pp. 189, 192; Fučíková 1984, pp. 56-7; Henning 1987, pp. 192-93; Kaufmann 1988, p. 269, cat. no. 20.60; Essen and Vienna 1988, cat. no. 160.

E.F.

I.92
Bartholomeus Spranger
Antwerp 1546–Prague 1611
Diana (Luna)
Oil on canvas
After 1600
Budapest, Szépmüvészeti Múzeum, inv. no. 73.12

Urbach's tentative attribution of this painting to Spranger in 1981 has since been generally accepted. In it Spranger returned to the figural style of his works from the 1580s, however the use of colour and light already anticipates late work, in which the forms of the figures are less

firm and the scene takes on the quality of a dramatic vision. The painting is not adversely affected by the change of format, as Henning suggested. The half-figure fills the surface, in keeping with the painter's intention to frame the composition for the viewer. In paintings composed of half-figures, Spranger often revolved the figures towards the viewer (e.g., the *Holy Family* from Braunschweig, *Venus, Mercury, and Amor* from Nürnberg). The Budapest *Diana (Luna)* is among his 'cabinet' pieces, collector's objects which were master examples of the painter's art for the galleries of the nobility. There is no need to assume that this work was part of

a larger cycle of allegories or mythologies. Budapest, 1981, p. 43, cat. no. 56 (S. Urbach's attribution to Spranger ?).

Urbach, S., (see preceding data); Kaufmann 1988, p. 273, cat. and ill. no. 20.72; Henning 1987, pp. 145-46, 189, cat. no. A55.

E.F.

I.93
Bartholomeus Spranger
Antwerp 1546–Prague 1611
Memento mori (Vanitas)
Oil on canvas
Lower right: *B. SPRANGERS.ANT.F*; on the plaque: *Hodie Mihi Cras Tibi*
After 1600
Acquired from the Miaczynski-Dzieduscszycki Collection, Lvov, in 1933
Cracow, Wawel Royal Castle – State Collection of Art, inv. no. 935

The putto with a skull represents Death (Thanatos), and this same theme is referred to by further attributes that appear

in the painting: the inscription on the plaque ('today me, tomorrow you') and the hour-glass. The *memento mori* is presented in the literature in connection with the graphic by Aegidius Sadeler after Spranger's allegory on the death of his wife Kristina in 1600. The painting, from Cracow, is admittedly from the same period and works with the same symbolism, but the allusion to a concrete person is missing here. In its composition the naked child closely resembles the mirrored, turned nude figure of the goddess in the Duchcov painting of *Venus and Adonis*, which is, in my opinion, a representation of the transitory nature of human

life. The putto points with its finger at the hour-glass, at Time, of which each person has a specific allowance. His expression and provocative posture, however, do not plainly signify anything of the painting's tragic message. This is a classic example of a cabinet painting in which elegant compositions are linked with sophisticated contents.

Oberhuber 1959, p. 222, with earlier literature; Henning 1987, pp. 146–147; Kaufmann 1988, p. 272, cat. and ill. no. 20.71.

E.F.

I.94
Bartholomeus Spranger
Antwerp 1546–Prague 1611
The Baptism of Christ (Epitaph of Simon Hannewald and His Wife Eva)
Oil on wood
102 × 88
Signed and dated on the back: *B./ SPRANGERS/ F. 1603*; the original date was 1604; when restored in 1911 the entire signature was removed and replaced by the text above
1604 or possibly 1603
Church of the Holy Trinity at Zurawina (Rothsürben), Silesia
Wroclaw, Muzeum Narodowe, inv. no. VI-
II-2252

The councillor to the imperial court and secretary Andreas Hannewald commissioned this epitaph, probably in 1604; for his parents, Simon, who died in 1599, and Eva, who died in 1600. From the year 1606, Andreas was to enjoy great favour with Rudolf II. The sculpture and the picture are rare examples of commissions undertaken by court artists for a customer other than the Emperor or indeed even outside the court. It is true that the two artists had met before during a similar exercise, when working on the epitaph for the goldsmith Muller, although this had been a family commission. The *Baptism of*

Christ is the oldest documented example of a freely painted chiaroscuro painting, in which the light disperses forms and transforms the scene into a celestial vision. De Vries was inpirsed by Spranger in this new style, of which the Zurawina *Flagellation* is, in fact, one of the first realizations.

Warsaw 1963–64, cat. no. 58.

Henning 1987, pp. 147–50, 189, cat no. A57; Kaufmann 1988, cat. no. 20.76.

E.F.

I.95
Bartholomeus Spranger
Antwerp 1546–Prague 1611
Allegory of the Turkish Wars
Oil on panel
165.1 × 104.5 cm
Ca. 1610
From Rudolf II's collection, 1648 to Sweden (?); Nils Rapp, Stockholm, 1929; Harry Wahlin, Stockholm, 1937; 1981 auctioned at Christie's
Münster, Stadtmuseum, on Loan from a Prviate Collection, inv. no. 601

This painting is the only one of Spranger's works to employ the theme of

the Turkish wars. It is full of tragedy and scepticism. The dark background, with its deserted landscape is lit by one or two fires. Victoria is depicted in a dominating pose beside the prostrate Turk, whom she approaches at the risk of being struck by his sword. The amoretto in the right corner holding the board without an inscription recalls the Cracovian allegory of Vanitas with the inscription *Hodie mihi cras tibi*. The Emperor's eagle is not flying heavenward as it is usually depicted, but is instead bound like the Turk to the earth. This painting evidently dates from the twilight years of Spranger's life. It clearly relates to the events that followed

the signing of the peace treaty with the Turks in 1606 and which prevented Rudolf II from pressing ahead for victory over the heathen in the 'Holy War', which he considered the most important aim of his reign.

Münster 1983, cat. no. 54; Essen and Vienna 1988, cat. and ill. 163.

Oberhuber 1958, pp. 200-01, 203; Kaufmann 1978, pp. 71, 74-75, ill. 6; Henning 1987, pp. 161-62, 191, cat. no. A62; Kaufmann 1988, cat. no. 20.86.

E.F.

See fig. 1.08

I.96
Bartholomeus Spranger
Antwerp 1546–Prague 1611
Allegory of Faithfulness Triumphant over Fate (Allegory of the Fate of Sculptor Hans Mont)
Oil on panel
52.5 × 43.5 cm
On the frame of the podium: *(A) DPIC-TUM ARCHETYPO IOH DE MONT GANDAVENSIS INTER PRIMOS AEVI HUIUS ET AUGUSTI CAES(ARIS) (S)TATUARIOS DESCRIPSIT B. SPRANGER A DCVII*; on the platform, bottom left: *INIQUA FATA (ITA) DECUS HOC/ ORBI ET BELGI/ EREPTUM ITTI?/ FIDES AEQUA/ QUAE ETIAM/*

NOCTA SUA (I)AM/ INVOLUTUM/ PA-TRIAE ET LUCI/ RESTITUTIS
1607
Probably part of Rudolf II's collection, appearing in Castle inventory records from 1685 onwards
Prague, Sbírky Pražského hradu, inv. no. O 259

Spranger worked with the sculptor Hans Mont in Italy and Vienna during the 1570s. Mont left the Emperor's services after suffering an eye injury in the early 1580s. The inscription states that the composition of this work was based on a design by Mont, which has not survived,

but several analogies can be seen in Mont's drawing of five marching figures (cat. no. I.219); this may have been intended as part of the decorations for the Vienna Neugebäude, on which both artists had worked some thirty or so years previously. The long inscription indicates that Spranger thought the picture important.

Essen and Vienna 1988, cat. no. 162; Vienna 1996, cat. no. 21.

Neumann 1966, pp. 268-70; Kaufmann 1988, cat. no. 20.65; Vienna 1996, p. 64, cat. no. 21, ill. 65.

E.F.

See fig. 1.07

I.97
Bartholomeus Spranger
Antwerp 1546–Prague 1611
Sophonisba
Oil on canvas
125.5 × 97 cm
1603-7
Purchased in 1938 from Dr O. Reichl
Prague, Národní galerie v Praze, inv. no. O 1 593

The painting belongs to the group of Spranger's paintings in which the human figures are depicted like phantasms emerging from the dark surface of the work. The light effects further add to this

impression and intensify the sense of drama. These visionary compositions are on the one hand 'Baroque' and expressive but on the other still Mannerist, in that the figures are just like those in Spranger's earlier works dating from the 1580s. The originally smooth surfaces of the bodies, however, have been blurred and lost most of their forms. Spranger first used this technique in the *Baptism of Christ* in Hannewald's epitaph (cat. no. I.94), dated 1603. The 1607 Bystad painting of *Venus at Her Toilet* (collection of Baron C. Grippenstedt), as well as several graphic prints, for instance two engravings of the *Holy Family* by Lucas Kilian

from 1605, also belong to this group of paintings. *Sophonisba* may be assumed to date from this period also. In Spranger's later works the calm, sculptural aspects of his works of the 1590s are recaptured.

Oberhuber 1958, pp. 173, 227, cat. no. 32; Neumann 1978, p. 319, ill. 5; Neumann 1984, p. 74, ill. 49; Kaufmann 1988, cat. no. 20.66.

E.F.

I.98
Bartholomeus Spranger
Antwerp 1546–Prague 1611
Venus and Adonis
Oil on canvas
118.5 × 175.5 cm
Between 1607 and 1611
Wallenstein's collection in Duchcov
Duchcov, Státní zámek, inv. no. 1079

Three well-preserved paintings by Spranger tell the story of Venus and Adonis and also highlight three stylistically different aspects of the painter's art. While the Amsterdam painting (Rijksmuseum, inv. no. N. 2224) representing a

wide range of Italian influences dates from around 1580, the large Vienna composition belonging to the Venus cycle of paintings dates from some time after 1590 and was clearly influenced by de Vries' sculptures. The Duchcov painting was executed during the last years of Spranger's life and is very much in accordance with his later style, in which the light blurs the forms and gives the figures a phantasmic appearance. The iconographic composition is also different in the three works. In the Amsterdam painting Spranger followed the descriptive topos of Ovid's *Metamorphoses* (Bk X). The other two works, however, deal with the

dead Adonis who, thanks to Venus' successful intervention, has been allowed to return from the underworld for a limited time each spring, but must then return to Persephone's kingdom. In the background arrangement of the Duchcov painting, Adonis' death is emphasized, as is the uninterrupted gloom of the underworld, which counterbalances the other compositional details in the work.

Fučíková 1972, pp. 347-62; Kaufmann 1988, cat. no. 20.90.

E.F.

I.99
Bartholomeus Spranger
Antwerp 1546–Prague 1611
Mars and Venus in the Smithy of Vulcan
Oil on canvas
140×95 cm
After 1607
From the collection of Rudolf II, imperial collection in Vienna
Vienna, Kunsthistorisches Museum, Gemäldegalerie, inv. no. 2 001

This painting is one of the most interesting works that Spranger created in the last years of his life. In contrast with the paintings dated before about 1607 (cat.

no. I.96), it shows that he had abandoned his free painting technique, which transformed figures into apparitions, and had returned to the statuesque conception of figures, carefully and smoothly painted, that appeared in his pictures in the 1590s. He had already had another stylistic 'proto-Baroque' period, under the influence of the Carracci, whose work he either saw in Rudolf's collection or had been made aware of by von Aachen. The picture portrays Venus' amorous adventure with Mars at the back of Vulcan's workshop, in which the deceived husband is forging a weapon for his rival. The painting illustrates how Spranger's style and concep-

tion of the scene (e.g. the dominant-female principle) had greatly altered in comparison with his *Mars, Venus and Amor* from Graz (Landesmuseum Joanneum, inv. no. 67), which belonged to the *Venus* cycle.

Essen and Vienna 1988, cat. no. 164; Vienna 1995, cat. no. 32.

Oberhuber 1958, pp. 202-03, 234; Henning 1987, pp. 164-66, 91, cat. no. A64; Kaufmann 1988, cat. no. 20.88.

E.F.

I.100
Pieter Stevens
Mechelen (?) ca. 1567–Prague (?) after 1624
Village Feast in a Landscape
Oil on wood
Lower left: PS 96
1596
Antwerp, Koninklijk Museum voor Schone Kunsten, inv. no. 998

Kaufmann has pointed out that Rudolf II acquired paintings with similar themes from Pieter Bruegel the Elder, after the death of his brother Archduke Ernest in 1595. Stevens could have been inspired by these, both their figural style and the

composition of the landscape, however similar themes had already appeared in his work in the two preceding years. Zwollo has noted a resemblance between this painting and the *Village Feast* (untraced; until 1945 Vienna, Kunsthistorisches Museum) dated to 1595. The *Village Feast* from the Fondation Custodia in Paris, dated to 1594, also belongs to this group. Although the first two include Roman architecture, the peasants are depicted in contemporary Bohemian dress. In the Antwerp painting the scene takes place in a natural setting, and the composition and high perspective are similar to the paintings executed at that time by Lucas

van Valckenborch for the Emperor and his brother.

Amsterdam, 1970, cat. no. 998; Essen and Vienna 1988, cat. no. 166.

Zwollo, 1968, p. 138, ill. 179; Franz 1968/69, tab. XXV, ill. 32; Kaufmann 1988, p. 282, ill. 21.7; Essen and Vienna, 1988, cat. no. 166.

E.F.

I.101
Pieter Stevens
Mechelen (?) ca. 1567–Prague (?) after 1624
Landscape with a Mill
Oil on canvas
60.5 × 103
After 1604
Warsaw, Muzeum Narodowe, inv. no. M.Ob. 2198 9

Once again in this picture Stevens uses light proceeding from the back through the branches of trees to suggest the depth of space and the quivering air under an overcast sky. His conception of landscape shows that he must have known by then

the inspirational work of Savery and Vianen, and he adapted to their manner of expression. In an attempt to attain a natural effect, he used many compositional motifs, which he had not yet managed to knit together. It would appear that this painting originated when Stevens was beginning to experiment with new conceptions of landscape, such as in his *Forest Landscape with Rocky Bridge* and the *Landscape with a Watermill* (cat. no. I.104) from Prague, which give the impression of an authentic record of nature. A comparison with *Landscape with Inn* reveals the use of similar motifs. In the Warsaw painting, however, he has still not managed to link

the various levels of terrain harmoniously or to place any restraints on his strikingly arranged array of captivating natural motifs.

Warsaw 1951, cat. no. 22, ill. XX; Rotterdam, cat. no. 296.

Zwollo 1968, p. 158, ill. 213; Kaufmann 1988, cat. no. 21.16.

E.F.

I.102
Pieter Stevens
Mechelen (?) ca. 1567–Prague (?) after 1624
Rocky landscape with Goat Hunt
Oil on wood
53 × 71.5 cm
After 1600
Acquired after 1955
Copenhagen, Den kgl. Malerei- og Skulptursamling Statens Museum for Kunst, inv. no. 4879

Zwollo has ascribed this picture to Stevens on the basis of a drawing in which may be seen the same expressive

motives of a rocky arch (Vienna, Albertina, inv. no. 13 396), at the Akademie der bildenen Künste (inv. nos. 9816, 9817) and in the collection of Prof. van Regteren Alten at Amsterdam. Closer examination also reveals a rocky bridge on an engraving by Sadeler, which identifies him as the author of the model on which Stevens' work is based. Unlike his more usual work, Stevens concentrated in this picture on a smaller piece of landscape of a natural-looking, albeit carefully composed, scene, in which figural pageantry plays only a subordinate role. The main subject is the bizarre rocky landscape in which a dark arch of rock and a brighter

backdrop permit the interplay of light and shadow. Stevens also demonstrated in this picture an ability to capture the atmosphere of a place, with the sun's rays remaining beyond the rocky gate and penetrating it on the leaves of trees and on the surface of the rivulet. It is one of the Stevens' most effective and purest landscapes.

E.F.

I.103
Pieter Stevens
Mechelen (?) ca. 1567–Prague (?) after 1624
Landscape with Roman Ruins
Oil on wood
1604-07
Ex Bautzen collection (as Hans Bol)
Dresden, Staatliche Kunstsammlungen, Gemäldegalerie Alte Meister, inv. no. 82/08

Zwollo attributed this painting to Pieter Stevens, noting that the vista of Rome in the background probably was not based on his own observation. She suggested that Stevens copied a view by Jan Bruegel

the Elder, who was in Prague briefly in 1604, at the imperial residence, and had a sizeable influence on Stevens and other Rudolfine landscape painters. Bruegel brought with him drawings, which Aegidius Sadeler had reproduced as prints, that included motifs of ancient ruins and Italian architecture. Stevens, who would have had access to the drawings, borrowed the background motif for his painting from Bruegel's *View of Rome* of 1594 (Darmstadt, Hessisches Landesmuseum). Jan Bruegel was also an influence, however, in the spatial construction and the rendering of light and atmosphere. A comparison with the *Flight Into Egypt* (untraced),

painted before 1594, shows that Stevens's style of landscape painting underwent a marked transformation during the first decade of the sixteenth century.

Essen and Vienna 1988, cat. no. 167.

Zwollo 1982, pp. 101-108, ill. 7, 12; Kaufmann 1988, p. 282, cat. and ill. no. 21.9; Essen and Vienna 1988, cat. no. 167.

E.F.

I.104

Pieter Stevens
Landscape with a Watermill
Oil on canvas
Ca. 1610
? From the collections of Rudolf II, Viennese inventory H, 1619, no. 208; Mechel, 174, no.3 (as Coninxloo); Depot (V, no. 24) inv. no. 2622 (as Valckenborch – art of); 1894 back to Prague as anonymous work
Prague, Sbírky Pražského hradu, inv. no. O 292 •

An Zwollo has linked this painting with an entry in Viennese inventory H dating

from 1619, where it is recorded as a work by Stevens. The *Landscape with Mill* occupies a significant place in the painter's work, not only because of its unusually large dimensions but also because of the conspicuous influence of the work of Roeland Savery, who was Stevens's new colleague at the imperial court. Rays of light passing over dramatic storm clouds into the branches of trees shine through to the back of the scene to create a deep space and evoke the atmosphere of the place. The apparent vibration of the light and the air in the foliage, attained by the contrast of light and shadow and executed with very delicate brushwork, could

not have been achieved unless Stevens had made a thorough study of Savery's drawings and pictures, which originated in connection with his journey to the Alps. This makes the dating of the picture at around 1610 the more probable.

Essen and Vienna 1988, cat. no. 170; Vienna 1996, cat. no. 23.

Neumann 1966, cat. no. 61; Zwollo 1968, p. 165, ill. 222; Kaufmann 1988, cat. no. 21.16.

E.F.

I.105

Hans Christoph Schürer
In Prague between 1609 and 1612
An Ill-Matched Couple
Drawing in pen-and-ink in brown tone, grey, black, and yellow-grey wash, underdrawing in red ochre
Below the cloth, the dedication: *Dieses hab ich dem Ehrenvesten unndt kunstreichen Nicolao Siertlebenn aus gutter gunst unndt freundtschaft gemacht. Zu gutter meiner Erinnerung gescheben In Prag d. 28. September Anno 1612. Hans Christoph Schurer f. 1612*
Ex Feldmann collection, Brno

In 1609 Schürer asked the Electress of Saxony, Hedvika, to intercede with her husband on his behalf for a stipend to train as a painter with Hans von Aachen at the imperial court in Prague. After Aachen's death in 1615, Schürer probably left Prague for Italy, with letters of introduction to the courts in Florence and Mantua from the Elector of Saxony. This is his only signed and dated drawing, and it demonstrates his devotion to Aachen's models, both in composition and technique. It resembles Aachen's late studies, composed of short lines and sharp breaks, although without his skilful drawing and use of foreshortening. Schürer became a

skilled painter in Aachen's workshop, and the Brno drawing is evidence for the ascription to him of a painting of the same composition.

Fučíková 1967, p. 130.

Schade, W., *Dresdner Zeichnungen 1550-1650: Inventionen sächsischer Künstler in europäischen Sammlungen*, Dresden: Kupferstichkabinett der Staatlichen Kunstsammlungen, 1969, p. 87; Fučíková 1979, p. 503, ill. 16; Fučíková 1966, ill.

E.F.

I.106

Paulus van Vianen
Paulus van Vianen Painting Hans von Aachen in the Presence of Adriaen de Vries
Oil on copper
d. 10 cm
After 1596
Purchased by Willem Vincent van Wittenhorst in 1654 and inherited by the Fürstenbergs in 1738
Münster, Westfälisches Landesmuseum für Kunst und Geschichte, inv. no. 42 (loan from private collection)

As already noted by An der Heiden and Kaufmann, this miniature is not by Hans

von Aachen. It is painted with a quite different technique and does not have the qualities normally associated with von Aachen's portraits. An der Heiden considers the work to be van Vianen's and regards it as a *Freundschaftsbild* depicting the three artists. The sculptor, Adriaen de Vries, is standing behind the easel, the painter, Hans von Aachen, is gazing out of the picture, and the goldsmith must be the man making the portrait. Von Aachen appears a lot younger than in Jan Sanraedam's engraving of 1601. De Vries and van Vianen also do not look the age they were in 1603, when van Vianen arrived in Prague. However, all three may have met

up in Bavaria, as from 1596 van Vianen is known to have been working in Munich, where in that same year von Aachen was married and where de Vries was working on the fountains of Augsburg.

Utrecht 1984-1985.

An der Heiden 1970, p. 225, ill. no. 195, for all earlier literature; Kaufmann 1988, cat. no. 23.1.

E.F.

I.107

Paulus van Vianen
The Invasion of Prague 15 February 1611
Oil on panel
24 × 34 cm
1611
From the collection of Willem Vincent van Wittenhorst, 1653, Gansoyen; inherited by the Fürstenbergs in 1738
Münster, Westfälisches Landesmuseum für Kunst und Geschichte, inv. no. 819
LG
(loan from private collection).

Willem Vincent van Wittenhorst purchased this painting in 1653, and it was

registered in his collection's inventory under no. CXXII as 'een cleyn stuckie van Paulus van Vianen, waer seer aerdig uutbelt is het inneemen van Praga met uutermating schoone teyckening ... ' (a small piece by Paulus van Vianen which is an extremely nice drawing depicting the capture of Prague). An engraving depicting the Passau troops' invasion of Malá Strana (Lesser Town) on 15 February 1611 shows that that the artist here must have been standing on what is today the bottom corner of Malostranské square, where the bell tower of the church of St Nicholas now stands, looking across the street towards Charles Bridge. It is the ex-

act opposite view to that captured by Savery (cat. no. I.70), who stood on the other side of the square and looked towards what was then the church of St Wenceslas. The brushwork in Savery's painting is different from that of the Münster painting, and its authorship as registered in the 1658 inventory of Wittenshorst's collection can therefore be accepted.

Ter Molen 1984, II, 79, cat. no. 401, for earlier literature; this painting, believed to be the work of van Vianen's son Paul, depicted the Swedish occupation of Prague.

E.F.

I.108

Hans Vredeman de Vries and Dirk de Quade van Ravesteyn
Palace Architecture with Musicians
Oil on canvas
135 × 174
Signed and dated on the plate in the middle of the column: HANS (lig) VREDEMAN (lig) VRIESE INV. 1596
1596
From the collection of Rudolf II; imperial collection in Vienna
Vienna, Kunsthistorisches Museum, Gemäldegalerie, inv. no. 2 336

Hans Vredeman de Vries painted this pic-

ture for the Emperor in Prague, together with two other Viennese paintings, which portray palace architecture with aristocratic visitors and people out strolling (cat. no. I.109). This occurred during a period of effective collaboration with his son Paul and with another Rudolfine painter, Dirk de Quade van Ravesteyn, to whom he entrusted the addition of figural pageantry to complete the pictures. The main task for the Vredemanns in Prague was to decorate the Emperor's palace, provide mural paintings and other more detailed architectural projects. But Rudolf II also admired their wall pictures, in which they gave vent to their fantasies

and created some remarkable historicizing architecture, which stood beyond time and space. It is interesting that this new genre in painting was not limited to the confines of Prague Castle, and that in the years that immediately followed, pictures of architecture can likewise be found in the works of other Prague town painters.

Essen and Vienna 1988, cat. no. 174.

Iwanoyko 1963, p. 189; Schneede 1967, p. 161; Fučíková 1979, pp. 493–94; Ehremann 1979, p. 24.
E.F.

I.109
Hans Vredeman de Vries
Palace Architecture with Strollers
Oil on canvas
137 × 174 cm
HANS (lig.) VREDEMAN (lig.) VRIESE
INV./ PAVL (lig.) VREDEMAN (lig.)
FEC. 1596 (to the left on the steps)
1596
Vienna, Kunsthistorisches Museum,
Gemäldegalerie, inv. no. 2335

E.F.

I.110
Paul Vredeman de Vries
Interior of a Gothic Church
Oil on canvas
108.5 × 115
Signed to the left on the plinth of a pillar:
PAVLUS FREDEMAN FRISE
? 1597–98
? From the collection of Rudolf II; impe-
rial collection in Vienna
Vienna, Kunsthistorisches Museum,
Gemäldegalerie, inv. no. 7 661

Comparison with the picture of the same
subject signed and dated by Hans and
from the same period (Wörlitz, Museum
Gotisches Haus), suggests that Paul's
paintings fall a long way short of his father's work. Hans was the leading personality in their studio; he painted church interiors and palace courtyards, managing
convincingly to create the illusion of a
deep space. He created well thought-out
compositions, not too crammed with details, out of the confusion of arcades and
open galleries. In the Wörlitz picture
Hans used only a few inconspicuous figures walking about the church in order to
emphasize the celestial character of perfect architecture. In the Viennese picture
by his son Paul the Gothic church is too
high, and there are a great number of
characters who disturb the dignity and
loftiness of the cathedral space. It was not
until Paul became independent and substituted fantastic architecture with natural-looking palace courtyards that he
found his own expression and style.

Essen and Vienna 1988, cat. no. 175.

Kaufmann 1988, cat. no. 25.7.

E.F.

I.111
Paul Vredeman de Vries
Esther Before Ahasuerus
Oil on wood
1612
Bratislava, Slovenská národná galéria,
inv. no. o 924

This painting was executed ten years after
Vries' stay in Prague, when he was already
a burgher in Amsterdam. In contrast to
his independent compositions executed
while he was still at the imperial court, in
which the architecture is the dominant element and the staffage acts somewhat independently, this work links both components in a harmonious whole. The meeting of Ahasuerus and Esther is confined
to the first picture plane, and the subtle
arcade architecture emphasizes the deep
space of the courtyard. The scene repeats
with a few variations the staffage in the
drawing of Solomon and the Queen of
Sheba by Hans Vredeman of Bremen
(1596). Vries replaced the coulisse-like architecture with a spacious, airy courtyard,
however. The central area, with a green
bower and a fountain, may be the trompe-
l'oeuil wall painting mentioned by van
Mander on the second floor of the Long
Wing, i.e., in the gallery at the entrance to
the Emperor's apartment. The staffage is
perhaps the work of Pieter Isaacs, who
was living in Amsterdam during this period.

Jaromír Neumann, *Rudolfinská Praha*,
Prague, 1984, p. 77, ill. 70.

E.F.

Introduction to Sculpture section

ELIŠKA FUČÍKOVÁ

Rudolf II had the New (i.e., Spanish) Hall built to house his collection of sculptures; when completed, the hall was twice as large as the imperial gallery. Since the court sculptors could hardly have been expected to fill its space with their works alone, the Emperor certainly anticipated installing there his collection of Classical sculptures, as well as the works of Giambologna and other sculptors he had acquired as purchases or gifts and stored in the Kunstkammer. He also wanted to have works created in the Prague Castle studios, where sculptors could avail themselves of the well-equipped foundry. Bringing capable sculptors to Prague was not easy, however. Hans Mont, who had worked at the court of Maxmilián II in Vienna, damaged one eye shortly after coming to Prague and was evidently unable to satisfy the Emperor's desire for a monumental sculpture. He did create a large bronze (*Venus and Adonis*, now at Drotningholm Castle) and possibly a few small sculptures. He then decided to leave the imperial services. During the initial stages of his patronage, Rudolf was apparently trying to engineer the acquisition of larger-than-life-size sculptures for Prague Castle and its ceremonial halls. Thus, when Giambologna's talented successor Adriaen de Vries appeared in Prague after Mont's departure, he began working on two monumental sculptural groups, one of the figures for which was *Psyche*, and, perhaps, other bronze sculptures which graced the halls of the Royal Summer Palace until the New Hall was completed. It seems that the Emperor altered the character of his commissions, reflecting a change of interest when de Vries settled in Prague. Although de Vries's portrait of Rudolf is monumental in character, and its dimensions correspond to the representative busts of the time, it was not placed on show in the Audience Hall, but in the Kunstkammer, where it could be admired only by a few privileged visitors. The

same applied to the reliefs showing Rudolf introducing art into Bohemia or the allegory of the Turkish Wars. As the *Kunstkammer* Inventory from 1607–11 makes clear, it contained other works by de Vries, for example, *Imperium triumphante* and sculptures of horses. The fact that his sculptures were small in size allowed them to be placed alongside the works of sculptors whose services Rudolf II was unable to secure, but whom he 'adopted as his own'. In addition to Giambologna, this included Hubert Gerhardt and other masters. These artists were generally pupils of Giambologna who based their work on his compositions and chose similar themes. This suggests that the comparison of artistic approaches must have been a subject of fascination for the Emperor.

The completion of the New Hall with its eleven tall niches rekindled the Emperor's interest in monumental sculpture. The new material chosen for the decoration of the hall, stucco, required specialists familiar with the technique. De Vries, undoubtedly well versed in stucco work, evidently wished to remain faithful to bronze or was busy with other commissions. The work of Giovanni Battista Quadri, who was called upon to supervise the relief ornamentation of the walls, much of which survives, and the monumental sculptures designed for the niches complemented that of de Vries. One cannot rule out the possibility that they may have worked together before they settled in Prague.

De Vries and Quadri remained in imperial service even after the death of Rudolf II, although they carried out commissions for other patrons. De Vries continued to use the Castle foundry, producing large works for Danish and German customers. His last monumental sculpture was crafted for Prague, although it was installed in the gardens of Wallenstein Palace and not at Prague Castle. While de Vries lived in Prague until his death in 1626 and created sculptures whose style could have influenced emerging early Baroque sculpture in the Czech lands in fundamental ways, he was unable to find a worthy successor there.

I.112
Hubert Gerhard
Amsterdam ca. 1540–Munich ca. 1622
Hercules, Deianeira and Nessus
Bronze, red-brown lacquer
58 cm
Ca. 1602
Kunstkammer of Emperor Rudolf II, inventory of 1607–11, no. 1890; Prague 1619; in the imperial *Schatzkammer* after 1750
Vienna, Kunsthistorisches Museum, Kunstkammer, inv. no. 5 979

This group shows Hercules rescuing his wife, Deianeira, from the centaur, Nessus,

who has abducted her. Part of Rudolf II's collection, it had probably been acquired by the Emperor about 1602 when he was considering whether to invite Hubert Gerhard to join the artists in the court in Prague. In this work, Gerhard takes up the themes of two works by Giambologna, his *Hercules Fighting with the Centaur* and his *Rape of a Sabine Woman*. Compared with the latter, Gerhard's work exhibits a certain stiffness in the figures and 'frontality' in the composition.

Essen and Vienna 1988, cat. no. 71 (with earlier literature).

Weihrauch 1967, pp. 351 and 359; Larsson 1982, pp. 227ff.

L.O.L.

I.113
Hubert Gerhard
Amsterdam 1550–Munich ca. 1622
Mars, Venus and Cupid
Bronze; Amor and Mars' right foot are cast separately, red-brown smoke glaze
41.4 cm
Ca. 1605
Matthias Inventory of 1619 (Köhler 1906/07, p. XV, no. 13); imperial *Schatzkammer* in 1750; after 1871 in Ambras.
Vienna, Kunsthistorisches Museum, Kunstkammer, inv. no. 5848

This sculpture clearly owes its existence to

sculptures *Theseus and Helena* by Vincenzo de Rossi in Florence or *Meleager and Atalanta* by Moschino now in the Nelson Gallery in Kansas City. Hubert Gerhard may well have seen this kind of work during his time in Florence where he is known to have stayed for a while before moving to Augsburg (Fock 1980, p. 327). But this work of Gerhard's, now held in Vienna, surpasses any such precursors in its complexity and beauty of movement and would seem more to be pointing forwards to the work of Bartholomeus Spranger (as Ilg has already shown). It would not be rash to assume from the style of this piece that Gerhard was also acquainted with the

refined courtly style of art at the court in Prague. It seems therefore likely that this item was made in 1605 for the Emperor Rudolf II through the good offices of the Archduke Maximilian III, in whose service Gerhard was employed at the time.

Essen and Vienna 1988, cat. no. 513

Leithe-Jasper 1986, pp. 26–66; Leithe-Jasper 1996, pp. 254–57, no. 74

M.L.J.

I.114
Giambologna
Douai 1529–Florence 1608
Mars
Bronze, black lacquer
39.5 cm
Ca. 1585
? Rudolf II; Christina (1652);
Drottningholm 1777, transferred into the
Nationalmuseum in 1865
Stockholm, Nationalmuseum, inv. no. 334

Mars was one of Giambologna's most frequently reproduced figures, but it is mentioned neither in Markus Zeh's list (1611) nor in Baldinucci's (1688). The oldest known example went in 1587 as a gift from the artist into the *Kunstkammer* of the young Elector Christian II in Dresden. Today it is in private ownership. Emperor Rudolf II probably also owned a reproduction of this figure. The version of *Mars* shown here, lively and precise, is one of the best. Indeed, its high quality suggests that it may well have been in the collection of Rudolf II before it went as spoils of war to Stockholm.

Stockholm 1984, cat. no. 6; Essen and Vienna 1988, cat. no. 54.

Avery 1987, p. 137; Larsson 1992, pp. 30ff.

L.O.L.

I.115
Giambologna
Douai 1529–Florence 1608
Mercury in Flight
Bronze, light brown patina, traces of
brown lacquer
62.7 cm
On the hat: *IB*
Ca. 1587
Kunstkammer of Emperor Rudolf II,
inventory of 1607–11, no. 1970
Vienna, Kunsthistorisches Museum,
Kunstkammer, inv. no. 5 898

Mercury in Flight must be Giambologna's best-known work. There are various versions of it in a variety of sizes, of which five known small-scale versions have fairly been attributed to Giambologna. Besides the statuette on show here, which was once in Rudolf II's own collection, there is a another example in Bologna (probably the oldest) and there are further examples in Naples, Florence and Dresden. The statue of *Mercury* in Dresden, which is documented there since 1587, was given by the artist to the Elector as a present. Among other surviving statues of *Mercury* by Giambologna, the one in Vienna seems most closely related to this one. It is not impossible that the artist also gave a statue of to Emperor Rudolf at much the same time.

His ennoblement in 1588 could have been the Emperor's appreciative response.

Florence 1980, cat. no. 676; Essen and Vienna 1988, cat. no. 48 (with earlier literature).

Dhanens 1956, pp. 125ff.; Avery 1987, p. 123, no. 73; Larsson 1984, pp. 117ff.

L.O.L.

I.116
Hans Mont
Mars and Venus
Marble (part of the left hand of Venus
and left hand of Mars are later additions)
Before 1580
Prague, Národní galerie v Praze,
inv. no. P 5820

The small-scale sculptural group *Mars and Venus* was first published by K. Chytil, who compared it to analogous compositions in paintings by B. Spranger and classified the work as belonging to the sphere of influence of Adriaen de Vries. J. Neumann raised doubts about de Vries's authorship by pointing out that not a single work in stone by this sculptor exists today. L. O. Larsson attributes the sculpture to Spranger's friend and collaborator Hans Mont, who worked in marble and alabaster. He compares it with the bronze group *Venus and Adonis*, which Mont created in Prague (Stockholm, Nationalmuseum) and which was part of Rudolf II's collection. There are many similarities to Spranger's works, for example, Salamakis from the painting *Salamakis and Hermaphrodite* (Vienna, Kunsthistorisches Museum). The spatial development of the group and the anatomical construction of the figures also clearly show the artistic influence of Mont's Florentine teacher, Giambologna, who recommended both Mont and Spranger to the Viennese imperial court in 1575.

Essen and Vienna 1988, cat. no. 73.

Neumann 1965, p. 72; Larsson 1967, pp. 4, 8; Larsson 1982, p. 217.

J.Ch.

I.117
Hans Mont
Mars and Venus
Bronze
37 cm
1575–80
Germany, private collection

This statue is the cast for some marble figural work by Hans Mont, carried out at the time when the left arms of Venus and Mars were still intact, in other words, before being attached. The inventory of the Nostitz collection provides no information about when the damage occurred nor when the statue was restored. It seems, however, that the addition is Baroque. Larsson believes that the bronze cast is old and could have arisen from as early as the Rudolfine period. Mont's sculptures became rare and unattainable when the sculptor left Prague. Documents can be found in the inventories of the *Kunstkammer* from 1607 to 1611, showing that some works were cast in another material (e.g., no. 767: 'one large Egyptian idol in silver, cast after a white marble of the Roman type, which also stands in the *Kunstkammer*'). The cast is important because it provided an unspoilt model for a work by Mont. The mounting for Venus' head is the original and the hands behind the backs of the two figures are particularly beautiful.

E.F.

I.118
Giovanni Battista Quadri
The Adoration of the Magi
Stucco with polychrome
167 × 118 cm
Before 1611
Brandýs nad Labem, in the chapel of the chateau; since 1965 on long-term loan to the Picture Gallery of Prague Castle, inv. no. P290

The original polychrome had been concealed until in 1965–66 the relief was restored, which brought out even more clearly the exceptionally captivating sculptural work that had led scholars to attribute the work to Adrian de Vries. Data in the inventory of the *Kunstkammer* from 1607 to 1611 permitted the sculptor at the imperial court, Giovanni Battista Quadri, to be identified. Quadri was a specialist in using stucco and oven-fired clay. This altarpiece was made as early as 1611. Quadri assuredly knew the work of de Vries, who in 1601 came to live in Prague. Quadri began to work at Brixen with stucco and clay under the leadership of Reichle. When the court was considering inviting an expert to carry out stucco decorations to the Nový Sál (New Hall), it may have been de Vries who recommended Quadri as the expert in this technique. A handwritten record of Quadri's work for the Emperor in the year 1611 lists other lifesize sculptures for the alcoves of Nový Sál and sculptural work for the *Kunstkammer*.

Essen and Vienna 1988, p. 164, cat. no. 70 (but the item was not displayed), for older relevant literature; Fučíková 1991, pp. 28–34

E.F.

I.119
Adriaen de Vries
Den Haag ca. 1545–Prag 1626
Faun and Nymph (*Venus ?*)
Bronze, yellow-brown patina shining through: section of mirror above the handle broken off; Pedestal: wood
Nymph: Height: 34.6 cm; Faun: Height: 48.2 cm
Before 1588
Italy, perhaps Turin
Probably bought by Giovanni Maria Nosseni during his stay in Italy in 1588. It went in 1622 from his estate to the Dresden *Kunstkammer*. Listed in the 1640 Inventory of the *Kunstkammer* under Bl. 502

Dresden, Grünes Gewölbe, inv. nos IX 20 and IX 36

This *Faun and Nymph* is among the most important early works by the Netherlandish artist Adriaen de Vries. With almost playful ease, he depicts the handsome youth's insistent attempts – charming and unmistakably erotic – to win Venus' favour. The faun, in an elegantly taut, dance-like pose seems almost weightless despite its physicality, which itself reflects Mannerist notions of 'figura serpentinata.' The Faun and Venus are connected almost magically through mime and gesture. In this all-round sculpture de Vries has created a masterly depiction of the eternal game of the two sexes with the delicate balance between the licentious seducer and the virtuous woman.

Berlin 1995, cat. no. 152

Baltische Studien 1834, II.2, p. 136; Holzhausen 1933, pp. 77–79; Larsson 1967, pp. 13f.; Meine-Schawe 1992, p. 25; Berlin 1995, exh. cat., cat. nos 152, 116 and p. 623

J.K.

See fig. 1.90

I.120
Adrian de Vries
Den Haag 1545–Prague 1626
Apollo
Bronze
47.3 cm
Ca. 1594–96
Bequeathed by G. Blumenthal in 1941
New York, Metropolitan Museum of Art, inv. no. 41.190.534

This statuette is stylistically similar to de Vries's Augsburg works and his *Dancing Faun* (Dresden), which means that it must have been made by 1602–3 at the latest. Jan Müller made an engraving of a very similar *Apollo*, saying it was after de Vries, which confirms that this piece is indeed de Vries's work. Jan Müller made several engravings after de Vries, which can be dated around 1594–96. The *Apollo* statuette goes back to the *Apollo Belvedere*. However, de Vries has altered the movement of the figure, changing the original *contrapposto* into a *figura serpentinata*. What may be a sketch for this work is at present held in Gdansk. No more is known about the history of this statuette, nor are there any records of it in Rudolf II's collection.

Essen and Vienna 1988, cat. no. 66.

Larsson 1982, pp. 231ff.; DaCosta Kaufmann 1984, pp. 203ff.

L.O.L.

I.121
Antonio Susini
Fl. in Florence 1580-1624
Nessus and Deianeira
Bronze, light brown natural patina and red-brown varnished patina
42.4 cm
Ca. 1600
Probably from the *Kunstkammer* of the Emperor Rudolf II, Inventory 1607-11 (no. 1882 or 1896); Matthias Inventory of 1619; imperial *Schatzkammer* Vienna in 1750; Ambras.
Vienna, Kunsthistorisches Museum, Kunstkammer, inv. no. 5847

Records show that Giambologna was working on this theme after 1575. Baldinucci's life of Giambologna (1688) reports that Antonio Susini made a bronze copy of one of Giambologna's works. Giambologna admired this copy so much that he sent Pietro Tacca to Susini to buy it for 200 scudi. But all this did was to encourage Susini to make an increasing number of replicas which he then sold for a high price. The Emperor Rudolf II owned several works of this kind of which at least one or the other may have come to the court in Prague as a present from the Medici family. The *Kunstkammer* Inventory of 1607-11 (Bauer-Haupt 1976, nos 1734, 1882, 1896) lists one example on silver: 'Den Centaurus mit dem weiblin and two examples in bronze: Item ein Centaurus, welcher ein weiblein rubirt und empfiert, von bronzo'. It is highly likely that the piece exhibited here is one of those listed in the inventory.

Essen and Vienna 1988, cat. no. 522; Vienna 1978–79, pp. 147-49 and pp. 150-59, nos 63–66

Leithe-Jasper 1986, pp. 206–09, no. 52

M.L.J.

I.122
Adriaen de Vries
Den Haag ca. 1545–Prague 1626
Rudolf II
Bronze; grey-brown natural patina
112 cm
signed: ADRIANVS FRIES HAGIEN FECIT 1603; inscribed on the armrests: RVD:II.ROM:IMP.CAES:AVG:/AET:SVAE LI.ANNO 1603
1603
Kunstkammer of the Emperor Rudolf II, Inventory of 1607-11, no. 1975; plundered from Prague in 1648 by Swedish militia; Queen Christina of Sweden, Inventory of 1652, no. 6; reacquired in 1803 from Sweden for the imperial collections in Vienna. Vienna, Kunsthistorisches Museum, Kunstkammer, inv. no. 5506

In 1600 the Emperor Rudolf II acquired a portrait bust of the Emperor Karl V by Leone Leoni, now held in Vienna. He had the court sculptor model this bust of himself as Emperor on that of Karl V, whom he admired so much. There are considerable similarities between the two portraits, but in its realization de Vries's work is far superior. The combination of heroic expression and psychological subtlety is unique. With the slight turn of the body and the somewhat raised glance of the Emperor this portrait expresses a degree of drama, pathos and majesty that far outstrips anything that sculpture had seen to date and which is already distinctly baroque in its aspect. This is reinforced by the virtuosic differentiation of detail and a painterly vibrato of surface values which add significantly to the sheer dynamism of the overall effect.

Essen and Vienna 1988, cat. no. 57

Larsson 1963, pp. 80–93; Larsson 1967, pp. 36–38 and p. 123

M.L.J.

I.123
Adriaen de Vries
Den Haag 1545–Prague 1626
Hercules, Nessus and Deianeira
Bronze, natural patina
82 × 50 × 37 cm
Ca. 1603
Probably from the *Kunstkammer* of Emperor Rudolf II
Paris, Musée du Louvre, Département des Objets d'Art, inv. no. OA 5 424

This sculpture depicts Hercules rescuing his wife, Deianeira, from the centaur Nessus. The sculpture on this theme, listed in the inventory of Rudolf II's *Kunstkammer*, is most probably the one on show here. In this work Adrian de Vries is referring to similar abduction scenes by Giambologna. The immediate inspiration for the work may have been the arrival in the imperial collection of Hubert Gerhard's bronze statuette on the same theme (see cat. no. 1/112). Adrian de Vries may well have wanted to outshine Gerhard with an even more virtuoso treatment of the theme in order to discourage the Emperor from inviting his rival to Prague. Several examples of this work are known, which is unusual for de Vries. They all seem to have been made in the nineteenth century.
Weihrauch 1967, pp. 358ff.; Zimmermann 1969, pp. 55ff.; Larsson 1982, pp. 227ff.; Larsson 1988, 1st edn, pp. 135, 155ff.

L.O.L.

I.124
Adriaen de Vries
Den Haag 1545–Prague 1626
Christian II
Bronze, dark brown lacquer
95.6 cm
ADRIANUS FRIES HAGENSIS FECIT
1603
1603
Gift from the Emperor to Christian II
Dresden, Skulptursammlung, inv. no. H 4 1/4

This portrait of Christian II and de Vries's busts of the Emperor are among the most impressive sculpted portraits from around 1600. Like the large bust of *Rudolf II* that Adrian de Vries had completed not long before, this piece is also carried by allegorical figures. Their gestures and the bundle of arrows below the coat of arms show that they embody the virtue Concordia. The reference is to the concord between the Emperor and the Elector Christian II, who is wearing a medallion with a bust of Rudolf on his chest. This sculpture is a good example of the important role that artworks could play at the time in politics and diplomacy. This flattering portrait was a gift to Christian from the Emperor, who was more than willing to invest whatever costs and effort were necessary to win the loyalty of the young Elector.

Dresden 1992, cat. no. 29; Berlin 1995, cat. no. 153.

Larsson 1967, pp. 38ff.; Larsson 1988, pp. 135ff.

L.O.L.

I.125
Adriaen de Vries
The Hague 1545–Prague 1626
The Christ from Zurawina
Bronze, black-brown lacquer
125 cm
ADRIANUS FRIES HAGIENSIS FECIT
1604
1604
From the tombstone of Adam Hannewald in Rothsürben in Silesia; transferred to the National Museum in Warsaw after the Second World War
Warsaw, Muzeum Narodowe w Warszawie, inv. no. 193 008

Until after the Second World War, this figure of Christ was in place on the marble tombstone of the imperial councillor Adam Hannewald in the parish church of Rothsürben in Silesia. Christ's calm pose and face marked with grief lend this sculpture a meditative quality rarely found elsewhere in de Vries's work. This sculpture was one of the few commissions that de Vries carried out during Rudolf II's lifetime for other patrons after his installation as court sculptor in Prague.

Larsson 1967, pp. 46–47; 123, no. 37.

L.O.L.

I.126
Adriaen de Vries
Den Haag 1545–Prague 1626
Allegeory of the Turkish Wars
Bronze
71 × 88.5 cm
ADRIANUS FRIES HAGENSIS FECIT
Ca. 1603
Kunstkammer of Emperor Rudolf II, inventory of 1607–11, no. 1982; Prague 1619, 1648; Christina 1652; P. Suther, reacquired for the imperial collection in 1803
Vienna, Kunsthistorisches Museum, Kunstkammer, inv. no. 5 474

This relief is listed in the Inventory of Rudolf II's *Kunstkammer* as an 'invention, die ungerische krieg und *impresa* bedeuttend'. Its theme is the war against the Turks that broke out in 1593 in Hungary and Transylvania. The scene in the left foreground shows the liberation of Hungary with specific reference to the recapture of Esztergom in 1595. The lion fighting the dragon and the eagle with the snake in its claws symbolize the fight of Good against Evil. The two river-gods in the foreground personify the Danube and the Save, representing Hungary as the theatre of war. The scene in the left background is a symbolical illustration of the recapture of the fortress of Raab, with the female figure as a symbol of Constantia, who has vanquished Fortuna, the goddess of good fortune. The capricorn, the monogram *R II* and the star in the sky all show that the Emperor is pursuing his campaign in the name of the Lord.

Vienna 1987, cat. no. IV:1; Essen and Vienna 1988, cat. no. 58.

Larsson 1967, pp. 39ff.; Ludwig 1978, pp. 43ff.; Kaufmann 1978, pp. 63ff.; Galavics 1986, pp. 27ff.

L.O.L.

I.127
Adriaen de Vries
Den Haag 1545–Prague 1626
Pacing Horse
Bronze, greenish natural patina
94 cm
ADRIANUS FRIES HAGENSIS FECIT
1607
1607
Kunstkammer of Emperor Rudolf II, inventory of 1607–11, no. 1976; Prague 1619, 1621; Christina 1652; Drottningholm 1726, 1744, 1777, 1867
Stockholm, Nationalmuseum, Royal Castle's collections, inv. no. Drottningholm 64

Bronze statues of horses were much in vogue during the sixteenth and seventeenth centuries. There seems to have been a virtual production line in Giambologna's workshop. Three signed horse sculptures by Adriaen de Vries are known and these are quite different in size and type from the work coming from the Giambologna workshop. This one, dated 1607, is the earliest and is probably the one referred to in the 1607–11 Inventory of the *Kunstkammer* (no. 1976) as 'so über die anderthalb Ellen hoch' (over one and a half ells high). This particular horse is so very different from Giambologna's horse statues and from the well-known horse sculptures from Antiquity that one wonders whether this might not in fact be the portrait of a horse from the Emperor's own famous stable.

Stockholm 1966, cat. no. 1328; Stockholm 1984, cat. no. 40; Essen and Vienna 1988, cat. no. 63.

Larsson 1967, pp. 52ff.; Larsson 1992, pp. 78ff.

L.O.L.

I.128
Adriaen de Vries
Pacing Horse
Bronze, original black lacquer and brown patina
54 cm
ADRIANVS FRIES HAGIENSIS FECIT
1610
1610
Prague, Národní galerie v Praze, inv. no. P 4605

The composition of this small sculpture is based on the monumental equestrian monument to the Tuscan grand duke Cosimo I de' Medici (Florence, Piazza della Signoria), created in 1587–93 by Giambologna. One source of inspiration for Giambologna's horse figure was the Classical sculptures preserved in Italy (the equestrian statue of *Marcus Aurelius* on the Capitoline in Rome, the four Hellenic horses on the façade of St Mark's Basilica in Venice). Of all Giambologna's works, the *Pacing Horse* most closely resembles the work in the Victoria and Albert Museum in London (height 23.5 cm, ill. on p. 174 in the Giambologna catalogue, 1973), dated between 1580 and 1590, and the *Walking Horse* of Queen Elisabeth II (height 24.2 cm; ill. on p. 175). Among de Vries's works, the Prague example bears the greatest formal similarity to the signed and dated horse from 1607 (Stockholm, Nationalmuseum, ill. 63 in exh. cat. *Prag um 1600*), which is larger (height 94 cm). The Prague sculpture, however, surpasses the examples above in its sculptural treatment, which is characteristically finer, with softer modelling that reacts to light and shadow, and a descriptive accuracy in the anatomical details such as veins, tendons and so on.

Larsson 1967, pp. 52–53, 122, no. 52.

J.Ch.

I.129
Adriaen de Vries
Den Haag 1545–Prague 1626
Imperium Triumphant
Bronze
77.3 cm
ADRIANUS FRIES FE 1610
1610
Kunstkammer of Emperor Rudolf II, inventory of 1607–11; ? Christina 1652; Blenheim Palace
Widener Collection
Washington, National Gallery of Art, inv. no. A-141

The 1607–11 inventory of Rudolf II's *Kun-* stkammer explains this allegorical sculpture. It shows 'imperium triumphante' – the victorious empire – and follows the conventions of the time with the superior figure of virtue (here representing the empire) treading the vanquished vice underfoot. Vice is characterized as *avaritia* – greed. Perhaps the implication was that the German nobility were not lending the Emperor the level of support he needed in his Turkish Wars. In any case, there is something moving about this monument to victory and personal success at a time when in reality Rudolf II had been stripped of his powers and no longer had any active part to play in the nation's poli- tics. This sculpture was for posterity, not for de Vries's contemporaries.

Essen and Vienna 1988, cat. no. 60; Amsterdam 1993, cat. no. 182.

Larsson 1967, pp. 51ff.; DaCosta Kaufmann 1978, pp. 63ff.; Larsson 1988 (1), pp. 134ff.

L.O.L.

I.130
Adriaen de Vries
Den Haag 1545–Prague 1626
The Smithy of Vulcan
Bronze, traces of gilding
47 × 56.5 cm (without frame)
ADRIANUS / FRIES / HAGIENSIS / BATAVVS. F 1611
1611
Acquired from private owner in 1969
Munich, Bayerisches Nationalmuseum, inv. no. 69/57

This relief shows Vulcan and four journey- men at work. In the background the naked Venus can be seen with a maidservant. The undulating, soft modelling of muscular forms releases a lively interplay of light and shadow, which is particularly typical of de Vries's late works and which here lends the scene a real sense of vitality. Nothing is known of the piece's prove- nance but its very fine craftsmanship would seem to indicate that it was at least intended for some princely *Kunstkammer*.

Berlin 1995, cat. no. 156.

Volk 1974, no. 34.

L.O.L.

I.131
Adriaen de Vries
Den Haag 1545–Prague 1626
Mercury
Bronze
45.5 cm (without base)
Ca. 1613–15
Found in a field near Schwanenstadt, Austria
Lambach, Stiftsbibliothek, without inv. no.

It would be impossible to imagine this statuette without its forerunner, *Mercury in Flight*, by Giambologna. And yet Adrian de Vries was still able to make this theme his own. Here Mercury is running rather than flying, rushing energetically towards some goal, whereas Giambologna's Mer- cury seems almost static in the perfection of his balance. The style of this work by de Vries dates it between 1613 and 1615. How the sculpture came to be in the field where it was supposedly found remains a mys- tery.

Giambologna 1978, cat. no. 35c; Stockholm 1984, cat. no. 39; Essen and Vienna 1988, cat. no. 67.

Larsson 1967, p. 57, 121, Cat. no. 28..

L.O.L.

I.132
Adriaen de Vries
Den Haag 1545–Prague 1626
Lazarus
Gilt bronze
65 cm
ADRIANUS FRIES HAGIENSIS BATAVVS FECIT. 1615
1615
Probably went to the king of Denmark in connection with de Vries's commission for the Neptune fountain for the castle at Frederiksborg; in the imperial *Kunstkam- mer* after 1749
Copenhagen, Statens Museum for Kunst, inv. no. 5493

This statuette recalls the parable of the rich man and Lazarus (Luke 16: 19ff.). The poor man, Lazarus, is sitting before the rich man's door and the dogs are licking his wounds. In this work de Vries demon- strates his virtuosity in his adaptation of various motifs from the *Laokoon*.

Copenhagen 1988, cat. no. 1121.

Weihrauch 1967, p. 358; Larsson 1967, p. 73; Olsen 1980, I, pp. 141ff.

L.O.L.

I.133
Adriaen de Vries
Den Haag 1545–Prague 1626
Hercules
Bronze
162.5 cm
1625–27
Prague, Celetná ulice (Celetná Street), 559/14; thence to the Muzeum Hlavního města Prahy (Museum of the City of Prague), inv. no. VP 400

This sculpture clearly does not belong to the group of statues on which de Vries worked for Albrecht von Wallenstein, but belongs to the sculptor's late work when he had changed from sculpting slim, Man- neristic figures to making stocky, muscu- lar statues, which might be thought to have more in common with a strapping country lad than with an elegant Olympian god. Larsson noted that while the statue was inspired by examples from antiquity (Rome, Palazzo dei Conserva- tori), it was not directly based on them. De Vries worked with a loose interpretation of the ancients' model, developing it in his own manner, and adding a striking sense of movement to its pose. The surface tex- ture, which looks as if it were modelled from wax, creates special light effects that serve to intensify the statue's expressive- ness. How the statue came to be in the house on Celetná Street has not been es- tablished, nor can it therefore be known who commissioned the work. The original verdigris would suggest that it was not one of the works that was left unfinished in de Vries's workshop at his death in 1626.

Prague 1898, cat. group G, no. 219.

Neumann 1966, pp. 286–87, cat. no. 74, for older literature; Larsson 1967, p. 97; Essen and Vienna 1988, cat. no. 69.

E.F.

Introduction to Drawings and Engravings section

ELIŠKA FUČÍKOVÁ

Drawing played an important role in the careers of all Rudolfine artists. Judging from period biographies, the childhood drawings of these future artists pointed to their developing talent and convinced their parents to entrust them to the care of capable teachers. Such stories, the accuracy of which should not be overestimated, at least tell us that mastery of drawing techniques was an important prerequisite for future painters, sculptors and masters of the decorative arts. The young novice learned to draw according to the models and designs of other masters, he acquired confidence and skill in various techniques and gradually developed his own characteristic style. To become a brilliant draughtsman was not easy, and not everyone was successful. The Rudolfine artists' juvenilia made it clear that they needed more than their native towns could provide.

As we know from their biographies, the majority of these artists chose to travel to Italy, to places which could provide them with sufficient inspiration and examples to complement their training and artistic development. They also learned how significant drawing was in the art theory of the time. It ceased being a mere workshop aid and, during the 1500s, began to receive the same recognition as painting or sculpture. Drawing was admired as the first, most immediate record of inspiration, and it provided first-hand testimony of the artist's creativity. Thus, in the sixteenth century, drawings also became a subject of interest on the part of collectors.

The moment they mastered the necessary techniques and found their own styles, Rudolfine artists began to use drawing for different purposes. Most important were quick sketches and studies recording spontaneous ideas or particular details. Sometimes these artists would draw models or in the open air; at other times, they were inspired by a well-known work which they transposed to reflect their own styles. Such drawings were chiefly intended as preparations for compositions which would later be developed into works in other media.

Drawing also played a role in portrait painting, serving either as a quick sketch of the subject or for the meticulous execution of a likeness on which a painting or engraving would be based; it might also have been given as a gift to the subject or set aside as a keepsake. This type of drawing as an independent work of art had its special charm and attraction for collectors and art lovers. They would create albums for which they would commission drawings, or they would acquire drawings often bearing not only the artist's signature but also the date and a dedication.

Prints were also designed for collectors which were crafted through the close cooperation of editors, draughtsmen and engravers. Aegidius Sadeler was one of those engravers who, apart from being able to reproduce perfectly all the stylistic finesse of foreign masters, worked following their own drawn designs. Prints also served as inspirational source material in the workshops of other masters and as information on what was happening in important cultural centres. Thanks to them, awareness of Rudolfine painting and sculpture spread all over Europe and beyond, to America and India, serving as a model for local artists.

All of the important themes in Rudolfine art appeared first in the medium of drawing. Drawings with religious themes were chiefly used as the basis for altar paintings. Certain Old and New Testament stories, however, provided attractive themes for works designed solely for collectors (Judith and Holofernes, Joseph and Potiphar's Wife, Bathsheba. Similarly, drawings with mythological themes would have been studies for murals and paintings or designs for prints. Of particular relevance were drawings with allegorical themes which equipped the Rudolfine artists with sufficient room to express their humanistic erudition and, above all, to comment on and celebrate human endeavour in the form of political and historical events. The Turkish Wars and the Emperor as protector of the Christian world against pagan onslaught provided the stimulus for a series of Hans von Aachen's drawings which he later transferred to canvas and which also served other artists as inspiration for reliefs and medals. With the arrival of Joris Hoefnagel into the imperial service, the art of miniature painting was afforded an exceptional position at the Rudolfine court, for the most part involving allegorical themes.

The Rudolfine landscape painters were also passionate draughtsmen. They did preparatory drawings for paintings and also drew designs for engravers. If, at the beginning, they composed their landscapes in their studios using motifs observed in nature but rendered according to certain customs of the period, they changed their habits with the arrival of goldsmith Paulus van Vianen, an excellent draughtsman who was not encumbered with the landscape-painting conventions of his time. His colleagues learned to make excursions into the countryside and record interesting scenery and fine details. They also discovered attractive motifs in the city, including panoramic views, secluded corners and the inhabitants themselves. Their sense of reality was also manifested in their drawings of animals; they had a great number of models at their disposal in the imperial menagerie, stables, aviaries and hunting enclosures.

Philipp van den Bossche, the imperial embroiderer, also regarded drawn designs as essential; he would mark future stitches in silk threads in fine strokes on his landscape drawings. His embroidery, demanding exceptional patience, predestined him for the huge task of creating the drawings for the monumental view of Prague of 1606.

Rudolfine sculptors were also capable draughtsmen whose studies served as preparation for sculptures or reliefs. Works in three dimensions required a different approach from that adopted by painters. Sculpted figures grew up from their bases, and a statue's stability relied upon a balanced design. Important for these artists was a clearly defined figural outline and an indication of the future shape through the use of light and shade.

In addition to prompting considerable interst on the part of collectors, the drawings of the Rudolfine masters also had major influence on the work of their contemporaries and on future generation. The distinctive style of Bartholomeus Spranger's drawings, reproduced in the prints of Hendrick Goltzius, Jan Muller, Aegidius Sadeler and others, influenced the style of many Dutch and German masters during the late sixteenth and early seventeenth centuries. Savery's landscape drawings, which even found their way into Rembrandt's collections, helped significantly to form the Dutch landscape tradition during the first few decades of the seventeenth century. For the Czech environment, it is undoubtedly worth noting the great influence of Rudolfine drawing on the development of the works of Václav Hollar and the inspiration it provided for Karel Škréta.

I.134
Hans von Aachen
Cologne 1551/52–Prague 1615
Part of the Frieze with the *History of Niobe*
Brown ink, brown wash, preliminary sketch in black chalk
18 × 42.4 cm
Signed on the left edge: *Johan ab Ach fecit Roma*
After 1575
Schwerin, Staatliches Museum, Kupferstichkabinett, inv. no. Hz 1 509

In this drawing too, von Aachen copied the chiaroscuro decoration that Polidoro da Caravaggio carried out at the Palazzo Milesi. This time he chose part of the frieze beneath the windows of the first floor, which depict the *History of Niobe*. This work is more commonplace and less assured than the drawing of *Romulus and Remus* and tends to lack clear definition. Only the two figures at the extreme right provide any sort of indication of von Aachen's drawing technique. It would seem, therefore, that the drawing is older than *Romulus and Remus*. At this stage von Aachen was merely a copyist, slavishly following the model with hard strokes of the brush. He learnt quickly, however, and was soon able to create his own individual compositions. The folio of *Romulus and Remus* is evidence of his progress towards mastery of the technique of drawing.

Fučíková 1971, pp. 120, 124, ill. 81.

E.F.

I.135
Hans von Aachen
Cologne 1551/52–Prague 1615
? *Romulus and Remus*
Drawing in brown ink, brown wash, preliminary underdrawing in black chalk
33.6 × 28 cm
Signed above right: *Johan ab Ach fecit / Roma*
After 1575
Schwerin, Staatliches Museum, Kupferstichkabinett, inv. no. Hz 1 507

After arriving at Rome, the young von Aachen began to dedicate himself in earnest to drawing, where he felt his greatest weakness to be. He found a teacher in Jan Speckaert, whose drawing technique he imitated and gradually transformed into a style of his own. But he also studied composition with other masters, above all, with Polidoro da Caravaggio, who was particularly popular at the time. In this drawing, von Aachen copied part of Polidoro's chiaroscuro decoration between the windows on the second floor of the Palazzo Milesi in Rome. The figures are seen from a sharply rising angle, which helps to capture their three-dimensionality. The drawing is indicative of von Aachen's style, although it lacks the rapidity and elegance of his later sketches. It was executed at the very beginning of the painter's stay in Italy and is, therefore, an important document of what he had learnt from his Flemish teacher in Cologne where he was born.

Fučíková 1971, pp. 120, 124; Fučíková 1986, p. 18, ill. 15.

E.F.

I.136
Hans von Aachen
Cologne 1551/52–Prague 1615
Judith and Holofernes
Drawing in brown ink, grey and brown wash
Ca. 1580
1963 Alfred Brod Gallery, ascribed to Bartolomeus Spranger; later in an art sale listed as a Netherlandish artist from the end of the sixteenth century; sold 1987 Washington, D.C., National Gallery of Art, Ailsa Mellon Bruce Fund, inv. no. 1987.31.1

In this secular drawing the influence of Jan Speckaert is still obvious, but the young von Aachen is already beginning to develop his own compositions. The drawings of the *Good Samaritan* and *Venus and Adonis* from the Louvre are the closest to the Washington sheet, not only in the style of drawing but also in their remarkably broad compositional development, and are influenced by Venetian art and particularly by the work of Veronese. Von Aachen returned to this subject several times. His sketch from the Florentine *Gabinetti disegni e stampe* (inv. no. S 7610 S, attributed to Spranger) and another variant (Salzburg, Stift St Peter, which Geissler attributed to von Aachen) are earlier than this drawing and they record the act of cutting off Holofernes' head. In the present folio Judith is shown just before this act. In later versions of this subject, the artist captured the moment when Judith was putting Holofernes' head into a sack, held by a servant. (See the picture in the Johnson Gallery, Middlebury College; two drawings in Dresden, Kupferstichkabinett, inv. nos C 1728 and C 1961–44; the drawing from Geiger's collection, Sotheby's auction 1920; the engraving by Aegidius Sadeler, Dom. Custos, Merlo 66.)

E.F.

I.137
Hans von Aachen
Cologne 1551/52–Prague 1615
Venus and Adonis
Pen drawing in brown ink, brown wash (verso: black chalk and pen drawing in brown ink)
1570–80
18.9 × 25.3 cm
Jabach Collection
Paris, Musée du Louvre, Département des Arts Graphiques, inv. no. 21 071

The work dates from the period when von Aachen was studying Speckaert's drawings in Rome, a time when he was improving his drawing skills and developing his own style. This composition attests to his stylistic development but lacks his later confidence in the depiction of physical forms. This drawing, with one or two changes, provided the basis for a later painting on the same theme (Cambridge, Mass., Busch-Reisinger Museum). It is the oldest surviving work which still contains elements of von Aachen's Flemish training and which is still nevertheless influenced by Venetian painting in its composition, and particularly in the connection of the figures with the landscape in the background. The drawing particularly highlights the influence on von Aachen of Venetian art, Veronese especially.

L. Demonts 1937–38, p. 90, cat. no. 445, ill. CXXXII; An der Heiden 1974, pp. 253–54, ill. 9 (picture).

E.F.

I.138
Hans von Aachen
Cologne 1551/52–Prague 1615
St Sebastian before Diocletian
Drawing in pen and brown ink, underdrawing in black and red ruddle, brown wash, white glaze on blue-green paper
Ca. 1585
Acquired in 1854
London, British Museum, inv. no. P. & D.1 854-6-28-10

In addition to the compositions of Polidora da Caravaggio that von Aachen copied, particularly at the beginning of his stay in Italy, this drawing after Paola Veronese occupies an exceptional position. The works of Titian, Tintoretto and Veronese had a profound effect on the young artist while he was living in Venice. The inspiration derived from their work markedly enriched his painting style. This drawing from London, however, is not from his first visit to Venice in the mid-1570s, but from the period when he was already making a name for himself as a skilled draughtsman with his own personal hand. As we may conclude from the drawings that he gave his assistants there (cat. no. 37 and *The Holy Family with the Young John and the Angel*, Dresden, Kupferstichkabinett, inv. no. C 1903-1950), he found opportunities for work around 1585 and he had an atelier of several people. The interesting composition was probably done for the purpose of copying Veronese's fresco from the church of San Sebastiano. Von Aachen even took note of the details of colour.

Fučíková 1986, p. 122, ill. 6.

E.F.

I.139
Hans von Aachen
Cologne 1551/52–Prague 1615
Cephalus and Procris
Drawing in pen and brown ink, brown
and orange-brown wash
On the back of the print, on the right: *Dis
hab ich Hans von achen gemacht zu gueden /
gedechtnis meinem guden gesellen Hans
Holtzma ... / In Venetia den 24 September ao
1585*; on the left, an added inscription in
another hand; on the front side at the left
edge is the notation: *Hans doo sompor
1585*
The Winkler Collection, Dresden; F. A. C.
Prestel, Frankfurt, 82 auction, 10–16

November, 1920, no. 1753; donated by A.
Voigtländer in 1920
Frankfurt am Main, Graphische Sammlung im Städelschen Kunstinstitut, inv.
no. 14 268

This drawing substantiates von Aachen's
stay in Venice in 1585 and introduces the
name of his journeyman, Hans Holtzmayr,
a native of Munich and active in Bavaria
between 1591 and 1602. Likewise it testifies to the fact that von Aachen had thoroughly absorbed the drawing lessons of
Jan Speckaert and had made a name for
himself through his own virtuosity. The
grand scene, two figures impeccably set in

a classical Italian landscape background,
makes this drawing one of the best from
von Aachen. Also working together with
Holtzmayr in Aachen's atelier was Pieter
Isaacsz, and perhaps even Joseph Heintz
the Elder.

Muchall-Viebrook 1925, 12, p. 49, ill. 3; Fischer 1951, p. 345, ill. 316; Schilling 1973, p.
16.

E.F.

I.140
Hans von Aachen
Cologne 1551/52–Prague 1615
A Deer Hunt
Drawing in pen and ink in brown tone,
wash in two tones of brown, underdraw-
ing in chalk on grey-blue paper
Below in the middle: *Hans vonach*
Ca. 1585 (?)
Dresden, Staatliche Kunstsammlungen,
Kupferstichkabinett, inv. no. C 1967-426

This drawing has a singular status among
von Aachen's early prints. When the
young painter came to Rome, Jan Speckaert became his `teacher' and model. Von

Aachen not only adopted his manner of
drawing but also his method of constructing a composition. Whereas in his first attempts at reproducing Speckaert's hand
von Aachen concentrated on acquiring
sureness in the execution of a line, command of the human figure and its complex motion, in this drawing from Dresden he measures up to his master.
Comparison with Speckaert's painting *The
Conversion of St Paul* (Paris, Louvre) suggests that von Aachen could have started
from some of Speckaert's designs. Several
figures are quite like Speckaert's, for example the prostrate male figure in a hat,
and do not appear elsewhere in von

Aachen's later work. The landscape however is drawn, or rather washed, unmistakably by von Aachen's method, so that
there may be some doubt whether this
work is from the final period of his stay in
Italy. Never in future work did von Aachen
again dedicate so much space in the composition to the landscape, nor did he ever
return to the theme of the hunt.

Fučíková 1986, p. 18, ill. 17.

E.F.

I.141
Hans von Aachen
Cologne 1551/52–Prague 1615
Lazarus Rising
Pen drawing in brown ink, brown wash,
chalk ground
27.7 × 43
1585–90
Purchased from E. Jabach's collection in
1671, inv. no. 259, under B. Spranger
Paris, Musée du Louvre, Département des
Arts Graphiques inv. no. 20 470

The drawing was originally attributed to
Speckaert by Lugt, but was later correctly
assigned to von Aachen by T. Gerszi and

dated between 1585 and 1590. The development of the composition of course has
a longer history. The earliest rough sketch
can be found in Amsterdam (Rijksprentenkabinet, inv. no. A 204 – under A.
de Weerdt) and dates from the time of von
Aachen's sojourn in Cologne in 1588. This
Paris drawing dates from a year later, some
time between his sojourn in Italy and his
stay in Bavaria. In Munich in 1590, von
Aachen painted *The Raising of the Young
Man from Naim* for Duke Wilhelm V of
Bavaria (Munich, Bayerische Staatsgemäldesammlungen, inv. no. 1463), which
with slight variations and a difference in
poise transferred the same figures from

the painting of *The Raising of Lazarus* into
the composition's elevation. The influence
of Venetian art on von Aachen's work during this period is unmistakable when compared to his painting *The Carrying of the
Cross* of 1587 (cf. Gerzsi 1971).

Lugt 1968, cat. no. 685 (under 'Speckaert');
Gerszi 1971, pp. 390-95, ill. 2; Gerszi, 1993,
pp. 21-30.

E.F.

I.142
Hans von Aachen
Cologne 1551/52–Prague 1615
Zeuxis and Parrhasios
Pen drawing in brown ink, grey-brown
wash, with a black chalk background
Below: *Hans von Aachen ao 89 di 5 decemb.
Ausporg*; above: *pictura mofa natora*
19 × 14.3 cm
1589
Maihingen, collection Ottingen-Waller-
stein; auction Karl und Faber 1936, cat.
no. 1190, tab. XXV; collection A. Gobiet,
Seeham bei Salzburg
Paris, Collection Frits Lugt, Institut Néer-
landais, inv. no. 7 186

This drawing is one of the rare works to
have been signed and dated by von
Aachen during his stay in Augsburg. At
that time he was painting portraits for the
Fugger family, was working for the Jesuits
in Munich, for Wilhelm V of Bavaria, and
at the same time he began making drawings for prints in collaboration with Joris
Hoefnagel and Aegidius Sadeler. The
learned Hoefnagel may well have drawn
his attention to this relatively uncommon
theme which appears twice among von
Aachen's works. The drawing relates the
story of Zeuxis, as recorded in Pliny the Elder's *Naturalis Historia* (XXXV, 65-66),

who was supposed to have painted so life-
like a picture of a boy carrying a bunch of
grapes that the birds swooped down and
tried to eat them. Zeuxis, however, was angered by this because it meant that his
painting of the boy had not been life-like
enough to scare them away. The meaning
of the picture, art imitating nature, is giv-
en in the inscription which should correctly read 'pictura mufa natura'.

Konečný 1988, pp. 147-55.

E.F.

I.143
Hans von Aachen
Cologne 1551/52–Prague 1615
Curriculum Vitae Christianae
Pen drawing in brown ink, brown wash,
white highlighting; the circle was cut from
a separate piece of paper and stuck on; inscription, text and signature are by the
artist
Bottom centre: *Hans von Aachen*
1589
Vojtěch Lanna's collection, dedicated to
the Society of Patriotic Art Lovers
Prague, Národní galerie v Praze, Grafická
sbírka, inv. no. K 1 157

This drawing served as a design for one of
Aegidius Sadeler's prints published in
1589 by Joris Hoefnagel, who was also responsible for its contents (Hollstein 113).
Hoefnagel also chose a different title for
the print as well as a different accompanying text (cf. Wilberg Vignau-Schuurman
1969, I, p. 236, ill. no. 128 for more detailed
information). In this work von Aachen
made use of all the Italian finesse of his refined handwriting, in particular with his
use of quick short strokes and rich washing technique, which not only gives life to
the faces but also provides striking light
effects. The figures in his composition are
characterized by similarly striking ges-

tures and a sense of complex theatrical
movement. This still very Mannerist style
remained an essential part of von
Aachen's work up until the mid-1580s.

Prague 1912, cat. no. 261; Dresden 1977,
cat. no. 15; Prague 1978, cat. no. 1; Essen-
Vienna 1988, cat. no. 176 (for earlier literature).

Pellau 1911-1912, p. 170; Fučíková 1986, p.
18, ill. V.

E.F.

I.144

Hans von Aachen
Cologne 1551/52–Prague 1615
The Adoration of the Magi
Pen and brown ink and wash
12 × 9.3 cm
Ca. 1590
Sir Hans Sloane Collection
London, British Museum, inv. no. Sloane
5227-78

In 1587, Hans von Aachen went to Bavaria to work for the Jesuits, the house of Fugger and Wilhelm V. This drawing by him, known to date from 1590, was in fact the preliminary drawing for an engraving by

Aegidius Sadeler (Hollstein 35). This is clear not only from the identical reversed image but also from the indentation of the outlines. Sadeler kept faithfully to the drawing of the main figures, and slight deviations from the original can be observed only in the face of the Madonna and in the mounted figures in the background. The preliminary drawing for the emblematic framework is perhaps by Joris Hoefnagel who also lived in Munich between 1587 and 1591. These three artists' names are linked together in several works executed in Munich – as, for example, in the series of prints depicting the Life of Christ, the *Salus generis humani*. In Hans von Aachen's

Adoration of the Kings, as in many of his other works, both the composition and the drawing of the figures show very clearly the powerful influence of Paolo Veronese. Von Aachen's graphic style shows a pronounced painterliness, evident in the subtlety of the rich wash contrasting with the clear outlines in the highly differentiated drawing of the inner areas.

Gerszi 1990, pp. 32–35.

T.G.

I.145

Hans von Aachen
Cologne 1551/52–Prague 1615
The Entombment of Christ
Drawing in pen and brown ink, gray wash, white glaze, underdrawing in black chalk
Lower left, a later inscription: *H.V. Aachen*
Ca. 1600
Purchased for the museum in 1895
Brno, Moravská galerie, inv. no. B 2 303

This drawing is one of a number of studies for a painting which has not survived, but for which the painter prepared more thoroughly than at other times. In Weimar

(not in Schwerin as H. Geissler mistakenly states) there is a study of the body of Christ which in its consistency and in its detailed execution could be a study after a model. In comparison with von Aachen's drawings on the same theme, the new approach of the painter to the construction of the scene surpasses the older by about a decade. Large figures step forth from the dark background, their bodies modelled by a dramatic light. This is one of the first of von Aachen's chiaroscuro compositions, in which he abandons elegant Mannerist formulae, aiming instead for natural forms and a naturally intensified, deeper space.

Stuttgart 1979, cat. no. B 15.

Peltzer 1911/1912, p. 170; Stuttgart 1979, pp. 60–62, cat. and ill. no. B 15.

E.F.

I.146

Hans von Aachen
Cologne 1551/52–Prague 1615
Pallas Athena Introduces Painting to Apollo and the Muses
Drawing in pen and ink in brown tone, brown wash, white glaze, underdrawing in chalk
Before 1595
Collection of Count Sternberg-Manderscheit; collection of Graf Rd. de V, auction in Berlin, Hollstein a Ruppel 4-6 May, 1931, cat. no. 1005 as H. Goltzius; auction H. Gilhofer and H. Ranschberg, Lucerne, 28 June, 1934; Feldmann collection, Brno
Brno, Moravská galerie, inv. no. 3 222

Aachen produced two versions of this popular theme. The first was executed before 1595, when Rudolf II by Imperial Charter elevated painting from a craft to an art. Thematic and compositional alterations in the second version reflected the new status of painting. The Brno example is characteristic of Aachen's drawing technique of the mid-1590s.

Essen and Vienna 1988, cat. no. 178.

Konečný 1982, pp. 237-39, ill. 2; Kaufmann 1985, ill. 33; Fučíková 1986, p. 19, ill. 22.

E.F.

I.147

Hans von Aachen
Cologne 1551/52–Prague 1615
The Resurrection
Pen-and-ink drawing in brown tone, brown and grey wash, the middle section pasted over and redrawn in his own hand
18.2 × 19.5 cm
1598
Brno, private collection
Brno, Moravská galerie, inv. no. B 9702

In 1598 Aachen, Spranger, Joseph Heintz the Elder, and both Vredemans worked on an altarpiece that was probably intended for the palace chapel. Although the wings

survive (Vienna, Kunsthistorisches Museum, inv. no. 6436), the central painting by Aachen is known only from his sketch. The drawing is a characteristic example of his working procedure. He first sketched out the composition in quick strokes, and if he was not satisfied, he would simply replace the offending portion with a new piece of paper and draw it again. The existence of a number of draughts is confirmed by a copy of one (Cologne, Wallraf-Richartz-Museum inv. no. Z 5663), which also includes a sarcophagus and a group of figures on the right. The engraving of Raphael Sadeler from 1614 may be a definitive likeness of the altarpiece (W., p.

7, Hollstein., p. 14).

Essen and Vienna 1988, cat. no. 180; Brno.

Kaufmann 1985, pp. 188-89, ill. 1.18; Fučíková 1986, p. 19, ill. VII; Essen and Vienna 1988, cat. no. 180

E.F.

I.148

Hans von Aachen
Cologne 1551/52–Prague 1615
Little Bacchus and Female Musicians
Black chalk and pen drawing in brown ink (partially discoloured)
18.9 × 24.4 cm
Ca. 1595
Baumgarten collection; Koller auction, Vienna 5 February 1866, cat. no. 257, Vojtěch Lanna's collection, donated to the Society of Patriotic Friends of Art
Prague, Národní galerie v Praze, Grafická sbíirka, inv. no. K 1 269

This drawing is a fine example of von

Aachen's ability to sketch out an idea quickly in chalk, and then to give it detail with the brush. Although it dates from the period when von Aachen had not yet renounced his Mannerist figurative style, the drawing, partially in its depiction of the young Bacchus, recalls the robust figures found in Flemish painting of the early seventeenth century. The two female musicians are mirror images of each other, a device also found in the drawing from Brno depicting *Minerva Ushering Painting before Apollo and the Muses* (cat. no. I.146), dating from before 1595. The Prague drawing no doubt dates from the same period, and was probably a study for a paint-

ing that has not survived. From the end of the sixteenth century onwards, Bacchus, depicted at various gatherings and in various poses, was the theme most commonly depicted in von Aachen's paintings.

Prague 1976, cat. no. 8; Dresden 1977, cat. no. 17; Prague 1978–79, cat. no. 3.

Fučíková 1967, p. 145; Fučíková 1986, p. 19, no. 25.

E.F.

I.149
Hans von Achen
Cologne 1551/52–Prague 1615
The Entombment of Christ
Pen-and-ink drawing in brown tone, brown wash
1590
Collection A. Skutezky, acquired in 1938
London, The British Museum, inv. no. 1895-9-5-1026

The Brno drawing is a preparatory study for *The Entombment* from the Christological cycle of prints, *Salus generis humani*, dedicated to Archduke Ferdinand II. Joris Hoefnagel composed the iconographic programme and accompanying text, which he published in 1590. Aachen used Hoefnagel's subject-matter in his drawings, which Aegidius Sadeler adapted to copper-plate engraving. The engraving (Hollstein 113) does not correspond exactly to this drawing nor to the other variant from an American private collection (Kaufmann 1982, cat. no. 53). Aachen evidently tried various solutions, in particular in the foreground of the composition. He also altered the viewpoint: in the drawings from the interior of a cave, in the engraving from the exterior. In the Brno example, the hand is sharp, rapid and linear, typical for his work from the late 1580s.

Washes are used to express form and the effects of light. The drawing is more worked up in the American example, representing a more advanced state of the composition. Aachen returned to it once more in an oval painting (untraced) for Wilhelm V of Bavaria, which Raphael Sadeler adapted for an engraving in 1593 (Hollstein). Its counterpart was the *Adoration of the Shepherds* (Munich, Bayerische, Staatsgemäldesammlungen).

Kaufmann 1982, cat. no. 53 (American drawing); Fučíková 1986, p. 19, ill. 19-21.

E.F.

I.150
Hans von Aachen
Cologne 1551/52–Prague 1615
Study of the Dead Christ
Black and white chalk on grey-blue paper
20.2 × 26.7
Ca. 1600
Kunstsammlungen zu Weimar, inv. no. KK 1

A similarly composed figure of the dead Christ, lying down, could be found on the altar painting with *Pietà* scene at the Herzog Max-Burg castle in Munich (destroyed during the Second World War) and in a series of drawings with *Lamentation* or with *Pietà* (for example, Vienna, Albertina, inv. no. 41700; Munich, Staatliche Graphische Sammlung, inv. nos 21215, 31706). In all stated works that originated before the mid-1590s, von Aachen used an expressively stylized figural canon. In the Weimar drawing, he had evidently studied a live model, and with great care he captured the modelling of the athletic body and indicated the reflection of light proceeding from the right. For von Aachen both to use model and to make so many drawings was quite exceptional. The reason he prepared so carefully this time is unclear, especially since at another level of preparation for this composition, in *Lamentation from London* (cat. no. I.149), he returned once again to a specific form of stylization.

Fučíková 1986, p. 19, ill. 24.

E.F.

I.151
Hans von Aachen
Cologne 1551/52–Prague 1615
Diana (Luna)
Drawing in black chalk
Ca. 1600
Dresden, Staatliche Kunstsammlungen, Kupferstichkabinett, inv. no. C 1967-433

This charming, almost Rococo drawing, long unattributed, was assigned to Aachen by Werner Schade. The motif of the female half-nude appears in Aachen's drawings and paintings around 1600. These tend to be tranquil, well-balanced compositions showing scenes of a sensual nature, and perfectly executed. In this drawing Aachen used chalk rather than wash, and the soft modelling of the forms by the powdered lines is closer to painting. The coquettishly turned young woman has a crescent moon in her hair, and a quiver with arrows is visible behind her. Thus, she may represent Diana or Luna. This could have been a preparatory study for the painting (untraced) that was listed in the inventory of the Vienna collection in 1610-19 under number 218 as '*1 stukkel mit Luna vom Hanss von Ach*'.

Fučíková 1986, p. 19, ill. 27.

E.F.

I.152
Hans von Aachen
Cologne 1551/52–Prague 1615
Sleeping Cupid (Amor)
Drawing in black chalk, light white glaze
Lower right: *Hans von Ach*
Ca. 1600
Nagler collection, acquired in 1835
Berlin, Staatliche Museen, Kupferstichkabinett, inv. no. KdZ 149

Aachen drew in chalk relatively rarely; for the most part he used pen-and-ink, which permitted the quick, sharp lines better suited to his natural draughtsmanship. His drawings in chalk are notable for their softness and an almost Rococo charm. He seems to have used chalk to create a 'painted' effect. Using a light hatching, he achieved ranges of dark shades, and by a fine application of white he amplified the effect of light and shade on the surface of forms. He also used chalk when he wanted to produce a drawing as an independent artistic work, e.g., as a commemorative sheet as is clearly the case here. *Sleeping Cupid* ranks with Aachen's compositions from the beginning of the seventeenth century in connection with his mythological paintings of *Bacchus, Venus, and Amor* or *Boy with Grapes*, in which he abandoned the elegant Mannerist figural canon. He simplified the composition, placing his figures before a neutral background. The figure of a sleeping *Amor* in the painting *Pan and Selene* (England, Private Collection) still has the subtlety of his earlier work. In this drawing there are indications of his move towards a new style.

Peltzer, 1911/12, pp.133, 169, ill. 54; Bock E., Staatliche Museen zu Berlin, Kupferstichkabinett, Die deutschen Meister, I, pg. 108, cat. no. 149; Essen and Vienna 1988, cat. no. 181.

E.F.

I.153
Hans von Aachen
Cologne 1551/52–Prague 1615
The Suicide of Lucretia
Drawing in black chalk and pen and ink on blue paper
Ca. 1600
Florence, Gabinetto Disegni e Stampe degli Uffizi, inv. no. 2 293 F

There is a graphic print of Aegidius Sadeler's (Holl. 146), the model for which is considered to be this Florentine drawing. It was evidently made, as were other earlier drawings of von Aachen, in the period when both artists were working together in Munich with Joris Hoefnagel (1588–91). The drawing clearly recalls other prints intended for graphic reproduction, e.g. *Curriculum vitae christianae*. Von Aachen drew the Florentine Lucretia about ten years later, after his engraving with fewer modifications, when it was prepared for a 1601 painting of the same theme. The figure of Lucretia is located more towards the centre. The left elbow is finished, but he has indicated what he intends to leave out of the future painting: drapery and a column in the left corner, a ribbon holding back a translucent veil. He has accentuated the background with a wash, enhancing the effect of the nude figure of Lucretia. Von Aachen had already completely abandoned the Mannerist canon of slenderness, preferring a more robust type of woman, and this was better rendered through the medium of chalk.

Peltzer 1911/1912, p. 170, ill. 5; Essen-Vienna 1988, cat. no. 551; Fučíková 1996, pp. 195–96.

E.F.

I.154

Hans von Aachen

Cologne 1551/52–Prague 1615

Tarquinius and Lucretia

Brown ink, grey wash on brownish paper

23.8 × 27.9 cm

Bottom right: *Spranger* (added later)

1600–05

Purchased in 1983 from a private collection

Stuttgart, Graphische Sammlung der Staatsgalerie, inv. no. C 83/3171

A Stuttgart drawing served as a study for this picture, which was recently sold to the Kunsthistorisches Museum in Vienna.

Von Aachen conceived a more dramatic scene here, depicting the moment of flagrant violence, perpetrated in the absence of witnesses. The preliminary sketch, composed of relatively thin lines, found definition in the sharply defined contours of this drawing. The generous use of wash has given the background a sombre hue, against which the application of light stands out more starkly. Von Aachen suggested the modelling of the bodies both with short, parallel brushstrokes and with the customary pencil crosshatching. The nature of the drawing suggests that it was a sketch, a quick rendering of an idea, which would undergo changes in other

phases. Von Aachen finally decided on a more static work and a more decoratively conceived scene.

Stuttgart 1984.

Essen and Vienna 1988, p. 218, cat. no. 101 – in the text about von Aachen's picture *Pan and Selene*.

E.F.

I.155

Hans von Aachen

Cologne 1551/52–Prague 1615

Rudolf II

After 1602

Ex Collection I. Delhaes

Budapest, Szépmüvészeti Múzeum, inv. no. 310

This rapid, cursory sketch for a full-length portrait of Rudolf II is the only surviving likeness of the Emperor drawn in Aachen's hand. Of the numerous portraits of Rudolf produced by Aachen and his workshop, very few of those preserved include a significant contribution from the

painter. Until recently only one of Aachen's painted full-length portraits of the Emperor (London, Wellington Museum) was known. The Budapest drawing is a study for it. The object on the table - the imperial crown, completed in 1602 - is important for its dating. As Rudolf attached great significance to the crown, it was moved to a more prominent position in the London painting. Whereas in the drawing the Emperor stands behind the crown, in the painting he has it next to him, holding it in his hand. The painter depicted the crown slightly over-sized to draw the viewer's attention to it. In the drawing, Rudolf has only a cuirass, mar-

shal's staff, and sword, in the painted portrait Aachen added a helmet and gloves. This portrait of Rudolf II is clearly connected to the group of works by Aachen, Vries, Ravesteyn and Vianen, dated between 1603 and 1604, commemorating Rudolf II as the bringer of peace and victor over the Turks.

Salzburg 1987, pp. 20-21, cat. no. I.

Gerszi 1958, p. 32, ill. 17; An der Heiden 1970, cat. no. B30, ill. 186; Essen and Vienna 1988, p. 216, cat. no. 98 (London painting).

E.F.

I.156

Hans von Aachen

Cologne 1551/52–Prague 1615

Venus and Cupid

Drawing in pen and grey-brown ink, brown wash, underdrawing in chalk, brown-toned paper

Ca. or before 1602

Munich, Staatliche Graphische Sammlung, inv. no. 1 021

Oberhuber (1968) considered this sheet to be the work of Spranger, and Wegner published it as such in a catalogue of Dutch drawings of the Graphic Arts Collection in Munich. The drawing does, however, have

all the traits of von Aachen's hand, closely connected with the sheet from the private German collection (Stuttgart 1979, cat. and ill. no. B16) on which appears the so-called identical figure of Amor. It seems that both drawings are preparatory works for a painting whose theme is twice listed in the inventory of the Rudolf collection from 1621 as numbers 890 and 1298; the painted version has not, however, survived. The same female figural type appears on the painting from St Petersburg, *Allegory of Peace, Science and Abundance*, dated to 1602. The 1607 sheet from Frankfurt is also close to this drawing in its draughtsmanship and content. The draw-

ing from Munich was made some time during this period.

Wegner 1973, p. 28, cat. no. 112, ill. tab. 41.

E.F.

I.157

Hans von Aachen

Cologne 1551/52–Prague 1615

Allegory of the Turkish Wars: Rudolf II as Imperator Romanorum

Drawing in pen and ink in brown tone, grey and red wash, an underdrawing in red ochre and chalk, the lower section of the piece pasted on

1603-04

Basel, Öffentliche Kunstsammlung Basel, Kupferstichkabinett, inv. no. Bi 376.104

The drawing is a proposal for the first sheet of a series of allegories on the Turkish War. It existed in two variants: in seven

original oils on parchment (five in Vienna, Kunsthistorisches Museum, on loan to Heeresgeschichtliches Museum; two in Budapest, Szépmüvészeti Múzeum) and in an album of thirteen drawings of Aachen's workshop, ca 172 from the Dresden Kupferstichkabinett where there are three more variants on loose sheets cat. no. 3, 5, 6). H. -J. Ludwig was not familiar with this drawing when he wrote his dissertation on Aachen's allegories on the Turkish war. The opening scene of the Dresden album was Aachen's starting point for the iconography. The sheet from Basil has a smaller square format, and the scene is more compact and dramatic. The

only explicit reference here to the Turkish war is in the upper right corner where an eagle battles with a basilisk. Rudolf II is represented as Imperator Romanorum. His new personal insignia, completed in 1602, is borne in a procession with three crowns; one of the reliefs on the original shows Rudolf as victor over the Turks. The Basle drawing was evidently a model for an oil on parchment, which is untraced. The Dresden piece is a weak workshop version.

Kaufmann, 1988, p. 150, ill. 1.48; for the workshop version see: Ludwig, 1978, pp. 33-36, with older literature.

E.F.

I.158

Hans von Aachen

Cologne 1551/52–Prague 1615

Allegory of the Turkish War: The Battle of Sissek, 22 June 1593

Drawing in ruddle and pen and black and brown ink, wash, underdrawing in chalk, on the upper and mid-right pasted and drawn over – changes by the artist

1603-04

Moscow, Vsjevolschskij Collection

Moscow, Pushkin State Museum of Fine Arts, inv. no. 7 456

The victory of the imperial forces at Sissek on 22 June 1593 induced the Turkish sul-

tan to declare a war which lasted thirteen years. In the sequence of von Aachen's cycle this is the third scene, capturing the first real battles, as opposed to the preceding two leafs on a general allegorical level. The Düsseldorf sketch (Kunstmuseum, inv. no. F.P. 5471) is a quick outline of the composition; the sheet from Moscow is the definitive model for the oil painting on parchment (Vienna, Kunsthistorisches Museum, inv. no. 1951). On the right of the figure of Victory, where the battle continued originally, is a rough underdrawing in grease chalk (in the Emperor's own hand ?). Von Aachen passed over this part and depicted the fortress that the empire

conquered. The appearance of this sheet is repeated on the sheet from Vienna and on the two workshop replicas from Dresden (Kupferstichkabinett Ca 172, sheet 3; C 5040).

Prague 1986, cat. no. 57; Essen and Vienna 1988, cat. no. 183.

Ludwig 1978, pp. 43-48 (neither this nor the drawing from Düsseldorf was known to him; see here for all earlier literature); Kaufmann 1988, cat. and ill. no. 1.50.

E.F.

I.159
Hans von Aachen
Cologne 1551/52–Prague 1615
Allegory of the Turkish Wars: The Battle of Mezö-Keresztes 26-28 October, 1596
Oil on parchment, mounted on canvas
1603-04
Kunstkammer of Rudolf II, the imperial collection in Vienna, Vienna, Kunsthistorisches Museum; transferred to Budapest in 1934
Budapest, Szépmüvészeti Múzeum, inv. no. 6 784

This, the fourth sheet of the series, is the only one depicting the battle in which the imperial army was defeated. At first, the Emperor's forces appeared to be winning, but the Turks' counter-attack under the leadership of Sinan Pasha dispersed the Christian army. As in the other examples, Aachen was attempting to represent the reality of the battle, however, the scene's symbolic aspects were also important. The helmet of the knight on horseback in the centre has two feathers from a peacock, a symbol of immortality and resurrection, and his lance bears the Austrian standard, which almost touches the figure flying down from the heavens. This figure is Justitia, whose appearance and attributes are also identified with the Archangel Michael. In this case, as H.-J. Ludwig has indicated in his iconographic analysis of this scene, the figure can be interpreted as Salvation, divine justice that saves the imperial forces from ultimate destruction.

Ludwig 1978, pp. 49-54; Kaufmann 1988, p. 151, cat. no. and ill. 1.51.

E.F.

I.160
Hans von Aachen
Cologne 1551/52–Prague 1615
Allegory of the Turkish Wars: The Conquest of Györ (Raab), 29 March 1598
Drawing in red ochre and pen and ink in a black tone, grey wash, white glaze; figures in the lower right corner and an eagle on the left pasted over the original drawing, correction by the artist
1603-04
Berlin, Staatliche Museen, Kupferstichkabinett, inv. no. KdZ 4 722

This is a model for the oil-on-parchment version, from Budapest, and the several pasted-over areas document Aachen's search for a definitive form for the composition. In addition to the Budapest painting, it is repeated in two workshop copies from Dresden (Album Ca 172, sheet 6 and inv. no. C 5043). The Berlin drawing has the same dimensions as the sheet from Basle, indicating that the format of Aachen's original design was almost square. One change in the final version was the replacement of the kneeling female figure by a male, an abased Turk. The female figure appears with the attribute of a wheel on Adrian de Vries' relief after Aachen's composition, leading H.-J. Ludwig to identify her as Fortuna. The drawing also includes an accurate likeness of the fortress, Adolf Schwarz-enberg as the commander of the imperial army, and an exploding *Raab* petard, the new weapon that humbled the Turks, as well as the lunar eclipse, which was interpreted as Divine assistance to the Christians.

Amsterdam 1955, cat. no. 126; Dresden 1982, cat. no. I.

Diez 1909-10, p. 126; Bock 1921, p. 107, ill. 138; Ludwig 1978, pp. 58-63; Dresden, 1982, cat. no. I; Kaufmann 1988, p. 151, cat. no. 1.53.

E.F.

I.161
Hans von Aachen
Cologne 1551/52–Prague 1615
Allegory of the Turkish Wars: The Conquest of Györ (Raab), 29 March, 1598
Oil on parchment, mounted on canvas
1603-04
Kunstkammer of Rudolf II, the imperial collection in Vienna, Vienna, Kunsthistorisches Museum; transferred to Budapest in 1934
Budapest, Szépmüvészeti Múzeum, inv. no. 6 710

On folio 381 of the Inventory of the *Kunstkammer* from 1607-11 is inscribed: '*Ihr.kay : Mt : impresabuch, so hat HVA (leg.) gemalt von olfarben auff pergamen, in rot leder gebunden*'. This somewhat imprecise description evidently related to the cycle of allegories of the Turkish war, which were painted in oil on parchment and originally bound in an album. Only seven examples survive, five in Vienna and two in Budapest. There were more, however, judging from the workshop replica transferred to the Elector of Saxony, Christian II, on 30 September, 1604 (Dresden, Kupferstichkabinett, Ca 172 and loose sheets C 5040-5043). If this date is the *ante quem* for the completion of the work, the depiction of the battle at Kronstadt, which took place 17 June 1603, is the *post quem*. The *Conquest of Raab* was a series of six sheets; in addition to the original drawings for it, two more Dresden examples are documented. Adriaen de Vries used part of the composition for a relief, and Paulus van Vianen used part for medals (Ter Molen 1984, cat. no. 199).

Dresden 1972, cat. no. I.

Dresden 1972, cat. no. I, with complete bibliography; Ludwig 1978, pp. 58-63; Kaufmann 1988, p. 151, ill. 1.53.

E.F.

I.162
Hans von Aachen
Cologne 1551/52–Prague 1615
Allegory of the Turkish Wars: the Conquest of Székesfehérvár (Stuhlweissenberg), 20 September 1601
Oil on parchment
1603-04
Kunstkammer of Rudolf II, the imperial collection in Vienna
Vienna, Kunsthistorisches Museum, Gemäldegalerie, inv. no. 5 842

The eighth sheet of the series commemorates the conquering of the city where the coronations and funerals of the Hungarian kings took place. Although the joy from the victory (20 September 1601) was short-lived - the Turks retook the city in August 1602 and held it until 1688 - Aachen commemorates it, emphasizing the affiliation of the imperial and Hungarian royal symbols. In the background of the scene a dramatic battle is taking place, based on descriptions by eye-witnesses. Two groups of figure in the foreground appear to have nothing to do with the battle, yet they symbolize its outcome. The Emperor is returning to Hungary its crown and the earth its peace; on the opposite side Mehmed II laments his defeat in a company of women. Opposite him there stands the pagan east and the Christian west. In the clouds is another coronation motif: the divine patroness (Juno=Virgin Mary) is crowning the matronly terrestrial sovereign (Hungary).

Permanently on display at Heeresgeschichtliches Museum in Vienna.

Ludwig 1978, pp. 66-71; Kaufmann 1988, p. 152, cat. and ill. no. 1.155.

E.F.

I.163
Hans von Aachen
Cologne 1551/52–Prague 1615
Portrait of an Unknown Nobleman (Hermann Christoph von Rusworm ?)
Drawing in black and red chalk
Ca. 1604
Budapest State Library
Budapest, Szépmüvészeti Múzeum, inv. no. K.58.1087

Among Aachen's portrait drawings this example is particularly significant, both for its virtuosity of execution and the realism of the portrayal. It was not intended as a model for an engraver, as the conspicuous framing of the oval drawing would suggest. If Hermann Christoph von Rusworm is the subject, it can be compared with his official portrait, for which Lucas Kilian used Aachen's model (Domenicus Custos illustrated it in *Atrium Herioicum*). The engraving presented a typical classical portrait of Rusworm, referring to his military success, particularly in the Turkish war, and showing him in his prime, younger than in the Budapest drawing. Rusworm, however, was a lover of duels, women and wine, as Aachen well knew for like Rusworm, he was a favourite of the Emperor. This 'unkempt' portrait was not meant for the public, but only for friends.

Salzburg 1987, cat. no. 23; Essen and Vienna 1988, cat. no. 184.

Fučíková 1986, p. 19, ill. 25; Salzburg 1987, p. 32, ill. 23; Essen and Vienna 1988, p. 334, cat. and ill. no. 184.

E.F.

I.164
Hans von Aachen
Cologne 1551/52–Prague 1615
A Nobleman (Portrait of Adriaen de Vries?)
Black and red chalk
Ca. 1605
Zurich, Graphische Sammlungen der
ETH, inv. no. 1925.36

Comparison with the portrait from the
Städtische Kunstsammlungen in Augsburg shows that this drawing could certainly represent the sculptor Adriaen de
Vries. The grandseigneurial aspect of the
man and his leisurely pose betoken a sophistication beyond what was customary

in that period and resemble elegant
Baroque portraits, although the rapidly
done drawing, complemented by some energetic hatching work, betray the inimitable style of Hans von Aachen. The nearest comparison would be Ruswurm's
portrait in Budapest (cat. no. I.163), which
is drawn with the same verve and likewise
goes beyond the contemporary type of
portrait. This drawing can be best explained as an attempt to create something
unusual for a friend, who, moreover,
would be skilled at evaluating a work of
originality since he himself was also an
artist. The friendly relations between von
Aachen and de Vries also form the back-

ground to their *Freundschaftsbild* (friendship painting), to which Paulus van Vianen (cat. no. I.106) had his own image
added, so as to be seen as one of their company.

Essen and Vienna 1988, cat. no. 185.

See the essay by L. Konečný in this catalogue.

E.F.

I.165
Hans von Aachen
Cologne 1551/52–Prague 1615
Venus Combing her Hair and Cupid
Drawing in chalk and pen and black ink,
white chalk glaze, pasted on brown paper
HVA (leg.) / F / 1607 (in different ink on
the pasted paper)
1607
From the Klein Collection, Frankfurt, in
1937
Frankfurt am Main, Graphische Samm-
lung im Städelschen Kunstintitut, inv. no.
15 910

Among the paintings in Rudolf's gallery

that were sold because of their unsuitable
erotic content in 1623 to Daniel de Bries
was, listed under #29, *Venus Combing her
Hair* by von Aachen. The Frankfurt drawing may provide some idea of this work,
now missing, and of its theme. After 1600
Aachen often used chalk in his preparato-
ry-drawings for his paintings. Its wide line
corresponded better to the more robustly
constructed figures and allowed for a richer gradation of tones by distribution of
the hatching. When von Aachen needed to
accentuate contours, he supplemented
the figures' outlines with several energetic
strokes of his pen. The date 1607, applied
in another pen on the pasted-on paper,

was perhaps not written by von Aachen
himself, but it does correspond to fact.
The drawing belongs to the last decade of
his life, a period when he chose only one
or two figures in his compositions and
was interested in natural body construction and tranquil movement.

Schilling, E., *Katalog der deutschen Zeichnungen: Alte Meister*, Städelsches Kunstinstitut, Frankfurt 1973, p. 17.

E.F.

I.166
Hans von Aachen
Cologne 1551/52–Prague 1615
Girl with a Fruit Bowl
Drawing in black chalk
Jo. ab ach.; *'fecit'* added later
After 1610
Ex Radowitz collection
Berlin, Staatliche Museen, Kupferstich-
kabinett, inv. no. KdZ 28 012

The female half-figure is among the
favourite motifs of Aachen's paintings and
also appears in two drawings. Whereas the
Dresden example, of ca. 1600, shows a sensual Mannerist half-nude of an almost Ro-

coco playfulness, the Berlin drawing appears to be a portrait in costume disguise,
like that of Aachen's wife and son as *Ceres
and Bacchus*. The closest analogy in the
painter's oeuvre seems to be the painting
Boy with Grapes, executed between 1600
and 1605. But the drawing technique suggests a later date, closer to two works from
Cologne executed in the last five years of
his life.

E.F.

I.167
Hans von Aachen
Cologne 1551/52–Prague 1615
Bordello Scene With an Ill-Matched Couple
Drawing in pen and brown ink, white
glaze, underdrawing in black chalk on
gray-brown paper
Upper left: *Hanss von Ach in Prag*
Ca. 1612
The collection of R. A. Peltzer, Cologne
(1912); the collection of Dr Kutter, Bad
Godesberg (1928); gift from the Freunde
des Wallraf-Richartz-Museums 1957
Colorne, Wallraf-Richartz-Museum, inv.
no. KK 57/4

The procurement scene was a favourite
subject in von Aachen's paintings. Two
paintings in Karlsruhe and in Linz (inv.
no. 1508, on loan from the Kunsthistorisches Museum, Vienna) attest to an
important source for its inspiration,
which were similar works by Cranach
(Stockholm, Nationalmuseum, inv. no.
258; Prague, Národní galerie, inv. no. O
455) and Massy (Stockholm, Nationalmuseum, inv. no. 508). The drawing from
Cologne probably represents a preparatory stage for a painting. In both paintings
the young girl is being tempted by expensive gifts, so she is in the centre and is being prevailed upon from both sides. In the

drawing the central figure is an old man
embracing his chosen one and the pro-
curess behind him is already depositing
her takings into a pouch. The draughtsmanship corresponds to von Aachen's later drawings dating from 612 and 1613.

Nürnberg 1952, p. 192, cat. no. W. 149;
Cologne 1965, p. 25, cat. no. 40.

Peltzer 1911/1912, pp. 136, 169, IV, no. 6;
Vey 1964, p. 80 (with earlier literature);
Cologne 1965, pp. 24–25, cat. no. 40.

E.F.

I.168
Hans von Aachen
Cologne 1551/52–Prague 1615
Female Musician
Drawing in pen and brown ink, gray-
brown wash, underdrawing in black and
red chalk; on the verso: drawing in black
and red chalk
Below: *Hanss von ach geschrieben in Prag
den 4 octobris Anno 1613*
1613
Old holdings
Cologne, Wallraf-Richartz-Museum, inv.
no. Z 152

On the back of the leaf is repeated von

Aachen's youthful composition, a self-portrait with Donna Venusta in which he has
modified his likeness to match his advanced age. This composition was the
source for the central scene on the side of
the leaf, on which one of the women is
likewise playing a lute and a second is raising a goblet of wine. Only the third woman is a new figure, and on the plate there
are apples instead of grapes. In the last
years of his life von Aachen intensively
pursued genre scenes, reflecting his
'Flemish' beginnings, although the figures no longer show slender forms and elegant curvilinear movement. They are thick
sc and more true to life. Also his draughts-

manship, with energetic and frequently
interrupted lines recalling his early studies, has been adapted to the rounded proportions of the figures. Von Aachen inti-
mates with his pen only what is
indispensable for comprehension, completing his modelling with copious wash.

Nürnberg 1952, p. 192, cat. no. W. 150;
Cologne 1965, cat. no. 39, ill. 39; Essen and
Vienna 1988, cat. no. 187.

Peltzer 1911/1912, pp. 139, 169, ill. 67; Vey
1964, p. 80; Essen and Vienna 1988, cat.
and ill. no. 187.

E.F.

I.169
Giuseppe Arcimboldo
Milan 1527–Milan 1593
Self-portrait
Pen and wash
23 × 15.7 cm
Signed upper left (in brown ink): *Ioseffi
Arcimboldi imago*
1570s?
Daniel Böhm Collection, 1820; Sale,
Dorotheum 1918; Prague, Jindřich Waldes
Collection
Prague, Národní galerie, Graficka sbírka,
inv. no. K 5338

Although Arcimboldo is first recorded in court office as a *Conterfetter* (portraitist) and as having executed portraits, no painted portrait of a member of the court can be definitively attributed to him. This drawing, inscribed in his hand, and two coronation sketches of Rudolf II (Prague, Národní muzeum) are the only surviving works in this genre surely attributable to his hand. Both the painting (present whereabouts unknown) and drawing show the same bearded countenance, with somewhat similar head covering. Arcimboldo is described in an account of a tournament held in Prague in 1570 as having a heavy beard. While Preiss (1986) dated this drawing ca. 1565, it possibly dates later, since it may be compared to the style of drawings from the 1570s.

Praha 1978, cat. no. 7, ill.; Venice ill.71; Essen 1988, no. 18, ill. 337.

Geiger 1954, 13, 149, ill. P 12; Alfons 1957, pp. 69-71, ill. 71; Preiss 1964, pp. 12-14; Preiss 1967, p. 7, frontispiece; Porzio 1979, ill. 89; Barthes, 1980, ill. 117; Neumann 1984, ill. 80; Fučíková 1986, p. 15, ill. 1; Fučíková 1988, p. 65, ill. 69; Kaufmann 1996, vol. 2, 374, ill. 373.

T.C.K.

I.170
Philipp van den Bossche
Fl. Prague and Augsburg 1604-15
Mountain Landscape with Hunters
Pen and brown ink
13.4 × 9 cm
Bottom left, in pen: *Philips / van den bosche
fecit / 1609*
1609
A. von Beckerath Collection
Berlin, Staatliche Museen, Kupferstich-
kabinett, inv. no. KdZ 12408

The books of the court treasury record the payment between 1604 and 1612 of relatively large sums to the *Camer-Seidenstich-*er Philipp van den Bossche. A letter written by Philipp Hainhofer in 1611 shows that van den Bossche made landscape pictures using silk threads, which fetched a high price. Only a very few of his works have survived. For a long time art historians were aware of only one drawing by him, but now ten surviving works are known. This signed and dated *Rocky Mountain Landscape*, held in the Kupferstichkabinett in Berlin, has been crucial in identifying unsigned works from his Prague period, particularly since it also clearly demonstrates his links with colleagues working as landscape artists. The rocky landscape with the *arco naturale* takes up a favourite theme in the drawings of Pieter Stevens, while the style of drawing is distinctly reminiscent of the pen-and-ink style of Paulus van Vianen.

Essen and Vienna 1988, cat. no. 194.

Bock and Rosenberg 1930, p. 90.

T.G.

I.171
Philipp van den Bossche
Fl. Prague and Augsburg 1604-15
Mountain Landscape with Ruins
Pen and brown ink
20.7 × 26.7 cm
1604-14
Berlin, Staatliche Museen, Kupferstich-
kabinett, inv. no. KdZ 27676

For a time this work was listed under Roelandt Savery's name. Then it was reattributed to Paulus van Vianen. However, the unbalanced conglomeration of motifs and the style of its linear structure do not resemble van Vianen's work. The less differentiated style of drawing and the somewhat schematic shading point rather to van den Bossche, and the work bears a distinct similarity to his signed and dated *Rocky Mountain Landscape* (Berlin, Staatliche Museen, Kupferstichkabinett). The Roman ruin on the mountain peak is, but for a few details, identical with pl. 43 in a series of engravings by Willem van Nieulandt II, *Ruinarum Antiquarum quae Romae sunt*. The same print was also the model for the verso of a drawing by Paulus van Vianen (Gerszi [1982], cat. no. 38v). The fact that these two artists based their work on the same original speaks for their close relationship.

Gerszi 1982, cat. no. F3.

T.G.

I.172
Philipp van den Bossche
Fl. Prague and Augsburg 1604-15
Ruined Wooden Mill in the Forest
Pen and brown ink
10.5 × 13.4 cm
1604-14
Weimar, Kunstsammlungen zu Weimar,
Schloßmuseum, inv. no. KK. 5 425

In the early seventeenth century Netherlandish art began to favour depictions of plain, modest buildings in a landscape context. Artists in Prague also portrayed houses and mills and it was probably van den Bossche's landscapist colleagues who inspired his interest in this type of subject-matter. In this example he not only took Paulus van Vianen's style as his model but also sought to achieve the same objective approach to reality. Thus this small section of landscape, with its convincing depiction of air and sunshine, seems to exude a sense of intimacy and realism.

Essen and Vienna 1988, cat. no. 195.

Wegner 1973, p. 11.

T.G.

I.173
Philipp van den Bossche
Fl. Prague and Augsburg 1604-15
Landscape in the Storm
Pen and black ink, grey and pink wash on parchment
11.7 × 21.8 cm
Bottom left, in pen: *philipp van den bossche
[fecit ?)]* 1615
1615
Rotterdam, Museum Boymans-van
Beuningen, inv. no. N 53

After the death of the Emperor, many artists left Prague, including van den Bossche, who then settled in Augsburg in 1614. Three landscapes by van den Bossche have survived from this period (Brussels, Bibliothèque Albert Ier, inv. no. F 20225; Dresden, Kupferstichkabinett, inv. no. C 1847; Rotterdam, Museum Boymans van Beuningen, inv. no. N-53). They are very similar, both in content and in composition. The example in Rotterdam showing a storm brewing is the most interesting. At the time it was still very rare for an artist to attempt to depict this form of natural phenomenon and the special atmospheric conditions that go with it. Van den Bossche is relatively successful here, showing the unusual light resulting from the fast-approaching storm clouds, with some areas already in dark shadow while others are still bathed in sunlight. Thus he dramatically heightens the effect of the storm hitting the land. He shows the particular tension induced by such a rapid change in the weather and demonstrates the terrifying effect of the storm, which is yet further emphasized by the incidental figures in the foreground.

T.G.

I.174
Daniel Fröschl
Augsburg 1563–Prague 1613
Madonna and Child with a Portrait of Dürer
Watercolours on parchment, stretched on
wood
Marked on the back: *Von Daniel Freschel*
43 × 32 cm
False date 1484; after 1604
From the collection of Rudolf II; inv. H
1619, no. 127; since 1772 in a gallery
Vienna, Kunsthistorisches Museum,
Gemäldegalerie, inv. no. 1932

This special transcription of two of Dürer's drawings originated after Fröschl had

definitely settled in Prague in 1604. Both
its models – *Madonna with Child* from 1512
(inv. no. 4848) and a *Self-portrait* dated
1484 (inv. no. 4839), which are today kept
in the Albertina in Vienna – formed part of
the imperial collection at Prague Castle.
Fröschl was able to study them, together
with other works by Albrecht Dürer, in the
rooms of the *Kunstkammer*. In 1607 he became an administrator of Rudolf's collections and had access to interesting material, which he used in his transcriptions of
well-known works into the form of miniatures. The linking of two of Dürer's works
that are significantly different in both
time and style is not clear: the *Self-portrait*

is the work of a thirteen-year-old boy,
whereas the artist painted the *Madonna* at
the peak of his glory. Without the inscription on the back of the parchment it
would be difficult to determine the author
of these copies as Fröschl held on to his
samples so faithfully. In Prague he gradually abandoned his habit of painting according to the models of others.

Prague 1912, cat. no. 120; Essen and Vienna 1988, cat. no. 117.

Fučíková 1972, pp. 150-51; Kaufmann
1988, cat. no. 3.2.

E.F.

I.175
Daniel Fröschl
Augsburg 1563–Prague 1613
*Two Satyrs and a Nymph (Jupiter and An-
tiope)*
Drawing in pen and ink in gray and
brown tones, ruddle, chalk and water-
colours on parchment
After 1604
Jourdeuil collection; donated by W. F.
Watson in 1881
Edinburgh, National Gallery of Scotland,
inv. no. D 3 071

As H. Geissler points out in the catalogue
to the Stuttgart exhibition, this print most

likely represents Jupiter, who in the guise
of a satyr seduced Antiope, daughter of
the king of Thebes (Propertius 3, 15).
Fröschl's works of this type basically constitute a transcription of designs by other
masters to the miniature format. Geissler
presumes that, in this case, the original
composition could have been the work of
Heintz, which seems to be likely. The attribution of this miniature to Fröschl was
generally accepted. Its `pointillistic' tech-
nique is the same as in Fröschl's signed
drawing in Vienna's Albertina dated to
1604, depicting – after Spranger's model
(cat. no. 3352) – Adam and Eve under the
tree of knowledge.

Stuttgart 1979/1980, cat. no. B28; Essen
and Vienna 1988, cat. no. 197.

Stuttgart 1979/1980, cat. no. B28; Kaufmann 1988, cat. and ill. no. 3.4; Essen
and Vienna 1988, cat. no. 197; Andrew 1991, pp.
6–7, ill. 24.

E.F.

I.176
Daniel Fröschl
Augsburg 1563–Prague 1613
Venus and Cupid
Watercolour on vellum
17.8 × 13.3 cm
Prague, 1613
Signed: *D.F.A. 1613*
Toronto, Frank and Marianne Seger
USA, private collection; with Paul Jero-
mack, New York, 1996

This unpublished miniature, which
Fröschl monogrammed and dated in the
last year of his life, complements the
handful of other miniatures known by

him. This composition of Venus coming
upon her son Cupid stringing his bow in a
woodland clearing is based on earlier imagery. Fröschl's setting in nature is shared
with Rubens's version dated 1614 (Schleis-
sheim, Schloss). That Venus is identical
with the figure of Diana (?) in a drawing
that has been attributed to Raffaellino da
Reggio in the British Museum (Gere and
Pouncey 1983, no. 239, ill.) was recently established by Paul Jeromack. The miniaturist may have known the drawing in Prague
and combined these sources; however, as
Zimmerman (1988, cat. no. E 41) has proposed that Heintz may have made a version of the British Museum composition,

it is likely that a lost composition by Heinz
combining these two figures was Fröschl's
source. A lost work by Heintz also can be
proposed as the source for the *Allegory of
Faith*, given its formal and stylistic connections with a *Gedenkblatt* by Anton
Gasser in honour of Heinz and based on a
lost work by this (Prague, Národní galerie;
Zimmerman 1988, fig. 11).

Gere 1983.

J.S.

I.177
Matthäus Gundelach
Kassel ? ca. 1565/67–Augsburg 1653/54
Minerva and Two Female Figures
Pen and brown ink and grey-brown wash,
heightened with white
15.6 × 10.7 cm
*Mattheus Gundelach / vonn Cassell
gesch[ehen] in Prag / 25. nouember / Anno.
93*
1593
Berlin art market 1933
Nürnberg, Germanisches Nationalmuseum, Graphische Sammlung, inv. no. Hz
41239 (Kapsel 568)

This little drawing is important as much
for what it tells us about Gundelach the
man as for what it shows of his development as an artist. It seems to be a drawing
for an album belonging to an otherwise
unidentified individual whom Gundelach
visited in Prague. The style of the drawing
shows that Gundelach was familiar with
Spranger's work and clearly admired it.
The drawing *Susanna and the Elders*, made
twelve years later, is in a style that is very
different but that does not usurp the earlier style; subsequently, these two styles together, plus the occasionally overriding
influence of Joseph Heintz, became the
mainstay of Gundelach's own personal

'style.' The actual iconography of this
small, oval piece has never been fully explained. This drawing is closely related to
a much more 'routine' drawing attributed
to Spranger, namely the *Young Painter with
Three Women*, now in Göttingen (Graphische Sammlung der Universität; see Wille
1963, p. 31, no. 86, ill. 33).

Nürnberg 1952, no. W 143; Essen and Vienna 1988, no. 203.

Bender 1981, pp. 290-91, no. ZA 15 (with
earlier literature).

J.Z.

I.178
Matthäus Gundelach
Kassel ? ca. 1565/67–Augsburg 1653/54
Apollo and Marsyas
Pen and brown ink, grey-brown wash over
chalk or pencil sketch on paper
30.9 × 20.8 cm
Mattheuus Gundelach. fe. / Ao: 1602
1602
Collection von Radowicz; acquired 1856
Berlin, Staatliche Museen zu Berlin,
Kupferstichkabinett, inv. no. KdZ 7 720

Only one small drawing by Gundelach has
an earlier date than this drawing of *Apollo
Flaying Marsyas* (see cat. no. I.177), which

was done when Gundelach was already
well into this thirties. The other drawing
was made eleven years earlier and there
are simply no works that can be located
with any certainty in the intervening years.
It is not possible to say whether this drawing was made in Prague or elsewhere. As
Bender has observed, it shows early evidence of Gundelach's contact with
Netherlandish landscape painting. It
clearly precedes his other two landscape
drawings (cat. nos I.180, I.181) and again illustrates an Ovidian narrative (*Metamorphoses*, VI, pp. 382-400; *Fasti* VI, pp. 703-8),
which in itself was one of the most popular motifs of the time. The relationship be-

tween figures and landscape is balanced
yet not without a degree of tension. The
landscape does not dominate. It stays as it
is, the scene of a cruel, mythical, yet 'real'
action. Although the two elements merge
into one another graphically, they are not
wholly integrated with each other.

Berlin 1996, no. 1.

Bender 1981, pp. 294-95 no. ZA 18; Groß
1996, pp. 8-10, no. 1.

J.Z.

I.179
Matthäus Gundelach
Kassel ? ca. 1565/67–Augsburg 1653/54
Joseph and Potiphar's Wife
Pen and grey-brown ink and wash, heightened with white on reddish-brown tinted paper
14.3 × 18 cm
M. / Gundolach F[ecit] P[ragae] / 1610
1610
Probably from the collection of the Emperor Rudolf II; 1934 ex Collection Graf de la Gardie, Borrestad (Sweden)
Berlin, Staatliche Museen zu Berlin, Kupferstichkabinett, KdZ no. 15 312

From the mid-sixteenth century right up until Rembrandt, there were numerous works depicting the Old Testament story of the failed attempted seduction and subsequent libellous accusation of Joseph by the wife of the Egyptian court official, Potiphar (Genesis 39:11–14). The story of Joseph and the Egyptian's wife was above all a worthy subject as a morally enlightening example of steadfastness and virtue, while at the same time it could strike a chord in the viewer's erotic imagination. This work shows Gundelach at his most successfully 'Rudolfine' and its artistic skill and refinement surpass, in my view, even that of the version of this story (see

cat. no I.790) made some decades before by his predecessor Joseph Heintz.

Stuttgart 1979–80, cat. no. F 14; Essen and Vienna 1988, cat. no. 201.

Bender 1981, pp. 236–37, no. ZA 1.

J.Z.

I.180
Matthäus Gundelach
Kassel ? ca. 1565/67–Augsburg 1653/54
Diana and Actaeon
Pen and brush and brown ink, wash, heightened with white on paper
17.2 × 11.9 cm
Probably between 1605 and 1615
Weimar, Kunstsammlungen zu Weimar, inv. KK 116

Countless artists, above all during the sixteenth and seventeenth centuries, have portrayed the fantastic tale of the hunter Actaeon's transformation into a stag (Ovid, *Metamorphoses*, III, 155ff.) because

he had observed the goddess and her companions as they bathed. However, Gundelach's drawing departs from the accepted iconography. He has transferred the mythical scene to a narrow gorge spanned by a primitive wooden bridge, which is Actaeon's vantage point. Thus the scene has both a realistic and a mythological level of meaning. The landscape is obviously of importance and dominates the picture space and is clearly influenced by Savery's landscape art, as in, for example, his series of engravings, the *Six Woodland Scenes* (see Essen and Vienna 1988, cat. no. 311) or his *Mountainous Landscape* of 1607–8 (*ibid.*, cat. no. 246, col. pl. 60).

Hämeenlinna/Turun 1960, no. 25; Venezia 1987, no. 17; Essen and Vienna 1988, cat. no. 200.

Bender 1981, pp. 291–92, no. ZA 16 (with earlier bibliography).

J.Z.

I.181
Matthäus Gundelach
Kassel ? ca. 1565/67–Augsburg 1653/54
Attack in the Forest
Pen and brown ink, bluish and brown wash, heightened with white on paper
15.9 × 20.5 cm
M / Gundolah
Probably between 1605 and 1615
Weimar, Kunstsammlungen zu Weimar, inv. no. KK 115

Landscape paintings by Rudolfine 'figurative' artists are a rarity (none by Heintz has survived for example). Painters Roelandt Savery and Pieter Stevens were the special-

ists in this genre. Thus it is surprising that Gundelach, who was still learning his trade in the early seventeenth century, should have taken up the form several times. In this landscape the somewhat indistinct ambush is no more than an iconographic pretext, as in *Diana and Actaeon*. Gundelach's landscape style in this work has echoes of Roelandt Savery's *Landscape with Stream* (Prague, Národní galerie v Praze, 0611). As his other 'early' drawings also show, Gundelach, although by now (presumably) into his fifties, was still keen to explore and expand his own repertoire as an artist.

Erfurt 1952, no. 9; Hämeenlinna/Turun 1960, no. 25; Weimar 1977, no. 12.

Bender 1981, pp. 308–9, no. ZA 29; Fučíková 1986, p. 21, pl. 36.

J.Z.

I.182
Matthäus Gundelach
Kassel ? ca. 1565/67–Augsburg 1653/54
Mercury and Herse
Pen and brush and brown ink, brown and bluish wash over red chalk sketch, heightened with white (partially blackened) on paper
23.9 × 16.8 cm
M / Gundelach / F. / 1613
1613
Ex István Delhaes Collection
Budapest, Szépmüvészeti Múzeum, Graphic Collection, inv. no. 81

It seems that Rudolf II owned a picture of

Mercury, Herse and Aglaurus (Ovid, *Metamorphoses*, II, 738ff.) by Veronese (now in Cambridge, Fitzwilliam Museum). However, when it came to Gundelach's strongly 'Rudolfine' *Mercury and Herse*, the Emperor was no longer alive to appreciate it, nor did he survive to see Gundelach's *Amor and Psyche* from the same year. Uncertainty surrounds the iconography of this relatively carefully finished work, as it does others. Thus in 1987 Gerszi (Salzburg 1987, p. 28) was still using the title *Jupiter and Kallisto*. However, since 1988 the title *Mercury Discovers Herse* (a name of unknown invention) has gained general acceptance, although not in the sense of an

'illustration' of any particular scene but more as a distillation of the spirit of the whole.

Budapest 1931, no. 239; Budapest 1961, no. 85; Vienna 1967, no. 55; Washington, Chicago and Los Angeles 1985, no. 54; Salzburg 1987, no. 5; Essen 1988, no. 202.

Bender 1981, pp. 293–94, no. ZA 17; *Prag um 1600*, 1988, vol. I, p. 346, no. 202, col. pl. 54 (Jürgen Zimmer, with earlier bibliography).

J.Z.

I.183
Matthäus Gundelach
Kassel ? ca. 1565/1567–
Augsburg 1653/1654
The Painter
Black chalk, pen and brown ink and wash on paper
16.6 × 12.1 cm, upright oval
Probably between 1615 and 1625
From the collection of Charles, Prince de Ligne
Vienna, Albertina, Graphische Sammlung, inv. no. 3 461

On 27 April 1595 Rudolf II issued a 'Letter of Majesty' officially raising the status of

painting from that of 'craft' to 'art'. In this work Gundelach shows his profession not only in its protected status but also on a more intimate level, framed by *Genius* and (possibly) *Eros*, with wings and clad in the clothes of antiquity. Genius is holding compasses and a straight-edge, the tools of architecture. The implied reference may be to the competition among the various arts (Paragone), and this may represent an attempt to assert the primacy of painting. Be that as it may, the subject of this small work was one that was frequently depicted at the time (see for example Hanna Peter-Raupp on the subject of 'art and artists' in German drawing between 1540 and 1640,

in *Zeichnung in Deutschland. Deutsche Zeichner 1540–1640*, ed. Heinrich Geissler, vol. 2 (Stuttgart, 1980), pp. 223–30). Joseph Heintz the Elder turned his attention to this theme in the 1590s, drawing on a more complex iconology.

Vienna 1998–89, no. 617.

Bender 1981, pp. 303–4, no. ZA 25; *Prag um 1600*, vol. 2, 1988, p. 153, no. 617 (Jürgen Zimmer).

J.Z.

I.184
Matthäus Gundelach
Kassel ? ca. 1565/67–Augsburg 1653/54
The Assembly of the Gods
Pen and brown ink over black chalk (or
charcoal?) underdrawing, brown and red
wash, heightened with white, on paper
36.8 × 51.2 cm
Dresden, Staatliche Kunstsammlungen,
Kupferstichkabinett, inv. no. 1967-460

Previously attributed to an otherwise unknown artist by the name of Matthias
Starsberg, this work has been reattributed
by Heinrich Geissler to Gundelach. The
drawing is in fact a fine example of Gun-

delach's style. In this rather unconventional *The Assembly of the Gods*, the artist
pays particular attention to the marginal
figures, gods and heroes alike. The right-
hand side is dominated by Hercules, with
Atlas behind him and Marsyas coming into the picture from the lower right. To the
left of Hercules is a satyr and a female
satyr with a jug. The real 'centre' of the
scene, surrounded by putti, where the
gods are actually gathering, is over in the
left half of the picture. It is also just possible to make out Neptune and Jupiter,
while Minerva and perhaps Ceres have
their place at the left-hand edge of the
scene. In the lower left corner of the pic-

ture there is a woman with the lid of a jug
or bowl. The overarching iconology of this
work has not yet been satisfactorily explained. It is also not clear whether this is
a drawing in its own right or, as seems
likely, intended as a design for a painting
or some other graphic treatment, but no
related painting or engraving has survived. Gundelach's 'handwriting' in this
work does not really give away the date
when it was made, so one can only assume
that this was at some point between 1605
and 1620.

J.Z.

I.185
Jeremias Günther
Fl. as painter to the court in Prague 1604–
19
Aristotle and Phyllis
Black and red chalk on paper
22.2 × 16.9 cm
IG (lig.) *inther F. 1600*
1600
Acquired 1926
Prague, Národní galerie, Grafická sbírka,
inv. no. K 4 510

This minutely precise copy after a work by
Heintz (likewise made in 1600; see cat. no
I.202) is the only known surviving drawing

by Günther. He was employed at both the
court of Rudolf II and the court of Emper-
or Matthias for many years as portraitist,
costume and ceremonial decorations designer, restorer and copyist, but there are
only two works documented in his name:
this drawing, which is also the earliest
record of his work, and a monogrammed
full-length portrait of *Empress Anna* made
in 1613 (Vienna, Kunsthistorisches Museum, inv. no. 3092).

Prague 1978–79, cat. no. 12; Essen and Vienna 1988, cat. no. 198.

Gerszi 1958, p. 58, ill. 21; Fučíková 1967, p.

156; Zimmer 1971, p. 25; Kaufmann 1988,
p. 178.

J.Z.

I.186
Joseph Heintz the Elder
Basel 1564–Prague 1609
Standing Soldier
Pen and brown ink and wash, minimally
heightened with white on paper
42 × 16.4 cm
Bottom left: *noch Tadeo Zuccero Jcseph
Heintz / Rom 1585*
1585
Darmstadt, Hessisches Landesmuseum,
Graphische Sammlung, inv. no. AE 359

This is one of Heintz's early copies, which
shows, along with many others, how intensively he studied the Old Masters in

Rome, having moved there from an apprenticeship in Basel with Hans Bock the
Elder. He was to stay in the metropolis,
then also the hub of the art world, for almost ten years. In this quite fastidious
work (evidently cut later), Heintz has
copied part of the famous wall painting by
Taddeo Zuccaro, who had died in 1566,
namely the soldier from the *Donatio Con-
stantini* of 1561 in the Sala Reggia in the
Vatican Palace. No doubt he was attracted
by the angle and the foreshortening of the
soldier's solid, yet pleasing, physical form.

Zimmer 1988, pp. 126–27, no. A 35, ill. 71
(with earlier bibliography).

J.Z.

I.187
Joseph Heintz the Elder
Basel 1564–Prague 1609
Rape of a Sabine Woman (after Giambologna)
Black chalk, drawn over (perhaps later)
with pen and black ink, on pale ochre-
coloured paper
34.4 × 22 cm
Probably ca. 1587
In 1770 ex Sammlung Friedrich, Armand
von Uffenbach, Frankfurt
Göttingen, Kunstsammlung der Universität, Graphische Sammlung, inv. no. H
650

This drawing after Giambologna's *Rape of
a Sabine Woman* of 1583 (Florence, Loggia
dei Lanzi) does not reproduce any of the
known graphic reproductions of the same
subject. This means it can only have been
made from the original in Florence.
Heintz evidently made this relatively large,
careful drawing at much the same time as
his drawing after Michelangelo's bozzetto
(see cat. no. I.189). The *Rape of a Sabine
Woman* is not signed, but a faithful copy of
it by Hans Friedrich Sch[r]orer (Dresden,
Kupferstichkabinett) is marked on the
back with the words 'nach des Joseph
Haintz', thus confirming that this is the
work of Heintz, as the style also suggests.

Zimmer 1988, p. 121, no. A 22, ill. 57.

J.Z.

I.188
Joseph Heintz the Elder
Basel 1564–Prague 1609
Group of Figures from the *Massacre of the
Innocents* (after Tintoretto)
Pen and brown ink and wash over faint
chalk sketch on paper; strip of paper at-
tached to top edge
29.5 × 42 cm
Monogram: *IOHE* (lig.), including num-
bers and indications of colours in the
artist's own hand
Ca. 1587–89
Moscow, Muzej Pushkina, inv. no. 13 365

This is another of the many copies the

young Heintz made as studies, now no
longer in Rome or Florence but in Venice,
where Tintoretto had just completed his
work in the Scuola di S. Rocco (lower
room). It is only the discreet numbers and
abbreviations of names of colours that
give Heintz's version away as a study. Other drawings by Heintz also show evidence
of his meticulous approach to his work
(see cat. no. I.191): *Two Riders Springing to
the Right*). No doubt the challenge of this
subject was the portrayal of violent movement within a limited space along with the
foreshortened perspective that this requires.

Zimmer 1988, p. 129, no. A 40, ill. 78.

J.Z.

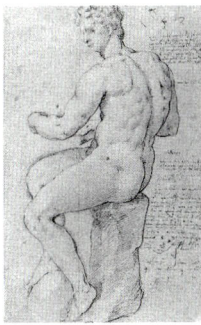

I.189
Joseph Heintz the Elder
Basel 1564–Prague 1609
Sitting Male Nude (after Michelangelo)
Black chalk, heightened with white on
blue tinted paper
31.3 × 19.2 cm
Monogram IOHE (lig.), inscribed: *MA*
(lig.) *ngl. / vom hals grub(en)...der fus 1/2*
Weimar, Staatliche Kunstsammlungen,
inv. no. KK 121

This is a study after a lost (? terracotta)
bozzetto by Michelangelo for the seated figure of *Giuliano de' Medici, Duke of Nemours*,
in the New Sacristy in S. Lorenzo in Florence (between 1520 and 1534) and can be
identified as such on the evidence of the
posture of the seated figure, but also by
other, quite different studies of Michelangelo's work (Oxford, Christ Church Library, no. 759rv, 760rv; and Rotterdam,
Museum Boymans-van Beuningen). This
work is good evidence of Heintz's diligent
application to his studies. In this case he
was less interested in creating a convincing copy of Michelangelo's *bozzetto* than in
discovering the proportions of such a
masterly piece, and thus by definition
learning specifically about Michelangelo's
principles of proportion. This is evident
from the detailed, unfortunately not entirely legible annotations on the right-
hand edge, which in themselves would be
worth closer study. This drawing on tinted
Venetian paper was clearly intended not as
an artwork *sui generis* but simply as a working document for the artist. While it
demonstrates his meticulous methods
and 'artistic zeal', it is not itself technically
perfect.

Gerszi 1988, p. 306 (only ill. 4); Zimmer
1988, pp. 121–22, no. A 23, ill. 58.

J.Z.

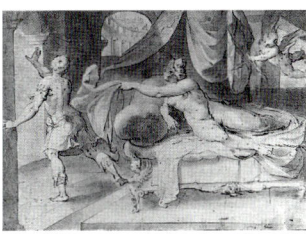

I.190
Joseph Heintz the Elder
Basel 1564–Prague 1609
Joseph and Potiphar's Wife
Pen and brown ink and wash on paper
23.1 × 33.3 cm
Lower right: *Joseph Heintz*
Probably after 1587
Vienna, Albertina, Graphische Samm-
lung, inv. no. 3 316

This accomplished pen-and-ink drawing
hardly looks like preliminary work for a
painting or an engraving: it is too 'pictorial,' too self-contained. It is in accord with
the iconography of the sixteenth century
(? Titian). The tension inherent in its subject-matter is expressed more on a formal
level in line and gesture than by the portrayal of mental conflict. On an emotional
level, this composition by Heintz, adhering to convention as it does, seems less
imaginative than the depiction of the
same Old Testament theme by Matthäus
Gundelach in 1610 (see cat. no. I.179).

Zimmer 1988, p. 127, no. A 37, ill. 72 (with
earlier bibliography).

J.Z.

I.191
Joseph Heintz the Elder
Basel 1564–Prague 1609
Descent From the Cross (after Tintoretto)
Pen and brown ink and wash, heightened
with white (some black) on paper
29 × 34.8 cm
Bottom left: *Joseph Heintz*
1588–95
Basel, Kunstmuseum, Kupferstichkabi-
nett, Öffentliche Kunstsammlung, inv.
no. 1910.66

Among the painters at the court of Rudolf
II, Heintz is notable for his copies of works
both by artists from previous generations
and by his own contemporaries, above all
by the most important Italian masters.
These have survived in large numbers and,
as far as one can tell, they served two purposes: first and foremost, to study and acquire various techniques; second, to 'reproduce' works that could be seen
elsewhere only as originals. Thus Heintz's
copies yield an unusually accurate picture
of the sources that he and his colleagues
at the court in Prague were drawing on,
and which, by definition, constituted the
substratum of art in the Rudolfine court.
This drawing, held in Basel, is a copy of
Tintoretto's *Descent of Christ* (Venice, Galleria dell'Accademia, inv. no. 217), painted
in 1559 for the Chiesa dell'Umiltà in
Venice, which was dissolved in 1824. It
must have been at about the same time
that the young Aegidius Sadeler II engraved the same work by Tintoretto (Hollstein 54) although there is no known connection between these two reproductions.

Zimmer 1988, pp. 129–30, no. A 42, ill. 79.

J.Z.

I.192
Joseph Heintz the Elder
Basel 1564–Prague 1609
Painter with Fame and Another Person
Pen and brown ink and wash, green and
red ink on paper
20.3 × 16.2 cm
*Simplicita et / Gusto con sincerita / a buon
fine conducero / Isepo Heintz Heluet(us). f.*
Probably ca. 1592–94
From the Wagner Collection in Leipzig in
1728, displayed in 1893
Dresden, Staatliche Kunstsammlungen,
Kupferstichkabinett, inv. no. C 6383

While Gundelach believed that the art of
painting was protected by *genius* (cat. no.
I.183), Heintz, by contrast, focuses on the
artist's fame and reputation (*fama*). A
painter, already crowned with a laurel
wreath, gives voice to his intentions and
hopes for fame and honour: 'Einfachheit
und Geschmack werden mich wahrhaftig
zu einem guten Ende führení (Simplicity
and taste will surely lead me to a good
end'). This drawing is in a quite different
style from other painstakingly executed
works by Heintz; this style crops up in various works throughout his career, for example in *Die Zeit bringt die Wahrheit ans
Licht* (Time brings the truth to light) of
1586 (Basel, Kupferstichkabinett, inv. no.
Bi.375.10) and in *Allegorie* of 1606
(Moscow, Muzej Pushkina, inv. no. 6964).
The characteristic of this style is not that it
portrays 'historias' but that it treats subjects on a different, often allegorical, level
of reality.

Zimmer 1988, p. 131, no. A 46, ill. 84 (with
earlier bibliography).

J.Z.

I.193
Joseph Heintz the Elder
Basle 1564–Prague 1609
Pan and Daphnis
Drawing with chalk and ruddle
37.9 × 25.9 cm
1593
Vienna, Graphische Sammlung Albertina,
inv. no. 3319

Essen and Vienna 1988, cat. no. 210.

E.F.

I.194
Joseph Heintz the Elder
Basel 1564–Prague 1609
Portrait of Aegidius Sadeler II
Black chalk over ? pencil sketch, on fine,
thin paper
16.5 × 12.7 cm
At one time accompanied by a strip of pa-
per with *Aegidius Sadeler, Kupferstecher* in a
later hand; this was removed in 1984
Probably ca. 1591–93
Munich, Staatliche Graphische Sammlun-
gen, inv. no. 34 825

It is clear that the name on the strip of paper, now removed from the drawing, was
indeed that of the sitter, for this subject's
features are indisputably those of Aegidius Sadeler, even as portrayed as late as
1629 by Pieter de Iode in his portrait engraving. Heintz made this portrait of the
twenty-two-year-old Aegidius Sadeler, the
most gifted of a whole family of engravers
from Antwerp – here seen in his fashionable *berretto a tozzo* – at around the time
when the two artists first met in Rome and
Sadeler was beginning to engrave works
after originals by Heintz. In 1597 Rudolf
himself issued an invitation to Sadeler to
come to the court in Prague. In its sensitivity and elegance this drawing has something about it of the portrait of Heintz by
Giovanni da Bologna, which had probably
been made a few years previously (Zimmer
1988, pp. 117–19, no. A 16, ill. 50). It is already evident from these drawings that
Heintz was a particularly gifted portrait
artist, as skilled in taking care over his sitters' features as in making the few deft
strokes that were all he needed to capture
the essence of the overall form.

Essen and Vienna 1988, no. 206

Zimmer 1988, pp. 132–33, no. A 49, ill. 91
(with earlier bibliography).

J.Z.

I.195
Joseph Heintz the Elder
Basel 1564–Prague 1609
Studies of Nymphs (recto and verso)
Red and black chalk on yellowish paper
21 × 18.3 cm
Probably ca. 1595–1600
From the Wiesböck and Delhaes
Collections
Budapest, Szépmüvészetí Múzeum, Col-
lection of Prints and Drawings, inv. no. 83

This virtuoso drawing hardly strikes one
as a sketch: the charming female figure
combing her hair is highly detailed. However, this well-known work by Heintz certainly is a sketch or a study in that it has
been executed on maculature, that is to
say, paper that has already been used for
some other purpose. In this case the paper
seems to have originated in the workshop
of a clockmaker in Augsburg or Prague
and bears the name of the president of the
Privy Council, Sixt Trautson.

Budapest 1931, no. 236; 1942, no. 89; 1961,
no. 93; Salzburg 1987, no. 6; Essen and Vienna 1988, no. 212.

Zimmer 1988, p. 142, nos 66, 67, ill. 107,
108.

J.Z.

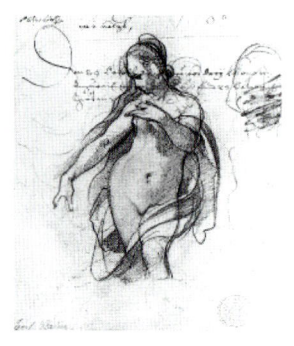

I.196
Joseph Heintz the Elder
Basel 1564–Prague 1609
Study of the Rape of Persephone
Light red chalk over pencil or chalk
sketch on thin, yellowish paper
18.2 × 17.7 cm
Stuttgart, Staatsgalerie, Graphische
Sammlung, inv. no. C 3761

At some point before 1605, Heintz painted
his *Rape of Persephone* (Dresden, Staatliche
Kunstsammlungen, Gemäldegalerie Alte
Meister, inv. no. 1971). This was then engraved in 1605 by Lukas Kilian (Zimmer
1971, no. A 21.0.1.1), which led to its becoming one of Heintz's best-known works.
This small drawing, a similar style of sketch
to *Mars and Venus* (see cat. no.I.197), could
be a preliminary study for the work now in
Dresden if the latter were the only work of
that kind by Heintz. However, in 1675 Sandrart reported that Heintz painted another work on this theme for the Emperor.
Only the work in Dresden has survived.
There are differences between the sketch
and the painting: on the sketch Pluto and
Persephone are travelling downwards, as
the narrative of the myth might lead one
to expect, whereas on the painting they
are moving upwards. The conflict between
Pluto and Persephone is more evident on
the sketch, where Persephone – understandably — is seen to be resisting more
strongly. Without knowing more about
the 'missing' second painting, it is not possible to be more precise about the original
purpose of this sketch.

Vienna 1988–89, no. 623.

Prag um 1600, vol. 2, 1988, pp. 157–58, no.
623 (Jürgen Zimmer); Zimmer 1988, pp.
149–50, no. A 78, ill. 120 (with earlier bibliography).

J.Z.

I.197
Joseph Heintz the Elder
Basel 1564–Prague 1609
Mars and Venus
Black chalk on paper
17.6 × 26 cm
Probably 1595–1605
? Collection Conte St Germain, Samm-
lung König, Gesellschaft patriotischer
Kunstfreunde, Prague
Prague, Národní galerie v Praze, Grafická
sbírka – inv. no. K 37 917

The attribution of this work has been
much discussed, but it is obviously the
work of Joseph Heintz.

Prague 1978, no. 14; Prague 1982, p. 97, no.
82

Fučíková 1986, pp. 21 and 231, pl. 34; Zimmer 1988, pp. 142–43, no. A 68, ill. 103
(with earlier bibliography).

J.Z.

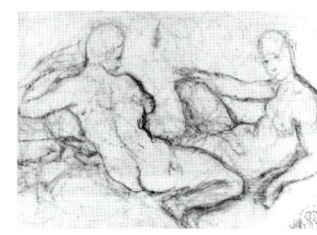

I.198
Joseph Heintz the Elder
Basel 1564–Prague 1609
Allegorical-Mythological Composition
Black and red chalk over faint pencil
38.3 × 23.4 cm
1595–1600
N. Esterházy Collection (L. 1965)
Budapest, Szépmüvészeti Múzeum, inv.
no. 82

The meaning of this allegory is not clear.
Various figures are grouped round a seated small child. Some of the figures are giving the child presents. The figures on the
right are personifications of the seasons.
The crouching female figure may be
Venus, with the Graces in attendance behind her, perhaps embodying the notion
of giving, receiving and replying. On the
version of this work held in the Albertina
in Vienna, these female figures are shown
in the traditional manner, but their arrangement in another version of this work
held in Gdansk, itself closely linked to the
Budapest version, is not readily comprehensible. All this suggests that the Viennese version was the first and that later
versions were altered for unknown reasons. The indented outlines of the Budapest version suggest that this was accepted as the final version and was
perhaps used for a relief or some other
purpose. Recently this work has been interpreted as an allegory of the New Year
(Geissler [1979], p. 80).

Budapest 1931, cat. no. 235; Washington
and Chicago 1985, cat. no. 53; Salzburg
1987, cat. no. 8; Essen and Vienna 1988,
cat. no. 621/2; Budapest 1991, cat. no. 28.

Gerszi 1958, pp. 36–40; Geissler 1979–80,
p. 65, cat. no. B21; Zimmer 1988, pp. 67–68,
no. A65.

T.G.

I.199
Joseph Heintz the Elder
Basel 1564–Prague 1609
Allegory of the Birth of a Prince
Dark red chalk, black chalk on fine, white paper
30.2 × 20.2 cm
Collection Jakob Kabrun, Gdansk
Gdansk, Muzeum Narodowe, Graphic Collection, inv. no. MNG/SD/866/R (Kbr. 8352)

This splendid drawing comes between two other drawings in Heintz's own hand on the same theme, although the theme itself has not yet been satisfactorily explained; examples of three works on the same theme are rare in Heintz's output. The progress of the work is shown at very different stages in the other two examples (Vienna, Albertina, inv. no. 3317, and Budapest, Szépmüvészeti Múseum, Collection of Prints and Drawings, inv. no. 83); both in Essen and Vienna contained no. 621/I.2). The drawing in Vienna is the richest, with countless figures and quite sketchlike in its style; the drawing in Gdansk has fewer figures and is in a somewhat looser style: with fewer motifs it is closer to the carefully worked-out version in Budapest. The generally accepted view that this work treats the birth of a prince is unsatisfactory, not least because it is impossible to say who the prince might be. Perhaps a more convincing, also more general, interpretation would be that this is a 'New Year's allegory', particularly in view of the presence of the seasons and the two 'nymphs' that are discernible in amongst the iconographic richness of the Viennese version.

Stuttgart 1979–80, cat. no. B 20.

Zimmer 1988, p. 141, no. A 64, ill. 106.

J.Z.

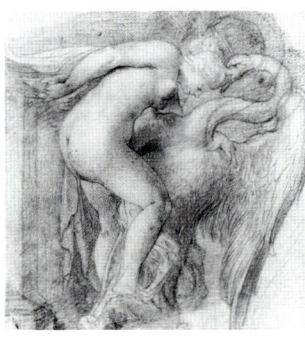

I.200
Joseph Heintz the Elder
Basel 1564–Prague 1609
Leda with the Swan
Red chalk on yellowish paper
19.8 × 17.9 cm
Probably ca. 1600
1949, from Vincene Karmář collection
Prague, Národní galerie v Praze, Grafická sbírka, inv. no. K 12 069

This story of Jupiter also comes from Ovid's *Metamorphoses* (VI, 109). It is one of three surviving versions of the story, and although it is the most carefully worked, it is not the most convincing, which distinction must go to the one now held in Vienna (cat. no. I.201). In terms of its form, this work draws on a long iconographic tradition. However, Heintz has taken the comparatively stiff, rather cool 'models' from Antiquity (see for example the copy after an Antique original in the so-called *Fossombron Sketchbook*, fol. 88v) and has transferred the scene into a more real, sensual world that is defined by the search for an aesthetically polished *maniera singolare*, although without completely abandoning the principles of antiquity.

Dresden 1977, no. 25; Prague 1978–79, no. 13; Stuttgart 1979–80, no. B 23; Paris 1981, no. 20; Prague 1982, no. 80; Essen and Vienna 1988, no. 209.

Zimmer 1988, p. 139, no. A 62, ill. 102 (with earlier bibliography).

J.Z.

I.201
Joseph Heintz the Elder
Basel 1564–Prague 1609
Leda with the Swan
Red chalk over black chalk or pencil sketch on paper
41.4 × 28.6 cm
Vienna, Graphische Sammlung Albertina, inv. no. 282

This tale of Jupiter's desire and his transformation into a swan comes from Ovid's *Metamorphoses* (VI, 109), where the poet describes the metamorphoses of the gods of antiquity and the gods, half-gods and humans that they desired, loved and hated. The Italian poet and near-contemporary of Heintz's, Andrea dall'Anguillara, took up and embellished Ovid's sparse account of the tale, and Heintz is known to have portrayed these events in a painting with which Sandrart was acquainted in 1675 but which has subsequently been lost. This drawing and two more related drawings (see also cat. no. I.200) are presumably chance survivors of Heintz's preliminary work on the painting. The one now held in Vienna is the most convincing of the three, although it is also the sketchiest; comments on cat. no. I.200 in this exhibition are particularly relevant here too.

Essen and Vienna 1988, cat, no. 208.

Zimmer 1988, pp. 138–39, no. A 60, ill. 100 (with earlier bibliography).

J.Z.

I.202
Joseph Heintz the Elder
Basel 1564–Prague 1609
Aristotle and Phyllis
Black and red chalk on thin, brownish paper
20.2 × 14.7 cm
Upper left: *Zu guter frindschaff vnd gedechtnus / hab ich Joseph Heintz dis / gemacht in prag* (?) / *Ano 160* (in the artist's own hand)
1600
From the István Delhaes Collection
Budapest, Szépmüvészeti Múzeum, Collection of Prints and Drawings, inv. no. 84

From the inscription it seems that this drawing, which has become one of Heintz's best-known works, was made for an album, with an unknown owner. Meanwhile, this drawing The coloured chalks, used here in the style of Raphael and Michelangelo, give the work a particular richness. The contents of the work take up a popular idea, namely the triumph of female charms over male wisdom. By the time of Rudolf II, this topic already had a long tradition on which Heintz could draw: while keeping within its bounds, Heintz lent a particular appeal to it in the shape of the beautifully proportioned back view of the nude, which in itself derived from even older traditions of Antiquity. Jeremias Günther (see cat. no. I.185) copied this small work by Heintz the very year it was made (1600). Comparison of these two works quickly shows how important art-historical criteria are in distinguishing an original from a copy.

Budapest 1931, no. 237; Budapest 1961, no. 91; Salzburg 1987, no. 7; Essen 1988, no. 204.

Gerszi 1958, p. 36, ill. 22; Zimmer 1988, p. 145, no. A 73, col. pl. VIII.

J.Z.

I.203
Joseph Heintz the Elder
Basel 1564–Prague 1600
Pietà with Angels
Black and red chalk, lightly gone over with pen, heightened with white, on paper
40.7 × 26 cm
IOHE (in ligature) *intz. F. 1607* (in the artist's own hand)
Acquired 1872
London, College Art Collections, University College London, inv. no. 3668

This splendid drawing, detailed and seemingly complete in itself, is only one of a group of works that has only survived by chance and even then is not complete. The group includes the altarpiece painting of 1607 in Augsburg in the Friedrichskapelle St Michael, Lukas Kilian's engraving of 1608 (Zimmer 1971, pp. 82–83, no. A 8, A 8.0.1, ill.) and two studies. Many artists made 'copies' from Kilian's engraving, with the result that this became one of Heintz's best-known works. This drawing is clearly not a design for the Augsburg work but served in its own right as the drawing for Kilian's engraving. The two other drawings were, however, clearly part of the design stage: one is lost and now known only as a photograph (previously in Aschaffenburg, Graphische Sammlung), while the other, with details of the heads of two putti, has survived (Zurich, Kunsthaus). The central figure of Maria is both a quotation of and a variation on a famous predecessor: the *Pietà* for Vittoria Colonna by Michelangelo.

Düsseldorf 1967, no. 11; London 1969–70; no. 25; Augsburg 1980, no. 626; Essen and Vienna 1988, no. 211.

Zimmer 1988, pp. 151–52, no. A 82, ill. 125.

J.Z.

I.204
Jacob Hoefnagel
Antwerp 1575–? Holland ca. 1603
Allegory of the Humanist Virtue
Red chalk, heightened with white
19.9 × 14.8 cm
On lower edge: *Jacobus Hoefnagel F. in
Praege An° 1559 Adiy 12 Augusty*
1599
I. Delhaes Collection
Budapest, Szépmüvészeti Múzeum, inv.
no. 1337

This seascape with a ship symbolizes the
view back over an illustrious past. The
storm and the rocks suggest threats to life,
the packets and barrels represent life's
trivia. The female figure who has escaped
danger and reached the shore is the personification of virtue. In her hand she
holds an olive branch encircled by snakes
– the attributes of Minerva and Mercury –
symbolizing the sciences and the arts, and
it is to these that the inscription refers
with the words 'All that I have I bear with
me.' The ox's hide on the figure's back – associated with Hercules – stands as a symbol of the diligence necessary to acquire
wisdom and knowledge, which the humanists believed could offer a bulwark for
the individual faced with the vicissitudes
of life. The late sixteenth century and the
early seventeenth century were racked by
historical catastrophes, and as a result the
humanists ascribed ever-increasing importance to the ideal of *virtus intellectualis*,
which was then taken up and further
propagated in visual terms by the artists
of the day.

Salzburg 1987, cat. no. 10; Essen and Vienna 1988, cat. no. 217; Budapest 1991, cat.
no. 18.

Gerszi 1971, no. 107; Gerszi 1972, pp. 755–
57.

T.G.

I.205
Unknown Artist (Jacob Hoefnagel?)
White Horse
Watercolour with body colour on parch-
ment
7.9 × 10.4 cm
Monogram below left: *JH* (?)(lig.)
Ca. 1600
Amsterdam, Rijksmuseum, Rijks-
prentenkabinet, inv. no. 05:161

The technique used here, along with the
monogram, led Boon to attribute it to
Joris Hoefnagel. However, there is no similar signature either by Joris Hoefnagel or
by his son Jacob. Both the landscape and
the horse are in keeping with German-
Netherlandish miniature painting from
around 1600. The particular configuration
of landscape, horse and the foreground
suggest that this could have been painted
after an engraving of a galloping horse
from the series *Pferde verschiedener Länder*
(*Horses from Different Lands*) by Antonio
Tempesta, which had been engraved in
1590.

Bartsch 36, pp. 196, 952 [161]; Boon 1978,
pp. 112ff., no. 319 (under the name of Joris
Hoefnagel).

Th.V.W.

I.206
Joris Hoefnagel
Allegory of Air
Watercolour with colours in the
parchment
12 × 17.3 cm
AIER (above); *Qui ponis nubem ascensum
tuum, qui/ambulas super pen/ nas vento-
rum/ Ps: 103 (below)*
Before 1600
New York, lent by the Metropolitan Museum of Art, Gift of Mrs Darwin, inv. no.
63.200.4

This cabinet miniature comes together
with others from the Lichtenstein collection at Vaduz (inv. no. GR 401) in the series entitled *The Four Elements*. While the
sheet from New York represents Air, the
Vaduz parchment is marked 'Terra' (earth).
The allegories of water and fire which belonged to the series have not been preserved. The surface of the picture is laden
with flying insects. Some of the specimens
depicted are taken from the work *Archetyp*
– for example, the large stag-beetle. Since
the composition of the miniature has not
been carried out to perfection, as is customary in Joris's work, and the depiction
of individual types from the insect world
has been superimposed, we cannot exclude the possibility that the work was
painted over by Jacob Hoefnagel.

Koreny 1985, p. 126 (listed as Joris Hoefnagel); Kaufmann 1988, cat. no. 10.2 (listed as Jacob Hoefnagel); Vignau-Wilberg
1989–90, pp. 70–71.

Th.V.W.

I.207
Joris Hoefnagel
Antwerp 1542–Vienna 1601
Allegory with a View of Munich and Landshut
Watercolour with body colour on parch-
ment, heightened with gold
23.5 × 18 cm
In the cartouche below: *Inventio opusque
Georgii Hoefnaglii natura magistra Monaci
Ao 1579*; on the two panels above: *Parcere
subiectis* and *et debellare superbos*; above the
view of Landshut: *Tibi lilia plenis ecce ferunt
nymphae calathis*
1579
Kunstkammer of Duke Wilhelm V of
Bavaria, Munich, inv. 1598, no. 2957; Na-
gler Collection (until 1835)
Berlin, Staatliche Museen, Kupferstichkabinett, inv. no. KdZ 4804

This cabinet miniature celebrates Duke
Albrecht V of Bavaria as a patron of the
arts. Hoefnagel had entered the service of
the Duke in spring 1578 and was then
completing a drawing of Landshut (Munich, Staatliche Graphische Sammlung,
preparatory drawing for Braun-Hogen-
berg, vol. 3, 45), where the fort of Trausnitz
had been transformed into a *Lustschloß* for
the relaxation of the owners and their
friends. The lines from Virgil's *Bucolica*
(*Ecloga*, vol. 2, 45f.) are intended here as a
reference to the fine gardens at Trausnitz.
The line from Virgil's *Aeneid* – 'Parcere
subiectis et debellare superbos' (vol. 6,
853) – was the Duke's own personal motto.
Symbols of wisdom and knowledge and attributes of the fine arts and music all refer
to Orlando di Lasso, the great composer to
the court of Albrecht V, and also to the
composer Cipriano Rore.

Munich 1980, vol. 1, no. 65.

Bock 1921, p. 46; Schilling 1956, pp. 233ff.,
ill. 4; Vignau-Wilberg 1985, pp. 117ff., ill.
99; Nuti 1988, pp. 214ff.

Th.V.W.

I.208
Joris Hoefnagel
Antwerp 1542–Vienna 1601
Sheet Dedicated to Johann Muisenhol
Watercolour with body colour on
parchment
8.9 × 12.3 cm
Above: *Neque navem una anchora neque vitam una spes fulciat / Mus non uni fidet
antro*; below: *Monument: amicitiae D: Ioan-
ni muisenhol / G: Houfna: D. genio duce Ao
1594*
1594
Amsterdam, Rijksmuseum, Rijksprentenkabinet, inv. no. RP-T-A 3115

This engaging print was a present from
Hoefnagel to his friend Johannes Muizenhol, whose name, 'mouse hole', explains
this picture of two mice on a wooden floor
filled with holes. The implication is that,
just as mice always keep more than one escape route in their sights, so too human
beings should not concentrate all their efforts in one direction. Hoefnagel accompanies the image with a quotation from
the *Adagia* by Erasmus (edition of 1551,
vol. 5, pt I, IV), which may well also have
been Muizenhol's own personal motto.
Mouse and *Adagium* are found together
again in the *Archetypa* (Part I, 10). A candle
end and a nutshell remind the viewer of
the transience of life, while the mouse itself seems to be gnawing away at our stock
of time.

Essen and Vienna 1988, no. 221; Frankfurt
1993/94, no. 106.

Bol [n.p., n.d.], p. 15, no. 2, ill.; Wilberg Vignau-Schuurman 1969, vol. 1, pp. 186ff; vol.
2, p. 118, list of works 11, ill. 112; Boon
1978, p. 112, no. 318, ill.; Kaufmann 1988,
pp. 205ff., no. 9/6; *Georg Flegel 1566–1638*,
exh. cat. ed. Kurt Wettengl (Stuttgart,
1993), pp. 208ff., no. 106.

Th.V.W.

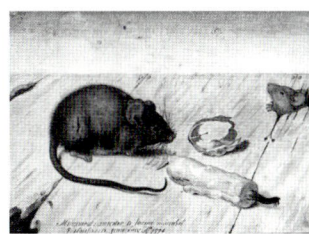

I.209
Joris Hoefnagel
Antwerp 1542–Vienna 1601
An Arrangement of Flowers with Insects
Watercolour with body colour on parch-
ment, heightened with gold
16.1 × 12.0 cm
The letter 'G' with a nail, and *1594*
1594
Art dealers, London
Oxford, Lent by the Visitors of the Ash-
molean Museum, Oxford, inv. no. 1951.49

Life-size, entomologically exact insects
surround a vase in the grotesque style
with columbines and rosebuds arranged

symmetrically around an unopened tulip –
two moths, a small dragonfly, a butterfly
caterpillar and a dead cockchafer. The subtle, delicately applied colouration of this
finely preserved cabinet miniature is characteristic of Hoefnagel's nature compositions, his *Blompottekens*. Although the
content of this still life is not constrained
by a text, the juxtaposition of buds and
flowers in full bloom on the one hand
with the dead cockchafer on the other
shows clearly that death is omnipresent,
even in the midst of blossoming life.

Munster and Baden-Baden 1979/80, no. 3;
Vienna 1985, no. 91; Essen 1988, no. 222.

Bergström 1973, p. 22, ill. 2; Bol 1980, p.
445; Koreny 1985, pp. 248ff, no. 91; Kaufmann 1988, pp. 206ff., no. 9.7; Gerszi 1988,
pp. 311ff.; Segal 1996, p. 127.

Th.V.W.

I.210
Joris Hoefnagel
Antwerp 1542–Vienna 1601
*Allegory of Life and Death: 'Vitam non
mortem recognita'*
Watercolour with body colour on parch-
ment, heightened with gold
16.8 × 23.7 cm
Above: *Pragae 1598. Joris Hoefnagel*; on the
paper strip below: *1598 Prague*
Rosi and Edmund Schilling Collection
London, British Museum, Rosi and Ed-
mund Schilling Bequest

In this cabinet miniature, both the medallion and the natural objects surrounding

it take up the theme of life and death. In
the centre a putto (Amor) with a skull
(possibly by Jacob Hoefnagel) personifies
vanitas. Budding and wilting flowers as
well as living and dead insects and small
animals – a mouse, a frog – frame the
medallion and again remind the viewer of
the transience of life. Many of these motifs
are also to be seen in the *Archetypa*, which
Jacob Hoefnagel engraved after his father
Joris.

London and Washington 1984, no. 57;
Nürnberg 1984, no. 57.

Chmelarz 1896, p. 287, n. 1; Kaufmann

1988, p. 208, no. 1.12; Vignau-Wilberg
1994, pp. 33ff., ill. 10.

Th.V.W.

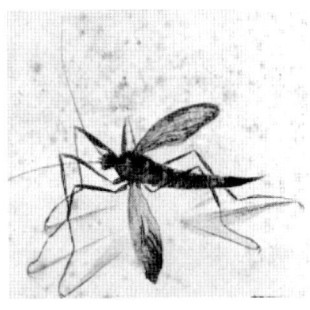

I.211
Hans Hoffmann
? Nürnberg ca. 1550–Prague 1591/92
Dragonfly
Brush and watercolour on paper
8.1 × 7.8 cm
Bottom centre: *Hb 1577*
1577
Esterházy, Praun Collection (L. 1965)
Budapest, Szépmüvészeti Múzeum, inv.
no. 185

Many of Hans Hoffmann's drawings
showing plants and animals reappear in
his larger compositions. However, this
dragonfly is nowhere to be seen on any

other of his extant works and it has only
one relation, in the upper left-hand corner
of his still-life *Hare in the Midst of Flowers*
(Koreny [1985], no. 47). To judge by the
way the insect's legs are turned inwards
and the back section of its body is curved,
this drawing was probably made from a
dead rather than a live insect.

Budapest 1931, cat. no. 192; Salzburg 1987,
cat. no. 27; Essen 1988, no. 231; Budapest
1991, cat. no. 4/D.

Schilling 1929, p. 36, no. 59; Pilz 1962, no.
6; Bodnár 1986, no. 21; Achilles-Syndram
1995, Z 345.

S.B.

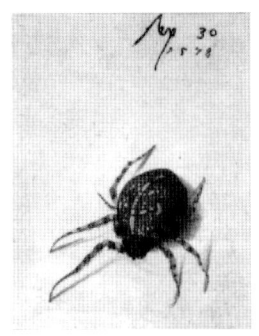

I.212
Hans Hoffmann
? Nürnberg ca. 1550–Prague 1591/92
Spider
Brush, watercolour and body colour on
paper
5.4 × 4.4 cm
Upper right: *Aug. 30 1578*
1578
Nürnberg, Praun Collection
Budapest, Szépmüvészeti Múzeum, inv.
no. 175

Hoffmann, probably inspired by Joris
Hoefnagel, used his studies of insects and
small animals in his still lifes. This study of

a female garden spider, completely accurate in both form and colour, might have
been made for use in a later work. Katrin
Achilles-Syndram (1994, p. 119) has suggested that this may in fact be the drawing
of a spider referred to as the verso of no.
102 in the 1616 inventory of the Praun
Collection in Nürnberg.

Budapest 1931, cat. no. 189/b; Washington, Chicago and Los Angeles 1985, cat.
no. 52/d; Essen 1988, no. 230; Budapest
1991, cat. no. 4/C.

Bodnár 1986, no. 23; Achilles-Syndram
1995, Z 348.

S.B.

I.213
Hans Hoffmann
? Nürnberg ca. 1550–Prague 1591/92
Frog
Brush, watercolour and white body colour
on paper
6 × 6.5 cm
Esterházy, Praun Collection (L. 1965)
Budapest, Szépmüvészeti Múzeum, inv.
no. 181

Two frog studies from the Hoffmann
drawings in the Praun Collection in Nürnberg are now held in Budapest. Hoffmann
used this true-to-life representation of a
young frog in his oil painting of a hare in a

clearing in a wood. Surviving documentation shows that Emperor Rudolf II bought
the Hoffmann oil painting (Koreny [1985],
no. 49). The other drawing shows a larger,
mature frog of the same species, used by
Hoffmann in one of his still-life compositions.

Budapest 1931, cat. no. 187/b; Washington, Chicago and Los Angeles 1985, cat.
no. 52/b; Essen 1988, no. 229; Budapest
1991, cat. no. 4/B.

Koreny 1985, ill. 49.1; Bodnár 1986, no. 24;
Achilles-Syndram 1995, Z 344.

S.B.

I.214
Hans Hoffmann
? Nürnberg ca. 1550–Prague 1591/92
Crane Fly
Brush and watercolour on paper
4.9 × 5.7 cm
Nürnberg, Praun Collection (L. 1965)
Budapest, Szépművészeti Múzeum, inv.
no. 179

As Katrin Achilles-Syndram has observed,
this same meadow crane fly also appears
in two miniatures by Joris Hoefnagel
(Berlin, Kupferstichkabinett; Münster and
Baden-Baden, 1980, ill. 24; New York,
Metropolitan Museum of Art; Koreny

[1985], ill. 39.1). The only difference is in
the length of the feelers and some other
details. One of the miniatures came from
Hoefnagel's volume of insect illustrations,
the first of four that he made for Emperor
Rudolf II. Many of Hoefnagel's illustrations of plants, insects and small animals
were published by his son Jacob in 1592 in
the form of a series of engravings, the
Archetypa studiaque. This meadow crane fly
appears on pl. 3 of the first part (see the
edition published by Vignau-Wilberg in
1994). Since Hoffmann was no longer
alive at the time, he must have either
known the miniatures by Joris or copied
Joris's originals. It seems likely that the

Nürnberg artist was in touch with Joris
Hoefnagel in Munich in 1584.

Budapest 1931, cat. no. 195/b; Essen 1988,
no. 228; Budapest 1991, cat. no. 4/A.

Bodnár 1986, no. 22; Achilles-Syndram
1995, Z 346.

S.B.

I.215
Hans Hoffmann
? Nürnberg ca. 1550–Prague 1591/92
Head of an Old Man
Red chalk with traces of black chalk on
paper
11.9 × 9.3 cm
Top centre: *Hb 1584*
1584
Nürnberg, Praun Collection (L. 1965)
Budapest, Szépművészeti Múzeum, inv.
no. 152

Amongst the drawings, more than fifty in
number, that found their way from the
Paulus II. Praun Collection in Nürnberg to

Budapest, there is a sequence of studies of
heads, which Hoffmann presumably made
partly as portraits and partly as studies for
works with biblical themes. In these predominantly small-scale works Hoffmann
generally concentrated, as here, on the facial expression of the subject, largely or
wholly ignoring the details of the upper
body. This is the latest of Hoffmann's dated Budapest drawings, completed shortly
before he moved to Prague.

Budapest 1931, cat. no. 145.

Pilz 1962, no. 30; Fučiková 1986, 26 and ill.
37; Bodnár 1986, no. 39; Achilles-Syndram

1995, Z 334.

S.B.

I.216
Hans Hoffmann
? Nürnberg ca. 1550–Prague 1591/92
Lion
Black chalk on paper
18.4 × 27 cm
Upper right: *Hb* (*HH* in a later hand)
Budapest, State Library Collection
Budapest, Szépművészeti Múzeum, inv.
no. K.67.27

Just as he copied and made variations on
Dürer's famous hares – with varying degrees of artistic licence (Koreny [1985],
nos 47–49, 52, 53) – so too Hans Hoffmann
copied Dürer's lion at least three times (Vi-

enna, Albertina). He made two copies very
close to the original: one of these he
signed *Hb 1577*, the other he marked *AD
1512* (Koreny [1985], no. 59 and ill. 59.1).
The lion held in the Szépművészeti
Múzeum, Budapest, which Teréz Gerszi
has shown to be by Hoffmann, is more of a
variation than a copy of Dürer's original,
as can be attested by the difference both in
technique and in the position of the lion's
tail and feet.

Essen 1988, no. 227.

Bodnár 1986, no. 16; Achilles-Syndram
1995, Z 349.

S.B.

I.217
Hans Hoffmann
? Nürnberg ca. 1550–Prague 1591/92
Resting Dog
Lead on paper
12.8 × 19.3 cm
Budapest, State Library Collection
Budapest, Szépművészeti Múzeum, inv.
no. K.58.1231

This drawing, which Teréz Gerszi has
shown to be the work of Hans Hoffmann,
is one of a number of copies he made of
pages in the sketch-book Dürer took on
his journey through the Netherlands
(London, British Museum). The fact that

he copied more than just this dog is
proved by the painting recently discovered by Koreny in Vienna (Koreny and Segal 1989/90, ill. 56) in which is depicted a
lion copied from a silverpoint drawing by
Dürer in the same sketch-book. Hoffmann's technique in his drawing of the
dog differs from that of the original, and
so the overall effect is accordingly altered.
Dürer's drawing has been cut into on
three sides, but Hoffmann's work still
shows the whole of the animal.

Essen 1988, cat. no. 226.

Bodnár 1986, no. 15; Achilles-Syndram

1995, A 350.

S.B.

I.218
Hans Hoffmann
? Nürnberg ca. 1550–Prague 1591/92
Head of a Roebuck with Deformed Antlers
Body colours on parchment
37.8 × 30.1 cm
Upper left: *Hhoffman Pictor Noric: ad
Vivum pinx Pragae. 1589*
1589
Von Nagler Collection
Berlin, Staatliche Museen, Kupferstich-
kabinett, inv. no. Hz. 2048

This body-colour painting made by Hans
Hoffmann in Prague in 1589 bears the
words *ad vivum pinx[it]*, but, as Heinrich

Geissler points out, these words must be
interpreted with caution. The head of a
roebuck with monstrous horns has all the
characteristics of a stuffed specimen and
cannot have been painted 'from nature' in
the modern sense of the word –particularly since there is an almost identical drawing signed with the initials *I.Z.* and dating
from the 1570s (Dresden, Kupferstichkabinett; Geissler [1986/87], ill. 94). There
is another representation of the same
beast by an unknown artist (Chatsworth,
Duke of Devonshire; Geissler [1986/87], ill.
94), which cannot be dated with any certainty and, as Lee Hendrix has pointed
out, the same roebuck appears again, al-

though in reverse, in Ulisse Aldovrandi's
nature studies, *Monstrorum Historia*
(Bologna, 1642). The Latin text accompanying the illustration in Aldrovandi's book
tells the reader that he received the drawing for his woodcut from a Bavarian duke:
Geissler dates this before 1590.

Nürnberg 1952, cat. no. W. 18; Essen 1988,
cat. no. 223.

Bock 1921, vol. 1, p. 46, no. 2048; Pilz 1962,
no. 31; Hendrix 1984, p. 113; Geissler
1986/87, pp. 101–5; DaCosta Kaufmann
1988, p. 216, no. 11.3.

S.B.

I.219
Hans Mont
Five Walking Figures
Drawing with brush in brown tone, brown wash, white glaze, under-drawing in chalk, blue paper
Lower right: *Hans Montes / van ghent*
Ca. 1577
Amsterdam, collection of A.L.W. van Regteren Altena-van Royen

This signed drawing has led to the recognition of the sculptor Hans Mont as a draughtsman. Mont's drawing technique, like Spranger's early work, was derived from the tradition of Parmigianino. He used mainly brush with a liberal wash, suppressed detail in favour of the summary delineation of volume, and followed the effect of light in the construction of relief in his compositions. It is difficult to determine whether Mont's drawings were sketches made for the realization of his work or to record a momentary idea. This drawing by Mont and the example from Budapest could be preparatory studies for work for Maximilian II in Neugebäude, possibly connected with the mock modelled ornamentation of the triumphal arch, on which he worked with Spranger, for the ceremonial entrance of Rudolf II to Vienna in 1577. This hypothesis is supported by the fact that Spranger employed a pattern very close to this drawing in the central group of a painting commemorating the memory of Mont, which was based on a composition by the sculptor.

Amsterdam 1955, cat. no. 223; Rotterdam 1977, cat. no. 90; Stuttgart 1979/80, cat. no. B13; Essen and Vienna 1988, cat. no. 232.

Regteren Altena 1939, pg. 160, ill. 6; Larsson 1967, pp. 7-8, ill. 8; Fučiková 1986, p. 18, ill. l1; Gerszi 1987, ill.

E.F.

I.220
Hans Mont
Sacrifice Scene
Brush drawing in gray tone, white glaze, underdrawing in black chalk on blue paper
1577 (?)
I. Delhaes collection
New York, The Metropolitan Museum of Art, Bequest of George Blumenthal, 1941, inv. no. 41.190.534

T. Gerszi credits this drawing to Hans Mont and suggests that it could have been a study for the ornamentation of the triumphal arch when Rudolf II made his ceremonial entrance into Vienna in 1577. For this occasion Mont created decorations for a larger-than-life sculpture and Spranger the images for the commemorative reliefs that depicted the monarch's virtue. The likely conclusion is that the theme of the drawing – the sacrifice of a bull – possibly better fits the ornamentation in the Neugebäude, the summer palace of Maximilian II, for which the sculptor also created smaller reliefs in addition to the large stucco sculptures. The pictures that G. Licinio created for this summer palace present a variety of scenes from Roman history. Mont's reliefs possibly could complement its ornamentation. His drawings have a marked painterly character. They adhere to the composition, never to the physical form. Light is implied in a manner similar to that seen in Italian chiaroscuro woodcuts.

Salzburg 1987, cat. no. 31.

Gerszi 1987, p. 58–59 cat. no. 31; Lietzmann 1987, pp. 151-55 (for the Neugebäude ornamentation).

E.F.

I.221
Dirk de Quade van Ravesteyn
Fl. 1589-99 and 1602-8 in Prague
Cupid Stung by Bees Running to Venus
Black and red chalk
19.8 × 15 cm
Theodorus Raffenstein ... fecit
Before 1608
I. Delhaes Collection
Budapest, Szépmüvészeti Múzeum, inv. no. 314

Amor (Cupid) has been plundering the beehive and is now seeking comfort from his mother for the stings he has received in the process: the moral is that there is no pleasure without pain (Alciati [1602], p. 505). Ravesteyn's drawing takes the figure of Amor and the shape of the beehive from a drawing by Dürer of 1514. This drawing by the great German master is from the so-called *Ambras Kunstbuch* (Vienna, Kunsthistorisches Museum), which at the time was in the possession of Archduke Ferdinand of Tyrol. The graceful female figure, on the other hand, is reminiscent of figures by Correggio, as is also the subtle shading that gives form to the figure.

Budapest 1967, cat. no. 81; Salzburg 1987, cat. no. 32; Essen and Vienna 1988, cat. no. 236; Budapest 1991, cat. no. 12.

Pigler 1948, pp. 74-77; Gerszi 1971, no. 217; DaCosta Kaufmann 1985, p. 95.

T.G.

I.222
Pieter Cornelis van Ryck
Delft 1568–? 1628
Allegory of Peace
Pen and brown ink
19.9 × 19 cm
PR F Prag; lower inscription: *in vreeden Ryk*
? 1606
I. Delhaes Collection (L. 665a)
Budapest, Szépmüvészeti Múzeum, inv. no. 385

An allegorical female figure holds an olive branch as the symbol of peace in her hand, at the same time burning the accoutrements of war with her torch. She recalls the allegorical figure of peace by Francesco Salviati in the fresco in the Palazzo Vecchio in Florence. Van Ryck spent a year and a half in Italy and the signature alone on this work shows that he also spent a short time in Prague. The inscription and the 'finished' feel of this drawing make it seem likely that it was part of an album. The inscription *in vreeden Ryk* (rich in peace) is a word play on the artist's name and underlines the economic advantages of peace. The underlying truth of this inscription was particularly topical at that time, when Prague was having to bear the financial burden of Rudolf II's campaign against Turkey.

Salzburg 1987, cat. no. 36; Essen 1988, cat. no. 237; Budapest 1991, cat. no. 19.

Gerszi 1971, no. 218; Fucíková 1979, p. 502.

T.G.

I.223
Aegidius Sadeler
Antwerp ca. 1568–Prague 1628
Angel with Cock, Armoured Gloves and Crown of Thorns
Pen and brush with india ink, over graphite
17.8 × 13.1 cm
Anton Neumann, Prague; Jirí Karásek ze Lvovic, Prague
Prague, Památník národního písemnictví, inv. no. I K 1298

Originally one of two drawings from the Neumann Collection, this sheet was paired with one (whereabouts unknown) showing an angel holding St Peter's sword, the torch carried by soldiers who came to seize Christ and the purse of gold coins given to Judas. These works belong to a popular Catholic tradition of images of the implements of Christ's Passion as objects of devotion. Probably during the 1580s, Sadeler engraved a series of Christ as the Man of Sorrows with six angels holding the Implements of the Passion (Hollstein 63-70). One of the prints corresponds closely to this drawing (cat. no. I.344). Unusual for its sketchy quality, this drawing displays several differences from the corresponding engraving. Scholars have differed on its role in relation to the print, suggesting that it is the first sketch for a more careful drawing for the print, or that it is a free reworking of a composition that dates from earlier in the artist's career. References to groups of two and four angels in early sales catalogues suggest that drawings of all six angels may have once existed.

Prague 1980, cat. no. 18.

Kuchynka 1905, pp. 149-54; Fučíková 1986, ills 89, 90.

D.L.

I.224
Aegidius Sadeler
Antwerp ca. 1568–Prague 1628
Allegory (Love Overcoming Deceit and Adverse Fortune?)
Pen with brown ink, brown wash, white heightening on blue paper
28.1 × 20.1 cm
Lower right corner: *Gilis Sadeler/fe: in veneti[a]*
Ca. 1595 (or 1592/3)
Canada, Frank and Marianne Seger

Recently discovered by J. Spicer, this drawing is exhibited for the first time in Prague. Its subject-matter is an open ques-

tion. The main characters, Cupid, Psyche (or Venus?), Natura, and a winged female figure with a sceptre, spear and helmet form a tetrad over a figure of Occasio/Fortuna, who has fallen back on to her spiked wheel and a discarded mask (a symbol of deceit). Two symbols of enduring love held by the central character suggest two possible identities. She raises in her left hand an anvil with two hearts forged into one (attributes of Venus, wife of Vulcan), and she and Cupid hold a heart-shaped vessel containing a lamp which sends rays of light from its twin spouts. The latter object may both reflect Pandora's vas and symbolize the love between Psyche and

Cupid. The type of allegory represented reflects Sadeler's contact with Joseph Heintz the Elder, whom he met in Rome in 1593, and also a familiarity with Bronzino and other Florentine Mannerists. Sadeler made his first trip to Italy between ca. 1591 and 1593, stopping in Venice early in his journey. In 1595 he returned to Venice in the company of his relatives, Jan and Justus Sadeler, who established a printing firm in that city. The sophistication of Sadeler's composition and drawing technique suggests that the drawing dates from his return journey to Venice in 1595.

D.L.

I.225
Aegidius Sadeler
Antwerp ca. 1568–Prague 1628
Pan and Syrinx
Black and red chalk
20.7 × 16 cm
Bottom left: *G.S.inv.*
Ca. 1595–1600
Basel, Öffentliche Kunstsammlung, Kupferstichkabinett, inv. no. Bi 376.60

This drawing is connected with an engraving (Hollstein 109), which shows the composition in reverse. Thus it is one of only two known Sadeler drawings of mythological or religious scenes that are preparato-

ry for prints. The composition is close to a print of the same subject by Marco Dente after Giulio Romano and a fresco of Pan and Syrinx by Raphael's followers in the Vatican *Stufetta* of Cardinal Bibiena. The materials and technique of the drawing reflect Sadeler's contact with Joseph Heintz, and the physiognomy of Syrinx is a Mannerist type that surfaces in Sadeler's work by 1600.

Limouze 1990.

D.L.

I.226
Aegidius Sadeler
Antwerp ca. 1568–Prague 1628
Venus with the Lute Player
Red and black chalk, underdrawing in graphite
19.7 × 21.5 cm
Bottom right: *gielio Sadelaer fecit*
Ca. 1600
Frits Lugt
Paris, Institut Néerlandais, Fondation Custodia, inv. no. 6965

On his appointment as court engraver to Rudolf II in 1597, Sadeler gained access to the rich collections of northern and Italian

paintings in the imperial *Kunstkammer*. Among these paintings was Titian's *Venus and the Lute Player* (now in Cambridge, Fitzwilliam Museum). In a joking reference to his source, Sadeler has signed his first name in an Italian form. Titian's allegory of physical love, symbolized by the analogy between the strummed lute and the aroused Venus, is here turned into a burlesque in which Cupid pulls away Venus' veil as the music progresses. This comic-erotic image mirrors Bartholomeus Spranger's mythological compositions, for example the drawings of *Mars and Venus* in Frankfurt and Northampton. The angularity of the drawn figures suggests

that Hans von Aachen was a key formal influence. The work also has motival connections with a painting of *Vanitas* (1602; Basle, Kunstmuseum) by von Aachen's pupil, Pieter Isaacz.

Paris 1980–81.

Limouze 1990.

D.L.

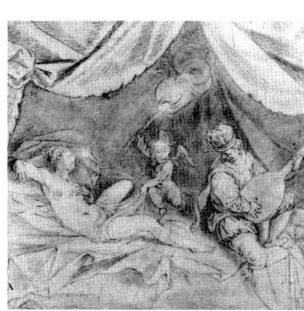

I.227
Aegidius Sadeler
Antwerp ca. 1568–Prague 1628
Venus and Cupid
Pen and brown ink with grey wash
13.9 × 8.9
Bottom left: *Egidius Sadeler/fecit 1600 (1606?)*
1600 or 1606
Moscow, Muzej Puskina, inv. no. 7634

This small and delicate drawing was one of three that came to the Pushkin Museum from an *album amicorum* belonging to the Munich art collector Emmanuel Schweigger. Its format and allegorical theme are

particularly suited for such an album. Jan, Aegidius and Raphael Sadeler all made album drawings with Venus and Cupid as their subject matter. The angular poses of the figures reflect Sadeler's exposure to the compositions of Bartholomeus Spranger, while the figural types themselves have been likened to the drawings of Anthonis Blocklandt and Friedrich Sustris. Cupid runs to Venus for shelter from the rays of the sun (i.e., the wrath of Apollo), at the same time coyly reaching for his bow. This scene may relate to the confrontation between Cupid and Apollo that led Cupid to wound both Apollo and Daphne (Ovid, *Metamorphoses*, I). Sadeler

not only drew scenes directly from Ovid, but also used the work as a starting point for free improvisations in his original prints and drawings.

Prague 1986–87, cat. no. 35.

Fučíková 1986, p. 33, ill. 88; Limouze 1990.

D.L.

I.228
Aegidius Sadeler
Antwerp ca. 1568–Prague 1628
Matthias Wacker von Wackenfels
Black chalk on grey prepared paper
14.8 × 12.6 cm
Ca. 1603–5
Copenhagen, Statens Museum for Kunst, Kobberstiksamling, inv. no. Tu 58.1

Published here for the first time, this delicate and spirited drawing portrays a humanist and adviser to the court of Rudolf II. Matthias Wacker von Wackenfels, an amateur scientist and neo-Latin poet, was a friend of Johannes Kepler and seems al-

so to have been a friend and patron of Aegidius Sadeler. Sadeler portrayed him in two separate engravings, included a poem by Wacker in his posthumous allegorical portrait of Rudolf II and dedicated to him his engraved series of ancient ruins, *Vestigi della antichità* (cat. nos. I.359–66). The drawing, which is connected with the earlier of the two engravings (cat. no. III.93), shows the likeness without the elaborate allegorical frame that appears in the print. Connections between figures in that frame and the *Allegorical Portrait of Rudolf II* (1603; cat. no. I.353) suggest that this drawing and print date from around the same time.

Limouze 1990.

D.L.

I.229
Aegidius Sadeler
Antwerp ca. 1568–Prague 1628
Synal Chaen
Black and red chalk on grey prepared
paper
15.4 × 12.1
1604
N. van Bremen, (sale, Amsterdam 1766);
private collection (sale, London, 1905);
Frederick Horne (Museo Horne, Flo-
rence)
Florence, Galleria degli Uffizi, Gabinetto
Disegni e Stampe, inv. no. 5574

This finely worked drawing is the prepara-

tory study for Sadeler's portrait engraving
of one of the Persian ambassadors who
visited the court of Rudolf II in 1604–5.
Identified as a Sadeler drawing by Carlos
van Hasselt and Werner Schade, and accepted by Limouze, it has only recently
been published in connection with the
print (Hollstein 281) by An Zwollo. While
it fits in with the group of portrait studies
on toned grounds, this drawing is the only
one in which the sitter is reversed in the final engraving. Further, unlike the other
drawings, this sheet bears signs of tracing
along the folds of the sitter's garments.
The features shown here are thus typical
of engravers' drawings of this period. In

fact, a few of Sadeler's other preparatory
drawings, such as those of *Carlo Madruzzi*
and of *Pan and Syrinx*, were reversed in
their corresponding prints. However, for
his other portraits, the technique of transfer that Sadeler used left the image in its
original direction.

Limouze 1990; Zwollo 1992, pp. 35–48.

D.L.

I.230
Aegidius Sadeler
Antwerp ca. 1568–Prague 1628
Arnold de Reyger
Brush in black, white heightening over
black chalk, on grey prepared paper
15.1 × 11.6 cm
1604
Arnold Ingen-Housz de Bréda (early nineteenth century); Joseph de Gréz and his
descendants, Brussels (given to the museum in 1913)
Brussels, Musées Royaux des Beaux-Arts
de Belgique, Collection de Gréz, inv. no.
4060/3115

This drawing is connected with a portrait
engraving from 1604 (Hollstein 319) of
the Brandenburg nobleman Arnold de
Reyger (Hollstein 319). It is typical of
Sadeler's preparatory drawings for portrait engravings in that the paper is prepared with a grey ground. The coating
seems to have provided Sadeler with a
medium tone, against which to build up a
range of darks and lights. These drawings
are, in effect, early examples of the grisaille technique that was commonly used
by Antwerp engravers of the second half
of the sixteenth and the seventeenth centuries. Whether using liquid media, as he
did here, or chalk, as in the portraits of

Synal Chaen, and Matthias Wacker, Sadeler focused on the details and shading of
the face, working out the surrounding values in the final engraving. The result is a
subtlety and precision in the engraved
likeness, which earned him much admiration from Baroque engravers and print
connoisseurs.

Limouze 1990.

D.L.

I.231
Aegidius Sadeler
Antwerp ca. 1568–Prague 1628
Georg Schrotl von Schrotenstain
Black chalk on grey prepared paper
16.1 × 13 cm
At bottom left: *Egidius Sadeler F.*
1610
Paris, Musée du Louvre, Cabinet des
Dessins, inv. no. 20 436

A preparatory drawing, this sheet shows
that Sadeler at first envisioned this portrait in a rectangular format, of a type developed by Albrecht Dürer and perpetuat-
ed by Hendrick Goltzius and other artists.

Light chalk lines indicate that the sitter
would be silhouetted against a light, rectangular background. At upper right, a
sketched-in oval indicates where Schrotl's
coat of arms might have been. The portrait
engraving (Hollstein 325) took on the
form of Sadeler's more typical oval, enframed by *putti*, garlands and unusual
mouldings in the then-fashionable auricular style. Schrotl was an Hungarian councillor to both Rudolf II and Matthias. This
sheet, one of the latest of Sadeler's known
portrait drawings, displays the relaxed,
rough-textured chalk technique that typifies his late drawing style. The economy of
line in the indication of facial features an-

ticipates Sadeler's *Self-portrait* of 1618 (cat.
no. I.235).

Paris 1949.

D.L.

I.232
Aegidius Sadeler
Antwerp ca. 1568–Prague 1628
Carlo Gaudenzio Madruzzi, Bishop of Trento
Black chalk, pen and brown ink, white
heightening, blue wash
(Oval) 9.8 × 7.5 cm
1610
Budapest, Szépmüvészeti Múzeum,
inv. no. 1 760

This drawing portrays a member of a
North Italian family of nobles and ecclesi-
astics that rose to special prominence
through its association with the Council
of Trent. Carlo Madruzzi (1562–1629),

grand-nephew of the bishop who presided
over that council, became in 1610 the
third member of his family to hold the title of Prince Bishop of Trento. The print
Sadeler made from this drawing (Hollstein 305) is dated to that year. While the
drawing has long been connected with
Sadeler, its appearance is compromised by
the clumsy coat of blue wash, which may
have been added by a later hand. However,
Sadeler's typically fine and exacting treatment of the details of the sitter's face and
costume is seen in the work in black chalk
and brown pen.

Limouze 1990; Dal Prà 1993.

D.L.

I.233
Aegidius Sadeler
Antwerp ca. 1568–Prague 1628
Allegory of Painting
Pen and brown ink, brown wash, red and
black chalk
13.1 × 8.5 cm
1610
J. Goll van Frankenstein and heir (sale,
Amsterdam, 1822);
Dr. A. Welcker
Leiden, Prentenkabinet der Rijksuniver-
siteit, inv. no. AW 1110

This drawing, in which Venus grinds pigments for painting before an easel, has

been interpreted as an art-theoretical allegory of Sadeler's own invention. The
themes of *grazia* and *bellezza* are played out
in the attributes and pose of the main figure, who is herself a model for the Cupid
drawing at bottom left. The image faintly
visible on the easel makes reference to history painting (paintings of historical, religious or mythological scenes) as the highest of artistic genres. The drawing is thus a
significant record of the theoretical discourses of Mannerist art as understood by
Sadeler and other artists at the Rudolfine
court. It was regarded with sufficient interest to be reproduced later in Antwerp,
with added text, by Cornelis I Galle, an en-

graver who worked for Pieter Paul Rubens.

Stuttgart 1979–80, cat. no. B30; Essen
1988, cat. no. 238.

Kaufmann 1982, pp. 119–148; Limouze
1990.

D.L.

I.234
Aegidius Sadeler
Antwerp ca. 1568–Prague 1628
Johannes Petrus Magnus
Brush in black and white heightening
over red chalk, on grey prepared paper
22.6 × 16.6 cm
1617
A. W. M. Mensing, Amsterdam (sale, 1939)
Amsterdam, Rijksmuseum, inv. no. 1941:3

Johannes Petrus Magnus, a councillor to Emperor Matthias, was portrayed by Sadeler in an engraving (Hollstein 306) for which this is a preliminary drawing. Of the various portrait drawings exhibited

here, this is a late example, unique for its architectural and allegorical frame. Although Sadeler designed elaborate surrounds for many of his oval portraits, no other example is seen in a preparatory drawing. The ornament surrounding the portrait includes a rooster (symbol of vigilance), garlands and trophy motifs, and Petrus Magnus's personal imprese at the bottom. The final engraving employed a much simpler frame, including only the sitter's impresa (a carpenter's level) and coat of arms.

Boon 1978, I, cat. no. 407; Limouze 1990.

D.L.

I.235
Joachim von Sandrart (after Aegidius Sadeler)
Frankfurt 1606–Nürnberg 1688
Portrait of Aegidius Sadeler
Black and white chalk on brown paper; partly traced
21.5 × 15.1 cm
At top (in brown ink): *Aegidius Sadeler Antuerpiensis/ Rudolphi II. et Mathiae Imperat Sculptor/ Delin:1618.*
Ca. 1675(?)
Vienna, Graphische Sammlung Albertina, inv. no. 17 539 (D 638)

Mounted with this drawing is a letter of

1685 from the art historian Joachim von Sandrart to a French-speaking collector, to whom he sent this work. In that letter, Sandrart relates that the drawing is by 'the hand of the great Egidius Sadeler'. Sandrart became a great admirer of Sadeler after visiting him in Prague in 1622. During that visit, Sadeler gave Sandrart many works of art, one of which may have been a drawn self-portrait of which this sheet appears to be a copy. Sandrart may have initially made this as a preparatory drawing for the identical engraved portrait of Sadeler in Sandrart's *Teutsche Academie* (Nürnberg, 1675). Evidence of its original use is seen in its tracing marks. Perhaps to

deceive the recipient, Sandrart or a contemporary penned the elaborate signature at the top, a text that may well come from Sadeler's original. The chalk technique of this drawing is unmistakably that of Sandrart drawings of the 1670s and 1680s, such as the scene of a *Defenestration by Night* (Vienna, Albertina, D 643), also in black chalk on brown paper. The portrait's oval format and iconography suggest that it is based on a lost original by Sadeler.

Limouze 1990; Tietze 1933, cat. no. 638.

D.L.

I.236
Aegidius Sadeler
Antwerp ca. 1568–Prague 1628
Woodland Scene with Bathing Nymphs, in the Distance Mercury and Two Satyrs
Brush in black, white heightening, grey-brown and brown wash
35.4 × 47.6 cm
At bottom left: *Es Sadeler Fecit/ 16(?)___P(?)_____*
Ca. 1619
Possibly Sébastien II LeClerc, Peintre du Roy (Sale, Paris, 1764)
Paris, Musée du Louvre, Cabinet des Dessins, inv. no. 20 485

The most unusual of Sadeler's works are the original drawings and prints from his late period in Prague (1618–28), following the death of Emperor Matthias. These show great freedom of invention and the clearest departures from the personal styles and genres of the Rudolfine artists. This drawing and a closely related sheet from 1619 in St Petersburg are clearly highly finished collectors' drawings, and they are noteworthy early examples of Baroque pastoral imagery. While Mercury and perhaps also Pan appear in this drawing, the overall scene has no clear mythological source. The languorous reclining nudes anticipate paintings of Arcadian

subjects by Rubens and other artists. Finally, the drawings reveal Sadeler's great skill in composing woodland scenes that are both reminiscent of and distinctive from those of Pieter Stevens and Roelandt Savery. The right-hand section of the Louvre drawing was copied in a painting by Johann Liss (Augsburg, Georg Schäfer Collection), a testament to Sadeler's importance for artists of the early Baroque.

Augsburg 1975, cat. no. E89.

Limouze 1990; Paris 1949.

D.L.

I.237
Aegidius Sadeler
Antwerp ca. 1568–Prague 1628
The Martyrdom of St Sebastian
Pen in brown ink, brown wash, white heightening, over black chalk
41.8 × 31.5 cm
Bottom, right: *EG: Sadeler Fecit.*
Ca. 1618–20
Van der Willingen; Gerlings; M. O. Brenner (sale, Amsterdam, 1911); private collection, Netherlands and France (sale, Amsterdam, 1989)
Washington, DC, National Gallery of Art, inv. no. 1992.18.1

This sheet is one of the two preparatory drawings known for prints of religious and mythological scenes (cat. no. I.378). It clearly involves a careful working out of the composition, with attention to ranges of dark and light. A pentimento is visible in the doubled eyes of Sebastian, and at lower left, the signs of a patch that covered the two angels, replacing them with angels in different poses. The drawing was not traced for transfer, and it is not reversed in the corresponding print. The religious subject-matter and chiaroscuro tonality of the drawing and print reflect new directions in Sadeler's late career. The young Joachim von Sandrart, who visited

Sadeler in 1622, noted a series of twelve grisaille paintings of the Passion of Christ that the Prague artist had just completed.

Limouze 1989; Limouze 1990.

D.L.

I.238
Aegidius Sadeler
Antwerp ca. 1568–Prague 1628
Europe and the Bull
Red chalk, white heightening (on pentimento, behind river god)
21 × 31.7 cm
Bottom, centre, in black chalk: *E G.S.*
Ca. 1619
Paris, Musée du Louvre, Cabinet des Dessins, inv. no. 21 726

While her companions tear their hair and fling themselves into the sea, Europa clutches the horns of her abductor Jupiter, who has changed himself into a

bull. Glancing coyly backward, she has no intention of being rescued from her plight. Sadeler's comic transformation of Ovid's tale (*Metamorphoses*, Bk II) is in the character of Sadeler's earlier drawing of *Venus and the Lute Player* and other Rudolfine mythologies. The chalk technique and proportions of the nude connect this drawing to other late drawings by Sadeler, especially the *Woodland Scene with Bathing Nymphs* (cat. no. I.236). It is not as thoroughly worked up as that drawing, but the signature and the artist's attempt to mask a pentimento with white heightening suggest that this was also meant for a collector. Sadeler made an ear-

lier finished drawing of this subject, following Ovid more closely. However, no engraving of this composition is known.

Limouze 1990; Lugt 1979.

D.L.

I.239
Jan Sadeler
Antwerp 1550–Venice 1600
Joris Hoefnagel
Red chalk with pen and brown ink
18.2 × 13.2 cm
At the end of the poem at bottom: *Hans Sadelers hant, d[e]n slechten naem*; bottom right: *Datum Monachij 1591 a di 21 July 1591*
Bremen, Kunsthalle Bremen, inv. no. 1262

Jan Sadeler, the elder cousin of Aegidius Sadeler, was probably Aegidius's teacher in engraving as well as his mentor and protector during the years in which the Sadelers emigrated from Antwerp to Germany. The Rudolfine artist Joris Hoefnagel may have come into contact with the Sadelers in the refugee community of Frankfurt around 1588, and he helped bring Jan Sadeler to Munich as engraver to the Wittelsbach court. The drawing is inscribed as having been given to Hoefnagel in Munich, and it bears an eight-line Flemish poem on the theme of friendship. Its size and inscriptions suggest that it may be connected with an *album amicorum*, an album of drawings and poems collected by a learned individual from friends and acquaintances. The motto at the top, *ars est contenta doceri*, art is content (i.e., lends itself) to be taught, has been seen by Limouze as a sign of the impact of artistic theory upon the Sadelers' image of themselves as artists. Jan Sadeler also used this motto for his page in the *Album Amicorum* of Jean de Seur (Amsterdam, Rijksprentenkabinett).

Vienna 1988, cat. no. 630.

Vignau Wilberg-Schuurman 1969; Limouze 1990.

D.L.

I.240
Roelandt Savery
Kortrijk 1576–Utrecht 1639
Inn and Cottages on the Outskirts of Prague
Brown ink with washes in rose, grey and light brown
22.8 × 23.7 cm
Later annotation on the verso: *No. 9 / M.N 8 / 2+ 731 (6)*
1603/5
David Laing; Royal Scottish Academy; transferred in 1910
Edinburgh, National Gallery of Scotland, inv. no. D. 1706

The fortified walls on the hill to the rear are those of Prague seen from the southern outskirts of the city. This and its companion drawing *Cottages by a Manor House* (inv. D. 1707; Spicer 1979, cat. no. 67), made from a vantage point a few metres to the left, depict the same cottages and inn displaying the traditional evergreen bough announcing the arrival of a new pressing of wine. The loose rendering lines link these two studies to the preceding two, also sketched directly with pen and ink.

Essen and Vienna 1988, cat. no. 252 (with further references).

Spicer 1979, cat. no. 67.

J.S.

I.241
Roelandt Savery
Kortrijk 1576–Utrecht 1639
Charles Bridge from Kampa Island
Brown ink
16.3 × 23.8 cm
In brown ink: *binnen praga nart leven*; annotation in brown ink: *R. Sauv*
1603/4
W. Kohler, 1868–72; A. von Lanna, Prague (L.2773) until 1910; *Aust. Kohler / 5 Feb' 19* (annotation in pencil on verso); C. Hofstede de Groot, until 1931; Dr. Wertheim; R. Morawetz, ca. 1933; F. Lugt, Paris until the Second World War
Prague, Národni galerie v Praze, inv. no. K

37.440

Savery must have begun making sketches of Prague almost immediately after arriving in the city in late summer (?) 1603. The earliest views, including also *Inn and Cottages on the Outskirts of Prague* (cat. no. I.240) and *Houses behind the Swarzenburg Palace* (cat. no. I.242), are drawn directly with the pen, without a preliminary sketch in chalk. They lack the greater sense of control that is characteristic of the pen drawings of a few years later, for example *Cottages by the Water* (cat. no. I.261). Viewed from the little island in the Moldau called Kampa, the two towers were intended to control access to the Charles Bridge from the Old Town. The inscription 'inside Prague, [drawn] from life' is the earliest (though undated) written reference to the artist's presence in the city and the earliest use of a version of the phrase so associated with Savery, 'naer het leven', on a landscape drawing.

Essen and Vienna 1988, cat. no. 250 (with further references).

Spicer 1979, cat no. 64.

J.S.

I.242
Roelandt Savery
Kortrijk 1576–Utrecht 1639
Houses behind the Schwarzenberg Palace
Brown ink
24.7 × 22.3 cm
1603/1604
Bought from Colnaghi's, London, in 1949
Ottawa, National Gallery of Canada, inv. no. 5524

Rather than show the façades of these buildings, Savery typically has chosen the irregular, anecdotal charms of the rear view, complete with pillows airing. Nevertheless, the Strahov monastery can be seen at the far left across the housetops of the Old Town below the Hradschin. The furthermost structure in the middleground, known since the eighteenth century as the Schwarzenberg Palace, was begun in 1545, passing eventually into the possession of Rudolf II. These same houses attracted the attention of Pieter Stevens; his study, known only in a later copy now in Prague, was typical for him in that it represented a much wider area. As in the preceding early pen sketch from the beginning of Savery's years in Prague, the contours are hesitant and surfaces are largely undifferentiated.

Ghent 1954, cat. no. 145; Florence 1969, cat. no. 20.

Boon 1961, pl. 46; Popham and Fenwich 1965, cat. no.137; Gerszi 1977, 122; Spicer 1979, cat. no. 66.

J.S.

I.243
Roelandt Savery
Kortrijk 1576–Utrecht 1639
Two Riders with Broad Hats
Black, red, ochre, and aqua chalk, light brown wash
12.8 × 14.1 cm
1604/1608
Von Nagler (L.2529); acquired in 1835
Berlin, Staatliche Museen Berlin, Kupferstichkabinett, inv. no. KdZ 3222

While cavalrymen similar to *Two Riders* plunge about in Savery's 1604 *Plundering of a Flemish Village* in Kortrijk (Kaufmann 1985) and his *Invasion of Prague on 15 February 1611* (cat. no. I.70), the absent rider of the *Saddled Horse* on the verso (Spicer 1979, cat. no. 131) carried a mace and may be presumed to be a Hungarian cavalry officer. Savery used a soft black chalk to bring out the solid, rounded forms of the horses on the recto and verso in the same way as he did the profile of a *Horse* also in Berlin (Spicer 1979, cat. no. 130; Münz cat. no. 64) which is the verso of a *naer het leven* study of a *Market Woman* datable to 1604–06 (Spicer 1979, cat. no. 180; Münz cat. no. 65). For Savery's military subjects see Spicer 1982.

Berlin 1975, cat. no. 219.

Erasmus 1908, cat. no. Z16; Bock and Rosenberg 1930, p. 270; Spicer 1970, p. 25; Spicer 1979, cat. no. 243; Liess 1981, p. 97; Spicer 1982, p. 461.

J.S.

I.244
Roelandt Savery
Kortrijk 1576–Utrecht 1639
Two Hungarian Cavalrymen
Brown ink and coloured washes
20.3 × 28.6 cm
1604–08
Lansing coll.; Royal Scottish Academy;
transferred to the National Gallery in
1966
Edinburgh, National Gallery of Scotland,
inv. no. RSA 7

The officer at the right carrying the war
hammer (a mark of rank) and protected by
chain mail appears again in *Hungarian*

Cavalrymen Riding through a Wood dated
161[1] (Paris, Musée du Louvre; Kaufmann 1985, cat. no. 19-16). The source is
Savery's black chalk and coloured wash
study of the same figure in *Two Hungarian
Cavalry Officers* (Paris, Institut Néerlandais; Spicer 1979, cat. no. 238). The rider seen from the rear must derive from a
similar chalk study made from life. Given
the angle of vision, it is likely that Savery
was mounted himself. Executed in water-
colors, this is a finished study comparable
to those in the British Museum (for example Spicer 1979, cat. no. 232). See preceding entry.

Edinburgh 1985, no. cat. no.

Andrews 1967, p. 381; Paszkiewicz 1973,
154; Spicer 1979, cat. no. 235; Spicer 1982,
p. 461; Andrews 1985, p. 78.

J.S.

I.245
Roelandt Savery
Kortrijk 1576–Utrecht 1639
Seven Hungarian Cavalrymen
Black, red, aqua and ochre chalk
19.7 × 32 cm
1604/1608
Georg John Earl Spencer (L. 1530)
Vienna, Graphische Sammlung Albertina,
inv. no. 8727

There are twelve extant drawings by Savery of these horsemen (Spicer 1979, cat.
no. 231-41, 131), and some of the figures
included in these were adapted for parallel
cavalrymen in his paintings. While the Al-

bertina drawing may be a composite study
bringing together several individual studies, it may also reflect the artist's attempt
to catch the movements of a group of hussars and cavalrymen milling around before moving out on the field. Although the
horses' legs disappear as if into ground
mist, the shading of the bodies and figures
is delicate and precise. The angle at which
the mounted cavalrymen are sometimes
depicted, particularly striking in the case
of left rider of *Two Hungarian Cavalrymen*
(cat. no. I.244), the notable absence of the
horses' feet in several studies, and the unprecedented subject matter of *Hungarian
Cavalrymen Riding through a Wood*, sug-

gests that Savery may actually have ridden
out into the field with them, indeed *Cavalrymen Riding through a Wood* is represented
as from the vantage point of a rider bringing up the rear.

Essen and Vienna 1988, cat. no. 631.

Schonbrunner and Meder 1896-1908, X,
cat. no. 1191 (J. Martsen); Spicer 1979, cat.
no. 236.

J.S.

I.246
Roelandt Savery
Kortrijk 1576–Utrecht 1639
Team of Horses and Rider
Shades of brown ink over black chalk
16.4 × 18.4 cm
In brown ink: *brúinockker / vil wit gris /
licht brúinockker / swart pert / rot pert /
nart leúen*
ca. 1604
Albert von Sachsen Teschen (L. 174)
Vienna, Graphische Sammlung Albertina,
inv. no. 7867

The more than eighty studies that Savery
made of Bohemian peasants, Jews and sol-

diers, among others, in the public spaces
of Prague in the years 1603 to ca. 1608 are
usually inscribed with colour notes on the
costumes and some variation of the
phrase 'naer het leven' (from life). While
Savery made them as a source for his
paintings of contemporary life, for example *Peasants Carousing before an Inn* of 1608
(cat. no. I.61), only a few can be identified
in specific compositions. His studies are
characterized by clearly delineated forms,
crisp contours and shading limited primarily to patches of hatching. The studies
were first sketched in chalk or perhaps
graphite or lead; most were then worked
up in detail with pen and brown ink. Here

the original chalk sketch is visible in the
pentimenti in the horse's legs.

Paris 1935, cat. no. 167 (as Pieter Bruegel);
Brussels 1935, cat. no. 468 (as P.B.); Vienna
1965, cat. no. 64 (as P.B.); Vienna 1986, by
V. Birke, cat. no. 26 (as P.B.); Amsterdam
1993-94, cat. no. 192 (R.S.).

Münz 1961, cat. no. 105 (P.B.); Spicer 1970,
17, 22 (R.S.); Spicer 1979, cat. no. 164 (R.S.);
Liess 1981, 91ff. (P.B.); Kaufmann 1988,
under cat. no. 19-9; Boon 1992, under cat.
no. 174.

J.S.

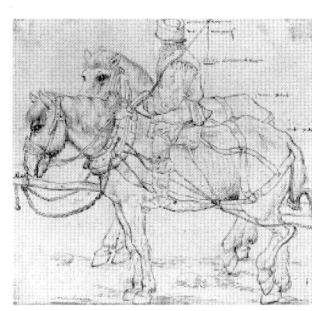

I.247
Roelandt Savery
Kortrijk 1576–Utrecht 1639
Peasant Seated on a Barrel
Brown ink over graphite or black chalk
15.2 × 10 cm
In brown ink over graphite or black chalk:
*[s]wartte / [br] >oeck / [sw] >wart lerse /
omber mús / brúinockker / Rock / rot / groen
/ gel / pers / nart leúen*
Ca. 1604
Private collection, Aerdenhout, Nether-
lands; purchased in 1969
Amsterdam, Rijksprentenkabinet, inv. no.
1969:210

Bohemian peasants drinking beer in casual outdoor settings, sometimes using barrels for furniture, abound in Savery's
scenes of contemporary peasant life, as in
Peasants Carousing before an Inn of 1608
(cat. no. I.61). This particular drawing was
not, however, used in any extant composition. Savery's 'naer het leven' figure studies are discussed in general under *Team of
Horses* (cat. no. I.246). In addition, stylistic
similarities with that drawing, which is
datable to ca. 1604, permit the present
work to be similarly dated. The present
study came to light in 1969, just as the attribution of the whole group to Pieter
Bruegel was being reassessed, and it was

identified from the onset as by Savery.

Amsterdam 1970, 76; Köln 1985, cat. no.
112.

Leeuwen 1970, 32; Spicer 1979, cat. no.
163; M. Schapelhouman 1987, cat. no. 71.

J.S.

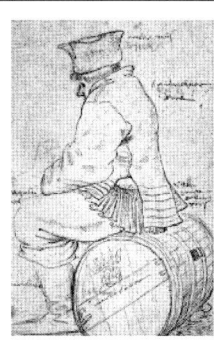

I.248
Roelandt Savery
Kortrijk 1576–Utrecht 1639
*Peasant Leaning on a Fence (recto); Woman
in a Cloak Seen from the Rear (verso)*
Brown ink over black chalk, grey wash
16 × 10 cm
In brown ink over traces of black chalk:
*ville swartte ombere mús / groen van binn /
en / ville brúinockkerre / Rock / swartte tas /
ville lichtte lere / broecke en swartte / lappen
dar op / nackten benen / swartte lerssen /
nart het leven*
1604-06
C. W. Klever 1892; Prince of Liechtenstein,
Feldsburg; with Colnaghi's, London,

1953; F. Springell, Portinscale; Sothebys,
London, 30.VI.1986, 26
Toronto, Frank and Marianne Seger

The woven 'shopping bags' carried by this
peasant on the verso point to Savery's tendency to make his studies in the open mar-
ketplace. The verso *Woman in a Cloak, Seen
from the Rear* (Spicer cat. no. 176; Münz cat.
no. 69) was likely the source for the parallel
figure in Savery's 1606 *Kermis* (St Petersburg, Hermitage; Spicer 1979, cat. no. 228)

Münz 1961, nr.70 (P. B., wash added later);
Spicer 1979, cat. no. 169 (R.S.).

J.S.

I.249
Roelandt Savery
Kortrijk 1576–Utrecht 1639
View of Prague Castle with Stag Moat (Jeleni prikop)
drawing in brown ink, washed orange, blue, brown and green
16.7 × 27.9 cm
Bottom right: *R. Saveri*
Cambridge, Fitzwilliam Museum, inv. no. 3 135

An engraving by F. Hoogenberghe with the title *PRAGA regni Bohemiae metropolis* launched countless views of Prague seen from the east, from where the characteris- tically narrow castle summit becomes ap- parent, separated from the north gardens by the Belvedere gorge, known as Stag Moat. Facing the lowest point at the very end of Stag Moat, Savery avoided the dom- inant White Tower of the Castle, hidden behind the prism of the east entry gate. The central prominence of the tower of St Vitus remains, just like its accompanying presbytery with the three characteristic bell-towers, subject to strict alignment. The cylindrical tower of Dalibor, lit up by morning sunlight, acquires importance from this viewing point, while the canon tower juts into the shadow beyond it. The central part of the composition encom- passes Prasny Bridge with the north outer gate and, on the right, it is possible to dis- cern the tennis hall, the summer house and the fig greenhouses. A drawing lost from the Prague City Museum, bore great resemblance to this scene from a higher position, capturing the White Tower still with its helmet-shaped roof, so that it can be reliably dated to before 1610. In the pre- sent work there is no mistaking Savery's masterly drawing technique.

I.M.

I.250
Roelandt Savery
Kortrijk 1576–Utrecht 1639
Houses by the Entrance to the Imperial Mill
Brown ink and red chalk, over traces of pencil (graphite?)
15.2 × 20 cm
In pencil: *R S*
1605/8
Leipzig, Museum der Bildenden Künste, inv. I.418

While the portal to the left is identifiable as that to the imperial mill just outside the city (which can be visited today), the hous- es are gone. The composition, centred on the various ramshackle structures at the back of the main house and viewed from a slightly elevated vantage point, is typical of Savery's drawings of Prague's neigh- bourhoods in that it is the reflection of a casual observer rather than a composition planned around a significant motif. This must result from Savery's intended use of such studies as a repertory of anecdotal detail for the background of paintings or formal drawings rather than as their pri- mary subject-matter. Nevertheless, no fur- ther use of the present study has been identified.

Krefeld 1938, cat. no. 125.

Spicer 1979, cat. no. 78; Fučíková 1986, pl. 66.

J.S.

I.251
Roelandt Savery
Kortrijk 1576–Utrecht 1576
Rocky Promontory in Bohemia
Brown and reddish brown ink over traces of black chalk (?), washes in blue and light brown
42 × 30.6 cm
Later annotation in brown ink: *P. Bril.*
Verso: see Schapelhouman
1605/6
Probably Rembrandt van Rijn (1606–69), Amsterdam; Lambert Doomer, Amster- dam (1624–1700); 'Oud bezit' Amsterdam, Rijksprentenkabinet, inv. no. 00:598

Before venturing into the Alps in 1606 or 1607, Savery spent time recording and in- terpreting the interesting rock formations of the mountainous regions of Bohemia. The drawings are all worked up in pen and ink. This is one of the landscape drawings by Savery that were copied in brown ink and wash by the Rembrandt follower Lam- bert Doomer, who apprently acquired an album of Savery's landscape drawings from Rembrandt's bankruptcy sale in 1658. He in turn may have sold several of these to Laurence van der Hem, who in- serted them in two volumes of his expand- ed version of Bluae's Atlas now in the Kartensammlung of the Nationalbiblio- thek, Vienna.

Ghent 1954, cat. no. 119; Amsterdam 1967, cat. no. V 51; Cologne 1985, cat. no. 95.

Schulz 1971, under cat. no. 3, p. 258 (with incorrect reference); Schulz 1972, under cat. no. 364; Schulz 1974, no. 254; Sumows- ki 1979, under no. 495x; Spicer 1979, cat. no. 14; Schapelhouman 1987, cat. no. 76.

J.S.

I.252
Roelandt Savery, with additions by Allart van Everdingen (1621–75)
Kortrijk 1576–Utrecht 1639
Mountain Landscape
Black chalk, red chalk in solution, washes in green, blue, grey; gouache and water- colour lower left added by Everdingen
38.2 × 41.2 cm
Inscription by Everdingen in brush and black ink: *AVE* ; verso: modern annotation in pencil: *R. Savery*; marks of C. Hofstede de Groot (L.561) and R. P. Goldschmidt (L.2926)
The Alps, 1606/7; Haarlem?, 1640s?
Allart van Everdingen; R.P. Goldschmidt (Prestel, Frankfurt, 4.X.1917, lot 533); C. Hofstede de Groot (Boerner, Leipzig, 4.XI.1931, lot 225)
Amsterdam, Rijksprentenkabinet, inv. no. 31:182

This alpine view is important as it pro- vides direct evidence for Allart van Everdingen's interest in Savery's render- ings of the alpine world. While Savery did not introduce real alpine vistas into his landscapes after he returned to the Netherlands in 1613, his drawings provid- ed a point of departure for Everdingen's own renderings of Scandinavia. We may suppose that Everdingen owned the pre- sent landscape, worked up the lower left corner, which he may have thought rather empty, with gouache and watercolour (a technique characteristic for him) and then placed his own monogram there.

The Hague 1930, cat. no 102; Ghent 1954, cat. no. 120; Amsterdam 1967, no. V50; Munich 1972-73, cat. no. 62; Cologne 1985, no. 96.

Schulz 1971, p. 255; A. Davies 1973 [1978], p. 117; Spicer 1979, cat. no. 19; Schapel- houman 1987, cat. no. 77.

J.S.

I.253
Roelandt Savery
Kortrijk 1576–Utrecht 1639
Village Street (Part of Prague)
Oily black and black chalk, smudged red chalk
12.6 × 16.3 cm
1605/1609
Göttingen, Kunstsammlung der Univer- sität, inv. no. H 172

This chalk study of a village street can be seen as a reflection of Savery's fascination with interesting perspectives rather than as a potential setting for a finished com- position. The artist apparently started working with chalk only after he had been in Prague for a few years, and the present study can be dated in conjunction with the *Farmyard* (cat. no. I.257).

Cologne 1985, cat. no. 99.

Bock-Rosenberg, 1930, 265 (as C. Saftleven ?); Spicer 1979, cat. no.85 (as R.S.).

J.S.

I.254
Roelandt Savery
Kortrijk 1576–Utrecht 1639
Peasant Woman in Half-length, Back of a Man's Head
Yellowish brown ink over lead (or black chalk or graphite)
12.5 × 10.1 cm
In brown ink over lead (or black chalk or graphite): *witten bandt / swart lifken / witte / hemt / swardtte hoedt / wit / 2) grisse / rock / grisse / shoed*; annotated in modern pencil on the back: *Brueghel*
1606–7
Sale Benoit Coster, C.F. Roos (Amsterdam), 1875; purchased as unidentified

sixteenth century (L.2228)
Amsterdam, Rijksprentenkabinett, inv. no. RP-T-1879-A-12

While the earliest 'naer het leven' drawings tend to avoid any intimacy with the subject, some of the later ones, such as this one of a weary market woman, are close-up studies demonstrating more interest in facial expression. Still, there is never any sense of interaction between the artist and subject. See *Team of Horses* (cat. no. I.246) for Savery's peasant studies in general and *Seated Peasant* (cat. no. I.255) for a characterization of the stylistic shifts in the later ones.

Cologne 1985, cat. no. 111.

Münz, 1961, cat. no. 123 (with further references); van Regteren Altena and Frerichs 1963, cat. no. 28; Van Leeuwen 1970, 29; Spicer 1979, cat. no. 205; Schapelhouman 1987, cat. no. 72.

J.S.

I.255
Roelandt Savery
Kortrijk 1576–Utrecht 1639
Seated Peasant with a Basket
Shades of brown ink over pencil (lead?)
15.8 × 15.2 cm
grisse roeck / swartte pantens / swardtte hoedt / swardtte broeck / swardtte le / nar hedt leúen
1606–08
Albert von Sachsen Teschen (L. 174)
Vienna, Graphische Sammlung Albertina, inv. no. 7866

This study and the other more mature *naer het leven* drawings are characterized

first of all by an increasing facility with the pen. The figures are on average larger than the earlier ones; some are only half-length and still fill the sheet. Rarely is anything now drawn on the verso. Billowing, volumetric forms with large hairpin folds are confined by large, confident, bold contours. The greater substantiality of the forms when compared with the *Team of Horses with Rider* is emphasized by the use of cross hatching, usually reinforced with short rhythmic hooks. There are parallels with the execution of *Cottages by the Water*, dated 1608(9?) (cat. no. I.261). Some parallels in the evolution of Savery's script are noted under *Blind Beggar* (cat. no. I.256).

The sheet has been trimmed, and the border is added. H. Saftleven made a copy of this figure (Amsterdam, Rijksprentenkabinet, inv. no. A 1485); the second figure on the copy sheet may reflect a lost study of the same man seen from the back.

London 1949, cat. no. 43 (P.B.); Vienna 1965, cat. no. 66 (P.B.).

Münz, 1961, cat. no. 125 (P.B.); Spicer 1979, cat. no. 210 (R.S.); Liess 1981, 91 ff. (P.B.); Spicer 1996, pp. 204-5 (R.S.).

J.S.

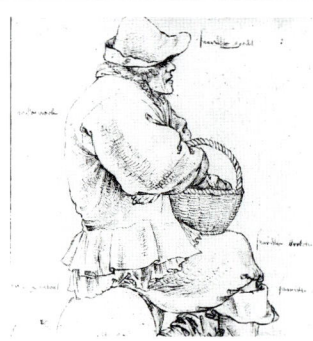

I.256
Roelandt Savery
Kortrijk 1576–Utrecht 1639
Blind Beggar with a Turban
Shades of brown ink over red chalk and possibly a trace of pencil (graphite ?) on the turban
14.3 × 13.6 cm
In brown ink over red chalk: *vÿllen wÿtten doeck / met ro strepen dar op / vÿlle lÿchdtte omberre / rock / grÿsen hoedt / vÿl swart lerre / broeck / vÿlle asgravve kovsen / vÿl / hoúdt / nart het leúen*; annotated in modern pencil on the back: *Bruegel / 34*
1607–8
Sale J. H. Cremer, Fr. Muller (Amsterdam),

15.VI.1886, under 47 (as Jan Brueghel); purchased from Fr. Muller 1888 (L.2228)
Amsterdam, Rijksprentenkabinett, inv. no. 1888 A 1449

The isolated head is that of the beggar without his turban. There are often beggars in Savery's paintings, but this study was not used directly in a known painting. Stylistically the study may be placed with the drawings datable to around 1607/8, for which see *Seated Peasant* (cat. no. I.255). In keeping with the shift towards elaboration seen in the stylistic evolution of these drawings, the script is now characterized by expressive uses of pressure on the nib

to achieve a flourish in the letters. The spelling is also more elaborate - 'ÿ' (or ij) replaces 'i,' and 'dt' or even 'dtt' replaces 't', as in *lÿchdtte* vs. the earlier *licht* (light, as in light brown).

Berlin 1975, cat. no. 221 (R.S. ?).

Münz 1961, cat. no. 117 (P.B.); Van Leeuwen 1970, 29 (R.S.); Spicer 1979, cat. no. 211 (R.S.); Liess 1981, 93 (P.B.),

J.S.

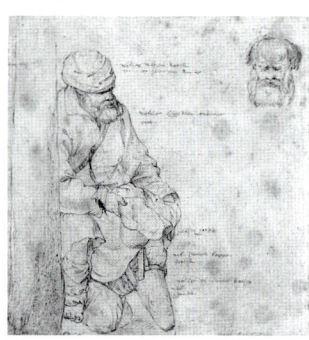

I.257
Roelandt Savery
Kortrijk 1576–Utrecht 1639
Farmyard
Black and red chalk, washes in light brown, green and grey heightened with white
42.3 × 29.3 cm
R S
1607–8
Rembrandt (?); Lambert Doomer; George John Earl Spencer (L.1530)
Vienna, Graphische Sammlung Albertina, inv. no. 9944

Later versions of this composition, includ-

ing paintings by Savery and a drawing by Lambert Doomer (Berlin, Kupferstichkabinett; Sumowski 1977, cat.no.498x), make it clear that Savery's drawing originally extended to the right, including a rearground view of a village. The sensitivity to the use of chalk in this softly modelled and articulated drawing prompts a comparison with Savery's rural studies and his chalk alpine landscapes as *Distant Valley* (cat. no. I.259). While the anecdotal quality of this setting suggests a study from life, there are surprising similarities between the present composition and the *Prodigal Son as a Swineherd* by Abraham Bloemaert, known in an undated engrav-

ing by Jan Saenredam (Hollstein: B1 528). As Saenredam died in 1607, his print and therefore the preliminary drawing must predate the proposed date of ca. 1607/8 for Savery's drawing. If the print was executed by 1603, Savery could have seen it before departing for Prague.

Essen and Vienna 1988, cat. no. 638 (with further references).

Spicer 1970, 6; Schulz 1971, 259; Schulz 1974, under no.252; Sumowski 1979, under no. 498x; Spicer 1979, no.89.

J.S.

I.258
Roelandt Savery
Kortrijk 1576–Utrecht 1639
Alpine Valley
Black chalk, red and ochre chalk in solution, washes in grey, green, and blue
37 × 55 cm
1607?
With Colnaghi's, London, 1956; bequest of Sir Bruce Ingram (L.1405a), 1963
Cambridge, Fitzwilliam Museum, inv. 696–1963

Although Savery's approach to the composition and execution of this mountain view are closely related to the preceding

landscapes, the inclusion of a sinuous, deciduous tree in place of the usual brace of unyielding pines creates a softer image. The washes in grey, green, and blue are applied somewhat carelessly; nevertheless they are autograph; Savery's characteristic use of chalk is found over as well as under the washes. In contrast, the ochre stroked into the foliage at the left may be an 'improvement' by a later hand.

Cambridge, Fitzwilliam Museum, *Old Master Drawings from the Collection of Sir Bruce Ingram*, 1958, cat. no. 46.

Spicer 1979, cat. no. 22.

J.S.

I.259
Roelandt Savery
Kortrijk 1576–Utrecht 1639
Distant Valley
Black chalk, oily black chalk, red chalk in
solution, washes in blue and brown
39.3 × 38.7 cm
The Alps, ca. 1607
Peter Sandby (cf. L.2112)
Hamburg, Kunsthalle, inv. no. 22490

Savery's travels in the Alps in 1606/7 and
more specifically his searching out of
bizarre rocks, rainbows and waterfalls is
discussed in the essay 'Roelandt Savery
and the "Discovery" of the Alpine Water-

fall'. Given the preferences evident in the
artist's choices of vantage points, this dramatic view may have been seen to combine the intimacy of the forest trail, the
thrill of the plunging waterfalls, the
rugged rocks and the changeable weather
conditions in the thin air. In working up
this breath-taking view between the re-
stricting side 'wings' over the valley to the
peaks beyond, Savery initially threw the
arch of a rainbow across this palest blue
sky, but he did not define the transitory
phenomenon more fully.

Essen and Vienna 1988, cat. no. 245 (with
further references).

Spicer 1979, cat. no. 38.

J.S.

I.260
Roelandt Savery
Kortrijk 1576–Utrecht 1639
Mountainous Stream with Travellers
Black chalk, red chalk in solution, blue
wash, traces of brown ink; partly incised
for transfer, verso rubbed red
19 × 26.5 cm
In black chalk: *R. SAVERY*; later annota-
tion in pencil: 3246
1607/8
Tessin collection; Royal Museum (L.1638)
Stockholm, Nationalmuseum, inv. no.
THC 3246/1863

Although related to the Alpine studies

such as *Distant Valley* (cat. no. I.259) in
terms of motifs and execution, this domesticated, highly structured view with its
many travellers is surely imaginary. It is a
characteristic example of the landscapes
(Spicer 1979, cat. no. 45-8) Savery composed around 1607/8, after returning to
Prague, as models for engravings to be
published by A. Sadeler. The present drawing is the same size as the engraving (Hollstein Sad 227; Spicer 1979, cat. no. Pr40;
see cat. for Sadeler's engravings). Some details of the foliage upper left are worked
up in pen and ink; this might be seen as a
guide to the printmaker, but other landscapes not meant for prints also exhibit

such passages. In addition it has been enlarged at top and bottom by a second
hand and incised for transfer (the verso
being rubbed red).

Essen and Vienna 1988, cat. no. 246 (with
further references).

Spicer 1979, cat. no. 42.

J.S.

I.261
Roelandt Savery
Kortrijk 1576–Utrecht 1639
Cottages by the Water
Brown ink with washes in blue, grey, and
brown
19.4 × 27.5 cm
In brown ink: *R SAVERY FC / 1609 (8?)*
1609(8?)
Alter Bestand
Stüttgart, Staatsgalerie, Graphische
Sammlung, inv. no. 1727

The pictorial quality of this composition
and the completeness, even to the rays of
light, of the consistently descriptive pen

work suggest that it was not executed in
preparation for a painting but rather as an
independent work of art or even as a potential model for a print. Dated 1609 (8?),
the drawing is contemporaneous with
other Savery landscapes that were engraved under Sadeler's supervision as
Mountain Stream with Travellers. While
Kurt Erasmus was not acquainted with
the present drawing when he finished his
dissertation on Savery in 1907, he later saw
it and made a notation in pencil in the
margin of page 174 of his personal copy of
his monograph published in 1908 (now in
the possession of the author) describing it
as 'echt' and the date as 1609.

Stuttgart 1979, cat. no. B38; Stuttgart,
Staatsgalerie Stuttgart 1984, cat. no. 105.

Zwollo 1968, n. 92; Spicer 1979, cat. no. 80;
Fučíková 1986, ill. 61; Essen and Vienna
1988, under cat. no. 254.

J.S.

I.262
Roelandt Savery
Kortrijk 1576–Utrecht 1639
Alley (in Prague)
Brown ink with washes in grey, light
brown and blue
22.2 × 16.6 cm
In black chalk: *R.S.*
1608/1609
Von Beckerath; acquired in 1902
Berlin, Staatliche Museen Berlin, Kupfer-
stichkabinett, inv. no. 13946

Bands of shadow and constricted spaces
resulting from the curving path of the re-
ceding archways provide the focal point

for this low-key but very original study of
an urban space. The execution bears comparison to that of the preceding drawing
dated 1609(8?).

Erasmus 1908, cat. no. Z13; Bock-Rosenberg 1930, p. 269; Spicer 1979, cat. no. 73;
Fučíková 1986, pl. 67.

J.S.

I.263
Roelandt Savery
Kortrijk 1576–Utrecht 1639
Roots over an Embankment
Black oily chalk, black and red chalk,
traces of green wash and oxidized white
on light brown paper
47.7 × 37.1 cm
In black chalk: *R S*
1607/1610
Acquired before 1930
Berlin, Staatliche Museen Berlin, Kupfer-
stichkabinett, inv. no. KdZ 13 865

Related to the preceding *Gnarled Roots*
even to technique, paper, and low viewing

angle, this is one of Savery's most flamboyant studies of an individual motif. The
softly curving contours, created by bold
single strokes, and the warm red tones set
off against the light brown paper give
these roots an animate qualtity at odds
with their static nature. It is this aspect of
Savery's oeuvre that Jacob Ruisdael most
admired.

Bock, Rosenberg 1930, 269; Spicer 1979,
cat. no. 58.

J.S.

I.264
Roelandt Savery
Kortrijk 1576–Utrecht 1639
Gnarled Roots
Black chalk, red chalk in solution, oily
black chalk, with green wash on light
brown paper
48.2 × 37 cm
Later annotation in black chalk, *not* a sig-
nature: *R. Sav.*
1608–10
K. E.van Liphart; with E.Parsons and Co.;
C. Hofstede de Groot; Professor J. Q. van
Regteren Altena
Netherlands, private collection

The extraordinary angle of vision, only
slightly above ground level, exaggerates
the swelling forms of the roots and lower
trunk. Savery is here working from life,
but his perspective, literally and figuratively, transforms his subject, bringing
out its dramatic expressiveness. The light
brown, slightly textured paper used here
and for the related tree studies including
Roots over an Embankment (Spicer 1979,
cat. no. 59-61) complements admirably the
warmth of the drawing media. As the model for the foreground thicket in the 1610
painting *Woodland with Deer Hunting* (untraced; Kaufmann 1985, cat. no. 19-44),
this study can be assigned to 1608 to 1610

and is therefore important for dating the
group as a whole. The Baroque qualities of
such flamboyant studies from nature in
the early seventeenth century and the significance of their popularity are addressed
in the concluding paragraphs of the essay
'Roelandt Savery and the "Discovery" of
the Alpine Waterfall' in this book.

Essen and Vienna 1988, cat. no. 249 (with
further references).

Spicer 1979, pp. 85-6, cat. no. 57; Kaufmann 1985, under cat. no. 19-44.

J.S.

I.265
Roelandt Savery
Kortrijk 1576–Utrecht 1639
Dapple-grey Horse, Seen from the Back
Soft black chalk; the orange chalk border
is a later addition
37.3 × 22.0 cm
Later annotation in pencil: *Stoop*
1608–10
Gottfried Wagner, Leipzig; purchased
from his estate in 1728
Dresden, Staatliche Kunstsammlungen,
Kupferstichkabinett, inv. no. C 1980-505

Horses appear everywhere in Savery's
paintings, in gatherings of animals such

as those soothed by Orpheus (cat. no. I.66),
or in Eden; as draught animals (e.g. *Team of
Horses with Rider* [cat. no. I.246]); or
mounts in a range of drawings and paintings of military life (cat. no. I.244, 245).
This sleek animal is very likely from
Rudolf's stable of the finest breeds from
Europe and Turkey. Savery depicted it in
graceful profile in his 1610 *Orpheus* (cat.
no. I.66), and it was also the subject of the
following study from the rear. One of the
drawings that Savery took back to the
Netherlands, the present study's only
known use is in a painting done after the
artist settled in Utrecht in 1618, an *Orpheus* from 1622 (Cambridge, Fitzwilliam

Museum). After the drawing left Savery's
shop, his authorship was forgotten; the
old attribution to 'Stoop' refers either to
Dirck or Maerten Stoop, later Utrecht
artists who both treated subjects with riders. In these two studies, chalk is used almost as a pencil for recording subtle detail, unlike the broad stroking of the lion
studies.

Salzburg 1966, cat. no. 84.

Spicer 1979, cat. no. 132; Fučíková 1986, pl.
70.

J.S.

I.266
Roelandt Savery
Kortrijk 1576–Utrecht 1639
Dapple-grey Horse, Seen from the Back
Black chalk with ochre chalk in solution
on greyish brown paper; 36.6 × 23.4 cm
In black chalk: *R S*
1608–10
Gottfried Wagner, Leipzig; purchased
from his estate in 1728
Dresden, Kupferstichkabinett, inv. no. C
931

This rear view of the dapple-grey depicted
in the preceding study was used in at least
two paintings, although with a darker

coat: *Animals near a Stream* (Oslo) and *Animal Kingdom* of 1619 (Amsterdam). The
present study, cut down at the left and
bottom edges, was begun from another
angle (leg lower right). The position of the
left rear leg has also been altered.

Essen and Vienna 1988, cat. no. 639 (with
further references).

Spicer 1979, cat. no. 133.

J.S.

I.267
Roelandt Savery
Kortrijk 1576–Utrecht 1639
Lion Stretched out on the Ground
Black chalk, ochre chalk in solution,
heightened with white, on greyish brown
paper treated with a blue tint
27.6 × 38.3 cm
Inscription in black chalk: *R.S.*
1606–10
Gottfried Wagner, Leipzig; purchased
from his estate in 1728
Dresden, Kupferstichkabinett, inv. no. C
924

Three studies of lions in Dresden and an-

other in the Historisch Museum, Amsterdam, must all have been made in Prague in
the imperial menagerie. While Savery's
Prague studies of animals from life, including the two Dresden studies of a *Dapple-grey Horse* (cat. no. I.265, 266), strikingly characterize the appearance of these
creatures, they show no attempt to capture
movement. This is in contrast to the frenzy
of his chalk drawing *Fight Between a Lion
and a Griffon* (Braunschweig, Herzog Anton Ulrich-Museum; Spicer 1979). Savery
apparently made his animal studies, from
exotic elephants to the more prosaic deer,
as part of a repertory of animal motifs for
paintings. This lion appears in the 1610

Orpheus in Frankfurt (cat. no. I.66) and the
1620 *Garden of Eden* at Buscot Park. The
broad strokes and use of rich coloured
chalks in the Dresden lion studies bring
out the rough flamboyance of the beasts.
The technique used here is comparable to
that of the alpine and woodland landscapes of 1606 to 1610 and points to a similar dating for the present drawing.

Essen and Vienna 1988, no. 240.

Erasmus 1908, cat. no. 46; Spicer 1979, cat.
no. 134; Fučíková 1986, pl. 71.

J.S.

I.268
Bartholomeus Spranger
Antwerp 1546–Prague 1611
Christ Crowned with Thorns
Pen and brown ink, with brown wash over
black chalk, with white highlights (body-
colour) on blue paper
28.5 × 24.4 cm
1572
Pope Pius V; Charles, Prince de Ligne
Vienna, Graphische Sammlung Albertina,
inv. no. 2010

This drawing was first identified by Konrad Oberhuber as one of a series of twelve
depictions of the Passion of Christ that ac-

cording to Karel van Mander (*Het Schilderboek*, Haarlem, 1604) Spranger executed in
a chiaroscuro manner for Pope Pius shortly before the pontiff's death. Oberhuber also associated another sheet representing
the *Mocking of Christ* (Munich, Staatliche
Graphische Sammlung, inv. no. 2795) with
this project. Most recently Sally Metzler
has found a third, hitherto unpublished
sheet (Stockholm, National Museum) that
also belong to the series. Van Mander reports that these were the first drawings executed by Spranger in pen and ink, and
Metzler's discovery bears out this point,
because the Stockholm drawing, although
belonging to the series, is more in chalk, a

medium in which Van Mander says the
artist had worked previously. This drawing
represents a turning point in Spranger's
career and must be considered one of his
more important early works. It exemplifies
his early style, before his service for the imperial court, at which both the subject-
matter and form of his inventions soon
took a different direction.

Essen and Vienna 1988-89, no. 640.

Metzler 1997, pp. 2-3, 10, 58ff., cat. A59, p.
240f.

T.C.K.

I.269
Bartholomeus Spranger
Antwerp 1546–Prague 1611
The Judgment of Paris
Pen and wash in grey, white highlighting
on blue-green paper
After 1575
Vojtěch Lanna's collection, donated in
1888
Prague, Národní galerie v Praze, Grafická
sbírka, inv. no. K 1 132

In Spranger's drawings, such striking use
of the brush is rare. It was perhaps inspired by Italian chiaroscuro woodcarvings. Hans Mont, Spranger's one-time

friend and colleague, particularly liked
this chiaroscuro style, and the work might
well have been made at the time when they
were working together on the Vienna
Neugebäude. It was probably a design for
a painting that has not survived or never
materialized, and it shows Spranger's
working methods in an interesting light.
The studies on the back are sketches for
the individual figures, which then appear
together in the main composition. Mont's
influence can be seen in the relief-like arrangement of the composition and in the
use of white to emphasize the facial features.

Prague 1912, cat. no. 261/5; Prague 1976,
cat. no. 5; Prague 1978–1979, cat. no. 20;
Dresden 1978, cat. no. 20; Stuttgart 1979–
80, cat. no. B 9; Essen and Vienna 1988, cat.
no. 257 for all earlier literature.

Oberhuber 1958, p. 254, cat. no. Z 47; Fučí-
cová 1986, p. 17, ill. II-I-III.

E.F.

I.270
Bartholomeus Spranger
Antwerp 1546–Prague 1611
The Circle of the Gods
Pen and grey-brown ink, watercolour and
white heightening on grey-green paper,
incised with circular holes
Diam: 37.3 cm
1576
Vienna, Graphische Sammlung Albertina,
inv. no. 11514

This sheet represents a number of the
Olympian deities seated in the clouds.
Since Otto Benesch first made the connec-
tion, the drawing has been associated with

the Neugebäude near Vienna, in which
van Mander reports that Spranger among
other works painted a ceiling: this description is also consonant with the view *di sot-
to in su*. The hole in the middle of the drawing, the circular lines impressed in it and
other circular holes at the edges indicate
that a compass was used to make the design. The use of such a device also points
to its connection with an architectural
project. The ample indications of colour
suggest that the drawing represents an advanced stage in the working out of the
composition. Documents for payment to
the artist allow a date of 1576 to be established for its execution. This drawing is

thus connected with the major project in
which Spranger was engaged when, on
the recommendation of Giambologna, he
was first called to the imperial court to
serve Maximilian II. This drawing displays
Spranger's capabilities as a designer of
fresco painting.

Essen and Vienna 1988, no. 641, with further references.

Metzler 1997, pp. 76, 242, cat. no. A60.

T.C.K.

I.271
Bartholomeus Spranger
Antwerp 1546–Prague 1611
Neptune and Caenis
Pen and brown ink and wash, heightened
with white on light brown paper
24.5 × 17.3 cm
Lower right (pen and brown ink): *Bar-
tolomeo Spranger mana propria* in another
hand
Before 1580
Antwerp, Stedelijk Prentenkabinet, Muse-
um Plantin Moretus, inv. no. 5

The inventory of 1621 lists a painting (no.
1214, now lost) of the same name, which

may have been Spranger's first picture after his move to Prague. It would seem
from the subject-matter that a drawing
and a print made by Jan Sadeler in 1580
were possibly after this same painting. The
two main figures on the engraving correspond to those on the drawing. However,
it is not possible to draw any final conclusions about the relationship of the three
works without more detailed knowledge
of the painting. All that is certain is that
they date from about the same time. The
painting may have been one of an erotic-
mythological series on the subject of the
gods and love, six of which have survived.
The drawing shows the scene described by

Ovid, in which Neptune takes the
renowned beauty Caenis (Ovid, *Metamorphoses* 12, 195–97). The extraordinarily dynamic yet decorative image of the two
bodies intertwined is an invention of
Spranger's, although his portrayal of Caenis clearly owes a debt of allegiance to the
engraving of *Venus and Mars* by Gian Giacomo Caraglio after Perino del Vaga.

Delen 1938, no. 116; Oberhuber 1958, pp.
103–4, no. Z.5; DaCosta Kaufmann 1985, p.
289.

T.G.

I.272
Bartholomeus Spranger
Antwerp 1546–Prague 1611
Venus and Cupid
Pen drawing in brown ink, grey wash,
with traces of black chalk and white and
red highlighting on a chalk ground
Between 1580 and 1585
Paris, Collection Frits Lugt, Institut Néer-
landais, inv. no. 1 205

Oberhuber considered this drawing to
have been made by Spranger while still in
Vienna, during the late 1570s. He pointed
out its connection with the composition
of *Mercury and Juno*, which was perhaps

engraved by Egbert van Panderen using
the artist's model. The same artist also
made a reproduction of Venus with Adonis, and a third composition of similar format by Panderen, depicting Minerva, may
also be connected with these. A comparison with Spranger's fresco in Prague Castle's White Tower provides a probable explanation for its intended use. The circular
format and the method employed in composing the figures within it would suggest
that it was a study for a fresco similar to
the one in the White Tower. To prove this
it is vital to date the drawings accurately. If
they were intended for this use then they
would have to have been made while

Spranger was still in Vienna or when he
was in Prague. The most similar drawing
to the one of Venus and Cupid is that of
Minerva and the Muses, the date for which
Gerszi sets at some time prior to 1580 (Essen and Vienna 1988, cat. no. 258). If we
consider the fact that Spranger's frescos
date from after 1585, then it would seem
that this series of circular compositions
originated roughly during his time in
Prague.

Oberhuber 1957, pp. 93–94, 254, cat. no. 45;
Neumann 1970, pp. 142–71.

E.F.

I.273
Bartholomeus Spranger
Antwerp 1546–Prague 1611
Ecce Homo
Ink drawing
29.4 × 19.1 cm
1580–85
Berlin, Staatliche Museen, Kupferstich-
kabinett, inv. no. KdZ 13 626

Bock 1930.

E.F.

I.274
Bartholomeus Spranger
Antwerp 1546–Prague 1611
Rest on the Flight to Egypt
Brush and grey ink, (white) body colour
on brown paper
11.6 × 8.9 cm
Before 1590
Florence, Galleria degli Uffizi, inv. no.
14715 F

The preliminary drawing for an engraving
by Aegidius Sadeler (Hollstein 36) was the
companion piece to another engraving by
Sadeler, which he made after the *Adoration
of the Kings* by Hans von Aachen (Hollstein

35). Hans von Aachen visited Prague in
1588 and it seems likely that he took
Spranger's drawing to Sadeler. Spranger's
fully three-dimensional figures are composed to form a self-contained triangle.
For their movements Spranger drew inspiration from works by earlier artists. The
seated pose of the Madonna, the position
of her head, her arm reaching out to the
fruit bowl and the movement of the Christ
child's arm as he helps her to the fruit are
all reminiscent of Correggio's painting
the *Madonna della Scodella* (Parma, Galleria
Nazionale). However, Spranger's characterization is stronger and weightier than
Correggio's graceful figures in all their

lyrical beauty. The distinct, stiff folds in
the figures' clothing and the contrasts of
light and shade are all the more pronounced on the reverse-image engraving.

Kloek 1975, no. 186; Gerszi 1990, p. 103.

T.G.

I.275
Bartholomeus Spranger
Antwerp 1546–Prague 1611
Sheet of Studies
Drawing in ruddle, white glaze (partially
oxidized)
Before 1597
Munich, Staatliche Graphische Samm-
lung, inv. no. 2195

Only seldom in Spranger's work do we
come across preparatory studies for his
paintings or drawings. But we know from
the engraving of Jan Muller from 1597
(Holl., p. 72) that Spranger made thorough preparations for the composition

depicting Fame introducing Painting,
Sculpting and Architecture on Mt Olympus. As can be seen on the leaf from Munich, in addition to studies for the central
figures of the composition he even drew
details of the hands and feet. Oberhuber
in his dissertation referred to this drawing
in connection with the paintings of
Spranger's Venus cycle; Muller's graphic
print is dated *ante quem*, but it seems that
this composition might have arisen in
connection with Rudolf's Imperial Decree
which elevated the status of painting to a
high art, and thus around 1595. The recalling of the Turkish wars on the engraving
may give a *post quem* date. The battle at Sis-

sek launched a thirteen-year war in 1593.

Oberhuber 1958, pp. 169–170, cat. no. Z
37, with the earlier literature; Wegner
1973, p. 28, cat. no. 109, ill. tab. 40/41.

E.F.

I.276
Bartholomeus Spranger
Antwerp 1546–Prague 1611
Minerva
Pen and brush in brown and grey ink,
heightened with white, on grey-grounded
paper
54.7 × 21.6 cm
Before 1600
E. J. von Dalberg Collection
Darmstadt, Hessisches Landesmuseum,
inv. no. AE 2138

Spranger often depicted Minerva, the patron of the sciences and the arts, alone or
in the company of other mythological fig-

ures. He wanted to emphasize the intellectual aspect of art. Here the goddess is presented in a statuesque pose. Spranger
brought out the figure's plasticity by using copious amounts of white body
colour, which is particularly effective on
the grounded paper. In contrast to some
of his earlier, more complicated figures,
Minerva is composed of simple, rounded
forms and her movements and gestures
are relatively restrained. This change in his
portrayal of the human form may have occurred under the influence of his colleague, the sculptor Adriaen de Vries.
Spranger probably made this drawing in
the late 1590s and it seems that Jan Müller

used it for an incomplete copper engraving he made in 1600 (Hollstein 60).

Darmstadt 1964, cat. no. 71.

Bergsträsser 1979, no. 88.

T.G.

I.277
Bartholomeus Spranger
Antwerp 1546–Prague 1611
The Triumph of Bacchus
Pen drawing in black ink, grey-blue wash,
with white highlighting
On the back: *Prago den 12 may anno 1524*
(according to Lugt, the third digit may
have been read incorrectly)
23.1 × 39.2 cm
Prior to 1600 (?)
Acquired from Mlle Boitte,
Fontainebleau, 1944
Paris, Musée du Louvre, Département des
Arts Graphiques, inv. no. R.F 29 452

K. Oberhuber, who found the drawing
among the anonymous works belonging
to the Fontainebleau School, correctly attributed it to Spranger. He believed it was
a sketch for a relief and dated it at around
1607. It is however very difficult to date accurately. It is a rough sketch, notable
mainly for its wash technique, brushwork
and highlighting with white pigment. Its
gloomy lighting led Oberhuber to date it
later than it in fact probably was. In its
brushwork and pen technique it would
seem to belong to those works which
Spranger made during the 1590s or perhaps even earlier. The wide, multi-figural
composition is not typical of Spranger's

oeuvre after 1600 and is mainly found in
works dating from his stay in Vienna and
the early period of his stay in Prague,
namely between 1575 and 1590. A more accurate dating of this exceptionally impressive drawing may be possible following a
careful re-examination of the date written
on the back.

Oberhuber 1958, pp. 199, 253, cat. no. 44;
Lugt 1986, p. 132, cat. no. 641, ill. tab. 184.

E.F.

I.278
Bartholomeus Spranger
Antwerp 1546–Prague 1611
Saint Martin with the Beggar
Later inscription, lower right: *Spranger*
Ca. 1600 or after
Auction of Jacob de Vos Jbzn., Amsterdam
22-24 May, 1883, no. 709, bought in 1884
from D. Dirksen, The Hague
Amsterdam, Rijksmuseum, Rijks-
prentenkabinet, inv. no. A 409

This drawing is probably a study for an altarpiece that does not survive. Niederstein
dated it from Spranger's first decade in
Prague; Oberhuber dated it ca.1604. How-

ever, it is closer to dated drawings from
1599, for example, *Hercules and Omphale*
or *Amor*, which have clearly delineated
contour lines, pronounced parallel hatching, and white heightening. The sheet
with *Minerva Triumphing over Ignorance
and Envy*, dated to 1604, is drawn by a
much more linear and economical hand
with a significant emphasis on washes,
which in effect define the forms. The
drawing became the model for the graphic
work of Zacharias Dolenda, which was
published by J. de Gheyn II (Le Bl.22, Hollstein 44). This led to Oberhuber's later
dating, but the drawing could have
reached the Netherlands when Spranger

was there in 1602 and could have been engraved over later.

Niederstein, 1931, p. 25, cat. no. 11; Oberhuber, 1958, pp.187-88, 244, cat. no. 2;
Boon K.G., 1978, II, p. 152, cat. no. 417; II,
p. 158, ill. 417.

E.F.

I.279
Bartholomeus Spranger
Antwerp 1546–Prague 1611
Young Artist before Minerva
Pen and brown ink, black chalk, grey-brown wash, white heightening
13.5 × 9.6 cm
Ca. 1590
Inscribed by the artist lower left: *cosi tratta Minerva 9?) La ser...*
Vienna, Graphische Sammlung Albertina, inv. no. 25437

The small scale and the inscription on this drawing suggest that it may have been presented as a gift or was originally a page

from a *Stammbuch*, or *album amicorum*. The subject, an allegory on the arts, fits either of these functions and is frequently found in the oeuvre of Rudolfine artists. Here Mercury, in the guise of an artist (he holds a maulstick), is being crowned by the bare-breasted. This discrepancy makes it unlikely that the drawing is directly connected with the print, although a dating of ca. 1590 on the basis of comparison with other drawings is still likely: Metzler (*Alchemy of Drawing*) however dates the sheet 1592. The theme can be related to numerous Hermathenic allegories in Rudolfine art. In particular the representation of Mercury/Hermes in the guise of an artist

points not only to the god's role as the protector of the arts, but suggests the ideal of the 'eloquent artist', which was espoused by Spranger and other artists at the imperial court, and gives a key to their attitude towards stylistics (see essay by Kaufmann in the catalogue above).

Essen and Vienna 1988, p. 176, cat. no. 646.

Metzler 1997, p. 134f., cat. no. A64, pp. 248f.

T.C.K.

I.280
Bartholomeus Spranger
Antwerp 1546–Prague 1611
Cybele and Minerva
Drawing in pen and brown ink, grey-brown wash, white glaze on paper coated with white paint
Ca. 1590
Collection of L. Krahe
Düsseldorf, Graphische Sammlung, Kunstmuseum Düsseldorf, Sammlung der Kunstakademie (NRW), inv. no. KA (FP) 4817

In the Essen catalogue, T. Gerszi points out that this drawing is from the begin-

ning of the 1590s when, in addition to the prevailing erotic tone of mythology, Spranger began to pursue allegorical scenes in his paintings, depicting moralizing or philosophical themes. In this drawing from Düsseldorf Cybele represents nature and fertility, Minerva's wisdom and knowledge. Their connection suggests an interpretation, often repeated in literature, that nature guides wisdom and knowledge is the path to success. Gerszi duly dates this drawing to the beginning of the 1590s, for both as a sculpturally conceived figural type and as an unbound composition it ranks with Spranger's paintings from the cycle of Venus, above

all the Hannover *Bacchus and Venus* (cat. no. 42).

Düsseldorf 1979/1980, cat. no. 136; Stuttgart 1979/1980, cat. no. B11; Essen and Vienna 1988, cat. no. 260.

Budde 1930, cat. no. 798; Niederstein 1931, pp. 3, 15, no. 16; Oberhuber 1958, p. 148, cat. no. Z 20; Oberhuber 1970, p. 221, ill. 10; Essen and Vienna 1988, cat. no. 260.

E.F.

I.281
Bartholomeus Spranger
Antwerp 1546–Prague 1611
Hercules and Omphale
Pen drawing in brown ink, brown wash, white highlighting, traces of red and white chalk
Above: *Bartolomeus Spranger fecit per lanno 1599 cio per compiaser*
1599
E. Šafařík's collection, Bratislava, 1928; acquired from an art dealer in Prague
Prague, Národní galerie v Praze, Grafická sbírka, inv. no. K 42 835

This theme recurs several times in

Spranger's work, notably in two paintings (one in Vienna, Kunsthistorisches Museum, inv. no. 1126, and another in a Swiss private collection currently on loan to the Prague, Národní galerie) This drawing was most probably inspired by *Mars and Venus* from the series painted by Paolo Veronese for Rudolf II in the late 1570s, with which Spranger would have been readily able to acquaint himself. He was clearly taken by the triangular composition of the three figures, the female body seen from the front and the male figure seen mostly from the back and side but with his head turned towards the viewer. The striking verticals of figures lend

Spranger's composition a sense of calmness and equipoise. The Vienna painting and composition, known from Sadeler's engraving, are more dramatic. 'He who overpowered all others was himself overpowered by love' provided the theme for this drawing probably intended as a keepsake.

Dresden 1977, cat. no. 20; Prague 1978-1979, cat. no. 22; Essen and Vienna 1988, cat. no. 263, for earlier literature.

Oberhuber 1958, p. 174, cat. no. Z 48; Fučíková 1986, p. 18, ill. IV.

E.F.

I.282
Bartholomeus Spranger
Antwerp 1546–Prague 1611
Cupid
Pen drawing in brown ink, grey wash, and highlights on pale-blue paper
18.6 × 14.6 cm
Bottom right: *Bartolomeo Sprangers fecit prag / del. 99*
1599
Nürnberg, Germanisches Nationalmuseum, inv. no. Hz. 28

T. Gerszi in the Essen catalogue claimed that this drawing was only connected with the painting of *Cupid Flees from Psyche*

(Oldenburg, Landesmuseum für Kunst und Kulturgeschichte) in its composition of the figure of Amor (Cupid) and, as the ostentatious signature would suggest, is in fact very much a work of its own. Spranger's copies of this drawing, drawn by himself (Erlangen, Universitätsbibliothek, inv. no. V. C. 11), attest to the painter's habit of making several versions of the same composition. Both works are signed, which would suggest that they were given to someone as a keepsake. The signature on the Nürnberg drawing is similar to the inscription on the drawing of *Hercules and Omphale* (cat. no. I.281) dedicating it to 'Spranger's friend'. The

Nürnberg *Amor* is also connected with this work, bearing the same date in its drawing style and in its use of whitening pigment.

Nürnberg 1952, cat. no. W. 134; Nürnberg 1955, cat. no. D. 25; Essen and Vienna 1988, cat. no. 262.

Kaufmann 1988, p. 272, cat. no. 20.69.

E.F.

I.283
Bartholomaus Spranger
Antwerp 1546–Prague 1611
Judith Lays the Head of Holofernes into a Sack
Pen and brown ink with brown wash, white heightening
32 × 21.2 cm
Inscribed in pen lower right: *Spranger 1/12f.*; on verso: *Spranger 1/12f.*
After 1600
Possibly Cabinet Paignon Dijonval, Paris (Catalogue, Paris, 1810, 62, no. 123); in the possession of the Louvre before 1727
Paris, Musée du Louvre, Cabinet des Dessins, inv. no. 20.474

While no painting exists by Spranger of the theme of Judith, from the Apocrypha, he is known to have depicted the subject at times throughout his career. The Louvre drawing represents Spranger's late drawing style. A more precise dating seems difficult, however: although plausible grounds have been advanced for a dating of 1606 (see Vienna 1988-89), Metzler dates the sheet ca. 1601. The repetition of the theme, while a frequent occurrence in Spranger's Prague oeuvre, suggests its attraction for him. It may be related to other themes representing the power of women, *Weibermacht*. Perhaps its attraction is also due to a piquant combination of elements

in the story of Judith, which seem common in Rudolfine art: eroticism, heroism and violence. It is not known what function this particular drawing served.

Essen and Vienna 1988, no. 647, p. 177.

Metzler 1997, pp. 220ff., cat. no. A46.

T.C.K.

I.284
Bartholomeus Spranger
Antwerp 1546–Prague 1611
Cupid and Psyche
Drawing in pen, brush and brown ink, underdrawn in charcoal on chalk-layered paper
After 1602
The art market in Lenz, Prague, 1939; collection of A. Welker, Amsterdam
Leiden, Prentenkabinet der Rijskuniversiteit, inv. no. 1070

Although this is only a cursory sketch composed of several quick lines and wide brushstrokes, it ranks among the most

beautiful and most impressive of Spranger's drawings. Gerszi correctly discerns in this work the influence of H. Goltzius, with whose drawings Spranger would have been able to accquaint himself during his journey to the Low Countries in 1602. Under Goltzius's influence Spranger abandoned for a short time the expressive stylization of human figures, striving for a natural physical form. The lying Eros could be a sketch of a just-sighted sleeping youth, and even the rounded shapes of Psyche have a quite natural effect. The drawing is a depiction of the story of Eros and Psyche, according to Apuleius. It captures the moment when Psyche is decid-

ing whether she should violate the prohibition and look at her husband while it is light. Spranger was most probably searching for an interesting solution to a composition. If a painted version had been produced, this drawing would never have been preserved.

Amsterdam 1955, cat. no. 60; Essen and Vienna 1988, cat. no. 265.

Oberhuber 1958, pp. 192–193, cat. no. Z 32; Fučíková 1986, p. 17, ill. 8; Essen and Vienna 1988, p. 392, cat. no. 4.265.

E.F.

I.285
Bartholomeus Spranger
Antwerp 1546–Prague 1611
Adam and Eve
Drawing in brown ink, brown wash, white hightening on grey paper
Signed bottom left: *B/ Spranger/ In*
Ca. 1610
? JHP 96 – an unknown collection from the ? eighteenth century; ? Association for the Support of Fine Arts; held in a museum since 1946
Warsaw, Muzeum Narodowe, inv. no. Rys. ob. d. 701

Spranger turned to the subject of Adam

and Eve several times and particularly in his drawings. The oldest recorded version is the model for Goltzin's engraving from 1585 (Bartsch 271, Hollstein 316). The Stuttgart drawing originated before 1598 (Staatsgalerie, inv. no. 1729), which Z. Dolendo reproduced in the same year (Hollstein 1). Oberhuber has dated the Vienna picture to ca. 1593, on the basis of an analogy between the figure of Eve and de Vries's *Psyche*. In the opinion of this author, the picture comes later; the artist's gentle technique suggests that it is related to pictures from the period before 1600, for example, the *Baptism of Christ*. The light transforms muscular human bodies

and figures into miraculous phantasms by the special play of projections and hollows. In the composition the figure of *Eve*, like Venus in the picture of Vulcan's workshop, represents the dominating female principle.

Warsaw 1963–64, cat. no. 101, pic 69b; London 1980, cat. no. and ill. 58.

London 1980, cat. no. 90, ill. 58, for older literature.

E.F.

I.286
Bartholomeus Spranger
Antwerp 1546–Prague 1611
St Sebastian (?)
Ink drawing in brown, brown wash, and white highlights on brownish paper
24.1 × 17.8 cm
Ca. 1610
E. Habich collection, Kassel
Stuttgart, Grapische Sammlung der Staatsgalerie, Sammlung Schloss Fachsenfeld, inv. no. II 284

In the catalogue to the exhibition *Prague um 1600*, T. Gerszi observed that it was very difficult to determine the subject of this

work: the man tied between two trees has not been wounded by an arrow as in the picture of St Sebastian at the church of St Nicholas in Prague, nor does he correspond to usual depictions of Prometheus or Mars. In his later drawings, Spranger often omitted attributes and concentrated on the cursory sketching of the composition with short, thick strokes. He made abundant use of white, emphasizing the modelling of the body and strong lighting. In the face, he indicated the nose by means of a light area set between the dark hollows of the eyes. Like Adrian de Vries, Spranger was passionately concerned with the play of light and shade. Two of Spranger's com-

positions, known only from graphic reproductions by Lukas Kilian, are particularly expressive: the *Struggle of Hercules with Anteus* and *St Jerome*, both dated at 1610. This drawing is therefore most reliably dated within the last years of Spranger's creative output.

Stuttgart 1967, cat. no. 128; Stuttgart 1984, cat. no. 21; Essen and Vienna 1988, cat. no. 266.

Essen and Vienna 1988, pp. 392–93, cat. no. 266.

E.F.

I.287
Pieter Stevens
? Mechelen ca. 1567–Prague after 1624
Landscape with Engagement Ceremony Outside the Chapel
Pen drawing in brown ink
18.2 × 30.2 cm
At the bottom right-hand edge: 95
1595
Prague, Národní muzeum
Prague, Národní galerie v Praze, Grafická sbírka, inv. no. K 26 068

An Zwollo attributed this work to Stevens on the basis of a comparison with his other works dated with two digits of the year

along the bottom edge. The closest analogy to this composition is a painting in the collection belonging to the Institut Néerlandais (Paris, inv. no. 1305), dated 1594, in which the figures occupy similar positions. In the drawing, however, Stevens abandoned the elevated view of the landscape, and substituted the fantasy Roman city for a village green and village buildings. The arrangement of the scene appears more natural but the composition itself is overburdened with detail. The striking linear technique, which uses only outlines and thick hachure, makes the work look ultimately flat and stiff. These and other similar drawings by Stevens lack

depth. Only his later use of washing succeeds in integrating the three parts that make up his landscapes, and provides a sense of depth.

Prague 1978–79, cat. no. 23.

Zwollo 1970, p. 245, no. 3; Fučíková 1986, p. 27, no. 54.

E.F.

I.288
Pieter Stevens
? Mechelen ca. 1567–Prague after 1624
Castle on River
1624
24 × 18 cm
Ca. 1597
Toronto, Frank and Marianne Seger

E.F.

I.289
Pieter Stevens
? Mechelen ca. 1567–Prague after 1624
Farmhouse and a Tower on a High River Bank
Pen and brown ink, brown and blue wash
21.7 × 33.7 cm
Monogram: *PS*
Late 1590s
O. Brenner and Duke de Solms Braunfels Collection
Amsterdam, Rijksmuseum, Rijksprentenkabinet, inv. no. RP-T-1922-12

Stevens always reacted positively towards artistic influences of all kinds and ab-sorbed a great variety of different elements into his work. This drawing is based fairly faithfully on a composition by Paul Brill, which today is known only as an engraving from the seventeenth century, published by Pierre-Jean Mariette together with other landscape works by Bril. An engraving by Isaac Major (Hollstein 18), which is known as an engraved version of this drawing by Pieter Stevens, is in fact a copy of the same lost drawing by Paulus Bril. The drawing by Bril may have been the model for Stevens, who merely changed some details. Stevens had already been influenced by Bril during his time in Rome, and he returned with renewed in-terest to Bril's work after 1597.

Zwollo 1968, p. 150; Boon 1978, no. 422.

T.G.

I.290
Pieter Stevens
? Mechelen ca. 1567–Prague after 1624
Cephalus and Procris
Drawing in pen and ink in brown tone, brown and blue wash
Ca. 1600
Ex Skutezky collection
Brno, Moravská galerie, inv. no. B 2 129

Stevens used a circular format for several landscape compositions, e.g., *Landscape with a Footbridge* and *The Flight into Egypt* (Brussels, Koninklijk Museum, coll. de Grez). The space is constructed slightly differently in each: in the Brussels and Prague examples it is symmetrically divided by a spreading tree; in *The Flight Into Egypt* the figures of the Virgin and Child occupy the left section, while on the right is a distant view of a wide valley. The overall effect is therefore unbalanced. In *Cephalos and Procris* the staffage occupies more space, and the composition is better adapted to the circular format. Two picture planes, two coulisses of trees create virtually a peephole view on to a landscape. Thus, the composition of the drawing is balanced, if somewhat decoratively. Figures were not Stevens's forte. In landscapes, as An Zwollo has pointed out, he had already demonstrated that he could capture natural detail and the atmosphere of a location. For this reason, she also dated the Brno drawing to around 1600.

Fučíková 1967, p. 181; Zwollo 1970, pp. 249-51, ill. 6; Fučíková 1967, p. 28, ill. 55.

E.F.

I.291
Pieter Stevens
? Mechelen ca. 1567–Prague after 1624
Landscape with a Bridge
Pen and brown ink, grey-brown and blue wash
17 × 17 cm
Ca. 1600
C. Wiesböck; J. A. Ruf; Vojtěch Lanna; Prague, Uměleckoprůmyslové muzeum v Praze
Prague, Národní galerie v Praze, Grafická sbírka, inv. no. K 36 805

Of several drawings with a circular format, this one, with its powerful and perfectly balanced composition, is one of the very best. Stevens's original linear style underwent a profound transformation in the course of the late 1590s: the sketch lines became softer, and much more washing was applied. The representation of light added a new dimension to his compositions in depicting changing atmospheric effects. The scenes became much smaller and appeared more natural even though they continued to be composed of the usual three parts. The pageant in the composition became of secondary importance. The distant buildings emerging from the haze over the two vistas running along the copses give the composition a sense of depth. This work belongs to the most powerful of Stevens's drawings from this period just before and at the turn of the seventeenth century.

Prague 1912, cat. no. 113/a; Prague 1978-79, cat. no. 24.

Fučíková 1967, pp. 178-79; Zwollo 1970, pp. 249-50, no. 5; Fučíková 1967, pp. 27-28, no. XIV.

E.F.

I.292
Pieter Stevens
? Mechelen ca. 1567–Prague after 1624
Woodland with Felled Trees
Pen drawing in brown ink, brown wash on the same-coloured paper
17.9 × 28.1 cm
After 1604
Prague, Národní galerie v Praze
Prague, Národní galerie v Praze, Graficá sbírka, inv. no. 24 801

For commentary, see cat. no. 293.

Prague 1976, cat. no. 2.

Zwollo 1970, p. 252, Gerszi 1977, pp. 108-9, no. 77; Fučíková 1986, p. 28, no. 56.

E.F.

I.293
Pieter Stevens
? Mechelen ca. 1567–Prague after 1624
Woodland with Stream
Pen drawing in brown ink, brown wash on the same-coloured paper
17.4 × 28.5 cm
After 1604
Prague, Národní galerie v Praze
Prague, Národní galerie v Praze, Graficá sbírka, inv. no. 24 802

These two forest still lifes are similar to drawings by Paulus van Vianen. In 1604 Stevens met two of the best landscape artists of his day, van Vianen and Jan Bruegel the Elder, who both had a lasting influence on his work. Breughel stayed a relatively short time in Prague, but long enough to influence Stevens's cityscapes. Van Vianen on the other hand was a long-time colleague of Stevens at the Emperor's court, and his fine, subtle drawings taught his friend to observe landscapes with a very different eye. Stevens never undertook naturalistic drawings, but succeeded in depicting the changeable atmospheric and lighting effects of nature. He began to concentrate on smaller areas of landscapes, capturing the particular beauty of a forest nook or a minor natural occurrence. He was indebted to van Vianen for his technique of short sketch lines, joined by rich washing to give them form. These two drawings from his time in Prague represent a daring excursion into van Vianen's style of landscape, such as is rarely seen in the rest of his work, for he later returned to his carefully and clearly formulated drawing style.

Prague 1967, cat. no. 3; Dresden 1977, cat. no. 19.

Zwollo 1970, p. 252, no. 8; Gerszi 1977, pp. 108-9; Fučíková 1986, p. 28, ill. 57.

E.F.

I.294
Pieter Stevens
? Mechelen ca. 1567–Prague after 1624
Moorland
Black ink on brown paper
After 1604
20.5 × 30 cm
Collection of V. Lanna; given in 1888 to
the Society of Patriotic Friends of Art in
Prague
Prague, Národní galerie v Praze, Grafická
sbírka, inv. no. K 1 286

When Paulus van Vianen came to Prague
in 1603, his studies of secluded forest
scenes and mountainside captivated

Stevens so much that he began to copy
them, and this gradually transformed not
only his drawing technique but also, particularly, his view of nature. This sheet
provides a rare opportunity to compare
the same motif as rendered by Stevens and
by van Vianen. T. Gerszi believes that the
Prague drawing is a copy and suggests another approach. In Stevens's drawing the
artist seems to be looking at the same spot
on the landscape as van Vianen but from a
slightly different viewpoint. If so, this suggests that Stevens was trying to see things
through the eyes of his colleague and to
capture his mode of expression. A comparison of the two folios side by side

seems to support this idea.

Prague 1976, cat. no. 12 (as for Vianen);
Dresden 1977, cat. no. 26 (as for Vianen);
Prague 1978–79, cat. no. 25, for older liter-
ature.

Gerszi 1977, pp. 107–8, ill. 75.

E.F.

I.295
Pieter Stevens
? Mechelen ca. 1567–Prague after 1624
Landscape with Pond
Pen and brown ink, wash in various wa-
tercolours
14.4 × 19 cm
After 1600
I. Delhaes Collection
Budapest, Szépművészeti Múzeum, inv.
no. 1382

From the 1590s onwards, Stevens had
been depicting atmospheric conditions.
His interest in this area was further
strengthened by his respect for Paulus van

Vianen and Jan Breugel. Most markedly
during and after 1610 he placed particular
emphasis on the sun and the air. In these
later works the whole landscape is bathed
in strong sunlight, forms are blurred, everything appears light and airy. Although
this masterly visual effect gives the image
a much greater realism than is found in
his earlier works, nevertheless the whole
also has a fairy-tale quality – the figures
are very small and the trees seem too large
in comparison. These prints from around
1600 already show Stevens' desire for a degree of monumentalism in the landscape,
which he then fully achieves in his later
works. This and other related works show

Stevens at the height of his powers as a
watercolour artist.

Budapest 1932, cat. no. 62; Salzburg 1987,
cat. no. 62; Essen and Vienna 1988, cat. no.
654; Budapest 1991, cat. no. 30.

Zwollo 1968, p. 166; Gerszi 1971, no. 250.

T.G.

I.296
Pieter Stevens
Rocky Landscape with Inn
Brown ink, brown wash and watercolours
After 1604
P. J. Mariette, Paris; auction, A. W. M.
Mensing, Amsterdam, F. Muller 1937, cat.
no. 737 with picture (like L. van Valcken-
borch)
Rotterdam, Museum Boymans van
Beuningen, inv. no. LvV 1

An Zwollo dates this drawing between
1601 and 1607 (Hollstein 248). It served
Aegidius Sadeler as a model for one of the
plates in the series *Eight Landscapes from*

Bohemia. However, this landscape, done in
short, gentle brushstrokes, richly watered
and with aquarelle added, could probably
not have originated before Stevens had
known the work of van Vianen and Savery,
that is, after 1604, when both of them had
permanently settled in Prague. From them
he learnt to reproduce the gleaming atmospheric phenomena inherent in a place,
and to construct a deep space, mostly with
two sharp vistas penetrating a barely recognizable background. A pageant of figures usually also became an integral part
of the composition, leading the viewer
through the terrain and animating the
scene. The use of colour suggests an in-

tention to a make a painting from the
drawing. The painting *Landscape with Mill*
from Prague Castle is stylistically very
close to this work, but in the former the
light effects are more meticulously graduated so that even their source is clearly indicated.

Essen and Vienna 1988, cat. no. 272 (for
older literature).

Zwollo 1968, p. 158, ill. 214.

E.F.

I.297
Pieter Stevens
? Mechelen ca. 1567–Prague after 1624
The Čertovka River under Charles Bridge
Pen drawing in brown ink; grey, red and
blue wash
Centre top: *46 te Praghe*
1604–1607
Vojtěch Lanna's collection, Prague (there
attributed to Savery)
Prague, Muzeum hl. m. Prahy, inv. no. 20
144

In 1969 A. Zwollo attributed this drawing,
which up until then had been considered
one of Savery's works, to Pieter Stevens. It

was originally part of an album of views of
various European cities, in particular
Prague and Rome, which had perhaps
been commissioned by Rudolf II to provide designs for his engravers. They were
not authentic records painted on the spot,
but rather studio drawings which gave a
'photogenic' appearance to these places.
The studies for them have not been preserved. Except for the view of Prague Castle seen from an equally unusual perspective, most of the places depicted were less
known and had a landscape-like appearance. Some of them were later used in
Aegidius Sadeler's graphic prints. One
such example is an adaptation of a draw-

ing using parts of Prague's Lesser Town
(Paris, Institut Néerlandais, inv. no. 5802)
to act as an allegory of October. The date
on that drawing (1607) must also have
been the date when the series of drawings
was completed.

Prague 1978–79, cat. and ill. no. 28; Essen
and Vienna 1988, cat. no. 275.

Zwollo 1970, p. 255, ill. 13 for earlier literature; Fučíková 1986, p. 28, ill.59.

E.F.

I.298
Pieter Stevens
? Mechelen ca. 1567–Prague after 1624
Landscape with Woodcutters (January)
Pen and brush drawing in brown ink,
grey-brown and red-brown watercolour,
white highlights, black chalk ground
20 × 28.75 cm
1607
Prague, Národní Galerie v Praze
Prague, Národní Galerie v Praze, Grafická
sbírka, inv. no. 26 962

In 1607, Aegidius Sadeler published a
graphic cycle of the twelve months based
on drawings by Pieter Stevens. The Al-

bertina in Vienna houses the designs for
March, July, and December (inv. nos 7962,
7963, 7961). The Prague design was used
for January. For the month of October
Sadeler chose a design from a cycle of city
views that now belong to the Institut
Néerlandais (inv. no. 5802). In view of this,
it may be assumed that Stevens's drawings
were not commissioned directly for the
engraver, but were taken from his existing
works and adapted as required. The
colouring of the present drawing suggests
that it was a study for a painting. The work
also attests to Stevens's gradual perfection
of the technique of integrating pageantry
into his compositions, serving not only to

enliven them, but passively to connect the
individual parts of the landscape.

Prague 1976, cat. no. 1; Dresden 1977 cat.
no. 1; Essen Vienna 1988, cat. no. 273.

Fučíková 1967, p. 177; Zwollo 1970, pp.
255–56, no. 14; Fučíková 1986, p. 28, ill. 60.

E.F.

I.299
Pieter Stevens
? Mechelen ca. 1567–Prague after 1624
Waterfall
Pen and dark grey ink, wash in various
watercolours
30.2 × 16.1 cm
After 1607
I. Delhaes Collection
Budapest, Szépmüvészeti Múzeum,
inv. no. 1375

Stevens's interest in this, for him, unusual
motif could have been inspired by Roelandt Savery's drawings from the Tyrol,
many of which show waterfalls plunging

down high, rocky mountain cliffs. Stevensí
work has, however, a completely different
feel: he shows a much smaller section of
landscape and from a much shorter distance; the rocks are so close that they cover the whole surface of the paper, restrict-
ing any broader view and thus conveying
the oppressive power of this rocky world.
The severity of the effect is mitigated
somewhat by Stevens' decorative linear
style and by his use of pastel shades for
the wash. The overall result is fantastic
and romantic.

Budapest 1932, cat. no. 56a; Salzburg 1987,
cat. no. 40; Budapest 1991, cat. no. 24.

Gerszi 1971, no. 251; Gerszi 1977, p. 114.

T.G.

I.300
Hans Christoph Schürer
An Ill-matched Couple
Oil on canvas
79 × 65 cm
1612
Leo Schidlof with the Kunstauktions-
haus, Vienna, auction on 12 March 1920:
Galerie ehem. Geza v. Osmitz und ander-
er Privatbesitz, 30, cat. no. 79 (like Hans
von Aachen)
Prague, Private collection

It is possible on the basis of a signed and
dated drawing (I.300) to ascribe this painting to Hans Christoph Schürer, who, since

1609, had been a student of Hans von
Aachen as a scholarship holder at the Saxon court. Judging by a Brno sheet, Schürer
had confidently acquired the drawing
technique of his master. This picture also
bears witness to the careful study he had
made of von Aachen's paintings. Schürer
was inspired by von Aachen's *Ill-matched
Couple* (Vienna, Kunsthistorisches Museum, inv. no. 1508, on loan to Linz) but simplified the scene to two figures, added the
defamatory gesture of the temptress and
allowed himself the introduction of some
decorative details to complete the composition. He was perhaps not as brilliant a
painter as Aachen, although in this pic-

ture he was still at the beginning of his career. Nevertheless the work demonstrates
that he was capable of creatively elaborat-
ing the stimuli contained in the work of
his master, and of finding his own expression.

Fučíková 1979, p. 503, ills 16, 17; Fučíková
1995–96, p. 40, ills 9, 10.

E.F.

I.301
Paulus van Vianen
Utrecht ca. 1570–Prague 1613
View of Prague Castle
Drawing in brown ink, lightly washed in
grey-white
13.4 × 30.7 cm
J. van der Heijden
Berlin, Staatliche Museen Berlin, Kupfer-
stichkabinett, inv. no. KdZ 11 935

This view of the Castle from the south
concentrates on the cathedral of St Vitus
with the tower and presbytery and the
three bell-towers and also on the old
palace where the Ludwig wing is situated.

On the right the span of the view ends approximately at the midway point of Rozmberk Palace, and on the left, by the White
Tower, thus exactly in the place where
Rudolf's residential buildings began. Several Rudolfine vistas concentrated on the
area between Maximilian's Kitchens
which had the characteristic double roof
and the White Tower. These views are in
greater detail than this drawing by Vianen.
Vianen's tends to confirm and verify the
reliability of the other views, which is of
no less importance since we are faced with
parts of the Castle which were later subject to alteration so that we may only
guess at their exact appearance. We may

think here of how the castle walls looked
in their worst section with a bridge and
small open windows and resembling a battle fortification. The White Tower in particular offers a definite starting point for
dating the drawing since it still has a bat-
tlement tower, which was removed some
time around 1608, and the clock which
was allegedly taken down in 1603.

Ter Molen, cat. no. 278, Essen 1988, cat. no.
289, Gerszi 1982, 203, cat. no. 57

I.M.

I.302
Paulus van Vianen
Utrecht ca. 1570–Prague 1613
Woodland Stream with a Bridge
Pen and brown ink and faint wash
19.2 × 19.6 cm
1601/3
N. Esterházy Collection (L. 1965)
Budapest, Szépmüvészeti Múzeum, inv.
1394

While in Salzburg, van Vianen had already
recognized that the thorough study of individual forms was the necessary first step
towards portraying the landscape with
authenticity. This explains why he made

so many nature studies between 1601 and
1603. At the time they were highly innovative: these studies with their fine, minutely precise lines are almost scientific in
their representation of trees, plants, rocks
and stones, as may be seen from the example here. In this work, van Vianen pays
particular attention to the bed of the
stream, where the force of the water
has brought various materials together.
This, together with the vegetation on the
banks of the stream, creates a picturesque
wealth and variety of forms. His work is
never simply an objective record, however, because his detailed representations of
landscape are also always pleasingly aes-

thetic in their effect.

Budapest 1932, cat. no. 65; Salzburg 1987,
cat. no. 54; Essen and Vienna 1988, cat. no.
288; Budapest 1991, cat. no. 27.

Gerszi 1970, pp. 265 and 269; Gerszi 1971,
no. 308; Gerszi 1975, p. 86; Gerszi 1982, no.
52; Ter Molen 1984, no. 272 (PDa);
Fučíková 1986, p. 32.

T.G.

I.303
Paulus van Vianen
Utrecht ca. 1570–Prague 1613
Forest Scene
Pen and brown ink and grey wash
19.3 × 28.1 cm
1601–3
N. Esterházy Collection (L. 1965)
Budapest, Szépmüvészeti Múzeum, inv.
1399

Van Vianen used to walk in the woods
around Salzburg with the keen interest of
a scientific researcher, making extremely
sensitive drawings of his 'discoveries' in
his sketch-books. The fine precision of his

pen work combined with generous yet
subtle washes produces drawings of captivating effect, here heightened by a great
variety of contrasts. Some of the detail in
the foreground is depicted with painstak-
ing care, while other elements are merely
hinted at with no more than a few lines.
The background and the foreground have
also been given different treatment. With
minimal use of the pen and the faintest of
washes, van Vianen creates a sense of free
space and airiness in the background.

Budapest 1932, cat. no. 55; Budapest 1967,
cat. no. 66; Salzburg 1983, cat. no. 30; Washington and New York 1987, cat. no. 116.

Gerszi 1970, pp. 266, 269; Gerszi 1971, no.
303; Gerszi 1982, no. 28; Ter Molen 1984,
no. 243 (PDa); Fučíková 1986, p. 32.

T.G.

I.304
Paulus van Vianen
Utrecht ca. 1570–Prague 1613
River Landscape with Raftsmen (verso: *Roman Ruins*)
Pen and brown ink and blue wash (recto)
19.7 × 29.7 cm
1603
N. Esterházy Collection (L. 1965)
Budapest, Szépmüvészeti Múzeum, inv. 1405

This drawing of a river landscape with high mountains in the background comes from van Vianen's time in Salzburg. In its composition this work is so similar to an engraving of a lost drawing by Pieter Bruegel that it seems van Vianen must have known it. Nevertheless, van Vianen's drawing is an outstanding masterpiece, in which the changes in atmospheric conditions are conveyed with an immediacy that was unrivalled at the time. In this work van Vianen used his brush more than his pen. The transience of the atmospheric conditions is conveyed above all by light and shade. The effect of the sun shining on the slope on the left somehow makes it seem weightless, as outlines dissolve in the sun's rays. Van Vianen also contrasts tactile forms, finely drawn with the broad sweep of painterly views of the landscape.

Budapest 1932, cat. no. 63; Budapest 1967, cat. no. 68; Vienna 1967, cat. no. 72; Munich 1972/73, cat. no. 64; Budapest 1974, cat. no. 23; Salzburg 1983, cat. no. 14; Washington, Chicago and Los Angeles 1985, cat. no. 71.

Wegner 1958, p. 223; Gerszi 1970, pp. 262, 266, 268–69; Gerszi 1971, no. 309; Gerszi 1976, no. 14; Gerszi 1982, no. 11; Neumann 1982, p. 30; Ter Molen 1984, no. 228 (PDa).

T.G.

I.305
Paulus van Vianen
Utrecht ca. 1570–Prague 1613
Landscape with Two Draughtsmen
Pen and brown ink and blue wash
19.2 × 28.2 cm
In red chalk on the reverse: *PV Pauvels von Vianen 1603*
1603
Berlin, Staatliche Museen, Kupferstichkabinett, inv. no. KdZ 13612

During his Salzburg years, van Vianen spent a great deal of time on woodland scenes, always experimenting with different artistic solutions to the problems these posed. All these drawings show his deep feeling for nature. Leaving behind the decorative fantasy landscapes of Mannerism, van Vianen discovered the beauty of unspoilt nature, which he sought to depict using a more modern style of drawing. The motifs of the artistís drawing also demonstrate how much emphasis he laid on actual field studies of nature. His drawings stand out among the work of his contemporaries – for their more realistic, less stylized mode of representation, on the one hand, and, on the other, because his motifs are arranged completely naturally. As in this work, a small number of simple motifs in natural sunlight serve to convey the fullness of life.

Salzburg 1983, cat. no. 20; Utrecht 1984/85, cat. no. 43.

Bock and Rosenberg 1930, p. 56; Gerszi 1975, p. 82, n. 21; Gerszi 1982, no. 10; Ter Molen 1984, no. 227 (PDa); Fučiková 1991, p. 136.

T.G.

I.306
Paulus van Vianen
Utrecht ca. 1570–Prague 1613
Peasant House with a Bridge (recto)
Pen and ink, grey and pink wash
12 × 19.2 cm
Bottom right (verso): *P.v: Vianen*
1603
Prague
Marquis of Cholmondeley Collection (L. 1149)
Private Collections, The Netherlands

The house with the bridge is one of a group of houses depicted in other drawings held in Budapest and Stockholm. Here van Vianen has drawn the house as seen from a slightly lower viewpoint, which makes it look bigger. Because of the plain wall in shadow on the right, the group seems more self-contained than in the other two versions. There is a similar sketch by Roelandt Savery (Amsterdam, J. P. de Boer), in which the artist's viewpoint is only a few paces away from that chosen by van Vianen. A watercolour in Oxford by Pieter Stevens takes up van Vianen's motif. Compared with these other versions of the subject, van Vianen's work with its finely shaded wash has all the appearance of a mature, painterly masterpiece. He again turned to this same motif for the relief on the foot of a drinking bowl made in 1607 (Frederiks [1961], p. 80).

London 1964, cat. no. 116a; Rotterdam, Paris and Brussels 1976/77, cat. no. 149; Utrecht 1985, cat. no. 42; Essen and Vienna 1988, cat. no. 287a.

Duyvené de Wit 1954, p. 83; Zwollo 1958, p. 176; Gerszi 1975, p. 74; Gerszi 1977, pp. 107, 121; Gerszi 1982, no. 54; Ter Molen 1984, no. 275 (PDa).

T.G.

I.307
Paulus van Vianen
Utrecht ca. 1570–Prague 1613
Landscape with Lovers
Pen and light and dark brown ink
20.1 × 29.2 cm
Ca. 1604
Oettingen-Wallerstein Collection and P. de Boer Collection
Amsterdam, Rijksmuseum, Rijksprentenkabinet, inv. RP-T-11937-24

Van Vianen's portrayal of lovers sitting by the banks of a meandering stream is a new approach to an old theme. The roots of this motif are found in the miniatures and prints of the fourteenth and fifteenth centuries, where the lovers are usually in a castle garden surrounded by walls or in the natural world outside the garden. In the sixteenth century the latter setting was favoured. Van Vianen may well have drawn his inspiration for this work both from the artists of the Dürer school and from the masters of the Danube school. The drawing comes from a sketch-book that van Vianen used both in Salzburg and in Prague, but it seems likely that this particular drawing was made in Prague. The tower in the background with three windows bears a strong resemblance to the architecture on the sketches of views of Prague held in Kassel. The immensely fine and detailed execution of this drawing indicates that it was made either as a present or to be sold.

Salzburg 1983, cat. no. 8.

Wegner 1956, p. 209; Gudlaugsson 1959, p. 138; Wied 1971, p. 224, no. G 39; Gerszi 1975, p. 88; Boon 1978, no. 467; Gerszi 1982, no. 33; Ter Molen 1984, no. 15 (PDa).

T.G.

I.308
Paulus van Vianen
Utrecht ca. 1570–Prague 1613
River Landscape with a Bridge
Pen and brown ink and blue wash
19.3 × 29.6 cm
1604–5
N. Esterházy Collection (L. 1965)
Budapest, Szépmüvészeti Múzeum, inv. 1404

This picturesque panorama is the subject of three drawings by van Vianen. He may have had some personal connection with the group of houses in the foreground, which was probably not far from Prague. The houses nestle in a mountainous landscape and the style is reminiscent of his mountain panoramas from Salzburg, although here the main emphasis is not on the scenery but on the house with the bridge in the centre foreground. The watermark in the paper shows that it came from one of the Salzburg sketch-books that he continued to use for some time after he had arrived in Prague.

Salzburg 1983, cat. no. 28; Salzburg 1987, cat. no. 53; Vienna 1988, cat. no. 657; Budapest 1991, cat. no. 25.

Gerszi 1970, pp. 265, 269; Gerszi 1971, no. 308; Gerszi 1975, p. 86; Gerszi 1982, no. 52; Ter Molen 1984, no. 272 (PDa); Fučiková 1986, p. 32.

T.G.

I.309
Paulus van Vianen
Utrecht ca. 1570–Prague 1613
Fishing Foot Bridge (Jetty on the River Moldau)
Pen and brown ink, grey and pink wash, black chalk
11.9 × 13.5 cm
1604/5
A. F. A. Reinicke Collection (1753–1838) and M. Reinicke 1978
Amsterdam, Rijksmuseum, Rijksprentenkabinet, inv. no. RP-T-1978-68 (r)

Wooden water-collection points along the banks of the Moldau permitted people to

collect pure water from the fast-moving sections of the river, as the figure in van Vianen's drawing is doing. These wooden constructions on the river-bank aroused the interest of various artists, including Pieter Stevens and Roelandt Savery, who also made drawings of them. However, all three artists approached the subject differently and in their own individual way. Van Vianen concentrated on depicting the misty air and the space around the wooden construction. His mastery of aerial perspective is revealed in this work, and on the low, faraway horizon it is just possible to make out the city of Prague with St Vitus' cathedral on the other side of the

Moldau.

Essen and Vienna 1988, cat. no. 292a.

Gerszi 1982, p. 208, no. 58; Ter Molen 1984, vol. 2, no. 279 (PDa); Schapelhouman 1987, no. 90.

T.G.

I.310
Paulus van Vianen
Utrecht ca. 1570–Prague 1613
Willows on the Moorland's Edge
Pen and light and dark brown ink, faint grey wash
14.7 × 19.7 cm
1604–10
Berlin, Staatliche Museen, Kupferstichkabinett, inv. no. 13618

This portrayal of nature, so organic and alive in its detail, does not immediately lead one to search for precursors. Nevertheless, both the theme and composition have their roots in tradition. There are

similar works with trees and plants near water by Lucas van Valckenborch, Jan Bruegel the Elder and Paul Brill, all of whom go back to Pieter Bruegel. In its motifs and composition this work by van Vianen is most closely related to Jan Bruegel's drawing *The Temptation of Christ* (Paris, Fondation Custodia), which is clearly the inspiration for the mighty, slightly leaning tree in the foreground with the small tree stump next to it and, diagonally opposite, the younger trees with their picturesquely irregular branches mirrored in the water. Jan Bruegel took his *Temptation of Christ* and other works with him when he visited Prague in 1604, in order to have

them engraved by Aegidius Sadeler who was living there at the time. With his masterly aerial perspective and painterly contrasts, which convey the magic of nature as experienced at first hand, van Vianen clearly surpasses even his inspiration, Jan Bruegel.

Essen and Vienna 1988, cat. no. 284.

Bock and Rosenberg 1930, p. 57; Gerszi 1975, p. 83; Gerszi 1977, p. 108; Gerszi 1982, no. 37; Ter Molen 1984, no. 253 (PDa).

T.G.

I.311
Paulus van Vianen
Utrecht ca. 1570–Prague 1613
House
Pen and brown ink and wash
10.6 × 19 cm
1604–10
Stockholm, Nationalmuseum, inv. no. NMH CC VI: 141

Versions of this group of houses in Prague are also held in Budapest and Amsterdam. The Stockholm version shows the houses closer to and from the opposite side to the Budapest version. All three versions have different artistic intentions and moods.

The Stockholm drawing, with its emphasis on the everyday aspect of the scene, is the most intimate. Here there are figures in the courtyard in front of the house, as well as a table and a seat and some fowl in the foreground, all of which lend realism to the scene. A pleasant, friendly mood is created by the subtle play of light and shade. This style of 'genre' drawing or painting was new both to van Vianen and to Prague. Human habitation became a major theme for van Vianen during his time in Prague.

Stockholm 1984/85, cat. no. 317; Essen and Vienna 1988, cat. no. 286.

T.G.

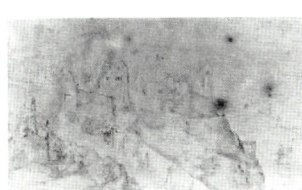

I.312
Paulus van Vianen
Utrecht ca. 1570–Prague 1613
Vyšehrad with Figures (recto)
Pen and brown ink and blue wash on brown paper (recto)
12.8 × 23.8 cm
1604–10
D. Franceschini and N. Esterházy Collection (L. 1965)
Budapest, Szépmüvészeti Múzeum, inv. no. 1406

It seems unlikely that van Vianen, who made several vedutas of the town of Salzburg, would not have attempted a

similar panorama of Prague during his time there. But only views of smaller sections of the town have survived, such as this partial view of the Vyšehrad, where the Bohemian princes first settled in Prague. It is possible to identify this view by comparing it with *Prague*, engraved by Johannes Wechter after a preliminary drawing by Philipp van den Bossche. It shows a part of the fort built on the steep hillside, in particular a section of the fortifications with bulwarks and towers that were already partially destroyed even then. In Wechter's engraving the same motifs are clearly visible to the right of the church of St Peter and St Paul. The figures

in the left foreground give an impression of the size of the fortifications.

Salzburg 1987, cat. no. 55; Essen and Vienna 1988, cat. no. 661.

Gerszi 1971, no. 310; Gerszi 1982, no. 56; Ter Molen 1984, no. 277 (PDa); Fučiková 1986, p. 33.

T.G.

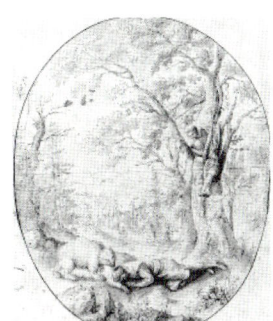

I.313
Paulus van Vianen
Utrecht ca. 1570–Prague 1613
Meeting of Two Pilgrims With a Bear
Pen and brown ink and grey wash
30.2 × 24.6 cm
Ca. 1608
K. E. von Liphart Collection (L. 1687)
Prague, Národní galerie v Praze, Grafická sbírka, inv. no. K 38 026

The moral that may drawn from the tale of the encounter between the walkers and the bear is that one should not forsake a friend in danger. Van Vianen probably turned to this theme under the influence

of the new edition of Aesop's *Fables* that had just come out in Prague at the time. In 1608 Paul Sesse published his *Theatrum Morum. Artliche Gespräch der Tier mit wahren Historien der Menschen zur Lehr.* The illustrations had been engraved by Aegidius Sadeler. These included some original compositions of his own and others after etchings by Marcus Gheeraerts from an earlier edition. In the University of Göttingen collection there is a copy of a lost van Vianen drawing, *The Deer at the Well,* illustrating one of Aesop's *Fables* after a print in Sesse's book. However, this drawing of the walkers and the bear is based on a model familiar in German art

in the sixteenth century, such as may be seen in the work of Augustin Hirschvogel (Budapest, Szépmüvészeti Múzeum).

Dresden 1977, cat. no. 25; Prague 1978/79, cat. no. 31; Essen and Vienna 1988, cat. no. 660.

Fučiková 1967, p. 181; Gerszi 1971, p. 98; Gerszi 1975, p. 90; Gerszi 1982, no. 25; Ter Molen 1984, no. 291 (PDa); Fučiková 1986, p. 32.

T.G.

I.314
Paulus van Vianen
Utrecht ca. 1570–Prague 1613
Four Landscape Sketches
Pen and brown ink and grey-brown wash
with pencil underdrawing
27.6 × 37 cm
1608–12
Prague
Collection of the Landgrave
Kassel, Staatliche Kunstsammlungen, inv.
no. 5064

The few extant views of Prague by van Vianen show his interest in individual buildings in the town and in the landscape im-

mediately outside it. This page of sketches shows two well-known architectural sights. In the top right there is a part of the 'Hunger Wall', begun for defensive purposes during the time of Karl IV. The name of the wall reflects the fact that the project was also designed to alleviate the plight of those without work or food. The sketch in the bottom right shows part of the Strahov monastery with the road known as the 'Hohlweg' leading to it. A town veduta by Roelandt Savery (Amsterdam, Rijksprentenkabinet) shows the monastery from the same side. Van Vianen depicts only the doorway and the choir of the church. The other two sketches – au-

tumn landscapes – are characteristic of van Vianen's late landscape style, simpler and with more of a sense of immediate reality than in his earlier works, in which aesthetic effect was the principal concern.

Essen and Vienna 1998, cat. no. 290.

Oehler 1979, no. 75; Gerszi 1982, no. 59; Fučíková 1983, p. 394; Ter Molen 1984, no. 280 (PDa).

T.G.

I.315
Adriaen de Vries
Den Haag ca. 1545–Prague 1626
Young Man Marching
Drawing in pen and brown ink, gray
wash, white glaze, underdrawing in chalk
Ca. 1594–96
Gdansk, Muzeum Naradowe, inv. no.
MNG/SD/848/R

This drawing differs markedly from de Vries's other sketches in that it almost gives the impression of a painting. It conspicuously resembles von Aachen's drawings in its figural style and in the manner in which the lines are drawn. This may be

interpreted by the fact that this drawing is much earlier than de Vries' group of studies of Hercules. It originated during the period of the sculptor's first stay at the Prague imperial court in the 1590s, when his painter colleagues made a considerable impression on him, and he in turn on them. Striking are the flowing contours, the soft modelling of the muscles, and the great attention paid to the face. Nevertheless, there can be no doubt that this drawing is intended for a sculpture. A straight line delineates the plinth of the future statue; the left leg is set back to maintain equilibrium, balancing the left arm which projects outwards. The figure of the

young man is seen from below, but the proportions of the head and body correspond to reality more than in later drawings. The Gdansk drawing was obviously a study for de Vries's *Apollo* in the Metropolitan Museum, New York.

'Rysunki z kregu manieristów niderlandzkich', Warsaw 1967, cat. no. 26, ill. 13, as an unknown master from the circle of B. Spranger.

Fučíková 1986, p. 24, ill. 43.

E.F.

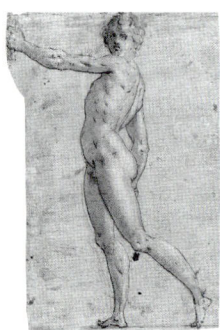

I.316
Adriaen de Vries
Den Haag ca. 1545–Prague 1626
Hercules and the Apples of the Hesperides
Pen drawing in brown ink, brown wash,
white highlights, black chalk undercoat
29.8 × 14.9 cm
Ca. 1615
Vojtěch Lanna's collection; The Society of
Patriotic Friends of Art
Prague, Národní galerie v Praze, Graficá
sbírka, inv. no. 1 967

This drawing has been attributed to Adriaen de Vries on the basis of a comparison with a similar signed and dated work from

Dresden (cat. no I.317). This Prague study is an interesting example of the sculptor's drawing skill, probably intended for a sculpture rather than a painting: the figure's knees, his club and his cloak are all touching the ground, which would have allowed a statue to stand unsupported. The outline, with its modified lines along the back, shows that it was conceived as a thin, tall, triangular form, into which the statue was to fit. The use of light effects and white highlighting is in line with contemporary sculptors' practices. The soft design on the surface of the body creates a complex interplay of light and shade, and the slight blurring of its form adds further

expressiveness. This drawing was probably a variant design for the *Standing Hercules* (cat. no. I.133), which was completed towards the end of the sculptor's life.

Prague 1976, cat. no. 9; Dresden 1977, cat. no. 22; Prague 1978–79, cat. no. 9; Essen and Vienna 1988, cat. no. 82.

Fučíková 1967, pp. 149–50; Larsson 1967, p. 59, ill. 120.

E.F.

I.317
Adriaen de Vries
Den Haag ca. 1545–Prague 1626
Hercules with a Club and A Lion's Hide
Drawing in pen and ink in brown tone,
brown wash, underdrawing in chalk
In the middle: *per compiacere lamicho /
Adriano de fries / Schultore 1615 / Prage*
1615
Laman collection, bought in 1937
Dresden, Staatliche Kunstsammlungen,
Kupferstichkabinett, inv. no. C 1937-650

This, the sole signed drawing by Adriaen de Vries, has enabled several others to be attributed to him. Four of them depict

Hercules – with a cudgel, with the apples of the Hesperides, wrestling with a centaur, and with Deianeira and the dead Nessus. Although they do not have identical dimensions, the group appears to be connected with the preparation of a sculpture, most likely with reliefs rather than stand-alone sculpted items on the theme of Hercules. De Vries's draughtsmanship is that of a sculptor rather than a painter. Sharp lines define the contours; the wash technique plays an important role in modelling the figures; marked depressions are indicated by short, energetic lines, dots and hooks. The figures are mostly viewed from below, so the small heads appear dis-

proportionate to the massive bodies with wide legs astride. De Vries dedicated this drawing from Dresden to an unnamed friend, whom L. O. Larson presumes could have been Nosseni, the court architect of Saxony. He worked with de Vries in 1615 on the mausoleum in Stadthagen.

Essen and Vienna 1988, cat. no. 82.

Larsson 1967, p. 58; Fučíková 1986, pp. 24-25, ill. 17; Essen and Vienna 1988, cat. no. 81.

E.F.

I.318
Adriaen de Vries
Den Haag ca. 1545–Prague 1626
Hercules and Nessus Fighting
Drawing in pen and brown ink, brown
wash
1615, possibly until 1620
I. Delhaes collection
Budapest, Szépmüvészeti Múzeum, inv.
no. 379

This drawing, again, could be a preparatory study for the Hercules cycle that was probably intended to be executed in relief. De Vries was inspired by similar Giambologno compositions. Yet its shaping

is distinctive in that it captures the moment of a contest whose outcome is still undecided. Another drawing – a print from the Albertina in Vienna – is devoted to the victory of Hercules. In this drawing it is also possible to follow better than in the others de Vries's working method: a quick sketch is drawn over in many places in an attempt to find a better solution. The strong contour lines that appear here emphasize a definitive solution.

Salzburg 1987, cat. no. 56; Essen and Vienna 1988, cat. no. 83.

Gerszi 1971, cat. no. 317; Larsson 1972, pp.

69–73.

E.F.

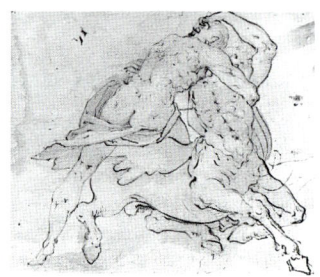

I.319
Hans Vredeman de Vries
Esther and Ahasuerus
Pen-and-ink drawing in brown tone, grey
and blue wash, traces of black chalk,
white glaze, perforated
27.2 × 47.1 cm
On the left: *Hans (leg.) EVR (leg.) 1589 in
septembri*; under this later added: *Martin
Devose fecit.*; under the figures:
ASSVUEROS, HESTER, HAMAN
1589
C. Morin, auction in Amsterdam, 10 May
1927, cat. no. 522
Amsterdam, Rijksprentenkabinet, Rijks-
museum, inv. no. RP-T-1927-13

Hans Vredeman de Vries worked until July
1589 as an architect for Duke Heinrich
Julie from Braunschweig-Lüneburg and
then went to Hamburg. This drawing was
probably made just before the move, while
he was still in Braunschweig. The architecture is drawn in his characteristic hand, as
is shown by a drawing of a slightly later
date from Bremen, but there is a difference in the drawing of the staffage. While
the Bremen drawing is certainly the work
of Vredeman, the Amsterdam drawing is
done with greater confidence and agility,
and there seem to have been insertions in
the architecture. Figures were not the
forte of either Hans or Paul Vredeman de

Vries, and the figural elements in their
paintings were usually entrusted to specialists such as Ravesteyn or Isaacs. It is
possible that a similar procedure obtained
in the preparatory drawings for them. Irmscher suggests that this sketch may have
been for a series of Old Testament scenes,
probably not executed.

Boon K.G. 1978, II, pp. 176-77, cat. no. 480,
ill. II, p. 181, 480; Irmscher 1985, p. 133;
Irmscher 1986, pp. 105-106, cat. no. 19,
with older literature.

E.F.

I.320
Hans Vredeman de Vries
King Solomon and the Queen of Sheba
Pen-and-ink drawing in brown tone, grey
and grey-blue wash, white glaze (partially
oxidized), perforated
28.3 × 44 cm
On the foot of the column, lower left:
*1596 HANS (leg.) EVR (leg.) VRISSE IN-
VEN e FEC; Salomon 3 Regü 10*; lower middle: *26*
1596
Acquired in 1937
Bremen, Kunsthalle, Kupferstichkabinett,
inv. no. 37/638

This drawing probably originated in
Prague, where the Vredemans, father and
son, began to work in 1596. In most of the
works they painted there the architecture
is dominant, but in this sheet there is unusual emphasis on the staffage, which extends into the foreground. As in the composition from 1589 depicting *Esther and
Ahasuerus* (Amsterdam, Rijksprentenkabinett), there is a much larger group of figures behind the high columns of the arcade. The stately architecture entirely
dominates the space. Hans Vredeman
used the group of Solomon, the Queen of
Sheba, and their escorts with minor variations in his painting *Ahaseurus Coming to

Meet Esther* from 1612. Irmscher suggested that this design could have been from a
set of prints, as there is a number 26 at the
bottom edge.

*Die schönsten Handzeichnungen von
Dürer bis Picasso aus dem Besitz der Kunsthalle Bremen, Bremen, 1964, cat. no. 36.*

Irmscher 1985, pp. 133, 135; Irmscher
1986, pp. 107-108, cat. no. 21, with older literature.

E.F.

I.321
Johannes Wechter (after Philipp van den
Bossche)
View of Prague
Copper engraving
*Philippus Vanden Bosche Sac. Caes. Mat./
phrygiarus desisnauit/ Johnnes Wechter aeri
incidit. SAC. CAES. MAI. PRIVILEGIO/
EIUSDEM MAI. SCULPTOR/ AEGID-
IUS/ SADELER EXCUDIT*; dedication:
*NOBILIBUS AMPLISSIMIS PRUDEN-
TISSIMIS / PRIMATIBIS CONSULIBUS
SENATORIBUS / METROPOLITANAE
TRIURIBUS PRAGAE / DEDICAT/ SAC.
CAES. MAI SCULPTOR AEG. SADELER/
M.D.C.VI.*

1606
Prague, Národní galerie v Praze,
inv. no. 78 031-78 039

Philipp van den Bossche, the court embroiderer to Rudolf II, and Johannes
Wechter, a Nürnberg engraver, originally
collaborated on this monumental vista of
Prague. Aegidius Sadeler, who issued the
imperial privelege, was too occupied to
participate in the actual engraving and
therefore entrusted the work to Wechter.
Philipp van den Bossche was not only an
excellent maker of embroidered pieces
and pictures but also outstanding at drawing. The *View of Prague* occupies a signifi-

cant place among the vistas of European
towns, not only for its remarkable proportions but also because of its ability to complement the architecture with scenes from
life in the metropolis at the time.

Edinburgh 1991, ill. between pp. 21 and
22.

Fučíková 1983, p. 395, pics 2 and 3;
Limouze 1990, pp. 356-58.

E.F.

I.322
Hendrik Goltzius (after Bartholomeus
Spranger)
Mühlbracht by Venlo 1558-Haarlem 1617
The Wedding of Cupid and Psyche
Copper engraving with three plates
43 × 85.4 cm
*Barto.us Sprangers Ant.us inven. Anno 1587
HGoltzius sculp. et excud.*
1587
Budapest, Szépmüvészeti Múzeum, inv.
no. 60.922

This copper engraving, made in 1587, is of
supreme importance in the oeuvres of
both Spranger and Goltzius. At the same

time it represents the high point of
Netherlandish Mannerism. It depicts the
glad outcome of the story of Amor and
Psyche, namely their nuptials, and shows
over seventy elegantly animated figures –
a magnificent achievement. Varied groups
of figures are arranged along two diagonal
axes, and the implied directions of their
movements create a strong sense of spatial tension and vigour. Spranger and
Goltzius first came into contact in 1585
through Karel van Mander and subsequently worked very productively together. At the time, Spranger was making
drawings specifically to be engraved and
the dynamism of his art clearly spurred

Goltzius on to a freer, positively virtuosic
style of engraving, which is seen at its
finest in this print.

Essen and Vienna 1988, cat. no. 312.

Bartsch 277; Hollstein A 322; Oberhuber
1958, p. 126, no. St.39; Reznicek 1961, pp.
75, 155, no. 403; Strauss 1977, no. 155.

T.G.

I.323
Lukas Kilian (after Joseph Heintz the El-
der)
Augsburg 1579-Augsburg 1637
The Triumph of Justice
Engraving (not in LeBL, Hollstein 541)
44.8 × 30.1 cm
*2) Germ⁰, suo Chariss.⁰ Danieli Heinz Mag:
Reip. Bern. architecto recreat et Solam. ergo
S.C.M. pictor Joseph Heinz delin. – Lukas
Kilianus Aug. Venetiis incisit.* [1), 3), 4) in
Zimmer 1971, p. 141, no. B 15]
1603
Stuttgart, Staatsgalerie, Graphische
Sammlung, inv. no. AN 1885

The drawing of 1602 by Joseph Heintz,
named on this Kilian print, has also survived (London, Courtauld Institute, Lul-
worth Collection, no. 231; Zimmer 1988,
pp. 146-47, no. A 74), although in very
poor condition with its 'darkened' white
heightenings. Heintz's design was made
to mark the appointment of his brother
Daniel Heintz (II) as chief master builder
to the town of Bern, and was frequently
copied and engraved. Larsson (1973-74)
has even detected its influence in Bernini's
tombstone design (Urban VIII, 1642-47)
and as late as 1674 the same print emerged
in Vienna. A detailed analysis of this
work's range may be pursued through the

bibliography provided.

Essen and Vienna 1988, cat. no. 302.

Zimmer 1988, pp. 146-47, cat. no. A75
(with further bibliography).

J.Z.

I.324
Lucas Kilian (after Bartholomeus Spranger)
Augsburg 1579–Augsburg 1637
Venus Is Bound by Cupid
Copper engraving
37.6 × 25 cm
S.C.M. Pictor B. Spranger pinxit (bottom left of picture); *L. Kilian. Aug.ae Sculps. et excudit.* (bottom right of picture)
Ca. 1610
Prague, Národní galerie v Praze, Grafická sbírka, inv. no. R 160 403

As the text to the engraving states, Kilian's model was Spranger's picture, painted

perhaps at the beginning of the seventeenth century. The subject of the work must be one of the most original iconographic 'inventions' of its time. At the behest of Venus, Mercury is bound by her son Amor (Cupid), while, in the background, Spranger has illustrated a sacrifice in front of Mercury's consecrated temple. The meaning of the composition seems clear: love is victorious even over eloquence. The beginning of the text beneath the picture, 'Cedit Amor nulli; Sapientia cedit Amori', alludes to Virgil's celebrated verse 'Omnia vincit Amor, et nos cedamus Amori', which, at around 1600, became the starting point for a series of

iconographically interesting works by Annibale and Agostino Carracci, Caravaggio and artists from their circles (Dempsey 1968; Rottgen 1993, 23–37).

Hollstein 553; Oberhuber 1959, p. 288, cat. no. 65; Rossacher 1981; Kaufmann 1988, cat. no. 20.77

L.K.

I.325
Lucas Kilian (after Bartholomeus Spranger)
Augsburg 1579–Augsburg 1637
Hercules and Anteus
Copper engraving
45.5 × 31.5 cm
S.C.M. pictor. B. Spranger pinxit (bottom left); *Lucas Kilianus Glyptes, civis August: Vindel. ... 1610* (bottom at the end of the dedication); *L. K. ex. cum. S.C.M. priulegie.* (bottom right)
1610
Prague, Národní galerie v Praze, Grafická sbírka, inv. no. R 726

The narrative in this composition begins at the back where Hercules is carrying out the first of his twelve (sometimes ten) labours: slaying the Nemean lion. In the central scene he is clad in the lion's skin, and to the rear he is with the giant Antaeus, who is invincible as long as he touches the ground. Hercules is depicted at the moment when he has severed the giant's connection to the earth. The earth mother, Gaia, who appears in the terrain to the bottom right, looks pained. Whatever Spranger's source, the significance of the composition is identified with the interpretation of the conflict between Hercules and Antaeus in the literature of the

period as a depiction of the battle between reason and desire.

Edinburgh 1991, cat. no. 27.

Hollstein 527; Herzog 1957–59, p.118; Oberhuber 1959, p. 282, cat. no. 41; Kaufmann 1988, cat. no. 20.87.

L.K.

I.326
Jan Muller (after Bartholomeus Spranger)
Amsterdam 1571–Amsterdam 1628
Oreada Pulling a Thorn from the Foot of a Faun
Copper engraving
26.7 × 20.7 cm
B. Sprangers Ant.us inven. Joan. Muller sculp: (to the bottom left of the picture); *Harman Muller excud.* (bottom right)
After 1590
Prague, Národní galerie v Praze, Grafická sbírka, inv. no. R 160 343

This iconographically unusual scene depicts a faun having a thorn removed from

his foot by a female with a goat's ears and legs, perhaps one of the oreads, mountain nymphs. While Oreada weeps over her friend's accident, a little satyr holds the wounded foot. The narrative apparently begins at the rear left of the picture, where the faun and Oreada are under in the trees, and continues into the central area with the wounded faun carried on the back of his companion. Spranger's composition represents an original parallel to the motif of the shepherd wounded by a thorn, known from the bucolic poetry of Antiquity. The famous antique sculpture of a boy extracting a thorn from his foot (known as the *Spinario*) was interpreted in

the sixteenth century as a depiction of Coridon (Schweikhart 1977, pp. 249–50). It seems, however, that the scene here has a comic intent: Oreada is performing the operation wearing a pince-nez due to short-sightedness.

Edinburgh 1991, cat. no. 22.

Bartsch 71; Hollstein 68; Oberhuber 1958, p. 286, cat. no. 57; Filedt Kok 1994–95, p. 233, 19.

L.K.

I.327
Jan Muller (after Bartholomeus Spranger)
Amsterdam 1571–Amsterdam 1628
Hercules at the Crossroads
Copper engraving
23.8 × 16 cm
B.us Sprangers inuentor. J. Muller sculpsit. (top right of the picture); *HMuller excud. Amster.* (bottom right of the picture)
Ca. 1591
Budapest, Szépmüvészeti Múseum, inv. no. 32 927

The main figure, Hercules, is at the crossing point of two paths. One, the path of joy and depravity, leads towards a group of

figures feasting at the bottom right of the picture. The other is the stony path of honour, which trails up to the left towards the temple of glory. The traditional iconography of Hercules at the crossroads is the starting point of this invention. Spranger's Hercules has already made his choice. Above him Genius, holding Mercury's stick, points the way to the temple of glory, and Minerva, the goddess of wisdom and the personification of honour, who bears a lance, accompanies Hercules on his journey. The Latin text beneath the picture recommends the viewer to follow the example of both Hercules and Scipio the Younger when making the correct

choice on the path of life. According to Cicero's work *Somnium Scipionis* and its commentators, this man of Rome also offered an example of choosing the true path through life.

Essen and Vienna 1988, cat. no. 320; Edinburgh 1991, cat. no. 21.

Bartsch 72; Hollstein 61; Oberhuber 1958, pp. 147–148, 282–83, cat. no. 42; Davis-Sacramento 1972, sub cat. no. 23; Filedt Kok 1994–95, p. 233, 20.

L.K.

I.328
Jan Muller (after Bartholomeus Spranger)
Amsterdam 1571–Amsterdam 1628
The Apotheosis of the Arts
Copper engraving
67.8 × 49.8 cm
B. Spranger inuen. (bottom left of the picture): *1610* (in the dedication); *Joannes Mullerus sculpsit* (below the dedication); *Harman Muller excudebat. Ger: Valk ex.* (bottom right)
1597
Prague, Národní galerie v Praze, Grafická sbírka, inv. no. 137 654

Spranger's composition is an allegory cre-

ated in the middle of the Turkish wars. A year later the imperial armies were defeated at the battle of Mezo-Kerszates near Gyor. Below to the right some Turks are approaching in a threatening manner; one of them even aims his bow at the personifications of the Muses in the centre of the print. Painting, Sculpture and Architecture are portrayed as the three Graces, the sisters (Sorores), and equipped with the attributes of these professions. The sisterly personifications hold in their arms the winged Fame with her trumpet, who is literally dragging them on to Olympus. Two deities are received by Jupiter, who bears the features of Emperor Rudolf. This pro-

fane 'Assumption' scene alludes to the text of an imperial decree from 27 April 1595, according to which painting was no longer to be considered an artisan trade but as an art form.

Berlin 1979, cat. no. 20; Essen and Vienna 1988, cat. no. 675; Edinburgh 1991, cat. no. 14.

Bartsch 76; Hollstein 72; Chytil 1918; Oberhuber 1958, pp. 169–70, 290, cat. no. 73; Winner 1962, p. 172; Herrmann-Fiore 1982, p. 249; Filedt Kok 1994–95, pp. 248–49, 20.

L.K.

I.329
Jan Muller (after Bartholomeus Spranger)
Amsterdam 1571–Amsterdam 1628
Bacchus and Ceres Abandoning Venus with Amor
Copper engraving
50 × 35 cm
Bart. Sprangers Ant.us inuentor. Johan. Muller sculpsit (bottom right); *Harman. Muller. excud. Amsterd* (bottom centre)
Ca. 1597
Prague, Národní galerie v Praze, Grafická sbírka, inv. no. R 160 577

Spranger's picture of this subject provided the model for the engraver in the mid-1590s in Vienna (cat. no. I.90). The source of the unusual iconography is verse 735 of Terence's comedy *The Eunuch*: '*Sine Cerere et Libero friget Venus*' (without Ceres and Bacchus Venus freezes), which may be interpreted as a simple statement or as a moralizing warning: Venus and physical desire exist only when one has sufficient food and drink. This iconography was employed in the plastic arts only from the mid-sixteenth century, but it rapidly became very popular, as it seems to have accorded with the hedonism of the period (Renger 1976–78; Kocks 1979). The counterpart to Spranger's Viennese picture, in which Bacchus and Ceres are abandoning Venus with Amor (Cupid) in flames to the rear left, is another picture by him at Graz, in which the three deities are represented together (cat. no. I.87). Spranger's composition became unusually popular due to Muller's engraving.

Berlin 1979, cat. no. 14. Prague 1982, cat. no. 72; Hamburg 1992, cat. no. 66.

Bartsch 74; Hollstein 49; Oberhuber 1958, p. 290, cat. no, 72: Kocks 1979; Filedt Kok 1994–95, pp. 250, 20.

L.K.

I.330
Jan Muller (after Adriaen de Vries)
Amsterdam 1571–Amsterdam 1628
Mercury Abducting Psyche
Copper engraving
51.5 × 26.2; 50.2 × 25.8; 50.3 × 26.1 cm
[Mercury in right profile] *IVSSV RHVDOLPHI. II. CAESARIS AVGVSTI, ADRIANVS DE VRIES HAGIENSIS FACIEBAT PRAGAE. PVS ALTITVDINIS PEDVM OCTO. 1503 In gratiam D: Adriani de Vries, Cognati sui chariss:mi sculpebat Iohannes Mullerus. Harman: Muller: excudebat.* (on the plinth of the sculpture in the illustration). [Mercury in frontal view] *IVSSV...excud.* (on the plinth of the sculpture in the illustration). [Mercury in left profile] *IVSSV... excudebat.* (on the plinth of the sculpture in the illustration)
Ca. 1597
Prague, Národní galerie v Praze, Grafická sbírka, inv. nos. R 233 696–698

These three prints [one shown here] represent a sculptural group made by Adriaen de Vries in 1593 for Emperor Rudolf II. As with de Vries' *Abduction of the Sabine Women*, Muller has recorded the model from three different viewpoints.

Berlin 1979, cat. no. 22; Essen and Vienna 1988, cat. no. 84; Edinburgh 1991, cat. no. 46; Hamburg 1992, cat. no. 67; Amsterdam 1993, cat. no. 180.

Bartsch 82–84; Hollstein 56–58; Reznicek 1956, pp. 68–69; Larsson 1967, pp. 14–15, 122, cat. no. 31; Filedt Kok 1994–95, pp. 236–37, 240, 373, 22; Krahn, in Berlin 1995, p. 32

L.K.

I.331
Jan Muller (after Adriaen de Vries)
Amsterdam 1571–Amsterdam 1628
The Rape of a Sabine Women
Copper engraving
42.5 × 28.5 cm
[Lateral] *Has effigies per Adrianum de Vries Haghien. e cera formatas, Joan Mullerus aeri incidit* (bottom left); *Harmannus Mullerus excudebat Amsterodamj.* (bottom right). [Frontal] *Adrianus de vries Hagien inuentor* (bottom left); *Jan Muller sculpsit* (bottom right). [View from behind] *Adrianus de vries Hagien inuentor* (bottom left); *Jan Muller sculpsit* (bottom right); *HMuller ex.* (bottom right)
Ca. 1598
Prague, Národní galerie v Praze, Grafická sbírka, inv. nos. R 165 879–881

According to the text on these three prints [one shown here], Muller based them on a wax sculptural group by Adriaen de Vries, and the ephemeral nature of the material may explain why the model has not survived. The theme of the abduction of the Sabine women had been relatively common in Italian sculpture of the sixteenth century since 1583, when de Vries's teacher, Giambologna, exhibited a glorious marble sculpture of the subject in Florence. According to Larsson, it is probable that the composition of de Vries' work derived from a lost bronze which originated in the workshop of Giambologna and, unlike the Florentine marble, it depicted only one Roman abducting a Sabine woman. Its Florentine provenance also included the idea of illustrating one sculpture from three different view points in three prints.

Berlin 1979, cat. no. 23; Essen and Vienna 1988, cat. no. 85.

Bartsch 77–79; Hollstein 65–67; Larsson 1967, pp. 18, 125, cat. no. 56; Larsson 1974, p. 45; Filedt Kok 1994–95, pp. 250, 20–21.

L.K.

I.332
Jan Muller (after Adriaen de Vries)
Amsterdam 1571–Amsterdam 1628
The Death of Cleopatra
Copper engraving
38 × 25.2 cm
Adrianus de Vries jnuent. Joan Muller sculp. (bottom right)
Ca. 1598
Prague, Národní galerie v Praze, Grafická sbírka, inv. no. R 165 883

As the text on the engraving states, Muller once again based a work on a sculpture by Adriaen de Vries. The specific model is unknown in this case, but the position of Cleopatra suggests that it was not a freestanding sculpture but a drawing or more probably a relief. In this case, the depiction of her bedchamber would also be the work of de Vries. Larsson states that the composition of the scene was inspired by the engraving of Agostino Veneziano (Bartsch 193), but this connection is very loose and it is possible at best to look at the use of drapery as the background for a female nude, which is, however, simply at variance with the work.

Bartsch 80; Hollstein 45; Larsson 1967, pp. 18, 125, cat. no. 58; Essen and Vienna 1988, p. 181; Filedt Kok 1994–95, p. 252 and 21.

L.K.

I.333
Jan Muller (after Adriaen de Vries)
Amsterdam 1571–Amsterdam 1628
Apollo Killing the Serpent Python
Copper engraving
40.6 × 30.4
Adrianus de vries inuent. Joan Muller sculp. Cornelis Danckertsz. Excud. (bottom right)
Ca. 1598
Prague, Národní galeri v Praze, Grafická sbírka, inv. no. R 143 333

Like several other copper engravings by Muller after works by Adriaen de Vries, this reflects a surviving sculpture. The model for the engraving was a bronze statue of *Apollo* made by de Vries between 1594 and 1596 (New York, Metropolitan Museum of Art, inv. no. 41, 190.534; Essen and Vienna 1988, cat. no. 66) based on the celebrated *Apollo Belvedere*. While de Vries's bronze represents the 'modern' transformation of an antique marble by radical contrapposto and more expressive movement, Muller's engraving, here displayed in a later edition by C. Danckertsz, places the figure of Apollo in a narrative context, provided by a mythological tale (Ovid, *Metamorphoses* I, pp. 438–51). In accordance with this, the deity is shown with a bow, quiver, arrows and a cloak, unlike the bronze model. The engraver has also added a landscape, and in it, to the left of centre, is the serpent Python. These differences between the engraving and the statue suggest that Muller did not base his work on de Vries' original, but on an unidentified drawing.

Essen and Vienna 1988, cat. no. 86.

Bartsch 81; Hollstein 47; Larsson 1967, pp. 18, 125, cat. no. 57; Kaufmann 1984, p. 205; Filedt Kok 1994–95, p. 252, 21–22.

L.K.

I.334
Jan Muller (after Bartholomeus Spranger)
Amsterdam 1571–Amsterdam 1628
Venus and Mercury
Copper engraving
40.2 × 27.9 cm
B. Sprangers Ant.us inuent. (bottom right of the picture); *Joan Muller sculp.* (bottom right of picture); *Muller excud. Amster.* (bottom right)
Ca. 1600
Prague, Národní galerie v Praze, Grafická sbírka, inv. no, R 59 441 (H 63)

The composition shows Venus and Mercury embracing, with a trio of winged Amors (Cupids). Amor draws an arrow in his left hand and pushes the goddess closer to Mercury, who yields his caduceus (winged staff) to Amor on the left edge of the folio. This iconography seems to be linked with a picture Spranger made after 1595 as part of a series of mythological works (Essen and Vienna 1988, cat. no. 580; Kaufmann 1988, cat. no. 20.42). The unusual combination of Venus and Mercury, the deities of love and eloquence, had been interpreted allegorically in a popular work by Vincenzo Cartari, *Le Imagini delli dei de gl'antichi* (Venice, 1556): love is ignited and animated by the gift of eloquence. Muller's print can be interpreted in the same sense.

Edinburgh 1991, cat. no. 24.

Bartsch 68; Hollstein 63; Oberhuber 1958, p. 288, cat. no. 84; Filedt Kok 1994–95, p. 250, 17.

L.K.

I.335
Jan Muller (after Bartholomeus Spranger)
Amsterdam 1571–Amsterdam 1628
After Bartholomaus Spranger
Perseus Being Armed by Minerva and Mercury
Copper engraving
56.5 × 39.5 cm
B. Sprangers jnentor. (bottom left of picture); *Ianus Muller Sculptor.* (bottom left at the end of the dedication); *JHMuller excud. Amstelodami, 1604* (bottom right)
1604
Prague, Národní galerie v Praze, Grafická sbírka, inv. no. R 112 449

Minerva and Mercury are arming for a confrontation with Medusa. Mercury fastens his winged sandals and Minerva attaches the glistening shield that will protect him from the gaze of the mythical monster (Ovid, *Metamorphoses*, IV, pp. 782–85). Perseus is armed with his curved sword. A covering for his head, to ensure that he does not see the creature, is provided by the Stygian Nymphs, who appear to the right above Minerva. The virtuoso element of this masterful print is the depiction of the shield, which is not just mirror-like but almost transparent. This refined composition was clearly intended as a moralizing lesson to the viewer, as Renaissance scholars have interpreted the conquest of Perseus over Medusa as the triumph of reason and wisdom over desire and sensuality.

Berlin 1979, cat. no. 19; Essen and Vienna 1988, cat. no. 315; Edinburgh 1991, cat. no. 25; Hamburg 1993, cat. no. III. 40.

Bartsch 69; Hollstein 59; Oberhuber 1958, pp. 186, 283–84, cat. no. 56; Muller 1981–82, p. 142; Filedt Kok 1994–95, p. 250, 17–18.

L.K.

I.336
Jan Muller (after Bartholomeus Spranger)
Amsterdam 1571–Amsterdam 1628
Cupid and Psyche
Copper engraving
36.7 × 52.6 cm
B. Sprangers in argilla.forma hemisphaerica. prius effinxit Joan: Mullerus in aere incidebat. (bottom right in the picture); *Harman Mul. excu.* (bottom right)
Ca. 1605–10
Prague, Národní galerie v Praze, Grafická sbírka, inv. no. R 160 576 (H 51)

The print depicts the moment when Amor catches sight of Psyche sleeping and falls in love with her. According to the text on the engraving, Muller's work was based on a terracotta relief made by the Spranger, who is also known to have worked as a sculptor. Although Spranger's relief of *Amor and Psyche* does not survive, another of his terracotta works is known: *Angelic Pietà* (formerly London, private collection). A copper engraving after it was made by Hendrick Goltzius in 1587 (Bartsch 273, Hollstein 320; Edinburgh 1991, cat. no. 30). The relief that provided the model for Muller must date from about two decades later, because similar facial types are found in Spranger's work from the last decade of his life. One of the painter's later works *Venus and Adonis* (cat. no. I.98) is a related composition, as is a bronze relief by de Vries of *Bacchus Finding Ariadne Asleep* (Amsterdam, Rijksmuseum, inv.no. RBK 14.692: Larsson 1967, 51; Amsterdam 1993, cat. no. 181), usually dated before 1610.

Berlin 1979, cat. no. 221; Essen and Vienna 1988, cat. no. 316; Edinburgh 1991, cat. no. 23.

Bartsch 70; Hollstein 51; Oberhuber 1958, pp. 182–83, 281, cat. no. 38; Reznicek 1968, p. 371; Filedt Kok 1994–95, p. 250,19.

L.K.

I.337
Aegidius Sadeler (after Hans von Aachen)
Antwerp ca. 1568–Prague 1628
The Holy Family with Angels
Copper engraving, etching
32.7 × 23.5 cm
Bottom left: *Ioan von Ach. Inue., G: sadl: sc:*
1588
Prague, Národní galerie v Praze, Grafická sbírka, inv. no. R 77 932

The painter Hans von Aachen arrived in Munich in 1587, after nearly 14 years in Italy. In September 1588 Jan Sadeler came to Munich to serve as engraver to the Wittelsbach court. He brought with him his younger cousin, Aegidius Sadeler. This print by Aegidius is one of many compositions by von Aachen that the Sadelers engraved. The print reproduces a drawing by von Aachen of his altarpiece for the church of Il Gesù in Rome. Fučíková has suggested that von Aachen's Jesuit patrons were instrumental in bringing him to Munich and that he had Sadeler engrave the Gesù composition in order to advertize his reputation and secure commissions for the Michaelskirche and other court projects. The collaboration involved a third party: Joris Hoefnagel, whose monogram and imperial privilegium appear on the ledge at lower right. The chance to work with two such talented artists helped Aegidius Sadeler to develop an original burin manner and to establish his own reputation at a young age.

Essen and Vienna 1988, cat. no. 297.

Hollstein 32; Fučíková 1970, pp. 129-42; Limouze 1990.

D.L.

I.338
Aegidius Sadeler
Antwerp ca. 1568–Prague 1628
Nicomaxia Vitae (The Three Fates)
Copper engraving
36.5 × 29.1 cm
In the picture, bottom: *1589*; beneath: *Inuent:Hoefnaglij a Joanne von Ach figuratu/ Scalpsit G.Sadeler.*
1589
Prague, Národní galerie v Praze, Grafická sbírka, inv. no. R 2 687

This product of the collaboration between Sadeler, Hans von Aachen and Joris Hoefnagel is a complex allegory of both biblical and classical derivation. Its title is translatable as 'victor in the battle of life', and the print represents the Three Fates, spinning the thread of life amid biblical symbols of death and reincarnation. The words at diagonal points of the circle refer to the entry and exit from life and to the attainment of grace and the fall from grace. The quotations from the Book of Job in each corner refer to human limitation in the face of the Almighty. Finally, the inscription beneath the sacrificial lamb, 'be in possession of your souls', is in keeping with contemporary *vanitas* allegories, which play on the theme of mortality. Collaborating with von Aachen and Hoefnagel provided Sadeler, then only twenty-one, with a series of sophisticated prints that launched his career. These inventive allegories also generated further imagery at the court of Rudolf II.

Essen and Vienna 1988, cat. no. 176 [the drawing]

Hollstein 113; Widerkehr 1988, cat. no. G 1; Limouze 1990.

D.L.

I.339
Aegidius Sadeler (after Hans von Aachen and Joris Hoefnagel)
Antwerp ca. 1568–Prague 1628
Title Page: *Salus Generis Humani*
Copper engraving
21.5 × 17.2 cm
At bottom of dedication: ... *Georgius Hoefnaglius Belga*; beneath: *Joannes ab Ach figura, Gilis Sadeler scalps.*
1590
Prague, Národní galerie v Praze, Grafická sbírka, inv. no. R 77974 A

The series *Salus Generi Humani* (The Salvation of Humankind) was dedicated to Archduke Ferdinand of Tyrol, a patron for whom Hoefnagel was engaged in preparing his ambitious illuminated *Missale Romanum*. Vignau-Wilberg has uncovered many comparisons between the two projects, which went on simultaneously. Each image in this print series contains elaborate figural borders designed by Hoefnagel, enframing von Aachen's narrative scenes. Vignau-Wilberg has connected this series with an imperial privilegium of 1590 that supported the publication of 'pulchras quasdam imagines, quae praeter elegantiam picturae plerumque hieroglyphicam quandam ac mysticam interpretationem aut moralem habeant ...' (many beautiful images ...with hieroglyphics, which have mystical or moral interpretations). These images were artfully conceived, both to appeal to the pious and sophisticated Munich court, with its support of Jesuit learning, and to attract a humanist audience interested in abstruse allegory.

Hollstein 18, Vignau-Wilberg 1985, pp. 103–67; Limouze 1990.

D.L.

I.340
Aegidius Sadeler (after Hans von Aachen and Joris Hoefnagel)
Antwerp ca. 1568–Prague 1628
The Adoration of the Magi, from *Salus Generi Humani*
Copper engraving
27.2 × 22.2 cm
1590
Prague, Národní galerie v Praze, Grafická sbírka, inv. no. 77 970

Here, von Aachen's scene of the visit of the Three Kings (cat. no. I/146) is framed by hieroglyphs designed by Hoefnagel. Motifs such as the Lamb of God above the gates of Jerusalem and the smoldering crosses in the tents of Abraham point to Christ as the descendant and salvation of Israel. The texts and images in this series work together, framing elements expounding upon the central scene. Even compositional devices and aspects of Sadeler's burin technique add levels of meaning. For example, the X-shaped configuration of figures in the central scene may symbolize the Greek initial for the word *Christos*. These youthful engravings by Sadeler already reflect a sophistication in the manipulation of tonal ranges. For each print in this series, he engraved the illusionistic central scene in a chiaroscuro tonality. The borders, however, were given lighter shading to de-emphasize their illusionistic aspects and call attention to their function as symbolic diagrams.

Hollstein 22, Vignau-Wilberg 1985, pp. 103–67; Limouze 1989; Limouze 1990.

D.L.

I.341
Aegidius Sadeler (after Hans von Aachen and Joris Hoefnagel)
Antwerp ca. 1568–Prague 1628
Hermathena
Copper engraving
39.9 × 29.3 cm
At bottom: *Ioannes ab ach Coloniensis fig: sculp: G. Sadler*
Ex: *Hoefnaglus auctor cum prae Cae: Mag:*
Ca. 1590
Budapest, Szépmüvészeti Múzeum, inv. no. 33.171

A work composed by Hans von Aachen and Joris Hoefnagel and engraved by Aegidius Sadeler while all three were working in South Germany, this print represents a key theme of late Renaissance and Baroque artistic allegories. The Hermathena, a conjunction of the two gods to represent the harmonious union of wisdom and eloquence, expressed a Ciceronian academic ideal that found widespread expression in the works of Rudolfine artists. The background figure of Perseus, the slayer of Medusa, symbolizes virtue, which together with wisdom formed the goals of a Renaissance education. That dual ideal is reflected by the title, *Cursus*, which may refer to the Ciceronian concepts of the *cursus honorum* and *cursus studiorum*. The Hermathena motif has antecedents in Achille Bocchi's emblem book, *Symbolicae Quaestiones* (Florence, 1555), and in paintings by Federico Zuccaro and Bartholomeus Spranger. In turn, this engraving engendered many related allegories in Munich and Prague.

Essen and Vienna 1988, cat. no. 314.

Hollstein 117; Gerszi 1972, pp. 755–62; Kaufmann 1986/7, pp. 163–77; Kaufmann 1988; Limouze 1990; Widerkehr 1988, cat. no. G10.

D.L.

I.342
Aegidius Sadeler (after Bartholomeus Spranger)
Antwerp ca. 1568–Prague 1628
Venus Receiving Gifts (Apostrophe ad Venerem)
Copper engraving
35.6 × 50.2
Bottom left: *Bartol; sprangers In: et figuravit, G: sadler scal*
Ca. 1592
Prague, Národní galerie v Praze, Grafická sbírka, inv. no. R 78 001

This work is placed by van den Brande on stylistic grounds in Sadeler's early period in Munich, and Spranger's model was dated by Diez and Oberhuber at ca. 1592. In fact it bears the monogram of Joris Hoefnagel, which sets it at the same time as the works that Sadeler engraved after Hoefnagel and von Aachen (*Hermathena*; *Salus Generis Humani*). The Sadelers began to make engravings after Spranger in the 1580s, well before Aegidius' arrival in Prague. Jan Muller engraved a different Spranger version of this subject around 1591 (Bartsch 73). The scene shows satyrs and nymphs presenting Venus with the first fruits of the season, in thanks for giving them fertility. Widerkehr has interpreted the poem beneath as an amplification of the narrative into an homage paid by Nature to Love. The gifts of fruits and flowers are bacchanalian and sexual symbols, respectively, and the doves are birds sacred to Venus, which recur as her attributes in Spranger's paintings.

Hollstein 110; Oberhuber 1958; van den Brande 1950; Widerkehr 1988, cat. no. G 2.

D.L.

I.343
Aegidius Sadeler (after Joseph Heintz the Elder)
Antwerp ca. 1568–Prague 1628
The Entombment of Christ
Copper engraving
52.5 × 39.4 cm
At end of dedication, bottom center: ..*Josephus Heintz Heluet:Inuen:/G: Sadler sculpt: Romae anno 1593*
1593
Prague, Národní galerie v Praze, Grafická sbírka, inv. no. R 157 365

This dramatic print is a youthful work of the engraver, Sadeler, who met the Rudolfine artist Joseph Heintz on his first trip to Italy. Heintz had been sent by Emperor Rudolf to Italy in 1592, to make drawn and painted copies of art works and antiquities and to act as a go-between in art purchases. The collaboration between Heintz and Sadeler produced a technical tour-de-force, unlike any prints then being made in Rome. With its striking chiaroscuro tonality, the print reflects an innovative direction of Northern Mannerist painting before Caravaggio. The torchlit scene has parallels in writings by Karel van Mander and other theorists on the expressive power of unusual lighting conditions and the science of shadow projection.

Hollstein 56; Zimmer 1971, cat. no. B3; Kaufmann 1988, cat. no. 7.3; Limouze 1990.

D.L.

I.344
Aegidius Sadeler
Antwerp ca. 1568–Prague 1628
*Angel with Cock, Armoured Gloves, and
Crown of Thorns*, from the series *Theatrum
Passionis Christi*
Copper engraving
15.2 × 10.9 cm
Bottom left: *EG: sadeler f.*
Ca. 1594/95
Prague, Národní galerie v Praze, Grafická
sbírka, inv. no. R 77 939

This print belongs to an undated series of
images of Christ as Man of Sorrows and
six angels with the Implements of Christ's

Passion. The angel in this print is also the
subject of a Sadeler drawing, which is either a preliminary sketch or a later reworking of the print composition. (cat. no.
I.223). The relationship of the drawing and
the engraving in part hinges upon the dating of the print series. Its subject-matter is
directed towards a Catholic audience and
belongs to the category of devotional
prints that the Sadelers were producing in
Antwerp and Munich. Sadeler's angels
show particular affinities with a group of
bronze angels from the mid-1590s by the
Munich artist, Hubert Gerhard (Munich,
Michaelskirche). In any case, a *terminus
ante quem* for his print series is provided

by an engraving by Jan Sadeler that incorporates Aegidius' angels in its border.
Dedicated to a patron in Venice, Jan Sadeler's print dates from his stay in that city,
between 1595 and his death in 1600.
Aegidius Sadeler revived themes of Passion iconography at later points in his career. An angel with Passion Implements
appears in the upper section of his portrait of *Ferdinand II* (cat. no. I.384).

Hollstein 65; Limouze 1990.

D.L.

I.345
Aegidius Sadeler (after Bartholomeus
Spranger)
Christ as Gardener with Mary Magdalen
Antwerp ca. 1568–Prague 1628
Copper engraving
29 × 23.8 cm
Inscribed, third line, bottom: *B. Spranger
Invent., Eg. Sadeler sculp.*
Ca. 1595?
Prague, Národní galerie v Praze, Grafická
sbírka, inv. no. R 9 745

The dating of this print is a puzzle. Both
Aegidius and Jan Sadeler made similar engravings of this composition by Bartholo-

meus Spranger. The print by Jan Sadeler
(Hollstein 255) probably dates from his
years in Italy (ca. 1595–1600). The burin
manner of Aegidius Sadeler's print likewise suggests a dating from the mid-
1590s. Nonetheless, the only model that
has been identified is a painting in Bucharest that was formerly in Emperor
Rudolf's collection. Both prints bear the
imperial privilegium, which the Sadelers
were allowed to use as early as 1580. Further, Aegidius's signature does not identify him as imperial engraver, a factor that
opens up other possibilities for the print's
date. Kaufmann, who notes that Aegidius
Sadeler's print may be based on another

composition by Spranger, also mentions
the existence of 'several painted versions'
of this composition. Perhaps another
version came to the notice of the Sadelers
between ca. 1595 and 1597, the years in
which Jan and Aegidius Sadeler were
working in North Italy. Paintings of the
same subject by artists like L'Ortolano and
Lavinia Fontana indicate that it was a popular theme in North Italian religious art.

Hollstein 61; van der Brande 1950;
Fučíková 1988, pp. 181–82; Kaufmann
1988, cat. no. 20.52.

D.L.

I.346
Aegidius Sadeler (after Albrecht Dürer)
Antwerp ca. 1568–Prague 1628
Head of the Twelve-Year-Old Christ
Copper engraving
36.4 × 23.1 cm
Inscribed under the picture: *Albertus.Dur-
er.Almanus.Fecit.Anno.M.D.VI, Egidius
Sadeler.Scalpsit.Anno.M.D.XCVII*
1598
Prague, Národní galerie v Praze, Grafická
sbírka, inv. no. R 179 444

The pendant to the *Head of an Angel* (cat.
no. I. 368), this print reproduces the other
side of Dürer's original drawing on blue

paper. Each has been related to a painting
that Dürer made in 1506: the *Head of an
Angel* to the *Feast of the Rose Garlands*, a
painting Rudolf II had acquired (Prague,
Národní galerie v Praze), and the *Twelve-
Year-Old Christ* to the painting of *Christ
Among the Doctors* (Thyssen Collection).
This study was also copied in a drawing by
the Rudolfine artist Hans Hoffmann (Budapest, Szépművészeti Múzeum). Dürer's
pairing on the same sheet of a head tilted
up with one looking down at an angle
would have pleased late Mannerist tastes.
So, too, the delicate calligraphy of the hair,
which Sadeler has translated into elegant
burin lines of varied thickness and tone.

Mungo Campbell notes that Sadeler
added Dürer's monogram at upper right
in each of the prints.

Edinburgh 1991, cat. no. 43.

Limouze 1989; Limouze 1990.

D.L.

I.347
Aegidius Sadeler (after Bartholomeus
Spranger)
Antwerp ca. 1568–Prague 1628
Wisdom Conquering Ignorance
Copper engraving
48 × 35.7 cm
Bottom, centre: *B: Spranger
inuent./Eg:Sadeler scalp:*
Ca. 1598–1600
Prague, Národní galerie v Praze, Grafická
sbírka, inv. no. R 160 579

This famous engraving reproduces a variant on the Spranger painting of the early
or mid-1590s that was in Emperor

Rudolf's collection (cat. no. I.84). It is one
of a group of compositions by Spranger
that Sadeler engraved soon after his arrival in Prague in 1597. Based in imagery
of the Resurrection and the Psychomachia
(battle between the virtues and the vices),
this image encompasses a number of key
allegorical motifs, such as the pairing of
Hermes and Athena as the union of eloquence and wisdom (see also the Hermathena print, cat. no. I.341), the nine Muses,
the implements of drawing, painting and
writing, and the armillary sphere, a traditional symbol of Neoplatonism. It is regarded as a political and humanist allegory of Rudolf II as protector of the arts and

sciences. To engrave Spranger's composition, Sadeler adopted the burin manner
associated with the Goltzius circle, with
swelling and tapering lines. The rich range
of values, which effectively captures
Spranger's chiaroscuro, reveals Sadeler's
superior abilities in achieving dramatic effects.

Essen and Vienna, cat. no. 159; Edinburgh
1991, cat. no. 12.

Hollstein 115; Widerkehr 1988, cat. no. G
18; Limouze 1990.

D.L.

I.348
Aegidius Sadeler (after Bartholomeus
Spranger)
Antwerp ca. 1568–Prague 1628
*Allegorical Portrait of Bartholomeus Spranger
and Christina Muller*
Copper engraving
29.3 × 41.8 cm
Below image: *Priuatas lacrymas Bart.
Sprangeri Egid. Sadeler miratus artem et
amantem redamans, publicas fecit:..*
1600
Prague, Národní galerie v Praze, Grafická
sbírka, inv. no. R 100 60

As with the portrait of *Pieter Brueghel the*

Younger (cat. no. I.358), no preparatory
study for this print has been found. The
full concept of this print is always attributed to Spranger, and Sadeler is credited
with skilfully engraving the artists's ideas.
However, the inscriptions are ambiguous
about their roles. The signature suggests
that two artists worked together to compose the allegory. The double portrait of
the grieving Spranger and his deceased
wife is a beautiful synthesis of symbolism
and exposition on the themes of mourning and the special role of the artist.
Spranger gestures toward his wife, who is
represented in her youth. Her portrait and
sarcophagus are framed by personifica-

tions of Faith, Death (Thanatos) and
Virtue (as represented by Minerva holding
the Medusa shield). Sadeler's engraving is
an extraordinary example of Mannerist illusionism. Different burin techniques distinguish the delicate and life-like portraits
from the personifications, which are engraved in a more mannered fashion.

Vienna 1967, cat. no. 347; West Berlin 1979,
cat. no. 42; Essen and Vienna 1988, cat. no.
313; Edinburgh 1991, cat. no. 9.

Hollstein 332; Limouze 1990.

D.L.

I.349
Aegidius Sadeler (after Bartholomeus Spranger)
Antwerp ca. 1568–Prague 1628
The Three Marys Returning from the Tomb
Copper engraving
On the picture, bottom right: *Bart. Sprangers Inuentor*; bottom centre: *Egidius Sadeler... Sculptor... anni 1600*
1600
Prague, Národní galerie v Praze, Grafická sbírka, inv. no. R 160 578

Sadeler's engraving reproduces the inner panel of the left wing of a triptych that was produced by four leading Rudolfine painters, Bartholomeus Spranger, Hans von Aachen, Joseph Heintz the Elder and Hans Vredeman de Vries, for the Chapel of All Saints in Prague Castle. Portions of the triptych, including Spranger's panel, are preserved in the Kunsthistorisches Museum, Vienna. Hans von Aachen's lost central panel of the Resurrection is recorded in an engraving of 1614 by Raphael II Sadeler (Hollstein 14). In this and other engravings after Spranger, Sadeler adopted a burin manner like those used by Goltzius, Jan Muller and Lukas Kilian in their reproductive engravings of works by Prague artists. The dramatically tapering burin lines give volume to the figures and call attention to the Manneristic elements of Spranger's design. Sadeler's print clearly influenced an etching by Jacques Bellange (Robert-Dumésnil, V, 9), in which the figural group is similarly composed.

Hollstein 60; Essen and Vienna 1988, cat. no. 589 (on Spranger's paintings); Kaufmann 1988, cat. no. 20.65; Limouze 1990.

D.L.

I.350
Aegidius Sadeler
Antwerp ca. 1568–Prague 1628
Ottavio Strada
18.4 × 11.8 cm
Copper engraving
Bottom right: *Eg. Sadeler sculp:*
1600
Prague, Národní galerie v Praze, Grafická sbírka, inv. no. R 155 117

Sadeler's engraving depicts Strada (b. 1550) at age fifty. It was used as an author's portrait in the first volume of *Symbola Divina*, a compilation of rulers' imprese which exploited Strada's vast knowledge of emblems and numismatics. The son of the famed court antiquarian Jacopo Strada, Ottavio carried on his father's profession, collaborating on many of his projects. He served Rudolf II as court antiquarian from 1581 until his death in 1606. His manuscripts include significant studies of antique coins and medals, the iconography of the Roman emperors, and Hapsburg genealogy, as well as designs for 'antique and modern' vases and drawings by Giulio Romano. However, new research has revealed Strada as an unscrupulous character, disinherited for absconding with his father's possessions and many times accused of failing to repay loans. His daughter, Anna Maria, was the mistress of Rudolf II.

Hollstein 335; Evans 1979; Bukovinská, Fučíková and Konečný 1984, pp. 61–190; Jansen 1988, pp. 132–46; van der Boom 1988, pp. 19–23.

D.L.

I.351
Aegidius Sadeler (after Bartholomeus Spranger)
Antwerp ca. 1568–Prague 1628
Hercules and Omphale
Copper engraving
43.8 × 31.5 cm
Bottom, right: *Bart. Sprangers Inuentor/ Eg. Sadeler Scalpsit*
Ca. 1600
Prague, Národní galerie v Praze, Grafická sbírka, inv. no. R 160.S71

Bartholomeus Spranger made various images of this subject, the misbegotten affair between Hercules and Omphale, queen of Lydia. A painting of the mid-1590s (Vienna, Kunshistorisches Museum), its preparatory drawing (Florence, Uffizi), and a drawing from 1599 (Prague, Národní galerie v Praze) (cat. no. I.281) all differ from the print. However, the model for Sadeler's engraving probably dates from the same time as the painting. The poem beneath relates that Hercules, 'who feared neither war (Mars) nor death', succumbed to love for Omphale. He is feminized by the pearls and silks that he wears and by his activity of spinning wool, a traditional symbol of the female sex. Kaufmann has observed that this image relates to the popular genre of the *Weibermacht*, themes reflecting the power of women over men.

Edinburgh 1991, cat. no. 18.

Hollstein 106; Kaufmann 1988, cat. no. 20.37; Essen and Vienna 1988, cat. nos 155, 263 (Spranger's painting and drawing); Widerkehr 1988.

D.L.

I.352
Aegidius Sadeler (after Adriaen de Vries)
Antwerp ca. 1568–Prague 1628
Emperor Rudolf II on Horseback
Copper engraving
49.5 × 38 cm
On the picture, bottom left: *Adrianus de Vries Hagiensis Inuent*; under the text, bottom right: *Eg. Sadeler Sculp.*
Ca. 1603
Prague, Národní galerie v Praze, Grafická sbírka, inv. no. R 16 967

An imaginary portrait of Rudolf II leading a victorious campaign against the Turkish invasions of Hungary. This engraving, like Sadeler's other portraits of the Emperor, makes allusions to ancient Roman themes of the emperor as military commander as well as a clear reference to Titian's portrait of *Charles V at the Battle of Mühlberg*. This is Sadeler's only engraving after Adriaen de Vries, and like Jan Muller, who made many more prints after this artist, he set De Vries' figures against a background of his own composition. To create this image, Sadeler seems to have placed De Vries' equestrian portrait (taken from a drawing which has recently surfaced in the art market) in a composition inspired by Antonio Tempesta's portrait engraving of *Henri IV of France*. The newly discovered drawing, which shows Rudolf holding a spear (rather than as here, a baton of rule), suggests that the impressions that include the spear come from the first state of the copper plate.

Essen and Vienna 1988, cat. no. 87; Edinburgh 1991, cat. no. 4.

Hollstein 321; Kaufmann 1988; Limouze 1990; Larsson, 1967.

D.L.

I.353
Aegidius Sadeler (after Hans von Aachen)
Antwerp ca. 1568–Prague 1628
Emperor Rudolf II
Copper engraving
33.6 × 25 cm
Bottom center: *S.C.M.tis pictor ab Ach Inventor*; in dedication: *..Aegidius sadeler Anno M.D.C.III.*
1603
Prague, Národní galerie v Praze, Grafická sbírka, inv. no. R 16 969

This engraving by Aegidius Sadeler preserves a lost design by Hans von Aachen, who created not only the portrait type of Rudolf II but possibly also the allegorical surround. Both Sadeler and von Aachen were designing such frames for title pages and portraits around the year 1600. The numerous references to ancient Roman iconography in this portrait include the Emperor's laurel crown, and the symbols of Augustus and Jupiter above (the sign of Capricorn and the eagle), as well as the three goddesses, Bellona, Roma and Fortuna. Below, bound captives and trophies of the Turkish Wars revive the symbolism of ancient Roman triumphs. A central image for Rudolfine iconography, this work was also pivotal for Sadeler's career as a portrait engraver. The series of prints of similar designs that this work inspired are among Sadeler's most celebrated achievements.

Edinburgh 1991, cat. no. 3.

Hollstein 323; an der Heiden 1970, pp. 191–98, cat. no. 25a; Kaufmann 1988, cat. no. I.43; Limouze 1990.

D.L

I.354
Aegidius Sadeler
Antwerp, ca. 1568–Prague, 1628
Anselm Boetius de Boodt, Physician to Rudolf II
Copper engraving
22.5 × 13.1 cm
Bottom, third and fourth lines: *Sculpsit et Dedicavit Aegidius Sadeler S.C.M. Sculptor.*
Ca. 1604
Prague, Národní galerie v Praze, Grafická sbírka, inv. no. R 155 110

The Brussels-born Anselm Boetius de Boodt (1550–1632) in 1604 became court physician to Rudolf II, the title he is given in Sadeler's print. De Boodt is best known for his treatise on gemstones, the *Gemmarum et Lapidum Historia* (Hanau, 1609). A major early lapidary text, it was a signficant contribution to science in its reclassification of minerals and observations on reflectivity. In addition, it reflects commonly held views on minerals as carriers of magical powers. De Boodt also provided explanatory texts for the third volume of the *Symbola Divina* (1603), after the death of the co-author Jacobus Typotius. His interest in imprese and herbals is reflected by two posthumously published treatises. Evans has characterized de Boodt's interests in herbals and gems as a parallel to the concept of the Kunstkammer itself. Like the system of collection, Boodt's knowledge was marked by an encyclopaedism and a belief in the study of nature as a path to understanding the Divine.

Essen and Vienna 1988, cat. no. 12 [not the Prague impression].

D.L.

I.355
Aegidius Sadeler
Antwerp ca. 1568–Prague 1628
Arnold de Reyger
Copper engraving
17.1 × 11.6 cm
On the picture, bottom right: *De Facie Faciem/Expressit Aeg. Sadel:/ Pragae 1604*; to right of text: *H.Treutlerus.F.*
1604
Prague, Národní galerie v Praze, Grafická sbírka, inv. no. R 77 956

This portrait engraving, for which the preparatory drawing is also exhibited (cat. no. I.230), depicts Reyger, the hereditary lord of Gladbeck (north of Essen) and councillor to the Elector of Brandenburg at Köln an der Spree. The finished engraving shows Sadeler fully in command of his burin technique, creating subtle tonal and textural variations. The poem beneath refers to the Spanish military campaigns in the Low Countries as events that affected Reyger, perhaps because of the proximity of his hereditary lands. The inscription above, 'my fate lies in the hand of god', similarly implies that his situation is uncertain. The sitter wears a portrait medallion of Rudolf II, a token of great honour. The signature to the right of the poem is that of its author, Treutler. This is one of very few cases in which an author of such a text is named on a Sadeler print.

Hollstein 319.

D.L.

I.356
Aegidius Sadeler (after Hans van Aachen and Martino Rota)
Antwerp ca. 1568–Prague 1628
Rudolpho II. Rom. imperator (Emperor Rudolf II in Armour)
Copper engraving
28.7 × 21.7 cm
Third line of text: ... *subiectissimvs cliens Aegidius Sadeler..*; fourth line: ... *dedicabat anno M.DC IIII Pragae:*
1604
Prague, Národní galerie v Praze, Grafická sbírka, inv. no. R 77 919

Crowned with laurel and wearing ornate parade armour, Rudolf stands against a masonry niche. The overall schema of this portrait is derived from a no-longer-extant Titian painting of Julius Caesar, which Sadeler later engraved (cat. no. I.380). As Larsson has observed, this print is a new version of Martino Rota's engraving of the Emperor from 1577. However, it does not appear that Sadeler used Rota's plate again, as Larsson suggested. Details across each print vary significantly, including the hatching of the backgrounds, a feature a later engraver might leave undisturbed. Further, the re-issuing of an older plate engraved with fine hatching shows plate wear that is impossible to disguise. Sadeler may never have had the opportunity to sketch Rudolf from life, although he was given that access for his portraits of Rudolf's successors, Matthias and Ferdinand II. The face of the Emperor is derived from a portrait type developed by Hans von Aachen in 1600–03.

Edinburgh 1991, cat. no. 5.

Hollstein 322; Kaufmann 1988, cat. no. I.64; Larsson 1988, pp. 161–70; Essen and Vienna, 1988, cat. no. 106 [the 1609 impression in Prague]; Limouze 1990.

D.L.

I.357
Aegidius Sadeler (after Albrecht Dürer)
Antwerp ca. 1568–Prague 1628
The Madonna with a Multitude of Animals (Virgin and Child in a Landscape)
Copper engraving with drypoint(?)
34.1 × 24.4 cm
At bottom: *Albertvs Dvrer Almanvs Inventor\S. C. Mtis. Scvlptor Aegid: Sadeler scvlpsit.*
Ca. 1605
Prague, Národní galerie v Praze, Grafická sbírka, inv. no. 236 740

Rudolf II, an avid collector of works by Dürer, was also a major force behind the movement of copying and emulating Dürer now referred to as the Dürer Renaissance. Recent scholars have seen in this movement a growing awareness of art-historical tradition and an interest in academic concepts of artistic imitation. Following his appointment as court engraver in 1597, Sadeler seems to have taken on the assignment of engraving four of Rudolf's works by Dürer, including the watercolour of *The Madonna with a Multitude of Animals* (Vienna, Albertina, inv. no. D50). In each case, the artist transformed Dürer's model into an exercise of virtuoso engraving. To capture the fine detail and gentle tonal ranges of the drawing, Sadeler may have used an etching needle to create much of his hatched shading.

Munich 1971; Edinburgh 1991, cat. no. 74.

Hollstein 72; Limouze 1990.

D.L.

I.358
Aegidius Sadeler (after Bartholomeus Spranger)
Antwerp ca. 1568–Prague 1628
Pieter Bruegel II
Copper engraving
30.4 × 21.3 cm
On the picture, bottom left: *Bar. Sprangers Inventor*; at end of text beneath: *Sac. Caes. Mai. Sculptor Egidius Sadeler, exhibet, 1606*
1606
Prague, Národní galerie v Praze, Grafická sbírka, inv. no. R 776

Ostensibly a portrait of the son and namesake of the painter Pieter Bruegel the Elder, this print was made to commemorate the one hundredth anniversary of the sitter's father. Hermes, Athena and Fama surround the portrait oval, beneath which a figure of Thanatos weeps, the skull he holds shattered and his torch extinguished by the rebirth of the elder Bruegel in his son. In their detailed explication of this print, Bedaux and van Gool discuss the themes of the regeneration of nature through art, as embodied in the work of Pieter Bruegel the Younger, which emulated that of his father. The accompanying poem also has connections with Seneca's famous letter on imitation. The print is significant as a document of attitudes to artistic imitation and the Bruegels as an important dynasty of artists within the Northern tradition. While Spranger is usually regarded as the inventor of this allegory, the present author sees it as a collaboration between Spranger, Sadeler, and probably a Latinist at the Prague court.

Edinburgh 1991, cat. no. 11.

Bedaux 1974, pp. 133–56; Limouze 1988, pp. 183–92; Limouze 1990.

D.L.

I.359
Aegidius Sadeler
Antwerp ca. 1568–Prague 1628
Title Page: *Vestigi della Antichità di Roma,
Tivoli, Pozzvolo Et Altri Lvochi*
Copper engraving
15 × 26.7 cm
Bottom: *Stampati in Praga da Aegidio Sadel-
er scultore di Essa Mae., dat.: 1606*
1606
Prague, Národní galerie v Praze, Grafická
sbírka, inv. no. R 160 515

In 1606, Sadeler, doubtless with the help
of Isaac Major and other assistants, issued
a series of forty-nine views of grandiose

Roman ruins and other curiosities. The
views numbered 1 through 9 and 11
through 39 were copied directly from the
famous series of Etienne Du Pérac, *I Vestigi dell'Antichità di Roma …* (Rome, 1575).
Plate number 10 is related to a drawing by
the Anonymous Fabricy (Stuttgart, Kupferstichkabinett). Later prints in the series reproduce drawings by Pieter I Bruegel (as
published by Hieronymus Cock), Jan
Bruegel and Pieter Stevens. No reference
to the inventors is made, a common practice within a genre in which artists and
publishers freely copied from one another. In this first page, designed by Sadeler
himself, the title, inscribed on the skin of

the she-wolf that nursed Romulus and Remus, hangs between terms bearing
philosopher portraits. These are flanked
by figures of Fame and Time.

Rome 1987.

Hollstein 151; Cammeti 1990; Limouze
1990.

D.L.

I.360
Aegidius Sadeler
Antwerp ca. 1568–Prague 1628
Dedication Page from *Vestigi della Anti-
chità*
Copper engraving
15 × 26.7 cm
Lower right: *AEgidio Sadeler*
1606
Prague, Národní galerie v Praze, Grafická
sbírka, inv. no. R 160 516

This second sheet bears a dedication to
Sadeler's patron Matthias Wacker von
Wackenfels, an intellectual at the Prague
court of whom Sadeler engraved two sepa-

rate portraits (see the drawing for the first,
cat. no. I.228). The lengthy, rhetorical address shows Sadeler's acquaintance with
the Italian language, gained on two trips
through Italy in the 1590s. A branch of
Sadeler's family settled in Venice by 1600
and appears to have maintained regular
contact with him. The pictorial details,
symbols of humanist learning, pay further
tribute to the dedicatee. The obelisks and
vases make particular reference to antiquarianism. The vases resemble those engraved by Sadeler and his assistants one
year earlier, copying a print series by
Cherubino Alberti after Polidoro da Caravaggio (Hollstein 377–86). The Italianate

form of Sadeler's name has a parallel in his
signature on the drawing of *Venus with the
Lute Player* (cat. no. I.226).

Rome 1987.

Hollstein 152; Cammeti, Falcucci, Mariani,1990; Limouze 1990.

D.L.

I.361
Aegidius Sadeler (after Etienne Du Pérac)
Antwerp ca. 1568–Prague 1628
View of the Arch of Constantine from *Vestigi
della Antichità*
Copper engraving
15 × 26.7 cm
1606
Prague, Národní galerie v Praze, Grafická
sbírka, inv. no. R 160 530

Sadeler's view of the Arch of Constantine
and the three prints that follow copy both
images and texts from the Du Pérac series.
Aside from liberties taken with small details, the prints vary mainly in their burin

technique. The burin manner in the 1606
engraving strongly suggests the participation of Isaac Major. This view has at its
centre the ruins of the *meta sudans*, a fountain constructed under Emperor Titus and
rebuilt under Constantine, and at far
right, labelled B, the Arch of Titus.

Rome 1987.

Hollstein 166; Cammeti, Falcucci, Mariani
1990; Limouze 1990.

D.L.

I.362
Aegidius Sadeler (after Etienne Du Pérac)
Antwerp, ca. 1568–Prague, 1628
View of Baths of Caracalla from *Vestigi della
Antichità*
Copper engraving
15 × 26.7 cm
1606
Prague, Národní galerie v Praze, Grafická
sbírka, inv. no. R 160 534

This view records a monumental archway
and two apsidal vaults from the famous
baths built by Emperor Caracalla between
212 and 216 C.E. The text, taken from
Du Pérac, describes grand columns of

coloured granite which were removed
from their original locations (marked A),
one of them a gift of Pope Pius IV to the
Grand Duke of Tuscany. The structure
had, as well, revetments in marble and
multicoloured stones, which were known
to Du Pérac but were clearly disappearing
from the site.

Rome 1987.

Hollstein 170; Cammeti, Falcucci, Mariani
1990; Limouze 1990.

D.L.

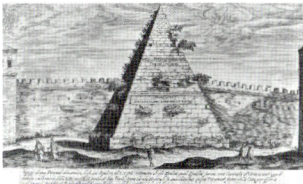

I.363
Aegidius Sadeler (after Etienne Du Pérac)
Antwerp ca. 1568–Prague 1628
View of the Pyramid of Caius Cestius from
Vestigi della Antichità
Copper engraving
15 × 26.7 cm
1606
Prague, Národní galerie v Praze, Grafická
sbírka, inv. no. R 160 537

This view depicts the funerary monument
of the Praetor Caius Cestius, identified by
the text as an Epulone, one of seven
priests of the cult of sacred banquets. The
inscription on the pyramid itself records

that it was built in three hundred and thirty days. Its probable date of construction
is ca. 12 C.E. As noted by previous writers,
the pyramid is shown framed by solid areas of wall, whereas it was actually alongside the gateway of the via Ostiense.

Rome 1987.

Hollstein 173; Cammeti, Falcucci, Mariani
1990; Limouze 1990.

D.L.

I.364
Aegidius Sadeler (after Etienne Du Pérac)
Antwerp ca. 1568–Prague 1628
View of the Ruined Amphitheatre by the Church of Sta Croce in Gerusalemme from *Vestigi della Antichità*
Copper engraving
15 × 26.7 cm
1606
Prague, Národní galerie v Praze, Grafická sbírka, inv. no. R 160 539

Again a copy after Du Pérac, this print depicts the Castrian Ampitheatre that was built along the Aurelian Wall by Heliogabalus in the third century C. E. Behind the

ampitheatre is the Monastery of Sta Croce in Gersalemme, with its basilican church and Romanesque bell-tower. Sadeler or his assistant has made Du Pérac's original foreground figures more picturesque, replacing a well-dressed young man by a limping beggar and a pair of women by a nun and a man kneeling before an elegant lady. Du Pérac augmented his images by descriptions of the original building materials, an effort to document Roman ruins at a time when their preservation was in great jeopardy.

Rome 1987.

Hollstein 175; Cammeti, Falcucci, Mariani,1990; Limouze 1990.

D.L.

I.365
Aegidius Sadeler (after Jan Bruegel?)
Antwerp ca. 1568–Prague 1628
Forum Vulcani from *Vestigi della Antichità*
Copper engraving
15.2 × 26.7 cm
1606
Prague, Národní galerie v Praze, Grafická sbírka, inv. no. R 160 563

This scene, for which no drawing is known, represents a volcanic field at Pozzuoli, by the Gulf of Naples. As the text beneath indicates, it was a famous natural curiosity, known to Pliny and Strabo, who called it the *campo flegrei* (Field of Flames)

and the *forum vulcani* (Forum of Vulcan). In Brueghel's time it was used as a quarry for white sulphur. The distant structures (marked F) are the shacks where labourers processed the sulphur for sale.

Rome 1987.

Hollstein 199; Cammeti, Falcucci, Mariani,1990; Limouze 1990.

D.L.

I.366
Aegidius Sadeler (after Jan Bruegel?)
Antwerp ca. 1568–Prague 1628
Vysehrad from *Vestigi della Antichità*
Copper engraving
15.2 × 26.7 cm
1606
Prague, Národní galerie v Praze, Grafická sbírka, inv. no. R 160 565

As a culmination to his series, Sadeler added two views of northern European ruins, one of Baerlandt, in the Netherlands, and the final print, a view of the medieval citadel of Vysehrad (cat. no. I.312). The accompanying text sketches its history, from

its founding under Prince Libuse, to its destruction by the followers of Jan Hus (referred to disrespectfully by Sadeler as *Zuccone*, or 'baldy'). Jan Bruegel visited Prague in 1605, and it is believed that he provided the sketch for Sadeler's view. However, no drawing of this scene is known, although its staffage is reminiscent of Bruegel drawings. Muchka has noted a few devices for dramatizing the scene that in the opinion of the present writer could have been created by Sadeler, who knew the locale, as easily as by Brueghel. These include the Italianization of the view through perspectival distortions and strong, dark-light contrasts, as well as the displacement

of the then-intact church on the site to one side, to increase the impression of a worldly Acropolis in ruins. Finally, in the distance at right is a detail of the Vltava and Petrín, a reference to Bossche and Wechter's *View of Prague* that was published by Sadeler in the same year (cat. no. I.321).

Rome 1987.

Hollstein 201; Cammeti, Falcucci, Mariani,1990; Limouze 1990.

D.L.

I.367
Aegidius Sadeler
Antwerp ca. 1568–Prague 1628
The Great Hall of Prague Castle
Copper engraving
57 × 61.5 cm
Last line, bottom: *SAC.CAES.SCVLPTOR EGIDIVS SADELER*
1607
Prague, Národní galerie v Praze, Grafická sbírka, inv. no. R 150 695

This ambitious engraving, printed from three copper plates, celebrates a major architectural monument within Prague Castle: the great hall with interlacing vaults

designed by Benedikt Reyt and built between 1493 and 1506, during the reign of King Vladislav Jagiellon. The accompanying text describes the hall in terms of ancient Roman grandeur, borrowed from Pliny the Elder, as '... a room of enormous size, a *Sala*, according to the measure of a basilica, a house of august splendor ...'. The print also documents court spectacle in its political and cultural dimensions. Clusters of nobles and delegates fill the fore- and middlegrounds, among them, the group of Persian ambassadors who visited in 1604–5, and the Emperor is in the left background. Finally, surrounding the room are stalls at which art objects are

being sold. At foreground right is a booth filled with prints and framed paintings. The representation of an art market in this diplomatic gathering place is seen as evidence of the centrality of the arts to the political life of the Rudolfine court.

Essen and Vienna 1988, cat. no. 678; Edinburgh 1991, cat. no. 39.

Hollstein 150; van den Brande 1950; Evans 1979; Fucíková 1983, pp. 391–99; Kaufmann 1988, cat. no. 678; Limouze 1990.

D.L.

I.368
Aegidius Sadeler (after Albrecht Dürer)
Antwerp ca. 1568–Prague 1628
Head of an Angel with Long Hair
Copper engraving
35.8 × 22.8 cm
Under the picture: *Albertus.Durer.Almanus.Fecit.Anno M.D.VI*
Egidius Sadeler.Scalpsit.Anno M.D.XCVIII.
1608
Prague, Národní galerie v Praze, Grafická sbírka, inv. no. R 9 737

The Dürer drawing on which this print is based was originally part of a larger sheet with the *Head of the Twelve-Year-Old Christ*

(cat. no. I.346). Sadeler made engravings after both drawings, which had been acquired by Rudolf II from the collection of Antoine Perrenot, Cardinal Granvelle. Engraving the heads separately in two prints of equal size, Sadeler added beneath each a panel suggestive of a stone plinth, in which the names of Dürer and Sadeler appear as if carved. The tonal ranges of Dürer's drawings, which were made with ink and white heightening on blue paper, would have posed a challenge to the engraver. Using fine horizontal hatching, Sadeler created a medium-grey background that approximated Dürer's toned paper. He then added a dark shadow to the

right of each head, to dramatize the highlighting that in the engraving technique can only be produced by blank areas in the plate. The resulting prints recapture some of the plasticity and animation of Dürer's originals.

Hollstein 98; Limouze 1990.

D.L.

I.369
Aegidius Sadeler (after Roelandt Savery)
Antwerp ca. 1568–Prague 1628
Six Landscapes in Tyrol – Three Hunters and Two Dogs near a Pool
Copper engraving
19.1 × 26.3
Bottom right: *R: Savery In: Aeg: S: ex 1609*
1609
Prague, Národní galerie v Praze, Grafická sbírka, inv. no. R 140 699

The landscapes engraved after drawings by Roelandt Savery and Pieter Stevens form a significant part of Sadeler's production of prints in Prague. The models for these prints were generally composed in the studio from diverse sketches made from nature, in keeping with the concept of drawing 'naer het leven'. In 1606–07, Savery was sent by Emperor Rudolf to the Tyrol to make drawings of the mountainous terrain. This print series may be the first to incorporate elements from the travels in the Tyrol, although it also includes motifs sketched in Bohemia (Hollstein 226). This print reproduces a drawing in black and coloured chalk (Paris, Fondation Custodia) signed and dated 1608. While the details of the drawing are faithfully reproduced, the engraver introduced starker tonal contrasts throughout the image. This creates a very different effect from the soft progressions of dark to light in Savery's chalk drawing.

Hollstein 225; Spicer 1979, cat. no. Pr 44, F 299; Limouze 1990.

D.L.

I.370
Aegidius Sadeler (after Roelandt Savery)
Antwerp ca. 1568–Prague 1628
Six Landscapes in Tyrol – Woodland Scene with a Waterfall
Copper engraving
20.1 × 26.7
Ca. 1609
Prague, Národní galerie v Praze, Grafická sbírka, inv. no. R 78 023

In line with contemporary practice, Aegidius Sadeler employed assistants for engraving and printing. The participation of assistants such as Johann Bara and Isaac Major is made evident by the large number of landscape prints that Sadeler signed as publisher, using the designation *excudit* (published) rather than *sculpsit* (engraved) or *fecit* (made). Such prints can be assigned to his print shop, but not necessarily to his hand. Nevertheless, the level of quality and the innovative range of burin technique in the landscapes published by Sadeler is characteristic of his overall print production. The prints that Major and Bara produced when no longer working for Sadeler differ markedly from these earlier print series. This suggests that Sadeler supervised the work of such assistants very closely. The drawing in the Nationalmuseum in Stockholm, on which this print is based, has been dated by Spicer at ca. 1607–08.

Hollstein 227; Spicer 1979, cat. no. Pr 40 F 295; Limouze 1990.

D.L.

I.371
Aegidius Sadeler
Antwerp ca. 1568–Prague 1628
Emperor Matthias
Copper engraving
67 × 41.5 cm
centre left: *SAC,CAES, EIVSDEM MAI. SCVLPTOR, EGIDIVS SADELER,AD VIVVM DELINEAVIT,../PRAGAE ANNO CHRISTIANO M. DC. XIIII.*
1614
Prague, Národní galerie v Praze, Grafická sbírka, inv. no. DR 3 755

In a document of December 1614, Sadeler mentions Matthias's recent praise of his efforts in the 'representation and ornamentation of the Emperor's likeness'. The reference is to this print, which Sadeler may have presented to the Emperor during his visit to the court at Linz earlier in the year. It is also the first portrait by Sadeler of a Habsburg emperor that he signed 'ad vivum delineavit' (drawn from life). All of Sadeler's portraits were taken from earlier representations of the Emperor. This exuberantly Baroque composition demonstrates Sadeler's awareness of and ability to adapt to new artistic currents. The image is filled with personfications and attributes, among them the figures of Intelligence and Fortitude, perched on the cornices, and the Three Graces, who shower their bounty upon Emperor. Earlier portraits and allegories, such as *Wisdom Conquering Ignorance* (cat. no. I.347), show the extent to which earlier motifs were re-used and at the same time transformed. This portrait was highly influential for later Hapsburg iconography.

Essen and Vienna 1988, cat. no. 677 [Vienna impression]; Brussels 1992, cat. no. 22.

Hollstein 310; Limouze 1989; Limouze 1990.

D.L.

I.372
Aegidius Sadeler (after Paul Brill)
Antwerp ca. 1568–Prague 1628
March/April
Copper engraving
1615
Prague, Národní galerie v Praze, Grafická sbírka, inv. no. 165.369

This print comes from a series of the Months after Paul Brill, a Flemish landscape painter who worked for over 50 years in Italy. Sadeler and Bril were in contact by the mid-1590s, and a series of landscapes after Brill was engraved by the Sadelers on their travels in North Italy around 1595–96. The present series was dedicated to Vincenz Muschinger, a Bohemian nobleman for whom Sadeler also engraved a portrait (Hollstein 313). Brill's views of the Labours of the Months are composites of his extensive studies of Italian landscapes. This scene of the delightful pastimes of nobles shows a common subject in images of the spring months. To engrave these Italian scenes, Sadeler used a lighter tonal range than employed for his contemporary prints after Pieter Stevens, bringing out the brighter lighting in Brill's drawings. However, parallels can be seen in such aspects as the engraving of figures in silhouette, and in Sadeler's clear delight in the abundant fruit and foliage, which express the rich bounty of nature.

Limouze 1990.

D.L.

I.373
Aegidius Sadeler (after Paul Brill)
Antwerp ca. 1568–Prague 1628
September/October
Copper engraving
Bottom left: *P: Bril Inve:*; bottom center: *EG : S. ex:*
1615
Prague, Národní galerie v Praze, Grafická sbírka, inv. no. R 165.368

A second print from the series of the Months, this engraving shows great interest in the particularities of apple and grape harvesting, barrel making and wine pressing. In passages where Brill may not have provided detail, additions by Sadeler can be seen. For example, the faces of the apple pickers show similarities to faces in Sadeler's original prints and drawings. Brill's design combines close study of nature with deliberate incongruities. The round temple on the Tiber (beside the Temple of Portunus), a favorite subject of Brill drawings, serves here as a country inn where an innkeeper waits on a guest.

Hollstein 127; Limouze 1990.

D.L.

I.374
Aegidius Sadeler (after Pieter Stevens)
Antwerp ca. 1568–Prague 1628
Eight Scenes in Bohemia – Gondolas on a Canal
Copper engraving
23.3 × 36
Ca. 1615–20
Prague, Národní galerie v Praze, Grafická sbírka, inv. no. R 156.153

Of the three landscapes exhibited from this series, this scene is distinguished by its Italianate elements, drawn either from Stevens' travels in Italy or from other artists' images. Such motifs frequently

have a fantastic character in Stevens's compositions. As with other prints from this series, the staffage seems to have been redesigned by Sadeler.

Hollstein 250; Zwollo 1968, pp. 399–412; Zwollo 1982, pp. 95–118; Kaufmann 1988; Limouze 1990.

D.L.

I.375
Aegidius Sadeler (after Pieter Stevens)
Antwerp ca. 1568–Prague 1628
Eight Scenes in Bohemia – Watermill on an Island in a River
Copper engraving
23.4 × 36.6
Below image at left: *Petrus Stephani Inven.; at right: Egid:Sadeler excud.*
Ca. 1615–20
Prague, Národní galerie v Praze, Grafická sbírka, inv. no. R 156.152

The court painter Pieter Stevens is documented as working in Prague in 1624, and he and Sadeler might have collaborated

on prints into the last decades of their careers. The models Stevens provided for this series are composites of his studies from life from Bohemia, with elements from his or other artists' landscapes from the southern Netherlands, Germany and Italy. He combined motifs in ways that create a deliberate and playful confusion in the objects and their surrounding space. The level of incongruity in these compositions seems to belong to the latest phase in the development of Stevens's painted landscapes. A closer study of the developments in Sadeler's landscape prints suggests a later dating than previously found in literature. The prints in this series cor-

respond closely to his prints and drawings from ca. 1615-20 in their dark tonal ranges with limited areas of contrast. This approach to chiaroscuro is very different approach from that found in the landscapes after Savery, from ca. 1609, or, for that matter, in Sadeler's prints after Spranger, from around 1600.

Hollstein 247; Zwollo 1968, pp. 399–412; Zwollo 1982, pp. 95–118; Kaufmann 1988; Koesslerová 1988; Limouze 1990.

D.L.

I.376
Aegidius Sadeler (after Pieter Stevens)
Antwerp ca. 1568–Prague 1628
Eight Scenes in Bohemia – A Forest with a Wooden Bridge on the Right
Copper engraving
23.5 × 36.5
Below image at right: *Egid.Sadeler. excud.*
Ca. 1615–20
Prague, Národní galerie v Praze, Grafická sbírka, inv. no. R 139.857

The composition of this print is perhaps the most innovative of this series. The visual field is filled almost completely with foliage, cutting down views into depth

and masking the incongruities that lie behind them. The engraver made use of this print to display his virtuosity at varying tone and texture within the limited range of the objects represented. The faces of the figures at left resemble those in Sadeler's late drawings. The incongruous motif of the timber bridge laden with packmules, at right, appeared in a more natural setting in an earlier engraving after Stevens (Hollstein 264).

Hollstein 253; Zwollo 1968, pp. 399–412; Zwollo 1982, pp. 95–118; Kaufmann 1988; Limouze 1990.

D.L.

I.377
Aegidius Sadeler
Antwerp ca. 1568–Prague 1628
Johannes Petrus Magnus, Count Palatine, Counsellor to Emperor Matthias
Copper engraving
17.8 × 13.3 cm
Bottom: *S.Caes.Mtis.sculp. Aeg. Sadeler ad vivum delineavit, et. D.D.Pragae. M.DC.XVII.*
1617
Praha, Národní galerie v Praze, Grafická sbírka, inv. no. R 119 769

The final stage of a project that began with an elaborate drawing (cat. no. I.234),

this portrait provides insights into Sadeler's working method. Although the drawing had an elaborate architectural frame, a more modest solution was chosen for the print, whether for reasons of cost or simply the sitter's taste. The marked decrease in Sadeler's official work following the death of Rudolf II suggests that Sadeler looked to private patronage, particularly portraiture, for more of his income. This may explain the increasingly elaborate formats of his portrait compositions from these years (e.g., Charles de Longueval, Emperors Matthias and Ferdinand, cat nos. I.383, I.371, I.384). The modest frame of the engraving gives greater emphasis to

the sitter's Jesuit badge, his coat of arms with its motto 'with counsel and speed', and his impresa, a carpenter's balance accompanied by the words, '[he] neither fails nor is failed'.

Hollstein 306; Limouze 1990.

D.L.

I.378
Aegidius Sadeler
Antwerp, ca. 1568–Prague, 1628
The Martyrdom of St Sebastian
Copper engraving
45.7 × 32.7 cm
Bottom left: *Aegidius Sadeler inuentor, et sculpsit*; bottom right: *Marcus Sadeler excudit*
Ca. 1618–20
Prague, Národní galerie v Praze, Grafická sbírka, inv. no. R 16 970

Connected with a preparatory drawing in Washington, DC (cat. no. I.237), this is a characteristic work from Sadeler's late ca-

reer. His late engravings seem to have been a reponse to the changing circumstances of patronage in Prague. Working for the intolerant Emperor Ferdinand II and for nobles who profited from the dispossession of the Bohemian Protestants, Sadeler shifted his imagery towards themes of Catholic piety. Some of the roots of his late style lie in religious works of other Prague artists, for example Joseph Heintz's *Pietà* of 1607 and Adriaen de Vries's large bronze statue of *St Sebastian*, completed in 1615 for the Catholic patron Prince Karl von Liechtenstein. At the same time, the figure of the saint is strikingly sensual. This is not out of keeping with

the iconographic tradition of St Sebastian, and it was doubtless inspired by the famous *Bound Captives* of Michelangelo. The smallest angels, who are in fact *amorini*, and the poem beneath the image also allude to erotic love.

Hollstein 95; Limouze 1990.

D.L.

I.379
Aegidius Sadeler
Antwerp ca. 1568–Prague 1628
Aelia Petina Clavdia Uxor 'Aelia Petina, Wife of Emperor Claudius'
Copper engraving
35.1 × 24.2 cm
Bottom left: *Aegidius Sadeler S.C.M. Sculp.*; bottom right: *Marcus Sadeler excud.*
Ca. 1618–22
Prague, Národní galerie v Praze, Grafická sbírka, inv. no. R 155 917

Seen together, this portrait and the print of Livia reveal a striking aspect of the empress engravings: they seem to have been a pretext for depicting a series of beautiful women in provocative costumes and mannered poses. In this regard, the empresses were very influential for painters of the seventeenth and eighteenth centuries, who appear to have copied them freely. Their inspiration can be found not only in Baroque Prague, but in portrait painting in England and the American colonies. The widespread copying of prints as a way of learning to draw made these popular models for drawing the female figure.

Rome 1977.

Hollstein 363; Limouze 1990.

D.L.

I.380
Aegidius Sadeler (after Titian)
Antwerp ca. 1568–Prague 1628
C. Iulius Caesar 'Gaius Julius Caesar'
Copper engraving
34.4 × 24 cm
Bottom left: *Aegidius sadeler S.C.M. Sculp.*; middle: *Titianus Inventor*; right: *Marcus Sadeler excud.*
Ca. 1618–22
Prague, Národní galerie v Praze, Grafická sbírka, inv. no. R 155 932

In a letter of December 1622, Sadeler petitioned Prince Karl von Liechtenstein to aid him in obtaining overdue payments from the court and a higher salary, so that he could complete three projects begun four years before. One of these projects was a series of 'zwölf antiquitetische kaisern und kaiserinnen', which he hoped to present to Emperor Ferdinand II. It is possible that the copper plates were nearly complete at the time of the petition, and that Sadeler needed money to cover the paper and ink needed for printing. The source for the Emperors is a series of paintings made by Titian and Bernardino Campi for Federico Gonzaga, Duke of Mantua. Although this print cycle dates from late in Sadeler's career, the image of Julius Caesar sheds light on the iconography of earlier imperial portraits. The portrait of *Rudolf II in Armour* (cat. no. I.356) was not only inspired by Martino Rota's engravings of the Emperor, but also by Titian's prototype.

Rome 1977.

Hollstein 347; Limouze 1990.

D.L.

I.381
Aegidius Sadeler
Antwerp ca. 1568–Prague 1628
Livia Drusilla D. Oct. Augusti Uxor 'Livia Drusilla, Wife of Augustus Caesar'
Copper engraving
35 × 24.1 cm
Bottom left: *Aegidius Sadeler S.C.M. Sculp.*; bottom right: *Marcus Sadeler excudit*
Ca. 1618–22
Prague, Národní galerie v Praze, Grafická sbírka, inv. no. R 155 911

Livia, the wife of Augustus Caesar, is represented in a manner that has little to do with traditional portraits of her. Her dress and hairstyle in fact recall the female figures in cameos made for Rudolf II by Milanese craftsmen. The sources of these figures are unknown. The models may have been Mantuan: a letter of 1603 from the Gonzaga archives mentions a gift of '24 imperatrices' (probably meaning emperors and empresses) to the court of Spain. On the other hand, Joachim von Sandrart, who knew Sadeler personally, referred to the empresses as engraved after inventions by Bartholomeus Spranger and Hans von Aachen. However, no model has been identified. This raises a third possibility, that the empresses are Sadeler's compositions. Like his other original works, these figures reflect the knowledge of a broad range of artistic imagery.

Rome 1977.

Hollstein 360; Sandrart 1675; Limouze 1990.

D.L.

I.382
Aegidius Sadeler (after Titian)
Antwerp ca. 1568–Prague 1628
D. Octavianus Augustus 'Augustus Caesar'
Copper engraving
35.1 × 24 cm
Bottom left: *Aegidius Sadeler S.C.M. Sculp.*; centre: *Titianus inventor*; right: *Marcus Sadeler excudit*
Ca. 1618–22
Prague, Národní galerie v Praze, Grafická sbírka, inv. no. R 155 933

Titian's and Campi's portrayals of the emperors were inspired by Suetonius' *The Twelve Caesars*. Suetonius' biographies of Julius Caesar and Augustus emphasize their exceptional gifts as rulers, whereas his lives of their successors call attention to their mental and physical weaknesses. Their portraits likewise provide heroic contrasts to the emperors that followed. The paintings in Mantua were part of a collection sold to Charles I of England. He presented the series as a diplomatic gift to Spain, where they were destroyed in a fire in the Alcazar in 1734. Titian's cycle of emperors inspired countless painted copies at courts across Europe. The 1621 inventory of Prague Castle lists one such set; another is in the Munich Residenz.

Rome 1977.

Hollstein 348; Limouze 1990.

D.L.

I.383
Aegidius Sadeler
Antwerp ca. 1568–Prague 1628
Charles de Longueval, Count of Buquoy, Baron of Vaux
Copper engraving
40.3 × 26.6 cm
Bottom: *S.C.M.tis sculptor Eg.sadeler ad/vivum delineauit et D.D.Pragae/M.D.C.XXI*
1621
Prague, Národní galerie v Praze, Grafická sbírka, inv. no. DR 1 763

This large and elaborate portrait engraving celebrates Charles de Longueval, the commander of the victorious imperial forces at the Battle of the White Mountain. Wearing the Order of the Golden Fleece, Longueval is further glorified by motifs found in Sadeler's portraits of Habsburg emperors. The oval portrait is enframed by war trophies and chained captives, Roman motifs which both link it with the 1603 portrait of *Rudolf II* (cat. no. I.353) and anticipate Sadeler's 1629 print of *Ferdinand II* (cat. no. I.354). The fictive torn paper curls back to uncover a battle scene, similar to that found in Sadeler's print, *Rudolf II on Horseback*. In this scene, imperial forces rout Bohemian insurgents on the outskirts of Prague. This grandiose print suggests many ironies of Aegidius Sadeler's late career. A member of a family that once was persecuted for religious reasons, he sought the patronage of the victors of White Mountain, and at one point even made a formal request for the estates of two dispossessed nobles.

Hollstein 304; Limouze 1990.

D.L.

1.384
Aegidius Sadeler
Antwerp ca. 1568–Prague 1628
Emperor Ferdinand II
Copper engraving
89.5 × 64 cm
Bottom left: *SAC. CAES. EIUSDEM MAI:SCVLPTOR EGIDIVS SADELER 1629*
1629 (completed posthumously)
Prague, Národní galerie v Praze, Grafická sbírka, inv. no. R 154 475

This engraving is the last and most powerful of Sadeler's imperial portraits, as well as the most extravagant of his original compositions. The printing if not the engraving of the work was completed posthumously. The Augsburg art agent Philipp Hainhofer conveyed news of the artist's death in a letter of 30 April 1628. As an equestrian portrait with much of the Roman symbolism revived in Rudolfine and earlier Habsburg art, this work nonetheless differs dramatically from these precedents. The allegory no longer praises the Emperor as ruler and patron: here he is newly defined as a soldier of the Catholic faith. Flanked by the words *immota* (unmoved) and *interrita* (undaunted), he bestrides a rearing horse beneath thunderclouds, a vision of terror. Of the numerous personfications, only two are Roman gods, both associated with warfare (Bellona and Jupiter). All the ancient Roman motifs are absorbed into the militant religious programme. The Emperor's horse tramples his foes, who are, with the exception of a turbanned Turk, Ferdinand's Protestant adversaries in the Thirty Years' War.

Brussels 1992, cat. no. 20.

Hollstein 287; Doering 1910; Limouze 1990.

D.L.

Section II: The *Kunstkammer* of Rudolf II

BEKET BUKOVINSKÁ

The exhibits in the Imperial Stables represent the part of Rudolf II's collections known as the *Kunstkammer*. It should be pointed out, however, that the exhibition itself is in no way identical to the *Kunstkammer*. The lamentable fate of the Prague collection after Rudolf's death ensured not only that original collections were broken up and scattered but also that a great part was lost forever. So a reconstruction was out of the question. In order to provide an impression of the *Kunstkammer*'s contents, a combination of two principles of selection and arrangement was adopted. The exhibition focuses on the most important works by prominent artists and craftsmen active in Prague at the imperial court. The various master workshops are represented by Anton Schweinberger, Nikolaus Pfaff, Paulus van Vianen, Ottavio Miseroni, Jan Vermeyen, Andreas Osenbruck, Cosimo and Giovanni Castrucci, Caspar Lehmann and Antonio and Alessandro Abondio. On the basis of this representative selection, the visitor will be able to gain some idea of the quality and significance of Rudolfine decorative art and see it in the context of art produced at the court. The exhibition also includes works and objects grouped in accordance with the 1607–11 inventory of the *Kunstkammer*.

This approach was adopted for several reasons. Firstly, the inventory itself is one of the most important sources which tell us about Rudolf's intentions in creating his collection. Secondly, it provides a graphic picture of this part of his collections and also contains a large amount of information about the objects themselves. In view of the fact that, unlike similar period inventories, the document is arranged thematically and not according to location, it was possible to make use of this division to create groupings of works to be exhibited together. While this is not a reconstruction, the order and groupings of the inventory have been followed. This provides an impression of the breadth, diversity and exceptional wealth of the collections based on precise data.

It would not be possible to assemble even the most modest profile of the collections included in the inventory merely with the aid of existing objects which could be linked with specific entries. Therefore, we have also included exhibits which are likely to have been part of the *Kunstkammer*, although this is not certain. The exhibition also contains pieces which probably did not find their way into the *Kunstkammer*, or which could never have been part of it, but which nevertheless represent an important or well-represented sphere of the collections described in the inventory. The authentic objects have been marked in the catalogue, and important data from the inventory have also been used in the exhibition.

Another part of the exhibition contains drawings, prints and literature. The selection of these exhibits was oriented towards the presentation of drawings, in particular those by goldsmiths, which most frequently capture the designs of works shown in the exhibition or listed in the inventory, but unavailable for inclusion in the show – for example, the famous vessel and bowl by Christoph Jamnitzer. Also included are prints which served as models for motifs. Several documents are evidence of the communication between artists and the imperial chamber, for the most part requests for payment for completed work.

The final part of the *Kunstkammer* section represents the works of artists active at the Prague court after the death of Rudolf II and during the period when the court moved to Austria. In this connection, Dionysio Miseroni is of particular importance, since he continued to make glyptic work with the same intensity until the 1660s. With his son Ferdinand Eusebio, Dionysio created the foundation for the development of Czech Baroque glass.

The original purpose of the Imperial Stables is indicated by the luxurious horse's harness which the Saxon elector Christian II commissioned from Prague goldsmith Johann Michael. On the basis of this work we can, at least in part, imagine what the harnesses for dozens of magnificent and highly valued horses owned by Rudolf II might have looked like. The saddle and accessories were stored in several tack rooms called *Sattelkammern* on the ground floor of the Corridor Wing.

Decorative Arts at the Rudolfine Court in Prague: The Key Figures

The most important recent discoveries in the field of Rudolfine art have been made in the area of the decorative arts. The discovery and publication of the authentic inventory of Rudolf's *Kunstkammer* brought with it vital information.[1] Not only individual artists but whole branches of the decorative arts have emerged from obscurity. When A. Lhotský published his major work on the Habsburg collections in 1943, he was still unaware of what was concealed, for example, behind the name 'Philip van den Bossche' – an individual who was paid an unusually high wage of 30 gulden. Lhotský explained this fact by stating that van den Bossche must have been an eminent specialist – 'ein Fachmann von Ruf, dem hauptsachlich Restaurierungsarbeiten oblangen ...' – and that he restored tapestries.[2] As the inventory explains, van den Bossche was an embroiderer, and his workshop, where his daughter Elisabeth and son-in-law H. Cappelmann also worked, produced the embroidered *Landscape with the Temptation of St Anthony* and a number of still lifes with flowers and birds for the *Kunstkammer*.[3] Despite the fact that none of these works had yet been identified with certainty, knowledge of them is basic to our being able to trace the development of silk embroideries from the Rudolfine era.[4]

The entries in the inventory also show that the *Kunstkammer* contained works by Jan Vermeyen, Antonio and Alessandro Abondio, Paulus van Vianen, Daniel Mignot and the sculptor Giovanni Baptista Quadri. They also document a whole area of the *Kunstkammer*, unknown until now, of which almost nothing remains. Almost all the works made from wax, fired clay or plaster have not survived. Sculptures in gold and silver also no longer exist, having evidently been melted down.

Where works did survive, information provided by the inventory helped to document them and to reconstruct and localize the entire oeuvre of certain artists, as in the case of Giovanni Castrucci. So-called Florentine mosaics were documented by E. Neumann, who stated that they were in fact made in Prague.[5] Nikolaus Pfaff, who until that time had been known as a wood-carver and joiner, has now been acknowledged as the creator of small virtuoso carvings in ivory, among the most important examples of Rudolfine art.[6]

The environment of the imperial court was exceptional, and the fact that the work of goldsmiths, engravers, cutters of precious stones, wood-carvers, embroiderers, joiners and other craftsmen was so highly valued was undoubtedly due to the Emperor himself. He carefully chose the artists who were active at his court and influenced their work. It is probable that he initiated a number of experiments and created the conditions in order that they be car-

ried out. We know that these artists were in close contact with each other, since we will find common motifs and solutions to similar artistic problems. Anton Schweinberger was one of the most important representatives of the Rudolfine goldsmith's trade. This craftsman, hailing from Augsburg, began to work for the Emperor as early as 1587, continuing until his death in 1607.[7] Although his name appears in nine entries in the Rudolfine inventory, only a fragment of his work has survived from what was indisputably a prolific 16-year period of imperial service. The significance of this artist, about whom we know so little, is, however, substantiated by the signed vessel made from a Seychelles-nut with its exquisite mount. It is a characteristic example of a luxurious cabinet piece linking an unusual and, at the time, highly valued gift of nature with the work of human genius. The dynamic sculpture of Neptune riding a sea-horse, crowned by a lid, is considered a significant forerunner of the Baroque (cat. no. II.1).

Nikolaus Pfaff, clearly a versatile artist, evidently shared in the work on the Seychelles-nut. Alongside his precise and detailed figural carvings in ivory – for example, *Venus and Amor* (cat. no. II.4), he also worked in amber[8] and undertook the demanding task of carving rhinoceros horn (cat. no. II.6). From the latter object, we can sense that he was a broad-minded artist; the gently modelled mascaron is closely connected with similarly conceived work by other Rudolfine artists, such as Paulus van Vianen or Ottavio Miseroni. Pfaff entered the imperial service in Prague on 1 January 1601; he died there in 1612.[9]

Fortunately, a good deal of the work of one of the most fascinating court artists, Paulus van Vianen, has survived.[10] We are familiar with him as an artist designing vases, reliefs, plaques and small sculptures, also as a sensitive renderer of designs for works in gold and intimate landscape studies. In a number of cases, the landscape backgrounds to his reliefs are, in fact, sculptures in themselves. Vianen's work culminated in a jug and bowl with finely modelled sculptural details which were an important impulse for so-called auricular ornament (cat. nos. II.15, II.16). This approach was later elevated to a fine art by Paulus's brother Adam and influenced the work of a number of artists, chiefly in the Netherlands. It is possible to imagine Paulus's sculptures by looking at the miniature figure of a Nereid set on to the lid of a jasper jug used on special occasions (cat. no. II.13). Van Vianen was employed at the imperial court in Prague with a regular wage until 1603; he died there in 1613.

Ottavio Miseroni, a member of the famous Milanese family of precious-stone cutters,[11] earned his reputation among the artists at the Prague court. He came to city at the end of the 1580s, severing his roots (he was one of the few to do so) and remaining there until his death in 1624. His son Dionysio and grandson Ferdinand Eusebio continued the family tradition in Prague until the last few decades of the seventeenth century.[12] Apart from his work carving vessels from precious stones, Ottavio also specialized in other fields, such as cameos and free-standing sculptures made of precious stones. It was evidently Ottavio who used the technique of so-called Florentine mosaic to create decorative reliefs. His main work consisted of vessels crafted around 1600 and during the following decade in which he developed his own distinctive approach. Probably through court commissions and under the influence of other court artists, Ottavio perfected his masterful treatment of raw materials, as if they yielded to his very touch. His works are gently contoured, the material shaped in such a way that we have the impression that the artist was working with soft

wax rather than stone. The staggering technical perfection and aesthetic impact, together with the splendour of the precious stones themselves, suggest that works from this branch of decorative art produced in these workshops had, in a certain sense, reached their peak.

The goldsmith's share in the creation of glyptic works gradually became essential to the success of the final product, and it would be extremely difficult to judge which of the two specialists was the leading craftsman in the field. At the Prague court of Rudolf II, In addition to the creation of sculptural mounts, settings had to be crafted for jewellery. Here brightly coloured enamel came into its own. Mounts surrounded the bases of vessels, linked the parts or formed rims and perhaps also lids. Small sculptural details often took the form of ornamental handles shaped like snakes and cornucopias or like small, precisely worked vases set atop lids. Sculptural ornaments in all manner of shapes with scrolls and fruit were most frequently used to enframe cameos, the whole complemented by decoration in transparent or opaque enamel. Motifs of tiny animals or insects were accompanied by an almost inexhaustible number of inspired variations on geometric patterns for which we would have difficulty finding a label. What is striking is that these combinations were almost never repeated. The themes were similar, but were used in an unending series of variations with new ideas being incorporated continually. Craftsmanship itself was of supreme quality, and details remained precise even when viewed through a magnifying glass.

The central works associated with these pieces are the imperial insignia – Rudolf II's crown, orb and sceptre. The crown has been attributed to Jan Vermeyen since the 1920s; the sceptre is signed and dated 1615 by Andreas Osenbruck.[13] Rudolf Distelberger has fairly convincingly documented an affinity between the reliefs of the Rudolfine crown and a large medal with the Emperor on horseback on the obverse and a crowned Rudolf on the reverse which bears the signature *J.Formaid* (a variant of Vermeyen) (cat. no. II.42).[14] We may, then, perhaps consider these two pieces as the basis of his oeuvre. Vermeyen probably contributed significantly to the making of the crown, but it is not clear whether he was responsible for the composition, the design, the relief ornamentation or all the jewellery and enamel work. Sources link his name specifically only with a few small sculptures and a portrait of Stefan Báthory with diamond-encrusted frame.[15]

The important fact remains that Vermeyen was frequently referred to as the *juwelier*.[16] He had been born in Brussels as the son of Jan Cornelisz. Vermeyen and had taken up his apprenticeship in Antwerp. Written sources tell us that he lived in Frankfurt in 1596. He entered the services of the Emperor in Prague in October of the following year and worked there until his death.[17] On the occasion of the 1988 exhibition held in Essen, Distelberger put together a large collection of works that he ascribed to Vermeyen.[18] The most important of these was the goblet made from narwhal horn, with its ornate mount studded with diamonds and rubies and sculptural decoration employing coloured enamel (cat. no. II.43), or the mount for a large bowl made from heliotrope (bloodstone) (cat. no. II.45). In the composition of the bowl, considered to be one of the greatest works by Ottavio Miseroni, it is clear that he intended using this setting since it complements the overall shape. The tiny figure of Bacchus, in all probability an example of the figurative ornamentation of Vermeyen, makes this one of the most important works from the imperial court in Prague.

The distinctive details and choice of motifs and their treatment

in many of the works which Distelberger has attributed to Vermeyen suggest that his was one of the larger workshops. Evidently under the watchful eye of this strong artistic personality, a number of goldsmiths, engravers and enamel workers were employed who greatly contributed to shaping the character of art in Prague at this time. These may have included lesser-known artists – for example, Herzich van Bein, court goldsmith and engraver, who also worked for the Roěmberk family and who was responsible for the mounts of vessels made from precious stones, or the monogramist GB, Hans de Bull and Mathias Beitler. Their series of tiny engravings and designs for work in gold certainly support such an assumption.[19] Examples of these prints (cat. nos. II.297–314) are shown in the present exhibition for the first time.

Also in the Essen exhibition, Distelberger grouped together a collection of works related to the signed sceptre by Andreas Osenbruck. Of particular importance is a collection of seventeen pendants that survived in the treasury at St Vitus' cathedral (cat. no. II.57). This artist based his work closely on that of Vermeyen and probably even assumed the imperial commissions after the latter's death. It is not entirely clear when he entered the services of Rudolf II, but it seems to have been earlier than the date asserted by A. Weixlgartner.[20] By shifting the date of Vermeyen's death to 1608, as M. Staudinger has done, the possibility that these two artists were in direct contact becomes more realistic. The works grouped around the imperial insignia are the basis for an extensive production linked with the Prague court for practically the whole of the reign of Rudolf II and continuing into the time of his successor. Osenbruck's workshop was perhaps one of the few which remained in Prague after the court moved to Vienna.

The idea to transform pictorial or graphic designs into a picture created from richly coloured and unusually structured layers of various precious stones is contained in the distinctive late Mannerist expression typical of the Rudolfine court in Prague. The works of Cosimo and Giovanni Castrucci give a vivid impression of the range and orientation of the Emperor's interests.[21] Members of this family originally from Florence worked in Prague during the course of three generations, developing a marked parallel to the well-known Florentine specialization. The *commessi di pietre dure* which originated in their workshop have their specific character. They are chiefly landscapes whose raw materials consist for the most part of precious stones from Bohemia. A telling feature is the fact that, in many cases, they were independent objects – i.e., the panels were not created as part of a certain item of furniture, but were artworks in their own right, 'pictures made from precious stones' in which the stones' structure was used as the raw material for art. We see examples of this in Cosimo's signed and dated *Landscape with Bridge and Chapel* (cat. no. II.62) and in *Landscape with the Sacrifice of Isaac*, which Distelberger has recently attributed to him Cosimo (compare cat. no. II.63). Similar unusual approaches to materials can be seen in the above-mentioned silk embroideries featuring landscapes or still lifes and in a form of collage by Jeremias Gunter made from multi-coloured pieces of silk, described in the *Kunstkammer* inventory as '1 quadretto von Jeremias Ginther, ist ein jungfraw in einem zimmer, die uff der lautten spilt, ist von lautter attlaʒfleckhlein von mancherley farben zusamengesetzt ...'[22]

Alongside the members of three generations of precious-stone cutters from the Milanese Miseroni family and the Castruccis from Florence, the work of Caspar Lehmann also made a profound impression on the artistic production of the day. This artist, originally from Uelzen, evidently took up apprenticeship at the Munich court and was in contact with the imperial court in Prague from the end of the 1580s. After engaging in a number of court functions, he became court precious-stone cutter in 1601. He was dismissed in June 1605 and left for the Saxon court, but was back in Prague three years later. After the death of Rudolf II, he was employed by Matthias. Lehmann used the technique of crystal-engraving on cheaper glass, for which he was granted an imperial privilege in 1609.[23] Apart from the renowned goblet with its allegorical figures (cat. no. II.69), which remained on Czech soil, the exhibition organizers were able to acquire a number of glass plates with figural ornamentation and portraits of important rulers from collections from all over the world. This unique opportunity for a direct comparison of works in a single location may help to solve the problems involved in ascertaining Lehmann's authorship of certain other works. A comparison of the glass-makers' raw material may inspire research into the imperial glassworks, which were to supply high-quality glass analogous with raw material from Italy.[24]

The last in this list of leading figures are medal-engravers Antonio Abondio and his son Alessandro.[25] Antonio had already worked for Maxmilian II, producing a great number of important portrait medals honouring members of the court and also designs for coins. His work, continuing the celebrated tradition of the North Italian medal-engravers, significantly influenced medal-engraving during the late sixteenth and early seventeenth centuries, particularly in Germany; his designs were also used as the basis for work in other fields. We are especially pleased to be able to show examples of Abondio's work in wax in the exhibition (Cat.no. II.248). The small medals executed as fine jewellery and adorned with precious stones and pearls were favoured artefacts of which the *Kunstkammer* inventory contains a great number. The Prague works of Alessandro, who was also active in Matthias's court, have yet to be fully researched.

Notes

1. The inventory was discovered in the library of the Prince of Lichtenštejn, G. Wilhelm, just after the Second World War. The first account of it was written by E. Neumann in 1966. It was published in its entirety in 1976 by Bauer – Haupt.
2. Lhotsky 1943, p. 273.
3. Bauer-Haupt 1976, n. 618, pp. 626, 632–34.
4. The exhibition includes a little altar with a Pietà whose background shows an embroidered landscape which E. Fučíková attributes to Philip van den Bossche.
5. Neumann 1957.
6. Distelberger 1985, p. 286; Essen and Vienna 1988, pp. 462–63, cat. nos 394–98, p. 734.
7. Distelberger 1985, pp. 275–76; Essen and Vienna 1988, p. 440, cat. no. 340. Important information came to light concerning Anton Schweinberger during archival research carried out as part of the OW Programme at the Austrian Academy of Sciences in 1991–95, in cooperation with the staff at the Institute of Art History, Czech Academy of Sciences. It was discovered that this goldsmith resided in rooms at the Castle and was included among those who received wood for heating free-of-charge. The results of this research will be published separately.
8. Bauer-Haupt 1976, n. 1031: 'schon geschirrlin hat M Nicolaus Pfaff von eim gantzen stuckh augstein geschnitten, mitsambt seinem deckhel.'
9. According to Z. Winter (1909, p. 55), Pfaff was still living in rented accommodation in the Old Town in 1608; he married Kateřina, the daughter of the wealthy baker Štefan, in 1609, and bought two houses. According to a 1611 testament, his mother and brother Pavel inherited the property from him.
10. Gerszi 1982; J. R. ter Molen 1984.
11. Bukovinská 1970, pp. 185–98; Urban 1976, pp. 88–90; Distelberger 1978, pp. 79–152; *idem* in Essen and Vienna 1988, pp. 457–59.
12. Distelberger 1979.
13. Regarding the attribution of the crown: Chytil 1921; *idem* 1928; attribution of the crown and sceptre: Weixlgärtner 1928, pp. 279–315.
14. This comparison was the theme of a paper which R.Distelberger gave at a conference organized at the close of the exhibition *Prag um 1600* in Vienna in 1989; it was not published, however.
15. Bauer-Haupt 1976, nos 2023–26,

2049–50, *JKSAKW*, vol. 10, 1889, reg. 5576.

16. For a summary of known sources on this artist, see Bukovinská 1989/90, pp. 126–27.

17. While the date of the artist's death was previously thought to be 1606 at the latest, M. Staudinger shifted it to 1608 on the basis of archival sources (Staudinger 1995, pp. 263–71).

18. Distelberger 1985, pp. 279–82; *idem*, Essen and Vienna 1988, pp. 449–52 and relevant cat. texts.

19. Compare Bukovinská 1982; Schutte 1988; Bukovinská 1989/90; Schutte 1989/90.

20. Weixlgärtner 1928, pp. 279–315; also compare Distelberger, Essen and Vienna 1988, p. 452, and, for example, cat. nos 714, 715, where he states that the mounts ascribed to Osenbruck had appeared by 1610.

21. Neumann 1957; most recently, Giusti 1992, pp. 134–76, which gives a summary of the literature.

22. Bauer–Haupt 1976, n. 625.

23. Meyer–Heisig 1967, pp. 117–29; Drahotová 1981.

24. Klante 1942, p. 302.

25. Katz 1928, pp. 30–44; Dworschak 1958; Schulz 1989/90, pp. 155–61.

The Evocation of Rudolf II's *Kunstkammer*

The second part of the exhibition is based entirely on what can be ascertained from the inventory,[1] which, with its heading 'Vonn Anno 1607. Verzeichnus, was in der Rom: Kay: May: *Kunstkammer* gefunden worden ...', was begun in 1607 and continues until 1611. The reason for beginning a new inventory was evidently the fact that it had become possible to transfer the collections to their new premises in the Corridor Wing, which had just been completed.[2] The imperial miniaturist Daniel Fröschl, who compiled the inventory, was also court antiquarian.

The objects are divided according to type into groups on separate sheets; for the sake of clarity, they are also marked in an index attached to the inventory. Spaces were left between these groups for new additions. The entries are extremely thorough; apart from detailed descriptions, they also present dimensions or weight, often including facts about the artist, the manner in which the work was acquired or – particularly in the case of the zoological exhibits – references to specialist literature. In several places, the entries are accompanied by drawings. The texts demonstrate not only profound interest in each object but also capture the extensive knowledge acquired in the field. The Rudolfine inventory is therefore a catalogue of collections that would have afforded readers a survey of the various sections and allowed them to be seen in their various contexts; it thus reflects the ideal of order on which the *Kunstkammer* itself was based.

The first to provide a precise account of the *Kunstkammer*'s composition was Erwin Neumann.[3] He outlined three basic categories, according to which the objects are grouped. The first group *naturalia*, things created by nature; the second is *artificialia*, human creations; the third is *scientifica*, products of human reason. Learning was, on one plane, oriented towards nature; thus the *Kunstkammer* contained objects from the spheres of mineralogy, palaeontology, zoology and botany. Attention was focused on natural products in their raw state; studies were also made of people's ability to provide faithful representations of nature and their ability to ennoble or dominate it with intellect and artistic skills.[4] On another level, the *Kunstkammer* was meant to embrace as large a territory as possible. Thus it contained objects from all accessible parts of the world, from East Asia and Africa to the Americas.

The exhibits in this section correspond to certain sections of the inventory. Hundreds of fascinating objects stored in the *Kunstkammer* sadly no longer exist.[5] Rudolf II's share in the consider-able progress achieved in all manner of artistic and scientific fields has yet to be fully appreciated. While his interests were in keeping with those of his period, their intensity and the concentrated efforts taken to ensure that these works were brought to fruition were unrivalled in his time. The responsibility which Rudolf II acknowledged as Holy Roman Emperor was closely linked with his yearning for knowledge. Francis Bacon's formulation that 'knowledge is power' conforms to the Emperor's designs. We must abandon the notion that Rudolf was an eccentric and look to the areas in which his endeavours left a major legacy. The evocation of his Prague *Kunstkammer* may provide a basis for this way of re-evaluation.

Notes

1. Bauer–Haupt 1976.
2. For a recapitulation of what is known about the location of the *Kunstkammer*, see the essay about it in the present catalogue.
3. Neumann 1966, pp. 2662–65.
4. Compare Bredekamp 1993.
5. We have tried to use exhibits from Czech collections as much as possible, even though there may be little likelihood that they ever passed through the Rudolfine *Kunstkammer*.

Sketches, Designs, Samples and Documents

The drawings executed mainly by goldsmiths reached a peak during the Rudolfine period. The purpose for which individual drawings were intended also determined their character.[1] The modest selection in this part of the exhibition suggests that they were independent works of art, ideas captured on paper, conveyers of motifs or designs for works which would have been crafted in specific material. At the court, the excellence and distinctive quality of the drawings were represented above all by the work of Paulus van Vianen, fascinating sketches by the work of Christoph Jamnitzer and designs for specific commissions by drawings ascribed to Christoph Lencker.

Designs and samples captured in print form served as the basis for workshop commissions, as samples for customers or as independent works for collectors. The works of Erasmus Hornick have their own individual character; Hornick was employed for a while as engraver at the Prague court, and his prolific work ensured that this specialization gained prominence in the decorative arts.

The miniature graphic designs known as *Schwarzornament* are presented here for the first time in connection with the production of the Prague court workshops. They served chiefly for ornamentation executed using coloured enamels on gold mounts for vessels and cameos.[2] The ties between hitherto little-known goldsmiths and engravers who carried out this work, such as Herzich van Bein, Hans de Bull, the monogramist GB, Corwinian Saur or Mathias Beitler, and representatives from the court workshops, such as Jan Vermeyen and Andreas Osenbruck, will perhaps provide a clearer picture of the way in which these workshops operated and the share individual artists had in their production.

Notes

1. Irmscher 1987, pp. 44–51.
2. Compare Bukovinská 1982; Bukovinská 1989/90; Schutte 1989/90.

II.1
Anton Schweinberger; reliefs on the nut
ascribed to Nikolaus Pfaff
Augsburg ca. 1550–Prague 1603; Nürn-
berg 1556 (?)–Prague (?) before 1612
Ewer made from a Nut
Half Seychelles-nut (*Lodoicea seychel-
larum*), silver, partially gilded
H: 38.5 cm
Inscribed on the underside of the foot: *A.
Schweinberger. f.*
1602
Kunstkammer of Emperor Rudolf II, In-
ventory of 1607-11, no. 296
Vienna, Kunsthistorisches Museum,
Kunstkammer, inv. no. 6872

Alluding to the nut's origins (inv. 6849),
Schweinberger chose the Triumph of Water as the theme for this work. The figure
of Neptune on the lid has the same movement in reverse as a North Italian bronze
statuette of a gladiator from the second
quarter of the sixteenth century (inv.
5583) that was also part of Rudolf II's collection and that Adriaen de Vries made a
version of in Prague (inv. 5819). Links with
works by de Vries make it seem all the
more likely that he may have been involved in the sculptural aspect of this
piece. The uncommonly fine reliefs on the
sides of the nut are the work of Nikolaus
Pfaff. Scheicher interprets the erotic

scenes with the sea-god couple as an allegory for water as an element that both
gives and sustains life. These reliefs are so
closely related to the style of the painter
Bartolomeus Spranger that it seems he
may have provided the designs. This jug
reflects the art of the Prague court and
stands as one of the finest examples of
Rudolfine work produced around 1600 for
the *Kunstkammer* in Prague.

Essen and Vienna 1988, cat. no. 340.

Scheicher 1995, pp. 115–16.

R.D.

II.2
? Ottavio Miscroni
Mount: ? Anton Schweinberger
Milan 1567–Prague 1624; Augsburg mid-
16th century–Prague 1603
Tazza
Jasper, gold
Height: 9.3 cm (without handles: 7.3 cm);
Width: 21.3 cm (without handles: 15.4
cm), Length: 21.7 cm
Between 1590 and 1600
From the imperial *Schatzkammer*;
Inventory of 1750, p. 234, no. 144
Vienna, Kunsthistorisches Museum,
Kunstkammer, inv. no. 1900

The shape of this simple oval sexfoil bowl
in particularly beautiful jasper is very
much in the Italian tradition. It gives the
impression of having been made from one
piece but, in fact, the hollow foot is actually a separate piece. This would hardly have
been contemplated in Milan where every
workshop had its own goldsmith. The foot
is constructed so that it does not need a
mount and, including the hollow underside, is almost identical to the foot on Ottavio Miseroni's oval jasper bowl (inv. no.
6866). This is a first indication that this
piece originated in Prague. A second is
provided by the gold handles which must
be by the Augsburg goldsmith Anton

Schweinberger (d. 1603), who was working in Prague after 1587. The work on this
piece is exactly like that signed by him on
the famous Seychelle-nut jug in Vienna
(inv. no. 6872). Taking all of this into account it is most likely that this bowl was
made early on in Ottavio's career, that is to
say during the 1590s.

Essen and Vienna 1988, cat. no. 696

R.D.

II.3
Unknown Master
Setting attributed to Anton Schweinberger
Augsburg, ca. 1550–Prague 1603
Agate Cup
Agate, silver gilt
8.8 cm; diam: 18.9 cm (incl. handle: 12.9 ×
24.7 cm)
Ca. 1500; mount ca. 1600
From the *Schatzkammer*; Inventory of
1750, p. 219, no. 81
Vienna, Kunsthistorisches Museum,
Kunstkammer, inv. no. 1646

Although this bowl offers practically no
clues as to its age, it is clear that it is con-

siderably older than its mount. The simple
outline and shallow base, with its somewhat 'wavy' interior, can be linked neither
to work being made in Milan nor in
Prague in the late sixteenth and early seventeenth centuries. There are no traces of
an older mount. Underneath, where one
of the ornamental handles joins the body,
there is evidence of an old crack which
clearly had to be hidden. The mount has
been fixed to the cup without harming the
agate – using a form of adhesive rather
than boring into the stone. A hinge above
the edge of the cup connects the interior
and the exterior of the structure of the
handle. Ernst Kris attributes this work to

Anton Schweinberger: there is a strong
stylistic affinity between this work and
Schweinberger's Seychelles-nut jug.

Essen and Vienna 1988, cat. no. 691.

Kris 1932, no. 81.

R.D.

II.4
Nikolaus Pfaff
Nürnberg ?1556–? Prague before 1612
Venus and Cupid
Ivory; ebony
H of statuette with base 19.5 cm; of fig-
ures 12.9 cm
Ca. 1601–7
Kunstkammer of Emperor Rudolf II,
Inventory of 1607–1611, no. 1786
Vienna, Kunsthistorisches Museum,
Kunstkammer, inv. no. 4658

This virtuoso pair of miniature figures is
remarkable for its sculptural self-assur-
ance and inner grandeur. Rudolf II partic-

ularly appreciated the sensual undertones
and implied eroticism of such delicate
ivory work. Tender expression and subtle
composition go hand in hand in this
piece. The harmony of the figures' glances
and movements binds them together. The
liveliness of the little figure of Amor is
reminiscent of the boys avidly picking up
gold coins on the early Danae relief, while
Venus is clearly related to the sea goddess
on the Seychelles-nut jug, as well as to
Danae. This delicate piece was made in the
rather competitive atmosphere that prevailed among artists at the court in
Prague. Thus the three-sided base – 'the
art of the goldsmith executed with the

skills of the ivory-carver' – is a conscious
artistic response to the mount made for
the Seychelles-nut jug. Like clasps for a
mount, a mascaron emerges from each
side. This treatment recalls work by the
goldsmith Schnabel for the large bowl on
which Anton Schweinberger and Nikolaus
Pfaff collaborated in Prague in 1602.

Essen and Vienna 1988, cat. no. 395.

Distelberger 1985, p. 286; Haag 1994, pp.
89ff.

S.H.

II.5
Nikolaus Pfaff
Nürnberg ?1556–? Prague before 1612
Danae
Ivory
19.5 × 14.5 cm
Ca. 1601–7
Kunstkammer of Emperor Rudolf II, In-
ventory of 1607–1611, no. 1785; Legat
Emile Baboin, 1931
Lyon, Musée Lyonnais des Arts Décoratifs,
inv. no. 1144

This small, intricately carved ivory panel is
the only relief that has so far been identified as part of the meagre surviving out-

put of Nikolaus Pfaff. Its pictorial quality
was most likely inspired by the *Venus* by
Lambert Sustris (Paris, Louvre), whose relaxed pose Pfaff has scarcely altered. Unlike in the preliminary drawing, now in
Stockholm, the movements, particularly
of the two main figures, have about them
an air of uncertainty that demonstrates
the distance between this and Pfaff's later
ivory statuettes. This would seem to indicate that *Danae* was made early in Pfaff's
career as an imperial stonecarver and cabinetmaker, for which he received a fixed
salary from 1601 onwards. The same figures emerge repeatedly in statuettes by
Pfaff, and as his career progresses, his

treatment of the human form, by preference nude, becomes increasingly more
confident and harmonious.

Essen and Vienna 1988, cat. no. 394.

Distelberger 1985, p. 286; Haag 1944, p. 90.

S.H.

II.6
Nikolaus Pfaff
Nürnberg ?1556–? Prague before 1612
Vessel from Rhinoceros Horn
Carved rhinoceros horn
H: 22.5 cm
1610
Kunstkammer of Emperor Rudolf II, Inventory of 1607–1611, no. 12
Vienna, Kunsthistorisches Museum, Kunstkammer, inv. no. 3737

Objects made from rhinoceros horn were immensely sought after by collectors from the early seventeenth century onwards. This was not only because of the scarcity of the material but also because of the magic properties attributed to it. (Hans Khevenhüller, writing from Madrid and hoping to persuade Emperor Rudolf II to purchase some exotica of this kind, stressed its potential to protect against poisons: 'Soll Wider Gifft far Guett sein'.) Nikolaus Pfaff, who strove for the highest possible standards in his work as a carver and who participated fully in the discourse of the artistic community at the court in Prague, was always searching for new ways to practise his art. The highly imaginative, lifelike acanthus and the mask on the front of this unusual cup, where horn is also seen in its original state, are perfect manifestations of these aspirations. The deep indentation between the slack lips of the mascaron was presumably intended for a mount which was never in fact made.

Essen and Vienna 1988, cat. no. 397; Bordeaux 1990.

Distelberger 1985, p. 286.

S.H.

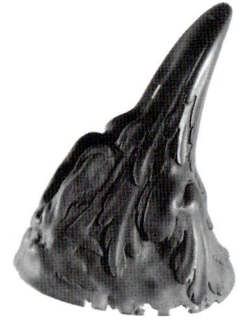

II.7
Nikolaus Pfaff
Nürnberg 1556 (?)-Prague (?) before 1612
Mercury in a Chariot Drawn by Cocks
Turned column of ivory; wooden lacquered base (modern)
36, Mercury 14 × 14 × 8 cm
Before 1612
Rudolf II's *Kunstkammer*, inv. 1635, no. 254 (?); acquired by Prof. Herget for the Stavovská inženýrská škola in Prague 1782; transferred 1832 to the Národní Muzeum v Praze in 1832
Prague, Narodni muzeum, inv. no. H2-3 685/a-b

When drawing up an inventory in 1635 a series of objects were found which Hans Karl König had neglected to register in the inventory of 1621. This particular object was found on the long green table in the *Kunstkammer* and registered under entry 254 as 'Ein hohe gedrähete saul von helfenbein, darauf ist ein Merkerius'. This statue can be found in castle inventories of the seventeenth and eighteenth centuries drawn up for treasure chambers, which were used as the old *Kunstkammer*, until it was decided in 1782 that it should be auctioned, along with some other art works. However, it was ultimately handed over to Professor Herget for teaching purposes, and later found its way to the Stavovská in Prague. The fine figurative carving style, carefully worked from hard material, and the striking fluid form of the mask on the chariot, all point to Nicolaus Pfaff, whose qualities and work were recorded in the *Kunstkammer* inventories between 1607 and 1611. The base seems, however, to have been the work of another sculptor. A more detailed study of this, the largest of Pfaff's known works, is preparation.

J. Koči 1989, no. 440.

E.F.

II.8
Paulus van Vianen
Utrecht ca. 1570–Prague 1613
Plaque with Cadmus Killing the Dragon
Cast lead
Diam: 16 cm
P. D. V. F. (= Paulus de Viana Fecit)
End of sixteenth century
Adalbert von Lanna collection, Prague; Berlin auction 9.11.1909, no. 321
Prague, Museum of Applied Arts, inv. no. 11491

In the foreground is a depiction of a winged monster about to bite off the head of a man leaning backwards; in its talons it holds another victim fast. On the left stands Cadmus, who manages to kill the dragon with a javelin (Ovid, *Metamorphoses* III, 30–94). The background consists of a landscape with a river and various Classical buildings. Both representations of the dragon in this composition are derived from an engraving by the Haarlem Mannerist Hendrick Goltzius which was produced after a model by Cornelius van Haarlem from 1588. The landscape resembles a graphic work by Hieronymus Cock dating from 1558. The execution of this plaque also shows a clear relationship with the work of the Nürnberg masters Hans Jamnitzer and Jonas Silber. After 1600 Paulus van Vianen's relief scenes acquire a more naturalistic character and his compositions are founded on his own open-air studies.

Essen–Vienna 1988, cat. no. 352.

Frederiks 1952, no. 68 J; Weber 1975, no. 924; Ter Molen 1984, no. 74.

J.R.tM.

II.9
Paulus van Vianen
Utrecht ca. 1570–Prague 1613
Plaque with Pan and Syrinx
Embosssed silver
17.5 × 19 cm
PVV (two last letters joined together) 1603
1603
Salzburg or Prague
Cologne auction, 28.4.1954, cat. no. 361
Amsterdam, Rijksmuseum, inv. no. RBK 1957-34

In the centre of the rectangular plaque is a depiction of Syrinx fleeing from her pursuer, Pan (Ovid, *Metamorphoses* I, 688–712). Amor is watching the couple from the clouds; on the right lies a naked river-god in front of a vessel from which water flows. Around him are several nymphs. On a rock overgrown with trees stands a watermill and several other buildings; behind the figure of Pan in the distance extends the Cathedral Square of Salzburg. Paulus van Vianen drew from his own sketches for this composition. Drawings by him are known of watermills (cat. no. II.292) and groups of trees growing among rocks. The cathedral of Salzburg is on one of his panoramas of the city. The classical complex behind the watermill depicts the ruins of the Temple of Sarapis on the Quirinale in Rome, with a loggia which was built later. This fragment is probably derived from a graphic work with a view of Classical Rome by Etienne du Pérac dating from 1575.

Utrecht 1984, cat. no. 10; Essen and Vienna 1988, cat. no. 528.

Frederiks 1961, no. 77; Weber 1975, no. 927; Ter Molen 1984, no. 76.

J.R.tM.

II.10
Paulus van Vianen
Utrecht ca. 1570–Prague 1613
Plaque with the Adoration of the Shepherds
Embossed and cast silver
31.8 × 22.9 cm
P V (one above the other) 1607
1607
Meyer collection, Munich 1817; Jane Starkey collection, London auction 21.3.1979, cat. no. 39
Amsterdam, Rijksmuseum, inv. no. RBK 1979-101

In the centre of the rectangular plaque is the Virgin Mary bending over the crib in which the baby Jesus lies; this scene is observed by a group of people, among whom in the foreground are Joseph and two shepherds. In the sky shines a great star surrounded by angels. In creating the characters Paulus van Vianen was inspired by the figures of countryfolk from the Prague region. For example, the figures of two women standing in the distance between high ruined walls can also be found on the back of one of his sketches (Ter Molen 1984, no. 238). To obtain the best possible suggestion of spatial depth, the figures of both shepherds were cast separately and then screwed on to the plate; the remainder of the scene is executed in exceptionally subtle and shallow relief. This composition was very often imitated by other goldsmiths, but usually in simplified form. A round silver platter produced in Antwerp in 1617 was used in the church of Aarschot as the back-plate for a candle.

Utrecht 1984, cat. no. 21; Amsterdam 1993, cat. no. 185.

Frederiks 1952, no. 78 T; Weber 1975, no. 935; Ter Molen 1984, no. 86; Baarsen 1989, pp. 141-147.

J.R.tM.

II.11
Paulus van Vianen
Utrecht ca. 1570–Prague 1613
Plaque with a Landscape
Embossed silver
8.3 × 12 cm
P V (one above the other) *1607*
1607
A. L. A. Gevers collection, auction in The
Hague, 19.3.1888, no. 1096
Amsterdam, Rijksmuseum, inv. no. NM
8478

The landscape with a wooden bridge
across a rivulet is executed in great detail
in low relief. A cart is crossing the bridge,

horses are wading through the water, and
on the banks women are washing their
laundry. On the left, on the far side of the
river, are the buildings of a tavern; on the
left by a shed stand several soldiers and
women, and a peddlar with his wares. The
outlines of a church tower and other
buildings in the distance suggest the form
of the city of Prague. For this composition
Paulus van Vianen used his own drawing
dated 1606 (cat. no. II.293); during the execution in silver he changed a few details.
According to the inventory of the imperial
treasury in 1750, cabinet 13 contained 'Ein
viereckiges deto [i.e. relief] von silber,
worauf eine landwürthschaft nebst der

jahrzahl 1607, in einem schwarzen rähmel
von ebenholz'. It is likely that the description refers to this plaque. Modern, however, refers to another possible landscape
from 1607 which was in the Günzburg
Collection in Petersburg at the end of the
last century (Modern 1894, p. 87).

Utrecht 1984, cat. no. 18; Essen and Vienna 1988, cat. no. 529; Amsterdam 1993, cat.
no. 188.

Frederiks 1952, no. 77 S; Weber 1975, no.
934; Ter Molen 1984, no. 87.

J.R.tM.

II.12
Paulus van Vianen
Utrecht ca. 1570–Prague 1613
Medal with the Allegory of the Turkish
Wars
Cast Silver
Diam: 8 cm
*SIGIS.BATH.TRANSYL.PRINC.AQVILAE
ET STELLAE CRINITAE
FOELICISS.PRAESAG.CAES.TVRCAS.IN-
TER DANVB: ET SAV FLU.AD TERGOV-
IST.FORTITER.FVGAVIT.A.MDVC.D.XVI-
II OCTOB.*, and *IAVARIN AVTORE
DEO.AVSPICIO RVDOLPH.II
CAES.NVBE OPPORTVNISS.LVNAM OB-
DVCENTAE DIRECTORE ADOLPH*

*COM.A SCHWARZENB.RECVPERATVR.
A.MDIIC.D.XXIX MART.*
Beginning of seventeenth century
Vienna, Kunsthistorisches Museum,
Münzkabinett, inv. no. 67 bß

One of two scenes on medals symbolizing
the capture of Tergowist by Sigismund
Báthory in 1595. In the centre Bellona sits
on a throne with a staff of command in her
hand; above her head Victoria holds a laurel wreath. In the foreground sit the gods
of the rivers Danube and Sava in front of a
bucket from which water is flowing. High
in the sky is the imperial eagle, guarding
the captured Turkish crescent. The reverse

of the medal, which describes the re-occu-
pation of Ráb by Adolf von Schwarzenberg in 1598, shows a Classical column
with an eagle; the whole structure is supported by a female figure, holding onto
the hair of kneeling Fortune with her left
hand. The warring armies are shown in the
background of both scenes. Both compositions are derived from oil sketches by
Hans von Aachen.

Essen and Vienna 1988, cat. no. 467.

Ter Molen 1984, no. 199.

J.R.tM.

II.13
? Ottavio Miseroni; Mount: Paulus van
Vianen
Milan 1567–Prague 1624; Utrecht ca.
1570–Prague 1613
Ewer
Gold; ewer in light-brown jasper streaked
with red
H: 36 cm; base diam: 13.5 cm
Under edge of base: *P. D. V. F 1608*
1608; ewer ca. 1600
Kunstkammer of Rudolf II, Inventory of
1607–1611, no. 1363
Vienna, Kunsthistorisches Museum,
Kunstkammer, inv. no. 1866

The jasper ewer, from which a dragon's
head protrudes was probably produced in
the Miseroni studio in Milan around 1590,
but it is also possible that it was produced
some years later by Ottavio Miseroni in
Prague. In 1608 Paulus van Vianen attached to this work a gold montage that
formed the ewer's lid and the rim of its
base. The lid has the form of a gracefully
floating nereid on a wavy water surface.
This womanly figure holds a chain in her
hand, which is linked to a collar on the
neck of the dragon. On the gold rim of the
base are depictions of four gods, symbolizing the four elements: Jupiter, Juno, Pluto
and Amphitrite. The gods are separated by

the heads of horned goats, a reference to
Rudolf's sign of the zodiac (Capricorn).
The work was taken to Vienna after
Rudolf's death. Sold or pawned by Ferdi-
nand II, it was reacquired for the imperial
collection by Maria Theresa.

Utrecht 1984, cat. no. 23; Essen and Vienna
1988, cat. no. 353.

Kris 1929, pp. 145, 191; Frederiks 1952, no.
78 U; Hayward 1976, p. 274, fig. 580; Distelberger 1978, pp. 126–128; Ter Molen 1984,
p. 23, no. 15.

J.R.tM.

II.14
Paulus van Vianen
Utrecht ca. 1570–Prague 1613
Dish of a Tazza with *Susanna and the Old
Men*
Gilded embossed silver
Diam: 20.5 cm
P V (monogram) *1612*
1612
Charles I's collection, London 1640;
Aarnout Stevens collection, Amsterdam
1706; Pierre Locquet collection, Amster-
dam auction 22.9.1783; D. G. van Beunin-
gen collection, Vierhouten 1937
Rotterdam, Museum Boijmans Van
Beuningen, inv. no. MBZ 198

The scene, framed by a leafy wreath, depicts Susanna bathing, observed by two elders (Daniel 13). The background is a
rocky landscape with several buildings, including Queen Anne's Summer House
from Hradčany in Prague. Paulus van Vianen composed a drawing on the same subject (cat no. II.289) and certain details from
the drawing are re-used in this relief. The
English text engraved on the bottom of
the platter indicates that the dish was supplemented in 1821 by a lower plate and
base; these mythological scenes were
probably the work of the London goldsmith William Elliott. Casts of this depiction of Susanna and the elders, which were

circulated widely and of which one was in
the collection of the English king Charles
I, were also used by other goldsmiths. This
can be seen, for example, in a silver platter
by the Amsterdam master Lucas Draef
from 1657, and on the lid of a beer tankard
produced around 1670 in Stockholm.

Utrecht 1984, cat. no. 29; Essen and Vienna
1988, cat. no. 534.

Frederiks 1952, no. 93 KK; Weber 1975, no.
942; Ter Molen 1984, no. 117; Ter Molen
1994, no. 7.

J.R.tM.

II.15
Paulus van Vianen
Utrecht ca. 1570–Prague 1613
Ewer
Embossed silver
H: 34 cm
PV 1613
1613
Nicolaes Snouckaert collection, Prague
1613; A. M. Hogguer-Ebeling collection,
Amsterdam auction 18.8.1817, cat. no.
160; Earl of Wemyss collection, London
auction 7.5.1947, cat. no. 144
Amsterdam, Rijksmuseum, inv. no. RBK
16089 a

On the front and back of the ewer are oval
low-relief scenes with the story of Diana
and her companion Callisto (Ovid, *Metamorphoses* II, 401–495). On one side of the
ewer is a depiction of Jupiter – in the form
of Diana – attempting to seduce Callisto;
in the wooded landscape in the background the following episode can be seen,
the moment when Diana discovers Callisto's pregnancy. On the other side is a depiction of Callisto's punishment by Diana,
who turns her into a bear. On the left, in
the distance, Arcas, the son of Callisto, is
shown trying to kill the animal, in reality
his mother, with an arrow. The son of the
original owner brought a lawsuit in 1637

against an individual in Amsterdam to
whom he had temporarily given the ewer
and the related platter (cat. no. II.016) for
safekeeping. This person had had a copy
made by the goldsmith Servaes Cocq and
sold it to the Polish king.

Amsterdam 1979, cat. no. 20; Utrecht 1984,
cat. no. 32; Amsterdam 1993, cat. no. 190.

Frederiks 1952, no. 96 NN; Duyvené de Wit
1955, pp. 185–190; Hayward 1976, pp. 290,
293, fig. 630; Ter Molen 1984, no. 19.

J.R.tM.

II.16
Paulus van Vianen
Utrecht ca. 1570–Prague 1613
Platter
Embossed silver
41×52 cm
PV (monogram) *1613*
1613
Nicolaes Snoukaert collection, Prague
1613; A. M. Hogguer-Ebeling collection,
Amsterdam auction 18.8.1817, cat. no.
159; Earl of Wemyss collection, London
auction 7.5.1947, cat. no. 144
Amsterdam, Rijksmuseum, inv. no. RBK
16089 b

On the bottom of the oval platter, the rim
of which is decorated with irregular masks
and other lobed ornaments, a rocky woodland landscape extends in relief. By a
stream Diana and her companions bathe;
the shepherd Actaeon watches them and
is later changed into a stag by Diana as a
punishment (Ovid, *Metamorphoses* III,
138–197). After this object, together with
the ewer which went with it (cat. no.
II.290), was taken from Prague to Holland,
it served as a model for other artists. The
platter is depicted in the painting *Glorification of the Christian Faith*, signed by
Claes Moeyaert and dated ca. 1650. On the
lower side of the platter, which rests on

four feet, is affixed an oval plate with a
scene in relief. This depicts the mountainous landscape in which Actaeon, transformed into a stag, is set upon by his own
dogs, while several hunters try to kill him
with darts.

Amsterdam 1979, cat. no. 20; Utrecht 1984,
cat. no. 32; Essen-Vienna 1988, p. 455, fig.
5; Amsterdam 1993, cat. no. 190.

Frederiks 1952, no. 96 NN; Duyvené de Wit
1955, pp. 185–190; Hayward 1976, p. 293,
figs. 631–632; Ter Molen 1984, no. 19.

J.R.tM.

II.17
? Ottavio Miseroni; mount: Jan Vermeyen
Milan 1567–Prague 1624; Brussels before
1559–Prague 1608
Cup with *Triton*
Bohemian moss agate, gold-enamelled
17.1 × 14 × 18 cm
Ca. 1600
From the *Schatzkammer*, inventory 1750,
p. 223, no. 99
Vienna, Kunsthistorisches Museum,
Kunstkammer, inv. no. 1987

Bukovinská attributed this bowl to Ottavio Miseroni, linking the triton's head
with the signed three-dimensional figure

of Mary Magdalen (Bukovinská 1970, p.
195). Although this is generally accepted,
there remains an element of doubt, although it is clear that the maker of this
bowl is working in the style of the Milan
Miseroni workshop. The doubt stems
from the fact that there is no other example of work by Ottavio Miseroni combining a fully three-dimensional human figure with a vessel. It is not impossible that
Giovanni Ambrogio played a part in the
conception and realisation of this bowl.
The pleasing modelling of the triton's
back and the precision of the mascaron
above the belt are superior to what is
known of Ottavio Miseroni up to this date.

The gold mount is clearly from Jan Vermeyen's workshop and is closely related to
that of the chalcedony bowl (inv. 1665).
This vessel, therefore, which may already
have been designed before 1600, was most
probably not mounted until the early
years of the seventeenth century.

Essen and Vienna 1988, cat. no. 365.

Kris 1929, pp. 145, 193, ill. 651; Bukovinská
1970, p. 195, ill. 5; Distelberger 1978, pp.
130–131, ill. 109; Bukovinská 1988, p. 163
(with ill.).

R.D.

II.18
Ottavio Miseroni; mount: Jan Vermeyen
Milan 1567–Prague 1624; Brussels before
1559–Prague 1608
Cup
Coloured Bohemian jasper, gold-enam-
elled
10 × 11 × 22.9 cm
Ca. 1600–1605
From the *Kunstkammer* of Emperor
Rudolf II, inventory of 1607–11, no. 1421
Vienna, Kunsthistorisches Museum,
Kunstkammer, inv. no. 6866

The wonderful colours of this piece are instantly captivating. Although there is sym-

metry in the arrangement of the motifs on
either side of the middle axis, the overall
form is not symmetrical. The side of the
bowl folds inwards as though the jasper
were soft and organic. This is the formal
language Ottavio Miseroni used in the
early seventeenth century, as in the large
heliotrope bowl of 1608 in the Galerie
d'Apollon at the Louvre. Although the
multicoloured jasper bowl is relatively
small, it is nevertheless one of Ottavio
Miseroni's most important works. Yet this
fine piece is not described in any great detail in the inventory of the *Kunstkammer*.
No other bowl has this combination of red
and green. The schematic mascarons

halfway along the long sides are like the
incunabula of the auricular style that was
later favoured in Prague. The mount in
enamelled gold has the same motifs as the
reverse of Masnago's cameo of the Madonna in the Clouds (inv. XII 815). This shows
that it is the work of Jan Vermeyen and can
be dated to the early seventeenth century.

Essen and Vienna 1988, cat. no. 371.

Bukovinská 1970, p. 192 und ill. 8; Bauer /
Haupt 1976, no. 1421 (not identified); Distelberger 1978, p. 136, ill. 114.

R.D.

II.19
Ottavio Miseroni; mount: workshop of
Jan Vermeyen
Milan 1567–Prague 1624; Brussels before
1559–Prague 1608
Cup
Green agate, gold-enamelled
10.1 × 13.3 × 16.7 cm
Ca. 1605
From the *Schatzkammer*
Vienna, Kunsthistorisches Museum,
Kunstkammer, inv. no. 1650

This simple, almost heart-shaped bowl
looks as though the artist used nothing
more than his bare hands to mould it. It is

as if this virtuoso handling of the material
is in itself part of the object's meaning. In
this sense, this green agate bowl is particularly closely related to the large heliotrope cup of 1608 in the Louvre. The
sides, left unadorned, look as though they
have simply been pressed inwards, and the
edge of the mouth curves inwards like soft
wax. The bowl flows forwards to form a
very fine lip. This bowl is typical of Ottavio
Miseroni's style in the first decade of the
seventeenth century. The mount is very
similar in much of its detail to that of the
large nephrite bowl (inv. 6846), showing
that it must be from the Vermeyen workshop in around 1605. The enamel work on

this agate bowl is closely related to enamel
work by Master G B, dated 1603.

Essen and Vienna 1988, cat. no. 368.

Bukovinská 1970, p. 192 and ill. 9; Distelberger 1978, p. 138.

R.D.

II.20
Ottavio Miseroni
Milan 1567–Prague 1624
Bowl with Rudolf II's Initials
Heliotrope, gilt silver
19 × 33 × 58 cm
I R I on the short end with a mitre crown
above
1608
Kunstkammer of Emperor Rudolf II,
inventory of 1607–1611, no. 1376
Paris, Musée du Louvre, Département des
Objets d'art, inv. no. MR 143 (MV.945)

This large bowl, cut from a single piece of
stone, is the only vessel listed and dated in

the inventory of 1607–11 under the name
of Ottavio Miseroni. This marks the bowl
as the key to Ottavio Miseroni's style in the
early seventeenth century. Its most striking feature is the tension between the
rigidity of the material and the disconcert-
ing 'softness' of the forms made from it.
The doughy scrolls and flat bands on the
outer walls of the vessel are repeated on a
number of other pieces. The edge of the
bowl looks almost as though it were made
out of some strangely viscous material.
Soft folds hang inwards, while mascarons
protrude from the outside as on the
coloured jasper bowl (inv. 6866). As elsewhere, Miseroni avoids strict symmetry

here. This extraordinary piece must have
occupied Miseroni for a period of years.
On 2 September 1608 Rudolf II elevated
Ottavio Miseroni and his three brothers –
Alessandro, Giovanni Ambrogio and Aurelio–to the nobility in recognition of their
twenty years of faithful service.

Essen and Vienna 1988, no. 372.

Alcouffe 1974, pp. 514, 517, fig. 21, no. 314;
Distelberger 1978, pp. 134–36.

R.D.

II.21
Ottavio Miseroni
Milan 1567–Prague 1624
Shell-Shaped Bowl
Heliotrope, gilt silver
8.3 × 13.7 × 12.7 cm
Between 1605 and 1620
From the *Schatzkammer*
Vienna, Kunsthistorisches Museum,
Kunstkammer, inv. no. 2019

This bowl is an example of how some pieces lay unfinished for over a decade in Ottavio Miseroni's workshop before they received their final polish and were delivered to the court. The flowing lines of the design place it amongst work that Miseroni was doing at the beginning of the seventeenth century. The two scrolls on the shell are reminiscent of the centre section of the coloured jasper bowl (inv. 6866), which also has a similar flat decorative band. Despite the fact that this work clearly dates from his middle period, Ottavio Miseroni did not take it to Vienna until 1622. It was in a batch of seventeen pieces and had no mount. The Viennese court treasurer, Nikolaus von Kurland, lists it under no. 5 as 'ein schallen samt den fues von elitropio, durchsichtig mit zwo rollen, auf der seiten ein ritz' (*Jahrbuch*, vol. 33, 1916, p. CXVI, Regest 20.608). The handles added by the Viennese goldsmith are superfluous and show how poorly he understood the subtlety of the stone carver's work.

Essen and Vienna 1988, cat. no. 703.

Distelberger 1978, pp. 144–45.

R.D.

II.22
Ottavio Miseroni
Milan 1567–Prague 1624
Tazza from Heliotrope
Green jasper with red patches (heliotrope), mounted in gold-bronze and silver gilt
17 × 21.3 × 44 cm
Bowl before 1621, mount after 1622
Carved in Prague, probably mounted in
Taken from Prague to Vienna in 1622.
Until 1944 in the Kunsthistorisches Museum, after that in private ownership. Old inventory no. from the Kunsthistorisches Museum, Vienna: 1875. Acquired in 1981 by the Museum für Kunst und Gewerbe, Hamburg
Hamburg, Museum für Kunst und Gewerbe, inv. no. 1981.235 / Campe's Historische Kunststiftung

The splendid, colourful appearance of the stone comes partly from the contrast of jasper green with the light, grey-blue clouds speckled with red dots (heliotrope), which bring the piece to life as they swirl across its surface. The shallow bowl sweeps upwards from its tiny oval base. Distelberger has shown the similarity between this bowl with its heavy handles and the monumental agate bowl from late Antiquity that was owned by the house of Habsburg. In 1621 Ottavio Miseroni listed the piece and in 1622 it was recorded among the items that he took to the court in Vienna. The mount, which had hitherto not been recorded, must have been made in two stages: the griffins' heads above the handles are made from a gold-bronze alloy, as are also the lizards. The foot, added even later, is in silver gilt.

Hamburg 1961, no. 292, pp. 102–3.

Distelberger 1982, pp. 154–56; Heitmann 1990, pp. 116ff.

B.H.

II.23
Ottavio Miseroni; setting: Jan Vermeyen workshop
Milan 1567–Prague 1624; Brussels before 1559–Prague 1608
Covered Vessel
Agate, enamelled gold
20.1 × 12.3 × 16.8 cm
Ca. 1603–07
Kunstkammer of the Emperor Rudolf II, Inventory of 1607-11, no. 1369
Vienna, Kunsthistorisches Museum, Kunstkammer, inv. no. 1624

The original shape of this rare rose agate with bluish clouds doubtless influenced the shape of this deep bowl. The discrepancy in size between the cover and the shape of the vessel is bridged by the broad gold mount: it arises from Ottavio Miseroni's practice of cutting the smaller form from the larger. The shape of the foot is found elsewhere as, for example, on the Bacchus bowl (CAT. NO. II.45). The low relief decoration is inspired by the Milan workshop of Ottavio's cousins. The mount is surprising in that it has a narrow band of landscape along the edge of the cover with wild animals and dogs and divided into sections by leaning trees. The same motifs are found on an ornament print from 1603 by the master GB (Schütte 1989/90, p. 186, illus. 152). Other prints by this particular engraver also depict the bat (Schütte 1989/90, p. 187, illus. 153) and the winged satyr's mask (Schütte 1991, vol. 2, 1, II. Monogr. GB 1./5), seen here on the inner edge of the cover and on the standing-ring at the bowl's base. The gold is worked in exactly the style of the Vermeyen workshop.

Essen and Vienna 1988, cat. no. 369

Kris 1929, pp. 145, 193, illus. 652; Bauer / Haupt 1976, no. 1369 (not identified); Distelberger 1978, pp. 139-141, illus. 117

R.D.

II.24
Ottavio Miseroni; mount: attributed to Jan Vermeyen
Milan 1567–Prague 1624; Brussels before 1559–Prague 1606
Footed Bowl with Lid
From the collections of Louis XIV
Paris, Musée du Louvre, Département des Objets d'Art, inv. no. MR 175 MV 975

The overall formal design, the treatment of the stone and other details (such as the gently curving lid, the low-relief decorative elements on the body of the vessel, etc.) identify this small agate vessel with an oval, shell-shaped lid and a foot with a low, compressed stem as a work from Ottavio Miseroni's peak period after 1600. The mount with coloured enamel on a gold background is directly related to works now attributed to Jan Vermeyen, such as the vessel with a small Bacchus (KK 1871) or the jasper bowl (KK 6866). The facing on the edge of the vessel and on the lid compensate for the difference in the size of the two parts, the lid having been carved from the inside of the vessel. The surface is decorated with engraved drawings that were once the base for a polychrome enamel, which is now missing on this part of the vessel. E. Kris has pointed out the bowl's similarity to Ottavio's pink agate vessel with lid from Vienna (cat. no. KK 1624).

Marquet de Vasselot 1914, no. 475; Kris 1929, no. 652, p. 177.

B.B.

II.25
? Ottavio Miseroni
Milan 1567–Prague 1624
Cup with Mascaron
Jasper; gold, enamel
12 × 19 cm
After 1600
From the royal collections
Paris, Musée du Louvre, Département des Objets d'Art, inv. no.OA 5 MV 949

Members of the Miseroni family of artists of Milan typically let the natural shape of precious stones inspire them and made use of these shapes in a masterly way. They then filled in the interesting outlines with expressive figural motifs, details of animals and monsters, which grow directly out of the shape of the vessel or form an inseparable part of it (the earliest examples of this type are several vessels by Gaspar, whose authorship was demonstrated in 1976 by W. Focková). This category also includes the green jasper vessel from Prague, which has an interesting shell shape and ends in an expressive, sculpturally rendered head of a monster. The smoothness of the form, the treatment of the surface, the illusion of the fantastic beast's softness and suppleness and the shape of the compressed stem all identify this as the work of Ottavio Miseroni. The gold mounts with coloured enamel are not typical of the Prague workshops, but a number of similarities in the colours of the enamel and in several decorative motifs can be found in other works from this circle.

Marquet de Vasselot 1914, no. 949; Kris 1929, p. 188, no. 594, ill. 594/176 (listed as 'Milan, ?late sixteenth century').

B.B.

II.26
? Ottavio Miseroni
Milan 1567–Prague 1624
Tazza
Rock crystal mounted in gold with enamel
14.7 cm
Early 17th century
Stockholm, The Royal Collections of Sweden, inv. no. HGS SS 196

This interestingly shaped vessel deserves attention because of the virtuoso treatment of the crystal. The extended and compressed volutes that form the handles also decorate several places on the edge of the vessel, and soft curves suggesting a pliable material extend from them. There are very few glyptic works in which the material is so treated. It is most similar to vessels carved from precious stone by Ottavio Miseroni, who, apparently influenced by Paulus van Vianen and Nikolaus Pfaff, or perhaps even at the request of the Emperor's buyer, imposed the appearance of a soft, malleable substance on the hard material. It is therefore assumed that this bowl is also the work of Ottavio Miseroni. The date of the work remains open to question, as does the introduction of the mounts, which were clearly not a part of the original design and date from a later period.

Poche 1979, p. 166, ill. no.149; Fogelmark 1982, p. 100, no. 196, ill. p. 101.

B.B.

II.27
Ottavio Miseroni
Milan 1567–Prague 1624
Cup
Smoky quartz, gilt silver
12.5 × 8.9 × 12.2 cm
Before 1622; mounting and foot later
From the *Schatzkammer*
Vienna, Kunsthistorisches Museum, Kunstkammer, inv. no. 1331

The archives show that this is definitely the work of Ottavio Miseroni. In the records of Emperor Ferdinand II's treasurer Nikolaus von Kurland, which list the pieces that Ottavio Miseroni brought with him to Vienna when he arrived from Prague on 5 September 1622, it is described as a 'thrinkgeschir von böhmischen topas mit einer großen doppelden rolln ohne fues' (*Jahrbuch*, vol. 33, 1916, p. CXVI, Regest. 20.608, no. 13). None of the vessels that Ottavio took to Vienna had mounts. The *großen doppelden rolln* is the double scroll on the 'hinge' of the shell. The foot in somewhat lighter smoky quartz originally belonged to a small bowl that had been sent – without a mount – to Rudolf's *Kunstkammer* from the Miseroni workshop in Milan. This shell-shaped bowl would have been much better suited to a flat base, and the foot was only added as the result of a mistake on the part of the Viennese goldsmith who, under Ferdinand II, mounted Ottavio's works in a particularly uncomprehending manner. The ornament added by the same goldsmith is just as superfluous.

Essen and Vienna 1988, cat. no. 373.

Distelberger 1978, pp. 146–48, ill. 130.

R.D.

II.28
Ottavio Miseroni
Milan 1567–Prague 1624
Cup
Burnt smoky quartz, gilt silver
9.9 × 6.1 × 9.7 cms
Before 1622
Prague
From the *Schatzkammer*
Vienna, Kunsthistorisches Museum, Kunstkammer, inv. no. 1475

The Kurland inventory of 1622 (inv. 1331) proves that this small bowl is by Ottavio Miseroni. Kurland described it as follows: 'Mehr von böhmischen gelbliche diemant ein weichkessel, ablanget famounted geschnitten, ohne fues, bedarf kheins'. *Weichkessel* is another name for this particular kind of bowl with a handle. Apart from a handle (now missing), all it would have needed was a circular stand around the base of the crystal, but the goldsmith devised an unnecessary foot which seriously undermines the proportions of the piece. As opposed to the 'soft style' of Ottavio Miseroni's middle period, in this cup he seems to be testing out the possibilities of strictly geometric forms. This delight in playing with logic and abstraction characterise his late period.

Essen and Vienna 1988, cat. no. 706.

Distelberger 1978, p. 150, ill. 133.

R.D.

II.29
Workshop of Ottavio Miseroni
Milan 1567–Prague 1624
Vase
Polished and cut smoky quartz; gold
9.8 × 6.4 × 5.8 cm
Copenhagen, De Danske Kongers Kronologiske Samling, Rosenborg, inv. no. 5228

The thicker a piece of smoky quartz, the more intense its colour, and this small vessel makes full use of this process of light absorption and reflection. The form is dynamic and yet controlled and self-contained. The decoration of faceted stones matches the simplicity of the gold mount.

In Vienna, there are a number of vessels with similarly sharp crystalline forms which Rudolf Distelberger has identified as late works by Ottavio Miseroni.

Copenhagen, Rosenborg 1986, no. 168; Rosenborg 1988, no. 651.

J. Hein 1985, p. 40; Copenhagen 1994, no. 4103.

J.He.

II.30
Ottavio Miseroni; mount: Prague Court Workshop
Milan 1567–Prague 1624
Rudolf II
Chalcedony, underlaid with black, gold-enamelled mount
4.1 × 2.7 cm; mount: 5.6 × 4.1 cm
OM on the arm; *R II* at top right on the mount
Ca. 1590; mount ca. 1600
From the *Schatzkammer*; inventory of 1750, p. 49, no. 250
Vienna, Kunsthistorisches Museum, Kunstkammer, inv. no. XII 58

This cameo is the earliest work that can definitely be attributed to Ottavio Miseroni. In the first place, it is signed and, in the second, Morigia reported in 1595 that Ottavio Miseroni had cut a portrait of the Emperor. The portrait is most probably based on a medallion by Antonio Abondio (see Essen and Vienna, no. 479). Miseroni's portrait cuts the figure of Rudolf in just the same way as Jacopo da Trezzo had done in an earlier work. However, while Miseroni is still formally bound by tradition, his work already displays his own personal artistic style; that is to say, all the forms are drawn very softly. In this piece there remains an element of uncertainty or inhibition in the flow of the lines. The shoulder with the mascaron falling sharply away is insubstantial. The head, rather cramped, seems to be lying on the ruffle around Rudolf's neck as though on a serving dish. As a result the Emperor appears to be rather withdrawn and constrained.

Essen and Vienna 1988, cat. no. 374.

Morigia 1595, p. 292; Eichler-Kris 1927, no. 301; Kris 1929, p. 140 and ill. 595; Bukovinská 1970, p. 187, ill. 1; Bukovinská 1988, p. 161 (with ill.).

R.D.

II.31
Ottavio Miseroni
Milan 1567–Prague 1624
Rudolf II
Onyx; Setting: silver gilt
4.8 × 4.2 cm
Monogram below the neckline: R·II·
Ca. 1606-1610
From the imperial *Schatzkammer*, Inventory of 1750, p. 49, no. 249
Vienna, Kunsthistorisches Museum, Kunstkammer, inv. no. XII 60

In comparison to the earlier portrait cameo of the Emperor (inv. no. XII 58) here the accent is on lordly dignity and de-termination. Rudolf II is portrayed here in advanced years as a Roman Imperator with a crown of laurel leaves. The narrow view go back to portraits of emperors from ancient times, but in this case, half of the neck has also been sacrificed. There has never been any doubt that Ernst Kris was right in attributing this cameo to Ottavio Miseroni. The way various details are carved – above all the formation of the eyes – is typical of Miseroni's work, notwithstanding the fact that he is evidently much more secure here than in the early cameo. Rudolf's features do not give away the date of this piece: for example, all three portraits of Rudolf II by Adriaen de Vries, dated 1603, 1607 and 1609, have the same prominent, bushy eyebrows. Perhaps in this case, the idealisation of Rudolf and his air of an Emperor from ancient times together point towards his death on 20 January 1612, particularly since, during his lifetime, he was invariably portrayed wearing armour.

Essen and Vienna 1988, cat. no. 718

R.D.

II.32
? Ottavio Miseroni
Milan 1567–Prague 1624
Rudolf II
Cameo, onyx
2 × 3 × 5 cm
After 1607
Vienna, Schatzkammer des Deutschen Ordens, inv. no. 3/6

Rudolf II is depicted in three-quarter profile with armour and a ruched collar. The artist used a layer of pink stone for the carving, as well as for the profiled oval frame. This type does not appear among the known cameo portraits of Rudolf II. The Emperor appears in three-quarter profile on the cameo from the Bibliothèque Nationale in Paris, but here he is quite a bit younger, and the type is different from the one in Paris. In his age and the design of the portrait, with the cheeks emphasized, the cameo most closely resembles the bust of Rudolf II sculpted by Adriaen de Vries in 1607. The type of carving is consistent with the work of Ottavio Miseroni, especially the rendering of the hair, the enlarged eyelids and the long, straight nose. This heretofore unknown piece adds another type to the repertoire of portraits of the Emperor carved in stone.

B.B.

II.33
Ottavio Miseroni
Milan 1567–Prague 1624
Mary Magdalen
Relief commesso in various agates and jaspers as well as carnelian on chalcedony plate; Setting: silver gilt
5 × 3.5 cm (7 × 6 cm)
Signed: Ott. M.
Ca. 1602-1605
From the imperial *Schatzkammer*; Inventory 1750, p. 50, no. 254
Vienna, Kunsthistorisches Museum, Kunstkammer, inv. no. XII 820

This lively three-quarter length portrait in the style of a *figura serpentinata* sits securely in its oval setting. Zimmer has pointed out the similarity between this figure and a picture in the Bayerische Staatsgemälde-sammlungen (Zweiggalerie Augsburg), showing the grieving Artemisia and which is attributed to Joseph Heintz the Elder (1564-1609, court painter in Prague after late 1591). Zimmer suggests that both works may be based on an as yet unidentified engraving. However, it is not impossible that Ottavio based his work on the picture itself or on a study for it. In Kris's opinion, the style of this commesso – made from 50 individual pieces – is very close to that of the signed oval commessi on two monstrances in the Geistliche Schatzkammer in Vienna which led him to date it at around 1620. However, the delicate shaping of the relief and other details, such as richer hair and fine hands, would seem to locate this Magdalena rather closer to the *Lady with Feather Fan* (inv. no. XII 140). Rudolf II's death must have intervened before a setting had been made for this piece.

Essen and Vienna 1988, cat. no. 378

R.D.

II.34
Ottavio Miseroni; mount: Prague Court Workshop
Milan 1567–Prague 1624
Lady with a Fan
Relief *commesso* of agate, jasper and carnelian on chalcedony underlaid with black; mount: gold-enamelled, with pearl
8.5 × 5.3 cm
Ca. 1610
Prague
From the *Schatzkammer*; Inventory of 1750, p. 48, no. 242
Vienna, Kunsthistorisches Museum, Kunstkammer, inv. no. XII 140

This piece has been attributed to Ottavio Miseroni because of its similarity to the *Mary Magdalen*. The hair is formed of carnelian, and the slim, almost three-dimensional hands in pink agate show the similarity. The slight anatomical inaccuracy of the left side of the lady's upper body makes it seem likely that Miseroni was not working from a painting or an engraving. The colourful grotesques enamelled on gold on the reverse of the mount are in the style of the Vermeyen workshop, but they do not have the 'body' and inner rhythm of earlier Vermeyen pieces. The goldsmith knew prints by Master GB from 1603, and also probably a series of etchings from 1609 by Esaias van Hulsen with various animals (Schütte 1991, vol. 2/2, V. E. v. Hulsen, 2/1, 2/2, 2/6). However, he distributes the various elements across the composition in the much freer, looser manner that is seen later in work by Mathias Beitler. Thus the goldsmith's work on this piece can have been carried out no earlier than 1610.

Essen and Vienna 1988, cat. no. 377.

Eichler-Kris 1927, no. 303; Kris 1929, pp. 141, 189, ill. 958.

R.D.

II.35
Ottavio Miseroni
Milan 1567–Prague 1624
Bust of *Diana* (?)
Carnelian, agate, jasper, chalcedony
5 × 3.5 cm (5.9 × 4 cm with frame)
Ca. 1605; mount: 1713-18
Rosenborg, inv. 1718, 26 no. 3
Copenhagen, De Danske Kongers Kronologiske Samling, Rosenborg, inv. no. 42142

Hair made from red carnelian (missing in the nape of the neck). Face of white agate with touches of pink. Green jasper garments. Lion's skin in yellow-green jasper (originally covering the right shoulder and breast). Ground in chalcedony painted black on the reverse. In her features and hair-style, this *Diana* is clearly related to the so-called 'Lady with a Feather Fan', which Rudolf Distelberger has dated around 1605 on the basis of its enamelled reverse. The blue enamelled reverse with the acanthus decoration in black and white was added to this *Diana* between 1713 and 1718.

Copenhagen 1994, no. 4142.

J.He.

II.36
Ottavio Miseroni
Milan 1567–Prague 1624
The Penitent Mary Magdalen
Agate
H: 16.4 cm
Inscribed *Ott. M. F.* on the lower front of
the base
Between 1590 and 1600
Inventory of Emperor Matthias 1619, no.
1496; from the *Schatzkammer*; Inventory
1750, p. 36, no. 188
Vienna, Kunsthistorisches Museum,
Kunstkammer, inv. no. 1723

Although the statuette is properly three-

dimensional, it is only intended to be
viewed from the front. The repentant figure's back is covered by broad waves of
hair. The side views show that Ottavio
Miseroni had problems depicting movement and draperies. Be that as it may, this
figure is an extraordinary achievement for
a stone carver, and Miseroni, who never
signed any of his wonderful vessels,
proudly put his name in a prominent position on the small rocky base. The statuette
was evidently appreciated as a rare work
of art because in the inventory from 1619
of Emperor Matthias' estate this work
has its own description: 'Gahr konstreich
gemacht'. Miseroni's small agate bust of

Mary Magdalen in Vienna is anatomically
similar but even more virtuosic in its execution, with one strand of hair floating
free. It is described in the Ambras inventory of 1596 and can therefore be dated before 1595 (the year of death of Archduke
Ferdinand). Thus the full-length *Magdalen*
clearly dates from Ottavio's early days in
Prague.

Essen and Vienna 1988, cat. no. 379.

Kris 1929, pp. 189–90, no. 611; Bukovinská
1970, p. 190, ill. 3.

R.D.

II.37
Ottavio Miseroni
Milan 1567–Prague 1624
Monstrance with *Madonna and Child*
Agate, jasper, carnelian, rock crystal, lapis
lazuli, diamonds, rubies, pearls, gold
enamelling, silver gilt
30 × 19 cm
Signed *Ott. M.* on the left edge of the oval
commesso below the Madonna's elbow
Ca. 1620
From the *Schatzkammer* of the Capuchins;
Inventory of 1626, no. A/4 (4)
Vienna, Kunsthistorisches Museum,
Geistliche Schatzkammer, inv. no. Kap.
219

Even if only the *commesso* is signed, one
may nevertheless safely assume that Ottavio Miseroni planned and carried out
this entire piece, together with a goldsmith, particularly since the node on the
shaft is typical of Ottavio Miseroni's style.
The flat stones may have been supplied by
the Castrucci workshop. Miseroni based
the structure of the aedicule on a little
ebony and jasper altar that Empress Anna
had sent to Prague in order to have a
matching altar made in the Miseroni
workshop. There is a companion piece to
this monstrance, containing relics of St
Anna and with a representation of the
saint in an oval *commesso*, signed by Ot-

tavio Miseroni. The order for these two
reliquaries formed part of the last will and
testament of Anna, the pious wife of Emperor Matthias, on 10 November 1618. It is
possible that the gold enamel work was
executed by Andreas Osenbruck.

Weixlgärtner 1932, p. 89, no. 48; Kris 1929,
pp. 142, 189, ill. 602; Fillitz 1961, p. 71, no.
55; Fillitz / Neumann 1964, pp. 275, 331, ill.
172; Bukovinská, 1970, pp. 189–90, ill. 4;
Krenn 1988, p. XX, no. A 4; *Weltliche und
Geistliche Schatzkammer*, 1991, p. 280, no.
95 (with ill.).

R.D.

II.38
Miseroni workshop in Prague
Venus with Cupid
Agate
8.3 × 10.1 × 11.4 cm
Between 1600 and 1610
Inventory of the Emperor 1619, no. 2184
Vienna, Kunsthistorisches Museum,
Kunstkammer, inv. no. 1730

This statuette, carved out of a single piece
of agate, is intended to be viewed looking
down from an angle. The artist has recreated human forms and movement with
great assurance. This alone casts doubt on
its having been made, as was previously

thought, by Ottavio Miseroni, maker of
the *Mary Magdalen Repentant* (inv. 1723).
In addition the facial details and the hair
do not correspond to Miseroni's usual
forms. On the other hand, they are to be
seen on the three herms in the Viennese
collection (cf. Essen and Vienna, no. 380),
so the master who made this piece was
definitely a Miseroni. Sources refer to two
of Ottavio's brothers, namely Giovanni
Ambrogio Miseroni and Alessandro Miseroni, as imperial stone carvers. Nothing is
known about precisely what they did, but
it could well be that one of them made this
very superior collector's item in Ottavio's
workshop. This statuette is typical of work

by artists at the Prague court and the subject very much reflects the Emperor's own
taste. It may have been made after a model
by Jan Vermeyen, who was in close contact
with the Miseroni workshop and who also
modelled in wax.

Essen and Vienna 1988, cat. no. 381.

Kris 1929, p. 190, ill. 613; Distelberger
1985, p. 283, ill. 271.

R.D.

II.39
? Giovanni Ambrogio Miseroni
Rudolf II
Cameo, agate
8.35 × 6.2 × 1.75 cm
After 1600
Purchased from a private collection 1980
Paris, Bibliothèque Nationale, inv. no.
1980/210

The cameo with a portrait of Rudolf II
was purchased in 1980 from a private collection and its provenance is not known. It is
remarkable for its quality, for the size of
the agate and for the unusual use the artist
made of the interestingly coloured layers

of the stone. He used a dark vein for the relief of the bust, including part of the face,
thus making the work as a whole especially
effective. The attribution of the work poses
a problem because there is no clear model
for this type of portrait or for its artisanal
execution. The artist was apparently intimately acquainted with the work of both
Antonio Abondio and the north Italian
medallion-makers, and that of Hans von
Aachen and Adriaen de Vries. He was undoubtedly active in the circle of the Prague
court, as is attested to by the use of Czech
garnet and agate, which most probably
came directly from Czech quarries. This
three-quarter portrait can be placed in the

same period as the portrait by Hans von
Aachen from ca. 1600. In the details of the
armour and in the facial features, however,
the cameo differs from the graphic work
engraved by Aegidius Sadler after Aachen's
portrait. Of the gem-cutters working in
Prague at the time, we can eliminate Ottavio Miseroni as the author of this work,
for his style is entirely different. The author
may have been the latter's brother, Giovanni Ambroggio, who received a salary in
Prague from 1598 until the Emperor's death

Bukovinská 1986, pp. 129–31.

B.B.

II.40
Miseroni workshop in Prague
Rosary with Double-Sided Cameo with a
Bust of *Christ and the Virgin Mary*
Lapis lazuli; gold, silk ribbon
92 cm, Cameo 6.2 × 4.5 cm (4.8 × 3.5 cm
without setting)
Early 17th century (mounted later)
Documented in the inventories of the St
Vitus' cathedral chapter since 1797
Prague, Treasury of St Vitus' cathedral

The two-sided carved medallion with the
head of Christ on the front side and the
Virgin Mary on the reverse is documented
in the inventories of the Svatovice Trea-

sure as of 1797. It is not known when and
under what circumstances it became a
part of the Treasure. This type of two-sided
medallion depicting this theme, which
took the work of Antonio Abondio as its
model, was very popular in the seventeenth century. It is highly probable that
the cameo was created in the circle of the
Miseroni workshop in Prague, possibly
even by Ottavio Miseroni himself, as is
suggested by a comparison of the reverse
side, showing the Virgin Mary, with his
signed works. The differences arise partly
from the use of an unusual material for
stone carving, because lapis lazuli does
not allow the modelling of more subtle de-

tails. This type of stone was apparently
chosen for some special reason, perhaps
the magical properties that were attributed to it, as Rudolf II's personal physician,
Anselmus Boetius de Boodt, mentions in
his book. The joining of the medallion to
the rosary probably occurred later.

Prague 1891, no. 56; Essen-Vienna 1988,
cat. no. 382.

B. Bukovinská 1974, pp. 58–64.

B.B.

II.41, II.42
Jan Vermeyen
Brussels before 1559–Prague 1608
Emperor Rudolf II on Horseback
Gold
Diameter: 7.9 cm
Circular inscription:
*RVDOLPHVS.II.ROM.IMP.AVG.REX.HV
NG.BOE.*
Ca. 1594
Collection of Rudolf II, Inventory of the
Duke August Library, Wolfenbüttel, Novi
370, fol. 63r.
Berlin, Bode-Museum. Acc. 1825, Fol. 17

Jan Vermeyen
Brussels before 1559–Prague 1608
Emperor Rudolf II on Horseback
Cast silver, no engraving
Diameter: 7.7 cm
Signed below on the edge: *IOHAN FOR-
MAI. F.*
Circular inscription:
*RVDOLPHVS.II.ROM.IMP.AVG.REX.HV
NG.BOE.*
1602–08
Vienna, Kunsthistorisches Museum,
Münzkabinett, inv. no. 22 bß

On the front the Emperor Rudolf II, accompanied by a flying Victoria, is seen on
horseback riding across and over the figure of Discord. On the reverse he is seated
on his throne flanked by allegorical figures of Victory (?) and Peace surrounded
by the six Electors. At his feet, there is a
naked, bound warrior and the trophies of
war. The signature *Johan Formai*, discovered by ter Molen on the edge of the unen-
graved silver version in Vienna is that of
the goldsmith and gemstone carver
known in the literature as *Vermeyen*. His
name appears in the sources in numerous
guises. The Frandfurt records call him,
amongst other things, *Hans Fermey,
Vormeyen* or *Vermeyen* (Zülch / Chytil 1929,
p. 272). The *Kunstkammer* Inventory of
1607-11 calls him *H. Formai*, *Formay* or
Formaiden. The court treasury even refers
to him as *von der Mayden*, *Formayden* and
more (see. Staudinger 1995, p. 263). The
finely engraved version of the medal held
in Berlin was once owned by Rudolf II, as
we know from the Wolfenbüttel Inventory
of the Prague collections: *Ein dito* (= gross
guldener pfening) *ist Kaysser Rudolphi rey-
tendt bildtnuss, auff der andern seyten
sitzendt* (ter Molen 1984). The piece can be
dated with the aid of the miniature by
Joris Hoefnagel in the Viennese *Musterbuch* showing the emperor on his throne
with his electors (DaCosta Kaufmann
1985, illus. on p. 15). The position of the
electors is virtually identical to that on the
medal. Vermeyen was resident in Frankfurt after 1589 at the latest and Hoefnagel
was working there on illustrations for the
Musterbuch between 1591 and 1594. Both
artists were from Antwerp and moved in
the same social circles in Frankfurt. The
occasion for the medal may have been the
Imperial Diet in Regensburg in 1594,
which Hoefnagel attended. Vermeyen
may have been attempting to win favour with
the Emperor with this medal. Although
Vermeyen's style was developed considerably by the time he created the mitre reliefs for the Rudolf crown, nevertheless
many of the details of this medal already
show clearly that it is his work. Vermeyen
was employed as court goldsmith in
Prague in 1597 and, as Staudinger has recently shown, died there in 1608 – not in
1606 as previously thought.

Essen and Vienna 1988, cat. no. 463

Ter Molen 1984, vol. 2, p. 53, no. 205;
Staudinger 1995 (publ. 1996), pp. 263-271
(on Vermeyen)

R.D.

II.43
Mount: Jan Vermeyen; Miseroni work-
shop (cameo)
Brussels before 1559–Prague 1608
Covered Goblet from the Horn of a Nar-
whal
Narwhal horn, enamelled gold, diamonds,
rubies, double cameo in agate
Height: 22.2 cm
Ca. 1600
Probably from the collection of the Em-
peror Rudolf II, Matthias Inventory of
1619, no. 899
Vienna, Kunsthistorisches Museum,
Kunstkammer, inv. no. 1113

In the inventory of the estate of the Emperor Matthias this cup is listed directly
after the insignia. It was one of the most
precious items in the *Schatzkammer*. The
most valuable part of the cup was the 'unicorn' horn itself, which was believed to
have immense healing powers and to be
more effective than anything else against
all manner of poisons. The working of the
gold bears such a striking resemblance to
that of the Rudolf crown that it must have
been carried out by Jan Vermeyen. The
bundles of fruit set into the lilies re-
emerge on the floor of the cup as festoons.
The enamel technique and the colours are
the same here as on the crown. The white
decorations around the diamonds and rubies match those flanking the ruby
obelisks in the small crown lilies. The edge
of the rim is decorated with a very similar
coloured translucent enamel on a white
ground as the bands on the mitre on the
crown. Instead of a knob, the lid has an
exquisite double cameo in the style of the
Miseroni workshop in Milan (see cat. nos
II.49, II.60).

Essen and Vienna 1988, cat. no. 342

Weixlgärtner 1928, pp. 297-299

R.D.

II.44
? Ottavio Miseroni; mount: Jan Vermeyen
Milan 1567–Prague 1624, Brussels before
1559–Prague 1608
Cup
Chalcedony, enamelled gold
Height: 8.2 cm (without handles, 10.2 cm
with handles); Diam: 12.2 cm (17.2 cm
across handles)
Ca. 1600/1605
Kunstkammer of the Emperor Rudolf II,
Inventory of 1607-11, no. 1341
Vienna, Kunsthistorisches Museum,
Kunstkammer, inv. no. 1665

Such a perfect balance of the work of the
stone carver and the goldsmith embodied
in such a fine vessel is truly rare. The simplicity of the shape of the bowl (by no
means common at the time) may well have
been inspired by an antique onyx bowl in
the Emperor's *Kunstkammer*, which was
marginally re-worked in the late sixteenth
century (Vienna, inv. no. 1808, Inventory
of 1607-11, no. 1360; not specified). The
form offers little that might help in determining the artist responsible other than
the fact that his technique was extremely
daring. Towards the rim, the walls are only
1.5 mm thick. In Prague, work of this calibre could only have come from Ottavio
Miseroni's workshop. The masterly gold
work has all the signs of Jan Vermeyen's
hand. The decoration on the base of the
mount is very similar both to that on Ottavio Miseroni's jasper bowl (inv. no. 6866)
and to that on the back of the setting for
Masnago's Madonna cameo (cat. no. II.50).
The enamel on the rim corresponds to the
enamel work on Rudolf II's crown.

Essen and Vienna 1988, cat. no. 343;
Antwerp 1993, p. 296, no. 149B

Distelberger 1985, p. 281, illus. 254

R.D.

II.45
Ottavio Miseron; mount: Jan Vermeyen
Milan 1567–Prague 1624, Brussels before
1559–Prague 1608
Heliotrope Vessel with a Statue of a Little
Bacchus
Heliotrope, enamelled gold
19.3 cm (with Bacchus figure); Width: 17.5
cm, Length: 19.9 cm
Ca. 1600-1605
Kunstkammer of the Emperor Rudolf II;
Inventory of 1607-11, no. 1386
Vienna, Kunsthistorisches Museum, Kun-
stkammer, inv. no. 1871

Ottavio Miseroni was clearly involved in
the design of this piece right from the
start. Instead of the usual folds of the
scroll, Miseroni created a small, flat area
for the green enamelled leaf on which the
little Bacchus figure sits. The mount is in
the style of the Vermeyen workshop as
many of its details show. The enamelled
designs on the outside of the lip were reminiscent of blackwork prints by Hertzich
van Bein and were presumably produced
in the workshop. The Bacchus figure is the
work of the master himself, skilled as he
was in figurative art. The meticulously
carved curls and eyebrows, the engraved
pupils and the fine facial features all set
this work apart from Vianen's nereid on
the jasper jug (inv. no. 1866) with its soft,
flowing lines and generous, almost
painterly, treatment of the hair. The four
small gold heads on the narwhale horn
cup by Vermeyen (cat. no. II.43) are just as
meticulous and detailed.

Essen and Vienna 1988, cat. no. 366;
Antwerp 1993, p. 296, no. 149A

Distelberger 1978, p. 136 -137; ter Molen
1984, no. 29; Distelberger 1985, p. 284;
Giusti 1992, p. 136

R.D.

II.46
Ottavio Miseroni; mount: Prague Court
Workshop
Milan 1567–Prague 1624
Goblet with a Swan
Agate; gold enamel
11.5 cm
Ca. 1600
Reclaimed from the collections of Ulrika
Eleonoras (1688–1741)
Stockholm, Husgerådskammaren, inv. no.
HGK SS 71

The tiny vessel is of a deep oval shell shape
and has a slightly crimped lip, which
forms a shell-shaped pocket on one side,

to which is affixed a small swan figurine
made of gold and decorated with coloured
enamel. This is a typical example of works
from the Prague court workshops and has
many characteristic signs of Ottavio Miseroni's work: the shape of the vessel, the
treatment of the stone, the typically gently
gathered edge and the manner in which
the surface is polished. In its choice of ornament and artistic quality, the gold
mount, with its precisely executed, subtle
decoration, relates to the circle of goldsmithing work that is now associated with
Jan Vermeyen, such as the mounts of the
large jade vessel (cat. no. KK 6846), the
agate vessels with lids (cat. no. KK 1624)

or the jasper bowl (cat. no. KK 1650) and
others. The swan figurine is a graceful detail of decoration, which is often missing
from modern vessels. It is also an isolated
example of a miniature sculptural work. It
is assumed that the bowl came to the royal
collection in Stockholm as part of the
Swedish plunders of war. The relevant
sources, however, do not cite any information that can be related definitively to this
work.

Fogelmark 1982, p. 95, no. 71.

B.B.

II.47
Miseroni workshop; mount: Jan Ver-
meyen
Brussels before 1559–Prague 1606
Covered Goblet
Heliotrope; gold, enamel
13 (8.7 without lid) × 12 × 10.3 cm
Ca. 1600
Rosenborg, inv. 1718, 54 no. 24. Probably
from the collection of the Duke of
Schleswig-Holstein-Gottorp, inv. 1694, 60
no. 24, perhaps from the estate of the
Dowager Duchess Marie Elisabeth, inv.
1689, Allerhandt Stein: no. 25
Copenhagen, De Danske Kongers Krono-
logiske Samling, Rosenborg, inv. no. 1 118

Both the harmonious and balanced form
and the strictly axial, symmetrical decorations point to the Miseroni workshop,
where the shell form was particularly
favoured. This covered bowl could have
been made by the Miseroni family either
in Milan or in Prague, but the sharp lip
makes Prague the more likely of the two.
The partly abstract decorations and the
range of colours of the enamel, as well as
various other features such as the vase-
shaped knob on the lid, are similar to
those on several other mounts assigned by
Rudolf Distelberger to Jan Vermeyen.

J. Hein 1985, p. 40; Copenhagen 1994, no.

4333.

J.He.

II.48
Ottavio Miseroni; mount: Jan Vermeyen
Milan 1567–Prague 1624; Brussels before
1559–Prague 1608
The Virgin Mary
Agate, gold-enamelled
4.3 × 2.2 cm; mount: 5.5 × 3.9 cm
Ca. 1600
From the Münz- und Antikenkabinett
Vienna, Kunsthistorisches Museum,
Kunstkammer, inv. no. XII 21

Like a vision wearing a white veil, the
Madonna stands in front of a white background with her head slightly turned
away. Only her flesh is lightly tinged with

pink. The artist has created this ethereal
effect by means of very shallow relief and
very soft lines. The generous folds of drapery lend the Madonna inner substance. The
details of the figure itself are similar
to those of the signed *Mary Magdalen* (cat.
no. 108, inv. XII 820) and show that this
cameo is the work of Ottavio Miseroni.
The exquisite mount matches the beauty
of the stone. The mount is particularly notable for the extremely high-quality enamel work on the back of the piece. For this
the goldsmith has drawn inspiration from
blackwork designs by Corvinian Saur
from ca. 1591, although without copying
them directly (see Schütte 1989/90, p.

184ff. and ill. 147). This immensely skilled
work is reminiscent of the enamel work on
the base of the mitre on the Rudolf crown.
This would seem to indicate with some
certainty that Jan Vermeyen made this
piece in around 1600.

Essen and Vienna 1988, cat. no. 375;
Antwerp 1993, p. 296, cat. no. 149 C (with
ill.).

Eichler–Kris 1927, no. 306; Distelberger
1985, p. 282 (with ill.); Schütte 1989/90, pp.
184–85 (with ill.).

R.D.

II.49
Miseroni Workshop in Milan; setting: Jan
Vermeyen
Brussels before 1559–Prague 1608
Moorish Girl
Agate, enamelled gold
Cameo: 4.8 × 3.5 cm; setting: 6.5 × 5.2 cm
Cameo: 1560–1600; setting: 1602–08
Probably from the Collection of the
Emperor Rudolf II; later in the Ambras
Collection
Vienna, Kunsthistorisches Museum,
Kunstkammer, inv. no. XII 806

This cameo is a masterpiece of Mannerist
gemmoglyptic art. With the utmost sensi-

tivity towards the character of the stone,
the artist has used the black of the stone
to bring the curve of the figure's shoulder
and her fascinatingly serious head. The
particular sensual charm of this wondrous
piece rests on the contrast between the
velvety, dully gleaming skin with its gentle
curves, the motion of the reddish
draperies that embrace her form and the
pale, finely worked head-dress. Style and
technique link this cameo to the signed
Portrait of a Woman with its reddish flesh
tones (cat. no. II.60) as well as to a second
Moorish Woman (cat. no. II.58). Thus this
piece was clearly also made in the Miseroni workshop in Milan.

The setting is a variation of the setting for
the cameo depicting *Jupiter und Io* and *Aurora* (cat. nos II.51, II.52) which both have
same decoratve inner band and which
have similar scroll work on the frame. This
piece must therefore also have been made
in the workshop of Jan Vermeyen, court
goldsmith to the Emperor Rudolf II.

Essen and Vienna 1988, cat. no. 349

Eichler–Kris 1927, Nr. 297

R.D.

II.50
Alessandro Masnago; setting: Jan
Vermeyen
Fl. in Milan after 1575 until after 1612;
Brussels before 1559–Prague 1608
Madonna with the Child in the Clouds
Agate cameo; setting: enamelled gold
Cameo: 3.3 × 4 cm; setting: 5.5 × 5.5 cm
Cameo: ca. 1590; setting: ca. 1602
Probably from the collection of the Em-
peror Rudolf II; *Schatzkammer* Inventory
1750, p. 6, no. 27.
Vienna, Kunsthistorisches Museum,
Kunstkammer, inv. no. XII 815

This stone, with natural markings that

seem to prefigure the Madonna, is typical
of many Kunstkammer pieces made from
rare or precious natural materials. Masnago worked in Milan predominantly for the
Emperor Rudolf II and was renowned for
his sensitive handling of the colour markings found in agate, which here produced
this remarkable mingling of Nature and
art. This cameo is documented as the work
of Alessandro Masnago by a report by Morigia in his 1595 *Nobilità di Milano*, which
refers to work carried out by the master
for Rudolf II. The setting can be identified
as the work of Jan Vermeyen on the
strength of the stylistic similarity with the
enamelled gold on Rudolf II's crown (com-

pleted in 1602). The central motif with
scrolls is found again both on the lower
band of the crown and on the setting of
the Lucretia cameo (cat. no. II.54), although in this case with small bunches of
fruit. The finely roughened ground and
band of black enamel are familiar from
several other settings by Masnago.

Essen and Vienna 1988, cat. no. 346; Darmstadt 1992, p. 179-180, no. 84 (with illus.);
Antwerp 1993, p. 296, no. 149C

Eichler–Kris 1927, no. 218

R.D.

II.51
Alessandro Masnago; setting: Jan Vermeyen
Fl. in Milan, after 1575–after 1612; Brussels before 1559–1608 Prague
Jupiter and Io
Agate Cameo, reverse painted black; Setting: enamelled gold, pearl
Cameo: 5.4 × 5.8 cm; setting: 7 × 7.5 cm
Cameo: ca. 1600; setting: 1600 until 1608
Probably from the Collection of the Emperor Rudolf II; Matthias Inventory 1619, no. 2227
Vienna, Kunsthistorisches Museum, Kunstkammer, inv. no. XII 15

Masnago's carving of Juno with features that are barely visible with the naked eye could hardly be finer. She holds the delicate peacocks' reigns in her hand. The vivid foreshortening of the figure of Io, transformed into a heifer, intensifies the sadness in the movement of her head towards Jupiter. The scene is lent great depth by the high relief of the carving. The stratification of the agate, its size and distinctly convex form mark it out as a companion piece to another cameo, namely *Jason's Fight for the Fleece* (also held in Vienna, Eichler–Kris 1927, no. 210), which is signed by Alessandro Masnago. In his design for the mount, Jan Vermeyen then takes up and develops these imaginative variations on an old theme, which started with *Lucretia* and the *Madonna in the Clouds* (cat. nos II.50, II.54). The scrolls on the main axis with the fine, small golden heads, the small bundles of fruit and the garlands along the lateral axis, heightened here largely with red and white enamel, are all typical of Vermeyen's repertoire.

Essen and Vienna 1988, cat. no. 348

Eichler–Kris 1927, no. 211

R.D.

II.52
? Alessandro Masnago; setting: Jan Vermeyen
Fl. in Milan after 1575–after 1612
Brussels before 1559–Prague 1608
Aurora
Agate Cameo, reverse painted black; Setting: enamelled gold
Cameo: 3.8 × 4.2 cm; setting 5.4 × 5.4
Cameo: late 16th century; setting: ca. 1605
Probably from the collection of the Emperor Rudolf II; from the *Schatzkammer*
Vienna, Kunsthistorisches Museum, Kunstkammer, inv. no. XII 134

Until now this cameo has generally been attributed to Jacopo da Trezzo (ca. 1514–1589), since the image is almost identical with that on the reverse of a medal signed by him in 1552 portraying the seventeen-year-old Ippolita Gonzaga. However, the style of this cameo is much closer to Alessandro Masnago's work. There are slight variations in the landscape. Where Trezzo has a river with a rower, here the water has become a bay pushing back the mountains on the right. Altogether the landscape on the cameo is cut off more distinctly from the dawn scene. Masnago added a small cloud above Pegasus. Minute details on the miniaturised objects are just as on other cameos known to be by Masnago. In addition, the high relief and the fondness for rose agate are wholly typical of Masnago. The setting was made in Jan Vermeyen's workshop in Prague, and is similar in technique to the cameo, *Jupiter and Io* (cat. no. II.51) and the large *Moorish Woman* (cat. no. II.49).

Essen and Vienna 1988, cat. no. 722

Eichler–Kris 1927, no. 202 (with older bibliography; Kris 1929, pp. 82, 172, illus. 325; Hackenbroch 1979, p. 199, illus. 555

R.D.

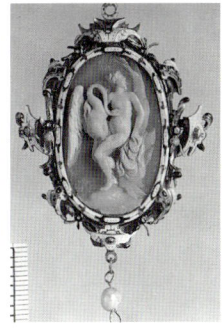

II.53
In the style of Alessandro Masnago; mount: Jan Vermeyen Workshop
Fl. in Milan, after 1575–after 1612
Brussels before 1559–Prague 1608
Leda and the Swan
Agate cameo, painted black on the reverse; setting: enamelled gold, pearl
Cameo: 3.4 × 2.3 cm; setting: 5.7 × 4.4 cm
Cameo: ca. 1600; setting: 1603 until 1608
Probably from the collection of the Emperor Rudolf II; *Schatzkammer* Inventory of 1750, p. 26, no. 144 (?)
Vienna, Kunsthistorisches Museum, Kunstkammer, inv. no. XII 14

Depicted here is the moment when Leda defends the swan from the eagle pursuing it (although the latter is not in the field of vision here). Some of the details of the carving seem a little hasty, which in itself links this cameo to a group of cameos attributed to the workshop of Alessandro Masnago and which are also made of rose quartz. The setting is in keeping with work from the Vermeyen workshop. The inner circle of white, red and blue is repeated only mildly varied on the foot-ring of the green jasper bowl by Ottavio Miseroni (inv. no. 1650). The translucent enamel design on the reverse clearly owes a debt to the blackwork prints from 1603 by the master known only as GB, which themselves show the influence of a print by Hans Hensel (Bukovinská 1982, pp. 78-79). This plate is, however, not as finely engraved as the one on the reverse of Ottavio Miseroni's *Madonna* (inv. no. XII 21). Other motifs by the master GB on similar mounts suggests that he may have been employed in the Vermeyen workshop.

Essen and Vienna 1988, cat. no. 350

Eichler – Kris 1927, no. 229; Hackenbroch 1979, no. 551; Bukovinská 1982, pp. 78-79

R.D.

II.54
? Alessandro Masnago; setting: Jan Vermeyen
Fl. in Milan after 1575–after 1612; Brussels before 1559–Prague 1608
Lucretia
Agate cameo; setting: enamelled gold
Cameo: 3.5 × 2.4 cm; setting: 5.8 × 5.2 cm
Cameo: ca. 1590-1600, setting: ca. 1602
Probably from the collection of the Emperor Rudolf II; Matthias Inventory of 1619, no. 926 (or 933?); *Schatzkammer* Inventory of 750, p. 10, no. 50
Vienna, Kunsthistorisches Museum, Kunstkammer, inv. no. XII 97

Ernst Kris attributed this cameo to Jacopo da Trezzo (ca. 1514–1589), basing his argument above all on the heavy-limbed forms and on the delicately gathered, close-fitting clothes. However, the depiction of draperies is the one area where Trezzo was more generous and imaginative, using these to lend his figures volume and inner stature. Furthermore, one could not fault with anatomy of his human figures, as is all too easy in the case of this Lucretia. These 'faults' suggest Masnago's work, as does the use of high relief, most noticeably here in the hands. The somewhat awkward movement of Lucretia's left arm recurs on the figure of Jupiter in the cameo depicting the story of Io (cat. no. II.51). Masnago used the same agate for other cameos, and it is also not unusual for his stones to have an irregular form. Kris identified the enamelled gold setting as the work of the master who made Rudolf II's crown (completed in 1602), whom we now know to have been Jan Vermeyen. The central motif on the lateral axis is used again with the double pearls on the crown.

Essen and Vienna 1988, cat. no. 345

Eichler–Kris, 1927, no. 204 (with older bibliography); Hackenbroch 1979, no. 556

R.D.

II.55
Jan Vermeyen (attr.)
Brussels before 1559–Prague 1606
Front: *Danae*; back: *The Judgment of Paris*
Chiselled cast silver
8.3 cm
After 1600
Vienna, Kunsthistorisches Museum, Münzkabinett, 582 bß
Recto: *FVLMINE NON POTVIT, POTVIT QVOD IVPPITER AVRO* ('What Jupiter could not accomplish with lightning, he achieved with gold'). Jupiter with the eagle and lightning is plunging down towards the recumbent Danae; a maidservant is catching the golden coins raining down from the sky. Verso: *APTA VENVS IVVENI MAGIS EST, IGNOSCATE DIVAE* ('Oh goddesses, do you not know that Venus is more suited to the youth?') Paris is giving Aphrodite the prize; to her left are Hera and Pallas Athene, there is a river god in front, Hermes is behind and Helios with his sun-chariot is up above the scene.

In the past this medal has been attributed to Paulus van Vianen. However, ter Molen (1984) has suggested that it is by the same artist who made the medal of Rudolf II on horseback. This medal, in the Vienna version, is signed 'IOHAN FORMEL' on the edge, which ter Molen has tentatively suggested may refer to Jan Vermeyen.

Essen and Vienna 1988, cat. no. 821

Dworschak 1926, 239; Habich 11/2 1934, no. 3566; ter Molen 1984, I, p. 26; II no. 206

K.Sch.

II.56
Unknown Master; mount: Andreas Osenbruck?
Fl. in Prague ca. 1610–after 1622
Round Covered Bowl
Agate, enamelled gold
14.5 × 17.2 cm (including handle);
Diameter: 11.4 cm
Ca. 1610
From the imperial *Schatzkammer*
Vienna, Kunsthistorisches Museum,
Kunstkammer, inv. no. 1985

This simple carved piece defies exact definition. It is not made to such a high standard as the similarly shaped chalcedony

bowl (cat. no. II.44). The only possible explanation is the fact that this bowl is made in a less precious stone, for this kind of work involved was supposed never to be more costly than the stone itself. However, it is clear that this piece was made in Prague because the handles are copies of the chalcedony bowl by Vermeyen, although not of the same quality as the work of the court gemstone carver. Here the branch-shaped clasps have been somewhat straightened and the vines have been slightly simplified. The dynamic sweep of the horn of plenty handle has been lost. The attribution of this work to Osenbruck is speculative. It is based on

the style of the work which bears a close resemblance to that on his signed sceptre. When Osenbruck was working on the insignia (the sceptre and the imperial orb) he had to match as closely as possible the style Vermeyen had created for the imperial crown. Bukovinská even suggests that Osenbruck may have worked in the Vermeyen workshop.

Essen and Vienna 1988, cat. no. 711

Distelberger 1985, p. 281

R.D.

II.57
Attributed to Andreas Osenbruck
Seventeen Pendants with Figural Motifs
Gold, enamel, diamonds, rubies, pearls
Early seventeenth century
Recovered from the inventories of the chapter in 1738
Prague, Treasury of St Vitus' cathedral

The set of seventeen pendants was placed on a monstrance, which is repeatedly listed in the Svatovice Treasure inventories from 1739 onwards as a gift of the provost Jan Dlouhoveský of Dlouhá Ves (1674–1701). According to the note that accompanied the reliquary, the jewels originally

decorated the wedding clothes of Johann Christian Eggenberg and Ernestina Schwarzenberg. It is possible that the pendants were originally part of a sumptuous chain. The largest piece with two female figures – possibly allegories of Peace and Justice – has a loop at the top and could have constituted the main pendant. The remaining pieces are related to Orpheus and are divided into two ensembles made up of mammals and birds, but the central ornamentation consists of precious stones in one series and a group of five pearls framed by a cornucopia in the other. In their secondary use on the monstrance, the jewels were adapted to their

new function, so that for example the main pendant was drastically shortened. On the basis of a comparison of the pendants with the imperial sceptre, which is a signed and dated work by Andreas Osenbruck from 1615, R. Distelberger has included them in the works of this court goldsmith. This set of jewels from the early seventeenth century is exceptional in the Czech collections for its size.

Essen and Vienna 1988, cat. no. 337.

Podlaha-Šittler 1903, no. 185.

B.B.

II.58
Miseroni workshop in Milan; setting:
Andreas Osenbruck
Fl. in Prague ca. 1610–after 1622
Moorish Girl
Agate, enamelled gold, diamonds, rubies
Cameo: 3.8 × 2.8 cm; setting: 6 × 5.1 cm
(with hook 5.95 cm)
Cameo: after 1575; setting: ca. 1610
Matthias Inventory of 1619, no. 941
Vienna, Kunsthistorisches Museum,
Kunstkammer, inv. no. XII 108

This cameo is carved from the same rare stone and in the same style as the larger *Moorish Woman* (cat. no. II.49). Thus it is

clearly also from the Miseroni workshop. It comes from a small group of female portraits in high relief, all distinctly anti-classical in aspect – although this is expressed in quite a different manner than in Masnago's work. Here, the artist is engaged in a lively 'conversation' with Nature, as it were, rather than setting out to emulate antiquity. This was the reason for working with a constantly expanding range of stones, even although this was also in part dictated by whoever had commissioned any given piece. In their handling of various motifs, the Miseronis always had one eye on developments in contemporary small-scale sculpture, as for example here

in the artful counter-motion of shoulders and head which calls to mind thoughts of the *figura serpentinata*, fashionable then in painting and sculpture. Only the smooth ground, which the figure is set against, recalls the traditions of antiquity. The setting is identical to that of the portrait of a woman (cat. no. II.60) and was also made by Andreas Osenbruck.

Eichler-Kris 1927, no. 298 (with older bibliography)

R.D.

II.59
Miseroni workshop in Prague; setting:
Andreas Osenbruck
Fl. in Prague 1612–after 1622
Madonna
Agate cameo; setting: enamelled gold, two rubies, two diamonds
Cameo: 3.5 × 2.2 cm; setting: 6.5 × 5 cm
Ca. 1610
From the imperial *Schatzkammer*; Inventory of 1750, p. 6, no. 23
Vienna, Kunsthistorisches Museum,
Kunstkammer, inv. no. XII 31

Not only did Ernst Kris show how close this cameo is in its style to work by Ottavio

Miseroni, but he also recognised that a second artist had a hand in this piece. This is most readily evident if this work is compared with Ottavio's Madonna cameo (inv. no. XII 21). The difference between the two pieces resides above all in the sharper and more telling carving of detail on this piece, which is thereby lent a deeper level of expression. The clear lines of the eyebrows, the precise lines of the eyelids and the clear articulation of the hand are not characteristic of Ottavio's style. The other artist involved here is more skilled in depicting human physiognomy. Since this other artist's style is not in keeping with Milanese glyptics, the piece must, there-

fore, have been made in Prague, perhaps by one of Ottavio's brothers: two of whom – Giovanni Ambrogio and Alessandro – worked as hardstone carvers. But so far it has not been possible to positively identify any single work by either. The setting is incomplete yet clearly one of a series by Andreas Osenbruck.

Essen and Vienna 1988, cat. no. 720

Eichler-Kris 1927, no. 315

R.D.

II.60
Miseroni workshop in Milan; setting:
Andreas Osenbruck
Fl. in Prague 1612–after 1622
Portrait of a Woman
Agate, enamelled gold, diamonds, rubies
Cameo: 3.5 × 2.8 cm; setting: 6.1 × 5.5 cm
(with hook: 6.3 cm)
Signed on the left arm: M
Cameo: 1570–1600; setting: ca. 1610
Matthias Inventory of 1619, no. 939 or 940; *Schatzkammer* Inventory of 1750, p. 16, no. 85
Vienna, Kunsthistorisches Museum,
Kunstkammer, inv. no. XII 149

This cameo is the key item in a small group of works. The letter M (not MI) on the left arm, barely visible through the setting stands, for the name Miseroni. However, it is not known which member of the family specialised in this particular form of glyptic art. Presumably it was one of the sons of Gasparo who died in 1573, none of whose names we know. Girolamo went to Spain in 1584, after his son had already gone there in 1582. This reading of the letter M is supported by the two cameos depicting Moorish women (cat. nos II.49, II.58), which are carved in the same style. Kris shows similarities in these rich draperies with those on medals by Gian

Antonio Signoretti (fl. in Reggio Emilia 1540–1602) (cf. Pollard 1984, pp. 1343–44, nos 785, 786). The setting comes from a group of works made in Andreas Osenbruck's workshop, which are clearly very closely related to his sceptre head of 1615 (Essen and Vienna 1988, p. 442, illus. 66).

Essen and Vienna 1988, cat. no. 714

Eichler-Kris 1927, no. 296; Kris 1929, pp. 88, 175, illus. 384; Steingräber 1956, p. 112 and illus. 184

R.D.

II.61
Ottavio Miseroni workshop; mount: Andreas Osenbruck (attr.)
Fl. in Prague 1612–after 1622
Jug with Cover
Jasper, enamelled gold, garnets
14.8 × 6.4 × 11.2 cm
Ca. 1615
Matthias Inventory of 1619, no. 3541
Vienna, Kunsthistorisches Museum, Kunstkammer, inv. no. 2026

This red jasper with green running through could well have come from the same location as the stone used for the oval jasper bowl (inv. no. 6866) and the ea-gle bowl (inv. no. 6831) by Ottavio Miseroni. The simple, turned, faintly conical form and two rings of moulding offer little to assist in its attribution. Only the lid, sinking slightly inwards towards the middle section might point towards Ottavio Miseroni's workshop, because exactly this feature is found on the foot of the monstrance (inv. Kap. 219). In addition, there is also the fact that Ottavio had this kind of jasper in his workshop. The flat base of this little jug has been glued and is further secured by the mount. The gold enamel work on the handle most closely resembles the strong scrolls both on the sceptre head by Andreas Osenbruck (1615) which is now in the Viennese *Schatzkammer* and those on his settings for cameos (cf. cat. nos II.58, II.60). The way the gold enamel work has been carried out is also identical with the work on these other pieces. Osenbruck was a court goldsmith to the Emperor Matthias.

Essen and Vienna 1988, cat. no. 383

R.D.

II.62
Cosimo Castrucci
In imperial service after 1592
Landscape with a Bridge and Chapel
Commesso of agate and jasper; wooden frame
18.3 × 24.5 cm (without frame)
Inscribed and signed on the reverse: *Cosimo Castrucci Flor(en)tino FEcit Anno 1596* (*F* and *E* upper-case with ligature)
1596
From the *Schatzkammer* (probably from the *Kunstkammer* of Emperor Rudolf II)
Vienna, Kunsthistorisches Museum, Kunstkammer, inv. no. 3037

This *commesso* is of key importance because it is the only one to be signed and dated, although there is debate as to whether the crucial numeral giving the decade should be read as a '7' or a '9'. Neumann, who discovered the signature, decided it must be 1576 (Neumann 1957, pp. 184, 199). Fock (Fock 1988, p. 56, n. 16) and Distelberger (Essen 1988, p. 460) agree. Vincent, Bukovinská und Giusti are instead inclined to read it as 1596 (Vincent 1987, p. 165, n. 37; Bukovinská in Essen 1988, no. 384; Giusti 1992, p. 138). Palaeographic examination of the two doubtful numerals comes down on the side of 9. While the Prague *commessi* are all fixed to slate, this landscape is mounted in a copper frame with considerable amounts of rust on the back. The panel was probably made as a piece in its own right in Florence.

Essen and Vienna 1988, cat. no. 384.

Neumann 1957, p. 184, 194–96, 199, no. 1, ill. 197; Vincent 1987, p. 165 (with ill.); Distelberger 1988, p. 460; Fock 1988, p. 52; Heikamp 1988, p. 232; Giusti 1992, p. 138, ill. 40.

R.D.

II.63
Cosimo Castrucci (attributed)
In imperial service after 1592
Landscape with the Sacrifice of Isaac
Commesso di pietre dure in agate and jasper on slate: Frame: gilded wood
43.3 × 57.7 cm
Ca. 1600
From the imperial *Schatzkammer*; Inventory of 1750, p. 611, no. 2
Vienna, Kunsthistorisches Museum, Kunstkammer, inv. no. 3411

The composition follows the same schema as *Landscape with Chapel and Bridge* (inv. no. 3037) which is signed by Cosimo Castrucci. A spatial diagonal crosses front left to back right, separating the strongly coloured, large-scale foreground from the paler, smaller-scale background. As on the *Landscape with Chapel and Bridge* a mighty tree provides a formal framework for the scene. This scene is no more than the setting for the most magnificent world-landscape of any *commesso* ever made. The right half of the picture opens the view to expanses of water, air and earth. The complexity of the design of this landscape is without equal. The artistic ideas underpinning Cosimo's small 1596 panel are taken here to their ultimate conclusion. No other artist shared Cosimo's ability to achieve such utterly painterly effects with coloured stones – even to the extent of creating aerial perspective. Landscapes were of particular interest to the Emperor Rudolf II. In 1595 he inherited the *Months* series by Pieter Breugel the Elder (1525/30–1569) from the Archduke Ernst.

Essen and Vienna 1988, cat. no. 390.

Neumann 1957, pp. 188, 200, no. 21; Przyborowski 1982, p. 257, no. 8.3f.

R.D.

II.64
Giovanni Castrucci
Fl. in Prague 1598–? 1615
Landscape with a Well and Dead Trees
Commesso di pietre dure in agate and jasper on slate; Frame: wood
14.7 × 20.1 cm
Before 1611
Kunstkammer of the Emperor Rudolf II; Inventory of 1607–11, no. 2812
Vienna, Kunsthistorisches Museum, Kunstkammer, inv. no. 3002

This small panel can be identified from the Inventory of the Emperor Rudolf II's Kunstkammer as the work of Giovanni Castrucci: *Ein Quadretto von Jo: Castruzio, ist ein Landtschafftl von hartten Stainen, darin ein Figürlin bey einem Schnellbrunnen, und drey dürre Bäum. Empfangen 23. Aug: A⁰. 1611.* Entry also provides a useful *terminus ante quem*. The way that somewhat simplified landscape elements are decoratively layered parallel to the picture plane, a characteristic of Giovanni's personal style. In fact his reductionism has led some to take this panel for a copy of the piece listed in the Inventory (González / Palacios / Röttgen 1982, p. 84). This is based on the idea that Giovanni Castrucci was a better artist than his father Cosimo, of whom less is known. In fact the opposite is the truth. This small panel has a companion piece of a very similar size in the Vienna collection, which is also framed in petrified wood.

Florence 1980, p. 244, no. 471; Essen and Vienna 1988, cat. no. 729

Neumann 1957, pp. 185, 186, 199, no. 4, illus. 203; González /Palacios / Röttgen 1982, p. 84; Vincent 1987, pp. 165f.; Giusti 1992, p. 164, illus. 43

R.D.

II.65
Giovanni Castrucci
Fl. in Prague 1598–1615
Landscape with an Obelisk and the Imperial Coat of Arms
Commesso di pietre dure in agate and jasper on slate; Frame: wood
34.2 × 49.3 cm
Before 1611
Kunstkammer of the Emperor Rudolf II; Inventory of 1607–11, no. 2813
Vienna, Kunsthistorisches Museum, Kunstkammer, inv. no. 3397

The Inventory of 1607–11 lists this piece as the work of Giovanni Castrucci: *Ein groß Quadretto von Joh: Castruzzi handt, von harten Stainen, darin ein Furman mit geladenem wagen und eine Gulia [Obelisk], daran des Römischen Kaysers wappen mit dem Adler, Kron und Flüß [Vlies].* This entry comes between two others referring to objects which come into the *Kunstkammer* in 1611. As Neumann has shown, it is based on an engraving of 1599 by Johann Sadeler I (1550–ca. 1600) after Lodewijk Toeput (who worked in Italy under the name Lodovico Pozzoserrato, ca. 1550–1603/05). A comparison with the engraving is revealing: Castrucci was simply not able to create an illusion of spatial depth. On the one hand, he changed the original composition, stacking the landscape as it were in layers parallel to the picture plane. On the other hand, he did not lighten the colours enough towards the background. Giovanni Castrucci joined his father Cosimo in Prague in 1598 and most probably ran the *commessi* workshop after 1602.

Essen and Vienna 1988, no. 388

Neumann 1957, pp. 185, 199, no. 3, illus. 201; Fillitz-Neumann 1964, pp. 275, 331, illus. 169; Vincent 1987, pp. 163–165; Giusti 1992, p. 140

R.D.

II.66
? Giovanni Castrucci
Fl. in Prag 1598–1615
View of Prague Castle
Commesso di pietre dure in agate and jasper
on slate; frame: wood
11.5 × 23.8 cm (without frame)
After 1606
From the imperial *Schatzkammer*
Vienna, Kunsthistorisches Museum,
Kunstkammer, inv. no. 3060

This *commesso* is based on two earlier
works. The first of these is the woodcut
from 1601, *View of Prague*, by Johann Willenberg (1571–1613). This woodcut gives

the *commesso* its main features and their
relation to each other, particularly the position of the belvedere and the sweep of
the river Moldau. The second work influencing this piece was the large engraving
by Johannes Wechter (ca. 1550–after
1606), which Aegidius Sadeler (1570–
1629) published in 1606. A total of three
commesso views of Hradčany have survived:
this one follows the graphical works most
closely; a second, like this one, is now also
held in Vienna, and a third in Prague.
There was a fourth variant in the Kunstkammer of the Elector Maximilian of
Bavaria but this is now lost (Neumann
1957, p. 188, n. 115). This panel may safely

be attributed to Giovanni Castrucci on
the strength of other items documented
as his work. It is typical of his style above
all in its lacking sense of space as well as in
the relatively dull range of colours.

Essen and Vienna 1988, cat. no. 726.

Neumann 1957, pp 187f., 200, no. 19, illus.
205; Fillitz-Neumann 1964, p. 331, illus.
168; Bukovinská 1972, p. 365; Poche 1979,
p. 170; Bukovinská 1983, pp. 444-446;
Bukovinská 1988, p. 166; Giusti 1992, p.
141, illus. 46.

R.D.

II.67
Giovanni Castrucci
Banquet of Abraham
16 × 44 cm
1610–1622
Florence, Museo dell' Opificio delle Pietre
Dure, inv. no. 1905, n. 460

After extensive research in the archives of
Florence, C. Przyborowski demonstrated
that this panel, which depicts Abraham receiving the three angels, was commissioned from Giovanni Castrucci in Prague
after 1606 by Grand Duke Ferdinand I de'
Medici for the altar of the family chapel in
San Lorenzo in Florence. After Castrucci's

death in 1615, Cosimo II de' Medici requested that the work be continued by
Cosimo Castrucci the Younger and Giuliano di Pietro Pandolfini. It was executed
according to coloured drawings by
Bernardino Poccetti between 1610 and
1622, and features the use of typical Czech
agates. The information discovered by
Przyborowski is important, for it pushes
the assumed date of Giovanni's death forward and documents the existence of his
son Cosimo and son-in-law Giuliano di
Pietro Pandolfini, whose activities in
Prague were heretofore completely unknown. It also sheds light on the activities
of the Castrucci workshop in Prague after

the Emperor's death and attests to the unusually close ties between Prague and Florence during this period.

Florence 1988, p. 118, no. 18 (see also older
literature here).

Przyborowski 1982, pp. 140 ff.; Giusti 1992,
pp. 169 ff., colour ill.

B.B.

II.68
Castrucci workshop
Altarpiece with St Jerome
Lacquered wood, silver; agate, amethyst,
garnet
64 × 45 × 10 cm
Early seventeenth century
Benediktinerstift Kremsmünster Kunst-
sammlungen, inv. no. N 31660

The miniature architecture of this altar for
the home has a panel depicting St Jerome
in the central field. The columns and some
of the panels are executed in agates of various colours; the central panel and the
oval panel on a pedestal with the attribute

of the saint are *commesso in pietre dure*. E.
Neumann has pointed out the work's connection to the small altar with *St Margaret*
from the Lobkowitz collection in Prague
and has attributed the work to the circle of
the Prague court workshops. The composition of the central panel with the kneeling penitent in a rocky landscape is based
on the same principle as the *commesso* with
the penitent Margaret, and its author was
a member of the circle of Giovanni Castrucci, whose work with figural themes
has been documented by C. Przyborowski
(1982). The issues of interconnection of
the workshops of the court gem-cutters in
Prague, the definition of their specializa-

tion, their mutual cooperation and the
role of individuals in the creation of specific works are far from solved. The participation of the Miseroni workshop in the
creation of this work cannot be ruled out,
especially if the various details, including
the small vases, are compared with the
miniature altars attributed to Ottavio Miseroni on the basis of a signed central
medallion.

E. Neumann 1963, p. 80; E. Neumann 1977,
no. 247, p. 52; Hagenmann-Bischof 1988,
pp. 84-104.

B.B.

II.69
Caspar Lehmann
Uelzen 1563/65–Prague 1622
Goblet with the *Coat of Arms of Wolf Sig-
mund of Losenstein and Susanna of Rogen-
dorf and Three Allegorical Figures*
Clear glass, engraved
H: 23 cm
On the lower part of the outer surface: *C.
LEMAN.F.1605*; above the figures are the
inscriptions *POTESTAS. NOBILITAS. LIB-
ERALITAS.*
1605
Hluboká Castle
Prague, Uměleckoprůmyslové Muzeum,
inv. no. Z–279/1

The conical beaker has a bell-shaped foot
and depictions of three seated female figures. Nobilitas holds the combined Losenstein and Rogendorf coats of arms, Potestas holds a sceptre and a palm branch, and
Liberalitas a globe and a purse full of
money. Wolf Sigmund von Losenstein was
the military and imperial counsel to
Rudolf II and the court marshal of
Matthias I and Ferdinand II. As his wedding took place in Linz in 1592, the beaker
cannot have been made for that occasion.
The model for the design was a bronze engraving by Johannes Sadeler on the title
page of the celebratory publication
Schema seu speculum principium from 1597,

dedicated to Karl Emanuel of Savoy and
Katerina of Austria. As the only piece bearing Lehmann's signature, this beaker has
become the defining piece used in the attribution of other works by Caspar
Lehmann.

Prague 1970 and 1984.

Chytil 1892, pp. 73–74; Schmidt 1922, p.
233; Jiřík 1934, pp. 58–59, 103–4; Hetteš
1953, p. 10; Meyer-Heisig 1963, p. 119;
Pešatová 1968, p. 55; Koula 1969, p. 546;
Drahotová 1981, p. 36.

O.D.

II.70
Caspar Lehmann
Uelzen 1563/65–Prague 1622
Covered Ewer with Caryatids
Polished and engraved crystal, gilded sil-
ver, garnets
H: 14.5 cm
Ca. 1605
From the *Kunstkammer*
Vienna, Kunsthistorisches Museum,
Sammlung für Plastik und Kunstgewerbe,
inv. no. 1.387

The cylindrical body of the vessel is concave in the lower part and is mounted with
flat garnets around the edge of the lid and

foot. The gilded silver handle is decorated
in a similar manner and has a maenad at
the top. The outer surface is decorated
with three caryatids in vertical fields between bunches of fruit. The female figures, flowers and bunches of fruit are
closely related to the 1605 beaker signed
by Lehmann (Prague, Uměleckoprůmyslové Muzeum), as well as to the Prague
panel with the *Portrait of Christian II*. Together with the Dresden goblet with Diana and Actaeon in the Grünes Gewölbe
collection, this jug is one of the only surviving works that demonstrate Lehmann's
ability to work in stone.

Vienna and Essen 1988, cat. no. 355; Darmstadt 1993, cat. no. 50.

O.D.

II.71
Caspar Lehmann
Uelzen 1563/65–Prague 1622
Portrait of Christian II, Elector of Saxony
Engraved clear glass
25 × 19 cm
On the upper part:
CHRIST:II:D:G:DUX:SAX:ELE:
Gift of Sir Vojtěch Lanna 1906
Prague, Uměleckoprůmyslové Muzeum,
inv. no. 10.341

The oblong panel is decorated with a bust of the Elector in right profile, enclosed in an oval medallion and crowned by an elector's hat. The medallion is framed on either side by caryatids and cornucopias. Under the medallion are the emblems of Saxony and Meissen under an olive tree. The panel with the *Portrait of Christian II* is one of Lehmann's finest works; the ornamental decor relates to the floral decorations from the circle of the Hoefnagels, and the portrait was undoubtedly engraved after a Saxon medallion. Given the excellent quality of the engraving and the detailed ornamental decoration, which was undoubtedly executed using a sketch by one of the Prague court artists, it is more plausible to assume that the work was created in Prague to mark the occasion in 1602 when Christian obtained the distinction of electoral rank, than to accept the later dating of the work to Lehmann's stay in Dresden in 1606 to 1607. The coloured glass frame dates from the nineteenth century.

Prague 1970, cat. no. 282; Corning 1981, cat. no. 11; Prague 1984, cat. no. 94.

Schmidt 1922, p. 234; Holzhausen 1934, p. 88; Jiřík 1934, p. 59; Meyer-Heisig 1963, p. 99; Drahotová 1981, p. 36.

O.D.

II.72
Caspar Lehmann
Uelzen 1563/65–Prague 1622
Panel with the *Portrait of Ludwig V. of Hessen-Darmstadt*
Clear glass, engraved
15.9 × 12 cm
Early seventeenth century
Prague
From the ducal collections of Darmstadt
Darmstadt, Hessisches Landesmuseum, inv. no. Kg.80:2

The oblong panel is decorated with a half-portrait of the Duke in profile, facing left. Dressed in armour and flaring trousers, he is leaning on a table and holds a marshal's staff in his left hand. Both the composition, and the careful rendering of the details of the armour closely relate this depiction to the portraits of Rudolf II (Vienna, Kunsthistorisches Museum) and to the somewhat later portrait of *Heinrich Julius of Braunschweig* (Dresden, Grünes Gewölbe). It is now possible, on the basis of the signed beaker from 1605, to attribute a number of works to Lehmann; the most important of these date to the years 1590–1605, during which he worked in close collaboration with the artists of the Prague court circle. Lehmann's portraits of Rudolf II's friends and political allies are generally more carefully engraved than his earlier mythological and allegorical scenes, which were modelled on contemporary illustrations. He was undoubtedly highly dependent on the quality of the model; accordingly, the quality of his own work varies markedly. His activities in Prague, however, certainly contributed to increasing the awareness and recognition of glyptic work on glass in the Czech milieu.

Meyer-Heisig 1963, p. 127; Meyer-Heisig 1967, p. 122.

O.D.

II.73
Caspar Lehmann
Ueizen 1563/65–Prague 1622
Portrait of the Duke Heinrich Julius of Braunschweig-Lüneburg
Glass: engraved; Frame: wood
20.7 cm x 15.5 cm (with frame): 16.2 cm x 11.3 cm (without frame)
Probably 1610
Acquired in 1884 for the Grünes Gewölbe from the art dealer Salomon in Dresden for only 60 Reichsmarks.
Dresden, Grünes Gewölbe. inv. no. 1884/3

There is widespread agreement that this portrait was engraved between 1610 and 1613, during Lehmann's last years as an artist to the imperial court. The year 1610 itself was particularly important for Duke Heinrich Julius of Braunschweig in his standing with the Emperor and the empire's nobility and saw him at the height of his political and diplomatic powers. This context more than explains the inclusion of his election slogan at the lower edge of the portrait: 'HONESTUM PRO PATRIA' (Honesty for the Fatherland). If 1610 is to be regarded as the most likely date of production for this glass portrait by Lehmann, then the 'Fürstenconvent' held in the same year, and attended by Christian II, will have been the last chance for the Duke to give it as a present to his close relative from Dresden before the latter's the following year.

Löbe 1883, p. 54; Meyer-Heisig 1967, p. 128; cf. Mol 1984, cat. no. 16 (Gold cup by van Vianen for the Duke); Brockmann 1985, pp. 53–55; Lietzmann 1993, pp. 26ff.

J.K.

II.74
Caspar Lehmann
Uelzen 1563/65–Prague 1622
Allegory Representing Peace Triumphant Over War
Engraved clear glass
23 × 18.9 cm
Ca. 1609
From a private collection in England, sold at auction at Christie's, London, 3 June 1986
The Corning Museum of Glass, inv. no. 86.3.100

A crowned female figure sitting on a globe holds a sceptre in her right hand and with her left hand takes a sword from a standing lion. An eagle rises above her and at her feet lies a knight with a broken sword and holding a severed head and two naked children. This is clearly an allegory of the victory of Peace over War. A small map of the provinces of Holland and West Frisia etched on to the globe makes the connection between the allegory and the armistice in the battle of the Dutch provinces against the rule of the Spanish Habsburgs in 1609.

Drahotová 1988, pp. 408–9; Strasser 1989, p. 56.

O.D.

II.75
Caspar Lehmann
Uelzen 1563/65–Prague 1622
Panel with *Children Embracing and Initials of Christian II and Hedvig of Denmark*
Engraved clear glass, slightly greyish
22.5 × 19 cm
Probably 1606-7
From a private collection in England, sold at auction at Christie's, London, 3 June 1986
Vienna, collection of Rudolf von Strasser

The panel with the symbol of conjugal love – two children embracing – has a lamb and an imperial apple on either side, flying cupids above them and the monogram *CH* (Christian and Hedvika) within a crowned heart. The panel was probably created during Lehmann's stay in Dresden in 1606-7, where he moved after falling from favour at Rudolf's court. Although the marriage of Christian II and the Danish princess Hedvika took place on 12 September 1602, it is possible to date the panel, as well as other small panels bearing the couple's monogram, to the period circa 1606-7. This is indicated by the monogram in a heart-shaped shield, which is also used on the gold medallions with portraits of the couple from 1606 (Tentzel 1705, tab. 372/3). Other panels from the series bearing the monogram CH are: the panel with *Perseus and Andromeda* in the Victoria and Albert Museum in London, the panel with *Diana and Actaeon* in Hamburg, and the panels auctioned in 1986 – the panel with *Cupid*, a pair of doves and a little boy, now in Corning, and the panel with the *Rape of Europa*, purchased by the British Museum in London.

Drahotová 1988, pp. 407 ff.; Strasser 1989, cat. no. 85.

O.D.

II.76
Antonio Abondio
Riva 1538–Vienna 1591
Plaque with Mars
Cast lead
9.9 × 6.3 cm
Göttweig, Kunstsammlungen des Stiftes
Göttweig, Sk 68 Gö

Mars is seen in the foreground in antique armour, with his left hand on a shield and a coat of chain mail by his right leg. This plaquette is one of a series of planet gods, of which *Mars, Mercury* and *Venus* have survived. It is not possible to say whether others are still in existence. It seems most

likely that it was made during Abondio's time in Prague and may or may not have been influenced by some earlier graphic depiction of Mars. Plaquettes of this kind served originally as decorations for various other objects. The Göttweig lead casts are angled at the corners and finished with baroque wooden frames.

Göttweig 1983, cat. no. 585; Essen and Vienna 1985, cat. no. 483

Dworschak 1954, p. 99; Weber 1975, no. 646,1

K.Sch.

II.77
Antonio Abondio
Riva 1538–Vienna 1591
Plaque with Mercury
Cast lead
9.6 × 5.8 cm
Inscribed below: *AN.AB*
Göttweig, Kunstsammlungen des Stiftes
Göttweig, Sk 67 Gö

Mercury is seen running on the right with winged hat, winged shoes and caduceus; there is a cockerel to the right of his legs. See commentary on *Plaque with Mars*.

Göttweig 1983, cat. no. 583; Essen and Vi-

enna 1988, cat. no. 484

Dworschak 1954, p. 99; Weber 1975, no. 646,2

K.Sch.

II.78
Antonio Abondio
Riva 1538-Vienna 1591
Plaque with Venus
Cast lead
10.1 × 6.2
Inscribed below: AN.AB
Göttweig, Kunstsammlungen des Stiftes
Göttweig, Sk 66 Gö

Venus stands naked in the foreground, with her left hand above the winged Amor.

Göttweig 1983, cat. no. 584; Essen-Vienna 1988, cat. no. 485

Habich 11/2 1933, no. 3471; Dworschak 1954, p. 99; Weber 1975, no. 646,3

K.Sch.

II.79, II.80
Antonio Abondio
Riva 1538–Vienna 1591
Medal of *Emperor Maximilian II*
Cast in silver
2.9
Undated, ca. 1567
MAXIMILI.II.ROM.IMP.SEMP.AVGV (obverse); DOMINVS PROVIDEBIT (reverse);
A.A. (signature by shoulder)
Prague, Národní muzeum, Numismatic Department, inv. no.H5-58225, H5-58436

Several versions exist of these medals, which were probably engraved after Maximilian's coronation. The motif of the ea-

gle clutching the globe is suggestive of the Habsburgs' expansionist plans. The design was taken from the coins of the Holy Roman emperors and was itself chosen as a base by French King Charles IX for a mint from 1573.

Fiala 1909; Habich 1934, II/2, no. 3401; *The Medal*, 1996, Autumn, p. 36, figs 13,14; Dworschak 1958, 5.62 (variant); Veillon 1996, 36, fig.13-14

Z.M.

II.80

See cat. no. II.79.

II.81
Antonio Abondio
Riva 1538–Vienna 1591
Medal of *Emperor Maxmilian II*
? 1575, undated
Prague, Národní muzeum, Numismatic
Department, inv. no. H5-150926

This is an example of a fine, one-sided cast taken from the original medal whose reverse side shows a portrait of Maxmilian's wife Maria, dated 1575. According to surviving sources, Antonio Abondio became court "conterfetter" for Emperor Maxmilian II in 1566. He developed the work of Leone Leoni and was his equal in the craftsmanship he applied to his portraits, although his style is distinctive.

Fiala 1909, pp. 4-5, tab.II, no. 6; Nohejlová 1963, p. 61/36; Schutte 1988, p. 578, no. 459

Z.M.

II.82
Antonio Abondio
Riva 1538–Vienna 1591
Medal of *Empress Maria*
1575
Prague, Národní muzeum, Numismatic
Department, inv. no. H5-58599

The medal is a cast of the reverse side of a double-sided medal which bears a portrait of Maxmilian II. Compare with preceding exhibit. This medal is set in a smooth frame intended to be worn with a chain.

Fiala 1909, p. 4-5, tab.II, no. 6; Habich 1934, II/2, nos 3412, 3447 ?; Schutte 1988, p. 578,

no. 459

Z.M.

II.83
Antonio Abondio
Riva 1538–Vienna 1591
Medal of *Empress Maria*
Undated, ca. 1564
Prague, National Musuem, Numismatic
Department, inv. no.H5-150930

This type of portrait of Empress Maria is similar to the oval, coloured wax relief from the numismatic cabinet collections in Munich, published by Fiala. It was evidently crafted shortly after the Emperor's coronation in 1564.

Fiala 1909; Habich 1934, II/2, no. 3408; No-

hejlová 1963, p. 62/42

Z.M.

II.84, II.85
Antonio Abondio
Riva 1538–Vienna 1591
Medal of *Archduke Matthias and Maxmilian; Albert and Václav*
1568
Prague, Národní muzeum, Numismatic
Department, inv. no. H5-58449,
H5-58451

This medal exists in a double-sided version. Our collections contain two one-sided casts using various metals. Both are signed A.A. Habich publishes examples dated 1568. The medals depict children's portraits of the sons of Maxmilian II,

Matthias (1557–1619), future emperor, Maxmilian (1558–1618), Albert (1559–1621) and Václav (1561–1578).

Habich 1934, II/2, no.3410; Schutte 1988, p. 579, no.462

Z.M.

II.85

See cat. no. II.84.

II.86
Antonio Abondio
Riva 1538–Vienna 1591
Medal of *Rudolf II*
After 1576
Prague, Národní muzeum, Numismatic
Department, inv. no. H5-58442

This is a single-sided cast of the obverse
side of a double-sided medal. The reverse
side of the original medal bears the portrait of Rudolf's brother, Archduke Ernst.
It was probably cast shortly after the imperial coronation of Rudolf II.

Domanig 1896, no. 104; Fiala 1909, p. 38,

no. 53; Habich 1934, II/2, no. 3418; Schutte
1988; p. 579, no. 461 obv.

Z.M.

II.87
Antonio Abondio
Riva 1538–Vienna 1591
Medal of *Rudolf II* to Commemorate his
Succession to the Throne
After 1576
Prague, Národní muzeum, Numismatic
Department, inv. no. H5-115047

The engraving of this medal is similar to
the portrait depicted on the thaler coin designed by Abondio some time during the
period 1576-77. The reverse side is an example of the use of emblems in medal-engraving. The symbolism contained in both
word and image was frequently difficult to

interpret and impossible without any
form of commentary. Rudolfine and other
emblems were collected and drawn by the
imperial antiquarian, Ottavio Strada; their
interpretation was formulated by Jakob
Typotius, the engravings by Aegidius
Sadeler. The sources used for Rudolfine
emblems were Classical coins, medallions,
cameos and gems. The flying eagle represents the monarch fulfilling God's wish
for general welfare – *saluti publicae*.

Strada-Typotius, Symbola Divina et Humana...I, tab.XXXIII/2, XXXIV/2; Habich
1934, II/2, no. 3419; Neumann 1977, pp.
400–41

Z.M.

II.88, II.89
Antonio Abondio
Riva 1538–Vienna 1591
Medal of *Rudolf II*
After 1576
Prague, Národní muzeum, Numismatic
Department, inv. no. H5-58441,
H5-58440

The design of both medals is based on an
original cast medal, similar to the preceding exhibit. They were reworked using
gold, chased and set in rhomboid frames.

Fiala 1909, tab.V, no. 1; Habich 1934, II/2,
no. 3419

Z.M.

II.89

II.90
Antonio Abondio
Riva 1538–Vienna 1591
Medal of *Rudolf II* to Commemorate the
Turkish Wars
After 1585
Prague, Národní muzeum, Numismatic
Department, inv. no. H5-58268

The medals commemorating the Turkish
wars are part of a large collection and document the significance Rudolf attributed
to every military success. The reverse side
of this medal again features period emblems. The legend is cautionary: Do not
succumb to evil. The shield and sword will

protect the Emperor from the assailing
Turkish hydra.

Typotius, Symbola Divina I, no. XXXVI/2;
Habich 1934, II/2, no. 3427; Schutte 1988,
p. 586, no. 476

Z.M.

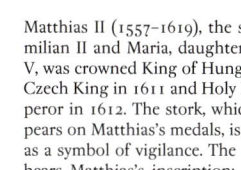

II.91
Antonio Abondio
Riva 1538–Vienna 1591
Medal of *Archduke Matthias*
1587
Prague, Národní muzeum, Numismatic
Department, inv. no. H5-58446

Matthias II (1557–1619), the son of Maxmilian II and Maria, daughter of Charles
V, was crowned King of Hungary in 1606,
Czech King in 1611 and Holy Roman Emperor in 1612. The stork, which often appears on Matthias's medals, is interpreted
as a symbol of vigilance. The reverse side
bears Matthias's inscription: *AMAT VIC-*

TORIA CVRAM – 'He loves victory, care'.
Fiala 1909, tab.V, no. 6; Habich 1934, II/2,
no. 3431; Schulze 812

Z.M.

II.92
Antonio Abondio
Riva 1538–Vienna 1591
Archduke Maximilian III
Cast gold, enamelled setting
Diameter: 3 cm; with setting: 5.2 × 4.3 cm
Recto: Bust of the Emperor Maximilian III
facing right. Verso: *MILITEMVS* (military
encampment)
1586
Vienna, Kunsthistorisches Museum,
Münzkabinett, 4365 bß

This bust of Maximilian goes back to an
earlier portrait on a medal signed by
Abondio in 1580. This later version, with

the signature being replaced by the date,
was made in 1583. The back with the military encampment was not made until 1586
and is connected with the election of the
Archduke as Coadjutor of the Grand Master of the Teutonic Order. Although other
examples of this 1586 medal have a retrospectively added Teutonic Order Cross on
the Emperor's chest, this is not so in the
case of this special edition which in fact
shows some signs of having been touched
up (particularly evident on the Emperor's
beard.) The medal was brazed into the setting which is itself has enamelled on it
four coats of arms: Hungary-Bohemia-
Austria-Burgundy, the Tyrol, Habsburg

and Old Austria. The four hooks in evidence were to hang the medal on a fine
chain or to hang a pearl from, as the case
may be.

Essen and Vienna 1988, cat. no. 813

Habich 11/2 1934, no. 3429; Börner 1981,
no 89

K.Sch.

II.93
Antonio Abondio
Riva 1538–Vienna 1591
Plaque of Caterina Riva
Ca. 1577
Prague, Národní muzeum, Numismatic
Department, inv. no. H5-115958

This plaque, bearing what is presumed to
be the portrait of Abondio's friend Caterina Riva, is a later cast of a medal which, according to Dworschak, appeared that
same year.

Fiala 1909, p. 32, no. 23, tab.1/8
Dworschak 1958, p. 64

Z.M.

II.94
Antonio Abondi
Riva 1538–Vienna 1591
Plaque of Madonna and Child
Last quarter of sixteenth century
Prague, Národní muzeum, Numismatic
Department, inv. no. H5-150928

This plaque from the workshop of Antonio Abondio exists in several versions and
sizes. It may have been copied from one of
the graphic sheets of Albrecht Dürer.

Habich 1934, II/2, no. 3469; Nohejlová
1963, p. 62/40; Weber I., Renaissance
Plaketten I and II, Munchen 1975, p. 287,

no. 651 B

Z.M.

II.95
Antonio Abondio
Riva 1538–Vienna 1591
Medal of *The Saviour*
Undated, latter half of the sixteenth cen-
tury
Prague, Národní muzeum, Numismatic
Department, inv. no. H5-150932

Abondio designed several signed variants
of Christ's portrait, both with a crown of
thorns and without, with a Hebrew text in
different parts of the field, etc. Habich and
other literature give a clear account of
these medals. An example of the use of
this medal to adorn clothing may be seen

in the painting by Gothard de Wedig, *Portrait of a Man*, 1627, at Orlík castle.

Fiala 1909, no. 55; Habich 1934, II/2, no.
3463; Bukovinská 1974, pp. 58–64

Z.M.

II.96
Antonio Abondio
Riva 1538–Vienna 1591
Rudolf II [recto] and *The Virgin Mary* [verso]
Gold
4.5 × 3.9 cm
AB
After 1585
Ex-Donebauer Collection, ? 1888
Staatliche Museen zu Berlin, Münzkabinett

This precious oval item belongs to a small group of three medallions with the identical bust of Rudolf II on the front.

The Order of the Golden Fleece worn by the Emperor serves as the *terminus post quem*, dating the piece after 1585. On view in the Münzkabinett in Berlin after 1904.

Habich 1929–34, no. 3422; Dworschak 1958, p. 107.

W.S.

II.97
Antonio Abondio
Riva 1538–Vienna 1591
Medal of *Jan Kalef*
Prague, Národní muzeum, Numismatic Department, inv. no. H5-150929

Jan Kalef (Calephus), Bishop of the Unity of Brethren, was born in 1522, worked in Mladá Boleslav and was later elected bishop. He died in 1588 in Brandýs nad Orlicí. With its complex symbolism, the medal represents the founding of the Unity of Brethren ("...it grew up like a tree from its roots..."), and the religious disputes of the period.

Fiala 1909, no. 70; Habich 1934, II/2, no. 3393; Nohejlová 1963, p. 62, no. 41.

Z.M.

II.98
Antonio Abondio
Medal of *Leonard Harrach and his Wife Barbora*
Undated, before 1585
Prague, Národní muzeum, Numismatic Department, inv. no. H5-150931

The Harrachs were members of the old Czech nobility. Leonard IV (1514-1590) worked for Maximilian II and Rudolf II in high positions; his last offices were that of Chief High Steward and Lord Chamberlain. He was awarded the Order of the Golden Fleece in 1585. His wife Barbora came from the Windischgratz family. Its

fine crafsmanship ensures this portrait a place among the most beautiful Czech medals of the 16th century.

Fiala 1909, no. 65; Habich 1934, II/2, no. 3362; Nohejlová 1963, p. 63/43.

Z.M.

II.99
Antonio Abondio
Medal of *Printer Michael Peterle*
Undated, ca. 1570s
Prague, Národní muzeum, Numismatic Department, inv. no. H5-115960

Michael Peterle, Prague woodcutter and printer, was born in 1537 in Annaberg in Saxony. He began working in Prague in 1562, was accepted into the Prague painting guild in 1565 and around the year 1570 he became a member of the Prague printing circle. He died at the age of 51 in 1588. Habich dates the medal around the year 1570 when Peterle became a Prague print-

er; the allegory on the reverse side would also suggest this. A one-sided version of this medal also exists, engraved to commemorate Peterle's 39th birthday, as the inscription indicates; thus the date of the medal may be set fairly reliably around the year 1576. The church of St Stephen in Prague contains a pictorial epitaph from the end of Peterle's life by painter Bartholomeus Spranger (1546-1611). The portrait of Peterle is a three-quarter profile and shares similar traits with the portrait depicted on the medal.

Habich 1934, II/2, no. 3354, 3381; Kneidl-Peterle 1995, pp. 107-133.

Z.M.

II.100
Alessandro Abondio
Medal of *Rudolf II*
Ca. 1608
Prague, Národní muzeum, Numismatic Department, inv. no. H5-58438

The portraits depicted in this and the following two medals were based on the portrait of Rudolf executed by Hans von Aachen, or perhaps more likely, they were taken from the engravings which were designed by the artist but crafted by Sadeler in 1603. This type of portrait was designed after the successful wars against the Turks and portrays the Emperor as

victor. The reverse side emphasises the symbolism of imperial might. This medal introduces another Rudolfine emblem, namely the astrological motif of Capricorn. Capricornus was Rudolf's constellation which he assumed as the star of Emperor Augustus. The imperial eagle and star also appear on the medal with the motto: *FVLGET CAESARIS ASTRVM* ('the imperial star shines'). The authorship of this group of medals is debatable. Certain authors ascribe the medal to Paulus van Vianen, a goldsmith and engraver who came to Prague around the year 1603 and died here in 1614. During the late 1920s Czech scholar Katz pub-

lished a study about Alessandro Abondio in which he attempts to establish its authorship.

Chytil 1904, p. 29, fig.15; Habich 1934, II/2, no. 3550; Katz 1928, p. 35, no. 1; Schutte 1988, p. 585, no. 473.

Z.M.

II.101
Alessandro Abondio
Medal of *Rudolf II*
Ca. 1608
Prague, Národní muzeum, Numismatic
Department, inv. no. H5-58443

In general terms, a medal featuring this
type of portrait testifies to the considerable skills of the artist and the clarity of
style. The catalogue published for the Viennese exhibition on Rudolfine art attributes these medals to an unknown
Prague artist. Which author of such
exquisite work could remain anonymous
if Rudolf is known to have secured the ser-

vices of Alessandro Abondio at his court
during this time? His authorship is more
probable than that of Paulus van Vianen,
also in light of the fact that the medal-engraving of the latter is close in style to his
original goldsmith work.

Katz 1928, p. 36, no. 18; Habich 1934, II/2;
Prag um 1600, Essen 1988.

Z.M.

II.102
Alessandro Abondio
Medal of *Rudolf II*
Ca. 1608
Prague, Národní muzeum, Numismatic
Department, inv. no. H5-59415

The medal depicts a different variant, with
Capricorn and the globe as included in Typotius's collection of Rudolfine emblems.

Katz 1928, p. 36, no. 15 – inscription variant; Habich 1934, II/2, no. 3553; Schutte,
no. 475 – inscription variant.

Z.M.

II.103
Alessandro Abondio
Galileo Galilei
Wax, slate
H: 9.5 cm
Ca. 1610 (?)
Acquired in 1905 from the Kunst-
auktionshaus Lempertz, Cologne, ex-Saf-
fé Collection
Staatliche Museen zu Berlin, Münzkabi-
nett, inv. no. 496/1905

This wax relief portrait of Galileo must
surely be one of the most beautiful surviving examples of this genre. It shows the
scholar in about his fifth decade, which

means that the piece may have been made
around 1610. The words *GALLILEO
GALLILEI* encircled by two fine lines on
the slate plate could mean that the piece
was made as a model for a medallion, but
this does not seem likely in view of the
range of colours used, from light brown
(Galileo's face) through dark brown (his
hair) to black (his clothes), and also in
view of the markedly painterly treatment
of the relief. Habich inclines to the view
that this is not the work of Alessandro
Abondio but originated in Italy.

Bonn, Gotha-Nürnberg 1995-96; Habich
1929–34, p. 534; Menadier 1910, col. 315;

Steguweit 1995, no. 86, ill. 46.

Berlin 1995, cat. no. 43.

Habich 1929-34, p. 534; Manadier 1910, Sp.
315.

W.S.

II.104, II.105
Alessandro Abondio
Medal to Commemorate Matthias's Turk-
ish Wars
1597
Prague, Národní muzeum, Numismatic
Department, inv. no. H5-150976,
H5-58445

Alessandro Abondio, son of Antonio
Abondio, worked for the court around the
period 1595-1612 in Vienna, Prague and
Innsbruck. He worked in the services of
Maxmilian I of Bavaria in Munich from
1619. His medals are difficult to
identify, unsigned and, in their design, are

often confused with the work of other
contemporary medal-engravers. The Turkish wars during the years 1593–1606 continued to pose a threat to the Hapsburg
monarchy. Archduke Matthias was appointed supreme military commander in
the Hungarian Lands where he faced Turkish expansion with varying degrees of success. In 1597 Rudolf II appointed Matthias
a member of the Order of the Golden
Fleece; it is conceivable that this medal
was cast in honour of this occasion.

Katz 1928, pp. 30-44; Habich 1934, II/2, no.
3586; Nohejlová 1963, p. 71, no. 2.

Z.M.

II.105

See cat. no. II.104.

II.106
Alessandro Abondio
Medal of *Matthias I after his Coronation as King of Hungary*
After 1606
Prague, Národní muzeum, Numismatic Department, inv. no. H5-150975

Matthias (1557-1619), brother of Rudolf II, was crowned King of Hungary in 1606, Czech King in 1611 and Roman-German Emperor in 1612. The medal evidently appeared for the Hungarian coronation in 1606 or shortly afterwards. The stork with the stone – symbolising vigilance – is a characteristic emblem on Matthias's

medals, together with the motto AMAT VICTORIA CVRAM ('He loves victory, care').

Don, 1862; Katz 1928, p. 36, no. 20; Nohejlová 1963, p. 71, no. 1.

Z.M.

II.107, II.108
Alessandro Abondio
Medal of *Matthias I as Czech and Hungarian King*
After 1611
Prague, Národní muzeum, Numismatic Department, inv. no. H5-58271, H5-58448

The medal symbolically documents the end of military hardship after the invasion of the Passau army but also clearly implies the conclusion to the drawn-out disputes between Matthias and Rudolf II over political succession which culminated after many years' endeavour in the acquisition

of the Czech crown in 1611.

Katz 1928, p. 37, no. 22; Habich 1934, II/2, no. 3588.

Z.M.

II.108

II.109
Horn of Indian Rhinoceros
Indian rhinoceros (*Rhinoceros unicornis*) horn
75 × 17 × 23 cm (including pedestal)
Presented 1884
Prague, Národní muzeum, Zoology Department, inv. no. P6V–54 481

The Indian rhinoceros was brought to Europe for the first time during the reign of the Roman emperor Titus (AD 79–81), and for the second time only in the sixteenth century, when it was painted by Albrecht Dürer. In contrast to the African rhinoceros, the Indian rhinoceros has only

one horn. The horns are not bony formations, but rather grow out of the skin and are replaced at infrequent intervals. They continue to play an important role in Asian medicine and are a commodity on the black market; these circumstances have brought the rhinoceros to the verge of extinction. The horn exhibited here has an overall length of 90 cm, making it one of the largest known trophies of its kind.

M.A.

II.110
Unknown Artist
Rhinoceros Horn
Rhinoceros horn, gold filigree, rubies, pearls
81 cm
Ca. 1582
Kunstkammer of the Emperor Rudolf II, Inventory of 1607-11, no. 29
Vienna, Kunsthistorisches Museum, *Kunstkammer*, inv. no. 3702

This horn was sent from Lisbon on 10 June 1582 by Rudolf II's mother, the Empress Maria (1528-1603), to the Emperor in Prague. It is an African rhino horn. In

the Inventory of 1607-11 it is listed under exotic natural objects as '*1 lang horn von asino indico von der kayserin Ihr Mt: verehrt, mit rubin und perlen indianischer arbeit durchbrochen, in gold gefast, geziert, in rot sametinen futral*'. The Emperor had this unusually large horn included in what amounts to an illustrated inventory that is known as 'Rudolf II's Museum' and which has a great many illustrations of exotic animals (Vienna 1996, cat. no. 47, Bestiaire 1990, pl. 11). According to this the rhinoceros horn originally had a band at the foot and in the middle. All the bands and the tip were connected by vertical bands. It is really not possible to say where

the gold work was carried out since Portuguese goldsmiths were working in Africa and India as were Indian goldsmiths in Portugal (cf. Lisbon 1996, p. 123, n. 45). Manfred Staudinger has documented the history of this piece right from its source to the present day (Bestiaire 1990, p. 118).

Essen and Vienna 1988, cat. no. 408.

Bestiaire 1990, p. 118, pl. 11.

R.D.

II.111
Nikolaus Pfaff; goldsmith unknown
Nürnberg ?1556–Prague before 1612
Covered Goblet Made from a Rhinoceros Horn
Rhinoceros horn, African wart-hog tusks, silver gilt
49.7 × 17.7 × 27.5 cm
1611
Kunstkammer of the Emperor Rudolf II, Inventory of 1607-11, no. 28
Vienna, Kunsthistorisches Museum, *Kunstkammer*, inv. no. 3709

A note added to the Inventory of 1607-11 details much except the artist's name: *Das grosse geschnittene geschirr von asino indico oder renotzerhorn, welches uff dem deckel zwey schlangenhörner hatt, in silber vergult gefasst und mit abgegoßnen thierlein von silber übermalt, geziert, verfertigt A⁰. 1611.* The tusks of the African wart-hog (the *Schlangenhörner*) are still in place in a tube-like upper jaw. This is contained within a mascaron with a fossilised shark's tooth in its mouth, which was believed to offer protection against poisons. The many details symbolise the positive and negative forces of Nature as well as pointing to India as the horn's place of origin (Scheicher 1995, p. 121). The fine carvings are so similar to the Rhinoceros Horn Cup with Satyrs (inv. no. 3701) and the base of the *Venus and Amor* statuette (inv. no. 4658) that they must have been made by the same artist, Nikolaus Pfaff. The moulds for the naturalistically painted small creatures (*Thierlein*) were most probably sent from Nürnberg. The gold work is also in keeping with Nürnberg style.

Essen and Vienna 1988, cat. no. 339.

Scheicher 1995, pp. 121-122.

R.D.

II.112
Unknown Artist
Goblet Made from a Rhinoceros Horn
Rhinoceros horn, enamelled gold
14.4 cm; Diameter 9.8 cm
Ca. 1600
Kunstkammer of the Emperor Rudolf II.; Inventory of 1607-11, no. 22 (?)
Vienna, Kunsthistorisches Museum, *Kunstkammer*, inv. no. 3736

The decoration of this delicate cup clearly marks it out as coming from Spain or the Iberian peninsula. The winged dragons on the band below the edge of the rim were commonly used by Spanish goldsmiths (cf. Hernmarck 1978, illus. 636; Fernández, Munoa, Rabasco 1985, p. illus. 62). The linear, graphic style of the decoration is also typically Iberian. The Kunstkammer Inventory of 1607/11 does not positively identify this cup although its number 22 is, in fact, a hidden reference to it: '*Ein klein niders renotzerkelchlein ohne deckhel, mit gantz guldenem und geschmeltztem füeßlein.*' The gold foot-ring may well have been added later in Prague.

Essen and Vienna 1988, no. 736.

R.D.

II.113
Emperor Rudolf II
Vienna 1552–Prague 1612
Covered Goblet
Rhinoceros horn turned on a lathe, mahogany, gold
H: 23 cm
On the cover: *Divi Rudolphi II. Rom: Imperat: Poculum deletorium ...* (see Scheicher, 341); on the foot: *Polydaedala manus Invicit: Imperat: Toreuma hoc finxit* (The cup of the sublime Rudolph II, which protects against poison, turned on the lathe by the hand of the invincible Emperor)
After 1599
Copenhagen, Königl. Kunstkammer, 1.8.1674, 20a
Copenhagen, Danish Národní muzeum, inv. no. D 406

In 1599 Rudolf had succeeded in 'borrowing' Georg Wecker – the famous Saxon court latheworker and pupil of Giovanni Ambrogio Maggiore – from Dresden along with the necessary equipment for his dilettante interest in the art. This drinking vessel is the only surviving certain evidence of the Emperor's skill in turning the lathe. The cup, first described by Philippovich in 1966, has recently been identified by Scheicher as the covered vessel that is illustrated on fol. 10r in the so-called *Museum* of Emperor Rudolf II (Vienna, Österreichische Nationalbibliothek, Cod. min. 129), along with a horn, a tooth and a piece of skin from an Indian rhinoceros horn. The metal setting with its all-important inscription is missing, however.

Philippovich 1966, p. 462; Staudinger 1990, p. 114; Gundestrup 1991,vol. 1, p. 301; Scheicher 1992, pp. 341ff.; Scheicher 1995, p. 123.

S.H.

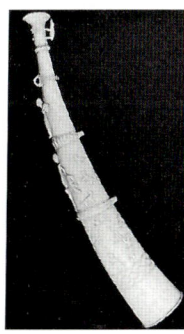

II.114
Oliphant
Carved ivory
54 cm
1490–1560
Sapi in the Portuguese zone, Sherbro Island, Sierra Leone
? From Rudolf II's collections
Discovered in Brandýs nad Labem near Prague and put in the Pachl collections. Bought by the Národní muzeum in the 1840s.
Prague, Národní muzeum, inv. no. 3.623

This oliphant was meant to be played vertically and was made for Europeans (Africans used transverse oliphants) to use while hunting. The two upper bands depict two European hunters with wild boar, accompanied by a pack of hounds and a small deer. The bottom band shows two Europeans, one with a longbow and one with a crossbow, shooting birds (perhaps parrots). The same motif of a hunter with a crossbow appears on one of the brass plaques that decorated the royal palace in Benin in the sixteenth century, and is evidence of the contemporary ties between Africa and Europe.

Prague 1983, ill. 1; New York 1988, no. 104.

Klar 1847, p. 501; Buchner 1956, figs 118-20; Klement-Kadlec 1972, p. 97; Kandert 1985, pp. 82-91; Herold 1990, figs 1-2.

J.Ka.

II.115
Spoon
Carved ivory
23.8 cm
Bini in the Portuguese zone, territory of the Bini Empire, southern Nigeria
In all probability comes from Rudolf II's collections. Discovered in Brandýs nad Labem and put in the Pachl collections. Bought by the Národní muzeum in Prague in the 1840s
Prague, Národní muzeum, inv. no. 3654

The handle of the spoon is decorated with a cockerel and an ibis (?), motifs peculiar to the Bini culutre, not ones ordered by European customers. Statues of cockerels and ibises, both carved in wood and cast in bronze, were common in Bini art of the sixteenth century and were connected with the state symbolism of power.

Prague 1983, not in cat.; New York 1988, fig. 169.

Klar 1847, p. 503; Kandert 1985, pp. 82-91; Herold 1990, fig. 3.

J.Ka.

II.116
Beak of a Dodo (*Raphus cucullatus*)
Bone, upper jaw
4.5 × 4.5 × 14.7 cm
Unmarked
1599–1609
Kunstkammer of Rudolf II
Prague, Národní muzeum, Zoology Department, inv. no. P6V-4389

This is a rare relic of the now-extinct dodo, a flightless bird which attained weights of 10–22 kg. The last reports of its existence date from 1665. The dodo that was kept in Rudolf II's menagerie in Prague Castle during the late sixteenth and early seven-teenth centuries was apparently the first living representative of the species to come to Europe. It is not unlikely that the Dutch painter Jakob Hoefnagel used the bird as a model for his painting of a dodo. At present, dodo remains are found in only twenty-two museums throughout the world. They were discovered in the collection of the Národní muzeum in Prague in 1847 or 1848 by Augustin Corda, the first custodian of the Zoology Department. In addition to the beak fragment, two long bones of one leg were also found. The beak is appreciably larger than that of other surviving pieces.

Reuss 1878, pp. 71–78; Wissen 1995, p. 102.

M.A.

II.117
Horn of a Narwhal
Dentine (upper left incisor)
123 cm, max. w: 4.5 cm
Unmarked
Prague, Národní muzeum, Zoology Department, inv. no. P6V-47 543

This is the exceptionally developed upper left canine of a narwhal, which can attain a length of up to three metres. The right canine remains of normal size and only rarely achieves the same proportions. The function of the horn, which is only found in males, is still the subject of debate. The narwhal is the most likely animal to have served as a model for the mythical unicorn (*Unicornis*), the symbol of indomitable strength, freedom and supreme power, which was a favourite subject in medieval art in particular.

M.A.

II.118
Daniel Fröschl (attr.)
Augsburg 1573–Prague 1613
Page with Dodo from 'Rudolf II's Museum'
Body colour on parchment
40.1 × 30.3 cm
1601–1609
Kunstkammer of the Emperor Rudolf II,
Inventory of 1607–11, no. 2689–90
Vienna, Österreichische Nationalbibliothek, Handschriften- und Inkunablensammlung, Cod. min. 130, fol. 31r.
L2

This and the following plate with the narwhal horn are from a compendium known as 'Rudolf II's Museum'; which was, in fact, an illustrated inventory of the Emperor's zoological collection. The dodo – *Raphus cucullatus* – was found on the Island of Mauritius in the southern Indian Ocean. After 1598 Netherlandish ships repeatedly visited the Mauritius Islands and stocked up with dodos as provisions. One of these was still alive on the ship's arrival in the Netherlands. It was then taken to Prague where this picture and the relevant study were made between 1601 and 1609. After its death this dodo was embalmed and put on display as a zoological specimen in the *Kunstkammer* in Prague Castle. It is listed in the *Kunstkammer* inventory and described in detail in a note added in 1609 (Inventory of 1607–11, no. 135).
Vienna 1996, *Thesaurus Austriacus. Europas Glanz im Spiegel der Buchkunst*, cat. no. 47/7

Staudinger 1990, pp. 344–349, II.199.

M.St.

II.119
Daniel Fröschl (attr.)
Augsburg 1573–Prague 1613
Page with Horn of a Narwhal from 'Rudolf II's Museum'
Body colour on parchment
40.2 × 30.4 cm
1598–1611
Kunstkammer of the Emperor Rudolf II,
Inventory of 1607–11, no. 2689–90
Vienna, Österreichische Nationalbibliothek, Handschriften- und Inkunablensammlung, Cod. min. 129, fol. 14r

The horn illustrated here is presumably the one given in 1540 by King Sigismund I of Poland (1506–1548) to King Ferdinand I. On the death of Ferdinand I it was excluded because of its inestimable value from the possessions that were to be divided up between his sons. On 11 August 1564 a contract was signed which agreed that these two treasures were to remain for all eternity with the house of Austria. On Maximilian's death in 1576 they went to the Archduke Ferdinand II who kept them in his residence, Schloß Ambras near Innsbruck. After Ferdinand II's death on 24 January 1595, Rudolf II took on the responsibility for these pieces and had the narwhal horn and agate bowl taken to Prague. Next the Emperor Matthias took the horn to Vienna and the inventory of his estate shows that it was ca. 2.37 metres long. Between 1755 and 1782 the horn, plus eight others, was handed over to the Naturalien-Kabinett, after which the trail runs dry.

Staudinger 1990, pp. 122–25.

M.St.

II.120
Unknown Master
Small Bucket from Coconut
Coconut, oriental bezoar, rhinoceros horn, silver gilt
H: 23.2 cm (overall; 11.5 cm to the edge); diam: 14.8 cm
Master mark: *ITB*
Ca. 1550–1600
Kunstkammer of Emperor Rudolf II,
Inventory of 1607–1611, no. 287
Vienna, Kunsthistorisches Museum, Kunstkammer, inv. no. 913

The Latin inscription on the rim refers to Psalms 41, 3, which points to the fact that this vessel was intended as a jug to hold holy water for liturgical use. In the centre there is a bezoar stone held by three clasps (a fourth clasp has been lost). The inventory of 1607–1611 wrongly describes this stone as a pit from the coconut fruit. Besides this there is a carrying ring made out of rhinoceros horn. Thus this vessel, probably carved by Indians in Goa with a Europeanized silver mount, uses three different natural materials, all of which were believed to react to and warn against the presence of poison and to possess healing properties. Daniel Fröschl, who compiled the inventory of 1607–1611, described all the coconuts as 'Indian nuts'. On the other hand, the description 'sea-nut' is only used by Fröschl for the '*cocco de maldiva*', the Seychelles-nut. (The compiler of the Ambras inventory of 1596 followed the same rule.)

Gaming 1991, cat. no. 12.37; Tokyo 1992, cat. no. 54; Utrecht 1993, cat. no. 255; Vienna 1996, cat. no. 3.26.

H.T.

II.121
Unknown Master
Vessel from Nut
Half of a Seychelles-nut, moulded and embossed silver, gilt
H: 41 cm; l: 34.3 cm; diam. of foot: 19.5 cm
Ca. 1575–1600
Kunstkammer of Archduke Ferdinand II, Ambras, inv. 1596, fol. 357v
Vienna, Kunsthistorisches Museum, Kunstkammer 6849

Nuts floating in the Indian Ocean, washed up on the shores of the Maldives, used to be called *cocco de maldiva* or 'sea-nuts' because people thought that they grew deep down in the ocean. In the sixteenth century Portuguese mariners brought back these strangely formed wonders, which were much prized, not least for their size. From Lisbon they found their way into the princely collections of Europe. Rudolf II owned a number of 'Indian sea-nuts', some in their natural state, some as artefacts with silver mounts. The pouring jug on exhibition here is from Archduke Ferdinand II's *Kunstkammer*, identifiable by a crowning swan, although this has now been lost. In response to the nut's supposed oceanic origins the mount has reliefs on the theme of the world of water. A similar item with only minor differences in the decorations, now in London (British Museum), came from the same workshop (possibly Augsburg?) in southern Germany.

Essen and Vienna 1988, cat. no. 687; Tokyo 1992, cat. no. 51; Neuhofen 1996, cat. no. 687.

Tait 1991, pp. 51ff.; Scheicher 1995, p. 116.

H.T.

II.122
Unknown Master
Vessel from Nut
Half Seychelles-nut, antelope's horn, silver gilt, traces of lacquer inside
37.1 × 34 × 22.2 cm
Ca. 1575–1600
Kunstkammer of Emperor Rudolf II, Inventory of 1607–1611, no. 298
Vienna, Schatzkammer des Deutschen Ordens, inv. no. 74/2/6

The bizarre appearance of this piece reveals significant information about its likely function. The body of the vessel, the *'cocco de maldiva'* and a bezoar stone (now lost), hanging into the vessel on a chain from the lid, were believed to have magical properties, neutralizing poisons and warding off illness. One of Fröschl's entries for a natural history item shows that he made the link between antelope horn and bezoar stone on the grounds of the 1605 *Exoticorum Liber septimus* by the botanist Carolus Clusius (Scheicher 1993, p. 116). Fröschl lists a horn that 'Carolus Clusius in his description believes comes from the bezoar animal'. Clusius in turn includes in that same book an illustration of a *cocco de maldiva* jug in the shape of a dragon and notes that he himself had seen something similar years before in Lisbon.

Essen and Vienna 1988, cat. no. 686; Nürnberg 1990, cat. no. 111.8.33; Lisbon 1996, 92.

Fritz 1983, cat. no. 254; Tait 1991, pp. 66f.; Scheicher 1995, pp. 116f.

H.T.

II.123
Eppendork Mandrake
Material unidentified, pearls
35 cm (without crown)
Ca. 1482; crown of pearls: sixteenth-seventeen-century.
From the *Geistliche Schatzkammer*
Vienna, Kunsthistorisches Museum, Kunstkammer, inv. no. D 148

According to legend in 1480 a woman in Eppendorf (in Hamburg) buried a host under a cabbage plant in the hope that her garden would flourish. But during the night the cabbage began to glow amazingly and when monks from Harvestehude came to investigate, they discovered that the root had assumed the form of Jesus on the cross. This miraculous object was taken to the monastery and in 1482 enclosed in a silver monstrance, in order that it might be displayed to the people as a holy object. The woman who had originally defiled the host confessed her sacrilege and was severely punished. Following the Reformation the root was taken to the Johanniskloster in Hamburg until, after lengthy negotiations, the Emperor Rudolf II bought it in 1602. The exact date of its delivery would seem to vouch for the authenticity of the historical background. There are several references to the root in seventeenth-century writings (Coburg 1983, no. 137). The natural form of the root has been slightly improved by human hand and a section of hair roots has been added. So far it has not been possible to make a botanical identification. The monstrance was melted down in 1810.

Essen and Vienna 1988, cat. no. 401; Coburg 1996, no. 137.

Hävernick 1966, p. 17-23.

R.D.

II.124
Unknown Master
Heart-Shaped Vessel
Tortoiseshell, embossed silver
26.3 cm
Ca. 1575–1600
Kunstkammer of Archduke Ferdinand II, Ambras, inv. no. 1596, fol. 457
Vienna, Kunsthistorisches Museum, inv. no. 4100

This, together with another, somewhat larger bottle of the same shape, was once in the Ambras *Kunstkammer*. Two very similar-sounding items are admittedly listed in the Prague inventory of 1607–1611, but since this bottle and its larger counterpart can be traced directly back to Ambras there is no doubt as to their provenance. Daniel Fröschl, who put together the Prague *Kunstkammer* inventory, was familiar with tortoiseshell as a material, whereas the writer of the Ambras inventory registers the work as either glass or clay. In both Prague and Ambras, tortoiseshell items were classed as 'Indian,' which could equally well mean from the Indian subcontinent or from the Americas. Tortoiseshell had been used in Gujarat since time immemorial and, as necessary, fitted by local craftsmen with Europeanized silver mounts, which nevertheless do still retain an unmistakably exotic feel. The foot added to this hanging bottle is European in origin. Tortoiseshell items of Indo-Portuguese origin have engravings on the highly polished surface of the tortoiseshell, which makes it seem likely that this bottle is from India and not the Americas.

Essen and Vienna 1988, cat. no. 404.

H.T.

II.125
Unknown Master
Tazza
Tortoiseshell
Diam: 42.7 cm
Ca. 1550–1600
Kunstkammer of Archduke Ferdinand II, Ambras, inv. no. 1596, fol. 467
Vienna, Kunsthistorisches Museum, inv. no. 4131

Rudolf II received a 'small Indian writing desk' from the regent of the Netherlands. Besides various other precious East Asian items, the list of contents of the table included this tortoiseshell bowl. However, other entries in the inventory make it clear that in fact this item came from Archduke Ferdinand II's *Kunstkammer* at Ambras. Whenever similar items of exotica turn up in either Habsburg collection this can generally be taken as an indication that they came from one of the overseas colonies belonging to Spain or Portugal. Tortoiseshell was highly prized for its smoothness and glowing colours and the main trading centre was Gambay, the capital of Gujarat. Precious materials such as tortoiseshell were still treasured in India and the Islamic world, just as they had been in antiquity, and the relevant craft skills had never been lost. With the discovery of the sea route to the Far East, Portugal entered a lucrative foreign trade in this kind of exotica. Soon the Netherlands and Spain emerged as trading rivals, with the latter 'manufacturing' tortoiseshell work in its Central American colonies; this was made from tortoiseshell hunted on the spot, but worked in an Indo-Portuguese style.

H.T.

II.126
Box
Wood, natural lacquer
Diam: 15cm
Sixteenth century
Prague, Náprstkovo muzeum, Národní muzeum, inv. no. A 19 333 a,b

Small round box, carving with natural black and red lacquer. Si Pi type, with a Zezla Zu I scroll motif.

Wang Shixiang, *Ancient Chinese Lacquerware* (Beijing, 1987).

Z.Č.

II.127
Bowl with wicker cover
Paint, clipped bamboo
4.9 cm; average 9.3 cm
Ca. 1600
Vienna, Kunsthistorisches Museum, Kunstkammer, inv. no. 6728

Food bowl on a circular base with extended rim. The bowl was made from a natural form of paint and has a covering of gently clipped bamboo strips. A large quantity of similar objects are recorded in the inventory of the *Kunstkammer* from 1607-11. They are identified as 'vom pintzen stro oder Reysewerck' (ff. 48-50), and perhaps evoked great interest at the time.

Z.Č.

II.128
European-style Chest
Wood covered with natural lacquer, painted with lacquer (gold and silver *makie* technique) and inlaid with mother-of-pearl. Original brass metalwork (lock and handles) with floral design
Momoyama period, end of the sixteenth century
Prague, Nåprstekovo Museum, inv. no. 20 611

The oldest Japanese lacquered chests produced for export to Europe come from the Momoyama period (1573-1615), when the numerous trading contacts between the Japanese and the Portuguese or Spanish, later the Dutch, were at their height. The Europeans were mostly attracted by valuable Japanese materials, the renowned sword-making, and not least by Japanese chests and jewel boxes, also exotic to the European eye and decorated with natural lacquer and inlay. Because lacquered objects produced for the Japanese market were completely different, European traders gave the manufacturers designs to copy. The lacquerers often developed and adapted the themes, producing a highly personal decoration. The Japanese called this European-influenced art Nanban ('southern barbarian'). This chest is one of the oldest examples of Japanese lacquerware in a Czech collection. The whole chest is decorated with tachibana and sakura flowers, maple leaves, wild vines, convolvulus flowers and tendrils.

Kyoto 1994, no. 1254.

F.S.

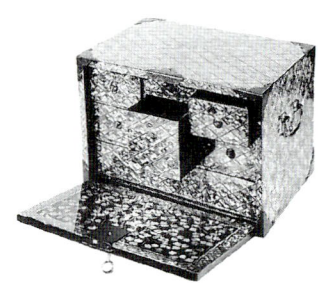

II.129
Rectangular Chest
Wood covered with natural lacquer, painted with lacquer (*makie* technique) and inlaid with mother-of-pearl. Brass metalwork with floral decoration
Momoyama period, ca. 1600
Prague, Nåprstekovo Museum, inv. no. 34 942

The outer sides of this Japanese jewellery box are decorated with a geometrical pattern of lozenge-shaped grilles, which the lacquerer has ingeniously composed in two dimensions – the larger lozenges are filled by smaller lozenges, and thus at first sight the simple pattern appears to have two planes. Jewellery boxes with completely geometrical designs on the outside are very rare in the Momoyama period and the decoration used is exceptional. On the inside of the hinged front panel is a more normal pattern of tendrils and flowers in a chequered frame, which can be found on other examples of Nanban art in Czech collections.

Kyoto 1994, no. 1256.

F.S.

II.130
Teke (?)
Cushion
Weaving and embroidery, raffia
50 × 72 cm
Ca. 1600
Taken from the Technical Institute to the Národní muzeum, from where it was taken to the Náprstkovo muzeum
Prague, Náprstkovo muzeum, Národní muzeum, Ethnographical Department, inv. no. NpM4-22.258

This cushion probably comes from Rudolf II's *Kunstkammer*. The cushion, decorated with what was called 'velvet' (a relief pattern embroidered on a canvas base) in geometrical patterns, is similar to the seventeenth-century raffia cushion in the Ethnographical Museum in Rome. Two seventeenth-century watercolours in the D'Este Library in Modena show cushions with similar patterns and with tassels on their corners. There are written reports from the sixteenth century on the production of 'velvet' in the Congo. During this period raffia fibres also began to appear on some European paintings.

Prague, 1983, fig. 2; New York 1988, pp. 202-8.

Bauer and Haupt 1976; Hanka 1832, Národní muzeum archive – N/3/86, box 12; Seydl 1951, pp. 1-59.J

J. Ka.

II.131
Philipp van den Bossche
Tabernacle with wax relief of the
Lamentation
Ebony case, wax, cloth, silk embroidery,
brass ornamentation, small tablets of
lapis lazuli (painted with oils), ivory
62.3 × 33.3 × 13 cm
Between 1604 and 1615
Rev. H. Crowe (1834); at his wish donated
in 1852 to the museum by the Rev.
George Murray
London, The Trustees of the British Museum, 1852,3-27,12

This tiny altar is quite extraordinary because of its ornamentation: the figures of the Virgin Mary and the body of Christ are modelled from coloured wax, the clothing is made from pieces of fabric and lace, and Jesus's hair is probably fine oakum. Thus far, the background of the relief, consisting of an fine silk embroidery depicting Golgotha and a far-off view of a landscape, has escaped notice. Its delicate stitching duplicates precisely the singular hand known from the drawings of the Emperor's court embroiderer Philipp van den Bossche. These were hitherto the sole known works of this master, about whom we know from the *Kunstkammer* inventory of 1607-1611 that he embroidered depic-

tions of landscapes and floral still-lifes. The landscape originated contemporaneously with the wax relief, for which it was composed. Its edges precisely fit the silhoutte of the Virgin's body. Bossche's authorship is verified by comparison with the drawing *Fluvial Landscape with Fishermen* (Mak van Waag, 301/1, 1979, p. 83, ill. 204), where there are similar figures, trees growing out of rocks, and a silhouette of a town with prominent towers. The maker of the wax relief, however, is still unknown.

Hagemann 1988, p. 85, note 18.

E.F.

II.132
Japanese Armour
Iron, leather, cords, flat sheet copper,
black lacquer, lacquer painting, cloth
35.8 × 100.8 cm; 36.5 × 107.7 cm
Ca. 1600
Vienna, Kaiserliches Zeughaus
Vienna, Kunsthistorisches Museum,
Schloß Ambras, inv. no. Pa 586/513

The 1607-11 inventory of Rudolf II's *Kunstkammer* (fol. 70' nos 746, 747) lists '1 indianische rustung, von leüchter materii, mit schwartzem glantzetem lacc uberzogen, brustharnisch, hutt und kinstuckh in einer grossen schiebladen oder trühlein. 1

andere dergleichen indianische rüstung, etwas stärcker und mehr geziert, von seydenwerck und etwas von metall oder messsing dabey, sonsten auch schwartz gelact, in gleichmessigem trülin mit eim fürschieber'. These descriptions of two boxed sets of 'Indian' armour sound very like armour now held in Schloß Ambras, which was probably made in Nara for the shogun Tokugawa Ieyasu. It seems fairly certain that these sets were not a gift to Rudolf II, but that they found their way to the Austrian court from Portugal via Spain, through Portugal's trade links with Japan.

Vienna 1990, p. 262; Tokyo 1992, no. 44; Nara 1995, no. 128.

Auer, Gamber 1981, pp. 58ff. and 82.

M.Pf.

II.133
Turkish Bow
Wood, horn, enamelled on both sides
155 cm
Schloß Ambras
Vienna, Kunsthistorisches Museum,
Hofjagd- und Rüstkammer, inv. no. C 93

The 1607-11 inventory of Rudolf II's *Kunstkammer* (f. 70' no. 746) lists '1 türkischer bogen mit 10 fitschpfeyl'. Along with the curved sword, the bow became in effect a symbol of Turkish armed power. Years were spent making these bows, using hard wood, buffalo horns, fish glue and cattle sinews. Turkish archers could shoot over

eight hundred metres with them. The Turkish bow was known in German as a 'reflex bow' because it always reverts to its natural curve when not in use: as soon as it is put under tension, however, the inside of the curve changes shape to become the outside.

Gamber and Beaufort 1990, p. 231.

M.Pf.

II.134
Bow Case
Brown leather, gilt brass, red, blue and
green silk
75 × 36 cm
Early seventeenth century
Vienna, Kaiserliches Zeughaus
Vienna, Kunsthistorisches Museum, Hofjagd- und Rüstkammer, inv. no. C 18

The 1607-11 inventory of Rudolf II's *Kunstkammer* (fol. 68' no. 743) lists '1 türkischer bogen mit 10 flitschpfeylí. There is no mention of a case for the bow or a quiver for the arrows. This brown leather case is decorated with perforated, gilt brass

mounts. The silk is appliquéd in red, blue and green to make rosettes and sweeping, stylized tulips, of the kind that were particularly favoured in Ottoman art. After use, the bow would be stored away in the bowcase (*sadak*), worn on the left-hand side. On the right-hand side, a Turk would have his quiver (*tirkes*). The bow could be a hindrance in close combat, and the bow-case thus served to store it neatly out of the way; it also protected the extremely sensitive bow from the damp. Since bows were in a certain sense a symbol of Turkish armed power, the Sultan often presented them as tokens of honour to visiting emissaries, even those from Europe. The

splendour of this bow-case, which was made with such skill in the early seventeenth century, would perhaps suggest that it was acquired by the Emperor not as spoils of war but as a diplomatic gift, as was the case with other oriental showpieces.

Essen and Vienna 1988, cat. no. 807.

Boeheim 1889, p. 166; Thomas 1963-64, p. 124.

M.Pf.

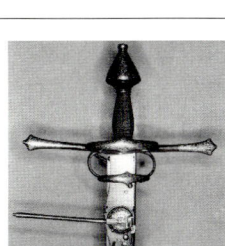

II.135
Combined Rapier and Wheel-lock Pistol
Iron, wood, wire
121 × 27 cm
Ca. 1560
Schloß Ambras
Vienna, Kunsthistorisches Museum, Hofjagd- und Rüstkammer inv. no. A 516

The 1607-11 inventory of Rudolf II's *Kunstkammer* (fol. 64' no. 705) lists '1 reitt oder schweinschwert, ist auch durchab mit einem rhor zum schiessen'. The weapon on show here largely fits the *Kunstkammer* description of a sword that also 'has a barrel for shooting'. The rise of the wheel-lock

led to a fashion for combination weapons, which were also often used for hunting. However, it is doubtful whether they were really practical: more likely, they were adult playthings kept for display rather than for actual use.

Schedelmann 1972, p. 22, ill. 39; Gamber and Beaufort 1978, p. 41; Gamber and Beaufort 1990, p. 177.

M.Pf.

II.136
Papal Ceremonial Sword
Gilt silver, iron
184 × 42 cm
1582
Schloß Ambras
Vienna, Kunsthistorisches Museum, Hof-
jagd- und Rüstkammer, inv. no. A 989

The 1607–11 inventory of Rudolf II's *Kunstkammer* (fol. 64' no. 686) lists '1 groß
langes baidenhändiges schwert, welches
babst Gregorius XIII. Ihrer k: Mt: verehrt,
alles mit silber vergultem gefäß und
schaiden'. This description of a large, two-
handed sword with silver gilt perfectly fits

a sword that Pope Gregory XIII gave to
Archduke Ferdinand II of Tyrol in 1581.
The custom of giving sanctified swords as
a sign of distinction seems to have started
under Pope Clement VI from Avignon.
These honours were bestowed each year
by the church on Christians who had
proved themselves particularly worthy.

*Fürstenhöfe der Renaissance, Giulio Romano
und die klassische Tradition* (Vienna, 1990),
no. 132.

Thomas, Gamber and Schedelmann, 1963,
pl. 55.

M.Pf.

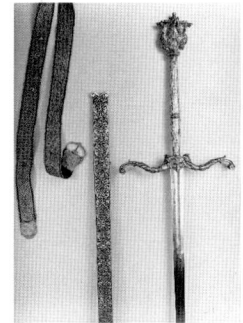

II.137
Estoc
Gilt silver, coloured stones, iron, wood
114 × 16 cm
Ca. 1550
Schloß Ambras
Vienna, Kunsthistorisches Museum, Hof-
jagd- und Rüstkammer, inv. no. C 78

The 1607–11 inventory of Rudolf II's *Kunstkammer* (fol. 62' no. 677) lists '1 stattlich-
er stecher mit vergulter schaiden und mit
stainen geziert' (1 mighty estoc, with a
gilded scabbard and decorated with
stones). This estoc from Lazarus Schwendi's Turkish booty broadly fits the descrip-

tion of the item in the *Kunstkammer*, with
its scabbard of gilt silver decorated with
turquoises and garnets. The estoc, a
thrusting weapon with a rhomboid blade
found mainly in eastern and south-eastern
Europe, was used primarily to pierce the
links of the opponent's chain mail.

Luchner 1958, pp. 104ff., 129; Gamber and
Beaufort 1990, p. 220.

M.Pf.

II.138
Ambrosius Gemlich, etcher
fl. 1527–42
Calendar Sword
Bright iron, wood, leather
88 × 20 cm
Ca. 1533
Vienna, Kaiserliches Zeughaus
Vienna, Kunsthistorisches Museum, Hof-
jagd- und Rüstkammer, inv. no. A 429

The 1607–11 inventory of Rudolf II's *Kunstkammer* (fol. 64' no. 693) lists '1. 2. kalen-
derklingen, darauff der gantze calender
geetzt'. On both sides of the blade there is
a blackened, etched calendar with saints'

names and movable feasts for the years
1533 to 1542. These calendar blades were a
popular extra in sixteenth-century
weaponry.

Seitz 1965, vol. 1, p. 343, ill. 22; Gamber
and Beaufort 1978, p. 38; Gamber and
Beaufort 1990, p. 73.

M.Pf.

II.139
Mace
Gilt silver, silver wire, wood
76 × 8 cm
Ca. 1550
Schloß Ambras
Vienna, Kunsthistorisches Museum, Hof-
jagd- und Rüstkammer, inv. no. C 135 g

The 1607–11 inventory of Rudolf II's *Kunstkammer* (fol. 62' no. 668) lists a mace with
the description 'gantz silber und vil daran
vergult' (all in silver and with much gilding). Although the weapon exhibited here
actually comes from the armoury of Archduke Ferdinand II, it is probably of exactly

the same type. The mace with a round or
pear-shaped head was widely used, particularly in eastern Europe, and known in
Polish as a *buzdygan*. Besides its combat
purpose, it also served as a badge of honour for officers on horseback or other
highly placed commanders. This weapon
for striking seems originally to have come
from the Far East and quickly found
favour with Turkish and Hungarian
troops, as well as with the Poles.

Luchner 1958, pp. 103ff., 129; Gamber and
Beaufort 1990, pp. 220ff.

M.Pf.

II.140
Battle-axe of the Bodyguard of Sultan
Mohammed III
Gilt steel, leather, chiselled and gilt silver
78 × 27 cm
Ca. 1600
Vienna, Kaiserliches Zeughaus
Vienna, Kunsthistorisches Museum, Hof-
jagd- und Rüstkammer, inv. no. C 119

The 1607–11 inventory of Rudolf II's *Kunstkammer* mentions (fol. 62í no. 673) '1
grosse türckische streitaxt'. The axe blade
is decorated on both sides with gilded Arabic lettering, which lists Ottoman sultans
up to Mehmed III, in no particular order

and missing some out. On the hammer is
the name of Sultan Mehmed III for whose
bodyguard this weapon was probably
made. The medallions in the middle of the
axe invoke the name of Allah, before the
writing dissolves into pure decoration.
Nothing is known of the means by which
this axe came into the Emperor's hands.
As the weapon belonged to the bodyguard
of a sultan who never set foot on the battlefield, this can hardly have been war
booty. Neither is it likely to have been a
diplomatic gift, since Mehmed III (reg.
1593–1603) was on the throne throughout
the long drawn-out Turkish Wars. It is possible that this axe was presented during

negotiations conducted by the Turks and
the Emperor's representatives between
the various campaigns of this war, or that
it was presented at the peace negotiations
at Zitvatorok.

Essen and Vienna 1988, cat. no. 806.

Boeheim 1889, p. 172; Thomas 1963–64, p.
123.

M.Pf.

II.141
Battle-axe
Gilt silver, coloured stones, blackened
iron, silver wire, wood
94 × 19 cm
Ca. 1550
Schloß Ambras
Vienna, Kunsthistorisches Museum, Hof-
jagd- und Rüstkammer, inv. no. C 135

The 1607–11 inventory of Rudolf II's *Kunstkammer* (fol. 62' no. 675) lists '1 strei-
thamer oder axtlin mit von silber geflocht-
nem stil und vil vergults daran' (1 battle
hammer or small axe with a silver woven
handle and much gold on it). This descrip-

tion largely tallies with the battle-axe exhibited here, which Lazarus Schwendi
brought with him as booty from Turkey
and which then found its way into the Am-
ras collection of Archduke Ferdinand II of
Tyrol. Like maces, these small battle-axes
were popular for mounted combat and also used by Turkish cavalry.

Luchner 1958, pp. 103ff., 129; Gamber and
Beaufort 1990, p. 220.

M.Pf.

II.142
Dagger with Curved Blade
Ivory, gilt silver, iron
L 37 cm
1549
Schloß Ambras
Vienna, Kunsthistorisches Museum, Hof-
jagd- und Rüstkammer, inv. no. C 199

The 1607–11 inventory of Rudolf II's *Kunstkammer* (fol. 66' no. 724) lists '1 ander
türckischer dolch mit glatt bainener handheb oder hefft, die klingen und die schaid
krumb zugespitzt, die schaid Silber vergult.' This description closely fits the dagger exhibited here, with its bone hilt, silver

gilt sheath and short, curved blade.

Munich 1910, cat. no. 350/1, tab. 242.

Gamber and Beaufort 1990, pp. 222ff.

M.Pf.

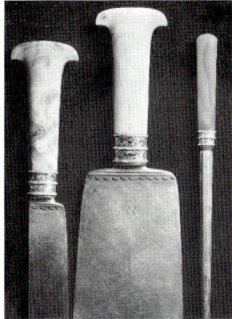

II.143
Serving Knife (Presentoir), Table Knife
and Fork of Rudolf II
Iron, agate, gold, silver gilt, enamel
Iron presentoir: L 49.5 cm; carving knife: L
39 cm; fork: L 30 cm
1580–1600
Vienna Hofjagd- und Sattelkammer
Vienna, Kunsthistorisches Museum, Hof-
jagd- und Rüstkammer, inv. no. D 209

The 1607–11 inventory of Rudolf II's *Kunstkammer* (fol. 68' no. 739) lists '1 gesteckh
vonn schönen grosser credentzmesser,
daran die hauben und schafft alles von
durchsichtigen augstein'. The precious set

on show here, consisting of a serving
knife, a so-called presentoir, a carving
knife and a fork, could be the same as the
one described in the *Kunstkammer* inventory. The handles are similarly made of
agate. The cutlery from the *Kunstkammer*
would have been used, if at all, only in the
court itself. The carving knife and fork
were used to cut up food, which would
then have been served with the serving
knife.

Essen and Vienna 1988, cat. no. 805.

Boeheim 1894, p. 23, pl. XLI/5; Thomas,
Gamber and Schedelmann 1963, no. 63.

M.Pf.

II.144
Lucio Piccino (attributed)
fl. Milan ca. 1550–89
Morion and Buckler
Embossed steel, damascened in gold and
silver
Buckler H: 7 cm, Diam: 53cm; Morion 22 ×
21 × 28 cm
Between 1585 and 1590
Vienna, Kunsthistorisches Museum, Hof-
jagd- und Rüstkammer, inv. no. A 1493

The 1607–11 inventory of Rudolf II's *Kunstkammer* (fol. 70' nos 748 and 749) lists '1
von eysen mit gold und silber eingesenck-
hte getribner künstlicher schöner helm.

sowie 1 sein darzugehorige, auch von eysen getribue rundartzen', describing a
peaked morion and a buckler that must
have closely resembled those worn by
Rudolf in his half-armour. In the middle of
the peaked morion there is a crown made
of foliage held up by two 'geniuses'. The
centre of the shield is occupied by the sea-
god Neptune, leading a crowned figure
across the waters in his seahorse-drawn
coach. The scene is framed by mythological creatures with trophies, mascarons
and garlands of fruit. Stylistically this
work looks much like that of Lucio Pic-
cinio, although it is not possible to be
more precise than this.

Schallaburg 1974, no. 408; Vienna 1987,
vol. 2, no. 23; Essen and Vienna 1988, no.
453.

Boeheim 1889, p. 129, no. 749; Boeheim
1898, p. 14, T XXXIX; Thomas and Gamber
1958, p. 791.

M.Pf.

II.145
Plate
Wood, upper side with decorative floral
lacquer painting in gold, red and green
on a black ground; underside decorated
with the so-called 'three-eyes motif' in red
and yellow on an orange ground
Diam: 22.5 cm, depth: 2 cm
16th century (?)
Vienna, Österreichisches Museum für
Angewandte Kunst, inv. no. KHM 500

Under the heading 'Türkische Sachen'
(Turkish items) in the catalogue of the
Ambras Collection there are several de-
scriptions that could apply to this plate.

No. 790, for example, is described as a
'small wooden bowl, green outside and red
inside, painted with gold and silver', while
no. 799 is described as a 'flat bowl or plate,
red and gold inside with painted flowers'.
Although it is not possible to be more precise in identifying this piece, it is fair to assume that it was indeed part of the collection in the *Kunstkammer* of Rudolf II.
Certainly it gives a good impression of the
type of object that would have been kept
there. The decoration is closely related to
that of the Iznik faiences from the second
half of the sixteenth century, and both
motifs are found in the standard repertoire of courtly book decoration.

J.W.

II.146
Vessel from Leather
Papier mâché, leather, decorated in silver and gold
4.6 cm; Diam. 15 cm
Ottoman Empire, sixteenth century
Imperial collections; 1940 from the Kunsthistorisches Museum
Vienna, Österreichisches Museum für Angewandte Kunst, KHM 496

In the chapter with Turkish items – 'Türkische Sachen' – in the 1607-11 Inventory of the Emperor Rudolf II's *Kunstkammer* (no. 800), the following entry refers to this bowl: '1 ander etwas dief-fer und von leder und allerley farben übernalt und gelacte und mit gold gezierte schüssel'. The structure of the papier maché is, in fact, so apparently similar to that of leather that it could only be identified under a microscope. Thus where the inventory entry refers to leather, it does in fact apply to this or similar objects, even if it is only the base, as the part that would be subjected to the heaviest wear, that was in fact made of leather. Stylistically the painted decorations on the bowl compare well with contemporary book decoration and above all with book-binding decorations, where leather was, of course, generally also used.

J.W.

II.147
Pin for a metal clasp
Jade, gold, rubies
5.7 × 4.2 cm
Ca. 1600, Osman era
1978, acquired by Náprstkovo muzeum
Prague, Národní muzeum, inv. no. A 15 009

This Jade plaque decorated in the 'Mehleme' technique (jade encrusted with precious stones) is typical of the High Osman period. Of the several hundred objects originating from outside Europe in Rudolf's *Kunstkammer* and which figure in the inventory of 1607-11, not one of them exists in Czech collections, about which it could be said with certainty that it could have come from the emperor's collection. A selection of exhibits of this nature, from Náprstkovo muzeum, however, strongly represents them.

Prague 1990, pic. VI.

H.Kn.

II.148
Portrait of Ibrahim 'Adil Shah II, Sultan of Bijapur
1019 hidjri (1610-1611), Mughal period
Prague, Náprstkovo muzeum, inv. no. A 12 182

A print from an album of miniatures, calligraphy and prints belonging to the Mughal emperor Jahangir, who ruled from 1604 to 1627. At the top there is an inscription in the nastaliq script: *Allahu akbar, shabih-i Ibrahim 'Adil Khan dakani tarafdar-i Bidjapur, ki dar 'lm-i musiki-i dakan khud ra saramad-i ahl-i an fann midanad* (Allah is great. A portrait of Ibrahim-'Adil Khan of Dakan, ruler of Bijapur, who is considered to have the greatest knowledge of Dakan music of all those who engage in this art). Inscription below: *va mal-i Farrukh Beg fi sana-i diulus-i mubarak mawafik-i sana-i 1019* ('and the work of Farrukh Beg in the happy year of his rule which corresponds to the year 1019'). There is a gap, followed by: *banda-i kamtarin Muhammad Husayn-i zarrin kalk-i Djahangirshahi, tahrir nimud* ('Written by his humble servant Muhammad Hussein with the golden pen of Shah Jahangir'). The portrait is complemented by two European prints representing Francis of Assisi (on the left) and St. Catherine (on the right). The album, together with other treasures, was taken by the Persian emperor Nadirshah to Iran in 1739. Today 129 sheets are owned by the imperial library in Teheran, while the others are scattered among various collections.

London 1982.

Hajek 1960, p. 10-14; Knizkova 1986, pp. 116-123; Nazir 1977, p. 24; Zebrowski 1981, fig. 414.

H.Kn.

II.149
Bowl for burning incense on zoomorphic legs
Bronze cast, engraved and stamped
8.7 cm average
Late twelfth–early thirteenth centuries, Seljuk period
Prague, Náprstkovo muzeum, Národní muzeum, inv. no. A 16 272

A fumigator was used for burning incense during festive occasions and to honour guests. The upper inside rim is decorated with medallions depicting birds and cartouches depicting animals (cheetah, fox, dog, hare) and the inscription in the duct reads 'empire, prosperity, happiness, affluence and assurance in the faith are from God'. At the bottom in the centre is the sovereign on his throne with guards to either side. The central band contains subjects from court life (lion, riding a horse, a game of polo); the outside central band contains medallions with an anthropomorphic zodiac, mythical animals including a gryphon and sphinx, as well as musicians. The central band contains animal motifs and a cartouche with somewhat illuminating inscriptions – 'robust health, abundant and big hearted...victorious... happy... secure... victorious... eternal'. The stand depicts the face of a lion and animals wearing a crown. Products from a certain periods cannot be distinguished so easily from those of an earlier period since in the Islamic world maintaining tradition is the basic means of judging the value of a work, and so, types of object with their decorative technique and motifs remain virtually unchanged for centuries. (Vahid Behmardi helped in rendering the Arabic inscriptions meaningful).

H.Kn., Ma.P.

II.150
Bronze jug, engraved
Decorations inlaid with gold and silver
14 cm max; average 12 cm
Ca. 1250
Acquired in 1975
Prague, Náprstkovo muzeum, Národní muzeum, inv. no. 46 443

On the outside neck a cartouche showing the planets (Mercury, Saturn, Mars, the Sun, Jupiter, Venus, the Moon); on the body is an inscription in the duct (uninterpreted), combined with an untangled knot. The main band of the jug is bordered by cartouches showing a geometric and plantlife pattern and the heads of animals. The centre shows an anthropomorphic zodiac. Inside on the rim of the neck is an inscription in the duct, "oh, drinker of pure water, say before drinking: cursed be the one who unjustly denies water to another; [made] for Ismail bin Ahmad of Wasiti. On the ring of the neck the inscription reads, "a long life to the one who has achieved lasting honour, and to him a peaceful life, long may he prosper in security with unlimited respect and lasting happiness". Other inscriptions have not been interpreted. The top of the handle shows the head of a dragon in a low relief and the bottom has the motif of a two-headed eagle.

H.Kn., Ma.P.

II.151
Magic water bowl
End of the sixteenth century,
Sophy period
Prague, Náprsteko Museum,
inv. no. A 12 957

A water bowl with healing and protective
qualities, which pilgrims brought home as
a souvenir or a talisman for luck from pilgrimages to Mecca (hadzdz).
(Inside) rolled edge: quotation from the
Koran in the naschi script, sura (chapter)
48; (Body) main band with twelve intersecting circles filled with numbers of a
mystic significance, with holy letters from

the Koran and inscriptions in naschi with
quotations from the Koran - sura 112, 113,
114, sura 9, verse 128, 129, sura 52, verse
68; Allah 'Ali Muhammad (God 'Ali
Muhammad; sura 33, verse 25, sura 36,
verses 1-40; (Convex middle) three inscriptions in the thuluth script: ya
Muhammad 'Ali (O, Muhammad 'Ali);
(Band around the centre) inscription in
the Persian thuluth script: bi-wilayatika ya
'Ali ya 'Ali ya 'Ali/mazar al-'adjayib kun
'awnan lana fi al-nawa '°b kullu hamm wa-
ghamm sayandjali (By your omnipotence,
O Ali, O Ali, O Ali/You, who are the manifestation of all wonders/help us in whatever happens to us/drive away from us all

worries and sadnesses); (Outside edge) a
band of numbers with a mystic significance and a band with an inscription in the
thuluth script, praising the prophet
Muhammad and twelve Shi'ite imams with
their official titles. (Main band) the signs
of the Zodiac in medallions on a background of carved numbers of mystic importance; (Inside the foot) three cartouches with numbers of mystic significance

On show at the Libechov chateau as part
of the Náprsteko muzeum's permanent
exhibition of Asian culture, 1977-96

H.Kn., Ma.P.

II.152
Unknown Artist
Vase
Smoky quartz
H: 16.6 cm; Diam: 9.5–9.7 cm
Ca. 1610
Kunstkammer of Emperor Rudolf II, In-
ventory of 1607–1611, no. 510, 1330
Vienna, Kunsthistorisches Museum,
Kunstkammer, inv. no. 1346

When Daniel Fröschl compiled the
Kunstkammer Inventory of 1607–11, he
avoided having to describe this – literally
incomparable – piece by making a small
drawing of it in the margin beside the rel-

evant entry, which reads as follows: 'Ein
vaso schwer und dickh in forma wie am
randt verzaichnet von topazio, hatt der
persianisch gesandte A° 1610 in namen
seines Konigs Ihr May: verehrt, ist nichts
von gold oder deckhel darbey' (Bauer–
Haupt, p. XXII, ill. 8 and no. 1330). That is
all the information there is about this
vase. So far it has not been possible to connect it to any particular artistic source or
to divine its original purpose. It is possible
that Shah Abbas the Great (1587–1628)
had it specially made in a supposedly 'Eu-
ropeanizing' style for Rudolf II, knowing
how much he loved fine stones. With their
shared political interest in the fight

against the Turks, the courts at Isfahan
and Prague exchanged several ambas-
sadorial missions between 1600 and 1609.

Essen and Vienna 1988, cat. no. 709.

R.D.

II.153
Hans (Johann) Wecker
fl. Prague and Dresden ca. 1600–1625
Box 'Pharmacy'
Turned ivory, gold, silver, steel
H: 18.1 cm
Ca. 1610
Kunstkammer of Emperor Rudolf II, In-
ventory of 1607–1611, no. 965
Vienna, Kunsthistorisches Museum,
Kunstkammer inv. no. 4697–4741

Nesting boxes were one of the earliest
popular forms of 'turned artwork'. They
were turned until the walls were extremely
thin, and usually the basic form was either

cylindrical or oblong, marked at intervals
with horizontal mouldings. The technique
had been invented around 1575 in Munich
by the Milan-born Giovanni Ambrogio
Maggiore, court latheworker to the dukes
of Bavaria. The boxes quickly became fashionable in other places too. Their accepted
form did not change until half-way
through the century. Hans (Johann) Wecker, whose father, Georg, had in 1599 installed a lathe in his workshop at the court
in Prague, was employed from 1601 onwards as imperial Kammerdrechsler, first by
Rudolf II and then by his successor,
Matthias, until he returned to the court of
the Electorate of Saxony in Dresden. This

Apotheke piece, which is technically perfect
but at the same time functional, is identified in the Kunstkammer inventory as the
only remaining piece from six listed as a
group of 'sechs gedrechselten sachen' by
the 'young Wecker'.

Essen and Vienna 1988, cat. no. 411.

Diemer 1985, p. 308; Maurice 1985, 34, no.
49.

S.H.

II.154
Georg Wecker
Munich ca. 1550–Dresden after 1626
Polyhedron
Ivory, turned; wood
H: 12 cm
Inscribed: GW 1581
1581
Listed in the 1587 Inventory of the Elec-
toral Kunstkammer, Bl. 106
Dresden, Grünes Gewölbe, inv. no. 11290

The art of ivory turning reached a high
point in Dresden when the Elector August
of Saxony appointed Georg Wecker to the
court on 13 January 1578. He had learnt

his art under his father Hans Wecker, himself appointed to the court of the Bavarian
Duke Albrecht V and most probably had
also met the inventor of oval turning, Giovanni Ambrogio Maggiore there between
1574 and 1577. Amongst the earliest
known turned artefacts by Georg Wecker
are two small polyhedrons, signed with
the initials "GW" and dated 1581. One of
these is on show in this exhibition. It
demonstrates geometrically perfect lathework which only a highly specialized master such as Georg Wecker could carry out
at this level. In 1584 when Egidius Lobenigk entered the Elector's service as court
lathe-worker in Dresden in 1584 he too

crafted a similar polyhedron, only 9 cm
high, to demonstrate his exceptional
skills. Even in the context of the turned
works in the Grünes Gewölbe, these three
polyhedrons are especially precious.

Cf. Menzhausen 1977, pp. 101–104;
Grünes Gewölbe 1994, pp. 101f., 122; Syndram 1995. pp. 6–13; Kappel 1995, p. 14–
19.

J.K.

II.155
Georg Wecker
Munich ca. 1550–Dresden after 1626
Covered Bowl
Ivory, turned
H: 28.3 cm
Inscribed: GW 1586
1586
A number of these turned vessels by
Georg Wecker is listed in the 1640 Inven-
tory of the Electoral Kunstkammer under
Bl. 443ff.
Dresden, Grünes Gewölbe, inv. no. II 169

Georg Wecker was active as court latheworker in Dresden from 1578 until his

death probably soon after 1626, and the
selection of ivory artefacts by him on display here is representative of his rich life's
work. A large proportion of this has been
preserved in the Grünes Gewölbe and was
restored between 1991 and 1996. The impressive total of over 70 turned works that
he had delivered to the Electoral Kunstkammer by 1595 reflects his immense
productivity. The turned cup of 1586 is
characteristic of Wecker's style. He
favoured clear-cut forms for his vessels,
which seem to combine elegance with stability and functionality.

Erbach 1995, cat. no. 21.

Cf. Menzhausen 1977, pp. 101–104;
Grünes Gewölbe 1994, pp. 101f., 122; Syndram 1995, pp. 6–13; Kappel 1995, pp. 14–
19.

J.K.

II.156
Georg Wecker
Munich ca. 1550–Dresden after 1626
Fourfold Cup
Ivory, turned
H: 22 cm
Inscribed: GW 1587
1587
This cup is listed in the 1610 Inventory of the Electoral *Kunstkammer* under Bl. 204. It originally had a cover (now lost).
Dresden, Grünes Gewölbe, inv. no. 1134

Georg Wecker's skills were not only appreciated in the court in Dresden. The Emperor Rudolf II was evidently also keenly impressed by Wecker's artistry. In 1599 Wecker was honoured with a commission to install a lathe on the Hradschin for the Emperor Rudolf II and duly travelled to Prague to fulfil this task. The Inventory of the Emperor's *Kunstkammer* lists five turned works by him: *vom altten Weckher*. Since the Elector August of Saxony also produced lathe-turned works in the courtly manner, pieces by him also found their way into Rudolf's *Kunstkammer*. A particularly original formal invention by Wecker is his cup on round feet dated 1587 and signed "GW ". It is made from one piece but creates the illusion of being four cups, one standing inside the other.

Erbach 1995, cat. no. 22.

Cf. Menzhausen 1977, p. 101–104, illus. 54; Grünes Gewölbe 1994, pp. 101f., 122; Syndram 1995, pp. 6–13; Kappel 1995, pp. 14–19.

J.K.

II.157
Georg Wecker
Munich ca. 1550–Dresden after 1626
Striated Covered Bowl
Ivory, turned
H: 21.9 cm
Inscribed: GW 1588
1588
A turned vessel, acquired for the *Kunstkammer* in 1588, is listed in the 1595 Inventory under Bl. 358.
Dresden, Grünes Gewölbe, inv. no. II 66

Two years after the death of the Elector August of Saxony, Georg Wecker – now court latheworker to Christian I – made this turned covered bowl. Its perfect execution demonstrates the stylistic continuity that Wecker preserved, however imaginative the form itself was. Georg Wecker retained his position in Dresden under both Christian II and Johann Georg I of Saxony. In 1601 Wecker travelled to the imperial court in Prague in order to deliver turned ivory artefacts from Christian II of Saxony to the Emperor Rudolf II. The latest known works by Georg Wecker include one which found its way into the Emperor's *Kunstkammer* having been given as a present to Duke Heinrich Julius of Braunschweig on his arrival in Prague in 1610, and four turned vessels that he delivered in 1619 to the Dresden *Kunstkammer*. Although Georg Wecker, as an old man, did not continue to work the lathe himself, he was still involved in design.

Erbach 1995, cat. no. 33.

Menzhausen 1977, pp. 101–104; Grünes Gewölbe 1994, pp. 101f., 122; Syndram 1995, pp. 6–13; Kappel 1995, p. 14–19.

J.K.

II.158
? Workshop of Georg Wecker
Small Cup
Ivory, turned
H: 12.9 cm
Ca. 1600
No verifiable provenance.
Dresden, Grünes Gewölbe, inv. no. II306

It is not possible to attribute this small cup definitively, although stylistically it bears a close resemblance to Georg Wecker's work. Presumably it is a product of Georg Wecker's workshop, which was situated on the top floor of the Dresden Castle not far from the *Kunstkammer*. Georg Wecker taught his sons the art of using a lathe. The only son of Wecker's whom we know of by name is Hans Wecker who was court latheworker both to the Emperor Rudolf II and the Emperor Matthias and after 1622 held the same position in the court of Johann Georg I of Saxony in Dresden, taking over from Georg Wecker.

Menzhausen 1977, pp. 101–104; Grünes Gewölbe 1994, pp. 101f., 122; Syndram 1995, pp. 6–13; Kappel 1995, pp. 14–19.

J.K.

II.159
Egidius Lobenigk
Cologne (?)–Dresden 1595, fl. after 1584 in Dresden
'Doppelscheuer' (one cup set above another)
Ivory, turned
H: 16.9 cm and 17 cm
EL 1590
1590
Listed in the 1595 *Kunstkammer* Inventory (Bl. 355) as being by Egidius Lobenigk and as having arrived in 1590.
Dresden, Grünes Gewölbe, inv. nos II 241 and II 266

For ten years Georg Wecker and Egidius Lobenigk's lives in Dresden were closely linked, until the latter's death in April 1595. Lobenigk, born in Cologne, was appointed as court latheworker on 20 November 1584, during the time of the Elector August of Saxony. This appointment also carried with it the duty to teach the young Duke Christian (I) the courtly skill of lathework. Christian had already been receiving the requisite instruction since 1576 in perspective and freehand drawing from the Nürnberg goldsmith and art theoretician Hans Lencker. Lobenigk's turned forms were both complex and bizarre: threaded pyramids, cups and bowls set one above the other, strange dice and balls. He also turned ivory vessels whose restrained beauty is close in style to the work of Georg Wecker. These two cups are a fine example of this.

Erbach 1995, cat. nos 10, 11.

Weber 1865, pp. 338, 351f.; Grünes Gewölbe 1994, pp. 101f., 122; Kappel 1995, pp. 14–16 (with further bibliography); Erbach 1995, exh. cat., cat. nos 10, 11.

J.K.

II.160
Unknown artist
Vase with Flowers
Turned and carved ivory
H: 36.8 cm (without flowers)
Early seventeenth century
Imperial *Schatzkammer*
Vienna, Kunsthistorisches Museum, Kunstkammer, inv. no. 4691

This superb piece, with its pronounced rectangles, is striking for its rhythmic interplay between horizontal mouldings and extremely finely turned, undecorated areas: the severe tectonics of the piece are softened only by the fragile bouquet of flowers that crowns it. This covered cup is typical of the turned artworks that were produced in the early seventeenth century, when large, simple, stereometric forms with unformed open areas were gradually being discarded in favour of the significantly more complex formal experiments that emerged in the second decade of the seventeenth century. Genuine *Kunstkammer* pieces of this kind were indeed being produced from the late sixteenth century onwards in response to the fascination felt by artists and collectors alike for 'the machine'. It was as though nature were being tamed by an act of human creativity, in the spirit of *Ars naturam superat*. Although it is not certain that this cup was listed in the inventory of Rudolf II's *Kunstkammer*, Fröschl does record some similar-sounding items, such as 'becherlin or blumenkrug mit vilen blumen', which also used a certain amount of fruitwood.

S.H.

II.161
Hans Wecker workshop
Three Small Pipes
Ivory, turned
L: between 5.4 and 5.8 cm
1622–40
Dresden, Grünes Gewölbe, inv. no. II 328e

According to the 1648 Inventory of the Electoral *Kunstkammer* the eighth room contained, besides various intricate clockwork mechanisms, the masterpieces of the ivory turners at the court in Dresden. Contrary to the usual practice in the *Kunstkammer*, these were not placed on long display tables with coloured cloth or marble panels. Instead they were presented in rectangular showcases constructed specifically for that purpose. These were made of wood stained black and glazed with large panes of glass forming eight doors on each of the long sides. The author of the Inventory reported all of this in great detail. The display of turned works – almost 300 in total – was arranged according to artist. First came Georg Wecker, followed by Egidius Lobenigk, then Jakob Zeller and his journeymen. Georg Friedel is also named. Last of all come the 'mehrentheils der Jungen Wecker, des alten Georg Weckers Sohnenn ihre gedroheten Kunststuckenn' (Bl. 459ff.). This last group included 42 ivory pipes, of which 23 still survive in the Grünes Gewölbe. Three of these are on show here: the finest of miniature works, constructed like little towers and, even today, still in perfect working order.

Inventory of the Dresden *Kunstkammer* of 1640, Bl. 439–465.

J.K.

II.162
Ag Achilles (attributed)
Hermansreyt, fl. ca. 1650
Writing Tools
Turned ivory
H: 41.5 cm
Ca. 1650
Imperial *Schatzkammer*
Vienna, Kunsthistorisches Museum, *Kunstkammer*, inv. no. 4916–4932

This ivory pillar, made purely for enjoyment, would reveal its contents to the astonished viewer only little by little. The mimetic qualities of such pieces exerted a huge fascination. On the one hand, technically perfect miniaturization of scientific and everyday objects demonstrated an interest in experiment that delighted in extremes of size and proportion. On the other hand, connoisseurs revelled as much in the ambiguity of strange artefacts and virtuoso displays as they did in real tools and instruments that had a practical application. Items such as this found their way not only into the *Kunstkammer* in Prague, but into many other collections besides, where princely 'machine art' was valued just as highly. A set of writing implements in the form of a pillar held in Dresden, marked and dated *Georg Wecker 1588*, is among the earliest such items and perhaps represents the incunabulum of the form. Comparison with a similar ivory pillar in Vienna by Achilles Ag suggests that the tools in the *Kunstkammer* in Vienna were not made until rather later, in the mid-seventeenth century.

Vienna 1978, 56; Vienna 1987, cat. no. VI-II/70.

S.H.

II.163
Hans Karl (mounting ascribed)
Cup with lid and leather case
Amber; gold, enamel; leather
23.5 (average 8.1 cm); case: 26.9 cm
Early seventeenth century
Gift from Melvin Gutman
Baltimore, The Baltimore Museum of Art, inv. no. 1964.13

The inventory of Rudolf's *Kunstkammer* contains an extensive group of objects fashioned from ivory or carved from amber. The gold-work mounting, ascribed to Hans Karl, bears interesting comparison with products from the Prague court workshops and demonstrates the close relations between the work of southern German goldsmiths and their mountings, which arose within the Prague circle of Rudolf's court. The leather case is an interesting example of a protective covering, which the majority of objects originally tended to have, especially those which were of greater weight.

Philippovich 1966, p.106, ill. 68

B.B.

II.164
Jug of Terra Sigillata
Baked clay
17.2 cm
Sixteenth century (?)
Vienna, Kunsthistorisches Museum, *Kunstkammer*, inv. no. 3128

The pitcher is made of a special kind of clay to which miraculous healing powers have been attributed since ancient times. In the sixteenth century, the interest in objects designated as 'terra sigillata' revived, and they once again became sought after as the cure for all kinds of illnesses. They also became collectors' items. A number of vessels of various shapes, most often small pitchers, goblets and bowls, can also be found among the entries in the 1607-11 Inventory of Rudolf II's *Kunstkammer* (nos 1061–81). A part of the collection is listed in the section labelled 'TERRAE SIGILLATAE GESCHIRRLEIN, TÜRKISCH'. One of the entries describes a small pitcher with lid: the piece exhibited here. The treatment of the unusual panel inserted into the neck of the vessel is striking, for it does not appear in any known European vessels. Its purpose was probably to permit the greatest possible contact between the liquid and the healing material. A similar pitcher is described among the other entries under the heading 'TERRAE SIGILLATAE GESCHIRLEIN VONN BRANDEIS': *Ein bachet nider geschierrlein oder krüglein auf die türkisch art, inwendig mit seinem erhebten aussgeschnittenen bödemlin, bandheh und deckel, welches wie auch nachfolgende Ihr May: aus der erden zu Prandeis Ao 1608 durch ihren damaln laibapotecher N. Hegenr machen lassen, ist von leibfarber erden.'* This tells us not only that terra sigillata was being produced in Bohemia as early as 1608, but also that some of the vessels imitated the Turkish models. At present no such vessel from Brandýs is known.

B.B.

II.165
Jug of Terra Sigillata
Baked clay
12.2 cm
Sixteenth century (?)
Vienna, Kunsthistorisches Museum, *Kunstkammer*, inv. no. 3178

This small pitcher, like the preceding one, is made of medicinal clay and has a mark with Arabic characters under the handle. It is decorated with carved ornaments and painted flowers. Objects designated as terra sigillata were produced both in Europe and in the Orient from the sixteenth century to the eighteenth; a large body of specialized literature exists from this period regarding the healing properties of this medicinal clay. In large part because of J. Horschik's 1966 article on the subject, terra sigillata has once again come to our attention, and several collections have been mapped out. Few objects have been preserved, and those outside the purview of Horschik's analysis are still waiting to be rediscovered. The collection housed in the Österreichisches Museum für Angewandte Kunst in Vienna has not been subjected to detailed study, and some of the pitchers may come from the collection of Rudolf II. Terra sigillata appears in the inventories of Rudolf's successor's inheritance among the objects that came in large part from Prague.

B. Bukovinská, *Terra Sigillata: Das vortrefflichste Mittel zu Pestzeiten* (in preparation).

B.B.

Chinese Porcelain

The export of Chinese porcelain to Europe increased considerably during the sixteenth century, when Europeans, above all the Portuguese, began to take advantage or trading opportunities. As the volume of trade grew, so it influenced production. In the first half of the century some Chinese porcelain factories were already starting to orientate themselves towards European export. During the Wanli era export grew so much that one consignment could number tens of thousands of each of the various pieces (saucers, plates, vases, jugs, etc.). Whole dinner services, with pieces completely alien to domestic Chinese tradition, began to be produced. Wanli is the name given to the reign of the Emperor (sometimes known as Guangzong) of the Ming period (1368-1644), a rival of Rudolf II, who ascended the throne in 1573 at the age of ten and ruled until 1620. A characteristic feature of Wanli porcelain is its cobalt underglaze decoration, especially in combination with overglaze decoration in enamel paints (red, green, yellow, a purplish tone, etc.). This technique is commonly known as 'five-

colour' (or *wu cai*) porcelain, and is fired twice (once at a high temperature before glazing, the second time at a low temperature after glazing). It was in the sixteenth century that this decorative technique was fully developed and mastered to perfection. By this time Chinese porcelain had already become an important part of rulers' collections. We know that Philip II, for example, owned over 700 pieces, and a total of 125 can be counted in Rudolf II's *Kunstkammer*. Three of the exhibits shown here come from the Habsburg collections, and it is not impossible that they originated in Rudolf's own collections. The other pieces on display belong to the in Prague, and represent typical products of the period. It should be added that in the sixteenth century porcelain was usually given ostentatious mounts, which in European eyes – entirely at odds with Oriental taste – enhanced and added to what were essentially very simple objects.

Z.Č.

II.166
Plate
Porcelain with cobalt-blue underglaze decoration
Diam: 30.3 cm, depth: 5.6 cm
Ming dynasty, Wanli period (1573–1619)
Vienna, Österreichisches Museum für Angewandte Kunst, inv. no. KHM 305

J.W

II.167
Plate
Porcelain with cobalt-blue underglaze decoration
Diam: 31.5 cm, depth: 5.5 cm
Ming dynasty (1368–1644)
Vienna, Österreichisches Museum für Angewandte Kunst, inv. no. KHM 305

J.W.

II.168
Vase
Porcelain with cobalt-blue underglaze decoration
Diam: 16 cm, h: 28 cm
Ming dynasty (1368–1644)
Vienna, Österreichisches Museum für Angewandte Kunst, inv. no. KHM 306

In the *Kunstkammer* inventories, foreign porcelains were categorized simply according to geographical origin ('türkisch', 'persisch', 'egiptisch', 'antiquitetisch', 'indianisch', 'chinesisch'), but without any further details, whereas the European mounts and decorations in gold and silver

were described relatively comprehensively. Items without mounts or without gold decorations were not mentioned at all, with the result that it is not possible to establish whether or not the above items were in Rudolf II's *Kunstkammer*. On the other hand, these are certainly typical of the porcelain objects exported from China that were so popular in the princely courts of Europe at the time.

J.W.

II.169
Vase
Porcelain, cobalt painting under glaze
40 cm
Sixteenth century
Prague, Náprstkovo muzeum, Národní muzeum, inv. no. 17 512

Flute-shaped vase with motif of Qi Lin meaning, 'May you have many sons' in landscape, pomegranate tree and leaf.

Bechyně 1989, cat. no. 165.

Z.Č.

II.170
Bowl
Beginning of seventeenth century
Prague, Národní muzeum, inv. no. 54 637

A flower-shaped bowl with a sea-horse motif in the upper band and clusters of flowers.

Ceramics of the Far East, Prague, Náprstkovo Museum, 1985; Bechyn-, Alčova jihoaesk galerie, 1989.

Z.Č.

II.171
Gu-shaped Vase
Porcelain decorated in coloured enamels
and blue underglaze (*wu cai*)
50cm
Ca. 1600
Prague, Náprstkovo muzeum, Národní
muzeum, inv. no. 29 147 17 605 a,b,

The basic motif of boys among lotus flowers, which has a congratulatory significance, is complemented by bands of floral
and geometric decoration and hanging
clouds.

Bechyně 1989, cat. no. 221.

Z.Č.

II.172
Wan Bowl
Porcelain decorated in coloured enamels
and blue underglaze (*wu cai*)
H: 10 cm; diam: 15 cm
Wanli era (1573–1620)
Prague, Náprstkovo muzeum, Národní
muzeum, inv. no. 17 522

Lotus petals enclose decorative motifs and
symbols of longevity.

Bechyně 1989, cat. no. 216.

Z.Č.

II.173
Ink Vessel
Wanli era (1573–1620)
Private collection

Dragons are shown playing with a pearl in
the clouds above stylized mountains in
the sea.

Ceramics of the Far East, Prague, Náprstkovo muzeum, 1985; Bechyně-Alčova jihoaesk galerie, 1989.

Z.Č.

II.174
Vase
Emerald-green glass, furnace-produced,
decorated with mould-blown ribbing,
with a forged and poured mounting, par-
tially pressed from tin, gilded
H: 16.5 cm; Diam: 14.7 cm
Ca. 1600
Prague, Uměleckoprůmyslové muzeum,
inv. no. 596

A round vase with a wide, six-lobed neck.
The mounting consists of a circular-pro-
filed foot, two S-shaped handles and a
band of pearl shapes with leaves and rings,
which is connected to a similar mounting

above the foot by four vertical bands decorated with angels' heads. R. Charleston
(1977, cat. nos 30–34) mentions several
similar vessels from the Rothschild collection in Waddeson Manor, which he identifies as seventeenth-century Italian, on the
basis of drawings by G. Ligozzi (ca. 1547–
1626) in the Uffizi. He enumerates similar
vases from the Museo Poldi-Pezzoli in Milan, the Veste Coburg and elsewhere. D.
Heikamp (1986, p. 319) mentions the Florentine drawings by G. Maggi in the Bic-
cheirografia, which include a similar
mounting. Heikamp first noted the possible connection between these works and
the glass listed as 'Pasta di Napoli' in the

1607 Inventory of Rudolf's collections (p.
63, no.1165). The works were thought to
be Neapolitan in origin because the
Neapolitan glass industry undoubtedly
modelled its products on those of Venice,
Florence and other places. The designation 'pasta' has to do with the fact that the
glass is made from a relatively heavy raw
material, which may originally have been
used to produce imitations of precious
stones. The unusually coarse mounting of
these artefacts also refutes a Florentine
origin.

O.D.

II.175
Oval Cup
Blue furnace-produced glass, mould-
blown ribbing
10 × 16.5 × 7.3 cm
Ca. 1600
Prague, Uměleckoprůmyslové muzeum,
inv. no. 9.789

An oval, vertically ribbed vase with an
open rim, compressed in the centre. A
coarse mounting of cut and pressed tin,
with poured handles in the shape of
winged snakes with birds' heads. The work
is related to the group of glass objects described in the preceding entry. R.

Charleston (1977, cat. no. 29) presented a
smooth blue vase of a similar shape together with a drawing by G. Ligozzi.

O.D.

II.176
Hans Jakob Sprüngli
Zurich 1559–Zurich 1637
Sleeping Venus and Cupid
Cold-painting on the back of the glass, lacquers, etched gold leaf with paper underlay, brown pigment paper (a technique known as *Amelieren*)
33.6 × 25 cm
Ca. 1610
Gift of Sir Vojtěch Lanna 1906
Prague, Uměleckoprůmyslové muzeum, inv. no. 10.376

The painting depicts an extensive indoor space articulated by pilasters; in the fore-ground, a nude Venus lies on gold draperies while Cupid, flying above her and to the left, shoots from a bow. A vase with flowers and a bowl of fruit stands on the chest in the front, and in front of the loge are a lute, a mandolin, musical scores, two gold ewers and the bust of a woman. *Amelieren*, the technique of applying an unfired painting to the back of the glass, came from medieval Italy and spread to Zurich from Nürnberg. Sprüngli was the best-known representative of this art during the early seventeenth century. He had many co-workers and students and worked often in Nürnberg, but always returned to Zurich, where he became a mas-ter in 1579. A number of his works have survived, painted on both blown and flat glass, and they include several pieces with the motif of *Venus and Cupid* (Berlin, Kunstgewerbemuseum, and Turin, Museo Civico). His works betray the influence of Spranger. For his scenes he used drawings by his Zurich contemporary Christoph Murer (1588–1614), whose works are mentioned in the Rudolfine Inventory.

Installation in the Uměleckoprůmyslové muzeum until 1975.

Ryser 1991, p. 101.

O.D.

II.177
Miseroni workshop in Milan(?)
Crystal Bowl
Rock crystal, enamelled gold, rubies
14.5 (without handle) × 25.4 × 27.8 cm
Ca. 1575/80
From the imperial *Schatzkammer*
Vienna, Kunsthistorisches Museum, *Kunstkammer*, inv. no. 2235

The base of this decafoil is decorated with spiral turned convex tongues. The hastily carved intaglios are mainly there to disguise imperfections in the rock crystal. Perseus and Andromeda are depicted along with Neptune and various sea-gods. The high value put on this rock crystal is evident from the precious mount. The golden semi-circular handle, like that on a lapis lazuli bowl from the Miseroni workshop in Vienna (inv. no. 1774; Fock 1974, pp. 115-117, illus. 91, 92; Fock 1976, pp. 129-131 and illus. 8, 9; mistakenly described as Florentine) consists of two horns of plenty facing each other. Where the handle is attached there are satyr masks on the outside, decorated with crowns of fruit and foliage, while on the inside there are acanthus leaves. The gold has been crafted by a master working for the Miseroni workshop in Milan and who may even have been a member of that same workshop. This bowl dates from between 1575 and 1580. In the *Kunstkammer* of the Emperor Rudolf II there was a similar bowl, which is described as 'ein großer kessel mit einer handheb von gold, der rest mit rubin und schmarall geziert'.

Cremona 1996, cat. no. XII. 14.

Leitner 1870-1873, p. 14 (with etching); Ilg 1895, p. 24, pl. 49; Strohmer 1947, pp. 27-28, illus. 10; Heinzl-Wied 1973, p. 48, illus. 21; Fock 1974, p. 116, illus. 93.

R.D.

II.178
Unknown Artist
Vessel with Two Handles
Rock crystal, enamelled gold
25.8 × 10.7 × 12.3 cm
Ca. 1565/70
From the Ambraß Collection
Vienna, Kunsthistorisches Museum, *Kunstkammer*, inv. no. 1490

This vessel is shaped somewhat like a pilgrim's flask, although instead of a narrow opening there is a broad round neck with a lid as on a vase. The oval body is decorated with a band showing the twelve signs of the zodiac, interspersed with four heads standing boldly out. These separate the four seasons. The figurative intaglios are of the highest quality and could be by the young Annibale Fontana (Milan 1540-1587). They share the same style and technique as his intaglios on the Persephone cup in Vienna (inv. no. 1415, Distelberger 1975, pp. 107-112, 117, 119-120, 144, illus. 121-127). The foliage intaglios with birds on the slightly concave neck, separated from the body by a ring of diamonds, has clearly been made by another artist. The golden semi-circular handle is fixed on to snakes. The base is decorated with the finest of enamel work and typical Milanese black foliage. Thus it is clear that this flask was been made by four artists altogether. The first created the vessel (arte grossa), the second created the foliage (arte minuta), the third created the signs of the zodiac (figurative arte minuta) and the fourth the mount. This is wholly typical of the degree of specialization amongst the hardstone carvers in Milan. In Rudolf II's *Kunst-kammer* there was a similar vessel, listed as no. 1244 in the Inventory of 1607–11.

R.D.

II.179
Gasparo Miseroni
Milan ca. 1518–? 1573
Rock Crystal Covered Bowl with Two Scrolled Handles
Rock crystal, enamelled gold, ruby
14.2 × 16.5 × 18.9 cm
Ca. 1565-1570
From the imperial *Schatzkammer*;
Inventory of 1750, p. 262, no. 58
Vienna, Kunsthistorisches Museum, *Kunstkammer*, inv. no. 2302

This very compact-looking bowl with a low foot is, on the one hand, positively sculptural, but does on the other hand have enough surfaces to show the immaculate clarity of the rock crystal and to accommodate some delicate intaglios. On the broad shoulder there are two spouts opposite each other on the same axis while the other has two masks. These latter have holes bored under the scrolls through the mouth for a handle to be attached, which has either been lost or was never made. A curved cover with a ruby knob completes the piece. Down to the last detail, this piece resembles work Gasparo Miseroni was producing by the 1560s at the latest (see Distelberger 1978, pp. 80-102). The golden foot-ring was made by the same hand that created the mounts for Gasparo Miseroni's large jasper bowl (inv. no. 1668) and the rock crystal dragon bowl (inv. no. 2268) which are both held in Vienna. Since it was the Emperor Maximilian II (1564-1576) who discovered Gasparo and was the first to collect his work, it is likely that this bowl was made in the 1560s after Maximilian II came to the throne.

Darmstadt 1992/93, pp. 153-154, no. 48.

Distelberger 1978, p. 94 and passim, illus. 67.

R.D.

II.180
Miseroni workshop in Milan
Amphora
Rock crystal, enamelled gold
33 × 22.1 cm; Diam: 13.4 cm
Ca. 1600
From the *Schatzkammer*
Vienna, Kunsthistorisches Museum, *Kunstkammer*, inv. no. 2311

Of all the many large vases that were made around 1600 in the Miseroni workshop in Milan, this is one of the most beautiful. The foliage intaglios on the sides take up and vary the scroll motif from the handles in a whole number of different ways. They are always symmetrical in their design and yet still manage to incorporate with the utmost virtuosity any imperfections in the crystal. The strong diagonal lines on one side are dictated by a strong streak in the crystal which had to be disguised. These taut lines do not recur on the other side which instead has a quite different design that nevertheless so closely resembles the other as it reaches the edge that a new symmetry is established. Stylistically this vase could hardly be more closely related to the small smoky quartz bowls that Ottavio Miseroni's cousins were sending to Prague in around 1610. The feathered twigs low down which are also there to hide imperfections in the crystal are almost identical to those on one of these smoky quartz bowls (Distelberger 1978, illus. 78), while the delicate festoons of fruit on the lip are clearly related to another (inv. no. 1370). The mount too links this vase with the Miseroni workshop in Milan.

Distelberger 1978, p. 117, illus. 93.

R.D.

II.181
Miseroni workshop in Milan
Tazza
Rock crystal, enamelled gold
12.2 cm; Diam: 15.3 cm
1580–1600
Kunstkammer of the Emperor Rudolf II,
Inventory of 1607-11, no. 1242
Vienna, Kunsthistorisches Museum,
Kunstkammer, inv. no. 1373

The name of this piece derives not from its function but from the Inventory of 1607-11 describing its ice-like appearance: 'geschnitten wie d'jacco oder sam wanns gfrorn wär'. Because of some impurity in the stone on the underside, this part is not polished, only grained. This makes it look as though this tazza is made of ice. The base of the foot echoes the same rough surface. In contrast, the stem and the upper surface are perfectly polished. No other vessel is known with a rough surface of this sort incorporated into the design, that is to say, left in the state it would be before the final polish. The shape of the foot is characteristic of work from the Miseroni workshop in Milan, as is also the precise carving of the fine tendrils along the rim.

Essen and Vienna, cat. no. 356.

R.D.

II.182
Unknown Artist
Covered Goblet
Rock crystal, enamelled gold, garnets
20.5 cm; Diam: 6.3 cm
Early seventeenth century
From the imperial *Schatzkammer*
Vienna, Kunsthistorisches Museum,
Kunstkammer, inv. no. 2367

On the underside of the foot there is a small gold enamelled plate with the Austrian coat of arms and the Archduke's crown which shows that this cup was not intended for Rudolf II although it is true that he did have a similar piece in his *Kunstkammer*. The Inventory of 1607-11 lists 'ein geschirr sambt deckel geschnitten auff diamant punt, mit einem fueß von gold' (Bauer-Haupt 1976, no. 1234). The style of decoration seen here on the walls, the lid and the stem is rare around 1600 although it is found on works (tankard, jugs and cups) by southern German goldsmiths. The rows of garnets on the various parts of the mount are typical of work produced in Prague but the connections to the Miseroni workshop are too vague for a definite attribution, particularly since there were other masters working with rock crystal in Prague at the time.

Essen and Vienna 1988, cat. no. 710.

Kris 1929, no. 657, pl. 199.

R.D.

II.183
Workshop of Ottavio Miseroni
? Milan–Prague 1624
Bowl with Festoons
Polished and engraved crystal
H: 15.5 cm
Late sixteenth century
From the property of the counts of Nostitz, 1945
Prague, Uměleckoprůmyslové muzeum, inv. no. 78.004

The slightly conical, flattened beaker is articulated by four pairs of horizontal ribs; the surfaces between them are decorated with fine garlands sparsely hung with fruits and leaves. The decoration is reminiscent of older works from the Miseroni workshop. It is possible that the beaker was made by a member of the Miseroni family who stayed briefly in Prague. A similar beaker is found in Vienna (Kunsthistorisches Museum), and the Dresden collections (Grünes Gewölbe) contain a barrel-shaped vessel with similar decorations, which was presented by Ferdinand III to the Saxon Elector George III in 1653 (Holzhausen 1934).

Corning 1981, cat. no. 10.

O.D.

II.184
Miseroni workshops in Milan and Prague; mount: attributed to Andreas Osenbruck
Active in Prague from 1610 to 1622
Covered Goblet
Smoky quartz, gold-enamelled
14.5 × 9.3 × 13.3 cm
1607-11; ca. 1625 (?)
Kunstkammer of Emperor Rudolf II, Inventory of 1607-11, no. 1333
Vienna, Kunsthistorisches Museum,
Kunstkammer, inv. no. 1370

This bowl is one of four listed in the Inventory of 1607-11 that a cousin of Ottavio Miseroni's brought unmounted from Milan. The less skilfully carved, darker lid is not mentioned in the Inventory and, although it uses Ottavio Miseroni's 'soft leaf' motif, it is not of the same standard as other work by him. This bowl could well be an early piece by his son Dionysio, who adopted his father's soft leaf motif (see inv. 1624) and in later works also included a relatively prominent disc below the node. The lid and the mount probably therefore date from the 1620s, during the reign of Emperor Ferdinand II (1619-37). The style of the mount is inspired by the Vermeyen workshop, while the details of the enamel work may well be from the Prague workshop of Andreas Osenbruck, who both adopted and adapted Vermeyen's style.

Essen and Vienna 1988, cat. no. 695.

Distelberger 1978, pp. 103–106.

R.D.

II.185
Miseroni workshop in Milan; mount: workshop of Jan Vermeyen
Brussels before 1559-Prague 1608
Vessel in the Shape of a Mascaron
Smoky quartz; mount: gold-enamelled
10.2 × 16.5 × 14 cm
Ca. 1600
Kunstkammer of Emperor Rudolf II, Inventory of 1607-11, no. 1328
Vienna, Kunsthistorisches Museum,
Kunstkammer, inv. no. 1347

This solid bowl in the form of a grotesque head with wide-open mouth is distinctly sculptural in its aspect. As a rule, stone-carvers made vessels with thick side walls in order to show the dark stone at its best. If the walls were too thin, the subtle shading of the stone would be lost. The convex mascaron and the tangled hair link this bowl closely with a similar item in the Wallace Collection (inv. no. I.A. 14) that is listed in the Inventory of 1607-11: 'hatt des Oct.(avian) Miserons vetter von Mayland ... gebracht' (no. 1331). Thus it may be assumed that this bowl was also made in the Miseroni workshop. The fine enamel work over a white ground on the golden base relates closely to work carried out in the Vermeyen workshop on the Rudolf crown, completed in 1602, which therefore dates this bowl to around 1600.

Essen and Vienna 1988, cat. no. 358.

Bauer-Haupt 1976, p. 72, no. 1328 (mistakenly listed there as 1331); Distelberger 1978, pp. 102–103, ill. 76.

R.D.

II.186
Ottavio Miseroni
Milan 1567-Prague 1624
Vessel in the Shape of Lion Skin
Smoky quartz
8.9 × 9.6 × 24.6 cm
Ca. 1590 until 1600
Kunstkammer of the Emperor Rudolf II,
Inventory of 1607-11, no. 1326
Vienna, Kunsthistorisches Museum,
Kunstkammer, inv. no. 2349

This remarkable design creates the illusion that an upside-down lion skin has been draped over an oblong bowl. Ottavio Miseroni made this bowl so that it would not need a mount. The position of the lion's head as well as the shape of its eyes and mouth are reminiscent of a mascaron on a shallow jade bowl now held in Vienna (inv. no. 1641). The young master demonstrates his technical skill by setting himself the additional challenge of having the lion's paws cross twice over the piece. In the *Kunstkammer* Inventory of 1607-1611 this piece is described as 'ein geschirrl von topazio, wie ein lewenhautt'. Nora Watteck's view that this piece comes from Salzburg is utterly without foundation.

Essen and Vienna 1988, cat. no. 364.

Distelberger 1978, p. 131.

R.D.

II.187
Miseroni workshop in Milan
Cup with a Mascaron
Smoke-quartz; gold, enamel
7.7 × 12 × 9.7 cm
1600–1610
Rosenborg, Inventory 1696, 64 no. 9.
Copenhagen, De Danske Kongers Kronologiske Samling, Rosenborg, inv. no. 5229

The soft, almost sensuous lion's mask is distinctly reminiscent of a mascaron bowl in Vienna (Kunsthistorisches Museum, inv. no. 1347) with a mount by Jan Vermeyen; according to Rudolf Distelberger, the Vienna bowl could have been made either in Prague or in Milan. The precise lines of the pipes, the tracery and the scrollwork are similar to other smoky-quartz vessels sent to Rudolf II from Milan between 1607 and 1611 (Vienna, Kunsthistorisches Museum, inv. nos 1338, 1370). The style of this bowl clearly marks it out as having been made in Milan.

Paris, Petit Palais, 1978, no. 35; Copenhagen, Rosenborg, 1988 no. 650.

J. Hein 1985, p. 40; Copenhagen 1994, no. 4102.

J.He.

II.188
Ottavio Miseroni; setting: Jan Vermeyen workshop
Milan 1567-Prague 1624
Violet Agate Covered Bowl
Agate, enamelled gold
14.8 × 10.1 × 12.7 cm
Ca. 1605
Kunstkammer of the Emperor Rudolf II,
Inventory of 1607-11, no. 1367
Vienna, Kunsthistorisches Museum,
Kunstkammer, inv. no. 1803

This stone probably comes from the same source as the larger rose agate covered bowl (cat. no. II.23). In both cases the cover is formed from the inside of the bowl. The vessel is shaped like a smooth shell, with strong lines rolling inwards at the hinge revealing the hand of Ottavio Miseroni. The foot is similar in form to the large nephrite bowl with scrolls (Vienna, inv. no. 6846; Essen and Vienna 1988, cat. no. 367). The Inventory of 1607-11 describes the piece as 'ein schön agatin geschirrlin und deckl gleich einer muschel, deckel und fueß mit gold und schwartz und weiß geschmeltzt, der stain ist bloblicht graw, mit rot vermischt'. The mount, in this case without any coloured enamel work, is indubitably from the Vermeyen workshop. The not very visible gold and the black and white enamel decoration form a harmonious whole together with the violet of the stone itself.

Essen and Vienna 1988, cat. no. 701.

Bauer-Haupt 1976, no. 1367 (not specified); Distelberger 1978, p. 139, illus. 117.

R.D.

II.189
Workshop of Ottavio Miseroni
Cup
Agate with gold and enamel mounts
7.5 × 8 × 11.5 cm
After 1600
Bought 1968
Berlin, Staatliche Museen, Kunstgewerbemuseum, inv. no. 1968/5

The smooth oval bowl made of beautiful moss agate has a high foot with a compressed stem and enamelled gold mounts. The treatment of the stone, the slightly raised oval on the bottom of the vessel and the shape of the stem indicate its relationship to the products of the Miseroni workshop in Prague.

Berlin 1970, cat. no. 39.

Dreier 1969, pp. 210 ff.

B.B.

II.190
Goblet
Bohemian agate (from the Kozákov); gold, enamel, rubies
16.4 × 14.1 × 10 cm (11.4 cm without lid)
1580-1590
Rosenborg, inv. 1718, 72 no. 26
Copenhagen, De Danske Kongers Kronologiske Samling, Rosenborg, inv. no. 194

In its proportions – the rotund oval of the bowl, the shallow curve of the lid and the baluster stem –this piece is reminiscent of Italian covered bowls from around 1550–60. Unfortunately, only the original mount for the lid has survived. The translucent grey and red agate with its mossy green veining can be identified as coming from Kozákov, but it is impossible to say where the enamelled mount was made. Anna Maria Giusti has shown that Bohemian hardstones were exported to Florence in 1589, if not earlier. Was this covered bowl made in Italy from imported Bohemian hardstones, or was it made in Prague in the early years after Rudolf II's move there in 1583?

Paris, Petit Palais 1978, no. 51.

Copenhagen 1994, no. 4463.

J.He.

II.191
Miseroni workshop in Prague; mount: Jan
Vermeyen workshop
Milan 1567–Prague 1624
Helmut-Shaped Bowl
Brown agate, enamelled gold
15 cm
Between 1600 and 1608
Inventory of 1776, no. 35
Madrid, Museo del Prado, Alhajas del
Delfin no. 18

This deep bowl prefigures the shape of later sauce-boats. The lip sweeping elegantly
upwards, the lower shoulders to the rear
and the high handle are all reminiscent of

the upper section of a jug, while the overall form derives from the shell-shaped
bowls. On the basis of the fine carving and
the Prague mount this piece could fairly
be attributed to Ottavio Miseroni without
further ado. However, the formation of
the rim and the scrolls turning outwards
on either side of the base of the handle do
not entirely match his style. On the other
hand, the flat disc at the foot joint and the
shape of the foot itself are quite clearly the
work of the Miseroni workshop in Prague.
The same shape of foot is found again in
Ottavio's covered agate bowl with a
Moor's head in the collection in Vienna
(inv. no. 1812; Distelberger 1978, illus.

118), which is listed in the *Kunstkammer*
Inventory of 1607-11 (Bauer–Haupt 1976,
no. 1342). This and the violet covered bowl
(inv. no. 1803) also have black enamel
work with similar decorations on their
mounts. Thus the gold work on this helmet-shaped bowl may be attributed to the
Jan Vermeyen workshop and dated before
1608.

Angulo Iñiguez, 1954 and 1989, no. 18.

R.D.

II.192
Ottavio Miseroni
Milan 1567–Prague 1624
Cup
Grey-black agate
7.2 × 10.3 × 13.4 cm
Ca. 1610–15
From the imperial *Schatzkammer*
Vienna, Kunsthistorisches Museum,
Kunstkammer, inv. no. 1640

This vessel in this rare stone is a variation
on the form of the brown helmet-shaped
bowl in Madrid (cat. no. II.191). On the
more shell-shaped Madrid bowl the back
edge stands out from the body: here the

lip is more prominent, while the shell-
hinge – as elsewhere in work by Ottavio
Miseroni – rolls inwards from the rim. The
master's hand is easily recognized in the
details of the piece. As in other shell-
shaped bowls by Ottavio, the stern rises
up more steeply than the prow. The scrolls
which are much more abstract here than
on the Madrid version are found again on
the shell-shaped green jasper bowl in Vienna (inv. no. 1962, Essen and Vienna, cat.
no. 698) and again, but considerably enlarged, on the Bacchus bowl (cat. no. II.45).
The walls are barely two millimetres thick
and perfectly polished. Between the scrolls
on the shell-hinge there is a square knob,

either the only point to attach a handle or
intended for some other decorative feature. Jan Vermeyen, who mounted most of
the pieces Ottavio made in the first decade
of the seventeenth century, died in 1608
which meant that this finest of pieces was
never completed.

R.D.

II.193
Miseroni workshop in Milan; mount: Jan
Vermeyen workshop
Shell-shaped Bowl
Red and green jasper, enamelled gold
11.9 × 13.3 × 16.5 cm
Ca. 1603
Kunstkammer of the Emperor Rudolf II,
Inventory of 1607–11, no. 1429 (or 1430?)
Vienna, Kunsthistorisches Museum,
Kunstkammer, inv. no. 1920

A broad spiral of red and green mixed together in the jasper here look more like a
painter's brushwork than stone. The carver then followed this colouration in his de-

sign for a bowl. It is possible to be misled
by the Prague mount into assuming this
to be a product of the Miseroni workshop
in Prague. However, it is too unlike their
work. The shape is an abstract reproduction of the dragon bowls made by Gasparo
Miseroni in Florence and Vienna. The animal in the latter is replaced here by a
raised rim. The swelling baluster foot
drawing in abruptly above the lower ring
of the mount is not found anywhere in Ottavio's output. Thus it is clear that this
bowl, like a number of others, arrived unmounted from Prague in Milan (for example inv. nos 1347, 1370). The enamelled
gold mount was most probably made in

the Vermeyen workshop. Details of the
decoration tie in as closely is possible with
the blackwork ornaments designed by the
Master GB in 1603, so it seems that the
piece was mounted in 1603 having been
made shortly before that.

Essen and Vienna 1988, cat. no. 693.

Bauer–Haupt 1976, no. 1429 (or 1430; not
indentified); Distelberger 1978, p. 132.

R.D.

II.194
Miseroni workshop in Prague; mount: Jan
Vermeyen workshop
Milan 1567-Prague 1624
Covered Goblet
Jasper; gold, enamel
14 cm (9.2 cm without lid)
Ca. 1600
Stuttgart, Württembergisches Landesmu-
seum, inv. no. grün 99

The small goblet with lid and gold mounts
with colourful enamel is a typical example
of the high-quality output of the Prague
court workshops. The vessel itself has a
simple shape complemented by precise

mounts, and the proportions of the work
as a whole are perfectly balanced. The goblet has been preserved undamaged and is a
vivid example of the care with which the
goldsmith shaped even a small piece of
precious stone into an exquisite display
piece. The lid is carved from the interior of
the goblet, and the difference in size is
compensated for by the mounts. These
can be compared with mounts attributed
to Jan Vermeyen (cat. nos KHM KK 1962,
6846, 1650 ad.).

Fleischhauer 1976, p. 30.

B.B.

II.195
Miseroni workshop in Prague; mount: Jan
Vermeyen workshop
Tazza
Jasper; gold, enamel
11 × 16.1 cm
Ca. 1600
Stuttgart, Württembergisches Landesmu-
seum, inv. no. grün 101

The six-lobed, shell-shaped bowl on a
high, slender baluster with an oval foot is
provided with coloured enamelled gold
mounts in three places. The beautiful
stone, precise carving, balanced composition and surface treatment of this work

make it one of the most outstanding items
produced by the Prague court workshops
in the late sixteenth century and the early
seventeenth century. The carving was
surely done by a member of the Miseroni
family, but it is not possible to determine
which one.

Fleischhauer 1976, pp. 114, 119.

B.B.

II.196
? Ottavio Miseroni
Milan 1567–Prague 1624
Cup with Cover
Jasper; gold, enamel
16 × 15 cm
After 1600
Skoklosterinventar 1728, 1793.
Bålsta, Skokloster, Castle, inv. no. 97

The footed vessel with lid is made of dark jasper and has a gold mount with sculptural ornaments and coloured enamel. The balanced proportions, graceful forms and interesting relief decoration of the outside and the lid make the vessel a high-quality example of glyptic items produced in the late sixteenth century and the early seventeenth. The closest analogues, particularly in the execution of the mount, are the three jadeite vessels (Vienna, KK 1651, 1641; Stuttgart, KK grün 34) attributed to Ottavio Miseroni. The flat relief seems to point to the authorship of Miseroni, who used different variations of it to decorate some of his vessels. The original case of stamped leather with gilded ornamentation and a black velvet interior has also been preserved in the Skokloster collections. It constitutes a rare example of the protective casings that were apparently used for all such vessels. Cases are often mentioned in Rudolfine inventories.

Skokloster 1995, p. 70, cat. no. 15.

B.B.

II.197
Ottavio Miseroni; mount: Jan Vermeyen workshop
Milan 1567–Prague 1624
Cup
Heliotrope, enamelled gold
6.5 cm
Ca. 1600–05
Inventory 1776, no. 58
Madrid, Museo del Prado, Alhajas del Delfin, inv. no. 17

Although this small bowl seems overall to be somewhat heavy and solid, it is nevertheless definitely the work of Ottavio Miseroni. It has much in common with Ottavio's green jasper bowl, now in the collection in Vienna (inv. no. 1962, Distelberger 1978, illus. 116). The same foot is also found on other pieces by Ottavio, for example, on the rose agate-covered bowl (cat. no. II.23) or the so-called Bacchus bowl (cat. no. II.45). And the mount resembles other Viennese mounts, the stem-ring being identical to that on a small moss agate bowl (inv. no. 2060). Thus it is clear that this small bowl was made, like these others, at some point after 1600.

Angulo Iñiguez, 1954 and 1989, no. 17

R.D.

II.198
Ottavio Miseroni (hardstone carver); mount: Jan Vermeyen
Milan 1567–Prague 1624; Brussels before 1559–Prague 1606
Bowl
Heliotrope, carved; Mount: gold, coloured enamel
Height: 10.5 cm
1600–05
Listed in the inventory of special valuables in the Grünes Gewölbe in 1733, Bl. 789, no. 33 and Bl. 791. This bowl came from the estate of the Duke Johann Adolf II of Sachsen–Weißenfels and went to the Grünes Gewölbe on 6 August 1746.
Dresden, Grünes Gewölbe, inv. no. V 19

This thin-walled oval bowl was made from heliotrope. Legend had it that the sprinklings of red in this dark-green form of jasper were petrified droplets of the blood of Christ, which is why this stone was also known as blood jasper and was believed to have special, magical healing powers. Stylistic comparisons with works known to be by Ottavio Miseroni in the Kunstkammer of the Kunsthistorisches Museum in Vienna suggest that this piece was by Miseroni, who had come at Rudolf II's behest to the court in Prague in 1588. The enamelled gold stem and foot-ring are by the imperial court goldsmith Jan Vermeyen from Brussels, who also fashioned the Rudolf crown. This bowl is clearly a masterpiece amongst the carved hardstone items produced in Prague around 1600. Combining the work of the hardstone carver Miseroni and the goldsmith Vermeyen, this piece constitutes the virtually perfect union of two virtuoso talents.

Sponsel 1921, p. 200; Menzhausen 1977, p. 187, illus. 117; Grünes Gewölbe 1994, p. 132

J.Kp.

II.199
Ottavio Miseroni
Milan 1567–Prague 1624
Cup
Jasper, stem heliotrope
8.5 × 15 cm
Early seventeenth century; stem and mounting later
Nostitz Collection. From 1945 in the State Monument Administration, transferred to the property of the Uměleckoprůmyslove Muzeum in Prague in 1963
Prague, Uměleckoprůmyslové Muzeum, inv. no. 78 008

This shell-shaped vessel of interestingly coloured jasper is actually the mouth of a monster, whose head forms the sculptural ornamentation at the cusp of the bowl. Objects shaped in this way were a favourite style of the Miseroni workshops, and a similar composition can be found on two vessels attributed to Ottavio Miseroni in the Österreichisches Museum für Angewandte Kunst in Vienna (KK 1651, cat. no. 1641). The vessel is damaged along the edge, and neither the foot nor the mounts are original, but it nonetheless constitutes an important example of this type of court artefact. It comes from the Nostitz Collection, along with other interesting pieces made of precious stones and crystal (Koula, 1913). How it became a part of these collections, however, is not yet known.

The Nostitz-Rienecke Property, exh. cat., 1891 (listed there without the foot); Ingelheim 1988, cat. no. 157; Prague 1993, no. V/3–22; Prague 1994, cat. no. 114.

Koula 1913, ill. p. 90 (without commentary or other information); B. Bukovinská 1971 p. 120.

B.B.

II.200
Jan Vermeyen (attr.); hardstone carver: Ottavio Miseroni
Brussels before 1559–Prague 1608; Milan 1567–Prague 1624
Tazza with Cover
Prase, enamelled gold, garnets, with a citrine on the tip of the cover and an amethyst inside the cover, garnets and a hyacinth in the base of the bowl
23.5 cm; Diameter 17.6 cm
Ca. 1600–1605
Kunstkammer of the Emperor Rudolf II, Inventory of 1607–11, no. 1437
Vienna, Kunsthistorisches Museum, Kunstkammer, inv. no. 1918

The form of the bowl which is made up of numerous sections of prase in a framework of gold suggests that the design was in fact by a goldsmith. The complexity of the cover is without parallel. And indeed, a number of details concerning the gold enamel work point to the hand of Jan Vermeyen as does the fine precision of the work itself. The extraordinarily fine, exact carving of the pieces of prase could only have been by Ottavio Miseroni, who also worked with Vermeyen on other pieces in the period after 1600 (cf. cat. nos II.44, II.45). In this case, unusually, the goldsmith was in charge, which explains the fact that this form is unique in Ottavio's œuvre, whose own vessels seem heavy and earthbound in comparison. The extremely slim stem above the high conical foot is only possible because it is hollow and held together with a pin: a practice otherwise quite unknown to the Italians. So far it has not been possible to identify any models for the design of the black translucent enamel work on the smooth gold bands on the underside of the tazza.

Essen and Vienna 1988, cat. no. 344

Distelberger 1985, p. 284

R.D.

II.201
Ottavio Miseroni
Milan 1567–Prague 1624
Shell-shaped Bowl Cup with Jade Mascaron
Jade, enamelled gold, rubies
10.9 × 20.4 × 22.4 cm
Ca. 1590–1600
Kunstkammer of the Emperor Rudolf II, Inventory of 1607–11, no. 1445
Vienna, Kunsthistorisches Museum, Kunstkammer, inv. no. 1641

The Inventory of 1607–11 describes this as 'ein ablang geschirrl von weißem igiada mit einem lewenkopf, handheb und fuß von gold mit rubin versetzt'. This bowl, the jade shell-shaped jade bowl in Stuttgart (inv. KK green 34; Essen and Vienna 1988, cat. no. 361) and the nephrite mascaron bowl with a high foot in Vienna (inv. no. 1651; Essen and Vienna 1988, cat. no. 362) are all products of Ottavio Miseroni's early period in Prague. All three have the same type of mount and in terms of their form are still close to the Miseroni workshop in Milan. It is not possible to say with any certainty whether or not Ottavio himself invented the motif of a large lion mascaron on the shell-hinge, found again on vessels from Milan around 1600 (cf. inv. 1347, and also the 'Lionskin' (cat. no. II.186). Typical of Ottavio is the way that he softens the solidity of the form of the vessel. The upper edge is not strictly horizontal while the scrolls on either side of the handle attachment are reminiscent of the scrolls on the somewhat more strictly composed moss agate bowl (inv. no. 1987).

Essen and Vienna 1988, cat. no. 363

Bukovinská 1970, p. 192 and illus. 7; Distelberger 1978, p. 130

R.D.

II.202
Prague court workshops; mount: after Mathias Beitler
Cup
Jade; gold, enamel, garnet
12.4 × 10.6 × 16.1 cm
Early seventeenth century
Schatzkammer
Vienna, Kunsthistorisches Museum, Kunstkammer, inv. no. 1727

The simple, oval-shaped vessel on a high foot has gold mounts, ornamented with Czech garnets along its edges and on the articulations of the individual parts of the foot. The matt surface, a characteristic treatment for jade work, differentiates the vessel somewhat from pieces more typical of the Prague workshops, such as jasper or agate objects characterized by their highly polished lustre. The shape of the vessel is not directly comparable with works from the circle of Ottavio Miseroni. The mounts on the edge of the work are interesting in that the smooth gold surface serves as a base for landscape and figural motifs executed in translucent enamel. These motifs relate to the graphic models of goldsmith and engraver Mathias Beitler, active after 1600 in Prague. The mounts point to the participation, so far unexplained, of other goldsmiths and engravers in the operation of the court goldsmithing workshops and their relationship to Jan Vermeyen personally. The pink jasper vessel with lid (cat. no. KHM 1624) has similar mounts.

Essen and Vienna 1988, cat. no. 370.

Distelberger 1978, p. 139; Bukovinská 1982, pp. 71–82; Schütte 1988, pp. 267–72.

B.B.

II.203
Gasparo Miseroni Workshop
Small Bowl
Lapis lazuli, enamelled gold
6 × 8.7 × 12.2 cm
Ca. 1560; mount: ca. 1550–75
Milan; Mount: Augsburg (?)
Kunstkammer of the Emperor Rudolf II, Inventory of 1607–1611, no. 1472
Vienna, Kunsthistorisches Museum, Kunstkammer, inv. no. 1818

The midpoint of each of the longer sides of this small bowl is decorated with a strong putto's head. One is surrounded with horns of plenty while the other is be-decked with grapes. The lip and the foot are mounted in a manner that was most likely not intended by the stone carver. The tapering lip is rounded from the inside but now this fine line is hidden by a band of enamel, flat on top and depriving the form of all its original elegance. This bowl had no need of a mount. In the Museo degli Argenti in Florence there is an oval bowl in lapis lazuli, which has very similar putti on its sides, one of whom is also a Bacchus figure with grapes (Inventory of 1921 no. 710, Height: 7.5 cm, Length: 21.5 cm, Breadth: 13 cm; Fock 1976, pp. 122–123, illus. 3). This bowl, which is already included in the Inventory of 1570, is rightly ascribed to Gasparo Miseroni. It had no mount from the outset. The similarity with the masks on the bowls in Vienna and Florence, right down to the eyes, is so striking that there is no doubt they came from the same workshop and the Florentine piece helps to establish the date.

Darmstadt 1992, p. 191, no. 101 (with illus.)

R.D.

II.204
? Miseroni workshop in Milan
Lapis Lazuli Basin
Lapis lazuli, agate; setting: silver gilt, enamelled gold, diamonds, rubies
Diam: 41.7 cm
Ca. 1575–1580
Kunstkammer of the Emperor Rudolf II; Inventory of 1607–11, no. 1474
Vienna, Kunsthistorisches Museum, Kunstkammer, inv. no. 963

This basin is not a pastiche, as was long thought to be the case, but complete in itself with each element relating closely to the others, both in the combination of silver gilt, enamelled gold and open-work on a blue ground, and in the details of the cameo setting in the Milan style. The design of radially arranged hermas is found again on a rock crystal bowl in Vienna that is attributed to the Miseroni workshop and which even has similar quatrefoil-shaped nuts on the reverse. The Leda cameo in the centre was much admired for its size but neither its circular composition nor the modelling of the figure is particularly successful. Details of the face, the hair, the draperies and the high relief all point to its possibly having been made in the Miseroni workshop. It is also likely that the work was coordinated there, including the goldwork, which looks to have been made in the late 1570s or around 1580. The Inventory of 1607–11, which only has five lapis lazuli pieces, describes this as 'ein gießbeckhen von lapis lazuli mit gold und silber gefasst, inmitten ein stuckh ist die Leda, 6 grosse rubin und 66 diamanten, 12 camehi, 12 kayser'.

Essen and Vienna 1988, cat. no. 357

Eichler–Kris 1927, p. 34 and no. 195; Rossi 1957, p. 46, pl. 56

R.D.

II.205
Jan Gregor van der Schardt; Wenzel Jamnitzer
Nijmegen ca. 1530–? Nürnberg after 1581; Vienna ca. 1508–Nürnberg 1585
Allegory of Spring (part of the *Fountain* of Wenzel Jamnitzer, no longer in existence)
Gilt bronze
H: 71.2 cm
Completed 1578
Kunstkammer of Emperor Rudolf II, Inventory of 1607–11, no. 1528; Inventory of Emperor Matthias of 1619; taken to Vienna in 1629; in the *Schatzkammer* in Vienna since 1640
Vienna, Kunsthistorisches Museum, Kunstkammer, inv. no. 1118

In 1568, Maximilian II commissioned the so-called 'Prague Pleasure Fountain' from Wenzel Jamnitzer. The 3-metre-tall silver fountain, completed in 1578, was in use for a short while only. In the mid-eighteenth century, the parts were melted down. However, the four gilt-bronze figures which originally carried the lowest dish have survived. These are allegories of the four seasons in the shape of gods from antiquity. The style of the caryatids shows them to be by van der Schardt, who must have worked as a sculptor with Jamnitzer. In her slim form, pose and gestures, *Spring* is clearly related to the now lost bronze figure of *Minerva*, which van den Schardt made for the Emperor Maximilian II, as can be seen from the mould, now in private ownership (see Berlin, 1995, cat. no. 93).

Essen and Vienna 1988, cat. no. 520a; Berlin 1995, cat. no. 94.

Pechstein 1988, pp. 232–35; Honnens 1991, pp. 97–101.

U.B.

II.206
Jan Gregor van der Schardt; Wenzel Jamnitzer
Nijmegen ca. 1530–? Nürnberg after 1581; Vienna ca. 1508–Nürnberg 1585
Allegory of Autumn (part of the *Fountain* of Wenzel Jamnitzer, no longer in existence)
Gilt bronze
H: 71.8 cm
1578
Kunstkammer of Emperor Rudolf II, Inventory of 1607-11, no. 1528; Inventory of Emperor Matthias of 1619; taken to Vienna in 1629; in the *Schatzkammer* in Vienna since 1640
Vienna, Kunsthistorisches Museum,

Kunstkammer, inv. no. 1 126

Like the figures of *Spring* (cat. no. II.205), *Summer* and *Winter* (Vienna, Kunsthistorisches Museum), *Autumn* is also from the otherwise destroyed 'Prague Pleasure Fountain'. A youthfully slim Bacchus wears vine leaves in his hair. In his right hand he has a grape and in his left hand he has a vine tendril. The Dutchman van der Schardt moved from Italy to Prague on his appointment as court sculptor to Maximilian II in 1569, and became one of the first exponents of Mannerist sculpture north of the Alps. The *Four Seasons* are notable for the elongated proportions and elegant

movements of the figures. Rudolf II did not keep van der Schardt on as court sculptor, preferring instead the more dynamic sculptural style of Adriaen de Vries.

Essen and Vienna 1988, cat. no. 520c; Berlin, 1995 cat. no. 96.

Pechstein 1988, pp. 232–35; Honnens 1991, pp. 97-101.

U.B.

II.207
Michael Schneeberger; goldsmith work: Jan Vermeyen
Fl. Prague 1602–1609; Brussels before 1559-Prague 1608
Table Clock
Gold, translucent enamel, rock crystal, garnet, gilded copper
H: 12.6 cm
MICHAEL SNEBERGER IN PRAG 1606
1606
Kunstkammer of Emperor Rudolf II, Inventory of 1607-11, nos 1495, 2190
Vienna, Kunsthistorisches Museum, Kunstkammer, inv. no. 1 148

This clock has three mechanisms built on top of each other (two are visible in the crystal cylinder): the main clockwork and one each for the quarter- and full-hour chimes. The face is under a crystal cover; it shows the minutes and the hours as well as the path and phases of the moon, the latter by means of a small, semi-gilded ball on the hour hand. The casing of this extraordinarily rich little clock is ascribed to Jan Vermeyen.

Essen and Vienna 1988, cat. no. 449.

J.H.L.

II.208
Unknown Artist
Table Clock
Silver, copper and brass, gilding, enamel, garnets, agate, smoky quartz, rock crystal
H: 21 cm
Ca. 1610; pendulum ca. 1700
Kunstkammer of Emperor Rudolf II, Inventory of 1607-11, no. 1506
Vienna, Kunsthistorisches Museum, Kunstkammer, inv. no. 1 144

This clock consists of two watchworks coupled together: the left face shows the hours and minutes, the right face shows the weeks and the phases of the moon.

The circle of animals in the centre of the face on the right suggests that originally the months of the year were also shown.

Essen and Vienna 1988, cat. no. 451.

J.H.L.

II.209
Christoph Lencker
Ludwigsorget ca. 1556–Augsburg 1613
Basin with the History of Europe
Silver, largely gilt, enamel, emeralds
7.8×68.5×57 cm
Inscribed: see Seling Supplement, no. 28* (ca. 1600-1610); Mz.: Seling Supplement no. 993h
Ca. 1600
Kunstkammer of Emperor Rudolf II, Inventory of 1607-1611, no. 1545
Vienna, Kunsthistorisches Museum, Kunstkammer, inv. no. 1110

The bowl portrays the rape of Europa by

Zeus in the Neo-Platonic interpretation. On the right Mercury drives the herd to the beach, with Zeus hidden amongst them; on the left the god – transformed into a bull – abducts the daughter of the Phoenician king. Lastly, we see the happy union of the couple in the clouds. In the foreground the mythological theme is developed in the struggle between Eros and Anteros and in the women on the right – all figures representing different shades of earthly and heavenly love. The emblem on the flag takes up the theme in the form of the swan fighting the snake: the conquest of worldly lust. In this work Christoph Lencker makes significant progress to-

wards visual unification. He draws the viewer's attention away from the centre of the bowl in order to minimize the disturbance to the image that will necessarily be caused by the foot of the jug.

Essen and Vienna 1988, cat. no. 684; Munich 1994, cat. no. 43.

Kris 1932, no. 77; Hayward 1976, pp. 234f.; Seling 1980, 1, pp. 65f; Müller 1983, p. 153; Irmscher 1989, pp. 32-37.

H.T.

II.210
Unknown Artist
The Table Bell of Rudolf II (so-called)
Alloy of metals; Hammer: iron
7.8 cm; Diam: 6.3 cm
Ca. 1575-1600
Kunstkammer of the Emperor Rudolf II, Inventory of 1607-11, no. 1613
Vienna, Kunsthistorisches Museum, Kunstkammer, inv. no. 5969

The key to the meaning of this bell is the pansophic view of the interconnection of all that the universe contains. On the outside of the bell are depicted astrological figures. The regent figures are arrived at

by dividing the year by 7: the remainder, then determines the regent for that year, namely the sun, Venus, Mercury, the moon, Saturn, Jupiter or Mars. This is the sequence in which the planet gods are depicted. In addition the sign of the zodiac that they rule is depicted with them: Leo with the sun, Taurus and Libra with Venus, Gemini and Virgo with Mercury, Cancer with Luna, Capricorn and Aquarius with Saturn, Pisces and Sagittarius with Jupiter, Aries and Scorpio with Mars. The seven fields at the top are filled with old chiromantic characters (from the realms of palmistry). The various metals associated in alchemical terms with each of the

planet gods are also depicted: the sun – gold, Venus – copper, Mercury – quicksilver, Luna – silver, Saturn – lead, Jupiter – tin, Mars – iron. The symbols on the large heptagonal node on the stem therefore refer both to gods and metals. Neither the Greek lettering engraved inside the bell nor the Hebrew inscriptions on the hammer have yet been deciphered.

Essen and Vienna 1988, cat. no. 407

R.D.

II.211
Ten-ducat Piece of *Rudolf II*
Struck in gold
0.41 cm, 34.331 g
1604
Prague mint (master of the mint: Jan Lasanz)
Prague, Národní muzeum, Numismatic Department, inv. no. H5-15 070

This second type of Prague ten-ducat piece of Rudolf II showing a bare-headed bust of the Emperor on the obverse side, and a heraldic eagle on the reverse, has survived from the years 1602 and 1604 only. Large gold coins bearing an image of

the standing monarch continued to be struck during the rest of the first decade of the seventeenth century. The die stamp from 1604 was crafted by Jan Konrád Greuter. The detail on the coin is proof of the high quality of the engraving work.

Halačka 1987, pp. 156–57, cat. no. 275.

E.Š.

II.212
Two-thaler Piece of *Rudolf II*
Struck in silver
4.04 cm, weight 57.788 g
1611
Prague mint (master of the mint: Benedikt Hubmer)
Prague, Národní muzeum, Numismatic Department, inv. no. H5-37 448

While the depiction of the bust of Rudolf II on the Prague ten-ducat pieces from the first decade of the seventeenth century was rather an exception, it was generally the rule for the large silver coins struck during the same period. Like the greater

denominations of the ducats, the denominations of the thalers were also produced in a limited edition. Thus they were owned by a small select group and were rarely used as legal tender. The minting in Prague of a number of two-thaler pieces began in 1587. After 1602 their engravings were designed by Jan Konrád Greuter.

Halačka 1987, pp. 168–70, cat. no. 308.

E.Š.

II.213
Anonymous artist – based on a design by ? Joachim Deschler
Model of a medal featuring a portrait of Ferdinand I
Mid-sixteenth century
Prague, Národní muzeum, Numismatic Department, inv. no. H5-59426

Set onto a black-stained circular base is the relief profile of a man in a natural wood colour. The profile is shown from the left side with smooth hair and pointed beard. The dress is decorated with an oval clasp. Habich ascribes the one-sided wooden model featuring Ferdinand's por-

trait to Deschler; it is currently stored in the Cabinet de Médailles in Paris. Typologically, this model is related to our wooden model and certain other period medals executed according to designs by Deschler. Joachim Deschler (ca. 1500–1571?) worked for Archduke Maxmilian in 1543 and also in Nürnburg and Vienna. He was appointed imperial sculptor and medal-engraver in 1566. Apart from small sculptures, he also crafted a large number of portrait medals during the years 1540–1569.

Habich 1929, 1/2, no. 1616; Katz 1932, p. 163, no. 318, tab.XLV/2

Z.M.

II.214
Gianpaolo Poggini
Medal of *Joanna*, daughter of Charles V
1564
Prague, Národní muzeum, Numismatic Department, inv. no. H5-57555

Gianpaolo Poggini, Italian goldsmith, gem-cutter and coin die-cutter, sculptor and medal-engraver, worked for Cosimo I de' Medici and later for Philip II in the Netherlands and Spain. The precision of the miniature relief is not simply proof of his exquisite portrait art but also assured the life-like expression of the symbols on the reverse side.

Joanna (1537–73), daughter of Charles V and Isabella of Portugal, was married off in 1552 to Johann, infante of Portugal, who, however, died in 1554. She later returned to Madrid and died in a Clare nunnery.

Armand 1883, I, p. 240, no. 17; Domanig 1896, p. 5, no. 50

Z.M.

II.215
Leone Leoni
Monaggio/Como 1509–Milan 1590
Medal of *Maximilian II*
Ca. 1554
Prague, Národní muzeum, Numismatic Department, inv. no. H5-59423, H5-57551

Leone Leoni, Italian sculptor and medal-engraver, was born into the large, artistically oriented family of Arezzo. He was active at the Milanese mint and worked for Emperor Charles V and for the court in Vienna. This excellent portrait artist applied his modelling skills in his highly realistic

symbolic depiction, often drawing from Classical mythology on the reverse sides of his medals.

Domanig 1896, no. 98; Forrer 1907, III, p. 404; Lanna 1911, no. 714; Nohejlová 1963, p. 42/10

Z.M.

II.216
Leone Leoni
Monaggio/Como 1509–Milan 1590
Medal of *Maximilian II*
Double-sided, cast in silver
6.6 cm
QUO.ME FATA.VOCANT (reverse)
Ca. 1554
Prague, Národní muzeum, Numismatic
Department, H5–57 551

See cat. no. II.215

Armand II., 237/4.

Z.M.

II.217
Circle of Leone Leoni
Medal of *Maxmilián II and his Wife Maria*
Ca. 1550
Prague, Národní muzeum, Numismatic
Department, inv. no. H5–57554

Maria (1528–1603), the daughter of
Charles V, married Maximilian II and she
became widowed in 1576. With her brother Philip II, she was appointed Vice-Regent in Portugal from where she travelled
to a convent in Madrid, where she died.
The authorship of this medal is unclear.
The characteristics of the portrait and
documents describing the activities of the

Viennese court at the time enable us to attribute this undated and unsigned medal
to the circle of Leone Leoni.

Armand 1883, II, p. 237, no. 8; Domanig
1896, p. 5, no. 53.

Z.M.

II.218
Jacopo da Trezzo or Pompeo Leoni?
Medal of *Maria, Wife of Maximilian II*
After 1550
Prague, Národní muzeum, Numismatic
Department, inv. no. H5–57553

Jacopo da Trezzo, Milanese sculptor, gem-
and medal-engraver, worked at the Spanish court of Philip II. He was an apprentice
under Leone Leoni and their work shares
many features which often makes identification difficult. Domanig attributes this
medal to da Trezzo; however, Forrer does
not agree. Armand publishes the motif on
the reverse side of the medal as the work

of Pompeo Leoni, sculptor and medal-engraver from the latter half of the sixteenth
century and son of Leone Leoni. He
worked for the Viennese court as assistant
to his father. For most of his life, however,
he was active in Spain where he also died.

Armand 1883, I, p. 239, no. 3,X; Armand
1883, II, p. 237, no. 6; Domanig 1896, no.
52; Forrer 1907, III, pp. 412–413; Forrer
1907, VI, p. 139.

Z.M.

II.219
Based on a design by Antonio Abondio
Wooden model of a medal of *Maximilian
II and Maria*
Undated
Prague, Národní muzeum, Numismatic
Department, inv. no. H5–59417

Both portraits show similar features to
those executed on coloured wax reliefs
from the numismatic cabinet collections
in Vienna (obverse) and in Munich (reverse).

Fiala 1909, tab.VIII, nos.1 and 3.

Z.M.

II.220
Antonio Abondio
Medal of *Rudolf II*
After 1576
Prague, Národní muzeum, Numismatic
Department, inv. no. H5–58233

The medal is set in a frame with two eyes
attached for the chain. This type of portrait of Rudolf II shares similar traits with
the previous medal; this unique example
was also worked and chased using gold ornamentation.

Nohejlová 1963, p. 61/39.

Z.M.

II.221
Valentin Maler
Medal of *Rudolf II*
After 1585–1589 ?
Prague, Národní muzeum, Numismatic Department, inv. no. H5-58469

Valentin Maler, born in Jihlava, Moravia, arrived in Nürnberg before 1568 and married Marie, the daughter of the eminent Nürnberg-based goldsmith Václav Jamnitzer, in 1569. During the early 1570s he worked for the Saxony court and later returned to Nürnberg to become a privileged medal-engraver for Emperor Rudolf II, creating a large number of both cast and struck medals. The portrait of Rudolf II on this medal is based on a design by Antonio Abondio. Habich presents both the obverse and reverse sides of the medal, the latter depicting a crowned double-headed eagle with the Austrian coat-of-arms and the Order of the Golden Fleece. Engraved round the edge of the medal are the 24 coats-of-arms of the individual countries and principalities of the Habsburg monarchy.

Forrer 1907, III, pp. 545–550; Habich 1927, 1/2, no. 2604.

Z.M.

II.222
Zacharias Kempf
Medal of *Rudolf II*
1590
Prague, Národní muzeum, Numismatic Department, inv. no. H5-150958

Zacharias Kempf was a medal-engraver and die-cutter in Jáchymov who worked for the imperial court during the latter half of the sixteenth century. His last dies date from the year 1606. The portrait depicted on the medal was evidently based on a painting by Josef Heintz or an engraving executed using his design. Kempf's portrait of Emperor Rudolf is stylized and manifests the skills acquired with long experience in the trade. The medal is fairly rigid in comparison with the picture used as a base design.

Katz, 1932, no. 514; Nohejlová 1963, p. 67/73.

Z.M.

II.223
Valentin Maler
Iglau (Moravia) 1540–Nürnberg 1603
Rudolf II
Silver-gilt, rubies (?)
Medallion: h: 2.4 cm; setting: 4.2 × 3.9 cm
VM (lig.)
Ex Donebauer Collection, ? 1888
Staatliche Museen zu Berlin, Münzkabinett

This rather standard portrait of Rudolf II on a ducat-shpaed medallion is lent additional charm and value by its gold setting. The medallion is held at the sides by two female figures while two putti hold a crown up above. Rubies and the remains of an eyelet show that this medallion was once a so-called *Gnadenpfennig*, which was a jewel or precious item given as a sign of favour to be worn by the recipient so honoured.

Habich 1929–34, no. 2607 (no setting); Börner 1981, no. 84.

W.S.

II.224
Unknown Artist
Miniature Portrait of *Rudolf II*
Oil on copper, gilt-bronze frame, oval-shaped
7 × 5.5 cm (with frame)
After 1602
Bought in auction ex co. Alb. Jaffé, Hamburg, at auction in Berlin 1912, Rudolf Lepke
Prague, Uměleckoprůmyslové Muzeum, inv. no. 12 715a

The miniature belongs to a late portrait type that drew on portraits of the Emperor by Hans von Aachen from 1600 to 1602. The miniature format is appropriate for civilian portraiture, concentrating on human physiognomy rather than imperial majesty and emphasizing the subject's ageing facial features.

Prague 1966, cat. no. 302; Prague 1985, cat. no. 268; Essen and Vienna 1988, cat. no. 295.

Lepke 1912, cat. no. 38; Larsson 1988), pp. 161–70.

R.V.

II.225
Unknown Artist
Rudolf II
Shell cameo on glass; gold, enamel, 24 rubies
2.3 × 2 cm (4.9 × 3.5 cm with frame)
After 1600; mounting ca. 1650
Rosenborg, inv. 1718, 27 no. 4. Perhaps from the Collection of the Duke of Copenhagen, De Danske Kongers Kronologiske Samling, Rosenborg, inv. no. 3140

Another version of the cameo in Vienna (Kunsthistorisches Museum, inv. no. XII 93) has been identified by Fritz Eichler and Ernst Kris as southern German from around 1605, but it could be later, because shell was a popular material during the time of Ferdinand III and Rudolf II is portrayed here in later life. The black-and-white painted enamel and the polished rubies are familiar from many other Viennese pieces from around 1650. Behind the black glass plate there is a medallion with an enamelled cover. On the outside, it has white flowers on a blue ground; the inside is green.

Copenhagen, Rosenborg 1988, no. 612.

J.He.

II.226
South German Goldsmith after
Giambologna
Giambologna: Douai 1529–Florence 1608
Allegory of the Reign of Francesco I de' Medici
Silver
29.7 × 43.3 cm
Before 1604
Kunstkammer of Emperor Rudolf II, Inventory of 1607-11, no. 1686
Vienna, Kunsthistorisches Museum,
Kunstkammer, inv. no. 1 195

According to reports by the Duke of Modena's envoy, Rudolf already owned this silver relief in 1604, when he was given the

bronze relief as a present by Cesare d'Este, duke of Modena. The *Kunstkammer* Inventory notes that this silver relief was a cast made from the bronze relief. These two facts would appear to contradict one another, unless one were to suppose that the bronze relief had already been in the imperial collection. The generally held view is that this was one of the works by Bologna that Cosimo de' Medici gave to Emperor Maximilian II in 1565 for the wedding of Francesco de' Medici and Johanna of Austria. It is possible that it found its way to Modena among the possessions of Barbara of Austria, who married Alfonso II. It is also possible that the silver relief was cast

from a bronze version in the imperial collection that has since been lost. The importance of this allegory for Medici propaganda is demonstrated by the fact that at least two versions are known: one in alabaster owned by the Spanish royal family (now in the Prado) and one that was owned by the Medicis (now in Florence).

Vienna 1978, cat. no. 120; Florence 1980, cat. no. 679; Essen and Vienna 1988, cat. no. 52.

Dhanens 1956, pp. 136ff.; Avery 1987, p. 179, no. 147.

L.O.L.

II.227
? Sylvester II. Eberlin; Hans Schlottheim
(musical box)
Ca. 1570–Augsburg 1639
Triumph of Bacchus
Silver gilt, partly painted
H: 43 cm
Hallmark: *Augsburg Pyr* (Seling 28 = 1600-10); master's mark: Seling 752c (ascribed to Sylvester Eberlin; however, since he died in 1592, it was more likely made by Sylvester Eberlin II)
Ca. 1605
Kunstkammer of Emperor Rudolf II, Inventory of 1607-161, no. 1735
Vienna, Kunsthistorisches Museum,

Kunstkammer, inv. no. 959

The automaton consists of two separate parts: the carriage that contains the works and the Bacchus group, which has an organ built into the base. The organ works were made by Hans Schlottheim, ca. 1605. A movable joint between the carriage and the fauns preceding it makes the fauns drag their steps: the head of the left faun and the arm of the right faun move. The organ, with six wooden pipes, also makes the figures move: Bacchus lifts his arm, the parrot flaps its wings and the musician blows down the mouthpipe of his bagpipes.

Essen and Vienna 1988, cat. no. 444.

J.H.L.

II.228
Paulus van Vianen
Utrecht ca. 1570–Prague 1613
Plaque with the Holy Family
Embossed silver
13.6 × 10.5 cm
PV (monogram) *1610*
1610
Kunstkammer of the Emperor Rudolf II, Inventory of 1607-11, no. 1693, Matthias Inventory of 1619, no. 290; A. M. Hogguer–Ebeling Collection; Amsterdam auction 18.8.1817, cat. no. 167
Weimar, Kunstsammlungen zu Weimar, Schloßmuseum, inv, no. A 248

This plaquette shows the Holy Family: Elisabeth and the young John the Baptist are seen kneeling on the right. A drawing by Paulus van Vianen has survived which could be a study for this work. A number of casts were made from this silver plaquette and Goethe owned a bronze version. Various other goldsmiths made copies of this plaquette although with varying degrees of success. It seems that the famous Amsterdam goldsmith Johannes Bogaert made a version in 1659 and Wilhelm Krüger incorporated the figure of the Virgin Mary with the Child on her lap into an ivory relief, now in the Grünes Gewölbe in Dresden.

Utrecht 1984–1985, cat. no. 25.

Frederiks 1952, no. 90 HH; Weber 1975, no. 938; Bauer-Haupt 1976, no. 1693; Ter Molen 1984, no. 107; Spicer 1988, pp. 274, 279, fig. 3.

J.R.tM.

II.229
Guglielmo della Porta (?)
Ca. 1510-Rome 1577
The Crucified
Gilded bronze, hollow cast
24.8 × 19.5 × 5.5 cm
Third quarter of the sixteenth century
Prague, Národní Galeri v Praze, inv. no. P 5187

The technically perfect gilded cast with its admirable modelling of Christ's body and minutely detailed head is an example of the *Cristo morto* type. The standard models were developed by Giambologna in Florence and Guglielmo della Porta in Rome.

These works, a number of which have been preserved, are sometimes so similar that their authorship is difficult to determine. Although there are formal analogies, Giambologna's works are somewhat more subtle than della Porta's more massive, athletic types. It is probable that della Porta's work influenced Giambologna during the latter's stay in Rome around the year 1500. Giambologna would not have been the only artist to come under the influence of the Roman master. The piece exhibited here has a number of traits in common with Giambologna's earliest works from Loreto (Palazzo Apostolico), as well as with della Porta's works, espe-

cially the *Crucified Christ* in Arezzo (Museo Civico), both in the modelling of the body and in the shaping of the *perizonio*.

Chlíbec 1992, p. 52, cat. no. 55; Chlíbec 1993-94, p. 42.

J.Ch.

II.230
Goldsmith at the court of Rudolf before 1587 and court goldsmith after 1600
Cross of Archbishop Medek
Silver body, cast and chased; silver stem, beaten; cross made of ? ebony
72.5 cm
On the trunk: *MARTINUS/ ARCHIEPIS/ PRAGENS/ 1587*; above this is the archbishop's coat of arms
1587
Since 1600 in the inventory of St Vitus' treasury
Prague, Metropolitní kapitula u sv. Víta

This crucifix is listed in the inventory of St

Vitus' treasury under the number 1, although there the body is described as made of ivory and the object is stated to have been kept in the archbishop's palace. Its present connection with a silver statue of *The Crucifixion* was not recorded in an inventory until 1615. Individual motifs on the stem of the cross, including lizards, frogs, little balls and the stylized depiction of the temple of the Lord's tomb, symbolize the death and resurrection of Christ and are associated with Easter rituals. The interest in naturalistic detail comes close to that of products of the Jamnitzer workshop. Giambologna's students, P. Tacci, A. Susini and others, made casts of this pop-

ular object of personal piety based on the master's models and on the tens of other pieces they had. These multiplications are distinguishable from their prototype mostly by the way the silver has been chased. The maker of the Prague statue could have been any one of a number of court sculptors or goldsmiths (see Essen and Vienna 1988, cat. no. 512), from Giambologna's workshop.

Podlaha–Šittler 1903, pp. 51–52; Podlaha–Šittler, pp. 272–73; Rouček 1948, p.56

E.F.

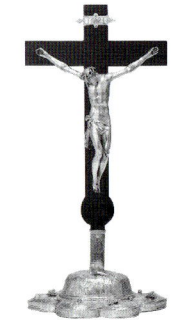

II.231
Nikolaus Pfaff
Nürnberg ?1556–? Prague before 1612
Cybele
Ivory, ebony
H of statuette 21.9 cm; of figure 15.7 cm
On the base: *VENERI VERTICORDIAE
SVLPITITA PATERC(VLI) F.(ILIA)
FVL(VII) FLACCI VXOR EX C(YBELAE)
PRAECIP(VO) ELEC(TA) CONSECRAVIT*
(Sulpici, daughter of Paterculus and wife
of Fulvius Flaccus, who was chosen by the
grace of Cybele, dedicates this [statuette]
to Venus, the mover of hearts)
Ca. 1605–12
Imperial *Schatzkammer*

Vienna, Kunsthistorisches Museum,
Kunstkammer, inv. no. 4621

Although it is not clear which of the goddesses in the Kunsthistorisches Museum,
Vienna, is being referred to in Rudolf II's
Inventory, both are certainly listed as being from the hand of 'N. Pfaffen'. In its
closeness to Classical ideals, its timeless
perfection and its air of sublime repose,
this late piece by Pfaff far surpasses his few
other surviving carved works and marks
the high point of his artistic career. While
his early works in ivory followed the lead
given by Lambert Sustris, it seems that
soon after his arrival in Prague Nikolaus

Pfaff succumbed to the influence of the
artists at Rudolf II's court, particularly that
of Bartholomeus Spranger – whose background in the principles of Mannerism he
shared. The way in which draperies gently
flow around the figure of Cybele is clearly
inspired by Spranger. The inscription on
the base is a tribute to the cultured intellectualism of Emperor Rudolf II.

Essen and Vienna 1988, cat. no. 396.

Distelberger 1985, p. 286; Haag 1994, pp.
87ff.

S.H.

II.232
Hans Daucher (attr.)
Ulm ca. 1485–Stuttgart 1538
The Emperor Maximilian I
Solnhofen stone, partially painted, silver
gilt setting
Diam: 9.0 cm; with frame: 9.9
Kunstkammer, Inventory of 1607–11 (no.
1790)
Vienna, Kunsthistorisches Museum,
Münzkabinett, H125

In the Inventory of the *Kunstkammer* of
the Emperor Rudolf II, this object is described as: Ein bildtnus kayser Maximilian
I., von stain erhebt geschnitten brustbild,

ist rund gefasst, in Silber vergult und hin-
den daruf gestochen wie er in kiris zu pfer-
dt sitzt. This bust of the Emperor looking
towards the right has been shown by Baldass to have been cut out of a (probably
rectangular) plate and set on a round,
pink-coloured stone. The silver setting,
which it is not possible to date with any
certainty despite the engraved date, consists of a frame with an engraved inscription reading CAES MAXIMILIANVS SEM-
PER AVG / 1516. The back plate has come
away from the frame. This plate is engraved with an image of the Emperor in
armour riding to the left after a woodcut
published by Hans Burgkmair in 1518.

The attribution of this work to Hans
Daucher is not definitive. It has been suggested that it could be 'in the style of Hans
Schwarz' or that it bears a certain resemblance to a wood relief by Hans Kels. Although the date is only in the frame,
which could have been made at some other time, this date is generally accepted as
applying to the stone as well in that it may
well have been taken from the stone's
original picture carrier.

Vienna 1959, cat. no. 659/664

K.Sch.

II.233
Hans Daucher
Ulm 1486–Stuttgart 1538
The Judgment of Paris
Solnhofn stone
22.9 × 17.2 cm
HD 1522 (beneath)
1522
Augsburg
From the *Kunstkammer*, Inventory
1607–1611 (no. 1801).
Vienna, Kunsthistorisches Musem,
Kunstkammer, inv. no. 4399

This miniature relief from the collection
of Rudolf II attests both to the Emperor's

interest in art of the Dürer period and to
his predilection for erotic subjects. In
spite of several small imperfections, the
relief is exceptional in the precision of its
execution, the sense of depth of the pictorial space and the gracefulness of the female figures and their gestures. Although
the goddesses at either side are characteristically robust, the nude figure of the central goddess is markedly Italianate. The
classicizing types of the female faces are
consistent with this tendency. Although it
is sometimes assumed that the model for
this relief was an unidentified engraving,
it is probable that Daucher was inspired
by several separate motifs in the graphic

art of the time. He was evidently familiar
with the woodcuts of Lucas Cranach the
Elder from 1508 (Bartsch 114) and Albrecht Altdorfer from 1511 (Bartsch 60).
Nonetheless, it is Daucher's own imagination that is the deciding factor in this gracious little work.

Primisser 1819, p. 180; von Sacken 1855,
vol. 2, p. 101; Bode 1887, p. 7; Schlosser
1910, vol. 1, p. 19; Halm 1920, p. 315 n.;
Halm 1927, pp. 220–24; Bange 1928, p. 18;
Schuselka 1966, p. 38, cat. no. 251.

J.Ch.

II.234
Unknown Artist
Matthias Corvinus
Marble, jasper
55 × 38.5 cm
Ca. 1485 or later
Burgpalast Buda (?), Maximilian II,
Kunstkammer of the Emperor Rudolf II,
Inventory 1607–11, no. 1803; Vienna,
Kunsthistorisches Museum, Kunstkam-
mer (until 1933)
Budapest, Szépművészeti Múzeum, inv.
no. 6712

II.235
Unknown Artist
Beatrix de Arragona
Marble, jasper
55 × 38.5 cm
Ca. 1485 or later
Burgpalast Buda (?), Maximilian II.,
Kunstkammer of the Emperor Rudolf II,
Inventory 1607–11, no. 1804; Vienna, Kun-
sthistorisches Museum, Kunstkammer
(until 1933)
Budapest, Szépművészeti Múzeum, inv.
no. 6712

These relief busts of Matthias Corvinus
(1443–1490) and Beatrix of Aragon (1457–
1508), whom Matthias married as his second wife in 1476, bear witness to the close
connections between the Hungarian court

and Italian Renaissance culture. Stylistically they are in keeping with artistic circles at the court in Milan, which, however,
gives no clear indication of whether they
were made in Italy or Hungary. Mention
has often been made in the literature of
two medals which may have served as
models for these reliefs (Schallaburg 1982,
nos 76 and 123). In the case of Matthias,
the relevant medal is only known in later
castings showing the Emperor in contemporary costume in the manner of a Roman
imperial portrait, with a wreath of oak
leaves in his hair. In the case of Queen
Beatrix the relevant medal come from the
circle of Giancristoforo Romano, which to
judge by the circular inscription – *DIVA
BEATRIX HUNGARIAE REGINA* – must
not have been made until 1508, that is to
say, after the death of Beatrix. These portrait reliefs are not dated, nor does their
provenance provide information that
would make it possible to date them with
any accuracy. They cannot have been
made on the occasion of the subjects' wedding since Beatrix is portrayed as clearly
being more than nineteen years old. It
seems more likely that these portraits are
connected with the defeat of Vienna by the
Emperor Matthias in 1485. This success
was the high point of Matthias' military
and political career. On the other hand, if
the head-dress worn by Beatrix is indeed a

widow's veil, then these portraits may not
have been made until after Matthias's
death in 1490, which would mean that the
crown of oak leaves should not be read as
a symbol of power *all'antice*.

Schallaburg 1982, no. 84

Zimmerman 1735, tab. 29; Balogh 1975,
nos 125, 126; Kruft 1995, nos 128, 138 f.

L.O.L.

II.236
Antonio Susini after Giambologna
Fl. in Florence 1580–1624
Lion Clawing a Horse
Bronze, light brown patina, red-brown
smoke glaze
21 cm
NM (lig., on the underside of the base)
Ca. 1600
Kunstkammer of the Emperor Rudolf II,
Inventory of 1607–11 no. 1878; Matthias
Inventory of 1619 no. 3; *Schatzkammer* Inventory of 1750, Vienna; 1871, Ambras.
Vienna, Kunsthistorisches Museum,
Kunstkammer, inv. no. 6018

This work is listed in the 1607–11 Inventory of Rudolf II's *Kunstkammer* as follows: 'Uff dem andern almar ist erstlich von metal gegossen das pferd, welches ein lew uberfellt und uff ein seitten reisst'. It goes back to a particular ancient sculpture, restored and 'completed' in 1594 and is an unusual variation on the theme. The extraordinarily precise modelling of this bronze, the taut, smooth animal skins and the meticulous sharpness of the details must be evidence enough that this was not cast after a model by Giambologna. It is very possible that this piece was a commissioned copy – carried out by Antonio Susini – of the by now famous sculpture

from antiquity.

Essen and Vienna 1988, cat. no. 523

M.L.J.

II.237
Antonio Susini after Giambologna
Fl. after 1580–Florence 1624
Sleeping Nymph
Bronze
20.5 × 32 cm
No. 37 (engraved)
Ca. 1575
1684 in the Inventaire des Mobiliers de la
Couronne Königs Ludwigs XIV., no. 37
Paris, Musée du Louvre, Département des
Objets d'Art, MR 3319

Amongst the sculptures listed in the 1607–11 Inventory of Rudolf II's collection there is a reference to one of the many versions of Giambologna's *Sleeping Nymph*, namely the version without the satyr gazing indiscreetly at the nymph. Yet it may be assumed that Giambologna's workshop also made its own versions of the *Sleeping Nymph* in its own right. The version shown here – 'standing in' for the *Sleeping Nymph* that was in the Rudolfine collection – is recorded in 1683 in the collection of Louis XIV. It also originally had a satyr but that has now been lost. The nymph's pose, half sitting, half lying, with her arm laid across her head was clearly inspired by the ancient marble sculpture of Ariadne in the Vatican Collection. The presence of this work in the Rudolfine

Kunstkammer was to have considerable significance for art in the court at Prague. Not only did it serve Bartolomeus Spranger as the basis of his *Amor and the Sleeping Psyche*, known to us through an engraving by Jan Muller, but it also inspired Adriaen de Vries in his bronze relief showing *Bacchus Finding the Sleeping Nymph*.

Essen and Vienna 1988, cat. no. 524

M.L.J.

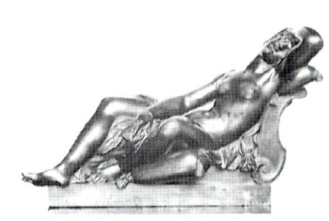

II.238
Unknown Artist
Hercules Resting
Marble
28.5 cm
1550–1600
Probably from the *Kunstkammer* of the
Emperor Rudolf II, Inventory of 1607–11,
no. 1935; later in Ambras.
Vienna, Kunsthistorisches Museum,
Kunstkammer, inv. no. 4439

This extraordinarily subtly worked little statuette is a typical *Kunstkammer* piece. It is based on the so-called *Hercules Farnese*, a colossal marble figure that is today in

the Museo Nazionale in Naples, by the Greek sculptor Clycon, after Lysippos. This had been discovered in 1540 during excavations at the Caracalla thermal springs in Rome and had come into the possession of the family of Pope Paul Farnese III. It rapidly became extremely famous and has been copied through the centuries in a variety of media and sizes. This little statuette is one of the earliest Renaissance copies. It is less monumental in aspect than the original – the figure is much more finely structured and the musculature much more detailed: all of which would indicate that this is not the work of an Italian artist but of an artist from the

north, presumably from the Netherlands. Beyond that, this Hercules statuette is reminiscent in its features and bearing of the Emperor Karl V, which is in keeping with the fact that the virtuous hero of the mythology of antiquity soon became a symbol for princely virtues and thus had a major part to play in allegorical portrayals of rulers and their domains.

Nara – Tokyo 1995, cat. no. 100

M.L.J.

II.239
Unknown Artist, probably from Northern
Italy
Gladiator
Bronze, black-brown varnish, natural
brown patina
17.3 cm
Ca. 1550–1600
North Italy
Probably from Rudolf II's *Kunstkammer*,
Inventory of 1607–11, no. 1900; later in
imperial ownership in Vienna
Vienna, Kunsthistorisches Museum,
Kunstkammer, inv. no. 5583

The composition of this figure caught in

motion is both exceptionally elastic and taut. The masterly modelling of slim, yet athletic, form would have been inconceivable without precursors from Antiquity such as the torso from Belvedere or the reliefs used to decorate sarcophagi. No less important as inspiration were the works of the young Michelangelo, for example the cartoons for the fresco, the Battle of Cascina, and the figures on the ceiling of the Sistine Chapel. Two rather weaker copies of this statuette are known today, as well as three variants, of which two seem to have been made in the region of Padua and Venice. Radcliffe has linked them with the work of Riccio, but there would, in

fact, seem to be a greater affinity with that of Vittore Gambello, also known as Camelio. The third variant, also in the collection of the Kunsthistorisches Museum (cat. no. II/240) is by Adriaen de Vries.

Vienna 1978, cat. no. 6; Washington D.C. 1986, cat. no. 39; Essen and Vienna 1988, cat. no. 77

Radcliffe 1979, pp. 24–27, no. 6; Leithe-Jasper 1986, pp. 160–62, no. 39

M.L.J.

II.240
Adriaen de Vries
Den Haag 1545–Prague 1626
Gladiator
Bronze, matt red-brown varnish over pale,
grey-brown natural patina
18.9 cm
Ca. 1603
Probably from Rudolf II's *Kunstkammer*,
Inventory of 1607–11, no. 1942; subsequently in the imperial *Schatzkammer* in
Vienna
Vienna, Kunsthistorisches Museum,
Kunstkammer, inv. no. 5819

This statuette is a version of another, pre-

sumably Upper Italian, figure of a gladiator which is also owned by the Kunsthistorisches Museum and exhibited here (cat. no. II.239). The modelling is softer and the surface values are more painterly. The warrior is wearing a fantasy helmet *all'antica*. This statuette was for a long time attributed to Leone Leoni. However, its very physicality, its vibrant forming, its ambivalent vacillation between positive and negative volumes, the face and the helmet are all characteristic of the hand of Adriaen de Vries. As a sculptor at the court of Rudolf II, he clearly had access to the imperial *Kunstkammer*, which apparently already included the gladiator statuette by a

North Italian artist (cat. no. II/239) that was to serve as the model for this work. The juxtaposition of these two statuettes is a striking demonstration of the inspirational function of the princely collections to contemporary artists at the court.

Vienna 1978, cat. no. 6; Washington D.C. 1986, cat. no. 6; Essen and Vienna 1988, cat. no. 61

Radcliffe 1979, pp. 24–27, no. 6; Leithe-Jasper 1986, pp. 163–65, no. 6

M.L.J.

II.241
Follower of Giambologna
Venus after her Bath
Bronze, black lacquer and brown patina, hollow cast
15.6 × 4.1 × 4.1 cm
Prague, Národní Galeri v Praze, inv. no. P 5802

Venus after the Bath was a very popular composition and exists in a number of different versions; Giambologna is generally considered to be the author of its prototype. It is formally related to his other small-scale works – sculptural studies such as *Apollo* (Florence, Museo Nazionale

del Bargello). A number of Giambologna's later works, such as the famous *La Fiorenza* (Florence, Villa Petraia) or *Venus after the Bath* and *Astronomia* (Vienna, Kunsthistorisches Museum), employ a similar compositional scheme. Most versions of *Venus after the Bath* have a more sketch-like character (and are more roughly cast) - that is, they take the form of a *bozzetto*. Some of them were probably cast by the artist himself (for example, the works in Cologne, Kunstgewerbe Museum; London, Wallace Collection; Florence, Museo Nazionale del Bargello), while others were made by his students or later imitators.

J. Chlíbec 1992, p. 47, cat. no. 50.

J.Ch.

II.242
Upper Italian Master
The Venus of Cardinal Granvella
Bronze and silver, green, artificial patina, silver plinth
18.5 cm without plinth
Master mark *CA* and the Besançon inspection mark (on the plinth)
Ca. 1500
Cardinal Antoine Perrenot de Granvella; Count Cantecroy; 1600 in the ownership of the Emperor Rudolf II, Inventory of 1607–11, no. 1943; later K.K. Münzkabinett; 1919 in the *Kunstkammer*.
Vienna, Kunsthistorisches Museum, Kunstkammer, inv. no. 7343

Rudolf II acquired this statuette from the collection of Cardinal Granvella and it is described in the *Kunstkammer* Inventory of 1607–11. With its apparently authentic provenance as a statuette from Antiquity and its unusual silver feet, this piece quickly achieved notoriety. As late as 1912 Schneider still regarded it as a work from Antiquity and it was not finally removed from the collection of antiquities until 1919. In fact, both the artificial patina *all'antica* and the silver feet clearly indicate that this was a conscious attempt to create a fake 'ancient' work of art. The feet, for example, join so seamlessly and smoothly to the legs that one can only assume they

were cast from the same model as the statuette, which means that the statuette was probably never in fragments but left the maker's studio complete. This intriguing piece is certainly from Upper Italy and was probably made in Padua or Venice around 1500.

Washington D.C. 1986, cat. no. 12; Essen and Vienna 1988, cat. no. 517

Leithe-Jasper 1986, pp. 91–93, no. 12

M.L.J.

II.243
Giambologna
Douai 1529–Florence 1608
Lion
Bronze, fire-gilded
13.1 cm (14 cm with base)
Ca. 1595
Kunstkammer of Emperor Rudolf II, Inventory of 1607–11, no. 1953
Vienna, Kunsthistorisches Museum, Kunstkammer, inv. no. 5 865

Rudolf II owned two almost identical statues of lions, both of which are now in the Kunsthistorisches Museum in Vienna. These statues are closely modelled on

their predecessors in antiquity. Baldinucci lists them among Giambologna's statuettes and they have been reproduced countless times. Their high technical quality suggests the artist's personal supervision. The present piece probably dates from around 1594-95, when the lions of Antiquity enjoyed particular favour in the Medici collection: in 1594 Flaminio Vacca made a companion piece to this lion and subsequently both were placed in front of the Villa Medici in Rome.

Vienna 1978, cat. no. 175a; Washington 1986, 218.

Avery 1987, p. 56; Larsson 1988, 1st edn, p. 142.

L.O.L.

II.244
Unknown Artist
Bowl Held by Siren
Bronze
12.8 × 11.8 × 21.8 cm
After 1550
Kunstkammer of the Emperor Rudolf II, Inventory of 1607–11, no. 1960; 1755 in the imperial *Schatzkammer*.
Vienna, Kunsthistorisches Museum, Kunstkammer, inv. no. 5 931

A siren, whose lower body consists of two snakes' tails crossed over each other, is holding a shell-shaped bowl in her arms. The zoomorphic form of the bowl is remi-

niscent of works by the hardstone carvers in the second half of the sixteenth century – which raises the question as to whether this might not be a hard-wearing, durable model for a vessel, perhaps made of rock crystal.

Planiscig 1924, p. 194, no. 318

M.L.J.

II.245
Giambologna
Douai 1529–Florence 1608
Allegory of the Reign of Francesco I de' Medici
Bronze
30.7 × 45.6 cm
1561–65
Kunstkammer of Emperor Rudolf II, Inventory of 1607–11, no. 1979
Vienna, Kunsthistorisches Museum, Kunstkammer, inv. no. 5 814

In 1604 Rudolf II was given this relief as a present by Cesare d'Este, duke of Modena. On receiving it he is supposed to have shouted out, 'and now it's mine' and car-

ried it with his own hands into his *Kunstkammer*. The subject's beardless face shows that it must have been made around 1560-61. The youth in the centre is Francesco de' Medici being led by Mercury to the woman lying down on the right of the picture. She is recognizable by her attributes as Abundantia and here personifies Florence. Above them hovers Amor, arrow at the ready. On the left of the picture are an old man and an old woman, symbols of age and winter. Beside them is a seated river-god and, as a symbol of all-devouring time, Saturn consuming his children. In the background is Hora with an hourglass in her hand. This work may

be interpreted as an allegory of the imminent accession to the throne of the young Francesco de' Medici. Youth takes over from age as spring takes over from winter and work can continue on the edifice of the state.

Vienna 1978, cat. no. 119; Florence 1980, cat. no. 678; Washington 1986, cat. no. 53; Essen and Vienna 1988, cat. no. 51.

Dhanens 1956, pp. 136ff.; Avery 1987, p. 179, no. 147.

L.O.L.

II.246
After Giambologna; casting: Antonio
Susini
Douai 1529–Florence 1608; fl. ca.1580–
Florence 1624
Walking Horse
Bronze, black-brown varnish, reddish-
brown natural patina
24.3 cm
Ca. 1605

II.247
Workshop of Adriaen de Vries
Walking Horse
Bronze, brown patina, hollow cast
27.5 cm
Early seventeenth century
Prague, Národní Galeri v Praze, inv. no.
P 351

The small statue of a horse is related to the
imposing prototype of the equestrian statue of Cosimo I de' Medici in the Piazza della Signoria in Florence, which came from
the workshop of Giambologna. The smaller piece from the Národni Galeri is treated
with less emphasis on the minute copying
of details – such as the modelling of the
musculature or the rendering of the veins
– which is typical of authentic works by de
Vries. The similarities with de Vries's horse
from Drottningholm (Essen, 1988, ill. 63),
particularly in the modelling of the head
and the rendering of the eyes, are so
strong that this work can be identified as a
workshop piece from his Prague studio.
Among other small bronzes depicting this
theme, the Prague statuette is closest to
the *Walking Horse* in the Szépmüvészeti
Múzeum in Budapest (Balogh, 1975, ill.
216, where the work is attributed to an unspecified follower of Giambologna and
dated as early seventeenth century), in the
overall modelling of the body and the
sculpting of the mane. Rudolf II's collection contained similar horse statuettes, as
the information from the inventories
shows (Inventory of 1607–11, no. 1955).

Chlíbec 1992, pp. 47–48, cat. no. 51;
Chlíbec 1993, p. 41.

J.Ch.

II.248
Antonio Abondio
Riva 1538–Vienna 1591
Mary, Wife of Maximilian II
Wax, pearls, glass, silver-gilt capsule with
glass lid
6×5 cm
On the rim of the capsule: *Alessandro
Abondio*
Ca. 1568
Acquired in 1905 from Dr J. Hirsch, Mu-
nich
Staatliche Museen zu Berlin, Münzkabi-
nett, inv. no. 151/1905

This enchanting wax relief in a silver-gilt
capsule was never intended as a relief for a
medallion but rather as a portable treasure. The naturalism and delicacy of this
work show Abondio's mastery. The very
physical nature of this polychrome portrait of Emperor Maximilian II's wife is
heightened by the string of pearls on her
lacy brocade dress and by the pearls and
precious stones in her blonde hair. Oddly
enough, the engraved rim of the capsule
with the words *Isotta da Rimini* has the
wrong name and the attribution to the
master *Alessandro Abondio* is also incorrect.

Berlin 1995, cat. no. 60.

Habich 1929–34, no. 3446; Menadier 1910,
col. 316.

W.S.

II.249
? Daniel Mignot
Rudolf II
Red-brown wax (gilded later, possibly
during the nineteenth century), ebony
base
27.8 cm; base 9.9×9.9 cm
Before 1607
Rudolf II's *Kunstkammer* (Inv. 1607–11,
no. 2107/341); handed over to Professor
Herget for the Stavovská inženýrská škola
in 1782; transferred to the Národní
Muzeum v Praze some time before 1855
Prague, Národní muzeum v Praze, inv. no.
H2–3 673

This miniature portrait was originally registered in the collection of the Národní
Muzeum v Praze as the work of Alexander
Collin. Two miniature bronze busts of
Rudolf II, cast from the same mould, were
shown at the exhibition *Prag um 1600* (Essen and Vienna 1988, cat. nos 79, 80). L. O.
Larsson noted the busts' similarity with de
Vries's 1607 portrait of the Emperor, but
dated the mould at around 1602, and considered it to have been made by one of
Rudolf's medallists. This wax bust also
cast from the same mould has shed new
light on its origin. It appears in *Kunstkammer* Inventory records between 1607 and
1611. The sculptor was registered as
Daniel Mignot (or Minnot), a copper engraver and goldsmith, possibly of French
origin, who worked at the Emperor's court
in Prague. The bust was clearly inspired by
de Vries's 1607 portrait of the Emperor, or
by one of its *bozzetti* and may have been intended for duplication and distribution as
gifts.

Křížek 1855, no. 50.

E.F.

II.250
Unknown Artist
Rudolf II
Bronze, fire-gilded
11.7 cm
Ca. 1602
Munich art market, acquired by the Muse-
um in 1916
Budapest, Szépmüvészeti Múzeum, inv.
no. 5 157

This small bust by an unknown artist
shows Emperor Rudolf in armour and
with a wide ruff around his neck. On a
band across his chest he wears the Order
of the Golden Fleece. In style, this work is
like the medallions with busts of the Emperor from around 1602 and after, and it is
also similar to the bust of 1607 by Adrian
de Vries (Vienna, Weltliche Schatzkammer), although there is no evidence that
permits a positive attribution to de Vries.
It seems more probable that the artist was
one of the medallion-makers at the court
in Prague.

Essen and Vienna 1988, cat. no. 79.

L.O.L.

II.251
David Altenstetter; Cornelius Groß, Hans Schlottheim (watch)
Master in 1573, d. 1617
Table Clock
Silver, brass, gilding, enamel, bronze, iron
H: 21.8 cm
DA (Seling 864 = David Altenstetter); hallmark: *Augsburg Pyr* (Seling 14 = 1580–90); master's mark: as Seling 1339, but in the form of a shield (= probably a member of the Gross family)
Ca. 1585
Kunstkammer of Emperor Rudolf II, Inventory of 1607–11, no. 2175
Vienna, Kunsthistorisches Museum, Kunstkammer, inv. no. 1 121

This clock has faces on four sides. Front: a large face with the hours and the position of the sun and the moon as well as the path of the moon and its phases. Back: a large face with the minutes and the hours with an alarm disc in the middle. The small faces on this side show the days of the week (left) and the months of the year (right). The narrow sides of the clock have the controls for the quarter- and full-hour chimes.

Essen and Vienna 1988, cat. no. 442.

J.H.L.

II.252
Unknown Artist
Wall Clock
Silver, copper and brass, gilding, enamel
H: 30 cm
Ca. 1600
Probably Augsburg
Kunstkammer of Emperor Rudolf II, Inventory of 1607–11, no. 2187
Vienna, Kunsthistorisches Museum, Kunstkammer, inv. no. 837

This clock shows the hours and the quarter hours: above the face; the phases of the moon are shown by means of a semi-gilded ball. The mechanism consists of clockwork plus full-hour chimes: the two rams above the clock butt the bell alternately as the hour chimes.

Essen and Vienna 1988, cat. no. 450.

J.H.L.

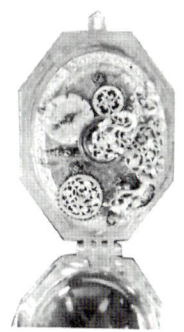

II.253
Johann Poestdorffer
Arrived from Prague in 1600, died in Dresden c. 1640
Oval Watch
Octagonal rock crystal casing, faceted; Clockwork: gilded brass, engraved, face with coloured enamel blossoms; red velvet cover 5.9 × 4.2 cm
Engraved signature on the back: *Johan poestdorffer fecit brag*
Probably ca. 1600.
Transferred in 1890 from the Historisches Museum to the Grünes Gewölbe : Cf. Zugangsverzeichnis 1890, no. 140. A number of 'little watches' with crystal casings are listed in the Elector's *Kunstkammer* of 1640 under Bl. 493/494.
Dresden, Grünes Gewölbe, inv. no. Vll 278

This watch with its fine clockwork in a crystal casing with a hook could be worn as a pendant. It is a spindle mechanism without a spiral spring, chimes hourly and has an alarm. The bell is located between the face and the clockwork. Practically nothing is known of Johann Poestdorffer's biography. He is thought to have come from Dresden, where he died, most likely in 1640. It is not possible to say with any certainty when he went to Prague and when he returned to Dresden, although it seems fair to assume that he returned from Prague in 1600 and at that point took up residence in Dresden again. The Grünes Gewölbe also has another signed octagonal pendant watch from his time in Dresden. The Mathematical-Physical Salon in Dresden also has a small table clock, inscribed with the words *Johan Postdorffer fecit in Dresden 1629.*

Sponsel 1923, p. 222; Menzhausen 1977, p. 99 (with mention of Jost Burgi in Prague); Abeler 1977, p. 487; Schardin 1989, p. 6, cat. no. 8

J.K.

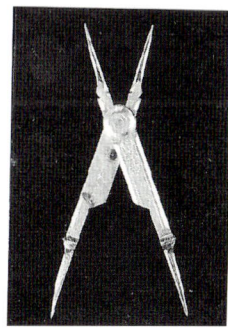

II.254
Erasmus Habermel
Died Prague 1606
Reductional Compasses (dividers)
? Gilt brass
15.2 × 1.7 × 1.0 cm
The owner's name is inscribed: *FRANci: D PADOAis: FOROLIis: M.D.*; and the number 2
Probably 1585–86
From the Strozzi collection in Florence; sold at the Muller auction in Amsterdam 1911
Prague, Národní Technické Muzeum, inv. no. 2 267

These conversion compasses with a ratio of 1:2 are made of gilt copper. The points are made of iron. The arms are fashioned in a decorative shape. One arm is decorated with engravings typical of Habermel and with the figure 2 appearing on both sides. The owner's name, Francisco Paduanio of Forli, is marked on the other arm.

Essen and Vienna 1988, cat. no. 418.

Prag um 1600 (Essen, 1988).

A.Š.

II.255
Mining Compass
Wood inlaid with bone ivory, engraved
2.3 × 14.5 × 14.5 cm
Ca. 1600
From the collection of R. Pfefferkorn
Prague, Národní Technické Muzeum, inv. no. 24 961

The compass is set in a plate made of hard wood, which is richly inlaid with bone ivory. The inlaid sections are decorated with engravings depicting botanical and hunting motifs and conveying scientific information. The compass itself with its magnetic needle measures about 4.5 cm across; on the base is a line with a small arrow and the markings 'M' and 'A' for 'Morgen' (morning) and 'Abend' (evening). The compass revolves and has an hour dial divided into twenty-four parts for telling the time. On the plate around the compass is another hour dial divided into two sections each of twelve hours. The edges of the plate contain the Latin names for the corners of the world: *SEPTENTRIO, ORIENS, MERIDIES, OCCIDENS.* On two sides there is a dial with inch markings divided into six inches (making one foot in total). The reverse side may have originally contained a clinometer. In the centre is some inlaid work with engravings of figures with a protractor and a sundial.

Horský and Škopová 1968, p. 169.

A.Š.

II.256
Markus Purmann
Scaphe
? Gilt brass, engraved
3.0 × 11.0 × 5.4 cm
On the circumference of the hemisphere cover: *1588* FECIT* DE* MONARCHIA* MARCVS* PVRMAN* HOROLOGIUM* SOLIS* ET* LUNAE*; on the inside of the hemisphere: *1588* M* P*
1588
Prague, State Observatory at the Clementine Library
Prague, Národní Technické Muzeum, inv. no. 17 189

This is a rare type of hemispherical sundial. The plate that forms the cover is connected to the hemisphere by a hinge. When functioning the instrument is opened and the circular plate is in the horizontal plane. In the middle is a compass, around which are several scales. The first of these can be used for adjusting to magnetic deviation. There is also a dial depicting the zodiac and the Gregorian calendar with the spring solstice. Descriptions of the months and their signs are given. On the outer side of the plate are the times of months with two dials each showing twelve hours twice. Inside is a movable disc showing the lunar month and phases

of the moon. The face markings on the sundial are located in the middle of the hemisphere. The equator is depicted in the hemisphere, as are the parallels as far as the tropics. At the ends of the parallels are the signs of the zodiac. The parallels are intersected by meridians, which carry hour markings. Inside the hemisphere is a tilted gnomon. The outer surface of the hemisphere is richly decorated with engravings.

Horský and Škopová 1968, p. 119.

A.Š.

II.257
Sundial on a Cube
Gilt brass, engraved
27.8 × 8.2 × 8.2 cm
Ca. 1600
From the collection of R. Pfefferkorn
Prague, Národní Technické Muzeum, inv. no. 24 863

The base consists of a circle with angle markings and four shaped legs. The faces of four sundials are on the block. The dial for eastern or oriental hours is marked *HORAE ORIENTALES*. The equator and the tropics are indicated and there is a dial for the afternoon hours from 4 to 11 and a

dial for the planetary hours from 1 to 6. The dial for the western or occidental hours is identically constituted but is marked *HORAE OCCIDENTALIS* and shows the afternoon hours from 1 to 8 and the planetary hours from 7 to 12. The dial for the southern hours spans the range 6–12–6. Planetary hours are also displayed. The dial also contains data for all the signs between the tropics of Cancer and Capricorn. There are markings for the hours relating to Earth latitutde, marked *ELEVATIO POLI 48 GRD 50 M*. In the lower part an inclined column carries a thread like a gnomon. On the block is a revolving barometer in the form of a mermaid

whose movement is transposed on to the hand of the dial of the north-facing side of the block and indicates the direction of the winds, for example *APARCTIAS, CIRCIVS, CORVS* and *FAVONIVS*. The instrument is both a piece of technology and a decorative item. In particular, the sundial and the dial for measuring wind on the vertical sides of the block have been accomplished with technical precision; while the base and the upper part are decoratively shaped and engraved.

Horský and Škopová 1968, p. 141.

A.Š.

II.258
Matthaeus Heintzius
Astronomical Compendium
Gilt brass, bone ivory, engraved
5.9 × 6.6 × 7.8 cm
At the back edge of the base of the plate: *Matthaeus Heintzius Fecit Lipsiae*
Beginning of the seventeenth century
Prague, State Observatory at the Clementine Library
Prague, Národní Technické Muzeum, inv. no. 17 188

This is a general-purpose instrument, composed of one basic and one tilted disc and connecting hinges. There is a square

grid with the markings of 12 × 12 parts. A slide-rule divided into seventeen parts is attached to the corner. There is a stereographic projection of the heavenly spheres for the geographical latitude of 51°25'. Symbols along the circumference of the dial allow for longitudinal readings. The bottom of the middle part of the compass is marked with the basic directions: SE, OR, ME, OC, a scale of 2 × 12 hours and the eastern magnetic deviation. Scale markings of 2 × 12 hours are marked around the circumference of the compasses and on the edge of the disc is a dial of horizontal lines for sundial markings III–XII–VIII. The indicating hand is the thread

passing through the eye on the compass and through an opening in a vertical plate. A latitudinal reading is recorded: *Elevatio Poli 51°25'*. There is a table with the astrological rulers of the hours for individual days in the week. The middle of the dial contains a table for monthly hours. The vertical side edges of the block are divided into ten parts with quarter divisions. The instrument is precisely made and decorated with Renaissance and early Baroque engravings.

Horský and Škopová 1968, p. 133.

A.Š.

II.259
European-Style Chest
Wood covered with black lacquer, painted with lacquer (gold and silver *makie* technique), mother-of-pearl inlay. Bronze metalwork on the edges, with two pins of the lock decorated with an engraved floral pattern.
Momoyama period, beginning of seventeenth century
The Imperial Collection
Prague Castle

The decoration of the lid consists in the upper part of two cartouches showing a landscape with peasants, water and archi-

tecture, complemented by zoomorphs and floral quotations. The sides of the lid contain lunette medallions with hares, Chinese greenfinches and herons. The inside of the lid is decorated with a pack-ox and hay under a pine tree with birds flying around. The front panel of the chest has two cartouches in the shape of clouds, one with an owl and a gate (*torii*) to the Shinto sanctuary, with huts and plants, the other with a draught ox and typical Oriental flowers. The sides are decorated with squares containing Chinese greenfinches, peach trees, bamboo, butterflies and birds, or with huts uder hortensia and chrysanthemums. The back panel has con-

volvulus winding round a low fence together with a vine. The chest also has a rectangular lacquered base with short legs, added in Europe and decorated with carved rosettes with golden pearl decoration.

F.S.

II.260
Raw Jasper
60 × 46 × 36 cm
Prague, Prague Castle Administration

A large quantity of precious stones was deposited in the *Kunstkammer* itself, as the inventories of 1619 and 1621 inform us. The largest pieces were in all likelihood those which served as a stock of raw material and were deposited on the ground floor in an area described in German as a 'vault known as the "stale beer" room'. A list, which was compiled after the inventory of 1635, mentions in German under item no. 509: 'A large pile of large and

small pieces of unused jasper and many other types of stone'.

P.Ch.

II.261
Raw Jasper
60 × 46 × 36 cm; 32 × 25 × 32 cm; 42 × 27 ×
21 cm
Prague, Prague Castle Administration

A large quantity of precious stones was deposited in the *Kunstkammer* itself, according to the Inventories of 1619 and 1621. The largest pieces were in all likelihood those that served as a stock of raw material and were deposited on the ground floor in an area described in German as a 'vault known as the "stale beer" room'. A list, which was compiled after the Inventory of 1635, mentions in German under item no.

509: 'A large pile of large and small pieces of unused jasper and many other types of stone'.

P.Ch.

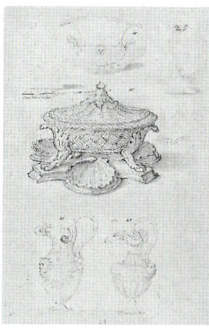

II.262
Giulio Romano and his workshop
Rome 1499–Mantua 1546
Selectarum inventionum collectaneum ex diversis auctoribus
Paper, 160 leaves with drawings attached on both sides; bound in pigskin with blind-stamp
30 × 20.5 × 7 cm
Signed *MK*, 1670s
Ca. 1524–50 (drawings); 1570–1580 (binding)
Ottavio Strada (ex libris on the title page); Premonstratensian monastery at Strahov, Prague, Premonstratensian monastery at Strahov, library, sign. DL III 3

With its 265 drawings, the Strahov album is one of the most remarkable documents of the decorative arts from the sixteenth century. The first part (fols 1–104) contains sketches for the decoration of buildings of the Duke of Mantua, particularly the Palazzo del Te, created by the Gonzagas' court painter Giulio Romano between 1524 and 1546. The drawings by Giulio and his workshop were probably acquired in Mantua by Jacopo Strada, who made this album out of them in the 1570s. Copies of Giulio's originals (fols 105–57) by the Stradas and their workshop are also bound into the album. They compiled several albums of this material, which they

dedicated to potential patrons (Brno, University Library, Sogn.Mk 4 [I.214]; Cambridge, Fitzwilliam Museum, inv. no. PD 6–1948; Florence, Museo delle Scienze, Antico 532).

Mantua 1989, 464; Vienna 1990, cat. no. V/27.

Strake 1916; Bukovinská-Fučíková-Konečný 1984; Fučíková 1987; Jansen 1989; Welzig 1990, p. 264.

L.K.

II.263
Ottavio Strada
? Vienna ?1550–Prague 1606
Symbola Romanorum Imperatorum Occidentis et Orientis, Regumque
Pseudo-Renaissance volume, according to a suggestion made by J. V. Spott at around 1900; 132 pages of which 109 are with drawings in brown and mauve ink
30 × 20.5 cm
Per Octauim de Strada Ciuem Romanum S. Caes: Mts: Aulicum, et Antiquarium (fol. 2r)
1596
Purchased in 1897 at Rosenthal's in Munich
Prague, Uměleckoprůmyslové muzeum v

Praze, inv. no. 7 627 Ck

This manuscript represents a further stage of the Stradas' plan to publish an edition of prints of imprese that were in their collection or 'museum'. After the death of his father, Ottavio concentrated on acquiring patrons who would provide financial support for this project. To this end, he had some manuscript versions in reduced form prepared for a planned printed edition and dedicated them to potential patrons. Today over thirty of these exemplars are known (Boom 1988,21). They vary somewhat in content but are closely related in appearance. According

to an inventory from between 1607 and 1611, it is most likely that at least one of them was in the imperial *Kunstkammer* (inv. no. 2397, 2398, 2601). The group of four imprese of Emperor Rudolf, including the one with the motto *ADSIT*, is on fol. 8r.

Prague 1904, cat. no. 278.

Chytil 1904, pp. 25, 44, 57, 63; Fučíková 1982, p. 351, n. 8; Konečný-Lencová 1997 (forthcoming).

L.K.

II.264
Ottavio Strada
? Vienna ? 1550–Prague 1606
De Vitis Imperatorum et Caesarum Romanorum, tam occidentalium quam orientalium Francofurti ad Moenum Johannes Bringerus, 1615
Paper, print, copper engraving; title page and 518 pages; smooth Renaissance binding, parchment
On the first plate *supralibros C H A T*; at the bottom: *1621*
30 × 20.5 cm
Piarist College at Benesov; Uměleckoprůmyslové Muzeum in Prague since about 1897, (additionally recorded in in-

ventory in 1938)
Prague, Uměleckoprůmyslové Muzeum, inv. no. 23 430 C

Like many humanist scholars and antiquarians in the sixteenth century, the Stradas were interested in numismatics (Weiss 1969, pp. 167–79). Jacopo assembled a large collection of Antique coins and wrote several scholarly treatises about them. His earliest printed work was *Epitome Thesauri Antiquitatum* (Lyon, 1553), in which numismatic portraits of Roman emperors from Julius Caesar to Charles V are reproduced and described. Ottavio Strada continued the tradition and in 1615

issued a book containing short biographies of the Roman emperors, their wives and descendants, accompanied by 533 illustrations of the corresponding coins. A biography of Emperor Rudolf and an illustration of a coin with his bust on the obverse and the motto *ADSIT* on the reverse are included (no. 529). Works devoted to numismatics are also found in the imperial *Kunstkammer* (inventory 1607–11, nos 2594–96).

Schultz 1950; Boom 1988, 21.

L.K.

II.265
Binding with Portrait of *Rudolf II*
Bartoloměj (Bartholomeus) Paprocký z Hlahol, *Diadochos id est successio: or the Succession of Czech Princes and Kings* (Prague, 1602)
Red-dyed leather on wood, blind stamping, gilding, goffered edges
32.4 × 20 cm
Middle book-plate marked *HG* at the bottom of columns (Haebler does not mention the plate)
1602; book-plate dates from 1576
Prague, Národní Knihovna, inv. no. 54 A 69

Master HG first appears on Czech bindings at the end of the sixteenth century. The Národní Knihovna binding features heraldic decoration in the corners of the internal frame (Czech and Lower Austrian emblem below, imperial and Hungarian above) and the goffering of the edges and gilding of the borders. The binding was probably made in the Prague workshops, as is indicated by the character of the binding and other analogies – the use of emblems and ornamental cylinders and the occurrence of the 'scaly' pattern reminiscent of the work of the so-called Master of the Dürer Sketch-book.

Prague 1891, no. 163; Brno 1898, no. 1054.

Hamanová 1959, pp. 116, 209, 262, ill. 89; Haebler 1928–29, vols 1 and 2; *Sammlung bibliothekswissenschaftlicher Arbeiten*, nos 41, 42, ser. 2, nos 24, 25, p. 445/II.

R.V.

II.266
Antonio Tempesta
Florence ca. 1550-Florence 1630
Landscape with Boar Hunt
Oil on stone with dendrites
40.7 × 31.2 cm
Before 1607
Kunstkammer of Rudolf II (inv. no. 1607-11, no. 955/2805 in recent numbering); imperial collection in Vienna
Vienna, Kunsthistorisches Museum, Kunstkammer, inv. no. 3 057

The authorship of this picture and its counterpart (inv. no. 3058) is documented in the 1607-11 Inventory of Rudolf's *Kun-*

stkammer, in which they are mentioned as 'Zwey grosse stuckh von Roma kommen, darein wie baub oder landschafften naturlich gewachsen und von Anthon: Tempest jagdlandschafften darein gemalt'. The Inventory very accurately describes the stone that was used as a foundation for the hunting scene. The dendrites are little tufts of growth that developed when foreign substances were deposited in the spreading cracks in the rock. Nature itself has also created an appealing 'drawing' reminiscent of a tree's leaves and branches. In the sixteenth century painters began to use natural structures and the colour of stones to complement and elevate their

work. They were thus linked to the traditions of Antiquity, when painters and sculptors endeavoured to compete with the products of nature and to cultivate them by means of creative intervention. Painting on stone, which fitted exceedingly well with the demands of Mannerist aesthetics, experienced a renaissance in the sixteenth century.

Essen and Vienna 1988, cat. no. 171.

Essen and Vienna 1988, cat. no. 171, for literature.

E.F.

II.267
Giovanni Castrucci
Fl. in Prag 1598-1615
Landscape with a Sitting Peasant
Commesso in agate and jasper; Frame: wood
21.2 × 27 cm
Before 1611
Kunstkammer of the Emperor Rudolf II, Inventory of 1607-11, no. 2811
Vienna, Kunsthistorisches Museum, Kunstkammer, inv. no. 3035

Until now the entry for this panel in the Inventory of Rudolf II's *Kunstkammer* has been overlooked (Bauer-Haupt 1976, no.

2811). According to Grimm's Dictionary a 'Stock' is a tree-stump plus roots that has been left in the ground. At the lower right edge of this scene a peasant is sitting all alone on a tree-stump; thus it is clearly the work of Giovanni Castrucci. It very noticeably bears all the hallmarks of his style. The individual elements of the landscape are schematic in the extreme, used like stage props for their decorative qualities and thus distributed somewhat incoherently across the picture plane. Spatial values are reduced to a minimum – all of which lead to a distinctly 'modern' picture with a considerable degree of abstraction.

Neumann 1957, pp. 188, 201, no. 30, illus. 211; Bauer-Haupt 1976, no. 2811 (not specified); Rossi 1969, p. 177 (col. pl. 99, p. 172)

R.D.

II.268
Giovanni Castrucci (attr.)
Fl in Prague 1598-1615
Landscape with a Church
Commesso in agate and jasper
18.2 × 23.5 cm
After 1604
From the imperial *Schatzkammer*
Vienna, Kunsthistorisches Museum, Kunstkammer, inv. no. 3049

The proximity to the landscape with chapel in the same frame brings out vividly the difference in the colours of the stones. In this panel agates with unusually lively markings have been used for the

foreground. Since the same stones were not always available in the workshop it is clear from the different stones that these two panels were made at different times. Neumann already suspected that the landscape and particularly the church might be based on reality (Neumann 1957, p. 188). The foreground with the mule-driver in the centre between two rocky hillsides, each with a single tree, is pure invention. However, An Zwollo has identified the church in the middle ground as a church in a forest near Brussels, going back to a drawing by Pieter Stevens dated between 1604 and 1607 (Zwollo 1968, pp. 177-179, illus. 243). It may be that the painter him-

self brought it to Prague. The composition of this panel with three zones layered parallel to the picture plane is typical for Giovanni Castrucci.

Neumann 1957, pp. 186, 188; 200, no. 18, illus. 207; Zwollo 1968, pp. 177-179, illus. 243-244

R.D.

II.269
Giovanni Castrucci (attr.)
Fl in Prague 1598-1615
Landscape with a Bridge and Chapel
Commesso in agate and jasper; Frame: wood
18.5 × 25.8 cm (without frame)
Ca. 1610
From the imperial *Schatzkammer*, Inventory of 1750, p. 611
Vienna, Kunsthistorisches Museum, Kunstkammer, inv. no. 3048

This *commesso* repeats a motif from the signed panel by Cosimo Castrucci which he made in 1596 (inv. no. 3037) and yet the

pictorial effect is utterly different. The outcrops of rock are less significant formally and the colours are not so carefully differentiated towards the distance. Thus the illusion of space is almost entirely negated. The considerable level of abstraction of the individual elements of the landscape creates a surface design based on layered segments stacked parallel to the picture plane. These are exactly the stylistic features found in the works that are known for certain to be by Giovanni Castrucci (cat. nos II.65, II.267). The comparison with Cosimo's original shows that Giovanni was simply not as skilled as his father.

Neumann 1957, pp. 186, 188; 200, no. 17, illus. 199

R.D.

II.270
Castrucci workshop
View of Hradčany and the Lesser Town
18.5 × 34 cm
After 1601, frame dated later
From the property of Count Clari-Aldrigen, transferred by the NKK to the property of the Národní Galeri in Prague in 1945. Transferred in 1962 to the Uměleckoprů-myslove Muzeum in Prague
Prague, Uměleckoprůmyslove Muzeum, inv. no. Z 314/30

The *View of Hradčany and Malá Strana* is one of the most famous motifs of the Castrucci workshops in Prague. The subject

and its execution must have won favour from the moment of its creation, because four variations of it are known. Two are in Vienna, one is in Prague and one is in Munich. In the Prague variant, the artist took some liberties in rendering the proportions of certain details, but otherwise worked with coloured structures and suppressed the larger surfaces. The work as a whole produces an uneasy impression. A graphic work from 1601 by Johann Willenberg and a well-known horizon of Prague, published by Aegidius Sadeler in 1606, have both been considered as models for the view, although the rendering of the White Tower, of which the cupola was re-

placed by a flat terrace ca. 1606, varies. The question of authorship also remains unresolved, and thus we must be satisfied with a general attribution to the Castrucci workshop.

Essen and Vienna 1988, cat. no. 389; Prague 1993, cat. no. I/2-1.

Bukovinská 1972, p. 365; Bukovinská 1983, pp. 444-46; Giusti 1992, pp. 152-53, ill. no. 80 (mirror image).

B.B.

II.271
Castrucci workshop
Landscape
Commessi di pietre dure, agate, jasper
17 × 23 cm
Early seventeenth century, frame dated later
Purchased from Mina Pächterová in 1931 for the collection of the Uměleckoprůmyslove Muzeum in Prague.
Prague, Uměleckoprůmyslove Muzeum, inv. no. 16 687

This landscape panel, along with the view of Hradčany and the cabinet from the Uměleckoprůmyslove Muzeum, are repre-

sentative of this aspect of the Castrucci workshop's production in the Czech collections. Its composition, its pictorial space centrally divided by a large rock with trees, can also be found in other landscapes, which are now in Vienna. This composition is repeated almost identically on the small board that forms the panel of the cabinet in the Grünes Gewölbe collection in Dresden, although the choice of detail alters the effect. In contrast to the calm atmosphere of the Prague landscape, the Dresden version is a dramatic scene with a gathering storm. P. Pries believes that the composition is a free transposition of the view of the Prague Castle from

Opyö, and L. Kybalová relates this landscape composition to the view of Český Krumlov (reproduced there in mirror image). It is most probable, however, that workshop craftsmen borrowed from various models.

Schallaburg 1989, cat. no. 15.

Bukovinská 1972, pp. 364–65; Pries 1980, p. 132; Kybalová 1988, pp. 156–58 (reproduced there in mirror image).

B.B.

II.272
? Giovanni Castrucci
Fl. in Prague 1598–1615
Imperial Eagle with the Bohemian Lion Coat-of-Arms
Commesso in agate, jasper, garnet, lapis lazuli, carnelian, chalcedony, gold; frame: wood
15.2 × 12.7 cm (without frame)
Ca. 1610
From the Ambras Collection; Ambras Inventory of 1788, vol. 2, p. 253, no. 1
Vienna, Kunsthistorisches Museum, Kunstkammer, inv. no. 3001

The coat of arms shows the Emperor as

the King of Bohemia, thus identifying Emperor Rudolf II. The panel was evidently intended as the centrepiece for a table but was not completed because of the death of Rudolf. The Prague Inventory of 1619 lists 'vier sechseckicht und ain rund stuck von jaspis zu aim tisch von Johan Castrucio'. In addition to this there are a further 100 small pieces. The supposition that the individual '*rund stuck*' (round piece) could be this coat of arms would, however, be overhasty since in 1621 it is described as a landscape. In 1648 there is a reference to '4 sechseckichte und 1 runde landtschafft' (four hexagonal landscapes and one round one) in a specification that the

Swedish General Königsmark made for Queen Christine (Dudik 1867, p. XLII, no. 10). However, these are not listed in a Swedish inventory from 1652. Although the coat of arms is therefore not the 'round piece,' this was not a *commesso* in its own right.

Essen/Vienna 1988, cat. no. 728

R.D.

II.273
Anonymous
Inventory of Rudolf II's Collections from 1619
Paper, leather binding - copy
32 × 21 cm
C. W. G. V. N.
1619
Prague Castle Archives, inv. no. Outside fund: safe no. 3

The manuscript contains 101 paper folios. The parchment binding has *13 (73)* on the spine, the original inscription. The whole inventory is written in one hand in German italics. The inventory was made on the orders of the directors just before

Frederick of the Palatinate ascended the throne. It contains descriptions of the objects in Rudolf II's collections and lists them according to subject (folios 2–81) and the place where they were kept (folios 82–98). In the first part a financial estimate of most of the objects is included. The Inventory is very similar to one made in 1621 and kept in the National Library in Vienna (published in 1905 by H. Zimmermann). The manuscript of the 1619 Inventory, bought at an antiquarian market in 1913, comes from the library of the chateau in Lobris (Silesia) and belonged to older Bohemian line of the counts of Nostitz.

Prague 1937.

Moravek 1937 (edition and commentary); Bauer–Haupt 1976 (gives further literature).

V.V.

II.274
Anonymous
Inventory of Prague Collections
Paper, sewn pages without binding, 16 pages, German language
32 × 20 cm
Title: *Den 31. Augusti – 10 Septembris anno 1648 ist die kunstkammer aufm königl. Schloß Prags inventiret und folgende maßen befunden werden*
After 1637 and before 1648
After 1648 Skokloster in Sweden
Stockholm, Riksarkivet, Skoklostersamlingen, inv. no. E 8578

These two of a series of inventories of the

imperial collections at Prague Castle were discovered in Sweden in 1851. The first list (A) may have been compiled before the Swedish attack on Prague and the second inventory (B) may give an overview of everything that remained in the Prague Castle Chamber of Arts after the ransacking of the castle by Swedish soldiers. It was probably compiled for use by the Swedes, whose aim was to take the greatest number of valuable objects from Prague, and who thus required a comprehensive summary of the actual state of the Chamber of Arts. It is hard to explain why so many rare and precious stones were left in Prague. Both inventories are probably contempo-

rary copies; frequent mistakes in the first inventory (A) suggest that it was copied by a scribe who was not quite sure of his German.

Prague 1937, no. I. / B.

Dudík 1867, XXXIII–XLIV; Zimmermann 1905, XVI–L; Morávek 1937, pp. 9–10; Larsson 1967, p. 124.

J.Ha.

II.275
Anonymous
Inventory of Prague Collections from 1648
Paper, sewn pages without binding, 62 + 10 pages, German language
31 × 20 cm
Title: *Verzeichniß, waß sich in Ihrer Kay. Mayt. Kunstkammer zu Prag befinden etc.*
? Before 1648
Prague; after 1648 Skokloster in Sweden
Stockholm, Riksarkivet, Skoklostersamlingen, inv. no. E 8578

Prague 1937, no. I. / C.

Dudík, 1867, pp. XXXIII-XLIV; Zimmer-

mann, 1905, p. XVI-L; Morávek, 1937, p. 9-10; Larsson, 1967, 124.

J.Ha.

II.276
David Hartmann
Active in Prague and Copenhagen (?) during the first quarter of the seventeenth century
The Crown of Rudolf II
Guache, watercolour, paper, glued on cardboard
39.3 × 30 cm
DH
1610
Copenhagen, Den Konigelige Kobberstiksamling, Statens Museum for Kunst, inv. no. 114.3

The graphic artwork with the crown of Rudolf II, dated 1610 and signed with the initials *DH*, was first published in 1950. Its author has been identified as David Hartmann, who in 1612 received 280 gold pieces for the creation of an 'abrizs von derosleven cron und halsband', although the disproportionate size of the sum suggests that the reference may not be to the present work. He is perhaps the same artist who was secured by the Danish court in 1616 as a drawing teacher for the Danish prince. The oldest pictorial depiction of the crown, which could have great documentary value, shows several marked discrepancies. The triangles with reliefs do not correspond to their actual arrangement on the crown, and the enamelled bands on the edges of the mitre have a completely different decoration. The reasons for these changes have not been convincingly explained so far, and thus we do not know for what purpose and under what circumstances this depiction of the crown was created.

Essen and Vienna 1988, cat. no. 336.

Fischer 1950, pp. 74–78; Fillitz 1950, pp. 79–83.

B.B.

II.277
Antonio Abondio
Riva 1538–Vienna 1591
Adam and Eve Plucking Fruit from the Tree of Knowledge
Pen and brown ink
26.6 × 19.6 cm
On the left: *o abbondio* (the left part is cut off); on the right: *Anto abbondio*
After 1586?
Ex cabinet of P. Praun; Esterhazy collection
Budapest, Szépmüvészeti Múzeum, 1786

This example from Budapest is the only surviving autograph drawing by Antonio Abondio, master medallist and creator of miniature wax sculptures. The simple, linear drawing, of confident execution, was probably a sketch for a wax relief rather than a medal. The forms are clearly marked by sharp contour lines. The inner modelling is indicated only with short lines and hooks, without washes, like the drawings of sculptors (e.g., Adriaen de Vries). The paper (water-mark Briquet 7106, Modena, Ferrara 1586) suggests that this was a late work of Abondio's.

Salzburg 1987, cat. no. 26; Essen and Vienna 1988, cat. no. 492

Murr, Ch.T, *Déscription du cabinet de Mr. Paul de Praun a Nuremberg 1797*, p. 37 (description of the drawing); Fučíková 1979, pp. 491–92, ill. 1; Fučíková 1986, pp. 15-16, ill. 7.

E.F.

II.278
Jan Vermeyen
Brussels before 1559-Prague 1608
Mother and Child
Drawing in black chalk on green paper
10.9 × 15.3 cm
On the back: *Ich ... S. Francisco van der minten den 5. Junio 1603 in Prag Hans van der meyden; Niet sonder moytte, op hope van gewin, Sietmen den Lantman den oogst verbeyden so oock de Liefhebbers der Consten met bert en sin*
1603
The collection of the Frankfurt alderman J. F. von Uffenbach; in 1769 to the university collection

Göttingen, Kunstsammlung der Universität Göttingen, H70

The son of the Dutch painter Jan Cornelisz, Vermeyen became a famous goldsmith, and for Rudolf II he created that most precious object, the Emperor's crown. He was probably trained in drawing by his father, so that, like Vianen, he was capable of preparing a drawn model for his work as a goldsmith. His draughtsmanship does not appear to have been influenced by the works of other Rudolfine masters as far as can be deduced from this, his only surviving signed and dated drawing. It was probably a study for an item of goldsmith's work which Vermeyen presented to one of his countrymen during his visit to Prague.

Essen and Vienna 1988, cat. no. 280.

Stechow 1930; Fučíková 1979, p. 496, ill. 8.

E.F.

II.279
Nikolaus Pfaff
Nürnberg ?1556–? Prague before 1612
Danae
Pen and brown ink and brown wash
21.4 × 16.3 cm
Ca. 1601-7
Albert von Sachsen–Teschen; Sammlung de la Gardie, Borrestad
Stockholm, Národní muzeum, inv. no. NMH 165/1973

This drawing, which once belonged to Duke Albrecht of Sachsen-Teschen, was made as a preparatory study for the ivory relief that Nikolaus Pfaff made as a response to Lambert Sustris's *Venus* (Paris, Louvre) and which is now held in Lyon. The contained outlines, the careful use of light and shade to create form and the exact delineation of space all leave the viewer in no doubt that this is a finished piece of work, as indeed are many of the Rudolfine drawings. This work is strikingly superior to the ivory relief based on it, notably in the lifeless hands of the two protagonists. Only two drawings by Nikolaus Pfaff have survived.

Essen and Vienna 1988, cat. no. 235.

Magnusson 1982, no. 165.

S.H.

II.280
Nikolaus Pfaff
Nürnberg ?1556–? Prague before 1612
Design for a Chandelier Adorned with Stag Heads and Figure of Actaeon with Dogs
Red chalk, brown ink; the paper has been trapezoidly trimmed at the top
17 × 11 cm
On the back: *niclas Pfaff*
Ca. 1605
Property from Nürnberg
Nürnberg, Germanisches Nationalmuseum, inv. no. STN 16585, Kapsel 566

This light and energetically drawn sketch shows that Pfaff, an excellent woodcarver, had also made himself into a fine draughtsman under the influence of his colleagues at the Emperor's court. This Stockholm drawing (Nationalmuseum, inv. no. NMH 165/1973) has the character of a perfect 'modeletto', and we know the later work based on it. In its technique and style it recalls some of Spranger's later drawings, and, as well as providing proof of Pfaff's masterful drawing ability, it also tells us something about the form of the woodcarver's work in wood and about the type of illuminations he designed for the Emperor's court.

Stuttgart 1979, cat. no. B29; Essen-Vienna 1988, cat. no. 234, for earlier literature.

Neuerwerbungen des Germanischen Nationalmuseums, 1921-1924, T. 123.

E.F.

II.281
Christoph Lencker
Ludwigsorget kolem ca. 1556–Augsburg
1613
The Rape of Europa
Lead pencil, pen and black ink, grey wash,
red chalk, white body colour
27.5 × 36.5 cm
1600/1605
Comte de Rey de Villette Collection; art
market, Berlin
Nürnberg, Germanisches Nationalmuseum, inv. no. Hz 4012, Kapsel 1552

This elliptical print shows three scenes
from the *Rape of Europa* after Ovid's *Meta-*

morphoses, ii, 845ff.: Mercury leads the bull
in, the bull rapes Europa, Europa is united
with Zeus in the heavens. This drawing is
generally accepted as a design by
Christoph Lencker for a lavabo bowl (now
in the Kunsthistorisches Museum, Vienna), which was at one stage in the *Kunstkammer* of Rudolf II and is listed in
Fröschl's Inventory of 1607. None of the
details of the drawing correspond to the
relief on the bowl, however, which means
that it could be the design for a bowl that
has since been lost. The drawing itself, in
the style of the school of Taddeo Zuccaro,
points to southern Germany as the place
of origin.

Berlin 1988, no. 75; Nürnberg 1992, cat. no.
51.

Hanke 1963, n. 259; Hayward 1976, illus.
167; Geissler 1978, pp. 65–91, n. 46; Seling
1980, I, illus. 81; Irmscher 1989, part 6, pp.
32–37.

I.G.

II.282
Christoph Lencker (attributed)
Ludwigsorget kolem ca. 1556–Augsburg
1613
Design for the Relief Ornament of a Bowl
Pen and black ink and grey wash
17.1 × 17.5 cm
Ca. 1600
Dr Helmut Seling, Munich

This circular drawing is without doubt a
design for the inside of the base of a bowl:
this is clear from the smooth line running
round the edge. John Hayward has identified it as the work of Christoph Lencker
on the strength of its stylistic similarity

with a particular basin in the Kunstkammer in Vienna showing Zeus abducting
Europa. Helmut Seling, whose publication on the Augsburg goldsmiths includes
an illustration of this design, is of the
same opinion. There are clear similarities
between the female figure riding a bull on
the left side of this drawing and the figure
on the left of the *Europa* basin. Both have
their bodies turned in the same way and
their heads thrown back, although in the
design by Lencker the head is proportionately a lot smaller. Other motifs, such as
the bank of clouds in the centre of the top
edge and the stylized trees, are common to
both.

Hayward 1976, pp. 234–35, pl. 166; Seling
1980, vol. 1, p. 69 (ill.), vol. 3, pp. 98ff., no.
993 (nos 993 f, l, m: salvers; no. 993h: *Europa* basin).

H.Sg.

II.283
Unknown Artist
Design for a Medal with the Portraits of
Rudolf II and *Matthias*
Pen and brown ink on very fine, thin paper
9.5 × 9 cm
Probably ca. 1612
J. M. von Radowitz (Lugt 2125), acquired
in 1856
Berlin, Staatliche Museen zu Berlin,
Kupferstichkabinett, KdZ no. 11 666

In the medallions Rudolf II is shown
above, turned slightly to the right and
with the motto *ADSIT*; below is Matthias

in profile with imperial insignia instead of
a motto or impress – the 'feuding brothers' together on one drawing. The work
has been ascribed to Paulus van Vianen,
but Gerszi quite rightly refutes this (not
published). This work is not, as one might
think, a design for a coin or a medallion
but is intended instead to be engraved as
an illustration of – fictive – coins and
medallions without impresses. The portrait of Rudolf II with his laurel wreath
clearly goes back to the alabaster work ascribed to Hans von Aachen in Nürnberg,
Germanisches Nationalmuseum, inv. no.
Gm 1235 (see Tacke 1996, pp. 26–28, no. 2,
ill. 2, col. pl. 2). This modest yet high-qual-

ity drawing can hardly have been made before 1612, but also not long after that date,
because it shows Matthias as yet without a
motto. In terms of quality, it may be compared with the drawings of Ottavio Strada
in Budapest, and one might be tempted to
see this as his work if he had not already
died in 1606 (see van der Boom 1988, p.
20). However, its provenance from the
Strada circle is self-evident.

J.Z.

II.284
? Rudolf II's goldsmith
Design for a Gold Goblet
Pen drawing in brown ink, brown wash,
coloured and gilded
24.4 × 10 cm
After 1600
Purchased 1956 from Heřman Štěpánek,
an art dealer based in Prague
Prague, Národní galeri v Praze, Grafická
sbírka, inv. no. 31 809

Both these drawings were the work of the
same person, most likely a goldsmith who
was also skilled at drawing. The unusual
theme of the design, depicting mining

scenes, would suggest that it may have
been connected with the gold wares that
were commissioned by the Salzburg archbishops and funded by the tithes paid to
them by the local mining fraternities. In
the light of this, the author of the work
may well be Hans Karl, to whom it is frequently attributed and who came to
Prague after having worked for Wolf Dietrich von Raitenau in Salzburg. This particular collection of gold wares was not however the work of one goldsmith. A number
of goldsmiths must have been commissioned to make the works, and given certain stylistic similarities some of the objects may well have been ordered from the

imperial workshops at Hradčany Castle. In
form, the design of the goblet is similar to
goldsmiths' works dating from the turn of
the seventeenth century, such as those by
Ch. Jamnitzer and H. Petzold. Whoever
made the drawing, it was clearly someone
skilled in the use of pen and chalk. The
drawing lacks the sharp linearity and
overdecoration often found in traditional
designs by other goldsmiths, and its technique is quite similar to that used by
Paulus van Vianen in his drawings.

Prague 1978, cat. no. 34.

E.F.

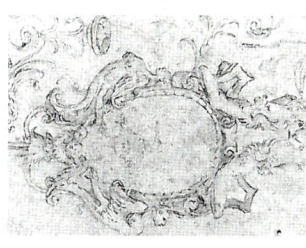

II.285
? Rudolf II's goldsmith
Design for a Mirror or Candlestick
Drawing in black chalk, brown wash on
grey paper (verso: ornament drawing in
black chalk, possibly from a later date)
13.5 × 9.1 cm
After 1600
Purchased 1956 from Heřman Štěpánek,
an art dealer based in Prague
Prague, Národní galeri v Praze, Grafická
sbírka, inv. no. 31 473

Prague 1978–79, cat. no. 35.

E.F.

II.286
Paulus van Vianen
Utrecht ca. 1570–Prague 1613
Design for a Covered Cup
Dark ruddle drawing, grey and pink wash
58.7 × 29.4 cm
Later inscription on verso: *Original von Paul von Fion*
Ca. 1610
Munich, Staatliche Graphische Sammlung, inv. no. 14704

A drawing of a goblet, the bowl of which is supported by two nude kneeling figures. Bizarre masks and anatomical motifs can be made out on the lobed ornamental dec-oration of the stem and lid of the goblet. The work is crowned on the lid with a female figure, who is probably a personification of Temperance or Continence: she is pouring a drink from an ewer on the dish of a tazza. In the circular cartouche on the bowl is an assembly of the gods, including Venus and Amor on the left and Minerva on the right. This design was once wrongly attributed to Adam van Vianen, who worked in Utrecht. However, the drawing is clearly linked to the work that his brother Paulus produced while active in Prague. The ornamentation draws on the decoration used by Paulus van Vianen in his Prague silver reliefs such as the ewer and platter from 1613 (cat. nos II.15, II.16), while the depiction of the assembly of the gods is also very close to his relief scenes and sketches.

Essen-Vienna 1988, cat. no. 294.

Gerszi 1982, no. 73; Ter Molen 1984, no. 306.

J.R.tM.

II.287
Paulus van Vianen
Utrecht ca. 1570–Prague 1613
Holy Family
Chalk drawing in brown with grey wash, greyish paper
50.3 × 40 cm
Ca. 1610
G. Huquier collection, Amsterdam auction 14.9.1761, no. 4327; Louis Metayer collection, Amsterdam auction 16.12.1799, no. 7; Frederik Muller, Amsterdam 1887
Amsterdam, Rijksmuseum, Rijksprentenkabinet, inv. no. A 1433

The drawing depicts the Madonna and Child, with Joseph standing next to her. On the right are Elizabeth and the young John the Baptist. In the background is the trunk of an old tree, and drapery hangs above the Holy Family. The composition can be considered a preliminary study for the silver relief which Paulus van Vianen created in 1610 (cat. no. II.228).

Utrecht 1984, cat. no. 49.

Boon 1978, no. 463; Gerszi 1982, no. 77; Ter Molen 1984, no. 300; Spicer 1988, pp. 274, 279, figs. 3, 10.

J.R.tM.

II.288
Paulus van Vianen
Utrecht ca. 1570–Prague 1613
Madonna and Child
Black and brown chalk drawing, grey wash, brown paper
49.4 × 39 cm
Ca. 1610
Paris, Musée du Louvre, Cabinet des Dessins, inv. no. 22359

In the centre of the scene sits the Virgin Mary with the frontally viewed infant on her knee. In the background are dilapidated buildings with ruined walls and a wooden ladder. A bearded man, who is doubtless intended to be Joseph, looks out from an open window. Paulus van Vianen probably based this composition on his impressions from the countryside around Prague, which he captured in his sketches. The pose of the Madonna and Child seems to have been influenced by Albrecht Dürer's graphic works depicting the same subject.

Utrecht 1984, cat. no. 48.

Gerszi 1982, no. 76; Ter Molen 1984, no. 299.

J.R.tM.

II.289
Paulus van Vianen
Utrecht ca. 1570–Prague 1613
Susanna in the Bath
Black chalk drawing, white-lead coating, grey-brown paper
45.8 × 36.6 cm
Ca. 1610
Prague
Legacy of Joh. Fr. Lahmann, Dresden 1937
Berlin, Staatliche Museen, Münzkabinett, inv. no. 37/638

Susanna, bathing by a stream in a wooded mountain landscape, is being watched by two men in the background. In the right in the distance are several buildings, among which is probably a part of Queen Anne's Summer Palace from Prague Hradčany. The theme of Susannah and the elders (Daniel 13) was also used by Paulus van Vianen for one of his silver reliefs. On the platter from 1612 (cat. no. II.14) he chose a different composition: the two old men are shown in the foreground of the relief on either side of the woman modestly bathing. However, it is noticeable that the artist did use some details from the drawing in the relief: the figure in the cloak and round hat leaning slightly forwards, and the group of buildings in the background. Nitze 1990, pp. 118–119, figs. 4–5.

J.R.tM.

II.290
Paulus van Vianen
Utrecht ca. 1570–Prague 1613
Diana and Actaeon
Black chalk drawing, grey wash
15.8 × 21.5 cm
Ca. 1610
Frankfurt, Städelsches Kunstinstitut, inv. no. 3144

On both sides of this drawing a number of naked women who belong to Diana's company turn their attention to the bathing goddess, who is changing Acteon into a stag as punishment for having watched her (Ovid, *Metamorphoses* III, 138–197). A mirror image of this composition, executed in far greater detail, was used by Paulus van Vianen for his silver plaque of 1612 (Ter Molen 1984, no. 118). In 1610 the subject had already appeared in the decoration of a gold goblet (Ter Molen 1984, no. 16) and again, in the year of Paulus van Vianen's death, on an oval platter (cat. no. II.16), where a few details have been changed as a result of the oval form.

Duyvené de Wit 1955, pp. 185–190; Gerszi 1982, no. 75; Ter Molen 1984, no. 304; Spicer 1988, pp. 277, 279, fig. 8.

J.R.tM.

II.291
Paulus van Vianen
Utrecht ca. 1570–Prague 1613
Study of a Tree
Grey pen drawing with wash
14.8 × 19.8 cm
On verso: *Paulus van Viane*
Early seventeenth century
Berlin auction 31.10.1929, no. 127; Hofstede de Groot collection, Leipzig auction 4.11.1931, no. 267
Amsterdam, Rijksmuseum, Rijksprentenkabinet, inv. no. 31:185

This drawing is one of a series of outdoor studies, which, given the fact that they have the same dimensions, paper type and technique, probably come from the same sketchbook. This sheet depicts a wooded and mountainous landscape through which a fast-flowing river winds its way. On the back is a depiction of a tree. This tree is found in almost identical form on the nodus of a silver platter with base, from 1607, which has the Judgment of Paris on the dish (Ter Molen 1984, no. 14).

Utrecht 1984, cat. no. 36.

Boon 1978, no. 466; Gerszi 1982, no. 18; Ter Molen 1984, no. 234.

J.R.tM.

II.292
Paulus van Vianen
Utrecht ca. 1570–Prague 1613
Water Mill; on verso: *Figures of Orientals*
Pen and black ink, grey wash; brush, brown pen
14.4 × 9.9 cm; verso 14.2 × 7.8
Beginning of seventeenth century
Salzburg or Prague
W. Bateson collection, London auction 23.4.1929, cat. no. 203; F. Koenigs collection
Rotterdam, Museum Boijmans van Beuningen, inv. no. N 128

This drawing shows a number of buildings, one of which has a water-wheel with above it a wooden construction leading water from a stream. Paulus van Vianen represented this mill several times on his silver plaques: in 1603 on the scene with Pan and Syrinx (cat. no. II.9), later on the large 1604 relief of the Assembly of the Gods (Ter Molen 1984, no. 78), and again in the Pursuit of Syrinx by Pan, produced in the year of the artist's death, 1613 (Ter Molen 1984, no. 119). On the back of the sheet in an oval frame are depictions of two Oriental figures with turbans on their heads, with a number of warriors in the background. On several plaques from the 'Martyrs' series (Ter Molen 1984, nos. 90–106) there are figures in similar dress.

Utrecht 1984, cat. no. 41.

Gerszi 1982, no. 53; Ter Molen 1984, no. 274.

J.R.tM.

II.293
Paulus van Vianen
Utrecht ca. 1570–Prague 1613
Landscape with Bridge; on verso: Figures and Ornaments
Brown pen drawing
18.2 × 26.7 cm
Pauwels van Vianen fecit 1606
1606
Joh. Chr. Endris collection, Vienna auction 4.5.1891, no. 151
Vienna, Museum für angewandte Kunst, inv. no. Hz.6512

Within a rectangular frame is a depiction of a river with a hilly landscape. The riverbanks are joined by a wooden bridge on which stands a cross. Paulus van Vianen used various details from this composition on the silver plaque from 1607 (cat. no. II.11). Around 1800 Joseph Burde of Prague produced an etching based on this drawing (Gerszi 1982, no. K 15). The back of the sheet is completely covered with small sketches by Paulus van Vianen, depicting nereids, figures riding dolphins, and winged putti. Among the individual drawings are designs for ornamental decorations and masks and models for cartouches and for goblet bases. Several of these decorations are used on the silver platter with base from 1607 (Ter Molen 1984, cat. no. 13).

Essen-Vienna 1988, cat. no. 659.

Ter Molen 1984, no. 292.

J.R.tM.

II.294
Christoph Jamnitzer
Nürnberg 1563–Nürnberg 1618
Design for the Triumph Ewer *Parade of the Allegory of Chastity*
Lead pencil, pen and brown ink and wash
16.8 × 19.6 cm
Ca. 1600
Budapest, Szépmüvészeti Múzeum, inv. no. 209

This sheet has, verso and recto, two different designs for the jug of the Trionfi lavabo depicting the Triumph of Chastity over Love. Slightly altered by Jamnitzer, the design is based on a woodcut on the same theme for Daniel Federmann's German translation of Petrarch's *Trionfi* (Basel 1578); the woodcut is generally accepted as the work of the young Christoph Murer. The figure bending over, burning Amor's weapons, was later replaced with a similar figure from the engraving *The Mother of St Lawrence* by Marcantonio Raimondi after Raphael, and the ermine on the flag was replaced with an elephant: both symbolize chastity. The studies of heads were also taken from engravings; thus the female head at the upper left comes – significantly – from Jan Sadeler's print *Hercules at the Crossroads* (after Friedrich Sustris).

Hoffmann 1935, illus. 15 and 16; O'Dell-Franke 1983, illus. 4–5; Angerer 1985, p. 134, illus. 107.

I.G.

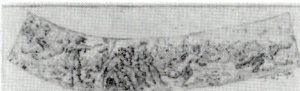

II.295
Christoph Jamnitzer
Nürnberg 1563–Nürnberg 1618
Four Sketches [two shown here] for the Decoration on the Border of the Triumph Basin (Charity, Death, Fame, Time)
Lead pencil, pen and brown ink and wash, heightened with gold
Ca. 4.8 × 29 cm
Monogram: *CI* (lig.); later inscription: *Bonasone*
Ca. 1600
London, Victoria and Albert Museum, inv. no. E 665-1929–E 668-1929

These are preliminary drawings for the immensely subtly worked mythological scenes around the edge of the Trionfi bowl, with the Triumph of Love in the centre. The four scenes are mythological interpretations of four *Trionfi* by Petrarch: 'Apollo and Daphne' (Chastity), 'Pluto rapes Persephone' (Death), 'The Race between Hippomenes and Atalanta' (Fame) and 'Venus mourns the Sleep of Amor' (Time). The figures are modelled on others from contemporary engravings. One weakness of Christoph Jamnitzer's compositions is the lack of any real middle ground. The gold heightening shows how greatly these works were valued by their owner.

Williams 1936, pp. 419–20, illus. 1–4; Williams 1937, p. 112; Hayward 1976, no. 137; Irmscher 1981, p. 91; O'Dell-Franke 1983, illus. 2; Irmscher 1988 (Beiträge), pp. 238 and 241, illus. 15.

I.G.

II.296
Christoph Jamnitzer
Nürnberg 1563–Nürnberg 1618
Minerva Teaches the Arts to Mankind
Lead pencil, pen and brown ink, pale blue
wash, heightened with white
14.3 × 9 cm
Cristoforo Jamnizer orofici da norimbergo
Ca. 1600
London, Victoria and Albert Museum, inv.
no. 2357-1928

This may well have been a leaf from a family album or register: on the back it is still
possible to make out the words 'Göttin
Pallaß der Weißheit' (Pallas, the Goddess
of Wisdom). The image depicts Minerva
instructing a man dressed in the clothing
of Antiquity: she is handing him tools
used in the arts, freeing him from heavy
work, symbolized by the yoke lying on the
ground. This is probably also a reference
to the artist being released from the restrictions of the guilds and worshipful
companies. In the upper right there are
birds harassing a donkey, an allusion to
the treatment meted out to the goldsmith
by those who envied him. Although this
print is much influenced by the conditions of art in the court at Prague, there is
perhaps also a source in Antiquity, namely
as the goddess of artists in Claudian, *De*
bell. Get. 15/16, *De Stil*, II, 340–347, and *In*
Eutrop, I, 271–276; as the inventor of tools
in the work of L. G. Giraldus, *De deis gen-*
tium varia et multiplex, 1548, pp. 466 and
479, and in the same work as a patron of
the arts (p. 465); and in the work of V. Cartari, *Imagini*, 1556, p. 188, as the inventor
of the arts. The Italianate inscription does
not mean that the work was produced in
Italy: Wenzel Jamnitzer's name also exists
in an Italian version.

O'Dell-Franke 1983, illus. 2; Angerer 1985,
p. 136, illus. 110.

I.G.

II.297
Hertzich van Bein
Fl. in Prague 1589–1617
Blackwork Print - Title
Etching
4.5 × 5.2 cm
HERTZICH VAN. BEIN. FE. (15)89
1589
Vienna, Museum für Angewandte Kunst,
inv. no. D 271 (1/1)

Hertzich van Bein was a court goldsmith
and engraver in Prague. Sources show that
he was active in Prague from 1589 to 1617
and had his own house there, where Mathias Beitler, the goldsmith and blackwork
engraver, was his lodger. This title page
with vases, fruit and insects was copied in
1590 by Corwinian Saur in Augsburg,
showing the considerable influence of the
style of van Bein's designs.

Bukovinská 1982, p. 78; Schütte 1989/90,
pp. 184, 188, I.1.

R.A.S.

II.298
Hertzich van Bein
Fl. in Prague 1589–1617
Blackwork Prints
Etching
Ca. 3.7 × 4.4 cm
HERZICH VAN BEIN FECIT 1592 (on ti-
tle page); *HVB* (on the other pages)
1592
Vienna, Museum für Angewandte Kunst,
inv. no. D 273 (2/1)

Title page of a set. Three are exhibited
here, all showing blackwork designs for
decorating rings.

Schütte 1989/90, p. 188, nos II.1, II.2, II.6.

R.A.S.

II.299
Hertzich van Bein
Fl. in Prague 1589–1617
Blackwork Prints
Etching
Approx. 5 × 4.1 cm
HVB (15)92; HVB.
1592
Vienna, Museum für Angewandte Kunst,
inv. no. D 270 (5/1)

Three plates from a set with two large
birds, insects and festoons and baldachins.

Schütte 1989/90, p. 189, nos V.1, V.2, V.4.

R.A.S.

II.300
Hertzich van Bein
Fl. in Prague 1589–1617
Blackwork Prints
Etching
4.2 × 5.2 cm
1592 HERTZICH VAN BEIN FECIT (title
page); *92 HVBF*
1592
London, Victoria and Albert Museum, inv.
no. E.1034-1923; E 1033-1923

Title page and another page from a set of
blackwork prints with birds, insects and
dragons. Designs of this nature were used
for the backs of cameos.

Schütte 1989/90, p. 189, nos IV.1, IV.2.

R.A.S.

II.301
Corwinian Saur after Hertzich van Bein
Fl. Augsburg 1590–Copenhagen 1635
Ornamental Pattern
Etching
4.3 × 5.1 cm
1590 CS
1590
London, Victoria and Albert Museum, inv.
no. E.2822–1910 (1/1)

Saur was a goldsmith and engraver of designs. Between 1590 and 1597 he published numerous sets of blackwork prints in Augsburg, which in some cases show considerable stylistic similarity to black-work designs from Prague. It is unfortunately not possible to establish whether Saur himself was ever in Prague. In 1606 Saur went to Copenhagen and from 1613 until his death was goldsmith to the Danish court. Blackwork print with birds, vases and festoons. The plate is a reverse image after an engraving by Hertzich van Bein of 1589.

Schütte 1989/90, p. 184, 185, illus. 145.

R.A.S.

II.302
Corwinian Saur
Fl. Augsburg 1590–Copenhagen 1635
Blackwork Prints
Etching
4.3 × 5.1 cm; diam: 5.1 and 4.1 cm
1591 CORWINIANVS SAVR FECIT (title page); *15 CS 91.*
1591
Probably Augsburg
London, Victoria and Albert Museum, inv.
no. E.2820–1910, E 2821–1910

Two plates from a series with four small rectangular plates with birds, festoons, various vases and grotesque figures.

Schütte 1989/90, p. 184, 185, illus. 146.

R.A.S.

II.303
Corwinian Saur
Fl. Augsburg 1590–Copenhagen 1635
Blackwork Prints
Etching
4 × 5 cm; diam: 5.1 and 4.1 cm
CSF; CS
Ca. 1591
Probably Augsburg
London, Victoria and Albert Museum, inv.
no. E.2823–1910, E 2824–1910, E 2825–1910, E 2826–1910

Four plates from a set with oval and round blackwork prints showing birds and insects amongst branches and fruits, predominantly used to decorate the backs of cameos.

See Schütte 1989/90, pp. 184–85, ills 147, 148.

R.A.S.

II.304
Johannes van Selen
Fl. last decade of sixteenth century, probably in Prague
Blackwork Print - Title
Etching
7 × 5.6 cm
IN DOMINO CONFIDEO. JOHANNES. VAN. SELEN. FECIT. ANNO. 1599
1599
Prague
Berlin, Kunstbibliothek, inv. no. 32 213 (pasp.733)

Like many other masters in Prague, Selen, a goldsmith and designs engraver, came from the Netherlands. Two sets of prints by Selen have survived, dated 1590 and 1599. The title page of the second set, decorated with numerous birds, is on exhibition here.

Ornamentstichsammlung Berlin 1939, 733; Schütte 1989/90, p. 186.

R.A.S.

II.305
Hans de Bull
Fl. in Prague ca. 1600
Blackwork Prints
Etching
5.7 × 4.4 cm
HDBF; HDB
Shortly after 1600
Prague
Berlin, Kunstbibliothek, inv. no. 728/8

Hans de Bull produced blackwork prints in Prague between 1592 and 1604. It is likely that he was also a goldsmith. Four plates (two shown here) from a set of oval blackwork prints with birds, fruits, a bat and weapons, used mainly for decorating the backs of cameos.

Ornamentstichsammlung Berlin 1939, 728/8; Bukovinská 1982, p. 78; Schütte 1989/90, pp. 185, 196, nos V.1–V.4.

R.A.S.

II.306
Hans de Bull
Fl. in Prague ca. 1600
Blackwork Prints
Etching
4.7 × 6.2 cm
IDB
After 1604
Berlin, Kunstbibliothek, inv. no. 90 296
(728/7)

Four plates from a set of blackwork prints: a winged, crowned heart pierced by two arrows beneath a baldachin. Other plates show weapons.
Ornamentstichsammlung Berlin 1939, 728/7; Schütte 1989/90, p. 196, no. VII.1–VII.4.

R.A.S.

II.307
Hans de Bull; engraved by Aegidius Sadeler
Fl. in Prague ca. 1600
Blackwork Prints
Etching
Between 7.2 × 6.4 and 6.4 × 5.5 cm
JOHAN D BVLL AEg Sadeler excudit Praga: 1604 (title page); *IDB* (other pages)
1604
Berlin, Kunstbibliothek, inv. no. 92 101
(728/5) (6/1)

Title page of a set of six blackwork designs for decorating rings: with a bat above and the inscription below. Subsequent plates show various fantasy creatures.
Ornamentstichsammlung Berlin 1939, 728/5; Schütte 1989/90, p. 196, nos VI.1–VI.6.

R.A.S.

II.308
GB (monogram)
Fl. ca. 1600, probably in Prague
Blackwork Prints
Etching
4.3 × 5.5 cm (4.3 × 5.9 cm)
1603 GB
1603
Vienna, Museum für Angewandte Kunst, inv. no. D 268

The artist who signed these prints with the monogram GB is known only for this set of blackwork prints. His designs have all the hallmarks of a master working in Prague, and five are on show here: dog and a hare, a bat and a phoenix, and long decorative strips from rings. This exhibition includes many vessels and cameos with mounts or settings influenced by these designs.

Florence 1975, no. 83.

Schütte 1989/90, 186, figs. 152–54.

R.A.S.

II.309
Mathias Beitler
Ansbach ca. 1560–Prague after 1617
Blackwork Prints
Etching
5.3 × 4.5 cm
MATHIAS BEITLER 1612 (title page); *MB* (other pages)
1612
Berlin, Kunstbibliothek, inv. no. 658/1

Mathias Beitler worked in Ansbach as a young man engraving designs. In 1600 he went to Prague, where he served as an imperial bodyguard (*Hartschier*) from 1601 to 1606. He lodged with the court goldsmith and blackwork engraver Hertzich van Bein. It is known that he was in Prague in 1617. Beitler's blackwork prints were immensely influential and his designs were copied repeatedly. The title page has an oval inscription and in the corners there are four water creatures. Each of the next four plates has three different figurative scenes.

Ornamentstichsammlung Berlin 1939, 658/1; Bukovinská 1982, p. 79, n. 34; Schütte 1988, p. 270, illus. 4–9.

R.A.S.

II.310
Mathias Beitler
Ansbach ca. 1560–Prague after 1617
Blackwork Print
Etching
4.5 × 7 cm
IRKMRII hartschier MATHIAS BEITLER 1614 (title page); *SMD MB; MB*
1614
Berlin, Kunstbibliothek, inv. no. 658/2
(5/1)

Here the title inscription, placed between two long-tailed, winged dragons, has been very much abbreviated. It may be read as: 'I(hrer) R(ömisch) K(aiserlichen) M(aje-stät) R(udolfs) II. hartschier' (bodyguard to His Imperial Roman Majesty Rudolf II). Here Beitler is alluding to his time between 1601 and 1606 as a bodyguard (*Hartschier*) to Rudolf II. Subsequent plates show imperial and ecclesiastical coats of arms, engravers' tools, gods, signs of the zodiac, and Diana and Acteon.

Ornamentstichsammlung Berlin 1939, 658/2; Schütte 1988, cf. pp. 267–68.

R.A.S.

II.311
Mathias Beitler
Ansbach ca. 1560–Prague after 1617
Prodigal Son (?)
Etching
3.8 × 6 cm
MATHIAS BEITLER 1616
1616
Berlin, Kunstbibliothek, inv. no. 658/5
(6/1)

Ornamentstichsammlung Berlin 1939, 658/5

R.A.S.

II.312
Mathias Beitler
Ansbach ca. 1560–Prague after 1617
Print with St. Jerome
Etching
5.6 × 3.6 cm
MB
Ca. 1616
Berlin, Kunstbibliothek, inv. no. 658/5

Ornamentstichsammlung Berlin 1939, 658/5.

R.A.S.

II.313
Mathias Beitler
Ansbach ca. 1560–Prague after 1617
Print with a Monkey
Etching
3.8 × 5.7 cm
MB
Ca. 1616
Berlin, Kunstbibliothek, inv. no. 658/5

Ornamentstichsammlung Berlin 1939, 658/5.

R.A.S.

II.314
Copyist after Mathias Beitler
Prague after 1616
Print with Susanna in the Bath
Etching
3.9 × 5.9 cm
MB
Ca. 1616
Berlin, Kunstbibliothek, inv. no. 658/5

Ornamentstichsammlung Berlin 1939, 658/5.

R.A.S.

II.315
Johann Sadeler the Elder after Jan van der
Straet, alias Stradanus
Brussels 1550–Venice ca. 1600
*Allegory of Power, Majesty and Freedom -
Model for the Design of the Lehman Cup*
Copper engraving
22.5 × 28.5 cm
Bottom left *Ioann Sadeler scalp. et exc.*; bottom right *Joan Stradan. Academic Floret fig.*; bottom centre *Venetis ex ofici Sadelery*
1597
Bought at Hanstein in 1904
Prague, Uměleckoprůmyslové Muzeum,
inv. no. 8818

This is the title page of the set *Schema seu speculum principum*, which includes five other pages by Johann Sadeler (*Arma, Litterae*) and Rafael Sadeler I (*Nuptiae, Pietas, Venatio*) after Stradanus. The set of allegories of power is dedicated to Duke Charles Emmanuel of Savoy (1562–1630) and his wife, the infanta Catherine (1567–1597), daughter of King Philip II of Spain and Rudolf II's cousin. Stradanus's original drawing, dated 1594, is in Haarlem (Teylers Museum). The title page served as model for the decoration of the Lehmann Bowl of 1605.

Hollstein a, XXI, no. 533, p. 171; Karel

Chytil, *Die Kunst in Prag zur Zeit Rudolf II.* (Prague, 1904), p. 69.

R.V.

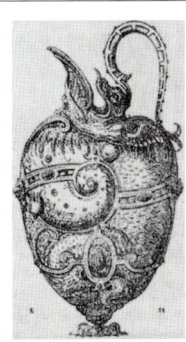

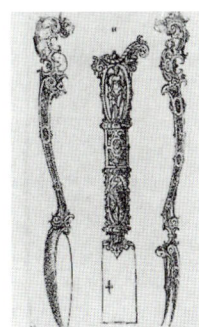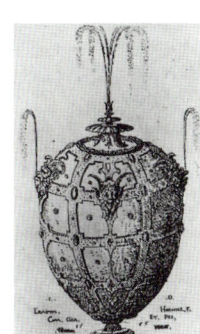

II.316
Erasmus Hornik
Antwerp ca. 1520–Prague (?) 1583
Sketches for Goldsmith's Works
Series of 21 etchings including title folio
[13 shown]
Ca. 14.2 × 8.0–8.6 cm (mostly cut at the edges); title folio 8.1 × 7.2 cm
All folios bear the monogram *EH*, title: *I, D, S, / ERASMVS, HORNICK, F / CUM, GRA, ET, PRI, / EH / NVREMBERG, / 1565*; one folio has the inscription *.L.D./ ERASMVS, HORNICK, F, / CUM, GRA, ET, PRI, 1565 / .NVREMBERG*
1565
Purchased from Taussig & Taussig book-

shop, Prague, in 1934
Prague, Uměleckoprůmyslové muzeum,
inv. no. 20 429/1–19, 20 430/1–2

Of the graphic works made by Erasmus Hornick, a goldsmith active in Augsburg and Nürnberg and then appointed goldsmith to the court of Rudolf II in Prague in 1582 shortly before his death, five series of designs for jewellery, medallions and plate are known today. The designs of vases and pots, especially the series of fantastic, sculpture-derived designs, constitute the highpoint of Hornick's Mannerist oeuvre. In specialist literature, this series has usually been described as comprising

eighteen folios, after a copy in the Albertina, Vienna (another copy is in the Kunstbibliothek Berlin). Hayward includes in the series the title folio in the form of stretched donkey skin with inscriptions.

Hollstein b, XV A, nos 42–59 (pp. 68–71); Nagler Mon., II, no. 1603, 1; Bartsch IX, 499, no. 1; Thieme–Becker, XVII, p. 521; Nürnberg 1985, pp. 387–90; Hayward 1968, pp. 200–206; Hayward; 1968, pp. 383 ff.; Hayward 1976, p. 351, ills 138ff.

R.V.

II.317
Virgil Solis
Nürnberg 1514–Nürnberg 1562
Models for Metal Works
Fifteen engravings from a series of 24
folios [8 shown here]
23.6 (24.1) × 12.2 (12.5) cm
All folios bear the monogram *VS* and are
numbered; the set comprises pages 2–8,
10–13, 15, 19, 22, 24
Ca. 1558
Unknown, taken over from the non-inventoried collection of ornamental engravings of the Uměleckoprůmyslové
muzeum, Prague
Prague, Uměleckoprůmyslové muzeum,

inv. nos G4 497-99, G5 1038/1-12

The stylistically varied series of Solis's
graphic originals reveals the influence of
Dutch and Italian works on Nürnberg
goldsmiths of the mid-sixteenth century.
The theory that Solis did engravings of
foreign originals, of W. Jamnitzer for example (see Bergau 1879 and, more recently, Hayward 1976), has not been confirmed. The numbered series of designs
for cups and pots has not been fully reconstructed; the copy in Prague's
Uměleckoprůmyslové muzeum contains
pages not recorded in the literature.

Nürnberg 1985, 369-70.

Bergau 1879, 4, Pl. B 4-15, 17, 18, 23, 41-3; B
525 (sheet 5); Nagler Mon., V, p. 265
(sheets 4, 7, 8, 11, 18-20, 22, 24); *Ornamentstichsammlung, Berlin* 1939, 133; Hayward 1976, p. 351, ill. 137 (sheet 3);
O'Dell-Franke 1977, i56-i79, pl. 112-17
(complete series).

R.V.

II.318
Paulus van Vianen
Request of the Goldsmith Paul von Vianen for Payment for Work Performed, Addressed to Rudolf II
Paper (colour photocopy)
31 × 20.5 cm
Autograph
Submitted July 28, 1610
Prague Castle Archives, Court Chamber,
inv. no. 685

In this document, Paulus van Vianen
asked the Emperor for payment in connection with his four-month journey to the
Netherlands. On the basis of this request

and an attached report from the court
treasurer, Rudolf II ordered in a document
dated November 2 that the Bohemian
Chamber ensure the jeweller Paulus van
Vianen was paid the 460 guilders he was
owed. Printed by F. Kreyczi in his
Jahrbuch, 1894, no. 11758

Jahrbuch der kunsthistorischen Sammlungen des Allerhochstens Kaisserhauses,
vol. 11, 1894, p. 38, Inventory of the Court
Chamber collection in the Prague Castle
Archives, reg. no. 11 758.

V.V.

II.319
Michael Schneeberger
Fl. in Prague 1602–? Prague 1616
Clockmaker Michael Schneeberg's Request for Payment for Works Performed
for the Emperor
Paper, double page and page (colour photocopy)
32 × 21 cm
September 23, 1614
Prague Castle Archives, Court Chamber
collection, inv. no. 748

Clockmaker and burgher of the Mala
Strana Michael Schneeberger asked the
Court Chamber for 230 thalers for watch-

es made for Rudolf II. In the attached list
he showed that on March 9, 1609 he supplied via a Mr Heyden two eight-chime
watches with topazes set in gold at a cost
of 200 thalers. Michael Schneeberger
made repeated requests for payment of
the money owed to him. After his death in
1616 the requests were continued by his
widow, Judita, who was left with four
young children. On January 1, 1616 Emperor Matthias asked the Court Chamber
to pay Schneeberger's widow 230 thalers
for the watches and other things supplied,
with a receipt from the debt-settling commissioners. The document provides new
information about Schneebergers's life,

such as the date of his death and his family situation. The description from 1619 of
work done for Rudolf II is also valuable.
The watches, signed by M. Schneeberger
and given in the Inventory of 1607-1611,
(no. 2175), are on show in the exhibition.

Inventory of the Court Chamber document collection in the Prague Castle
Archives

V.V.

II.320
Ottavio Miseroni
Ottavio Miseroni's Request for Payment
of Money the Emperor Owes Him
1614
Prague Castle Archives, Court Chamber,
inv. no. 731

In a document dated August 7, 1614 in
Linz, Emperor Matthias ordered the Bohemian Chamber to pay Ottavio Miseroni,
Rudolf II's stone cutter, 2,000 guilders
from the pension which the Chamber had
established. This sum was meant to be
subtracted from his request for 570
guilders and 11 groschen, with the rest to

be paid when the Land parliament next
met. This decision by the Emperor was
preceded by a request from Miseroni and a
memo from the Court Chamber dated July 29, 1614, in which it is said that Miseroni, his wife and eight children were in
great need. Miseroni's request and Emperor Matthias's decision were printed in full
by F. Kreyczi in his Jahrbuch, 1894, no.
11772 and 11773

Jahrbuch der kunsthistorischen Sammlungen des Allerhochstens Kaisserhauses,
vol. 15, 1894, pp. 40-61; Inventory of the
Court Chamber collection in the Prague
Castle Archives, reg. no. 11 772, 11 773.

V.V.

II.321
Ottavio Miseroni
Ottavio Miseroni's Request for Payment
of Money the Emperor Owes Him
Paper (colour photocopy)
31.6 × 38.5 cm and 31.6 × 22.7 cm
Signed in own hand
September 25, 1621
Prague Castle Archives, Court Chamber,
inv. no. 784

Ottavio Miseroni here asked Emperor Ferdinand II to pay him 13, 701 guilders which he was owed for work carried out for Rudolf II. He attached a list of objects (dated September 18, 1621) protected from the rebellious nobles with debts for this work outstanding from his last invoicing of Rudolf II. In a document dated October 5, 1621 the Bohemian vice-governor, Karl of Liechtenstein, advised the Emperor to pay the stone-cutter at least half of what he was owed. The Emperor asked the court accountant to submit a report on what was owed to Miseroni. Printed in full by G. Bodenstein in the Jahrbuch 1913/1914, no. 20 316

Jahrbuch der kunsthistorischen Sammlungen des Allerhochstens Kaiserhauses, vol. 36, 1913/1914, pp. 4–5; Inventory of the Court Chamber collection in the Prague Castle Archives; Bukovinska 1970, pp. 185–198; Distelberger 1979, pp. 109–188

V.V.

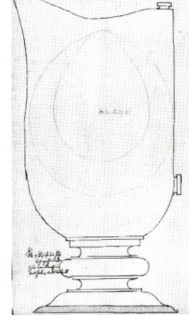

II.322
Eusebio Ferdinand Miseroni
Four Sketches for Crystal Cups
Paper, ink, pencil (photocopy)
1672
Prague
Prague, Státni ústřední archiv v Praze, inv. no. I, 1673, I.–IV. box 621

The sketches are inserted into the records from January 1673 and are part of a letter by Ferdinand Eusebius Miseroni. The letter is undated, but the official letter from the Court Chamber in which it is enclosed bears the date 8 November 1672. The letter informs us that the writer obtained several pieces of crystal from the Emperor, and that part of the application consists of designs for their treatment, which Miseroni submitted to the Emperor for his opinion. The simple drawings delineate the outlines of the four vessels, apparently in their actual size, and with the planned mounts sketched in yellow, most probably to indicate silver gilt. The drawings are interesting because they are the only surviving designs of actual vessels from the Miseroni workshop; this is why they were included in the exhibition in spite of the fact that they do not belong to the time period that it covers.

Urban 1973, ills 1–5; Urban 1976, p. 97 and ill.

B.B.

II.323
Castrucci workshop
Cabinet with *Pietre Dure* Mosaics
Ebony wood, rosewood, oak, pine, ash, *pietra dura*, silver gilt, gilt bronze
109 × 99 × 55 cm
Early seventeenth century
1624 Medici collection
Florence, Museo dell' Opificio delle Pietre Dure, inv. no. 1905, n. 567

The cabinet features rich decoration, which makes use of the magnificence of precious stones in panels of *commessi in pietre dure*, arranged to form landscape motifs; it is a luxury collector's piece and gives us an idea of the appearance of some of the pieces, most often identified as *Schreibtisch*, that furnished Rudolf's *Kunstkammer*. The cabinet can be attributed to the Castrucci workshop on the basis of its *commessi*. The compositional scheme of the landscape and its colour arrangement, which makes abundant use of jasper from Czech quarries, are closely related to works that can be documented and localized in Prague. The horizontal panel to the right of centre on the base of the cabinet contains a composition similar to the landscape cut-out on the panel of the table in the Palazzo Pitti (Florence, Muzeo degli Argenti), placed within an irregular polygon above a central landscape. The cabinet comes from the property of the Medicis and is included in the inventory of the Villa del Poggio Imperiale from 1624. The literature of the time assumes that it was a gift to Emperor Ferdinand I de' Medici.

Florence 1988, p. 240, cat. no. 72 (see older literature there).

Giusti 1992, pp. 144ff., colour ills 84–85; Bohr 1993, cat. no. XI, ill. 107.

B.B.

II.324
Castrucci workshop
Cabinet
Ebony, commessi in pietre dure, agate and jasper
46 × 61 × 38 cm
Early 17th century
Prague
Purchased for the Uměleckoprůmyslove Muzeum in Prague from the collection of Marie Pelcová in 1915
Prague, Uměleckoprůmyslove Muzeum, inv. no. 14018

The cabinet of ebony wood in the form of a miniature piece of architecture is decorated with panels with *commessi in pietre dure*. It was bought for the Uměleckoprůmyslove Muzeum in 1915 and its provenance is unknown. The composition and choice of precious stones are typical of *commessi* from the Prague Castrucci workshops. The uneven quality of the individual panels points to the rather extensive operation of the workshop, which is also evidenced by the frequent repetition of various details and entire compositions. The small panels with stereometric elements are an interesting addition, for this motif is also found on the cabinet in the Österreichisches Museum für Angewandte Kunst, Vienna (no. 3392), or on the table with the coat of arms of Karl of Liechtenstein (Vaduz). The Prague cabinet dates from the period after Rudolf's death, during which the workshops evidently took commissions from a wider circle of buyers.

Florence 1988, p. 238, cat. no. 71.

Bukovinská 1972, pp. 363–70.

B.B.

II.325
Castrucci workshop in Prague
1596–? 1622
Casket with *Pietre Dure* Mosaics
Softwood, ebony, mahogany, elm, gilt-iron fittings, silver, *commessi in pietre dure*, inlays of semi-precious stones
24.6 × 41.3 × 27.3 cm; *commessi* (visible dimensions) 19 × 7.1 cm (lid), 18.6 × 11.3 cm (front), 7 × 11.9 cm (sides)
1610–15
Present from Duke Johann Ernst I the Younger of Sachsen-Weimar (1594–1626, came to power in 1615) to Johann Georg I, elector of Saxony (reg. 1611–56). Then in the *Kunstkammer* in Dresden. From 1832 in the Dresden armoury. Taken as spoils of war to the USSR in 1945, returned in 1959 and made over to the Kunstgewerbemuseum, Dresden.
Dresden, Kunstgewerbemuseum, inv. no. 46 152

This hitherto barely known casket in an architectural design has a *pietra dura* panel on each of three sides and on the lid. Tuscan columns flank the panels at the corners. The lid, which projects over the sides, opens upwards. The back of the casket has no hardstone decoration, indicating that it was intended to be placed against a wall. The four *commessi*, framed by fine mouldings, depict rocky ideal landscapes with water, trees, forts, churches, ruins and other architectural constructions. The choice of motifs, the composition and the colouration are in keeping with the work of the Castrucci workshop in Prague, as can be seen also on the cabinet cupboard and the large, sectioned table-top in the collections of the ruling dukes of Liechtenstein in Vaduz.

Ehrenthal 1899.

G.H.

II.326
Castrucci workshop
Landscape with the Penitent Mary Magdalen
Commesso in pietre dure in agate, jasper,
horn stone, amethyst on slate; Frame:
wood
21.8 × 30.7 cm
Ca. 1615–22
Ambras Collection; Ambras Inventory of
1788, vol. 2, p. 258, no. 10
Vienna, Kunsthistorisches Museum,
Kunstkammer, inv. no. 3006

II.327
Castrucci Workshop
Landscape with Sky on Fire
Commesso in pietre dure in agate, jasper
and horn stone on slate: Frame: wood
21.5 × 30.0 cm
Ca. 1615–22
Ambras Collection; Ambras Inventory of
1788, vol. 2, p. 258, no. 11
Vienna, Kunsthistorisches Museum,
Kunstkammer, inv. no. 3039

These two panels are companion pieces
which demonstrate a third Castrucci
workshop style, in addition to those of
Cosimo and Giovanni. The master who
made this piece has adopted Cosimo's illusion of space. Props to the left and right
in the foreground frame a view with
strong colour contrasts between distance

and proximity. From Giovanni he adopted
the layering of spatial zones. The 'building
block' town in the background is almost
identical on the two panels and is found a
third time to the right in the background
in the centre of the large table top in the
Museo degli Argenti in Florence (Giusti
1992, pp. 166/167, pl. 90). The dramatic sky
is particularly striking and even surpasses
the sky in Giovanni's *Landscape with Seated
Peasants.* (cat. no. II.267). These two
commessi are already in the new landscape
style that had been introduced to Prague
by Paulus van Vianen (resident in Prague
after 1603) and Jan Bruegel the Elder (in
Prague in 1604). This style was quickly
adopted by Pieter Stevens (resident in
Prague after 1594) and Roelandt Savery
(in Prague after 1603). In these landscapes
the viewer is led towards a small section of
Nature. The town in the background is
taken from an ideal landscape by Paul Brill
(1554–1626) (Vincent 1987, p. 171, illus.
23). A print from the series of Roman ruins by Willem van Nieulandt II (ca.1584–
1636) provided the model for the ruin in
the middle ground of the Magdalena panel, consisting of a pillar and two arches,
one above the other (Hollstein XIV, 1956,
pp. 164f., nos. 2, 6 or 8). The same motif is
found to the left of the central axis on a
cabinet in the Museo dell'Opificio delle
Pietre Dure in Florence (Giusti 1992, p.

158, pl. 84). As yet it is not known for certain whether the commessi for this cabinet, which are made in Bohemian hardstone were created in Prague or Florence.
The modern landscape style of these
tableaus and their links with individual
motifs from commessi in Florence dates
them as late products of the Prague workshop. The leading masters at that stage
were Cosimo di Giovanni Castrucci (Giovanni's son) and Giuliano di Piero Pandolfini, Giovanni's son-in-law. It has been
shown that Pandolfini took many of the
Prague motifs with him when he went to
Florence in about 1622.

Essen and Vienna 1988, cat. no. 730 and
731.

Neumann 1957, pp. 188, 200, no. 23 and 26
illus. 209 and 210.

R.D.

II.328
Karel Škréta
Prague ca. 1610-Prague 1674
Portrait of Dionysio Miseroni and Family
Oil on canvas
185 × 251 cm
1653
In 1684 in the estate of Dionysio's son
Ferdinand Eusebius, 1747 in the estate of
Dionysio's grandson Jan Pavel, 1796 lent
to the Picture Gallery of the Association
of Patriotic Friends of Art by Ignác Vesely,
1886 bought by the Picture Gallery collec-
tion.
Prague, Národní galerie v Praze, inv. no. O
560

The work depicts Dionysio Miseroni (ca.
1600–1661), son of the Rudolfine gem-cutter Ottavio Miseroni. In 1623, Dionysio became the head of the Prague engravers'
workshop and the Schatzmeister and administrator of the art collections of the
Prague Castle. The family is gathered
around a table on which rings and gemstones are displayed, and Dionysio himself
holds a large onyx goblet. To the left, his
son and later successor reaches for a large
crystal vessel, the so-called pyramid that
Dionysio carved for Ferdinand III in 1651–
1653. The Miseroni gem-cutting workshop on Prague Castle is depicted in the
background. The emphasis in this work,

which, unusually, shows the artist in his
working environment, is on the relationships between family members and on realistic details.

Prague 1974, no. k. 89.

Národní galerie v Praze 1984, pp. 294–95.

M.Š.

II.329
? Dionysio Miseroni
Prague 1607 (?)-Prague 1661
*Coat-of-arms of the Šotnovský family of
Závořice*
Commesso in pietre dure, artificial marble
9.4 × 7.6 oval
Ca. 1650
Acquired from an unknown source by the
Gallery of the Society for the Patriotic
Friends of Art
Prague, Národní galerie v Praze, inv. no. o
85

Jan Škréta, grandfather of artist Karel
Škréta, acquired the title Šotnovský of Zá-

vořice with the issue of an Imperial Charter by Maxmilián II dated 24.1.1570. His
coat-of-arms was embellished by Rudolf II
on 12 March 1580 with the addition of a
crown. The coat-of-arms has been exhibited on several occasions in connection
with the artist's work, most recently at an
exhibition of his collected works held in
1974, where the coat-of-arms is attributed
to Dionysio Miseroni. While a link with
Miseroni (first indicated by K.Chytil (1933,
78) was based merely on the fact that the
two artist were in close contact, it cannot
be entirely ruled out.

Prague 1974, no. 100a (previous exhibi-

tions summarized here).

Pries 1986, p. 75, ill. VI.

B.B.

II.330
Dionysio Miseroni
Prague 1607 (?)-Prague 1661
Tabernacle
Agate, jasper, araucarit, silex, Czech gar-
net, slate, oak, gilded copper
92 × 65 × 47 cm
1644-50
Property of the chapter since 1680
Prague, Treasury of St Vitus' cathedral,
K574

The earliest mention of the intention to
make the tabernacle, which is the representative work of Dionysio Miseroni,
comes from a letter dated 3 December

1644. Its completion was delayed by the
Swedish invasion, but in 1650 the prestigious tabernacle was ready. Urban believes that it was intended for the new
chapel of St Wenceslas in Prague Castle,
but in the end it was never placed there. In
1680, on the orders of Emperor Leopold I,
Dionysio's son Ferdinand Eusebius offered it as a gift to the Prague chapter. In
1836 the tabernacle stood on the altar of
St Wenceslas in the cathedral of Svatovice.
The tabernacle was originally intended to
be viewed from all sides, but it was seriously damaged in the early twentieth century, and a decision was made during its
restoration to sacrifice the back in order to

replace the missing parts. The crucifix in
the frontal niche may also have been replaced. In 1965 the forgotten
piece was found in very poor condition
and restored. The finely rendered miniature architecture is an eloquent testimony
to the importance of glyptic work at the
Prague court as late as the mid-seventeenth century, as well as to the exceptional standing of its foremost representative
at the time, Dionysio Miseroni.

Podlaha-Šittler 1903, no. 294; Urban 1975,
pp. 526-35.

B.B.

II.331
Dionysio Miseroni
Prague 1607 (?)–Prague 1661
Shell-Shaped Cup
Heliotrope, enamelled gold
12.3 × 7.7 × 21.6 cm
Ca. 1635/45
From the imperial *Schatzkammer*;
Schatzkammer Inventory of 1750, p. 190,
Kasten IV, no. 35
Vienna, Österreichisches Museum für
Angewandte Kunst, inv. no. LKH 553

The decorative style of this bowl is similar
to works that Ottavio Miseroni left behind
unfinished and which Dionysio then com-

pleted in the mid 1630s. Thus this vessel
could have been made by Ottavio Miseroni during his early period, when he also
held the position of treasurer in Prague.
The low reliefs on both of the longer sides
each form abstract mascarons towards the
centre. This long, rather than round, vessel is structured along the same lines as
Ottavio's oval coloured jasper bowl (inv.
no. 6866), yet all the shapes are harder and
less refined. The foot in the shape of a dolphin is made from green jasper and not
out of heliotrope like the bowl itself. The
mount has to accommodate the difference
between the cross-section of the bowl and
the pedestal which reinforces the notion

that this too might be a bowl started by
Ottavio, with Dionysio then finishing it
and adding the foot.

Distelberger 1979, p. 118.

R.D.

II.332
Dionysio Miseroni (attributed)
Prague 1607 (?)–Prague 1661
Tulip-shaped Vase with Cover
Jasper, enamelled gold
Height: 19.2 cm
Ca. 1647
From the imperial *Schatzkammer*; Invento-
ry of 1750, p. 190, Kasten IV, no. 36
Vienna, Kunsthistorisches Museum,
Kunstkammer, inv. no. 1661

In 1647 Dionysio finished his largest citrine flower vase and in 1648 he saved it
from the plundering Swedish troops. (Distelberger 1979, pp. 132-133, illus. 104). It

seems that, presumably according to the
master's instructions, a certain Paul Pertz
carved the agate, jasper, chalcedony and
rock crystal flowers. The flower motif may
have been the inspiration for Miseroni to
create this very 'modern' vessel in the
shape of an opening tulip. The delicate
lines of the cup are echoed in various flowers in the citrine vase. Even the lid, the
knob and the foot are in the form of flowers or blossoms. The diagonally hatched
black enamel of the mount is seen again
on the foot-ring of the citrine vase and
shows clearly that the two pieces are from
the same period.

Distelberger 1979, p. 133.

R.D.

II.333
Dionysio Miseroni
Prague 1607 (?)–Prague 1661
Covered Vessel
Smoky quarz, silver gilt, partially enam-
elled
16.6 × 9.9 × 16.3 cm
1648/49
Prague
Schatzkammer
Vienna, Kunsthistorisches Museum,
Kunstkammer, inv. no. 1344

This bowl, with its irregular shape, is decorated with a relief consisting entirely of
vine leaves and grapes. The leaves running

round either side of the bowl to the point
where it dips inwards again grow out of a
handle at the back carved from the same
piece. The narrow front section is occupied by one large grape. The lid is also decorated with a grape and a leaf. Dionysio
Miseroni charged 200 thalers for the vessel. The goldsmith who made the silver
mount which is also decorated on the underside of the cover with flowers and birds
in translucent enamel only received 16
thalers for his work and had to cover the
cost of the silver himself. This bowl is included in a list compiled on 2 February
1650 of Dionysio's works during the previous years: 'Ein ander geschier von Topäss,

wie eine Wein Traub geschniten, samt dem
Teckhel und fuess' (Klapsia 1944, pp. 349-
50, Regest 128; not identifed there). By this
time Miseroni was already active as an en-
trepreneur in his own right, paying his
own assistants and goldsmiths.

Distelberger 1979, p. 134.

R.D.

II.334
Dionysio Miseroni
Prague 1607 (?)–Prague 1661
Vessel in the Shape of a Shell
Citrine, silver gilt, partially enamelled
14.4 × 12.9 × 17.2 cm
1650
From the imperial *Schatzkammer*
Vienna, Kunsthistorisches Museum,
Kunstkammer, inv. no. 1366

This bowl comes second on a list compiled
on 27 February 1651 of all the vessels
Dionysio made in 1659 (see cat. no. II.336).
The price for this piece was 300 thalers,
which included the cost of the stone itself.

Prominent mouldings curl round the
hinge and up and over the edge. The base
and the walls are decorated with leaves
and fruit. This kind of low relief, also seen
on the covered bowl with grapes (cat. no.
II.333), is typical of Miseroni's work
around 1650. It allows the citrine and the
smoky quartz, much used at this period, to
come fully into their own. In the list of
works the bowl is described as 'ein ander
Geschier von dergleichen Topassi in form
einer muschel mit erhobener arbeitt
geschnietten, darbey ein fuess' (Klapsia
1944, p. 350, Regest 146, not identified
there).

Darmstadt 1992/93, cat. no. 69.

Distelberger 1979, p. 136.

R.D.

II.335
Dionysio Miseroni
Prague 1607 (?)–Prague 1661
'Groppo'
Citrine (fired smoky quartz)
5.4 × 9.4 × 11.4 cm
1650
From the imperial *Schatzkammer*
Vienna, Kunsthistorisches Museum,
Kunstkammer, inv. no. 1447

The greatest variety of vessels from Dionysio Miseroni's workshop come from the
time around 1650. Although at the time
the business and its output was continually increasing Miseroni still seems to have

had a hand in each individual piece. This
unusually distinctive item comes fourth
on the list of 27 February 1651, and is described as a 'Geschirl von schön weissen
gebrenten Topassi oder bömischen diamant wie ein groppo geschnietten'. A
'groppo' is something entwined in itself, a
knot – and that is what this irregular, basically triangular bowl most resembles.
There seem to be no rigid surfaces and it is
as though the whole form is caught up in
some whirling movement. This relatively
small bowl cost 110 thalers because of its
complex form. The entry for this bowl in
the 1651 list also makes it clear that 'Bohemian diamond,' which is often men-

tioned elsewhere, is in fact fired smoky
quartz. Many beautiful citrine vessels were
made by firing smoky quartz.

Distelberger 1979, p. 137.

R.D.

II.336
Dionysio Miseroni
Prague 1607 (?)–Prague 1661
Oval Cistrine Bowl
Citrine
8 × 10.9 × 18.5 cm
1650
From the imperial *Schatzkammer*
Vienna, Kunsthistorisches Museum,
Kunstkammer, inv. no. 1367

This bowl comes at the top of a delivery list dated 27 February 1651 made out by Dionysio Miseroni recording pieces he made in 1650: 'Ein geschier von schön gelben böhmischen Topassi, wie ein schieffel

mit dem fuess undt handthaben, von einem stuck, mit erhobener arbeitt geschnietten' (Klapsia 1944, p. 350, Regest 146, not identified). The price, including the cost of the hardstone, was 400 thalers. The shape with the mask in the centre is, like the heliotrope bowl (cat. no. II.331), another variation on Ottavio Miseroni's coloured jasper oval bowl. Soft scrolls form the eyes of the mask while the nose is a simple quatrefoil. Below the heart-shaped mouth there are handles in the form of deep-cut shells. The edge of the bowl curves in again towards the centre. The parallel decorative grooves go back to Ottavio in his late period and his late

shell-shaped smoky quartz bowl also has the spiral design. Thus motifs were passed down over a long period in the Miseroni workshop, the coarser, heavier overall form showing just how long it had in fact been since his father's day.

Distelberger 1979, p. 121.

R.D.

II.337
Dionysio Miseroni
Prague 1607 (?)–1661 Prague
Ewer
Jasper
H: 24.3 cm
1652
From the imperial *Schatzkammer*, Inventory of 1750, p. 190, Kasten IV, no. 36
Vienna, Kunsthistorisches Museum, Kunstkammer, inv. no. 2064

The beauty and quality of this reddish stone seems to have inspired Dionysio create an extremely demanding piece. Rich decorations, with soft lines and shapes,

contrast with the rigour of the overall form. Slightly conical in form, the vessel is fixed without a mount on the foot. On the back there is a square knob for a handle which was never made. The rim is virtuosic in its technique, reaching out inwards over the opening and sinking down in the middle before swinging lightly outwards toward the lip which has a flat mask below it. Individual motifs used to decorate the jug have a long history in the Miseroni workshop and the soft leaves on the lower half of the wall are already familiar from Ottavio's day, as are the parallel flutings – although never together as here. In 1653 Dionysio made a variation of the scrolls on

either side of the acanthus leaves on the reverse of the jug for his famous pyramid. On 7 September 1652 Miseroni received 450 guilders for his work: 'wegen verfertigung aines geschirs von diaspis'. Since no other vessels in this material are listed in the accounts, the payment must have been for this piece.

Klapsia 1944, p. 319; Distelberger 1979, pp. 145–46.

R.D.

II.338
Dionysio Miseroni
Prague 1607 (?)–1661 Prague
Covered Goblet
Rock crystal, gold, enamelled
H: 44.9 cm; Diam: 13.7 cm
Ca. 1653–56
From the imperial *Schatzkammer*; Inventory of 1750, p. 221, Kasten IV, no. 9
Vienna, Kunsthistorisches Museum, Kunstkammer, inv. no. 2256

This large vase is one of the six that were carved from the Swiss rock crystal that was delivered to the court in Vienna in 1651. It is based on a quatrefoil. The lid and the

base are carved as abstract flowers. The knob on the lid is a flower bud. Rich foliage intaglios grow out symmetrically from the two main axes of the piece. On the one side there is the imperial eagle with the Habsburg coat of arms in a heart-shaped shield (the only polished intaglio). On the other side is the Bohemian coat of arms. In this piece Dionysio, or his specialist in the workshop, has drawn on a style of decoration from sixteenth-century Italy. He clearly had understood that unpolished intaglio is all the decoration rock crystal needs and did not use any of the relief decorations on the curved walls of the vase. In comparison to the jug (cat. no.

II.339) these intaglios are freer and more elastic. From piece to piece the intaglio work becomes increasingly free and yet this somewhat backward-looking form of decoration is no more than an episode in Miseroni's work, for more modern intaglios were by now already being used for glass.

Kris 1929, p. 191, no. 637; Klapsia 1944, pp. 332–333; Strohmer 1947, p. 32, no. 37; Distelberger 1979, p. 160.

R.D.

II.339
Dionysio Miseroni
Prague 1607 (?)–Prague 1661
Ewer
Rock crystal
26.5 × 17.9 × 18 cm
1653–56
From the imperial *Schatzkammer*
Vienna, Kunsthistorisches Museum, Kunstkammer, inv. no. 1412

Dionysio used rock crystal more than any other stone in his late period. In 1651 the Emperor Ferdinand III gave him six large rock crystals from Switzerland weighing 300 Viennese pounds. All six vessels which

were made from these between 1651 and 1656 have survived to this day. This jug, which was never mounted, is one of the six. Its irregular angular form still reflects the shape of the original stone. As on the jasper jug (cat. no. II.337) the foot is jointed and glued and, again, like the jasper jug, below the spout, there is a flat mask. The shoulder and the area around the spout are decorated with a relief, while the surfaces and edges of the body are covered with simple intaglios. The decorations are diverse and mix tendrils in an old Italian style with polished bands of leaves, cornucopia and vine branches. It is possible that Dionysio had a craftsman specialising in

these in his workshop, which had 14 workers at the time. The individual pieces from this period are the more remarkable for their size than for their forms or complexity of design. In form and design Dionysio's skills are seen at their best in his smaller citrine and smoky quartz vessels from around 1650.

Klapsia 1944, pp. 329–330; Strohmer 1947, p. 32, no. 36; Distelberger 1979, p. 157.

R.D.

II.340
Georg Schwanhardt; mount: Esaias Linden
Nürnberg 1601– Nürnberg 1667
Covered Goblet with a *Portrait of Emperor Ferdinand III as King of Bohemia and Hungary*
Polished and engraved crystal, mounted in gilded silver
17.6 × 7.1 × 5.9 cm
FERDINAND II.D.G.R.H.B.REX./ UT VIVAT; mounting marked with the goldsmith's mark of *Jesiais zur Linden of Nuremberg*
Between 1637 and 1641
Vienna, Kunsthistorisches Museum, inv.

no. 2378
Installation, Germanisches Nationalmuseum, Nürnberg

The goblet has an oval bowl that widens slightly, a flat lid, flat foot and a low stem. On the front is a medallion with a bust of Ferdinand III and his titles in an inscription, wreathed by linear foliage. On the sides are candelabra with fruit and on the back is a sunflower and a phoenix rising from the flames. The goblet was created some time between the coronation of Ferdinand as the Czech and Hungarian king and his elevation to the rank of Emperor. The C-shaped leaves are typical of the ear-

ly work of Lehmann's student Georg Schwanhardt the Elder, active in Nürnberg. The portrait is comparable with other portraits engraved by Schwanhardt during this period, such as the portrait of *Gustavus Adolphus* (Nürnberg, Germanisches Nationalmuseum) and the portrait of *Emperor Ferdinand II* from Trachtenberg Castle in Silesia (New York, Metropolitan Museum of Art).

Meyer-Heisig 1963, 28, 35, 78.

O.D.

II.341
Georg Schwanhardt
Nürnberg 1600–Nürnberg 1661
Panel with *Three Lions under the Elector's Hat*
Clear engraved glass
23.2 × 18.7 cm
Ca. 1632
From a private collection in England, sold at auction at Christie's, London, 3 June 1986
Corning, The Corning Museum of Glass, inv. no. 86.3.28

The panel depicts three crowned lions under a figure '8' woven from laurel leaves and an elector's hat. The meaning of these contemporary allegories can be interpreted more precisely only in the context of the specific political situation. It most probably symbolizes the short-term ambition of the Saxon elector Johann Georg I to become the leader of the Protestant camp during the Thirty Years' War. In 1631 he became the head of Convent of Protestant princes, which took place in Leipzig and formulated the Protestant demands in a letter to the Emperor. The plausibility of dating the panel to the 1630s is supported by the marked similarity between several engraved details and the beaker with the *Judgment of Paris* in the collection of R. von Strasser in Vienna, which can also most probably be attributed to Georg Schwanhardt the Elder. The beaker, too, relates to Johann Georg I and commemorates the celebration of his silver wedding to Magdalena Sibylla in 1632.

Drahotová 1988, pp. 410 ff.

O.D.

II.342
Johann Michael
Fl. early seventeenth century in Prague
Saddle, Shabrack, Headband, Halter and Bit, Tassel for the Neck, Stirrup Strap, Stirrup, Spurs, Sword, Sabre, Scabbard, Mace
Saddle, shabrack and riding tackle: leather and velvet; decorations in gold and silver plate, enamelled and set with topaz, garnets and other stones, silver relief embroidery underlaid with parchment; sword and sabre; blades: blued, damascened with gold and silver; hilts: silver gilt, enamelled and set with stones; wooden scabbards, covered with silver plate, gilded and decorated to match the hilt; mace: brass shaft, gilded, partially enamelled, set with precious stones; head made from faceted rock crystal
Shabrack: 70 × 135 cm; sword: total L: 103 cm; blade: 86 cm; weight 2000 gm; sabre: total L: 98 cm; blade; 85 cm; weight 1600 gm; mace: total L: 61.5 cm; weight 1800 gm
On the shabrack: *CHRISTIAN DER AN-DER HERTZOG ZV SACHSEN GVLCH KLEVF VNND BERG DES HEILIGEN ROMISCHEN RIECHS ERTZ-MARSCHALCK VNND CHVRFVRST*
Before 1614
Inventory of the Armoury, 1606, S. 1599, and Inventory of the Elector's Stables, 1627, Bl. 2, no. 1
Dresden, Rüstkammer, inv. nos L 1 (riding tackle) and Y 353a–c (weapons)

Parade weapons *à la turca* for court occasions and an 'oriental' garniture, probably ordered by Elector Christian II of Saxony.

Dresden 1991, p. 28, no. 42; Dresden 1995, p. 145, cat. no. 143.

Ehrenthal 1899, pp. 111, E 731; 193, K 4; Haenel 1923, p. 122, pl. 61; Thomas-Gamber-Schedelmann 1963, pl. 67.

H.Sch.

Section III: History, Architecture and Funeralia

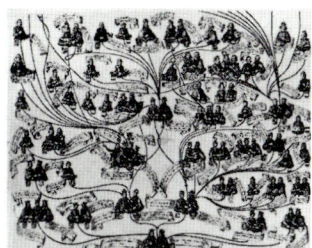

III.1
Aegidius Sadeler
Antwerp ca. 1568–Prague 1628
Family Tree of the Austrian Royal Family
Copper engraving
40.7 × 57.7 cm
First page, bottom: *Sac. Caes. Eiusdem Mai: Sculptor Egidius Sadeler fecit ... Pragae, Anno MDCXXIX*; right: *Marco Sadeler excudit*
1629 (posthumous)
Prague, Národní galerie, Grafická sbírka, inv. no. R 170 253, R 170 254, R 170 255

Sadeler's letter of December 1622 to Karl von Liechtenstein indicates that this large,

three-plate genealogical table was under way by that time, but it was printed posthumously, if not finished by assistants. Some impressions include a fourth sheet with further generations of the Habsburg dynasty. The third sheet of the *Family Tree* may have been conceived during the reign of Emperor Matthias (d. 1618), as he and Empress Anna appears at the top, whereas a portrait of his successor and cousin, Ferdinand II, is not included. Nonetheless, the sheet is designed to place greatest emphasis on Rudolf II. Rudolf appears as a larger figure than his siblings, at the top centre and at the uppermost point of a vertical axis which con-

nects him to his namesake, Rudolf I, at the bottom of the first page. The format and decorative motifs of this geneaology come from the earlier history of printing.

Doering 1910; Limouze 1990.

D.L.

III.2
? Martino Rota
Sebenico ca. 1520–Vienna 1583
Ferdinand I, Holy Roman Emperor with the Order of the Golden Fleece
Copper engraving
19.4 × 13.9 cm
Title: *FERDINAND D. G. ROMAN IMPER. AUG.*; in the lower part of the illustration: *CHRISTO, DUCE.*; under the illustration: *Par animo, morum par integritate fuisti Materno, par ut nomine, prorsus auo.*
? After 1556
Prague, Národní galerie v Praze, inv. no. Clementinum – 5920

Ferdinand I (1503–64), grandson of Emperor Maximilian I, was educated in Spain and the Netherlands. He became the founder of the Austrian branch of the Habsburgs and in 1526, after an agreement with the noble estates in Bohemia he was proclaimed Czech King. His opponent in Hungary in the election of 1526 was Jan Zapolský. The consequent division of Hungary between the two opponents was the reason for the military conflicts which the Turkish Sultan used to increase his influence in the eastern part of Hungary. In 1526 Ferdinand made peace with the Turks. The long drawn-out

arguments with his brother Karl V over succession in the Empire finally ended in 1556 with Karl's abdication and the proclamation of Ferdinand as Holy Roman Emperor. The Augsburg peace of 1555, achieved by Ferdinand and Karl, guaranteed the free profession of several different non-Catholic faiths in the Empire. Ferdinand himself, however, was awarded the Order of the Golden Fleece for his services to the Catholic church.

J.Ha.

III.3
Dominicus Custos (?)
Antwerp 1550/60–Augsburg 1612
Emperor Maximilian II with the Order of the Golden Fleece
Engraving
22 × 12 cm
MAXIMILIANVS II. D[EI] G[RATIA] ROMAN[ORUM] IMPERATOR SEMP[ER] AVG[USTUS] PATER PATRIAE; the Emperor's motto at the foot of the medallion: *Deus Providebit*; the legend *Nomen idem ... ipse tuis* takes up the Emperor's motto, praising the ruler's concern for peace in the empire
Prague, Narodni galerie v Praze, Grafická

sbírka, inv. no. DR 1 655

Maximilian II (1527–76) was the the first son of Ferdinand I and Anna of Hungary. In 1548, he married his cousin Maria, the daughter of Emperor Karl V, and stood in for his father-in-law while the latter was in Spain. Karl V's intention was that Maximilian should inherit the throne in Spain, while his own son Philipp was to become Emperor. However, this was not to be, since Ferdinand I had disposal of the inheritance. Thus Maximilian received Bohemia and Hungary as well as the lands along the Danube. Maximilian, whose son Rudolf (b. 1552) was later to become Em-

peror Rudolf II, was crowned king of the Romans in 1562 and, after his father's death, elected emperor in 1564. During the religious wars, Maximilian II attempted to reconcile Lutherans and Catholics. His restrained and tolerant attitude to the Protestants led in 1571 to the so-called 'assecuration' which granted freedom of religious observance *de facto* to the Lutherans.

Essen 1988, cat. no. 21, p. 106.

Bibl 1929.

H.H.

III.4
Martino Rota
Sebenico ca. 1520–Vienna 1583
Archduke Ferdinand of Tyrol as Hercules
Engraving
21.6 × 13.6 cm
On the plinth: *FERDINANDVS II. Archidux Austriae*
Prague, Národní galerie v Praze, Grafická sbírka, inv. no. 72 161

This full-length portrait shows the Archduke in a niche, half in armour, half as Hercules with his club and lion-head helmet at his feet. On his breast, he wears the insignia of the Order of the Golden Fleece.

Born in 1529 as the second son of Ferdinand I and Anna of Hungary, Archduke Ferdinand was an imperial governor in Bohemia from 1547 to 1563 and then regent in the Tyrol for 30 years (1565–95). Ferdinand acquired Schloß Ambras near Innsbruck for his wife Philippine Welser and, after her death in 1580, installed there the contents of the *Kunstkammer* collection which he had started in Bohemia.

Essen and Vienna 1988, cat. no. 35, p. 112.

Bruck 1953, ill. 228; Hirn 1981.

H.H.

III.5
Aegidius Sadeler
Antwerp 1570–Prague 1629
Portrait of Emperor Rudolf II in Armour
Engraving
30.5 × 22.1 cm
Inscribed and dated: *AVGVSTISSIMO ET GLORIOSISSIMO ROM[ANORUM] IMPERATORI RVDOLPHO II., GERMANIAE, HUNGARIAE, BOHEMIAE ETC. REGI, D[OMI]NO SVO CLEMENTISSIMO, SVBIECTISSIMVS CLIENS AEGIDIVS SADELER IN DEMISSAE ET DEBITAE OBSERVANTIAE SIGNVM DECICABAT ANNO M. DCVIIII PRAGAE*; publisher named lower right: *Dankkert Danckerts*

exc[ulpsit]; confirmation of imperial approval at left edge: *CVM PRIVIL[EGIO] S[UAE] C[AESAREAE] M[AIESTATIS]*
1609
Prague, Národní galerie v Praze, Grafická sbírka, inv. no. R 16 968

Essen and Vienna cat. no. 22, p. 106.

Vocelka 1985, 41; Trunz 1986, ill. 1.

H.H.

III.6
Anonymous
Matthias as King of Hungary
Copper engraving
188 × 145 cm
SERENISS[i]mus POTENTISS[i]musque
PRINCE. AC DOM. D. MATHIAS CORO-
NATUS REX HUNGARIAE DESIGNA-
TUS BOHEMIAE ARCHIDUX AUSTRI-
AE, DUX BURGUNDIAE, STYRIAE,
CARINTHIAE, CARNIOLAE, ET
WIRTEMB. MARCHIO MORAVIAE,
COMES HABSPURG. ET TYROLIS
1608–12
Prague, Národní galerie v Praze, Grafická
sbírka, inv. no. Clementinum – 8945

Matthias (1557–1619), third son of Maximilian II and Maria of Spain, was from
1593 the Protector of Upper and Lower
Austria. After the death of his brother
Arnošt in 1595 he became first in the line
of possible successors to the imperial
throne and heirs to regal titles after his
oldest brother Rudolf. After peace was
made with the Hungarian rebels and after
the peace agreement with Turkey (1606),
which he signed as representative of the
Emperor, Matthias joined with the Protestant nobilities of Upper and Lower Austria, Hungary and Moravia, promising
them aristocratic and religious freedoms.
They tried unsuccessfully to gain the sup-

port of the Czech nobility. In a treaty concluded between Rudolf and Matthias on
24 June 1608, Rudolf relinquished the
throne of Hungary and the title of Margrave of Moravia, giving up the lands of
Austria to his brother at the same time;
Matthias was also given the Hungarian
crown jewels. The illustration is evidently
related to Matthias's election as King of
Hungary on 1608.

J.Ha.

III.7
Aegidius Sadeler
Antwerp 1570–Prague 1629
Empress Anna of Austria, Wife of the Emper-
or Matthias
Copper engraving
302 × 210 cm
Under the illustration: *SERENISSIMA*
AVGVSTISSIMA OPTIMA PRINCEPS
DOMINA DOMINA ANNA RO-
MANORVM IMPERATRIX GERMANIAE
HVNGARIAE BOHEMIAE DALMATIAE
CROATIAE SCLAVONIAE ETC: REGINA
ARCHIDVC: AVSTRIAE DVC: BVRGVN-
DIAE ETC: COM: TYROLIS ETC:; also:
Sacrae Caesareae Majestatis Sculptor Egidius

Sadeler de facie expressit et in deuoti animi
signum humilis obtulit Pragae Anno Chris-
tiano MDCXVI. Cum privil. S. C. Mtis.
1616
Prague, Národní galerie v Praze, Grafická
sbírka, inv. no. R-105.061

This is a portrait of Anna of Austria (of Tyrol, 1585–1618), daughter of Ferdinand of
Tyrol and Anna Katharina of Gonzago,
and from 1611 wife of the King of Hungary and later Czech and Roman King
Matthias. The image shows Anna with the
attributes of the Holy Roman (German)
Empress, which she became in 1612.

Hollstein 21, no. 273.

J.Ha.

III.8
Anonymous
Ferdinand II with the Order of the Golden
Fleece
After 1619
Copper engraving
31 × 20 cm
Under the illustration: *FERDINANDVS*
II, D. G. IMPERATOR ROMANORVM,
SEMPER AVGVSTVS, GERMANIAE
HVNGARIAE, BOHEMIAE, DALMATIAE,
CROATIAE, SCLAVONIAE, ETC. REX,
ARCHIDVX AVSTRIAE, DVX BVRGVNDI-
AE, STIRIAE, CARINTHIAE, CARNIOLAE
ET WIRTEMPERGAE ETC. COMES
TIROLIS ETC.; on the border: *LEGITIME*

CERTANTIBVS
After 1619
Prague, Národní galerie v Praze, Grafická
sbírka, inv. no. Clementinum – 5917

Ferdinand II (1578–1637), son of Archduke Karl of Styria and Maria of
Bavaria, assumed power in Styria, Carniola
and Carinthia, where he continued his father's anti-reform politics. As neither Emperor Rudolf II nor his successor Matthias
had a direct descendant, Archduke Ferdinand of Styria became the heir of the Habsburg line on the Czech (1619), Hungarian (1618) and German (1619) imperial
thrones. In 1619 Ferdinand was unseated

from the Czech throne and Frederick V,
the Palatine Elector, was appointed in his
place. In Hungary Gabor Bethlen was appointed in Ferdinand's place. With the renewal of the Land Order in Bohemia in
1627 (and in Moravia in 1628) Ferdinand II
proclaimed Catholicism as the only permitted religion and at the same time restricted the rights of the parliament and
the aristocracy. In 1628 he passed a resolu-
tion making Catholicism the only permitted religion in lower Austria.

J.Ha.

FERDINANDVS II.D.G. IMPERATOR
ROMANORVM, SEMPER AVGVSTVS, GERMANIAE HVN-
GARLÆ BOHEMIÆ, DALMATIÆ, CROATIÆ, SCLAVONIÆ, ETC. REX,
ARCHIDVX AVSTRIÆ, DVX BVRGVNDI, STIRIÆ, CARINTHIÆ,
CARNIOLÆ ET WIRTEMPERGÆ ETC. COMES TIROLIS ETC.

III.9
Crispyn Passe the Younger
Cologne 1597/1598–Amsterdam 1670
Frederick of the Palatinate as King of Bo-
hemia
Copper engraving
277 × 196 cm
Title: *FREDERICUS D. G. REX BO-*
HEMIAE MORAVIAE ET SCHLES.
COMES PALA.; Vtriusq[uae] Baua. Dux.; in-
scription: *Crisp. Passae junior figu: et sculp.*
? 1619
Prague, Muzeum Hlavního Města Prahy,
inv. no. 485/c

Frederick V, King of Bohemia (1596–

1632), son of Frederick IV, the Palatine
Elector, and Luisa Juliana of Nassau-Or-
ange, became Palatine Elector in 1614. In
1613 he married Elizabeth, daughter of
the English King James I. The culture of
the court and the architectural design of
his newly built seat in Heidelberg were influenced by French style. In 1619 he was
appointed King of Bohemia by the rebellious Czech nobility in place of the de-
throned Ferdinand II. The same year he
moved his seat to Prague. His name is
linked with the completion of the Catholic
cathedral of St Vitus in Prague castle, for
which he gave his agreement as a Calvinist. He fled from Prague after the Battle of

the White Mountain (8 November 1620),
in which the noble factions were heavily
defeated by the combined imperial and
Bavarian armies. The image of the ruler
with the Czech crown jewels is probably
related to the Czech coronation of Frederick the Palatine in 1619. The military trophies and the lions, symbols both of
Czech bravery and of the Palatine Elector,
celebrate the initial military successes of
the armies of the nobility.

J.Ha.

III.10
Anonymous
Emperor Ferdinand III
Copper engraving
145 × 117 cm
Title: *FERDINANDus III. D. G. ROMAN.*
IMPER. SEMPER AVGVS.; motto below
the illustration: *PIETATE ET IVSTITIA*
After 1634
Prague, Národní galerie v Praze, Grafická
sbírka, inv. no. Clementinum – 5.908

Ferdinand III (1608–1657), son of Emperor
Ferdinand II and Marie Anna of Bavaria,
was appointed and crowned King of Hungary in 1625, and King of Bohemia in 1627.

His love of military matters took him to
the command of the united armies of the
Emperor and the Catholic League in the
victorious battle against the Swedish at
Nördlingen. Having assumed power on
the death of his father in 1637, he dedicated himself exclusively to state duties. He
tried to achieve peace in the long-lasting
European military conflict, finally managing to do so in 1648 with the Peace of
Westphalia. After 1648 he rewarded the
citizens of Prague for their successful defence of the city against the Swedish
armies and gained recognition for his renewal of Prague Castle, destroyed in the
Swedish attack. He continued his father's

recatholicising politics but in a more moderate form. He is known to have been a
lover of music, even composing some
himself. His successor was his son
Leopold by his first wife, Maria Anna,
daughter of Philip III of Spain.

J.Ha.

III.11
Jáchymov Mint
Beginning of sixteenth century–after 1550
Ferdinand I and his Son Maximilian
Struck in silver
4.3 cm
Obverse: *FERDINAND9.
D.G.RO.HVNG.BO.REX.ARCHIDVX.AVS.
1549.*; bust of the Emperor with the Order
of the Golden Fleece, inscribed with the
year *15–49* on either side; reverse: *MAXI-
MI.D.G.REX.BOHE. ET. ARCHIDVX.AVS-
TRIA.ETA.SV.*; bust of the Grand Duke
with the Order of the Golden Fleece, *15–
49* in the field; Maximilian's age on the
bottom edge of the medal: *21*

1549
Prague, Národní muzeum, Numismatic
Department, inv. no. H5-57 694

This medal was struck in the Jáchymov
mint, which was founded in 1519 in
Krušné Hory. The dies for it were engraved by the Kraslice goldsmith and engraver Hieronymus Dietrich who designed a number of portraits, as well as a
collection of distinctive medals with biblical themes, which originated in the mint.
The face of the medal shows a portrait of
the Czech and Hungarian King Ferdinand
I, before he was elected Holy Roman Emperor. On the reverse side is a rather bland

portrait of the then 21-year-old Grand
Duke Maximilian who was elected Czech
King in 1549 but was not crowned until
1562. The medal is dated 1549 and was
probably struck as a tribute to the future
Czech King.

Katz, no. 536; Nohejlová 1962, p. 50, no. 47.

Z.M.

III.12
Leone Leoni
Arezzo 1509–Milan 1590
Ferdinand I and his Son Maximilian
Cast in bronze
3.9 cm
Obverse: *FERDINAND./ROM.IMP.
ELECTVS.*; portrait; reverse: *MAXIMIL-
IANVS.D.G.BOHE.REX.*; portrait
After 1556
Prague, Národní muzeum, Numismatic
Department, inv. no. 150 918

Ferdinand I became King of Bohemia and
Hungary in 1526 and Roman King in 1530
and was elected Holy Roman Emperor in

1556, but he was not able to assume power
until 1558, after the death of his brother,
Karl V. The atypical portrait of Ferdinand I
complements a portrait of Maximilian on
the reverse side, which is entirely identifiable with the type of portrait featured on
other medals by Leoni (compare *Kunstkammer* exhibition). The medal was
probably struck to commemorate the election of Ferdinand I as Emperor.

Don. 1023, var.; Fiala, p. 25.

Z.M.

III.13
Joachim Deschler
First half of the sixteenth century–Vienna
1571
*Commemorative Coin of Maximilian II Is-
sued on His Wedding to Maria of Spain and
Election as King of Bohemia*
Struck in silver
3.1 cm
Obverse: *DIVA.MARIA.DIWS.MAXIMIL.
REG.BOHE.CONIVG.*; busts of the King
and his wife; reverse: *A.CONCORDIB-
VS.MAIORA.*; putti holding a shield be-
neath a crown which bears the Czech coat
of arms, monogram *MM*
After 1548

Prague, Národní muzeum, Numismatic
Department, inv. no. H5-50 130

Joachim Deschler worked for Maximilian
II at the Viennese court and in Nürnberg.
He was also an imperial sculptor and engraver of a number of superbly executed
portrait medals. Maximilian was in Spain
with his family when he was elected Czech
king. He returned alone to Vienna in 1550
and, a year later, travelled via Genoa to
Spain with a retinue of Czech noblemen
to bring back his family. The journey
home was postponed until 1552 and they
reached Vienna in May of that year. Deschler's medal of Maximilian and his wife

was probably not made until this time; it
represents part of a unique collection of
medals celebrating Maximilian's ascent to
the Czech throne.

Domanig, no. 101; Lanna 1911, no. 727;
Janáček, pp. 20–25.

Z.M.

III.14
Jacopo da Trezzo
Madrid 1515–Madrid 1589
Maria of Spain and Maximilian II
Cast in silver
3.6 cm
Obverse: *MACIMILIANVS.D.G.BOHE.
REX.*; bust with the Golden Fleece; re-
verse: *MARIA.AVSTR.REG.BOEM.*; bust
with veiled hair
Ca. 1548
Prague, Národní muzeum, Numismatic
Department, inv. no. H5-57 552

The dynastic policy of the Habsburgs,
which was oriented towards attaining the

greatest possible expansion of their power
in Europe, gained fresh momentum during the mid-sixteenth century with the
marriage of the Spanish Infanta, Maria, to
Grand Duke Maximilian. The two brothers
Karl V, Emperor and Spanish king, and
Ferdinand I, at that time Czech and Hungarian King, were instrumental in bringing about the union. The marriage was
publicly announced on 24 April 1548 at
the Augsburg Diet, and the ceremony took
place on 13 September 1548 in Valladolid
in Spain. Shortly after the marriage, Maximilian and Maria were apppointed vice-re-
gents of Spain; Maximilian remained
there until 1550 when he was summoned

by his father to the diet in Augsburg. He
had intended to return to Vienna since he
had been elected Czech king by the Czech
Estates in 1549. With its characteristic portraits of Maximilian and Maria, Trezzo's
medal is an example of the outstanding relief work characteristic of medal engraving at that time. It was probably struck
shortly after Maximilian was elected
Czech King.

Katz 1929, pp. 125–26; Nohejlová, p. 60,
no. 27; Janáček, pp. 20–25.

Z.M.

III.15, III.16
? Valentin Maler
Jihlava ca.1540–Nürnberg 1603
Peacock Thaler of Maximilian II
Struck in silver, 5.5 cm; struck in bronze,
5.4 cm, variant
Obverse: *IVSTICIAN VINDICA - DA
PACEM PATRIAE / VNO ANNO REGEM
BOHEMIA / MAXMILIANVM / VECTVE
ROMANVM VIDIT ET VNGARICUM /
M.D.LXIII.*; Maximilian II sitting on the
throne, holding a sceptre and imperial
orb; personifications of justice and peace
crown him on either side; reverse: pea-
cock in the medal's field with the Austrian
coat of arms on its breast; the 22 coats of

arms of the imperial lands and inherited
Austrian lands are displayed on the peacock's fanned tail
1563
Prague, Národní muzeum, Numismatic
Department, inv. nos H5-150 965, H5-114
794

The authorship of this medal is uncertain,
since Valentin Maler signed the majority
of his works. Habich places it among the
medals produced in the Valentin Maler
workshop. The image of the seated Maximilian being crowned by Justice and
Peace, with its minute, precise detail, suggests that this is the work of a highly expe-

rienced engraver. The medal was made to
celebrate Maximilian's ascent to the
throne: he was crowned Czech King on 20
September 1562, Roman King on 24
November 1562, Hungarian King on 8
September 1563 and Holy Roman Emper-
or on 25 July 1564, when he assumed power after the death of his father, Ferdinand
I. The medal was struck and cast in several
variations.

Don. 1223; Domanig D.M. no. 455; Habich,
vol. 2/1, no. 2629a.

Z.M.

III.16

See cat. no. III.15

III.17
Valentin Maler based on a design by Antonio Abondio
Ca. 1540–Nürnberg 1603
Commemorative Coin of Maximilian II on his Ascent to the Throne
Struck in silver
2.6 cm
Obverse:
MAXIMILI.II.ROM.IMP.SEM.AVG.; portrait, sign. *VM* on shoulder; reverse: *DOMINVS.PROVIDEBIT.*; flying eagle holding the globe
Around 1564
Prague, Národní muzeum, Numismatic Department, inv. no. H5-50 119

Maximilian's portrait on this medal was engraved according to a design by Antonio Abondio; the eagle holding the globe on the reverse side symbolizing power is also based on this model. This expression of the desire to rule the world, however, originated during the Classical era (compare with *Kunstkammer*). Several variants exist of these small medals, which differ chiefly in the design chosen for the reverse side. The inscription on the reverse of this medal, *DOMINVS PROVIDEBIT*, despite its symbolism, suggests the certain humility and faith of the young Emperor: 'God will provide.'

Fiala, p. 30, nos 14, 16 var.; Don. 1229; Habich, vol. 2/1, no. 2601 var.

Z.M.

III.18
Workshop of Nickel Milicz
First half of the sixteenth century–1570
Emperor Maximilian II
Struck in silver
5.2 cm
Obverse:
MAXMILIANVS.II.D.G.ROMA.IMERI.SE M.AVO.GER.HV.BO.ETZ.REX.; bust of the Emperor with a laurel wreath; reverse: *ARCHI.DVX.AVSTRI.DVX.BVRG.MAR-CA.MOR.1566*; double-headed eagle in the field
1566
Prague, Národní muzeum, Numismatic Department, inv. no. H5-58 481

Nickel Milicz worked as a die cutter for the Jáchymov mint from approximately 1545. Apart from portrait medals, his workshop also produced dies for a large quantity of medals with biblical motifs, and dies for the Prague mint. The portrait for the medal of Maximilian II was crafted by an experienced engraver, probably for presentation purposes at court.

Fiala, *Stempelsammlung*, nos 103–4; Domanig, D.M. no. 230; Lanna, p. 719; Katz 1932, no. 326.

Z.M.

III.19
Valentin Maler
Jihlava ca.1540–Nürnberg 1603
Commemorative Coin of Maximilian II on his Fortieth Birthday
Struck in silver
3.7 cm
Obverse:
MAXIMILIANVS.II./RO.IM.AE.XXXX; bust of the Emperor with laurel wreath; reverse: *DOMINVS PROVIDEBIT*; double-headed eagle holding a sceptre and sword, beneath it the imperial orb
After 1567
Prague, Národní muzeum, Numismatic Department, inv. no. H5-50 122

Maximilian II was born 1 August 1527, the first-born son of Ferdinand I and Anna of Jagellon. The medal commemorating his fortieth birthday was evidently made after 1567 and the engraved portrait was based on a design by Antonio Abondio. The insignia on the reverse side highlight his status as emperor.

Don. 1231; Katz 1929, p. 119.

Z.M.

III.20
Prague mint
First half of the seventeenth century
Matthias II - Commemorative Coin Issued for his Coronation as King of Bohemia
Struck in silver
2.6 cm
Obverse: *MATTHIAS II. / D.G.HVNG.REX.CO / RONAT IN REG / EM BOHEMIA / AN.1611 DIER / 23.MAY*; reverse: bust of the King in Hungarian national costume with a cap and Golden Fleece
1611
Prague, Národní muzeum, Numismatic Department, inv. no. H5-58 277

Don. 1877 obv.; 1881 rev.; ES, vol. 1, 122.

Z.M.

III.21
Prague mint
First half of the seventeenth century
Matthias - Commemorative Coin Issued for his Coronation as King of Bohemia
Struck in silver
2.8 cm
Obverse: *MATTHIAS II. / D.G.HVNG.REX.CO / RONAT IN REG / EM BOHEMIA / An.1611.DIE / 23 MAY*; reverse: *SALVTEM EX INIMICIS NOS-TRIS*; stork devouring a snake
1611
Prague, Národní muzeum, Numismatic Department, inv .no. H5-50 182

From the earliest times, it was customary to throw coins among the people during coronations. Originally they were ordinary coins; later, from the time of Matthias's coronation in 1611 onwards, they became special commemorative coins bearing the date and place of the coronation with the sovereign's motto, and frequently also his portrait or symbolic motifs generally relating to the motto's contents. Matthias's insistence over many years that Rudolf II surrender the Czech throne ended with Rudolf's abdication on the day of Matthias's coronation. The reverse side of one of the coronation jettons depicts a stork devouring a snake, which expresses

the symbolism contained in the words *Salutem ex inimicis nostris* ('prosperity from the defeat of our enemies'). The choice of this motto does not reflect well on Matthias's personality since it openly expresses his satisfaction in the political defeat of his brother, Rudolf II.

Don. 1878; ES, vol. 1, 122.

Z.M.

III.22
Anonymous (monogram *CA.H.*)
First half of the seventeenth century
Commemorative Coin Issued for the Marriage of Matthias II and the Archduchess Anne of Tyrol (Austria)
Struck in gilded silver
3.4 cm
Obverse: *MATTHIAS II.REX.HVNGARI-AE CORONATVS MDCVIII*; bust of the King with his crown; reverse: *ANNA AVS-TRAE ARCHID: VIENAE NVPTIAS CELE-BRAVIT.4.DEC:QVI/CVM*; bust of the Queen with the inscription *ANNO – 1611* on either side
1611

Prague, Národní muzeum, Numismatic Department, inv. no. H5-58 276

Matthias II (1557-1619), the brother of Rudolf II, was vice-regent in the Netherlands during the years 1577-81, then later in the Tyrol, the Hungarian and the Austrian lands. He was also supreme field sheriff of the Habsburg army during the Turkish Wars. At the instigation of his family, he became regent in 1606 and in 1608 he was elected Hungarian King. He increased pressure on the ailing Rudolf II to retreat from the Austrian lands and Bohemia, but his wish was not granted until 1611. He was elected Holy Roman Emperor on 3

June 1612 after Rudolf's death, and crowned on 24 July that same year. In 1611 Matthias married Grand Duchess Anna (1585-1618), the daughter of Ferdinand of Tyrol. The medal struck for the occasion shows, on the obverse side, the date 1608 when Matthias became King of Hungary. His portrait and the letter type around the perimeter of the medal are distinctive. The reverse side shows his wife and the year of their marriage, 1611.

Don. 1854; Huszár, p. 98.

Z.M.

III.23
Christian Maler
Nürnberg ca.1584–Nürnberg ca.1648
Matthias - Commemorative Coin Issued for the Imperial Coronation
Struck in silver
5.2 cm
Obverse: *MATTHIAS MVNDI MODERA-TOR MAGNIFICATVS*; one segment bears the inscription: *CVM_PRIVIL.CAES*; depiction of the Emperor on horseback with crown and sceptre; reverse: *R.K.V.K.W.VNGARN.DALMACI...*; eagle surrounded by the coats of arms of the inherited lands
No date (1612)

Prague, Národní muzeum, Numismatic Department, inv. no. H5-50 179

Wellenheim, vol. 2/1, 7021.

Z.M.

III.24
Christian Maler
Nürnberg ca. 1584–Nürnberg ca.1648
Commemorative Coin Issued for the Imperial Coronation of Matthias and Anne
Struck in silver
4 cm
Obverse: *MATTH.ROM.IMP.CAES.ET AN-NA AVSTR.AVG.*; busts of the Emperor and his wife in ceremonial dress; the Emperor is wearing a laurel wreath and the Order of the Golden Fleece; reverse: *MATTH. / IMP.CAES.PP.AVG. / ELIG-ITVR EIDIB.IVNI / CORONATVR IIX.KAL / QVINCT.BIDVO POST / ANNA AVGVSTA CORO / NATA ANo.SAL.M. /*

D.CXII.FRANCOF / - CVM PRIVILEG./ CA.M.
1612
Prague, Národní muzeum, Numismatic Department, inv .no. H5-150 980

Christian Maler, the son of Valentin Maler, was a highly productive and superbly skilled goldsmith and medal engraver who worked for Emperors Rudolf II, Matthias II and Ferdinand II, from whom he acquired permission to strike medals in his own house ('cum privilegio'). Most of his work involved striking medals that document political events during the first half of the seventeenth century. On the death

of Rudolf II, Frankfurt – the coronation city of German emperors since medieval times – witnessed the coronation of his brother Matthias and his wife, Anna of Tyrol, on 24-26 June 1612. A large number of ceremonial medals was struck for the occasion; as their dies were often crossed, several variants exist.

Montenuovo, p. 717; Forrer, vol. 3, pp. 540–44; Nohejlová, p. 71, no. 7; Joseph and Fellner, no. 319.

Z.M.

III.25
Christian Maler
Nürnberg ca.1584–Nürnberg ca.1648
Ferdinand II – Commemorative Coin Issued for his Coronation as King of Bohemia
Struck in silver
4.2 cm
Obverse: *FERDINAND II.D.G.BOH.REX.ARCHIDV.AVSTR.*; bust of the King with the Order of the Golden Fleece, sign.*CM.*; outer inscription: *AMORE FIDEQ-PATERNA*; reverse: *STARTAM HIS / VIRTVTIBVS ORNO*; shield with the Czech lion on the base, allegorical figures *Charitas* and *Fides* on either side, beneath them the motto *LE-*

GITIME CERTANTIBVS and the Czech crown
No date (1617)
Prague, Národní muzeum, Numismatic Department, inv. no. H5 58 173

Since Emperor Matthias II did not have an heir, he secured succession to the Czech throne for Grand Duke Ferdinand of Styria, who was the son of Karl of Styria and Maria of Bavaria. Like Ferdinand II, he was crowned Czech King while Matthias was still alive, on 29 June 1617. In honour of the occasion several types of coronation coins were struck, in sizes similar to that of the thaler, quarter-thaler and groschen.

The reverse side of most of these coins depicts a crown in the field bearing the legend *Legitime certantibus* (Fighting for one's legal right). This motto also appears on the medal by Christian Maler, but the text and coronation date are missing.

ES, vol. 1, 239; MZE 28/5, tab. IV.

Z.M.

III.26
Christian Maler
Nürnberg ca.1584–Nürnberg ca.1648
Commemorative Coin Issued for the Bohemian Coronation of Frederick of the Palatinate and Elizabeth of England
Struck in silver
4.2 ×3.5 cm, oval
Obverse: *FRIDERICVS ET ELISABETHA D.G.R.R.BOHEMIAE*; two busts of the royal couple, sign.*CM; reverse: FRIDERI:/D.G.COM.PALAT...*; oval depicting five hands holding up the Czech crown, inscription on either side; legend: *DANTE DEO ET ORDINVM*
1619

Prague, Národní muzeum, Numismatic Department, inv. no. H5-150 982

ĽS vol. 3, 375; Nohejlová, p. 72, no. 9.

Z.M.

III.27
Anonymous
Seventeenth century
Frederick of Palatinate - Commemorative Coin Issued for the Bohemian Coronation
Struck in gold
4.5 × 3.6 cm (oval)
Obverse: reclining Czech lion with the insignia of royal might; above it, five hands holding the Czech crown are depicted breaking through the clouds
No date (1619)
Prague, Národní muzeum, Numismatic Department, inv. no. H5-150 993

ĽS, vol. 3, 379 ; Nohejlová, p. 73, no. 20.

Z.M.

III.28
Christian Maler
Nürnberg ca.1584–Nürnberg ca.1648
Commemorative Coin of the Anti-Habsburg Uprising
Struck in gilded silver, chain attached
3.6 cm,
Obverse: *PRVDENS CONCORDIA VICTRIX*, sign.*CM*; three allegorical female figures; reverse: *PRO ARIS ET POCIS*; two knights in armour. One segment bears the inscription *CA.MALER*
Prague, Národní muzeum, Numismatic Department, inv. no. H5-58 263

The uprising of the Czech Estates, begun in 1618 by the Prague defenestrations, continued during the following year when Ferdinand II succeeded to the throne in March 1619 after the death of Matthias. In July the Estates summoned a general assembly of the lands of the Czech crown to secure religious freedom. The confederation of the lands of the Czech crown was enacted here, as was also a change to the consitution of the Czech kingdom in favour of the Estates and a restriction of the power of the King. A law was also passed stating that the King could ascend the throne only by election. Frederick Palatine was accordingly elected Czech King on 26 August 1619. The Czech confedera-tion was also supported by the evangelical estates of the Austrian and Hungarian lands, which led to the culmination of anti-Habsburg resistance. The medal commemorates this era in two variants. The allegorical figures on the obverse side complement a second design of Frederick Palatine on horseback, while the figures of the two knights in armour remain on the reverse side of both types.

ĽS 387.

Z.M.

III.29
? Andreas Peter
First half of the seventeenth century
Ferdinand III as King of Bohemia
Struck in silver
3.9 cm
Obverse: *FERDINANDVUS III.D.G.HVNG.BO.REX.ARCHID.AVSTRIAE*; bust of the King above the inscription AP 1630; reverse: *PIETATE ET IVSTITIA*; scales with crucifix above an engraving of the city
1630
Prague, Národní muzeum, Numismatic Department, inv. no. H5-151 011

Ferdinand II reigned until 1637, but, after the declaration of the Renewed Constitution on 25 November 1627, he had his son and successor Ferdinand III crowned Czech king, later Hungarian king and Roman king in 1636. His commemorative coronation medals bear the motto *Pietate et justitia* (Piety and justice), hence the symbolic engravings of scales and crucifix on the reverse side. The medal, which is dated 1630, also has an image of a city divided by a river engraved on the reverse side. The artist who designed it, Andreas Peter, was probably active in the Kladno region during the first half of the seventeenth century.

ĽS 624; Nohejlová, p. 77, no. 43.

Z.M.

III.30
Ten-ducat Coin of Rudolf II
Struck in gold
4.01 mm, weight 34.508 g
1599
Prague mint (master of the mint: Zuzana Erckerová)
Prague, Národní muzeum, Numismatic Department, inv. no. H5-15 069

During the last few decades of Rudolf II's reign, the Prague mint began striking denominations of larger ducats and thalers for the first time, in addition to ordinary coins. Two-, three-, four-, five- and ten-ducat pieces were produced in gold; most of the coins date from after 1600. The coins of the highest values are exceptional mints, which were acquired only by the most discerning collectors in the highest stratum of society. The oldest ten-ducat piece was struck in Prague during the time of master of the mint Lazer Ercker in 1589. The mint engraving used at that time – the figure of the monarch with his crown, sceptre, imperial orb and sword standing between shields with the Czech and Hungarian coats of arms on the obverse side and a crowned imperial eagle with a shield bearing the Austrian-Burgundian coat of arms and the Order of the Golden Fleece on the reverse side – also appeared on the Prague ten-ducat pieces from the 1590s and, in a slightly modified form, on the larger gold coins from the beginning of the seventeenth century. The first design of this type is attributed to the engraver Wolf Wirth who worked in Prague during the period 1587–89. The die stamp for the 1599 issue was designed by David Engelhart, who worked at the Prague mint during the years 1593–1601.

E.Š.

III.31
Two-thaler Coin of Rudolf II
Struck in silver
4.26 cm, weight 57.797 g
1602
Prague mint (master of the mint: Jan
Lasanz)
Prague, Národní muzeum, Numismatic
Department, inv. no. H5-34 064

E.Š.

III.32
Ten-ducat Coin of Matthias
Struck in gold
4.06 cm, weight 34.483 g
1612
Prague mint (master of the mint:
Benedikt Hubmer)
Prague, Národní muzeum, Numismatic
Department, inv. no. H5-15 075

The reign of Matthias II (1612–19) occasioned several issues of larger denominations from the Prague mint. Exceptional coins include the gold cast of the silver thaler weighing the same as the twenty-ducat piece, and a coin known as the

hranáč, klipa or útes, which had four sides and weighed the same as the twenty-five-ducat piece. The design of the ten-ducat piece from 1612 links it to the previous issue struck during the reign of Rudolf II, and was engraved by Jan Konrád Greuter.

E.Š.

III.33
Five-ducat Coin of Matthias
Struck in gold
4.04 cm, weight 17.195 g
1612
Prague mint (master of the mint:
Benedikt Hubmer)
Prague, Národní muzeum, Numismatic
Department, inv. no. H5-15 074

The Prague five-ducat pieces bearing the portrait of Matthias II were similar in design to those minted during the time of Rudolf II, most frequently bearing an engraving of the monarch in a standing position. The issue surviving from 1612 bears

an exceptional design of the bare-headed monarch with the Czech lion in the area below his bust reserved for the legend; this design was thus identical to that used for the last five-ducat piece of Rudolf II, marked as gold casts of the Rudolfine silver thalers. This issue also documents the work of Jan Konrád Greuter.

E.Š.

III.34
Five-ducat Coin of Matthias
Struck in gold
3.495 cm, weight 17.325 g
1612
Prague mint (master of the mint:
Benedikt Hubmer)
Prague, Národní muzeum, Numismatic
Department, inv. no. H5-15 076

At the beginning of the reign of Matthias II, in 1611 and 1612, the Prague mint introduced new types of large gold and silver coins showing the crowned bust of the ruler on the obverse side and a large crowned coat of arms on the reverse. An

important element of the design on the reverse side was the depiction of the Order of the Golden Fleece, engraved next to the coat of arms. Other royal mints in Bohemia produced similar designs (Kutná Hora, Jáchymov). The dies for these coins were crafted by Jan Konrád Greuter.

E.Š.

III.35
Two-ducat Coin of Matthias
Struck in silver
4.07 cm, weight 58.27 g
1611
Prague mint (master of the mint:
Benedikt Hubmer)
Prague, Národní muzeum, Numismatic
Department, inv. no. H5-36 363

While the higher denominations of Prague thalers (two-and-a half-, three-, four- and five-thaler pieces) are known exclusively to have depicted the standing monarch on the obverse side and the heraldic eagle on the reverse, the two-

thaler and one-thaler pieces chiefly portrayed the monarch wearing a crown or bare-headed. The issue from 1611, one of the earliest of the coins commemorating Matthias II, is remarkable for the rich detail of the coat of arms on the reverse side. No similar design is to be found on any other coins depicting this monarch.

E.Š.

III.36
Two-thaler Coin of Matthias
Struck in silver
4.23 cm, weight 57.63 g
1618
Prague mint (master of the mint:
Benedikt Hubmer)
Prague, Národní muzeum, Numismatic
Department, inv. no. H5-35 934

This type of two-thaler piece (the bare-
headed bust of the monarch on the obverse side, a heraldic eagle on the reverse)
was issued at the Prague mint from 1613.
Two years later this issue was joined by
two-thaler pieces featuring the ruler

standing between two shields, bearing
coats of arms on the obverse side and a
heraldic eagle on the reverse.

E.Š.

III.37
Ten-ducat Coin of Frederick of the Palatinate
Struck in gold
4.0 cm, weight 33.58 g
1620
Prague mint (master of the mint: Pavel
Škréta)
Prague, Národní muzeum, Numismatic
Department, inv. no. H5-35 769

Jan Konrád Greuter, who received a commission from the court to design coins
bearing the images of Rudolf and
Matthias, also struck a special edition of
rare coins for Frederick Palatine. The design incorporates the traditional depic-

tion of the standing monarch, this time
accompanied by different coats of arms
and legends. The obverse side bears the
Czech and Palatine coats of arms and on
the reverse side are the coats of arms of all
five lands of the Czech Crown: Bohemia,
Moravia, Silesia, Upper and Lower Lusatia.

E.Š.

III.38
Ten-ducat Coin of Ferdinand II
Struck in gold
4.23 cm, weight 34.48 g
1630
Prague mint (master of the mint: Eliseus
du Bois)
Prague, Národní muzeum, Numismatic
Department, inv. no. H5-34 444

The standing monarch remained the typical image for the obverse sides of the large
gold coins and silver thalers, even during
the reign of Ferdinand II. The coin exhibited here was minted for a period of ten
years, from 1627 to 1637, although data re-

lating to its production in 1629 and 1632
are missing. The reverse side is notable for
displaying the trademark of master of the
mint Eliseus du Bois – a boar's head. The
die stamp was made by Donát Starck who
worked in Prague in 1626–35.

E.Š.

III.39
Ten-ducat Coin of Ferdinand III
Struck in gold
4.10 cm, weight 34.528 g
1648
Prague mint (master of the mint: Jakub
Wolker)
Prague, Národní muzeum, Numismatic
Department, inv. no. H5-15 105

Five types of ten-ducat pieces are known
to have existed during the reign of Ferdinand III. Their obverse sides depict either
the bare-headed bust of the monarch or
his bust decorated with a laurel wreath,
while the reverse side bears the heraldic

crowned eagle with a crowned Czech coat
of arms on its breast. The engraving of the
bare-headed bust was cut by medal-engraver Šalamoun Škultét, who worked at
the Prague mint (he lived in Prague during the period 1638–56), based on a medal
design by Alessandro Abondio. The former's design was, however, simplified and
its relief shallower. The influence of Abondio's portrait is also evident in the design
of the bust with the laurel wreath. From
the long succession of annual issues, the
years 1649, 1650 and 1653 are missing.

E.Š.

III.40
Ten-ducat Coin of Ferdinand III
Struck in gold
4.78 cm, weight 34.56 g
1641
Prague mint (master of the mint: Jakub
Wolker)
Prague, Muzeum Hlavniho Mešta Prahy,
inv. no. 15 931

E.Š.

III.41
Nicolas Neufchatel (workshop)
Mid-sixteenth century–ca. 1600
Emperor Maximilian II
Oil on canvas
81 × 65 cm
After 1566
From 1816 in the Kunsthistorisches
Museum, Vienna
Vienna, Kunsthistorisches Museum,
Gemäldergalerie, 374

This portrait of Maximilian II comes from
a model preserved only in a miniature
copy in the 'Portrait Book' of H. Beck. The
original was the work of Nicolas Neufcha-

tel who painted it in 1566 in three sessions
(*JKSAK*, VII, 1888, reg. 5032). Neufchatel's
workshop produced a series of originals to
which belongs the picture on display. The
Emperor is dressed in the Spanish fashion
of the 1560s.

Schallaburg 1974, cat. no. 280.

Heinz 1963, p. 186, no. 4.

E.F.

III.42
Follower of Sánchez Alonso Coello
*Empress Maria of Spain (Mother of Rudolf
II)*
Oil on canvas
103 × 97 cm
Last third of the sixteenth century
This picture of Pernštejn origin became
part of the famous Pernštejn-Rožmberk-
Lobkowicz gallery at Roudnice Castle. After nationalization in 1948, the painting
was hung in Nelahozeves Castle from
1951 to 1968, and when the Středočeská
galerie was established in 1965, it was included in its collection of old artworks. In
1992, the work, along with the rest of the

Roudnice collection, was returned in
restitution to the Lobkowicz family. It is
now part of the Roudnice-Lobkowicz collection at Nelahozeves
Martin and William Lobkowicz, Nelahozeves Castle, Lobkowicz 5490 (SG O–
2065; Roudnice 269/1003)

The portrait entered the Pernštejn collection as a gift from Maria Marique de Lara,
who was *camarera mayor* of the Spanish Infanta Maria, future wife of Maximilian,
and who accompanied Maria on a visit to
Austria. This so-called 'black portrait' of
Empress Maria (Dvořák 1918, p. 46) is traditionally attributed to Sánchez Coello,

but a contemporary monograph (*Alonso
Sánchez Coello*, 1990) refutes its direct execution by this artist.

Nelahozeves Castle, 1965–92 (rm. x).

Madrid 1990, p. 79, ill. 25; Bukolská 1980,
ill. 23; Dvořák 1980; Dvořák 1907, p. 42, no.
69 (inv. no. 251); Dvořák 1907, pp. 13–18;
Dvořák 1910; Dvořák 1918, pp. 10–11,
21–23, 33, 46–47, 57–58, 97; Dvořák 1929,
pp. 28ff.; Fučíková–Bukovinská–Muchka
1991, ill. 5; Janáček 1987, ill. 19; Matějček
1948, pp. 84ff.; Mikovec 1852, pp. 638ff.

M.Mž.

III.43
Martino Rota
Sebenico ca. 1520–Vienna 1583
Archduke Ernst
Oil on canvas
51 × 42.5 cm
1577–80
Imperial Portrait Gallery; since 1781 in
the Kunsthistorisches Museum
Vienna, Kunsthistorisches Museum,
Gemäldegalerie, 2588

This portait of Archduke Ernst belongs to
a series of portraits of Maximilian's sons.
The prince is wearing armour belonging
to the so-called 'Dreiprinzengarnitur' Waf-

fensammlung, inv. no. 1281), which is the
only detail to distinguish it from a similarly composed portrait of Rudolf II (cat. no.
I.156). Martino Rota's workshop produced
other variants in a series of portraits of
three-quarters the size. Both versions have
survived with the portrait of archduke
Ernst. The majority of collection is housed
at the Hispanic Society in New York.

Graz 1964, cat. no. 590; Schallaburg 1974,
cat. no. 365; Essen and Vienna 1988, cat.
no. 570.

Heinz 1963, pp.115, 192, cat. no. 40; Kaufmann 1988, cat. no. 17.2.

E.F.

III.44
Follower of Alonso Sánchez Coello
Portrait of the Young Rudolf
Oil on canvas
45.5 × 41.5 cm
1570s
Martin and William Lobkowicz, Nela-
hozeves Castle
Lobkowicz 7247 (SG O 2062; R 111 391,
Roudnice 196/256)

The painting is usually attributed to Alonso Sánchez Coello, court painter to Philip
II. According to M. Dvořák (1918, p. 46), it
dates from the time of Archduke Rudolf's
residence in Madrid, where he and his

brother Ernst were educated from 1563 to
1571 at the Spanish royal court. A recent
monograph questions attribution of the
painting to Coello owing to the somewhat
schematic nature of the portrait and the
lack of elaboration (Alonso Sánchez Coello 1990, p. 79, ill. 25).

Nelahozeves Castle, 1965–92, rm. x).

Madrid 1990, p. 79, ill. 25; Prague 1985, ill.
p. 275; Bukolská 1968; Bukolská 1980, ill.
23. Dvořák 1980; Dvořák 1907, p. 42, no. 69
(inv. no. 251). Dvořák 1907, pp. 13–18;
Dvořák 1910; Dvořák 1918, pp. 10–11,
21–23, 33, 46–47, 57–58, 97; Dvořák 1929,

pp. 28ff.; Fučíková–Bukovinská–Muchka
1991, ill. 5; Janáček 1987, ill. 19; Matějček
1948, pp. 84ff; Mikovec 1852, pp. 638ff.

M.Mž.

III.45
Lucas van Valckenborch
*Emperor Rudolf II at the Spa in
the Schwalbach*
Oil on oak
After 1593
? From the collection of Archduke Ernst;
? collection of Rudolf II; from the collection of Archduke Leopold Wilhelm, inv.
no. 1659, no. 333 or 334; imperial collection in Vienna

This scene evidently represented a
favourite theme in the work of Lucas van
Valckenborch because the painter returned to it repeatedly with tiny alter-

ations. Apart from the works known in the
Herzog Anton Ulrich-Museum in Braunschweig and in a private collection (Vienna 1971, cat. no. 70), there is another work
from the chateau at Hrádek u Nechanic.
Only one of the three noblemen in the Viennese picture held the Order of the Gold-
en Fleece and that could be Rudolf II, although it could also be Archduke Ernst to
whom the Emperor bore a striking resemblance. It was also more probable that
Ernst made a visit to the spa at Schwalbach than that the Emperor did. In 1594
the Archduke had Lucas paid 36 guilders
in Frankfurt for a view of Linz, and, several
months later, as much as 200 thalers for an

unspecified work. Valckenborch's pictures
may have come into the Rudolfine collections with the collection of Archduke
Ernst's pictures, and through further separation, later to Archduke Leopold Wilhelm.

Vienna 1935, cat. no. 181; Vienna 1964, cat.
no. 39; Essen and Vienna 1988, cat. no. 597.

Essen and Vienna 1988, cat. no. 597, for
older related literature.

E.F.

III.46
Giuseppe Arcimboldo
Milan 1527-Milan 1593
Portrait of Rudolf II as Holy Roman Emperor; Portrait of Rudolf II as King of Bohemia
Pen and black ink
16.5 × 16.5cm; 15.5 × 15.5 cm
Inscribed and signed: *La corona doue si corono Re de Romano Rodolbpo el primo di Nouembro 1575 in Ratisbona corna cher in quiserana che feco far Carlo Magno et erta di tanta larchezzza che gli auanzaua doi dita per parte era tutt a oro e della medema fattura. Io Guisseppe Arcimboldo fui presente*; Inscribed and signed: *la corona doue si corono Rodolhpo Re di bouemia de medomo garbo*

come si uede nel presente sisegno 1575 il Giorgno de Santo Mati di Settembre. Io Giuseppe Arcimboldo fui presente 1576; 1575
Prague, Národní muzeum, inv. no. 40155

Lengthy inscriptions on these drawings establish them as portraits of Rudolf II at his coronation in Regensburg as Holy Roman Emperor, 1 November 1576 (not 1575), and in Prague as King of Bohemia, 22 September, 1575.

Prague 1978, no. 5, 6; Venice 1987, ill. 71; Essen and Vienna 1988, no. 191.

Additional literature to Essen and Vienna 1988: Fučí-ková 1986, pp. 14-15 ill. 4-5; Fučíková in Dvorský, et. al, 1988, pp. 65-6, fig. 52 on p. 68.

T.C.K.

III.47
Anonymous after Anthoni Bays
The Solemn Conferment of the Order of the Golden Fleece on Rudolf II, Karl of Styria, Ernst, Vilém of Rožmberk and Leonard of Harrach in Prague and Maximilian of Bavaria in Landshut
Paper on canvas, coloured pen drawing
310 × 6000 cm
After 1585
From the archive of Archduke Ferdinand of Tyrol in Ambras
Vienna, Kunsthistorisches Museum, Sammlung für Kunst und Kunstgewerbe, inv. no. 5348

In 1585 the highest award for meritorious service in the protection and proliferation of Catholicism, the Order of the Golden Fleece, was awarded to Emperor Rudolf II, to his brother Archduke Arnošt, Archduke Karl of Styria, to the Supreme Burgrave of the Bohemian kingdom Vilém of Rožmberk, to the court adviser Vilém of Harrach and to the Bavarian Duke William V. At that time it was the Spanish King Philip who decided on the recipients ofthe Order, while the actual giving of the award was entrusted to Archduke Ferdinand of Tyrol. Illustrations 1-10 document the celebrations connected with the giving of the Order at Prague Castle. Illustrations 11-13

depict the awarding of the Order to William of Bavaria in Landshut. The model for the cycle of pictures was provided by an illustration by A. Bays in a book by P.Zehendtner, *Ordentliche Beschreibunge* (Dillingen, 1587).

Essen and Vienna 1988, cat. no. 8; Innsbruck 1995, cat. no. 29 (also a source of other literature).

J.Ha.

III.48
Anonymous after Hoogenbergh
Reges Bohemiae (Chronology of the Bohemian Princes and Kings from Bořivoj to Rudolf II)
4. 1591 to 1611
Copper engraving
57.5 × 43.0 cm
On the right: *Reges BOHEMIAE Sacratissimo ac Potentissimo Romanor. IMPERATORIS AVG. RVDOLPHO II. GERMAN. HVNG. BOHEM. etc. REGI: consecrat.*; on the left: *BOIEMI NOMEN ROMANA POTENTIA NORAT, MARBODVO HOSPITIVM QVANDO RAVENNA DEDIT. TEMPORE ROMANAS QVO CAESAR GESSIT HABENAS ANTELVLIT PVLCHRAE QVI*

*CAPREAS PATRIAE.*in the upper right corner: *Fol. XVIII 1591-1611*
Originally part of a larger whole; on the reverse side a text explaining the history of the royal succession in Bohemia.
Třeboň, State Regional Archive; Schwarzenburg family archive, Sekundogenitura, Graphic Collection, no.5

An illustration of the line of succession of the Czech Kings from the time of Prince BoŸivoj up to Emperor Rudolf II, who was crowned Czech King in 1575 and ruled in Bohemia from 1576 to 1611. The line of succession is pictured as a tree inscribed with the names of the Czech rulers and

their wives, and rudimentary biographical information. The family tree culminates in a portait of Rudolf placed in a cartouche carried by a female eagle with the imperial crown, sceptre and an inscription with Rudolf's motto, *ADSIT*. On the left side of the paper are the insignia of the Moravian margravate, the Bohemian kingdom and of Upper and Lower Hungary.

Hlavsa 1971, p. 148.

J.Ha.

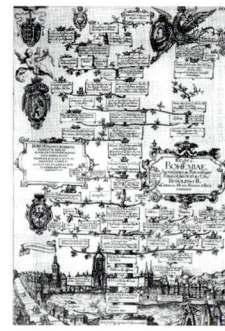

III.49
Unknown engraver from the fourth quarter of the sixteenth century
Rudolf II in Imperial Vestment and with Coats of Arms of Seven Electors
Copper engraving
Before 1583
Roudnice, Lobkowicz Collection, inv. no. LR 9855

In 1979 H. Geissler published a drawing in the catalogue of the exhibition *Zeichnung in Deutschland*, which portrayed Rudolf II wearing his imperial robes and with the emblems of the Electors. He ascribed the drawing to Arcimboldo. An engraving,

which is a precise copy of this composition, however, casts doubt on that attribution. In its basic scheme, it resembles an etching made from an engraving, around which someone had begun, but not finished, tracing with a quill pen. The engraving is much more certain and exact in its details. Rudolf is portrayed without the Order of the Golden Fleece, which means that this portrait originated before 1585. Here he has a beard and looks older than he did in 1576. The creator of the model may well have been Martino Rota.

Essen and Vienna 1988, cat. no. 325.

E.F.

III.50
Domenicus Custos
Fl. Antwerp after 1550–died Augsburg 1612
Portrait of Emperor Rudolf II with a Spanish Hat and the Order of the Golden Fleece
Copper engraving
174 × 123 cm
RUDOLF: II. A DEO DAT. AETERN. PRINC. REIQ. ROM. D[OMI]N[U]S, FVNDATOR PUBL. QVIETIS: ET EXTINCTOR TVRCAE FERAE TYRANNDIS. PATR. PAT. SEMP. AVGVST. REX BOHEM. REX HVNGARIAE etc. ARCHID. AVSTR. etc.; motto under the illustration: *ADSIT*

? After 1600
Prague, Národní galerie v Praze, Grafická sbírka, inv. no. R-1741

The portrait of Rudolf II in a Spanish hat and with the Order of the Golden Fleece is set in an oval cartouche bordered with a wreath of plants. On the left-hand side is Jupiter with an eagle and a crane – the symbol of vigilance – on the right an allegorical female figure with wings and a branch as a symbol of victory over the Turks. In the middle is the imperial symbol, and along its sides the emblem of Rudolf II – an eagle flying to the sun with the motto *SALVTI PUBLICAE*, after J. Ty-

potio, *Symbola divina et humana* (Prague, 1601-3). On the left is the Hungarian seal and on the right the Czech seal.

J.Ha.

III.51
Anonymous Master
Portrait Medallion of Emperor Rudolf II
Mother-of-pearl
RVDOLPHVS II. ROM.IMP.AVG.REX.HV
Opava, Slezské muzeum, inv. no. U 458 L

There are three known versions of the portrait of Rudolf II carved in mother-of-pearl. The treatment of each version is different. It seems that in the early seventeenth century this material was already popular, but no artist is known with whom the works can be associated. The profile portrait from Darmstadt is signed *D. M.*, but the monogram has not been deciphered. The remaining two portraits from Prague and Opava depict the Emperor in three-quarter profile, which seems to have been in fashion after 1600 and is used in a number of portraits executed in various materials and different versions. The most famous is a medallion whose author has not been definitively identified. Paulus van Vianen and Alessandro Abondio have been considered, but vanVianen's authorship was refuted by J. R. ter Molen (1984). The closest model for this type of portrait seems to be the portrait of the monarch painted by Hans von Aachen and engraved by Aegidius Sadeler in 1604; the Opava medallion also bears the closest resemblance to this work.

Fučíková, Bukovinská, Muchka 1988, ill. without text.

B.B.

III.52
Portrait Medallion of Emperor Rudolf II
Engraved mother-of-pearl, wood rough-cut and stained black
Oval 4.2 cm, width 3.5 cm
RVDOLPHVS II ROM. IMP. AVG. REX HVNG.BOE
Ca. 1609
1893 from the Frederica Spitzera collection in Paris
Prague, Uměleckoprůmyslové muzeum v Praze, inv. no. 5209

This portrait of a bust in cuirass with a laurel wreath in the third quarter enface bears similarity to the obverse side of a medal by an unknown master from 1600. Related facial features and a similar costume in the copper engravings by Aegidius Sadeler, particularly if made in 1609 (Prague, Národní galerie v Praze, inv. no. R-9.738), point to a later date of origin.

D.S.

III.53
Anton Peffenhauser (attributed)
Augsburg 1525–1603
Rudolf II's Armour on the Occasion of his Coronation as King of Bohemia
Bright iron, etched, gilded and blackened
1575
Vienna, Bürgerliches Zeughaus
Vienna, Historisches Museum der Stadt Wien, inv. nos 127.123–127.141

The maker of this tilt armour can be clearly identified, on stylistic grounds, as Anton Peffenhauser, from Augsburg, and the date some time in the 1570s. On the chest and on the back there is a mighty, two-tailed, etched lion, sitting upright. This two-tailed lion is found on the coat of arms of the king of Bohemia. Maximilian II was emperor in the 1570s and died in 1576. As emperor he naturally also had his imperial emblem added to his own armour. This armour can therefore have belonged only to a King of Bohemia who was not yet Emperor, which would mean Archduke Rudolf, Maximilian II's son, who was crowned King of Bohemia in Prague in 1575. Thus, although no records of an order for this armour exist, we can say with certainty that it was made for Rudolf II in 1575 and would have been worn by him for his Bohemian coronation.

Schallaburg 1977, cat. no. 635; Vienna 1988, cat. no. 793.

M.Pf.

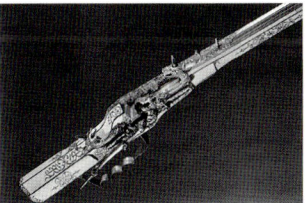

III.54
Daniel Sadeler and Hieronymus Borstorffer the Elder
Sadeler: Antwerp before 1602–Munich 1632; Borstorffer: Munich before 1589–Munich 1637
Rifle
Iron, chiselled, blued and gilded, wood, bone, horn
115 cm
1605–10
Vienna, Kaiserliches Zeughaus
Vienna, Kunsthistorisches Museum, Hofjagd- und Rüstkammer, inv. no. D 86

The iron parts of this weapon were chiselled by Daniel Sadeler. The barrel with grooved rifling and the lock are decorated with ornamental foliage and tritons. The two cocks are in fantastic animal forms. The raised parts are blued while the background is gilded. The stock with German butt is in a style consistent with the initials *HB*, identifying the stockmaker Hieronymus Borstorffer. The decoration is striking in its simple elegance, relying as it does purely on colour contrasts. The whole stock is veneered with white bone plates with black horn or ebony inlays. The decoration consists of arabesques and tracery that Borstorffer presumably took from ornamental prints. Hieronymus Borstorffer worked primarily for the court at Wittelsbach. It is possible that between 1605 and 1610 he collaborated with Daniel Sadeler, then working in Prague, on work for the court in Prague. This highly decorated gun was thus probably made around this time for Emperor Rudolf II.

Vienna 1988, cat. no. 796.

Boeheim 1889, p. 184, no. 56; Stöcklein, Eisenschnitt 1922, p. 65, pl. 2359; Hayward 1963–64, p. 288; Hoff 1963, 149; Schedelmann 1972, pp. 67, 72.

M.Pf.

III.55, III.56
Zachariáš Kempf
Second half of the sixteenth century–ca. 1606
Rudolf II – Commemorative Coin Issued on the Ascension to the Throne
Struck in gilded silver, 4 cm, metal loop for chain; struck in black metal, 4.4 cm, gilded setting with chain
Obverse: *RVDOL.DER AN.V.G.G. - ER.ROM.KAISER*; bust with the crown of the Holy Roman Emperor; inscription *AETA.SVE.25* on either side; reverse: *AVCH + ZV + VNGERN + VNND + BEHAIM + KO + 76N*; double-headed eagle 1576
Prague, Národní muzeum, Numismatic Department, inv. nos H5–58 494 and H5–58 270

In May 1575 the parliamentary debates of the Czech Estates in Prague opened with two important issues: the Bohemian Confession and Rudolf's succession to the Czech throne; by this time Rudolf had become King of Hungary. To the frequently ailing Emperor Maximilian, his son's succession as Czech King was of extreme importance. Maximilian II promised to fulfil the proposed Confession and tolerate freedom of faith, and the issues of the succession were also resolved. Rudolf became Czech king and Roman King in 1575. Emperor Maximilian II died on 12 October 1576, and Rudolf subsequently became Holy Roman Emperor. The Jáchymov die cutter Zachariáš Kempf crafted a medal to commemorate this occasion. Rudolf's portrait with the imperial crown emphasizes his majesty, and the inscription tells us his age at the time – 25 years. The black metal alloy from which one of the medals was crafted was unique in medal engraving at that time.

Don. 1393; Katz, no. 506.

Z.M.

III.56

See cat. no. III.55.

III.57
Valentin Maler
Jihlava ca. 1540–Nürnberg 1603
Medal of *Rudolf II*
After 1585
Prague, Národní muzeum, Numismatic
Department, inv. no. H5-58500

The medal is attached to three chains
joined together, and has a pearl ornament at the bottom. The reverse depicts
Rudolf's well-known emblem – an eagle
flying up to the skies and a laurel
wreath.

Habich 1/2, no. 2605, 2607.

Z.M.

III.58
Anonymous
After 1585
Medal of *Rudolf II and Archduke Ernst*
Cast in silver, chain
3.3 cm
Obverse:
RVDOLPHVS.II.IMP.AVGV.H.B.R.; bust
with the Order of the Golden Fleece; re-
verse: *ERNESTVS.ARCHI.D.AVSTRIAE*;
bust with the Order of the Golden Fleece
Prague, Národní muzeum, Numismatic
Department, inv. no. H5-58 498

In 1563 Archduke Ernst, son of Maximilian II and Maria of Spain, was sent with his

elder brother Rudolf and a large retinue to
be educated at the Spanish court, at the request of their mother and her brother,
King Philip II of Spain. The children remained there until 1571, when they returned to Vienna. During the reign of
Rudolf II, Ernst was appointed vice-regent
in the Austrian lands, later in the Netherlands. He died in Brussels on 20th February 1595. The medal, which presents both
brothers with the Order of the Golden
Fleece, was evidently produced after 1585,
when they received this most valuable of
Habsburg orders from their uncle Philip
II.

MZČ, tab. IV-21-4; Katz 517.

Z.M.

III.59, III.60
Valentin Maler
Jihlava ca. 1540–Nürnberg 1603
*Commemorative Coin of Emperor Rudolf II
issued for the Imperial Diet*
Struck in silver
4.2 cm
Obverse: *RVDOLPHVS
II.D.G.RO/MA:IMPERA:SEM.AV*; the Emperor standing in his coronation cloak
with the imperial insignia, sign.*VM*; reverse: double-headed eagle, the year *15–
89*, twenty-four coats of arms of the lands
of the Habsburg crown around the
perimeter
1589

Prague, Národní muzeum, Numismatic
Department, inv. nos H5-50 172 and H5-
58 240

Don. 1396; Habich, vol. 2/1, no. 2610.

Z.M.

III.60

See cat. no. III.59.

III.61
Valentin Maler
Jihlava ca. 1540–Nürnberg 1603
Commemorative Coin of Emperor Rudolf II Issued for the Imperial Diet
1590
Struck in silver
4 cm
Obverse: *RVDOLPH.II.D.G.ROM: IMP.S.A.GER: VNG:BOH:REX ARCH: AV*; the Emperor on horseback, sign.VM; legend on the edge of the medal: *A DOMINO REGNVM VENIT...*; reverse: letter *R* decorated with a crown set between two coats-of-arms and allegorical female figures. *1590*. Initials of the names of twelve

previous emperors round the perimeter.
Prague, Národní muzeum, Numismatic Department, inv. no. H5-58 242

Don. 1398; Habich II/1, 2609; Wurzbach II, 8031.

Z.M.

III.62, III.63
Valentin Maler
Jihlava ca. 1540–Nürnberg 1603
Commemorative Coin of Rudolf II Issued for the Imperial Diet
Struck in silver
4 cm
Obverse: *RVDOLPH.II.D.G.ROM: IMP.S.A.GER: VNG:BOH:REX ARCH: AV:*; the Emperor on horseback, sign.*VM*; legend on the edge of the medal: *A DOMINO REGNVM VENIT ...*; reverse: letter *R* decorated with a crown set between two coats of arms and allegorical female figures; inscription: *1590*; initials of the names of twelve previous Emperors

round the perimeter
1590
Prague, Národní muzeum, Numismatic Department, inv. nos H5-58 242 and H5-58 241

Don. 1398; Habich, vol. 2/1, 2609; Wurzbach, vol. 2, 8031.

Z.M.

III.63

See cat. no. III.62

III.64
Valentin Maler
Jihlava ca. 1540–Nürnberg 1603
Commemorative Coin of Rudolf II and the Electors
Struck in silver; 3.1 cm; struck in gilded silver, 3.3 with setting
Obverse: *RVDOLPHVS II ROM IMP.SEM.AVG.*; bust of the Emperor; reverse: *MANE NOBISCVM DNE QVONOAM ADVESPERASCIT:ET INCLINA: IAM DIES.LVC* ; the seven Electors' coats of arms
Prague, Národní muzeum, Numismatic Department, inv. nos H5-59 508, H5-58 253

Don. 1402; Habich, vol. 2/1, 2603.

Z.M.

III.65, III.66
Valentin Maler
Jihlava ca. 1540–Nürnberg 1603
Commemorative Coin of Emperor Rudolf II Issued for the Imperial Diet
Struck in silver
2.5 cm
Obverse: *RVDOLPHVS II.D.G.ROM.IMP.AVGV.*; bust with spiked crown (*Zackenkrone*), sign. *VM*; reverse: *REX.BO.PALA.SAXO.BRAN.TREVI.COLO.MOGVN:* ; coats of arms of the Electors in each polygonal segment
Prague, Národní muzeum, Numismatic Department, inv. nos H5-58 252 and H5-50 165

Horský, 1209; Habich, vol. 2/1, 2607.

Z.M.

III.66

See cat. no. III.65.

III.67
Valentin Maler
Jihlava ca. 1540–Nürnberg 1603
Apostolic Medal of Rudolf II
Struck in silver
Diam: 3.7 cm
PETR.:ANDR.:IOAN.:IACO.:THOM.:IAC:
M:PHILI.:BART.:MATHE.:SIMO.:IV:TA.:M
ATHI: - Below the names of the apostles:
twelve symbols of the government in-
signia and symbols of the offertory and
Christ's martyrdom. A circular field bears
Christ as ruler and judge holding an olive
branch and bolts of lightning. The four
Evangelists are engraved around the em-
blems; (obverse):

GERM:HVNG:BOHE:POLO:GALL:SCHW:
DENM:SCHO:HISPA:ANGL:PORT:NEAP:
The relevant state coats of arms are depicted beneath the legend. The inner field
contains a standing figure of the Emper-
or personified by Jupiter; beneath him a
double-headed eagle. Sign:
CVM/PRI:CAES: - signed VM. (reverse)
1592
Purchased in an auction of the Lanna collections, Berlin 1911; from the Montenu
collection, no. 650
Prague, Uměleckoprůmyslové muzeum v
Praze, inv. no. 12 189

The symbolism on the obverse side is ori-

ented towards religious themes, the reverse depicts worldly might. The figure of
Christ, the Judge, with an olive branch in
his right hand and lightning bolts in his
left, symbolizes victory over Death. The
figure of Jupiter (?) on the reserve side
holds the symbols of power – the imperial
sceptre and orb. It is not known for certain
why or for whom this medal was engraved.

Wellenheim, II/1, 1844, no. 7022; Fiala
1888, no. 1419; Domanig 1907, no. 812;
Lanna 1911, no. 740.

Z.M.

III.68
Christian Maler
Nürnberg ca.1584–Nürnberg ca.1648
*Medal Commemorating the Congress of the
Electors in Nürnberg*
Struck in silver
3.6 cm
Obverse: *MEM.REV.ET
SERENISS.S.R.I.VII – VIRVN
ELECT.NVREMBERGAE. /
FELICA.CONGRESSORVM Ao MD-
CXI.M.IIX BRI.*; the seven Electors' coats
of arms; reverse: *IVSTITIA.SOPHIA ET
CONCORDIA.*; three allegorical female
figures, sign.*CM*
1611

Prague, Národní muzeum, Numismatic
Department, inv. no. H5-50 171

This medal commemorating the assembly
of Electors in Nürnberg in 1611 provides a
valuable document of this undeniably important event. The Electors would also
have resolved the disputes over Matthias's
assumption of power from the ailing
Rudolf II. The allegory on the reverse side,
depicting justice, wisdom and unity, was
evidently a memento of the assembly of
the most powerful men in the empire.

Z.M.

III.69
*Letter of Archduke Rudolf to his Father Maxi-
milian II from Spain*
Ink on paper, two sheets; watermark:
hand with a star (see Briquet, Les Fil-
igranes, no. 10 719), seal pressed
30.5 × 21 cm
13 September Madrid 1567
Secret family archives
Vienna, Haus- Hof- und Staatsarchiv,
Familienkorespondenz A, Kart. 2, fol. 308-
9.

Between the ages of twelve and nineteen
(1563–71), Emperor Rudolf lived with his
brother Ernst at the Spanish court of King

Philip II. He was to be receive his education from this strictly catholic king. The
nobleman Adam of Ditrichštejn accompanied the archduke to Madrid, as did, after a
short period, the celebrated diplomat Ogi-
er Ghiselin de Busbecq. Their instructor
was Dr Johann Tonner of Trubbach. During their stay in Spain the two brothers
wrote letters regularly of about one or two
pages. Thirty letters were written in Latin
in Rudolf's own hand have remained, except one in German. In the letters he
writes about his studies and everyday
events. He also describes hunting, journeys by horse, fencing and dances. In this
letter he writes that to become proficient

in reading and writing Latin he is reading
the works of Sallust and Horatio. The letter is neat and clear, and in comparison
with earlier letters, his handwriting is now
well-formed.

E.Sp.

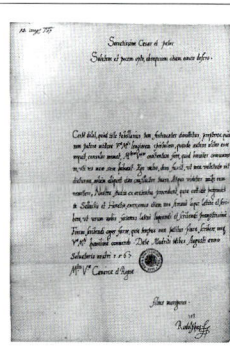

III.70
Hans Stromair
Augsburg 1524/25–Augsburg after 1583
*Glaive of the Bodyguard of Emperor
Rudolf II*
Iron, etched, gilded and blackened
220 cm
1577
Vienna, Kunsthistorisches Museum, Hof-
jagd- und Rüstkammer, inv. no. A 1505

The glaive, a pole weapon with a knife-
shaped blade, was part of the equipment
of the Hartschier corps of bodyguards
who were recruited from the nobility to
serve Emperor Rudolf II. The German

name *Kuse* comes from the French word
for knife, *couteau*. It may have been from
the court in Burgundy that this weapon
was introduced into Austria where it became a standard part of the weaponry of
the Habsburg bodyguards. This glaive has
a knifelike blade of about 50 cm in length
for strike and thrust. At the centre of one
side it has the emblem of the Emperor
Rudolf II, the imperial eagle with an arrow
in its claws and Rudolf's motto, *ADSIT*. On
the other side is the quartered coat of
arms of Hungary and Bohemia below the
monogram surrounded by imperial insignia. The date of this piece would suggest that it was ordered for the swearing of

the oath of allegiance by the nobility from
the lands south of the Enns. It may have
been worn by the captain of the
Hartschiers, Konrad zu Pappenheim.

Augsburg 1980, inv. no. 923; Vienna 1988,
inv. no. 799.

Boeheim 1889, p. 130, Thomas 1969, pp.
64ff.

M.Pf.

III.71
Schulzhuber (manufacture), Hans
Stromeir (decoration)
Herald's Glaive from Rudolf II's Court
Guard
Beaten iron, wood, etching, chasing
Length (including eye) 69.3 cm, maxi-
mum width 9 cm, length of shaft 160 cm
On the front: *HS*; above the eye: *OS*; on
the reverse: *1577*
1577
Bought by the Národní muzeum in 1954
Prague, Národní muzeum, inv. no. 334
925

The glaive preserves the medieval shape of

the fifteenth century. It was used by the
heralds in Rudolf II's court guard. Its
court origin is shown by the decorative 'R'
under the imperial crown between a
sword and a sceptre, an orb and the Hun-
garian-Bohemian crest on the front, and
the Austrian (Babenberg) crest pierced by
an arrow under the imperial eagle on the
reverse side, as well as the rich etched decoration of ribbons and tendrils.

Koci-Vondruska 1989, no. 442.

E.Šn.

III.72
Halberd of the Bodyguard of Rudolf II
Light, polished iron with engraved and
etched decoration
On the obverse, the imperial
monogram:*R II*, with the imperial crown,
sword and sceptre; on the reverse: *1577*
1577
Prague, Muzeum Hlavniho Mešta Prahy,
inv. no. 12875

Halberd used by personal guards. Finely
carved, arched axe blade with rhomboid
opening. The flat of the halberd is decorated with floral and geometric ornamentation.

L.Č.

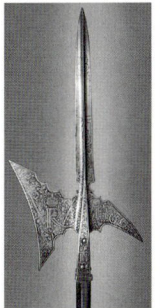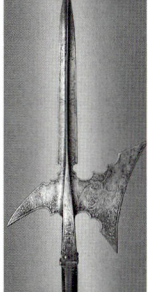

III.73
Hans Stromair
Augsburg 1524/25–Augsburg after 1583
Halberd of the Guard of Rudolf II, Etched
and Blackenend Iron
220 cm
1577
Vienna, Kaiserliches Zeughaus
Vienna, Kunsthistorisches Museum, Hof-
jagd- und Rüstkammer, inv. no. A 1555

An essential part of ceremonial life at
court was the Emperor's magnificently
equipped bodyguard, the so-called *Tra-
bante*. They were responsible for the Emperor's personal safety and on court occa-

sions surrounded him in substantial numbers to underline his superiority and immense power. The basic halberd with its
spike and fluke was still in use in the sixteenth century. The spike became very
narrow after the mid-sixteenth century.
The axe blade became smaller and the cutting edge became concave. Now the halberd was better suited to the thrust than
the blow. The axe blade withered away and
the half-moon cutting edge lost much of
its effectiveness. However, as the halberd
forfeited its fatal potential so it gained in
decorative value. The halberdiers' pole
weapons were etched with coats of arms
and their lord's mark, in this case Rudolf

II's monogram with the imperial insignia
round about it. The initials *HS* on the
weapon itself allow the etchings to be
identified as the work of the Augsburg
painter Hans Stromair.

Vienna 1960 (Bürgerliches Zeughaus I),
cat. no. 115; Vienna 1988, cat. no. 800.

Thomas 1969, pp. 64ff.

M.Pf.

III.74
Hu(e)ber Joachim, Imperial Councillor
and Master of the Treasury
Book of the Court Disbursement Office
Manuscript, bound in brown leather with
rich blind stamping, 34 and 331 leaves
Volume: 44 × 32 × 9 cm; block: 43 × 30 7 cm
Author and title, fol. 1r: *Mein Joachim
Huebers Röm(isch): Kay(serlicher):
May(es)t(ä)t: Rath und Hoffzalmeisters
Geldt Raithung über alle meine Empfäng vnd
Außgaben in Ihrer Maytt: Hoffzablmeister-
ambt von aimen ganzen Jahr, Alß vom Er-
sten Januarij biß endlezten Tag Decembris
diß ausgebnuden Sechzehenhundert vnd Ne-
unden Jahr*; fol. 331r: *Actum den 20 Maij:*

Ao. 1616
Treasury, under the Lord Chamberlain
Vienna, Finanz- und Hofkammerarchiv,
inv. no. HZB 60 (1609)

The archive of the *Hofkammer* in Vienna
holds court treasury records from the
years 1542 to 1714. These were kept by the
master of the treasury, who customarily
gave his own name at the beginning of the
entries, which were kept year by year. The
records show the income and expenditure
for the court and for the main organs of
the state. Thus these volumes are a valuable source of information not only about
political and economic developments but

also about cultural matters.

Sapper 1982, pp. 404–55.

G.M.

III.75
Unknown Copyist
*The Session of the Great Land Court in
Prague in the Presence of Rudolf II in 1593*
Oil on canvas, in a new frame
Inner frame 105.3 × 130.3 cm, outer frame
106.6 × 131.6 cm
No inscription by the artist; in the inscrip-
tion band in front of the Emperor: *TITO
SAV NEYWIZSSY PANII AUýZEDNICZY
A SAUDCZOWE, ZEMSSTII, KRALE
CZESKEHO, AN/N/O. D/OMI/NI
MDLXXXXIII.*; there are cartouches by
most of the officials and judiciary indicat-
ing their names and functions
Baroque copy of an original made after

1594
Unknown, in the Národní muzeum collection before 1862
Prague, Národní muzeum, inv. no. H2–22
555

The Supreme Provincial Court met regularly three times a year in the old Diet Hall
next to Vladislav Hall in Prague Castle. Until the Battle of the White Mountain, foreigners were not allowed to be judges and
the official language of the Diet was Czech
until 1627. The painting has two objec-
tives, which it was not possible to reconcile without certain compromises. It
shows the general scheme of the session

agenda, and records a specific session of
1593, attended by Rudolf II at which the
trial was taking place of two people accused of trying to incite resistance to
Rudolf.

Prague 1990.

Sršeň 1975, pp. 167–72.

L.Sr.

III.76
Seal of the Land Court
Copy, bronze
7.5 × 0.3 × 12 cm
Late nineteenth century
Prague, Státní ústřední archív v Praze,
fond Sbírka typářů, inv. no. 340

The bronze sealing-stick, known as a citational or summons sealing-stick, was used by the Provincial High Court from the thirteenth century onwards to confirm documents issued, and the red wax imprint on parchment served as the official certification of the chamberlain when delivering a summons. It was entrusted into the keeping of the deputy copyist. The handle consists of a hollow bronze jug in the form of a single-tailed lion with a thick mane. The earliest surviving imprint dates from the year 1284. After the Battle of the White Mountain, the Wenceslas seal was used instead of the provincial seal, for which the Estates had to give consent to the Diet. The sealing-stick remained in the keeping of the Provincial High Court even after its re-organization, but the original is not on record.

Jireček 1874; Demuth 1843, 308; Šarek 1938, 32; Beneč 1868, 484–85; Beránek 1989, pp. 71–77.

P.B.

III.77
Liber Memorabilis of the Clerks of the Land Court in Bohemia (depicted 1605)
Manuscript, leather binding, painting on parchment
36.5 × 45 cm (opened manuscript 36.5 × 90 cm)
Late eighteenth century
Prague, Státní ústřední archiv v Praze; fond Archiv českých stavů, inv. no. 7

The manuscript contains twenty-two sheets of parchment with paintings of the coats of arms and the names and titles of the clerks of the Provincial High Court from the sixteenth to the eighteenth century. The white leather binding is decorated with linear friezes and mountings with clasps. A lion in a decorative field is depicted in brown paint in the centre of the front and back panels. The depictions of the coats of arms were executed by an anonymous painter in watercolours combined with white paint and vivid gold paint. The manuscript was commissioned in the late eighteenth century, during the reorganization of the Provincial High Court for the Estates. According to the wording of the introductory Latin quotation, it was meant to serve as a symbol of the prestige which the clerks of the Provincial High Court enjoyed. In 1870, the manuscript was transferred from the Provincial High Court to the Archive of the Czech Lands, where it was filed under various names.

Burdová 1981, 207–26.

P.B.

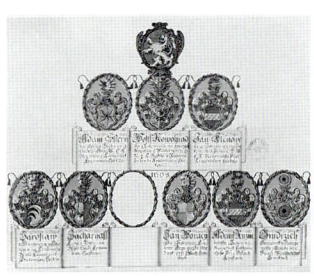

III.78
The Estates of the Kingdom of Bohemia Permit 5 Groschen to be Collected from the Houses of their Subjects over a Period of 3 Years for the Building of Prague Castle. The Collection Is also to Be Made on the King's Estates. The Royal Cities Promise that Instead of this Collection they Will Pay for the Same Purpose over a Period of Three Years a Quarter of the Border Tax in the Amount of 3,125 (kopa) Bohemian Groschen
Original, paper, printed, Czech, bound, 26 fols, paper binding from mid-nineteenth century
15 × 19 cm
18 November–14 December 1583

Prague, Státní ústřední archív v Praze, Assembly articles section, inv. no. 20

Taxes and collections were permitted by the Land Assembly at the request of the ruler, who used them to finance wars, coronations and weddings. Before the Battle of the White Mountain in 1620, the Assembly was attended by lords, knights and representatives of royal cities. It was chaired by the ruler or, in his absence, by the highest-ranking burgrave.

Gindely 1868, pp. 89–167; Janaček-Hledékov 1989, p. 111 nn.; Maly-Sivék 1988, p. 120 nn.; Janaček 1987, p. 203 nn.

Be.

III.79
Aegidius Sadeler
Antwerp 1570–Prague 1629
Anselmus Boetius de Boodt, Physician to Rudolf II
Engraving
22.1 × 11.9 cm
Dedication: HANC EFFIGIEM ... SCVLPSIT ET DEDICAVIT AEGIDIUS SADELER S[UAE] C[AESAREAE] M[AIESTATIS] SCULPTOR; inscription: ANSELMUS BOETIVS DE BOODT BRVGENSIS BELGA I.V.L. RVDOLPHI II. ROMAN[ORUM] IMPERATORIS CVBICULARIVS MEDICVS; slogan at the foot of the medallion: VNO SVMES STABILE; motto above: OBSTANDO DELEMVS; title inscription combining both mottos: OBSTANDO, SORTIS ...SVMES STABILE VNO
Prague, Národní galerie v Praze, Grafická sbírka, inv. no. R 7339

Having studied law and medicine, Anselmus de Boodt (1550–1632) went to live in Bohemia in 1583. His first position was with Wilhelm von Rosenberg. In 1604, de Boodt was appointed personal physician to Emperor Rudolf in Prague. In 1609, he published *Gemmarum et lapidum historia*, the first 'scientific' attempt at establishing a systematic mineralogy. The study describes and classifies around 600 stones, most of which de Boodt was able to observe in the collection of the Emperor in their natural state. He was also interested in botany and in 1603 edited the third part of the famous *Symbola divina et humana*. After the death of Rudolf II, de Boodt returned to his native land.

Essen and Vienna 1988, cat. no. 12, p. 101.

Hollstein 21; De Hoop Scheffer 1980, no. 278; Trunz 1986, ill. 9.

H.H.

III.80
Lucas Kilian
Augsburg 1579–Augsburg 1637
Count Heinrich Julius of Brunswick
Engraving
19.7 × 12.2 cm
Below the medallion: S[uae] C[aesareae] M[aiestatis] pict[or] Ioa[nes] ab Ach ad viun(m) depinxit; lower right: Lucas Kilia(n) Aug(ustaneus) F[ecit]; inscription: HENRICVS IVLIVS D[EI] G[RATIA] POSTVLAT[US] EPISCOPVS HALBERSTADENS[IS], DVX BRVNSVICE(N)S[IS] et LVNEBVRGENSIS; motto on the plinth: PRO PATRIA CONSVMOR (I am consumed by love of my fatherland)
Vienna, Graphische Sammlung Albertina, inv. no. HB 50(2), p. 31, no. 83

Along with Moritz von Hessen, Heinrich Julius, Duke of Braunschweig (1564–1613), was regarded as a scholar amongst German nobles. As a young man, he was the first rector of the university in Helmstedt, and later he became the postulate bishop of Halberstadt. In 1587, he took over the regency in Brunswick and turned Gröningen, his residence, into a much-admired centre for science and the arts. Heinrich Julius spent much time during 1602 and 1604 at the court in Prague and was almost constantly there after 1607. As the leader of the Privy Council, he was the driving force behind imperial politics between 1607 and 1611. Like the Emperor, he encouraged and collected around himself leading artists, scholars and men of letters.

Essen and Vienna 1988, cat. no. 17, p. 104.

Knight 1948; Lietzmann 1993.

H.H.

III.81
Adam of Dietrichstein, Imperial Ambassador to Spain and Royal Steward
Engraving
16.1 × 11.6 cm
At foot of the medallion: *Adam Her von Dietrichstain Kaysers Max/imiliani II. Rath, Cammerer, und Gesandter / in Spanien, und Kaysers Rudolphi II. obri[ster] Hofmaister und geh[eimer] Rath*; on the setting: the figure 7.
Early seventeenth century
Prague, Národní galerie v Praze, Grafická sbírka, inv. no. R 20 799

From 1547 until his death, Adam von Diet-

richstein (1527–1590) was continuously employed in a series of important positions in the Emperor's service. He enjoyed particular influence as principle tutor and educator to the archdukes Rudolf and Ernst during their stay at the court of King Philipp II in Spain between 1564 and 1571. After Maximilian II was elected emperor, Dietrichstein was called as principle tutor to Vienna; he continued to occupy this position under Rudolf. As an intelligent man of noble birth, Dietrichstein was trusted implicitly by Emperor Maximilian II, despite the fact that he never made a secret of his strict Catholicism and loyalty to the pope. Dietrichstein spent the last years

of his life on the estates at Nikolsburg (Mikulov) given to him by Maximilian II, devoting his time to the pursuit of his scientific and spiritual interests.

Essen and Vienna 1988, cat. no. 34, p. 112.

H.H.

III.82
Domenicus Custos
Antwerp 1550/60–Augsburg 1612
Zacharias Geizkofler, Imperial Treasurer
Engraving
19.2 × 13 cm
Below: *S[uae] C[aesareae] M[aiestatis] pictor Ioa[nnes] ab Ach ad vivu(m) pinxit a[nn]o M.DC.*; dedication by Dominicus Custos: *Eidem Generos[is simo] ... D[e]D[ic]at Aug[ustae] Vind[elicorum]*; inscription: *GENEROSO ET NOBILISS[IMO] VIRO D[OMI]N[O] ZACHARIAE GEIZCOFLERO DE GAILENBACH etc., EQV[ITI] AVRA[TO], IMP[ERATORIS] RVDOL[PHI] II. A[ULI-*

CO] CONSIL[ARIO], SVM[M]O PER HUNGAR[IAM] ET AVSTR[IAM] ANNONAE PRAE[SIDI], S[ACRI] R[OMANI] IMP[ERII] THESAVRAR[IO]; motto above: *VINCIT TANDEM VERITAS* (Truth always wins)
1600
Prague, Národní galerie v Praze, Grafická sbírka, inv. no. R 181 017

In 1585 Zacharias Geizkofler (1560–1617) went to serve Archduke Ferdinand of Tyrol. He proved to be a skilled diplomat, particularly in the negotiations regarding Habsburg claims to the Polish throne, and was rewarded by Emperor

Rudolf II, who made him an adviser and in 1589 conferred upon him the office of *Reichspfennigmeister*. In 1600, he was granted the title 'von Reiffenegg, von und zu Gailenbach' and made a knight of the empire.

Essen and Vienna 1988, cat. no. 33, p. 111.

Peltzer 1911/12, ill. 44; Müller 1938; Vocelka 1985, p. 79.

H.H.

III.83
Anonymous
Johann Count Khevenhüller, Imperial Ambassador in Spain
Engraving
19.7 × 12.2 cm
At the foot of the medallion: *Hanns Kheuenhüller Zu Aichelberg, Freyherr Graff Zu Franckenbürg*
Prague, Národní galerie v Praze, Grafická sbírka, inv. no. Clementinum 8 746

Count Johann Khevenhüller (1538–1606) was active as a diplomat in the service of the emperors Ferdinand I, Maximilian II and Rudolf II. He spent almost 33 years at

the Spanish court and after the death of Adam von Dietrichstein took on the role of imperial ambassador. His extensive correspondence provides much information on his activities at the court of Philipp II. In recognition of his faithful and successful services, in 1586 Khevenhüller received the Order of the Golden Fleece from Rudolf II. In 1592, Khevenhüller travelled to Prague in order to arrange the marriage of Rudolf II with the Spanish Infanta Isabella. Negotiations had been going on for years, but Rudolf's indecision eventually put paid to the project. In 1593, the Emperor elevated Johann Khevenhüller to the hereditary imperial nobility.

Czerwenka 1867.

H.H. and J.Ha.

III.84
Anonymous
Georg Ludwig of Leuchtenberg, Imperial Privy Councillor
Copper engraving
17.9 × 14.0 cm
Inscription: *GEORGE LUDOVICUS D. G. IANTGRAVIUS LEUCHTENBERG COMES HALS. DOM. PEREIMBDT ...*; below the illustration: *LUVCHTENBERGAm tenes qui nunc LVDOVICE GEORGI, Princeps arva, tuo est talis in ore vigor.*
Prague, Národní galerie v Praze, Grafická sbírka, inv. no. Clementinum - 9151

George Ludvig, Landgrave of Leuchtenberg, is known primarily as a confidant and adviser to Rudolf II. From 1594 he was President of the imperial court Council. His influence in court grew especially after 1608 when, as Lord Chamberlain, he headed the court offices. Between 1611 and 1612, when he was Chairman of the Secret Council, he and Arnoöt Mollart had a significant influence on Emperor Rudolf II's decision-making. During the occupation of the Lesser Town (Malá Strana) and Hradčany by the armies of the aristocracy in 1611 both politicians represented the Emperor at all the important political meetings with the Czech nobility, the pa-

pal nunciate and with the Hungarian King Matthias. Leuchtenberg mostly promoted a position of compromise during the political crisis. It is likely that he accepted the title of Chamberlain in the court of King Matthias while Emperor Rudolf was still alive.

J.Ha.

III.85
Anonymous
Zdeněk Vojtěch Popel of Lobkovic, Chancellor of the Kingdom of Bohemia
Copper engraving
15.1 × 12.4 cm
Stencko Popel Furst von Lobkowitz Rom: Kay: May: Rath vnd Gros Cantzler in Böheimb auch Ritter des gulden Fluss...
After 1621
Prague, Národní galerie v Praze, Grafická sbírka, inv. no. R-90 318

Zdeněk Vojtěch Popel of Lobkovic (1568–1628), member of the Bohemian nobility, studied at the Jesuit Academy and at

Prague University. After completing the 'gentleman's' tour of Europe he entered the Emperor's service in 1591 as court councillor. A great change in his life came when he was named as Supreme Chancellor of the Kingdom of Bohemia in 1599. BY virtue of his education and his abilities he was able to turn the Bohemian regal chancellery into an office defending the interests of the Catholics, and his uncompromising stand in matters of belief quickly brought him to the head of the Catholic aristocratic clique. In 1609 he refused to add his signature to an imperial charter with which Rudolf II guaranteed religious freedom in the Czech lands. He

continued in the chancellor's office until his death in 1628, with a short interval during the uprising of the Czech nobility (1618–20) when he was deprived of his position and expelled from the country. For his services to Catholicism he was awarded the Order of the Golden Fleece in 1621, and in 1623 he was raised to the rank of imperial prince for his fidelity to the house of Habsburg.

Essen and Vienna 1988, cat. no. 20.

Stloukal 1931; Kutiöová 1995.

J.Ha.

III.86
Dominecus Custos
Antwerp 1550/60–Augsburg 1612
Dr Johannes Pistorius, Imperial Confessor
Engraving
15.4 × 11.4 cm
Lower left: *Do[mi]inic[us] [?] Cust[os] scalp[sit]*; inscription: *EFFIGIES REVER[ENDISSIMI] NOBILIS[SIMI] ET CLARISS[IMI] VIRI D[OMINI] IO[AN-NI]IS PISTORII NIDANI, S[ANCTIS] S[IMAE] THEOLOGIAE D[OCTORIS], PROTONOT[ARII] AP[OSTO]LICI AET[ATIS] SVAE XLIX A[NN]O VERO 1594*; the legend *Vis scire ... corde, scriptionibus* alludes to the importance of Pisto-

rius's theological writings in the debates between Catholics and Lutherans and Calvinists
1594
Prague, Národní galerie v Praze, Grafická sbírka, inv. no. R 133 369

Johannes Pistorius (1546–1608) studied theology, medicine and jurisprudence. His adoption of Calvinism in favour of Lutheranism in 1575 engendered just as heated debate as his subsequent conversion to Catholicism in 1588. As the result of detailed studies of Jewish mysticism and secret doctrines, in 1587 Pistorius published in Basel the first volume of a

planned comprehensive compendium of cabbalistic texts. However, this first volume was to remain the only one, owing to its author's summons to the imperial court in Prague. As Emperor Rudolf's father confessor, Pistorius succeeded in somewhat alleviating the severe bouts of depression that afflicted the Emperor around 1600.

Essen and Vienna 1988, cat. no. 29, p. 109.

Vocelka 1985, 81.

H.H.

III.87
Pieter II de Jode (after Aegidius Sadeler)
Antwerp 1606–England(?) after 1674
Aegidius Sadeler, Court Copper Engraver
Copper engraving
16.5 × 11.6 cm
Bottom left: *AEgidius Sadeler pinxit.*; centre: *Pet.de Iode sculpsit.*; right: *Io. Meyssens excudit.*
By 1661
Prague, Národní galerie v Praze, Grafická sbírka, inv. no. R 49 494

Impressions of this print appear in editions of Cornelis de Bie's *Het Gulden Cabinet van de edel vry Schilderconst* (1661),

along with portraits of Aegidius' cousins, Jan and Raphael Sadeler. De Bie's book contains celebratory poems about artists from the Southern Netherlands. A descendent of an Antwerp family of engravers, De Jode illustrated many books of this genre, beginning with Antonie van Dyck's *Iconographia* (1636). *Het Gulden Cabinet*, which is distinctive in this genre for its literary content, is also an important document of Aegidius Sadeler's early reputation and activity as a painter. The print itself records a now lost self-portrait by Sadeler. He is shown here in middle age, one hand holding a triple chain with a medallion portrait of Rudolf II. Such

chains were tokens of great honour among artists at the Rudolfine court. Sadeler's prominent hand is a symbol of artistic virtuosity, which is often found in Renaissance self-portraits.

Cornelis de Bie 1661; Limouze 1990.

D.L.

III.88
Aegidius Sadeler
Antwerp 1570–Prague 1629
Georg Schrotl von Schrotenstain, Imperial Court Chancellor
Copper engraving
At lower left and lower right:
Sac.Caes.Mtis Sculptor Egidius Sadeler./ officio et obseruantiae ad viuum expressit et D.D.
1610
Prague, Národní galerie v Praze, Grafická sbírka, inv. no. R 7341 (Hollstein 325)

A comparison between the preparatory drawing and this print reveals that the

portrait of the Hungarian councillor Schrotl grew in complexity as it progressed. Sadeler's drawing follows a traditional rectangular composition of a bust portrait behind a stone plinth. He translated this formula into the oval type that had become one of his trademarks, adding *putti*, garlands, the sitter's coat of arms, and a frame in the then-fashionable auricular style. His skill at designing ornament is revealed by the humourous references in the frame to human torsos and to the features and moustache of the sitter. While the ornamental surround was engraved in a manner typical of Sadeler's first years in Prague, the hatching in the

treatment of the sitter's costume is first found in portraits from 1610 and 1611. A reflection of Sadeler's interest in diverse burin techniques, this may also reveal that he had assistants engrave the frames of some portraits.

Limouze 1990.

D.L.

III.89
? Dominecus Custos
Fl. Antwerp after 1550–died Augsburg 1612
Otto Henry of Schwarzenburg, Marshal of the Imperial Court
Copper engraving
23.0 × 15.6 cm
OTT HAINRICHUS COMES A SCHWARZENBERG LIB. BARO IN HOHENIANSPERG RANDECK...; *Cernis OTHERNRICVM Schwarzenbergo stemmate cretum: Qui Boio placuit per bene gesta Duci.*
? After 1588
Prague, Národní galerie v Praze, Grafická

sbírka, inv. no. Clementinum – 6.551

Otto Henry of Schwarzenburg (1535–1590), son of Prince Cristof of Schwarzenburg, was the founder of the younger branch of the Bavarian Schwarzenburgs. From 1571 he was adviser to Philip II, Margrave of Baden, who was still a minor, and Governor in Baden, where the recatholicization of the country was carried out under his leadership. In 1576 he was named court marshall and adviser to Emperor Rudolf II. As Commissar he defended the Emperor's interests at the Imperial Congress of 1579 which was summoned after the declaration of the Utrecht Union

in the northern Netherlands. In 1588 he inherited the Schwarzenburg and Hohenlandsburg family estates. He was known as a patron of the sciences and arts and as a collector. The inscription below the illustration, *Tális OTH. HENRICIÖ hunc Ducibus. PETRVS*, celebrates his virtues and merits.

J.Ha.

III.90
Jan Muller (after Hans von Aachen)
Amsterdam 1571–1628
Bartholomeus Spranger, Court Painter
Copper engraving
26.7 × 18.7 cm
BARTHOLOMAEVS SPRANGER S. CAES: M. PICTOR CELEBERRIMVS; (in the cartouche) *D. D. Ioannes ab Ach S. Caes. Mtis Pictor. Ao 1597*; (below) *In perpetuam amici memorians Joan. Mullerus...*
1597
Prague, Národní galerie v Praze, Graficka sbírka, R 206 256

An interesting document about the origin

of this print has been preserved at the Rijksprentenkabinet in Amsterdam (inv. no. A 10 486). According to Aachen's model, possibly a drawing, Muller carved a cursory effort at Aachen's portrait, printed it, cut it into an oval and then stuck it to a different piece of paper. Since he himself was an outstanding draughtsman, he drew the corresponding allegorical framework in ink. Only then did the sheet serve as the actual model for the engraving.

Essen and Vienna 1988, cat. no. 300.

E.F.

III.91
Domenicus Custos (?)
Antwerp 1550/60–Augsburg 1612
Paul Sixt, Count Trautson, Marshal of the Imperial Court
Engraving
16 × 12.5 cm
IILLVSTRISS[IMUS] AC GENEROSISS[IMUS] D[OMINUS] PAVLVS SIXTVS TRAVTHSON LIBER BARO IN SPRECHENSTEI[N], SCHROVENSI[EIN] ET FALCKENSI[EIN] etc. S[UAE] C[AESAREAE] M[AIESTATIS] INTIIM[U]s CONSIL[IARIUS], CAMERAR[IUS] et SVP[REMUS] MARESCALC[US]; the leg-

end *TRAUTSONIAE PAVLLUS ... bonore viget* praises the subject's noble origins and achievements
Prague, Národní galerie v Praze, Grafická sbírka, inv. no. DR 5786

Paulus Sixtus von Trautson (1550–1621) was in imperial service as 'Hofrat' after 1576 and between 1582 and 1594 as the president of the Imperial Court. Soon he established himself as one of Emperor Rudolf II's most trusted confidants. Trautson, a master of extravagant display, occupied the position of chief lord chamberlain and between 1589 and 1600 had immense influence on the Emperor's po-

litical decisions. Favoured by Rudolf II, Sixtus was elevated to the hereditary nobility in 1598. However, in 1600 Trautson was stripped of all his duties and privileges at court because of the Emperor's suspicions that Trautson might be part of a Spanish plot to force him to abdicate because of his ill health. Although Trautson then established a position of trust with Archduke Matthias during the feud between the two brothers, he never really entered the political limelight again.

Essen and Vienna 1988, cat. no. 24, p. 107.

H.H.

III.92
Wolfgang Kilian (?)
Augsburg 10 May 1581–Augsburg 1662
Adam of Waldstein Privy Councillor and Land Steward in Bohemia, Imperial Equerry
Bronze engraving, paper
Frame 12 × 14.8 cm; engraving 18 × 26 cm
Ca. 1640–50
Wallenstein library in Doksy
Prague, Central State Archives, collection of Wallenstein engravings, inv. no. 129

Adam of Wallenstein the younger (died 24 August 1638) was a civil servant. From 1603 he was a counsellor in the office which administered the king of Bohemia's

property and from 1608 to 1611 he was the Bohemian chief justice. On the accession of Emperor Matthias to the throne in 1611, Adam of Wallenstein was appointed head steward of the royal household, a post which he held until 1619. At the court of Rudolf II he had been imperial chamberlain and for a short time he had also fulfilled the important function of chief equerry. After Rudolf II abdicated in 1611 he appointed him his privy counsellor. During the stormy years of Rudolf's rule, Adam of Wallenstein was a tolerant Catholic, and he enjoyed the favour of both Rudolf and his brother Matthias. On 3 March 1611, as spokesman for the Bo-

hemian Estates, he made a speech welcoming Matthias on his victorious arrival in Prague. Adam of Wallenstein spent the period of the Estates' revolt in exile in Bautzen.

Toman 1947, pp. 481–82; Janáček 1987; Prague 1993 (manuscript, first sect.).

L.G.

III.93
Aegidius Sadeler
Antwerp 1570–Prague 1629
Matthaeus Wacker von Wackenfels, Scholar and Diplomat, Imperial Court Councillor
Engraving
24.5 × 16.2 cm
ILLVSTR[ISSI]mus ET GENEROS[ISSI]mus D[OMINUS] D[OMI]N[U]S MATHEVS WACKERVS A WACKENFELS, SAC[RAE] CAES[AREAE] MAI[ESTA]tis CONSILIARIVS AVLICVS; below, a small medallion with two dogs and the Greek motto: *Epiméleia kai áskes[is]* (Care and Practice)
Prague, Národní galerie v Praze, Grafická

sbírka, inv. no. R 155 120

Johann Matthäus Wacker von Wackenfels (1550–1619) settled in Breslau, where he became a councillor and representative of the Emperor in the Silesian parliament. In 1592, he converted to Catholicism and was instrumental in the election of a new bishop of Breslau acceptable to Rudolf II. In 1594, he was rewarded for this and other successes by being elevated to the imperial nobility and honoured with the title 'von Wackenfels'. After 1599, Wacker lived permanently in Prague, where he was in friendly contact with Kepler and many other scholars at the court of the Emperor.

He served Rudolf as a councillor in the imperial court after 1597, and as late as 1611 he was still personal adviser to Rudolf and took notes during negotiations between the Emperor and Matthias. After Rudolf's death, Matthias took Wacker into his own service.

Essen and Vienna 1988, cat. no. 30, pp. 109–10.

Lindner 1867, pp. 319–51.

H.H.

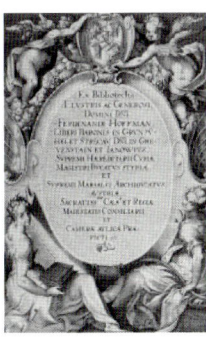

III.94
Lukas Kilian after Matthäus Gundelach
Augsburg 1578–Augsburg 1637
Ex Libris of Ferdinand Hoffmann of Grünbüchl, President of the Court Chamber
Copper engraving
25.5 × 16.8 cm (cut)
Bottom centre *M: Göndelach. f*:; bottom right *L: Kilian A. sia*
Early seventeenth century (before 1607)
Prague, private collection

To mark the volumes in his library, Ferdinand Hoffmann von Grünbüchl (1540–1607) used an oval heraldic *supralibros* and

four types of engraved ex libris (this one being biggest in format). Ex librises allowed a newly acquired book to be marked without the need for rebinding. We find parallel occurences of both kinds of ownership markings in the Czech lands at the end of the sixteenth century only with a few leading bibliophiles, including Hoffmann and his fellow pupil from Italian studies Petr Vok z Rožmberk.

Hollstein b, XVII, no. 777, p. 162 Thieme-Becker, vol. 20, 1927, p. 298; Scapinelli 1927–28, pp. 13–14 (two types of ex-libris by Kilian); Lifka 1980, pp. 75, 78; Hamanová 1959, pp. 123, 212; Obrátil 1932, pp.

107–10.

R.V.

III.95
Binding with an Ex Libris of F. Hoffmann of Grünbüchel
Dark green parchment, gilded
21.5 × 17 × 4.5 cm
Prague (?), end of the sixteenth century
Before 1607 in the library of F. Hoffmann, later possessed by Ferdinand of Ditrichštejn; after 1669 in the library of the Jesuit College in Brno
Olomouc, Státní vědecká knihovna, inv. no. 29 898

President of the court chamber Ferdinand Hoffmann of Grunbuchl and Střechov, lord of Gravenstein and Janovitz (1540–

1607), was one of the foremost book collectors in Rudolf II's court. His library numbered over four thousand volumes of mainly religious and historical literature. This binding shows the dominant type of composition, with a heraldic supralibros positioned conspicuously in the centre of the field, which is framed by triple lines and a narrow cylinder and S-shaped ornamentation. The elegant composition is the work of the court workshops of Prague; the fact that these bookbinders worked for Hoffmann was first proved by I. Schunke. Also characteristic of this type of bookbinding is the choice of green parchment, an allusion to the owner's ti-

tle, 'von Grünbüchl'.

Schunke 1942, pp. 75–80; Hamanová 1959, pp. 123, 211–12, ill. 93; Lifka 1980, pp. 75, 78.

R.V.

III.96
Severin Brachmann
Medal of *Jan of Valdštejn*
1565
Prague, National Museum, Numismatic
Department, inv. no. H5-150 936

Jan of Valdštejn (Wallenstein), son of
Vilém of Lomnice was the supreme judge
during the period 1554-1570 and Lord
High Chamberlain of the Czech Kingdom
in the years 1570-1576. This distinguished
representative of old Utraquism died in
1576. The medal, dated 1565, bears an inscription on the reverse side stating
Valdštejn's rank as Lord High Chamber-

lain, although he was not appointed to
this office until 1570. Nohejlová explains
this discrepancy maintaining that the
medal must have been struck at a later
date.

Habich 1934, II/2, no. 3271; Nohejlová
1938, pp. 83-85; Nohejlová 1963, p. 62/48.

Z.M.

III.97
Unknown Artist
Jetton of *Vratislav of Pernštejn*
After 1566
Prague, Národní muzeum, Numismatic
Department, inv. no. H5-55 643

Vratislav of Pernštejn (1530-1582), a member of an ancient Bohemian and Moravian
noble family, held high offices during the
reigns of Maxmilián II and Rudolf II and
finally became supreme chancellor of the
Czech Kingdom (1566-1582). He was honoured as a knight of the Order of the Gold-
en Fleece in 1556. This jetton, probably
struck in the Prague mint, was issued to

commmemorate his appointment to the office of supreme chancellor.

MN 1852-70, no. 306; Don.1889, no. 3649
AE.

Z.M.

III.98
Jan of Liboslavě
Died 1557
Medal *Wolf of Vřesovice, Supreme Scribe of
the Kingdom of Bohemia and President
of the Bohemian Chamber*
Struck in silver
2.7 cm
Obverse: WOLF Z WRZESOWIC:ANA
DAVBRAW:HORZE; bust; reverse: NEI-
WISSI:PISARZ:KRALO:OZIE:PRESIDE:N
T KRA:GE:KOMORI:CZIESK.; coat of
arms
Beginning of the second half of the six-
teenth century
Prague, Národní Muzeum, Numismatic

Department, inv. no. H5-150 947

Jan of Liboslavœ, a goldsmith in Kutná
Hora, was a distinguished die engraver,
chiefly of jettons and the first thalers from
Kutná Hora. To him is also attributed the
medal of Wolf of Vřesovice, whose character typologically corresponds to the technique he used. The line of the lords of
Vřesovice originally came from a family of
Moravian freemen, which expanded during the fifteenth century and was elevated
to the nobility. Wolf (Vlk) of Vřesovice was
sheriff of Prague Castle from 1542 and
during the years 1547-69 he was the highest scribe and president of the Bohemian

Chamber. He led the commission for the
reform of the constitution from 1557. He
died on 21 March 1569 and was buried in
the castle chapel in Teplice.

MN 1852-70, no. 655, pp. 698-99; Katz
1929, p. 114, Nohejlová 1952, pp. 55, no. 61.

Z.M.

III.99
Severin Brachman
Medal of *Heřman Varlich of Bubno*
1572
Prague, Národní muzeum, Numismatic
Department, inv. no. H5-115 049

The precise birthdate of Heřman Varlich
of Bubno, famous for his valour and military successes in the Turkish wars during
the reign of Rudolf II, cannot be stated
with accuracy. He died, however, in 1602.
The medal, set in a frame decorated with
green, blue and white enamel, somewhat
differs from other medals designed by
Brachmann. The portrait of this sover-

eign military figure is highlighted by additional engraving and distinctive chasing
work.

Habich 1934, II/2; Nohejlová 1938, pp. 95-
97; Nohejlová 1963, p. 63/52.

Z.M.

III.100
Severin Brachmann
Medal of *Bohuslav Felix Hasištejn*
1575
Prague, Národní muzeum, Numismatic
Department, inv. no. H5-150 943

Bohuslav Felix Hasištejn of Lobkovic
(1517-1583) was a member of the Czech
nobility and an educated man who held a
number of important offices during his
lifetime. In 1544 he was associate judge at
the chamber court, in 1547 supreme sheriff in Jáchymov, in 1570 he was appointed
supreme judge and, six years later, the
Lord High Chamberlain of the Czech

Kingdom. His participated in the negotiations of the Czech Confession in 1575
where, as a Protestant, he was a leading
member of the Czech estates. This portrait
medal also dates from this period.

Habich 1934, II/2, no. 3294; Nohejlová
1938, p. 109, no. 31; Nohejlová 1963, p. 64,
no. 57; Polívka 1991, pp. 26-27, no. 7.

Z.M.

III.101
Valentin Maler
Medal of *Jiří Pichl of Pichlperk*
Ca. 1576
Prague, Národní muzeum, Numismatic
Department, inv. no. H5-51 443

Jiří Pichl of Pichlperk (ca. 1545) was a
representative of the line of aldermen
from northern Bohemia. He was an official in the imperial office, he received
his coat-of-arms in 1579 which was embellished in 1582. He became the highest court postmaster around the year
1598. He died on 1 January 1611.

MN 1852-70, p. 407; Habich.

Z.M.

III.102
Severin Brachmann
Medal of *Albrecht Kapoun of Svojkov*
1579
Prague, Národní muzeum, Numismatic
Department, inv. no. H5-150 944

Albrecht Kapoun of Svojkov (August
1523) was appointed burgrave of Prague
Castle in 1557 and subsequently burgrave
of the Hradec region in 1570. He held this
office until his death in 1591. He took his
seat in the state assembly from 1556 and
often represented the estates during critical negotiations. Although childless, he
supported the education of the younger

members of his line abroad "...since a
knowledge of letters and language signifies great enhancement" as Nohejlová noted in a text taken from the land records.

1934, II/2, no. 3300; Nohejlová 1938, pp.
110-112; Nohejlová 1963, p. 64/58.

Z.M.

III.103
Severin Brachmann
Medal of *Adam Huber of Meziříčí*
? 1580
Prague, Národní muzeum, Numismatic
Department, inv. no. H5-51 226

Adam Huber Meziříčí of Rysenpach was
born in 1546 in Meziříčí nad Oslavou
and studied philosophy and medicine in
Wittenberg. He taught regularly at the
Prague university from 1567 and was appointed its rector in 1612. He was an advocate of communion in both kinds. His
renown earned him a position as personal physician to Rudolf II and he also

wrote a number of specialist publications. He died on 23 June 1613.

Habich 1934, II/2, no. 3301; Nohejlová
1938, pp. 112-114; Nohejlová 1963, p.
64/59.

Z.M.

III.104
Zacharias Kempf
Medal of *Florian Griesbeck*
1582
Prague, Národní muzeum, Numismatic
Department, inv. no. H5-150 957

Florian Griespek of Griesbach and Na
Kačerov (1509-1588) was the founder of
the Czech branch of this family of knights.
He arrived in Bohemia with Ferdinand I
and soon became royal secretary, later royal counsel and finally counsel for the
Czech chamber. He owned a vast estate in
western Bohemia and was known for his
specialist library, art collections and ar-

moury. He died at his castle in Nelahozeves. A large number of medals and
jettons appeared during his lifetime covering the period from the 1530s to the 1580s.
The medal by Jáchymov die cutter Zacharias Kempf is distinctive for its characteristic stylization.

MN 1852-70, p. 85, no. 106; Katz 1932, no.
520; Nohejlová 1963, p. 66/72.

Z.M.

III.105
Unknown Artist
Medal of *Vilém of Rožmberk*
After 1585
Prague, Národní muzeum, Numismatic
Department, inv. no. H5-59 422

Vilém of Rožmberk (1535–92), a member
of an ancient Czech noble line, was appointed Lord High Chamberlain in 1560
and highest burgrave of the Czech Kingdom in 1570. He served under Maximilian
II and Rudolf II and was often chosen to
represent his sovereign during important
negotiations abroad. He supported mining, science and the arts, and also con-

struction development on his own estates.
He received the Order of the Golden
Fleece from the Spanish King in 1585.
This medal commemorates the occasion.

MN 1852-70, no. 351.

Z.M.

III.106
Antonio Abondio
Riva 1538–Vienna 1591
Medal of *Leonard IV of Harrach*
Struck in bronze
3.8 × 3.2 cm (oval)
Obverse: *LEONAR:AB HARRACH:B:AVR:VELLE:EQVES D: FERDI:MAXIMIL:II:ET RVDOL:II:IMP:INTIMVS CONS:*; bust with high collar and Order of the Golden Fleece; reverse: *ET EIVSDEM MAXIM-ILI:II:SVP:AVIAE / ET CVBIS:PRAE-FECTVS AETATIS SVAE / LXXI*; the Order of the Golden Fleece draped over a richly decorative coat of arms

After 1585
Prague, Národní muzeum, Numismatic Department, inv. no. H5-51 148

As a high official at the court of Maxmil-ián and Rudolf II, Leonard IV of Harrach (1514–1590), along with the Emperor him-self, received the Order of the Golden Fleece in 1585, at the age of seventy-one. The order was conferred at the instigation of the administrator of the orders, King Philip II of Spain. Compare the Harrach medal by Antonio Abondio in the *Kun-stkammer* section.

Don. 1888, no. 3391; MN 1852–70; Habich,

vol. 2/2, no. 3390.

Z.M.

III.107
? Thomas Stor
Second half of the sixteenth century–1611
Mdeal of *Bernhard Elsaaser, Court Gun-smith of Rudolf II*
Cast in silver
4.8 cm
Obverse: *SENHARDTIN.ELSASSER.AE-TA:39.1593*; bust, bearded face, high collar; reverse: coat of arms with richly ornamen-tal plume
1593
Prague, Národní muzeum, Numismatic Department, inv. no. H5-59 416

Thomas Stor, who worked in Nürnberg

and possibly also Jáchymov, was a mem-ber of the goldsmiths' guild. Habich pre-sents a group of medals he attributes to Stor, which share a characteristic design on their reverse sides featuring various coats of arms. This medal of Elsasser be-longs in this group. Bernhard Elsasser (1554–), a burgher from Prague Old Town, was court gunsmith to Rudolf II during the years 1578–1612.

MN 1852–70, p. 47 / XXXIV; Habich 1932, vol. 2/1, no. 2770.

Z.M.

III.108
Jiří Starší the Elder
Died 1599
Medal of *Jan Erasmus of Švamberk, Master of the Mint of the Kingdom of Bohemia*
Struck in silver
2.4 cm
Obverse: *HANS.ASMVS - H.V.SVHWAN*; bust; reverse: *BERG OBERSTER - MVNCMEI.K.B.*; coat of arms
1560s
Prague, Národní muzeum, Numismatic Department, inv. no. H5-51 530

Jiří Starší the Elder, active from 1557 to 1599, worked as an engraver of dies chiefly

for the mint in Kutná Hora, but also for Prague and Jáchymov. He is particularly known for his designs of a number of jet-tons for private and sovereign commis-sions. The medal of Jan of ävamberk, the highest master of the mint of the Czech kingdom during the years 1561–66, is clos-er from a formal point of view to the jet-tons of Jiří Starší the Elder. The portrait is skilfully crafted and betrays the hand of an experienced engraver. The coat of arms on the reverse side typologically corresponds to works designed by Jiří Starší the Elder.

MN 1852–70, no. 518; Katz pp. 4–5; Nohe-jlová 1963, p. 65, no. 62.

Z.M.

III.109
Unknown Artist
Medal of *Petr Vok of Rožmberk*
1611
Prague, Národní muzeum, Numismatic Department, inv. no. H5-150 998

Petr Vok of Rožmberk (1539-1611), the younger brother of Vilém, was appointed royal chamberlain in 1560 and in 1594 he became sheriff of the Czech army fighting against the Turks. He was an advocate of the Czech Confession. He died as the last of his line and was buried in Vyšší Brod. The medal, whose original was struck and not cast, appeared poshumously and was

commissioned in honour of Petr Vok by Jan Jiří of Švamberk, chamberlain during the years 1609-11. After the Rožmberk family died out, the Švamberks inherited part of their estate. The medal depicts a swan, the bird featuring on the Švamberk coat-of-arms, with the Rožmberk rose on its breast.

MN 1852–70, no. 369, pp. 480-82; Don 1888, no. 3720; Nohejlová 1963, p. 74, no. 26.

Z.M.

III.110
Zellerfeld workshop for Master of the Mint Heinrich Deckeler
First half of the seventeenth century
The Broad Five-thaler Coin of *Heinrich Julius, Count of Braunschweig*
Struck in silver
8.1 cm
Obverse: *HENRICUS.JULIUS.DEI.GRA.P OSTULAT.EPISCOPUS.HALBERSTAD.D UX. BRUNSVICA.ET.LUNE.*; portrait of the Duke on horseback, castle of Wolfen-büttel depicted in the background; re-verse: *HONESTUM.PRO - 5 PATRIA.1609*; coat of arms
1609

Prague, Národní muzeum, Numismatic Department, inv. no. H5-115 961

Jindřich Julius (1564-Prague 1613), duke of Braunschweig-Wolfenbüttel and Bish-op of Halberstadt, was an educated advo-cate and poet. He came to Prague in 1607 and worked at the court where he gained the trust of Emperor Rudolf II. He became a mediator in negotiations between the sovereign and Matthias, particularly con-cerning the Protestant Estates.

Fiala 1806, no. 698.

Z.M.

III.111
Liber Memorabilis of Caspar Raif, Court Cup-Bearer
1606–26
Paper, leather binding, engravings and watercolours
Closed 13 cm × 15.5 cm; open 13 cm × 33.5 cm
Decorated with a coat of arms, name and the year *1610* (fol. b)
Prague
Prague, Národní Muzeum, Archive, shelf mark B. no. 11 (H3-B 11)

The album of the royal junior cup-bearer, Kašpar Reiff, contains entries by various courtiers. Besides the entries and accompanying coats of arms, there are a large number of decorative engravings, some directly bound between the album's pages, and others which have been cut out of Theodore de Bra's book *Emblematika saecularia* (Frankfurt, 1596) and pasted in. A series of miniatures taken from another manuscript has also been pasted in. Particularly worth mentioning is the depiction of Renaissance cavaliers and a lady in Renaissance dress, a miniature landscape (pasted in) and a pen-and-wash drawing of Bacchus sitting on a wine cask. A picture of servants carrying various articles of service ware, accompanied by an entry by the royal silver-cleaner Hans Lehner, brings to life the day-to-day routine of the court.

B. Hertlová 1975, pp. 117–46.

J.Kr.

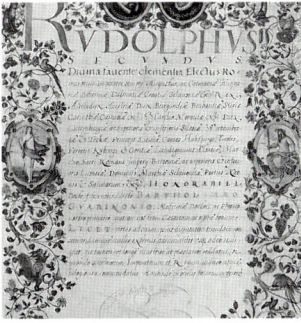

III.112
Anonymous, Central Europe
Heraldic charter of Bartholomeus Guarinoni
Gouache on parchment
49 × 29.5
1590s
Munich antiquarian G. Hess before 1898, purchased for the Museum of Decorative Arts in Brno in 1898.
Brno, Moravian Gallery in Brno–Museum of Decorative Arts, inv. no. 9192

The first page of the parchment charter contains a Latin text within an ornate floral border with allegorical figures of humans and animals and two miniature portraits of Emperors Maximilian II and Rudolf II. Bartholomeus Guarinoni (1534-1616) was personal physician to Rudolf II; he lived in Prague until 1604. The average quality of the artwork on this document suggests it was executed by an unknown painter and scribe who worked in the imperial court office.

Holešovský 1988, nos. 43, 33–36.

K.H.

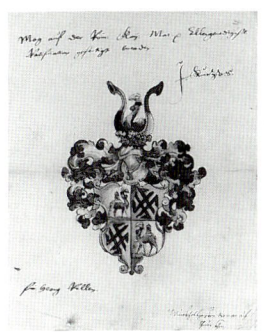

III.113
Unknown Artist
The Improvement of the Coat-of-Arms of Jiří Roll, Court Clock-Maker
Ink and watercolours on paper
20.5 × 32.5 cm
28 February 1589
Reichskanzlei
Vienna, Österreichisches Staatsarchiv/Allgemeines Verwaltungsarchiv, inv. no. Adelsarchiv, RA Roll, 28.II.1589

After an apprenticeship in Augsburg, Georg Roll (ca. 1546–1592) set himself up as a horologist without being a master. This was tolerated because he was mainly dealing in clocks. He turned his attention to a problem that loomed large at the time, namely determining how an astral body revolves around its own axis. He was interested in mechanisms that could show the daily revolution of the celestial globe, the paths of the sun and the moon, the months of the year, saints' days and movable religious feasts. Roll travelled several times to the court of Rudolf II, who, as a passionate collector, acquired several clocks and celestial globes from him. Clocks of this kind were favoured also among imperial emissaries as gifts to take to the Sublime Porte in Turkey, hence perhaps the camel carrying a clock on Roll's coat of arms. The second unusual heraldic item (lower right) most probably represents the tools of his trade. Above the illustration of the coat of arms is a stamp signed by the deputy imperial chancellor, Jakob Kurtz von Senftenau, confirming imperial approval of the design.

Bobinger 1969.

Gbl.

III.114
Unknown Artist
The Granting of a Coat-of-Arms to Christof May, Court Baker
Ink and watercolours on paper
32 × 21 cm
3 May 1593
Reichskanzlei
Vienna, Österreichisches Staatsarchiv/Allgemeines Verwaltungsarchiv, inv. no. Adelsarchiv, RA May, 3.V.1593

On 3 May 1593 the Emperor awarded to Christoph May, imperial baker, and his brothers Georg and Lorenz the coat of arms previously used by their late brother, Sebastian. Sebastian May, who had himself been imperial baker for many years, had received the coat of arms in 1574 from Emperor Maximilian II, but had died without male heirs. On receipt of the coat of arms Christoph May applied for it to be improved, but this was rejected, as can be seen from the correction to the illustration on his application ('Neu', lower left). Ennoblement did eventually come to him, but not until 1604.

Johann Siebmachers Wappenbuch.

Gbl.

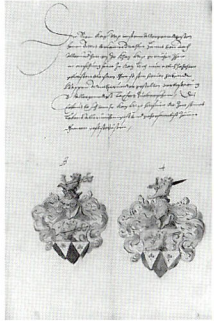

III.115
Unknown Artist
The Improvement of the Coat-of-Arms of Hans von Aachen, Court Painter
Ink and watercolours on paper
32.5 × 21 cm
1 November 1594
Reichskanzlei
Vienna, Österreichisches Staatsarchiv/Allgemeines Verwaltungsarchiv, inv. no. Adelsarchiv, RA Aach, 1.XI.1594

Johann von Aach (Aachen), history, genre and portrait painter (Cologne 1552–Prague 1615) bore the name of his father's place of birth. Emperor Rudolf II greatly admired Hans von Aachen's work and was keen to attract him into service at the court in Prague: hence von Aachen's appointment as court painter in 1592 and his ennoblement and the improvement to his coat of arms on 1 November 1594. He was ennobled for 'die angenemen, getreuen, gehorsamen und willige dienst, so er uns nun etliche jahr hero als unser camer maller vleissig, unverdrossenlich erzaiget und bewaist und hiefüro zu thuen sich underthänigst erpeut' (the pleasant, faithful, obedient and willing service which he has given to us for some years as court painter diligently and tirelessly and which he has humbly promised to give in the future). Von Aachen's application for a new coat of arms (B) adds elements reserved for the nobility alone to his former bourgeois coat of arms (A). In addition, he changed the sword carried by the lion into a caduceus, probably as an allusion to his work as an artist, for at the time Mercury was seen as the protector of artists and scholars.

Peltzer 1911/12, pp. 59–82.

Gbl.

III.116
Unknown Artist
The Granting of a Coat-of-Arm to Johan Plumberger, Court Embroiderer
Ink and watercolours on paper
31.5 × 20.5 cm
29 January 1609
Reichskanzlei
Vienna, Österreichisches Staatsarchiv/Allgemeines Verwaltungsarchiv, inv. no. Adelsarchiv, RA Plumberger, 29.I. 1609

According to the text of this application, Plumberger had supplied beadwork to the court for 16 years. For the last 6 of these he had received a fixed salary from the court.

Thus on 29 January 1609 he was awarded a diploma plus the coat of arms, along with his deed of enfeoffment. Although this was in fact a bourgeois coat of arms and he was not being ennobled, he was nevertheless being awarded some of the rights of the lower nobility.

Gbl.

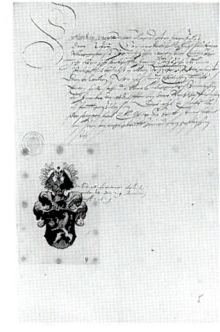

III.117
Oath of Allegiance of Painter Bartholomeus Spranger
Original, parchment, in Czech, on parchment strip to which is attached seal of red wax in a small bowl of natural wax
41.5 × 24.5 – 7.5 cm
2 November 1593
Prague, Státní ústřední archiv, Declarations of Allegiance, inv. no. 151

Bartolomeus Spranger (1546–1611), resident artist in the imperial court of Rudolf II,
was one of the most significant artists of the Mannerist period. Although he evidently lived in Prague from 1580, married there, and later owned several houses in the Lesser Town (Malá Strana), he was accepted among the inhabitants of the Czech kingdom relatively late, as his Declaration of Allegiance testifies. This legal act was the precondition for adding estates bought in Bohemia to the Land Archives.

J.Ha.

III.118
Oath of Allegiance of Karl of Lichtenstein
Original, parchment, Czech; stamp of the issuer in red wax in a bowl of natural wax attached to parchment strip
42.5 × 26–6.5 cm
29 April 1602
Prague, Státní ústřední archiv, inv. no. RkZ 199

A Pledge to the Land is an undertaking by the issuer, for himself and on behalf of his descendants, to recognize the Czech king as his sole sovereign, to satisfy all his obligations, like other members of his Estate in the kingdom, and to abide by the provincial constitution. From the sixteenth century onwards the issuing of such pledges was one of the conditions of admittance to the Estate of Czech gentlemen or knights for nobles whose fathers had not had such standing. In 1591 the 22-year-old Karl von Liechtenstein acquired the estates of the Lutheran branch of the old noble family of Liechtenstein. From 1600 to 1603 and again from 1606 to 1607 he was chairman of the secret council in the Prague court. In the conflict between Rudolf II and his brother Archduke Matthias he considerably aided Matthias, the future emperor. In 1608 he was accorded the title of knight. He took part personally in the military crusade against the Elector Palatine Frederick, the 'Winter King', in 1620. By the time of his death on 12 February 1627, Karl von Liechtenstein had amassed a considerable fortune, but he was tainted with the suspicion that he was responsible for the so-called 'long coin' affair and the subsequent confiscations, which damaged him financially.

Falke 1877; Klecanda 1931, pp. 456–67; Klecanda 1928, pp. 1–125; Janáček 1978; Stloukal 1912, pp. 21–37, 153–69, 389–434.

P.S.

III.119
Oath of Allegiance of Filip Lang of Langenfels, Emperor's Chamberlain
Original, parchment, Czech; issuer's seal of red wax in a bowl of natural wax, attached to golden string
15 March 1607
Prague, Státní ústřední archiv, inv. no. 226

In 1606 Philipp Lang, chamberlain to the Emperor and one of the most influential men at court, and his sons Ferdinand and Andreas were made Czech knights by the provincial Diet. Lang, who issued a Pledge to the Land (for discussion of these pledges, see cat. no.) on 15 March 1607, came from a Tyrolean Jewish family; he converted to Catholicism and having served Archduke Ferdinand of Tyrol was appointed private chamberlain to Emperor Rudolf II, whose confidence he gained to a remarkable degree. On 24 March 1601 he acquired the title of Langenfeld. After his predecessor, Jeroným Makovský, was imprisoned, he attained a position of such influence that he effectively spoke for the Emperor, whose favour he exploited, accepting bribes or gifts to feed his insatiable desire for riches. In June 1607, however, he lost the Emperor's confidence and was thrown into prison, accused, among other things, of plundering the imperial collections. A provincial decision of 5 November 1609 expelled Lang's sons from the knightly estate and he died in prison not long afterwards.

Hurter 1851; Janáček, 1987.

P.S.

III.120
Oath of Allegiance of Octaviano Roboreta, Physician of Rudolf II
Original, in Czech, on parchment strip to which is attached the publisher's seal of red wax in a small bowl of natural wax
27.5 × 17.5 – 3.5 cm
22 April 1608
Prague, Central State Archive, Declarations of Allegiance, inv. no. 232

Oktavian Roboreta was resident physician to the imperial court from 1600 and personal physician to Rudolf II, whom he looked after until his death on 20 January 1612. According to surviving documents, he also supervised a post mortem carried out on the Emperor's body that same day, and gave the main causes of death as gangrene, damaged lungs, liver and spleen, and dropsy (Janáček 1987, p. 503). Oktavian Roboreta lived inside the precincts of Prague Castle, where he had a house not far from the Emperor's palace. In 1605 he was accepted by the Czech Land Assembly as a knight of the Bohemian kingdom and in 1608 he deposited in the Land Archives his *Declaration of Allegiance*, in which he promised to keep the laws and customs of the Bohemian kingdom.

Klecanda 1928, p. 117.

J.Ha.

III.121
The Bohemian Chancery issues a report in the form of a decree on the arrest of Jeronym Makovský of Makov, Rudolf II's Valet, including the indictment, confession and verdict of loss of honour, life and property
Original, paper, Czech, given the seal of Emperor Rudolf II under a paper covering
21 × 32 cm
23 October 1603
Prague, Státní ústřední archiv, inv. no. M 51/1, fols 30-37

During the reign of Ferdinand I, a fourth type of document, the decree, was added to the three kinds already issued by the royal office – deeds, letters patent and rescripts. Decrees contained various recommendations, orders or information. Jeroným Makovský of Makov, originally chamberlain to Petr Vok of Rožmberk, became chamberlain to Emperor Rudolf II, who in 1598 promoted him to the status of Golden Knight. In 1603 he was arrested, accused of trying to gain the post of under-chamberlain of the royal cities, of obtaining a book about fiefs and of using it to try and secure fiefs and estates that had become free. He was further accused of taking bribes and of divulging secrets from the Emperor's milieu, of keeping instruments of sorcery in a chest, of consorting with witches and living with the wife of another man. He confessed, was sentenced and imprisoned for years in royal castles.

Sedlaek, p. 297; Světek 1883, pp. 231–39; Stloukal 1931, pp. 78–80; Janaček 1987, p. 393.

Be.

III.122
Aegidius Sadeler and Adriaen de Vries
Antwerp 1570–Prague 1629; Den Haag ca. 1560–Prague 1626
Emperor Rudolf II with a Laurel Wreath on Horseback / Equestrian Portrait of Rudolf II
Copper engraving on paper
Plate 49.6 × 38.6 cm; in all 52.1 × 40.1 cm
Adrianus de Vries Hagiensis Jnvent, Marco Sadeler excudit, Eg: Sadeler Sculp:.
Ca. 1603
Donated by Uměleckoprůmyslové Muzeum v Praze in 1965
Prague, Národní muzeum, inv. no. H2-109227

The sculptor Adriaen de Vries settled permanently in Prague only after 1601. For Rudolf II he made three bronze busts and a portrait on horseback. The heroizing portrayals of Rudolf were rhetorical exaggerations: none of the Viennese Habsburgs ever showed much zest for warfare, and martial élan was least in evidence in Rudolf II, who never went near actual battle until he was forty. At the time of the wars against the Turks, everybody was notified in advance of the Emperor's absence from the field. After 1598 Rudolf II began to take pleasure in allegorical paintings depicting heroism in war and his own supposed accomplishments, and he enjoyed posing in his cuirass before court portraitists as the heroic victor over the Turks. The perception of Rudolf II as a proud and stately emperor derived from old sculptures of Charles IV by Leoni. Sadeler made the copper engraving from an original by Adriaen de Vries, probably in connection with work on portraits of the Emperor.

Essen 1988, p. 176.

V.P.

III.123
Anonymous
The Turkish Sultan Ahmed I
Copper engraving
10.0 × 10.5 cm
ACHMET IEZIGER TÜRKISCHER SULTAN
After 1603
Prague, Národní galerie v Praze, inv. no. Clementinum – 11706

Sultan Ahmed I ruled Turkey from 1604 to 1617, during which time years of military conflict contributed to the internal collapse of the Turkish Empire and its foreign policy. Immediately after ascending to the Turkish throne on the death of Mehmed III, Ahmed I commenced peace negotiations with ambassadors of the Emperor Rudolf II. Despite initial disagreements the negotiations ended with a peace agreement in 1666 in the town of Šitva-Torok. Under this agreement Rudolf II made a single payment in compensation to Turkey of 200,000 ducats; this concession absolved him from the annual obligation to pay 50,000 ducats, to which Ferdinand I had been bound since the peace of 1547. In 1612 Ahmed I concluded a peace agreement with Persia under the terms of which he had to withdraw from Georgia, Tabriz and Baghdad.

J.Ha.

III.124
Lukas Kilian
Augsburg 1579–Augsburg 1637
Portrait Medallion of the Imperal General Georg Count Basta
Engraving
18.5 × 12.6 cm
Inscribed lower right: *S[uae] C[aesareae] M[aiestatis] Pictor / Ioan[nes] ab Ach pinx[it]*; dedication by Dominicus Custos (lower right): *GEORGIUS BASTA D[OMI]N[U]S IN SVLT, EQVES AVRAT[US], SAC[RAE] CAES[AREAE] MA[IEST]ATis AC CATHOLICI REGIS HISPANIAE CANSIL[IARIUS] BELLICVS NEC NON PARTIVM REGNI*

HVNG[ARIAE] SVPERIORIS GENERAL[IS] PROCAPITAN[EUS]
Publ. Dominicus Custos
Prague, Národní galerie v Praze, inv. no. R 41 214

Count Georg Basta (1550–1606 or 1612?) began his military career in the army of Alessandro Farnese in the Netherlands. In 1598/99, Basta entered the service of Emperor Rudolf II and played a decisive role as a commander in the bloodshed during the next years in Transylvania and Hungary. In 1602, Basta gained the upper hand in the eventful campaign against the Transylvanian prince Sigismund Báthory. The legendary cruelty of his soldiers was no doubt one reason why, after his departure, the Transylvanian aristocracy proclaimed Stephan Bocskay their new prince. Basta's attempts to subdue Transylvania once again proved fruitless. Despite considerable successes in the years 1604-5 as the commander in chief of the imperial troops in Hungary, he had to recognize the superiority of the Turkish forces.

Essen 1988, cat. no. 10, p. 100.

Peltzer 1911/12, ill. 42; Vocelka 1985, p. 79.

H.H.

III.125
Aegidius Sadeler
Antwerp 1570–Prague 1629
Báthory Sigismund, Prince of Transylvania
Copper engraving
323 × 125 cm
SERENISSIMUS SIGISMUNDUS BATHORI TRANSULVANIAE ... PRINCEPS ...; signature: *Eg. Sadeler fecit*; dating: *Serenissimo principio Sac. Caes. Mai. Sculptor Egidius Sadeler dedicat MDCVII*
1607

Portait of Sigismund Báthory (1572–1613) assumed power in Sedmihrad in 1581. In 1595 he married Maria Kristina, daughter of the Archduke Karl of Styria. The same year he signed a peace agreement with Rudolf II under whose terms Sedmihrad was to pass to the Emperor in the event of Báthory's death without heir. In 1598 he decided to follow a spiritual path and left Sedmihrad – which was constantly under threat from the Turkish army – in the control of the Emperor's officials. He returned to Sedmihrad twice more after he failed to receive the promised rank of Cardinal in order to take power again. He left the princedom finally in 1602 and settled in Bohemia where he had been promised the vacant estate of Libochovice by the Emperor as well as a regular annual allowance. In 1610 he was accused of dishonest actions against the Emperor and imprisoned. While Rudolf II was still alive Batory was cleared of the allegation. The portrait shows the prince in an oval cartouche, in armour and with the Order of the Golden Fleece.

Essen and Vienna 1988, cat. no. 11.

J.Ha.

III.126
Domenicus Custos
Antwerp after 1550–Augsburg 1612
Stefan Báthory, King of Poland
Copper engraving
169 × 123 cm
After 1576
Prague, Národní galerie v Praze, inv. no.
Clementinum – 6326

Stefan Báthory (1533–1586), Prince of Sedmihrad, King of Poland, was an outstanding statesman and military commander.
He succeeded to the Polish throne in May
1576. The same year he gave up the Sedmihrad throne to his brother Kristof (or

Christopher). During his reign Báthory attempted to strengthen the power of the
monarch in Poland. Báthory's reign saw
the flowering of humanism in Poland and
reform of the judicial and financial systems. His expansionist foreign policy was
mainly directed towards the east. Three
campaigns against Russia (1578–81) ended in 1582 with the absolute victory of the
Polish–Lithuanian armies and the
armistice of Jama Zapolsk, at which
Poland retained the occupied lands of
Polock and Vžlič. After Stefan Báthory 's
death in 1586 the struggle for the Polish
throne began again.

J.Ha.

III.127
Aegidius Sadeler
Antwerp 1570–Prague 1629
*Ollibeag Cuchein Persian Ambassador in
Prague*
Engraving
19.5 × 13.2 cm
Inscribed and dated below: S[uae]
Caes[areae] M[aiesta]tis sculptor Aegidius
Sadeler ad viuum delineauit Pragae 1601; in-
scription: CVCHEINOLLIBEAG IN-
CLYTVS DOMINVS PERSA SOCIVS
LEGATONIS MAGNI SOPHI REGIS
PERSARVM; confirmation of imperial ap-
proval at the foot of the medallion: cum
priuil[egio] S[uae] Cae[sareae] M[aiesta]tis;

name and title of the sitter in Arabic below
1601
Prague, Národní galerie v Praze, Grafická
sbírka, inv. no. R 20 771

In 1600, for the first time, a Persian emissary arrived in Prague, and this led to
diplomatic contacts in the early seventeenth century between Emperor Rudolf
II and Shah Abbas I of Persia, also known
as Abbas the Great (1587–1629). The Persian mission was led by the Englishman
Sir Anthony Sherley. The delegation
stayed at the court in Prague until February 1601. Rudolf II's aim was to establish

an alliance with the Persians against the
Ottoman Empire which would put a stop
to the Turks' lucrative role as middlemen
in the trade in much-sought-after Persian
silks. However, no such treaty was agreed,
neither then nor on subsequent visits by
two further delegations which visited
Prague in 1602 and 1604–5.

Essen 1988, cat. no. 19, p. 105.

Kurz 1966, pp. 462–89; Kurz 1966, ill. 2;
Hollstein, p. 21, De Hoop Scheffer 1980,
no. 314; Vocelka 1985, p. 201.

H.H.

III.128
Aegidius Sadeler
Antwerp 1570–Prague 1629
The Persian Ambassador, Mahdi Quli Bega
Engraving
25.7 × 18.8 cm
Below: S[uae] Caes[areae] M[aiesta]tis
sculptor Aegidius Sadeler ad viuum delin-
eauit. Cum Priuil[egio] S[uae] Cae[sareae]
M[aiesta]tis Anno Pragae 1605; inscription:
MECHTI KVLI BEG ENNVG OGLY IL-
LVSTRIS D[OMINVS] IN PERSIA
LEGATVS REGIS PERSAR[UM] AD
IMP[ERATOREM] ROMAN[UM]; in-
scription in Arabic giving the sitter's
name, title and role

1605
Prague, Národní galerie v Praze, Grafická
sbírka, inv. no. R 155 122

Essen 1988, cat. no. 36, pp. 112, 121.

Hollstein 21; De Hoop Scheffer 1980, no.
275; Vocelka 1985, p. 201.

H.H.

III.129
Anonymous
István Bocskay, Prince of Transylvania
Copper engraving
28.7 × 16.2 cm
Stephanus Botskay
After 1606
Prague, Národní galerie v Praze, inv. no.
Clementinum – 7660

Stefan (or István) Bocskay (1555–1606) assumed the leadership in 1604 of rebels
fighting for religious freedom and against
the restriction of the rights of the nobility
in Hungary. After several successful military actions, in which he managed to occu-

py a large part of Upper Hungary, Bocskay
was proclaimed Prince of Hungary by the
nobility. In the Vienna Peace of 1606,
which Emperor Rudolf II concluded with
Bocskay with the help of the Archduke
Matthias, Bocskay was made a hereditary
Prince of Sedmihrad and religious freedom was guaranteed to the Hungarian
Protestants.

J.Ha.

III.130
Anonymous
Philip II, King of Spain
Seventeenth century
Engraving
16.4 × 12 cm
At foot of the medallion: *Philippus II. dises
Nahamens König / auss Hispanien Ertzher-
zog zu Öster/reich.RR.*
Prague, Narodni galeri v Praze, Grafická
sbírka, inv. no. R 97 718

King Philipp II (1527–1598) was the son of
Emperor Karl V and Isabella of Portugal
and in 1556 succeeded to the throne in
Spain after his father's abdication. His

reign was a high point in Spanish history
during which his country became the
undisputed dominant force in European
power politics. Individual setbacks such as
the loss of the northern provinces in the
Netherlands in 1579–81 and the defeat of
the Spanish Armada in 1588 did not seriously affect Spain's position. Philipp II was
above all aware of his duty to protect
Christianity and felt personally responsible for ensuring the final victory of
Catholicism in the religious struggles of
the time. His intolerance in matters of religion was as characteristic as his own unyielding self-discipline.

Essen 1988, cat. no. 41, p. 123.
Prescott 1856–59; Pfandl 1938.

H.H.

III.131
Anonymous
Isabella (Eugenie Clara), Daughter of Philip II
Copper engraving
19.2 × 12.5 cm
ISABELLA AUSTRIA, PHILIPPI II. REGIS CATHOLICI FILIA HISPANIARUM PRINC. INFANS ...
? After 1599
Prague, Národnié galerie v Praze, inv. no. Clementinum - 6194

Isabella Clara Eugenia (1566–1633), daughter of the Spanish King Philip II and Elisabeth de Valois, was offered in mar-riage, while aged two, to Archduke Rudolf, later Emperor, who at that time was living with his brother Ernst in the Spanish court. Rudolf II, however, never took up the offer of marriage to Isabella Clara, nor indeed of offers of marriage to the daugh-ters of other leading European ruling fam-ilies. The issue of betrothal dragged on until 1592 when the Spanish princess's hand was offered to Rudolf's brother Ernst. On his death in 1595 the problem of betrothal began again, to be resolved with Isabella's marriage to Archduke Albrecht (or Albert, 1559–1621). The couple were named hereditary governors of the Span-ish Netherlands and their court in Brus-sels became a centre of social and cultural contacts, but also the place from which the renewal of the Catholic church in the country was conducted. Both Isabella and her husband Albrecht are mentioned among the donors of artistic objects in Rudolf's *Kunstkammer*.

Vocelka 1976; Janáček 1987.

J.Ha.

III.132
Anonymous
Johann Georg, Margrave of Brandenburg
Copper engraving
19.5 × 14.3 cm
Motto below the illustration: *IVSTE ET CLEMENTER*; below the portrait: *IOANNES GEORGIVS DIVINA CLEMENTIA. MARCH. BRANDENB. S. R. IMP. CAMERARIVS. ET NVNC TEM-PORIS ARCHIGERON ELECTOR, VII ORDIN. DVCENS. DUX BORUSS. ...*
After 1571
Prague, Národní galerie v Praze, Grafická sbírka, inv. no. Clementinum - 7782

Johann Georg, Brandenburg Elector (1525–1598), was the son of the Branden-burg Elector Joachim II and Magdalena of Saxony. The illustration represents the Elector surrounded by military trophies – an uncharacteristic setting, as he was known as a man who preferred family life and managing his own estates and who had a keen interest in alchemy and astrol-ogy.

J.Ha.

III.133
Anonymous
Juan of Austria, General
Copper engraving
19.1 × 14.1 cm
IOANN DE AUSTRIA
? After 1571
Prague, Národní galerie v Praze, Grafická sbírka, inv. no. Clementinum - 8495

Johann (Juan) of Austria (1547–1578) was the illegitimate son of Karl V and Barbara of Blomberg, and half-brother to the Spanish King Philip II. This outstanding military commander was especially cele-brated for the Battle of Lepant (7 October 1571) where the combined navies of the Holy League (Spain, Venice, Florence and the Pope) under his command defeated the Turks. The image of Johann of Austria in the dress and emblems of the Order of Maltese Knights is probably linked to this victory. After the victory, however, the League fell apart and the occupied lands were gradually lost. In 1573 Johann of Aus-tria gained Tunis, but the following year Turkey occupied it again and kept both it and Cyprus. In 1576 he was named Gover-nor of the Spanish Netherlands, where an uprising had broken out before his arrival. Its immediate result was the Pacification of Ghent, by which the nobility of the north and the south Netherlands agreed to fight together against Spain. After his arrival in Brussels in 1576 Ferdinand passed the Perpetual Edict in which he confirmed the laws of the Netherlands, recognized William of Orange as the rep-resentative of the northern Netherlands and guaranteed the protection of non-Catholic religions. The following year, 1577, he broke the peace and defeated the army of William of Orange at the battle of Gembloux.

J.Ha.

III.134
Anonymous
Christian I, Elector of Saxony
Copper engraving
205 × 148 cm
CHRISTIANVS I. IX. DVX SAXONIAE ELECTOR.; below the portrait: *Cui mater-nus auus dat rex sua nomina Danus. Condi-tor hoc Saxo Caesaris ore fuit.*
After 1586
Prague
Prague, Národní galerie v Praze, Grafická sbírka, inv. no. Clementinum - 12.125

During the short rule of Christian I, Elec-tor of Saxony between 1586 and 1591, a radical change in the course of Saxon pol-itics took place in the Saxon princedom, which had traditionally been oriented against the Calvinist Palatinate and thus had supported the Emperor's position in the Empire. The political events moving towards a settlement with Calvinism cul-minated in the meeting of the representa-tives of Saxony and the Palatinate, togeth-er with the French King Henry IV in 1591 in Torgava. Here the possibility was raised of creating a defensive confederation against the Catholic-oriented party in the Empire and against Emperor Rudolf II. The danger from this party for the Emper-or was warded off by the unexpected death of the Saxon Elector. His successor Chris-tian II returned to the original direction of Saxon politics in supporting the Emperor and opposing Calvinism.

J.Ha.

III.135
Domenicus Custos
Antwerp 1550/60–Augsburg 1612
The Turkish Commander Süleiman Pasha
Engraving
15.1 × 11.8 cm
Partly dated: *CAPT[U]S A CAESAREANIS DIE XVII. MENS[IS] AVG[USTAE]* (Süleiman, Pasha of Buda, was taken pri-sioner by imperial troops on 17 August (?) 1599); title: *SOLIMANVS BASCHA VON OFEN*
Prague, Národní galerie v Praze, Grafická sbírka, inv. no. Clementinum 6 730

The capture of the highest representative of Constantinople in Hungary on 17 Au-gust 1599 was a triumph for the Emperor at the time of the Turkish Wars. The Pasha was sent to Vienna as a 'present' to Arch-duke Matthias by Nikolaus Pálffy II, the commander of the fort at Gran.

J.Ha. and H.H.

III.136
Lukas Kilian
Augsburg 1579–Augsburg 1637
The Imperial General Hermann Christoph Rusworm
Engraving
18.2 × 12.6 cm
Inscribed lower left: *L[ukas] K[ilian] F[ecit]*; lower right: *S[UAE] C[AE-SAREAE] M[AIESTATIS] PICTOR IO[ANNES] AB ACH PINXIT*; inscription: *HERMANNVS CHRISTOPH[ORUS] RVESWORMB S[UAE] CAEES[AREAE] MAI[ESTATIS] CONSIL[IARIUS] BEL-LICVS ET COPIAR[UM] PRAEFECTVS, SER[ENISSIMI] BOIOR[UM] DVCIS*

MILITIAE DVCTOR ET CVBICVL[ARIUS]; the legend *Antiquis dominus ... Boiaricamque, Domos*' praises the subject's heroic deeds in the Turkish wars, the mark of true nobility
Publ. Dominicus Custos
Prague, Národní galerie v Praze, Grafická sbírka, inv. no. R 136 752

Hermann Christoph Rusworm (1565–1605) played a significant part in the 1594-98 imperial victories in the Turkish Wars. Rudolf II admired Rusworm for his personality and soon made him imperial general, but it was these same qualities which inspired hostility on the part of Adolph

von Schwarzenberg and, above all, Arch-duke Matthias. The result was Rusworm's arrest in 1599, although he was later freed. After 1602, he was given overall command of the imperial troops in Hungary. When Francesco Belgiojoso was murdered in 1605 by one of Rusworm's servants, he was again arrested, tried and executed.

Essen 1988, cat. no. 31, p. 110.

Janko 1869; Stauffer 1884; Peltzer 1911-12, ill. 41; Hollstein 17; Zijlma 1976, no. 401; Schwarzenfeld 1979, ill. 22; Vocelka 1985, p. 79.

H.H.

III.137
Aegidius Sadeler
Antwerp 1570–Prague 1629
Guillén de Sanclemente, the Spanish Ambas-sador in Prague
Engraving
18.3 × 12.3 cm
At the foot of the medallion: *S[UAE] C[AESAREAE] M[AIESTA]tis SCVLPT[OR] EG[IDIUS] SADELER FECIT ET DEDICAVIT*; inscription: *D[OMINUS] D[OMINUS] GVILIELM[US] A S[ANC]to CLEMENTE, ORDINIS S[ANC]ti IACOBI DE SPATA EQVES AC COMENDATOR NEC NON CATH[OLI]cae MAIESTATIS A[ULICUS]*

CONS[ILIAR]is EIVSDEMQ[UE] APVD CAES[ARE]am MAIES[TA]tum ORATOR; upper right: *Invenient fata.*; the legend *Qui Celebri ... orbis honores* alludes, as do the attributes to left and right, to the sub-ject's travels and experience of war
Prague, Národní galerie v Praze, Grafická sbírk, inv. no. R 78 000

Sanclemente is portrayed with the shell-shaped sign of the Order of the Knights of St Jacob with the Sword, also known as the Order of Compostela. He spent the years 1581–1608 in Prague as the ambassador of King Philipp II and then of King Philipp III of Spain. Rudolf II appreciated his abil-

ities, and Sanclemente acted as a skilful and successful mediator between King Philip II and the Emperor. Letters from Sanclemente show his realistic attitude to the Protestant question. He died in Prague in 1608.

Essen 1988, cat. no. 42, p. 124.

Trunz 1986, ill. 2.

H.H.

III.138
Lukas Kilian
Augsburg 1579–Augsburg 1637
Adolf Count of Schwarzenberg, Imperial Gen-eral
Engraving
19 × 12.8 cm
Lower left: *S[uae] C[aesareae] M[aiestatis] Pictor Ioan[nes] ab Ach ad Viuu(m) depinxit*; and: *L[ukas] K[ilian] f[ecit]*; inscription: *ILLVSTRISS[IM]o ADOLPHO COMITI AC D[OMI]NO IN SCHWARZENBERG etc. S[UAE] C[AESARAE] M[AIESTA]ti (?) CONSIL[IARIO] AVL[ICO] BELLIC[O], SVM(M)O HUNG[ARICO] BEL[LO] EQVIT[UM] MAGISTRO, VR-*

BAN[ARUM] VIENNAE ET PRAE-SIDIAR[IARUM] IAVARINI COPIAR[UM] DVCI SVP[REM]
Prague, Národní galerie v Praze, Grafická sbírka, inv. no. 54 803

Adolf von Schwarzenberg (1547–1600) first served in the armies of King Philipp II of Spain and King Henry III of France. The Elector of Cologne made von Schwarzen-berg a member of the Privy Council and a general. In 1594 he joined the imperial troops in Hungary. His recapture of Raab proved to be the most significant victory by the imperial army during the 'long' Turkish Wars., which also brought him

fame. Emperor Rudolf II personally knighted him in Prague, gave him lands and money and finally, in 1599, made him a member of the hereditary imperial nobil-ity. On 26 July 1600, von Schwarzenberg was shot whilst attempting to subdue mutinying imperial mercenaries who were trying to hand over the fort of Pápa to the Turkish forces.

Essen 1988, cat. no. 25, pp. 107–8.

Peltzer 1911/12, ill. 39; Hollstein 17; Zijlma 1976, no. 421; Schwarzenfeld 1979, ill. 23.

H.H.

III.139
Anonymous
Sigismund III, King of Poland
Copper engraving
19.7 × 15.0 cm
SERENISS[IM]O AC POTENTISS[IM]O PRINCIPI SIGISMUNDO III. REGI POLONIAE, MAGNO DUCI LITHUANI-AE, RUSSIAE, PRUSSIAE, MASOVIAE, SAMOGICIAE, LIVONIAEQUE ETC. NEC NO SVECORUM, GOTTHOR[UM], VANDALOR[UM]Q[UE] HAEREDI-TARIO REGI DUCIQUE FILANDIAE.
After 1587
Prague
Prague, Národní galerie v Praze, Grafická

sbírka, inv. no. Clementinum – 6681

Zikmund (or Sigismund) III Vasa (1566–1632), son of the Swedish King Jana III Vasa, King of Poland and Sweden, was pro-claimed Polish King in 1587 after the death of Stefan Báthory. The other con-tender for the Polish throne was Archduke Maximilian, brother of Emperor Rudolf II. In the struggle between the two rivals Zik-mund's army was victorious and Maximil-ian was captured (1588). Despite this con-flict Zikmund married the Archduchess Anna (1593) and after her death her sister Konstanze (1605). His rule in Poland can be characterized as a time of trying to

strengthen the position of the Catholic church in the country and of military con-flicts with Sweden, Russia and Turkey. As King of Sweden between 1592 and 1599 he supported the return to Catholicism. The portrait shows Zikmund III as King of Poland with the Order of the Golden Fleece, surrounded by allegories of Reli-gion, Justice, War and Wisdom.

Sieniawski 1874.

J.Ha.

III.140
Aegidius Sadeler
Antwerp 1570–Prague 1629
Michael the Brave
Engraving
23.6 × 15.5 cm
Below: *S[uae] Caes[areae] M[aiesta]tis sculptor Aeg[idius] Sadeler ad viuum deline-auit, et D[ono] D[edit] Pragae MDCI*; inscription: *MICHAEL WAIVODA WALACHIAE TRANSALPINAE VTRAQ[UE] EADEM VIRTVTE AET[ATE] XLIII*; at the foot: *cum priu[i]l[egio] S[uae] Cae[sareae] M[aiesta]tis*, the legend *Tanti facit ... obruens factis* alludes to the sitter's importance in the Turkish Wars and in

Transylvania
1601
Prague, Národní galerie v Praze, Grafická sbírka, inv. no. R 77 955.

Michael the Brave, Prince of Wallachia (a Danube princedom situated near Transyl-vania), created a strong position for him-self by engaging in a shrewd form of poli-tics during the early years of the Turkish Wars. In 1595, the vaivode entered the war on Rudolf II's side together with Sigis-mund Báthory and helped to drive Turkish forces out of Transylvania. When Sigis-mund ceded Transylvania to Rudolf II in 1598, Michael agreed a special contract

with the Emperor and swore an oath of al-legiance to him as his lord and protector. In 1599, Michael entered Transylvania with his army and on the strength of his position as an imperial governor took command of the region. After the decisive defeat at Mirizsló in 1600, he sought refuge in Prague and was murdered by sol-diers of General Basta, a personal enemy.

Essen 1988, cat. no. 38, pp. 121, 122.

Goellner 1943; Michai 1975.

H.H.

III.141
Samuel Suchuduller
Arrival of the Turkish Embassy in Prague
1609
Copper engraving on paper
8.9 × 201.2
Samuel Suchuduller
Bought in 1959
Prague, Národní muzeum, inv. no. H2–
59257

The end of the sixteenth century saw a change in relations between the Habsburg monarchy and the Ottoman Empire. After representatives of the most militant wing of Sinan Pasha came to power the sit-

uation at the borders worsened to the point of open hostilities. Early military defeats forced Rudolf II to change his supreme commander and his deputy. As a result, skilled professional soldiers entered the Habsburg army and enabled it to win some partial victories. Peace talks began in 1606 and dragged on until 1608, when a peace treaty was signed. A copper engraving from the period shows the procession of the Ottoman delegation, which arrived in Prague on 12 October 1609.

V.P.

III.142
Garments of the Elector Johann Georg of Saxony
Coat and trousers: outer material – silver-white stripes with gold brocade; coloured figures, silk and gold fibres; under-stitching: sewn and quilted; linen of natural colour; white taffeta, silk white atlas, partly new, sides: threaded with gold and silver material, dressing cords: with gold fibres; Coat: length of front: 27 cm; length of tails: 11 cm; length of collar: 9.5, 7.5 cm; length of sleeve: 61; trousers: 58, 32, 81
1604
Inventionskammer Kleider 1711, 85 no. 13; Kleiderkammer 1785, 5, no. 6;

Kleiderkammer 1821, 28, no. 29; Kostumzimmer 1838, 213, no. 26
Dresden, Staatliche Kunstsammlungen
Dresden, Rustkammer, inv. no. I 9.

Georg I of Saxony wore these exquisite garments at his wedding with Sibylla Elisabetha von Wurttenberg on 16 September 1604 in Dresden. The bridegroom was very conscious of fashion and had these garments made especially for his wedding night, for which a richly ornate bed was placed in the large hall of the château. He also attended many of the ceremonies of the first day of his marriage celebrations.

Bm

III.143
Valentin Maler
Nürnberg, ca. 1540–1603
Rudolf II – Commemorative Coin of Ten Emperors at the Diet of Regensburg 1594
Struck in silver
3.8 cm
Overse: *DOMO ININVICTI RVDO.ROM.IMP.EX SERENI.AVSTRIA-CA*; five medallions bearing Emperors' portraits: Rudolf I, Albrecht I, Frederick III, Albrecht II and Frederick IV, with an eagle and the year *15–94* in the middle; reverse: *LPHI.II.EI/DEMQ DOM/HON-OREM/NORI.F.V.M./CA.PRIVIL.*; five medallions with the portraits of Maximil-

ian I, Charles V, Ferdinand I, Maximilian II and Rudolf II with crowned letter R in the middle
1594
Prague, Národní muzeum, Numismatic Department, inv. no. H5–59 512

The collection of medals made for Rudolf II to honour the Imperial Diets, also as a tribute to the Electors, originated in the workshop of Valentin Maler (ca. 1540–1603), privileged imperial medal engraver from Nürnberg. His appointment as court medal engraver also gave him the right to design the official monarchical medals, to which group those commemorating the

imperial diets undoubtedly belonged. These medals had a chiefly political function. The Imperial Diet was a legislative body within the Roman–German empire, and a forum of discussion by an assembly of religious and lay Estates. The body of Electors had its specific role – namely the exclusive right to elect the Holy Roman Emperor.

Don. 1400; Wurzbach, vol. 2, 8037.

Z.M.

III.144
Medals of *The Conquest of Raab*
Struck in silver
2.7 × 2.7 cm
Second half of the sixteenth century
Obverse: R with crown on top – legend *29.M – ARCI / IAVRINVM / ERIDITVR VIVIT / VIRTVTE RV / DOLPH / I*; reverse: Christ with the Apostles in front of a closed gate; bottom edge: *FAX / V*
1598
Prague, Národní muzeum, Numismatic Department, inv. no. H5–58 243

After a quarter of a century of peace with the Turks secured by Emperor Maximilian

II in 1568, the Turkish army began to threaten the Habsburg empire once more in 1593. Grand Duke Matthias was appointed supreme commander of the imperial army in Hungary, but he was unable to devise an effective military strategy. After various battles the Turks concentrated their efforts on laying siege to the fortress at Györ, the commander of which surrendered on 28 September 1594. It took several years before Emperor Rudolf II acquired the services of experienced commanders – in particular, Adolf Schwarzenberg – who would be able to return the fortress to the Christians. Schwarzenberg, along with other commanders, launched a sudden

atttack on the fortress and regained it on 29 March 1598 after fierce fighting. A number of medals and jettons were struck to celebrate this conquest. On the reverse side this particular medal (*klippe*) bears a symbolic portrayal of Christ and his apostles in front of closed gates. This represents the actual conquest of the fortress, where a petard was used to blow open the gates.

Wellenheim, vol. 2/1, no. 6955; Montenuovo, no. 661; Janáček, pp. 320–27.

Z.M.

III.145, III.146
Unknown Artist
Medal of *Martin Schlumberger*
1592
Prague, Národní muzeum, Numismatic Department, inv. no. H5-51 527,
H5-59 224

The ancestors of Martin Schlumberger originally came from Germany. Schlumberger himself joined his cousins in their crusade against the Turks in the Hungarian Lands and became renowned as a courageous warrior. For his services he was honoured with a noble title from Emperor Rudolf II with the appropriate

decoration of his coat-of-arms; this portrait medal was produced in honour of the event.

MN 1852-70, pp. 527-528

Z.M.

III.146

See cat. no. III.145

III.147
Memorial Volume of Sebald Plano, Member of the Imperial Embassy to Constantinople
Bound book of paper, leather binding, watercolours, drawings
19 × 12.5 (opened 19 × 28)
On fol. 1a: *Der Besitzer dieses Albums war Sebald Plan*
1571–93
Prague, Premonstratensian monastery at Strahov, library, sign. DG IV 25

This album was owned by Sebald Plan, who came from Schleswig-Holstein and worked as a cook for the imperial envoy in Constantinople. It contains a number of writings recalling the period spent in Turkey. Of particular value are the pictures, such as the watercolours depicting Turkish men (the sultan's courtiers) and women or Persians in period dress. Other drawings represent the travellers' stay in Constantinople, for example, the mosques they saw there. A significant number of pages were made using the so-called Turkish silhouette or marbled paper, which was popular at that time. Those who contributed to the album chiefly include members of the imperial delegations; members of the Czech nobility are also represented, such as Zachariás Slavata of Chlum and Kosumberk and Václav Budovec of Budov (Constantinople, 1578). According to the testimonies contained in the album, Plan lived in Salzburg, Vienna and Prague when he was not travelling as part of the delegations.

Hertlová 1975, pp. 117–46; Rataj 1995, pp. 7–12.

L.A.

III.148
Ratification of the Peace Treaty with Turkey (Treaty of Zsitvatorok)
Oriental paper; gold and black ink; gold *tugra*; script: *sülüs* and *divani*
297 × 54
25 April–4 May 1610
Constantinople
Military Council
Haus-, Hof- und Staatsarchiv, Vienna, Türkische Urkunden und Staatsschreiben, 1606 XI 11

On 11 November 1606, the 'Long Turkish Wars' which had raged since 1593 came to an end. By 9 December, Rudolf II was already signing the treaty (in Latin). In some passages, this translation departed from the Ottoman Turkish text, although nobody noticed this at the time. However, the contractually agreed dispatch of an emissary with a 'gift' of 200,000 thalers as a 'one-off' payment never took place, thus accounting for the fact that the treaty was not ratified from the Turkish side. After the treaty was renewed in 1608 and the gifts had also arrived, Sultan Ahmed I ratified the peace. It was only at this point that the Ottoman Turkish version was translated and numerous discrepancies in the text came to light. After violent protests by King Matthias, the treaty shown here was rewritten. It only later became clear that the new version still did not tally with the Emperor's version and was hardly an improvement on the first Ottoman ratification.

Vienna 1983.

Rudolf Neck 1950, pp. 166–95.

Ptr.

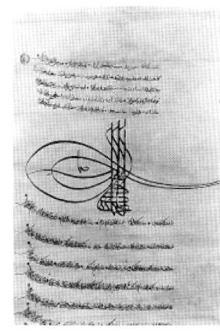

III.149
Directions issued by Rudolf II on the behaviour the horsemen and foot soldiers going to Hungary against the Turks in places set aside for mustering and disbandening troops
Original, paper, German, print, bound, 7 fols
21.5 × 30 cm
20 March 1601
Prague, Státní ústřední archiv (Patents collection), inv. no. 169

Patents were at first issued in the form of a letter, often in large format, written or printed on one side. It soon became the practice, however, to bind longer texts, often made up of several points. Before long this became the dominant form, and until 1849 was also used for laws. It is used for this extensive patent giving orders for the cavalry riding to Hungary against the Turks. The royal office was continually issuing new decrees concerning the war with the Turks and the troops marching against them, and the war was the subject of a large number of the military documents issued by the royal chamber and office in Bohemia. Emperor Rudolf II led a war against the Turks between 1595 and 1606. Soldiers at this time were mercenaries. They were hired by miltary contractors (the owners of regiments), who had sovereign's or officer's patents issued by the Estates. Because enlisting and discharging troops had in the past often involved the oppression and plundering of the local population, the Emperor issued an order designed to prevent such excesses, and also by appointing commissars to take charge of provisions and accommodation. This order says that officers are to pay for their own food and are not to extort anything from their underlings.

Loebl 1899+, pp. 1–136, 10 (*1904+), pp. 1–151.

Be.

III.150
Anonymous
The Invasion of the Lesser Town by Leopold of Passau
Coloured copper engraving
23.3 × 30.8 cm
Title: *EINFAHL DES PASSAWischen Krigvolcks, in die kleine Statt Prag. Anno MDCXI. Den 15. Februarii.*; cut into the lower frame: *ÒannoÓ*
? 1611
Prague
Třeboň, State Regional Archive, Schwarzenburg family archive, Sekundogenitura, Graphic collection, no. 17

J.Ha.

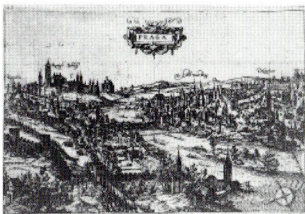

III.151
Anonymous
The Invasion of the Lesser Town by Leopold of Passa, vista of Prague
Copper engraving
230 × 343 cm
? 1611
Prague
Třeboň, State Regional Archive, Schwarzenburg family archive, Sekundo-genitur, Graphic collection, no.18

Both illustrations document the events of 1611 when the army of Duke Leopold, Bishop of Passau, attacked Prague in a lightning strike. The action took place with the agreement of Emperor Rudolf II, who hoped that by this means he would recover from the dire position into which his brother Matthias had cast him in 1608 (see cat. no. III.6) and at the same time settle the problem of the opposition of the Czech nobility (see cat. no. III.153). The armies of the Czech nobles and the citizens of Prague stood against the Passau mercenaries. Reliable witnesses claimed that around 200 people died in the street fighting. The attackers did not manage to capture Prague's right bank, that is, the Old and New Towns. The Passau armies withdrew from Prague on 8 March after long discussions conducted with the leaders of the Czech nobility and the Emperor at the Old Town Hall. King Matthias, whose Czech political leaders had asked for help, came immediately to Prague as a conqueror. The legend in the left-hand corner illustrates the most important strategic points in the Lesser Town (Malá Strana) where battle was waged, and the figures of the commanders.

Novák 1935.

J.Ha.

III.152
The Letter of Majesty of Rudolf II: Rudolf II Grants Religious Freedom to the Protestant Estates of the Kingdom of Bohemia
Original, parchment, Czech text; the Czech Imperial Charter seal of Rudolf II, made of wax, has been removed, along with pendant and gilded silver box; facsimile 1986
72.8 × 60.1 × 5.4 cm
1609, 9 July, Prague Castle
Státní ústřední archiv v Praze, fond Národní kulturní památka Archiv České koruny, inv. no. 2293 (within the N.k.p., inv. no. 2306)

The so-called 'Imperial Charter' is the most important document in religious and political history from the reign of Rudolf II. Its issue served as the culmination of the fundamental power struggle between the opposing Protestant Estates and the Emperor, and the remaining Catholic powers within the kingdom of Bohemia. The Imperial Charter declared the necessity of 'friendly', tolerant cohabitation; it granted freedom of religion to the Protestants united under the Czech Confession of 1575 and guaranteed them equal status with Catholics. The Imperial Charter guaranteed religious freedom even for the serfs and explicitly forbade religious persecution and forced conversion. After the defeat of the revolt of the Czech Estates, the Imperial Charter and other written documents were taken to Vienna, probably in late November 1620; there the seal was destroyed, and the text and the signatures of Rudolf II and of Adam of Šternberk were annulled.

Prague 1958; Prague 1979; Prague 1988.

Gindely 1858; Gindely 1878, pp. 273-74; Krotta 1919; Glücklich 1917, pp. 110-28; Janáček 1956, pp. 226-51; Janáček 1987, pp. 437-48.

D.Č.

III.153
Contemporary Tracing of the Engraved Heraldic Decoration of the Recto and Verso of the Gilded Silver Box for the Czech Imperial Charter Seal of Rudolf II, Appended to the Imperial Charter of 9 July 1609
Paper, pen and ink drawing in grey (recto) and brown (verso) ink, Czech commentary. Both reversed drawings are part of a manuscript which was re-bound in the eighteenth century
In-folio manuscript 30.1 cm
Signature *B I F 82* (the drawings are found in the non-foliated portion of the manuscript)
Prague, Státní ústřední archiv, inv. no. B 1 F 82

The only known depiction of the decoration on the case has been preserved in the manuscript from the abovementioned episcopal library. The manuscript contains the somewhat shortened (modified) texts of two historico-political writings by Václav Budovec of Budov on the events of the years 1608-10. The last pages contain an abstract of the important documents pertaining to Bethlehem chapel in Prague. The creation of the manuscript can be dated to 1612 or the years immediately following. The gilded and decorated silver case was commissioned by the body of Estate directors

Prague 1866 (ed. J. Jireèek), p. 380; Nováček 1896, 1897, Prague 1897, pp. 260-61; Krofta 1909, pp. 29-30; Glücklich 1911, pp. 15-16; Burdová 1981, pp. 207-26; Čumlivski (in publication).

D.Č.

III.154
Aegidius Sadeler
Antwerp 1570–Prague 1629
Matthias as Holy Roman Emperor
Copper engraving
30.2 × 20.8 cm
Bottom: ... *sculptor Egidius Sadeler de facie expressit ... Pragae Anno Christiano MD-CXVI.*
1616
Prague, Národní galerie v Praze, Grafická sbírka, inv. no. R 9 736

A request for a privilegium from December 1614 mentions both this portrait and its pendant, the engraving of Empress Anna (Hollstein 273), as works in progress. Sadeler expressed concern that other artists, on seeing these fine portraits from life, would copy them for portraits of other rulers. The date of 1616 on both prints suggests that Sadeler issued them to coincide with the entry and coronation of Anna in Prague in that year, a stratagem for attracting the patronage of the imperial couple. In both prints, Sadeler used the formula of the half- or three-quarter-length figure by a table, seen in a number of other portrait engravings. Standing on either side of a table on which are imperial regalia, the couple share a more or less continuous space. This is a similar schema to that of the painted portraits from 1616 of Jan and Klara Minckwitz, works that are here re-attributed to Sadeler.

Hollstein 309; Limouze 1990.

D.L.

III.155
Frieze with Plant Tendrils
Sandstone, grey polychromy
22 × 147 × 15 cm
Ca. 1550
Prague, Prague Castle, Prague Castle Administration, inv. no. 2 970

The centre of this symmetrical ornamental composition is formed by plant life from which long stalks uncoil on both sides with a large quantity of leaves and tendrils to create a complex leafy motif. Two birds with outstretched wings are sitting on the suckers (or sprouts) nearer the centre. The delicate execution of the relief betrays the work of an Italian mason. The place where it was discovered (the lower Stag Moat below the Royal Summer House) demonstrates its relations to an older phase in the construction of the summer house. The frieze was part of a portal.

P.Ch.

III.156
Fragment of an Archivolt from Pernštejn Palace
Terracotta
21 × 53 × 27 cm
Ca. 1555
Prague Castle
Prague, Pražský hrad, Správa Pražského hradu, inv. no. PHLPT 22

This was originally a segment of some size. Its surface face, skirted at the upper edge by a sculpted cornice or fillet with a leaf mould, had a rich decorative relief. Five incomplete small figures of children have been preserved, of which one is rid-ing on a billy-goat which another holds by the tail and beats with a rod. This object formed part of a large arch, possibly for one of the main portals.

P.Ch.

III.157
Fragment with a Relief of an Old Crone from Pernštejn Palace
Terracotta
35 × 27 × 19.5 cm
Ca. 1555
Prague Castle
Prague, Pražský hrad, Správa Pražského hradu, inv. no. PHA 19/500

A prism forms the base of this article. On the front it bears the relief of a winged mermaid, who is holding her S-shaped fish-tail. Most of the edging is broken off. This item was probably part of a frieze.

Chotebor 1989, pp. 112–127.

P.Ch.

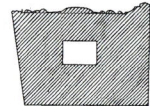

III.158
Jamb of a Large Window of Pernštejn Palace (partial reconstruction)
Terracotta, supplements from a resin base
Ca. 1555
Prague Castle
Prague, Pražský hard, Správa Pražského hradu

This window jamb is made up of parts and fragments found in Baroque stonework, used as a secondary form of building material. It is assumed that large window openings of this type lightened dwelling and occasional rooms on the larger floors of the palace. Their presence can be ascer-tained only on the first floor of the divid-ing wing between the large and small court. At the site, only sizeable parts of the parapet ledge have been preserved, out of which had been cut all kinds of profile pieces and ornamental work. The width of the window could be determined by the brickwork and by the preserved graffito, which originally went all the way to the jamb. The jamb consists of three elements: the parapet ledge, the vertical parts (the stand), and the curve above the window. The ledge has a richly articulated profile, ornamented with egg and leaf moulding. The vertical parts have the appearance of a prism, the frontal wall of which is richly decorated. Two S-shaped tendrils, which cross in the middle, form the basis and leaves, protracted clusters or ears of corn fill up the surface. The decorative work was continuous which, where necessary, enabled a section to be shortened. Two dragons (or serpents) in the relief band between the profiles at the edge are at-tacking a two-headed eagle in the middle. The outer sides were furnished with an ex-tension rod for joining the vertical part of the jamb.

P.Ch.

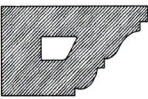

III.159
Jamb of a large opening from Pernštejn Palace (partial reconstruction)
Terracotta, supplements from a resin base
Ca. 1555
Prague Castle
Prague, Pražský hard, Správa Pražského hradu

The jamb is composed of fragments which were used as secondary building material during the Baroque reconstruction of the palace. Pieces of the vertical section and of the bow of the window form a trapezoidal profile. The bevelled front panel is skirted by sculpted fillets and embellished with a rich decorative relief. A candelabrum with twin putti serves as the axis for the decora-tion of the vertical section, with two half-figures with a winged head and wearing the armour worn in Antiquity. An op-posed lion and dragon embellish sections of the window's bow. Wedge-shaped ex-tensions are attached to both parts for joining the base and the bow. An incom-plete pilaster has been inserted between the two jambs, decoraed by a candelabrum with little figures of putti and with leaf moulding.

P.Ch.

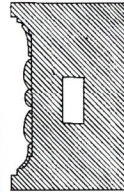

III.160
Panel with Figural Ornaments from Pern-stejn Palace (fragments of an original and overall reconstruction)
Terracotta
86 × 62.5 × 10 cm (whole panel)
Ca. 1555
Prague, Prague Castle
Prague, Pražský hard, Správa Pražského hradu, inv. nos. 19/330, 19/361, 19/356, 19/397, 19/458

A relief of two putti appears on the princi-pal panel with a thickness of 5 cm; they are bearing plates of fruit on their head and carry yet more fruit in their hands. In the background posts can be seen, around which vines are entwined. A goat is stand-ing on its hind legs to eat the grapes. As numerous fragments demonstrate, two oblong panels of the same proportions and with a similar decorative relief reoccur in the palace decorations. They might have been put to use in the wall panels be-tween the wainscot or the pilasters.

P.Ch.

III.161
Fragment of Ornamental Mural Painting
Painting on lime stucco
30 × 14 × 7 cm
Second half of sixteenth century
Prague, Prague Castle
Prague, Pražský hard, Správa Pražského hradu, inv. no. 1 866

The brick with a layer of plaster, on which there is a fragment of pearl or beadwork and plant-life ornamentation, comes from the second storey of the South Wing. It is very poor in terms of colouring; its black and white contrast is reminiscent of graffito.

P.Ch.

III.162–165
Ferdinand of the Tyrol
Hvězda Summer Palace (Prague–Liboc): basement, ground-floor, first-floor plans and section
Photographic reproduction
28.8 × 39.5 cm
Ca. 1555 (original)
Vienna, Österreichisches Nationalbibliothek, cod.min. 108. fols 2, 4–6

This collection of plans of the four floors and a sectional view of the building attests to the competence of the designer, who was none other than Archduke Ferdinand Tyrolský himself. This has been confirmed by comparing the plans with technical drawings dating from 1780, more than two hundred years later. Both collections are identical but for very slight changes in some details. The sectional plan of the building has more of a schematic character; it is of course very valuable since it presents us with the original shape of the roof, including its height. The Archduke drew his inspiration mainly from Pietro Cataneo's *L'architettura*, the first part of which was published in 1554; he had acquired a copy for his library. The Archduke was not only a keen builder, he was also a very erudite scholar in the field of architecture. He was well informed about all the latest artistic opinions being formulated in Italy, the centre of architectural innovation at that time; he was familiar, for instance, with the theoretical designs of ideal cities and fortification architecture, as drawn up by the likes of Filarete, Maggi and Vasari. Their designs often included polygonal structures and star shapes.

Morávek 1955, pp. 199–211; Muchka 1969, p. 85; Krčálová 1976, illus. no. 34.

I.M.

III.166–169
Adolf Hilscher
Hvězda Summer Palace (Prague–Liboc): Basement, ground-floor, first-floor and second-floor plans
Drawing in Indian ink
38 × 52
1780
Prague, Ústav dějin umění, Archive of Plans, inv. no. 05248 W-D-IX/1818-21

This collection of plans were drawn up when the Hvězda residence was to be converted into a munitions house. It provides vivid evidence of both how minor the changes to the ground plan were over a period of more than two hundred years, and how resistant the building's internal structure, which remains one of the finest examples of European Mannerism, turned out to be. The juxtaposition of all four floors shows the designer's unusual use of space, particularly in the dramatic change to the ground plan with its concentric corridor in the basement and the radial corridors on the ground floor. Resonances of the basement corridor are only found in the location of the doors connecting up all the rooms on the ground floor. The first floor which had essentially the same ground plan as the ground floor, was given a different design consisting of a more intimate, private style with only one entrance to each of the rooms. On the second floor the designer finally made allowance for the star-shaped design of the ground plan, and did not undermine it with the introduction of any divisions. The principle of the maximum partition (Alberti uses the term 'partitio') of the ground plan in the basement area, is shown to be in absolute opposition to the ground plan on the second floor, which highlights the complex spiritual climate of the Manneristic period.

I.M.

III.170–171
Hvězda Game-Park (Prague–Liboc): plan
Ink drawing
Plan von dem unweit Prag in dem Königl. Thirgarten befindlichen Lustgebäude des Sterns, gegenwärtiges Pulfer Despositorium Aufgenomen von denen Frequentanten Math. Schule des l'Feld Archite Picquinto von Pentzerstein, gezeichnet... 1790
Prague, Ústav dějin umění, Archive of Plans, inv. no. 05247 W-D-IX/1817

Obora Hvězda is often referred to in the sources of the period as Nová (New), to distinguish it from Stromovká, correspondingly referred to as Stará obora (Old obora). The area was developed during the period when the Emperor had bought the forest called Malejov. The roughly oblong-shaped area was gradually developed between 1546 and 1563, when it was enclosed and provided with entrance archways, which to a certain degree fitted in with the basic urban planning and gave the area a definite outline. The lengthways axis of the area began by the archway in the east and continued in the opposite direction to the monastery of Saint Margaret. This axis was crossed by a second north-south axis, which again ran between archways, the northern one of which, with its stone embossed portal, has survived. A further two axes ran diagonally through the intersection point of the lengthwise and crosswise axes, dividing the area up into an eight-pointed star. This unique example of urban planning may be considered one of the period's supreme examples of artificially shaped landscapes in Central Europe.

I.M.

III.172
Hvězda Summer Palace (Prague–Liboc): site plan
Ink drawing
59 × 42
Stern Pulver Magasin
Prague, Ústav dějin umění,, Archive of Plans, inv. no. 05186 W-D-IX/1756

The Hvězda summer residence forms the heart of the complex, which includes the ball-games court on the slope to west, referred to in the documentation of the period as the 'galleria'. Both buildings, the court and the residence, were enclosed by a perimeter wall, which as can be seen in eighteenth- and nineteenth-century plans, had an unusually interesting ground plan. The section to the east of the area where the summer residence is located, has the 'perfectly' centralized proportions of a square with each side approximately sixty-three metres long, with the residence positioned at its very centre. Also of interest is the fact that each corner of the square was originally occupied by a bastion extension. The symmetry of the area cannot be readily taken in when at the site itself, given that the symmetry is provided only by the depth of the axis. This plan is similar to others which were commonly used as something of a building aid. The illusion of a fortified appearance was also aided by the undecorated, austere-looking brick masonry, which was only partially plastered over during pointing so as to leave the unusually thin brick work showing. A working building fitted out with kitchens, and with no special architectural features, was erected just beyond the area and positioned so as not to interfere with the urban-planning arrangement of the complex as a whole.

I.M.

III.173
Johann Heinrich Dienebier
Hvězda Summer Palace (Prague–Liboc): section
Colour reproduction (washed pencil and paper drawing)
67 × 53
Prague, Archiv Pražského hradu, inv. no. 171/7

The silhouette of the building which was important from an urban-planning aspect, was originally not so crude and inelegant as it is today, given that the roof was drastically lowered during reconstruction work in the 1950s. If the plans dating from 1555 are to be believed, then originally the pointed roof stood out above the crown gable of the rest of the building. Even on this 1737 sectional view by Dienebier, by which time the pinnacle of the roof had been given a cupola finish, the roof can still be seen markedly extending above the height of the main body of the building. The fate of the building in the latter half of the eighteenth century, when as with the ball-games court it was reconstructed for use as a munitions house, was in the 1950s again changed for social use. Unfortunately the reconstruction work which was then carried out on the building by Pavel Janák, left much to be desired, par-

ticularly with regard to the roof and from the point of view of historical accuracy of the restoration work.

Lietzmann 1987, 178–79, ill. 50; Morávek 1955, ill. p. 203.

I.M.

III.174
Anonymous
Prague Castle: the oldest extand plan
Photocopy
42.5 × 35 cm
Latter half of sixteenth century
Florence, Galleria degli Uffizi, inv. no. 4521-A

This outstanding source document recording the development of the Castle's construction was only published recently. It is a schematic plan of the type normally used in the sixteenth and early seventeenth century, which mostly provides only the perimeter demarcations but occa-

sionally particular ground-plan features as well. For the purposes of dating the document, it should theoretically be possible to use an *ante quem* method: in other words, examine which buildings are absent: in this respect, the chapel of St Adalbert. The plan shows that there was an interesting array of buildings where the 'fraucimor' wing was later constructed around 1640.

Brykowska 1979, pp. 65–71.

I.M.

III.175
Prague Castle: ground-floor plan
Colour reproduction
61 × 182 (possibly made up of two parts glued together)
Ca. 1760
Prague, Archiv Pražského hradu, inv. no. 157 A/1

This ground plan of Hradčany Castle before the rebuilding undertaken during the reign of Queen Maria, begins in the west by the drawbridge between the house of the administrator responsible for the armoury. In the south it includes the residential wing including the quarters be-

neath the Vladislavský sál, without however the Královské zahrady. In the north it includes the stables, and ends in the east by the so-called secret armoury (no. 40), but does not include Jelení přikop and the foreground area to the north.

Podlaha 1929-1921, 89, no.14, picture and tab. X.

I.M.

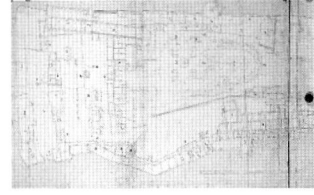
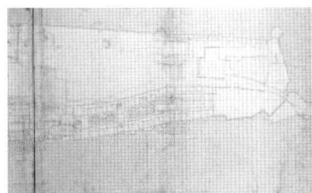

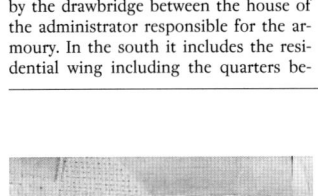
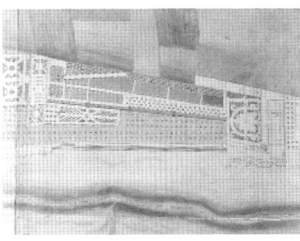
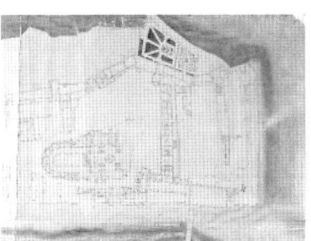

III.176
Prague Castle: first-floor plan
Paper, colour photographic reproduction
147 × 212 (162 × 216) cm
1760, according to the plan (A. Masák's copy)
Prague, Archiv Pražského hradu, inv. no. 157/35

This modern, redrawn plan of the whole of Hradčany Castle before the changes implemented during the reign of Maria Theresa includes the interior of the first floor. The plan of the rest of the grounds includes St Vitus' cathedral, the Rajské zahrady, the Rožmberk's palaces, Jižské

monasteries, and all the foreground to the north. The section extends to Queen Anna's summer residence in the east and to the middle of the pheasant breeding area in the west. Some of the buildings which had other owners (chapter, 'Lobkovický Palace') are shown only in silhouette.

Podlaha 1920–21, p. 89, no. 13, ill. and tab. VI-IX.

I.M.

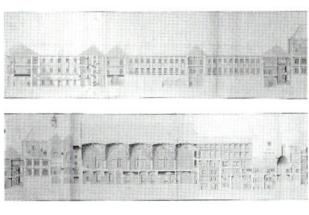

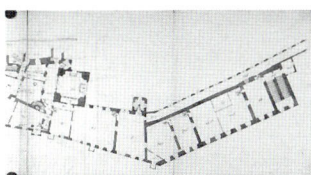

III.177
Prague Castle: longitudinal section of the South Wing (1723–44), including the Institute of Noblewomen
Pasted onto a canvas base, facsimile (?), colour photographic reproduction
28 × 273
Ca. 1756
Prague, Archiv Pražského hradu, inv. no. 112/2

Comparisons between the actual layout of the buildings and the outlines and sectional drawings on plans, dating from before the architectural changes introduced during the reign of Queen Maria in the latter half of the eighteenth century, are essential to researching the earlier architectural development of the Castle. As no sixteenth-century plans have survived, this collection of plans drawn up before Maria Theresa's reign are the only aid we have for studying Rudolf's architecture. Sixteenth-century plans would allow us to re-create a picture of the residential section in the south which was established during Rudolf's reign (cf. the double windows on the third floor roughly by the extension to the central wing). Unfortunately there is no other way of determining the precise appearance of the courtyards' façades, and of demarcating exactly where the seventeenth-century building work (the so-called Empress's wing dating from around 1640, between the residential quarters to the right of the plan, and the kitchens) begins and ends.

Podlaha 1920–21, 100, no. 15, ill. and tab. XI/1.

I.M.

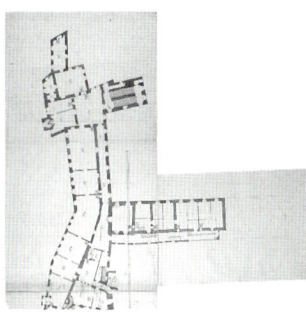

III.178
Johann Heinrich Dienebier
Prague Castle: ground-floor plan of South Wing (1723–44)
Colour reproduction
46 × 153 cm
Liter. A. Grundt-Reiss des königl. Schlosses ebner Erden gegen der Statt; Liter. A Grundt Ryss ebner Erden untter den Ertz-Hertzoglichen Stock A∞1744
1744
Prague, Archiv Pražského hradu, inv. no. 109/2

The development of the ground plan for the residential south wing is documented in a series of six plans attributed to the building scribe Jan Jiří Dienebier which, according to the inscriptions, date from 1744. The second floor is outlined both as a whole and in two separate parts divided into east and west. These more detailed plans are made even more valuable by the additional descriptions which are important for determining the intended use to which the individual rooms were to be put. The basic problem of research, however, arises when trying to determine when the section on the east side of the wing – where Giuseppe Mattei later designed the so-called Empress's palace, with five rooms on the ground floor and an early Baroque double-flight stairs – was completed. According to archival records, Rudolf's residential rooms were most likely to have been located on the second floor, the first floor being reserved for his future wife. On the plans the floors are connected by a winding staircase leading to where Rudolf's bedroom would have been.

Podlaha 1920–21, p. 77, no. 1, ill. 37; Muchka 1988, pp. 193–196; Muchka 1992, pp. 95–98.

I.M.

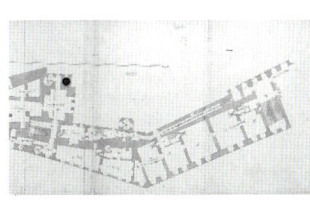

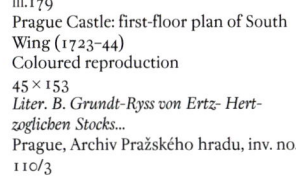

III.179
Prague Castle: first-floor plan of South Wing (1723–44)
Coloured reproduction
45 × 153
Liter. B. Grundt-Ryss von Ertz- Hertzoglichen Stocks...
Prague, Archiv Pražského hradu, inv. no. 110/3

See cat. no. III.178

Podlaha 1920–21, p. 83, no. 3, ill. 39.

I.M.

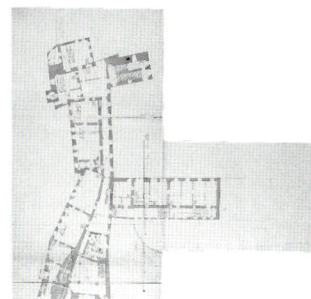

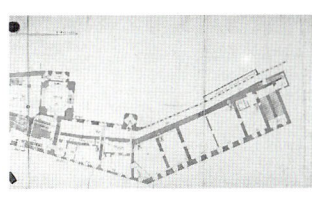

III.180
Prague Castle: second-floor plan of South Wing (1723–44)
Coloured reproduction
45 × 156
Liter. C. .Kayserl. Zimmer 2 Stiegen hoch...1723–44
Prague, Archiv Pražského hradu, inv. no. 111/2

See cat. no. III.178

Podlaha 1920–21, p. 81, no. 4, ill. 40.

I.M.

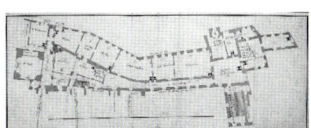

III.181
Prague Castle: second-floor plan of west wing (1723–44)
Coloured reproduction
37 × 98 cm
Kayserliche Zimmer in koniglichen prager Schloss...
Prague, Archiv Pražského hradu, inv. no. 111/4

See cat. no. III.178

Podlaha 1920–21, p.81, no. 5, ill. 41.

I.M.

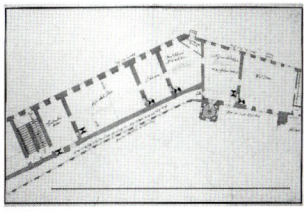

III.182
Prague Castle: second-floor plan of South Wing's eastern section (1723–44)
Coloured reproduction
42 × 66
Prague, Archiv Pražského hradu, inv. no. 111/3

See cat. no. III.178

Podlaha 1920–21, p.84, no. 6, ill. 42.

I.M.

III.183
Prague Castle: third-floor plan of South
Wing's western section (1723-44)
coloured reproduction
40 × 118
Liter. D. Jesuviter Stock, 3 Stugen hoch...
Prague, Archiv Pražského hradu, inv. no.
112/1

See cat. no. III.178

Podlaha 1920–21, p. 84, no. 7, ill. 43.

I.M.

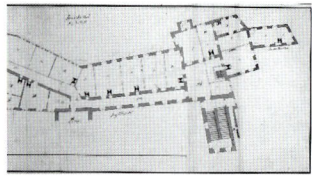
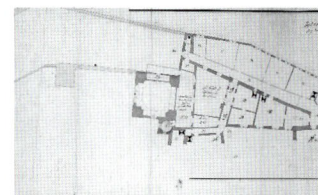

III.184
Johann Heinrich Dienebier
Prague Castle: ground-floor plan of
Central Wing
Colour reproduction
51 × 76 cm
*Zu Liter. A. den Grund Ryss gehörig. Ebner
Erd untter dem Fraw-Zimmer Stock, vor die
Officianten. Nebst der A∞1723 neugebauthen
Munth-Kochel un Bawambte*
1723
Prague, Hradčany Castle Archive, inv. no.
113/1

This collection of seven ground plans, sectional views and outlines allows us men-
tally to reconstruct the so-called central or
transversal wing, referred in the sources of
the period as the '*Gangbau*' because it provided what was in a sense a series of connecting corridors between the south and
north sections. This particular part of
Hradčany Castle contained Rudolf's famous *Kunstkammer* (on the first floor) as
well as part of his picture gallery. The
structural development of the section is
very complicated, owing to the fact that
the southernmost part provided a passageway to the centre of the Castle, guarded by the so-called White Tower, part of
the masonry of which has survived. Another tower, known as the Mathematical
Tower and no longer extant, was built
against the powerful castle wall at roughly
the midway point. In the section between
the White Tower and the Mathematical
Tower there must have been in total three
Kunstkammer rooms which were vaulted
over. To the north of the Mathematical
Tower was the main *Kunstkammer*.

Podlaha 1920–21, p. 86, no. 8, ill. 44; Muchka 1988, pp. 196–99.

I.M.

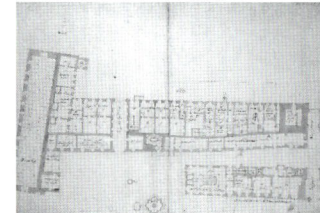

III.185
Johann Heinrich Dienebier
Prague Castle: first-floor plan of South
and Central wings
Coloured reproduction
39 × 50 cm
*Nr.1. Eine Stiegen Hoch. Ertzherzoglicher
Stock...*
Prague, Archiv Pražského hradu, inv. no.
113/7

See cat. no. III.184

Podlaha 1920–1921, p. 86, no. 10 ill. 46.

I.M

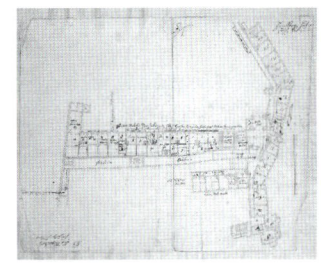

III.186
Johann Heinrich Dienebier
Prague Castle: second-floor plan of
central extension
Coloured reproduction
51 × 75 cm
Nr.2. Koniglicher Stock...
Prague, Archiv Pražského hradu, inv. no.
113/11

See cat. no. III.184

Podlaha 1920–1921, p. 89, no. 11, ill. 47.

I.M.

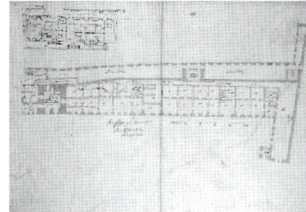

III.187
Prague Castle: partial profile of central
extension
Coloured reproduction
24 × 88 cm
Ca. 1756
Prague, Archiv Pražského hradu, inv. no.
113/17

See cat. no. III.184

Podlaha 1920–1921, p. 86, no. 9, ill. 45.

I.M.

III.188
Prague Castle: cross section and western
façade of central extension
Coloured reproduction
56 × 97 cm
Late eighteenth century
Prague, Archiv Pražského hradu, inv. no.
113/15

See cat. no. III.184

Podlaha 1920–1921, p. 100, no. 20, ill. 53.

I.M.

III.189
Prague Castle: western façade of central
extension
Facsimile
46 × 71 cm
Late eighteenth century
Prague, Archiv Pražského hradu, inv. no.
113/14

See cat. no. III.184

Podlaha 1920–21, p. 103, no. 21, ill. 54.

I.M.

III.190
Prague Castle: eastern façade of central
extension
Coloured reproduction
31 × 89 cm
Late eighteenth century
Prague, Archiv Pražského hradu, inv. no.
113/16

See cat. no. III.184

Podlaha 1920–21, p. 103, no. 22, ill. 55.

I.M.

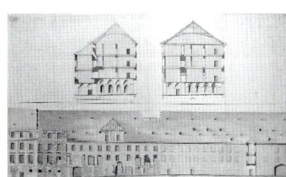

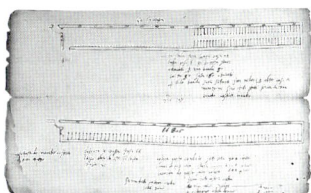

III.191
Report on the Bohemian Chamber on the Construction of the Stables below the later Kunstkammer
Paper, pen and ink drawing
32.5 × 19.5 cm
1576-01/04
Prague
Prague, Central State Archive, inv. no. ČDKM IV., P, Praha-Hrad, Kart. 192

The plan is a good example of a sketched plan for the construction of stables, containing two ground plans and accompanying descriptions in Italian as well as the estimated costs. As the text only provides the length and width given in the unit 'passo' (66 × 5 in the upper ground plan) and the number of horses in a single row (80 in the upper ground plan, making 160 in total, and 66 in the lower plan), it is very difficult to determine the intended location. Given the characteristic quadrant entrance corridors to the left of the plans, the fifteen windows or vents in each, and the fact that they are of the same length, this may indicate that they were variants of each other. However, the difference in width in each of the plans would seem to throw doubt on this theory. Both types of stables, with stalls along both sides or on only one side, were built in the Castle. The estimated length of the stables (ca. 110–120 metres) could well link it in length to the central wing.

I.M.

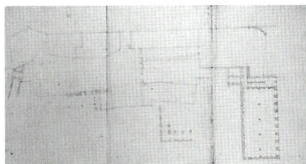

III.192
Prague Castle: plan of Spanish (New) Hall and part of Arcade
Colour reproduction (pencil drawing)
50 × 98 cm
Seventeenth century
Prague, Archiv Pražského hradu, inv. no. 115/100

The uses to which Rudolf intended the Castle to be put led to the decision to build two large halls, one a picture gallery, the other a sculpture gallery. The size of the latter hall was such that it could also be used for banquets and other celebratory occasions. In initiating the project Rudolf made himself the Castle's greatest ever secular contributor to the erection of new buildings in its grounds. In terms of housing for art treasures, there was little in the rest of Europe to compare with Rudolf's galleries.

Krčálová 1975, pp. 512 and 522 (footnote 80), picture 10; Muchka 1988, pp. 199–202.

I.M.

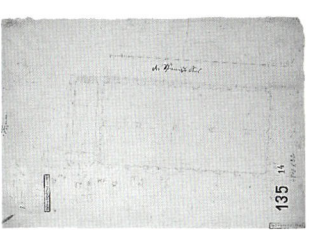

III.193
Prague Castle: plan of Spanish (New) Hall and part of Arcade
Colour reproduction (pencil drawing)
50 × 98 cm
Seventeenth century
Prague, Archiv Pražského hradu, inv. no. 115/101

See cat. no. III.192

I.M.

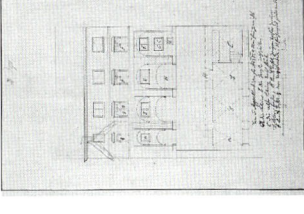

III.194
Prague Castle: north-western façade of the Court of Appeal, with partial plan
Black-and-white reproduction
38 × 24.5
? 1724, post 1728
Prague, Archiv Pražského hradu, inv. no. 102/5

This palace wing where the state records were housed provides us with one of the few clear examples of the appearance of the Castle during the Renaissance period. Even here, however, the today's seemingly authentic appearance is not complete. Compared with the plan, we no longer see the last northern line of windows, which were covered over by extensions at a later date, and which undermine the harmonious and overall uninterrupted appearance of the original design. According to the plan it would appear that not even the hipped roof is original. In the case of the ridged roofs we can reasonably assume that they were covered from the north side by a first-floor gable, which as a common feature of renaissance buildings would have lent the silhouette a picturesque and lively appearance. Another detail which was important for the morphological appearance of the building, was the series of tiny roofs above the straight mouldings above the semicircular coupled windows. Today these rooflets are missing.

Podlaha 1920–21, 167, no. 28, ill 95.

I.M.

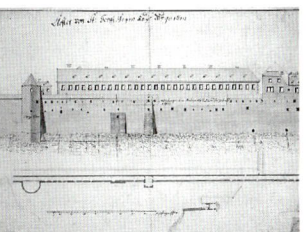

III.195
Prague Castle: view of north turret wall
Coloured reproduction
36.5 × 50.5 cm
Ca. 1733
Prague, Archiv Pražského hradu, inv. no. 126/1

See cat. no. III.196

Podlaha 1920–21, p. 175, no. 33, ill. 103.

I.M.

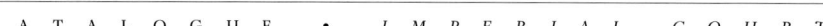
III.196
Prague Castle, House of the Castle Captain: façade and longitudinal section
colour reproduction
43 × 62 cm
1824
Prague, Archiv Pražského hradu, inv. no. 127/7

The palace house of this high-standing Castle functionary was built on a steeply sloping terrain. This view shows an extensive basement area. On the ground floor spherical sections of the vaulting can be seen, and on the floor above the decorative details of the fireplace. However, it is

necessary to take great care in defining the style of the rest of the building. We know for certain that the windows had stone frames and straight ledges dividing them from the floor above. One feature particular to the period was the embossed portal with its relatively large latitudinal proportions and a two-floor voluted gable, bordered at both ends by a somewhat ambiguous form, which look like small pointed volutes. The various obelisk forms were not common to the Renaissance in Bohemia. The plan does not show whether or not the rendering had a graffito finish, although it is likely that it did. The overall composition of the façade is

interesting in that the strictly symmetrical gable, with its regularly positioned windows, has little in common with the asymmetrical design of the first and ground floors. Nevertheless the overall impression of the façade is calm, balanced and harmonious.

Podlaha 1920–21, 176, no. 35, ill. 105, tab. XVI.

I.M.

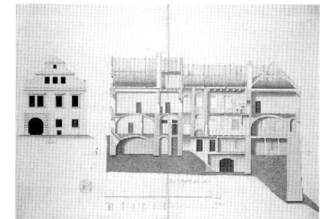

III.197
Antonín Haffenecker
Prague Castle: façade, partial cross section and plan of the armoury
Coloured reproduction
64 × 19 cm
Late eighteenth century
Prague, Archiv Pražského hradu, inv. no. 129/4

See cat. no. III.196

Podlaha 1920–21, p. 176, no. 36. ill. 106.

I.M.

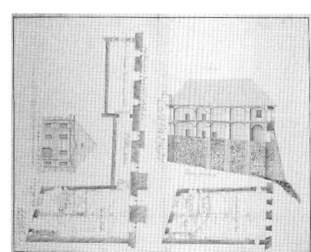

III.198
Antonín Haffenecker
Prague Castle: cross section with artillery workshop
Coloured reproduction
25 × 19 cm
Early eighteenth century
Prague, Archiv Pražského hradu, inv. no. 134/1

See cat. no. III.196

Podlaha 1920–21, p. 178, no. 37, ill. 107.

I.M.

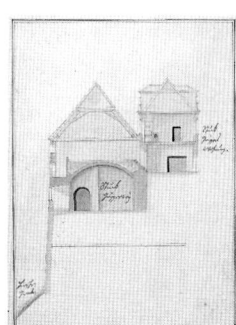

III.199
Antonín Haffenecker
Prague Castle: cross section and plan of artillery workshop
Coloured reproduction
38.5 × 65 cm
End of eighteenth century
Prague, Archiv Pražského hradu, inv. no. 134/7

See cat. no. III.196

Podlaha 1920–21, p. 178, no. 38, ill. 108.

I.M.

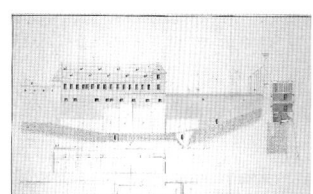

III.200
Antonín Haffenecker
Prague Castle: main armoury
coloured reproduction
21.5 × 36 cm
Prager Schloss - Zeughausz gegen der Ertzbischoffl....
Early eighteenth century
Prague, Archiv Pražského hradu, inv. no. 122/1

See cat. no. III.196

Podlaha 1920–21, p. 180, no. 40. ill. 108.

I.M.

III.201
Prague Castle: view and section of tower of St Vitus Cathedral
Colour reproduction
52.5 × 36 cm
Latter half of the eighteenth century (1768?)
Prague, Archiv Pražského hradu, inv. no. 131/3

We know that the tower of the Cathedral of Saint Vitus was roofed some time before 1562, thanks to the so-called Vratislavský view depicted by Kozel and Petrle in that year, in which the roof is almost certainly featured, and which ap-

pears in a series of graphic prints up until the latter half of the eighteenth century. The sectional view of the roof on the right-hand side of the plan highlights the fine carpentry involved in making the 23-metre-high spire, which consisted of three helmet-shaped constructions fitted one on top of the other. The two open levels at the top, were fitted with bells and bell-ringing equipment connected to the clock on the floor decorated with trefoil-shaped double windows. The helmet design was in effect a Classical circle eccentrically elongated by one sixth of its length above its upper ledge. The size of the uppermost helmet was equal with that of the four hel-

mets found above the gallery. This in essence was based on a simple mathematical formula. In contrast to the taller bell-shaped profile of the late baroque helmet, which was based on the amalgamation of the two variants seen on the left-hand side of this depiction, the Renaissance roof was far less 'refined', but thereby more momentous and effective.

Podlaha 1920–21, 180, no. 41, ill. 110.

I.M.

III.202
Prague Castle, St George's Convent: plan
Paper
41 × 59 cm
1627-28
Prague, Central State Archive, inv. no. ČDKM IV., Praha–Hrad, fol. 187

This plan of the benedictine monastery of Saint George and its surrounds is of immense worth in that it was made both before the monastery was reconstructed and before the extensive modifications were made to the area behind the monastery to the east. Although it is only a sketched diagram which does not allow us to verify

the dimensions, angles and other such architectural data, it does nevertheless, by comparison with the Popis Pražského Hradu of 1620, and thanks to the fact that the buildings behind the monastery have inscriptions providing information about their owners, allow us to reconstruct the building development in this part of Hradčany Castle.

I.M.

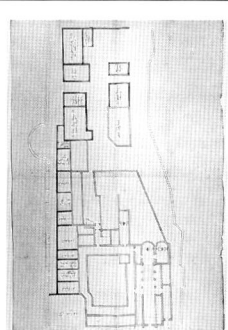

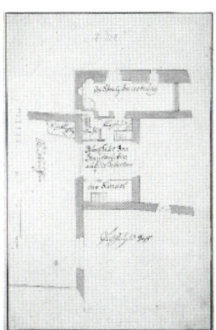

III.203
Prague Castle: plan of the gate to the northern bridgehead of Prašný most (Dusty Bridge)
Colour reproduction
27 × 40 cm
Early eighteenth century
Prague, Archiv Pražského hradu, inv. no. 135/2

In contrast to the summary plans of the Castle as a whole, there is also a sectional plan depicting part of the all-important archway at the north end of the bridge. Its outline was preserved in a woodcut in a publication by M. Albrecht's printed some time after 1600. The woodcut is of immense importance in determining the appearance of the Castle during Rudolf's reign, in spite of the fact that it is in essence a simple depiction of the equestrian training area around what is today the terrace of the riding school. The reason for this is that it also includes a lengthwise depiction of the two-storeyed Prašný most archway with the hipped roof, lunette ledge, and the two windows above the embossed portal, with its alternating long and short bosses. Other than providing valuable information about the proportions and physical dimensions of the archway, the ground plan tells us little about its Renaissance design other than that in the northern corner of the room on its west side, it had two deep refuge holes, which were a particular characteristic of the architecture of that period, which as well as being a feature of the staircase in the Nový sál (New Hall) and elsewhere, would also have been seen in the unpreserved Mathematical Tower.

Podlaha 1920–21, 184, no. 46, ill. 113; Krčálová 1975, 514; Muchka 1988, 187.

I.M.

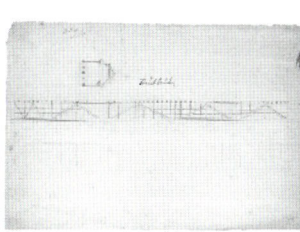

III.204
Prague Castle: Prašný most (Dusty Bridge)
Coloured reproduction
Early eighteenth century
Prague, Archiv Pražského hradu, inv. no. 115/101

See cat. no. III.203

Krčálová 1975, pp. 512, 522 (n. 80).

I.M.

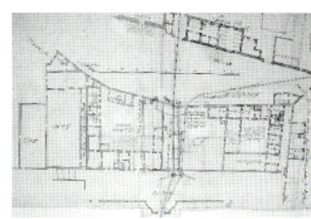

III.205
Prague Castle: plan of buildings entering into Royal Garden
Coloured reproduction
44 × 72.5 cm
Early eighteenth century
Prague, Archiv Pražského hradu, inv. no. 141/5

Podlaha 1920–21, p. 184, no. 47, ill. 114.

I.M.

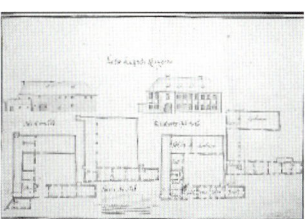

III.206
Antonín Haffemecker
Prague Castle: plan of the Lion Court
Colour reproduction
32 × 50.5 cm
Kaiserl. Königliches Löwenhaus
Late eighteenth century (1785)
Prague, Archiv Pražského hradu, inv. no. 141/8

Although details of the Lion's Court and the fate of animals kept there abound in archival documents relating to the period, and in reports by individuals who travelled to Prague and who were impressed by Rudolf's menagerie, we have by contrast very little information about its architectural design. The reconstruction of the original is based on the northernmost part of the floor plan which can be seen at the very left of this ground plan. The long corridor provided entrance to six caged areas, which roughly corresponds to the masonry divides on the Baroque plan. The spiral staircase in the most easterly section provided access to the first floor, where there was a terrace above the corridor for viewing the animals.

Podlaha 1920–21, 185, no. 48, ill. 115; Vilímková 1970, 34–41, ill. on p. 35; Muchka 1992, 228.

I.M.

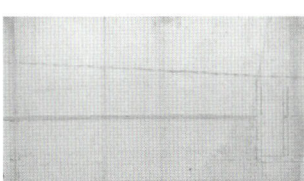 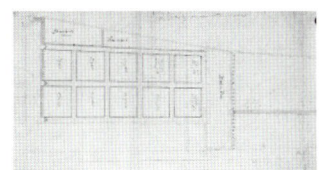

III.207
Prague Castle: plan of Royal Garden – Renaissance layout
47 × 167 cm
Early eighteenth century
Prague, Archiv Pražského hradu, inv. no. 142/5

I.M.

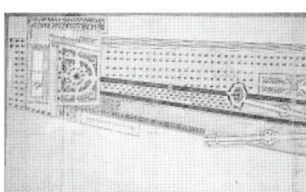 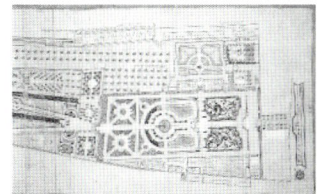

III.208
Johann Michael Zieglmayer
Prague Castle: plan of Royal Garden
Facsimile
41.5 × 128 cm
Delinieation von Ihro konigl. May / Prager Schlos Lustgarten. 1744. Fecit Joh. Mih. Ziegelmayer
1744
Prague, Archiv Pražského hradu, inv. no. 142/36

Podlaha 1920–21, p. 185, no. 49, tab. XVIII/1.

I.M.

III.209
Prague Castle, Chapel of Saint Adalbert:
plan
33.7 × 44 cm
Latter half of the nineteenth century
Prague, Archiv Pražského hradu, The Association for the Completion of the Cathedral of Saint Vitus

At the beginning of his reign Rudolf contributed 135 kopa1 to the construction of the Chapel of Saint Adalbert on the site of the Saint's tomb. At roughly the same time his mother, the Empress Maria, also made a contribution of 300 gulden to the construction of a new sanctuary for their pa-

tron saint, actually a paltry sum. The Archbishop Antonín Brus of Mohelnice was given charge of the funds and made responsible for the building of the chapel. It is quite probable in view of this, that it was in fact he who approved the architectural design. Bonifác Wohlmut, the leading builder on Hradčany Castle, was engaged in the Archbishop's services, as was the Castle's master brick mason Ulrico Aostalli. A very advanced feature was the ground plan of an elongated decagon. The chapel was eventually demolished to make way for the neo-Gothic completion of the Cathedral.

Krčálová, 1976, 66; photographic documentation in Friedrich made before its demolition in 1879; Merhout-Wirth 1946, ills 17–19.

I.M.

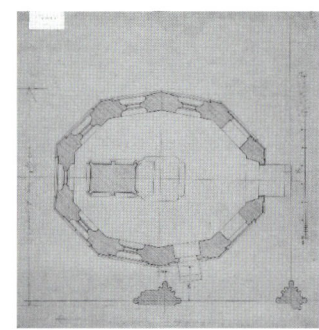

III.210
Prague Castle, Chapel of Saint Adalbert:
façade
Colour reproduction
62.5 × 48.5
Latter half of the nineteenth century
Prague, Archiv Pražského hradu, Association for the Completion of the Cathedral of Saint Vitus, 384

Although the chapel had relatively small interior dimensions (approximately 7.5 × 10 m, 4 × 5 and 2/6 of a cord with 4 cords including the height up to the crown cornice), it was impressive for its line of Tuscan-Doric pilasters, which mark out areas

for monumental, extremely shallow recesses. The combination of a recess with pilasters recalls Wohlmut's other earlier building in the Castle, the Large Ball-Game Court in the Royal Garden. The chapel's main portal was of particular importance to architectural development in Prague. In effect it was a segmented aedicule where the gable did not rest on the column or pilaster supports, but only on sections of the wall highlighted with geometrical panels. To hold the weight of the gable, two voluted consoles were added as supports at the sides of the portal. This gave birth to a design which later spread both in Prague and the rest of Cen-

tral Bohemia (cf. the church in Hospozín). However, precisely by viewing these later derivations, one is made aware of just how elegant nd gracious the Castle portal is.

Podlaha 1910, 119.

I.M.

III.211
Prague Castle, Chapel of Saint Adalbert:
section
Coloured reproduction
63.5 × 44
Latter half of the nineteenth century
Prague, Archiv Pražského hradu, Association for the Completion of the Cathedral of Saint Vitus, 387

While the location of the chapel in these nineteenth-century records is exact, there are certain inconsistencies as far as the architectural details are concerned, which for instance can be seen in the difference in poise between the angels on the vault in

the photograph, which are full of life, and the stiff, lifeless figures depicted in the sectional drawing. The faces of the vault are shown to be empty, where as in fact they were adorned with figurative frescos. This decoration more than likely dated back to the early Baroque, a hypothesis supported by the basic architectural division of the chapel and its architectonic details, such as consoles on the arcades.

Krčálová 1976, ill. 41.

I.M.

III.212
Anonymous
Rožmberk Palace: Jiřská-street façade
Artistic copy
28.5 × 103.5 cm
Notes by the architect's clerk,
J.H. Dienebier
1738
Prague Castle Archives, old plans collection, inv. no. 125/13

The façade of the Rožmberk Palace on Jiřská street still had Renaissance pediments until the 1730s. It had one on the east wing and three on the north wing, and the pediments of the former Švam-

berk House could also be seen. Alterations were made in 1680 when a wooden gallery was put in front of the façade in the direction of Jiřská street. After 1738 not only this wing was altered, but also the side wing, and further interior alterations were also made. The architect K.I Dienstenhofer participated in them.

Prague-Royal Summer Palace, 1979, cat. no. 44.

Krčalova 1970, pp. 469–85; Krčalova 1989, pp. 6–61; SURPMO and APH KPR, manuscript, 1992.

V.V.

III.213
Tomas Haffenecker
Haldensee 1669–Prague 1730
Rožmberk Palace: south façade
Colour reproduction
25.6 × 64 cm
Notes by the architect's clerk,
J.H. Dienebier
1722
Prague Castle Archives, Old plans c ollection, inv. no. 125/1

Alterations to the Rožmberk Palace started to be made in the 1720s because of its bad condition. Until then the palace had been Renaissance in appearance. During

the next thirty years the dormer windows and towers were gradually removed, and interior alterations were also made, with the large palace rooms being divided up. The roof of the palace was gradually raised, to a design by T. Haffernecker, and instead of the attic demi-storey a whole new storey was created.

Prague-Royal Summer Palace, 1979, cat. no. 41.

Krčalova 1970, pp. 469–85, Krčalova 1989, pp. 6–61; SURPMO and APH KPR, manuscript, 1992; *Nova encyklopedie...* 1995, pp. 238–39.

V.V.

III.214
Franz Haffl
Prague Castle, House of the Imperial
Chancery: façade
Colour reproduction
43 × 28
Prague, Hradčany Castle, inv. no. 177/4

In the latter half of the sixteenth century a
Renaissance-style building was erected on
the spot previously occupied by a mediae-
val building. In 1602 it was purchased by
Rudolf II and converted for use as the
headquarters of the Imperial Court Office.
This plan dates from shortly after 1806
when the institute's activities had been

comprehensively concluded with Franz I
surrendering his title of Holy Roman Emperor. The plan provides a diagram of the
south-facing façade towards Úvoz (including the noticeably disfigured two-floor
gable), but not of the façade on Loretán-
ská street where it was actually located.
Owing to the sloping terrain the ground
floor of the building had to be raised up
on a series of high arcade pilasters. However, the main feature of the street-facing
façade in all three plans (the cellar complex, ground floor, and first floor), is a centrally positioned oriel extension or 'rizalit'.
To the left of the façade there was also a
triple window, and inside the building on

the first floor, the oriel made up two sides
of the cross vault. As with many other
buildings dating from the Rudolf's reign,
the building's precise architectural style
and detail is unknown.

Podlaha 1920–21, ill. 117; Vilímková-Poko-
rný 1985, 5.

I.M.

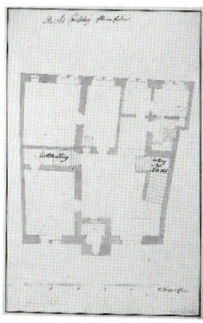

III.215
Prague Castle, House of the Imperial
Chancery: ground-floor plan
Coloured reproduction
43 × 28
Prague, Archiv Pražského hradu, inv. no.
177/3

See cat. no. III.214

Podlaha 1920–21, p. 190, no. 56, ill. 117.

I.M.

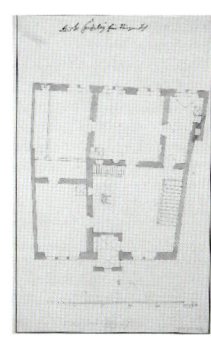

III.216
Prague Castle, House of the Imperial
Chancery: first-floor plan
Coloured reproduction
43 × 28 cm
Prague, Archiv Pražského hradu, inv. no.
177/2

See cat. no. III.214

Podlaha 1920–21, p. 190, no. 56, ill. 117.

I.M.

III.217
Chapel of St Rochus (Prague–Strahov):
longitudinal section and plan
Colour reproduction
42 × 34
First half of the eighteenth century
Prague, Archiv Pražského hradu, inv. no.
178/6

This plan of the chapel, which is one of the
most interesting examples of Central European church architecture, was published for the first time (cf. literature) in
1969. At that time the particular stylistic
importance of Gothic styles on Mannerism was pointed out both in the context of

Europe and Bohemia itself. Along with a
number of other buildings the Church of
Saint Peter and Paul in Kralovice were
built on the basis of this Mannerism, and
in no way could be described as representing the tail end of the late Gothic period.
As in the rest of Europe, where there were
many instances of the use of Gothic
ground plans and morphological elements and details (such as many-sided
chapels, supporting arches, tracery windows and so forth), so too in Bohemia,
where in the case of the Chapel of Saint
Rochus, the Gothic style clearly suited the
architect's own personal and artistic ends.
The structure is based on an elongated oc-

tagon to the sides of which fine, very elegant, vertically dominant pentagonal
chapels were built. The interior was given
a 'modern' finish, with slim colossal pilasters mounted with Ionian capitals. The
Chapel of St Rochus shares a surprising
number of features with the Church of St
Salvador.

Muchka 1969, 105–06, ill. 74; Krčálová
1976, ill. 49.

I.M.

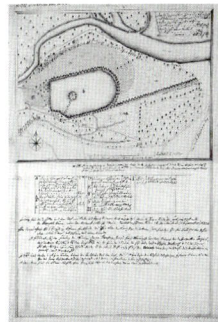

III.218
Stromovka Park (Prague–Bubeneč): plan
Coloured reproduction
62.5 × 42.2 cm
Prague, Archiv Pražského hradu, inv. no.
165/2

See cat. no. III.224

Podlaha 1922–23, no. 17, ill. 18.

I.M.

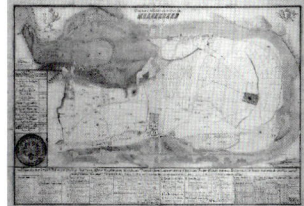

III.219
Johannes Glocksperger
Stromovka Park (Prague–Bubeneč): plan
Photo reproduction
69 × 100 cm
Prague, Archiv Pražského hradu, inv. no.
165/1

See cat. no. III.224

Podlaha 1922–23, no.16.

I.M.

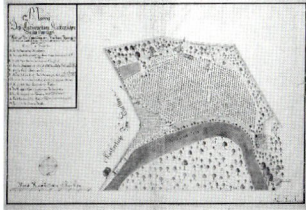

III.220
Stromovka Park (Prague–Bubeneč): plan
Coloured reproduction
47.5 × 70 cm
In the upper left corner:*Mappa des
aufgemessenen kayserlichen Baumbautens...*
early eighteenth century
Prague, Archiv Pražského hradu, inv. no.
164/1

See cat. no. III.224

Podlaha 1922–23, no.15.

I.M.

III.221
Franz Bretschneider
Stromovka Park (Prague–Bubeneč): site plan
Colour reproduction
68.6 × 48.8
Geometrischer Grund-Riss... Thiergarten, Fasan-Gartl, Baum-Garten, Kays-Insl, Mahl-Mühl
1775
Prague, Archiv Pražského hradu, inv. no. 165/10

The area of Hradčany Castle reserved for hunting included the Královská obora (the Royal Park) founded by Jan Lucem-

burský in the parish of Zadní Ovenec, today known as Bubeneč, in the early fourteenth century. At one point destroyed by the Hussites it was restored and extended during the fourteenth and fifteenth century. During Rudolf's reign it was divided into two parts, the smaller western part being reserved as a 'tree-garden' and a hunting area. In the northern part of the park there was perhaps already an area preserved for pheasant hunting and breeding during the reign of Rudolf II. A roughly oblong-shaped lake was located at the centre of the park, a section of which in the east was vaulted over. In the centre of the lake near to the summer resi-

dence there was a circular island. In the eighteenth century the lake was partially removed in connection with alterations to the park as a whole, and the island was turned into a natural elevation. Stromovka was connected to the Castle by a 1.7-kilometre-long direct route. In 1616 an avenue of trees (willows and lindens), inspired by a similar avenue in the Pratr in Vienna, was planted along the route

Wirth 1943, ill. 44.

I.M.

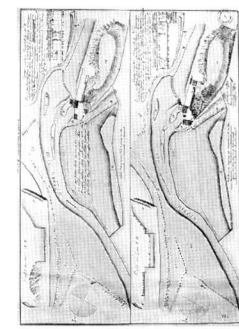

III.222
Stromovka Park (Prague–Bubeneč): plan
44.3 × 65.6 cm
Plan der nachst Prag liegenden Kaiser Muhle und der dazu gehorigen Realitaten
1834
Prague, Státní ústav památkové péče, sbírka pláný, inv. no. PPOP 9965198

See cat. no. III.224.

I.M.

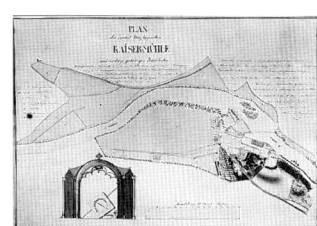

III.223
Summer Palace in Stromovka Park (Prague–Bubeneč): plan of basement, ground and first floors, and eaves
Coloured reproduction (drawing washed dark brown)
74.5 × 52 cm
Mid-nineteenth century
Prague, Archiv Pražského, inv. no. 165/79

See cat. no. III.224.

Podlaha 1922-23, tab. XXXI.

I.M.

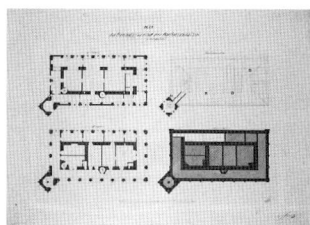

III.224
Summer Palace in Stromovka Park (Prague–Bubeneč): plan
Drawing on paper, colour photographic reproduction
42 × 24.5 cm
GrundtRieß und Profill von dem Kayl Bubentscher Thiergartten Obern Lusthauß 1726 gezeichnet, 59 Ellen lang, 29 Ellen Breith, 28 Ellen Hoch
1726
Prague, Archiv Pražského hradu, inv. no. 165/3

This summer residence in what was then known as Stará obora, today's Stromovka,

was Rudolf II's first building project and had perhaps already been prepared before his accession to the throne. The design made the greatest possible use of the existing building structures dating from the Jagello period. It was rebuilt between 1578 and 1579 by Ulrico Aostalli. The slanting corner tower was of unusual compositional importance in that it created an optical endpoint to the avenue of trees which led from Hradčany Castle to Stromovka, probably from the foreground area at the northern end, from the Lion's Court, and later on from the bastion to the north of it. The existence of the avenue is documented from 1616. The summer residence was

extremely important in that it marked the entrance way to the area. The natural terrain played a significant role in the design: in particular the steep slope on which the buildings stands. This was felt to be the ideal location for the summer residence, which looks out over an astounding natural landscape at a point where the river Vltava (Moldau) bifurcates.

Krčálová 1975, p. 501 (nn. 23-25), ill. 1 (APH); Krčálová 1976, ill. 32; Preiss 1986, ill. on p. 61.

I.M.

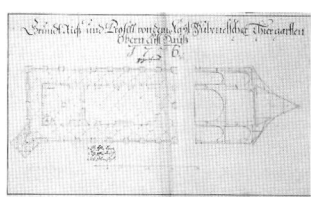

III.225
The Imperial Mill in Stromovka Park (Prague–Bubeneč): ground-floor plan
46.2 × 67.2
Alter Grund-Riss des Kayß. Bubentsch. Mül. (written in red ink) *A 308* (on back) *Kays. Müller in Bubentsch A 1730*
1730
Prague, Archiv Pražského hradu, inv. no. 168/1

A man-made cave by the east entrance to the complex, partially chiselled out of the cliff face. It formed the heart of the design, emphasized not only by the circular composition of its plan, but also by the origi-

nality of the design as a whole, which was created by a terrace originally fenced around with a balustrade. On the terrace was the two-storey façade of the grotto with the second floor also on a terrace. The façade's main feature is the semicircular hollowed-out recesses, which alternate at regular intervals with flat recesses. The mill can be attributed to the stone mason Antonio Brocco who received a payment of five hundred thalers for his work in 1594. Stone was the only material used inside the grotto, which has much in common with Serlio's designs, and in the use of bossage in the interior it may well have taken its inspiration from the work of

Hans Vredeman de Vries, in particular his *Variae Architecturae Formae*. Eighteenth-century plans which feature the grotto would seem to suggest that it housed a circular fountain, or perhaps a circular water cistern, and thus that it may have been used for bathing.

Krčálová 1972, ill. 1; Podlaha 1922, ill. 14b.

I.M.

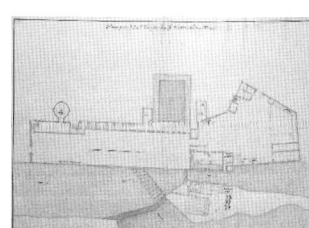

III.226
The Imperial Mill in Stromovka Park (Prague–Bubeneč): ground-floor pla
Photocopy
32.4 × 46.7
Alter grund Riss des Kayß. Bubentsch. Mül. Lit A
Vienna, Kriegsarchiv
Prague, National Institute for the care of Historical Monuments, collection of plans, inv. no. PPOP-996-5-199

In 1584 the Bohemia Office purchased the existing mill located at a point where the Bubeneč stream ran into one of the branches of the Vltava (Moldau). Work

was immediately begun on Rudolf's project of turning the site into a garden court area. To allow access to the area from the summer residence at the centre of Stromovka, the cliff face of the hill known as Pecka, the contour of which dropped in a sheer descent to the stream, was partially quarried away. Earlier sources state that the area was greatly favoured by the Emperor, who was able to walk there unaccompanied and undisturbed beside the beautiful scenery. The design of the recreational part of the site is very simple and consists of a two-storey L-shaped building, the longer side of which on both floors forms a corridor of arcade columns end-

ing in the west by the shorter wing. On the ground floor of this wing a passageway provided access to the working part of the mill. In the eighteenth century the open arcades were walled up, and in the first half of the nineteenth century another floor was added. At the turn of the twentieth century the river was canalized. Recently the area was reconstructed to serve a completely different purpose.

Muchka 1969, pp. 88-92; Fučíková-Bukovinská-Muchka 1988, pp. 202-209.

I.M.

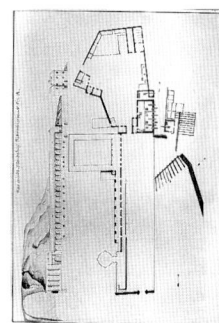

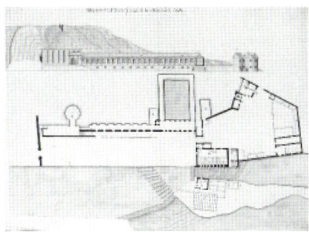

III.227
Antonín Haffenecker
The Imperial Mill in Stromovka Park
(Prague–Bubeneč): ground-floor plan
(1776 measurements)
Facsimile
50 × 70 cm
Prague, Archiv Praěského hradu, inv. no.
168/11

See cat. no. III.226.

Podlaha 1922–23, no. 14a, ill. 16,
Krčálová 1976, ill. 2.

I.M.

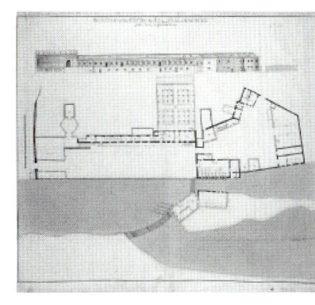

III.228
Antonín Haffenecker
Imperial Mill in Stromovka Park (Prague–
Bubeneč): view and ground-floor plan af-
ter renovation
Colour photo-reproduction
59.5 × 66.3 cm
*Alt und Neuer grund Riss des Königl.
Bubentscher Mühl. Lit B Erste Stock za
Ebener Erden, 1776*
Prague, Archiv Praěského hradu, 168/10

See cat. no. III.226.

Podlaha 1922,23, no. 14c, ill. 17.

I.M.

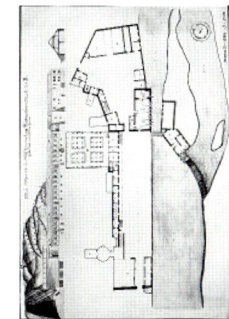

III.229
Imperial Mill in Stromovka Park (Prague–
Bubeneč): ground-floor plan after
renovation
34 × 46 cm
*Alt und Neuer grund Riss des Kayl.
Bubentscher Mühl. Lit B Erste Stock zu
Ebener Erden*
Prague, Státní ústav památkové péče,
sbírku plánů, inv. no. 996 5 201

See cat. no. III.226.

I.M.

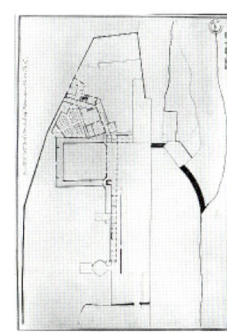

III.230
The Imperial Mill in Stromovka Park
(Prague–Bubeneč): first-floor plan after
adaptations
32.5 × 45.4 cm
*grund Riss des 2 Stocks von der Kayl.
Bubentscher Mühl. Lit C*
Prague, Státní ústav památkové, sbírku
plánů, inv. no. 996 5 201

See cat. no. III.226.

I.M.

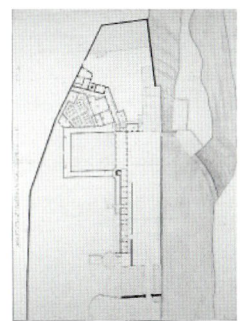
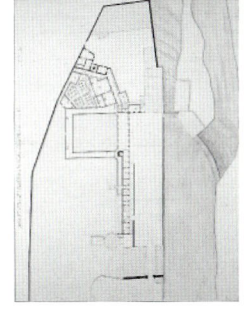

III.231
The Imperial Mill in Stromovka Park
(Prague–Bubeneč): second-floor plan af-
ter adaptations50 × 68 cm
Prague, Archiv Praěského hradu, inv. no.
168/9

See cat. no. III.226

I.M.

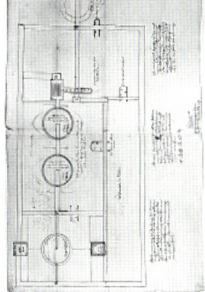

III.232
*Report by a building scribe on the establish-
ment of a cutting room for precious stones at
the Imperial mill* (plan).
Paper, pen drawing
41 × 62.5 cm
1602 (1607 ?)
Prague, Archiv Pražského hradu, SM B
110/1/1., fol. 1, inv. no. 291

The plan provides an outline of part of the
Imperial Mill, with its cutting room. It
combines both the ground plan with outline details of doors and polishing wheels.
The shaft leading from the mill is connected to a system of gears which increases the
speed of its rotation, while on a second
shaft two polishing stones (*Schleifstein*) are
then set in a room marked as the
Stainkammer, and a third stone at the end
of the shaft is located in a separate room
of its own. Another room at the bottom of
the plan, referred to as the *Stuben*, which is
in fact on the east side, is not fitted out
with any equipment.

I.M.

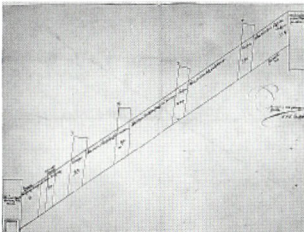

III.233
Rudolf's underground passage:
longitudinal sketch
Prague, Central State Archive, SM B 110/8

This profile of the Letenská underground passage shows both the distances between the individual air ducts,
referred to in the plan as *Liechtloch*, and
the overall distance of the passage. In
contrast to Phendler's plan, which depicts all five air ducts, including the unfinished central one, this diagram corresponds to the actual state of construction, which accounts for the fact that
the length between the second and third
air duct is almost twice as long compared with the other intervals. The segments at the Vltava (Moldau) and Stromovka are described as the vault *Gewelb*.
The plan was intended to serve as an aid
when carrying out maintenance work on
this unique construction.

I.M.

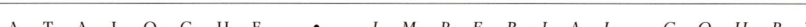
III.234
Jan Kozel, Michael Petrle of Annaberg
View of Prague
Photolithograph from 1904, coloured woodcut in five pages
62 × 192 (77 × 207) cm
In the upper part: *Praga Bohemiae metropolis accuratissime expressa 1562*
1562 (print Unie 1904)
Prague, Archives of the City of Prague, inv. no. AMP -1

This wide vista begins a period when graphically produced views were becoming irreplaceable as a source of identifying the exact appearance of the urban land-scape and the architecture of the city. The schematic and symbolic means of capturing reality is replaced by what could be called a 'photorealistic' view, in which details of individual buildings can be discerned. The significance of the vista from 1562 consists in that it captures the Castle before the decisive building activity of the Rudolfine era and offers an accurate view of the state of building at that time, at least concerning the Castle's south side which faces the town. In this view, we see both the extent of the south rampart and the palace by the south tower with three roofs, with the vertical axis towards the front and also the chisel-shaped roof of the gate along the White Tower, by which entry to the Castle from the west was gained.

Essen, cat. no. 1.

Novotny 1946, p. 15; Hlavsa 1971, p. 147, Muchka 1983, p. 449.

I.M.

III.235
Joris Hoefnagel
Antwerp 1542–Vienna 1600
View of Prague
Copper engraving, coloured
36.2 × 49.3 cm
Praga regni Bohemiae metropolis
Ca. 1591
Prague, Museum of the City of Prague, inv. no. 9 994

The author of the proposals marked 'de-lineator' for Hoefnagel's views was Franz Hoogenbergh, whose merit rests on his new view of Prague from Letna which appeared in opposition to the older viewing points onto Petrin Hill. In this case, the river divides the vista on the left and the Old Town can been seen beyond the 'me-andering' river in the place today known as Parizska Street. The picturesque and dramatic right-hand side shows the pro-portions of the relations between the Cas-tle and settlement around it known as Malá Strana (the Lesser Town).

I.M.

III.236
Joris Hoefnagel
Antwerp 1542–Vienna 1600
View of Prague
Copper engraving
18 × 46 cm
Praga, Bohemiae metropolis accuratissime espressa Franz Hoogenberghe (Delineator)
1572
Prague, Museum of the City of Prague, inv. no. 8 613

The importance of Hoefnagel's views of Prague consists particularly in that he catches Prague Castle as it gradually took shape during the 1570s and 1580s. Admit-tedly, they are not as precise as the some-what earlier views by Willenberg or the so-called Sadeler's Prospect, but with their clear arrangement, cogency and meticu-lous construction, unencumbered by ex-cess details, they are of fundamental im-portance in presenting Prague at that time. They formed part of a voluminous work entitled *Civitates orbis terrarum* and helped to popularize Prague and place it in the context of other metropolises in Eu-rope.

Essen, cat. no. 2.

I.M.

III.237
Johann Willenberg
View of Prague
Woodcut
14 × 60 cm
Jo. Willenberg fecit 1601
1601
Prague, Printing press of Johann Ssuman
Prague, Museum of the City of Prague, inv. no. 27 739 AMP 2f 104

In the artistic production of the Czech Lands, Willenberg can be regarded as a specialist whose skill in the art of the vista was outstanding. It is really due to him that the face of Czech and Moravian towns at around 1600 is known to us. A large number of artists created vistas of Prague and Prague Castle. Nevertheless, his persistent interest, expressed in vistas from 1601, 1604 (the Pilsen Calendar) and 1610 brings the opportunity for extensive comparisons to be made. A detail of the White Tower clock serves as an example: portrayed in 1601 and 1604, it is absent from the view of 1610 (for that matter, it is missing in Sadeler's Prospect from 1606).

Essen, cat. no. 4

Straka 1913, tab. II; Hlavsa 1971, p. 149, Muchka 1983, pp. 447–50.

I.M.

III.238
Vaclav Hollar
View of Prague in 1636 (from M. Zeiller's book Topographia Bohemiae, Moraviae et Silesiae durch Matteum Merian zu Frackfurt a. M. 1650)
Etching
27.2 × 108.7 cm
Lower centre of the picture: *Wenceslaus Hollar...1636 exactissime delineavit Aqua for-ti in hac forma... in sculpsit, Antwerpiae A. o 1649*
Prague, Národní galerie v Praze, Grafická sbírka, inv. no. DR 13 833

Hollar's view is, after the so-called Sadel-er's Prospect, another actually presentable depiction of Prague after an approximate-ly thirty-year caesura. From the point of view of the iconography of the Castle it-self, he does not introduce any revolution-ary 'innovations', but rather a confirma-tion, a petrification of the state which was reached during the reign of Rudolf II. Since he captures the Castle as if from a higher point than Sadeler's prospect, how-ever, we can see the west entrance to the Castle, the roofs of the north assembly rooms and the towers of the central tract, known as the Mathematical and the White towers, both of which have terraces for viewing. The likeness to the residential buildings, east of the White Tower, contin-ues to remain somewhat uncertain; this is where the Empress's Palace originated at about the end of the 1630s, between the actual sketch of the vista and it being pub-lished.

Novotny 1946, pp. 31-34; Muchka 1983, p. 448.

I.M.

III.239
Prague Castle: view of western entrance
Photo reproduction
32 × 41 cm
1649
Vienna, Österreichisches Staatsarchiv,
Kriegsarchiv, K VII C 89 - 178 E

I.M.

III.240
Antonín Pucherna
Imperial Mill in Stromovka (Prague–
Bubeneč): view
Photographic reproduction
19 × 26
Die Kaisermühle, A. Pucherna del.
Ca. 1800
Prague, Archiv Pražského hradu, Collec-
tion of engravings APH, inv. no. VI/68

The archway providing access to the Imperial Mill faces the eastern approach from
the summer residence, and together with
the perimeter wall is practically the only
purpose-built construction capable of

preventing an unwanted visitor from entering. This was the mill was guarded by
its geological location, from the south by
the sheer drop of Pecka hill, and from the
north by the river. In the west, where the
commercial section of the mill was located, it was also guarded. The archway was
constructed out of brick and given an
identical design on either side, consisting
of a Tuscan aedicule framing a semicircular arch. The design of the archway was in
essence based on a combination of two designs which can be found in the works of
the architectural theoretician Sebastiano
Serlio. Rudolf's architecture developed in
an intellectually dramatic and fertile con-

text, the principal features of which also
served to articulate the sophisticated principles underlying the Manneristic painting and sculpture of the period.

Muchka 1969, ill 46.

I.M.

III.241
Sebastiano Serlio
*Architettura si Sebastian Serlio in sei libri di-
visa*
Prague, ÚDU, F 345 (22386/63)

In the history of the theory of architecture,
Serlio occupies a unique position, entirely
different from that occupied by systema-
tists such as Vitruvius, Alberti, di Giorgio
and Filarete. Serlio's theorctical interest
was of secondary importance: he sought
rather to provide practical instruction on
how to build. This consisted of presenting
selected examples, particular patterns,
ideal designs, and pointing out examples

of the buildings and architectural feats of
Antiquity. The universal influence of Serlio's work on Central Europe is attested to
by numerous buildings based on his designs. Oskar Pollak was the first to point
out Serlio's influence on Renaissance
Prague in his study completed in 1910,
and since then a number of other similar
studies have been made. Serlio's work was
published in a steady stream beginning
with his *Book IV* in 1537, entitled *Regole
generali Di Architettura Sopra Le Cinque
Maniere De Gli Edifici*. By 1551 his *Books I -
V* had been published and another book
which he did not not number, *Extraordinario libro... nel Quale Si Dimostrano Trenta*

*Porte di Opera Rustica... Et Venti Di Opera
Dilicata'*. Since his *Book VII* was published
in Frankfurt by Jacopo Strada in 1575, it
was thought that the *libro extraordinario*
referred to the sixth book. However, at different times during the 1930s two
manuscripts were discovered of the real
sixth book, which was devoted to residential buildings. In view of the fact that there
are known woodcuts which were made for
this book, the possibility that it drew on
this source in the sixteenth century cannot be ruled out.

I.M.

III.242
Sebastiano Serlio
Il settimo libro di architettura (titulus)
Prague, National Library, 17 A 11

Serlio's work became a limitless source of
inspiration for architecture in northern
Europe, a point stressed by the fact that
his seventh book was published by
Rudolf's own antiquarian, Jacopo Strada,
as well as by the fact that his influence
could already be seen in the design of the
so-called Queen Anna summer residence
built before the mid-point of the century.
Serlio's designs were used in all aspects of
the architectural design, including the

ground plan and choice of location (cf. the
ground plan of the country estate in Nelahozeves), the designs of the façade (cf. the
courtyard façade of the country estate in
Moravská Třebová), and even in the individual features and details, a point attested to by the fact that almost all surviving
Renaissance ceilings in the present-day
Czech Republic, are based on Serlio's designs. There is even a rather curious example of one of Serlio's designs for a panelled
ceiling being used for a geometrical graffito pattern. Serlio's designs were also used
in like measure for the construction of
archways and portals, one such example
being the archway to the Imperial Mill,

which was based on a combination of two
designs, the lower section being based on
a design for a portal taken from his fourth
book, and the curved gable being based on
a design printed on the title page of the
seventh.

I.M.

III.243
Pietro di Giacomo Cantaneo
*L'Architettura Di Pietro Cantaneo Senese...
Sono aggiunti di piu il Quinto, Sesto, Settimo
e Ottava libro*
Prague, Národní muzeum, Nostická
Library, E 27

Cantaneo's tract was published beginning
in 1554 with *I Quattro Primi Libri Di Achi-
tettura Di Pietro Cantaneo Senese*. It was later published in its entirety (eight books)
in Venice in 1567, and in 1572 *Opera del
misurare* was also published. The most interesting of the works is the fourth book
on palace plans. These plans may well

have influenced Ferdinand Tyrolský, who
owned one of the first edition copies of
Cantaneo's tract, in his choice of design
for his Hvězda summer residence in 1555.
Cantaneo was considered one of the leading theoreticians on fortification architecture of his day. As he himself makes clear,
he was indebted to Serlio's work, and
aimed rather to supplement it in the area
of fortification theory and its connected
area of urban planning, the latter of which
he considered the architect's most important task.

I.M.

III.244
Walther Herm Rivius
Bawkunst... aller fürnemsten... angehörigen Mathematischen und Mechanischen Künsten, eygentlicher Bericht ... in Truck verordnet, Durch Gualtherum H. Rivium
Prague, Národní muzeum, Nostická Library, D 49

Walther Rivius (Ryff), by vocation a doctor and mathematician living in Nürnberg (post-1548), was an important figure in the theory of architecture in the German-speaking parts of Europe before the mid-sixteenth century. His major achievement lay in the introduction of the writings of the architect Vitruvius to trans-alpine Europe, first in a Latin edition published in 1543, and later in a critical edition in German published in 1548. In 1547 Ryff published another book on architecture entitled *Der furnembsten... der ...Architectur angehörigen Mathematischen und Mechanischen Künst, eygentlicher bericht ...* (published by Johann Petreius in Nürnberg), which was devoted in particular to aspects of perspective and geometry, and which made much use of Sebastiano Serlio's first two books on architecture. It was normal for books on geometry and perspective in this period to also provide instruction on making technical drawings and using measuring and orientation equipment. Ryff, as well as being very erudite and well-read, was also very adept at collating and compiling information drawn from numerous sources, some of which he introduced the preface (Pacioli, Cesarian, Philander, Serlio, and Tartaglio). The volume in the Nostická library is a copy of his translation of Vitruvius, published in an extensive edition by Sebastiano Henricpetri in Basle, with 681 pages and numerous illustrations.

I.M.

III.245
Hans Blum
Ein kunstrych Buch von allerley antiquitetn, so zum verstand der fünff Seulen der Architectur gehörend. Getruckt zu Zürich in der Froschow bey Chrystofell Froschower
Prague, Národní muzeum, Nostická Library, E 26

This textbook on column orders, originally in Latin, was first published in Zurich in 1550, and entitled *Quinque columnarum Exacta descriptio....* A German version was later published in 1555, entitled *Von den fünff Süllen, Grundtlicher Bericht*. The same publishing house which had first published the Latin version in 1550, published a new edition together with examples of ancient architecture. This was followed by yet another edition, and Dutch, English, and French translations. From the point of view of Central Europe it is interesting to note that over a century after the first Latin edition, Abraham Leuthner, an architect of the early Baroque period, borrowed freely from Blum's text in his work similarly entitled *Grundtliche Darstellung der fünff Seylen*, published in Prague in 1677. In the hope of making life easier for constructors and craftsmen, Blum sought to present the most precise calculation possible for the proportions of columns, pedestals and entablature. Blum borrowed many illustrations from Serlio, but his system differed from his predecessor's in that the individual proportions of a pedestal, column with base and capital, and entablature used set measurements by which the size of a feature belonging to an order could be determined. These perhaps seemingly minor technical details were of immense importance in the Renaissance, as was attested to by the publication of Vignoli's *Regola delle cinque ordini* which presented the 'definitive' version of the proportions of the five orders.

I.M.

III.246
Hans Vredeman de Vries
Architectura oder Bauung der Antiquen
Prague, National Library

Hans Vredeman de Vries encapsulated in this complex theoretical work the requirements for an all-round architectural grounding in 'construction' (*Lehrgebäude*). As is justly claimed in the book itself, theoretical writings of precisely this kind had to a certain degree begun to replace specialized study, and were rapidly becoming the real 'academies of the north'. Vredeman, as Serlio before him, understood that simple objective illustrations were of the utmost importance in conveying architectural theories and principles. In many seminal works by figures such as Vitruvius, such illustrations had been wholly lacking, and attempts to add them at a later date in new editions ran the risk of deviating from what had originally been intended. Dozens of Vredeman's engravings presented elementary designs of columns, pedestals and entablature, together with instructions for how they were to be constructed, an approach referred to in the sixteenth century as a *Säulenbuch*. Other engravings were much more complex, presenting designs of façades, town squares and even entire streets. Vredeman's personal choice of style can be particularly seen in the rustic designs and the bossage, often composed in encircling bands, a motif which was intended to lend symmetry to portals, window jambs, gables attic gables, and so forth. Vredeman's designs include the conical baluster pillar, positioned 'head-down' towards its cone centre.

I.M.

III.247
Hans Vredeman de Vries
Caryatidum (Vulgus Termas Vocat) Sive Athlantidum...
Prague, Premonstratensians monastery in Strahov, library, AY XI4

Vredeman was an unusually productive author, both of general compilations on the theory of column styles and particular architectural schools of thought, and of monothematic works devoted to individual elements of architecture and themes such as fountains, tombs and tombstones, military trophies (panoplia), 'rolwerk' frames, different types of vessels, and so forth. The undated sixteen-part series published by Gerard de Iode in Antwerp around 1560, is particularly impressive for its rich variations in articulating the basic relation between the human half-figure form, and the wedge-shaped pillar. The scrawny figures with the recognizable parts of the pillar capitals in the uppermost sections can be linked to particular column styles, even though, as is usually the case, Vredeman himself does not expressly draw the connection. This is often the case even where it would least be expected, as for instance in the case of gardens or the five senses, or the allegories of the ages of man. His scrawny figures stand in complete contrast to the guards or Perseuses depicted on dozens of portals in transalpine Europe as good omens symbolizing the protection and security of property or homes. The portal of house number '19' on the main square in Jihlava took its inspiration from the herma of the young man with 'shorn-off' arms depicted in print no. I of Vredeman's undated series.

I.M.

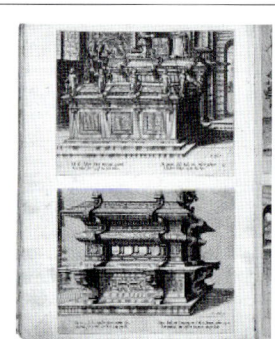

III.248
Hans Vredeman de Vries
Den Eersten Boeck... Colomnen Dorica en Ionica
Prague, Premonstratensians monastery in Strahov, library, AY XI 4

The basic theory of column orders based on a knowledge of the architectural principles of Antiquity consisted of the gradual movement from columns of large robust proportions to proportions that were increasingly refined and slender. The three basic types of column used in the architecture of antiquity, namely Doric, Ionian, and Corinthian, were increased in number by the European humanist order of architecture to include the Tuscan and composite orders. Sebastiano Serlio invented a simple mathematical formula for the Tuscan column, its base-to-capital length measuring a total of six times the diameter of its lowest column shaft. Each of the other orders was then one unit thinner, with the height of the last (the composite), measuring ten times the diameter of its base column shaft. A similar system, using different proportions was also used for the plinth. Each column order, however, had an autonomous 'existence', and as result Vredeman was able to publish his architecture works based on each different architectural style. His book on the Doric and Ionic order was published in 1565, *Architectura 3ᵒᵒ stuck. De Oorden Tvschana* was published in 1578, and 'das ander Buech', dealing with the Corinthian and composite orders, in 1581.

I.M.

III.249
Hans Vredeman de Vries
Perspective, Id est Celeberrima ars inspicientis aut transcipientis oculorum aciei, in pariete, tabula aut tel depicta...
Prague, Národní muzeum, Nostická
Library, E 64

The importance of this universal artist, theoretician and active architect of the sixteenth century is well attested to by his last book on perspective, published in 1604 with an engraving of the artist in his seventy-seventh year. In its range and depth of content, there is no other sixteenth-century work by any other theoreti-

cian of architecture and ornamentation to compare this book and the corpus of work to which it belongs. It is interesting to compare the work with other works which sought to deal with the same theme, such as Cantaneo's eighth book published in Venice in 1567. Cantaneo's book presents the reader with a very simplified explanation of the principles of perspective using a series of drawings, the two most complex of which are diagrams of a cylinder and an octagon. The book does not try to analyse a complete interior or exterior design. In the preface Vredeman refers to different predecessors, such as Albrecht Dürer, Hieronymus Cock, Gerardi de Iode,

Philippi Galle and Petri Baltens. The complete first volume of Vredeman's publication in the Nostická library has a total of forty-nine illustrations accompanied by fourteen pages of explanatory notes in Latin. The second volume entitled *Perspective pars altera ...* was much shorter, with only twenty-four illustrations.

I.M.

III.250
Hugues Sambin
Oeuvre de la Diversité des Termes, dont on use en Architecture, reduict en ordre: Par maistre Huges Sambin, demeurant a Dijon
Prague, National Library, 6 B 48

This publication on caryatids was unusual for the theoretical literature published on architecture during this period. Architectonic features such as a capitals, column bases, cornices and so forth had often been the subject of monothematic publications during the first half of the sixteenth century (Peter Flötner, cf. Schmitz 1939, cat. no. 3900;

Agostino Veneziano, cf. Schmitz 1939, cat. no. 3899, or Heinrich Vogtherr: Kunstbüchlein 1537), and in the latter half of the century this move towards greater specialization increased still further. An interesting example of this could be seen in the publications on the architectural feature which appeared under the various titles of herma, terma, Perseus, Atlas, caryatid, to name but a few. In view of the culminating Mannerism of the period this anthropomorphic feature with its particularly unstable, grotesque and obscure features, was particularly popular, because it fitted in well with the then need to 'psycholo-

gize' architecture by making it express a particular 'character'. These publications appeared in almost all languages.

I.M.

III.251
Daniel Meyer
Architectura Oder Verzeichnus allerhand Eynfassungen
Paris, Bibliothèque Nationale

The full title of the book, which was first published in 1609 by the prestigious publishing house of the de Bra family, read as follows: *Architectura Oder Verzeichnuß allerhand Eynfassungen an Thüren, Fenstern un Decken, sehr nützlich und dienlich allen Mahlern, Bildthawern, Steinmetzen, Schreinern, und andern Liebhabern dieser Kunst, Alles erstlichen new erfunden und geetzt Durch Daniel Meyern, Mahlern und Bürgern*

zu Franckfurt am Mayn. The index of architectural features was not quite complete, with such items as 'rolwerk' cartouches, frames and panelling missing. In 1612 Meyer published another book with a slightly modified title, which also included fountains, fireplaces, tombs and headstones, and so forth. Though not specified in the title, folio forty-nine included a section on hermae, which were used in the design of portals and furniture. The fantastical couple depicted in this print is a perfect analogy of one of Giuseppe Arcimboldo's playful fancies, the figure on the left identifiable as female by the two apples in place of breasts, and the figure on

the right recognizable as male by the laurel leaves which have replaced its moustache. The composition of the leaves, flowers and fruit motifs recalls Vertumno, even though in its pose it is more rustic, and more naively narrative.

I.M.

III.252
Pirro Ligorio
Libro delle antichita di Roma
Prague, National Library, 23 G 60, No 1

Ligorio, who as an architect found a place in history thanks to his design for Pius IV's Casino in the Vatican gardens, also wrote a seminal work on Roman Antiquity, which included a section on architecture. His theories were founded on principles similar to those shared by the Vitruvius school (cf. Kruft 1993, 97). However, the work is not primarily concerned with the theoretical issues of architecture. Various copies of this manuscript can be found in

collections in Naples, Oxford, Paris, and Turin.

I.M.

III.253
Jean Jacques Boissard
Topographia urbis Romae, Das ist Eygentliche Beschreibung der Statt Rom
Prague, Národní muzeum, Nostická
Library, E 13

Besides textbooks, professional literature on the subject of architecture also included the genre of artistic 'topography', which should of course be understood in the broadest sense of the word and in the context of the period. Compared with tracts which in addition to their main content often included a section on ancient architecture and monuments, and very oc-

casionally on modern architecture and monuments as well, topographic literature and guidebooks were solely geared to the purpose of acquainting the reader with the riches of a particular area or city, depending on its chosen subject. In the sixteenth century Rome was the most commonly selected city for such books. From 1510 onwards a whole stream of such books were published on the city by different authors, beginning with Francisco Albertini, and followed by Andrea Fulvius, Bartolomeo Marliani, Jacques Ducerceau, Martin Heemskerck, Andrea Palladio, Antonio Lanbacco, Stefan Duperac and Pirro Ligorio. In addition to

obelisks and sites and monuments of architectural interest, Boissard's *Topography* also includes sections on themes such as sculpture. The rather curious claim that Rome could be viewed in four days was made in the full title and repeated in the preface. The book has seventy-eight pages of text and 104 illustrations, including a plan of the city.

I.M.

III.254
Christoph Jamnitzer
Neüw Grotteßken Buch, Inventirt radirt und verlegt Durch Christoph Jamnitzer Bürg: und Goltsch: in Nürnberg
Prague, Národní muzeum, Nostická Library, bg 338

Jamnitzer's series is interesting for a number of reasons. It documents the transformation the concept of the grotesque underwent during the sixteenth century. This type of ornamentation, which had often been linked with Antiquity in general, as examples of it had been found in the so-called 'Nero's House' or Golden House (*casa aurea*), began its development in the Vatican's loggias, where it consisted of clear geometrical designs. In a series of peripeteias during the pinnacle of the Renaissance and late Renaissance period, it began to take on bizarre forms, finally blending with ornamentation that was both anthropomorphic and zoomorphic. There were a number of noteworthy graphic series published on the theme of the grotesque during the sixteenth century, both in Italy and in transalpine Europe. In this series Jamnitzer, a well-known goldsmith in Nürnberg, not only made the designs and engravings but also acted as his own publisher, a point stressed in the title. His series presented a style of ornamentation referred to in German as *schweifwerk*. The series is divided into three parts, each with its own title page. The first contains eighteen engravings, the second nineteen engravings, and the last twenty-one.

I.M.

III.255
Giovanni Battista Montano
Architettura
Prague, National Library, 17 A 14 (FFUK, S 70)

This theoretical work tends to be thought of as simply a source of inspiration for Borromini, an architect of the subsequent Baroque period. Borromini can be shown to have used Montano's proto-Baroque designs, but there is a slight problem for historians of architecture in asserting this claim in view of the fact that all Borromini's works were published after Montano's death. The most likely explanation in the light of this is that Montano had prepared his designs with a view to publishing them, and that long before their posthumous publication they had already become known in certain circles. As evidence of this his Ionian column capital in folio twenty of his *Architettura*, which appears beneath the heading 'Capitelli varij, cavati da diversi Edifici antichi', has an acanthus design on the opening page which is very similar to the ornamentation featured on the column capitals in the Church of St Rochus. Further indirect evidence of Central European interest in Montano's work can be found in Abraham Leuthner's tract on architecture published in 1677, which contains illustrations quite literally lifted (appearing as mirror inversions of their originals) from Montano's 'Raccolta di tempii' of 1638.

I.M.

III.256
Hans Vredeman de Vries and Dirk de Quade van Ravesteyn
Palace Architecture with Aristocratic Visitors
Oil on canvas
Signed bottom right at the edge of the fountain: HANS (leg) VREDEMAN (leg) VRIESE IN
Ca. 1596
From the collection of Rudolf II; imperial collection in Vienna
Vienna, Kunsthistorisches Museum, Gemäldegalerie, inv. no. 2 334

Together with pictures depicting musicians and people out walking, the *Palace Architecture with Noble Visitors* forms a trio of works, which Hans Vredeman de Vries with the help of his son Paul and Dirk de Quade van Ravesteyn painted for Rudolf II, and which were never allowed to leave the imperial collections. The striking signature of Hans can with difficulty be understood as merely demonstrating an admission of authorship, although his intentions for the painting were carried out by Paul, as is sometimes mentioned in the literature. It is not easy to distinguish the shares contributed by father and son in the light of the fact that they lived and worked together for many years. On the other hand, if Paul's signature were to be found on one of those paintings, notably *Palace Architecture with People out Walking*, that would undoubtedly mean that his contribution to the work was substantial. The figural pageantry, painted in the inimitable style of Ravesteyn, was, however, not considered worthy of a signature and it was only recently that this painter was identified as the expert who assisted on the figures.

Kaufmann 1988, cat. no. 25.3 (see also 25.1, for relevant literature).

E.F.

III.257
Paul Vredeman de Vries and
Pieter Isaacsz
King Solomon and the Queen of Sheba
Oil on canvas
Herdringen, Fürstenberg Collection
Münster, Westfälisches Landesmuseum für Kunst und Geschichte, inv. no. 1889
LG

While the architectural paintings made by Hans Vredeman de Vries and his son for Rudolf II have secular themes, depicting the high society of the nobles at ease in the palace courtyards, works commissioned by others were often livened up with themes from the Old Testament. Paul also used the theme of the meeting between Solomon and the Queen of Sheba to enliven several of his architectural paintings, which in this particular case was done for him by Pieter Isaacsz. Paul used various well-known motifs in his depiction of the palace architecture, taken for instance from Hans' drawings of Bremen and Amsterdam. It is interesting to note that Isaacsz also took a degree of inspiration from them. This painting dates from between 1601 and 1607 when both artists were based in Amsterdam. Isaacsz went later to the royal court of Denmark.

E.F.

III.258
Epistle of the Bohemian Chamber to the Imperial Chamber on the Matter of Settling the Outstanding Amount of 2000 Thalers with Adriaen de Vries for Work on 'New Hall'
Colour reproduction
32 × 20.5 cm
1614
Prague, Archiv Pražského hradu, inv. no. Dvor. komora. 738

Original, in German, double page.

I.M.

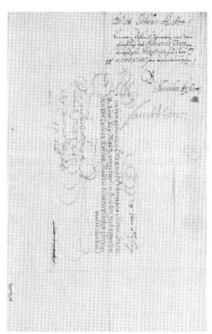

III.259
The Elders and Masters of the Painters'
Guild of the Prague Municipalities Assess
Work Carried out During the Painting of
the Ceiling of the Palace above the Stables
in Prague castle, 27 November 1579
Paper
32 × 21 cm
Modern date in upper left corner, different from text
1597
Prague, Archiv Národního muzea, inv. no. H3-F 178, box 142

I.M.

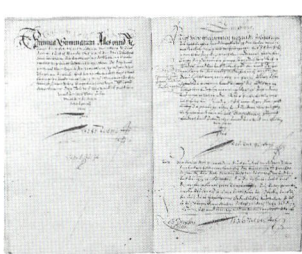

III.260
Ulrico Aostalli de Sala
Savosa 1525 (?)–Prague 1597
Invoice for Building Construction at Prague Castle
Artistic copy, paper, leather binding
31.5 × 20.5 cm
Own signature
1580s–90s
Prague Castle Archives, Court Building Office inventory, inv. no. 53

Accounts from the administrator of the Emperor's building office and from master builder Ulrico Aostalli de Sala, containing accounts for several buildings in the Castle and its surroundings, which Rudolf II paid for with his own money via his highest chamberlain, Jeronim Gaberin. They concern the definitive completion of the royal tomb in the Cathedral of St Vitus in 1589-90, the Melantrich vineyard, the building of a new wall under the Royal Garden, the building of the Imperial Mill, the creation of a fishpond in Bubenec in 1589-90 and the building of a new wall round the expanded Old Enclosure in 1583-84.

Moravek 1959 pp. 52-53, Krčalova 1989, pp. 160-81, Nova encylopedie česke vytvarneho umění 1995, pp. 31-32.

V.V.

III.261
Anonymous
Gargoyle
Sandstone
65 × 52 × 30 cm (mounting board: 16 cm; depth of relief: 14 cm)
Ca. 1590
Spanish Hall in the north wing of Hradčany Castle
Prague, Hradčany Castle, Hradčany Castle Administrative Authority

This gargoyle was found in a walled-up recess in the so-called Spanish Stables, where it evidently functioned as a water spout for the trough. In the catalogue printed for the Essen exhibition the gargoyle was presented as possibly being based on designs seen in the work of Frans Huys. His works can be found in Prague on the doors that were later transferred to the Old Town Hall, and in the voussoir of the courtyard porticos in a palace in the Lesser Town. Also linked with these works in terms of their design and period is the group of gargoyles found in the entrance ways, which are hypothetically linked with the stonemason Antonio Brok and attest to the high standard of masonry around the turn of the seventeenth century.

Essen, cat. no. 7.

Muchka 1969, p. 91, illus. 56–58.

I.M.

III.262
Inventory of the Tomb of Anna of Jagellon: Robe
Silk, tailored velvet, trimmings of warp rep decorated with weft loops in the shape of lozenges, bobbin-shaped decorations with ribbons wound round and a wooden core.
Fragmentary state and bad reconstruction make it difficult to gauge the original measurements. Trimmings are 2 cm wide.
Probably 1547
Velvet probably fom Italy or Germany, trimming from Bohemia, sewn probably in Prague
Archiv Pražského hradu, inv. no. PHA 25/1

This dress, now brown, was inexpertly restored and reconstructed without its original cut being documented, and so only probable details of the original can now be given. The bodice and skirt were cut separately. The bodice was low-cut, so a blouse must have been worn under it, and the neckline was edged with two (?) rows of braid. The bodice was laced at the front. The sleeves were slashed, with braid sewn between the rows of diagonal slashes. The belt was made of two cords ending in tassels and knotted at intervals into medallions, in between which there were large beads. The skirt was wide and gathered at the top. The dress is a typical Renaissance model, popular above all in Germany from 1530 onwards.

M.Br.

III.263
Inventory of the Tomb of Anna of Jagellon: Cloak
Velvet and trimmings made from the same material and with the same technique as the dress
Fragmentary state - bottom hem ca. 240 cm, velvet strips 60 cm wide, trimmings 2.5 cm wide
Probably 1547
Velvet probably from Italy or Germany, trimmings probably from Bohemia, sewn probably in Prague
Archiv Pražského hradu, inv. no. PHA 25/10

A cloak, today brown, of which as a result of inexpert treatment immediately it was taken out of the grave there remain only six (?) fragmentary strips of velvet from the lower part, decorated with three rows of trimmings, and several independent fragments. The cloak probably had no sleeves, but only holes for the hands. The bottom of the cloak was finished in a curve, and there was perhaps a train. This is the type of cloak in which Anna of Jagellon is portrayed in a relief in the Belvedere summer palace.

M.Br.

III.264
Inventory of the Tomb of Anna of Jagellon: Cap and Veil
Silk, gold thread, drawn-work, twill-weave ribbon, sewn lace, veil of tabby-weave silk muslin
22 cm high, bottom circumference 53 cm, bottom band 1 cm wide, veil 35 cm long, 116 cm wide
Probably before 1547
Material probably Italy, Germany or Austria, made up probably in Vienna or Prague
Archiv Pražského hradu, inv. no. PHA 25/2

A cap made of gold thread with a bottom band of woven cloth from which there is a sewn central medallion, made in open-work from 'columns' of thread. Gold thread is fixed around the circumference, and out of it the cap is made in knot-work. It is given shape by stiffener inside. A veil was affixed to the cap, tied into a bow at the side. The wearing of caps was one of the rights and also duties of married women. Analogous to Anna of Jagellon's cap is a Renaissance hair net found in the well near the All Saints' chapel in Prague Castle (1550–80, Prague, Archiv Pražského hradu). Both head coverings have a similar decorative medallion above the forehead, called an eye.

M.Br.

III.265
Inventory of the Tomb of Anna of Jagellon: Slippers and Stockings
Slippers: silk, cut-pile velvet, cork. Hose: wool, three-weave weft twill
Fragmentary state – slippers impossible to measure, hose 31 cm from instep to upper hem, 27 cm from heel to upper hem, circumference of upper hem 32 cm
Probably 1547
Velvet probably from Italy or Germany, cork from Portugal, wool probably from Austria or Bohemia, probably made in Prague
Archiv Pražského hradu, inv. no. 25/11, 12

The knee-high hose had a seam at the back, while the front came up in an arch underneath the knee. Only one of the soles has been preserved. Cloth hose was typical in the period before knitted stockings became fashionable in the middle of the sixteenth century. It is clearer what the original appearance of the queen's shoes was than those of the other Habsburgs buried in Prague, because they were not subjected to a bad restoration attempt on being taken out of the grave. The uppers were made of velvet. The insoles above the cork undersoles were also made of velvet, while the undersoles were covered on the bottom and sides with leather. Not exhib-ited.

Bravermanova–Kobrlova–Samohylova 1994, vol. 19, pp. 437-461; Bravermanova–Samohylova (in preparation).

M.Br.

III.266
Inventory of the Tomb of Anna of Jagellon: Pall
Silk, tabby-weave muslin
Fragmentary state – 44 cm long, 35 cm wide
Probably 1547
Material probably from Italy or Germany
Archiv Pražského hradu, inv. no. PHA 25/7

A muslin shroud, today copper-coloured, which covered Anna of Jagellon's face in the coffin.

M.Br.

III.267
Inventory of the Tomb of Anna of Jagellon: Pall
Silk, tabby-weave
214 cm long, 53 cm wide
Probably 1547
Material probably from Italy or Germany
Archiv Pražského hradu, inv. no. PHA 25/13

A shroud, now brown in colour, which covered the dead queen's body.

M.Br.

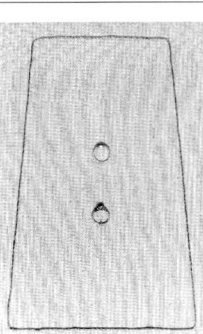

III.268
Anonymous Goldsmith
Active in the second quarter of sixteenth century
Inventory of the grave of Anna Jagellonská: a braided gold cord
Purity of the gold: 915/1000 (22 carat), braided wire
D: 102
Before 1547
Found in coffin on chest of the deceased
Prague, Sbírky Pražského hradu, PHA 25/3

Mihulka, up to 1993.

III.269
Anonymous Goldsmith
Active in the second quarter of sixteenth century
Inventory of the grave of Anna Jagellonská: ring with miniature glass eye
Purity of the gold: 965/1000 (23.2 carat), cast
D: 1.75; glass: 0.5 × 0.7 (measured as set in ring)
Found where hands are clasped
Prague, Sbírky Pražského hradu, PHA 25/4

Mihulka, up to 1993.

III.270
Anonymous Goldsmith
Active in the second quarter of sixteenth century
Iventory of grave of Anna Jagellonská: ring with ruby
purity of gold 875/1000 (21.0 carat), cast, engraved, chased, ruby, cut
D: 1.75, ruby 0.4 × 0.5
Before 1547
Found among fingers
Prague, Sbírky Pražského hradu, PHA 25/5

Mihulka, up to 1993.

D.St.

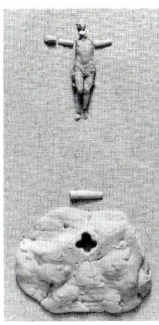

III.271
Anonymous Master
Working in first half of sixteenth century
Inventory of grave of Anna Jagellonská:
table crucifix
Alabaster, engraved
Fragmented state: alabaster part in 12
pieces (7 the largest), part of wooden
cross
Base: 9.7 × 12.8 × 2.2
Before 1547
Found in coffin of the deceased
Prague, Sbírky Pražského hradu, PHA
25/6

D.St.

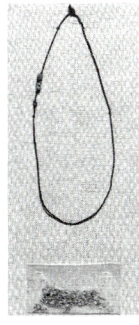

III.272
Anonymous
Inventory of grave of Anna Jagellonská:
fragment of rosary
Cloth string, wood and stone
? 1547
Found in coffin of the deceased
Prague, Sbírky Pražského hradu, PHA
25/9

D.St.

III.273
Inventory of the Tomb of Ferdinand I:
Cloak
Silk, tabby weave (longitudinal rep), decorative strips made out of silk cut-pile velvet, bordered with a cord woven on tablets.
Fragmentary state – sewn from strips of material 50 cm wide, ca. 82 cm long, collar 16 cm high, balloon sleeves made from a rectangle 109 cm long and 29 cm wide, bottom part of sleeves 52 cm long
Probably 1564
Rep and velvet probably from Italy or Germany, trimmings probably from Austria, probably sewn in Vienna

Archiv Pražského hradu, inv. no. PHA 24/1

After being reconstructed the cloak has the shape of a segment of a circle, with balloons in the upper part of the sleeves. The balloons are formed out of rectangles with most of the length gathered up and sewn into the armhole. The two ends of each rectangle, 9 cm long, were not sewn into the armhole but hung loose. In the tight lower part of the sleeves there were holes for the arms in two places. The whole circumference of the cloak, including the slit at the back, was edged with slashed velvet strips which ended with a cord and binding. The lining of both front parts and the underside of the high collar were trimmed in the same way. The cut of the cloak is influenced by Spanish fashion, but brought into a German context. It is highly reminiscent of the preserved funeral garb of Elector Moritz of Saxony (1540–50, Dresden, Rustkammer).

M.Br.

III.274
Inventory of the Tomb of Ferdinand I:
Cloak
Same material as larger cloak, textile-covered buttons with wooden core
Fragmentary state – length ca. 73 cm, collar 8 cm high, balloon sleeves made from rectangle 66 cm long and 21 cm wide
Probably 1564
Rep and velvet probably Italy or Germany, trimming probably Austria, sewn probably in Vienna
Archiv Pražského hradu, inv. no. PHA 24/2

A smaller cloak in the form of a segment of a circle with a high collar. From reconstruction it can be seen that it buttoned at the front with six buttons, and that it had balloon sleeves. The whole of its circumference, including the slit at the back, was edged with slashed velvet strips finished off with binding. The cloak was originally belted with a strip of material. Its cut is influenced by Spanish fashion, brought into a German context.

M.Br.

III.275
Inventory of the Tomb of Ferdinand I:
Tabard
Silk, eight-thread warp-faced satin, material-covered buttons with wooden core
Fragmentary state – extension on the front part 36 cm long, collar 8 cm high, skirt a maximum of 9 cm long, sleeves 68 cm long
Before or in 1564
Satin Italy or Germany, sewn probably in Vienna
Archiv Pražského hradu, inv. no. PHA 24/3

From reconstruction it seems the doublet had twelve buttons down the front. The left front piece had an extension. A skirt of four overlapping pieces of trapezoid-shaped material was fixed to the waist. Above the waist eighteen holes have been preserved, through which a lace which held together the doublet and hose once passed. The sleeves are widened into balloons in the upper part but are not slashed. They and the high collar were edged with a tooth-cut strip of material. The cut of the doublet shows Spanish influence, and it may be that the Emperor wore it while still alive. A doublet with balloon sleeves has been preserved as part of the uniform ascribed to Andreas Wild of Wynigen (second half of sixteenth century, Berne, Historisches Museum).

M.Br.

III.276
Inventory of the Tomb of Ferdinand I:
Short Breeches
Slashed silk cut-pile velvet, base material not preserved, likely to have been silk rep.
Fragmentary state, strips 6 cm wide
1564
Velvet probably from Italy or Germany, probably sewn in Vienna
Archiv Pražského hradu, inv. no. PHA 49/4

Of the trunk hose only five slashed velvet strips have been preserved. They were originally sewn horizontally on to a base material. In the velvet strip which formed the waistband there were holes

for the lace which held the doublet and hose together. At the front there was a velvet codpiece. The trunk hose were probably narrower and longer than the Spanish melon-shaped ones. Spanish influence is still visible in them, but modified by the German context. On the other hand, the Emperor's trunk hose did not have the same cut as the typical German breeches. Don Garzio of Medici was dressed in similar trunk hose when he was buried, although the strips were sewn on vertically (1562, Florence, Pitti Palace).

M.Br.

III.277
Inventory of the Tomb of Ferdinand I:
Stockings
Wool, tabby weave
Fragmentary state – height ca. 8 cm, length 16 cm
1564
Wool probably from Austria, probably sewn
Archiv Pražského hradu, inv. no. PHA 24/13

These wool hose were originally black and reached to above the knee. The soles were cut separately, and there were gussets at the ankles. There were seams at the back.

The hose must have originally been held up by garters. Anna of Jagellon was dressed for the grave in similar hose (1547, Prague, Archiv Pražského hradu). Not exhibited.

M.Br.

III.278
Inventory of the Tomb of Ferdinand I:
Shoes
Silk cut-pile velvet, cork soles
Fragmentary state – soles 17 cm long, uppers from instep to toe 16 cm
1564
Velvet probably from Italy or Germany, cork from Portugal, probably made in Vienna
Archiv Pražského hradu, inv. no. PHA 24/5

Ferdinand's shoes were made out of two parts, of a heel part and an upper with a rounded toe. The cork undersole must

originally been covered by a leather sole. Cork shoes were designed mostly for indoor wear, or were worn over light leather shoes. All the Habsburgs buried in Prague Castle were buried in them.

M.Br.

III.279
Inventory of the Tomb of Ferdinand I:
Pillow
Silk cut-pile velvet, tassels of silk cord
50 × 50 cm
1564
Velvet probably from Italy or Germany, tassels probably from Vienna, sewn probably in Vienna
Archiv Pražského hradu, inv. no. 24/6

Originally there were two cushions in the coffin, one underneath Ferdinand's head and one under his feet. Only the first has been preserved, however. Of four tassels only one is original. It was usual to put

cushions in coffins in the Middle Ages, and all the Habsburgs buried at Prague Castle had them.

M.Br.

III.280
Inventory of the Tomb of Ferdinand I:
Palls
Silk cut-pile velvet
Upper shroud 50 cm wide, 210 cm long, lower shroud 49 cm wide, 210 cm long
1564
Velvet probably from Italy or Germany, sewn probably in Vienna
Archiv Pražského hradu, inv. no. PHA 24/7,8

Lining the coffin with shrouds was one of the normal funeral customs of the Middle Ages. At Prague Castle, the bodies of Anna of Jagellon and Rudolf II, for example,

were covered by velvet shrouds in the coffin.

M.Br.

III.281
Anonymous
Inventory of the Tomb of Ferdinand I:
Visceral Vessel
Gilded silver
15.05 cm; average 11.83 cm; lid: 5.4 cm
Before 1564

The utensil tended to be employed as a pharmaceutical measure in the imperial pharmacy. It is numbered at the bottom XXIII.

Prague, Sbírky Pražského hradu, inv. no. PHA 24/9

M.Pe.

III.282
Inventory of the Tomb of Maximilian II:
Cloak
Silk damask; base: five-thread weft-faced satin; pattern: five-thread warp-faced satin, decorative strips of cut-pile velvet, woven trimmings and ties; lining: cut-pile plush; material-covered buttons with wooden core
135 cm long, bottom hem 288 cm wide, sleeves 75 cm, collar 25 cm high
Before or in 1576
Damask probably from Italy, velvet probably from Italy or Germany, trimmings probably from Austria or Germany, sewn probably in Vienna or Regensburg, possi-

bly Hungary
Archiv Pražského hradu, inv. no. PHA 26/1

This long damask cloak, today nut-brown in colour, had a large floral and geometric pattern, dominated by pomegranates and crowns. The hem, including the slits at the side, the bottom of the sleeves and the high standing collar were edged with slashed velvet strips, trimmed with two rows of braid. The front was fastened with 29 buttons and loops. The upper part of the sleeves was slashed, the slashings being similarly edged. Broad, long cloaks were worn especially by older people and

apprentices all over Europe. However, the decoration of Maximilian's cloak is connected with Hungarian, Polish and Russian fashion, which spread over Europe in the second half of the sixteenth century. In inventories of the time this type of cloak is described as a Hungarian cloak. The burial cloak of Rudolf II (1612) is similar, as is that of Zdenek Popel of Lobkowicz, who was buried in Brno (1604, Prague, Archiv Pražského hradu).

M.Br.

III.283
Inventory of the Tomb of Maximilian II:
Tabard
Silk, eight-thread warp-faced satin, textile-covered buttons with wooden core
Length 44 cm, bottom hem 100 cm, sleeves 65 cm long, skirts 5.5 cm long, two lines of embroidery 7mm apart, each of the two lines 2 mm from the other.
Before or in 1576
Satin probably Italy or Germany, sewn probably in Vienna or Regensburg
Archiv Pražského hradu, inv. no. PHA 26/2

The doublet, today nut-brown in colour,

was decorated all over by two rows of embroidery in back stitch, with deep slashing in between. The front part of the doublet is formed into a 'goose stomach,' which was probably stuffed. It was fastened by 20 buttons. A short skirt was set into the waist. The collar, sleeves and skirt were edged with tooth-cut strips of material. The cut of the doublet shows Spanish influence. Count Alwig IX of Schulz was dressed in a similar doublet for the grave (1572, Stuttgart, Landesdenkmalamt Baden-Württemberg)

M.Br.

III.284
Inventory of the Tomb of Maximilian II:
Breeches
Silk, satin identical to that of the doublet, one lace, textile-covered buttons with wooden core
Fragmentary state, 78 cm long
Before or in 1576
Satin probably Italy or Germany, points lace probably from Austria or Germany, textile buttons with wooden core
Archiv Pražského hradu, inv. no. PHA 26/3

The trunk hose, reaching to below the knee, were gathered at the waist and a

tube was sewn there, through which originally the lace probably passed. A codpiece was inserted between the front parts, with a fly buttoned with six buttons. At the knee the hose were gathered in to a strip of material. The seams were decorated with backstitch. Trunk hose reaching to the knee began to be worn in Europe in the 1560s alongside the still-popular Spanish melon-shaped hose. There is a western European influence on the cut of Maximilian's trunk hose, but also that of Hungarian fashion. In addition to the grave clothes of Rudolf II, trunk hose of a similar style have been preserved as part of men's costume in Germany (beginning

of seventeenth century, Dresden, Staatliche Kunstsammlungen).

M.Br.

III.285
Inventory of the Tomb of Maximilian II:
Hat
Silk, the same velvet as the strips on the cloak, cord woven on tablets
Lower circumference: 59 cm; H: 21 cm; cord 2 cm wide
Before or in 1576
Velvet probably from Italy or Germany, cord probably from Austria or Germany, sewn probably in Vienna or Regensburg, possibly in Hungary
Prague Castle Administration, inv. no. PHA 26/4

The hat was made from four parts. The

bottom edge was turned up and decorated with cord, ending in tassels. High and pointed, the hat was influenced by Hungarian fashion. A similar hat was laid in the grave of Tycho Brahe (1601, Prague, Museum of the City of Prague)

M.Br.

III.286
Inventory of the Tomb of Maximilian II:
Stockings
Silk, hand-knitted using stocking stitch,
upper edge only plain stitch.
81 cm long, sole 27 cm long, upper edge 1
cm wide
Before or in 1576
Probably Vienna or Regensburg
Archiv Pražského hradu, inv. no. PHA
26/8

These stockings, now ochre in colour, had
a seam at the back sewn by hand. Triangular gussets were sewn into the sides of the
soles. The garters have been made from

new material. The stockings were hand-
knitted, because machine-knitted stockings did not begin to appear until after
1589. Renaissance knitted stockings are
found relatively frequently by archaeolo-
gists. The stockings in the grave of Count
Alwig IX of Schulz (1572, Stuttgart, Lan-
desdekmalamt Baden-Württemberg) are
similar.

M.Br.

III.287
Inventory of the Tomb of Maximilian II:
Slippers
Silk, the same velvet as the strips on the
cloak, cork
26 cm long, length of uppers from toe to
instep 17 cm
Probably 1576
Velvet probably from Italy or Germany,
cork from Portugal, made probably in Vienna or Regensburg
Archiv Pražského hradu, inv. no. PHA
26/7

These velvet slippers, now brown in
colour, have uppers with tooth-cut edges.

The cork sole is new. Slippers were worn
indoors, or were worn outside as light
leather shoes. They were probably made
for the burial of the Emperor.

M.Br.

III.288
Inventory of the Tomb of Maximilian II:
Pillow
Silk, the same velvet as the velvet strips
on the cloak, tassels
50 cm × 75 cm
1576
Velvet probably from Italy or Germany,
tassels probably from Austria or Germany, sewn probably in Vienna or Regensburg
Archiv Pražského hradu, inv. no. PHA
26/6

The cushion, now brown in colour, was
edged with cord, which was replaced by

modern cord during restoration.

M.Br.

III.289
Inventory of the Tomb of Maximilian II:
Blanket
Wool, tabby weave, woven edging with
the weft pulled out and cut into a fringe
230 cm long, 151 cm wide
Before or in 1576
Wool probably from Austria or Germany,
edging probably from Austria or Germany, made probably in Vienna or Regensburg
Archiv Pražského hradu, inv. no. PHA
26/5

A green woollen blanket with edging all
round,

Bravermanova–Kobrlova–Samohylova 1995,
pp. 497-521.

M.Br.

III.290
Inventory of the Tomb of Maximilian II:
Viscera Vessel
Wrought; inside: tin-coated bronze
16 cm; average 14.5 cm
1576
Prague, Sbírka Pražského hradu, PHA
26/11

M.Pe.

III.291
Inventory of the Tomb of Maximilian II:
Torse of a Sword
Carburized iron, gilded, wood, velvet
H: 120 cm
After 1550
Prague, Sbírky Pražského hradu, PHA
26/12

M.Pe.

III.292, III.293
Inventory of the Tomb of Maximilian II:
Miniature of the Order of the Golden
Fleece
Between 1546 and 1576
Gold (purity: chain 945-22.7, pendant 885-21.2), black and transparent enamel
Length of chain: 3 × 98, height of pendant
4.8 × 2.4
Vienna (?)
Prague, Správa Pražského hradu, inv.n.
PHA 26/9

This chain with its Order of the Golden
Fleece is made from 28 oval firestones
with black and enamel dots. The stones

are finished with short gold flame decorations with little beads. The stones are interwoven with 28 linked flame ornaments.
The Golden Fleece is crafted in the shape
of a three-dimensional rhombus. Its head
is turned to the right side. The Order of
the Golden Fleece was founded by Filip
Dobrý in 1431. Charles V became its fifth
sovereign who conferred it upon Maximilian II on 15 January 1546. Since the decoration had to be returned to the sovereign
of the order after the death of its wearer,
and because it was large and heavy to
wear, its wearers had copies made for everyday use. The miniature of the Order of
the Golden Fleece, which was taken from

the grave of Maximilian II, is an example
of one of these copies. It is reminiscent of
a copy of the Order conferred upon Vilém
of Rožmberk in 1585.

M.Br.

III.293
Unknown Goldsmith
Active in the 1560s and 1570s
Inventory of the Tomb of Maximilian II:
Pendent Cross
Gilded silver, cast, engraved, chased,
malachites apparently from the Urals
H: 8.8 cm; width: 5.8 cm; stones: central 1
× 1.2, on the beams: 1.1 × 2 cm
1562/64–76
Found in the coffin at the left side of the
deceased
Prague, Sbírky Pražského hradu PHA
26/10

M.Pe.

III.294
Funerary Shield of Maximilian II
Larch and lime wood, polychromy
170 × 190 cm
1576
Prague, Archiv Pražského hradu, inv. no.
PH 13 275

The oval panel of blue-grey wood is firmly
supported on the reverse side by two
cross-pieces. Fixed to the facing side is a
relief cutting and lettering in lime wood.
The edges of the panel are fringed with a
stylized laurel wreath with two mascarons
above and below. A ring with an inscription, bearing abbreviations of Maximil-

ian's titles and the year of his death, is divided by beadwork of which only the cylinders/rolls have been preserved; the beads
are all missing. Originally there were emblems of the Lands in a further ring. Out
of eleven such emblems, only that of the
Slavonic kingdom with a damaged crown
and a further crown bearing the emblem
of another land, possibly Hungary, have
been preserved. The centre of the shield,
limited by a small fillet with leaf motif,
completes the field with a two-headed imperial eagle borne by two gryphons. The
imperial crown above the shield has not
survived. The divided emblem of Austria–
Castille appears on this shield. The date of

death is given beneath the suspended Order of the Golden Fleece. The sculptural
ornamentation of the funeral shield has
been preserved in an incomplete state;
several missing parts were added later.
Restorative research has ascertained the
original colouring, which was likewise
substantially modified. The principal panel was dark grey, almost black, on an
ochre–red base. The lettering was gilded,
and the inscriptive band had a grey-blue
ground. Both gryphons were gilded.

M.Br.

III.295a–c
Augsburg or Prague Metalworker
Funeral Regalia in the St Vitus Treasure:
The Imperial Crown, Orb and Sceptre
Prague, Chapter of St Vitus' cathedral,
inv. nos 277–79

The funeral regalia are first mentioned in
the inventory of the Svatovice cathedral in
1635 and were apparently used as part of
the funeral rites of the cathedral chapter
until the early twentieth century. The jewels were found during the late 1980s in
very bad condition and were restored. At
that time the missing lilies were added to
the crown and the globe, which dated

from a later period, was replaced by an apple surmounted with a cross. During
cleaning it was found that the original
high-quality gilding had remained almost
intact. The crown and apple are closely related in all their decorative elements and
most probably come from the same workshop. The characteristic moresque motif
with a wide band bordering a field with
miniature ornaments was widely used in
the 1660s and 1670s. The sceptre features
richer sculptural decoration. The shape of
the crown clearly identifies it as the imperial one and therefore inseparable from
the mitre, which is also made of metal. It is
highly probable that the regalia were also

created in a metalworking shop and that
they are copies of the pieces created for
the funeral of Maximilian II in Prague in
1577. However, it is also possible that they
were commissioned for the funeral ceremonies after the death of Ferdinand I in
1564. Stylistically, the crown forms an interesting chapter in the presently accepted line of development.

Essen 1988, cat. no. 454.

Bukovinská 1988, pp. 24-26 (here the older literature).

B.B.

III.296
Second half of the sixteenth century
Obituary Medal of *Maximilian II*
Struck in bronze
2.9 cm
Obverse: *MAXIMIL II D G - AVG IMP CAES*; bust with laurel wreath, sceptre and imperial orb; reverse: *DOMINVS / VIVIFICAT ME / SECVNDVM VER / BVM SVVM*
No date (1576)
Prague, Národní muzeum, Numismatic Department, inv. no. H5-50 141

Emperor Maximilian II travelled with his retinue from Vienna to the Roman Diet in

Regensburg at the beginning of June 1573. His physicians were increasingly alarmed at his state of health, which worsened during the course of the assembly. Finally, exhausted after numerous illnesses, the Emperor died in Regensburg on 12 October. This bronze medal, apparently issued to mark the event, is a valuable example of the commemorative coins and medals minted at this time, although the medal itself bears no date. Other types of jettons tell us more, featuring the portrait of the emperor, the imperial insignia and the exact date of his death. The provenance of these medals cannot be determined with certainty. Katz (1929) provides

evidence that they were crafted by the Viennese engravers M. Engl and J. J. Knifer.

Katz 1929, p. 122; Janáček, pp. 151–53.

Z.M.

III.297
Prague mint
Funerary Coin of *Maximilian II*
Struck in gilded silver
2.7 cm, setting on a chain
Obverse: *DIVI.MAXI ? ILI.II.CAESAR.AVG.P.F.*; bust with crown; reverse: *MEMORIA / FVNEBRIS / PRAGAE / BOHANN.LXXVII*
1577
Prague, Národní muzeum, Numismatic Department, inv. no. H5-50 116

Maximilian II was buried in a monastery near Linz. At that time it was decided that his remains would subsequently be trans-

ferred to St Vitus' cathedral at Prague Castle. At the beginning of February 1577 a procession set off on a journey from Linz to Prague where the remains were stored for a short time at the church of St James in the Old Town. The funeral, long in preparation, took place on 22 March 1577 and was attended by a great number of illustrious guests. Small commemorative burial jettons were scattered along the funereal procession, which caused considerable chaos among the onlookers who fought among themselves for possession of the coins. Although the jettons have more the character of coins produced on the dies of the Prague mint, today they are

considered a rare document of this important historical event.

Don. 188, no. 1244; Ľermák-Skrbek, vol. 1, p. 30; Janáček, pp. 158–59, 162–67 g.

Z.M.

III.298
Funerary Coin of *Maximilian II*
Struck in silver
2.7 cm
Obverse: *DIVVS.MAXIMILIANVS.SECVNDVS.CAES.P.F.*; bust of the emperor; reverse: *DVM.SVPER.ASTRA.FEROR / .NII.HVMANA.MOROR.*; eagle flying up to the skies above the imperial insignia; shield with the inscription: *OBIIT.RATISB / 12.OCTOB / AN 1576* at the bottom
1576
Second half of the sixteenth century
Prague, Národní muzeum, Numismatic Department, inv. no.H5-50 115

One of the jettons commemorating the death of Emperor Maximilian II, crafted using the technique adopted by mints typical for that time. Compare previous catalogue entry.

Don. 1240.

Z.M.

III.299
Inventory of the Tomb of Eleonora, Daughter of Maximilian : Robe
Silk, damask - base: five-thread warp-faced satin; pattern: five-thread weft-faced satin; iron hooks and eyes
117 cm high, bottom hem 284 cm long, sleeves 55 cm long, collar 7 cm high
Probably 1580
Prague Castle Administration, inv. no. PHA 49/2a

This child's dress, now a golden-brown colour, was sewn from two damasks with similar stylized plant and geometric patterns. The dress had long sleeves, balloon-

shaped at the top. It was bell-cut, with the two front pieces fastened by hooks and eyes. The collar and sleeves were edged with a tooth-cut band of material. Children's clothers were a faithful copy of adult dress, and Eleonora's were made according to the Spanish fashion. From an engraving of 1572 it seems that the Archduchess may have been buried in a cloak, which in a source of the time was described as red, and a ruff. Small fragments of linen which may come from the ruff have been preserved in the coffin. However, no traces of any top garment have been found. Given Eleonora's youth and her bad health it may be assumed that the

clothes were made either as burial garments or shortly before her death. A rosary, a wreath and a garland of rosemary and orange-tree leaves were also found in the coffin.

Bazantova–Bravermanova–Koblova 1993, pp. 154–160. Detailed information on the restoration in Abegg-Stiftung will be published in the Riggisberger Berichte.

M.Br.

III.300
Inventory of the Tomb of Eleonora, Daughter of Maximilian II: Wreath
Wire, berries, remains of leaves from an orange tree and rosemary leaves
1580
Found in the coffin of the deceased
Prague, Sbírka Pražského hradu, inv. no. PHA 49/2

D.St.

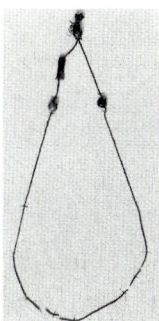

III.301
Inventory of the Tomb of Eleonora,
Daughter of Maximilian II: Rosary
Twisted thread of textile materials, turned
wood
L: 54 cm
1580 (?)
Discovered in the tomb of the deceased
Prague, Sbírky Pražského hradu, inv. no.
PHA 49/2e

D.St.

III.302
Inventory of the Tomb of Rudolf II: Cloak
Silk, velvet looped (ground) and cut-pile
(pattern), binding in tabby weave with
rep effect, cord in diagonal twill weave,
decorative wound buttons with wooden
core
Length 140 cm, bottom hem 388 cm long,
sleeves 82 cm long, collar 9 cm high,
length of side slits 29 cm, strips of cloth
55 cm wide
Probably 1612
Prague, Sbírky Pražského hradu, inv. no.
PHA 27/1

A long coat, today nut-brown in colour

(but this was also the description of its
colour in 1612). It was decorated with a
small diagonal plant pattern whose repeats went opposite ways. The cloak was
made out of four straight strips of material, with gussets at the side. The whole of
its bottom hem was edged with a rep
braid. In the upper part of the sleeve there
was a T-shaped opening fastened by buttons and loops, from which went twill-
weave cords ending in tassels. The front of
the cloak was fastened in the same way (37
buttons) and so were the side slits (8 buttons). This type of cloak decoration originates in the east, in Hungary, Poland and
Russia. In the second half of the 16th cen-

tury this fashion, which also took on
Spanish features, caught on all over Europe. Similar elements are found at
Prague Castle in the grave clothes of Maximilian II (1576) and Vojtech Popel of
Lobkowicz (1604), originally buried in the
church of St. Peter in Brno). Juraj Thurz's
burial cloak was made of satin and velvet
with a similar pattern (1611, Orava, P.O.
Hviezdoslav Museum).

M.Br.

III.303
Inventory of the Tomb of Rudolf II:
Tabard
Silk, eight-thread warp-faced satin,
clipped, tabby-weave cord, tabby-weave
lining, decoratively wound buttons with
wooden core
Length 50 cm, bottom hem 116 cm long,
shoulders 16 cm wide, collar 4 cm high,
skirt 3 cm long, sleeves 52 cm long, cord
3.2 cm wide
Probably 1612
Prague, Sbírky Pražského hradu, inv. no.
PHA 27/2

A satin doublet, today golden-brown in

colour, decorated with a close pattern of
lines of clipped holes. The front pieces (in
the shape of a 'goose stomach') and the
slits on the sleeves were fastened by rows
of buttons. The short skirt had seven pairs
of holes below the waist, originally for the
cord keeping the doublet and hose together. The hem was decorated with pearl
stitch. The back of the doublet was cut to
enable it to be put on to the dead body
more easily, the hole being edged and fastened with seven laces. The same thing
was done in the case of Count Anton Gunther (1667, Oldenburg, Landesmuseum).
The cut of the doublet was influenced by
Spanish fashion. There is a similar one in

the museum in Munich, for example
(1615-1625, Munich, Bayerisches Nationalmuseum).

M.Br.

III.304
Inventory of the Tomb of Rudolf II:
Breeches
Silk, velvet the same as that of the cloak,
codpiece partially lined with satin like
that of the doublet, edging tabby-weave
with rep effect, lining tabby weave, deco-
ratively wound buttons with wooden core
Length 71 cm, waist 108 cm
Probably 1612
Prague Castle Administration, inv. no.
PHA 27/3

Wide hose ending below the knee, sewn
from the same material as the cloak. The
gusset-shaped codpiece was fastened to

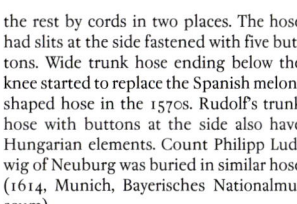

the rest by cords in two places. The hose
had slits at the side fastened with five buttons. Wide trunk hose ending below the
knee started to replace the Spanish melon-
shaped hose in the 1570s. Rudolf's trunk
hose with buttons at the side also have
Hungarian elements. Count Philipp Ludwig of Neuburg was buried in similar hose
(1614, Munich, Bayerisches Nationalmuseum).

M.Br.

III.305
Inventory of the Tomb of Rudolf II: Hat
Silk, canvas binding with the effect of
warped repp, strip of fabric around the
lower part of the helmet, belt and under-
stitching from a fabric sewn into canvas
binding; cockade from a thinly sewn
thread of canvass binding, woolen felt as
a base, embroidery with chain stitch, knitted lace
H: 18 cm; average 17cm; length of strip
from which is formed the face of the helmet: 53 cm; brim of hat: 4.5 cm
Repp probably from Italy or Germany,
probably made in Prague
Probably before 1612

Prague, Sbírky Pražského hradu, inv. no.
PHA 27/16 (originally 399)

M.Br.

III.306
Inventory of the tomb of Rudolf II:
Stockings
Silk, single-faced knit; rear seam hand-
sewn with mattrass stich
Length: 76.5 cm; length of sole: 27 cm
Probably made in Bohemia, before 1612
Prague, Sbírky Pražského hradu, inv. no.
PHA 27/5

Essen and Vienna, cat. no. 455.

M.Br.

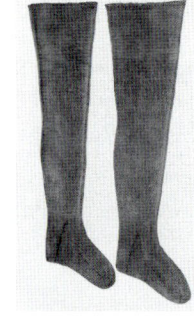

III.307
Inventory of the tomb of Rudolf II:
Stockings
Silk, woven with linen binding
Length 76 cm, length of sole 30 cm
Material probably from Italy or Germany,
probably sewn in Bohemia
Probably 1612
Prague, Sbírky Pražského hradu, inv. no.
PHA 27/4

Essen and Vienna, cat. no. 455.

M.Br.

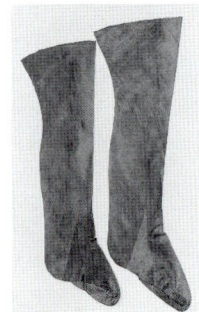

III.308
Inventory of the tomb of Rudolf II:
Slippers
Velvet, cork, tanned cowhide
Length 22.5 cm, length of uppers 14.5 cm
Velvet probably from Italy or Germany,
cork from Portugal, hide probably from
Bohemia, probably made in Bohemia
Probably 1612
Prague, Sbírky Pražského hradu, inv. no.
PHA 27/6

Essen and Vienna, cat. no. 455.

Bravermanová–Čierna 1997 (in preparation).

M.Br.

III.309
Inventory of the tomb of Rudolf II: Pillow
Silk, plain velvet
Length 55 cm, width 49 cm
Material probably from Italy or Germany,
sewn in Prague
Probably 1612
Prague, Sbírky Pražského hradu, inv. no.
PHA 27/7, 17

Essen and Vienna, cat. no. 455.

Bravermanová–Čierna 1997 (in preparation); Bukovinská 1988, p. 570.

M.Br.

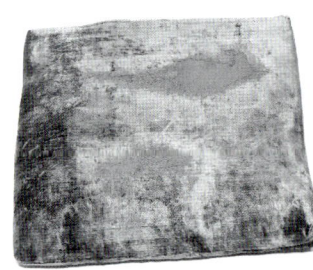

III.310
Inventory of the tomb of Rudolf II: Veil
Silk, plain velvet
Length 146 cm, width 52 cm
Material probably from Italy or Germany,
sewn in Prague
Probably 1612
Prague, Sbírky Pražského hradu, inv. no.
PHA 27/8

Essen and Vienna, cat. no. 455.

Bravermanová–Čierna 1997 (in preparation).

M.Br.

III.311
Inventory of the tomb of Rudolf II: Veil
Silk, fabric woven with linen binding
Length approx. 170 cm, width 104 cm
Material probably from Italy or Germany
1612
Prague, Sbírky Pražského hradu, inv. no.
PHA 27/10

Essen and Vienna, cat. no. 455.

Bravermanová–Čierna 1997 (in preparation).

M.Br.

III.312
Inventory of the tomb of Rudolf II:
Ribbon
Silk, fabric woven with linen binding
Length 162 cm, width 15 cm
Material from Italy or Germany
1612
Prague, Sbírky Pražského hradu, inv. no.
PHA 27/9

Essen and Vienna, cat. no. 455.

Bravermanová–Čierna 1997 (in preparation).

M.Br.

III.313
Inventory of the Tomb of Rudolf II:
Viscera Vessel
Gilded silver
16.9 cm; average: 11.5cm; lid: 12 cm
Stamped with the sign of Munich,
stamped with the sign *HS* beneath crossing hammers
1577 (?), 1597 (?)
Prague, Sbírky Pražského hradu, inv. no.
PHA 27/11 (originally 399)

M.Pe.

III.314
Inventory of the Tomb of Rudolf II:
Viscera Vessel
Gilded silver, silver
15.1 cm; average: 12 cm; lid: 3.9 cm
Stamped with the sign of two towers with
open gate; (beneath the sign) *PH-HIERIN. LIGT.IHR MAYTT.GEHIRN.*
1580, 1612
Prague, Sbírky Pražského hradu, inv. no.
PHA 27/12

M.Pe.

III.315
Inventory of the Tomb of Rudolf II:
Three Rings
Removed in 1975
Prague, Sbírky Pražského hradu,
inv. no. 27/15–17

The oldest report of the existence of the three rings worn by Rudolf II at the time of his death is given by Abraham Hosmannus, a writer in the service of Emperor Matyáö: '... an den fingern sind drey Ringe / einer von Bein / in dem andern is ein Demant / Saphír / Rubin / und Smaragd / zu andeutung der 4 elementen/' (Vocelka [1981], p. 329). In the documentation of the first opening in 1928 of the coffin containing Rudolf's remains, published that same year in *Památky archeologické* (vol. 36, pp. 250–51), there is no mention of the rings. One of the rings is in fact set with the four gemstones mentioned above, but the second is not of ivory but of nephrite, and the third is made of gold and wood. The nephrite ring is smooth, rather wide and thick-walled, and the stone is dark green. The second, most exquisite ring is made up of several parts. Segments with subtle, sculpturally treated zodiac signs are inserted between the stones in their rectangular mounts. Capricorn is between the diamond and the sapphire, Libra between the sapphire and the emerald, Cancer between the emerald and the ruby, and Aquarius between the ruby and the diamond. Capricorn is coloured with blue enamel, Libra and Aquarius with green enamel, and Cancer with white enamel. A smaller gold ring with the carved inscription *GABRIEL, MICHAEL, VRIEL, ANAEL* is inserted into the inner circle of the ring. The choice of gemstones and zodiac signs, the colours and the references to the cabbala have deeper meanings.

Essen and Vienna 1988, cat. no. 456.

B.B.

III.316
Inventory of the Tomb of Rudolf II:
Cross in the Hands of the Deceased
Prague, Sbírky Pražského hradu,
inv. no. PHA 27/20

M.Pe.

III.317
Anonymous
Inventory of the Tomb of Rudolf II:
Rosary
Wood, copper, silver
L: 60 cm; average beads: 0.5-1 cm; average
medallion: 1.2 cm
1612 (?)
Prague, Sbírky Pražského hradu, inv. no.
PHA 27/16

M.Pe.

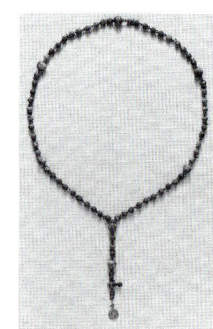

III.318
Funerary Shield of Rudolf II
Larch and lime wood, polychromy
170 × 190 cm
1612
Prague Castle Administration, inv. no. PH
13 274

An oval panel of larch wood is held firm
on the reverse side by two cross-pieces and
on its face has a carved relief of lime wood
secured to it. The incorporation of the
panel is basically the same as in the funeral shield of Maximilian II. The difference is
in the lettering, which was not sculpted
(perhaps with the exception of the date of
death given beneath the Order of the
Golden Fleece) but gilded on a panel on
the grey-blue foundation. Not a single emblem of the land has been preserved. Only
the remains of the imperial crown appear
on the central shield. Research has shown
that the remains have their original polychromy and gilding and that there are a
number of later additions. The most outstanding of these is the figure of the
gryphon sinister, which is new as far as the
hind legs. The figure opposite was created
as a mirror image; its original face, however, was significantly different.

M.Br.

III.319
Rudolf II on his Death-bed in the Audi-
ence Hall of Prague Castle
Copper engraving
*Aigentliche Abcontrafactur wie die Rom. Kay.
Rudolphus 2. nach dem dieselbe den 20. Jan-
uarij An 01612 todts verschieden in der audi-
ents stuben sey offentlich sey gesehen worden.
Hie siehst du des Kaisers leich*
Prague, Museum of the City of Prague,
inv. no. 892

The engraving is anonymous. Its unique
significance for our knowledge of the
Rudolfine era consists in that it is almost
the only illustrated interior of the period
which could be instantaneously related to
the area on the second floor of the south
residential wing, since according to the
engraving, that area was the emperor's audience hall as is identified by the text. Giv-
en the purpose of the engraving, unfortunately, the artist showed less interest in
depicting the details of the environment
in comparison with the care and accuracy
taken with Rudolf's garment and insignia.
The awkwardly folded materials and car-
pet can therefore be considered an inevitable part of an inventory of the rooms,
where we would either have expected a
tapestry or leather wall hangings, according to sources.

Vienna 1988, cat. no. 680

Janáček 1973, pic. pp.198-99; K. Vocelka
1985, 212-13, Muchka 1988, 203.

I.M.

III.320
Unknown Master
*Castrum doloris Rudolfa II (Rudolf's Dolour
Turret)*
Copper engraving
16.8 × 27.3 cm
1612
Prague, Muzeum hl. m. Prahy,
inv. no. 25 919

In the catalogue of the Essen exhibition,
several similar items were exhibited
demonstrating the stylistic nature and
artistic significance of this type of
'ephemeral' architecture. The *Castrum doloris* of Ferdinand I of Tuscany may be listed as a building which closely features
those examples. It was designed by L. Co-
goli. It has an identical ground-plan to the
Prague building but with more columns
in place. The fronton, however, is not broken but worn down and subsiding. The octagon of the dome is also identical, articulated horizontally within the columns and
perhaps even with small lamps. It has,
however, only three storeys and makes a
much smaller impression in comparison
with the coffin inside. For closer identification, it would be desirable to reconsti-
tute the dimensions of individual buildings to answer better one of the most
engaging questions on which the *Castrum*
doloris balances, namely that of construction technology.

Essen, cat. no. 326

Helfertova 1974, 292-94, Popelka 1994,
p.35.

I.M.

Section IV: Science and Music
'The Merchants of Light'

JAMES BRADBURNE

The Habsburg court in the late Renaissance, in Vienna under Ferdinand I and Maximilian II, and later in Prague under Rudolf II, has excited the interest of scholars and the general public alike. Whether it is through the astronomical observations of the silver-nosed Tycho Brahe, or through tales of the golem who haunted the streets of Prague at the behest of the Rabbi Löw, the period is known to have been one of intense intellectual, artistic and political ferment. On the other hand, compared to the same period in other European countries such as France, Spain or Italy, little is known about Rudolf's court in Prague, which for over three decades was a well-spring of Neo-Platonic studies in alchemy, astrology, allegorical painting and technology, and attracted such scholars and artists as Arcimboldo, Savery, Bruno and Kepler. Certainly what we do know is tantalizing.

The climate of Renaissance humanism nourished the belief that Man could operate not only in the physical realms, but in the intellectual and divine realms as well, by means of the correspondences operating at different levels of the angelic hierarchy. Renaissance Neo-Platonism, conflated with the so-called 'prisca theologica' of Hermes Trismegistus, provided the philosophical underpinning to the pursuit of most natural philosophy into the mid-1600s. In this hybrid, text, image, objects and number provided privileged insights into the natural world, and into the world of the spirit, as defined by the humanist doctrine of the microcosm and the macrocosm, and by the Hermetic three worlds of the terrestrial (man), celestial (cosmic correspondences) and super-celestial (the angelic).

The principal goal of this part of the exhibition is to provide an insight into the late Renaissance, in particular the world of Central Europe, and its focal point, the Habsburg court at Prague. The exhibition suggests that the epicentre of the propagation of the last rays of Renaissance light was not Atlantis, but Rudolfine Prague. It sets out to show that one of the brightest 'lights' of the late Renaissance was Neo-Platonism, that this light was carried from court to court by artists and scholars, that it was fostered by enlightened rulers such as the Austrian Habsburg emperors, and that the material traces of this culture can be put in context in order to reveal and recover some of their original meaning. Moreover, the exhibition intends to show how the light of the late Renaissance was driven underground after the victory of the Counter-Reformation in 1620, to reappear in England, Italy and France decades later via other 'merchants of light', such as Comenius, Kircher, Drebbel, Fludd and Maier.

According to scholars such as Yates, Gombrich, and Vasoli, the predominant world view of the late Renaissance court was a Christian Cabalist hermetic Neo-Platonism, in which the primary task of the scholar was to establish correspondences between the ideal and real worlds in order to better understand the workings of nature, which was God's book, on the one hand, and to control nature by means of these correspondences, on the other. The world view was profoundly magical, and the Renaissance scholar believed that by creating the correct correspondences between objects, images, texts and the greater worlds of the angels, he would be able to participate in divine, or quasi-divine powers. In this framework, the distinction between art, as the expression of an individual creator's emotional state (an idea born in a much later period) and science,

the disinterested analysis of the behaviour of matter, was not one that made sense. The Renaissance scholar, artist or alchemist would draw equally on classical texts, both those within the Christian canon and texts newly introduced with the collapse of Byzantium in 1453, and on the evidence of the senses, be it in the form of astronomical observations, meticulous drawing, alchemical experiments or Cabalistic numerical manipulations.

Thus what we would now term art, science, literature and history were all closely linked under the rubric of natural philosophy, and we find artists such as Arcimboldo working with humanist scholars such as Fonteo to enrich the symbolism of his paintings, humanist scholars-cum-artists such as Joris Hoefnagel incorporating meticulous drawings of snakes, beetles and lizards in textbooks on handwriting, astronomers such as Johannes Kepler preparing elaborate horoscopes while compiling detailed astronomical tables, and mathematicians such as John Dee invoking the powers of the angels by means of Cabalistic formulae and geometrical shapes. The intellectual world of the Renaissance court was profoundly different from our own, and the distinctions we treat as self-evident either did not exist or were viewed very differently. To understand the Renaissance and the world of Rudolf II we must research, and thereby attempt partially to restore, or at least re-imagine, the intellectual context in which its material culture made sense, with all the critical problems that this attempt poses.

The Neo-Platonism of the late Renaissance, while it influenced thinkers across the span of religious confessions, fostered tolerance, and the desire to heal the rifts that had begun to tear apart the fabric of the universal Catholic Church with the reforms of Luther, Calvin and Wyatt in the early sixteenth century. Many neo-platonists favoured a form of universal Christianity – pansophia – based on the Holy Scriptures, the Jewish Cabala put to use to prove the divinity of Christ, and the writings of Hermes Trismegistus, supposed contemporary with Moses, which spoke of Man's ability to use the powers of the angels. What was the cultural expression of this outlook?

Since the beginning of the sixteenth century, the Habsburg court was an important locus of late Renaissance culture. In Vienna, concerned with reconciling a state increasingly riven by religious conflict, Rudolf's grandfather, Ferdinand I (brother of the Emperor Charles V) assembled an important collection; Rudolf's father, Maximilian II, enlarged the collection significantly, created a humanist court of scholars and artists from across the spectrum of religious belief and vastly increased the size and variety of the imperial collections of naturalia, artificialia and books.

By the 1570s, Habsburg tolerance had brought peace to their lands in Austria and Hungary, and the Habsburg court became a magnet for not only German-speaking intellectuals from the North and West, but Italians, French and Dutch. By the end of his reign, Maximilian's court had hosted the composer Philip de Monte, the humanist Blotius, the Milanese artist Arcimboldo, the Anglo-Welsh mathematician John Dee, the Dutch diplomat Busbecq (who would return to Vienna from Constantinople with tulips and lilacs), the moral philosopher Lipsius, and the natural philosophers Fabritius and Clusius. These travellers of immense erudition and experience, these 'merchants of light', all found in the Habsburg court the highly refined late Renaissance culture.

Maximilian died suddenly in 1576 and rule fell to his son Rudolf II. Perhaps in emulation of his uncle, Philip II of Spain, Rudolf immersed himself in the creation of the ideal Renaissance court, the material traces of which were his vast collections and *Kunstkammer*, gardens and zoo. At his court in Prague, Rudolf was the model of an enlightened Renaissance monarch, gathering around him the brightest lights of his generation, Spranger, de Vries, Hoefnagel, Lehman, Brahe, Kepler, Habermel, Burgi. Their works – in the form of books, paintings, metalwork, sculptures and instruments – continued to enrich Rudolf's famous *Kunstkammer*, while within the castle walls were encyclopedic medicinal gardens, mechanical marvels and a well-stocked menagerie.

Seen in the with modern eyes, the *Kunstkammer* was merely a proto-museum, a place where the traces of the past could be brought together, studied and organized. Seen in the context of Neo-Platonism, the context of its creation, the *Kunstkammer* was much more. It was an instrument of power, and thus played a role every bit as important, and entirely consistent with Rudolf's occult and alchemical investigations. By bringing together objects, images, and texts representing in miniature the vastness of the world at large, by means of these correspondences the Emperor established dominion over the world. Thus the collection functioned as a powerful new text, drawing down astral influences, evoking the glories of classical civilization, proclaiming the equivalence between the Emperor and his mythical predecessors. Complex and mannered images alluded to classical texts, now woven together in new and modern forms by accomplished allegorists such as Spranger or Arcimboldo. To view a painting, an object, an emblem, a flower or a shell was to participate in the decoding of secret messages and the unveiling of hidden meanings. Sometimes, to amuse the court, these meanings could be ribald or humorous, complex allegories based on the works of Ovid or Apuleius. Just as often these images could also have alchemical and occult import, their meanings obscure and powerful, such as the Monas of Dee or the alchemical diagrams of Count Michael Maier.

Central to this courtly culture was the Neo-Platonic concept that the world was a whole – that all elements of the world revealed some aspect of the mystery of the whole. Moreover, by examination of the parts, one could find in them clues to the whole. These correspondences, between the world of Man, the microcosm, and the World at large, the macrocosm, which included the realms of the angels and ultimately of God, were a central preoccupation of the late Renaissance, and central to understanding the material culture of the Austrian Habsburg court. In the Renaissance Neo-Platonic view, the world was God's book, and his answers were written in it for all to seek. God's immanence in the world meant, among other things, that all relations were real relations, that mathematical truth, the behaviour of the stars and planets and the characteristics of natural phenomena were all presentations of God's mind in the world. There was no question of a proportion adequately representing beauty, it *was* beauty. In the same way, neither did a talisman need to represent an abstract quality, it *was* the quality. It must be emphasized that in the Renaissance there are no gaps between thought and signs and between signs and reality, as there was later to be in Descartes. To the Renaissance thinker, relations between objects, numbers and images were real relations, and they did not stand for relations in an arbitrary way. Equally, words and signs were knowledge, they did not stand for knowledge. This approach thereby avoids one of the key problems of modern epistemology, that of the adequacy of relation between ideas and things, words and ideas. This adequation between sign and signified underpinned the intellectual edifice on which was founded the intellectual practice of Rudolfine Prague.

Since Ficino and Pico della Mirandola translated the works of Hermes Trismegistus and the Cabala in Florence in the late fifteenth century, the philosophy of Neoplatonism had a decisive impact on the intellectual life of Europe. From the Venice of Francesco Giorgi to the London of Robert Fludd, the theory of the microcosm and the macrocosm spans one of the most significant moments of modern European history.

IV.1
Nikolaus Pfaff and Benedikt Wurzelbauer
Venus and Amor with Dolphin
1599
Prague, Národní galeri v Praze, inv. no. P 4606

The fountain that was topped by this sculptural group was cast in Nürnberg in 1599 by Benedikt Wurzelbauer, who (as Doppelmayer indicates) officially installed it in Prague the following year. It was commissioned by Kryštof Popel of Lobkovic and was possibly related to his appointment as chief steward of the kingdom of Bohemia. He had it placed in the garden of his residence on Hradčany Square in Prague, which stood on the site of the present Šternberk Palace. The bronze fountain consisted in ensemble of a pedestal from which caryatids arose supporting a massive bowl: the sculptural group exhibited here was placed in the centre of the bowl. The author of the actual design was probably Nikolaus Pfaff, also a native of Nürnberg. The creator of the fountain could have been influenced by the Classical *Venus* from the Capitoline (Louvre) or by one of its copies.

Neumann 1964, p. 232, cat. no. 74; Weihrauch 1967, pp. 325, 327, 353; Weihrauch, *Umění*, vol. 18 (1970), pp. 60–68; Fučíková 1982, p. 95, cat. nos 77, 78.

J.Ch.

IV.2
Hans von Aachen
Young Couple and the Reaper (Vanitas)
Oil on slate
1580s
Purchased from a private collection in 1986
Prague, Národní galerie v Praze, inv. no. O 14 811

Von Aachen became familiar with the technique of painting on stone while in Italy, where it had enjoyed a renaissance. This medium permitted the expression of a human desire to outdo nature, to employ human creativity to perfect nature's creations. In Italy, where stone had been used as a base for paintings since the early sixteenth century, the most commonly used material was *paragone* (black marble). Later other types of stone were also used, in particular those with an interesting colour or design, which could itself be used as part of the composition. In von Aachen's work two stages can be observed: the first, making the difficult surface fit for use, and the second, refining it by painting. The present work was painted on slate, which has a colour very similar to *paragone*, and its dark surface creates an ideal background for a scene of light and shade. It was painted either when von Aachen was still in Italy, or else shortly afterwards. Von Aachen later made some paintings on alabaster for Rudolf II, which successfully incorporated the material's translucence, fine colouring and texture into the compositions (Vienna, Kunsthistorisches Museum, inv. no. PA 941, 943, exhibited in Ambras).

Essen and Vienna 1988, cat. no. 90.

E.F.

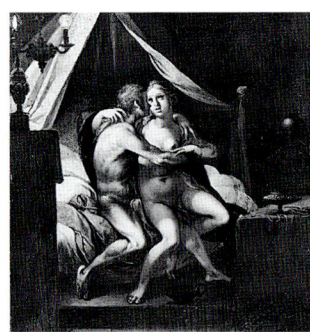

IV.3
Hans von Aachen
Johannes Kepler
Oil on canvas
51.5 × 38.5 cm
Before 1612
For many years the property of the
Kolowrat family, inv. no. Rk 186/365

This portrait in the Kolowrat collection
was originally thought to be a portrait of
Albrecht Liebstein of Kolowrat by Bartolomeus Spranger. Comparison with an
engraving by Jacob Heyden or with the title page of *Tabullae Rudolphinae* demonstrates, however, that it is a portrait of Jo-

hannes Kepler, the celebrated astronomer
and mathematician who worked at the
court of Rudolf II. Whether Aachen and
Kepler together were merely contemporaries in court service or whether they
were also friends is not known. A portrait
of the astronomer could even have been
commissioned by the Emperor, to be
placed among the portraits of his celebrated colleagues past and present in the royal
summer house.

Essen and Vienna 1988, pp. 223–24, cat. no.
109, for all older literature.

E.F.

IV.4
Giuseppe Arcimboldo
Milan 1527–Milan 1593
Winter
Oil on linden wood (limewood) panel
66.5 × 50.5 cm
Signed lower right: *GIUSEPPE ARCIM-
BOLDO F.*; date and title on the
back: *1563 Hjems*
1563
Vienna, Kunsthistorisches Museum,
Gemäldegalerie, inv. no. 1590

This version of *Winter* belongs to the same
series as *Summer*. Like *Summer*, it was also
probably later in Prague, listed under no.

901 in the 1621 inventory. The collar of the
figure of Winter bears the letter *M* surmounted by a crown, and the fire iron,
from the chain of the order of the Golden
Fleece. The *M* stands for Maximilian, and
the fire iron is a Habsburg emblem, marking the season as the Emperor's own.

Venice 1987, p. 78; Essen and Vienna 1988,
cat. no. 112, ill. 204; Vienna 1995, p. 63, cat.
no. 7, ill. 25; Cremona 1996, cat. no. 1.2, pp.
52-4, ill. 53.

Legrand and Sluys 1955, p. 50, no.2; Alfons
1957, pp. 35-6; Preiss 1967, p. 12, colour ill.
I; Kaufmann 1976, pp. 275-96; Kaufmann

1978, pp. 76-102; De Mandiargues pp.
50ff.; Porzio 1979, p. 30, 34, 35, ill. 58;
Barthes 1980, p. 16, 50, 54, ill. 7; Kaufmann
1985, no. 2-2; Kaufmann 1988, pp. 29-30,
cat. no. 2.2; Kriegeskörte 1988, pp. 54, 55,
ill.; Maiorino 1991, p. 32, ill. 33 (fig. 1);
Kaufmann 1993, pp. 100-126, 197-205, ill.
112.

T.C.K.

IV.5
Giuseppe Arcimboldo
Milan 1527–Milan 1593
Water
Oil on linden wood panel
Title on the back: *AQUA*
1566
Vienna, Kunsthistorisches Museum,
Gemäldegalerie, inv. no. 1586

This belongs to a series of the four elements painted by Arcimboldo as complements to the depictions of the four seasons. Thus since Winter faces towards the
right, Water faces towards the left. Where
Winter is depicted in the guise of an elder-

ly male, the pearl necklace indicates that
Water is to be identified as a female. The
composite head of Water may thus on the
one hand appear grotesque, or a *grillo*, as
Fonteo says. The close relation between
Fonteo's poems, Arcimboldo's paintings
and their collaborative project for tournament designs is demonstrated by the appearance of figures with similar costumes
in the 1571 tournament held in Vienna.

Venice 1987, pp. 94-5, 96-7; Essen and Vienna 1988, cat. 113, ill. 205; Vienna, Kunsthistorisches Museum, 1995, p. 63, cat.
no. 9, 27, ill. 25; Cremona 1996, cat. no., 1.3,
pp. 52-54, ill. 55.

Legrand and Sluys 1955, p. 51, plate 3; Alfons 1957, pp. 48-9; Preiss colour ill.; Kaufmann 1976, pp. 275-96; Kaufmann 1978,
pp. 76-102; De Mandiargues 1978, pp. 74-5,
ill. 68-9, 71; Porzio 1979, pp. 30, 34, ill 64;
Barthes, 30, 31, 52, ill. 62; Kaufmann 1985,
cat. no. 2-4; Kaufmann 1988, cat. no. 2,4;
Kriegeskörte 1988, pp. 16, 22, ill. 23; Maiorino 1991, p. 40, ill. 42 (fig. 8); Kaufmann
1993, pp. 100-126, 197-205, ill. 113.

T.C.K.

IV.6
Giuseppe Arcimboldo
Milan 1527–Milan 1593
Rudolf II as Vertumnus
Oil, wood
68 × 56 cm
Ca. 1590
Imperial collections, Prague, Inventory
1621, no. 1062, Inventory 1635, no. 582;
Königsmarck, Inventory 1648, no. 318(?);
Sklokoster, Collection of Gustav Carl
Wrangel; Skokloster, Collection of Baron
Rüdiger von Essen
Bålsta, Skokloster Slott, inv. no. 11615

Although the painting may at first seem

humorous it was an imperial allegory with
a serious meaning (and the ability to tell
and take a joke was regarded as an imperial virtue in any instance). Culminating the
artist's series of the seasons, it depicts the
Emperor as ruling over them. Since fruits
and flowers of all seasons are shown, it be-
tokens a golden age that has returned
with the Emperor's beneficent rule.

Bordeaux 1957; Stockholm 1966, no. 1274,
pl. 73; Munich 1980, cat. no. 479, ill.; Venice
1987, ill.; Essen and Vienna 1988, cat. 111,
colour ill. p. 203.

Granberg 1911, no. 322; Granberg 1929, pp.
100, 129; Legrand and Sluys, pp. 10, 56, no.

18; Alfons 1957, pp. 134–39, ill. 137; Preiss
1967, pp. 21–22, ill. 63, 64; Neumann 1977,
pp. 436–38; Kaufmann 1976; De Mandiargues 1978, 100ff.; Kaufmann 1978, pp. 99-
102; Porzio 1979, pp. 39-45, ill. 74; Barthes
and Oliva 1980, pp. 59, 107; Klemm, pp. 157-
60; Vocelka 1985, ill. 87; Kaufmann 1985, pp.
117-23; Berra 1988, pp. 11–39; Fučíková
1988, pp. 65-68, ill. 67; Kaufmann 1985, pp.
79-82, ill. 41, 80, cat. no. 2-22; Kriegeskörte
1988, pp. 44ff., ill.; Kaufmann 1990, pp. 59-
86; Kaufmann 1993, pp. 100, 126-35, ill. 101;
Kaufmann 1995, p. 191, ill. 184; Kaufmann
1996, vol. 2, p. 374, fig. 2; vol. 13, p. 914.

T.C.K.

IV.7
Giuseppe Arcimboldo
Milan 1527–Milan 1593
Allegorical Figure
Pen and brown ink, black chalk
18.6 × 26.7 cm
Budapest, Szépmüvészeti Múzeum, inv.
no. K.58.6

Between 1570 and 1585, Arcimboldo regularly advised the Habsburgs on allegorical
programmes for their many ceremonial
processions and tournaments. Many of his
designs now held in the Uffizi in Florence
were made for the wedding in 1571 of
Archduke Karl II of Styria and María of

Bavaria. The festivities included a ceremonial procession to the scene of the 'tilling
at the ring' and the procession itself was
based on the notion of the *harmonia mundi* (DaCosta Kaufmann [1978], pp. 35-40).
Among the allegorical figures symbolizing the various components of the microcosm were some representing water or
particular rivers. This recently identified
drawing of a figure riding a fantastic fish
may well have been drawn for one of the
processions and could have an allegorical
connection with water.

Bodnár 1992.

S.B.

IV.8
Giuseppe Arcimboldo (circle of?)
Milan 1527–Milan 1593
Costume Design
Pen and brown ink, brown wash, over
black chalk
274 × 155 cm
Dr F. Machßček, Prague
Prague, Národní galerie v Praze, Grafická
Sbírka, inv. no. K 9405

The fantastic attire, mask and torch all
suggest that this is a festive costume.
Since the drawing was first published, it
has been compared to similar designs for
tournaments by Arcimboldo, and indeed

it is known that figures carried torches in
balls where Arcimboldo acted as designer
(e.g. in 1571). It has also been noted that
the drawing differs in style from Arcimboldo, as it does in technique, and therefore the sheet has been assigned to a follower or a member of his workshop.
Jacopo Strada and Arcimboldo's associate
Fonteo provided drawings for imperial
festivals, but their designs are not comparable to this one. It also cannot be determined that this drawing is a further elaboration of Arcimboldo's ideas, since some
of his designs are equally elaborate, and
this sheet also is worked up from a chalk
underdrawing (cf. Fučíková 1986).

Prague 1978, no. 8.

Preiss 1964, p. 12, fig. 2; Prague 1968, pp.
140, 145, fig. 62; Fučíková 1986, p. 15, ill. 6.

T.C.K.

IV.9
Giuseppe Arcimboldo
Milan 1527–Milan 1593
Costume Design: *Companions of Arith-
metic*
Pen and blue ink and wash
30 × 20 cm
At top: *Arithmetica condotta da Pitagora
italiano et Euclide Greco/ Vesta verde*; at up-
per right: *11*
1571
Imperial Collections, Prague
Florence, Galleria degli Uffizi, Gabinetto
Disegni e Stampe, inv. no. 3153F

As in most of the designs of the series, the

inscription pairs a Greek and an Italian,
only here both the figures are famed
mathematicians (and in the case of
Pythagoras, also philosopher) who spoke
Greek. Using the hand language of the Renaissance, the mathematician makes the
sign for the number three. The drawing
can be identified with costumes described
by Fonteo as being for the *patrones* who accompanied the personification of Arithmetic in the suite of Europa at the tournament held in Vienna in 1571 to celebrate
the marriage of Archduke Karl. Fonteo describes the costume as very ancient (*an-
tiquissima*) and the headdress as a *ricinium*,
an ancient veil worn by the Romans. All

the Liberal Arts wore different-coloured
costumes, perhaps an effort further to associate them with the elements, planets,
rivers, countries, etc., that appeared in the
tournament procession.

Venice 1987, p. 149, ill.

Kaufmann 1978, p. 55, ill. 21; Beyer 1983, p.
74, no. 4, ill. 18.; Kriegeskörte 1988, pp. 72-
4, ill. 75.

T.C.K.

IV.10
Giuseppe Arcimboldo
Milan 1527–Milan 1593
Costume Design: *Companion of Astrology
(Astronomy)*
Pen and blue ink, blue wash
30 × 20 cm
At top: *Astrologia condotto da Ptolomeo
Alexandrino et da Iulio Hygino Romano/ Ves-
ta biancha le fase cose con le stelle d'oro*; at
upper right: *14*
1571
Imperial Collections, Prague
Florence, Galleria degli Uffizi, Gabinetto
Disegni e Stampe, inv. no. 3156 F

Arcimboldo's inscription at the top of this
drawing identifies the figure as one of the
companions of Astrology, to be taken in
the Renaissance sense as astronomy, one
of the seven liberal arts. The figures mentioned are Ptolemy of Alexandria, the
famed author of the *Almagest*, and Gaius
Julius Hyginus, a Roman freedman believed to have written a work entitled *De
Astronomia*. The item held aloft is an armillary sphere, an astronomer's device. A description of this costume in Fonteo's account of the 1571 tournament in Vienna
confirms its identification with one of the
patrons of astronomy in the train of the
liberal arts in the suite of Europe in that

celebration. Fonteo says that the decoration of the border of the costume with
stars was appropriate for a magus: the turban worn would also be suitable.

Venice, Palazzo Grassi 1987, p. 149, ill.

Kaufmann 1978, p. 55, ill. 24; Beyer 1983,
75, no. 7, ill. 21; Kriegeskörte 1988, pp. 72-
4, ill. 75; Kaufmann 1993, ill. 159.

T.C.K.

IV.11
Giuseppe Arcimboldo
Milan 1527–Milan 1593
Costume Design: *Companion of Diana*
Pen and blue ink, blue wash
31 × 21.50 cm
Upper right: *45*
1571
Florence, Galleria degli Uffizi, Gabinetto
Disegni e Stampe, inv. no. 3185F

The festival designed by Arcimboldo in
1571 and held in Vienna to celebrate the
marriage of Archduke Karl with Maria of
Bavaria is the most extensively recorded of
any such inventions by the artist. The

tournament was mentioned by Lomazzo
and described in several manuscript and
printed festival accounts; many drawings
by Arcimboldo connected with the event
also survive, including several exhibited
here. As in another drawing in this exhibition, the crescent-moon diadem worn by
this figure associates her with the moon
and its goddess, Cynthia, or Diana. She is
thus to be identified with one of the companions of Diana from the cortège of Europa in the 1571 tournament. The identification is made definite by comparison
with illustrations seen in an account of
this festival, Heinrich Wirrich's *Ordentliche
Beschreibung...*, where figures in Diana's

suite holding bows and with quivers of arrows have almost identical costumes. Like
other females in the tournament, Diana
was personified by a knight, and members
of her suite were also probably enacted by
men *en masque* and *en travestie*.

Venice 1987, p. 152, ill.

Preis 1967, ill. 25; Kaufmann 1978, pp. 55-
6, ill. 26; Beyer 1983, p. 87, no.48, ill 62.

T.C.K.

IV.12
Giuseppe Arcimboldo
Milan 1527–Milan 1593
Costume Design: *Diana or her Companion*
Pen and blue ink, blue wash
30.5 × 20.5
Upper right: *44*
1571
Florence, Galleria degli Uffizi, Gabinetto
Disegni e Stampe, inv. no. 3184

The diadem with crescent moon worn by
this figure associates her with the goddess
of the moon Diana, otherwise known as
Cynthia. Alfons, followed by Beyer, suggested that she was a member of the suite

of Diana who belonged to the cortège of
Europe appearing in the *Ringlrennen* that
constituted part of a tournament held in
Vienna in 1571 to celebrate the wedding of
Archduke Karl. Comparison with illustrations of the entry of figures to the
Ringlrennen confirms this identification. A
figure in very similar costume bearing a
spear appears in the illustrations to Heinrich Wirrich's *Ordentliche Beschreibung* (Vienna, 1571) of this event. Probably neither
of the figure designs exhibited here is for
Diana, however, as she is described as riding on a unicorn.

Venice 1987, p. 152, ill.

Alfons 1957; Preiss 1967, ill. 24; Kaufmann
1978, p. 56, ill. 31; Beyer 1983, p. 88, no. 50.
ill. 62; Kaufmann 1985, ill. 40; Kaufmann
1988, p. 29, ill.

T.C.K.

IV.13
Giuseppe Arcimboldo
Milan 1527–Milan 1593
Costume Design: *Companion of Geometry*
Pen and blue ink, blue wash
30 × 20 cm
At top: *Geometria condutta [sic] da Arcimede Siciliano et Archita calabrese/ Vesta morella*; at upper right: *13*
1571
Imperial Collections, Prague
Florence, Galleria degli Uffizi, Gabinetto Disegni e Stampe, inv. no. 3155F

The inscription identifies the drawing as a design for a costume for the companions of Geometry, the famed mathematician Archimedes of Syracuse in Sicily and the Pythagorean philosopher and geometer Archytas of Taranto. Hence the figure in the drawing holds a rectangle. Fonteo identifies the costume as a *pallium*, known by the Romans as the mantle of philosophers, particularly Greek philosophers. Fonteo cites as his sources Gellius, and Heroes Atticus, whom he also probably found cited in Gellius. Fonteo's description allows for an identification with one of the costume designs for the companions of the liberal arts in the train of Europe, from the 1571 tournament held in Vienna.

Venice 1987, p. 149, ill.

Kaufmann 1978, p.55, ill. 22; Beyer 1983, pp. 74-5, no. 6, ill. 19; Kriegeskörte 1988, pp. 72-4. ill.

T.C.K.

IV.14
Giuseppe Arcimboldo
Milan 1527–Milan 1593
Costume Design: *Companion of Music*
Pen and blue ink, blue wash
30 × 20 cm
Inscribed by artist, above: *Musica condotta da Boetio latino et Arione greco/vesta gialda traversata di roso le Bolle al petto d'oro/ e le altre per la vest d'argento*; inscribed upper right: *12*
1571
Imperial Collections, Prague
Florence, Galleria degli Uffizi, Gabinetto Disegni e Stampe, inv. no. F 3154

The lengthy inscription in Italian by Arcimboldo allows for its precise identification as a costume for one of the patrons (seconds) of Music, present in the train of Europe at the tournament held in Vienna in 1571 to celebrate the marriage of Archduke Karl. This inscription corresponds to the description given in Latin by Arcimboldo's collaborator, Fonteo (ÍNB Cod. 10106). According to Fonteo, the costume is a *syrma*, worn at poetic recitations. Fonteo correctly indicates the Roman authors Seneca and Martial as sources for citation of this costume. The exemplars are the philosopher and music theorist Boethius and the semi-mythical poet Arion. The shape of the body and particularly the head of the musical instrument suggests that it is not a violin (cf. Beyer), but a *lira da braccio*, a symbol of noble 'mathematical music' (Winternitz 1979).

Venice 1987, p. 148, ill; Essen and Vienna 1988, no. 189.

Alfons 1957, p. 112, ill.; Kaufmann 1978, p. 55, ill. 23; Porzio 1979, ill. p. 93; Beyer 1983, p. 75, no. 6, ill. 20; Kriegeskörte 1988, pp. 72-4, ill.

T.C.K.

IV.15
Giuseppe Arcimboldo
Milan 1527–Milan 1593
Costume Design: *The Cook*
Pen and blue ink, blue wash
30.5 × 20 cm
Upper right: *57*
Imperial Collections, Prague
Florence, Galleria degli Uffizi, Gabinetto Disegni e Stampe, inv. no. 3197 F

This drawing derives from the book of tournament designs presented to Rudolf II by Arcimboldo in 1585 Among Arcimboldo's surviving costume designs, it is the unique invention that recalls his composite heads, best known from his paintings: it is composed out of cooking implements. Composite pictures of a cook and a waiter are known to have existed (see Kaufmann 1988, no. 1.15 and 1.16). These paintings probably came from the Saxon collections, and another painting of the waiter adorned with the royal arms of Spain, probably from Arcimboldo's workshop, was recently offered at auction (Christie's, London, 1993). A drawing of a head composed out of cooking utensils (Paris, Ecole des Beaux Arts) and a Venetian print designed similarly are also known. None of these precisely resembles the Uffizi drawing, however. This drawing is done in a similar manner to that of other tournament inventions by Arcimboldo, so that its attribution is secure. Since, however, no similar figure is mentioned in any surviving tournament account, nor shown in other illustrations, the occasion for which it was made remains unknown.

Venice 1987, p. 142, ill.

Preiss 1967, ill. 27; Beyer 1983, p. 88, no. 52, ill. 66; Kriegeskörte 1988, title page ill.

T.C.K.

IV.16
Giuseppe Arcimboldo
Milan 1527–Milan 1593
Costume Design: *Necromancer*
Pen and blue ink, blue wash
21 × 16.5 cm
At bottom: *abito de negromante*; upper right: *84*
Florence, Galleria degli Uffizi, Gabinetto Disegni e Stampe, inv. no. 3217 F

The inscription at the bottom of the drawing indicates that this is a costume designed for a magician or necromancer. As in Arcimboldo's drawing of the companions of astronomy, the turban worn by this figure may also associate him with a magician. The dimensions, execution largely in brush, and figure-ground relation of this drawing differ from those of the designs for the 1571 ceremony, where no such character appeared. A necromancer was, however, one of the central personages in a tournament held in Bratislava in 1572 to celebrate the coronation of Rudolf II as king of Hungary, and Beyer has associated this drawing with this event. A magician, or *negromante*, also appeared at a tournament held in Prague in 1570, that Fonteo's account (ONB cod. 10206) indicates Arcimboldo definitely invented. In fact another published description of the 1570 tournament is written by 'Zirfeo Schwartzkunstler', who from his *nom de plume* may very have been the *negromante* dressed up for this event. The dating of the drawing must thus remain open.

Venice 1987, p. 152, ill.

Alfons 1957, p. 113, ill; Preiss 1967, p. 11, ill. 35; Kaufmann 1978, pp. 54, 56, ill. 29; Beyer 1983, p. 83, no. 32, ill. 46.

T.C.K.

IV.17
Giuseppe Arcimboldo
Milan 1527–Milan 1593
Costume Design: *Sleigh*
Pen, blue ink, blue wash
19 × 23 cm
Upper right: *123*
Imperial Collections, Prague
Florence, Galleria degli Uffizi, Gabinetto Disegni e Stampe, inv. no. 3278AF

This sheet comes from a volume in the collections of the Uffizi that contained 148 drawings with a title page dated 1585, bearing a dedication to Rudolf II from Arcimboldo. The drawings are described by the artist as being inventions for tournaments (*hastiludis*). This book is most likely identifiable with one of three similar volumes (inv. no. 2581, 2765, 2766) of drawings by Arcimboldo for *mascherate* that are listed in the 1607-11 Inventory of the Prague *Kunstkammer*. It is possible that the drawings were given in connection with a ceremony for the Golden Fleece in 1585 at which event a tournament is known to have taken place, but many other drawings from the volume can be associated with other, earlier tournaments. Although it is not necessary to assume sleighs were used exclusively for tournaments held during the winter, the long garments of the driver and especially the way in which the capes are wrapped around the men seated on a sleigh in a related drawing (inv. no. 3278) do suggest that the event took place in winter.

Venice 1987, ill. 150.

Preiss 1967, ill. fig. 43; Porzio 1979, ill. p. 92.

T.C.K.

IV.18
Giuseppe Arcimboldo
Milan 1527–Milan 1593
Costume Design: *Sleigh*
Pen, blue ink and wash
30 × 20 cm [Beyer gives 23 × 19]
[Imperial collection, Prague}
Florence, Galleria degli Uffizi, Gabinetto
Disegni e Stampe, inv. no. 3278BF

The decoration of this sleigh with a figure
of Cupid shooting an arrow, two dolphins
and a shell, might associate it with Venus
(Marina), or with Galatea, as Beyer also
noted. The unusual detail of the paddle
wheels seen below the shell is also found

in other representations of the *carro* of
Galatea, first invented by Raphael in a ceiling painting in the Villa Farnesina, Rome,
dated 1513. The wheels are taken from a
mode of land transport, transferred to the
sea; in Arcimboldo's drawing the motif is
simply readapted, and peculiarly appears
again on land, where the sleigh would actually be employed to transport the car
(see M.Meiss, in *The Painter's Choice*, New
York, 1976). Like inv. no. 3278AF, with
which it shares a watery theme, this drawing cannot be identified with any known
descriptions of Arcimboldo's festivals or
depictions of the vehicles used therein.
Since tournaments known from his period

of imperial service took place earlier in the
year, the date of these drawings is unsure.

Preiss 1967, ill. no. 39; Beyer 1983, p. 80, no.
22, ill. 36.; Kriegeskörte 1988, ill. 70; Bod-
nar 1992, p. 64, fig. 38.

T.C.K.

IV.19
Giuseppe Arcimboldo
Milan 1527–Milan 1593
Elephant
Pen and blue ink
24 × 18.75 cm
[Imperial Collections, Prague]
Florence, Galleria degli Uffizi, Gabinetto
Disegni e Stampe, inv. no. 3225F

Chroniclers of a tournament held in
Prague in 1570 describe the appearance of
a live elephant there as the most spectacular aspect of the event (see Kaufmann
1978, p. 31). This was the first such beast
to be seen in Bohemia, if not in Central

Europe: one had been seen in Vienna earlier, and its bones were eventually made into a chair for Emperor Maximilian II (see
U. Giese, *Wiener Menagerien*, Vienna,
1962). Beyer has proposed that this is a
drawing of the elephant that appeared in
the 1570 tournament, but an inscription
by Ottavio Strada on a drawing by (or copy
after) Jacopo Strada indicates that Strada
also made a design for the elephant for the
1571 tournament in Vienna (Kaufmann
1978, p. 63 and fig. 45), so the date cannot
be made exact. Since no such attire appears in this sheet and it is known that
Arcimboldo designed a pyramid for it in
1570, it can be inferred that this drawing is

a sketch from the actual beast. The quality
of the drawing, which has not been
worked up with wash— unusual in Arcimboldo's oeuvre – also argues for its character as a sketch.

Beyer 1983, p. 89, no. 53, ill. 67;
Kriegeskörte 1988, p. 72, ill. 73.

T.C.K.

IV.20
Daniel Fröschl
Satyr, Bacchante, and Old Man
Pen and brush, with additional colouring
on parchment; grid is visible
After 1603
Bequeathed to the Society of Patriotic Art
Lovers by J. Hlávka on 25 January 1904
Prague, Národní galerie v Praze, Gráficka
sbírka, inv. no. K 4 239

Fröschl often used compositions taken
from well-known masters as the basis for
his mimiatures on parchment. In addition
to his most famous work based on a design by Dürer (cat. no. I.174), he also made

paintings based on works by Bartolomeus
Spranger (Vienna, Albertina, inv. no.
3352), Hans von Aachen (Florence,
Church of San Lorenzo, treasure) and
many famous Italian painters, although
the evidence that remains is mostly in the
form of documents. The grid beneath the
colour would suggest that this Prague
drawing was based on a foreign composition. It as yet has not come to light, but the
more robust figurative forms would suggest it was of Flemish origin. Like all
Fröschl's miniatures, this work was painted with his characteristic technique of using fine lines and points to create a subtle
coloured relief on the surface of the parch-

ment. The closest of Fröschl's other works
to this one is his miniature from Edinburgh depicting *Satyrs and a Nymph* (cat.
no. I.175).

Prague 1978–79, cat. no. 10.

Fučíková 1967, p. 151; Prague 1978–79, cat.
no. 10; Fučíková 1986, p. 23, no. X; Kaufmann 1988, p. 174, cat. no. 3.3.

E.F.

IV.21
Matthäus Gundelach
Kassel ? ca. 1565/67–Augsburg 1653/54
Allegories of Fire and Air
Pen and brown ink and grey wash over
pencil underdrawing, on paper
30.4 × 29.5 cm
Below centre: *M. / Gundelach / F
Probably 1605–30*
From the Alexander Fioring Collection,
Kassel; acquired in 1939 from the
Staatliche Kunstsammlungen in Kassel
Kassel, Staatliche Kunstsammlungen,
Graphische Sammlung, inv. no. 2 194

This circular image with allegorical per-

sonifications of the elements shows fire
(male, on the right) and air (female, on the
left) working together: fire holds a candle
in his right hand while smoke rises from
his head. Air has the attributes of a bird
(possibly a raven) on her head and, operating a bellows with her right foot, she is
feeding (or extinguishing) the candle with
her breath. In the background there are
ruins that have fallen victim to these two
elements. There was probably also a work
showing the other two elements, water
and earth. The function of this drawing is
unknown. Gundelach was called to
Stuttgart in 1617–18 and there received
payment, perhaps for a ceremonial deco-

ration of this kind. The work is important
for what it reveals about the understanding of the elements in the 'holistic' cosmological teachings, embracing both philosophy and science, that were crucial in
defining the cultural atmosphere at the
court of Rudolf II.

Essen and Vienna 1988, no. 199.

Bender 1981, pp. 299ff., no. ZA 22.

J.Z.

IV.22
Matthäus Gundelach
Kassel ? ca. 1565/67–Augsburg 1653/54
Allegory of Mining and the Earth
Oil on canvas
133 × 83 cm
M GONDOLACH / (probably not the
artist's own hand)
Traditionally dated 1610
Before 1889 in the collection of Carl Rit-
ter von Klinkosch, after that in the collec-
tions of A. Spitzer and Matsvansky, all in
Vienna; 1955 sold on the open market, ac-
quired by the mining firm of Dortmunder
Bergbau AG
Dortmund, Museum für Kunst und Kul-

turgeschichte, inv. no. C 518

Up until now the iconology of this work
has received less attention than its iconography: the question is whether this is an allegory of mining or of the Earth. There is
of course no reason why it could not be an
allegory of both, that is to say, that mining
is being used here as a symbol for the
earth. This would after all correspond to
the iconology inherent in what looks like a
companion piece, Gundelach's *Allegory of
Water and Fishing* (Friedrichshafen, Städt-
isches Bodensee-Museum; Essen and Vienna 1988, p. 232, no. 123). Gundelach
presumably painted these for a patron of

the arts in Augsburg. The loss of a puta-
tive original signature and date may have
occurred during restoration. According to
Frimmel, writing in 1908 (p. 9), this read
M. Gundelach f. 1620.

Augsburg 1968, no. 107; Essen and Vienna
1988, no. 122.

Bender 1981, pp. 170–73, no. GA6.

J.Z.

IV.33
Northern Netherlandish painter ca. 1600
Warning of Syphilis
Unmarked, undated
In 1827 lent from the castle in Duchcov by Count Arnošt of Valdštejn to the Picture Gallery of the Society of Patriotic Friends of the Arts in Bohemia (as Christoph Schwarz)

The theme of this painting of cabinet size is an ironic warning of the dangers of love. Venus lactans is presented with Cupid above an allegorical female figure with a lute, sitting behind a small table spread with delicacies. There is a young man who is eagerly drinking the cup of love, an unkempt dog in front of him, a young hunter with a lance, and the central figure of a philosopher with a book, pointing out the foolishness of the lover's behaviour. The idea came from Girolamus Francastoro da Verona, doctor, natural philosopher and poet (his didactic poem *Syphilis sive morbus Gallicus* was printed in Verona 1530) and had been portrayed in the engraving by Jan I. Sadeler after Christoph Schwarz (Panofsky: 'Hommage to Francastoro in a German-Flemish Composition of about 1590?', Nederlands kunsthistorisch Jaarbeek, XII, 1961, 1-33.) This painting has been reworked in lively and expressive colour. There are more compositions inspired by this print; one is in Potsdam (Bildgalerie), and a variation by Otto van Veen is in Stockholm (Nationalmuseum).

J.V.

IV.34
Central European Master from the early–mid-seventeenth century after a model by Jacob de Weert
Allegorical Procession I: Spring
Oil on canvas
110 × 150 cm
1625-50
Property of the Bees family of Chrostin at the Hnojnik chateau. After being seized in 1948 it was taken to Sternberk Castle in Moravia.
Local History Museum in Olomouc, located at Sternberk Castle in Moravia, 52.773
inv. no. St 282

The significance and moralizing aspect of the triumphal processions of antiquity inspired the Italian Renaissance artists Titian and Romano, the German masters Dürer, Altdorfer, Burkmaier, Holbein, and Kolderer as well as the Dutch masters de Vos, van Heemskerck, Cock, Galle, Volkert-sz Coornhert, Vorsterman II and de Bry. The picture was produced after a copper engraving model and was issued by the engraver and printer J. Weer, a pupil of H. Wierix. The procession features the signs of Aries, Taurus and Gemini as an allegory of Early Age, Childhood, but also of Time (the beginning of the year and the day). A two-wheeled cart symbolizes the triumph of life, yet also has the appearance of a sarcophagus, i.e. a grave. The three horses bear joy (Laetitia) with a lute (here the attribute of Hearing), Nature (Natura), nourishing all that is living, and Safety (Securitas). On the cart are toddlers – the Dawn (Aurora) awakening and disturbing 'the peace', but symbols of Vanity (Vanitas) are not missing from the scene. Peace (Pax) wearing the garb of antiquity is conversing with Innonce (Inocentia) whose consort is Chastity (Castitas).

Mžykova 1997 (in preparation).

M.Mž.

IV.35
Central European Master from the early–mid-seventeenth century after a model by Jacob de Weert
Allegorical Procession II: Summer
Oil on canvas
110 × 50 cm
1625-50
Local History Museum at Olomouc, located at Sternberk Castle in Moravia, 52.772
inv. no. St 283

Unlike Weert's copper-engraving, which provided the model, the allegorical procession of Maturity (Spring and Summer) in the signs of Virgo, Leo and Cancer was created as a mirror image (i.e, reversed): here three horses are bearing completely contradictory company – strong-willed ambition (Ambitio) with Aesculapius's stick, lofty Art (Ars) and negligent frivolity (Temeris). On the way to a mature, active age, also identified with Meridian or Noon (Meridies), the children's toys end underneath the wheels of the cart. The time for study has begun, but also for deciding between life and Virtue (Virtus), or the enticing Voluptuousness (Voluptas), shown with the phallic attribute of depravity. Amor in the guise of Desire (Cupid) triumphs alongside Frivolity, managing to overturn even the course of the world (a globe with a cross). This compact painting is replete with central tonality and reflects the Venetian use of colour (russet, purple, ochre-brown). Even the schematization of the execution and the heavy-going characterisation of the figures, in terms of their rural aspect, is at variance with the richness of the work, which betrays being been made after a model.

Mžykova 1997 (in preparation).

M.Mž.

IV.36
Central European Master from the early–mid-seventeenth century after a model by Jacob de Weert
Allegorical Procession III: Autumn
Oil on canvas
110 × 150 cm
1625-50
Local History Museum at Olomouc, located at Sternberk Castle in Moravia, 52.771
inv. no. St 284

As an expression of moral strength and the norms marked out on the quest for the meaning of human existence, this allegorical 'pilgrimage' also points to a natural, cosmological regularity: the parade has grown sad as it reaches the autumn of life. An enormous zebra bears a banner with the signs of Libra, Scorpio and Sagittarius. Three horses draw a two-wheeled cart – Evening or Dusk (Vesper), the Age of Man. An ass, the beast of impoverished folk, carries Affliction (Luctus), next to which is seated Anxiety (Cura) with an accumulation of useless things. Age rings in, in the spirit of Horatio's Odes (1, 7, 31:1, 18, 4), relieved by wine. On the horse, in a cajoling way nearest to the viewer, a coquette is being carried, introducing herself with the intention of Moses' utterances (22, 17-41, 49 etc) representing Deceit (Fraus). Her steed is draped with symbols of depravity (Hercules, 21), masks and allusions to Night. On the cart a scholar is studying and a chronicler is recording the 'shades' of life. Discord (Discordia) with synonyms of Satan (Ovid's *Metamorphoses* IV:769-803), Avarice (Avaritia) and Covetousness (a sycophantic toad) are storing up gold pieces. In the background, Ill-health (Aegritude) underlines the scene of grimness with quack potions.

Mžykova 1997 (in preparation).

M.Mž.

IV.37
Central European Master from the early–mid-seventeenth century after a model by Jacob de Weert
Allegorical Procession IV: Winter
Oil on canvas
110 × 150 cm
1625-50
Local History Museum at Olomouc, located at Sternberk Castle in Moravia, 52.770
inv. no. St 285

In an atmosphere of swarming demons emanating from man's last efforts, the standard-bearer carries a flag with the signs of Capricorn, Pisces and Aquarius. Accompanied by weeping people, the coach, sacred Night, moves across the carrion of horses and all the bodies. Fate (Fatus), i.e, Death, with frantic impatience comes to its final aim and is already letting fly its arrow. In the spirit of Petrarch's *Triumphs*, it sits on a black bullock. Without sorrow, another horseman, Chronos or Time (Tempus), manages to mow in the lives. Moirae, the Fates (Parcae) sit by the wheels with an impenetrable back, while Clotho spins the thread of life. Lachesis twines the propitiousness of fate and the span of life. Moira, the Irreversible, cuts the thread of Life and extinguishes the splinter of wood by her. Over the coffin on a gloomily covered globe is winged Myth (Fama) who proclaims the merits of the dead as well as their guilt. The Sternberk paintings have, after Weert's models, a meditative, sullen, dwindling, moralizing aspect. They are built on the principle of allegory, which was still naive in a medieval way and consisted of a repertoire constructed in various layers.

Mžykova 1997 (in preparation).

M.Mž.

IV.38
Lucas van Valckenborch
Louvain ca. 1535–Frankfurt am Main ca. 1597
Spring (?) (March or April)
1584–87
Imperial collection in Vienna; together with the painting Autumn transferred to the monastery by the Empress Maria Theresa in exchange for a debt
Brno, Klášter augustiniánů na Starém Brně, inv. no. 1584LVV

This broad view of a landscape with the planting of saplings and the setting of vine supports in the foreground was (to-

gether with the painting *Autumn*) part of the cycle *The Months*, of which there must have been twelve to start with. Seven have survived, dated between 1584 and 1587, of which five are in the Kunsthistorisches Museum in Vienna. However, it is not certain whether the remaining paintings have not survived, or whether the cycle was ever completed. The inspiration was *The Months* by Pieter Bruegel the Elder, which the painter must have known either by 1566 or during his second stay in Antwerp (1574–81). Although *Spring* is reminiscent of Bruegel's *Early Spring*, it maintains the tradition of Joachim Patenier and Herri met de Bles in its clear, dry

colour. The figures are reminiscent of the type produced in Antwerp by Gillis Mostaert, with whom Valckenborch sometimes worked. From the viewer's angle his cycle may have been intended to be hung high up in the style of a frieze.

Brünn 1925, cat. no. 118.

Kratinová, 1957, p. 86. Wied 1971, p. 170, cat. no. 38, ill. 126. Seifertová 1974, p. 329 (31). Vacková 1989, pp. 339–40, ill. 294, 376 (32). Wied 1990, p. 153, cat. no. 46, ill. 46.

J.V.

IV.39
Lucas van Valckenborch
Louvain ca. 1535–Frankfurt am Main ca. 1597
Autumn (?) (Return of the Herds and the Cattle Market)
1584–87
Imperial collection in Vienna; together with the painting Autumn transferred to the monastery by the Empress Maria Theresa in exchange for a debt
Brno, Klášter augustiniánů na Starém Brně, inv. no. 1585LVV

Together with the painting *Spring (?)*, part of the cycle *The Months*. The painting is

reminiscent of Bruegel's *Autumn* (or *The Return of the Herds*, Vienna, Kunsthistorisches Museum), adding to its theme with the scene of a cattle market in the middle ground of the composition.

J.V.

IV.40
Lucas van Valckenborch, Georg Flegel
Louvain ca. 1535–Frankfurt am Main ca. 1597; Olomouc 1566–Frankfurt am Maine 1638
Feast
After 1593
Bought by W.H. Braun, director of the museum for the Dukes of Lichtenštejn and donated to the museum in 1926.
Opava, Slezské muzeum, inv. no. U2036 A

The composition of restrained colourfulness (grey, black, white and gold) links in an individual way the genres of large figure painting, still life and portraiture. The

feast of the young couple (marriage partners?) served to them by an old man of dignified deportment, presents in addition to its main actors, actions fulfilling their functions according to the etiquette of the time. The dainties laid on the table – which, covered both by flowers and sweet-smelling herbs and by valuable china and glasses, is in a niche in the left background – are the work of a specialist. They are probably – in spite of some roughness in the painting – the first evidence of cooperation between the young Flegel and Lucas van Valckenborch. Either the whole possesses an allegorical meaning and serves as a warning against enjoyment and sen-

sual delights (the young couple in the park in the vista on the right), or in its restraint is intended for the decoration of a dining room (clearly a commission from members of the upper bourgeoisie). This picture is a simplified version of an analogous unsigned painting with many more figures *Celebration Feast* (with musical accompaniment, Austria, private collection) from the late 1590s, and was probably painted in Frankfurt, where the painter lived from 1593.

J.V.

IV.41
Lucas van Valckenborch
Louvain ca. 1535–Frankfurt am Main ca. 1597
Taking the Waters and Schwalbach Spa
Ca. 1597
Castle of Hrádek u Nechanic, earlier origin unknown
Castle of Hrádek u Nechanic, inv. no. 150

The forest scenery with the distant view of the countryside on the right shows the figure of Archduke Matthias in the middle ground, surrounded by members of the nobility. The picture is linked with two smaller panel paintings on this theme.

The older of them, with the title *Rudolf II Taking the Drinking Cure* (Vienna, Kunsthistorisches Museum) dating from after 1593 (when Valckenborch left Matthias's service and moved to Frankfurt) shows the same surroundings of the spring with its visitors, including Rudolf II with Ernst and Matthias. In the other, modified, composition with a small number of figures, signed and dated 1596 (Braunschweig, Herzog Anton Ulrich-Museum), Ernst is no longer portrayed. The painting *Spring Countryside with Elegant Company* has features in common with the preceding paintings (beside the lake in Oye near Brussels?), is signed and dated 1597 (un-

known private collection) and must have originated in January of that year, for news of the artist's funeral is dated 2 February. Similar dating is valid for our picture, carried out – despite its size – with detailed exactitude. A simplified reproduction, obviously made in the workshop, was recorded (1990) in the collection of P. P. M. Boer in Amsterdam.

J.V.

IV.42
Jacob Hoefnagel after Joris Hoefnagel
Antwerp 1572–Holland between 1632 and 1635
Archetypa studiaque patris Georgii Hoefnagelli Iacobus Fil: genio duce ab ipso scalpta, omnibus philomusis amict' D: ac perbenignt' communicat Frankfurt 1592
Engraving on paper
15 × 20.4 cm
1592
Prague, Národní galerie v Praze, Prints and Drawings section, inv. nos R 146 8785, R 146 877, R 146

In 1592 the young Jacob Hoefnagel en-

graved his *Archetypa* after designs by his father, Joris Hoefnagel, who used the same designs for the *Mira calligraphiae monumenta* (Los Angeles, J. Paul Getty Museum) and for other works. In 1591 Joris moved with his family to Frankfurt. The *Archetypa* is the first printed work that contains entomologically precise illustrations of insects. Numerous wild or exotic plants that Hoefnagel sketched on his travels are also seen here for the first time in print. The items are accompanied by a whole variety of relevant sayings and quotations. The *Archetypa* was intended as a handbook for other artists and as an encouragement to viewers to look more

closely at images. It was continuously in print right up until the late eighteenth century.

Wilberg Vignau-Schuurman 1969, vol. 2, p. 118, list of works 17; Hollstein 1949, nos 17–64; Bergström 1985, pp. 177ff., ills 5–9; Vignau-Wilberg 1994 (with additional bibliography).

Th.V.W.

IV.43
Painted Shield
D: 48 cm
Prague, Muzeum, inv. no. H2-418

The body of this circular, convex shield is constructed from two interconnected layers of poplar wood covered with a binding of hemp fibres. The painting represents a fantastic array of monstrous beings and animals, linked to the work of Hieronymus Bosch. The intense colours and compact modelling of forms that have replaced the sublime limpidity of Bosch's conception are close in style to his Antwerp imitator Pieter Huys (ca. 1519–

84). The inscription on the shield refers to St James the Great, who was traditionally honoured as the defender against the Moors in Spain, where the call of 'Santiago' (St James) was also a battle cry. During the sixteenth century, wooden, painted or otherwise embellished shields often used celebratory and triumphant processions as a decorative theme. All known examples to date of painted shields, however, were executed by Italian artists, or by artists from north of the Alps but in the Italian spirit. This is the only example of a shield with Dutch painting.

Prague 1994; Uhersky Brod 1996.

Snajdrova, Berger, T., Berger, V., Vackova and Royt 1994; Snajdrova 1994, p. 16; Hronsky 1995, p. 17.

M.M.

IV.44

See cat. no. III.236.

IV.45
Jacob de Gheyn
Antwerp 1565–The Hague 1629
Tycho de Brahe
Engraving
18.7 × 13.6 cm
On plinth: *EFFIGIES TYCHONIS BRAHE OTTONIDIS DANI D[OMI(NI DE KNVDSTRVP ET ARCIS VRANIENBVRG IN INSVLA HELLISPONTI DANICI HVAENA, FVNDATORIS MACHINARVMQAE ASTRONOMICARVM IN EADEM DSPOSITARVM INVENTORIS ET STRVCTORIS AETATIS SVAE ANNO 40. ANNO D[OMI]NI. 1586 COMPL[ETAE]*; motto next to the in-

scription: *NON HABERI SED ESSE*
1586
Prague, Národní galerie v Praze, Collection of Prints and Drawings, inv. no. R 102191

Tycho Brahe (Knudstrup auf Schonen 1546–Prague 1601) enjoyed widespread recognition after his discovery in 1572 of a new star, the Nova Cassiopeia. In 1576 he built the Uranienborg observatory on Ven im Sund, an island given to him by King Frederick II of Denmark. In 1597, after Frederick's death, Brahe left Denmark and in 1599 entered the service of Rudolf II as his astronomer. Brahe founded the Prague

observatory and gathered scholars and friends around himself, including Christian Ljönberg and Johannes Kepler. Brahe, who calculated Rudolf II's horoscope, laid the basis for Kepler's ground-breaking work on the planets and their orbits. This portrait shows Tycho Brahe wearing the Danish Order of the Elephant.

Essen and Vienna 1988, cat. no. 13, pp. 101–2.

Dreyer 1890; Hauser 1872.

H.H.

IV.46
Aegidius Sadeler (after Hans von Aachen)
Antwerp 1570–Prague 1629
Portrait of Rudolf II (and an allegory his rule)
Copper engraving
33.1 × 24.8 cm
(bottom centre – in the dedication)
S.C.M. tis pictor Iohan ab Ach Inventor, Aegidiussadeler. Anno M.D.C.III.
1603
Prague, Národní galerie v Praze, Grafická sbírka, inv. no. 778.

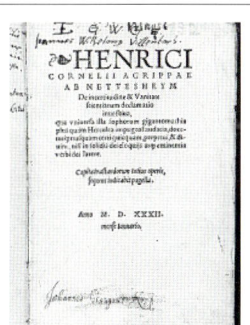

IV.47
Henry Cornelius Agrippa of Nettesheim
1486–1535
De incertudine et Vanitate scientiarum declamatio
Prague, Národní knihovna České republiky, inv. no. 2L91

De incertudine et Vanitate scientiarum declamatio was written in 1530, and follows the conventional pattern of dismissing human ability to comprehend nature in general, and disparaging the vain pursuit of the occult sciences in particular. Only theology and religion can bring Man closer to God, and all else is worthless. Given the

publication of *De occulta philosophia* three years later, this denial of the value of the occult sciences has puzzled scholars. Yates suggests that the stance was adopted as a 'safety device' in anticipation of his magnum opus, to protect him against possible accusations of black magic.

J.B.

IV.48
Henry Cornelius Agrippa of Nettesheim
(1486–1535)
De occulta philosophia libri tres
Prague, Národní knihovna České republiky, inv. no. 12H154

The three books of *De occulta philosophia* are among the most influential occult texts of the sixteenth century, and the recipes therein were consulted by virtually every leading late Renaissance intellectual and practitioner of the occult arts, including Dee, Camillo, Maier, and Sambucus, to name only a few. The three books of the *De occulta philosophia* are deeply imbued

with the Neo-Platonic theory of the microcosm and the macrocosm, the theory of celestial correspondences, and cites the Hermetic belief in the power of astral influences to animate statues.

J.B.

IV.49
Bonancina
Treatise on Drinkable Gold
Prague, Národní knihovna České republiky, inv. no. 49C145

A central preoccupation among the alchemists at Rudolf's court was the search for an elixir that would grant eternal life. This, and the related search for the Philosopher's Stone that would transform base metals into gold, could be seen either as a practical or a spiritual quest. In both cases, many works were published treating the issues, including this work in 1603, by the Florentine Bonancina.

J.B.

IV.50
Tycho Brahe
Knudstrup auf Schonen 1546–Prague 1601
Astronomiae instauratae mechanica
33.5 × 23.5 cm
1598
Facsimile edition: Wandesburgi M.D. IIC (1598) (the first edition was coloured by hand, with a portrait of Tycho Brahe on the front cover and an escutcheon in the lower part of the illustration)
Brussels, Culture et Civilisation 1969. (84), 32 pp., illustrated in the text, initialled, labelled
Prague, Národní technické muzeum, inv.

no. C 3783

A jewel of astronomical literature and one of the most important works written by Tycho Brahe, *Astronomia...* was published in 1598 (Wandesburg), 1602 (Nürnberg) and 1603 (Prague). The contents include a description of the instruments Brahe used for taking his readings and extraordinarily beautiful illustrations of them. It presents the main instruments (sextants, quadrants, semicircles), armillary spheres, and parallactic rulers, as well as a description of a large globe and other directional and reading aids. A section of the publication is devoted to Hven Island (a map of the is-

land) and the observatories located there, Uranienborg and Stjerneborg. The instruments, which Brahe constructed with the help of various mechanics, are among the best of that period. Designed to obtain the most accurate measurements, they were very large, made mostly of brass and richly ornamented. After his arrival at the court of Rudolf II in 1599, Brahe gradually moved his instruments and aids to Bohemia.

Gruss 1901; Thoren 1990.

Kc.

IV.51
Anselm Boethius de Boodt
Ca.1570–1634
Gemmarum et Lapidum Historia
Prague, Národní knihovna České republiky, inv. no. 16H73 Rd-43

Born in Bruges, Anselm Boethius de Boodt was an emblematist and herbalist of deep learning, and Rudolf's court lapidary, or specialist in precious stones. Stones and jewels played an important part in the life of Rudolf's court, not only as the visible signs of power, but as an essential part of alchemical investigations. His own magnum opus, the *Gemmarum et Lapidum His-*

toria, has been described as 'the most important lapidary of the seventeenth century', and outlines the classification of stones according to their properties, their origins, and their powers to bring about good or evil effects. As a member of Rudolf's circle of iconographers, he also worked on Typotius's *Symbola Divina et Humana*, a compendium of imperial symbolism. As keeper of the imperial gem collection, he provided materials to alchemists for their experiments, and is said to have performed transformations himself.

J.B.

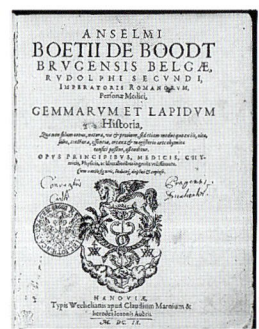

IV.52
John Dee
1527–1608
Monas Hieroglyphica
Prague, Národní knihovna České republiky, inv. no. 14H352,14J97

John Dee was the foremost mathematician of the Elizabethan age, and was responsible in part for shaping the English imperial culture. Confidant of Cecil and the Queen, tutor to Sir Philip Sidney, he had a panoramic education and possessed the largest library in England, with books and manuscripts representing the full range of late Renaissance learning. As a mathe-

matician he introduced Vitruvius to the English-reading public, and helped prepare navigational tables for the English Navy. He was also an exemplary Renaissance magus, and embraced the occult arts of angelology, white magic, and alchemy. In 1583, he appeared before Rudolf II with a message of eirenic salvation, but was soon exiled with his assistant Edward Kelley due to the influence of the Catholic faction at court, who treated his message with grave suspicion. The *Monas Hieroglyphica* was first published in 1564 and dedicated to Rudolf's father, Maximilian II, and is among the most influential, and opaque, of his writings. The Monas is a

symbol composed of the astrological characters for each of the seven planets, based on the character for Mercury and infused with astral powers, to be used by the adept. Dee's writings, and his extensive travel throughout Europe, are said to have sown the seeds for later spiritual and political movements, culminating in the Rosicrucian manifestos of the early seventeenth century, and in the abortive attempt on the part of Frederick V to claim the Bohemian crown.

J.B.

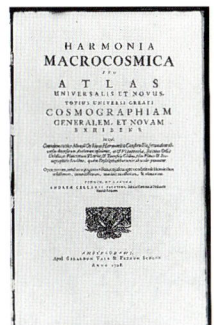

IV.53
Andreas Cellarius
Harmonia macrocosmia
Prague, Národní knihovna České republiky, inv. no. 19ZZ12

By the end of the sixteenth century, the intellectual life of Europe, and its cultural and spiritual centre, Prague, had been profoundly shaped by the conflation of Neo-Platonism, rekindled by an influx of new texts following the fall of Constantinople and the collapse of the Byzantine Empire, and Hermeticism, by way of the translations of Ficino and the writings of Pico della Mirandola and Cabala, which had

been introduced into the mainstream with the expulsion of the Jews from Spain. Within this framework, the philosophy of the microcosm and the macrocosm, wherein all that takes place in the 'little world' of Man is a reflection of aspects of the greater world of the Cosmos, had assumed a central position in late Renaissance thought. Most of the intellectual output of the late Renaissance was influenced by the idea that there was a deep and non-trivial correspondence between the order of things on earth and the divine order ordained by the Almighty, mediated by influences from the stars. In this context Andreas Cellarius's book the *Harmo-*

nia macrocosmia fits as part of the spectrum of intellectual activity that characterized Rudolf's court.

J.B.

IV.54
Oswald Croll
Ca.1556–1609
Basilica Chymica . . .
1608
Prague, Národní knihovna České republiky, inv. no. D IV 62

Oswald Croll was an important Paracelsan alchemist, and physician to the Protestant activist Christian of Anhalt, who engineered the abortive attempt to claim the Bohemian throne for Frederick V. His exact role is not always clear, although it seems he was Anhalt's agent at Rudolf's court. There he was a confidant of both

Rudolf and Peter Vok Rozmberk, an important Czech noble, and actively participated in the intellectual life of the Castle. His *Basilica Chymica* was published in 1608, a year before his death, dedicated to Anhalt with a printer's privilege from Rudolf II. It includes illustrations by the court engraver Aegidius Sadeler and poems by the Anglo-Czech poetess Westonia (step-daughter of John Dee's notorious medium, Edward Kelley). The text celebrates the Paracelsan use of herbal and homeopathic remedies, and is deeply imbued with the Neo-Platonic doctrine of the microcosm and the macrocosm, in which the virtues of plants correspond to

astral influences. Associated with the *Basilica Chymica* is the text *De Signaturis internis rerum*, a treatise on astral signatures dedicated to Peter Vok, which mentions certain herbs received from Rudolf II's estate at Brandeis.

J.B.

IV.55
Sign. Mladá Vozice 13 A 2512
Marsilio Ficino
MARSILII FICINI, PHILOSOPHI, PLATONICI, MEDICI ATQUE THEOLOGI OMNIUM PRAESTANTISSIMI, OPERUM: IN QUO COMPRAEHENDUNTUR EA, QUAE EX GRAECO IN LATINUM SERMONEM DOCTISSIMĚ TRANSTULIT, EXCEPTIS PLATONE, ATQUE PLOTINO PHILOSOPHIS, QUORUM TAMEN EPITOME, ...TOMVS SECVNDVS. BASILEAE, (EX OFFICINA HENRICPETRINA, ANNO M. D. LXXVI. MENSE MARTIO.) (=1576), /3/ ff., 1013–1979 pp.

32 × 21 cm
Binding: white leather, ornament, in gold letters V H 1593
Tovacova and Mladť Vozice

Marsilio Ficino (1433–1495) was a leading figure at the Academy which was founded in 1459 under the patronage of Cosimo Medici in Florence. As a translator of Plato's works into Latin, Ficino understood Plato as an interpreter of hermetic truths.

Verzeichnis der im deutschen Sprachbereich erschienenen Druckes des XVI. Jahrhunderts (Stuttgart, 1983), F 926; Ferguson 1906, p. 269.

L.A.

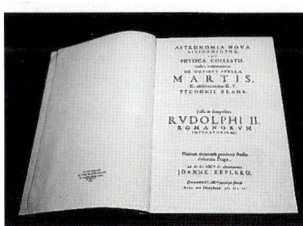

IV.56
Johannes Kepler
Weil der Stadt 1571–Regensburg 1630
Astronomia nova Aitiologetos, seu physica coelestis, tradita commentariis de motibus Stellae Martis, ex obsevationibus G.V. Tychonis Brahe ...
36.5 × 24.5 cm
1609
Facsimile edition: Prague, 1609
Brussels, Culture et Civilisation 1968.
(37), 337 pp., with illustrations and tables in the text, (1) tab. suppl.
Prague, Národní technické muzeum, inv. no. D 537

This new astronomy was Kepler's most significant work, written in Prague during his stay at the university residence. The title states what the work includes and how it came about. In *Astronomia nova* Kepler summarized the results of many years of research and explained in detail how he had derived his three astronomical laws, the first two of which were:
1. The planets revolve in elliptical orbits, not unlike circles, of which the common focus is the sun.
2. The radius vector (the straight line joining a planet to the sun) circumscribes equal surfaces in equal times.
The work, which contains seventy chap-

ters, has a remarkable introduction. In one passage, concerning the causes of planetary motion, Kepler challenged the contemporary Aristotelian theory of weight. He also attempted to determine the principles of the theory of gravity, anticipating Newton.

Caspar 1948 (1st edn); Horský 1980; Janáček 1987.

Kc.

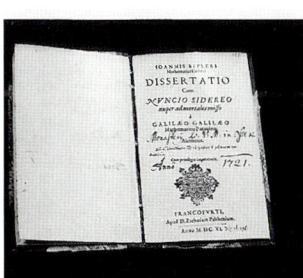

IV.57
Johannes Kepler
Weil der Stadt 1571–Regensburg 1630
Ioannis Kepleri Mathematici Caesarei Dissertatio cum Nuncio Sidereo nuper ad mortales mizzo a Galilaeo Galilaeo Mathematico Patauino ...
15.5 × 9 cm
1611
Frankfurt, D. Zachariam Palthenium, 1611, 53.1 pp.
Prague, Národní technické muzeum, inv. no. A 17648

In this work (Treatise on Starry Messenger, sent among the mortals by Galileo Galilei,

the mathematician of Padua), Kepler was the first among his contemporaries in the scientific world to give a positive response to Galileo's *Nuncius Sidereus...*, published in Venice in 1610. The discoveries Galileo made using a telescope, which he called a perspicillum, including the satellites of Jupiter, a description of the surface of the moon, and the composition of the Milky Way, and a confirmation of Copernicus's theory that the system was heliocentric. Kepler's treatise, which was published as early as mid-1610 in Prague, was actually an open letter to Galileo, and to support it he immediately wrote another work, *Narratio...* (A commentary on the observation

of Jupiter's four satellites), summarizing his own observations by telescope and confirming Galileo's discoveries. In the treatise Kepler expressed his enthusiasm for the new possibilities of astronomy, but also his disagreement with the views of his friend Jan Matouš Wacker von Wackenfels, an adherent of Giordano Bruno's concept of a limitless universe.

Caspar 1948 (1st ed.); Horský 1980; Janáček 1987.

Kc.

IV.58
Michael Maier
1568–1622
Secreta Natura Chymica
Prague, Národní knihovna České republiky, inv. no. 15H92

One of the most enigmatic of Rudolf's court physicians, Michael Maier served in Prague as Rudolf's private secretary from 1608 until Rudolf's abdication in 1611, and was granted the title of Count Palatine for his services. He returned only in 1617, possibly in anticipation of a golden age of Rosicrucian enlightenment heralded by the prospect of the Bohemian throne being offered to the Elector Palatine, Frederick V. He was an accomplished emblematist, and his *Secreta Natura Chymica* is one of several symbolic texts written by Maier that combine careful observation and penetrating analysis with explanations influenced and to a large extent defined by the interest in the occult that characterized the late Renaissance court of Rudolf II – Neo-Platonism, Cabala, Hermeticism and alchemy. In his best-known works, such as *Atalanta Fugiens*, Maier seems to propose that the processes underlying the world are fundamentally alchemical, and that alchemical transformations offer a means of approaching the truth about the world, a view that places him in both the Paracelsan and occult intellectual concerns of the late sixteenth century. In the political realm, his association with the court of Rudolf II and with Christian of Anhalt implicate him in the attempt to weaken the Habsburg powers by putting Frederick V on the throne of Bohemia in 1619.

J.B.

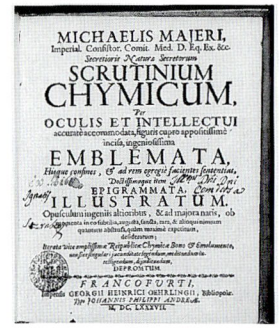

IV.59
Jan Marek Marci z Kronlandu
Lanškroun 1595–Prague 1667
Idearum operatricium idea
Book, print on paper, copper engraving title page with 20 illustrations and text, woodcut initials and vignettes
1635
Bought in 1985 at the antiquarian bookshop at Karlova 2 in Prague
Prague, Uměleckoprůmyslové Muzeum, inv. no. Gk-10.975 E

This first scientific publication by Jan Marek Marci, professor of medicine at Prague University, was a novel study of fertilization and the development of the human foetus from the perspective of philosophy and the natural sciences. He defended and expanded the theory that the embryo developed from a fertilized seed (egg) and that organs gradually emerged within the embryo. He wrote the work in 1631 in honour of his pregnant wife and the 'creative force that perfected a first-born son in the maternal womb'. His views, derived from Neo-Platonist tradition, were vehemently criticized by the Prague Jesuits (particularly Rodrigo Arriaga), who denounced the book as heretical. Marci was supported by Cardinal Harrach and the Jesuit polyglot Anthanasius Kircher.

Servít 1989, pp. 144ff.

R.V.

IV.60
Jan Marcus Marci from Kronland
Lanškroun 1595–Prague 1667
Labyrinthus in quo via ad circuli quadraturam pluribus modis exhibetur ...
(On the second (title?) page: *Circulo archetypo immenso absque mole, cuius centrum ubique peripheria nusquam ...*)
18.5 × 15 cm
1654
Prague, printed by Urbani Goliasch, 1654, 4⁰ XVI, 120 pp. (2) supp., copper-engraving on title page, marginalia
Prague, Národní technické muzeum, inv. no. A 17149

Labyrinthus... contains the results of Marci's work over many years. The problem of the quadrature, constructing a square equal in area to a given circle, had engaged scholars since Antiquity. Based on his knowledge of Archimedes, Marci presented twelve approaches to the problem, without claiming to have found a definitive solution. The quadrature of the circle can be accomplished only with the aid of a compass and ruler. Such a geometric construct is called Euclidean, and even methods that give a satisfactory result by accuracy of design or computation are taken as the quadrature. The attempts of to find a solution contributed to the development of numerical methods, the theory of numbers, integral calculus, and other fields.) The high regard in which Marci's work was held by his contemporaries is borne out by this publication: before the author's forward are five poems, written by two physicians and two professors at the university of Prague, which celebrate the solution of the problem, a claim not made by the author.

Studnička 1988; Smolík 1871; *Jan Marek ...* papers 1996; *Johannes Marcus ...* papers 1997.

Kc.

IV.61
Pierandrea Mattioli and Daniel Adam of Veleslavín
1501–1577
Herbalist
Book, print on paper, woodcut illustrations, partly coloured
1596
Acquired by transfer from the library of the Uměleckoprůmyslové Muzeum
Prague, Uměleckoprůmyslové Muzeum, inv. no. G 109-B

The famous Czech re-edition of Mattioli's herbal, based on the Frankfurt edition of 1586 with illustrations by Konrad Gesner, and supplemented by Daniel Adam and the translator Adam Huber.

Knihopis, 2/5, 5417

R.V.

IV.62
Paracelsus
1493–1541
Astronomia Magna ...
Prague, Národní knihovna České republiky, inv. no. 15A53

Theophrastus Bombast von Hohenheim, known as Paracelsus (and also as Theophrastus), was one of the most influential writers of the late Renaissance, and, owing to his strident nationalism, is often spoken of as the Luther of natural philosophy. He was hailed by his supporters as a prophet, a visionary and a genius for his rejection of the Scholastic medical tradition based on Aristotle and Galen, and his belief in the importance of first-hand observation, herbal and homeopathic remedies and the philosophy of Hermetic Neo-Platonism. His enemies branded him as a charlatan, a heretic and a revolutionary. As he wrote in a crude Swiss-German vernacular, few of his works were published during his lifetime, save for a short work (suppressed by the Fugger family) on the dubious effects of guaiacum as a treatment for syphilis, a work on mineral waters and a work on surgery based on his own experience as an army surgeon. The *Astronomia Magna* was written during his most productive period, while he was physician to Erasmus in Basel in the late 1520s and was published much later, in the 1570s, when a surge of Latin translations of Paracelsan works came off the presses in Basle.

J.B.

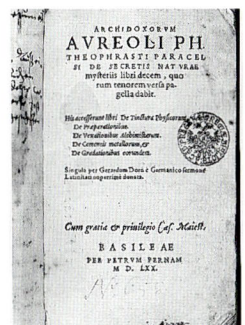

IV.63
Paracelsus (1493–1541)
De secretis naturae mysteriis 1570
Prague, Národní knihovna České republiky, inv. no. 15J122 Bf607

De secretis naturae mysteriis was among the many works published in Latin in the years following Paracelsus's death in 1541. More than the original works, these Latin translations ensured the diffusion of Paracelsan ideas throughout Europe, and their acceptance by the educated. This acceptance among certain groups of intellectuals carried a high price. Paracelsus represented a deep threat to the faculties of Medicine and to Galenic physicians, who spent much ink denouncing Paracelsan practices and listing casualties to Paracelsan cures, especially those using antimony, known to be toxic. As the century progressed, and his works associated with another vituperative German vernacular writer, Luther, Paracelsan medicine acquired the even more serious taint of heresy.

J.B.

IV.64
Paracelsus
Domain of the Holy Rood Sign. 3521/1
ERSTER (ANDER) THEIL DER BUCHER VND SCHRIFTEN DES EDLEN, HOCHGELEHRTEN VND BE-WEHRTEN PHILOSOPHI VNND MEDICI PHILIPPI THEOPHRASTI BOMBAST VON HOHENHEIM PARACELSI GENANNT: JETZT AUFF AUSS DEM ORIGINALIEN, VND THEOPHRASTI EIGNER HANDSCHRIFFT, SOUIEL DERSELBEN ZUBOKOMMEN GEWESEN, AUFFS TREWLICHST VND FLEISSIGST AN TAG GEBEN DURCH IOHANNEM HVSERVM BRISGOIVM. BASEL,
DURCH CONRAD WALDKIRCH, ANNO M. D. LXXXIX. (=1589), /9/ ff., 426 S., 342 S., index
24 × 17 cm
Binding: leather
On title page: *CASPAR SCHVENCKFELT D.HIRSCHBERGA*

Woodcut portrait of the author is illustrated here.

Allgemeine Deutsche Biographie 1880, pp. 675–83; *Verzeichnis der im deutschen Sprachbereich Erschienenen Druckes des XVI. Jahrhunders* 1983, p. 365.

L.A.

IV.65
Giovanni Battista Porta
1535–1615
Magia Naturalis
Prague, Národní knihovna České republiky, inv. no. sign. 15J35

In 1558 Giovanni Battista Porta, magus and proto-scientist, published the *Magia Naturalis*, which was to become, along with Agrippa's *Occulta philosophia*, one of the most influential books of the late Renaissance, with a profound impact on both Tommaso Campanella and Francis Bacon. In this essential text, Porta describes the values and virtues of plants and stones, and sets out a detailed system of correspondences between the stars and the world below, mediated by astral influences. In 1560 Porta founded the Academia Secreterum Naturae, a precursor of the early scientific societies such as the Lincei which shaped much of the later development of Renaissance science.

J.B.

IV.66
Giovanni Battista Porta
1535–1615
Phytognomica
Prague, Národní knihovna České republiky, inv. no. 12H126

Among Porta's many interests was physiognomy, especially the similarities between human and animal facial features. His book the *Phytognomica* is devoted to describing the correspondences between human and animal faces.

J.B.

Science and Instruments

Antonín Švedja

The sixteenth century was a period of unprecedented economic development in Bohemia. A great upsurge was recorded in mining, thanks to the discovery of silver ore in Jáchymov, and work continued in Kutná Hora and other areas. In mining a significant role was played by surveying, both in surveying drifts and in mapping out sites. The Institute of Bona Fide Provincial Surveyors was created at this time. Among the best surveyors were Matouš Ornys of Lindperk (1526–1600) and Šimon Poldolský of Podolí (1561–1617). In addition to surveying terrain and mine sites, surveyors took part in laying the groundwork for and maintaining fish ponds, which were constructed primarily in southern Bohemia in the Rožmberk domain and in eastern Bohemia in the Pernštejn domain. A notable water shaft was the so-called 'Rudolf's adit' in Prague, under Letna Hill, which conducted water to the pond in the Royal Game Preserve. This structure and its design provide convincing evidence of the high skill levels of surveying in Bohemia at that time.

In the mid-sixteenth century, besides practical and scientific questions related to economic growth, cosmological questions also received a great deal of attention. This interest was initiated by Nicolaus Copernicus, who in 1543 promulgated his heliocentric notion in the book *De revolutionibus orbium coelestium*. The noted Czech astronomer and mathematician of this period was Cyprián Lvovický of Lvovic (1514–74), who taught astronomy in Bavaria (Lauingen) to – among others – Tycho Brahe. A distinctive scientific personality in Bohemia in the second half of the sixteenth century, Tadeáš Hájek (1525–1600), was a polymath who studied astronomy, mathematics and medicine, among other subjects. He maintained personal contacts and kept up a written correspondence with the foremost European scientists, among them Tycho Brahe. It was Hájek who arranged for Brahe to come to Prague. Brahe arrived at the imperial court after many years of activity in Denmark, where he had built a remarkable observatory, the first modern scientific institute. He capped his scientific activity in Prague, in particular collaborating successfully with his eventual successor, Johannes Kepler. During his activity in Prague, Kepler elaborated on Brahe's wealth of observation material to derive his famous laws of planetary motion. He published the first two of these in 1609 in the work *Astronomia nova*.

In addition to astronomers, geometricians and mathematicians, instrument-makers also had a strong presence at the time. Similar methods were employed to measure terrain, mines and the stars; quantities were assessed in the same way and the instruments used were similar, as were the calculations. Several of the measuring instruments produced in sixteenth-century Bohemia are mentioned in the contemporary literature: Jan Dubravius (1486–1553) describes three types of levelling instruments employed in laying the groundwork for fish ponds; Agricola gives an account of an instrument used for mine measurements; and other accounts speak of compasses and measuring cords. Active in Prague in the 1560s was a native of Jáchymov, Johannes Praetorius (1537–1616), a mathematician and mechanic who worked for Emperor Maximilian II.

The manufacture of scientific instruments spread all across Europe in the sixteenth century. Craftsmen and artisans found new applications, new workshops emerged, and numerous new instruments were invented and constructed. The instrument-maker com-

bined both the mechanic and the artist in one person. His work had to be precisely executed so that it would be functional, but a concern for aesthetics also played an important part: it characterized its producer and helped to determine the value of the product. The objects produced were artistic creations in their decorative modelling, engraving and selection of materials. Instruments were constantly being perfected. Sometimes this involved the complex combination of several individual parts. The producer was usually a skilled designer, but also a mathematician so that he could accurately calculate the parameters of the instrument. Often, two people were involved – the scientist as creator and the mechanic as producer. There were changes in technology and in the materials used. The original wooden, coarse, imprecise aids gave way to metal instruments, primarily of brass and copper, with a fire-gilt or silver-plated surface finish. The selection of materials influenced an instrument's longevity, durability and accuracy of measurement. Among the non-metals used were ivory tusks and high-grade timber. At the same time there were developed inexpensive, less accurate instruments of wood that were ornamented with paper impresses and were intended for a wider usage, in particular as sundials and quadrants.

By the end of the sixteenth century Prague had become the centre for the production of instruments, taking over the traditions of Germany (Nürnberg, Augsburg, Munich) and the Low Countries (Antwerp, Louvain). The best scientists were active in Prague, as were the best mechanics, clockmakers, goldsmiths and engravers. Erasmus Habermel, Jost Bürgi and Heinrich Stolle worked at Rudolf's court over a fairly long time. Other masters were active in Prague only for shorter periods or worked at the specific behest of the Emperor. The most prominent imperial supplier was the Augsburg mechanic Christoph Schissler I. Additional specialists who satisfied the Emperor's craving for collecting were Gerhard Emmoser, Hans Christoph Schissler II and Wenzel Jamnitzer. It is possible to classify the masters according to their activity as goldsmiths and copper engravers, the most prominent of whom was Habermel, and as mechanics and clockmakers, among whom Bürgi was the dominant figure. Their output was used in various ways. Some items were produced for Rudolf II, whose vast collection contained astronomical and mathematical instruments, clocks, globes and armillary spheres. Other objects were produced for the courts of the aristocracy or for scientists, astronomers and surveyors.

Erasmus Habermel was among the most accomplished masters of the sixteenth century. According to written accounts, he worked as a 'producer of astronomical and geometrical instruments' at the court of Rudolf and for the Rožmberks, Vilém and Petr Vok. A set of about twenty surviving instruments bears the inscription '*Francisci de Padoanis Foroliviensis M.D.*' and specify this Italian physician as their owner. Habermel's activities were extremely wide-ranging. He produced primarily sundials in a variety of types, as well as instruments for surveying and for astronomical and mathematical calculations. Outstanding are his theodolitic, trigonometric and levelling instruments. His astrolabes, torques and demonstrational instruments are exceptional in the field of astronomy. More than a hundred of Habermel's works have been preserved to this day, but it is estimated that he may have manufactured as many as three hundred. In addition to those already mentioned, a sextant that has survived is clearly among the greatest of Habermel's works. It originated during the period of Brahe's and Kepler's activities and under the direct influence of their research in astronomy. Among

Habermel's preserved instruments is the 'transom of telescopes', which testifies to the existence of an optical instrument at the onset of the optical era (Habermel died in 1606).

Another of Kepler's close collaborators was the clockmaker and mathematician Jost Bürgi (1552–1632). He moved from Kassel in 1604 to Prague, where he stayed almost until his death. He had already worked for Rudolf II while at the court in Hesse of Wilhelm IV and his successor Moritz. Bürgi constructed remarkable instruments – Tycho Brahe called him a 'second Archimedes'. The majority were original inventions that served as aids to demonstrate the motion of the planets according to Brahe and Copernicus, or they involved globes driven by clockwork, geometrical instruments and timepieces. Bürgi's mathematical research was also extremely important. For Kepler he devised aid charts and computation methods, e.g. for the sine function, and he introduced the use of decimals. His greatest achievement in mathematics was to compile the tables that were later termed 'logarithmic'. He compiled these tables around 1610, but since he hesitated over their publication for some ten years Napier (or Neper) was published first in 1614. Bürgi took part in astronomical observations in Kassel and in Prague, where he collaborated with Kepler, who used a high-quality sextant designed by Bürgi during his tenure in Prague. His observation timepiece with cross-movement, which until the introduction of the pendulum was the most precise method, served to determine the position of the stars with accuracy. To the advancement of geometry he contributed several innovative products. A trigonometrical instrument was based on the similarity of triangles, while an instrument for perspective drawings emanated from the princi-

ple of the theodolite and was useful in cartography. He also constructed a conversion compass with a sliding head which bears his name. Bürgi's partner in 1607 was the clockmaker Heinrich Stolle, whose activity appears to have been limited to Prague. All of his known work is signed, but never dated. He produced Bürgi's trigonometrical instrument, as well as semicircular instruments, compasses and direction-finding aids for artillery. Outstanding among these objects is the theodolite, which it was possible to use as a sundial. On this multi-purpose apparatus there are graphs and scales of mathematical functions.

At the beginning of the seventeenth century the telescope expanded human knowledge in a revolutionary manner. The Prague milieu, as the paramount location of science in Europe, did not stay aloof from employing and perfecting the new apparatus. The telescope was invented around 1600. Galileo Galilei is considered to have been the first person to use it for astronomic observation in 1609. Kepler responded to his notes entitled *Nuncius sidereus* (Herald of the Stars) with three publications, the largest of which is *Dioptrice*, where he describes a new type of telescope that later was given his name and has continued in use to the present day. Kepler himself had already used a telescope for observation in 1610. His telescopes have not survived, but two well-known instruments originated in Prague during this period. One is the aforementioned 'transom of telescopes' of Habermel, which was constructed at least three years prior to Galileo's instrument. The second is a small telescope that Stolle constructed around 1612 along the lines of Galileo's; given the royal crown on the casing, it was clearly intended for Rudolf II.

IV.67
Willem Janszoon Blaeu
Alkmaar 1571–Amsterdam 1638
Celestial Globe
Wood, paper, brass
50 × 48 × 48 cm
In the cartouche of the globe: *1603*
1603
Amsterdam
Prague, Národní Technické Muzeum, inv. no. 25 482

The printed astral globe itself measures about 33.7 cm in diameter. The colours that once enhanced its figurative and decorative elements have now faded. Stars are

differentiated on a scale of brightness from one to six. The depiction of the northern hemisphere is based on the observations of Tycho Brahe, the southern hemisphere on those of Frederic Houtman. The position of the nova from 1600 is shown on the globe. A portrait of Tycho Brahe with his motto *Non haberi Sed esse* appears next to the cartouche in the representation of the northern hemisphere. The base is composed of a horizontal circle, four legs and a plinth. Attached to it is a paper guide on which are marked degrees of direction and wind and a scale decorated with the Gregorian, lunar, Julian and ecliptic calendars. The globemak-

er was the celebrated cartographer, engraver and printer Willem Janszoon Blaeu. He was a student of Tycho Brahe, and portrayed him on the globe out of gratitude. He founded a cartographical company in Amsterdam, which printed maps, atlases and globes.

Horsky–Skopova 1968; Muris–Saarman 1961.

A.Š.

IV.68
Jost Bürgi
Lichtensteig 1552–Kassel 1632
Globe-shaped Clock
Brass, silver, iron
H: 44 cm; diam. of globe: 23 cm
Ca. 1585
Prague
In Dresden *Kunstkammer* from 1660
Dresden, Mathematisch-Physikalischer Salon, inv. no. E II 30

The instrument is composed of a four-legged shaped base and a globe. The sphere is formed by two brass hemispheres that are connected by a bayonet

socket along an ecliptic. On the surface of the sphere there are stars engraved from the first to sixth magnitude and with an explanation. The names are affixed to individual constellations. Highlighted on the globe is an ecliptical and equatorial grid. The ecliptical is divided into the twelve signs of the zodiac, 12 × 30 degrees; the equatorial is graduated by 360 degrees. The horizontal ring is composed of two sections: an outer movable calendar ring and, inside, a fixed reading ring with gradations by azimuth. The calendar ring is divided into 365 days, further demarcated into months, holy days, days of the week and important Christian festivals. The

clock engine that drives it is solidly built into the interior of the globe and comprises an operating and striking mechanism that strikes on the hour.

Uhren–Globen 1993.

A.Š.

IV.69
Jost Bürgi
Lichtensteig 1552–Kassel 1632
Sextant
Instrument: iron, brass, engraved scale;
stand: iron, wood
251 × 114 × 66 cm
Ca. 1600
Prague, State Observatory at the Clemen-
tine Library
Prague, Národní Technické Muzeum, inv.
no. 17 195

This sextant is fundamental to the history
of astronomical knowledge, being both
solidly constructed and capable of giving

accurate readings. It is a precise measuring
instrument without any decoration. The
body of the sextant is formed by the limb
(an arc in the circumference) and by the
terminal borders of a sixth of the circle.
Two vertical braces have been attached to
the internal section of the arc to strength-
en it. A ruler, known as the alidade, which
serves to determine directions, moves
along the limb. A complete dioptric system
serves to fix the line of sight; the objective
dioptre only has been preserved on the alidade. Aids such as the transversals, circle
and scale on the alidade permit readings
accurate to one minute of a degree. This
instrument, evidently manufactured in

Prague in 1600, is probably the one that
Baron Hofmann had made to give to astronomer Johann Kepler. Kepler would
have worked with this sextant between
1602 and 1604 and in 1628. This sextant
and the one made by Habermel are among
the most valuable astrometrical instruments to have been preserved from the
turn of the seventeenth century.

Essen and Vienna 1988, cat. no. 433;
Bochum 1992; Landskrona 1996.

Horsky–Skopova 1968;

A.Š.

IV.70
Erasmus Habermel
Died Prague 1606
Astronomical Compendium
Copper gilding, silver, engraved
17 × 15.5 × 15.5 cm
Inventvm Jacobi Cvrtii á Senftenav and
Erasmus Habermel sculpsit
Before 1595
Prague
Acquired from Karl Ullmayer in Vienna,
1913
Vienna, Kunsthistorisches Museum, inv.
no. 7246

An instrument with a square base on four

feet. Below is a wind rose, around which is
the zodiac and the Gregorian calendar.
Above is an azimuthal projection of the
Earth's northern hemisphere centred on
the pole. It is possible to tilt over this a
cogged quadrant (the plumbline is missing) to designate the height of the pole.
The upper sliding panel bears a geographical map of the southern hemisphere underneath, prepared in the same manner as
the northern hemisphere, with a compass
and the symbol of Bavaria. On the upper
surface are two revolving discs for con-
verting the hours. The compendium has
multiple functions. It is possible to determine the times of sunrise and sunset, and

thus the length of the day and night, as
well as calculate the conversion of German, Czech and Babylonian hours. The inventor of this instrument is said to have
been Jakob Kurtz (Curtius) from Senfte-
nava, who was vice-chancellor at the Emperor's court and a lover of astronomy. He
died in 1594.

Essen and Vienna 1988, cat. no. 432.

Zinner 1967.

A.Š.

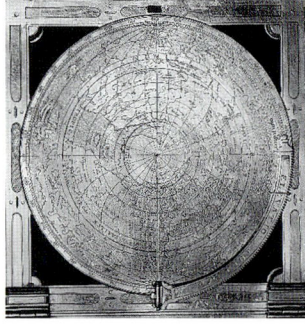

IV.71
Erasmus Habermel
Died Prague 1606
Nocturnal Clock and Sundial
Gilt copper, engraved
15.5 × 12.8 × 1.4 cm
On the back the motto: *Septa licet spinis
tamen Efflorescere quaerit*; and the dedica-
tion: *Clar:mo. Artiu et Med:ne Doc: D.Fran-
cisco de Padoais Erasmus Habermel animj
Grati: Ergo D. D.*
1585–86
From the Strozzi collection in Florence;
bought at the Muller auction in Amster-
dam 1911
Prague, Národní Technické Muzeum, inv.

no. 2 262

The layout of this instrument is unusual,
combining altitude sundials with nocturnal clocks. This instrument type may be
designated the invention of Habermel
since he alone was making it. The circular
plate in the instrument is about 12.8 cm in
diameter. On the face of it is an nocturnal
clock, which contains hour markings and
the degrees of angles around the circumference. Inside is a turning circular plate
with the Gregorian calendar and two tables for determining the astrological
rulers of the hours and days of the week.
The internal disc is connected to the sus-

pension of the clock. A movable index extending beyond the edge of the large disc
is used for telling the time. An elevated
sundial appears on the back of the instrument. The disc is divided like rays of the
sun into the twelve signs of the zodiac.
The hand of the sundial is tilted and is
connected to the suspension.

Essen and Vienna 1988, cat. no. 414.

Horsky–Skopova 1968.

A.Š.

IV.72
Erasmus Habermel
Died Prague 1606
Horizontal Sundial
Gilt brass, engraved; iron
1.5 × 10.2 × 9.4 cm
Ca. 1600
From the collection of R. Pfefferkorn
Prague, Národní Technické Muzeum, inv.
no. 24 891

The sundial is made from a solid, almost
square plate, which stands on four circular
iron legs. A circular socket for a compass
has been hewn out from the plate. A wind
rose is formed by a cross of the four main

directions, marked *SE, OR, ME, OC* and an
arrow marking the magnetic deviation to
the west. The wind rose is engraved much
more crudely than the dial. The lettering
has been stamped. The dial around the
compass has quarter-hour markings in
the range V–XII–VII. The number *48* suggests that the hours were probably related
to the 48th parallel of latitutde. The
gnomon has not been preserved, but there
may have been a fixing point for it near
the figure XII. The upper side with a dial
and a plate are decorated with typical
Habermel engravings, but there is no
maker's signature.

Horsky–Skopova 1968.

A.Š.

IV.73
Erasmus Habermel
Died Prague 1606
Equatorial Sundial
Gilt copper, engraved
5 × 19.4 × 10.5 cm
On the underside of the frame: *E. Haber-
mel fecit*
1585–86
From the Strozzi collection in Florence;
sold at the Muller auction in Amsterdam
1911
Prague, Národní Technické Muzeum, inv.
no. 2 260

The base plate consists of a rectangular

frame and is supported on four low legs.
In the centre stands the circular socket for
a compass with hour markings. The movable socket of the compass, inscribed *HO-
RAE AB ORTU OCCASU SOLIS*, allows for
Czech and Babylon clocks to be modified
into German ones. The compass, measuring about 5.2 cm across, are fixed into the
centre; they retain the original magnetic
needle. On the shorter sides of the frame
are two compatible scales marked *ALTI-
TUDO POLI* for determining geographical latitude. A frame of the same dimensions as the base, marked with the dial for
equatorial hours, is hinged to the base. A
semicircular dial with alidade indicates

the time to an accuracy of within five minutes. Only one dioptre is on the alidade,
the other is missing. On the edges of the
frame are the scales *Vmbra Uersa* and *Vmbra Recta*. The lower side of the tilted
frame contains two small supports for positioning the elevation of the poles. The
instrument was made for Francisco Paduanio of Forli.

Essen and Vienna 1988, cat. no. 415;
Bochum 1992.

Horsky–Skopova 1968.

A.Š.

IV.74
Erasmus Habermel
Died Prague 1606
Equatorial Ring-dial with Stand
Gilt brass, engraved
26.3 × 38.5 × 26.3 cm
On the circle of the meridian: *Erasmus Habermel fec:*
Ca. 1600
From the collection of R. Pfefferkorn
Prague, Uměleckoprůmyslové Muzeum, inv. no. 30 457

The size, the formation of the base, the richly decorative engravings and the precision of workmanship make this highly functional cabinet piece extremely rare and valuable. It is one of the finest from Habermel's Prague workshop to have survived. The base is formed by four legs with scrolled braces and sculpted acanthuses, with fixing screws and compasses for the calibration of measuring planes. The degree of magnetic destination is marked and the base also carries a sundial. A meridian circle about 26 cm in diameter, marked with the signs of the zodiac and the Gregorian calendar and inscribed *MERIDIANVS*, is attached to the vertical column of the base. In its upper quadrant is a protractor with markings and the inscription *Elevatio eqvinoctialis Poli*. In the lower part is the maker's signature. A horizontal circle of the same proportions and with appropriate scale markings is attached to this circle. Inside the fixed meridian circle is a movable circle, which allows lines of latitude to be determined.

Essen and Vienna 1988, cat. no. 425.

Lenfeld 1984.

A.Š.

IV.75
Probably Erasmus Habermel or associates
Planetolabium to Demonstrate the Course of the Planet Jupiter
Brass, gilded; some gilding worn away
Outer ring system: 21.8 cm; second ring system: 20 cm; third ring system: 18.8 cm; fourth (broad, eccentric) ring system 17.2 cm; inner ring system: 9.8 cm; outer measurements of the discs of the epicycle system on the fourth ring: 2.7 cm; height of (not original) stand: 17.8 cm; height of whole instrument including guard ring: 44.9 cm
Ty. de Brahe 1599
1599

Auctioned in 1852 by the Prague Observatory (Clementinum); purchased by Ritter Gabriel von Max; purchased in 1909 by the Deutsches Museum, Munich
Munich, Deutsches Museum, inv. no. 19641

The date 1599 and the inscription *Ty. de Brahe* point towards Prague and the court of Rudolf II, and suggest that this instrument was made by E. Habermel or his circle. This is confirmed by similarities between the style of engraving on this and other items known to be by Habermel. This measuring instrument, consisting of five spheres made of brass rings, demonstrates the course of the planet Jupiter around the Earth according to the Ptolemaic system.

Permanent display of the Deutsches Museum, Munich.

Fuchs 1905–1925, *Deutsches Museum ... 1955*, pp. 17–20; Horsky–Skopova 1968, pp. 138f.

Hr.

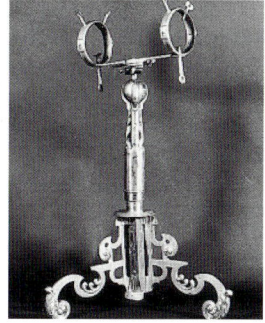

IV.76
Erasmus Habermel ?
Telescope beam
Gilded brass
30 × 30 cm
Observatoire de Paris, inv. no. I.A.15.20

A.Š.

IV.77
Erasmus Habermel
Died Prague 1606
Sextant
Instrument: iron, gilt brass; stand: engraved iron
244 × 134 × 88 cm
On the engraving at the ocular end of the instrument: *Pragae fecit Erasm9 habermel 1600*
1600
Prague, State Observatory at the Clementine Library
Prague, Národní Technické Muzeum, inv. no. 24 551

In the sixteenth and seventeenth centuries sextants were used to determine the position of the planets in the sky. Measurements of angles from known constellations could be taken at any favourable level and used to calculate the coordinates of a planet. The sector proper is formed by the girth of the limb and two arms from which three supports rise into the centre. A movable measure for taking sights is attached to the top of the angle, to the limb and to a guiding arc-shaped belt. Scales on the limb and the alidade enable angles to be read to an accuracy of one minute. This sextant is the largest of Habermel's instruments to have survived: most were removed from Prague during the Thirty Years' War. The sextant remained because of its size. The instrument was probably inspired by the work of Tycho Brahe or one of his colleagues. The sextant is positioned on an iron tripod, which enables the instrument to be set up inside a cabin. The tripod originates from the mid-eighteenth century and is in a Baroque style.

Essen and Vienna 1988, cat. no. 413; Bochum 1992.

Horsky Skopova 1968.

A.Š.

IV.78
Probably from the workshop of Erasmus Habermel
Died Prague 1606
Torquetum
Brass, fire-gilded
Base: 20.8 × 20.5 cm; h: 32 cm
Ca. 1585
From the collection of the Bayerische Akademie der Wissenschaften
Munich, Deutsches Museum, inv. no. 1687

This torquetum bears a striking resemblance to that owned by the Museum für Kunst und Gewerbe in Hamburg. The latter is signed with the initials *EH*. The torquetum is a versatile measuring instrument. The derivation of the name of this instrument, probably invented during the early Renaissance, is not entirely certain. It is often translated as 'Turkish instrument', but the term is more likely to be linked to the word *torque,* which would make this a 'turning instrument.' By means of the compass, the instrument can be trained towards the north. The various plates (equatorial and ecliptic) and the circular diagrams with alidades represent the coordinate systems of the Earth and the heavens. The plates can be turned to set the width of the area to be observed.

Röde 1923, p. 79; Eckhart 1977, pp. 13ff.; Zinner 1979, pp. 177ff., 329f., 338.

Hr.

IV.79
Erasmus Habermel
died Prague 1606
Theodolite
gilded copper
30 × 30 cm
Observatoire de Paris, inv. no. I.A.16.24

A.Š.

IV.80
? Erasmus Habermel
Died Prague 1606
Clinometer
Gilt copper
10.5 × 20.8 × 0.7 cm
On the face: *HALBE LENG STRASBVRG-ER. V. STAT WERCK SCHUH; V: HALBE LENG NVRENBERGER WERCK SCHUH; VMBRA VERSA VMBRA RECTA;* on the back: *LENGE DER STAT AVGSPVRG V WERCK SCHVCH. V. VND ZOL; VMBRA RECTA; VMBRA VERSA*
Probably 1585–86
From the Strozzi collection in Florence; sold at the Muller auction in Amsterdam
1911
Prague, Národní Technické Muzeum, inv. no. 2 263

This is a multi-purpose instrument, which is used (like a spirit level) to determine horizontal positions, to measure the incline of a plane and to measure angles as well as the parts of a shadow quadrant for *Vmbra Versa* and *Vmbra Recta* (of the goniometric functions of tangent and subtangent). A hinge shaped like a pendulum acts as the indicating hand. One side of a right-angled triangle is used for measuring distances. The Strasbourg and Nürnberg half-foot measures are used, divided into six

inches. Individual inches are divided into parts, the first into halves and the second into thirds. Identical angular scales and a complete Augsburg foot, which comprises twelve inches, appear on the reverse. Each inch is further divided: the first is into one part, the second into two, and so on. The instrument is pleasingly shaped and decorated with engravings of plant motifs. It is unsigned but belongs to the collection of Habermel's instruments made for Francisco Paduanio of Forli.

Essen and Vienna 1988, cat. no. 416.

A.Š.

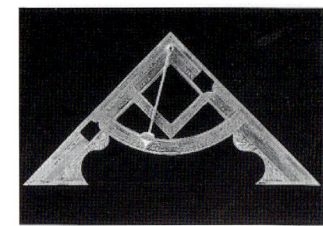

IV.81
Erasmus Habermel
Died Prague 1606
Case with Compass
Gilt brass, engraved
15.5 × 5.7 × 11.5 cm
End of the sixteenth century
Sold at the K. Therwall auction in Cologne
Prague, Uměleckoprůmyslové Muzeum, inv. no. 8 691

This box contains instrumentation and data relevant to both chronology and geography. On the upper side of the lid is a set of oval-shaped compasses with an

eight-scale wind rose and initials in German (*N, S, O, W*) of the main directions (east and west are reversed). The magnetic needle and the glass are missing. On the lower side of the lid is a Gregorian calendar, the markings of the zodiac, the four seasons of the year designated in Latin. The names of outstanding saints or church feast days are written against each month on the scale. The lower part of the case contains a nomogram, inscribed *OCCASVS SOLIS,* for determining the time of sunset in various places in the northern hemisphere during the year. The nomogram consists of a geometric projection of the northern hemisphere and a dial with

the signs of the zodiac. A movable finger screwed to the centre of the semicircle sets the position of the sun in the zodiac, and relevant data can be read off from the geographical grid. The box stands on four rounded legs. Its upper side is richly ornate, with illustrations of flowers. It is without doubt an unsigned work by Habermel.

Essen and Vienna 1988, cat. no. 427.

Lenfeld 1984.

A.Š.

IV.82
Erasmus Habermel
Died Prague 1606
Compasses with Quadrant
Gilt copper, engraved
23.8 × 17.7 × 12.0 cm
Probably 1585–86
From the Strozzi collection in Florence; sold at the Muller auction in Amsterdam
1911
Prague, Národní Technické Muzeum, inv. no. 2 269

The compass is of a very unusual shape. The shorter arm is bent into proximity with the connecting joint and has a special

prong at its tip for the attachment of a drawing instrument. The longer arm is equipped with a small plate and a screw. A quadrant is screwed on to the shorter arm and fits between the groove of the second arm and the plate. The quadrant is divided into individual degrees, which are numbered in tens from ten to ninety. The compass could have been used for measuring gradients, perhaps within the context of a sundial. The entire instrument is decorated with Habermel's engravings but it is unsigned.

Essen and Vienna 1988, cat. no. 419.

A.Š.

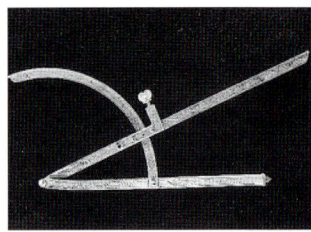

IV.83
Erasmus Habermel
Died Prague 1606
Reduction Compasses
Gilt copper, engraved, steel
15.4 × 1.7 × 1.0 cm
Owner's name engraved: *FRAN ci: D PADOA is: FOROLI is: M.D.* and the number 3
Probably 1585–86
From the Strozzi collection in Florence; sold at the Muller auction in Amsterdam
1911
Prague, Národní Technické Muzeum, inv. no. 2 266

This pair of reduction compasses is made from gilt copper; with points made of iron and engravings in keeping with the ornamental aspect of its purpose. Such engraved ornaments comport entirely with the methods used by Erasmus Habermel. The number '3' appears on the arm with ornamentations. This indicates the ratio of length to the points of the frame – 1:3. The compasses were made for Francisco Paduanio of Forli, whose name is inscribed on the second arm. These conversion compasses are comparable in shape, ornamentation, size and function with the compasses at inv. no. 2 267. Only the proportions differ.

Essen and Vienna 1988, cat. no. 417.

A.Š.

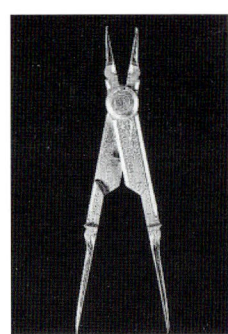

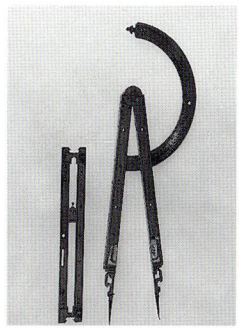

IV.84
Erasmus Habermel
Died Prague 1606
Compasses with Semicircle
Gilt brass, engraved, iron-tipped
23.2 × 12.0 × 9.5 cm
Pragae fecit E habermel
Ca. 1600
Acquired from Popper
Prague, Uměleckoprůmyslové Muzeum,
inv. no. 2 064

The instrument may be used in two ways:
as compasses and as a multi-purpose protractor for artillery. It is very similar to the
instrument in Vienna (Kunsthistorisches

Museum, inv. no. 8 869). One side of the
compass with the inscription *AD LINEAS*
was equipped with a stand, which is now
missing. This side is set in the horizontal
plane and attached to it is a semicircular
arch, which is divided into 180 degrees
and has three scales for cannon balls of
stone (Lapis), iron (Ferrum) and lead
(Plumbum). The maker's signature also
appears on the arch. The movable side
bears the inscription *CIRCVLA*. On the
other side are two inscriptions: *RECTAS*
on the fixed part and *AD LINEAS* on the
movable part. Both sides have irregular
scale markings displaying the ranges of 7
to 16 and 2 to 12 respectively, as well as

purpose-made sighting notches.

Essen and Vienna 1988, cat. no. 426.

Lenfeld 1984.

A.Š.

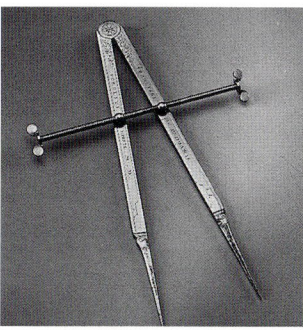

IV.85
Erasmus Habermel
Died Prague 1606
Compasses with Fixed Screw
Gilt copper, engraved; steel
25.2 × 16.2 × 1.5 cm
The name of the owner appears on the
front of both arms: *FRANCISCI DE
PADOANIS FOROLIVIENSIS. M.D.*; and
the initials of the manufacturer are *E.H.*
Probably 1585–86
From the Strozzi collection in Florence;
sold at the Muller Auction in Amsterdam
1911
Prague, Národní Technické Muzeum, inv.
no. 2 270

These calliper compasses end in a screw
with an anticlockwise thread, which allows them to be opened. They are made of
heat-gilded copper, with points of steel,
and decorated with a subtle design by
Habermel. They formed part of the collection of Francisco Paduanio of Forli, whose
name is engraved, along with the initials
of the maker, *E. H.*, on the front part of the
arms.

Essen and Vienna 1988, cat. no. 420.

A.Š.

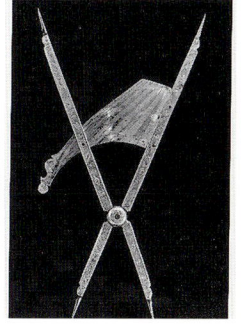

IV.86
? Erasmus Habermel
Died Prague 1606
Reduction Compasses with Nomogram
Copper, heat-gilded, engraved; steel
33.5 × 10.0 × 1.3 cm
1585–86
From the Strozzi collection in Florence;
sold at the Muller auction in Amsterdam
1911
Prague, Národní Technické Muzeum, inv.
no. 2 265

The compasses are contructed as a reduction type with a ratio of 1:2. The arms of
the rectangular cross-section have been

finished with steel prongs. One of the
arms is connected to the surface by a
small, irregular-shaped plate which comes
through a groove in the other arm. The
nomogram is divided into twelve fields,
nine of which are on the other side and are
listed along the frame. The scales on both
sides are cut into six little circles. The
meaning of the nomogram is still unclear.
The compass is richly ornamented with
engravings.

Essen and Vienna 1988, cat. no. 422.

A.Š.

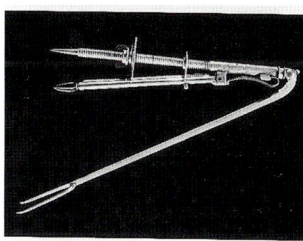

IV.87
Erasmus Habermel
Died Prague 1606
Three-armed Compasses
Gilt copper, engraved; steel
19.5 × 16.3 × 3.0 cm
1585–86
From the Strozzi collection in Florence;
sold at the Muller auction in Amsterdam
1911
Prague, Národní Technické Muzeum, inv.
no. 2 268

The compasses consist, unusually, of
three arms, which could serve to draw a
spiral shape, as well as models and orna-

ments. The central (main) arm contains a
point for fixing the compasses. This arm
has a coil across which move two small
plates for controlling and altering the radius of the drawing arm. This arm is attached to the main one and is equipped
with a pen which presses down. The drawing arm has a movable point, which can be
dipped into ink. The top of the principal
arm contains a joint to which is attached
the third supporting arm and which ends
in a two-pronged fork.

Essen and Vienna 1988, cat. no. 421.

A.Š.

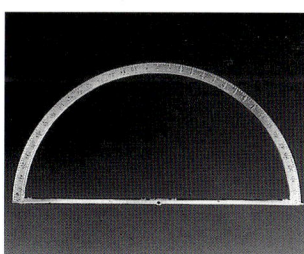

IV.88
? Erasmus Habermel
Died Prague 1606
Protractor
Gilt copper, engraved
8.7 × 17.4 × 0.2 cm
1585–86
From the Strozzi collection in Florence;
sold at the Muller auction in Amsterdam
1911
Prague, Národní Technické Muzeum, inv.
no. 2 264

This semicircular protractor with a radius
of 8.6 cm is divided into two sections each
of ninety degrees. Nought is at the centre

of the semicircle; the degrees are numbered in fives. In the middle of the base is
a small opening for hanging a plumb-line
or for extending the tip of the angle. The
instrument is very simple, and possibly
only part of another instrument. Decorations appear on the back and at the base of
the instrument.

Essen and Vienna 1988, cat. no. 423.

A.Š.

IV.89
Erasmus Habermel
Died Prague 1606
Universal Land-Surveying Instrument
Brass, gilded
79.3 × 1.8 × 5 cm
Erasmus Habermel, bei der Bussole Jakobus Curtius / A. Senfftenau
Ca. 1600
Probably Prague
Königliche Ludwig-Maximilians-Universität Munich, donated to the Deutsches Museum, Munich, in 1905
Munich, Deutsches Museum, inv. no. 2578

A versatile surveying instrument which not only measured angles and distances but also calculated the amount of powder needed to propel lead or iron shot of any particular calibre to the target. In addition, measurements could be made in different units *Schuh* and *Zoll* for Rome, Prague, Nürnberg and Vienna.

Exhibited until 1967 in the Deutsches Museum, Munich.

Eckardt 21 (1976); 22 (1977); Zimmer 1979.

Seeberger

IV.90
Johannes Klein
1684 Kamenický Šenov–1762 Prague
Astronomical Clock Using Tycho Brahe's System
Iron, brass, wood, gold, silver, enamel
120 × 75.5 × 39.5 cm
1751
Matematické muzeum in the Clementinum, Prague
Prague, Národní knihovna, inv. no. P/804

The clock presents the solar system and planetary motion according to Tycho Brahe. On the front is a large dial, with hours and minutes, and the hands. The details appear in slots: a gold number, a solar ring, the phases of the moon, the full moon preceding Easter, and Roman numerals. In the lower slot are shown fixed festivals, the month, the sign of the zodiac, the length of day and night, sunrise and sunset. In the upper section of the dial is a calendar of years from 1700 to 3200 – the clock was designed for this epoch. In addition we find Sunday readings and New Year's day. On the back there is a depiction of the motion of the planets according to Tycho Brahe. Revolving around a small disc of the earth with coloured pictures of Europe, Asia, Africa and America are the moon, sun, stars and the rings of the zodiac with a cal-

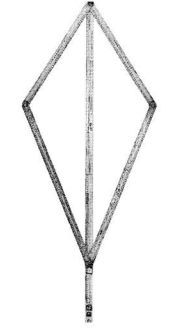

endar. An illustration of the stars is set around the sun, around which revolve hands with the planets Mercury, Venus, Mars, Jupiter and Saturn. Around them are the rings of the zodiac. The clock is housed in an opulently carved wooden Baroque cabinet, the surface of which is finished with a black burnish and gilding. The clock's maker, Father Johannes Klein, belonged to a Jesuitical order; he studied astronomy and mathematics and was an outstanding mechanic and designer.

Böhm 1908; Slouka.

A.Š.

IV.91
Heinrich Stolle
Telescope
Brass
1.3 × 10.5 × 1.3 cm
Henr. Stolle Vbrm. prag fec.
Ca. 1612
Prague
Acquired from A. W. Franks, 1890
London, British Museum, inv. no. 90 2-9 2

A small telescope of the Galileo type with two protective coverings. The diameter of the telescope is 13 mm, the length is 63 mm, closed, and 105 mm, extended. The diameter of the objective lens is 12 mm, the eyepiece is 4.5 mm, and there is a two-fold enlargement in sharpening the image. The telescope is housed in a metal casing 82 mm in length with a cap. Mounted on the cap is a silver coronet, clearly the sign of ownership by Emperor Rudof II. On the bottom of the casing is engraved the signature of the instrument's maker: 'Henr. Stolle Vbrm. prag fec'. The telescope and casing are contained in a red leather étui lined with parchment – diameter 25 mm, length 87 mm.

Ward 1981; Zinner 1967.

A.Š.

IV.92
Heinrich Stolle
Theodolite
Gilt brass, engraved
12.5 × 24.0 × 17.5 cm
Engraved below the index, visible only if the instrument is dismantled: *Henr. Stolle Vbrm. prag.fec.et.Inuet*
1600–13
Prague
From the collection of R. Pfefferkorn
Prague, Národní Technické Muzeum, inv. no. 24 868

This instrument is a theodolite of classic design for measuring horizontal and verti-cal angles. But it is also an extraordinary general-purpose device which can be used for telling the time and performing many kinds of calculations. The theodolite has a measuring arm, known as an alidade, which is fixed in the middle column and allows for measurement of height and direction. The alidade is equipped with two pairs of dioptres, a suspended semicircle and a plumbline for calculating angles. The suspended semicircle is divided into half degrees. In the lower part of the column is an auxiliary pipe-shaped direction-finder. The column is connected to a little hand, which enables horizontal angles to be read off from the circumference of the

horizontal circle. The facilities for taking measurements, including circles and tranversal lines, enable angles to be determined to within ten degrees. Heinrich Stolle was a mechanic and clock-maker who worked in Prague and was a contemporary of Jost Burgi.

Essen and Vienna 1988, cat. no. 424.

Horsky-Skopova 1968.

A.Š.

IV.93
Heinrich Stolle
Measuring Instrument for a Cannon
Gilt brass
10.5 × 13.2 × 2.0 cm
On the face: *Prager Zoll*; on the back: *Henr. Stolle Vbrm. prag*
1600–13
Prague, Národní Technické Muzeum, inv. no. 24 902

On the base with a plate positioned lengthwise is a groove with scale markings. A slide-valve, which can move in this groove thanks to a screw with a light thread, has a vertical part for measuring. The horizontal scale is divided into two sections each of thirty-two parts and is numbered on both sides 0-8-16-24-32. The vertical frame has a scale on both sides of the groove, which measures three Prague inches, the so-called *Prager Zoll*. The left-hand scale is evenly divided, each inch having twelve markings. The right scale is irregularly marked into twelve, fourteen and eighteen parts. The slide-rule moves in the groove with an irregular scale-marking in nine sections, the first of which is divided into thirty-two parts. The slide-rule has two eye-hole visors and bears the inscription *blei*. A sextant is attached to the vertical part, which is divid-

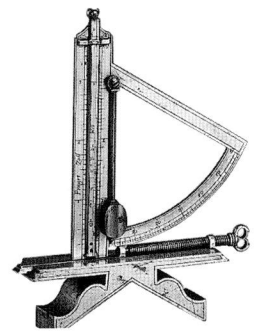

ed into degrees and has a hinge of the same shape as in the theodolite at inv. no. NTM 24 868. The instrument was used for fixing the parameters of artillery fire, mainly the angle of tilt and the range. The engraved markings and the ornamental shapes of some parts of the instrument are the only decorative features. Heinrich Stolle was an assistant to Burgi, later becoming an independent Prague clock-maker.

Zinner 1967.

A.Š.

IV.94
Armillary Sphere
Gilt brass, engraved
34 × 21 × 21 cm
1560–80
From the collection of R. Pfefferkorn
Prague, Národní Technické Muzeum, inv.
no. 24 860

The armillary sphere is set in an articulated base, consisting of three feet in the form of lion's paws. On this stands a circular plate holding the compass, which has a diameter of 60 mm. On the circular plane around the compass is a dial with markings for directions, winds and angles. An-

other part of the base is formed by two times four quarter circles of a brace, which is linked to the central support. On the horizontal circle of the base is a dial for reading off calendrical, ecliptic and directional information. An actual armillary sphere with a geocentric model of the universe is positioned in the base. It consists of astral, sun and moon systems. The celestial system is formed by two colures, the equator, the tropics, the polar circles and the ecliptic belt. Attached to the colures are points that depict the positions of eight stars. The sun sphere is formed by three rings with a picture of the sun. The third system is lunar and is formed by

three rings with a depiction of the moon. In the centre of the armillary sphere sits a globe averaging 38mm. Its cartographical representation comports with other maps and globes made in the second half of the sixteenth century. The precisely accomplished work and the manner of its engraving and the shapes of the lettering are reminiscent of the work of Erasmus Habermel.

Bochum 1992.

Horsky–Skopova 1968.

A.Š.

IV.95
Armillary Sphere
Brass, engraved
23.7 × 18.2 × 18.2 cm
Ca. 1600
From the collection of the Zamberk chateau
Prague, Národní Technické Muzeum, inv.
no. 15 081

The instrument comprises a base and its own armillary spheres. The base is formed by a ring supported by four legs and itself bearing a four-part strut to which is attached an octagonal horizontal plate. This measures internally about 14.6 cm and is

divided into sections of one degree each. The base is richly shaped and decorated with early Baroque engravings. Engravings of the eight allegorical heads of the winds are depicted on the horizontal circle. The outside part of the armillary sphere represents the celestial sphere, which is composed of colures, an equator, the tropics, polar circles and an ecliptic belt. All the circles are divided into degrees. In the ecliptic section they are marked with both representations and descriptions of the constellations. The eclipse axis is inside the celestial sphere, around which rotate two rings with symbols of the sun and the moon. A globe representing the Earth is in the centre of the armillary sphere.

Horsky–Skopova 1968.

A.Š.

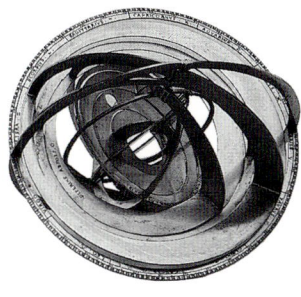

IV.96
Planetarium
Brass, engraved
21.5 × 21.5 × 21.5 cm
Sixteenth century
Prague, State Observatory at the Clementine Library
Prague, Národní Technické Muzeum, inv.
no. 17 148

The planetarium is constructed, unusually, of armillary spheres, here of equal strength and separated by quite a lot of free space. Flat discs fill up almost the entire surface at the same level. Gaps between the discs enable each disc to turn

freely with the one before it. Another equally large disc connects to each of the discs on the vertical plane, and is fastened on its axis by the preceding and succeeding disc. The planetarium is of the geocentric type and represents the orbit of the moon and the sun around the Earth. Three systems are depicted in the planetarium. The outer one is the sphere of fixed stars and is represented by a single centric circle, which is divided into panels depicting the twelve signs of the zodiac, identified by their Latin titles and their pictorial symbols. The central sphere of the sun comprises three discs, two of which are eccentric and one centric. A ring

with the axis inclined at twenty-three and a half degrees is located in this sphere, where the internal sphere of the Earth and the moon is represented on the third disc. The first two discs rotate around an ecliptic axis, while the system of the Earth and its moon rotates around the axis of the globe.

Horsky–Skopova 1968.

A.Š.

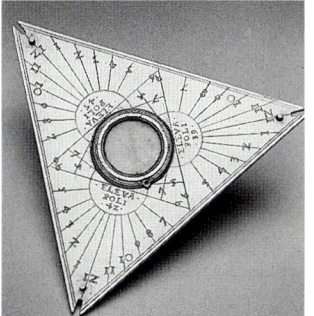

IV.97
Horizontal Sundial
Gilt brass, engraved
0.7 × 8.0 × 7.1 cm
On each dial is an inscription with the corresponding geographical width, for example: *ELEVA. POLI. 48*
Ca. 1600
From the Strozzi collection; sold at the Muller auction in Amsterdam 1911
Prague, Národní Technické Muzeum, inv.
no. 2 261

This is an unusual type of sundial. It is made from a plate in the form of an equilateral triangle, equipped with simple legs

for portability. The disc has dials of three horizontal clocks across both sides: on one side for the geographical measurements of 39, 42 and 45 degrees, and on the other for 48, 51 and 54 degrees. All the dials are the same for the whole clock with numbering shown as 5 – 12 – 7. In the centre of the disc is an unusual type of compass, by which it is possible to turn to each dial. The gnomon, which was set in slots at the corners of the triangle and at the opening to the casing of the compass, has not been preserved. The gnomon was probably adjustable to the appropriate geographical width, as in the Butterfield type of instrument. The instrument has no dec-

oration. It is usually considered to be the work of Erasmus Habermel or F. M. Mass.

Horsky–Skopova 1968.

A.Š.

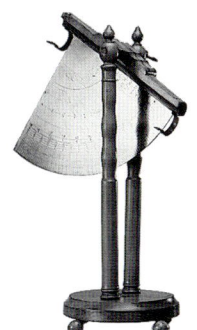

IV.98
Quadrant
Brass, engraved; wood
60.7 × 34.3 × 25 cm, radius 28.5 cm
End of the sixteenth century
From the inventory of the State Czechoslovak Secondary School in Litomysl
Prague, Národní Technické Muzeum, inv.
no. 11 809

The quadrant consists of two parts: a stand and a measuring device. The wooden stand is formed by a circular plate on four ball-shaped legs and two vertical columns; a brace with a horizontally re-

volving axis is attached. The instrument itself has two basic functions: to measure altitude and to tell the time, by means of a sundial. On the face in the middle of the quadrant is a square showing the degree markings of the goniometric functions of *Vmbra Versa* and *Vmbra Recta*. In the middle of the plane are the markings of a sundial (IV–XII) as well as a marking named *Hores Vulgares* for the latitude of 51°10'. A planetary clock is marked *Horae Planetarum* and has divisions from one to twelve. Along the borders is a scale of ecliptic lengths with markings and descriptions in German. A scale for measuring angles is around the circumference;

degrees are divided into ten minutes. Each individual degree is divided into double transversal lines and it is possible to count off minutes in twos in the fifteen circles. Two scales appear on the back of the instrument. One is for measuring angles from 0 in fives up to 45 degrees. The other is a clinometer divided into 100 parts. The instrument is incomplete in that it lacks additional viewing holes as well as a telescope and dioptres. It is undecorated.

Horsky–Skopova 1968.

A.Š.

IV.99
Compasses
Burgi type – engraved brass
steel 40.5 × 2.5 × 3.5
early seventeenth century
Provenance: from the collection of František Fiala
Prague, Národní technické muzeum, inv. no. 1211

Burgi type of reductive compasses with variable ratio of division. The positioning of the arms in the required ratio is fixed by a sliding head. The compasses function by means of a technical aid, which is decorated minimally. Only the finishing on the

arms with the tips and sliding head have been made decoratively. The compasses are of use in solving mathematical problems, both graphical and numerical: multiplication (division) of arcs and numbers, the construction of set-squares in the circle, the calculation of the surfaces of figures, the volumes of bodies, the diameter of a circle, etca.

Mackensen 1979.

AŠ

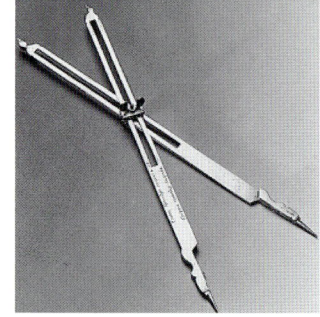

IV.100
Scales
Silver-plated brass, engraved, cornelian
49x 55 × 7 cm
1607
Ca. 1607
Bought by UPM at an auction of the collection of V. Lanna in Berlin 1909. Collection of the baronet V. Lanna, Prague; Uměleckoprýmyslové muzeum v Praze, 11 488

Berlin 1909, cat. no. 306; Essen and Vienna 1988, cat. no. 428; Prague 1996, cat. no. 545

D.K.

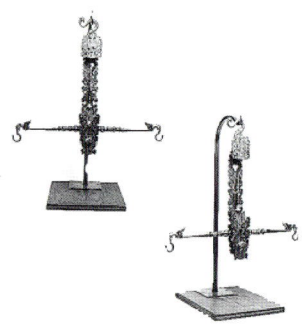

IV.101
Isaac Phendler
Plan of Rudolf's Tunnel (the 'Gallery)
Painting on parchment, gilded ornaments
248 × 20 cm
Isaac Phendler
1593 (dated according to data stated in the designs)
End of the nineteenth century discovered in Paris, where Dr Schebek purchased it for the collection of Vojtěch Lanna. The latter donated the design to Uměleckoprůmyslové muzeum, Prague, in 1911, whose director, František Borovský passed it on to the Technical

Museum on behalf of the Czech Republic.
Prague, Národní technické muzeum, inv. no. 1848

Hz.

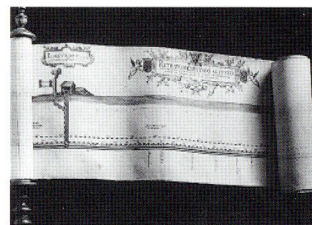

IV.102
Anonymous
Portrait of Tycho de Brahe
Copper alloy, black opaque enamel, gold foil
Oval 15 × 11.2 cm
On the front: *TYCHO BRAHE*; on the back: *Ne a Knutstrup pres Helsinborgen Dannemark 1 jullie/1546 mort a Prague le 24 octobre 1601*
After 1601
1894 sold C. Altmann, Frankfurt
Prague, Uměleckoprůmyslové muzeum Belvedere, Prague 1967, cat. no. 269, inv. no. 5.457

On the basis of a drawing in ruddle (graphics collection of the University of Copenhagen, cf. Zeeberg 1994, p.19), signed L.S. but ascribed to Jacob de Gheyn the Elder (Antwerp 1565-Den Haag 1629), de Gheyn made two signed variations of copper engravings. The composition of the second variant more closely resembles the medal at hand. This one differs from both engravings in that it is missing the structurally designed frame with caption and the sixteen coats-of-arms of the subject's ancestors. The portrait is of a ceremonial nature, unlike the Wandsbek coloured engravings from 1598 (Strahov Library, Prague). Enamellers from Limo

ges were using heat-gilded black enamel (cf. the beret and the eyes); a gleaming reverse side and caption in gold with a French text is typical of their work. Technical experimentation sits well with the court of Rudolf. One maker comes into consideration, for example, the francophone Jacobo de Gheyn, who made another oval portrait medal in black and gold in 1596 using the technique of verre eglomise (Nagler, 1837, V, p.130).

D.S.

IV.103
The burial garb of Tycho Brahe: Hat
Silk, cut-pile velvet, lining and band at bottom made of tabby-weave material
Bottom circumference 59 cm, height 17 cm, band 3.5 cm high
Before or in 1601
Velvet and lining probably Italy or Germany
Museum of the City of Prague, inv. no. 86562

Tycho Brahe died on 24 October 1601. On 4 November he was buried with great ceremony in the Týn Church in Prague's Old Town. In 1604 the coffin of Tycho's wife

was added to the grave. The stone tomb was built by their children. The tomb was opened on the 300th anniversary of the astronomer's death in 1901. While in the coffin of Tycho's wife nothing had been preserved but the skeleton and a few beads, Tycho was dressed. The crown of the hat, which is today dark brown in colour, was made up of four parts. The bottom band was decorated with a strip of material which was the same as the lining, but turned upwards. In 1901 a pin, which could have been used to attach a feather, was taken out of the tomb but is now missing. The shape of the hat is influenced by Hungarian fashion. A similar hat, but a lit-

tle taller, was put in the tomb of Maximilian II (1576, Prague Castle Administration).

M.Br.

IV.104
The burial garb of Tycho Brahe:
Fragment of Doublet
Silk, eight-thread, warp-faced satin
Length 62 cm, width of armholes 60 cm,
of cuffs 12 cm
Before or in 1601
Satin probably from Italy or Germany
Museum of the City of Prague, inv. no.
86563

Only the right sleeve of the doublet was
taken from the tomb. Today it is ochre
brown in colour. The cuff was edged with
a strip of satin. In 1901 mention was made
of the doublet, but it was probably con-

fused with the fragment of the cloak. Satin
doublets were a normal part of male costume in the Renaissance era.

M.Br.

IV.105
The burial garb of Tycho Brahe:
Cloak
Silk, damask, background five-thread,
weft-faced satin, pattern five-thread warp-
faced satin
Two fragments: one 16 × 18 cm, the other
26 × 18 cm
Probably before or in 1601
Damask probably from Italy
Museum of the City of Prague, inv. no.
86564/1-2

Two fragments of material with a large,
stylized plant and geometrical pattern.
The material is today brown in colour, but

in 1901 its colour was given as dark red.
The larger fragment, made up of two
pieces, has a selve edge and the remnants
of stitches. Given that the material shows
signs of having originally been cut as a
gusset, from other examples of the period
it can be assumed that the fragment was
originally part of the triangle which was
sewn into the sides of large and voluminous cloaks, such as those in which Maximilian II and Rudolf II were buried. Similar damask was used to make the burial
clothes of Archduchess Eleonora (1580,
Prague, Prague Castle Administration).

M.Br.

IV.106
The burial garb of Tycho Brahe: Stocking
Linen, hand-knitted using stocking stitch,
upper border only plain stitch
64 cm long; sole: 24 cm long
Before or in 1601
Probably made in Germany or Bohemia
Museum of the City of Prague, inv. no.
86565

Only one stocking was taken from the
grave. It is hand-knitted and now ochre
brown in colour. Gussets were inserted
from the sole to the ankles, and there was
a seam behind. Similar stockings formed
part of the burial garb of Maximilian II

(1576, Prague, Prague Castle Administration).

Landskron 1996.

Herain 1901, vol. XI, pp. 105–29.

M.Br.

IV.107
Shoe
Silk, velvet, the same as that used for the
hat, tanned ox-hide
Length 24.5 cm; length from toe to instep:
21 cm; heel: 8 cm high
Before or in 1601
Velvet probably from Italy or Germany,
leather probably from Germany or Bo-
hemia
Museum of the City of Prague, inv. no.
86566/1-3

Only one shoe and a piece of velvet, probably from the heel of the other shoe, was
taken from the grave. The velvet shoe is

now dark brown, and had a leather sole
made of two layers sewn together. In
restoration a copy of the sole was attached
to the shoe. The original is stored separately. The velvet upper was completely
lined with leather, and so it seems as if the
shoe was not made just for the burial. The
velvet slippers and shoes with cork soles
of all the Habsburgs buried at Prague Castle are similar, but in their case the velvet
uppers were not lined with leather.

M.Br.

IV.108
Nikolaus Pfaff
Nürnberg ? 1556–? Prague before 1612
Rhinoceros-horn Cup with Satyrs
Carved rhinoceros horn
H: 29.6 cm
Ca. 1610–12
From the imperial *Schatzkammer*
Vienna, Kunsthistorisches Museum,
Kunstkammer, inv. no. 3701

Distelberger has convincingly shown that
this subtly carved cup is from the refined,
courtly oeuvre of Nikolaus Pfaff. In creating this piece for the imperial *Kunstkammer*, Pfaff drew inspiration from both the

origins and the supposed potent magical
powers of the horn: at the time there was a
widespread belief that rhinoceros horn,
like bezoar stone or, as people thought,
like the even rarer unicorn, had the power
to ward off poisons. Since the days of Marco Polo, descriptions of rhinoceroses, as
yet unseen by Europeans, had frequently
been illustrated with a picture of a unicorn. After all, Aristotle had referred to an
Asinus indicus, a one-hoofed, one-horned
Indian donkey, which he said was identical
to the mythical unicorn. Since Ctesias, in
particular since Pliny, and right into the
seventeenth century, satyrs were believed
to be hybrid creatures living in India.

Rhinoceros horn had long been valued as
an aphrodisiac and it was thought that the
satyrs drew substances from the rhinoceros horn that allowed them totally to
fulfil their unfettered desires.

Salzburg 1987, cat. no. 297; Essen 1988,
cat. no. 398; Cremona 1996, cat. no. XII.16.

Kris 1932, under nos 80, 51; Scheicher
1995, pp. 122ff.

S.H.

IV.109
John Dee's crystal ball and wax tablet
Sixteenth century
London, The Trustees of the British Museum, inv. no. 1735
SL.232 OA. 106

D.T.

IV.110
Bill Presented by the Imperial Barber, Matěj Nicolai, and the Imperial Physician, Martin Piatowski, for Medicines and Remedies Supplied to the Chamber between 16 January 1603 and 24 December 1611
The bill and the request for its payment are countersigned by Oktavián Roboretus and Hektor Moscalea, formerly physicians to Emperor Rudolf II
Original on paper, in Latin, 2 fols
20 × 32 cm
After 20 January 1612
Prague, Státní ústřední archiv v Praze, archivní fond Stará manipulace, Signatura P 118/15, carton 1835

This bill is one of the many outstanding debts which the Czech Chamber had to pay after Rudolf's death. It documents the administration of the health of the sovereign and his court. In 1596, for example, Rudolf had four personal physicians, one surgeon and one court doctor. During the reigns of Ferdinand I and Maximilian II, Mattioli, the famous author of the *Herbarium*, had served as the court doctor, while under Rudolf the post was held by Quarinoni. The Roboretus mentioned here was the father of Roboreti, professor of the Prague law faculty after the Battle of the White Mountain. The bill lists pills, quack medicines, waters, gruels, candies or 'sugars', and sugarplums, made mostly of plants and roots Also listed are glass and ceramic apothecary jars. A total sum for all expenses incurred between 16 January 1603 and 10 October 1607 is calculated, and the detailed list of items is continued until 24 December 1611, less than one month before the Emperor's death. The total sum is 888 zlatys and 31 crowns.

Mattioli 1596; Winter 1909, pp. 717-24; Vojtová 1970.

K.B.

IV.111
Hans Wecker ?
Active in Prague in 1599 until after 1610
Syringe
Turned (or rough-hewn) ivory, felt; box: rough-cut (or unpolished) wood
Length max. 23.3 cm; average 2.5 cm
First quarter of the seventeenth century
Prague ?
Ca. 1610 in the *Kunstkammer*, Prague Castle (?), until 1957 in a private collection in Prague
Prague, Uměleckoprůmyslové muzeum, inv. no. 43.777

The only convertible syringe to be preserved intact in Czech collections. A needle extension is located beneath the screw-off stopper inside a piston, which is extended and rounded at the mouth with an internal average size of 1 mm. This shows that it was used to apply curative solutions from the outside, for example to the eyes, ears or nose. Hans Wecker the Younger, the Prague court ivory-turner, is mentioned in the inventory of Rudolf's *Kunstkammer* (see Bauer-Haupt, 1976, no. 965) as the maker of a set of miniature medical utensils from 1610 (Kunsthistorisches Museum, Vienna). We may ascribe this syringe to the same group of medical and technical miniatures since the same inventory apparently under entry no.930 mentions a 'a subtly made syringe' ('von helffenbain ein spritzerlin, gar subtil gedreht') and a set of instruments with a little table (ibid. 921, 924 or 944), both of which entries are now in the museum of Decorative Arts in Prague.

D.S.

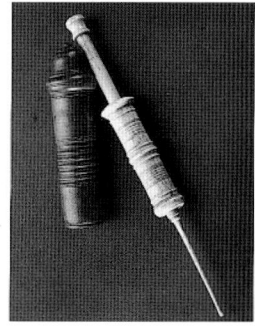

IV.112
Philippe de Monte
Malines 1521–Prague 1603
Liber I. Missarum
Print, paper
1587
Antwerp, Christophor Plantin's printing house
From the possessions of Jiří Bartholdt of Braitenberk
Prague, Library of the Metropolitan Chapter

A preserved manuscript from the imperial *Kapellmeister* Philippe de Monte still surprises with its legibility and quality. Although de Monte working duties were quite onerous, he produced 1,073 secular madrigals to Italian texts, 144 sacred madrigals, 45 French chansons, 319 motets and 38 masses. Most of de Monte's masses were preserved only in copies. The workshop of Christophor Plantin in 1579 was responsible for printing this exception, which contains a mass of *Benedicta es* in six voices and a volume of masses which came out from the same printing house eight years later. The volume encompasses two masses for five voices, four for six voices and one for eight voices. The edition is dedicated to Emperor Rudolf II in an undated preface. The typography is ingeniously furnished with an engraved title page with stylized musical scenes. This edition was probably the model for a volume of masses for the imperial organist Charles Luython, which came out in 1609 at the Prague printing works of Mikulas Strauss.

Essen and Vienna, cat. no. 775.

Doorslaer 1921, pp. 167-68; Stellfeld 1949; Monte de P., Opera, Series B Masses vol. 1, 1976; Lindell 1982; Comberiati 1987, pp. 58-61; Przywecka-Samecka 1987, pp. 124-45.

P.D.

IV.113
Charles Luython
Antwerp 1556/7–Prague 1602
Liber l. Missarum
Printed work, paper, wooden cover bound in leather
1609
Prague, Mikulas Strauss printing press
Usti nad Labem, Municipal Museum, inv. no. St 1298

In 1609 the printing works of Mikulas Strauss issued a mass composed by Charles Luython, the imperial organist and composer of *Sacrae Caesa, Maiest, Organistae et Componistae*. Mikulas Strauss tended to produce small and occasional printed works. This type of book, however, is in the folio format of a choirbook in which all the voices are printed spread out on two pages. In the choice of lettering and pictorial design of the title page, it is apparent that the printer devoted great attention to the whole work. The collection of Luython's compositions contains nine arrangements of a mass ordinary. The masses are composed for various combinations of voices: one mass is intended for seven voices, three for six voices, two for five voices and there are also two masses for four voices and one for three. The entire collection of masses is dedicated to Emperor Rudolf II. An exceptionally large quantity of specimens of Luython's work has been preserved to this day. In the same year in which the first edition of Luython's masses came out, Strauss also issued the Magnificat of Nicolaus Zangia. The typography of this work has been designed in a similar way to the editions of Luython's compositions.

Smijers 1923; Comberiati 1987, pp. 62-77; Danek 1990, pp. 219-238.

P.D.

IV.114
Various authors
Kutná Hora (Gutenburg) Volume of
Masses
Manuscript, paper
57.5 × 43 cm
End of sixteenth century
Kutna Hora, St James' cathedral
Prague, Národní muzeum v Praze, Museum of Czech Music, AZ 33

An affluent burgher, Zikmund Kozel of Ryzntal, had this manuscript volume of polyphonic masses made for the needs of the Kutná Hora Literates choir. The possibility that it originated in the copying

clerks' workroom of the court Kapelle cannot be excluded. It contains ten polyphonic mass ordinaries, none of whose authors – with one exception – we know. Dominant among them are composers from the Rudolfine Kapelle. Giuli Belli is the only composer among the circle of court composers not to be mentioned in the volume. He was 'maestro di cappella' to Alfonso II d'Este in Ferrara. The manuscript is an example of a so-called choirbook, in which individual voices in the composition are located next to each other on two pages of basically simultaneous music sheets, although not in the modern sense of that of a music stand. The singers sang from an

opened book which was placed in front of them on a pulpit (or stand), according to the instructions of the cantor. The Kutna Hora volume is an example of lively music by Rudolfine composers in a Czech environment.

Comberiati 1987, p. 221; *Rukovet humanistickeho ...* 1969, pp. 79–80; Snizkova 1971, pp. 278–80; Snizkova 1972, p. 49.

P.D.

IV.115
Mathias de Sayve
Ca. 1540/50–1619
Liber primum motectorum quinque vocum
Print, paper
16.4 × 18.8 cm
1595
Prague, Národní muzeum, Museum of Czech Music, sign. IV E 87

Jiří Nigrin practically had the monopoly on typesetting for vocal polyphonies during the Rudolfine era in Prague. Other printers also produced books and used relief printing blocks for musical notation. Only one printer, however, could tackle

large-scale projects comparable to those of Nigrin's edition of Handl's *Opus musicum*, and that was Mikulas Strauss. Three years after Nigrin's death, he printed a mass by the imperial organist Charles Luython which was very successful in terms of its typography. Jan Othmar, who inherited a printing business from his father, Jiří Dacicky, concentrated particularly on high-selling calendars and news articles. In 1595, however, he printed a collection of motets by the imperial chorister Mathias de Sayve, entitled *Liber primum motectorum*, which is dedicated to the highest Hofmeister, Wolfgang Rumpf. The composer belonged to the prosper-

ous and talented musical de Sayve family, which came from France. Most of its members were active in the service of the Habsburgs in Central Europe. Apart from the Prague print, only three other compositions have been preserved in collections by various authors (RISM 1604/7, 1610/18).

Winter 1613, pp. 585–86; Schenk 1961, p. 103; Quitin 1973, p. 451; Comberiati 1987, pp. 21–22, 44, 55; Danek 1990, p. 225.

P.D.

IV.116
Franz Sale
Namur ca. 1550–Prague 1599
Dialogismus de amore Christ sponsi erga ecclesiam sponsam
Print, paper
1598
Prague, Jiří Nigrin printing works
Library of the evangelical church of St Mary Magdalene in Wroclaw, afterwards in the city library of Wroclaw
Prague, Národní knihovna Čekské republiky, hudební oddělení, inv. no. 59 E 710

On 1 May 1591 Franz Sale, a chorister and composer, entered the service of Emperor

Rudolf II. He was a tenor in the imperial Kapelle and remained there for the rest of his life. In the course of his eight years' activity in Prague, he had seven volumes of compositions comprising various genres printed at Jiří Nigrin's printing works. Nigrin produced Sale's collection of motets in five- and six-voice arrangements that was dedicated to Wolfgang Rumpf in 1593, as well as three books of minor propria, which were dedicated to Zikmund III, King of Poland, and to Bishop Stanislav Pavlovsky (1594-96). The *Dialogismus* is dedicated to the council and people of Wroclaw and was composed for a spiritual text by Johannus Linckius, a humanist po-

et and cantor from Linz, who identifies himself as Silesius. The entire piece is conceived as a debate between the church, Christ and the angels.

Mares 1894, pp. 217, 232; Senn 1938, pp. 150, 176–81, 332–33; Senn 1954, pp. 124–25; *Rukkovet humanisticke ...*1969, p. 163; Danek 1987, pp. 121–36; Sale 1991.

P.D.

IV.117
Franz Sale
Namur 1550–Prague 1599
Canzonette, Vilanelle et Neapolitane, per cantar
Print, paper
15.5 × 16.5 cm
1598
Prague, Jiří Nigrin printing works
Originally in the library of the evangelical church of St Mary Magdalene in Wroclaw
Wroclaw, Bibl. Uniwersytecka, inv. no. 50 776 Muz.

The list of documents and printed works of the Rožmberk library has an entry un-

der the letter 'S', 'Francisci Sale Cantiones Italice trium vocum. Partes III. In red leather with the emperor's coat of arms'. This undoubtedly concerned the printing of a work for a tenor in the Rudolfine Kapelle by Franz Sale, *Canzonette, Vilanelle et Neapolitane*, from 1598. Sale, a versatile and gifted musician in terms of compositional abilities, had this opus printed at Jiří Nigrin's Prague printing works and dedicated it to Count Albert of Furstenberk. In it he compiled eleven songs for three voices set to an Italian text. This type of secular polyvocal song, simple in form and known as *canzonette* or villanelles, was particularly fa-voured among Rudolfine

composers. Jacobus Regnart was its main pioneer in Central Europe, but other Rudolfine authors composed canzonette. Sale, who is identified on the title page as 'Musico della Sacra Caesarea Maesta, del' Imperatore Rodolfo Secondo', emphasizes in the introduction to the collection that these vocal compositions may be accompanied by an instrument. Similar notes may be found in other printed works by this author.

Vogel 1977, no. 2535; Zackova 1996; see also cat. no. III.116.

P.D.

IV.118
Giovanni Battista Pinello
Genoa 1544–Prague 1587
Primo libro delle Neapolitane
1584

The Italian composer and singer Giovanni Battista Pinello di Ghirardi died in Prague in 1587 as a chorister in the imperial choir. By 1580 that he had spent thirty years singing. From 1576 he served as a tenor in the court choir of Archduke Ferdinand of Tyrol at Innsbruck. While living in Prague around 1580, he applied for the position of *Kapellmeister* at the court of the Elector August of Saxony at Dresden. His applica-

tion was successful. Because of conflicting personalities, however, he had only a short spell in that position. He spent the last three years of his life in Prague. He is the author of several collections of Italian canzoni, secular songs, six masses, two 'Magnificats' and some sacred motets (printed by Jiří Nigrin in Prague). Some loose unbound and virtually uncut pages of Pinello's choir books are uniquely preserved in the archives of the State Conservatory in Prague, although the edition of Primo libro delle neapolitane for five voices has not been completely preserved. This was printed in 1584 by the Dresden printer Matthauss Stoeckel. The introduction to

the collection contains a portrait of the authors and a dedication which is intended for Ottavius Spinolius, who held the position of equerry at Rudolf's court in Prague.

Nemcova 1588; Danek 1987, p. 131; Prispevek k poznani ... 1996.

P.D.

IV.119
Charles Luython
Antwerp 1556/57–Prague 1620
Riccercar and Fantasy for Keyboard
Paper, manuscript – facsimile
29.5 × 19.5 cm
Ad usum Pris Alexandri Geissel Ord: Min: S: Fran: Convent
1620–30
Vienna
Vienna, Minorite Convent, sign. XIV.714

Within the structure of the imperial court, the position of court organist was honoured throughout the sixteenth century. They usually accompanied the choristers during court masses, but also gave solo performances and played for various instrumental combinations. They performed outside the framework of court services and obligations. Almost all the imperial organists were also active composers, but little of their compositional output has survived. One of the most important sources of organ music from the Rudolfine era is a manuscript which is preserved in the library of a Minorite convent in Vienna. It was written at some time around 1630, partly in the new German style of tablature for organ but predominantly in the form of the ten-lined stave notational system. It contains over five hundred compositions by a number of authors from the peak of the Renaissance and the early Baroque, among which we find individually preserved compositions by Charles Luython, Liberale Zanchi, Franz Sale, Philippe de Monte and Jacobus Regnart.

Schierning 1961; Riedel 1963; *Vienna, Minoritenkonvent, Klosterbibliothek und Archiv* 1988; Freren, 1988, p. 282; Padrta 1989, p. 35.

P.D.

IV.120
Various authors
Tabulature for Organ
Manuscript on paper, after conservation kept in transparent pasted covers
31 × 24 cm
Ca. 1600
Straz n. Nisou, afterwards Liberec, district archives
Liberec, State District Archives

In comparison with vocal music, very few documents concerning the performance of instrumental music emanating from the Rudolfine period have been preserved on Czech territory. One of these rare documents is a German-style tabulature for organ, which comes from Zahořany u Vintiřova. It consists of fourteen sheets which had been used as cast-off material in making plates for a register at the end of the seventeenth century. The tabulature was discovered when the bindings were removed in 1966. The sheets of the tabulature bear their original foliation (70–93) and must have formed part of an extensive manuscript volume of compositions for organ. The authors are given for the majority of the compositions (Tiburtio Massiani, Anibale Paduano, Leonhard Lechner, Orlando di Lasso, Hans Leo Hassler, Phillippe de Monte and others). On the sheet that probably formed the inside page of the whole manuscript, periodic notes appear for the acolyte or altar-server. All the compositions in question present an intabulation of religious compositions for voice, particularly in the motets and the mass parts. The possibility cannot be excluded that the manuscript was a copy of some sort of printed anthology of compositions for organ from the period.

Ryba 1970, pp. 67–85.

P.D.

IV.121
Fragment of a Score for Lute
Paper
18 × 24 cm
Ca. 1610
Prague, Národní muzeum v Praze, Museum of Czech Music, XIII B237

This fragment of a score for lute contains dances and the transcripts of songs written down according to the German notation system. The compositions are interpolated with quotations from Classical literature. For the most part, the score is marked for a six-stringed lute with strings tuned to A–D–G–B–E♯–A♯ or G–C–F–A–D♯–G♯. Some compositions assume the use of a ten-stringed lute. It is apparent from this that the manuscript originated at the beginning of the seventeenth century when such an instrument came to be used more frequently. Among the purely instrumental compositions for dance and performance we encounter arrangements of villanelles by the imperial under-choirmaster Jacobus Regnart which were very popular at the time. The work was first printed in 1583 and copies of it, as well as reprints and alterations, spread afterwards. Some of the scores to Regnart's songs in the fragment have been supplied with a textual incipit in Czech, for example, 'Maiden', 'Your fickleness', 'She will marry me', 'My good fortune will harm no one'. It can therefore be supposed that these songs were sung even in Czech. The fragment contains a preamble of an otherwise unknown Czech composer, Stephan Laurentio Jacobides.

Osthoff 1938; Pohanka 1958, nos 96, 97; Vogel 1964, pp. 11–19; Tichota 1965, pp. 139–49; Vogel 1965, Heft 3, pp. 281–96; Tichota 1967, pp. 63–69.

P.D.

IV.122
Various authors
Selectae aliqout cantiones piae sex quinque vocibus
Manuscript of miscellaneous volume of motets containing compositions by court musicians
Five volumes of manuscripts, paper, bound in parchment
15.5 × 21 cm
Ca. 1600
Benedictine monastery at Rajhrad
Brno, Moravske zemske museum, Department of Musical History, inv. no. A 7077

The manuscript is one of the best-preserved sources for the history of music in the Rudolfine period that is of Czech provenance. The manuscript originally comprised a set of six vocal scores (*Discantus – Altus – Tenor – Bassus – Quinta vox – Sexta vox*) which contained parts from seventy polyphonic compositions. Compositions for six voices dominate the first part of the manuscript, while the second part comprises compositions for five voices. The final part of the document contains a mass, greatly favoured in its day, by the imperial choirmaster, Philippe de Monte, entitled *Nasce la pena mia*, as well as a secular song, *Einstmals in einem tiefen Tal*, by the under-choirmaster Jacobus Regnart. Apart from these, the manuscript also contains records of spiritual motets, and an anonymous five-voiced arrangement of a Czech text entitled *Milosrdny Boze, prosim za to* (Merciful God, I beg). An interesting note by the manuscript's compiler in the introduction informs us that these works may be accompanied by instruments. In the composition with the text 'Carole Salve Imperatorum generosa', the bar lines were added at a later date.

Strakova 1893, pp. 149–80.

P.D.

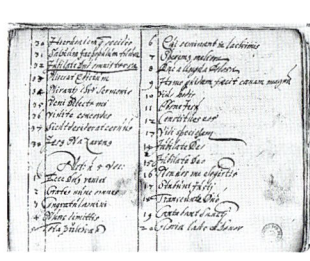

IV.123
Nicolaus Zangius
Died ca. 1618/19
Magnificat anima mea Dominum
Print, paper, wooden covers covered with leather, clasps
47.5 × 36 cm
1609
Prague, Mikulas Strauss printing works
Ústi nad Labem, Muzeum mešta Ústi nad Labem, inv. no. ST 1 298

Nicolaus Zangius probably originated from Walterdorf. In 1594, he brought out his first edition of musical works (*Schoene newe ... Weltliche Lieder*). From not later than 1597 he worked as a choirmaster at the ducal bishop's court of Philippe Sigismund in Iburg. From 1599 to 1602 he was choirmaster in Gdansk, before trying to establish himself in Rudolfine Prague. He dedicated certain compositions to the Emperor, for which he was remunerated. In 1603 his collection *Kurtzweilige ... Weltliche Lieder* appeared. Documents preserved from the offices of the court demonstrate that the composer, a Protestant, was employed in the service of the court without being a member of the court chapel. During his stay in Prague, he had an edition of *Magnificat anima mea Dominum* for six voices printed at the printing works of Mikulas Strauss. In 1612 he entered the service of the Brandenburg Elector in Berlin, probably his last engagement. Zangius was an extraordinarily prolific composer. His activities in Prague – about which unfortunately very little is known – demonstrate that even artists of the Protestant persuasion were able to work for the court without actually being servants of the court.

Rauschning 1931, p. 33; Zangius 1951; Lindell 1989, p. 104; Danek 1990, pp. 219–38.

P.D.

IV.124
Tiburtio Massaini
Ca. 1550–ca. 1609
Liber primus cantionum ecclesiasticarum
Print, paper
15 × 19.6 cm
1592
Prague, Jiří Nigrin's printing works
Originally from the library of the Národní muzeum
Prague, Národní muzeum, Museum of Czech Music, inv. no. AZ 36/7

The Italian composer and Augustinian friar Tiburtio Massaini arrived in Prague at the end of 1591, having been released from the services of the bishop of Salzburg, Wolf Dietrich of Reitenau, on account of some terrible 'offence against nature'. In Prague, he hoped to gain a place in the imperial *Kapelle*. Massaini printed an edition of motets for four voices, dedicated in 31 May 1592 and is addressed to the imperial *Kapellmeister*, Phillipe de Monte. Even this attention, however, did not guarantee Massaini any favour among those with influence at the court and so, after a year, he left Prague and returned to his native Italy. Lack of success in Central Europe did not discourage him from other attempts at composition. In the course of his life he printed a series of masses, motets, litanies and other forms of religious music as well as several volumes of madrigals and some outstanding instrumental *canzone*. The exhibited model is part of a bundle of prints, in which Jacobus Handl Gallus and Orlando di Lasso appear next to Massaini's representation.

Senn 1954, pp. 129–30; Monterosso 1964; Comberiati 1987, pp. 56–57; Danek 1987, pp. 121–36; Hintermaier 1987, pp. 296–302; Lindell 1988, pp. 75–83; Lindell 1989, pp. 99–111.

P.D.

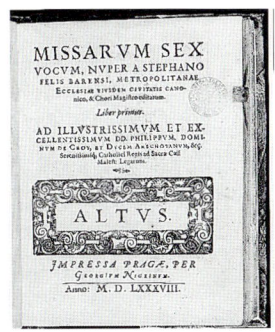

IV.125
Stefano Felis
Ca. 1550-1603
Missarum sex vocum ... Liber primus
Paper, set of manuscripts and prints
1588
Prague, Premonstratensian monastery at Strahov, library, D.H.V. 25

Stefano Felis was an Italian composer who went to Prague in 1587 as part of the entourage of the papal nuncio Antonio Puteo. He added the title 'Barensis' to his name on account of his birthplace. In 1588 he published a mass for six voices, *Missarum sex vocum ... Liber primus*, at the printing works of Jiří Nigrin. Evidently, even composers who were only passing through Prague made use of the local facilities to print their work. This shows too the existence of a local market for sheet music and the affiliation of the Prague printers to the European distribution network. Not all the scores for voice in Felis's Prague volume were preserved. The exhibited exemplar demonstrates the part for alto, which forms part of the set. In addition to Stefano Felis' mass, two printed motets by Jacobus Reiner (1600 and 1603) as well as a manuscript of Czech motets (the vast majority of which are psalms put to music) have been put into this volume.

One of the introductory compositions in the manuscript is dedicated to Jan Hus, and the penultimate composition has been ascribed to the Pavel Spongopae Jistebnicky. The bundle thus represents a curious combination of a repertoire from the Czech Utraquists with a mass by a composer whose orientation lay closer to the Italian Counter-Reformation.

Racek 1973, p. 34; RISM A/I/3/315; Comberiati 1987, p. 17; Danek 1987, no. 2, p. 132; Lindell 1988, p. 81; Lindell 1989, no. 2, p. 105; Fojtikova, p. 136.

P.D.

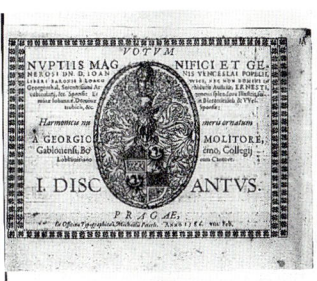

IV.126
Georg Molitor
Ca. 1600
Votum nuptiis magnifici et generosi Dn. D. Joannis Venceslai Popelii
Bundle of printed matter, paper
16.5 × 21 cm
1586-99
Wroclaw, Bibliotheke Uniwersytecka, inv. no. 51222-51235 Muz.

One of the means by which musicians were able to gain the favour of influential people and thereby acquire financial reward was by dedicating to them a collection or, at least, an individual composition. The musical press at the peak of the Renaissance rarely went without a dedication to a prominent character, town council or influential institution. The bundle of printed matter from the Wroclaw University library contains a number of compositions which were intended for secular celebrations. Composers who were active in Silesia, northern Bohemia and Saxony are dominant among such authors: Reiner, Hausmann, Gesius, Demantius, Pencun, Pittanus etc. The author of two printed works is the composer Georg Molitor, who came from Jablonec and worked for the Lobkowicz family. The composition *Votum nuptiis* was created on the occasion of the wedding of Jan Vaclav Popel of Lobkowicz, who was chamberlain to Archduke Arnost, and Johanna of Beronic. It was issued in Prague by the printing works of Michael Peterle in 1586. The second composition by the same author, which is also bound with the bundle, was printed in the same year at the Jiří Nigrin printing works for the marriage of Victorin Henrico of Frankenstein with Anna Hungerin.

Molitor 1913; Danek 1987, p. 131; Kolbuszewska 1992, pp. 63–64.

P.D.

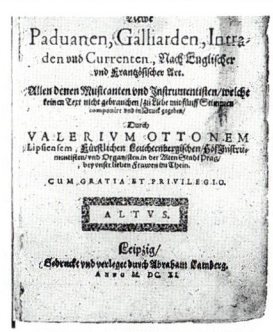

IV.127
Valerius Otto Lipsiensis
Lipsko 1579–ca. 1620
Newe Paduanen, Galliarden, Intraden und Currenten ... a 5
Printed, paper
20.5 × 17 cm
1611
Lipsko, the Abraham Lamberg printing works
Wroclaw, Bibliotheka Uniwersytecka, sign. 50 671

Instrumental music underwent a period of great emancipation at the beginning of the seventeenth century. While in previous decades instruments were used, above all, to accompany voices, and separate instrumental companies for the most part played arrangements of vocal motets and madrigals, the beginning of the century brought an upsurge in original instrumental music. Changes in style that gradually came to dominate the work of the up-and-coming generation of composers, and the requirements of society, gave rise in about 1600 to a series of new collections of original compositions for various types of instrumental use. The author of one of these collections of instrumental works was a German composer and organist, Valerius Otto, whose fate was linked with that of Prague at the time of Rudolf. The collection *Newe Paduanen ...* contains sixty-two dances for five voices. According to practices at the time, they could have been played with various arrangements of instruments.

Bohn 1883, p. 300; Buchner 1954, p. 82, no. 339; Danek 1993, IV-XII; Kolbuszewska 1992, no. 169; Otto 1993.

P.D.

IV.128
Jan Sixt of Lerchenfels
Ca. 1560-1629
Triumphus et victoria ... Ioannes Sterclaes comitis de Tilli
Print, paper
29 × 18.5 cm
1626
Strahov, monastery library
Prague, Národní muzeum, Museum of Czech Music, AZ 19

Jan Sixt of Lerchenfels was the author and publisher of the print *Triumphus et victoria*. He was an outstanding figure in Rudolfine and pre-White Mountain Bohemia. He came from Prague. In 1584 he allegedly became a chorister in the imperial *Kapelle*, and he made progress in his church and courtly career with great tenacity. Between 1599 and 1602 he held the position of court chaplain. He had studied in Prague and at the Jesuit university in Olomouc, where he obtained his Master's degree. At the beginning of the seventeenth century he became the dean of Vysehrad, a Prague scholastic, the canon of Stara Boleslav, and the provost of Litomerice. In 1625 he established a printing works in Litomerice, where he printed this volume, which contains several compositions. The spiritual compositions are a *Te Deum*, a *Magnificat* and a *Da pacem*. Other works are arrangements for three Italian sonnets and a remarkable text, *Un altro Sonetto degla Bataglia di Praga*, which celebrates the victory of the Habsburgs at the Battle of White Mountain. From a musical point of view, it is merely the arrangement of a favourite madrigal by Giovanni Gastoldi entitled *Tuti venite armati*.

Sclenz 1911; Smijers 1919, pp. 148, 150, 155; Haas 1923, p. 106; Knihopis 15 878; Pohanka 1959, no. 105; *Rukovet humanisticke ... 1982*, pp. 111-14.

P.D.

IV.129
Jiří Bartholdus Pontanus of Braitenberk
Most 1555 (?)–Prague 1614
Episcoporum ... Pragensium historia brevissima
Print, 28 folios
1593
Prague, Jiří Nigrin printing works
Prague, Narodni knihovna, inv. no. 49 C 81

Jiří Bartholdus, the author of this edition about Prague bishops and archbishops, is one of the undervalued personalities of Rudolfine Bohemia in terms of his historical and cultural significance. The breadth and formal perfection of his literary legacy is remarkable, whether in the form of poetry or prose. Conceptually and in terms of content and formal technique Bartholdus practically anticipated what would become Baroque literature. His numerous printed works and particularly well-preserved notes in manuscript form demonstrate that he was an especially active and inventive artist of Catholic orientation, who worked with other artists during the era of Prague's Rudolfine culture. He was an active writer throughout his life, despite holding a series of important functions in the church hierarchy, where he led an unusually high-principled career. His collaborative work with the imperial under-*Kapellmeister* Jacob Regnart is of significance, since Regnart set music to a number of texts by Bartholdus. This edition of *Episcoporum ... historia* was dedicated to the Archbishop of Prague, Zbynek Berka of Duba.

Tumpach 1912, p. 942; Smijers 1923; *Rukovet humanistickeho ...* 1966, pp. 137–67.

P.D.

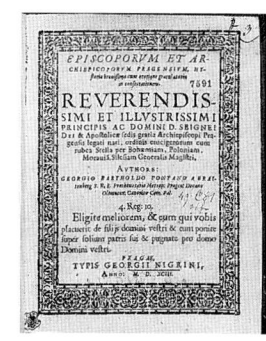

IV.130
Elizabeth Ionna Westonia
1582–1612
Parthenicon Elisabethae Ionnae Westoniae ... liber I
Print, paper
1606
Prague, the Pavel Sessius printing works
Prague, Národní muzeum, library, inv. no. 49 E 17

The poet Alzbeta (Elizabeth) Westonia was a legendary figure in Prague at the time of Rudolf. In many respects she seems to have defied the conventions of her time. Unlike her female peers, she had received an extraordinary education through which her literary and linguistic talents became manifest. These brought dividends in the form of social relations and literary conversation. She came from England, but emigrated to Bohemia with her stepfather Eduard Kelly, who was an alchemist. She and married the court advocate Jan Leon of Eisenach. She is revealed to have been an adroit humanist poet in her collections, the majority of which were printed in Prague (by Nigrin, Bohutsky and Sessius). The individual collection entitled *Parthenicon*, which most probably appeared in 1606, contains a poem in honour of the composer Phillipe de Monte, who is called 'musico nostro seculo principi'. The poem serves both as a celebration of music as an art form and as a means of thanking Phillipe de Monte for some unspecified act of kindness.

Celakovsky 1832, p. 131; Kolar 1926, pp. 12, 33; Patzak 1943, p. 102; *Rukovet humanistickeho ...* 1982, pp. 470–77; Bassnett 1988, pp. 9–15; Zwollo 1988, pp. 326–33; Svitak 1992; Ticha 1992.

P.D.

IV.131
Aegidius Sadeler
Antwerp 1570–1629 Prague
Portrait of Jacobus Chimarrhaeus
Copper engraving
19.5 × 12.1 cm
1601
Prague, Národní galerie v Praze, Grafická sbírka, inv. no. R 16 971

Jacobus Chimarrhaeus is an example of a musician who had a highly remarkable career in the service of the court. He began as a bass and went on to become the court *Kapellmeister*. He was nominated a court beneficiary and a count palatine by the Emperor. In 1585 he received the title 'comes Palatinus' and a coat of arms. Sadeler's portrait states that he was also a Knight of the Golden Spur and a vice-notary. He also attained high office in the church, becoming a provost in Cologne and Ratibor and a canon at Bautzen and in Olomouc. He succeeded Frantisek of Ditrichstejn to become Provost of Litomerice, where he died in 1614. In the 1580s he founded the Confraternitas Sanctissimi Corporis Christi (Brethren for the Celebration of the Body of Christ), to which were affiliated various distinguished members of the imperial court. Throughout his numerous offices he maintained relations with the court Kapelle and its members. It was the latter who commemorated him by producing a volume of compositions entitled *Odae suavissimae*, to which contributions were made by almost all the musicians of the Rudolfine Kapelle who were active as composers: Philippe de Monte, Charles Luython, Camillo Zanotti, Philippe Schoendorf (who compiled the volume), Stefano Felis, Lucas Zigotta and others.

Essen and Vienna 1988, p. 14.

P.D.

IV.132
Franz Sale
Namur ca. 1550–Prague 1599
Request for the Granting of a Privilege to Issue Compositions
Manuscript, paper
21.5 × 33.5 cm; 16.5 × 21 cm
1592
Vienna, Haus, Hof- und Staatsarchiv, Impressorien Kart. 61, fols 5, 7, 8

In 1592 the imperial chorister Franz Sale requested the office of the court to issue a decree to print his collection of sacred motets. He enclosed with the request a proposal for the title page and a list of compositions which were to have been included in the collection. The court *Kapellmeister*, Philippe de Monte, expressed an opinion about the request; his note is entered on the back and signed in his own hand. The office of the court dispatched the request with a postscript dated 30th March 1592. Sale's collection of motets, *Sacrarum cantionum omnis generis instrumentis musicis, et vivae voci accomodatarum...liber primus*, was his first musical work to be printed in Prague at the workshop of Jiří Nigrin in January 1593. It is interesting that the author's proposal for a design on the title page and in the set of motets met later with interference, which became apparent in various sorts of deletions: the author's name was incorporated more modestly and also some motets were discarded. The edition itself also contains authorial suggestions for a means of interpreting them, e.g. alternating solo and choir, the use of organs, repetitions).

Truhlar 1897, pp. 79–82; *Rukovet humanistickeho ...* 1966, pp. 384–85; Niemoller 1973, pp. 520–22; Lindell 1989, pp. 99–111; Lindell 1988, pp. 79–88; *Prag um 1600* 1988, p. 102; Niemoller 1994, pp. 359–74; see also cat. no. iv.116.

P.D.

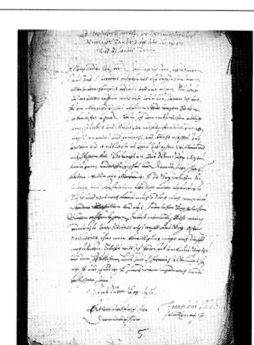

IV.133
Prague Old Town Book of Testimonies
Entry in the town records: the imperial musician Waynand de Hodege intervened for a woman who had been assaulted
Paper
33.5 × 21 × 7 cm
1602
Prague, Archives of the City of Prague, MS 1064, fol. 55b

In 1602 the imperial musician Waynand de Hodege intervened when an old woman was assaulted in the street by a baker of some description. The two men came to blows and fought 'like cocks', and, had it not been for the intervention of the imperial musician, the quarrel might have ended tragically. Waynand de Hodege was an alto in the court *Kapelle*. He is listed in the register of its members for 1600. We do not, however, have much information about his activities in the service of the court. He was a paid member from 1 April 1580 until his death in 1603. We also know that in 1589 he took Anna di Horetta to be his wife. Together with their children, she was still receiving payments for her husband's services from the court offices two years after his death.

Smijers 1919–22, pp. 155, 184; Doorslaer 1931, pp. 481–91; Doorslaer 1933, pp. 148–61; Comberiati 1987, p. 206.

P.D.

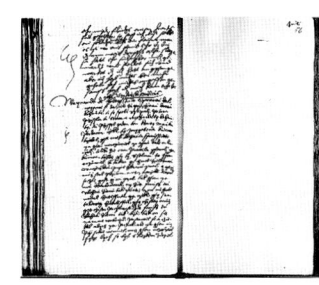

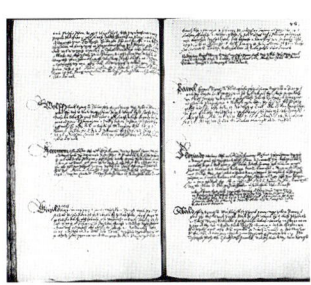

IV.134
Book of the Town Rights of Malá Strana
Florindo Sartorio, chamber musician, received the rights of township
Paper
33.5 × 21.5 × 6 cm
1596
Prague, Archives of the City of Prague, MS no. 567, fol. 45a

'For his excellence, the imperial chamber musicus', in 1596 Florindo Sartorio obtained the rights to dwell and practise a livelihood in the Lesser Town of Prague. Despite designating himself an imperial chamber musician, which was a particu-

larly prestigious position to hold within the hierarchy of the court Kapelle, Sartorio was actually a court trumpeter. In this function, he formed part of the entourage of Rudolf II when a session of the Imperial Council was convened at Augsburg in 1582. He was also given a similar opportunity around twelve years later at another session in Regensburg. He lived in the Lesser Town district of Prague on Vlasska Street, area code 361, that is, in the place where the Rudolfine era had more or less created an Italian colony. The witnesses to the conferment of the rights of township on Florindo Sartorio were also Italian: the stone-cutter Antonio Brocko and the

painter Marian de Marianis were present. The name of Florindo Sartorio often turns up in the city's books in connection with the transfer of possessions and the payment of debts.

Hojda 1987, no. 2, pp. 162-67; Janacek 1983, pp. 77-118; Pietzsch 1934, pp. 171-76.

P.D.

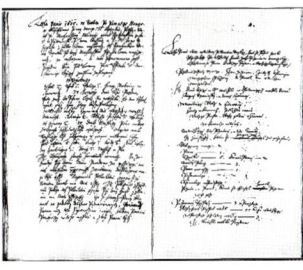

IV.135
Book of Inventories
List of inheritance left by Alzbeta Zachova dating from 15 November 1603
Paper
33.5 × 22 × 5 cm
1603
Prague, Archives of the City of Prague, MS 1214 fols 11a-b, 12a

This list, left by Alzbeta Zachova and dated 15 November 1603, contains an extensive collection of musical instruments which were used at the peak of the Renaissance. Alzbeta Zachova owned a house in the Zderaz area within the parish of St

Michal v Opatovicich. Five books of vocal scores from choristers in this church serve as one of the most important sources for the history of Czech musical culture at the end of the sixteenth century. Alzbeta Zachova was the sole owner of the collection of musical instruments. The will lists almost ninety varied instruments: among the wind instruments it includes several trombones, dulcians, Renaissance-style wooden recorders with eight notes, krummhorns, shawms, pommers, a few unspecified horns, as well as recorders and flutes. Other instruments include violins and Italian drums. The collection contained in the document would easily suf-

fice to equip an entire company of musicians. Surprisingly, the inventory contains no mention of musical printed works or manuscripts.

Cerny 1982; Pesek 1983, 3, pp. 242-56.

P.D.

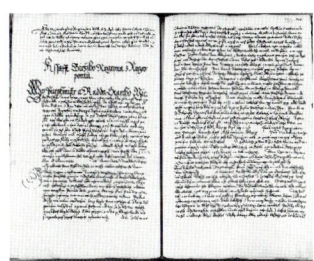

IV.136
Book of Testaments from Prague's Old Town
The testament of Jiří Nigrin
Paper
38.5 × 28 × 11 cm
8.12.1606
Archives of the City of Prague, no. 2205, fols 300b-301b

Jiří Nigrin of Nigropont was one of the most outstanding printers of the Rudolfine era in Prague. He worked in this profession from 1571 until his death in 1606. Nigrin issued almost six hundred printed works of sundry content from his printing works. He printed works for all

strata of society including topical items such as a newspaper, calendars, miscellaneous writings on meteorology, reading for amusement and recipe books. Nigrin also printed serious works drawn from all the known fields of science of the time. The university authorities commissioned the printing works to produce declarations, salutations, disputations, official speeches and teaching aids. In a certain respect Nigrin was also the court printer, since he was sought out by court functionaries to carry out demanding typesetting work. He was the most important pre-White Mountain music printer, since he published over sixty printed works in

which he typeset musical notation.

Five Hundred Years of Printing in Prague, Archives of the City of Prague, 1987-88.

Bohatcova and Hejnic 1981-82; Danek 1987, no. 2, pp. 121-36; Danek 1990, pp. 219-38; Teige 1915, p. 468; Winter 1909, p. 281.

P.D.

IV.137
Inventarium musicum. Directory of musical works from the library of Petr Vok
Manuscript, paper
1610

The musical instruments and sheet music in the possession of Petr Vok were recorded on 19 August 1610 by his secretary Theobald Hoeck, his librarians Matej de Cara and Vit Vostiralek and his chronicler Vaclav Brezan. Thus originated this remarkable inventory which records that the extensive and systematically built-up Rožmberk library contained countless representations and editions of musical

works and manuscripts of European provenance. The inventory provides a document of the largest pre-White Mountain private musical library in Bohemia and stands up to comparison with similar European directories on account of the structure of its assembled repertoire and the number of composers represented therein. The inventory is no less a document of the extent to which the Czech lands were linked to the European distribution network and it confirms that during the Rudolfine era even the latest innovations in European music reached the Czechs shortly after coming into existence.

Horyna 1993, pp.257-64; Jedlickova 1962, pp.187-214; Mares 1894, pp.209-36

P.D.

IV.138
Ca. 1590
Coloured Portrait of Jacobus Handl
Paper, four books of vocal scores bound in leather
19.5 × 16 cm
Ca. 1590
Brno, Moravské muzeum v Brne, Department of Musical History, inv. no. A 20 530
Tenor

Jacobus Handl Gallus (Ribnica 1550-Prague 1591) was a composer of Slovene origin who spent the last six years of his life in Prague as a cantor at the church of St John on the Bank, which is no longer

extant. He published eleven volumes of spiritual compositions at the printing house of Jiří Nigrin, including sixteen masses, 380 motets for the entire liturgical year and lamentations on the Passion. He is also the author of two books of moralia, in which he set Latin humanist texts in the form of madrigals. His compositions were particularly favoured and countless copies have been preserved, including his arrangements for instruments. He was one of the most outstanding composers to have been active at the peak of the Renaissance. His portrait, which portrays him at forty years of age, was painted by an unknown artist in association with the publi-

cation of the fourth volume of Handl's work *Opus musicum* (Prague, 1590).

Cvetko 1972; Racek 1970, p. 195; Snizkova 1985, p. 138ff; Strakova 1982, pp. 85-98; Skulj 1991.

P.D.

IV.139
Imperial Privilege Granted to Print Compositions by Jacob Handl
Manuscript, paper
21 × 32.5 cm
10 March 1588
Vienna, Haus-, Hof- und Staatsarchiv, Impression Kart 27, fols 481–82

At the request of the composer, Rudolf II through the agency of the imperial office granted a privilege to print a collection by Jacob Handl entitled *Opus musicum*. The privilege ("Impressorium pro Cantibus Ecclesiasticis Jacobi Handl) is dated 19th March 1588 and was printed in shortened form in the introduction to the fourth part of Handl's Opus musicum, which was issued by the printing works of Jiří Nigrin in 1590. The imperial privilege banned the printing and duplication of this work for a period of ten years in all the countries where the Emperor was sovereign and in the Roman empire. The granting of a printing privilege in this way functioned like an early form of copyright. Handl's interest in the privilege and his probable personal efforts to obtain it illustrate that as an author he was aware of the substantial popularity of his work and was anxious to limit further dissemination of the work in the form of copies and reprints.

Mantuani 1991, 106; Skulj 1991, 86-89.

P.D.

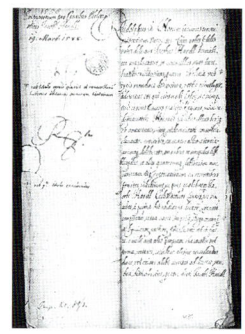

IV.140
Jacobus Handl Gallus
Ribnica 1550–Prague 1591
Moralia
Printed, paper
1596
Nürnberg, Alexander Theodoricus
Prague, Knights' Order of the Crusaders with Red Star, U:N:2, U:N:4

The *Moralia*, a collection by Jacobus Handl, was issued five years after the composer's death by the printing works of Alexander Theodoricus in Nürnberg. It contains forty-seven polyphonic secular compositions of the madrigal type, which the author himself called 'moralia'. The collection is basically related to the content of Handl's edition of *Harmoniae morales* for four voices, which was printed in 1590 at Jiří Nigrin's printing works in Prague. The *Moralia* are intended for eight, six or five voices. Handl's brother, Jiří, who worked as a printer, prepared this edition. The compositions make use of antiquated and medieval aphorisms, which, in Handl's day, were known mostly from anthologies.

Cvetko 1991; Cvetko 1972; Gallus 1995; Gallus 1968; Gallus 1970; Krones 1991/9, pp. 459–70; Lanzke 1964; Skei 1966, pp. 431–47; Skulj 1992.

P.D.

IV.141
Jacobus Handl Gallus
Ribnica 1550–Prague 1591
Copy of *Musica noster amor*
1550–91
Manuscript counterweight to the edition by O. Vecchi: *Piu e diversi Madrigali e Canzonette*, 1594
Book bound by hand in medieval parchment
19 × 16.2 cm; two volumes
Ca. 1600
Jan Jetrich of Zerotin, Benedectine monastery at Rajhrad
Brno, Moravské muzeum v Brne, Department of Musical History, inv. no. A 369

The bundle of prints from Vecchi and the manuscript are a primary source of information. Of the original collection of six volumes of vocal works, only two voices have been preserved to this day: the tenor and the bass. The source has been preserved in its original form, the plates of which comprise parchment leaves of an older antiphonary. The bundle originally belonged to the Straznice branch of the Zerotin family. This edition of Italian secular compositions is regarded as the manifestation of preferred fashion and the establishment of Italian song forms in Central Europe at the end of the sixteenth century. It was published in Nürnberg at the printing house of Theodor Gerlach in 1594. The manuscript part of the bundle contains twenty-two compositions. The fourth and fifth compositions in the manuscript provide the only evidence of the occurrence of *quodlibet* in the Czech lands. The remaining compositions, except the last, are all spiritual motets.

Danek, *Nezname quidlibety ceskeho puvodu, v tisku*; Strakova 1983, pp. 149–80.

P.D.

IV.142
Anonymous copper engraver
Portrait of Jacobus Handl Gallus
Engraving
13.5 × 11 cm
IACOBVS HÄNDL GALLVS DICTVS CARNIOLVS AETATIS SVAE XL ANNO MD.CX.
1590
Prague, Národní galerie v Praze, Collection of Prints and Drawings, inv. no. R 90
158

The musician and composer Handl Gallus first translated his name from Slovenian into German and then Latinized the result. Little is known of his life. He was born in Reifnitz (Ribnica), and sources show that around 1570 he was singing in the chapel in Melk. It seems likely that he was a member of the imperial court orchestra after 1574, and that from 1575 to 1585 he was also a diocesan *Kapellmeister*. Handl Gallus spent his last years at the imperial court in Prague, where he enjoyed a high reputation. In 1588, Rudolf II issued a ten-year decree allowing the publication of his compositions. He is now regarded as one of the most important exponents of the German school of music of the second half of the seventeenth century.

Essen 1988, cat. no. 27, p. 108.

H.H.

IV.143
Commemorative Volume by Vacláv Dobrenský
A Commemorative Piece on Jacobus Handl
Facsimile
1591
Prague, printing press of Jiří Nigrin
Prague, Premonstratensian monastery at Strahov, library, inv. no. f.100

A one-page work was issued by the printing press of Jiří Nigrin shortly after the death of the composer Jacobus Handl on 18 July 1591. The document verifies Handl's friendly relations with the capitular provost, the imperial alms-giver, the poet Salomon Frenzeli and others. A portrait of the composer appears in the left corner. The portrait is known from Nigrin's print of Handl's *Opus musicum*. The authors, who are mentioned only by their initials (M.I.K. Pls., Mart. Gal., J.S.C., J.M.V.), contributed five humanist poems to the volume. The first author is probably Jan Khernerus, the Pilsen rector of a humanist school at St Henry's in Prague. The second is Martil Galli (Havlik), who was the trustee of a school in Zatec and, in 1591, at St Henry's in Prague, then afterwards at Hradec Kralove. The third author was most likely to be Jan Matthiolus Vodnanský, assistant cantor at St Henry's. The last contributor is the brother of Martin Galli, Jan Sequenides Cernovicky, a burgher from Prague's Old Town.

Cvetko 1972, pp. 34–35, 112; *Rukovet humanistickeho basnictvi v Cechach a na Morave*, 2, Prague, 1966, pp. 254–55; Snizkova 1985; Snizkova 1957, pp. 907–908; Skulj 1991, pp. 118–23; Zibrt 1909, p. 100.

P.D.

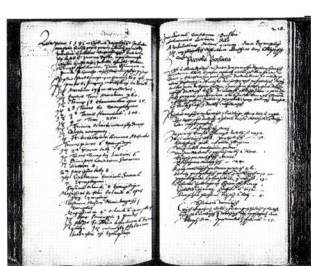

IV.144
Book of Inventories from the Old Town, Prague
List of Unpublished Works by the Composer Jacobus Handl
Paper
33 × 23 × 8 cm
24.7.1591
Prague, Archives of the City of Prague, MS 1173, 235b–236a

Handl died in Prague on 18 June 1591 at the age of forty-one. Shortly after his death, the list of his inheritance appeared, which also served as a list of the musical scores preserved after his death. Jacobus Handl Gallus is identified in the introduction to the list as the cantor at the church of St John on the Bank (thought to have been on the site of what is now the Nazabradli Theatre). The inventory was compiled in the presence of Handl's brother Jiří, who later worked as a printer in Olomouc, and in front of the burghers Tomas Folckman, Jan Suman and the town scribe Pavel Pihavy. It is clear from the list that Handl also traded in musical literature, since a number of titles from his published works have been preserved in many exemplars. The publication of his work runs into hundreds of copies. It was apparently the practice that the author would receive printed copies of his work and would then have to distribute them himself.

Cvetko 1991, pp. 34–36; Cvetko 1972, p. 113; Pesek 1983, no. 3, pp. 242–56; Snizkova 1985, pp. 134–41; Skulj 1991, pp. 140–49.

P.D.

IV.145
Aegidius Sadeler
Antwerp 1570–Prague 1629
Portrait of Kryštof Harant of Polzice and Bezdruzic
Copper engraving
18.3 × 13 cm
Bottom right
1608 (?)
Prague, Národní galerie v Praze, Graphics Collection, inv. no. R 119 770

The versatility and talent of Kryštof Harant of Polzice and Bezdruzic, together with his tragic fate, have ensured this Czech nobleman a place in the annals of Czech history. He was brought up at the court of Ferdinand of the Tyrol in Innsbruck. In 1598 he undertook a hazardous journey to the Holy Lands. On the intervention of Rudolf II he was received into the Estates in 1607. Two years after the death of Rudolf he personally carried the Order of the Golden Fleece to King Philip III of Spain. Between 1618 and 1620 Harant became involved in the uprising of the Estates, for which he was executed at the Old Town Square on 21 June 1621. His mass for five voices has been preserved. This portrait shows Harant, approaching the age of forty, clad in cuirass and wearing a Renaissance collar. His motto is below is portrait: *Virtus ut sol mi chat* (Virtue glows like the sun).

Essen 1988, no. 18.

Buzek 1995, pp. 94–105; Erben 1854, 1855; Nejedly 1921; *Prag um 1600*, Essen, 1988, no. 18; Quoika 1954/4, p. 414; Racek 1970, 1972, 1973; Schebek 1873, pp. 273–86; Volek 1977, p. 118.

P.D.

IV.146, IV.147
Kryštof Harant of Polžice and Bezdružice
Klenove 1564–Prague 1621
Travels or A Journey from the Kingdom of Bohemia
Print, paper, hard plate
1608
Prague, heirs of M. Adam of Veleslavin
Prague, Národní knihovna, inv. no. LIV C 21; Národní muzeum, library, inv. no. 29 D 1

In 1608 a travelogue in two parts entitled *Travels or A Journey from the Kingdom of Bohemia to the City of Venice: From There across the Sea to the Holy Lands* was printed at the workshop owned by the heirs and successors to Daniel Adam of Veleslavin. The travelogue is a compilation of the experiences and incidents of the Czech nobleman Kryštof Harant during his travels in 1598. He undertook the journey with Herman Cernin of Chudenice to see distant lands, and he was able to make use of his experiences in the service of the court. They set out in March 1598 and travelled across Bavaria, the Tyrol and northern Italy to Venice. There they took a boat, sailing across the Adriatic and Ionian seas and the Mediterranean around Crete and Cyprus to reach Jerusalem. They stayed there for some two weeks. In October of the same year they visited the Red Sea and Suez, where they paid a visit to the monastery of St Catherine and went to Mount Horeb. For the return journey, they embarked at Alexandria and reached Venice before Christmas. Harant assembled a great quantity of geographical, historical and ethnological information in his travelogue as well as data on the natural sciences. His narrative even includes music. A print of a motet for six voices provides a special appendix to the first volume, entitled *Qui confidunt in Domino*, which he composed during his stay in Jerusalem.

P.D.

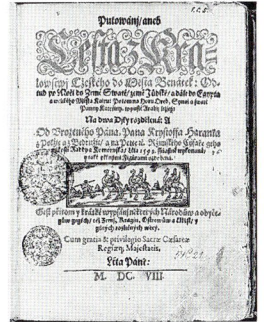

IV.147

See cat. no. IV.146.

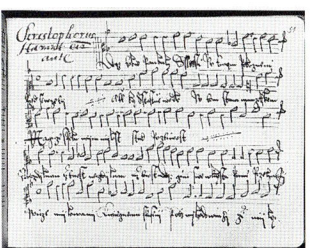

IV.148
Kryštof Harant of Polžice and Bezdružice
1564–1621
Record of a Composition by Kryštof Harant
Paper, leather-bound in pigskin
15 × 21 cm
Beginning of seventeenth century
Ondrej Hornik collection, Civic Depository in Karlin, since 1918 at the Národní muzeum
Prague, Národní muzeum, Museum of Czech Music, inv. no. AZ 37

This slender and inconspicuous manuscript tends to be known by its old designation XIV C 141 and provides one of the most interesting sources of vocal polyphony of Czech provenance. It belonged to an alto who lived in Bohemia, more than likely in Prague, around 1600. The manuscript is a particularly outstanding composition of a repertoire consisting of a set of forty-eight motets and one mass. Two composers are prominent among the authors it contains: the imperial *Kapellmeister* Philippe de Monte, who is represented by fifteen compositions, and the court organist Charles Luython. Four of de Monte's works are uniquely preserved compositions. The last part of the manuscript lists four compositions by Kryštof Harant of Plozic.

Danek 1983, p. 261; Berkovec 1966; Nejedly 1921; Quoika 1954/4, p. 414; Racek 1970, 1972, 1973; Snizkova 1958, p. 16; Snizlova 1980, p. 56; Steinhardt 1979/3, pp. 163–71.

P.D.

IV.149
Kryštof Harant of Polžice and Bezdružice
Klenove 1564–Prague 1621
Der Chrystliche Ulysses
Print, paper
Title page: *Catalogo Collegii Societatis Jesu
Egra inscriptus 1704*
1678
Nürnberg, Wolfgang Moritz Endter
Prague, Národní knihovna, inv. no. 51 B
51

The German translation of the travelogue
*Putovani aneb Cesta z kralovstvi ceskeho
(Travels or a Journey from the Kingdom of Bo-
hemia)* by the Czech nobleman and com-

poser Kryštof Harant, which was originally printed in Prague in 1608, was arranged
by the author's brother Jan Jiří thirty years
after the Czech edition. The edition that
came out in 1673 in Nürnberg at the printing works of Wolfgang Endter contains a
dedication to Leopold I. The translated
version of the travelogue has been supplemented with a chapter that deals with the
life of Kryštof Harant after his return
from his travels up until the fateful year of
1621, when he was executed.

Racek 1973, pp. 181–82; Schebek 1874, pp.
275–77; Zibrt 1890, pp. 363–64.

P.D.

IV.150
Kryštof Harant of Polžice and Bezdružice
Klenove 1564–Prague 1621
Missa quinis vocibus super Dolorosi martir
Manuscript, paper, bundle, two volumes
33 × 21 cm
Beginning of seventeenth century
Wroclaw, Biblioteka Uniwersytecka 50145
Muz.

In 1905 Zdenek Nejedly noticed that a
mass for five voices by Kryštof Harant, entitled *Missa quinque vocum super Dolorosi
martir*, had been preserved in the University Library of Wroclaw. It had been written down in manuscript form at the begin-

ning of the seventeenth century, together
with compositions by Mathias de Sayve,
Philippe de Monte, Charles Luython,
Lodovic Viadana and Orlando di Lasso.
This manuscript was bound with an edition of motets which had been printed at
Magdeburg in 1602 under the title *Opus
melicum*. Harant's mass belongs to the
composition type 'missa parodia'. It was
used as a model for a particularly popular
madrigal, *Dolorosi martir*, by the Italian
composer Luca Marenzia. Harant's mass is
the longest known composition by him
and reveals his undoubted talent. Of the
original collection of vocal scores, only
the tenor and the bass are still extant.

Berkovec 1966; Bohn 1890; Nejedly 1905,
pp. 138–50, 405-415; Prague, 1906, pp.
140–147, 353–56; Racek 1970, 1972, 1973;
Sychra 1910.

P.D.

IV.151
Bundle of Papers from the Library of
J. Carolides
Prague, National Library Se 1337

Four song books from a six-volume set of
vocal polyphonic compositions are held in
the manuscript department of the National Library in Prague. They are part of the
bundles of two Nürnburg musical printed
works from the printing press of Katerina
Gerlach from 1585 and 1588 and a
manuscript. According to a note, the bundles belonged to the library of Jiří Carolides of Carlsberg, who was a humanist
poet. The manuscript part of the bundle

provides a remarkable document of the
repertoire of vocal polyphony cultivated
on Czech territory at the end of the sixteenth century. It contains two motets by
the possessor of the bundles, Jiří Carolides. Compositions by H. L. Hassler,
Chas. Luython, R. Giovanelli and G. Croce
are also represented in the manuscript.
Several anonymous compositions of
Czech origin are recorded there, of which
three are musical arrangements of texts
relating to the characters of Jan Hus and
Jerome of Prague. A number of compositions are of a secular nature. In three cases
a typically humanist text has been set to
music, which is demonstrated not by the

content but by the metrics. The entire
manuscript evidently originated and
served as a private collection of motets for
various – extraliturgical -purposes.

Danek 1983, pp. 257–65; Danek 1981; Fojtikova 1981, pp. 51–145.

P.D.

IV.152
Jiří Carolides of Carlsberg
Prague 1569–Prague 1612
Farrago symbolica sententiosa
Print, paper
16.5 × 20 cm
1597
Prague, printing works of Daniel Adam of
Veleslavin
Prague, Národní muzeum, library, inv. no.
49 F 4

Jiří Carolides, a humanist poet, enjoyed
great popularity among literary and cultural circles in Prague at the time of
Rudolf. He has long been recognized as

the most capable Latin poet of the period,
and his post-war and commemorative
verses spread beyond the borders of the
kingdom of Bohemia. Carolides cultivated
personal relations with a number of characters who were prominent in public life.
His friendly relations with the Literates in
a number of Czech towns are on record. In
Carolides's collections of epigrams, epitaphs, insignia, funebrialia and prefaces
dedicated to his contemporaries we also
find poems which were dedicated to
Czech composers and musicians. Carolides himself was an active composer. A
bundle of printed works and manuscripts
has survived from his library, which con-

tain a motet that he composed. Other
works can be found in Literate manuscripts stored in Rokycany and Rakovnik.
Unfortunately, his works have survived
without a complete set of voice scores.

Branberger 1948, p. 12; Danek 1983/3, pp.
257–65; Danek 1981; Snizkova 1958, p. 14;
Snizkova 1980/1, p. 58; *Poselstvi ducha.
Latinska proza ceskych humanistu*, ed. D.
Martinkova, Prague, 1975, Ziva dila minu-
lost 75, pp. 259–260; *Renesancni poesie*, ed.
H. Businska, Prague, 1975, pp. 164–69;
Trolda 1933, nos 5–6, p. 53.

P.D.

IV.153
Jan Campanus Vodnansky
Vodnany 1572–Prague 1622
Sacrarum odarum libri duo
Printed work, paper, leather bound
1618
Prague, National Library, inv. no. 52 H 2

Jan Campanus Vodnansky became one of
the symbols of pre-White Mountain Bohemia. His entire productive life was
linked to the activities of the University of
Prague and Czech schools. In 1603 he was
called to the university to take up the position of professor of Greek and Latin poetry. He was an active writer even as a stu-

dent and quickly acquired an unprecedented reputation as a poet. He produced
a number of poetry collections, which confirmed his literary talent and composed
music: his *Sacrarum odarum libri duo*, printed by Erasmus Kempffer, appeared at
Frankfurt in 1618. The collection contains
a reprint of his earlier volumes of poetry,
Psalmi davidici and *Odae sacrae*.

Branberger 1942, esp. p. 96; Campanus
Vodnansky 1978; Capek 1942; Kouba
1989, p. 137; Pohanka 1958, no. 94; Postolka 1988, pp. 127–135; Postolka 1970, pp.
107-52; RISM A/I/2, C614; Rukovet humanistickeho basnictvi v Cechach a na

Morave 1, Prague, 1966, p.273.

P.D.

IV.154
Claude Goudimel
1514–72
Psalms or the Songs of St David
Print, paper, covers covered in leather
1618
Prague, the printing press of Daniel
Carolides of Carlsberg
Prague, National Library, inv. no. 54 E 1

In 1564 the French composer Claude Goudimel had an adaptation printed of 150 psalms from the Geneva Psalter, arranged for four voices. His simple, syllabic musical rendering of a Huguenot psalter became a particular favourite and quickly spread throughout the Protestant world. In Bohemia the Prague printer Daniel Carolides of Carlsberg printed this work in 1618. He was the brother of the poet and composer Jiří Carolides. The printing house of Daniel Carolides printed a series of works, remarkable both for their content and their typography. In 1614 he printed *Písně duchovní křestanské* (*Songs Spiritual and Christian*), in 1617 *Nešpory česke* (*Czech Vespers*) and, in 1620, a new edition of a popular hymnbook by Tobias Zavorka. Apart from printing musical works, he also printed political tracts, and as a result of his political involvement at the time of the anti-Habsburg uprising, was forced to leave the country after the Battle of the White Mountain.

Bohatcova 1990, p. 158; Danek 1981; Kouba 1989, p. 115; Kucerova 1986, pp. 71–81; Richter 1933, typewritten; Snizkova 1958, p. 103; Winter 1909, pp. 308, 316.

P.D.

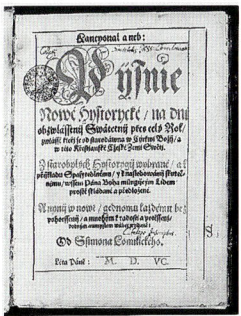

IV.155
Šimon Lomnický of Budeč
Lomnice 1552–Prague ca. 1623
Hymnbook or Songs, New and Old
4#, print, paper
1595
Prague, Jiří Nigrin printing house
Prague, Národní knihovna, inv. no. 54 C37

The hymnbook of Šimon Lomnický is one of the most significant works produced by this versatile pre-White Mountain author. It was printed by Jiří Nigrin in 1595 and dedicated to Zbynek Berk of Duba, who was Archbishop of Prague.

Bohatcova and Hejnic 1981, no. 2, p. 118; Danek 1987, p. 134; *Rukovet humanistickeho basnictvi v Cechach a na Morave* 3, Prague, 1969, p. 208; Knihopis, 4946.

P.D.

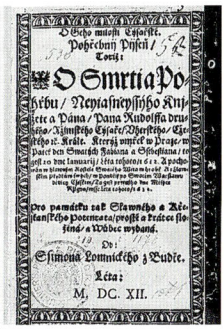

IV.156
Simon Lomnicky of Budec
Lomnice 1552–Prague ca. 1623
Funeral Song for His Imperial Majesty
Print, paper
1612
Prague, Národní knihovna, inv. no. 54 K 1504

Shortly after the death of Rudolf II, Simon Lomnicky of Budec had this title printed at the printing house of Jonatan Bohutsky. It is dedicated to the influential Zdeněk Popel of Lobkowicz, who held the office of high chancellor. In accordance with the tradition of rhyming ditties and ornamental pieces, even the tune to the song has been printed. It was brought out to commemorate 'such a Glorious and Christian Potentate'. The work also contains a portrait of Rudolf II and the coat of arms of Zdenek Popel. The quality and originality of these lines of verse by no means deviate from those of the author's other produced work, although historians of literature have been very critical in evaluating his work's literary merits.

Danek 1990, p. 230; Flajshans 1901, pp. 358–64; Knihopis, 4967; *Rukovet humanistickeho basnictvi* 3, Prague, 1969, p. 208.

P.D.

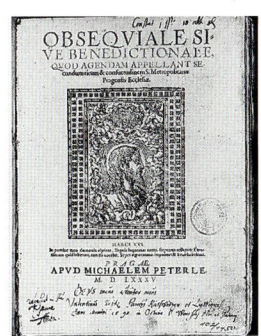

IV.157
Obsequiale sive benedictionale ... s.Metropolitanae pragensis ecclesiae
Print, paper
29 × 21.5 cm
1585
Library at Brevnov monastery
Prague, Národní muzeum, Museum of Czech Music, AZ 55

For almost the whole of the sixteenth century, books in manuscript form had to suffice throughout Bohemia for coverage of this Catholic plainsong. In view of the non-Catholic orientation of the population there was little demand for such a work. Books had been designed for other localities, or liturgical works intended for a Czech diocese but printed at foreign printing houses, were frequently used in the Czech Lands. *Obsequiale sive benedictionale* was one of the first liturgical works of musical notation to be printed in Prague. It was produced by Michael Peterle in 1585. He came from Annaberg in Saxony and had already written himself into the annals of printing history in 1562 when, together with his partner, Jan Kozel, he printed a particularly successful panoramic picture of Prague. He died on 12 September 1588, and his epitaph is preserved at the church of St Stephan in Prague. It was produced at the workshop of Bartholomeus Spranger.

Danek 1990; Janacek 1995, p. 97; DaCosta Kaufmann 1988, p. 264; *Umeni na dvore Rudolfa II.*, Prague, 1988; Novotny 1945; Winter 1613.

P.D.

IV.158
Filip Leuconius
End of the sixteenth century
18.5 × 14.5 cm
Prague, Museum of the City of Prague, inv. no. 10 598

Very little is actually known about the life of the parish priest and composer, Filip Leuconius. Only his work in Sobechleby at around 1590 is documented. We also know that he was the author of a work which came out under the title *Seven Ways of Singing the Litany* in 1608 under the "impress of Nigrin". This edition seems to have been intended as a song for the community and was very popular in its time.

Danek 1987, 135; Knihopis 4.819.

P.D.

IV.159
Song Books of the Rokycany Literates
Paper, manuscript, bundle, bound in parchment
15.3 × 20.5 cm
Front inside page: *Alta Deus frangit, franget quoque mente superbum Franget crede mihi corda superba Deus.* Back inside page: *O: B: M: D: T:, Qui pro vobis effunditur, in remissionem peccantorum, Animas. Requiem aeternam Dona eis Domine Miserere miserere mwi autem vos Amici mei, Smilugte se smilugte se nade mnou aspon wi przatele mogi* (Mercy upon me, have mercy ye who are my companions)
Ca. 1600–1610

Property of the Literate Brethren in Rokycany
Rokycany, Dean's Office, A V 24a – altus

The manuscript comes from a collection of song books which the Literates Brethren in Rokycany used during the pre-White Mountain era. The volume is marked for an alto and is associated with editions of polyphonic compositions for voice (Lasso, Sale). It contains a number of mostly anonymous Czech spiritual motets. The authors listed for some of the compositions were active in Literate Brethren circles. These include Jiří Carolides of Karlsperk, who was also a hu-

manist poet, poet laureate and a former burgher Literate in Prague during the time of Rudolf. He is represented in the manuscript by the two-part motet *Veselte se, křestané, pamatujíc hody slavné* (Rejoice Christians, remember the hour of glory).

Mayrova 1980; Snizkova 1958, p. 14; Snizkova 1980, p. 58; Trolda 1933, p. 53.

P.D.

IV.160
Charles Luython
Antwerp 1556/7–Prague 1620
Introitus; Rorate coeli de super (Chlumec hymnbook)
Paper, manuscript, wooden covers bound in leather, blindstamp, remains of a clasp and sheath
30 × 45.5 cm
On the covers: *Kancional literatsky konwentv chlvmeckeho M: CH: S: VHL: Kvrv borzeyssiho W B L Anno 1593 (?)* (Hymn book of the Literate convent of Chlumec); oldest postscript: *Tento kancionalek ge Wazaney 1593* (This hymn book was bound in 1593); a number of later

postscripts from 1595, 1638, 1639, 1654, 1882. The manuscript was reconstituted evidently for the State Jubilee Exhibition.
1593
Literate Brethren at Chlumec n. Cidlinou, Municipal Museum of Chlumec n. Cidlinou, Prague
Prague, Národní Muzeum, Museum of Czech Music; reg. no. 1/95

The hymnbook was supplied for the Literate Brethren and used up to the nineteenth century. It contains mostly spiritual songs set to Czech texts for five voices. Exceptionally, another repertoire has been recorded here: choral antiphons in

several places, the copy of a song by Simon Lomnicky of Budec and, in one case, an *introit* or entry antiphon for four voices entitled *Rorate coeli de super* by Charles Luython, the imperial organist and composer. Luython's composition was written in the hand of a scribe. The *introit* recorded in the Chlumec hymnbook has survived only in this source.

Trolda 1934, nos 5–6.

P.D.

IV.161
Gradual from the Literates of St Havel
Paper, manuscript
56 × 38.5 cm
1576
Prague, the scriptorium of Jan Kantor the Elder
Prague, Národní knihovna, inv. no. XVII B 19

Apart from printed works and manuscripts which served as songbooks, the Literate brethren also made use of graduals and hymnbooks. These originated in the workshops of professional copy clerks. From the point of view of creativity as well

as their musical and historical iconography, they are among the most fascinating sources from the era before the Battle of the White Mountain. They demonstrate the relatively high standard of illumination work in Bohemia, while providing realistic portraits of burghers and Literates, and documentation of customs, way of life and manner of dress.

Chytil 1906, pp. 191–95; Pesina 1954, p. 279; Jares 1979, pp. 165–75; Urbankova 1975, plate 43; Volek 1977, no. 68; Winter 1909, pp. 196–97.

P.D.

IV.162
Fabián Puléř
Ústí n. Labem ca. 1520–Prague 1562/1563
First Part of the Gradual for the Metropolitan Cathedral of St Vitus
Hymn book in Latin, 273 pages, parchment, original leather binding adorned with ink stamps
Pages 62.8 × 41.0 cm; binding 66.0 × 43.0 cm
1551–52
The Library of the Metropolitan Chapter of St Vitus, MS shelf mark P-10

The large, illuminated hymn books be-

longing to the choir associations of the period, commissioned by both Utraquists and Catholics, are among the most important sources of documented urban culture to have survived from the latter half of the sixteenth century. The gradual was commissioned by members of the St Vitus Chapter and created in the workshop of the humanist Jan Táborský of Klokotská Hora (Tábor 1500–Prague 1572), who was also responsible for looking after the clock on the Old Town Square. At some point during the latter half of the century his workshop began to produce by far the largest number of hymn books. Puléř, the leading illuminator of the day, reportedly

painted fascicules and also collaborated on projects with Táborský, his work representing both a late offshoot of the Danube school of art and a prefiguration of early Mannerist style. The gradual contains nineteen large initials, comprising figurative scenes, ornamental decoration along the edges and a twin portrait of scribe and painter, complete with monograms in the manner of an epitaph (fol. 30).

Kropáček 1988, pp. 199, 203; Vacková 1989, p. 94 (with a review of recent literature).

J.V.

IV.163
A Rebuke by a Literate Choir to Those Who Do Not Know How to Sing, Issued from the Capital City of Prague by the Choir of Tyn Church
Paper glued on to wooden panel
Ca. 1580
Church of St Nicholas in Jaromer
Jaromer, Mestske muzeum

The *Napomenutí literátské* contains principles for singers wittily written in verse form. The singers were from the Literate choir of the church of St Nicholas in Jaromer. The preface to the text was evidently in the form of a set of rules or *Reg-*

ule for choristers and was mentioned by Jan Blahoslav in his work *Musica, to jest knížka zpévákům náležité zprávy v sobé zavírající (Music: A Little Book Containing the Proper Rules for Choristers)* (Olomouc, 1558). The *Rebuke* contains the principles actually used at the time of performing this vocal music. According to the message in the inscription (' ... issued from the capital city of Prague by the choir of Tyn church ... '), it is clear that the principles of interpretation that they elaborated spread and were applied among Czech Literate choirs. They most probably originated from the circle of Literates at the Prague church of Our Lady before Tyn. Various ar-

rangements of them were mentioned in hymnbooks printed in Czech.

110 Years of the Museum of Jaromer.

Danek 1986, pp. 233–43; Hostinsky 1986; Exner 1935, pp. 7–10.

P.D.

IV.164
Song Books of the Rakovnik Literates
Manuscript, paper, leather covers with
blind-stamp
1580–1590
Literate Brethren in Rakovnik
Rakovnik, Okresní muzeum, inv. no. Pr.c.
1967, 1968

The Rakovnik song books were compiled
in the 1580s for the requirements of the
Czech Literate choir there. They were written with great care, and it is probable that
the composer Jan Stefanides Peldrimovsky had a share in initiating them,
since his compositions – with detailed

dedications – dominate the second part of
the manuscript. The texts which lay under
the notation for the majority of compositions were written with remarkable accuracy. Compositions for a Czech text and
by Czech authors dominate the manuscript. The Czech authors are Pavel Spongopaeus Jistebnicky, Jiří Tachovsky, Jan
Stefanides Peldrimovsky and Jiří Cari-
olides. Compositions for six voices were
customary, although in the manuscript we
also find works for two choirs. Detailed
columns of information list the name of
the author, the date of writing, dedications, the number of voices and a series of
other notes. The manuscripts contain only

tenor and bass parts (the remainder of the
voice parts have not survived). The overwhelming majority of the works are spiritual motets, but the manuscript also contains individually preserved secular
motets composed in honour of Rudolf II.

Danek 1981; Konrad 1893.

P.D.

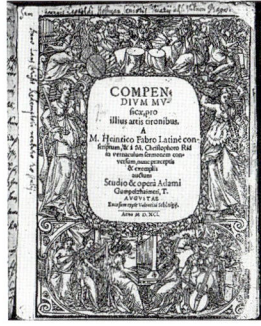

IV.165
Heinrich Faber
Ca. 1500–52
Compendium musicae pro incipientibus
Print, paper
1591
Prague, Metropolitní kapitula u sv Víta,
sign. D.b.s.60

This book by the Wittemberg theorist
Heinrich Faber was one of the most popular practical text books on musical theory
in the sixteenth century. The first issue appeared in 1548. It was mostly used in
schools for the middle grades and was still
in print in the seventeenth century. In

1572 Faber's work was translated into German. That it was twice revised attests to its
popularity: once in 1591 by Adam
Gumpelzhaimer and in 1620 by Melchior
Vulpius.

Meier 1974.

P.D.

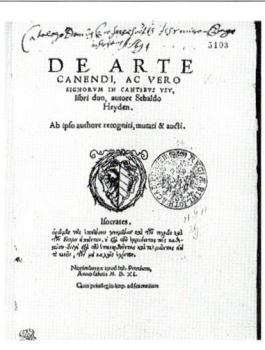

IV.166
Sebald Heyden
Bruck 1499–Nürnberg 1561
De arte canendi
Print, paper
1540
Catalogo Dominus Jessae Societas Jesu ...
Pragae inscriptus 1691
Prague, Národní kníhovna, inv. no. 11 G
11

The musical tract *De arte canendi, ac vero
signorum in cantibus usu, libri duo* was printed in Nürnberg in 1540 at the printing
works of Johannus Petreus. It served as a
popular and much used textbook for

singing, musical theory and composition
throughout the sixteenth century. Its author, the Nürnberg writer, educationalist,
musical theorist and perhaps also composer, Sebald Heyden, came from a flourishing musical family. During his lifetime
Heyden printed several works of musical
theory. The earliest was *Rudimenta* (1529),
which was reworked about three years later and issued under the title *Musicae sto-
icheiosis* (1532). A conceptually more varied
work, *Musicae, id est Artis canendi* (1537),
introduced a series of practical demonstrations as well as a theoretical treatise on
music. *De arte canendi* from 1540 is a reworked version of an earlier work. It con-

tains practical demonstrations from the
work of Ghiseline, Obracht and Senfl as
well as other examples of which it might
be supposed that Sebald Heyden himself
was their author.

Heyden 1972; Riemann 1920.

P.D.

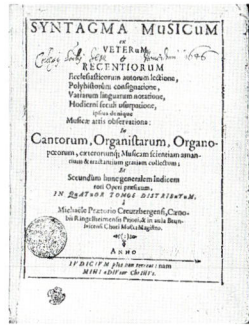

IV.167
Michael Praetorius Creuzburgensis
Creuzburg 1571–Wolfenbüttel 1621
Syntagma musicum
Print, paper, leather plate
22.5 × 17 cm
Collegii Socii Jesu Nova domi 1646
1615–19
Library of the Jesuit College, Jindřichův
Hradec
Prague, Národní kníhovna, inv. no. 11 G 6

Michael Praetorius was one of the most remarkable representatives of that generation of composers who lived and worked
during the transition between the Renais-

sance and the Baroque, observing and
helping to create this stylistic transformation. Praetorius spent almost all his productive life in the service of the arts connoisseur Duke Jindrich Julius of
Brunswick, with whom he often visited
Prague. In the imperial city he came to
know a host of musicians and composers.
He included the most impressive pieces of
information in his work on musical instruments. The first part of his collection
Musae Sioniae appeared in 1605. It was
conceived on a monumental scale and
contained 1244 spiritual compositions of
the motet type. Apart from this, he dedicated himself to writing an extensive theo-

retical work which he called *Syntagma musicum*, arranged into four sections, wherein he attempted to reflect the musical theory, means of composition and praxis of
performance of the period.

Gurlitt 1915; Praetorius 1985; *Prag um
1600*, Freren, 1988, no. 760.

P.D.

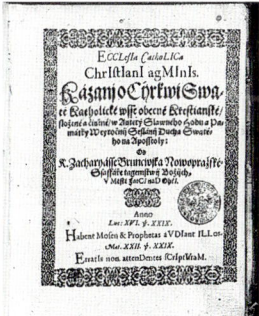

IV.168
*Song on the glorious arrival of Matthias in
Prague*
Paper, print
20 × 16 cm
1611
Prague, Národní knihovna České repub-
liky (National Library), inv. no. 54 B 99

Daněk 1990, p.230.

P.D.

IV.169
Probably from the Schnitzer family workshop
Tenor Shawm with Pirouette
Light-brown polished maple wood (in one piece)
L: 75 cm, diam. of bell (excluding pirouette): 7.8 cm
Two branded symbols
Sixteenth century
Discovered 1812 in Jindřichův Hradec, stored at the Národní muzeum in Prague from 1862
Prague, Národní muzeum, Museum of Czech Music, inv. no. 484 E

Example of a Renaissance woodwind instrument with seven fingerholes, originally with a single key. The note was produced by the vibration of air through a double reed, which was mounted on to a staple and inserted into a pirouette. This tenor shawm produces nine notes from f to f^I.

Permanent exhibition of musical instruments at the Národní muzeum, 1954–90.

Buchner 1952.

B.C.

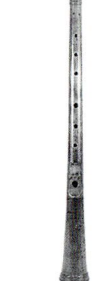

IV.170
Probably from the Schnitzer family workshop
Bass Shawm with Crook
Light-brown polished maple wood (in two sections), brass
L: 106 cm, diam. of bell: 7.2 cm (with more recent crook)
Two branded symbols
Sixteenth century
Discovered 1812 in Jindřichův Hradec, stored at the Národní muzeum in Prague from 1862
Prague, Národní muzeum, Museum of Czech Music, inv. no. 486 E

Example of a Renaissance woodwind instrument with seven fingerholes and one brass key covered originally by a decorative *fontanelle*. The underside of the instrument features brass work. This shawm produces nine notes from d to d^I.

Permanent exhibition of musical instruments at the Národní muzeum, 1954–90.

Buchner 1952.

B.C.

IV.171
Probably from the Schnitzer family workshop
Tenor Shawm with Pirouette
Light-brown polished maple wood (one piece), brass
L: 84 cm, diam. of bell: 7.8 cm (with more recent pirouette)
Two branded symbols
Sixteenth century
Discovered 1812 in Jindřichův Hradec, stored at the Národní muzeum in Prague since 1862
Prague, Národní muzeum, Museum of Czech Music, inv. no. 485 E

Example of a Renaissance woodwind instrument with seven fingerholes and one brass key covered originally by a decorative *fontanelle*. The note was produced by the vibration of air through a double cane reed, fixed on to a staple and inserted into a pirouette. This tenor shawm produces the same number of notes as its twin (inv. no. 484 E) – nine notes in a small octave; it is not possible to overblow this instrument to produce higher notes.

Permanent exhibition of musical instruments at the Národní muzeum, 1954–90.

Buchner 1952.

B.C.

IV.172
Probably from the Schnitzer family workshop
Great Bass Shawm with Pirouette
Light-brown polished maple wood, brass
L: 139.5 cm, diam. of bell: 8.6 cm (with more recent pirouette)
Two branded symbols
Sixteenth century
Discovered 1812 in Jindřichův Hradec, stored at the Národní muzeum in Prague from 1862
Prague, Národní muzeum, Museum of Czech Music, inv. no. 487 E

Example of a Renaissance woodwind instrument with seven fingerholes and a single brass key covered by a decorative brass *fontanelle*, surviving only on this instrument. The double cane reed (staple) was inserted into a pirouette, a wooden lip rest designed to ease playing. The result – as with all shawms featuring pirouettes – was a rather dull-sounding tone. This bass shawm produces nine notes (without overblowing) from B to c^I.

Permanent exhibition of musical instruments at the Národní muzeum, 1954–90.

Buchner 1952.

B.C.

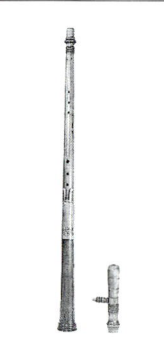

IV.173
Probably from the Schnitzer family workshop
Great Bass Shawm with Pirouette
Light-brown polished maple wood, brass
L: 140 cm, diam. of bell: 9 cm (with more recent pirouette)
Two branded symbols
Sixteenth century
Discovered 1812 in Jindřichův Hradec, stored at the Národní muzeum in Prague from 1862
Prague, Národní muzeum, Museum of Czech Music, inv. no. 488 E

Example of a Renaissance woodwind instrument with a pirouette and double cane reed (staple). This great bass shawm, one of a pair with the instrument registered under inv. no. 487 E, also produces nine rather dull-sounding notes, chiefly in the small octave. Along with seven fingerholes it also has one key, which replaced the damaged or missing original, probably during the nineteenth century.

Permanent exhibition of musical instruments at the Národní muzeum, 1954–90.

Buchner 1952.

B.C.

IV.174
Anonymous
Alto Pommer
Red-brown stained maplewood, brass
L: 75 cm, diam. of the bell: 12 cm
Branded on to the wood: letter 'W' with a little crown
Sixteenth century
Discovered 1812 in Jindřichův Hradec, stored at the Národní muzeum in Prague from 1862
Prague, Národní muzeum, Museum of Czech Music, inv. no. 483 E

Also known as a bombarde, this is an example of a Renaissance double-reeded

wind instrument with six fingerholes and a double brass extension key, which operates inside a slide-on wooden barrel (*fontanelle*) perforated by groups of small holes. The brass S-shape and original double reed, which would have been inserted on to the staple, have not survived as is the case with all the Prague pommers from the sixteenth century. The reconstructed instrument produces eight notes ranging from f to e^I.

Permanent exhibition of musical instruments at the Národní muzeum, 1954–90.

Buchner 1952.

B.C.

IV.175
Probably from the Schnitzer family workshop
Sixteenth century
Tenor Pommer, known as the Nicolo Pommer
Red-brown stained maple wood, brass
L: 108.9 cm, diam. of bell 13 cm
Two branded symbols
Sixteenth century
Probably Nürnberg
Supposedly discovered before 1820 in a parish church in Jindřichův Hradec, stored at the Národní muzeum in Prague after 1820
Prague, Národní muzeum, Museum of

Czech Music, inv. no. 474 E

Example of a Renaissance double-reeded wind instrument with six fingerholes and one double brass extension key covered with a wooden, barrel-shaped *fontanelle*. The corpus is lathed from two sections of red-brown stained maple; the edge of the funnel-shaped bell is finished with a decorative iron ring. The Nicolo tenor Pommer produces eight notes in a small octave: c – c^I.

Permanent exhibition of musical instruments at the Národní muzeum, 1954–90.

Buchner 1952.

B.C.

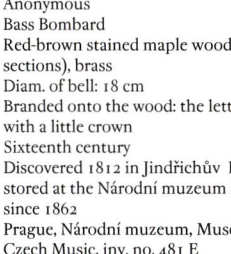

IV.176
Tenor Pommer, known as the Nicolo Pommer
Red-brown stained maple wood, brass
L: 108 cm, diam. of bell: 13 cm
Branded on to the wood: letter 'W' with a little crown
Sixteenth century
Discovered 1812 in Jindřichův Hradec, stored at the Národní muzeum in Prague from 1862
Prague, Národní muzeum, Museum of Czech Music, inv. no. 482 E

Example of a Renaissance double-reeded wind instrument with six fingerholes and

one double brass key covered by a wooden *fontanelle*. Like its twin (with different markings, inv. no. 474 E), this instrument produces eight notes, chiefly in a small octave. The edge of the bell is finished with a decorative brass ring.

Permanent exhibition of musical instruments at the Národní muzeum, 1954–90.

Buchner 1952.

B.C.

IV.177
Anonymous
Bass Bombard
Red-brown stained maple wood (in two sections), brass
Diam. of bell: 18 cm
Branded onto the wood: the letter 'W' with a little crown
Sixteenth century
Discovered 1812 in Jindřichův Hradec, stored at the Národní muzeum in Prague since 1862
Prague, Národní muzeum, Museum of Czech Music, inv. no. 481 E

A unique example of a Renaissance dou-

ble-reeded wind instrument with five fingerholes; the sixth has a key originally covered by a brass *fontanelle*. Another four keys are located on the underside of the instrument, also beneath a large wooden *fontanelle*, part of which has broken off. Although – as elsewhere – the S-shaped staple has not survived, it was still possible to reconstruct the series of notes the instrument would have produced, namely eleven notes, from e^I to a.

Permanent exhibition of musical instruments at the Národní muzeum, 1954–90.

Buchner 1952.

B.C.

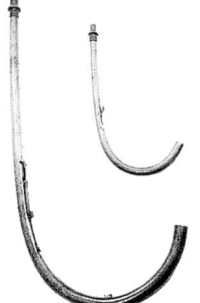

IV.178
Close-coiled Alto Horn
Light brown boxwood, brass
60 × 76 cm
Imprinted on the wood: symbol of a backwards 'S'
Sixteenth century
From a collection of musical instruments housed at the Premonstratensian monastery in Teplá near Mariánské lázne, stored at the Národní muzeum during the years 1950–94
Teplá near Mariánské lázne, Premonstratensian monastery, inv. no. 827

An example of one of the rarer Renais-

sance wind instruments featuring a crook whose corpus is designed in a coil shape. It has six fingerholes on the upper side and one on the underside; the instrument also has a key covered by a brass *fontanelle* beneath which two more air holes are located. The air channel is missing. The reconstructed series of nine notes range from d to e^I.

Permanent exhibition of musical instruments at the Národní muzeum, 1954–90.

Buchner 1952.

B.C.

IV.179
Probably Jörg Wier
Close-coiled Great Bass Horn
Gold-brown polished maple wood, brass
118 × 157 cm, diam. of bell: 5 cm
Branded inscription: two designs of the
German letter 'F'
First half of the sixteenth century
Discovered in 1812 in Jindřichův Hradec;
stored at the Národní muzeum in Prague
since 1862
Prague, Národní muzeum, Museum of
Czech Music, inv. no. 489 E

The distinguishing features of this unique
example of a Renaissance wind instrument with crook are its coiled shape and
six fingerholes in front and one thumb-
hole at the back. It originally had two keys
and pads over the air holes. Only a fragment has survived and a copy was made of
the original. The original crook has not
survived. The reconstructed twelve-note
series covers a range from g¹ to d.

Permanent exhibition of musical instruments at the Národní muzeum, 1954–90.

Buchner 1952.

B.C.

IV.180
Regal
Hard and soft wood, leather, lead, brass
110 × 130 × 90 (including base)
Late sixteenth - early seventeenth century
Originated in Trebon, where it evidently
once served the local church; has been
stored in the Národní muzeum in Prague
since 1951
Decanal office in Trebon; Prague, Národní
muzeum, Museum of Czech Music, inv.
no. 1 330 E, depository inv. no. 982

The regal is a small reed organ from the
Renaissance and Baroque periods whose
sound was produced with a current of air
running through reed pipes ('beating
reeds'), which vibrated against an air slot;
these reeds were housed in lead or pewter
cases. The instrument on display has two
fan bellows marked on the surface with
the capital letters 'A' and 'B'. The keyboard
spans a short octave in the bass and produces a vibrating chromatic series in the
treble, that is, C/E–g², a². This is a unique
example of a portable regal with its stand.

Permanent exhibition of musical instruments at the Národní muzeum, 1954–90.

Hradecky 1974.

B.C.

IV.181
Great Bass Viola da Gamba
Spruce and maple wood
209 × 73 × 24 cm
On upper part of back of instrument:
three rose-shaped carved ornaments resembling the Rožmberk rose
Sixteenth century (supposedly 1579)
The instrument was found in a decanal
office in Trebon after the Second World
War in a bad state of repair. In the Národní muzeum collection since 1951
Decanal office in Trebon; Prague, Národní
muzeum, Museum of Czech Music, inv.
no. 1 329 E, depository inv. no. 981

This great bass viola da gamba, known as
the Rožmberk Bass, represents a unique
example of Renaissance musical culture in
Bohemia. The three Rožmberk roses on
the back of the instrument (upper part)
loosely place it among the group of so-
called Rožmberk *kapelle* – that is, other,
chiefly wind, instruments from this period
of southern Bohemian provenance. This
instrument, originally in an extremely bad
state of repair, was restored by violinmak-
er Karel Pilar in 1952. It has four strings
and F-holes like a violin.

Permanent exhibition of musical instruments at the Národní muzeum, 1954–90.

Buchner 1952.

B.C.

IV.182
Anthoni Bays
*The Conferring of the Order of the Golden
Fleece in Prague, 1585*
Print, paper
1587
Prague, Muzeum hl. m. Prahy, inv. no. 20
859

In 1585 Philip II, King of Spain, conferred
the exceptional title 'Sovereign of the Order of the Golden Fleece' upon Emperor
Rudolf II. The conferment ceremony took
place in Prague and shortly afterwards in
Landshut and the title was bestowed by
King Philip's representative, Archduke
Ferdinand of the Tyrol, who had already received the honour. The ceremony consisted of a number of magnificent and solemn
events which took place in the palace at
the Castle, St Vitus' cathedral, the Castle
Riding School and in specific courtyards.
There was also a great banquet, some
jousting, a firework display and a series of
balls. Archduke Ferdinand was the main
organizer of the event. The entire ceremonial was recorded on paper. A print entitled *Ordenliche Beschreibung mit was stat-
tlichen Ceremonien ...* is of a similar nature
to the present one. It was issued in 1587 by
the printing works of Joannes Mayer in
Dillingen. The course of the entire ceremonial and succeeding events has been
captured in great detail and in a number
of commentaries. The illustrations portray
with remarkable accuracy court musicians
engaged in various musical activities.

Janacek 1987, pp. 255–68; *Prag um 1600*, Essen, 1988, p. 99, cat. no. 8; Vocelka 1985, pp.
84–85; Volek 1977, no. 117.

P.D.

IV.183
Brikcí of Cimperk
Praguc ca. 1530–1599
Table Bell
13 cm, diam: 10 cm
Bronze, cast and chiselled
*IAN ALBIN Z GREIFBERKU, BRYKCY
ZVONARZ Z CYNPERKU* / coat-of-arms
1590
1892 ex coll. Jan Neuberg, Prague
Prague, Uměleckoprůmyslové muzeum,
inv. no. 4521

This table bell with a female nude (and a
pair of shield-bearing knights) is unique
in the thematic repertoire of Czech bell-
making. It was commissioned by Jan
Šturm Albin of Greifenberk, a sometime
teacher at the private school of St Michael
in the parish of Opatovice (from 1564). Of
the three bell-makers who bore the name
Brikcí (father, son, and nephew), the probable creator of the bell is the oldest of the
three masters, who was Albín's coeval and
fellow town councillor of the New Town.
From 1589 onward they were neighbours
in Mikulandská street, and around the
year 1599 they both died of the plague.
The coat of arms with the Czech lion that
appears on the bell was granted to Brikcí
in 1571. In his will, such small table bells
are called *poultry*.

Teige II, 1902; Winter 1909, p. 343 (on
Šturm, see Martínek-Hejnic).

Prague 1891, cabinet XLVI, cat. no. 374;
Prague 1967, cat. no. 264.

D.St.

IV.184
Small Bell
10 cm, diam: 6.2 cm
Cast bronze
Late seventeenth century
1889 gift of A. Borovsky
Prague, Uměleckoprůmyslové muzeum,
inv. no. 3203

A cast bronze bell used for mass, with ornaments and birds.

D.St.

IV.185
Nicolaus Siebenhaer
Ca. 1600
Travel Alarm Clock
Prague, Uměleckoprůmyslové muzeum,
inv. no.32 162

Hour-striking clock with spring-driven escapement and balance wheel set into a
spherical case decorated with stylized, tendril-like floral motifs. The top of the case
has twenty-four little windows displaying
tin rings with two sets of dials I–XII and 1–
12. The rings contain three turning gilded
discs. The outer disc shows two sets of dials 1–12, the central disc with a fixed hand

on the perimeter indicates the date and
the inner disc shows the phases of the
moon.

Prague 1977, cat. no. 15.

Baillie 1969, pp. 291, 357; Uresová 1986, p.
189, fig. 137.

L.U.

IV.186
Master JS
Beginning of the seventeenth century
Clock in the Shape of a Crucifix
Prague, Uměleckoprůmyslové Muzeum,
inv. no. 13 337

Crucifix with chased festoons and rosettes
set on to a rectangular wooden base with
small elliptical windows, supported by
sculptural, tendril-like floral motifs at the
base of the clock. The cross is crowned
with a revolving sphere with a ring showing Roman numerals. The clock is of iron,
with a chiming mechanism and spring-
driven escapement. The inscription *JS* in-

dicates that the clock is the work of Augsburg clockmaker Johannes Schneider, or
of Jobst Schmeller, who travelled from
Augsburg to Prague, where, at the beginning of the seventeenth century, he became a member of the clockmakers' guild.

Prague 1977, cat. no. 19.

Fischer 1963; Baillie 1969, pp. 285, 357.

L.U.

IV.187
Master ZO.MAſ ANO
Tabernacle-style Table Clock
1588
Prague, Národní technické muzeum v
Praze, inv. no. 24 864

A clock dial I–XII, 1–24, is carved on to the
front of the rectangular case; a second dial
for hourly chiming marked 1–12 is carved
on the opposite side with an external pendulum. Each corner is decorated with half
columns and little vases. These surround
an iron bell positioned beneath two cross-
strips with decorative leaves and a little
turret crowning the whole timepiece. Vas-

es and floral motifs are carved beneath the
dials; the sides of the clock depict Adam
and Eve and an allegory of Justice. The
clock is crafted in iron with a spring-driv-
en escapement; the pendulum was added
later. There is an hour-striking mechanism.

Tardy III (1964), pp. 298–318; Michal 1974,
p. 35, figs 10, 11, cat. no. 18; *Katalog Expozice Mereni Casu*, exh. cat. by Michal and
Laboutková (Prague, Národní technické
muzeum v Praze, in preparation).

L.U.

IV.188
Nicolas Plantart
Hexagonal Table Clock
1590
Prague, Národní technické muzeum, inv.
no. 24865

Six-sided clock with pilasters carved in the
corners, a French coat of arms below the
dial, an iron ring with the numerals I–XII,
13–24 and an iron hour hand. The clock
features an ornamental carved dome with
a figure of Judith at the top concealing the
bell. Other decorations include cast figures of the four Evangelists, the Apostle
Paul and King David. This clock is made of

iron with a spring-driven escapement and
balance wheel and it has an hour-striking
mechanism.

Tardy I (1961), pp. 10–22; Baillie 1969, p.
254; Bertele 1969, p. 71; Michal 1974, pp.
34, 35, cat. no. 19.

Michal and Laboutková, *Katalog expozice
merení casu* (Prague, Národní technické
muzeum, in preparation).

L.U.

IV.189
Turret Table Clock
1560
Prague, Uměleckoprůmyslové muzeum, inv. no. 5216

A figure of Diana sitting against a background depicting a castle is carved on the front of a hexagonal case below a dial showing the numerals I–XII. There is an iron hour hand. Other figures of Greek gods – Mars, Pluto, Venus, Saturn and Apollo – are carved on the other sides, set in oval medallions. Amoretti and Greek soldiers are also depicted around the medallions. The clock bell is positioned beneath the ornamental carved dome with a small figure of Cupid at its top. A wreath and cartouche with the year 1560 are carved on the base. This iron clock has an hourly chiming mechanism with a spring-driven escapement. The dial shows a later inscription: *REISS PRAG*. This type of turret table clock began to establish itself in France at the beginning of the sixteenth century. The type was crafted in Paris, Abbeville, Blois, Aix-en-Provence, Beauvais and especially in Lyon, and the masters at all these workshops strove to achieve a perfect mechanism. The hexagonal shape and filigree ornamentation of the dome are typical of the French style; the sides of the case are covered with skilfully carved compositions, based chiefly on the graphic designs of Etienne Delaune.

Prague 1977, cat. no. 3.

Bertele 1969, p. 74, depiction of a similar design bearing the signature of Pierre de Fobis, Lyon; Uresová 1986, p. 99, fig. 53; Poche and Uresová 1987, pp. 30, 161, fig. 5.

L.U.

IV.190
Turret Table Clock
First quarter of the seventeenth century
Prague, Uměleckoprůmyslové Muzeum, inv. no. 606

This clock is rectangular with fluted pilasters, set on a slightly larger base. The base and casing feature carved and embossed floral ornamentation surrounding three rings with numerical inscriptions – 1–12, 13–24 and I–XII – and a chiming mechanism. On the opposite side is a silver ring with a quarter-hour dial and external pendulum. A little gable with corner obelisks is secured to the ledge of the case; inside, a dome with scaled ornamentation is set on to an arcaded tambour, which conceals the bell. This chiming clock is crafted in iron with a spring-driven escapement. Turret table clocks became a tradition in Augsburg and Nürnberg from the mid-sixteenth century until the end of the seventeenth century. They were typical for having the character of miniature works of architecture, with little corner pillars or columns and entablatures, gables and walls covered with floral and figural motifs.

Prague 1977, cat. no. 5.

L.U.

IV.191
Master DK
Table Clock with *Calvary*
Beginning of the seventeenth century
Prague, Uměleckoprůmyslové Muzeum, inv. no. 8420

Cast and chased depiction of the *Calvary* set on a wooden rectangular base which conceals an iron chiming clock with a spring-driven escapement and balance wheel. A revolving sphere with a silver-plated ring carved with the Roman numerals I–XII is secured to the top of the cross. The maker's fondness for astronomy inspired him to connect the clock mechanism with the inside of the globe which, turning by itself, would indicate the current situation of the Earth within the universe. Thus the hour indicator (an arrow) points to the revolving spheres positioned above the slender trunk of a tree, the crucifix or the crown of the Madonna.

Prague 1977, cat. no. 18.

Bertele 1969, p. 238.

L.U.

IV.192
Konrad Seifert of Freibitz – probably
Torsoe of organ cabinet
wood painted and polychrome
268 × 214 × 58 cm
*Lavdate dominum in tympano et choro lavdate cvm in chordis et organo = PSL . CL .
=1606* (text on the carved parapet)
1606
Originally in the château chapel at Krásné Březno, ca. 1900 a gift from Malvin Kolowrat to the Muzeum at Ustí nad Labem. Muzeum města ústí nad Labem, Uÿ 238

Permanent exhibition at Muzeum města ústí nad Labem

Hf.

IV.193
Picture of the Literate Brethren in Prachatice
Oil on canvas
147 × 200 cm
1664
Property of the Office of the Dean in Prachatice, inv. no. 93
Prachatice, Okresni muzeum

The *Picture of the Literate Brethren in Prachatice* shows the choir of the decanal church of St James the Greater. Jan Kulisek, a Prachatice burgher and member of the Literate choir, commissioned it. It presents a very faithful portrayal of the interior of the church as well as portraits of individual Literate members. The choristers are uniformly dressed in fashionable, Spanish-style black cloaks with a frilled collar. The choristers are dispersed into individual vocal groups clustered around one vocal score. At the time of Rudolf, the Prachatice Literates were one of the most renowned choirs in Bohemia. They enjoyed the favour and patronage of Vilem of Rožmberk, who in 1569 conferred guild privileges upon them. At the time of the picture's origin, the Prachatice Literates were divided into choirs singing in Latin and in Czech. The Prachatice fraternity was one of the largest choirs in Bohemia, and it was probably also able to sing arrangements of the multi-choral music of the late Renaissance. The painting also shows two organs, which have not survived.

Die Musik in Geschichte und Gegenwart, vol. 13, Kassel, 1966, p. 800; Emingerova 1909; Jares 1979, p. 2; Padrta and others, *Jihoceska vlastiveda – Hudba*, Ceske Budejovice, 1989; Pesina 1954, p. 279; Volek and Jares 1977, no. 73; Winter 1913, p. 173.

P.D.

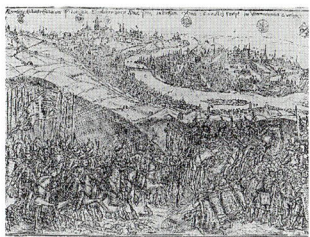

IV.194
*Aingentliche Abkunterfactus der weit-
berumte kunglichen Haupt Stadt Prag ...*
1608
Paper
21.2 × 30.8 cm
1608
Prague, Muzeum hl. m. Prahy, inv. no.
1914

This anonymous copper engraving portrays the arrival of the Hungarian king
Matthias in Prague in 1608. Matthias is
accompanied by a group of Hungarian
lords. The Czech Estates, one of whom
bears the royal crown, are welcoming

him. There are military heralds on horseback between the two groups. At the back
of the scene there is a view of Prague
from Strahov all the way to Vysehrad.
This view is a copy of Willenberg's *View of
Prague* dating from 1601. The emblems of
the individual Prague townships are set
below the inscription. The scene acts as a
successful demonstration of the use of
so-called signal music.

Hlavsa 1971, pp. 145–83.

P.D.

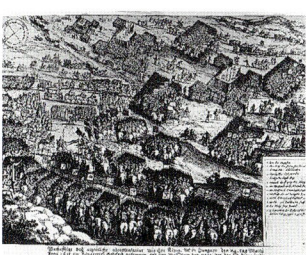

IV.195
Rafael (?) Sadeler
Welcoming of King Matthias
Copper engraving, paper
29.5 × 43 cm
Description of events at the bottom be-
low the small frame; explanations in the
lower right corner
1611
Prague, Archives of the City of Prague,
AMP 1603

This engraving depicts King Matthias being welcomed to Prague on 24 March
1611. The entire scene is filled with military units paying homage to Matthias.

Shortly after this portrayal of Matthias's
arrival in Prague, an assembly of the Estates of the Bohemian Crown took place,
which led to the abdication of Rudolf II,
thereby putting an end to the dynastic
dispute between the Habsburgs.
Matthias was crowned Czech king in May
of the same year. Several groupings of
military trumpeters and drummers can
be made out among the military units.
The largest group is situated in the centre of the action. According to Zibrt's *Bibliografie ceske historie* (*Bibliogaphy of Czech
History*), this engraving was used to illustrate a publication by Jiří Zaveta of Zavet-
ic, *Vypsani slavneho prijezdu knizete*

Matyase do Prahy (*Excerpts of the Glorious
Arrival of Prince Matthias in Prague*).

Hlavsa 1971, p. 161 and photo.

P.D.

IV.196
Matthäus Gundelach
Kassel ? ca. 1565/67–Augsburg 1653/54
Adoration of the Shepherds (after
Bartholomeus Spranger and Jan Muller)
Oil on beechwood panel
49.5 × 34.3 cm
Monogram on a stone in the lower cen-
tre: *M.G.*
1606
1912 in the collection of Graf Buquoy in
Prague; 1945 from Rožmberk castle in
southern Bohemia.
Prague, Národní galerie v Praze, inv. no.
DO 4 577

Gundelach's painting was made after a
relatively large engraving (1606) by Jan
Muller, which in turn was after a design
by Spranger that has survived and is now
in the Albertina in Vienna (inv. no. 13
260). Other artists were attracted by the
atmospheric lighting of this work and
made many copies. This colourful version
by Gundelach was presumably a commission. Whatever the case, this painting
provides valuable information on Gundelach's development as an artist, while
at the same time also indicating the level
of cross-fertilization that prevailed
among the various artists at the court of
Rudolf II. There are records of a compan-

ion piece, *The Adoration of the Kings*, in
Rožmberk castle in southern Bohemia,
but this has apparently been lost since
1945 (Bender 1981, p. 216, no. GC 17).

Prague 1912, no. 44; Prague 1938, no. 981;
Essen 1988, no. 120.

Bender 1981, pp. 157ff., no. GA 1 (with
earlier bibliography); Kaufmann 1985,
pp. 221ff., no. 5–1 with ill.; Kaufmann
1988, p. 180, no. 6–2; *Prag um 1600*, vol. 1,
1988, pp. 230ff., no. 120 (Jürgen Zimmer).

J.Z.

IV.197
Paulus van Vianen
Utrecht ca. 1570 – Prague 1613
Concert on Mt Parnassus
Pen drawing in brown with black-brown
wash
14.6 × 19.8 cm
Beginning of seventeenth century
Vienna, Albertina, Graphische Samm-
lung, inv. no. 8389

On Mt Parnassus the nine Muses are
playing musical instruments; similar instruments are also lying on the ground.
In the hilly landscape we see listeners, including Apollo, Orpheus, Pan and one of

his companions. From below the clouds
Juno, Minerva and Venus are watching
together with Amor; winged Pegasus
hovers in the sky. This sheet is very characteristic for van Vianen's style of drawing after 1600. The elongated figures with
their graceful posture meet the ideals of
Mannerism, which Rudolf II particularly
appreciated and which were also applied
by other contemporary artists at the imperial court. The landscape is depicted
very naturalistically; Paulus van Vianen
drew intensively from sketches he had
made. Although it is possible to see a
clear stylistic relationship between the
drawings and the silver plaques, the lat-

ter are often executed in a more traditional way. A good example of this is the
relief with *Minerva and the Muses* (ca.
1604), where the figures still show the
typical features of the Italian Renaissance
(Ter Molen 1984, no. 79).

Utrecht 1984–85, cat. no. 34; Essen and
Vienna 1988, cat. no. 658.

Gerszi 1982, no. 66; Ter Molen 1984, no.
287.

J.R.tM.

IV.198
Paulus van Vianen
Utrecht ca. 1570 – Prague 1613
The Judgment of Midas
Chalk drawing, white-lead coating, grey
wash, grey paper
39.7 × 49.2 cm
Ca. 1605
Everard Jabach collection
Paris, Louvre, Cabinet des Dessins, inv.
no. 21449

The subject of the painting is the judgment of Midas (Ovid, *Metamorphoses* XI,
146–193). In a rocky landscape, Apollo
plays a zither. Among the listeners are

Midas, turned towards Pan, and the God
of the Mountains Tmolus, who holds a
sceptre in his hand. In the left foreground are depictions of the Muses with
their attributes, and also of the goddess
Minerva. Although the conception of the
characters and of the group of trees is
characteristic for Paulus van Vianen's
style of drawing after 1600, the composition itself is clearly influenced by the
graphic work on the same subject by the
Haarlem Mannerist Hendrick Goltzius.
Various components of this composition
appear in identical form on a 1605 plaque
of the same subject (Ter Molen 1984, no.
80). Since the drawing is stylistically very

close to the artist's work from the following years, it is quite possible that it is not
a sketch for the silver relief, but a later
variation on it.

Utrecht 1984–85, cat. no. 47; Essen and
Vienna 1988, cat. no. 662.

Gerszi 1982, no. 74; Ter Molen 1984, no.
293.

J.R.tM.

IV.199
Rudolfine Master (? Alexander Wiskemann)
Minerva and the Muses
Oil on canvas
132.7 × 205.5
Ca. 1609
Since 1841 in the Premonstratensians' collection
Prague, Picture Gallery of the Monastery of the Premonstratensians at Strahov, inv. no. 0999

This voluminous picture stems from Spranger's composition of the same subject, documented in a drawing at the Albertina museum in Vienna, although mediated through a workshop replica from Düsseldorf. The painter set the scene in a charming landscape, animated by painstakingly painted animals, flowers and even fruit. It seems that at the imperial court he acquainted himself not only with Spranger's work but also Aachen's and Stevens' landscapes. He paid great attention to musical instruments: apart from the four Muses, a further two putti are devoted to making music. The picture is a possible allegory of Music or Sound. He displays all he is capable of in this picture: he has mastered the human form, the face and the treatment of drapery. He is also a

competent landscape painter. It could have benn Alexander Wiskemann, a painter from Eschwege whose two drawings (Kunsthalle Bremen, inv. no. 771, Perseus with the Head of Medusa, signed and dated in Prague; inv. no. 336, Allegory of Painting) bear a striking resemblance to the Strahov picture, in the aspects of the face, the sharply curving drapery and in the well accomplished landscape background.

Fučíková 1979, p.503, ills 18, 19.

E.F.

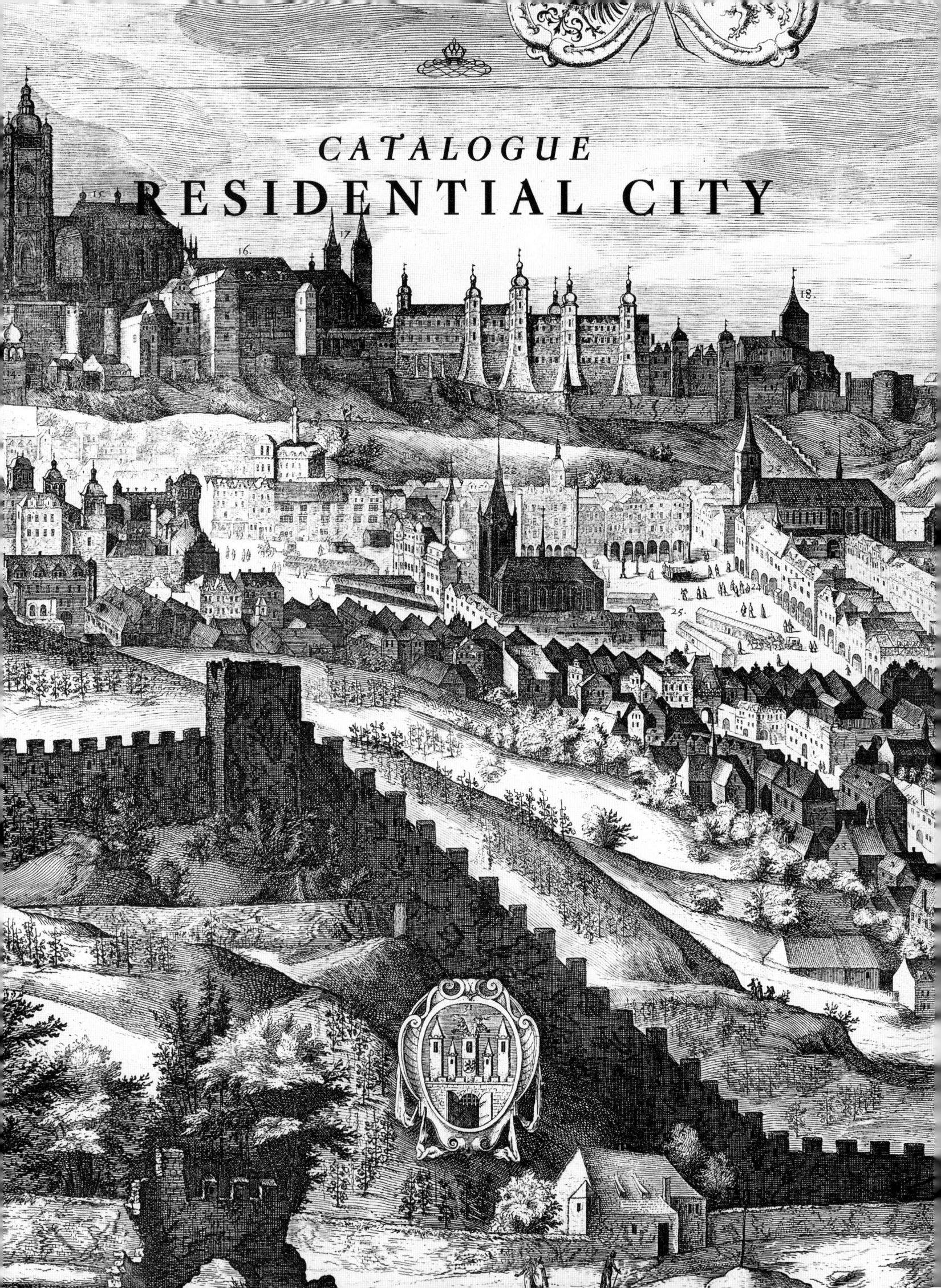

CATALOGUE
RESIDENTIAL CITY

Section V: Prague – Residential City, 1550–1650

HELENA KÖNIGSMARKOVÁ

During the course of one century the three Prague towns experienced unprecedented development, from the arrival of the Renaissance when the city's horizons were broadened under the Italian influence and the universal richness of culture during the Rudolfine era, to the radical political, religious and social changes after the Battle of the White Mountain. This exhibition at the Wallenstein Palace was conceived from a cultural-historical point of view; it should bring to life the most important historical events, characterize the individual strata of society and outline the development of learning, culture and art from the Renaissance to the early Baroque. It brings together works of art and objects which were part of the everyday life of the burghers, the largest stratum of this society, the nobles, who were the politically most important figures, and the Protestant churches and the reforming and gradually more aggressive Catholic church which finally became the main bearer of approaching Baroque culture.

The multi-functional nature of Prague was a specific feature of the city during the reign of Rudolf II. It was the seat of the Holy Roman Emperor and the Czech King, the central offices of the Utraquist and Catholic churches within the re-established archbishopric and the centre for both university and Jesuit education.

Prague at that time was a city which welcomed people of different nationalities. Apart from Czechs and Germans, there was also a fairly large Italian community and a number of Dutch representatives. The Jewish community in the Prague ghetto fulfilled a considerable economic and intellectual role. Thanks to an earlier tradition, the Prague environment was relatively tolerant to differing religions until the dispute between the ruler, the estates and the towns escalated into open conflict.

The cultural life of Prague, however, was greatly influenced by the art and learning of the artists and scientists gathered around the imperial court whose activities also spread to the noble and burgher environments with which they had daily contact. After the unsuccessful rebellion of the Czech estates against the Habsburgs, the country was marked by a radical re-Catholicization and restructuring of the whole of society. One of the results of this phenomenon was heightened cultural activity on the part of the Catholic church, which governed the university and chose to present its important social role through the fine arts. The objects exhibited from museum and castle collections today provide us with a three-dimensional picture of an eventful era in whose animated cultural life Czech culture of the following centuries laid its roots.

V.1
Aegidius Sadeler
Antwerp 1570-Prague 1629
Hans van Aachen
Portrait of the Emperor Rudolf II
Copper engraving
34 × 25 cm
S. C. Mtis. pictor Iohan ab Ach Inuentor;
AVGVSTISSIMO, INVICTISSIMO, SAPI-
ENISSo, ET FELICISSo ROM: IMPERA-
TORI, RVDOLPHO II. DNO SVO
CLEMENTISSIMO, GRATVLATIONIS,
FIDEI, ET SVBIECTIONIS SPECIMEN
HVMILLIME DICAT, CONSECRAT, PER-
PETVVS CLIENS AEGIDIVS SADELER.
ANNO M.D.C.III.; RVDOLPHVS II. RO-

MANORVM IMPERATOR AVGVSTVS:
REX HVNGARIAE, BOHE: ETC.
1603
Prague, Národní muzeum, inv. no. H2-26
646

See cat. no. I.353.

V.P.

V.2
A Central European Artist
Portrait of Ferdinand II
Oil on canvas
Before 1604
Private collection, USA

This portrait depicts Ferdinand II when he was still Archduke and a representative of the Styrian branch of the Habsburg royal family. He became head of the family in 1596 and remained so until elected Emperor in 1619. (He became King of Bohemia in 1617 and King of Hungary in 1618). This very dignified portrait is the work of a painter who was well acquainted

with court art. It is conspicuously reminiscent of Aachen's portraits and is painted in a spare and reserved manner without being too preoccupied with the subject. It lends itself to comparison in particular with a portrait of Ferdinand by Joseph Heintz the Elder from 1604, with its excellently painted details in a classic exquisite portrait (Vienna, Porträtgalerie, inv. no. 3480).

E.F.

V.3
Lukas van Valckenborch
Panorama of Prague from Petřín Hill
Oil on wood
62 × 89 cm
Ca. 1580
Prague, Muzeum hl. m. Prahy, inv. no. 20
685

This depiction of Prague is known as the Vratislav Prospect, i.e. from the hills over Smíchov. The first such view appeared in 1562. This spot offers a vivid view of the River Vltava meandering in three bends, and unambiguously emphasizes their function in shaping the city. The entire

southern edge of the territory is shown, with the cathedral of St Vitus jutting out against the background of the hilly regions of Bohnice and Dáblice. The Prague Lesser Town and the boroughs on the eastern bank of the Vltava are seen less clearly. The picture provides an overall view of the city in the landscape with more than documentary accuracy and detailed information.

Kropáček 1995, 5.

I.M.

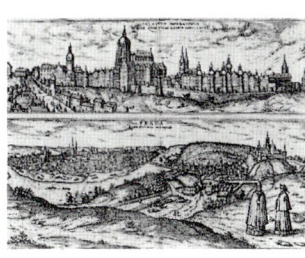

V.4
Jan Kozel and Michael Peterle
View of Prague
Woodcut
55.7 × 196.5 cm
Praga Bohemiae metropolis accuratissime expressa 1562
Prague, Správa Pražského hradu, b. č.

This wide vista is an irreplaceable source of information about the exact appearance of the urban landscape. It depicts the Castle before the decisive building action of the Rudolfine era and gives an accurate view of the state of building at that time, at least concerning the Castle's south side

which faces the town. Certainly, in this view, we see both the extent of the south rampart and the palace by the south tower with three roofs, with the vertical axis towards the front and also the chisel-shaped roof of the gate along the White Tower, by which entry to the Castle from the west was gained.

Essen and Vienna 1988, cat. no. 1.

Novotný 1946, 15; Hlavsa 1971, 147.

I.M.

V.5
Franz Hogenberg, after Joris Hoefnagel
1540-90
Prague Castle and a View of Prague from Letná Plain
Copper engraving
51.2 × 38.8 cm
1598
Above: *PRAGA*, the coats of arms of the empire, the kingdom of Bohemia and the individual municipal boroughs of Prague; in cartouche form, bottom left: *NO-*
BILIBUS AMPLISSIMIS PRUDENTIS-
SIMIS PRIMATIBUS CONSULIBUS
SENATORIBUS METROPOLITANAE
TRIURBIS PRAGAE DEDICAT SAC.

CAES MAI. SCULPTUR AEG SADELER
MDCVI; bottom left: *SAC. CAES. EXCU-*
DIT. PHILIPPUS VAN DEN BOSCHE Sac.
Caes. Mai. phrygiarius designavit. Johannes
Wechter aeri icidit.
Purchased in 1958 in Prague
Prague, Uměleckoprůmyslové muzeum, 47 790
Prague, Archiv hl. mesta Prahy AMP 26

For discussion see cat. no. III/235-236

Kozák 1983, 381-390.

R.V.

v.6
Jan Willenberg
Trzebenice, near Wroclaw 23 June 1571–
Prague 1613
View of Prague
Woodcut on paper
Drawing 13.7 × 37.8 cm; sheet 19.9 × 37.8
cm
J. Willenberg fecit 1601
1601
Prague, Národní muzeum, H2-63 707

See cat. no. III.237

Novotný 1945, 20; Essen and Vienna 1988,
cat. no. 4.

V.P.

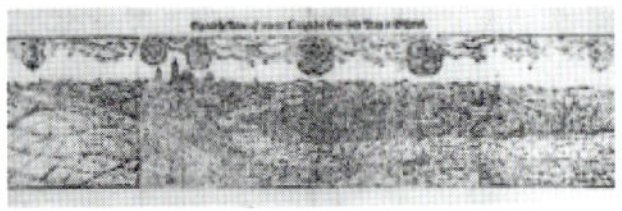

---

v.7, a
Johannes Wechter and Philipp van den
Bossche
View of Prague (known as Sadeler's
Prospect)
47.3 × 316.8 (48.5 × 317.8) cm
*NOBILIBUS AMPLISSIMIS PRUDEN-
TISSIMIS PRIMATIBUS CONSULIBUS
SENATORIBUS METROPOLITANAE
TRIURBIS PRAGAE DEDICAT SAC.
CAES. MAI. SCULPTOR AEG. SADELER
MDCVI, vlevo dole: SAC. CAES. MAI. PRIV-
ILEGIO EIUSDEM MAI. SCULPTOR
AEGEDIUS SADELER EXCUDIT. Philip-
pus Van den Bosche Sac. Caes. Mai. phrygiar-
ius designavit. Johannes Wechter aeri icidit.*

1606
Prague, Archiv hl. města Prahy, sbírka
grafiky, 26

See cat. no. I.321

v.7, b
Philipp van den Bossche
View of Prague (fragment)
Göttingen, Kunstsammlung der Univer-
sität

This drawing of part of the New Town was
a study for Sadeler's Prospect, made by
van den Bossche, the court embroidery
artist. He applied his ability to capture the
minute details of individual buildings.
The view is a detailed and faithful study of
Prague from around 1600. The artists Johannes Wechter, who was an engraver,
and van den Bossche, who drew the model, chose the same angle for the view from
Smíchov as Peterle and Willenberg, who
were view artists. Unlike the views of Jan
Willenberg and Joris Hoefnagel, this one
portrays the ground-plan of the town.

Essen and Vienna 1988, cat. no. 5.

Novotny 1946, p.22; Hlavsa 1971, p.149.

J.R.

---

v.8
Roelandt Savery
Kostrijk 1576–Utrecht 1639
View of Prague
Pen drawing in brown ink, green, brown,
blue, pink and yellow wash
37 × 49.6 cm
Copenhagen, Statens Museum for Kunst,
Kobberstiksamling, inv. no. Tu 86/4

Savery chose an unusual position for this
view of the Prague Lesser Town, from Letná Plane. From there he portrayed the
Písek Gate, on which stood what is today
known as Klárov. Behind this lies part of
the Lesser Town, where the Valdštejn
Palace was built in the 1620s. The left is
dominated by the enormous church of St
Thomas's, which was an important centre
for the Lesser Town catholics at the time.

M.Š.

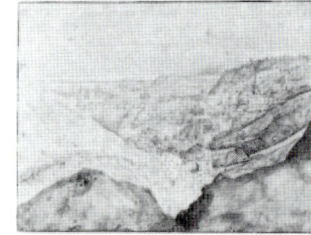

---

v.9
Roelandt Savery
The Vicinity of the Lesser Town Square
Drawing in ink, wash
16.8 × 23.8 cm
Ca. 1608
Leipzig, Museum der Bildenden Kunste,
1417

In his drawings Savery depicted the interi-
or of Rudolfine Prague in detail. In this
drawing he portrayed the site of what is today called Malostranské náměstí (Lesser
Town Square) from its south-western aspect and looking north-east. Merchants'
stalls are positioned in the foreground; in
the centre the narrow tower of St
Nicholas' church is perceptible. The ostentatious house, depicted in images of the
fall of the Pasovsky family in 1611, contrasts with the untidy surface of the
square.

Essen and Vienna, cat. no. 254.

M.Š.

---

v.10
View of Prague
Copper engraving on paper
Print 22.2 × 33.2; sheet 29.4 × 35
After 1611
Prague, Národní muzeum, H2-27 128

The reduced copy of Sadeler's Prospect,
the closest in time to its model, shows the
Malá Strana, Hradčany and part of the
New Town. The artist did not use the view
from the original prospect showing the
layout of the city. A drawing of the Passau
foot and mounted company heading towards the city gate can be seen in the lower left-hand corner. Unlike in the original,
a rectangular plate with the name of the
city, in the style of Benedetto Battini, is positioned in the centre and the wind rose
has been moved to the lower right-hand
corner.

Novotný 1945, 23-24.

V.P.

V.11
Václav Hollar
Prague 1607–London 1677
Four Early views of Prague: Below Letná
Plain, Prague's Old Town, Šítkovské Mills in
Prague, A Prague Neighbourhood
Etching
5.1 × 7.1 cm; 4.9 × 7.2 cm; 4.2 × 6.1; 4.1 × 5.9
cm
Na R 50 765 datace 1626
Prague, Národní galerie v Praze, R 50 765
- R 50 768

These views are among the earliest depictions of some Prague nooks and corners. They were etched before the artist left Prague. The landscape they depict is accurate in its topographical details and is still of an ideal nature. The artist depicted some Prague motifs in a similar way in the series known as *Ten Small Views* from 1628.

Hollar NG 1969; Hollar NG 1983.

Parthey 1853; Hollar 1858; Borovsky 1898.

J.R.

V.12
Václav Hollar
Prague 1607–London 1677
Two Views of Prague, Etchings from the Cycle
'Amoenissimae Aliquot Locorum'
Etching
6.2 × 10.1 cm.
First sheet marked: *WHollar Pr: Boh. inv. I.*
Heyde exc.
1629-1634?
Prague, Národní galeri v Praze, R 50882,
50887

First sheet: The first etching from the cycle *Ten Small Views*, published by Abraham Hohenberg. The engraver must have mechanically copied the drawing on to the plate, because the image is reversed on the engraving. Hollar etched this engraving during his stay in Strasbourg or in Cologne. The models for it were probably drawn during the artist's stay in Prague in 1626.

Second sheet: Hollar's etching from the cycle *Ten Small Views* shows the Smíchov Mills in Prague. The author has clearly drawn on a graphic work with a similar subject from the so-called *Seven Views* cycle (R 50874, P 776).

Prague 1969; Prague 1983.

Parthey 1853; Hollar 1858; Borovský 1898.

J.R.

V.13
Václav Hollar
Prague 1607–London 1677
View of Prague
Pen drawing with watercolour. Nineteenth-century montage.
12 × 27.9 cm; 12.1 × 28.1 cm
At bottom left: *W. Hollar delin. in Augusto*
1636. Praga Bohemiae Metropolis.
1636
Praha, Národní galeri v Praze, K 33 360
(Spr 273)

The view is taken from the summit of Petřín. The drawing was produced by Hollar on the basis of the sketches which he had made during his stay in Prague in July 1636. The foreground of the drawing is brought to life by two men, observers in period costume. The brilliant and lively drawing captures the whole panorama of the city with a certain nostalgia. In 1649 Hollar issued an etching in Antwerp based on this drawing, but with several changes: for instance, he chose a view from a higher point, omitted the figures in the foreground and added topographic information.

Prague 1977; Prague 1983.

Sprinzels 1938; Kesnerová 1977; Denkstein 1977.

J.R.

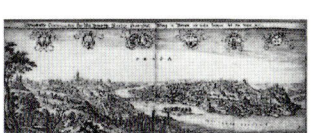

V.14
View of Prague
Copper engraving on paper
25.0 × 69.7 cm
Wahrhaffte CONTRAFACTUR Der Weit
Berühmbten Königlichen Haupt Statt Prag
in Böhmen, wie solche Jetziger Zeit Im wesen
steht
1649
Prague, Národní muzeum, Department of
Early Czech History, inv. no. H2-27 094

Sadeler's Prospect (cat. no. V.7/1-2) was copied many times. In 1649 *Archontologia cosmica* by Johann Ludwig Gotofred (real name Johann Philipp Abelin) was published by M. Merian in Frankfurt. It included the present reduced and slightly revised copy made by an unnamed artist.

Novotný 1945, 22-31.

V.P.

V.15
Fall of the Passau Army
Copper engraving and etching
29 × 37.3 cm
Einfahl des Passavischen Kriegsvolcks in die
Kleine Statt
Prag Anno MDCXI den 15. Februarii
1611
Prague, Národní galeri v Praze, inv. no.
DR 4806

The work appeared in an edition by Wilhelm Peter Zimmermann: *Relatio, Ausführlicher Bericht, was sich mit dem Passavischen Kriegvolk* (Augsburg, 1611) and later in the seventh volume of Khevenhüller's *Annales Ferdinandai* (Regensburg, 1643). Both variants concur in the basic composition of the scene and in their documentary details but significantly vary in the level of artistic treatment of the subject, which is much greater in the Regensburg print. The light on the engraving is actually imaginary, since, although it comes from the south, it falls from a disproportionate height. The engraving is of significant documentary value, as proved by the legend in the bottom left corner, which contains twenty-six entries. The view includes the area around the main square and illustrates well how it was originally closed off on the southern side on the site of what is today a dilapidated house. It accurately depicts the south-facing façades of Mostecká, Trziste, Ostruhová and Thunovská streets. Unfortunately, however, almost nothing of the original estate of Valdštejn Palace is portrayed. Nevertheless, it is possible to compare the engraving with the view known as Sadeler's Prospect from 1606.

Essen and Vienna 1988, cat. no. 6.

Novotny 1946, p.22; Hlavsa 1971, pp. 157-8; Spicer 1982, pp. 544-562.

I.M.

V.16
The Desolation of the Church of Charlemagne and the Monastery on Karlov in 1611 (Engravings).
16.5 × 18.3; 21 × 18.5 cm.
Prague, Archiv hl. mesta Prahy, inv. no. 359.

In the series of engravings of events from the invasion by forces from Passau in February 1611, the view with the monastery at Karlov is notable for its full portrayal of the stormy times. Under the Latin title 'Representatio excidii Caes. Regiaeque Canoniae Canonicorum Regul Later. Ord. S. Augusti Neo Pragae in Car-

low' there is an explanatory inscription in Czech, in which the author's gloss is put on the event, when 'this canonry of Karlov with the canons of the Lateran Order of St Augustus was by the heretic horde utterly surrounded and destroyed...' In addition there is a German text on the engraving. The same scene is depicted in the Church of Our Lady of the Snows, but here the church is moved back in order to develop more fully the scene of the plunder of the church possessions, the torture of Abbot Kašpar Tschepl and the killing of monks. These horrors are offset by a celebration with a barrel of wine, and the demolition of the monastery buildings. Here too

there is a sharp discrepancy in proportions between the figures depicted and the size of the architectural forms.

Hlavsa 1971, 159.

J.R., I.M.

V.17
Plundering the Church of St Mary of the Snows and the Franciscan Monastery in 1611
Copper engraving
17.5 × 26 (18 × 28.2) cm
Adii den 15 Februari Anno 1611 ist zwischen 16 und 17 Uhr in der Neustatt Prag das Kloster S. Maria nivis geplindert und gestirmet worden von gemeinem Pefel oder leichtfertigen gesindl, auch deren 14 Priedern erbermbliche ermertet worden, wie ordentlichen verzeichen ist; bottom right corner: *S.A.S.*
1611
Prague, Archiv hl. mesta Prahy, inv. no.

AMP 1704

Prague engravings show the significant events in the turbulent life of the city after 1600. During the attack by the Passau troops there was plundering in St Agnes' Convent and in the convent at Karlov, but most attention was provoked by the attack on the church of St Mary of the Snows, where fourteen Franciscan brothers were killed. The engraving shows them being thrown from the roof and the tower. The drama is increased by the vertical format, which allows good use of the surface to be made for the heightened construction of the church's choir. For the publication by

Wilhelm Peter Zimmermann, *Relatio, Ausfuhrlicher Bericht, was sich mit dem Passavischen Kriegsvolk, Augsburg 1611*, the scene was modified into a horizontal format, showing the surroundings and even more distant parts of Prague. The composition and perspective of the engraving are subordinated to a convincing portrayal of the dramatic event, with the proportion between the figures and the building being considerably exaggerated.

Hlavsa 1971, 159.

I.M., Prk.

V.18
The Sacking of the Convent of St Agnes in Prague, 15 February 1611
Copper engraving on paper
Engraving 20 × 19.4 cm; sheet 22.1 × 19.8 cm
1611
Prague
Prague, Národní muzeum, inv. no. H2-26 666

Soukupová 1989, 233-34.

V.P.

V.19
Allegory of the Counter-Reformation
Oil on canvas
70.5 × 83.0 cm
On the book at bottom right (in ligature): *HVA* (Despite the inscription, the painting is not by Hans von Aachen)
Between 1610 and 1620
Graz, Landesmuseum Joanneum

The silhouette of Hradčany Castle in the background is evidence that the artist responsible for this painting must have been working in Prague during the first decade of the seventeenth century. Neither the style of brushstroke nor the man-

ner of the composition would suggest that the work was by Hans von Aachen. The artist was probably a city painter who had adopted the figurative styles and compositions used by the court painters. The painting is very interesting from the point of view of its iconography. As long as the main figures depicted in it remain unidentified, it is not possible to discover the precise message the painting was intended to convey. However, it appears to be an allegory in which both the empery and the papacy are represented as the guardians of peace, prosperity and art. Although imperial allegories were relatively common in court art, references to the church were

rare. The painting must have been made during the reign of Matthias, who acquired the crown thanks to an alliance with the papal court.

Suida 1923, p. 52, no. 117.

E.F.

V.20
Defenestration of the Imperial Governors on 23 May 1618
Etching
30.4 × 37.5 cm
Wahre Contrafactur wie die Kayserl: Räthe zum Fenster...
1646
Prague, Památník národního písemnictví, GKF 7304

This anonymous engraving, illustrating Khevenhüller's *Annales Ferdinandei IX* from 1646, shows the defenestration of the imperial governors William Slavata of Chlum and Košumberg and Jaroslav

Bořita of Martinic on 23 May 1618 from the Czech Chancellery. The engraver reproduces the historical event without too much precision, as the protagonists are not individualized in the engraving. He selected the most dramatic moment of the whole event, the defenestration itself, which representatives of the Estates are performing from two windows. The third man being held in the middle of the room by two members of the Estates opposition should be the secretary Filip Fabricius, who followed his superiors out of the window because of disrespectful behaviour. However, his dress suggests that he could be one of the other two governors present

(Adam of Šternberg or Děpolt Matthew of Lobkovicz), who were spared defenestration by the Estates. The drama of the event is underlined by the armed and active groups of Estates representatives in the doors of the room.

Janáček 1978, 145.

J.R.

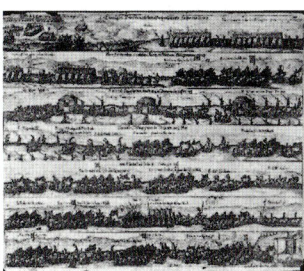

V.21
E. Kieser
Triumphant Entry of Frederick of the Palatinate into Prague, 31 October 1619
Copper engraving
29.8 × 36.5 cm
Centre bottom: *Eb. Kieser f.; Einzug des Durchleuchtigsten Grossmächtigen Fürsten und Herren...*
Praha, Muzeum hl. města Prahy, inv. no. 1910

This engraving from the book *Gewisse Beschreibung dess... Einzug zu Prag* depicts in four strips the triumphal entry of the 'Winter King' Frederick Palatine and his wife into Prague on 31 October 1619. In the first strip we see three companies of soldiers dressed in the spirit of the Kingdom in 'Hussite' style, with flails and longshields. In the second are cuirassiers' and arquebusiers' cornets, in the third the coach of the Empress and her retinue and in the fourth the Directors of the Kingdom and the Bohemian knights.

J.R.

V.22
E. Kieser
The Coronation of Frederick Palatine on 4 November 1619
Copper engraving
26.7 × 36.8 (30.3 × 36.8) cm
Eigentliche Contrafactur aller enderschiedlichen Acten, wie der Durchleuchtigste und Grossmachtige Furst und Herr, Herr Friedrich der 5. Pfalzgrave bey Rhein, Churfurst, Hertzog in Bayern etc. den 4. Nov. Anno 1619, zum Konig Boheim ist gekront worden.
Prague, Archives of the City of Prague, 1608b

This appeared in an edition entitled *Gewisse Beschreibung des Ansehnlichen Einzugs zu Prag, so geschehen den 21. altes n. 31 Octobris Newes Calenders. Praag 1619.* The author divided the sheet into ten unequal sections. In the centre is a view into St Vitus' Cathedral during the coronation. Individual details of the coronation with a brief commentary are depicted in seven smaller sections around the central scene. Portraits of Frederick Palatine and his wife, Elizabeth, are located in the left and right corners at the bottom. The lower part of the field contains a description of the coronation and an enumeration of the most important figures present.

Hlavsa 1971, p.179.

Prk.

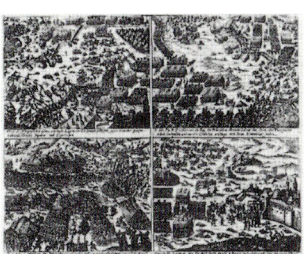

V.23
Battle of the White Mountain, 8 November 1620
Etching
27.5 × 33.1 cm
Albie in A. ist Eigentlich Zusehen
1627
Prague, Památník národního písemnictví, GKF 7287

This engraving (published by R. Sadeler) comes from the work of Caspar Entz, *Fama Austriaca...,* published in Cologne in 1627. The Battle of the White Mountain, with its onset and its results, is shown in four fields: in the first is the arrangement of the enemy camps before Rakovník, in the second and third is the Battle of the White Mountain itself and in the last is the entry of the Imperial troops into Prague. The Battle of the White Mountain is also to be found on other engravings, such as the illustrations in the publication *Ober und Nieder Enserisch wie auch Böhemisch Journal* (published by Rafael Sadeler, engravings attributed to Jan Sadeler) or on an anonymous engraving with the inscription *DELINIATIONIS ACIEI ET PUGNA AD PRAGAM BOHEMIAE METROPOLIM FACTAE* (after the engraving of Jan Sadeler from 1621).

J.R.

V.24
Rafael Sadeler
The Carmelite General Dominic de Jesu Maria and the Battle of the White Mountain
Copper engraving
28.8 × 15.4 cm
REVERENDUS PATER, FRATER DOMINICUS DE IESU - MARIA TARRACONENSIS. Ord. B. Virg de Monte Carmelo fratrum Carmel. praep. gener. qui pugna Pragensi interfuit Ao. SaC. MDCXX. VIII
Ca. 1624
Prague, private collection

The General of the Carmelite Order, Father Dominic Scalza de Jesu Maria, was confessor to the imperial army which took part in the Battle of White Mountain. According to legend, before the crusade on White Mountain in 1620 he found a desecrated picture of the *Adoration of Christ* in the courtyard of Strakonice Castle, which was in Protestant hands. He stirred the imperial generals to courageous action just before the battle by hanging the picture on his chest. Father Dominic took the picture to Rome in 1622 where, unfortunately, it was destroyed by fire in 1833. Numerous copies succeeded it and may be found, for example at the pilgrim church of Our Lady on White Mountain, at Our Lady of Victories in the Lesser Town or at the church of St Prokopius in Strakonice. Father Dominic was often painted, for example in the picture by Matyáš Mayer dating from 1627-37 in the church of Our Lady of Victories or in the fresco of Václav Vavrinec Reiner (1728) on the dome of the chapel of St Felicián in the pilgrim church of Our Lady the Victorious on White Mountain.

Royt 1996.

J.R.

V.25
Execution on Old Town Square, 21 June 1621
Etching; trimmed paper
27.8 × 31.5; picture 27.3 × 31 cm
EXECUTION. So zu Prag den 21. Junii 1621...
1626
Prague, Památník národního písemnictví, GKF 7288

This engraving from the book *Österreichischer Lorberkrantz Oder Kayser, Victori ...,* published in 1626 in Frankfurt, shows the main events connected with the execution, on 21 June 1621, of participants in the anti-Habsburg revolt. The engraving is divided into three strips. The first, narrower, strip depicts the transmission of the verdict to the condemned men by Prince Charles of Liechtenstein, and their wives and children begging for mercy. The action continues in the bottom strip, where the condemned are taken from Prague Castle to Old Town Square and imprisoned there. The central strip then depicts the execution itself in two episodes, and, in the third box, the heads of the executed men, placed on the Old Town bridge tower as an example.

Petráň 1971.

J.R.

v.26
M. Merian, after Karel Škréta
1610-74
The Siege of Prague by the Swedish Army in 1648
Copper engraving
29.7 × 58.5; 33.5 × 59.4 cm
1662
Prague, Národní galeri v Praze, inv. no. R88 929

A period print documenting the political events of the Thirty Years' War at the Battle of the White Mountain. In *Theatrum Europeum*, his sixth work, Merian issued two engravings after a design by Karel

Škréta entitled *Wahrer Abriss...der beyden Koniglichen Haubt-Alt und Newstatt Prag....* The second engraving bears a more laconic title in its upper part: *Besturmbung der Prager Statte 1648.* The elevated viewpoint of the engraver from the site of what is today called Vinohrady corresponds with the direction of the attack but it also provides the opportunity to show the entire defence lines of eastern Prague from the Porícská Gate as far as Karlova street. Unlike the print of White Mountain, which is rather concentrated on the schematic composition of the main armies and their positions, the view taken at the threshold of the Baroque is much more dramatic. It

makes use of a more vigorous perspective and contains sharper contrasts in the depiction of individual moments of the battle, including details of soldiers and weapons.

Hlavsa 1971, p.177.

I.M.

---

v.27
Figures of a Drummer, an Officer, and a Musketeer from the Thirty Years' War
Pen-and-ink drawing on paper
10,1 × 20,6 cm
After 1633
Původ: recorded into the files from the old, unregistered funds of the Národní muzeum in 1965.
Prague, Národní muzeum, inv. no. H2-125 821

The drawing, which depicts typical figures of soldiers in the Thirty Years' War, imitates the small copper engravings of the *Military Exercises* cycle by Jacques Callot,

1631-1632. Callot depicted the various mercenaries who were training with weapons in the area of Nancy at the time with documentary and didactic objectivity. The cycle of thirteen small works of graphic art, each of which depicts a trio of individual figures about 2 centimetres high, was perhaps intended for use in instructing children. The Museum's drawing appropriates and slightly modifies figures from various works in the cycle and is also executed on a larger scale. It is not a work by Callot himself, for his sketches are executed mostly in white or red chalk. It was apparently drawn by one of Callot's students or imitators fairly soon after the

creation of the cycle itself.

L.Sr.

---

v.28
Václav Budovec z Budova
28 August 1551–21 June 1621
Diarium
Paper codex, 1247 ff., decorated cover in white leather with imprint date 1617, damaged in places
17 × 21 × 13 cm
Původ: Originally in the private library of Václav Budovec. Reached the collections of the Národní muzeum as a gift. Flyleaf contains an ex-libris of the owner, Jan Jůsko, chaplain in Krumlov, dated 20 September 1882
Prague, Národní muzeum, inv. no. H3– Rkp, 28

Diary of the famous humanist, traveller and theologian of the Unitas Fratrum, who was executed in Old Town Square on 21 June 1621 for his part in the Estates Revolt. In the journal Václav Budovec recorded events, especially those concerning religious matters, along with theological tracts ('What is the Antichrist?', 'On six common causes of heresy'). Important, for example, are his notes on proceedings concerning the Imperial Charter on Religious Freedom and the subsequent settlement (f. 560 ann.: 'Acta, or a sure and truthful record of all matters occurring with regard to religion in the presence of all three Utraquist estates at the Old Town

Rathaus in the year of our Lord 1609').

I.Č.

---

v.29
Mikuláš Dačický of Heslov
1555–1626
Memoirs
Autograph, 155 pages in fol., paper; original parchment binding (fragment of Czech missal)
28.5 × 18 cm (closed book)
1619–20
Prague, Národní muzeum, inv. no. VC 11

Athough an Utraquist, M. Dačicky of Heslov, an arms-bearing burgher from Kutná Hora, received a Latin education at the monastery in Kladruby. In his native town he lived from his family estate and

held no office. Towards the end of his life he dedicated himself to his handwritten book, in which he include both an 'extract for the notes of his ancestors' and his own chronicles and extensive memoirs. The collection is made up of an introduction and 15 sections; it does not proceed in a consistently chronological order. It included Czech, Central European and Kutna Hora information and events from the period 929 - 1626. The most recent records are valuable for their characterful perceptions, judgments and fears about the future of the kingdom; they are an expression of patriotism. The many parts of the text which are crossed out testify to the author

and his descendants' fear of divulging its contents. The greater part of the manuscript is carefully corrected and includes attempts at initialling.

Bartoš, 1926, 258, č. 1361.

J.Kr.

---

v.30
Abraham Bruyn
Antwerp 1538/39-Cologne? 1587?
Imperii ac Sacerdotii Ornatus
Album of 50 copper engravings on paper, neo-renaissance binding (design by Karel Spott 1902)
35 × 25 cm
1578
From the collection of Jan v. Spott, donated by Spott to the museum collection in 1934
Praha, Uměleckoprůmyslové muzeum, inv. no. 20 329

The album is made up of two collections

of 24 and 26 pages, depicting the dress mainly of German and south European noblemen, burghers, monks and representatives of secular and church powers, proceeding to the vestments of the Roman Emperor and King, the Spanish King Philip II, and others. The copy in the Museum of Decorative Arts has lost its title page with the impress and Bruyn's dedication to the Archbishop of Cologne. Some pages were included in other editions of Bruyn's costume pictures; we can find for example the dress of Czech and Silesian burghers in the Brussels publication of 1581, *Habitus varriarum gentium.*

Saur, 614; Wurzbach I, 214; Hollstein IV, 7.

R.V.

V.31
Bartoloměj Paprocký of Hloholy and of Paprocká Vůle
1540/43-1614
Diadochos, id est Successio, jinak Poslaupnost knížat a králův českých, biskupův i arcibiskupův pražských a všech třech stavův slavného Království českého, to jest panského, rytířského a městského, krátce sebraná a vydaná
Print on paper, woodcut decoration, binding originally pigskin
33 × 20.5 cm
Inscriptions and notes: woodcuts with the monograms *VS* (Virgil Solis junior ?), *CE*, *JW* (Jan Willenberg)

1602
Obtained through transfer from the Museum of Decorative Arts Library (inv. no. 1400/1892).
Prague, Uměleckoprůmyslové muzeum, inv. no. G 110 B

The author was of Polish origin, arriving in Moravia in 1588 as a political refugee and later moving to Bohemia. He dedicated his best-known historical and educational work to the Emperor Rudolf, from whom he received financial support. The book is richly provided with illustrations (symbols of countries, pictures of rulers, battles and historical scenes, coats of arms and portraits of noblemen and church dignitaries).

Knihopis 6843.

R.V.

V.32
After conferring with the imperial ministers at the Czech congress, Rudolf II decrees that all purchases of gold and silver goods, precious stones and furs be taxed in the amount of one-tenth their purchase price to help fund the war against the Turks
30 June, 1601
Paper, original, printed seal of Rudolf II under paper cover
52 × 37 cm
Prague Castle
Prague, Státní ústřední archiv, Sbírka patentů, 171

Patents, or 'open papers', were something between documents and letters. They were used primarily for issuing orders (mandates). Owing to the numbers of patents required, they were printed on the printing press shortly after it was invented. Printed patents were secured with a printed seal and many examples bore the signature of the monarch, chancellor, vice-chancellor and secretary; others had a printed signature, if only as a facsimile. From the beginning, patents were used by the financial offices responsible for taxes, which were collected in the war effort against the Turks in the amount of ten per cent on the purchase price on luxury goods. Various jewels and precious metals were documented in the texts, as were pearls and precious stones, medals and buttons, 'trinkets', glass ornaments which today would be considered costume jewellery, crystal and jasper tableware, fabrics of woven gold and silver, and even lynx and reindeer pelts. This patent features the signature and seal of Emperor Rudolf along with the signatures of Stephen [Jiří] of Šternberk, Chamber President; Kašpar Kaplíř of Sulevic, Chamber vice-president and their secretary.

Kulířová–Sander 1956.

K.B.

V.33
Document by Which Rudolf II Declares his Abdication
Czech, original, parchment, seal of the printer originally attached to a chord has come apart and been lost.
42 × 31.5 cm
23 May 1611
Prague, Archiv hl. města Prahy, inv. no. AMP PGL 1-62A

A result of the power struggle within the Habsburg family first came with the fall of the faction of the Rudolf II's cousin, Leopold, Bishop of Passau, from January–March 1611. The latter had a secret pact with Rudolf to weaken the unified uprising of the Czech Estates and to bring an end to the aspirations of Rudolf's brother Matthias. This unsuccessful act ended with Bohemia being plundered. In Prague only the Lesser Town and the Castle were occupied and the action provoked a decisive rejection of the Estates' position towards Rudolf. Matthias exploited the opposition of the Estates to denounce Rudolf, who finally abdicated. After his death on 20 January 1611, Matthias ascended to the throne. The abdication took the form of documents, which were sent to the most important members of the nobility and the largest towns. In the document Rudolf II steps down from the throne and relieves all three Estates in the kingdom of Bohemia of their subjection to the king. It is recalled that he had spent his best years among them, that for thirty-six years he had governed them and been resident in the kingdom and that 'during the time of his kingship the kingdom had enjoyed long and prosperous peace and had greatly flourished'.

Prague 1938, cat. no. 361; Prague 1966, cat. no. 116.
Čelakovský 1886, p. 503,

J.Hr.

V.34
Halberd
Weaponry work, steel, wood
total length: 213 cm; axe with hook: 20 cm
Producer's trademark branded on to the wood
End of the sixteenth century - beginning of the seventeenth
Plzeň, Západočeské muzeum v Plzni
inv.n. Z 542

Long weapon of the imperial guard, also used by the Plzeň town guard.

F.F.

V.35
Flag of the municipal militia of Prague New Town
Oil painting on silk damask
105 × 91 cm
1604
Presumably produced in 1604 in Prague, where it was later looted by the Swedish army during their attack on the city in 1648. Later it was deposited in the Swedish royal palace. From 1817 it was in the Riddarholmskyrkan, from 1907 in the Livrustkammaren and from 1960 in the Armémuseum.
Statens trofesamling, Armémuseum, Stockholm, inv. no. ST 8: 107

A fragment of a cavalry flag, probably two-pointed (known as a swallowtail). The original flagpole and spike have been lost. The front of the flag has the motif of the two-headed imperial eagle, while its upper edge has the legend: RUDOLPH II IMP: SEMP (sempiternus = eternal) and the year 1619. Immediately under the heads of the eagle is Rudolf's device AD SIT (Auxilium Domini Sit Inquis Terror). On the back of the flag, bearing the arms of the New Town, is the incomplete text: [IN-GIG]NIA NOVAE VRBIS PRAGENSIS and again 1619. On both sides of the flag the year 1619 has been painted over the original year 1604, which suggests that the old Rudophine flag became relevant again during the short rule of Frederick of the Palatinate.

Stockholm 1992.

Turek 1991.

E.T.

V.36
Standard of the Malá Strana cavalry
Silk, embroidery, appliqué
55 × 55 cm
1637-46
Acquired from the presidium of the
Prague Council
Prague, Muzeum hlavního města Prahy,
inv. no. 2 268

The standard of the Prague Malá Strana
cavalry reflects the organization of the
military defence of the Prague towns.
From the early Middle Ages Prague defence had been organized according to
town quarters: in Old Town there were the

quarters of Týn, Linhart, Mikuláš and Havel. Malá Strana had its own military organization. This dispersion of forces of the
town was in effect well into the seventeenth century. Monogram *F III* (Ferdinand III) has provided a reliable date for
the Malá Strana standard.

Schallaburg 1989, cat. no. 4, 11.

J.D.

V.37
Master of the mint Konrád Sauermann
Ducat of Ferdinand I
Gold, coinage
2.14 cm, 3.505 g
1541
Prague, Národní muzeum, inv. no. H5-14
879

On 21 September 1537 Ferdinand I pronounced his basic agreement with the setting up of a royal mint in Prague. Work began there in 1539. Gold was minted for the
first time in 1540. Because of a shortage of
rare metals, the operation of the mint was
closed down in 1542. According to the ac-

counting of Konrád Sauermann, master of
the mint, between 1539 and 1542 a total of
15,263 ducats, 1,367 thalers and 12,936
Prague groschen were issued by their
workshops in the Hankas House on the
corner of Celetná Street and the Fruit
Market in the Old Town of Prague.

Nohejlová 1929, pp. 82-104; Nohejlová
1929; Nohejlová 8, 1932, pp. 74-78; Halačka 1987, pp. 32-33 (no. 6).

E.Š.

V.38
Master of the mint Konrád Sauermann
Prague groschen of Ferdinand I
Silver, coinage
2.12 cm, 2.308 g
1539
Prague, Národní muzeum, inv. no. H5-34
670

Silver coins - Prague groschen, thalers and
quarter-thalers dated 1539 - are the oldest
coinage of the Prague mint set up in the
time of Ferdinand I. According to the accounts of Konrád Sauermann, master of
the mint, during the first period of activity
by the mint (up to 1542), 305 talents and

13 half-ounces (approximately 77 kilo-
grams) of silver were obtained for the
minting of silver coins. This explains the
meagre number of coins produced, and
their present value.

Nohejlová 1929, pp. 82-104; Nohejlová
1929; Halačka 1987, p. 41 (no. 27).

E.Š.

V.39
Master of the mint Ludvík Neufahrer
Thaler of Ferdinand I
Silver, coinage
4.05 cm, 28.723 g
1557
Prague, Národní muzeum, inv. no. H5-38
136

No coins have survived from between
1542 and 1557 which would be evidence of
the activity of a Prague mint, apart from
ducats which, as before 1540, were minted
under the administration of the supreme
master of the mint or other royal official
(not the Prague master of the mint). It was

not until 1557 that the mint came into operation again. The minting of thalers and
their parts (half-thaler, quarter-thaler)
took place yearly until the introduction of
gulden currency in 1561. The silver from
which they were made came from mines
around Příbram, České Budějovice, Tábor,
Ratibořice, Nalžov, Slavkov and Stříbrná
Skalice. Apart from silver from the mines,
varied pagament (precious metal from
jewelry and outdated currency) came to
the mint from a number of individuals.
The die for the first minted thaler of this
period was made by Michal Hohenhauer.

Nohejlová 1929; Halačka 1987, p. 36

(no. 12).

E.Š.

V.40
Master of the mint Ludvík Neufahrer
Half-thaler of Ferdinand I
Silver, coinage
3.49 cm, 13.973 g
1558
Prague, Národní muzeum, inv. no. H5-38
149

Halačka 1987, pp. 37-39 (no. 20).

E.Š.

V.41
Master of the mint Ludvík Neufahrer
Quarter-thaler of Ferdinand I
Silver, coinage
2.87 cm, 7.036 g
1558
Prague, Národní muzeum, inv. no. H5-37
332

Halačka 1987, pp. 39-40 (no. 25).

E.Š.

V.42
Master of the mint Jan Harder
Gulder (60 kreutzers) of Ferdinand I
Silver, coinage
3.64 cm, 24.473 g
1561
Prague, Národní muzeum, inv. no. H5-34
687

After the passing of what is known as the third imperial regulation of coinage in Augsburg on 8 August 1559, which became applicable in Bohemia on 1 August 1561, the Prague mint, as the first in Bohemia, began to strike - in place of the hitherto leading silver nominal, the thaler (mass 29.40 g; quality 0.930; silver content 27.37 g) and its parts - the gulder (60 kreutzers; mass 24.62 g; quality 0.931; silver content 22.89 g) and its parts (30-kreutzer and ten-kreutzer pieces). Their issue marked the peak of Ferdinand I's attempts to unify minting in the lands of the Habsburg confederation and in the wider area of central Europe. Between 1562 and 1564 Czech gulders and their parts were issued in Prague to a value of 72,132 × three score of groschen. The die for minting was supplied by Mates Doctor of Linz.

Nohejlová 1929; Halačka 1987, pp. 42-43

(no. 30).

E.Š.

V.43
Master of the mint Jan Harder
Half-gulder (30 kreutzers) of Ferdinand I
Silver, coinage
3.11 cm, 12.091 g
1564
Prague, Národní muzeum, inv. no. H5-37
334

The half-gulders of Ferdinand I, like the gulders, were made continuously in the Prague mint from 1561 to 1564.

Halačka 1987, pp. 43-44 (no. 34).

E.Š.

V.44
Master of the mint Jan Harder
Ten-kreutzer piece of Ferdinand I
Silver, coinage
2.61 cm, 4.038 g
1564
Prague, Národní muzeum, inv. no. H5-37
335

Ten-kreutzer pieces of Ferdinand I from the Prague mint are known from 1562, 1563 and 1564.

Halačka 1987, pp. 45 (no. 35).

E.Š.

V.45
Master of the mint Jan Harder
Two-kreutzer piece of Ferdinand I
Silver, coinage
1.96 cm, 1.559 g
1562
Prague, Národní muzeum, inv. no. H5-37
826

At the same time as the striking of gulders and their parts, the Prague mint began to include new small kreutzer nominals: the two-kreutzer piece (mass 1.504 g; quality 0.500; silver content 0.752 g) and the kreutzer (mass 0.960 g; quality 0.380; silver content 0.373 g). Whilst two-kreutzer pieces are known from 1561, 1562, 1563 and 1564, the kreutzers were struck without a date. Gulders and their parts and the small kreutzer coins were the first coins in this country to be issued with a numerical value marked on them.

Halačka 1987, pp. 45-46 (no. 37).

E.Š.

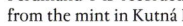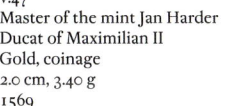

V.46
Master of the mint Jan Harder
White coin of Ferdinand I
Silver, coinage
1.26 cm, 0.413 g
1561
Prague, Národní muzeum, inv. no. H5-38
082

Between 1561 and 1564 some small one-sided white coins were struck in Prague, whose abundant issue during the reign of Ferdinand I is recorded as being mainly from the mint in Kutná Hora.

Halačka 1987, p. 47 (no. 39).

E.Š.

V.47
Master of the mint Jan Harder
Ducat of Maximilian II
Gold, coinage
2.0 cm, 3.40 g
1569
Prague, Muzeum hl. města Prahy, inv. no.
18 087

Prague ducats from the reign of Maximilian II are known only from a few years (1566, 1568, 1569 and 1574). Like the ducats of Ferdinand I from the beginning of the 1560s, they do not bear the portrait of St Václav with the corresponding legend SANCTUS WENCESLAUS DUX BOEMIE, which had been used on Czech gold coinage from the time of Václav IV. Instead of this the reverse bears the quadripartite Czech-Hungarian symbol with the Czech lion in the centre of a scutcheon (on a ducat from 1574 with the divided scutcheon of Austro-Burgundy) and in the case of dies from 1569 (and similarly on a Ferdinand ducat of 1562) surprisingly bear the legend SANCTUS LADISLAUS REX, which is the typical symbol of the Hungarian ducat. But we also find this on dies from mints in Vienna, Linz and Graz, which simulate Hungarian ducats. Mates Doctor, when he prepared the die for the ducat of 1562, clearly kept to these models, as did the Jáchymov cutter Nikl Milicz, in preparing the stamp for the reverse side of the ducat in 1569.

Nohejlová 1930, pp. 74-79; Halačka 1987, pp. 103-104 (no. 169).

E.Š.

V.48
Master of the mint Jan Harder
Gulder (60 kreutzers) of Maximilian II
Silver, coinage
3.75 cm, 24.45 g
1566
Prague, Muzeum hl. města Prahy, inv. no.
19 024

During the reign of Maximilian II the minting of gulders in the Prague mint continued to 1569. None is known from later years. The production of the mint was ensured in the 1560s mainly by a supply of silver from the southern Bohemian mines in Rudolfov. As soon as the provi-

sion of Rudolfov silver ran out (from 1569 it was used exclusively by the newly set-up royal mint in České Budějovice) the production of the Prague mint fell substantially.

Nohejlová 1929; Halačka 1987, pp. 104-106 (no. 173).

E.Š.

V.49
Master of the mint Jan Harder
Half-gulder (30 kreutzers) of Maximilian II
Silver, coinage
3.21 cm, 12.304 g
1567
Prague, Národní muzeum, inv. no. H5-37
393

Half-gulders (30 kreutzers) of Maximilian II from the Prague mint are known only from the years 1567 to 1569.

Halačka 1987, pp. 106-107 (no. 175).

E.Š.

V.50
Master of the mint Jan Harder
Two-kreutzer piece of Maximilian II
Silver, coinage
1.81 cm, 1.442 g
1566
Prague, Národní muzeum, inv. no. H5-38
383

In the early 1570s there was a change in the composition of the production of the Prague mint. From 1570 to 1572 small kreutzer nominals only were minted.

Halačka 1987, pp. 107-108 (no. 178).

E.Š.

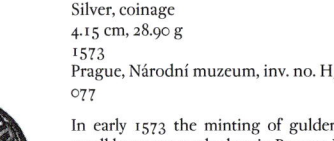

V.51
Master of the mint Jan Harder
Kreutzer piece of Maximilian II
Silver, coinage
1.55 cm, 0.768 g
1570
Prague, Národní muzeum, inv. no. H5-38
479

Halačka 1987, pp. 108-109 (no. 182).

E.Š.

V.52
Master of the mint Jan Harder
Thaler of Maximilian II
Silver, coinage
4.15 cm, 28.90 g
1573
Prague, Národní muzeum, inv. no. H5-30
077

In early 1573 the minting of gulders and small kreutzers took place in Prague, Kutná Hora, Jáchymov and České Budějovice. In 1573, 15,901 items were struck in Prague.

Nohejlová 1929; Halačka 1987, p. 110.

E.Š.

V.53
Master of the mint Jan Harder
White groschen of Maximilian II
Silver, coinage
2.17 cm, 2.294 g
1574
Prague, Národní muzeum, inv. no. H5-38
427

The minting of the white groschen was renewed in 1573. It was the most frequently produced coin of the Prague mint until the end of the 1570s.

Halačka 1987, pp. 111-112 (no. 189).

E.Š.

V.54
Master of the mint Jan Harder
White groschen of Maximilian II
Silver, coinage
2.2 cm, 1.46 g
1574
Prague, Národní muzeum, inv. no. H5-30
059

Halačka 1987, pp. 111-112 (no. 189).

E.Š.

V.55
Master of the mint Lazar Ercker
Ducat of Rudolf II
Gold, coinage
2.27 cm, 3.50 g
1584
Prague, Muzeum hl. města Prahy, inv. no.
17 248

The production of the Prague mint during the 1570s was in a gradual decline. A solution to this difficult situation was to lie in the agreement of the master of the mint Tobiáš Gebhart with the Nürnberg merchant Bartoloměj Albrecht in April 1580 to mint ducats out of gold provided by Al-

brecht, at a charge of one and a half kreutzers per item. For fifteen years from the second quarter of 1580 (with an interruption in 1591) the provision of gold and (from 1588) silver from Bartoloměj Albrecht ensured the running of the mint and an increase in its production.

Nohejlová 1928, pp. 11-24; Nohejlová 1929; Halačka 1987, pp. 164-167 (no. 294).

E.Š.

V.56
Master of the mint Lazar Ercker
Ducat of Rudolf II
Gold, coinage
2.27 cm, 3.50 g
1588
Prague, Muzeum hl. města Prahy, inv. no.
12 998

The extent of the minting of ducats in Prague between 1580 and 1595 can be compared with the production of such an important central European centre for the minting of gold coins as the Kremnica mint. More than a million ducats were minted in Prague for Bartoloměj Albrecht.

Nohejlová 1928, pp. 11-24; Halačka 1987, pp. 165-167 (no. 295).

E.Š.

V.57
Master of the mint Jan Lasanz
Ducat of Rudolf II
Gold, coinage
2.25 cm, 3.51 g
1606
Prague, Muzeum hl. města Prahy, inv. no.
17 254

After the massive increase in minting in the 1580s and in the first half of the 1590s, contingent on the work for Bartoloměj Albrecht, a sharp decline occurred after 1595 and for many subsequent years. Gold was further minted according to previously established practice at the ruler's direction,

or at the cost of a few private providers of gold. Although it is impossible to identify these individuals precisely, it is supposed that they were mostly members of the Prague Jewish community.

Šimek 1977, pp. 235-238; Halačka 1987, pp. 164-167 (no. 301).

E.Š.

V.58
Master of the mint Benedikt Hubmer
Ducat of Rudolf II
Gold, coinage
2.24 cm, 3.49 g
1610
Prague, Muzeum hl. města Prahy, inv. no.
17 256

Halačka 1987, pp. 164-167 (no. 302).

E.Š.

V.59
Master of the mint Samuel Salvart
Ducat of Rudolf II
Gold, coinage
2.23 cm, 3.51 g
1610
Prague, Muzeum hl. města Prahy, inv. no.
17 259

Halačka 1987, pp. 164-167 (no. 302).

E.Š.

V.60
Master of the mint Lazar Ercker
Thaler of Rudolf II
Silver, coinage
4.18 cm, 28.22 g
1585
Prague, Národní muzeum, inv. no. H5-37
433

The minting of thalers in the Prague mint was from the 1580s to the end of the century completely overshadowed by the minting of ducats. None was struck during the first years of Rudolf II's reign. In 1585 they were struck only for the second time (the first Rudolf thaler is dated 1580)

during his reign. On the reverse is a design by Abondio bearing a non-heraldic eagle. Abondio's design was cut in Prague by the iron cutter Michal Stolz.

Nohejlová 1929; Halačka 1987, pp. 171-173 (no. 310).

E.Š.

V.61
Thaler of Rudolf II
Struck in silver
4.14 cm; 28.8 g
1601
Prague, Národní muzeum, inv. no. H5-37
442

1592 saw the beginning of a continuous series of thalers, struck in Prague, that depicted Rudolf II in a standing position. This type of coin was only produced by the Prague mint. It was apparently struck by the die-cutter Worf Wirth. These coins first appear in 1588 and finally in 1602.

Halačka 1987, pp. 171-73 (312).

E.Š.

V.62
Master of the mint Jan Lasanz
Thaler of Rudolf II
Silver, coinage
4.16 cm, 28.97 g
1608
Prague, Muzeum hl. města Prahy, inv. no.
17 144

In 1601 the iron-cutter Jan Konrád Greuter began to work for the Prague mint. His work may be the uniform design for a Czech coin, carried out at the end of 1602, on the obverse the bare-headed older ruler with, on the circumference under his bust, a small Czech lion, on the reverse

a heraldic eagle.

Nohejlová 1929; Halačka 1987, pp. 171-173 (no. 313).

E.Š.

V.63
Master of the mint Benedikt Hubmer
Thaler of Rudolf II
Silver, coinage
4.09 cm, 29.13 g
1611
Prague, Muzeum hl. města Prahy, inv. no.
9395b

A ten-ducat impress was clearly used for the preparation of this thaler. The ordinary type of thaler with the bust of the ruler was also struck bearing the year 1611. In the last year of Rudolf`s reign 15,401 × three score of groschen and Czech thalers, their multiples and parts,

were struck.

Šimek 1977, no. 4, supplement; Halačka 1987, pp. 171-173 (no. 314).

E.Š.

V.64
Master of the mint Zuzana Erckerová
Half-thaler of Rudolf II
Silver, coinage
3.56 cm, 14.32 g
1598
Prague, Národní muzeum, inv. no.
H5-111 772

Halačka 1987, pp. 173-176 (no. 316).

E.Š.

V.65
Master of the mint Samuel Salvart
Half-thaler of Rudolf II
Silver, coinage
3.56 cm, 14.37 g
1610
Prague, Národní muzeum, inv. no. inv. no.
H5-37 446

The first evidence of Prague half-thalers of Rudolf II with the bust of the ruler is from 1606, if we do not count the solitary type from 1585.

Halačka 1987, pp. 173-176 (no. 320).

E.Š.

V.66
Master of the mint Benedikt Hubmer
Half-thaler of Rudolf II
Silver, coinage
3.56 cm, 14.44 g
1610
Prague, Národní muzeum, inv. no.
H5-37 447

Halačka 1987, pp. 173-176 (no. 320).

E.Š.

V.67
Master of the mint Jan Lasanz
Quarter-thaler of Rudolf II
Silver, coinage
3.0 cm, 6.495 g
1601
Prague, Národní muzeum, inv. no. H5-36
311

Rudolf quarter-thalers from the Prague mint are known mainly from the early seventeenth century. They resemble thalers bearing the years 1598, 1601 and 1602.

Halačka 1987, pp. 176-177 (no. 322).

E.Š.

V.68
Master of the mint Jan Lasanz
Quarter-thaler of Rudolf II
Silver, coinage
3.1 cm, 6.657 g
1605
Prague, Národní muzeum, inv. no. H5-37
445

Halačka 1987, pp. 176-177 (no. 323).

E.Š.

V.69
Master of the mint Jan Lasanz
White groschen of Rudolf II
Silver, coinage
2.1 cm, 1.93 g
1601
Prague, Národní muzeum, inv. no. H5-30
746

The white groschen of Rudolf II was first struck in 1578 and 1579. The Prague mint issued it again in the first decade of the seventeenth century.

Halačka 1987, pp. 178-179 (no. 327).

E.Š.

V.70
Master of the mint Jan Lasanz
White groschen of Rudolf II
Silver, coinage
2.1 cm, 1.57 g
1604
Prague, Národní muzeum, inv. no. H5-30747

Halačka 1987, pp. 178-179 (no. 328).

E.Š.

V.71
Master of the mint Jan Harder
Small groschen of Rudolf II
Silver, coinage
1.71 cm, 1.04 g
1578
Prague, Národní muzeum, inv. no. H5-35883

On 4 February 1577 Rudolf II added to the existing system of coinage with the small groschen, which were the most consistently issued silver coin under Rudolf's reign.

Halačka 1987, pp. 179-184 (no. 331).

E.Š.

V.72
Master of the mint Tobiáš Gebhart
Small groschen of Rudolf II
Silver, coinage
1.74 cm, 1.13 g
1580
Prague, Národní muzeum, inv. no. H5-93134

Halačka 1987, pp. 179-184 (no. 334).

E.Š.

V.73
Master of the mint Zuzana Erckerová
Small groschen of Rudolf II
Silver, coinage
1.73 cm, 1.071 g
1598
Prague, Národní muzeum, inv. no. H5-93300

Halačka 1987, pp. 179-184 (no. 352).

E.Š.

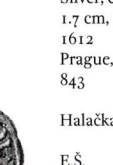

V.74
Master of the mint Benedikt Hubmer
Small groschen of Rudolf II
Silver, coinage
1.7 cm, 1.05 g
1612
Prague, Národní muzeum, inv. no. H5-36843

Halačka 1987, pp. 179-184 (no. 356).

E.Š.

V.75
Master of the mint Benedikt Hubmer
Ducat of Matthias II
Gold, coinage
2.18 cm, 3.47 g
1612
Prague, Muzeum hl. města Prahy, inv. no. 17 260

Gold minting in Prague was at its highest level in Matthias II's reign. The figure of St Václav appeared for the first time in sixty years. The stamps are by Greuter.

Nohejlová 1929; Halačka 1987, p. 251.

E.Š.

V.76
Master of the mint Benedikt Hubmer
Ducat of Matthias II
Gold, coinage
2.18 cm, 3.48 g
1612
Prague, Muzeum hl. města Prahy, inv. no. 17 261

Halačka 1987, p. 251 (no. 487).

E.Š.

V.77
Master of the mint Benedikt Hubmer
Ducat of Matthias II
Gold, coinage
2.24 cm, 3.51 g
1615
Prague, Národní muzeum, inv. no. H5-39653

In 1613, St Václav was replaced by the imperial eagle with the Austro-Burgundian heraldic scutcheon on its breast.

Nohejlová 1929; Šimek 1977, no. 4, supplement 1; Halačka 1987, p. 251 (no. 488).

E.Š.

V.78
Master of the mint Benedikt Hubmer
Thaler of Mathias II
Silver, coinage
4.19 cm, 28.79 g
1612
Prague, Muzeum hl. města Prahy, inv. no. 13 259

In the years 1611 and 1612, the time of Mathias II, a pictorially new type of Prague groschen was introduced, with a crowned bust of the ruler on the obverse and a large heraldic shield and the Order of the Golden Fleece on the reverse. This type is also known from the Kutná Hora and

Jáchymov mints. The greater number of the Prague coins bear the year 1612. The value of the Prague thaler coin then equalled 24,614 × three score of Czech groschen (49,228 thalers). In Kutná Hora thalers were struck to the value of 27,370 × three score Czech groschen (54,740 thalers) and in Jáchymov to a value of 2,878 × three score (5,756 thalers). The die was made by Jan Konrád Greuter.

Nohejlová 1929; Simek 1977, no. 4, supplement 1-3; Halačka 1987, pp. 256-259 (no. 500).

E.Š.

V.79
Master of the mint Benedikt Hubmer
Half-thaler of Matthias II
Silver, coinage
3.6 cm, 14.10 g
1616
Prague, Národní muzeum, inv. no. H5-34 232

From 1613 thalers with the bust of the ruler and the imperial eagle continued to be minted. Half-thalers are known from every year of Matthias's reign.

Halačka 1987, pp. 260-261 (no. 509).

E.Š.

V.80
Master of the mint Benedikt Hubmer
Quarter-thaler of Matthias II
Silver, coinage
2.99 cm, 6.90 g
1618
Prague, Národní muzeum, H5-35 747

Quarter-thalers of Matthias II from the Prague mint come from the same operation as the thalers and half-thalers. No quarter-thaler is known from 1615.

Halačka 1987, p. 262 (no. 512).

E.Š.

V.81
Master of the mint Benedikt Hubmer
White groschen of Matthias II
Silver, coinage
2.09 cm, 1.40 g
1617
Prague, Národní muzeum, inv. no. H5-35 746

White groschen of Matthias II from the Prague mint are known bearing the years 1615, 1616, 1617, 1618 and 1619. The level of minting of this coin nominal was decisive for the complementing of the reserves of money in circulation. Only a small quantity of white groschen were struck in Kutná Hora during these years, and none in Jáchymov. From 1617 to 1619 56,229 × three score of Czech groschen were issued (that is, around 3,373,740); thalers were issued to a value of 51,716 × three score Czech groschen.

Šimek 1977, no. 4; Halačka 1987, pp. 263-264 (no. 514).

E.Š.

V.82
Master of the mint Benedikt Hubmer
Small groschen of Matthias II
Silver, coinage
1.64 cm, 0.94 g
1618
Prague, Národní muzeum, inv. no. H5-39 731

The Prague production of small groschen in the time of the reign of Matthias II visibly fell behind the production of white groschen and behind the Kutná Hora production. They were struck in the years 1615 to 1618.

Šimek 1977, no. 4; Halačka 1987, pp. 264-165 (no. 520).

E.Š.

V.83
Master of the mint Benedikt Hubmer
Twenty-four-kreutzer piece of the Bohemian Estates
Silver, coinage
2.98 cm, 7.7 g
1619
Prague, Národní muzeum, inv. no. H5-39 931

Minting of the first decades of the seventeenth century was marked by a grave currency and coinage crisis and was a time of chronic inflation. It originated in central Germany and peaked in the Czech lands at the beginning of the Thirty Years' War. The Bohemian Estates - who with their coinage order of 28 June 1619 returned after more than half a century to the minting of kreutzer coins whose enforcement was in 1561 the peak of the centralizing efforts of Ferdinand I - began to strike coins of a reduced grade.

Šimek 1977, no. 4; Halačka 1987, pp. 292-293 (no. 571).

E.Š.

V.84
Master of the mint Pavel Škréta
Twenty-four-kreutzer piece of the Bohemian Estates
Silver, coinage
3.15 cm, 6.80 g
1620
Prague, Národní muzeum, inv. no. H5-34 322

During the maintenance of the thaler as the popular tender of the Czech coinage system during the period of the Estates uprising there were made: the 24-kreutzer piece (mass: 7.97 g; quality: 0.625); the 12-kreutzer piece (mass: 4.66 g; quality: 0.531); the 3-kreutzer piece (mass: 1.43 g; quality: 0.422) and the kreutzer (mass: 0.65 g; quality: 0.313); and from the old nominal, the white coin (mass: 0.36 g; quality: 0.195) and the small coin (mass: 0.30 g; quality: 0.133). Of these coins the Prague mint in the second half of 1619 issued 24-kreutzer pieces and 12-kreutzer pieces with the mark of the master of the mint Benedikt Hubmer and in the following year 24-kreutzer pieces with the mark of the master of the mint Pavel Škréta.

Nohejlová 1930, pp. 107-123; Halačka 1987, pp. 292-293 (no. 568).

E.Š.

v.85
Master of the mint Benedikt Hubmer
Twelve-kreutzer piece of the Bohemian Estates
Silver, coinage
2.9 cm, 3.64 g
1619
Prague, Národní muzeum, inv. no. H5-31
131

Halačka 1987, p. 293 (no. 572).

E.Š.

v.86
Master of the mint Pavel Škréta
Ducat of Fridrich Falcky
Gold, coinage
2.26 cm, 3.44 g
1620
Prague, Národní muzeum, inv. no. H5-35
766

According to the coinage regulations of the Czech Estates in 1620 even coins of the Winter King Fridrich Falcky were struck in Prague in 1620. During his short reign, which ended with the Battle of Bílá Hora on 8 November 1620, the Czech coinage system increased by further nom-inals: the 48-kreutzer piece was added on 7 August 1620, and subsequently there were trial strikings of 60- and 70-kreutzer pieces, which had the same mass and quality as the 48-kreutzer piece (mass: 15.34 g; quality: 0.563). Fridrich ducats were also struck in Prague.

Nohejlová CSPS 1930, pp. 107-123; Halačka 1987, pp. 329-330 (no. 651).

E.Š.

v.87
Master of the mint Pavel Škréta
Forty-eight-kreutzer piece of Fridrich Falcky
Silver, coinage
3.7 cm, 15.054 g
1620
Prague, Národní muzeum, inv. no. H5-37
133

Halačka 1987, pp. 331-332 (no. 654).

E.Š.

v.88
Master of the mint Pavel Škréta
Twenty-four-kreutzer piece of Fridrich Falcky
Silver, coinage
3.14 cm, 7.58 g
1620
Prague, Národní muzeum, inv. no. H5-35
763

Halačka 1987, pp. 332-333 (no. 658).

E.Š.

v.89
Master of the mint Pavel Škréta
Twenty-four-kreutzer piece of Fridrich Falcky
Silver, coinage
3.1 cm, 7.70 g
1620
Prague, Národní muzeum, inv. no. H5-35
765

Halačka 1987, pp. 332-333 (no. 656).

E.Š.

v.90
Master of the mint Pavel Škréta
Twelve-kreutzer piece of Fridrich Falcky
Silver, coinage
2.67 cm, 3.84 g
1620
Prague, Národní muzeum, inv. no. H5-35
762

Halačka 1987, pp. 333-334 (no. 659).

E.Š.

v.91
Master of the mint Benedikt Hubmer
150-kreutzer piece of Ferdinand II
Silver, coinage
4.16 cm, 24.780 g
1621
Prague, Národní muzeum, inv. no. H5-95
026

The process of devaluation of the currency in circulation was far from over with the issue of Fridrich's 60- and 70-kerutzer pieces. The months immediately following were to bring its peak with results which were to affect the economic life of the country and the life of individuals for decades to come. Although at the beginning the minting under the reign of the victorious Ferdinand II merely continued as before, under the Estates and Fridrich Falcky, it was soon marked by by a long-lasting decline in the mass and quality of minted coins. Further devaluation was achieved by the issue of thaler coins with higher numerical value.

Nohejlová-Prátová 1945/46, pp 29-35; Halačka 1988, p. 366 (no. 695).

E.Š.

V.92
Master of the mint Benedikt Hubmer
Forty-eight-kreutzer piece of Ferdinand II
Silver, coinage
3.5 cm, 8.32 g
1622
Prague, Národní muzeum, inv. no. H5-34
418

On 18 January 1622 Ferdinand leased the
minting of coinage in Bohemia, Moravia
and Silesia for 6,000,000 gulders to what
was known as the de Witte consortium
(members included the financier Jan de
Witte, the governor Charles of Liechtenstein, the commander of Prague at that

time, Albrecht of Waldstein, Pavel Michna
of Vacínov and Jakub Basevi), which, by
the issue of a great quantity of coins of
low quality with a stamped higher nominal number, impoverished all levels of the
population for nearly a year and a half and
even damaged the state exchequer.

Nohejlová-Prátová 1945/46, pp 29–35; Halačka 1988, p. 371 (no. 703).

E.Š.

V.93
Master of the mint Benedikt Hubmer
Fifteen-kreutzer piece of Ferdinand II
Silver, coinage
2.58 cm, 2.34 g
1622
Prague, Národní muzeum, inv. no. H5-35
774

During the period of the de Witte consortium's minting all the mints issued a great
many devalued coins, for which metal
from the old full-value coins and rare metal obtained from any source was used as
raw material. In 1622 the Prague mint
alone accepted 240,083 talents of silver

(approximately 60,000 kg) for minting.
During the year`s lease new coins to a val-
ue of 42,000,000 gulders were minted.

Nohejlová-Prátová 1945/46, pp 29–35;
Šimek 1986, pp. 351–71; Halačka 1988, pp.
372–73 (no. 705).

E.Š.

V.94
Master of the mint Benedikt Hubmer
3-kreutzer piece of Ferdinand II
Silver, coinage
1,84, 0.90 gm.
Prague mint, 1620
Prague, Národní muzeum, inv. no. H5-34
421

Halačka 1988, pp. 373-374.

E.Š.

V.95
Master of the mint Benedikt Hubmer
Ducat of Ferdinand II
Gold, coinage
2,25, 3.45 gm.
Prague mint, 1627
Prague, Muzeum hl. města Prahy, inv. no.
15 513

The production of ducats by the Prague
mint during the 1620s and 1630s was
higher than before the Thirty Years' War.

Šimek 1986, pp. 351-371; Halačka 1988, pp.
381-383 (no. 728).

EŠ

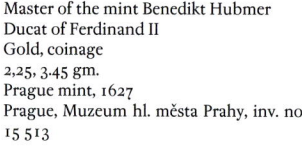
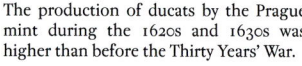

V.96
Master of the mint Jan Suttner
Thaler of Ferdinand II
Silver, coinage
4,19, 29.038 gm.
Prague mint, 1623
Prague, Národní muzeum, inv. no. H5-95
088

On 31 March 1623 Ferdinand II decided
not to renew the contract with the de
Witte consortium for the lease of the
mints. The state administration took the
striking of coinage under its own control.
The issue of so-called 'long coins' ended
on 2nd June 1623. On 1st August 1623 the

minting of good coins of the thaler
coinage system was renewed by retaining
the small kreutzer nominals. The disparity
between these and the 'long coins' was
equalized by the state devaluation (kala-
da) of 28 December 1623, by which the value of currency was lowered by 86.76-
91.89%.

Nohejlová-Prátová 1945/46 pp 29–35; Halačka 1988, pp. 386–90 (no. 741).

E.Š.

V.97
Master of the mint Tobiás Schuster
Thaler of Ferdinand II
Silver, coinage
4,45, 28.300 gm.
Prague mint, 1632
Prague, Národní muzeum, inv. no. H5-34
449
The need for a sufficient amount of good
coins placed increased demands on the activity of all the mints after 1623. However,
a decline in their production soon occurred and even the domestic composition of production changed. The Prague
mint was not an exception in this respect.
It is clear from surviving accounts of mint-

ing that the beginning priority minting of
large thaler coins was replaced from 1627
by the minting of small coins, abouve all
the 3-kreutzer piece. This formed 85% or
more of the Prague production, whose value after the marked decline in the second
half of the 1620s settled in the 1630s to
roughly 100,000 guilders.

Šimek 1986, pp 351-371; Halačka 1988, pp.
386-390 (no. 749)

E.Š.

V.98
Master of the mint Jakub Wolker
Half-thaler of Ferdinand II
Silver, coinage
3,62, 14.41 gm.
Prague mint, 1637
Prague, Národní muzeum, inv. no. H5-34
451

Prague half-thalers of Ferdinand II do not survive in such rich profusion as the thalers. We do no know from surviving accounts how many were struck in each year.

Halačka 1988, pp. 390-391 (no. 751).

E.Š.

V.99
Master of the mint Jan Suttner
Quarter-thaler of Ferdinand II
Silver, coinage
3.07 cm, 6.928 g
1624
Prague, Národní muzeum, inv. no. H5-95
103

Prague quarter-thalers survive from 1623-25, 1630-33, 1635 and 1637. The gaps in time curiously coincide with the interruptions in the minting of half-thalers.

Halačka 1988, pp. 392-93 (no. 755).

E.Š.

V.100
Master of the mint Benedikt Hubmer
Three-kreutzer piece of Ferdinand II
Silver, coinage
2.08 cm, 1.458 g
1628
Prague, Národní muzeum, H5-95 346

After 1625 the small 3-kreutzer piece became decisive for the whole value of the coin production. In 1628 they were struck in Prague to a value of 53,227 gulders.

Šimek, 1986, pp. 351-71; Halačka 1988, pp. 393-95 (no. 760).

E.Š.

V.101
Master of the mint Jakub Wolker
Three-kreutzer piece of Ferdinand II
Silver, coinage
2.02 cm, 1.600 g
1637
Prague, Národní muzeum, H5-34 452

Halačka 1988, pp. 393-95 (no. 763).

E.Š.

V.102
Master of the mint Jakub Wolker
Kreutzer piece of Ferdinand II
Silver, coinage
1.5 cm, 0.471 g
1637
Prague, Národní muzeum, inv. no. H5-95
551

During the time of Ferdinand II kreutzers were struck only exceptionally. Two types have survived, from 1627 and 1637. Half-kreutzer pieces were struck only in 1626.

Halačka 1988, pp. 395-96 (no. 765).

E.Š.

V.103
Master of the mint Jakub Wolker
Ducat of Ferdinand III
Gold, coinage
2.29 cm, 3.470 g
1638
Prague, Muzeum hl. města Prahy, inv. no.
15 414

These were the most frequent coin struck in Prague during the Thirty Years' War. Portraits were cut to the pattern of Abondio.

Šimek 1986, pp 351-71; Halačka 1988, pp. 567-68 (no. 1166).

E.Š.

V.104
Master of the mint Jakub Wolker
Thaler of Ferdinand III
Silver, coinage
4.33 cm, 29.01 g
1639
Prague, Muzeum hl. města Prahy, inv. no.
14 875

These thalers were struck in the Prague in the years 1638-44, 1646-50, 1653 and 1656.

Šimek 1986, pp 351-71; Halačka 1988, pp. 568-69 (no. 1171).

E.Š.

V.105
Master of the mint Jakub Wolker
Half-thaler of Ferdinand III
Silver, coinage
3.6 cm, 13.91 g
1648
Prague, Národní muzeum, inv. no. H5-35
963

Prague half-thalers of Ferdinand III survive from the years 1638-41, 1644, 1646-49, 1653, 1655 and 1656. From 1641 the bust was replaced by a head with a laurel wreath.

Halačka 1988, pp. 570-71 (no. 1175).

E.Š.

V.106
Master of the mint Krystof Margalík
Quarter-thaler of Ferdinand III
Silver, coinage
2.9 cm, 7.20 g
1656
Prague, Národní muzeum, inv. no. H5-35
911

Prague quarter-thalers of Ferdinand III survive from the years 1638-42, 1646-48, 1653 and 1655-57.

Halačka 1988, pp. 571-72 (no. 1177).

E.Š.

V.107
Master of the mint Jakub Wolker
Three-kreutzer piece of Ferdinand III
Silver, coinage
2.05 cm 1.722 g
1640
Prague, Národní muzeum, inv. no. H5-111
586

The small silver 3-kreutzer coin was in the time of Ferdinand III the most frequent and the most consistent coin issued by the Prague mint.

Halačka 1988, pp. 573-74 (no. 1180).

E.Š.

V.108
Master of the mint Jakub Wolker
Kreutzer of Ferdinand III
Silver, coinage
1.54 cm, 0.729 g
1641, Prague mint
Prague, Národní muzeum, inv. no. H5-111
601

The Prague mint struck the smallest coin
nominal – the kreutzer – in the years 1637–
42, 1645 and 1653.

Halačka 1988, pp. 574–75 (no. 1183).

E.Š.

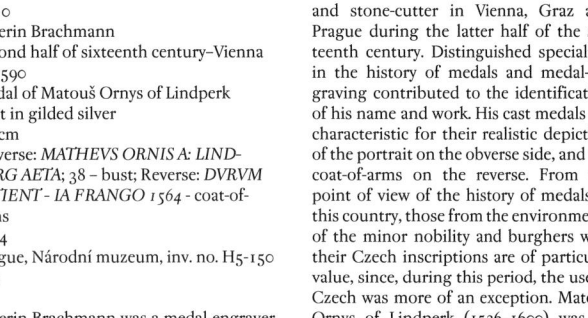

V.109
Master of the mint Krystof Margalík
Half-kreutzer of *Ferdinand III*
Silver, coinage
1.48 cm, 0.557 g
1655, Prague mint
Prague, Národní muzeum, inv. no. H5-111
673

During the reign of Ferdinand III half-
kreutzers were struck by the Prague mint
only in 1655.

Halačka 1988, p. 575 (no. 1185)

E.Š.

V.110
Severin Brachmann
Second half of sixteenth century–Vienna
ca.1590
Medal of Matouš Ornys of Lindperk
Cast in gilded silver
2.9 cm
Obverse: *MATHEVS ORNIS A: LIND-
PERG AETA*; 38 – bust; Reverse: *DVRVM
PATIENT - IA FRANGO 1564* - coat-of-
arms
1564
Prague, Národní muzeum, inv. no. H5-150
934

Severin Brachmann was a medal-engraver
and stone-cutter in Vienna, Graz and
Prague during the latter half of the sixteenth century. Distinguished specialists
in the history of medals and medal-engraving contributed to the identification
of his name and work. His cast medals are
characteristic for their realistic depiction
of the portrait on the obverse side, and the
coat-of-arms on the reverse. From the
point of view of the history of medals in
this country, those from the environments
of the minor nobility and burghers with
their Czech inscriptions are of particular
value, since, during this period, the use of
Czech was more of an exception. Matouš
Ornys of Lindperk (1526–1600) was an
artist, illuminator and surveyor active in
Prague during the years 1549–1600. He
served the court and the nobility. He is
particularly known for his illumination of
the Litomyšl gradual and Třebenice hymnbook. He became a land surveyor around
the year 1570. He acquired the title 'of
Lindperk' and a coat-of-arms from Ferdinand I in 1562.

Dworschak, 1923-1924, p. 63; Habich
1929-34, no. 3269; Nohejlová 1938, pp. 80-
82.

Z.M.

V.111
Severin Brachmann
Second half of sixteenth century–Vienna
ca.1590
Medal of Adam Horký of Vysoký
Cast in gilded silver
3.4 cm
Obverse: *ADAM HORKY Z WYSO-
(K)EHO AETA:S:41* – bust; Reverse: *SOLI
DEO GLORIA - 1565* – coat-of-arms
1565
Prague, Národní muzeum, inv. no. H5-150
935

Adam Horký of Vysoký (1524–ca.1567) was
a Prague burgher and merchant. He was
elected to the Land Assembly by the collector of taxes in 1565.

Habich 1929–34, no. 3270; Nohejlová 1938,
p. 82.

Z.M.

V.112
Severin Brachmann
Second half of sixteenth century–Vienna
ca.1590
Medal of Jan Škréta Šotnovský of
Závořice
Cast in gilded silver
3.3 × 3.6 cm (oval)
Inscription: *IAN.SSKRETA.SSOT-
NOWSKEY.Z ZAWORICZ.* - bust with the
year 1570; Reverse: coat-of-arms
1570
Prague, Národní muzeum, inv. no. H5-150
939

Jan Škréta Šotnovský of Závořice (died
1587) was a burgher and alderman of the
Prague Old Town. He also traded in wines
and leather. He was presented with a coat-
of-arms and the title 'of Zavořice' by Max-
omilian II in 1570. Rudolf II sanctioned
the conferment of this title in 1580 and
commissioned a grander coat-of-arms in
his honour. His grandson was the artist
Karel Škréta.

Habich 1929–34, no. 3278; Nohejlová 1938,
p. 88.

Z.M.

V.113
Severin Brachmann
Second half of sixteenth century–Vienna
ca.1590
Medal of *Adam Myslík of Hyršov*
Cast in silver
3.4 cm
S B; Obverse: *ADAM MYSLIK Z
HYRSSOWA . AETA: 53*; Bust with the date
1573; *S B* by the shoulder of the bust; Re-
verse: coat-of-arms
1573
Prague, Národní muzeum, inv. no. H5-115
050

One of the few signed works by Severin
Brachmann is this medal of Adam Myslík
of Hyršov (1520-1581) who was a burgher
and, around the year 1570, magistrate of
the Prague New Town, later alderman of
the supreme burgraviate. In 1553 he was
accepted to the knights' Estate and participated in the general land assemblies during the period 1567–71. He is buried in the
church of St Stephen in Prague.

Habich 1929–34, n. 3288; Nohejlová 1938,
p. 99.

Z.M.

V.114
Severin Brachmann
Second half of sixteenth century–Vienna
ca.1590
Medal of Prudencie Myslíková
Cast in silver
3.4 cm
Obverse: *PRVDENCZY MYSLIKOWA - Z DOVBRAWY - AETA 48*; bust; Reverse: coat-of-arms
1573
Prague, Národní muzeum, inv. no. H5-150 940

The maiden name of Prudencie, wife of Adam Myslík, as the legend on the medal suggests, was 'of Doubrava' (born. ca.1525). Miltner–Neumann presents a medal comprising both portraits of husband and wife bearing the inscription 1573.

Miltner–Neumann 1852-1870, no. 286; Habich 1929-34, no. 3289; Nohejlová 1938, pp. 99-101.

Z.M.

V.115
Severin Brachmann
Second half of sixteenth century–Vienna
ca.1590
Medal of Bohuslav Mazanec of Frimburk
Cast in silver
3.4 cm
Obverse: *BOHVSLAV MAZANECZ Z FRIMBVRKV AN. 1573* – bust; Reverse: coat-of-arms, on either side: *W.P. - C.S.*
1573
Prague, Národní muzeum, inv. no. H5-150 941

Bohuslav Mazanec of Frimburk (died 1589) was a burgher of Prague and a scrivener of minor land records. He was awarded a coat-of-arms in 1557 and was accepted to the knights' Estate in 1561.

Miltner–Neumann 1852-1870, no. 262; Habich 1929-34, no. 3291; Nohejlová 1938, pp. 105.

Z.M.

V.116
Balduin Drentwett
Frisk 1545-1627
Medal with Likeness of Thomas Schweicker
Minted silver, gilt
Average 3.9 cm
Obverse: *THOMAS SCHWEICKER AE-TA(TIS). SU(AE). 41 1582*; reverse: MIRABILIA OPERA TUA ET ANIMA MEA COGNOSCET NIMIS. PSA(LM). 138 1582
1887, Lann collection; a gift to the Uměleckoprumyslové Muzeum
Prague, Uměleckoprumyslové muzeum, inv. no. 1874/1887

The only clear-cut mint of quality among the exemplars on record (cf. Cahn 1927, no. 1344, tab. 22) and a rare variant with complete dating (Domanig: the figure '2' is missing on the obverse). Drentwett did not sign the medal; he can be recognized by his personal manuscript (rugged surfaces, especially the writing). The character in the portrait is Thomas Schweicker (1540-1602), who came from a prominent family from Halle in Swabia. He was born without any hands and learned to write, draw and carve with his feet. He earned his living as a circus performer and artisan at the courts of the emperors Maximilian II and Rudolf II among others.

Prague 1995, cat. no. 29.

Domanig 1907, no. 852; Habich, 1916, pp. 232-33.

D.S.

V.117
Jiří Starší of Řásná
Died 1599
Medal of Petr Keck of Schwarzbach
Struck in silver
3.1 cm
Obverse: *PETER KECK VON SCHWAR-CZPACH - GWARDEIN VND MVNTZ - GEGENHANDLER.ZV PR - / R:K:M:* - portrait; Reverse: *GWARDEIN VND MVNTZ - GEGENHANDLER.ZV PR* - coat-of-arms
Ca. 1585
Prague, Národní muzeum, inv. no. H5-150 949

Petr Keck of Schwarzbach was an official at the Prague mint in 1584–91, responsible for assessing the value of precious metals, later an official at the Czech Chamber. During the period 1601-04 he worked in Kutná Hora, and then returned to Prague after 1610.

Miltner–Neumann 1852-70, pp. 222-23; Katz 1929, p. 116; Nohejlová 1963, 65, cat. no. 63.

Z.M.

V.118
Jiří Starší of Řásná
Medal of Václav Krocín of Drahobejl
struck in silver
3.2 cm
Obverse: *WENCES:SE:CROCINVS A DRAHOBEYL AE:57* - bust; Reverse: *CIB-VS IN ORE - PSAL:IN CORDE*
1589
Prague, Národní muzeum, inv. no. H5-150 950

Jiří Starší of Řásná was a die engraver in Kutná Hora where he worked from 1557 until his death in 1599. He designed the dies for a number of jettons, both for the court and for private customers; however, no detailed records of his medal-engraving activities have survived. Certain similar characteristics may be found both in his medals and his jettons, specifically the treatment of the coats-of-arms; the decoration on the edge of the coins and medals suggests that he was responsible for their design. Václav Krocín of Drahobejl (1532-1602) was an alderman from 1579 and Lord Mayor of the Prague Old Town from 1584.

Miltner–Neumann 1852-70, pp. 264-65; Katz 1929, p. 116.

 Z.M.

V.119
Bonifac Riedel
Medal Portrait of Vilém of Rožmberk
(1536–1592)
Silver, cast, chased; silver partially gilt, old cast
Average 3.9 cm
Obverse: portrait in profile with chain and order of distinction around subject's neck, *WILHELM REGIERENDER HER DES HAVS ROSENBER*; Reverse: bearshield bearer with the Rozmberk coat of arms, *FORTITVDO MEA ET LAVS MEA DOMINVS*
Ca. 1585
1911 auction of the Lanna collection, Berlín 1911, cat. no. 1233.
Prague, Uměleckoprůmyslové muzeum, inv. no. 12 216(also 12.217)

The medal was evidently prepared for conferment of the Order of the Golden Fleece (3 June 1585). Miltner and Neumann have ascribed its authorship to Riedel, and say it was made at České Budějovice in the 1580s or 1590s.

Miltner–Neumann 1859, p. 359; Donnebauer 1889, no. 3704; Nohejlova 1963, p. 66, no. 67.

D.S.

V.120
Medal Portrait of Jan Albin of Greifenberk
Silver, cast, chased
H: 3.6 cm; w: 2.8 cm
Obverse: *IAN ALBIN Z GREIFENBERK v. AETAT.58. 1597*; Reverse: *SCIO QVOD SALVATOR MEVS VIVIT*
1597
1911 auction of the Lanna collection, Berlín 1911, cat. no. 1173
Prague, Uměleckoprůmyslové muzeum, inv. no. 12 211

The humanist Jan Albin Sturmius of Greifenberk worked as a teacher at the preparatory school beside the church of St Michal in Opatovice in Prague's New Town. He was the father-in-law of the cutter of precious stones Ottavio Miseroni. The portrait is of high quality. In the third quarter en face and in its execution, the nearest parallels in relief portraiture are by the Prague court medallists Wenzel and Valentin Maler.

Fiala 1888, no. 3253, tab. 48; Hirsch 1908, p. 416.

D.S.

V.121
Valentin Maler
Jihlava ca.1540–Nürnberg 1603
Medal of Gottfried Raab
Struck in silver
3.2 cm
Obverse: *VND DER KONIG WIRD THVN WAS ER WIL VND SICH ERHEBEN VND / AVFWERFEN WIDER ALLES WAS GOTT IST DANI.12.2.THE 2*; The field of the medal is divided horizontally. The upper part depicts a goose and swan sitting opposite each other; beneath them is a raven standing on the papal symbols. The segment bears the inscription: *C.PRIVI.C.*; Reverse: *ANNO 1414. / ZV COSTNITZ*

DIE / GANS GEBRATEN WARD / A.1521 DEN SCHWANEN ZV / WURMS GOT BEWARDT: / A.1601 GEN WITEMBERG GEFLOGEN KAM. EIN RAB / WELCHER OHN ALLE SCH / AM.SEIN HESLICH GSCH: / REI VERLASSEN HADT / ITZT LIEBLICH SINGT / DVRCH GOTES GNAD / GODEFRID.RAB. / D.D. v.M.
1601
Prague, Národní muzeum, inv. no. H5-51 473

Valentin Maler, goldsmith and medal engraver, worked in Nürnberg, where he married the daughter of goldsmith Václav Jamnitzer. He worked in the imperial services – chiefly for Maximilian II and Rudolf II. This medal represents those that document important events of the time and are distinctive for their remarkable portraits. Gottfried Raab was an Augustinian monk and preacher in Prague. In 1601 he adopted the evangelical denomination in Wittenberg and was later a preacher in Dresden. His conversion is symbolized on the obverse side of the medal by the depiction of Hus and Luther standing in opposition to papal might.

Miltner–Neumann 1852–70, no. 331; Fiala 1888, no. 3679 var.

Z.M.

V.122
Rafael Ranghieri (?)
Second half of sixteenth century
Medal of Adam Linhart of Nienpergh
struck in silver
3.2 cm
Obverse: *ADAM.LINHART. - Z NAIENPERGKU - AET 37* - bust; Reverse: *PAN.BVOH.SPOMOCNIK.MVY.* - coat-of-arms
1602
Prague, Národní muzeum, inv. no. H5-51 355

It is not documented that Rafael Ranghieri designed this medal, but Dworschak states that he worked in Prague, also in connection with the activities of Antonio Abondio. The typical design of the coat-of-arms on the reverse side indicates the possibility that either Ranghieri or an artist from his workshop was responsible for the engraving. Adam Linhart of Nienpergh (Neuenberg) was a Prague burgher in imperial services, regional prosecutor of the Czech kingdom, the legal representative of Petr Vok of Rožmberk and also, from 1600, defender of the feuds of the Old Town burghers.

MN 1852–70, p. 228; Dworschak 1926, p. 229; Katz 1929, pp.105-138.

Z.M.

V.123
Jan Konrad Greuter
Died 1625
Medal to Commemorate the Founding of the Church of the Holy Saviour in Prague
Struck in silver
3.6 cm
Obverse: *AB HOC SOLO SEMPITERNA SALVS.* - the bust of Christ; Reverse: *TEMPLVM / SALVATORIS / G.D.ET.CAES.RVD.II / SVB BOHE.REGE.MA / THIAE II. FVNDARVT / GERMA / EVANGELI / CI PRAGAE IN VRBE / VETERIDIE CA / ROLI.A.1611*
1611
Prague, Národní muzeum, inv. no.

H5-115 153

Jan Konrád Greuter, an engraver of mint dies in the Rheinish Palatinate, worked at the Prague mint from 1601. The German evangelists in Prague founded the church of the Holy Saviour in 1611. In honour of the celebrations that took place at this time, the Prague mint struck this medal with its characteristic shallow relief, in both gold and silver.

Fiala 1888, n. 4761; Nohejlová 1963, p. 75, n. 29.

Z.M.

V.124
Commemorative Medal of the Bohemian Confederation
Silver, struck medal
5.3 × 4.3 cm
Obverse: PIA ET RELIGIOSA ORTHODOXORVM LIGA – Below the crown five pillars represent the lands under the crown of Bohemia; on the rim of the crown UNG.BOH.MOR; around the pillars reads: ARA/ PRO/ LEGE/ REGE/ GRECE; a segment of the edge is inscribed: C.PRIVIL./ S.R.M.; Reverse: SI DEVS PRO NOBIS QVIS E HOMINIBVS CONTRA NOS; The field of the medal is divided by an oval-shaped shield with

VER/ BVM/ DEI; above is a group of people with a banner marked: SVB/ VTRA/QVE; below is a group with the words: S.VNA
1619
Prague, Národní muzeum, inv. no. H5-150 991

The Confederation of Bohemia came into law at a general assembly in July 1619. The confederation altered the Czech constitution and limited royal power to the benefit of the Estates. It also set out that the King of Bohemia could come to the throne only by being elected. Thus, in August 1619 Frederick Palatine was elected. The medal

evidently came into being a short time after these events.

Fiala 1888, no. 2039; Čermák–Skrbek 1891–1931, I, p. 157.

Z.M.

V.125
Jetton with Portrait of Kryštof Harant of Polžice
Silver, cast, chased
Average 2.5 cm
Obverse: KRYSSTOF HARRANT Z POLCZICZ; reverse: KOM. KR. CZESKE. NA PECCE PRES. 1620
1620
1911 auction of the Lanna collection
Prague, Uměleckoprůmyslové muzeum, inv. no. 12 214

Krystof Harant of Polžžce, Bezdružice and na Pecce (1564–1621) had been in the service of Archduke Ferdinand of the Tyrol

and then served as chamberlain to Emperor Rudolf II. After the Turkish War (1591–97) and travelling to Palestine and Egypt (1598–1600), he wrote a travelogue and became a privy councillor to Emperor Matthias. In 1618 he converted from Catholicism to join the Hussite Church and in 1619 he was at the forefront of the Estates' opposition. In 1620 he became the highest chamberlain in the Bohemian Chamber during the reign of Emperor Frederick of the Palatinate (for which occasion this playing token was struck). On 21 June 1621 Harant was beheaded in Prague.

Auction of A. Lanna collection, Berlin 1911, cat. no. 1182.

D.S.

V.126
Pietro de Pomis
Ca. 1565 Lodi–1633
Medal of Ferdinand II to celebrate his victory over Frederick Palatine after 1620.
cast in lead
4.75 cm
Obverse: FERDINANDVS.II.ROM.IMP. SEM.AVG. - bust; Reverse: LEGITIME - CERTANTI - bBattle scene symbolizing the defeat of Frederick Palatine
Prague, Národní muzeum, inv. no. H5-58 539

Pietro de Pomis, born in Lodi, Italy, initially worked at the court of Ferdinand of Ty-

rol in Innsbruck. After the latter's death he entered the services of the Styrian court under Archduke Ferdinand, the future Emperor Ferdinand II. The medals which he designed in the imperial services to celebrate the defeat of Frederick Palatine at the Battle of the White Mountain are remarkable for their detail of the portrait and the figural composition on the reverse side.

Domanig 1896, no.174; Forrer IV, pp. 648-49.

Z.M.

V.127
Donát Starckh
Early seventeenth century
Medal to Commemorate the Transfer of the Relics of St Norbert
Silver, struck medal
2.6 cm
Obverse: S:NORBERTE. O-RA.PRO. NOBIS; Semi figure of St Norbert; Reverse: TRANS/ FERTVR IN/ METROPOLIM/ BOHEMIAE/ SECVNDA.MAY/ ANNO 1627
1627
Prague, Národní muzeum, inv. no. H5-54 269

In 1627 celebrations to welcome the relics of St Norbert were held at the Premonstratensian monastery at Strahov in Prague. St Norbert had founded the order. The relics were taken from Magdeburg and placed in the cathedral of The Assumption of Or Lady at Strahov. Some jetons in gold and silver were struck at the Prague mint to commemorate this event. Silver coins were distributed among the people.

Miltner–Neumann 1852–70, no.738; Přibil 1931–37/38, no. 676.

Z.M.

V.128
Donát Starckh
Early seventeenth century
Medal to Commemorate the First Procession to Our Lady's Church in Jílové.
Silver, struck medal
2.8 cm
Obverse: B.M.V. Lavre – TANA – GILOVY – Loretto hut at which sits the Virgin mary with child; Reverse: FIT. PRIMA/ PROCESSIO ANN/ DNI. MDCXXVII/ DIE XII/ MENSIS/ SEPTEMBRIS
1627
Prague, Národní muzeum, inv. no. H5-54 643

Jílové was a royal mining town south of Prague. Pilgrimages began taking place here in 1626 to the church of Our Lady of Loretto at the Minorite monastery.

Literature: Miltner–Neumann 1852-1-70, no. 823; Přibil 1931–37/38, no. 108; Nohejlová 1963, p. 31.

Z.M.

V.129
Donát Starckh
First half of seventeenth century
Medal of Zdeněk Popel, Prince of
Lobkovic
Struck in gold
3.7 cm
Obverse: *SDENCO AD DG SRI PRINC D
LOBCO.* - bust; Reverse: The Lobkovic
coat-of-arms entwining the Order of the
Golden Fleece
After 1621
Prague, Národní muzeum, inv. no. H5-115
052

Donát Starckh worked as a medal-en-

graver at the Prague mint during the years
1626–35 where, apart from coins, he also
designed the dies for several medals. A
characteristic feature of his medals is their
very shallow reliefs, reminiscent of those
crafted for coins. The medal of Zdeněk Vojtěch of Lobkovic is attributed to Starckh,
although his authorship has not been
documented. Zdeněk Vojtěch of Lobkovic
(1568–1628) was a representative of the
old Czech noble family: he was appointed
imperial counsel by Rudolf II in 1591, and
in 1599 he became supreme chancellor of
the Czech Kingdom. Because of his
Catholic orientation he fell into dispute
with the Protestant estates and was ex-

pelled from the land in 1618. After the Battle of the White Mountain he was appointed a knight of the Order of the Golden
Fleece by Spanish King Philip IV in 1621,
and Ferdinand II awarded him the status
of a member of the royal Estate. These important events in the life of Lobkovic are
reflected in this commemorative medal,
struck in gold, silver and bronze.

Miltner–Neumann 1852-1870, n. 738; Fiala
1888, n. 4709; Polívka 1991, pp. 45-47.

Z.M.

V.130
Hans Rieger
1580–1653
Medal of Ernst Count Harrach
Gold, stamped medal
4,1 × 5 (ovál)
Obverse: *ERNESTVS .S.R.E. PRESB.
CARD. AB. HARRACH.* - bust; Reverse
*ARCHIEPS. PRAG.AC.REGNI. BOHAE.
PRIMAS. ET. PRINCEPS*
1629
Prague, Národní muzeum, H5-151 009

Miltner–Neuman 1852-70, p. 701; Přibil
1931–38/39, p. 494; Katz–Rieger 1934, p.
71.

Z.M.

V.131
Donát Starckh
Medal of Ferdinand II to Commemorate
the Founding of the Servite Monastery
and the Church of Our Lady at the White
Mountain outside Prague
Struck in silver
3.3 cm
First half of the seventeenth century
Obverse: *SVB TVVM PRAESIDIVM 1628 .
25 APR* - Ferdinand II in a kneeling posi-
tion, being crowned Czech King; Reverse:
*S.MARIA.DE.VICTORIA.A.FERD.II.PAR-
TA.PRAGAE 8.NO V.1620* - the two armies
facing each other in battle positions
1628

Prague, Národní muzeum, H5-58 539

The mint character of this medal suggests
that it originated in the Prague mint. It is
one of the few examples of Czech coinage
which commemorate the Battle of the
White Mountain, although it was struck
eight years later on the occasion of the
founding of the monastery and church in
1628.

Fiala 1888, n. 4722; Katz 1926, p. 121; Přibil
1931-1937/38, n. 740.

Z.M.

Public and Private Life in the City

V.132
Circle of Bartholomeus Spranger
Antwerp 1546–Prague 1611
The Procession of Bacchus
Dark green tempera on a white background, with light green highlights, on 20 pinewood cover panels
103 × 592.5 (height of painted band 74), max. thickness of panels 3.5
Ca.1600
The ceiling was discovered underneath a later plaster ceiling from the late eighteenth century in house no. 200 in Thunovská Street in Prague's Malá Strana during reconstruction in 1932; it was dismantled, wrapped and temporarily stored in the house on Thunovská street. In 1947 is was given by Tomáš Šašek to the Národní muzeum.
Prague, Národní muzeum, inv. no. H2-26 578/8-27

This is the first band in the ceiling which measures about 7 × 7 metres, with seven beams and seven bands of cover panels. The central part of the ceiling (five beams and four bands) has been displayed since 1986 in the Národní muzeum in the Lobkowitz Palace at Prague Castle. The ceiling comes from a bourgeois house in Malá Strana which was sold in 1596 by Linhart Hechle, a wealthy court tailor, to Laurenzio Nerro, a court gilder and swordmaker. It is thought that Laurenzio Nerro decided to have the ceiling, with its painted floral decor, repainted and probably enlisted the help of his neighbour in the same street, Bartholomeus Spranger. Six rather elongated fields were painted with figural mythological scenes. It seems likely that Spranger designed the iconographic content and composition but left the actual execution to his routine assistants.

Matyášová–Lejsková 1963, 195; Poche–Preiss 1973, 132; Matyášová-Lejsková 1973, 168.

L.Sr.

V.133
I Was Naked And You Clothed Me
oil on a circular wooden board with remnants of gilding on the edges of the front side
Diam:13.6 cm; thickness: 1.4 cm
Late sixteenth century
registered in the records of the Národní muzeum in 1928 without mention of its provenance.
Prague, Národní muzeum, inv. no. H2-14 548

The small tondo of unknown attribution bears a painting of a subject taken from the New Testament (Matthew 25:40). According to the Evangelists, Christ says 'I was naked and you clothed me' or 'Whatsoever you do unto these, my humble brothers, you also do unto me'. It is likely that the painting was originally part of a larger cycle of a moralistic nature.

L.Sr.

V.134
The Virgin Mary with the Infant Jesus and the Child John the Baptist
Oil on copper sheet
Sheet 25.1 × 19.5 cm, frame 29.5 × 42.1 cm
Unsigned. The reverse side of the copper sheet is marked in the centre with two punched marks, 7 and 5 mm high. Both marks have shields with indented edges; the larger mark bears a heart-shaped motif and the letters PS pierced by a vertical ending in a figure '4' shape; the smaller mark depicts the motif of the open palm of a right hand.
Late sixteenth century
Bequeathed to the Národní muzeum in 1909 from the estate of Josef Koptík, the owner of a house in Nerudova street in Prague's Malá Strana quarter.
Prague, Národní muzeum, inv. no. H2-7 012

Considering the work's last private owner, it is highly probable that this small painting originated in Prague. The identification of the two maker's marks on the copper plate would have aided in establishing a more precise place of origin, but they have not been identified as yet. The standard theme is depicted using a basically classical Renaissance composition consisting of a balanced pyramid which deviates only slightly to the right of the vertical axis. This irregularity is balanced by the placement of the bowl of fruit and the foot of the column into the left half of the pictorial surface.

L.Sr.

V.135
Christ before the Crucifixion
Oil on copper plate
47.3 × 32.6 cm
Unsigned. The letters *P.Q.R.* are painted on a pennon. The date *18 1/ 3 38* is carved into the back of the panel
Late sixteenth century
Church in Rataje nad Sázavou
Given to the Národní muzeum by Josef Balabán, the parish priest at Saint Bartholomew in Kyje (now Prague 9), with the information about its provenance from the church (of Saint Matthew) in Rataje nad Sázavou, where he had worked before. It was registered in the Museum's files only on 27 October 1908, after a necessary restoration by Pavel Bergner, the gallery inspector of the Association of Patriotic Friends of Art
Prague, Národní muzeum, inv. no. H2-6 998

The painting undoubtedly came to the Baroque church of Saint Matthew (1675-1691) in Rataje nad Sázavou secondarily; given its high quality, it most probably came from Prague. It is notable for the refined spatial composition based on several intersecting diagonals, the dramatic alternations of warm and cold colour tones, the complex positions of the figures, the smooth, blended painting technique, and above all the typology of the refined, round faces and only slightly elongated heads. The strong foreground figure of the bailiff with the rope kneeling in the lower left recalls the young man who often appears in various forms in von Aachen's paintings; it is widely thought that the artist's son served as the model for this figure.

L.Sr.

V.136
Portrait of an Anonymous Burgher
Oil on fragmentary wooden panel
15.1 × 9.8 cm, thickness 0.5 cm
Ca. 1600
Given to the Národní muzeum in late
1868 – early 1869 by Antonín Pavan, a
locksmith in Prague
Prague, Národní muzeum, inv. no. H2-3
926

When the academic painter Milan Kadavý
restored this fragmentary painting in
1996, the results confirmed the hypothesis
that this work, like the corresponding portrait of a woman (Inv. n. H2-3 927) is actu-

ally a cut-out from an epitaph rather than
an independent portrait. Given the slight
thickness of the board, it must have been a
relatively small epitaph. The extremely refined, almost glazed painting is of fairly
good quality and depicts an anonymous
burgher, apparently from Prague, and successfully incorporates portrait-like traits
into the painting. The traditional short-
cropped hair and beard and the shape of
the small frilled collar suggest a date in
the late sixteenth to early seventeenth centuries.

L.Sr.

V.137
*Portrait of an Anonymous Burgher Woman
and Female Relatives*
Oil on fragmentary wooden panel
17.4 × 12.7 cm, thickness 0.5 cm
Ca. 1600
Given to the Národní muzeum in late
1868; early 1869 by Antonín Pavan, a locksmith in Prague
Prague, Národní muzeum, inv. no. H2-3
927

The portrait of a woman with fragments
of two other women's heads, uncovered
during the restoration of the work in 1996,
is a fragment cut from the same epitaph as

the preceding portrait of a man. The face
of this woman (the wife, perhaps) is depicted in a much more summary manner
and with downcast eyes, thus it is possible
that the portrait was painted immediately
following her death. The diagonal arrangement of the other female figures is
proof that this work was originally an illustration for an epitaph, of which there
are numerous other examples from the
time.

L.Sr.

V.138
*Portrait of Matyáš Devoty, Head of the Reg-
istry Office of the Vice-Regency on Prague
Castle*
Oil on canvas, affixed to a wooden panel
panel
26.7 × 19.6 cm, frame 29.8 × 23.2 cm
Unsigned. On the back of the panel there
is the following addition in brown pen
and ink from the year 1626 or thereafter:
Matias Devoty bei der Staat / Halterei zu
Prag Registrator 1620 / Gestorben Anno
1626 Aetatis Suae 99 annoru/m/ et 9 Men-
sibus".
1620
1877 gift of Václav Diviš of Pardubice,

known as Čistecký of Šerlink, a supporter
and correspondent member of the
Muzeum království českého (Museum of
the Kingdom of Bohemia), along with
portraits of the Hradec Králové wood-
carver Karel Devoty (1738-1817) and his
son, the canon Devoty (1780-1865). It is
most probable that Diviš obtained the
paintings from J. F. Devoty, who spent the
last part of his life in Pardubice.
Prague, Národní muzeum, inv. no. H2-3
978

The portrait of the Registrar (who was responsible for registering any written documents received as well as any messages

received verbally) is artistically mediocre,
but this does not lessen its historical interest. It depicts the face of an energetic old
man who was active in the bureaucratic
service as late as the age of 93. The technique of painting on a board covered with
canvas continues the medieval and early
Renaissance tradition of panel painting,
although oil binding media are used here.
Because of the low quality of standard
bourgeois portraits of the time, they were
often destroyed: that this one was not was
probably due to the strong sense of tradition in the Registrar's family.

L.Sr.

V.139
Portrait of an Anonymous Priest
Oil on an oval iron sheet, with oval brass
frame with a handle
Oval: 16.4 × 12.1 cm; frame 14.9 × 12 cm
1625-50
'Purchased in Prague' for the collections
of the Národní muzeum. Registered in
the records on 6 April 1928 along with a
larger collection of other objects of various provenance.
Prague, Národní muzeum, inv. no. H2-
14.547/a-b

The miniature portrait was painted, surprisingly, on an iron rather than a copper

sheet, as was customary. It was subsequently fitted into a glass covered brass
frame with a handle during the late nineteenth century. The anonymous, mediocre
artistic work depicts an authentic portrait
of an unknown man who can be identified
as a Catholic priest by his cassock, pectoral cross and book. The work is one of
the few extant miniature portraits from
the post-White Mountain period.

L.Sr.

V.140
Anonymous Painter
*Christ on the Cross between the Virgin Mary
and Saint John*
Oil on copper
22.2 × 16.9 cm
Second quarter of the seventeenth centu-
ry
Prague, Národní galerie v Praze, inv. no. O
1 326

This small painting of the Crucifixion,
which is now housed in the Národní galerie in Prague, is a work of unknown origin but is exhibited as an example of lesser domestic painting and was most

probably made to decorate a bourgeois interior. Similar paintings, mostly the work
of domestic guild masters, are documented in great numbers in the inheritance inventories of the Prague bourgeoisie, but
these lists have not yet been identified
with a specific extant work.

M.Š.

V.141
Karel Škréta
Prague 1610 (?) –Prague 1674
Portrait of 'the Mathematician' and his Wife
Oil on canvas
93.5 × 73.5 cm
Before 1640
The portrait comes from the collection of Count Vrtba, and lent in 1796 to the Picture Gallery of the Society of Patriotic Friends of Art, where it was exhibited and subsequently purchased into the collection in 1887
Prague, Národní galerie v Praze, inv. no. O 21

This painting was excluded several times from Škréta's oeuvre, but today its authorship is undisputed. The attribution is confirmed by the comparison with several early works by Škréta (*The Birth of the Virgin Mary*, in the Národní galerie in Prague), as well as by a technical analysis. The work was apparently executed soon after Škréta's return to Bohemia from Italy and is evidence of his acclimatization to the somewhat conservative environment of the Czech lands. The figures portrayed here have never been identified, and the work's title is based on a drawing of almost illegible geometric figures on a piece of paper that the man holds in his hand. Recently,

two interesting but unproved hypotheses have been advanced, according to which the portrait depicts one of the painter's friends – either the mathematician Marcus Marci of Kronland or the provincial land surveyor Rafael Globitz of Bučín, whose son studied in Škréta's workshop during the 1750s.

Prague 1974, cat. no. 76.

M.Š.

V.142
Karel Škréta
Prague 1610 (?)–Prague 1674
Portrait of Bramberger of Bramberg
Oil on canvas
83 × 50 cm
On the right, next to the figure, his coat-of-arms; on the shield a lion in a greenish-grey field, with a black eagle with outspread wings as the jewel
After 1640
The painting was purchased by the Society of Patriotic Friends of Art in 1836 from the estate of J. Bergler, the Director of the Academy
Prague, Národní galerie v Praze, inv. no. O

103

The painting demonstrates the shift in Škréta's artistic views which occurred several years after his return to Bohemia. *If the Portrait of the 'Mathematician' and his Wife* shows Škréta's compromise, as it were, with the Czech Renaissance tradition, then this painting attests to his extraordinary ability to arrive at a deep psychological characterization of the model and to grasp the serious atmosphere of the moment, all using very simple means. The attitude of the figure, the work with light and shadow, and the simple but effective use of gesture indicate that Škréta

was inspired mainly by Venetian portrait painting to introduce new approaches into early Baroque Czech painting.

Prague 1974, cat. no. 78.

M.Š.

V.143
Karel Škréta
Prague 1610 (?)–Prague 1674
Portrait of a Man with Long Blond Hair
Oil on canvas
114.5 × 87 cm
1640s
The portrait comes from the collection of Count Vrtba, from which it was lent in 1796 to the Picture Gallery of the Society of Patriotic Friends of Art, where it was exhibited and subsequently purchased into the collection in 1887
Prague, Národní galerie v Praze, inv. no. O 10

The painting is the portrait of an unknown man who was thought to be Václav Michna of Vacínov. The work demonstrates Škréta's ability to depict the psychological characteristics of the subject: the seemingly relaxed attitude of the figure contrasts sharply with the man's confident, direct gaze and his facial expression. The composition and colour scheme attest to Škréta's deep knowledge of Northern Italian painting techniques (T. Tinelli, B. Strozzi), but the subject's clothing is of Central European origin. The painting's composition, its perfect grasp of the subject, and the treatment of the colour scheme make it one of Škréta's most outstanding works.

Prague 1974, cat. no. 80.

M.Š.

V.144
Emblem (coat-of-arms) of Jiří Melantrich from Aventinum
Relief of fine-grained sandstone with painted fragments
94 × 82 × 15 cm
1563
Transferred to the Lapadarium probably after 1895; listed in the register in 1982
Prague, Národní muzeum v Praze, inv. no. H2-180 490

The tablet with escutcheon was originally part of the semicircular tympanum of the main portal of house no. 471-I in Prague's

Old Town. In the 1660s, the printer Jiří Melantrich from Aventinum gave it a Renaissance make-over. The artistic quality and execution of the relief correspond to this singular type of portal, which in the environs of Prague is distinguished by its stylistic purity. The stonemasonry reveals a refinement and sureness of touch that is especially evident in the figural component of the escutcheon – a bearded man dressed in armour with a flaming torch in his right hand. The depth of the relief of the cartouche's curled ornament and of the overlapping plantlike ornamentation avoids sharp contrasts.

Líbal 1988, p. 105.

M.P.

V.145
Torso of Justice
Cut from Slivenec marble
83 × 49.5 × 29 cm
1591–96
Came to the Lapidarium after the destruction of the Žižkov gasworks in 1932
Prague, Národní muzeum v Praze, inv. no. 2/96

The allegorical figure Justice, along with figures of the other Virtues (by two flanking half-columns), adorn the small pillars of the thirteen-sided frame of the monumental Krocín Fountain, which Mayor Vá-

clav Krocín from Drahobejle had built during the years 1591–96, and on whose front field his coat of arms appeared. The torso of one of the main virtues – Justice – is presented with its usual attributes. The iconographic scheme of the fountain, with the signs of the zodiac in relief in the cartouches of the frame, with statues of the four elements, represented by figures from ancient mythology, by Neptune supported by a pair of dolphins and by the figure of St Wenceslas, issues from the idea of a close relationship between human fate and the immutable laws of the cosmos. In comparison with the figures on the central pillar of the fountain, the lower

artistic standard of the figure of Justice betrays the participation of a less capable stonemason.

M.P.

V.146
Sandstone Console Ornamented by
a Mask
Sandstone
48-48.5 × 14-15 × 28-38.5 cm
After 1600
Prague, Národní muzeum v Praze,
inv. no. H2-dep. 39, 43, 45, 46, 48

Voluted consoles, ornamented on the
front side by masks and below the smaller
scrolls by an acanthus leaf. Originally they
buttressed the upper window-sills of the
first floor of the house known as The Emperor's house, no. 832-II, which stood until 1895 at the corner of Václavské náměstí
(Wenceslas Square) and Jindříské Street.
The sculptor of the consoles has made a
characteristic attempt at expressive indi-
vidualization of the masks, capturing the
variable gestures of the face that reflect
various psychic sensations. Contrasting
with this intention is the uniform representation of the eyes, which produces a
certain degree of tension. Motifs from
components of costumes of the period integrate the individual masks. It is probable
that there was also originally colour on
the very lively relief surface of the consoles. The Late Renaissance adaptations to
the house manifested the need to apply a
more expressive proportion of figural elements, even to the city's architectural
façades. The numerous graphic designs
played an inspirational role in the use of
these decorative motifs.

Denkstein-Drobná-Kybalová 1958, pp. 69,
130, cat. no. 94; Kybalová 1985, p. 248;
Libal 1988, p. 130.

M.P.

V.147
The Book of Citizens' Rights of the Old Town in
Prague
Paper
32.5 × 22 × 6 cm
1550–1600
Prague, Archiv hl. města Prahy
inv. no. sign. 535

In the Old Town in Prague, the books of
citizens' rights began to be kept separately
beginning in the year 1550. The books
contain information on the origins and
previous residences of new citizens. One
of the most prominent politicians of the
city was M. Pavel Kristián Koldín of
Koldín. He came to Prague from Klatov
and, after working in municipal schools
and at the university, he obtained a place
in the municipal government as the chancellor of the Old Town office. He was an
outstanding lawyer and the author of legal codes of citizens' rights, which were
published and adopted in 1563. The
manuscript contains his acceptance into
the bourgeois estate. Kristián of Koldín
received citizenship in the Old Town in
Prague on 16 July 1563. His guarantors in
this transaction were the politician Sixt of
Ottersdorf and the publisher Jiří Melantrich of Aventin.

Teige I (1901), (1902), VI. (1903), VII.
(1904); VIII (1905); Pešek–Svatoš 1987.

J.Me., Sm.

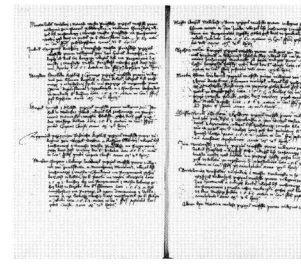

V.148
Confirmation of the Privilege of Ferdinand I
Granted to the Inhabitants of the Old Town
Czech, original, parchment document in
book form, four folios, in a parchment
cover from a later period. A seal originally
attached by the issuer has been lost.
27.5 × 35.1 cm
Prague 1558, 3rd December, Prague
Castle
Prague, Archiv hl. města Prahy, inv. no.
AMP PGL I-48

In 1558, during a period of retrenchment,
the sovereign reinstated privileges which
he had removed from the citizens of
Prague as a punishment for their part in
the unsuccessful Uprising of the Estates
in 1547. Documents which set out the
most fundamental political and commercial rights. Twenty-two documents were
returned three months later, but at the
same time, Ferdinand I declared unambiguous measures by which these rights
were expressly limited and put into effect
some sanctions of an explicitly commercial nature (of which he revoked part because of their catastrophic consequences
on the general economy in 1549). The majority of limitation measures were incorporated into documents, in which he confirmed the privileges of the former
sovereigns to the primate, the burgrave,
councillors and the general community of
the Old Town of Prague. The privilege was
issued as part of other favours which the
sovereign had bestowed on the Czech
subjects during a stay in Prague. Judging
by his ceremonial entrance into the city,
his stay was devoted mostly to celebrating
and presenting his recently acquired rank
of the Holy Roman Emperor.

Prague 1966, cat. no. 97.

Carek 1966, p. 19; Celakovsky 1886, pp.
420–25.

J.Hr.

V.149
Confirmation of a Privilege Granted by Fer-
dinand II to the Old Town of Prague
Czech, original, parchment document in
book form, fourteen folios in brocade
binding. The seal of the issuer, originally
attached to a chord, has been lost.
31 × 35 × 1.5 cm, binding fabric 40 cm
8 April 1627
Prague, Archiv hl. města Prahy, inv. no.
AMP PGL I-66

In this document Ferdinand II confirmed
in detail the privileges of former sovereigns to the magistrates, burgomasters,
primates, councillors and general community of Prague's Old Town, who had remained faithful during the uprising and
had remained within the catholic faith. Insofar as the rights had once been approved by Emperor Ferdinand I, Ferdinand II stipulated further that a
non-catholic was not permitted to take
part in any of the city's guilds and nor
could he be accepted as a citizen or
burgher; also that church property remained in the administration of the councillors, that the community's debts incurred during the uprising should be
considered cancelled and that houses registered in the city records would henceforth not have to be registered in the state
records. The text is richest on the title
page where it has been supplemented by
heraldic decorations arranged in order of
hierarchy with the imperial coat-of-arms,
under which is the emblem of the Chancellor, Zdenek Popel of Lobkowicz (i.e.
representing the office of the Czech court
where the privilege originated) and the
lowest position is the recipient - the Old
Town of Prague.

Prague 1938, no. 396; Prague 1966, no. 131.

Carek 1966, p.23; Celakovsky 1886, pp.527-
540; Vojtisek 1938, p.108.

J.Hr.

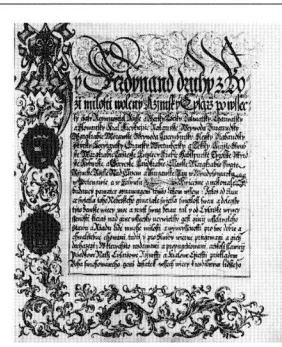

V.150
A Book of Decrees for Prague's Old Town
Paper, bound in parchment originating
from an older manuscript
32 × 20 × 3 cm
Prague, Archiv hl. města Prahy, inv. no.
744, F. 126-129 b

Among other documents the Old Town
book of decrees contains a list of post-
White Mountain emigrées who returned
to Prague after the defeat of Saxony in
1631. The register shows the estate of nobles and knights as well as burghers from
the boroughs of Prague. All were pe-
nalised by the 'Friedland' commission for
confiscation with new fines and by having
their former property confiscated. An entry was recorded as a transcript of the decision of the commission for confiscation
held on 13 December 1633, on the basis of
which the townspeople of the Prague boroughs were to bear witness about the activities and behaviour of those who were
listed in the register.

Bílek, 1882–83; Líva 1930, p. 357.

J.Me., Sm.

V.151
Sealing-stick of Prague's Old Town
Silver
4.5 cm
Copy: *SECRETUM. CIVIUM PRAGENSI-UM*; Inscription: *BOHEMIE REX*
1570
Prague, Archiv hl. města Prahy, Collection of Sealing-sticks and Stamps I/5

The field of the seal bears the royal torso like the seals from the fourteenth century and from the mid-fifteenth century. The head wears a crown. The arms, head and neck are concealed by a wire shirt and the chest by armour-plate. In his right hand

the king holds a sword and, in his left, the apple of the empire with a small cross. The seal has a semi-circular movable casement with a little tab for hanging up. It is ornamented and dated.

Vojtisek 1928, pp.147-48.

J.M.

V.152
Sealing-stick of Prague's Old Town
Silver
Average size 9.0 cm
Copy: *SIGILLUM MAIUS CIVIUM VET-ERIS PRAGAE*
1570
Prague, Archiv hl. města Prahy, Collection of Sealing-sticks and Stamps I/6

The field of the seal bears the Old Town coat-of-arms and resembles an old sealing-stick from 1477. Artistically, however, it corresponds to the period in which it originated. The escutcheon has been rounded off. The helmet and the imperial

crown as well as the lions, the bearers of the coat-of-arms, have been altered. The sealing-stick has a graduated edge comprising several circles. A movable casement which is decoratively wrought is attached to the reverse side; it has a little tab for hanging up.

Prague 1991/92, cat. no. 12.

Vojtisek 1928, p. 147.

J.M.

V.153
Sealing-stick of Malá Strana (Lesser Town) Iron
2.7 cm
PECZET AURZEDN. DO. MEN. MES. PRAZSKEGO
First half of seventeenth century
Prague, Archiv hl. města Prahy, Collection of Sealing-sticks and Stamps

The picture on the seal bears the unusual emblem of a coat-of-arms with a tower and battlements where two trumpeters are playing. A scutcheon of a two-tailed lion appears beneath the window of the tower.

Vojtisek 1928, p. 157.

J.M.

V.154
Sealing-stick of Prague's New Town
Bronze with iron handle
8.8 cm
SIGILLUM. MAIUS. NOVAE. URBIS. PRAGENSIS
1649
Prague, Archiv hl. města Prahy, Collection of Sealing-sticks and Stamps, I/23

This sealing-stick was created and redesigned to mark the successful defence of the New Town during the Swedish siege in 1648. On this occasion Emperor Ferdinand III reformed the town's coat-of-arms, which is borne on the body of the seal of

that impression. The impression has a semicircular holder.

Prague 1991/2, p. 30.

Vojtisek 1928, p. 165.

J.M.

V.155
Privilege of a Coat-of-arms Granted by Ferdinand I to Wolfgang Zach
German, original, parchment document. Border foldd with appended seal has become detached. Coat-of-arms in miniature in the centre of the document
66.5 × 35.5 cm
15 November 1553
Prague, Archiv hl. města Prahy, inv. no. AMP PGL II-200

A personal privilege in which Ferdinand I, by the power of the German King, granted a coat-of-arms to Wolfgang Zach and all his descendants through marriage. The

emblem is reserved for privileged social strata, which thereby satisfies the recipient's desire for greater exposure of himself or of his entire family, while the sovereign's treasury receives much needed income in the form of payments of office taxes for issuing the appropriate privilege, and considering the numerousness of such operations in the sovereign's office, this was not negligible. Even the formal and general justification of unspecified loyal service to the king, the Austrian ruling house and the entire Holy Roman Empire and, by unwritten convention, the use of less ostentatious heraldic components such as a jousting helmet, all comport well

with this type of endowment. The general justification in these documents is stereotypically repetitive. Representation in black and gold colouring is usual, i.e. the colours assumed to be of the imperial coat-of-arms. It was fashionable to make use of a so-called pagan crown, although its combination with twisting drapery is unusual.

Kneschke 1859–70, IX. p.622-623; Hefner 1857, p.6, table 5.

J.Hr.

V.156
Privilege of Nobility Granted by Rudolf II to Veith, Iheremias, Christoff and Balthasar von Gagers zu Rohr
German, authenticated copy, parchment document with coat-of-arms in miniature in the centre, 106 × 130 mm. The seal is in a wooden box attached to a black and gold chord. The copy was obtained in Bruneck on 21 April 1679 and authorized with the seal of the town.
75.7 × 49.1 - 13.5 cm
26 August 1578; copy: 21 April 1679,
Prague, Archiv hl. města Prahy, inv. no.
AMP PGL V-84

By issuing this document, Rudolf II elevated the brothers Veith, Iheremias and Christoff as well as their uncle Balthasar Gagers to the nobility and reformed their old coat-of-arms, with which they had acquired the predicate von Gagers zu Rohr. The privilege was bestowed for the family's many years of service to the Austrian archdukes and the Roman Emperors beginning with Maximilian I and ending with the issuer of this document, mostly for services during the wars with the Turks. Today, the original is not known, so that the exhibit on display is a younger official copy of the first by a hundred and one years. In this regard, the systematical-

ly designed figural miniature, (allegorical figures of Justice and Piety) in the official copy is for the most part a loyal copy of the original miniature. Actually accomplishing the miniature was merely a question of the heraldic and entirely unfinished parts of its decorations in which the town coat-of-arms of Bruneck is illustrated. The Bruneck town council issued the seal for the official copy in 1679.

J.Hr.

V.157
Privilege of a Coat-of-arms Granted by Rudolf II to Petr, Hans, David and Christoff Plintnhofer
German, original, parchment document, coat-of-arms in miniature in the centre of the document, 82 × 108 mm. Originally attached seal of the issuer has been lost
62.5 × 42.5 (border drapes 12 cm)
12 April 1579
Prague, Archiv hl. města Prahy, inv. no.
AMP PGL V -37 11

The coat-of-arms contained in miniature of the privilege granted by Rudolf to the Plintnhofer brothers is a successful exam-

ple of numerous applications of the components of the imperial coat-of-arms and thereby of the sovereign (and later state) to the symbolic repertoire of the townspeople. The entire coat-of-arms is in the traditional colours of black and gold. The figure in the scutcheon is jewelled and portrays the mythical gryphon, which had been the shield bearer of the imperial emblem since the time of Maximilian I. Part of the miniature was filled in a year after being issued, after having been left out by the scribe from the imperial office when writing the text of the document. It is a product of the miniature painting work of the time and represents a combination of

simple, ornamental, systematically designed and figurative types of decoration, the last of which is the most expressive, even though it is limited merely to mythological (seraphim and amorets) or entirely general motifs, and these, moreover, are only in part likenesses of a human and a lion's head.

J.Hr.

V.158
Privilege of a Coat-of-arms Granted by Rudolf II to Johan and Karl Winderbach
German, original, parchment document with miniature coat-of-arms in the centre, 123 × 128 mm. The issuer's attached seal has been lost
74.5 × 43 cm (border folds 13.5 cm)
5 April 1600
Prague, Archiv hl. města Prahy, inv. no.
AMP PGL V-41

The document contains a figurative coat-of-arms in miniature of allegorical figures of Wisdom and Justice. The miniature excels particularly for its very well accom-

plished secondary decorative work which is introduced by an elaborated, systematically designed ornament at the base and especially by the garlands around the edges. The depiction of a river on the scutcheon is an allusion to one of the recipients, Johan Winderbach, who was a burgomaster of the imperial town of Rottenburg, which extends as far as the banks of the River Tauba.

Hrdlicka 1993, p.167, pic. no. 50.

J.Hr.

V.159
Rudolf II's Privileges of Nobility Granted to Conrad Koch
German, original, parchment document. Coat-of-arms in miniature is in the middle of the document, 143 × 150 mm. Seal in a wax bowl, attached to a gold chord
75.5 × 53.5 cm (seal border 11 cm); seal average size 17.5 × 2 cm (body), pendant 7 +24
1 October 1602
Prague, Archiv hl. města Prahy, inv. no.
AMP PGL V 42

This document concerns the elevation of an ordinary and unknown servant of the

imperial court of Rudolf II, who served for twenty-two years as a body-guard, to the rank of nobleman. The coat of arms incorporated certain reference to the recipient's name and profession (e.g., 'Koch' in German = cook).

Hrdlicka 1993, p.167, n., ill. 51.

J.Hr.

V.160
Charter by which Emperor Rudolf II Raises Šimon Podolský and Martin Fruwein to the Nobility and Awards Them an Illustrated Coat of Arms
Original parchment, text in Latin; seal and tassel missing
62.8 × 50 - 11.5 cm
24 February 1603
Prague, Státní ústřední archiv, Archivní fond Guberniální listiny, inv. no. 3416

This heraldic charter is an example of the type of document with which a monarch (or a person empowered by him, known as a palatine) awarded a new coat of arms, or

confirmed or improved an existing one. In some cases the document may also include a promotion to the nobility or to a higher level of the nobility and the right to further privileges, such as the use of red wax seals. The damaged document, with unusually fine decoration, originated in the Hungarian royal chancery. Emperor Rudolf II, acting as King of Hungary, raised Šimon Podolský and his relative Martin Fruwein to the nobility of the Hungarian kingdom and its attached lands, and awarded them an illustrated coat of arms. Šimon Podolský of Podolí (1562–1617) was a painter, provincial and imperial land surveyor, engineer and representa-

tive of the Old Town painters' guild, who worked for Emperor Rudolf II, the City of Prague and the community of the Estates. Martin Fruwein of Podolí, Prague burgher and Old Town procurator, was elected Defensor in 1609. A leading participant in the resistance to the Emperor, he was imprisoned after the Battle of the White Mountain and died tragically as a result of a fall from the White Tower of Prague Castle on 7 June 1621.

H.S.

v.161

Privilege of a Coat-of-arms Granted by udolf II to the Brothers Jirik, Jan Mikulas, Vaclav and Pavel Zaluzsky
Czech original, parchment document, coat-of-arms in miniature in the middle of the document, 102 × 104 mm; Attached seal has been lost
72 × 54 (border folds 11 cm)
13 November 1606
Prague, Archiv hl. města Prahy, inv. no. AMP PGL V 46

Emperor Rudolf II conferred a coat-of-arms by his majesty, issued at his summer residence at the chateau in Brandýs nad Labem, to the brothers Zaluzsky, and the predicate name of Helfenstejn. Of the merits of the family, only the many years' service of Pavel Zaluzsky, along with father of the recipients, was expressly cited in his function of imperial burgomaster of the royal town of Tabor.

Sedlacek 1925, p. 683-684; Kral 1900, p. 283; Schimon 1859, p.197; Kral 1904, p.302; Doerr 1900, p.76

J.Hr.

v.162

The Privilege of Rudolf II Granted to the State Guild of Dyers and Linen Pressers in the Czech Kingdom
Czech original, parchment document in the form of a bundle, six folios; the spine is pulled taut by a yellow chord, from which the seal of the printer has come apart and been lost. Coat-of-arms in miniature on folio 1b.
32.5 × 41.5 × 0.5 cm
On the back section of folio 6b: the name of *Jirik Perger*. This perhaps concerns one of the persons from the circle of those in receipt of the document.
26 June 1596

Prague, Archiv hl. města Prahy, inv. no. AMP PGL II - 54

Although the colouring of linen belongs to the venerable professions, information about the origin of the guild for this trade, which was later to become independent, does not appear until 1518. In view of marked specialization in Czech towns, this activity provided additional work carried out mostly by the journeymen to drapery and linen masters. The number of pure master dyers who pressed linen in their workshops was never great in the capital, let alone in the other towns, and this was evidently one of the reasons that the guild of pressers and linen dyers became established for the country as a whole. Being founded so late meant that it was not endowed with a guild symbol in heraldic form until the time of Ferdinand I when the guild was restored in 1562.

Prague, 1966, no. 101; Prague, 1991, no. 8/2

Carek 1966, p. 19; Carek 1973, pp. 9, 11, 16; Diviš 1984, p. 31, Diviš 1992, p. 21; Hrdlicka 1993, p. 78 n., ill. 19; Husa 1967, ill. 64; Jasek 1980, p. 54; Jasek 1981, p. 18; Mendelova 1991, p. 13; Muller 1987, p. 134; Rybicka 1881, pp. 459, 460; Sedlak 1977, March.

J.Hr.

---

v.163

Old Masters of Embroidery Describe Their Work
Paper, single sheet, original, Czech language
32.5 × 20.5 cm
Ca. 1600
Prague, Archiv hl. města Prahy, inv. no. PPL 133/38

The embroiderers (users of gold and silver thread, pearls and silk) belonged after 1600 to the third largest craft in the Prague Old Town and Malá Strana Guild of St Luke – the association of painters, glassworkers, embroiderers, cabinet-makers, gold-beaters and carvers. From approximately 1577 the embroiderers maintained a guild with the ornamenters – a craft concerned primarily with the decoration of hats. Both crafts worked with similar materials and on analogous orders. In 1594 conflicts over the monopoly in the craft in the Prague townships brought the embroiderers over to the numerically strong and professionally respected Guild of St Luke. The document dates from around 1600 and is addressed to the Town Council of Prague Old Town. It gives a picture of the articles made by the embroiderers: '...everything which is from pearls, drawn gold and silver, similarly gold and silver thread and beaten gold and silver, whether pictures, foliage, flowers or herbs, also with black enamel and silk, in sum all those items of woven materials embroidered in a frame, to whatever they belong, to altar covers or to vestments, to clothes, hats or ornaments, all that is connected with the art of the sewer in precious materials'. Conflicts between the embroiderers and ornamenters continued into the first decade of the seventeenth century and grew in intensity between 1603 and 1609.

Winter 1909, p. 246.

M.H. and J.H.L.

---

v.164

Confirmation of Privilege Granted by King Matthias to the Prague Swordsmen for Plume and Long Sword
German original, parchment document, original seal of the issuer attached by chords has been lost.
80 × 56.5 cm (border folds 13 cm)
4 March 1613
Prague, Archiv hl. města Prahy, inv. no. AMP PGL II-72

The swordsmen's schools in Rudolfine Prague crystallized around several groups whose position approximated that of the trade guilds, but which were far more freely organised in the specific details of their activities and which enjoyed a special superior form of jurisdiction. Their regulations were evidently frightening in origin and are contained in the first preserved and, at the same time, specially established privilege for them by Emperor Rudolf II, which Matthias had received without any changes to their confirmation. The vast majority of Prague swordsmen came from the Italian school, which was opposed to the Spanish conception which drew on the social hierarchy and in being put into practice made use of an accurately calculated geometry of movements. The Italian school was noted for its vigour and elegance (for example, the regulation of constantly touching the blade of the weapon when practising for a fencing competition).

J.Hr.

v.165

Privilege of Ferdinand II Granted to the State Guild of Dyers and Linen-pressers in the Kingdom of Bohemia
In German, the original parchment document is in the form of a scroll of 10 folios. A miniature of the coat-of-arms is on folio 1b, 213 × 266 mm. The relatively damaged seal of the issuer in black wax is appended to partially broken gold-black chords in a wooden box, the lid of which has been lost and replaced by a paper one from a later period.
27 October 1628
Prague, Archiv hl. města Prahy, inv. no. AMG PGL II-51

The systematic figural design of the miniature is complemented by symbols of power with reminders of the military events which took place during the Thirty Years' War. Emperor Ferdinand II, the issuer of the document, is portrayed on the right side, wearing the usual majestic cloak with the insignia of his high office and the Order of the Golden Fleece. The allegorical figure of Victory (bearing the attributes of a laurel wreath and a sprig of palm) stands as his counterpart. The hierarchically ordered decorations for coats-of-arms are brought to mind by the issuer. Next to the most highly positioned imperial coat-of-arms, situated on the right are the emblems of the church electors of the Roman Empire in Spanish scutcheons with golden cartouche, under the red hats of priestly office (those of the archbishop of Mainz, Cologne and Treves). On the left are the secular electors in the same arrangement as the emblems of the church electors.

Carek 1973, pp.9, 11, 16; Diviš 1984, p.31; Diviš 1992, p.21; Hrdlicka 1993, p.78, n., pic. no. 20; Husa 1967, pic. no.64; Jasek 1980, p.54; Jasek 1981, p.18; Muller 1987, p.134; Rybicka 1881, pp.459-460; Sedlak 1977, March.

J.Hr.

V.166
Privilege Granted by Ferdinand II to the Old Town Cobblers of Prague
Czech original, parchment document in book form, 11 folios. On the inside page of the plates appears the paper diploma of graduation from Leipzig University, dated 20 May 1602 of Georgius Valgrist. The paper binding of the book is covered with black velvet and completed by binding strings made of silk. A coat-of-arms in miniature appears on folio 7a, 144 × 151 mm. The seal of the issuer has been lost.
30 × 34.5 × 1.5 cm; binding strings max 28.5 cm
28 February 1629

Prague, Archiv hl. města Prahy, inv. no. AMP Cechy, sevci 1

A series of privileges issued at the end of the 1620s by Ferdinand II reflected social changes which were enacted in the revised state constitution. Confirmation was also issued of appropriate alterations to the older statutes of the cobblers' guild in Prague's Old Town, including the wording of two decrees which were issued in the name of the Emperor between 1624 and 1626 by his power of attorney and Vice-regent in Bohemia, Charles of Lichtenstein. Their emblem was also confirmed and renewed. The Old Town cobblers, like the

majority of servants of this trade throughout Europe, had been using a white shield with red top boots since the Middle Ages. Top boots were one of the items a novice had to submit to a master for examination, but setting them into an anchor is remarkable.

Prague 1991, no.6/3.

Carek 1930, pp.54, 59, 61, 63, tab. I, no. 1, III, no.8, IV, no. 5; Carek 1973, pp.11, 16; Diviš 1984, pp.62-63; Diviš 1992, pp. 109-116; Harlas 1903, pp.126-127, tab. X. Harlas 1912, pp.23-46

J.Hr.

V.167
Privilege Granted by Ferdinand II to the Lesser Town Cobblers
Czech original, parchment document in book form, five folios. Brown binding, leather with gold embossed decoration, on the main plate of which in the middle is the imperial coat-of-arms with the figures of the evangelists in the frame. The Czech emblem is on the back plate in the frame with the figures of Mercury and Helius. Eight purple silk strings were originally attached to the binding, the majority of which have come apart or been inserted inside the document. A coat-of-arms in miniature appears on fo-

lio 5a, 149 × 133 mm
35 × 40 2 cm; the seal is of average size 14.5 × 3 cm (body), pendant 12 +7.5 cm
Vienna, 1631, 22nd December
Prague, Archiv hl. města Prahy, inv. no. AMP, Sevci 10

As in the case of the Old Town cobblers, those of the Lesser Town obtained confirmation and revision of their statutes and emblem a little later from Emperor Ferdinand II. The emblem was particularly different in that it was only codified by this privilege. Given that the Lesser Town had been destroyed during the Hussite Wars and was not reconstructed until the Jagel-

lonian era, it was thereby subject to the Old Town for administration, which lasted until the sixteenth century. The shield-bearers are constituted as an analogy of the Old Town, as contemporary men-at-arms and not in the Renaissance style.

Prague 1991, no. 6/4.

Carek 1930, pp.54, 59, 61,63, tab. I, no.1, III, no.8, IV, no.5; Carek 1973, pp.11, 16; Diviš 1984, p.62-63; Diviš 1992, pp.109-116; Harlas 1903, pp.126-127, tab. X; Harlas 1912, pp.23-46.

J.Hr.

V.168
Document by which the Palatine Jan Steinmerz of Lilienstein, Confers an Emblem on the Barbers of Prague
German original, parchment document in book form, seven folios. Binding in dark brown leather with embossed ornamental models on the edges. The foremost is further completed by the date 1632. The imperial emblem is on both plates in the oval and in the middle of a wormwood cartouche. A coat-of-arms in miniature appears on folio 4b, 84 × 113 mm. The issuer's seal, mentioned in corroboration on folio 6b, as of great nobility, has come apart from its chord, which has been lost.

22 × 31 × 1.5 cm; binding strings 26.5 cm
Prague, Archiv hl. města Prahy, inv. no. AMP PGL II -75

For a long time the barbers were in the shadow of their more numerous and often more affluent colleagues, the barber-surgeons. Just about all the activities which a barber carried out as his independent trade, i.e. mostly shaving chins, washing, cutting hair and other improvements to hair as well as all the medical operations they performed at the time, could only make them second to the profession of barber-surgeons. The main difference, which perhaps led to the division of the two

trades, was that a barber with his surgical and healing treatment, carried out all this in his own workplace, which was equipped specifically for these purposes. Minimum medical treatment included opening veins for bleeding and the extraction of gunshot caused by light weaponry (hand fire-arms) with the help of special screws.

Carek 1973, p.16; Diviš 1984, p.44; Diviš 1992, p.55, 143; Hrdlicka 1993, p. 88, pic. no. 24; Husa 1967, pic. no. 106; Muller 1987, p.132; Palivec 1972, pp.11-13; Palivec 1974, pp.41-43.

J.Hr.

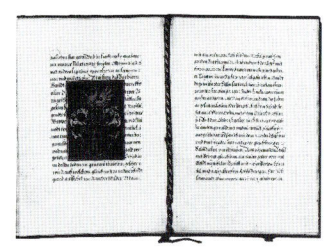

V.169
Visitors' Book of the Prague Store-house of Salted Fish
paper, initial illumination on parchment
32 × 22 × 4 cm
1600–79
Prague, Archiv hl. mďsta Prahy, inv. no. 7962

The fish picklers were part of a brotherhood of merchants whose activities were centred in Prague's New Town on the cattle market near the 'Underlák'. The storehouse had an exclusive right to store salted fish for the entire kingdom of Bohemia from the fourteenth century onwards. The

manuscript is some sort of commemorative book which includes various texts for light reading as well as visitors' records. In addition to genre pictures relating to the business, the book also contains the coats-of-arms of individual burghers - salted fish traders - and merchants' emblems.

Janáček 1972, pp. 154–57.

J.Me., Sm.

V.170
Sealing-stick of the Vysehrad Butchers' Guild
Silver
4 cm
RZEMESIA RZEZNICKEHO PORZADKU. MIESTA HORY VISSEHRADU.
1576
Prague, Archiv hl. města Prahy, Collection of Sealing-sticks and Stamps III/99

The seal bears the emblem of the guild: a coat-of-arms with a two-tailed lion with crown. The butchers' guild was the oldest in Vysehrad. Its statutes were renewed in 1613.

Exhibitions: Prague guild souvenirs from the collection of the Archives of the City of Prague, Prague, 1990

Ruffer Historie ... 1861, p. 288.

J.Me.

V.171
Sealing-stick of the Guild of Prague
Soapmakers
Brass
3.4 cm
*SIGILLUM MINUS SAPONUM PRA-
GENSIUM*
1579
Prague, Archiv hl. města Prahy, Collection
of Sealing-sticks and Stamps III/20

The body of the seal bears the sign of the
guild: soap-makers' tools and a bar of
soap. The first mention of a guild of soapmakers does not appear until 1464. It was
apparently common to the city of Prague.

Apart from soap, the soapmakers produced tallow and wax candles.

Diviš 1992, p. 61 nn.

J.Me.

V.172
Sealing-stick of the Old Town Guild of
Innkeepers
Silver
3.5 cm
*STARSSY A VSSICNI. PIVNI. SSENKIRRY
V STAREM MIESTE PRAZ.*
1603
Prague, Archiv hl. města Prahy, Collection
of Sealing-sticks and Stamps III/20

The seal bears the emblem of the guild.
Citizens who had the right to brew beer
hired innkeepers to sell their beer for a
payment or they themselves hired a tap-
room. In the fourteenth century, councillors and later an office of six masters supervised their activities. In 1357 they
founded a brethren which was common to
the entire city of Prague. As can be seen
from the dating of the sealing-stick, an independent guild already existed in 1603 in
the Old Town of Prague. From 1620 this
guild served under the jurisdiction of the
council of eight masters - purveyors of
brewed beer.

Diviš 1992, p. 125 nn.; Winter 1909, p. 705
nn.; Mendelova 1984, p. 90 nn.

J.Me.

V.173
Sealing-stick of the New Town Guild of
Leather-tanners
Silver
3.7 cm
*S. SECRETUM PELIFICUM. NOVAE.
CIVITATIS. PRAGEN.*
1651
Prague, Archiv hl. města Prahy, Collection
of Sealing-sticks and Stamps III/166

The seal bears the emblem of the guild: a
coat-of-arms with a slanting strip of
leather and a dove with a twig as it was reformed by Vladislav II in 1473. The dove
with twig appears again in the jewellery
where it is supplemented by a coat-of-
arms with the letter 'W' to indicate
Vladislav's name. The emblem is adorned
with a Baroque cover. The guild was
founded in Prague's New Town in 1396
and was among the most affluent.

Prague 1990.

J.Me.

V.174
Sealing-stick of the Soapmakers' Guild
Brass
3.9 cm
Copy: *PECET. MENSSI. PORATKU.
MYDIARSKE A SWIZNIZKE. M.
PRAZSKE* 1655
Prague, Archiv hl. města Prahy, Collection
of Seals and Stamps III/21

The body of the seal bears an emblem of
the guild: a bar of soap and the soap-makers' implements with some Baroque elements.

Diviš 1992, p. 61 nn.

J.Me.

V.175
Sealing-stick of the Old Town
Beer Suppliers
Silver, iron handle
3.6 cm
*P. PAN STARSS. NAKIADN. PIW. WAR-
RENI. STARIHO M.P.*
1657
Prague, Archiv hl. města Prahy, Collection
of Sealing-sticks and Stamps III/23

The body of the seal bears the emblem of
the guild: the figure of St Wenceslas between two brewing implements with
crowns. The guild, the Order of the Old
Town purveyors of brewed beer, was a society of carriers who were at the same time
maltsters and who owned store-houses,
malting houses and breweries and who financed the produce of beer. The guild's
members also included brewing masters,
malt grinders and later tavern-keepers.
The oldest and foremost amongst them
administered the guild's activities and at
the beginning of the sixteenth century,
eight of the foremost and oldest members
acted as a lower delegated court (court of
the eight masters) to deal with debts. The
order was revived at the same time as the
town council. It had an office with scribes
and servants.

Prague 1990.

Holec 1972-4, p. 5.

J.Me.

V.176
The Guild Strong-box for the Prague
Shearers
Wood, veneer of maple and walnut, mar-
quetry, carvings
H: 47.8 cm; W: 58.7 × 39.3 cm
1609
Acquired by the Museum from the Asso-
ciation of Shearers in Prague
Prague, Muzeum hlavního města Prahy,
inv. no. 8.780

The cash-box of the shearers represents
the beginning of a new artistic outlook.
With the coming of early Baroque elements borrowed from architecture began

to dominate in the ornamentation of
strong-boxes. This manifested itself in the
plasticity of the ground plan and the walls
of the box. The marquetry, up till that time
the dominant element of the ornamentation, was now consigned to an ornamental
role. Even the lid, with its raised mid-sec-
tion, underscores the entire architectural
conception of the work.

Schallaburg 1989, no. 1, 8.

Diviš, 1984, p. 51; Diviš 1991-1992, p. 106
Hálová 1955, p. 116; Harlas 1903, p. 125;
Herain 1930, p. 152; Novotný 1948, p. 11

J.D.

V.177
Guild Coffer
Carved wood, inlaid, painted, gilded
60 × 71 × 51 cm
8 November 1612
1911 purchased in Berlin at the Lepke
auction of the Lanna collection
Prague, Uměleckoprůmyslové muzeum
inv. no. 11 953

This coffer (treasury) of the Prague glove-
makers' guild bears the carved, polychromed and gilded coat-of-arms of the
guild, with inlaid inscriptions and a date.
It was bought from the Lanna collection
and is similar to the 1609 guild coffer in

the Muzeum hlavního města Prahy; it evidently came from the same workshop. It is
one of the finest examples of Prague artisanal work, which by the early seventeenth
century was comparable to late Renaissance Italian jewel boxes.

Prague 1955, ill. no. 3; Prague 1965, ill. no.
20; Prague 1975, cat. no. 37; Prague 1985;
Prague 1995; Auction of the Sammlung
Lanna, Berlin 1911, cat. no. 1320, ill. 103

Herain 1930, p. 152; Cimburek, 1950, ill.
1127; Kreisl, 1968, 199, ill. 435.

D.K.

V.178
The Guild Strong-box of the Bakers of
Prague's Old and New Towns
Wood, marquetry
40.2 × 71 × 51.5 cm
On the lid the date 1636 and *Táto pokladna
gest vdelana Za P. ten cass starssich ...*
1636
Acquired by the Museum from the the As-
sociation of Bakers in Prague I and
Prague II
Prague, Muzeum hlavního města Prahy,
inv. no. 34 518

This bakers' strong-box embodies the
changes in the function of guild strong-

boxes that took place over the course of
the second half of the sixteenth century,
when the strong-box vaults, retained by
iron bands able to withstand rough treatment, changed into a chest of ornamental
veneer with marquetry and carvings. The
bakers' strong-box was itself an ostentatious representative of the guild. Unless it
were opened at the beginning of a meeting the proceedings of the guild would
not be valid.

Schallaburg 1989, no. 9, 4.

Diviš 1984, p. 48; Diviš 1991-1992, p. 70;
Harlas 1903, p. 126; Herain 1930, p. 154;

Novotný 1948, p. 13, ill. 5.

J.D.

V.179
An Anonymous Goldsmith
Goblet of the Malá Strana Guild of Gold-
smiths
Gilt copper, coconut, cast, engraved,
wrought, chasing
H: 22.4 cm, Diam: 9.5 cm, the total H: 30
cm
On the lid is an emprinted seal of the
Mala Strana guild of goldsmiths
ca. 1600
Prague, Národní muzeum, dept. of older
Czech history, inv. no. H2-60 761/ab

Goblet of a metal foot and stem with a
body of smooth coconut, embellished by

an engraving and wrought ornamentation
On the lid is the scene of a wild boar hunt.
The metal gilt impress of the guild's seal
on the inner side of the lid gives evidence
of the origin of the goblet. In the seal's picture we are able to recognize the seated
figure of Saint Eligia, patron of goldsmiths and the Latin transcript makes
more specific that this involves a group of
goldsmiths from Prague's Lesser Town. Inside at the bottom of the goblet is a gilt
medallion depicting the Crucifixion, a
borrowing from Renaissance medallions.

Prague 1987 (entry by D. Stará), cat. no.
488.

J.D.

V.180
Window disc with the Sign of the Tailor's
Guild
Glass, painting
Diam: 26 cm
1561
Prague, Muzeum hlavního města Prahy,
inv. no. 14.851

Clearly this item is a fragment of a larger
window whole, of origin and location unfortunately nothing has been passed
down. Yet, it is evident that in the sixteenth century artisans in Bohemia could
bear the expense of such a financially demanding work of art as a painted window.

Thus there had obviously been a significant change in the prestige of crafts in the
Czech lands of that century.

Diviš 1991-1992, p. 48.

J.D.

V.181
Window Roundel with the Emblem of the
Czech Butchers
Clear greenish glass, enamel painting
WOLF.ANDRES.PHILIP.A.RICHTER
1.5.7.9.
Diam: 12.7 cm
1579
Prague, Uměleckoprůmyslové muzeum,
inv. no. 8 340

The divided roundel features crossed axes
and a knife in a blue field on the upper
part, the head of a bull in a white field in
the lower half, and an inscription around
the circumference. It is the counterpart to

the roundel with the emblem of Albrecht
Kolovrat. Based on the analogy with the
pair of roundels showing Christ and the
emblem of Jan of Vartemberg, we can assume that retainers put not only their own
emblems but those of their lord into the
windows of newly-built houses.

Prague 1984.

Jiřík 1933, p. 33; Drahotová-Hejdová 1989,
cat. no. 75.

O.D.

V.182
Beaker with Portraits of Members of the
Winter Family of Tanners
Greenish glass, enamel-painted
H: 25 cm
JACOB WINTER 43, BARTHOL. KNABE
35, MICHAEL WINDER 33, DANIEL
WINTER 35
1614
1939 gift of Hedvika Schicková, Prague
Prague, Uměleckoprůmyslové muzeum,
inv. no. 24 662

The cylindrical beaker has a massive rib
around the bottom. On the surface, between the lines and friezes of white dots,

are four men in black clothing, one with a
staff and beaker, the second with a beaker,
the third with a violin and the fourth with
cards and a handkerchief. Between them
are depictions of tanning implements.

Prague 1984.

Drahotová-Hejdová 1989, cat. no. 68.

O.D.

V.183
Tankard with the Sign of the Cobbler's
Guild
Pewter
H: 17 cm with lid; Diam at bottom: 12.4
cm
1651
Purchased on the antique market
Prague, Muzeum hlavního města Prahy,
inv. no. 3.860

Analogous tankards belonged to the customary equipment of guilds. An integral
part of every guild meeting was what was
known as the 'snack' at the conclusion of
all proceedings. The names engraved on

the tankard's casing do not record its
users, but those who donated the tankard
to the guild for general use.

Schallaburg 1989, no. 9, 36

Diviš 1991–92, p. 110

J.D.

V.184
Ferule of the Guildmaster of Butchers in
Prague's Nové Město
Wood
43.3 cm
1626
Acquired from the Association of Butch-
ers in Prague's Nové Město
Prague, Muzeum hlavního města Prahy,
inv. no. D-1.223

The ferule was the symbol of the guildmasters and its form consciously imitated
the royal sceptre. The the guildmaster's
ferule of individual trades differed in ornamentation, be it painted or engraved, but

not in shape, which remained unaltered
up until the abrogation of the guilds in
the mid-nineteenth century. The ferule
played an important role during various
guild festivals, particularly during the reception of trainees among the journeymen.

Diviš 1991–92, p. 91.

J.D.

V.185
Beaker of Tannery Journeymen of
Prague's Nové Město
Light silver gilding, engraved, hallmarked
H: 13.5 cm; Diam at top: 8.2 cm
On the upper border, *Tento koflík spusobu*
gest od towarissov porzadku kosieluskoho v
NoMIE. Prah. ('this cup was produced by
the journeyman's order of tanners in New
Town, Prague'), the Augsburg mark of in-
spection and the mark of master *NL*; the
marks were re-hallmarked and assessed in
1806/7 and 1810 for the silver.
1627 (end of the sixteenth century)
Acquired from the collection of Dr. J.
Plaček in Kutná Hora

Prague, Muzeum hlavního města Prahy,
inv. no. 27.125

An important component of guild life was
the emergence of journeyman's organizations, known as 'lesser orders', were set up,
despite the opposition of the masters, in
the early sixteenth century. The journeymen's organizations had a parallel structure to the masters' guilds, including their
own treasury and specific powers. The inscription on the beaker bears witness not
only to a strong journeymen's organization, but also to a certain self-reliance of
the journeymen's order, because the
beaker was obviously intended as a gift.

Diviš 1991–92, p. 44

J.D.

v.186
Cask
Silver
11.4 cm
1636
Purchased for the museum in the auction of the Lanna collection, Lepke Berlin, 1911, no. 481
Prague, Muzeum hlavního města Prahy, inv. no. 18 265

The artistic and technical skill of Prague goldsmiths was always very highly valued. Unfortunately, few of the objects made from precious metals have come down from private possessions, because in the early nineteenth century residents had to hand over by government decrees articles made of precious metals, without regard to their antiquity or artistic value, for smelting down in the mints. The cask, which it is possible to break down into two beakers, is a rare preserved object from the property of a Prague burgher.

Schallaburg 1989, cat. nos 10, 1, 17.

J.D.

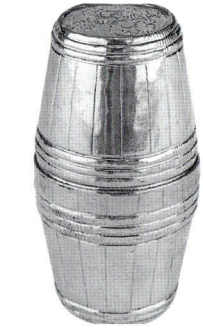

v.187
Drum of the Brewers' Guild
Wood, leather, paint
H: 80.5 cm, Diam: 65 cm
Leopoldus Kubeczius : fecit
16 August 1639
Donated to the museum by Mr. Batula , Prague
Prague, Muzeum hlavního města Prahy, inv. no. 10.318

This drum of the brewers is unique in the general holdings of the collection of guilds in the Museum of the City of Prague, being the sole musical instrument to have survived to the present. Yet guild celebrations undoubtedly were accompanied by music, whether played by the actual members of the guild or by invited professionals. The exact dating and the signature of the instrument's creator have not been established because the drum has received attention hitherto primarily from specialists.

Schallaburg 1989, no. 9, 55.

Diviš 1991–92, p. 100; Valenta, 1918, p. 29.

J.D.

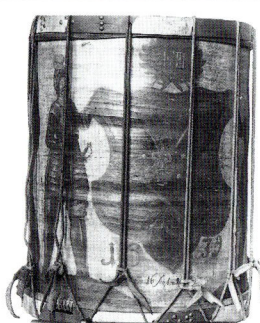

v.188
Sign of the Painters' Guild of Old Town and Malá Strana
Paint on wood, carving
Oval 94 × 85 cm
1604
Acquired from the holdings of a Prague church
Prague, Muzeum hlavního města Prahy, inv. no. 8.950

It is unfortunately not possible to say with certainty from which Prague church the sign came because no precise records of this nature were kept. The sign was most likely originally located on the altar of Saint Luke in the church of Our Lady before Týn. The impetus to produce the shield undoubtedly came from Emperor Rudolf II from 1595 by which the Emperor – bestowing on the guild even further privileges – upgraded the status of the painter's sign used up till then. This upgrade is also rendered precisely on the sign.

Schallaburg 1989, no. 9, 58.

Diviš, 1991–92, p. 56.

J.D.

v.189
The Imperial Charter of 27 April 1595 of Rudolf II
Document parchment, Czech language; seal of Rudolf II in a wooden case; casing of the document black leather
Document 65 × 70 cm; seal diam: 16 cm; casing 28.5 × 29.0 cm, H: 9 cm
On the casing: *MH, 1598* (embossed, gilded); miniature of the coat of arms, marked on the lower right *G.G. Meiier*
27 April 1595; documented in written records 1626–31
1595 Old Town and Malá Strana Painters' Guild; 1812 Archive of the Society of Patriotic Friends of the Arts, Prague
Prague, Národní galerie v Praze, archive, inv. no. AA1 208

By the Imperial Charter of 27 April 1595 Rudolf II confirmed for the Old Town and Malá Strana guild of painters and other crafts the previous privileges of Ludvík Jagellonský (1523) and Ferdinand I (1562); raised painting to an art; accepted the inclusion of a new craft – embroidery – in the guild; and revised the old painters' emblem. According to the document the jewel above the tournament helmet was supplemented with a golden crown, set with two diamonds at the sides and a ruby in the middle; the Moorish woman above the crown was replaced by Pallas Athena in armour as the defender of artistic and educational insitutions. The document was handed over to the association signed and sealed, but with an empty space into which the revised emblem could later be painted. The design for the emblem was executed by the painter Bartolomeus Spranger (1564–1611)

Vienna and Essen 1988, cat. no. 88, p. 209.

Chytil 1904, pp. 22–23; Chytil 1906, pp. 310–14; Halata (ed.).

M.H. and J.H.L.

v.190
Seal of the Guild of Old Town and Malá Strana Painters, Glaziers and Embroiderers
Brass, engraved
Oval, H: 4 cm, W: 3.8 cm, length of the handle 1.9 cm
On the perimeter of the sealing tablet: *SIGILLUM PICTORUM VETERIS PRAGAE*, in the field of the seal: the emblem of the guild from the period after 1595; engraved on the handle: 1601
1601
Prague, Národní galerie v Praze, archive, inv. no. H3-B 819

The brass seal of 1601 was the second seal to belong to the guild of Malá Strana and Old Town painters, glaziers and embroiderers. The emblem on the sealing tablet corresponds to the revised emblem of the guild, as documented in the charter of Rudolf II of 27 April 1595. In the new emblem the jewel above the tournament helmet was supplemented by a golden crown, set with two diamonds at the side, and above the crown were added the figure of the defender of artistic and educational institutions, the goddess Pallas Athena in armour. Until the new seal was made the guild members used the old pewter seal (now in the Archive of the Národní Muzeum v Praze), which represented the first stage in the evolution of the painters' emblem – three badges in a heraldic field. The second stage, involving the addition of the jewel, described in the charter of Rudolf II (cat. no v.189), has not been preserved either as a seal or as its consequent stamp, nor is it documented in other written sources. It is probable that such a seal never even existed.

Chytil 1906, pp. 310–14; Stará 1965, pp. 4, 9–10; Halata (ed.)

M.H.

V.191
Book of Protocols of the Painters' Guild 1600–56
Handwritten on paper, 179 pages, 1 missing (fol. 162); the minutes in the book are written in Czech and German with some individual words in Latin; binding ochre-coloured pigskin, without flaps, openings for leather straps (not preserved) to bind the boards; front cover decorated with stamped arabesques forming two fields
Paper and boards 32.2 × 20.6 cm; spine H: 4 cm
A paper label is glued on the upper field: *Numero 3. Prothocoll von A(nn)o 1600 bies A(nn)o 1656*

1598–99
1598–99 the Old Town and the Malá Strana Painters' Guild, 1812 the Society for the Patriotic Friends of the Arts in Prague
Prague, Národní galerie v Praze, archive, inv. no. AA 120

Altogether the book contains 245 protocols concerning the guild meetings and occasional earlier meetings of members of the Old Town and Malá Strana guild of painters, glassworkers, embroiderers, cabinet-makers, goldbeaters, finishers and carvers. The minutes concern questions such as the presentation of an apprentice

and his acceptance for training; his proclamation as journeyman; records of the acceptance of a guild master and the deposit of examples of his work; records of a newly proclaimed master in the craft; and so on.

Kuchynka 1915, pp. 24–46; Halata 1992, pp. 58–61, Halata (ed.)

M.H.

V.192
Stein with St Luke's Painters' Guild Emblem
Pewter, engraved.
H 22 cm
On handle: tinsmith's emblem, beside the letters *IS VAI*; on the lid: the letters *AM.L* (perhaps *ISS* as well)
1599
Bought in 1932 from J. Bělík in Prague. According to him the stein was previously owned by Josef Nostic from the castle in Horká nad Jizerou. (Although there are no records of ownership at the castle, it is likely that the stein became part of the collection when Josef II dissolved the

guilds.)
Prague, Uměleckoprůmyslové muzeum, inv. no. 16,837

Cylindrical in shape, the stein widens at the bottom and has a leather handle. The lid is flat with a protruding handle and is provided with a finger tab for opening the lid. On the nine facets in the mantle are engraved personifications of the sun and moon and of the planets Venus, Mercury, Jupiter and Mars. On the front is engraved the guild's emblem with the year 1599 and the letters *IS VAI*; beneath the handle is an engraved personification of the Timur Domini ('fear of God'). However, members of

the guild were exhorted to 'be joyous together in the fear of God' and that 'the young [to] show care for the old' (Chytil, p. 318). Such lightness of heart is evident in the comic engraving on the bottom of the stein, which can be seen when the vessel is upturned.

Pewter NM 1972; Uměleckoprůmyslové Muzeum 1975; Uměleckoprůmyslové Muzeum 1985.

Stará 1965, p. 3; Volavková 1969, p. 62.

H.K.

V.193
Window Roundel with the Coat of Arms of Matěj Hutský of Křivoklát
Clear, greenish glass painted with translucent enamel and yellow lazule
Diam: 20 cm
MATIAS HUTSKI OD KRZIWOKLATU MIESTENIN STAR.O MIESTA PRAZSKEO LETHA PANI 1595
1595
Franciscan monastery in Bechyně
Premonstraterian monastery in Teplá, stored in the Uměleckoprůmyslové muzeum in Prague, inv. no. 64 349

The roundel has an inscription and a di-

vided emblem depicting a walking lion in a blue field in the upper half and three shields in a red field in the lower part. There is a standing lion in the jewel. Matěj Hutský of Křivoklát (1546 Křivoklát–1599 Prague) was a painter and illuminator of contemporary Psalters. He studied in the Tyrol and became court painter to Archduke Ferdinand of the Tyrol. He worked in Prague from 1568 onwards and became a member of the Prague painters' guild in 1572. The roundel could have been produced by the glassworks in Broumy on the Křivoklát estate, of which Hutský – the son of a miller – was a native. Window roundels painted with translucent enamel

combined with yellow lazule were quite rare in Bohemia in the late sixteenth century. One of the best-known analogues is the window roundel with the emblem of Petr Vok of Rožmberk in the Uměleckoprůmyslové muzeum in Prague.

Prague 1984.

Drahotová-Hejdová 1989, cat. no. 79.

O.D.

V.194
David Norbert Altman
? Prague–Prague 1656
Madonna with the Infant Jesus, Saint Joseph, Elizabeth and Saint John the Baptist
Oil on canvas
Bottom left: a dedication in Latin to F. Fuk, the abbot of the Premonstratensian monastery in Strahov, dating from 1644. On the back: a guild evaluation of the work certifying that it was received as a master work by the then head of the Old Town painters' guild; also eighteenth-century inscriptions.
1644
Austria, private collection

This painting is the only known work by the Prague painter David Norman Altman. It is a typical example of early Bohemian painting influenced in its depiction of detail by Rudolf's Mannerism, but overall unmistakably a work belonging to the early Baroque. The work conforms to the requirements for a master work set down in the guild's rules of 1589, 'an apprentice in the art of painting... is to paint a picture, using permanent and fine oils, of the Virgin Mary in a red skirt and with a blue cloak wrapped around her, in a seated pose with the infant Jesus in her lap or in her arms, with a building in the foreground and a landscape or land with hill-

tops, forests, mountains and a building in the distance, ... and ... [all] must be painted appropriately and positioned in such a way as to prove a masterly sense of depth and space.' Altman deviated from the requirements in his representation of the background landscape, which is intimated rather than accurately depicted. He often worked on commissions from the monastery between the 1630s and the 1640s.

Chytil 1906, pp. 319–20; Šroněk 1992, pp. 155–61; Šroněk 1996 (under 'D. N. Altman').

M.Š.

V.195
Privilege of Ferdinand I Granted to the Potters of the Old Town and Lesser Town
In Czech, authenticated copy, parchment document. A coat-of-arms in miniature is in the middle of the document, 124 × 128 mm. The issuer of the copy's seal, which was originally attached, has come apart and has been lost with the chords. The copy was supplied by the council of Prague's Old Town in that place on 3 July 1567 and confirmed by the official seal of that town.
66.5 × 43.5 cm (seal border 8.5 cm)
A note on the translation of the document: *Anno 1733 dne 5. Marti tento Vidimus*

Copia jest k J[eho] Vys[oke] Hrab[eci] Exc[elenci] k nejmil[ovstivejsimu] Cis[arskemu] potvrzeni odeslan
17 September 1562
Prague, Muzeum hlavního města Prahy, inv. no. AMP PGL II-109

One of many sanctions against the Prague towns for their participation in the Estates' uprising in 1547 was the termination of commerce organisations or guilds which had existed at the time. Eleven years later and at the same time as the confirmation of privilege was issued by Ferdinand I, which once again laid down this sanction in Prague's Old Town, on 5 December 1558

Prague's citizens attained at least the possibility of revising their trade.

Prague 1991, no. 12/3

Carek 1930, pp. 58, 63, tab. II, no. 4, IV, no. 2, VI, no. 2; Carek 1973, pp. 8, 12, 16; Diviš 1984, p. 33; Diviš 1992, pp. 27–28; Holec 1972, no. 4, p. 53; Holec 1982, p. 34; Hrdlicka 1993, p. 92, n., ill. 95; Husa 1967, pp. 89, 97, 98, ills 99–101; Chromy 1980, p .45 n; Jasek 1980, p. 54; Jasek 1981, pp. 18, 19; Jasek 1989, pp. 88-9; Mendelova 1991, p. 15; Mendl 1947, p. 28; Moschkau 1852, p. 507.

J.Hr.

v.196
Prague Master
Signboard of Prague Potters and Stove-makers
Relief in glazed baked clay; set in wooden frame with two painted sidepanels.
68.5 × 48 cm; Frame 88 × 55 cm with side-panels closed, 88 × 110 cm with panels open.
Ca. 1550
Prague, Muzeum hlavního města Prahy, inv. no. 1554, 34262

The first sign, an image of paradise with the small figure of a potter at the base of the tree, is a guild emblem, referring to the

creation of Adam from the dust of the earth (Gn 2, vii). Iconographically it alludes to Albrecht Dürer (Adam and Eve, 1504; B. 1). In terms of motif and style, however, the relief is related to the carvings of the monogrammist IP (who may, according to some sources, have been the woodcarver Jan-Hanslis of Passau), who represents the Danube school of small-scalle sculptures around 1520; the relief demonstrates the striking influence of this style as late as the middle of the century. The paintings on the side panels, with figures of guildmasters, belong to the same period. They were repainted after 1600 and again in the second quarter of

the eighteenth century. The identity of the painter is not known.

Hálová-Jahodová 1955, no. 134; Kutal 1956, p. 35 n.; Legner 1956, p. 681; Kropáček 1965, p. 35; Müller 1982, p. 279.

J.Kr.

v.197
Burial Shield of the Prague Guild of Cobblers of Malá Strana and Hradčany
Textile, embroidery, appliqué
Oval 43 × 42
1591
Donated to the Museum by the Association of Shoemakers in Prague III and IV
Prague, Muzeum hlavního města Prahy, inv. no. 33 863/2

The burial shield of the cobblers belongs to the oldest preserved in the museum's holdings. It is evidence that Czech cobblers' guilds evidently used from the oldest periods the sign of the so-called 'trivet',

i.e., the motif of three concentrically placed high boots on a shield. The cobblers' guilds in neighbouring lands had one boot in their sign, sometimes shot through by an arrow. The origin of the Czech cobblers' sign has so far not been satisfactorily explained.

Schallaburg 1989, nos 1, 4.

Diviš 1991–92, p. 114; Hálová 1955, p. 209; Harlas 1911, p. 33; Harlas 1914, p. 619.

J.D.

v.198
Burial Shield of the Prague Guild of Furriers
Textile, embroidery
Oval 45.4 × 43.4 cm
Ca. 1600
Donated to the Museum by the Association of Furriers in Prague
Prague, Muzeum hlavního města Prahy, inv. no. 34 442/3

The original sign of Prague furriers was a red shield through which was placed a sash of white fur. In 1473 King Vladislav II augmented the sign by a white dove with a golden sprig in its beak, located on the

transverse strip of fur. The colour of the shield was changed from red to blue. Furriers used this manner of the sign's design for the entire period of the guild's existence.

Diviš, 1991–92, p. 45; Hecke, addend. III, ill. 1.

J.D.

v.199, 1–4
Oval Burial Shields of the Guilds of Malá Strana Locksmiths, Clockmakers, Gunsmiths and Spurmakers
Textile, embroidery and appliqué
Oval 37.5 × 33 cm
1611
Acquired from the property of the Association of Locksmiths in Prague
Prague, Muzeum hlavního města Prahy, inv. nos. D-832/1-4

Burial shields were hung on the displayed coffin of the deceased member of the guild. Guild funerals were known for their ostentation and reflected the economic

and social advancement of the guilds in the sixteenth century. Thus many a wealthy man, without being an artisan, prepaid a guild funeral, even to the extent of furnishing the guilds for public presentability. The textile embroidery and appliqué ornamenting these shields are among the most demanding examples of this type.

Diviš, 1991-92, p. 128.

J.D.

v.200
Funeral Shield of Blacksmith's
Textile, embroidery
Oval 39 × 35.5 cm
1630
Acquired by the Museum from the Association of Blacksmiths in Prague
Praha, Muzeum hlavního města Prahy, inv. no. D-618

Blacksmiths were always esteemed and necessary artisans, which is proven by the fact that the so-called 'due mile' did not apply to them. In Prague's Old Town the guild had already established themselves by 1418, later in New Town in 1446. The

Prague guild was obviously also a regional guild for other Czech blacksmith guilds it was the higher guild. This respect for the Prague guild was reflected in the costly and technically sophisticated execution of the set of funeral shields, such as the one displayed here.

J.D.

V.201
Credenza
Wood, brown stained and carved
100 × 176 × 53 cm
Second half of the sixteenth century
Prague, Uměleckoprůmyslové muzeum
inv. no. 82 857

A prismatoid credenza on low carved feet, with two doors in the lower part and a band of drawers on the upper part, separated by a cornice. The lower part is articulated by vertical bands with scale pattern motifs and tongues. The door panels have lathe-turned handles which are decorated with articulated leaves in a circular field

and in the corners. The band of drawers id divided by three panels with an acanthus motif. The front surface of the drawers is decorated with a horizontal band with scale pattern motifs, and a handle in the centre. The band of drawers is edged with gradated mouldings. The credenza was a favourite element of the aristocratic and bourgeois interior - it was a dining room piece which served to store table dishes and utensils (inside), as well as for serving and for displaying fine dishes (above).

Castle of Trojá (Uměleckoprůmyslové muzeum, Prague) 1989.

D.K.

V.202
Washstand (lavabo)
Inlaid spruce wood
217 × 80 × 42 cm
Second half of the sixteenth century
Prague, Uměleckoprůmyslové muzeum
inv. no. 71 453

A vertical storage piece, the lower part of which is made up of a small five-sided cabinet with doors. The central part has three shelves fixed between two pilasters which support the upper, prismatoid cabinet with doors and console moulding with tooth ornament. The edicule of the doors is inlaid with a flower with birds and a

brickwork motif, and the other panels feature simple geometric inlay. The washstand, a specialized part of the furnishings of the Renaissance interior, developed out of Gothic furniture which was built directly into the wooden wall panelling. The upper cabinet was used to store a water vessel with a spigot; the board held a pewter or ceramic wash basin, and the lower cabinet held a vessel for the used water. Typologically, the lavabo corresponds to the Renaissance sideboard on high legs. It later developed into separate pieces: washstands, commodes, and tables.

Permanent exhibition at the Umělecko-

průmyslové muzeum, Prague.

D.K.

V.203
Chest (cabinet) Table
Brown-stained wood, carved
76 × 109 × 83 cm
First half of the seventeenth century
Central Europe (Bohemia)
Transferred from the castle at Kunratice
Prague, Uměleckoprůmyslové muzeum
inv. no. 78 513

The table has a rectangular upper board (not original) which folds out, and the strip of wood below it contains a storage place with a drawer from a later period. The arched, carved legs are affixed with two wedged crossbars and are connected

below by a parallel crossbar. The strip of wood and the legs are decorated with ornamental carvings of foliage motifs. This type of table with a storage space in the wood below the board, and sometimes with a drawer in the lower part, is related to the Gothic cabinet table which appeared in aristocratic and bourgeois households during the Renaissance and early Baroque periods in Germany, Bohemia, and other parts of Europe.

Lemberk Castle (Uměleckoprůmyslové muzeum, Prague) 1992.

D.K.

V.204, a
Chair
wood, dark stained, carved, turned
92.5 cm
Ca. 1600
From Lemberk castle, obtained in 1953 by the Uměleckoprůmyslové muzeum
Prague, Uměleckoprůmyslové muzeum
inv. no. Z-275/77

The chair is late Renaissance and has lathe-turned front legs joined below by a crossbar. The back legs extend into the chair back, which has carvings with mascarons on the upper part. The middle bar of the back features a cutwork rosette in

the middle. This is a characteristic type of chair from Northern Italy (from the region of Florence) which was used and later manufactured throughout Europe.

V.204, b
Chair
Wood, dark stained, carved, turned
100 cm
Late sixteenth century
From Lemberk castle, obtained in 1953 by the Uměleckoprůmyslové muzeum
Prague, Uměleckoprůmyslové muzeum
inv. no. Z-275/76

The chair is late Renaissance and has

lathe-turned front legs which are joined in the middle and lower parts by a crossbar. The back legs extend into the chair back, which has carvings with mascarons on the upper part. The frame of the back is decorated with carved scale-pattern ornaments, and the central bar features cutwork ornaments with tendrils and a cartouche with a bird and the initials I.V. (the owner's initials).

Lemberk Castle 1992 (Uměleckoprůmyslové muzeum, Prague).

D.K.

V.205, a
Small Jug
Terracotta, light distemper painting, transparent glaze
H: 4.7 cm; diam: 17 cm
1550–1625
Found in 1925 in Prague's Old Town, ul. 17. listopadu, at the construction site for the Law Faculty of Charles University
Prague, Národní muzeum, inv. no. H2-62665

v.205, b
Pitcher with Deer
Terracotta, light distemper painting, transparent glaze

H: 17.5 cm; max. diam: 9.2 cm
1550–1625
Found in Prague's Old Town, Kozí ul.; purchased in 1904 from Mr Steuera
Prague, Národní muzeum, inv. no. H2-5935

V.205, c
Pitcher with Geometric and Stylized Plant Ornamentation
Terracotta, light distemper painting, transparent glaze
H: 17.5 cm
1550–1625
Found in Prague's Old Town, Kozí ul.; purchased in 1904 from Mr Steuera

Prague, Národní muzeum, inv. no. H2-5936

The importation of so-called 'Beroun' wares to Prague has been identified from archaeological finds in the strata of the early modern era. Particularly characteristic are the transparent glaze both inside and out and the ornamentation painted in distemper on contrastingly tinted, hard-fired earthenware.

Matouček, Scheufler, 1988, pp. 189–196; Žegklitz, Zavél, 1990, pp. 95–126.

P.B.

V.206, a
Ball-shaped Jug
Green glass decorated with applied glass thread
H: 19 cm
First half of the seventeenth century
1890 purchased by Chaura
Prague, Uměleckoprůmyslové muzeum, inv. no. 3 777

Prague 1984, cat. no. 91.
Drahotová-Hejdová 1989, cat. no. 91.

V.206, b
Goblet in the Shape of a Female Figure
Muddy green glass with ribbed bowl, fur-

nace-made
H: 19.5 cm
Late sixteenth–early seventeenth century
1906 gift of Sir Vojtěch Lanna
Prague, Uměleckoprůmyslové muzeum, inv. no. 9 760

V.206, c
Conical Goblet with Rings
Green glass, glassworks-decorated
H: 16.5 cm
1600–50
Gift of Sir Vojtěch Lanna
Prague, Uměleckoprůmyslové muzeum, inv. no. 9 843

Prague 1984.
Drahotová-Hejdová 1989, cat. no. 89.

V.206, d
Kuttrolf
Greenish glass, glassworks-produced
H: 23.5 cm
1625–50
1906 gift of Sir Vojtěch Lanna
Prague, Uměleckoprůmyslové muzeum, inv. no. 2 401

O.D.

V.207
Tankard
Clear greyish-green glass, threaded, pewter lid
H: 25.5 cm without lid
Ca. 1600
Purchased at auction in 1888
Prague, Uměleckoprůmyslové muzeum, inv. no. 2 915

The slim, conical tankard features alternating smooth and intertwining stripes which are fused into the material. A horizontal filament has been applied under the rim of the vessel, and the handle is in the shape of a 'C'. Threaded, or filigree,

glass has been documented in archaeological finds at Prague Castle, in the accounts of the glassworks near Vilémov during the years 1608-14, in the Brandenburg glassworks in Grimitz, founded by glassmakers from Chřibská, and in the business reports of Petr Hille of Chřibská at the turn of the seventeenth century.

Prague 1984.

Drahotová-Hejdová 1989, cat. no. 86.

O.D.

V.208
Beaker with a Man Filling a Cup from a Barrel
Clear greyish glass, enamel-painted
H: 24.5 cm; diam: 10 cm
1597
1906 gift of Sir Vojtěch Lanna
Prague, Uměleckoprůmyslové muzeum, inv. no. 9 889

On the front of the cylindrical beaker with a massive foot is a depiction of a man bending over a barrel and filling his cup. Above him is the inscription: *Trinck und ihs / Gott deines Herren / nicht vergiß / 1597.* The other side bears the following rhymed

inscription:

*Der wilkommen bin ich genand
und werd darumb hie her gesandt
so ausgefüttert mit guttem bier oder wen
das wer zum esten mahl kompt erin
dem wirdt man mich so setzem fuhr
damit ein ider sehs und spuhr
was Standes auch dieselben seindt
das se der wirdt mit im meindt*

*Wer Mich williglich nimet an
der thutt alls ein vorstendiger man
und thutt dich nichts sehr dafür wehren
solchs gereich im und dem wirdt zu ehren
wer mich aus trinckt zu Zeit*

dem gesenes die heylige dreyfaltigkeit

Below the rim there is a border of painted white, blue and green pearls; the foot is decorated in a similar manner. With the expansion of the production of enamel-painted glass in the late sixteenth century came an increase in work motifs related to the guilds and the urban patrician class.

O.D.

V.209
Heimeran Wildner the Younger
Aldermen's Kettle
Pewter cast, engraved
H: 51 cm
Pewter founder's marks
1550–80
Vienna, Kunsthistorisches Museum, Sammlungen Schloss Ambras, inv. no. PA 322

The kettle on a high stem with a depressed, globular body, elongated underspout, and rounded handle is in shape closer to the late Gothic period than the Renaissance. According to its heraldic

tablet with a relief of the town emblem of Cheb located on the casing of the vessel, we may assume that the exemplar was originally used at the town hall in Cheb. The kettle is the work of the prominent Cheb master Heimeran Wildner the Younger, a member of a pewter founder's family who became famous particularly for ornamentally reliefed tankards and plates. During the production of the kettle here displayed he respected the older habitual type of aldermen's kettle, which remained in its designed form of that period, with its analogous function, well into the seventeenth century.

Innsbruck 1967, cat. no. 268.

D.St.

V.210
Unknown Master and S. B. Rudolfov
Kettle with Lid
Pewter, engraved; handle repaired in the seventeenth century
H: 37 cm
Engraved 1578
1575–1600
Benedictine monastery in Broumov
Prague, Uměleckoprůmyslové muzeum, inv. no. 64 673

Cylindrical and slightly indented vessel, engraved with bands of stylized leafy patterns. In the centre are vertical oval shapes alternating with S-shaped floral designs in

two rings. Engraved on the flat lid is the date 1578. On the inside bottom is a relief medallion of the Crucifixion. Most likely used in liturgical celebrations, this kettle's design and shape typifies craftsmanship of the second half of the sixteenth century. This kettle already needed repair in the seventeenth century, as is evident from deformations of the body and from the trademark of a younger master on the handle

Hrubý Rohozec.

H.K.

V.211
Jan Slepička the Younger
Active in the last quarter of the sixteenth
century
Smooth Plate
Pewter
Diam: 21.5 cm
On the bottom of the plate: tinsmith's
emblem (Tischer, no. 1236)
1575–1600
Bought in a shop 1958
Prague, Uměleckoprůmyslové muzeum,
inv. no. 45,396

Winter mentions that Jan Slepička frequently visited and often stayed in Prague.

In 1580 he made a pewter coffin for Vilém
of Rožmberk's wife, Anna Bádenská.

Winter 1909, p. 376.

H.K.

V.212
SSG – Master 1597
Decorative Plate
Pewter, engraved
Diam: 27.5 cm
On the bottom: tinsmith's emblem, dated
1599; on the bottom edge: monogram
J.A.N.
1599
Property of Vojtech Lanna 1861 (exhibit
Arkadia Association, no. 269), bought at
auction of Lanna's collection in Berlin
1909
Prague, Uměleckoprůmyslové muzeum,
inv. no. 11 070

The inside bottom features a twelve-point-
ed rosette with floral design and blooms
along the side. Between them is a plate
with an engraved deer, under which is the
date 1599.

Prague 1996, cat. no. 529.

Verzeichnis 1910, cat. no. 79; Stará 1974, p.
13.

H.K.

V.213
Václav Macek, pewterer
Died in Prague ca. 1609
Bowl
Pewter, cast, engraving, hallmarked
Diam: 48.5 cm
Two signs on the bottom: the master's in-
tersected by the initials WM under a coro-
net; the town's is that of Prague's New
Town
Ca. 1600
Discovered during excavation of a house
in Prague's Royal Vineyards. It was pur-
chased by the museum in 1885
Prague, Národní muzeum, inv. no. H2-
1407

An example of Prague pewter production
in the period preceding the Battle of the
White Mountain. Of particular note is the
use of punches in ornamenting the surface of the bowl. This method was more
often applied to the decoration of kettles
and tankards. They largely had expressive
hallmarks in the form of leaves, crosses,
little bells and the like. This technique, frequently used only to complement engraved ornamentation, was at its flourishing peak in Bohemia during the sixteenth
century and the first half of the seventeenth century.

Prague 1972/73.

D.St.

V.214
Master M
Active ca. 1600
Plate
Pewter, engraved
Diam: 27.5 cm
On the border: an emblem
Beginning of the seventeenth century
Bought from Mr Sternschusse 1886
Prague, Uměleckoprůmyslové muzeum,
inv. no. 1,175

On the border of this plate is a wide band
of stylized stems and blooms amid a series
of wavy lines. This pattern is reproduced
on the slightly convex bottom. The central

band features an engraved plate with the
monogram WM. The emblems of Master
M and of Prague's New Town can also be
found on a plate in the museum in Plzeň
upon which is engraved the year 1668 (Tischer, entry 980). D. Stará indicates that the
emblem could be that of a counterfeiter,
even though items with this monogram
appear in distinguished collections. The
characteristic flower motif also appears on
a plate of Prague origin dated 1599
(Prague, Uměleckoprůmyslové muzeum,
inv. n. 11070). This type of 'M' monogram
is typical of craftsmen from the Mrkvička
family: Václav (1560), Jan (1580) and Václav the Younger (1580). The WM mono-

gram may indicate that the plate belonged
to the maker's family.

Permanent collection Prague, Uměleckoprůmyslove Muzeum since 1985.

Tischer p. 223, no. 980; Stará p. 50, no. 64.

H.K.

V.215
Stein with Lid
Ca. 1600
Central Europe
Pewter
H: 22.5 cm
Illegible emblem on handle; on lid: mono-
gram AK
Donated to the Uměleckoprůmyslové
muzeum, Prague, by the castle at Roud-
nice 1950; restored in 1991
Lobkovicz family and Prague, Umělecko-
průmyslové muzeum

A cylindrical vessel, which narrows in the
middle and has a flat lid decorated with

engraved finger-holds. A medallion on the
inside bottom features a relief of a lady in
Renaissance clothing. This is a typical
drinking vessel of the kind seen in paintings in the sixteenth century and the first
half of the seventeenth century. Significantly restored in 1978 by František Jánský.

Permanent collection Prague, Uměleckoprůmyslove muzeum since 1985.

H.K.

V.216
Nicolaus Hirsch
Kettle (Pot) with Lid
Pewter, engraved
H: 44cm
On the handle: tinsmith's emblem (Tischer, no. 100) engraved 1609
After 1600
Bought in Prague from a private collection 1957; previously owned by the church in Chvalšiny
Prague, Uměleckoprůmyslové muzeum, inv. no. 45 312

This cylindrical vessel widens at the bottom and rests on three legs. The flat lid has a handle in the shape of three sitting lions. The centre of the mantle features two rings in a cartouche with an engraved Rožmberg rose and the date. On either side are engraved bearded men in contemporary dress with large canes. On the side bands are blooms and fantastic animal heads. This large stein, which was most likely used as a serving vessel during cermonies at the imperial court, eventually became the property of the church in Chvalšiny.

Permanent exhibit Prague, Uměleckoprůmyslove Muzeum, since 1985.

Historical Register, Krumlov region, Chvalšiny.

H.K.

V.217
Paulus Munch (Münch, Mönch), bell-founder and pewterer
Tankard
Pewter, cast, engraved
H: 30 cm
Two tinsmith's symbols on the handle: the master's with the initial *M*; the town's with the symbol of the town of Louny
After 1608
Louny
After discovery in the Oh'e River, entered the collection of Mr Říha in Počedělnice; in 1953/1954 in the museum at Louny
Louny, Okresní muzeum, inv. no. 8987

A conical tankard decorated on the casing by an engraved plant motif and furnished with three feet in the likeness of sitting lions. On the lid the initials of the owner's name are engraved – MA – and a circular medallion with an illustration of a bouquet in a vase is set in the base of the interior. It is an example of the pewter vessels used for drinking and, if need be, for pouring, which on a reduced scale repeated the shape of the large guild kettles and was utilized predominantly in the milieu of the town inhabitants.

Prague 1972/73.

J.St.

V.218
Unknown master
? According to F. Floris
Four Moulds with Allegories of the Seasons
Pewter
Diam. 15.3 cm
Early seventeenth century
Bought at auction of the Lannov collections 1909
Prague, Uměleckoprůmyslové muzeum, inv. no. 11 498

These round moulds with raised edges feature inverted scenes framed with laurel wreaths. Each season is personified by a woman in a different guise: spring, as a gardener; summer, in a field; autumn, in a vineyard; winter, by the hearth. Moulds of this quality and sharp detail may have been used in forging pewter emblems that were made to decorate other items; other sources indicate they were used for making gingerbread. The engravings of Frans Floris, distributed by the Dutch publishing house of Hieronymus Cock, may have served as models for these moulds.

Ingelheim 1988, cat. no. 108; Prague 1996, cat. no. 523.

H.K.

V.219
Hans Wildt the Younger
Drinking Jug with Relief Decoration
Cast pewter
H: 17.2 cm
Ca. 1600
Bequest of H. Demiani of Dresden in 1911
Dresden, Kunstgewerbemuseum, Schloss Pillnitz, inv. no. 30 282

Hans Wildt, like his father of the same name, made not only bells but also pewter tableware with relief decoration. He used plates produced in Nürnberg as patterns for the casting moulds. On the jug is the unusual motif of the winged evangelists, which had appeared for the first time on the heads of romanesque columns and after that only shortly before 1600. Embossed additions dated 1594 in the corners of the Lindau evangeliary from 810–20 depict similar winged evangelists sitting on plinths opposite their particular symbolic figures. The blocks from which Wildt cast are the work of Hans Peisser of Nürnberg (born ca. 1530). Both works may have been inspired by a series of woodcuts of the evangelists by Hans Sebald Beham, dated 1541, on which however the evangelists are represented as standing figures in heavy, flowing cloaks.

Dresden 1983.

Reinheckel 1983, p. 8, no. 7, ill. 6.

I.J.

V.220
Hans Wildt the Younger
Drinking Jug with Relief Decoration
Cast pewter
H: 19 cm
Ca. 1600
Bequest of H. Demiani of Dresden in 1911
Dresden, Kunstgewerbemuseum, Schloss Pillnitz, inv. no. 30375

The identity of the creator of the plates used by Wildt for this small lidded jug is unknown. The main motif of figures of women set into an arch was created by the repetition of three motifs. The allegorical Faith holding a chalice over which the Host is raised is bordered on one side by Cleopatra with the serpent and on the other by Judith with the head of Holofernes and a sword. The combination of allegory with classical characters is unusual in the humanist iconography of the time. One would perhaps expect to find instead Sofonisba or Artemisia. Sofonisba, the daughter of the King of Carthage, drank poison to escape being taken into capitivity by the Romans. Artemisia was the widow of King Mausolus who demonstrated her fidelity to his memory not only by building his famous tomb but also by daily mixing a little of his ashes into her drink, so that she would be one with him.

Both these historical figures were heorized in the sixteenth century. It is not known whether the maker of the plates represented the figure of Faith in this unusual way deliberately or out of ignorance. Identical plates were made by Hans Wildt's brother, Master C. George Wildt, who was based in Annaberg. The large jug with his mark in the Louvre even has two corresponding rows of characters.

Dresden 1983.

Reinheckel 1983, p. 6, no. 3, ill. 5.

I.J.

V.221
Anonymous Pewterer
Tankard
Pewter, cast
H: 14.5 cm
Second half of sixteenth century
Donated in 1873 by Josef Kofránek, curate in Véstary (in the Hradec Králové region)
Prague, Národní muzeum, inv. no. H2-1375

On the front of the tankard is a relief of the Crucifixion with the kneeling figure of a knight; along the sides are allegorical figures after the designs of Petr Flötner of Nürnberg (1485–1546). On the base of the interior there is a cast of the Jáchymov medal from Wolfe Milicz, dating from 1539, and on the lid an impress of a Saxony medal. The tankard is the sole surviving evidence in the museum's collection of the technology employed on both the Saxonian and Bohemian sides of the Kruňo Mountains in the sixteenth century, during which period the bodies of tankards and kettles were shaped from tin plates and simultaneously cast with relief ornamentation.

Prague 1972/73.

Pewter 1972, p. 19.

J.St.

V.222
Master LG
Dish with Allegorical Asia
Pewter, cast, engraved and embossed
Diam: ca. 45.5 cm
Ca. 1622
Dresden, Kunstgewerbemuseum, Schloss Pillnitz, inv. no. 30 374

Two techniques of execution (casting and this combination of engraving and embossing), typical of pewter from the Jihlava foundry, can be found on the series of plates showing the continents. This combination was widespread in Silesia and Moravia, just as cast relief work was in neighbouring Saxony. In all these districts the patterns for plates that were used apparently came from Nürnberg, and these were then combined in different products. Reliefs used on the plates came from the Netherlandish artist Marcus Geeraerts.

Demiani–Briot 1897.

Haedeke, p. 196.

I.J.

V.223
Master MZ
Dish with Allegory of Europe
Pewter, cast, engraved and embossed
Diam: ca. 47.5 cm
First quarter of the seventeenth century
Dresden, Kunstgewerbemuseum, Schloss Pillnitz, inv. no. 30 373

Demiani–Briot 1897; Haedeke 1973, pp. 196–97.

I.J.

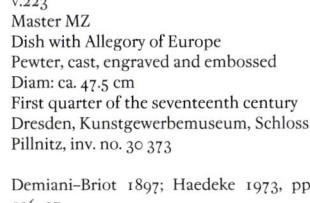

V.224
Decorative Nuptial Plate
Pewter, engraved
Diam. 25.5 cm
On the bottom: tinsmith's emblem (Tischer, entry 976); on the edge: a joint emblem
After 1653
Gift of Mrs M. Bondy 1907
Prague, Uměleckoprůmyslové muzeum, inv. no. 10 684.

On the inside bottom are two rings in which a couple in contemporary dress is embracing. The edge features floral patterning with wavy lines and a stamped joint trademark with the letters *WMZMB* (Matěj Miller Vojtech from Mildenberg, councillor of Prague's New Town) and *KAMRZRS* (his wife, née Rittersfeld). Jan Holub was a prominent Prague tinsmith.

Ingelheim 1988, cat. no. 108; Schallaburg 1989, cat. no. 10.4.15 (trademark indentified by P. Pokorný, 1988).

Stará 1974, p. 50, entry 77; Hráský 1989, p. 77.

H.K.

V.225, a–o
a: Starý, Jiřík (master in Sušice, 1614): Kettle, pewter cast, engraved; 1614–20; Sušice, Muzeum Šumavy, no. 504

b: Master AK: Cistern, lavabo; Sušice, Muzeum Šumavy, inv. no. 509; 7 449

c: Bottle with a screw-on cap, pewter cast; 1620; Sušice, Muzeum Šumavy, inv. no. 511

d: Salt shaker, pewter cast; ca. 1600; Sušice, Muzeum Šumavy, inv. no. 512

e: Table candlestick, pewter cast; ca. 1600; Sušice, Muzeum Šumavy, inv. no. 514

f: Starý, Jiřík (master in Sušice, 1614): Tankard, pewter cast, engraved; 1614–20; Sušice, Muzeum Šumavy, inv. no. 501

g: Anonymous Master: Tankard Pewter cast, engraved, hallmarked; Late 17th century; Sušice, Muzeum Šumavy, inv. no. 498

h: Mistr PP: Tankard, pewter cast, engraved; early 17th century; Sušice, Muzeum Šumavy, inv. no. 503

i: Starý, Jiřík (master in Sušice, 1614): Plate Pewter cast, engraved; 1616; Sušice, Muzeum Šumavy, inv. no. 487

j: Starý, Jiřík (master in Sušice, 1614): Bowl with relief of St Mark, pewter cast, engraved; end of 16th century; Sušice, Muzeum Šumavy, inv. no. 446

k: Mrkvička, Václav (?): Bowl with deer engraving, pewter cast, engraved; ca. 1600; Sušice, Muzeum Šumavy, inv. no. 443

l: Laufer, Matěj (?): Bowl, pewter cast; 1586–1620; Sušice, Muzeum Šumavy, inv. no. 454

m: Starý, Jiřík (master in Sušice, 1614): Plate, pewter cast, engraved; 1614–20; Sušice, Muzeum Šumavy, inv. no. 484

n: Starý, Jiřík (master in Sušice, 1614): Plate, pewter cast, engraved; Sušice, Muzeum Šumavy, inv. no. 480

o: Master PP: Plate on three feet, pewter cast, engraved; 1607; Sušice, Muzeum Šumavy, inv. no. 468

J.St.

V.226
Candlestick
Bronze
H: 36 cm
Ca. 1600
1960, from the property of the V. A. But-
tový family
Prague, Uměleckoprůmyslové muzeum,
inv. no. 52 834

A round bronze candlestick with a profiled baluster stem. The conical centre is
made of iron. This type of candlestick was
produced mainly in southern Germany
and Holland.

J.N.

V.227
Mortar
Bronze
H: 15 cm
Sixteenth century
Obtained in 1935 from the so-called 'mili-
tary patriotic metal collection'
Prague, Uměleckoprůmyslové muzeum,
inv. no. 20 632

A bronze, bell-shaped mortar decorated
with small animal figures and two shields.
The monogram F.B. appears in one of
them, and the other bears the emblem of
the founders' guild. Around the shields
are griffins and, above them, eagles. Gift

of Josefov.

J.N.

V.228
Balthazar Hofman, bell-founder
Documented in Prague's New Town 1607–
30
Mortar
Bronze or bell-metal, cast
H: 42.5 cm
On the casing the legend: *UDIELAN
GEST ODE MNE (BALTHAZARA HOF-
MAN) ZWONARZE MIESSTIENINA/
N.M.P. W SLOWANECH* ('made by me
[Baltazar Hofman] bell-founder
burgher/Nové Město Prague in Slovany')
1621
Deposited in the museum by 1887
Prague, Národní muzeum, inv. no. H2-
1312

The mortar apparently originates from a
Prague apothecary. The owner's sign is on
the casing between horizontal bands in relief, and on the opposite side is the maker's legend. An illustration of the New Testament story of the return of the prodigal
son recurs four times on the upper relief,
which comes from models by Leonhard
Danner of Nürnberg (1507–85) from the
period around 1540. On the lower relief
there is the story of Orpheus enchanting
the animals with his music. This mortar
from 1621 is the sole surviving 'smaller'
example of the bell-founder's work.

Among Hofman's bells, the one at
Vy'ehrad (SS Peter and Paul) was cast in
the same year. The fate of Balthazar Hofman is unknown; he continued the work
of the highly reputed Brikcius of Cimperk
(died 1599).

J.St.

V.229
Hans Weinhabt
Mortar
Bronze
H: 17 cm; D: 16 cm
HANS WEINHABT 1656
1656
Purchased in 1948 at the auction of
Zdeněk Jeřábek
Prague, Uměleckoprůmyslové muzeum,
inv. no. 30 449

A bell-shaped bronze mortar with a single
rectangular handle with horizontal notching. The engraved inscription runs around
the circumference.

J.N.

V.230
Tile with a Likeness of Charles V
Terracotta, unglazed, relief ornamenta-
tion
Front: 22.5 × 17 cm; depth of affixed
frame: 6 cm
CARILVS KEISSER
Ca. 1550
A gift from Franti'ek Pěkny in 1850; un-
published
Prague, Národní muzeum, inv. no. H2-
2556

Known as the 'noble' or 'princely' tile,
named after the depictions of often histor-
ically important noblemen and noble-

women (in this case Emperor Charles V,
1519–1556), it represents a remarkable feature of the Renaissance. Tiles with figures
of the leading representatives of the
Catholic and Protestant camps illustrate a
wide and heterogeneous range of motifs.
The recurrence of entire series of the same
motifs in the Central European region
(and elsewhere) is evidence not only of the
period's predilection for this fashionable
theme (without excluding the primary political purpose) but also, above all, of an
internationalization of tile production in
the Renaissance period. This made possible the circulation of graphic patterns
and, undoubtedly, even of readymade

moulds for tile production.

Hazlbauer–Špaček, 1986, pp. 146–65, 151–
55.

P.B.

V.231
Tile with a Likeness of Rudolf II
Terracotta, unglazed, relief ornamentation; broken fragments replenished by plaster and cardboard (museum adjustment in the nineteenth century)
Original fragment: 15.5 × 10 cm; overall: 21 × 18 × 3.5 cm
Front: *RVDOLPH/ROM(ISCH) K(AISER)*
Ca. 1600
A gift from Marie Matiegková, registered in the collection in 1910; unpublished
Prague, Národní muzeum, inv. no. H2-7246

This is one of the few preserved likenesses

of Rudolf II. Executed in relief on the front of the tile, it renders the monarch in a similar manner to Joseph Heintz's oil painting or to Domenicus Custos' copper engraving of 1594. The pattern for preparing the wooden matrix for the mould was most probably one of the graphic prints of these works. The individual features of Rudolf's face – given the limited scope provided by the material employed – testify to the accomplished level of craftsmanship achieved by the maker of the matrix. Its prototype could have been one of a series of analogous tiles with portraits of the Emperor and the Danish queen known from Ústí nad Labem (an unpublished

find of M. Cvrková), which suggests Saxony (the workshop of Master M F ?) or, even more likely, northern Germany as the region of production.

Strauss 1983, p. 128, tab. 102.

P.B.

V.232, a
Tile with a Scene of Christ Entering Jerusalem
Terracotta, transparent green lead glaze, relief ornamentation
Front: 26 × 23 cm; depth of frame: 5 cm
After 1550

V.232,b
Corner Tile with a Scene of the Capturing of Christ and the Kiss of Judas
Terracotta, transparent green lead glaze, relief ornamentation
Front: 26 × 24 cm and 25.5 × 12.3 cm; depth of frame: 5.5 cm
After 1550

V.232, c
Tile with a Scene of Christ Collapsing under the Cross
Terracotta, transparent green lead glaze, relief ornamentation
Front: 26 × 23 cm; depth of frame: 5.2 cm
After 1550

V.232, d
Tile with a Scene of the Crucifixion
Terracotta, transparent green lead glaze, relief ornamentation
Front: 26 × 23.2 cm; depth of frame: 5 cm
After 1550

Prague, Narodní muzeum, inv. nos H2-144072-4, H2-5810

Religious themes typical of medieval tilework also occur on Renaissance tiles. Their characteristic features are a more sophisticated composition of figural scenes with a large number of figures and, in particular, the use of entire series of semantically connected motifs. One example is this unpublished set of tiles ornamented with scenes of the Passion that have close analogies in the Alpine region.

Strauss 1940, tab. IX; Gutin, Horvath, 1994, pp. 81–82.

P.B.

V.233, a
Tile with Allegorical Figure of Mars
Terracotta, transparent green lead glaze, relief ornamentation
Front: 34.6 × 22.2 cm; depth of frame: 5 cm
1550–1600

V.233, b
Tile with Allegorical Figure of Mercury
Terracotta, transparent green lead glaze, relief ornamentation
Front: 35 × 22 cm; depth of frame: 5.5 cm
1550–1600

V.233, c
Tile with Allegorical Figure of Jupiter

Terracotta, transparent green lead glaze, relief ornamentation
Front: 35 × 22 cm; depth of frame: 5.5 cm
1550–1600

V.233, d
Tile with Allegorical Figure of Saturn
Terracotta, transparent green lead glaze, relief ornamentation
Front: 34.6 × 22.2 cm; depth of frame: 5 cm
1550–1600

Prague, Národní muzeum, inv. nos H2-144075, H2-5811, 5812, 5816

The Renaissance predilection for symbol-

ism and metaphorical expression influenced even the relief ornamentation of tiles. Here we have personifications of the planets. An entire stove survives that is ornamented by allegories of the planets and the liberal arts in polygonally extended sections and by scenes of the Passion. It comes from the Styrian castle of Schönberg (today the Landesmuseum Joanneum Graz) and indicates the likely origin of two analogous series of tiles in the National Museum.

Strauss 1940, p. 45, tab. IX–X.

P.B.

V.234, a
Tile with a Representation of a Roman Heroine
Terracotta, multicoloured glaze – transparent green, white, black, blue, opaque yellow, gilding, relief ornamentation
Front: 29.5 × 29.7 cm; depth of frame: 6 cm
1550–1600

V.234, b
Tile with a Representation of a Roman Empress
Terracotta, multicoloured glaze, gilding, relief ornamentation
Front: 29.5 × 29.5 cm; depth of frame: 6.5 cm

1550–1600

Prague, Národní muzeum, inv. no. H2-2615-16

Ornamentation that draws on Classical mythology and history is an integral attribute of Renaissance tilework. These tiles contain medallions with idealized portraits of the Roman heroine Susanna and the empress Julia. Inscriptions identify the person depicted on each tile. For the time being it is not possible to differentiate conclusively between tiles produced in Nürnberg (e.g., compare the intact stove at Castle Coburg) and Salzburg (work-

shop of Hans Resch ?). The perfect carving and ceramic workmanship and the use of demanding technology involving majolica glazing and gilding place these previously unpublished examples at the summit of contemporaneous production. The customers for these products undoubtedly belonged to the social elite.

Walcher 1906, pp. 67–68, tab. XIX; Hackenbroch 1963–1964, pp. 309–316; Franz 1969, pp. 77–78, ill. 180–183.

P.B.

V.235
Tile with a Medallion-shaped Recess and Figural Motifs
Terracotta, transparent green lead glaze, relief ornamentation
Front: 30 × 18.5 cm; depth of frame: 6.5 cm
1550–1600
Registered in the museum's collection 1940–1942; unpublished
Prague, Narodní muzeum, inv. no. H2-103848

An example of a simple but effective artistic solution to the Renaissance stove is tiles whose front side is divided up by shallowly recessed geometric configurations,

very often in the form of circular medallions. A more exacting variant of the type with a medallion-shaped recess is represented by this tile complemented with figural ornamentation (putti, a female and a male atlas [?] half-figure) and plant motifs – predominantly foliage. It represents a characteristic work of the second half of the sixteenth century. In Rudolfian Prague the recurrence of large oblong tiles with a medallion-shaped recess is documented by archaeological finds from various social milieux: from the town as well as from the Castle area.

Brych, Stehlíková, Žegklitz, 1990, pp. 145–

146.

P.B.

V.236
Tesselated Tile with Plant Decoration
Terracotta, unglazed, relief ornamentation
Front: 25.5 × 21.3 cm; depth of affixed frame: 5.9 cm
Second half of sixteenth to beginning of seventeenth century
Registered in the museum's collection in 1914; unpublished
Prague, Národní muzeum, inv. no. H2-2553

One of the innovations of the Renaissance period was the emergence of so-called 'mosaic' or 'decor-covered' tiles with an 'endless' pattern passing from one tile to the other. Geometric figures in combination with rich plant ornamentation became the dominant elements of decoration, which in their continuity covered the entire surface of the stove.

Brych, Stehlíková, Žegklitz, 1990, pp. 166–70.

P.B.

V.237
Tile with the Imperial Eagle
Terracotta, unglazed, relief ornamentation
Front: 21.7 × 21.8 cm; depth of affixed frame: 6.8 cm
Seventeenth century
Transferred from the Náprstkovo muzeum to the collection in 1969; unpublished
Prague, Národní muzeum, inv. no. H2-144044

This tile bearing the emblem of the Habsburg emperor of the Holy Roman Empire represents the highest stratum of signifi-cation in the group of heraldic tiles from the period under consideration. As surprising as the ordinary, stylistically insignificant and noticeably rustic execution, which somewhat complicates an interpretation of the emblem, is the fact that in the tile material so far there is no comparable analogy to the abovementioned type. The split heart-shaped tablet on the breast of the double-headed eagle bears the symbol of the ancestral Habsburg domains: on the right half is the emblem of Burgundy (reversed) and a figure; on the left half, where we would expect to find the old emblem of Austria, is that of Babenburg (properly on the right), which is not decipherable. The heart-shaped tablet with the Habsburg emblem usually includes other motifs, such as the emblem of Castile – the tower – together with the beam of Babenburg in the most austere variant of the two fields. A lack of adherence to the rules of heraldry (in no way unusual on tiles) is another possible interpretation.

Posse 1909–13; Miller, Loehr, Holzmair, 1948; Kasík 1995, pp. 15–20.

P.B.

V.238
Stove Extension with a Blank Cartouche and Figural Motifs
Terracotta, transparent lead glaze, partially broken relief ornamentation
Front: 20.8 × 31 cm; width of support rib: 6.8 cm
1550–1600
Registered in the collection in 1904; unpublished
Prague, Národní muzeum, inv. no. H2-5814

The decorative extension, which would have completed the crown cornice of the stove, is a little-known component of the production of stovemakers. Openwork ornamentation has been applied: in this instance a pair of angels, supporting the blank cartouche and urn, and a pair of sea horses. They underline the predilection of the period for mythical motifs, often of bizarre creatures whose world became a source of inspiration in the Renaissance, even for tile reliefs. An analogy to the item in question can be found on the stove at Šternberk Castle in Moravia, most likely dating from the second half of the sixteenth century. According to the old inventory of the museum, this extension comes from the same stove as the set of tiles depicting the planetary signs and scenes from the Passion.

Plechačková 1975.

P.B.

V.239
Treasury
Iron
32 × 34 × 80.5 cm
Early sixteenth century
Purchased in 1954 from Karel Fera
Prague, Uměleckoprůmyslové muzeum, inv. no. 35 994

The treasury with key is plated with iron bands and reinforced with crossed bands. There is one keyhole in the centre of the lid, and a second, with two clasps, on the front of the treasury. On the bottom of the lid there are four brackets with engraved decorations. There are two oval handles on the shorter sides.

Moscow 1975.

J.N.

V.240
Furniture Door Lock
Malleable wrough iron, filed and nielled*
13.6 × 30 cm
3rd quarter of the 16th century.
Bought in 1893 from the collections of Architect G. Hering of Munich.
Liberec, Northern Bohemian Museum, inv. no. OK 1902

This furniture lock with ordinary locking mechanism is covered in floral and animal designs common in the third quarter of the sixteenth century. The nielle design used on the lock is not a common feature.

Liberec 1988

Pazaurek 1895, tab. IX; Semerk-Bohmann 1977, p. 90, fig. 69; Mohr 1985, cat. no. 19.

J.M.

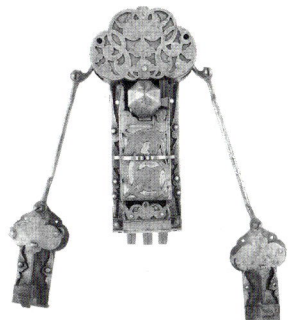

V.241
Group of Furniture Locks
Malleable wrought iron, filed, engraved
and scored.
Total size 84.5 cm (central lock 14.6 × 31.5
cm)
1597
Bought from Heinrich von Liebieg of
Liberec
Liberec, Northern Bohemian Museum

Dated example of a uncommon door lock
controlled from the sides from the central
piece (?). Wavy lines and comic charica-
tures are carefully engraved.

Liberec 1989.

Hanl 1897, p. 33 fig. 14, n. 6, 6a.

J.M.

V.242
Lock
Iron
31 × 20 cm
Seventeenth century
Purchased in 1893 from J. Růžička
Prague, Uměleckoprůmyslové muzeum,
inv. no. 5 119

An upper door lock made of iron, with cutwork and engraving. The labyrinth is in
the shape of a trefoil.

J.N.

V.243, a–d
Padlock
Iron
7.5 × 5 cm
Sixteenth–seventeenth century
Prague, Muzeum hl. m. Prahy, inv. no. 5
248

Padlock with key
Iron
30 × 17.5 cm; key 15 cm
Seventeenth century
Prague, Muzeum hl. m. Prahy, inv. no. 5
990

Padlock
Iron
17 × 13 × 14 cm
Seventeenth century
Prague, Muzeum hl. m. Prahy, 2 085

Padlock
Iron
10 × 8 × 8 cm
Seventeenth century
Prague, Muzeum hl. m. Prahy, inv. no. 2
087

This set of four padlocks represents the
work of Prague locksmiths working at the

turn of seventeenth century. These purely
functional objects, to whose manufacture
almost no attention was paid, remained
basically unchanged in their form from
the fifteenth to the nineteenth century.
They provide clear evidence of the level of
skill among locksmiths whose function
was purely practical.

J.D., J.Ps.

V.244, a-d
Doorkey
Iron
12.5 cm, average of eye 6.5 cm
Gift fromt the archives of A. Wiehl.
Prague, Muzeum hl. m. Prahy, inv. no. 12
710

Doorkey
15.5 cm, average of eye 6.4 cm
Seventeenth century
Prague, Muzeum hl. m. Prahy, inv. no. 9
839

Doorkey
Iron

21 cm, average of eye 8.4 cm
Early seventeenth century
Prague, Muzeum hl. m. Prahy, inv. no. 2
100

Doorkey
14.5 cm, average of eye 5.2 cm
Ca. 1600
Prague, Muzeum hl. m. Prahy, inv. no. 2
094

This set of keys documents the attempt
not only to improve the level of technology and security of a lock (with a hollow pin
inside the lock and a complex labyrinth of
grooves) but also to improve the artistic

design of keys. This is manifest by the
shape of the eye of the key but also often
in its carved decorative work. The keys become works of art without losing any of
their functional value.

J.D., J.Ps.

V.245
Window grill
Wrought iron
97 × 62 cm
Beginning of the seventeenth century
Acquired by the museum from the house
'U minuty', Prague, Old Town no. 3
Prague, Muzeum hl. m. Prahy, inv. no. 11
409

The house 'U minuty', located at the heart
of the town's Gothic centre since the beginning of the fifteenth century, was
transformed into the Renaissance style in
the late sixteenth century. At the beginning of the seventeenth century its façade

was decorated with figural grafitti. The
grill in the shape of the figure '8' was prepared from a circular segment and ornamented by small leaves and little heads, to
create a concept which is completely fitting for the period of the house.

J.D., J.Ps.

V.246
Tombstone cross
Iron, gilded
108 × 58 cm
1600–50
Prague, Muzeum hl. m. Prahy,
inv. no. 8 985

Considering that iron is liable to corrode when exposed to the elements, examples of an iron tombstone cross do not survive from before the beginning of the seventeenth century. This item is one of the oldest and demonstrates the skill and artistic certainty of the maker, a metalsmith who made use of almost all the technological

advancements of his trade to create a work which is indeed presentable.

J.D., J.Ps.

V.247
Tombstone cross
Iron, gilded
158 × 92 cm
Seventeenth century
Prague, Muzeum hl. m. Prahy, inv. no. 14 517

Making this tombstone cross was a monumental challenge to the metalsmith, who demonstrated his creative sensitivity as well as his dexterity as a tradesman. The cross is adorned with spirals that are set in place with rosettes and wrought gilded leaves, the surface of which is highlighted with engravings. The decorative work is

completed by a figure of the crucified Christ with skull, both of which have been made from metal-plate. It may be presumed that the surface of the cross had been treated with colour as was the custom at the time.

J.D., J.Ps.

V.248
Acta Collegi Carolini
Paper codex in plain parchment binding
32.5 × 24 × 6.5 cm
1583–95
Originally in the Carolinum archives, later in those of its successor, the archives of the Charles University. Manuscript catalogued by Adolf Bachmann, the keeper of the archives in the second half of the nineteenth century.
Prague, Archiv Univerzity Karlovy, inv. no. A 13 a

Records of the academic and more generally political affairs of the Utraquist

Charles College of the academy in Prague, the oldest university in Central Europe, drawn up by the provosts of the college. Also includes the correspondence of the provosts with important individuals of the period.

Kučera-Truc 1961

I.Č.

V.249
Acta Universitatis Pragensis
Paper codex in plain parchment cover
32 × 21 × 11.5 cm
1619–22
Originally in the Carolinum archives, later in those of its successor, the archives of the Charles University. Book catalogued by Adolf Bachmann, the keeper of the archives in the second half of the nineteenth century.
Prague, Archiv Univerzity Karlovy, inv. no. A 14 b

Records of important events at the Utraquist academy in Prague. Apart from

records of academic events, most common are references to political events during the Estates Revolt and responses to debates on the future of the Utraquist academy after the Battle of the White Mountain. Included also are notes on the transfer of the former Utraquist academy to the Jesuits and, for example, a record of the death of Jan Kampanus Vodňanský.

Kučera-Truc 1961.

I.Č.

V.250
Variae epistulae scriptae
Paper, parchment binding, partially damaged
29.5 × 20 × 3.5 cm, 206 pages including back endpapers and end leaf
Initials *SP*, date 1598, supralibros of Simon Proxen of Sudeten
After 1658
Plzeň, Archiv města Plzné, inv. no. 353

The manuscript was owned and largely compiled by the humanist poet Šimon Proxen of Sudeten (ca. 1532–1575). He was a professor at Prague University from 1556 to 1562, then travelled abroad as a

preceptor from 1562 to 1566. He was Imperial counsel in the dispute between the Kingdom of Poland and the Duchy of Silesia over the border of the Hlohow princedom in 1567, and participated in the protest of the Czech Estates. The manuscript contains copies of papers and documents, mostly dating from the second half of the sixteenth century, which were important in his personal and official life; documents on the establishment of the Czech state; documents of a more personal nature; and a number of records penned by later owners.

Strnad 1908, 27 (manuscript); Bolohlávek

1954, p. 276; Hejnic–Martínek 1973, pp. 255- 264 (lists other sources).

I.v.M.

V.251
Old University Treasury
Iron
69 × 40 × 39 cm
Second half of the sixteenth century
Prague, Archiv Univerzity Karlovy

The five-part university treasury is made of wrought iron plated with iron bands and reinforced with crossed bands. On the front there are two clasps and a keyhole with an engraved plate around the opening. The coffer was used to store money and especially important documents. In addition to the elected council and the chancellor of the university, two money

collectors (collectores) were elected as keyholders.

Prague 1992–95.

Dějiny Univerzity Karlovy 1995, I, p. 36.

J.N.

V.252
Album academiae Pragensis Societatis Iesu
Paper codex, 111 ff., wooden covers bound in yellowed and untreated leather with relief decoration from the second half of the sixteenth century
20.5 × 30 × 5 cm
1573–1618
Originally in the archives of the Jesuit college of the Clementinum. Placed after the dissolution of the Jesuit order in the university archives, filed by the keeper of the archives, Prof. Adolf Bachmann, in the second half of the nineteenth century. Prague, Archiv Univerzity Karlovy, inv. no. M 19

This book is the oldest surviving register of the Jesuit Ferdinand academy, containing in chronological order the names of the graduates and students in higher and basic studies at the academy. This is the only source of information on the activities of the Jesuit university in the period before the Battle of the White Mountain.

Truc 1968.

I.Č.

V.253
Memorandum of Prague Archbishop and Cardinal Arnošt Vojtěch Harrach, to the Propaganda Committee of Czech Affairs in Rome concerning matters of Charles University, which in 1622 was given by Emperor Ferdinand II to the Jesuit college in Prague's Old Town
22 August 1639
Rough direct copy, paper; In Italian. 3 fols
27.7 × 20 cm
Prague, Státní ústřední archiv, APA I, inv. no. 3356, karton 2044, sign. C 110/2 (a)

In 1622 Emperor Ferdinand II gave the estates and colleges of Charles University to

the Jesuit Order of St Clement in order to augment their philosophical and theological colleges with the faculties of law and medicine. As Archbishop of Prague, Cardinal Harrach was given the office of University Chancellor. He led a dispute with the Propaganda Committee in Rome, which was temporarily settled by an agreement signed in Vienna in 1623, but renewed several years later when the Propaganda Committee prohibited graduation ceremonies. Ceremonies were re-established in 1638, when Emperor Ferdinand III took Charles University into his own hands and established a Rector appointed from the higher echelons of Czech nobility. Negotiations

between the Jesuits, the Propaganda Committee, the Emperor and the Archbishop lasted until 1654, when the ruler finally unified the schools. The contents of Archbishop Harrach's memorandum indicate the state of negotiations in 1639: a copy of his case, thoughts on Charles University, copies of documents from a meeting with Cardinal Pasman 19 June 1632, an essay by Cardinal Pasman and a decree from a conference of 13 May 1632.

Bernek 1971, pp 185-234; Čornejová et al. 1995.

K.B.

V.254
Samuel Weishun
Johan van Bolen
Doctoral thesis of Count Ferdinand Leopold Benn of Martinitz with an Engraving Depicting the Glorification of Ferdinand III
Copper engraving
11.2 × 7.8 cm
1637
Prague, Národní muzeum, inv. no. 425

This doctoral thesis was defended by Count Ferdinand Leopold Benn of Martinitz, the provost of the Vyšehrad chapter, canon of Passau, Halberstadt, Olomouc and Prague before the praesidium,

a Jesuit named father Martin Benedict who was also Ferdinand's ordinary. As a high-ranking church dignitary, Count Martinitz sought to pay homage to his sovereign, Ferdinand III. Martinitz celebrates the honour, justice and piety of the Emperor in the introduction to the thesis, which is emphasized in the iconographic concept of Weishun's engraving.

Fechtnerová 1984, Th 425.

J.R.

V.255
Karel Škréta
Theseus
Drawing in ink with graphite undersketch
27.8 × 17.1 cm
1654
Berlin, Staatliche Museen Berlin, Kupferstichkabinett, inv. no. 79 D 8, Kdz 26 394

This depiction of Theseus coming out of the labyrinth with Adrian's thread in his arms is a design for a university thesis entitled *Ariadnae suae Logica Pragensis*, which S. Weishun (print PNP 20 944) etched in 1645 after a model by Škréta. After Ferdinand Count Martinitz's thesis (cat. no.

V.254), this is the second oldest thesis of Prague University and, respectively, design by Škréta. The latter was later to return often to designing and making these proportional-sized prints.

Prague 1974, cat. no. 170.

M.Š.

V.256
Letter of Thanks from Ferdinand III to the University and its Students for their Defence of Prague against the Swedes
Originally in the Carolinum archives, later in those of its successor, the archives of the Charles University. Document already filed in inventories from the eighteenth century.
22 September 1648
Prague, Archiv Univerzity Karlovy, inv. no. 95/I b

Letter of thanks from the Emperor and Czech King Ferdinand III, in appreciation of the contribution of the academic com-

munity to the defence of Prague against the mercenary division of the Swedish troops in 1648. The combined action of Prague students and teachers in the defence of the town not only contributed to the preservation of the centre of the Czech Kingdom but also became one of the impulses behind the definitive unification of the Jesuit academy of St Clement with the Charles Academy.

Kučera-Truc 1961.

I.Č.

V.257
Letter from Ferdinand III Notifying the Deans and Professors of the Charles University of their Future Amalgamation with the Jesuit Ferdinand Academy
Originally in the Carolinum archives, later in those of its successor, the archives of the Charles University. Document already filed in inventories from the eighteenth century.
23 February 1654
Prague, Archiv Univerzity Karlovy, inv. no. 96/I a.

Letter from Emperor Ferdinand III notifying the Prague Charles University – which

had since 1638 again existed as an independent university with two faculties (medicine and law) – of the decision to unify it with the philosophy and theology faculties of the Ferdinand Jesuit Academy of St Clement. This is the original rescript from 1654 that led to university union.

Kučera-Truc 1961.

I.Č.

V.258
Matricula Universitatis Pragensis, rectorum, decanorum, professorum et specialim in facultate philosophica graduatorum ab Anno 1654
Paper codex in paper-board cover, bound in plain parchment
30 × 22 × 6.5 cm
1654–1730
Originally in the Jesuit archives of the philosophy faculty. After the dissolution of the order in 1773, transferred to the university archives.
Prague, Archiv Univerzity Karlovy, inv. no. M 20

Following the losses suffered by the

archives of the Charles University during the evacuation of the German University in April 1945, this is one of the oldest surviving registers of the Prague university. It records the Masters and Bachelors of the philosophy faculty from the date of university union, the definitive unification of the Charles and Ferdinand Academies in 1654. The document is an important source of information about students and graduands of the Prague university in the period after the Battle of the White Mountain.

I.Č.

V.259
Liber privilegiorum, rescriptorum ... statuorum
Paper codex, 230 fol., wooden covers bound in plain brown leather (binding from the eighteenth century)
41.5 × 28.5 × 3.5 cm
End of seventeenth century or beginning of eighteenth century
Originally in the possession of Jan František Löw of Erlsfeld, professor of the Prague University faculty of medicine, then in the possession of Vilém MacNeven, famous professor of the same faculty. The book probably reached the museum later as a gift.

Prague, Národní muzeum, inv. no. H3–F 191

A book containing copies of the most important privileges, rescripts and statutes of the university in Prague (from 1654 the Charles-Ferdinand University) and its faculty of medicine, with references to important documents of the Charles Academy before the Battle of the White Mountain. The author was Jan František Löw of Erlsfeld, an important professor of the Prague faculty of medicine, long-standing dean and twice rector of the university. He was a patron of the Arts, renowned for having examined the remains of John Nepomuk

before his beatification.

I.Č.

V.260
Chains with Thalers of *Ferdinand I and III*
Gilded silver
Chain lengths 65cm; average size of thalers 6 cm
Mid-sixteenth and mid-seventeenth centuries
Initially in the university treasury, later (precise date not known) deposited in the archives of the Charles University.
Prague, Archiv Univerzity Karlovy, not numbered

Chains with thalers, later with medals depicting monarchs, were decorations for university dignitaries, but were not actual-

ly part of their insignia. Experts subscribe to the view of Václav Vojtíček, who concluded that chains with medals were not worn to comply with any binding university regulations, but rather from a habit of medieval times, when the various dignitaries wore chains with hanging sealing-sticks or other emblems as proof of their rank.

Herber 1987.

I.Č.

V.261
Album of Václav Dobřenský
Leather-bound book, paper
16 × 11 cm (16 × 25 cm open)
After the death of Václav Dobřenský 'Ionnes Drescher' (died 1702) to Tobias Schmid (1714), W. de Veidenthal, 1774 the Prague collector, public servant Jan Heidel, whose extensive library was bought by Strahov library in 1780.
Prague, monastery of the Premonstratensions at Strahov L II 3

The album of the Prague burgher Václav Dobřenský is in one of the most widely available books of emblems, a classic work

entitled *Liber emblematum Andrei Alciati* (Frankfurt 1580), alongside a book by Johann Hoffer, *Icones catecheseos et virtutum ac vitiorum illustratae numeris* (Wittenberg 1557). The album contains records of various characters such as Daniel Adam of Veleeslavín from 1582 as well as some unattributed Czech proverbs. This manuscript is remarkable for its binding from 1571 with an illustration of Martin Luther at the front and of Phillip Melanchton at the back.

Urban 1786, p. 153; Straka 1909, pp. 141-45; Ryba 1971, p. 257; Hertlová, pp. 117-46.

M.R.

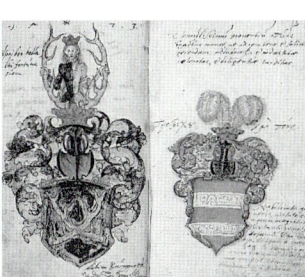

V.262
Album of Isak Aschpan von Hag
Leather bound, paper
18 × 12 cm (open 18 × 24 cm)
erb (sheet 1b)
1572–80
Prague, Národní knihovna, XXIII F 17

The album of Isak Aschpan contains the signatures of Václav Budovec of Budov (1572), Michal Slavata of Chlum and Košumberk, Heník and Zdeněk of Wallenstein, Ondřej and Jiří Šternberk, Jaroslav of Vartenberk and the brothers Erich, Mikuláš and Jan Špánovský of Lisov, from the period of his studies at Wittenberg.

Urbánková 1957, p. 53 (no. 380); Hertlová 1975, pp. 117-46.

M.R.

V.263
Album of Oldrich and Jan Zahrádecký of Zahrádek
Leather-bound book, paper (with gilt remains)
6.5 × 12.5 cm (open 16.5 × 26 cm)
1587-91, 1593, 1595
Prague, Premonstratension monastery at Strahov, inv. no. DG IV 18

The album came to belong to three owners: Oldřich Zahrádský of Zahrádek (1587-1591), Jan Zahrádský (1593) and finally Petr Číčkovský the Younger (1595). It contains a series of miniatures that recall Oldřich's journey to Italy from 1587-88

and his stay in Padua and Venice, referring in particular to the countless popular depictions of women wearing the garments of the time and to depictions of the Venetian doge, as well as the scene of a masked ball an a gondola with a pair of lovers.

Hertlová 1975, pp.117-46.

M.R.

V.264
Album of Zikmund Válek and Kryštof Adam Holbeck
Leather-bound book, paper, print, watercolour
15 × 10.5 cm (open 15 × 23 cm)
1580-02
Godefridus Daniel Liber Baro de Wunschwitz, 1724.
Prague, Národní muzeum, inv. no. H3-B 17

The album of Zikmund Válek and Kryštof Adam Holbeck is an example of where various prints were used to present the records, in this case *Iohan. Posthii Germer-*

shemii Tetrasticha in Ovidii Metamorphoses Libri XV., quibus accesserunt Vergilii Solis figurae...(1563). Many engravings are to be found in the book, often coloured and on loose pages appears a series of coats-of-arms and various records. The scene of parting with a woman was resonant for a good deal of the nobility. Even the motif of winning over a woman between a monk and a nobleman may be found.

Hertlová 1975, pp.117-46.

M.R.

V.265
Album of Adam of Egg
Leather-bound book, paper, watercolours
15 × 10.5 cm (open 15 × 23 cm)
Adama z Eggu památník
1593-1620
Prague, Národní muzeum, inv. no. H3-B 24

Along with a coats-of-arms, the album of Adam of Egg contains a number of quality miniatures that recall the cavalier's journey to Italy from 1593-96, taking in Padua, Sienna, Rome, Venice, Verona, Bologna and Naples. It contains illustrations of the carneval in Venice (including masked fig-

ures and jugglers), portraits of the Venetian doge, dignitaries of the University of Padua, Venetian ladies and prostitutes, a depiction of several boats including the doge's gallery, an audience with the Pope, almost photographic scenes of the Italian landscape by a canal of the River Brenta and genre pictures of journeys (a stagecoach, vegetable seller). The album also contains lists of various outings of the nobility, whether a night-time dual or the 'gallant' visit of a prostitute when a young nobleman is accompanied by an angel and the devil.

Hertlová 1975, pp.117-46.

M.R.

v.266
Album of Jiří Kryštof of Ursenbeck,
Knight of St John
Bound, paper, leather binding
15 × 10 cm (open 15 × 23 cm)
later inscription on end-paper
1596–1605
Prague, Premonstratensian monastery at
Strahov, inv. no. DG IV 10

This album contains a number of entries
in the form of coats-of-arms and several
miniatures, in particular, two favourite depictions of galleys in memory of his voyage to Italy during the years 1596–97,
when he visited Rome, Naples, Padua and

Sienna. The nobility were especially fond
of falconry, a sport represented in one of
the miniatures.

Hertlová 1975, pp. 117-46.

M.R.

v.267
Album of Adam Lehner of Kouba
Paper, leather binding with supralibros
20 × 16 cm (open 20 × 34.5 cm)
*Adamus Lehnerus de Cauba, 8.Novemb.
1598, Pragae Bohemus*(fol .20r)
1598–1616
Prague, Premonstratensian monastery at
Strahov, inv. no. DF IV 24

This album contains engravings of Austri-
an Archdukes and Tyrolean Counts
Ernest, Maximilian and Matthias, Polish
King Zikmund III, Danish King Kristian
IV, Turkish Sultan Mahmed III and others,
with an entry by Jan Jesenský, rector of the

Wittenberg Academy (1598), and several
other entries (some with coats-of-arms) to
commemorate the owner's visit to Wittenberg. Other entries were added in Prague,
including several by members of the
Platýz family of Platenštejn.

Hertlová 1975, pp. 117-46.

M.R.

v.268
Album of Matyáš Gunther of Jihlava
Paper, leather binding
21 × 17 cm (open 21 × 37.5 cm)
1599–1612
Prague, Premonstratensian monastery at
Strahov, inv. no. DG IV 27

Two publications were used for the purposes of this album: *Sphera Ciuitatis*
(Frankfurt, 1593), with various excerpts
and notes on the text; and *David, virtutis
exercitatissimae probatum Deo spectaculum...*
(1597). The second work contains single
sheets bearing a number of coats-of-arms
and entries by Czech nobles (Krakovský of

Kolowrat, Libštejnský of Kolowrat,
Vratislav of Mitrovice) and several miniatures depicting a fall from a horse and an
audience with King Midas.

Hertlová 1975, pp. 117-46.

M.R.

v.269
Album of Michal the Elder of Stubenvol
Paper, leather binding with supralibros
20.5 × 13.5 cm (open 20.5 × 28 cm)
1602–30
Prague, Premonstratensian monastery at
Strahov, inv. no. DG IV 26

This album contains several anonymous
drawings in sepia, pencil or ink without
any accompanying text, which would suggest it served partly as a sketchbook (there
are depictions of the Lord, Madonna, the
head of Christ, cherubim, St Christopher).
There are a number of coats-of-arms and
entries describing a journey through Eu-

rope during the period 1602–03 (Milan,
Florence, Naples, Verona, Paris, Lyon), and
entries from Prague and Vienna from
1630. This manuscript is also remarkable
for its coloured Turkish silhouette paper
(*Silhouettenpapier*) with the floral motifs
that were fashionable at the time and often appeared in albums.

Herlová 1975, pp. 117-46.

M.R.

v.270
Album of Vilém Kunáš of Machovice
Paper, leather binding, engravings, watercolours
18 × 14 cm (open 18 × 30 cm)
In pencil: *Vilém Kunáš z Machovic* (fol. 1a)
1603–20 (1692)
Prague, Národní muzeum, inv. no. H3-B 1
166

This album belonged to a southern Bohemian nobleman and is one of the most
valuable, most richly decorated and most
fascinating manuscripts of its type. Apart
from the numerous customary entries
with coats-of-arms, proverbs, mottos and

engravings, it also contains a great number of miniatures covering a broad range
of themes: Classical motifs (Diana and Actaeon, Amor and Venus, Perseus and Andromeda), several hunting scenes and fine
executions based on military themes or allegorical depictions of the Christian
virtues, as well as adventures with prostitutes or noblemen fencing or drinking together, and the favoured scenes of fare-
well. The exquisite depiction of Fortuna is
evidently the work of the young Václav
Hollar, with whose father the owner of the
album was acquainted. The sheets of the
album are inset with several leaves of marbled paper.

Hertlová 1975, pp. 117-46; Denkstein
1981, pp. 377-94.

M.R.

V.271
Album of Jiří Leopold von Stadl
Bound, paper, leather
21.5 × 18 cm
1606–14
Lobkowicz library in Roudnice
Prague, W.Lobkowicz collection, deposited in the National Library, inv. no. VI Fe 64

This album comprises two volumes containing cut-out and rebound album leaves probably originating from a larger single album. The first volume exclusively contains illustrations, the second features written entries with painted coats-of-

arms. This album commemorates a journey to Venice and Naples, and depicts men and women in period dress. There are also landscapes, illustrations of stage-coaches, peasants and a figure of a Turk. Mythological themes are well represented (Marcus Tulius, Cleopatra, Mars, Pyramus and Thisbe, etc.), along with several allegories.

Hertlová 1975, pp. 117–46.

M.R.

V.272
Album of Jindřich Biesenroth
Paper, velvet binding
18.5 × 11 cm (open 18.5 × 23.5 cm)
1612–17
Prague, National Library, inv. no. VII G 28

This album contains entries chiefly from Paris and Bourges, for the most part coats-of-arms. Czech entries include those by Jan of Vchynice and Tetov, and Zdeslav Hrzán of Harasov; also represented in the album is Tycho Brahe the Younger, son of the famous astronomer. Several miniatures (pen drawings) depict idyllic pastoral scenes and a fight with a dragon, as

well as a watercolour with an allegorical scene of a girl being fished out of the sea.

Urbánková 1957, p. 54 (n. 384); Hertlová 1975, pp. 117–46.

M.R.

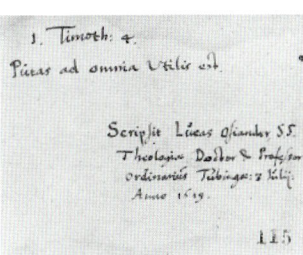

V.273
Album of counsellor Kryštof Scheutzlich
Paper, leather binding, water-colours
10 × 17 cm (open 10 × 36 cm)
The coat-of-arms of the owner without any further text or inscription (fol. 1a)
1617–27
Prague, Národní muzeum, inv. no. H3-B 19

This album is an example of a student manuscript containing various entries by students and professors from Tubingen, Leyden, Strasbourg and Heidelberg.

Hertlová 1975, pp. 117–46.

M.R.

V.274
Album of Jiří Jindřich of Reifenberg
Paper, leather binding
8 × 13 cm (open 8 × 26 cm)
1619–25
Purchased in 1895 from Count Boos-Waldeck of Voselec
Prague, Uměleckoprůmyslové muzeum, inv. no. E 6 048

This album, featuring entries acquired in Strasbourg and other university towns where Reifenberg studied, is in miniature version for use during travels. In addition to coats-of-arms and mottos and entries written by professors and students, the al-

bum also contains several miniatures: the symbol of two columns with interwoven laurel wreaths and two fasces, a picture of a horserider and two men carrying a wooden tub. The album also contains a depiction of female figures in different Renaissance dress, which ornament an entry by Reifenberg's Strasbourg teacher, Vavřinec Auinerer, from 1623.

Hertlová 1975, pp. 117–46.

M.R.

V.275
Album of Jakub von Zinnenburg
Paper, leather binding, water-colours
10.5 × 15.5 cm (open 10.5 × 34 cm)
Coat-of-arms of the Zinnenburgs - engraving (fol. 1a)
1620–33
Prague, Národní muzeum, inv. no. H3-B 7

Along with a number of coats-of-arms and miniatures depicting a hunting scene (of a hare), an allegorical scene of a man with a cock and mouse and a woman with a parrot, an hour-glass, several military scenes and a lady with three cavaliers, this album also features the favoured depiction of

Fortuna on a winged sphere with a sail, symbolizing her capriciousness; a little boat carrying lovers; the expulsion of witches, and a theme on the choice between the paths that life offer – a career in the military or the church, or marriage.

Hertlová 1975, pp. 117–46.

M.R.

V.276
Album of Jan Kulík
Paper, leather binding, miniatures
9.5 × 16 cm (open 9.5 × 33.5 cm)
1588–1653
Prague, Národní muzeum, inv. no. H3-B 6

The painter Jan Kulík's album is an example of a rather non-traditional work found outside noble circles; it was also used as a sketchbook, to which Kulík's colleagues contributed. Jan Vojtěch Kulík worked as an artist in Prague from 1644, where he apprenticed under Matyáš Mayer. He was honoured with the title of burgher in 1653. The album originally belonged to

someone else and Kulík began using it in 1645, testified by his dated drawing of an angel with a trombone (fol. 5a). Also notable are the miniature of a castle landscape executed by his teacher Antonín Stevens (fol. 97a) and the landscape by Pieter Stevens (fol. 96a). Some of the entries originated from the owner's journeys to Vienna and Styria in 1650–52.
Prague 1993, cat. no. II/3-3.

Hertlová 1975, pp. 117–46; Fučíková 1979, pp. 489-519 (Kulík p.504); Šroněk 1992, pp. 148-161.

M.R.

V.277
Album of Kryštof Vilém Harant of Polžice and Bezdružice
Paper, leather binding, watercolours
13 × 16 cm (open 13 × 54.5 cm)
1631–38
Prague, Národní muzeum, inv. no. H3-B 10

Kryštof Vilém Harant of Polžice and Bezdružice (1617–1691) was the nephew of the famous Kryštof Harant, who was executed on the 21 June 1621 on the Old Town Square in Prague. After his emigration from Bohemia, Kryštof Vilém served in the Saxon and Swedish army during the

Thirty Years' War, was in imperial services from 1642 and he became a colonel in 1648. His album contains entries by numerous military figures, particularly Italian noblemen, from 1643, and by relatives and Czech noblemen from the beginning of the emigration period in 1631. A detailed family tree beginning in 1346 appears in the albums' introduction and includes the condemned Kryštof Harant and contemporaries of the album's owner. His occupation is evident from the entries and illustrations of various military figures and battle scenes. The album also contains the motif of a fight taken from the book of emblems by Theodor de Bry

(Frankfurt 1592) and other emblematic miniatures.

Prague 1993, cat. no. II/3-2.

Hertlová 1975, pp. 117–46.

M.R.

V.278
Album of Kryštof Vilém Harant of Polžice and Bezdružice
Paper, leather binding, water-colours
9 × 12.5 cm (open 9 × 27.5 cm)
Introductory text featuring the name of the owner and the year 1648 (fol. 3b)
1631–68
Prague, Národní muzeum, inv. no. H3-B5

This is the second album owned by Kryštof Vilém Harant, which he kept during the period 1648–86. It contains entries chiefly from military figures, during later years from Czech noblemen, many with coloured coats-of-arms. The favoured mo-

tif of Fortuna appears here in connection with the theme of life's choices, represented by a monk and a woman with a lute. Miniature emblems and a symbol of death in the form of a skull are also included.

M.R.

V.279
Binding with initials BC
1586
Brown kidskin on wooden boards, gilded, blind-stamped, brass clasps
27 × 19 cm
On the front cover, supralibros with the initials *BC*, panel-stamp with the mark *A* (Adam?)
Donated to Uměleckoprůslové muzeum in 1900 by Dr. J. Zahradník.
Prague, Uměleckoprůslové muzeum, inv. no. 8 139 C

Both in composition and in ornament the binding follows the traditional framed de-

sign – rectangular panel-stamp in the middle of the panel (in this case with the gilded imperial symbol), the frame ornamented by a roll with the half-figure of Virtue. The framed composition is typical of the production of all the Prague city workshops of the second half of the sixteenth century and was particularly common for blind-stamped bindings. This binding for the unidentified BC was carried out in a workshop which we know used tools belonging to the bookbinder Adam.

Prague 1912, cat. no. 247.

Nuska 1966, p. 381 (anonymous workshop

1560s–90s).

R.V.

V.280
Pavel Gutsch
Active 1558–1590/1595?
Binding with the supralibros of Jiří Mehl of Střelice
Pale leather on wooden boards, blind-stamped, gold-tooled, brass clasps (incomplete); 18 × 12.5 cm, central panel-stamp 8.9 × 5.2 cm.
Contents: Dominicus Aegidius Topiarus, Conciones in epistolas et evangelia, Antwerp 1573
Panel-stamp dated 1578, binding possibly from the 1580s
Blind-stamped roll with signature plate with the monogram *PG* (Pavel Gutsch),

the Mehl heraldicsupralibros on the front cover, on the title page the owner's note 'Collegii Novodomensis Soctis JESU. Ex libte Illssi D. Fund: Catalogo Inscriptus 99'
After the death of Jiří Mehl the volume probably came into the possession of Adam of Hradec who presented it to the Jesuit house he had founded in Jindřichův Hradec. Bought by the Uměleckoprůslové muzeum in 1907 from the secondhand bookshop Steuer in Prague
Prague, Uměleckoprůslové muzeum, inv. no. 10 537 E

The binding for the royal counsellor and

German vice-chancellor in Bohemia, Jiří Mehl of Střelice (d. 1589 in Rumburk) came from the workshop of a leading Prague bookbinder of the 1560s–80s. Pavel Gutsch came to Prague from Wroclaw and in 1558 obtained citizen's rights in the Old Town of Prague. Between 1571 and 1590 he was often mentioned as a member of the guild.

Decorated binding see Lifka 1962, pp. 38–39, ill. 11; further Prague 1966, pp. 14, 17, 39; for Gutsch's tools see Nuska 1966, p. 380, ill. VII/1-7.

R.V.

v.281
Kryštof Meyšnar
Active during the 1570s–90s, died 1599)
Binding with the initials ICVZ
Pale pigskin, blind-stamped, brass corner-mountings and clasps
Contents: Biblí České, Díl druhý, Kralice 1580
25.5 × 18 cm; panel-stamps 8.9 × 5.3 cm.
Supralibros with the initials *ICVZ* on the front cover
1585
Added to the Uměleckoprůslové muzeum inventory in 1940.
Prague, Uměleckoprůslové muzeum, inv. no. 25 192/1

The original assumption that this binding for the unidentified nobleman ICVZ was made in one of the bookbinding workshops of the Unitas Fratrum was overturned by Bohumil Nuska in his comparison of the rolls and panel-stamps known from other bindings of the Prague bookbinder Kryštof Meyšnar. The motifs on the panel-stamps (portraits of Luther and of Melanchthon) reflect the contents bound within – the Kralice, i.e., the evangelical translation of the Bible.

Prague 1912, cat. no. 252; Prague 1995, cat. no. 18.

Herain 1933, p. 557 (ill.); Hamanová 1959, p. 105; Vávra 1970, p. 88; Nuska 1970, p. 128; for Meyšnar's tools, see Nuska 1966, p. 381–82, 387–88, ill. XI/1-5.

R.V.

v.282
Binding for the Prague Archbishop Martin Medek
Brown calfskin on pasteboard, gold-tooled, blind-stamped, ties (not original), gold-tooled edges, gauffered
Contents: Valentinus Leuchthius, Ein Christliche Catholische in Gottes Wort wolgegrundte Predigt..., Mohuč 1583
On the front cover: an inscribed supralibros with the legend: *MARTINUS°DEI°ET°APOST°SEDIS°GRATIA°ARCHIEPISCOPVS°PRAGENSIS°1583*
20.5 × 15.7 cm
1583

Purchased from an shop in Prague, in 1905
Prague, Uměleckoprůslové muzeum, inv. no. 8 983

This, the only binding for Martin Medek (1583–90, Archbishop of Prague from 1581), displays a number of features exceptional in Czech bookbinding, for example, a circular inscription and, for domestic conditions, an early use of a dominant composition with an arabesque oval and corner panelling. In Prague at that time the traditional framed composition still held sway. The central die almost corresponds to the German tools used in

the Wurzburg binding in the library in Gotha (see Walde 1930). However, it cannot be ruled out that the binding was carried out in a Prague workshop based on foreign patterns.

Analogy of the dies: Walde 1930, p. 27, ill. 4c.

R.V.

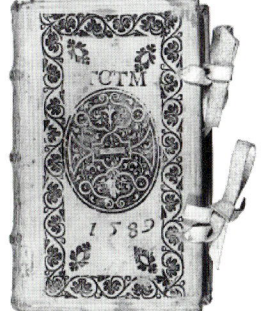

v.283
Binding for Tomáše Cropacius Třebíčkého
Pale calfskin on pasteboard, gold-tooled, blind-stamped, gold-tooled edges, gauffered, leather laces (not original)
Contents: Jan van Boeckel (Iohann Bokelius), Anatome vel descriptio partium humani corporis..., Helmstedt 1585, De divinatione, quae fit per astra, ... Cologne, 1580
Supralibros with the initials *TCTM*; owner's note on title pages: *sum ex libris Thomae Cropacii Trebiceni, G.K.P. 1626* (= Georgius Kule Pardubicensis), *Ex Bibliotheca Monserratensi Pragae in Emmaus.*

15.7 × 10 cm
1589
In the possession of Tomáš Cropacius (d. 1614 in Pardubice), in 1626 obtained by the Pardubice town clerk Jiří Kule (d. 1647), subsequently passing into the possession of the Emaus monastery in Prague and in 1902 purchased in a shop in Prague.
Prague, Uměleckoprůslové muzeum, inv. no. 8 370 E

The binding was made for Tomáš Cropacius (Kropáček), a priest working in Prague, in Vysoké Město and in Písek, and from 1611 Dean in Pardubice. The binding

was probably made during his period in Prague in the 1580s (in 1586 he received his bachelorship). The non-figurative ornamental decoration of the covers with the moresque dominant reveals a stylistically advanced product, even though the disproportionate size of the central die and the not altogether certain execution lead one to believe that the workshop was not yet fully prepared for such orders.

R.V.

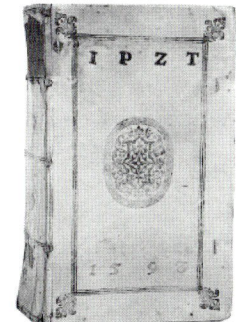

v.284
Binding for Jan Píseckého of Třebska
Parchment on pasteboard, gold-tooled, sprinkled edges, traces left from green laces
Contents: Johannes de Spina, Tractatus de providentia Dei, s.l. (Geneva) 1591
On the front cover: a supralibros with the initials *IPZT* and the owner's note on the title page *Ioannes Piscenus a Trzebska civis in Rakownik*
17.8 × 11.1 cm
1593
Prague, Uměleckoprůslové muzeum, inv. no. 36 C 179

The mayor of Rakovník Jan Píseckého probably ordered this binding from one of the Prague bookbinders, since at that time Rakovník did not have its own bookbindery. The newly discovered type of parchment binding also points to a Prague workshop, as does the dominant composition with an arabesque oval, characterizing the change in style which took place in Bohemia in the last quarter of the century.

Hamanová, ill. 20, p. 108.

R.V.

v.285
Binding with the supralibros of Václav Budovec of Budov
White pigskin on pasteboard, blind-stamped, gold-tooled, sprayed edges
Contents: Iunius, Exposition prophetae Denielis, s.l. 1594
Supralibros inscribed *W BUDOWECZ* on the front cover
16.5 × 21.5 cm
1595
Purchased from Twietmeyer in Leipzig in 1891
Prague, Uměleckoprůslové muzeum, inv. no. 3 903 D

An elegant bibliophile binding from the library of Václav Budovec of Budov (1551–1621) with rollwork cartouches and moresque ovals in the middle of a lightly framed open plate, from the circle of the Rudolfine court workshop (or workshops). The ornamentation we find here is denominationally neutral and does not betray the fact that it was an order made for a leading representative of the protestant opposition. It confirms the opinion that the creation of a new ornamental style in the second half of the sixteenth century is apart from anything else connected with the effort of the workshops to establish themselves with both parties,

catholic and protestant.

Prague 1912, cat. no. 253.

Chytil 1909, p. 86; Herain 1933, p. 555 (ill.); Hamanová 1959, p. 110.

R.V.

v.286
Binding with supralibros of Rudolf of Teuffenbach
Red morocco leather, gold-tooled, gold-tooled edges, gauffered
Contents: Sacrorum bibliorum Tomus Primus... Antwerp 1572
41.7 × 31 cm
On the half-title page the owner's note *Collegii Societ JESU...Ex Munificentia...Rudolphi L B a Teuffenpach 20. Octob. 1638*
End of sixteent–beginning of seventeenth century
Teuffenbach presented the book to the Jesuit house in Jičín in 1638, from whence it

found its way into the Prague Klementinum
Prague, National Library, inv. no. 26 A 11 (Tres Na S sv. 1)

Ilse Schunke gave the name 'Master of the Dürer Sketchbook' (after the binding of the famous sketchbook in the Rudolfinian library) to the bookbinder working at the Prague court of Rudolf II for the most demanding bibliophiles amongst the courtiers, and for the Emperor himself. From this court workshop, so far anonymous, originated luxurious bindings for such as Zdeněk Popel of Lobkovice, Jiří Bartold Pontanus of Breitenberk, Hoff-

mann of Grünbüchl, Tycho Brahe and likewise several bindings for the young Rudolf of Teuffenbach (1582–1653), later General and friend to Emperor Ferdinand III.

R.V.

v.287
Binding for Rudolf of Teuffenbach
eddish-brown morocco leather, gold-tooled, blind-stamped, gold-tooled edges, gauffered, traces from laces;
Contents: Biblia sacra. Vol. I, II, Heidelberg 1580, 1586
In both volumes the owner's note *Collegii Societatis JESU Gictinii Ex munificentia Excel. D.D. Rudolphi L.B. a Teuffenbach 20. Octobris 1638.*
40 × 28 cm
End of sixteenth–early seventeenth century
In 1638 the bible was presented to the Jesuithouse in Jičín, whence it later passed

to the Prague Klementinum
Prague, National Library, inv. no. 26 B 14 (Tres Na 19)

The richly gold-tooled binding with semis design decoration is unquestionably the work of the Rudolfine court workshop. We find the parallel decorative design, not usual in Bohemia, corresponding to the corner panelling and other stamps, in the binding of the Dürer sketchbook and other bindings of this workshop. Unlike the preceding binding for Rudolf of Teuffenbach, his heraldic supralibros is not used here; an oval with a moresque and another with an arabesque have been placed in the

centre of the front and back covers.

Hamanová 1959, p. 82, 257, ill. 55.

R.V.

v.288
Binding with the supralibros of Zden?k Popel of Lobkovice
Red stained kid, gold-tooled, gold-tooled and gauffered edges
Contains: Aristoteles, Operum Arisotelis Stagiritae philosophorum omnium longe principos, nova edition. Geneva 1605
40 × 26.5 cm
Heraldic supralibros with the initials *SAP* (Sidonius Adalbertus Popel); on the flyleaf, the ex libris of Ferdinand August Leopold of Lobkovice (1655–1715)
After 1605
From the seventeenth century in the Lobkovice library, from 1657 held in

Roudnice nad Labem
Prague, collection of W. Lobkowicz, deposited in the National Library, Prague, inv. no. II Aa 2 (Tres. Ro A 43)

This binding for the Czech chancellor and leading representative of the catholic party Zdeněk Vojtěch Popel of Lobkovice (1568–1628) belongs to the most splendid bibliophile orders carried out at the beginning of the seventeenth century in the Prague court workshop. The exceptional binding with a rollwork cartouche, semicircular segments in the internal corners and a wonderfully decorated spine and edges, anticipates Baroque composition

and ornamentation (compare, for example, the filigree projections of stylized flowers).

Chytil 1899, p. 333, tab. XIII; Straka 1922, p. 129, picture 151; Hamanová 1959, p. 111; Nuska 1965, p. 42 and 143; Lifka 1980, p. 85, 97.

R.V.

v.289
Binding with the Lobkowicz supralibros
Brown kid, gold-tooled, gold-tooled edges, gauffered
Contents: Tabula aura Magistri Petr De Borgomo, Venice 1613
34.7 × 25 cm
On the front cover, the Lobkowicz supralibros; the owner's note on the title page *Conventus Pragensis Carmelitanu Discalceatorum*
1613
After 1613 in the Lobkowicz library, then in the library of the monastery of the Barefoot Carmelites in Prague in the Malá Strana, whence it entered the Prague

Clementinum
Prague, National Library, inv. no. 31 C 53

The common symbol of the Lobkowicz bindings, originating in the Prague court workshop, is an articulated rollwork cartouche with coat of arms inside, adorned with festoons, fruit, mascaroons or allegorical characters – in this case the allegories of Justice and Faith. According to Hamanová, the binding, with an exceptionally delicately carried out ornamental border, probably comes from the library of Zdeněk Popel of Lobkovicě.

Hamanová 1958, p. 110–11, ill. 22.

R.V.

v.290
Binding with the painted supralibros of the Lords of Pernštejn
Parchment covers with coat of arms painted in gouache and gold
Contents: John Leslie, De titulo et iure serenissimae principis Mariae Scotorum reginae..., Rheims 1580
22 × 16 cm
On the title page, the note *Caesar Collegii Societatis Jesu Pragae Ex Liberalitate D. Mariaemanrique Seniorae de Pernstein...*
After 1580
Originally in the Pernštejn library, it passed in 1608 from the estate of Marie Manrique the Elder de Lara, wife of

Vratislav of Pernštejn, to the library of the Jesuit house in the Prague Clementinum
Prague, National Library, inv. no. 25 H 145

The binding displays a rarely found type of painted decoration on soft parchment covers. The library of the Czech chancellor Vratislav of Pernštejn (1530–1582), from which the binding possibly originates and which was inherited by Vratislav's wife, Marie Manrique de Lara, reflected the extravagant life style of its owner, a well-known lover of Renaissance luxury.

Hamanová 1959, pp. 112, 207, 275, ill. III;

Urbánková 1957, p. 58; Lifka 1980, pp. 94, 100.

R.V.

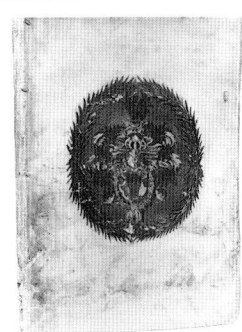

V.291
Binding with the supralibros of Leopold Stralendorf
Pigskin on pasteboard, gold-tooled, blind-stamped
Contents: Jakob Feucht, Wintertheil Der Kleinen Catholischen Postill, Cologne 1595
Binding from the turn of the seventeen century, panel-stamp with supralibros dated 1593
Prague, Premonstrarian Monastery, Strahov, inv. no. B T VI 45

Leopold Stralendorf belonged to the highest dignitaries of the court (from 1603 privy councillor, from 1606 vice-chancellor). However, his heraldic supralibros originates from the time that Stralendorf spent in the service of the Elector of Mainz, when he was steward of Eisfeld. The binding itself is from a later date, probably after Stralendorf's arrival in Prague. Evidence of its Prague origin is in the decoration of the frame (a roll with an undulating ornament) and the stamps on the corners, which occur in the bindings of the Rudolfine court workshops (compare, for example, the binding for Tycho Brahe, Strahov V 5).

Hamanová 1965, pp. 16, 178, ill. 10.

R.V.

V.292
Binding with the supralibros of Jan Chrystof of Hornštejn
White calfskin, gold-tooled and blind-stamped, edges coloured blue-green, metal clasps;
Contents: William Rainolds (Gulielmus Reginaldus), Calvino-Turcismus id est, calvinisticae perfidae, cum mahumetana collatio,...Quatuor libris explicata, Antwerp 1597
18.2 × 11.4 cm
On both covers, the Hornštejn heraldic supralibros, on the flyleaf the ex libris of Ferdinand Filip Josef, Duke of Lobkovice (1724–1784) from the 1740s, engraved by David Coster.
End of the 16th century; older tools – roll dated 1566
In the seventeenth or early eighteenth century the volume passed from the Hornštejn library to the Lobkowicz library in Roudnice.
Prague, collection of W. Lobkowicz, deposited in the National Library, inv. no. Sign.IV Fe 45

This binding for the privy counsellor of Rudolf II, Jan Kryštof of Hornštejn (1542-1606) bears a panel with a coat of arms framed by a roll with the half-figures of Prudence, Judith, Venus and Lucrezia, a common motif in German and Czech Renaissance bindings.

Hamanová 1965, pp. 14-15, ills 6 and 7. For the analogical supralibros dated 1591 see Haebler II, p 54.

R.V.

V.293
Binding from the workshop of the Czech Brothers
Reddish-brown kidskin on pasteboard, gold-tooled, blind-stamped, gold-tooled eges, gauffered, clasps and corner-mountings in bronze, embossed
Contents: manuscript of the genealogical book of the Silber (Zylvár) family of Silberstein, written in 1602 by Salomon Wenczký, later records relating to the period up to 1622 written in another hand.
21 × 16.8 cm; panel-stamp on the front cover 4.8 × 3.5 cm; panel-stamp on the back cover 7.1 × 5 cm
Supralibros with the initials KLVA (Katarina Log con Altendorf?), metal mark WS 1604
From the collection of Vojtěch Lanna, in 1911 sold in the auction house of Gilhofer-Ranschburg, Vienna
Prague, Uměleckoprůslové muzeum, inv. no. 11 906 D

The commission for the binding may have been given by Kateřina Loková, daughter of Kryštof Zylvár and wife of Jiří Lok of Altendorf and Kynšperk. Folios with the manuscript genealogical data and emblems of the knights of Lok (Log) of Altendorf were bound into the front of this genealogical book of the east Bohemian family, the Silbers. The binding is evidence of the high craftsmanship and stylistic level of some of the bibliophile bindings of the bookbinding brothers.

Prague 1912, cat. no. 248; Prague 1996, cat. no. 554.

Auction cat. Vienna 1911, cat. no. 21; Cat. Prague 1912, p. 78, cat. no. 248; on the decoration of the covers, see Vávra 1970, pp. 121, 133 an., ill. 25; Hamanová 1959, p. 110, ill 84 (stamp on the Borbonius binding).

R.V.

V.294
Blind-stamped binding (from stock)
Pale pigskin on wooden boards, blind-stamped, brass clasps
Contents: Basilius Faber, Dictionarium linguae Latinae, Prague 1579
22.5 × 17.5 cm
Owner's notes on the flyleaf and the title page Pris Bartholomai Amardani Parochi.., Post mortem P.Benigni Kinsky Bibl. Beneschov. S.P., remainder crossed out
End the sixteenth century
In the eighteenth century it passed from the ownership of the Kinský family to the Piarist house in Beneřov, from which it was purchased by the Uměleckoprůslové muzeum in 1896
Prague, Uměleckoprůslové muzeum, inv. no. 6 992 D

The stylistic changes of the last quarter of the sixteenth century affected not only the gold-tooled bindings prepared to order but also the ordinary blind-stamped bindings intended for sale in the bookbinders' shops. The central plate, until now completely filled by a panel-stamp or a roll, frees its surface for the placing of an ornamental dominant.

Herain 1933, p. 557 (ill.).

R.V.

V.295
Blind-stamped binding (from stock)
Contents: Bartoloměj Paprocký, Zrdcadlo slavného margkrabství Moravského, Olomouc 1593
Roll with the half figures of the evangelists marked BM (possibly Bartoloměj Metzger)
Ca. 1600
Provenance: added to the inventory of the Uměleckoprůslové muzeum in 1938
Prague, Uměleckoprůslové muzeum, inv. no. 23 421 C

Haebler attributed the mark BM to the Saxon bookbinder Bartoloměj Metzger. His instruments were also used by his son Valentin, working for the Elector of Saxony in the 1560s. The occurrence of the symbols BM and VM on Czech blind-stamped bindings gives credence to the view that the inheritor of the Metzger workshop (Valentin Metzger junior) worked in Prague. The binding witnesses to an effort to 'improve' the conservative decorative design typical for a publisher's binding prepared for stock - an oval with flowers, fashionable at that time, is stamped into the centre of the framed layout, whilst on the back is an oval with an arabesque.

Concerning the occurrence of the tools belonging to the bookbinder BM, see Nuska 1961a, pp. 327-328, Nuska 1961b, p. 489.

R.V.

V.296
Binding for Pavel Pistorius of Lucko
Pale pigskin on wooden boards,
blind-stamped, brass clasps (incomplete)
Contents: Felippe Diez, Concionum qua-
druplicium dominicarum, et festorum
omnium, Lyons 1596
18 × 12.3 cm
On the front cover supralibros with the
initials *DPPAL* (Dominus Paulus Pistorius
a Luczka); owner's note also on the title
page
1598
Originally in the library of Pavel Pistorius,
in the eighteenth-nineteenth centuries in
the library of the Piarist house from

which the volume was purchased by the
Uměleckoprůmyslové muzeum in 1896.
Prague, Uměleckoprůmyslové muzeum,
inv. no. 6 994 E

Pavel Pistorius of Lucko (1552-1630), dean
of Karlštejn and a Vyšehrad canon, owned
a sizeable library, which in 1622 he donated to the Jesuit house in the Prague
Clementinum (where dozens of bindings
bearing his supralibros have been preserved). Most of Pistorius's bindings belong to the conservative framed type,
whilst the binding from the Uměleckoprůmyslové muzeum displays a stylistic
synthesis – a miniature dominant compo-

sition is stamped into the central panel
of the traditional blind-stamped panel–
stamp.

None published. For other Pistorius bindings see Hamanová 1959, pp. 114-16, and
Nuska 1965, p. 179, picture 27.

R.V.

V.297
Early Baroque binding with portrait of
Ferdinand II
1625-50
Gold-tooled parchment; 29.5 × 19.5 cm
Purchased in 1895 from the shop of S.
Kende, Vienna
Prague, Uměleckoprůmyslové muzeum,
inv. no. 5 952 C

This ceremonial binding whose contents
have not been preserved answers in both
style and quality to the production of the
court workshop. The late Renaissance rollwork cartouche is placed in the middle of
what is called a sunken internal field, en-

countered often in Czech Baroque bindings of the seventeenth century.

Hamanová 1959, pp. 151, 68, picture 127.

R.V.

V.298, a
Bottle
Earthenware
H: 5.8 cm; diam. of rim: 3.4 cm
First third of seventeenth century
Prague, Muzeum hl. města Prahy, inv. no.
104-3

The bottle set is on a conical stand and
decorated on its lower half, with a light
yellow surface glaze. The bottom of the
vessel has traces indicating that a chord
had originally been attached.

V.298, b
Small jug
Earthenware
H: 2.3 cm; diam. of base 8.5 cm; diam. of
rim 6.2 cm; diam. of body 1.5 cm
First third of seventeenth century
Prague, Muzeum hl. města Prahy, inv.
no. 119-4

Barrel-shaped jug with rounded neck and
oval rim. Disk-shaped base. The neck is
decorated with the Austrian eagle and
medallions with sculptural ornamentation.

V.H.

V.299
A follower of Anthonis Mor (Moro, Moor)
von Dashorst
Utrecht 1519–Antwerp 1575
*Vratislav of Pernštejn, Known as the Magnifi-
cent, the Highest Chancellor in the Kingdom
of Bohemia, Dressed in the Order of the Gold-
en Fleece*
Oil on canvas
117.8 × 93.2 cm (after restoration to the
sides the field increased by 0.2 cm)
1555-75
When the state had confiscated the
renowned Roudnice (Pernštejn-
Rožmberk-Roudnice) picture gallery in
1951, with the greater part of it being lo-

cated at the Nelahozeves chateau, the
gallery became incorporated in the collections of the newly instituted Central Bohemian Gallery in 1965. In 1992 the picture with the Roudnice collection was
returned to the Lobkowicz family.
Prague, collection of W. Lobkowicz, inv.
no. L 4377

Vratislav of Pernštejn (9 or 15 July 1530-27
October 1582, the highest Chancellor in
the kingdom of Bohemia, was one of the
most distinguished personages who was
regulating political events at the time of
Maximilian. His marriage to the Spanish
noblewoman Marie Manrique de Lara had

influence on the formation of Czech-
Spanish political and cultural relations
and on forming the religious climate in
the Czech Lands before the time of
Rudolf. After returning from Spain, Mor
worked at Antwerp in 1555, precisely
where Pernštejn received the Order of the
Golden Fleece, the first Czech knight in
that order.

Dvorak–Matejka 1907, p.82; Bukolska p.
33, cat. no. 2; Janacek 1976, pic. 2, II edition
1995; Janacek 1987, pic. 43; Panek 1989,
pic.6; Mzykova 1997 (for other literature).

M.Mž.

V.300
Unknown Artist
Portrait of Zachariáš of Hradec
Oil on canvas
200 × 85 cm
15 BH 70; and signed with the monogram: *BH*
1570
State-owned country estate of Telč

Zachariáš of Hradec (1527/8-1589) was
descended from the Hradec branch of the
house of the Vítkovci. Following the death
of his father, Adam I of Hradec, he inherited the Moravian estates and as a young
noble joined the famous excursion of Bo-

hemian lords to Genoa. Upon his return
he initiated the redecoration of the country estate in Telč, using the new Renaissance styles then in fashion. He held a
number of high offices including chamberlain and ultimately chief regional administrator for Moravia. Portraits of his
parents, Adam I and Anna of Hradec (the
latter formerly 'of Rožmitál'), painted by J.
Seisenegger in 1529, make up part of the
decoration in the so-called Golden Hall.
The twin portrait of Zachariáš and his
brother Jáchym as children, painted by the
same artist in the same year, can be found
in the country estate in Červená Lhota.

Křížová 1979/9, pp. 534-40; Křížová 1997
(in preparation).

K.K.

V.301
Unknown Artist
Portrait of Kateřina of Hradec (formerly von Wallenstein)
Oil on canvas
200 × 84 cm
15 BH 70; and signed with the monogram: *BH*
1570
State-owned country estate of Telč

Kateřina of Hradec (ca. 1535–71), was the first wife of Zachariáš of Hradec (1527/8–89), who held noble title over Telč, and the daughter of Karel and Eliška von Wallenstein (the latter formerly 'of Postupice').

Following the death of her father, her mother became deranged and she suffered a difficult childhood with her in Polná u Přibyslavi. Her marriage to Zachariáš of Hradec in 1553 doubtless brought her a welcome breath of freedom. The portrait was made when Kateřina was expecting her son, Lev Menhart, who should have been the family heir but who died in infancy. His mother took to her deathbed later in the same year, 1971, evidently from complications following the birth. The portrait of Kateřina was twinned with another of her husband. In the country estate at Telč there are nineteenth-century copies of both paintings.

Křížová 1979/9, pp. 534–40; Křížová 1997 (in preparation).

K.K.

V.302
Anthoni Bays
1543–1615
Jakub Hannibal I. of Hohenems with his Wife, Hortensia neé Boromejská of Arona, with the court steward Hartmann Bappus of Trazberg and the chamber-maid Pausánia Miniconá
Distemper on canvas
110 × 187.5 cm
HARTMANNVS BAPPVS A TRAZBERG SERVVS FIDELIS IACOBVS HANIBAL COMES IN ALTA EMPS ETC – ANTHONI BAIIS PANCEBAT ANNO 1577 – HORTENSIA COMITISSA IN ALTA EMPS NATA COMITISSA DE BOROMEA – PAVSANIA MINICONA SERVA FIDELISSIMA 1577
Polička, Městská galerie

Anthoni Bays, a Dutch portrait and landscape artist, had entered the service of Archduke Ferdinand of Tyrol and accompanied him and Emperor Rudolf II on a journey from Prague to Landshut on the occasion of the Order of the Golden Fleece being conferred. The result of this excursion was a remarkable reportage of drawings (preserved in the form of coloured drawings and printed in a book by P. Zehendtner). This picture originated on the twelfth wedding anniversary of the couple. They are holding a carnation,

which was still a rare and precious flower at that time, having been brought to Europe by the crusaders. It tended to be a symbol of independence and of masculine ageing. (The botanist Bocke wrote about it in 1546 that it was a 'diversion for the rich'). Bays also painted portraits of children and wedded couples. He used these portraits in the composition of his magnificent voluminous canvas – *Garden Party at the Hohenems Family*, painted a year later.

K.K.

V.303
Portrait of Albrecht of Fürstenberg
Oil on wood
24.5 × 19.0 cm
AETATIS SUAE 19: MEN 10 ANNO DNI 1577
1577
State-owned castle of Křivoklát

This portrait of Albrecht of Fürstenberg (1577–1599) is the oldest portrait in the extensive collection of the Fürstenberg gallery in the Křivoklát Castle. The modestly sized oil painting on wood (later restored) portrays the face of the young magnate, one-time imperial chamberlain,

adviser and highest-ranking equerry, a year before his marriage into the powerful family of the Pernštejns, to the daughter of Vratislav Pernštejn, who died in 1610. Thirteen children resulted from the marriage, and some of their portraits can be found in the Křivoklát Fürstenberg gallery, for instance that of Anna Marie who married Vilém Popel of Lobkovic, and of Františka, who married Lev Buriánek Berka of Dubá. Albrecht of Fürstenberg is portrayed in black Spanish dress with a pleated lace collar, and wearing a gold chain, attached to which is a medallion with a portrait of Emperor Ferdinand I.

Křížová 1996.

K.K.

V.304
School of Sánchez Alonso Coello
Benifairů dell Valls, ca. 1531/32–Madrid 158
Polyxena of Rožmberk, later Lobkowiczová of Pernštejn
Oil on canvas
192.7 × 102 cm
After 1587
Until 1948 in the Roudnice-Lobkowicz collection; later confiscated, from 1965 in the Středočeské galerie in Prague (inv. no. o 2185). Restored in 1992.
Prague, W. Lobkowicz collection, SG–o 2185

This representative portrait of 'the first lady of the kingdom' – daughter of the highest chancellor of the kingdom of Bohemia, Vratislav of Pernštejn and of the Spanish noblewoman Marie Manrique de Lara – portrays a socially important character who influenced political and religious relations in Rudolfine Prague. Polyxena (1566–1642) was married twice: in 1587 to Vilém of Rožmberk (died 1592) and in 1603 to Zdeněk Vojtěch of Lobkowicz (1568–1628), who was the highest chancellor in the kingdom of Bohemia. Among others she set the foundation in place of the Pernštejn-Rožmberk-Lobkowicz art collection. Her portrait was traditionally

ascribed to Sánchez Coello, court artist to Philip II, without having taken into consideration that in the year of Coello's death (1588), Polyxena was only twenty-two, while in the picture she is considerably older. Moreover, it is not documented that she would have travelled to Spain or Flanders, where Sánchez had been active for some time.

Dvořák-Matějka 1907, p.42; Bukolská-Štěpánek 1980, p.34; Sánchez Coello 1990, ill. 60; Bastl 1990.

M.Mž.

V.305
Unknown Artist
Portrait of Kateřina of Hradec
Oil on canvas
50 × 37 cm
Ca. 1591
State-owned country estate of Telč, inv. no. 2684/1857

This portrait of the only daughter of Zachariáš of Hradec, from his second marriage, to Anna of Šlejnice, may well have been a wedding portrait. Kateřina of Hradec married Ladislav Berka of Dubá in 1591. The wedding was held at the estate in Jindřichův Hradec. The cook Achásius

is reported to have made for the banqueting hall two enormous sugar trees, the branches of which could scarcely support the weight of all the sugar birds of many different colours that were perched on them. The tree trunks and all the twigs were made out of gingerbread and the whole cascaded with the finest Italian sweetmeats. This was disapprovingly recorded as 'grandiose and unnecessary feasting. Nothing but luxury, grandeur and waste'. Later, however, a protracted dispute concerning an inheritance, which had eventually to be settled by the Emperor himself, arose between Kateřina and the Lord of Jindřichův Hradec, Adam II.

The portrait belongs to the decorations of the Telč estate's main Renaissance hall, known as the Golden Hall.

Křížová 1979/9, pp. 534–40.

K.K.

V.306
Jakub Ludvík of Furstenberg
Oil on canvass
220 × 130 cm
Ca. 1625
Křivoklát, statní hrad

This picture is one of the oldest portraits from the extensive Furstenberg family picture gallery at Křivoklát. Jakub Ludvík of Furstenburg (1592–1627) was a former field chief armourer and artillery general in the services of the Catholic League. The warrior's right side consists symbolically of heavy artillery. On the ground lies a cuirass, richly plumed helmet and seven canon balls. Jakub Ludvík has a chord at his side, a red embroidered sash; across his chest is a gold-tinted embroidered bandoleer; on his legs are high leather boots with spurs

Křížová 1996.

K.K.

V.307
Seventeenth-century Czech Painter
Heřman Černín
Oil on copper
Oval 10 × 9 cm
Der hoch und ... geborene Her Herman Graf Cschernin Aeta: Sue 78
Second half of the seventeenth century
Praha, Národní galerie v Praze, sbírka starého umění, inv. no. DO 5 372

The miniature portrait depicts Heřman Černín of Chudenice in Hungarian dress. Černín was among the members of the old Czech aristocracy who joined the Habsburg side during the rebellion of the Czech Estates. Before 1618 Černín served King Matthias. In 1620 he took part in the Battle of the White Mountain, and later fought in other battles of the Thirty Years' War. For his services, he was elevated to the rank of Count and his coat of arms was improved to the form depicted in the portrait. He died in 1651, while performing the function of highest steward. The miniature portrait is a type of painting which was very popular during the sixteenth and seventeenth centuries, but few examples of such work have been preserved in Bohemia.

M.Š.

V.308
Unknown Artist
Portrait of Albrecht Wenzel Eusebius von Wallenstein
Oil on tin
23.0 × 17.5 cm
On the back: *ALBERTS WENCESLAUS E. DE WALDSTEIN NAT. 1579 PRINC. SAGAN. 1624. DUX MEK(L)EENB. 1628.*
First half of the seventeenth century
USA, private collection

General Albrecht von Wallenstein (1583–1634) is here depicted in a dark garment with a lace collar and sleeves with open slits. With his right hand he leans on a table on which there is a pair of gloves, and at his left side can be seen the basket hilt of his sword. The face is identical to that in his full-length portrait housed in the museum in Cheb. The features also resemble those of the bellicose figure in allegorical guise in the fresco on the ceiling of the main hall in the Wallenstein Palace in Prague, which is alleged to have been a portrait of the General himself. The artist is unknown but was probably Central European. The work itself, of chamber format, is restrained rather than ostentatious, and while not exceptional is certainly admirable.

K.K.

V.309
Unknown Artist
Portrait of Albrecht Wenzel Eusebius von Wallenstein
Oil on canvas
105 × 81 cm
Prague, Wallenstein Palace (the Senate of the Czech Republic)

This portrait of Albrecht Wenzel Eusebius von Wallenstein belongs to the series of Wallenstein family portraits housed in the Wallenstein Palace collection in Prague. The General is portrayed holding a marshal's cane, decorated with the Order of the Golden Fleece, and wearing the red imperial sash. A sword hangs at his left side. To the right, beneath a cliff-top castle, the artist has depicted a raging battle, perhaps intended to recall the famous Battle of Wolgast, in which the Emperor's forces eventually proved victorious on 22 August 1628.

Křížová–Krutinová 1982/3, pp. 321–33; Muchka–Křížová 1996.

K.K.

V.310
Matthäus Merian
Basel 1593–Frankfurt 1650
The Murder of Albrecht of Wallenstein
Drawing in pencil, pen, bistre, ink wash
26,3 × 34,5 cm
On the reverse: *Mathäus Merian fec.*
1634–35
Bought from František Lašan 1982
Prague, Národní galerie v Praze, Grafická sbírka, inv. no. K 52 181.

A direct model for the graphic published by Merian as part of the Theatrum Europeum, which his workshop produced from 1635 onwards. The drawing is a mirror image of the graphic, and is blackened on the reverse side; etching strokes are visible. The drawing, one of the few by Merian to have survived, shows his skill as a draughtsman, in this case disciplined to fit the drawing's aim.

Eisenstadt 1992, nos 3, 11; Basel 1993, no.107.

Eisenstadt cat. 1992, pp.241–43; Basel cat. 1993, pp.158–59.

A.V.

V.311
Jewellery Box of the Type Known as a Wrangler Case
Inlaid work of heterogeneous, predominantly domestic light-coloured types of wood (according to the restorer, mostly pine, which becomes deeply shaded when scorched in earth). Pear has been used, being applied in the belt (alternating in checks with the maple), with the greenish tinge of birch and seasoned with birch (in the smaller panels of the inlaid work), tinged with oak (brown on the device for opening the hatch) and to a slight extent ebony. Iron-engraved mounting.
H: 48.5 cm; W: 65.5 cm; depth 34 cm

Ca. 1600
From the property of the Waldstein family of Valdštejn Palace in Prague; confiscated after the Second World War, the case was then incorporated into a exhibition at the Veltrusy Palace which comes within the administration of the Museum Institute of Central Bohemia in Prague
Veltrusy House, near Prague, Museum Institute of Central Bohemia
Inv. no. VE 48/816, svoz, Valdštejn palace, Veltrusy 7 916

This double-sided jewellery case was one of a number of so-called Wrangler cases (Wrangelschrank) identified after an item

of furniture from 1566 in the Landesmuseum at Münster in Westphalia), which according to tradition belonged to a Swedish general Carl Gustav Wrangler. The panels of all these jewellery boxes are covered with inlaid objects from the fragmentary structures of Antiquity mostly of gates and other architectural motifs.

Prague, Pilsen, Cheb 1986; Prague 1986; Pilsen 1986; Cheb 1986.

Mzykova 1997.

M.Mž.

V.312
Tapestry of the Death of Decius Mus, from the Series Decius Mus
Tapestry, woven rep, wool, silk
Reed density 8cm; 322 ¥ 598 cm
1625-50
Presumably from the collection of Albrecht of Waldstein, kept at the Waldstein Palace until 1906
Veltrusy Palace, VE 3837

In the centre of this battlefield scene are Decius Mus and a group of mounted soldiers. Decius Mus, fatally injured by an enemy's lance, is falling from his horse and is about to be struck by another sabre-wield-

ing enemy. Casualties and groups of fighting soldiers, both mounted and infantry, surround the central group. A tree stands by the left border. In the right-hand corner is the weaver's emblem. The scene depicted on this tapestry is taken from Tita Livia's book *The History of Rome* (vol. 8/9), in which six significant episodes of Roman consul Decius Mus' life are depicted. The night before the battle at Veseris two Roman consuls, Titus Manlius and Decius Mus, shared the dream that victory would come to the army whose general would perish in battle. Decius Mus, who was blessed by the gods of the underworld as well as the goddess of Earth, was slain the

next day on the battlefield and his army went on to victory. Studies of this scene made between 1616 and 1618 by P. P. Rubens were woven immediately upon completion into tapestries by a number of Flemish textile shops.

Baroque Tapestries from the Collections of ČSR (Hluboká nad Vltavou, Alšová Jihočeská galerie, 1974).

Blažková 1974, cat. no. 13; Blažková 1978, pp. 49-74.

N.B.

V.313
Privilege of a Coat of Arms Granted by Ferdinand I to Ludvik and Gabriel von Taxis
German, original, parchment document; attached seal has been lost. Coat of arms in miniature in the centre of the document, 104 × 118 mm
69 × 46.5 cm (border drapery 13.5 cm)
27 March 1564
Prague, Muzeum hlavního město Prahy, inv. no. AMP PGL V -34

The Holy Roman Emperor Ferdinand I reformed the old coat of arms of his noble uncles Ludvik and Gabriel von Taxis. The privilege for ancestors of the latter prince-

ly line of Thurn-Taxis was issued, above all, as recognition of the many years' service of this family, which in times of war and peace organized the operations of the court mail service throughout the whole of the Roman Empire. The motivation for issuing this is quite different from issuing simple heraldic privileges (without entitlement to nobility) of which a commoner would have been the recipient.

Kneschke 1859-70, IX. pp.152-3; Kral 1900, p.94; Schimon 1859, p.170; Kral 1904, p.265; Hefner 1856, p.23, tab. 18; Hefner 1857–Tirol, pp. 16-17, tab. 19; Hrdlička 1993, p.167, pic. no. 49; Starkenfels-Kirn-

bauer 1885-1904, pp. 452-456, tabs. 110-111.

J.Hr.

V.314
Document of Georgio and Leonhard Korku Cholowskych de Korkyna et Cholowitcz Concerning the Avuncular Coat of arms in Relation to Michael Bohuslav Zniowsky
Latin original, parchment document, miniature coat of arms in the centre of the document, 82 × 106 mm. Attached seal of Jiři Korka in a wooden box on a blue and orange chord; the seal of Linhart Korka has been lost.
54 × 40 cm (border folds- 7.5 cm); seal average size: 6 × 2 cm (body), 9 + 26.5 cm
4 January 1616
Prague, Muzeum hlavního město Prahy, inv. no. AMP PGL II-220

In the sixteenth century, apart from royal conferment, there was another widespread method by which burghers could acquire a significantly cheaper coat-of-arms without mediators and access to the sovereign's environment and offices. This was by means of the avuncular coat-of-arms, which originally served to preserve the coat of arms of a family which was dying out, by leaving it to another family.
The actual document committing this was always on parchment and confirmed in accordance with the customs of the time by a various number of seals of members of the nobility. This document from 1616 serves as an example, whereby Jiři and Lin-

hart Korka Cholovsti of Korkyn and Cholovice admitted Michael Bohuslav Zniovsky to their own coat of arms and predicate name, which they had acquired in 1609 from the late Emperor Matthias

Hrdlička 1993, p.169, pic. no. 53; Sedlaček 1925, p.687-88; Schimon 1859, p. 201; Kral 1904, p.307; Pilnaček 1930, p.294; Meraviglia 1886, p.96, tab.144; Kadich 1899, p. 190, tab. 132; Blazek 1885, p. 110, tab. 58.

J.Hr.

V.315
By his Imperial Power Ferdinand II Elevates Jaroslav Bořita of Martinic to the State of Count of the Empire and Reforms his Coat-of-arms by Inserting a Red Shield with White Bar and the Letters F.M.R. Between the Red Wings of a Jewel
Copy, paper notebook, Latin
10 April 1621
Prague, Státní ústřední archiv
Bohemia Office of the Court, sign. IV D 1 Martinic, kart.417

Since the fourteenth century, sovereigns had been awarding certificates of nobility, which were usually known as letters of a

coat-of-arms. As Roman Emperor and King of Hungary and Bohemia, Ferdinand II issued certificates of nobility from the three appropriate offices often as a reward to subjects of the empire or to regional officials for their services. Jaroslav Bořita of Martinic (1582–1649) was made a count of the empire by Ferdinand II on 10 April 1621 and confirmed on 6 January 1622 by the Bohemian Office. A copy of the confirmation, with an illustration of the coat-of-arms in the same style as the original, was provided. Known for being a fierce opponent of non-Catholics, Martinic had been a member of the Imperial Council since 1603 and from 1609-18 was Marshall to

the Court. From 1616–18 he was Burgrave of Karlštejn and royal governor. With other officials he was thrown out of the window of the Bohemia Office on 23 May 1618 by representatives of the rebellious Estates. He went on to hold other high offices and was the highest regional judge. From 1625 he was Lord High Chamberlain, and once again royal governor and president of the Czech chamber. From 1638–49 he was the highest burgrave.

K.B.

v.316
Eggenberg tapestry of coat-of-arms
Web of wool, weft wool, silk, gold and silver material
6 threads per cm
215 × 200 cm
Ca.1600
Woven for Ruprecht Eggenberg, originally at Český Krumlov.
Hluboká n. Vltavou, château, inv. no. 65

Evidently commissioned by Ruprecht of Eggenberg, this tapestry has been made as a table cover. In the middle of the picture surface is the Eggenberg coat-of-arms: three ravens bearing a crown; in the jewel is the Bosnian flag. Around the emblem is a broad circular frame filled with flowers. An S-shaped motif appears on the border ending in fantastic heads. The surface of the tapestry is filled with a dense pattern of leaves, flowers and fruit; the border is formed by flowers, leaves and fruit; in the centres of all the borders are two sphinxes. The basic colour of the surface is black, in the central field it is green and in the decorative work green, blue and a sandy colour are dominant. The emblem is in heraldic colours and uses metals.

Prague 1975, cat. no. 33.

K.C.

v.317
Armour with a Depiction of the Virgin Mary
Light, polished iron decorated with engravings, etchings and gilding
1580-85
Originally housed in the armoury of the Italian ducal estate Este in Modena. After 1868 transferred by the last Duke of Modena to the Modena palace in Vienna. Inherited by Archduke Franz in 1875.
Konopiötž castle, Prague, Památkový ústav středních Čech, inv. no. K 11750

Richly decorated cavalry armour with a closed helmet and two-part movable visor.

Decorative features include vertical bands lined with polished metal fillets; figural ornamentation, ornate braiding work and central medallions complement strips with stylized trophies. The figural designs incorporate complex symbolism with Classical (Medusa), Old Testament (David playing the Psalms), New Testament (the Virgin Mary) and apocalyptic motifs (Archangel Michael), in combination with motifs from the legend of St George and allegories of the Virtues, Justice and Fortune.

Vienna, Neue Hofburg, 1904; Ferrara, Castello Estense, 1986-87.

L.Č.

v.318
Morion
Light, polished iron with engraved and etched ornamentation
max. height 35 cm; width: 24 cm; max. length: 38 cm
Ca. 1590
Originally housed in the armoury of the Italian ducal estate of Este in Modena. In 1868 transferred by the last Duke of Modena to the Modena palace in Vienna. Inherited by Archduke Franz in 1875.
Konopiötž castle, Prague, Památkový ústav středních Čech, inv. no. K 10519

Morion with half-ball-shaped bell with a row of rivets along the lower edge; also features a high crest and turned-down brim with raised points. The ornamentation is created from shallow engraving and carved relief work. The main area of the helmet is covered with a broad, tendril-like, plaited design which frames central medallions with figural decoration on both sides. The bell of the helmet shows a duel in progress between two naked men (Hercules and Antaeus?); the crest depicts the figure of Fortuna with a sword and veil. The remainder of the main body of the helmet is covered with Pisan-style motifs – trophies, griffins, supernatural beings and mascarons. The top of the morion is decorated with acanthus leaves, a polished metal band and carved rim. The inside still bears the remainer of the soft lining – a strip of leather fixed round the edge by rivets.

Vienna, Neue Hofburg, 1904.

L.Č.

v.319
Protective Shield
Light, polished iron with engraved and relief ornamentation; decorated with etchings
Diam: 65 cm
End of the sixteenth century
Originally housed in the armoury of the Italian ducal family Este in Modena. After 1868 transferred by the last Duke of Modena to the Modena palace in Vienna. Inherited by Archduke Franze in 1875.
Konopiötž castle, Prague, Památkový ústav středních Čech, inv. no. K 10524

An iron shield with sculptural decoration and medallions depicting the heads of mascarons in the form of the devil, an imp and a king. Palmetto ornamentation and landscape motifs designed below the little heads. Architecture and pine trees are visible in the landscape. The individual vignettes are decorated with little fruit and floral festoons. The area between the vignettes in the middle of the shield forms a six-pointed ornamental star set around an elongated tip which used to hold a spike, now missing. The main area of the shield is polished metal, the vignettes are blackened by the engravings. The edge of the shield is bent over twice and creates a wide groove which is decorated with rivets. The edge itself is pulled out and rolled back again with carvings which gives the illusion of a twisted design. A rectangular construction with rounded corners is screwed onto the back of the shield using four screws, for securing the elbow rest.

Vienna, Neue Hofburg, 1904.

L.Č.

v.320
Protective Shield
Light, polished iron with engraved and beaten ornamentation, etched and gilded decoration with rivets filled with mother-of-pearl and silver rosettes.
Diam: 60 cm
End of sixteenth century
Originally from the armoury of the ducal line of Este in Modena. After 1868 moved by the last Duke of Modena to the Modena palace in Vienna. Inherited by Archduke Franz in 1875.
Konopiötž castle, Prague, Památkový ústav středních Čech, inv. no. K 10528

An iron shield comprising three parts: the centre of the shield is concave, the two-part borders are composed of semicircular sections of metal plate secured by rivets to the central section; originally with spikes screwed on to the shield, which are now missing. The main motif of the ornamentation comprises four half-figures – warriors armed with a lance, axe, cudgel and sword with protective helmets and shields. Leafy ornamentation grows out from the middle entwining the individual warrior figures; etched tendril-like motifs also frame the whole central section of the shield spreading to the border among the rivets. The border itself is much more ornate, decorated with black-etched foliage and beaten granulation. The leaf ornamentation cuts through the stylized rosettes and flowers created from rivets set with mother-of-pearl. The rim of the shield is curved back, the surface covered with more floral decoration and gilding. The back of the shield still has its original silver rivets in the shape of rosettes for securing the elbow rest.

Vienna, Neue Hofburg, 1904.

L.Č.

V.321
Cuirass
Light, polished cut iron, decorated with engravings, etchings and gilding
Max. height: 35 cm; max. width: 29 cm
Ca. 1640
Originally housed in the armoury of the Italian ducal estate of Este in Modena. After 1868 transferred by the last Duke of Modena to the Modena palace in Vienna. Inherited by Archduke Franz in 1875. Konopiötž castle, Prague, Památkový ústav středních Čech, inv. no. 1022

A decorative piece of armour symbolizing the apocalyptic theme of the duel between St Michael and Satan. The lower-middle section of the breast plate features a palmetto leaf, above it the mask of a lion's head personifying the Devil. The remainder of the surface is decorated with palmetto tendrils and other floral, tendril-like ornamentation – a symbol of angels' wings – set within two tripartite fields on each side. The tendril ornamentation is etched and the area between the ornaments are beaten to create a fine granulation effect, then etched and finally gilded. The band is cut through to form a twisted shape. The lower section of the back of the plate bears an unintelligible symbol (lion?).

Vienna, Neue Hofburg, 1904; Ferrara, Castello Estense, 1986-87.

L.Č.

V.322
Italian (?) Weapon-smith
Sheath for a Sword or Rapier
Copper alloy, cast
Average 9 cm
End of sixteenth century
Prague, Uměleckoprůmyslové muzeum, inv. no. 90 215

The 'endless' battle scene of Antiquity was among the most widespread subjects of Renaissance decoration (cf. a stone relief from the second half of the sixteenth century in the collection of the Vatican Museum in Rome). Variations of the composition may also be encountered among Prague products from the last quarter of the sixteenth century: for example, in a series of glazed cornice tiles from the potter's workshop in the Jindrisska quarter (Brych–Zegklitz–Stehlikova 1990, nos 305–12) which are linked to the decorative work (no longer extant) on the façade of St Henry's presbytery.

D.S.

V.323
Gentleman's garments: coat and trousers
Silk brocade, grass green with Maloport design
Alternating gold and silver material (model contains a motif of lillies between rows of wavy lines)
Circumference of band: 68 cm; length: 67 cm
End of sixteenth century
Český Krumlov, château
Český Krumlov, château, inv. no. CK 5042

Coat: slim outline, divided by vertical seams extending from the belt line towards the lower border. The sleeves are narrow and inset. A thick row of buttons (little wooden balls sewn on with gold thread); the sides are bound together in the same way; high slits in the dividing seams of the trunk and the lower seam of the sleeves. The arm and neck-holes are emphasized by a strip of fabric in counter composition to the pattern. The lining is of green silk repp.

Trousers: are of the ragged type with richly pleated legs as far as the knees; the hip seams have the same buttons as the coat; two vertically loose-cut pockets are to the front with two pockets at the side seams. They are tied at the waist and knees by two golden chords.

Vienna 1990, 193.

K.C.

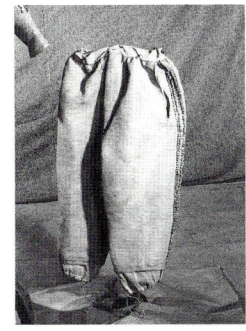

V.324
Gentleman's garments
Gold-tinted silk repp; the edging is of a colour formed by three rows of tiny silk straps, circular buttons hand-wound with silk
Coat: length 52 cm, width of shoulder 42 cm; Trousers: length 80 cm, waist 76 cm
Ca 1630
Český Krumlov, château 1630
Český Krumlov, château, inv. no. 5041

Coat: one row of buttons on concealed hooks; the high standing collar has holes for four buttons. The boddice is shaped at the front and back by vertical seams; it has a slightly raised waist and spreads out considerably towards the bottom. Ball-shaped sleeves become narrow at the wrists and the strip for four buttons has a narrow border of taffeta. The dividing seams of the bodice and sleeves are adorned by straps like the button strip. The lining is of gold-tinted silk taffeta (even inside the dividing seams in part of the waist, which is made firm from the lining material of a narrow hem with three openings above it connecting the trousers with hooks – the height of the trouser waist provides three variable sizes).

Trousers: above the knee are of a more free cut, becoming slightly tucked in towards the bottom. To the front there are two vertically loose-cut pockets, a narrow taffeta band to the front is tied by a chord. The band at the back and front is across two hooks. The side vertical seams are adorned by edge straps. A taffeta lining reaches up from the bottom edge, the hem of which is pulled back by a chord. The trouser lining is of plain linen.

K.C.

V.325
The So-called livery of Trabant
Black silk velvet, gold-threaded edging, applied with gold thread
Coat: width of shoulders 44 cm, circumference of belt 69 cm, length 69 cm; Trousers: waist 75 cm, length 73 cm; waistcoat: shoulders 43 cm, waist 88, length 94 cm
1638
Český Krumlov, château, inv. no. CK 5044

Coat: slim outline, divided by vertical seams spreading out from the waist line towards the lower hem; narrow sleeves set in. Strip for one thick row of circular buttons wound with gold thread; high slits on both the front and central back parts. The arm-holes are emphasized by epaulettes. Along the button strip, side seams and on the edges of the sleeves is a band with an ornamental design, made from several types of gold thread.

Trousers: ragged; Pleated at the waist towards the knees. At the waist and knees tied by gold threads. Decorative work along the side seams as on the coat; two vertical loose-cut pockets. The lining is of linen.

Waistcoat: cut with a raised waist, divided by vertical seams and spreading out downwards to become bell-shaped; a thick button strip from the neck to the waist. Ornamental plantlife design of gold thread around the button strip and to the back at the high waist.

The livery also contains an oval-shaped black hat with a circular crown and a gold-thread border. Six runners wore the livery and accompanied the coach of Jan Antonín Eggenberk in glorious procession when, in 1638, he went to report to Pope Urban VIII for the election of Ferdinand III as Holy Roman Emperor.

České Budějovické 1988.

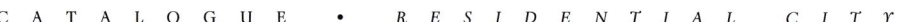

V.326
Neckerchief and cuffs
Linen, cambric, linen bobbin-lace
Neckerchief 43 × 18.5 cm; cuffs 15.5 × 10 cm
End sixtenth–early seventeenth century
According to tradition, these belonged to Vilém Slavata of Chlumec and Košumberk (1572-1652)
Jindřichův Hradec, château, inv. no. JH 3776, JH 3773

Tradition has it that the neckerchief and the cuffs were part of the wardrobe of Vilém Slavata of Chlumec and Košumberk and were allegedly stained by blood from a wound which he suffered when he was defenestrated from the Bohemia Office in 1618. The noticeable browned stain on the neckerchief was subjected to chemical analysis when being restored, which proved its non-albuminous nature. The stain, therefore, was decidedly not from blood. Another fact that strongly casts doubt on the direct connection between Vilém Slavata and the outfit is its very subtle dimensions, according to which it may be judged that the wearer was a woman or a child.

České Budějovické 1988; cat. no. 15.

K.C.

V.327
Anonymous Shoemaker
Lady's Slipper
Leather, wood, embroidery
24 × 10 cm, height of heel 4.5 cm
1610–30
This formal noblewoman's shoe comes from the collections of Buchlov Castle.
Zlín, Obuvnické muzeum, inv. no. 2433 entry 31

The upper part of the shoe was originally made of black silk, which has now disintegrated. Only the sole has survived and is made of a material known as Hungarian leather (i.e. the hide was tanned using aluminium salts, the oldest method of tanning. A characteristic trait of this method of leather preparation is the white colour of the surface). The instep is richly decorated with embroidery featuring silver and gold coloured metal threads and copper strips. A slightly raised platform forms the symmetrical sole and ends in a low heel. The hollow wooden heel and the platform are covered in brown leather.

Wilson 1969.

Št.

V.328
Woman's Shoe
Leather, hand-sewn
16 × 7.5 × 21.5 cm
Ca. 1620
Prague, Národní muzeum, Department of Early Czech History, inv. no. H2-3 430

The shoe is typical of footwear of the first quarter of the seventeenth century. It is characterized by the rounded toe and a heel and sole that are rather wide and high, supported by strong strips of leather. The tongue on the vamp is tied to the extended end with decorative ribbons, such as often covered the uppers of the shoe. The entire sole is raised on a red platform, which could indicate that the owner belonged to the court circle.

V.P.

V.329
Woman's Shoe
Leather, hand sewn
14.5 × 6.5 × 25 cm
1630–50
Donated to the Národní Muzeum in 1856 by the court jeweller, Jeroným Grohmann
Prague, Národní muzeum, Department of Early Czech History, inv. no. H2-3 429

The shape of the toe in footwear changed before the middle of the seventeenth century: it was lengthened and often squared off at the end. The decorative holes cut into the upper are typical of shoes of this period. Traces of red can be found on the sole of this shoe.

V.P.

V.330
Cover
White linen, colourful silk embroidery, coloured bobbin-lace
Length: 81 cm; width: 89 cm
1550–1600
Bought from Dr Bocek's collection in 1888
Prague, Uměleckoprůmyslové muzeum, inv. no, 2 692

E.U.

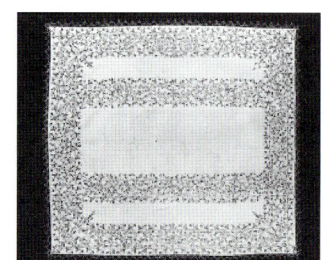

V.331
Towel with the Emblem of the Salviati
Family
White linen, colourful silk embroidery,
coloured bobbin-lace
Length: 155 cm; width: 75 cm
End of the sixteenth century
Bought in 1909 at the Helbing auction in
Munich, from the collection of Fr v. Lip-
perheide
Prague, Uměleckoprůmyslové muzeum,
inv. no, 11 279

Embroidery with surface and chain stitch.
The emblem is sewn to the lower border
with three bars, discerned by Dr J. Vydrová

as the coat-of-arms of the Salviati family.

E.U.

V.332
Pillow case
Interlaced linen, sewn with bobbin-lace
Length: 47 cm; width: 35 cm
Ca. 1600
Bought in 1968 from Marie Umlaufová
Prague, Uměleckoprůmyslové muzeum,
inv. no. 72 533

The lace is of the reticella type with a s-
tandard star pattern. The front and back
parts are linked by inter-lining from the
bobbin lace with a rhomboid pattern
running through.

E.U.

V.333
Cover
Interlaced linen, white embroidery, sewn
with bobbin-lace
64 × 64 cm
1600–30
Bought in 1944 from Sofia Andrejevská
Prague, Uměleckoprůmyslové muzeum,
inv. no. 28 880

The surface is divided into quarters alternating between full white sewn and cut
out with grotesque zoomorphic motifs
from the lace sewing of the 'punto tagliato'
style (a technique of making double holes,
filled in with stitch work). The hems are
bobbin-laced.

E.U.

V.334, a
Reticella lace
Linen yarn, sewn
Length: 31 cm; width: 20 cm
Ca. 1600
Bought in 1892 from I of Kaan
Prague, Uměleckoprůmyslové muzeum,
inv. no. 5 032

Reticella lace (made with holes and sewn
lace in a geometrical pattern) with a standard pattern of circles and stars.

V.334, b
Reticella lace
Linen yarn, sewing, bobbin-lace
Length: 40 cm; width: 14 cm

Beginning of the seventeenth century
Bought in 1888 from I of Kaan
Prague, Uměleckoprůmyslové muzeum,
inv. no. 2 783

Reticella lace border with a geometrical
pattern, hems bobbin-laced.

V.334, c
Lace
Linen yarn, sewn
Length: 40 cm; width: 6 cm
1620–50
Bought in 1888 from I of Kaan
Prague, Uměleckoprůmyslové muzeum,
inv. no. 3 756

Laced hem with a pattern of symmetrically
ordered flowers. The border has a pattern
of leaves of flower vases.

V.334, d
Lace
Linen yarn, sewing
Length: 40 cm; width 8 cm
1620–50
Bought in 1888 from I of Kaan
Prague, Uměleckoprůmyslové muzeum,
inv. no. 2 956

Laced hem with a pattern of symmetrical
twigs with flowers. The 'punto in aria' type.

E.U.

V.335
Credenza
Oak and maple wood, carved and inlaid
126 × 152 × 61 cm
Second half of the sixteenth century
In Uměleckoprůmyslové muzeum since
1954 (transferred from the Ministry of
Foreign Affairs)
Prague, Uměleckoprůmyslové muzeum,
inv. no. Z–290/a,b

A low, prismatoid cabinet with two doors,
on a high, full pedestal resting on lens-
shaped feet. The front surface of the cabinet is richly articulated with architectural
forms. The edicules of the doors are inlaid

with the figures of the Apostles Peter and
Paul, and the pilasters and moulding panels feature ornamental inlay. The sides are
smooth, with bands of geometric inlay.
The locks and keys are wrought iron. Typologically, the credenza represents a transition from the storage chest to the shelved
cabinet and a predecessor of the com-
mode with drawers. The combination of
sculpturally carved architectonic divisions
with flat inlay (both ornamental and figural) is characteristic of Southern German
and Czech Renaissance furniture of the
second half of the sixteenth century.

Permanent Exhibition of the Umělecko-

průmyslové muzeum since 1985; Rosenburg, Austria, 1990.

Adel im Wandel cat. 1990; Uměleckoprůmyslové muzeum 1885-1995 cat.; Prague,
ill. 40.

D.K.

V.336
Chest
Wood, carved, inlaid and painted
96 × 190 × 77 cm
Late sixteenth century
From the estate of Dr. Stupecky, court counsel, gift to the Uměleckoprůmyslové muzeum, 1908
Prague, Uměleckoprůmyslové muzeum, inv. no. 10 978

A prismatoid chest on a high, full pedestal, with drawers; the front piece is divided by pilasters and pillars into five fields which are richly decorated with ornamental and floral inlays (flowers in vases, and masks in cartouches in the two larger panels). The tendril inlay appears on all three coffered panels on the lid and on the sides, which also have wrought iron handles. Inside the chest are compartments with inlaid motifs of heraldic lions and smaller compartments with a polychromed grille. JUDr. Stupecky was a member of the Board of Directors of the Royal and Imperial Austrian Museum, which sent him to the Board of Directors of the Prague Uměleckoprůmyslové muzeum (1900-07). From 1906 onwards, he was a member of the purchasing committee, was responsible for obtaining a great deal of financial resources for the museum and left many collector's objects to the museum in his will.

Exhibition of the Uměleckoprůmyslové muzeum, Duchcov.

Prague 1995, 24.

D.K.

V.337
Cabinet
Wood, tortoise shell, enamelled panels, mother-of-pearl, ivory, silver, and brass
130 × 105 × 30 cm
First half of the seventeenth century
At the Ursuline Convent in Kutná Hora until 1950
Prague, Uměleckoprůmyslové muzeum, inv. no. 64 846 Vk 815

The piece features tiered Renaissance cabinet architecture with doors and inner drawers. The brown stained wood on the frontal surface is covered with tortoise shell and silver guilloche mouldings which line the edges of the panels of the drawers and doors. The lower part is articulated with vertical columns with silver pedestals and capitals, and the lateral enamelled panels feature the allegories of war and peace. The upper part is divided by columns into three edicules: the ones on either side depict figures with the inscriptions Providentia and Justitia (God's Providence and Justice), while the central one bears the figure of the Emperor and his emblem. Inside, behind the doors, are drawers inlaid on the front with mother-of-pearl and tortoise shell (ornamental and plant motifs). On the inner side of the doors is a glass-covered watercolour depicting the Holy Family, with a German inscription. The niche contains a cube-shaped pull-out panel with gilded columns, mirrors and a balustrade, behind which are twenty miniature secret drawers.

Permanent Exhibition of the Uměleckoprůmyslové muzeum since 1985.

D.K.

V.338
Adam Eck (?)
1604–64
Cabinet
Wood, black-stained, with relief inlay
93 × 98 × 45 cm
Ca. 1650
1896 purchased in Berlin at the Louis Gottschaeck auction (R. Lepke)
Prague, Uměleckoprůmyslové muzeum, inv. no. 7 063

The prismatoid cabinet with doors, numerous drawers, and metal handrails on the sides stands on a black-stained table base with turned feet. The panels on the outer and inner sides of the doors and on the front of the drawers are decorated with hunting scenes, themes from the return of the prodigal son and from commedia dell'arte and are edged with guilloche mouldings. On the inner side of the tabernacle doors of the cabinet is a scene with musicians in masks, based on a copper engraving by J. de Gheyn the Younger. The cabinet, with its opulent workmanship techniques, is one of the largest and most richly decorated works from among thirty such objects in the Uměleckoprůmyslové muzeum. The probable authorship of Adam Eck or his workshop is supported by the work's similarity to the cabinet from Skokloster, Sweden, attributed to the workshop of Eck by H. O. Boström.

Permanent Exhibition of the Uměleckoprůmyslové muzeum since 1985; Prague 1986.

Sturm 1961; Bunte Welt 1982, ill. 17; Mžyková 1986, cat. n. 47.

D.K.

V.339
Coffer
Wood, relief inlay
20 × 28 × 43.5 cm
First half of the seventeenth century
1976 purchased from a wood processing plant, Prague
Prague, Uměleckoprůmyslové muzeum, inv. no. 84 726

A prismatoid coffer on four flattened feet, with a fold-out lid. The rectangular panels are framed by guilloche mouldings and contain figural reliefs – the allegories of earth and water and of war and peace. The lid features the allegory of time on the outside surface and a relief with Saint John the Baptist in the wilderness on the inner side, in a guilloche and dotted frame with floral motifs. The mounting is engraved brass. This is a standard type of casket found in aristocratic and bourgeois households; it is unique because of the decoration which features the technique of Cheb relief inlay.

Lemberk Castle 1992; Prague 1995.

D.K.

V.340
Plate with Gold Heraldic Device
Majolica, painted with high-temperature colours
Diam: 28 cm
1570–90
Auction of the Lanna Collection, Berlin 1909, R. Lepke cat. no. 504
Prague, Uměleckoprůmyslové muzeum, inv. no. 11 572

A deep plate with a smooth, narrow rim. Decorations are painted in white, yellow and gold on the dark blue glaze. The cartouche contains a heraldic emblem; leaves and rosettes frame the emblem and decorate the rim of the vessel. The earlier designation of Venice or Faenza as the vessel's place of origin was disproved at the comprehensive exhibition in Castelli in 1989.

Le maioliche cinquecentesche di Castelli 1989, cat. no. 545.

Vydrová 1955, cat. no. 128; Kybalová 1992, cat. no. 17.

J.Ky.

V.341
Plate in the *Istoriati* Style
Majolica, painted with high-temperature colours
H: 6.2 cm; diam: 31.5 cm
Ca. 1500
1936, from Vinoř Castle
Prague, Uměleckoprůmyslové muzeum, inv. no. 78 417

The deep plate has a low foot and a wide rim. The entire bottom is painted with a scene from the tale of Diana and Acteon (Ovid, *Metamorphoses*, Book III): Diana and her maids are surprised during their bath by Acteon, and she changes him into a

stag. The predominant colours are cobalt blue, followed by yellow, ochre, green and terracotta. The back of the plate is painted with yellow lines and the inscription in cobalt *AKTEON MVTATO IN CERVO DA DIANA*.

Troja 1992–96.

Vydrová 1973, cat. no. 45; Kybalová 1992, cat. no. 11.

J.Ky.

V.342
Apothecary Ewer
Majolica, painted with high-temperature colours
H: 24.5 cm
1550–70
1903 gift of Vojtěch Lanna
Prague, Uměleckoprůmyslové muzeum, inv. no. 5 107

A round vessel on a high foot with a spout and a wide, flat handle. Paintings of trophies in ochre, cobalt and white. The precisely painted figure of an angel appears on the handle. The text plate bears the inscription *SY.D.AGR.D.C.*

Prague 1973; Bechyně 1983–86; Troja 1992–96.

Vydrová 1973, cat. no. 44; Kybalová 1992, cat. no. 14.

J.Ky.

V.343
Salt-cellar in the Form of a Conch Shell
Majolica, painted with high-temperature colours
H: 12.5 cm
1570–90
Auction of the Lanna Collection, Berlin 1909, R. Lepke cat. no. 421
Prague, Uměleckoprůmyslové muzeum, inv. no. 11 583

An asymmetrical vessel in the form of a conch shell held by a naiad. The motif is known from other Italian centres of majolica production. It was used in the same form in the cutting of precious stones in

the workshops of the Miseroni family after 1600. Analogues are found in the Victoria and Albert Museum in London (Rackham, Catalogue of Italian Maiolica, 1940, no. 850, ill. 135) and the Innsbruck Fernandeum ('Tiroler Tafelgeschirr aus Faenza', in *Alte und moderne Kunst*, 1962/6).

Vydrová 1973, cat. no. 105; Vojtěch Lanna and Fronek cat. 1996.

J.Ky.

V.344
Gourd in the *bianchi di Faenza* Style
Majolica, painted with high-temperature colours
H: 30.7 cm
1560–80
Auction of the Lanna Collection, Berlin 1909, R. Lepke cat. no. 508
Prague, Uměleckoprůmyslové muzeum, inv. no. 11 565

The bottle has a profiled, pear-shaped form with an extended neck, handles on the sides, and a tin foot and screw cap. The surface is sculpted into scrolled shapes and small sculptural heads, with shallow

grooving and twisting. The front bears a pair of unknown alliance coats of arms and the monogram C.V.K. in light blue, yellow and orange with a red outline.

Vydrová 1955, cat. no. 93; Kybalová 1992, cat. no. 20.

J.Ky.

V.345
Hans Hilgers
Active 1569–95
Tankard
Earthenware, pewter
H: 28.4 cm; base diam: 10.6 cm
On the tankard's side: the initials *HH* in relief; on the band: the legend *SALVATOR MONDE 1577*
1577
Donated to the Národní museum in 1824 by Mr Vojtěch Juhn from Českych Budějovice or in 1829 by Mikuláš Straka from Prague
Prague, Národní muzeum, inv. no. H2-3099

Situated in the Rhineland, Siegburg was one of the oldest and most important German centres of earthenware production. Since the Middle Ages the products of Siegburg manufacturers had been highly popular throughout Europe for their quality of material and the refined creamy white colour, which did not require any additional surface treatment. The use of these products is also documented in Bohemia. This tankard, of a type of an elegantly slender shape which is usually designated in German as a 'Schnelle', originated during the peak of this ware's production, which in Siegburg took place in the sixteenth century. At that time, ele-

ments of Renaissance decoration, applied to the decorative reliefs of earthenware, made their way there via Cologne. The customary graphic patterns of Nürnberg origins subsequently served as a model.

Die archaeologische Sammlung im Museum des Königreichs Böhmen zu Prag, Abt. II (Prague, 1862), p. 2, cat. no. 12; *Archaeologické sbírky v museum kralovství Českého v Praze* (Prague, 1863), p. 37, cat. no. 12.

P.B.

V.346
Tankard with the Hohenlohe Coat of Arms
Hard, greyish-white stoneware, with salt glaze and relief decoration
H: 34.5 cm
1573
Auction of the Lanna Collection, Berlin 1909, R. Lepke cat. no. 644
Prague, Uměleckoprůmyslové muzeum, inv. no. 11 531

The cylindrical shape of this high tankard (*Schnelle*) is conically narrowed near the top and has a flattened handle and three horizontal rings under the neck. The rich relief decoration is divided vertically into three stripes. The central one bears the princely Hohenlohe coat of arms and allegories of the months of March and April in medallions arranged one above the other. The identical side strips bear hexagonally framed depictions of Judith with the head of Holofernes and Christ and the Samaritan woman, and on the bottom is Susanna in her bath. The vessel bears the signature *SPVRKEL L. W.* The surface between the medallions is filled with grotesques. Each figural depiction is accompanied by an imprinted text.

Prague 1996.

Lanna Collection auction, Berlin 1909, cat. no. 644; Prague 1910, cat. no. Vojtěch 88; Lanna cat., Fronek.

J.Ky.

V.347
Small Jug with Heads in Medallions
Hard stoneware, salt glaze
H: 23 cm
1589
Raeren, Belgium
1886 gift of Vojtěch Lanna
Prague, Uměleckoprůmyslové muzeum, inv. no. 663

A spherical vessel on a low foot, with a high, slender neck and an arched handle. The neck features four relief-carved medallions with the heads of ancient warriors, and the two central medallions contain the divided date 1589. The greyish-white surface is divided horizontally; the upper part is decorated with vertical cobalt stripes, and the lower part is cannelated. The handle has an opening for the tin mount (not extant).

J.Ky.

V.348
Jan Emens
Jug with Medallions of Sovereigns
Hard stoneware, salt glaze, cobalt
H: 32 cm
1589
Auction of the Lanna Collection, Berlin 1909, R. Lepke cat. no. 706
Prague, Uměleckoprůmyslové muzeum, inv. no. 11 529

An ovoid shape with a high, narrow neck and an arched handle. Relief-carved medallions of kings and princes are arranged in a horizontal band around the centre of the surface and are accompanied by the texts *KVINNINCK IN SVEDEN / 1589 / KVINNINCK FILIPPVS D.G. PRINSE DE PARMA HENRICVS DER 3 IN FRANKRICH / HENRI DE GVISE / CHARLES DE LORRAIN / ROBERTVS COMES.* In the centre of the frieze and on its end are the initials of Jan Emens, *I.E.* The neck is decorated with a relief of festoons and medallions. The lower part of the surface above the low foot is grooved. The grey stoneware is glazed with salt glaze and cobalt.

Prague 1996.

Lanna Collection auction, Berlin 1909, Lepke, cat. no. 706; Lanna cat., Fronek.

J.Ky.

V.349
'TEYLOR' Apothecary Jar
Hard stoneware, grey salt glaze decorated with cobalt
H: 19 cm
1590
Purchased in 1887
Prague, Uměleckoprůmyslové muzeum, inv. no. 2451

A cylindrical albarello with a narrowed foot and neck. The dark grey surface contoured with cobalt is divided horizontally into three bands and features Renaissance geometric and plant ornamentation. The front bears a horizontal cartouche with the inscription *TEYLOR / ICH HEB EMPOR* and the divided date 1590. The relief is deep, and the cobalt colour has bled into the grey background.

J.Ky.

V.350
Tankard
Earthenware with a brownish-grey glaze, pewter
H: 40 cm; base diam: 17 cm
On the pewter lid are impressed the initials *LC* and three indecipherable signs
Beginning of seventeenth century
Waldenburg
Prague, Národní muzeum, inv. no. H2-2995

The tankard cames from Waldenburg in Saxony. In the sixteenth and seventeenth centuries in particular this area was known for its production of brown-glazed earthenware, used widely for scientific purposes. Agricola expressed his very high opinion of it before the mid-sixteenth century in his work *De natura fossilum*. Such crockery was also employed by Czech apothecaries. Examples in the archaeological and apothecary collection of the Department of Ancient Czech History at the Národní muzeum, as well as archaeological finds of earthenware fragments at house number 837 on Wenceslas Square in Prague, are evidently from Waldenburg. During the years 1612–21 the house belonged to the regional apothecary Matthias Borbonius from Borbenheim. In addition, exclusive wares with elements of Renaissance ornamentation, emblems of the nobility, and figures and portraits (among others, of Emperor Rudolf II) originated from the Waldenburg workshops. Included in this group is the tankard provided with a pewter fitting and ornamented by a decorative impress of a cylindrical die, with the heads of lions and cherubim, columns, the figures of pipers and the coats of arms of the noble families von Steinbach, Gruna, Hertwig and Konarski (?).

Horschik 1978, p. 79, nn. 152, 153.

P.B.

V.351
Jug with Half-portraits of Nobles and
Coats of Arms
Hard stoneware, salt glaze, relief decoration
H: 22 cm
1603
Purchased in 1887 at the Seyffer auction
Prague, Uměleckoprůmyslové muzeum,
inv. no. 2441

An ovoid vessel with a low foot, high neck
and arched handle. A frieze with seven
half-portraits of nobles and their coats of
arms within arcades runs horizontally
across the centre of the outer surface. The

neck and foot feature engraved and relief-
carved Renaissance ornamentation consisting of medallions, hearts and leaves.
The salt glaze is light brown and slightly
spotted. Raeren, in modern-day Belgium,
was after Siegburg and Cologne the most
important manufacturing centre of hard
Rhineland stoneware.

J.Ky.

V.352
Tankard with a Portrait of Rudolf II
Hard, light brown hard earthenware, salt
glaze
H: 25.5 cm
1604
1981 gift of Hermína Dušková as part of
the bequest of the collection of Bohuslav
Dušek
Prague, Uměleckoprůmyslové muzeum,
inv. no. 89 978

A slender, cylindrical vessel (*Schnelle*)
which narrows at the top and has a widely
arched, flat handle. Rings in relief are
found on the foot and under the neck. The

front bears an oval, relief-carved medallion containing a half-portrait of Rudolf II
with the imperial emblem and the year
1604. The medallion is framed by a Latin
inscription. The neck is damaged.

Kybalová 1984, cat. no. 11.

J.Ky.

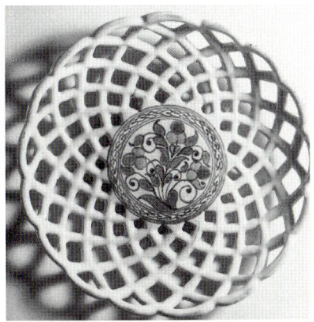

V.353
Bowl with Openwork Rim
Faience, painted with high-temperature
colours
Diam: 21.5 cm
Ca. 1600
Purchased in 1903
Prague, Národní muzeum, oddělení
starších českých dějin, inv. no. 5 509

The circular bowl with openwork diamonds on the rim has been preserved
without the bell-shaped foot. In the white
glaze on the bottom is a spray of berry
plants framed by a cobalt blue wreath. The
bowl is one of the oldest Habaner faience

pieces from the pre-White Mountain period of 1590–1620.

Prague/Brno 1981–82.

Černohorsky 1931, ill. 5, 6; Černohorsky
1941, colour ill. I; Kudělková-Zeminová
1955, cat. no. 11; Kybalová-Novotná 1981,
cat. no. 12, ill. p. 98.

J.Ky.

V.354
Bowl with Alliance Coat of Arms
Faience, painted with cobalt
H: 6.3 cm; diam: 22.5 cm
1602
Acquired by Hugo Vavrečka at the Vienna
antique market in 1929; deposited in the
Uměleckoprůmyslové muzeum since
1952, restituted to the heirs in 1991
Prague, keramická sbírka Hugo Vavrečký,
deposited in the Uměleckoprůmyslové
muzeum under inv. no. 56 766

The round, flat bowl on a bell-shaped foot
has a wide rim with subtle, heart-shaped
openwork ornamentation. The white-

glazed full bottom features a pair of
cobalt-blue coats of arms with initials *GZ-
ZAGKZW*, the date *1602* and a scribe's 'illumination'. This piece was probably part
of a wedding service. This and another
bowl from Vavrečký's collection are
among the most outstanding and most intricate works of Habaner faience from its
earliest period, 1590–1620.

Brno 1955; Prague/Brno 1981–82;
Bern/Zürich 1986; Troja 1992–96; Prague
1995–96.

Koula 1903, p. 29; Černohorsky 1931, ill. 8;
Černohorsky 1940, p. 16; Kudělková-Zemi-

nová 1955, cat. no. 21; Hejdová 1962, ill. 18;
Lessner 1967, p. 21; Vydrová 1973, cat. no.
139; Kybalová 1978, ill. 291; Kybalová-
Novotná 1981, cat. no. 9, ill. p. 99; Kybalová
1986, cat. no. 2; Kybalová 1992, ill. p. 8; Kybalová 1995, cat. nos 1–2.

J.Ky.

V.355
Cask for Spirits
Faience, painted with high-temperature
colours
H: 20 cm; diam: 19 cm
1600–10
Purchased from an antique shop, 1961
Prague, Uměleckoprůmyslové muzeum,
inv. no. 52 635

The horizontal cask on four round legs is
spanned by four triplets of iron bands
with relief decoration. The openings for
the tin stopper (on the upper surface) and
the spigot (on the side) are missing. The
white glaze on the side walls is decorated

with soberly painted bouquets in blue, yellow and green with manganese drawing.
Both the shape and the treatment of the
floral decoration make the cask one of the
most typical examples of Habaner incunabula from the period 1590–1620.

Prague/Brno 1981–82; Troja 1992–96.

Kybalová-Novotná 1981, cat. no. 24, ill. p.
103; Kybalová 1992, cat. no. 48.

J.Ky.

v.356
Wine Cask
Faience, painted with high-temperature
colours
H: 30 cm; diam: 29.5 cm
1610–20
1957 from Červený Hrádek Castle
Prague, Uměleckoprůmyslové muzeum,
inv. no. 83 798

The vessel in the form of a horizontal cask
has four rows of sculptural iron bands and
stands on four round legs. There is a tin
stopper in the top wall and a tin spigot in
the side. The glaze is white, and both side
walls are painted with yellow, blue and

green flowers. Similar casks (of smaller dimensions) were also made of glass and
wood at the time. Of the group of extant
faience casks, this is the largest. It was evidently used for wine rather than for spirits.

Brno 1955; Prague/Brno 1981–82.

Kudělková-Zeminová 1961, cat. no. 13, ill.
5; Kybalová-Novotná 1981, cat. no. 44, p.
109.

J.Ky.

---

v.357
Plate with the Coat of Arms of the Trček
of Lípa
Faience, painted with high-temperature
colours
H: 4.5 cm; diam: 29.7 cm
1610–20
1957 from the Lobkowitz collection, at
the castles of Roudnice and Mělnice until
1951, then at the Uměleckoprůmyslové
muzeum in Prague, inv. no. 83 591; restituted in 1991
Prague, Uměleckoprůmyslové muzeum,
inv. no. Lobkowitz

The plate has a deep shape with a round

bottom and a narrower, octagonal rim. It
is glazed in white and features the painted
coat of arms of Jan Rudolf Trček of Lípa in
manganese purple and yellow, with the
initials I.R.T / Z.L. on the sides. Based on
other extant Habaner faiences, it is clear
that Jan Rudolf Trček's wife, Magdalena
Trčková, had her own dining service, with
a less ostentatious coat of arms and the
initials M.T.Z.L. on the rim.

Prague-Brno 1981–82; Bern–Zürich 1986.

Soupis památek (Roudnice), p. 247 ff, ill.
163; Poche 1955, ill. 69; Koula 1888, pp. 35–
36; Kybalová-Novotná 1981, cat. no. 46, ill.

p. 110.

J.Ky.

---

v.358
Platter with the Vrtba Coat of Arms
Faience, cobalt glaze, yellow and white
paint
H: 6.3 cm; diam: 21.5 cm
1613
1910 gift of F. A. Borovsky
Prague, Uměleckoprůmyslové muzeum,
inv. no. 11 718

The platter is round and flat and has a
raised rim with a bell-shaped profiled foot.
The glaze is blue-grey and the primitive
painting depicts white tendrils with yellow
flowers. The coat of arms has three horns
painted in manganese and the date 1613.

The initials W.B.S.N.S. / A.M.W.R.Z.W. are
in yellow. The platter represents the oldest
Habaner faience with a cobalt glaze. The
bottom row of initials can be interpreted
as 'Anna Markéta Vítová rozena z Wrbny'.
Another platter from this service is in the
collection of the Uměleckoprůmyslové
muzeum, and yet another is in the museum in Týn nad Sázavou.

Brno 1955; Prague/Brno 1981–82; Troja
1992–96.

Kudělková-Zeminová 1955, cat. no. 30, and
1961, cat. no. 8, ill. 6; Kybalová-Novotná
1981, cat. no. 31, ill. p. 104; Kybalová 1992,

cat. no. 49.

J.Ky.

---

v.359
Pitcher Painted with Cobalt
Faience, white glaze with cobalt painting
H: 26 cm; diam: 15.4 cm
1616
Auction of the Lanna Collection, Berlin
1909, R. Lepke, cat. no. 775
Prague, Uměleckoprůmyslové muzeum,
inv. no. 11 554

The pitcher is egg-shaped and has a massive, scrolled, sessile handle. The surface
of the tin lid is relief-decorated, and there
is a tin spout with a stopper. On the front,
the monogram HSFVTG and the date 1616
are drawn in cobalt and manganese on

white glaze and surrounded by a circular
frame. At the summit, there is a crown
with three rosettes.

Praha/Brno, 1981–82; Troja 1992–96.

Poche 1955, ill. 70; Kudělková-Zeminová
1961, cat. no. 10; Encyclopédie des antiquités
1978, p. 245, ill. 288; Kybalová-Novotná
1981, cat. no. 33, ill. p. 106; Kybalová 1992,
cat. no. 50, ill. p. 10.

J.Ky.

---

v.360
Bowl with Openwork Rim
Faience, painted with high-temperature
colours
H: 5.4 cm; diam: 19 cm
Ca. 1620
1952, Hugo Vavrečka deposit
Prague, keramická sbírka Hugo Vavrečka,
deposited in the Uměleckoprůmyslové
muzeum, inv. no. 56 726

The round-footed bowl has a wide rim
with subtle openwork in the form of
heraldic lilies. White glaze. On the bottom
is a depiction of a yellow and cobalt
rosette framed by two cobalt circles. The

bowl is one of the finest early Habaner
faiences. Both this bowl and its counterpart (inv. no. 56 725) are part of the ceramics collection of Hugo Vavrečka. Both
pieces were bought in Budapest. Evidence
of a similar style of painting dating from
around 1630 was found among the archaeological findings of W. Landsfeld.

Brno 1955; Prague-Brno 1981–82; Bern–
Zürich 1986; Troja 1992–96.

Umění na Slovensku 1938, p. 324, ill. 926;
Černohorsky 1940, p. 16; Kudělková-Zeminová 1955, cat. no. 15; Kybalová-Novotná
1981, cat. no. 16, ill. p. 53; Kybalová 1986,

cat. no. 3; Kybalová 1992, ill. p. 9; Kybalová
1995, cat. nos 7–8.

J.Ky.

V.361
Light Blue Glazed Bottle
Faience, light blue lead-tin glaze
H: 23.5 cm
1620–50
Moravia or Slovakia, Anabaptist workshop
1950, from the collection of Hermína Sr-
bová
Prague, Uměleckoprůmyslové muzeum,
inv. no. 79 556

The surface of the melon-shaped bottle
features inconspicuous diagonal ribbing.
The vessel has a low pewter foot and a
neck with a scroll; the stopper is missing.

During the first half of the seventeenth
century, some pastel glazes were used, although very infrequently, on Habaner
faience. These colours – yellow, a light
verdigris green and light blue (e.g. the
pitcher in the Uměleckoprůmyslové muzeum, inv. no. 11 552) – come from a weak
admixture of antimony oxide, copper and
cobalt.

Brno 1955; Prague–Brno 1981–82; Bern–
Zurich 1986; Troja 1992–96.

Kudělková-Zeminová 1955, cat. no. 62; Kybalová-Novotná 1981, cat. no. 59, ill. p. 113;
Kybalová 1986; Kybalová 1992, cat. no. 52;

J.Ky.

V.362
Pitcher with Pewter Lid
Faience, painted with high-temperature
colours
H: 21.5 cm
1635
South-western Slovakia, Anabaptist work-
shop
Vysoké Mýto, Okresní muzeum A. V. Šem-
bery, inv. no. 10 C–34

The round, white-glazed pitcher has a
massive handle, a tin lid and tin mounting.
Between two blue horizontal lines (double
circles), leafy spirals with lilies painted in
green, yellow and cobalt with manganese

outlines run from the front wall down the
sides. The divided date *16 / 35* features calligraphic ornamentation. The initials *M.
H.* are engraved on the lid. The pitcher is
part of a group of exceptionally finely
painted faiences from the Slovak settlement which date from the second half of
the 1630s. The same painter, apparently
with the same attention (judging by the
lustre of the high-temperature colours),
also executed the pitcher dated 1635 in
the Institute of Ethnography (Etno-
graficky ústav) of the Moravské muzeum
in Brno, inv. no. 20 454, and the tankard in
the Uměleckoprůmyslové muzeum in
Prague, dated 1636, inv. no. 82 752.

Prague–Brno 1981–82.

Kybalová-Novotná 1981, p. 34, cat. no. 54.

J.Ky.

V.363
Albarello with Cobalt Cartouche
Faience, painted with high-temperature
colours
H: 23 cm
1640
South-western Slovakia, Anabaptist work-
shop
Purchased from Rudolf Just in 1958
Prague, Uměleckoprůmyslové muzeum,
inv. no. 47 948

The vessel is barrel-shaped with a bent
and turned-up rim. On the front, the white
glaze is painted with a horizontal cartouche bordered with blue striped scroll-

work, in the centre of which is a Renaissance fruit platter. The sides feature blossoms painted in yellow, green and blue.
Apothecary vessels made by Anabaptist
and Italian faience makers often featured
blank labels, indicating that the Latin
names of medications were added later using cold-painting techniques.

Prague–Brno 1981–82.

Kybalová-Novotná 1981, cat. no. 63, ill. p.
115.

J.Ky.

V.364
Bowl with the Dietrichstein Coat of Arms
Faience, painted with high-temperature
colours
Diam: 41 cm
Ca. 1650
South-western Slovakia, Anabaptist workshop
From the Lobkowitz collection, at the castles of Roudnice and briefly at Mělník until 1952, then at the Uměleckoprůmyslové
muzeum in Prague, inv. no. 83 504, restituted in 1992
Prague, Uměleckoprůmyslové muzeum,
inv. no. Lobkowitz

The bowl is shallow and round with a deep
bottom and wide rim. It is white-glazed
with the family emblem of the Dietrich-
steins on the rim: two vines on a diagonally divided background. It is painted in yellow and manganese purple. The bowl is
part of the remnants of a large dining service comprised of eighteen plates, ten
bowls, three standing bowls, two platters
and a spice set.

Prague/Brno 1981–82; Bechyně 1983–86;
Troja 1992–96.

Soupis památek (Roudnice), p. 248, ill.
164; Kudělková-Zeminová 1955, cat. no.

70; Kudělková-Zeminová 1961, cat. nos
223–24; Kybalová-Novotná 1981, cat. no.
90; Kybalová 1992, cat. no. 54.

J.Ky.

V.365
Bowl with Ecclesiastical Emblem
Faience, painted with high-temperature
colours
H: 7.5 cm; l: 39 cm
1650
South-western Slovakia, Anabaptist workshop
1940 gift from Miss Šittlerová of Mezi-
mostí
Prague, Národní muzeum, oddělení
starších českých dějin, inv. no. 18 520

The bowl has an oval, rather deep shape
with a wide, radially ribbed and serrated
rim. The bottom of the vessel has a ring in

relief with a convex centre. The date and
the letter 'L' are framed by a yellow leafy
frame on white glaze. At the top is a mitre
painted in high-temperature colours. The
bowl is evidently part of the same service
as the four-sided bottle in the Okresní
muzeum in Česká Lípa (Kybalová-Novotná, cat. no. 78).

Prague/Brno 1981–82.

Kybalová-Novotná 1981, cat. no. 77, ill. p.
119.

J.Ky.

v.366
Bottle with Ecclesiastical Emblem
Faience, painted with high-temperature colours
H: 18 cm; base 8.5 × 8.5 cm
1650
South-western Slovakia, Anabaptist workshop
Česká Lípa, Okresní vlastivědné muzeum, inv. no. 18 401

The simple shape of a four-sided prism ends in a circular neck with a tin screw top and a circular handle. The white glaze is painted on the front with a circular wreath with a date and the initial 'L' in pale high-temperature colours. At the top is a mitre with fluttering lappets. The bottle is one of the few extant pieces from the same service as the bowl with the ecclesiastical emblem (Kybalová-Novotná, cat. no. 77). It demonstrates that, even after the Battle of the White Mountain, the Catholic clergy did not stop ordering functional faience from the Moravian and Slovak Anabaptists.

Prague/Brno 1981–82.

Kybalová-Novotná 1981, cat. no. 78, ill. p. 119.

J.Ky.

v.367
Tankard with Silesian Eagle
Ceramic with coloured glazes and a sand-polished surface
H: 16 cm
1550–1600
Silesia
Auction of the Lanna Collection, Berlin 1909, R. Lepke
Prague, Uměleckoprůmyslové muzeum, inv. no. 11 534

A barrel shape with a massive flattened handle. The neck is graduated with two rings in relief. On the front is a Silesian eagle in relief in manganese purple with a yellow crown and blue wing tips. Both sides of the crudely sand-polished surface have blue applications interrupted by a relief of Diana with a stag on a blue background. The rings are blue, white and yellow, and the top of the neck and the handle are green.

J.Ky.

v.368
Jug with the Coat of Arms of Jan Vojtěch Šlik
Fired clay, painted with coloured enamel
H: 29.5 cm
Ca. 1610
Auction of the Lanna Collection, Berlin 1909, R. Lepke
Prague, Uměleckoprůmyslové muzeum, inv. no. 11 553

An ovoid shape with a flattened handle. The sculptural, colour-glazed heraldic alliance emblems of Count Jan Vojtěch Šlik and his spouse, Johanna of Wildenfels, are depicted in oval, horizontally arranged fields. The emblems are framed by yellow and green circles with sculptural rosettes.

Lanna Collection auction, Berlin 1909, cat. no. 597; Prague 1910, cat. no. 121; Lanna cat., Fronek.

J.Ky.

v.369
Tankard with Figures of the Apostles
Ceramic with coloured glazes
H: 20.5 cm
Ca. 1600
Silesia, Wroclaw or Osoblaha (Hotzenplotz)
Auction of the Lanna Collection, Berlin 1909, R. Lepke
Prague, Uměleckoprůmyslové muzeum, inv. no. 17 543

A barrel shape on a higher, expanded foot. The mounting of the handle and the lid bear the engraved initials V. M. A geometric motif of alternating blue and white triangles appears on the foot and neck. The central, widest part is glazed in manganese purple. The bas-relief figures of the Apostles in yellow, green, blue and white stand in seven yellow relief arches. In the arcade on the right side of the handle is a circular medallion with a yellow Renaissance vase. The handle and neck are noticeably abraded, and part of the upper rim is missing. The vessel's Silesian origin is indicated by its conspicuous artistic and technical similarity with the well-known bowls with the portrait of Rudolf II in the Slezské muzeum in Opava and in the Victoria and Albert Museum in London. The geometric decoration, separated by deeply engraved lines, was not produced in any other ceramics centre in Europe at the time.

J.Ky.

v.370
Terra Sigillata Vessel with Lid
Red-brown terra sigillata, undecorated
H: 16 cm
1639
From the Lobkowitz collection, at the castles of Roudnice and Mělník until 1951, then at the Uměleckoprůmyslové muzeum in Prague, inv. no. 83 450 a, b; restituted in 1992
Prague, Uměleckoprůmyslové muzeum, inv. no. Lobkowitz 11 644

A small, cylindrical vessel on a low, narrow base with a simple, deep-fitting lid with a lenticular handle. Two horizontal ridges run across the middle of the surface. Both the vessel and the lid are imprinted with a circular stamp with the initials KB (Königreich Böhmen) and the coat of arms of the Berka family – two small knolls and crossed logs – and bear the inscription TERRA SIGILLATA, dated 1639. The inside of the vessel has a sculptural structure, indicating that it was made on a potter's wheel. During the years 1630–1860, a special type of thin-walled pottery marked with a stamp was produced on the estate of Jindřich Berka of Dubá in Jablonné; the material used resembled Roman terra sigillata and was thought to have healing powers against poison, snakebites and some illnesses. The privilege for its production was issued by the Emperor on the basis of the expert opinions of mineralogists and physicians. Thus an ancient tradition became of interest to the members of the Rudolfine court. Terra sigillata was much sought after by collectors and appears in all the famous inventories of the time, including that of the Rudolfine collections.

Horschik 1966, pp. 3–55; Kybalová 1996.

J.Ky.

V.371
Terra Sigillata Bowl
Whitish terra sigillata, undecorated
Diam: 15.4 cm
1639
Jablonné v Podještědí
From the Lobkowitz collection, at the castles of Roudnice and Mělnice until 1951, then at the Uměleckoprůmyslové muzeum in Prague, inv. no. 83 451; restituted in 1992
Prague, Uměleckoprůmyslové muzeum, inv. no. Lobkowitz 11 646

A somewhat deep, conical bowl with a narrow, smooth rim. The distinct circular

stamp of the Berkas of Dubá with the initials *KB* and the text *TERRA SIGILLATA* appear in the centre of the bottom, along with the date *1639*. The date on the stamp refers to the date of the renewal of the privilege. Certain areas on the smooth surface of the vessel are markedly abraded.

J.Ky.

V.372
Small Terra Sigillata Pitcher
Reddish-brown terra sigillata, unfired enamel painting
H: 13 cm
1639
Jablonné v Podještědí
1892 bequest of Sir V. Neuberg
Prague, Uměleckoprůmyslové muzeum, inv. no. 4 826

The pear-shaped vessel has a high neck and an arched handle with an opening for the mounting. The smooth, shiny surface of the pitcher features painted leafy spiralling with red carnations and black-and-

white tulips. Between the horizontal white lines on the neck of the vessel are the remnants of an inscription. A green frame with the visibly imprinted stamp of Jindřich Berka of Dubá, the year and the initials *KB* appears on the front side. The unfired painting has washed away to a large extent.

J.Ky.

V.373
Small Terra Sigillata Tankard
Whitish terra sigillata, unfired enamel painting
H: 9.2 cm
1642
Jablonné v Podještědí
Auction of the Lanna Collection, Berlin 1909, R. Lepke
Prague, Uměleckoprůmyslové muzeum, inv. no. 11 512

A low, barrel-shaped tankard with a subtle handle and notching on the foot and upper edge. The whitish-grey surface features unusually fine and precisely painted

scrolling green leaves with lily-like flowers and rosettes in purple, orange and yellow. To the left of the handle is a half-portrait of St Elisabeth in an oval medallion. Under the neck, between horizontal red lines, is the inscription in black *SPES MEA CHRISTVS / 1642*. There is an imprinted stamp. The unfired painting has been partially washed away. The tankard is the most intricately painted terra sigillata vessel in the collections of the Uměleckoprůmyslové muzeum.

J.Ky.

V.374
Conical bowl of smooth form with three horizontal grooves
Whitish terra sigillata
stamp of Berk of Dubá family
Jablonne v Podještědí, seat of the Berk of Dubá family, 1625-1650
Lobkowicz collection, Roudnice
Prague, W. Lobkowicz collection, inv. no. 11 643 and 11 646 (formerly UPM 83 451ab)

This medium-depth bowl has a narrow, smooth rim. At the centre of the bottom is the pronounced stamp of the Berk of Dubá family with the initials *KB*, a text

with the words *TERRA SIGILLATA* and the dating to 1639. The year of the stamp shows the date of a privilege being conferred. The once smooth surface of the vessel is noticeably worn. (For the text on the production and history of terra sigillata and for further literature see cat. no. V.370).

J.Ky.

V.375
Small Terra Sigillata Pitcher
Whitish terra sigillata, unfired enamel painting
H: 12.6 cm
1651
Jablonné v Podještědí
Auction of the Lanna Collection, Berlin 1909, R. Lepke
Prague, Uměleckoprůmyslové muzeum, inv. no. 11 511

The slender, pear-shaped pitcher has a wide, flattened handle with an opening for the mounting and two horizontal protrusions on the neck. The whitish-grey sur-

face is painted with Renaissance vines outlined in black, with large red rosettes and tulips. To the left of the handle are the remnants of a standing (female?) figure, possibly a saint. Below the neck of the vessel, half of the distinct inscription *WIE GOTT ...* has been preserved. The usual stamp of the Berkas of Dubá on the front wall of the vessel bears traces of yellow, green and red polychromy. The unfired painting has been washed off to a large extent, particularly on the part to the left of the handle.

J.Ky.

V.376
Small Terra Sigillata Pitcher
Whitish terra sigillata, unfired enamel
painting
H: 16.7 cm
1651
1950, from Doksa Castle
Prague, Uměleckoprůmyslové muzeum,
inv. no. 79 417

The round pitcher has a high neck with a
tin top which is attached to the handle.
The smooth surface of the vessel features
painted black leafwork with red, green and
yellow flowers. The neck bears the inscription in black *SOLI DEO GLORIA* between

painted red lines. The colour has washed
away to a significant extent, and the side is
pierced by a small hole; the mounting of
the lid is damaged.

J.Ky.

V.377
Terra Sigillata Bowl
Reddish-brown terra sigillata, cold-paint-
ed with enamel
Diam: 18 cm
1653
From the Nostitz collection
Prague, Uměleckoprůmyslové muzeum,
inv. no. 78 027

A conical vessel with two flat, indented
handles. The entire interior surface bears
traces of finely painted leafy spirals with
flowers in yellow, white and blue. In the
centre of the bottom is the conspicuous
stamp of the Berkas of Dubá and the des-

ignation *TERRA SIGILLATA*.

J.Ky.

V.378
Beaker with the Emblems of Vratislav of
Pernštejn and Marie Manrique de Lara y
Mendoza
Clear glass, enamel paint
H: 24 cm
Before 1572
At the castle of Buchlov at least since the
nineteenth century
Buchlov Castle, inv. no. SZ Buchlov 701

The conical beaker on a bell-shaped foot
bears the coat of arms of Vratislav of
Pernštejn on the front and the coat of
arms of Marie Manrique de Lara y Mendoza on the opposite side. There is a bor-

der of white and red dots along the upper
rim. Vratislav of Pernštejn, who became
the highest chancellor of the kingdom of
Bohemia in 1567, was, along with Vilém of
Rožmberk, one of the wealthiest magnates
and most important figures on the Czech
political scene during the second half of
the sixteenth century. The beaker cannot
be dated to the time of the marriage in
1555 because we do not know of any
Czech enamel-painted glass from that period. The *datum ante quem* is the death of
Vratislav of Pernštejn in 1582, or rather the
awarding of the Order of the Golden
Fleece by Philip II in 1572. The beaker is
unrelated to the history of Buchlov. It is

possible that it was created as a welcoming beaker for the castle in Lytomyšl,
which was obtained from the King in 1567
and remodelled at great cost during the
years 1568–73. It most probably entered
the Buchlov Castle collections as part of
the collecting activities of the Berchtolds,
as did the beaker of Archduke Maximilian,
dated 1582.

Permanent exhibition of Buchlov Castle.

Jiřík 1934, ill. 5; Medková 1957, pp. 148ff.

O.D.

V.379
Beaker with the Coats of Arms of Zdeněk
of Valdštejn on Brtnice and Sádek and of
Magdalena Valdštejn, née Thurn
Clear greenish glass, enamel-painted
H: 29.8 cm
Above the coats of arms in inscription
bands: *Zdeniek Z Waltsteyna na Brtnicz a
Sadku, Mandalena Waldsteinska rozena Hra-
binka z Turnu na Brtnici a Sad*
1610
1906 gift of Sir Vojtěch Lanna
Prague, Uměleckoprůmyslové muzeum,
inv. no. 10 399

The cylindrical beaker has a cylindrical

foot which expands into a bell shape at the
bottom. The surface is decorated with the
coats of arms of the Waldsteins
(Valdštejns) and Thurns and a border of
white and red dots and small apples. Jiřík
(1934, p. 102, n. 158) astutely points out
the frequent contact between the lords of
Brtnice and the lords of Hradec and
Rožmberk and thus does not rule out the
possibility that the beaker could have
come from a southern Bohemian glassworks in spite of the fact that the Brtnice
estates are located in the Jihlava region of
Moravia. The engagement of the pair occurred in 1603. The accounts of the
Rožmberk glassworks above Vilémov

from 1608 to 1614 document the production of enamel-painted glass, especially of
beakers with one or two coats of arms.

Prague 1984.

Jiřík 1934, p. 102; Drahotová-Hejdová
1989, cat. no. 65.

O.D.

V.380
Pitcher with a Scene from the Fable of the
Fox and the Geese
Dark blue cobalt glass, enamel-painted
H: 20 cm
1595
1906 gift of Vojtěch Lanna
Prague, Uměleckoprůmyslové muzeum,
inv. no. 9 894

A round pitcher with a high, cylindrical
neck. The rounded bulge of the vessel features two geese leading the captured fox
on a leash; on the other side of the vessel,
the geese hang the fox on a tree. The neck
of the pitcher features a rich frieze with

stylized flower ornamentation and intersecting arches between two bands of
wreaths. The animal fables of Aesop and
other authors were very popular in the sixteenth century. The fox in particular often
appears as a thief or as an erotic symbol.
The closest analogue to this pitcher is the
one in the Landesmuseum Johanneum in
Graz (see Saldern 1965, p. 119, ill. 163).

Prague 1984.

Drahotová-Hejdová 1984, cat. no. 49.

O.D.

v.381
Beaker with Card and 'Triktrak' Players
Clear, greyish glass, enamel-painted
H: 24.5 cm; diam: 11.1 cm
Gregorius Kamsetzer
1596
1906 gift of Sir Vojtěch Lanna
Prague, Uměleckoprůmyslové muzeum,
inv. no. 9 887

The cylindrical beaker has a massive rib around the bottom. The surface decoration is comprised of wide borders made up of bands of intersecting arches, oval ornaments, wreaths and dots. Between these borders there are two scenes: 'triktrak' players and card players sitting at a table. Bunches of flowers are painted on the sides. The borders repeat motifs which appear on many Czech painted glass vessels – intersecting arches and coloured oval ornaments. The beaker features the only extant depiction of the iconography of contemporary games and amusements on glass. As game players were often the targets of sharp criticism, these scenes, which are based on engravings by J. T. de Bry, are essentially satirical critiques of society.

Prague 1984.
Drahotová-Hejdová 1989, cat. no. 51.

O.D.

v.382
Bottle in the Shape of a Pistol with Ornamental Decoration
Clear, greyish glass, shaped in a glassworks, enamel-painted
Diam: 41 cm
Late sixteenth to early seventeenth century
1596
1906 gift of Sir Vojtěch Lanna
Prague, Uměleckoprůmyslové muzeum,
inv. no. 9 963

One end of the pistol ends in a tin screw valve. The trigger and lock ring are welded on to the other, ball-shaped, end, and the rest of the mechanism is painted, along with accompanying flower and leaf motifs on both sides. The pistol was formerly in the collection of H. Krug, Mülheim (see Klesse 1965, cat. no. 519). Pistol-shaped bottles continued to be produced in Bohemia until the eighteenth century.

Prague 1984.

Drahotová-Hejdová 1984, cat. no. 67.

O.D.

v.383
Humpen with a Maiden, Three Cavaliers and Saint George
Enamelled glass
H: 24.8
1604
Dresden, Staatliche Kunstsammlungen, Historisches Museum, inv. no. 37 088

According to the inscription, this vessel served as a welcoming beaker of the Ölbing Brotherhood. One of the illustrations on the sides depicts Saint George battling with the dragon, accompanied by the text *Ritter S. Georgius B. H.*, and the other is a dance scene with an elegant lady and three cavaliers, all dressed according to the fashion of the time. Next to the cavaliers is the inscription *Spaniger, Franzos, tetscher,* and above them we read, *Die Jungfrau sagt mit füs tretten Hand drücken und lachen kan ich sie alle drei zu narren machen.* The tankard comes from a group of glass vessels from the late sixteenth to mid-seventeenth centuries. The illustrations are a moralizing depiction of the power of the coquettish woman over men. According to A. von Saldern (German Enameled Glass, New York, 1965, 106-108; with other illustrations), the scene is taken from the decoration of a copper engraving by the monographist *B K G F*, or rather *K G H S B F*, from 1590.

G.H.

---

v.384
Beaker with Hunting Scenes
Clear glass, enamel-painted
H: 31 cm
1627
1906 gift of Sir Vojtěch Lanna
Prague, Uměleckoprůmyslové muzeum,
inv. no. 9 906

The cylindrical beaker has a massive rib around the bottom. The surface features friezes of lines, dots and arches; between these are depictions of stylized vegetation and the figures of hunters with crossbows, lances, a gun and sticks, attacking dogs, a fox, a wolf, rabbits and a lynx. The composition is freely adapted from both older and contemporary engravings. Related motifs are found in the engravings of Virgil Solis, Hans Weiditz, Erhard Schoen, H. Brosamer and others (see Saldern 1965, p. 112).

Prague 1992.

Brožková 1992, cat. no. 2.

O.D.

v.385
Beaker with Dancing Couples and Inscription to Archduke Maximilian
Clear, slightly greyish glass, diamond-engraved
H: 40 cm
MAXIMILIANO SERENISSIMO ARCHIDUCI AVSTRIAE LIBATA SVNTO
1582
1582
At Buchlov since at least the nineteenth century
Buchlov Castle, inv. no. SH Buchlov 427

The cylindrical beaker on a cylindrical foot with an open, bell-shaped bottom is decorated with dancing and promenading couples in two horizontal bands. The lower band includes a brass band and a timpanist. The upper rim is decorated with a border of foliage ornamentation between hatched bands of goose-necked zigzags, and above that a band of trefoils and the inscription. The use of the brass band and the timpani is significant here, for they symbolized military and worldly power; in addition to being used in battle, they were exclusively a part of aristocratic representation. None of the extant sources demonstrates the beaker's historical relationship to Buchlov Castle. It may have reached the castle only in the nineteenth century, intended perhaps as a gift for Archduke Maximilian's visit to Bohemia, a journey that was never made because of the sudden death of Vratislav of Pernštejn in 1582. The technique of diamond-point engraving is mentioned in Bohemia as early as 1562, and by the late sixteenth century had become widespread in Bohemia, particularly at the Rožmberk glassworks near Vilémov or the glassworks in Chřibská.

Permanent installation in Buchlov Castle.
Jiřík 1934, p. 47, ill. 2; Medková 1957, pp. 148ff; Sehna 1958, pp. 75-77.

O.D.

V.386
Beaker with the Allegory of Caritas and
the Žerotín Coat of Arms
Clear, slightly greenish glass, diamond-
point engraving, cold painting
H: 45.5 cm
CARITAS in an inscription frame
Late sixteenth to early seventeenth century
Possibly the glassworks at Vilémov on the
Nové Hrady estate in southern Bohemia
Purchased in 1955 from a private collec-
tion
Prague, Uměleckoprůmyslové muzeum,
inv. no. 39 654

The slender, cylindrical beaker has a taller

bell-shaped foot. On the surface, between
the painted and diamond-point-engraved
friezes, we find the Žerotín coat of arms
and the remnants of the monogram *I.D.S.*;
the opposite side features a woman with a
child seated on a throne under the inscription frame. The sides are decorated with
leaves. The shape, technique and decoration of the goblet relate it to the Tyrolean
glass manufactured in Innsbruck for
Archduke Ferdinand of Tyrol in the period
1570–90. The allegory of Caritas was executed according to an engraving by Jost
Amman. The coat of arms probably refers
to Jan Diviš of Žerotín (d. 1616), of the
Náměšt branch of the family, son of Jan

the Elder of Žerotín and his cousin Karel
the Elder of Žerotín, who inherited Židlo-
chovice (Selowitz) and married Veronika
of Žerotín in 1601. As a fellow member of
the Moravian Brethren, Petr Vok of
Rožmberk had a close relationship with
both Jan the Elder and Karel the Elder of
Žerotín. Cold painting on glass is documented from the beginning of the sixteenth century onwards in the accounts of
the Rožmberk glassworks near Vilémov.

Prague 1984.

Drahotová-Hejdová 1989, cat. no. 81.

O.D.

V.387
Beaker with Dancing Couples
Clear greenish glass, diamond-point en-
graved and cold-painted
H: 39 cm; diam: 10 cm
1621
Probably southern Bohemia, glassworks
near Vilémov on the Nové Hrady estate
(Gratzen)
Gift of Sir Vojtěch Lanna
Prague, Uměleckoprůmyslové muzeum,
cat. no. 10 041

The cylindrical beaker stands on a taller
cylindrical foot with a bell-shaped bottom.
The surface features two dancing couples

between diamond-point-engraved borders and gilded bands, with engraved
ornamental foliage on the sides. The techniques of cold painting and diamon-point
engraving were documented beginning in
the early seventeenth century at the
Rožmberk glassworks near Vilémov on
the estate of Nové Hrady. After the
Rožmberk family died out and after the
forfeiture of their heirs, the Švamberks, in
February 1620 – that is, before the Battle
of the White Mountain – the estate fell to
the decorated general Karel Bonaventure
de Longueval de Buquoy. The beaker
clearly continues the tradition of works
from the Rožmberk glassworks. The bor-

ders bear a similarity, albeit as a rougher
version, to the beaker with the allegory of
Caritas and the Žerotín coat of arms in the
Uměleckoprůmyslové muzeum in Prague
(cat. no.). The unfired figural painting,
however, is no longer Mannerist in character.

Corning 1981, cat. no. 9; Prague 1984, cat.
no. 84.

Drahotová 1981, p. 53; Drahotová-Hejdová
1989, cat. no. 84.

O.D.

V.388
Dolls' House
Wood, metal, textiles and other materials
85 × 129 × 51 cm
Seventeenth century, with later additions
Prague, Památkový ústav středních Čech,
inv. nos JE 13 333–JE 13 337

One of the oldest European items of this
kind, with four interior rooms: a drawing
room, bedroom, kitchen and dining room,
made and arranged in the style of the late
Renaissance and early Baroque. In the
drawing room is a figure of a woman with
an ivory head. Tin, copper and tiny silver
utensils in other rooms bear the mark of

Amsterdam, Augsburg and Nürnburg
workshops. Some parts of the furnishings,
e.g., the book and table, come from an earlier period. The composition was produced for children of the Wallenstein family and comes from the collection at
Wallenstein Palace in Prague. In the 1950s
this arrangement of rooms was found at
an exhibition at the Jemniště château and
in the 1980s it became part of a survey of
historical toys and curiosities at the
Hořovice château. It later went to the Ursuline convent in Kutná Hora. Drs Ludiše
Letošníková and Alena Horynová have devoted particular attention to this item in
the past. Another preserved historical toy,

for a boy, also comes from the Wallenstein
Palace: a model of a knight in full Renaissance armour on horseback made of lime
wood.

Muchka–Křížová 1996, p .128.

K.K.

V.389
Adam Eck
Game Box
Wood, relief inlay
8.5 × 53 × 53 cm
Ca. 1650
1965 transfer from the ONV Benešov,
Jemniště Castle
Prague, Uměleckoprůmyslové muzeum,
inv. no. 65 997

A coffer for storing chess and dice games.
On the lid are two scenes in relief: the upper one depicts a family kneeling in a landscape and looking up at the clouds, in
which the initial *A* appears. The lower im-

age features the same landscape with the
theme of the inconstancy of fortune symbolized by a broken column and the date
1618 (the beginning of the Thirty Years'
War) in the lower part, while a human face
looking out from a cloud blows powerfully on to the column. The lid and lower part
of the coffer are set into a dotted frame
with a relief of the coat of arms of the Los
family of Losinthal (a swan and an eagle),
and tulip, carnation and narcissus blossoms. The chessboard on the bottom of
the coffer is decorated with inlaid rosettes,
and the interior part for dice games is decorated with inlaid obelisks and other symbols (fire, grapevines, streams of water).

The scenes of a Swiss city on the coffer
were carved according to models by M.
Merian the Elder and W. Dilich. Adam Eck
worked for the Los family of Losinthal and
created a similar coffer to celebrate the
victory of Ferdinand II in the Battle of
Nordling. Game boxes were also decorated with relief inlay.

Prague 1986, cat. nos 52, 52a, 52b.

Sturm 1961, ill. 107; Mžyková 1986, cat.
nos 52, 52a, 52b.

D.K.

V.390
Compass–Pointer
Wrought iron, scored
32.1 cm
Mid-17th century.
Bought in 1893 from the collections of
Architect G. Hering of Munich.
Liberec, Northern Bohemian Museum,
inv. no. OK 1975

The technique of cutting reliefs on the
surface of metal was used since the middle
ages but it was only in the seventeenth
century that it became common in ornamental ironwork when the relative difficulty of nielloing became less commonly

used in ornamental works and more frequent in locksmithing.

Liberec 1989, no. 5.

Pazourek 1985, tab. XXIX; Mohr, 1989, no. 5.

J.M.

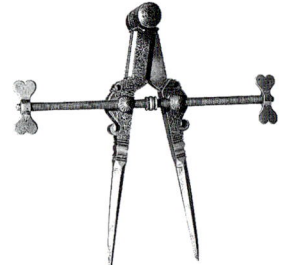

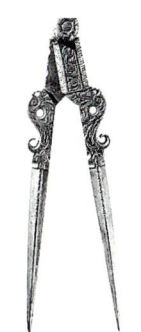

V.391
Compass – Pointer
Wrought iron, scored, nielloed
32.2 cm
Second half of the sixteenth century
Bought in 1894 from Joseph Grger of Munich.
Liberec, Northern Bohemian Museum, inv. no. OK 1041

Richly nielloed and decorated, this tool is amongst the best preserved of its kind. Decor and shape indicates southern German handiwork from around 1600. Tools with niello decoration were used for demanding customers, usually from the

court.

Prague 1984, no. 281; Liberec 1989, no. 1.

MNGM 1894/3, p 46 ; MNGM 1898/3, pp 61–62, fig.; Rasl-Mohr, 1984, attachment cat. p. 23; Mohr, 1989, n. 1.

V.392, a–f

a: Blacksmith's Pliers [shown here]
Malleable wrought iron, filed; 31.5 cm, second half of sixteenth century
Liberec, Northern Bohemian Museum, inv. no. OK 1976.

b: Hammer [shown here]
Malleable wrought iron, nielloed, lathed wood; 23.7 cm; ca. 1600
Liberec, Northern Bohemian Museum inv. no. OK 2639.

c: Combination Tool
Malleable wrought iron, filed brass; 18.5 cm; beginning of the seventeenth century

Liberec, Northern Bohemian Museum, inv. no. OK 1974.

d: Gavel
Iron; 5.6 × 19.7 cm; sixteenth century
Prague, Uměleckoprůmyslové muzeum, inv. no. 8 877

e: Goldsmith's Saw with Frame
Malleable iron, wrought and engraved, lathed tortoiseshel; 29.3 cm; seventeenth century
Liberec, Northern Bohemian Museum, inv. no. 1970

f: Ironsmith's Pliers
Malleable iron, wrought and filed; 27.3

cm; ca. sixteenth century
Liberec, Northern Bohemian Museum inv. no. OK 1974

h: Cork Holer (Spoon Screw)
Malleable iron, wrought and engraved, carved wood; 28.8 cm; end of sixteenth century
Liberec, Northern Bohemian Museum inv. no. OK 1979

Prague 1984, Liberec 1989.

Pazaurek 1895, Rasl-Mohr 1984, Mohr 1989.

J.M.

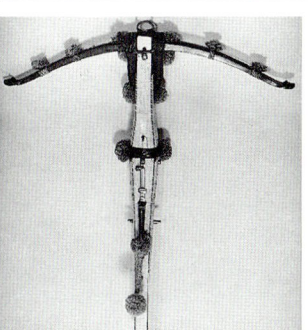

V.393
Hunting Crossbow with Lever
Wood, ivory, rope, iron, mounting, etching, turned carving
Crossbow: length 65 cm, span of bow 70 cm; lever length 35 cm
On the bow set in quartered circles beneath the crown, on the rod of the lever, IH with a six-pointed star between the letters, above which is a half moon and two stars
Ca. 1600
Prague, Národní muzeum, inv. no. H2-197

The emblem on the lower surface of the statue indicates that this is probably a

weapon produced for servants of the noble family of Daun, who had seats in Bítov, Skalice, Horní Kounice, Halinkov and other places in Moravia. Made with superb mastery, it is of exquisite character, is demonstrated particularly by the exceptional quality of its bas-relief carving in ivory (stag hunt, boar hunting, the coat-of-arms) that envelopes the entire bow. The lever is used to wind the bow, and was probably not made for this bow and acquired independently later. Apart from its utilitarian function, it is of exceptional value for the history of decorative crafts, as cann be seen in the quality of the etchings of animals.

E.Sn.

V.394
Hunting Crossbow
Weaponry (gunsmith's?) work, steel, wood, bone
Length: 64.9 cm; bow span 53.5 cm
Branded producer's symbol
Late sixteenth and early seventeenth centuries
Plzeň, Západočeské muzeum v Plzni, inv. no. Z 66

Hunting crossbow with a metal construction, designed for hunting small birds.

F.F.

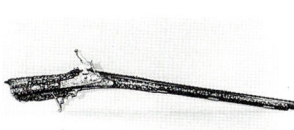

V.395
Hunting Rifle with Wheel Lock
Iron, bone, ebony, ivory, inlaid with mother-of-pearl
Total length: 122.5 cm, length of the barrel: 89.0 cm; calibre: 14 mm
Sixteenth to mid-seventeenth century
Plzeň, Západočekské muzeum v Plzni inv. no. Z 650

Hunting rifle with wheel lock, German butt, richly inlaid bone with hunting scenes and tendril-like leaf ornamentation. The lock plate is also decorated with tendrils and a picture of a reclining dog. The case for the butt is decorated with

ebony and ivory. The bone inlay is complemented with mother-of-pearl. The butt runs the whole length of the octagonal barrel.

F.F.

V.396
Cinquedea Small Hunting Knife
Cutler's work, steel, wood
Length: 66 cm; length of the blade: 45 cm;
width of the blade: 11.6 cm
Sixteenth century
Plzeň, Západočeské muzeum v Plzni,
inv. no. Z 151

Sidearm for mercenaries and members of
the middle social strata.

F.F.

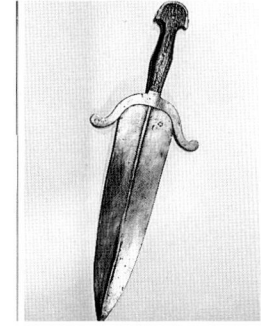

V.397
Dagger with Sheath, Sculptural Decoration
Swordsmith's work
Length: 38 cm; length of blade: 24.3 cm
Relief of the year 1656 designed on the
border of the sheath
1656
Plzeň, Západočeské muzeum v Plzni, inv.
no. Z 776

A type of small hunting knife, which became more widely used chiefly in Germany at the end of the sixteenth century
and during the first half of the seventeenth century.

F.F.

V.398
Gun-powder Holder
Ox horn, iron plate, engraving
Height 26 cm, below 9.8, above 6.5 cm
Ca. 1600
Property of the National Museum of the
kingdom of Bohemia in Prague, 1863,
no.168
Prague, Národní muzeum, inv. no. H2-326

A kind of hunting-bow-shaped gun-powder holder, with a hunting scene engraved
on the outer side and a concentrated arrangement of circles on the inside, used in
central and western Europe. In Prague
such items are represented at the Military

Museum at the Castle and beyond Prague
in large number at the state-run château
of Konopiště.

E.Sn.

V.399
Gun-powder Holder
Ivory, gilded brass, turned, engraved
Average size 13–15 cm
1600–50
Confiscated property in 1945, taken from
the local council in Cheb
Prague, Národní muzeum, inv. no. H2-32
260

This exceptional work is turned in ivory,
which is especially apparent on the relief
of the rosette on the flat part of the holder
and on the cartouche with a stylized flower on the bulging side. The figures of the
ornate little dragons on the attached

loops are also of artistic interest. Similar
gun-powder holders can also be found at
the Historical Museum in Dresden, at the
museum in Budapest or at the state-run
château at Cheb.

E.Šn.

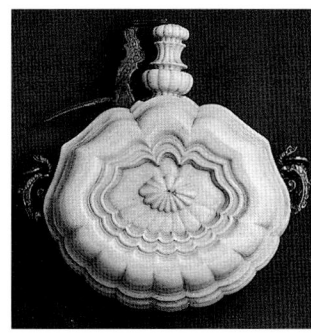

V.400
Workshop of Castrucci
Small Home Altar with the Coats of Arms
of the Pernštejn and Lobkowitz Families
Ebony, commessi in pietre dure
64 × 46 cm
1603 (?)
From the collections of the Lobkowitz
family at Roudnice Castle
Prague, collection of W. Lobkowicz, Inv.
no. XI.Ea.LR 5272

The inventory of the collection drawn up
by M. Dvořák and B. Matějka attributes the
altar correctly to the Rudolfine period and
indicates that it was a gift from Rudolf II

to Zdeněk Vojtěch of Lobkowitz and
Polyxena of Pernštejn on the occasion of
their wedding in 1603. The work is an
exquisite example of miniature altar architecture and brilliantly contrasts the rather
austere ebony construction with the mosaic of colourful gemstones that make up
the central image. Work on the attribution
and iconography of the central panel has
to date proved inconclusive. The female
figure with a crown and halo may be Saint
Margaret or Saint Helena. C. Przborowská
has argued convincingly for an attribution
to the Castrucci workshop. If the work
predates 1603, then the motif of the kneeling woman will be one of the first known

figural compositions executed using this
technique.

Essen 1988, cat. no. 393.

Dvořák-Matějka 1910, p. 214, ill. 128;
Bukovinská 1972, pp. 365-66, ill. 6; Poche
1979, p. 170, ill. 146; Preiss 1986, p. 132, ill.
133; Hagemann 1988, pp. 84-104, ill. 1;
Bukovinská 1988, p. 166, ill. 131.

B.B.

V.401
Czech or South German Goldsmith
Household Altar
Bronze, gold, diamonds, two green beryls,
two turquoise tourmalines, four rubies,
crystal, river pearls, converse enamel en
ronde basse
H: 24 cm; W: 11.5 cm
1570–80 figures, stones and balusters;
base, corpus and medallion Vienna (?),
late nineteenth century
Germany
1948–50 seized from an unknown Czech
castle; 1950 Uměleckoprůmyslové
muzeum, Prague
Prague, Uměleckoprůmyslové muzeum,

inv. no. 83 211 (Z-CXC)

Renaissance pieces can be identified by
the types of enamel and stones used. The
original figures of SS Peter and Paul, God
in an edicule and the angels, as well as a
cross with shroud, are analogous to handstein pieces from Jáchymov; in Czech and
south German jewellery little figural
heads, rosettes, rollwork, small garlands of
flowers, stones and frames in profile are
also similar. Cut rings in crystal columns
represent traces of the original setting.
The metal plinths and the outer frame are
probably from a later period. The age of
the stones can be determined by the

method by which they were set and by
mineralogical analysis: the majority of Renaissance stones cut into tabular form (diamonds) and graded form (two beryls and
two tourmalines) have older small mountings with enamel leaves. Some of these
have been set deeply into the frame. A
locket with radial beams proceeding from
it acts as a replacement for a larger octagonal tablet on which the Risen Christ
would originally have been placed.

Prague 1970; Prague 1975, suppl. III.

D.S.

V.402
Daniel Fröschl (?)
1573–1613
Altarpiece of the Family of Christ
Soft wood coated with ivory, marble, thir-
ty-seven cut stones, brass, gouache on paper; repaired 1915 by a cabinet-maker
named Mlch and a goldsmith named Ne-
mec
H: 54.8 cm in total; w: 32.4 cm; miniature
15.3 × 11.7 cm
1600–10
1915 from the collection of Vaclav Stepan,
Stara Boleslav; by tradition from the
property of the Valdštejn family

This type of altarpiece, with a portal construction, is analogous to the Stará
Boleslav altarpiece used for the Paleadi-
um. The interior contains scenes of specific genres: the Virgin Mary rocks the Infant
Jesus and reads to him from a book; St
Joseph has left his workbench and is opening a curtain to welcome visitors – John
the Baptist as a little boy with his family. In
1995 Eliška Fučíková ascribed the painting to Daniel Fröschl at the Uměleckoprůmyslové muzeum.

Brandýs nad Labem 1995, cat. no. 9.

D.S.

V.403
Anonymous Florentine Master
Frame in the Shape of an Edicule
Ebony, rosewood, pewter, gilded silver,
lapis lazuli, amethyst, marble, coloured
glass
65 × 45 cm
Early seventeenth century
Purchased in Prague, 1982
Prague, Uměleckoprůmyslové muzeum,
inv. no. 90 276

The frame, which was purchased by the
Uměleckoprůmyslové muzeum only in
1982, is made in the form of a refined architectural miniature. It has not been pos-

sible to document the purpose that it
served nor its ownership history, but it
represents an example of the artisanal
work of the circle of Florentine artists of
the late sixteenth and early seventeenth
centuries. Given the close ties that existed
between Prague and Florence during the
reign of Rudolf II, we must assume that
such objects would have been found not
only in imperial and aristocratic collections, but also in the households of the
community of Italian artists living in
Prague. This fact is evidenced, among other things, by the very interesting and recently analyzed inventories of Prague
households.

B.B.

V.404
Dionision Miseroni workshop
Three-lobed Boat with Sprigs
Lead crystal, cut
Height: 12cm
1625–50
From the estate of the Counts of Nostic,
Prague, Uměleckoprůmyslové muzeum,
invl. no. 78 006

A boat has two rings in the lower part and
on a smaller oval-shaped foot. On the
dome are the symmetrically cut leaves of a
sprig with berries, which project under the
lock to the flowers with polished centres
and into the heads of dolphins. The sim-

plicity of the decoration is proved by it
later origin; the quality does not prove
that the piece might have been made for
the court. The decorative carvings are
more recent, perhaps from the late seventeenth century. Nevertheless, a number
of undecorated pieces of varying sizes
have been preserved at the Kunsthistorisches Museum in Vienna. They are of
the same form and are from the imperial
collection.

Prague 1993, cat. no. V.3-55.

Drahotová 1970, pp. 7–13.

O.D.

V.405
Shell on a Baluster Stem
Cut smoky quartz, smooth gilt-silver
mount
H: 15 cm
1625–50
Prague
From the estate of the counts of Nostitz,
Prague
Prague, Uměleckoprůmyslové muzeum,
inv. no. 77 990

The deep, oval, rounded bowl with an
openwork rim opens up to the height of
the shell, which culminates in two volutes
at the top. Smooth relief ridges run from

the volutes down the sides of the bowl.
Each side of the rounded lower part features six vertical grooves ending in arches.
The stem is a smooth baluster between
two flat nodes. The foot is new.

Prague 1993, cat. no. V.3-31. Permanent
installation in the Uměleckoprůmyslové
muzeum, Prague.

O.D.

V.406
Workshop of Dionysio Miseroni
Prague 1607 (?)-Prague 1661
Beaker with Lid, Decorated with a Landscape
Cut and engraved crystal, gold mounts
28 cm, 17 cm without lid
Mount is marked with a lion on a shield
1625-50
1945, from the collections of the counts of Nostitz, Prague
Prague, Uměleckoprůmyslové muzeum, inv. no. 78 009 ab

The beaker has a flat foot, a bi-conical stem, a barrel-shaped bowl with a rounded

bottom and an arched lid which ends in a metal grip in the form of Athena with a lance and shield. The sheath of the bowl features a running landscape with trees, hunters and a dog. On the bottom of the bowl and the foot there is a margin with a cut border with flowers and twigs with small leaves. The goldsmith's mark is indeterminate, perhaps Czech. The engraved decoration is similar to the Nürnberg style of work from the circle of Georg Schwanhardt the Elder but is of an inferior quality. Based on the fairly rustic engraving work and the Mannerist style of the metal figure of Athena, it is possible that the beaker was created in Prague, outside the

circle of the Miseroni workshop. A number of stone-cutters were active there in addition to the court artists.

Prague 1993.

Prague 1993, cat. no. V.3-27.

O.D.

V.407
Prague Cutter of Precious Stones
Candlestick
Agate, cut and polished, brass
1600-50
Nostic collection, Prague; 1945 Uměleckoprůmyslové muzeum in Prague
Prague, Umeleckoprumyslove muzeum, inv. no. 77 995

This pair of cut table candlesticks belonged to the inventory of noble and burgher family interiors from the end of the sixteenth century to the end of the seventeenth century. Based on the shape, choice of stone and type of setting, it is of

Czech origin. It is analogous in Prague collections, for example, to candlesticks made from Jestedsky jasper (cf. UPM inv. no. 4 704 from the Neuberg collection; UPM inv. no. 13 061 from the Ritter collection).

Prague 1938, no. 172c, d; Ingelheim 1988, no. 160.

D.S.

V.408
Martin Dumling
Pineapple Goblet
Silver, cast, beaten, gilt
H: 22 cm
Ca. 1590
1945 confiscated property, Lisno chateau; in the collection of Cenek Danko von Esse; State Heritage Board; 1963 transferred to the Uměleckoprůmyslové muzeum, Prague
Prague, Uměleckoprůmyslové muzeum, inv. no. 82 905

This pineapple goblet is a typical piece by a Nürnberg goldsmith to be imported into

Bohemia (as are cups in the shape of a cockerel). In common with the Augsburg, Kraków and Vratislav workshops, they evidently provided for the majority of requirements. Domestic production had not yet been established.

Prague 1995, cat. no. 30.

D.S.

V.409
Jerg Marquart
Born Augsburg-died 1622
Pineapple Goblet
Beaten silver, trimmed, gilt
28 cm
Hallmark Augsburg, maker's emblem (Seling 1980, no. 996), re-hallmarked 1806 Graz (R 7806)
Early seventeenth century
In the collection of a country house in Bohemia; 1951 State Heritage Board (SPS); 1962 Uměleckoprůmyslové muzeum in Prague
Prague, Uměleckoprůmyslové muzeum, inv. no. 83 742

A typical import of table silver for a Czech nobleman's residence from the foremost central European centre of production.

Prague 1994, cat. no. 109.

D.S.

V.410
Czech Master Identified as IZ
Cup for Matej Kolowratek (Kolowrat)
Silver, cast, beaten, engraved, gilded in parts
H: 14.5 cm; average upper W: 7.5 cm
Engraved inscription: MATEG KOLOWRATEK MEZRICKY LETHA 1642; the monogram IZ is cut into the edge of the cupola
1642
Prague, the Lann collection; 1909 the Uměleckoprůmyslové muzeum bought it at auction
Prague, Uměleckoprůmyslové muzeum, inv. no. 11 927

Insofar as the buyer was of noble birth, this brings into consideration the last male descendant of the Moravian noble family of Meziricsky of Mezirice. He was the son of Tas (died 1603), but neither the name nor the date of his death is known. In the genealogy of the Kolowrat family for the period given there is no mention of a Matej (OSN XVII, p. 240). It is more probable that the cup belonged to a burgher with the surname Kolowratek, evidence for which comes from the absence of a family emblem on the cup.

Prague 1996, cat. no. 410; New York 1996.

Berlin auction, 1911, cat. no. 474, tab 37.

D.S.

V.411
Prague Goldsmith
Goblet with Coconut
Cut coconut shell, polished; copper mounting, cast, chased, beaten
H: 22.5 cm; average W: 9.5 cm
1575–1600
1892 bequeathed from the collection of Jan of Neuberg, until 1898; Prague, Uměleckoprůmyslové muzeum, inv. no. 4 690/182

Goblets with a dome made of coconut shell were not merely to be found in the inventory of a nobleman's collection. By 1587 the Prague burgher Pavel Sturm of

Firstenfeld had bequeathed his 'cup made of Indian nut [coconut] and the rim of another cup is also gilded' (AhMP, manuscript 2205, fol. 75v; cit. Teige II 1915, p. 169). The shape of the stem and the decoration, especially the ornamentation, most closely resemble the guild goblet of the Prague Lesser Town goldsmiths in the Národní muzeum.

Prague 1994, cat. no. 110; Prague 1995, cat. no. 318.

D.S.

V.412
Central European Goldsmith and Engraver
Nautilus with Engraved Battle Scenes
Cut and polished shell, engraved, blackened furrows
25 × 16 × 9.5 cm
First half of seventeenth century
Central Europe
1896 from the chateau at Nova Bystrice near Jindřichův Hradec
Prague, Uměleckoprůmyslové muzeum, inv. no. 7 095

Scenes of various genres (marine, rustic, animals and flowers) engraved on the nau-

tilus shell tend to be inspired by Netherlandish and German graphic models. The battle scene depicting the Thirty Years' War attests to the Central European origin of the piece, as does the coat of arms with the spread-eagle. Nautilus shells are recorded in the inventories of Prague burghers as early as the last quarter of the sixteenth century; for example, Pavel Sturm in 1587 bequeathed a 'sea-snail of pearl' (AhMP, manuscript 2205, fol. 75v; cit. Teige II, 1915, p. 169).

D.S.

V.413
Candlesticks of Amber with Silver Sheathing
Amber, silver gild
H: 31 cm
Ca. 1600
Tradition has it that it was found in a back recess during the demolition of house no. 1107 and 1109 in Prague's New Town. It comes from the collection of Dr J. Plaček in Kutná Hora.
Prague, Muzeum hlavního města Prahy, inv. no. 26.368, 26.367

The candlesticks are undoubtedly evidence of the high cultural level of Prague

burghers at the close of the sixteenth century. In the disturbances that befell the first half of the seventeenth century, the value of the candlesticks rose, which made the owner brick them up. Their preparation corresponds to analogous metal products of this period.

Schallaburg 1989, no. 1, 6.

J.D.

V.414
Goblet of Rhinoceros Horn
Carving: late Ming period (1368–1644), China
Setting: first half of seventeenth century,
Carved horn, silver filigree
H: 14 cm; average size of stem 9.5 cm; cupola 19.2 × 11.5 cm
Until 1945 Nostic Palace, Prague
Prague, Uměleckoprůmyslové muzeum, inv. no. 77 997

The cupola is shaped like a magnolia, on the outer side of which, in a semi-sculpted relief, an ornamental flowering magnolia (a symbol of joy) contrasts with a type of

fungus of Asian origin (from which a curative tea is brewed), here a symbol of immortality. On the inner side, an uncovered screw projects from the bottom and would originally have been concealed by a bezoar globule. A silver filigree setting was possible both in southern Europe and in Bohemia, where preserved examples can be dated within the first and second decades of the sixteenth century (cf. the clasp from the tomb in Polna and caskets from the Loretto church in Prague). There was a robust trade importing such goblets from China and India into Europe in the second half of the sixteenth century and up to the seventeenth century, since the horn was

respected as a magical symbol of masculinity. Insofar as this goblet came into being before 1612, it could be related, for example, to records in the inventory of Rudolf's *Kunstkammer* (Bauer–Haupt, 1976, no. 9, no. 11).

Prague 1993a, cat. no. V.3-21; Prague 1995, cat. no. 278.

D.S.

V.415
Central European Turner
Goblet
Turned horn, carved and adhered
H: 27 cm
End of sixteenth century–first half of seventeenth century
Linz, in the collection of L. Blumauer; 1886 bought for the Uměleckoprůmyslové muzeum in Prague
Prague, UPM, inv. no. 1 488

Prague 1995, cat. no. 259.

D.S.

V.416
Czech Turner
Small Goblet
Turned horn, carved, adhered
H: 10.9 cm; average dome max. 11.5 cm
Beginning of seventeenth century
Until 1945 in the Nostic collection,
Prague; 1946 UPM
Prague, Uměleckoprůmyslové muzeum,
inv. no. 78 023

The profile of the goblet allows it to be
dated among the oldest objects in the
Nostic collection. This piece is not recorded in the first inventory.

D.S.

V.417
Central European Wood-carver
Goblet
Ivory turned on a lathe
H: 17 cm; average W: 6 cm
Ca. 1600
Until 1886 in the collection of L.
Blumauer, Linz
Prague, Uměleckoprůmyslové muzeum,
inv. no. 1 462

Prague 1995, cat. no. 218.

D.S.

V.418
Central European Wood-carver
Goblet
Ivory turned on a lathe
H: 17.5 cm; average W: 6 cm
Ca. 1600
Until 1886 in the collection of L.
Blumauer, Linz
Prague, Uměleckolprůmyslové muzeum,
inv. no. 1 463

Prague 1995, cat. no. 219.

D.S.

V.419
Central European Master
Goblet with Lid
Ivory turned on a lathe, cut, adhered
H: 22 cm; average upper W: 8.5 cm
1600–50
1886 M. Blum, Vienna
Prague, Uměleckoprůmyslové Muzeum,
inv. no. 589

Prague 1995, cat. no. 217.

D.S.

V.420
Central European Turner
'Counterfeit' Ball with the Afflicted Christ
and the Virgin Mary in Lockets
Turned ivory, bored, adhered; gouache on
paper underlaid with silk rep
H: 27.2 cm; average max. W: 7.2 cm
Beginning of seventeenth century
Until 1886 in the collection of L.
Blumauer, Linz
Prague, Uměleckoprůmyslové muzeum,
inv. no 1459

This detailed and not wholly preserved
ball is not signed. Analogous examples
come from both the Nürnberg workshop
of Zickova (Kunsthistorisches Museum
Viden) and from Marek Heiden in Coburg
(Kat. Dresden 1995, cat. no. 52). A Czech
origin cannot be excluded in view of the
painting on the lockets.

D.S.

V.421
Rudolfine Master after Crispin de Passe II
(1593–1670)
Construction of a Colossus of Rhodes
Carved ivory
18 × 11.5 cm
COLOSSVS SOLIS
1600–1650
1896 purchased from the Ehrlich business in Prague
Prague, Uměleckoprůmyslové muzeum,
inv. no. 6 908

This tablet belongs to a series of the *Seven Wonders of the World*. The model was apparently by Maarten de Vos (1532–1603),
transferred to copper engravings by members of the de Passe family, who were mostly active in Cologne and Amsterdam. The engraving is signed by Crispijn de Passe II (cf. Hollstein, XLV, 168, no. 1308). His father, Crispijn de Passe I, and his uncle Simon de Passe carved others. Unlike the print, the tablet has been cut by two groups (sculptors and chisellers alter the head). The carver has changed the face of the sun god to that of a boy and left out the nimbus. The tablet probably served as one of the panels for a wooden cabinet or the casing of a small chest. A tablet of the *Tower of Babylon* (cat. no. v.422) belongs to the same series.

D.S.

V.422
Unknown Engraver
Tablet with the *Tower of Babylon*
Engraved ivory
9 × 14.6 cm
BABYL.MVRI
1600–50
Purchased from the F. Benda collection at Valašske Měříčí.
Prague, Uměleckoprůmyslové muzeum,
inv. no. 14 904.

See cat. no. v.421.

D.S.

V.423
Nicolaas Daems
Active from 1611; died 1633
Adoration of the Magi
Alabaster, touches of gilt
H: 13.5 cm; W: 17 cm
NHD
Before 1633
Until 1952 in the collection of Vojtěch Mastny, doctor of law; 1952 bequeathed to the Uměleckoprůmyslové muzeum, Prague
Prague, UPM, inv. no. 32 256

Analogous to the *Nativity* from Antwerp (Kat. Trier 1967, cat. no. 15), but a compo-
sitional variation of less refined accomplishment. Jan Rudolf Spork in around 1740 recorded another variation in terms of the format for the height and the original frame (PNP, MS commemorative volume of drawings, vol. 5, document no. 14). Two small tablets with a different subject bear the signature *ND* (Kat. Trier, cat. nos 32 and 62). The Prague exemplar has preserved the highest-quality carvings from the work of Daems and about a quarter of the larger format, albeit incomplete – the upper edge with parts of the stable roof has broken away. This is a case of the only example of a typical artefact to have emerged from the *Kunstkammer* between
the sixteenth century and the first half of the seventeenth. It was imported from the northern Netherlands, from the one creative centre in Mechelen (cf. a relief in the Buquoy collection, today held at the state-owned castle of Rozmberk). See also Theuerkauff, 1995.

Prague 1995, cat. no. 128.

D.S.

V.424
Hans Jamnitzer
1539–1603
Nürnberg
King Minos and Princess Scylla
Cast lead
Average diam: 17.2 cm
HG 1569
1569
1892, ex. coll. Neuberg, Prague
Prague, Uměleckoprůmyslové muzeum,
inv. no. 4 512

One of Ovid's tales from the *Metamorphoses* begins with the arrival of King Minos of Crete and his army at Megaris and
his meeting with Scylla, the daughter of King Niss (chap. VIII, 6–151), as portrayed in a copy by Virgil Solis. Scylla waits on the ramparts. She has cut off a miraculous lock of hair from her father's head and gives it with love to Minos so that he may enter the town without fear. Minos conquers the town, but Scylla treacherously abandons him. As a result of her father's curse, Scylla is changed into a seabird and must continually flee from her father, who has been transformed into an eagle. Authorship of the plate had earlier been ascribed to Paul van Vianen. The plate is missing in Jamnitzer's monograph (cat. Nürnberg 1985). Weber has assembled
eleven model lead casts, of which the Prague relief is the best-preserved. Copies apparently came into being on account of a silver tazza at the Kunsthistorisches Museum in Vienna.

Prague 1995, cat. no. 98.

Zprava Kuratoria 1893, p. 9; Braun 1918, pp. 19–21, no. 114; Weber 1975, p. 159, tab. cat. no. 271.

D.S.

V.425
Hans Jamnitzer
Born 1539–died Nürnberg 1603
Vulcan's Workshop
Lead, cast, chased
Average diam: 16.5 cm
HG
Ca. 1573
1894 C. Altmann, Frankfurt
Prague, Uměleckoprůmyslové muzeum,
inv. no. 5 458

The coming of Venus, according to Virgil's description (*Aeneas*, chap. VIII, pp. 416–53). A group of four metalworkers domi-
nates the scene. A certain Ant. Berka bought the oil painting by the Netherlandish painter Maarten van Heemskerck (1498–1574) between 1536 and 1571. From 1706 it was held at the Nostic Gallery in Prague. In 1546 Cornelis Bos transformed the content into a copper carving. The plates appeared ca. 1570: bronze (BNM, Munich, GNM, Nürnberg, Amberbach's cabinet, Basel) and a strip of silver at the bottom of a tazza.

D.S.

V.426
A Czech Mould Founder
Plaque of the Holy Trinity
Bronze cast, chased, frame of wood, black paint, velvet
31.5 × 25 cm; frame: 46.3 × 38.5 cm
1580–1611
Until 1945 held by Ant. Widmann-Sednitzský, château Luka nad Jihlavou, 1946 Uměleckoprůmsylové muzeum Prague, Uměleckoprůmsylové muzeum, inv. no. 82 990 (Z-CLIX/91)

The basis of the Holy Trinity as the Throne of Divine Wisdom was determined by the woodcarver Albrecht Dürer (1511) and from him were taken the medallions of Hans Reinhardt. Three variations of the more complicated scene after the model by Martin de Vos in copper were carved by Adriaen Collaert and Johann Sadeler I (1550–1600) at Antwerp around 1585–90 (Hollstein, XLV, no.679, 681/1. 482/II). Christ, as based on Luther's interpretation of Paul's Epistle to the Hebrews (9:5), is not crucified but dead and suffering, therefore angels accompany him with Arma Christi. This is a frequent subject of epitaphs and altar pieces. In view of the Utraquist owners' orientation, it may have been an altarpiece. Sources indicate that it was part of funereal decorations, for example, for a shield on a catafalque, as was fashionable during the Baroque. The frame bears coats-of-arms of the last descendant of the Rožmberk family, Petr Vok (1539–611) and his wife Kateřina of Ludanic (died 1601).

D.S.

V.427
? Czech Goldsmith
A Penitent Mary Magdalene
Beaten silver
12.8 × 10 cm; frame 26 × 24 cm
Unmarked; in the book is an engraving: *Ave Maria gratia plena dominus tecum, benedicta inter.mulieribus, benedictus fructus fuit Jesus Cristus*
1600–25
Nostic collection, Prague; 1945 to the Uměleckoprůmyslové muzeum (UPM), Prague, UPM, inv. no. 78 443

Mary Magdalene is praying in the wilderness with the attributes of a pilgrim (crucifix, skull, rosary, book and scourge) and tending to Christ's body (with a vessel containing ointment). This represents a modified composition taken from a copper plate in the Bayersiches Nationalmuseum, Munich. It was hypothetically regarded as a Spanish work of the seventeenth century (Weber 1975, cat. no. 1044). The silver relief has been executed to a higher standard, distinguishing between the design of the cloak, the details of the landscape, the ruins and, especially, the modelling of the face (which is a typical product of the Prague van Vianen circle and also south German plates; cf. also a bronze relief of the same subject in the Victoria and Albert Museum, London). Analogous compositions are known from the engravings of Lukas Kilian and Jacopo de Gheyn from 1617. The torso cannot be definitively identified in the Nostic inventories. It probably formed the centre of a votive tablet or a household altarpiece, often as the counterpart to the contrition of St Jerome.

D.S.

V.428
Nude Reclining Woman
Statuette made of (linden?) wood, unfinished surface, on a lathe-turned pedestal of brown-stained beech wood
14.5 × 19.7 × 9 cm; diam of pedestal 5.2 cm
Late sixteenth century
State-confiscated German property from the castle in Jindřichovice in 1945
Prague, Národní muzeum, inv. no. H2-32 128

The statuette came into the museum's collections along with other luxury objects from various European countries, so that the localization of its origin in Central Europe or in Prague itself is not certain. P. Preiss's hypothesis that it was perhaps a rococo model for a porcelain figure can, however, be refuted with certainty. It seems more likely that it could have been a model for goldsmithing work (note a certain similarity with the allegory of the Earth on Cellini's famous salt cellar from 1540–43). Many of the work's traits indicate that it was an individual Mannerist wood-carving intended for display in a cabinet collection. Its placement in this time period is supported by the deliberate composition of the slender, erotically attractive female nude, her refined, elongated limbs and lovely head with a typical period hairstyle. Nor is its dating to the late sixteenth century contradicted by the somewhat neutral form of the veil around the figure's sides. The technical details further support this argument: the nipples are made of a different, harder wood as was customary until the mid-Mannerist period. The turned pedestal, although it is probably not original, bears numerous formal similarities to small sculptural works from the Master HG.

L.Sr.

V.429
Case with Scissors
Ivory, steel, gold, Bohemian garnets, carving, engraving, gold-plating, embossing
L: 8 cm
Ca. 1600
Prague, Loretto treasury; after the Capuchin monastery was dissolved at the beginning of the 1950s the exhibit was administered by the Prague Information Service, between 1962 and 1990 the City of Prague Museum; it is included only in later inventories (1850, 1914, 1925 and 1956)
Order of the Capuchins, Loretto treasury, inv. no. P 210

Gold-plated steel scissors decorated with an etched-on arabesque, in a two-part ivory case with appliqué gold-leaf montage and large rhomboids of Bohemian garnet, and with eyelets at the sides for attachment to the waist.

Prague 1984, no. 6.

Poche–Hejdova 1956; Vokacova 1984.

V.Vo.

V.430
Hans Steinmeissel
Turret Table Clock
Brass and engraved copper, gilded
Height: 24.5 cm
Signature engraved on the upper part of the clock by the bell: *HANS STEIN MEISSEL VRMACHER ZV PRAGH DOMINI 1549 IAR*, and the master's initials *HS 1549*
From the Minutoli collection, acquired at the Felix auction in 1886
Prague, Uměleckoprůmyslové muzeum, inv. no. I 295

Concentric dial on the face; the outer dial round the rim reads 1-24, with tiny metal studs for reading the time at night; the middle dial reads 2 × 1-12. A ball is set above the dial showing the phases of the moon. The hand is made of iron. The other sides of the clock feature carved figures of elegant knights in arcades. The striking mechanism is iron with wooden perpetual screws and a spring-driven escapement. This clock is the oldest example of a Central European turret table clock representing a definitive type crafted in gilded brass and copper, similar to the French quadratic clocks. Hans Steinmeissel was an apprentice in the workshop of Jakub Čech (Czech, Zech) in Platnéřská street no.121 in the Prague Old Town which he took over after the latter's death in 1540. He became a burgher of the Old Town in 1547 and married Jakub Čech's daughter in 1548. From 1551 he was the custodian of the astronomical clock in the Old Town Hall.

Prague 1975, cat. no. 20; Prague 1977, cat. no. 2.

Urešová 1986, pp. 95 and 98, figs 23 and 52; Poche-Urešová 1987, pp. 31 and 161, fig. 4; Poche 1989, p. 138, fig. 94.

L.U.

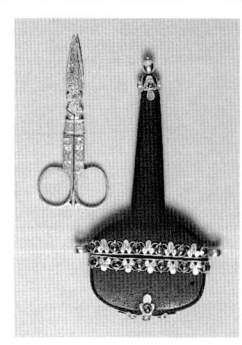

V.431
Master GIG
Box-shaped Table Clock
Chased, carved and engraved in brass;
gilded
Height: 8 cm
The clock bears a shield with the master's
inscription GIG
After 1560
From the collection of Dr L. Plick, pur-
chased via Mrs Brunnerová, Prague 1902
Prague, Uměleckoprůmyslové muzeum,
inv. no. 8 419

Double dial I-XII and 13-24 on the upper
part of the clock. The hand is made of iron

in the shape of a sceptre. The mechanical
part is made of iron with a spring-driven
escapement and balance wheel set beneath a bridge carved into a leaf design,
features striking mechanism. The sides of
the clock feature six-pointed stars carved
into the main body of the clock, designed
to make the striking more audible. This
type of travel clock with its dial on the upper section belongs to a large group of
box-shaped clocks produced throughout
the sixteenth and seventeenth centuries.

Prague 1977, cat. no. 9.

L.U.

V.432
Anonymous
Turret Table Clock with Astronomical
Calendar
Beaten, engraved and gilded brass and
copper, silver, enamel
Height: 52 cm
Last quarter of the sixteenth century
Donated by Richard Pfefferkorn from
New York in 1948
Prague, Uměleckoprůmyslové muzeum,
inv. no. 30 458

The face features a clock dial with two sets
of numerals I-XII, surrounded by a calendar with the names of saints. Further as-

tronomical and planetary numerals and
regulators cover the other sides of the
clock which is crowned with a three-
storeyed arbour and a double gong. The
mechanical part is made of iron with a
spring-driven escapement and striking
mechanism. The ring-shaped oscillator
was later replaced with a pendulum. Turret table clocks of this type were important for the development of clock-making
for their complex mechanism which not
only gave the hour but also provided calendar and astronomical information.

Prague 1977, cat. no. 6.

Bertele 1969, p. 84; Urešová 1986, p. 62, fig.
24; Poche-Urešová 1987, p. 32, fig. 6.

L.U.

V.433
Georg Wildt
Turret Table Clock
Brass and engraved copper, gilded
Height: 15.5 cm
Signature engraved on the upper section
of the clock around the bell: IEORG 1589
WILDT ZVO FRANCKFORT
1589
From the collection of Dr L Plick, pur-
chased via Mrs Brunnerová, Prague, 1902
Prague, Uměleckoprůmyslové muzeum,
inv. no. 8 412

A double concentric dial with an Italian
and Central European readings on the

face. The hand is made of iron. A further
dial is located on the opposite side for the
regulation of the striking mechanism. The
sides of the clock feature the figure of a
Classical man-at-arms and a woman with a
palm branch set in bossed arcades. Made
of iron with a spring-driven escapement,
striking mechanism. This type of table turret clock represents a craft in which the
technical perfection of the mechanism developed along with its external presentation during the last quarter of the sixteenth century. The corners of the tower
are decorated with half-columns or pilasters; a further dial is located on the back
of the prism.

Prague 1966/67, cat. no. 251; Prague 1977,
cat. no. 4.

Baillie 1969, p. 342; Urešová 1986, p. 92.

L.U.

V.434
Andreas Plenninger
Born Regensburg
Horizontal Table Sundial
Solnhofen limestone (lithographic stone),
etched, polychrome, partially gilded
36.5 × 25.5 cm
Signature in the left inner ring of the lu-
nar clock: ANDREAS PLENINGER OR-
GANIST; in the bottom right corner of
the plate: the monogram LS
End of the sixteenth century
From the collection of Vojtěch Lanna,
purchased at the Lepke auction in Berlin
1909
Prague, Uměleckoprůmyslové muzeum,

inv. no. 11 481

The centre of the dial 5-12-7 features a
polychrome scene of Jason fighting a
dragon. On either side are the Latin names
of the months accompanied by the symbols of the signs of the zodiac and the
number of days. The clock also features 2 ×
6 holes for moving a peg which indicated
the month. A lunar clock is located in the
centre of the face to the left; to the right is
a calendarium with the inscription Im
Schalt Jahr hat der Februarius 29 Tag, and
the names of the days. The times of sunrise and sunset are indicated on a vertical
band located between the circles. The low-

er field of the clock face features two dials:
6-12-6 and 9-23 in Czech, and 6-12-6 and 1-
15 in Italian. Andreas Pleninger crafted
sundials, perpetual calendars and maps;
his known works date from 1590 to 1605;
some bear the monogram AP.

Prague 1966/67, cat. no. 253.

Rhode 1923, pp. 23-24; Zinner 1967; pp. 85,
470-71, 492; Lenfeld 1984, pp. 43-48;
Urešová 1986, p. 33, fig.6.

L.U.

V.435
Thomas Fridl
Figural Table Clock
Engraved and gilded bronze and copper,
partially enamelled
Height: 30 cm
Signature on the striking wheel mecha-
nism: THOMAS FRIDL
Ca. 1620
Purchased in a jewellery and antiques
shop in Prague 1952
Prague, Uměleckoprůmyslové muzeum,
inv. no. 32 823

A revolving sphere with a ring dial 1-12 is
set in the crown of a stylized tree; a negro

in Classical armour points to the time
with his lance. Beside him is a moving
jumping dog. The clock has a spring-driv-
en escapement and striking mechanism.
The internal movement of the instrument
transferred the illusion of movement and
life to its external decoration, thus inspiring a great number of clock-makers to introduce sculptural figural expression into
the design of their works, a phenomenon
which was marked because of the large
number of south German goldsmiths
working at the end of the sixteenth century and throughout the seventeenth.

Prague 1977, cat. no. 17.

Maurice 1968, fig. 57; Urešová 1986, p. 108,
fig. 61; Poche-Urešová 1987, p. 162, fig. 7.

L.U.

V.436
Melchior Zinng
Pendant Watch
Engraved and carved in brass and silver
Height: 6.5
Carved signature on the back plate of the
instrument: *Zinng Augspurk*
Ca. 1580
From the Thun-Hohenstein collection in
Karlovy Vary 1949
Prague, Uměleckoprůmyslové muzeum,
inv. no. 83 119

The case opens on both sides, the whole
area of which is carved with scenes of the
Calvary and the Resurrection of SS Peter

and James. The dial on the front shows I-
XII with carved depictions of Adam and
Eve and the expulsion from the Garden of
Eden. The original hand has survived and
the mechanism itself is made of brass with
a perpetual screw, spring-driven escapement and balance wheel. Workshops in
Paris, Strasbourg, Lyon and Augsburg became famous for their production of this
type of watch, to be worn as a pendant in
the style of a cross.

Prague 1966/67, cat. no. 204.

Baillie 1969, p. 353; Urešová 1986, p. 170,
fig. 122; Poche-Urešová 1987, p. 170, fig. 58

L.U.

V.437
Pendant Watch
Silver, enamel, gilded brass
Diam: 7 cm
Symbol struck on the back: two little
shields, in the first a galloping horse, in
the second, the initials *GK*, set in between
three little stars
End of the sixteenth century
Found near the village of Slíčany in the
Kromžříč region, 1840. Transferred from
the Moravian Regional Museum in 1929.
Brno, Moravian Gallery , Museum of Dec-
orative Arts, inv. no. 24 201

The carved case with its lid contains a

watch mechanism with a silver dial and
dark blue enamel digits I-XII and 13-24.
The rim features 12 metal studs around
the rim for reading the time in the dark.
The mechanical part of the watch is made
of brass with a spring-driven escapement.
The centre of the dial and the hand are
missing. The primary box-shaped 'tambour' pendant watch became more spherical around the year 1580 and assumed a
shape known as the 'cushion' (*Wulstform*).

Brno 1975/76, cat. no. 118.

Baillie 1969, p. 355.

L.U.

V.438
Pendant Watch
Chased and engraved silver, cut crystal,
enamel
Height: 7.5 cm
Ca. 1600
From the Thun Hohenstein collection in
Karlovy Vary 1949
Prague, Uměleckoprůmyslové muzeum,
inv. no. 83 118

Oval case with crystal lids, engraved with
the Crucifix and tendril ornamentation.
The centre of the dial shows an image of
the Resurrection, with original brass
hands. The brass mechanism features a

perpetual screw, spring-driven escapement and balance wheel. The bridges inside the watch are carved with floral motifs. The watch's mechanism was mounted
into crystal cases or was given crystal lids
around the year 1560. Cases like this were
made in Switzerland, Germany, England
and Bohemia, which became famous for
its crystal reserves in the region of Turnov.

Prague 1966/67, cat. no. 205; Prague 1975,
cat. no. 35.

Urešová 1986, p. 172, fig. 124; Poche-
Urešová 1987, p. 170, fig. 60.

L.U.

V.439
Pendant Watch
Horn, bone, silver and gilded brass
Height: 9.5 cm
First quarter of the seventeenth century
Transferred from Uměleckoprůmyslové
muzeum in Prague in 1963.
Brno, Moravian Gallery, Museum of Dec-
orative Arts, inv. no. 17 843

Octagonal case with two lids with hunting
scenes carved in bone, the whole set in a
frame made of dark grey horn. Engraved
floral motifs and birds surround the silver
dial with its Roman numerals and one
iron hand. The back of the watch features

floral ornamentation in a similar design to
the carved motifs on the sides of the case.
The mechanism of made of brass with a
spring-driven escapement, including later
modifications. A rare example of a clock
casing carved from horn and bone.

Brno 1975/76, cat. no. 126.

L.U.

V.440
Watch Set in a Ring
Gold, enamel
Diam: 2.2 cm
First half of the seventeenth century
Transferred from a Postal Savings Bank in
1949
Prague, Uměleckoprůmyslové muzeum,
inv. no. 83 021

The ring's fan-shaped enamel sides enclose an oval engraved casket containing a
brass mechanism with a lid, a spring-driv-
en escapement and balance wheel. The
hand is missing. Technical progress in
watchmaking during the latter half of the

sixteenth century influenced the design of
the mechanisms which decreased in size,
thus also altering the external appearance
of these watches. Miniature gold and
enamel watches set into rings were already
appearing in Lyon in 1562. In Augsburg
these watches were being produced from
1585.

Urešová 1986, p. 173, fig. 125; Poche-
Urešová 1987, pp.170–71, fig. 64.

L.U.

V.441
Hans Butz
Pendant Watch
Engraved and gilded brass, inset with silver
Height: 4.5 cm
Signature engraved on the back of the lower lid: *Hans Butz*
Ca. 1630
From the collection of J.R.Neuberg, a legacy from 1892
Prague, Uměleckoprůmyslové muzeum, inv. no. 4 578

A brass mechanism, with a perpetual screw, spring-driven escapement and balance wheel, is suspended in a shell-shaped case with a lid. Decorative silver fauna and floral motifs surround the dial I-XII. The centre of the watch contains a relief engraving of a coastal scene. The original brass hand is present.

Baillie 1969, p. 48; Urešová, p. 174, fig. 127.

L.U.

V.442
Melchior Hager
Died Frankfurt 1657
Pendant Watch
Gilded bronze, crystal
Height: 5.3 cm
Engraved signature on the back: *Melchior Hager in Frfurt*
Ca. 1640
From the Thun-Hohenstein collection in Karlovy Vary 1949
Prague, Uměleckoprůmyslové muzeum, inv. no. 11 926

This watch features a cut crystal case with lid set in an octagonal bronze frame decorated with floral engravings. The case contains a brass mechanism with its perpetual screw, a spring-driven escapement and steel balance wheel. The bridges are gently carved in the shape of tendrils. A steel dial I-XII is set onto the oval plate featuring an engraved landscape scene with a mill in the centre. The hands are made of iron. Melchior Hager lived and worked in Frankfurt from 1632. He arrived as a Protestant from Steyer an der Enns via Regensburg and Augsburg.

Poche-Urešová 1987, p. 170, fig. 59.

L.U.

V.443
Spoon
Silver; beaten, engraved
16.6 cm
Crest and monogram *GP*
Second half of sixteenth century
Bought in 1903 in an auction held by Karl Thewalt, Cologne
Prague, Uměleckoprůmyslové muzeum, inv. no. 8 692

A short spoon of an earlier type, which was held in the fist. A crest and the monogram *GP* are engraved on the underside of the bowl. Thewalt's auction catalogue number 1388 cites another spoon with the same crest as made in Nürnberg. The Uměleckoprůmyslové muzeum in Prague has a similar spoon (inv. no. 67 664), which is stamped (Rosenberg IV 8707 gives under the same indefinite stamp a spoon from the Historical Museum in Stockholm, inv. no. 2 703 in 1906).

Prague 1966, no. 219; Prague 1981, no. 10.

Urešová 1966; Vokacová 1981.

V.Vo.

V.444
Mikulas Smolik (?)
Active Prague, Old Town, 1567–1590
Wedding Spoon
Beaten silver, engraved and gilded
16 cm
Hallmark: *Stare Mesto prazske* (Old Town, Prague); maker's hallmark *MS*; engraved associated coats of arms with the initials *IWZ* and *EWZ*
1570–80
The Wiederspergers; 1825–92 in the collection of Jan Neuberg of Neuberg
Prague, Uměleckoprůmyslové muzeum, inv. no. 4 626

The two associated coats of arms with the initials *IWZ* and *EWZ* belonged to Jan Wiedersperger of Wiedersperger and na Mutenine (died 1590) and his wife Eliska (née Cerninova of Chudenic). The spoon entered the Neuberg Collection with the marriage of Zofie Wiederspergova and Jan Norbert Neuberg around the year 1825, and the Neuberg Collection was later bequeathed to the Umeleckoprumyslove Muzeum, Prague. According to the goldsmith's hallmark, *MS*, the piece can be ascribed to Mikulas Smolik, made between 1567 and 1590. A 'waistband with chain and lions' heads' was also among the works by Smolik (AhMP, rkp. 1049, fol. 99, excerpted by V. Vojtisek). In 1583 Smolik sold a 'spoon of fake silver' to the prior of St Agnes's, for which he was fined (Winter 1909, p. 411). Identification of the Master MS with the poor goldsmith Matyas Strniste is improbable; he is placed from 1580 to 1581 in the parish of St Nicholas in the Old Town.

Prague 1981, cat. no. 21; Prague 1994, cat. no. 106; Prague 1995, cat. no. 26.

Teige, II, 1902, pp. 15, 16, 621, 626, 834; Winter 1909, pp. 411, 444.

D.S.

V.445
Spoon
Silver, partially gold-plated; cast engraved
17 cm
Monogram *CSD* and date *1596* in wreath with crest, monogram *AK*
1596
Bought in 1903 at an auction held by Karl Thewalt, Cologne
Prague, Uměleckoprůmyslové muzeum, inv. no. 8 693

A spoon with a shell-shaped bowl with the monogram *CSD* and the year *1596* engraved in a wreath with a crest showing a bent arm and a sabre. On the underside is the monogram *AK*. The handle is in the form of a profiled column with leaf decoration in relief, modelled on fairly old designs by Heinrich Aldegrever (viz. Benker, ill. 13).

Prague 1981, no. 16.

Vokacová 1981.

V.Vo.

V.446
Spoon
Silver, partially gold-plated; casting, beating, engraving
18 cm
Crest, initials *GS*
Late sixteenth century
Left by Jan Neuberg, knight, of Prague, in 1892
Prague, Uměleckoprůmyslové muzeum, inv. no. 4 627

A spoon with a woman's mascaron on the upper side of the prismoid handle and an oval medallion on the underside of the bowl, with an engraved crest and the initials *GS*. It is a free variation on another spoon (inv. no. 590) in the Uměleckoprůmyslové muzeum, Prague.

Prague 1981, no. 17.

Vokacová 1981.

V.Vo.

V.447
Apostle Spoon
Silver, partially gold-plated; casting, beating, engraving
20.2 cm
S: Jan, TRPIEL POD PONSKYM. PILATEM UKRZISOWAN. UMRSEL A POHRZBEN, crest, monogram *RH*; subsequent stamp: *Brno 1806* and the letter *K*
Late sixteenth century
Acquired in 1945 when transferred by the state from unknown property
Prague, Uměleckoprůmyslové muzeum, inv. no. 78 307

A spoon with a shell-shaped bowl and a slender prismoid handle with the engraved inscription *S: Jan, TRPIEL POD PONSKYM. PILATEM* (St John, He suffered under Pontius Pilate) and, on the underside, *UKRZISOWAN. UMRSEL A POHRZBEN* (was crucified, dead and buried). At the end of the handle is a figure of St John with a chalice, in a relief cartouche frame. On the upper side there is a moulded figure of Christ the Saviour. On the underside of the bowl there is an engraved crest with the monogram *RH* and a relief crest on a cartouche. In Poland this type of spoon was still being made in the eighteenth century.

Prague 1981, no. 14.

Vokacová 1981; Petneki 1977, pp. 127–40; Bobrow 1977, p. 10.

V.Vo.

V.448
Apostle Spoon
Silver, partially gold-plated; casting, engraving, beating
17.3 cm
Crest of Stehlik of Cenkov
Ca. 1600
Bought in 1912 from Frantisek Richter, Karlin, Prague
Prague, Uměleckoprůmyslové muzeum, inv. no. 12 461

This ornate spoon with a figure of St Andrew and the engraved crest of Stehlik of Cenkov is one of the apostle spoons which were made all over Europe. In Poland this type of spoon was still being made at the beginning of the eighteenth century. The crest engraved, as was usual, on the underside of the bowl belongs to Bartolomej Stehlik of Cenkov, who was ennobled in 1598.

Prague 1981, no. 19.

Vokacová 1981.

V.Vo.

V.449
Spoon
Silver; casting, beating, engraving
20.5 cm
D Sigmunt Stezicze/darowal ty lizicze and the monogram *SO*
Ca. 1600
Bought in 1886 from M. Blum, Vienna
Prague, Uměleckoprůmyslové muzeum, inv. no. 590

This spoon with a slender prismoid handle ending in a profiled head bears the inscription *D Sigmunt Stezicze/darowal ty lizicze* (D Sigmunt Stezicze gave these spoons) and the monogram *SO*. Inscriptions or short prayers are not uncommon on Renaissance spoons. The plural in the inscription indicates that there were several spoons. The high-quality craftsmanship shows the raised social standing of both donor and recipient. There were many such spoons in noble families; at the beginning of the seventeenth century Albrecht of Wallenstein had hundreds of them.

Prague 1981, no. 19.

Vokacová 1981.

V.Vo.

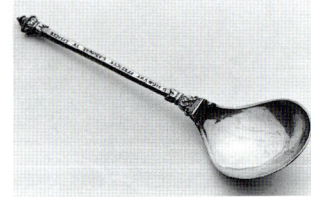

V.450
Spoon
Silver, partially gold-plated; casting, beating
18.7 cm
After 1600
Bought in 1928 from Gisela Lobkovicova's collection, Prague
Prague, Uměleckoprůmyslové muzeum, inv. no. 16 299

A spoon with a pear-shaped bowl and a carefully crafted handle with a winged mascaroon of a child (with bat's wings on the back). The handle ends in a woman's head (on the back a bearded mascaron). Acquired from the collection of Gisela Lobkovicova, it has a counterpart in the Uměleckoprůmyslové muzeum's collection (inv. no. 67 121) which was obtained in 1963 from Plana near Marianske Lazne in western Bohemia and is stamped *RC*, with a small branch.

Prague 1981, no. 20.

Vokacová 1981.

V.Vo.

V.451
Spoon
Silver; beating, cutting
18 cm
Early seventeenth century
Bought in 1928 from Gisela Lobkovico-
va's collection, Prague
Prague, Uměleckoprůmyslové muzeum,
inv. no. 16 304

This spoon, with a large oval bowl and a
slender, twisted handle pinched three
times at the end is a simple piece of cutlery
of the time. It comes from Gisela Lobkovicova's collection, which contained mostly
spoons from the sixteenth and seven-

teenth centuries, mainly from Bohemia.

Prague 1981, no. 22; Prague 1994, no. 104.

Vokacová 1981; Flegel 1994.

V.Vo.

V.452
Wedding Spoon
Silver, partially gold-plated; casting, engraving
19 cm
Monograms *IDD* and *VH*, 1616; unclear
stamp with letter *D*
1616
Bought in 1888 from Mr Hak, Petrovice
Prague, Uměleckoprůmyslové muzeum,
inv. no. 2 792

The straight handle with a profiled end
and a solid rib with an oval bowl is characteristic of late Renaissance spoons. That it
is a wedding spoon can be seen by the

monograms *IDD* and *VH* with the year,
1616.

Prague 1966, no. 219; Prague 1981, no. 25;
Prague 1994, no. 105.

Urešová 1966; Vokacová 1981; Flegel 1991.

V.Vo.

V.453
Czech (?) master
Cutlery Case
Leather, tanned, carved, inscribed, wire
20 cm; average w: 8.5–9 cm
1624
1982 bought by UPM in Prague
Prague, Uměleckoprůmyslové Muzeum,
inv. no. 93 456

This case for an eight-piece cutlery set is
appropriate for the contemporary urban
production. Judging from the two hearts
with which it is decorated, it may have
been meant as a wedding gift. Leather cases are not generally dated. Stylistic ambi-

guities in the decorative work of the first
half of the seventeenth century as regards
stamping in leather and silverware may er-
roneously indicate a datre of eighteenth or
even nineteenth century.

D.S.

V.454
Spoon
Silver; beating, casting, engraving
15 cm
AR VA 1625; subsequent stamp: *1806 Lvov*
1625
Bought in 1928 from Gisela Lobkovico-
va's collection, Prague
Prague, Uměleckoprůmyslové muzeum,
inv. no. 16 298

Spoons with a round bowl and a relatively
short handle started to be produced in the
sixteenth century. This one has a gently
bent handle ending in a scroll, which indicates that it was made in the seventeenth

century. It is decorated with the monogram of its owner, *AR VA*, and the date,
1625. At that time each person still owned
his own knife and spoon and carried them
around with him.

Prague 1981, no. 26.

Vokacová 1981.

V.Vo.

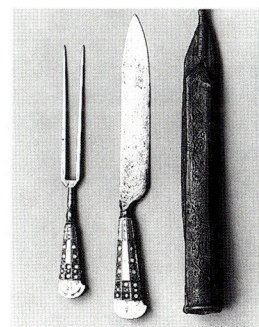

V.455
Knife and Fork with Case
Steel, brass, mother-of-pearl, horn; case
made of black leather with blind stamp-
ing; cutting, inlaying
Knife 22 cm; fork 18.5 cm; case 22.5 cm
Cutler's stamp
First half of seventeenth century
Area settled by Haban Anabaptists in
western (former) Hungary
Bought in 1988 in the Roesch-Zimmer-
mann auction
Prague, Uměleckoprůmyslové muzeum,
inv. no. 2 916

In addition to faience, cutlery-making was

one of the most notable crafts of the Haban Anabaptists. Mother-of-pearl, brass
and horn were the most frequently used
materials for inlay decoration of the handles, with a fine plant engraving sometimes being added. In European collections this work is wrongly said to be
German. However, the characteristic decoration and the use of materials allow it to
be safely distinguished from cutlery made
elsewhere. One of the main centres of Haban cutlery-making was Velke Levary (now
in eastern Slovakia).

Prague 1966, no. 221; Prague 1981, no. 59;
Prague 1982 exhibition of Haban faience

in the Belvedere; Nelazoheves 1988–89, no.
73; Prague 1994, no. 102.

Urešová 1966; Vokacová 1980, 1981; Vlk
1988.

V.Vo.

V.456
Knife, Fork and Spoon
Silver, Bohemian garnets, filigree, steel
Knife 17 cm; fork 15 cm; spoon 14 cm
Spoon has a Viennese stamp added later:
1806
First half of seventeenth century
Transferred by the State Monuments Office from the chateau at Bludov in 1963
Prague, Uměleckoprůmyslové muzeum,
inv. no. 67 360-361, 67 120 (spoon)

The two-pronged fork and the knife handle are steel, with the handles covered in silver filigree and Bohemian garnets. The spoon is all of silver and has a different fil-

igree decoration – the same as the cutlery from the Loretto (P 104, P 105). Silver filigree work from Bohemia can be seen on other objects, such as the jewel box from the Loretto (P 7).

Pforzheim 1968, no. 108; Prague 1981, nos 69 and 79; Prague 1984, no. 9.

Vokacová 1968, 1981, 1984.

V.Vo.

V.457
Knife and Fork
Filigree, silver, steel, Bohemian rhomboid-cut garnets
Knife 16 cm; fork 14 cm
First half of seventeenth century
Bohemia
Prague, Loretto treasury (shown in inventories from 1850, 1914 and 1925)
Prague, Order of the Capuchins, Loretto,
inv. no. P 104, P 105

The two-pronged fork and the blade of the knife are steel. The silver filigree handle with Bohemian garnets is the same as the handle of the spoon from the Umělecko-

průmyslové muzeum in Prague (inv. no. 67 120). The cutlery is part of a larger set numbering eighteen pieces.

Prague 1984, no. 8.

Poche–Hejdova 1956 (unpub.), p. 14; Vokacová 1984.

V.Vo.

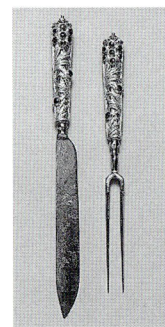

V.458
Knife and Fork
Steel, crystal, enamel, Bohemian garnets and turquoises; polishing, cutting
Knife 19.5 cm; fork 18 cm
Mid-seventeenth century
Bought in 1903 from Karl Thewalt in Cologne
Prague, Uměleckoprůmyslové muzeum,
inv. no. 8 694

The knife and fork have the same rolled, conical ribbed handles of polished crystal mounted in enamelled silver, decorated by rhomboid-cut Bohemian garnets and round turquoises. The decoration sug-

gests the cutlery comes from Bohemia.

Pforzheim 1968, no. 108; Prague 1981, no. 10; Prague 1984, no. 72; Ramat Gan 1994, no. 38.

Vokacová 1968, 1981, 1984; Stehlíková 1994.

V.Vo.

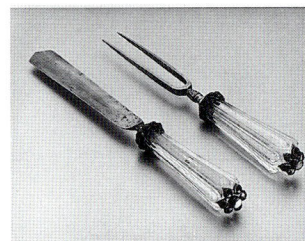

V.459
Knife and Fork in Case
Steel, silver, jasper; leather with blind stamping, gold stamping; polishing, cutting, mounting
Knife 21 cm; fork 20.5 cm; case 24 cm
Cutler's stamp
Mid-seventeenth century
Transferred by the State Monuments Office from the castle at Buchlovice in 1963
Prague, Uměleckoprůmyslové muzeum,
inv. nos 67 499, 67 500

A steel knife and two-pronged fork with conical handles of polished jasper, mounted in silver. The craftsmanship is probably

Bohemian, because from the Rudolfine period onwards the production of cutlery from crystal and coloured opaque precious stones is documented several times, including manufacture outside Prague such as that by Jan Jiří Rhabenhaupt in Česky Krumlov.

Prague 1981; Ingelheim 1988, no. 159.

Vokacova, 1981, 1988.

V.Vo.

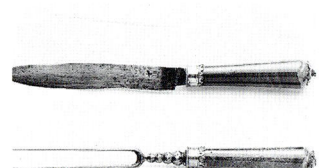

V.460
Fork
Steel, brass, jasper; cutting, polishing, mounting
18.2 cm
Mid-seventeenth century
Bought in 1895 from A. Morawitz, Prague
Prague, Uměleckoprůmyslové muzeum,
inv. no. 5 945

A close variant on inv. no. 67 500, bought in Prague. There is more than one example of cutlery from semi-precious stones still being made in Bohemia after the second half of the sixteenth century. In the Rožmberk accounts there is a record of a

payment in 1614 to the widow of the Rožmberk cutler J. J. Rhabenhaupt (see Mares, *Materialie*).

Prague 1981, no. 73.

Vokacová 1981.

V.Vo.

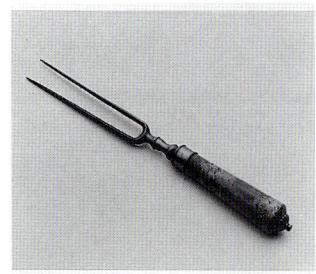

V.461
Toothpick
Ivory; carving
L: 13 cm
First half of seventeenth century
Bought from the Hruby collection from
Jeleni in 1977
Prague, Uměleckoprůmyslové muzeum,
inv. no. 85.914

It is rarely that this sort of hygienic cos-
metic implement – a toothpick combined
with a little spoon for cleaning out the
ears – is preserved. This exhibit is carved
from ivory. The handle is in the shape of
two entwined snakes, with a satyr sitting

on a goat. The relatively coarse work and
the origin in a Bohemian noble family suggest that the object is of Bohemian provenance.

Prague 1979, no. 100; Doudleby 1985–91.

Vokacová 1979.

V.Vo.

V.462
Pendant with St George
Gold; beating
3.7 cm
Mid-sixteenth century
Left by Jan Neuberg, knight, Prague, in
1892
Prague, Uměleckoprůmyslové muzeum,
inv. no. 4 593

An oval medallion with St George on
horseback, beaten in high relief in gold. It
looks like the work of Italian jewellers, not
only because of the appearance of the
horse – after Leonardo da Vinci – but because of the exceptional quality of the

craftsmanship. The simple, rope-like border makes an earlier date in the sixteenth
century more likely.

Prague 1966, no. 185.

Urešová 1966.

V.Vo.

V.463
Pendant Showing Daniel
Gold, pearl, mother-of-pearl, casting,
enamelling, mounting
Diam: 5.15 cm
Second half of sixteenth century
Bought from Frantisek Zapletal, Karlovy
Vary, in 1935
Prague, Národní muzeum, inv. no. H2-17
436

The Old Testament subject of the pendant, Daniel in the lion's den, was a
favourite Renaissance theme. The placing
of cast scenes on a shell background is
used in Dutch and South German jew-

ellery, as are misshapen pearls. The influences of both regions made themselves
felt in Rudolfine Prague, so it is not impossible that the jewellery was produced
there.

Johnova 1989, no. 460.

V.Vo.

V.464
Pendant
Silver, lens-shaped crystal; casting, polish-
ing
3.5 cm
Second half of sixteenth century
Bought in 1887 from the collection of
Daniel Penther, a painter in Vienna
Prague, Uměleckoprůmyslové muzeum,
inv. no. 2 478

Pendants like this, with a solid surround
decorated with female figures around a
lens-shaped crystal, feature in a number
of pictures by the Kleinmeisters, as well as
by René Boyvin and Mathias Zundt (q.v.

Hackenbroch 1979, pp. 134–35).

Prague 1966, no. 190.

Urešová 1966; Stará 1968, ill. 374.

V.Vo.

V.465
Pendant (Incomplete) in the Shape of a
Portal
Diamonds, pearls; casting, enamelling
H: 6.8 cm
After 1580
Bought in 1936 from Frantisek Zapletal,
Karlovy Vary
Prague, Národní muzeum, inv. no. H2-17
680

Pendants with an architectural theme, in
the shape of a portal with a niche which
usually contains a figure or a group of figures, are typical of South German jewellery. Most of them were modelled on a

design by Hans Collaert the younger. That
his graphic designs were used in Bohemia
is shown, for example, in wall painting
(the castle at Rožmberk). It can be assumed that he influenced Prague jewellers
at the end of the sixteenth and the beginning of the seventeenth century.

Johnova 1989, no. 458.

V.Vo.

v.466
Pendant with St George
Gold, mother-of-pearl, pearls, rubies, emeralds, diamond rhomboids and tablets; casting in the round, enamelling
H: 10.1 cm
End of sixteenth century
From 1893 onwards in the Town Museum in Chrudim, eastern Bohemia; previously owned alternately by the town and the Deanery Church of the Assumption of the Virgin Mary in Chrudim; allegedly found on the altar underneath a painting of St Saviour in the church; mentioned in the eighteenth century; copy made in 1968

Chrudim, Vlastivědné muzeum, inv. no. 23

St George in triumph, kneeling down and leaning on his lance with the dragon tied up by a chain. Excellent craftsmanship and materials. Exhibited at the Jubilee Exhibition in 1891, where it aroused the interest of theorists, who believed it to have been made in Bohemia, and collectors such as Baron Rothschild and Ferdinand d'Este, both of whom tried to buy it. Although the model for the pendant is not known, it is possible that the jeweller was inspired by the work of Hans Collaert.

Prague 1891; Prague 1892 (temporarily in the Uměleckoprůmyslové muzeum).

Chytil 1891, 1905; Labler 1897; Vokacová 1969; Burdychová 1992.

V.Vo.

v.467
Pendant with Hunter
Gold-plated silver, precious stones; casting, enamelling
H: 7.5 cm
End of sixteenth century
South Germany or Bohemia
Acquired from O. Gross's collection in Prague in 1960
Prague, Uměleckoprůmyslové muzeum, inv. no. 50 291

A pendant with a hunter, hare and dog. Hunting was a favourite subject in Renaissance art. Although such jewellery is usually of South German origin, it is not im-

possible that it was made in Bohemia. Similar subjects feature in the collection of the Victoria and Albert Museum in London (see Lanllier-Pini, p. 41) and in the Rothschild collection (Kunstwerke ... Rothschild, ill. 78).

Prague 1966, no. 189; Milan 1983–84, no. 6.

Urešová 1966; Rubesova 1983–84.

V.Vo.

v.468
Pendant Medallion
Gold, enamel, crystal; beating, polishing
H: 5 cm
Sixteenth century
France (?) or Spain (?)
Bought in 1888 from Rosenberg in Paris
Prague, Uměleckoprůmyslové muzeum, inv. no. 2 546

The pendant is incomplete. Its second crystal is missing, as are the contents of the locket, probably a biblical scene cast in the round (see Hackenbroch 1979, no. 884, and Somers Cocks 1980, ill. 26).

Prague 1966, no. 191.

Urešová 1966; Stará 1968, no. 373.

V.Vo.

v.469
Pendant with the *Head of Christ*
Painting on parchment, gold, polished crystal, blue and white enamel
H: 7.7 cm
Sixteenth or early seventeenth century
Prague (?), Spain (?)
Bought in 1935 from František Zapletal, Karlovy Vary
Prague, Národní muzeum, inv. no. H2-17 434

Miniature head of Christ in gold, with an enamelled medallion on the back, set in a double crystal frame with large facets. This makes it more likely to be of Spanish

provenance, as does its devotional nature (see Hackenbroch 1979, ill. 875 and 878).

Johnová 1989, no. 455.

V.Vo.

v.470
A Czech Goldsmith
Brooch with the Virgin Mary and Child
Gold, enamel, crystal, three cut rubies, glass, gouache on paper
H: 3.3 cm; W: 3 cm
Beginning of seventeenth century (latter part of nineteenth century)
Prague
Bought in 1961
Prague, Uměleckoprůmyslové Muzeum, inv. no. 49 924

The technical features of a painting on paper in place of enamel, as with sketched renditions, demonstrate the occasional

nature of an artist's work when he is not accustomed to producing decorative work as a goldsmith. The technical accomplishment of the enamelling and the artist's use of colour (blue and green droplets are surrogates for lapis lazuli and chrysoprase) attest to the piece having originated in a Prague goldsmith's workshop. Customers included both burghers and the nobility (cf. the garment ornaments from Polna).

Milan 1994, cat. no. 17; Ramat Gan 1995, cat. no. 20.

D.S.

V.471
Cameo of *Christ with Our Lady*
Jasper, carved, polished, gold mounting
Height: 4.5 cm
1600–50, frame early eighteenth century
Ca. 1870–94
Augsburg, Museum August Riedinger;
1894 purchased at auction: H. Helbing
Munich, cat. no. 978
Prague, Uměleckoprůmsylové muzeum,
inv. no. 5 859/1894

This cameo, which has a bust of the suffering Christ on the obverse side and with the Mother of God on the reverse, is taken from models by Ottavio Miseroni in a less

accomplished work from a Prague epigone of the Miseroni family.

Ingelheim 1989, cat. no. 158; Prague 1995, cat. no. 33.

D.S.

V.472
Czech Goldsmith
Pectoral Crucifix with Corpus
Silver cast, gilt, cut
H: 10 cm
INRI
1600–50
1950 unidentified Czech piece confiscated from the Church; 1970 transferred to the State Laboratory for Precious Metals
Prague, Uměleckoprůmyslové Muzeum,
inv. no. 74 599

A typical small piece of personal jewellery with domestic analogies in the first half of the seventeenth century (cf. the sepulchral

inventory of Empress Eleonor at Prague Castle and the tombs of the Zejdlic family in Polna).

D.S.

V.473
Czech Goldsmith
Pectoral or Breast Crucifix with Corpus
Silver, cast, gilt; sixteen diamond rhombs
H: 8.7 cm
Ca. 1630–50
1950 unidentified Czech piece confiscated from the Church; 1970 UPM, Prague; transferred to the State Laboratory for Precious Metals
Prague, Uměleckoprůmyslové Muzeum,
inv. no. 74 598

Pendant of unknown origin, which may have served as the insignia of a priest or as a personal secular piece of jewellery.

D.S.

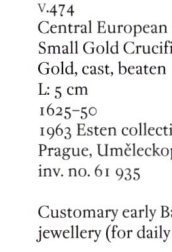

V.474
Central European Goldsmith
Small Gold Crucifix
Gold, cast, beaten
L: 5 cm
1625–50
1963 Esten collection of Konopiste
Prague, Uměleckoprůmyslové Muzeum,
inv. no. 61 935

Customary early Baroque item of personal jewellery (for daily or funereal use).

D.S.

V.475
Pendant in the Shape of a Pelican
Gold, crystal underlaid in red, diamonds, pearls; casting in the round, enamelling
H: 9.6 cm
Late sixteenth century
Bought in 1936 from Frantisek Zapletal, Karlovy Vary
Prague, Národní muzeum, inv. no. H2-17 681

A pelican in black, white and purple enamel with a large stone heart on its throat, hanging on three short chains. This is one of numerous depictions of pelicans, a symbol of Christ. It is different from South

German jewellery and seems more likely to come from Spain, or to have been made in Bohemia under Spanish influence. The pelican has no young, which makes it possible that this might instead be an eagle, something also suggested by the crown on its head.

Johnová 1989.

V.Vo.

V.476
Pendant in the Shape of a Dove
Gold, rubies; casting, enamelling
H: 3.2 cm
Late sixteenth century
Bought in 1936 from Frantisek Zapletal,
Karlovy Vary
Prague, Národní muzeum, inv. no. H2-17
577

A dove, the symbol of the Holy Spirit, is portrayed in flight with wings outstretched; it was cast in the round. The tablet-cut rubies cover the surface of the piece, which is clearly incomplete. Hackenbroch (no. 533) gives a similar pendant with a crowned eagle from a private collection as an example of Prague work from 1600 to 1610.

Johnová 1989, no. 457.

V.Vo.

V.477
Locket with *Mary Magdalen*
Gold, pearls, cast, enamelled
4.5 × 2.7 cm
Sixteenth century; mounting eighteenth century
1950 purchased from Dr Neumann, Prague
Prague, Národní muzeum, inv. no. H2-26 588

This oval cast medallion with coloured enamel depicts the scene of the penitent Mary Magdalen, semi-prostrate on the ground with a skull and a jar of ointment, and Christ on the cross. It has been mounted in a relief frame with pearls appended and bound by a ribbon to short chains. The composition of the scene and the figure indicate that, contrary to the date it has been ascribed, it did not originate until the first half of the seventeenth century.

Prague 1989.

V.Vo.

V.478
Czech (?) Goldsmith
Medal with the Head of Christ
Cast silver, chased, gilt
H: 3.5 cm; w: 3 cm
Early seventeenth century
Ex. coll. Daniel Penther, Vienna, 1887
Dorotheum auction
Prague, Uměleckoprůmyslové muzeum, inv. no. 2 846

This one-sided medal with the head of Christ in profile was taken originally from the reverse of two-sided Italian medallions from the second half of the sixteenth century: for example, Christ the Saviour from the reverse of the papal medallion by Giambattista Gelli (1498–1563) (cf. Armand I, p. 244) or from the Redeemers with 'blunt profile' by Leone Leoni and his successor, Antonio Abondio. Particularly favoured were models with a votive purpose, which penetrated the German and Czech production of medals and jewellery design (cf. Domanig 1907, no. 760: oval medal with the Redeemer, a variant without the crown of thorns). The displayed medal is cast in one piece with the frame. It would have originally served as a burgher's jewellery locket. The medal's frame also attests to its Czech provenance.

D.S.

V.479
Ring
Gold, Bohemian garnet; carving, engraving, enamelling
H: 2.2 cm
Mid-sixteenth century
Bought from Otto Morawitz in Prague in 1892
Prague, Uměleckoprůmyslové muzeum, inv. no. 4 948

Lady's ring with relief band decorated with white enamel. It has a high crown with four supports of the Gothic type. The rhomboid cut of the Bohemian garnet suggests it may be of secondary quality.

Prague 1966, no. 202; Pforzheim 1968, no. 1; Prague 1984, no. 3; Trencin 1985.

Urešová 1966; Vokacová 1968, 1984.

V.Vo.

V.480
Hand-in-hand Ring
Gold; casting, engraving
Diam: 2.3 cm
CZO PAN BUH SPOGIL TO CZLOWIEK NEROZLUCZUG
Second half of sixteenth century
Brought to the Uměleckoprůmyslové muzeum in 1963 from the State Research Institute for Precious Stones
Prague, Uměleckoprůmyslové muzeum, inv. no. 61 929

Engagement rings known as 'hand-in-hand' rings originated in ancient Rome and in a simpler form appeared in the Middle Ages. The Renaissance form is documented by a number of examples in European collections. The inscription means: What God hath joined together, let no man put asunder. The flat bands widen into shaped hands, with a heart carved on one of them.

Milan 1993–94, no. 12.

Rubesová, 1993–94.

V.Vo.

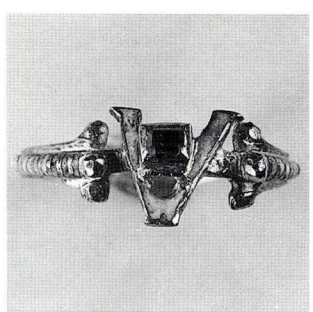

V.481
Engagement Ring with Letter 'A'
Gold, diamonds, cutting, carving, enam-
elling
H: 2 cm
A
Second half of sixteenth century
Excavated in Prague, bought from Mr
Bolehlav (?) in 1889
Prague, Uměleckoprůmyslové muzeum,
inv. no. 3 173

Engagement rings with clasped hands exist in a number of forms. This exhibit is
decorated with white enamel on a carved
band with diamanté and a shaped letter 'A'

on the crown, given emphasis by a tablet-
cut diamond. Initials appear in jewellery,
not just as engraved inscriptions or a detail but also as an obligatory decorative
motif, from the end of the fifteenth century.

Milan 1993–94, no. 20.

Rubesová 1993–94.

V.Vo.

V.482
Ring with *Naked Girl*
Sardonyx, partially enamelled gold, crys-
tal; carving
Diam: 1.9 cm
Ca. 1600
Bought in 1893 in Paris from the Spitzer
collections (no. 1946)
Prague, Uměleckoprůmyslové muzeum,
inv. no. 5 208

This carved ring, originally thought to be
of ivory, was assumed to come from Bohemia. The fine carving suggests an Italian craftsman, while the Mannerist-style
figure is typical of the Prague circle.

Prague 1966, no. 200; Milan 1993–94, no.
16; Ramat Gan 1994, no. 19.

Urešová 1966; Stará 1968, p. 371; Rubesova 1993–94; Stehlíková 1994.

V.Vo.

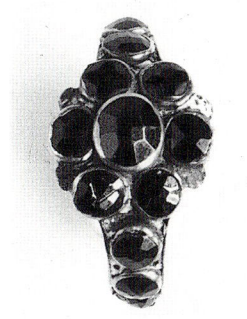

V.483
Ring
Gold, beating, enamelling, Bohemian gar-
nets
Diam: 1.8 cm
Ca. 1600
Given by Karel Rummel, court jeweller in
Prague, in 1894
Prague, Uměleckoprůmyslové muzeum,
inv. no. 5 604

A ring of Bohemian origin with a wide
band set with Bohemian garnets and with
a crown in the shape of a rose, with additional black and white enamelling. The
form is unusual in European jewellery.

Pforzheim 1968, no. 1; Prague 1984, no. 4;
Trencin 1985.

Vokacová 1968, 1984.

V.Vo.

V.484
Ring in the Shape of an Armillary Sphere
Gold; beating, carving, assembling
Diam: 1.8 cm
*V.L. W F I O G. I.N.E.S. K.R. V.G. SIDM
HLO NMIVMN.W*
Ca. 1600
Bought from Prague jeweller Jan Eckert
in 1896
Prague, Uměleckoprůmyslové muzeum,
inv. no. 6 774

A puzzle ring in the shape of an armillary
sphere, engraved with signs of the zodiac
and initials on the inner bands. There are a
number of similar examples in European

collections. Some researchers consider the
incomprehensible inscriptions to be ama-
tory, an interpretation supported by the
appearance of an engraved heart. It is
more likely, however, that they have an astrological meaning.

Prague 1966, no. 197; Milan 1993–94, no.
26; Ramat Gan 1994, no. 22; Prague, Kabinety 1995, no. 32.

Stehlíková 1995.

V.Vo.

V.485
Bracelet
Silver; casting
L: 20.5 cm
End of sixteenth century
Anonymous gift in 1897
Prague, Uměleckoprůmyslové muzeum,
inv. no. 7 552

A bracelet composed of roughly cast
openwork links with diamanté in the centre. Simple work, probably by a girdler for
a bourgeois customer.

Prague 1966, no. 196.

Urešová 1966.

V.Vo.

V.486
Pin with Pelican Motif
Gold, pearl, emerald, spinel; carving,
enamelling, casting in the round
L: 7 cm
End of sixteenth century
Transferred by the State Monuments Ad-
ministration from Zleby castle in 1962
Prague, Uměleckoprůmyslové muzeum,
inv. no. 67 594

A pelican feeding its young with its own
blood was a favourite Renaissance motif
symbolizing Christ and Charity and is
seen fairly often in jewellery. The exhibit
seems to have formed part of a pendant – a

pin of different metal added to the eyelet
from which the pendant was hung.

Milan 1993–94, no. 5; Ramat Gan 1995, no.
5.

Rubesová 1993–94; Stehlíková 1994.

V.Vo.

V.487
Bracelet Clasp
Gold, rubies, enamel
Diam: 2.3 cm
Early seventeenth century
Bohemia (?)
Bought in Vienna in 1909 at the
Dorotheum auction entitled 'Ringe,
Uhren, alter Schmuck aus polnischem
Privatbesitz', lot no. 409
Prague, Uměleckoprůmyslové muzeum,
inv. no. 11 055

A clasp, probably made out of a sew-on
decoration. The pin is made of cheap metal and added separately. There is a consid-

erable quantity of similar pieces in Central
European jewellery, for example some of
the decorations of the Jewel Monstrance
in the Loretto treasury, in which the jeweller, in addition to the well-known
cameos of Habsburg emperors and kings,
also used jewels given ex voto to the
monastery.

Prague 1966, no. 195.

Urešová 1966.

V.Vo.

V.488
Earrings
Gold; casting
L: 3.3 cm
Second half of sixteenth century
Bought in 1887 from Daniel Penther in
Vienna
Prague, Uměleckoprůmyslové muzeum,
inv. no. 2 482

These earrings moulded in the shape of a
cartouche are simple but represent stylistically pure craftsmanship from the Central European region.

Prague 1966, no. 184.

Urešová 1966.

V.Vo.

V.489
Woman's Girdle
Partially gold-plated silver; beating,
mounting
L: 104.2 cm
Stamp illegible
Sixteenth century
Given in 1905 by Anna Jandova from Bu-
dohostice near Melnik, central Bohemia
Prague, Narodni muzeum, inv. no. H2-7
225

The Národní muzeum v Praze alone has
several variations of this type of girdle,
with plaited chains separated by larger,
rectangular links decorated in relief, and

with a horseshoe-shaped hook for trinkets
to be hung from. Some of them come
from the same donor. Another girdle from
the Melník area has a Prague Old Town
stamp and the craftsman's initials, A.L. It is
mistakenly dated to the middle of the seventeenth century by Podlaha.

Podlaha 1899, pp. 171–72, ill. 269; Johnová
1989.

V.Vo.

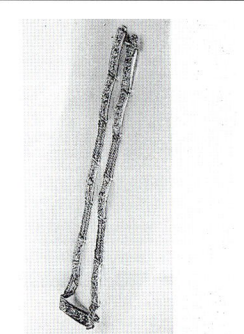

V.490
Woman's Girdle
Silver, partially gold-plated; beating, cast-
ing, mounting
78 cm
Two encircled stamps, unknown
Second half of sixteenth century
Bohemia
Found in 1904 by a forester in a forest
near Suvec, Turnov; in 1905 bought from
F. Mares of Suvec
Prague, Narodni muzeum, inv. no. H2-6
022

A girdle composed of a plaited chain and
six larger rectangular links with relief dec-

oration and a rosette in the middle, with a
cast horseshoe-shaped hook with a
cherub's head. It is an accessory of a type
which appears with considerable frequen-
cy in the wills of Czech bourgeois families.
They have also been preserved in various
forms in Czech museum collections.

Johnová 1989.

V.Vo.

V.491
Woman's Girdle
Gold-plated silver; casting, chasing, mounting
L: 101 cm
Later Austrian stamp *1806* with the letter *K* for Ljubljana
Late sixteenth century
Held in the Waldes Museum in Prague until its closure, when it was transferred to the Uměleckoprůmyslové muzeum; in 1967 returned to Koh-i-noor and given to the Museum of Glass and Jewellery in Jablonec nad Nisou; currently the subject of a claim for restitution
Jablonec nad Nisou, Muzeum skla a bižuterie, inv. no. 16 368

An ostentatious girdle displaying high-quality jeweller's work. Pairs of short plaited chains are joined by rectangular links with applied openwork decoration topped by diamanté. The polygonal buckle has a stylized figure of a two-headed eagle. Only good-quality girdles like these were made by jewellers, the others being produced by girdlers.

V.Vo.

V.492
Woman's Girdle with Pomander
Silver, partially gold plated; casting, assembling
L: 78 cm; hanging chain l: 84 cm; pomander h: 7.5 cm
End of sixteenth century
Found in 1970 during work on the house at U modré hvězdy, no. 252, Týn nad Vltavou, together with other items
Muzeum Týn nad Vltavou, inv. no. 8.738

A girdle composed of six rectangular pieces with a relief portrait of a woman and a floral decoration, alternating with series of four openwork links with scrolls, with a small gold-plated ball in the middle. Next to the hook clasp is a long chain with shaped oval links and a gilded vase-shaped link with cherubs' heads on either side. At the end of the chain is a pomander with embossed bunches of fruit and cartouches, joined by a coil in the middle. This kind of girdle with pomander, rarely preserved, was worn throughout the sixteenth century; the decoration on this one puts it at the end of the century. It is part of the Týn nad Vltavou treasure.

Pletzer, Týn nad Vltavou, n.d., p. 12.

V.Vo.

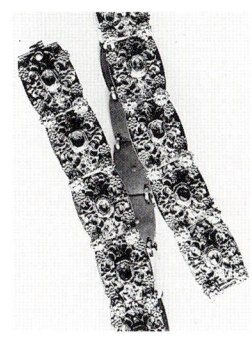

V.493
Woman's Girdle
Gold-plated silver, partially enamelled, crystal, emeralds, rubies; casting, assembling
L: 94 cm; individual links 3.8 × 3.1 to 3.9 × 3.3 cm
Ca. 1600
Found in 1970 during work on the house U modré hvězdy, no. 252, Týn nad Vltavou, together with other items
Muzeum Týn nad Vltavou, inv. no. 8.737

A girdle made up of twenty-three rectangular, slightly segmented tablets with cast cartouche, floral decoration and medium-high border containing crystals, emeralds and rubies cut into faceted rectangles, underlaid with coloured metal foil. The links are connected by pairs of carved oval pieces with cast silver flowers. The sliding clasp is damaged, and three precious stones are missing. The 'Týn treasure' has not yet featured in specialist literature. The girdle is one of the ostentatious accessories which can be seen on sixteenth-century portraits of women. The decor and the cut of the stones place it at the end of the century. The treasure was stored together with some gold coins minted in Hungary and dated 1589. It is likely that the treasure was walled up in 1619 when the town was occupied by Estates troops (cf. Karel Pletzer, Týn nad Vltavou, n.d., p. 12).

V.Vo.

V.494
Pomander
Gold-plated silver; casting, engraving
H: 4.2 cm
Ca. 1600
Germany (?)
Brought from the castle at Zleby by the State Monuments Office in 1963
Prague, Umeleckoprumyslove muzeum, inv. no. 67.583

Pomanders, for holding solid scented material, appear frequently in Czech inventories of estates from the fifteenth century onwards, but above all in the sixteenth century. Pomanders were used not only for personal enhancement but for hygienic purposes. They were hung round the waist and might contain balsam, ambergris or civet. The receptacle has seven parts, joined by a screw. It seems that the balsam holder which the Rozmberk jeweller Abraham Schmelzer made in 1613 for Jan Jiri of Svamberk was the same (with seven parts which screw together, in gold-plated silver).

Prague 1979; Doudleby 1985–91.

Mares 1898–99, p. 96; Vokacová 1979, p. 214.

V.Vo.

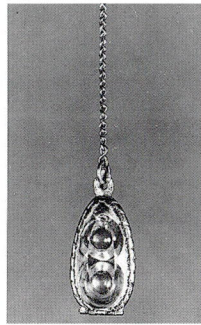

V.495
Scent Locket
Crystal and gold-plated silver; polishing, mounting
H: 3.8 cm
Mid-seventeenth century
Prague (?)
Left to the museum by Jan Neuberg, knight, Prague, in 1892
Prague, Uměleckoprůmyslové muzeum, inv. no. 4 596

An egg-shaped locket in two parts with a hollow interior for solid scent, used as a pomander. Similar lockets from the seventeenth and eighteenth centuries were also used as amulets. The lockets were worn on a necklace or girdle. The Uměleckoprůmyslové muzeum has another variation, also from Neuberg's collection. The materials and craftsmanship suggest a Bohemian origin.

Prague 1979, no. 127; Doudleby 1985–91.

Vokacová 1979.

V.Vo.

V.496
Perfume Bottle in the Shape of a Vase
Gold, pearls; casting, enamelling
H: 7.4 cm
Late sixteenth or early seventeenth century
Bought in 1936 from Frantisek Zapletal, Karlovy Vary
Prague, Národní muzeum, inv. no. H2-17 579

A scent bottle in the shape of a vase with a stopper, with short chains and pearls attached, is a rare item for this period, since pomanders containing solid perfume were more common up to the seventeenth century.

Johnová 1989, no. 456.

V.Vo.

V.497
Perfume Bottle
Silver, partially gold-plated and enamelled; casting, engraving
H: 7.2 cm
Mid-seventeenth century
Brought from Teplice, north Bohemia, in 1963 by the State Monuments Office
Prague, Uměleckoprůmyslové muzeum, inv. no. 66.791

A pear-shaped flask with a figure of an eagle at the top, carved plant decoration and two round medallions with a double-headed eagle. Its lower part is fixed in an openwork enamelled basket. The bottle, which contained liquid scent, was fixed at the waist by a short chain. Although liquid scents were well known in Italy and France in the sixteenth century, they did not advance further until the seventeenth century. Flasks from the beginning of this period have only rarely been preserved.

Prague 1979, no. 235; Doudleby 1985-91.

Vokacová 1979.

V.Vo.

V.498
Miniature Cabinet (Jewel Box) with Glass Panels with Birds
Black stained wood, clear glass, lacquer painting on gold leaf
28 × 33 × 25.2 cm; panels 8.5 × 7 and 3 × 7 cm
Ca. 1580
Antique shop, Prague, 1975
Prague. Uměleckoprůmyslové muzeum, inv. no. 75 435

The jewel box has six small drawers and one large drawer, which are framed by inlays and profiled fillets. The panels bear depictions of exotic birds among leafs with flowers and pomegranates. Ryser has published similar panels from his own collection (Ryser 1991, p. 318, ills. 92-94). The paintings are based on models by V. Solis and are of very high quality. The painting technique used (the colour is applied over the gold) leads Ryser to suggest that this work comes from Nürnberg.

Ryser 1991, pp. 93, 316, ills. 96-97.

O.D.

V.499
Workshop of Jost Amman
Zürich 1539-Nürnberg 1591
Casket for Jewellery with Allegories of the Virtues
Wood, glass painted from the back
9 × 7 × 11 cm
SPES, FIDES, CHARITAS, FORTITUDO, PATIENTIA, JUSITTIA, TEMPERANTIA, PRUDENTIA
Ca. 1580
Purchased from the Egger company, Paris
Prague, Uměleckoprůmyslové muzeum, inv. no. 2 073

An oblong casket, made of glass and wood saturated with black stain, with an arched lid, front and back sides. The allegories of the Virtues stand in arcades and are identified by inscriptions. The technique of painting from the back of the glass, called amelieren at the time, spread from Italy to southern Germany and Switzerland. The figures active in this field in Nürnberg were Virgil Solis (1514-1562), Nicolaus Solis (1542-1584) and Jost Amman (1539-1591). Of the many analogous works listed in the literature, the casket most closely resembles the jewel box with allegories of the Virtues in the Bayerisches Nationalmuseum (see Ryser 1995, cat. no. F 5).

Murnau 1995.

Ryser 1991, pp. 81, 318, ills. 86-88; Ryser 1995, cat. no. F 6.

O.D.

V.500
Nürnberg Master
Casket for Jewels with Allegories of the Five Senses
Wood, glass painted from the back
16 × 18 × 7 cm
Ca. 1600-1625
1906 gift of Sir Vojtěch Lanna
Prague, Uměleckoprůmyslové muzeum, inv. no. 10 535

The four-sided jewel box is made of black stained wood and four glass panels on the sides, and stands on a wide base. The panels are decorated with allegories of the Five Senses in cartouches. The techniques used are similar to those of the preceding work.

Murnau 1995.

Ryser 1991, pp. 81, 318, ills. 89-91; Ryser 1995, cat. no. F 8.

O.D.

V.501
Coffer
Iron
13 × 8.5 × 15.5 cm
Sixteenth century
Prague, 1890, B. Bondy
Prague, Uměleckoprůmyslové muzeum,
inv. no. 3 804

The oblong, wrought-iron coffer is painted and has bronze rosettes. A lord and lady
in period dress are painted on the front
wall of the box. On the bottom of the lid
there are two brackets and two rosettes
made of hammered bronze plate. In the
early sixteenth century, carnation blos-

soms and rosettes became a popular motif
used to decorate rivet heads.

Exhibition of the Uměleckoprůmyslové
Muzeum, Lemberk Castle, 1993.

J.N.

V.502
Jewellery Box
Malleable iron, nielloed, wrought and
filed
22.6 × 31 × 23 cm
End of the sixteenth century
Bought in 1895 by the Northern Bohemi-
an Museum in Liberec from Architect G.
Hering of Munich.
Liberec, Northern Bohemian Museum,
inv. no. OK 850

Among the many works of this type, this
jewellery box from Liberec is an excellent
example of high-quality southern German
ironwork. The design features the fre-

quently used image of a man, framed in a
niche with a moorish frame. The locking
mechanism on the inside of the lid works
on one key. The keyhole on the front is
covered by a small plate.

MNGM 1898/3; illustrated example, Pazourek, 1989, n. 6

J.M.

V.503
Coffer
Etched iron
9.5 × 9 × 15.8 cm
Early seventeenth century
Bequest of Sir Jan Neuberg 1892
Prague, Uměleckoprůmyslové muzeum,
inv. no. 4 570

The oblong coffer is made of etched
wrought iron and has a hinged lid and a
handle. It rests on four round legs. Four
square fields with etched leafwork and
birds run around the perimeter. On the lid
there are brackets with a slanted striking
surface. Inside the lid are a lock and key.

New decorating techniques appeared in
the mid-sixteenth century in regions of
southern Germany – particularly the techniques of etching and niello – in addition
to the already popular techniques of flut-
ing and cutwork.

J.N.

V.504
Casket
Engraved bronze
4 × 4.7 × 7.2 cm
First quarter of the seventeenth century
Germany
Purchased in 1960 from Artia
Prague, Uměleckoprůmyslové muzeum,
inv. no. 49 351

The oblong bronze casket stands on four
lens-shaped legs with engravings of couples in costumes from the early seventeenth century. Caskets, used for storing
small jewels, were very popular, particularly in bourgeois circles.

Exhibition of the Uměleckoprůmyslové
muzeum, Doudleby, 1985–91.

J.N.

V.505
Coffer
Iron
11 × 10 × 18 cm
1630
Purchased from Artia in 1958
Prague, Uměleckoprůmyslové muzeum,
inv. no. 45 391

An oblong coffer on four legs, with engraved figures, a hinged lid and a handle.
The lid and walls are divided into two oblong fields with depictions of standing figures in period dress against a background
of leafy and flowering stems. Inside the lid
are a lock and key.

J.N.

V.506
Jewellery box
Silver filigree, enamel
5 × 11 cm
Seventeenth century
Prague, Loreta, inv. no. P-99

This box, clearly designated for jewels, is evidence of the quick mastering of filigree techniques by Czech, in this case Prague, workshops. The green emerald petals only underscore the exacting work of the craftsmanship that used a thin silver wire. This time-honoured technique again found favor in Central Europe during the course of the seventeenth century and lived on until the nineteenth century in folk art.

Diviš, 1972, pg. 207, ill. 56.

J.D.

V.507
Jewellery box
Gilded silver, Czech garnet, crystal, filigree, watercolour
9.8 × 13 cm
Seventeenth century
Prague, Loreta, inv. no. P-07

The Loreta treasury arose from the gifts of admirers of the Loreta *Virgin Mary*. Thus the objects have come down from the treasure troves of a wide variety of provenances. The origin of the jewel box, however, is certainly Czech as is evidenced by its embellishment of Czech garnets, which in the seventeenth century were already very popular and highly valued. The filigree testifies to the fact that the creator of the box had already mastered the revamped technique that made its way to Bohemia through southern Germany, particularly via the Augsburg goldsmiths' workshops.

Diviš, 1972, pg. 206, ill. 50.

J.D.

V.508
Burial Scutcheon of Adam of Dietrichštejn
Without fringe: 81 × 67 cm
Around the perimeter in letters cut from serrated material and sewn with gold thread, and set in a border of double twisted cord: *ADAMUS A DIETRICH-STAIN LIBER BARO COMMENDATOR MAYOR IN ALCANITZ ORDINIS CALA-TRAVA.*
After 1590
Prague, Treasury of St Vitus' cathedral
Prague, Prague Castle, inv. no. 10105-K132
The burial scutcheons are outstanding artistic relics, which are nowadays often the only testimony to the splendid ceremonials of death among the high aristocracy. Five scutcheons were usually made: four were laid in pairs at the sides of the catafalque, and the fifth, known as the large scutcheon, at the feet of the deceased. The burial scutcheon of the powerful catholic politician Adam of Dietrichštejn (died 5 February 1590) bears the distinguishing marks of the deceased. The red cross with arms of equal length of the Spanish Order of Calatrava was sewn on to the field of the scutcheon, with four horses' bits placed obliquely to the centre of the cross. Adam of Dietrichštejn, faithful servant of the Emperors Ferdinand I, Maximilian II and Rudolf II, acquired the cross during his diplomatic service as Maximilian's ambassador to the court in Madrid. His political career reached its peak in the 1570s: in 1572 he undertook a diplomatic mission to Hungary to negotiate with the Estates the coronation of Rudolf II.

Podlaha-Šittler, Soupis (register), pp.186-87.

M.H., J.H.L.

V.509
Burial Scutcheon of Jiří Bořita of Martinice
Without fringe: 77.5 × 67 cm
On cream silk satin between laurel wreaths: *.GEORGIVS.BORZITA.DE.MAR-TINIZ.IN.SMETZNA.S(ACRAE).C(ESARE AE).M(AJESTA)TIS.CONSILIARIVS.ET.S VPREMVS.REGNI.BOHEMAE.CANCEL-IARVS.*
1598
Prague, Treasury of St Vitus' cathedral.
Prague, Prague Castle, inv. no.10105-K130

Jiří Bořita held the post of honorary chamberlain to Rudolf II, then from 1584 to 1585 he held the office of courtier and afterwards of regional judge. In 1597 he became Supreme Chancellor of the country. He died childless on 22 January 1598. In the main field of the scutcheon is the Martinice family emblem, in high relief on blue silver-brocade. The vizor of the tournament helmet is made of silver wire. The date 1598 is sewn in silver thread beside of the jewel. The coat of arms is bordered by a three-dimensional laurel wreath of silver-brocade with leaves edged in gold thread. Fringes, not part of the original work, are attached round the perimeter of the scutcheon with silver thread.

Prague, 1891, p. 242, no. 36.

Podlaha-Šittler 1903, p. 307; Podlaha-Šittler, Soupis (register), pp. 187-88; Borovský-Chytil 1892, sheet no. 10; Janáček 1987, p. 224.

M.H.

V.510
Jan Blumberger
Cvikov; fl. Prague 1596-1628 Burial Scutcheon of Kryštof Popel of Lobkovic
Without fringe: 79 × 73 cm
Sewn in black thread on cream-coloured silver-brocade: *CHRISTOPHO. POPELI(US).BARO.A.LOBKO(WIZ).D(O MI)N(US).IN.PK.ET DIWITZ.S(ACRAE). C(ESAREAE).M(AJESTATIS).RV(DOLPH O).II.CONSI(LLIARIUS).INTIM(US).SVP (RE)M(US).P(RE)FECT(US).CVRIAE.R(EGNI).BOH(EMIAE).*
1609
Treasury of the chapel of the Holy Rood
Prague, Prague Castle, inv. no. 10105-K131

The burial scutcheon of Kryštof Popel of Lobkovic (1549-1609) is a piece of embroidered work of a typically high standard. The Lobkovic coat of arms, in high relief on a base of dark red silver-brocade, is bordered by three-dimensional laurel wreaths. Lobkovic became Supreme Controller/Chamberlain of the Household in 1599. Like all the funeral shields now held at the cathedral of St Vitus, it is representative of what is known as the heraldic type, in this case bearing the coat of arms of the deceased aristocrat. This scutcheon has many features in common with the funeral shield of Petr Vok of Rožmberk (now in the Národní muzeum in Prague). That is the only funeral embroidery from the first two decades of the seventeenth century of which the making is documented and which bears the signature in his own hand of the eminent Prague embroiderer Jan Blumberger.

Prague 1891, no. 35, p. 242.

Borovský-Chytil 1892, sheet 11; Podlaha-Šittler, 1903, p. 308; Podlaha-Šittler, Soupis (register), p. 187.

M.H., J.H.L.

V.511
Jan Blumberger
Burial Scutcheon of Petr Vok of Rožmberk
Embroidery and appliqué; wood, textile, silk and metal thread, gold thread
100 × 90 cm
1612
Prague, Nádodní muzeum, inv. no. H2-3493

After the burial of Petr Vok of Rožmberk the scutcheon hung for several decades above his tomb in the monastery of Vyšší Brod. During repair work to the building it was taken down and kept in the mona-stery museum. Valentin Schopper, abbot of the monastery, donated it in 1843 to what is now the Národní muzeum
Prague, Národní muzeum, Department of Early Czech History, inv. no. H2-3493

The scutcheon is made up of an oval piece of wood covered with material interwoven with metal threads, on which has been created in embroidery and appliqué a three-dimensional coat of arms of Petr Vok of Rožmberk (1539-1611). A Latin phrase is embroidered round the edge. The scutcheon was made, along with oth-er mourning coats of arms in Prague, by Master Hans Blumgarten at the expense of Jan Jiří of Švamberk, the inheritor of the Rožmberk estates. It formed part of the decorations used at the burial of Petr Vok on 30 January 1612 in the former mona-stery church at Vyšší Brod.

Prague, Lobkovic Palace, since 1987, cat. no. 469.

Pletzer 1964, year 133, issue 2, pp. 91–96.

V.P.

V.512
Polyxena Ejdlicov of Enfeld's Coffin
Pewter, Chromed and gilded
107 × 52 × 56 cm
619
Originally entombed in the deacon's church in Poln. The tomb was opened for the second time in 1959 (the first was in 1916) and the coffin moved to the muse-um. Restored in 1997 by F. Jnsk, Prague. inv. no. Po-Fs 48 962 (H 538)

One of a group of eight pewter coffins (six large and two small) from the ejdlice's tomb in Poln, which can be dated from 1603 (Hartvik Ejdlices' coffin the plaque and family herald of which is displayed in the museum) to 1622 (Rudolf Ejdlice's coffin; the museum features reliefs of the apostles taken from the coffin). The ejdlice family, particularly Rudolf, took part in the Estates revolt and the church was led by Protestant priests in the years 1597 to 1623. The relief ornamentation on the coffins of Polyxena and Rudolf feature similar themes to those on the church baptismal dated 1617. The pewter crafts-manship is of a very high quality, not only in the clarity of the tin poured from the moulds, but also in the designcomposi-tion and final colour. This is the first ex-ample of work of this caliber (Rudolf II's coffin from 1612 is also polychromed pewter) Similar design element reliefs of the apostles in *rolwerk* cartouches, wavy bands with pear designs with birds and angel's heads indicate that both coffins were made around the same time by a sin-gle tinsmith between the years 1617 and 1622.

D.S.

V.513
Bartholomeus Spranger
Antwerp 1546–Prague 1611
Epitaph for Michael Peterle of Annaberk
Oil on wood
150 × 120 cm
On the cloud on the right:
B./SPRANGERS/ANTus/F.
1587-88
According to K. van Mander, originally housed in the Church of Saint Giles
Prague, Church of Saint Stephen, 265

In 1584 the book illuminator (*Briefmaler*), woodcut artist and printer Michael Peterle of Annaberg, bought a house on Zámecké schody, becoming Spranger's neighbour. He ordered the epitaph prior to his death in 1587. Spranger's work was exceptional in terms not only of its skill and technique but also of its choice of theme. Both Spranger and Peterle were Protestants. For the central panel the artist therefore chose an image of Christ on the Cross tri-umphing over sin and death, and for the epitaph's extension piece an image of God the Father. The complex composition, densely filled, corresponds with Sprang-er's mythological paintings dating from the same period. The main scene is a clas-sic example of his extreme Mannerist style of the fifteen-eighties. The portraits of the members of Peterle's family, however, ap-parently added later by another artist, are stiff, two-dimensional and schematically devised. Nevertheless, the fact that Spranger saw fit to mention this work to Karel van Mander means that he must have taken some personal pride in it.

Prague 1912, cat. no. 68.

Mander (ed.) 1906; Oberhuber 1958, pp. 132–34, 228, cat. no. 36, for older literature; Henning 1987, pp. 78–81, 183–84, cat. no. A32; Kaufmann 1988, cat. no. 20.46.

E.F.

V.514
Circle of Bartholomeus Spranger
Antwerp 1546–Prague 1611
Epitaph of Unknown Family with the Trans-figuration of Christ
Oil on wood
159.5 × 118.5 cm
1610-20
Hung in the cloister of the Strahov monastery until 1950. After the dissolu-tion of the monastery in 1950 it was kept elsewhere. Restituted to the monastery in 1992.
Prague, Picture Gallery of the Strahov Premonstratensian Monastery, inv. no. O 707

The painting is attributed in the old cata-logue of the Strahov Picture Gallery, and by J. Vacková, to Spranger himself. It is structured in three bands, each of which has a distinct signification. In the lowest band we see the donor with his wife and two daughters. It has not been possible to identify him, despite the accomplishment of his depiction; he holds in his left hand a commemorative medal, evidently with a portrait of Rudolf II. In terms of both style and subject the painting can be placed in the artistic circle of the Rudolphine Man-nerists, and is particularly close to the work of B. Spranger (*Epitaph of the Gold-smith Müller*, ca. 1592, Prague Národní ga-lerie) and of M. Gundelach (*Ezekiel's vision*, ca. 1614-17, Žebrák, Cemetery Church). While the link to Spranger's work is more general, the artist is linked to Gundelach's work particularly by the conception of the central figure and its composition within the painting surface, the distaste for ex-cessive spatial development and the paint-ing's organization into horizontal rather than perspective-based planes.

Haupt-Catalog 1841, no. 823; Vacková 1969, p.146.

I.Ky.

V.515
Pupil of Hans von Aachen
The Entombment
Oil on wood
Ca. 1600
Prague, Národní galerie v Praze, collec-tion of old art , inv. no. O1277

While Aachen was working in Bavaria, he gradually began to abandon his elegant Mannerist style, with its radiant colours and compositions, no doubt to conform with the more conservative tastes of the Munich Jesuits, the Wittelsbachs and the Fugger family who commissioned works from him. At that period Aachen also com-pleted some unfinished paintings by Christoph Schwarz, or made counterparts to them, adapting and basing his style on Titian's Venetian style of painting, and us-ing subject-matter that was strictly in keeping with the spirit that prevailed after the Council of Trent. A whole series of Aachen's pupils from Central Europe drew their inspiration from these works. The unidentified pupil of the present work had an eye for fine detail, in his treat-ment of the bodies and the drapery, and a good sense of light and depth. His compo-sition was an adaptation of one R. Sadel-er's engravings designed by Hans von Aachen.

Fučíková 1979, p. 504, ill. 21.

E.F.

V.516
Copy after Hans von Aachen
The Crucifixion
Oil on copper
Ca. 1600
Prague, Národní galerie v Praze, collection of old art, inv. no. 01355

At the time when this painting was made, this subject-matter was very popular and frequently copied. Another of Aachen's pupils, Hans Holzmayr, also made a copy of the same work but as a drawing (Vienna, Albertina, inv. no. 3309). Aachen himself returned to the composition a number of times (*The Crucifixion*, oil on copper,

signed and dated 1602, private German collection; drawings in the Getty Museum, Malibu, inv. no. 92.GA.83; Munich, Staatliche Graphische Sammlung, inv. no. 1928: 102). Differences between this and Aachen's treatment, such as the absence of the figure of the rider on the right of the composition and the pose of Saint John, may be accounted for by the artist's free interpretation or by his possible reference to one of Aachen's versions of the subject that is now unknown. Although both of Aachen's drawings were made around 1590, the painting that has survived was made more than ten years later, in 1602. The present Prague painting was painted

either by one of Aachen's pupils or by one of the helpers in his workshop who had access to his designs.

Fučíková 1979, p. 504, pic. no. 22.

E.F.

V.517, a–d
Ecce Homo, The Last Supper, Christ Carrying the Cross, The Entombment
Oil on wood
19.2 × 24.5-24.7 cm
All four signed bottom right with the monogram (in ligature): *CS*
Ca. 1600
Kozel country estate, inv. nos KZ 2075, 2070, 2076, 2079

In Italy Hans von Aachen already had a workshop and apprentices, who helped him with his large-scale commissions and who under his guidance developed into competent artists. This was also the case

while he was in Bavaria, and later on in Prague at the emperor's court, where he received and taught students from other nobles' courts in the vicinity. These four paintings, evidently belonging to a larger series of paintings depicting scenes from the Passion, must have been originally intended for a either a palace or a monastery chapel. The work was painted by an artist who must have been in close contact with Aachen, most likely one of his workshop team, possibly in Bavaria. This is suggested by slight changes to Aachen's compositions in particular scenes, primarily in *The Carrying of the Cross* and *Jesus in the Tomb*, dating from the late 1580s and the 1590s.

Aachen's artistic and figurative style is preserved, but the artist has employed a free and unusual form of painting, which does not clearly distinguish lines. The unidentified artist was probably one of those who, although trained at the court, later practised the techniques and skills of Rudolf's art in the city and on noble estates, and who restrained their own artistic virtuosity the better to emphasize the more devotional aspects of their works.

Fučíková 1979, p. 504, ill. 20.

E.F.

V.518
Anonymous, probably Northern Italian Painter
The Vision of Saint Ignatius of Loyola in La Storta
Oil on canvas
Ca. 1610
Prague, Church of Saint Salvator in the Clementium

This extremely high-quality painting is the work of an as yet unidentified Mannerist, probably from northern Italy. The heads of the putti recall the work of the Venetian painter P. Piazza, who worked in Prague in the early seventeenth century at

the church of The Angelic Virgin Mary, which belonged the Capuchin order, of which Piazza himself was a member. However, the overall colour scheme of the work, which is dominated by blue and violet tones, is different from that of the known works by P. Piazza. The work depicts a scene from the life of Saint Ignatius, who had a vision on his way to Rome to request the Pope's consent to found the order of the Society of Jesus. In the vision, he saw Christ with a cross, and Christ said to him *Ego vobis propitius ero*, which was taken as the expression of God's approval of Saint Ignatius' plan. The scene thus depicts the founding of

the Society of Jesus; its illustration in a monumental painting was explicitly intended as a demonstrative anti-reform statement in pre-White Mountain Prague.

M.Š.

V.519
Sustris, Friedrichor, or circle Schwartz, Christoph
1540-1599; ca. 1545-1594
The Virgin Mary with the Instruments of Christ's Suffering
Oil painting on copper plate
53.2 × 43.1 cm
On the reverse side of the painting, the Helfenburg coat of arms with inscription: *Illustri venerabili ac generose Sophyae Albinae de Helfenburg abatissae sancti Georgii Martyris in arce Pragensis sorori in Christo dilectissimae. Nobilis Abrahamus Albinis de Helfeburk fieri curavit ano 1613 mense marty 1613*

Probably originally from the Convent of St. George in Prague Castle, apparently bought in 1842 for the Strahov Monastery Picture Gallery from the collection of the Government Council of Janek. After the dissolution of the monastery in 1950 kept outside Prague. Restituted to the monastery in 1992.
Prague, Picture Gallery of the Strahov Premonstratensian Monastery, inv. no. O 933.

The picture is attributed to Friedrich Sustris in the old catalogue of the Strahov Picture Gallery; however, in terms of composition, the painting resembles the works of

Sustris's contemporary and colleague Christoph Schwartz. Given the difficulty in distinguishing the works of these two painters it is possible to support an attribution to either of these two famous Bavarian Mannerists. The composition of the whole painting and of the individual figures is relatively simple, the central figure of the Virgin Mary rather stiff and the painter's treatment quite poor.

Haupt-Catalog 1841, no. 972; Parthey 1864, p. 600, no. 2.

I.Ky.

V.520
Matyáš Mayer
In Prague 1604-1648
St Wenceslas between Two Angels
Oil on canvas
148 × 247 cm with frame
1629
Prague, rectory office of Saint Nicholas in Malá Strana, inv. no. D-M/31/431

The work comes from the now-desanctified church of St Wenceslas in Malá Strana in Prague. The rectory was transferred here in 1629 (it was originally located at the Church of St Nicholas, which, however, devolved upon the Jesuit order that year). In

1629 the church of St Wenceslas was rebuilt and redecorated. It is highly probable that this work was also painted at that time and was meant to hang above the main altar of the church. Mayer depicted St Wenceslas as an earthly patron standing between two angels, pronouncing a blessing and carrying a shield and banner. The painter based the design of St Wenceslas between two angels as well as certain details of the armour on medieval models (*Liber Viaticus, St Wenceslas between Two Angels*, on the eastern wall of the chapel of St Wenceslas in St Vitus' cathedral). The scene at the bottom of the painting depicts the transfer of the body of St Wenceslas

from Stará Boleslav to Prague just at the moment when the cortege with the body of the saint stopped in front of the Malá Strana prison and would not move until all of the prisoners were set free. The model for this illustration were the text and illustrations of the *Hájek Chronicle* of 1540. With his depiction of St Wenceslas Mayer introduced a theme into Czech Baroque painting which would later be taken up by other Czech Baroque artists.

Šroněk 1992, p. 148–52; Šroněk 1996 (under the heading M. Mayer).

M.Š.

V.521
Jan Jiří Hering
Eschwege in Hesse 1547–Prague 1648
St Evermod
Oil on canvas
183 × 152 cm
Inscribed in the lower left part of the painting *HHering Inu: Pinxit* and in the lower left part *B. Evermodus ex / Praeposito Ecclesiae B.M. / Magdeburgen.Race / burgen.episcopus, / Miraculis clarus / moritur A:1177*
After 1620
Probably originally for the Strahov Monastery. Hung in the cloister of the monastery until 1950. After the dissolu-

tion of the monastery in 1950 kept outside Prague. Restituted to the monastery in 1992.
Prague, Picture Gallery of the Strahov Premonstratensian Monastery, inv. no. O 75.

St Evermod, friend of the founder of the Premonstratensian Order St Norbert, became bishop of Ratzenburg in 1154. He is known as the apostle of the Lusatians (the Wends). He died in 1178, and his cult was authorized by Pope Benedict XIII in 1728. The kneeling figure of the saint fills almost the entire foreground of the painting. In the clearly traditional spatial organisation

of the background, scenes from the life of the saint take place in smaller scale. The painting belongs to a series of Premonstratensian saints, including St Evermod, the Blessed Rudolf, Reiner, Milo and Gottfried, and is first mentioned by G. J. Dlabacz. These paintings resemble each another in dimensions and style, and clearly all came from the hand of Hering. The Strahov cycle of Premonstratensian saints is more extensive than this.

Haupt-Catalog 1841, no. 972; Parthey 1864, p. 600, no. 2.

I.Ky.

V.522
Jan Jiří Hering
Eschwege in Hess 1587–Prague 1648
The Visitation of the Blessed Virgin Mary
Oil on canvas
207 × 118 cm
J. Häring Pinxit
Ca. 1630
St Vitus' Cathedral, inv. no. V–119

The painting was most probably intended for the altar of the Visitation of the Blessed Virgin Mary in the Cathedral of Saint Vitus; the altar was built as a part of the renovation of the cathedral decoration following the Calvinist iconoclasm of the

year 1619. Caspar Arsenius of Radburza noted that the altar of the Visitation was created in 1621, but apparently this was only the temporary version of the altar, and Hering's work was added to it only later. The work represents an interesting amalgamation of Hering's painterly experiences. The composition is based on the model of F. Barocci's painting in the Church of Santa Maria in Valicella in Rome, which Hering undoubtedly knew from the autopsy, because he copied the painting's colours scheme as well as its composition. The design of the landscape in the background attests to the influence of the Italian landscape painter G.

Muziano, as well as that of the Rudolfine landscape painters Peter Stevens and Paul van Vianen. Hering himself is a remarkable figure: on the one hand, he is unusually close to the Rudolfine artists in his drawings, but on the other hand his numerous extant altar paintings are typical examples of early Baroque Czech painting in their realism, narrative and dramatic light effects.

Neumann 1951, p. 71; Šroněk 1988, p. 325; Šroněk 1996 (under the heading H. G. Hering).

M.Š.

V.523
Antonín Stevens
Ca. 1610–Prague 1673/4
St Sebastian
Oil on canvas
204 × 171 cm
1740s
Česky Šternberk, castle, inv. no. 63-373/9

This is the earliest known work by Antonín Stevens, a descendant (the son, apparently) of the Rudolfine landscape painter Pieter Stevens. In the painting of *St Sebastian*, the artist takes up the tradition of his Rudolfine predecessors. The treatment of the figure of the saint tied to

a tree is evidently inspired in particular by the work of Bartholomeus Spranger (compare, for example, Spranger's treatment of the same subject in the church of Saint Thomas in Prague's Malá Strana). The conception of the landscape in the background is influenced by the work of Pieter Stevens. The painting of *St Sebastian* is an important demonstration of the connection between early Baroque painting and the work of the Rudolfine court artists.

Šroněk 1988, p. 337; Šroněk 1996 (under the heading A. Stevens).

M.Š.

V.524
Karel Škréta
Prague 1610 (?)–Prague 1674
St Thomas Aquinas
Oil on linden wood
87 × 74 cm
1740s
Originally intended for use in decorating the library of the Barefoot Augustine Monastery in Prague, later stored in the sacristy of the church of St Gallus (Havel); now at the Parish Office at the Church of Our Lady before Týn in Prague.
Prague, Rectory Office at the church of Our Lady before Týn

The painting of St Thomas Aquinas was originally part of the interior decoration of the library of the Monastery of the Barefoot Augustines in na Zderaze street, where it was part of a cycle of works depicting the Church Fathers and the Evangelists, which also included a painting of Moses and the Virgin Mary with Jesus on a throne (*SEDES SAPENTIA*). Škréta maintained active ties with the Augustine monks of na Zderaze. During the late 1730s and early 1740, Škréta and several other painters executed a large set of paintings known as the St Wenceslas Cycle for the Augustines. The decorative programme of the library, executed during

the 1740s, illustrates the idea of Christian wisdom. The painting of St Thomas represents one of the most outstanding works in the ensemble of Škréta's paintings for the monastery library, some of which are now partially destroyed and scattered. The work is noteworthy for the extraordinary concentration of the saint, the sculpturally modelled depiction of the figure and his markedly portrait-like traits.

Prague 1974, cat. no. 68.

M.Š.

V.525
Karel Škréta
Prague 1610–Prague 1674
St Charles Borromeo Visiting Victims of the Plague
Oil on canvas
210 × 247.5 cm
An inscription on the altar at the back on the wall identifies the donor: *Ego Max Antonius Cassinis/ F/C/ 1647*
1647
The work was on the main altar of the church of the Blessed Virgin and St Charles Borromeo in a spital in Malá Strana. Following the closure of the spital the painting remained where it was until

it was purchased in 1943 by the Národní galerie, collection of old art.
Prague, Národní galerie v Praze, Collection of old art, inv. no. o 2 579

Having studied in Italy and forged a friendship with Dionysio Miseroni, Karel Škréta maintained close contact with the Italians in Prague. The style of this painting was particular to Lombardy in the early seventeenth century. The Saint is depicted entering the spital in the company of several men among whom the artist has painted his own self-portrait. Škréta's debt to the Carracios and to Venetian artworks by the Bassano family, is evident in this

monumental work. The influences of Michelangelo and S. Voueto are also visible. The artist has with great skill woven a multiplicity of influences into a unified work, which moreover is a key to the activities of the Italians in Prague at this period and shows how much Italian Counter-Reformation iconography had become an accepted feature of early Baroque painting in Bohemia.

Prague 1974, cat. no. 12.

M.Š.

v.526
The Scourged Christ Standing by a Column
Small polychrome statue made of linden wood
H: 29.9 cm, w: 9 cm; diam. of pedestal
7 6 × 6 8 cm
1550–1600
Purchased in Prague, registered in the records in 1928
Prague, Národní muzeum, odd. starých Ženskych, inv. no. H2-14 551

The high quality of the artistic treatment suggests that this small statue originated in Prague. The gracious refinement of the carving, the sensitive polychroming, and the noble fragility of the scene, whose theme is highly dramatic, localize the work fairly convincingly within the cultural centre which was Prague. The statue must have been part of a larger whole. Three openings for pins in the base indicate that it was at some point attached to a small pedestal. The figure of Christ was evidently the centre of a more extensively narrative composition which was supplemented by two additional bailiffs, as we know from a later work, the popular and often copied gilded bronze group of the *Scourging* by Alessandro Algardi (Vienna, Kunsthistorisches Museum). The small scale and minutely detailed execution attest to the statue's intended use in the home. The mixture of Gothic residues (the subject, the shape of the loin-cloth, the naturalistic bulging of the veins) with elements of the Renaissance (the refined head with ornamentally carved hair and beard) and Mannerist (the spiral winding of the figure) styles is characteristic of the Czech milieu.

L.Sr.

v.527
Prague Woodcarver
St Wenceslas
Woodcarving
1600–10
St Wenceslas Church in Prosek
Prague, Muzeum hl. m. Prahy, inv. no. 9 661

The carving demonstrates the change in the representation of St Wenceslas during the period of Utraquism, prior to the Battle of the White Mountain, and in the hands of a local artist. At that time, the Patron of the Bohemian Lands lost his religious function and, for the most part (as in Krocín's fountain from 1591–96), is transformed into the political representative of these lands. In essence, this type was later adopted even by J. Bendl, and survived throughout the entire Baroque period.

I.K.

v.528
Daniel Altmann of Eidenburg
Active in the Bohemian Lands from the end of sixteenth century until 1625, Prague
St Peter and Paul
Wood, larger-than-life size, originally polychrome, gilded in Baroque style after 1711
From group of four statues (*St Peter, Paul, Augustine, Norbert*) on main altar of the Church of the Assumption of the Virgin Mary in Milevsko. The statues obviously come from the original main altar of the monastery church in Strahov, for which, according to an agreement still preserved, D. Altman carved them from the year 1618. His brother David had them gilded by 1633. They were probably moved to Milevsko after 1711 during the construction of the main altar of that town
Milevsko, kostel Navštívení P. Marie

As far as we can tell, D. Altman was influenced by the tradition of Augsburg woodcarving at the turn of the sixteenth and seventeenth centuries (main altar of the Church of St Ulric and Afra in Augsburg), and developed it in the Bohemian Lands. His strictly sculptural carvings (decoration of the altar in Litice near Pilsen from 1600) are only occasionally enlived by a late gothicizing deviation of drapery or a movement of the hand or head; they are not, however, lacking in grandeur.

Kořán 1988, p. 438.

I.K.

v.529
Prague woodcarver of first quarter of seventeenth century
Assumpta
Wood, polychrome from second quarter of eighteenth century, larger-than-life size
1626
Prague, kostel P. Marie Vítězné (Church of Our Lady of Victories), Talmberská chapel, 013585

The kind of the Assumpta, already known in the Bohemian Lands by the fourteenth century, is copied in the driest manner of Central European late Renaissance woodcarving, without artistic aspirations. The importance of the carving (as in the case of the contemporaneous relief of the Assumpta on the gable of the Church of the Our Lady before Týn) consists in the demonstrative and opportunist conversion of the donor to Catholicism. He converted when the church of the German Lutherans of the Lesser Town, consecrated to the Holy Trinity, became the Church of the Our Lady the Victorious.\

Blažíček 1958, p. 60.

I.K.

v.530
Ernst Heidelberger
St Francis of Paula
Wood, slightly larger-than-life size
Ca. 1627
Originally from the Pauline church in the Old Town; after 1780 moved to the Church of Our Lady before Týn
Prague, kostel P. Marie před Týnem, inv. no. 257 D (010003)

The statue in the Pauline church of the Holy Saviour stood either on the main altar, installed in 1627, or on the altar of St Francis of Paula, installed before 1659 by Daniel Pachta von Rayhofen and his wife. The likeness of the founder of the order is carried out as a 'vera effigies' of the saint, with the utmost noble restraint, and yet it impresses one as monumental and majestic. In a certain sense it is a muffled echo of the mystical verism of contemporaneous Spanish woodcarvings and definitely (besides the *Head of the Crucified Christ from Charles Bridge*, cat. no. v.531) the greatest artistic work of the first half of the seventeenth century in the Bohemian Lands.\

Blažíček 1958, p. 61; Kořán 1988, p. 440.

I.K.

V.531
Arnošt Heidelberger
Died Prague ca. 1657
Head of Crucified Christ from Charles Bridge
Wood, slightly larger-than-life size,
with frame 58 × 55 × 14
From the group *Crucifixion* on Charles
Bridge
1629
Prague, Arcibiskupský seminář, inv. no.
3158

The cross on Charles Bridge was already
standing in the fourteenth century; it was
taken down during the Calvinist iconoclasm in the reign of Friedrich Palatine
(Frederick V) in the years 1619–20 and re-
installed by Ferdinand II in 1629. In 1648 it
was destroyed by a shot during the
Swedish siege of the Prague Old Town, but
the head of the Crucified Christ was pi-
ously preserved by the Jesuits in the
Church of the Holy Saviour and, after the
dissolving of the order, in the Archiepiscopal seminary. After 1950 it was placed in
the Church of St Gothard in Bubeneč and
following the revival of the Archiepiscopal
seminary in Prague in 1990, it was returned. Despite the restraint in the expression, the carving allows for a whole range
of views, demonstrating the absolute
sculptural vision of its creator. In the transition from late Mannerism to the
Baroque, has emerged one of the most noble and artistically pure works of the seventeenth century in the Czech lands.

Kořán 1991, p. 41.

I.K.

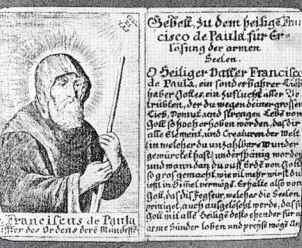

V.532
*Devotional image with Saint Francis of Paula
and a German prayer*
Copper engraving on paper
57.6 × 10.5 cm
Under the illustration *H. Franciscus de
Paula /St/üfter des Ordens dere/n/ Mün-
deste/n/*; Incipit of the prayer *Gebett zu
dem heilige/n/ Francisco de Paula /.../*.
Before 1650
From the collections of the sometime museum in Doupov; transferred to the collections of the Národní muzeum by the
museum in Karlovy Vary in 1957.
Prague, Národní muzeum, inv. no. H2-50
215

This small devotional work of graphic art
is most probably associated with the post-
White Mountain Prague milieu. In spite of
its primitive presentation and the mirror
image reversal, the picture clearly depicts
the venerated statue of St Francis of Paula,
to which numerous miracles were attributed and which stood in the Church of
St Salvatór (not far from the Old Town
Square), which belonged to the order of
Minimes after 1626. The statue is a characteristic example of early Baroque carving
in Prague from the circle of Arnošt Heidelberg (perhaps Abraham Melber?) and was
later transferred to the church of the
Blessed Virgin before Týn, where it still
stands.

L.Sr.

V.533
The Scourging at the Pillar
Rosy black alabaster, pedestal of
Slivenec marble
70 cm
1620–40
Prague, Jemniště, castle, Památkový ústav
středních Čech, inv. no. 104 JE 9 985

The statuette of the Flagellation comes
from the castle in Jemniště, but its Czech
origin has not been conclusively demonstrated. Only a definite analogy to the
work of Adriaen de Vries and the pedestal
of Slivenec marble suggest that the work
did emerge from a Czech (Prague) setting.

Comparable material, however, has not
been preserved and thus even the dating is
problematic.

Registration, in the Benešov district,
1911

M.Š.

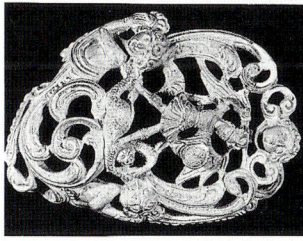

V.534
Archangel Michael
Carved calcite, repaired at the top with
plaster
H: 16 cm; w: 13 cm
QUIS UT DEUS
1525–50
Prague (?)
Jan Neuberg collection, the Neuberg fam-
ily seat (Cejeticky); 1892 bequeathed to
the Uměleckoprůmyslové muzeum
Prague, Uměleckoprůmyslové muzeum,
inv. no. 4 727

The model for a cast-metal appliance,
probably for a door knocker. The figure of
Michael, portrayed like a knight in armour
and a helmet and with a circular shield, is
taken from an Italian Renaissance model.
Two putti function as caryatids, and the
amorphous pixie-devil is derived from
Mannerism. This composition and the
Baroque calcite relief of the archangel
Michael from the collection of the
Carmelite monastery at Hradčany in
Prague (UPM, inv. no. 64 613, without accompanying figures) were taken from the
same model, which might provide evidence for the Czech origin of both variants.

D.S.

V.535
Jan Jiří Bendl
Ca. 1620–1680
Archangel Raphael
Wood
176.5 cm
1650
The carving came to the Národní galerie
from the dead-house of the church in Zlí-
chov, but one can assume that originally
it was a part of the main altar of the Old
Town Servit Church of St Michael, founded around the middle of the seventeenth
century by the Emperor Ferdinand III
Prague, Muzeum hl. m. Prahy, inv. no. 26
623

Because of its rotary movement, this statue is exceptional in this early period. The
sculptor successfully united Baroque dynamism with a Classical tendency. The relation to the stone angels of *Mariánská*
statue in Old Town Square is also certain;
the carving, however, is more delicate and
more successful in its entire execution.

Blažíček 1982, cat. no. 6.

Kořán 1991, p. 504.

I.K.

V.536
Jiří Gabriel Majer (Mayer)
In Prague 1613–1648
Landscape with a River
Pen-and-ink drawing in black shade, grey, greyish-black and greyish-green
14.7 × 18.7 cm
Girg Gabriel Meyer Maller gesel von Eger geschehen in Prag 1613; dedication on reverse: *Zu Ehrenn und freindlichere Gedechnis schreibe Ich dies G. G. Meyer von Eger meinem guden Freidnt Jobst Mˆllr von Stadt Hagen zu guden gedechnis im Prag Anno 1613 m.*
1613
Purchased for the Národní galerie collection in 1925
Prague, Národní galerie v Praze, inv. no. K 4495

E. Fučíková, who published Mayer's drawing, pointed out that in addition to landscape painters working in Rudolf's court, there were also other artists in Prague pursuing this genre. One of these was Mayer, whose presence in Prague is noted in 1613, when he is mentioned as a painter's journeyman. In 1617 he became a burgher of the Lesser Town, and a year later, a member of the Old Town painters' guild. This drawing evinces Mayer's knowledge of the works of Pieter Stevens. The next,

and thus far the last, known work by Mayer is the coat-of-arms painted in 1627-31, allegedly in accordance with Bartholomeus Spranger's proposal for Rudolf II's privilege to the painters' guild in 1595.

M.Š.

V.537
Jan Jiří Hering
Eschwege 1587–Prague 1648
Minerva (Sapentia) and the Muses
Drawing in brown ink, washed grey, white highlights with undersketch in black chalk
12.8 × 17.8 cm
1610–20 (?)
Acquired by the Národní muzeum in Prague
Prague, Národní galerie v Praze, inv. no. K 28 761

The drawing was ascribed to Hering by E. Fučíková, who drew attention to the equipoise of landscape and figural components of the artist's work. The drawing bears Hering's characteristic mark economical drawing in ink, which defines the size, and is completed in its lighting effect by a rich wash. In its subject-matter and in its composition (cf. *Minerva Introducing Painting to the Liberal Arts* by Aegidius Sadeler after Hans von Aachen), Hering's drawing approaches the quality of work associated with the Rudolfine court circle. Hering was evidently at the beginning of his acitivity in Prague and at that time in uncertain contact with the court artists. After 1620, however, he worked, as far as we know, exclusively for church commis-

sioners, for whom he made sizeable altar pictures.

Prague 1978-79, cat. no. 15.

Šroněk 1996 (entry for H.G. Hering).

M.Š.

V.538
Karel Škréta
Prague 1610–Prague 1674
Madonna with Child and Book
Drawing in brown pen; underdrawing graffitoed on yellowed, watermarked paper.
12.1 × 13 cm
After 1640
Transferred from the Národní museum in 1949
Prague, Národní galerie v Praze, Grafická sbírka, inv. no. K 27 932

The emblematic character of this small-scale drawing suggests that it may have

been a design for a graphic. In composition it slightly resembles the centre of the commemoration of the Stará Boleslav Palladio, with a Madonna in the middle surrounded by angels. However, no final version of the drawing, either as a graphic or as a painting, is known. It is definitely an early sketch, as can be seen both from the monumental conception, particularly of the head of the Virgin Mary, and from the rapid brushwork; authorship was attributed to Škréta particularly because of the character of the drawing, which is consistent with an Italian schooling.

Unpublished.

A.V.

V.539
Karel Škréta
Prague 1610–Prague 1674
The Czech Lands Commemorate Palladio – Virgin Mary of Stará Boleslav
Drawing in brown pen and brush; underdrawing graffitoed on yellowed, watermarked paper
30.8 × 38.2 cm
Before 1650
Prague, Národní galerie v Praze, Grafická sbírka, inv. no. K 1 642

Design for unrealised graphic. The aim of the drawing is confirmed by the fact that Palladio's figures are in mirror image, and

by the simple and 'readable' central composition. The Madonna is adored by angels bearing stars. The illustration was clearly ordered by members of the Šternberg family, recalled by the stars in the angels' hands, which do not here have a Marian signification, or at least have a double signification. The shaping of the subject is linked to the concrete event of the reacquisition of the Palladio by Bohemia in 1650.

Prague 1934, cat. no. 32; Milan 1966, cat. no. 25; Prague, Národní galerie 1974, cat. no. 175; Prague, Národní galerie 1976, cat. no. 34.

Kramář, Novotný 1934, cat. no. 32; Loriš 1949, p. 189, Neumann 1951, pp. 87, 132, fig. 161; Milan 1966, cat. no. 25; Neumann 1974, cat. no. 175; Neumann 1976, cat. no. 34.

A.V.

V.540
Karel Škréta
Prague 1610–Prague 1674
Study for the Figure of Virgin Mary Dolorosa and of an Angel in Flight
Drawing in brown-grey pen; underdrawing graffitoed
26.4 × 18.8 cm
Ca. 1645
Placed in the Národní galerie as a deposit of the Czechoslovak State Bank, which acquired the work in 1956
Prague, Národní galerie v Praze, Grafická sbírka, inv. no. DK 4 631.

These versions of figures of suffering

saints on a previously unpublished sketch page (confirmed by M. Zlatohlávek) are clearly studies for the *Virgin Mary Dolorosa* from the painting *Crucifixion with the Dolorosa and Angels* in the chapel of St Barbara in St Nicholas' church in Malá Strana. The outstretched figure of the angel is also reused in the same painting; it can be compared with the angel floating over the souls in purgatory in the background of the painting. The very sharpened pen gave the artist's hand a somewhat dry appearance.

Unpublished.

A.V.

V.541
Karel Škréta
Prague 1610–Prague 1674
St Sigismond
Drawing in brown pen and brush; under-drawing graffitoed on yellowed, water-marked paper
15.7 × 10.2 cm
1640-50
Transferred from the Národní museum, Prague, Národní galerie v Praze, Grafická sbírka, inv. no. K 24 539.

Design for graphic. From the overall conception, the iconography of the subject and the small scale it can even be assumed

that this was to be one image from a planned cycle, either of the life of the saint, or of a collection of saints. The drawing lacks the usual certainty both in the pen and brushwork and in the structure of the figures, particularly that of the Saint. In the group of figures kneeling on the left we also fail to find the qualities we know from Škréta's drawings. This may be an early work by the young artist.

Unpublished.

A.V.

V.542
Karel Škréta
Prague 1610–Prague 1674
St Charles Borromeus Visiting Plague Victims
Drawing in brown pen, grey brush; underdrawing graffitoed on yellowed, water-marked paper
28.1 × 16.9 cm
Ca. 1647
Prague, Národní galerie v Praze, Grafická sbírka, inv. no. K 1 645.

This drawing, which may have been a sketch for the well-known painting of the same theme, differs from it markedly both in format and in the conception of the

subject. The drawing has a tense and excited atmosphere: from amongst the endless and tortuous coils of bodies of the sick rises the figure of the Saint, who looks ecstatically towards a vision of Madonna and Child in the clouds. The formation of space using pleats of drapery fluttering from the sky – unique in Škréta's work – is one of the techniques of illusion used frequently in the later Czech Baroque painting of the eighteenth century.

Prague 1910, cat. no. 72a; Prague 1912/1169/1; Prague 1934, cat. no. 43; Milan 1966, cat. no. 24; Prague 1974, cat. no. 115; Prague 1976, cat. no. 31; Essen 1977,

cat. no. 79; Paris 1981, cat. no. 163.

Bergner-Herain 1910, p. 5, no.10, tab. XVI-II; Rouček 1943, p. 235; Loriš 1947, pp. 189-90, pl.102; Loriš 1947/A, pl.1; Loriš 1949, p.189, pl.102; Neumann 1951, pp. 87, 131, pl.160; Neumann 1970, p. 205; Neumann 1974, p. 203, pl.139; Blažíček, Preiss, Hejdová 1977, pp. 151, 153; Preiss 1979, pp. 34-35.

A.V.

V.543
Karel Škréta
Prague 1610–Prague 1674
The Assumption of the Virgin Mary
Drawing in brown pen and brush; under-drawing graffitoed on yellowed, water-marked paper
22.9 × 17.5 cm
Signed in the bottom left: *Screta del.*
Ca. 1649.
Transferred from the Národní museum in 1949
Prague, Národní galerie v Praze, Grafická sbírka, inv. no. K 27 922

The study of the *Assumption of the Virgin*

Mary was done for the altar painting in the church of the Virgin Mary before Týn. This sketch is very close to the final form of the painting in the arrangement of its basic components. Stylistically it differs from the majority of Škréta's drawings: here the broader, soft penmarks and vigorous brushstrokes give a greater succulence. The author was probably interested primarily in a study of the distribution and contrasts of light. He uses fuller tones than is usual in his drawings. It is evidently the difference in the draughtsman's expression that has led other researchers to be cautious in attributing the work to Škréta.

Prague 1974.

Neumann 1974.

A.V.

V.544
Karel Škréta
Prague 1610–Prague 1674
The Resurrection of Christ with Armour-bearers
Drawing in brown pen, grey brush; under-drawing graffitoed on yellowed, water-marked paper
31 × 20.4 cm
Before 1650
Prague, Národní galerie v Praze, Grafická sbírka, inv. no. K 1 647

The painting or graphic for which this drawing was the model is unknown in Škréta's oeuvre. The care taken with the

drawing and its elaborateness suggest that the artist probably intended to use it as a model for a more serious work. (The same can be said of the version with angels.) This version with armour-bearers, where the artist attempts to depict a moment of surprise, of fright, even of terror, allows the use of several striking short-cuts in the figures of the soldiers. Their small size is thus emphasized in contrast with the monumental frontality of the ascending figure of the risen Christ, who is, in addition, the only source of light for the entire scene.

Bergner-Herain 1910; Prague 1934; Milan

1966, cat. no. 23; Prague 1974, cat. no. 117; Sarasota 1972, cat. no. 24; Prague 1974, cat. no. 116; Dresden 1977, cat. no. 35; Prague 1976, cat. no. 29; Essen 1977, cat. no. 78; Paris 1981, cat. no. 164.

Bergner 1910, p. 91; Bergner-Herain 1910, p.5, cat. no. 8; Central Europe 1972, p.17, cat. no. 24; Loriš 1949, p. 190; Neumann 1951, pp. 87, 131; Sobotík 1972, p. 17; Neumann 1974, cat. no. 117; *Meisterzeichnungen* 1977; Preiss 1979, pp. 36-37; Blažíček, Preiss, Hejdová 1977, pp. 148, 150, 154, cat. no. 78; Paris cat. 1981.

A.V.

V.545
Karel Škréta
Prague 1610–Prague 1674
The Resurrection of Christ with Angels
Drawing in brown pen, grey brush; under-drawing graffitoed on yellowed, water-marked paper
31.2 × 20.3 cm
Before 1650
Prague, Národní galerie v Praze, Grafická sbírka, inv. no. K 1 984

In comparison with the relatively simple, rectangular composition of the version with armour-bearers, the *Resurrection of Christ with Angels* is more elaborate and, at

the same time, more rhetorical. While the figure of Christ in the upper part is similar to the previous version rotated in the framework of a diagonal composition, a complicated story is played out in the lower part of the drawing. Worthy of attention are the figures of angels lifting away a heavy tombstone next to the unsuspecting sleeping soldiers, who are masterly depictions of different types of human figures. The source of light in this composition is less specific; the light is more diffused.

Prague 1934, cat. no. 42; Milan 1966, cat. no. 22; Prague 1974, cat. no. 116; Prague

1976, cat. no. 30; Essen 1977, cat. no. 80; Paris 1981, cat. no. 165.

Bergner 1910, p. 71; Dolenský 1911; Kramář, Novotný 1934, no. 42; Loriš 1947, fig. 3; Loriš 1949, p. 190; Neumann 1951, pp. 87, 131, fig. 161; Milan cat. 1966; Neumann 1974, cat. no. 116; Preiss 1979, pp. 38-39; Prague catalogue 1976, cat. no. 30; Blažíček, Preiss, Hejdová 1977, cat. no. 80; Paris catalogue 1981, cat. no. 165.

A.V.

V.546
Karel Škréta
Prague 1610–Prague 1674
The Martyrdom of St Lawrence
Drawing in brown pen and brush, under-drawing graffitoed
26.3 × 34.5 cm
In the bottom left-hand corner: *C. Screta*
Before 1650
Gift of Vojtěch Lanna
Prague, Národní galerie v Praze, Grafická sbírka, inv. no. K 1 287

Probably a design for an altarpiece. The painter's Italian experience is quite clear in this drawing. As P. Preiss has pointed out, it is most influenced by the work of Titian (see literature). However, the artist's preoccupation with the nude, the striking shortenings and shaping are close to his other works of the period. In the otherwise relatively traditional iconographic composition of the subject, there is an interesting gesture by one of the men in the background who points at the statue of a pagan god, perhaps to show the Christian the 'true faith' to which he should have confessed.

Prague 1934, no. 39; Milan 1966, cat. no. 39 Prague 1974, cat. no. 118; Prague 1976, cat. no. 32; Essen 1977, cat. no. 81; Prague 1996.

Neumann 1951, pp. 88, 132, fig. XIX; Preiss 1979, pp. 38-39; Blažíček, Preiss, Hejdová 1977; Sobotík 1972, p. 17; Neumann 1974, cat. no. 118; Preiss 1996.

A.V.

V.547
Acta Consistorii sub utraque
Paper codex, 327 ff., with paper-board cover. Cloth binding combined with brown polished leather dates from restoration of the manuscript in the second half of the twentieth century. Original binding of brown polished leather with embossed pattern dates from the end of the sixteenth century or the start of the seventeenth century. Pattern preserved on raincover.
32.5 × 24 × 6.5 cm
1539-54
Prague, Lower Consistory of the church of Our Lady before Týn

Originally in the document collection of the Utraquist Consistory. After its liquidation in 1621, the documents of the Lower Consistory were presumably transferred to Vienna. Later this was in the Jesuit collections and, after the dissolution of the order, in the property of the philosophy faculty, in its doctoral collegium. At the time of the organization of the university archives by Adolf Bachmann, the manuscripts of the Utraquist Consistory were in the provincial archives. Later these manuscripts, which did not belong to the university, were assembled by Bachmann into a separate group called, quite inappropriately, *Economica*.

Prague, Archiv Univerzity Karlovy, Economica, inv. no. B 2

Kučera–Truc 1961.

I.Č.

V.548
Fabián Puléř (Pulíř)
Ústí nad Labem c. 1520–Prague 1562 or 1563.
Gradual of the Metropolitan Church of St Vitus, first part
Latin Catholic hymnbook, 273 pages, parchment. Original leather cover with die-stamp decoration
62.6 × 43 cm; cover 66 × 43 cm
1551-52
Prague, Library of the Metropolitan Chapter of St Vitus, Ms. sign. P-10

Large illuminated hymnbooks by the Literary Brethren, ordered by Utraquists as well as Catholics, are still an important source of documentation about burgher culture in the second half of the sixteenth century. The Saint Vitus hymnbook was produced in the workshop of the scribe, humanist and custodian of the Old Town clock Jan Táborský z Klokotská Hora (Tábor 1500–Prague 1572), as a result of an order from the members of the chapter. Táborský's workshop was responsible for the greater part of hymnbook production in the middle of the sixteenth century. The distinguished illustrator, and apparently also painter, Puléř, and his assistant collaborated with Táborský. Puléř's work is both a late offspring of the art of the Danube school and an early example of the impact of international Mannerism. The gradual contains 19 large initials with figural scenes, ornamental decoration of the borders, and monograms marked with the double-portrait of scribe and artist in the manner of an epitaph (f. 30).

Kropáček 1988, pp. 199, 203; Vacková 1989, p. 94.

J.Kr.

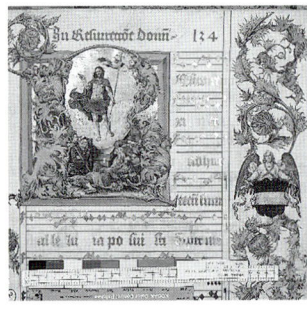

V.549
Czech Master
Hymnbook of the Church of the Virgin Mary before Týn, second part
249 pages, parchment. Original leather cover with die-stamp decoration showing busts of saints, humanists and reformers
57 × 37.8 cm; cover 60.5 × 40 cm
Ca. 1570
Prague, National Library, Křižovnická knihovna, Ms. XVII A 6

The second part of the hymnbook of the Literary Brethren from the choir of the principal church in the Old Town was moved, along with the first part, during the reign of the Emperor Josef, to the Library of the Order of the Knights of the Cross with the Red Star; for this reason both are often referred to in older literature as the Hymnbooks of the Knights of the Cross (*křižovnické kancionály*). The decoration of the second consists only of six initials and ornaments on the edges of the pages. It is related to the style of Fabián Pulíř, who, with his assistants, created the basic illustration for the first part in 1559 (there is also supplementary decoration from 1575 and 1592). On folio 1 is the large initial *P* (for *poslal*, 'transmitted'), and a picture of the Angel of the Annunciation.

Chytil 1906, p.184.

J.Kr.

V.550
Matouš Ornys of Lindperk
Died Prague 1600/01
Section II of the Lesser Town Czech Utraquist Gradual
Hymnbook, 311 pages, parchment; original leather binding, decorated with ink stamps portraying half-length pictures of the saints and reformers
Pages 58.2 × 38.5 cm; binding 61.8 × 40 cm
Decorated between 1561 and 1573
Prague, Archiv hl. města Prahy, RKP č. 1869

This second section of the St Vitus choir association's hymnbook is a standard example of Bohemian book illumination in the last quarter of the sixteenth century. It was produced in the workshop of Jan Kantor the Elder (died Prague 1582). Several city craftsmen collaborated on creating the miniatures and M. Ornys, a book illuminator, portrait artist and land surveyor, was responsible for the overall decoration. His choice of motifs and use of colour are closely linked with northern Mannerism. St Wenceslas and King Charles IV are depicted on the title page, accompanied by the trademark of the maltsters' guild (fol. 1).

Kropáček 1988, pp. 199, 201; Vacková 1989, p. 95 (with a review of recent literature).

J.Kr.

V.551
Matouš Ornys of Lindperk (Ptáček)
Died Prague 1600/01
Old Town Gradual
340 pages, parchment; original leather
cover decorated with impressions showing busts of prophets, saints and personifications of the Virtues
57.8 × 38.5 cm; cover 60.3 × 40 cm
Incription: *Jan Komor.../ knihař 1565*.
1561-67
Prague, National Library, Manuscript MS
XVII A 40

Written from 1561 in the workshop of Jan
Táborský of Klokotská Hora (died 1582).

The rich set of painted illustrations, rich
from the point of view both of ornamentation and of its colouring and stylization,
show how the Mannerist style found
favour in the work of Matouš Ornys and
his assistant. It includes initials, marginal
decorations and large figural scenes,
whose conception recalls altar paintings.
From the point of view of cultural history
fol. 78v, CVI, is significant. The large initial *D* (for *Dítě*, 'child'), with an image of
the Nativity, and the marginal decoration
with the monogram of Christ's *IHS* was
ordered by Jan Mystopolus, dean of St
Apollinaire's in Prague New Town, preacher in the Bethlehem Chapel in Prague Old

Town and administrator of the Utraquist
Archbishopric of Prague.

Vacková 1989, p. 95.

J.Kr.

V.552
Tadeáš Aquilinus
Gradual Latin-Czech for Five Voices
31 × 20.5 cm
1578
Prague, monastery of the Premonstratensians at Strahov, inv. no. DA II 3

Tadeáš Aquilinus was a typical representative of the burgher intelligentsia of the
early New Age. He represents that quiet
but essential level of educated people for
whom a universal education enabled them
to find work not only as tutors at the primary schools and in the offices of the
towns, but also to become associated, al-

beit on the periphery, with the cultural activities of Prague. Aquilinus's religious tolerance is typical: his beliefs did not prevent him from working as a clerk in the
service of Catholic institutions. Born during the first half of the sixteenth century,
probably into a family of Prague burghers,
he became one of the many figures who
formed the inconspicuous activities of intellectual spawn into Renaissance Bohemia. In the early 1560s he was employed
at the Premonstratensian monastery in
Strahov as a guard and later as a financial
clerk. He became the author of a land and
duties register in 1564 and instituted a
thorough specialized book about vine-

yards. He was a member of the Literate
Brethren choir at St Michael in Opatovice,
whose members composed the five-voice
gradual which has been preserved. In autumn 1586 he wrote his will and died on 7
May of the following year.

J.P.

V.553
The Resurrection of Our Lord
Miniature tempera painting, gilded in
places, on parchment
18.1 × 18.4 cm
Unsigned; on the back are the music and
text from a Czech hymnal, with the words
/.../ ú geum na demi diwněyssi /etc/.
1575-1600
Purchased for the Národní muzeum in
1902, probably from the Prague business-
man Vincene Artur Duda
Prague, Národní muzeum, inv. no.
H2-5 298

The miniature was cut out of a Czech

hymnal with a fairly large format. The
scene of Christ's Resurrection is executed
in a standard form which became fixed
during the sixteenth century. The work's
somewhat inferior artistic quality, evident
mainly in the primitive depiction of the
sleeping centurions, indicates that it was
executed by a less successful minaturist
working for the bourgeois milieu. The
most interesting aspect of the entire
painting is its setting into a profiled, purple sort of picture frame which is covered
abundantly with white flowering columbine. The columbine (aquilegia), which
appeared in Christian art until the end of
the sixteenth century as a symbol of the

Holy Spirit, is intended in this case as an
allusion to the eagle, the symbol of eternal
life and of Christ's Crucifixion (Psalms
103:5).

L.Sr.

V.554
*Document by which Pope Pius IV Confirms
the Appointment of Antonín Brus of Mobel-
nice as Archbishop of Prague and Thus Re-
news the Occupancy of the Prague Archbishopric*
Original parchment, Latin text, lead seal
(bull) on hemp tassel (string)
55.3 × 76.7 × 6.2 cm
5 September 1561
Prague, Státní ústřední archiv, archivní
fond Archiv pražského arcibiskupství-
listiny (depository of the Prague archbishopric), inv. no. 84, sign. C 103/1 and 2, box
2002a

The re-establishment of the Prague archbishopric was the result of extremely complicated private negotiations between Emperor Ferdinand I and the papal Curia in
1560 and 1561, in connection with the intensive preparations for the third session
of the Council of Trent. Pope Pius IV, in a
bull of 5 September 1561, confirmed Antonín Brus's appointment as Prague Archbishop, and accorded to Ferdinand I and
his successors, the Bohemian Catholic
Kings, the rights of patronage and presentation over the Prague archbishopric.
These were based on the Emperor's pledge
that he would secure the finances of the
metropolitan seat. In compensation for

damages incurred by the church, the Emperor designated a yearly sum of nearly a
million Meissen groschen from the kingdom's funds, of which 350,000 were for the
Archbishop. The yearly salary was to be
paid by the Bohemian chamber out of barrel tax. For his residence, the Archbishop
received the house of Florián Gryspek of
Gryspach in Hradčany.

Kávka-Skýbová 1969; Skýbová 1994.

D.Č.

V.555
*Document by which Rudolf II Raises the
Archbishop of Prague, Zbyněk Berka of Dubá
and Lipá, and his Successor Archbishops of
Prague, to the Nobility*
Original parchment, Latin text (part of
the entitlement and several words and letters of the text written in gold tincture),
wax seal on a tassel with a string of gold
thread. Lower part of circular box also
preserved.
55.3 × 65 × 12.1 cm
15 June 1603
Prague, Státní ústřední archiv, archivní
fond Archiv pražského arcibiskupství-
listiny, (depository of the Prague arch-

bishopric), inv. no. 154

The Privilege is important both for its content and for the broader circumstances of
its origin. Rudolf II had tried until 1599 to
preserve the status quo in the religious relations of the Czech kingdom, and paid no
particlular attention to the problems or
tangible needs of the Catholic church in
Bohemia. In conflicts of interest with the
Prague archbishopric he stressed his own
sovereign interests. Archbishop Zbyněk,
advocate of Catholic reforms, was Archbishop from 1592 to 1606, a period that
saw ever-worsening political and religious
conflicts in his diocese. The act of eleva-

tion to the nobility was thus undertaken
primarily with an eye to the domestic political scene, and had the effect of raising
the prestige of the Archbishop and of the
Roman Catholic church in Bohemia and
the other lands of the Crown, and of en-
couraging the radical Catholic group in its
chosen direction.

Vacek 1896, pp. 25-45; České 1900, pp.
482-84; Podlaha 1905, pp. 1-5, 108-13; Do-
biáč 1919, pp. 70-71; Stloukal 1925; Matouček 1931, pp. 16-41, 252-92; Sakař
1935, p. 78.

D.Č.

V.556
Inventory of the Archbishop's House
(Palace) from 30 March 1606 – 'Inventory
of all things for the sometime good memory of His Gracious Lord Zbyněk Berka of
Dubá and Lipá, Archbishop of Prague, of
all effects, carried out on Thursday after
Easter 1606'
Original paper, Czech text
33.1 × 21.3 cm
30 March 1606
Prague, Státní ústřední archiv, Stará manipulace, inv. no. 872, sig. E 32/48/I, box
714, ff. 127r-159v (text only to f. 156v; also
includes three original supplements, ff.
129r-130v, 139r-140v)

Zbyněk Berka, the first member of the
Czech high nobility to occupy the Prague
metropolitan see after 1561, led an active
social life despite his very limited financial
means. The Archbishop's house served as
headquarters for the Prague diocese: it
was both the Archbishop's residence and
his office. It also, however, served his social life, for example, in 'lunches' given by
the Archbishop, at which high radical
Catholic politics was created. The inventory testifies to Zbyněk's efforts to adapt the
residence for the requirements of pomp
and state. The inventory demonstrates the
interests of Zbyněk Berka as a collector, a
fact not recorded by any other source. The

house contained, or temporarily stored, almost sixty portraits of important people –
emperors, popes, cardinals, archdukes,
Bavarian princes, French kings and so on.
Despite the influences of the culture and
lifestyle of the court, he preferred objects
with a superficial showpiece function, and
had little regard for artistic quality.

Tischer 1905, pp. 299-301; Tischer 1908,
pp. 1-56; Muchka 1988, p. 108; Krčalová
1989, pp. 76, 83, 84.

D.Č.

V.557
Prague Painter (?)
*Portrait of Jiří (Georg) Barthold Pontanus of
Breitenberg*
Oil on canvas
92 × 75 cm.
In the upper right a Latin inscription with
the name of the portrait subject and the
year, accompanied by a coat of arms. The
carved polychrome, edicule-type frame
(not exhibited) culminates in a cleft fron-
ton. At the bottom is a commemorative
inscription in Latin and Czech.
Ca. 1600
Most, Church of the Assumption of the
Virgin Mary

Most, Deanery Church, II./2

The Catholic priest, poet and playwright
Jiří Barthold (Berthold) Pontanus (named
after his birthplace, Most) of Breitenberg,
who died in 1614, was a teacher of poetry
and rhetoric and a canon in St. Vitus's
cathedral, raised to the nobility in 1588,
and head of the Chapter in St Vitus from
1593. In the cultural circles of the Premonstratensian order, he was the principal
representative of late Latin humanism. In
his hymns he made new contributions to
the fame of the Czech patrons, including
St Ivan (1592). He dedicated a selection of
his sermons to Rudolf II. The collection

Poetický kalendář (*Poetic Calendar*) from
1608 is the literary counterpart to the
landscapes and miniature still-lives of the
Rudolfine painters. The as yet unidentified painter of the formal portrait was undoubtedly influenced by the early court
paintings of Bartholomeus Spranger and
his followers.

Bitnar 1939, p. 87n.; Hejnic and Martínek
Prague 1966, p. 137n.; Poche 1978, p. 434.

J.Kr.

V.558
Goblet with the Coat of Arms of Jiří
(Georg) Pontanus of Breitenberg
Clear, greenish filigree glass, enamel-
painted
18.5 cm
Remnants of the inscription: *de Breiten-
berk ... Pragensis ... 1595*
1595
Archaeological find from the waste pit in
Vikářská street at Prague Castle (I.
Borovsky 1957); reconstruction by E.
Vosátková 1982
Prague, Správa Pražského hradu, inv. no.
PHA 8

The mould-blown goblet has a cylindrical
bowl and a relief-decorated stem with lion
mascarons. The bowl and foot are decorated with alternating white and intertwining
vertical stripes. The humanist poet Pontanus of Breitenberg (d. 1614) was a canon
of the Svatovice chapter and became
cathedral provost in 1593. He was the
protonotary and general vicar of the archbishops of Prague (Martin Medek, Zbyněk
Berka of Dubá, Karel Lamberk and Jan Lohelius). The goblet was most probably
made by one of the glassworks that produced glass for Prague Castle during the
time of Rudolf II, either the Schürer glassworks in Falknov or the glassworks in

Broumy. The shape and technique of the
goblet relate it to Venetian models, but the
quality and colouration of the raw material bear the characteristics of domestically
produced glass.

Prague 1984.

Hetteš 1964, pp. 39-53; Drahotová-Hejdová 1989, cat. no. 30.

O.D.

V.559
Jiří (Georg) Barthold Pontanus of Breiten-
berg
*Life of St Ivan, whose Body Rests the in Lord
in the Church of St John beneath the Rock*
1592
Prague, Premonstratensian Monastery at
Strahov, Library, inv. no. DQ IV 4, op. 8.

The publication of the *Life of St Ivan*, written by the provost of the St Vitus Chapter,
Jiří Pontanus of Breitenberg, in 1592 (also
in Latin and German) was linked to the
growing cult of the Saint in St John beneath the Rock towards the end of the sixteenth century. For his translation into

Czech, Pontanus used a latin text of the
legend of St Ivan contained in manuscript
in the chapter library. The Latin and German editions have a syncretic character,
because the author combined in them the
text of a Latin legend with the narrative of
Václav Hájek of Libočany. The engraving
on the title page of Pontanus's book depicts the legendary meeting of the hermit
Ivan with John the Baptist.

Kořán 1987, pp. 219-37.

J.R.

V.560
Jiří (Georg) Barthold Pontanus of Breitenberg
Spiritual Occupation for the Czech Crown
14 × 21 cm (open book)
1599
Prague, Národní museum library, inv. no.
36G

The Czech version of Pontanus's prayers
contains, alongside prayers to traditional
Czech patrons, a prayer to John Nepomuk,
referred to as 'holy John, confessor to
queen Johanna, wife of King Wenceslas'.
The woodcut with the canon at prayer
used to be considered the oldest known

depiction of John Nepomuk. However,
given that the same block was used by the
printer before the title of the book was
known, and that the canon's face has striking features which recall known likenesses
of Pontanus, the picture is probably a depiction of the author himself. The publisher's use of this woodcut for the prayer
to John Nepomuk testifies to the fact that
the martyr's iconographic appearance had
not yet been constituted.

J.R.

V.561
Jiří (Georg) Barthold Pontanus of Breitenberg
Hymnorum sacrorum de B. M. V. Mariae et S. Patronis S. R. Bohemiae Libri tres, Pragae 1602
1602
Prague, Premonstratensian Monastery at Strahov, Library, inv. no. FP VI, 23.

The Provost of the St Vitus metropolitan chapter, Jiří Barthold, named Pontanus after his birthplace, Most, is the principal representative of early Catholic history writing in the religious divisions of Bohemia in the period before the Battle of the White Mountain. Pontanus's anti-Baroque patriotism was expressed in his programmatic renewal of the cults of the patron saints of Bohemia, and even by its extension with the addition of other individuals (St Zdislav of Lemberg and so on). It is not by chance that Barthold introduces into the assembly of patron saints of Bohemia John Nepomuk. Although the text of the Latin hymn speaks of John as a martyr, the accompanying illustration is conceived principally as an image of a confessor. This is the first programmatic depiction of John Nepomuk.

Prahou ve stopách baroka, Museum of National Literature, 1978.

Petráň 1971.

J.R.

V.562
Platter
Wood, inside surface inlaid with mother-of-pearl, outer surface painted with coloured lacquers
Diam: 71.5 cm
1598?
Jiří Barthold of Breitenberg, provost of the metropolitan capitula (1594–1614)
Prague, Treasury of Saint Vitus Cathedral, inv. no. 260, now K-259

Inside surface: around the large, central roundel are six smaller roundels with the motif of a blossoming lotus on a background of leafwork with small and large flowers. A band of scale pattern decoration runs around the oval rim. Outer surface: a flowering bush appears on the bottom, and the edges feature bands of geometric, stylized floral motifs. According to A. Podlaha, one of the mother-of-pearl petals was carved with an emblem (the archangel Michael above a tower) and the letters *G.B.A.B.* – the initials of Georgius Bartholdus Braitenberg – along with the date *1598*, which is no longer extant.

Podlaha and Šittler 1903, 194, no. 296, ill. 175; Podlaha and Šittler 1903, 124; Podlaha 1948, 41, no. 78.

H.Kn.

V.563
Register of Births and Marriages at the Church of St Thomas in the Lesser Town
Book made of paper, semi-leather bound
32.5 × 21.5 × 6.5 cm
1588–1632
Parish office
Prague, Archives of the City of Prague, inv. no. TO N1 O1

The parish house of St Thomas' in Lesser Town was one of the most affluent at the end of the sixteenth century. Among its baptism and marriage records may be found some of the most prominent personalities of Rudolfine Prague. The majority of entries are recorded in Latin. The exhibit documents the marriage of one Italian builder: 'Dominicus de Bossi von Monte from Italy concludes a marriage with the widow of Jakub de Bossi (circa 1603)'.

Hlavsa 1954; Cakrtova 1979; Bartunek 1938), pp.58-61, 119-121; Podlaha 1916, p.36, roc. XXX (1930) p.53.

J.Me.

V.564
Register of Births from the Church of St Henry in Prague's New Town
Paper book, leather bound, restored.
31 × 10 × 1.2 cm
1584–1600
Parish office
Prague, Archives of the City of Prague, inv. no. JCH N 1

The oldest Prague register contains notes of baptisms held at the parish church of St Henry in Prague's New Town. At the time when the register was founded, the church belonged to the Utraquists, a reformist group of Christians who took communion in both kinds. The parish boundaries reached as far as Porice, and the parish communities of Kyje, Malesice, Sterboholy, Hostivice, Hostivicky and Hrdlorezy, which were sold to the church authorities in 1520, held their baptisms here. In the fourteenth century a school here had been administered by the parish office, where such sixteenth-century characters as M. Pavel Kristian of Koldin and Jan Kampanus Vodnánsky would be active. The church also had a choir of Literate Brethren. The records are written in Czech. Exhibited here is folio 1 from 1584.

Mendelova 1992; Mendelova 1987, DP.

VII/2, pp. 340-355, AMP, 1987; Hlavsa 1954; Cakrtova 1979.

J.Me.

V.565
Prague Goldsmith
Crown of the Abbess of St George's
Gilt silver, stones; centre: thirty diamonds (five with tabulated cut, two rhombs, seventeen baguettes and six small rhombs); on the fibula: four emeralds, four rubies on the baldaquin, an opal, above a large garnet of rhodolite; diadem: four amethysts, two garnets of hessonite, two garnets of rhodolite, four citrines, two orange chalcedonic stones, four blue doublets; upper series: four olivines, four garnets of rhodolite, one turquoise; forty-three bored river pearls of an average 4–6 mm in length (mineralogical determination by Dr Jaroslav Hyrsl). Red velvet, pounded gold thread
1553, biretta 1836
VIRGO LUDMILLA A BLYZYW ABBATISSA ME FECIT MDLIII
1553–1782
Benedictine convent of St Jiri; Prague Castle, 1782–1803, Marie Terezie Harnach of Harnach, Prague; 1803 Adam Count Dohalsky, Prague; 1803–1836 St Vitus' treasury, Prague; 1836–1918 Noblewomen's Institute, Prague Castle, 1918–50, St Vitus' Chapter, Prague
Prague, Administration of Prague Castle; location: Národní galerie, St George's monastery, chapel of St Anna; (on long-term loan) inv. no. K 362

The crown was completed for Abbess Ludmila Blizivska of Bliziva (who was abbess from 1541 to 1562), using stones from older crowns. This magnificent crown represented not only the distinction of the order for the abbess of St George's, but also the highest position among the Czech orders of nuns, carrying equal rank with the Archbishop of Prague.

Zap 1857, pp. 89–90; Podlaha; Poche 1974, ill. 16; Poche 1983.

D.S.

v.566

Prague Goldsmith
Crozier of the Abbess of St George's
Copper and gilt silver, black and red
paint, stones: nine amethysts (taken from
older jewellery), two rhombs of garnet-
rhodolite, two citrines, ten crystals, two
pieces of green glass, two carnalites, two
yellow chalcedonic stones
Scroll: H: 23 cm; max. W: 14 cm
1303, stick ca. 1533, extended ca. 1553, additions 1836
Prague
1553–1782
Benedictine convent of St George, Prague
Castle; 1782–1803 Marie Terezie Harnach

of Harnach, Prague; 1803 Adam Count
Dohalsky, Prague; 1803–1806 St Vitus'
treasury, Prague; 1836–1918 Noblewom-
en's Institute, Prague Castle; 1918–1950
St Vitus' Chapter, Prague
Prague, Administration of Prague Castle;
location: Národní galerie, St George's
Convent collection of old Czech art (on
long-term loan), inv. no. K 123, (formerly
VP 499)

The pedum, as the only insignia of the
continuity of the abbot's office, was always
handed down. Therefore, when it was restored in about 1553, fragments of a Gothic stick were used (three inscribed bands)

dating from 1303, from the time of Abbess
Kunhuta Premyslovna. In 1836 the restorer J. Friedrich replaced the green enamel
on the serpent's body with black and dis-
lodged the red enamel cross from the
shield of St George. The original use of
colour is recorded in a wooden copy of the
crozier in the coffin of Abbess Mlada from
1670. The crozier was wrapped in the kerchief of the Abbess Anna Mechtilda
Schoenweiss of Eckstein together with
embroidery dating from 1691.

Poche 1974, no. 8b; Poche DCVU 1/2,
1983.
D.S.

v.567

*General Journeyman of Jesus, Ignatius of
Loyola, Responds to Emperor Ferdinand I
Regarding the Posting of Twelve Jesuits to the
Prague College and Hospital.* In an attached
letter to the Emperor, Loyala describes
the Jesuits who will be arriving in Prague
12 February 1556
Paper, original. In Latin. 2 folios, the rest
sealed in red wax on the bottom of the
second sheet
35.5 × 22 cm
Prague, Státní ústřední archiv, Fond
Česká dvorská kancelář, IV B 100 jezuité v
Praze, karton 387

The Jesuit order was founded by the
Basque noble, courtier and soldier Ignatius of Loyola in 1534 in Paris. The order
focused on the education of youth for
monastic activities. Jesuit monasteries,
called colleges, were divided: the lower
part comprised five to six grade courses,
and a higher one included three years'
study of philosophy and four years of theology, as well as academic subjects. When
Emperor Ferdinand I's attempts to have
Catholics admitted to Prague University
failed, he summoned the Jesuits to Prague,
and in 1556 he opened a college for them
in the Dominican monastery of St
Clement, now known as the Clement-

inum. Two documents from the correspondences of the Emperor and Ignatius
survive in the Czech Court Office: one a
registered copy, the other (shown here) in
the original, with Ignatius' own signature,
*Humillimus ac perpetuus servus in Domino
Ignatius* (Most humble and constant servant of the Lord, Ignatius).

Blek 1893; Blek 1896; Winter 1897; Flp-
Miller 1929; Ornejov 1995; Svato et al.
1995.
K.B.

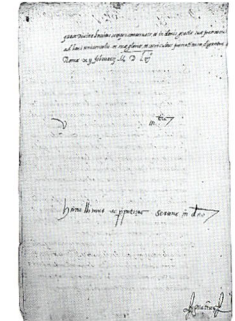

v.568

*Charter by which Ferdinand I Founds the Je-
suit College of St Clement in Prague*
Original parchment, text in Latin; copy-
book, 6 ff., black wax seal attached on
black and yellow silk string, protected by
small bowl of natural wax
26.5 × 34 cm
15 March 1562
Prague, Státní ústřední archiv, Archivní
fond Guberniální listiny, inv. no. 2193

In this charter, Ferdinand I, acting as
Czech King, demonstrates his objective of
gradually re-Catholicizing the Czech
lands. This was supported by the arrival of

the Jesuit order in Prague in 1556. The Emperor, with the previous agreement of
Pope Julian III and of Ignatius Loyola,
founder of the Society of Jesus, established
a college in Prague for the education of the
youth and clergy of the order. One of his
gifts to it was St Clement, while financial
security was to come principally from revenue from the former Upper Lusatian
monastery in Oybin. The document also
confirms the privileges of the college in
the areas of sanctity, preaching and education. Graduates of the college were entitled
to the same degrees as those awarded by
universities in Holland, Italy, Spain or
France. The college was to enjoy all free-

doms in litigation and other legal matters,
and was released from provincial taxes.
This privilege was drafted in three copies.
One was kept by the Emperor, one by the
college and the third was committed to the
chamber. This act of foundation practically
represents the birth of the Jesuit University
in Prague. The academy was officially raised
to the status of a university by Emperor
Matthias only on 27 August 1616.

Bílek 1896; Beránek 1972, pp. 209–36;
Čornejová 1995; Kavka-Petraš 1995;
Brauerová 1997.
H.S.

v.569

*Historia Collegii S. I. ad s. Clementem et
totius Provinciae Bohemiae 1556–1689*
Paper codex in parchment cover, using
scraps of manuscript from the fifteenth
century (Latin liturgical text)
30.5 × 19.5 × 5 cm
1556–1689
Originally in the archives of the
Clementinum. After the dissolution of
the order in 1773 its history is not known.
It probably reached the museum later as a
gift.
Prague, Národní muzeum, inv. no. H3–
XXIII D 147, inv. no. 1335

Official history of the oldest Czech Jesuit
college, written contemporaneously and
retrospectively by college historiogra-
phers according to the regulations of the
order. Includes the period from the arrival
of the first Jesuits in Prague until the end
of the seventeenth century, the culmination of the first phase of re-Catholicization. The history ends the year after the
death of probably the best-known Czech
Jesuit, Bohuslav Balbín, who died in the
buildings of the college itself.

I.Č.

v.570

Czech (?) goldsmith
Seal from the Jesuit College in Prague's
New Town
Red wax, imprint, small wooden bowl
with lid, turned on a lathe
Average 4.5 cm
*SIGILLVM COLLEGII. SOCIETATIS.
IESv. NEO. PRAGAE*
1630–50, imprint 1653
Prague, University Library; from 1950
SUA Prague
Prague, State Central Archives, Order Je-
suits Prague – documents; sign. L IV JS -6

Christ's monogram with the cross issuing

from the beam of the letter 'H' and with
the three holy nails inside a circular disc
with a beaming halo is among emblems
used frequently, in this case to indicate the
transformation of the host into the body
of Christ. The Franciscan St Bernardino of
Sienna introduced the emblem without
nails in about 1440. From the mid-sixteenth century a standard reproduction of
it began to spread. Jesuits and Franciscans
used it as an emblem of their orders. The
seal of the New Town Jesuit College is daring in its engraving design and differs
from the seal of the Lesser Town college
only in the little bow at the foot of the
cross. The seal of the college rector and

Provincial of the order at the time, Jan
Molitorov, is differentiated by another detail in the emblem. Similar seals (though
engraved without skill) were used at the
same time by Minorites and Clare nuns
(State Central Archives, Collection of Seal
Imprints, sign. SPR 320 and SPR 210).

D.S.

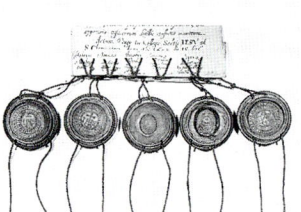

V.571
Prague engraver
The Imprint of a Seal for the Dominicans'
Provincial
Second half of sixteenth century
London, Victoria and Albert Museum

The Prague exemplar pertains to material
of a form used in goldsmiths' work. It is
the sharpest of the preserved reliefs and
freely reproduces figures: the male figures
are entirely naked and have individualized
faces. The view into the furnace has been
deepened, and a detailed landscape depiction has replaced the interior of the metal
forge by which O. von Falke ascribed the

plates to Hans Jamnitzer (1926, p. 205).
Fuhse and Braun have ascribed it to Master H G. Berlin authorship is disputed on
account of some Munich plates which are
inscribed *AZ 1573*. This author's opinion
is that various goldsmiths revised the Jamnitzer model and sometimes even signed
it.

Prague 1967, cat. no. 248 (ascribed to Hans
Junder Gar).

Braun 1918 II, p. 17, note 3; Falke 1926, p.
205; Fuhse, cat. no. 6; Weber 1975, p. 187,
cat. no. 475; Nürnberg 1992, cat. no. 11.

D.S.

V.572
Prague Engraver
Seal Imprint for the Convent of Barefoot-
ed Carmelites at the Church of Our Lady
of Victories in Prague
Brass
4.7 × 3.85 cm
*CONVENTVS. S. MARIAE. DE. VICTO-
RIA. CARMELITAR/ORVM/. DISCAL-
CEAT/ORVM/. PRAGAE.* In the saint's ha-
lo: *S. ANT. DE. PA.*
After 1624
1950 confiscated
Prague, State Central Archives, Collection
of seal imprints, inv. no. SPR 373

The Adoration is a variation of the so-
called Strakonice picture, in which, according to legend, Dominik, a Lesser Town
Carmelite, and Jesu Maria blessed the
Catholic armies and thus contributed to
their victory at the Battle of the White
Mountain. A copy of the picture has been
venerated on the church altar of Our Lady
of Victories since 1622; the church on
White Mountain obtained a second copy.
The original was destroyed by fire in Rome
in 1833. The seal's illustration varies from
the original composition in its background, where one shepherd figures has
been replaced by St Anthony of Padua,
who was a fellow patron of the order.

D.S.

V.573
Prague Engraver
Seal Imprints for the College of Hiberni-
an Franciscans in Prague
Brass, cast, engraved
Oval: H: 7.4 cm; W: 4.4 cm; main bridge: 2
cm
*SIG/ILLUM/: COLLEGII/: PRAG/EN-
SIS/: IM/MACULATAE/ CONCEPTION-
IS/. AD S/ANCTUM/. AMBRO/SIUM/.
F/RATRORUM/. MIN/ORUM/:
STRICT/U/. OBS/ERVANTIAE/: PRO
V.INCIAE/ HIBERNIAE.;* on the band:
NODVS. ORIGINALIS. NON EST. IN TE.
1631
Prague, State Central Archives, collection

of seal imprints, inv. no. SPR 380

The illustrated prelate, without nimbus or
halo, is represented merely by his insignia
of mitre and crozier as well as a scourge
(symbol of penance – also an attribute of
St Ambrose) on the altar table. He may be
interpreted by these attributes as the patron of the Hibernian order, the holy bishop Ambrose, to whom tends to be ascribed
a theological disputation concerning the
Immaculate Conception. As he is shown
without a halo, and according to his physiognomy and beard, the possibility that
this is a portrait of Malachias Full cannot
be excluded. The latter brought the Hiber-

nians to Prague in 1629 and was their
spokesman until his death. The friar ven-
erates the Immaculate Conception of Our
Lady with words from the Loretto litany
on the inscriptive band. Our Lady is depicted as the Apocalyptic Virgin in the
Sun, that is without child but with five
stars above her – a symbol of the Immaculate Conception. The spectacle is accompanied by the emblem of the order: a heart
between the four wounds of Christ.

D.S.

V.574
Prague Engraver
Seal Imprint for the Franciscan
Monastery at Hajek
Wrought iron, engraved
Oval: H: 5 cm; W: 4.4 cm; length of stem:
10.5 cm
*SIGILLVM MONASTERII. S.DOMVS.
LAVRETANAE. HAGECENSIS*; coat of
arms of the Counts Zdarsky of Zdar with
the initials *F:AE:S:R:I:C:D:SORA* (Francis-
cus Adamus Eusebius Sacri Romani Im-
perii Comes de Sara)
Ca. 1659
Until 1785 at Hajek; from 1953 at the
State Central Archives

Prague, State Central Archives; Order of
the Franciscans, Prague

The oldest Loretto chapel in Bohemia was
founded in 1623 by Florian Dietrich
Zdarsky of Zdar. His son, Adam Eusebius,
extended it in 1659, putting it into the
charge of four Franciscan friars. A wooden
provisorium served them as a monastery
until a stone building was constructed in
the 1670s. Franciscans came to use three
different seal imprints. This one probably
belonged to the first community before
the priory was established in 1663 because
it does not use the word 'conventus'. The
depiction of a field contains a likeness of

the founder kneeling and praying in front
of three trees, which represent Hajek (the
sacra silva or sacred grove), where the
Loretto chapel was founded. The Zdarsky
family's coat of arms, a Moravian spread-
eagle, lies in the middle of the cartouche
together with an earl's coronet. The Loretto hut together with the Virgin Mary and
the Infant Jesus rise up into the clouds,
adored by St Francis Seraphine and St Anthony of Padua.

Directory XXVI, p. 39.

D.S.

V.575
Tadeáš Aquilinus
*Land and Duties Register of the Monastery
of Premonstratensians at Strahov*
Paper, parchment binding
30.9 × 11.1 cm
1564
Prague, Monastery of the Premon-
stratensians at Strahov (SŘA deposits),
Strahov, book no. 178

A land and duties register of the Premonstratensians at Strahov was written by T.
Aquilinus, a representative of the Literate
Brethren church of St Michael in Opatovice (cat. no. V.552). The register sets out

a record of payments and subject obligations.

J.P.

V.576
Pewterer from Prague's Lesser Town
Bowl
Pewter, cast, engraved ornamentation
Diam: 55.3 cm
Two tinsmith's symbols on the rim of the bowl: the master's with an illustration of a kettle; and that of Prague's Lesser Town
1594
Donated to the Muzeum Království českého (Museum of the Kingdom of Bohemia), Prague, in 1853 by Jerome Zeidler, abbot of the Strahov monastery (1834–70)
Prague, Národní muzeum, inv. no. H2-1406

The only sample of pewter work from Prague in the period preceding the Battle of the White Mountain. On the wide rim is the engraved sign of the original owner, Johannes Lohelius, the abbot of the Strahov monastery from 1586 to 1612; and in the upper part the initials ILAMS (Johannes Lohelius Abbas Montis Sion) and the year 1594. This form of Lohelius's sign began to appear after 1591, after the incorporation of the Želiv monastery into Strahov. It is found on book supralibros until 1596. The pewter bowl represents the first documented use of this sign on a household item.

Prague 1972/73.

Die archäologischen Sammlungen, 1862, Abt. II-VIII, p. 12, cat. no. 186; Archeologické sbírky, 1863, p. 47, cat. no. 186; Kočí-Vondruška 1989, pp. 140, 142, ill. 489.

D.St.

V.577
Martinus Mertz
Norbertus Triumphans in Vita Translatione... descriptus Ravensburg
Partially coloured print, leather binding
15 × 9.5 cm (opened 18.5 × 9.5 cm), octavo format
1627
Prague, Premonstratensian Monastery of Strahov, Library, inv. no. FD IV 38

Through the efforts of Kašpar Questenberg, the abbot of the Strahov monastery, the remains of Saint Norbert, the founder of the Premonstratensian order, were removed from the Protestant town of

Magdeburg to Doksany in 1626 and then to Strahov on 1 April of the following year. The monastery thus became the centre of the entire order, and the new saint was soon accepted as one of the patrons of the Kingdom of Bohemia. The event itself aroused interest throughout Europe. Descriptions of the translation were published not only in Prague, but in Antwerp, Paris, and Ravensburg. Martin Mertz, the prior of the Premonstraterian monastery in the Swabian town of Roth published a life of Saint Norbert accompanied by a description of the triumphal translation; he dedicated the coloured print to Kašpar Questenberg.

Straka 1927, 112.

Straka 1927, v. III, 333-35.

P.P.

V.578
Jan Sixt of Lerchenfels
Apologia for St Norbert
Quarto format
1628
Prague, Premonstratensian Monastery of Strahov, Library, inv. no. FK V 6

Jan Sixt of Lerchenfels was the provost of Litomerice, the dean of Vysehrad and canon of the chapters of St Vitus at Stara Boleslav and Budysin. He duplicated literature in Czech concerning the translation of the relics of St Norbert, in which he assembled arguments to confirm the authority of the translation with countless

examples from Czech and Church history. While Latin works were being issued directly from Strahov (*Amandus Fabius Octiduum s. Norberti triumphantis, Pragae, 1627*) which concentrated on describing St Norbert's personality itself, the author of this text resorted to an apology, aimed at domestic circumstances which had become splintered in their profession of faith.

Knihopis no. 15870; Straka 1927, TIII, pp. 333-35.

P.P.

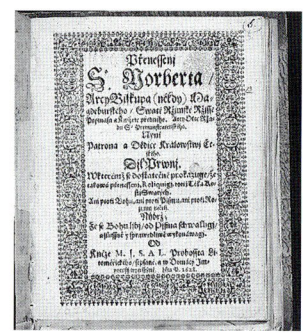

V.579
P. Aegidius, Joanne Baptista
D. Wenceslao Bohemorum duci ac martyri...
Print and copper engraving
1644
Prague, Národní knihovna, inv. no. 65 E 4837 (BY II 41 BZ VII 46)

The book of the prior of the monastery of Barefooted Augustinians by P. Aegidius and Joanne Baptista (under the name of Daniel Václav Himmelstein) is accompanied by thirty-two decorative printed illustrations of the legend of St Wenceslas by P. Henrica based on models by Karel Škréta. Since the subjects of the illustrations al-

most correspond to what has been preserved of Škréta's pictures for the St Wenceslas series, we may reconstruct the entire series quite reliably. At the monastery of the Barefooted Augustinians there was a deeply honoured St Wenceslas tradition and a manuscript of the St Wenceslas legend, *Ut annuncietur*, was preserved there; Jan of Středa was considered the author. The first edition of Aegidius's book appeared in Czech in 1643 and about a year later, a Latin and German version appeared.

Prague 1994, no. 26.

J.R.

V.580
The Book of Founders of the Flagellant Brotherhood of Don Guillén de San Clemente (Spanish Ambassador) and Don Baltasar Marradas, with miniatures of their Coats-of-arms
Parchment, beaten binding covered with red velvet
30 × 35 cm
1606
Prague, Státni ústřední archiv, Kapuciný, inv. no. 66

The book, founded as early as 1606 (from which period come the title records with emblems) and translated in 1628 for Em-

peror Ferdinand II, was originally for records of the foundation for building a chapel for the brotherhood at the Capuchin monastery in Hradčany, Prague. The founders of the fraternity were the Spanish ambassador to Prague and a member of the Johanite order of Guillén de San Clemente (died 1608) and Baltazar de Marradas (ca. 1560-1638), later to become an imperial general. Although the Emperor signed over six hundred gold pieces as a gift and the Empress one hundred gold pieces, the chapel was never constructed and the brethren did not come into being (further records in the book are missing). The book is remarkable

for its miniatures, i.e., for the two emblems of both founders and three miniatures of the emblem of the future brethren of flagellants, with a scene of Chist suffering as he is being scourged. The authors of these quality miniatures are unknown. The most abundant is the emblem of Baltazar de Marradas, after which comes the introductory record of instituting the brethren written in Latin, Czech and German.

L.G.

v.581
Jeremias II Flicker and ? Matthias Walbaum
Before 1590–Augsburg 1647; Kiel 1554–Augsburg 1632
Altarpiece of the *Virgin Mary, Mother of God*
Silver, cast, hammered, gilded in parts; oak with ebony panelling; crimson velvet
H: 60 cm; W: 25 cm
1610–20
To the right at the bottom of the Virgin's cloak: hallmark: Augsburg 1610-25 (R 137), master's hallmark *IF* (Seling 1980, no. 1246); on the sash: *S. Maria Mater Dei*; on scutcheon: TAB 1695 / *Thomas abbas*

Brevnoviensis /
From before 1638 until 1950 at Brevnov Monastery; 1950–93
Uměleckoprůmyslové muzeum, inv. no. 64 668, inv. no. UPM 64 667 1950–93
Prague, Benedictine Arch-abbacy of SS Marketa and Vojtech at Brevnov
Prague, Uměleckoprůmyslové muzeum, depository inv. no. 64 667

Flicker marked the plaque with a figure of the Mother of God in prayer. This is completed by the standing figures of the evangelists Mark and Luke as well as figures of piety. It has been struck from the same matrix as in the Walbaum altarpiece from

Lambach (Lowe 1975, cat. no. 11). The adornments concur with a series of pieces from the Walbaum workshop and those who collaborated there, among whom was Jeremias II Flicker. The altarpiece was apparently commissioned by Wolfgang Selender of Prosovice, prior of St Emmeram at Regensburg until 1602.

Uměleckoprůmyslové muzeum, Prague 1974, cat. no. 89; Prague 1993, cat. no. IX.05; Prague 1994, cat. no. 97.

Cechner 1930, pp. 97–98; Stehlikova 1993, p. 188.

D.S.

v.582
Jeremias II Flicker and ? Matthias Walbaum
Before 1590–Augsburg 1647; Kiel 1554–Augsburg 1632
Altarpiece with *Ecce Homo*
Silver, cast, hammered, gilded in parts, oak panelling with ebony, crimson velvet
H: 60 cm; W: 25 cm
On the plaque: *Ecce homo*; plaque added later: *T.A.B. 1695* (Tomas abbas Brevnoviensis)
1610–20
From before 1638 to 1950 Brevnov Monastery; 1950–93
Uměleckoprůmyslové muzeum, Prague,

inv. no. 64 668
Prague, Benedictine Arch-abbacy at the church of SS Marketa and Vojtech at Brevnov; not numbered (former UPM inv. no. 64 668)

In the middle of the votive tablet is a plate depicting the afflicted Christ, identical to a section from a scene of *Christ the Sufferer* between two soldiers on an unsigned altarpiece from Schwerin, which R. Lowe has ascribed to Walbaum (Lowe 1975, cat. no. 23). To the sides there is a series of embossed reliefs which depict the standing figures of the evangelists Matthew and John. In the extension there is an impres-

sion of some missing figures of piety. This is the counterpart to the previously discussed altarpiece, cat. no. 64 667.

Cat. Prague 1974, cat. no. 89; cat. Prague 1993, cat. no. IX/06.

Cechner 1930, pp. 97–99; Stehlikova 1993, p. 188.

D.S.

---

v.583
Abraham II Lotter
1580-1614
Household Altarpiece with *Adoration of the Shepherds*
Silver, cast, hammered, beaten, partially gilded, ebony and soft black madder, ivory, paint on sheet metal
89 × 44 × 25 cm
Hallmark of the town of Augsburg; the maker's monogram appears in five places: *AL* (Seling, no. 1278); two plates bearing a coat of arms with the initials *MFBVS-GHVM, SCFBVS*; inscriptive band: *Gloria in excelcis deo*
Before 1626

1951 confiscated; 1953–90 Museum of Prague; exposition at the Loretto church in Prague; monastery of the lesser brothers of Capuccin, Loretto, inv. no. P 41
Munich, Bayerisches Nationalmuseum

This 'spectaculum' is the oldest Mannerist type of courtly nativity scenes in the form of a miniature altarpiece. Thomas Muller has traced its genesis from the inventory of the Brugge Carmelites (1537), via the Loretto's silver tabernacle brought to Prague by Katerina Benigna of Lobkowicz, right up to its current location. This altarpiece decoration bears the traditional hierarchy of christological subjects: Birth –

Pietà – Resurrection. The spacious development of the viewing stage with shepherds on a staircase forms the typological first stage of miniature cabinets that reached their peak in the Baroque and the Rococo.

Dvorak 1893; Podloha 1901, p. 5; Muller 1966, pp. 159–66; Divis 1972, pp. 113–16, no. 44; Seling 1980, vol. III, no. 1278.

D.S.

---

v.584
Anonymous Court Artist
Small Altar with the *Annunciation* and *Visitation of the Virgin Mary*
Wooden body faced with enamel, gilded and engraved silver, enamels, semi-precious and precious stones, pearls, mountain crystal, oil painting on copper
72 × 47 × 14.8 cm
Stará Boleslav, Church of the Assumption of the Virgin Mary, treasury

The small altar was used in Stará Boleslav until the beginning of this century as the frame for one of the most important Marian cult images of the Czech Counter-Re-

formation, which was led by the Jesuits of the 'Palladium Boemiae'. Thanks to the famous image, the city became one of the most popular Baroque places of pilgrimage in Bohemia from the first half of the seventeenth century. Thus far it has not been possible to determine the circumstances under which this bejewelled retable was created. The heterogeneous state of the material and the sources give contradictory results. The work shows several traces of later, non-professional interventions, such as the fixture for displaying the painting, which was not included in the original design of the altar. Eight decorations of various styles, some dating

from a much later period, are hung on the front part of the altar as votive gifts. It seems that even the coats of arms were later additions. The hypothesis that the altar was a gift of Empress Maria Anna, the wife of Ferdinand III, cannot be confirmed. Although no altars comparable to this one, which is an example of Mannerist court art, have survived in the Prague area, we can assume that the work originated in Prague because of the Rudolfine style of both paintings and because of the use of domestic semi-precious stones.

H.B.

---

v.585
Crucifix
Varnished wood, carved ivory, bored
H: 75 cm; body 33 cm
Ca. 1600
1950–93 Uměleckoprůmyslové muzeum, Prague; Premonstratensian abbey at Tepla u Touzimi; item deposited at Prague, Uměleckoprůmyslové muzeum, inv. no. 64 243

Restored in 1995 by P. Spacek. The larger of a pair of carved ivory bodies from the original inventory of the Tepla monastery (Annales Teplenses, II). The figure of the Crucified Christ has been modelled freely

according to an ivory model by Benvenuto Cellini (1500–71). It was made for the royal palace of the Escorial. Scaled-down variations of it held in collections throughout the world (e.g. at the Walters Art Gallery, Baltimore) date from the last quarter of the sixteenth century to the beginning of the seventeenth century. The face of the Tepla Christ is reminiscent of the sculptural work of Giambologna. The more compact material of the barely anatomically articulated body is also close to the corpora of southern Germany.

D.S.

v.586
Augsburg Goldsmith from the circle of
Matthias Walbaum and Jeremias II Flicker
Table Cross
Corpus of cast silver, tempered; oak cross
and base; casing of ebony with silver
adornments, restored 1995)
H: 27.5 cm; W: 11.4 cm
1600–25
From ca. 1625 probably held at Brevnov
or Broumov Benedictine monasteries;
from 1950 at the Uměleckoprůmyslové
muzeum, Prague
Prague, Uměleckoprůmyslové muzeum,
inv. no. 52 574

Restoration confirmed the first-class quality of this hitherto unnoticed work. The
significantly protracted and limp body
with rigid legs is taken from the sculptural
work of Giambologna (1529–1608), from
which were derived a number of Central
European variations (e.g. Vienna, Kunsthistorisches Museum, inv. no. E 34). It is
generally feasible that the table cross of
the Czech Benedictines is related to the
Walbaum Calvaries originating between
the first and third decades of the seventeenth century (Lowe 1975, cat. nos 1, 3, 4).
Compare also the plaque by Walbaum's
pupil and companion Jeremias Flicker
from the collection of the Maximilian Mu-

seum in Augsburg (Lowe 1975).

Prague 1938, cat. no. 150.

D.S.

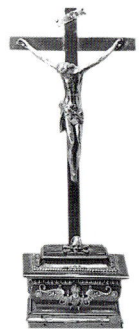

v.587
Chasuble
Patterned silk, gold and silver purl em-
broidery (1625)
Diam: 109 cm; W: 72 cm
1550–1600
Obtained from the church in Budětice
Prague, Uměleckoprůmyslové muzeum,
inv. no. 7 971

The sides of the chasuble are brocaded,
the centre is embroidered velvet. A recurring design of red pointed oval medallions
with stylized artichokes and woven arabesques appears on a gold-ochre silk background. The very fine embriodery, which

covers the central posterior and anterior
band, features a floral design of twisting
stalks and fine blooms. The chasuble is
separated into panels by gold ribbons and
is lined with pink canvas. The vestment is
made from two materials of separate origin. The patterned fabric is Italian, most
probably woven in Tuscany between 1550
and 1560. It a good example of the oriental
influence in Italian textiles, particularly in
the form of Moorish arabesques, which
can be seen in a number of variations on
velvets and brocades in the Prague
Uměleckoprůmyslove Muzeum (inv. nos
844, 845, 56,561) and in other European
collections. The design is interrupted in

the front of the chasuble where a section
of previously used fabric was later sewn in.
The breadth of the spiralling stalks radiat-
ing out horizontally on both sides indicates an intended design of larger proportions, perhaps that of a portière. A
chasuble from Bubovice (Prague, Uměleckoprůmyslové muzeum, inv. no. 5,035)
and two portières from the Prague Ghetto,
gifts from Jakub Bashevi and Mose
Chafan in 1623, feature designs similar to
those on the chasuble.

N.B.

v.588
Chasuble
Textile appliqué; light blue, red, white and
yellow atlas cord; brocade
103 × 70 cm
1575–1610
Purchased from the Cantoni collection at
an auction in Milan, 1891
Prague, Uměleckoprůmyslové muzeum,
inv. no. 4,238

The chasuble is made from a textured silk
fabric. Embroidered floral and herbal designs are arranged in a network of large
medallions. The pectoral and dorsal crosses feature a fabric appliqué. Contoured

motifs made from light blue, yellow and
white atlas cord are applied to a red atlas
background. The lining is blue oilcloth
(waxed canvas). These textile ornaments
were made in Tuscany. Similar fabric designs can be found in the collections
of the Prague Uměleckoprůmyslové muzeum, inv. no. 4,216. The fabrics were
made in Milan. Although not of Bohemian
origin, this chasuble is included in this exhibition because the fabric and embroidery are similar to those that were made in
Bohemia at the turn of the century. Towards the second half of the sixteenth century features such as acanthus leaves, carnations, daffodils, lilies and later even

tulips were appearing on brocaded fabrics
and in embroidered appliqués: these
demonstrate the growing influence of
both western and eastern Islam on textile
craftsmanship.

Renaissance Art and Craftsmanship,
Belvedere 1966–67.

Renaissance Art and Craftsmanship, Prague
1996, exh. cat., p. 15.

N.B.

v.589
Chasuble
Blue-grey silk atlas with coloured silk bro-
cade and embroidered gold purl
Design 13cm and 101 cm
1600–25
Prague, Loreta, 1950
Prague, Uměleckoprůmyslové muzeum,
inv. no. 65,401/1

The chasuble is made from patterned silk.
Horizontal rows feature spiral leaves and
geometrically stylized stems with tiny floral blooms. The design motifs alternate
from left to right. The chasuble is fringed
with a silver band; the lining is green can-

vas. Associated with the chasuble are a
stole, maniple, veil and burse. All except
the stole are made of the same fabric. Brocaded atlases were apparently very popular in Italy and many of them have been
preserved. Such atlases often appear in
contemporary Italian portraiture, for example the portrait of Margaret Gonzaga
(Florence, Palazzo Pitti) painted in 1605 by
Franz Pourbous the Younger. Also very
similar are two textile fragments found in
the collections of the Museum für Angewandte Kunst in Cologne (B. Markowsky,
Europäische Seidengewebe (Cologne,
1976), inv. nos 285, 286) and a fragment
dating from the turn of the seventeenth

century from the Gandini collection, now
housed in the Archivio di Stato de Modena (D. Devoti and M Cuoghi Costantini,
La collezione Gandini. Tessuti dal XVII al
XIX secolo (Modena, 1993), inv. no. 34).

Prague 1974.

Zeminová 1974, cat. no. 1.

N.B.

v.590
Chasuble
Gold and silver thread embroidery, paita
cotton, gold bullion, cording; red silk at-
las
Diam. 108 cm; W: 70cm
Ca. 1630
Bubovice, district of Příbram
The chasuble's origins are not certain but
can be attributed to the local church of St
Václav (Wenceslas), reconstruction of
which was begun by Přibík Jeníšek of
Újezd in 1629.
Prague, Uměleckoprůmyslové muzeum,
inv. no. 5 035

The vestment is made of a red atlas and is
ornamented with three embroidered vertical bands. The centre band features a
heart-shaped cartouche filled with floral
designs, leaves and stalks – the centre stalk
is topped with a crown. The top centre half
of the dorsal band features a a wreath of
laurel with four rosettes, the letters *IHS*, a
cross and three combs. The sides, separated from the central band by a narrow floral border, feature twisting, S-shaped
stems with thin, swordlike leaves, tiny floral designs and large rosettes. The whole
area is trimmed with wavy floral lines scattered with tiny rosettes. The yellow silk
taffeta lining is patched in a few places

with a floral-patterned silk damask. From
the end of the sixteenth century until well
into the first quarter of the seventeenth
century printed patterns issued in Germany, Italy and later throughout central
Europe were the favoured models for embroidery and textile appliqués.

Milan 1966; Bucharest 1971; Prague 1974.

Siena 1994, cat., fig. 62; Zeminová 1974.,
cat. no. 4.

N.B.

V.591
Omophorion
Gold purl embroidery, blue and green silk, braided filament, gold silk fringes, red silk atlas, yellow packcloth(canvas) lining
H: 15.5 cm; W: 57cm
Early seventeenth century
A. S. Drey, auction, Munich, 1895
Prague, Uměleckoprůmyslové muzeum, inv. no. 5,962

The red silk atlas has gold purl embroidery of fine lily blooms. Red and gold cord fringes the omophorion. The richly embroidered stiff collar was originally a part of the trim of the linen kerchief, which was altered later in the seventeenth century. Patterns most frequently used in such embroidery were fine floral designs and medallions with holy figures. Examples of similar designs can be found in Italian and Spanish handiwork of the first half of the seventeenth century (J. Braun, *Die liturgischen Paramente in Gegenwart und Vergangenheit* (Freiburg im Breisgau, 1924), p. 72, fig. 38; auction in Munich at the Galerie Helbing, 25–30 October 1909, Section I, Textiles, pl. 34, 20360).

N.B.

V.592
Stole, Maniple
Textile appliqué, red fabric, blue silk velvet, green and beige silk atlas, silk cords, rep (type of canvas) band, silk fringes
Stole 190 cm; maniple 36 cm
Ca. 1600
Tranferred from the Chodské muzeum in Domažlice, 1980
Prague, Uměleckoprůmyslové muzeum, inv. nos 87 855; 87 856

The stole and maniple are made from red cloth and feature textile appliqués made from multicoloured fragments of velvet and atlas. Cherubs and figures of nude young women holding palm leaves are depicted on a background of symmetrical floral motifs. Both items have trimming of a green rep band with blue fringes. The textile applications are a good example of the practice of reusing material in creating liturgical vestments. Multicoloured fabric cuttings were widely used in domestic design. Not only was this practice aesthetically pleasing and effective but it also made use of fabric remnants that would otherwise have been wasted. Motifs of human figures or events frequently decorated interior portières and covers, book casings, mirror frames and cabinets with writing implements. Although international in design, the stole and maniple were most likely made from an old curtain or table covering.

N.B.

V.593
Velum with the name of Jesus embroidered
White canvas, red bead, stitching with coloured silk and gold and silver thread, coloured bobbin-lace
525 × 52 cm
Ca. 1600
Purchased at Helbing auction in 1909, Munich; from the collection of Fr. v. Lipperheide
Prague, Uměleckoprůmyslové muzeum, inv. no. 11 302

N.B.

V.594
Veil
Silk atlas with silver and gold brocade
Pattern 31cm; Diam: 57cm; W: 55cm
1600-25
Prague, Loreta, 1950
Prague, Uměleckoprůmyslové muzeum, inv. no. 65 508

Made of a violet-blue silk atlas, the veil is embroidered with a textured silver and gold design. A fine floral design is arranged in a diamond-shaped pattern covering the entire fabric. The diamonds are formed by double twigs entwined with leaves and accentuated in each corner by a rosette. In the centre of the veil is a symmetrical cross of gold lace. The veil is also trimmed with gold lace. The inner lining is blue canvas. Symmetrical floral patterns were popular in the first half of the seventeenth century. Floral designs were incorporated into symmetrical networks of either pointed ovals or diamond shapes. At the end of the sixteenth century an asymmetrical element of undulating floral stems and plant stalks was introduced into established designs. This fabric is an example of the combination of symmetrical and asymmetrical design elements. Similar undulating floral stems are featured on the colours (flag) of the imperial ride from Domažlice inscribed 1621, which can be found in the Military Museum in Prague. A similar example can be found on the velvet of a contemporary suit of clothes in Siena (*Drappi, velluti, taffeta et altre cose, Antichi tessuti a Siena a nel suo territorio*, Siena, Chiesa di Sant'Agostino, exh. cat. (Siena, 1994), fig. 58).

Prague 1974.

Zeminová 1974, cat. no. 2.

N.B.

V.595
Veil (on chalice)
Green silk damask
Pattern 23cm; Diam: 51cm; W: 50cm
1625-40
Private collection of Mr Duda, 1886
Prague, Uměleckoprůmyslové muzeum, inv. no. 686

The veil is made from light-green damask with a dense floral pattern. Stylized chrysanthemums and dahlia blooms are arranged into alternating horizontal rows. Stems with symmetrically opened leaves are intertwined in a kidney-shaped motif featuring the stem of a pomegranate. The veil is trimmed with silver lace. Damasks featuring this type of floral patterning were first made in Italy in the mid-1720s. A number of fabrics featuring variations of similar floral patterns have been preserved in Czech and other collections worldwide. The Prague Uměleckoprůmyslové muzeum owns identical and related examples of this type of patterning (inv. nos 55,087; 907; 1656; 48,444), as does the Muzeum Narodowe w Krakowie in Kraków (M. Taszycka, *Wloskie jedwabne tkaniny odzieżowe w Polsce w pierwszej polowie w XVII* (Wroclaw, Warsaw, Kraków and Gdansk, 1971), figs 7, 8 and 9). Virtually identical examples can also be found in Germany, in the collections of the Museum für Angewandte Kunst in Cologne (B. Markowsky, *Europäische Seidengewebe* (Cologne, 1976), inv. nos 274, 275, 278) and on the velvet cloak of Swedish King Adolf II (died 1632) (P. Thorton, *Baroque and Rococo Silks* (London, 1965), fig. 3c, dated 1625-32; fig. 4b, dated ca. 1640).

Prague 1974.

Zeminová 1974, cat. no. 3.

N.B.

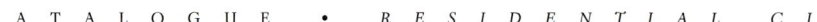

V.596
Dutch Master
Embroidery with the *Annunciation to the Virgin Mary*
Coloured silk (needle painting), relief embroidery with gold spangles, coils of gold thread, and silver sequins
68.6 × 77 cm
1610–20
1978 gift
Prague, Uměleckoprůmyslové muzeum, inv. no. 86 713

An oval medallion with a depiction of the *Annunciation* and a relief-decorated frame with four masks, palmettes, and bunches

of fruit, between which are colourful flowers and exotic birds. The discovery of the inventory of Rudolf II's *Kunstkammer* from 1607–11 brought revolutionary information to numerous fields of scholarship. One such new discovery was the existence of embroiderers. The documents indicate that at least three specialists were active in the field of silk embroidery in Prague; these were Philip van den Bossche, his daughter Elisabeth and his son-in-law Cappelmann. Bossche's oeuvre is represented by the *Landscape with the Virgin Mary and Joseph*, *The Temptation of Saint Anthony*, and two still lifes. His daughter and son-in-law embroidered the *Still Life*

with Flowers. The impetus for the later flowering of embroidery work in the Netherlands must evidently be sought in Rudolfine Prague. The figure of Philip van den Bosche has remained unnoticed thus far in the scholarly literature. The embroidery with the exquisitely framed scene of the Annunciation from the Uměleckoprůmyslové muzeum may bear some relation to embroidery work from Prague, and its publication will perhaps serve as an impulse for further research in this field.

B.B.

V.597
North Rhenish (?) Goldsmith
Monstrance
Brass, cast, hammered; cut glass
H: 62 cm; stem 20.5 cm
HERMAN° GRAVE° ZW. MANDER-SCHEID° VND° BLANCKENHEIM HERR° ZW° IVNCKERDODT° DHAVN° VND° ERPP° DERO° ROM° KAY° MAT° RHAT (engraved on the stem and a coat of arms); dated year *1601° A.G.B.* (Arnold II. Count Blankenheim)
1601, nineteenth and twentieth-century additions (barrel, lunula, IHS disc, glass gilding)
After 1612 a dedication by Herman Man-

derscheid-Blankenheim during the time of Rudolf II; Privy Council of Emperor Matthias; came into possession of the Lobkowicz family via the Sternberg-Manderscheids (?); until 1957 remained in the castle chapel at Krimice in Pilsen, then at the Roman Catholic parish council offices at Vejprnice, Pilsen

A uniquely documented example of a monstrance of the North Rhenish type designed at the peak of the Renaissance.

D.S.

V.598
Monstrance
Silver gilded, beaten, chased and cut
H: 56 cm, max. W: 25
On the oval-shaped node is an engraved emblem with: *MARIA MAXIMILIANA A STERNBERG COMITIS AB HOHEN-ZOLLERN FUNDATRIX COLLEGII SOC...*
1633, base after 1809
Prague, New Town, church of St Ignatius
Prague, church of St Ignatius, A-24 18c (437)

This period monstrance combines structural form with the rays of the sun. The

frame with lunula across the sides is decorated with two naked women's torsos, which is incomprehensible from the point of view of post-Tridentine dogma. Busts of SS Ignatius and Francis Xavier, the co-patrons of the college, are located on the canopy. The engraved dedication, with date at the node, determines that the monstrance was a gift from Marie Maximiliána of Šternberk, née princess Hohenzollern, which is linked to the death of her only son, Vojtěch, in the same year and with her foundation of the New Town College of Jesuits. The base, with course reliefs of the the evangelists' torsos, was added in 1809.

D.S.

V.599
Andreas Kynne the Elder
Chalice
Silver, cast, chased, gilded
H: 24 cm; average max. 17.5 cm; wt: 1,640 g
AK; P in the oval; inscription: *IM 1575 IAR HAB ICH VRSVLA FRAW VON/ PRVSKAW GEBORNE VON/ LOBKOW-ICZ AVF ALTENBVRG DISEN KELCH ZVR EHR GOTTES VND MEYNER GEDECHTNVS MACHEN LASSEN.*
1575
Lobkowicz collection, Roudnice nad Labem; auctioned Vienna 1898
Berlin, Kunstgewerbemuseum, inv. no. 9 827

Associative markings and inscriptions show that the piece was commissioned for Vorsila of Lobkowicz, who in 1573 married Jiří Proskovsky of Proskov, the highest-ranking chamberlain in the Kingdom of Bohemia. Lessing, Rosenberg, Pechstein and Bursche designated the piece as an anonymous work from Prague. Pechstein interpreted the chalice's decoration of a vine tree for the liturgy from the Gospel of John (15:1–3,5). The depiction of the vine tree as a maze of severed branches is adhered to in the naturalism of the Prague Jagellonian Gothic (e.g. the royal oratory in the dome of St Vitus' cathedral). Authorship of the chalice may be ascribed to

a single master by means of the monogram AK, which was inscribed in Prague in the 1570s: Andres Khynne worked for the Lobkowicz family on many occasions.

KGW 1963, 1, cat. no. 108; *KGW* 1971; Pechstein, cat. no. 34; *KGW* 1989; Bursche, p. 81, cat. no. 99.

AhMp, rkp. 1289, 12; Lessing 1907, p. 42; Creutz 1909, p. 256; Winter 1909, p. 441; Teige 1915, II, pp. 388, 441; Braun 1932, p. 117.

D.S.

V.600
Czech Goldsmith
Chalice
Engraved silver, gilt
H: 18.5 cm
IHESVS
After mid-sixteenth century
1950 confiscated from the Church, of unknown origin; 1963 transferred from the State Heritage Board
Prague, Umelückolprůmyslové muzeum, inv. no. 68 017

Most frequently occurring form of Central European Renaissance chalice without decoration. From the same set come

works analogous to those both of Augsburg origin (UPM inv. no. 68 016, with the markings of Bartolome Koch, between 1580 and 1590) and of Czech origin.

D.S.

V.601
Czech Goldsmith
Chalice
Cast silver, hammered, gilt; brass
H: 23 cm; average of dome 10 cm
Second half of sixteenth century; stem
eighteenth century
Prague (?)
1891, from the church at Kadov u Blatne
Prague, Uměleckoprůmyslové muzeum,
inv. no. 4 272

D.S.

V.602
Czech Goldsmith
Chalice
Beaten silver, engraved
H: 18.8 cm; lower average 12.3 cm
S:VRSLA ORA P/RO/ N/OBIS/ F.E. FABI-
AN KLAPBSCHE ANNO DOM 1629; on
stem: MRA, IHS
1629
The chapel of Kladruby (Kladersal) near
Marienbad; 1951 State Heritage Board;
1962 UPM, Prague
Prague, Uměleckoprůmyslové muzeum,
inv. no. 67 301

A typical chalice of Renaissance structure,

preserved intact and dated. The only object of art which has been preserved from
the chapel of the monasterial court of the
Tepla Premonstratensians before its destruction by armies during the Thirty
Years' War (1645), apparently held in storage at Tepla.

D.S.

V.603
Court Goldsmith
Chalice
Cast silver, hammered, gilt
H: 27 cm; average W: 12.5 cm
1637
Prague (?) or Italy
Emaus Benedictine monastery, Prague;
1950-95 confiscated property; since 1995
in the depository of UPM, Prague
Emaus Benedictine monastery, Prague,
held in the depository of Uměleckoprů-
myslové muzeum, Prague, inv. no. 65 196a

The stem of the chalice is embellished
with three personifications of the Chris-

tian virtues. Their nodal point is enclosed
by the Old Testament patriarchs Moses,
Abraham and David between depictions
of sacrifice. These correspond to the eu-
charistic function of the chalice. Sculptural figures, functioning as caryatids,
were already known from about the mid-
sixteenth century from graphic models
(Hans Mielich, Virgil Solis) as were scrolls
appearing on secular vessels, for example,
in the work of Wenzel Jamnitz, which date
from the fourth quarter of the sixteenth
century. Mass-produced chalices of the
'sculpted' type spread particularly in Italy
from the mid-seventeenth century. The
miniatures of the patriarchs displayed on

the chalice derive from Michelangelo, but
the reliefs also have German parallels. The
appearance of the chalice is related to a
donation made by Ferdinand III: he
wished to have the imperial chapel decorated in accordance with the iconographic
scheme of his own ruling house: the paintings and murals represented the Old Testament patriarchs Moses, Abraham and
David.

Prague 1974, cat. no. 116 (Augsburg, ca.
1650); Milan 1993, cat. no. 21; Ramat Gan
1994, cat. no. 24.

D.S.

V.604
Hans Michael Stotz
Fl. Regensburg 1632-1643
Chalice
Beaten silver, perforated, gilt
H: 21 cm; lower average W: 15.2 cm
Maker's monogram: HMS; Regensburg
town coat of arms (R 4441)
Ca. 1640
1951-52 confiscated and held at the
Uměleckoprůmyslové muzeum; 1992 re-
stored, UPM depository
Franciscans, Tachov Franciscan
monastery; Prague UPM, depository no.
65 129

The quality work of a master who, in 1643,
produced a processional cross for the Regensburg dome (Hubel 1976, cat. no. 57,
ill. 89). This master cannot be identified
with H. M. Schober, who was working in
the third quarter of the seventeenth century (identified in a Prague catalogue from
1974 at R 4461). The chalice is a typical example from the Thirty Years' War of a directly imported liturgical vessel from the
nearest centre of gold production in
Bavaria.

Prague 1974, cat. no. 115.

D.S.

V.605
North Italian Master
Case for Chalice or Cup
Leather, carved, tailored and stamped decorations; soft wood kernel
28.4 cm; average lower section 24 cm; average upper section 28.4 cm
B. BLASI. PACHAGNI. ARCHIP. BAZANI.
1637
1637
Lombardy or Emilia Romagna
1885 bought at M. Salmoun in Dresden
Prague, Uměleckoprůmyslové muzeum,
inv. no. 310

Displays an illustration of the archdeacon

St Blasius exposing the stigmata in his
hand. St Blasius is the Christian patron of
Blasius Pachagmi, an archminister of the
Church (no such record of an archbishop
of this name exists in the registers of archbishops from either Europe or Asia Minor), more probably from Bassano near
Venice than from the Latin-named Basat-
um. The design of the case conforms to
that of a chalice and paten used in the
mass. Leather cases of this type, with
carved and tailored figural work as well as
a stamp, were traditionally produced in
northern Italy and exported in great quantities. This case of unknown origin is characteristic of those leather products which

were imported into Bohemia and which
have been ruined through use.

D.S.

V.606
Czech Goldsmith
Ciborium with Lid
Beaten copper, gilt
H: 20 cm; average w: 9 cm
Ca. 1600
Until 1895 held at the church in Chrast u Chrudimi
Prague, Uměleckoprůmyslové muzeum, inv. no. 6 738

The make and decorative elements usual for a secular goblet have been adopted for this ciborium; the permeation of various stylistic forms is characteristic for the Mannerist period.

Prague 1994a, cat. no. 107.

Chytil, Directory XL, p. 23.

D.S.

V.607
Czech (?) Goldsmith
Ciborium
H: 34.5 cm; lower average 13.5 cm; max. W: 14.5 cm
IHS
Ca. 1650
1948 bequeathed from the collection of Hermina Srbova, Prague
Prague, Uměleckoprůmyslové muzeum, inv. no. 80 343

Christ's monogram with the cross issuing out of the beam of the letter 'H' and with the three holy nails inside the radial beams of a halo is among symbols fre-

quently used, in this case for the transformation of the host into the body of Christ. The Franciscan friar Bernadin of Sienna introduced the emblem without nails in about 1440. From the mid-sixteenth century it spread generally to become the definitive form. Jesuits and Franciscans used it directly as an emblem of their orders.

D.S.

V.608
Czech Goldsmith
Mass Cruets with Tray
Cast silver, beaten, gilt
H: 9.4 cm; tray: 23.7 × 17.5 cm
Maker's monogram CR in the plate with three spikes; a town's coat of arms with two towers (R 9451), re-hallmarked to twelve half-ounce silver, Brno 1806–07; two coats of arms with the year 1630 almost worn away; the coat-of-arms placket bears the monogram OCAR (Othmarus Conrad Praepositus Raygraydenis)
1630
1785–1950 Rajhrad; 1950–90 held at the Uměleckoprůmyslové muzeum; Rajhrad

near Brno, Benedictine monastery
Prague, Uměleckoprůmyslové muzeum depository. inv. no. 65 353/1–3

The decorations on the tray contain four emblems of Arma Christi with an auricular ornament between the heads of the angels. It is the oldest liturgical cruet set of this formation in current Czech collections. Cruets from the Rajhrad inventory date from 1645 and are missing from later inventories (Dudik II 1868, p. 195). The Provost of Rajhrad, Otmar (1764–1812), acquired them and affixed his monogram to them. The worn-away coats of arms may be hypothetically identified as the em-

blems of the abbot and the convent monastery of Plase, which was dissolved in 1784. Another work ascribed to this maker is a monstrance, dated 1628, from the Cistercians at Plase with a dedication by the Abbot Jiří Wasmuth, today housed in the parish of Kralovice (Register XXXVII, p. 67); Rosenberg has recorded both signs on the cup in the Kremlin (?) treasury in Moscow (R 9482, R9483).

Prague 1974, cat. no. 158; Prague 1994a, cat. no. 107.

D.S.

V.609
Czech Goldsmith
Fumigator (Incense Cask)
Copper, gilt, silver
H: 36 cm; w: 16 cm
Second third of seventeenth century
Until 1905 in the collection of Anton Scharf, Vienna-Prague
Prague, Uměleckoprůmyslové muzeum, inv. no. 9 183

This less typical ciborium form of incense cask conforms to the Mannerist period, as does the Blessed Virgin, who holds an apple as though it were her bared breast. The figures and the ornamental decorations

are already Baroque (cf. the ciborium here from Chrast; also Italian works, Faranda 1990, no. 69). The iconographic grouping of the figures (at the foot of the Virgin, between the figures of St Francis Seraphim and the holy Bishop Vojtěch [?]; on the cupola the Blessed Virgin is between two sinners who have been cast into the fires of hell, and St Onufrius is also depicted; St Jerome appears on the lid) accentuates the spiritual cleansing of the pious person and the sinner. The ascetics Francis, Onufrius and Jerome are renowned for their contemplation in the wilderness, while the two sinful mortals are returning to the faith (they are at prayer!) in the fire.

The theme of cleansing by fire corresponds to the function of the vessel: the smoke from burning incense likewise symbolizes prayers ascending to heaven (Psalms 141:2). The form of the reliefs and the iconography of the saints does not exclude the possibility that this may have had its origin in the Czech monastic environment of the Benedictines (the Emaus church, the church of St John below the Rock), the Franciscans or the Capuchins.

D.S.

V.610
Unknown Czech or German Goldsmith
Aspersorium
Silver 800/1200, cast, chased
H: 13.8 cm
Hallmark: illegible; plate with the letter r (R 4483 ?), a quality hallmark from the end of the eighteenth century
Until 1950 probably held by the Benedictines at Brevnov; 1967 Uměleckoprůmyslové muzeum, Prague; transferred from the State Laboratory for Precious Metals
Prague, Uměleckoprůmyslové muzeum, inv. no. 72 154

The ornamental frame of the edicule contains two winged female torsos with bared breasts, which contrast with the religious function of the aspersorium. The position of the Virgin Mary (the twisting curve of the raised left leg) also attests to the secular nature of the workshop's products in the late Mannerist style. (See the related figures of two female saints on the Brevnov altarpiece requested by Abbot Sartorius, as well as the silver ladies' waistband at Uměleckoprůmyslové muzeum, inv. no. 97 937.)

Prague 1974, cat. no. 90.

D.S.

V.611
Unknown Pewterer
Pair of Candlesticks
Pewter, cast, engraved
H: 45.5 cm
1644
Bohemia
Bought in 1901
Prague, Národní muzeum, inv. nos H2–1535, H2–1536

According to the symbol engraved on the stem, the candlesticks were once the property of the Bohemian Order of Knights of the Cross with a Red Star. The shape, with a horizontal triangular base, is rarely seen in pewter. During the seventeenth century, this shape alternated with candlesticks of circular section. It was the first stage of altar-light fixtures with a smooth or relief, ornamented, three-sided base, which began to gain recognition following the model of silversmiths' products in the second half of the seventeenth century.

Prague 1972/73.

D.St.

V.612
Matouš Voříšek, Bell-founder and Pewterer
In Roudnice nad Labem 1590–1619
Baptismal Font
Pewter, cast, engraved
H: 144 cm; dome 52 cm
The author's legend is on the casing, and the sign and bell-founder's monogram, *MW*
1595
From the cemetery of the church of Saint Rochus in Prague's Ol'any; it was purchased by the museum in 1900
Prague, Muzeum hlavního město Prahy, inv. no. 12617

The casing of the baptismal font is demarcated by two encircling bands in relief. On the upper relief there recur four scenes from Genesis, following models of Saxonian or Bohemian origin from the second third of the sixteenth century. On the lower relief, an ornamental motif of German authorship from the third quarter of the sixteenth century alternates with impresses of Saxonian medals. In the middle, in the space between the bands, there is a relief of a chalice with the Host and an inscription in Czech concerning the creator of the font. On the opposite side is a cartouche with a dedication. Heimeran Wildner the younger from Cheb and Hans Wildt the younger from Jáchymov, among other pewterers, applied analogous models from Genesis to ornamentation.

Prague 1972/73; Prague 1994.

D.St.

V.613
Chest
Brown-stained wood, inlaid, with oak, maple and walnut veneer
Ca. 1600
Stará Boleslav, Church of Saint Wenceslas, obtained in 1907 in exchange for another chest owned by the Národní muzeum.
Prague, Národní muzeum, inv. no. H2-6 898

A prismatoid chest on a high, full pedestal and with a fold-out lid. The upper part of the front piece is articulated by pilasters into three fields with rich inlaid ornamentation, which is repeated on the sides and the lid. This is an exceptional example of Renaissance furniture as it occasionally appeared in the ecclesiastical and secular (aristocratic or bourgeois) interior in Prague. The chest was formerly part of the sacristy furnishings in the Church of Saint Wenceslas in Stará Boleslav, where it was used for storing ecclesiastical paraments. It attests to the high quality of the cabinetmaker's art.

Prague 1986.

Herain 1930, p. 149; Cimburek et al., p. 970, ill. n. 1125.

D.K.

V.614
Priedieu with Coat-of-arms
Walnut and linden wood, carved and polychromed
100 × 73 × 60.5 cm
Early seventeenth century
Transferred from Zbraslav Castle (monastery) in 1967
Prague, Uměleckoprůmyslové muzeum, inv. no. 73 180

The priedieu has doors in the central part, a fold-out upper board, and a surface for kneeling. The front side is decorated with polychromed carving, and the doors feature a carved and polychromed coat-of-arms with a stag leaping across a divided red and white field with a half figure of a man in the jewel – the coat-of-arms of the Württemburg aristocrat Ludwig Michael of Schorndorf (?). The monogram CGK is burned into the right side of the priedieu. A cartouche with scrollwork motifs appears above the doors. Along the sides of the cabinet are vertical relief bands with female half figures, grotesque masks, and heads with scrollwork. The surface of the priedieu and the carving are polychromed in the basic blue-green tone and shades of red. During the Renaissance, the priedieu was a standard part of the interior furnishings of the aristocratic interior. The Mannerist grotesque decoration with the family coat-of-arms confirm the work's Renaissance origin.

Rosenburg 1990; Trója 1992.

D.K.

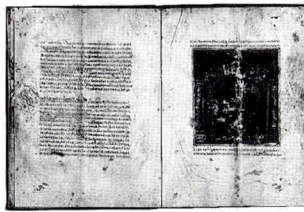

V.615
Confirmation of Privilege Granted by Ferdinand II to Jacob Bassevi von Treyenberg
German, authenticated copy (or authenticated copy in the form of a translation of the original Czech)
Parchment, newer yellow leather binding. form, ten folios.
Miniature of the original coat-of-arms on folio 5a, 147 × 153 mm, revised on folio 8a, 144 × 158 mm. The seal attached by the verifier has been lost.
25 × 32 × 1 cm
12 April 1628
Prague, Muzeum hlavního město Prahy, inv. no. AMP PGL I-68A

The document is a verified copy of the confirmation of imperial privileges to the renowned Jewish financier Jacob Bassevi von Treyenberg. With this document of 1648, Ferdinand II confirms not only the title of Court Jew already conferred by Rudolf II in 1599 and by Matthias in 1611, undoubtedly for his credit services, but also two other documents from 1622 by which Bassevi was acknowledged as the first Jew to be granted a name predicate by the Emperor. Further such elevations to subjects from Prague's Jewish community were not made until the very end of Josef II's rule; thus, not for another 160 years. Bassevi participated in the activities of a banking consortium. It was not until the death of his powerful protector, Valdstejn, which signalled a marked deterioration in his wealth, the remainder of which he transferred to his family and withdrew into retirement.

Hrdlicka 1993, p.193; Sedlacek 1925, p.365; Schimon 1859, p.6; Kral 1904, p.91; Stafl 1974, p. 59–61.

J.Hr.

v.616
Confirmation of a Privilege Granted by Ferdinand II to Jacob Bassevi von Treyenberg
German authentic copy (or authentic in the form of a translation of the Czech original); parchment document in book form; twelve folios with black velvet binding. Miniature of an original coat-of-arms on folio 6b, 154 × 129 mm, semi-grain on folio 10a, 153 × 130 mm. The bulk of the seal authenticating the copy (of the translation) is of red wax appended to a black and yellow cord. The translation was authenticated by Ilter; a copy of the translation was authenticated by the registrar of the Czech Chamber, Daniel Ambler von

Friedenfels.
28.5 × 31 × 1.5 cm; average size of the trunk of the seal: 6.5 cm ; pendant 22.5 + 16 cm
12 April 1628
Prague, Muzeum hlavního město Prahy, inv. no. AMP PGL 1 – 68 B

This second specimen, compatible in content, of a privilege granted by Ferdinand II to the Jewish financier Bassevi is again in the form of an authentic copy. It contains two miniatures with an original and a revised coat-of-arms, in which the depiction of the ruling sovereign is taken to extremes. In the usual two-fold heraldic expression of the imperial office (the imperial coat-of-arms and the scutcheon of the imperial electors) even the figural pieces (of the Emperor seated on the throne in the middle surrounded by the figures of the electors in the manner of an ideal but not realistic portrait), were both supplemented by the coat-of-arms and the figure of the King of Hungary. This leads, particularly in the figurative decorations

Hrdlicka 1993, p.193, pic. no. 55; Sedlacek 1925, p.365; Schimon 1859, p.6; Kral 1904, p.9; Stafl 1974, p. 59–61

J.Hr.

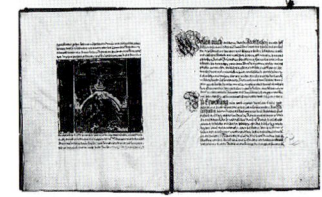

---

v.617
Curtain from the Old-New Synagogue
Velvet, silk, appliqué and embroidery in gold and silver thread
230 × 163 cm
1592
Prague, Židovské muzeum, inv. no. 27 365

The work of two generations of the Prague family embroiderers Perlsticker is the oldest preserved Torah curtain in Central and Eastern Europe. As the Hebrew inscription says: 'The Lord gave Solomon wisdom so that he could make designs for work with gold and silver and every kind of craft and embroidery and weaving from figures of blue and crimson' (Ex 31.4 and 35.5) The text recalls an older curtain donated by the Perlstickers in 1547. The tessalated embroidery, which produces a portal design on the central field of the curtain, is dated 1592 and signed by Pinchas and his wife Gunzi. The columns form a portal and repeat in the upper central field along the sides of the Torah crown, which is a frequent motif in synagogal art, expressing the majesty of the Law.

Essen and Vienna 1988; Jerusalem, 1990; Prague 1992.

J.Š

---

v.618
Curtain from the Maisel Synagogue
Silk, velvet and appliqué, river pearl beads
230 × 163
Mordecai ben Solomon Maisel and his wife Frumet, daughter Yitzhaka Rofe
1592
Donated by Mordecai Maisel and his wife Frumet
Prague, Židovské muzeum, inv. no. 31 749

As the donor's inscription attests, the curtain belongs to the original furnishing of the synagogue, for the consecration of which on the holy day of Simchat Torah in 1592 it was made in a Prague Jewish embroiderer's workshop, most likely the workshop of the Perlstickers. In the portal design of its ornamentation the crown of the Torah directly rounds off the columns by a method that is repeated by a succession of textiles that have been fabricated up until modern times. The Maisel Torah curtain together with the one donated to the Old-New Synagogue by the Perlstickers represent the oldest ceremonial synagogal textiles from the Renaissance period.

Essen and Vienna 1988, cat. no. 497; permanent exhibition in the Jewish Museum, Prague.

J.Š

---

v.619
Curtain from the Old-New Synagogue
Velvet, silk, appliqué, embroidery with silver and gold threads and pearl beads
215 × 132 cm
1602
Donated by Nathan Karpl-Zaks and his wife Hadasi
Prague, Židovské muzeum, inv. no. 27 391

The curtain is one of four large Renaissance textiles donated to the Old-New Synagogue in the sixteenth and seventeenth centuries that were ornamented by appliqué. The medallion at top of the trimming above the donor's inscription bears the emblem of three fish (small carps) symbolizing the donor's family name.

USA-Canada, 1983–85; Essen and Vienna 1988; Prague 1991.

J.Š

---

v.620
Curtain from the Old-New Synagogue
Velvet, silk brocade, embroidery, pearl beads
215 × 133 cm
1609
Donated by Moses Epstein and his wife Sara
Prague, Židovské muzeum, inv. no. 27381

In place of a portal type of ornamentation is a composition of two rare fabrics with an emphasis on the large central field. The distinctive framed donor's inscription in the upper strip is complemented by realistically executed Levitical services - a laver and basin that symbolize the traditional family membership of the donor as of the tribe of Levi.

Prague 1984–85; permanent exhibition of the Jewish Museum, Prague.

Vilímkova 1993, p. 188.

J.Š

V.621
Curtain from the Old-New Synagogue
Velvet, embroidery in gold and silver, bells
235 × 170 cm
1623
Donated by Jacob Bat Sheva-Bashevi and his wife Hendl
Prague, Židovské muzeum, inv. no. 27 396

An opulent Renaissance embroidery of an architectural design and vegetal motifs is executed in contours by silver and gold thread. The bells under the inscribed band accentuate by their ring the solemnity of the moment when during the religious service the curtain is drawn aside and from the Holy Ark a scroll of the Torah is taken out. The curtain was donated to the synagogue in the period when Jacob Bashevi was acting as head of the Prague ghetto and was approaching the height of his career.

Jerusalem 1990; permanent exhibition in the Jewish Museum, Prague.

Muneles 1965, p. 58, ill. 3; Volavková 1949, ills 16-19.

J.Š

V.622
Synagogue Pulpit Cover
Velvet, silk, embroidery
155 × 146 cm
1638
Donated by Zalman ben Azriel and his wife Rachel
Prague, Židovské muzeum, inv. no. 40 974

The centre of this textile, used as a covering on the high pulpit for the reading of the Torah in the *bimah* (the platform of the synagogue) and considerably later even as a curtain, is made of Florentine brocade from the fifteenth century. It is one of the oldest pieces of textile preserved in the collection of the Jewish Museum. It was donated to the Old School, the oldest synagogue of the Prague ghetto.

Permanent exhibition of the Jewish Museum, Prague.

Muneles 1965, p. 102; Volavková 1949, ills 1-5.

J.Š

V.623
Torah mantle
Velvet, brocade, embroidery with gold thread
96 × 49 cm
1661
Donated by Yokev Popper and his wife Jutl
Prague, Židovské muzeum, inv. no. 27 405

The centre of the mantle is composed of the oldest, precious patterned fabric, likely of Florentine origin. The ornamentation is complemented at top with a Levitical laver as a symbol of the donor's belonging to the tribe of Levi. Jacob or Yokev Popper was the head of the Old-New Synagogue.
Permanent exhibition of the Jewish Museum, Prague

Kybalová 1973, p. 38; 1975, p. 66

J.Š

V.624
Kiddush Cup
Silver, gilding
H: 24.5 cm; Diam: 8 cm
Early seventeenth century
Prague, Židovské muzeum, inv. no. 3939

The Renaissance kiddush cup decorated by scaled ornaments was used for the holy and ceremonial blessing of the wine (kiddush), and according to tradition it belonged to Rabbi Löw. The cup is one of the small ceremonial objects used both during religious services in the synagogue and in the home. They frequently did not bear the donor's inscription nor other text that would indicate its function. Objects of precious metals were kept in families for a succession of generations.

Essen and Vienna 1988, cat. no. 508; permanent exhibition of the Jewish Museum, Prague.

J.Š

V.625
Wild, Jeremias
Levite Service: Laver and Basin
Silver
Pitcher: H 15 cm, diam 8 cm; laver: diam. 28.5 cm
Ca. 1590
Prague, Židovské muzeum, inv. no. 3804, 3825

A Levite laver and basin serves the ritual washing of the hands of the priests (Cohanim) before the benediction to the community on holy days, according to Old Testament precepts with the assistance of ancillary priests (Levites). The service was produced by J. Wild and it is the oldest silver utensil in the collection of the Jewish Museum. The coat-of-arms, engraved onto the outer side of the pitcher and in the middle of the basin suggests that the service was originally in the possession of a noble family and was purchased for the Jewish community.

Essen and Vienna 1988, cat. no. 506; permanent exhibition of the Jewish Museum, Prague

J.Š

v.626

Jehudah Loew ben Bezalel (Maharal Rabbi Löw)
Worms 1520–Prague 1609
Gur Arye (Young Lion)
Print, paper, leather binding
30 × 18.5 cm (open 30 × 39 cm); 228 fols.
1578
By the data on the title page, it was published in Prague during the reign of Rudolf, Emperor of Rome by Bezales ben Mordecai Katz in the home of Mordecai ben Gershom Katz
Prague, Židovské muzeum, inv. no. 3578

The book contains the first published commentary of Rabbi Löw to the explication of the Pentateuch from Solomon ben Yitzhak from Troyes (Rashi, 1040–1105). It is a characteristic product of the Prague Hebrew printing house of the Gersonide family with a clear typeface and woodcut embellishment. The ornamentaion is concentrated primarily on the title page and its basis is an architectonic portal-style frame complemented by period motifs, traditional Judaic fine arts motifs, and miniature typographical trimmings typical for the Gersonide printers (lime-tree leaves, clover leaves, four-leafed rosettes). The ornamentation of this edition distinctly follows the pattern of Renaissance Jewish book-printing in Italy.

Essen and Vienna, 1988, cat. no. 503; Prague, 1992; permanent exhibition of the Jewish Museum, Prague.

J.Š.

v.627

Jehudah Loew ben Bezalel (Maharal, Rabbi Löw)
Worms 1520–Prague 1609
Derush Na'e u-Meshubbah (Beautiful and Delightful sermon ... for the weekly section 'Command' on the High Sabbath in the year 349 according to the small dating)
Print, paper, leather binding
19 × 15 cm (open 20 × 31 cm); 30 fols.
1589
According to the data on the title page, it was published in the city of Prague during the reign of the Emperor of Rome Rudolf by the printer Bezalel ben Mordechai Katz in the home of Mordechai ben Gershom ha-Kohen
Prague, Židovské muzeum, inv. no. 12210

The tiltle page of the sermon for the High Sabbath preceding the holiday of Passover is embellished with a typical portal styled frame with columns and frieze filled out by floral motifs. An interesting addition is the inconspicuous figure of a man with a shield.

Essen and Vienna, 1988, cat. no. 504; permanent exhibition of the Jewish Museum

J.Š.

v.628

Jehudah Loew ben Bezalel (Maharal, Rabbi Löw)
Worms 1520–Prague 1609
Derush al ha-Tora ve-al ha-Mitzvot (sermon on the Torah and the Precepts)
Print, paper, paper binding
19 × 15.5 cm (open 19 × 30.5 cm); 40 folios
1593
According to the data on the title page and in the colophon, the work was published by two associate Gersonide family book-printers, Solomon ben Mordecai ha-Kohen Katz and Moses ben Joseph Bezalel ha-Kohen
Prague, Židovské muzeum, inv. no. 4727

Ethical commentaries delivered in Poznan in May 1572. The text on the title page has a simple frame composed of graphic trimming without sophisticated decorative elements. Fol. 2a contains a woodcut illustrating the ancient temple in Jerusalem after the conceptions of the day.

Exhibition of the Jewish Museum in Prague.

Nosek, 1974, p. 34.

J.Š.

v.629

Rabbi Jacob Pollak
Died Lublin 1530
Responsum Concerning the Teshuva al Aguna (abandoned wives)
Print, leather binding
18 × 14 cm (open 18 × 28 cm); 20 fols.
1594
According to the data on the title page it was published in Prague during the reign of the Emperor of Rome Rudolf by Moses ben Bezalel Katz, printer
Prague, Židovské muzeum, inv. no. 4778

The author of the responsa was active in Prague at the beginning of the sixteenth century as rabbi and rector of the yeshivah. In his replies, printed with an extensive commentary by Rabbi Löw, he pursued the frequent legal problem of the *agunoth*, women abandoned by their husbands. Regardless of the circumstances of a particular case, a woman is not allowed to remarry without obtaining a divorce permit or a statement of the husband's death. The title page is embellished by Renaissance figural woodcuts: in addition to animal motifs there is also a portrait of a man and the figures of Adam and Eve who obviously have a relationship to the subject-matter of the responsa. The signet of the Gersonides on fol. 20b has an inscription on the periphery with the name of the then owner of the printing house, Solomon ben Mordecai ha-Kohen.

USA–Canada, 1983–85, cat. no. 279; permanent exhibition of the Jewish Museum in Prague.

Altshuler 1983, p. 272.

J.Š.

v.630

David Gans ben Solomon
Lippstadt 1541–Prague 1613
Zemah David (Offspring of David)
Print, paper, half-leather binding
18.5 × 15 cm (open 19 × 34 cm)
1592
According to the data on the title page, it was published in the city of Prague during the reign of Emperor Rudolf by two associate book-printers, Solomon ha-Kohen and the son of his brother Moses ha-Kohen
Prague, Židovské muzeum, inv. no. Jc 4279

This two-part chronicle, which covers the history of the Jews and general history from the creation of the world up until the year 1592, was the first written Hebrew work of this genre in Central Europe. In it the author applied an array of principles of Renaissance historiography. The graphic embellishment of the chronicle is not sophisticated. The text on the title pages of both parts is set in a simple frame and a few paragraphs of the world chronicle dedicated to the prominent sovereigns are indicated by a woodcut of the royal crown.

Essen and Vienna 1988, cat.no. 500; Prague 1971; permanent exhibition of the Jewish Museum in Prague.

J.Š.

v.631
David Gans ben Solomon
Lippstadt 1541–Prague 1613
Nehmad ve-Na'im (*Pleasant and Lovely*)
Print, paper, half-leather binding
21.5 × 15.5 cm (open 21.5 × 33 cm)
1743
According to the data on the title page, the work was printed in Slavkov (Austerlitz) by Joel ben Yekutiel, who came from Hlohov (Glogau).
Prague, Židovské muzeum, cat. no. 12600

An astronomical-geographical-mathematical work in which the author communicates to his contemporaries the then present state of knowledge in these disciplines. Commentary accompanies an array of sketches including instructions on the use of measuring apparatus, sundials, etc. The portal trimming of the title page is composed of a frequently applied Baroque schematic of tortile columns with Corinthian capitals bearing an open segmented arch with complementary architectonic elements.

Prague 1971; permanent exhibition of the Jewish Museum, Prague.

Alter 1958.

J.Š.

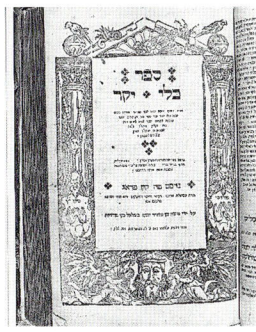

v.632
Mordecai Jafe ben Abraham
Vesture of Cambric and Crimson, Vesture from the City of Shushan
Print, paper, leather binding
31 × 19.5 cm (open 31 × 46 cm); 117 and 210 fols.
1609
According to the date on the title page, it was published in Prague during the reign of Rudolf, Emperor of Rome by Moses Bezalel Katz, printer
Prague, Židovské muzeum, inv. no. 2891a

The fourth and fifth volumes of the collection of writings *Levush ha-malchut* (*Royal Vesture*) which contains an elaboration of the religious-legal codex of Joseph Kara (1488-1575) *Shulchan Aruch* (*A Laid Table*). The Gersonides published all ten volumes in the same design and almost all with the same graphic ornamentation. The title list is composed as a compact portal frame, complemented by Renaissance architectonic elements and vegetal and figural motifs including human figures and mascarons. Located at the feet of the columns, the signet of the Gersonide printers – priestly hands in blessing – repeats in the end of the books as an emblem with a crown of the priesthood buttressing angels and with the inscription *Mishpahat ha-Gershoni* (*The Gersonide Family*).

Essen and Vienna 1988, cat. no. 501; permanent exhibition of the Jewish Museum.

J.Š.

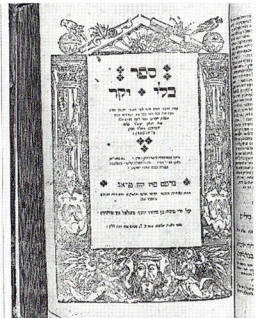

v.633
Mordecai Jafe ben Abraham
Levush ha-Butz ve-Argaman (*Vesture of Cambric and Crimson*)
Print, paper, leather binding on wood
31 × 19.5 cm (open 31 × 46 cm); 117 fols
1609
According to the data on the title page, it was published by Moses ben Bezalel Katz, printer
Prague, Židovské muzeum, inv. no. Jc 14 703

The fourth volume of the collection of writings *Levush ha-Malchut* (*Royal Vesture*).

Nosek 1974, p. 36.

J.Š.

---

v.634
Solomon Ephraim Luntschitz
Died in Prague 1619
Keli Yakar (*Precious Vessel*)
Print, paper, leather binding on wood
33 × 22 cm (open 33 × 45.5 cm); 141 fols
1608
According to the data on the title page it was published by Moses ben Joseph Bezalel Katz. Scroll: *Sefer Sheelot u-Teshuvot* (*Responsa*), Gersonide, Prague, 1608
Prague, Židovské muzeum, inv. no. 33 562 II A 5064

Solomon Ephraim Luntschitz was active in Prague from 1604 as the successor of Rabbi Löw in the function as Chief Rabbi. He became renowned mainly as a lecturer. The Prague publication of his well-known and often cited commentary to the Pentateuch has the same ornamentation on the title page as a series of other folio printings by the Gersonides's offices of the same period. In a further text there are found Renaissance designed initials and characteristic typographic trimming, and the end of the work bears the Gersonides' signet.

Prmanent exhibition of the Jewish Museum, Prague

Nosek, 1974, pg. 35

J.Š.

---

v.635
Joseph Ber Miklis ben Yitzachar
Sefer Josef Daat (*The Book Furnishing Knowledge*)
Print, paper, half-leather binding
18.5 × 15 cm (open 18.5 × 31.5 cm); without title page; 148 fols
1609
Prague, Židovské muzeum, inv. no. 1157

Commentary to the Pentateuch contains explications of the medieval authors Rabbi Löw, Mordecai Jaffe and others. The text is accompanied by tiny sketches and several full-page descriptive woodcuts (symbolizing Jacob's ladder with the rungs as the twelve tribes of Israel, fol. 25b; a seven-armed menorah from the temple in Jerusalem, fol. 58b; the plan of the Temple district, fol. 73b; a map of the land of Israel, fol. 128a). The author of the work acted as a proof-reader and co-publisher in the Bak printing house.

Permanent exhibition of the Jewish Museum, Prague.

Nosek 1974, pg. 36; 1975, pp. 47-48

J.Š.

v.636
Petahia Yitzacher ben Moses
Imre Bina (Words of Wisdom)
Print, paper, paper binding
18 × 14 cm (open 18 × 28 cm); 44 fols
1610
According to the data on the title page
the book was published by Moses ben
Bezalel Katz
Prague, Židovské muzeum, inv. no. 12248

A work on ethics containing commentary
to the cabbalistic book *Zohar*. The rich Renaissance embellishment of the title page,
in which figural motifs are set in an architectonic portal schematic, complement

traditional motifs of the hexagram and
the hands of the Cohanim in blessing - the
symbol of the family name and signet of
the Gersonides book printers.

Permanent exhibition Jewish Museum,
Prague.

Nosek 1974, p. 37; Sadek 1992, p. 58.

J.Š.

v.637
Shem Tov ben Joseph
Spain 1225–1290
Cori ha-Yagon (Balm for Woe)
Print, paper, paper binding
17 × 13.5 cm (open 17 × 28 cm)
1612
According to the data on the title page it
was published for the second time in
Prague by Jacob ben Gershom Bak,
printer
Prague, Židovské muzeum, inv. no. 13214

An ethical work about the resignation of
the soul in sorrow. The text of the title
page enframes loosely composed plates,

two with a vegetal frieze and two with figures of the Old Testament prophets
Habakkuk and Zephaniah. A description
of both figures in a Latin legend suggests
that these plates were obtained from a
Christian printing house.

Essen and Vienna, cat. no. 502; permanent
exhibition of the Jewish Museum, Prague.

J.Š.

v.638
Yom Tov Lipmann Heller
Wallerstein 1579–Cracow 1654
Mishna, the passage on Purity; with a commentary of the learned Obadiah Bertinoro
and with Addenda by Yom Tov ...
Print, paper, half-leather binding
21.5 × 18.5 cm (open 21.5 × 37 cm); 167 fols
(torso)
1614
From the data on the title page, it was published in Prague during the reign of Emperor Matthias by Moses ben Joseph Bezalel Katz, printer
Prague, Židovské muzeum, inv. no. 1899

The print has a typical design for a commentary of Talmudic text with a basic explication in the middle of the printed page
and commentary arranged around it. This
edition contains, in addition to the classic
commentary of the Italian scholar Obadiah da Bertinoro (1440–1516), a corresponding section of the most significant
work of Yom Tov Lipman Heller, which
was first published in Prague in 1597 and
to this day is a part of all great editions of
the Talmud.

Muneles 1952, no. 95

J.Š.

v.639
*Megillat Vorhangpurim (Scroll on a Curtain
Purim)*
Ink on parchment
26 × 76 cm
1623
Prague, Židovské muzeum, inv. no. Ms
254

A commemorative scroll written in Hebrew or in Judeo-German, which arose in
the seventeenth century after the model of
the Biblical Book of *Esther*, and was in Bohemia a popular form of vernacular town
chronicle-writing. Such works narrated
the fortunate ending of threatening

events and they were read out at annual
family celebrations, organized to commemorate deliverance from danger. The
story of the *Vorhangpurim* coincides with
the dramatic period of Thirty Years' War
and recounts the preservation of the synagogal servant Hanoch ben Moses Altschul
who was accused of the purchase of expensive drapes stolen from Lichtenstein
Palace.

USA–Canada, 1983–85, cat. no. 250.

Altshuler 1983, p. 268.

J.Š.

v.640
Yom Tov Lipmann Heller
Wallerstein 1579–Cracow 1654
Megillat Eva (Scroll of Hatred)
Ink, paper
22 × 18.5 cm (open 22 × 37 cm); 31 fols (14
in Hebrew, 17 Judeo-German)
1773
The manuscript was produced for Lezer
Zekeles
Prague, Židovské muzeum, inv. no. Ms 29

An autobiographical work of the Prague
Rabbi, the contents of which bear a resemblance to a family scroll, originated in
1628. It recounts the dangers that later

threatened Heller who was accused by the
authorities in Vienna of attacking the
Catholic faith and was imprisoned. Although Heller demonstrated his innocence and was freed, he had to pay a fine of
10,000 tolars (which was partially defrayed
by the head of the Prague ghetto and
Court Jew Jacob Bashevi), and he left
Prague where he had been engaged for almost thirty years. His *Scroll of Tribulation*
was popular reading for a century, disseminated in transcriptions in Hebrew and
Judeo-German, as was the case with the
present manuscript.

Sadek 1973, pp. 16-17.

J.Š.

Exhibitions

Amsterdam 1906
Werk van Pieter Brueghel den Oude, Amsterdam, Rijks Prentenkabinet, 1906

Amsterdam 1912
Nederlandsche Volkskleederdrachten van de XVIde tot in de XXste eeuw, Amsterdam, 1912

Amsterdam 1955
De triomf van het manierisme: De europese stijl van Michelangelo tot El Greco, Amsterdam, Rijksmuseum, 1955

Amsterdam 1965
J. Q. van Regteren Altena-L. C. J. Frederichs, *Selected Drawings from the Printroom*, Amsterdam, Rijksmuseum, 1965

Amsterdam 1967
Grafiek van Hercules Segbers, Amsterdam, Rijksprentenkabinet, 1967

Amsterdam 1970
Keuze uit de aanwisten 1969 van het Rijksprentenkabinet, Amsterdam, 1970

Amsterdam 1979
Nederlands zilver/ Dutch silver 1580-1830, Amsterdam, Rijksmuseum, 1979

Amsterdam 1993
Dawn of the Golden Age: Northern Netherlandish art 1580-1620, ed. G. Luijten-A. van Suchtelen, Amsterdam-Zwolle, 1993

Antwerpen 1993
Antwerpen: Story of a metropolis 16th - 17th century, Antwerp, Hessenhuis, 1993

Basel 1967
Unbekannte Handzeichnungen alter Meister 15. - 18. Jahrhundert: Sammlung Freiherr Koenig-Fachsenfeld, Basel, Kunsthalle, 1967

Berlin 1912
R. Lepke, *Sammlung Alb. Jaffé, II: Miniaturbildnisse*, Berlin, 1912

Berlin 1963
Ausgewählte Werke, Berlin, Kunstgewerbemuseum, 1963

Berlin 1968
K. Pechstein, *Bronzen und Plaketten vom ausgehenden 15. Jahrhundert bis zur Mitte des 17. Jahrhunderts*, Berlin, Kunstgewerbemuseums, 1968

Berlin 1970
Europäisches Kunsthandwerk: Neuerwerbungen 1959-1969, Berlin, Kustgewerbemuseum, 1970

Berlin 1975
Pieter Bruegel d. Ä. als Zeichner, Berlin, Staatliche Museen Preussischer Kulturbesitz, Kupferstichkabinett, 1975

Berlin 1979
H. Mielke, *Manierismus in Holland um 1600: Kupferstiche, Holzschitte und Zeichnungen*, Berlin, Staatliche Museen Preussischer Kulturbesitz, Kupferstichkabinett, 1979

Berlin 1979
Klaus Pechstein, *Goldschmiedewerke der Renaissance*, Berlin, Kunstgewerbemuseum, 1979

Berlin 1982
Mythen der neuen Welt, Berlin, 1982

Berlin 1983
Kunst der Reformationszeit, Berlin, Staatliche Museen der DDR, 1983

Berlin 1988
Die Verführung der Europa, Berlin, 1988

Berlin 1995
W. Steguweit, *Europäische Medaillenkunst von der Renaissance bis zur Gegenwart*, Berlin, 1995

Berlin 1995
Von allen Seiten schön: Bronzen der Renaissance und des Barock, ed. V. Krahn, Berlin, 1995

Bern-Zürich 1986
J. Kybalová, *Fayencen aus der Tschechoslowakei*, Bern-Zürich, 1986

Bordeaux 1957
Bosch, Goya et les fantastique, Bordeaux, 1957

Brandýs nad Labem 1995
D. Stehlíková, *"Paládium a pokladnice": Poutě do Staré Boleslavi*, Brandýs nad Labem, 1995

Bremen 1964
Die schönsten Handzeichnungen von Dürer bis Picasso aus dem Besitz der Kunsthalle Bremen, 1964

Brno 1898
Katalog der Buch-Ausstellung, Brno, Mährisches Gewerbemuseum, 1898

Brno 1925
Alte Meister im mährischen Privatbesitz, Brno, Künstlerhaus, 1925

Brno 1955
A. Kudělková, *Moravská a slovenská habánská keramika*, Brno, 1955

Brno 1961 (Liberec 1962)
Škola vidění, Brno, 1961 (Liberec, 1962)

Brno 1975
L. a K. Holešovští, *Historické hodiny 15.-19. století ze sbírek Moravské galerie v Brně*, Brno, 1975

Brussels 1935
Cinq siecles d'Art, Brussels, Mussées Royaux des Beaux-Arts, 1935

Bucharest 1979
Catalogue of the Universal Art Gallery, The Museum of the Socialist Republic of Romania: German and Austrian Painting, Bucharest, 1979

Budapest 1931
E. Hoffmann, *Deutsche Zeichnungen 1400-1650*, Budapest, Szépmüvészeti Múzeum, 1931

Budapest 1961
A manierismus korának mıveszete, Budapest, Szépmüvészeti Múzeum, 1961
T. Gerszi, *Von Bruegel bis Rembrandt*, Budapest, Szépmüvészeti Múzeum, 1967

Budapest 1974
A. Czobor, *Aquarelle aus sieben Jahrhunderten*, Budapest, Szépmüvészeti Múzeum, 1974

Budapest 1991
T. Gerszi-S. Bodnár, *Müvészet II. Rudolf Prágai udvarában: Rajzok és metszetek a budapesti Szépmüvészeti Múzeum és a bécsi Albertina anyagából*, Budapest, Szépmüvészeti Múzeum, 1991

Coburg 1983
Illustrierte Flugblätter aus den Jahrhunderten der Reformation und der Glaubenskämpfe, Coburg, Kunstsammlungen der Veste Coburg, 1983

Copenhagen-Rosenborg 1994
J. Hein, *Guide 1994*, Copenhagen, Rosenborg, 1994

Copenhagen-Rosenborg 1986
J. Hein, *Sophie Amalie (1628 - 85) - den onde dronning*, Copenhagen, Rosenborg, 1986

Copenhagen-Rosenborg 1988
Christian IV og Europa/Christian IV and Europe, Copenhagen, 1988

Cologne 1965
Handzeichnungen des 15. und 16. Jahrhunderts und Miniaturen aus den Sammlungen des Wallraf-Richartz-Museum Köln, Cologne, 1965

Cologne 1985
Roelandt Savery in seiner Zeit, Cologne, Walraf-Richarts-Museum, 1985

Corning 1981
A. Adlerová, *Bohemian Glass 1350-1980*, Corning, The Corning Museum of Glass, 1981

Corning 1981
O. Drahotová, *Czechoslovakian Glass 1350-1980*, Corning, The Corning Museum of Glass, 1981

Cremona 1996
Immagini del sentire: I cinque sensi nell'arte, Milan, 1996

Darmstadt 1964
G. Bergsträsser, *Zeichnungen alter und neuer Meister aus dem Hessinschen Landesmuseum in Darmstadt*, Darmstadt, 1964

Darmstadt 1992
Faszination Edelstein. Aus den Schazkammern der Welt: Mythos-Kunst-Wissenschaft, Darmstadt, 1992

Davis-Sacramento 1972
S. Howard, *Classical Narratives in Master Drawings Selected from the Collections of the E .B .Crocker Art Gallery*, Davis-Sacramento, 1972

Dresden 1972
Europäische Landschaftsmalerei 1550-1650, Dresden, Albertinum, 1972

Dresden 1977
Meisterzeichnungen aus der Graphischen Sammlung der Nationalgalerie Prag, Dresden, Albertinum, 1977

Dresden 1979
Gemäldegalerie Alte Meister, Dresden: Katalog der ausgestellten Werke, Dresden, 1979

Dresden 1991
Die Kurfürsten von Sachsen: Repräsentation in Bildnis und Rüstung, Dresden, 1991

Dresden 1992
Verborgene Schätze der Skulpturensammlung, Dresden, Albertinum, 1992

Dresden 1995
Im Lichte des Halbmonds: Das Abendland und der türkische Orient, Dresden, 1995

Duisburg 1987
Von der Kunstkammer zum Museum: Plastik aus dem Schloßmuseum Gotha, Duisburg, Wilhelm-Lehmbruck-Museum, 1987

Duisburg 1987
Die Beschwörung des Kosmos: Europäische Bildwerke der Renaissance, Duisburg, Wilhelm Lehmbruck-Museum, 1987

Düsseldorf 1969
Meisterzeichnungen der Sammlung Lambert Krabe, Düsseldorf, Kunstmuseum, 1969

Edinburgh 1985
K. Andrew, *Some Netherlandish Drawings in the National Gallery of Scotland*, Edinburgh, 1985

Edinburgh 1991
The Stylish Image: Printmakers to the Court of Rudolf II., Edinburgh, 1991

Eisenstadt 1992
Triumph des Todes, Eisenstadt, 1992

Erbach 1995
Wiedergewonnen: Elfenbeinkunststücke aus Dresden - Eine wiedergewonnene Sammlung, Erbach, Deutsches Elfenbeinmuseum, 1995

Essen and Vienna 1988
Prag um 1600: Kunst und Kultur am Hofe Kaiser Rudolfs II., Freren, 1988

Essen 1977
Barock in Böhmen, Essen, 1977

Florence 1969
Da Dürer a Picasso, Florence, Uffizi, 1969

Florence 1975
Grafica per Orafi: Modelli del Cinque e Seicento. Mostra di incisioni da collezioni italiane, Florence, 1975

Florence 1979
Gli Uffizi: Catalogo generale, Florence, 1979

Florence 1980
Firenze e la Toscana dei Medici nell'Europa del Cinquecento, Palazzo Vecchio: Committenza e collezionismo medicei, Florence, 1980

Frankfurt 1926
Meisterwerke alter Malerei aus Privatbesitz, Frankfurt, 1926

Frankfurt 1993
K. Wettengl, *Georg Flegel 1566-1638: Stilleben*, Frankfurt, Schirn Kunsthalle, 1993

Frankfurt 1993
Mathaeus Merian des Aelteren, Frankfurt, 1993

Ghent 1954
P. Eeckhout, *Roelandt Savery*, Ghent, Museum voor Schone Kunsten, 1954

Gloggnitz 1992
Eroberung der Landschaft, Gloggnitz, 1992

Göttweig 1983
Jubiläumsausstellung 900 Jahre Stift Göttweig, 1083-1983, Gottweig, 1983

Hamburg 1961
Sechs Sammler stellen aus, Hamburg, Museum für Kunst und Gewerbe, 1961

Hamburg 1992
E. Schaar-H. Broeker, *Invenit et sculpsit: Zeichnung und Graphik des niederländischen Manierismus*, Hamburg, Museum für Kunst und Gewerbe, 1992

Hamburg 1993
Pegasus and the Arts, Hamburg, Museum für Kunst und Gewerbe, Munich, 1993

Heidelberg 1986
Die Renaissance im deutschen Südwesten, Heidelberg, 1986

Ingelheim 1988
Kunsthandwerk in Böhmen, Ingelheim, 1988

Innsbruck 1967
Essen und Trinken, Innsbruck, 1967

Karlsruhe 1986
Die Renaissance im deutschen Südwesten: Zwischen Reformation und Dreißigjährigem Krieg, Karlsruhe, 1986

Krefeld 1938
Deutsche Landschaften und Städte in der niederländischen Kunst des 16. bis 18. Jahrhunderts, Krefeld, Kaiser Wilhelm Museum 1938

Krems 1983
900 Jahre des Stiftes Göttweig, Krems, 1983

Kyoto 1994
Catalogue of Japanese Art in the Náprstek Museum, Kyoto, 1994

Lanškroun 1996
Jan Marek Marci z Kronlandu: Život, dílo, doba, Lanškroun, 1996

Liberec 1988
Zámky 15. - 19. století, Liberec, Severočeské muzeum, 1988

Liberec 1989
J. Mohr, *Historické nářadí a nástroje*, Liberec, 1989

Lisbon 1996
A Heranca de Rauchluchantim, Lisbon, Museu de Sao Roque, 1996

London 1949
Art Treasures from Vienna, London, Tate Gallery, 1949

London 1953
Flemish Art 1300-1700, London, Royal Academy, 1953

London 1964
The Orange and the Rose, London, Victoria and Albert Museum, 1964

London 1982
Facets of Indian Art, London, Victoria and Albert Museum, 1982

London 1986
M. Leithe-Jasper, *Renaissance Master Bronzes from the Collection of the Kunsthistorisch Museum in Vienna*, London, 1986

London 1984
J. Rowlands, *German Drawings from a private collection*, London, British Museum, 1984

Madrid 1985
Catalogo de las pinturas, Madrid, Museo del Prado, 1985

Madrid 1990
Alfonso Sánchez Coello y el retrato en la corte de Felippe II, Madrid, Museo del Prado, 1990

Mantova 1989
Giulio Romano, Milan, 1989

Milan 1966
L'Arte del Barocco in Bohemia, Milan, 1966

Milan 1992
Ori e tesori d' Europa: Mille anni di oreficeria nel Friuli e Venezia Giulia, Milan, 1992

Murnau 1995
F. Ryser, *Amalierte Stuck uff Glass: Hinder Glas gemalte Historien und Gemäld*, Murnau, 1995.

Munich 1910
C. List, *Die Waffen*, Munich, 1910

Munich 1972
Das Aquarell 1400-1950, Munich, Haus der Kunst, 1972

Munich 1980
Um Glauben und Reich, Munich, 1980

München 1980
Wittelsbach und Bayern, Munich, 1980

Munich 1994
Silber und Gold: Augsburger Goldschmiedekunst für die Höfe Europas, Munich, Bayerisches Nationalmuseum, 1994

Münster-Baden Baden 1980
Stilleben in Europa, Münster, Westfälisches Landesmuseum für Kunst und Kulturgeschichte; Baden-Baden, Staatliche Kunsthalle, 1980

Nara/Tokyo 1995
Treasures of the Habsburgs: Masterpieces of the Kunsthistorisches Museum, Wien, Nara, 1995

Neuhofen 1996
Ostarrichi: Österreich 996-1996, Neuhofen a. d. Ybbs, 1996

New York 1988
Africa and the Renaissance: Art in Ivory, New York, 1988

Nürnberg 1952
Aufgang der Neuzeit: Deutsche Kunst und Kultur von Dürers Tod bis zum Dreißigjährigen Kriege, 1530-1650, Nürnberg, Germanisches Nationalmuseum, 1952

Nürnberg 1955
Kunst und Kultur in Böhmen, Mähren und Schlesien, Nürnberg, Germanisches Nationalmuseum, 1955

Nürnberg 1984
Deutsche Zeichnungen aus einer Privatsammlung, Nürnberg, Germanisches Nationalmuseum, 1984

Nürnberg 1985
Wenzel Jamnitzer und die Nürnberger Goldschmiedekunst 1500-1700, Nürnberg, Germanisches Nationalmuseum, 1985

Nürnberg 1990
800 Jahre Deutscher Orden, Nürnberg, Germanisches Nationalmuseum, 1990

Nürnberg 1992
R. Schoch, *Meister der Zeichnung*, Nürnberg, 1992

Pardubice 1972
L.Machytka, *Malířství 17. a 18. století ve Státních zámcích východních Čech*, Pardubice, KSPPOP a Východočeská galerie v Pardubicích, 1972

Pardubice 1973
L.Machytka, *Výstava málo známých obrazů z východočeských zámků*, Pardubice, KSPPOP a Východočeská galerie v Pardubicích, 1973

Paris 1893
Collection Fréderic Spitzer, Paris, 1893

Paris 1935
De Van Eyck a Bruegel, Paris, Orangerie, 1935

Paris 1952
Nature morte de l'antiquité a nos jours, Paris, 1952

Paris 1981
Baroque en Bohéme, Paris, 1981

Paris 1978
H. D. Schepelern, *Tresor des Rois de Danemark*, Paris, Petit Palais, 1978

Prague 1862
Die Archeologischen Sammlungen im Museum Königreichs Böhmen in Prag, Prague, 1862

Prague 1891
Katalog retrospektivní výstavy: Všeobecná zemská výstava v Praze 1891, Prague, 1891

Prague 1898
Výstava architektury a inženýrství, Prague, 1898

Prague 1904
K. Chytil, *Umění v Praze za Rudolfa II.*, Prague, 1904

Prague 1910
Výstava děl Karla Škréty, Prague, Krasoumná jednota pro Čechy a Kroužek přátel umění malířského, 1910

Prague 1912
K. Chytil, *Rudolf II.: Výstava děl jeho dvorních umělců a podobizen osobností jeho dvora*, Prague, 1912

Prague 1912
Rudolf II. Eine Ausstellung von Werken seiner Hofkünstler und Bildnissen von Persönlichkeiten an dessen Hof, Prague, 1912

Prague 1912
Obrazárna v Rudolfinu v Praze, Prague, 1912

Prague 1912
K. Chytil, *Rudolf II.: Umění na jeho dvoře*, Prague, Rudolfinum, 1912

Prague 1934
Albrecht z Valdštejna a doba bělohorská, Prague, Valdštejnský palác a Uměleckoprůmyslové muzeum, 1934

Prague 1934
V. Kramář, *Výstava kreseb starých českých mistrů XVII. a XVIII. stol.*, Prague, 1934

Prague 1938
Staroměstská radnice a její památky, Prague, 1938

Prague 1938
Pražské baroko 1620-1800, Prague, 1938

Prague 1955
J. Vydrová, *Italská majolika v Uměleckoprůmyslovém museu v Praze*, Prague, 1955

Prague 1958
Celostátní výstava archivních dokumentů, Prague 1958

Prague 1962
Výstava přírůstků 1957-1962: Obrazy, Prague, Národní galerie, 1962

Prague 1966
Minulost Prahy v dokumentech Archivu hlavního města Prahy, Prague, 1966.

Prague 1966
L. Urešová, *Renesanční umělecké řemeslo ze sbírek Uměleckoprůmyslového musea v Praze*, Prague, 1966

Prague 1966
Vojtěch svobodný pán Lanna, sběratel, mecenáš a podnikatel, Prague, Uměleckoprůmyslové museum, 1966

Prague 1966
B. Nuska, *Knižní vazba sedmi století z fondů Strahovské knihovny*, Prague, 1966

Prague 1968
Z. Míková-J. Hlinka, *Česká a slovenská medaile 1508-1968*, Prague, 1968

Prague 1969
Václav Hollar 1607-1677: Lepty a kresby, Prague, 1969

Prague 1970
E. Poche, *České sklo 17. a 18. století*, Prague, Uměleckoprůmyslové muzeum, 1970

Prague 1970
Prahou ve stopách baroka: Výstava grafiky v Památníku národního písemnictví na Strahově, Prague, 1970

Prague 1971
Kepler a Praha, Prague, Židovské museum, 1971

Prague 1972
Cín-z dějin českého konvářství, Prague, 1972

Prague 1973
J. Vydrová, *Velká doba italského umění ohně: Italská majolika z československých sbírek*, Prague, 1973

Prague 1974
J. Neumann, *Karel Škréta 1610-1674*, Prague, Národní galerie, 1974

Prague 1974
Barokní zlatnictví ze sbírek Uměleckoprůmyslového muzea v Praze, Prague, 1974

Prague 1975
Mistrovská díla UPM, Prague, 1975

Prague 1976
100 starých českých kreseb z Grafické sbírky v Praze, Prague, 1976

Prague 1977
L. Urešová, *Hodiny ze sbírek Uměleckoprůmyslového muzea v Praze*, Prague, 1977

Prague 1978
E. Fučíková, *Rudolfínská kresba*, Prague, Národní galerie v Praze, 1979

Prague 1978
Doba Karla IV. v dějinách národů ČSSR, Prague, 1979

Prague 1981
Věra Vokáčová, *Nože, lžíce, vidličky*, Prague, 1981

Prague-Brno 1981-82
J. Kybalová, *Hábánská fajáns*, Prague-Brno, 1981-82

Prague 1982
Antické tradice v českém umění, Prague, 1982

Prague 1982
Věra Vokáčová, *Lavabo-flakón*, Prague, Uměleckoprůmyslové muzeum, 1982

Prague 1983
E. Herold, *Africké umění v Československu*, Prague, 1983

Prague 1983
Václav Hollar: Kresby a grafické listy ze sbírek Britského muzea v Londýně a Národní galerie v Praze, Prague, 1983

Prague 1984
Český granát, Prague, 1984

Prague 1984
P. Štěpánek, *Španělské umění 14. - 16. století z československých sbírek*, Prague, Středočeská galerie, 1984

Prague 1984
Z. Rasl, *Černé řemeslo v průběhu staletí*, Prague, Národní technické muzeum, 1984

Prague 1984
H. Brožková, *České sklo*, Prague, Uměleckoprůmyslové muzeum, 1989

Prague 1985
Miniatura drobný portrét z českých a moravských sbírek, Prague, Středočeská galerie, 1985

Prague 1985
Uměleckoprůmyslové muzeum v Praze 1885-1985, Prague, 1985

Prague 1985-Bechyně 1989
Keramika Dálného východu, Prague, Náprstkovo museum; Bechyně, Alšova jihočeská galerie, 1989

Prague 1986
M. Mžyková, *Chebská reliéfní intarzie a grafika*, Prague, 1986

Prague 1988
Poklady Archivu České koruny, Prague, 1988

Prague 1990
Desky zemské - Klenoty Království českého, Prague, 1990

Prague 1991
Pražské cechovní památky ze sbírek Archivu hl. města Prahy, Prague, 1991

Prague 1991
Sedm století pražské heraldiky, Prague, 1991

Prague 1992
J. Chlíbec, *Italské renesanční bronzy*, Prague, Národní galerie, 1992

Prague 1992
J. Kybalová, *Evropská fajáns- European Faience*, Prague, 1992

Prague 1993
A. Rollová, *Nizozemské kresby 16. a 17. století*, Prague, Národní galerie, 1993

Prague 1993
Johannes von Nepomuk 1393-1993, Prague-Mnichov, 1993

Prague 1993
Tisíc let kláštera benediktinů v Břevnově, Prague, 1993

Prague 1993
Artis pictoriae amatores: Evropa v zrcadle pražského barokního sběratelství, Prague, Národní galerie,1993

Prague 1994
H. Seifertová, *Georg Flegel (1566-1638): zátiší*, Prague, Národní galerie, 1994

Prague 1994
Proti silám temnot, Prague, Národní muzeum, 1994

Prague 1994
Svatý Václav v umění 17. a 18. století, Prague, 1994.

Prague 1994
Vše pro dítě, ze sbírek Uměleckoprůmyslového muzea v Praze, Prague, 1994.

Prague 1994
M. Mžyková, *Navrácené poklady: Restitutio in integrum*, Prague, 1994

Prague 1995
V. Huml, *Rudolfínská lékárna Matyáše Borbonia z Borbenheimu na Koňském trhu očima archeologa*, Prague, 1995

Prague 1995
I. Janáková, *Knižní vazba 15.-20. století*, Prague, Uměleckoprůmyslové muzeum, 1995

Prague 1995
D. Stehlíková et al., *Kabinety umění a kuriozit: Pět století sběratelství uměleckého řemesla*, Prague, 1995

Prague 1995
110 let UPM, Prague, 1995

Prague 1996
Vojtěch Lanna, sběratel, mecenáš a podnikatel, Prague, Uměleckoprůmyslové muzeum, 1996

Prague 1996
Obrazárna v Čechách 1796-1918, Prague, Národní galerie, 1996

Roma 1977
M. C. Isola, *Immagini da Tiziano*, Rome, Gabinetto Nazionale delle Stampe, 1977

Roma 1991
A. Moltedo, *La Sistina riprodotta: Gli affreschi di Michelangelo dalle stampe del Cinquecento alle campagne fotografiche Anderson*, Rome, 1991

Rosenburg 1990
Adel im Wandel: Politik-Kultur-Konfession 1500-1700, Rosenburg, 1990

Rotterdam 1976
J. Giltay, *Kabinet van Tekeningen: XVI en XVII eeuwse Hollandse en Vlaamse tekeningen uit een Amsterdamse verzameling*, Rotterdam, Museum Boymans-van Beuningen, 1976

Salzburg 1966
100 Handzeichnungen alter Meister aus der Dresdener Kupferstichkabinett, Salzburg, Residenzgalerie, 1966

Salzburg 1983
T. Gerszi, *Die Salzburger Skizzenbücher des Paulus van Vianen: Landschaftszeichnungen und Stadtansichen des Hofgoldschmiedes von Erzbischof Wolf Dietrich von Raitenau*, Salzburg, Salzburger Barockmuseum, 1983

Salzburg 1987
T. Gerszi-S. Bodnár, *Meisterzeichnungen des Künstlerkreises um Kaiser Rudolf II. aus dem Szépművészeti Múzeum in Budapest*, Salzburg, Salzburger Barockmuseum, 1987

Sarasota 1972
Central Europe 1600-1800, Sarasota, John and Mable Ringling Museum, 1972

Schallaburg 1974
Das Wiener Bürgerliche Zeughaus: Rüstungen und Waffen aus 5 Jahrhunderten, Schloß Schallaburg, 1974.

Schallaburg 1974
Renaissance in Österreich, Schloß Schallaburg, 1974

Schallaburg 1982
Österreichisches Landesmuseum, Vienna, 1982

Schallaburg 1989
Prager Barock, Schallaburg, 1989

St. Florian-Linz 1956
Die Kunst der Donauschule, St. Florian-Linz, 1956

Stockholm 1966
Christina, Queen of Sweden, Stockholm, Nationalmuseum, 1996

Stockholm 1984
G. Cavalli-Björkman, *Bruegels Tid: Nederländsk konst 1540-1620*, Stockholm, Nationalmuseum, 1984

Stuttgart 1979
H. Geissler, *Zeichnung in Deutschland: Deutsche Zeichner 1540-1640*, Stuttgart, Staatsgalerie, 1979

Stuttgart 1984
Zeichnungen des 15. bis 18. Jahrhunderts der Graphischen Sammlung, Stuttgart, 1984

Tokyo 1992
Der Glanz des Hauses Habsburg, Tokyo, Tobu Museum of Art, 1992

Trieste 1996
L. Daniel, *Tesori di Praga: La pittura veneta del '600 e del '700 dalle collezioni nella Republica Ceca*, Milan, 1996

Uherský Brod 1996
Cesty dvou poutníků, Muzeum J.A. Komenského, Uherský Brod, 1996

USA-Kanada 1983-85
The Precious Legacy: Judaic Treasures from the Czechoslovac State Collections, [USA-Canada], 1983-85

Utrecht 1996
M. van Hongarije, *Konigin tussen keizers en kunstenaars*, Utrecht, Rijksmuseum Het Catharijneconvent, 1993

Utrecht 1984
I. van Zijl, *Zeldzaam Zilver uit de Gouden Eeuw: De Utrechtse edelsmeden Van Vianen*, Utrecht, Centraal Museum Utrecht, 1984

Venice 1987
The Arcimboldo Effect: Transformations of the Face from the Sixteenth to the Twentieth Century, Venice, Palazzo Grassi, 1987
Warszawa 1963
Sztuka czasów Michala Aniola, Warsaw, Muzeum Narodowe w Warszawie, 1963

Vienna 1959
Maximilian I., 1459-1519, Vienna, Österreichische Nationalbibliothek, 1959

Vienna 1960
Das Wiener Bürgerliche Zeughaus: Gotik und Renaissance, Vienna, 1960

Vienna 1965
Hundert ausgewählte Zeichnungen, Vienna, Graphische Sammlung Albertina, 1965

Vienna 1967
I. Fenyö, *Meisterzeichnungen aus dem Museum der Schönen Künste in Budapest*, Vienna, Graphische Sammlung Albertina, 1967

Vienna 1967
K. Oberhuber, *Zwischen Renaissance und Barock: Das Zeitalter von Brueghel und Bellange*, Vienna, Graphische Sammlung Albertina, 1967

Vienna 1978
Giambologna 1529-1608: Ein Wendepunkt der europäischen Plastik, Vienna, Kunsthistorisches Museum, 1978

Vienna 1982
Porträtgalerie zur Geschichte Österreichs von 1400 bis 1800, Vienna, 1982

Vienna 1983
Österreich und die Osmanen, Vienna, 1983

Vienna 1985
Fritz Koreny, *Albrecht Dürer und die Tier- und Pflanzenstudien der Renaissance*, Vienna, Graphische Sammlung Albertina, 1985

Vienna 1986
V. Birke, *Zeichenkunst aus sechs Jahrhunderten*, Vienna, Graphische Sammlung Albertina, 1986

Vienna 1987
Zauber der Medusa: Europäische Manierismen, Vienna, Künstlerhaus, 1987

Vienna 1990
Roberto Capucci, *Roben wie Rüstungen: Mode in Stahl und Seide einst und heute*, Vienna, 1990

Vienna 1990
Fürstenhöfe der Renaissance: Giulio Romano und die klassische Tradition, Vienna, Kunsthistorisches Museum, 1990

Vienna 1995
Eros und Mythos: Kunst am Hof Rudolfs II., Vienna, Kunsthistorisches Museum, 1995

Vienna 1996
Thesaurus Austriacus: Europas Glanz im Spiegel der Buchkunst, Vienna, Österreichische Nationalbibliothek, 1996

Vienna 1996
Mäßig und gefräßig, Vienna, Österreichisches Museum für angewandte Kunst, 1996

Vienna 1996
Meisterwerke der Prager Burggalerie, Vienna, Kunsthistorisches Museum, 1996

Vienna Neustadt 1966
Friedrich III., Wiener Neustadt, 1966

Warsaw 1967
Rysunki z kręgu manieristów niderlandzkich, Warsaw, 1967

Warsaw 1976
M. Mrozinska, *Risunki szkol obcych w Zbiorach polskich*, Warsaw, 1976

Washington 1986
J. O. Hand, *The Age of Bruegel: Netherlandish Drawings in the Sixteenth Century*, Washington, The National Gallery of Art, 1986

Washington 1985
Leonardo to Van Gogh: Master Drawings from Budapest, Museum of Fine Arts, Washington, National Gallery of Art, 1985

Zürich 1994
Ein Blick auf Amor und Psyche um 1800, Zürich, Museé de Carouge-Kunsthaus, 1994

Literature

Abeler 1977
J. Abeler, *Meister der Uhrmacherkunst*, Wuppertal, 1977

Adler 1958
G. Adler, *Two Renaissance Astronomers: David Gans, Josef Delmedigo*, Prague, 1958 (Rozpravy Československé akademie věd, 68)

Achilles-Syndram 1994
K. Achilles-Syndram, *Die Kunstsammlung des Paulus Praun: Die Inventare von 1616 und 1719*, Nürnberg, 1994

Achilles-Syndram 1995
K. Achilles-Syndram, *Die Zeichnungsammlung des Nürnberger Kaufmanns Paulus II. Praun (1548-1616): Versuch einer Rekonstruktion*, Berlin, 1995 (Microfiche edition)

Album 1573-1617 (1968)
Album Academiae Pragensis Societatis Iesu 1573-1617 (1565-1624), Prague, 1968

Alciati 1602
A. Alciati, *Omnia Andreae Alciati V.C. Emblemata*, Paris, 1602

Alcouffe 1974
D. Alcouffe, 'The Collection of Cardinal Mazarin's Gems', *The Burlington Magazine*, CXVI, 1974, 514-26

Alfons 1957
S. Alfons, *Giuseppe Arcimboldo*, Malmö, 1957 (= *Symbolister: Tidskrift for Konstvetenskap*, XXXI)

ADB 1880
Allgemeine Deutsche Biographie, Leipzig, 1880

Andrews 1991
K. Andrews, *Catalogue of German Drawings in the National Gallery of Scotland*, Edinburgh, 1991

Andrews 1967
K. Andrews, 'Recent Acquisitions at the National Gallery of Scotland', *Master Drawings*, V, 1967, 379-81

Angerer 1985
M. Angerer, 'Über Nürnberger Goldschmiedezeichnungen', Nürnberg 1985, 123-39

Angulo Iniguez 1989
D. Angulo Iniguez, *Catalogo de las Albajas del Delfin, Museo del Prado*, Madrid, 1989

Anon 1967
anon., 'A propos de l'exposition Seghers de K.G. Boon', *Gazette des Beaux-Arts*, CIX, 1967, 312

Archeologické sbírky 1863
Archeologické sbírky v museu království Českého, Prague, 1863

Armand 1883
A. Armand, *Les médailleurs italiens*, Paris, 1883

Auer-Gamber 1981
A. Auer-O. Gamber, *Sammlungen Schloß Ambras: Die Rüstkammern*, Vienna, 1981

Auer-Irblich 1995
A. Auer-E. Irblich, *Natur und Kunst: Handschriften und Alben aus der Ambraser Sammlung Erzherzog Ferdinands II. (1529-1595)*, Innsbruck, 1995

Avery 1987
C. Avery, *Giambologna: The Complete Sculpture*, Oxford, 1987

Baarsen 1989
R. J. Baarsen, 'Paulus van Vianen: De aanbidding der herders, Praag 1607', *Bulletin van het Rijksmuseum*, XXXVII, 1989, 141-47

Baillie 1969
G. Baillie, *Watchmakers and Clockmakers of the World*, London, 1969

Balabán-Nytrová-Pokorný 1995
M. Balabán-O. Nytrová-R.P. Pokorný, *Starý zákon v knižní kultuře v Čechách*, Prague, 1995

Balbín 1673
B. Balbín, *Epitomes rerum Bohemicarum, seu: Historiae Boleslaviensis Libri duo: VI et VII.*, Prague, 1673

Baldass 1913-14
L. von Baldass, 'Die Bildnisse Kaiser Maximilians I.', *JKSAK*, XXXI, 1913-14, 247-334

Balogh 1975
I. Balogh, *Katalog der ausländischen Bildwerke des Museum für bildenden Künste in Budapest: IV.-XVIII. Jahrbundert*, Budapest, 1975

Bange 1928
E. F. Bange, *Die Kleinplastik der Deutschen Renaissance in Holz und Stein*, Leipzig, 1928

Barthes-Oliva 1980
R. Barthes-A. B. Oliva, *Arcimboldo*, Milan-Paris, 1980

Basnett 1988
S. Basnett, 'Elizabeth Jane Weston-the hidden Roots of Poetry', *Prag um 1600: Beiträge zur Kunst und Kultur am Hofe Rudolfs II.*, Freren, 1988, 9-15

Basserman-Jordan 1969
B. Basserman-Jordan, *Uhren*, Brunswick, 1969

Bastelaer-Loo 1907
R. von Bastelaer-G. Hulin de Loo, *Peter Bruegel l'ancien, son oeuvre et son temps*, Brussels, 1907

Bastl 1990
B. Bastl, 'Adeliger Lebenslauf: Die Riten um Leben und Sterben in der frühen Neuzeit', Rosenburg 1990, 377-89

Bauer-Haupt 1976
R. Bauer-H. Haupt, 'Das Kunstkammerinventar Kaiser Rudolfs II. 1607-1611', *JKSW*, LXXII, 1976

Bäumel 1993
J. Bäumel, 'Kleidung und Ausstattung zu den Hochzeiten des Herzogs Johann Georgs I. von Sachsen 1604 in Dresden und 1607 in Torgau', *Jahrbuch der Staatlichen Kunstsammlungen Dresden*, 1993

Bäumel 1995
J. Bäumel, 'Fürstliche Bräutigamskleidung - Kunstwerk des Monats in der Rüstkammer', *Dresdener Kunstblätter*, XXXIX, 1995, 186-89

Bažantová-Bravermannová-Kobrlová 1993
N. Bažantová-M. Bravermannová-J. Kobrlová, 'Textilie z hrobu arcikněžny Eleonory, dcery Maxmiliána II.', *Musejní a vlastivědná práce*, XXXI, 1993

Becker 1854
C. Becker, *Jobst Amman*, Leipzig, 1854

Bedaux-Gool 1974
J. B. Bedaux-A. van Gool, 'Brueghel's birthyear, motive of an ars/natura transmutation', *Simiolus*, VII, 1974, 133-56

Bělohlávek 1954
M. Bělohlávek, *Městský archiv v Plzni: Průvodce po archivu*, Plzeň, 1954

Bender 1981
E. Bender, *Matthäus Gundelach: Leben und Werk*, Diss., Frankfurt, 1981

Benesch 1928
O. Benesch, *Die Zeichnungen der Niederländischen Schulen des XV. und XVI. Jahrhunderts*, Vienna, 1928

Beneš 1868
F. Beneš, 'Památky kultu Svatováclavského', *Památky archeologické*, VII, 1868, 484-85

Benker 1978
G. Benker, *Alte Bestecke*, Munich, 1978

Beránek 1959
K. Beránek, 'Kancelář university pražské na zlomu XVI.a XVII.věku', *Sborník archivních prací*, IX, 1959, 220-39

Beránek 1972
K. Beránek, 'Statuta univerzity sv. Klimenta v Praze', *Acta Universitatis Carolinae-Historia Universitatis Carolinae Pragensis*, Prague, 1972, 209-36

Beránek 1989
K. Beránek, 'Příspěvek k dějinám české

zemské pečeti', *Právně-historické studie*, XXIX, 1989, 71-77

Bergamini 1992
G. Bergamini, *Ori e tesori de Europa: Mille di oreficeria nel Friuli e Venezia Giulia*, Milan, 1992

Bergau 1879
R. Bergau, *Wenzel Jamnitzers Entwürfe zu Prachtgefäßen in Silber und Gold*, Berlin, 1879

Bergau 1880
R. Bergau, 'Die Nürnberger Erzgiesser Labenwolf und Wurzelbauer', *Zeitschrift für bildende Kunst*, XV, 1880

Bergner-Herain 1910
P. Bergner-J. Herain, 'Karel Škréta (1610-1674): Příspěvek k ocenění jeho díla', *Časopis společnosti přátel starožitností českých*, XVIII, 1910, 41-51

Bergner 1910
P. Bergner, *Seznam výstavy děl Karla Škréty*, Prague, 1910

Bergner 1912
P. Bergner, *Obrazárna v Rudolfinu v Praze*, Prague, 1912

Bergsträsser 1979
G. Bergsträsser, *Niederländische Zeichnungen, 16. Jahrhundert, im Hessischen Landesmuseum Darmstadt*, Darmstadt, 1979

Bergström 1963
I. Bergström, 'Georg Hoefnagel, le dernier des grands miniaturistes flamands', *L'Oil*, 101, 1963, 3-9, 66

Bergström 1973
I. Bergström, 'Flower Pieces of Radial Composition in European 16th and 17th Century Art', *Album Amicorum J. G. Van Gelder*, The Hague, 1973, 22-26

Berkovec 1966
J. Berkovec, 'Kryštof Harant z Polžic a Bezručic', *Opera musica*, 1966

Bernt 1948
W. Bernt, *Die Niederländischen Maler des 17. Jahrhunderts*, Munich, 1948

Bernt 1977
W. Bernt, *Altes Werkzeug*, Munich, 1977

Berra 1988
G. Berra, 'Allegoria e mitologia nella pittura dell'Arcimboldi', *Acme*, XLI, 1988, 11-39

Le Bestiaire 1990
Le Bestiaire de Rodolphe II: Cod. min. 129 et 130 de la Bibliotheque national d'Autriche, Paris, 1990

Beyer 1983
A. Beyer, *Arcimboldo Figurinen: Kostüme für böfische Feste*, Frankfurt, 1983

Bialostocki 1958
J. Bialostocki, 'Les betes et les humains de Roelant Savery', *Bulletin des Musees des Beaux-Arts de Belgique*, VII, 1958, 69-92

Bibliografie 1979
Bibliografie k dějinám pražské univerzity do roku 1622, Prague, 1979

Bie 1661
C. de Bic, *Het Gulden Cabinet van de edel vry Schilder-Const*, Antwerp, 1661

Bilderlexikon 1968
Das grosse Bilderlexikon der Antiquitäten, Prague, 1968

Bílek 1882-83
T. V. Bílek, *Dějiny konfiskací v Čechách*, Prague, 1882-83

Bílek 1893
T. V. Bílek, *Statky a jmění kolejí jesuitských, klášterů, kostelů, bratrstev a jiných ústavů v království českém od císaře Josefa II. zrušených*, Prague, 1893

Bílek 1896
T. V.Bílek, *Dějiny řádu Tovaryšstva Ježíšova*, Prague, 1896

Birnbaum 1924-25
V. Birnbaum, 'Původní průčelí kostela P. Marie Vítězné na Malé Straně', *Památky archeologické*, XXXIV, 1924-25, 219-21

Birnbaumová 1948
V. Birnbaumová, *Tyršův dům v Praze*, Prague, 1948

Blatný 1993
R. Blatný, 'Albrecht z Valdštejna a ženy', *Naše rodina*, 1993, 12-13

Blättel 1992
H. Blättel, *International Dictionary: Miniature Painters, Porcelain Painters, Silhouettists*, Munich, 1992

Blažíček 1958
O. J. Blažíček, *Sochařství baroku v Čechách: Plastika 17.a 18. věku*, Prague, 1958

Blažíček-Preiss-Hejdová 1977
O. J. Blažíček-P. Preiss-D. Hejdová, *Barock in Böhmen*, Essen, 1977

Blažíček 1982
O. J. Blažíček, *Jan Jiří Bendl: Výběr řezeb*, Prague, 1982

Bobinger 1969
M. Bobinger, *Kunstuhrmacher in Alt-Augsburg*, Augsburg, 1969

Bobrow 1977
R. Bobrow, *Dawne stucce*, Warsaw, 1977

Bock-Rosenberg 1920
E. Bock-J. Rosenberg, *Staatliche Museen zu Berlin. Die Zeichnungen alter Meister im Kupferstichkabinett: Die deutschen Meister (Beschreibendes Verzeichnis sämtlicher Zeichnungen)*, Berlin, 1920

Bock 1921
E. Bock, *Staatliche Museen zu Berlin. Die Zeichnungen alter Meister im Kupferstichkabinett: Die deutschen Meister*, Berlin, 1921

Bock-Rosenberg 1930
E. Bock-J. Rosenberg, *Staatliche Museen zu Berlin. Die Zeichnungen alter Meister im Kupferstichkabinett: Die Niederländischen Meister (Beschreibendes Verzeichnis sämtlicher Zeichnungen)*, Berlin, 1930

Bode 1887
W. von Bode, 'Ein Altar in Kelheimer Stein vom Augsburger Meister Hans Daucher', *Jahrbuch der Königlich Preussischen Kunstsammlungen*, VIII, 1887

Bode 1930
W. von Bode, *Die italienischen Bronzen. Königliche Museen zu Berlin (Beschreibung der Bildwerke der christlichen Epochen)*, Berlin, 1930

Bodnár 1986
S. Bodnár, 'Hans Hoffmanns Zeichnungen in Budapest', *Acta Historiae Artium*, XXXII, 1986, 73-121

Bodnár 1992
S. Bodnár, 'Un dessin d`Arcimboldo', *Bulletin du Museé Hongrois des Beaux-Arts*, 75, 1992, 57-65

Boeheim 1889
W. Boeheim, *Führer durch die Waffensammlung, Kunsthistorische Sammlungen des Allerhöchsten Kaiserbauses*, Vienna, 1889

Boeheim 1894-1898
W. Boeheim, *Album hervorragender Gegenstände aus der Waffensammlung des Allerhöchsten Kaiserbauses*, Vienna 1894-98

Bohatcová 1981
M. Bohatcová, 'Knihtiskař Jiřík Nigrin a jednolistové `Proroctví' Jindřicha Demetriana', *Sborník Národního muzea v Praze, řada A-Historie*, XXXV:2, 1981

Bohatcová 1990
M. Bohatcová, *Česká kniha v proměnách staletí*, Prague, 1990

Böhm 1908
J. Böhm, *Die Kunstuhren auf der k.k. Sternwarte zu Prag*, Prague, 1908

Bohn 1883
E. Bohn, *Bibliographie der Musik-Druckwerke bis 1700, welche in der Stadtbibliothek... zu Breslau aufbewahrt werden*, Berlin, 1883

Bohn 1890
E. Bohn, *Die musikalische Handschriften des XVI. und XVII. Jahrhunderts in der Stadtbibliothek zu Breslau*, Wroclaw, 1890

Bohr 1993
M. Bohr, *Die Entwicklung der Kabi-
nettschränke in Florenz*, Frankfurt, 1993

Boom 1988
A. C. Boom, 'Tra Principi e Imprese: The
Life and Work of Ottavio Strada', *Prag um
1600: Beiträge zur Kunst und Kultur am Hofe
Rudolfs II.*, Freren, 1988, 19-23

Boon 1961
K. G. Boon, 'Roelandt Savery te Praag', *Bulletin van het Rijksmuseum*, IX, 1961, 145-48

Boon 1978
K. Boon, *Netherlandish Drawings of the Fifteenth and Sixteenth Centuries (Catalogue of
the Dutch and Flemish Drawings in the Rijksmuseum)*, The Hague, 1978

Börner 1981
L. Börner, *Deutsche Medaillenkleinode des 16.
und 17. Jahrhunderts*, Leipzig, 1981

Borovička 1922
J. Borovička, 'Pád Želinského (Obsazení nejvyšších zemských úřadů v Čechách 1597-
1599)', *Český časopis historický*, XXVIII, 1922,
277-304

Borovský 1891
F. A. Borovský, *Výběr umělecko-průmyslových
předmětů z retrospektivní výstavy Všeobecné
zemské jubilejní výstavy v Praze 1891*, Prague,
1892

Borovský 1898
F. A. Borovský, *Wenzel Hollar: Ergänzungen
zu G. Partbey`s beschreibenden Verzeichniss*,
Prague, 1898

Borový 1868-69
K. Borový, *Jednání a dopisy konsistoře katolické a utrakvistické*, Prague, 1868-69

Borový 1873
K. Borový, *Antonín Brus z Mohelnice,
arcibiskup Pražský*, Prague, 1873

Borový 1877
K. Borový, *Martin Medek, arcibiskup Pražský:
Historicko-kritické vypsání náboženských
poměrů v Čechách od roku 1581-90*, Prague,
1877

Boström 1988
H. O. Boström, *Ett tyrolerskap pa Skokloster*,
Skokloster, 1988

Bott 1963
G. Bott, 'Der Lobkowitzsche Kaiserpokal
und verwandte Arbeiten des Goldschmieds
Hans Reinhardt Taravell vom Prager Hof
Ferdinands III.', *Festschrift für Harald Keller*,
Darmstadt, 1963, 301-34

Branberger 1942
J. Branberger, 'Kampanovy harmonie poet-
ické', *Lyra Kampanova*, Prague, 1942, 96 ad.

Branberger 1948
J. Branberger, 'Hudební úvahy o české hu-
manistické poesii', *Věstník královské
společnosti nauk*, 1948, 12

Brande 1950
R. van den Brande, *Die Stilentwicklung im
graphischen Werke des Aegidius Sadeler*, Diss.,
Vienna, 1950

Braun 1914
E. Braun, 'Eine buntglasierte schlesische
Hafnerschüssel mit dem Brustbilde Kaiser
Rudolf II. in Kaiser Franz Josef-Museum zu
Troppau', *Der Cicerone*, VI, 1914, 1-3

Braun 1918
E. Braun, 'Die deutschen Renaissanceplaketten der Samlung Alfred Walcher Ritter von Moltbein in Wien', *Österreichische
Privatsammlumgen*, Vienna, 1918

Braun 1920
E. Braun, 'Weitere signierte Arbeiten des
Joachimsthaler Goldschmiedes Concz Wel-
cz', *Kunst und Kunsthandwerk*, XXV, 1920

Braun 1923
E. Braun, *Die Silberkammer eine Reichs-
fürsten*, Leipzig, 1923

Braun 1923
J. Braun, *Das christliche Altargerät in seinem
Sinn und Entwicklung*, Munich, 1923

Brauerová 1997 (in preparation)
H. Brauerová, 'Císařský typ pečeti Ferdinanda I. z české kanceláře', *Sborník P. Burdové*, Prague, 1997 (v tisku)

Bravermanová-Kobrlová-Samohýlová 1994
M. Bravermanová-J. Kobrlová-A.
Samohýlová 'Soubor textilních fragmentů
ze studny u kostela Všech svatých na
Pražském hradě', *Muzejní a vlastivědná
práce*, XXXII, (= Časopis Společnosti přátel
Starožitností, CII), 1994, 151-66

Bravermanová-Kobrlová-Samohýlová 1994
M. Bravermanová-J. Kobrlová-A.
Samohýlová, 'Textilie z hrobu Anny Jagcl-
lonské z Colinova mauzolea v katedrále sv.
Víta na Pražském hradě ', *Archaeologia histor-
ica*, XIX, 1994, 437-61

Bravermanová-Kobrlová-Samohýlová 1995
M. Bravermanová-J. Kobrlová-A.
Samohýlová 'Textilie z hrobu Maxmiliána
II. Habsburského z Colinova mauzolea v
katedrále sv. Víta na Pražském hradě ', *Ar-
chaeologia historica*, XX, 1995, 497-521

Bravermanová-Čierná 1997
M. Bravermanová-A. Čierná 'Pohřební oděv
Rudolfa II. z královské hroby v katedrále
sv. Víta na Pražském hradě', *Archaeologia historica*, XXII, 1997, 151-66

Bravermannová-Samohýlová 1997
M. Bravermanová-A. Samohýlová 'Textilie z
hrobu Ferdinanda I. Habsburského z Colinova muzolea v katedrále sv. Víta', *Castel-
lologica bohemica*, 1997

Breitenbacher-Dostál 1930
A. Breitenbacher-E. Dostál, *Katalog
arcibiskupské obrazárny v Kroměříži*,
Kroměříž, 1930

Brinckmann 1919
A. E. Brinckmann, *Barockskulptur*, Berlin-
Neubabelsberg, 1919

Bristot 1980
A. Bristot, 'Un artista del secondo Cinquecento: Giovanni Contarini', *Saggi e memorie
di storia dell'arte*, XII, 1980, 33-136

Brockmann 1985
G. Brockmann, *Die Medaillen der Welfen, I:
Linie Wölfenbüttel*, Cologne, 1985

Brožková 1993
H. Brožková, *Myslivost v uměleckém řemesle
čtyř století*, Hluboká n.Vl., 1993

Brych-Stehlíková-Žegklitz 1990
V. Brych-D. Stehlíková-J. Žegklitz, *Pražské
kachle doby gotické a renesanční*, Prague, 1990

Brykowska 1979
M. Brykowska, 'Nieznany plan zamku
praskiego w zbiorach Uffizi we Florencji',
Biuletyn Historii Sztuki, XLI, 1979, 65-71

Březan 1985
V. Březan, *Životy posledních Rožmberků*,
Prague, 1985

Budde 1930
I. Budde, *Beschreibender Katalog der Handze-
ichnungen in der Kunst - akademie Düsseldorf*,
Düsseldorf, 1930

Buchler 1956
A. Buchler, *Musical Instruments through the
Ages*, London, 1956

Buchner 1952
A. Buchner, 'Zaniklé dřevěné dechové
nástroje 16. století', *Sborník Národního
muzea*, 1952

Buchner 1954
A. Buchner, *Hudební sbírka E. Troldy*,
Prague, 1954

Buchwald 1896
C. Buchwald, 'Zwei Bronzebildwerke des
Adriaen de Vries in Schlesien', *Zeitschrift des
Vereins für das Museum schlesischer Al-
tertümer*, VI, 1896, 53

Bukolská 1965
E. Bukolská, *Renesanční portrét v Čechách.
1520-1620*, Dis., Prague, 1965

Bukolská-Štěpánek 1980
E. Bukolská-P. Štěpánek, *Španělské
podobizny*, Prague, 1980

Bukovinská 1970
B. Bukovinská, 'Anmerkungen zur Persönlichkeit Ottavio Miseronis', *Umění*, XVIII,
1970, 185-98

Bukovinská 1971
B. Bukovinská, *Příspěvek k problematice
rudolfínské glyptiky*, Dis., Prague, 1971

Bukovinská 1974
B. Bukovinská, 'Rudolfínská kamej ze sva-
tovítského pokladu', *Umění*, XXII, 1974, 58-
64

Bukovinská 1982
B. Bukovinská, 'Zu den Goldschmiedearbeiten der Prager Hofwerkstätte zur Zeit
Rudolfs II.', *Leids Kunsthistorisch Jaarboek*, I,
1982, 71-82

Bukovinská 1983
B. Bukovinská, 'Pražský hrad na
'florentských mozaikách' z rudolfínských
dílen', *Umění*, XXXI, 1983, 444-46

Bukovinská-Fučíková-Konečný 1984
B. Bukovinská-E. Fučíková-L. Konečný, 'Zeichnungen von Giulio Romano und seiner
Werkstatt in einem vergessenen Sammel-
band in Prag', *JKSW*, LXXX, 1984, 61-186

Bukovinská 1986
B. Bukovinská, 'Neznámá kamej s
portrétem Rudolfa II.', *Umění*, XXXIV, 1986,
129-31

Bukovinská 1988
B. Bukovinská, 'Die Funeralkrone aus dem
Domschatz in Prag', *Prag um 1600: Beiträge
zur Kunst und Kultur am Hofe Rudolfs II.*, Freren, 1988, 24-26

Bukovinská 1988
B. Bukovinská, 'Kunsthandwerk', *Die Kunst
am Hofe Rudolfs II.*, Prague, 1988, 141-77

Bukovinská 1989
B. Bukovinská, 'Umělecké řemeslo na dvoře
Rudolfa II.', *Dějiny českého výtvarného umění,
II/1: Od počátků renesance do závěru baroka*,
Prague, 1989, 223-47

Bukovinská 1989/90
B. Bukovinská, 'Prager Hofwerkstatt':
Einige Erwägungen mit vielen Fragen', *JK-
SW*, LXXXV/LXXXVI, 1989/90, 123-30

Burdová 1981
P. Burdová, 'Zemský soud v malbách na
Pražském hradě a v rukopisu Stavovského
archivu', *Sborník archivních prací*, XXXI,
1981, 207-26

Burdová 1986
P. Burdová, 'Úřad desek zemských', *Sborník
archivních prací* , XXXVI, 1986, 273-381

Burdová 1990
P. Burdová, 'Desky zemské 1541-1869', *Inventáře a katalogy fondů Státního ústředního
archivu*, 18, 1990, 253-55

Burdová 1993
P. Burdová, 'Desky zemské', *Sborník
archivních prací*, XLIII, 1993, 347-439

Burdychová 1992
M. Burdychová , 'Závěsek sv. Jiří', *Chrudim-
ské vlastivědné listy*, I:6, 1992

Burdychová 1992
M. Burdychová, *Kopie závěsku sv. Jiří*, 1992

Bůžek 1995
V. Bůžek, *Rytíři renesančních Čech*, Prague,
1995

Cammeti-Falcucci-Mariani 1990
C. Cammeti-C. Falcucci-G. Mariani, *Etienne
Du Pérac e altri: Veduti di Roma nel 1500*,
Rome, 1990

Campanus Vodňanský 1978
J. Campanus Vodňanský, *Carmina festiva,
MAB II/9*, Prague, 1978

Caroselli 1993
S. L. Caroselli, *The painted Enamels of Limo-
ges*, Los Angeles, 1993

Caspar 1848
M. Caspar, *Johannes Kepler*, Stuttgart, 1848

Cavalli-Björkmann 1988
G. Cavalli-Björkmann, 'Mythologische The-
men am Hofe des Kaisers', Essen-Vienna,
1988, 61-68

Cechner 1930
A. Cechner, *Soupis památek v politickém
okresu Broumov*, Prague, 1930

Cesnaková-Michalcová 1968
M. Cesnaková-Michalcová, 'První jezuitská
představení v českých zemích', *Dějiny
českého divadla, I: Od počátku do sklonku osmnáctého století*, Prague, 1968, 132-39

Cimburek-Halák-Herain-Wirth 1950
F. Cimburek-J. Halák-K. Herain-Z. Wirth,
Dějiny nábytkového umění, Brno, 1950

Císařová-Kolářová 1939
A. Císařová-Kolářová, 'Několik supralibros
z doby české reformace', *Český bibliofil*, XI,
1939, 114-15

Charleston 1968
R. Charleston, *World Ceramics*, New York,
1968

Charleston-Archer 1977
R. Charleston-M. Archer, *Glass and Stained
Glass: The James R. de Rothschild Collection at
Waddesdon Manor*, Fribourg, 1977

Charleston-Archer 1980
R. Charleston-M. Archer, *Masterpieces of
Glass: A World History from the Corning Mu-
seum of Glass*, New York, 1980

Cherry 1994
J. Cherry, 'Medieval and Later Antiquities',
*Sir Hans Sloane: Collector, Scientist, Anti-
quary, Founding Father of the British
Museum*, ed. A. Gregor, London, 1994, 198-
221

Chlíbec 1993-94
J. Chlíbec , 'Small Italian Renaissance
Bronzes in the Collection of the National
Gallery in Prague', *Bulletin of the National
Gallery in Prague*, III-IV, , 1993-94, 36-52

Chmelarz 1896
E. Chmelarz, 'Georg und Jakob Hoefnagel',
JKSAK, XVII, 1896, 275-90

Chotěbor 1989
P. Chotěbor, 'Terakotové architektonické
články z pernštejnské stavební etapy
Lobkovického paláce na Pražském hradě',
Umění, XXXVII, 1989, 112-27

Chytil 1892
K. Chytil, *Výběr uměleckoprůmyslových předmětů z Retrospektivní výstavy 1891*, Prague,
1892

Chytil 1892
K. Chytil, *Umělecký průmysl na výstavě retrospektivní*, Prague, 1892

Chytil 1899
K. Chytil, *Dějiny českého knihařství*, Prague,
1899

Chytil 1902
K. Chytil, *Pražská Venušina fontána od B.
Wurzelbauera*, Prague, 1902

Chytil 1904
K. Chytil, *Umění v Praze za Rudolfa II.*,
Prague, 1904

Chytil 1906
K. Chytil, *Malířstvo pražské XV. a XVI. věku a
jeho cechovní kniha staroměstská z let 1490-
1582*, Prague, 1906

Chytil 1909
K. Chytil, *Führer durch die Sammlungen:
Kunstgewerbliches Museum der Handels- und
Gewerbekammer in Prag*, Prague, 1909

Chytil 1912
K. Chytil, *Umění a umělci na dvoře Rudolfa
II.*, Prague, 1912

Chytil 1918
K. Chytil, 'Apotheosa umění od B.
Sprangera', *Ročenka krubu pro pěstování
dějin umění za rok 1918*, 3-10

Chytil 1924-25
K. Chytil, 'O posledních umělcích Rudolfa
II. v Praze', *Dílo*, XVIII, 1924-25, 26-28, 33-34

Chytil 1932
K. Chytil, 'Dionys Miseroni, pražský řezáč
drahých kamenů a jeho vztahy k malířům',
*Ročenka krubu pro pěstování dějin umění za
rok 1932*, 67-79

Clouzot 1910
H. Clouzot, 'Les Émailleurs verriers en
France au XVIIe et XVIIIe siécles', *La Revue
de l'Art*, 1910, 285

Clulee 1988
N. Clulee, *John Dee's Natural Philosophy Between Science and Religion*, London-New York, 1988

Comberiati 1987
C. P. Comberiati, *Late Renaissance Music at the Habsburg Court*, New York, 1987

Creutz 1909
M. Creutz, *Kunstgeschichte der edlen Metalle*, Stuttgart, 1909

Cuming 1850
H. S. Cuming, 'On Crystals of Augury', *Journal of the British Archaeological Association*, V, 1850, 52

Cvetko 1972
D. Cvetko, *Jacobus Gallus: Sein Leben und Werk*, Munich, 1972

Cvetko 1991
D. Cvetko, *Jacobus Händl Gallus vocatus Carniolanus*, Ljubljana, 1991

Czerwenka 1867
Czerwenka, *Die Khevenhüller: Geschichte eines Geschlechts mithaupt besonderer Berücksichtigung des 17. Jahrhunderts*, Vienna, 1867

Čapek 1942
J. B. Čapek, *Lyra Kampanova*, Prague, 1942

Čarek 1930
J. Čarek, 'Příspěvky k cechovní sfragistice', *Časopis Společnosti přátel starožitností českých*, XXXVIII, 1930, 52-79

Čarek 1938
J. Čarek, 'O pečetech českých knížat a králů z rodu Přemyslova', *Sborník příspěvek k dějinám hl.m. Prahy*, VIII, 1938

Čelakovský 1886
J. Čelakovský, *Codex juris municipalis regni Bohemiae, I: Privilegia civitatum pragensium*, Prague, 1886

Čermák-Skrbek 1891-1931
B. Čermák-Skrbek, *Mince království českého za panování rodu Habsburského*, Pardubice, 1891-1931

Černohorský 1931
K. Černohorský, 'Počátky habánských fajansí', *Sborník k 60. narozeninám E. W. Brauna*, Augsburg, 1931, 103-43

Černohorský 1941
K. Černohorský, *Moravská lidová keramika*, Prague, 1941

Černý 1982
J. Černý, *Hudba české renesance: (Výběr polyfonních skladeb 16. století z rukopisů Státní knihovny ČSR [XI B 1 a,b,c,d] a Památníku národního písemnictví [DA II 3])*, Prague, 1982

Čornejová 1990
I. Čornejová, 'Jezuitské školství a Jan Amos Komenský', *Pocta Univerzity Karlovy J. A. Komenskému*, Prague, 1990, 74-87

Čornejová 1992
I. Čornejová, *Kapitoly z dějin pražské univerzity 1622-1773*, Prague, 1992

Čornejová 1995
I. Čornejová, 'Jezuitská akademie do roku 1622', *Dějiny Univerzity Karlovy*, I, Prague, 1995, 247-68

Čornejová 1995
I. Čornejová, *Tovaryšstvo Ježíšovo: Jezuité v Čechách*, Prague, 1995

Čumlivski (v tisku)
D. Čumlivski, 'K symbolické funkci schránky na pečeť Majestátu Rudolfa II. z 9.7.1609', *Sborník k 70. narozeninám Pavly Burdové* (v tisku)

Dalton 1905-1907
O. L. Dalton, *Proceedings of the Society of Antiquaries, Second Series*, 1905-1907

Daněk 1981
P. Daněk, *Rukopisná část konvolutu Se 1337*, Dipl. práce, Prague, 1981

Daněk 1983
P. Daněk, 'Málo známý pramen vokální polyfonie rudolfínské éry', *Hudební věda*, XX, 1983, 257-65

Daněk 1986
P. Daněk, 'Literátské bratrstvo v Jaroměři v době předbělohorské', *Muzikologické dialogy 1984*, Hradec Králové, 1986, 233-43

Daněk 1987
P. Daněk, 'Nototiskařská činnost Jiřího Nigrina', *Hudební věda*, XXIV, 1987, 121-36

Daněk 1988
P. Daněk, 'Neznámý pramen vokální polyfonie české provenience', *Nové poznatky o dějinách starší české a slovenské hudby*, Prague, 1988, 71-76

Daněk 1990
P. Daněk, 'Tisky vokální polyfonie pražské provenience do roku 1620', *Documenta pragensia*, X, 1990, 219-38

Daněk 1993
P. Daněk, 'Valerius Otto Lipsiensis-"Fürstlich Lichtenbergischer Organist in Prag", Otto V., Newe Paduanen..., Editio similiae ludentes 3*, IV.-XII., Prague, 1993

Daněk (in preparation)
P. Daněk, *Neznámé qudlibety českého původu* (in preparation)

Daněk (in preparation)
P. Daněk, *Rukopis Národního muzea IV H 64 jako pramen k dějinám české polyfonie 16. století* (in preparation)

Davies 1973
A. Davies, *Allart Van Everdingen*, Ph.D. Diss., Harvard University, Cambridge, 1973

Deacon 1968
R. Deacon, *John Dee: Scientist, Geographer, Astrologer and Secret Agent to Elizabeth I*, London, 1968

Dějiny 1995
Dějiny Univerzity Karlovy, Prague, 1995

Delen 1938
A. J. Delen, *Catalogue des Dessins Anciens: Écoles Flamande et Hollandaise*, Brussels, 1938

Demiani-Briot 1897
H. Demiani-F. Briot, *Caspar Enderlein und das Edelzinn*, Leipzig, 1897

Demiani 1897
H. Demiani, 'Sächsisches Edelzinn', *Neues Archiv für sächsische Geschichte und Althertumskunde*, 1897

Demonts 1937/38
L. Demonts, *Musée du Louvre, Inventaire General des Dessins des écoles du Nord: Ecoles Allemande et Suisse*, Paris, 1937/38

Dempsey 1968
C. Dempsey, 'Et nos cedamus Amori: Observations on the Farnese Gallery', *Art Bulletin*, L, 1968, 363-74

Demus 1981
Kunsthistorisches Museum: Katalog der Gemäldegalerie, ed. K. Demus, Vienna, 1981

Demuth 1843
K. J. Demuth, 'Das böhmische Landes- oder Sct. Wenzels Siegel', *Libussa*, 1843

Denkstein 1977
V. Denkstein, *Václav Hollar: Kresby*, Prague, 1977

Denkstein 1981
V. Denkstein, 'K prvním počátkům Hollarova uměleckého růstu: Nově zjištěná miniatura Fortuny - nejčasnější iuvenilie Václava Hollara', *Umění*, XXIX, 1981, 377-94

Dhanens 1956
E. Dhanens, *Jean Boulogne: Giovanni Bologna Fiamingo, Douai 1529 - Florence 1608*, Brussels, 1956

Diemer 1985
D. Diemer, 'Giovanni Ambrogio Maggiore und die Anfänge der Kunstdrechselei um 1570', *Jahrbuch des Zentralinstituts für Kunstgeschichte*, I, 1985, 295-342

Diez 1909-10
E. Diez, 'Der Hofmaler Bartholomäus Spranger', *JKSAK*, XXVIII, 1909-10, 93-151

Distelberger 1975
R. Distelberger, 'Die Saracchi-Werkstatt und Annibale Fontana', *JKSW*, LXXI, 1975, 95-152

Distelberger 1978
R. Distelberger, 'Beobachtungen zu den Steinschneidewerkstätten der Miseroni in Mailand und Prag', *JKSW*, LXXIV, 1978, 79-152

Distelberger 1979
R. Distelberger, 'Dionysio und Ferdinand Eusebio Miseroni', *JKSW*, LXXV, 1979, 109-88

Distelberger 1985
R. Distelberger, 'Gold und Silber, Edelsteine und Elfenbein', *Renaissance in Böhmen*, Munich, 1985, 255-87

Diviš 1964
J. Diviš, *Pražská Loreta*, Prague, 1964

Diviš 1984
J. Diviš, 'Pokladny pražských cechů', *Acta Musei pragensis*, 1984

Diviš 1992
J. Diviš, *Pražské cechy*, Prague, 1992

Dlabacž 1815
J. G. Dlabacž, *Allgemeines historisches Künstler-Lexikon für Böhmen und zum Teil auch für Mähren und Schlesien*, Prague, 1815

Dobiáš 1919
J. Dobiáš, 'Usilování arcibiskupů pražských o znovuzískání panství někdy Řečického', *Český časopis historický*, XXV, 1919, 70-71

Dodgson 1923
C. Dodgson, 'Valentin Sezenius', *The Print Collector's Quarterly*, 1923, 89-93

Doer 1900
A. von Doer, *Der Adel der böhmischen Kronländer*, Prague, 1900

Doering 1910
O. Doering, *Hainhofers Reisen nach Innsbruck und Dresden*, Vienna, 1910

Dolenský 1911
A. Dolenský, *Výstava obrazů Karla Škréty*, Nymburk, 1911

Domanig 1896
K. Domanig, *Portraitmedaillen des Erzhauses Österreich von Kaiser Friedrich III. bis Franz I.*, Vienna, 1896

Domanig 1907
K. Domanig, *Die Deutsche Medaille*, Vienna, 1907

Donzelli-Pilo 1967
C. Donzelli-G. M. Pilo, *I pittori veneti del Seicento*, Florence, 1967

Doorslaer 1921
G. van Doorslaer, *La vie et les oeuvres de Philippe de Monte 1521-1603*, Brussels, 1921

Doorslaer 1931
G. van Doorslaer, 'Die Musikkapelle Kaiser Rudolfs II. i. J. 1582 unter der Leitung von Ph. de Monte', *Zeitschrift zur Musikwissenschaft*, XIII, 1931, 481-91

Doorslaer 1933
G. van Doorslaer, 'La Chapelle musicale de l'empereur Rudolphe II, en 1594 sous la direction de Philippe de Monte', *Acta Musicologica*, V, 1933, 148-61

Dopisy 1610-19 (1917)
Dopisy konsistoře podobojí z let 1610 - 19, Prague, 1917

Doppelmayer 1730
J. G. Doppelmayer, *Historische Nachrichten von den Nürnbergischen Mathematicis und Künstlern*, Nürnberg, 1730

Drahotová
O. Drahotová, 'Renesanční křišťály a počátky českého řezaného skla', *Umění a řemesla*, 3, 1970, 6-13

Drahotová 1981
O. Drahotová, 'Comments on Caspar Lehmann, Central European Glass and Hard Stones Engraver', *Journal of Glass Studies*, XXIII, 1981, 34-45

Drahotová 1988,1990
O. Drahotová, 'Ikonographie, Autorenschaft und Provenienz der neugefundenen geschnittenen Glasplatten vom Beginn des 17. Jahrhunderts', *Annales du 11e Congres de L'Association internationale pour l'Histoire du Verre, Basel, 1988, Amsterdam, 1990, 407-16

Drašarová 1989
E. Drašarová, 'Dvůr Rudolfa II.: Příspěvek k organizaci a personální skladbě dvora středoevropských Habsburků v 16.a na počátku 17.století', *Sborník prací Státního ústředního archivu v Praze*, 1989, 42-86

Dreier 1969
A. Dreier, 'Neuerwerbungen des Kunstgewerbemuseums', *Preußischer Kulturbesitz*, VI, 1968, 210

Dreyer 1890
J. L. E. Dreyer, *Tycho Brahe*, Edinburgh, 1890

Dudík 1867
B. Dudík, 'Die Rudolfinische Kunst- und Raritätenkammer in Prag', *Mittheilungen der Cetralkommission für Erforschung und Erhaltung der Baudenkmale*, VII, 1867, XXXIII-XLIV

Dudík 1868
B. Dudík, *Geschichte des Benediktiner-Stiftes Raygern im Markgrafthum Mähren*, Brünn, 1868

Duyvené de Wit-Klinkhamer 1954
Th. M. Duyvené de Wit-Klinkhamer, 'Een Drinkschaal van Paulus van Vianen', *Bulletin van het Rijksmuseum Amsterdam*, II, 1954, 75-83

Duyvené de Wit-Klinkhamer 1955
Th. M. Duyvené de Wit-Klinkhamer, 'Diana en Actaeon door Paulus van Vianen', *Nederlands Kunsthistorisch Jaarboek*, VI, 1955, 185-90

Dvořák 1860
M. Dvořák, *Raudnitzer Schlossbilder nach ihren letzten Austellung im Jahre 1860 beschreiben*, Prague, 1860

Dvořák 1907
M. Dvořák, 'Spanische Bilder einer Österreichischen Ahnengalerie', *Kunstgeschichtlicher Jahrbuch der k. k. Zentral Kommission für Kunst-und Historische Denkmale*, I, 1907, 13-18

Dvořák-Matějka 1907
M. Dvořák-B. Matějka, *Soupis historických a uměleckých památek-okres Roudnický, II: Zámek roudnický.*, Prague, 1907

Dvořák-Matějka 1910
M. Dvořák-B. Matějka, *Topographie der Historischen und Kunst-Denkmale-Der politische Bezirk Raudnitz, II: Raudnitzer Schloss*, Prague, 1910

Dvořák 1918
M. Dvořák, 'Španělské obrazy roudnické galerie předků', *Zlatá Praha*, XXXV, 1918, 10-11

Dvořák 1929
M. Dvořák, 'Spanische Bilder einer Öesterreichischen Ahnengalerie', *Gesamelte Aufsätze zur Kunstgeschichte*, Munich, 1929

Dworschak 1923-24
F. Dworschak, 'Bemerkungen und Nachträge zum Meister des Heidegger und zum Monogrammisten S. B.', *Archiv für Medaillenkunde*, III, 1923-24, 63

Dworschak 1926
F. Dworschak, 'Die Renaissancemedaille in Österreich', *JKSW*, I, 1926, 213-44

Dworschak 1954
F. Dworschak, 'Unbekannte Plaketten von Antonio Abondio', *Blätter für Münzfreunde und Münzforschung*, LXXVIII, 1954, 97-99

Dworschak 1958
F. Dworschak, *Antonio Abondio-medaglista e ceroplasta*, Trento, 1958

Eckardt 1976
W. Eckardt, 'Erasmus Habermel: Zur Biographie des Instrumentenmachers Kaiser Rudolfs II.', *Jahrbuch der Hamburger Kunstsammlungen*, XXI, 1976, 55-92

Eckhardt 1977
W. Eckhardt, 'Erasmus und Josua Habermel: Kunstgeschichtliche Anmerkungen zu den Werken der beiden Instrumentenbauer', *Jahrbuch der Hamburger Kunstsammlungen*, XXII, 1977, 13-74

Ehrenthal 1899
M. von Ehrenthal, *Führer durch das Königliche Historische Museum zu Dresden*,

Dresden, 1899.

Ehrmann 1979
J. Ehrmann, 'Hans Vredemann de Vries', *Gazette des Beaux-Arts*, XCIII, 1979, 13-26

Eichler-Kris 1927
F. Eichler-E. Kris, *Die Kameen im Kunsthistorischen Museum*, Vienna, 1927

Ekert 1883
F. Ekert, *Posvátná místa král. hl.m. Prahy a obcí sousedních*, Prague, 1883

Emingerová 1909
K. Emingerová, 'Z pamětní knihy literátů prachatických', *Časopis českého muzea*, LXXXIII, 1909

Encyklopedie 1995
Nová encyklopedie českého výtvarného umění, Prague, 1995

Epekhoff-Winzer 1968
H. Epekhoff-F. Winzer, *Das grosse Buch der Graphik*, Braunschweig, 1968

Erasmus 1908
K. Erasmus, *Roelant Savery, sein Leben und seine Zeit*, Halle, 1908

Erben 1854-55
K. J. Erben, *Krištofa Haranta z Polžic cesta do země svaté a do Egypta*, Prague, 1854-55

Erbstein 1888
J. Erbstein, *Erörterungen aus dem Gebiete der Sächsischen Münz- und Medaillen-Geschichte*, Dresden, 1888

Evans 1970
R. J. Evans, *A History of Jewellery 1100 - 1870*, London, 1970

Evans 1979
R. J. Evans, *Rudolf II and His World: A Study in Intellectual History 1576-1612*, Oxford, 1979

Exner 1935
V. Exner, 'Literátský konvent v Jaroměři', *Ročenka městského muzea v Jaroměři*, 1935, 7-10

Falke 1877
J. Falke, *Geschichte des fürstlichen Hauses Liechtenstein*, Vienna, 1877

Faranda 1990
F. Faranda, *Argentieri e argentaria sacra in Romagna*, Rimini, 1990

Fechtnerová 1984
A. Fechtnerová, *Katalog grafických listů univerzitních*, Prague, 1984

Fellner-Kretschmayer 1907
T. Fellner-H. Kretschmayer, *Die Österreichische Zentralverwaltung*, Vienna, 1907

Ferguson 1906
J. Ferguson, *Bibliotheca Chemica: A Catalogue of the alchemical, chemical and pharmaceutical books in the collection of the late James Young of Kelly and Durris, Esq.*, Glasgow, 1906

Fernández-Munoa-Rabasco 1985
A. Fernández-R. Munoa-J. Rabasco, *Enciclopedia de la plata espanola y virreinal americana*, Madrid, 1985

Fiala 1888
E. Fiala, *Beschreibung der Sammlung Max Donebauer*, Prague, 1888

Fiala 1901-06
E. Fiala, *Katalog der Münzen und Medaillen-Stempel Sammlung des k.k. Hauptmünzamtes in Wien*, Vienna, 1901-06

Fiala 1907-09
E. Fiala, *Münzen und Medaillen der Welfischen Lande: Haus Braunschweig zu Wolfenbüttel*, 1907-09

Fiala 1909
E. Fiala, *Antonio Abondio*, Prague, 1909

Filedt Kok 1994-95
J. P. Filedt Kok, 'Jan Harmensz. Muller as Printmaker', *Print Quarterly*, XI, 1994, 223-64, 351-78; XII, 1995, 3-29

Fillitz 1950
H. Fillitz, 'Studien zur Krone Kaiser Rudolfs II.', *Kunstmuseets Aarsskrift*, 1950, 79-93

Fillitz 1961
H. Fillitz, *Katalog der Weltlichen und Geistlichen Schatzkammer*, Vienna, 1961

Fillitz-Neumann 1964
H. Fillitz-E. Neumann, 'Kunstgewerbe', *Barock in Böhmen*, Munich, 1964, 273-88

Fischer 1951
H. Fischer, *Geschichte der deutsch´n Zeichnung und Graphik*, Munich, 1951

Fischer 1963
K. Fischer, 'Die Uhrmacher in Böhmen und Mähren zur Zeit der Gotik und Renaissance', *Neue Uhrmacher- Zeitung*, Ulm, 1963

Flade 1986
H. Flade, *Intarsia: Europäische Einlegekunst aus sechs Jahrhunderten*, Dresden, 1986

Flajšhans 1901
V. Flajšhans, *Písemnictví české slovem i obrazem*, Prague, 1901

Fleischhauer 1976
W. Fleischhauer, *Die Geschichte der Kunstkammer der Herzöge von Württemberg in Stuttgart*, Stuttgart, 1976

Fock 1974
C. Fock, 'Der Goldschmied Jacques Bylivelt aus Delft und sein Wirken in der Mediceischen Hofwerkstatt in Florenz', *JKSW*, LXX, 1974, 89-178

Fock 1976
C. Fock, 'Vases en lapis-lazuli des collections médicéennes du seiziéme siécle', *Münchener Jahrbuch der bildenden Kunst*, XXVII, 1976, 119-54

Fock 1988
C. Fock, 'Pietre Dure Work at the Court of Prague and Florence: Some Relations', *Prag um 1600: Beiträge zur Kunst und Kultur am Hofe Rudolfs II.*, Freren, 1988, 51-58

Fogelmark 1982
S. Fogelmark, *Den svenska stattsammlingen*, Stockholm, 1982

Fojtíková
J. Fojtíková, 'Hudební doklady Husova kultu z 15.a 16.století', *Miscellanea musicologica*, XXIX, 136

Forrer 1902-30
L. Forrer, *Biographical Dictionary of Medallists*, London, 1902-30

Forssman 1956
E. Forssman, *Säule und Ornament: Studien zum Problem des Manierismus in den nordischen Säulenbüchern und Vorlageblättern des 16. und 17. Jahrhunderts*, Stockholm, 1956

Franz 1968-69
H. G. Franz, 'Meister der spätmanieristischen Landschaftsmalerei in den Niederlanden', *Jahrbuch des Kunsthistorischen Instituts der Universität Graz*, III/IV, 1968-69, 19-71

Franz 1969
R. Franz, *Der Kachelofen*, Graz, 1969

Frederiks 1952
J. Frederiks, *Dutch Silver*, The Hague, 1952

Frederiks 1961
J. W. Frederiks, *Dutch Silver*, The Hague, 1961

Friederichs 1960
J. W. Friederichs, 'Die ältesten Darstellungen des Aartales: Letzte Gemälde des Lucas van Valckenborch (1595)', *Heimat: Jahrbuch des Untertaunuskreises*, Bad Schwalbach, 1960, 96-100

Frimmel 1908
T. von Frimmel, 'Ein allegorisches Gemälde von Matthäus Gundelach', *Blätter für Gemäldekunde*, IV, 1908, 9-11

Frinta 1961
A. Frinta, 'O prvním vydání Blahoslavovy 'Musiky'', *Časopis Národního musea*, 1961, 41-42

Fritz 1983
R. Fritz, *Die Gefäße aus Kokosnuß in Mitteleuropa 1250-1880*, Mainz, 1983

Fronsperg 1571-73
L. Fronsperg, *Kriegsbuch*, Frankfurt, 1571-73

Fučíková 1967
E. Fučíková, *Kresby z doby mezi renesancí a barokem*, Dis., Prague, 1967

Fučíková 1970
E. Fučíková, 'Rudolf II. - Einige Bemerkungen zu seinen Sammlungen', *Umění*, XVIII, 1970, 128-33

Fučíková 1970
E. Fučíková, 'Über die Tätigkeit Hans von Aachens in Bayern', *Münchener Jahrbuch der bildenden Kunst*, XXI, 1970, 129-42

Fučíková 1971
E. Fučíková, "Quae praestat iuvenis vix potuere viri': Hans von Aachens Selbstbildnis in Köln', *Wallraf-Richartz-Jahrbuch*, XXXIII, 1971, 115-21

Fučíková 1972
E. Fučíková, 'Sprangerův obraz Venuše a Adonis v zámecké galerii v Duchcově: K výkladu a ikonografii adónisovského mýtu v 16. století', *Umění*, XX, 1972, 347-66

Fučíková 1979
E. Fučíková, 'Studien zur Rudolfinischen Kunst: Addenda et Corrigenda', *Umění*, XXVII, 1979, 489-519

Fučíková 1980
E. Fučíková, 'Zur Zeichnung am Prager Hof unter Kaiser Rudolf II.', Stuttgart 1980, II, 187-92

Fučíková 1982
E. Fučíková, 'Einige Erwägungen zum Werk des Jacopo und Ottavio Strada', *Leids Kunsthistorisch Jaarboek*, I, 1982, 339-53

Fučíková 1983
E. Fučíková, 'Veduta v rudolfínském krajinářství', *Umění*, XXXI, 1983, 391-99

Fučíková 1986
E. Fučíková, *Die Rudolfinische Zeichnung*, Prague, 1986

Fučíková 1986
E. Fučíková, *Rudolfínská kresba*, Prague, 1986

Fučíková 1987
E. Fučíková, 'Giulio Romano and His Workshop: Designs for Artisans', in *Drawings Defined*, ed.W.Strauss-T.Felker, New York, 1987, 217-28

Fučíková 1988
E. Fučíková, 'Die Malerei am Hofe Rudolfs II', in Essen-Vienna 1988, 177-92

Fučíková-Bukovinská-Muchka 1988
E. Fučíková-B.-I. Muchka, *Die Kunst am Hofe Rudolfs II.*, Prague, 1988

Fučíková-Bukovinská-Muchka 1990
E. Fučíková-B. Bukovinská-I. Muchka, *Monarque et mécène: Rodolphe II*, Paris, 1990

Fučíková-Bukovinská-Muchka 1991
E. Fučíková-B. Bukovinská-I. Muchka, *Umění na dvoře Rudolfa II.*, Prague, 1991

Fučíková 1995-96
E. Fučíková, 'New Rudolfine Paintings in Prague Collections', *Bulletin of the National Gallery in Prague*, V-VI, 1995-96, 36-45

Fučíková 1996
E. Fučíková, *Hans von Aachen: Bakchus a Silén*, Prague, 1996

Fuchs 1955
F. Fuchs, 'Der Aufbau der Astronomie im Deutschen Museum, 1905-1925', *Deutsches Museum-Abhandlungen und Berichte*, XXIII:1, 1955, 17-20

Fülöp-Miller 1929
R. Fülöp-Miller, *Macht und Geheimnis der Jesuiten*, Berlin, 1929

Galavics 1986
G. Galavics, *Kössünk Kardot Az Pogány Ellen: Török Háorúk És Képzömüvészet*, Budapest, 1986

Gallus 1968
I. Gallus, *Moralia*, Ljubljana, 1968

Gallus 1970
I. Gallus, 'The Moralia of 1596', in *Recent Researches in the Music of the Renaissance*, ed. A.B. Skei Madison, 1970

Gallus 1986
I. Gallus, *Opus musicum, I/3: A Dominica septuagesima per quadragesimam de poenitentia*, Ljubljana, 1986

Gallus 1995
I. Gallus, 'Moralia', *Monumenta artis musicae Sloveniae*, XXVII, 1995

Gamber 1961
O. Gamber, 'Die mittelalterlichen Blankwaffen der Wiener Waffensammlung', *JKSW*, LVII, 1961

Gamber-Beaufort 1978
O. Gamber-Ch. Beaufort, *Curiositäten und Inventionen aus Kunst- und Rüstkammer*, Vienna, 1978.

Gamber-Beaufort 1990
O. Gamber-Ch. Beaufort, *Katalog der Leibrüstkammer, II: Der Zeitraum von 1530-1560*, Busto Arsizio, 1990

Geiger 1954
B. Geiger, *I pitturi ghiribizzosi di Guiseppe Arcimboldo, pittore illusionista del cinquecento*, Florence, 1954

Geissler 1978
H. Geissler, 'Neues zu Friedrich Sustris', *Münchner Jahrbuch der bildenden kunst*, XXIX, 1978, 65-91

Geissler 1986-87
H. Geissler, 'Ad vivum pinxit: Überlegungen zu Tierdarstellungen der zweiten Hälfte des 16. Jahrhunderts', *JKSW*, LXXXII/LXXXIII, 1986-87, 101-14

Gellner 1938
G. Gellner, *Životopis lékaře Borbonia a výklad jeho deníků*, Prague, 1938

Gere-Pouncey 1983
J. A. Gere-P. Pouncey, *Italian Drawings in the Department of Prints and Drawings in the British Museum: Artists working in Rome c. 1550 to c. 1640*, London, 1983

Gerszi 1958
T. Gerszi, 'Contribution a l'art des peintres allemands de la cour de Rodolphe II.', *Bulletin du Musée National Hongrois des Beaux-Arts*, 13, 1958, 21-43

Gerszi 1970
T. Gerszi, 'Die Landschaftskunst von Paulus van Vianen', *Umění*, XVIII, 1970, 260-69

Gerszi 1971
T. Gerszi, 'Beiträge zur Kunst des Hans von Aachen', *Pantheon*, XXIX, 1971, 390-95

Gerszi 1971
T. Gerszi, *Netherlandish Drawings in the Budapest Museum: Sixteenth Century Drawings*, Amsterdam-New York, 1971

Gerszi 1972
T. Gerszi, 'Die humanistischen Allegorien der rudolfinischen Meister', *Evolution générale et développements régionaux en historie de l' art: Actes du XXIIe Congres international d'histoire de l'art*, Budapest, 1972, I, 755-62

Gerszi 1975
T. Gerszi, 'Les attaches de Paulus van Vianen avec l'art allemand', *Bulletin de Musée Hongrois des Beaux-Arts*, 44, 1975, 71-90

Gerszi 1977
T. Gerszi , 'Le Problòme de l' influence réciproque des paysagistes rodolphins', *Bulletin du Musée Hongrois des Beaux-Arts*, 48-49, 1977, 105-28

Gerszi 1982
T. Gerszi, *Paulus van Vianen: Handzeichnungen*, Hanau, 1982

Gerszi 1987
T. Gerszi, 'Dessins de Jan de Mont', *Bulletin du Musée Hongrois des Beaux-Arts*, 68-69, 1987, 131-38

Gerszi 1988
T. Gerszi, 'Zeichnungen und Druckgraphik', Essen-Vienna 1988, 301-27

Gerszi 1990
T. Gerszi, 'Nouvelles attributions aux maitres de la cour de Rodolphe II.', *Bulletin du Musée Hongrois des Beaux-Arts*, 73, 1990, 32-34

Gerszi 1993
T. Gerszi, 'Italian Impulses in Newly Identified Drawings by Bartholomeus Spranger and Hans von Aachen', *Nationalmuseum Bulletin*, XVII:2, 1933, 21-30

Gindely 1858
A. Gindely, *Geschichte der Ertheilung des böhmischen Majestätsbriefs von 1609*, Prague, 1858

Gindely 1878
A. Gindely, *Dějiny českého povstání léta 1618*, Prague, 1878

Gindely 1968
A. Gindely, *Geschichte der böhmischen Finanzen von 1526 bis 1618*, Vienna, 1968

Giusti 1992
A. M. Giusti, *Pietre dure: Hardstone in furniture and decorations*, London, 1992

Glücklich 1904
J. Glücklich, 'Mandát proti bratřím z 2. září 1602 a jeho provádění v letech 1602-1604', *Věstník Královské české společnosti nauk*, 1904

Glücklich 1911
J. Glücklich, 'O historických dílech Václava Budovce z Budova z let 1608-1610 a jeho poměru k Slavatovi, Skálovi a neznámému dosud diariu lutheránu Karla Zikmundova', *Rozpravy České akademie pro vědy, slovesnost a umění*, 42, 1911, 15-16

Glücklich 1917
J. Glücklich, 'Koncept Majestátu a vznik Porovnání', *Český časopis historický*, XXIII, 1917, 110-28

Glücklich 1930
J. Glücklich, 'Majestát Rudolfa II. z roku 1608 o nekonfiskování statků', *Od pravěku k dnešku: Sborník prací k šedesátým narozeninám Josefa Pekaře*, Prague, 1930, 15-29

Goellner 1943
C. Goellner, *Michael der Tapfere im Lichte des Abendlandes*, Hermannstadt, 1943

Goldberg 1971
G.Goldberg, *Dürer Renaissance*, Munich, 1971

Gonzales-Palacios - Röttgen 1982
A. Gonzales-Palacios - S. Röttgen, *The Art of Mosaics: Selection from the Gilbert Collection*, Los Angeles, 1982

Granberg 1911-13
O. Granberg, *Inventaire Général des trésors d'art: Peintures & sculptures principalement de maitres étrangers en Suede*, Stockholm, 1911-13

Granberg 1929
O. Granberg, *Svenska konstsamlingarnas historia fran Gustav Vasas tid till vara dagar*, Stockholm, 1929

Gregor 1969
V. Gregor, 'O první českou Muziku', *Opus musicum*, V, 1969, 135-38

Gronský 1995
R. Gronský, 'Neznámý dárce boschovského štítu', *Starožitnosti*, 11, 1995, 17

Groß 1996
S. Groß, *Zeichnungen des deutschen Barock*, Berlin, 1996

Grossmann 1954
F. Grossmann, 'The Drawings of Pieter Bruegel the Elder in the Museum Boymans and some problems of attribution', *Bulletin Museum Boymans-van Beuningen*, V, 1954, 44-63

Gruss 1901
G. Gruss, *K třistaleté památce Tyge Braha*, Prague, 1901

Gschwend 1996
A. V. Gschwend, 'The Marvels of the East: Renaissance Curiosity Collections in Portugal', Lisbon, 1996

Gualandi 1856
M. Gualandi, *Nuova raccolta di lettere,*

Bologna, 1856

Guardia 1987
G. Guardia, *Vestigi delle antichita di Roma ... et altri luochi*, Rome, 1987

Gudlaugsson 1959
S. J. Gudlaugsson, 'Het Errera-schetsboek en Lucas van Valckenborch', *Oud-Holland*, LXXIV, 1959, 118-38

Gumppenberg 1659
G. Gumppenberg, *Atlas Marianvs sive de imaginibus Deiparae per orbem Christianum miraclosis*, Ingolstadt, 1659

Gumppenberg 1673
G. Gumppenberg, *Marianischer Atlaß Von Anfang Vnd Vrsprung Zwölffhundert Wundertbätiger Maria-Bilder*, Munich, 1673

Gurlitt 1915
W. Gurlitt, *Michael Praetorius Creuzburgensis: Sein Leben und seine Werke*, Leipzig, 1915

Guštin-Horvat 1994
M. Guštin-M. Horvat, 'Ljubljanski grad: Pečnice-Ljublana Castle. Stove tiles', *Archaelogia Historica Slovenica*, I, 1994

Haas 1923
R. Haas, 'Ein leitmeritzer Musikdruck von 1626', *Auftakt*, III, 1923

Habich 1916
G. Habich, *Deutsche Medailleure des 16. Jahrhunderts*, Halle a.d. Saale, 1916

Habich 1929-34
G. Habich, *Die Deutschen Schaumünzen des XVI. Jahrhunderts*, Munich, 1929-34

Hackenbroch 1963-64
Y. Hackenbroch, 'Stove Tiles from Austria', *The Metropolitan Museum of Art Bulletin*, XXII, 1963-64, 309-16

Hackenbroch 1979
Y. Hackenbroch, *Renaissance Jewelry*, New York-Munich, 1979

Haebler 1928-29
K. Haebler, *Rollen und Plattenstempel des XVI. Jahrhunderts*, Leipzig, 1928-29

Haedecke 1963
H. U. Haedecke, *Zinn*, Braunschweig, 1963

Haenel 1911
E. Haenel, 'Hofkleider Johann Georgs I. im Historischen Museum Dresden', *Mitteilungen aus den sächsischen Kunstsammlungen*, II, 1911, 41-53

Haenel 1923
E. Haenel, *Kostbare Waffen aus der Dresdener Rüstkammer*, Leipzig, 1923

Hagenmann 1988
M. Hagenmann, 'Aspekte religiöser Kleinkunst im rudolfinischen Milieu am Untersuchungsgegenstand der kleiner Altärchen', *Prag um 1600: Beiträge zur Kunst und Kultur am Hofe Rudolfs II.*, Freren, 1988, 84-104

Hainhofer 1617 (1834)
Philipp Hainhofers Reise-Tagebuch, enthaltend Schilderungen aus Franken, Sachsen, der Mark Brandenburg und Pommern im Jahr 1617, Stettin, 1834

Hájek 1960
L. Hájek, *Indian Miniatures of the Mughal School*, Prague, 1960

Halačka 1987-88
I. Halačka, *Mince zemí Koruny české*, Kroměříž, 1987-88

Halada 1996
J. Halada, 'Polyxena z Perštejna - první dáma království', *Květy*, VI: 9, 1996, 22-23

Halata 1992
M. Halata, 'Das St. Lukas-Zunftbuch der Prager Altstadt aus den Jahren 1600-1656 und Ergebnisse seiner letzten Untersuchung', *Bulletin Národní galerie v Praze*, II, 1992, 58-61

Halata 1996
M. Halata, *Kniha protokolů pražského malířského cechu z let 1600-1656*, Prague, 1996

Hall 1991
J. Hall, *Slovník námětů a symbolů ve*

výtvarném umění, Prague, 1991

Halm 1920
P. M. Halm, 'Studien zur Augsburger Bildnerei der Frührenaissance', *Jahrbuch der Preussischen Kunstsammlungen*, XLI, 1920, 315

Halm 1927
P. H. Halm, *Studien zur Süddeutschen Plastik*, Augsburg-Cologne-Vienna, 1927

Hálová-Jahodová 1955
C. Hálová-Jahodová, *Umění a život zapomenutých řemesel*, Prague, 1955

Hamanová 1959
P. Hamanová, 'O několika vazbách ze 16.-18.století', *Ročenka Univesitní knihovny v Praze 1958*, Prague, 1959, 107-19

Hamanová 1959
P. Hamanová, *Z dějin knižní vazby od nejstarších doby do konce XIX. století*, Prague, 1959

Hamanová 1965
P. Hamanová, 'Příspěvek k dějinám české vazby', *Historická knižní vazba 1964-1965*, Liberec, 1965

Hanke 1963
H. R. Hanke, *Die Entführung der Europa: Eine ikonographische Untersuchung*, Diss., Cologne, 1963

Harant z Polžic a Bezručic 1966
K. Harant z Polžic a Bezručic, *Opera musica*, 1966

Harksen 1970
J. Harksen, *Deutsche Malerei von der zweiten Hälfte des 16. Jahrhunderts bis 1700 im Schloß Georgium*, Dessau, 1970

Harksen (ca. 1968)
J. Harksen, *Die flämische Landschaftsmalerei des 16. und 17. Jahrhunderts im Schloss Georgium*, Dessau (ca. 1968)

Harlas 1903
F. X. Harlas, 'Cechovní pokladny v Museu král. hl. m. Prahy', *Časopis Společnosti přátel starožitností českých*, XI, 1903, 122-25

Harlas 1912
F. X. Harlas, 'Cechovní památka v Městském museu pražském', *Zpráva kuratoria Městského musea za rok 1911*, Prague, 1912

Haupt 1990
H. Haupt, 'Neue Ergebnisse archivalischer Forschung zu Kunst und Handwerk am Hofe Kaiser Rudolfs II.', *Umění*, XXXVIII, 1990, 27-38

Hausenblasová 1996
J. Hausenblasová, 'Seznamy dvořanů císaře Rudolfa II. z let 1580, 1584 a 1589', *Paginae historie*, IV, 1996, 39-151

Hausner 1872
I. von Hausner, *Tycho Brahe und Johann Kepler in Prag: Eine Studie*, Prague, 1872

Hävernick 1966
W. Hävernick, 'Wunderwurzeln, Alraunen und Hausgeister im deutschen Volksglauben', *Beiträge zur deutschen Volks- und Altertumskunde*, X, 1966, 17-23

Hayward 1963
J. F. Hayward, *The Art of the Gunmaker, I: 1500-1660*, London, 1963

Hayward 1968
J. F. Hayward, 'The Goldsmith's Designs of the Bayerische Staatsbibliothek reattributed to Erasmus Hornick, *The Burlington Magazine*, CX, 1968, 201-06

Hayward 1968
J. F. Hayward, 'The Drawings and Engraved Ornament of Erasmus Hornick', *The Burlington Magazine*, CX, 1968, 383-93

Hayward 1976
J. F. Hayward, *Virtuoso Goldsmiths and the Triumph of Mannerism 1540-1620*, London, 1976

Hazlbauer 1986
Z. Hazlbauer, 'Poznámky k výrobě reliéfních renesančních kachlů s přihlédnutím k nálezům ve středním Polabí', *Časopis Národního muzea - řada historická*, CLV, 1986, 146-65, 151-55

Hecke 1920
J. Hecke, *Sbírka historických památek kožešnických*, Prague, 1920

Hederich 1770
B. Hederich, *Gründliches mythologisches Lexicon*, Leipzig, 1770

Hefner 1857
O. T. von Hefner, *J. Siebmachers grosses und allgemeines Wappenbuch in Verbindung mit mehreren neu herausgegeben mit historischen, genealogischen und heraldischen Notizen begleitet*, Nürnberg, 1857

Heiden 1970
R. an der Heiden, 'Die Porträtmalerei des Hans von Aachen', *JKSW*, LXVI, 1970, 135-226

Heiden 1974
R. an der Heiden, 'Zu neu aufgefundenen Gemälden Hans von Aachens', *Pantheon*, XXII, 1974, 249-54

Heiden 1976
R. an der Heiden, 'Bartholomäus Sprangers Lukas-Madonna Bild', *Pantheon*, XXIV, 1976, 34-37

Heiden 1979
R. an der Heiden, 'Eine Zeichnung Hans von Aachens: Selbstbildnis mit Donna Venusta', *Weltkunst*, 5, 1979, 452-53

Heikamp 1986
D. Heikamp, *Mediceische Glaskunst*, Florence, 1986

Heikamp 1988
D. Heikamp, 'Opere di commesso di pietre dure a Praga', *Splendori di Pietre Dure: L'Arte di Corte nella Firenze dei Granduchi*, Florence, 1988, 232-37

Hein 1985
J. Hein, 'Versteinertes Eis: Gefässe aus Bergkristall und Halbedelstein aus dem Grünen Kabinett', *Kunst & Antiquitäten*, 1, 1985, 34-45

Heinz 1963
G. Heinz, 'Studien zur Porträtmalerei an den Höfen der österreichischen Erblande', *JKSW*, LIX, 1963, 99-224

Heinzl-Wied 1973
B. Heinzl-Wied, 'Studi sull'arte della scultura in pietre dure durante il Rinascimento: i fratelli Sarachi', *Antichita viva*, XII: 6, 1973, 37-58

Heitmann 1982
B. Heitmann, 'Erwerbungsbericht', *Jahrbuch des Museums für Kunst und Gewerbe Hamburg*, I, 1982, 154-56

Heitmann 1990
B. Heitmann, *Kunst für Hamburg: Erwerbungen in der Zeit des Direktors Axel von Saldern 1971-1988*, Hamburg, 1990

Heitz 1906-42
P. Heitz, *Einblattdrucke des 15. Jahrhunderts*, Strassburg, 1906-42

Helfert 1923
V. Helfert, 'Muzika Blahoslavova a Philomatova', *Sborník Blahoslavův*, Přerov, 1923, 121-51

Hendrix 1984
M. L. Hendrix, *Joris Hoefnagel and Four Elements: A Study in Sixteenth Century Nature Painting*, Ph.D. Diss., Princeton, 1984

Henning 1987
M. Henning, *Die Tafelbilder Bartholomäus Sprangers (1546-1611): Höfische Malerei zwischen 'Manierismus' und 'Barock'*, Essen, 1987

Herain-Matiegka 1901
J. Herain-J. Matiegka, 'Tycho Brahe', *Společnost přátel starožitností českých v Praze*, IX, 1901, 105-29

Herain 1930
K. Herain, 'Z minulosti pražského nábytku', *Kniha o Praze*, I, 1930, 130

Herain 1933
K. Herain, 'Knižní vazba', *Československá vlastivěda*, Prague, 1933, 553-64

Hernmarck 1978
C. Hernmarck, *Die Kunst der europäischen Gold- und Silberschmiede von 1450-1830,*

London-Munich, 1978

Herold 1884
E. Herold, *Malerische Wanderungen durch Prag*, Prague, 1884

Herold 1990
E. Herold, *African Art*, London, 1990

Herrmann-Fiore 1982
K. Herrmann-Fiore, 'Disegno and Giuditio: Allegorical Drawings by Federico Zuccaro and Cherubino Alberti', *Master Drawings*, XX, 1982, 247-56

Hertlová 1975
B. Hertlová, 'Úvod do problematiky památníků raného novověku', *Acta Universitatis Carolinae - Philosophica et Historica*, V (*Z pomocných věd historických*, 3) 1975, 117-46

Herzog 1957-59
E. Herzog, 'Zwei philostratische Bildthemen der venezianischen Malerei', *Mitteilungen des Kunsthistorischen Instituts in Florenz*, VIII, 1957-59, 112-23

Hetteš 1953
K. Hetteš, *Böhmisches Glas*, Prague, 1953

Hetteš 1963
K. Hetteš, 'Venetian Trends in Bohemian Glass-making in the Sixteenth and Sevententh Centuries', *Journal of Glass Studies*, V, 1963, 39-53

Heyden 1972
S. Heyden, 'De arte canendi, ac vero signorum in cantibus usu, libri duo', *MSD*, XXVI, 1972

Hintermaier 1987
E. Hintermaier, *Die Kirchenmusik und Liturgie-Reform Wolf Dietrichs*, Salzburg, 1987

Hintze 1921-26
E. Hintze, *Die Deutschen Zinngiesser und ihre Marken*, I: *Säschsische Zinngiesser; IV: Schlesische Zinngiesser*, Leipzig, 1921-26

Hirn 1981
J. Hirn, *Erzherzog Ferdinand II. von Tirol*, Innsbruck 1885-88

Hirsch 1908
J. Hirsch, *Sammlung Löbbecke*, Munich, 1908

Hirschmann 1916
O. Hirschmann, 'Die Handzeichnungen Sammlung Dr. Hofstede de Groot im Haag', *Cicerone*, VIII, 1916, 402

Hlavsa 1954
V. Hlavsa, *Pražské matriky farní 1584-1870*, Prague, 1954

Hlavsa 1971
V. Hlavsa, 'Praha a její život do poloviny 17. století v grafických listech', *Pražský sborník historický*, VI, 1971, 161

Hobson 1962
R. L. Hobson, *The Wares of the Ming Dynasty*, Tokyo, 1962

Hoff 1969
A. Hoff, *Feuerwaffen*, Braunschweig, 1969

Hoffmann 1935
E. Hoffmann, 'Iparművészeti és egyéb Rajzok a Szépművészeti Múzeumban', *Az Országos Magyar Szépművészeti Múzeum Eokönyvei*, VII, 1935

Hojda 1987
Z. Hojda, 'Hudebníci Rudolfova dvora v ubytovací knize Malé Strany a Hradčan z roku 1608', *Hudební věda*, XXIV, 1987, 162-67

Holec 1972
F. Holec, 'Pečetidla pražských cechů', *Umění a řemesla*, 4, 1972, 53-60

Holešovský 1988
K. Holešovský, 'Rudolfinský rukopis ze sbírek Moravské galerie', *Bulletin Moravské galerie*, 43, 1988, 33-36

Hollstein 1949 ad.
F. W. H. Hollstein, *Dutch and Flemish Etchings, Engravings and Woodcuts ca. 1450-1700*, Amsterdam, 1949 ad.

Hollstein 1954 ad.
F. W. H. Hollstein, *German Engravings, Etchings and Woodcuts ca. 1400-1700*, Ams-

terdam, 1954 ad.

Holzhausen 1931
W. Holzhausen, 'Ein Bronzepferd des Giovanni da Bologna im Grünen Gewölbe', *Das schöne Sachsen*, VI, 1931, 129-30

Holzhausen 1933
W. Holzhausen, 'Die Bronzen der Kurfürstlich-Sächsischen Kunstkammer zu Dresden', *Jahrbuch der Königlich-Preußischen Kunstsammlungen*, LIV, 1933, 45

Honl 1947
I. Honl, *Z minulosti karetní hry v Čechách*, Prague, 1947

Honl-Procházka 1980
I. Honl-E. Procházka, *Úvod do dějin zeměměřictví*, Prague, 1980

Honnens de Lichtenberg 1991
H. Honnens de Lichtenberg, *Johan Gregor van der Schardt: Bildhauer bei Kaiser Maximilian II., am dänsischen Hof und bei Tycho Brahe*, Copenhagen, 1991

Hopper 1988
F. Hopper, 'Jacques de Gheyn II and Rudolf II's Collection of Nature Drawings', *Prag um 1600: Beiträge zur Kunst und Kultur am Hofe Rudolfs II.*, Freren, 1988, 124-31

Horáková 1994
M. Horáková, *Čínská keramika ze sbírek NG v Praze*, Prague, 1994

Horschik 1966
J. Horschik, 'Die deutschen Terra-sigillata-Gefäße des 17. und 18. Jahrhunderts und ihre Siegelmarken', *Keramos*, XXXIII, 1966, 3-54

Horschik 1978
J. Horschik, *Steinzeug*, Dresden, 1978

Horský-Škopová 1968
Z. Horský-O. Škopová, *Astronomy Gnomonics: A catalogue of instruments of the 15th to the 19th centuries in the collections of the National Museum, Prague*, Prague, 1968

Horský 1980
Z. Horský, *Kepler v Praze*, Prague, 1980

Hostinský 1896
O. Hostinský, *Jan Blahoslav a Jan Josquin*, Prague, 1896

Hradecký 1979
E. Hradecký a kol., *Výstavní katalog hudebních nástrojů*, 1979

Hráský 1987
J. Hráský, *Zlatníci pražského baroka*, Prague, 1987 (Acta UPM, XVII-Řada D, Supplementa 5)

Hrdlička 1993
J. Hrdlička, *Pražská heraldika*, Prague, 1993

Hrejsa 1912
F. Hrejsa, *Česká konfese, její vznik, podstata a dějiny*, Prague, 1912

Hubel 1976
A. Hubel, *Der Regensburger Domschatz*, Munich-Zürich, 1976

Hubel 1979
A. Hubel, *Diözesanmuseum Regensburg*, Munich-Zürich, 1979

Hurter 1851
F. Hurter, *Philipp Lang*, Schaffhausen, 1851

Husa-Petráň-Šubrtová 1967
V. Husa-J. Petráň-A. Šubrtová, *Homo faber: Pracovní motivy ve starých vyobrazeních*, Prague, 1967

Huszár-Prokopius 1932
L. Huszár-B. Prokopius, *Medaillen und Plakettenkunst in Ungarn*, Budapest, 1932

Ilg 1895
A. Ilg, *Album von Objecten aus der Sammlung kunstindustrieller Gegenstände des Allerhöchsten Kaiserhauses: Arbeiten der Goldschmiede- und Steinschlifftechnik*, Vienna, 1895

Irmscher 1981
G. Irmscher, 'Motiventlehnungen in neuentdeckten und bekannten Handzeichnungen Christoph Jamnitzers', *Anzeiger des Germanischen Nationalmuseums*, 1981, 84-106

Irmscher 1983
G. Irmscher, 'Goldschmiedezeichnungen: Eine Reihe von Beispielen aus Mitteleuropa 1540-1650', *Kunst & Antiquitäten*, 3, 1983, 44-51

Irmscher 1985-86
G. Irmscher, 'Hans Vredeman de Vries als Zeichner', *Kunsthistorisches Jahrbuch Graz*, XXI, 1985, 123-45; XXII, 1986, 79-117

Irmscher 1989
G. Irmscher, 'Schlange und Schwan: Christoph Lenckers 'Europa'-Becken im Kunsthistorischen Museum Wien', *Kunst & Antiquitäten*, 6, 1989, 32-37

Irmscher 1989
G. Irmscher, 'Christoph Jamnitze: Neue Zeichnungen und ein Globuspokal', *Anzeiger des Germanischen Nationalmuseums*, 1989, 117-29

Iwanoyko 1963
E. Iwanoyko, *Gdafski okres Hansa Vredemana de Vries*, Poznaj, 1963

Janáček 1956
J. Janáček, 'Královská města česká na zemském sněmu r. 1609-1610', *Sborník historický*, IV, 1956, 226-51

Janáček 1966
J. Janáček, *Jan Blahoslav*, Prague, 1966

Janáček 1972
J. Janáček, 'Poznámka k obrazové příloze', *Pražský sborník historický*, VII, 1972, 154-57

Janáček 1973
J. Janáček, *Pád Rudolfa II.*, Prague, 1973

Janáček 1976
J. Janáček, *Ženy české renesance*, Prague, 1976

Janáček 1978
J. Janáček, *Valdštejn a jeho doba*, Prague, 1978

Janáček 1983
J. Janáček, 'Italové v předbělohorské Praze (1526-1620)', *Pražský sborník historický*, XVI, 1983, 77-118

Janáček 1987
J. Janáček, *Rudolf II. a jeho doba*, Prague, 1987

Janák-Hledíková 1989
J. Janák-Z. Hledíková, *Dějiny správy v českých zemích do r. 1945*, Prague, 1989

Janko 1869
W. von Janko, *Der k.k. FM Christof Herman von Russworm: Ein Beitrag zur Kenntnis der Regierungs-Periode, Cultur und Sittengeschichte unter Kaiser Rudolf II.*, Vienna, 1869

Jansen 1988
D. J. Jansen, 'Exemple and Examples: The Potential Influence of Jacopo Strada on the Development of Rudolfine Art', *Prag um 1600: Beiträge zur Kunst und Kultur am Hofe Rudolfs II.*, Freren, 1988, 132-46

Jansen 1989
D. J. Jansen, 'Jacopo Strada antiquario Mantovano e la fortuna di Giulio Romano', *Giulio Romano: Atti del Convegno Internationale di Studi su 'Giulio Romano e l'espansione europea del Rinascimento'*, Mantua, 1989, 361-74

Jareš 1979
S. Jareš, 'Literátská bratrstva z hlediska ikonografických pramenů', *Hudební věda*, XVI, 1979, 165-75

Jásek 1980
J. Jásek, 'Cechovní symbolika na sfragistickém materiálu', *Sborník I. setkání historiků a genealogů*, Ostrava, 1980, 53-54

Jásek 1981
J. Jásek, 'Pokladnice cechovní symboliky', *Heraldická ročenka*, 1981, 2-22

Jásek 1986
J. Jásek, 'Heraldika a technika', *Sborník příspěvků III. setkání heraldiků a genealogů*, Ostrava, 1986, 72-76

Jásek 1992
J. Jásek, 'K symbolu boty prostřelené šípem', *Heraldická ročenka*, 1992, 38-40

Jireček-Jireček 1882

J. Jireček-H. Jireček, *Zřízení zemská Království českého XVI. věku*, Prague, 1882

Jirka 1985
A. Jirka, 'Poznámky k nové instalaci kroměřížské obrazárny', *Historická Olomouc a její současné problémy*, V, Olomouc, 1985, 249-58

Jiřík 1934
F. X. Jiřík, *České sklo*, Prague, 1934

Jixian 1987
L. Jixian, *Zhongguo gudai taoci bai tu*, Peking, 1987

Jonas 1888
E. Jonas, *Die Bronzegruppe von Wurzelbaue: Venus und Amor mit Delphin*, 1888

Jonas 1890
E. Jonas, 'Wurzelbauers Bronzegruppe Venus und Amor mit Delphin', *Zeitschrift für bildende Kunst*, 1890, 299

Joseph-Fellner 1896
P. Joseph-E. Fellner, *Die Münzen von Frankfurt am Main*, Frankfurt, 1896

Kadich 1899
H. Kadich, J. Siebmachers grosses und allgemeines Wappenbuch in einer neuen, vollständig geordneten und reich vermehrten Auflage mit heraldischen und historisch-genealogischen Erläuterungen, Nürnberg, 1899

Kadlec-Kotyk 1990
G. Kadlec-J. Kotyk, 'Perštejnové', *Heraldika a genealogie*, XXIII, 1990, 181-224

Kadlec 1991
J. Kadlec, *Přehled českých církevních dějin*, Prague, 1991

Kandert 1985
J. Kandert, 'Exotické slonovinové řezby 16. a 17. století', *Čas*, CLIV, 1985, 82-91

Kappel 1992
J. Kappel, 'Steinintarsien aus der kaiserlichen Hofwerkstatt zu Prag', *Dresdner Kunstblätter*, XXXVI, 1992, 80-88

Kappel 1995
J. Kappel, 'Die Elfenbeindrechsler am kurfürstlichern Hof zu Dresden', Erbach, 1995, 14-19

Kasík 1993
S. Kasík, 'Marie Pernštejnská Manrique de Lara y Mendoza', *Heraldika a genealogie*, XXVI, 1993

Kasík 1995
S. Kasík, 'Kachel s císařským orlem', *Děčínské vlastivědné zprávy*, IX, 1995, 15-20

Katz 1928
V. Katz, 'Kutnohorské medailérství v XVI. století', *Kutnohorské příspěvky k dějinám vzdělanosti české*, Kutná Hora, 1928, 1-14

Katz 1928
V. Katz, 'Alessandro Abondio', *Numismatický časopis československý*, IV, 1928, 30-44

Katz 1929
V. Katz, 'Bílá Hora na medaili', *Numismatický časopis československý*, V, 1929, 105-38

Katz 1929
V. Katz, 'Prvních sto let české portrétní medaile', *Numismatický časopis československý*, V, 1929, 105-38

Katz 1932
V. Katz, *Die Erzgebirgische Prägemedaille des XVI. Jahrhunderts*, Prague, 1932

Katz 1934
V. Katz, 'Hans Rieger, Siegel-und Stempelschneider zu Breslau', *Numismatische Zeitschrift*, 1934, 71-82

Kaufmann 1986-87
T. Da Costa Kaufmann, 'The Nature of Imitation: Hoefnagel on Dürer', *JKSW*, LXXXII/LXXXIII, 1986-87, 163-77

Kaufmann (v tisku)
T. Da Costa Kaufmann, 'Drawings by Bartholomäus Spranger in the Hermitage', *Essays in Memory of Dmitri Shelest* (v tisku)

Kaufmann 1976
T. Da Costa Kaufmann, 'Arcimboldo's Imperial Allegories', *Zeitschrift für Kunstgeschichte*, XXXIX, 1976, 275-96

Kaufmann 1976
T. Da Costa Kaufmann, 'Hand-coloured Prints and 'Pseudomanuscripts': The curious case of Codex 7906 of the Österreichische Nationalbibliothek', *Codices manuskripti*, II:1, 1976, 26-31

Kaufmann 1978
T. Da Costa Kaufmann, 'Empire Triumphant. Notes on an Imperial Allegory by Adrian de Vries', *Studies in the History of Art*, VIII, 1978, 63-75

Kaufmann 1978
T. Da Costa Kaufmann, *Variations on the Imperial Theme in the Age of Maximilian II and Rudolf II*, New York-London, 1978

Kaufmann 1982
T. Da Costa Kaufmann, 'The Eloquent Artist: Towards an Understanding of the Stylistics of Painting at the Court of Rudolf II', *Leids Kunsthistorisch Jaarboek*, I, 1982, 119-48

Kaufmann 1982
T. Da Costa Kaufmann, *Drawings from the Holy Roman Empire, 1540-1680*, Princeton, 1982

Kaufmann 1984
T. Da Costa Kaufmann, 'A Drawing by Adrian de Vries in Gdańsk', *Biuletyn Historii Sztuki*, XLVI, 1984, 203-09

Kaufmann 1985
T. Da Costa Kaufmann, 'Arcimboldo and Propertius: A Classical Source for Rudolf II as Vertumnus', *Zeitschrift für Kunstgeschichte*, XLVIII, 1985, 117-23

Kaufmann 1985
T. Da Costa Kaufmann, *L'École de Prague: La peinture a la cour de Rodolphe II*, Paris, 1985

Kaufmann 1988
T. Da Costa Kaufmann, *The School of Prague: Painting at the Court of Rudolf II*, Chicago-London, 1988

Kaufmann 1990
T. Da Costa Kaufmann, 'Arcimboldo's Serious Jokes: Mysterious but Long Meaning', *The Visual and the Verbal: Essays in Honor of William Sebastian Heckscher*, New York, 1990, 59-86

Kaufmann 1995
T. Da Costa Kaufmann, *Court, Cloister, and City: The Art and Culture of Central Europe 1450-1800*, Chicago-London, 1995

Kaufmann 1996
T. Da Costa Kaufmann, 'Arcimboldo, Giuseppe', in *The Dictionary of Art*, II, London-New York, 1996, 374

Kaufmann 1996
T. Da Costa Kaufmann, 'Habsburg, Rudolf II', in *The Dictionary of Art*, XIII, London-New York, 1996, 914

Kavka-Skýbová 1968
F. Kavka-A. Skýbová, *Husitský epilog na koncilu tridentském a původní koncepce habsburské rekatolizace Čech*, Prague, 1968

Kayser 1983
H. Kayser, *Niederländische und flämische Malerei des 16. und 17. Jahrhunderts*, Osnabrück, 1983

Kesnerová 1977
G. Kesnerová, *Kresby Václava Hollara*, Prague, 1977

Keutner 1984
H. Keutner, *Giambologna: il Mercurio volante e altre opere giovanili*, Florence 1984

Klapsia 1944
H. Klapsia, 'Dionysio Miseroni', *JKSW*, XIII, 1944, 301-58

Klar 1847
P. A. Klar, 'Einige, in neuester Zeit in Böhmen aufgefundene alte Gefässe, Aschenkrüge und Kunstgegenstände', *Libussa*, 1847

Klecanda 1928
J. Klecanda, 'Přijímání do rytířského stavu v zemích českých a rakouských na počátku novověku', *Časopis archivní školy*, VI, 1928, 1-125

Klecanda 1931
V. Klecanda, 'Přijímání cizozemců na sněmu do Čech za obyvatele', *Sborník G. Friedrichovi*, Prague, 1931, 456-67

Klement-Kadlec 1972
M. Klement-M. Kadlec, *Hudební nástroje*, Prague, 1972

Klemm 1980
C. Klemm, 'Weltdeutung', Münster-Baden-Baden 1980, 157-60

Klingen 1996
S. Klingen, *Anhaltische Gemäldegalerie Dessau: Die deutschen Gemälde des 16. und 17. Jahrhunderts*, Weimar, 1996

Kloek 1975
W. Th. Kloek, *Beknopte catalogus van de Nederlandse tekeningen in het Prentenkabinet van de Uffizi te Florence*, Utrecht, 1975

Kneidl 1995
P. Kneidl, 'Michael Paterle, přední pražský dřevorytec a tiskař 16. století', *Bibliotheca Strahoviensis*, I, 1995, 107-19

Kneschke 1859-70
E. H. Kneschke, *Neues allgemeines Deutsches Adels-Lexikon*, Leipzig, 1859-70

Knight 1948
A. H. J. Knight, *Heinrich Julius, Duke of Brunswick*, Oxford, 1948

Knihopis 1925-67
Knihopis českých a slovenských tisků od doby nejstarší až do konce XVIII. století, ed. Z. Tobolka-F. Horák, Prague, 1925-67

Kocks 1979
D. Kocks, 'Sine Cerere et Libero friget Venus: Zu einem manieristischen Bildthema, seiner erfolgreichsten kompositionellen Fassung und deren Rezeption bis in das 18. Jahrhundert', *Jahrbuch der Hamburger Kunstsammlungen*, XXIV, 1979, 113-32

Koči-Vondruška 1989
J. Koči-V. Vondruška a kol., *Památky národní minulosti*, Prague, 1989

Koesslerová 1988
D. Koesslerová, *Aegidius Sadeler's Prints in the National Gallery of Scotland*, M. Litt. thesis, University of St. Andrews, 1988

Kohlhaussen 1968
H. Kohlhaussen, *Nürnberger Goldschmiedekunst des Mittelalters und der Dürerzeit (1240-1530)*, Munich, 1968

Kolář 1926
A. Kolář, 'Humanistická básnířka Vestonia', *Sborník Filosofické fakulty University Komenského*, Bratislava, 1926, 12-33

Kolbuszewska 1992
A. Kolbuszewska, *Katalog zbiorów muzycznych biblioteki ksiecia Jerzego Rudolfa 'Bibliotheca Rudolphina'*, Legnica, 1992

Konečný 1982
L. Konečný, 'Hans von Aachen and Lucian: an Essay in Rudolfine Iconography', *Leids Kunsthistorisch Jaarboek*, I, 1982, 237-58

Konečný 1988
L. Konečný, 'Zeuxis in Prague: some Thoughts on Hans von Aachen', *Prag um 1600: Beiträge zur Kunst und Kultur am Hofe Rudolfs II.*, Freren, 1988, 147-55.

Konečný 1995-96
Konečný, 'Arcimboldo, Christ, and Dürer', *Bulletin of the National Gallery Prague*, V-VI, 1995-96, 132-37

Konečný-Lencová 1997
L. Konečný-J. Lencová, 'Rudolfinské emblémy na habánské fajánsi', *Umění a řemesla*, XXXIX:2, 1997, 65-67

Konrád 1893
K. Konrád, *Dějiny posvátného zpěvu staročeského od XV. věku do zrušení literátských bratrstev*, Prague, 1893

Koreny 1985
F. Koreny, *Dürer und die Tier- und Pflanzenstudien der Renaissance*, Munich, 1985

Koreny-Segal 1989/90
F. Koreny-S. Segal, 'Hans Hoffmann: Entdeckungen und Zuschreibungen', *JKSW*, LXXXV/LXXXVI, 1989/90, 57-65

Kornel ze Všehrd 1874
V. Kornel ze Všehrd, 'O práviech země české knihy devatery', *Codex juris Bohemici*, III, 1874

Kořán 1987
I. Kořán, 'Legenda a kult sv. Ivana', *Umění*, XXXV, 1987, 219-39

Kořán 1988
I. Kořán, 'Sochařství', *Praha na úsvitu nových dějin*, Prague, 1988, 433-518

Kořán 1991
I. Kořán, 'Tři pražské barokní oltáře na Karlovarsku', *Umění*, XXIX, 1991, 503-11

Kořán-Suchomel 1991
I. Kořán-M. Suchomel, *Karlův most*, Prague, 1991

Košnář 1905
J. Košnář, *Stará Boleslav a její památky*, Prague, 1905

Kotrba 1959
V. Kotrba, *Frýdlant: Státní hrad a památky v okolí*, Prague, 1959

Kotrba 1962
V. Kotrba, *Frýdlant*, Prague, 1962

Kouba 1962
J. Kouba, 'Blahoslavův rejstřík autorů českobratrských písní a jeho pozdější zpracování', *Miscellanea musicologica*, XVII, 1962

Kouba 1989
J. Kouba, 'Od husitství do Bílé Hory', *Hudba v českých dějinách*, Prague, 1989, 115

Koula 1890
J. Koula, 'Nové dílo Lehmannovo', *Památky archeologické a místopisné*, XV, 1890, 545

Koula 1891
J. Koula, 'Naše jubilejní výstava', *Osvěta*, 1891, 953

Koula 1902
J. Koula, *Památky umělecko-průmyslové v Čechách*, Prague, 1902

Koula 1903
J. Koula, 'Několik dat o české majolice', *Dílo*, I, 1903, 29-36

Koula 1913
J. Koula, 'O křišťálech doby rudolfinské a vzniku broušení českého skla', *Dílo*, XI, 1913, 77-100, 113-19

Kostbarkeiten 1979
Kostbarkeiten aus Kirchlichen Schatzkammern, Regensburg, 1979

Kowalczyk 1973
J. Kowalczyk, *Sebastiano Serlio a sztuka polska*, Wroclaw 1973

Kozák 1983
J. Kozák, 'Civitates orbis terrarum: 'Pana Francise kniha měst'', *Umění*, XXXI, 1983, 381-90

Král z Dobré Vody 1900
V. Král z Dobré Vody, *Heraldika: Souhrn pravidel a předpisů znakových*, Prague, 1900

Král von Dobrá Voda 1904
A. Král von Dobrá Voda, *Der Adel von Böhmen, Mähren und Schlesien*, Prague, 1904

Kratinová 1957
V. Kratinová, 'K brněnské výstavě Evropské malířství 16.-18. století', *Umění*, V, 1957, 86

Krämer 1984
S. Krämer, *Deutsche Barockgalerie: Katalog der Gemälde*, Augsburg, 1984

Krčálová 1970
J. Krčálová, 'Palác pánů z Rožmberka', *Umění*, XVIII, 1970, 469-85

Krčálová 1970
J. Krčálová, 'Italští mistři Malé Strany na počátku 17. století', *Umění*, XVIII, 1970, 545-81

Krčálová 1975
J. Krčálová, 'Poznámky k rudolfinské architektuře', *Umění*, XXIII, 1975, 499-526

Krčálová 1976
J. Krčálová, *Centrální stavby české renesance*, Prague, 1976

Krčálová 1981
J. Krčálová, 'Kostely české a moravské renesance, příspěvek k jejich typologii', *Umění*, XXIX, 1981, 1-37

Krčálová 1989
J. Krčálová, 'Renesanční architektura v Čechách a na Moravě', *Dějiny českého výtvarného umění, II/1: Od počátku renesance do závěru baroka*, Prague, 1989, 6-61

Krčálová 1989
J. Krčálová, 'Architektura doby Rudolfa II.', *ibidem*, 160-81

Kreisel 1968
H. Kreisel, *Die Kunst des deutschen Möbels: Von den Anfängen bis zum Hochbarock*, Munich, 1968

Krenn 1988
S. Krenn, 'Der kaiserliche Schatz bei der Kapuzinergruft und seine Inventare: Die Stiftung der Kaiserin Anna', *JKSW*, LXXXIV, 1988, 1-127

Kriegeskörte 1988
W. Kriegeskörte, *Giuseppe Arcimboldo*, Cologne, 1988

Kris 1929
E. Kris, *Meister und Meisterwerke der Steinschneidekunst in der italienischen Renaissance*, Vienna, 1929

Kris 1932
E. Kris, *Goldschmiedearbeiten des Mittelalters, der Renaissance und des Barock: Beschreibender Katalog*, Vienna, 1932

Krofta 1909
K. Krofta, *Majestát Rudolfa II.*, Prague, 1909

Krofta 1911
K. Krofta, 'Boj o konzistoř podobojí v letech 1562-1575 a jeho historický základ', *Český časopis historický*, XVII, 1911

Krones 1991
H. Krones, 'Musik und Humanismus im Prag Kaiser Rudolfs II. Am Beispiel der 'Moralia' von Jacobus Gallus', *Österreichische Musikzeitschrift*, VIII, 1991, 459-70

Kropáček 1953
J. Kropáček, *České kancionály 16. století a iluminátor Fabián Puléř*, Dis., Prague, 1953

Kropáček 1965
J. Kropáček, 'Arbeiten des Monogramisten IP in Bohmen', *Alte und moderne Kunst*, X, 1965, 34

Kropáček 1988
J. Kropáček, 'Malířství', *Praha na úsvitu nových dějin*, Prague, 1988, 179-201

Kropáček 1995
J. Kropáček, *Pražské veduty: Proměny obrazu města (1493 - 1908)*, Prague, 1995

Kruft 1993
H.W. Kruft, *Dějiny teórie architektury od antiky po současnost*, Bratislava, 1993

Kruft 1995
H. W. Kruft, *Francesco Laurana: Ein Bildhauer der Frührenaissance*, Munich, 1995

Krutinová-Křížová 1984
A. Krutinová-K. Křížová, 'Historický mobiliář Valdštejnského paláce v Praze: Zpráva o novém soupisu', *Památky a příroda*, IX, 1984, 321-33

Křížek 1855
V. Křížek, 'Archeologické sbírky Musea království českého', *Památky archeologické a místopisné*, I, 1855, 330

Křížová 1979
K. Křížová, 'K některým částem výzdoby renesančních interiérů zámku v Telči', *Památky a příroda*, IX, 1979, 534-40

Křížová 1981
K. Křížová, 'Anthoni Bays und die Bildergalerie der Hohenemser', *Montfort: Vierteljahresschrift für Geschichte und Gegenwart Vorarlbergs*, XXXIII, 1981, 134-44

Křížová 1981
K. Křížová, 'Anthoni Bays a jeho dílo v Čechách', *Umění*, XXIX, 1981, 347-59

Křížová 1996
K. Křížová, *Obrazárna-Národní kulturní památka-hrad Křivoklát*, 1996

Kubátová 1954
T. Kubátová, 'Roudnická galerie v Nela-hozevsi', *Zprávy památkové péče*, XIV, 1954, 142-43

Kučera-Truc 1961
K. Kučera-M.Truc, *Archiv University Karlovy: Průvodce po archivních fondech*, Prague, 1961

Kučera-Rak 1983
J. P. Kučera-J. Rak, *Bohuslav Balbín a jeho místo v české kultuře*, Prague, 1983

Kučerová 1986
M. Kučerová, 'La tabulature d'épinette de Samuel Mareschal', *Revue Musicale de Suisse romane*, 1986, 71-81

Kudělková-Zeminová 1961
A. Kudělková-M. Zeminová, *Habánská fajans v Uměleckoprůmyslovém museu v Praze a v Brně*, Prague-Brno, 1961

Kuchynka 1915
R. Kuchynka, 'Manuál pražského pořádku malířského z let 1600-1656', *Památky archeologické*, XXVII, 1915, 24-46

Kulířová-Sander 1956
K. Kulířová-R. Sander, *Patenty: Katalog sbírky patentů Státního ústředního archivu v Praze*, Prague, 1956

Kunstwerke 1933
Kunstwerke aus dem Besitz Baron Albert von Goldschmidt-Rothschild, Berlin, 1933

Kurz 1996
O. Kurz, 'Umělecké vztahy mezi Prahou a Persií za Rudolfa II. a poznámky k historii jeho sbírek', *Umění*, XIV, 1996, 462-89

Kutal 1956
A. Kutal, 'O mistru zlíchovského epitafu', *Časopis Národního muzea-oddělení věd společenských*, CXXIV, 1956, 24-52

Kutišová 1995
Š. Kutišová, 'Zdeněk Vojtěch Popel z Lobkovic. Pokus o profil osobnosti', *Opera historica*, 4, 1995

Kybalová 1984
J. Kybalová, 'Sbírka Bohuslava Duška', *Acta UPM*, Prague, 1984

Kybalová 1995
J. Kybalová, *Keramická sbírka Hugo Vavrečky*, Prague, 1995

Kybalová 1996
J. Kybalová, 'Terra sigilata ze severních Čech', *Umění a řemesla*, XXXVII, 1996, 12-15

Kyzourová-Kalina 1993
I. Kyzourová-P. Kalina, *Strahovská obrazárna: Od gotiky k romantismu*, Prague, 1993

Lábek 1967
L. Lábek, 'Sušický poklad cínového nádobí z doby předbělohorské', *Minulostí západočeského kraje*, 1967, 143-62

Lábler 1897
K. Lábler, 'Závěsek zdobený soškou sv. Jiří v Chrudimi', *Časopis přátel starožitností českých*, V, 1897, 17-18

Laboutková (v tisku)
M. Laboutková, *Národní technické muzeum v Praze: Katalog expozice měření času* (v tisku)

Lanllier-Pini 1971
J. Lanllier-A. Pini, *Fünf Jahrhunderte abendländischer Schmuck*, Munich, 1971

Lanzke 1964
H. W. Lanzke, *Die weltlichen Chorgesange (Moralia) von Jacobus Gallus*, Mainz, 1964

Larsson 1963
L. O. Larsson, 'Adrian de Vries Porträtbüsten', *Konsthistorisk Tidskrift*, XXXII, 1963, 80-93

Larsson 1967
L. O. Larsson, *Adrian de Vries: Adrianus Fries Hagiensis Batavus 1545-1626*, Munich-Vienna, 1967

Larsson 1968
L. O. Larsson, 'Adrian de Vries v Praze', *Umění*, XVI, 1968, 255-95

Larsson 1972
L. O. Larsson, 'Eine neuentdeckte Zeichnung von Adrian de Vries', *Bulletin du Museé Hongrois des Beaux-Arts*, 38, 1972, 69-73

Larsson 1974
L. O. Larsson, *Von allen Seiten gleich schön: Studien zum Begriff der Viellansichtigkeit in der europäischen Plastik von der Renaissance bis zum Klassizismus*, Uppsala, 1974

Larsson 1975
L. O. Larsson, 'Gianlorenzo Bernini und Joseph Heintz', *Konsthistorisk Tidskrift*, XLIV, 1975, 23-26

Larsson 1982
L. O. Larsson, 'Bildhauerkunst und Plastik am Hofe Kaiser Rudolfs II.', *Leids Kunsthistorisch Jaarboek*, I, 1982, 211-35

Larsson 1985
L. O. Larsson , 'Zwei Frühwerke von Adrian de Vries', *Netherlandish Mannerism*, Stockholm, 1985, 117-26

Larsson 1988
L.O. Larsson, 'Bildnisse Kaiser Rudolfs II.', *Prag um 1600: Beiträge zur Kunst und Kultur am Hofe Rudolfs II.*, Freren, 1988, 161-70

Larsson 1992
L. O. Larsson, *Swedish National Art Museums: European Bronzes 1450-1700*, Stockholm, 1992

Le Blanc 1970
C. Le Blanc, *Manuel de l'amateur d'estampes*, Amsterdam, 1970

Leeuwen 1970
F. van Leeuwen, 'Iets over het handschrift van de 'naer het leven' tekenaar', *Oud Holland*, LXXXV, 1970, 25-32

LeGrand-Sluys 1955
F. C. LeGrand-F. Sluys, *Arcimboldo et les Arcimboldesques*, Paris, 1955

Leiching 1909
J. Leiching, *Sammlung Lanna Prag*, Leipzig, 1909

Leithe-Jasper - Distelberger 1982
M. Leithe-Jasper -R. Distelberger, *Kunsthistorisches Museum*, Vienna, 1982

Leitner 1870-73
Q. Leitner, *Die hervorragendsten Kunstwerke der Schatzkammer des österreichischen Kaiserhauses*, Vienna, 1870-73

Lejsková-Matyášová 1971
M. Lejsková-Matyášová, 'Z valdštejnského nábytku v pražském paláci', *Stoletá Praha*, V, 1971, 210-16

Lenfeld 1984
J. Lenfeld, *Sluneční hodiny ze sbírek UPM v Praze*, Prague, 1984 (Acta UPM, XVI-Řada D, Supplementa 5)

Lessing 1907
J. Lessing, 'Gold und Silber', *Handbücher des Kgl. Museen zu Berlin*, Berlin, 1907

Líbal 1977
D. Líbal, 'Dvě dávno zaniklá architektonická díla české renesance', *Staletá Praha*, VI-II, 1977, 267-73

Liess 1981
R. Liess, 'Die kleinen Landschaften Pieter Bruegels d. A. im Lichte seines Gesamtwerkes (2.Teil)', *Jahrbuch des kunsthistorischen Institutes der Universität Graz*, XVII, 1981, 35-150

Lietzmann 1987
H. Lietzmann, *Das Neugebäude in Wien: Sultan Suleymans Zelt, Kaiser Maximilian II. Lustschloß. Ein Beitrag zur Kunst- und Kulturgeschichte der zweiten Hälfte des sechzehnten Jahrhundert*, Munich-Berlin, 1987

Lietzmann 1993
H. Lietzmann, *Herzog Heinrich Julius von Braunschweig und Lüneburg (1564-1613): Persönlichkeit und Wirken für Kaiser und Reich*, Braunschweig 1993

Lifka 1962
B. Lifka, 'Vazby se supralibros v českých, moravských a slezských zámeckých knihovách', *Historická knižní vazba*, Liberec, 1962

Lifka 1980
B. Lifka, *Exlibris a supralibros v českých korunních zemích v letech 1000 až 1900*, Prague, 1980

Limouze 1988
D. Limouze, 'Aegidius Sadeler (1570-1629): Drawings, Prints and the Development of an Art Theoretical Attitude', *Prag um 1600: Beiträge zur Kunst und Kultur am Hofe Rudolfs II.*, Freren, 1988, 183-92

Limouze 1989
D. Limouze, 'Aegidius Sadeler, Imperial Engraver', *Bulletin of the Philadelphia Museum of Art*, LXXXV:362, 1989

Limouze 1990
D. Limouze, *Aegidius Sadeler (1570-1629): Drawings, Prints and Art Theory*, Ph.D. Diss., Princeton, 1990

Lindell 1982
R. Lindell, 'Filippo di Montes Widmungen an Kaiser Rudolf II.: Dokumente einer Krise?', *Festschrift Othmar Wessely zum 60. Geburtstag*, Tutzing, 1982

Lindell 1989-90
R. Lindell, 'Relations between Musicians and Artists at the Court of Rudolf II', *JK-SW*, LXXXV/LXXXVI, 1989-90, 79-88

Lindell 1988
R. Lindell, 'Das Musikleben am Hofe Rudolfs II.', *Prag um 1600: Kunst und Kultur am Hofe Rudolfs II.*, Freren 1988, 75-83

Lindell 1989
R. Lindell, 'Hudební život na dvoře Rudolfa II.', *Hudební věda*, XXVI, 1989, 99-111

Lindner 1867
T. Lindner, 'Johann Matthäus Wacker von Wackenfels', *Zeitschrift des Vereins für Geschichte und Altertum Schlesien*, VIII, 1867, 319-51

Líva 1930
V. Líva, 'Studie o Praze předbělohorské, I: Emigrace', *Sborník příspěvků k dějepisu hl. m. Prahy*, VI, 1930

Líva 1933
V. Líva, 'Studie o době pobělohorské, II', *Sborník k dějinám hlavního města Prahy*, 1933, 1-71

Löbe 1883
M. Löbe, *Wahlsprüche, Devisen und Sinnsprüche deutscher Fürstengeschlechter*, Leipzig, 1883

Lobkowicz 1991
F. Lobkowicz, 'Zlaté rouno v Čechách', *Heraldika a genealogie*, XIV, 1991, 206-08

Loebl 1899
A. H. Loebl, 'Zur Geschichte des Türkenkrieges 1593-1606', *Prager Studien*, VI, 1899, 1-151

Löcher 1962
K. Löcher, *Jacob Seisenegger, Hofmaler Kaiser Ferdinands I.*, Munich-Berlin, 1962

Loriš 1947
J. Loriš, *Česká barokní kresba*, Prague, 1947

Loriš 1949
J. Loriš, 'Datování kreseb Karla Škréty', *Cestami umění: Sborník k poctě šedesátých narozenin Antonína Matějčka*, Prague, 1949, 188-91

Löwe 1975
R. Löwe, *Die Augsburger Goldschmiedewerkstatt des Mathias Walbaum*, Munich, 1975

Lübke 1882
W. Lübke, *Geschichte der Renaissance in Deutschland*, Berlin, 1882

Ludwig 1978
H. J. Ludwig, *Die Türkenkrieg-Skizzen des Hans von Aachen für Rudolf II.*, Diss., Frankfurt, 1978

Lugt 1931
F. Lugt, 'Beiträge zu dem Katalog der niederländischen Handzeichnungen in Berlin', *Jahrbuch der Preussischen Kunstsammlungen*, 1931

Lugt 1968-86
F. Lugt, *Musée du Louvre: Inventaire général des dessins du Nord: Maitres des Anciens Pays-Bas nés avant 1550*, Paris, 1968-86

Luchner 1978
L. Luchner, *Denkmal eines Renaissancefürsten: Versuch einer Rekonstruktion des Ambraser Museums vor 1583*, Vienna, 1958

Mackensen 1979
L. von Mackensen, *Die erste Sternwarte Europas mit ihren Instrumenten und Uhren: 400 Jahre Jost Bürgi in Kassel*, Munich, 1979

Magnusson 1982
B. Magnusson, 'The De la Gardie (Borrestad) Collection of Drawings', *Nationalmuseum Bulletin*, VI, 1982, 113-41

Machytka 1977
L. Machytka, 'Nová instalace obrazárny zámku Hrádku u Nechanic', *Památky a příroda*, II, 1977, 322

Maiorino 1991
G. Maiorino, *The Portrait of Eccentricity: Arcimboldo and the Mannerist Grotesque*, University Park - London, 1991

Malý-Sivák 1988
K. Malý-F. Sivák, *Dějiny státu a práva v Československu do r. 1918*, Prague, 1988

Mander 1906
C. van Mander, *Das Leben der niederländischen und deutschen Maler* (Übersetzung und Anmerkungen von Hanns Floerke), Munich-Leipzig, 1906

Mandiargues 1978
A. P. de Mandiargues, *Arcimboldo the Marvelous*, New York, 1978

Mantuani 1991
J. Mantuani, *Gallusov zbornik*, Ljubljana, 1991, 90-135

Manýrová 1980
K. Manýrová, *Hudební prameny literátského bratrstva v Rokycanech ze XVI. a ze začátku XVII. století*, Dipl. práce, Prague, 1980

Mareš-Březan 1880
F. Mareš-V. Březan, *Život Petra Voka z Rosenberka*, Prague, 1880

Mareš 1894
F. Mareš, 'Rožmberská kapela', *Časopis Musea království českého*, 1894

Mareš 1898-99
F. Mareš , 'Materiálie k dějinám umění, uměleckého průmyslu a podobným', *Památky archeologické*, XVII, 1898-99

Marquet de Vasselot 1914
J. J. Marquet de Vasselot, *Catalogue sommaire de l'orfévrerie, de l'émaillerie et des gemmes du moyen age au XVIIe siecle*, Paris, 1914

Martels 1992
Z. von Martels, 'On his Majesty's service: Augerius Busbequius, Courtier and Diplomat of Maximilian II', *Kaiser Maximilian II.: Kultur und Politik im 16. Jahrhundert*, ed. F. Edelmayer-A. Kohler, Vienna, 1992, 169-81

Martin 1995
A. J. Martin, 'Eine unbekannte Sammlung bedeutender Portraits der Renaissance aus dem Besitz des Hans Jakob König', *Kunstchronik*, XLVIII, 1995, 46-54

Masner 1900
K. Masner, 'Zur schlesischen Keramik der Renaissancezeit', *Jahrbuch des Schlesischen Museums für Kunstgewerbe und Altertümer*, I, 1900, 122-32

Massaino 1964
T. Massaino, *Motetten und Instrumentalcanzonen*, DTÖ 110, Graz-Vienna, 1964

Massinelli-Tuena 1992
A. M. Massinelli-F. Tuena, *Treasures of the Medici*, Milan, 1992

Matějček 1948
A. Matějček, 'Španělské podobizny v zámku roudnickém', *O umění a umělcích*, Prague, 1948, 84

Matoušek 1931
J. Matoušek, 'Kurie a boj o konsistoř podobojí za administrátora Rezka', *Český časopis historický*, XXXVIII, 1931, 16-41, 252-92

Matoušek-Scheufler 1988
V. Matoušek-V. Scheufler, 'Raně novověké berounké zboží ve světle archeologických výzkumů v Berouně', *Archaeologia historica*, VIII, 1988, 189-96

Mattioli 1596
P. O. Mattioli, *Herbář neb bylinář...*, Prague, 1596

Maurice 1968
K. Maurice, *Von Uhren und Automaten: Das Mesen der Zeit*, Munich, 1968

Mayer 1958
J. Mayer, 'Dům u dvou zlatých medvědů', *Umění*, VI, 1958, 389-95

Mayer 1971
J. Mayer, 'Architektonické dílo Jana Dominika de Barifis', *Staletá Praha*, V, 1971, 199-209

Mayer-Löwenschwert 1927
E. Mayer-Löwenschwert, 'Der Aufenthalt der Erzherzoge Rudolf und Ernst in Spanien 1564-1571', *Akademie der Wissenschaften in Wien, Philos.-hist. Klasse, Sitzungsberichte*, CCVI, 5. Abhandlung, 1927, 1-64

Mazerolle 1902
L. Mazerolle, *Les médailleurs francais du XVe siécle a midi du XVIIe siecle*, Paris, 1902

McAllister Johnson 1969
W. McAllister Johnson, 'Prolegomena to the 'Images ou Tableaux de Platte Peinture', with an excursus on two drawings of the School of Fontaineblau', *Gazette des Beaux-Arts*, LXXIII (CXI), 1969, 227-304

Medková 1957
J. Medková, 'Renesanční sklenice ve sbírkách státního hradu Buchlova', *Zprávy památkové péče*, XVII, 1957, 148

Meine-Schawe 1992
M. Meine-Schawe, *Die Grablege der Wettiner im Dom zu Freiberg*, Diss., Munich, 1992

Menclová 1972
D. Menclová, *Státní zámek Bučovice*, Brno, 1972

Mendelová 1984
J. Mendelová, 'Osmipanský úřad na Starém Městě pražském do roku 1636', *Pražský sborník historický*, 1984, 90

Mendl 1947
B. Mendl, *Vývoj řemesl a obchodu v městech pražských*, Prague, 1947

Menzhausen 1977
J. Menzhausen, *Dresdener Kunstkammer und Grünes Gewölbe*, Leipzig, 1977

Meraviglia-Crivelli 1886
R. J. Meraviglia-Crivelli, *J. Siebmachers grosses und allgemeines Wappenbuch in einer neuen, vollständig geordneten und reich vermehrten Auflage mit heraldischen und historisch - genealogischen Erläuterungen*, Nürnberg, 1886

Merhaut 1955
C. Merhaut, *Valdštejnský palác*, Prague, 1955

Metzler 1997
S. Metzler, *The Alchemy of Drawing: Bartholomäus Spranger at the Court of Rudolf II.*, Ph.D. Diss., Princeton, 1997

Meyer-Heisig 1963
E. Meyer-Heisig, 'Caspar Lehmann: Beitrage zur Frühgeschichte des deutschen Glasschnittes', *Anzeiger des Germanischen Nationalmuseum*, 1963,Nürnberg, 116-31

Meyer-Heisig 1963
E. Meyer-Heisig, *Der Nürnberger Glasschnitt des 17.Jahrbunderts*, Nürnberg, 1963

Meyer-Heisig 1967
E. Meyer-Heisig, 'Caspar Lehmann', *Kunstjahrbuch der Stadt Linz*, 1967, 117-29

Michai 1975
V. Michai, *Culegere de studii*, Bucharest, 1975

Mikovec 1852
F. B. Mikovec, 'Obrazárna knížat z Lobkovic na Roudnici', *Lumír*, II, 1852, 638

Mikovec 1861
F. B. Mikovec, *Seznam českých starožitností ve výstavě uspořádané od jednoty Arkadie v Praze*, Prague, 1861

Miller zu Aichholz-Loehr-Holzmair 1948
V. Miller zu Aichholz-A. Loehr-E. Holzmair,

Österreichische Münzprägungen 1519-1938, Vienna, 1948

Miltner-Neumann 1852-70
J. O. Miltner-J. Neumann, *Beschreibung der bisher bekannten böhmischen Privatmünzen*, Prague, 1852-70

Modern 1894
H. Modern, 'Paulus van Vianen', *JKSAK*, XV, 1894, 60-102

Mohr 1985
J. Mohr, 'Zámky pěti století', *Umění a řemesla*, 3, 1985, 38-45

Mohr 1985
J. Mohr, *Zámky 15.-18. století ze sbírek Severočeského muzea v Liberci*, Liberec, 1985

Mohr 1989
J. Mohr, *Historické nářadí a nástroje*, Liberec, 1989

ter Molen 1984
J. R. ter Molen, *Van Vianen: Een Utrechtse familie van zilversmeeden met internationale faam*, Diss., Leiden, 1984

ter Molen 1994
J. R. ter Molen, *Zilver: Catalogus van voorwerpen van edelmetaal in de collectie van het Museum Boymans-van Beuningen*, Rotterdam, 1994

Molinier 1886
E. Molinier, *Les plaquetes: Catalogue raisonné*, Paris, 1886

Molitor 1913
G. Molitor, *Votum nuptiis*, Prague, 1913

Möller 1956
L. Möller, *Der Wrangelschrank und die verwandten süddeutschen Intarsiemöbel des 16. Jahrbunderts*, Berlin, 1956

Monte 1976
P. de Monte, *Opera, Series B: Masses*, I, Kleuven, 1976

Morávek 1937
J. Morávek, *Sbírky Rudolfa II. a pokus o jejich identifikaci*, Prague, 1937

Morávek 1954
J. Morávek, 'Ke vzniku Hvězdy', *Umění*, II, 1954, 199-211

Morávek 1959
J. Morávek, 'Královské mauzoleum v chrámu sv. Víta a jeho dokončení', *Umění*, VII, 1959, 52-53

Morigia 1595
P. Morigia, *La nobilita di Milano*, Milan, 1595

Muchall-Viebrook 1925
T. Muchall-Viebrook, *Deutsche Barockzeichnungen*, Munich, 1925

Muchka 1969
I. Muchka, *Stylové otázky v české architektuře kolem roku 1600*, Dipl. práce, Prague, 1969

Muchka 1983
I. Muchka, 'Podoba Pražského hradu v rudolfinské době z hlediska veduty', *Umění*, XXXI, 1983, 447-50

Muchka 1988
I. Muchka, 'Rudolf II. jako stavebník', *Umění na dvoře Rudolfa II.*, Prague, 1988, 179-213

Muchka 1989-90
I. Muchka, 'Die Prager Burg zur Zeit Rudolfs II.-Neue Forschungsergebnisse', *JKSW*, LXXXV/LXXXVI, 1989-90, 95-98

Muchka 1992
I. Muchka-K. Schwarzenberg-I.Hlobil-L. Kesner-T.Vlček, *Der Hradschin: Die Prager Burg und ihre Kunstschätze*, Freiburg-Basel-Vienna, 1992

Muchka-Křížová 1996
I. Muchka-K. Křížová, *Valdštejnský palác*, Prague, 1996

Müllenmeister 1988
K. J. Müllenmeister, *Roelandt Savery: Die Gemälde mit kritischem Oeuvrekatalog*, Freren, 1988

Muller 1967
M. Muller, 'Hercules Seghers, weergaloos grafisch experimentator', *Ons Amsterdam*,

1967, 222

Muller 1981-82
J. M. Muller, 'The 'Perseus and Andromeda' on Rubens's House', *Simiolus*, XII, 1981-82, 131-46

Müller 1938
J. M. Müller, *Zacharias Geizkofler (1560-1617), des Heiligen Römischen Reiches Pfennigmeister und oberster Proviantmeister im Königreich Ungarn*, Vienna, 1938

Müller 1982
J. M. Müller, 'Oltář sv. Anny v hradní kapli na Českém Krumlově', *Umění*, XXX, 1982

Müller 1983
H. Müller, 'Errare humanum est, oder: Das von Scheurlische Taufbecken', *Studien zum europäischen Kunsthandwerk: Festschrift Yvonne Hackenbroch*, Munich, 1983

Müller 1987
K. Müller, 'Soupis typářů v archivech Severomoravského kraje, I: Typáře obecní a cechovní', *Sborník Státního oblastního archivu v Opavě 1981-1985*, Opava, 1987, 73-141

Müller 1966
T. Müller, 'Ein Augsburger Silberaltarchen in Prag', *Opuscula in honorem C. Hernmarck*, Copenhagen, 1966, 159-61

Muneles 1952
O. Muneles, *Bibliografický přehled židovské Prahy*, Prague, 1952

Muneles 1965
O. Muneles, *Prague Ghetto in the Renaissance Period*, Prague, 1965

Münz 1961
L. Münz, *The Drawings of Bruegel*, London, 1961

Mžyková (v tisku)
M. Mžyková, 'Obrazy alegorických průvodů ze Sbírek hradu Šternberka na Moravě', *Acta Universitatis Palackianae Olomucensis, Facultas Philosophica-Aesthetica, Historia artium*, (v tisku)

Mžyková 1985
M. Mžyková, 'Díla českých malířů 19. a 20. století v zámeckých sbírkách', *Památky a příroda*, X, 1985, 84-90

Mžyková 1987
M. Mžyková, 'Helmut Flade: Intarsia', *Památky a příroda*, XII, 1987, 412-13

Mžyková 1990
M. Mžyková, *Chebské reliéfní intarzie 1630-1730*, Dis., Prague, 1990

Mžyková 1990
M. Mžyková, *Valdštejnský palác*, Prague, 1990

Mžyková (v tisku)
M. Mžyková, *Chebská reliéfní intarzie*, Brno, (v tisku)

Mžyková (v tisku)
M. Mžyková, 'K podobiznám Albrechta z Valdštejna v českých sbírkách', *Zprávy památkové péče* (v tisku)

Nagler 1837
G. K. Nagler, *Neues allgemeines Künstler Lexicon*, Munich, 1837

Nagler 1858-79
G. K. Nagler, *Die Monogrammisten und diejenigen bekannten und unbekannten Künstler aller Schulen...*, Munich-Leipzig, 1858-79

Nachträge 1858
Nachträge und Verbesserungen zum Verzeichniss der Hollarschen Kupferstiche, Berlin, 1858

Národní galerie 1984
Národní galerie v Praze, I: Sbírka starého evropského umění. Sbírka starého českého umění, Prague, 1984

Nazir 1977
A. Nazir, 'Jahangir's Album of Art-Muraqqa-i Gulshan and Its Two Adilshahi Paintings', *Indo-Iranica*, XXX, 1977, 24

Neck 1950
R. Neck, 'Andrea Negroni: Ein Beitrag zur Geschichte der österreichisch-türkischen Beziehungen nach dem Frieden von Zsitvatorok', *Mitteilungen des Österreichischen Staatsarchivs*, 1950, 166-95

Nejedlý 1905-06
Z. Nejedlý, 'Mše Krištofa Haranta z Polžic', *Časopis musea království českého*, 1905, 138-50, 405-15; 1906,140-47, 353-56

Nejedlý 1921
Z. Nejedlý, *Kryštof Harant z Polžic*, Prague, 1921

Némethy 1818
F. Némethy, *Das Schloss Friedland in Böhmen, und die Monumente in der Friedlander Stadtkirche, nebst einingen alten Urkunden und eigehändigen Briefen des Herzog Waldstein*, Prague, 1818

E. Neumann 1957
E. Neumann, 'Florentiner Mosaik aus Prag', *JKSW*, LIII, 1957, 157-202

E. Neumann 1963
E. Neumann, 'Zur Neueinrichtung der Kunstkammer des Stiftes Kremsmünster', *Österrechische Zeitschrift für Kunst und Denkmalpflege*, XVII, 1963, 69-81

E. Neumann 1966
E. Neumann, 'Das Inventar der rudolfinischen Kunstkammer von 1607/11', *Queen Christina of Sweden: Documents and Studies*, Stockholm, 1966, 262-65 (Analecta Reginensia, I)

E. Neumann 1977
E. Neumann, 'Die stiftlichen Sammlungen und die Bibliothek', *Die Kunstdenkmäler des Benediktinerstiftes Kremsmünster (Österreichische Kunsttopographie, XLIII)*, Vienna, 1977, 17-57

J. Neumann 1951
J. Neumann, *Malířství 17. století v Cechách: Barokní realismus*, Prague, 1951

Neumann 1956
J. Neumann, 'Aachenovo Zvěstování Panny Marie', *Umění*, IV, 1956, 119-32

J. Neumann 1964
J. Neumann, *Obrazárna Pražského hradu: Soubor vybraných děl*, Prague, 1964

J. Neumann 1970
J. Neumann, 'Kleine Beiträge zur rudolfinischen Kunst und ihre Auswirkungen', *Umění*, XVIII, 1970, 142-71

J. Neumann 1977-78
J. Neumann, 'Rudolfinské umění', *Umění*, XXV, 1977, 400-48; XXIVI, 1978, 303-47

J. Neumann 1979
J. Neumann, 'Die Kunst am Hofe Rudolfs II.', *Die Kunst der Renaissance und des Manierismus in Böhmen*, Prague, 1979, 172-217, 232-33

J. Neumann 1982
J. Neumann, 'Die rudolfinische Malerei und ihre Entwicklung', *Leids Kunsthistorisch Jaarboek*, I, 1982, 12-34

J. Neumann 1984
J. Neumann, *Rudolfinská Praha*, Prague, 1984

J. Neumann 1985
J. Neumann, 'Die rudolfinische Kunst und Niederlanden', *Netherlandish Mannerism*, Stockholm, 1985, 47-60

Niederstein 1931
A. Niederstein, 'Das graphische Werk des Bartholomäus Spranger', *Repertorium für Kunstwissenschaft*, LII, 1931, 1-35

Niemoller 1973
K. W. Niemoller, 'Die musikalische Festschrift für den Direktor der Hofkapelle Kaiser Rudolfs II: 1602', *Kongressbericht Bonn, 1970*, Kassel, 1973

Niemoller 1994
K. W. Niemoller, *Jacob Chimarrhaeus: Ein Kolner Musiker am Habsburger Hof Rudolfs II. in Prag*, Cologne, 1994

Nicht 1962
J. Nicht, 'Das Bräutigamskleid Johann Georgs I.', *Dresdener Kunstblätter*, VI:4, 1962, 59-62

Nitze 1990
I. Nitze, 'Erhalten und Restaurieren, Zeichnungen, Aquarelle, Graphik', *Weltkunst*, LX, 1990, 116-19

Nohejlová-Prátová 1963
E. Nohejlová-Prátová, *Výstavní sbírka medailí Národního muzea*, Prague, 1963

Nohejlová 1928
E. Nohejlová, 'Příspěvek k otázce Bartoloměje Albrechta', *Numismatický časopis*, IV, 1928, 11-24

Nohejlová 1929
E. Nohejlová, 'Počátky pražské mincovny za Ferdinanda I.', *Numismatický časopis*, VIII, 1929, 82-104

Nohejlová 1929
E. Nohejlová, *Z příběhů pražské mincovny: Nástin jejich osudů v letech 1537-1618*, Prague, 1929

Nohejlová 1930
E. Nohejlová, 'Poznámky o ražbách pražské mincovny, I: Dva dukáty s opisem S. Ladislaus', *Numismatický časopis*, VIII, 1930, 74-79

Nohejlová 1930
E. Nohejlová, 'Podzim roku 1620 v pražské mincovně', *Časopis Společnosti přátel starožitností českých*, XXXVIII, 1930, 107-23

Nohejlová 1932
E. Nohejlová, 'Poznámky o ražbách pražské mincovny, III: Zlatá ražba Konráda Sauermanna', *Numismatický časopis*, VIII, 1932, 74-78

Nohejlová 1938
E. Nohejlová, 'České medaile Severina Brachmanna', *Sborník Národního muzea*, 1938, 61-119

Nohejlová 1945-46
E. Nohejlová, 'Dlouhá mince v Čechách v letech 1621-1623', *Numismatické listy*, I, 1945-46, 29-35

Nosek 1974
B. Nosek, 'Katalog mit der Auswahl hebräischer Drucke Prager Provenienz, I. Teil: Drucke der Gersoniden im 16. und 17.Jahrhundert', *Judaica Bohemiae*, X, 1974, 13-41

Nosek 1975
B. Nosek, 'Katalog mit der Auswahlter hebräischer Drucke Prager Provenienz, II. Teil: Drucke der Familie bak. Die Buchdruckerei des Abraham ben Schimon Heida, gennant Lemberger', *Judaica Bohemiae*, XI, 1975, 29-53

Nováček 1897
V. Nováček, 'Schránka na pečeť majestátu', *Památky archeologické a místopisné*, XVII, 1897, 260-61

Novák 1935
J. B. Novák, *Rudolf II. a jeho pád*, Prague, 1935

Novotná 1992
J. Novotná, 'Vícehlasná zpracování mešního propria v období české renesance', *Miscellanea musicologica*, XXXIII, 1992, 9-31

Novotný 1945
A. Novotný, *Grafické pohledy na Prahu*, Prague, 1945

Novotný 1946
A. Novotný, *Grafické pohledy Prahy 1493-1850*, Prague, 1946

Novotný 1948
A. Novotný, *Pražské cechovní truhlice a korouhve*, Prague, 1948

Nuska 1958
B. Nuska, 'Vazba soboteckého graduálu', *Sborník Severočeského musea-Historia*, I, 1958, 146-67

Nuska 1961
B. Nuska, 'Böhmische Buchbinder in Haeblers Werk', *Gutenberg-Jahrbuch*, 1961, 323-28

Nuska 1961
B. Nuska, 'Die Beziehungen des böhmischen Renaissance-Bucheinbandes zu den Nachbarländern', *Zentralblatt für Bibliothekwissenschaft*, LXXV, 1961, 481-94

Nuska 1965
B. Nuska, 'Typologie českých renesančních vazeb', *Historická knižní vazba 1964-65*, Liberec, 1965

Nuska 1966
B. Nuska, 'Prager Buchbinderwerkstätten aus der Mitte und zweiten Hälfte des 16. Jahrhunderts', *Gutenberg-Jahrbuch*, 1966, 378-89

Nuska 1970
B. Nuska, 'Meyšnarova knihařská dílna', *Knihtisk a kniha v českých zemích od husitství do Bílé Hory*, Prague, 1970

O'Dell-Franke 1977
I. O'Dell-Franke, *Kupferstiche und Radierungen aus der Werkstatt des Virgil Solis*, Wiesbaden, 1977

O'Dell-Franke 1983
I. O'Dell-Franke, 'Zu Zeichnungen von Christoph Jamnitzer', *Niederdeutsche Beiträge zur Kunstgeschichte*, XXII, 1983, 91-112

Oberhuber 1958
K. Oberhuber, *Die stilistische Entwicklung im Werk Bartholomäus Sprangers*, Diss., Vienna, 1958

Oberhuber 1970
K. Oberhuber, 'Anmerkungen zu Bartholomäus Spranger als Zeichner', *Umění*, XVIII, 1970, 213-22

Obrátil 1932
K. J. Obrátil, 'Exlibris moravských knihoven', *Vitrinka*, IX, 1932, 107-10

Oehler 1979
L. Oehler, *Niederländische Zeichnungen des 16. Jahrhunderts*, Fridingen, 1979

Olsen 1980
H. Olsen, *Statens museum for kunst; Aeldre udenlandsk skulptur*, Copenhagen, 1980

Oman 1927
C. C. Oman, 'A Note on a design by Valentin Sezenius', *Apollo*, VI, 1927, 149-150

Ornamentstichsammlung Berlin 1939
Katalog der Ornamentstichsammlung der staatlichen Kunstbibliothek Berlin, Berlin, 1939

Osthoff 1938
H. Osthoff, *Die Niederländer und das deutsche Lied*, Berlin, 1938

Otto 1993
V. Otto, 'Newe Paduanen, Galliarden, Intraden und Currenten, Nach Englischer und Frantzosischer Art. a 5', *Editio simiae ludentes*, 1993

Padrta 1989
K. Padrta a kol., *Jihočeská vlastivěda: Hudba*, České Budějovice, 1989

Palacký 1832
F. Palacký, *Přehled současný nejvyšších důstojníků a úředníků ve Království českém*, Prague, 1832

Palivec 1972
V. Palivec, 'Medickoheraldické symboly', *Genealogicko-heraldické listy*, 1972, 11-13

Palivec 1974
V. Palivec, 'Pušťadla a baňka v erbu', *Heraldika*, VII, 1974, 41-43

Pallucchini 1969
R. Pallucchini, *Tiziano*, Florence, 1969

Pallucchini 1981
R. Pallucchini, *La pittura veneziana del Seicento*, Rome, 1981

Pánek 1982
J. Pánek, *Stavovská opozice a její zápas s Habsburky*, Prague, 1982

Pánek 1989
J. Pánek, *Poslední Rožmberkové: Velmožové české renesance*, Prague, 1989

Pánek 1991
J. Pánek, *Zápas o Českou konfesi*, Prague, 1911

Panofsky 1930
E. Panofsky, *Hercules am Scheidewege und andere antike Bildstoffe in der neueren Kunst*, Leipzig-Berlin, 1930

Parthey 1853
G. Parthey, *Wenzel Hollar: Beschreibendes Verzeichniss seiner Kupferstiche*, Berlin, 1853

Parthey 1863-64

G. Parthey, *Deutscher Bildersaal: Verzeichnis der in Deutschland vorhandenen Oelbilder verstorbener Maler aller Schulen*, Berlin, 1863-64

Paszkiewicz 1973
M. Paszkiewicz, 'Roelant Savery: "Jezdzcy Polscy"', *Museum Polskie*, III, 1973, 154

Patzak 1943
I. Patzak, 'Eine Prager Dichterin im Zeitalter Rudolfs II.', *Prager Jahrbuch*, 1943, 102-06

Pazaurek 1895
G. E. Pazaurek, *Kunstschmiede- und Schlosserarbeiten des 13. bis 18. Jahrhunderts aus den Sammlungen des Nordböhmische Gewerbemuseums in Reichenberg*, Leipzig, 1895

Pazaurek 1898
G. Pazaurek, 'Alte Eisenätzkunst', *Mittheilungen des Nordböhmischen Gewerbe-Museums*, XVI, 1898, 60

Pazaurek 1898
G. Pazaurek, *Ausgewählte Sammlung-Gegenstände*, Reichenberg, 1898

Pazaurek 1905
G. Pazaurek, *Schloss Friedland*, Reichenberg, 1905

Pechstein 1971
K. Pechstein, *Goldschmidewerke der Remaissance. Kataloge des Kunstgewerbemuseum in Berlin*, Berlin, 1971

Pechstein 1988
K. Pechstein, 'Kaiser Rudolf II. und die Nürnberger Goldschmiedekunst', *Prag um 1600: Beiträge zur Kunst und Kultur am Hofe Rudolfs II.*, Freren, 1988, 232-43

Peltzer 1911-12
R. A. Peltzer, 'Der Hofmaler Hans von Aachen, seine Schule und seine Zeit', *JK-SAK*, XXX, 1911-12, 59-182

Pernštejnové 1995
Pernštejnové v českých dějinách: Sborník příspěvků z konference v Pardubicích, ed. P. Vorel, Pardubice, 1995

Pešatová 1968
Z. Pešatová, *Böhmische Glasgravuren*, Prague, 1968

Pešek 1977
J. Pešek, 'M. Martin Bacháček z Nauměřic, rektor university pražské', *Acta Universitatis Carolinae-Historia Universitatis Carolinae Pragensis*, XVII, 1977, 73-94

Pešek 1980
J. Pešek, 'Knihy a knihovny v kšaftech a inventářích pozůstalostí Nového Města pražského v letech 1576 -1620', *Folia historica bohemica*, III, 1980, 247-77

Pešek 1982
J. Pešek, 'Pražské knihy kšaftů a inventářů: Příspěvek k jejich struktuře a vývoji v době předbělohorské', *Pražský sborník historický*, 1982, 63-90

Pešek-Svatoš 1982
J. Pešek-M. Svatoš, 'Mistr Koldín a právní kultura pražských měst', *Městské právo v 16.-18. století v Evropě*, Prague, 1982, 289

Pešek 1983
J. Pešek, 'Z pražské hudební kultury měšťanského soukromí před Bílou Horou', *Hudební věda*, XX, 1983, 242-56

Pešina 1954
J. Pešina, 'Skupinový portrét v českém renesančním malířství', *Umění*, II, 1954, 269-95

Petneki 1977
Á. Petneki, 'Silberlöffer aus Polen', *Ars Decorativa*, 1977, 127-40

Petráň 1971
J. Petráň, *Staroměstská exekuce*, Prague, 1971

Pfandl 1938
L. Pfandl, *Philipp II: Gemälde eines Lebens und einer Zeit*, Munich, 1938

Philippowich 1966
E. Philippowich, *Kuriositäten und Antiquitäten*, Braunschweig, 1966

Pietzsch 1934
G. Pietzsch, 'Zur Musikkapelle Kaiser Rudolfs II.', *Zeitschrift für Musikwissenschaft*,

1934, 171-76

Pigler 1948
A. Pigler, 'Notice sur Dirck Quade van Ravesteyn', *Oud-Holland*, LXIII, 1948, 74-77

Pilnáček 1930
J. Pilnáček, *Staromoravští rodové*, Vídeň, 1930

Pilz 1962
K. Pilz, 'Hans Hoffmann, ein Nürnberger Dürer-Nachahmer der 2. Hälfte des 16. Jahrhunderts', *Mitteilungen des Vereins für Geschichte der Stadt Nürnberg*, LI, 1962, 236-72

Planiscig 1924
L. von Planiscig, *Kunsthistorisches Museum in Wien: Die Bronzeplastiken, Statuetten, Reliefs, Geräte und Plaketten*, Vienna, 1924

Planiscig 1942
L.von Planiscig, *Katalog der Kunstsammlungen in Stift Klosterneuburg, III: Die Bronzen*, Vienna, 1942

Plecháčková 1975
M. Plecháčková, *Renesanční kamna na českých a moravských hradech a zámcích*, Prague, 1975

Pletzer 1964
K. Pletzer, 'Posmrtné štíty Petra Voka z Rožmberka a Jana Zrinského z roku 1612', *Časopis Národního muzea*, CXXXIII, 1964, 91-95

Plocek 1973
V. Plocek, *Catalogus codicum notis musicis instructorum qui in Bibliotheca universitatis Pragensis servantur*, Prague, 1973

Poche 1955
E. Poche, *Uměleckoprůmyslové muzeum v Praze*, Prague, 1955

Poche-Hejdová 1956
E. Poche-D. Hejdová, *Inventář pokladu loretánskkého*, 1956 (nepubl.)

Poche 1974
E. Poche, *Bazilika sv. Jiří na Pražském hradě*, Prague, 1974

Poche 1979
E. Poche, 'Die angewandte Kunst am Hofe Rudolfs II', *Die Kunst der Renaissance und der Manierismus in Böhmen*, Prag-Hanau, 1979, 159-71

Poche 1988
E. Poche, 'Umělecké řemeslo', *Praha na úsvitu nových dějin*, Prague 1986, 613-47

Poche 1989
E. Poche, 'Renesanční umělecké řemeslo v Čechách', *Dějiny českého výtvarného umění*, II/1: *Od počátků renesance do závěru baroka*, Prague, 1989, 136-49

Poche-Urešová 1987
E. Poche-L. Urešová, *Hodiny a hodinky*, Prague, 1987

Podlaha 1899
A. Podlaha, *Soupis památek historických a uměleckých v politickém okrese Mělnickém*, Prague, 1899

Podlaha-Šittler 1903
A. Podlaha-E. Šittler, *Topographie der Historischen und Kunst-Denkmale im Politischen Bezirke Karolinenthal*, Prague, 1903

Podlaha-Šittler 1903
A. Podlaha-E. Šittler, *Chrámový poklad u Sv. Víta v Praze: Jeho dějiny a popis*, Prague, 1903

Podlaha 1905
A. Podlaha, *Illustrierter Katalog des Prager Domschatzes*, Prague, 1905

Podlaha 1909
A. Podlaha, 'Dějiny kolejí jesuitských v Čechách a na Moravě', *Sborník historického kroužku*, 1909

Podlaha 1920-21
A. Podlaha, 'Plány a kresby chované v kanceláři správy hradu Pražského', *Památky archeologické*, XXXII, 1920-21, 77-103,165-201

Podlaha 1922-23
A. Podlaha, 'Plány a kresby chované v kanceláři správy hradu Pražského', *Památky archeologické*, XXXIII, 1922-23, 44-54, 286-318

Podlaha 1948
A. Podlaha, *Ilustrovaný katalog pokladu chrámu sv.Víta*, Prague, 1948

Podlaha
A. Podlaha, 'Z prvých let činnosti arcibiskupa pražského Zbyňka Berky z Dubé', *Sborník historického kroužku*, I-V, 108-13

Pohanka 1958
J. Pohanka, *Dějiny české hudby v příkladech*, Prague, 1958

Polívka 1991
E. Polívka, *Pět století lobkowiczkých numismatických památek 1547-1958*, Prague, 1991

Pollak 1910-11
O. Pollak, 'Studien zur Geschichte der Architektur Prags 1520-1600', *JKSAK*, XXIX, 1910-11, 85-170

Pollard 1985
J. G. Pollard, *Medaglie italiane del Rinascimento nel Museo Nazionale del Bargello*, Florence, 1985

Popham-Fenwick 1965
A. E. Popham-K. M. Fenwick, *European Drawings in the Collection of the National Gallery of Canada*, Toronto, 1965

Port 1968
J. Port, 'Divadlo řádových škol a náboženských bratrstev', *Dějiny českého divadla, I: Od počátků do sklonku 18. století*, Prague, 1968, 136-54

Porzio 1979
F. Porzio, *L'universo illusorio di Arcimboldi*, Milan, 1979

Poselství ducha 1975
Poselství ducha: Latinská próza českých humanistů, Prague, 1975

Posse 1909-13
O. Posse, *Die Siegel der deutschen Kaiser und Könige von 751 bis 1913*, Dresden, 1909-13

Poštolka 1970
M. Poštolka, 'Die 'Odae Sacrae'des Campanus (1618) und des Tranoscius (1629): ein Vergleich', *Miscellanea musicologica*, XXI-XXII, 1970, 152-70

Poštolka 1988
M. Poštolka, 'Barokní slohové prvky v Campanových ódách', *Nové poznatky o dějinách starší české a slovenské hudby*, Prague, 1988, 127-35.

Praetorius 1985
M. Praetorius, *Syntagma musicum, I: De organographia*, Kassel, 1985

Preiss 1964
P. Preiss, 'Prager Marginalien zu Guiseppe Arcimboldo', *Alte und Moderne Kunst*, IX:77, 1964, 12-14

Preiss 1967
P. Preiss, *Guiseppe Arcimboldo*, Prague, 1967

Preiss 1979
P. Preiss, *Barokní kresby*, Prague, 1979

Preiss 1986
P. Preiss, *Italští umělci v Praze*, Prague, 1986

Prescott 1856-59
W. Prescott, *Geschichte Philips II.*, Leipzig, 1856-59

Pribramenus 1615
J. Pribramenus, *Haustus aeviterni nectaris*, Prague, 1615

Primisser 1819
A. Primisser, *Die Kaiserlich-Königliche Ambraser Sammlung*, Vienna, 1819

Prinz 1971
W. Prinz, *Die Sammlung der Selbstbildnisse in den Uffizien*, Berlin, 1971

Przywecka-Samecka 1987
M. Przywecka-Samecka, *Drukarstwo muzyczne w Europie do konca XVIII wieku*, Wroclaw, 1987

Přibil 1931-1937/38
B. Přibil, 'Soupis československých svatostek, katolických medailí a jetonů', *Numismatický časopis československý*, VII, 1931, 1-83; XIII/XIV, 1937/38, 5-96

Quitin 1973
J. Quitin, 'A propos de trois musiciens liégeois du 16e siécle: Petit Jean de Latre, Johannes Mangon et Mathieu de Sayve', *Musica scientiae collectanea: Festschrift Karl Gustav Fellerer* - Cologne, 1973

Quoika 1954
R. Quoika, 'Christophorus Harant von Polschitz und seine Zeit', *Die Musikforschung*, 1954, 414

Racek 1970
J. Racek, *Kryštof Harant z Polžic a jeho doba*, Brno, 1970

Radcliffe 1979
A. Radcliffe, *Sculptures from the David Daniels Collection*, Minneapolis, 1979

Raine 1856
J. Raine, 'Divination in the fifteenth century by aid of a magical crystal', *Archaeological Journal*, XIII, 1856, 372

Rak 1977
J. Rak, 'Karlova univerzita v pravomoci defenzorů 1609-1622', *Acta Universitatis Carolinae-Historia Universitatis Carolinae Pragensis*, XIX, 1977, 33-46

Rak 1979
J. Rak, 'Vývoj utrakvistické organizace v době předbělohorské', *Sborník archivních prací*, 1979, 179-204

Ramaix 1992
I. de Ramaix, *Les Sadeler: Graveurs et éditeurs*, Brussels, 1992

Randa 1870
A. Randa, *Přehled vzniku a vývinu desk čili knih veřejných hlavně v Čechách a na Moravě*, 1870

Rasl-Mohr 1984
Z. Rasl-J. Mohr, *Černé řemeslo v průběhu staletí*, Prague, 1984

Rataj 1995
T. Rataj, 'Císařská poselstva v Cařihradě ve druhé polovině 16.století', *Dějiny a současnost*, 4, 1995, 7-12

Rauschning 1931
H. Rauschning, *Geschichte der Musik und Musikpflege in Danzig*, Gdansk, 1931

Regteren Altena-Frederichs 1963
J A. van Regteren Altena-L. C. J. Frerichs, *Keuze van tekeningen bewaard in het Rijksprentenkabinet, Rijksmuseum Amsterdam*, Amsterdam, 1963

Reinheckel 1981
G. Reinheckel, *Sächsisches Zinn im Museum für Kunsthandwerk Dresden*, Dresden, 1981

Renesanční poesie 1975
Renesanční poesie, Prague, 1975

Renger 1976-78
K. Renger, 'Sine Cerere et Baccho friget Venus', *Gentse Bijdragen tot Kunstgeschiedenis*, XXIV, 1976-78, 190-203

Reuss 1878
A. E. Reuss, 'Paläontologische Miscellen I: Über ein Schädelfragment der Dronte im Prager Museum', *Denkschr. K. K. Akad. Wiss. Wien*, X, 1878, 71-78

Reznicek 1956
E. K. J. Reznicek, 'Jan Harmensz. Muller als tekenaar', *Nederlands Kunsthistorisch Jaarboek*, VII, 1956, 65-120

Reznicek 1961
E. K. J. Reznicek, *Die Zeichnungen von Hendrick Goltzius*, Utrecht, 1961

Reznicek 1968
E. K. J. Reznicek, 'Bartholomäus Spranger als Bildhauer', *Festschrift Ulrich Middeldorf*, Berlin, 1968, 370-75

Riedel 1963
F. W. Riedel, *Das Musikarchiv im Minoritenkonvent zu Wien*, Kassel, 1963 (Catalogus Musicus, I)

Riegger 1793
J. A. Riegger, 'Aula Rudolphi II. Kayserlicher Hoffstatt', *Archiv der Geschichte und Statistik insbes. von Böhmen*, II, Dresden, 1793

Riemann 1920
H. Riemann, *Geschichte der Musiktheorie im IX.-XIX. Jahrhundert*, Berlin, 1920

Richter 1933
E. Richter, *Geschichte des Musiknotendrucks in den böhmischen Ländern bis 1618*, Diss., Prague, 1933

Rohde 1923
A. Rohde, *Geschichte der wissenschaftlichen Instrumente vom Beginn der Renaissance bis zum Anfangs des 18. Jahrhunderts*, Leipzig, 1923

Rosenberg 1922-28
M. Rosenberg, *Der Goldschmiede Merkzeichen*, Frankfurt, 1922-28

Rossacher 1981
K. Rossacher, 'Die Weisheit beugt sich den Fesseln der Liebe: Eine verschollene Allegorie des Prager Hofmalers Batholomäus Spranger', *Alte und moderne Kunst*, XXVI:197, 1981, 1-6

Rossi 1957
F. Rossi, *Malerei in Stein: Mosaiken und Intarsien*, Stuttgart, 1957

Rossi 1957
F. Rossi, *Italienische Goldschmiedekunst*, Munich, 1957

Röttgen 1993
H. Röttgen, *Caravaggio: Der irdische Amor oder Der Sieg der fleischlichen Liebe*, Frankfurt, 1993

Rouček 1948
R. Rouček, *Chrám sv. Víta: Dějiny a průvodce*, Prague, 1948

Royt 1996
J. Royt, *Poutní místo Panny Marie Vítězné na Bílé Hoře*, Prague, 1996

Ruffer 1861
V. Ruffer, *Historie vyšehradská, neb vypravování o hradu, kapitole a městu hory Vyšehradu u Prahy v království Českém*, Prague, 1861

Rukověť 1966-82
Rukověť humanistického básnictví v Čechách, Prague, 1966-82

Ryantová 1995
M. Ryantová, 'Polyxena z Lobkovic, rozená z Pernštejna a její hospodářská činnost', *Pernštejnové: Sborník příspěvků z konference v Pardubicích*, ed. P. Vorel Pardubice, 1995, 105-14

Ryba 1970
B. Ryba, 'Dva nálezy z vnitřku starých vazeb', *Historická knižní vazba*, 1970, 67-85

Ryba 1971
B. Ryba, *Soupis rukopisů Strahovské knihovny Památníku národního písemnictví v Praze*, Prague, 1971

Rychnovský 1972
J. Rychnovský, *Missa super 'Et valde mane'*, Chorwerk, Wolfenbuettel, 1972

Ryneš 1948
V. Ryneš, *Paladium země české*, Prague, 1948

Ryser 1991
F. Ryser, *Verzauberte Bilder: Die Kunst der Malerei hinter Glas*, Munchen, 1991

Sacken 1855
E. von Sacken, *Die Ambraser Sammlung*, Vienna, 1855

Sadek 1973
V. Sadek, 'From the MSS Collection of the State Jewish Museum in Prague (MSS of Historical Content)', *Judaica Bohemiae*, IX, 1973, 16-22

Sadek 1992
V. Sadek, *Židovská mystika v Praze*, Prague, 1992

Sakař 1935
J. Sakař, *Dějiny města Týna nad Vltavou a okolí*, Týn nad Vltavou, 1935

Saldern 1965
A. von Saldern, *German Enameled Glass*, Corning, 1965

Sale 1994
F. Sale, *Dialogismus octo vocum de amore Christi, Musica temporis Rudolphi II.*, (CD Supraphon 11 2176-2 231), Prague, 1994

Sammlung Horský 1910
Sammlung des Herrn Johann Horský, Frankfurt, 1910

Sammlung Lanna 1910
Sammlung des Freiherrn Adalbert von Lanna: Auktionskatalog der Sammlung, Berlin, 1910

Sammlung Lanna 1911
Sammlung Freiherr v. Lanna-Prag: Manuscripte und Bücher

Sammlung Löbbecke 1908
Sammlung Löbbecke, Munich, 1908

Sandrart 1675
J. von Sandrart, *Teutsche Academie der edlen Bau-, Bild- und Mahlerey-Künste*, Nürnberg, 1675

Sapper 1982
C. Sapper, 'Die Zahlamtsbücher im Hofkammerarchiv 1542-1825', *Mitteilungen des Österreichischen Staatsarchivs*, XXXV, 1982, 404-55

Sasaki 1980
H. Sasaki, *Le Nu féminin dans l'art, IV: Mythologies. Feés et Nymphes*, Tokyo, 1980

Saur 1992
K. G. Saur, *Allgemeines Künstler-Lexikon*, Munich-Leipzig, 1992

Saxl-Nosková 1972
M. Saxl-L. Nosková, *Renesanční portrét*, I, Roudnice nad Labem, 1972

Sborník 1923
Sborník Blahoslavův (1523-1923), Přerov, 1923

Scapinelli 1927-28
P. Scapinelli, 'Die Exlibris des Freiherrn Ferdinand Hoffmann', *Österreichisches Jahrbuch für Exlibris und Gebrauchsgraphik*, 1927-28

Sedláček 1925
A. Sedláček, *Českomoravská heraldika*, Prague, 1925

Sedlák 1945
V. J. Sedlák, *O počátcích erbů pražských cechů*, Prague, 1945

Sedlák-Konopásek 1977
V. J. Sedlák-E. Konopásek, *Jílovská minucí*, Jílové u Prahy, 1977

Segal 1984
S. Segal, 'Georg Flegel as a flower painter', *Tableau*,V:3, 1984, 73-86

Sehnal 1958
Sehnal, 'Hudba 16. století na číši buchlovského hradu', *Zprávy krajského vlastivědného ústavu v Gottwaldově*, 1958, 75

Seifertová 1974
H. Seifertová, 'Tempores anni Lucas van Valckenborch', *Umění*, XXIII, 1974, 324-40

Seifertová 1981
H. Seifertová, 'Poznámky k výstavě Stilleben in Europa', *Umění*, XXIX, 1981, 164-77

Seifertová-Šroněk 1995-96
H. Seifertová-M. Šroněk, "'Gestraift doppelt Bild' from Prague's Rudolfine Collections', *Bulletin of the National Gallery in Prague*, V-VI, 1995-96, 138-45

Seitz 1965
H. Seitz, *Blankwaffen*, Braunschweig, 1965

Seling 1980-94
H. Seling, *Die Kunst der Augsburger Goldschmiede 1529-1868*, Munich, 1980-94

Semerák-Bohmann 1977
G. Semerák-K. Bohmann, *Umělecké kovářství a zámečnictví*, Prague, 1977

Senn 1938
W. Senn, *Musik, Schule, und Theater der Stadt Hall in Tirol in der Zeit vom 15. bis 19. Jahrhundert*, Innsbruck, 1938

Senn 1954
W. Senn, *Musik und Theater am Hof zu Innsbruck*, Innsbruck, 1954

Servít 1989
Z. Servít, *Jan Marek Marci z Kronlandu, zapomenutý zakladatel novověké fyziologie a mediciny*, Bratislava-Prague, 1989

Seydl 1951
O. Seydl, 'Dějiny jesuitského 'musea matematického' v koleji sv. Klimenta na Starém městě v Praze ', *Věstník král. české spol. nauk, tř. matem.-přír.*, 1951

Shixiang 1987
W. Shixiang, *Ancient Chinese Lacquerware*, Peking, 1987

Schade 1969
W. Schade, *Dresdner Zeichnungen 1550-1650: Inventionen sächsischer Künstler in europäischen Sammlungen*, Dresden, 1969

Schapelhouman 1987
M. Schapelhouman, *Nederlandse tekeningen omstreeks 1600 (Catalogus van de Nederlandse tekeningen in het Rijksprentenkabinet, Rijksmuseum, Amsterdam, III)*, The Hague-Amsterdam, 1987

Schardin 1989
J. Schardin, *Kunst- und Automatenuhren (Katalog der Großuhrensammlung, Staatlicher mathematisch - physikalischer Salon, Dresden, Zwinger)*, Dresden, 1989

Schardin 1989
J. Schardin, *Kunst-Automatenuhren*, Dresden, 1989

Schebek 1873
E. Schebek, 'Aus dem Leben des Christoph Harant von Polzitz', *Mitteilungen des Vereins fuer Geschichte Deutschen in Boehmen*, XII, 1873, 273-86

Schedelmann 1972
H. Schedelmann, *Die großen Büchsenmacher*, Braunschweig, 1972

Scheiger 1825
J. Scheiger, 'Museum technologicum ab Equite de Schoenfeld Vindobonae fundatum. Conspectus rerum ibi visendarum brevi, amicisque artium et antiquitatum dedicatus', *Ex typographia Equitis de Schoenfeld*, Prague, 1825

Scheicher 1995
E. Scheicher, 'Zur Ikonologie von Naturalien im Zusammenhang der enzyklopädischen Kunstkammer', *Anzeiger des Germanischen Nationalmuseums*, 1995, 115-25

Schenk 1961
E. Schenk, 'Zur Lebens-und Familiengeschichte von Lambert de Sayve', *Festschrift Helmuth Osthoff*, Tutzing, 1961

Scheybal 1994
J. V. Scheybal, *Státní hrad a zámek Frýdlant*, 1994

Schierning 1961
L. Schierning, *Die Uberlieferung des deutschen Orgel- und Klaviermusik aus den ersten Halfte des 17. Jahrhunderts*, Kassel, 1961

Schilling 1929
E. Schilling, *Die Meisterzeichnung: Nürnberger Handzeichnungen des XV. und XVI. Jahrhunderts*, Freiburg i.B., 1929

Schilling 1973
E. Schilling, *Städelsches Kunstinstitut, Katalog der deutschen Zeichnungen: Alte Meister*, Frankfurt, 1973

Schimon 1859
A. Schimon, *Der Adel von Böhmen, Mähren und Schlesien*, Böhmisch Leipa, 1859

Schlenz 1911
J. Schlenz, *Johann Sixt von Lerchenfels, Propst von Leitmeritz*, Prague, 1911

Schlosser 1910
J. von Schlosser, *Werke der Kleinplastik in der Skulpturensammlung des A.H. Kaiserhauses*, Vienna, 1910

Schmidt 1922
R. Schmidt, *Das Glas*, Berlin, 1922

Schnackenburg 1970
B. Schnackenburg, 'Beobachtungen zu einem neuen Bild von Bartholomäus Spranger', *Niederdeutsche Beiträge zur Kunstgeschichte*, IX, 1970, 143-60

Schneede 1967
U. Schneede, 'Interieurs von Hans und Paul Vredeman de Vries', *Nederlands Kunsthistorisch Jaarboek*, XVIII, 1967, 127-66

Schönbrunner-Meder 1896-1908
J. Schönbrunner - J. Meder, *Handzeichnungen alter Meister aus der Albertina und anderen Sammlungen*, Vienna, 1896-1908

Schulz 1950
E. J. Schulz, 'Jakub a Octavius Strada', *Numismatický časopis*, XIX, 1950, 131-50

Schulz 1971
W. Schulz, 'Doomer und Savery', *Master Drawings*, IX, 1971, 253-59

Schulz 1974
W. Schulz, *Lambert Doomer: Sämtliche Zeichnungen*, 1974

Schulz 1989-90
K. Schulz, 'Bemerkungen zu Antonio Abondio', *JKSW*, LXXXV/LXXXVI, 1989-90, 155-62

Schunke 1942
I. Schunke, 'Der Dürerbuch-Meister: Ein Buchbinder aus dem Rudolfinischen Prag', *Archiv für Buchbinderei*, XLII, 1942, 75-80

Schuselka 1966
E. Schuselka, *Kunsthistorisches Museum Wien, Katalog der Sammlung für Plastik und Kunstgewerbe, II: Renaissance*, Vienna, 1966

Schütte 1988
R. A. Schütte, 'Medaillen, Münzen und Wachsbossierungen am Hofe Rudolfs II.', Essen-Vienna 1988, 575-77

Schütte 1988
R. A. Schütte, 'Mathias Beitler - Ornamentstecher in Ansbach und Hartschier in Prag', *Prag um 1600: Beiträge zur Kunst und Kultur am Hofe Rudolfs II.*, Freren, 1988, 267-73

Schütte 1989-90
R. A. Schütte, 'Hertzich van Bein und Hans de Bull: Zu den Bildformeln der Prager Schwarzornamentstecher', *JKSW*, LXXXV/LXXXVI, 1989-90, 183-202

Schütte 1991
R. A. Schütte, *Geschichte der Schwarzornamente: Entwicklung und Ausprägung einer Gruppe von Vorlageblättern für Goldschmiede von 1585 bis ca. 1635*, Diss., Kiel, 1991

Schütz 1976
K. Schütz, *Porträtgalerie zur Geschichte Österreichs von 1400 bis 1800*, Vienna, 1976

Schwarzenfeld 1979
G. von Schwarzenfeld, *Rudolf II. Ein deutscher Kaiser am Vorabend des Dreißigjährigen Krieges*, Munich, 1979

Schweikhart 1977
G. Schweikhart, 'Von Priapus zu Coridon: Benennungen des Dornausziehers in Mittelalter und Neuzeit', *Würzburger Jahrbücher für Altertumswissenschaft*, N.F.III, 1977, 243-52

Siebmacher 1906
Johann Siebmachers Wappenbuch des abgestorbenen Bayerischen Adel, Nürnberg, 1906

Skei 1966
A. B. Skei, 'Jacob Handl's Moralia', *The Musical Quarterly*, 1966, 431-447

Skýbová 1966
A. Skýbová, 'Obnovení pražského arcibiskupství v letech 1561-1562 a jeho vztah k pražské universitě', *Acta Universitatis Carolinae-Historia Universitatis Carolinae Pragensis*, XII, 1966, 2-11

Slavata 1608-19 (1866)
Paměti nejvyššího kancléře království českého Viléma hraběte Slavaty z Chlumu a Košumberka ... od 1608 do 1619, Prague, 1866

Smijers 1919-22
A. Smijers, *Die kaiserliche Hofmusik-Kapelle von 1543-1619*, Vienna, 1919-22

Smijers 1923
J. Smijers, *Karl Luython als Motetten-Komponist*, Amsterdam, 1923

Smolík 1871
J. Smolík, 'Jan Marek Marci a jeho spisy', *Živa: Sborník vědecký Musea král. Českého*, VII, 1871

Sněmy 1877-1954
Sněmy české od léta 1526 až po naši dobu, Prague, 1877-1954

Snížková 1957
J. Snížková, 'Sborník Dobřenského', *Hudební rozhledy*, VIII, 1957, 907-08

Snížková 1971
J. Snížková, 'Einige Bemerkungen zur Mehrstimmigkeit in Böhmen', *Die Musikforschung*, XXIV, 1971, 278-80

Snížková 1972
J. Snížková, 'Kutnohorský sborník mší ze sklonku 16. století', *Časopis národního muzea*, CXLI, 1972, 49

Snížková 1980
J. Snížková, 'Málo známí čeští skladatelé konce 16. století', *Hudební věda*, XVII, 1980, 53-59

Snížková 1982
J. Snížková, *Česká vokální polyfonie*, Prague, 1982

Snížková 1985
J. Snížková, 'Jacobus Handl Gallus und Prag in drei Dokumenten', *Jacobus Handl Gallus and his Time*, Ljubljana, 1985, 138

Somers Coks 1980
A. Somers Coks, *Court Jewellery*, London, 1980

Soušková 1983
D. Soušková, *Pavel Spongopaeus Jistebnický: Příspěvek k poznání života a tvorby*, Dipl. práce, Prague, 1983

Spicer 1970
J. A. Spicer, 'The 'Naer het leven' Drawings: By Pieter Bruegel or Roelandt Savery?', *Master Drawings*, VIII, 1970, 3-30

Spicer 1979
J. A. Spicer, *The Drawings of Roelandt Savery*, PhD. Diss, Yale University, New Haven, Conn., 1979

Spicer 1982
J. Spicer, 'The Defence of Prague 15 February 1611', *Umění*, XL, 1982, 454-62

Spicer 1988
J. Spicer, 'Adam and Eve after the Fall by Paulus van Viannen and the Interrelationship of the Arts', *Prag um 1600: Beiträge zur Kunst und Kultur am Hofe Rudolfs II.*, Freren, 1988, 273-83

Spicer 1996
J. Spicer, 'The Star of David and Jewish Culture in Prague around 1600, Reflected in Drawings of Roelandt Savery and Paulus van Vianen', *The Journal of the Walters Art Gallery*, LIV, 1996, 203-24

Spickernagel
E. Spickernagel, *Roelandt Savery: Orpheus unter den Tieren 1610*, Frankfurt, s.d. (Kleine Werkmonographie 17)

Sponsel 1921
J. L. Sponsel, *Führer durch das Grüne Gewölbe zu Dresden*, Dresden, 1921.

Sponsel 1923
J. L. Sponsel, 'Kostbare Uhren im Grünen Gewölbe', *Die Uhrmacherkunst*, 1923, 221-24

Sprinzels 1938
F. Sprinzels, *Hollar Handzeichnungen*, Prague, 1938

Srurm 1961
H. Srurm, *Egerer Reliefintarsien*, Munich, 1961

Stará 1965
D. Stará, 'Tři památky pražského malířského bratrstva', *Časopis Národního muzea*, CXXXIV, 1965, 3-13

Stará 1995
D. Stará, 'Sušická cínová mísa s reliéfem evangelisty sv. Marka', *Vlastivědné zprávy muzea Šumavy*, III,1995, 80-83

Starkenfels-von Kirnbauer 1885-1904
A. von Starkenfels-J.E.von Kirnbauer, J. *Siehmachers grosses und allgemeines Wappenbuch in einer neuen, vollständig geordneten und reich vermehrten Auflage mit heraldischen und historisch-genealogischen Erläuterungen*, Nürnberg, 1885-1904

Staudinger 1990
M. Staudinger, 'Études descriptives de zoologie historique', *Le Bestiaire de Rodolphe II, Cod. min. 129 et 130 de la Bibliotheque national d'Autriche*, Paris, 1990, 91-493

Staudinger 1995
M. Staudinger, 'Hans Vermeyen, Kammer-goldschmied Kaiser Rudolfs II. in Prag', *JKSW*, XCI, 1995, 263-71

Staudinger-Irblich 1996
M. Staudinger-E. Irblich, 'Naturstudien Kaiser Rudolfs II. (1576-1612): Zur Kunstkammer auf der Prager Burg.', in Vienna, 1996, 228-86

Stauffer 1884
A. Stauffer, *Hermann Christoph Graf von Russworm*, Munich, 1884

Steenbock 1965
F. Steenbock, *Der kirchliche Prachteinband in frühen Mittelalter von den Anfänge bis zum Beginn der Gotik*, Berlin, 1965

Stehlíková 1993
D. Stehlíková, 'Zlatnické práce z břevnovské pokladnice', *Zprávy památkové péče*, LIII, 1993, 187-91

Stehlíková 1994
D. Stehlíková, *From the Golden Treasury of Prague*, Ramat-Gan, 1994

Stechow 1930
W. Stechow, 'Eine Zeichnung von Hans Vermeyen', *JKSW*, IV, 1930, 267-68

Steingräber 1956
E. Steingräber, *Alter Schmuck: Die Kunst des europäischen Schmuckes*, Munich, 1956

Steinhardt 1973
M. Steinhardt, 'A Musical Fragment from Prague: Národní muzeum XIV C 149', *Fontes artis musicae*,1973

Stellfeld 1949
J. A. Stellfeld, *Bibliographie des Editions Musicales Plantiniennes*, Brussels, 1949

Stloukal 1912
K. Stloukal, 'Karel z Lichtenštejna a jeho účast ve vládě Rudolfa II. (1596-1607)', *Český časopis historický*, 1912, 153-69, 389-434

Stloukal 1925
K. Stloukal, *Papežská politika a císařský dvůr pražský na předělu XVI a XVII. věku*, Prague, 1925

Stloukal 1930
K. Stloukal, 'Portrét Rudolfa II. z roku 1600', *Od pravěku k dnešku: Sborník k 60. narozeninám J. Pekaře II.*, Prague, 1930

Stloukal 1931
K. Stloukal, *Česká kancelář dvorská 1599-1608*, Prague, 1931

Stloukal 1940
K. Stloukal, 'Polyxena z Lobkovic, rozená z Pernštejna ', *Královny, kněžny a veliké ženy české*, ed.P.Vorel, Prague, 1940

Stöcklein 1922
H. Stöcklein, *Meister des Eisenschnittes*, Esslingen, 1922

Straka 1909
C. Straka, 'Památník Václava Dobřenského', *Časopis Českého musea*, LXXXIII, 1909, 141-45

Straka 1916
C. Straka, 'Stradové z Rosbergu', *Památky archeologické*, XXVIII, 1916, 18-24

Straka 1922-23
C. Straka, 'Přehled historického vývoje knižních vazeb', *Náš směr*, IX, 1922-23, 116-27

Straka 1927
C. Straka, *Přenesení ostatků sv. Norberta z Magdeburku na Strahov (1626-1628)*, Prague, 1927

Strakov á 1982-83
T. Straková, 'Vokálně polyfonní skladby na Moravě v 16. a na začátku 17. století', *Časopis Moravského muzea*, LXVII, 1982, 85-97; LXVIII, 1983, 149-80

Strasser-Spiegl 1989
R. von Strasser-W. Spiegl, *Dekoriertes Glas: Renaisance bis Biedermeier*, Munich, 1989

Strauss 1940
K. Strauss, *Kacheln und Öfen der Steiermark*, Graz, 1940

Strauss 1977
W. L. Strauss, *Hendrick Goltzius 1500-1617: The Complete Engravings and Woodcuts*, New

York, 1977

Strauss 1983
K. Strauss, *Die Kachelkunst des 15. bis 17. Jahrhunderts*, Munich, 1983

Strohmer 1947
E. V. Strohmer, *Prunkgefäße aus Bergkristall*, Vienna, 1947

Strohmer 1947-48
E. V. Strohmer, 'Bemerkungen zu den Werken des Adriaen de Vries', *Nationalmusei arsbok*, 1947-48

Studnička 1898
Studnička, 'Marcus Marci, český Galileo Galilei', *Bohatýrové ducha*, Prague, 1898

Sumowski 1979
W. Sumowski, *Drawings of the Rembrandt School*, New York, 1979

Svatoš 1995
M. Svatoš, 'Pokusy o reformu a zánik karolinské akademie', *Dějiny Univerzity Karlovy*, I, Prague, 1995, 269-89

Sviták 1992
I. Sviták, *Malostranská Sapfo*, Prague, 1992

Sychra 1910
J. C. Sychra, *Christophorus Harant: Missa quinis vocibus*, Prague, 1910

Syndram-Kappel-Arnold 1994
D. Syndram-J. Kappel-U. Arnold, *Das Grüne Gewölbe zu Dresden: Führer durch seine Geschichte und seine Sammlungen*, Munich-Berlin, 1994

Syndram 1995
D. Syndram, 'Die Elfenbeindrechseleien im Grünen Gewölbe: Von der Maschinenkunst zum fürstlichen Sammlungsgegenstand', *Erbach*, 1995, 6-13

Šafránek 1913
J. Šafránek, *Školy české: Obraz jejich vývoje a osudů*, I, Prague, 1913

Šimek 1977
E. Šimek, 'Česká mince v prvních desetiletích 17. století', *Sborník Národního muzea-řada A (Historie)*, 1977, 235-38

Šimek 1986
E. Šimek, 'Zásobování pražské mincovny drahým kovem v době třicetileté války', *Folia Historica Bohemica*, X, 1986, 351-71

Široká 1995
E. J. Široká, *Northern Artists in Italy ca. 1565-85: Hans Speckaert as a draughtsman and a teacher*, PhD. Diss., Princeton, 1995

Šittler-Podlaha 1898-99
E. Šittler-A. Podlaha, 'Loretánský poklad v Praze na Hradčanech', *Památky archeologické*, XVIII, 1898-99, 41-48,133-40, 281-88, 427-32

Šittler-Podlaha 1903
E. Šittler-A. Podlaha, *Poklad svatovítský*, Prague, 1903, (Soupis památek historických a uměleckých II/1)

Škulj 1991
E. Škulj, *Gallusovi predgovori in drugi dokumenti*, Ljubljana, 1991

Šnajdrová 1994
E. Šnajdrová, 'Proti silám temnot', *Starožitnosti*, 1994, 16

Šroněk 1989
M. Šroněk, 'Barokní malířství 17. století v Čechách', *Dějiny českého výtvarného umění*, II/1: *Od počátků renesance do závěru baroka*, Prague, 1989, 324-55

Šroněk 1992
M. Šroněk, 'Matyáš Mayer, Oldřich Musch a David Altmann - pražští malíři první poloviny 17. století', *Umění*, XL, 1992, 148-62

Šroněk 1996
M. Šroněk, *Pražští malíři 1600-1656: Mistři, tovaryši, učedníci a štolíři v Knize Staroměstského malířského cechu. Biografický slovník*, Prague, 1996

Sršeň 1975
L. Sršeň, 'Větší zemský soud v Čechách ve vyobrazení 16.století', *Časopis Národního muzea*, CXLIV, 1975, 167-72

Štafl 1974
I. Štafl, 'J. Bassewi z Treuenburgu, první

pražský židovský erbovník', *Heraldická ročenka*, 1974, 59-61

Tacke 1996
A. Tacke, *Die Gemälde des 17. Jahrhunderts im Germanischen Nationalmuseum: Bestandskatalog*, Mainz, 1996

Tait 1967
H. Tait, "The Devil's Looking-Glass': the Magical Speculum of Dr. John Dee', *Horace Walpole: Writer, Collector and Connoisseur*, New Haven-London, 1967, 195-212

Tait 1991
H. Tait, *Catalogue of the Waddeston Bequest in the British Museum, III: The 'Curiosities'*, London, 1991

Tardy 1961-69
J. Tardy, *Le pendule francaise des origines a nos jours*, Paris, 1961-69

Teige 1902-03
J. Teige, *Základy starého místopisu pražského*, Prague, 1902-03

Tentzel 1705 (1981)
W. E. Tentzel, *Saxonia Nummismatica* (Leipzig, 1705), Berlin, 1981

Theuerkauff 1986
C. Theuerkauff, *Die Bildwerke in Elfenbein des 16.-19.Jahrhunderts (Die Bildwerke der Skulpturen Galerie, Staatliche Museen Preussischer Kulturbesitz)*, Berlin, 1986

Thomas-Gamber 1958
B. Thomas-O. Gamber, 'L'arte milanese dell`armatura', *Storia di Milano*, XI, Milan, 1958, 698-841

Thomas-Gamber-Schedelman 1963
B. Thomas-O. Gamber-H. Schedelmann, *Die schönsten Waffen und Rüstungen aus europäischen und amerikanischen Sammlungen*, Heidelberg-Munich, 1963

Thomas 1963-64
B. Thomas, 'Aus der Waffensammlung in der Neuen Burg zu Wien: Orientalische Kostbarkeiten', *Zeitschrift Bustan*, 1963-64

Thomas 1969
B. Thomas, 'Zwei Vorzeichnungen zu kaiserlichen Garde Stangenwaffen von Hans Stromair 1577 und Johann Bernhard Fischer von Erlach 1705', *JKSW*, LXV, 1969

Thomas-Gamber 1976
B. Thomas-O. Gamber, *Katalog der Leibrüstkammer, I.: Der Zeitraum von 500 bis 1530*, Vienna, 1976

Thoren 1990
V. E. Thoren, *The Lord of Uraniborg: A Biography of Tycho Brahe*, New York, 1990

Tietze 1933
H. Tietze et al., *Beschreibender Katalog der Handzeichnungen in der Graphischen Sammlung Albertina, IV: Die Zeichnungen der deutschen Schulen*, Vienna, 1933

Tichá 1984
Z. Tichá, *Cesta starší české literatury*, Prague, 1984

Tichota 1965
J. Tichota, 'Tabulatury pro loutnu a příbuzné nástroje na území ČSSR', *Acta Universitatis Carolinae-Philosophica et historica*, 1965, 139-49

Tichota 1967
J. Tichota, 'Deutsche Lieder in Prager Lautentabulaturen des beginnenden 17. Jahrhunderts', *Miscellanea musicologica*, XX, 1967, 63-69

Tischer 1905
F. Tischer, 'Bartoloměj Paprocký', *Časopis Musea království Českého*, LXXIX, 1905, 299-301

Tischer 1908
F. Tischer, 'Uvedení řádu Kapucínů do Čech okolo 1600', *Věstník Královské české společnosti nauk, třída filosoficko-historicko-jazykozpytná*, 1908, 1-56

Tischer 1928
F. Tischer, *Böhmisches Zinn und seine Marken*, Leipzig, 1928

Tobolka-Horák 1939-67
Z. Tobolka-F. Horák, *Knihopis českých a slovenských tisků od doby nejstarší až do konce

XVIII. století*, Prague, 1939-67

Tolnay 1952
C. de Tolnay, *Die Zeichnungen Pieter Bruegels*, Zürich, 1952

Toman 1947-50
P. Toman, *Nový slovník československých výtvarných umělců*, Prague, 1947-50

Toranová 1980
E. Toranová, *Cínárstvo na Slovensku*, Bratislava, 1980

Trevor-Roper 1976
H. Trevor-Roper, *Princes and Artists: Patronage and Ideology at four Habsburg courts, 1517-1633*, London, 1976

Trolda 1933
E. Trolda, 'Kapitoly o české mensurální hudbě', *Cyril*, LIX,LX, 1933, 4-7, 27-31, 52-56

Trolda 1934
E. Trolda, 'Česká církevní hudba v období generálbasu', *Cyril*, LX, 1934

Truhlář 1897
A. Truhlář, 'Jakub Chimarrhaeus', *Časopis českého muzea*, 1897

Truhlář 1905-06
J. Truhlář, *Catalogus codicum manu scriptorum qui in c.r. bibliotheca publica atque universitatis Pragensis asservatur*, Prague, 1905-06

Trunz 1986
E. Trunz, 'Pansophie und Manierismus im Kreise Kaiser Rudolfs II.', *Die österreichische Literatur: Ihr Profil von den Anfängen im Mittelalter bis ins 18. Jahrhundert (1050-1750)*, ed.F. P. Knapp-H. Zeman, Graz, 1986, 865-986.

Tumpach-Podlaha 1912
J. Tumpach-A. Podlaha, *Český slovník bohovědný*, Prague, 1912

Turek 1991
E. Turek, 'Böhmiska fanor i Statens trofésamling', *Armémusei Arsbok-Meddelande*, LI, Stockholm, 1991

Urban 1786
A. Urban, *Merkwürdigkeiten der Strahöfer Bibliothek*, Prague, 1786

Urban 1973
J. Urban, 'Poslední řezáč z rodu Miseroniů. K životu a dílu F.E. Miseroniho', *Umění*, XXI, 1973, 515-27

UPČ 1977-82
Umělecké památky Čech, Prague, 1977-82

Urban 1975
J. Urban, 'Tabernaculum ex gemmis Bohemicis', *Umění*, XXIII, 1975, 526-36

Urban 1976
J. Urban, *Řezáči drahých kamenů v Čechách v 16. a 17.století*, Prague, 1976 (Acta UPM, IX-Řada D. Supplementa 2)

Urbánková 1975
E. Urbánková, *Rukopisy a vzácné tisky pražské Universitní knihovny*, Prague, 1975

Urešová 1986
L. Urešová, *Alte Uhren*, Prague, 1986

Urešová 1986
I. Urešová, *European Clocks*, Prague, 1986

Urešová 1989
L. Urešová, *Montres et Horloges*, Prague, 1989

Urešová 1990
L. Urešová, *El Arte de la Relojeria*, Prague, 1990

Urešová 1991
L. Urešová, *Orologi di tutti tempi*, Prague, 1991

Urešová 1991
L. Urešová, *Zegary*, Prague, 1991

Vacek 1896
F. Vacek, 'Diecézní synoda pražská z r. 1605: Život církevní v Čechách z počátku sedmnáctého století', *Sborník historického kroužku*, Prague, 1896, 25-45

Vacková 1968
J. Vacková, 'Podoba a příčiny anachronismu', *Umění*, XVI , 1968, 379-93

Vacková 1969
J. Vacková, 'Epitafní obrazy v předbělohorských Čechách', *Umění*, XVII, 1969, 131-56

Vacková 1972
J. Vacková, 'Obrazový cyklus od Fredericka van Valckenborch', *Umění*, XX, 1972, 370-75

Vacková 1989
J. Vacková, *Nizozemské malířství 15. a 16. století: Československé sbírky*, Prague, 1989

Vacková 1989
J. Vacková 'Závěsné malířství a knižní malba v letech 1526 až 1620', *Dějiny českého výtvarného umění*, II/1: *Od počátku renesance do závěru baroka*, Praha, 1989, 93-106

Valenta 1918
J. Valenta, *Tam, kde se zpívalo*, Prague, 1918

Vávra 1970
I. Vávra, 'Knižní vazby bratrské dílny ivančicko-kralické (1562-1620)', *Historická knižní vazba*, 1966-70, 86-160

Veillon 1996
M. Veillon, 'Influences de l'antiquité romaine sur les médailles des Rois de France (1450-1589)', *The Medal*, 1996, 30-38

Veldman 1983
I. M. Veldman, 'De macht van de planeten over het mensdom in prenten naar Maarten de Vos', *Bulletin van het Rijkmuseum*, XXXI, 1983, 21-53

Verzeichniss 1844
Verzeichniss der Münz- und Medaillen-Sammlung des L. W. von Wellenheim, Vienna, 1844

Verzeichnis 1983
Verzeichnis der im deutschen Sprachbereich erschienenen Druckes des XVI. Jahrhunderts, Stuttgart, 1983

Vey 1964
H. Vey, 'Kölner Zeichnungen aus den 16.,17., und 18. Jahrhundert', *Wallraf-Richartz-Jahrbuch*, XXVI, 1964, 75-166

Vignau-Wilberg 1969
T. Vignau-Wilberg Schuurman, *Die emblematischen Elemente im Werke Joris Hoefnagels*, Leiden, 1969

Vignau-Wilberg 1985
T. Vignau-Wilberg, 'Joris Hoefnagel's Tätigkeit in München', *JKSW*, LXXXI, 1985, 103-67

Vignau-Wilberg 1994
T. Vignau-Wilberg, *Archetypa studiaque patris Georgii Hoenagelii: Natur, Dichtung und Wissenschaft in der Kunst um 1600*, Munich, 1994

Vilímková 1993
M. Vilímková, *Židovské Město Pražské*, Prague, 1993

Vilímková-Kašička 1970
M. Vilímková-F. Kašička, 'Lví dvůr Pražského hradu', *Památková péče*, XXX, 1970, 34-41

Vilímková-Kašička 1976
M. Vilímková-F. Kašička, 'Křídlo Španělského sálu ve stavebním vývoji Pražského hradu', *Památky a příroda*, I, 1976, 385-91

Vilímková-Kašička 1976
M. Vilímková-E. Kašička, 'Císařská kuchyně Pražského hradu', *Památky a příroda*, I, 1976, 67-70.

Vilímková-Kašička 1977
M. Vilímková-F. Kašička, 'Stavební proměny Středního křídla Pražského hradu', *Památky a příroda*, II, 1977, 129-39

Vilímková-Líbal 1988
M. Vilímková-D. Líbal, 'Architektura', *Praha na úsvitu nových dějin*, Prague, 1988, 43-124

Vilímková 1995
M. Vilímková, 'Dějiny Lobkovického paláce na Pražském hradě', *Umění*, XLIII, 1995, 395-410

Vincent 1987
C. Vincent, 'Prince Karl I of Liechtenstein's Pietre Dure Tabletop', *Metropolitan Museum Journal*, XX, 1987, 157-78

Vlček 1989
P. Vlček, "Dientzenhoferův skicář' a česká architektura 1640-1670', *Umění*, XXXVII,

1989, 473-97

Vlk-Assman 1988
M. Vlk-J. Assman, *Stolničení a výtvarné umění pěti staletí*, Nelahozeves, 1988

Vocelka 1981
K. Vocelka, *Die politische Propaganda Kaiser Rudolfs II. (1576 bis 1612)*, Vienna, 1981

Vocelka 1985
K. Vocelka, *Rudolf II. und seine Zeit*, Vienna-Cologne-Graz, 1985

Vogel 1964
E. Vogel, 'Loutnová hudba v Čechách', *Časopis Národního muzea*, CXXXIII, 1964, 11-19

Vogel 1965
E. Vogel, 'Lautenisten der böhmischen Spätrenaissance', *Die Musikforschung*, XVIII, 1965, 281-96

Vogel 1977
E. Vogel a kol., *Bibliografia della musica italiana vocale profana pubblicata dal 1500 al 1700*, Pomezia, 1977

Vojenské dějiny 1986
Vojenské dějiny Československa, II: 1526-1918, Prague, 1986

Vojtíšek 1928
V. Vojtíšek, *O pečetech a erbech měst pražských a jiných měst českých*, Prague, 1928

Vojtová 1970
M. Vojtová a kol., *Dějiny československého lékařství*, Prague, 1970

Vokáčová 1957
V. Vokáčová, *Renesanční interiérová výzdoba zámku Rožmberk*, dipl. práce, Prague, 1957

Vokáčová 1968
V. Vokáčová, *Böhmischer Granatschmuck*, Pforzheim, 1968

Vokáčová 1969
V. Vokáčová, 'Svatojiřský závěsek z Chrudimi', *Umění a řemesla*, 1969

Vokáčová 1980
V. Vokáčová, 'Habánské příbory ve sbírce UPM v Praze', *Acta UPM*, XV, Prague, 1980, 114

Vokáčová 1985
V. Vokáčová, *Český granát*, Prague, 1985

Vokáčová 1985
V. Vokáčová, *Český granát*, Trenčín, 1985

Volavková 1969
H. Volavková, s.t., *Výtvarné umění*, 2/3, 1969, 62

Volek-Jareš 1977
T. Volek-S. Jareš, *Dějiny české hudby v obrazech*, Prague, 1977

Volk 1974
P. Volk, *Bronzeplastiken: Erwerbungen von 1956-1973 (Bayerisches Nationalmuseum)*, Munich, 1974

Vorel 1993
P. Vorel, 'O rodu s erbem zubří hlavy', *Dějiny a současnost*, 4, 1993, 19-24

Vorel 1993
P. Vorel, *Páni z Pernštejna: Českomoravský rod v zrcadle staletí*, Pardubice, 1993

Walde 1930
O. Walde, 'Die herzogliche Bibliothek in Gotha und die literarische Kriegsbeute aus Würzburg', *Nordisk tidskrift för bok och biblioteksväsen*, XVII, 1930, 14-30

Walcher von Molthein 1906
A. Walcher von Molthein, *Bunte Hafnerkeramik der Renaissance in den Österreichischen Ländern*, Vienna, 1906

Ward 1981
F. A. B. Ward, *A Catalogue of European Scientific Instruments in the Department of Medieval and Later Antiquities of the British Museum*, London, 1981

Weber 1865
K. von Weber, *Anna-Churfürstin zu Sachsen: Ein Lebens- und Sittenbild aus dem sechzehnten Jahrhundert*, Leipzig, 1865

Weber 1975
I. Weber, *Deutsche, Niederländische und Französische Renaissanceplaketten 1500-1650*, Munich, 1975

Wegner-Klein 1956
W. Wegner-H. Klein, 'Skizzenbuchblätter von Paulus van Vianen mit einer Ansicht von Salzburg', *Mitteilungen der Gesellschaft für Salzburger Landeskunde*, XCVI, 1956, 207-16

Wegner 1973
W. Wegner, *Kataloge der Staatlichen Graphischen Sammlung München: Die niederländischen Handzeichnungen des 15-18. Jahrhunderts*, Berlin, 1973

Weihrauch 1937-38, vi-ix
H.R. Weihrauch, 'Röttel- und Kreidezeichnungen Barth. Sprangers', *Münchner Jahrbuch der bildenden Kunst*, XII, 1937-38, vi-ix

Weihrauch 1967
H. R. Weihrauch, *Europäische Bronzestatuetten 15.-18.Jahrhundert*, Braunschweig, 1967

Weihrauch 1970
H.R. Weihrauch, 'Příspěvky k dílu Benedikta Wurzelbauera a Adriaena de Vriese', *Umění*, XVIII, 1970, 60-68

Weiss 1969
R. Weiss, *The Renaissance Discovery of Classical Antiquity*, London, 1969

Weixlgärtner 1928
A. Weixlgärtner, 'Die weltliche Schatzkammer in Wien: Neue Funde und Forschungen II', *JKSW*, II, 1928, 267-315

Weixlgärtner 1932
A. Weixlgärtner, *Führer durch die Geistliche Schatzkammer*, Vienna, 1932

Weltliche und Geistliche Schatzkammer.1991
Weltliche und Geistliche Schatzkammer: Bildführer, Vienna, 1991

Welzig 1990
M. Welzig, 'Prunkgefässe', Vienna, 1990, 250-64

Wenping 1990
C. Wenping, *Zhongguo gu taoci jian shang*, Shanghai, 1990

Wethey 1975
H.E. Wethey, *The paintings of Titian. Complete edition, III: The Mythological and Historical Paintings*, London, 1975

Wettengl 1983
K. Wettengl, *Die Mahlzeitstilleben von Georg Flegel*, Diss., Osnabrück, 1983

Widerkehr 1988
L. Widerkehr, *Contributions éssentiellement iconographiques a l'étude de quelques gravures d' Egidius Sadeler*, These du Maitrise, Strasbourg, 1988

Wied 1971
A. Wied, 'Lucas van Valckenborch', *JKSW*, LXVII, 1971, 119-231

Wied 1990
A. Wied, *Lucas und Marten van Valckenborch (1535-1597 und 1534-1612): Das Gesamtwerk mit kritischem Oeuvrekatalog*, Freren, 1990

Wille 1965
H. Wille, *Handzeichnungen alter Meister aus dem Besitz der Kunstsammlungen der Georg-August-Universität Göttingen*, Duisburg, 1965

Williams 1936
H. W. Williams, 'Four drawings attributed to Christoph Jamnitzer', *The Art Bulletin*, XVIII, 1936

Williams 1937
H. W. Williams, 'Supplementary note regarding four drawings attributed to Christoph Jamnitzer', *The Art Bulletin*, XIX, 1937

Wilson 1969
E. Wilson, *A History of Shoe Fashions*, London, 1969

Winner 1962
M. Winner, 'Gemalte Kunsttheorie: Zu Gustave Courbets 'Allégorie réelle' und der Tradition', *Jahrbuch der Berliner Museen*, IV, 1962, 151-85

Winter 1895
Z. Winter, *Život církevní v Čechách: Kulturně historický obraz XV. a XVI. století*, Prague, 1895

Winter 1897
Z. Winter, *Děje vysokých škol pražských od secesí cizích národů po dobu bitvy běloborské*, Prague, 1897

Winter 1897
Z. Winter, 'Konec samostatné university Karlovy', *Časopis českého musea*, LXXI, 1897, 3-35, 97-109

Winter 1906
Z. Winter, *Dějiny řemesel a obchodu v Čechách v XIV. a XV. století*, Prague, 1906

Winter 1909
Z. Winter, *Řemeslnictvo a živnost XVI. věku v Čechách (1526-1620)*, Prague, 1909

Winter 1909
Z. Winter, *Umělecký průmysl v Čechách v 16. věku*, Prague, 1909

Winter 1912
Z. Winter, *Řemeslnictvo a živnosti české v 15. a 16. věku*, Prague, 1912

Winter 1913
Z. Winter, *Zlatá doba měst českých*, Prague, 1913

Winter 1913
Z. Winter, *Český průmysl a obchod v XVI. věku*, Prague, 1913

Winter 1985
Z. Winter, *Život církevní v Čechách: Kulturně-historické vypsání náboženských poměrů v XV. a XVI. století*, Prague, 1985

Wirth 1932
Z. Wirth, *Praha v obraze pěti století*, Prague, 1932.

Wissen 1995
B. van Wissen, *Dodo Raphus cucullatus (Didus ineptus, ISP)*, Amsterdam, 1995

Wostry 1938
W. Wostry, *Die Geschichte des Friedländischen, III: Der Herzog von Friedland*, Friedland, 1938

Wurzbach 1906-11
A. von Wurzbach, *Niederländisches Künstler-Lexikon*, Vienna-Leipzig, 1906-11

Wurzbach-Tannenberg 1943
A. von Wurzbach-W. Tannenberg, *Medaillen, Plaketten und Jetons*, Zürich-Leipzig-Vienna, 1943

Zangius 1951
N. Zangius, *Geisitliche und weltliche Gasange*, DTO 87, Vienna, 1951

Zap 1857
K. V. Zap, 'Berla a koruna někdejších abatyší u sv. Jiří na hradě Pražském', *Památky archeologické a místopisné*, II, 1857, 89-90

Zebrowski 1981
M. Zebrowski, 'Transformations in Seventeenth Century Deccani Paintings at Bijapur', *Chhavi*, 1981

Zeeberg 1994
P. Zeeberg, *Tycho Brahes Urania Titani*, Copenhagen, 1994

Zeminová 1974
M. Zeminová, *Barokní textilie*, Prague, 1974

Zíbrt 1890
Č. Zíbrt, *Bibliografie české historie*, Prague, 1890

Zíbrt 1909
Č. Zíbrt, 'Strahovský sborník vzácných tisků přiležitostných Václava Dobřenského z druhé polovice věku XVI', *Časopis českého muzea*, 1909, 100

Zimmer 1967
J. Zimmer, *Joseph Heintz der Ältere als Maler (1564-1609)*, Diss. Bamberg, 1967

Zimmer 1969
J. Zimmer, 'Iosephus Heinzius Architectus cum antiquis comparandus: Příspěvek k poznání rudolfínské architektury mezi lety 1590-1612', *Umění*, XVII, 1969, 217-46

Zimmer 1971
J. Zimmer, *Joseph Heintz der Ältere als Maler*, Weißenhorn, 1971

Zimmer 1979
J. Zimmer, 'Joseph Heintz der Ältere: Neue Ergebnisse zum Werk des Malers', *Alte und moderne Kunst*, XXIV:163, 1979, 9-13

Zimmer 1980
J. Zimmer, 'Joseph Heintz und die Fugger', *Alte und moderne Kunst*, XXV:168, 1980, 17-23

Zimmer 1985
J. Zimmer, 'Joseph Heintz in Augsburg und Haunsheim: Überblick und neue Aspekte', *Zeitschrift des Historischen Vereins für Schwaben*, 1985, 163-65

Zimmer 1988
J. Zimmer, 'Giovanni Contarini - ein 'rudolfinischer' Künstler?', *Prag um 1600: Beiträge zur Kunst und Kultur am Hofe Rudolfs II.*, Freren, 1988, 314-25

Zimmer 1988
J. Zimmer, *Joseph Heintz der Ältere: Zeichnungen und Dokumente*, Munich-Berlin, 1988

Zimmermann 1905
H. Zimmermann, 'Das Inventar der Prager Schatz - und Kunstkammer vom 6. Dezember 1621', nach den Akten des k.u.k. Reichsfinanzarchiv, *JKSW*, XXV/2, 1905, XIII-LXXV

Zimmermann 1969
E. Zimmermann, 'Herkules, Deianeira und Nessus: Eine Bronzeskulptur des Adrian de Vries im Badischen Landesmuseum', *Jahrbuch der Staatlichen Kunstsammlungen in Baden-Württemberg*, VI, 1969, 55-78

Zinke 1990
D. Zinke, *Augustinermuseum: Gemälde bis 1800*, Freiburg i. Br., 1990

Zinner 1967
E. Zinner, *Deutsche und niederländische astronomische Instrumente des 11.-18. Jahrhunderts*, Munich, 1967

Zhongguo 1982
Zhongguo taoci guixuan xuehui, Zhongguo taoci shi, Peking, 1982.

Zülch-Chytil 1929
W. K. Zülch-K. Chytil, 'Archivalische Beiträge zu Hans Vermeyen und Andreas Osenbruck, den Verfertigern der österreichischen Kroninsignien', *JKSW*, III, 1929, 271-74

Zuwachs 1894
'Zuwachs der Sammlungen', *Mittheilungen des Nordböhmischen Gewerbe-Museums*, XII, 1894, 46

Zwollo 1968
A. Zwollo, 'Pieter Stevens, ein vergessener Maler des Rudolfinischen Kreises', *JKSW*, LXIV, 1968, 119-80

Zwollo 1970
A. Zwollo, 'Pieter Stevens: Neue Zuschreibungen und Zusammenhänge', *Umění*, XVIII, 1970, 246-59

Zwollo 1982
A. Zwollo, 'Pieter Stevens: Nieuw werk, contact met Jan Brueghel, invloed op Kerstiaen de Keuninck', *Leids Kunsthistorische Jaarboek*, I, 1982, 95-118

Zwollo 1988
Z. Zwollo, 'Pieter Stevens, Addenda zu seinem Werk, mit einem Anhang iber ein Porträt der Westonia', *Prag um 1600: Beiträge zur Kunst und Kultur am Hofe Rudolfs II.*, Freren, 1988, 326-33

Zwollo 1992
A. Zwollo, 'Kaufmann 1985 & 1988', *Oud Holland*, CVI, 1992, 35-48

Žáčková 1996
M. Žáčková, *Gregorio Turini (1553-1596): Příspěvek k životu a dílu rudolfinského budehníka*, Dipl. práce, Prague, 1996

Žegklitz-Zavřel 1990
J. Žegklitz-J. Zavřel, 'Geochemical and petrographical studies of the post-medieval pottery of the Prague and Beroun regions', *Studies in post-medieval archaeology*, 1990, 95-126

Index

The essays in this book were originally written in numerous languages and translated into English by several translators. As a result there is some variation in the rendering of names. Both generally accepted and frequently recurring variants are given in this index.